THE HARVARD CONCISE DICTIONARY

OF MUSIC AND MUSICIANS

HARVARD
UNIVERSITY
PRESS
REFERENCE
LIBRARY

EDITED BY

DON MICHAEL RANDEL

THE HARVARD
CONCISE
DICTIONARY
OF MUSIC
AND MUSICIANS

The Belknap Press of Harvard University Press

Cambridge, Massachusetts, and London, England

Portions of this book were previously published in *The New Harvard Dictionary of Music,*
edited by Don Michael Randel, copyright © 1986 by the President and Fellows of Harvard
College, and *The Harvard Biographical Dictionary of Music,* edited by Don Michael
Randel, copyright © 1996 by the President and Fellows of Harvard College.

Library of Congress Cataloging-in-Publication Data

The Harvard concise dictionary of music and musicians /
   edited by Don Michael Randel.
       p.   cm.
    ISBN 0-674-00084-6 (cloth)
    ISBN 0-674-00978-9 (paper)
     1. Music—Dictionaries.   2. Music—Bio-bibliography.
   I. Randel, Don Michael.
   ML100.H36   1999   99-40644
   780′.3—dc21

Preface

This book, like its predecessor, the *Harvard Concise Dictionary of Music* (1978), is intended to serve the needs of a variety of readers, including students of music history, theory, and performance; amateur musicians; and those who simply listen to music and occasionally read about it. Its coverage, however, is somewhat expanded. It remains primarily a book devoted to concert music in the Western tradition from the earliest times, but it treats many of the terms and the people in this domain in greater detail. And, unlike its predecessor, it includes entries for performers of Western concert music, jazz, and popular music. In addition, there are entries for a number of terms and instruments (some of which are illustrated under the heading Instrument) belonging to non-Western musical traditions and to Western popular music.

In all of this, conciseness continues to be prized. I have avoided evaluative and emotive language that, in this context, is likely to be either misleading or merely superfluous. For every music lover, listening ought to come before taking anyone else's word about how to feel or what to like. That said, this book inevitably reflects in considerable degree what serious students of music have found valuable over the years. Especially with biographical entries, however, the relative lengths of entries should not be taken as an index of the relative importance of their subjects. It simply takes less space to say that Domenico Scarlatti wrote 555 sonatas than to list even a few of the works of a less well-known composer who wrote for unusual combinations of instruments and employed fanciful titles.

Readers in search of greater detail and guidance to the larger literature on music should turn first to *The New Harvard Dictionary of Music* (1986) and *The Harvard Biographical Dictionary of Music* (1996), on which the present book is based. It is to the many collaborators on these books that I owe my thanks in the first instance for the present one. Of particular importance in the production of this book, however, were Ronald Rabin and Julia Randel. Special thanks are also due the staff of the Harvard University Press, most notably Jennifer Snodgrass and Margaretta Fulton.

Don Michael Randel
Ithaca, New York

Abbreviations

General

An asterisk (*) before a term indicates a separate article on that subject.

Middle C is designated c′, the C's below that c, C, C_1, etc. The C's above middle C are designated c″, c‴, etc. See Pitch names.

A	alto	ill.	illustration
abbr.	abbreviated, abbreviation	incl.	inclusive, including
anon.	anonymous	movt.	movement
B	bass	no.	number
b.	born	N.S.	New Style
bapt.	baptized	op.	opus (plural opp.)
B.C.E.	before the common era	O.S.	Old Style
bk.	book	p.	page (plural pp.)
ca.	circa	perf.	performance, performed
C.E.	of the common era	pl.	plural
cent.	century	Ps.	Psalm
d.	died	publ.	published by
ex.	example (plural exx.)	R:	reprint
f.	and following (plural ff.)	rev.	revised, revised by
fig.	figure	S	soprano
fl.	flourished	T	tenor
fr.	from	Univ.	University

Languages

Ar.	Arabic	Jav.	Javanese
AS	Anglo-Saxon	Kor.	Korean
Brit.	British usage	Lat.	Latin
Bulg.	Bulgarian	ME	Middle English
Cat.	Catalan	MHG	Middle High German
Chin.	Chinese	Nor.	Norwegian
Cz.	Czechoslovakian	OE	Old English
Dan.	Danish	OFr.	Old French
Du.	Dutch	OHG	Old High German
Eng.	English	ON	Old Norse
Finn.	Finnish	Per.	Persian
Fr.	French	Pol.	Polish
Gael.	Gaelic	Port.	Portuguese
Ger.	German	Prov.	Provençal
Gr.	Greek	Rom.	Romanian
Heb.	Hebrew	Russ.	Russian
Hin.	Hindi	Serb.-Cro.	Serbo-Croatian
Hung.	Hungarian	Skt.	Sanskrit
Icel.	Icelandic	Sp.	Spanish
IE	Indo-European	Swed.	Swedish
It.	Italian	Tel.	Telugu
Jap.	Japanese	Turk.	Turkish

THE HARVARD CONCISE DICTIONARY
OF MUSIC AND MUSICIANS

A. (1) See Pitch names, Letter notation, Hexachord, Pitch. (2) An abbreviation for *alto or *altus. (3) *A* [It.], *à* [Fr.]. To, at, with, for; *a 2* [etc.] *voci*, for two [etc.] voices. Phrases beginning with this word should be sought under the word immediately following, e.g., *Battuta, Beneplacito, Cappella, Deux, Due, Peine entendu, Piacere, Tempo*.

Ab [Ger.]. Off, as for a mute or an organ stop.

Abaco, Evaristo Felice dall'. See Dall'Abaco, Evaristo Felice.

Abandonné [Fr.], **abbandonatamente, con abbandono** [It.]. With abandon, unrestrained.

Abbado, Claudio (b. Milan, 26 June 1933). Conductor. Studied piano at the Milan Conservatory and with Gulda in Salzburg; conducting with Swarowsky at the Vienna Academy. Principal conductor (from 1968) and artistic director (1976–86) of La Scala; principal conductor of the Vienna Philharmonic from 1971; of the London Symphony, 1979–86; music director of the Vienna State Opera, 1986–91; chief conductor of the Berlin Philharmonic from 1990.

Abbassare [It.]. To lower, e.g., the pitch of a string.

Abbatini, Antonio Maria (b. Città di Castello, 1609 or 1610; d. there, ca. 1679). Composer, teacher, and theorist. *Maestro di cappella* at St. John Lateran in Rome, 1626–28; at the cathedral in Orvieto in 1633; and at S. Maria Maggiore in Rome (1640–46, 1649–57, 1672–77). Cesti was among his pupils. His *Dal male il bene* (Rome, 1653; libretto by Giulio Rospigliosi; act 2 by Marco Marazzoli) is an important early example of comic opera. Also composed Latin church music.

Abbellimento [It.]. Ornament.

Abdämpfen [Ger.]. To damp, to mute.

Abduction from the Seraglio. See *Entführung aus dem Serail, Die*.

Abegg Variations. Schumann's variations for piano op. 1 (1829–30), dedicated to his friend Meta Abegg, whose name is represented in the first five notes of the theme: a', bb', e'', g'', g''.

Abel, Carl Friedrich (b. Cöthen, 22 Dec. 1723; d. London, 20 June 1787). Composer and viola da gamba player for whose use J. S. Bach's three gamba sonatas may have been composed. Probably joined Bach's Collegium musicum in 1737. Settled in London, giving his first concert there in 1759. In 1764 gave his first joint concert with J. C. Bach, both serving as chamber musicians to Queen Charlotte from about this time. Together they established the Bach-Abel concerts, a series of 10 to 15 concerts given each year from 1765 until 1781. Works include symphonies, concertos, overtures; string quartets, string trios, sonatas; pieces for viola da gamba.

Abendmusik [Ger.]. An evening concert in a church; specifically the performances at the Marienkirche in Lübeck, north Germany, begun in the 17th century and lasting until 1810. They came to prominence under Dietrich Buxtehude (organist at Lübeck from 1668 until 1707), who established them on five Sundays preceding Christmas.

Abgesang [Ger.]. See Bar form.

Abgestossen [Ger.]. *Staccato.

Abnehmend [Ger.]. *Diminuendo*.

Abravanel, Maurice (de) (b. Thessaloniki, of Sephardic parents, 6 Jan. 1903; d. Salt Lake City, Utah, 22 Sept. 1993). Conductor. Studied composition with Weill in Berlin. Conducted in Germany; moved to Paris in 1933. On the staff of the Metropolitan Opera in New York, 1936–38; thereafter conducted Broadway shows (including Weill's *Knickerbocker Holiday* and *Street Scene*). Conductor of the Utah Symphony, 1947–79.

Absetzen [Ger.]. (1) To separate; to articulate. (2) To intabulate, i.e., to transcribe in *tablature.

Absil, Jean (b. Bon-Secours, Hainaut, Belgium, 23 Oct. 1893; d. Brussels, 2 Feb. 1974). Composer. Studied organ and composition at the Brussels Conservatory beginning in 1913; studied composition with Gilson in 1920–22. Director of the Etterbeek Music School in 1922; faculty, Brussels Conservatory (from 1930), subsequently professor of fugue there (1939–59). The works of Schoenberg, Berg, Stravinsky, and Milhaud were important influences, as was his study of folk music from Romania and other countries. His *Postulats de la musique contemporaine* (1937) advocated his own brand of polytonality and pointed to its historical roots.

Absolute music [fr. Ger. *absolute Musik, absolute Tonkunst*]. Instrumental music that is "free of" [Lat. *absolutus*] any explicit connection with words beyond simple indications of tempo and genre. The dichotomy between absolute and *program music is essentially misleading, for it obscures the complex intertwining of extramusical associations and "purely" musical substance that can be found even in pieces that bear no verbal clues whatever.

Absolute pitch. (1) *Pitch as defined both by its name and by the specific frequency that produces it rather than by its name alone. (2) The ability to name a pitch or produce a pitch designated by name without recourse to any external source or standard, as distinct from *relative pitch. Theories of absolute pitch assume that individuals with this ability possess an internal standard pitch in long-term memory, and some maintain that the ability is largely innate. There is no general agreement as to whether absolute pitch is continuously distributed in the population, and underlying neurological mechanisms have not been identified.

Abstossen [Ger.]. (1) To detach; to play *staccato. (2) In organ playing, to take off a stop.

Abstract music. *Absolute music.

Abstrich [Ger.]. Down-bow. See Bowing (1).

Abt, Franz Wilhelm (b. Eilenburg, 22 Dec. 1819; d. Wiesbaden, 31 Mar. 1885). Composer. Studied in Leipzig; conducted in Zurich and at the court in Brunswick; traveled widely as a choral conductor and toured America very successfully in 1872. Composed over 3,000 works, including numerous choral works (many for male chorus) and many songs.

Abwechseln [Ger.]. To alternate, as when a single player alternates in playing two instruments.

Abzug [Ger.]. (1) *Scordatura tuning, especially on the lute; by extension, in the writings of Praetorius, additional open bass strings. (2) The softening of an *appoggiatura as it tapers into its resolution; a *Schneller.

Academic Festival Overture [Ger. *Akademische Festouvertüre*]. An orchestral composition by Brahms, op. 80 (1880), dedicated to the University of Breslau in recognition of the honorary doctorate awarded him in 1879. It makes free use of several German student songs, notably "Gaudeamus igitur."

Academy. A scholarly or artistic society. The term first referred to a grove in Athens sacred to the mythological hero Academus, where Plato established a school as early as 385 B.C.E. It gained new currency with the revival of Platonic and Neoplatonic thought in the Renaissance. In some academies musical composition and performance were the primary or even sole aims, such as the Accademia filarmonica of Verona (established 1543) and the Accademia degli elevati of Florence (established 1607). Numerous informal groups of learned aristocrats gathered at private palaces in the 16th and 17th centuries, and many of these *camerate* or *ridotti,* such as those meeting in late 16th-century Florence at the palaces of Giovanni de' Bardi and Jacopo Corsi, featured musical discussion and experimentation.

The first French academy officially instituted by royal decree was the Académie de poésie et de musique, established in 1570 by the poet Jean-Antoine de Baïf and the musician Joachim Thibault de Courville. The Académie aimed to rediscover the legendary effects of ancient music [see *musique mesurée à l'antique*].

In 1669 the Académie royale de musique was founded, with letters patent granted to the poet Pierre Perrin and composer Robert Cambert (the patent passing to Jean-Baptiste Lully in 1672). This was an opera company with royal sponsorship, and it survives as the Paris Opéra, the official title of which through most of its history has included the term *académie.* By 1800 almost any concert with aristocratic support might be termed an academy. Musical academies since that time have included schools of music, groups promoting musical performance, and learned associations devoted to studies of music theory and history.

A cappella [It.]. See *Cappella.*

Accelerando, accelerato [It., abbr. *accel.*]. Becoming faster; faster.

Accent. (1) Emphasis on one pitch or chord. An accent is dynamic if the pitch or chord is louder than its surroundings, tonic if it is higher in pitch, and agogic if it is of longer duration. In measured music [see Meter], the first beat of each measure is the strong beat and thus carries a metrical accent. The creation of regularly recurring metrical accents depends on the manipulation of groups of pitches or chords (e.g., according to the principles of tonality) and not solely on the placement of dynamic, tonic, or agogic accents. Thus, the strong beat in a measure need not be louder, higher, or longer than the remaining weak beats in order to retain its quality of strength with respect to its surroundings. When the regular recurrence of metrical accents is contradicted by means of loudness, pitch, or duration, *syncopation results. In vocal music, the coordination of musical accent with the various sonorous characteristics (including accent) of a text is termed *declamation. For the role of tonic accent in Gregorian chant, see Cursive and tonic, Gregorian chant.

A dynamic accent on a single pitch or chord may

be specified with the symbols > and ^, the second calling for greater loudness and sharper attack than the first. See also *Sforzando, sforzato;* Dynamic marks; Notation.

(2) [Fr., Ger.; It. *accento*] From the late 16th through the 18th century, any of various ornaments such as the *springer, *appoggiatura, *Schneller,* and small groups of notes.

(3) [Fr.] In the 17th and 18th centuries, a type of *Nachschlag* in which the upper neighbor is added to the very end of the main note. The following note most often lies below the main note or is a return to the pitch of the main note. It is also called an *aspiration* and sometimes a *plainte.* See Ornamentation.

(4) For the signs associated with Greek prosodic accents and with cantillation of Semitic texts, see Ecphonetic notation.

Acciaccatura [It., perhaps from *acciaccare,* to crush]. An ornament of 17th- and 18th-century keyboard playing, particularly in the Italian style of accompanying recitatives, consisting of a nonharmonic tone (either a whole tone or a semitone below the main note) that is sounded simultaneously with a harmonic tone or tones but that is neither prepared nor resolved and usually released almost immediately; sometimes referred to as a *Zusammenschlag* and by extension as a simultaneous appoggiatura. See Ornamentation.

Accidental. In musical notation, any of the symbols used to raise or lower a pitch by one or two semitones or to cancel a previous sign or part of a *key signature. The five symbols used for this purpose are given in the table with their names in English, French, German, Italian, and Spanish.

A sharp raises and a flat lowers a pitch by one semitone. A double sharp raises and a double flat lowers a pitch by two semitones. A natural cancels any preceding sign, including an element of the prevailing key signature. The combinations ♮♯ and ♮♭ are sometimes used to cancel one element of the double sharp and double flat, respectively, and ♮♮ is sometimes used to cancel the double sharp or double flat altogether. The simple forms ♯, ♭, and ♮ suffice for these purposes, however. An accidental is placed on a line or space of the staff immediately to the left of the

note to which it applies. According to modern notational practice, an accidental remains in force for all notes occurring on the same line or space in the remainder of the measure in which it appears. This practice is not well established until the 19th century.

In tonal music, certain conventions govern the choice between enharmonically equivalent sharps and flats, e.g., between F-sharp and G-flat. In general, if the note to be altered is followed by a higher pitch it is altered by means of a sharp; if followed by a lower pitch, a flat is used. Alterations to the pure minor *scale result from "raising" the sixth and seventh scale degrees, with the result that a natural note is used to substitute for a prevailing flat and a sharped note to substitute for a prevailing natural. In some atonal music, in order to avoid ambiguity, accidentals are applied to every note and thus apply only to the note immediately following.

The sharp, flat, and natural derive from the two forms of the letter b employed to represent B-natural and B-flat in the medieval *Gamut. For B-natural, a square-shaped b, called *b quadratum* (square b) or *b durum* (hard b), was used. For B-flat a rounded b, called *b rotundum* (round b) or *b molle* (soft b), was used. This terminology is reflected in the terminology still in use for flats and naturals in German and the Romance languages as well as in the German *Dur* for major and *Moll* for minor. Because of the early shapes of these signs, German pitch nomenclature still refers to B-flat as B and to B-natural as H. For the use of unnotated accidentals in some early music, see *Musica ficta.*

Accolade [Fr.]. *Brace.

Accompagnato [It.]. Accompanied. See Recitative.

Accompanied keyboard sonata. A sonata for harpsichord or piano with one or more accompanying melodic instruments such as violin or flute, the keyboard part being written out in full rather than realized from a thoroughbass part. A product of the middle third of the 18th century with both French and German antecedents, it was a widely cultivated and very prominent form through the 1770s, and its influence was felt into the 19th century in the standard repertory of solo sonatas, trios, and the like. It was not an outgrowth of the sonata with thorough-

	♯	♭	𝄪	♭♭	♮
Eng.	sharp	flat	double sharp	double flat	natural
Fr.	dièse	bémol	double dièse	double bémol	bécarre
Ger.	Kreuz	Be	Doppelkreutz	Doppel-Be	Auflösungszeichen, Quadrat
It.	diesis	bemolle	doppio diesis	doppio bemolle	bequadro
Sp.	sostenido	bemol	doble sostenido	doble bemol	becuadro

bass accompaniment, but rather coexisted with it for several decades.

Accompaniment. The musical background for a principal part or parts. This term is used in two somewhat different ways, one referring to manner of performance, the other to texture. The first is appropriate when the performers of a musical work are divided into two components of contrasting and complementary function: a principal part in which musical interest and the listener's attention are mainly centered, and the accompaniment, subordinate to it, whose main purpose is in some sense supportive. The principal part may be one or more solo performers, vocal or instrumental, or a group of performers, such as a chorus. The accompaniment is usually instrumental, either a single instrument (usually one capable of chords), an ensemble, or an orchestra. The relation between accompaniment and principal part can vary from a completely and unobtrusively subordinate role for the accompaniment, like that of guitar chords strummed with a song or that of the church organist in congregational singing, to what is usually called *obbligato accompaniment, found in more complex music, where the accompaniment is an essential part of the texture. Obbligato parts can remain in a subordinate relation to the principal part, as in much Baroque music, or can interact with it to varying degrees, as in much music from the Classical period onward. It is in such music that accompaniment makes its greatest artistic demands on performers.

By extension the term has also been applied to musical textures, as in the phrase "melody and accompaniment," when one or more primary melodic parts are supported by other material subordinate in musical interest, often of a primarily harmonic rather than melodic character, commonly chords or chordal figuration, e.g., the *Alberti bass and similar formulas. Melody and accompaniment may be performed on a single instrument or by different performers in an ensemble. In many cases these two uses of the term are both applicable at the same time.

Instruments and voices were frequently used together in the Middle Ages and Renaissance, as documentary evidence shows, but the reconstruction of accompanimental practice is difficult because the written music lacks precise indications of when instruments were used, and which ones. Very likely this lack reflects a degree of flexibility on both points [see Performance practice].

Until the decline of the *thoroughbass at the end of the Baroque period, improvisation played a prominent role in accompaniment. Since that time, it has been restricted within art music to a few domains, notably organ accompaniment of congregational singing, where improvisation is sometimes quite elaborate. In folk and popular music, accompaniment is often improvised, though ensembles may rely on written *arrangements for the purpose. There is a centuries-long tradition of providing composed accompaniments for folk songs that includes not only works by composers such as Haydn and Ives, but also what are now regarded as the misguided efforts of some 19th- and 20th-century collectors. In some non-Western musics, *heterophony is a prominent feature of accompaniment. See also Additional accompaniment.

Accoppiare [It.]. In organ playing, to couple.

Accord [Fr.]. (1) Chord; *accord parfait,* triad. (2) The set of pitches to which an instrument such as the lute is tuned. Various tunings have been used for a single instrument. See also *Accords nouveaux,* Scordatura.

Accordare [It.]. To tune.

Accordatura [It.]. The set of pitches to which an instrument, especially a stringed instrument, is tuned; in stringed instruments, often the usual as opposed to some less common set. See also Scordatura.

Accorder [Fr.]. To tune.

Accordion. A bellows-operated, hand-held wind instrument sounded by free reeds. It consists in effect of two reed organs, each with its own keyboard, joined by a rectangular bellows. The organ in the player's right hand is the higher pitched, and in the

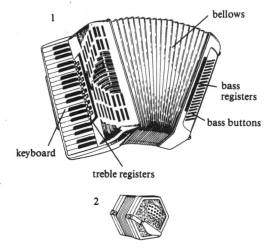

1. Accordion. 2. Concertina.

prevalent design, its reeds are sounded by means of a piano keyboard. The left-hand organ, designed for accompaniment, is played on rows of buttons, some sounding single bass notes, others producing major, minor, diminished, and seventh chords. In standard double-action models, the steel reeds are arranged in pairs, one reed sounded by pressure (pushing), the other by suction (pulling). Supplementary sets of reeds in the right-hand organ are activated by register switches above the keyboard and provide a variety of tone colors.

Related instruments like the *concertina and *mouth organ were developed in the early 19th century, inspired by the Chinese *sheng. The first instrument of this type to incorporate bellows and a button keyboard was patented as the Handäoline in 1821 by Friedrich Buschmann of Berlin. The first instrument with the name accordion was patented in 1829 by Cyrillus Demian in Vienna and included a button keyboard and chords for accompaniment. The piano keyboard and steel reeds were introduced in the 1850s.

Accordo [It.]. Chord.

Accords nouveaux [Fr., new tunings]. The various 17th-century tunings for the lute and related instruments. To facilitate playing in diverse keys, at least 25 tunings appear in manuscript and printed sources of lute music, particularly in the French repertory.

Accoupler [Fr.]. In organ playing, to couple.

Accusé [Fr.]. Marked, emphasized.

Achron, Joseph (b. Lozdzieje, Poland, 13 May 1886; d. Hollywood, 29 Apr. 1943). Violinist and composer. In 1898 entered the St. Petersburg Conservatory, studying violin with Auer and composition with Lyadov. In 1911 joined with other Jewish musicians in the study of Jewish folklore, which played a continuing role in his compositions thereafter. Moved to Palestine (1924) and then the U.S. (1925), settling in Hollywood in 1934; played violin in film studio orchestras while continuing to compose and to perform as a soloist. His best-known work is *Hebrew Melody* for violin and orchestra (1911); later works employ principles related to those of the music of Schoenberg.

Achtel, Achtelnote; Achtelpause [Ger.]. Eighth note; eighth rest. See Note.

Achtfuss [Ger.]. Eight-foot stop.

Acid rock. A genre of American *rock music often meant to evoke or to accompany an experience on psychedelic drugs such as LSD (termed acid). Performances were sometimes combined with lightshows to enhance this effect. Most songs combined blues-derived song forms with heavy amplification and distortion. The genre emerged in San Francisco in the late 1960s; its originators include Jimi Hendrix, the Jefferson Airplane, and the Grateful Dead. The term lost currency in the early 1970s.

Acis and Galatea. Handel's two-act dramatic work, variously described as a *masque, *pastorale, or *serenata, to a libretto by John Gay with additions by Pope and Dryden, composed and first performed in 1718 at Cannons, the estate of the future Duke of Chandos. It was revived in London in 1732 with additions from his cantata *Aci, Galatea e Polifemo,* completed in Naples in 1708.

Acoustic. (1) Not electric, especially with reference to the guitar or double bass (acoustic guitar, acoustic bass). (2) The acoustical character of a space.

Acoustic bass. An effect comparable in pitch to that of a 32-foot stop on an organ, obtained by playing a 16-foot stop with a stop pitched a fifth above. Also termed resultant bass or harmonic bass, the effect is produced by the acoustical phenomenon of *combination or resultant tones. See also Acoustic (1).

Acoustics. (1) The science of the production, propagation, and perception of sound. Sound will be taken here in the physical sense and will refer to mechanical vibrations or pressure oscillations of various sorts. The production of musical sound entails mechanical vibrations such as those of stretched strings (violin or piano), wooden or metal plates (violin body, piano soundboard, or cymbal), stretched membranes (vocal cord or drumhead), wooden or metal bars (marimba or celesta), and the oscillatory motion of air columns (the vocal tract, trumpet, clarinet, or organ). The propagation of sound involves pressure oscillations and associated vibrational motion of a medium, usually air but sometimes a liquid or solid material, that carries the vibrational energy, or sound, from source to listener. The perception of sound requires the transmission of sound energy, again as mechanical vibrations, by the eardrum via the small bones of the middle ear to the fluid of the inner ear and finally to the hair cells of the inner ear where the information contained in the details of the vibrational motion is encoded into patterns of nerve impulses. The brain interprets these impulses, with extremely subtle discrimination, as the psychological sound of which we are consciously aware.

It is convenient to represent the physical sound as a graph that records the variation with time of the vibration, perhaps the displacement from its resting position of a particular point on a violin string or the air pressure at a particular position within a trumpet. Fig. 1a represents such an oscillatory motion for a string vibrating in a particularly simple way; the associated sound is called a pure tone, and its graph is a sine wave. The frequency, f, of this pure tone is the number of full oscillations that occur each second. For example, since there are 4 full oscillations occurring in the duration .0091 second of the graph, the frequency is (4 cycles/.0091 second) = 440 cycles

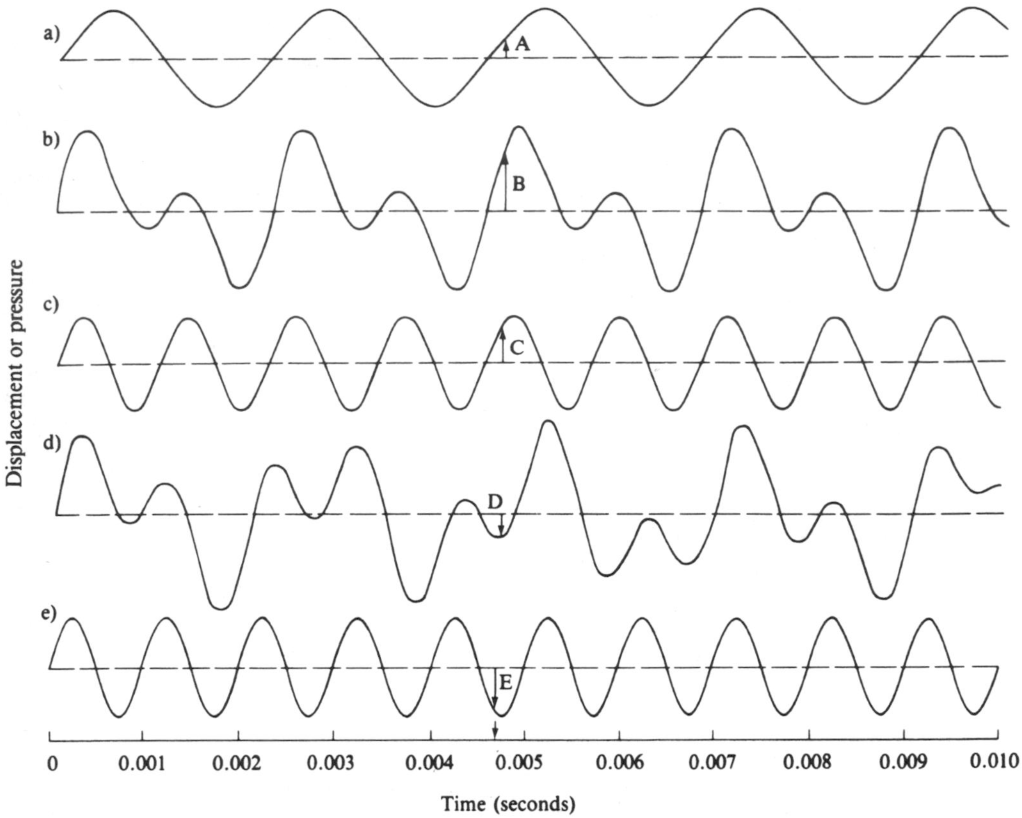

Fig. I

per second (cps or Hertz, abbrev. Hz). The approximate range of frequencies to which the human ear is sensitive, 20 to 20,000 cps, defines the frequencies of interest in musical acoustics. As is discussed more fully below, the frequency of a pure tone determines its *pitch, higher frequencies corresponding to higher pitches. The frequency 440 cps corresponds to the "concert A" produced when the tines of the tuning fork vibrate back and forth 440 times each second. Doubling frequency raises the pitch by one octave. The maximum displacement or pressure of the vibration, as recorded on the vertical axis of the graph, is the amplitude of the vibration and represents the amount of energy in the vibrating system and available to be transmitted to the surrounding medium. The amount of energy reaching any point in the surrounding medium is the intensity of the sound at that point. An increase in the intensity of a sound is heard as an increase in loudness. The relationship between intensity and perceived loudness is rather more complex than that between frequency and pitch.

I. *The representation of complex sounds and its relation to pitch.* Almost all musical sounds have

a much more complex graph than Fig. 1a. Figs. 1b and 1d represent two examples of more complicated forms. An important mathematical theorem (Fourier's theorem) states that any such graph may be represented as the superposition or sum of sine waves such as 1a. In fact, 1b is obtained by adding together 1a and 1c. For example, the vertical displacement B at the time 0.0047 second is the algebraic sum of the displacements A and C at that same time. Similarly, the displacement D is the sum of A and E. Quite generally, any complex musical tone may be represented as the sum of a number of pure tones of different frequencies and different amplitudes. If one strikes a metallic lampshade or pan lid and listens carefully, one can hear at least a couple of the distinct frequencies that make up the full complex tone. These different components, which together make up the sound produced by the flute, violin, or cymbal, are called partials, and their individual frequencies are called partial frequencies. For many practical purposes, the complete specification of a continuously sounding musical tone, and to a fair approximation decaying tones as well, requires only the enumeration of the frequencies and amplitudes (strengths) of the different partials. The partial frequencies are typically listed in order, the lowest first, as a series of numbers f_1, f_2, f_3, ... The sound represented by graph 1b has partial frequencies $f_1 = 440$ and $f_2 = 880$ cps; 1d reflects partials with frequencies $f_1 = 440$ and $f_2 = 573$ cps.

For many musical sounds, specifically those that are continuously produced by a single source such as the bowed violin, trumpet, oboe, or voice, a special relationship exists among the partial frequencies: they are all equal to an integer times a single frequency, called the fundamental. The partial frequencies f_1, f_2, f_3, ... of the A played by the oboist will be 440, 880, 1320, 1760, ... cps, or $1f_1$, $2f_1$, $3f_1$, $4f_1$, ... , where $f_1 = 440$ cps. A convenient statement of the relationship, assuming none of the partial frequencies in the simple sequence happens to be missing, is that the frequency of the nth partial is n times the frequency of the fundamental. A set of frequencies related to one another in this way is called a harmonic set. Continuously produced musical tones are characterized by a harmonic set of partial frequencies.

The pitch of such a musical tone is well defined (identifiable without difficulty by a musician) and is related to the frequency of the fundamental of the harmonic set making up that tone. Although the frequencies making up the complex oboe tone when it is playing a "concert A" are 440, 880, 1320, ... cps, the pitch is unambiguously concert A or 440 cps. Equally important in the composition of the tone nevertheless are the 880 cps partial (pitch an octave higher), the 1320 cps partial (pitch an octave and a fifth higher), etc. The tone is heard as a single entity, not as a chord corresponding to the various individual partials. So important is the psychological identification of the pitch of a tone with the fundamental of the harmonic set of partials making up that tone that the pitch remains identified with the fundamental even if the partial at the fundamental happens to be completely absent from the tone.

Musical sounds that are percussively produced, such as the tones of the bell, piano, cymbal, guitar, marimba, pizzicato violin, and drum, will have partial frequencies that are not harmonic sets. In some instances, for example the middle range of the piano or the guitar, the partial frequencies so nearly approximate a harmonic set that they may be considered harmonic, and the remarks of the preceding paragraphs are relevant; in particular, the pitch of such sounds is well defined. At the other extreme are the tones of the cymbal, gong, and many drums, in which there is a rich set of partials with no simple relationship among the partial frequencies and for which there is no defined pitch. Intermediate are some of the instruments of the percussion section, e.g., marimba, timpani, and some bells, which are constructed so that several of the lowest partial frequencies are harmonically related. The harmonically related partials establish a well-defined pitch, while additional partials, which are not harmonically related to the pitch, contribute importantly to the tone quality of the instrument. There are also examples such as the bass strings on small pianos, from which one hopes to hear a defined pitch but for which the partial frequencies are so far from harmonic that no meaningful pitch is established.

Figs. 1b and 1d illustrate the contrast between the wave forms characteristic of continuously produced sound and those of percussively produced sound. The continuously produced sound, Fig. 1b, is the sum of two pure tones, or partials, of frequency 440 and 880 cps (Fig. 1a plus Fig. 1c), which are the first two members of a harmonic set; the wave form shows a clear pattern that repeats at the fundamental frequency of the partials that combine to make the full tone. The percussively produced sound of Fig. 1d is the sum of two partials (Figs. 1a and 1e) with frequencies 440 and 573 cps, frequencies not harmonically related to one another. The wave form now does not show a repeating pattern, a consequence of the anharmonic relation between the two partials.

II. *Sound production.* The first essential in the sound production by a musical instrument is the vibration of some part of the instrument. The simplest mechanisms to excite such motion are those used in the percussion instruments, plucking or hammering, for which the excitation is of short duration. The subsequent motion of the vibrating part is usually quite complex, but may be represented as the superposition or sum of many simple motions all taking place concurrently. Figs. 2a, b, and c represent some of the simple kinds of motion, or normal modes of motion, possible for a stretched string. The solid and dotted lines are meant to represent the extremes of the motion. Any point on the string oscillates back and forth between the extremes in a fashion similar to the graph of Fig. 1a. Each normal mode of motion, i.e., each pattern of Fig. 2, has associated with it a characteristic frequency. For the "ideal" stretched string, these frequencies happen to form a harmonic set. For modes other than the first, such a string vibrates in segments of equal length termed loops; the stationary points between loops are termed nodes. A drumhead, a straight wooden bar, or a cymbal also has a series of normal modes of vibration, or "ways in which it can vibrate," but in these examples the frequencies of the normal modes are not harmonically related. When an instrument is percussively excited, many normal modes of the instrument are set into vibration, and the partial frequencies of the tone produced by the instrument are just the frequencies characteristic of the normal modes of motion of the instrument.

The excitation of vibrations in instruments such

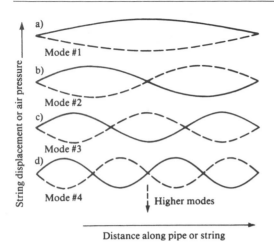

Fig. 2

as the winds and the bowed strings is a continuous rather than an instantaneous process and is more complicated to describe. Essential is some device to convert continuous motion, such as airflow from the lungs or the movement of a bow, into the oscillatory motion of an air column or a string. As noted already, the partial frequencies of the sound produced by such an instrument will be a harmonic set of frequencies, and although the partials are often approximately equal to the normal mode frequencies of the instrument, that relationship is less direct than in the case of the percussively produced sound.

Understanding the determining factors in the pitch produced by an instrument requires a knowledge of the natural or normal-mode frequencies of the pitch-determining element, often a stretched string or an air column. As noted above, the natural modes of vibration of an ideal stretched string, represented schematically in Fig. 2, have frequencies that are a harmonic set, $f_n = nf_1$, with a fundamental frequency given by the following:

$$f_1 = \sqrt{(\text{tension})/(\text{mass per unit length})}/2(\text{length})$$

This equation is used intuitively by all string players, who tune their instruments by increasing the tension in the strings to raise the frequency f_1 and hence the pitch. The strings intended to sound at higher pitch are thinner and hence have smaller mass per unit length. The effective length of a string is shortened, and the pitch raised, by stopping the string against the fingerboard. The equation gives quantitative expression to these principles.

In a wind instrument, the vibration is an oscillatory motion of the air along the instrument pipe. For the lowest mode of oscillation in the flute, for example, the air flows alternately from both ends toward the middle of the instrument and back toward the ends.

At the middle, the air is not moving, but the pressure rises as the air flows in from both ends, then falls as the air flows away. There are large pressure oscillations at the center of the instrument. Fig. 2a may in fact be interpreted schematically as representing the pressure variation along the flute, the solid line corresponding to the time when the pressure at the center is maximum, the dotted line a half cycle later when some of the air has moved out of the ends, leaving decreased pressure at the center. Similarly, Figs. 2b and c may be interpreted as the pressure variations for the second and third modes of oscillation of the air column of the flute. Again, as in the case of the string, a formula something like the one above is appropriate to describe the dependence of the fundamental-mode frequency upon the physical parameters of the instrument; and again the higher mode frequencies are (approximately) members of the harmonic set based upon the fundamental, although for certain instruments only the odd-numbered harmonics are present. The proportionality of the fundamental frequency to the inverse of the effective length of the instrument is again essential to the idea of controlling the sounding pitch by varying, in one way or another, the effective length of the air column.

For most percussion instruments, stretched membranes, metal plates or bars, bells, etc., the formulas giving the natural frequencies are more complicated than those for strings or air columns.

A second essential feature of musical instruments is a mechanism to transfer the energy of the vibrations within the instrument to the surrounding air. This occurs naturally with an instrument such as a drum, in which the vibrations are set up in the drumhead, which provides a large moving area that is relatively efficient in forcing vibrational motion into the surrounding air. By contrast, a vibrating string, rigidly fixed at each end, is extremely inefficient in transferring the energy to the surrounding air. The purpose of the bridge and soundboard of the piano, or of the bridge and thin wooden body of the violin or guitar, is to provide the needed transfer. The bridge of the violin transfers the vibrational energy to the belly and via the sound post to the back; the motion of these front and back plates transfers the sound to the surrounding air. The efficiency of energy transfer and its variation with the frequency of vibration depend critically upon the thickness and shape of the walls of the stringed instrument or the construction of the piano or harpsichord soundboard. These parts of the instrument are important in determining such properties of the instrument as tone quality, ease of playing, and carrying power.

III. *Tone quality.* The timbre or tone quality of an instrument is determined by many properties of the sound. Probably the most important properties—certainly the ones the scientist can most easily measure, characterize, and discuss—are the number, frequencies, and amplitudes of the various partials. One important characteristic of timbre is the number of partials that make up the tone. The tone of the flute, for example, has very few partials, while that of the violin has many.

The characteristic sound of some instruments results from the relative intensities of the partials. The clarinet, played in the low register, has strong odd-numbered partials and weak even ones. In the electronic synthesis of instrumental sounds, the first step in imitating a clarinet is to assure this alternation in the relative amplitudes of successive partials.

A special quality may also be provided by one or several relatively narrow ranges of frequency in which the coupling from the instrument to the surrounding air is stronger than at other frequencies. These ranges in frequency are referred to as formants. In the human voice, the several formant frequencies are varied by adjusting the shape of the vocal tract, and in speaking, the distinction among the various vowel sounds is made by appropriate subconscious adjustment or tuning of the various formant frequencies. In the singing voice these same adjustments are heard not only as differences among vowel sounds but also as changes in vocal timbre or tone quality.

Nevertheless, the specification of frequencies and relative amplitudes, though easy to measure, is by no means the only clue used by the ear and brain in identifying instrumental sounds. The way in which tones start and end in different instruments is characteristic and important in the identification of those instruments. The way in which a tone starts and reaches a steady state is its attack. The way in which a tone ends or dies away is its decay. The combination of characteristics defining the attack, steady state, and decay of a tone taken together constitute its envelope. The envelope, attack, and decay controls on an electronic synthesizer regulate these essential transient characteristics of the synthesized tones.

(2) The characteristics of a physical space affecting the perception of sound within it. The two most important and relevant physical phenomena are the reflection of sound and the finite speed of propagation of sound. The phenomenon of reflection implies that in the concert hall the sound is heard both as it comes directly, by line of sight so to speak, from the performer and in addition as it propagates to a side wall or ceiling and is reflected to the listener from those surfaces. There are many paths, a direct one and ones involving one, two, or more reflections from walls and ceilings, by which any feature of the musical performance reaches the ear. Because of the finite speed of sound, about 350 meters per second, and because the various paths by which the sound reaches the ear involve different distances, each feature of the music in fact reaches the ear many times in close succession. A "live" room is one in which the reflected sound is very apparent, though not as a series of discrete echoes, and contributes in a major way to the total sound heard. A "dead" room is one in which most of the sound reaching the surfaces of the room is absorbed, perhaps by carpeting, drapes, or sound-absorbing ceiling tiles, and the reflected sound is only a minor contributor, compared with the direct sound, to the perceived sound. Other considerations in architectural acoustics include freedom from extraneous noise, even distribution of sound throughout the hall, good balance between high and low frequencies, and a sense of acoustic intimacy.

Action. (1) In keyboard instruments, the mechanism that causes a string or pipe to sound when a key is depressed [see Piano, Organ, Harpsichord, Clavichord]. (2) In the *harp, the mechanism that alters the pitch of strings when a pedal is depressed.

Act tune. A composition played between acts of an opera or play. See also *Entr'acte.*

Actus musicus [Lat.]. In German Protestant music of the late 17th and early 18th centuries, a dramatic vocal work on a Biblical subject. Like the less elaborate *historia,* it is an antecedent of the German Protestant *oratorio.

Actus tragicus. Bach's Cantata no. 106, *Gottes Zeit ist die allerbeste Zeit* (God's Time Is Best), perhaps composed in Mühlhausen in 1707 and performed at the funeral of his mother's uncle.

Acuff, Roy (Claxton) (b. Maynardville, Tenn., 15 Sept. 1903; d. Nashville, 24 Nov. 1992). Country-and-western singer, fiddler, songwriter, and publisher. His performances of "The Wabash Cannon Ball" and "The Great Speckled Bird" were extremely popular, as was his own song "Precious Jewel."

Adagietto [It., diminutive of *adagio*]. (1) A tempo slightly faster than *adagio. (2) A movement in a slow tempo, but shorter or less somber in character than the typical *adagio.

Adagio [It.]. (1) A slow tempo, often said to be slower than *andante* but not as slow as *largo.* Some writers of the 18th and 19th centuries, however, regarded the term as designating the slowest of all tempos, though the term itself could be modified to call for still slower tempos, e.g., *adagissimo.* In the 18th century, the term sometimes implied the need for ornamentation. See also Performance marks. (2) A composition with a slow tempo (perhaps, but not necessarily, specified by the term *adagio* itself), especially the slow movement of a sonata, symphony, or similar multimovement work.

Adagissimo [It.]. Extremely slow. See also *Adagio* (1).

Adam, Adolphe (Charles) (b. Paris, 24 July 1803; d. there, 3 May 1856). Composer. Entered the Paris Conservatory and studied organ with Benoist, counterpoint with Reicha, and composition with Boieldieu, his principal mentor. Professor of composition there from 1849. Composed more than 50 operas and over a dozen ballets. Now best known for his ballets *Giselle, ou Les Wilis* and *Le corsaire* (1856) and the Christmas carol "Cantique de Noël" ("O Holy Night").

Adam von Fulda (b. Fulda, ca. 1445; d. Wittenberg, 1505). Composer and theorist. At first a Benedictine, he married and entered the service of Frederick the Wise of Saxony in 1490. Wrote a treatise titled *De musica* (1490). Composed a Mass, hymns, antiphons, and other sacred music, and 3 secular songs.

Adam de la Halle [Adan le Bossu, Adan le Boscu d'Arras] (b. Arras, 1245–50; d. Naples, 1285–88? or England, after 1306?). Trouvère poet and composer. In the late 1270s went to Italy in the service of Robert II, Count of Artois, and there entered the service of Robert's uncle Charles of Anjou (d. 1285). Works include monophonic chansons and *jeux-partis;* polyphonic *rondeaux* and motets; and 3 plays, of which one, a pastoral work titled *Le jeu de Robin et de Marion,* makes considerable use of music.

Ádám, Jenő (b. Szigetszentmiklós, 12 Dec. 1896; d. Budapest, 15 May 1982). Composer, conductor, and educator. Studied composition with Kodály in Budapest and conducting with Weingartner in Basel. Conductor and teacher at the Academy of Music in Budapest (1929–59). Collaborated with Kodály in the reform of music education in Hungary. Works include 2 operas, orchestral works, choral works (some with orchestra); 2 string quartets and other chamber music; numerous arrangements of folk songs.

Adam of St. Victor (d. St. Victor, Paris, late 1140s). Poet and composer. Probably identical with Adam Precentor, canon of the Cathedral of Notre Dame of Paris in the early 12th century; canon of and resident at the Abbey of St. Victor from 1133 or shortly thereafter. Wrote many *sequences.

Adamis, Michael (b. Piraeus, Greece, 19 May 1929). Composer and musicologist. Studied Byzantine chant and composition (with Papaioannou) in Greece and then at Brandeis Univ. (1962–65). At Pierce College, Athens, from 1968. Early works employ twelve-tone techniques; more recent ones often draw on Byzantine chant and include a *Byzantine Passion* (1967); electronic works include music for classical Greek and other plays.

Adams, John (Coolidge) (b. Worcester, Mass., 15 Feb. 1947). Composer, clarinetist, and conductor. Studied composition at Harvard with Kirchner, Kim, and Sessions (1965–71). On the faculty of the San Francisco Conservatory and director of the New Music Ensemble there, 1972–82; composer in residence with the San Francisco Symphony, 1982–85. Winner of the 1995 Grawemeyer Award for his violin concerto (1993). Has employed a wide variety of media, including electronics and video, and often makes repetitive use of relatively simple tonal materials. Works include operas (*Nixon in China,* 1987; *The Death of Klinghoffer,* 1991); orchestral music (*Shaker Loops, for 7 Strings,* 1978; *Harmonielehre,* 1985; *Fearful Symmetries,* 1988; *Short Ride in a Fast Machine,* 1986); other instrumental (*Light over Water* [*Symphony for Brass and Synthesizers*], 1983); choral (*Harmonium,* 1981); songs; piano music.

Added sixth. A sixth added above the root of a triad, or the chord thus produced; thus, f–a–c′–d′. The traditional theory of chord *inversion derived from Rameau requires such a structure to be viewed as the first inversion of a *seventh chord (the root in this example being d, making the chord a ii^7 in the context of C major and implying a resolution to the dominant). But Rameau himself observed that the chord can also function as an embellished triad (usually, as in this example in C major, the subdominant) and thus resolve in different ways. Such chords are often used in jazz and popular music as embellished triads and are specified by the letter indicating the root of the triad followed by the arabic numeral 6 (e.g., F6), as distinct from what is termed the minor seventh chord (specified, in the example above, Dm7).

Adderley, Cannonball [Julian Edwin] (b. Tampa, 15 Sept. 1928; d. Gary, Ind., 8 Aug. 1975). Jazz alto saxophonist and leader of small groups. In 1955 left a career as a high school music teacher to join Oscar Pettiford's bop group in New York. After leading a quintet (1956–57) with his brother Nat (b. 1931), a cornetist, he joined Miles Davis's sextet (1957–59). From 1959 to 1975 led groups with Nat.

Addinsell, Richard (Stewart) (b. London, 13 Jan. 1904; d. there, 14 Nov. 1977). Composer. Studied at the Royal College of Music and in Berlin and Vienna. Best known for his *Warsaw Concerto,* a work for piano and orchestra from the film *Dangerous Moonlight* (1941, released in the U.S. as *Suicide Squadron*). Other film scores include *Goodbye, Mr. Chips* (1939), *Blithe Spirit* (1945), *A Tale of Two Cities* (1958), *The Roman Spring of Mrs. Stone* (1961), and *The Waltz of the Toreadors* (1962).

Addison, John (b. Chobham, Surrey, 16 Mar. 1920). Composer. Studied at the Royal College of Music (composition with Gordon Jacob; oboe, Leon Goossens; clarinet, Frederick Thurston) and was a member of its staff from 1951 until 1958. His more than 60 film scores include *A Taste of Honey* (1961), *Tom Jones* (1963), *The Loved One* (1965), *Torn Curtain* (1966), *The Charge of the Light Brigade* (1968), *Sleuth* (1972), and *The Seven Per Cent Solution* (1976).

Additional accompaniment. The reworking of the accompaniments of older vocal works to fit them to later concepts of sonority and orchestration. The practice began with the continued performance of works by Handel in the changed musical conditions of the late 18th century. Mozart rescored, sometimes radically altering, *Messiah, Alexander's Feast, Acis and Galatea,* and the *Ode for St. Cecilia's Day.* His *Messiah* became the basis for several 19th-century versions.

Addolorato [It.]. Pained, afflicted.

Adelaide. A song by Beethoven, op. 46 (1794–95), to a poem by Friedrich von Matthisson.

Adélaïde Concerto. A Concerto in D major for violin and orchestra attributed to Mozart, K. Anhang 294a. The work exists in a simple two-stave sketch, supposedly written in 1766, and dedicated to the French Princess Adélaïde. Although a letter exists in which Mozart dedicates such a work to the Princess, it is almost certainly not this concerto. The sketch was completed and published by Marius Casadesus in 1933.

Adeste fideles [Lat.]. A hymn often sung in the English translation beginning "O come, all ye faithful" by Frederick Oakeley (1802–80). The Latin text and the well-known tune have been dated ca. 1740 and attributed to John Francis Wade (d. 1786). It was published in 1751 and used thereafter in the Portuguese Embassy Chapel in London, whence the title "Portuguese Hymn" by which it is also known.

Adieux, Les [Fr.]. Beethoven's Piano Sonata no. 26 in E♭ major op. 81a (1809–10), titled *Das Lebewohl, Abwesenheit und Wiedersehn* and subtitled *Les adieux, l'absence, et le retour* (The Farewell, Absence, and Return). It was inspired by the departure from Vienna of Beethoven's patron the Archduke Rudolph, to whom the work is dedicated.

Adler, Kurt Herbert (b. Vienna, 2 Apr. 1905; d. Ross, Calif., 9 Feb. 1988). Conductor and administrator. Studied at the conservatory and the university in Vienna. Conducted in Austria, Germany, Italy, and elsewhere; assisted Toscanini in Salzburg in 1936; conducted at the Chicago Opera in 1949. At the San Francisco Opera he became chorusmaster in 1943,

artistic director in 1953, and general director in 1956, retiring in 1981.

Adler, Larry [Lawrence Cecil] (b. Baltimore, 10 Feb. 1914). Harmonica player. The first well-known performer of concert music on the harmonica. Milhaud, Vaughan Williams, and Gordon Jacob composed works for him. Blacklisted by militant anticommunists, he was effectively forced to reside and perform in England for a number of years beginning in 1949.

Adler, Peter Herman (b. Jablonec, Czechoslovakia, 2 Dec. 1899; d. Ridgefield, Conn., 2 Oct. 1990). Conductor. Studied at the Prague Conservatory with Fidelio Finke, Vítězslav Novák, and Alexander von Zemlinsky. Emigrated to the U.S. in the late 1930s. Artistic director of the NBC Opera Company (commissioned *Amahl and the Night Visitors*), 1949–59; music director of the Baltimore Symphony, 1959–68; music and artistic director of National Educational Television from 1969; director of the American Opera Center at Juilliard, 1973–81.

Adler, Richard (b. New York, 3 Aug. 1921). Composer and producer of musicals. Graduated from the Univ. of North Carolina in 1943. His most successful works were *Pajama Game* (1954) and *Damn Yankees* (1955), both in collaboration with Jerry Ross (1926–55).

Adler, Samuel (Hans) (b. Mannheim, 4 Mar. 1928). Composer and conductor. In 1939 emigrated with his family to the U.S.; studied composition in Boston with Herbert Fromm (1943–47); for the B.Mus. at Boston Univ. with Hugo Norden, Karl Geiringer, and Paul Pisk; at Harvard (1948–50) with Piston, Thompson, and Hindemith; at Tanglewood (1949, 1950) with Copland and Koussevitzky. Director of music at Temple Emanu-El in Dallas (1953–56); faculty member, North Texas State Univ. (1957–66) and the Eastman School (from 1966). Works include operas; symphonies, concertos, and other orchestral works; several synagogue services and other choral music; much chamber music, including 6 string quartets; songs; piano pieces.

Adlgasser, Anton Cajetan (b. Inzell, Bavaria, 1 Oct. 1729; d. Salzburg, 22 Dec. 1777). Composer and organist. Studied with Eberlin in Salzburg, succeeded him as court and cathedral organist there in 1750. After his death in 1777, was succeeded as cathedral organist by Mozart, who praised him as a master of counterpoint. He collaborated with Mozart and Michael Haydn on the oratorio *Die Schuldigkeit* (1767). Composed oratorios, much Latin church music, symphonies, organ music.

Ad libitum [Lat.]. At the pleasure of the performer. The phrase may indicate that a part for voice or an instrument may be omitted (in contrast to *obbli-*

gato); that the performer is to improvise either orna-ments or altogether new material such as a *cadenza; or that the tempo may be varied.

Adriana Lecouvreur. Opera in four acts by Francesco Cilea (libretto by Arturo Colautti after Eugène Scribe and Ernest Legouvé), produced in Milan in 1902. Setting: Paris, 1730, the year of the death of the celebrated French actress of this name.

A due [It.]. See *Due*.

Aeolian, aeolian mode. See Mode.

Aeolian harp. A zither whose strings are set in motion by the wind. A variable number of strings of varying thickness but equal length are stretched over a sound box (usually rectangular and as much as a meter or more in length) and tuned to the same fundamental pitch. The wind generates different harmonics in each string, producing a chord whose texture changes as the wind rises and falls. Instruments of this type were known in antiquity. It was popular in late 18th- and early 19th-century Europe and was a frequent subject of Romantic literature. See also Anémocorde.

Aeoline. A free-reed keyboard instrument invented by Bernhard Eschenbach ca. 1810. An antecedent of the *harmonium, it incorporated knee-operated bellows and permitted variations in loudness.

Aeolodicon. Any of several free-reed keyboard instruments developed from the *aeoline.

Aeolo melodicon. A reed organ patented in Warsaw in 1824 with tubes attached to the reeds and permitting variations in loudness.

Aeolopantalon. An instrument combining the *aeolo melodicon and the piano, patented in Warsaw in 1824, and on which Chopin performed in 1825.

Aequal [Lat.], **Aequalstimmen** [Ger.]. See *Equale;* Equal voices.

Aerophon. See Aerophor.

Aerophone. An instrument in which a column of air is the primary vibrating system. In most cases the player sets the air in motion by blowing. There are three main categories of aerophone: *flutes, in which the turbulence produced by blowing across a sharp edge sets the air column in motion; lip-vibrated aerophones (primarily *brass instruments), in which the air is set in motion by the vibration of the player's lips; reedpipes (most *woodwinds), in which air is set in motion by a vibrating *reed. In addition there are free aerophones, in which the vibrating air is not confined to a column (e.g., the *accordion, *bull-roarer, *mouth organ, *harmonium) or in which the

column serves merely as a *resonator (e.g., the *sheng). See also Instrument.

Aerophor. A device permitting the player of a wind instrument to sustain a tone indefinitely. A foot-operated bellows pumps air to the player's mouth through a tube, thus maintaining air pressure to the instrument while allowing breathing through the nose. Invented ca. 1912 by Bernhard Samuel, it was prescribed by Richard Strauss (incorrectly as an "aerophon") in his *Alpensinfonie*.

Aevia. An abbreviation for *alleluia consisting of its vowels (*v* representing *u*), sometimes used in manuscripts of liturgical chant. See also *Euouae*.

Affabile [It.]. Affable, pleasing.

Affannato, affanoso [It.]. Breathless, anxious, excited.

Affections (affects), doctrine of [Ger. *Affektenlehre*]. The belief, widely held in the 17th and early 18th centuries, that the principal aim of music is to arouse the passions or affections (love, hate, joy, anger, fear, etc., conceived as rationalized, discrete, and relatively static states). By the later 17th century, the view also included the notion that a composition (or at least a single movement or major section of a larger work) should have a unity of affection.

Affektenlehre [Ger.]. See Affections, doctrine of.

Affetto [It., pl. *affetti*]. An affection or passion such as, in the view of 16th-, 17th-, and 18th-century writers, could be aroused or moved by music. See Affections, doctrine of.

Affettuoso [It.]. Affectionate, tender.

Affrettando [It.]. Hurrying.

Africaine, L' [Fr., The African Woman]. Opera in five acts by Meyerbeer (libretto by Eugène Scribe; final revisions to libretto following Scribe's death in 1861 and to music following Meyerbeer's death in 1864 by François-Joseph Fétis), produced in Paris in 1865. Setting: Lisbon and Madagascar at the end of the 15th century.

Afro-Cuban jazz. A jazz style that flourished first in the late 1940s combining elements of *bebop with the rhythms and percussion instruments of Afro-Cuban popular music such as the *mambo, especially as arranged for big bands. The Latin American musicians who most directly inspired it were trumpeter Mario Bauza, percussionist Chano Pozo, and bandleader Frank Grillo ("Machito"). Dizzy Gillespie was its most prominent non-Latin exponent, and Charlie Parker also played some music of this type.

Afterbeat. A beat falling after a metrically stronger beat, especially the second and fourth quarter notes in a measure of 4/4 and, by extension, the second and fourth eighth notes in a measure of 2/4.

After-dance. The second of a pair of dances, in a fast tempo, danced with skips, hops, and leaps that contrast with the slow, elegant steps of the preceding dance [see also *Nachtanz*]. As a rule, the melodic or the harmonic materials or both of the first dance are used in the second, but in a different meter. The earliest extant examples are in a 14th-century manuscript. In the 15th century, the most common pairings were the *bassadanza* with the *saltarello* in Italy, the *basse danse* with the *pas de Brabant* in France, and the *bassadanza* with the *alta* in Spain. In the 16th and 17th centuries, it was the *pavana* and *saltarello*, the *pass'e mezo* and *saltarello*, the *pavana* and *gagliarda*, and the *pass'e mezo* and *gagliarda* that were most commonly paired.

Afternoon of a Faun. See *Prelude to "The Afternoon of a Faun."*

Agazzari, Agostino (b. Siena, 2 Dec. 1578; d. there, 10 Apr. 1640). Composer and organist. Worked in Germany; then *maestro di cappella* at the German College in Rome (1602–3) and at the Jesuit Roman Seminary (1606); returned in 1607 to Siena, where he was organist and then *maestro di cappella* at the cathedral until his death. Published an early and widely influential treatise on thoroughbass, *Del sonare sopra 'l basso* (Siena, 1607).

Agende [Ger.]. In the German Protestant (Evangelical) Church, the formularies for divine service; synonymous with *Kirchenordnung, Kirchenamt.*

Ager, Milton (b. Chicago, 6 Oct. 1893; d. Inglewood, Calif., 6 May 1979). Composer of popular music. At first, pianist in silent film theaters and in vaudeville; composed music for films and numerous songs, including "Happy Days Are Here Again" (1930), "Ain't She Sweet?" (1927), and "Hard-Hearted Hannah" (1924).

Agevole [It.]. Easy, unconstrained.

Aggradevole [It.]. Pleasing.

Agiato, agiatamente [It.]. Sedate, with ease.

Agile, agilmente [It.]. Agile, with agility.

Agitato [It.]. Agitated.

Agnesi, Maria Teresa (b. Milan, 17 Oct. 1720; d. there, 19 Jan. 1795). She composed several operas (some to her own librettos) that were performed in Milan, Naples, and Venice; arias; keyboard concertos; keyboard pieces.

Agnus Dei [Lat., Lamb of God]. The fifth item of the *Ordinary of the Roman *Mass, the received form consisting of three acclamations, each beginning "Agnus Dei" and derived from John 1:29. It was apparently added to the Mass late in the 7th century as a chant associated with the breaking of the communion bread. The Agnus Dei has been widely used, though not prescribed, in the Anglican service of Holy Communion. For the complete text with translation, see Mass.

Agogic. (1) An agogic *accent is one created by duration rather than by loudness or metrical position. (2) In the plural form, *agogics,* those aspects of performance related to duration, and by extension tempo, in the way that *dynamics* are related to loudness; thus, the use of *rubato or other departures from strictly notated durations.

Agon [Gr., contest]. A ballet by Stravinsky (choreography by George Balanchine) composed in 1953–54 and 1956–57, and first produced in New York in 1957.

Agostini, Paolo (b. Vallerano, ca. 1583; d. Rome, 3 Oct. 1629). Composer and organist. Studied in Rome with Nanino; *maestro di cappella* of the Cappella Giulia at St. Peter's from 1626 until his death. Composed much Latin church music, some for elaborate polychoral forces.

Agréments [Fr.]. Ornaments introduced in French music of the 17th century and soon widely used throughout Europe. They were generally indicated by stenographic signs or notes in small type. See Ornamentation.

Agricola, Alexander (b. 1446?; d. Valladolid, Aug. 1506). Composer and singer. Described in his epitaph as Belgian and in Italian documents as "alemanno." Sometime after 1476 joined the French royal chapel; singer at the cathedral in Florence, 1491–92. Returned to the French court in 1492; in 1500 entered the service of Philip the Fair, Duke of Burgundy and King of Castile, with whom he traveled through France and, on two occasions, to Spain. Composed Latin church music; over 40 French chansons.

Agricola, Johann Friedrich (b. Dobitschen, Saxe-Altenburg, 4 Jan. 1720; d. Berlin, 2 Dec. 1774). Composer, organist, singing teacher, and writer on music. Studied with Bach in Leipzig and later with Quantz in Berlin; court composer to Frederick the Great (1751); in 1759 succeeded Graun as director of the royal opera. Took up the cause of Italian music against Marpurg's advocacy of French taste. Composed 11 Italian operas or other dramatic works produced in Potsdam and Berlin; German sacred oratorios and cantatas; many songs in the style of the First Berlin School; keyboard pieces; chorale preludes for organ.

Agricola, Martin [Martin Sore] (b. Schwiebus, 6 Jan. 1486; d. Magdeburg, 10 June 1556). Theorist and composer. Music teacher in Magdeburg in 1519 and choirmaster of the Lutheran Latin school there from 1525 or 1527. His writings include *Musica instrumentalis deudsch* (Wittenberg, 1529). Composed Latin motets; German Protestant songs for 2 and 3 voices; over 50 3- and 4-voice instrumental pieces.

Aguiari [Agujari], **Lucrezia** ["La bastardina"] (b. Ferrara, 1743; d. Parma, 18 May 1783). Singer. Allegedly a foundling; sang throughout Italy and, in 1775, in London. In the mid-1760s settled in Parma, where she met the composer Giuseppe Colla, to whose works she devoted her singing career almost entirely after 1769. Leopold and W. A. Mozart wrote of the remarkable range and flexibility of her voice.

Aguilera de Heredia, Sebastián (b. Zaragoza, bapt. 15 Aug. 1561; d. there, 16 Dec. 1627). Composer. Organist at Huesca Cathedral from 1585 to 1603; then chief organist at the Cathedral of La Seo, Zaragoza, until his death. Wrote sacred music for organ and for choir.

Aguinaldo [Sp.]. A traditional religious song, most characteristically associated with the Christmas season, found in Iberia and in several countries of Latin America.

Ähnlich [Ger.]. Similar, like.

Aichinger, Gregor (b. Regensburg, 1564–65; d. Augsburg, 20–21 Jan. 1628). Composer. The official organist to the Fugger household and hence of the Church of St. Ulrich, Augsburg, from 1584. Made two trips to Italy, the first (at some time between 1584 and 1588) including study with Giovanni Gabrieli in Venice. Composed mostly sacred vocal works with Latin texts.

Aida. Opera in four acts by Verdi (libretto by Antonio Ghislanzoni from the French prose version by Camille du Locle of a scenario by Auguste Mariette Bey), produced in Cairo in 1871. Setting: Memphis and Thebes during the time of the pharaohs.

Air. A tune, whether vocal or instrumental. In the 16th century in France and England [see Ayre], the term applied essentially to vocal melodies, but its meaning was soon loosened. In opera, airs are distinguished from *recitatives, but in French Baroque style they are more declamatory than Italian *arias. Instrumental operatic excerpts are *airs à jouer* (as against *airs à chanter*), including dances (*airs de mouvement*). Seventeenth-century French serious songs (**airs de cour*) are a separate category from light ones (*airs à boire,* drinking songs). In Baroque suites, the practice of transcribing operatic airs resulted in the use of the title for newly composed tuneful movements that did not fit any dance category.

Air de cour [Fr., court air]. A type of French secular vocal music prominent in the last quarter of the 16th century and the first half of the 17th. The first published collection (1571) contains works for solo voice with lute accompaniment by Adrian Le Roy, who remarks in his preface that such pieces were formerly known as *voix de ville* [see *Vaudeville*]. Pieces for four or five voices predominate in the later 16th century and exist alongside the accompanied solos that predominate in the 17th. They are generally syllabic, homophonic, and without fixed meter, resembling in this respect *musique mesurée*.

Air on the G String. Popular name for the second movement of Bach's Orchestral Suite no. 3 in D major BWV 1068, composed ca. 1729–31. In 1871, August Wilhelmj published an arrangement of the air for violin and piano, transposing it to C major in such a way that the tune could be played solely on the violin's lowest string, the G string.

Ais [Ger.]. A-sharp. See Pitch names.

Aisé [Fr.]. With ease.

Aisis [Ger.]. A-double-sharp. See Pitch names.

Ajouter [Fr.]. To add, e.g., an organ stop.

Akeroyde, Samuel (b. Yorkshire, ca. 1650; d. London, 1706 or later). Composer and violinist. During the 1680s, one of the king's musicians. Composed more than 100 songs, many for plays produced on London stages between 1685 and 1706, including D'Urfey's *Commonwealth of Women* (1685) and *Don Quixote III* (1695).

Akimenko [Yakimenko], **Fyodor Stepanovich** (b. Kharkov, 20 Feb. 1876; d. Paris, 8 Jan. 1945). Composer, pianist, and writer. Studied at the St. Petersburg Conservatory with Rimsky-Korsakov, Lyadov, and Vitols; professor there from 1919 until 1923, after which he moved to Paris. Stravinsky's first composition teacher.

Akiyoshi, Toshiko (b. Dairen, China, 12 Dec. 1929). Jazz composer, pianist, and bandleader of Japanese parentage. After World War II lived in Japan, where Oscar Peterson set up her first bop recording with his rhythm section (1953). Worked with Charlie Mariano and Charles Mingus. With Lew Tabackin she led a big band in Los Angeles (1973–84); from 1985 she led a big band in New York.

Akkord [Ger.]. Chord.

Akutagawa, Yasushi (b. Tokyo, 12 July 1925; d. there, 31 Jan. 1989). Composer. Studied composition with Hashimoto and Ifukube. In 1953 formed, with Ikuma Dan and Toshiro Mayuzumi, the "Group of Three." His music shows the influence of Soviet composers such as Shostakovich and Khachaturian, with whom he established ties during the 1950s and 1960s.

Al [It.]. To the, at the; e.g., *al *fine, al *segno.* See also *All', alla.*

À la, à l' [Fr.]. To the, at the; in the manner of, e.g., *à l'espagnol,* in the Spanish manner.

Alabado, alabanza [Sp.]. A religious song of praise originating in Spain and brought to the New World by Spanish missionaries.

Alain, Marie-Claire (b. St. Germain-en-Laye, 10 Aug. 1926). Organist. Sister of composer and organist Jehan Alain. Studied with Duruflé (harmony) and Dupré (organ) at the Paris Conservatory. Has specialized in music of the 17th and 18th centuries; recorded complete works of her brother Jehan and of J. S. Bach.

Alalá. A type of folk song from the Spanish province of Galicia, examples of which use syllables such as *la-la* and *ai-le-lo-la,* especially as refrains.

A la mi re, Alamire. See Hexachord.

Ālāp, ālāpa(na) [Hin., Skt., Tel.]. An unmetered and unpulsed, improvised prelude or vocalise in Indian music. Broadly speaking, it may include types of pulsed music, but drum accompaniment and meter are now rarely used. An abbreviated *ālāp* (*āocār ālāp*) normally precedes lighter forms of Hindustani instrumental music and performances of *khyāl* in which *ālāp* types of improvisation figure prominently.

Alard, (Jean-) Delphin (b. Bayonne, 8 Mar. 1815; d. Paris, 22 Feb. 1888). Violinist and teacher. Studied at the Paris Conservatory under Habeneck (violin) and Fétis (composition); active as a soloist and in chamber music; professor at the conservatory, 1843–75, where he taught Sarasate. His *École du violon* (1844) was widely used.

Alba [Prov., white (of dawn)], **aube** [Fr.]. In the troubadour and trouvère repertories, a song portraying the parting of two lovers, who, after a secret, often illicit, nocturnal tryst, are awakened at sunrise and lament the too sudden arrival of day. A night watchman—at times the lovers' friend and ally—often plays a significant role. The *Tagelied* (or *Wächterlied*) is the medieval German counterpart.

Albanese, Licia (b. Bari, 22 July 1913). Soprano. Studied voice with Emanuel De Rosa in Bari and

Giuseppina Baldassare-Tedeschi in Milan. Operatic debut 1935 at Parma; both there and in her American debut (1940) played Cio-cio-san in *Madama Butterfly.* Other roles included Mimi, Tosca, Susanna, Donna Anna, Zerlina, Gounod's Marguerite and Massenet's Manon. Verdi's Violetta was perhaps her most famous role.

Albani [Lajeunesse], **(Marie Louise Cécile) Emma** (b. Chambly, near Montreal, 1 Nov. 1847; d. London, 3 Apr. 1930). Soprano. Studied in Paris with Duprez in 1868, then with Lamperti in Milan, and began an opera career in Italy in 1870, taking the name Albani. She sang often in London opera 1872–96 and also in oratorios. Toured widely. Sang Oscar in *Un ballo in maschera* and Amina in *La sonnambula* in her first season, then heavier dramatic roles, including Eva, Desdemona, and Isolde.

Albéniz, Isaac (Manuel Francisco) (b. Camprodón, Lérida, Spain, 29 May 1860; d. Cambô-les-Bains, 18 May 1909). Composer and pianist. Began lessons with Narciso Oliveras at age 5; two years later studied in Paris with Marmontel. In 1869 entered the Madrid Conservatory but soon ran away. Traveled widely; studied with Reinecke in Leipzig; returned to Madrid in 1877 and was given a scholarship to study composition in Brussels with Gevaert and Dupont; also studied piano with Liszt. By 1890 had quit concertizing and studied composition with Dukas and d'Indy. In 1891 started a lucrative operatic collaboration with amateur librettist Francis Money-Coutts (*The Magic Opal,* 1893; *Pepita Jiménez,* 1896). His best-known works are for the piano (*Iberia*) and often evoke Spanish scenes through the use of melodic and rhythmic gestures derived from Spanish folklore.

Albert, Eugen [Eugène] **(Francis Charles) d'** (b. Glasgow, 10 Apr. 1864; d. Riga, 3 Mar. 1932). Pianist and composer. Studied in London with Pauer (piano), Prout, Stainer, and Sullivan, arousing much attention with London concerts in 1880–81; studied with Liszt from 1882. At his peak regarded as one of the principal successors of Liszt. Became director of the Berlin Hochschule für Musik in 1907. Composed 21 operas, including the Italianate verismo *Tiefland* (1903).

Albert, Heinrich (b. Lobenstein, 8 July 1604; d. Königsberg, 6 Oct. 1651). Composer. A musician under Schütz in Dresden (1622); settled in Königsberg around 1630 and was organist at its cathedral. Best known for his 170 songs; also composed dramatic allegories, motets, and many other vocal and instrumental works.

Albert, Stephen (Joel) (b. New York, 6 Feb. 1941; d. Truro, Mass., 27 Dec. 1992). Composer. Studied with Siegmeister (1956–58), Milhaud (1958), Bernard Rogers at Eastman (1958–60), Joseph Castaldo at the Philadelphia Music Academy (1962), and Rochberg (1963). Held positions at the Philadelphia Music Academy (1968–70), Stanford (1970–71), Smith College (1974–76), and Juilliard (1988–1992). Composer-in-residence with the Seattle Symphony and Seattle Opera (beginning 1985). Adopted a highly expressive, neoromantic idiom for which Mahler was a principal inspiration. Much of his music was inspired by literary sources, especially the works of James Joyce: *To Wake the Dead,* soprano and chamber ensemble (1977–78); *RiverRun,* orchestra (1983–84; Pulitzer Prize, 1985).

Albert Herring. Comic opera in three acts by Britten (libretto by Eric Crozier adapted from the short story "Le rosier de Madame Husson" by Guy de Maupassant), produced in Glyndebourne in 1947. Setting: a small market town in East Suffolk, 1900.

Alberti, Domenico (b. Venice, ca. 1710; d. Rome, 1740). Composer and harpsichordist. A nobleman, he studied counterpoint with Antonio Biffi and Antonio Lotti. Praised by Farinelli for his singing. Best known for his two-movement keyboard sonatas, which make use of a familiar arpeggiated accompaniment figure (Alberti bass); also composed 3 operas, arias, and keyboard pieces.

Alberti bass. An accompaniment figure, found frequently in the left hand of 18th-century keyboard music, in which the pitches of three-pitch chords are played successively in the order lowest, highest, middle, highest, as in the accompanying example by Mozart (Sonata in C major K. 545). The figure takes its name from the composer Domenico Alberti (ca. 1710–40), who employed it frequently. The term is sometimes inappropriately extended to refer to any arpeggiated accompaniment figure in the left hand.

Albicastro, Henricus [Weissenburg, Heinrich] (b. probably Switzerland, fl. 1695–1705; d. Netherlands, ca. 1738). Composer. Apparently served in the Spanish War of Succession. Around 1700 in Amsterdam, published a number of his virtuosic works for strings, including concertos and more than 50 sonatas for violin (some with viola or cello) and continuo.

Albinoni, Tomaso (Giovanni) (b. Venice, 8 June 1671; d. there, 17 Jan. 1751). Composer. Born into a wealthy family; perhaps studied with Legrenzi. First attracted attention with his op. 2 (*Sinfonie e concerti a cinque,* 1700) and with a prodigious number of operas, first for Venice, then in other Italian cities including Naples and Florence. In 1722 he was invited to Munich to conduct his *I veri amici* and *Il trionfo dell'amore* as part of a wedding celebration. He appears to have stopped composing around 1740; his last years were spent in Venice. Composed more than 50 works for the theater (*Vespetta e Pimpinone,* 1708?; *Didone abbandonata,* Venice, 1725); the music for most of these is lost. Other works include some 50 *Concerti a cinque* (including opp. 5, 7, 9, and 10); 79 solo and ensemble sonatas; *balletti;* solo cantatas (including the 12 cantatas op. 4); a three-voice Mass; and a Magnificat.

Albisiphone [It. *albisiphon, albisifono*]. A metal *Boehm-system flute of large bore invented in 1910 by Abelardo Albisi of Milan.

Alboni, Marietta [Maria Anna Marzia] (b. Città di Castello, 6 Mar. 1823; d. Ville d'Avray, 23 June 1894). Contralto. Had singing lessons with Rossini in Bologna; made her opera debut there, then appeared all over Europe with great success; toured the U.S. in 1852–53. Retired in 1863 but later sang occasionally in concert. Also sang soprano parts.

Alborada [Sp., dawn]. (1) Music performed at dawn, especially on a festive occasion or to honor an individual, as on a bride's wedding day. Other terms used in various regions of Spain include *alba, albae,* and *albará.* (2) A type of Spanish folk music accompanied by the *dulzaina* (a double-reed instrument) and *tamboril* (drum). Some examples employ 6/8 meter in a way that is perhaps echoed in Ravel's composition for piano *Alborada del gracioso* (The Fool's Dawn Song, 1905) from *Miroirs.*

Albrechtsberger, Johann Georg (b. Klosterneuburg, 3 Feb. 1736; d. Vienna, 7 Mar. 1809). Theorist, organist, and composer. Studied at Melk Abbey (from 1749) and at the Jesuit seminary in Vienna (1754); organist at Raab (from 1755), at Maria Taferl (from 1757), and at Melk (1759–65); assistant at St. Stephen's (1791) in Vienna; Kapellmeister there from 1793 until his death. A master of counterpoint and of the organ; perhaps best known as Beethoven's teacher. Compositions include 300 sacred works and more than 450 instrumental pieces. Also authored treatises.

Albright, William (Hugh) (b. Gary, Ind., 20 Oct. 1944; d. Ann Arbor, 17 Sept. 1998). Composer, pianist, and organist. Studied at the Univ. of Michigan (1963–70) and the Paris Conservatory; teachers included Finney, Bassett, Rochberg, and Messiaen (composition) and Marilyn Mason (organ); faculty member, Univ. of Michigan (from 1970) and associate director of its electronic music studio. His performances and recordings of classical ragtime and his own rag compositions helped spur the revival of the music of Scott Joplin. Works include the opera *The Magic City* (1978); theater and mixed media works; music for chamber ensembles (*Sphaera*, 1988) and band; choral music; piano works (*Piano-agogo*, 1966; *Grand Sonata in Rag*, 1968; *Five Chromatic Dances*, 1976); organ works.

Albumblatt [Ger., album leaf]. A fanciful title in the 19th century for short pieces, usually for piano, of a type once inscribed in autograph albums. The name does not imply any particular character or musical form.

Alceste. Opera in three acts by Gluck (Italian libretto by Raniero de Calzabigi after Euripides) produced in Vienna in 1767. A revised French version (translated by François Louis Gaud le Bland du Roullet) was produced in Paris in 1776. Gluck's dedication to the first edition (1769) sets out his views on the reform of opera. Setting: Thessaly in ancient times.

Aldrich, Henry (b. Westminster, London, bapt. 22 Jan. 1648; d. Oxford, 14 Dec. 1710). Composer and music scholar. Educated at Oxford (from 1662); traveled to Germany, France, and Italy in the 1670s; canon at Christ Church, Oxford (1681), dean of the college (1689), vice-chancellor of Oxford (1692–95). His music collection formed the basis for the Christ Church library. Compositions include services, anthems, and motets; also adapted and translated Italian and Latin works by Byrd, Palestrina, and others.

Aleatory music. Music in which deliberate use is made of chance or indeterminacy; the term chance music is preferred by many composers. The indeterminate aspect may affect the act of composition, the performance, or both. In the first instance, some random process, such as throwing dice (the original meaning of aleatory being "according to the throw of a die"), is used to fix certain compositional decisions: e.g., the choice of pitches or rhythmic values. In the second, the performer (or performers) makes certain compositional decisions in a given realization of a piece: e.g., the number of segments played or the order in which they are played (for which the terms open form and mobile form are sometimes used) or the specific pitches or durations used. Although aleatory music, especially in its more extreme forms, is principally a phenomenon of the later 20th century, precedents are found throughout Western musical history.

The major figure in the evolution of modern aleatory music is John Cage, whose *Music of Changes*, a piano piece composed in 1951, was the first compo-

sition to be largely determined by random procedures.

Alessandri, Felice (b. Rome, 24 Nov. 1747; d. Casinalbo, 15 Aug. 1798). Composer. Studied music in Naples and wrote operas and oratorios for various Italian cities; composed *La moglie fedele* (1768) and *Il re alla caccia* (1769) for London. Shared direction of the Concert spirituel in Paris (1777); singing teacher at the St. Petersburg court; assistant to Reichardt at the Berlin court opera (1789). Works include serious and comic operas as well as sacred and instrumental music.

Alexander Nevsky. Music by Prokofiev for a film directed in 1938 by Sergei Eisenstein. In 1939, Prokofiev reworked it as a cantata for mezzo soprano, chorus, and orchestra with text by himself and Vladimir Lugorsky.

Alexandrov, Alexander Vasilevich (b. Plakhino, district of Riazan, 13 Apr. 1883; d. Berlin, 8 July 1946). Composer, conductor, and teacher. Studied with Glazunov and Lyadov at the St. Petersburg Conservatory and with Vasilenko at the Moscow Conservatory, where he taught from 1918; choral conductor in Tver (1906–9, 1913–16) and later in Moscow (from 1922). In 1928 founded the Soviet Army Song and Dance Ensemble, which achieved international acclaim and which now bears his name. Composed choral songs and patriotic music. His "Hymn of the Bolshevik Party" became, with a new text, the Soviet national anthem.

Alfano, Franco (b. Posilippo, Naples, 8 Mar. 1875; d. San Remo, 27 Oct. 1954). Composer. Studied at the Conservatorio di S. Pietro a Maiella and with Jadassohn in Leipzig; lived in Paris (1899–1905), Milan, and San Remo (1914); taught composition (from 1916) and served as director (1918–23) of the Liceo musicale, Bologna. Subsequently director of the Liceo musicale (later Conservatory) of Turin (1923–39); superintendent of the Teatro massimo, Palermo (1940–42); acting director of the Liceo musicale, Pesaro (1947–50). His opera *Risurrezione* (1902–3) was widely celebrated; also known for completing *Turandot*.

Al fine [It.]. See *Fine*.

Alfvén, Hugo (Emil) (b. Stockholm, 1 May 1872; d. Falun, 8 May 1960). Composer and conductor. Studied at the Stockholm Conservatory; won several scholarships for European study. Director of music at Uppsala Univ. (1910–39). His music was influenced by Wagner and Richard Strauss as well as by Swedish folk music; *Midsommarvaka* (Midsummer Vigil, the first of 3 Swedish Rhapsodies, 1903), for example, embroiders a native melody within an orchestral fabric. Other works include 5 symphonies (no. 4,

Från havsbandet [From the Outskirts of the Archipelago], 1918–19); ballets (*Bergakungen,* 1916–23; *Den förlorade sonen* [The Prodigal Son], 1957); other orchestral works; vocal music; chamber works.

Algarotti, Francesco (b. Venice, 11 Dec. 1712; d. Pisa, 3 May 1764). Poet and music scholar. Studied mathematics and philosophy in Bologna and Rome; met Voltaire in Paris during the 1730s. Wrote, arranged, and translated opera librettos for the court of Frederick II in Berlin (from 1740) and Augustus III in Dresden (1742–47). Returned to Italy (1753) and wrote his influential *Saggio sopra l'opera in musica* (1755), in which he criticized the "abuses" of contemporary Italian opera and held up the operas of Lully and Quinault as models.

Aliquotstimmen [Ger.]. Organ stops sounding intervals above the unison other than the octave (i.e., twelfth, 2 2/3′; seventeenth, 1 3/5′; etc.).

Aliquot string. A *sympathetic string. The terms aliquot stringing and aliquot scaling are applied to pianos (such as those by the firm of Blüthner) that employ such strings or that arrange the strings of the upper register in such a way that the portion of each string between the bridge and the hitch pin will act as a sympathetic string.

Alison, Richard (fl. England, 1592–1606). Composer. Wrote sacred and secular instrumental and vocal works. Provided simple harmonizations and, in some cases, optional instrumental accompaniments for a number of Psalm tunes (mostly from the Sternhold and Hopkins psalter); set some secular poetry similarly. Contributed compositions to Thomas Morley's *First Book of Consort Lessons* (London, 1599; 2nd ed., 1611); various other instrumental pieces survive in prints and in manuscript.

Alkan [Morhange], **(Charles-Henri-) Valentin** (b. Paris, 30 Nov. 1813; d. there, 29 Mar. 1888). Composer and pianist. A child prodigy, entered the Paris Conservatory at 6, studying piano with Zimmermann; published piano music from 1828. A friend of Chopin, he performed in Paris concerts and salons but after 1838 became increasingly reclusive; gave public concerts only in 1844–45, 1853, and 1870, after which he played regularly in public until his death. Nearly all of his music is for solo piano. Earlier works are related to fashionable salon styles; later compositions are more individual, ranging from collections of short pieces and etudes to a Grande Sonata op. 33 (1848) and a long symphony and concerto included in the etudes of op. 39 (1857).

All', alla [It.]. To the, at the; in the manner of. See, e.g., *Ongarese, Ottava, Unisono, Turca, Zingarese.*

Alla breve [It., at the breve]. The *meter indicated with the sign ¢, in which each measure is conceived as consisting of two half notes, each given one beat, rather than the four quarter notes indicated with the sign C. It is thus the equivalent of 2/2 as compared with 4/4. It is sometimes referred to as cut time. In modern practice this implies relatively rapid tempo, as in military marches, which often employ this meter. But its use with respect to tempo varied considerably from the 17th through the 19th century. Historically *alla breve* derives from the system of *proportions, in use in the Middle Ages and Renaissance, in which it indicated that the *tactus* or metrical pulse was to be "at the breve" rather than "at the semibreve" [see Mensural notation]. Thus it represented in theory, as it still does, a diminution of the duration of any note value by one-half, given a fixed tempo or rate of beats, and was known as *tempus imperfectum diminutum* or *proportio dupla.*

Allant [Fr.]. (1) Going, stirring; continuing. (2) *Andante.*

Allargando [It.]. Broadening, becoming slower, sometimes with an accompanying *crescendo.*

Alle [Ger.]. All, *tutti.

Allegramente [It.]. *Allegro.*

Allegretto [It.]. (1) Slightly less fast than *allegro, often implying lighter texture or character as well. See Performance marks. (2) A short piece with the tempo mark *allegro* or *allegretto.*

Allegri, Gregorio (b. Rome, ca. 1582; d. there, 7 Feb. 1652). Composer. A choirboy in Rome (1591–96), studied counterpoint with Nanino (1600–7); tenor soloist at San Luigi dei Francesi (from 1604); sang in cathedrals at Fermo and Tivoli; from 1629 a member of the papal choir. A composer of sacred music, best known for his *Miserere,* probably composed in the 1630s and performed regularly during Holy Week at the papal chapel ever since.

Allegro [It., merry, lively]. (1) Fast. Although the term has been used since the 17th century to indicate a fast or moderately fast tempo and is the single most. widely used term for such a tempo since the 18th century, it continued to be used into the 18th century as an indication of character or mood without respect to tempo. See Performance marks. (2) A movement in a fast or moderately fast tempo, especially the first movement, in *sonata form (whence sonata-allegro), of a sonata, symphony, or similar work.

Allein [Ger.]. Alone.

Alleluia [Lat., fr. Heb. *hallelujah, praise ye the Lord]. (1) An expression of praise to God occurring in Psalms 110-18 (111-13, 115-17) and in the Book of Revelation (19:1, 3, 4, 6), in the latter case as the cry "of a great multitude" in heaven. In *Gregorian chant, it is found in different types of chants especially for the Easter season, which celebrates the resurrection. It is absent from seasons of somber character such as Lent.

(2) In Gregorian chant, the item of the *Proper of the *Mass sung before the reading of the Gospel except in the period from Septuagesima Sunday through Lent to Holy Saturday, when the *tract is sung instead, and in three of the four groups of Ember Days [see Liturgy]. From Saturday after Easter to Friday after Pentecost two alleluias are sung, one substituting for the gradual. Its texts consist of the word alleluia followed by a verse often drawn from the Psalms. Its melodies are *melismatic, and a characteristic feature is the melisma, called the *jubilus*, with which the setting of the word alleluia itself concludes. This melisma often recurs at the end of the verse and may include internal repetitions in various forms. The first part of the alleluia itself is sung by soloists, after which the choir repeats the first part and continues with the *jubilus*. The soloists then sing the verse except for the conclusion, which is sung by the choir, and repeat the alleluia, the concluding *jubilus* again being sung by the choir. The alleluia is thus usually regarded as an example of responsorial *psalmody.

Allemande [Fr., German; It. *alemana, allemanda;* Eng. allemand, almain, alman]. (1) A Renaissance and Baroque dance that was cultivated as an independent instrumental piece ca. 1580-1750. It became the first of the four core movements of the solo *suite. In its mature Baroque form (ca. 1660-1750), its characteristics had more to do with idiomatic instrumental writing than dance rhythms. In solo harpsichord, lute, and viol music, it ordinarily has quadruple meter and binary form, beginning with one or more upbeats and proceeding to cadences on downbeats in phrases of irregular lengths. Its texture is permeated with imitation and *style brisé* figures that obscure a sense of clear-cut melodic phrases; its mood is serious and its tempo moderately slow. The allemande originated in the early or mid-16th century as a "German dance" *(Teutschertanz, bal tedesco).* It was a fast dance in duple meter often followed by a triple-meter *Nachtanz.* It continued to be danced throughout the 17th and 18th centuries.

(2) A dance in triple meter originating in the mid-18th century. It involved the giving of both hands to the partner, from which evolved the American square-dance call. The name was applied loosely to a number of waltzlike dances through the 19th century as an equivalent of "German Dance."

Allen, Henry "Red" [Henry James, Jr.] (b. New Orleans, 7 Jan. 1908; d. New York, 17 Apr. 1967). Jazz trumpeter, singer, and bandleader. Joined King Oliver (1927), worked on Mississippi riverboats (1928-29), then joined Luis Russell (1929-32), Fletcher Henderson (1932, 1933-34), the Mills Blue Rhythm Band (1934-37), and Russell again (1937-40). Second only to Louis Armstrong among contemporary jazz trumpeters, was often cast in the role of accompanist to Armstrong while with Russell in 1929 and 1937-40. From the 1940s led traditional and mainstream jazz combos, holding a long engagement at the Metropole in New York; toured internationally as a soloist during the 1960s.

Allende (Sarón), Pedro Humberto (b. Santiago, Chile, 29 June 1885; d. there, 16 Aug. 1959). Composer. Studied violin and composition at the National Conservatory in Santiago; also studied in France and Spain (1908-10). The first to make recordings of the Mapuche music of Chile's Araucanian Indians, his interest in folk music is reflected in his own compositions; the symphonic poem *La voz de las calles* (1920) incorporates the melodies of city street vendors. Taught composition at the National Conservatory (1930-50). Other works include the opera *La cenicienta* (1948); a symphony (1910) and piano concerto (1945); choral music; chamber music; vocal works.

Allentando, allentamente [It.]. Slowing down.

Alliteration. The use of two or more words in close succession that begin with (or include) the same sound, usually a consonant. It is an important feature of the oldest poetry in all of the Germanic languages (in which context it is known as *Stabreim*) and was taken up by Wagner in imitation of this tradition in his *Der Ring des Nibelungen.*

Allmählich [Ger.]. Gradually.

Allo. [It.]. Abbr. for *allegro.*

All' ottava [It.]. See *Ottava.*

All' unisono [It.]. See Unison.

Almain, alman. In early English sources, the *allemande.

Alma Redemptoris Mater [Lat., Nourishing Mother of the Redeemer]. One of the four *antiphons for the Blessed Virgin Mary. Formerly attributed to Hermannus Contractus (d. 1054), it is sung in modern practice at Compline through Advent to the Purification (February 2).

Alpaerts, Flor (b. Antwerp, 12 Sept. 1876; d. there, 5 Oct. 1954). Composer. Studied violin with Coligns and composition with Blockx and Benoit at the

Flemish School of Music and Antwerp's Royal Flemish Conservatory, where he taught (from 1903) and served as director (1933–41). His music frequently emulates the orchestral color of Debussy. Works include opera (*Shylock*, 1913); orchestral music (*Psyche*, 1899–1901); incidental music; 4 string quartets; piano music

Alpensinfonie, Eine [Ger., An Alpine Symphony]. A symphonic poem by Richard Strauss, op. 64 (1911–15), describing a day in the Alps. The work is in 22 short, continuously connected sections and requires an orchestra of over 150 players.

Alphorn. A long wooden trumpet of the Alps made in various forms, usually straight with a small upturned bell, but also S-shaped. It ranges in length from 1.5 to 4 m. and is characteristically a shepherd's instrument, used for signaling over long distances. It is known by various names elsewhere in Europe. See ill. under Brass instruments; see also Lur (2).

Alpine Symphony, An. See *Alpensinfonie, Eine.*

Al segno [It.]. See *Segno.*

Alsina, Carlos Roque (b. Buenos Aires, 19 Feb. 1941). Composer and pianist. Studied with Kröpfl at the National Univ. in Buenos Aires (1962–64); assistant conductor of Teatro Colón (1960–64) and of the Deutsche Oper, Berlin (1966); taught at SUNY Buffalo (1966–68). In 1969 co-founded the improvisation group New Phonic Art. His music embraces atonality as well as triadic harmonies, and employs aleatory techniques, taped sounds, and extreme instrumental virtuosity; Berio is a clear influence. Works include *Überwindung,* orchestra with soloists (1970); the opera *La muraille* (1981); a piano concerto (1985).

Also sprach Zarathustra [Ger., Thus Spake Zarathustra]. A symphonic poem by Richard Strauss, op. 30 (1896), based on Friedrich Nietzsche's prose work of the same title.

Alt. (1) [Ger.] *Alto, as a designation both for voices and (in compounds such as *Altklarinette, Altsaxophon*) instruments. (2) [fr. It. *in alto*] In the phrase *in alt,* the range of pitches lying one octave above the treble staff, from g'' to f'''. The pitches of the next higher octave are said to be *in altissimo.*

Alta [It., Sp.]. (1) A 15th-century dance that was the Spanish equivalent of the *saltarello* or the *passo brabante* [Fr. *pas de Brabant*]. An *alta* could be danced to any of the *bassedanze* (*basse danse*) tunes. (2) In the 15th century, an ensemble of loud instruments, usually two or three *shawms and a *sackbut.

Altenberg Lieder [Ger., Altenberg Songs]. Five songs with violin and orchestra by Berg, op. 4 (1912). The full title is *Fünf Orchesterlieder nach Ansichtskartentexten von Peter Altenberg* (Five Orchestral Songs on Picture-Postcard Texts by Peter Altenberg).

Altenburg, Johann Ernst (b. Weissenfels, 15 June 1734; d. Bitterfeld, 14 May 1801). Trumpet player, organist, and composer. From 1757 served as field trumpeter in the Seven Years' War; returned to Weissenfels in 1766 and served as organist at nearby Landsberg. Wrote a treatise on playing trumpet and kettledrums, which discusses the social milieu of the court trumpeter as well as trumpet technique.

Alteration. (1) The raising or lowering of a pitch by means of an *accidental, also termed chromatic alteration. (2) See Mensural notation.

Altered chord. In tonal harmony, a chord in which one or more pitches has been altered by an accidental and thus does not belong to the scale of the operative key, e.g., the Neapolitan and augmented *sixth chords. See Harmonic analysis.

Alternatim [Lat., alternately]. The practice of two or more contrasting forces taking turns in performing music for a liturgical text, each taking only one verse or short section at a time. The contrast might be of soloists (*cantores*) versus choir (*schola*), polyphony versus monophonic plainchant, organ *versets versus vocal plainchant, or more complicated juxtapositions of any of these elements. In the later Renaissance, vocal polyphony for use in alternatim performance was quite significant, especially for the Magnificat, sequences, and hymns.

Alternative, alternativement [Fr.], **alternativo** [It.]. Eighteenth-century indications to play two movements as a pair in alternation, that is, to repeat the first one after playing the second. The terms are attached to either member of a pair of dances such as minuets, bourrées, passepieds, etc. The second is often labeled trio and is generally in the opposite mode or in a related key. In modern tradition, documented rarely in the 18th century, the internal repetitions of the first dance are often omitted during its second playing. *Alternativo* was used by Schumann to designate the middle sections of intermezzos in his op. 4.

Altgeige [Ger.]. (1) *Viola alta. (2) Viola (now rarely).

Althorn [Ger.]. See Alto horn.

Altissimo [It.]. See *Alt* (2).

Altistin [Ger.]. A contralto singer.

Alto [It.]. (1) A low female voice, also called a contralto. For its approximate range see Voice. (2) A high male voice, sung with *falsetto, often called a countertenor. (3) The second highest part (thus lying below the soprano and above the tenor) in the normal four-part vocal texture. (4) [It., Fr.] Viola. (5) In families of instruments such as the flute, clarinet, and saxophone, the second, third, or even fourth highest member, depending upon whether there are members higher than the soprano (e.g., sopranino, piccolo). See also Clef.

Alto horn [Ger. *Althorn;* Fr. *saxhorn tenor;* Eng. also tenor horn; It. *flicorno contralto;* Sp. *bugle contralto*]. A valved brass instrument in E♭, a fifth lower than the modern cornet or trumpet. It has about 2.1 m. (7 ft.) of tube length, usually folded in an upright tuba form with the bell straight up or turned partly forward. Small circular models called mellophones, large circular ones called cavalry horns, as well as trumpet, oval, and over-shoulder shapes are also encountered. All of these instruments came into being as members of various families of brass instruments invented during the 1830s and 1840s. Their written range is that of the cornet (f♯ to c′′′), and they sound a major sixth lower than written. Their proportions are based on those of the *bugle-*flugelhorn family. See ills. under Brass instruments.

Alto moderne [Fr.]. *Viole-ténor.

Alto Rhapsody. See *Rhapsodie (Fragment aus Goethe's Harzreise im Winter).*

Altra volta [It.]. *Encore.

Altus [Lat.]. *Alto (3). See also Contratenor.

Alwyn, William (b. Northampton, 7 Nov. 1905; d. Southwold, 11 Sept. 1985). Composer, flutist, writer, and painter. Studied (1920–23) and taught composition (1926–55) at the Royal Academy of Music; flutist with the London Symphony and other orchestras. Works include the opera *Miss Julie;* 5 symphonies (1950–73); 3 concerti grossi (1942, 1950, 1964); more than 60 film scores; 3 string quartets (1955, 1976, 1984), and other chamber music; piano pieces; songs.

Alzato, alzati [It.]. Raised, removed (e.g., a mute or mutes).

Amabile [It.]. Amiable, lovable.

Amadei, Filippo (b. Reggio, ca. 1670; d. Rome?, after 1729). Cellist and composer. Instrumentalist to Cardinal Pietro Ottoboni in Rome, 1690–96, serving under Corelli; after 1700 cellist in the Società del centesimo and trumpeter for the Campidoglio. Spent the 1720s in London, played in the orchestra of the Royal Academy of Music. In 1721 composed act 1 of *Muzio Scevola;* the other acts were supplied by Bononcini and Handel.

Amahl and the Night Visitors. Opera in one act by Gian Carlo Menotti (setting his own libretto), composed for and produced on television in New York in 1951; first produced on the stage at Indiana University in 1952. Setting: near Bethlehem at the time of the birth of Jesus.

Amaro, amarevole [It.]. Bitter, bitterly.

Amat, Joan Carlos [Carles y Amat, Joan] (b. Monistrol de Montserrat, Catalonia, 1572; d. there, 10 Feb. 1642). Physician, guitarist, and writer on guitar playing, medicine, astrology, and other subjects. In 1596 published *Guitarra española de cinco ordenes* (numerous editions through 1819), the earliest treatise on the five-string guitar.

Amati, Nicola [Nicolo] (b. Cremona, 3 Dec. 1596; d. there, 12 Apr. 1684). Violin maker. Both his grandfather Andrea (b. before 1511) and his father Girolamo (b. 1561) were path-breaking instrument makers, but Nicola was the finest craftsman of the family. After 1640 produced a large quantity of instruments—mostly violins—and passed on the Cremonese legacy through his pupils Guarneri and Stradivari, and his own son Girolamo (b. 1649).

Ambitus [Lat.]. The range of pitches employed in a melody or voice. It is an important determinant of mode in the usual description of the system of church modes employed in liturgical chant and in some repertories of early polyphony. For the ambitus of individual modes, see Mode.

Amboss [Ger.]. *Anvil.

Ambrose (b. Trier, ca. 340; d. Milan, 397). Saint. Bishop of Milan from 7 Dec. 374; credited with the establishment of the Milanese or Ambrosian rite and chant. Medieval tradition also assigned to him the introduction of hymns and antiphonal psalmody into the Western church from Eastern models. Six hymn texts are now generally attributed to him; neither the *Te Deum* nor any melodies can be attributed to him with certainty.

Ambrosian chant. The Latin liturgical chant of Milan, preserved in about 300 north Italian manuscripts, mostly of the late 12th century. Though it is named for the great Milanese bishop St. Ambrose (ca. 340–97), most of the repertory developed after his time. He did, however, write a few of the numerous *"Ambrosian" hymn texts attributed to him.

Ambrosian hymns. The hymns of the Gregorian and Ambrosian chant repertories attributed to St. Ambrose (ca. 340–97). Although a great many hymns were formerly attributed to him, only six can be so ascribed with any confidence: four ("Aeterne rerum conditor," "Deus Creator omnium," "Jam surgit hora tertia," and "Veni Redemptor gentium") on the basis of statements by St. Augustine and two ("Illuxit orbi" and "Bis ternas horas") on the basis of statements by Cassiodorus. It is not certain that any of the surviving melodies is by Ambrose. See also Hymn, *Te Deum*.

Âme [Fr., soul]. *Sound post.

Ameling, Elly [Elisabeth] **(Sara)** (b. Rotterdam, 8 Feb. 1934). Soprano. Studied with Jo Bollenkamp in Dresden and Pierre Bernac in Paris; debut recital in Amsterdam, 1961; U.S. debut in 1968. Best known for performing lieder and concert arias by Mozart, Schubert, Schumann, and Wolf, cantatas by Bach, oratorios by Handel; in 1995 gave several farewell recitals.

Amen [Heb., so be it]. An expression used variously by Christians, Jews, and Muslims as an affirmative response to prayers, readings, hymns, or other texts. In the Roman rite and the liturgical music associated with it, Amen occurs at the end of the lesser *doxology and at the end of the Gloria and Credo of the Mass. In polyphonic settings of the Gloria and Credo, it is often set as a separate section, and from the 17th century onward, settings of it are often in fugal style.

Amen cadence. A plagal *cadence, frequently sung to the word Amen at the conclusion of Protestant hymns.

Amener [Fr., from *branle à mener*]. A Baroque dance movement in moderate triple time with phrases of six measures (3+3 or 4+2). Like a sarabande, it tends to have accented dotted notes on the second beat. In the first half of the 17th century, it was a type of *branle, similar in style to early versions of the *minuet.

American in Paris, An. A symphonic poem by George Gershwin, composed in 1928, describing a sightseer's day in Paris. The work makes use of automobile horns, bluesy tunes, and the rhythms of the Charleston.

American organ. A *harmonium operated by suction rather than by compression.

Amfiparnaso, L'. See Madrigal comedy.

Am Frosch [Ger.]. At the *frog; hence, an instruction to bow the violin or other stringed instrument with that portion of the bow nearest the hand.

Am Griffbrett [Ger.]. At the *fingerboard; hence, an instruction to bow the violin or other stringed instru-

ment near or above the fingerboard. See Bowing (12).

Amirkhanian, Charles (Benjamin) (b. Fresno, Calif., 19 Jan. 1945). Composer. Studied electronic music and sound recording techniques at Mills College; lecturer at San Francisco State Univ. (1977–80). Early works are mostly for percussion and were influenced by Cage and Harrison. After 1970 turned mostly to tape composition. Works for synthesizer include *Metropolis San Francisco* (1985–86) and *Pas de voix*, "Portrait of Samuel Beckett" (1987).

Ammerbach, Elias Nikolaus (b. Naumburg, ca. 1530; d. Leipzig, buried 29 Jan. 1597). Organist and intabulator of music for keyboard. Organist at the Thomaskirche in Leipzig (1561–95); his *Orgel oder Instrument Tabulatur* (1571; 2nd ed., 1583) is the first published German organ music and the first example of the so-called new German organ tablature.

Ammons, Albert (C.) (b. Chicago, 23 Sept. 1907; d. there, 2 Dec. 1949). Boogie-woogie pianist. Played in bands in Chicago; his Rhythm Kings (1934–38) recorded *Boogie Woogie Stomp* (1936). A central figure in the popularization of boogie-woogie; moved to New York in 1938 to perform and record in trios with Pete Johnson and Meade "Lux" Lewis, in duos with Johnson, and as a soloist.

Amner, John (b. Ely, bapt. 24 Aug. 1579; d. there, buried 24 July 1641). Organist and composer. Studied at Oxford; choirmaster at Ely Cathedral from 1610 until his death. Works include services and full and verse anthems; one set of keyboard variations also survives.

Amor brujo, El [Sp., Love the Sorcerer]. A ballet by Manuel de Falla, composed in 1914–15 and produced in Madrid in 1915 (choreography by Pastora Imperio), on a gypsy subject, and including numerous folk-inspired dances, the best known of which is the "Ritual Fire Dance." The work includes several songs originally intended to be sung by the ballerina, but now most often sung from the orchestra pit by a singer.

Amore, con; amorevole; amoroso [It.]. With love, lovingly. Instruments with names including the phrase *d'amore* are usually thought to have an especially mellow tone; in the case of stringed instruments this is usually attributable to the presence of *sympathetic strings in addition to the strings actually played upon.

Amorschall [Ger.]. A French horn having two side holes with keys and some kind of cover or insert for its bell, invented by a Bohemian horn player named Kölbel, ca. 1766. It was one of the first attempts to complete the scale of the horn, and Kölbel, employed in St. Petersburg, attracted considerable attention performing on it.

Amour des trois oranges, L'. See *Love for Three Oranges.*

Amplitude. See Acoustics.

Amram, David (Werner, III) (b. Philadelphia, 17 Nov. 1930). Composer, horn player, and conductor. Studied horn at Oberlin (1948), then attended George Washington Univ. In 1955 enrolled at the Manhattan School of Music, where he studied with Mitropoulos, Giannini, and Schuller and performed in the Manhattan Woodwind Quintet; from 1956 composed incidental music for Joseph Papp and the New York Shakespeare Festival. Composer in residence, New York Philharmonic (1966–67); conductor of the Brooklyn Philharmonia's youth concerts from 1972. His experience as a jazz performer has influenced his music, which includes theater and film music as well as works for orchestra, chorus, and jazz ensemble.

Am Steg [Ger.]. At the *bridge; hence, an instruction to bow the violin or other stringed instrument near or on the bridge. See Bowing (11).

Amy, Gilbert (b. Paris, 29 Aug. 1936). Composer and conductor. Studied at the Paris Conservatory, 1955–60, with Milhaud (composition), Messiaen (analysis), and Loriod (piano and harmony); attended Darmstadt summer courses, 1959–61. Studied conducting with Boulez in Basel (1965) and succeeded him as conductor of the Domaine musicale (1967). Musical adviser to the French national radio and television network (ORTF) from 1973. The strict serial orientation of his early music (Piano Sonata, 1957–60), polyphonic rigor, and interest in mobile forms developed to encompass exploration of spatial effects (*Antiphonies* for 2 orchestras, 1960–63), concertante style, and subtlety of tone color.

Anacrusis [fr. Gr.]. One or more notes preceding the first metrically strong beat of a phrase; upbeat, pickup.

Analysis. The study of musical structure applied to actual works or performances. In ethnomusicology, analysis includes the study of the relation among musical structure, performance, and culture. The analysis of Western art music deals substantively with questions of technique and is therefore considered a branch of music *theory, but it is distinct in that it addresses music already composed or performed. Much analysis aims to demonstrate the organic unity of a work or works. Many practitioners see it as having no bearing on larger aesthetic issues, such as expressiveness, or on questions of the value of individual works. With respect to these and many other topics, the relationship between analysis and *criticism of music is not well defined.

The analysis of any repertory of music necessarily rests on some view (whether or not expressed) about which features of the repertory are significant as well as on the aims of the analyst. It may rest on a widely shared theory of a repertory and simply describe the work in terms of that theory, or it may be advanced as evidence for the correctness of a theory. Its aim may be to elucidate the individual work in strictly technical terms without direct reference to other works, or it may seek to situate the work in a larger theoretical, biographical, historical, or cultural context. In Western art music, the aim of analysis is sometimes to guide the performer's interpretation. At issue with respect to every repertory is the extent to which analysis can or should be carried out in terms that do not form an explicit part of the musical and cultural traditions of the repertory itself. This issue is forcefully present in *ethnomusicology, where, for example, the study of non-Western musics in analytical terms derived from Western art music poses serious risks of distortion. Similarly, the study of the history of Western art music requires choosing an analytical vocabulary appropriate to the period and repertory in question, though the vocabulary need not be restricted to that of contemporaneous theorists.

The analysis of Western tonal music may deal comprehensively with all of the structural aspects of a work, including identification of its larger outlines or *form, variability within types of form, specific gestures, special devices, and relationship to a text. The analysis of form may subsume motivic analysis [see Motive] and *harmonic analysis, which considers aspects of *tonality, *modulation, function (determined in turn by root analysis, or, less accurately, "roman-numeral analysis"), and *harmonic rhythm. The analysis of melody, rhythm, and instrumentation may be applicable to larger questions of structure. *Schenker analysis is a technique that stresses the linear motions of tonal works.

The analysis of works from before the period of tonality is often carried out in terms of concepts such as *mode that form a part of contemporaneous theory, though considerable study (and some controversy) surrounds the relationship of this music to the emergence of the tonal system. The aim of such analysis is often historical. Some styles of art music of the 20th century, notably *twelve-tone and *serial music, have developed along with a related body of theory that provides terms for analysis. This theory has inspired the development of techniques for the analysis (principally of pitch relations) of other atonal music as well. In contrast, *aleatory music, by undermining the fixity of the individual work, radically calls into question analysis as traditionally conceived.

All of the techniques of analysis may be subsumed under *style analysis, which usually has aims reaching beyond the individual work. It may concern itself with a composer's growth and evolution; with the similarities and differences between the works of a single composer or between those of one composer and those of another; with the trends and idiosyncrasies of musical eras and national heritages; with the humanistic aspect of music and the relationship between music and other arts and human activities. Some analysis has used the techniques of information theory, linguistics, semiotics, and computer science. See also Criticism, Theory.

Anapest, anapaest. See Prosody.

Ančerl, Karel (b. Tučapy, Bohemia, 11 Apr. 1908; d. Toronto, 3 July 1973). Conductor. Studied with Vaclav Talich at the Prague Conservatory, then with Hermann Scherchen in Strasbourg. Led the Prague Radio Orchestra from 1933 until 1939, when he was removed by the Nazis, who in 1942 sent him to Theresienstadt and Auschwitz. Led the Prague Opera, 1945–47; Czech Radio Orchestra, 1947–50; Czech Philharmonic, 1950–68. After the Russian invasion of Czechoslovakia, conductor of the Toronto Symphony from 1968 until his death.

Anche [Fr.]. *Reed. The plural, *anches,* denotes the reed stops of the organ.

Anchieta, Juan de (b. Urrestilla?, near Azpeitia, Spain, 1462; d. Azpeitia, 30 July 1523). Composer. A singer in the court chapel of Queen Isabella (1489–1504); after her death joined the chapel of Isabella's daughter Joanna and Philip the Fair; remained with the royal chapel until being pensioned off by Charles V on 15 Aug. 1519. Surviving works include 2 Masses, 2 Magnificats, several motets, and a few *villancicos.*

Ancia [It.]. *Reed.

Ancora [It.]. (1) Again, often as a request to repeat a performance. (2) Still, more; *ancora più forte,* still louder.

Anda, Géza (b. Budapest, 19 Nov. 1921; d. Zurich, 13 June 1976). Pianist. Studied with Ernst von Dohnányi at the Budapest Academy; 1939, debut with Budapest Philharmonic; moved to Switzerland in 1943. Best known for his interpretation of Bartók and for a cycle of 25 Mozart concertos recorded 1961–70.

Andacht, mit; andächtig [Ger.]. With devotion, devoutly.

Andamento [It.]. (1) A fugue subject of some length, often consisting of more than one phrase, as distinct from the *attaco and *soggetto. (2) *Sequence (2). (3) An episode in a *fugue.

Andante [It., walking]. (1) Moderately slow, and since the late 18th century, usually regarded as a tempo lying between *adagio and *allegro. The term was first used as a performance instruction independent of tempo, particularly with reference to bass lines with a steadily moving or "walking" character in even note-values. Its position between tempos that are thought of as clearly slow and clearly fast leads to some ambiguity when the term is combined with others, as in the phrases *molto andante, più andante,* and *meno andante.* Although the first two are probably most often intended to call for a tempo slower and the last to call for a tempo faster than *andante,* the reverse may be true in some cases. A similar ambiguity exists with respect to *andantino. See Performance marks. (2) A movement in moderately slow tempo, perhaps not as slow as an *adagio* and in any case less somber in character.

Andante con moto [It.]. See *Moto.*

Andantino [It.]. In present usage, usually slightly less slow than *andante. The term is ambiguous, however, in part because of the ambiguity associated with andante. In the late 18th century, *andantino* seems to have called for a tempo slower than *andante.* See Performance marks.

Anderson, Cat [William Alonzo] (b. Greenville, S.C., 12 Sept. 1916; d. Norwalk, Calif., 29 Apr. 1981). Jazz trumpeter. Trained with other future jazzmen in bands at Jenkins's Orphanage in Charleston. Joined Hampton (1942, 1944), then Ellington (1944–47, 1950–59, intermittently 1961–71); in the intervals led bands and freelanced. Best known for high register playing with Ellington ("Trumpet No End") but a growling muted solo on "A Gatherin' in a Clearin'" demonstrates his versatility (both 1946). Also recorded as a leader (1947–79) and with Johnny Hodges (intermittently 1956–67) and Hampton, with whom he toured in the 1970s.

Anderson, Laurie (b. Chicago, 5 June 1947). Composer and performer. Trained as a violinist, moved to New York in 1966 and attended Barnard and Columbia; studied privately with minimalist painter Sol LeWitt; wrote art criticism and taught art history. In 1974 started making her own instruments, including a tapebow violin. Performed at the Museum of Modern Art and at Berlin Festival of 1976. Compositions include the two-evening performance art work *United States* (1983); the song "O Superman (for Massenet)" from this was a commercial success.

Anderson, Leroy (b. Cambridge, Mass., 29 June 1908; d. Woodbury, Conn., 18 May 1975). Composer, arranger, and conductor. Studied with Piston and Enesco at Harvard; director of the Harvard Band and an organist and conductor in Boston (1931–35); subsequently worked as an arranger and orchestrator. Composer primarily of light music for orchestra (*The Syncopated Clock,* 1945; *The Typewriter,* 1950; *Sandpaper Ballet,* 1954).

Anderson, Marian (b. Philadelphia, 27 Feb. 1897; d. Portland, Ore., 8 Apr. 1993). Contralto. Debut recital in New York, 1924; soloist with the New York Philharmonic, 1925. Her American career was restricted by barriers against black artists. London debut in 1930; tours of Scandinavia (1931, 1933) established her career in Europe. In 1939 she was banned on racial grounds from singing at Constitution Hall in Washington, D.C.; an outpouring of public sympathy led to her Easter concert at the Lincoln Memorial, attended by 75,000 people and broadcast nationally. Operatic debut at the Met in 1955; retired in 1965.

An die ferne Geliebte [Ger., To the Distant Beloved]. A cycle of six songs by Beethoven, op. 98 (1815–16), on poems by Alois Jeitteles.

André, Johann (b. Offenbach, 28 Mar. 1741; d. there, 18 June 1799). Composer and music publisher. His first original stage work, the singspiel *Der Töpfer* (1773), was admired by Goethe. In 1774 gave up the family silk business in favor of his own music publishing firm. From 1776 to 1784 conductor at Döbbelin's Berlin theater; returned to Offenbach in 1784 to look after his firm, which flourished during the 1780s and 1790s. Composed numerous stage works and lieder.

André, Johann Anton (b. Offenbach, 6 Oct. 1775; d. there, 6 Apr. 1842). Composer and publisher, son of Johann André. Took charge of the family firm in 1799 and introduced lithography. In 1800 bought Mozart's papers from his widow and devoted much time to cataloguing and publishing Mozart's works. Compositions include 2 operas and instrumental music.

André, Maurice (b. Alès, France, 21 May 1933). Trumpeter. Studied at the Paris Conservatory, where he began teaching in 1967. A widely recorded proponent of Baroque music, he favors a custom-made four-valved piccolo trumpet in this repertory.

Andrea Chénier. Opera in four acts by Umberto Giordano (libretto by Luigi Illica), produced in Milan in 1896. Setting: Paris before, during, and after the French Revolution.

Andriessen, Hendrik (b. Haarlem, 17 Sept. 1892; d. Heemstede, 12 Apr. 1981). Organist and composer. Studied at the Amsterdam Conservatory; organist at St. Joseph's Church, Haarlem (from 1916); faculty, Amsterdam Conservatory (from 1926). Served as di-

rector of the conservatories at Utrecht (1937–49) and The Hague (1949–57); professor of musicology at the Catholic Univ. at Nijmegen (1952–63). His musical style is eclectic, a mix of romantic harmony and atonal melody (*Symphonic Etude,* orchestra, 1952), of church modes and polyphony in the style of Notre Dame (*Missa in honorem Sacratissimi Cordis,* 1919), of sonata form and Baroque dances (Third Symphony, 1946).

Andriessen, Jurriaan (b. Haarlem, 15 Nov. 1925; d. 23 Aug. 1986). Composer, son of Hendrik Andriessen. Studied at the Utrecht Conservatory, in Paris (1947), and at the Berkshire Music Center (1949–51). In 1954 made resident composer of The Hague Theater Company. Works include incidental music, film scores, operas, ballets, instrumental music.

Andriessen, Louis (b. Utrecht, 6 June 1939). Composer, son of Hendrik Andriessen. Studied at the Utrecht Conservatory (from 1957) and with Berio in Milan and Berlin (1962–65). A leading Dutch avant-gardist, he employed electronic and collage techniques and jazz idioms. His works include *De Tijd* [Time] (1981); *De Snelheid* [Velocity] (1984); *Die Matiere* [Matter], music theater (1984–88).

Andriessen, Willem (b. Haarlem, 25 Oct. 1887; d. Amsterdam, 29 Mar. 1964). Pianist and composer; brother of Hendrik Andriessen. From 1900 studied at the Amsterdam Conservatory; taught piano at the conservatories in The Hague (1910–17) and Rotterdam; director of the Amsterdam Conservatory from 1937. His works include a Mass in F minor (1914–16); other choral works; a piano sonata (1938) and concerto (1908).

Anémocorde [Fr.]. A mechanical *aeolian harp invented by Johann Jacob Schnell in Paris in 1789. Wind was supplied by bellows and channeled past tuned strings by a mechanism activated by a keyboard. See also Sostenente piano.

Anerio, Felice (b. Rome, ca. 1560; d. there, 26 Sept. 1614). Composer, brother of Giovanni Francesco Anerio. Sang in a succession of choirs in Rome; *maestro di cappella* of the Collegio degli Inglesi (1584–85); in 1594 succeeded Palestrina as composer to the papal choir; also directed the chapel choir of Duke Giovanni Angelo Altaemps. In 1611–12 worked with Soriano on a reformation of the Roman Gradual. Works include numerous madrigals and canzonettas, 4 Masses and other sacred music.

Anerio, Giovanni Francesco (b. Rome, ca. 1567; d. Graz, buried 12 June 1630). Composer, brother of Felice Anerio. During the 1590s was apparently organist for services at S. Marcello; also served at St. John Lateran from around 1600. In 1608 became *maestro di cappella* at Santo Spirito in Sassia, and from 1609 of the Verona Cathedral as well. In 1611 settled again in Rome, where he served as *maestro* at S. Maria dei Monti (1613–20); during his last years directed the choirs for Sigismund III in Poland. Both sacred and secular works include examples of the modern monodic style and the use of basso continuo.

Anfang [Ger.]. Beginning; *vom Anfang,* from the beginning, and thus the equivalent of **da capo.*

Anfossi, Pasquale (b. Taggia, 5 April 1727; d. Rome, Feb. 1797). Composer. During the 1750s and early 1760s studied composition with Sacchini and Piccinni; composed operas for Naples and Rome. Director, King's Theatre in London (1782–86); from 1792 until his death *maestro di cappella* at St. John Lateran in Rome. Composed over 60 operas, sacred music, chamber music.

Angelica [It.; Fr. *angélique;* Eng. angel lute]. An archlute of the 17th and 18th centuries with 16 or 17 single gut strings tuned diatonically, D to e'. Played like a harp, it was popular with amateurs because of the full, clear, sustained tone of the open plucked strings.

Angenehm [Ger.]. Pleasant.

Angklung [Jav.]. An Indonesian instrument made of tuned lengths of bamboo. In East Java, 12 to 14 tubes are set on a frame and struck with mallets. In West Java and in Bali, 2 or 3 tubes tuned in octaves are fastened loosely to a frame and shaken by hand like a **rattle.

Anglaise, anglois [Fr.]. A fast, late Baroque dance movement in a harpsichord or orchestral suite (Bach, Telemann). The term was used loosely to refer to any of the English dance types whose popularity spread from the court of Louis XIV across Europe [see *Contredanse,* Country Dance, Hornpipe, *Écossaise*]. Anglaises usually have folkish simplicity and are strongly accented. They continued to be written until the end of the 18th century.

Angle harp. A **harp in which the neck forms an angle (usually acute) with the sound box and which lacks a pillar, thus having only two sides. Angle harps are now common only in Africa, having been replaced elsewhere by *frame harps. See also Arched harp.

Anglican chant. Harmonized formulas for singing Psalms and canticles in the daily Offices of the Anglican Church. Before the Restoration (mid-17th century), simple harmonizations of Gregorian *psalm tones with the chant in the tenor were used (examples in Thomas Morley's *A Plaine and Easie Introduction,* 1597). After the Restoration, the connection between Anglican chant and the Gregorian psalm tones became gradually less direct. The mel-

ody was moved to the top voice, but the bipartite form of the Gregorian tones was retained. Eventually Anglican chant came to be a small binary form, each part opening with an expandable, unmeasured reciting chord (to accommodate the varying number of syllables per verse in the prose texts) and closing with a measured cadential pattern.

Angosciosamente [It.]. With anguish.

Ängstlich [Ger.]. Anxiously.

Anhalt, István (b. Budapest, 12 Apr. 1919). Composer, conductor, and pianist. Studied composition under Kodály at the Royal Hungarian Academy; subsequently at the Paris Conservatory and with Boulanger. Assistant conductor, Hungarian National Opera (1945); joined the faculty of McGill Univ. in Canada, where he founded the electronic music studio; faculty member, SUNY Buffalo (1969); head of the music department, Queen's Univ., Ontario (1971–84). Early works were influenced by the dodecaphonic techniques of Schoenberg; his electronic studies and works for prepared tape and live media (*La tourangelle,* 3 sopranos, 2 speakers, 15 instrumentalists, tape, 1974) were significant in the development of electronic music in Canada.

Anhalten, anhaltend [Ger.]. To hold or continue (e.g., sounding, as when a tone is not damped); continuing.

Anhemitonic. Lacking semitones; e.g., the whole-tone scale or the pentatonic scale c d e g a.

Anima [It., soul]. **Sound post.

Animando, animandosi, animato [It.]. Animating, becoming animated, animated; usually with the implication of (increasingly) rapid tempo.

Animé [Fr.]. Animated; thus, in a moderately fast tempo.

Animo, animoso [It.]. Spirit, spirited.

Animuccia, Giovanni (b. Florence, ca. 1500; d. Rome, 20 Mar. 1571). Composer. In 1555 became director of the choir of the Cappella Giulia, succeeding Palestrina and remaining there until his death. The most prominent and prolific of Palestrina's contemporaries in Rome, his elaborate sacred music includes one book each of Masses, Magnificats, and motets; also composed four books of madrigals, including extended madrigal cycles, the first such works by a composer from Florence.

Anmutig [Ger.]. Graceful.

Anna Amalia [Amalie] (1) (b. Berlin, 9 Nov. 1723; d. there, 30 Mar. 1787). Composer, patroness of music, and Princess of Prussia. A sister of Frederick II, she studied music with her brother and with Hayne;

around 1735 established a private library, eventually amassing some 600 compositions (including autographs) by J. S. and C. P. E. Bach, Handel, Hasse, Telemann, and many others. Musicians and literati gathered at her soirees in the royal palace; in the 1750s she studied composition with Kirnberger.

Anna Amalia [Amalie] (2) (b. Wolfenbüttel, 24 Oct. 1739; d. Weimar, 10 Apr. 1807). Musician and patroness of music. She married the Duke of Saxe-Weimar in 1756; reigned over the duchy from the duke's death two years later until 1775, during which time the Weimar court was an important literary and musical center. The poets Wieland, Herder, and Goethe gathered there, and singspiels by Hiller and Schweitzer received first performances at her court. Goethe wrote singspiel texts for her, including *Erwin und Elmire,* which she set in 1776, and *Das Jahrmarktsfest zu Plundersweilern,* set in 1778.

Années de pèlerinage [Fr., Years of Pilgrimage]. Three volumes of piano music by Liszt, composed during the years 1835–77. The first (published in 1855) is titled *Suisse,* the second (1858) *Italie,* and the third (1883) is untitled. Each contains pieces with descriptive titles. Many of the pieces in the first volume were composed in 1835–36, published in 1840 as *Album d'un voyageur,* and later revised.

Anreissen [Ger.]. In string playing, to pluck forcefully.

Ansatz [Ger.]. (1) In the playing of wind instruments, *embouchure. (2) The adjustment of the organs contributing to vocal production. (3) *Attack.

Anschlag [Ger.]. (1) In piano playing, touch. (2) An ornament mainly associated with German music of the mid-18th century and consisting most commonly of two notes, the first a step below the main note and the second a step above. These notes precede the main note and take their value from it; they are executed more lightly than the main note, however, unlike an *appoggiatura.

Anschwellend [Ger.]. Becoming louder.

Ansermet, Ernest (Alexandre) (b. Vevey, 11 Nov. 1883; d. Geneva, 20 Feb. 1969). Conductor. Studied composition with Gédalge in Paris (1905–6) and with Bloch (ca. 1907) in Geneva; in Berlin (1909) observed the conducting techniques of Nikisch, Richard Strauss, and Weingartner. Conductor, Montreux Kursaal Orchestra (1912–14); Stravinsky assisted his appointment as conductor for Diaghilev's Ballets russes (1915–23), where he premiered Satie's *Parade* (1917) and Stravinsky's *Les noces* (1923). Ansermet founded the Orchestre de la Suisse Romande, leading it from 1918 until his retirement in 1966. His recorded repertory includes the Russian Five, Debussy, Ravel, Honegger, and Stravinsky.

Anspach, Elizabeth, Margravine of [Craven, Elizabeth] (b. London, 17 Dec. 1750; d. Naples, 13 Jan. 1828). Composer and playwright. During the 1780s and 1790s wrote plays performed in London theaters, as well as music for operas such as *The Silver Tankard* (1781) and *The Princess of Georgia* (1794). Her only surviving work is a madrigal setting from Shakespeare ("O Mistress Mine").

Answer. In a fugue, a statement of the subject immediately following its statement in the prevailing key. Answers usually result from imitation of the subject at an interval other than the unison or octave, most often the perfect fifth above or the perfect fourth below, and the term is sometimes reserved for only such cases. Depending on the nature of their similarity to the original subject, answers may be either tonal or real [see Tonal and real].

Antara [Quechua]. Andean *panpipes of cane or clay.

Antecedent, consequent. Two musical phrases, the second of which is a concluding response to or resolution of the first. The two phrases often have the same or similar rhythms, but have complementary pitch contours and/or tonal implications, e.g., a rising contour in the first and a falling contour in the second, or a conclusion on the dominant in the first and a conclusion on the tonic in the second. In the accompanying example from the first movement of

Antecedent, consequent.

Mozart's Symphony no. 40 in G minor K. 550, this relationship obtains at two levels simultaneously. Phrases c and d form one antecedent-consequent pair, as do phrases e and f. At the same time, the two pairs, understood as phrases A and B, respectively, are also related to one another as antecedent and consequent.

Antes, John (b. Frederick, Pa., 24 March 1740; d. Bristol, England, 17 Dec. 1811). Composer, instrument maker, and minister. Early training by the Moravians in Pennsylvania was followed by missionary service in Egypt during the 1770s; soon after 1781 took up residence among the Moravians in Fulneck, England. Compositions include hymn tunes, anthems, songs, and 3 string trios op. 3 (1790). Also invented a mechanism that automatically turns pages on a music stand.

Antheil, George [Georg] (**Johann Carl**) (b. Trenton, N.J., 8 July 1900; d. New York, 12 Feb. 1959). Composer and pianist. Studied piano from age 6; had composition lessons with Bloch in New York (1919–21). Settled in Berlin in 1922 to pursue a career as concert pianist. Stravinsky's influence is apparent in *Airplane Sonata* (1921); moved to Paris (1923), became a leading spokesman of the avant-garde; the percussion score *Ballet mécanique* (1923–25; rev. 1952–53) marked the high point of his iconoclastic prestige. In subsequent works (Piano Concerto, 1926) employed a neoclassic idiom. Moved to Vienna (1928), then to the U.S. (1933), wrote scores for Balanchine and Graham and composed film music. Other works include Symphony no. 5, "Joyous" (1945–46) and the opera *Volpone* (1949).

Anthem [fr. *antiphon*]. A choral composition with a sacred or moralizing text in English, performed in a liturgical or ceremonial context. In the worship of Protestant churches, it is the analogue of the *motet* in the Roman Catholic Church. In a verse anthem, sections or "verses" for one or more soloists with instrumental accompaniment alternate with sections for full chorus; a full anthem is entirely choral.

Anticipation. See Counterpoint, *Nachschlag.*

Antienne [Fr.]. *Antiphon.

Antill, John Henry (b. Sydney, 8 Apr. 1904; d. there, 29 Dec. 1986). Composer. Studied at St. Andrew's Cathedral Choir School in Sydney and at New South Wales State Conservatorium of Music; in 1936 began a long association with the Australian Broadcasting Commission. His early interest and extensive research in Aboriginal music led to the orchestral suite *Corroboree* (1946), which fostered the notion of a specifically Australian music; also composed operas, ballets, symphonic works, vocal music.

Antimasque. See Masque.

Antiphon. A type of liturgical chant common to the *Gregorian and other Western chant repertories and associated principally with antiphonal psalmody. It is generally a relatively short melody in a simple, syllabic style that serves as a refrain in the singing of the verses of a Psalm or canticle. For the relationship of antiphon to accompanying verses and the methods of performing these, see Psalmody, Latin, and Psalm tone. Of the Marian antiphons (antiphons for the Blessed Virgin Mary), the most important are the four sung at the end of Compline, one for each season of the year: *"Alma Redemptoris Mater," *"Ave Regina caelorum," *"Regina caeli laetare," and *"Salve Regina." These date from the 11th century and after, are rather more elaborate than the antiphons of the Psalms and canticles, and have been set polyphonically by numerous composers, especially in the 15th and 16th centuries.

Antiphonal singing. Singing in which two choirs alternate. In liturgical chant it is present in one of the three basic forms of *psalmody. The term is also applied to any *polychoral music.

Antiphoner, antiphonal, antiphonary [Lat. *antiphonale, antiphonarium, antiphonarius*]. The *liturgical book of the Western Christian rites containing the chants for the Office and thus antiphons as well as responsories and other types of chant. The comparable book for the Mass is the *gradual.

Antiphonia [Gr.]. In Greek theory, the octave.

Antiphony. The use of two (or more) spatially separated performers or ensembles that alternate or oppose one another in a musical work or performance. Music employing choirs in this way is said to be *polychoral.

Antoniou, Theodore (b. Athens, 10 Feb. 1935). Composer and conductor. Studied at the National Conservatory in Athens, 1947–58; at the Hellenic Conservatory, 1956–61, and at the Munich Musikhochschule, 1961–65; taught at Stanford (1969–70), the Univ. of Utah (1970), the Philadelphia Musical Academy (1970–77), the Univ. of Pennsylvania (1978), and Boston Univ. (since 1979). A prolific composer of stage works (*Bacchae*, 1991–92); orchestral music (*Paean*, 1989); choral and solo vocal music; music for chamber ensembles, and tape music.

Antony and Cleopatra. Opera in three acts by Samuel Barber (libretto by Franco Zeffirelli after Shakespeare), produced in New York in 1966; a revised version (libretto revised by Gian Carlo Menotti) was produced at the Juilliard American Opera Center in

1975. Setting: Alexandria and Rome in the first century B.C.E.

Anvil [Fr. *enclume;* Ger. *Amboss;* It. *incudine;* Sp. *yunque*]. A percussion instrument, often intended to represent the sound of the metal-working tool, consisting of a small metal bar struck with a hard wooden or metal mallet. It may or may not be of definite pitch. Sometimes the blacksmith's anvil itself is used. Works calling for one or more anvils include the "Anvil Chorus" in Verdi's *Il trovatore,* Wagner's *Das Rheingold,* and Varèse's *Ionisation.*

Anwachsend [Ger.]. Growing, swelling.

À peine entendu [Fr.]. See *Peine entendu, à.*

Aperto [It., open]. (1) In horn playing, with the bell open, i.e., not stopped (*chiuso*) [see Horn, Stopped tones]. (2) In 14th-century music, the first of two endings for a section of a piece; thus, equivalent to the French *ouvert.*

A piacere [It.]. See *Piacere, a.*

Aplvor, Denis (b. Collinstown, near Dublin, of Welsh parentage, 14 Apr. 1916). Composer. Studied privately with Rawsthorne and Patrick Hadley from 1937 to 1939 while studying medicine in London. Works include operas (*She Stoops to Conquer,* 1943–47, rev. 1976–77); 5 ballets; choral music (cantata *The Hollow Men,* 1939); 4 symphonies and other orchestral works; chamber music.

Apollo. See *Apollon Musagète.*

Apollo Club. Any of a number of choral societies, at first usually all male, founded in the late 19th century in American cities, including Boston (1871), Chicago (1872), Brooklyn (1878), Cincinnati (1882), and St. Louis (1893).

Apollonicon. A large organ built by Flight and Robson of London between 1812 and 1817 that attempted to imitate the sound of an orchestra and that could be played either manually by five players or automatically by means of three pinned barrels, each 2.4 m. (8 ft.) long. See also Automatic instrument.

Apollon Musagète [Fr., Apollo, Leader of the Muses]. A ballet, scored for string orchestra, by Stravinsky. It was produced in Washington, D.C., in 1928 (with choreography by Adolph Bolm) and in Paris later the same year (with choreography by George Balanchine). Stravinsky revised the work in 1947 and published it two years later; at some later time it was renamed simply *Apollo.*

Apostel, Hans Erich (b. Karlsruhe, 22 Jan. 1901; d. Vienna, 30 Nov. 1972). Composer. Studied at the Munz Conservatory in Karlsruhe, subsequently conductor at the Badisches Landestheater there. Moved to Vienna in 1921 and studied privately with Schoenberg (1921–25) and Berg (1925–35). A dissonant, expressionistic style and free use of dodecaphonic procedures (*Variations on a Theme of Joseph Haydn,* orchestra, 1949) eventually led to a more systematic application of serial techniques (*Paralipomena dodekaphonika* op. 44, orchestra, 1970).

Apothéose [Fr.]. Apotheosis, sometimes used as a title for works glorifying a deceased composer, e.g., François Couperin's *L'Apothéose de Corelli.*

Appalachian dulcimer. A plucked *zither of European derivation found chiefly in the Appalachian mountains. The narrow sound box is 70 to 100 cm. (ca. 3 ft.) long and gently bulging, often in the shape of a figure 8. Three or four metal strings, often tuned c′ g′ g′, run the length of the instrument over a fingerboard with 13 or 14 frets. It is held horizontally in the player's lap and strummed with a quill or the thumb of the right hand. The string nearest the player (g′) is the melody string and is stopped either with a finger or with a wooden bar, called a noter, held in the left hand. The remaining strings are drones. It is used today principally to accompany folk singing. See ill. under Zither; see also *Hummel, Langleik, Scheitholt.*

Appalachian Spring. A ballet, scored for 13 instruments, by Copland (choreography by Martha Graham, who chose the title of the work from a Hart Crane poem and to whom the piece is dedicated), produced in Washington, D.C., in 1944. Its setting is a pioneer wedding at a Pennsylvania farmhouse. Much of the music is incorporated in a suite for full orchestra of the same name completed in 1945. The work includes variations on the Shaker hymn "Simple Gifts."

Appassionata; Sonata appassionata [It., impassioned]. Beethoven's Piano Sonata no. 23 in F minor op. 57 (1804–5). The title was first added to the work in 1838 by the publisher of an arrangement of it for piano four-hands.

Appassionato [It.]. Impassioned.

Appena [It.]. Scarcely.

Applied dominant. The *dominant of a pitch other than the tonic. See also Tonicization.

Appoggiando [It., leaning]. With succeeding notes stressed and closely connected.

Appoggiatura [It.]. (1) A dissonant pitch occurring in a strong metrical position and resolving by ascending or descending step to a consonance in a relatively weaker metrical position. See Counterpoint 4.

(2) An ornamental note falling on the beat, that is, one that replaces the main note at the moment of its attack, then resolves to the pitch of that note. The

meaning of the word itself, "a leaning," suggests that the ornament should be accented relative to its resolution; the term is often used for unaccented, single-note ornaments that anticipate the beat, however.

Apprenti sorcier, L' [Fr., The Sorcerer's Apprentice]. A symphonic poem by Paul Dukas composed in 1897 and based on Goethe's ballad "Der Zauberlehrling."

Appuy [Fr.]. An 18th-century term for a note having the quality of an appoggiatura. It usually refers to the appoggiatura that constitutes the first note of the *tremblement* or *cadence* [see Trill].

Appuyé [Fr.]. Accented.

Après-midi d'un faune, L'. See *Prelude to "The Afternoon of a Faun."*

Aquitanian neume, notation. See Neume.

Arabella. Opera ("lyrical comedy") in three acts by Richard Strauss (libretto by Hugo von Hofmannsthal after his short novel *Lucidor*), produced in Dresden in 1933. Setting: Vienna, 1860.

Arabesque [Fr.], **Arabeske** [Ger.]. An ornament characteristic of Arabic art and architecture; hence, similarly decorative or florid musical material or a composition employing such material. As a title, the term is used by Schumann (op. 18), Debussy, and others.

Aragonesa [Sp.], **aragonaise** [Fr.]. From Aragón [see *Jota*].

Araia [Araja], **Francesco** (b. Naples, 25 June 1709; d. Bologna, ca. 1767–70). Composer. Best known for a comic opera in Neapolitan dialect, *Lo matremmonejo pe' vennetta* (1729). Appointed *maestro di cappella* at St. Petersburg (1735); in 1740 returned to Italy briefly but went back to Russia to serve Empress Elizabeth. Composed *Cephalus and Procris* (1755), considered the first opera on a text in Russian (by Sumarokov). Retired to Bologna after 1762.

Arará [Sp.]. A Cuban cult drum.

Arban, (Joseph) Jean-Baptiste (Laurent) (b. Lyons, 28 Feb. 1825; d. Paris, 9 Apr. 1889). Cornetist, conductor, and teacher. Studied trumpet at the Paris Conservatory (1841–45); professor of saxhorn at the École militaire from 1857; taught cornet at the conservatory 1869–74 and, after a period conducting in Russia, again from 1880. Called the founder of modern trumpet playing; wrote the standard cornet method.

Arbós, Enrique Fernández (b. Madrid, 24 Dec. 1863; d. San Sebastián, 2 June 1939). Violinist, conductor, and composer. Studied violin with Monasterio at the Madrid Conservatory; subsequently with Vieuxtemps, Gevaert, and Joachim. Concertmaster, Berlin Philharmonic (from 1882); professor of violin in Madrid (1884) and at London's Royal College of Music (1894); from 1904 conductor of the Madrid Symphony Orchestra; from 1913 assistant conductor of the Boston Symphony. His own works include a comic opera; orchestral works; songs.

Arcadelt [Archadelt], **Jacques** (b. 1505?; d. Paris, 14 Oct. 1568). Composer. Although probably French by birth, lived and worked chiefly in Italy (Florence, Venice, and Rome) from 1532 to 1551. From 1540 to 1551 connected with the papal chapel, later a member of the chapel of Charles of Lorraine and moved to France. Over 200 madrigals (most for four voices) are extant, published in Venice between 1537 and 1559; the majority of his 126 extant chansons were written after he left Italy. Although his music is predominantly secular, motets and other sacred music survive.

Arcata [It.]. Bow stroke; *a. in giù,* down-bow; *a. in su,* up-bow.

Arcato [It.]. Bowed.

Archduke Trio. Popular name for Beethoven's Piano Trio in B♭ major op. 97 (1810–11), dedicated to his patron the Archduke Rudolph.

Arched harp. A *harp with a curved neck, usually forming a continuous line with the sound box. The arched harp thus resembles a musical bow with several strings instead of one. Such instruments are depicted in the third millennium B.C.E. in Mesopotamia and Egypt. They are important today in Burma and sub-Saharan Africa.

Archer, Violet (Balestreri) (b. Montreal, 24 Apr. 1913). Composer. Studied with Champagne at McGill, with Bartók in New York, and with Hindemith at Yale; taught at McGill (1944–47), North Texas State (1950–53), the Univ. of Oklahoma (1953–61), and the Univ. of Alberta (1962–78). Her works include operas (*The Meal*, 1983); orchestral music; chamber music (2 string trios, 1953, 1961); keyboard works.

Archet [Fr.], **archetto** [It.]. The bow of a stringed instrument.

Archi [It.]. Bows; hence, an instruction to resume bowing after a passage marked *pizzicato.

Archlute [Fr. *archiluth;* Ger. *Erzlaute;* It. *arciliuto, liuto attiorbato;* Sp. *archilaúd*]. A small, six- or seven-course lute to which an extended pegbox has been added to hold six or seven unfretted bass courses. Used in Italy for solo and continuo in the 17th and 18th centuries, it retained the Renaissance tuning with added basses, $F_1 G_1 A_1 B_1 C D E F G c f a d' g'$. Alessandro Piccinini (1623) claimed its invention.

Arco [It.]. The bow of a stringed instrument; hence, also an instruction (sometimes in the phrase *col arco,* with the bow) to resume bowing after a passage marked *pizzicato.

Ardévol, José (b. Barcelona, 13 Mar. 1911; d. Havana, 7 Jan. 1981). Composer. Emigrated to Cuba (1930); directed the Orquesta de cámara de la Habana (1934–52); from 1936 to 1951 taught at universities in Havana and Oriente; taught at the Havana Conservatory (from 1965) and at the National School of Music (from 1968); conducted the orchestra of the Ministry of Education. The neoclassicism of his early works was abandoned for aleatoric and serial techniques.

Arditamente, ardito [It.]. Boldly.

Arditi, Luigi (b. Crescentino, Piedmont, 16 July 1822; d. Hove, near Brighton, 1 May 1903). Conductor and composer. Studied at the Milan Conservatory; active as an opera conductor in Havana (from 1846), at Her Majesty's Theatre, London (1858–69), on the Continent, and in Mapleson's U.S. tours (1878–94). Composed the once very popular song "Il bacio."

A re, are. See Hexachord.

Arel, Bülent (b. Constantinople, 23 Apr. 1918; d. Stony Brook, N.Y., 24 Nov. 1990). Composer. Studied composition with Akses at the Ankara Conservatory (1941–47); worked at the Columbia-Princeton Electronic Music Studio (1959–63); taught at Yale (1961–62, 1965–70) and SUNY Stony Brook (from 1971). His later style embraced twelve-tone techniques and free atonality; works include tape pieces (*Impressions of Wall Street,* 1961) and video (*Capriccio for TV,* 1969).

Arensky, Anton Stepanovich (b. Novgorod, 12 July 1861; d. Perkiarvi?, near Terioki, Finland, 25 Feb. 1906). Composer, pianist, and conductor. Studied with Rimsky-Korsakov at the St. Petersburg Conservatory; taught at the Moscow Conservatory until 1895, where his students included Rachmaninoff, Scriabin, and Glier. Directed the concerts of the Russian Choral Society (1888–95) and headed the Russian imperial chapel (1895–1901); after 1901 concertized widely as pianist and conductor. Works include operas (*Rafael,* 1894), a ballet (*Egyptian Nights* (1900); 2 symphonies (1883, 1889); choral

and vocal works; Piano trio no. 1 in D minor (1894) and other chamber music; numerous piano pieces.

Argenta (Maza), Ataúlfo (b. Castro Urdiales, Spain, 19 Nov. 1913; d. Los Molinos, 21 Jan. 1958). Conductor and pianist. Studied at the Royal Conservatory in Madrid and conducting with Carl Schuricht; taught piano at the Kassel Conservatory. Debut with Orquesta nacional (1945), subsequently music director (1947–58).

Argento, Dominick (b. York, Pa., 27 Oct. 1927). Composer. Studied with Nabokov and Weisgall at Peabody; subsequently with Dallapiccola in Italy, and with Hanson, Hovhaness, and Rogers at Eastman. Taught at the Univ. of Minnesota (from 1958). His song cycle *From the Diary of Virginia Woolf* (1974) was awarded a Pulitzer; other works include the operas *Postcard from Morocco* (1971) and *The Dream of Valentino* (1994); *6 Elizabethan Songs* (1958); *The Mask of Night* (soprano, orchestra, 1965).

Argerich, Martha (b. Buenos Aires, 5 June 1941). Pianist. Studied with Vincente Scaramuzza, Friedrich Gulda, Madeleine Lipatti, Arturo Benedetti Michelangeli, and Nikita Magaloff. Debut in Buenos Aires, 1946; European tour, 1955; first prize at Chopin Competition in Warsaw, 1965; U.S. debut, 1966. Well known as a soloist for the earlier Romantics, has also accompanied (e.g., Rostropovich, Kremer) in this repertory.

Arghūl [Ar.]. A Middle Eastern *double clarinet made of cane. The shorter pipe has six finger holes; the longer is a drone.

Aria [It.]. A self-contained composition for solo voice, usually with instrumental accompaniment and occurring within the context of a larger form such as opera, oratorio, or cantata.

The term first appeared at the end of the 14th century signifying a manner or style of singing or playing. This meaning continued into the 15th and 16th centuries (when the word was joined to certain place names, as in *aria veneziana* or *aria napoletana*), but the term came increasingly to mean tune or lyrical piece. Aria could also refer to a melodic scheme or pattern used for singing texts of similar poetic structure, such as the sonnet, *terza rima,* or *ottava rima,* and was sometimes used to designate strophic pieces for three or four voices in homophonic texture— pieces that might otherwise be called *canzonetta or *villanella. The term was further attached to instrumental pieces, either accompaniments of songs or independent works such as the *romanesca and *ruggiero.

In the 17th century, the aria existed as a portion of a larger work, such as an opera, or as an independent piece. The forms favored were strophic or strophic-bass [see Strophic variations]. In many cases the strophes were separated by a *ritornello played either by strings or by the basso continuo. Although arias at this time differed from recitative in their formal organization, they could be similar to recitative in melodic style. By the second third of the 17th century, triple meter became a characteristic feature of arias. About that time, ostinato arias—arias over a *ground bass—also came into use, particularly for laments.

In the later 17th century, the da capo aria became increasingly important, and this became the dominant form in the first decades of the 18th century. The text for a da capo aria, as seen in the librettos of Zeno and Metastasio, was typically a poem in two strophes, each strophe normally containing three to six lines. The first strophe of the poem provided the text for the first section of the da capo aria. By the 1720s and 1730s, a typical scheme for the first part had emerged: an instrumental ritornello; a full statement of the first strophe with a harmonic movement from tonic to dominant; a further ritornello in the dominant; a second full statement of the first strophe either beginning in the tonic or moving quickly back to it; a final statement of the ritornello in the tonic. The second strophe provided the text for the middle section of the da capo aria. This section usually provided harmonic contrast by avoiding the tonic, often using the relative key. The middle section might be more lightly scored than the outer sections and generally presented the full strophe only once, although internal text might be repeated. Then came the return of the first strophe and its music, a repetition that the singer was usually expected to vary with improvised ornamentation. But the form of the da capo aria was predictable only on the largest level: ABA. Matters such as the relation of the melodic material of the ritornello to that of the voice, the orchestration of the ritornello, the balance of the tonic- and dominant-controlled sections within the first part, and the degree of contrast between the first and second sections were all variable.

The da capo aria came under increasing criticism from Gluck and others by the final third of the 18th century, for both musical and dramatic reasons. In the second half of the 18th century, a number of alternative forms for the aria emerged. One possibility was an abridgment of the da capo—the dal segno aria, in which the return was not to the beginning of the aria but to a point marked by a sign after the ritornello, often the beginning of the second full statement of the first strophe. Arias were also constructed along the lines of instrumental movements, in binary, sonata, or rondo forms. New procedures emerged, such as the intrusion of a chorus or another soloist. Nevertheless, the form of the da capo aria was still to be found, though fully written out, in the early *opere serie* of Mozart. Comic opera in particular showed a notable variety of formal procedures during the 18th century. One particularly striking innovation was the "double" aria, in which two tempos (usually slow–fast) outlined two contrasting emotions.

In 19th-century Italian opera, at least from Rossini onward, this double aria became the norm and was typically expanded into an entire scene. First came the *scena,* an orchestrally accompanied recitative setting of unrhymed lines of variable length; then the first lyrical section, sometimes called *cantabile* and usually slow; then the *tempo di mezzo,* effecting a change of mood, usually by the arrival or interjection of secondary characters or the chorus; and finally the *cabaletta,* usually faster and more energetic than the *cantabile,* nearly always repeated literally with choral interjections. Each of these last three sections was set to rhymed, metrically stable verse, though typically the line length and syllabic stress changed from section to section. This double aria remained the standard form for Bellini, Donizetti, and early Verdi, and was even extended to duets and larger ensembles, usually with an added confrontational movement (the *tempo d'attacco*) between the *scena* and *cantabile.* After *La traviata* (1853), however, Verdi became increasingly wary of the *cabaletta,* often preferring to end his scenes with a *coup de théâtre* at the *tempo di mezzo* stage.

In French grand opera, as represented by the works of Meyerbeer, the aria plays a less significant role. The variety of terms used for arialike pieces in German romantic opera before Wagner is a reflection of the variety of formal procedures used. The terms *arie, arietta, solo, Lied, romanza, rondo, cavatina* are present in the works of Spohr, Schubert, Weber, and Marschner. In the course of Wagner's life work, the aria, understood as a lyric, self-sufficient piece, gradually became less and less important, a reform whose impact was felt well beyond the bounds of German opera.

The aria has had a restricted role in 20th-century opera.

Ariadne auf Naxos. Opera in one act and a prologue by Richard Strauss (libretto by Hugo von Hofmannsthal). In its original form, produced in Stuttgart in 1912, the opera was in one act only and was performed together with a condensed version of Molière's *Le bourgeois gentilhomme* (translation by Hofmannsthal, incidental music by Strauss). In 1916, it was produced in Vienna as an independent work with the addition of a prologue establishing a dramatic situation similar to that in Molière's play, whereby an *opera seria* is interwoven with the antics of a *commedia dell'arte* troupe. Setting: Vienna in the 18th century and Naxos, ancient Greece.

Arietta [It.]. A small aria or a song, less elaborate than an aria, sometimes sung by a secondary character in an opera. The term was in use by the middle of the 17th century.

Ariette [Fr.]. (1) In French opera of the first half of the 18th century, a virtuoso aria, written in imitation of the Italian style. It might contain runs, trills, or long sustained notes in the vocal part, and was frequently in da capo form. (2) In French comic opera of the second half of the 18th century, simply a song. The *comédie mêlée d'ariettes* is thus a spoken play with added songs.

Arioso [It.]. A lyrical manner of setting a text, usually a recitative text, in an opera, cantata, or oratorio. The term was in use in Italy by the 1630s. An *arioso* may grow directly out of recitative and be distinguished from it by text repetition, more florid or expressive melodic line, melodic sequence, or a more regular harmonic rhythm. For such a passage, *recitativo arioso* may be a more accurate designation. *Arioso* may also indicate a small aria that, although songlike and tonally self-contained, does not have the formal shape of a regular aria (e.g., strophic or *da capo,* depending on the period). Handel's operas and oratorios contain numerous examples of such pieces, "Ombra mai fù" from *Serse* being one of the best known. The term may also be applied to instrumental movements in *arioso* style, as in Beethoven's Piano Sonata op. 110.

Ariosti, Attilio (b. Bologna, 5 Nov. 1666; d. ca. 1730?). Composer. Joined the Order of S. Maria de' Servi (1688); left the order and served the Duke of Mantua (by 1696) and at the Berlin (1697–1703) and Austrian (1703–11) courts; in 1712 returned to his order. During two visits to London (1716–17 and 1723–27) his operas, cantatas, and chamber works brought him much success. Compositions include 22 stage works; 5 oratorios; some 45 solo cantatas; many chamber works, including nearly 60 pieces for viola d'amore with continuo.

Arizaga, Rodolfo (b. Buenos Aires, 11 July 1926; d. there, 1985). Composer. Studied at the National Conservatory in Buenos Aires and with Boulanger and Messiaen in Paris (from 1954); resettled in Argentina in 1960, teaching music at Buenos Aires Univ. and writing music criticism. Compositions include cantatas; orchestral works; chamber music; piano pieces; songs.

Arlen, Harold [Arluck, Hyman] (b. Buffalo, 15 Feb. 1905; d. New York, 23 Apr. 1986). Composer of popular songs, musicals, and film scores. In 1929 began to compose songs for the Cotton Club Revue in Harlem, including "Get Happy" (1929) and "Stormy Weather" (1933); in films collaborated with lyricists E. Y. Harburg (*Wizard of Oz,* 1939, including "Over the Rainbow") and Ira Gershwin (*A Star Is Born,* 1954), and in musicals with Johnny Mercer (*St. Louis Woman,* 1941) and Truman Capote (*House of Flowers,* 1954).

Arlésienne, L' [Fr., The Woman of Arles]. Incidental music by Bizet, composed in 1872, to Alphonse Daudet's play of the same name. Bizet arranged an orchestral suite from this work in 1872. A second suite was arranged posthumously by Ernest Guiraud in 1879.

Armonica. *Glass harmonica.

Armonica a bocca [It.]. *Mouth organ.

Armstrong, Louis [Pops; Satchmo] (b. New Orleans, 4 Aug. 1901; d. New York, 6 July 1971). Jazz trumpeter and singer. Replaced King Oliver in Kid Ory's band (1919?) and played with Fate Marable on riverboats based in New Orleans (1918–19) and St. Louis (1919–21); second cornet in Oliver's Creole Jazz Band in Chicago (1922–24). In New York became featured cornet soloist with Fletcher Henderson's big band (1924–25), then in Chicago made seminal recordings with his Hot Five, Hot Seven, and Savoy Ballroom Five; switched to trumpet around 1927. He was accompanied by big bands until 1947, when he formed the All Stars which toured internationally until 1971. Also made a number of films. Armstrong redefined notions of trumpet virtuosity not only for jazz but for all genres. He was also the first great jazz singer, often combining lyrics with scat singing. Recordings include *Heebie Jeebies, Cornet Chop Suey* (both 1926), *Potato Head Blues* (1927), *Weather Bird* (1928), *Black and Blue* (1929), *Rockin' Chair* (1947), the album *Louis Armstrong Plays W. C. Handy* (1954), and *Hello Dolly* (1963).

Armure [Fr.]. *Key signature.

Arne, Michael (b. London, ca. 1740; d. Lambeth, 14 Jan. 1786). Composer and keyboard player, perhaps the adopted son of Thomas Arne. Performed as a singer, harpsichordist and organist; during the 1750s and 1760s contributed a large number of songs to stage plays for London theaters. Composed 9 operas, collaborated on at least 15 others, and published 7 song collections.

Arne, Thomas Augustine (b. London, 12 Mar. 1710; d. there, 5 Mar. 1778). Composer. His *Rosamond* (1733) and masque *Dido and Aeneas* (1734) were the first in a long series of extraordinary stage successes; until well into the 1760s he was England's leading stage composer. Named D.Mus. in 1759, thereafter commonly called "Dr. Arne." Stage works include *Comus* (1738); *Thomas and Sally, or The Sailor's Return* (1760); *Artaxerxes* (1762); *Love in a Village*

(1762); also composed individual songs and chamber works.

Arnold, Eddy [Richard Edward] (b. Henderson, Tenn., 15 May 1918). Country singer and songwriter. After early performances on radio stations and with the Grand Ole Opry as the "Tennessee Plowboy" he began recording for RCA Victor; songs include "I'll Hold You in My Heart" (1948), "Cattle Call" (1955), and "Anytime" (1958). Appeared on national television shows.

Arnold, Malcolm (Henry) (b. Northampton, 21 Oct. 1921). Composer. Studied with Gordon Jacob (composition) and Ernest Hall (trumpet) at the Royal College of Music (1938–40); first trumpet in the London Philharmonic and the BBC Symphony (1942–48); subsequently devoted himself to composing. Works are firmly diatonic, with elements of 19th-century orchestral lushness; they include operas; ballets; film scores (*Bridge on the River Kwai,* 1957); 9 symphonies; many chamber works (*Trevelyan Suite,* 1968).

Arnold, Samuel (b. London, 10 Aug. 1740; d. there, 22 Oct. 1802). Composer, organist, and scholar. Harpsichordist at Covent Garden (from 1764); during the 1760s his pastiche operas were highly successful there. Contributed works to London theaters throughout the 1770s. Organist of the Chapel Royal (1783); director of the Academy of Ancient Music (1789); organist at Westminster Abbey (1793); also a music editor.

Arpa [It., Sp.]. Harp.

Arpanetta [It.; Ger. *Spitzharfe*]. A double *zither popular in Italy and Germany in the 16th, 17th, and 18th centuries. It has strings on both sides of its trapezoidal sound box: steel strings on one side for the melody and brass strings on the other for accompaniment. The player sets the instrument upright with the steel strings on the right and plucks it like a harp with the fingers of both hands.

Arpège [Fr.]. *Arpeggio; in earlier writing also *arpègement, arpégé.* See also *Acciaccatura.*

Arpeggiando, arpeggiato [It.]. See Bowing (9).

Arpeggiate, arpeggiation. To sound the pitches of a chord successively, as in an *arpeggio, rather than simultaneously; the sounding of a chord in this way.

Arpeggio [It., fr. *arpa,* harp; Fr. *arpège;* Sp. *arpegio*]. A chord whose pitches are sounded successively, usually from lowest to highest, rather than simultaneously. In current notational practice, it may be indicated by any of the methods shown in Ex. 1, all of which should be interpreted to mean performance from lowest to highest pitch unless the contrary is specifically indicated by additional signs or the

reversal of the order of the smaller notes. A distinction between simultaneous arpeggios in the two hands in keyboard music and a single arpeggio in which the two hands play successively is often indicated by the distinction between separate wavy lines for the two hands [Ex. 2a] and a single wavy line spanning the chords of the two hands [Ex. 2b]. Although some modern authorities insist that arpeggios should always begin on the beat, the treatises on *ornamentation of the 17th and 18th centuries do not explicitly state any such rule, and musical context often suggests the contrary.

Although the arpeggio is particularly associated with plucked instruments, such as the harp, lute, and guitar, and stringed keyboard instruments, it is common also in music for bowed instruments, such as the members of the violin and viol families, where, however, it is often a technical necessity deriving from the limited ability of such instruments to sustain three or more pitches simultaneously [see Bowing].

Arpeggione. (1) A bowed guitar invented by J. G. Staufer in 1824. It is the size of a cello, its bridge and fingerboard are curved, its neck is fretted, and its six strings are tuned like those of the guitar, E A d g b e'. (2) A sonata in A minor by Schubert, D. 821 (1824), for arpeggione and piano, now often played on the cello.

Arpicordo [It.]. In early 16th-century Italy, a gut-strung harpsichord or virginal; later, ordinary wire-strung instruments.

Arraché [Fr., torn]. Forceful pizzicato.

Arrangement [Ger. *Bearbeitung*]. (1) The adaption of a composition for a medium different from that for which it was originally composed, usually with the intention of preserving the essentials of the musical substance; also the result of such a process of adaptation. The practice is widespread at least as early as the 14th through the 16th century, when numerous vocal works (both sacred and secular) were arranged for keyboard instruments and the lute [see Intabulation]. Bach provides the most celebrated examples from the Baroque era in his arrangements of works by Vivaldi. Mozart in turn arranged some fugues by Bach for string trio and quartet.

Numerous works from the 18th and 19th centuries were arranged for piano, often, in the case of operas, orchestral works, and some chamber music, to aid the study and dissemination of the works. Some such arrangements, however, notably those of Liszt, were clearly intended to have artistic merit in their own right as well as to serve as vehicles for the display of virtuosity by performers. Earlier in the 20th century, there was a considerable vogue for arranging works (including keyboard works) by Bach for the modern symphony orchestra. There are also numerous examples from the 18th century to the present of composers arranging their own works for a new medium of performance.

The terms transcribe and transcription are sometimes used interchangeably with arrange and arrangement. Often, however, the former imply greater fidelity to the original. Transcription also means the translation of works from earlier forms of musical notation into the notation now in use. See also Additional accompaniment, Orchestration.

(2) In popular music and jazz, a specific version, including orchestration if for an ensemble, of a tune and its harmonies. In such repertories, it is usually assumed that the composer's role has been to specify the melody and to name the accompanying harmonies in a rather straightforward way, leaving the arranger complete freedom with respect to performance medium and orchestration, and considerable latitude with respect to rhythmic and harmonic detail. An arrangement is in general something written down or at least preserved essentially unchanged from performance to performance rather than improvised.

Arrau, Claudio (b. Chillán, Chile, 6 Feb. 1903; d. Mürzzuschlag, Austria, 9 June 1991). Pianist. Studied with Bindo Paoli (1910–12) and Martin Krause in Berlin (1912–18); debut in Berlin, 1914; U.S. debut, 1923; taught at Stern's Conservatory (1924–40). Performed recital cycles devoted to all of Mozart's and Schubert's solo keyboard music (1930s) and all of Beethoven's sonatas (1953–54); world tours (1968, 1974–75, 1981).

Arriaga (y Balzola), Juan Crisóstomo (Jacobo Antonio) de (b. Rigoitia, near Bilbao, 27 Jan. 1806; d. Paris, 17 Jan. 1826). Composer. Entered the Paris Conservatory at age 15; studied counterpoint with Fétis and violin with Baillot; composed sacred works, orchestral music, and 3 string quartets that are still performed. His death at age 19 prompted romanticized assessments of his life and music.

Arroyo, Martina (b. New York, 2 Feb. 1936). Soprano. Studied with Marinka Gurewich and Josef Turnau; debuted in 1958; Met debut the following year. From 1963 to 1968 performed with the Zurich Opera. After 1965 sang major roles at the Met. Repertory includes Aida, Tosca, Elsa *(Lohengrin),* and Donna Anna, as well as 20th-century music.

Ars antiqua, ars vetus [Lat., previous technique, old craft]. The era of 13th-century French polyphony (beginning with the school of *Notre Dame in Paris), in contrast to the 14th century, which is often termed the *ars nova;* also the notational and compositional practices of 13th-century French polyphony. Compositional genres associated with the *ars antiqua* include *organum, *clausula, *motet, *hocket, *conductus, *rondellus, *estampie.* See also Middle Ages.

Arsis and thesis [fr. Gr., raising, lowering]. (1) Originally, the raising and lowering of the foot in ancient Greek dance. By extension with respect to Greek verse, thesis referred to the long syllable of the poetic foot and arsis to the remainder of the foot. (2) Among Roman writers, who associated the rise and fall with the voice, and for many writers since then, the reverse of (1), i.e., arsis referring to the long syllable of the foot and thesis to the remainder; with respect to accentual verse, the accented and unaccented parts of the foot, respectively. (3) In musical usage, the metrically unaccented and accented parts of a measure, respectively [see Accent, Meter]; hence, often the equivalent of upbeat and downbeat, respectively.

Ars nova [Lat., new technique, new craft]. (1) A stylistic era of European (especially French and Italian) art music beginning around the time of a manuscript copy dated 1316 of the *Roman de *Fauvel* and extending through most or all of the 14th century. See also *Ars subtilior.*

The association of the term with 14th-century France is due to the prestige of Philippe de Vitry's treatise *Ars nova.* It is particularly associated with advances in the notation of rhythm. The leading French composer of the period was Guillaume de Machaut. In Italy, 14th-century music was seen more as a continuation of than a departure from the music of the 13th century. In light of this, many authors believe that the era is more justly known by its literary designation, *trecento.* The leading Italian composer of the period was Francesco Landini. See also *Ars antiqua,* Middle Ages.

(2) Two related but autonomous 14th-century repertories, centered in France and northern Italy, that are characterized by new conventions of notation and a new emphasis on polyphonic song (in France principally the *ballade, *virelai, and *rondeau; in Italy the *madrigal, *caccia, and *ballata). The French

repertory further gives prominence to polyphonic settings of Mass movements and *isorhythmic principles of construction, chiefly in motets.

Ars subtilior [Lat., more subtle art]. The intricate style of late 14th-century music by composers after Machaut. The term is a modern coinage and refers to a repertory whose notation combines features of French and Italian notation and can be extremely complex. The compositions, usually in one of the French *formes fixes,* often exhibit textures that are very complicated rhythmically. The repertory seems to have been centered in southern France and northern Spain

Artemov [Artyomov], **Viacheslav Petrovich** (b. Moscow, 29 June 1940). Composer. Studied at the Moscow Conservatory; particularly interested in musical folklore and improvisational techniques; collaborated with composers Sofia Gubaidulina and Viktor Suslin in the experimental ensemble Astrea (1975–81). Works include *Way to Olympus* (1978–84) and a Requiem (1986–88).

Articulation. (1) In performance, the characteristics of attack and decay of single tones or groups of tones and the means by which these characteristics are produced. Thus, for example, *staccato and *legato are types of articulation. In the playing of stringed instruments, this is largely a function of *bowing; in wind instruments, of *tonguing. Groups of tones may be articulated (i.e., "phrased") so as to be perceived as constituting phrases [see Phrase, Phrasing]. Notational symbols for articulation first occur around 1600, are not uncommon in compositions from ca. 1620 to 1750, and occur with increasing attention to detail in works thereafter. See also Performance practice.

(2) In the analysis of musical form, a boundary or point of demarcation between formal segments, e.g., that produced by a cadence or rest. As a compositional process, articulation is comparable to punctuation in language.

Art of Fugue, The [Ger. *Die Kunst der Fuge*]. A didactic keyboard work by Bach, BWV 1080 (ca. 1745–50), first published in 1751, though the publication was partly overseen by Bach before his death in 1750. This printed edition contains 14 fugues, called *contrapuncti* (numbers 12 and 13 being completely invertible and thus in two versions each), 4 canons, 2 mirror fugues arranged for two keyboards, and an incomplete quadruple fugue, all based on the same theme [see Ex.]. The work exploits a wide variety of contrapuntal devices—inversion, stretto, augmentation, diminution, canon, double fugue, triple fugue, and quadruple fugue. A concluding chorale prelude, "Wenn wir in höchsten Nöten sein" BWV 668, was added to the work by its editors to "com-

pensate" for missing and incomplete material. The printed edition, however, represents a reordering of Bach's extant autograph score and adds several movements. Consequently, extended controversies have arisen as to the proper order of the *contrapuncti* and canons, the intended medium for performance (Bach having had the work engraved in open score without specifying the medium), the added chorale, and the role of the last fugue.

Art song. A song intended for the concert repertory, as distinct from a folk or popular song. An art song traditionally is a setting of a text of high literary quality and, unlike most folk and popular songs, includes an accompaniment that is specified by the composer rather than improvised or arranged by or for the performer. See also Song.

Artusi, Giovanni Maria (b. Bologna ca. 1540; d. there, 18 Aug. 1613). Theorist. In 1562 entered the Order of S. Salvatore (Bologna), where he spent most of his life. Studied with Zarlino, whose views he defended and amplified in the influential treatise *L'arte del contraponto* (1598). In his *L'Artusi* (Venice, 1600) he spoke out against abuses in the "modern" style of Monteverdi.

Arutiunian, Alexander Grigorevich (b. Yerevan, 23 Sept. 1920). Composer. Graduated from the Yerevan Conservatory in 1941; continued study in Moscow at the House of Armenian Culture under Litinsky. His style is influenced by the melodic and rhythmic inflections of Armenian folk music. Works include the opera *Saiat-Nova* (1963–67); concertos for piano (1941), coloratura soprano (1950 and 1959), trumpet (1950), French horn (1962), woodwind quintet (1964), oboe (1979), and flute (1980); chamber music; songs; incidental and film music.

As, ases [Ger.]. A-flat, A-double-flat. See Pitch names.

Asafiev, Boris Vladimirovich [literary pseud. Igor Glebov] (b. St. Petersburg, 29 July 1884; d. Moscow, 27 Jan. 1949). Musicologist and composer. Studied with Lyadov (composition) and Rimsky-Korsakov (orchestration) at the St. Petersburg Conservatory (1904–10); taught at the Leningrad (1925–43) and Moscow (from 1943) conservatories. Wrote on contemporary Western and Soviet music as well as on 19th-century Russian music; his major theoretical studies formed the cornerstone of the Soviet analytic method.

Ashkenazy, Vladimir (Davidovich) (b. Gorki, 6 July 1937). Pianist and conductor. Studied piano with

Anaida Sumbatian (1945–55) and Boris Zemlyianski and Lev Oborin (1955–63). U.S. debut, 1958; first prize (shared with John Ogdon), Tchaikovsky Competition at Moscow, 1962. Moved to London, 1963; to Reykjavík, 1968; to Lucerne, 1978. Guest conductor, the London Philharmonic, 1981; principal guest conductor Philharmonia Orchestra, 1982–83; music director Royal Philharmonic, 1987–94; principal guest conductor Cleveland Orchestra from 1987; chief conductor (West) Berlin Radio Orchestra from 1989. His repertory includes Mozart, Beethoven, Chopin, Rachmaninov, Sibelius, and Scriabin.

Ashley, Robert (Reynolds) (b. Ann Arbor, 28 Mar. 1930). Composer. Studied theory, composition, and acoustics at the Univ. of Michigan, 1948–52 and 1957–60; piano and composition at the Manhattan School (1953); from 1969 to 1981 directed the Center for Contemporary Music at Mills College. A pioneer in the development of mixed-media performance art, turning his attention in the 1970s to televised opera (*Perfect Lives (Private Parts)*, 1977–83; *Yellow Man with Heart with Wings*, 1989–90)

Asioli, Bonifazio (b. Correggio, 30 Aug. 1769; d. there, 18 May 1832). Composer, theorist, and harpsichordist. Studied in Parma; composed church works and comic operas. *Maestro di cappella* in Correggio (1786); in 1808 became the first director of the Milan Conservatory. Published a series of theoretical works; returned to Correggio and established a music school there (1814).

Asola, Giammateo [Giovanni Matteo] (b. Verona, ca. 1532; d. Venice, 1 Oct. 1609). Composer. Probably studied with Vincenzo Ruffo in Verona; became a chaplain at S. Severo in Venice in 1588 and remained there until his death. Composed much conservative sacred music and several books of secular and spiritual madrigals.

Aspiration [Fr.]. (1) The French *accent. (2) A one-finger vibrato (*plainte*) on the viola da gamba. (3) The substitution of silence for the last part of a note-value, indicated by a vertical stroke over the note.

Asplmayr [Aspelmayr], **Franz** (b. Linz, bapt. 2 Apr. 1728; d. Vienna, 29 July 1786). Composer. Beginning in 1759 served in the imperial court at Vienna, eventually as composer for the Kärntnertortheater; in 1776 he brought to the stage *Pygmalion* (after J. J. Rousseau), possibly the first German-language melodrama; subsequently composed singspiels and incidental music for the Viennese court.

Assai [It.]. Much, very much, e.g., *allegro assai,* very fast. Some 18th-century writers, however, use the term to mean *rather* and thus in a way similar to the French *assez*.

Assez [Fr.]. Sufficiently, rather, e.g., *assez vite,* rather fast.

Astorga, Emanuele (Gioacchino Cesare Rincón) d' (b. Augusta, Sicily, 20 Mar. 1680; d. Madrid?, ca. 1757). Composer. Born of Spanish nobility, moved with his family to Palermo (1693). His opera *Dafni* (1709) caught the attention of Charles III, whom the composer apparently followed to Vienna (1712–14); he subsequently returned to Italy, became a senator of Palermo (1718), and later (1720s) traveled to Sicily, Lisbon, and possibly also to London. His life was the subject of highly romanticized accounts (and of Abert's opera *Astorga,* 1866). Remembered mainly for a *Stabat Mater* that was popular during the 19th century.

Asuar, José Vicente (b. Santiago, Chile, 20 July 1933). Composer. Studied at the National Conservatory in Santiago and with Blacher in Berlin; later with Hiller (1970). Directed electronic studios in Chile and in Karlsruh (1958–65), and established the first such studio in Caracas (1965). Has taught acoustics and electronic music at the Univ. of Chile and elsewhere.

Atabal [Sp.]. (1) *Kettledrum. (2) A cylindrical drum; in Spain a large bass drum, in Central America and the West Indies a smaller drum sometimes played in sets of three. (3) In Cuba, a *slit drum. (4) In the Dominican Republic, a single-headed frame drum, also called a *palo*.

Atabaque [Port.]. A single-headed, barrel-shaped drum used in Afro-Brazilian cults and generally played in sets of three.

Atem [Ger.]. Breath; *Atempause,* breathing pause, usually indicated in musical notation with an apostrophe and often a guide to phrasing as much as an indication of where wind players or singers should take a breath.

A tempo [It.]. In *tempo; hence, an instruction to return to the original tempo after some deviation from it.

Atkins, Chet [Chester Burton] (b. Luttrell, Tenn., 20 June 1924). Country guitarist and record producer. After early work as a backup musician became manager of RCA Victor's Nashville studio in 1957, where he produced and appeared on many country albums that established the "Nashville Sound." Recorded many solo albums and some with guitarists Jerry Reed (1972) and Les Paul (1976).

Atonality. The absence of *tonality, the absence of key. The term is most often applied to music of the 20th century in which pitches are not treated in accordance with the particular principles of tonal centers, consonance and dissonance, and harmony and counterpoint that prevailed in various forms in Western music from the end of the 17th century through the 19th and into the 20th. Thus, the term generally refers to the absence of a particular kind of tonality, sometimes called tonic-dominant or triadic tonality. Many works that are "atonal" in this sense do in fact treat pitches in a hierarchical fashion in which one or a few pitches play a central role. Sometimes included in the category of atonal works are those based on the *twelve-tone system, in which the creation of tonal centers is often rigorously avoided. A more precise use of the term restricts it to works such as Arnold Schoenberg's op. 11 (1909) through op. 22 (1913–14) and contemporaneous works by Berg and Webern, which are examples of neither triadic tonality nor the twelve-tone system.

Attacca, attacca subito [It.]. Attack, attack immediately; hence, when placed at the end of one movement, an instruction to begin the next movement immediately without the customary pause.

Attacco [It., attack]. A short motive that is treated imitatively, either as the subject for a fugue or within a work using imitation. It is to be distinguished from the *andamento and *soggetto.

Attack. The characteristics of the beginning of a sound, either as described technically by the science of *acoustics or more loosely as a function of *articulation in performance; also the degree of precision with which members of an ensemble coordinate the beginnings of pitches.

Attaingnant, Pierre (b. ca. 1494; d. Paris, late 1551 or 1552). Printer and publisher. Son-in-law and heir of the printer-engraver Philippe Pigouchet (fl. 1490–1514). Beginning with a collection of chansons dated 1527/28, used movable type and a single impression, a method that was probably his invention; eventually named *imprimeur et libraire du Roy en musique.* His publications include several books of pieces in lute tablature or keyboard score, 7 books of Masses, 14 books of motets, and over 36 books of chansons, plus numerous re-editions. New music by French composers dominates most of these books.

Atterberg, Kurt (b. Göteborg, 12 Dec. 1887; d. Stockholm, 15 Feb. 1974). Composer, conductor, and critic. Studied composition and instrumentation under Hallén at the Stockholm Conservatory (1910–11) and in Berlin between 1911 and 1915; from 1912 to 1968 made a career in Sweden's national patent office. Conducted the premiere of his first symphony (1909–11) in 1916 at Göteborg, and from 1916 to 1922 was *kapellmästare* at the Royal Dramatic Theater in Stockholm; also a music critic. Composed 5 operas; 3 ballets; 9 symphonies; choral and chamber music.

Attwood, Thomas (b. London, bapt. 23 Nov. 1765; d. there, 24 Mar. 1838). Composer and organist. Studied in Naples with Latilla (1783–85). His studies in Vienna with Mozart (1785–87), containing Mozart's corrections to his exercises, have been published. He returned to England in 1787 and became music instructor to the royal family. Subsequently organist at St. Paul's (1796) and composer and organist (1836) for the Chapel Royal. During the 1790s composed music for London comedies and farces.

Aubade [Fr.]. Originally, music played in the morning for a specific person or persons, as opposed to the *serenade, which is intended for the evening. In the 17th and 18th centuries, such music was often played for members of the royalty or civil authorities. More recently, composers (e.g., Bizet, Rimsky-Korsakov, Poulenc) have sometimes used the term as a title for instrumental works. See also *Alba, Alborada.*

Auber, Daniel-François-Esprit (b. Caen, 29 Jan. 1782; d. Paris, 12 or 13 May 1871). Composer. Studied in Paris with Ignaz Ladurner and later with Cherubini. His first work for the Opéra-comique was a failure, but *La bergère châtelaine* (1820) was successful; subsequently produced from one to three new stage works nearly every year until the early 1850s, almost all (from 1823) written in collaboration with Scribe (often with other librettists also involved) until Scribe's death in 1861. Their 36 works together included some of the greatest successes in opéra comique of the time. *La muette de Portici* (1828) established the model for French grand opera; *Gustave III* (1833) was on a similar scale. Auber served as director of the Paris Conservatory from 1842 to 1870.

Aubert, Jacques ["le vieux"] (b. Paris, 30 Sept. 1689; d. Belleville, nr. Paris, buried 19 May 1753). Composer and violinist. From 1719 in the service of the Duke of Bourbon; in 1727 joined the Vingt-quatre Violons du Roy; also played with the Académie royale de musique (from 1728), the Opéra (1728–52), and at the Concert spirituel (1729–40). His violin concertos are known as the first published in France (1734). Also composed chamber music and stage works.

Aubin, Tony (Louis Alexandre) (b. Paris, 8 Dec. 1907; d. there, 21 Sept. 1981). Composer and conductor. Studied with Dukas at the Paris Conservatory (1925–30) and conducting with Gaubert (1934–35). Conductor, French radio (1945–60); professor at the Paris Conservatory (from 1945). His music was influenced in its harmonic and coloristic palette by Ravel and Dukas.

Au chevalet [Fr.]. At the bridge; hence, an instruction to bow the violin or other stringed instrument near or on the bridge. See Bowing (11).

Auctoralis [Lat.]. Authentic as opposed to plagal. See Mode.

Audition. (1) A hearing given to a performer, often for the purpose of determining the performer's level of ability and therefore admissibility to a particular school, class, or ensemble; to perform for such a purpose; to listen to or preside over such a performance. (2) The sense of hearing.

Audran, Edmond (b. Lyons, 11 or 12 Apr. 1840; d. Tierceville, Seine-et-Oise, 17 Aug. 1901). Composer. Studied at the École Niedermeyer until 1859, then worked as a church musician in Marseilles. Produced his first comic operas in Marseilles; in 1879 began to work for the Bouffes-Parisiens in Paris, and with *La mascotte* (1880) had a worldwide success. He remained one of the genre's leaders through the 1890s.

Auer, Leopold (von) (b. Veszprém, Hungary, 7 June 1845; d. Loschwitz, near Dresden, 15 July 1930). Violinist and teacher. Studied at the conservatories in Budapest (1853–56) and Vienna (1857–58) and with Joachim (1863–64). Concertmaster in Düsseldorf and Hamburg (1864–68); court violinist and professor at the St. Petersburg Conservatory (1868–1917), where his pupils included Elman, Zimbalist, and Heifetz. Moved to the U.S. (1918), taught at Curtis in the 1920s. The Tchaikovsky violin concerto was written for him, but he declined to perform it.

Aufforderung zum Tanz [Ger., Invitation to the Dance]. A composition for piano by Carl Maria von Weber, J. 260 (1819), consisting of an introduction (the "invitation"), a waltz, and an epilogue. It was arranged for orchestra by Berlioz and by Felix Weingartner.

Aufführungspraxis [Ger.]. *Performance practice.

Aufgeregt [Ger.]. Excited.

Auflösung [Ger.]. (1) Resolution, as of a dissonance. (2) Cancellation of an accidental or element of a key signature; *Auflösungszeichen,* the natural sign.

Aufstrich [Ger.]. Up-bow.

Auftakt [Ger.]. Upbeat.

Auftritt [Ger.]. Entrance; scene, as of a dramatic work.

Aufzug [Ger]. (1) An act of an opera, play, etc. (2) In ceremonial trumpet music of the 18th and 19th cen-

turies, a processional fanfare, sometimes followed by a *Tusch.

Augenmusik [Ger.]. *Eye music.

Augmentation and diminution. The statement of a theme in uniformly longer or shorter note-values, respectively, than those originally associated with it. Thus, if the ratio between old and new values is 2 to 1, in augmentation what was originally a quarter note becomes a half note, etc., whereas in diminution what was originally a quarter note becomes an eighth note. Other ratios may apply as well. These devices are particularly characteristic of music based on imitation, such as the *fugue, *canon (including especially the augmentation canon), *ricercar, and early *fantasia. In fugues, augmentation of the subject is most likely to occur near the end (e.g., in Bach's *Well-Tempered Clavier* vol. 1 no. 8; for an example of diminution see vol. 2 no. 9). Complex examples such as are found in Bach's *The Art of Fugue* nos. 6 and 7 may include simultaneous use of augmentation and diminution at various ratios.

Music of the Middle Ages and Renaissance based on a *cantus firmus* (including *clausulae* of the Notre Dame repertory) also sometimes makes use of these devices, as do some *isorhythmic works, and they are important in the ricercars and fantasias of composers such as Andrea Gabrieli, Sweelinck, and Frescobaldi. In the 15th and 16th centuries, the system of *proportions employed in musical notation embodied augmentation and diminution. See also Diminutions.

Augmented. See Intervals, Sixth chords, Triads.

Aulos [Gr., also *kalamos;* Lat. *tibia*]. The most important wind instrument of ancient Greece. The aulos of classical times (600–300 B.C.E.) was a slender pipe made of cane, wood, bone, or ivory with three to five finger holes plus a thumb hole and a reed affixed to the top. Auloi were always played in pairs. The player put both reeds in the mouth and held the pipes apart in a V shape, with the left hand fingering one pipe and the right hand the other. They ranged from 30 to over 60 cm. (2 ft.) in length. There is much debate over whether the aulos had a single or double *reed. Aulos players are often depicted wearing a halter (*phorbeia*) fitted around the head and passing across the cheeks, but the purpose of this device is not known.

Auric, Georges (b. Lodève, 15 Feb. 1899; d. Paris, 23 July 1983). Composer. In 1913 studied with Caussade at the Paris Conservatory, continuing his studies with d'Indy at the Schola cantorum (1914–16). One of "Les six," he had contact with Stravinsky, Diaghilev, and the Ballets russes; wrote several ballets for Diaghilev and music for the theater, as well as songs and film scores for Cocteau. His Piano Sonata in F moved away from the straightforwardness of his earlier style; *Chemin de lumière,* a ballet of 1951, includes serial writing and the juxtaposition of tonality and atonality. From 1962 to 1968 he served as director of the Paris Opéra and the Opéra-comique.

Aurresku, auṙesku [Basque]. A Basque dance consisting of several sections (including a *zortziko*) that takes its name from the leader of a line of dancers. It is accompanied by the *txistu* and *tamboril,* the Basque equivalent of the *pipe and tabor.

Ausdruck, mit; Ausdrucksvoll [Ger.]. With expression.

Aushalten [Ger.]. To sustain.

Aus Italien [Ger., From Italy]. A symphonic fantasy, op. 16, composed in 1886 by Richard Strauss and inspired by his trip to Italy in that year.

Auslösung [Ger.]. The escapement of the *piano.

Äusserst [Ger.]. Extremely.

Austin, Larry (Don) (b. Duncan, Okla., 12 Sept. 1930). Composer. Studied at North Texas State Univ., Mills College, and Berkeley (1955–58); teachers included Imbrie, Milhaud, and Shifrin. Taught at the Univ. of California, Davis (1958–72); the Univ. of South Florida, Tampa (1972–78); North Texas State (from 1978). His experience as a modern jazz improviser contributed to the success of *Improvisations for Orchestra and Jazz Soloists* (1961); later music left areas of improvisational choice open to the performer within a controlled context. Other works include *Sinfonia concertante: A Mozartean Episode* (chamber orchestra, computer, 1986).

Auszug [Ger.]. Extract, excerpt; *Klavierauszug,* a reduction for piano of a work for larger forces such as an opera.

Authentic. (1) Of a musical text, unequivocally linked with the composer to whom the work is attributed. (2) In the study of folklore and folk music, belonging to a living, continuous folk tradition (often orally transmitted), as opposed to the corruption, imitation, or revival of a tradition. (3) In *performance practice, instruments or styles of playing that are historically appropriate to the music being performed. (4) See Cadence. (5) See Mode.

Auto [Sp.]. A Spanish dramatic work in one act with a prologue, often on a sacred or allegorical subject. By the middle of the 16th century, *autos* were performed especially on the feast of Corpus Christi and dealt in one way or another with the miracle of transubstantiation in the sacrament of communion, whence the term *auto sacramental.* They were writ-

ten in verse and made use of music in varying degrees. Such plays were taken by missionaries in the 16th century to the Spanish and Portuguese colonies of Latin America, where there are accounts of *autos* performed with music.

Autograph. A manuscript of a musical work written in its composer's hand, as opposed to music in the hand of a copyist or printed music; also holograph. The term usually refers to the score of an entire piece or movement, although a composer's corrections in a copy or print may be "autograph" in an adjectival sense. There are very few autographs of musical works from as early as the 16th century. From the 18th century on, autographs survive in considerable quantity and have played an important role in 20th-century efforts to produce reliable editions.

Autoharp. A *zither on which chords are produced with the aid of dampers mounted on a set of bars above the strings. The dampers are mounted on each bar in such a way as to allow only the strings for a designated chord to sound when that bar is depressed. The player plucks or strums the strings with the right hand while depressing the bars with the left. Invented in Germany in the late 19th century, it was patented in the U.S. in 1881 by C. F. Zimmermann. See ill. under Zither.

Automatic instrument. An instrument that plays itself without the agency of a living performer; also automatophone. Instruments are also called automatic if the sounding of the notes is caused by a self-actuating mechanism, even if the motive power is supplied by someone who turns a crank or treads on pedals and who also may have control over such aspects of the music as tempo, dynamics, or registration. Some instruments can be played either manually or automatically. The most common are player pianos and player organs, which have a normal keyboard as well as a built-in mechanism that can operate it. Another type of automatic device is the accessory mechanism applied to a normal instrument; for example, the Pianola and *Vorsitzer,* which stand in front of a piano keyboard and play upon it automatically.

In principle, any instrument can be played automatically, given the technology, and from the early 19th century, attempts have been made to simulate whole orchestras, using organ pipes and automatic percussion instruments. For such a machine (Maelzel's Panharmonicon) Beethoven wrote his *Wellington's Victory* (1813).

In the simplest automatic instruments, pins on the cylinder or projections from the disc engage the teeth of a metal comb, sometimes through the intermediary of a star wheel, causing them to vibrate and make a sound. No mechanism is needed beyond that required to rotate the cylinder. This is the principle of the music box, and it goes back to the 18th century. Sometimes, as in carillons, spinets, harp clocks, or barrel pianos, the motion of the cylinder acts directly through a mechanical linkage to strike or pluck. In wind instruments—pipe or reed organs, accordions, etc.—valves must be opened to admit or exhaust wind. In the simplest kind, holes in a paper roll pass over openings to become valves themselves. Most, however, employ a mechanical or pneumatic action.

The history of automatic instruments may extend, via Byzantine and Arab civilization, back to antiquity. In more recent times, it is closely bound up with the history of clockwork and automata (mechanical birds, moving figures, etc.). Most recently it has been affected by the use of electronic and, especially, digital technologies, which may be employed to sound a conventional instrument such as the piano or to produce wholly synthesized music.

Autry, (Orvon) Gene (b. Tioga, Tex., 29 Sept. 1907; d. Studio City, Calif., 2 Oct. 1998). Country and popular singer, songwriter, and actor. Through radio performances and appearances in over 100 western musical films, popularized the image of the singing cowboy that facilitated the national acceptance of country music. From 1939 to 1956 he hosted the CBS radio show *Melody Ranch*. His many successful recordings included "Rudolph the Red-Nosed Reindeer" (1949), which sold over 7 million copies.

Auxiliary tone. Neighbor note [see Counterpoint].

Ave Maria [Lat., Hail, Mary]. (1) A prayer of the Roman Catholic Church. Its text begins with parts of two verses of Scripture (Luke 1:28, 42) and concludes with a petition added in the 15th century. The melody associated with the first part of the text as an antiphon for the Annunciation dates from the 10th century. There are numerous polyphonic settings of the text from the Renaissance, some based on the melody, and there are Renaissance Masses based on this material as well. (2) A song by Schubert, D. 839 (1825), based on verses from Sir Walter Scott's *Lady of the Lake*. (3) A song by Gounod (1859) in which Bach's prelude in C major from *The Well-Tempered Clavier* vol. 1 provides the harmonic background for a new melody.

Ave maris stella [Lat., Hail, Star of the Sea]. A hymn of the Roman Catholic Church sung to several different melodies. These were frequently used during the Renaissance as the basis for polyphonic settings of the text.

Ave Regina caelorum [Lat., Hail, Queen of Heaven]. One of the four *antiphons for the Blessed Virgin Mary, sung in modern practice at Compline from the Purification (February 2) until Wednesday

in Holy Week. During the Renaissance it was often set polyphonically and used as the basis for polyphonic Masses.

Avidom [Mahler-Kalkstein], **Menahem** (b. Stanislav, Ukraine, 6 Jan. 1908). Composer. Emigrated to Palestine in 1925; studied in Beirut at the American Univ. (1926–28) and in Paris at the conservatory (1928–31); from 1935 lived in Tel Aviv, where he taught music theory at the conservatory. Works include 9 operas; choral works; 10 symphonies; chamber music (*Suite on B-A-C-H,* 1964).

Avison, Charles (b. Newcastle upon Tyne, bapt. 16 Feb. 1709; d. there, 9 or 10 May 1770). Composer and writer on music. Burney states that he traveled to Italy and later was a pupil of Geminiani. Organist at St. John's, Newcastle (1735) and at St. Nicholas's (1736); in 1738 became director of the town's concert series. In 1752 he published the treatise for which he is best known, the *Essay on Musical Expression;* Burney called it the first piece of English music criticism.

Avni, Tzvi (Jacob) (b. Saarbrücken, 2 Sept. 1927). Composer. In 1935 he emigrated to Palestine; studied composition in Tel Aviv with Ehrlich, Seter, and Ben-Haim (1954–58). In the U.S. (1962–64) worked with Copland and Foss, and studied electronic music with Ussachevsky at Columbia and with Myron Schaeffer at the Univ. of Toronto. Since 1971 has taught at Jerusalem's Rubin Academy. Works include ballets; instrumental music (*Al naharot Bavel* [By the Rivers of Babylon], 1971; *Mashav,* concertino for xylophone, 10 winds, percussion, 1988); works with tape (*Synchromotrask,* 1976).

Ax, Emanuel (b. Lvov, Poland, 8 June 1949). Pianist. Moved to Canada, 1959; studied at Juilliard (1961–66). New York debut, 1973; Avery Fisher Award, 1979. Plays the established repertory from Mozart to Ravel plus a few conservative moderns; often collaborates with Yo-Yo Ma and others.

Ayala Pérez, Daniel (b. Abalá, Yucatán, 21 July 1906; d. Veracruz, 20 June 1975). Composer and conductor. From 1929 studied at the conservatory in Mexico City; violinist in the Mexico Symphony. In 1940 returned to Yucatán; directed the Mérida Symphony (from 1944) and the Yucatán Conservatory. In 1955 became director of the Music School at Veracruz. His compositions evoke Mayan music.

Ayler, Albert (b. Cleveland, 13 July 1936; d. New York? between 5 and 25 Nov. 1970). Jazz tenor saxophonist. Played alto saxophone in rhythm-and-blues bands, switching to the tenor while serving in army bands. Stationed in France (1960–61), played with Cecil Taylor in Copenhagen (1962–63). Based in New York from 1963, led groups which performed and recorded irregularly, owing to the challenges his music presented listeners. Among the originators of free jazz saxophone playing, Ayler was the most unusual, combining wild swooping lines with rhythm-and-blues honks and squeals, and an old-fashioned wide vibrato.

Ayre. (1) The English lute-accompanied song of the late 16th and early 17th centuries. Such pieces were often published with an optional bass viol part or with three additional vocal parts printed in such a way that they could be read from a single copy by singers seated around a table. They range in style from serious songs with contrapuntal texture to lighter, homophonic, strophic songs. The first published collection was John Dowland's *First Booke of Songes or Ayres* of 1597. (2) In the 17th century, a movement in a suite [see Air]. (3) [also aire, air] In 17th-century English writers, mode or key; also the general character of a work.

Aznavour [Aznavurian], **Charles** (b. Paris, 25 May 1924). Popular songwriter, lyricist, singer, and actor. Closely associated with Edith Piaf, who supported his early partnership with composer Pierre Roche; in 1955 achieved success as a singer with "Sur ma vie." In America he was popular in nightclubs with songs such as "On ne sait jamais" and "Ce jour tant attendu."

B

B. (1) See Pitch names, Letter notation, Hexachord, Pitch. (2) In German nomenclature for pitch, B-flat. (3) An abbreviation for *bass, or *bassus.*

B fa. See Hexachord.

B mi. See Hexachord.

Baaren, Kees van (b. Enschede, Netherlands, 22 Oct. 1906; d. Oegstgeest, 2 Sept. 1970). Composer. Studied at the Berlin Hochschule and with Willem Pijper; appointed director of the Music Lyceum in Amsterdam (1948), the Utrecht Conservatory (1953), the Royal Conservatory, The Hague (1958). Works include *Variazioni per orchestra* (1959); *Sinfonia,* orchestra (1956).

Babbitt, Milton (Byron) (b. Philadelphia, 10 May 1916). Composer and theorist. Studied music at New York Univ. and at Princeton with Sessions; wrote criticism for the *Musical Leader;* taught mathematics, later music (1948–86) at Princeton; also taught at Juilliard, the Berkshire Music Center, New England Conservatory, Harvard Univ., the Salzburg Seminars on American Music, and Darmstadt. Directed the Columbia–Princeton Electronic Music Center beginning in 1959; awards include the New York Music Critics' Circle award (*Composition for 4 Instruments,* 1948; *Philomel,* soprano, tape, 1964) and a Pulitzer Prize Special Citation for "a life's work as a distinguished and seminal American composer." His work has formulated and extended twelve-tone music, which takes much of its analytical vocabulary from Babbitt; *3 Compositions for Piano* (1947) was one of the first pieces to extend Schoenberg's method. In addition to pitch class Babbitt has serialized register, dynamics, duration, and timbre; he relies on extensive precompositional planning but his compositions are not predetermined in every respect. Awarded a Guggenheim Fellowship (1960–61) to study electronic music, Babbitt worked with RCA's newly developed Mark II synthesizer, producing *Composition for Synthesizer* and *Vision and Prayer* (soprano and synthesizer, both works 1961); many of his compositions combine live performers with tape. He believes the university to be the proper home for the contemporary composer; in his 1958 essay, "Who Cares If You Listen?," he argued that the concertgoing public is not the proper audience for the serious composer. Other works: *All Set,* jazz ensemble, 1957; *Con-*

sortini, 5 instruments, 1989; *Correspondences,* tape, string orchestra, 1967; *None but the Lonely Flute,* solo flute (1993).

Bacchetta [It.]. (1) *Baton. (2) The stick of the *bow of a stringed instrument. (3) Drumstick; *b. di legno,* wooden; *b. di spugna,* sponge-headed.

Bacewicz, Grażyna (b. Łódź, 5 Feb. 1909; d. Warsaw, 17 Jan. 1969). Composer and violinist. Studied violin and piano at the Kijeska-Dobkiewiczowa and Warsaw Conservatories, and with Boulanger in Paris (1932–34); from 1934 toured Europe as a violinist; during the 1950s began devoting herself chiefly to composition. Professor of composition at the Warsaw Conservatory from 1966; works include 5 symphonies (*String Symphony,* 1946); 15 concertos; chamber works; vocal works; songs for voice and piano.

B-A-C-H. The letters of J. S. Bach's surname. If read in the context of German nomenclature for pitch (in which B denotes B-flat and H denotes B-natural), these letters represent the succession of pitches B♭–A–C–B♮, which has been used in works (especially as a fugue subject) by various composers, including Bach himself *(The *Art of Fugue),* Albrechtsberger, Schumann, Liszt, Reger, Piston, Casella, and Busoni.

Bach, Carl Philipp Emanuel (b. Weimar, 8 Mar. 1714; d. Hamburg, 14 Dec. 1788). Composer, keyboard player, and writer on music. Second son of J. S. Bach, who was his principal teacher. Became chamber musician to Prince Frederick of Prussia in 1738; remained with him after Frederick's accession to the throne in 1740, when court moved to Berlin; had contact with Quantz, the Graun brothers, the Benda brothers, and literary figures such as Ramler and Lessing; published several path-breaking sets of keyboard works during this period (Prussian Sonatas Wq. 48, 1743; Württemberg Sonatas Wq. 49, 1744; later the Sonatas with Varied Reprises Wq. 50, (1760). Underpaid at court, he left to become Telemann's replacement in Hamburg, where he remained the rest of his life; as music director at five churches and Kantor at the Johanneum, wrote much sacred vocal music. Central to his oeuvre of nearly 900 works is solo keyboard music, including sonatas, fantasies, rondos, variations, and fugues; also wrote symphonies, concertos, trio sonatas. Author of the important treatise *Versuch über die wahre Art das Clavier zu spielen,* 2 vols. (Berlin, 1753–62; facs., Leipzig, 1957); trans. William J. Mitchell as *Essay on the True Art of Playing Keyboard Instruments* (New York, 1948).

Bach, Johann Christian (b. Leipzig, 5 Sept. 1735; d. London, 1 Jan. 1782). Composer, youngest surviving son of J. S. Bach. Studied with his father and his half-brother Emanuel, and in Italy with Padre Martini; became cathedral organist in Milan (1760), where he wrote some operas; moved to London and created operas for the King's Theatre (1763); also composed operas for Mannheim and Paris. With Abel began the Bach–Abel concerts (1765), which helped establish public concerts in London. Composed 13 operas, sacred vocal works, nearly 50 symphonies, 15 *symphonies concertantes,* some 30 concertos, and much chamber and solo keyboard music.

Bach, Johann Christoph (b. Arnstadt, 3 Dec. 1642; d. Eisenach, 31 Mar. 1703). Composer and organist; first cousin of J. S. Bach's father, Johann Ambrosius Bach. Organist of the Arnstadt court chapel (1663) and the Georgenkirche in Eisenach (1665); from 1700 a chamber musician for the Duke of Eisenach. He composed motets, cantatas and vocal concertos, arias, and organ music; J. S. Bach admired his works.

Bach, Johann Christoph Friedrich (b. Leipzig, 21 June 1732; d. Bückeburg, 26 Jan. 1795). Composer, eldest surviving son of J. S. and Anna Magdalena Bach. Studied with his father; from 1750 until his death served as chamber musician at the Bückeburg court of Count Wilhelm of Schaumburg-Lippe; collaborated with the poet Herder on opera and sacred music; also composed 20 symphonies, 6 keyboard concertos, solo keyboard music, many chamber works.

Bach, Johann Sebastian (b. Eisenach, 21 Mar. 1685; d. Leipzig, 28 July 1750). Composer and organist. Went to Ohrdruf following the death of his parents; sang in the church choir in Lüneburg; subsequently became organist in Arnstadt and then in Mühlhausen (1707); appointed court organist to Duke Wilhelm Ernst of Weimar (1708), later *Konzertmeister* (1714); in 1717 accepted a position at the court of Prince Leopold in Cöthen, where he composed a great deal of chamber music (3 sonatas and 3 partitas for solo violin BWV 1001–6, 1720; 6 suites for solo cello BWV 1007–12, ca. 1720; 6 sonatas for violin and continuo BWV 1014–19, 1720s) and didactic keyboard music (the *inventions; 15 sinfonias BWV 787–801, 1723; the *French suites). The *Brandenburg Concertos also date from this time. In 1721 married Anna Magdalena, who would become the mother of 13 of his children; his first

wife, Maria Barbara, had died the previous year. In 1723 accepted the post at which he was to spend his final, most productive years: Kantor of the Thomasschule in Leipzig. His first years at Leipzig saw the composition of some 200 cantatas, the *St. Matthew and *St. John Passions, and numerous motets and instrumental works; produced music for nearby courts as well (on the death of the Elector of Saxony composed the Kyrie and Gloria that were later to become part of the *B-minor Mass). Works from the latter 1730s include the *Christmas Oratorio, the harpsichord concertos, and the *Clavier-Übung. In 1736 he obtained an appointment as *Hofcompositeur for the Dresden court. His final creative years were occupied chiefly with "private" works such as the Canonic Variations for Organ on *Vom Himmel hoch* BWV 769, the *Musikalisches Opfer, and the *Art of Fugue.

Works: *Vocal music.* About 200 known sacred cantatas, including *Christ lag in Todes Banden* BWV 4 (1707–8?); *O Ewigkeit du Donnerwort* BWV 20 (1724); *Jauchzet Gott in allen Landen!* BWV 51 (1730); *Jesu, der du meine Seele* BWV 78 (1724); *Ein feste Burg ist unser Gott* BWV 80 (1724); *Ich habe genug* BWV 82 (1727); *Gottes Zeit ist die allerbeste Zeit* [Actus tragicus] BWV 106 (1707?); *Wachet auf, ruft uns die Stimme* BWV 140 (1731); *Herz und Mund und Tat und Leben* BWV 147 (1723); *Mein Herze schwimmt im Blut* BWV 199 (1714). Secular cantatas include *Weichet nur, betrübte Schatten* [Wedding Cantata] BWV 202 (1718–23?); *Coffee Cantata; *Bauernkantate. Other large-scale sacred vocal works include *Magnificat; 4 Kyrie-Gloria Masses BWV 233–36; 8 motets. Nearly 200 chorale settings; some 100 sacred songs.

Instrumental music. Includes 4 suites for orchestra BWV 1066–69 (1720s and 1730s); Concerto no. 1 in A minor, violin, orchestra BWV 1041 (1730s); no. 2 in E; Concerto in D minor, 2 violins and orchestra BWV 1043 (1730s); 14 concertos for harpsichord and orchestra BWV 1052–65 (1730s, mostly arrangements of earlier works); 4 sonatas for flute and harpsichord BWV 1030, 1032, 1034, 1035 (1717–23 and 1730s).

Nearly 250 works for organ: preludes and fugues, toccatas, fantasias, 6 trio sonatas BWV 525–30 (ca. 1727); *Das *Orgel-Büchlein.

Other keyboard. The *Well-Tempered Clavier; *Goldberg Variations; *Italian Concerto; *English suites; many other fantasias, preludes, fugues, sonatas.

Bach, Wilhelm Friedemann (b. Weimar, 22 Nov. 1710; d. Berlin, 1 July 1784). Composer. Eldest son of J. S. and Maria Barbara Bach. Studied with his father, who composed the *Clavier-Büchlein* and the first volume of the *Well-Tempered Clavier* chiefly for him; served as organist in Dresden and Halle (1746); accompanied his father on the famous "Musical Offering" visit to Frederick II in 1747. Resigned his Halle post in 1764 and would never again hold a permanent job; moved to Berlin in 1774. Compositions include more than 40 keyboard works, 7 concertos, chamber music, 10 symphonies, 33 sacred cantatas, other vocal works.

Bachauer, Gina (b. Athens, 21 May 1913; d. there, 22 Aug. 1976). Pianist. Studied with Ariadne Casasis and Waldemar Freeman at the Athens Conservatory; with Alfred Cortot at the École normale in Paris; with Sergei Rachmaninoff privately (1932–35); debut with the Athens National Symphony (1935); toured the U.S. annually from 1950. Performed virtuoso repertory from Scarlatti to Rachmaninoff, as well as music of J. S. Bach.

Bacilly, Bénigne de (b. Normandy?, ca. 1625?; d. Paris, 27 Sept. 1690). Composer and writer. Ordained to the priesthood; lived mostly in Paris, where he was a respected singing master. Published one of the most significant 17th-century treatises on singing, *Remarques curieuses sur l'art de bien chanter* (1668; R: 1971; 4th ed., 1681); trans. Austin B. Caswell as *A Commentary on the Art of Proper Singing* (Brooklyn, 1968); also published some 15 collections of his own sacred and secular songs.

Bäck, Sven-Erik (b. Stockholm, 16 Sept. 1919). Composer. Studied with Hilding Rosenberg and in Rome with Petrassi (1951–52); also took courses at the Schola cantorum in Basel; led the "Kammarorkestern–1953" beginning in 1953, and in 1959 became director of the Swedish radio's music school near Stockholm. Began composing in the late romantic tradition, but subsequently assumed terse, Webern-like serialism and electronic techniques.

Backbeat. In *rock and related genres, a sharp attack on beats two and four of a 4/4 measure, often sounded continuously on the snare drum.

Backer-Grøndahl, Agathe. See Grøndahl, Agathe.

Backfall, forefall. In 17th-century England, two types of *appoggiatura, the former approaching the main note from above, the latter from below, notated and played as in the accompanying example.

Backhaus, Wilhelm (b. Leipzig, 26 Mar. 1884; d. Villach, Austria, 5 July 1969). Pianist. Studied with

A. Reckendorf and Eugene D'Albert; debut in Leipzig, 1892. Taught at the Royal College of Music in Manchester, 1905; won the Rubenstein Prize, Paris, 1905. U.S. debut 5 Jan. 1912; toured extensively; moved to Lugano, Switzerland, in 1930. Best known for his performances of Beethoven.

Bacon, Ernst (b. Chicago, 26 May 1898; d. Orinda, Calif., 16 Mar. 1990). Composer and pianist; teachers included Goossens (conducting), and Karl Weigl and Bloch (composition). Assistant conductor of the Rochester Opera Company; taught piano at the Eastman School of Music (1925–28); dean and professor of piano at Converse College (from 1935); director of the School of Music at Syracuse Univ. (1945–64). His Symphony in D (1932) was awarded the Pulitzer Prize; best known for settings of American texts and arrangements of American folk music.

Badinage, badine, badinerie [Fr., banter]. A playful or coy movement. It was both a descriptive title and a category in 18th-century suites (Bach, Telemann, Claude-Bénigne Balbastre).

Badings, Henk (b. Bandung, Java, 17 Jan. 1907; d. Maarheeze, Netherlands, 26 June 1987). Composer. Studied with Willem Pijper during the 1930s; lectured on music theory and composition at the Rotterdam Conservatory (1934–37); directed the Amsterdam Music Lyceum (from 1937) and the State Conservatory at The Hague (1941–45); taught acoustics at Utrecht Univ. (from 1961); professor of composition at the Hochschule für Musik in Stuttgart (1962–72). His music employs electronic elements and makes use of a 31-note scale.

Badura-Skoda, Paul (b. Vienna, 6 Oct. 1927). Pianist. Studied with Viola Thern at the Vienna Hochschule für Musik (diploma, 1948) and with Edwin Fischer (1949); won major competitions in Austria, Budapest, and Paris; U.S. debut, 1953; artist-in-residence, Univ. of Wisconsin, 1966–71. Often plays core repertory of Mozart, Beethoven, and Schubert on historic instruments.

Baez, Joan (Chandos) (b. Staten Island, N.Y., 9 Jan. 1941). Folksinger and songwriter. Following successful appearances at the Newport Folk Festival (1959–60) performed and recorded a repertory of ballads, original songs, and works by others (including Bob Dylan); performances often associated with political causes, including the movement opposing the war in Vietnam. Her recordings of Robbie Robertson's "The Night They Drove Old Dixie Down" (1971) and of her own "Diamonds and Rust" (1975) were very popular.

Bagana, beganna [Amharic]. An Ethiopian *lyre with a large, rectangular frame, a rectangular sound

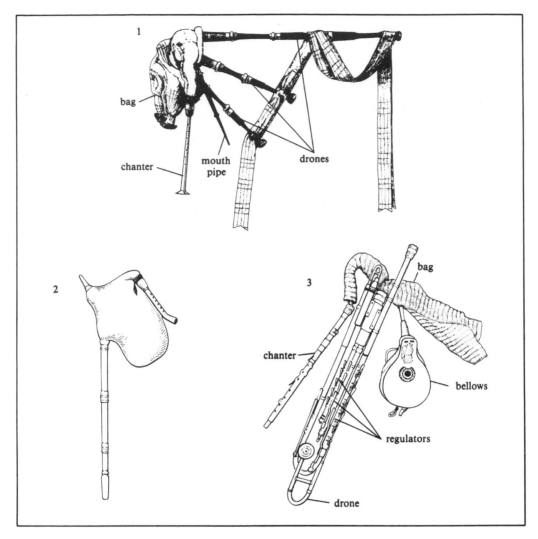

1. Highland bagpipe.   2. Bulgarian gaida.   3. Union pipe.

box, and up to ten gut strings, plucked with the fingers of both hands.

Bagatelle [Fr., trifle]. A short, unpretentious piece, often for piano and often presented in sets with contrasting tempos and moods. The title has been used by François Couperin (*Ordre* 10), Beethoven (three sets for piano opp. 33, 119, and 126), Sibelius (opp. 34 and 97), and Anton Webern (*Six Bagatelles* for string quartet, 1913).

Bagpipe. Any of a family of wind instruments in which one or more reedpipes are attached to a windbag, usually made of animal skin. The player holds the windbag under the arm and squeezes it with the elbow to provide a steady stream of air to the pipes. The windbag is filled by means either of a mouth

pipe or a set of bellows operated by the player's free elbow. One or two of the pipes, called *chanters, have finger holes and play a melody. The other pipes, called *drones, have no finger holes and sound a single pitch.

The bagpipe is, or has been, a popular instrument in Europe, North Africa, the Middle East, Central Asia, and India, taking on various forms in different regions. Broadly speaking, Eastern European and Asian bagpipes have single-reed, cylindrical-bore chanters, while Western European bagpipes have double-reed, conical-bore chanters. Most North African and Middle Eastern bagpipes have no drone pipes, and their chanter consists of two pipes side by side like a *double clarinet. The French *cornemuse,* Spanish *gaita,* Irish *union pipe, and Scottish *highland pipes all combine a double-reed, conical-bore chanter with one or more single-reed, cylindrical-bore drones. See also *Biniou, Gaita,* Highland bagpipe, Union pipe, *Zampogna.*

Baguette [Fr.]. (1) *Baton. (2) The stick of the *bow of a stringed instrument. (3) Drumstick; *b. de bois,* wooden; *b. d'éponge,* sponge-headed.

Bahr-Mildenburg [née von Mildenburg], **Anna** (b. Vienna, 29 Nov. 1872; d. there, 27 Jan. 1947). Soprano. Studied with Rosa Papier and in 1895 sang in Hamburg under Mahler; subsequently sang under him at the Vienna Opera (1898–1916), also appeared at Bayreuth (1897–1914) and Covent Garden (from 1906); retired in 1917. Her repertory included all the leading Wagner roles.

Baïf, Jean-Antoine de (b. Venice, 19 Feb. 1532; d. Paris, Oct. 1589). Poet, associate of the literary group known as the Pléiade. Beginning in 1567 he developed *vers mesurés à l'antique* (French poetry set to *musique mesurée*). Such verse and music were cultivated at Baïf's Académie de poésie et de musique (meeting from 1571) and the Académie du Palais (which met until 1584)

Bailey, Pearl (Mae) (b. Newport News, Va., 29 Mar. 1918; d. Philadelphia, 17 Aug. 1990). Jazz and popular singer; performed in New York with the Noble Sissle Band and with Count Basie during the 1930s and 40s; also appeared on Broadway; her most successful recordings include "Tired" (1947) and "Takes Two to Tango" (1953). Bailey appeared in films and hosted her own television show (1970–71).

Baird, Tadeusz (b. Grodzisk Mazowiecki, 26 July 1928; d. Warsaw, 2 Sept. 1981). Composer. Studied with Woytowicz and Sikorski; after the war, with Rytel and Perkowskati at the Warsaw Conservatory; with composers Serocki and Krenz founded the "Group 1949"; in 1956 helped found the "Warsaw Autumn" International Festival of Contemporary Music. His earlier neoclassical style became more experimental and avant-garde in the late 1950s. Works include the opera *Jutro* [Tomorrow] (1966); orchestral music; vocal music; chamber music.

Baisser [Fr.]. To lower, e.g., the tuning of a string.

Baker, Chet [Chesney Henry] (b. Yale, Okla., 23 Dec. 1929; d. Amsterdam, 13 May 1988). Jazz trumpeter. Worked with Charlie Parker's bop quintet (1952) before joining Gerry Mulligan's pianoless quartet ("Bernie's Tune," "My Funny Valentine," 1952); left Mulligan in 1953 to lead groups. Following a European tour (1955–56), addiction to heroin repeatedly disrupted his career, much of which was spent in Europe, especially Italy, after 1959; played

flugelhorn in the late 1960s; performed regularly in the 1970s and 1980s and made many albums.

Baker, Janet (Abbott) (b. Hatfield, Yorkshire, 21 Aug. 1933). Mezzo-soprano. Studied with Helene Isepp, master classes with Lotte Lehmann, also studied at the Mozarteum in Salzburg. Covent Garden debut as Britten's Hermia (1964), U.S. debut singing Mahler (1968). Repertory included operas by Monteverdi, Purcell, Rameau, and especially Handel, but also performed Gluck, Mozart, Donizetti, Berlioz, Gounod, and Strauss. Retired from the operatic stage July 1982, but continued to perform in recital; made Dame of the British Empire in 1976.

Baker, Julius (b. Cleveland, 23 Sept. 1915). Flutist. Studied with William Kincaid at the Curtis Institute; principal flutist, Pittsburgh Symphony (1941–43), CBS Symphony (1943–50), Chicago Symphony (1951–53), New York Philharmonic (1964–83); member of the Bach Aria Group (1947–65); taught at Juilliard (from 1954) and the Curtis Institute (from 1980).

Balakirev, Mily Alexeyevich (b. Nizhny-Novgorod, 2 Jan. 1837; d. St. Petersburg, 29 May 1910). Composer. In 1855 he went to St. Petersburg, where he met Glinka; the following year made his debut there as soloist in his Piano Concerto in F♯ minor op. 1; attracted a number of disciples in the early 1860s, including Mussorgsky, Rimsky-Korsakov, and Borodin. In 1863 began conducting at the newly opened Free School of Music in St. Petersburg; also collected Circassian, Georgian, and Persian tunes, an influence evident in his songs. Succeeded Anton Rubinstein as conductor of the Russian Musical Society concerts (1867), became director of the Free School; in 1883 appointed director of the imperial court chapel; his often stormy relationship with Rimsky-Korsakov was all but severed in 1890. Spent the last decade of his life in retirement, completing among other projects the Symphony no. 2 in D minor (1908). One of Russia's "moguchaya kuchka" or "Mighty Five," his impact on a generation of composers rivals Glinka's. The piano works (*Islamey* and the B♭ minor Sonata) are of greatest interest.

Balalaika [Russ.]. A *long-necked lute of Russia with three strings, a fretted neck, and a flat-backed triangular body. It has been popular in accompaniment for song and dance since the 18th century, when it replaced its antecedent the *dömbra.* See ill. under Guitar.

Balancement [Fr.]. In singing, a rather slow vibrato of loudness, not pitch; sometimes used synonymously with *Bebung.*

Balbastre, Claude-Bénigne (b. Dijon, 22 Jan. 1727; d. Paris, 9 May 1799). Composer and organist. Studied with his father and with Pierre Février in Paris; had composition lessons with Rameau. From 1755 until the 1780s performed frequently at the Concert spirituel, often his own works; organist at St. Roch (1756) and Notre Dame Cathedral (1760); from 1776 employed at the French court as organist and harpsichord teacher to Marie Antoinette. Composed chiefly keyboard works.

Balfe, Michael William (b. Dublin, 15 May 1808; d. Rowney Abbey, Hertfordshire, 20 Oct. 1870). Composer. Following a singing career in Italy returned to London and had great success with English operas *The Siege of Rochelle* (1835) and *The Maid of Artois* (1836); an Italian opera, *Falstaff* (1838), was commissioned for Her Majesty's Theatre; other operas include *Keolanthe* and *Les puits d'amour* (1843), but best known for *The Bohemian Girl* (1843) and *The Rose of Castile* (1857).

Ballabile [It.]. In 19th-century opera, a piece suitable for dancing. Such pieces may be purely instrumental or performed with chorus.

Ballad [fr. Lat. *ballare,* to dance]. (1) A strophic narrative song. The English term refers most commonly to the traditional Anglo-American ballads, a large body of narrative songs passed down orally from as early as the Middle Ages. Similar traditions exist in German and the Scandinavian languages, however. Ballads are less prominent in the Romance languages except for Spanish [see *Romance* (1)] and should not be confused with poetic forms of the 14th century and later that have similar names in these languages [see *Ballade* (1), *Ballata*]. The subject matter of ballad texts ranges widely from history and legend to domestic affairs, often with elements of the supernatural. They employ a variety of meters and rhyme schemes, including what is called ballad or common meter: a four-line strophe with alternating lines of eight and six syllables (8.6.8.6) having four and three stresses, respectively. Refrains and nonsense lines are common. Ballad tunes are typically cast in regular two-bar phrases, with four phrases to the strophe. Because ballads have been transmitted orally for generations, neither text nor tune has a unique or definitive form; it is more appropriate to speak of families of texts and tunes.

The broadside ballads of England and America, from the 16th to the 19th century, were narrative verses printed on one side of a folio page. Their subjects were usually topics of current and ephemeral interest: politics, personalities, notorious crimes, natural disasters. Usually only the ballad text was printed and was intended to be sung to a known tune that fit the words. Many broadside ballads passed into oral tradition, but some were also incorporated into art music, especially in the *ballad opera of the

18th century. Translations of traditional English ballads enjoyed a vogue in late 18th-century Germany, inspiring a genre of poetry and music cultivated well into the 19th century [see *Ballade* (2)].

(2) In English and American popular music of the late 19th and early 20th centuries, a song with sentimental text, usually in moderate or slow tempo, and often in a form consisting of two or more 16-measure strophes, each followed by an 8-measure (or multiple thereof) refrain, the whole sometimes referred to as a ballad and refrain or a song and chorus.

(3) In English and American popular music from the 1920s on, a song in a slow tempo. Many such songs consist of an introductory "verse" of 16 or 32 measures followed by a chorus or refrain of 32 measures made up of four 8-measure phrases arranged AABA. Phrase B in such a scheme is called the bridge or release. The verse is often omitted in performance, and some songs lack it altogether.

Ballad of Baby Doe. Opera in two acts by Douglas Moore (libretto by John Latouche), first produced in Central City, Colorado, in 1956. Setting: Colorado and Washington, D.C., 1880–99.

Ballad opera. A musico-dramatic genre popular in England, Ireland, and the American colonies in the 18th century in which spoken dialogue alternates with songs consisting of new words fit to traditional or familiar tunes. Such works draw variously on collections of dance tunes; English, Irish, Scottish, or French folk tunes; instrumental or vocal music by composers such as Purcell, Handel, Corelli, and Geminiani; as well as the broadside *ballads that gave the genre its name. The texts are often satirical, taking as their targets aspects of English political, social, or economic life; the conventions of Italian opera, very popular in London at that time, are also a favorite target.

The first and most famous ballad opera was *The *Beggar's Opera* (1728). Ballad opera flourished for about a decade, after which the earlier works continued to be played, but none of the new works written was successful. It was probably influenced by the French *comédie en *vaudeville*. The ballad opera, in its turn, influenced the development of north German *Singspiel. Kurt Weill's *Die *Dreigroschenoper* (1921) is a modern reworking of *The Beggar's Opera*.

Ballade. (1) [Fr.] One of the three *formes fixes* prominent in the poetry and music of France in the 14th and 15th centuries. In the variety usually set to music, the poem has three seven- or eight-line stanzas, all with the same metrical and rhyme scheme; most often the stanzas also share a *refrain, consisting of one or (occasionally) two lines. The poetic form of the stanza may be ababcdE or ababcdeF (capital letters denoting the refrain) or any of a number of other patterns. Two or more of the lines after the second b often rhyme with each other; one or more may rhyme with a or b, as in the very common ababbcC. The whole of the poem sometimes concludes with an *envoi.

The music of a *ballade* stanza is in two sections (X and Y), the first setting the initial couplet ab and repeated for the next couplet, the second setting the remainder. The musical form can be described as XXY. When the latter portion of a stanza is made up of an even number of lines, Y may be used twice, each statement providing music for half of the relevant section, the musical form then being XXYY. Any repeated music may have first and second endings. Subsequent stanzas have the same music as the first.

In the monophonic *ballades* of Jehannot de l'Escurel (d. 1304), the form is completely distinct from the other *formes fixes* for the first time. Guillaume de Machaut (ca. 1300–1377) composed settings of 42 *ballades,* most of them courtly love songs. He usually employed one-line refrains and set *ballades* polyphonically. In these compositions, most often one part carries the text and is evidently meant to be sung, while the other parts (up to three) are seemingly instrumental. In the early 15th century, the *ballade* receded in importance in music, although as poetry, the form continued to be cultivated. See also Chanson, Bar form, *Ballata,* Trouvère, Troubadour.

(2) [Ger.] A narrative poem or song in German, or an instrumental work associated with a narrative poem. Related to the folk *ballad, the German *Ballade* flourished as a literary and musical genre in the last quarter of the 18th and first half of the 19th century. Its subjects, usually drawn from popular (often medieval) history and legend, are largely serious, even tragic (though sometimes light or even comic), frequently with supernatural elements. The tale is told suspensefully but impersonally, often employing dialogue. In imitation of its folk model, the *Ballade* is cast in strophic form; quatrains with three- and four-stress lines and simple rhyme (sometimes with refrains) are common. As a musical work, the *Ballade* is most often a solo song with piano accompaniment. Settings may be *strophic (like traditional folk ballads) or modified strophic, or they may be *through-composed. The stylistic development generally parallels that of the *lied.

Precursors of the musical *Ballade* are found in the "Fabelr" and "Erzählungen" of Johann Ernst Bach (1683–1739) and Valentin Herbing (1735–66). Other composers, such as Johann Friedrich Reichardt (1752–1814) and Carl Friedrich Zelter (1758–1832) of the second *"Berlin school," numbered *Balladen* among their songs, but the most important *Ballade* composer of the 18th century was Johann Rudolf

Zumsteeg (1760–1802). Schubert developed a more economical and integrated style in his famous setting of Goethe's "Erlkönig" (1815), but this is an exceptional work even within his own output. Carl Loewe (1796–1869) set the same poem (op. 1, 1818), and he became the most productive (17 vols.) and most celebrated *Ballade* composer of the 19th century.

Some purely instrumental compositions are entitled *Ballade,* with sometimes explicit, sometimes inferable relation to the literary genre. Chief among them are piano works, the best known being Chopin's four *Ballades* (thought by some to be based on poems by Adam Mickiewicz), but also including the *Balladen* of Liszt and Brahms.

Ballade style. The style of the polyphonic *ballade* [see *Ballade* (1)] of the 14th century. Such pieces typically employ three-part texture (cantus, tenor, and contratenor) with the text carried only in the uppermost part, which is also the most animated part of the three. Other forms, both sacred (*Mass, *motet) and secular (*formes fixes), were composed in the same style, which has also been termed *cantilena style and treble-dominated style.

Ballata [It., fr. *ballare,* to dance]. A principal Italian musical and poetic form of the mid-13th to 15th centuries. The *ballata* was intensely cultivated as art music, usually polyphonic, in the 14th century [see *Ars nova* (2)].

The *ballata* of the 14th century is formally similar to the contemporaneous French *virelai (not *ballade). The poetic form of a single stanza with refrain can be outlined AbbaA (capital letters indicating the refrain), and the musical form XYYXX. Each letter may stand for one or several lines. The refrain (A) is called the *ripresa,* the other sections *piedi* (b) and *volta* (a). Most *ballate* have three stanzas; it is not clear whether the refrain should always be repeated between them. Many *ballate,* however, have only one stanza.

Although the musical style of early *ballate* resembles that of the Italian *madrigal, the style of later *ballate* approximates that of French polyphonic songs of the period. The *ballata* was cultivated by such composers as Niccolò da Perugia, Andreas de Florentia, Bartolino da Padova, Johannes Ciconia, and Francesco Landini. See also *Barzelletta, Lauda.

Ballet de cour [Fr., court ballet]. The chief French courtly amateur entertainment of the 16th and 17th centuries, succeeding the 15th-century *entremet* and influenced by the Italian *intermedio, mascherata,* and *trionfo.* Produced in a decorated hall, the ballet consisted of up to five mythological or allegorical *entrées* (sets of dances and choruses) with corresponding *vers* (verses printed and distributed to participants), each introduced by a spoken or sung *récit.*

The whole commenced with an *ouverture* and concluded with a *grand ballet* in which at least once a year the king himself danced. The *ballet de cour* reached its apogee in the 1650s with the poet Isaac de Benserade and the young Florentine musician Giambattista Lulli (Lully). From the 1660s, the autocratic and influential Lully transformed the ballet, first with Molière into the professional *comédie-ballet,* finally with Quinault into the operatic *tragédie-lyrique.*

Ballett. See *Balletto* (2).

Balletto [It.]. (1) A 15th-century choreographed Italian dance using pantomimic gesture; the term was also used for composed dances, for dance groups, and for dance in general in the 16th and 17th centuries. See *Ballo.*

(2) In the 16th and 17th centuries, a vocal piece in homophonic, dance-rhythm style, with strophic texts punctuated by nonsense refrains such as "fa-la-la." The earliest known collection (1591) is by Giovanni Gastoldi; Adriano Banchieri, Orazio Vecchi, Sigismondo d'India, and others continued writing *balletti* in the early 17th century. The *balletto* was taken up in Germany by Hans Leo Hassler (1601) and especially in England by Thomas Morley (1595) and Thomas Weelkes (1598).

(3) An instrumental dance, mainly for lute in the late 16th century, and for guitar, keyboard, and chamber ensemble (especially strings and continuo) throughout the 17th century. In Italy the term was often used for a foreign dance, especially one of German origin (hence its close relationship with the *allemande).*

Ballo [It., sometimes also *bal, balletto,* dance, ball]. (1) In the late Middle Ages, any social dancing. (2) In the 15th century, a lively dance that contrasted with the slower-moving *bassadanza* [see *Basse danse*]. (3) In the 15th and 16th centuries, a professionally choreographed dance performed socially or as an entertainment. (4) In the titles of 16th-century collections of instrumental music, any of various specific dances (e.g., *pavana, *gagliarda). (5) Around 1600, a stage work in which dance is of central importance (e.g., Monteverdi's *Il ballo delle ingrate,* 1608) or a dance forming a part of a larger stage work.

Ballo in maschera, Un [It., A Masked Ball]. Opera in three acts by Verdi (libretto by Antonio Somma, based on Eugène Scribe's libretto for Auber's opera *Gustave III, ou Le bal masqué* of 1833), first produced in Rome in 1859. It was originally to be set in Stockholm at the end of the 18th century. In order to appease government censors, who objected to the staged portrayal of a successful assassination of a king, the setting was transferred to Boston and its surroundings at the end of the 17th century. Modern productions may use Boston, Stockholm, Naples, or other cities; the epoch is also variable.

Balsam, Artur (b. Warsaw, 8 Feb. 1906; d. New York, 1 Sept. 1994). Pianist. Studied at the Łódź Conservatory and the Berlin Hochschule für Musik; emigrated to U.S. (1933) and taught thereafter at Eastman, Boston Univ., and the Manhattan School of Music; performed and recorded chamber music with Menuhin, Milstein, Oistrakh, and Rostropovich and as a member of the Balsam–Kroll–Heifetz Trio.

Banchieri, Adriano (Tomaso) (b. Bologna, 3 Sept. 1568; d. there, 1634). Composer, organist, and writer on music. In 1587 joined the order of the Olivetans, subsequently lived and worked at its monasteries; in 1609 settled for good at S. Michele in Bosco; founded the Accademia dei Floridi in Bologna (1615). An associate of Monteverdi; his writings (*L'organo suonarino,* Venice, 1605; *Cartella* series, Venice, 1601ff.) are important works of early Baroque music theory. Compositions include sacred music, madrigals, and theater works.

Band [Fr. *bande;* Ger. *Kapelle;* It., Sp. *banda*]. (1) Any instrumental ensemble larger than a chamber ensemble, including, especially in British usage, the orchestra. Early ensembles bearing the name include the 17th-century *Vingt-quatre violons du roi (La grande bande)* and the 24 fiddlers of Charles II (The King's Private Band). (2) An ensemble of wind instruments, sometimes also with percussion. See Brass band. (3) Any ensemble other than one of the traditional combinations of Western art music, sometimes identified by the type of instrument(s) included or by the repertory performed, e.g., accordion band, jazz band, dance band, *big band, string band, *jug band. (4) [It.] The brass and percussion sections of the orchestra.

Bandoneon. A square, entirely button-operated *accordion invented in the 1840s by Heinrich Band, after whom it is named. It is used in Argentine popular music. David Tudor and Gordon Mumma have played and composed music for it, sometimes modifying the sound electronically.

Bandora [Fr. *bandore, pandore, pandura;* Ger. *Pandora, Bandoer;* It., Sp. *pandora*]. A wire-strung plucked instrument with a festooned outline invented by John Rose of London in 1562. A bass instrument with six courses, tuned C D G c e a, it was used to accompany the first printed English solo songs (1596) and was one of the continuo instruments in a mixed consort. See ill. under Lute.

Bandurria [Sp.]. A small Spanish plectrum instrument found also in Latin America [see ill. under Guitar]. The modern instrument has six courses of metal strings tuned in fourths. It often plays the treble part in small ensembles, producing sustained tones by means of a tremolo with the plectrum.

Banister, John (b. London, ca. 1625; d. there, 3 Oct. 1679). Composer and violinist. Sent to France in 1661 to observe Louis XIV's Violons du Roy; on his return to London directed a 12-member ensemble extracted from the King's Violins; remained in the royal service until his death. In 1672 began a popular series of concerts in his home and in various concert halls, some of the first public concerts in Europe. Composed sacred music; songs for plays; chamber music.

Banjo. A plucked stringed instrument with a long, fretted neck and a circular body in the form of a shallow, one-headed drum. The five-string banjo has four strings (often metal) running the length of the neck plus a shorter fifth string placed next to the lowest string and fastened to a peg at the fifth fret [see ill. under Guitar]. The most common tunings are g′ c g b d′ and g′ d g b d′. Tenor banjos and plectrum banjos have four strings. The former is tuned c g d′ a′, the latter d g b e′. Four-string banjos are strummed with a plectrum. Five-string banjos may be plucked with the thumb and forefinger, the thumb and first three fingers, or the thumb and first two fingers, often using finger picks. The fifth string serves primarily as a drone.

The earliest banjos were brought by slaves from Africa to the U.S. and Caribbean islands. The instrument was given its modern form with five strings and flat, circular body in the first half of the 19th century by white minstrel-show performers like J. W. Sweeney and Dan Emmett.

Banks, Don(ald Oscar) (b. South Melbourne, 25 Oct. 1923; d. Sydney, 5 Sept. 1980). Composer. Studied with Seiber in London; other teachers included Babbitt, Dallapiccola, and Nono. Returned to Australia in 1971 and headed the composition and electronic music studies at Canberra School of Music (1974); subsequently head of the School of Composition Studies at the Sydney Conservatorium (1978). Banks's compositions usually employ serial procedures; other works were influenced by jazz or are recognizably Australian.

Bantock, Granville (b. London, 7 Aug. 1868; d. there, 16 Oct. 1946). Composer. Studied with Frederick Corder at the Royal Academy of Music (1889–92); his first opera, *Caedmar* (1892) was performed at the Crystal Palace; in 1894 launched a successful conducting career, subsequently appointed conductor of "The Tower" orchestra of New Brighton (1897); an early champion in England of the music of Sibelius; in 1908 succeeded Elgar as professor of music at the Univ. of Birmingham;

knighted in 1930. His music shows influences of Berlioz, Brahms, and early Wagner.

Bar. (1) *Measure. (2) *Bar line. (3) *Bar form.

Bar form [Ger. *Barform*]. In musicology, the formal design AAB, common to music and poetry of many times and places, but particularly associated with German strophic song (both secular and liturgical) from the late 12th century onward.

Among the German *Meistersinger (from whom the term bar is borrowed), the strophe of a new song was typically written to one of the preexisting *Töne* (authoritative tunes with associated verse forms). The organization into two *Stollen* (AA, making up one *Aufgesang*) and an *Abgesang* (B) is typical of most Meistersinger *Töne*.

The form AAB also describes the sequence of strophe, antistrophe, and epode found in the Greek *ode as cultivated by Pindar and later imitated by Horace. Medieval songs with an AAB arrangement include many 12th- and 13th-century Provençal *canzos* and French *chansons* (sources for the bar form of the Minnesinger and Meistersinger), as well as 14th- and 15th-century French *ballades* [see also Troubadour, Trouvère, *Formes fixes*].

Bar line [Fr. *barre de mesure;* Ger. *Taktstrich;* It. *stranghetta;* Sp. *barra de compás*]. A line drawn vertically through one or more staves to mark off a *measure [see also Meter]. In the modern sense, it is not a regular feature of musical notation until the 17th century. Prior to that time, it is found most frequently in *tablatures for keyboard and fretted instruments (particularly the Spanish *vihuela*) and in keyboard music produced in *score (from ca. 1400). Here, however, it may serve primarily to aid in the alignment of the parts and not as a guide to the metrical organization of the music. The bar line is in general absent from vocal or ensemble music that is presented in *partbooks and becomes a regular feature of notation only with increasing use of the score in the late 16th century.

Barber, Samuel (b. West Chester, Pa., 9 Mar. 1910; d. New York, 23 Jan. 1981). Composer. Entered Curtis when it opened (1924), studying composition (Scalero), piano (Boyle, Vengerova), conducting (Reiner), and voice (Emilio de Gogorza); taught briefly there (1939–42) but otherwise devoted himself to composition; early works include *Dover Beach* (voice and string quartet, 1931), the Cello Sonata (1932), and *The School for Scandal* (awarded the Bearns Prize in 1933). During the 1930s his works were performed by major orchestras and soloists, including the famous Adagio for Strings (an arrangement of the second movement of his String Quartet, 1936) and the first *Essay for Orchestra* (1937). His songs (including *Knoxville: Summer of*

1915, 1948; *Hermit Songs,* 1953) were particularly well received; he won Pulitzer Prizes for the opera *Vanessa* (1958) and the Piano Concerto (1962). Often described as a romanticist in expression and a classicist in his use of form, Barber wrote in a consistently lyrical vein; in works composed after 1939 his style became more dissonant. Other works include the opera *Antony and Cleopatra* (1966); the ballet *Medea* (1946); 2 symphonies (1936; 1944, rev. 1947), other orchestral music (violin concerto, 1940; cello concerto, 1945; piano concerto, 1962); choral works; chamber music; piano pieces (piano sonata, 1949–50); many songs.

Barber of Seville, The. See *Barbiere di Siviglia, Il.*

Barbershop singing. A style of popular singing for four unaccompanied male voices, arranged from highest to lowest as tenor, lead, baritone, and bass. The melody is almost always sung by the lead and harmonized in characteristically "close" part writing in which triads and seventh chords predominate, with frequent chromatic passing tones.

Barbiere di Siviglia, Il [It., The Barber of Seville]. (1) Opera in two acts by Rossini, produced in Rome in 1816. The libretto by Cesare Sterbini, based on Beaumarchais's *Le barbier de Seville* and on the libretto for Paisiello's opera [see (2) below], was originally titled *Almaviva, ossia L'inutile precauzione,* possibly to avoid direct comparison with Paisiello's opera. Setting: 18th-century Seville. (2) Opera in four parts by Giovanni Paisiello with a libretto by Giuseppe Petrosellini (after Beaumarchais), produced in St. Petersburg in 1782. Setting: 18th-century Seville.

Barbieri, Francisco Asenjo (b. Madrid, 3 Aug. 1823; d. there, 17 Feb. 1894). Composer. Studied at the Madrid Conservatory, then lived a wandering life; returned to Madrid in 1846 and devoted himself to furthering Spanish music; established the periodical *La España musical.* His most important scholarly work was an edition, *Cancionero musical de los siglos XV y XVI* (Madrid, 1890; 2nd ed., 1945; facs., Málaga, 1987); also composed 72 zarzuelas.

Barbieri, Gato [Leandro J.] (b. Rosario, Argentina, 28 Nov. 1934). Jazz tenor saxophonist and bandleader. In Buenos Aires played alto saxophone with Lalo Schifrin; switched to tenor, joined Don Cherry's free jazz group in Paris (1964–66), recording the album *Complete Communion* (1965). In the late 1960s led groups that combined free jazz improvisation with dance rhythms and simple melodies from Latin American popular music; performed in the movie *Last Tango in Paris* (1972).

Barbirolli, John [Giovanni Battista] (b. London, 2 Dec. 1899; d. there, 29 July 1970). Conductor and cellist. Following studies and career as a cellist became conductor of the Chenil Orchestra (1925); the National Opera Company (1926); guest conductor, London Symphony and the Royal Philharmonic (1927); the Royal Opera at Covent Garden (1928). Conducted the Scottish Orchestra in Glasgow (1933–36); guest conducted the New York Philharmonic (1936–37) and became its music director (1937–42); permanent conductor of the Hallé Orchestra in Manchester (1943–58), then principal conductor (1958–68); conductor-in-chief of the Houston Symphony (1960–66). Knighted in 1949. His repertory ranged from Bach to Berg, with special sympathy for Elgar and Vaughan Williams.

Barcarole [Fr. *barcarolle;* It. *barcarola*]. A song of the Venetian gondoliers, or a vocal or instrumental composition modeled on such a song. In the latter, a rhythmically repetitive accompaniment, usually in moderate 6/8 or 12/8 meter, evokes the motion of a boat in the waves. Well-known examples for piano include three from Mendelssohn's *Songs without Words* (op. 19 no. 6; op. 30 no. 6; op. 62 no. 5) and Chopin's *Barcarolle* op. 60.

Barce, Ramón (b. Madrid, 16 Mar. 1928). Composer and critic. Chiefly self-taught as a composer; founded Spanish new music groups including the Nueva música (1958), the Aula de música del Ateneo (1959), and the "Zaj" group (1964). As a critic founded the journal *Sonda* and, from 1971, wrote for the newspaper *Ya* in Madrid. His compositions, which employ serial and nonserial atonality, include the opera *Los bárbaros* (1965–73); theater music; choral music; orchestral works (*Las cuatro estaciones,* 1967; *Concierto de Lizara* no. 1, oboe, trumpet, percussion, string orchestra, 1969); chamber music; piano music.

Bard. A poet-musician of the Celts, especially of Wales, Ireland, and Scotland. Greek and Roman writers mention the bards as early as the 2nd century B.C.E., and in the 1st century B.C.E., Diodorus Siculus reports that they used an instrument similar to the lyre. They were later associated with the *harp and, especially, the *crwth. In the 10th century, their position in Welsh society was fixed in the laws of King Howel the Good. They held high rank in noble households, where they played and sang verse of various kinds, including elegies, eulogies, and sagas. They also gathered for an annual competition, known from the 18th century as an *eisteddfod, at which their elaborate procedures and regulations were discussed.

Bardi, Giovanni de' (b. Florence, 5 Feb. 1534; d. Rome, Sept. 1612). Poet and writer on music; from 1592 *maestro di camera* at the papal court; helped fund the education of Galilei, Caccini, and possibly others. During the 1570s and 1580s his home became a gathering place for Florentine composers and poets; Caccini called the group "Bardi's camerata" in his preface to *Le nuove musiche* (1601). Bardi's criticicisms of complex contrapuntal music are set forth in a discourse addressed to Caccini.

Barenboim, Daniel (b. Buenos Aires, 15 Nov. 1942). Conductor and pianist. Studied piano with his father and with Edwin Fischer, conducting with Igor Markevitch at the Mozarteum in Salzburg (1952); attended the Santa Cecilia Academy in Rome. U.S. debut with Stokowski (1957), conducting debut with Melbourne and Sydney Symphony Orchestras (1962); in 1964 began a close association with the English Chamber Orchestra. Music director of the Orchestre de Paris (from 1975), the Bastille Opéra in Paris (1988–89), the Chicago Symphony (from 1991), the Deutsche Staatsoper in Berlin (from 1993). As a pianist devoted particular attention to Mozart and Beethoven.

Bargiel, Woldemar (b. Berlin, 3 Oct. 1828; d. there, 23 Feb. 1897). Composer and teacher. The son of Clara Schumann's mother and her second husband; studied with his parents and at the Leipzig Conservatory (1846–50) with Moscheles, Hauptmann, Rietz, and Gade; in 1859 became professor of theory at the Cologne Conservatory; Kapellmeister in Rotterdam and directed the Association for the Furthering of Music (1865–74); from 1874 professor of composition at the Berlin Hochschule für Musik. His compositions, highly esteemed during his lifetime, include a symphony, chamber music, piano music.

Bariolage [Fr.]. In the playing of bowed stringed instruments such as the violin, an effect produced by playing in rapid alternation on two strings, one open and the other stopped, with a resulting contrast in tone color. The type of bowing required is termed *ondeggiando* or *ondulé*.

Baritone [Fr. *baryton;* Ger. *Bariton;* It. *baritono;* Sp. *barítono*]. (1) The male *voice lying below the tenor and above the bass. (2) In families of instruments such as the saxophone, the member pitched below the tenor and above the bass. (3) The baritone horn. See Euphonium.

Barnet, Charlie [Charles Daly] (b. New York, 26 Oct. 1913; d. 4 Sept. 1991). Jazz bandleader and saxophonist. Led big bands regularly from 1933 to the 1950s and intermittently thereafter. Billy May's arrangement of *Cherokee*, recorded in 1939, shows off the band's swinging dance riffs. Barnet admired the leading African American bands and imitated Duke Ellington's orchestra; furthered integration in jazz by hiring many prominent African American musicians, including Benny Carter, as early as 1935.

Baroque. The period of Western music history extending from the end of the 16th century to ca. 1750; also the musical styles of that period.

Two contrasting derivations of the word were posited already in the 18th century: (1) from the Portuguese *barroco,* describing an irregularly shaped pearl; and (2) from the Italian *baroco,* a logical term referring to an extraordinary type of syllogism. The first derivation is now generally accepted. Both etymologies suggest the bizarre, unnatural, and strained as connotations of the term; it was used in the 18th and 19th centuries (and still is occasionally in the 20th) with pejorative intent. The term Baroque is best employed to connote the stylistic features of music from a period whose borders, by now, have been set largely by scholarly convention.

Baroque music typically shows a homophonic texture in which the uppermost part carries the melody over a bass line with strong harmonic implications. The resulting soprano-bass polarity leads from around 1600 to the employment of the *thoroughbass (*basso continuo* or figured bass), an instrumental bass line with the inner parts improvised chordally above it. The division of labor implied in this melody–bass line dichotomy manifests itself also in the *stile *concertato* (concerted style), in which performing forces diverse in function and timbre are united, and later in the *concerto, with its functional contrast of soloist(s) and *ripieno. Throughout the period, stylistic diversity is enhanced by a pervasive feature of Baroque musical thought (one clearly anticipated in the late Renaissance): the self-conscious discrimination of separate styles for separate musical functions. Baroque theorists often recognized three such styles, destined for church, chamber, and theater, though these distinctions embraced important subdivisions (e.g., concerted church music vs. that in the Palestrinian *stile antico* or "old style"; see Palestrina style) and were often blurred in practice (e.g., in the *oratorio; that is, theatrical church music).

The Baroque period is usually divided into three subperiods. The early Baroque (ca. 1590–1640) is a period of experimentation characterized by the new hegemony of monodic styles (which had persisted, if not predominated, throughout the Renaissance; see Monody) in such genres as solo *madrigal and *aria, *opera (uniting aria and dramatic monody or *recitative), sacred vocal concerto, and the nascent solo and trio *sonatas. The pitch hierarchies of modern tonality begin to emerge from the freer tonal practices of the polyphonic madrigalists. This process is aided by the new importance, in the monodic texture, of bass-line structures with clear tonal implications, especially repeating bass lines [see Ground bass] and *strophic variation forms taken over from 16th-century dances and poetic reciting formulas.

The middle Baroque, from around 1640 to 1690, is a period of consolidation. Dissonance is more strictly controlled than in the early Baroque. The expressive recitative of earlier years declines in importance, while the lyrical, *bel canto* aria, in new, regularized forms (one of them the da capo form, ABA), takes on greater expressive weight. Operatic features appear in other vocal genres: the *cantata, built from a simple alternation of aria and recitative, displaces earlier lyrical monody, and the oratorio and (in Protestant countries) church cantata transform the sacred concerto. Solo and especially trio sonatas are standardized in movement order and style.

In the late Baroque, from ca. 1690 to the mid-18th century, the tonal regularity attained gradually through the preceding century generates large formal patterns: the grand da capo aria, and *ritornello form in the concerto. The moderate, triple-time motion typical of the *bel canto* style gives way to insistent, motoristic rhythms that emphasize motives designed to project a single, static affection.

Barraine, Elsa (b. Paris, 13 Feb. 1910). Composer. Studied with Dukas (composition), Caussade (fugue), and Jean Gallon (harmony) at the Paris Conservatory; won the Prix de Rome in 1929; choral director for French Radio (1936–39); taught at the conservatory (1954–75). She composed a comic opera (*Le roi bossu,* 1932); *Claudine à l'école* (1950) and several other ballets; incidental music and film scores; 2 symphonies (1931, 1938); chamber music; several piano and organ works.

Barraqué, Jean (b. Puteaux, Seine, 17 Jan. 1928; d. Paris, 17 Aug. 1973). Composer. Studied at the Paris Conservatory with Langlais and Messiaen (1948–51); worked with the Groupe de musique concrète at French Radio (1951–54), where he produced his only electronic piece (*Étude,* 1954). His compositions employ serial procedures in the service of a lyrical style. Early works include Sonata for Piano (1950–52) and *Séquence* (soprano and instrumental ensemble, 1950–55); a large work based on Hermann Broch's *The Death of Virgil* remained unfinished at his death.

Barraud, Henry (b. Bordeaux, 23 Apr. 1900). Composer. Entered the Paris Conservatory in 1926 and studied with Dukas, Caussade, and Aubert; in the early 1930s Pierre Monteux conducted two of his orchestral works (*Finale of a Symphony* and *Poème*); in 1933 Barraud cofounded with Rivier the Triton Concerts for performance of contemporary works; after the war joined Radiodiffusion française, from which he retired in 1965. Works include operas, ballets, film and radio scores, chamber music, large-scale choral works.

Barre de mesure [Fr.]. *Bar line.

Barré, grand-barré [Fr.; Sp. *ceja, cejilla*]. In guitar and lute playing, the stopping of all strings with the forefinger at some specified fret; sometimes termed in English capotasto, which, however, also refers to a device [see Capotasto (1)]. In the *petit-barré* [Sp. *media ceja;* Eng. half-capotasto], the forefinger stops only the highest-pitched three, four, or five strings.

Barrel. (1) In some *automatic instruments, including the most common variety of music box, a cylinder studded with pins or pegs that engage the sound-producing mechanism (often a metal comb) when the cylinder is made to rotate. (2) The short section of the clarinet that connects the mouthpiece to the first section or joint with finger holes. Barrels of differing length are sometimes used to adjust pitch.

Barrel organ [Fr. *orgue à cilindre, o. à manivelle, o. de Barbarie;* Ger. *Drehorgel, Leierkasten;* It. *organetto;* Sp. *organillo*]. A small organ in which a *barrel with pins or staples is made to rotate by a hand crank (which also operates a bellows), the pins or staples engaging a mechanism that causes individual pipes to sound [see also Automatic instrument]. A barrel might have eight or ten tunes encoded on it side by side, each tune requiring one complete revolution. Such instruments were developed in the 18th century and were widely used in English parish churches into the 19th. Smaller instruments that could be supported by a strap over the shoulder were also developed in the 18th century and survived into the 20th, along with instruments on wheels, as the street organs (sometimes also termed hand organs) of itinerant "organ grinders." See also Barrel piano.

Barrel piano. An upright piano operated by a barrel-and-pin mechanism and used especially by itinerant street musicians; sometimes also called a hand organ or street organ. See also Barrel organ.

Barrelhouse. In early jazz, raucous piano playing; also a style of piano playing, related to *boogie-woogie, that developed in the noise of barrooms (barrelhouses).

Barrett, Syd [Roger] (b. Cambridge, England, 6 Jan. 1946). Rock singer, songwriter, and guitarist. In 1965 founded the band Pink Floyd with David Gilmour, Roger Waters, Richard Wright, and Nick Mason; composed much of their early album *Pipers at the Gates of Dawn* (1967), gaining recognition for his surrealistic and mystical lyrics. After his 1968 departure from the band his work was released by Harvest Records as *The Madcap Laughs* (1974).

Barsanti, Francesco (b. Lucca, 1690; d. London, 1772). Composer. From 1714 played oboe and flute with the Italian opera in London; in 1724 had his first solo sonatas published there; was in Edinburgh by 1735, where he published 10 concerti grossi (1742) and 9 overtures (1743). Returned to London in 1743, took a job as orchestral violist, and continued to compose (6 *antifoni*, ca. 1750; 6 solo sonatas, op. 6, 1769; violin concertos).

Bartered Bride, The [Cz. *Prodaná nevěsta;* Ger. *Die verkaufte Braut*]. Opera in three acts by Smetana (libretto by Karel Sabina), produced in Prague in 1866 in a version with spoken dialogue and two acts, revised three times, and produced in the definitive version in three acts with recitatives instead of spoken dialogue in 1870. Setting: a village in Bohemia in the middle of the 19th century.

Bartók, Béla (b. Nagyszentmiklós, now Sînnicolau Mare, Romania, 25 Mar. 1881; d. New York, 26 Sept. 1945). Composer and ethnomusicologist. Entered the Budapest Academy of Music in 1899, where his teachers included Thomán (piano) and Koessler (composition); in 1901 made his Budapest debut as a pianist; around 1906 he and Kodály began collecting folk songs in Hungarian villages (later in Romania, Slovakia, Bulgaria, and Serbo-Croatia); Bartók assimilated the spirit and substance of these melodies in his own music. Works from this time include String Quartet no. 1 (1908) and Piano Quintet (1903–4, rev. 1920); during World War I composed Piano Suite (1916) and the Second String Quartet (1915–17); soon after the war completed the ballet *The Wooden Prince* (1914–17), which unlike *Bluebeard's Castle* was an immediate success in Budapest; by 1918 began to achieve international renown. In 1926 composed, for his own concert tours, a number of large piano works, including the First Piano Concerto and the Sonata (both 1926); toured the U.S. (1927–28). The years 1927–33 were prolific: works from this period include the String Quartets nos. 3 and 4 (1927, 1928), *Cantata Profana* (1930), and the Piano Concerto no. 2 (1930–31). The war drove him out of Budapest in 1940; arrived in New York and received a stipend to transcribe and classify Yugoslav folk song recordings. His last compositions were the Concerto for Orchestra (1943, rev. 1945), the Piano Concerto no. 3 (1945), and the Viola Concerto (1945). Other works include the *Miraculous Mandarin, Music for Strings, Percussion, and Celesta* (1936); string quartets nos. 5 and 6 (1934, 1939); 2 sonatas, violin and piano (1921; 1922); 44 duos, 2 violins (in 4 vols., 1931); *Contrasts,* violin, clarinet, piano (1938); Sonata, solo violin (1944). Piano music includes: *Allegro barbaro,* 1911; *Szabadban* [Out of Doors], 1926; *Mikrokosmos,* in 6 vols., 1926–39. Many original songs and folk song arrangements.

Bartolozzi, Bruno (b. Florence, 8 June 1911; d. there, 12 Dec. 1980). Composer and theorist. Studied violin and composition (Fragapane, Dallapiccola) at the Florence Conservatory and at the Accademia Chigiana in Siena; played violin in the Maggio musicale fiorentino (1941–65); from 1964 taught at the Florence Conservatory. Edited a series of string and wind methods; his compositions employ serialism, aleatoric methods, quarter tones, and speech-song, as well as new playing techniques for most instruments.

Baryton [Ger.; It. *viola di bordone*]. An 18th-century bowed stringed instrument similar to the bass viol, with six bowed strings and seven fingerboard frets, but with a festooned body outline and a very broad neck hollowed in the rear to accommodate as many as twenty *sympathetic strings [see ill. under Viol]. The baryton enjoyed its greatest popularity in Austria and southern Germany and has been often likened to a bass form of the *viola d'amore. The bowed strings are commonly tuned like those of the bass viol, D G c e a′ d′, with sympathetics in diatonic or chromatic progression. While fingering the six fretted bowed strings, the left hand is also required to pluck with the thumb the exposed sympathetics behind the neck. Haydn composed about 170 chamber works requiring baryton for his patron Prince Nikolaus Esterházy.

Barzelletta [It.]. The most often used verse form in the 16th-century *frottola. Like the *ballata,* it consists of a *ripresa* (refrain) followed by *piedi* or *mutazioni* and a *volta* leading back to the *ripresa.* A typical rhyme scheme is abba *(ripresa)* cdcd *(piedi)* d(ee)a *(volta).* In meter (usually a jingly eight-syllable trochaic) and lightness of subject matter, it differs from the *ballata.* A common musical form (one stanza) is AB *(ripresa)* AA *(piedi)* (A)B *(volta).*

Bas [Fr.]. See *Haut.*

Basie, Count [William] (b. Red Bank, N.J., 21 Aug. 1904; d. Hollywood, Fla., 26 Apr. 1984). Jazz bandleader and pianist. In Kansas City formed a 9-piece group that expanded to 14 musicians in 1936; his band favored a repertory of head arrangements that combined swing riffs with strong soloists, including Lester Young, Buck Clayton, and Herschel Evans. Basie developed the most economical piano style in jazz, supplying sparse accentuations as an accompanist and varying simple motives as a soloist. In 1950–52 led small groups; later reformed a big band, with which he toured internationally into the 1980s.

Bass [Fr. *basse;* Ger. *Bass;* It. *basso;* Sp. *bajo*]. (1) The lowest-sounding male voice [see Voice]. (2) The *double bass. (3) In families of instruments such as the clarinet or trombone, the lowest sounding member. (4) The BB♭ *tuba. (5) From the 15th century (when it emerged as the *contratenor bassus*), the lowest part in a polyphonic composition; by extension, the lowest pitch of any single chord and the succession of such lowest pitches even if produced by different voices or instruments in turn. In music composed in the language of triadic *tonality, the bass part (or line, if not confined to a single instrument or voice) is usually regarded as having a primary structural role in determining *harmony; *harmonic analysis takes it as fundamental, though the bass is subject to the principles of *counterpoint as much as is any other part. The role of the bass part becomes particularly important around 1600 with the advent of the *thoroughbass (or *basso continuo*). See also Clef; Ground bass; Bass horn.

Bass horn. (1) An English variety of the *serpent, invented in the 1790s and made of two sections of conical brass tubing joined to form a tall, narrow V. The larger section is topped with an expanded opening or bell, the other with a long, looped mouth pipe. It has six finger holes, three or four keys, approximately 2.45 m. (8 ft.) of tube length, and is in the key of C. (2) In modern high school band usage, a *tuba or *sousaphone.

Bassa [It.]. Low; *ottava bassa* (abbr. *8va bassa*), an octave lower than notated; *con ottava bassa*, an instruction to double the notated pitches with those an octave lower.

Bassadanza [It.]. *Basse danse*.

Bassani, Giovanni Battista (b. Padua, ca. 1657; d. Bergamo, 1 Oct. 1716). Composer and violinist. Studied in Venice, possibly with Legrenzi (composition) and Vitali (violin); *Maestro di cappella* at the Confraternità del finale in Modena from 1677; at the court of Duke Alessandro II from 1680; at the Accademia della morte in Ferrara from 1684; and at the cathedral in Ferrara from 1686. In 1712 went to Bergamo, where he taught music and directed at S. Maria Maggiore. Composed operas, oratorios, sacred music.

Bass-bar [Fr. *barre*; Ger. *Bassbalken*; It. *catena*; Sp. *cadena, barra*]. In the violin and other bowed stringed instruments, a long vertical strip of even-grained spruce glued under tension to the inside of the table beneath the bass foot of the bridge. It strengthens the table and aids the distribution and amplification of string vibrations, especially those of the lower register.

Bass-course. On some plucked stringed instruments, a low-pitched *course or string that is not over the fingerboard and thus cannot be stopped.

Basse [Fr.]. *Bass; *b. à pistons*, *euphonium; *b. chiffrée*, *figured bass; *b. continue*, *thoroughbass; *b. contrainte*, *ground bass; *b.-contre*, an especially deep bass voice or the lowest member of the *viol family; *b. d'harmonie*, *ophicleide; *b. fondamentale*, *fundamental bass; *b.-taille*, in the 18th century, the baritone voice. For *b. chantante, profonde*, see Voice.

Basse danse [Fr.; It. *bassadanza*]. A family of related dances including the *basse danse* proper (*bassadanza*), the *quaternaria*, the *pas de Brabant (*saltarello), and the *piva*, widely cultivated in the courts of Europe in the 15th century and, because of early literary sources, thought to be of French origin. The *basse danse* itself was a sedate dance performed by couples. It was danced with slow, gliding steps that contrasted with the livelier movements of the *pas de Brabant* or the *saltarello*. The music of the *basse danse* consists of a series of long-note tenors that served as *cantus firmi*. One step was danced to each note, and, as with the sequence of steps, it took several notes to make up a measure. For the rest of the music, the dance band, usually consisting of two or three *shawms and a *sackbut, improvised livelier parts around the tenor [for the ensemble see *Alta*]. More than 50 such tenor melodies are preserved (the most famous of which is the *Spagna*). Many of these tenors find their origin in French chansons.

In 16th-century Italy, the *bassadanza* was superseded by the *pavana. In France, it continued well into the 16th century. Sometimes a *basse danse* is followed by a *tourdion and sometimes by a *recoupe and a *tourdion* to form an embryonic suite. In Germany, the 16th-century counterpart is the *Hoftanz with its accompanying *Nachtanz.

Basset horn [Fr. *cor de basset*; Ger. *Bassetthorn, Bassettklarinette*; It. *corno di bassetto*]. A form of *clarinet developed by Anton and Michael Mayrhofer of Passau about 1770. The instrument is usually in F, a fourth lower than the normal B♭ clarinet. Its key mechanism usually includes "basset" keys, operated by the right thumb, that extend the written range down to c by opening three parallel internal-bore channels housed in a wooden box [Ger. *Kasten*] connecting the bell and body. The earliest form of the basset horn seems to have been a curved wooden tube covered with leather, ending with a flared metal bell. Later the curved body was replaced by a bent one in which two straight sections are connected by a short (often ivory) elbow section [see ill. under Reed]. Modern basset horns are usually made in a shape similar to the modern alto or bass clarinet. The instrument is called for in works by Mozart (e.g., *Die Zauberflöte*, the Requiem, and the Serenade K. 370a [361]), Mendelssohn (opp. 113, 114), and Richard Strauss (e.g., *Elektra*).

Bassett, bassetgen, bassettl [Ger.], **bassetto** [It.]. (1) In the 18th century, the *violoncello. (2) In the Baroque era, a part exercising the function of the bass part, but sounding in a higher register than normal.

Bassett, Leslie (Raymond) (b. Hanford, Calif., 22 Jan. 1923). Composer. Teachers included Honegger, Boulanger (1950–51), Gerhard (1960) and Davidovsky (electronic music, 1964); from 1952 on the faculty of the Univ. of Michigan; received the Pulitzer Prize for *Variations for Orchestra* (1963); other works include *Echoes from an Invisible World* (1976). Composed a few serial and electronic pieces in the 1960s, but most compositions are for conventional instruments and focus on orchestral color.

Bassist. (1) In jazz and popular music, a player of the *double bass or *electric bass. (2) [Ger.] A bass singer.

Basso [It.]. *Bass; *col basso,* with the bass.

Basso buffo [It.]. See Voice.

Basso cantante [It.]. See Voice.

Basso continuo [It.]. *Thoroughbass.

Basso ostinato [It.]. See Ground, *Ostinato.*

Basso profondo [It.]. See Voice.

Basso ripieno [It.]. In a *concerto grosso, a bass part for the **ripieno* or tutti passages only.

Basso seguente [It.]. In the late 16th and early 17th centuries, a part composed of the lowest-sounding pitches of a composition and played on the organ or some other instrument in the fashion of a *thoroughbass (or *basso continuo*).

Basson [Fr.]. *Bassoon; *b. quinte,* *tenoroon; *b. russe,* *Russian bassoon.

Bassoon [Fr. *basson;* Ger. *Fagott;* It. *fagotto;* Sp. *fagot*]. A conical-bore, double-reed woodwind instrument that has its bore folded in the center in order to reduce its exterior dimensions. To further aid in making the finger holes reachable, several of them are drilled at an extreme angle into the bore. The bassoon has been made in a variety of sizes, but the only instruments that have survived in current use are the normal bassoon (range B♭₁ to e″, written at pitch) and the *contrabassoon (range A₂ or B♭₂ to g, usually written an octave higher). From the Baroque period to the present, bassoons have been built in four sections, usually called the wing (or tenor), the boot (or butt), the long (or bass), and the bell. The reed is connected to the wing by an S-shaped tube called a *bocal. Modern bassoons may be divided into two types, the French and the German, which differ in design and in fingering. The German instrument is usually made of maple, the French instrument of rosewood. The German instrument dominates most of Europe and the U.S., while the French instrument remains solidly entrenched in France, with a few adherents in French Canada as well. See ill. under Reed.

The bassoon is descended from the various folded-bore instruments of the Renaissance, such as the

*curtal and the *sordone.* Besides those in current use, there have been instruments pitched an octave higher (octave bassoon, *fagottino*), tenors pitched a fifth higher (often called *tenoroons; also *basson quinte*), and instruments a fourth or a fifth below the normal bassoon *(Quartfagott, Quintfagott).* Subcontrabass instruments have also been constructed, but have never achieved much use.

Bassus [Lat., fr. *contratenor bassus*]. *Bass (5).

Bastien und Bastienne. *Singspiel in one act (libretto by Friedrich Wilhelm Weiskern after Favart's parody of Rousseau's *Le devin du village*) composed by Mozart at the age of 12 and first performed, probably, at the home of Anton Mesmer in Vienna in 1768.

Bateson, Thomas (b. Cheshire County, 1570–75?; d. Dublin, Mar. 1630). Composer. Organist of Chester Cathedral from 1599; from 1609 organist and vicar-choral at Christ Church Cathedral, Dublin; received B.Mus. and M.A. from Trinity College, Dublin. Extant compositions include one anthem and two books of madrigals.

Bathyphone [Ger. *Bathyphon*]. A type of contrabass clarinet designed in 1839 by Wilhelm Wieprecht (1802–72). It was built in bassoon shape of either metal or wood, with a metal bell. It was pitched two octaves lower than the normal clarinet and was usually constructed in C.

Baton. (1) A thin, tapered stick, about 45 cm. (18 in.) in length, often colored white, used in *conducting. (2) The stick, nearly a meter (3.25 ft.) or more in length, often ornamented with braid, used by the drum major in a military or other marching band.

Battaglia [It., battle]. A composition that depicts a battle, sometimes with quite naturalistic attempts to imitate the cries and noise of the battlefield. There are examples from as early as the late 14th century, and a rather large repertory of such pieces was composed in the second half of the 18th century and in the first half of the 19th, e.g., Beethoven's *Wellingtons Sieg.*

Battement [Fr.]. (1) An acoustical *beat. (2) In Baroque music, a *mordent, or a two-finger gamba vibrato, or a trill beginning on the main note, or a multiple mordent beginning on the lower auxiliary; also the separate oscillations of a trill or multiple mordent. See Ornamentation.

Batterie [Fr.]. (1) The percussion section of the orchestra. (2) In jazz, a drum set. (3) A formulaic drum pattern used as a military signal. (4) In the 18th century, an arpeggiated or broken chord repeated several times. (5) In guitar playing, strumming the strings rather than plucking.

Battery. (1) The percussion section of the orchestra. (2) *Batterie (4).

Battistini, Mattia (b. Rome, 27 Feb. 1856; d. Collebaccaro, near Rieti, 7 Nov. 1928). Baritone. Made his debut as a replacement in *La favorita* at the Teatro Argentina, Rome (1878); appeared in opera houses throughout Europe and in Russia; sang primarily in 19th-century Italian and French (also a few German and Russian) works; a notable Don Giovanni. His many recordings (1903–25) are prized as models of 19th-century Italian singing technique and style.

Battle of the Huns, The. See *Hunnenschlacht, Die*.

Battle of Victoria, The. See *Wellingtons Sieg*.

Battle pieces. See *Battaglia*.

Battle, Kathleen (Deanne) (b. Portsmouth, Ohio, 13 Aug. 1948). Soprano. Studied with Franklin Bens (1972); appeared at Spoleto Festival (1972) and with the Cincinnati Symphony. Coached by James Levine (1973); Young Artist Award (1975); operatic debut in 1976, Covent Garden debut in 1985. Roles include Mozart's Susanna and Despina, Rossini's Rosina, Strauss's Zerbinetta, Zdenka, and Sophie.

Battre [Fr.]. To beat, with respect to both time in conducting and percussion instruments.

Battuta [It.]. Beat; measure; *a battuta*, return to a strict tempo after some deviation from it. Beethoven's direction "ritmo di tre [quattro] battute" in the scherzo of his Symphony no. 9 indicates that measures, each of which takes only a single beat, should be grouped in threes (or fours).

Baudrier, Yves (Marie) (b. Paris, 11 Feb. 1906; d. there, 9 Nov. 1988). Composer. Studied with Georges Loth; after 1935 associated with Messiaen, Jolivet, and Daniel-Lesur in the group called "La Jeune France" which championed a return to a more lyrical style; his music reflects his admiration for Debussy. Taught at the Institut des hautes études cinématographiques (1945–60); compositions include many film scores, a ballet, and music for theater and television.

Bauer, Harold (b. Kingston-on-Thames, 28 Apr. 1873; d. Miami, 12 Mar. 1951). Pianist and violinist. Following career as a violinist switched to piano in 1892 with Paderewski's encouragement; debut in London, 1892; U.S., 1900; based in Paris, 1893–1913. Moved to the U.S. in 1913, where he helped found Manhattan School of Music. Repertory included Beethoven, Brahms, Chopin, and especially Schumann, whose music he also edited.

Bauer, Marion (Eugenie) (b. Walla Walla, Wash., 15 Aug. 1887; d. South Hadley, Mass., 9 Aug. 1955). Composer, pianist, teacher, writer on music. Her teachers included Campbell-Tipton, Boulanger, and Gédalge in Paris (1923–26); her compositions are often cast in smaller forms and in an impressionist idiom, sometimes incorporating exotic elements (*Lament on African Themes*, chamber orchestra, 1928). Later works adopted a neoclassical approach (Prelude and Fugue, flute and strings op. 43, 1948). Taught at New York Univ. (1926–51) and at Juilliard (1940–44) and gave lectures at Chatauqua from 1928. An important advocate for new music in numerous articles; author of several books on music.

Bauernkantate [Ger., Peasant Cantata]. A secular cantata by Bach, BWV 212, setting a text by Picander in Saxon dialect ("Mer hahn en neue Oberkeet"; We have a new magistrate) and performed in 1742 on the installation of a new magistrate in the rural town of Klein-Zschocher, Saxony. It makes use of several popular tunes.

Bax, Arnold (Edward Trevor) (b. Streatham, 8 Nov. 1883; d. Cork, 3 Oct. 1953). Composer. Following early instruction at the Hampstead Conservatory enrolled at the Royal Academy of Music in 1900, where his teachers included Corder (composition) and Matthay (piano); traveled to Dresden in 1906 and to Russia in 1910, in addition to frequent visits to Ireland. Compositions from this period include the tone poems *In the Faery Hills* (1909) and *The Garden of Fand* (1913), and a piano quartet (1915). Lived in Ireland from 1911 until the beginning of World War I, when he returned to Hampstead; knighted in 1937 and in 1941 became Master of the King's Music. His music includes elements of Irish and folk song and of the tonal palette of early 20th-century France. Works include ballet and incidental music (*The Truth about the Russian Dancers*, 1920; rev. 1926); film scores; 7 symphonies (1922–39) and 9 symphonic poems (*Christmas Eve on the Mountains*, 1911–12; *November Woods*, 1917; *Tintagel*, 1917; *Summer Music*, 1920); choral and vocal works (*This Worldes Joie*, 1922); chamber works (3 string quartets); more than 125 songs; much piano music (6 sonatas, 1898–32).

Bay Psalm Book. *The Whole Booke of Psalms Faithfully Translated into English Metre*, the first book printed in North America (Cambridge, Mass., 1640). Subsequent editions were spread over more than a century. The first edition employed only six metrical patterns for the entire Psalter (common meter being used for three-fourths of the Psalms) and referred its users to 48 tunes for the singing of them. Some later editions into the mid-18th century were called the *New England Psalm Book*. The ninth edition (Boston, 1698) included settings in two parts for 13 tunes, the first music printed in America. See also Psalter.

Bayadère, La [Fr., The Indian Dancing Girl]. A ballet in three acts by Léon Minkus, first produced in St. Petersburg in 1877 with choreography by Marius Petipa.

Bazelon, Irwin (Allen) (b. Evanston, Ill., 4 June 1922; d. New York, 2 Aug. 1995). Composer. Studied with Leon Stein at DePaul Univ., with Milhaud at Mills College, and with Hindemith and Bloch; composed concert and film music; taught film music at the School for Visual Arts in New York (1968–73), authored *Knowing the Score* (1975) on the same topic. In the 1960s experimented with twelve-tone techniques (Symphony no. 5, 1966); some works show jazz influence (Chamber Concerto no. 2, Churchill Downs, both 1970).

Bazzini, Antonio (b. Brescia, 11 Mar. 1818; d. Milan, 10 Feb. 1897). Violinist, composer, and teacher. Encouraged by Paganini, became a soloist and toured widely in Europe; composed much music, including violin concertos and character pieces (*La ronde des lutins*); settled in Brescia in 1864 to compose full-time. Became professor of composition (1873) and then director (1882) of the Milan Conservatory; pupils included Catalani, Mascagni, and Puccini.

BB♭ bass [pronounced "double-B-flat"]. See Tuba.

B.c. Abbr. for *basso continuo*. See Thoroughbass.

Be [Ger.]. The flat sign, ♭ [see Accidental, Pitch names].

Beach, Amy Marcy Cheney (b. Henniker, N.H., 5 Sept. 1867; d. New York, 27 Dec. 1944). Composer and pianist. A virtuoso pianist and largely an autodidact in composition, she often played her own music in the U.S. and Europe; limited her appearances during her marriage; after her husband's death (1910) resumed performing in the U.S. and in Europe, composing during the summers (from 1921 at the Mac-Dowell Colony). A prolific composer who favored rich chromatic textures; works include the opera *Cabildo* (1932); orchestral music; chamber music; piano works. Best known for her songs.

Beak(ed) flute [Fr. *flûte à bec;* Ger. *Schnabelflöte*]. A *duct flute with beak-shaped upper end; specifically the *recorder.

Beardslee, Bethany (b. Lansing, Mich., 25 Dec. 1927). Soprano; married Jacques-Louis Monod, with whom she gave many recitals; has premiered works of her second husband, Godfrey Winham, as well as compositions by Stravinsky, Berg, Webern, Babbitt, Krenek, Boulez, Dallapiccola, Peter Maxwell

Davies, and others; commissioned and performed Babbitt's *Philomel*. Taught at Univ. of Calif., Davis; Univ. of Texas (1981–82); Brooklyn College (from 1983).

Beaser, Robert Harry (b. Boston, Mass., 29 May 1954). Composer and conductor. Studied at Yale and at the Berkshire Music Center; teachers include Jacob Druckman, Yehudi Wyner, Betsy Jolas, Gofreddo Petrassi and Arnold Franchetti. Assistant conductor, Norwalk Symphony (1975–77); composer-in-residence, American Composers Orchestra (1988–93); member, Juilliard faculty from 1993. Works include *The Seven Deadly Sins* (1979); *Variations* (flute and piano, 1983); *Psalm 150 for Chorus* (1995).

Beat [Fr. *temps;* Ger. *Zählzeit, Schlag;* It. *battuta;* Sp. *tiempo*]. (1) A metrical pulse; also the marking of such a pulse by movements of the hand in *conducting. For the grouping of beats in recurring patterns of strong and weak beats, see Meter. For metrical pulse in early music, see *Tactus*. See also Accent (1), Downbeat, Upbeat, Afterbeat, Backbeat. (2) The English term for *mordent, indicated by a wavy line without a stroke through it and, by the 18th century, other signs [see Ex.]. A "shaked beat" is a mordent with several repercussions. (3) See Beats.

Béatitudes, Les [Fr., The Beatitudes]. An oratorio by César Franck for soloists, chorus, and orchestra, op. 53 (1869–79), a setting of texts adapted from the Beatitudes of the Sermon on the Mount (Matt. 5:3–12).

Beats. A slight, steady pulsation in intensity that results from the interference between two sound waves of slightly different frequencies. The frequency of the beats will be equal to the difference between the frequencies of the sound waves.

Beaujoyeux [Beaujoyeulx, Belgioioso], **Balthasar de** [Baldassare de; "Baltazarini"] (b. before ca. 1535; d. ca. 1587). Ballet master and violinist. About 1555 left Italy to serve French royal court; creator, organizer, and participant in various court entertainments, including the elaborate *Magnificences* of 1581; only surviving work is *Balet comique de la Royne,* for which he was stage manager and choreographer; it was an influential predecessor of the *ballet de cour* and of French opera.

Bebop, bop. A jazz style that flourished between about 1944 and 1958, stressing melodic improvisation. Among its leading exponents were Charlie Parker and Dizzy Gillespie. See also Jazz.

Bebung [Ger.; Fr. *balancement*]. A *vibrato produced on the clavichord by varying the pressure with which a key is held and thus varying the tension of the string that has been struck [see Clavichord], notated thus:

Bec [Fr.]. The *mouthpiece of a clarinet or recorder; *flûte à bec*, recorder.

Bécarre [Fr.]. The natural sign, ♮ [see Accidental, Pitch names].

Becerra (-Schmidt), Gustavo (b. Temuco, Chile, 26 Aug. 1925). Composer. Studied composition with Pedro Allende at Santiago's National Conservatory (from 1933); graduated from the Univ. of Chile and became professor of composition there (1952); after two years in Europe returned home to to serve as director of the Extensión musical (1960–62) and of the composition department at the State Conservatory. Works conform chiefly to classical structures, with the addition of aleatoric and electronic elements.

Bechet, Sidney (Joseph) (b. New Orleans, 14 May 1897; d. Paris, 14 May 1959). Jazz clarinetist and soprano saxophonist. Moved to Chicago (1917), played clarinet with Freddie Keppard and King Oliver; toured England and France; in London acquired a soprano saxophone. In New York recorded with Louis Armstrong and joined Duke Ellington (1924); toured Europe, including Russia, 1925–30, playing in revues, leading bands, and working with Noble Sissle. In the U.S. rejoined Sissle (intermittently 1931–38) and with the trumpeter Tommy Ladnier led the New Orleans Feetwarmers (1932–33), recording "Maple Leaf Rag" (1932). From 1939, when he recorded "Summertime," active in the New Orleans jazz revival, performing in New York, Boston, and Chicago. He recorded with Jelly Roll Morton (including "High Society," 1939) and the clarinetist Mezz Mezzrow (1945–47); from 1951 lived in France. He played with a wide vibrato and an extremely passionate, powerful sound.

Beck, Conrad (b. Lohn, Schaffhausen, Switzerland, 16 June 1901; d. Basel, 31 Oct. 1989). Composer. Studied at the Zurich Conservatory and then in Paris and Berlin; lived in Paris (1923–32), where he associated with Boulanger, Ibert, Honegger, and Roussel; moved to Basel (1932), where he eventually became director of Radio Basel (1939–62). His style combines an austere polyphony with clarity of form, later works exhibiting a freedom from tonality and a simplification of texture. His Concerto for String Quartet (1929) won the Coolidge Prize.

Becken [Ger.]. Cymbals.

Beckwith, John (b. Victoria, B.C., 9 Mar. 1927). Composer. Studied at the Toronto Conservatory and the Univ. of Toronto (Mus.B., 1947) and in Paris with Boulanger (1950–52); worked for CBC Radio (1953–65) and wrote music criticism for the *Toronto Star* (1959–66); edited the *Canadian Music Journal* (1956–62); wrote program notes for the Toronto Symphony (1966–71); taught at the Univ. of Toronto (assistant professor, 1961; dean of the faculty, 1970–77). Early works are neoclassical; later made use of serial and collage techniques. Compositions include operas, orchestral works, choral works (*Harp of David*), chamber music, piano music.

Becuadro [Sp.]. The natural sign, ♮ [see Accidental, Pitch names].

Bedächtig [Ger.]. Deliberate, slow.

Bedeckt [Ger.]. With respect to the kettledrum, muffled.

Bedford, David (Vickerman) (b. London, 4 Aug. 1937). Composer. Studied at Lancing College in Sussex (1951–55) and the Royal Academy of Music (1956–60) with Berkeley; also with Nono in Venice (1960); after 1963 taught secondary school in London, from 1968 taught as well at Queen's College; especially interested in working with children and musicians not classically trained. His works often employ indeterminate compositional and improvisatory performance techniques and graphic notation; some are scored for unusual instruments (*100 Kazoos,* 1971), and others employ new instrumental techniques.

Bedrohlich [Ger.]. Threatening.

Bedyngham [Bedyngeham, Bedingham, Benigun], **Johannes** (d. Westminster?, London, reported between 3 May 1459 and 22 May 1460). Composer. Verger at the chapel of St. Stephen, Westminster, a position generally held by a notable composer; works survive in numerous, widely distributed sources, attesting to his reputation. Probably spent his entire life in England, though his fame reached as far as Italy. Works (some with conflicting attributions) include 2 Mass cycles, 2 Mass movements, 3 motets, and 8 songs (with texts in English, French, and Italian).

Beecham, Thomas (b. St. Helens, Lancashire, 29 Apr. 1879; d. London, 8 Mar. 1961). Self-taught as a conductor; founded the Beecham Symphony Orchestra (1909) and conducted operas at Covent Garden and Drury Lane; during World War I conducted the Hallé Orchestra, the London Symphony, and the Royal Philharmonic Society; in 1932 formed the London Philharmonic; artistic director, Covent Garden (1932–39); conducted the Seattle Symphony, Metropolitan Opera, and New York Philharmonic (1940–45); subsequently conducted the London Philharmonic and formed the Royal Philharmonic (1946); knighted in 1916.

Beecroft, Norma (Marian) (b. Oshawa, Ont., 11 Apr. 1934). Composer. Studied at the Toronto Conservatory (1950–58), in Rome with Petrassi (1959–61), with Copland and Foss (1958), Maderna (1960 and 1961), Schaeffer (Univ. of Toronto, 1962–63), and Davidovsky (1964); worked for CBC Radio and Television. Debussy, Hindemith and Stravinsky are influences on her style; also interested in electronic music and twelve-tone methods. Works include orchestral music; chamber music for traditional ensembles and for ensembles with tape; choral music (Requiem Mass, soloists, chorus, orchestra, 1989–90).

Beeson, Jack (Hamilton) (b. Muncie, Ind., 15 July 1921). Composer. Studied with Phillips, Rogers, and Hanson at Eastman, with Bartók in New York (1944–45), and then at Columbia Univ. (musicology, 1945–48), where he subsequently taught (from 1945); supervised the publication of new music by Columbia Univ. Press. A lifelong interest in opera is reflected in stage works including *Lizzie Borden* (1965).

Beethoven, Ludwig van (b. Bonn, 15 or 16 Dec., bapt. 17 Dec. 1770; d. Vienna, 26 Mar. 1827). Composer. Studied with his father and with Neefe, the Bonn court's opera director; appointed deputy organist by elector Maximilian Franz (1784); visited Vienna in 1787 where he might have studied with Mozart; returned to Vienna in 1792 to study with Haydn but also had lessons from Schenk, Albrechtsberger, and Salieri; quickly became known as a composer and pianist-improviser in the homes of Viennese aristocrats. In 1795 published three brilliant piano trios (op. 1) and a set of piano sonatas (op. 2); during 1796 embarked on concert tours that included Prague, Dresden, Berlin, and Pressburg; 1797–98 saw the publication of opp. 7 and 10 piano sonatas; in 1800 gave a concert that included his First Symphony; other works from this time include the Septet op. 20, String Quartets op. 18, the *Pathétique* Sonata, and 2 violin sonatas. Around 1801 he began to acknowledge to close friends that he was going deaf; spending the summer and early fall of 1802 in the village of Heiligenstadt, he completed the Second Symphony and penned the "Heiligenstadt Testament," an expression of despondence brought about

by encroaching deafness; continued to complete works at a remarkable rate, including the *Kreutzer Sonata and third piano concerto (1803). The years 1802–3 are often considered the onset of Beethoven's "middle" or "heroic" period; works from this time include the *Waldstein Sonata, the *Triple Concerto, and especially *Eroica; the period culminated in his only opera, *Fidelio. A number of large, path-breaking works date from between 1806 and early 1809: Symphonies 4 and 5, the *Pastoral Symphony, the Piano Concerto no. 4, the Violin Concerto, three *Rasumovsky String Quartets op. 59, two Piano Trios op. 70, the Cello Sonata op. 69, and the Mass in C op. 86. Support from noble patrons continued: in 1809 the Archduke Johann Joseph Rudolph and two other patrons agreed to provide the composer with an annuity and, upon his retirement, a pension; Beethoven dedicated a number of works to the Archduke, including the *Emperor Concerto and the *Archduke Trio. In 1812 he completed work on the Seventh and Eighth Symphonies; the same year wrote a love confession that has come to be known as the (never delivered) letter to the "immortal beloved." The years 1812–13 mark the beginning of a "spiritual" late period; the first large work, ironically, was the bombastic *Wellingtons Sieg. The years 1815–17 were relatively unproductive ones, marred largely by a bitter custody battle over his nephew Karl. Early in 1818 Beethoven again began composing large-scale works, beginning with the *Hammerklavier and the onset of work on the *Missa solemnis; the last three piano sonatas (opp. 109–111) were begun in 1820; the *Diabelli Variations also date from this period, as does the Ninth Symphony (1822–24). The last four years were devoted entirely to string quartets: opp. 127, 130, 131, 132, 135 and *Grosse Fuge presented a challenge to audience and players alike. An attempted suicide by Karl in the summer of 1826 dealt a severe emotional blow to his uncle, who died in March, leaving his whole estate to Karl. Other works include:

Orchestra. *Leonore overtures; *Coriolan Overture; Piano Concerto no. 1 in C, op. 15 (1795); no. 2 in B♭, op. 19 (1795, but begun before 1793)

Chamber music. String quartets: opp 74 (*Harp*, 1809), 95 (*Serioso*, 1810); piano trios op. 70 (2, 1808), 10 violin sonatas (including *Spring Sonata); cello sonatas op. 5 (2, 1797); cello sonatas op. 102 (2, 1815).

Piano. 32 sonatas, including *Moonlight, *Tempest, *Appassionata.

Incidental music. *Egmont, op. 84 (1809–10).

Vocal music. Choral Fantasy, piano, chorus, orchestra, op. 80 (1808). Songs: *"Adelaide" op. 46 (1794–95); Six Gellert Songs op. 48 (1802); "An die Hoffnung" op. 32 (1805); Six Songs op. 75 (1809);

Three Goethe Songs op. 83 (1810); *An die ferne Geliebte* op. 98 (cycle, 1815–16). Nearly 60 canons and "jokes"; 172 folk song arrangements.

Beggar's Opera, The. A *ballad opera with music arranged by Johann Christoph Pepusch (libretto by John Gay), produced in London in 1728. It presents a satirical view of 18th-century London (including the fashion for Italian opera) through a cast of criminals and harlots. A work based on the libretto but with new music is Kurt Weill's *Die *Dreigroschenoper.*

Begleitung [Ger.]. Accompaniment.

Béguine [Fr.]. A social dance popular in Europe and America from the 1930s, with a rhythm similar to that of the *bolero.

Behende [Ger.]. Agile, quick.

Behrens, Hildegard (b. Varel, West Germany, 9 Feb. 1937). Soprano. Studied with Ines Leuwen at the Freiburg Conservatory (1966–71), coached by Jerome Lo Monaco; 1971 debut with the Deutsche Oper am Rhein in Düsseldorf; her 1975 Leonore *(Fidelio)* with the Zurich Opera made her famous, and U.S. debut followed the next year. Roles include Mozart's Electra, Weber's Agathe, Strauss's Salome, Janáček's Katya, and Berg's Marie; especially prized for her Wagner heroines.

Beiderbecke, (Leon Bismarck) Bix (b. Davenport, Iowa, 10 Mar. 1903; d. New York, 6 Aug. 1931). Jazz cornetist. Toured the Midwest with the Wolverines (1923–24), with Frankie Trumbauer played in Jean Goldkette's orchestra (1924, 1926–27); recorded under pseudonyms and Trumbauer's name (1924, 1927–29); joined Paul Whiteman's orchestra (1927–29). Recordings include "Singin' the Blues" and "Riverboat Shuffle" with Trumbauer, "At the Jazz Band Ball" and "Royal Garden Blues" as leader, and "In a Mist" as an unaccompanied pianist (all 1927).

Beissel, (Johann) Conrad [Konrad] (b. Eberbach, near Mannheim, 1 Mar. 1691; d. Ephrata, Pa., 6 July 1768). Composer. Religious intolerance drove him to Pennsylvania, where he settled among Baptists in 1720; founded the Ephrata Cloister (1732); Benjamin Franklin published three collections of his hymns (1730–36), and Christopher Sauer published his *Zionistischer Weyrauchs Hügel* (1739). In 1747 the monastic group issued a hymn collection, *Das Gesang der einsamen und verlassenen Turtel-Taube,* which contains a preface by Beissel outlining his singing method.

Beisser [Ger.]. In the 18th century, *mordent.

Beklemmt [Ger.]. Anxious, oppressed.

Bel. See Decibel.

Bel canto [It., beautiful singing]. A manner of singing that emphasizes beauty of sound, with an even tone throughout the full range of the voice; fine legato phrasing dependent on a mastery of breath control; agility in florid passages; and an apparent ease in attaining high notes. The period from the middle of the 17th century to the beginning of the 19th is thought of as the golden age of *bel canto.*

Belcher, Supply (b. Stoughton, Mass., 29 Mar. 1752; d. Farmington, Maine, 9 June 1836). Chief magistrate, schoolteacher, choirmaster, and violinist in Farmington; leading figure in the development of American psalmody; in 1794 published *The Harmony of Maine.*

Belebend, belebt [Ger.]. Lively, animated.

Bell. (1) Any of a variety of objects that, when struck, emit a ringing sound. There are three basic types of bell: open, cup-shaped bells, usually made of metal, that are struck at the rim; closed, spherical *pellet bells; and *tubular bells (orchestral chimes).

Open bells may be hemispheric, quadrilateral, or beehive-shaped, but the characteristic bell of the Occident is tulip-shaped or "campaniform," with a well-defined shoulder and flaring sides. Quadrilateral bells (e.g., the *cowbell) are typically made of sheet metal, hammered and soldered. Other metal bells are cast, most often of bronze. The smallest bells, such as those hung on clothing or animal harnesses, may weigh only a few grams. The largest bell ever cast weighed approximately 200,000 kg. Church tower bells generally weigh from 4,000 to 10,000 kg., though a few approach 20,000 kg. (44,000 lb.).

Bells are struck either from the inside by a *clapper or from the outside by a hammer or a mechanical striking device. Chiming consists in swinging a bell so as to cause the clapper to strike it. Ringing consists in rotating a bell vertically through a full circle, causing the clapper to strike it more forcefully. Clocking consists in moving a bell's clapper so as to cause it to strike the stationary bell. Open bells produce a complicated, nonharmonic vibrational pattern [see Acoustics]. See also Carillon, Celesta, Cymbalum, Gong, Idiophone.

(2) [Fr. *pavillon;* Ger. *Schallbecher, Schallstück, Schalltrichter, Stürze;* It. *padiglione, campana;* Sp. *pabellón, campana*]. The opening, usually flared, of a wind instrument at the end opposite the mouthpiece.

Bell harp. A type of zither invented ca. 1700, perhaps by John Simcock of Bath, with 14 to 24 courses of 3 or 4 strings. It was held in both hands, plucked with the thumbs, and swung back and forth while being played. A form manufactured in the 19th century was known as fairy bells.

Bell lyra, bell lyre. A portable *glockenspiel in the shape of a lyre, used principally in marching bands.

Bell ringing. See Change ringing.

Bellini, Vincenzo (Salvatore Carmelo Francesco) (b. Catania, 3 Nov. 1801; d. Puteaux, near Paris, 23 Sept. 1835). Composer. Entered the Naples Conservatory in 1819; composed the opera seria *Bianca e Gernando* (1826) for the Teatro San Carlo; collaborated with the librettist Felice Romani on *Il pirata* (1827) for Milan. This work established Bellini's reputation in Italy and internationally; until their rupture in 1833, Romani would supply the texts of all his operas.

La straniera (1829) soon followed; the opera marked an important stage in Bellini's freeing himself from Rossinian influences. For Carnival 1830 Bellini revised *Il pirata* for Venice, and on short notice composed a new opera there, *I Capuleti e i Montecchi*; it was a great and widespread success, as was *La *sonnambula*. *Norma*, coldly received at first, quickly achieved its standing as Bellini's finest work. His last opera composed in Italy, *Beatrice di Tenda* (1833), had an unfriendly reception due to delays; the resulting bitterness between Bellini and Romani ended their collaboration. Bellini spent part of 1833 in London directing productions of his operas at the King's Theatre, then settled in Paris where he produced his last opera, *I *Puritani di Scozia*.

Bells. In the context of music for orchestra or band, either the *glockenspiel or the *tubular bells.

Bellson, Louie [Louis Paul; Balassoni, Luigi Paulinho Alfredo Francesco Antonio] (b. Rock Falls, Ill., 6 July 1924). Jazz drummer and bandleader. Played with Goodman (1942–43, 1946) and Tommy Dorsey (1947–49), then led a sextet with Charlie Shavers; joined Harry James (1950–51) and Duke Ellington (1951–53); beginning 1953 accompanied Pearl Bailey, whom he had married a year earlier. Bellson toured with Jazz at the Philharmonic (occasionally 1954–1970s); joined the Dorsey brothers (1955–56). From 1967 led a big band based in North Hollywood; in the late 1980s led a big band in New York and combos drawn from both ensembles.

Belly [Ger. *Decke;* Fr. *table (d'harmonie);* It. *tavola armonica;* Sp. *tapa (tabla) de armonía*]. (1) On stringed instruments such as the violin or lute, the upper face of the body or sound box, over which the strings pass and which plays a major part in transmitting the vibrations of the strings to the surrounding atmosphere; also called the table. See ill. under Violin. (2) The soundboard of the *piano.

Bémol [Fr.], **bemol** [Sp.], **bemolle** [It.]. The flat sign, ♭ [see Accidental, Pitch names].

Ben, bene [It.]. Well; as in *ben marcato*, well marked.

Benda, Franz [František] (b. Staré Benátky [Altbenatek], Bohemia, bapt. 22 Nov. 1709; d. Nowawes, near Potsdam, 7 Mar. 1786). Composer and violin virtuoso. Ran away to Dresden and sang in the court chapel choir there; in 1723 returned to Prague, where he was a chorister and seminary student; employed in Frederick II's orchestra (from 1733), a position he held until his death; had close contact with C. P. E. Bach, Quantz, and the Graun brothers. Famous for his cantabile playing; composed symphonies, concertos, sonatas, and other chamber music.

Benda, Georg (Anton) [Jiří Antonín] (b. Staré Benátky [Altbenatek], Bohemia, bapt. 30 June 1722; d. Köstritz, 6 Nov. 1795). Composer. In 1742 moved to Potsdam and joined his brother Franz in the court orchestra of Frederick II; became Kapellmeister at Frederick III's ducal chapel at Gotha (1750); after 1772 devoted much effort to theater music, including the melodramas *Ariadne auf Naxos* (1775) and *Medea* (1775); both were praised by Mozart. Benda moved to Hamburg in 1778 and then to Vienna, but received no appointment at either court

Bendl, Karel (b. Prague, 16 Apr. 1838; d. there, 20 Sept. 1897). Composer. Studied at the Prague Organ School (1855–58); conductor and chorusmaster in Brussels, Amsterdam, and Paris (1864–65); returned to Prague and conducted the Hlahol Choral Society for 12 years, for which he composed much music. Assistant conductor at the Provisional Theater (1874); in 1894 succeeded Dvořák as professor of composition at the conservatory. Works include 9 Czech operas.

Benedicamus Domino [Lat., Let us bless the Lord]. A *versicle sung or recited at the end of the hours of the *Office of the Roman rite and in place of the *Ite, missa est* at the conclusion of Masses in which the Gloria is omitted or which are followed by a procession. It is followed by the response "Deo gratias" (To God be praise). Its melodies often served as tenors of polyphonic compositions in the repertories of *St. Martial and *Notre Dame.

Benedicite [Lat., Bless ye (the Lord)]. The *Canticle of the Three Children in the Fiery Furnace (Vulgate, Daniel 3:57–88 and 56).

Benedict, Julius (b. Stuttgart, 27 Nov. 1804; d. London, 5 June 1885). Composer and conductor. Studied with Hummel and Weber (1821–24); conductor at the Teatro San Carlo and Teatro del Fondo in Naples (1825–34), also composed Italian operas; moved to Paris in 1834, to London in 1835; from 1836 conducted at the Opera Buffa at the Lyceum Theatre and in 1838–48 at Drury Lane; toured the U.S. with

Jenny Lind (1850–52); conductor, Norwich Festival (1845–78) and the Liverpool Philharmonic (1876–80). Best known for his opera *The Lily of Killarney* (1862); knighted in 1871.

Benediction. (1) A blessing, especially one pronounced on the congregation at the conclusion of a service of worship. (2) In the Roman Catholic Church and some communities of the Anglican Communion, a service in which the congregation is blessed with the Host.

Benedictus Dominus Deus Israel [Lat., Blessed be the Lord God of Israel]. The *Canticle of Zachary on the birth of his son St. John the Baptist (Luke 1:68–79). In the monastic Office of the Roman Catholic Church it is sung at Lauds; in the Anglican Church at Morning Prayer.

Benedictus (qui venit) [Lat., Blessed is he who comes in the name of the Lord]. Matthew 21:9, the second part of the *Sanctus of the *Mass, usually set as a separate composition in polyphonic works.

Beneplacito, A [It.]. At the pleasure of the performer, especially as regards tempo.

Benevoli, Orazio (b. Rome, 19 Apr. 1605; d. there, 17 June 1672). Composer. Choirboy at S. Luigi dei Francesi in Rome (1617–23), thereafter *maestro di cappella* at S. Maria in Trastevere (from 1624), at Santo Spirito in Sassia (from 1630), and eventually at S. Luigi dei Francesi (from 1638). Served the Archduke Leopold Wilhelm in Vienna (1644–46) but returned to Rome to serve at S. Maria Maggiore and at the Cappella Giulia (St. Peter's); composed Masses, motets, Magnificats, and other sacred vocal works; famous for a work he probably didn't compose, the 53-part *Missa salisburgensi* perhaps by H. J. Biber.

Ben Haim, Paul (b. Munich, 5 July 1897; d. Tel Aviv, 14 Jan. 1984). Composer and conductor. Studied at Munich's Akademie der Tonkunst; assistant conductor to Bruno Walter and Hans Knappertsbusch in Munich (1920–24), subsequently conducted in Augsberg until 1931. Forced to leave Germany in 1933, settled in Palestine and assumed the surname Ben Haim to replace the original Frankenburger; taught and conducted in Tel Aviv and Jerusalem. After the 1940s his music, characterized by a late romantic style, showed influence from Yemenite folk music; in 1957 won the nation's State Prize for *The Sweet Psalmist of Israel* (harpsichord, harp, and orchestra, 1956); other works include a violin concerto (1962) and unaccompanied sonata (1952); 2 symphonies (1940; 1945); choral and other vocal works; chamber music.

Benjamin, Arthur (b. Sydney, 18 Sept. 1893; d. London, 10 Apr. 1960). Composer and pianist. Studied with Charles Stanford (composition) and Frederick Cliffe (piano) at London's Royal College of Music (1911–14); returned to Australia and taught at the Sydney Conservatory (1919); then a professor at London's Royal College of Music (1926). Best known for his operas (*The Devil Take Her*, 1931; *The Tale of Two Cities*, 1949–50; *Mañana*, 1956) and for the Concerto for Oboe and Strings (1942), an arranged pastiche of one-movement keyboard sonatas of Cimarosa.

Bennet, John (b. ca. 1575–80?; fl. 1599–1614). Composer. Probably from northwestern England. His works consist of a book of madrigals for 4 voices (London, 1599), 1 madrigal in *The Triumphes of Oriana* (1601), 2 consort songs, 4 Psalm settings and a prayer in Barley's psalter of ca. 1599, a verse anthem, and 6 secular vocal pieces in Ravenscroft's *A Briefe Discourse* (1614).

Bennett, Richard Rodney (b. Broadstairs, Kent, 29 Mar. 1936). Composer and pianist. Studied with Lennox Berkeley and Howard Ferguson at the Royal Academy of Music (1953–56) and in Paris with Pierre Boulez (1957–58); taught at the Royal Academy (1963–65) and at the Peabody Conservatory (1970–71). His early works employed twelve-tone methods; after the Paris years this was combined with a postromantic lyricism; some of his music has been compared to that of Berg. Works include a number of film scores; an alto saxophone concerto (1988); *Concerto for Stan Getz,* sax, orchestra (1992); 2 symphonies (1965, 1967); choral and other vocal works; some 40 chamber works (4 string quartets, 1952–64); keyboard works.

Bennett, Robert Russell (b. Kansas City, Mo., 15 June 1894; d. New York, 18 Aug. 1981). Composer, orchestrator, and conductor. By age 16 was in New York working as a dance band musician and music copyist; in 1919 began orchestrating songs for the publisher T. B. Harms; lived in Europe from 1926 to 1931. By the end of his career had orchestrated over 200 musicals by all the major Broadway composers including Berlin, Gershwin, Kern, Loewe, Porter, Rodgers, and Weill; also worked in Hollywood on more than 30 film scores (1936–40); wrote a book on orchestration. Much of his concert music makes use of popular idioms or Americana.

Bennett, Tony [Benedetto, Anthony Dominick] (b. New York, 3 Aug. 1926). Popular singer. Sang in American military bands during World War II, then returned to New York where he came under the tutelage of comedian Bob Hope and Mitch Miller; greatest success came with "I Left My Heart in San Francisco" (1962); has performed with swing bands, popular orchestras, and jazz artists.

Bennett, William Sterndale (b. Sheffield, 13 Apr. 1816; d. London, 1 Feb. 1875). Composer. Studied at the Royal Academy of Music; became a virtuoso pianist and from 1832 began to be known as a composer, especially through his first piano concerto. The period 1832–38 was especially productive, and included 5 piano concertos and symphonies, as well as a piano sonata. He appeared frequently as a pianist and was enthusiastically received in Germany by Mendelssohn and Schumann (1836–37); taught at the Royal Academy (1837–1858); founded the Bach Society (1849); conductor, Philharmonic Society (1856–66); professor of music at Cambridge (from 1856); principal, Royal Academy. Knighted in 1871.

Benoit, Peter (Léonard Léopold) (b. Harlebeke, Belgium, 17 Aug. 1834; d. Antwerp, 8 Mar. 1901). Composer and teacher. Studied at the Brussels Conservatory (1851–55); in 1856 became conductor at the Park Theater in Brussels; after a year in Germany went to Paris, conducting at Offenbach's Théâtre des Bouffes-Parisiens (1862–63). Returned to Brussels, where his growing reputation was fully established with the oratorio *Lucifer* (1866); became the central figure of Flemish musical nationalism; in 1867 founded the Flemish Music School and headed it until his death. Best known for his oratorios and cantatas.

Benson, Warren (Frank) (b. Detroit, 26 Jan. 1924). Composer. Studied at the Univ. of Michigan (1943–51); timpanist in the Detroit Symphony (1946). Taught in Greece (1950–52), in North Carolina, at Ithaca College (1953–67), and at the Eastman School (from 1967). At Ithaca he founded the College Percussion Ensemble and developed musicianship courses; the author of *Compositional Processes and Writing Skills* (Washington, D.C., 1974). Many of his own works reflect interests in timbre and a montage technique that may include quotations. He has composed works for orchestra, band (*The Leaves Are Falling*, 1963), chamber ensembles, piano, choir, and solo voice.

Bentzon, Niels Viggo (b. Copenhagen, 24 Aug. 1919). Composer and pianist; cousin of composer Jørgen (Liebenberg) Bentzon (1897–1951). Studied composition with Knud Jeppesen at the Royal Conservatory in Copenhagen (1939–42); in 1949 joined the staff of the Copenhagen Conservatory. His music contains elements of Bartók, jazz, nonserialized atonality, and aleatory processes. Works include operas (*Faust III*, 1964); ballets; orchestral works (15 numbered symphonies, 1942–80; *Feature Article on René Descartes* 1975); concertos; choral music; chamber music (11 string quartets, 1940–76).

Benvenuto Cellini. Opera in two acts by Berlioz (libretto by Léon de Wailly and Auguste Barbier, after Cellini's autobiography), first produced in Paris in 1838. It was revised in three acts for performance in Weimar in 1852. Setting: Italy in the 16th century.

Bequadro [It.]. The natural sign, ♮ [see Accidental, Pitch names].

Berberian, Cathy (b. Attleboro, Mass., 4 July 1925; d. Rome, 6 Mar. 1983). Mezzo-soprano. Soloist with New York's Armenian Folk Group (1950), studied in Italy with Giorgina del Vigo. Her 1958 performance of Cage's *Aria with Fontana Mix* established her as a major presence in contemporary vocal music; Stravinsky and Henze wrote for her, as did Berio, her husband from 1950 to 1966. She has taught at the Univ. of Vancouver and Cologne's Rheinische Musikschule.

Berceuse [Fr.; Ger. *Wiegenlied*]. Lullaby. In instrumental works, especially for piano, 19th- and early 20th-century composers (including Chopin, Schumann, Brahms, Liszt, Grieg, Debussy, Ravel, Busoni, and Stravinsky) captured the steady rocking of the lullaby through an ostinato accompaniment in compound meter or triplets. Chopin's Berceuse op. 57 in particular provided a model for others.

Berchem, Jacquet de (b. Berchem-lez-Anvers, near Antwerp, ca. 1505; d. ca. 1565). Composer; often confused with his contemporaries Jacquet of Mantua, Jacques Buus, and Jacques Brunel. In Venice by the 1530s and had much music published there beginning in 1538; *maestro di cappella* of Verona Cathedral from 1546 until perhaps 1550; may have visited Ferrara thereafter. Many of his madrigals published in Rome between 1555 and 1563; they played an important role in the history of the genre. The earliest are in a Franco-Flemish contrapuntal style; later works are more animated, chordal, and syllabic.

Berezowski, Nicolai (Tikhonovich) (b. St. Petersburg, 17 May 1900; d. New York, 27 Aug. 1953). Composer and violinist. Studied at the imperial chapel in St. Petersburg (1908–16); arrived in the U.S. in 1922, played in the New York Philharmonic (1923–29) and studied composition and violin (Goldmark, Kochanski) at Juilliard; spent two years in Europe, where his violin concerto was premiered by Carl Flesch (1930). After his return to the U.S. his compositions were widely performed, especially by Koussevitzky with the Boston Symphony; played in the Coolidge String Quartet (1935–40). His works, in a mildly dissonant Russian Romantic idiom, include 4 symphonies, several concertos, chamber music, piano pieces.

Berg, Alban (Maria Johannes) (b. Vienna, 9 Feb. 1885; d. there, 24 Dec. 1935). Composer, along with Webern the most prominent student of Schoenberg.

Studied with Schoenberg without fee beginning in 1904; wrote the *Seven Early Songs,* which reflect the German lied tradition (1905–8); the Piano Sonata op. 1 (1907–8); the *Four Songs* op. 2, in which tonality is in question and the final song is clearly atonal (completed in 1910); and the String Quartet op. 3 (1910). With Schoenberg's move to Berlin in 1911 lessons ended but devotion to and reliance upon his teacher continued. Between 1912 and the onset of the war Berg produced a set of orchestral songs, *Four Pieces* for clarinet and piano, and *Three Orchestral Pieces* (1914); after World War I was heavily involved, along with Schoenberg, in the creation of the Society for Private Musical Performances in Vienna. Between 1917 and 1922 was involved with *Wozzeck.* It was during these years that Schoenberg formulated his twelve-tone method, first employed by Berg in his second setting of "Schliesse mir die Augen beide" (1925); the *Lyric Suite* displays various features that distinguish his personal use of the method; while Schoenberg and Webern were avoiding implication of tonality in their rows, the row in Berg's Violin Concerto (1935) has been called a search for a twelve-tone tonality. At his death Berg had not completed the orchestration of the last act of *Lulu;* vocal techniques in the opera include normal and rhythmic speech, rhythmic declamation in which pitch is only suggested, "half-sung" rhythmic declamation in which pitch is clearer, and traditional singing.

Bergamasca [It.]. (1) A dance, dance song, or popular poem with a real or fancied relationship to the district of Bergamo in northern Italy. The title occurs in works from the 16th through the 19th centuries and into the 20th. For Claude Debussy's work with this title, see *Suite bergamasque.*

(2) Late in the 16th century, any of a number of pieces composed on repetitions of the harmonic pattern [Ex.]: I–IV–V–I. In the 17th century, hundreds of compositions, largely for the guitar but also for other instruments and ensembles, were composed throughout Europe (in England as the "Bergomask"). Early in the 17th century, a single discant began to be associated with the harmonic pattern and in some cases supplanted the pattern itself. Both persisted through the 18th and 19th centuries.

Berganza (Vargas), Teresa (b. Madrid, 16 Mar. 1935). Mezzo-soprano. Studied at the Madrid Conservatory, debut as Dorabella at Aachen (1957); her Cherubino (Glyndebourne, 1958), Cenerentola (Glyndebourne, 1959), and Rosina (Covent Garden, 1960) launched an international career; has also sung roles by Monteverdi, Cesti, Purcell, Bellini, and Massenet; performs popular Spanish songs.

Berger, Arthur (Victor) (b. New York, 15 May 1912). Composer and critic. Studied at New York Univ., the Longy School of Music, at Harvard under Piston, and with Boulanger; during the 1930s met Cowell, Ives, and Varèse; wrote music criticism supporting the avant-garde; taught at Mills, Brooklyn College, Juilliard, Brandeis, and New England Conservatory; music critic, *New York Herald Tribune* (1946–53); cofounder, *Perspectives of New Music* (1962). After an early interest in twelve-tone procedures, abandoned composition until his contact with Milhaud (1939–42), when his interest in Stravinsky's neoclassicism emerged in his own works; returned to serial procedures in works from 1956 and later.

Bergerette [Fr.]. (1) In the 15th century, a form related to the *formes fixes* that dominated French poetry and music of the period. The *bergerette* appeared early in the century, experienced a surge in popularity in the latter half, and then largely died out by about 1500. The form is often described today as a one-stanza *virelai,* but was commonly defined by 15th- and early 16th-century writers in terms of the *rondeau.* (2) In the 18th century, a French *air* with frequent pastoral references.

Bergonzi, Carlo (1) (b. Cremona?, 1683; d. there, 1747). Violin maker. A leading figure among Cremonese instrument makers; probably spent his early years in the Guarneri workshop. Not until the 1720s did he put his own labels on his violins; the best of the instruments date from the 1730s.

Bergonzi, Carlo (2) (b. Polisene, near Parma, 13 July 1924). Baritone and tenor. Studied at Parma's Conservatorio di musica Arrigo Boito, made his debut as Rossini's Figaro (1948); three years later made second debut as tenor. La Scala debut in 1953, U.S. debut 1955; after 1956 appearance with Metropolitan Opera remained with that company until 1983; farewell recital in New York in 1994. His repertory centered on Rossini, Donizetti, Bellini, Verdi, Massenet, and Puccini.

Bergsma, William (Laurence) (b. Oakland, Calif., 1 Apr. 1921; d. Seattle, 18 Mar. 1994). Composer. Attended Stanford (1938–40), studied under Hanson and Bernard Rogers at Eastman (1940–44); taught composition at Juilliard (1946–63), then became director of the School of Music at the Univ. of Washington. Works, consistently tonal and lyrical, include 2 ballets, 2 operas (*The Wife of Martin Guerre,* 1951–56); pieces for orchestra (*Chameleon Variations*);

chamber and piano music (5 string quartets, 1942–82); choral works; songs.

Berigan, Bunny [Rowland Bernart] (b. Hilbert, Wis., 2 Nov. 1908; d. New York, 2 June 1942). Jazz trumpeter and bandleader. He joined Benny Goodman (1935), recording "King Porter Stomp," and Tommy Dorsey (1936–37), recording "Marie" (1937); formed a big band (1937–39) known for its driving swing and for Berigan's sumptuous reading of the ballad "I Can't Get Started," recorded in 1937. After rejoining Dorsey briefly in 1940 he formed new bands, but alcoholism impeded further success.

Berio, Luciano (b. Oneglia, Imperia, Italy, 24 Oct. 1925). Composer. Studied in Milan with Ghedini and Paribeni and at the Berkshire Music Center with Dallapiccola (1951); with Maderna opened the Studio di fonologia in Milan (1955); lived in the U.S. (1963–72) and taught at Mills, Harvard, and Juilliard before returning to Italy; Charles Eliot Norton Lecturer at Harvard (1993–94). His works before 1962 explore serialism, electronic music, and aleatory procedures: *Serenata I* (flute and 14 instruments, 1958) applied serial procedures to tone color, pitch, and duration; in *Thema (Omaggio a Joyce)* (1958) he had Cathy Berberian (to whom he was married in 1950) record an excerpt from Joyce's *Ulysses,* then electronically transformed it to produce a choral-instrumental work. As early as *Sequenza I* (flute, 1958) used proportional notation to indicate relative durations; in the solo cantata *Epiphanie* (1959–61) 6 instrumental and 5 vocal sections can be performed separately or combined in any order. Later compositions exhibit an even more eclectic and personal style, particularly in treatment of the voice as pure timbre, the text as "verbal material," and in more and more complex collage and quotation techniques (e.g., *Sinfonia,* 1968–69). *Chemins* for orchestra treats his own *Sequenza* series (for soloists including flute, harp, voice, etc., 1958–) as raw material for new works.

Bériot, Charles-Auguste de (b. Louvain, 20 Feb. 1802; d. Brussels, 8 Apr. 1870). Violinist and composer. Studied at the Paris Conservatory with Baillot; performed and taught in Paris and Belgium; London debut in 1826, six years later appeared in concert with his best-known pupil, Henri Vieuxtemps, aged 8. Often performed with singer Maria Malibran, principally in Paris, Italy, and England; taught at the Brussels Conservatory (1843–52). Works include 10 concertos and a *Méthode du violon* (1857–58).

Berkeley, Lennox (Randall Francis) (b. Boar's Hill, near Oxford, 12 May 1903; d. London, 26 Dec. 1989). Composer. Studied at Merton College, Oxford (1922–26) and in Paris with Boulanger (1927–33); in 1946 he was appointed professor at the Royal Academy of Music; knighted, 1974. His early music

followed the neoclassicism prevalent in France during the 1920s; later formed a neoromantic style characterized by lush textures and by a diatonic tonal idiom. His works include 4 operas, ballets, incidental music, film scores; orchestral works (4 symphonies, 1940, 1956–58, 1969, 1976–77; *Mont Juic,* 1937; *Serenade,* string orchestra, 1939; Divertimento in B♭, 1943); much choral music (*Missa brevis* op. 57, 1960; Magnificat op. 71, 1968); chamber and solo instrumental works (*Theme and Variations,* guitar, 1970); many songs and solo vocal works.

Berlin, Irving [Baline, Israel] (b. Mogilev, 11 May 1888; d. New York, 22 Sept. 1989). Popular songwriter. Emigrated to New York with his family in 1893; hired as a lyricist by Snyder Publishing in 1909 but soon began writing his own music as well; notable early successes include "Alexander's Ragtime Band" (1911). From 1911 contributed to the Ziegfeld Follies and other Broadway revues; formed his own publishing company in 1919 and established the Music Box Theatre in 1921. Composed some 1,500 songs; many (particularly "Blue Skies," 1927; "God Bless America," 1938; "White Christmas," 1942; "There's No Business Like Show Business," 1946) have become defining elements of American culture.

Berlin school. A group of composers, also known as the North-German School, working in Berlin in the second half of the 18th century, principally at the court of Frederick the Great (reigned 1740–86). They included Johann Joachim Quantz (1697–1773), Johann Gottlieb Graun (1703–71), Carl Heinrich Graun (1704–59), Franz Benda (1709–86), C. P. E. Bach (1714–88), Christoph Nichelmann (1717–62), Friedrich Wilhelm Marpurg (1718–95), Johann Philipp Kirnberger (1721–83), and Johann Friedrich Agricola (1720–74). As song composers (sometimes called the Berlin Lieder School), they sought a folklike quality in their works. A younger generation (called the Second Berlin Lieder School), which included Johann Abraham Peter Schulz (1747–1800), Johann Friedrich Reichardt (1752–1814), and Carl Friedrich Zelter (1758–1832), turned away from the folklike element to the poetry of Klopstock and Goethe. See Lied.

Berlioz, (Louis-) Hector (b. La Côte St.-André, near Grenoble, 11 Dec. 1803; d. Paris, 8 Mar. 1869). Composer. Moved to Paris in 1821 to study medicine but was intoxicated by the Opéra, where he formed a lifelong devotion to Gluck; in 1822 began lessons with Lesueur; formally enrolled at the Conservatory in 1826. In 1827 was elated by a performance of *Hamlet* and *Romeo and Juliet* by a British company that included Harriet Smithson as leading lady; to further his pursuit of her gave an 1828 concert consisting of the premieres of his most recent works.

That year he first became acquainted with Beethoven's *Eroica* and Fifth Symphonies and with Goethe's *Faust;* these joined Gluck, Spontini, Weber, Virgil, and Shakespeare as central influences. Berlioz's unrequited passion for Smithson helped precipitate an emotional crisis that found release in the composition of the **Symphonie fantastique,* whose program was in many respects a turning into art of what he perceived as his own situation and state of mind. Left for Italy at the end of 1830; in Nice composed the *King Lear Overture* and began his sequel to the *Symphonie fantastique, Lélio, ou Le retour à la vie* and the *Rob Roy Overture.* Returned to Paris in 1832, where he courted and married Smithson (they separated in 1844). From 1833 regularly wrote music criticism for Paris newspapers and organized three or four concerts of his works every year. In 1834 composed **Harold en Italie,* the first of a series of major works over the next few years, including **Benvenuto Cellini,* Requiem (1837), **Romeo and Juliet, Grande symphonie funèbre et triomphale* (1840), and the songs of *Les nuits d'été* (1840–41). In 1842, by this time a virtuoso conductor, Berlioz undertook the first of many foreign concert tours; published a book on orchestration (1843) and an account of his German tour and of a holiday trip to Nice (1844); also toured Vienna, Prague, Pest, and other cities (1845–46), Russia (1847), and London (1847–48, returned in 1850s). During this period devoted less energy to composing: major works were *La *Damnation de Faust,* Te Deum (1849), and *L'*Enfance du Christ.* From 1853 spent several summers conducting concerts at Baden-Baden; this led to the commissioning of his last opera, *Béatrice et Bénédict* (1862); the monumental *Les *Troyens* was begun in 1856. Berlioz conducted in Vienna and Germany (1866–67) and in Russia (1867–68); he returned home exhausted, and his health declined quickly.

Bernardi, Stefano (b. Verona, ca. 1585; d. Salzburg?, 1636). Composer. Early music training at the Verona Cathedral; in 1610 *maestro di cappella* at Madonna dei Monti in Rome, but returned the following year to Verona; served the Archduke Carl Joseph in Breslau (1622–24), then moved to Salzburg, where he apparently remained until his death; composed mostly sacred music, including a Te Deum for 12 choirs.

Bernart de Ventadorn (b. Ventadorn, 1130–40?; d. Dordogne?, ca. 1190–1200). Poet and composer, one of the most important members of the second generation of troubadours. Biographical information comes from his *vida;* born in the province of Limousin, he spent time in northern France and perhaps even in England in the middle of the 12th century. Forty-five of his poems survive; 19 have melodies extant, 18 complete and 1 fragmentary; the wide diffusion of his music and his travels to northern Europe suggest that he may have been instrumental in the spread of the art of the troubadours to the North, prompting the development of the trouvère tradition.

Berners (Gerald Hugh Tyrwhitt-Wilson), Lord (b. Arley Park, Shropshire, 18 Sept. 1883; d. Faringdon House, Berkshire, 19 Apr. 1950). Composer and writer. Schooled at Eton, studied music and art in Vienna and Dresden. His music is often of a whimsical nature; he gained some success as a musical satirist, as well as the admiration of Stravinsky and others. Works include an opera; ballets (*Les sirènes,* 1946); film scores (*Nicholas Nickleby,* 1946); orchestral works (*3 Pieces,* 1919); piano works.

Bernhard, Christoph (b. Kolberg, Pomerania [Kolobrzeg, Poland]?, 1 Jan. 1628; d. Dresden, 14 Nov. 1692). Theorist and composer. Studied in Danzig, from 1649 in the employ of the Elector of Saxony at Dresden, where he had lessons from Schütz; studied briefly in Rome; in 1655 appointed Vice-Kapellmeister at Dresden; Kantor at St. John's School in Hamburg (1663). Highly regarded by his contemporaries as a composer of sacred vocal works but best remembered today for his theoretical treatises, especially the *Tractatus compositionis augmentatus.*

Bernstein, Elmer (b. New York, 4 Apr. 1922). Composer and conductor. Studied at Juilliard and with Stefan Wolpe and Roger Sessions; after World War II commissioned to score radio dramas; began to compose for film in the 1950s. Among his many scores are those for *Sudden Fear* (1952), *The Man with the Golden Arm* (an early and influential use of jazz, 1955), *Walk on the Wild Side* (1962), *True Grit* (1969), and *Ghostbusters* (1984). Active in advancing the legitimacy of film music.

Bernstein, Leonard (b. Lawrence, Mass., 25 Aug. 1918; d. New York, 14 Oct. 1990). Composer, conductor, pianist; lectured worldwide and on television; author of several books, made signal contributions to musical theater. He studied at Harvard (1935–39) and at Curtis with Vengerova (piano), Reiner (conducting), and Thompson (orchestration); from 1940 associated with Koussevitzky as student and then assistant at the Berkshire Music Center. Assistant conductor of the New York Philharmonic; his substitution for the ill Bruno Walter in a nationally televised concert (1943) immediately launched his conducting career. Conducted the New York City Center Orchestra (1945–58); took over conducting classes at the Berkshire Center after Koussevitzky's death in 1951; taught at Brandeis Univ. (1951–55). In 1957 named codirector of the New York Philharmonic (with Mitropoulos); director of that orchestra from 1958 through 1969, retiring as conductor laureate; under his direction the orchestra toured extensively and was nationally prominent as a result of recordings and concerts on television (Young People's Concerts, 1958–73). As a conductor Bernstein premiered more than 40 new works but his views of nontonal music did not always please the avant-garde; in the 1970s and 1980s focused on the standard repertory; worked closely with European orchestras, notably the Vienna Philharmonic, and gave a prominent place to the German symphonic tradition from Beethoven through Mahler. Throughout his conducting career continued to perform as a pianist. His first large orchestral work, *Jeremiah* (1942), won the New York Critics' Circle Award in 1944; he explored serial methods of composition but retained his commitment to tonality and regarded his own music as eclectic, with roots in jazz, Hebrew liturgical music, and the standard concert repertory (as in *Mass: A Theater Piece for Singers, Players, and Dancers*, 1971). Perhaps best known as a composer of dramatic works: *West Side Story* (1957) profoundly affected the course of American musical theater. Other works include ballets (*Fancy Free*, with Jerome Robbins, 1944), musicals (*On the Town*, 1944; *Wonderful Town*, 1953), operas (*Trouble in Tahiti*, 1951; *Candide*, 1956), a film score (*On the Waterfront*, 1954), orchestral music (Second Symphony, "The Age of Anxiety," with solo piano, 1949), vocal works (Symphony no. 3 [Kaddish], speaker, soprano, chorus, boys' chorus, orchestra, 1963; *Chichester Psalms*, tenor, chorus, orchestra, 1965), chamber music, songs.

Berry, Chu [Leon Brown] (b. Wheeling, W. Va., 13 Sept. 1908; d. Conneaut, Ohio, 30 Oct. 1941). Jazz tenor saxophonist. Worked in the big bands of Benny Carter (1932; 1933, recording under Spike Hughes's name), Charlie Johnson (1932–33), Teddy Hill (1933–35), Fletcher Henderson (1935–36), and Cab Calloway (1937–41), with whom he recorded "A Ghost of a Chance" the year before his death in an automobile accident.

Berry, Chuck [Charles Edward Anderson] (b. San Jose, Calif., 15 Jan. 1926). Rock guitarist, singer, and songwriter. Muddy Waters helped him secure a recording contract with the rock-and-roll label Chess; "Maybelline" (1955) was the first rock-and-roll song to reach the top of popular, country, and rhythm-and-blues sales charts; achieved similar success with "Roll Over Beethoven" (1956) and "Johnny B. Goode" (1958). The influence of his early work was acknowledged by rock groups including the Beatles and the Rolling Stones.

Bersag horn. A type of military *bugle adopted by the Bersaglieri corps of the Italian army in 1861. The soprano was similar to a three-valve *flugelhorn. The

contralto, tenor, baritone, and bass had one valve lowering the pitch a fourth. Modern versions of this instrument often have two valves and are seen in drum and bugle corps.

Berton, Henri-Montan (b. Paris, 17 Sept. 1767; d. there, 22 Apr. 1844). Composer. Son of Pierre-Montan Berton, conductor and later director of the Paris Opéra. Wrote opéras comiques for Paris; appointed harmony professor at the new Paris Conservatory (1795); music director at the Opéra-bouffe (1807–9); succeeded Méhul as composition professor (1818). Published *Traité d'harmonie* (1815) and other writings, including an attack on Rossini.

Bertoni, Ferdinando (Gasparo) (b. Salò, 15 Aug. 1725; d. Desenzano, 1 Dec. 1813). Organist and composer. Studied in Bologna with Giovanni Battista Martini; his first opera, *La vedova accorta* (Venice, 1745), was a great success throughout Italy; during the next decade composed opere serie, oratorios, and solo motets; in 1785 became *maestro di cappella* at St. Mark's (he had already served as principal organist since 1752); held this position until his retirement in 1808. Between 1778 and 1783 created operas and pastiches for London.

Bertrand, Anthoine [Antoine] **de** (b. Fontanges, Auvergne, 1530–40; d. Toulouse, 1580–July 1582). Composer. His 3 books of secular polyphony (1576, 1578, 1578) include mostly chansons; his compositions contain much chromaticism and make some use of microtones; also composed sacred music.

Beruhigend, beruhigt [Ger.]. Calming, calm.

Berwald, Franz (Adolf) (b. Stockholm, 23 July 1796; d. there, 3 Apr. 1868). Composer. Taught the violin by his father; member of the Stockholm court orchestra (1812–28); toured Finland and Russia (1818–20). Began to compose in this period, including instrumental and chamber works. Went to Berlin in 1829, where he worked on several operas; composed most of his surviving music in the 1840s, including 4 numbered symphonies (the first 3 subtitled *Sérieuse, Capricieuse,* and *Singulière*), other orchestral pieces, 2 string quartets, a cantata, and several large choral works. In 1867 appointed composition professor at the Swedish Royal Academy of Music.

Bes [Ger.]. B-double-flat. See Pitch names.

Besard, Jean-Baptiste (b. Besançon, ca. 1567; d. Augsburg?, 1625). Studied music in Rome until ca. 1595; in 1597 was in Hesse, where he perhaps taught lute; lived for a period in Cologne, where in 1603 published *Thesaurus harmonicus* (R: 1975), primarily arrangements for lute of contemporary instrumental works. In 1617 published another collection in Augsburg, *Novus partus, sive Concertationes musicae.*

Beschleunigend, beschleunigt [Ger.]. **Accelerando, accelerato.*

Besetzung [Ger.]. Setting, scoring, orchestration.

Bestimmt [Ger.]. Decisively.

Bethune (Green), Thomas [Blind Tom] (b. Columbus, Ga., 25 May 1849; d. Hoboken, 13 June 1908). Pianist and composer. Born blind to slave parents, he was bought with his parents in 1850 by General James Bethune of Columbus; Bethune began exhibiting him for profit, first locally, then in 1857 throughout Georgia, and in 1860 leased him for $15,000 for 3 years to another entrepreneur, who toured him widely in the slave states; he was also exhibited in Europe (1866–67). His performances included the classics, his own compositions, and demonstrations of his extraordinary aural abilities and recall.

Betont [Ger.]. Accented, stressed.

Betrothal in a Monastery. See *Duenna, The* (2).

Bevin, Elway (b. ca. 1554; d. Bristol, buried 19 Oct. 1638). Composer and theorist. Said to have studied with Tallis; vicar-choral at Wells Cathedral (1579–80), chorusmaster and later organist at Bristol Cathedral (from ca. 1585), and Gentleman Extraordinary at the Chapel Royal (1605). His best-known work is the "Dorian" or "Short" Service, in four voices; his primer *A Briefe and Short Instruction in the Art of Music* (London, 1631) was praised by Purcell and Christopher Simpson.

Beweglich [Ger.]. Nimbly.

Bewegt [Ger.]. Agitated.

Bezifferter Bass [Ger.]. Figured bass, **thoroughbass.*

Bharata-nāṭyam [Skt.]. A major solo dance tradition of South India performed by women. The standard recital contains pieces that range from abstract dance to mime; some mix the two. The dancer is accompanied by a vocalist, a wind instrument, a drum, and a dance master who recites rhythmic compositions.

Biber, Heinrich Ignaz Franz von (b. Wartenburg, Bohemia, bapt. 12 Aug. 1644; d. Salzburg, 3 May 1704). Composer and violinist. From around 1665 a member of the court of Prince-Bishop Karl of Olomouc (Count Liechtenstein-Kastelkorn) at his castle in Kroměříž; joined the chapel forces at the Salzburg court of the Archbishop Maximilian Gandolph (1670); promoted to Vice-Kapellmeister (1679) then court Kapellmeister (1684) there. Admired by Em-

peror Leopold I, who bestowed the title of nobility on him in 1690. Best known for his violin music, including the Mystery Sonatas and the *Harmonia artificiosa-ariosa* (Nuremberg, 1712); many of these works employ *scordatura* tunings.

Bicinium [Lat.]. A two-voice composition for voices, instruments, or keyboard without further accompaniment, especially one from the 15th through the early 17th century.

Big band. A large jazz or popular music ensemble of the type that dominated American popular music of the period 1935–45. Typically, a rhythm section of piano, double bass, drums [see Drum set], and guitar accompanies five saxophones (two altos, two tenors, and one baritone, some of whom double on clarinet and perhaps flute), three or four trumpets, and three or four trombones. A male or female vocalist frequently performs with such a group. Such ensembles, now often called stage bands, have enjoyed a considerable revival in high schools and colleges in the U.S. in recent decades. See also Jazz.

Bigard, Barney [Albany Leon] (b. New Orleans, 3 Mar. 1906; d. Culver City, Calif., 27 June 1980). Jazz clarinetist. Played tenor saxophonist with Albert Nicholas in New Orleans (1922–23, 1923–24), then joined King Oliver in Chicago (1924–27) and concentrated on clarinet. Worked with Charlie Elgar in Milwaukee, then joined Duke Ellington (1927?/28?–1942; recordings include "Mood Indigo," 1930; "Clarinet Lament," 1936); subsequently performed with Louis Armstrong's All Stars (1947–52, 1953–55, 1960–61).

Biggs, E(dward George) Power (b. Westcliff-on-Sea, Essex, 29 Mar. 1906; d. Boston, 10 Mar. 1977). Organist. Studied at the Royal Academy of Music (1924–29); emigrated to the U.S. (1930), eventually settled in Cambridge, Mass; New York debut in 1932. Weekly series of broadcasts for CBS (1942–58) made him a household name; recorded extensively for Columbia Records; performed cycles of Bach's complete organ works and commissioned new works.

Billings, William (b. Boston, 7 Oct. 1746; d. there, 26 Sept. 1800). Most important American composer of the 18th century. Taught in Boston, Providence and Stoughton, Mass; in 1770 published his first tune collection, *The New-England Psalm-Singer,* probably the first published collection of the music of a single American composer; other collections followed. During the 1770s and early 1780s singing master for the Brattle Street Church and the Old South Church; final published collection was *The Continental Harmony* (1794; R: 1961). Individual compositions include "Lamentation over Boston," "David's Lamentation," "I Am the Rose of Sharon," and "Modern Music."

Billington, Elizabeth [née Weichsel] (b. London, 27 Dec. 1765; d. near Venice, 25 Aug. 1818). Soprano. Had singing lessons with J. C. Bach and later with James Billington, whom she married in 1783; debut at Dublin's Crow Street Theater (1784); subsequent success at Covent Garden, at Milan, and at the San Carlo Theater in Naples, where Bianchi, Paisiello, and Paer composed operas for her. Much admired by Haydn.

Billy Budd. Opera in four acts by Britten (libretto by E. M. Forster and Eric Crozier, adapted from the story by Herman Melville), produced in London in 1951. A two-act revision was completed by Britten in 1960. Setting: aboard H.M.S. Indomitable, 1797.

Billy the Kid. A ballet in one act by Copland (choreography by Eugene Loring, book by Lincoln Kirstein on the American West and the outlaw of the same name), first produced in Chicago in 1938. An orchestral suite derived from it has become part of the concert repertory.

Bilson, Malcolm (b. Los Angeles, 24 Oct. 1935). Pianist. Studied in Vienna, with Grete Hinterhofer in Berlin, and Reine Gianoli in Paris; also with Stanley Fletcher and Webster Aitken at the Univ. of Illinois. Joined the faculty of Cornell Univ. in 1968. A champion of late 18th- and early 19th-century instruments; recordings include the complete sonatas and concertos of Mozart.

Bīn [Hin.]. A North Indian *stick zither. Four playing strings and three drone strings are stretched over a fretted fingerboard with a gourd resonator attached at either end. Tuning and playing techniques are similar to those of the South Indian *vīṇā. See ill. under Instrument.

Binary and ternary form. Two fundamental musical forms, the first consisting of two parts, the second of three.

Binary form. A movement in binary form contains two parts, each usually repeated. The first generally modulates from the tonic to a related key, ordinarily the dominant if the tonic is major, the relative major (less often the dominant minor) if the tonic is minor. In short binary movements there is often no modulation, the first part merely ending with a half *cadence. The second part reverses this motion, progressing back to the tonic either directly or via one or more additional keys. Binary form is thus an archetypal example of *open* tonal structure at the large scale, in which motion away from the tonic in one

part requires a complementary return to the tonic in a second.

The accompanying diagram (Fig. 1) presents the most important characteristics of a typical simple (nonrounded) binary structure in major (roman numerals symbolize keys, arrows indicate modulations, "Cl." = closing material).

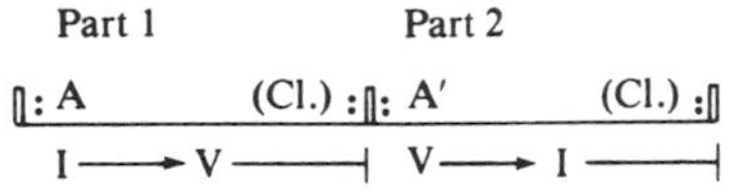

Fig. 1.

Binary form in which part 2 is significantly longer than part 1 may be referred to as asymmetrical binary form, in contrast to the symmetrical type just described. In one scheme common in the late Baroque, part 2 is divided into two sections, each approximately equivalent in length to part 1. The first half of part 2 begins as usual in the dominant or relative major, but cadences in a related key (in major, usually a modal degree such as the submediant or mediant); the second half begins in or leads to the tonic, but without a decisive return to the principal theme.

Binary form already appears with some frequency in dances of the 16th century, and it becomes increasingly common in dance movements of the early Baroque. The high point in the cultivation of simple binary form comes in the middle and late Baroque periods, which utilize it in most dance movements and in many other movement-types. Simple binary form (both symmetrical and asymmetrical) is still the most common form in dance movements of the early Classical period, and it survives in the later 18th and 19th centuries as a frequent choice for short character pieces and for themes of theme-and-variation movements (as in the finale to Beethoven's Piano Sonata op. 109).

Rounded binary form. In the early 18th century, composers began frequently to introduce a coordinated return of the main theme and the tonic key within part 2 of binary forms, producing a rounded or recapitulating binary form that may be diagrammed as shown in Fig. 2. The idea of a return to primary material at this point in the form probably originated in ternary forms such as the da capo *aria and especially in the ritornello form of the *concerto, one version of which, tri-ritornello form, closely resembles rounded binary form without repeat signs. Rounded binary form is common in late Baroque dance and sonata movements and is found in most minuets, scherzos, and trios of later Classical symphonies and other instrumental works. Equally important, it serves as the principal structural basis for the emerging *sonata form, part 1 becoming the (repeated) exposition, the first half of part 2 the development, and the second half of part 2 the recapitulation.

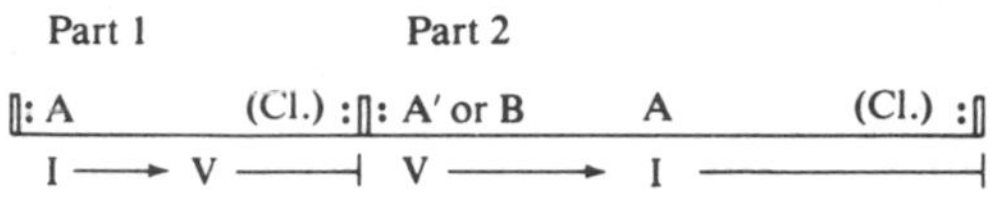

Part 1   Part 2

‖: A   (Cl.) :‖: A' or B   A   (Cl.) :‖

I ⟶ V ⟶⊣ V ⟶ I ⟶⊣

Fig. 2.

Ternary form. Movements in ternary form consist of three parts, the first and third identical or closely related, the second contrasting to a greater or lesser degree. The form may therefore be symbolized ABA. Both A parts end in the tonic key, usually after a central modulation to a related key or keys. The B part generally begins in a related key and cadences in the same or another related key before the reentry of the A part. Thus, in contrast to binary form, ternary form is *closed* in structure; the two A parts, and often the B part, are complete within themselves, not interdependent or complementary like the parts of a binary movement. It should be noted that the return of the A part in a ternary form is often indicated by placing a *da capo or *dal segno marking at the end of the B part rather than writing it out in full. A typical ternary movement proceeds as shown in Fig. 3 (N = new key or keys).

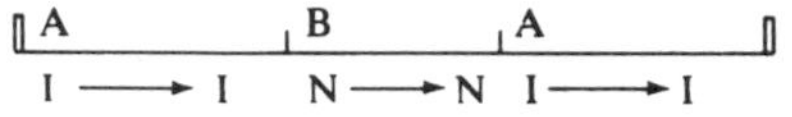

‖ A   ┊ B   ┊ A   ‖
I ⟶ I   N ⟶ N   I ⟶ I

Fig. 3.

The basic ternary principle of return after contrast occurs throughout music history. It appears most prolifically and characteristically, however, in the da capo *aria of the late 17th and 18th centuries, the minuet (or scherzo)–trio–minuet alternation of the symphony and other instrumental genres, and the *character piece of the Romantic period (e.g., Chopin's nocturnes and Brahms's intermezzos).

Binchois, Gilles de Bins [Binch, Binche] **dit** (b. Mons?, ca. 1400; d. Soignies, 20 Sept. 1460). Composer. Organist at Ste. Waudru in Mons (1419–23); in the 1420s perhaps in the service of William Pole, Earl of Suffolk, an Englishman resident in France; by about 1427 joined the Burgundian court chapel, remaining there until retiring in 1453 to Soignies. Known to have met Dufay at Mons in 1449; the two probably had other meetings, the first perhaps as early as 1434. The 15th-century author Martin le Franc began the tradition that paired Binchois and Dufay as leading composers of their age and found the influence of Dunstable in the works of both; laments on Bichois's death written by Ockeghem and Dufay attest to the high regard of contemporaries.

Known chiefly for his secular music, about 60 rondeaux and 7 ballades, almost all for 3 voices with only the top voice texted. Sacred compositions are almost as numerous and incorporate both more complex and simpler styles: they include approximately 20 Mass movements or pairs. Many pieces are in fauxbourdon or a fully written out approximation.

Bind. *Tie.

Bingham, Seth (Daniels) (b. Bloomfield, N.J., 16 Apr. 1882; d. New York, 21 June 1972). Composer and organist. Studied with Parker at Yale and in Paris with d'Indy, Widor, and Guilmant; taught at Yale (1908–19) and Columbia (1920–54), lectured at Union Theological Seminary until 1965; organist and choirmaster at Madison Avenue Presbyterian Church (New York) for most of his career. His compositions are in a conservative and lyrical vein.

Biniou [Fr.]. A small, mouth-blown *bagpipe of Brittany, usually played in ensemble with the *bombarde.

Binkerd, Gordon (Ware) (b. Lynch, Nebr., 22 May 1916). Composer. Educated at South Dakota Wesleyan Univ., Eastman, and Harvard, where he worked with Piston and Fine; professor, Univ. of Illinois (1949–71). Gave up serial techniques (employed in his sonata for cello and piano, 1952) midway through his first symphony (1954) when he experienced "an intense revulsion away from the system . . . " Tonal organization often depends on tritone polarities; motivic development on "backtracking," the relentless reiteration and gradual transformation of minuscule units. Works include symphonies; chamber music; organ service music; piano works; choral works; many songs.

Bird, The. Popular name for Haydn's String Quartet no. 32 in C major Hob. III:39, published in 1782. The grace notes in the main subject of the first movement and the duet in dialogue between the violins in the trio of the scherzando suggest the chirping of birds.

Birtwistle, Harrison (Paul) (b. Accrington, Lancashire, 15 July 1934). Composer. Training as a clarinetist at the Royal Manchester College (from 1952), also studied composition there with Richard Hall; taught at the Cranborne Chase School (1962–65), visiting fellow at Princeton (1966–67), visiting professor at Swarthmore (1973). With Davies in 1967 founded the Pierrot Players; more recently has composed for the group Matrix; in 1975 became music director at the South Bank Theatre, London; knighted in 1987. His music shows influences from medieval music and from Stravinsky, and is often marked by florid contrapuntal lines and fragmented textures. Works include opera (*Punch and Judy,* 1966–67; *The Mask of Orpheus,* 1973–84; *The Sec-*

ond Mrs. Kong, 1994); orchestral music (*The Triumph of Time,* 1972; *Nomos,* amplified flute, clarinet, bassoon, horn, and orchestra, 1968); other ensembles (*Carmen arcadiae mechanicae perpetuum,* 1977); choral (*The Fields of Sorrow,* 2 sopranos, chorus, instruments, 1971; *Tombeau: In memoriam Igor Stravinsky,* 1972); chamber music (*Three movements for string quartet,* 1993); works for soprano with instruments.

Bis [Lat., twice]. (1) An instruction to repeat a passage. (2) [Fr., Ger.] Said by an audience as a request for an *encore.

Bisbigliando [It., whispering]. In harp playing, a rapid, back-and-forth motion of the fingers producing a soft tremolo.

Biscroma [It.]. Thirty-second note. See Note.

Bishop, Henry R(owley) (b. London, 18 Nov. 1786; d. there, 30 Apr., 1855). Composer. Studied music with Francesco Bianchi and began to write for the stage in 1804; composed operas, leading to appointment as music director at Covent Garden (1810–24); produced tremendous output of stage music for this theater during his tenure; founded the Philharmonic Society (1813) and conducted some of its concerts. In 1824 became music director at Drury Lane; also music director at Vauxhall Gardens. Held the Reid professorship at Edinburgh (1841–43) and the music chair at Oxford (from 1848). Many of his songs and glees were extremely popular; knighted in 1842.

Bitonality, polytonality. The simultaneous use of two or more tonalities or keys. This may occur briefly or over an extended span. (When two tonal triads or other chords are combined, the result is said to be a bichord or polychord.) The device was widely used in the first half of the 20th century by Richard Strauss, Stravinsky, Prokofiev, and many others, but is particularly characteristic of the music of Darius Milhaud (1892–1974).

Biwa [Jap.]. A Japanese lute, similar in form and playing technique to the Chinese *p'i-p'a.* See ill. under Instrument.

Bizet, Georges (Alexandre César Léopold) (b. Paris, 25 Oct. 1838; d. Bougival, near Paris, 3 June 1875). Composer. Entered the Paris Conservatory in 1848, studying with Marmontel (piano), Zimmerman (counterpoint), Benoist (organ), and Halévy (composition); Gounod's influence is apparent in the most important of Bizet's student compositions, the Symphony in C (1855); in 1857 he won the Prix de Rome, and during his three years in Italy composed a Te Deum, an opera buffa, and an ode-symphony. Returned to Paris and composed a string of unsuccessful operas; *Les *pêcheurs de perles* had only moder-

ate success. In 1871 composed *Jeux d'enfants* for piano four-hands, five selections of which were orchestrated as *Petite suite;* also composed *L'*arlésienne. **Carmen* was received with outrage at the earthiness of its subject; the work's rise to universal popularity began with its very successful Vienna production in Oct. 1875, several months after Bizet's death.

Björling, Jussi [Johan] **(Jonaton)** (b. Stora Tuna, Sweden, 2 Feb. 1911; d. Siarö, near Stockholm, 9 Sept. 1960). Tenor. Studied with John Forsell; debut with the Royal Swedish Opera in 1930. After singing Puccini's Rodolfo in New York (1938) was a fixture at the Metropolitan Opera; remained in Sweden during World War II, returned to the Met as the Duke in *Rigoletto* in 1945, and sang with that company in 1947, 1948, and 1950.

Bkl. [Ger.]. Abbr. for *Bassklarinette,* bass clarinet.

Blacher, Boris (b. Niu-chang, China, of German-Russian parents, 19 Jan. 1903; d. Berlin, 30 Jan. 1975). Composer. Studied with Koch at the Hochschule für Musik; also with Schering, Blume, and von Hornbostel at the Univ. in Berlin (1927–31); in 1938 appointed to teach composition at the Dresden Conservatory but resigned because of conflict with the Nazis; by 1948 was teaching at the Berlin Hochschule für Musik, which he later directed (1953–70); also taught at the Berkshire Music Center (1955). Until the late 1940s works were tonal and often witty; Satie, Milhaud, and Stravinsky were influences, along with jazz idioms. In works of the early 1950s developed a means of relating varying meters systematically in relation to the twelve-tone idea. Many of his works, especially his operas, contain social criticism.

Black-Key Etude. Popular name for Chopin's Etude op. 10 no. 5 in G♭ major (1830), for piano, in which the right hand plays only on the black keys.

Blackwood, Easley (b. Indianapolis, 21 Apr. 1933). Composer and pianist. Studied with Messiaen (Berkshire Music Center, 1949), Hindemith (Yale, 1950–54), and Boulanger (Paris, 1954–57); joined faculty at the Univ. of Chicago in 1958. As a pianist has actively promoted contemporary repertory including Ives, Boulez, and the second Viennese School. His works employ polyrhythmic textures and wide-ranging melodic contours; in the 1980s he became interested in equal-tempered tuning systems of more than 12 pitches per octave.

Bladder pipe. A wind instrument consisting of a short blowpipe, an animal bladder, and a *chanter whose reed is enclosed in the bladder. The bladder acts as a reservoir to enable continuous playing.

Bladder pipes have been played in Europe since at least the 13th century. See also Bagpipe.

Blades, Rubén (b. Panama City, Panama, 16 July 1948). Popular singer, songwriter, and actor. Went to New York City to pursue a music career, appearing first as a soloist with Ray Barretto's band at Madison Square Garden; later associated with Willie Colón, with whom he recorded "Siembra" and "Tiburón." His albums *Buscando America* (1984) and *Escenas* (1985) continued to explore social and political themes and established him with a wider audience in both the United States and Latin America; in 1985 began career as an actor; returned to Panama in 1994.

Blake, Blind (Arthur) (b. Jacksonville, Fla., ca. 1890–95; d. Florida? ca. 1933–35). Blues singer and guitarist. Blake's career is obscure; he made just over 80 recordings as Blind Blake, or under identifiable nicknames (1926–32), and several more as accompanist to other musicians, including Ma Rainey (1926) and Gus Cannon (1927). A technically accomplished guitarist; repertory included blues, country dance songs, and songster or medicine show pieces.

Blake, Eubie [James Hubert] (b. Baltimore, 7 Feb. 1883; d. New York, 12 Feb. 1983). Ragtime and revue pianist and composer. Worked as a pianist, mainly in Baltimore; in partnership with Noble Sissle wrote for musical revues from 1915. Their hit show *Shuffle Along,* the first African American musical, included the song "I'm Just Wild about Harry" (1921); with Andy Razaf wrote the popular song "Memories of You"; during this period made records and piano rolls; involved as a performer and lecturer in the first ragtime revival (1950s). Reached his widest audience after recording the album *The Eighty-Six Years of Eubie Blake* (1969).

Blakey, Art [Buhaina, Abdullah ibn] (b. Pittsburgh, 11 Oct. 1919; d. New York, 16 Oct. 1990). Jazz drummer and bandleader. Played with Mary Lou Williams (1942), Fletcher Henderson (1943–44), and Billy Eckstine's bop big band (1944–47); recorded with Thelonious Monk (intermittently 1947–54), then formed the definitive hard bop combo, the Jazz Messengers, initially sharing leadership with Horace Silver (until 1956). His recordings include *Art Blakey's Jazz Messengers with Thelonious Monk* and with Johnny Griffin (1957), and *Album of the Year* with Wynton Marsalis (1981); also toured with the Giants of Jazz, including Dizzy Gillespie, Sonny Stitt, and Monk (1971–72).

Blanche [Fr.]. Half note. See Note.

Bland, James A(llen) (b. Flushing, N.Y., 22 Oct. 1854; d. Philadelphia, 5 May 1911). Minstrel performer and composer. Raised in Washington, D.C., from 1875 performed in all-black minstrel groups and composed popular songs, including "Carry Me Back to Old Virginny" (1878) and "Oh, Dem Golden Slippers" (1879); in 1881 journeyed with Haverly's Genuine Colored Minstrels to England, where he remained until 1890. Returned to the U.S. to find the popularity of the minstrels diminished; the remainder of his work was unsuccessful.

Blanton, Jimmy [James] (b. Chattanooga, Tenn., Oct. 1918; d. Monrovia, Calif., 30 July 1942). Jazz double bass player. Based in St. Louis, played in the Jeter–Pillars Orchestra and on riverboats with Fate Marable; toured with Duke Ellington from 1939 to 1941. The most important jazz bassist of his era; recordings with Ellington include "Plucked Again" (1939), "Pitter Panther Patter," and "Sophisticated Lady," and the big band pieces "Jack the Bear," "Ko-Ko," and "Harlem Air Shaft" (all 1940).

Bläserquartett, -quintett, -trio [Ger.]. Wind quartet, quintet, trio.

Blasinstrument [Ger.]. Wind instrument.

Blasmusik [Ger.]. Music for wind instruments.

Blatt [Ger.]. (1) Sheet, as of music. (2) Reed *(Rohrblatt).*

Blavet, Michel (b. Besançon, bapt. 13 Mar. 1700; d. Paris, 28 Oct. 1768). Flutist and composer. A self-taught musician, moved to Paris (1723) and became the most admired French flutist of the time, appearing at the Concert spirituel from 1726; first flute of the Musique du roi (1738) and at the Opéra (1740). Works include 3 sets of 6 flute sonatas, one surviving concerto, many arrangements for flute, 4 stage works (1752–53).

Blech, Blechinstrumente [Ger.]. Brass instruments.

Blechmusik [Ger.]. Music for brass instruments.

Bledsoe, Jules [Julius] (b. Waco, Tex., 29 Dec. 1898; d. Hollywood, Calif., 14 July 1943). Baritone. Debut recital in New York (1924); performed in Harling's opera *Deep River* (1926); played Joe in Kern's *Showboat* (1927) and sang the role in the 1929 film version. The first black to perform Amonasro in *Aida* on a first-rate musical stage (Municipal Stadium in Cleveland).

Blegen, Judith (Eyer) (b. Lexington, Ky., 27 Apr. 1940). Lyric soprano. Studied voice and violin at Curtis (1959–64); 1963 debut with the Philadelphia Orchestra. After an apprenticeship at the Santa Fe Opera, went to Spoleto in 1964 and worked with Luigi Ricci; joined the Nuremberg Opera (1965). Success as Mélisande at the 1966 Spoleto Festival led to her debut with the Vienna Staatsoper as Rossini's Rosine; debuted as Papagena at the Met (1970);

also sang at the Salzburg Festival (1974), Edinburgh Festival (1976), and with the Paris Opera (1977).

Bley, Carla [née Borg] (b. Oakland, Calif., 11 May 1938). Jazz composer, bandleader, and entrepreneur. In the early 1960s began composing for her first husband, Paul Bley, who recorded "Around Again" and "Ida Lupino"; she also composed "Sing Me Softly of the Blues." With second husband Mike Mantler formed the Jazz Composers Guild Orchestra (1964), from which grew the Jazz Composers Orchestra Association (1966–), through which in turn developed the New Music Distribution Service (1968–), a principal outlet for independent record labels. From 1976 played keyboard in and composed eclectic pieces for her own bands; albums include *Dinner Music* (1976) and *Social Studies* (1980).

Blind octaves. A technique of piano playing in which the two hands alternate playing octaves in such a way that the thumbs of the two hands combine to produce a scale, trill, arpeggio, etc., alternating notes of which are doubled at the octave above or below [see Ex.].

Bliss, Arthur (Edward Drummond) (b. London, 2 Aug. 1891; d. there, 27 Mar. 1975). Composer. Attended Cambridge Univ. and studied conducting with Stanford at the Royal College of Music (1913–14); works after World War I show influences of Stravinsky, Ravel, and jazz. Professor of composition at the Royal College of Music (1921); in the U.S. between 1923 and 1925; taught at Berkeley (1934–41); returned to England and served as music director of the BBC (1942–44). Knighted in 1950, Master of the Queen's Music from 1953. Works include operas (*The Olympians,* 1948–49); ballet scores (*Checkmate,* 1937; *Adam Zero,* 1946); incidental music; film scores; orchestral music (*Mêlée fantasque,* 1921, rev. 1965; *A Colour Symphony,* 1922, rev. 1932; *Hymn to Apollo,* 1926, rev. 1966; *Music for Strings,* 1935; *Metamorphic Variations,* 1972); choral works (*Morning Heroes,* 1930); other vocal works (*Rout,* soprano, chamber ensemble, 1920; *Serenade,* baritone, orchestra, 1939); many songs with piano; chamber and piano works; *Belmont Variations,* brass, 1963.

Blitzstein, Marc (b. Philadelphia, 2 Mar. 1905; d. Fort-de-France, Martinique, 22 Jan. 1964). Composer. Attended Univ. of Pennsylvania (1921–23) and Curtis (1924), studying composition with Scalero and continuing piano study in New York with Siloti; also studied in Paris with Boulanger (1926–28) and in Berlin with Schoenberg. Premiered his own sonata for piano (1928); a one-act opera (*The Harpies,* 1931) parodies his own Parisian neoclassical style. After 1935 turned to producing dramatic music, often with a leftist political message (*The Cradle Will Rock,* 1936–37). Widest fame came from his translation and adaptation of *Die *Dreigroschenoper.*

Bloch, Ernest (b. Geneva, 24 July 1880; d. Portland, Ore., 15 July 1959). Composer and teacher. Studied violin and composition Geneva; further studies in Brussels (including violin lessons with Ysaÿe), Frankfurt am Main, Munich, and Paris; lectured on aesthetics at the Geneva Conservatory (1911–15). Early works are in a German Romantic or French impressionist vein; their modal cast and cyclic construction became consistent features of Bloch's style. Emigrated to the U.S. and taught at Mannes (1917–19); several works from the period 1911–16 constitute a "Jewish Cycle" (*Schelomo*): large in scale and often on biblical subjects. Served as director of the Cleveland Institute of Music (1920–25) and the San Francisco Conservatory (1925–30). Most of the works from the 1920s are in a neoclassic style (the first piano quintet, 1921–23, which uses quarter tones; violin sonatas); more Jewish works appeared as well (*Baal shem,* violin and piano, 1923; *Méditation hébraïque,* cello and piano, 1924). Spent the 1930s in Europe and returned to large-scale works, including a violin concerto (1937–38) and a Jewish sacred service (*Avodath hakodesh,* 1930–33); returned to the U.S. to teach at Berkeley (1940–52). Late works range in style from the neoclassic Concerto Grosso no. 2 (1952) to the neoromantic *Concerto symphonique* (piano and orchestra, 1947–48) to the twelve-tone *Sinfonia breve* (1951).

Block chords, harmony. (1) Chords played in such a way that all pitches are attacked simultaneously, especially on the keyboard, as in the simplest hymn settings. The resulting texture is described as *homophony. (2) *Parallel chords.

Blockflöte [Ger.]. *Recorder.

Blockx, Jan (b. Antwerp, 25 Jan. 1851; d. Kapellenbos, near Antwerp, 26 May 1912). Composer. Studied briefly with Benoit at the Flemish Music School in Antwerp, then with Reinecke at the Leipzig Conservatory; taught harmony at the Flemish Music School from 1885, succeeding Benoit as director in 1901 (by then the Royal Flemish Conservatory). Composed 7 operas, mostly in Flemish; a symphony and other orchestral pieces; chamber music; songs; piano pieces.

Blomdahl, Karl-Birger (b. Växjö, 19 Oct. 1916; d. Kungsängen, near Stockholm, 14 June 1968). Composer. Studied composition and conducting at the conservatory in Stockholm; later studied conducting with Wöldike. Traveled to France and Italy (1946–47) and to the U.S. (Tanglewood, 1954–55; Princeton, 1959); taught at Stockholm's Royal College of Music (from 1960), music director of Swedish Radio (from 1964). Early music manifests influence of Hindemith and neoclassical experiments; later explored twelve-tone and electronic techniques. Works include operas (*Herr von Hancken*, 1962–65); ballets (*Sisyfos*, 1954); incidental music; orchestral works (3 symphonies); choral and vocal music; music with tape; chamber music.

Blondel de Nesle (fl. 1180–1200). Trouvère. The language of his poetry reveals that he was from Picardy; no other biographical details are available. Some of his songs survive in an uncommonly large number of sources; many were used as models for later chansons.

Blow, John (b. Newark, Nottinghamshire, bapt. 23 Feb. 1649; d. Westminster, 1 Oct. 1708). Composer and organist. A choirboy at the Chapel Royal; appointed organist at Westminster Abbey in 1668; subsequently Gentleman of the Chapel (1674) and Master of the Children, a position he held for the rest of his life. Choirmaster at St. Paul's Cathedral (1687); in 1699 or 1700 became the official Chapel Royal composer, the first to hold such a post. Works include anthems with string accompaniment, the masque *Venus and Adonis,* 11 services, some 115 anthems, 10 Latin church works, 36 known odes, many songs and catches, organ works; also authored thorough-bass treatises. His pupils included William Croft and Henry Purcell.

Blue note. In Afro-American music, especially in *blues and *jazz, the lowered third, seventh, and sometimes fifth scale degrees of the otherwise major scale. The degree of inflection may vary considerably.

Bluebeard's Castle [Hung. *A Kékszakálld Herceg Vára*]. Opera in one act by Bartók (libretto by Béla Balázs, after Maeterlinck), produced in Budapest in 1918. Setting: Bluebeard's castle.

Bluegrass music. A style of *country and western music brought to prominence in the mid-1940s, first on broadcasts of the Grand Ole Opry, by Bill Monroe and his Blue Grass Boys. The term refers to Monroe's native state, Kentucky (the Bluegrass State). The style is formed principally from the Anglo-American traditions of white musicians of rural Appalachia and was seen from the beginning as consciously preserving those traditions in the face of the increasing commercialization of what was termed hillbilly music generally. Monroe himself, however, recognized the influence of black musicians. Bluegrass is typically performed by a "string band" consisting of a combination of nonelectric instruments such as violin, mandolin, guitar, five-string banjo, and double bass, with some or all of the instrumentalists also singing.

Blues. (1) A body of 20th-century black American poetry; also a verse form in that poetry. Poems range from coherent, composed stories to discontinuous, improvised stanzas drawn from a common pool of formulas. Delivered in black American dialects, lyrics address day-to-day concerns, with love life the ubiquitous subject. By far the most common form is a rhymed couplet with the first line repeated, yielding the structure AAB. Line B, which rhymes with A, usually resolves A with a humorous or ironic twist. In one alternative structure, each stanza ends with a refrain.

(2) A standard rhythmic-harmonic structure in which the 12-bar progression I–I–I–I–IV–IV–I–I–V–IV–I–I is tied to the AAB couplet of (1) in three 4-bar phrases. Although 8- and 16-bar patterns occur, the 12-bar blues predominates and is highly flexible. It may be rendered literally, as in *boogie-woogie, or radically altered, as in modern jazz improvisation. Secondary dominants and dominant substitutions are common in jazz styles, and the use of the lowered seventh degree in bar 4 (producing the dominant seventh of the IV of bar 5) is especially common.

(3) A secular, 20th-century black American vocal genre, and a vital component of related genres. As a genre, blues "proper" falls into three general categories.

In *country (or downhome) blues,* a male singer plays an acoustic steel-stringed guitar. All singers use blues inflections [see above], but timbre, enunciation, contour, and range vary greatly, individuality being especially prized. Lyrics are highly flexible; many titles refer to one or two traditional verses rather than to a fixed text, and verses migrate from one melody to another. Accompaniments exhibit an often intentional freedom from the underlying 4/4 meter and 12-bar structure. String bending and *bottleneck techniques may be used to produce nondiatonic pitches in melodies that parallel or answer the vocal line. Country blues originated ca. 1890–1905 in the Mississippi delta and east Texas. Wide dissemination of downhome blues began only with Blind Lemon Jefferson's emergence as a recording star in 1926.

In *classic blues,* a *ragtime or *stride pianist or a *New Orleans style jazz band accompanies a female singer. Designed for formal presentation on stage, a song pursues a coherent theme through stanzas divided into introductory verse and chorus; 12-bar

AAB structures provide only one element of the multithematic repertory. The style derives from country blues through performers (e.g., Ma Rainey, whose black minstrel band toured the South in the early 1900s) and composers (e.g., W. C. Handy, who began to publish and popularize "blues" in 1912).

In post–World War II *Chicago and urban blues,* which employ electronic amplification, a male singer leads an instrumental group. Composed lyrics frequently tell a story. In Chicago blues, a sound and style associated with Howlin' Wolf, Muddy Waters, Little Walter, and Sonny Boy Williamson (Rice Miller), harmonica, piano, and especially electric guitar improvisations rival *gospel-influenced, melismatic vocal lines. Usually adhering to 12-bar, AAB forms, drums and bass establish strong dance rhythms with ostinato patterns. In urban blues groups, saxophones or brass sustain chords and play accompanimental *riffs. Widely influential in the creation of the style were singer–electric guitarists T-Bone Walker and B. B. King.

The entire genre of blues proper stands in complex relationship to *jazz, *boogie-woogie, *jug band music, *rhythm and blues, *rock, *soul, and white American folk music.

Blumen [Ger.]. Coloratura passages in the music of the *Meistersinger.

B-minor Mass. A Latin Mass by Bach, BWV 232, for soloists, chorus, and orchestra, assembled in the years 1747–49. The principal parts of the Ordinary are subdivided into many sections treated as choruses, arias, duets, etc. Some of these are reworkings of material from earlier cantatas, among them the *Crucifixus* (from BWV 12, *Weinen, Klagen, Sorgen, Sagen*). The Sanctus was first performed in 1724. The Kyrie and the Gloria were sent by Bach to the Catholic Elector of Saxony in 1733 as part of a request to be appointed court composer, a request granted only in 1736.

BMV. Abbr. for *Beatae Mariae Virginis,* of the Blessed Virgin Mary; used to designate feasts as well as the four Marian *antiphons.

Bo Diddley [McDaniel, Elias] (b. McComb, Miss., 30 Dec. 1928). Rock-and-roll singer. Moved to Chicago as a boy and taught himself guitar; played with several rhythm-and-blues groups in the 1950s. Walked into Chess and Checker Records to audition and was given the name Bo Diddley; the song that was a takeoff on this name reached no. 2 on the R & B charts in 1955; other songs include "I'm a Man," "Bring It to Jerome," and "Diddley Way Diddley." His music had a big influence on pop musicians, including the Yardbirds, the Rolling Stones, and Jimi Hendrix.

Boatwright, Helen (Strassburger) (b. Sheboygan, Wis., 17 Nov. 1916). Soprano. Studied with Anna Shram Irving and at Oberlin with Marion Simms; debut at the Berkshire Music Festival (1942); New York recital debut in 1967; from 1964 taught voice at Syracuse Univ. Performed with orchestras and in recital, giving important performances of works by Hindemith and Ives; often appeared with husband Howard Boatwright.

Boatwright, Howard (Leake, Jr.) (b. Newport News, Va., 16 Mar. 1918; d. Syracuse, 20 Feb. 1999). Composer and violinist. Studied violin with Israel Feldman in Norfolk and taught violin at the Univ. of Texas (1943–45); studied composition with Hindemith at Yale; taught there (1948–64); directed music at St. Thomas's Church in New Haven (1949–64); concertmaster of the New Haven Symphony (1950–62). In 1964 became Dean of the School of Music at Syracuse Univ.; beginning in 1971 taught composition and theory there. His early choral music is frequently modal and sometimes makes use of Anglo-American folk tunes; the second string quartet (1974) shows influence of Hindemith and twelve-tone techniques.

Bobization. See Solmization.

Bocal. (1) The curved metal tube to which the reed of the bassoon, English horn, or similar instrument is attached; sometimes also called the crook. (2) [Fr.] Mouthpiece.

Bocca chiusa [It.]. *Bouche fermée.*

Bocca ridente [It., laughing mouth]. In singing, a smiling position of the lips.

Boccherini, (Ridolfo) Luigi (b. Lucca, 19 Feb. 1743; d. Madrid, 28 May 1805). Composer and cellist, prolific composer of chamber music. After studies in Lucca and Rome received an appointment at the Viennese court theater; in 1766 joined violinist Filippo Manfredi on a tour that took him to Paris and then to Madrid in 1768 or 1769; received a post there as composer and cellist at the court of the Infante Don Luis. Following the Infante's death in 1785 became a chamber musician at the Berlin court of Frederick William of Prussia. Works include 125 string quintets (nearly all for 2 cellos rather than 2 violas), about 100 string quartets, more than 50 string trios, 11 cello concertos, 29 symphonies, other orchestral music, as well as vocal music.

Bocedization. See Solmization.

Bock, Jerry [Jerrold Lewis] (b. New Haven, Conn., 23 Nov. 1928). Popular composer. Moved to New York City where he collaborated with lyricist Larry Holofcener on songs for television and Broadway revues and on a full-length musical, *Mr. Wonderfi*

(1956); subsequently composed musicals with lyricist Sheldon Harnick (*Fiorello!*, 1959; *Fiddler on the Roof*, 1964). Produced 2 concept albums in the 1970s.

Bockstriller [Ger.]. *Goat's trill.

Bodley, Seóirse (b. Dublin, 4 Apr. 1933). Composer. Studied at the Royal Irish Academy, at University College, Dublin, and in Stuttgart; lecturer at University College since 1959. His interest in Gaelic folk song is reflected in his music, which also uses serial techniques.

Boehm system. A system of fingering for woodwind instruments developed starting in the 1830s by Theobald Boehm (1794–1881) of Munich. The system attempts to place the holes at their most acoustically advantageous positions, to provide a separate hole for each chromatic pitch so that all notes on the instrument will be of the same tone quality, and to construct a key mechanism that provides full venting (in which all holes below the first open hole are open) and that brings distant holes under easy control by the fingers. Boehm himself applied his system primarily to the flute; others have applied it successfully to the clarinet, oboe, bassoon, and other instruments.

Boehm, Theobald (b. Munich, 9 Apr. 1794; d. there, 25 Nov. 1881). Flutist and flute designer. Became a virtuoso flutist and received a musical appointment at court (1818); established a flute factory (1828). Instruments heard in London while touring in 1831 led to production of a redesigned instrument in 1832 with a new kind of key mechanism; in 1847 produced a new flute, distinguished by a cylindrical bore and holes of a size and placement determined by acoustical considerations, to which his earlier key mechanism was now adapted.

Boëllmann, Léon (b. Ensisheim, Alsace, 25 Sept. 1862; d. Paris, 11 Oct. 1897). Composer and organist. Studied organ with Gigout at the École Niedermeyer, Paris (1871–81); organist at St. Vincent-de-Paul, Paris; married Gigout's niece in 1885 and began teaching at Gigout's new organ school. Highly regarded as an organist and improviser, was also a prolific composer.

Boëly, Alexandre-Pierre-François (b. Versailles, 19 Apr. 1785; d. Paris, 27 Dec. 1858). Composer. Probably studied at the Paris Conservatory until he was 15; thereafter largely self-taught; became a good pianist, and much of his earlier music was for that instrument, including 2 sonatas op. 1 (1810) and many etudes and other short pieces. Around 1830 devoted himself primarily to the organ, becoming acting organist at St. Gervais (1834–38) and organist St. Germain l'Auxerrois (1840–51). Much admired by Saint-Saëns and Franck.

Boësset, Antoine de (b. Blois, 1586; d. Paris, 8 Dec. 1643). Composer. At the court of Louis XIII served as music master for the royal children (from 1613), as the queen's music teacher (from 1615), and in other administrative positions, including *surintendant de la musique du roy* (from 1623). Best known as composer of a large number of *airs de cour*, also composed at least 9 *ballets de cour* and sacred music including Masses and motets. Some of the *airs* were published in the collection *Airs choisis à 1, 2 et 3 voix* (Paris, 1738).

Boethian notation. See Letter notation.

Boethius, Anicius Manlius Severinus (b. Rome, ca. 480; d. ca. 524). Writer. Acted as an adviser to Emperor Theodoric, first through Cassiodorus, then directly from 510 until 523; soon thereafter was imprisoned and executed for treason. Writings include texts on the Quadrivium; much music theory of the later Middle Ages is based on ideas set forth in his *De institutione musica*, a treatise little known until the 10th century but then widely copied and disseminated.

Bogen [Ger.]. (1) The bow of a bowed stringed instrument; *Bogenführung*, bowing; *Bogenstrich*, bow stroke; *Bogenflügel, Bogenklavier*, *bowed keyboard instrument [see also Sostenente piano]. (2) [also *Haltebogen*] *Tie.

Bogenform [Ger.]. Bow or arch form, i.e., a musical *form that is roughly symmetrical; thus, ABA, ABCBA, etc.

Bohème, La. Opera in four acts by Puccini (libretto by Giuseppe Giacosa and Luigi Illica, after Henri Murger's novel *Scènes de la vie de Bohème*), produced in Turin in 1896. Setting: the Latin Quarter in Paris, 1830.

Böhm, Georg (b. Hohenkirchen, near Ohrdruf, 2 Sept. 1661; d. Lüneburg, 18 May 1733). Composer and organist. Studied at the Gymnasium at Gotha and from 1684 at the Univ. of Jena; may have had contact with Reincken or Buxtehude when he was in Hamburg in 1693. From 1698 until his death organist at the Johanniskirche in Lüneburg; perhaps had contact with J. S. Bach during Bach's Lüneburg years (1700–1703). Works include cantatas and motets; two passions; organ chorales and chorale preludes.

Böhm, Karl (b. Graz, 28 Aug. 1894; d. Salzburg, 14 Aug. 1981). Conductor. Studied music theory with Mandyczewski in Vienna (1913); conducting debut in Graz (1917), became the company's chief conductor in 1920. On the recommendation of Bruno Walter went to Munich to conduct in 1921 and remained there after Walter's departure; in 1927 became music director in Darmstadt. Director of the Dresden

Staatsoper (1934–42), where he led premieres of 2 Richard Strauss operas; in 1938 began a lifelong association with the Salzburg Festival. Director of the Vienna State Opera (1942, 1954–56). First conducted at La Scala in 1948; at the Met in 1957; at Bayreuth in 1962; at Covent Garden in 1977. Excelled at Schubert, Wagner, Bruckner, Strauss, and Berg, but particularly esteemed for his Mozart.

Böhm system. See Boehm system.

Boieldieu, (François-) Adrien (b. Rouen, 16 Dec. 1775, d. Jarcy, near Paris, 8 Oct. 1834). Composer. A choirboy at Rouen cathedral; composed two opéras comiques for Rouen; in 1794–95 began to publish music in Paris, then moved there, where he had success with one-act opéras comiques; in 1798 became professor of piano at the Conservatory. Became director of French opera at the Russian court (1803–12); reestablished himself on the French stage with *Jean de Paris* (1812), a great success that was, however, not repeated until *Le petit chaperon rouge* (1818). Professor of composition at the Conservatory (1817–26), composed little after this until *La *dame blanche,* which had worldwide success.

Bois [Fr., wood]. (1) Woodwind instruments. (2) *Avec le bois,* an instruction to bow or strike the strings of a violin or similar instrument with the wood or stick of the bow.

Boismortier, Joseph Bodin de (b. Thionville, 23 Dec. 1689; d. Roissy-en-Brie, 28 Oct. 1755). Composer. Around 1700 moved from his birthplace to Metz, then to Paris, where he spent much of the rest of his life; his op. 1 (6 sonatas for 2 flutes) appeared there in 1724. During the next 20 years issued more than 100 publications; orchestral director of the Foire St. Laurent (1744) and of the Foire St. Germain (1745); often cited as having composed the first solo concerto in France (Concerto for Cello or Bassoon op. 26, 1729). Remembered today chiefly for his large and varied instrumental output (nearly 500 instrumental pieces); the flute is of special importance.

Boîte [Fr.]. (1) *Swell box. (2) *Boîte à musique,* music box [see Automatic instruments].

Boito, Arrigo [Enrico Giuseppe Giovanni] (b. Padua, 24 Feb. 1842; d. Milan, 10 June 1918). Librettist and composer. Studied composition at the Milan Conservatory (1853–61); provided texts for two works by fellow student Franco Faccio. Went to Paris, where he wrote for Verdi the text of the *Inno delle nazioni* (1862); worked on *Amleto,* a libretto for Faccio; traveled in England, Belgium, and Germany. Returned to Milan in 1862; composed text and music for opera *Mefistofele* (1868, rev. 1875). Operatic collaboration with Verdi began with the revision of *Simon Boc-

canegra,* continued with *Otello* and *Falstaff;* also wrote the libretto to Ponchielli's *La *Gioconda.*

Bolcom, William (Elden) (b. Seattle, 26 May 1938). Composer and pianist. Attended the Univ. of Washington (1955–58); studied with Milhaud at Mills (1958–61); with Milhaud and Messiaen in France; and with Leland Smith at Stanford (1961–64); taught at the Univ. of Washington (1965–66), Queens College (1966–68), Univ. of Michigan (beginning 1973). As a performer particularly interested in ragtime and American popular song of the late 19th and early 20th centuries, which he has performed and recorded with wife Joan Morris. As a composer juxtaposes ragtime and electronic music (*Black Host,* organ, percussion, and tape, 1967); popular song, chromatic tonal melody, and *Sprechstimme* (*Open House,* tenor and small orchestra, 1975); microtones, polyrhythm, and pointillism (Piano Quartet, 1976); jazz, blues, serial methods, and Ivesian collages. Other works include theatre piece *Casino Paradise* (1990); 4 symphonies; choral works; chamber music; piano music; songs.

Bolden, Buddy [Charles Joseph] (b. New Orleans, 6 Sept. 1877; d. Jackson, La., 4 Nov. 1931). Jazz cornetist and bandleader. Led bands from at least 1895 and by 1901 had a sextet, which became the Eagle Band after he was committed to the State Insane Asylum at Jackson (1907). Admired for his powerful sound, his ability to "rag" (to improvise a paraphrase of) a tune, his propulsive sense of rhythm, and his blues playing.

Bolero [Sp.]. (1) A Spanish dance in moderate triple meter traditionally said to have been invented by the dancer Sebastián Cerezo of Cádiz in about 1780. It is most often danced by a couple with castanets, includes a variety of intricate steps, and is in three parts, each of which concludes with the characteristic gesture (termed *bien parado*) formed with one arm arched over the head and the other crossed in front of the chest. Art music evoking this dance includes Beethoven's "Bolero a solo" WoO 158a no. 19 and "Bolero a due" WoO 158a no. 20; numbers in operas by Weber *(Preciosa),* Auber *(La muette de Portici),* and Berlioz *(Benvenuto Cellini);* Chopin's *Boléro* op. 19 for piano (1833); and Ravel's *Boléro* for orchestra, composed as a ballet in one act (choreography by Bronislava Nijinska), produced by Ida Rubinstein in Paris in 1928.

(2) A Cuban song and dance-music form, of 19th-century origin, and an element important in the repertories of Afro-Cuban urban dance ensembles as well as in most of the rest of Latin America. The *bolero* is in slow to moderate duple meter, with characteristic bass and accompanying percussion figures. It sets sentimental texts and plays a role in Latin

American urban popular music closely analogous to that of the North American ballad [see Ballad (3)].

Bolet, Jorge (b. Havana, 15 Nov. 1914; d. Mountain View, Calif., 16 Oct. 1990). Pianist. Debuted as a prodigy in 1924; studied at Curtis (1925–36) with David Saperton, Leopold Godowsky, and Maurice Rosenthal; also worked with Emil von Sauer in Vienna. New York debut 1937; Rudolf Serkin's assistant at Curtis (1939–42); joined the faculty of Indiana Univ. (1968). Best known for performances of Beethoven, Chopin, Reger, and Liszt.

Bolling, Claude (b. Cannes, France, 10 Apr. 1930). Pianist and composer. A child prodigy; played with Roy Eldridge, Lionel Hampton, Paul Gonsalves, and others; formed his own orchestra in 1955. Best known for his semiclassical works, which include Suite for Flute and Jazz Piano Trio (1975); *Toot Suite* (1981); *California Suite* (flute and jazz piano, 1976); Suite for Cello and Jazz Piano Trio (1984).

Bologna school. A group of composers active in Bologna, Italy, in the second half of the 17th century and associated with one or both of the city's two principal musical institutions: the church of San Petronio and the Accademia filarmonica. Especially characteristic of instrumental music at San Petronio were works for trumpet and strings, the first of which were sonatas by Maurizio Cazzati (ca. 1620–77). Later works for this combination, including some of the earliest examples of the Baroque concerto grosso style, were by Domenico Gabrielli (1651–90), Giacomo Antonio Perti (1661–1756), Giuseppe Aldrovandini (1672–1707), and Giuseppe Torelli (1658–1709). Other composers associated with musical styles developed there include Giovanni Battista Vitali (1632–92), Giovanni Paolo Colonna (1637–95), Pietro Degli Antoni (1648–1720), Giovanni Battista Bassani (ca. 1657–1716), Tomaso Antonio Vitali (1663–1745), and Giovanni Bononcini (1670–1747). Arcangelo Corelli (1653–1713) is also sometimes associated with the Bologna school, though he was active in Rome from perhaps as early as 1671.

Bombard [Ger., also *Bomhardt, Bombhardt, Pomhart, Pommer;* Fr. *bombarde;* It. *bombarda*]. The tenor or bass member of the *shawm family of woodwinds, named after a type of artillery.

Bombardon. (1) In Germany in the 1820s, an early *ophicleide. (2) In the 1830s, a military valved *tuba designed and made in Berlin by Wieprecht and Moritz

Bombo. (1) [It.] In the 17th century, a figure of repeated notes. (2) [It.] In the 17th and 18th centuries, a string *tremolo.

Bomhardt [Ger.]. *Bombard.

Bomtempo, João Domingos (b. Lisbon, 28 Dec. 1775; d. there, 18 Aug. 1842). Composer. Went to Paris in 1801, published 2 piano concertos and a sonata there (1803–5); became friendly with Clementi, who published most of his later music. Moved to London (1810), to Lisbon (1811), back to London (1816), settling finally in Lisbon in 1820. In 1822 founded a Philharmonic Society which gave Lisbon's first public concerts, and in 1835 became director of the new conservatory.

Bonang [Jav.]. A Javanese *gong set employed in a *gamelan* ensemble. Ten to fourteen kettle-shaped, knobbed gongs are set open-side down in two rows on taut cords in a wooden frame. The player strikes the kettles with two padded sticks. See ill. under Instrument.

Bond, Capel (b. Gloucester, bapt. 14 Dec. 1730; d. Coventry, 14 Feb. 1790). Composer and organist. Apprenticed to the organist at Gloucester Cathedral; moved to Coventry in 1749, where he held positions at St. Michael's (beginning 1749), All Angels (1749), and Holy Trinity (1752); composed concerti grossi, concertos for trumpet and bassoon, and anthems.

Bones. European and American *clappers originally made of animal ribs and later of hardwood. The player holds a pair in one hand and clicks them together. They figured prominently in 19th-century *minstrel shows.

Bongos, bongo drums. A permanently attached pair of small, single-headed, cylindrical or conical drums of Afro-Cuban origin. One drum of slightly larger diameter is tuned about a fifth below the smaller, and the pair is held between the knees and struck with both hands. They are widely used in the urban popular music of Latin America. See ill. under Percussion instruments.

Bonno, Giuseppe (b. Vienna, 29 Jan. 1711; d. there, 15 Apr. 1788). Composer. Studied with Johann Georg Reinhardt, from 1726 with Durante and Leo in Naples. Returned to Vienna 10 years later and became court composer (from 1739); in 1749 became Kapellmeister to Joseph Frederick of Sachsen-Hildburghausen; in 1774 appointed imperial Kapellmeister. Was well acquainted with the Mozarts, among others.

Bononcini, Antonio Maria (b. Modena, 18 June 1677; d. there, 8 July 1726). Composer and cellist. Like his brother Giovanni studied in Bologna with Colonna; played in the orchestra of Cardinal Pamphili (1690–93); in Vienna became Kapellmeister for the court of the emperor's brother Charles, composed the opera *Tigrane* (1710). In 1713 accompanied

Giovanni to Italy, where he spent the rest of his life, mostly in Milan, Naples, and (from 1715) Modena, where he was named *maestro di cappella* in 1721. Composed some 24 stage works; 40 cantatas; sacred vocal works.

Bononcini, Giovanni (b. Modena, 18 July 1670; d. Vienna, 9 July 1747). Composer and cellist. Studied with his father and (from about 1678) in Bologna with Colonna; entered the Accademia filarmonica in 1685, two years later appointed *maestro di cappella* at S. Giovanni in Monte; fulfilled commissions in Modena and Bologna and published a number of vocal and instrumental pieces; chamber musician for Filippo Colonna and his family in Rome (1692–97). Bononcini's opera *Il trionfo di Camilla* (1696) enjoyed success in Naples and other cities; he served Leopold I (from 1698) and his successor, Joseph (from 1705) in Vienna; from 1714 to 1719 he was in the service of Johann Wenzel in Rome. His string of London successes began in 1720 with *Astarto;* his operas often competed with Handel's. In 1733 was in Paris; in 1741 pensioned in Vienna by Maria Theresa. Compositions include some 62 stage works, nearly 300 cantatas, sacred vocal works, and instrumental works.

Bononcini, Giovanni Maria (b. Montecorone, near Modena, bapt. 23 Sept. 1642; d. Modena 18 Nov. 1678). Composer and theorist, father of Giovanni and Antonio Maria. Studied with Agostino Bendinelli and possibly with Uccellini in Modena; from 1671 court musician for Duchess Laura d'Este and violinist at the Modena Cathedral; in 1673 published a widely used treatise, *Musico prattico* (facs., 1969). Best known for his chamber and church sonatas.

Bonporti, Francesco Antonio (b. Trent, bapt. 11 June 1672; d. Padua, 19 Dec. 1748). Composer. After early studies in Trent and Innsbruck studied for the priesthood at Rome's Collegium germanicum (from 1691); allegedly had instruction from Corelli (violin) and Ottavio Pitoni (composition); in 1696 published 10 trio sonatas op. 1; ordained to the priesthood and appointed cleric to the Trent Cathedral in 1697. The bulk of his output was instrumental music: he published at least 12 sets of trio sonatas, *invenzioni*, violin concertos, and other instrumental chamber music.

Bontempi [Angelini], **Giovanni Andrea** (b. Perugia, ca. 1624; d. Brufa, Torgiano, 1 July 1705). Composer and writer on music. Studied with Virgilio Mazzocchi in Rome, and in 1643 became a singer at St. Mark's, Venice; from 1650 served Johann Georg I at Dresden, after 1656 appointed Kapellmeister (with Schütz). Returned to Italy (1666–70), was again in Dresden (1671–80), and in 1680 settled again in Perugia; from 1686 *maestro di cappella* at the College

of S. Maria. In 1695 published *Historia musica,* for which he is best known today.

Bonynge, Richard (Alan) (b. Sydney, 29 Sept. 1930). Conductor and pianist. Studied piano at the Sydney Conservatory and privately in London; London debut as pianist, 1954; married Joan Sutherland the same year; their careers have been intertwined ever since. Debut as an opera conductor, Vancouver 1963; subsequently conducted opera at San Francisco (1963), Covent Garden (1964), the Met (1970); artistic director, Vancouver Opera (1974–78); musical director, Australian Opera (1975–86).

Boogie-woogie. A piano blues style featuring percussive ostinato accompaniments such as that of the accompanying example. The steadily repeated bass patterns, one or two bars long, delineate the 12-bar blues progression, sometimes with IV in measure 2 or 10 [see Blues]. The piano style flourished from around 1936 through the early 1940s with the rediscovery of performers from the 1920s such as Meade Lux Lewis and Albert Ammons.

Book of Common Prayer. The basic Anglican liturgical book. See Liturgical books.

Boone, Charles (b. Cleveland, 21 June 1939). Composer. Studied composition under Karl Schiske at the Academy of Music in Vienna (1960–61); attended the Univ. of Southern California and San Francisco State; studied also with Krenek and Adolf Weiss. Lived in Berlin (1975–77); directed the Mills College Tape Music Center and Performing Group (1966–68); founded the Bring Your Own Pillow concert series in San Francisco in the early 1970s. His early pointillistic style evolved into what he called "serial music without the aid of the techniques of serialism."

Boone, Pat [Charles Eugene] (b. Jacksonville, Fla., 1 June 1934). Singer and actor. Became popular for performing country, rock-and-roll, and Tin Pan Alley songs in a diluted version of emerging rock-and-roll styles; successful recordings included "Ain't That a Shame" (1955), "Long Tall Sally" (1956), and "Love Letters in the Sand" (1957); also acted in movies.

Bop. *Bebop.

Bordone [It.], **Bordun** [Ger.]. (1) Drone. (2) Drone bass strings that do not pass over the fingerboard on plucked stringed instruments such as the theorbo.

Bordoni [Hasse], **Faustina** (b. Venice, ca. 1700; d. there, 4 Nov. 1781). Mezzo-soprano. Raised in

Venice under the protection of the Marcello brothers and under the musical tutelage of Michelangelo Gasparini. From 1716 to 1723 sang throughout Italy, then in Munich (1723), Vienna (1725–26), and London (from 1726), where she created several Handel roles (Alcestis in *Admeto*, 1727; Emira in *Siroe*, 1728). Her rivalry with the soprano Cuzzoni culminated in 1727 when the two traded onstage blows. Returned to Italy and married Hasse in Venice in 1730; the following year both were engaged at the Saxon court at Dresden; during the next two decades sang in most of Hasse's operas and appeared frequently in Venice, Naples, and Paris; by 1751 had retired. Highly praised for both her singing and acting.

Bore. The cross section of the column of air contained in the tube of a *wind or *brass instrument. If the bore is of uniform size over most of the length of the tube, it is said to be cylindrical; if it increases in size over a significant part of the length of the tube, it is said to be conical.

Bore, borea, boree. *Bourrée.

Boris Godunov. Opera by Mussorgsky (libretto by Mussorgsky after a play by Pushkin and Karamazin's *History of the Russian State*). The first version consisted of seven scenes and was composed in 1868–69 but not produced until 1928 in Leningrad. The second version, which has a prologue and four acts, was composed in 1871–72, revised in 1873, and produced in St. Petersburg in 1874. In 1896, Rimsky-Korsakov thoroughly revised the work, reorchestrating it and making both major omissions and additions. This version was produced in Russia a number of times in the years following. Rimsky-Korsakov prepared yet another version in 1906–8; this version was produced in Paris in 1908, the work's first production outside of Russia. Setting: Russia and Poland, 1598–1605.

Bořkovec, Pavel (b. Prague, 10 June 1894; d. there, 22 July 1972). Composer. After World War I studied with Joseph Foerster and Jaroslav Křička; later with Joseph Suk at the Prague Conservatory (1925–27). His music from the 1930s shows the influence of Hindemith and Stravinsky; after the Second World War became professor at the Prague Academy of Music (1946–63). Works include operas (*Satyr,* 1937–38; *Paleček,* 1945–47); orchestral works (3 symphonies); vocal works; chamber music (5 string quartets, 1924–61); songs.

Borodin, Alexander Porfir'yevich (b. St. Petersburg, 12 Nov. 1833; d. there, 27 Feb. 1887). Composer, one of the "Mighty Five." Had early lessons on the flute and piano but developed an interest in chemistry, subsequently receiving a doctorate and continu-

ing scientific studies in Europe (1859–62), primarily in Germany and Pisa; a few chamber works date from this time (Piano Quintet in C minor, 1862). In 1862 returned to St. Petersburg and taught at the Academy of Medicine; under Balakirev's guidance started working on his Symphony no. 1 in E♭ (completed 1867). In 1869 began two new compositions, the Symphony no. 2 and *Prince Igor (which contains the famous *Polovtsian Dances) but large-scale works often took him years to complete, and his lecturing and administrative duties took up considerable time. During an 1877 business trip to Germany visited Liszt in Weimar; *In Central Asia is dedicated to the Hungarian composer, who championed Borodin's music; the String Quartet no. 2 in D was completed in 1881; the lyrical third movement (Nocturne) has been arranged by many composers. Borodin's works were performed with increasing frequency in Europe toward the end of his life; a Third Symphony in A minor was begun in 1886 but remained incomplete at his death.

Borowski, Felix (b. Burton, Westmorland, 10 Mar. 1872; d. Chicago, 6 Sept. 1956). Composer and critic. Studied music in London and Cologne; taught violin and composition at the Chicago Musical College (from 1897), subsequently served as its president (1916–25); professor of musicology at Northwestern Univ. (1937–42); staff member of the Newberry Library until 1956.

Bortniansky, Dmitry Stepanovich (b. Glukhov, Ukraine, 1751; d. St. Petersburg, 10 Oct. 1825). Composer. A choirboy at the court chapel in St. Petersburg, he studied with Galuppi; from 1769 to 1779 continued his studies in Italy where his operas *Creonte* (1776), *Alcide* (1778), and *Quinto Fabio* (1778) were produced. Appointed Kapellmeister on his return to St. Petersburg; from 1796, director of vocal music at the court chapel. Works include more than 50 sacred concerti; other choral music; operas on French texts; instrumental music.

Boskovich, Alexander Uriah (b. Kolozvár, Hungary [Cluj, Romania], 16 Aug. 1907; d. Tel Aviv, 5 Nov. 1964). Composer. Studied at the Budapest Academy and later in Vienna (1924) and in Paris with Dukas and Boulanger (1925); afterward conducted the State Opera in Cluj. In 1938 emigrated to Palestine and began teaching at the Tel Aviv Academy of Music. His compositions often integrate diatonic art-music idioms with Eastern Mediterranean elements. Composed orchestral works (*Semitic Suite,* 1946–47, rev. 1959; *Adayim* [Ornaments], flute, orchestra, 1964); vocal music (*Ha'or haganuz* [The Hidden Light], oratorio, 1964); chamber music; piano works.

Bossa-nova [Port.]. A style of *samba pioneered by Antonio Carlos Jobim, João Gilberto, and others in the late 1950s. Characteristics, some of which reflect the influence of *cool jazz styles of the period, include increased harmonic and melodic complexity, a detached, unemotional singing style, the acoustic guitar as principal accompanying instrument, and a departure from the older samba's emphasis on percussion.

Bossi, Marco Enrico (b. Salò, Lake Garda, 25 Apr. 1861; d. aboard ship on the Atlantic Ocean, 20 Feb. 1925). Composer, organist, and pianist. Studied organ in Bologna and Milan with Ponchielli; in 1881 appointed organist at the Como Cathedral; from 1890 taught harmony and organ at the conservatory in Naples; directed the conservatories in Venice (1895–1902), Bologna (1902–11), and Rome (1916–23). An active participant in the revival of nonoperatic composition at the turn of the century in Italy, his own style drew on the late German Romantic tradition. Works include 5 operas; an organ concerto (1895); *Intermezzi goldoniani* (1905), and other orchestral works; chamber music; many organ and other keyboard works.

Bostic, Earl (b. Tulsa, 25 Apr. 1913; d. Rochester, 28 Oct. 1965). Jazz and rhythm-and-blues alto saxophonist and bandleader. Played on riverboats in the band of Charlie Creath and Fate Marable (1935–36); in New York played in big bands with Don Redman (1938) and Lionel Hampton (1943–44), led his own bands (1939–42?), and worked with Hot Lips Page (1941, 1943). From 1944 led groups, achieving considerable popularity with his recording of "Flamingo" (1951).

Boston dip waltz, Boston waltz. Dances to popular songs in 3/4 meter. Americans introduced the former in the 1870s, the latter in 1913. The terms have been used rather casually with resulting confusion in their relation to the hesitation waltz (further confused with the Viennese hesitation waltz). In general, the Boston dip featured a dip on the first beat of one-bar patterns; the Boston and hesitation waltzes featured three steps syncopated through two-bar patterns, a hemiola rhythm that Paul Hindemith used in the "Boston" of his *Suite 1922* for piano.

Bottesini, Giovanni (b. Crema, 22 Dec. 1821; d. Parma, 7 July 1889). Double bass player, conductor, and composer. Studied the double bass at the Milan Conservatory (1835–39) and eventually became a concert soloist and conductor, mostly of opera, throughout Europe and America; chosen by his friend Verdi to conduct the premiere of *Aida;* appointed director of the Parma Conservatory in 1889. Extended the technique of the double bass.

Bottleneck. A *blues guitar technique. Holding a bottleneck or metal tube on either the ring or the little finger of the left hand and tuning to an open major chord, the player produces a vibrato by shaking the device above a fret, or a wail by running it along the steel strings. The effect is sometimes produced with a knife instead.

Bouché [Fr.]. In horn playing, *stopped tones.

Bouche fermée [Fr. closed mouth; It. *bocca chiusa;* Ger. *Brummstimme*]. Singing with the mouth closed, i.e., humming.

Boucourechliev, André (b. Sofia, Bulgaria, 28 July 1925; d. Paris, 1998). Composer, critic, and musicologist. Studied piano at the Sofia Conservatory (1946–47) and the École normale de musique in Paris (1949–51); began composing in 1954, attended the Darmstadt summer courses, and worked with Berio and Maderna at the Milan Radio electronic music studio. Compositions explore not only electronic music but also indeterminacy (*Texte 2,* 1960; *Archipels,* 1967–72) composed several works for orchestra (*Amers,* 1973). Wrote books and articles on various composers, including Schumann, Stravinsky, and Messiaen.

Bouffons [Fr.]. Costumed dancers of the 15th and 16th centuries who danced the *moresca or *matasin.

Bouffons, Querelle (guerre) des [Fr., Quarrel (War) of the Buffoons]. A dispute, carried on principally in an exchange of several dozen published letters and pamphlets in Paris in the years 1752–54, over the relative merits of French and Italian music. It was occasioned by the appearance in Paris in 1752 of a troupe of Italians who performed Pergolesi's *La serva padrona* and other examples of *opera buffa* and who became known as the Bouffons. The Italian partisans included Rousseau, D'Alembert, and Diderot. Composers associated with the defense of French music included Rameau, Destouches, and Mondonville.

Boughton, Rutland (b. Aylesbury, 23 Jan. 1878; d. London, 25 Jan. 1960). Composer. Studied with Stanford and Walford Davies at the Royal College of Music (1898–1901), taught at the Midland Institute in Birmingham (1905–11). Influenced by Wagner's ideals coauthored *Music Drama of the Future* (1911) with Reginald Buckley; three years after its publication presented the first Glastonbury Festival, with aim of providing a forum for his own Wagnerian "choral dramas." *The Birth of Arthur* (1909) became the first of his 5-opera "Arthurian cycle"; *The Immortal Hour* (1914) achieved more than 200 consecutive performances in Birmingham. Around 1930 retired to Gloucestershire, where he completed the Arthur cycle and mounted festivals at Stroud and Bath.

Boulanger, Lili (b. Paris, 21 Aug. 1893; d. Mézy, 15 Mar. 1918). Composer. Her study of music was at first guided by her sister Nadia, then by Caussade and Vidal at the Paris Conservatory (1912); her compositions reflect the mainstream of French music in its subtle chromaticism and contrapuntal character. Works include *Poème symphonique* for orchestra (1917); Nocturne for violin and piano (1911); Psalm settings and other works for soloists, chorus, and orchestra; cantatas and songs.

Boulanger, Nadia (b. Paris, 16 Sept. 1887; d. there, 22 Oct. 1979). Teacher, conductor, and composer. Studied organ (Vierne, Guilmant) and composition (Fauré, Widor) but stopped composing before World War I. Conducted performances of and recorded much early music between the wars; conducted symphony orchestras in London and in Washington, D.C. Remembered primarily as a teacher: taught harmony at the École normale in Paris (1920–39) and accompanying at the Paris Conservatory (from 1946); associated with the American Conservatory at Fontainebleau from 1921, becoming its director in 1950; during the Second World War taught at Wellesley, Juilliard, and Radcliffe. Her American students included Copland, Carter, Harris, Piston, Thomson, and many others.

Boulevard Solitude. Opera in seven scenes by Hans Werner Henze (libretto by Grete Weil, based on the Manon Lescaut story), produced in Hanover in 1952. Setting: Paris, 1950.

Boulez, Pierre (b. Montbrison, 26 Mar. 1925). Composer, conductor, and writer on music. Entered the Paris Conservatory in 1942; studied harmony under Messiaen and counterpoint with Andrée Vaurabourg-Honegger; later studied twelve-tone composition under Leibowitz. By the early 1950s at the center of the avant-garde, in close touch with Cage, Pousseur, and Stockhausen; in his famous "Schönberg est mort" (1952) announced that Webern was the most fertile source of the new approach, one that would serialize other aspects of sound in addition to pitch. Earliest published compositions already reflected his interest in serialism (*Polyphonie X,* 18 soloists, 1951). Composed electronic pieces (*Étude sur un son, Étude sur sept sons,* 1952) but he did not abandon live performers; in *Le *marteau sans maître* Boulez was in control of a sufficiently well-developed method to write what has become a classic of serialism. Also explored indeterminacy (Third Piano Sonata, 1955–57); continued combining improvisatory and fixed elements (*Pli selon pli* (1957–62); in other works combined taped and live sounds and explored the spatial distribution of performers or loudspeakers. For many decades has had a successful career as a conductor; founded the Domaine musical series of concerts in Paris (1954); in 1963 led the first French performance of *Wozzeck* at the Opéra; guest conductor of the Cleveland Orchestra (1967), and in 1971 became principal conductor of the BBC Symphony Orchestra and the New York Philharmonic. In 1977 returned to Paris to assume the direction of IRCAM, retiring in 1992; in 1995 appointed principal guest conductor of the Chicago Symphony.

Other major works include *Le visage nuptial,* vocal soloists and chamber orchestra (1946; rev. for soloists and orchestra, 1950–51); 3 piano sonatas (no. 1, 1946; no. 2, 1948, withdrawn; no. 3, 1955–57); *Structures II,* 2 pianos (1956–61); *e. e. cummings ist der Dichter,* 16 voices and 24 instruments (1970–).

Boult, Adrian (Cedric) (b. Chester, 8 Apr. 1889; d. Tunbridge Wells, 22 Feb. 1983). Conductor. In Leipzig (1912–13) studied theory with Reger and observed Nikisch's rehearsals; joined Beecham's staff at Covent Garden (1914), conducting debut with the Liverpool Philharmonic (1915). Led London productions by Diaghilev's Ballets russes (1918–19); guest conductor with Beecham's Royal Philharmonic (1919). Conductor of the City of Birmingham Orchestra (1924–30); assistant music director of Covent Garden (1926). Created and led the BBC Symphony Orchestra from its first concert in 1930 until his retirement in 1950. Guest conductor, New York Philharmonic (1938–39); led the London Proms Concerts (1942–50), the London Philharmonic (1950–57), the City of Birmingham Orchestra (1959–60). Taught conducting at London's Royal College of Music (1919–30, 1962–66). A committed champion of British composers; knighted in 1937.

Bourdon [Fr.]. *Drone; a string or pipe that produces a drone. See also *Burdo.

Bourgault-Ducoudray, Louis-Albert (b. Nantes, 2 Feb. 1840; d. Vernouillet, Yvelines, 4 July 1910). Composer. Entered the Paris Conservatory, winning the Prix de Rome in 1863; from 1878 taught music history at the Conservatory; composed prolifically until about 1890, including several operas, choral music, songs, chamber music, and piano pieces, many of them using exotic or folk material.

Bourgeois, Loys [Louis] (b. Paris, ca. 1510–15; d. in or after 1560). Composer and theorist. Between 1545 and 1552 active in Calvinist Geneva as singer and teacher of choristers; contributed to the Huguenot Psalter; moved to Lyons in 1552, to Paris by 1560. Of his numerous polyphonic settings of Psalms, most incorporate the Genevan melodies. Author of the singing and sight-reading treatise *Le droict chemin de musique* (Geneva, 1550).

Bourrée [Fr.]. A Baroque dance movement in moderately quick duple meter and binary form. It usually has four-measure phrases in ¢ (or 2), a quarter-note upbeat, dactylic figures in quarters and eighths, and syncopations in quarters and halves (especially in the second or fourth measures of phrases). It was danced frequently at the court of Louis XIV and in Lully's operas, and it was an independent instrumental form throughout the Baroque era.

Nicolas-Antoine Lebègue, Bourrée (1687).

Bout. (1) A curve in the side of a stringed instrument such as the violin, including the outward curves at the upper and lower parts of the body and the inward curves forming the waist. (2) [Fr.] The point of the bow.

Boutade [Fr.]. In the 18th century, a dance or ballet of improvisatory character; also an instrumental piece of similar character, such as might otherwise be called a *caprice* or *fantaisie.*

Bouzouki [Gr.]. A *long-necked lute of modern Greece. Developed in the early 20th century from the Turkish *saz,* it has a fretted neck, a pear-shaped body, and metal strings in courses of two. It is the leading instrument in some forms of Greek urban popular music.

Bow [Fr. *archet;* Ger. *Bogen;* It. *arco, archetto;* Sp. *arco*]. A device for setting in motion the strings of some types of stringed instruments. It consists of a stick that is shaped (often simply curved) to permit a string or fibers such as horsehair to be attached at both ends and held away from the stick itself. When the bow string or hair is drawn across a string of an instrument, the instrument's string is made to sound by being repeatedly displaced slightly and released by the friction between the two. See also Musical bow.

The violin bow was given its present form in about 1785 by François Tourte (1747–1835). The stick curves slightly inward toward a ribbon of horsehair or similar synthetic material that is held away from the stick at one end by the head and at the other by the frog. The tension of the hair is adjusted by means of a screw mechanism that moves the frog along the stick. The stick, the best examples of which are made of Pernambuco wood, is usually octagonal in cross section at the frog and round and tapering slightly above

the frog. The frog is of ebony, sometimes inlaid with mother-of-pearl. At the head, the hair passes through an ivory or metal plate; at the frog, it passes through a metal ferrule that spreads it evenly. According to Tourte's specifications, the stick is about 75 cm. (29.5 in.) long and the hair about 65 cm., with the center of gravity 19 cm. above the frog. Viola and cello bows are 74 and 73 or 72 cm. long, respectively. For the double bass, the French style of bow (held with the palm down) is about 71 cm. long, the German or Simandl bow (with a higher frog and held with the palm up; see Bowing) about 77 cm. long.

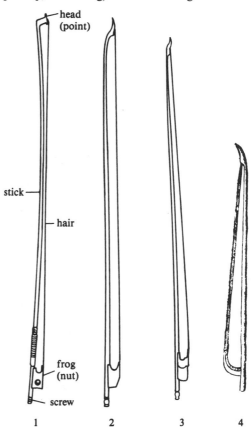

Bows: 1. Tourte, ca. 1800. 2. Thomas Smith, 1760–70. 3. Anonymous, 1694. 4. Marin Mersenne, *Harmonie universelle,* 1636–37.

The earliest bows, illustrated beginning in about the 10th century, were convex like the hunting bow, the stick curving away from the hair. The gradual straightening of the stick in the 16th and 17th centuries made necessary the creation of a horn-shaped frog and, subsequently, a distinct head to hold the hair away from the stick. Movable frogs for adjusting the tension of the hair by means of a screw mechanism were first introduced around 1700. In the decades preceding, this purpose was sometimes served by a metal catch on the frog that could be engaged in one or another of a set of teeth (dentated or *crémallère* bow). By about 1700, the stick was straight or only very slightly curved outward and had increased in length to between 60 and 70 cm. or more. Eighteenth-century bows before Tourte were in general lighter and more flexible than the modern bow, with the center of gravity closer to the player's hand. These features contributed to a lighter style of articulation in the playing of that period than has since prevailed. As bows became increasingly concave after 1750, a more pronounced head was required.

Bow harp. See Arched harp.

Bowed keyboard instrument. A stringed keyboard instrument in which the strings are bowed mechanically rather than being struck or plucked. See Sostenente piano.

Bowie [Jones], **David** (b. London, 8 Jan. 1947). Rock singer, songwriter, and actor. From 1972 released many successful albums (*The Rise and Fall of Ziggy Stardust and the Spiders from Mars,* 1972; *Young Americans,* 1975, including "Fame"; *Let's Dance,* 1983; *Black Tie White Noise,* 1993), each of which embodied an abrupt stylistic shift between various genres of pop music (psychedelia, punk, soul, etc.); also acted in films.

Bowing. The technique of using the *bow on stringed instruments such as the violin. Instruments of the violin family are bowed overhand, i.e., with the palm downward. The most important bowing techniques are briefly described below.
(1) *Legato* [It.]. Legato bowing consists of two basic strokes: down-bow [Fr. *tiré;* Ger. *Abstrich, Herabstrich, Herstrich, Herunterstrich, Niederstrich;* It. *arcata in giù;* Sp. *arco abajo*] and up-bow [Fr. *poussé;* Ger. *Aufstrich, Heraufstrich, Hinstrich;* It. *arcata in su;* Sp. *arco arriba*]. During the down-bow, indicated by the sign in Ex. 1, the hand moves away from the violin; during the up-bow [Ex. 2], the hand moves toward the violin. The slur [Ex. 3] indicates the number of notes to be taken in a single stroke.
(2) *Détaché* [Fr.]. The basic stroke in which notes are taken one per bow. Lines appearing above or below the notes [Ex. 4] indicate a broad, vigorous stroke.
(3) *Martelé* [Fr., hammered; It. *martellato*]. An effect obtained by releasing each stroke forcefully and suddenly. It can be played in any section of the bow and is indicated by an arrowhead [Ex. 5].

(4) *Sautillé* [Fr., bounced; It. *saltando;* Ger. *Springbogen;* Sp. *saltillo*]. A short stroke played at rapid tempos in the middle of the bow so that the bow bounces slightly off the string. It is indicated by dots [Ex. 6]. The same indication is used for the *spiccato* [It., detached], in which the bow is dropped on the string and lifted again after each note.
(5) *Ricochet* [Fr., also *jeté*]. The upper third of the bow is "thrown" on the string so that it bounces a series of rapid notes on the down-bow [Ex. 7]. Usually from two to six notes are taken in one stroke, but up to ten or eleven can be played.
(6) *Louré* [Fr.], *portato* [It.]. A stroke in which each of several notes is separated slightly within a slur [Ex. 8], i.e., without a change in the direction of the bow. It is used for passages of a *cantabile* character.
(7) *Staccato* [It.]. A solo effect theoretically consisting of a number of *martelé* notes taken in the same stroke. It can be executed either up- or down-bow, but the latter is more difficult. When the bow is allowed to spring slightly from the string, it is known as *staccato volante* (flying staccato) [Ex. 9]. See also Staccato.
(8) *Viotti-stroke.* A variant of the staccato, attributed to Giovanni Battista Viotti (1755–1824). It consists of two detached and strongly marked notes, the first of which is unaccented and given very little bow, while the second comes on the accented part of the beat and takes much more bow. Its use is practically limited to the works of Viotti, Rodolphe Kreutzer (1766–1831), and Pierre Rode (1774–1830) [Ex. 10].
(9) *Arpeggio, arpeggiando* [It.]. A bouncing stroke played on broken chords in such a way that successive bounces fall on different strings [Ex. 11].
(10) *Tremolo* [It.]. An effect much used in orchestral music and produced by playing extremely short, rapid up- and down-strokes on one note [Ex. 12]. See Tremolo.
(11) *Sul ponticello* [It.; Fr. *au chevalet;* Ger. *am Steg;* Sp. *sobre el puentecillo*]. A nasal, brittle effect produced by bowing very close to the instrument's bridge.
(12) *Sul tasto, sulla tastiera* [It.; Fr. *sur la touche;* Ger. *am Griffbrett*]. A flutelike effect (hence also called *flautando*) produced by bowing over the end of the fingerboard.
(13) *Col legno* [It.]. Striking the string with the stick rather than the hair.
(14) *Ondulé* [Fr.; It. *ondeggiando*]. A stroke in which the bow alternates between two adjacent strings, either in the same bow-stroke or within a slur. *Bariolage is a form of *ondulé* in which the same pitch is thus alternated, generally using one stopped and one open string. See Tremolo.

Earlier styles of bowing differed considerably from present-day methods. Violin treatises of the 19th century stress the use of a higher wrist and a lower arm; the arm was used less to control the stroke. The lighter, more flexible bows of the 17th and 18th centuries, with their natural clarity of articulation, made a non-legato the customary stroke; on rapid notes, the effect is similar to the modern *sautillé*. The Italian bow grip was not too unlike the modern grip, but the hand was usually held several inches above the frog; the style of bowing involved less pressure and arm movement. The 17th-century French violin bow grip, used to emphasize the metric accents in dance music, placed the thumb on the playing hair; strong beats were played with a downbow.

Viols are bowed underhand, i.e., with the palm upward. The double bass, a hybrid of the viol and violin families of instruments, may be played with either of two styles of bow. The French or Bottesini bow is held in a manner similar to the bows for other instruments of the violin family; the German or Simandl bow, with its high frog producing a considerable distance between stick and hair, is held with the fingers parallel to the stick and the palm upward.

Bowles, Paul (Frederic) (b. Jamaica, N.Y., 30 Dec. 1910). Composer and writer. In the 1930s studied with Copland, Boulanger, Thomson, and Sessions; wrote ballets and incidental music for more than 20 plays of Williams (*The Glass Menagerie*, 1945), Welles, Hellman, Saroyan; his music reflects his interests in Moroccan folk song, Mexican music, and jazz. Works include ballets; 3 operas (*The Wind Remains*, 1943); orchestral music; chamber music; piano music (Preludes, 1934–45); cantatas; and songs.

Boyce, William (b. London, bapt. 11 Sept. 1711; d. Kensington, 7 Feb. 1779). Composer and organist. A choirboy at St. Paul's, studied organ and harmony with Greene; organist at the Earl of Oxford's chapel in London; composer to the Chapel Royal and organist at St. Michael's, Cornhill (1736). Probably during the late 1730s composed the masque *Peleus and*

Thetis; in 1747 his trio sonatas op. 1 were greeted with wide public acclaim. Master of the King's Music (from 1757); in 1758 named one of the organists of the Chapel Royal. As a result of growing deafness, dismissed from his duties at All Hallow's Church (1764) and resigned from St. Michael's (1768). Compiled an important collection of music by Purcell, Gibbons, Blow, and others entitled *Cathedral Music* (1760, 1768, and 1773). Compositions include 17 stage works (most for Drury Lane); other vocal works, including services, anthems, and odes; instrumental music (8 symphonies op. 2, publ. 1760).

Boykan, Martin (b. New York, 12 Apr. 1931). Composer. Studied conducting with Szell at Mannes (1943); composition with Piston at Harvard and with Hindemith in Vienna (1951–52) and at Yale; further studies in Vienna (1953–55); from 1957 taught composition at Brandeis. Later works are in an atonal idiom influenced by Webern and late Stravinsky. In his first mature string quartet (1967) adopted the serial methods that characterize his later compositions.

Braccio [It.]. Arm; **viola da braccio,* a bowed stringed instrument held on the arm rather than on or between the knees [cf. *Viola da gamba*]. The German term *Bratsche* for the viola is a corruption of this term.

Brace [Fr. *accolade*]. The bracket connecting two or more staves to form a *score; also the staves so connected, for which the term system is sometimes used.

Bradbury, William Batchelder (b. York, Maine, 6 Oct. 1816; d. Montclair, N.J., 7 Jan. 1868). Teacher and composer. Studied in Boston with Lowell Mason, also in Europe, primarily Leipzig (1847–49); from 1836 taught singing in Machias, Maine, and St. John's, New Brunswick; from 1840 a church musician in New York, where he organized free singing classes for children in churches. An influential figure in American musical education; published collections of educational material and music; composed over 800 hymns.

Braga, (Antônio) Francisco (b. Rio de Janeiro, 15 Apr. 1868; d. there, 14 Mar. 1945). Composer. From 1885 studied with Moura (clarinet) and Mesquita (composition) at the Rio Conservatory; in 1889 composed *Hino à bandeira* [Hymn to the Flag] which later became the national anthem. Studied with Massenet at the Paris Conservatory (1890–94); in Germany composed *Episódo sinfônico* and the symphonic poem *Marabá*, and in Italy the opera *Tupira*. Returned to Rio around 1900, professor at the National Institute of Music (1902–38).

Braga Santos, (José Manuel) Joly (b. Lisbon, 14 May 1924; d. there, 18 July 1988). Composer and conductor. Studied with Luis de Freitas Branco at the Lisbon Conservatory (1934–43); also conducting with Scherchen, electronic techniques at the Gravesano Acoustic Studio (1957–58), and composition with Mortari in Rome (1959–60); assistant conductor at Oporto and at the National Radio Symphony. His early music adheres to a late Romantic style; he subsequently assimilated electronic and aleatory techniques.

Brahms, Johannes (b. Hamburg, 7 May 1833; d. Vienna, 3 Apr. 1897). Composer. Brought up in poverty near the Hamburg waterfront. In 1853 toured as pianist with violinist Reményi; Joachim recognized Brahms's abilities and recommended him to Liszt and Schumann. Though welcomed by Liszt, did not stay long in Weimar; revisited Joachim and then met the Schumanns in Düsseldorf (Schumann's resulting excitement was conveyed in his famous article "Neue Bahnen"). In 1854 Brahms received news of Robert's attempted suicide; went at once to Düsseldorf and remained with the family until Robert's death in 1856; formed a close but platonic friendship with Clara Schumann that was to endure until her death. Between 1857 and 1859 Brahms spent part of each year at the court of Detmold; the two serenades for orchestra (No. 1 in D major; no. 2 in A major) date from this time; the major work of the period was the Piano Concerto no. 1. In 1859 organized a women's chorus in Hamburg but failed to get a desired post as conductor of the Hamburg Philharmonic; named director of the Vienna Singakademie (1863), settled permanently in Vienna in 1868 although he was often away touring as a pianist and conductor. Produced chamber works, songs, the *Hungarian Dances, and Ein *Deutsches Requiem; the series of large vocal works continued with the *Rhapsodie (Fragment aus Goethe's Harzreise im Winter)* and *Schicksalslied* (1868–71). From 1872–75 conducted concerts of the Gesellschaft der Musikfreunde, and concentrated energy on symphonies, concertos (violin, 1878; violin and cello, 1887) and chamber music. Composed relatively little in 1888–89, and retired from composition in 1890, although later composed the Clarinet Trio and Clarinet Quintet (1891), two clarinet sonatas (1894), and the *Vier ernste Gesänge* (1896) occasioned by the final illness of Clara Schumann. Other works include: *Orchestra.* Symphonies: no. 1 in C minor (1855–76); no. 2 in D major (1877); no. 3 in F major (1883); no. 4 in E minor (1884–85); *Haydn Variations; *Academic Festival Overture; *Tragische Ouvertüre.* 2 Piano concertos (1854–58, 1878–81). *Chamber music.* 3 String quartets (1865–75); 2 String quintets (1882, 1890); 2 String sextets (1859–60, 1864–65); 3 Piano trios (1853–86); 3 Piano quartets (1855–75); Piano Quintet (1861?–64); Trio for violin, horn or viola, and piano in E♭ major (1865). 3 Violin sonatas (1878–79, 1886, 1886–88). 2 Cello sonatas (1862–65). *One or more voices with piano.* 196 solo songs in 32 published collections, including *Liebeslieder. Piano.* 3 Sonatas (1852–53). 5 variation sets, including *Handel Variations; *Paganini Variations; 34 piano pieces in 7 published sets (1878–92).

Brailowsky, Alexander (b. Kiev, 16 Feb. 1896; d. New York, 25 Apr. 1976). Pianist. Studied with Pukhal'ski at the Kiev Conservatory and with Leschetizky in Vienna. Spent World War I in Switzerland, where he worked with Busoni; toured Europe. Gave a series of six all-Chopin recitals in Paris (1924), performed similar series in the U.S. (1937–38, 1960). Also played Liszt, Schumann, and Ravel.

Brain, Dennis (b. London, 17 May 1921; d. on the Barnet bypass near Hatfield, 1 Sept. 1957). Horn player. Studied horn with father Aubrey Brain at the Royal Academy of Music; after the war founded and led the Dennis Brain Wind Ensemble, which in 1955 enlarged to a chamber orchestra; first horn with Royal Philharmonic, then the Philharmonia Orchestra. Died in an automobile accident returning from the Edinburgh Festival; considered the founder of the British school of horn playing.

Brand, Max (b. Lvov, 26 Apr. 1896; d. Langenzersdorf, 5 Apr. 1980). Composer. Studied with Schreker in Vienna; emigrated to the U.S. in 1940. Worked with twelve-tone composition in the 1920s; during the 1960s experimented with electronic media. His opera *Maschinist Hopkins* (1929) was very successful.

Brandenburg Concertos. Six concertos (BWV 1046–51) composed by Bach beginning perhaps as early as 1708 and dedicated to Christian Ludwig, Margrave of Brandenburg, on 24 March 1721. Nos. 2, 4, and 5 are most closely related to the concerto grosso, though the treatment of the violin in no. 4 and of the harpsichord in no. 5 links these works to the solo concerto as well.

Branle [Fr.; It. *brando;* Eng. brawl, brall, brangill]. In the 15th century, one of the steps of the *basse danse,* indicated in dance notation by the letter *b*. In the 16th century, the *branle* was a popular French group dance. A characteristic motion was a side step as the group, holding hands, moved in a large, perhaps circular pattern. As the century progressed, a large number of local varieties developed.

Brant, Henry (Dreyfuss) (b. Montreal, 15 Sept. 1913). Composer. Studied at McGill (1926–29), at New York's Institute of Musical Art (1930–34), and Juilliard (1932–34, under Rubin Goldmark); studied composition privately with Riegger, Antheil, and Fritz Mahler; taught at Columbia (1945–52), Juilliard (1947–54), and Bennington (1957–80). Compositions include works limited to one family of instruments (*Angels and Devils,* flute and flute orchestra, 1931; rev. 1956, 1979); after the 1953 *Antiphony I* for 5 orchestral groups, usually incorporated a spatial element in his music and often presented markedly contrasting styles simultaneously (*Meteor Farm,* orchestra, 2 choruses, 2 percussion groups, jazz orchestra, Javanese gamelan, West African drums and voices, Indian ensemble, and 2 sopranos, 1982).

Brass band. An ensemble composed entirely of brass instruments; especially one consisting of 24 or 25 players including 1 E♭ soprano cornet; 1 *repiano, 4 or 5 solo, 2 second, and 1 or 2 third B♭ cornets; 1 B♭ flugelhorn; 3 E♭ tenor horns (solo, first, and second); 2 B♭ baritones (first and second); 2 B♭ euphoniums; 2 B♭ tenor trombones (first and second); 1 B♭ bass trombone; 2 E♭ basses; and 2 BB♭ basses. Percussion instruments are sometimes added.

Such bands came to prominence in the 1830s not only as military bands, especially for cavalry units, but also as groups of amateurs. In Great Britain, where the tradition of such bands has remained strong, they have often been established as part of recreational and educational programs offered by industry, religious groups, and schools. The Salvation Army has played an especially prominent role in this tradition. In the U.S., such bands were popular through the mid-19th century, but began to decline thereafter in favor of ensembles that mixed brass and reed instruments, as did the bands of John Philip Sousa. See also Symphonic band.

Brass instruments. A family of tubular wind instruments or aerophones most often made of brass and sounded by the buzzing of the player's lips. Each consists of a more or less expanding length of tube with a mouthpiece at one end and a rapidly enlarging or flared opening called a bell at the other end. Common members of this family are the *trumpet, *cornet, *horn, *trombone, *euphonium, and *tuba of European and American bands and orchestras. Not all brass instruments are made of brass. Other materials commonly used are German silver, silver, and copper. Since the middle of the 19th century, brass has also been electroplated with nickel, silver, and gold. Unusual instruments in this family have been made of ceramics, glass, tortoise shell, and solid gold. Recently sousaphones have also been made of fiber glass. Most of the metals used tarnish rapidly, but are kept shiny today by a coating of lacquer.

Simple brasses such as military *bugles will sound only a limited number of tones spaced approximately

according to the *harmonic series. In order to produce additional tones, most brasses are fitted with *valves or a *slide, either of which can lengthen the instrument and provide an additional series of tones with fundamentals on each of several successive half-steps lower. Earlier brasses changed their sounding length by adding sections of tubing called crooks (*natural horn, trumpet) or by opening side holes similar to those on flutes or saxophones (*cornett, *serpent, keyed trumpet, *keyed bugle, *ophicleide).

Bratsche [Ger., fr. It. *braccio*]. Viola.

Braunfels, Walter (b. Frankfurt, 19 Dec. 1882; d. Cologne, 19 Mar. 1954). Composer and pianist. Studied piano with Leschetizky in Vienna and with Thuille and Mottl in Munich; established and directed the Cologne Hochschule für Musik (1925–33); after the war returned to Cologne to reorganize the Hochschule, from which he retired in 1950. His works, which belong to the Romantic tradition, were most popular in the 1920s; they include 10 operas, about 15 orchestral works, chamber music, and songs.

Brautlied [Ger.]. Bridal song.

Bravura [It., skill, bravery]. Virtuosic display of skill by a performer; a composition requiring such display, as in the type of aria known in the 18th century as an *aria di bravura.*

Brawl. *Branle.

Braxton, Anthony (b. Chicago, 4 June 1945). Jazz and avant-garde alto saxophonist, contrabass clarinetist, and composer. As an alto saxophonist played free jazz in Chicago with members of the Association for the Advancement of Creative Musicians (1966–69), including the trio Creative Construction Company; joined Chick Corea's quartet Circle (1970–71). Recorded the album *For Alto* (1968), began giving unaccompanied concerts in 1972; also led groups, recording bop as a contrabass clarinetist and his own compositions; in 1985 joined the faculty of Mills College.

Break. (1) In jazz, a brief, fast-moving, improvised solo, usually played without any accompaniment, that serves as an introduction to a more extended solo or that occurs between passages for the ensemble. (2) In *bluegrass and related styles, an improvised instrumental solo occurring within the framework of an ensemble performance. (3) In singing, the point in the vocal range at which the shift from one register to another takes place.

Breakdown. In U.S. folk music of the rural South beginning about 1850, an animated instrumental (especially fiddle) tune in duple meter, often to accompany dancing; also the associated lively dance.

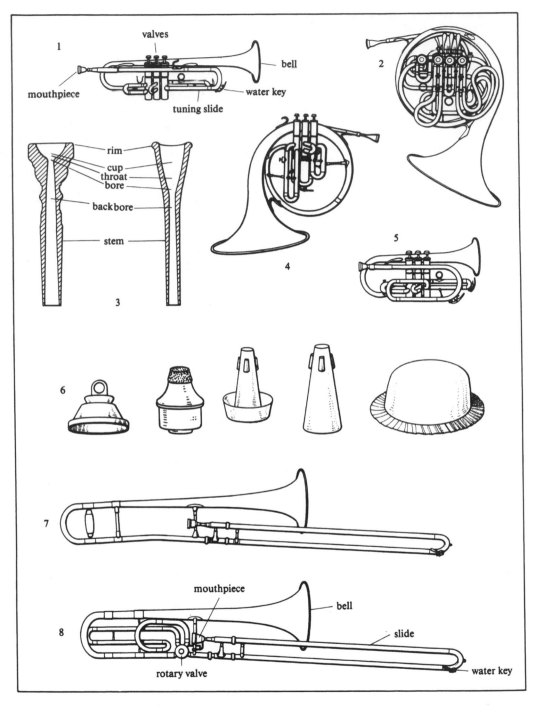

Brass instruments: 1. Trumpet in B♭.   2. French horn.   3. Mouthpieces (not to scale): left, trumpet; right, French horn.
4. Mellophone.   5. Cornet in B♭.   6. Mutes for trumpet (not to scale): plunger, Harmon or wow-wow, cup, straight, hat.
7. Tenor trombone.   8. Bass trombone.

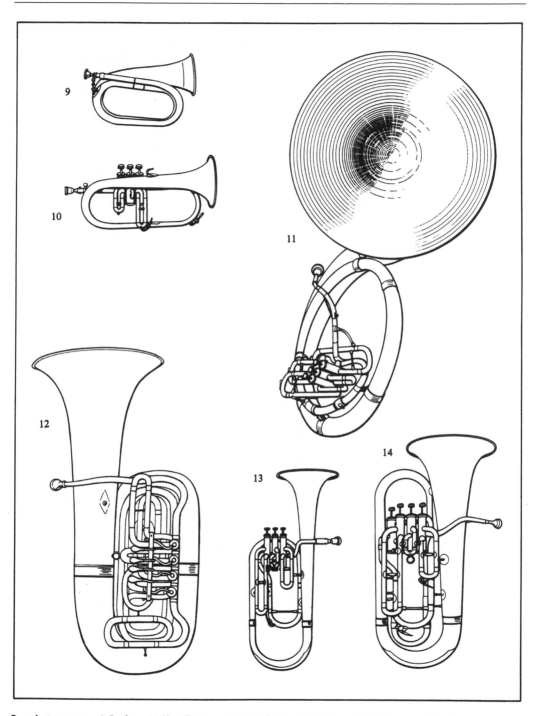

Brass instruments: 9. Bugle. 10. Flugelhorn. 11. Sousaphone. 12. Tuba. 13. Alto horn. 14. Euphonium.

Brass instruments: 15. Ophicleide.   16. Sackbut.   17. Natural horn.   18. Serpent.   19. Natural trumpet.   20. Buisine.
21. Lur.   22. Cornetto.   23. Alphorn (shown half size in relation to others).

Bream, Julian (Alexander) (b. Battersea, London, 15 July 1933). Guitarist and lutenist. Studied at the Royal College of Music; became Segovia's student in 1947. London debut, 1948; subsequently took up the lute. Began a long association with Peter Pears in 1952; toured internationally during the 1950s and after; formed the Julian Bream Consort in 1961.

Brecker, Michael [Mike] (b. Philadelphia, 29 Mar. 1949). Jazz tenor saxophonist. In 1969 formed the jazz-rock group Dreams with his brother Randy and Billy Cobham; worked with Horace Silver (1973–74) and Cobham (1974), then with Randy led The Brecker Brothers (1974–77), whose album of the same name (1975) combines jazz and funk. In 1979 helped form Steps (from 1982, Steps Ahead), a fusion quintet; toured the U.S. and Japan with Herbie Hancock and recorded the album *Michael Brecker* (both 1987).

Breit [Ger.]. *Largo,* broad.

Brel, Jacques (b. Brussels, 8 Apr. 1929; d. Paris, 9 Oct. 1978). Popular singer and songwriter, actor, film director. Began performing in clubs in Paris in 1953; authored and recorded popular songs concerning current social issues, love, and death. Between 1967 and 1973 appeared in 10 films and a musical; his music became widely known in America through Mort Schuman's revue *Jacques Brel Is Alive and Well and Living in Paris* (1968; film version, 1977).

Brendel, Alfred (b. Wiesenberg, Moravia, 5 Jan. 1931). Pianist. Studied with Sofija Dezelic in Zagreb, Ludovica von Kaan in Graz, Paul Baumgartner in Basel, and Edwin Fisher in Lucerne; debut in Graz, 1948. Twice recorded the 32 sonatas of Beethoven; his core repertory includes Mozart, Schubert, and Liszt; also a notable interpreter of Schoenberg and writer of essays on music.

Bresnick, Martin (b. New York, 13 Nov. 1946). Composer. Attended Hartt College; studied with Chowning and Ligeti at Stanford; further studies in Vienna with Einem and Cerha (1969–70); taught at the San Francisco Conservatory, Stanford, and Yale (from 1976). His compositions are often programmatic and explicitly political; his concern with timbre has led to works for multiples of one instrument treated heterophonically or contrapuntally (*Conspiracies,* 5 flutes, 1979); some pieces incorporate electronic music in which a spatial element is important (*Der Signal,* 3 voices, tape, and chamber ensemble, 1982). Other works: *Lady Meil's Dumpe,* synthesizer, computer, 1987; Piano trio, 1988.

Bretón (y Hernández), Tomás (b. Salamanca, 29 Dec. 1850; d. Madrid, 2 Dec. 1923). Composer and conductor. Studied music in Salamanca and at the Madrid Conservatory; beginning in 1874 composed more than 40 zarzuelas; also composed operas (*Los amantes de Teruel).* His most successful zarzuela was *La verbena de la paloma* (1893); his most important opera, *La Dolores* (1895). Taught at the Madrid conservatory from 1901.

Bréval, Jean-Baptiste Sébastien (b. Paris, 6 Nov. 1753; d. Colligis, Aisne, 18 Mar. 1823). Cellist and composer. After study of cello with (Jean-Baptiste?) Cupis taught cello in Paris in the early 1770s. In 1775 published *Six quatuors concertants* op. 1; from 1778 performed frequently as soloist at the Concert spirituel. He was engaged by several Paris orchestras, including the Concert spirituel (1781–91), Théâtre Feydeau (1791–1800), and the Opéra (1801–14, intermittently); published the treatise *Traité de violoncelle* (Paris, 1804).

Breve, brevis [Lat., short]. At the time of the first systematization of *mensural notation in the 13th century, the prevailing short note-value, as distinct from the *longa* or long note-value; now the equivalent of two whole notes or semibreves. See also Note, *Alla breve.*

Breviary [Lat. *breviarium*]. See Liturgical books.

Bréville, Pierre (Eugène Onfroy) de (b. Bar-le-Duc, 21 Feb. 1861; d. Paris, 24 Sept. 1949). Composer. Studied harmony under Dubois at the Paris Conservatory, then worked privately with Franck; taught counterpoint at the Schola cantorum (1898–1902). Composed one opera; much sacred music; secular choral works; songs; orchestral, chamber, and keyboard pieces; a longtime journalistic music critic.

Brian, Havergal (b. Dresden, Staffordshire, 29 Jan. 1876; d. Shoreham, Sussex, 28 Nov. 1972). Composer. As a youth was organist for the church at Meir; around 1907 began composing the large-scale choral and orchestral works that were to occupy him for the next 65 years. Early style showed admiration for Richard Strauss; later formed an individual style marked by late Romantic tonality and dense textures. Works include 5 operas (*Agamemnon,* 1957), 32 symphonies, 1919–68, also *In memoriam* (1911–12); large scale vocal-orchestra works; smaller choral works; songs; chamber music.

Bridge. (1) [Fr. *chevalet;* Ger. *Steg;* It. *ponticello;* Sp. *puente*]. In bowed stringed instruments, a slender wedge-shaped wooden device, usually of unfigured maple, that holds the strings in place and transmits string vibration to the table for amplification by the body of the instrument [see ill. under Violin]. The bridge, with two feet, is held in place on the table between the sound holes by string pressure alone.

(2) A transitional passage whose primary function is to connect two passages of greater weight or importance in the work as a whole. Such passages often embody a modulation, as between the keys of the first and second themes of a work in sonata form.

(3) In jazz and popular music, the 8-bar B section of a tune in 32-bar AABA form; also release or channel.

Bridge, Frank (b. Brighton, 26 Feb. 1879; d. Eastbourne, 10 Jan. 1941). Composer. Studied composition with Stanford at the Royal College of Music (1899–1903); violist with the Joachim Quartet and the English Quartet; also conducted at the Savoy Theatre (1910–11) and Covent Garden (1913). During the late 1920s taught the young Britten, who later became a strong advocate of his music. His compositions are characterized by a highly expressive Romantic idiom, later on approached atonality. Works include an opera (*The Christmas Rose*, 1919–29); orchestral music (*The Sea*, 1911); chamber music (*Elegy*, cello and piano, 1911; 4 string quartets, 1905–37; string sextet, 1906–12); choral and vocal music; Piano Sonata (1926).

Bridgetower, George (Augustus) Polgreen (b. Biala, Poland, 11 Oct. 1778; d. Peckham, Surrey, 29 Feb. 1860). Violinist; son of a black servant, apparently of West Indian origin, and a possibly Polish or German mother. His father toured him as a child prodigy at the Concert spirituel, Paris, then in England; due to mistreatment by his father taken under the protection of the Prince of Wales around 1791; played in London orchestras and as a soloist; served as first violinist in the prince's private music (1795–1809), becoming a respected figure in English musical life. In Vienna met Beethoven, with whom he gave a concert in 1803 which included the premiere of the Kreutzer sonata.

Brillante [It.]. Brilliant.

Brindisi [It.]. In 19th-century Italian opera, a drinking song, most often set for a soloist with a choral response. Examples are found in Verdi's *Macbeth, La traviata,* and *Otello.*

Brio, con; brioso [It.]. With vivacity, spirited.

Brisé [Fr.]. Broken, as in the arpeggiation of chords or detached bowing.

Bristow, George Frederick (b. Brooklyn, 19 Dec. 1825; d. New York, 13 Dec. 1898). Composer. Had some violin lessons from Ole Bull and played in the New York Philharmonic Society (1843–79); also a church organist and choirmaster, conducted choral societies including the New York Harmonic Society (1851–63) and the Mendelssohn Society (1867–71). Best remembered for efforts to establish a school of American serious music; the Americanness of his own music limited largely to some of its subject matter.

Britten, (Edward) Benjamin (b. Lowestoft, Suffolk, 22 Nov. 1913; d. Aldeburgh, 4 Dec. 1976). Composer. As a youth studied harmony and composition with Bridge and piano with Harold Samuel; from 1930 continued studies with Samuel, Ireland, and Arthur Benjamin at the Royal College of Music. In 1933 his *Sinfonietta* (1932) was performed; first popular success was Variations on a Theme of Frank Bridge (1937); began series of collaborations with W. H. Auden (*Ballad of Heroes,* 1939). In 1939 emigrated to the U.S. with tenor Peter Pears; there composed his *Sinfonia da requiem* (1940) and the First String Quartet (1941). Returned to England in 1942; with Pears was active giving concerts during the war years. Pears sang the title role of **Peter Grimes,* which established Britten as one of England's great musical dramatists; it was followed by a number of important instrumental works (*The Young Person's Guide to the Orchestra,* 1946) and by two chamber operas (including **Albert Herring*). In 1948 the first Aldeburgh Festival was mounted; this festival became the center of Britten's activities as composer and performer; works premiered there include *Lachrymae,* viola and piano, 1950; the 3 suites for cello (1964–72); and *A *Midsummer Night's Dream.* The stream of major theater works continued in the 1950s with **Billy Budd* and *The *Turn of the Screw.* The 1960s marked new directions, including a thinning of orchestral textures possibly under the influence of Asian music. With the **War Requiem* he again attracted popular acclaim; his final stage work was **Death in Venice.* Other works include operas (*Gloriana,* 1953; *Owen Wingrave,* 1971); orchestral music (*Simple Symphony,* 1933–34; Piano (1938) and violin (1939) concertos; *Four Sea Interludes* from *Peter Grimes; Suite on English Folk Tunes,* 1974); choral works (*A Boy Was Born,* 1932–33, rev. 1955; Te Deum, 1934; *A *Ceremony of Carols,* 1942; *Rejoice in the Lamb,* 1943; *Missa brevis,* 1959); solo voice (5 Canticles, 1947–75; *A Chain of Lullabies,* 1948); chamber music (3 string quartets, 1941, 1945, 1975; Cello sonata, 1961; *Nocturnal after John Dowland,* guitar 1963).

Brixi, František [Franz] **Xaver** (b. Prague, bapt. 2 Jan. 1732; d. there, 14 Oct. 1771). Composer. In 1749 received a post as organist at St. Gallus Church in Prague; later organist at the Cathedral of St. Vitus (1759); oeuvre comprises nearly 500 works, including oratorios, dramatic cantatas, school dramas, symphonies, and many works for keyboard.

Broadwood, John (b. Cockburnspath, Scotland, Oct. 1732; d. London, 1812). Piano maker. Went to London in 1761 and worked for harpsichord builder Burkat Shudi, with whom he formed a partnership (1770); started own firm in 1773. In the early 1780s produced first grand pianos of his own design; by 1790 had nearly perfected the triple-strung instrument with greatly increased dynamic range that was to become a favorite of Haydn, Clementi, Beethoven, and others.

Brod, Max (b. Prague, 27 May 1884; d. Tel Aviv, 20 Dec. 1968). Composer and writer on music. Translated Janáček's operas into German, promoting international interest in them; emigrated to Palestine (1939), artistic adviser to the Habimah Theatre in Tel Aviv until he died; composed music, wrote books on Janáček and Mahler.

Broderie [Fr.]. (1) Ornament; [pl. *broderies*] vocal ornaments. (2) Auxiliary tone, neighboring tone. See Counterpoint.

Brodsky, Adolph (b. Taganrog, Russia, 2 Apr. [O.S. 21 Mar.] 1851; d. Manchester, England, 22 Jan. 1929). Violinist. Studied under Hellmesberger at the Vienna Conservatory (1860–63); played in the Vienna court orchestra (1866–68); from 1873 studied with Laub at the Moscow Conservatory, succeeding him in 1875. In 1881 premiered Tchaikovsky's Violin Concerto, which was dedicated to him; taught at the Leipzig Conservatory (1883–91, 1891–94), concertmaster of the New York Symphony and the Hallé orchestra (1894–96), violin teacher at the Royal Manchester College of Music.

Broken chord. *Arpeggio; also any figure in which the pitches of a chord are stated successively rather than simultaneously, e.g., the *Alberti bass.

Broken octave. The lowest octave of a keyboard, with one or more accidentals omitted; rare after 1800. See Short octave.

Brookmeyer, Bob [Robert] (b. Kansas City, Mo., 19 Dec. 1929). Jazz valve trombonist, arranger, and pianist. Initially a pianist, concentrated on trombone after working with big bands; joined Stan Getz (1952–53), Gerry Mulligan's combos (1953–57, 1962–64), Jimmy Giuffre's trio (1957–58), and Mulligan's Concert Jazz Band (1960–61). With Clark Terry led a quintet (1961–66), recording the album *The Power of Positively Swinging* (1964). He played in and arranged for the Thad Jones–Mel Lewis Orchestra (1965–68), became its music director in the 1980s when Lewis was the sole leader; from 1968 worked as a studio musician.

Broonzy, Big Bill [William Lee Conley] (b. Scott, Miss., 26 June 1893; d. Chicago, 14 Aug. 1958). Blues singer and guitarist. Recorded as a singer and guitarist from ca. 1926 and with jazz band accompaniment from ca. 1937. Identified with the folk blues revival, Broonzy became one of the first blues musicians to tour regularly in Europe (from 1951); many of his songs became blues standards, including "Big Bill Blues" (1932), "Keep Your Hands Off Her" (1935), and "Too Many Drivers" (1939).

Broschi, Carlo. See Farinelli.

Brott, Alexander (b. Montreal, 17 Mar. 1915). Composer, conductor, and violinist. Studied at McGill Conservatorium (1928–35) and joined Montreal Symphony; continued studies at Juilliard; joined the faculty of McGill University. Concertmaster and assistant conductor of the Montreal Symphony (1945–58).

Brouwer, Leo (b. Havana, 1 Mar. 1939). Composer and guitarist. Studied at Juilliard with Wolpe and Persichetti (1960–61), later with Isadore Freed at Hartt College of Music; assistant music director at Radio Havana (1960–61), professor of composition at Havana Conservatory (1961–67), music director for the Institute of Arts and Cinematographic Industry (from 1969). His early music draws on native popular music; more recently has employed graphically notated aleatory and electronic sound. Works include *La espiral eterna,* guitar (1970); Guitar Concerto (1972); *Homage to Mingus,* jazz ensemble, orchestra (1965).

Brown, Clifford (b. Wilmington, Del., 30 Oct. 1930; d. Pennsylvania Turnpike, 26 June 1956). Jazz trumpeter. Played bop with Charlie Parker (1951) and Tadd Dameron (1953), then toured Europe with Lionel Hampton (1953). After working briefly with Art Blakey, he and Max Roach led a quintet (1954–56) that included Sonny Rollins. Arguably the greatest bop trumpeter; albums include *Clifford Brown and Max Roach* (1954–55, including his compositions "Joy Spring" and "Daahoud"), *Study in Brown* (1955), and *At Basin Street* (1956).

Brown, Earle (Appleton, Jr.) (b. Lunenburg, Mass., 26 Dec. 1926). Composer. Studied at the Schillinger School of Music in New York (1946–50); in the 1950s active at the Darmstadt summer courses and worked for Capitol Records; from 1968 to 1973 taught at Peabody Conservatory; visiting professor at Berkeley, Buffalo, Yale, and in Europe; taught at Aspen in 1975 and 1981. Early compositions are organized serially and are pointillistic in texture; from the early 1950s produced music in which spontaneity and mobility of form are paramount. In 1952 became associated with Cage and Tudor; began to use his "time notation," a graphic notation in which durations are flexible, and to design pieces in "open form."

Brown, James (b. Augusta, Ga., 3 May 1928). Soul singer, songwriter, and bandleader. Sang with the vocal gospel group Famous Flames ("Please, Please, Please," 1956), later toured with a large musical and dance troupe (*Live at the Apollo,* 1963); instrumental in popularizing soul (of which he is often described as the godfather) and funk music. Eexperienced a resurgence of popularity in the 1980s, in part due to appearance in the movies *Blues Brothers* and *Rocky IV.*

Brown, Ray(mond Matthews) (b. Pittsburgh, 13 Oct. 1926). Jazz double bass player. Joined Dizzy Gillespie's bop quintet with Charlie Parker, Bud Powell, and Max Roach (1945), then played in Gillespie's big band, recording "One Bass Hit" (1946) and "Two Bass Hit" (1947); from 1948 accompanied Ella Fitzgerald. Joined Milt Jackson's quartet with Kenny Clarke and John Lewis (1951) and played with Oscar Peterson (1950–66); in 1966 became a studio musician but continued playing jazz as a free-lance; recorded duos with Duke Ellington (1972) and helped form the L.A. Four (1974–ca. 1985).

Browning. Any of a number of 16th- and 17th-century English sets of variations for keyboard, lute, or instrumental ensemble, based on a melody associated with texts such as "The leaves be greene, the nuts be browne." Examples include a set of 20 variations for five parts by William Byrd.

Browning, John (S., Jr.) (b. Denver, 22 May 1933). Pianist. Made his debut at age 10, later worked with Lee Pattison at Occidental College and Rosina Lhévinne at Juilliard; New York debut in 1956. Premiered Barber's Concerto (1962); taught at Northwestern Univ. (975–80) and the Manhattan School (1980–85); repertory includes Mozart, Beethoven, Chopin, Schumann, Debussy, and some American composers.

Brubeck, Dave [David Warren] (b. Concord, Calif., 6 Dec. 1920). Jazz pianist, composer, and bandleader. While studying with Milhaud at Mills College led an octet (1946–49), then formed a trio (1949–51) and a quartet which included Paul Desmond and for which Brubeck composed "In Your Own Sweet Way" (ca. 1952) and "The Duke" (ca. 1954). Later, with Joe Morello (from 1956) and Gene Wright (from 1958) it achieved great success with recordings of Desmond's "Take Five" and Brubeck's "Blue Rondo à la Turk" on the album *Time Out* (1959); the quartet also recorded the album *At Carnegie Hall* (1963). It disbanded in 1967; from the mid-1970s one or more of Brubeck's sons have been among his sidemen.

Bruch, Max (Christian Friedrich) (b. Cologne, 6 Jan. 1838; d. Friedenau, near Berlin, 2 Oct. 1920). Composer. Studied with Ferdinand Hiller in Cologne (1853–57) and with Reinecke (to 1854) and Ferdinand Breunung; taught music in Cologne (1858–61); in 1862–64 lived in Mannheim, where he composed the popular secular cantata *Frithjof.* Music director in Koblenz (1865–67), court Kapellmeister in Sondershausen (1867–70); in 1878 director of the Sternschen

Gesangsverein in Berlin, in 1880–83 conductor of the Liverpool Philharmonic, and after conducting his music in the U.S. in 1883, conductor of the Breslau Orchestra (1883–90). From 1891 to 1910 professor at the Hochschule für Musik, Berlin. Best known in his own time for his choral music, now remembered for works for soloist and orchestra, especially the first (1867) of his 3 violin concertos, the *Scottish Fantasy* (1880) for violin and orchestra, and the *Kol Nidrei.*

Bruckner, Anton (Joseph) (b. Ansfelden, near Linz, 4 Sept. 1824; d. Vienna, 11 Oct. 1896). Composer. Assistant schoolmaster in Windhaag; in 1842 transferred to Kronstorf near St. Florian. In 1845 appointed first assistant teacher at St. Florian; subsequently acting organist (1850); the following year became cathedral organist in Linz. Beginning 1855 had lessons with Simon Sechter, later continued his studies with Otto Kitzler; during this time composed his first orchestral music, including an Overture in G minor (1862–63) and the Symphony "no. 0" (1863–64); became acquainted with Wagner's music. The Mass in D minor, called no. 1 (1864) is often considered his first fully mature work; it was followed by the Mass no. 2 in E minor (1866) and the Symphony no. 1 (1865–66). Bruckner had a nervous breakdown in 1867 and spent three months in a sanatorium at Bad Kreuzen, then composed his last Mass, no. 3 in F minor (1867–68). After Sechter's death in 1867 applied for his posts of court organist and professor at the Univ. of Vienna but was rejected; eventually appointed acting court organist and teacher of harmony and counterpoint at the conservatory; from 1870 to 1874 also taught piano at the teachers' college of St. Anna. Lectured at the university (1876–94), retired from the court chapel in 1892. He composed the first version of his Second Symphony in 1871–72, the Third mostly in 1873, the Fourth ("Romantic") in 1874, the Fifth in 1875. Performances of such large works were not easy to obtain, and audience response was mixed; the balance shifted with the successful premiere of the Seventh in Leipzig in 1884 under Nikisch, who became a champion of Bruckner's work. He died working on his Ninth Symphony (begun 1887), leaving the finale uncompleted. Other works include the Symphonies no. 6 (1879–81) and no. 8 (1884–87); Te Deum (1881–84); many Latin motets and German part songs.

Brueggen, Frans [Franciscus] **(Josef)** (b. Amsterdam, 30 Oct. 1934). Flutist, recorder player, and conductor. Studied transverse flute and recorder at Amsterdam's Vereniging Muzieklyceum (diploma, 1952), then musicology at the Univ. of Amsterdam (1952–56). Founded the Brueggen-Consort (1967); professor of recorder and 18th-century music at Royal Conservatory at The Hague. A leader in the performance of 18th-century music on period instruments; founded the Orchestra of the 18th Century in 1981.

Brüll, Ignaz (b. Prossnitz, now Prostějov, Moravia, 7 Nov. 1846; d. Vienna, 17 Sept. 1907). Composer. Lived in Vienna from 1850, studied piano with Julius Epstein and composition with Otto Dessoff; toured Germany and beyond as concert pianist; a close friend of Brahms; later active as a composer. Works include 10 operas (*Das goldene Kreuz,* Berlin, 1875); a ballet; a symphony; chamber music; part songs; solo songs.

Brumel, Antoine [Anton, Anthonius] (b. 1460, perhaps near Chartres; d. after 1520). Composer. Sang at Chartres Cathedral from 1483; from 1486 until 1492 Master of the Innocents at St. Peter's, Geneva; subsequently a canon at Laon Cathedral; from 1498 to late 1500 Master of the Children at Notre Dame in Paris; for one year a singer at the ducal court in Chambéry; finally *maestro di cappella* at the court of Ferrara from 1506 until 1510, when the chapel was disbanded. Praised by Gaffurius, Zarlino, and others. Works consist chiefly of sacred vocal music with Latin texts, including about 15 complete Masses; secular compositions are probably settings of preexisting melodies.

Brummen, Brummstimme [Ger.]. To hum; **bouche fermée.*

Brün, Herbert (b. Berlin, 9 July 1918). Composer. Studied composition under Wolpe at the Jerusalem Conservatory (1936–38) and at Columbia (1948–49). In Germany and Israel composed for theatrical productions, radio, and TV; lectured on German radio at Darmstadt and on tours in the U.S.; from 1955 to 1961 conducted research on electronic music in Paris, Cologne, and Munich; from 1963 taught electronic and computer music at the Univ. of Illinois, where he composed *Gestures for 11* (1964); other works include ballets, orchestral works, many electronic and computer works.

Bruneau, (Louis-Charles-Bonaventure-) Alfred (b. Paris, 3 Mar. 1857; d. there, 15 June 1934). Composer. Studied cello (under Franchomme), theory (under Savart), and composition (under Massenet) at the Paris Conservatory (1873–81); most famous for *Le rêve* (Opéra-comique, 1891) based on a novel by Zola, who wrote the librettos for *Messidor* (1897) and *L'ouragan* (1901). Bruneau conducted at the Opéra-comique; from 1889 to 1933 wrote music criticism.

Brunette [Fr.]. A type of French song of the 17th and 18th centuries for one to three voices, with or without accompaniment, and with pastoral or amorous texts. A few examples are incorporated in works for harpsichord by Chambonnières and D'Anglebert and in later comic operas.

Brunswick, Mark (b. New York, 6 Jan. 1902; d. London, 26 May 1971). Composer. Studied with Rubin Goldmark, Sessions, and Bloch, and with Boulanger in Paris (1925–29); lived in Vienna in the 1930s, where he was influenced by the twelve-tone method, although continued to favor the tonal music of Bartók and Stravinsky. Returned to the U.S. in 1937 to teach at Greenwich House Music School; taught at Black Mountain College, Kenyon College, and City College of New York (1946–67). Works include a symphony (1945), a choral symphony (*Eros and Death,* 1932–54), chamber music, choral music and songs.

Brush. A fan-shaped array of relatively flexible wires bound together in a retractable handle and used in pairs in playing principally the snare drum and cymbals in jazz and popular music, especially in pieces with slow tempo [see ill. accompanying the drum set under Percussion instruments]. See also *Rute.*

Bruson, Renato (b. Este, 13 Jan. 1936). Baritone. Studied with Elena Fava Ceriati in Padua, debut as Verdi's Count di Luna at Spoleto (1961); subsequently performed at the Met, La Scala, the Edinburgh Festival, and Covent Garden; repertory includes over 80 roles in operas by Rossini, Verdi, Puccini, earlier Wagner, Donizetti, and others.

Bryn-Julson, Phyllis (Mae) (b. Bowdon, N.D., 5 Feb. 1945). Soprano. Studied singing at the Berkshire Music Center, where she worked with Erich Leinsdorf; also with Helen Boatwright at Syracuse Univ.; gave the American premiere of Sessions's *Montezuma* (Boston, 1976). Has taught at the Univ. of Maryland, Kirkland-Hamilton College (N.Y.), and at Peabody. Best known for her performances of 20th-century music, but repertory includes many earlier works as well.

Buccina [Lat.]. A Roman horn or trumpet. Its precise appearance is unknown, but it is described by Latin authors as curved. It was used primarily for military signaling and is not to be confused with the **cornu.* In medieval Latin, *buccina* denoted the straight trumpet [see Tuba (1)]. See also *Buisine.*

Buchner, Hans (b. Ravensburg, 26 Oct. 1483; d. Konstanz?, mid-Feb., 1538). Organist and composer. May have been organist at the court of Emperor Maximilian I; cathedral organist in Konstanz from 1506. Around 1520 wrote a *Fundamentum* which treats aspects of playing the organ, including fingering.

Bucht, Gunnar (b. Stocksund, Sweden, 5 Aug. 1927). Composer. From 1947 studied composition with Blomdahl; in 1953 earned a doctorate in musicology from Uppsala Univ; studied in Germany with Orff, with Petrassi in Rome (1954–62), and with Max Deutsch in Paris; in 1975 became professor of composition at the Stockholm Conservatory; director of the Musikhögskolan in Stockholm from 1987. Composed operas (*Jerikos murar* [Walls of Jericho], 1966–67); orchestral music (7 symphonies, 1952–71); chamber music (2 string quartets, 1951, 1959); *Unter vollem Einsatz,* organ, 5 percussion (1986–87).

Buck, Dudley (b. Hartford, 10 Mar. 1839; d. West Orange, N.J., 6 Oct. 1909). Composer and organist. Educated in Leipzig (1858–59), Dresden (1860–61), and Paris (1861–62). Teacher and church organist in Hartford from 1862; in 1872–75 organist in Boston and teacher at the New England Conservatory. Toured extensively as concert organist until the mid-1870s; from 1875 assistant conductor of the Theodore Thomas orchestra; conductor of a male chorus, the Apollo Club, until retirement in 1903. Organ works include Variations on "The Star Spangled Banner" (1868); also composed sacred and secular cantatas.

Buckwheat note. See Shape-note.

Budd, Harold (b. Los Angeles, 24 May 1936). Composer. Studied at Los Angeles City College (1957–59), San Fernando Valley State College (1961–63), and with Dahl at the Univ. of Southern California (1963–66); faculty member, California Institute of the Arts. Influences on his music include jazz, works of Feldman and Cage, and the minimalists in the graphic arts of the 1960s. Works include *Coeur d'Orr* (tape, soprano saxophone, and/or voices, 1969) and *The Candy Apple Revision* (1970); beginning 1979 abandoned notation, composing and modifying electronic works directly in the studio (*Abandoned Cities,* 1984).

Buff stop. See Harpsichord, Harp stop.

Buffo [It.]. Comic; *opera buffa,* comic opera; *basso buffo,* a male singer of comic roles. A *buffo* role (e.g., Bartolo in Rossini's *Il barbiere di Siviglia*) may call for rapid-fire enunciation of texts. See Patter song.

Buffoons. See *Bouffons.*

Bügelhorn [Ger.]. Bugle.

Bugle [Fr. *bugle, clairon;* Ger. *Signalhorn, Bügelhorn;* It. *cornetta segnale;* Sp. *bugle, corneta*]. (1) A very large-bore soprano brass instrument in *trumpet form. It was used in the 18th century as a signaling instrument, first for hunting and later by military units. Early in the 19th century, the addition of keys [see Keyed bugle] and then *valves gave it a complete chromatic scale and a place as the solo voice of early *brass bands. Complete sets of valved bugles

patterned after the *saxhorns of Adolphe Sax (1814–94) filled out the instrumentation of brass bands of the 1850s and 1860s. Usual sizes ranged from E♭ soprano to E♭ contrabass, alternating at E♭ and B♭ pitches.

(2) A soprano brass signaling instrument without valves used by the military. The most common type in the United States is proportioned like a *trumpet or *cornet. It is pitched from B♭ to F (the same or lower than the B♭ trumpet), is 1.4 to 1.8 m. (4.5 to 6 ft.) in tube length, and usually only plays pitches two through six of the *harmonic series.

(3) An instrument with one or two valves made in various sizes for modern drum and bugle corps [see Bersag horn].

Bühne [Ger.]. Stage. *Bühnenmusik,* *incidental music for a play; also music played on stage in an opera.

Buisine [OFr., also *busine, buysine, buzine,* etc.; related terms are *buccina* and *Posaune*]. From the 12th through the 16th centuries, a trumpet, especially a ceremonial and military signaling instrument. See ill. under Brass instruments.

Bull, John (b. Old Radnor?, 1562–63?; d. Antwerp, 12–13 March 1628). Composer, virginalist, and organist. Lived and worked in both England (at Hereford Cathedral and the royal court in London) and the Low Countries; from 1573 a chorister in both places, organist and master of the choristers in Hereford; from 1586 a Gentleman of the Chapel Royal, serving the royal household in various capacities, especially as composer and organist. In 1613 legal difficulties forced him to leave England, a flight which took him first to Brussels, where Archduke Albert gave him a position in his chapel for a year. Assistant organist (1615), then cathedral organist (1617) at Antwerp Cathedral. Composed keyboard works, sacred vocal works, some compositions for instrumental consort, and over 200 canons.

Bull, Ole (Bornemann) (b. Bergen, 5 Feb. 1810; d. Lysøen, near Bergen, 17 Aug. 1880). Violinist. From 1828 a musician in Christiania (now Oslo); in 1831 went to Paris, where he won attention with an 1833 concert featuring his *Souvenirs de Norvège* with folk tunes played on Norwegian peasant fiddle; toured widely, arousing considerable acclaim in Italy, Britain (1836), northern Europe (including Russia and Scandinavia), and the U.S. (first of many tours, 1843–45). In 1849 founded the Norwegian Theater in Bergen, which was to advance the careers of Ibsen and Bjørnson. A national cultural figure in Norway.

Bull-roarer. An instrument made by attaching a flat, narrow, elongated object to a string and whirling it overhead. As it circles the player, it rotates on its own axis, causing the air to vibrate and producing a roaring or screaming sound. Examples have been discovered in paleolithic excavations and are distributed worldwide.

Bülow, Hans (Guido) von (b. Dresden, 8 Jan. 1830; d. Cairo, 12 Feb. 1894). Conductor and pianist. Studied with Wieck (piano) and Eberwein (harmony) in Dresden, later with Plaidy (piano) and Hauptmann (theory) in Leipzig; Wagner helped his conducting career. After piano study with Liszt (from 1851) toured as a pianist; married Liszt's daughter Cosima. Appointed by Ludwig II court pianist and conductor, director of the conservatory in Munich, where he conducted the premieres of *Tristan und Isolde* and *Die Meistersinger.* In 1869 Cosima left him for Wagner; they divorced in 1870. Bülow resumed touring in 1872, including the U.S. (1875–76, 1889–90); conducted at the court theater in Hannover (1878–80) and Meiningen (1880–85); became close to Brahms and encouraged the young Richard Strauss; conducted the Berlin Philharmonic (1887–93).

Bumbry, Grace (Melzia Ann) (b. St. Louis, 4 Jan. 1937). Soprano and mezzo-soprano. Studied with Lotte Lehmann at Northwestern Univ. and the Music Academy of the West, 1955–58; in London with Lehmann gave a successful debut recital as mezzo-soprano; operatic debut with the Paris Opera in 1960, the same year she joined the Basel Opera. In 1961 became the first black performer to sing at Bayreuth; subsequent debuts at Covent Garden, La Scala, and the Met. In 1970 appeared for the first time as a soprano; within the year had sung Strauss's Salome at Covent Garden and Tosca at the Met. Has also performed roles in operas of Janáček and Dukas.

Bund [Ger.]. *Fret; for *bundfrei,* see Clavichord.

Buonamente, Giovanni Battista (b. Mantua, late 16th century; d. Assisi, 29 Aug. 1642). Composer and violinist. In the service of the Gonzagas at Mantua until at least 1622; served the emperor in Vienna (1626–ca. 1630); violinist at Parma's Madonna della Steccata church (1632); *maestro di cappella* at Assisi from 1633 to his death. Best known for violin ensemble music, which cultivates the "new violin style" that he is credited with having brought to Austria.

Burden. (1) Refrain, especially that of the 15th-century *carol. (2) In 14th- and 15th-century England, the lowest part in a polyphonic complex, whence perhaps the term *faburden.

Burdo [Lat.]. From the late 13th century, *drone, including the sustained tenors of *organum and the pipes and strings producing invariable pitches on instruments. See also *Bourdon.*

Burge, David (Russell) (b. Evanston, Ill., 25 Mar. 1930). Composer and pianist. Studied at Northwest-

ern, at Eastman (1956), and at the Cherubini Conservatory in Florence (1956–57). Taught at Northwestern (1949–52), Whitman College (1957–62), and the Univ. of Colorado (1962–75); chairman of the piano department at Eastman beginning 1975. Conducted Boulder Philharmonic Orchestra (1965–72). Compositions include *Sources,* flute and piano (1964); *that no one knew,* violin, orchestra (1969).

Burgmüller, Johann Friedrich Franz (b. Regensburg, 4 Dec. 1806; d. Beaulieu, near Paris, 13 Feb. 1874). Composer. Settled in Paris around 1832 as pianist, teacher, and composer of salon music for piano and of progressive piano etudes, which remained standard teaching material almost to the present; also composed ballets.

Burgundian school. A group of composers of the 15th century with ties of varying kinds to the court of the Dukes of Burgundy, especially Philip the Good (1419–67) and Charles the Bold (1467–77), or born or active at some time in the duchy of Burgundy, which included eastern France and the Low Countries. Composers loosely grouped under this rubric, the usefulness of which may be doubted, have included Guillaume Dufay (1397 or 1398–1474), Gilles Binchois (ca. 1400–1460), Hayne van Ghizeghem (ca. 1445–between 1472 and 1497), Pierre Fontaine (d. ca. 1450), Nicolas Grenon (ca. 1380–1456), Robert Morton (ca. 1430–ca. 1476), and Antoine Busnois (ca. 1430–92). Particularly characteristic of the period were three-voice *chansons with French text in the uppermost part alone, especially settings of *rondeaux. a form cultivated and circulated internationally. Most of these composers also composed Latin sacred music, however. See also Chanson, Middle Ages, Renaissance.

Burian, Emil František (b. Plzeň, 11 Apr. 1904; d. Prague, 9 Aug. 1959). Composer and stage director. Studied at the Prague Conservatory during the 1920s; also directed and acted on several local stages. In 1924 founded a group for modern music, Přítomnost [Presence]; in 1927 began the Voice Band; during the 1930s directed theaters in Brno and Olomouc and established his own theater, D-34. After the war resumed his theater activities in Brno and Prague. His music shows influences from a variety of sources including jazz, his French contemporaries, Richard Strauss, Janáček, and Czech folk music.

Burkhard, Willy (b. Evilard-sur-Bienne, 17 Apr. 1900; d. Zurich, 18 June 1955). Composer. Studied in Bern, Leipzig, Munich, and Paris; taught composition, theory, and piano and was active as a conductor in Bern (1924–33); lived for a few years in the U.S., but returned to Switzerland and taught at the conservatory in Zurich (1942–55). Wrote in a contrapuntal and modal style, influenced by Scriabin, Stravinsky,

Bartók, and the French impressionists; his liturgical music often used Renaissance and Baroque models.

Burla [It.]. (1) In 18th-century Italian opera, a colloquial term for a comic work. (2) In instrumental music, a humorous piece, for example the "Burla" in Schumann's *Albumblätter* op. 124.

Burleigh, Harry [Henry] **T(hacker)** (b. Erie, Penn., 2 Dec. 1866; d. Stamford, Conn., 12 Sept. 1949). Baritone and composer. Studied at National Conservatory of Music in New York (1892–95); baritone soloist at St. George's Church in New York (1894–1946); soloist at Temple Emanu-El (1900–25). Music editor at Ricordi from 1913 to his death. Wrote over 265 vocal compositions, made 187 choral arrangements of spiritual melodies; published collections of black ministrel melodies.

Burlesca [It.]. A playful or comical piece. Examples of instrumental burlescas include the fifth movement of Bach's Partita in A minor, Richard Strauss's *Burleske* for piano and orchestra, and works by Hiller, Heller, Paderewski, Reger, and Bartók, among others.

Burlesque [Fr.]. (1) *Burlesca. (2) In England beginning in the late 17th century, a satirical parody of a stage work, often of an opera or *ballad opera. (3) In America until about 1860, works similar to those of (2) above; after about 1860 and up to the present, a variety show likely to include comedians and other entertainers, but the principal ingredient of which is striptease.

Burletta. In England in the late 18th and early 19th centuries, an Italian comic opera such as Pergolesi's *La serva padrona* or an English imitation of such a work.

Burmeister, Joachim (b. Lüneburg, 5 Mar. 1564; d. Rostock, 5 May 1629). Theorist and composer. Studied at the Johannisschule in Lüneburg and at the Univ. of Rostock (1586); three years later became Kantor at that town's Nikolaikirche, later at the Marienkirche. Best known for his theoretical writings, especially *Musica autoschediastikē* (1601) and *Musica poetica* (1606; facs., 1955). Rejecting a notion of affections conveyed by mode, adopted instead a theory in which melodic "figures" established the affections; his labels for these figures were widely used and discussed during the 17th century.

Burney, Charles (b. Shrewsbury, 7 Apr. 1726; d. Chelsea, 12 Apr. 1814). Music historian and composer. Apprenticed to Thomas Arne, 1744–46; organist at St. Dionis's Backchurch, London (1749) and at King's Lynn, Norfolk (1751); returned to London in 1760 and taught music to the well-to-do. In 1770 embarked on his brilliantly chronicled travels; although his tours of Italy and France (1770) and of Germany, Austria, and the Netherlands (1772) were made chiefly to gather information for his *General History of Music* (London, 1776–89; R: London, 1937; 1957), the chronicles themselves are immensely valuable, for they detail the author's personal contacts with figures such as Gluck, Hasse, C. P. E. Bach, Quantz, and others.

Burrell, Kenny [Kenneth Earl] (b. Detroit, 31 July 1931). Jazz guitarist. In Detroit played in a bop group with Tommy Flanagan, Pepper Adams, Paul Chambers, and Elvin Jones, and also briefly with Dizzy Gillespie (1951); toured with Oscar Peterson, then settled in New York (1956). Recordings include *Kenny Burrell and John Coltrane* (1958) and *Midnight Blue* (1963), as well as sessions with Billie Holiday, Jimmy Smith, and Stanley Turrentine. Also worked as a soloist and leader, recorded with Mercer Ellington (1984), toured with the Philip Morris Superband (1985–86).

Burt, Francis (b. London, 28 Apr. 1926). Composer. Studied with Howard Ferguson at the Royal Academy of Music and with Blacher in Berlin; in the 1950s settled in Vienna; from 1973 professor at the Hochschule für Musik there. His music shows influence of the late Romantics as well as of African drumming. Works include operas (*Volpone,* 1952–58; rev. 1960–66; *Barnstable, or Someone in the Attic* 1967–69); a ballet; orchestral and vocal music.

Busch, Adolf (Georg Wilhelm) (b. Siegen, Westphalia, 8 Aug. 1891; d. Guilford, Vt., 9 June 1952). Violinist, composer, conductor, brother of Fritz Busch. Studied violin at the Cologne Conservatory; concertmaster of Vienna's Konzertverein Orchestra (1911); professor at Berlin's Musikhochschule (1918); founded the preeminent Busch Quartet. With the rise of the Nazis moved to Switzerland, then to London, and continued to tour widely; moved to the U.S. (1939); established the Marlboro Festival (1950).

Busch, Fritz (b. Siegen, Westphalia, 13 Mar. 1890; d. London, 14 Sept. 1951). Conductor and pianist. Studied conducting at the Cologne Conservatory (1906); conductor at Riga's Deutsches Theater (1909); toured as a pianist (1911–12). In 1918 music director of the Stuttgart Opera, in 1922 appointed general music director of the Dresden Opera; led premieres of works by Busoni and Richard Strauss. Opposition to Hitler led to his dismissal; subsequently divided time between leading the Danish State Radio Symphony (from 1934), directing the Teatro Colón of Buenos Aires (1934–36; 1940–47), and serving as music director of Glyndebourne

(1934–39); also conducted the Stockholm Philharmonic (1937–40). After the war conducted at the Met (1945–49), led the Chicago Symphony (1948–50), and resumed his work in Copenhagen, Stockholm, and Glyndebourne.

Bush, Alan (Dudley) (b. Dulwich, South London, 22 Dec. 1900; d. Watford, England, 31 Oct. 1995). Composer. Studied with Corder at the Royal Academy of Music (1918–22); later studied piano with Schnabel, composition in Ireland (1921–27), musicology in Berlin (1929–31); from 1925 taught composition at the Royal Academy. During the 1950s and 1960s received commissions from East German opera houses and orchestras. His music is marked by a sophisticated but harmonically simple style, which, along with the subjects of his works, reflects his leftist political beliefs.

Busnois [de Busne], Antoine (b. probably Busnes, ca. 1430; d. Bruges, before 6 Nov. 1492). Composer. Before 1467 was in the service of Charles the Bold; shortly after Charles became Duke of Burgundy (1467) Busnois joined his chapel at Dijon; when Charles died his daughter Mary of Burgundy took Busnois into her chapel (1477–82). Little is known about what he did thereafter. Contemporaries considered him second only to Ockeghem as a composer. Sacred compositions comprise 2 complete Masses and about a dozen other works of various types; more prominent are his more than 60 chansons, nearly all with French texts or incipits and mostly in the *formes fixes*.

Busoni, Ferruccio (Dante Michelangiolo Benvenuto) (b. Empoli, near Florence, 1 Apr. 1866; d. Berlin, 27 July 1924). Composer, pianist, writer on music. Grew up in Austria, studied composition with Wilhelm Mayer; in 1881 admitted to the Accademia filarmonica in Bologna. Before settling in Berlin (1894), lived in Vienna, Leipzig, Helsinki, Moscow, Boston, and New York, pursuing career as a virtuoso pianist and teaching. With the Second Violin Sonata (1898) claimed to have "first found his way as a composer": Schoenberg, Bartók, and Varèse replaced Bach, Mendelssohn, and Schuma as influences. Busoni pointed to his *Elegien* for piano (1907) as an expression of his vision of the nature and direction of music. His writings discussed a series of innovatory ideas including microtones, a new style of polyphony, and the abolition of consonance and dissonance. Works include the opera *Doktor Faust* (1916–24); incidental music to *Turandot* (orchestral suite, 1904; basis of his 1917 opera); *Konzertstück,* piano and orchestra, 1890); *Fantasia contrappuntistica,* 4 versions, 1910–22; arrangements and editions of works by Bach, Beethoven, Brahms, Chopin, and others.

Büsser [Busser], (Paul-) Henri (b. Toulouse, 16 Jan. 1872; d. Paris, 30 Dec. 1973). Composer, conductor, organist, and writer. Lived in Paris from 1885, studied at the Conservatory with Franck, Widor (organ), and Guiraud (composition); organist at St. Cloud, near Paris (1892); conductor of the Opéra (from 1905); professor of composition at the Conservatory (1931). Composed prolifically in the French 19th-century tradition but also influenced by Debussy, several of whose works he orchestrated.

Bussotti, Sylvano (b. Florence, 1 Oct. 1931). Composer. At the Florence Conservatory studied violin, harmony, and piano (from 1940); pursued his interest in composition independently (1949–56); met Cage in Darmstadt (1958). Organized exhibition with Chiari, *Musica e segno* (1962), which toured in Europe and the U.S; professor of the history of music drama at L'Aquila Academy of Fine Arts (1971–74); artistic director of La Fenice, Venice (1975). Early works were serial, but in late 1950s turned to aleatoric composition, new vocal techniques, and graphic scores; from 1965 involved with theater, including sets, direction, choreography, and costumes (*L'ispirazione,* 1988).

Butterley, Nigel (Henry) (b. Sydney, 13 May 1935). Composer. From 1952 studied composition at the New South Wales Conservatory; from 1962 took private composition lessons in London with Priaulx Rainer. Received the Italia Prize in 1966 for *In the Head the Fire,* an oratorio-like work for radio, employing aleatory, tape tracks, and various mystical and religious texts. Also composed ballets; orchestral works; chamber and instrumental works; vocal works; piano works (*Letter from Hardy's Bay,* 1971).

Butterworth, George (Sainton Kaye) (b. London, 12 July 1885; d. Pozières, 5 Aug. 1916). Composer. Attended Oxford, wrote music criticism for the London *Times* and later entered the Royal College of Music. Around 1910 befriended Vaughan Williams, whose lost *London Symphony* he helped reconstruct; died in battle in World War I. English folk song played an important role in his music. Works include orchestral pieces (*A Shropshire Lad,* rhapsody, 1912; *The Banks of Green Willow,* idyll, 1913–14); vocal music (*Love Blows as the Wind Blows,* baritone, string quartet, 1914); arrangements.

Butting, Max (b. Berlin, 6 Oct. 1888; d. there, 13 July 1976). Composer. From 1908 studied in Munich at the Akademie der Tonkunst; private composition lessons with Courvoisier. Active in broadcasting in the 1920s; in 1933 began to teach composition for radio plays in Berlin. After the war became adviser to the state broadcasting committee of the German Democratic Republic and a founding member of the

German Academy of Arts. His compositional style was influenced especially by Reger.

Buus, Jacques (b. Ghent? ca. 1500; d. Vienna, between 18 Aug. and 1 Sept. 1565). Composer. May have begun his career in France and certainly maintained French connections throughout his life; organist of St. Mark's, Venice (1541); in 1550 entered the imperial chapel in Vienna, where he remained until his death. He composed motets, chansons (especially Protestant *chansons spirituelles*), and ricercars.

Buxtehude, Dietrich (b. Helsingborg, Denmark, ca. 1637; d. Lübeck, 9 May 1707). Composer and organist. Details of his early life are uncertain. In 1657 or 1658 became organist at Helsingborg; in 1660 was back in Helsingør as organist for the Marienkirche; in 1668 appointed to the prestigious post at the Marienkirche in Lübeck, where he remained the rest of his life. The *Abendmusik* concerts he gave were famous throughout northern Germany, and probably the reason for J. S. Bach's lengthy musical sojourn to Lübeck in 1705–6. Buxtehude's compositions include 114 sacred vocal works (cantatas and motets: *Jesu meine Freud und Lust; Jesu, meines Lebens Leben);* 10 secular vocal works; 89 organ works including toccatas and fugues, preludes and fugues; canzonettas, many chorale preludes ("Ich ruf zu dir, Herr Jesu Christ"); 19 keyboard suites, and chamber works, including trio sonatas opp. 1 and 2.

Buzuq [Ar.]. A *long-necked lute of Syria, Lebanon, and northern Iraq. It has a fretted fingerboard and two or three courses of two or three strings, and it is played with a plectrum. Similar instruments are the Turkish *saz and Greek *bouzouki.

B.V.M. Abbr. for Blessed Virgin Mary [Lat. *B.M.V., Beatae Mariae Virginis*].

BWV. Abbr. for *Bach-Werke-Verzeichnis,* the short title of Wolfgang Schmieder's *Thematisch-systematisches Verzeichnis der musikalischen Werke von Johann Sebastian Bach: Bach-Werke-Verzeichnis* (Leipzig: Breitkopf & Härtel, 1950; 3rd ed., 1961), a thematic catalog of the works of J. S. Bach.

Byard, Jaki (John Anthony, Jr.) (b. Worcester, Mass., 15 June 1922; d. Hollis, Queens, N.Y., 11 Feb. 1999). Jazz pianist, saxophonist, bandleader. Worked widely as a solo pianist, as sideman with Earl Bostic (1949–50), Herb Pomeroy (1955–57), Maynard Ferguson (1962–64 and 1968–70), and with several innovative groups of the 1960s; taught at the New England Conservatory, the Hartt School, and elsewhere. In the late 1970s formed two big bands in Boston and New York, both named the Apollo Stompers.

Byas, Don [Carlos Wesley] (b. Muskogee, Okla., 21 Oct. 1912; d. Amsterdam, 24 Aug. 1972). Jazz tenor saxophonist. Played alto saxophone in the big bands of Bennie Moten and Walter Page. After switching to tenor joined Lionel Hampton (1935), Eddie Barefield, Buck Clayton (1936), Don Redman, Lucky Millinder, Andy Kirk (1939–40), Edgar Hayes, Benny Carter (1940), and Count Basie (1941–43); a sideman with Dizzy Gillespie and Coleman Hawkins. With Redman's band traveled to Europe in 1946, settling in France, and later in the Netherlands and Denmark; toured widely and recorded regularly as a soloist in Europe, making the album *Don Byas Meets Ben Webster* in 1968.

Byrd, Donald (son Toussaint L'Ouverture, II) (b. Detroit, 9 Dec. 1932). Jazz trumpeter. Studied at the Manhattan School of Music, joined Art Blakey (1955) and recorded with many other hard bop groups, playing with John Coltrane on Red Garland's album *All Mornin' Long* (1957). With Pepper Adams led a quintet (1958–61). After studying composition in Europe (1962–63) taught at colleges and universities and continued working as a leader, turning to African American dance music upon the success of his album *Black Byrd.*

Byrd, William (b. Lincoln?, 1543; d. Stondon Massey, Essex, 4 July 1623). Composer. Raised in London and taught by Tallis; organist and Master of the Choristers at Lincoln Cathedral (from 1563); in 1570 became a Gentleman of the Chapel Royal and shared organ duties with Tallis, but connections with Lincoln continued until 1581. In 1593 moved to Stondon Massey, Essex but maintained ties with London. At the Lincoln Cathedral produced most of his English liturgical music; some organ music; some Latin motets; much consort music; and the beginnings of his large body of virginal music. In London after 1570 produced more songs and consort music, a quantity of virginal music, and additional Latin motets. After 1580 wrote Latin motets at a greatly increased rate; also produced a number of consort songs; polyphonic songs; carols; at least one major verse anthem; and more music for virginals. With the move to Stondon Massey turned his attention to writing Catholic liturgical music for practical use, including 3 settings of the Mass Ordinary and the *Gradualia,* 2 books of settings of the Propers of the Mass for all major feasts, Marian feasts, and Marian votive masses; also continued to write consort and polyphonic songs, full and verse anthems, consort pieces for instruments alone, and keyboard music. After 1587 became very active as a publisher, and contributed pieces to several other printed or manuscript books, including My Ladye Nevells Booke (1591) and the *Fitzwilliam Virginal Book (1609–19).

Byrne, David (b. Dumbarton, Scotland, 14 May 1952). Rock songwriter, singer, and guitarist. In 1974 formed the Talking Heads with Tina Weymouth and Chris Frantz (Jerry Harrison joined in 1975); their albums feature his eclectic songwriting, which draws on elements of American minimalism, African polyrhythm (*Remain in Light,* 1980) and country music (*Little Creatures,* 1985). He coproduced their concert film *Stop Making Sense* (1984) and has written for dance and the stage.

Byzantine chant. The medieval sacred music of the Christian churches following the Eastern Orthodox rite. This tradition, principally encompassing the Greek-speaking world [see also Russian and Slavonic chant], developed in Byzantium from the establishment of its capital, Constantinople, in 330 until its conquest in 1453. It is undeniably of composite origin, drawing on the artistic and technical productions of the classical age and on Jewish music, and inspired by the plainsong that evolved in the early Christian cities of Alexandria, Antioch, and Ephesus.

Byzantine chant manuscripts date from the 9th century, while lectionaries of Biblical readings with *ecphonetic notation begin about a century earlier. In common with other dialects in the East and West, Byzantine music is purely vocal and exclusively monodic. The most ancient evidence suggests that hymns and Psalms were originally syllabic or near-syllabic in style. Later, with the development of monasticism, at first in Palestine and then in Constantinople, and with the augmentation of rites and ceremonies in new and magnificent edifices (such as Hagia Sophia), trained choirs, each with its own leader, assumed full musical responsibilities. Consequently after ca. 850 there began a tendency to elaborate and to ornament, and this produced a radically new melismatic style. Fully diastematic Byzantine notation, which can be readily converted into the modern system, surfaces in the last quarter of the 12th century.

Byzantine psalmody and hymnody were systematically assigned to the eight ecclesiastical modes that, from about the 8th century, provided the compositional framework for Eastern and Western musical practices. A special position was accorded to non-Biblical hymnody, within which the generic term *troparion* came to signify a monostrophic stanza, or one of a series of stanzas, in poetic prose of irregular length and accentuated patterns.

C

C. (1) See Pitch names, Letter notation, Hexachord, Pitch. (2) Abbr. for *con (col, colla)*, with, as in **c.a., *c.b., *c.d., *c.o., *c.s;* for *capo*, as in *D.C.* for **da capo;* in guitar music, for *ceja* or *cejilla* [see *Barré*]; for **cantus;* for **contralto*. (3) In modern musical notation, a sign used to specify 4/4 meter. Though it is sometimes said to be an abbreviation for "common meter," it derives from the incomplete circle (C) used in **mensural* notation to specify imperfect *tempus* with minor prolation.

C.a. [It.]. Abbr. for *col arco*, with the bow.

Caamaño, Roberto (b. Buenos Aires, 7 July 1923). Composer and pianist. Studied at the National Conservatory in Buenos Aires; toured Latin America and the U.S. as a pianist; faculty member, the Catholic Univ. (1955), and Buenos Aires Conservatory (from 1956). Artistic director of the Teatro Colón (1960–64).

Cabaça [Port.]. An Afro-Brazilian **rattle consisting of a small gourd covered with a loose network of strung beads. It is held by a handle and shaken with a rotating motion. See ill. under Percussion instruments.

Cabaletta [It.]. In 19th-century Italian opera, the concluding portion of an aria or a duet with several sections. Cabalettas are usually in a rapid, audience-rousing tempo with regular phrase structure. The usual order in the operas of Rossini, Bellini, Donizetti, and their contemporaries (including Verdi through the 1850s) is orchestral introduction; vocal statement; orchestral or orchestral and choral interlude; literal repetition of vocal statement; coda in faster tempo.

Caballé, Montserrat (b. Barcelona, 12 Apr. 1933). Soprano. From 1942 studied at Barcelona's Conservatorio del Liceo. Joined the Basel Opera in 1956, moved to the Bremen Opera in 1960–61. Her 1965 success in Donizetti's *Lucrezia Borgia* led to engagements the same year at Glyndebourne and the Met. In 1972 made her debut at La Scala (as Norma) and Covent Garden (as Violetta).

Cabanilles [Cavanilles], **Juan Bautista José** [Juan Bautista Josep] (b. Algemesí, near Valencia, 4 Sept. 1644; d. Valencia, 29 Apr. 1712). Composer and organist. Moved to Valencia, where he became second organist in 1665 and first organist the following year. Compositions include sacred vocal works and many organ works, especially *tientos*.

Cabezón [Cabeçón], **Antonio de** (b. Castrillo de Matajudíos, near Burgos, 1510; d. Madrid, 26 Mar. 1566). Composer and organist. Blind from infancy; appointed organist to Queen Isabella (1526), subsequently served Prince Philip (later King Philip II). From 1548 to 1556 traveled widely in Europe with the king but settled in Madrid when it became the home of the Spanish royal court. Numerous compositions for organ and stringed keyboard instruments, including *glosas, diferencias* (of which he was a pioneer), *tientos*, and various liturgical pieces such as hymns.

Caça [Sp.]. **Chace.*

Caccia [It., hunt]. An Italian poetic and musical genre of the 14th and early 15th centuries. The texts usually deal with hunting scenes or with similar realistic subjects (e.g., a fire, cries of street vendors, market scenes), often in dialogue. Most of the 25 surviving musical works have two texted upper voices in canon and a textless (and hence presumably instrumental) tenor that does not participate in the canon. Composers of *cacce* include Magister Piero, Giovanni da Cascia, Gherardello da Firenze, Jacopo da Bologna, and Francesco Landini. See also *Chace*.

Caccini, Francesca ["La Cecchina"] (b. Florence, 18 Sept. 1587; d. there? after 1637). Singer and composer, daughter of Giulio Caccini. In 1607 was officially appointed to the service of the Medicis, chiefly as singer, though she also played harpsichord, wrote poetry, and composed. Works include an opera and a collection of solo songs, *Il primo libro delle musiche* (1618).

Caccini, Giulio (b. probably Tivoli, 8 Oct. 1551; d. Florence, buried 10 Dec. 1618). Composer and singer. Studied with Animuccia in Rome and with Scipione delle Palle in Florence; a singer at the Medici court (by 1579) and the Este court in Ferrara (by the 1580s). During the 1570s and 1580s associated with the Camerata of Florence; began composing in a vocal style that closely approximated speech. After a brief appointment in Rome returned to Florence; during the 1590s served the Medici court, from 1600 as music director. That year discussed his new vocal style in the preface to *Euridice. In 1602 (1601 old style) published the epoch-making *Le nuove musiche;* its preface discusses monody in detail. Other works include arias and 2 choruses for the opera *Il rapimento di Cefalo* (1600); *Nuove musiche e nuova maniera di scriverle* (1614).

Cachucha [Sp.]. A popular dance of Andalusia in triple meter, related to the *fandango. Fanny Elssler included an example in the ballet *Le diable boiteux* (1836).

Cadence. (1) [Fr.] In the 17th and 18th centuries, *trill.

(2) [Fr. *cadence;* Ger. *Kadenz, Schluss;* It. *cadenza;* Sp. *cadencia*]. A melodic or harmonic configuration that creates a sense of repose or resolution. Cadences thus most often mark the end of a phrase, period, or complete composition. The strength or finality of cadences varies considerably, however. The cadences of Western tonal music [see Tonality] are usually classified through the *harmonic analysis of their constituent elements and, to a lesser extent, according to the voice leading of the highest and lowest parts. The names that have been assigned to these cadences are for the most part an accumulation of historical accidents. Cadences are the principal means by which tonal music projects the sense of one pitch as a central or tonic pitch in a passage or work.

The strongest cadence in tonal music is the progression from the dominant harmony to the tonic harmony, V–I, and is termed an authentic cadence [Ex. 1]. Other terms for the authentic cadence are final cadence, full cadence, and full close [Fr. *cadence parfaite, c. authentique;* Ger. *Ganzschluss, authentische Kadenz, vollkommene K.;* It. *cadenza perfetta;* Sp. *cadencia perfecta*]. The force of this cadence derives in large measure from the presence in the dominant harmony of the supertonic and the leading tone [see Scale degrees], both of which have functioned historically as tending toward the tonic pitch. This cadence is a microcosm of the tonal system and is the most direct means of establishing a pitch as tonic. It is virtually obligatory as the final structural cadence of a tonal work. When a seventh is added to the dominant harmony, the result is a dominant seventh cadence, V⁷–I [Ex. 2].

The progression IV–I is termed a plagal cadence [Ex. 3; Fr. *cadence plagale;* Ger. *plagale Kadenz, unvollkommene K., Kirchenschluss;* It. *cadenza plagale;* Sp. *cadencia plagal*]. Because it is sung to the word amen at the conclusion of Protestant hymns, it is also termed an amen cadence. As at the conclusion of hymns, it often follows immediately on an authentic cadence and is interpreted in this context as elaborating or prolonging the tonic harmony by means of neighboring-tone motions to the sixth and fourth scale degrees from the fifth and third, respectively.

A deceptive cadence (also termed interrupted) is one in which the dominant is followed by a harmony other than the tonic, most often VI [Ex. 4], but sometimes IV or some other harmony instead [Fr. *cadence interrompue, c. évitée;* Ger. *Trugschluss;* It. *cadenza evitata, c. d'inganno;* Sp. *cadencia evitada, c. interrumpida*]. In the great majority of deceptive cadences, the leading tone in V resolves normally to the tonic pitch, which is contained in the following chord (V–VI, V–IV, V–V⁷/♭ II, etc.), but is harmonized as the third or fifth of the chord rather than as the root. Such cadences can serve to establish or maintain clearly the identity of the tonic while avoiding full closure on the tonic harmony itself.

A half cadence (also termed a half close or an imperfect cadence) ends on the dominant [Ex. 5; Fr. *demi-cadence, cadence suspendue;* Ger. *Halbschluss;* It. *cadenza imperfetta, c. sospesa;* Sp. *semicadencia, cadencia suspendida*]. The dominant is most often preceded by the tonic. The dominant frequently follows a six-four chord with the same bass note, the so-called cadential tonic six-four. When the dominant is preceded by its own dominant [see Tonicization], a half cadence, in which the final harmony must be heard as the dominant, may be difficult to distinguish from a cadence that effects a modulation to the dominant, which is then heard as the local tonic. The half cadence is frequently encountered at the conclusion of the first part of shorter pieces in *binary form.

In the context of tonal music, a Phrygian cadence is one in which the root of the final chord is approached from a semitone above, most often in the form IV⁶–V in minor [Ex. 6]. A Phrygian cadence is thus a type of half cadence, concluding as it does on the dominant. It is a characteristic gesture of Baroque music and often concludes a slow movement that is to be followed immediately by a faster one.

In terms of voice leading, authentic and plagal cadences are termed perfect if both harmonies are in root position and the tonic pitch is sounded in the uppermost voice; otherwise they are imperfect. If one or both harmonies is sounded in inversion rather than root position, a cadence may be termed medial or inverted rather than radical [fr. Lat. *radix,* root].

In polyphonic music, the 13th century saw the emergence of those elements that make up the familiar cadences of tonal music. Principal among these is the approach to a perfect consonance (either perfect fifth or perfect octave) by stepwise contrary motion in two voices, one voice moving a whole tone, the other a semitone. Thus, for example, a major third expands to a perfect fifth and a major sixth to an octave [Ex. 7]. In three-voice music of the 14th century, these two may be combined in the most characteristic cadence of the period [Ex. 8]. Since in this example, both the fifth and the octave are approached by semitone from below, this cadence is sometimes termed the double leading-tone cadence. Because these semitone relationships occur naturally in the Lydian mode with final on F, it is also termed a Lydian cadence. If some other pitch is the final or cadential goal, accidentals are required, though they may not be explicitly notated in contemporaneous sources [see *Musica ficta*]. The same principles also apply in the Phrygian cadence, however, in which the lowest voice moves down a semitone and the upper two upward by a whole tone [Ex. 9]. This occurs naturally in the Phrygian mode with final on E and by means of accidentals on other pitches. When combined with motion in the uppermost part to the sixth scale degree above the cadential goal [Ex. 10], the double leading-tone cadence is sometimes termed a Landini cadence, after Francesco Landini (ca. 1325–97), in whose music it occurs frequently. Cadences of this general type, often including motion to the sixth in one form or another, remained prominent through the 15th century.

The form given in Ex. 11 is sometimes termed Burgundian because of its regular occurrence in the so-called Burgundian chanson of the middle and late 15th century. In this three-voice cadence, the stepwise descent to the cadential goal occurs in the tenor and the ascent to its octave in the uppermost part. If the penultimate simultaneity is to be wholly consonant, the third voice must sound either the third above the tenor or the fifth below. The latter, followed by a leap up a fourth to the cadential goal or up an octave to the fifth [Ex. 12], begins to occur regularly in music of the second half of the 15th century at about the same time that four-voice texture begins to be the norm in sacred music. In four-voice texture, harmonization of the sixth to octave progression with the fifth below the tenor is the only practical alternative if the fourth voice is to avoid parallel fifths or octaves or the awkward voice leading that would result from the doubling of one of the two leading tones or of the supertonic of the double leading-tone cadence. The harmonization with the fifth below the tenor in either three or four voices of course results in a cadence identical in structure to the V–I of tonal harmony, but through the end of the 16th century, theorists such as Gioseffo Zarlino continue to describe it as deriving from the combination of pairs of voices, one of which is the soprano and tenor pair moving from a major sixth to an octave. Only with the advent of the *thoroughbass in the 17th century and the development of harmonic theory by Rameau and others in the 18th does this cadence come to be understood as arising from the root motion V–I in the bass.

Cadenza [It., cadence]. In music for soloist, especially a *concerto or other work with accompanying ensemble, an improvised or written-out ornamental passage performed by the soloist, usually over the penultimate or antepenultimate note or harmony of a prominent cadence. During a cadenza the accompaniment either pauses or sustains a pitch or a chord.

Although a cadenza may occur elsewhere, it most typically ornaments a prominent tonic cadence, such as one before a final *ritornello or *coda. If improvised, it may be indicated by a *fermata in all parts. The typical principal cadenza in the Classical concerto is an elaboration of the progression from the tonic second-inversion or six-four chord, on which the orchestra pauses, to the dominant, the conclusion of which is often marked by a trill by the soloist, to the tonic, with which the orchestra reenters to begin the coda. An *Eingang* is a passage of similar character but smaller dimensions that introduces a section of a work, such as the recurring material in rondo form. If improvised, it may be indicated by a fermata over a dominant seventh chord.

As cadenzas became more elaborate in the 18th and 19th centuries, their thematic reference to the composition increased. Mozart wrote optional cadenzas to many of his concertos for friends and students. Beethoven integrated obligatory cadenzas in his Piano Concerto no. 5. In the 19th century, obligatory cadenzas, often placed in unorthodox positions, became a common feature of vocal and instrumental music, notably in piano works of Chopin and Liszt and the later operas of Verdi. Beethoven, Brahms, and others wrote out cadenzas to earlier composers' concertos, often in anachronistic style. Performers today generally use cadenzas already composed for the standard repertory, though some create their own.

Cadenzato [It.]. Rhythmical.

Cadman, Charles Wakefield (b. Johnstown, Pa., 24 Dec. 1881; d. Los Angeles, 30 Dec. 1946). Composer. Studied music from the age of 13. An interest in American Indian music and culture led to very popular arrangements of American Indian songs ("From the Land of Sky Blue Water," 1909), visits with various tribes and recordings of their music, and lecture-recitals in the U.S. and Europe with the Indian mezzo-soprano Tsianina Redfeather (1913–23). Best known for his parlor songs but also composed stage, orchestral, choral, and chamber works.

Cafaro, Pasquale (b. S. Pietro, near Lecce, 8 Feb. 1716; d. Naples, 25 Oct. 1787). Composer. Studied with Leo and with Nicola and Lorenzo Fago at the Naples Conservatory from 1735. Appointed *secondo maestro* at the conservatory (1759) and *maestro di cappella* of the royal chapel (1771), after which he composed only sacred music. A 4-voice Stabat Mater (1784) became well known outside of Italy; also composed operas.

Caffarelli [Majorano, Gaetano] (b. Bitonto, 12 Apr. 1710; d. Naples, 31 Jan. 1783). Mezzo-soprano castrato. Studied in Naples with Porpora during the early 1720s; in 1726 made his debut in Rome. His fame spread rapidly throughout Italy during the 1730s. Sang at the King's Theatre, London (1737–38), where he created the role of *Serse*, and at Madrid (1739), Vienna (1749), Versailles (1754), and Lisbon (1755). Sang little after 1756.

Cage, John (b. Los Angeles, 5 Sept. 1912; d. New York, 12 Aug. 1992). Composer and writer on music. His influence was achieved less through his academic positions (Wesleyan Univ., 1960–61; Univ. of Cincinnati, 1967; Univ. of Illinois, 1967–69; Univ. of California at Davis, 1969; Norton Lectures at Harvard, 1988–89) than through his explorations of new sounds, indeterminacy, graphic notations, live electronics, and mixed-media events in numerous compositions and writings about music. Visited Paris, Berlin, and Madrid; in 1933 attended Cowell's classes in non-Western, folk, and contemporary music; studied counterpoint with Schoenberg (1934–35). *Imaginary Landscapes* no. 1 (1939) illustrates

his concern with time as a structural unit and with timbre. In 1940 composed his first piece for prepared piano (*Bacchanale,* 1940); used the instrument in dance music from this period. Indeterminacy became important in the compositions of the 1950s, which include the well-known *4'33''* (tacet for any instrument or instruments, 1952) as well as *Imaginary Landscape* no. 5 (1952); the *I Ching* plays a central role in *Music for Piano* (1952–56). In the late 1950s and 1960s theatrical and multimedia events became more frequent and were combined with indeterminacy (*4'33''* no. 2, 1962). In the 1970s Cage became interested in Thoreau (*Renga,* 1976) and in the transformation of literature into music (*Roaratorio, an Irish Circus on Finnegans Wake,* 1979). Writings include *Themes and Variations* (1982) and *I–VI* (1990).

Caisse [Fr.]. Drum.

Caix d'Hervelois, Louis de (b. Amiens, ca. 1680; d. Paris, 1760). Composer and bass viol virtuoso, one of the leading French viol players of his era. May have studied with Sainte-Colombe and Marais. Works include 8 published collections of pieces, 6 for 1 and 2 viols with basso continuo and 2 for transverse flute and continuo.

Caja [Sp.]. Any of a variety of two-headed drums of Spain and Latin America. They are most often played with sticks and are sometimes struck on the frame as well as the heads.

Cakewalk. (1) A dance originating among plantation slaves in the 1840s as a strutting promenade mocking the owner's manners. It became a commercial entertainment in the 1890s and an international hit in social dancing in the period 1898–1903. (2) During the period in which the dance of the same name was popular, a multithematic instrumental march with syncopated melodic rhythms, the simplest of which became a trademark: ♪♩♪ in 2/4. Cakewalks formed a subgenre of *ragtime and American marching band repertories.

Calando [It.]. Decreasing in loudness and often also in tempo.

Caldara, Antonio (b. Venice, ca. 1670; d. Vienna, 28 Dec. 1736). Composer. A chorister at St. Mark's, Venice; was probably educated by Legrenzi. In 1699 appointed *maestro di cappella* to Duke Ferdinando Carlo of Mantua, and composed operas that received lavish productions. Composed 150 solo cantatas during his tenure as *maestro* for Prince Ruspoli in Rome (beginning 1709). In 1716 appointed Imperial Vice-Kapellmeister.

Caldwell, Sarah (b. Maryville, Mo., 6 Mar. 1924). Conductor. Studied at the New England Conservatory. Head of Boston Univ. opera workshop, 1952;

debut as director, 1953. In 1957 formed Opera Group (later the Opera Company of Boston) and acted as producer, director, and conductor for most productions. In 1976 became the first woman to conduct at the Met. Artistic director of the New Opera Company of Israel (from 1983).

Calendric Song. A song associated with a particular time of year (harvest, planting, solstice, equinox) or the life cycle (birth, puberty, marriage).

Call and response. Alternation between two performers or groups of performers, especially between a solo singer and a group of singers. Diverse African musics employ such exchanges between a lead singer's improvisations and a group's recurring response, or between two vocal groups. Black American work songs and gospel music make use of this device.

Callas [Kalogeropoulos], **(Cecilia Sophia Anna) Maria** (b. New York, 2 Dec. 1923; d. Paris, 16 Sept. 1977). Soprano. Moved to Greece (1937), studied voice with Maria Trivella and at the Athens Conservatory with Elvira de Hidalgo. Joined the Athens Royal Opera (1940–45). Debut at the 1947 Verona Festival in La Gioconda launched her international career. After performing dramatic roles (Turandot, Brünnhilde, Kundry) switched to the bel canto roles for which she is best remembered. Debuted as Norma, her most acclaimed role, at Covent Garden (1952), Chicago (1954), and New York (1956); La Scala debut as Aida (1950); other roles included Cherubini's Medea and Donizetti's Lucia. Taught at Juilliard, 1971–72.

Callcott, John Wall (b. Kensington, 20 Nov. 1766; d. Bristol, 15 May 1821). Theorist and composer of glees. From 1784 contributed glees to the Catch Club competitions, composing some 200 during the subsequent decade. Organist at St. Paul, Covent Garden (1789), and at the Female Orphan Asylum (1792). Authored several treatises.

Calliope [the Muse of epic poetry]. An instrument consisting of tuned steam whistles played from a keyboard or operated by a barrel-and-pin mechanism. Patented in 1855, it soon became a feature of showboats, carnivals, and circuses.

Callithump. *Charivari.

Calloway, Cab [Cabell] (b. Rochester, N.Y., 25 Dec. 1907; d. Hockessin, Del., 18 Nov. 1994). Jazz singer and bandleader. Sang with the Alabamians in Chicago, then joined the Missourians at the Cotton Club in Harlem (1931–32). From the late 1930s until 1948 led his own band, which featured Dizzy Gillespie, Cozy Cole, and Milt Hinton, among others; later ap-

peared on Broadway, singing in *Porgy and Bess* (1952–54).

Calmando, calmato [It.]. Becoming calm, quiet.

Calm Sea and Prosperous Voyage. See *Meeresstille und glückliche Fahrt.*

Calore, con; caloroso [It.]. With warmth, passionately.

Calvé (de Roquer), (Rosa-Noémie-) Emma (b. Décazeville, 15 Aug. 1858; d. Millau, Avignon, 6 Jan. 1942). Soprano. Studied with Puget, Marchesi, and, later, Laborde; opera debut in Brussels (1881); subsequently performed in Paris, Milan, New York (the Met, 1893–1904), and London. Best known for her verismo roles.

Calypso. A song style of Trinidad, also established in Jamaica and elsewhere in the Caribbean. Calypso is most distinctive in its texts, which are topical and witty. Calypso singer-composers are specialists esteemed for their verse-making ability, colorful figures with grandiose names (Lord Executor, Atilla the Hun, Mighty Sparrow), frequently enjoying national and sometimes international recognition. Even though modern calypso performance by singers with small, conventional dance bands is common, the traditional percussion accompaniment of older calypsos remains important and today is most characteristically performed by steel bands [see Steel drum].

Calzabigi, Raniero [Ranieri] **(Simone Francesco Maria) de** (b. Livorno, 23 Dec. 1714; d. Naples, July 1795). Author and librettist. In Paris in the 1750s collaborated with Metastasio on an edition of the latter's works. Beginning in 1761 collaborated with Gluck on "reform" operas, which included *Orfeo ed Euridice* and *Alceste.*

Cambert, Robert (b. Paris, ca. 1627; d. London, Feb. or Mar. 1677). Composer and organist. Studied with Chambonnières in Paris; from 1652 to 1673 organist at St. Honoré there; appointed *maître de musique* in 1662. From the mid-1650s collaborated with librettist Pierre Perrin on a series of stage works (*La pastorale*, 1659; *Pomone*, 1671). In London from 1673, where *Ariane* (1674) was performed.

Cambia, cambiano, cambiare [It.]. Change, to change, as when a player is instructed to change instruments or tuning. See also Muta.

Cambiata, nota cambiata [It.; Fr. *note de rechange;* Ger. *Wechselnote;* Sp. *nota cambiada*]. See Counterpoint.

Cambini, Giuseppe Maria (Gioacchino) (b. Livorno, 13 Feb. 1746; d. Bicêtre, 29 Dec. 1825). Composer and violinist. May have studied with Manfredini. Arrived in Paris in the early 1770s; played solo violin at the Concert spirituel and published his op. 1 string quartets (1773). In all, some 600 published instrumental works are attributed to him; also wrote sacred and secular vocal music and stage works. Authored a violin treatise (ca. 1795).

Camera [It.]. Chamber, as in *chamber music *(musica da camera)*. In the Baroque period (ca. 1600–1750), the term identifies music intended for performance outside the church *(*chiesa)*, especially the *concerto da camera* and the *sonata da camera.*

Camerata [It.]. An informal gathering, usually for the purposes of literary, philosophical, or artistic discussion. Specifically, a group of noblemen and musicians who met in the salon of Giovanni de' Bardi in Florence from ca. 1573 to ca. 1582 to discuss poetry, music, and other subjects. The only known participants are the noblemen Bardi and Piero Strozzi, and the musicians Vincenzo Galilei and Giulio Caccini. The influence of the Camerata on the first operas (written in the 1590s) was of a general, indirect nature, and took the form of a desire to recreate the expressive power of ancient Greek music through a new manner of solo song and a belief that ancient Greek drama was sung throughout. These positions reflect the views of the philologist and antiquarian Girolamo Mei, the mentor of the Camerata.

Camidge, Matthew (bapt. York, 25 May 1764; d. there, 23 Oct. 1844). Organist and composer. Appointed organist at York Minster (1799); compiled collections of psalms *(Psalmody for a Single Voice,* 1789). Works include sacred vocal works, chamber music, secular songs, psalm and hymn tunes.

Camminando [It.]. Walking, moving along.

Campana [It., Lat., Sp.]. *Bell (1) (2).

Campane [It.]. *Tubular bells.

Campanelli [It.]. *Glockenspiel.

Campion [Campian], **Thomas** (b. London, bapt. 12 Feb. 1567; d. London, buried 1 Mar. 1620). Poet and composer. Raised in affluence, his masques and other music was performed for noble and royal audiences, including Queen Elizabeth. His first published poems appeared in the early 1590s; his first published songs in 1601. Studied medicine abroad but returned to England by 1607. Works include some 120 songs (most for solo voice) with lute accompaniment; nearly all the texts are by him.

Campo (y Zabaleta), Conrado del (b. Madrid, 28 Oct. 1879; d. there, 17 Mar. 1953). Composer and conductor. Studied with Hierro, Monasterio, and Serrano at the Madrid Conservatory; joined the faculty there in 1915. His music shows the influence of Beethoven and of folk and popular music of Spain; his stage works show the marks of Wagner and Strauss.

Campos-Parsi, Héctor (b. Ponce, Puerto Rico, 1 Oct. 1922). Composer. Attended the Univ. of Puerto Rico at Río Piedras (1934–44) and New England Conservatory (1947–50); also studied with Copland at Tanglewood (1949, 1956) and with Boulanger in Paris (1950–53). Returned to Puerto Rico in the mid-1950s. His music has embraced native popular music and neoclassicism, as well as electronic and aleatoric techniques. Works include ballets *(Urayoan,* 1958); orchestral music *(Tiempo sereno,* strings, 1983); chamber music; keyboard music (Piano Sonata, 1953).

Campra, André (b. Aix-en-Provence, bapt. 4 Dec. 1660; d. Versailles, 29 June 1744). Composer. Entered the choir of the Church of St. Sauveur (1674). After posts as *maître* in Arles (1681–83) and Toulouse (1683–94) became *maître de musique* at Notre Dame; perhaps served in the same capacity at the Collège Louis-le-Grand. Due to contemporary moral strictures governing the production of operas, many of his works were published anonymously *(L'Europe galante,* opera-ballet, 1697). In 1700 gave up his post at Notre Dame and assumed theatrical composition full-time. From 1722 served the Prince of Conti, Louis-Armand de Bourbon; later appointed *sous-maître,* along with Bernier and Gervais, of the royal chapel. Other works include *Iphigénie en Tauride,* 1704; *Idomenée,* 1712; cantatas, over 100 motets and *grands motets;* songs and airs; other sacred vocal works.

Can. [Lat.]. Abbr. for *cantoris.* See *Decani and cantoris.*

Canarie [Fr.; Eng. canary; It., Sp. *canario*]. A very fast Baroque dance movement in duple-compound or triple meter, a fast and heavily accented French *gigue in style. It usually begins with an upbeat and has a dotted note on most strong beats, with regular four-measure phrases and little counterpoint. It was particularly popular in French stage and harpsichord music (Lully, Louis and François Couperin), as well as in German *suites for orchestra or harpsichord (Georg Muffat, J. C. F. Fischer, Telemann). The dance originated in the Canary Islands.

Cancan [Fr.]. A French dance of the 19th century in a fast duple meter and derived from the quadrille. It is most characteristically danced by a line of female dancers in full skirts and ruffled petticoats, with much kicking and thus exposure of the legs. The most celebrated example is in Offenbach's *Orphée aux enfers* (1874).

Canción [Sp.]. (1) Song. (2) In the 15th and early 16th centuries, a type of *villancico. (3) After about

1530, a type of Spanish poem, largely derived from Italian models (particularly the *canzone* stanza), in which 7- and 11-syllable lines alternate freely and which makes use of freely invented rhyme schemes; also a musical setting of such a poem.

Cancionero [Sp., fr. *canción*, song]. A collection of lyric poems, often poems intended for singing, and sometimes including music. In the history of music, the term is often specifically applied to collections of Spanish secular polyphony from the 15th through the early 17th centuries [see also *Romance* (1), *Villancico*].

Cancrizans [Lat., crabwise]. *Retrograde.

Cannabich, (Johann) Christian (Innocenz Bonaventura) (b. Mannheim, bapt. Dec. 1731; d. Frankfurt am Main, 20 Jan. 1798). Composer and violinist. Studied violin with Johann Stamitz and joined the Mannheim orchestra (1744); in the 1750s studied with Jommelli in Rome, and later in Stuttgart and Milan. By 1757 had returned to Mannheim to assume Stamitz's post as first violinist (together with Carl Joseph Toeschi). During the 1760s and 1770s often visited Paris, performing his own works at the Concert spirituel and publishing symphonies and chamber works. In 1774 became director of instrumental music at Mannheim. Composed more than 40 ballet scores, over 75 symphonies and other instrumental music.

Canntaireachd [Gael.]. The notation used for a *pibroch.

Canon [Lat.; fr. Gr. *kanōn*, rule, precept]. (1) The *monochord of ancient Greece, used for acoustical experiments, not for music making. (2) In medieval Europe, a *psaltery. See also *Qānūn.* (3) In the Roman Catholic Mass, the prayer consecrating the elements of communion, said immediately following the Sanctus. (4) A rule or instruction for realizing a composition. In the Middle Ages and Renaissance, such rules were sometimes stated in cryptic fashion and might entail a variety of ways of interpreting a composition's notation, only one of which is the strict form of imitation with which the term has since come to be almost exclusively associated [see (5) below].

(5) Imitation of a complete subject by one or more voices at fixed intervals of pitch and time. If each successive following voice *(comes)* follows the leading voice *(dux)* in every detail, the canon is strict; if, however, the *comes* modifies the *dux* by minor changes in accidentals, the canon is free. Originally, canon referred to the verbal motto or rule by which the *comes* could be derived from the *dux.* In such cases only the *dux* would be notated. Canons may be self-contained entities or may occur within larger pieces (canonic imitation). They may also be combined with independent lines (mixed or accompanied canons) or even with other canons (group or compound canons). In the simple two-part canon of Ex. 1, Bach wrote the *dux* on a single staff and marked the entry of the *comes* with a sign *(signum congruentiae* or *presa).*

Canons are usually classified on the basis of the following elements.

1. The time between entries—*canon ad minimam* (at the half note), *ad semibrevem* (at the whole note), etc.

2. The interval between entries—*canon ad unisonum* (at the unison), *ad epidiapente* (at the fifth above). For example, Bach's *Goldberg Variations* (BWV 988) include nine canons at increasing intervals from a unison to a ninth, and the fifth of Bach's *Canonic Variations on Vom Himmel hoch* (BWV 769) contains four canons by inversion on the chorale theme at the sixth, third, second, and ninth [see Ex. 2].

3. Transformations of the subject, as follows: (a) Inversion *(canon per motu contrario, per arsin et thesin* [see also Arsis and thesis]), in which the *comes* imitates the *dux* upside down [Ex. 2]. (b) Retrograde *(canon cancrizans, al rovescio,* crab canon), in which the *comes* gives the *dux* backwards [Ex. 3]. (c) Retrograde inversion *(canon al contrario riverso),* in which the *comes* gives the *dux* upside down and backwards. (d) Augmentation, in which the note-values of the *comes* are longer by a fixed ratio. (e) Diminution, in which the note-values of the *comes* are shorter [Ex. 4]. (f) A mensuration canon is one in which the *dux* is interpreted simultaneously in different mensurations or *proportions [see also Mensural notation], with the result that the temporal relationship between the voices may shift because of the different interpretation of individual note-values.

4. Ending. Finite canons have a definite ending that may either add notes to the *dux* to make up the time lag between the first and last entries or perhaps add a short coda; infinite canons (perpetual canon, circle canon, *round, *rota) lead straight back to the beginning with an arbitrary ending shown by a fermata *(corona).* In the case of the modulating canon (spiral canon), the *dux* ends in a key different from the one in which it begins; a specific case is the *canon per tonos,* in which the *dux* ends in a key a whole tone higher than the key in which it begins, returning to the original key only after six statements, as in the example in Bach's *Musical Offering* (BWV 1079).

5. Number of canons. Canons combined with other canons (group or compound canons) are indicated by the number of canons (double canon has two, triple canon has three, etc.) and by the number of parts. A two-part double canon has four parts and is thus a canon "four-in-two" [Ex. 5].

1. Canon. Bach, BWV 1075.   2. Canon by inversion. Bach, *Canonic Variations on Vom Himmel hoch* BWV 769, var. 5.
3. Retrograde canon. Bach, *Musical Offering* BWV 1079.   4. Canon by diminution. Bach, 14 canons BWV 1087.
5. Double canon at the octave. Bach, Chorale prelude *In dulci jubilo* BWV 608.

The term mirror canon normally refers to canons by inversion but may also denote canons by retrograde or retrograde inversion. Canons that are fully transcribed are said to be resolved canons whereas those that must be deciphered (i.e., in which only the *dux* is written out) are unresolved. Unresolved canons inscribed with cryptic instructions for resolution are called riddle or enigmatic canons. If a canon is capable of more than one solution it is termed polymorphous. Accompaniments to mixed canons may be based on freely composed melodies (*Goldberg Variations*, canons 1–8), preexistent *cantus firmi (Musical Offering)*, or a ground bass (14 canons BWV 1087).

Canonic imitation can be traced back at least to the 13th century and was possibly related to the principle of *voice exchange as found, for example, in motets and the three-part English *rondellus*. The earliest known canon is the 13th-century English round *"Sumer is icumen in," a four-part infinite canon sung over a two-voice *pes*. Fourteenth-century genres related to the canon are the French *chace and the Italian *caccia*.

Canonic imitation. Strict *imitation, as in a *canon.

Canonical hours. The services making up the *Office.

Canso [Prov.]. *Canzo.

Cantabile [It.]. Singable, songlike.

Cantando [It.]. Singing, *cantabile.

Cantata [It.]. A composite vocal genre of the Baroque era, consisting of a succession of *recitatives, *ariosos, and set-pieces (e.g., *arias, duets, and choruses). A cantata may be either secular or sacred in subject matter and function, and its treatment may be lyrical, allegorical, or dramatic (although almost never actually staged). Cantatas range from intimate, small-scale works for solo singer or singers and restricted accompanimental forces (sometimes called chamber cantatas) to large ones with chorus and orchestral accompaniment. Such large cantatas were often composed to celebrate or commemorate specific events. The cantata originated early in the 17th century in Italy, where the term was first used simply to indicate a piece to be sung (as opposed to *sonata, to be played on instruments). The most frequently performed cantatas today are those of Bach; they are sacred works with German texts and were intended for performance during Lutheran church services. The typical Bach cantata employs several soloists and chorus and is accompanied by a small orchestra.

The 17th-century Italian cantata was a distinctly secular work intended for performance at private social gatherings; and it was composed, most often, for a solo voice accompanied by only *basso continuo*

[see Thoroughbass]. The evolution of the Italian cantata can be roughly divided into three periods. In the first period, through about 1620, the repertory was usually published, a circumstance suggesting that this music was apt for both professional singers and competent amateurs. It includes simple strophic arias, *strophic variations, and monodic *madrigals [see also Monody]. Generically this early published repertory is known to historians as monody, although that term rarely appears in the prints. Its leading composers include Giulio Caccini (ca. 1550–1618), Sigismondo d'India (ca. 1580–1629), and Stefano Landi (ca. 1590–1639).

In the second period—the 1630s and 40s—this monodic repertory was printed with decreasing regularity, a circumstance indicating that amateur performers were leaving it to professionals—opera singers in particular. The principal locale for the cultivation of the cantata during this period was Rome. The forms of cantatas during this period are, like those of monody, characterized by amazing variety. Arias grew in size, and in the latter half of the century a new form-dynamic reigned briefly, the aria in two strophes. Among the composers of this rich period are Luigi Rossi (1598–1653), Marco Marazzoli (ca. 1602–62), Giacomo Carissimi (1605–74), Antonio Cesti (1623–69), Alessandro Stradella (1644?–82), and Agostino Steffani (1654–1728).

The third period is characterized by the prevailing use of the da capo *aria. A typical early 18th-century Italian cantata involves a sequence of two or three da capo arias, each of which is prepared by a recitative. In the 18th century, composers produced a large repertory of cantatas that, though still involving solo voices and lacking choruses, now had rather ample orchestral accompaniments. The demand for Italian cantatas in the first half of the 18th century stimulated prodigious output by, among others, Alessandro Scarlatti (1660–1725), Giovanni Bononcini (1670–1747), Handel (1685–1759), Benedetto Marcello (1686–1739), Nicola Porpora (1686–1768), and Johann Adolf Hasse (1699–1783).

During this same period, there appeared numerous composers in northern Europe (England and France as well as the German-speaking countries) who set texts in their own languages, producing cantatas that were inspired by the Italian models. Among the French composers were André Campra (1660–1744), Michel Montéclair (1667–1737), Louis-Nicolas Clérambault (1676–1749), and Jean-Philippe Rameau (1683–1764). Among the English composers were John Pepusch (1667–1752), John Stanley (1713–86), and Thomas Arne (1710–88).

As the Lutheran motet developed in the 17th century, it became longer, often expanding into a work with many sections. Along with the chorus, it frequently employed solo singers as well as instruments. This extremely varied repertory came under the influence of the Italian cantata as it began to include passages of recitative and arias in da capo form. Within the Lutheran service, these often quite lengthy sacred cantatas functioned as sermons in music, preceding the actual sermon itself.

The approximately 200 surviving cantatas of Bach (out of a substantially greater number that he is thought to have composed) embody much of this long tradition. Most of Bach's cantatas employ a chorus, but a few are for solo singers only. Chorales are also employed in a variety of ways, many works concluding with a largely homophonic four-part setting of one strophe. See also Chorale cantata.

During the latter half of the 18th century and continuing into the 19th and 20th centuries, the cantata evolved into a miniature *oratorio, usually secular and frequently involving classical or allegorical motifs. Such works, requiring the forces of an orchestra, a chorus, and soloists, were often produced on special commission to celebrate some important occasion. Many cantatas composed to meet the academic requirements of the French *Prix de Rome (the most celebrated of which is Debussy's L'enfant prodigue, 1884) emphasize tradition. In England the 19th and 20th centuries have seen a steady cultivation of the cantata, including works by Parry, Sullivan, Stanford, Elgar, Vaughan Williams, and Britten.

Cante flamenco, cante hondo, cante jondo [Sp.]. See Flamenco.

Cantelli, Guido (b. Novara, Italy, 27 Apr. 1920; d. Orly Airport, near Paris, 24 Nov. 1956). Conductor. Artistic director of Novara's Teatro Coccia (1943). Spent 1943–45 in concentration camps and (after his health collapsed) Stettin, and (after his escape) in Milan. Debut with La Scala, 1945; U.S. debut with NBC Symphony, 1949. Led other major orchestras, active at La Scala (1954–56). Died in a plane crash.

Canteloube (de Malaret), (Marie) Joseph (b. Annonay, 21 Oct. 1879; d. Grigny, Seine-et-Oise, 4 Nov. 1957). Composer and writer. Studied at the Schola cantorum with d'Indy from 1901. Most of his music reflects either his interest in depicting his native landscape in the Auvergne region or his activities as a folk song collector and arranger. Works include 2 operas, a symphonic poem and other orchestral music, chamber music, songs, choral and solo arrangements of folk songs.

Canti carnascialeschi [It.]. Any of various kinds of Florentine carnival part songs sung by masquers on foot or by costumed performers on decorated carts, as part of the festivities at pre-Lenten Carnival, at Calendimaggio (1 May), and on the feast of San Giovanni (24 June). The surviving repertory comes chiefly from the first 20 years of the 16th century and

is homophonic, rhythmically crisp, and of appropriately choral, "outdoor" character.

Canticle [Lat. canticum, dim. canticulum]. A song or lyrical passage from a book of the Bible other than the Book of Psalms; sometimes also the *"Te Deum." Canticles play an ancient and important role in the liturgies of both the Eastern and Western Christian churches. In the Roman rite, three canticles from the New Testament, *"Benedictus Dominus Deus Israel," *"Magnificat," and *"Nunc dimittis," are sung daily at Lauds, Vespers, and Compline, respectively [see Office]. In the Anglican rite, the first of these is sung at Morning Prayer, and the last two at Evening Prayer. In Gregorian chant, canticles are sung with *antiphons and *psalm tones similar to those employed with the Psalms.

Canticum [Lat.]. Song, *canticle.

Cantiga [Sp., Port.]. A medieval monophonic song of the Iberian peninsula. Although the term is generic and may refer to both sacred and secular poems (including, e.g., cantigas de amigo, love poems in feminine voice), it is most often used to refer to the Cantigas de Santa María of Alfonso el Sabio (Alfonso the Wise, 1221–84, King of Castile and León from 1252). This repertory of more than 400 songs has texts in Galician-Portuguese, cast in the form of the zajal (hence the family of the *villancico and *virelai), most of which narrate miracles of the Virgin Mary.

Cantilena [Lat.]. (1) In the Middle Ages, song, melody, including liturgical chant as well as secular song. (2) From the 13th through the 15th century, polyphonic song, especially the French *chanson. (3) In the 19th century and since, a lyrical vocal melody or an instrumental melody of similar character.

Cantillation. The speechlike chanting of a liturgical text. The term is used especially, though not exclusively, with respect to Jewish music. For the notation used for such chanting, see Ecphonetic notation.

Cantino [It.; Fr. chanterelle; Ger. Sangsaite]. The highest-pitched string of a stringed instrument, especially the E string of the violin.

Cantio [Lat.]. Song, especially the monophonic song of the Middle Ages with Latin, sacred, nonliturgical, strophic text, often with a refrain. See also Cantio sacra.

Cantio sacra [Lat., pl. cantiones sacrae]. Sacred song; especially in the 16th and 17th centuries, the *motet.

Cantionale [Lat.; Ger. also Kantionale]. A collection from the late 16th or early 17th century of chorales or hymns intended for German Protestant liturgical use, especially one containing homophonic settings in four parts with the melody in the uppermost part.

Cantique [Fr.]. Canticle; hymn; any religious song with French text.

Canto [It.; Sp.]. (1) Song, melody; *c. piano* [It.], *c. llano* [Sp.], plainsong; *c. fermo, *cantus firmus; col c.*, an instruction for the accompanist to follow the lead of the singer of the melody. See also *Bel canto, Canti carnascialeschi, Canto de órgano.* (2) The soprano or highest part in vocal music. (3) The art of singing.

Canto de órgano [Sp.]. In Spain from the 14th through the 18th centuries, measured or *mensural music, especially vocal polyphony, as distinct from plainsong *(canto llano).*

Cantor [Lat.; Heb. *chazzan*]. (1) In Jewish and Latin-Christian liturgical music, a solo singer. (2) In the Lutheran Church, the director of music of a church [see Kantor].

Cantoris [Lat.]. See *Decani and cantoris.*

Cantus [Lat., song, tune, melody]. (1) Chant, liturgical plainsong; i.e., a single piece of chant, or a repertory of such pieces, such as *cantus gregorianus, ambrosianus, romanus,* etc.; in *Ambrosian chant, the equivalent of the Gregorian *tract. (2) In 9th- to 13th-century polyphony, a chant or a portion of a chant to which an added voice *(discantus)* was improvised or composed. (3) In 14th-, 15th-, and especially 16th-century polyphony, the topmost part (abbr. C.) of a polyphonic work, regardless of vocal range. (4) Any song or vocal work.

Cantus firmus [Lat., pl. *cantus (canti) firmi;* It., *canto fermo*]. A preexistent melody used as the basis of a new polyphonic composition. A *cantus firmus* may be derived from sacred or secular music or may be freely invented; its pitch content may be preserved intact or elaborated in the new composition; its rhythm or phrase structure may or may not be retained. It is often stated in long notes. The use of *cantus firmi* is common throughout the Middle Ages and Renaissance.

Perhaps the most important use of preexistent melodies after the 16th century was in Lutheran organ and vocal music, commonly based on chorale melodies [see Organ chorale]. The employment of given melodies for instruction in counterpoint, still common today, is probably most firmly linked to the name of Johann Joseph Fux (1660–1741) [see Species counterpoint].

Cantus prius factus [Lat., previously made song]. *Cantus firmus.*

Canzo, canso, chanso [Prov., song; Fr. *chanson*]. In the *troubadour repertory, the principal vehicle for the expression of *fin' amor* [Prov., refined love]. The melody of the *canso* is often cast in an AAB musical form [see Bar form].

Canzona [It., song; see also *Canzone*]. An instrumental composition of the 16th and 17th centuries having as its prototype the French *chanson [It. *canzona francese*]. The ensemble canzona *(canzona da sonare)* eventually influenced and gave way to the *sonata, *concerto, and other multimovement genres of the Baroque, while the keyboard canzona, along with the *ricercar, laid a foundation for the *fugue.

The Italian vogue for transcriptions of chansons began in the 1530s and lute transcriptions remained a staple throughout the century, although they seldom spawned original works, as did transcriptions in the keyboard and ensemble repertories. The independently conceived keyboard canzona reached its culmination early in the 17th century in the works of Girolamo Frescobaldi. The ensemble canzona grew in directions quite separate from the keyboard one. Original ensemble canzonas antedate those for solo instruments by nearly two decades.

In some 40 canzonas (published in Venice in 1597, 1615), Giovanni Gabrieli absorbed the legacy of the ensemble canzona and realized its potential in works that exploit the color contrasts of the *cori spezzati* tradition at the Basilica of St. Mark. His canzonas and sonatas *a 4* to *a 22* for cornetts, violins, trombones, and organ continuo divide into sections, some very short, almost "quiltlike," that pit from two to five groups of instruments *(cori)* against one another in alternation, one group echoing another, or repeating or contrasting textures of sound in a spatially oriented style. His canzonas were imitated by German composers, such as Hans Leo Hassler (Nuremberg, 1601), Johann Hermann Schein (Wittenberg, 1609; Leipzig, 1615), and especially Samuel Scheidt (Hamburg, 1621).

Tarquinio Merula (Venice, 1615, 1637), Maurizio Cazzati (Venice, 1642), and others wrote canzonas for two violins and continuo that trace the gradual fusion of the canzona and the trio sonata. Frescobaldi's (Venice, 1635) canzonas mark formal changes toward the *sonata da chiesa,* with expanded chordal adagios separating spirited fugal sections in a variety of meters and tempos, unified by thematic variation. By the second half of the 17th century, sonata had virtually ousted canzona as a name for the central tradition of ensemble music.

The earliest original keyboard canzonas include 13 by Vincenzo Pellegrini (Venice, 1599) and 5 by Giovanni Gabrieli, both of whom worked within the northern Italian milieu of the ensemble canzona. A southern school of Giovanni de Macque (Rome,

1586; Basel, 1617), Ascanio Mayone (Naples, 1609), and Giovanni Maria Trabaci (Naples, 1603, 1615) provides a link with Frescobaldi. Neapolitan canzonas lace together one to three ingeniously combined and varied subjects (some use contrary motion) in contrasting sections with sudden changes of meter, tempo, and figuration, providing examples of both the "quilt" and variation canzona. Frescobaldi's (Rome, 1615, 1627, 1628, and Venice, 1635, 1645) are essays concentrated in three to six sections of imitation connected with toccatalike flourishes or *adagio* interludes. The canzona declined in Italy after Frescobaldi, being sustained through the 17th century and into the 18th mainly by south German composers such as Johann Kaspar Kerll, Gottlieb Muffat, and Frescobaldi's student Johann Jacob Froberger,whose canzonas feature a succession of fugal expositions in which a subject is recast in fresh rhythmic guises.

Toward the 17th century's end, differences began to widen between the canzona and the ricercar, capriccio, and fantasia, which all draw upon similar constructive principles. By the early 18th century, the fantasia and capriccio had become freely organized, nearly improvisational structures, whereas the ricercar and canzona had merged into the fugue. Nevertheless, the slower-moving *alla breve* meter and archaic contrapuntal devices of the ricercar distinguish it from the faster, lighter subjects and moods of the canzona.

Canzone [It., pl. *canzoni*]. (1) A poetic form defined by Dante and made popular by Petrarch, having five to seven stanzas of identical scheme and often ending with a shorter final stanza *(commiato)*. Iambic lines of seven and eleven syllables are freely mixed. Petrarch's *canzoni* are love lyrics; they were popular with 16th-century madrigalists, who set whole *canzoni* as cycles or, more often, chose individual stanzas. *Canzone* was used as a general term for serious madrigals; it was also employed for lighter forms, with words such as *villanesca* attached. The instrumental genre now known as the *canzona* was often spelled *canzon* or *canzone* in the 16th century.

(2) Song. In the 18th and 19th centuries, the term (sometimes spelled *canzona*) was occasionally applied to songlike works for voice (e.g., "Voi che sapete" in Mozart's *Le nozze di Figaro*) or instruments (e.g., the slow movement of Tchaikovsky's Symphony no. 4).

Canzonet [Eng.], **canzonetta** [It.]. A light vocal piece popular in Italy from the 1560s, in England at the end of the 16th century, and in Germany in the early 17th century. The first examples are homophonic in style but of greater refinement than the *villanella,* which employs similar texts. Later the

term came to mean, in England and Germany, a strophic solo song.

Caoine [Gael., pronounced *keen*]. In Ireland from the 8th to the 20th centuries, a lament sung at a funeral or wake. See also Coronach.

Cape, Safford (b. Denver, 28 June 1906; d. Brussels, 26 Mar. 1973). Conductor. In 1925 moved to Brussels and studied musicology under Charles van den Borren; in 1933 founded the Pro Musica Antiqua to perform medieval and Renaissance music in accordance with the latest scholarship. Composed chamber music and songs.

Capet, Lucien (b. Paris, 8 Jan. 1873; d. there, 18 Dec. 1928). Violinist and composer. Studied violin at the Paris Conservatory (1888–93); founded the Capet Quartet (1893–1921) which did much to promote the Beethoven quartets in France. Concertmaster of the Concerts Lamoureux (1896–99); taught in Bordeaux (1899–1903) and at the Paris Conservatory (1907–28); wrote monographs on the Beethoven quartets and on violin technique. Composed 5 string quartets, other chamber and orchestral music.

Capitolo [It.]. A verse form used by the frottolists [see *Frottola*], consisting of three-line stanzas of eleven-syllable iambic meter in an interlocking rhyme scheme (aba bcb cdc; the last stanza sometimes had a fourth line).

Caplet, André (b. Le Havre, 23 Nov. 1878; d. Neuilly-sur-Seine, 22 Apr. 1925). Composer and conductor. Entered the Paris Conservatory in 1896. By 1899 was director of music at the Odéon Theater; conducted the Boston Opera orchestra (1910–14). His early compositional style is related to that of Debussy; at Debussy's request he orchestrated part of *Le martyre de Saint-Sébastien* and conducted the premiere. Later compositions became more innovatory. Works include *Septet* (3 voices and string quartet, 1909); *Conte fantastique* (harp and string quartet, 1919), *2 Divertissements* (solo harp, 1924).

Capo, capotasto [It.]. (1) A device for transposing on a fretted stringed instrument such as a guitar. It consists of a bar that can be affixed to the fingerboard by means of a spring mechanism or elastic, thereby stopping all strings at a desired fret and raising the pitch by a desired number of semitones without requiring a change in fingering by the player. (2) *Barré*. See also *Da capo*.

Cappella [It.]. *Chapel; a cappella* (in the manner of a chapel), pertaining to choral music without instrumental accompaniment.

Capriccio [It., whim; Eng., Fr. *caprice*]. A humorous, fanciful, or bizarre composition, often characterized by an idiosyncratic departure from current stylistic norms. The capriccio has been closely allied with pieces called *fantasia but is more extreme in contrasts and more daring in deviating from conventions of harmony and counterpoint.

The term is first used in the 16th century for vocal works, but it more frequently identifies instrumental pieces. In the 17th and 18th centuries, the capriccio may also be a dance-song or movement in a suite, partita, or *sonata da camera*. One type of capriccio, a precursor of the fugue, draws upon the abstract contrapuntal learnedness of the contemporaneous fantasia and canzona [see Fantasia]. Another type of Baroque capriccio is programmatic.

The instruction *a capriccio* indicates a passage played in free tempo, e.g., a cadenza. This leads to a tradition of virtuoso technical etudes, including sets by Veracini (in op. 2, 1744), Rodolphe Kreutzer (*40 Études ou caprices,* 1796), Paganini (24 Caprices op. 1, ca. 1805), and Pierre Rode (*24 Caprices en forme d'études* op. 22, ca. 1815). The title was also used for fanciful pieces by Weber, Mendelssohn, Brahms, Stravinsky, and Penderecki.

(2) Opera in one act by Richard Strauss (libretto by Clemens Krauss, with contributions by the composer and others), produced in Munich in 1942. The authors call the work "a conversation piece for music." Setting: near Paris, around 1775.

Capriccio espagnol [Fr., Spanish Capriccio]. A symphonic suite in five sections, op. 34 (1887), by Rimsky-Korsakov employing some characteristic Spanish rhythms and melodic figures.

Capriccio italien [Fr., Italian Capriccio]. A symphonic poem by Tchaikovsky, op. 45 (1880), composed during a visit to Italy and employing Italian folk songs.

Capriccioso, capricciosamente, a capriccio [It.]. Capricious, capriciously, at the player's whim. See Capriccio.

Caprice [Fr.]. *Capriccio.

Cara, Marchetto [Marco, Marcus, Marchettus] (b. in or near Verona, ca. 1470; d. Mantua, 1525?). Composer, lutenist, and singer. With Tromboncino one of the foremost composers of frottolas. From 1494 or earlier until 1525 served the Gonzaga court in Mantua; from 1502 traveled to numerous cities in northern Italy to perform. His compositions attracted attention from central and southern Italy as well. Many of his more than 100 frottolas were published by Petrucci; others appeared in later anthologies. Also composed a Salve Regina (probably his earliest work) and 7 *laude.*

Carafa (de Colobrano), Michele (Enrico Francesco Vincenzo Aloisio Paolo) (b. Naples, 17 Nov. 1787; d. Paris, 26 July 1872). Composer. Studied music with Ruggi and later Fenaroli in Naples and in 1806 with Cherubini and Kalkbrenner in Paris. From 1806 to 1814 served in military campaigns, then became a professional composer, from 1814 producing operas for Italy and (from 1821) for Paris. Taught at the Conservatory (from 1840).

Card Game, The. See *Jeu de cartes.*

Cardew, Cornelius (b. Winchcombe, Gloucester, 7 May 1936; d. London, 13 Dec. 1981). Composer. Studied with Ferguson and Percy Waller at the Royal Academy of Music (1953–57), and with Stockhausen in Cologne (1958) and Petrassi in Italy (1963–65). Professor at the Royal Academy (from 1967). His massive Confucian work *The Great Learning* (1968–70) manifested interests in graphic notation, improvisation, electronic music, and indeterminacy. A turn to socialist thought around 1970 is reflected in his writings.

Cardillac. Opera in three acts by Hindemith (libretto by Ferdinand Lion after E. T. A. Hoffmann), produced in Dresden in 1926; produced with libretto revised by the composer in Zurich in 1952. Setting: Paris, 17th century.

Carestini, Giovanni (b. Filottrano, Ancona, ca. 1705; d. there? ca. 1760). Alto castrato singer. In 1721 debuted in Rome. From 1723 to 1725 held an appointment at the Viennese imperial theater, subsequently established his career with works by Hasse, Vinci, Scarlatti, and Porpora. Between 1733 and 1740 appeared in London on three separate occasions, singing works by Handel and others.

Carey, Henry (b. probably Yorkshire, 1687; d. London, 4 Oct. 1743). Poet and composer. Studied in London with Olaus Linnert and with Geminiani. Wrote plays, burlesques (*Nancy, or The Parting Lovers,* 1739) and ballad operas. The librettist for Lampe's *The Dragon of Wantley* (1737), a highly successful parody of Handel, Farinelli, and the machinery of Italian opera. His most popular song (for which he composed both words and music) was "Sally in Our Alley."

Carezzando [It.]. Caressingly, soothingly.

Carillon. A set of large, tuned *bells, usually hung in a tower and played from a keyboard and pedalboard. A carillon may contain anywhere from 25 to 40 bells, tuned chromatically and covering from two to four octaves. The bells, the largest weighing as much as 10,000 kg., do not move but are fixed to beams and struck by moving clappers. The keyboard consists of two rows of wooden batons arranged like a piano keyboard but played with the fists rather than the fingers. The batons are attached to the clappers by a system of wires, springs, and counterweights.

Carissimi, Giacomo (b. Marini, bapt. 18 Apr. 1605; d. Rome, 12 Jan. 1674). Composer. A singer and organist at Tivoli, he was appointed *maestro di cappella* at the S. Rufino Cathedral in Assisi in 1628. The following year was called to Rome to fill the prestigious post of *maestro* at the German College there, where he spent the rest of his life. During the 1650s composed and conducted for the Oratorio del S. Crocifisso. The first major composer of oratorios (*Jephte*, before 1650; *Jonas; Judicium Salomonis*), also composed hundreds of motets and cantatas in addition to Masses and other sacred works. His pupils include Charpentier, Kerll, and Bernhard.

Carlos, Wendy [formerly Walter] (b. Pawtucket, R.I., 14 Nov. 1939). Composer. Studied with Ron Nelson at Brown and with Luening, Ussachevsky, and Beeson at Columbia. Aided Moog in improving the synthesizer (1964); *Switched on Bach,* produced on that synthesizer, was very successful. She has written many film scores (*A Clockwork Orange,* 1971) and other works using synthesizer, digitally synthesized orchestral sounds, or both (*The Shining,* 1978–80).

Carmen [Lat., pl. *carmina*]. (1) Song, poem. (2) In Germany in the late 15th and early 16th centuries, compositions for instrumental ensemble, often in three voices. (3) [Sp. proper name]. Opera in four acts by Bizet (libretto by Henri Meilhac and Ludovic Halévy, after Mérimée), produced in Paris in 1875. Setting: Seville and environs, about 1820.

Carmichael, Hoagy [Hoagland Howard] (b. Bloomington, Ind., 22 Nov. 1899; d. Rancho Mirage, Calif., 27 Dec. 1981). Popular songwriter. Around 1930 moved to New York, spending his career there and in Hollywood. His songwriting was strongly influenced by experiences with jazz musicians; worked with numerous lyricists and wrote songs for films (*To Have and Have Not,* 1944; *Here Comes the Groom,* including "In the Cool, Cool, Cool of the Evening," 1951) and one full-length Broadway musical (*Walk with Music,* 1940). His most famous composition was "Stardust" (1929); others include "Georgia on My Mind" (1931), "Heart and Soul" (1938), and "Skylark" (1942). Acted in 14 films.

Carmina burana [Lat., songs of Beuren]. (1) A title given in the 19th century to a collection of over 200 Latin secular poems preserved in a manuscript of the 13th century. The great majority are love poems (often obscene) belonging to an international repertory reaching back to the 12th century and beyond and preserved also principally in French and English manuscripts. Some poems are provided with musical notation. See also Goliards. (2) A scenic oratorio (1937) by Carl Orff for soloists, choruses, and orchestra, based on 24 Latin poems from the collection described under (1).

Carnaval des animaux, Le [Fr., The Carnival of the Animals]. A "Grand Zoological Fantasy" composed in 1886 by Saint-Saëns for chamber orchestra and two pianos. It consists of short descriptive pieces named for various animals.

Carnaval romain, Le [Fr., The Roman Carnival]. An overture ("ouverture charactéristique") by Berlioz, op. 9 (1844), based on themes from his opera *Benvenuto Cellini* (produced in Paris in 1838).

Carnaval: Scènes mignonnes sur quatre notes [Fr., Carnival: Dainty Scenes on Four Notes]. A work for piano by Schumann, op. 9 (1833–35), consisting of 21 short pieces bearing programmatic titles. The notes in question are derived from the name of a Bohemian town, Asch, the home of the young Schumann's sweetheart Ernestine von Fricken, by means of German *pitch names. The results are a four-note group—A, E♭ (from the *S* interpreted as *Es*), C, and B♮ (called *H* in German)—and a three-note group—A♭ (from *As*), C, and B♮. See also *Davidsbündlertänze*.

Carneyro, Cláudio (b. Oporto, 27 Jan. 1895; d. there, 18 Oct. 1963). Composer. Studied at the Oporto Conservatory and with Widor and Dukas at the Paris Conservatory. After two years in the U.S. (1928–30) returned home to teach composition at the Oporto Conservatory, which he directed from 1955 to 1958. His music is in an essentially neo-Romantic idiom and contains some Portuguese folk and native materials.

Carnicer (y Batlle), Ramón (b. Tárrega, near Lérida, 24 Oct. 1789; d. Madrid, 17 Mar. 1855). Composer. Studied in Barcelona and spent the war years teaching on Minorca; visited London (1815–16), then recruited an opera company in Italy for Barcelona. Conductor at the Coliseo theater, Barcelona, 1818; director of opera in Madrid, 1827; from 1831 professor at the new Madrid Conservatory. Works include many once-popular Spanish songs.

Carnival songs. *Canti carnascialeschi.

Carol. In the Middle Ages, a song of English origin, with text in English or Latin (or a mixture of the two) and dealing with any subject, but most often having to do with the Virgin Mary or some aspect of Christmas. The medieval carol began with a burden (refrain), which was followed by verses (stanzas) of uniform structure; the burden was repeated after each verse. In present-day usage, the term designates a strophic song, often traditional and usually (but not always) connected with the celebration of Christmas. Informally, similar songs not of English origin (such as the French *noël or the German *Weihnachtslied*) are sometimes called carols. For Spanish songs associated with Christmas, see *Villancico*.

Caron, Philippe (fl. 2nd half of 15th century). Composer. His identity and even his first name are uncertain, and all information about his life is conjectural. Tinctoris linked him with Busnois, Regis, and Ockeghem as among the "most excellent" composers. He may have served Charles the Bold and perhaps spent time in Italy. Composed about 20 chansons, 2 motets, and 5 Masses (including a *Missa super L'homme armé*, modeled on a chanson by Morton).

Carpenter, John Alden (b. Park Ridge, Ill., 28 Feb. 1876; d. Chicago, 26 Apr. 1951). Composer. Studied with Paine at Harvard, with Elgar in Italy (1906), and with Bernhard Ziehn in Chicago (1908–12). *Skyscrapers* (1923–24) was commissioned by Diaghilev for a projected U.S. tour; its orchestra included saxophone, tenor banjo, traffic lights, on- and offstage choir; its style incorporated jazz idioms and allusions to popular song. After 1926 wrote in an impressionist style evident in his tone poems for orchestra (*Sea Drift*). Other works include ballets (*Krazy Kat,* 1921), orchestral music (*Adventures in a Perambulator,* 1914), chamber music, choir works, many songs.

Carpentras [Genet, Elzéar] (b. Carpentras, ca. 1470; d. Avignon, 14 June 1548). Composer. Active in Rome (1508–?; master of the papal chapel, 1514–21; 1524–26), in the French royal chapel (sometime between 1508 and 1514), and in Avignon (1505–ca. 1508; 1521–24; 1526–48). Eventually became dean of St. Agricole, where he remained until his death. The majority of his extant music, almost entirely sacred, was published in Avignon between 1532 and ca. 1539.

Carr, Benjamin (b. London, 12 Sept. 1768; d. Philadelphia, 24 May 1831). Composer, organist, and publisher. Studied music in London; moved to Philadelphia in 1793 and opened a music publishing business. The first important American music publisher. Issued *Musical Journal for the Piano Forte* (1800–1804) and *Carr's Musical Miscellany in Occasional Numbers.* More than 350 of his works survive.

Carrée [Fr.]. A double whole note or breve. See Note.

Carreño, (María) Teresa (b. Caracas, 22 Dec. 1853; d. New York, 12 June 1917). Pianist. Studied with Gottschalk, Mathias, and Anton Rubinstein. Began concert career in 1866; also occasionally sang in opera; ran an opera company in Venezuela. From 1889 until World War I lived mostly in Berlin; active as a performer and teacher.

Carreras, José (b. Barcelona, 5 Dec. 1946). Lyric tenor. Studied in Barcelona. Sang with Caballé at Barcelona's Teatro del Liceo, 1970. London debut in 1971 in concert version of Donizetti's *Maria Stu-*

arda. U.S. debut as Pinkerton with the New York City Opera, 1972; debut with San Francisco Opera, 1973; Covent Garden and the Met, 1974; La Scala, 1975. The telecast in 1994 of the second "Three Tenors" concert (with Pavarotti and Domingo) was seen by over a billion people worldwide.

Carrillo (Trujillo), Julián (Antonio) (b. Ahualulco, San Luis Potosí, 28 Jan. 1875; d. San Ángel, 9 Sept. 1965). Composer and theorist. Studied with Melesio Morales at the National Conservatory in Mexico City, continuing his studies in Leipzig. Around 1900 began to formulate a theory using microtones, promoting his ideas through compositions and writings; central to the system was the sonido trece. Returned to Mexico in 1905, served as professor and later director (1913–14, 1920–24) at the National Conservatory. Lived in the U.S., then formed the "Orquesta sonido 13" in Mexico (1930). His works, about half of which are microtonal, include operas, symphonies (1924–31), choral works, chamber music, works for solo instruments.

Carter, Benny [Bennett Lester] (b. New York, 8 Aug. 1907). Jazz alto saxophonist, trumpeter, composer, arranger, and bandleader. Played with and arranged for Fletcher Henderson (1930–31), McKinney's Cotton Pickers (1931–32), and his own big band (1932–34). Moved to Europe in 1935 and arranged for big bands; returned to the U.S. in 1938 and led big bands and combos. From the 1930s also made many recordings playing alto saxophone, trumpet, or clarinet as a free-lance. Settled in Los Angeles in 1942 and increasingly devoted himself to writing for films and television. Toured with Jazz at the Philharmonic (intermittently, 1950s and 1960s) and arranged for an all-star group on his album *Further Definitions* (1961).

Carter, Betty [Jones, Lillie Mae] (b. Flint, Mich., 16 May 1930; d. New York, 26 Sept. 1998). Jazz singer. As a teenager sang with Charlie Parker and other bop musicians; earned the nickname "Betty Bebop" while singing with Lionel Hampton's big band (1948–51). Based in New York, worked intermittently, touring (1960–63) and recording (1961) with Ray Charles. From 1969 led groups.

Carter, Elliott (Cook) (b. New York, 11 Dec. 1908). Composer and writer on music. Studied at Harvard and with Boulanger (1932–35). Taught at Columbia (1948–56), Yale (1960–62), and Juilliard (from 1967); also at the Dartington and Tanglewood summer courses. Numerous awards and honors include 2 Pulitzer Prizes (String Quartet no. 2 and no. 3). His compositions favor large-scale integration of tempo relationships and harmonic material. In the Piano Sonata (1945–46) his conception of meter in terms of steady rhythm combined with a changing pulse is already clear; in the Cello Sonata (1948) this conception led to the technique of metric (or time) modulation, for which he has been most widely known. Works include Concerto for Orchestra (1968–69); *Partita,* orchestra (1994); Sonata for Flute, Oboe, Cello, and Harpsichord (1952); 5 string quartets (1951–95); a woodwind quintet (1948); *Of Challenge and of Love,* soprano, piano (1995).

Carter, Ron [Ronald Levin] (b. Ferndale, Mich., 4 May 1937). Jazz double bass player. Studied at Eastman and the Manhattan School of Music. Recorded with Eric Dolphy and Don Ellis (both 1960) and worked with Jaki Byard, Thelonious Monk, and Cannonball Adderley among others. Recorded with Miles Davis's quintet (1963–68); played in the New York Jazz Quartet, Herbie Hancock's V.S.O.P. (1976–77, 1980s), the Milestone Jazzstars (1978), and duos with Cedar Walton and Jim Hall. From 1972 also led groups.

Carulli, Ferdinando (b. Naples, 20 Feb. 1770; d. Paris, 17 Feb. 1841). Guitarist. Largely self-taught in music, developed his own technique of playing; settled in Paris in 1808 and became the leading guitarist and teacher there. Published a famous guitar method and hundreds of guitar pieces, transcriptions and etudes, and chamber pieces with guitar.

Caruso, Enrico (b. Naples, 25 or 27 Feb. 1873; d. there, 2 Aug. 1921). Lyric and dramatic tenor. His 1895 debut in Morelli's *L'amico Francesco* led to a string of engagements in Caserta and Naples, and later in Egypt. His performances during the 1897 season in Milan elevated him to the front rank of tenors. Nerves and poor health contributed to a disastrous debut at La Scala (1900) but he quickly recouped his position. Debuts at Monte Carlo and Covent Garden (both 1902) in *Rigoletto* were triumphs, and he returned to La Scala the world's preeminent star. After his 1903 New York debut he sang every season for the Met. His final performance in Italy was in 1915, at the Met in 1920. His enormous repertory included Verdi's Radames, Riccardo, Duke of Mantua, and Alfredo; Bizet's Don José; and Puccini's Rodolfo, Pinkerton, and Cavaradossi. His most famous role was Canio in *Pagliacci.*

Cary, Tristam (Ogilvie) (b. Oxford, England, 14 May 1925). Composer. Studied at Trinity College of Music (A.Mus., L.Mus, 1949–51) and founded an electronic music studio at the Royal College of Music (1967). Senior lecturer (1974) and dean of music (1982) at Univ. of Adelaide, his works include music for stage, film, and television.

Casadesus, Robert (b. Paris, 7 Apr. 1899; d. there, 19 Sept. 1972). Pianist and composer. Studied at the Paris Conservatory. Toured as a soloist and played under Toscanini in New York in 1935; performed in duos with his wife Gaby (piano) and with Francescatti (violin). Professor and later director at the American Conservatory at Fontainebleau. Composed a number of piano works and concertos for 2 and 3 pianos.

Casals, Pablo [Pau] **(Carlos Salvador Defilló)** (b. Vendrell, Catalonia, 29 Dec. 1876; d. San Juan, Puerto Rico, 22 Oct. 1973). Cellist, conductor, and composer. Studied at Barcelona's Escuela municipal de música (from 1888) and at the Madrid Conservatory (from 1890). Played in the Paris Opéra's orchestra; returned to Barcelona in 1897 and taught at the conservatory until 1899, the year of his Parisian solo debut and acceptance as one of the era's elect virtuosi. Toured the U.S, South America, and Russia; from 1905 performed frequently in a trio with Thibaud and Cortot. After the Spanish Civil War settled in the French Catalan village of Prades and conducted festivals (1950–66). Made Puerto Rico his home in 1956; annual festivals bearing his name were begun there in 1957.

Cascabeles [Sp.]. Sleigh bells.

Casella, Alfredo (b. Turin, 25 July 1883; d. Rome, 5 Mar. 1947). Composer, conductor, pianist, and writer. At age 12 studied in Paris (piano with Diémer, composition with Fauré); by 1902 had begun career as a pianist; taught a piano class at the Paris Conservatory (1912–15). Early compositions influenced by Fauré, Debussy, Mahler, Strauss, and the Russian nationalists. Taught at the Liceo musicale di Santa Cecilia in Rome (1915–22) and became more receptive to the music of Bartók, Stravinsky, and Schoenberg. By 1920 was making use of earlier Italian instrumental music and folk song style. Taught piano master classes at the Accademia di S. Cecilia in Rome and at summer courses at the Accademia Chigiana in Siena. Works include operas; ballets; many orchestral works (*Paganiniana,* 1942; *Scarlattiana,* piano and orchestra, 1926); chamber music (Serenade for clarinet, bassoon, trumpet, violin, cello, 1926); piano works (Sonatina, 1916); solo vocal music; orchestral arrangements of folk songs.

Cassa [It.]. *Drum.

Cassadó (Moreu), Gaspar (b. Barcelona, 30 Sept. 1897; d. Madrid, 24 Dec. 1966). Cellist and composer. Entered Barcelona's Conservatorio Las Mercedes in 1905; studied with Casals in Paris (1908–14), subsequently established a career as soloist. Played with Bauer and Rubinstein; later formed trio with Menuhin and Kentner. U.S. debut, 1936. Taught at Siena's Accademia musicale chigiana (1946–52 and 1955–63). Composed orchestral works, an oratorio, a cello concerto, chamber music.

Cassation. An informal instrumental genre of the Classical period, usually intended for performance outdoors as a kind of street serenade. Cassations were most common in Austria and its dominions. The term was often used interchangeably in the 18th century with *serenade and *notturno. Cassations are normally in multiple movements, one or more of which is a minuet, march, or other light movement-type.

Casse-noisette. See *Nutcracker, The.*

Castaldo, Joseph (b. New York, 23 Dec. 1927). Composer. In 1947 studied at the Accademia di S. Cecilia in Rome; then at the Manhattan School (with Giannini) and the Philadelphia Conservatory (with Persichetti); taught at the Philadelphia Conservatory and chaired its department of composition and theory from 1960; retired in 1983. Works include a cello concerto (1984); *Lacrimosa,* strings (1976–77); other chamber music and piano works; a cantata and choral works.

Castanets [Fr. *castagnettes;* Ger. *Kastagnetten;* It. *castagnette, nacchere;* Sp. *castañuelas*]. A percussion instrument of indefinite pitch consisting of two shell-shaped pieces of wood, the hollowed sides of which are clapped together. They are widely used in Spanish music, especially to accompany dancing. When played by dancers, they are loosely joined by a string that is looped over the thumb, permitting the remaining fingers to strike them together against the palm of the hand. For orchestral use they are often mounted on either side of a piece of wood that is held by the player and shaken. See ill. under Percussion instruments.

Castelnuovo-Tedesco, Mario (b. Florence, 3 Apr. 1895; d. Beverly Hills, 16 Mar. 1968). Composer and pianist. Studied with Pizzetti in Florence. Early orchestral works were impressionistic, depicting his native Tuscany (*Cipressi,* piano, 1920; orchestrated, 1921). Neo-Romantic compositions on Jewish themes include the violin concerto *The Prophets* (1933), *Le danze del Re David* for piano (1921) and oratorios. Moved to the U.S. in 1939, composing over 100 film scores (*Tortilla Flat,* 1942; *The Day of the Fox,* 1956) as well as more orchestral and chamber music. Made a significant contribution to the contemporary literature for guitar, much of it commissioned by Segovia.

Castrato [It.]. A male singer, castrated as a boy so as to preserve his soprano or alto range after his chest and lungs had become those of an adult; also *evirato.* Castration for this purpose was practiced in Italy in the 16th through 18th centuries and into the 19th century. They were especially important in *opera *seria,* where they sang the leading male roles and were international stars.

Castro, Jean de (b. Liège, ca. 1540; d. ca. 1611). Composer. Lived and had works printed in Antwerp, Düsseldorf, and Cologne; also lived in Lyons. An exceptionally prolific composer, his works were among the most popular of his time. Compositions include 3 parody Masses, 7 books of other sacred music, about 28 books of secular songs (both chansons and madrigals), and sacred and secular pieces in anthologies or manuscript sources.

Castro, Juan José (b. Avellaneda, near Buenos Aires, 7 Mar. 1895; d. Buenos Aires, 3 Sept. 1968). Composer and conductor. Studied in Buenos Aires and with d'Indy at the Schola cantorum in Paris. Conductor of the Renacimiento Chamber Orchestra (1928) and of the ballet at the Teatro Colón (1930) in Buenos Aires. From 1947 conducted the Havana Philharmonic, from 1949 the Sodre Orchestra in Uruguay, from 1952 the Victorian Symphony in Melbourne, and from 1956 to 1960 the National Symphony in Buenos Aires. Directed the Puerto Rico Conservatory until 1964. Works include operas, ballets, 5 symphonies (1931–56); choral music; chamber music.

Castrucci, Pietro (b. Rome, 1679; d. Dublin, 29 Feb. 1752). Violinist and composer. Reportedly a violin student of Corelli, he came to London around 1715 and became concertmaster of Handel's opera orchestra, a position he maintained until 1737. Partly responsible for the development of the violalike "violetta marina," which Handel employed in *Sosarme* and *Orlando.* Castrucci's compositions include violin sonatas and concerti grossi.

Cat's Fugue. Popular name for a keyboard sonata in G minor by Domenico Scarlatti (L. 499, K. 30), so called because the theme consists of wide and irregular skips in ascending motion, as if produced by a cat bounding across the keyboard.

Catalani, Alfredo (b. Lucca, 19 June 1854; d. Milan, 7 Aug. 1893). Composer. Studied at the conservatories in Lucca and Milan (1873–75); appointed professor of composition at the latter (1886). His first two operas were not successful, but *Edmea* (1886) was, and led to a close friendship with Toscanini. *La Wally* (1892) became his most enduring work, although not in the regular repertory.

Catalani, Angelica (b. Sinigaglia, 10 May 1780; d. Paris, 12 June 1849). Soprano. May have been taught by the castrato Marchesi; she debuted with him in 1797. Sang in many leading Italian houses and toured across Europe. Based in London (1806–13), later at the Théâtre-Italien, Paris (1814–17). Retired in 1832.

Catch. A kind of English *round for three unaccompanied male voices, usually with lighthearted words. It was popular from the late 16th century into the 19th. The 17th-century catch became a sophisticated and often intricate genre, developing the manner of treating the words that was to remain characteristic. This involved calculating the words so that the interplay among the parts produced new combinations, usually comic or (especially during the Restoration period) bawdy in effect.

Catel, Charles-Simon (b. Laigle, Normandy, 10 June 1773; d. Paris, 29 Nov. 1830). Composer and theorist. Studied theory and composition in Paris with Gossec (1780s); in 1795 became professor at the Conservatoire. During the 1790s composed revolutionary hymns and marches. After 1800 concentrated on works for Paris theaters (*Sémiramis,* 1802; *Wallace, ou Le ménestrel écossais,* 1817), many of which look toward the large-scale grand opera of the 19th century. Wrote a highly popular *Traité d'harmonie* (Paris, 1802).

Catoire [Katuar], **Georgy (L'vovich)** (b. Moscow, 27 Apr. 1861; d. there, 21 May 1926). Composer and musicologist. Studied piano with Klindworth at the Moscow Conservatory. In 1885 went to Berlin, where he worked with Tirsch and Rüfer and continued with Klindworth. Studied briefly with Rimsky-Korsakov and Lyadov. Professor of composition at Moscow Conservatory. Compositions include vocal and instrumental music.

Caturla, Alejandro García (b. Remedios, Cuba, 7 Mar. 1906; d. there, 12 Nov. 1940). Composer. Studied in Havana with Sanjuán (1926–27) and in Paris with Boulanger (1928). In 1932 founded the Orquesta de conciertos de Caibarién, the same year he was appointed district judge in Remedios. He was shot to death by a criminal whom he had sentenced in his courtroom. His music explores Afro-Cuban rhythms and folk tunes and also employs Cuban popular tunes.

Cauda [Lat., tail]. (1) In *mensural notation, an ascending or descending stem attached to any of various note shapes. (2) A textless passage such as often occurs at the ends of lines in *conductus.*

Caustun [Causton], **Thomas** (b. ca. 1520–25?; d. London, 28 Oct. 1569). Composer. Gentleman of the Chapel Royal from ca. 1550 until his death. Wrote mostly 4-voice, primarily chordal English cathedral music (anthems and services).

Cavaco [Port.]. A Portuguese fretted stringed instrument related to the guitar and the mandolin, with four or six strings. See also *Cavaquinho.*

Cavaillé-Coll, Aristide (b. Montpellier, 4 Feb. 1811; d. Paris, 13 Oct. 1899). Organ builder. From a family of organ builders; at Rossini's urging settled in Paris in 1833, joined by his father and brother, forming a company that was to build more than 500 organs in western Europe, representing the perfecting of the French romantic organ.

Caval, kaval [fr. Turk. *qawul*]. An *end-blown flute of the Balkans and Turkey made of cane or softwood. In construction and playing technique it is similar to the *nāy.* It is characteristically a shepherd's instrument.

Cavalieri, Caterina [Kavalier, Franziska Helena Appolonia] (b. Vienna, 19 Feb. 1760; d. there, 30 June 1801). Soprano. Studied with Salieri in Vienna and debuted at the Kärntnertortheater in 1775. One of the principal sopranos of the National-Singspiel, she created the roles of Costanze in Mozart's *Die Entführung aus dem Serail* and Mlle. Silberklang in *Der Schauspieldirektor.* Also the first Viennese Donna Elvira in *Don Giovanni;* the composer added the aria "Mi tradì" for her.

Cavalieri, Emilio de' (b. Rome, ca. 1550; d. there, 11 Mar. 1602). Composer, organist, and diplomat. Ferdinando de' Medici, upon becoming Grand Duke of Tuscany in 1588, hired him as overseer of musical activities at his court. Best known for his *Rappresentatione di Anima, et di Corpo,* an important early work in the development of the new recitative style and in the history of the oratorio.

Cavalleria rusticana [It., Rustic Chivalry]. Opera in one act by Pietro Mascagni (libretto by Guido Menasci and Giovanni Targioni-Tozzetti, after Giovanni Verga's play), produced in Rome in 1890. Setting: a Sicilian village in the late 19th century. See *Verismo.*

Cavalli [Caletti, Caletti-Bruni], **(Pietro)** [Pier] **Francesco** (b. Crema, 14 Feb. 1602; d. Venice, 14 Jan. 1676). Composer and singer. As a boy was brought to Venice by a nobleman to further his musical studies; taken into the choir of St. Mark's (Monteverdi was *maestro*), where he remained for a decade; from 1620 was also an organist at SS. Giovanni e Paolo. Appointed second organist at St. Mark's in 1639, the same year his first opera was performed in Venice. It was followed by a number of successes throughout the 1640s (*Egisto,* 1642); in the 1650s composed operas for Venice, Naples, Milan, and Florence. Spent two years in Paris (1660–62) composing *Ercole amante;* returned to Venice in 1662 and took up his organ duties at St. Mark's; in 1668 appointed *maestro di cappella.* Composed, in addition to 33 verifiable operas and 2 published collections of sacred music, cantatas, arias, a Magnificat (1650), and a Cantate Domino (1625).

Cavaquinho [Port., dim. of *cavaco*]. A small, four-stringed, guitarlike instrument of Portugal and Brazil; also called a *machete*. It was taken by Portuguese sailors to Hawaii, where it became known as the *ukulele.

Cavata [It.]. A short, epigrammatic arioso found at the end of a long recitative *(recitativo con cavata)*. Popular in 17th-century chamber cantatas, the procedure is also found in Bach's cantatas, although he does not use the term as such.

Cavatina [It.; Fr. *cavatine;* Ger. *Kavatine*]. A type of *aria. In 19th-century Italian opera, the cavatina is the entrance aria of a principal singer. It is in all formal ways identical to pieces labeled aria. In this repertory, the cavatina is distinguished only by its position in the opera, that is, in the first act. In 19th-century French and German opera, a *cavatine* or *Kavatine* is a short aria in a moderate or slower than moderate tempo. In the second half of the 18th century, a cavatina is a short aria, simpler than the da capo aria.

Cavazzoni, Girolamo [Hieronimo d'Urbino] (b. Urbino, ca. 1520; d. ca. 1577). Composer, son of Marco Antonio Cavazzoni. Worked in Mantua from at least 1565 until 1577, supervising the construction of the organ at S. Barbara and then serving as organist there. Wrote mostly for keyboard.

Cavazzoni, Marco Antonio [Marco Antonio da Bologna, Marco Antonio da Urbino] (b. Bologna, ca. 1490; d. Venice, ca. 1570). Composer. Spent much of his adult life, from 1517 or perhaps earlier, in or near Venice: as a singer at St. Mark's; perhaps organist at St. Stephen's and then at Treviso Cathedral and Chioggia Cathedral. Also lived and worked (usually as an organist) in Padua, Urbino, Ferrara, and Rome. Wrote only keyboard works, all but one ricercar published in Venice in 1523.

Cavendish, Michael (b. ca. 1565; d. London, 5 July 1628?). Composer. Little is known of his life. He served Prince Charles, son of James I. Wrote a book of lute songs and madrigals published in London in 1598; also contributed to The *Triumphes of Oriana* and The *Whole Booke of Psalmes* (1592).

Cazden, Norman (b. New York, 23 Sept. 1914; d. Bangor, Maine, 18 Aug. 1980). Composer, pianist, musicologist. Studied at the Institute of Musical Arts in New York (Newstead, Seeger), at the Juilliard Graduate School (1932–39), and at Harvard in 1948 (Piston, Copland). Taught at the Univ. of Illinois (1950–53) and the Univ. of Maine (1969–80). Wrote strongly contrapuntal and rhythmic music in ex-

panded tonality that often reflected his interest in folk music of the Catskills (*3 Ballads from the Catskills,* orchestra, 1949); as a scholar challenged Helmholtz's theories of consonance and dissonance.

Cazzati, Maurizio (b. Lucera, near Reggio Emilia, ca. 1620; d. Mantua, 1677). Composer. In 1641 appointed organist and *maestro di cappella* at S. Andrea in Mantua; from ca. 1647 *maestro* at Ferrara (Accademia della Morte), and during the 1650s at Bologna—first at S. Maria Maggiore and later (from 1657) at S. Petronio, where he served for nearly 15 years. From 1659 was engaged in a famous quarrel centering on his *Missa primi toni* (1655), which was attacked for "musical errors" by Arresti. Around 1665 began his own music publishing shop; in 1671 returned to Mantua, where he spent his remaining years as *maestro* for Anna Isabella Gonzaga.

C.b. [It.]. Abbr. for *col basso,* with the bass, or *contrabasso,* double bass.

C.d. [It.]. Abbr. for *colla destra,* with the right hand.

Cebell. *Cibell.

Cedendo [It.]. Becoming slower.

Cédez [Fr.]. Yield, slow down.

Ceja, cejilla [Sp.]. *Barré.

Celere, celermente [It.]. Quickly, swiftly.

Celesta [Eng., Ger., It., Sp.; Fr. *célesta*]. An instrument in the form of a small upright piano in which the action causes hammers to strike metal bars suspended over resonators. Dampers for the bars are controlled by a damper pedal. The celesta has a range of five octaves upward from c and is notated on staves in the fashion of piano music, sounding an octave higher than notated. See ill. under Percussion instruments. See also Dulcitone.

Celibidache, Sergiu (b. Roman, Romania, 28 June 1912; d. Paris, 14 Aug. 1996). Conductor, musicologist, composer. Studied composition and conducting at the Berlin Hochschule. As conductor pro tem of the Berlin Philharmonic (1945–48) rebuilt that orchestra into a world-class ensemble; co-conductor with Furtwängler, 1948–51. Music director, Swedish Radio Symphony, 1964–71. Permanent conductor of the Stuttgart Radio Orchestra, 1971–77; of the Munich Philharmonic, 1979–84. Taught at the Curtis Institute, 1983–84.

Cello. *Violoncello.

Cellone [It.]. A large violoncello, tuned a fourth lower than the normal cello (G_1 D A e), designed by Alfred Stelzner of Dresden about 1890 to provide a bass part in chamber music.

Cembal d'amour. A type of *clavichord invented by Gottfried Silbermann about 1721. According to an engraving published in 1723 it had the shape of an irregular trapezoid and had a 51-note compass (C to d‴). Its strings were approximately twice normal length and were struck near the middle, so that both segments of each string sounded the same pitch. The central tangent that struck the string also raised it off a damping block, which replaced the usual clavichord damper listing.

Cembalo [It., abbr. of *clavicembalo;* Ger.]. *Harpsichord. On the piano, a cembalo or harpsichord stop is a device intended to imitate the sound of the harpsichord.

Cencerro [Sp.]. *Cowbell.

Cenerentola, La [It., Cinderella]. Opera in two acts by Rossini (libretto by Jacopo Ferretti, after Charles Perrault's fairy tale *Cendrillon,* Charles-Guillaume Étienne's libretto *Cendrillon,* and Felice Romani's libretto *Agatina*). First produced in Rome in 1817. Setting: Salerno in the 18th century (although the specific time and place have no great bearing on the work).

Cent. On the logarithmic scale used in measuring the size of the *interval between two pitches, 1/100 of a semitone in equal *temperament. The octave in this scheme is equal to 1,200 cents, since each of the twelve equally tempered semitones is equal to 100 cents.

Centitone. A unit of measurement equal to 1/100 of a whole tone in equal *temperament and thus equal to two *cents.

Centonization [fr. Lat. *cento,* patchwork]. The creation of a work from preexisting elements. The term has been much used in connection with liturgical chants that make use of melodic formulas shared with other chants, usually of the same liturgical type and in the same mode. Such a chant is said to be centonate.

Cercar la nota [It., to seek the note]. In singing, a slight anticipation of the following pitch before pronouncing the syllable assigned to it.

Ceremony of Carols. A setting of nine medieval *carols in Middle English for treble voices and harp by Benjamin Britten, op. 28 (1942). The carols are framed by a Latin plainsong processional and recessional.

Cererols, Joan (b. Martorell, Catalonia, 9 Sept. 1618; d. Montserrat, 28 Aug. 1676). Composer. His entire life was devoted to the Montserrat Monastery near Barcelona, first as chorister, then (from 1636) as novice, and later as monk; for 40 years directed the musical activities at the monastery. Extant works include sacred vocal music and secular *villancicos.*

Cerha, Friedrich (b. Vienna, 17 Feb. 1926). Composer and conductor. In Vienna studied violin and composition at the academy and philosophy and musicology at the university. With Kurt Schwertsik founded the chamber ensemble Die Reihe, noted for its performances of contemporary music. From 1960 taught composition at the Vienna Academy, where he was made professor in 1969 and directed the electronic music studio. Prepared the third act of *Lulu* for its 1979 premiere at the Paris Opéra. His own style is concerned with sonority and timbre. Compositions include opera (*Baal,* 1973–81); orchestral music (flute concerto, 1986); vocal music; chamber music; piano music.

Certon, Pierre (b. ca. 1510; d. Paris, 23 Feb. 1572). Composer. Worked as a clerk at Notre Dame de Paris from 1529; assumed a similar post at the Sainte-Chapelle in 1532. From 1536 until his death master of the choristers there. Among his close friends was Sermisy, whose death in 1562 prompted the composition of a *déploration* modeled on Josquin's for Ockeghem. Extant sacred works include 8 Masses and over 40 motets. The majority of his compositions, however, are secular chansons, works which contributed substantially to the stylistic transformation of the chanson in the third quarter of the 16th century.

Cervantes (Kawanag), Ignacio (b. Havana, 31 July 1847; d. there, 29 Apr. 1905). Composer and pianist. Studied with Gottschalk and with Espadero in Havana, and with Alkan and Marmontel at the Paris Conservatory. Returned to Havana in 1869 or 1870 but was forced to leave in 1876; gave concerts in the U.S. and lived for a time in Mexico. Considered one of the pioneers of Cuban music, especially for his 21 *Danzas cubanas* for piano (1878–95); also composed 3 operas, a symphony, and much piano music.

Cervelas, cervelat [Fr.]. *Racket.

Ces, ceses [Ger.]. C-flat, C-double-flat. See Pitch names.

Cesti, Antonio [Pietro] (b. Arezzo, bapt. 5 Aug. 1623; d. Florence, 14 Oct. 1669). Composer and singer. After joining the Franciscan order (1637) was sent to Florence (S. Croce, ca. 1638–40), then back to Arezzo (ca. 1640–43). During the late 1640s served members of the Medici family. His first opera, *Orontea* (Venice, 1649) was a sensational success; it was followed by a number of other successes, including *Il Cesare amante* (1651). Served as Chor-Kapellmeister at the Innsbruck court of Archbishop Ferdinand Karl (1652–65); in 1658 sang at the papal chapel. When the archbishop's court disbanded in

1665 Cesti followed it to Vienna. His last opera for Vienna, *Il pomo d'oro* (1668), was a pinnacle of Baroque opera on the gigantic scale.

Cetera [It.]. *Cittern.

Ceterone [Fr. *cisteron;* Ger. *gross Zittern*]. A large *cittern of the 17th century with an extended pegbox similar to the *theorbo. Wire strung, it was used for *thoroughbass.

Cetra [It.]. (1) *Zither. (2) *English guitar.

C.f. Abbr. for *cantus firmus.*

Chabrier, (Alexis-) Emmanuel (b. Ambert, Puy-de-Dôme, 18 Jan. 1841; d. Paris, 13 Sept. 1894). Composer. The family moved to Paris in 1856; Duparc and d'Indy were close friends, as were Verlaine and Manet, who painted his portrait. A clerk in the Ministry of the Interior, Chabrier composed little before the opéra comique *L'étoile* (1877), which made his reputation. In 1881 published *10 pièces pittoresques* for piano, a landmark in French music. A visit to Spain in July–Dec. 1882 led to his most popular work, the rhapsody *España*, originally for piano and a tremendous success in its orchestral version (1883). Much of Chabrier's efforts in the 1880s were devoted to grand tragic opera. Other works include *scène lyrique; Joyeuse marche*, piano (1888; later orchestrated); *6 mélodies* (1890); *Bourrée fantasque*, piano (1891).

Chace [Fr., hunt]. A type of French composition of the 14th century employing canon in the setting of a text that includes naturalistic sounds, in one case, as in some examples of the Italian *caccia*, those of the hunt. Unlike the *caccia*, it does not include an untexted, noncanonic tenor part. The term for similar works from Spain is *caça.*

Chachachá, cha cha cha [Sp.]. A Cuban dance-music genre, developed by traditional urban ensembles known as *charangas* in the early 1950s and popular throughout Latin America.

Chaconne. A continuous variation form of the Baroque, similar to the *passacaglia, based on the chord progression of a late 16th-century dance imported into Spain and Italy from Latin America. Usually in triple meter and major mode, the dance had a few stereotyped bass lines and a basic series of chords (I–V–IV–V) that acted as melodic or melodic-harmonic *ostinatos. Other chords were possible, especially vi and iii, just before IV.

The first written versions in Spanish guitar books of the early 17th century show a simple progression sometimes repeating often enough over the bass line to create a set of ostinato variations; this suggests an originally improvised practice. By 1627, the first chaconne variations for keyboard appeared (Frescobaldi, *Partite sopra ciaconna*) and joined the growing body of keyboard variations on dance basses and progressions (e.g., the *folia, *passamezzo, *romanesca, *ruggiero). The French chaconne of the same period, rather more sedate than its southern counterpart, often was presented "en rondeau," the first section returning as a refrain after couplets that may modulate or alter refrain material. By the late 17th century, instrumental chaconnes on both the variation and *rondeau* schemes were popular in England, Germany, and Austria, and they remained so until around 1750.

Although 18th-century theorists attempted to distinguish between the chaconne and the *passacaglia, no consistent differences are readily apparent from the 18th century onward, except that the chaconne was more frequently in major. Some pieces called passacaglia were actually closer to the original progressions of the chaconne. Unlike the passacaglia, the chaconne had few adherents after the Baroque.

Chadwick, George Whitefield (b. Lowell, Mass., 13 Nov. 1854; d. Boston, 4 Apr. 1931). Composer. Studied at the New England Conservatory (1872–76); taught music at Olivet College (1876–77), then studied with Jadassohn at the Leipzig Conservatory (1877–79); further study with Rheinberger in Munich. Returned to Boston in 1880; from 1882 taught at the New England Conservatory, from 1897 as director. One of the most important American composers of the late 19th century. His style is based on European models but often has a recognizably American flavor. Works include operas; 3 symphonies (1882, 1885, 1894); 5 string quartets; piano pieces; songs.

Chaillou de Pesstain [Chaillou, Raoul] (d. before spring 1336). Writer and perhaps composer. Member of the French royal court. Revised and completed the *Roman de *Fauvel*, adding both poetry and music to the work. Much of the music consists of preexisting compositions of the 13th and 14th centuries, adapted as necessary; other pieces may have been written by Chaillou, although his authorship cannot be proved.

Chailly, Riccardo (b. Milan, 20 Feb. 1953). Conductor. Studied at the Conservatorio Giuseppe Verdi in Milan, continuing his studies in Perugia, Milan, and Siena. Conducting debut in Milan, 1970. Abbado's assistant at La Scala, 1973–74. Principal guest conductor, London Philharmonic, 1980; principal conductor, West Berlin Radio Symphony, 1982–88; artistic director, Teatro communale, Bologna, 1986–89; principal conductor, Amsterdam Concertgebouw, from 1988.

Chaleur [Fr.]. Warmth, passion.

Chaliapin, Feodor (Ivanovich) [Shalyapin, Fyodor Ivanovich] (b. Kazan, Russia, 13 Feb. 1873; d. Paris, 12 Apr. 1938). Bass. After Caruso the best-known male opera singer of his time. Debut in Tiflis as Gounod's Mephistopheles (1893). Sang in St. Petersburg, 1894–95; with Marmontov's company in Moscow, 1896–98. Sensational debut at La Scala in 1901 (as Boito's Mefistofele); returned 1904, 1908, 1912, 1929–30, and 1933. Sang nearly every year at the Monte Carlo Opera, 1905–37. His forceful acting did not appeal to audiences at the Met, 1907–8, but proved as successful there in 1921–29 as it always had in Europe. Also performed at Covent Garden, 1926–29. His success in the title role of Massenet's *Don Quichotte* led to a starring nonsinging role in the 1933 film.

Chaloff, Serge (b. Boston, 24 Nov. 1923; d. there, 16 July 1957). Jazz baritone saxophonist. Played with Boyd Raeburn (1945), Georgie Auld (1945–46, ca. 1947), and Jimmy Dorsey (1946) before joining the saxophone section of Woody Herman's big band (1947–49). Played in Count Basie's octet (1950). As a leader of bop combos recorded "Gabardine and Serge" (1947) and the album *Blue Serge* (1956).

Chalumeau [Fr.]. (1) A shepherd's reed pipe. (2) A single-reed woodwind instrument, with cylindrical bore and usually two keys, that appeared in the late 17th century. The profile of the *chalumeau* resembles that of the baroque *recorder. The terms *chalumeau* and clarinet were often used interchangeably until the former disappeared about 1770. (3) The lowest register of the clarinet, from written g' downward. This is approximately the range of (2).

Chamber music. In present usage, music written for and performed by a small ensemble, usually instrumental, with one performer on a part. The term has been defined or delimited differently in various periods, reflecting changing social and musical conditions. For the 19th century and much of the 20th, it meant instrumental music for small ensembles in the tradition deriving from the Viennese Classical masters, Haydn, Mozart, and Beethoven. Much of this music is in four-movement *sonata format and bears abstract titles reflecting the number of instruments employed (*trio, *quartet, *quintet, *sextet, *septet, *octet, *nonet). Chamber music has most often been written for strings in standard groupings, most prominently the *string quartet, but piano and strings, mixed winds and strings, winds alone, and other combinations are often employed. Music for a solo performer, with or without accompaniment, is often excluded from this definition, because interplay of parts is considered an essential element of it.

From the 16th to the late 18th century, the term was used differently, with all music classified in three large categories: chamber, church, and—after the rise of opera—theater. This classification was based primarily on the music's social function and only secondarily on differences of style, form, or performing forces. The *sonata da camera* (chamber sonata) and *sonata da chiesa* (church sonata), the two main types of trio sonata, therefore fell into different categories. Chamber music included whatever secular music might be performed in the musical establishment of a private household, whether vocal or instrumental, solo or ensemble, including music for orchestra.

Mid-18th-century orchestras often were not much larger than solo ensembles with only one player on each part, and it is sometimes not easy to distinguish, on the basis of style, music written for one or the other. Some was intended to be suitable for either type of ensemble. Later in the century, there was an increasing divergence between the two in size and the style of their music, as the transference of the orchestra's center of activity to the public concert hall created conditions for its rapid growth. Small solo ensembles remained popular, especially with the period's growing numbers of musical amateurs. Of the large quantities of music produced for this market, much tended to be easy to play and simple in style, texture, and expression.

As the orchestra grew in size and coloristic possibilities in the 19th century, chamber music with its more restricted scope came to be seen in a somewhat reverential light as the most intellectual and the most profound and purest of the instrumental genres (especially after the late quartets of Beethoven). With the increasing complexity of compositional styles, demands on performers rose; chamber-music concerts by professionals became more frequent, amateur performances less so.

The Classical tradition remained strong in chamber music in the 20th century, with the string quartet much cultivated by composers of otherwise very different stylistic tendencies. At the same time, there was wide-ranging experimentation with unusual combinations of instruments, the participation of voices, electronic elements, new forms, and compositional methods that expanded the boundaries of the genre and made necessary a broader definition of it.

Chamber opera. An opera of small dimensions, of an intimate character, using relatively small performing resources.

Chamber orchestra. A small orchestra, often of around 20 or 25 players, as distinct from the modern symphony *orchestra. This was, however, about the normal size for orchestras in the 18th century.

Chamber organ. An organ of modest size (usually four to seven stops), with a single keyboard, intended for use in domestic rooms or other small spaces.

Chamber pitch. See Pitch.

Chamber sonata. See *Sonata da camera.*

Chamber symphony. A symphony intended for performance by a *chamber orchestra rather than by a modern symphony orchestra. The term is not normally applied to works from earlier periods in which the normal size of the orchestra was that of what is now often termed a chamber orchestra.

Chambers, Paul (Laurence Dunbar, Jr.) (b. Pittsburgh, 22 Apr. 1935; d. New York, 4 Jan. 1969). Jazz double bass player. Played bop with Kenny Burrell, Pepper Adams, Tommy Flanagan, and others (1949–55); toured with Paul Quinichette. After touring the South with Bennie Green, played briefly with Sonny Stitt and J. J. Johnson. A member of Miles Davis's quintets and sextets (1955–63), recorded with Sonny Rollins, John Coltrane, and many others. In 1963 joined Wynton Kelly's trio.

Chambonnières, Jacques Champion Sieur de (b. Paris, 1601 or 1602; d. there, Apr. 1672). Composer and harpsichordist. By 1632 was a chamber musician at the court of Louis XIII. From 1643 to 1656 served as court clavecinist. Like Couperin, spent his final years preparing his own music for publication. Compositions include *Les pièces de clavessin . . . livre premier* and *livre second* (Paris, 1670) and a large number of keyboard suites in all "white" keys, most in manuscript.

Chaminade, Cécile (Louise Stéphanie) (b. Paris, 8 Aug. 1857; d. Monte Carlo, 13 Apr. 1944). Pianist and composer. Made her debut as a pianist at age 18; subsequently toured France and England. Compositions include an opera (unpublished) and a ballet (1890); *Concertino,* flute, orchestra, 1902; 2 piano trios; piano works; songs.

Champagne, Claude (Adonai) (b. Montreal, 27 May 1891; d. there, 21 Dec. 1965). Composer. Studied with Gédalge in Paris (1920–28), where he was influenced by music of Fauré and Debussy. Taught at the McGill Conservatory (1930–42) and the École Vincent d'Indy (1930–62); in 1942 helped found the Montreal Conservatory. Most compositions reflect French Canadian folk elements, his own Irish heritage, and the Canadian landscape (*Images du Canada français,* 1946; *Altitude,* 1958–59; both for chorus and orchestra).

Chance music. See Aleatory music.

Chandos Anthems. Twelve anthems for soloists, chorus, and orchestra by Handel, composed in the years 1717–18 for James Brydges, later Duke of Chandos. Included are a *Te Deum* and a *Jubilate.*

Change ringing. The English practice of ringing tower *bells (or, more recently, handbells) in a methodical order, the changes in the ringing sequence prescribed by arithmetical permutations. For instance, a set, or "ring," of six bells, 1 2 3 4 5 6, may be played in the orders, or "changes," 2 1 4 3 6 5, or 2 4 1 6 3 5, etc. The "peal," or total number of permutations, for six bells is 720 (6!, i.e., $6 \times 5 \times 4 \times 3 \times 2 \times 1$; for twelve bells, 479,001,660), but in actual performance, usually a limited selection of changes is played in succession, the main principle being the course, or path, of a bell among the other bells, effected chiefly by the exchange of pairs of bells. A complete system of changes, called a "method," always begins and ends with "rounds," the ring rung in order from highest to lowest pitch. Methods, some of which are extremely complicated, are known by such traditional names as "Grandsire Triple," "Treble Bob," and "Plain Hunt."

Changes. In jazz and popular music, a harmonic *progression; also the entire series of chords or harmonies making up a piece.

Changing note. Cambiata. See Counterpoint.

Chanler, Theodore (Ward) (b. Newport, R.I., 29 Apr. 1902; d. Boston, 27 July 1961). Composer. Studied at the Institute of Musical Art in New York with Buhlig (piano) and Goetschius (counterpoint); a meeting with Bloch led to study at the Cleveland Institute (1920–23); also studied at Oxford and with Boulanger in Paris (1924–27). Taught briefly at Peabody (1945–47) and at the Longy School in Cambridge, Mass. Best known for his songs, including settings of texts by De la Mare (*Eight Epitaphs,* 1937; *Three Epitaphs,* 1940), Blake, and Feeney composed in the tradition of Fauré.

Channel. In popular music and jazz, *bridge.

Chanson [Fr.]. (1) Song. The term has been in use since the Middle Ages and has referred to a very wide range of both poetry and music cultivated by all classes of society, including the medieval epic (*chanson de geste),* the *troubadour and *trouvère repertories, secular polyphony and the related poetry of the 14th through 16th centuries [see (2) below], the *air de cour of the late 16th and early 17th centuries, the *brunette of the 17th and 18th centuries, the *vaudeville originating in the 16th century and spawning a tradition lasting into the 19th, the art song of the 19th and 20th centuries (more often referred to as the *mélodie), and folk and popular song of all periods up to the present.

(2) French secular polyphonic song of the 14th through 16th centuries; sometimes, more narrowly, a

late 15th- or 16th-century setting of a text not in one of the *formes fixes*. Chansons setting one or another of the *formes fixes* are first encountered at the end of the 13th century. It is in the works of Guillaume de Machaut (ca. 1300–77), however, that the tradition that dominated chanson composition until near the end of the 15th century was established. His chansons, among which the *ballade* predominates, are most often for three voices, the uppermost voice being the leading melodic part and the only one provided with text, the lower two voices, termed tenor and contratenor, being less animated, close together in range (though the tenor is the lowest voice at structurally important points), and perhaps intended for instruments. His poems treat the themes of courtly love and are the finest lyrics of their age.

Rhythmic complexity characterizes many of the chansons by the generation of composers immediately following Machaut. The notation of these works has been termed mannered [see Mensural notation], and their style has been described as the *ars subtilior*. By about 1400, a simpler style seems to have emerged, and the *rondeau* begins to be favored. Of composers born around 1400, Guillaume Dufay (ca. 1400–74) and Gilles Binchois (ca. 1400–60) were preeminent in establishing the character of what has been termed the *Burgundian chanson. The themes of courtly love are prominent among their texts, but other poetic registers are explored as well, especially in works by Dufay. Three parts continue to make up the usual texture, only the uppermost part of which is regularly texted in the sources. This music is overwhelmingly consonant compared with that of the 14th century. Later composers, who brought this tradition of chansons in the *formes fixes* largely to an end, include Johannes Ockeghem (ca. 1410–97), Antoine Busnois (ca. 1430–92), and Hayne van Ghizeghem (ca. 1445–between 1472 and 1497). In this period, the *bergerette* assumed a place in the repertory, without rivaling the *rondeau,* however.

Only at the end of the 15th century does a significant transformation of the chanson begin to take place, a transformation embodied in the works of Josquin Desprez (ca. 1440–1521) and his contemporaries. Although the *formes fixes* continued to be set, these composers turned increasingly to texts of popular character, often in strophic form. Such texts were often set with their associated melodies either paraphrased or treated in canon (a favorite device of Josquin) in a complex of three, four, or more voices employing extensive imitation. Remnants of this style—notably its continuously imitative polyphony in four or more voices—persist through the mid-16th century.

A somewhat different style, or group of styles, was cultivated by composers from Paris and surrounding territories and published in Paris. Prominent within this repertory is a largely homophonic style associated with the Parisian composer Claudin de Sermisy (ca. 1490–1562) and sometimes termed the Parisian chanson. This style also suggests a relationship with Italian music, notably the *frottola,* and Italian musicians active in France. The second half of the 16th century saw further interpenetration of regional and national styles as new printers in France and the Low Countries became active. A radically simple, chordal style had emerged in Paris by mid-century, termed the *voix de ville* or *vaudeville,* and this became the *air de cour,* the principal type of French secular vocal music of the late 16th and early 17th centuries. It bore, too, on the efforts of the poet Jean Antoine de Baïf (1532–89) to recapture the character of the music of antiquity through quantitative poetry and music termed *musique mesurée.* The principal composer associated with this particular enterprise, and France's most distinguished chanson composer of the later 16th century, was Claude Le Jeune (ca. 1530–1600). See also *Chanson spirituelle.*

Chanson balladée [Fr.]. See *Virelai.*

Chanson de geste [Fr., fr. Lat. *gesta,* actions]. A type of medieval French epic poetry of which the most famous example, and probably the oldest preserved, is the *Chanson de Roland.* The genre recounts the exploits of historical or legendary heroes and seems to have flourished as a written form in the late 11th and 12th centuries. Examples are most frequently divided into *laisses* (or sections) of variable length. It has generally been assumed that the *chansons de geste* were sung, perhaps to some recitational melodic formula, but none of the poems is preserved together with its music.

Chanson de toile [Fr.]. A type of northern French narrative poem of the 13th century practiced by the trouvères in which the singer, a young woman, relates in simple style a tale of disappointed love, often with a tragic ending. The woman is frequently portrayed as sewing, weaving, or spinning, hence its name.

Chanson mesurée [Fr.]. See *Musique mesurée.*

Chanson spirituelle [Fr.]. In the middle and late 16th century, a polyphonic *chanson with a religious or moralizing text in French. Such pieces often resulted merely from the substitution of a new text for the original one in a secular chanson, the music remaining unchanged.

Chansonnier [Fr., fr. *chanson*]. A manuscript or printed collection of French lyric poetry or musical settings of such poetry. Although the term may be applied to sources for the whole range of repertories, both text and music, referred to as *chansons [see, for example, *Troubadour, Trouvère], it is especially applied to manuscript anthologies containing predominantly polyphonic chansons of the 15th century [see Chanson (2)].

Chant. (1) *Plainsong, e.g., *Gregorian chant, *Byzantine chant. See also Anglican chant. (2) To sing plainsong or in the style of plainsong; to sing a single pitch or a limited range of pitches repetitively. (3) [Fr.] Song, melody; the voice part as distinct from the accompaniment.

Chantant, chanté [Fr.]. Singing, in a singing style.

Chanter. A pipe with finger holes for playing melody on a *bagpipe; as distinct from a drone, which sounds only a single pitch.

Chanterelle [Fr.]. *Cantino.

Chantey, chanty. *Shanty.

Chapel [Lat. *cappella, capella,* dim. of *cappa,* cloak; Fr. *chapelle;* Ger. *Capelle, Kapelle;* It. *cappella;* Sp. *capilla*]. (1) A place of worship within or dependent upon a larger church, institution, or residence; often small or private, though sometimes large and quite elaborate. (2) The staff of a chapel, including clergy and musicians, if any; also the specifically musical establishment of any church or chapel. In the later Middle Ages and Renaissance, such institutions might include up to 20 or 30 singers (both men and boys), an organist, and, especially later, other instrumentalists. The musical director of such an institution was called the *chapel master. (3) In Germany beginning in the 17th century, the entire musical establishment of a court, including the opera. (4) In Germany by the 19th century, any orchestra. See also *Kapelle, Kapellmeister.*

Chapel master [Fr. *maître de chapelle;* Ger. *Kapellmeister;* It. *maestro di cappella;* Sp. *maestro de capilla*]. The leader of a musical *chapel. In France, Italy, and Spain, this remained the title of the leader of a sacred institution. For German usage, see *Kapelle, Kapellmeister.*

Chapí (y Lorente), Ruperto (b. Villena, near Alicante, 27 Mar. 1851; d. Madrid, 25 Mar. 1909). Composer. Studied composition at the Madrid Conservatory; played cornet in a theater orchestra and conducted a military band. In 1873 the first of his more than 100 zarzuelas was produced; his most popular included *La tempestad* (1882), *La bruja* (1887), and *Curro Vargas* (1899).

Character (characteristic) piece [Ger. *Charakterstück;* Fr. *pièce caractéristique*]. In the late 18th and 19th centuries, any of a wide variety of kinds of *program music; now principally a short, lyric piano piece. The individual piece usually evokes a particular mood or scene, suggested more often than not by

a descriptive title. The Romantic lyric piano pieces generally thought of as character pieces frequently appeared in sets or cycles bearing titles such as *Handstücke, Kinderszenen, Albumblätter, Bagatelles, Nocturnes, Impromptus, Intermezzi, Capriccios, Rhapsodies, Eclogues,* and *Novelletten.* Virtually every 19th-century keyboard composer from Beethoven to Richard Strauss wrote such pieces. Forms varied from Schumann's musically unified sets of miniatures to Chopin's large independent works, but song forms (ABA) were most common for individual pieces.

Character notation. *Shape-note.

Characteristic note. *Leading tone, note.

Charanga [Sp.]. A Cuban dance ensemble, characteristically consisting of flute, two or three violins, piano, double bass, *timbales with *cencerro, and *güiro. Traditionally a prominent exponent of the Cuban *danzón,* the *charanga* was also principally responsible for the development of the *chachachá in the early 1950s.

Charango [Sp.]. A small guitar of the Andes with five double courses of strings. The back of the soundbox is characteristically of armadillo shell.

Charivari [Fr.; Ger. *Katzenmusik;* It. *scampata;* in the U.S., shivaree]. Deliberately cacophonous music, often including the use of pots and pans; especially music of this type played outside the home of newlyweds or of an unpopular person.

Charles, Ray [Robinson, Ray Charles] (b. Albany, Ga., 23 Sept. 1930). Rhythm-and-blues and soul singer, pianist, and songwriter. Blinded by glaucoma as a child, he performed with jazz trios in Seattle and participated in the rising popularity of rhythm-and-blues with recordings of original songs ("I've Got a Woman," 1955; "What'd I Say," 1959). Incorporated elements of gospel singing into songs dealing with standard blues topics and themes. His eclectic repertory includes several albums of country music.

Charleston. (1) A fast, American dance that flourished in the 1920s. Said to have originated among southern blacks, it became a commercial hit with James P. Johnson's song "Charleston," composed for the show *Runnin' Wild* (1923). Subsequent Charlestons borrowed the catchy rhythmic motive of Johnson's melody: ₵ ♩ ⅋ ♪ (2) [archaic] *Hi-hat cymbals.

Charpentier, Gustave (b. Dieuze, Lorraine, 25 June 1860; d. Paris, 18 Feb. 1956). Composer. Studied at the Lille Académie de musique and with Massart (violin) at the Paris Conservatory. Won the Prix de Rome in 1887; it was in Rome that he conceived most of his important compositions, including the *symphonie-drame La vie du poète* (1889), the orchestral suite *Impressions d'Italie* (1889–90), and the opera *Louise* (1900). Produced 4 sets of songs (*Poèmes chantés,* 1894; *Impressions fausses,* 1895). *La couronnement de la muse* (chorus and orchestra, 1897) was the realization of a festival imagined in *Louise,* featuring the crowning of a working girl. Founded the Oeuvre de Mimi Pinson (later called the Conservatoire populaire) which taught music to working-class women.

Charpentier, Marc-Antoine (b. Paris, 1643; d. there, 24 Feb. 1704). Composer. Apparently studied with Carissimi in Rome, probably from around 1662; returned to Paris before 1670 and became *maître de musique* at the residence of Marie de Lorraine, Mademoiselle de Guise. During his years at this post (which lasted until 1688) composed motets, Psalms, and other sacred music. In 1672 became Molière's musical collaborator, composing prologues, entr'actes, and other music for *Mariage forcé* (1672) and *Malade imaginaire* (1673). During the 1680s served as *maître* of the Jesuits' St. Louis church and as music teacher to Philippe, Duke of Chartres. In 1698 appointed *maître de musique des enfants* at the Sainte Chapelle; composed a large number of sacred works and music for special occasions (a Te Deum and the *Judicium Salomonis*). He died leaving few published works (*Médée,* 1694; selections from *Circé,* 1676) but a great many works in manuscript. Sacred works include 11 Mass settings, a large number of Psalms, antiphons, sequences, and lessons, and more than 200 motets; also composed cantatas and instrumental music for the church. Stage works include *David et Jonathas* (1688) and *Les Arts Florissants* (1685–86).

Chasins, Abram (b. New York, 17 Aug. 1903; d. there, 21 June 1987). Pianist and composer. Studied composition at Juilliard with Rubin Goldmark and piano with Ernest Hutcheson, subsequently with Josef Hoffman at Curtis, where he taught piano (1926–35). Musical director of WQXR, New York, 1943–65; musician-in-residence, Univ. of Southern Calif., 1972–77. Best known for 2 concertos (1928, 1931) and *Three Chinese Pieces* (piano, 1928; orchestrated, 1929).

Chasse, La [Fr., the hunt]. A title sometimes given to compositions imitating the sound of hunting horns or some other aspect of the hunt. See *Hunt Quartet, Hunt Symphony.*

Chasseur maudit, Le [Fr., The Accursed Huntsman]. A symphonic poem by César Franck, op. 44 (1882), based on the ballad "Der wilde Jäger" by Gottfried Bürger (1747–94).

Chausson, (Amédée-) Ernest (b. Paris, 20 Jan. 1855; d. Limay, near Mantes, Yvelines, 10 June 1899). Composer. Studied at the Conservatory with Massenet in 1879–81 and unofficially with Franck; made Wagnerian pilgrimages to Munich and Bayreuth (1879–82). Traveled extensively in Europe; maintained a Paris salon frequented by leading artistic figures and young artists whose careers he encouraged (including Debussy). Works include Symphony in B♭ (1889–90); *Poème,* violin and orchestra (1896); concerto for piano, violin, and string quartet (1889–91); orchestral song cycle, *Poème de l'amour et de la mer* (1882–90; rev. 1893); 36 published songs. His magnum opus was the opera *Le roi Arthus* (1886–95) to his own libretto.

Chávez (y Ramírez), Carlos (Antonio de Padua) (b. Mexico City, 13 June 1899; d. there, 2 Aug. 1978). Composer and conductor. Studied piano with Pedro Luís Orgazón (1915–20) and theory with Juan Fuentes and Manuel Ponce. Traveled to Europe (1922–23); formed ties with Cowell, Persichetti, and others in New York (1926–28). In 1928 helped found the Symphony Orchestra of Mexico (later National Symphony Orchestra) and became its principal conductor; director, National Conservatory (from 1928) and National Institute of Fine Arts (1947–52). After 1948 concertized extensively in the U.S. and Europe. Charles Eliot Norton Lecturer at Harvard (1958–59). His music often strives for the simplicity of native Indian tunes but rarely uses actual folk melodies. Works include an opera, ballet scores, 7 symphonies, choral and vocal works, much chamber and keyboard music, songs.

Chaykovsky. See Tchaikovsky.

Cheatham, Doc [Adolphus Anthony] (b. near Nashville, 13 June 1905; d. Washington, D.C., 2 June 1997). Jazz trumpeter. Originally a soprano saxophonist, also played trumpet and joined the big bands of Chick Webb (1928), Sam Wooding (touring Europe, 1928–30), and Cab Calloway (1933–39). Played with Eddie Heywood's sextet (1943–46) and from 1948 played with Latin big bands, touring internationally with these as well as with the trombonist Wilbur De Paris (1957, 1960) and the pianist Sammy Price (1958). From 1960 led a band in New York; also joined Benny Goodman (1966–67) and toured widely as a free-lance.

Check, check head. Back check. See Piano.

Checker, Chubby [Evans, Ernest] (b. Philadelphia, 3 Oct. 1941). Rock-and-roll singer and dancer. His 1960 recording "The Twist" and performances of the accompanying dance inspired a national craze; other popular songs included another dance number, "Limbo Rock" (1962).

Chef d'attaque [Fr.]. *Concertmaster; the leader of a section.

Chef d'orchestre [Fr.]. *Conductor.

Cheironomy. See Chironomy.

Chekker [Fr. *échiquier, eschaquier, eschiquier;* Ger. *Schachtbrett;* Lat. *scacarum;* Sp. *esaquier*]. An early stringed keyboard instrument mentioned, but not described, in various 14th- to 16th-century literary sources.

Chelys [Gr.]. The Greek *lyra, so called because its soundbox was often made from a turtle shell. From the Middle Ages through the 17th century, the term could refer to lutes, viols, and violins.

Cheng (zheng) [Chin.]. A Chinese zither with 10 to 17 silk strings, each with its own movable bridge. The modern version has 16 metal strings tuned to three pentatonic octaves. Its playing technique is similar to that of the Japanese *koto. See also *Ch'in;* see ill. under Instrument.

Cherry, Don(ald Eugene) (b. Oklahoma City, 18 Nov. 1936; d. near Malaga, Spain, 19 Oct. 1995). Jazz cornetist and bandleader. Played with Ornette Coleman (1957–61), Steve Lacy (1961), Sonny Rollins (1962–63), the New York Contemporary Five including Archie Shepp (1963–64), Albert Ayler (1964), and Dollar Brand, then led a group including Gato Barbieri. Also played wooden flutes and the doussn' gouni and sang. Formed Old and New Dreams (1976–95) and the trio Codona (1976–84). After playing in the all-star sextet The Leaders (1984–86) he formed Nu, including Vasconcelos and the tenor saxophonist Carlos Ward.

Cherubic Hymn. The offertory chant of the Byzantine *Divine Liturgy. For ordinary celebrations the text begins "Oi ta cherubim," but during Lent and Holy Week other hymns are used.

Cherubini, Luigi (Carlo Zanobi Salvadore Maria) (b. Florence, 8 or 14 Sept. 1760; d. Paris, 15 Mar. 1842). Composer. Studied with Sarti and began a career as an opera composer; 1784–86 composer to the King's Theatre, London. Settled in Paris, became music director of the Théâtre de Monsieur (1789–92); *Lodoïska* (1791) was his first French operatic success, followed by *Eliza* (1794) and *Médée* (1797). *Les *deux journées,* his most popular opera, was given at the Opéra-comique until 1830 and widely performed elsewhere. After *Faniska* (1805) his opera activity declined, and he turned increasingly to sacred music; his appointment as superintendent of the royal chapel (1816–30, jointly with Le Sueur) led to many Masses and motets (Requiem in C minor, 1816; Requiem in D minor, 1836, intended for himself). In 1793 began teaching at the Institut national

de musique, which in 1795 became the Conservatory; subsequently served as director (1822–42).

Chest of viols. In England in the 16th and 17th centuries, a matched (in size, shape, wood, and color) set of viols, usually two trebles, two tenors, and two basses, kept in an appropriately partitioned chest. See also Consort.

Chest voice, chest register. See Voice.

Cheute [Fr.]. See *Chûte.*

Chevalet [Fr.]. The *bridge of a bowed stringed instrument; *au chevalet,* an instruction to bow at or near the bridge. See Bowing (11).

Cheville [Fr.]. In stringed instruments, a tuning peg; in the piano, a tuning or wrest pin.

Cheviller [Fr.]. *Pegbox.

Chevreuille, Raymond (b. Watermael-Boitsfort, Brussels, 17 Nov. 1901; d. Montignies-le-Tilleul, 9 May 1976). Composer. Studied briefly at the Brussels Conservatory; had an extremely large output but destroyed many of his early works. Surviving compositions include 8 symphonies, 3 violin concertos, 3 piano concertos, 2 cello concertos, 6 string quartets, ballets, operas, radio works, and other dramatic works.

Chevrotement [Fr.]. *Goat's trill.

Chiaro, chiaramente [It.]. Clear, clearly.

Chiave [It.]. (1) *Clef. (2) On woodwind instruments, a key.

Chiavette [It.]. In 16th-century vocal polyphony, a coordinated collection of clefs (G2 C2 C3 F3/C4; Ex. 1) that locates the staves of individual parts (or the ten-line staff used by composers and theorists) a third lower on the gamut than do the usual *chiavi naturali* [It., natural clefs] (C1 C3 C4 F4; Ex. 2). A third common clef grouping (C2 C4 F3 F5; Ex. 3), sometimes termed *chiavi trasportati* [It., transposed clefs] or "low *chiavette,*" locates most staves a third higher on the gamut than do the *chiavi naturali.*

Transposition of staves on the gamut admits of two different interpretations. One claims that when clefs shift, pitch associations shift correspondingly, but vocal ranges remain the same. The alternative interpretation holds that when clefs shift, vocal ranges shift correspondingly, but pitch associations remain the same.

Several central sources for 16th-century Italian polyphony use a systematic association of modes with clef groupings and system signature [see Mode]. In these sources, the *chiavette* grouping is in principle reserved for authentic (odd-numbered) modes, and the *chiavi naturali* for the plagal (even-numbered)

1. *Chiavette.* 2. *Chiavi naturali.* 3. *Chiavi trasportati.*

modes. This suggests that in such sources, the first priority of the *chiavette* is to signal a feature of the modal system rather than to accommodate ranges.

Chiavi naturali, trasportati [It.]. See *Chiavette.*

Chicago jazz. A modification of *New Orleans jazz made in the 1920s by white musicians in the Midwest. While retaining collective improvisation among trumpet, trombone, and clarinet in climactic endings, they increasingly emphasized solos, arrangements including accompanimental figures, a string bass playing on each beat in 4/4, and popular song forms.

Chiesa [It.]. Church. In the Baroque period (ca. 1600–1750), in which music was classified as belonging to the style of church, chamber *(*camera),* or theater, the phrase *da chiesa* identifies music appropriate for use in church, especially the *concerto da chiesa* and the *sonata da chiesa.*

Chihara, Paul (Seiko) (b. Seattle, 9 July 1938). Composer. Studied with Boulanger (1962–63) and with Palmer at Cornell (1965); further study with Pepping and Schuller. Taught at UCLA (1966–74); composer-in-residence with the San Francisco Ballet (1980). Wrote a series of tone pictures of trees in static textures (*Forest Music,* orchestra, 1970) as well as a Ceremony series. Other works include Symphony no. 2 (Birds of Sorrow), 1981; *Sequoia,* string quartet and tape, 1984; film and TV scores; arrangements for musicals.

Child, William (b. Bristol, 1606; d. Windsor, 23 Mar. 1697). Organist and composer. Studied at Oxford; in 1632 appointed organist at St. George's Chapel, Windsor. Expelled from the chapel during the Interregnum, given back his post after the Restoration and eventually made musician to the chapel royal. Composed some 20 services and 80 anthems, as well as instrumental music.

Childhood of Christ, The. See *Enfance du Christ, L'.*

Children's Corner. A suite of six piano pieces composed by Debussy in 1906–8 and dedicated to his daughter Claude-Emma, who is referred to in the dedication as "Chouchou." The original English titles of the pieces are "Doctor Gradus ad Parnassum" (a humorous allusion to Clementi's *Gradus ad Parnassum*), "Jimbo's Lullaby," "Serenade for the Doll," "The Snow Is Dancing," "The Little Shepherd," and "Golliwogg's Cake-Walk."

Childs, Barney (Sanford) (b. Spokane, 13 Feb. 1926). Composer. Studied literature at Oxford and Stanford; teachers included Ratner, Chávez, Copland, and Carter; continued to compose during his career as professor of literature (1956–69). Composer-in-residence at the Wisconsin College-Conservatory (1970); professor of composition at Johnston College, Univ. of the Redlands. Has employed indeterminacy and improvisation (*The Roachville Project,* 1967), and composed more traditional multisectional pieces whose structures he calls "self-generating."

Chimes. (1) A set of tuned *idiophones (e.g., *gong chimes, stone chimes). (2) The *tubular bells of the orchestra and similar sets of struck tubes (e.g., doorbell chimes, wind chimes). (3) A set of stationary *bells or a small *carillon. Clock chimes, sounded by automatic mechanisms, have been popular in the West since the 15th century.

Chiming. See Bell (1).

Ch'in (qin) [Chin.]. A Chinese *zither made from a hollowed, slightly convex board approximately 120 cm. (4 ft.) long, 20 cm. wide, and 8 cm. deep, over the length of which are stretched seven silk strings of varying thickness. The most common tuning pattern is C D F G A c d. It has neither frets nor bridges. Inlaid along one edge of the instrument are 13 small disks of ivory or mother-of-pearl marking points at which a string is to be fully stopped or touched lightly to produce harmonics. The strings are plucked with the fingers in a variety of ways.

The instrument may have existed as early as the 15th century B.C.E. Archeological remains date from the 3rd century B.C.E. The earliest surviving work for it is thought to date from the 6th century and is preserved in tablature in a manuscript from the T'ang dynasty (618–906). See ill. under Instrument.

Chin rest [Fr. *mentionnière;* Ger. *Kinnhalter;* It. *mentoniera;* Sp. *mentonera, barbada*]. A holding device for the violin and other bowed stringed instruments played on the arm, allowing the player to grip the instrument firmly between chin and shoulder for ease of left-hand shifting without damping the sound by touching the table of the instrument with the chin. The modern chin rest was developed in the first quarter of the 19th century. Prior to that time, musicians placed their chins usually above or to the right side of the tailpiece, or supported the instrument mainly on the shoulder.

Chinese block [Fr. *bloc de bois, caisse chinoise;* Ger. *Holzblock, Holzblocktrommel;* It. *cassettina, blochetto;* Sp. *caja china*]. A percussion instrument consisting of a partially hollowed rectangular block of wood that is struck with wooden drumsticks or other beaters; also wood block. See ill. under Percussion instruments.

Chinese crescent, Chinese pavilion. *Turkish crescent.

Ch'ing (qing) [Chin.]. A Chinese sounding stone used in Confucian temple rituals. The *t'e ch'ing (te qing)* is a single thin piece of limestone or jade cut in an L-shape, hung from a frame, and struck with a wooden mallet. The *pien-ch'ing (bien qing)* is a set of such stones (usually 16) hung in two rows and carefully tuned. See ill. under Instrument.

Ching-hu [Chin.]. A Chinese *spike fiddle similar in construction and playing technique to the *erh-hu,* though only about 45 cm. tall; also called *hu-ch'in.* It is the principal melodic instrument in *Peking opera, where it plays along with the singer, ornamenting and elaborating the vocal line.

Chirimía [Sp.; Cat. *xirimía*]. A *shawm of Spain and Latin America. The keyed *chirimía* is important in the *cobla* bands of Catalonia. In some Indian communities of Mexico, Guatemala, and Colombia, an ensemble of two *chirimías* and a drum plays for public processions. See also *Dulzaina, Tiple, Zūrnā.*

Chironomy [fr. Gr. *cheir,* hand]. The use of movements of the hand to indicate approximate pitch or melodic contour to singers. The practice is evidently of great antiquity and is widely distributed. According to one of several competing hypotheses, the notations developed in the traditions of Jewish music, *Byzantine chant, and Western plainchant [see Neume] derive from the written tracing of hand gestures.

Chiroplast. A sliding frame attached to a piano keyboard for guiding and training the hands, patented in 1814 by Johann Bernhard Logier (1777–1846).

Chisholm, Erik (b. Glasgow, 4 Jan. 1904; d. Rondebosch, Cape Town, South Africa, 7 June 1965). Composer and conductor. Studied at the Scottish Academy of Music and with Tovey at Edinburgh Univ. Conducted the Glasgow Grand Opera (1930–39) and the Anglo-Polish Ballet (1940–43); while touring abroad founded the Singapore Symphony. From 1946 professor of music at the South African College of Music (Univ. of Cape Town). His own music em-

ploys relaxed twelve-tone techniques and includes Celtic and Hindu elements.

Chitarra [It.]. *Guitar.

Chitarra battente [It.]. A five-course (often with three strings per course), wire-strung, Italian folk guitar played with a plectrum and used for accompaniment. Developed in the 18th century, it resembles the 17th-century round-back guitar, with which it is often confused.

Chitarrone [It.]. (1) In 16th-century Italy, a large bass *lute whose fingerboard strings were tuned like those of the descant lute, but with the first two courses tuned an octave lower than lute pitch, and with seven or eight contrabasses tuned diatonically. See ill. under Lute. (2) In the 17th century, the *theorbo.

Chiterna [It.]. *Gittern.

Chiuso [It., closed]. (1) In horn playing, stopped [see Horn, Stopped tones, *Aperto*]. (2) In 14th-century music, the second of two endings for a section of a piece [see also *Ouvert* and *clos*].

Choeur [Fr.]. (1) *Choir. (2) *Course.

Choir. (1) A group of singers, especially one dedicated to the performance of sacred music [see also Chorus]. (2) A group of instruments of similar type, sometimes forming part of a larger ensemble, e.g., brass choir, woodwind choir. (3) That part of a church in which the choir (1) is placed.

Choirbook. A manuscript of dimensions large enough and in a format designed to permit an entire choir (of 20 or more singers) to sing from it; any manuscript in such a format, regardless of size. Such manuscripts were especially characteristic of the late 15th and early 16th centuries and could be as large as 75 × 50 cm. Manuscripts (including much smaller ones) containing polyphony of the period were generally copied in choirbook format, in which all parts appear separately on a single opening. The norm in four-part polyphony was for the superius to be copied above the tenor on the left-hand page (verso) of the opening, with the alto above the bass on the right-hand page (recto). See also Partbook, Score.

Choir organ. (1) A secondary division of English and American organs with its wind-chest often located behind the Great organ. (2) A small organ with a single keyboard, located in the choir of a church.

Choir pitch. See Pitch.

Chopin, Fryderyk (Franciszek) [Frédéric François] (b. Żelazowa Wola, near Warsaw, 1 Mar. 1810; d. Paris, 17 Oct. 1849). Composer and pianist. Studied piano with Adalbert Żywny and began to compose piano pieces, few of which have survived; played at charity concerts and private salons. In 1826 began courses in counterpoint and harmony at the conservatory, and in 1827–28 composed a number of larger works (Variations on Mozart's "Là ci darem," piano and orchestra; Piano Sonata op. 4; Fantasy on Polish Airs, piano and orchestra). In 1829 reached a new stage of maturity as a composer, producing works that remain among his most popular (the op. 9 Nocturnes, the Piano Concerto in F minor, the first of the op. 10 Etudes). That same year Chopin made an excursion to Vienna and gave several successful concerts there. In 1830 he left Warsaw forever, but his attempt to establish himself as a professional musician in Vienna was unsuccessful. Arrived in Paris in September 1831, where he found a much more hospitable atmosphere. Became friendly with Liszt, Berlioz, and the pianist Kalkbrenner, who helped arrange his first Paris concert (1832) which was well received; Schumann had already hailed him as a genius. Chopin gave very few of his own concerts, preferring to appear as guest in those of others; was more amenable to playing in private salons, often late at night, when he would sometimes improvise for hours. Much of his composing seems to have been done in the summer, which he spent in the country or on excursions. In 1838 began a liaison with George Sand, and that November accompanied her and her two children to Majorca. But his health suffered greatly from the Majorcan winter, and the diagnosis of tuberculosis only increased their difficulties. Chopin reached the mainland in February 1839 hemorrhaging badly but improved rapidly in Barcelona and then Marseilles. Spent the summer recuperating and composing at Sand's country estate at Nohant, returning to Paris in October, a pattern that he maintained until his break with her in 1847. In February 1848 Chopin gave his last Paris concert, and in April went to England, where he was heard at soirees and by Queen Victoria; also gave expensive lessons and private concerts for small audiences; concerts in Glasgow and Edinburgh followed. In November returned to Paris and resumed teaching. In summer 1849 moved to Chaillot but in September returned to the center of Paris, where he died on 17 October. Works include:

Piano and orchestra. 2 concertos: no. 1, op. 11 (1830), no. 2, op. 21 (1829–30); Variations on "Là ci darem" op. 2 (1827); Fantasy on Polish Airs op. 13 (1828); Krakowiak, rondo op. 14 (1828); Grand Polonaise op. 22 (1831).

Chamber music. Piano Trio op. 8 (1829); Cello Sonata op. 65 (1846); Introduction and Polonaise, cello and piano, op. 3 (1830).

Piano solo. Andante spianato op. 22 (1834); 4 ballades op. 23 (1835), op. 38 (1839), op. 47 (1841), op. 52 (1843); Barcarolle op. 60 (1846); Berceuse

op. 57 (1844); 27 etudes: 12 op. 10 (1829–32), 12 op. 25 (1832–36), 3 (1839); Fantaisie-impromptu op. 66 (1835); Fantasy op. 49 (1841); 3 impromptus op. 29 (1837), op. 36 (1839), op. 51 (1842); 59 mazurkas (1830–46, some posthumous); 21 nocturnes (1830–46, some posthumous); 15 polonaises (1817–42, some posthumous); Polonaise-fantaisie op. 61 (1846); 26 preludes: 24 op. 28 (1839), op. 45 (1841), 1 posthumous; 4 scherzos: op. 20 (1832), op. 31 (1837), op. 39 (1839), op. 54 (1842); 3 sonatas: op. 4 (1828), op. 35 (1839), op. 58 (1844); 19 waltzes: op. 18 (1831), 3 op. 34 (1831–38), op. 42 (1840), 3 op. 64 (1846–47), others posthumous.

19 Polish songs (1829–47), all posthumous.

Chor [Ger.]. *Chorus, *choir.

Choral. (1) Of or pertaining to a choir or chorus. (2) [Ger.] Plainchant. (3) [Ger.] *Chorale.

Choral cantata. A *cantata employing a chorus, as distinct from one for soloist only. See also Chorale cantata.

Choral Symphony. Popular name for Beethoven's Symphony no. 9 in D minor op. 125 (1822–24). The fourth and final movement, the introduction to which quotes themes from the preceding movements, is a setting for four soloists, chorus, and orchestra of Schiller's ode "To Joy" [Ger. "An die Freude"]. The first movement is an allegro, the second a scherzo with trio, and the third an adagio, all for orchestra alone.

Choralbearbeitung [Ger.]. A composition based on sacred melody, whether a plainchant or a chorale. Examples thus include Notre Dame *organum, many *motets, *chorale cantatas, and *organ chorales (including chorale preludes).

Chorale. The congregational song or hymn of the German Protestant (Evangelical) Church. The term derives from the German *Choral* (i.e., plainsong, in turn derived from the Latin *cantus choralis*) and first referred to the style of performance (as in plainsong, unison, and unaccompanied, i.e., *choraliter* as opposed to *figuraliter*). Only later, in the 17th century, did the word denote the tune and subsequently the text and tune together. Luther's Latin terms *canticum vernaculum* and *psalmus vernaculus* clearly refer to the text, as do the German *Lied* and *Kirchenlied*. *Kirchengesang* and *Gemeindegesang* (church song and congregational song) are later terms, the latter being current.

Martin Luther (1483–1546), like Calvin, insisted upon the value of congregational singing in the vernacular as part of the liturgical action. He provided the prototypes by adapting texts and tunes from a variety of sources and composing some few of them himself. The texts of Luther's 34 chorales are drawn from Psalms ("Ein' feste Burg," from Psalm 46), Gregorian seasonal hymns ("Nun komm' der Heiden Heiland," from "Veni Redemptor gentium," for Advent), antiphons ("Mitten wir im Leben sind," from "Media vita in morte sumus"), the Mass Ordinary ("Jesaia, dem Propheten," from the Sanctus), German sacred song ("Christ lag in Todesbanden," from "Christ ist erstanden"; see *Leise*), and nonliturgical Latin hymns ("Wir glauben all an einen Gott," from "Credo in unum Deum patrem omnipotentem"), with tunes adapted and readapted from these and secular sources or composed on similar models.

Bach composed many four-part harmonizations (still often regarded as paradigms of tonal harmony) and employed chorale melodies in very diverse and often elaborate ways in works for voices and for organ [see Chorale cantata, Chorale concerto, Chorale fantasia, Chorale fugue, Chorale motet, Chorale variations, Organ chorale]. See also Hymn, Organ chorale.

Chorale cantata [Ger. *Choralkantate*]. A *cantata based on the words or on both words and melody of a German Protestant *chorale. Several types are found among the works of Bach: (i) Every movement is based on both words and melody of the chorale (*Christ lag in Todesbanden* BWV 4). (ii) The first and last strophes of the chorale text are retained, but some others are paraphrased poetically and set as arias and recitatives (*Ach Gott vom Himmel* BWV 2). (iii) The first and last strophes of the chorale text are retained, but some others are replaced by poetry that is set as arias and recitatives (*Wachet auf* BWV 140 and *Ein' feste Burg* BWV 80). The final strophe of all three types is characteristically a relatively simple four-part setting of the melody.

Chorale concerto [Ger. *Choralkonzert*]. A setting for voices and instruments of a German Protestant *chorale, arising, like the *geistliches Konzert* of which it is a type, in the early 17th century under the influence of the Italian *concertato* style [see also Concerto (1)].

Chorale fantasia [Ger. *Choralfantasie*]. (1) A composition for organ in which a *chorale melody is treated freely. Successive phrases of the melody may be ornamented, broken into smaller motives, paraphrased, imitated, and the like. The genre was developed and cultivated by north German organists from the middle 17th century through the middle 18th, including Heinrich Scheidemann (ca. 1595–1663), Franz Tunder (1614–67), Dietrich Buxtehude (ca. 1637–1707), Vincent Lübeck (1654–1740), Georg Böhm (1661–1733), and Bach. In the later part of his career, Bach applied the term fantasia to large-scale organ works in which the chorale melody is treated as a *cantus firmus* in the bass. See Organ chorale.

(2) An elaborate choral movement based on a chorale melody, such as often occurs as the first movement of a Bach *chorale cantata.

Chorale fugue, chorale fughetta [Ger. *Choralfuge*]. A work for organ in which the first phrase of a *chorale is made the subject of a fugue. Such works were composed principally by middle-German composers of the later 17th and early 18th centuries, including Johann Pachelbel (1653–1706), and J. S. Bach. See also Organ chorale, Chorale motet.

Chorale motet [Ger. *Choralmotette*]. (1) A polyphonic vocal work in the style of a motet and based on a German Protestant *chorale melody. Examples from the early part of the 16th century usually treat the chorale melody as a *cantus firmus*. The term is most often applied, however, to settings from the later 16th century through the 18th in which successive phrases of the chorale are treated in imitation. Such works were often accompanied by instruments doubling the vocal parts. (2) A work for organ in the style of (1), also termed a chorale ricercar. See also Organ chorale.

Chorale partita. See Chorale variations.

Chorale prelude [Ger. *Choralvorspiel*]. A composition for organ based on a German Protestant *chorale melody and intended to serve as an introduction to the singing of the chorale. See Organ chorale.

Chorale ricercar. See Chorale motet.

Chorale variations. A composition for organ or harpsichord in which a German Protestant *chorale is made the basis of a set of variations. The genre was developed, under the influence of English keyboard variations, by Jan Pieterszoon Sweelinck (1562–1621), in whose works the chorale melody is presented in long notes, sometimes slightly ornamented, in a series of *cantus firmus* settings of varying texture and number of voices connected by transitional passages. In the second half of the 17th century, compositions of this type give way to settings, often termed chorale *partitas, in which each variation retains the basic structural (including rhythmic) properties of the chorale in the fashion of what are now normally thought of as sets of *variations. Bach's contributions include three early sets and the monumental *Canonic Variations on Vom Himmel hoch* BWV 769. See also Organ chorale.

Choralis constantinus. A three-volume collection of four-voice polyphonic settings of *Mass Propers for the liturgical year composed by Heinrich Isaac (ca. 1450–1517), completed and edited by his pupil Ludwig Senfl (ca. 1486–1542 or 1543), and published in Nuremberg in the years 1550–55 by Hieronymus Formschneider.

Choraliter [Lat.]. In the manner of *plainsong, as distinct from measured music.

Choralvorspiel [Ger.]. *Chorale prelude.

Chord [Fr. *accord;* Ger. *Akkord, Zusammenklang;* It. *accordo;* Sp. *acorde*]. Three or more pitches sounded simultaneously or functioning as if sounded simultaneously; two such pitches are normally referred to as an *interval. The most basic chords in the system of tonic-dominant or triadic *tonality are the major and minor *triads and their *inversions (the *sixth or six-three chord and the *six-four chord). Other chords that play an important though subordinate role are the *seventh chord (especially the dominant seventh), the augmented *sixth chord, the ninth chord, and the diminished triad, each of which is regarded in this context as dissonant [see Consonance, dissonance]. In the analysis of tonal music [see Harmonic analysis], all chords may be regarded as consisting of or deriving from two or more thirds (whether major or minor; see Interval) arranged one above another (e.g., G–B–D–F). When a chord is arranged in this most compact form containing only thirds, the lowest pitch is the root. A chord in which the root is the lowest pitch is said to be in root position regardless of the spacing of the pitches that lie above the root. The superposition of thirds may be extended to include ninth, eleventh, and thirteenth chords, each of which takes its name from the interval that separates the lowest and highest pitches when the chord is in the most compact form of root position. All such chords can be inverted, and, in some circumstances, one or more pitches other than the highest may be omitted.

In works of the 20th century not based on the tonal system, chords of numerous types are used, the concepts of consonance and dissonance being often irrelevant [see also Fourth chord, Tone cluster, Atonality, Twelve-tone music]. Discussions of such music often prefer the term simultaneity to chord, though the latter may appear in such compounds as trichord, tetrachord, pentachord, and *hexachord for collections of three, four, five, and six pitches, respectively, that may or may not be sounded simultaneously. Two pitches may be referred to as a dyad.

Chordal style. A style or texture consisting of *chords whose pitches are sounded simultaneously. Such texture is also described as homophonic or *homorhythmic. In strict chordal style, the number of pitches in each chord (and thus the number of parts making up the texture) remains constant (most often four, as in the Protestant chorale or hymn). In free chordal style, the number of pitches may vary.

Chordophone. Any instrument in which sound is produced by the vibration of a *string. Strings may be set in motion by plucking (as in the guitar), by striking (piano), or by bowing (violin). In some chordophones (such as the piano), strings are tuned to fixed pitches in advance and not normally altered during performance. In others (such as the violin), different pitches are produced in performance by altering the effective length or tension of a string. [For a discussion of the relationship of length, tension, and thickness of strings to their pitch, see Acoustics.] Many chordophones are provided with a *sound box or *resonator to amplify and prolong the sound. Chordophones are classified on the basis of their shape and construction into the following families: *harps, *lutes (including violins and guitars), *lyres, *musical bows, and *zithers (including pianos and harpsichords). See also Instrument.

Chorister. A singer in a choir, especially a boy singer.

Chorlied [Ger.]. A choral song, especially one without accompaniment.

Chôro [Port.]. An ensemble of serenaders of the type established in the later 19th century in Rio de Janeiro consisting of guitars, *cavaquinhos* (small, four-string guitars), flute and other winds, and percussion and dedicated to the polka and other dances of European derivation. In the early 20th century, it became prominently associated with such distinctive Brazilian popular dances as the *maxixe* and *samba*. The term *chôro* is also applied to various kinds of instrumental music that reflect the virtuosic, contrapuntal, and improvisatory character of the ensemble's typical performance and has been used in art music by Heitor Villa-Lobos, among others.

Chorton [Ger.]. See Pitch.

Chorus [fr. Gr. *choros;* Fr. *choeur;* Ger. *Chor;* It., Sp. *coro*]. (1) A body of singers who perform together, either in unison or in parts, usually with more than one on a part. A body of church singers is a choir, a term also sometimes used for a secular chorus. Other names for a secular chorus include glee club, choral society, and chorale. The most common kind of chorus at present, but not always in the past, is the mixed chorus of male and female voices, usually distributed soprano, alto, tenor, and bass, although other numbers of parts are not uncommon. Choruses of exclusively male, female, or boys' voices are also found. An a *cappella* chorus sings without instrumental accompaniment.

(2) A piece intended to be sung by a chorus, often a movement within a larger work.

(3) The *refrain, or *burden, of a strophic song, both text and music of which are repeated after each verse, or stanza, of changing text.

(4) In jazz, a single statement of the harmonic-melodic pattern (as of a 32-bar popular song in AABA form or the 12-bar *blues chord progression)

whose varied repetition constitutes a performance of a piece. The first and last choruses will usually be the same or similar in presenting the least varied statement of the given melody and harmonies. Intervening choruses are usually improvisations based on the pattern. To "take a chorus" is to improvise in this way.

(5) In organ registration, the combined sound of unison- and fifth-sounding stops of the same tone family. See *Plein jeu.*

(6) [Lat.]. In the Middle Ages, any of several instruments including the *bagpipe, *crwth, and *string drum.

Chou Wen-Chung (b. Chefoo, China, 29 July 1923). Composer. Came to the U.S. in 1946, studied composition at the New England Conservatory (Slonimsky) and Columbia (Luening); a student and associate of Varèse, whose *Nocturnal* he completed. Taught at Columbia from 1972. His style reflects an interest in the application of Asian concepts to Western music.

Chrétien [Crétien] **de Troyes** (b. Troyes; fl. ca. 1160–90). Trouvère, earliest known French poet-composer. Also wrote the Arthurian romances *Perceval* and *Lancelot*. Educated in Troyes, spent time at the court of Henry the Liberal, Count of Champagne. Five chansons, without music, are attributed to him in at least one manuscript source. Of these, only 2 (1 with and 1 without music) are now generally accepted as authentic.

Christ on the Mount of Olives. See *Christus am Ölberge.*

Christian, Charlie [Charles] (b. Bonham, Texas, 29 July 1916; d. New York, 2 Mar. 1942). Jazz guitarist. Played guitar and double bass with Trent (1938), then joined Goodman's sextet (1939–41), recording "Seven Come Eleven" (1939) and "Breakfast Feud" (1941) as well as "Solo Flight" with Goodman's big band (1941). Participated in jam sessions during the development of bop, including sessions with Thelonious Monk and Kenny Clarke recorded informally at Minton's Playhouse in New York (1941).

Christmas Concerto. Popular name for Corelli's Concerto Grosso in G minor op. 6 no. 8 (first printed in 1714), headed "Fatto per la notte di Natale" (made for Christmas night). The last movement is a *pastorale.

Christmas Oratorio. (1) [Ger. *Weihnachts-Oratorium;* Lat., *Oratorium tempore Nativitatis Christi*]. A work by Bach, BWV 248 (performed in 1734/35), consisting of six church cantatas intended to be performed on six successive days between Christmas Day and Epiphany. It includes a number of pieces used in earlier cantatas. (2) [Ger. *Historia, der freuden- und gnadenreichen Geburth Gottes und*

Marien Sohnes, Jesu Christi, Story of the Joyful and Merciful Birth of the Son of God and Mary, Jesus Christ]. A work by Heinrich Schütz, SWV 435, published in 1664. See also Cantata, Oratorio.

Christoff, Boris (b. Plovdiv, Bulgaria, 18 May 1914; d. Rome, 28 June 1993). Bass. Studied voice with Riccardo Stracciari in Rome, 1942–43. Operatic debut in Reggio Calabria as Colline in *La bohème.* Debut as Boris at Covent Garden, 1949; at La Scala, 1950; at San Francisco (U.S. debut), 1956. Especially praised for his Boris; other roles included Verdi's Philippe II, Handel's Giulio Cesare, and Wagner's King Marke.

Christophe Colomb [Fr., Christopher Columbus]. Opera in two parts by Darius Milhaud (libretto by Paul Claudel) composed in 1928 and first produced in Berlin in 1930. Setting: Spain at the end of the 15th century. Milhaud also composed substantially unrelated incidental music for Claudel's play.

Christou, Jani (b. Heliopolis, Egypt, 9 Jan. 1926; d. Athens, 8 Jan. 1970). Composer. Studied at Victoria College in Alexandria, with Hans Redlich in Letchworth, and at the Chigiana in Siena (1949–50). His varied oeuvre embraces serialism, aleatory techniques, and metaphysical texts. Works include much incidental music for classical Greek plays and 33 works from the genre he termed *anaparastis* (re-enactments), which attempt to re-create primitive rituals for modern uses.

Christus. (1) An oratorio by Liszt with texts from the Bible and the Roman Catholic liturgy, composed in 1862–67 and first performed in Weimar in 1873. (2) An unfinished oratorio by Mendelssohn.

Christus am Ölberge [Ger., Christ on the Mount of Olives]. An oratorio by Beethoven, op. 85 (libretto by Franz Xaver Huber), first performed in Vienna in 1803, and revised in 1804.

Christy, Edwin Pearce (b. Philadelphia, 28 Nov. 1815; d. New York, 21 May 1862). Entertainer. Considered the inventor of the minstrel show. Assembled and led the first company in Buffalo (1842); played almost continuously in New York City, also sending touring companies under his name throughout the country and in 1857 to Great Britain. From 1847 introduced many Stephen Foster songs.

Chromatic [Gr., colored]. (1) The *scale that includes all of the 12 pitches (and thus all of the 12 semitones) contained in an octave, as distinct from the *diatonic scale. (2) Harmony or melody that employs some if not all of the pitches of the chromatic scale in addition to those of the diatonic scale of some particular key, whether or not the harmony or melody in question can be understood within the context of any single key. See Chromaticism. (3) An instrument capable of playing a chromatic scale, e.g., *brass instruments with valves as distinct from natural instruments [but see also Harp]. (4) One of the three genera (the other two being *diatonic and *enharmonic) of the music of ancient Greece. It employs a *tetrachord bounded by a perfect fourth and in which the lower two intervals are both semitones. (5) [It. *cromatico.*] In the 16th century, works notated with black notes. See *Note nere.*

Chromatic Fantasy and Fugue. A composition for harpsichord in D minor by Bach, BWV 903 (ca. 1720, rev. ca. 1730). The fantasy makes extensive use of chromatic harmonies, and the fugue is based on a chromatic subject.

Chromaticism. The use of at least some pitches of the *chromatic scale in addition to or instead of those of the *diatonic scale of some particular key. It can occur in limited degrees that do not detract from the sense of key or tonal center; thus it can function fully within the system of tonic-dominant *tonality. The term may also refer, however, to the procedures employed in music in which no single diatonic scale or key predominates and in which, therefore, chromaticism cannot be regarded as the elaboration of an underlying diatonic structure [see also Atonality; Twelve-tone music].

In tonal music, chromaticism may occur as a surface detail or on a deeper structural level. At the surface or foreground, it may result simply from the filling in of whole steps with half steps. Chromatic pitches introduced in this way can usually be understood as resulting from an extension of the principles of *counterpoint or voice leading that produce *nonharmonic tones in general: passing tones, neighboring tones, suspensions, and the like, each of which may thus have both diatonic and chromatic forms. Chromaticism may also be associated at this level with modal mixture, i.e., the introduction of pitches from the parallel major or minor of the prevailing key. At a somewhat deeper level of musical structure, chromatic tones may bring about the *tonicization of a pitch other than the prevailing tonic. In this context, they most often occur as either the leading tone or the fourth scale degree of some key other than the prevailing tonic. The resulting harmonies are usually described as applied or secondary dominants. At the deepest level of structure, chromaticism is associated with *modulation from the prevailing tonic to other keys, especially keys whose tonics do not occur as diatonic pitches in the original key.

The harmonies resulting from chromatic voice leading, whether or not for the sake of modulation to remote keys, are often described as altered chords. Among the most prominent of these are various types of *sixth chords, including the Neapolitan sixth,

formed on the flatted supertonic, and the several augmented sixth chords. The diminished *seventh chord is inherently chromatic, since it cannot be constructed from the diatonic pitches of a single key (though it can occur on the raised leading tone in the harmonic minor scale). Also inherently chromatic, though much less prominent in tonal music, is the augmented *triad. See also Harmonic analysis.

From the mid-19th century onward, increasing amounts of music deploy the resources of chromaticism at all structural levels. The result sometimes undermines the procedures of tonality to such a degree that individual works are not easily described as belonging to a single key. Examples of such works include Chopin's Prelude op. 28 no. 2 and the prelude to Wagner's *Tristan und Isolde.* Wagner's opera is sometimes seen as marking a crisis in the tonal language, leading ultimately to its abandonment in the 20th century in the atonal works of Schoenberg and others. Of at least equal historical importance, however, is the rather different chromaticism of Debussy, which is not satisfactorily explained as resulting from an organic process of unchecked and ultimately destructive growth of the chromaticism latent within tonality.

Notable examples of chromaticism occur in some works from before the establishment of the tonal system in the late 17th century such as the madrigals of Marenzio and Gesualdo. See also *Musica ficta.*

Chronos, chronos protos [Gr.]. In ancient Greek music, the temporal unit. Theoretically indivisible, it takes the time of a short syllable of text.

Chrotta [Lat.]. See *Rote.*

Chueca, Federico (b. Madrid, 5 May 1846; d. there, 20 June 1908). Composer. Began as a cafe pianist and theater orchestra conductor, then composed zarzuelas, often in collaboration with Joaquín Valverde. *Agua, azucarillos y aguardiente* (1897), considered by many his best work, is still performed; also wrote very popular dance music.

Chung, Kyung Wha (b. Seoul, 26 Mar. 1948). Violinist. Debut in Seoul, 1957; studied with Galamian at Juilliard, 1960–67; joint winner (with Pinchas Zukerman) of the Leventritt Competition, 1967. U.S. debut, 1968; subsequently performed and recorded 19th- and 20th-century concertos with the world's major orchestras, resuming her career after a break in the mid-1980s to marry and have a child.

Church mode. See Mode.

Church sonata. *Sonata da chiesa.*

Chûte [Fr.]. In the 17th and 18th centuries, (1) an *appoggiatura, falling or rising; (2) a figured *arpeggio with one or two inserted dissonances.

Ciaccona [It.]. *Chaconne.

Ciampi, Vincenzo (Legrenzio) (b. Piacenza, 1719?; d. Venice, 30 Mar. 1762). Composer. May have studied with Rondini in Piacenza and with Durante and Leo in Naples. Composed several successful comedies in Naples and an opera seria, *Artaserse*, for Palermo (1747). Also composed choral music for the Ospedale degli incurabili in Venice, where he was choirmaster from 1747. During the 1750s was frequently in London, where his were among the first Italian comic operas performed.

Ciaramella [It.]. A south Italian *shawm, usually played in ensemble with the *zampogna.

Cibell, cebel. An English harpsichord or ensemble piece ca. 1680–1710 in imitation of the *gavotte "Descente de Cybelle" in Jean-Baptiste Lully's opera *Atys* (1676), act 1. Henry Purcell's version (an "old cibell") was itself imitated, creating a second generation of the genre.

Ciccolini, Aldo (b. Naples, 15 Aug. 1925). Pianist. Studied at the Naples Conservatory and subsequently taught there (1947–49). Moved to Paris in 1949, U.S. debut in 1950; professor at the Paris Conservatory from 1971. Recordings include the 5 concertos of Saint-Saëns as well as complete piano works by Satie and Massenet.

Ciconia, Johannes [Jean] (b. Liège, ca. 1335; d. Padua, between 15 and 24 Dec. 1411). Composer and theorist. From at least 1401 until his death associated with the cathedral of Padua; may have spent time in Avignon. His works are rooted in the musical traditions of northern Italy, but many also incorporate features typical of the French *ars nova* and *ars subtilior*. Secular compositions include 4 Italian madrigals, 9 *ballate*, 2 French virelays, and 1 Latin canon; sacred works include 10 Mass movements, 8 motets, and 2 Latin *contrafacta*. Two theoretical treatises survive: *Nova musica* and *De proportionibus*.

Cifra, Antonio (b. near Terracina, 1584; d. Loreto, 2 Oct. 1629). Composer. Director of music at various institutions in Rome; in 1609 became *maestro di cappella* of the Santa Casa, Loreto, holding this post for most of the rest of his life. Briefly (1623–26) *maestro* at St. John Lateran, Rome. The most prolific composer of the Roman school in the early 17th century; works include motets, Masses, 5-part madrigals, and ricercars.

Cikker, Ján (b. Banská Bystrica, Slovakia, 29 July 1911; d. Bratislava, 21 Dec. 1989). Studied at the Prague Conservatory and with Weingartner at the Vienna Academy (1936–37). From 1938 professor at the Bratislava Conservatory, and from 1951 professor of composition at the Bratislava Academy; stage

director for the Slovak National Opera (1944–48). Works are generally diatonic, though during the 1960s he experimented with twelve-tone composition, often within a diatonic context. Compositions include stage works (*Coriolanus*, 1972); orchestral works (Symphony "1945," 1974–75); choral and other vocal works; piano music.

Cilea, Francesco (b. Palmi, Calabria, 23 July 1866; d. Varazze, near Genoa, 20 Nov. 1950). Composer. Studied at the Naples Conservatory, 1881–89, taught piano there and theory and composition at the Florence Conservatory (1896–1904). Director of the Palermo (1913–16) and Naples (1916–35) Conservatories. His opera *L'arlesiana* (1897) was Caruso's first great success but the opera did not maintain itself without him; *Adriana Lecouvreur*, however, is still performed.

Cima, Giovanni Paolo (b. Milan, ca. 1570; d. after 1622). Composer and organist. By 1610 organist and *maestro di cappella* at S. Celso in Milan; a leading musical figure in Milan well into the 17th century. Published sacred collections (*Concerti ecclesiastici*, 1610, including 6 sonatas for 2–4 instruments with continuo, 2 of which represent the earliest known examples of solo sonatas and 2 of which are early examples of trio sonata texture) and keyboard collections (*Ricercate per l'organo*, 1602).

Cimarosa, Domenico (b. Aversa, 17 Dec. 1749; d. Venice, 11 Jan. 1801). Composer. Studied in Naples at the Conservatorio di Santa Maria di Loreto. Appointed second organist at King Ferdinand's royal chapel at Naples (1785); during the 1780s music master at Venice's Ospedaletto. From 1787 *maestro di cappella* at Catherine's court at St. Petersburg, from 1791 Kapellmeister in Vienna. Returned to Naples in 1794. Imprisoned in 1799 for antiroyalist tendencies; released the following year and went to Venice. Composed some 76 operas, which include the very popular *Il *matrimonio segreto* as well as *Giannina e Bernardone* (1781), *L'impresario in angustie* (1786), and *Gli Orazi ed i Curiazi* (Venice, 1797). Also composed sacred music and keyboard sonatas.

Cimbal d'amou. *Cembal d'amour.

Cimbalom [fr. Gr. *kymbalon*]. Either of two types of Hungarian *dulcimer: a smaller instrument similar to the Middle Eastern *santur or a larger instrument developed in the 1870s in Budapest by Joseph Schunda. The larger instrument has a large sound box and is set on legs. Metal strings arranged in courses of three or four and tuned chromatically run over individual bridges. A pedal mechanism operates dampers. This is a favorite instrument in Hungarian Gypsy orchestras and has also been used in orchestral works by Liszt, Kodály, Bartók, and Stravinsky. See ill. under Zither.

Cimbasso [It.]. (1) A bass or contrabass valve trombone, widely used in Italy in the 19th century. It is the bass of the brass group in all of Verdi's operas except *Otello* and *Falstaff* (which call for bass trombone). Whether the first uses of the term apply specifically to this instrument rather than to the serpent, ophicleide, or tuba remains in doubt. (2) A slide bass trombone with two valves, designed by Hans Kunitz in 1959.

Cinderella. (1) *Cenerentola, La.* (2) Ballet in three acts by Prokofiev (book by Nicolai Volkov, choreography by Rostislav Zakharov), composed in 1940–44 and first produced in Moscow in 1945. Prokofiev's music (with some omissions) was also used in a production with book and choreography by Frederick Ashton in London in 1948. Prokofiev employed music from the ballet in three orchestral suites and other works.

Cinelli [It.]. *Cymbals.

Cinque passi [It.; Fr. *cinq pas;* Eng. cinque pace, sinkapas, sink-a-pace, sink a part, etc.]. Five basic steps of the Renaissance *saltarello and *gagliarda, consisting of a forward thrust of alternate legs (L R L R) on the first four beats of the measure (coincidentally with each thrust the other foot executed a bounce), a leap on the fifth beat, and a resting stance (posture) on the sixth.

Cinti-Damoreau [née Montalant], **Laure (Cinthie)** (b. Paris, 6 Feb. 1801; d. Chantilly, 25 Feb. 1863). Soprano. Studied at the Paris Conservatory; opera debut in 1816; sang in opera mostly in Paris but also London and Brussels, in 1826–35 at the Opéra. Specialized in florid, Italianate singing. Moved to the Opéra-comique in 1836, where Auber wrote leading roles for her; retired from the stage in 1843; toured Europe and the U.S.; taught at the Paris Conservatory (1833–56).

Circle of fifths [Ger. *Quintenzirkel*]. The arrangement in a closed circle of all 12 pitch names in such a way that, when proceeding clockwise along the circle, any pair of adjacent pitch names represents the *interval of a perfect fifth [see fig.]. Thus, C to G is a perfect fifth, as are G to D, D to A, A to E, E to B, etc. Literal closure of the circle requires the substitution of an enharmonically equivalent pitch name at some point; otherwise, extending the series of fifths from C results in arrival at B♯ rather than C. Thus, B to F♯ is a perfect fifth; F♯ is enharmonically equivalent to G♭; G♭ to D♭ is a perfect fifth. Closure also requires the use of tempered tuning [see Temperament; Tuning; Interval]. Acoustically pure fifths (i.e., the fifths that occur in the harmonic series and that

equal 702 *cents) are larger by 2 cents than equally tempered fifths (700 cents). Thus, a succession of 12 acoustically pure fifths produces a pitch 24 cents (about one quarter of a semitone) higher than the starting point.

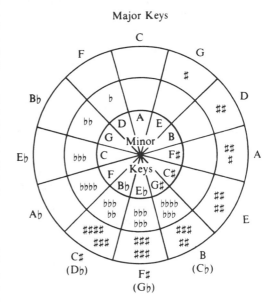

Major Keys

When each pitch name is taken to represent the tonic of a major *scale, the circle arranges keys in such a way that, beginning with C and proceeding clockwise, the number of sharps in each succeeding key increases by one; proceeding counterclockwise from C, the number of flats increases by one. The order in which sharps are added to a *key signature remains the same for all sharp keys, and this can be seen to be represented on the circle proceeding clockwise from F. Similarly, the pitches that must be flatted in the flat keys lie along the circle proceeding counterclockwise from B. The same relationships hold for minor keys, A minor (the relative minor of C major) being the minor key with no sharps and no flats in the key signature.

Because of the way in which sharps or flats are added to key signatures along the circle, the number of pitches in common between the starting key and each successive key outward in either direction decreases by one. Thus, the circle of fifths also illustrates the degree of relatedness of keys. The farther apart on the circle of fifths, the more distant in a musical sense are two keys from one another, since they will have fewer pitches in common.

Circular breathing. A technique employed in the playing of wind instruments, especially Western and non-Western woodwinds. The mouth is used to maintain a continuous stream of air through the instrument in such a way as to permit the player to draw breath through the nose.

Cis, cisis [Ger.]. C-sharp, C-double-sharp. See Pitch names.

Cister [Ger.], **cistre** [Fr.]. *Cittern.

Cithara [Lat.]. See Kithara.

Cither. *Cittern.

Cithrinchen [Ger.]. See Cittern.

Citole [Fr.; Eng. cythol, sitole, sytholle, etc.; Ger. *Zitole;* It. *cet(e)ra, cetula;* Sp. *citola*]. A wire-strung, plucked-string instrument; the medieval form of the Renaissance *cittern.

Cittern [Fr. *cistre, sistre;* Ger. *Cister, Cither, Zither;* It. *cetula;* Sp. *cistro, cedra*]. A small, wire-strung, quill-plucked instrument of Renaissance Europe, second in popularity only to the lute. It was developed late in 15th-century Italy from the *cetra (*citole)* to fill again the role of the ancient *kithara. The body of the 16th-century cittern is usually pear-shaped, with a flat back and a top bearing an ornate rosette, often of Gothic design. Before 1570, the body and its neck were carved from one piece of wood. By 1600, a standardized form, built up from pieces, had emerged. See ill. under Guitar. It remained popular into the 18th century when it was supplanted by such regional derivatives as the *English guitar, Portuguese *guiterra,* Spanish *bandurria,* and German *Cithrinchen.*

Cl. Abbr. for *clarinet.

Clair de lune [Fr., Moonlight]. The third movement of Debussy's *Suite bergamasque.*

Clairon [Fr.]. *Bugle.

Cláirseach [Gael.]. *Harp; especially the *Irish harp.

Clapisson, (Antoine-) Louis (b. Naples, 15 Sept. 1808; d. Paris, 19 Mar. 1866). Composer. From 1830 studied at the Paris Conservatory (violin with Habeneck, counterpoint with Reicha), taught there from 1862. Composed salon romances and 19 opéras comiques, of which *La perruche* (1840), *La promise* (1854), and *La fanchonnette* (1856) were especially popular.

Clapp, Philip Greeley (b. Boston, 4 Aug. 1888; d. Iowa City, 9 Apr. 1954). Composer and teacher. Studied at Harvard with Spalding, Converse, and Hill, and with Max von Schillings in Stuttgart; taught at Dartmouth (1915–18); after the war became director of music in the School of Fine Arts, Univ. of Iowa. His compositions, which include 3 symphonic po-

ems and 12 symphonies, are in a German Romantic idiom.

Clapper. (1) Any instrument consisting of two or more similar objects that are struck together; hence, a concussion idiophone, e.g., the *claves or the *bones. Vessel clappers, in which two convex objects are struck, include *castanets and *cymbals. Clappers are distributed worldwide and are extremely ancient. (2) The tongue of a *bell.

Clapton, Eric (b. Ripley, Surrey, 30 Mar. 1945). Rock guitarist, singer, and songwriter. Founding member of the Yardbirds (1963); played with John Mayall's Bluesbreakers (1965–66). His blues-oriented guitar technique was exhibited in his work with the bands Cream (1966–68), Blind Faith (1969), and Derek and the Dominoes (1970–72). In the 1970s recorded solo albums, achieving success with the song "Lay Down Sally" (1977).

Claquebois [Fr., obs.]. *Xylophone.

Clarín [Sp.]. *Clarino.

Clarin trumpet. A modern term for a natural trumpet on which the *clarino register or style of playing is exploited.

Clarinet [Fr. *clarinette;* Ger. *Klarinette;* It. *clarinetto;* Sp. *clarinete*]. A family of single-reed woodwind instruments with predominantly cylindrical bore. The modern instrument is generally made of grenadilla (African blackwood), less often of materials such as ebonite, plastic, and metal. See ill. under Reed.

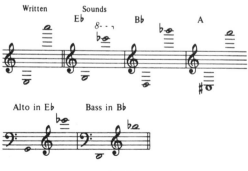

Ranges.

The complete family usually comprises the following instruments: high Ab, Eb, Bb, A, alto in Eb, bass in Bb, contrabass in Eb, and contrabass in Bb. All clarinets have approximately the same written range, e to c'''' in the treble staff; but the lower instruments seldom use their higher octaves. They are notated as *transposing instruments. Some scores notate the bass instruments in the bass clef, one octave below the written range given above. Of the instruments listed, the clarinet in B♭ is the most common. Orchestral parts often call for the clarinet in A. The player is expected either to double on this instrument or to transpose the part.

The clarinet is descended from the European *chalumeau* around 1700. It steadily acquired additional keys during the 18th century. By about 1750, the five-key clarinet (E/B, F♯/C♯, G♯/D♯, A, B♭/*speaker) had become standard. The instrument was built in several sections: mouthpiece, barrel, left-hand section, right-hand section, lower section, and bell. Sometimes the lower section and the bell were made in one piece. Near the end of the 18th century, a sixth key (C♯/G♯) was added. Additional keys continued to be added to facilitate trills and the slurring of difficult intervals. Today two principal systems of keys survive: the *Boehm system, used throughout the French- and English-speaking worlds, and the descendants of the older five-key system, used in German- and Russian-speaking countries. Clarinets of various types and pitch are also widely used in the folk music of eastern Europe, India, and especially Turkey.

Clarino [It.]. (1) The upper range of the Baroque *trumpet, from the eighth through the twentieth pitch of the *harmonic series or higher. (The lower range was called the *principale.*) (2) The style of trumpet playing that uses the natural trumpet in its highest register, where the diatonic scale is possible. (3) In the Middle Ages and Renaissance through the 18th century, a trumpet.

Clarion. In the Middle Ages and Renaissance, a *trumpet.

Clarke, Henry Leland (b. Dover, N.H., 9 Mar. 1907). Composer and scholar. Studied with Holst at Harvard, with Boulanger (1929–31), and with Weisse and Luening in New York (1932–38). Taught at UCLA, Vassar, and the Univ. of Washington (1958–77). Composed in a tonal style, in which line and lyricism outweigh vertical elements; used unusual scales (String Quartet no. 3, 1958, uses no semitones) and "wordtones," in which the repetition of a word necessitates the repetition of its associated pitch in the same octave (*Lysistrata,* opera, 1968–72).

Clarke [Clark, Clerk], **Jeremiah** (b. London, ca. 1673; d. London, 1 Dec. 1707). Composer. Chorister of the Chapel Royal in London by 1685; organist at Winchester College (1692–95). From 1699 vicar-choral, then organist, then almoner and Master of the Choristers at St. Paul's Cathedral, London. From 1700 Gentleman Extraordinary of the Chapel Royal, and from 1704 until his death (by suicide) organist there (jointly with Croft). Composed services and anthems; psalms and hymns; much music for plays

and other stage works; instrumental music. Best known for a *Trumpet Voluntary.

Clarke, Kenny [Kenneth Spearman; Klook] (b. Pittsburgh, 9 Jan. 1914; d. Montreuil-sous-Bois, near Paris, 26 Jan. 1985). Jazz drummer and bandleader. Played in big bands from 1935, then helped create the bop style in jam sessions with Gillespie, Monk, and Christian (1940–43). Recorded as a leader, including *Epistrophy* (1946, with Fats Navarro and Bud Powell), which he composed with Monk, and joined Gillespie's big band (1946–48). Helped form the Modern Jazz Quartet, then settled in Paris where he played with Powell (1959–62). With Francy Boland led an octet and big band (1960–73).

Clarone [It.]. (1) Bass *clarinet. (2) *Basset horn.

Clàrsach, clarsech, clarseth [Gael.]. *Cláirseach.

Classical [fr. Lat. *classicus,* Roman citizen of the highest class; Fr. *classique*]. (1) In popular usage, art or "serious" music as opposed to "popular" music.

(2) In French writings about music, the period or style of Louis XIV (ruled 1643–1715), often extended to include the music of Jean-Philippe Rameau (1683–1764).

(3) The period or style that has its tentative beginnings in Italy in the early 18th century and extends through the early 19th century. In most periodizations of music history, the Classical period therefore succeeds the Baroque and precedes the Romantic, in both cases with sizable chronological overlaps. The basic components of the new style of the early 18th century were homophonic texture and simpler, more "natural" melody. (This style was labeled the *galant style by theorists of the time.) To these characteristics may be added the development of hierarchical phrase and period structure (at first generally based on phrases of two bars, later of four), introduction of a greater degree of affective and stylistic contrast within sections or movements, use of graded dynamics such as the *crescendo,* choice of more differentiated and contoured rhythmic values (as opposed to the more continuous beat-marking, unicellular rhythms of the late Baroque), simplification of the harmonic vocabulary, and slowing of the harmonic rhythm (the latter two points related to the growing preference for harmonic rather than linear bass lines).

Elements of the new style appear decisively in Italian instrumental music somewhat later than in opera, from ca. 1730 on [see Symphony, Overture, Sonata, Concerto].

In addition to the characteristics already noted, orchestral music saw the development of various principles of *sonata form as well as a more idiomatic approach to orchestration. Music for soloists during the early part of this period tended to cultivate a highly ornamented melodic style based on constant subdivision of the beat and half-beat levels; figures involving triplet sixteenth notes, dotted sixteenths and thirty-seconds, and the like are ubiquitous. This tendency toward rhythmic intricacy reached its peak in the keyboard works of the north German *empfindsam* style.

The wide range of styles characteristic of the period from ca. 1720 to ca. 1765 has led some scholars to consider it a separate "Pre-Classical" period preceding what they regard as the "true" classicism of Haydn and Mozart. [For another frequent designation of this period, see Rococo.] Many scholars now prefer to designate the period from ca. 1720 (later in other countries than Italy) through approximately the 1760s as simply the "early Classical period," in full realization of the oversimplification all such labels entail.

The period from approximately the 1760s until the end of the century brought a synthesis of the disparate idioms of the early phase into a more cosmopolitan "middle" style, one that was basically Italianate but that also increasingly introduced stylistic and formal complexity and expressive depth. The culmination of this approach is represented by the mature works of Haydn and Mozart.

The description "late Classical" is appropriate for those successors of Haydn and Mozart who generally avoided the new Romantic currents of the early 19th century. In the case of Beethoven, however, there has long been disagreement as to whether he is best regarded as a Classical or Romantic composer. Much of Beethoven's style may be viewed as fundamentally an extension and expansion of the styles of Haydn and Mozart. Nevertheless, many of Beethoven's late works are too personal and idiosyncratic to relate directly to either a Classical or Romantic tradition.

Classical Symphony. Prokofiev's Symphony no. 1 in D major op. 25 (1916–17), composed in a style sometimes called *neoclassical. It is scored for a relatively small orchestra of strings with pairs of wind instruments reminiscent of the works of Haydn and Mozart.

Clausula [Lat., fr. *claudo, claudere,* to conclude]. (1) From the 11th to the 15th century, a cadence. The word *clausula* was largely replaced in the 16th century by *cadentia.*

(2) In the 12th and 13th centuries, a passage of (Parisian) liturgical polyphony, most often in *discant style. The tenor (the voice on which the piece is based) is typically a melismatic fragment from one of the responsorial chants of the Mass or the Office. The principal source for the *clausula* is the *Notre Dame repertory, which includes more than 900 pieces for two voices plus a handful for three and four. Many

of these are embedded in larger organal settings of chants [see Organum]; many others are copied separately. The rhythm of these pieces is characterized by the rhythmic *modes.

The *clausula* as such, which seems to have attracted little attention after ca. 1230, survived to the end of the century as the basis of the enormously popular *motet.

Clavecin [Fr., occasionally *claveçin, clavessin*]. *Harpsichord.

Clavecín [Sp.]. *Harpsichord.

Clavecin d'amore. *Cembal d'amour.

Claves [Sp.]. A Cuban *clapper consisting of a pair of solid, hardwood cylinders, each approximately 20 cm. long; see ill. under Percussion instruments. One cylinder rests against the fingernails of a loosely formed fist (cupped to act as a resonator) and is struck with the other. They are widely used in the urban popular music of Latin America. The most characteristic rhythmic figure played on the *claves* is shown in the accompanying example.

Clavessin [Fr.]. *Harpsichord.

Clavicembalo [It.], **clavicémbalo** [Sp.]. *Harpsichord.

Clavichord [Fr. *clavicorde, manicorde;* Ger. *Clavichord, Klavichord, Clavier;* It. *clavicordo, manicordo, sordino;* Sp. *clavicordio, manicordio, monacordio*]. A stringed keyboard instrument in use from the 15th to 18th centuries and revived since the 1890s. It consists of a rectangular case with its keyboard projecting from or set into one of the long

Clavichord.

sides. The soundboard is to the right of the keyboard and the strings traverse the case from right to left. When a key is depressed, a brass blade or tangent at the far end strikes a pair of strings, remaining in contact until the key is released. To the left of the tangent, the strings are damped by a strip of cloth (or listing). But at the right, where they pass over a bridge that transmits their vibrations to the soundboard, the strings are sounded by the blow of the tangent [see ill.]. When the key is released, the listing silences the strings immediately. Since the tangent's striking point determines the strings' vibrating length, several different pitches can be produced on a single pair of strings by causing various tangents to strike at different points. But as one pair of strings can sound only one pitch at a time, keys whose tangents strike the same pair cannot be sounded simultaneously. Thus, from the earliest times makers took care that only notes forming dissonances with each other would be sounded on the same strings. Clavichords in which pairs of strings are struck by more than one tangent are called fretted [Ger. *gebunden*]; those in which each key has its own pair are termed unfretted or fret-free [Ger. *bundfrei*].

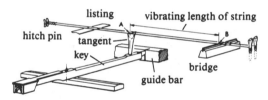

Clavichord mechanism.

The sound of the clavichord is relatively small and soft, but it has a wide dynamic range: variations in the force with which the keys are depressed produce corresponding variations in loudness, much as on the piano. A special effect unavailable on any other keyboard instrument, is the **Bebung,* a kind of vibrato produced by varying finger pressure on the key.

The precise role of the clavichord in the history of keyboard music is difficult to establish. Although the word *Clavier* appears frequently on the title pages of German publications, the term means keyboard instrument as well as clavichord. The clavichord, however, was the usual domestic instrument of the 16th, 17th, and 18th centuries in Germany, and its value as an instrument for teaching and practice had been emphasized from the early years of the 16th century.

Clavicor [Fr.; It. *clavicorno*]. An alto or tenor brass instrument in a tall, upright shape. It has a very narrow bore and three Stölzel **valves, one for the left hand and two for the right. Patented in 1837, it was designed to replace the **ophicleide and was made in five sizes (alto in F and E♭; tenor in D♭, C, and B♭).

Later models had all three valves together in the usual right-hand position.

Clavicylinder. A keyboard instrument invented by Ernst Friedrich Chladni ca. 1800. Depressing a key pressed a tuned metal bar against a revolving glass cylinder, thus causing the bar to sound by friction. See also Sostenente piano.

Clavicytherium [Fr., also *clavecin vertical;* Ger. *Klaviziterium;* It. *claviciterio, cembalo verticale;* Sp. *claveciterio*]. An upright harpsichord and hence one in which the plane of the strings is vertical. Because such instruments required relatively little space, they were widely used in the 17th and 18th centuries.

Clavier [Eng., Fr., Ger.]. **Keyboard; in English, widely used to mean stringed keyboard instrument (harpsichord, clavichord, piano, etc.) in contradistinction to the organ; there is no instrument called in English clavier. In the second half of the 18th century, *Clavier* was the normal German word for clavichord, though it was not rigorously confined to that meaning; in the 19th century, *Klavier* became the normal word for piano.

Clavier-Übung [Ger., Keyboard Study]. Bach's title for four publications of his keyboard music. *Clavier-Übung* I (published 1731) contains six partitas BWV 825–30; II (published 1735) the **Italian* Concerto BWV 971 and an *Ouvertüre nach französischer Art* (Overture in the French Manner) BWV 831; III (published 1739) nine chorale preludes for Mass and twelve for the catechism BWV 669–89 and four duets BWV 802–5 framed by the Prelude and Fugue (**St. Anne's Fugue*) in E♭ major BWV 552; IV (published 1741–42) the **Goldberg Variations.* Parts I, II, and IV are for harpsichord, whereas part III is for the organ. The term had earlier been used in the titles of Johann Kuhnau's *Neue* [New] *Clavier-Übung* (1689, 1692) and Johann Krieger's *Anmuthige* [Charming] *Clavier-Übung* (1698).

Clavilux. A **color organ introduced in 1925 by Thomas Wilfrid. It projected moving colors and shapes on a screen, but did not produce sounds.

Claviorgan [Lat. *claviorganum;* Fr. *clavecin organisé;* Ger. *Orgelklavier;* It. *claviorgano;* Sp. *claviórgano*]. A keyboard instrument combining a harpsichord or piano and an organ. Such instruments were described in the late 15th century, and examples survive from the 16th. They were built in the late 18th century by some of the best makers of stringed keyboard instruments, including Stein, Taskin, and Broadwood.

Clavis [Lat., key, as of a lock; pl. *claves*]. (1) **Clef. (2) Pitch, especially any of the pitches making up the **gamut.

Clayton, Buck [Wilbur Dorsey] (b. Parsons, Kans., 12 Nov. 1911; d. 8 Dec. 1991). Jazz trumpeter and arranger. Joined Count Basie (1936–43), recorded often as a soloist with him, Billie Holiday (1937–39), and Lester Young (1938–39, 1944). Led groups as a trumpeter (into the early 1970s) and arranger (through the 1980s) and worked with Jazz at the Philharmonic (from 1946).

Clef [fr. Lat. *clavis,* key; Fr.; Ger. *Schlüssel;* It. *chiave;* Sp. *clave*]. A sign placed at the beginning of a staff to indicate the position of some particular pitch and, by extension, the pitches represented by all of the staff's lines and spaces. There are three types of clefs now in general use: the G-clef, the C-clef (of which there are several shapes), and the F-clef [see Ex. 1]. The spiral of the lower part of the G-clef locates the position of g′ (the G above middle C) on some line, now almost exclusively on the second line from the bottom, in which case it is termed the treble or violin clef. The C-clef is now placed on either of two lines so as to locate the position of c′ (middle C): when placed on the third line it is termed the alto or viola clef; when placed on the fourth line it is the tenor clef. The F-clef locates f (the F below middle C) and is today employed almost exclusively on the fourth line, in which case it is termed the bass clef.

4a. French violin clef.   b. Treble clef, violin clef.
c. Soprano clef, descant clef.   d. Mezzo-soprano clef.
e. Alto clef.   f. Tenor clef.   g, h. Baritone clefs.
i. Bass clef.   j. Subbass clef.

The three clefs in their most common positions are illustrated in Ex. 2. The combination of clef and posi-

tion is sometimes indicated by the letter of the clef followed by the number of the line; hence, the treble clef is G2, the alto clef C3, the bass clef F4.

The treble clef is now used for the violin, woodwinds, higher brasses, and the right hand in keyboard music. Some wind instruments so notated, however, may actually sound in higher or lower octaves [see also Transposing instruments]. The alto clef is employed principally for the viola, for which it is the normal clef. The tenor clef is occasionally used for the cello, bassoon, and trombone, the normal clef for all of which is the bass clef. The bass clef is employed, in addition, for lower brasses, the double bass, and the left hand in keyboard music. The G-clef on the second line is also regularly used for the tenor part in choral music and in this context is understood to represent transposition down one octave from the normal treble clef. This is sometimes made explicit, especially in editions of early music (where it may serve for parts other than the one actually called the tenor), in the ways shown in Ex. 3. Historically, all three clefs have been used in a variety of positions, as illustrated and identified in Ex. 4.

Clefs were first used with regularity in the 12th century, F- and C-clefs being by far the most common. The modern form of the G-clef came into use in the 16th century. In the 17th and 18th centuries, G1 was more often used than G2, with the result that G1 is still sometimes termed the French violin clef. In the course of the 20th century, the use of the C-clef has steadily declined except in the music of a few instruments, principally the viola and, to a lesser extent, the tenor trombone and bassoon. Thus, even in modern editions of earlier music that employed a variety of clefs, the treble, octave-treble, and bass clefs are now used almost exclusively. For the use in the Renaissance of certain standard combinations of clefs, see *Chiavette,* Mode. See also Notation.

Clemencic, René (b. Vienna, 27 Feb. 1928). Recorder player, composer, and musicologist. Studied recorder, keyboard instruments, and musicology and philosophy at Univ. of Vienna, Collège de France, and the Sorbonne. Founded *Musica antiqua,* 1958, known as *Ensemble musica antiqua* from 1959. Professor at the Musikhochschule in Vienna, 1961. Since 1969 his Clemencic Consort, based in Vienna, has performed and recorded music from the Middle Ages to the avant garde.

Clemens (non Papa) [Clement, Jacob] (b. probably in Ieper, ca. 1510; d. Dixmuiden, near Ieper, 1555 or 1556). Composer. Bruges Cathedral employed him as succentor, 1544–45; motet texts suggest a connection with Charles V between 1544 and 1549. Surviving manuscripts indicate some relationship with Leiden; little else is known of his life. One of the most prolific composers of the early 16th century, wrote both sacred and secular music but is chiefly known for the former, which include 15 Masses, 2 Mass fragments, over 230 motets, 2 Magnificats, and 3-part polyphonic settings of the Psalms in Dutch.

Clementi, Aldo (b. Catania, 25 May 1925). Composer. Studied with Sangiorgi and Petrassi and at the Santa Cecilia Conservatory in Rome. Attended Darmstadt summer courses (1955–62); worked under Maderna's guidance at the Milan Radio electronic music studio (1956–57). Taught composition at the Milan and Bologna conservatories. Mature compositions are organized around variations in the density of a set of interchangeable events (*Sette scene*). Other works include *Collage,* stage, 1961; *O Du Selige,* orchestra, 1985; concerto for piano and 11 instruments, 1986.

Clementi, Muzio [Mutius Philippus Vincentius Franciscus Xaverius] (b. Rome, 23 Jan. 1752; d. Evesham, England, 10 Mar. 1832). Composer, music publisher, and pianist. An Englishman who heard him play in 1766 took the boy to his English country estate for intensive musical studies and to serve as his house musician. After seven years in Dorsetshire Clementi moved to London and began concertizing; in 1780 began a concert tour that included Paris and Vienna, where he engaged in the famous keyboard contest with Mozart in 1781. Returned to London in 1783 and settled permanently there, becoming a successful pianist, pedagogue, and music publisher; from the 1790s concentrated on teaching and publishing. In 1802 embarked on a concert tour to Paris, Vienna, and St. Petersburg with his pupil John Field. During the 1820s continued directing concerts of his works and made other tours of the Continent. The 3 volumes of his highly successful pedagogical work *Gradus ad Parnassum, or The Art of Playing on the Piano Forte* appeared in 1817, 1819, and 1826. Works include more than 100 piano sonatas (many accompanied) and many works for 4-hand piano.

Clemenza di Tito, La [It., The Clemency of Titus]. An *opera seria* in two acts by Mozart. The libretto, by Caterino Mazzolà, is an abridgment and adaptation of one by Pietro Metastasio. The simple recitatives were perhaps composed by Mozart's student Franz Xaver Süssmayr. The work was first produced in Prague in 1791 at the coronation of Emperor Leopold II as King of Bohemia. Setting: Rome, ca. 80 C.E.

Clérambault, Louis-Nicolas (b. Paris, 19 Dec. 1676; d. there, 26 Oct. 1749). Composer and organist. Studied music with Raison and Moreau, and around 1705 was appointed *surintendant* for Louis XIV. In 1704 published the *Premier livre de pièces de clavecin.* Around 1710 assumed the post of organist at St. Sulpice; in 1714 was also appointed organist at the

convent at St. Cyr, and in 1719 at the church in the rue St. Jacques. Later vocal and instrumental works show the increasing presence of Italian elements. Works include cantatas (*Orphée,* 1710; *La muse de l'opéra,* 1716); motets; collections for harpsichord (1704) and organ (ca. 1710).

Cliburn, Van [Lavan, Harvey, Jr.] (b. Shreveport, La., 12 July 1934). Pianist. Studied with his mother, Rilda Bee O'Bryan. Performed with the Houston Symphony, 1947; New York debut, 1948; subsequently studied with Lhevinne at Juilliard. Won the Tchaikovsky Competition in Moscow in 1958, returned to the first New York ticker-tape parade for a musician. His international career includes 4 tours of the U.S.S.R., 1960–72. Took a leave of absence from public performance, 1978–89; a U.S. tour in 1994 met with little critical success.

Cliquet-Pleyel, Henri (b. Paris, 12 Mar. 1894; d. there, 9 May 1963). Composer. Studied with Gédalge at the Paris Conservatory; belonged to the École d'Arcueil, a group founded by Satie in 1923. His own compositions were rarely performed; they include film scores; orchestral and chamber music; piano works.

Cloche [Fr.]. *Bell; cloches tubulaires,* *tubular bells.

Clock Symphony. Popular name for Haydn's Symphony no. 101 in D major Hob. I:101 (1793–94; one of the *London Symphonies), so called because of the ticking motif in the second movement (Andante).

Clocking. See Bell.

Clockwork instruments. See Automatic instrument.

Clos [Fr.]. See *Ouvert* and *clos.*

Close. *Cadence.

Close harmony, position. In harmony in four voices, the placement of the three uppermost voices as close together as possible, i.e., without the omission of a chord tone between soprano and alto or alto and tenor. See also Spacing.

Closing theme. A theme occurring at the end of the exposition in *sonata form.

Cluster. See Tone cluster.

Clutsam keyboard. See Keyboard.

Cluytens, André (b. Antwerp, 26 Mar. 1905; d. Neuilly, 3 June 1967). Conductor. Studied at the Conservatoire royal flamand (1914–22); choral coach with the Théâtre royal français d'Anvers (1921–32). Theater conductor in Toulouse, 1932–35; at Lyons, 1935, becoming music director, 1942. Music director of the Opéra-comique, Paris, 1947–53.

Frequent conductor at Vienna State Opera from 1959; music director of the Orchestre national de belgique from 1960.

C.O. Abbr. for *Coll' *ottava.*

Coates, Albert (b. St. Petersburg, Russia, of English parents, 23 Apr. 1882; d. Milnerton, South Africa, 11 Dec. 1953). Conductor and composer. Studied with Nikisch at the Leipzig Conservatory, 1902; a coach at the Leipzig Opera. Conductor at the Elberfeld (1906), Dresden (1909), and Mannheim (1910) operas. Music director, St. Petersburg Opera, 1911–17. Led Rochester Philharmonic, 1923–25. Moved to South Africa in 1946; taught at the Univ. of South Africa at Cape Town and led the Johannesburg Symphony. Compositions include operas and the symphonic poem *The Eagle* (1925).

Coates, Eric (b. Hucknall, England, 27 Aug. 1886; d. Chichester, 21 Dec. 1957). Composer and violist. Studied at the Royal Academy of Music. Joined the Hamburg String Quartet (1908); founding member of the Beecham Symphony Orchestra; played in the Queen's Hall Orchestra (1910–19). Composer of light music: the ballet suite *Snow White and the Seven Dwarfs* (1930; rev. as *The Enchanted Garden,* 1938); the fantasy *Cinderella* (1929); marches; other orchestral music; and over 100 songs.

Coclico, Adrianus Petit (b. Flanders, 1499 or 1500; d. Copenhagen, 1563). Composer. Originally a Flemish Catholic, converted to Protestantism and moved to Germany, first teaching privately at the Univ. of Wittenberg in 1545. From late 1547 to 1550 served in the chapel of the Duke of Prussia; in Nuremberg in 1552 published a collection of motets and the treatise *Compendium musices;* both are prominent in their use of the term *musica reservata.* Subsequently was a musician at the Danish royal court and in the service of Marcellus Amersfortius.

Coda [It., tail]. In instrumental music following regular musical forms, a concluding section extraneous to the form as usually defined; any concluding passage that can be understood as occurring after the structural conclusion of a work and that serves as a formal closing gesture. Although codas may on occasion consist of only a few perfunctory chords, they may on other occasions assume considerable dimensions and cannot always be regarded as essentially superfluous. Beethoven used codas most notably to delay or interrupt a final resolution, often with highly dramatic effect. In some cases, they may approach the weight and technical resources of a development (e.g., the first movements of Symphony nos. 3, 5, and 9). See also Codetta.

Codax [Codaz], **Martin** (fl. ca. 1230). Composer and poet. His extant works are 7 poems, 6 with musical settings. The poems are *cantigas d'amigo* and are the only secular medieval Galician–Portuguese lyrics with music that have survived.

Codetta [It., little tail]. (1) In *sonata form, a brief coda concluding the exposition. (2) In an exposition of a *fugue, a modulatory passage connecting the end of a statement of the subject in the dominant with the beginning of the next statement in the tonic. (3) A brief coda concluding an inner section of a movement or piece as opposed to a coda at the end of the movement or piece as a whole.

Coelho, Rui (b. Alcácer do Sal, Portugal, 3 Mar. 1891; d. Lisbon, 5 May 1986). Composer and pianist. Studied in Lisbon, with Bruch, Humperdinck, and Schoenberg (1910–13) in Berlin, and with Vidal in Paris. His music employs folklike themes and was important in establishing a national style in Portugal. Works include some 20 operas (*Auto da barca da glória,* 1970); ballet scores; orchestral works, many on Portugese themes (*Retábulo português,* 1960); vocal music; chamber works.

Coerne, Louis (Adolphe) (b. Newark, N.J., 27 Feb. 1870; d. Boston, 11 Sept. 1922). Composer, conductor, and teacher. Studied with Payne at Harvard (1888–90) and with Rheinberger in Munich (1890–93); received the first American Ph.D. in music (Harvard, 1905). Director of the School of Music at the Univ. of Wisconsin (1910–15) and professor at Connecticut College for Women (1915–22). His more than 500 compositions include many dramatic works (*Zenobia,* 1905); orchestral music; chamber music; songs; incidental music.

Coffee Cantata. Popular name for Bach's secular cantata *Schweigt stille, plaudert nicht* [Ger., Be quiet, don't prattle] for soloists and orchestra BWV 211 (ca. 1734–35). The cantata relates the predicament of a burgher's daughter whose coffee habit her father wishes to break.

Cog rattle. An instrument consisting of a grooved cylinder attached to a handle and a wooden tongue, both set in a frame; also ratchet. The frame is whirled around the cylinder, causing the tongue to strike the cogs in rapid succession. See also *Matraca.*

Cohan, George M(ichael) (b. Providence, R.I., 3 July 1878; d. New York, 5 Nov. 1942). Popular songwriter, actor, and producer. In the early 1900s in New York wrote several musical shows that prefigured the Broadway musical comedy; continued to write, appear in, and produce shows on Broadway. His best-known songs were patriotic ("You're a Grand Old Flag," 1906; "Over There," 1917). The subject of a biographical movie (*Yankee Doodle Dandy,* 1942) and musical (*George M!,* 1968).

Col, coll', colla, colle [It.]. With, with the. For phrases beginning with these words, see the word following, e.g., *arco, punta d'arco, destra, legno, ottava.*

Colascione [It.; Fr. *colachon*]. A fretted, *long-necked lute of Eastern origin introduced first into 16th-century Italy and into France and Germany in the 17th century. Its two or three metal or sometimes gut strings were tuned (E) A d and played with a plectrum. It may have been used as a drone in popular and amateur ensembles, and according to Johann Mattheson (1713), it was used as a continuo instrument in Germany. See ill. under Lute.

Colbran, Isabella [Isabel] **(Angela)** (b. Madrid, 2 Feb. 1785; d. Castenaso, near Bologna, 7 Oct. 1845). Soprano. From 1807 a leading prima donna in Italy; between 1811 and 1821 a fixture at the San Carlo, Naples; Rossini wrote many parts for her there (from 1815). In 1822 she and Rossini married; his last role for her was in *Semiramide*. By their joint engagement in London, 1824, her voice was so far gone that she had to be replaced, and she retired. The couple separated in 1837.

Cole, Cozy [William Randolph] (b. East Orange, N.J., 17 Oct. 1906; d. Columbus, Ohio, 29 Jan. 1981). Jazz drummer. Recorded with Jelly Roll Morton (1930) and belonged to Benny Carter's big band (1933–34) and Stuff Smith's combo (1936–38) before joining Cab Calloway (1938–42). Led groups intermittently, then joined Louis Armstrong's All Stars (1949–53). Toured with Earl Hines and Jack Teagarden (1957) and then as a leader following the success of "Topsy" (1958). Joined Jonah Jones's quintet in 1969 and later toured as a free-lance.

Cole, Nat "King" [Coles, Nathaniel Adams] (b. Montgomery, Ala., 17 March 1917; d. Santa Monica, Calif., 15 Feb. 1965). Singer and pianist. Moved to Los Angeles, 1937; formed King Cole Trio with guitar and bass. Hits included "The Christmas Song" (1946), "Straighten Up and Fly Right" (1943), and "Mona Lisa" (1950). Remembered as a singer, but his piano style was very influential.

Coleman, Ornette (b. Fort Worth, 9 Mar. 1930). Jazz alto saxophonist, composer, and bandleader. While in Texas, Natchez, New Orleans, and Los Angeles, developed a new way of playing from a background of bop and rhythm-and-blues. His quartet recorded in Los Angeles (1958–59); Coleman led a trio with double bass player David Izenzon and drummer Charles Moffett (1962, 1965–67) and taught himself trumpet and violin. In 1975 formed Prime Time; recorded separately on a double album with both Prime Time and colleagues from the early quartets (1987). Albums include *Virgin Beauty* (1988).

Coleridge-Taylor, Samuel (b. London, 15 Aug. 1875; d. Croydon, 1 Sept. 1912). Composer. Studied with Stanford at the Royal College of Music (1890–97); in 1898 produced the popular cantata *Hiawatha's Wedding Feast*, which led to other cantatas based on Longfellow's poem. Much of his considerable output was devoted to the cantata and choral genres. Other works include *Symphonic Variations on an African Air*, 1906; *24 Negro Melodies*, 1908. The son of an Englishwoman and an African, he was very conscious of his African blood and of having a mission and responsibility as a black artist, often using Negro themes in his music.

Colgrass, Michael (Charles) (b. Chicago, 22 Apr. 1932). Composer and percussionist. Studied composition with Milhaud, Riegger, Weigel, Foss, B. Weber; active as a percussionist in New York (1956–66). Received the Pulitzer Prize for his *Déjà Vu*, a concerto for 4 percussionists, in 1978. Earlier works were in an atonal avant-garde idiom; from the mid-1960s his music was more accessible, featuring the juxtaposition of various musical styles.

Coll', colla [It.]. See *Col.*

Collasse [Colasse], **Pascal** (b. Rheims, baptized 22 Jan. 1649; d. Versailles, 17 July 1709). Composer. Worked closely with Lully at the Paris Opéra from 1677; after Lully's death in 1687 acted as a composer for the Académie royale de musique; also a *sous-maître* at the French royal chapel (1683–1704). Of some 15 stage works by far the most successful was *Thétis et Pélée*, a *tragédie lyrique*. Other compositions include a number of airs and many *grands motets* for the royal chapel (most lost).

Collect [Lat. *oratio, collecta*]. A short prayer consisting of an invocation (e.g., "Almighty God, who hast . . ."), a petition ("Grant that . . ."), and a pleading of Christ's name or ascription of glory to God ("through the same our Lord Jesus Christ, who . . ."). In the Roman rite, it is either sung to a simple recitation tone or recited.

Collegium musicum [Lat., musical guild]. One of various types of musical societies arising in German and German-Swiss cities and towns during the Reformation and thriving into the mid-18th century. Generally the *collegium musicum* performed for pleasure both vocal and instrumental music, especially the latter as it rose in stature during the Baroque era. From the 1660s, their functions largely constituted the beginnings of public concert life in Germany. Leipzig *collegia musica*, consisting mostly of university students, enjoyed a succession of particularly illustrious directors, including Johann Kuhnau (1688), Telemann (1702), and Bach (1729–37). With the Moravian emigration, American *collegia* sprang up beginning in 1744 in Pennsylvania, Maryland, Ohio, and the Carolinas. Since the early 20th century, the term has come to be associated in large measure with university ensembles that perform early music, though from a historical perspective, the term need not imply any restriction in repertory.

Colonna, Giovanni Paolo (b. Bologna, 16 June 1637; d. there, 28 Nov. 1695). Composer. From 1659 organist at S. Petronio in Bologna (first organist from 1661) and from 1674 until his death *maestro di cappella* there. A founding member and a prominent official of the Accademia de filarmonica. In 1685 was involved in a debate by correspondence with Corelli (in Rome) over part-writing. Recognized in his time as one of the best Italian composers of church music, his output also includes cantatas and operas.

Colonne, Eduard [Judas] (b. Bordeaux, 23 July 1838; d. Paris, 28 Mar. 1910). Studied at the Paris Conservatory; from 1873 conducted the Concert national at the Odéon, then from 1875 the Concerts du Châtelet, later known as the Concerts Colonne. During the 1870s Colonne gradually overtook the initially greater popularity of Pasdeloup's Concerts populaires. Made frequent appearances elsewhere in Europe, including London (1896); in 1905 conducted the New York Philharmonic.

Colophony. *Rosin.

Color [Lat.]. In the Middle Ages, embellishment of various kinds, including especially repetition, but also the use of *musica ficta.* In modern discussions of *isorhythm, the term refers specifically to a repeated series of pitches as distinct from a repeated series of rhythmic values (known as *talea*). See also Coloration, Coloratura.

Color organ. An instrument for manipulating colors in a fashion analogous to that in which an organ manipulates sounds. The earliest instrument of this type, built in the first half of the 18th century, was Louis-Bertrand Castel's *clavecin oculaire,* in which depressing a key plucked a string and at the same time projected a color on a screen. Examples from the first part of the 20th century usually manipulate color alone and include the Clavilux (1925) by Thomas Wilfrid, who sought to develop a new and independent visual art by analogy with music. Scriabin's *Prometheus: Poem of Fire* (1910) specifies the use of a keyboard instrument (It. *tastiera per luce*) for projecting colors. The development of digital technologies in the later 20th century vastly increased the possibilities for manipulating sound and visual images in relation to one another.

Coloration. (1) In *mensural notation, the use of colored notes (red or white in black notation, black in white notation). (2) Florid ornaments of a type written out in keyboard and lute music of the 15th and 16th centuries [see Colorists, Intabulation, Diminutions, Ornamentation]. (3) Any elaborate *ornamentation or figuration, whether written or improvised, of the type common in the 17th and 18th centuries and in some singing styles of the 19th. See Coloratura.

Coloratura [It.]. (1) Elaborate ornamentation or embellishment, including running passages and trills, whether written or improvised, and common in 18th- and 19th-century singing, e.g., that occurring in the arias for the Queen of the Night in Mozart's *Die Zauberflöte.* (2) A soprano with a high range who sings in the style of (1). (3) *Coloration (2).

Colorists [Ger. *Koloristen,* fr. med. Lat. *color,* embellishment]. A group of north German organists of the late 16th century who transcribed polyphonic vocal works for keyboard, embellishing them heavily with formulaic ornamental figures in the style of Italian instrumental *divisions or *coloraturas. The colorists include Elias Nikolaus Ammerbach (ca. 1530–97), Bernhard Schmid Sr. (1535–92) and Jr. (1567–1625), and Jakob Paix (1556–after 1623).

Colpo d'arco [It.]. Bow stroke.

Coltrane, John (William) (b. Hamlet, N.C., 23 Sept. 1926; d. Huntington, Long Island, 17 July 1967). Jazz tenor and soprano saxophonist, bandleader, and composer. Played alto or tenor saxophone in various groups before settling on the tenor as a member of Johnny Hodges's septet (1953–54). Played in Davis's quintets and sextets (1955–57, 1958–59) and with Monk's quartet (1957), also recording extensively as a leader. After taking up the soprano saxophone in 1960, formed a quartet that soon included McCoy Tyner (–1965), Elvin Jones (–1966), and Jimmy Garrison (1961–66); Eric Dolphy was an intermittent fifth member (1961–63), and Roy Haynes substituted for Jones; other members included Alice Coltrane, Pharoah Sanders, and Rashied Ali. Coltrane was the most influential saxophonist since the 1940s. Albums with Davis include *'Round about Midnight* (1955–56); as a leader, *Ascension* (1965) and *Live at the Village Vanguard Again* (1966).

Combattimento di Tancredi e Clorinda [It., The Duel between Tancred and Clorinda]. A dramatic scene composed by Monteverdi, first performed in 1624 and published in his eighth book of madrigals (1638). Partly acted and partly narrated, it is based on a passage from Torquato Tasso's *Gerusalemme liberata.* See *Concitato.*

Combination pedal. A mechanical device for bringing on or retiring a group of organ stops. As used by the 19th-century French builder Cavaillé-Coll, these were preset and not adjustable.

Combination piston. In electric-action organs, a device for changing combinations of stops, operated by small buttons (pistons) below the keyboards.

Combination tone [also resultant tone, obs.; Fr. *son combiné;* Ger. *Kombinationston;* It. *suono di combinazione;* Sp. *sonido de combinación*]. A tone produced by a nonlinear system (one that introduces distortion during transmission) when it is supplied with two tones having sufficient and similar intensities as well as a frequency difference that is itself an audible frequency. Examples of nonlinear systems include the resonating masses of musical instruments, certain electric circuits in receivers and transmitters, and—of particular importance—the cochlea of the inner ear, where perceived combination tones are produced. These include difference tones and summation tones.

Difference tones are the easiest to hear. For example, if a pitch of frequency 500 Hz is sounded with a pitch of frequency 400 Hz, a pitch of frequency 100 Hz (the difference between 500 and 400) will be heard even though it is not physically present outside the ear. Tartini, employing the term *terzo suono,* claimed in 1754 to have discovered them in 1714, and the effect is sometimes termed Tartini's tone.

Summation tones, which are perceived at a frequency that is the sum of two sounded frequencies, can be heard only in very favorable circumstances because lower frequency tones mask higher ones much more strongly than the reverse. Summation tones were discovered by Helmholz under laboratory conditions and were first discussed by him in 1856.

Combinatoriality. See Twelve-tone music.

Combo. In jazz and popular music, a small ensemble (i.e., "combination" of instruments or players).

Come [It.]. As, like; *c. prima,* to be performed as on the first playing; *c. sopra,* as above; *c. stà,* as it stands, as written.

Comédie mêlée d'ariettes [Fr.]. A type of *opéra comique* appearing toward the middle of the 18th century in which spoken dialogue alternates with newly composed songs, duets, and, occasionally, larger ensembles.

Comes [Lat.]. See *Dux, comes.*

Comic opera. Opera with humorous or lighthearted subject matter. In this sense, comic opera stands in direct and simple analogy with spoken comedy and includes works in a wide range and variety of styles, e.g., Mozart's *Le nozze di Figaro,* Smetana's *The Bartered Bride,* Wagner's *Die Meistersinger,* and Britten's *Albert Herring.* The term is also applied,

however, to opera with certain musical or structural characteristics, regardless of subject matter. The most important of these characteristics is the use of spoken dialogue in place of *recitative. French *opéra comique,* German *Singspiel,* English *ballad opera,* Spanish *tonadilla escénica,* and *operetta in whatever language all employ spoken dialogue in alternation with musical numbers. Italian *opera buffa,* on the other hand, uses recitative. Until the end of the 18th century, works called comic operas were usually comic both in sentiment and in structure, though Mozart's mature operas blend comic and serious elements. The 19th century, however, offers many examples of works that alternate music with spoken dialogue but are nevertheless serious or even tragic. Notable examples are Beethoven's *Fidelio* and Bizet's *Carmen* (in its original version). See Opera.

Comissiona, Sergiu (b. Bucharest, 16 June 1928). Conductor. Studied conducting at the Romanian Conservatory. Directed the Romanian State Ensemble, 1948–55. Principal conductor of the Romanian State Opera and frequent guest conductor of the Georges Enesco Philharmonic, 1955–58. Music director of the Haifa Symphony, 1959–64; founder and leader of the Israel Chamber Orchestra, 1960–64. Frequent guest conductor of the London Philharmonic (1960–63), Stockholm Philharmonic (1964–66), and Berlin Radio Orchestra (1965–67). Chief conductor of the Göteborg Symphony, 1966–72. Music director of the Baltimore Symphony, 1969–84. Artistic director (from 1980) then music director of the Houston Symphony, 1982–87. Chief conductor of the New York City Opera, 1987–88; of the Helsinki Philharmonic from 1990.

Comma, schisma. Minute differences that exist between two relatively large, nearly identical intervals that have been obtained by different methods. These include the Pythagorean and syntonic commas, the schisma, and the diaschisma.

Commedia dell' arte [It., comedy by profession as distinct from amateur courtly theater]. A genre of improvised theater parodying Venetian and northern Italian society, arising in the early 16th century, and flourishing throughout Europe until the early 18th. Its stock characters included lecherous Pantalone, gullible Dottore Graziano, boastful Capitano or Scaramuccia, the ingenue Columbina, clown Pedrolino (Pierrot), and base comedians or *zanni* Arlecchino (Harlequin) and Pulcinella (Punch), each with stereotyped mask, costume, and accessories. Performances intermingled stock dramatic situations with improvised singing, dancing, and acrobatics.

Commedia per musica, commedia in musica, commedia musicale [It.]. An *opera buffa* [see Opera] in two or three acts. The terms were used most frequently in Naples from the 1720s through the 1790s.

Commiato [It.]. See *Envoi.*

Common chord. Major *triad.

Common meter. In *prosody, a four-line strophe alternating lines of eight and six syllables. See also Ballad.

Common time. The *meter 4/4. For the use of **C** to designate this meter, see Mensural notation.

Commosso [It.]. Moved, excited.

Communion [Lat. *communio*]. In *Gregorian chant, the final item of the *Proper of the *Mass, sung during communion. It belongs to the category of antiphonal *psalmody.

Como, Perry [Pierino Ronald] (b. Canonsburg, Pa., 18 May 1912). Popular singer. From 1943 hosted several radio and television shows and made many popular recordings, including "'Till the End of Time" (1945), "Catch a Falling Star" (1958), and "It's Impossible" (1970).

Comodo, comodamente [It.]. With respect to tempo, comfortable, easy.

Comparsa [Sp.]. See Conga.

Compass. The complete range of pitches from lowest to highest of an instrument, voice, or part.

Compère, Loyset (b. Hainaut, ca. 1450; d. St. Quentin, 16 Aug. 1518). Composer. In the chapel of Galeazzo Maria Sforza, Duke of Milan, in the mid-1470s; left Milan in about 1477. By 1486 was in the service of the French royal court. Held church posts in Cambrai (1498–1500) and Douai (1500–1503 or 1504). During his last years, a canon at the collegiate church in St. Quentin. Among his extant sacred works are about 15 motets, 2 Mass ordinaries, and 3 cycles of *motetti missales.* The finest of the secular works are the over 45 chansons.

Complement. (1) Of an *interval, the difference between that interval and the octave, i.e., its *inversion. (2) Of a hexachord in *twelve-tone music, the six remaining pitch classes not included in that hexachord. (3) Of any set of pitch classes, all of the remaining pitch classes.

Compline [Lat. *completorium*]. See Office.

Composition [fr. Lat. *componere,* to put together]. The activity of creating a musical work; the work thus created. The term is most often used in opposition to improvisation, implying an activity carried out prior to performance or a work whose features are specified in sufficient detail to retain its essential

identity from one performance to another. This opposition, however, is not entirely clear-cut, and the status of the concepts varies widely with time and place. Non-Western cultures vary considerably in the extent to which the concepts implied by the term composition are applicable.

Composition pedal, stop. A foot- or hand-operated button on the *organ permitting a preset selection of several stops to be drawn at once.

Compostela. See Santiago de Compostela, repertory of.

Compound interval. An *interval that exceeds an octave.

Compound meter, time. A *meter that includes a triple subdivision within the beat, e.g., 6/8.

Compound stop. Any organ stop with two or more pipes per note, sounding the unison or octaves along with the fifth. *Sesquialtera and *Cornet stops also include the third. *Mixtures contain only octaves and fifths.

Comprimario [It.]. In opera, a singer of secondary roles.

Computers, musical applications of. See Electro-acoustic music.

Con [It., Sp.]. With. For phrases beginning with this word, see the word following.

Concert. A public performance of music before an audience that has assembled for the purpose of listening to it. A performance by a soloist, with or without an accompanist, is usually called a *recital.

Until the 18th century, most secular music-making was private, confined to those households, usually royal or aristocratic, that could afford a musical establishment. The rise of public concerts was concomitant with that of a general public sufficiently knowledgeable and prosperous to support them, and so is first found primarily in cities with a well-developed middle class.

The origin of concerts is usually held to lie in the musical activities of *academies in Italy and *collegia musica in Germany, beginning in the 16th and 17th centuries. Although both were private societies and so did not give public concerts in the modern sense, their musical performances were a move away from individual patronage to collective support. (Academy was long to be synonymous with concert.) Concerts with paid admission began in London by 1664. In the 18th century, numerous concert organizations were active in London, including that managed jointly by Johann Christian Bach and Carl Friedrich Abel (1765–81) and that of Johann Peter Salomon (1791–95). Beginning with the famous

Concert spirituel (1725–90), 18th-century Paris also had several concert societies. Many of those in German cities grew out of *collegia musica*. The famous and still-continuing *Gewandhaus* concerts of Leipzig began in 1781.

Concert grand. The largest size of grand *piano, measuring approximately 2.75 m. (9 ft.) in length.

Concert pitch. The pitch at which the piano and other nontransposing instruments play. See Transposing instruments, Pitch.

Concert spirituel [Fr., sacred concert]. A series of concerts founded in Paris by Anne Danican Philidor (1681–1728) in 1725 and extending to 1790. Their purpose was to provide concerts on religious holidays when opera was not performed. The series was revived in 1805.

Concertant [Fr.], **concertante** [It.]. Beginning in the 18th century, adjectives applied to works for two or more performers (including orchestral works) in which one or more of the performers is called upon for soloistic display, e.g., Mozart's *Sinfonia concertante* K. 364 (320d) for violin, viola, and orchestra, and Weber's *Grand duo concertant* op. 48 for clarinet and piano. The form *concertante* has also been used as a noun to refer to pieces of this kind, particularly in the 18th century. See *Symphonie concertante,* Concerto, String quartet.

Concertato [It., concerted]. Of or pertaining to works of the early 17th century that combine and contrast vocal and instrumental forces, especially through the introduction of the *thoroughbass.

Concertgebouw [Du.]. Concert building, specifically the one constructed in Amsterdam in 1888 and from which The Netherlands' foremost orchestra takes its name.

Concertina. A free-reed [see Reed], bellows-operated instrument similar to the *accordion but hexagonal in shape and with a button keyboard for each hand. See ill. under Accordion; see also Bandoneon.

Concertino [It., dim. of *concerto*]. (1) The soloists in a concerto grosso [see Concerto]. (2) In the early and mid-18th century, a multimovement work for orchestra or chamber ensemble. Orchestral concertinos do not usually feature soloists, and they are generally lighter and less formal in style than early symphonies. See also String quartet. (3) In the 19th and 20th centuries, a work in the style of a concerto, but freer in form and on a smaller scale, sometimes for one or a few instruments without orchestra and usually in a single movement. A common German title for works of this type is *Konzertstück.* (4) [Sp.] *Concertmaster.

Concertmaster [Brit. leader; Fr. *chef d'attaque, de pupitre;* Ger. *Konzertmeister;* It. *primo violino;* Sp. *concertino*]. The principal first violinist of an orchestra and as such the person responsible for coordinating the bowing and attack of all strings and for playing solo violin passages. The concertmaster usually comes to the stage after the remainder of the orchestra is seated, oversees tuning, and takes his or her place on the conductor's immediate left.

Concerto [fr. It. *concertare,* to join together; pres. part. *concertante,* past part. *concertato;* related to Lat. *concertare,* to fight or contend]. (1) In the 16th through the early 18th centuries, a diverse ensemble of voices, instruments, or both, or a composition for such an ensemble. The performers in an early concerto are usually heterogeneous in some sense: soloists and chorus, two separate choruses, different instruments, or (most commonly of all) voices and instruments. In the 17th century, sacred works for voices and instruments were typically called concertos; secular works of similar character were more often entitled airs *(arie), musiche,* cantatas, and so forth [see Cantata]. See also Chorale cantata, Chorale concerto.

(2) From the latter part of the 17th century to the present, a multimovement (occasionally multisectional) work for soloist or soloists and orchestra. The instrumental concerto of the middle and late Baroque comprised three types. The earliest of these was the concerto grosso, in which a small group of soloists opposes a larger orchestra. The smaller group, consisting most often of two solo violins and continuo, is known as the concertino (little ensemble). The larger group, generally a string orchestra plus continuo, is known variously as the concerto grosso (large ensemble), grosso, tutti, or—perhaps least confusingly—ripieno (from *concerto ripieno,* full ensemble, i.e., with doubled parts).

Arcangelo Corelli's concertos resemble others of the period ca. 1680 in that the alternation of tutti and solo follows no preconceived plan; the effect is generally that of a *trio sonata in which additional contrast has been provided by entry of the ripieno at various points. Beginning with Giuseppe Torelli and Antonio Vivaldi, the concerto grosso came more and more under the domination of the solo concerto in matters of form and instrumental treatment. While this tendency is most obvious in the so-called double concerto—less a concerto grosso than a concerto for two individual soloists—it may also be seen in concerti grossi such as Bach's *Brandenburg* Concertos (dedication dated 1721), the greatest works in this genre.

A somewhat later type of concerto is the ripieno concerto, known in the Baroque as the *concerto ripieno* or *concerto a 4* (or *a 5* if the orchestra included two viola parts, a standard 17th-century scoring). These are merely compositions for the ripieno alone (i.e., for string orchestra and continuo), with either no solo parts or clearly subsidiary ones. Beginning with the six ripieno concertos of Giuseppe Torelli's op. 5 (1692), this genre enjoyed an efflorescence that extended until about 1740. Most ripieno concertos fall into one of two distinct classes: a sonata type and a sinfonia type. The sonata type generally mirrors the form and style of the *sonata da chiesa* in its use of four-movement slow–fast–slow–fast cycles and predominantly fugal texture. The more modern sinfonia type was firmly established in Torelli's second publication to include concertos, op. 6 (1698), which turn to the three-movement (fast–slow–fast) pattern and more homophonic texture familiar to us from the solo concerto and opera sinfonia. The opening movements also parallel the solo concerto in utilizing ritornello form (without solo sections), in which the opening material recurs from one to several times in various keys, the last statement normally in the tonic. Finales are most often binary in form and dancelike in style.

The last type of concerto to develop, and the one with the most far-reaching influence, was the concerto for a single soloist (most often violin during the Baroque) and orchestra. The earliest known solo concertos are nos. 6 and 12 of Torelli's op. 6 of 1698. These works employ both a three-movement cycle and clear (if diminutive) ritornello form, like that of the ripieno concerto except that sections for the soloist and continuo now separate the various orchestral ritornellos.

The most influential and prolific composer of concertos during the Baroque period was the Venetian Antonio Vivaldi (1678–1741), who composed nearly 60 ripieno concertos, approximately 425 concertos for one or more soloists, including about 350 solo concertos (two-thirds for solo violin) and 45 double concertos (over half for two violins). Vivaldi's concertos firmly establish the three-movement cycle as the norm. The virtuosity of the solo sections increases markedly, especially in the later works, and concurrently the texture becomes more homophonic.

Ritornello form in Vivaldi is often a fairly standardized scheme of four or five regularly recurring tutti sections or ritornellos (hereafter symbolized R_1, R_2, etc.). The first and last ritornellos are in the tonic, the second in the dominant or relative major, and the remainder in related keys, including the dominant minor in a minor-key work. Central (and often final) ritornellos are usually shorter than the opening one,

merely stating material selected from it and frequently omitting the opening theme. The intervening solo sections (symbolized S_1, S_2, etc.), which may or may not incorporate material from the ritornello sections, normally have the function of carrying out the modulations from key to key, each new key being confirmed and stabilized by the eventual entry of the tutti. In many other Vivaldi concertos, however, the entire middle area from the beginning of S_2 to the final ritornello is more varied, often simply alternating brief tutti and solo statements.

The Classical period brought the final triumph of the solo concerto over the group or multiple concerto; the only important manifestation of the latter type during this period was the *symphonie concertante,* a variety of concerto for two or more instruments fashionable after ca. 1770. The Classical period also witnessed the coming of age of the keyboard concerto. Until about 1770, the preferred instrument was generally the harpsichord, but thereafter the piano rapidly came to the fore.

Most of the concertos of this period are in three movements, though a significant minority adopt such lighter two-movement patterns as Allegro–Minuet and Allegro–Rondo. Dance and rondo finales are also frequent in three-movement concertos. Nearly all first movements during this period are in some variety of ritornello form, as are many finales. This form shows great fluidity until late in the Classical period. The number of ritornellos is most often three or four, and most sections tend to be longer and more variegated than in the Baroque. One particularly common plan illustrates the tendency of Classical ritornello form to assimilate principles of structure evident in *sonata form.* This design is a modified version of the Vivaldi type with four ritornellos (R_1–R_4) and three solo sections (S_1–S_3). Here the final solo, S_3, begins and ends in the tonic and tends to parallel S_1 thematically. Thus, S_3 now resembles the recapitulation of a sonata-form movement. Moreover, S_1 had always been comparable to an exposition and S_2 to a development section, owing to their modulatory schemes (e.g., I–V for S_1, V–vi for S_2; real thematic development is uncommon in S_2 during the 18th century, however).

The most variable element of 18th-century concerto form was the penultimate tutti, R_3 in a movement with four ritornellos. Many early Classical movements deemphasize this section, reducing it to a brief interpolation before the final solo. Other movements either omit it entirely, proceeding directly from S_2 to S_3, or else assign it the function of a

$$\| R_1/\text{Orch. exp.}/\text{Intro.} \quad | S_1/\text{Solo exp.} \qquad R_2 \quad | S_2/\text{Dev.} \qquad (\text{Retr.}) | R_3/S_3/\text{Recap.} \qquad | R_4 \quad (\text{Cad.}) \|$$

$$\text{I (i)} \longmapsto \text{I (i)} \longrightarrow \text{V (III, v)} \longmapsto \text{V (III, V)} \;\rightsquigarrow\; \text{I (i)} \longmapsto$$

Ritornello-sonata form of the late 18th and the early 19th century.

retransition. But the most influential approach, found in most of Mozart's piano concertos, was to accentuate the coordinated return of the main theme and the tonic key by assigning it to the orchestra rather than to the soloist, who then reenters at some convenient spot. The section thus combines the functions of R$_3$, S$_3$, and recapitulation [see fig.].

By approximately 1760, up-to-date composers had begun to introduce into R$_1$ and S$_1$ the kind of thematic contrast already common in expositions of sonata-form movements, including use of a secondary theme or themes. The relationship between the two sections themselves, however, remained flexible throughout the century. The accompanying figure presents an overview of concerto first-movement form of the late 18th and early 19th centuries, showing how it synthesizes the structural principles of both ritornello and sonata forms. (Roman numerals indicate keys, those in parentheses referring to minor-key movements; arrows indicate modulations.) It should be noted in regard to the accompanying figure that Mozart usually places a *cadenza within R$_4$, as indicated, whereas in earlier concertos it normally occurs in S$_3$ (or often not at all). In addition, Mozart frequently utilizes an *Eingang* (entry), a brief cadenzalike passage for the piano leading to the beginning of S$_1$ proper.

A predominantly conservative tradition of the concerto after Beethoven can be traced from Mendelssohn's two piano concertos (1831–37) and his important Violin Concerto (1844) to concertos by Schumann (piano, cello, violin, 1841–53), Brahms (two for piano, one for violin, one for violin and cello, 1854–87), Grieg (piano, 1868), Max Bruch (three for violin, 1868–91), and Dvořák (piano, violin, cello, 1876–95). In France this tradition is represented primarily by Camille Saint-Saëns (ten concertos for piano, violin, and cello, 1858–1902), in Russia by Anton Rubinstein, Tchaikovsky (three piano concertos, one for violin, 1874–93), and Rachmaninoff (four piano concertos, 1890–1926).

Mendelssohn initiated a formal type for the first movement of concertos in which the opening ritornello and first solo section are merged into one unrepeated exposition; presentation of the themes is now shared by soloist and orchestra. Development, recapitulation, and coda follow as in the usual Romantic versions of sonata form, material again being assigned to tutti and solo at the discretion of the composer (though vestiges of ritornello procedure are often apparent). This structure may be considered a final stage in the previously described assimilation of sonata-form elements within the first-movement form of the concerto.

Numerous works of the 20th century basically continued the 19th-century concept of the concerto (and often its forms and styles). And the *neoclassi-

cal movement of the period after World War I produced a long series of works that returned to pre-Romantic conceptions of the concerto.

A special class of 20th-century concerto is the "concerto for orchestra." These works are not for the most part ripieno concertos in the Baroque sense but rather display pieces in which the orchestra itself is the virtuoso—from soloists to sections to choirs to tutti, as in Bartók's popular work of 1943.

Concerto grosso [It., large concerto]. A concerto for a small group of soloists (the concertino) and orchestra (the tutti or ripieno). See Concerto (2).

Concerto for Orchestra. See Concerto (2).

Concerto ripieno [It.]. See Concerto (2).

Concitato [It., agitated]. A style *(stile concitato)* defined by Monteverdi and employed in his *Combattimento di Tancredi e Clorinda* (1624) and *Madrigali guerrieri ed amorosi* (1638) to express anger and warfare. By analogy with classical Greek poetic meters, it was based on a division of the whole note into 16 sixteenth notes repeated on single pitches.

Concord, discord. *Consonance, dissonance.

Concord Sonata. Charles Ives's second piano sonata, composed in 1910–15. Its complete title is "Concord, Mass., 1840–1860," and its four movements are titled, respectively, "Emerson," "Hawthorne," "The Alcotts," and "Thoreau." The last movement includes an optional part for flute.

Concrete music [Fr. *musique concrète*]. See Electro-acoustic music.

Condon, Eddie [Albert Edwin] (b. Goodland, Ind., 16 Nov. 1905; d. New York, 4 Aug. 1973). Jazz guitarist, banjoist, bandleader, and entrepreneur. Recorded "Sugar" and "China Boy" leading McKenzie and Condon's Chicagoans in 1927. Toured with Red Nichols (1929) and the Mound City Blue Blowers (1930–31, 1933) and with the clarinetist Joe Marsala led a band; recorded extensively as a rhythm guitarist accompanying prominent jazzmen. Organized performances mixing traditional and swing musicians at Nick's (1937–44), then at his own club, Eddie Condon's (1945–67), and on international tours.

Conducting [Fr. *direction;* Ger. *Dirigieren* (v.), *Taktschlag;* It. *direzione, concertazione;* Sp. *dirigir* (v.)]. Leading and coordinating a group of singers and or instrumentalists in a musical performance or rehearsal. Conducting includes indicating the meter and tempo; signaling changes in tempo and dynamics; cueing entrances; adjusting timbral balances; identifying the source(s) of performance errors and helping to resolve these; demanding clear articulation and enunciation; and, generally, bearing responsibility for the coherent interpretation of musical works. A conductor may also serve in an administrative role (often with the title music director) and in this capacity reviews and revises the membership of the orchestra or chorus, selects repertory and guest artists, and participates in fund-raising and public-relations events.

The conductor's skills seen by audiences are chiefly time-beating and expressive gesture, for which many conductors (especially of instrumental ensembles) use a baton. In the past, different patterns have been used to beat time in different meters. Patterns in current use for both choral and instrumental conducting are shown in the accompanying figure.

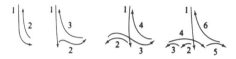

In the 17th and 18th centuries, leadership of instrumental ensembles was generally exercised by either the principal violinist or the keyboard continuo player. Mozart sometimes conducted opera performances from the keyboard, as Haydn did his symphonies. In the early 19th century, orchestral and opera performances were often conducted by the first violinist using the bow and the first violin part with a few annotations, a practice that lasted well into the second half of the century. The rise of the modern orchestral conductor can be attributed in part to increased attention to elements of timbre, texture, and dynamics in music. Beginning with the later works of Mozart and especially the works of Beethoven, the tendency in orchestral scores to fragment a single melodic line among two or more leading instruments (or an accompanimental figuration between different sections) demands levels of ensemble precision that were previously unknown.

The first well-known conductors were highly regarded composers: Weber, Spohr, Spontini, Mendelssohn, Berlioz, and Wagner. Carl Maria von Weber is sometimes credited with being the first (in 1817) to assume the role of the conductor in the modern sense. Berlioz's essay on conducting (1855) was the first to treat the conductor as a specialist in his own right. By 1880, conductors were accorded the same recognition as instrumental virtuosos.

Conductor. A person who, principally by means of gestures of the hands and arms, leads the performance of a musical ensemble. See Conducting.

Conductor's part. A condensed (as distinct from a full) *score, in which the entrances and principal parts of a composition are indicated, usually at actual pitch, on relatively few staves, for use by a conductor; also short score.

Conductus [pl. *conductus* or *conducti,* fr. Lat. *conducere,* to escort]. A medieval song for one or more voices with a serious, most often sacred, text in rhythmical Latin verse.

The term first appears in manuscripts of the mid-12th century (including the repertory of *Santiago de Compostela), where it is written above a number of monophonic songs used as processional introductions to liturgical readings. The musical style of these songs is akin to that of one type of verse composition (*versus) found in Aquitanian manuscripts dating from the end of the 11th century to the turn of the 13th.

The largest repertory of *conductus* is from Notre Dame of Paris (ca. 1150/60–ca. 1240). Like the Aquitanian *versus,* the majority celebrate the great feasts of the church year; a goodly number, however, refer to contemporary events, and many decry the vices of simony and sloth, said to be rampant among clerics of every rank. These are *discant compositions, but they differ from other types of Parisian polyphony in that the tenor or principal voice is almost always original rather than drawn from liturgical chant. The tenor is also usually similar in both melodic and rhythmic character to the other voice(s). Such pieces are notated in score with the tenor occupying the lowest position and underlaid with the text. Many end with long melismas. Although the *conductus* is included by 13th-century theorists among the categories governed by the rhythmic *modes, and the reading of the melismas, which are notated in ligature, is largely unproblematical, the rhythm of the texted portions is not made clear by their notation and has been the subject of considerable scholarly debate. The composition of new *conductus* essentially ended with the 13th century.

Cone, Edward T(oner) (b. Greensboro, N.C., 4 May 1917). Composer and writer on music. Studied composition (Sessions) and piano (K. U. Schnabel) at Princeton, and musicology (Lang) at Columbia (1939–41). Began teaching at Princeton in 1945; lectured widely in the U.S. and Europe. His compositions employ expanded tonality and often structure harmonic and tonal relations in terms of hexachordal properties (String Sextet, 1966). Highly regarded as an analyst of music (*The Composer's Voice,* 1974; *Music: A View from Delft: Selected Essays,* 1989).

Confinalis [Lat.]. The pitch lying a fifth above the final of a *mode.

Conflicting signatures, partial signatures. In early music, "key" signatures with differing numbers of flats in the several voices of a polyphonic composition. As a rule, upper voices carry fewer flats than do lower voices. Common patterns include the following (top voice listed first; "-" indicates the absence of a flat): - ♭; - - ♭, - ♭ ♭, ♭ ♭♭ ♭♭; - - ♭ ♭. Such signatures occur as early as the 13th century and as late as the 16th century, but are most common in music of the 15th century. Early theorists seldom mention them, and modern scholars have differed widely in their attempts to explain them.

Confrey, Zez [Edward Elezear] (b. Peru, Ill., 3 Apr. 1895; d. Lakewood, N.J., 22 Nov. 1971). Popular composer and pianist. In 1918 his "My Pet" (published on piano roll) made popular the style of "novelty piano" playing, which combined elements of contemporary popular and classical musical genres including ragtime and impressionism. Other successful pieces include "Kitten on the Keys" (1921) and "Nickel in the Slot" (1923).

Conga [Sp.]. (1) An Afro-Cuban dance-music genre and an essential element in the performances of *comparsas*—groups of masqueraders that dance during the celebration of Carnival in Latin American countries. In the 1930s, it became popular as a ballroom dance in North America and Europe. The characteristic dance consists of three short steps and a forward leap, coordinated with the following continuously repeated rhythmic figure:

(2) A long, single-headed, Afro-Cuban drum played with bare hands. The head is generally larger than the open end, and the shell may bulge slightly below the head. See ill. under Percussion instruments.

Conjunct, disjunct. Types of melodic *motion. Conjunct motion proceeds by step from one scale degree to the next (i.e., by the *interval of a second), and disjunct motion proceeds by leap (i.e., by intervals larger than a second). *Tetrachords in the music of ancient Greece and the Middle Ages are conjunct if the last pitch of one is the first pitch of the other, and otherwise disjunct.

Conlon, James (b. New York, 18 Mar. 1950). Conductor. Studied at Juilliard; debut as an opera conductor at the Spoleto Festival (1971); engagements with the New York Philharmonic (1974) and the Met (1976). Music director of the Cincinnati May Festival, 1979; of the Rotterdam Philharmonic, 1983–91; of the Cologne Opera from 1991.

Consecration of the House. See *Weihe des Hauses, Die.*

Consecutives. See Parallel fifths, octaves; Counterpoint.

Consequent. See Antecedent, consequent.

Conservatory [Fr. *conservatoire;* Ger. *Konservatorium* or *Hochschule für Musik;* It., Sp. *conservatorio*]. A school for the practical and theoretical training of musicians of all types and grades. Pupils can receive training in composition, individual instruments, voice, conducting, music education, and church music. In the U.S., conservatories are generally independent private institutions. Public and private universities have schools and departments of music that combine professional and academic education in varying degrees; some university schools of music offer programs similar in every way to those of conservatories.

Conservatories originated in the 16th century in Italy, where the term (from the Latin *conservare,* to keep or preserve) designated an orphanage. The orphans received special training in music so that they could be employed in church choirs and later in opera. One such institution was the Conservatorio Santa Maria di Loreto, founded in 1537 in Naples. Numerous 17th- and 18th-century Italian composers were associated with conservatories, either as students or teachers, most notably Vivaldi, who was employed from 1703 on by the Pio Ospedale della Pietà, a Venetian orphanage for girls. In France, the government, rather than the church, established the Conservatoire national de musique et de déclamation in Paris in 1795. Other nations followed this example of a state conservatory or a network of them.

Console. (1) In organs, the key desk, containing one or more manual keyboards, pedalboard, and the knobs controlling all of the stops. (2) A small upright *piano.

Consonance and dissonance. The perceived stability or instability of a complex of two or more sounds. When this perception depends only on sounds simultaneously present to the ear or the mind, it is usually explained by acoustics and psychoacoustics. When it depends on a context of sounds employed in some musical repertory, it is explained by some set of syntactical rules that describes (or prescribes) the ways in which sounds function in that context. It is in the latter sense that the concepts consonance and dissonance are most often employed in discussions of Western music: as indices of the ways in which intervals or chords are treated in this music rather than as acoustical properties inherent in the sounds themselves.

In Western tonal music, consonant *intervals (pairs of pitches) are those that are treated as stable and not requiring resolution. Dissonant intervals are those regarded as having an instability that requires resolution to a consonance. In most theories of Western tonal music, the intervals unison, perfect fifth, and octave (plus their octave multiples) are always perfect consonances. Since ca. 1320, whenever the interval of the perfect fourth (or its octave multiple) occurs in a simultaneity of three or more pitches but does not include the lowest sounding pitch, it too is a perfect consonance; otherwise it is a dissonance. The minor third, major third, minor sixth, and major sixth are always imperfect consonances. All other intervals are dissonances. Consonant intervals are thus those that can be derived from the major or minor *triad. Conversely, the major and minor triads are the only combinations of more than two pitches that are wholly consonant. Chords (collections of three or more pitches) are dissonant if they include even a single dissonant interval. For an account of the basic principles regulating the use of dissonance and its resolution to consonance in Western tonal music, see Counterpoint, Harmony.

Consort [perhaps fr. Fr. *concert* and It. *concerto,* or fr. Lat. *consortio,* fellowship]. In 16th- and 17th-century England, an instrumental ensemble, usually of two to eight players, or a composition for such an ensemble. In the late 17th century, the term consort gave way to such foreign terms as concert, concerto, and sonata, as a preference for imported music and terminology took hold.

English consorts were principally of two types. One type combined instruments of only one family, such as viols, violins, recorders, shawms, or sackbuts; for example, a usual consort of six viols included two treble, two tenor, and two bass viols. The other type mixed families; a standard six-part mixed consort included recorder, treble viol, bass viol, lute, cittern, and bandora. In the late 17th century, and even more in modern times, these two types have come to be called whole and broken consorts, respectively.

Constant, Marius (b. Bucharest, 7 Feb. 1925). Composer. Studied in Paris with Enescu, then at the Conservatory with Messiaen and Aubin. In 1950 joined Groupe de recherches musicales studying *musique concrète* at French Radio; music director of the VHF network (1953), of ORTF (1970), of the ballet company of Roland Petit (1957–63). Works reveal influence of aleatory music and of timbre; sometimes calls for unusual instruments.

Consul, The. Opera in three acts by Gian Carlo Menotti (libretto by the composer), produced in Philadelphia in 1950. Setting: a police state in the 20th century.

Contant, (Joseph Pierre) Alexis (b. Montreal, 12 Nov. 1858; d. there, 28 Nov. 1918). Composer. Worked with Calixa Lavallée. Taught at Collège de l'Assomption, 1880–81. Organist at the church of St. Jean-Baptiste (Montreal) from 1885. Taught at Collège de Montréal, 1883–90; Collège de Mont-St.

Louis, 1900–18; Conservatoire nationale, 1905–17. Works include many vocal and choral compositions.

Contes d'Hoffmann, Les [Fr., The Tales of Hoffmann]. An "opéra fantastique" in three acts with prologue and epilogue by Jacques Offenbach (libretto by Jules Barbier and Michel Carré, on three stories by E. T. A. Hoffmann), completed after the composer's death in 1880 by Ernest Guiraud, and first produced in Paris in 1881. Setting: Germany and Italy in the 19th century.

Conti, Francesco Bartolomeo (b. Florence, 20 Jan. 1681; d. Vienna, 20 July 1732). Composer. From 1701 until 1726 associate then principal theorbist at the Habsburg court in Vienna; from 1713 court composer. By 1729 had gone to Italy; returned to Vienna in 1732. Composed mostly dramatic works, both operas (*Griselda,* 1725) and oratorios (*David,* 1724); also numerous chamber cantatas.

Continuo [It., abbr. for *basso continuo*]. *Thoroughbass.

Contra [Lat., It.]. (1) Against, counter to, as in compounds such as *contratenor (sometimes referred to simply as the contra), *contrapunctus* or *contrappunto* (*counterpoint), *contralto, and, in French, *hautecontre. (2) With respect to pitch, lower octave. Thus, the contra-octave is the octave below the great octave [see Pitch names]. The names of instruments formed with this prefix are normally the lowest members of their families (though there are a few subcontrabass instruments).

Contrabass. (1) The lowest pitched member of some families of instruments, such as the *clarinet, often with a range extending down to around C_1 (three octaves below middle C). See also Contra. (2) *Double bass.

Contrabassoon. See Bassoon.

Contrabbasso [It.]. *Double bass.

Contradanza [It.]. *Contredanse.

Contrafactum [Lat.]. A vocal work in which a new text has been substituted for the original one. The substitution of new texts in preexisting works was common through the 16th century, was restricted to fewer genres in the 17th and 18th centuries, and, in art music, largely disappeared in the 19th century. See also Parody.

Contrafagotto [It.]. Contrabassoon. See Bassoon.

Contralto [fr. Lat. *contratenor altus*]. (1) The lowest female voice, as distinct from the soprano and mezzo-soprano [see Voice], also called an alto. Through the 18th century, the term could refer to male altos (including *castrati*) as well as to females.

(2) A large viola (67.5 cm. in length), but with the range of the normal viola, designed by Jean-Baptiste Vuillaume in about 1855.

Contra-octave. The octave below the great octave and thus the third octave below middle C (C_1 to B_1). See Pitch names.

Contrappunto [It.]. *Counterpoint.

Contrapunctus [Lat.]. (1) *Counterpoint. (2) A contrapuntal composition, especially one employing *imitation.

Contrapuntal. (1) Of or pertaining to *counterpoint. (2) With respect to musical *texture, exhibiting counterpoint, i.e., a degree of independence among the lines or parts making up the texture; in this sense roughly synonymous with *polyphonic, as distinct from *homophonic.

Contrary motion. See Motion, Counterpoint.

Contratenor [Lat.]. In music of the 14th and 15th centuries, a part written "against" the tenor part. The contratenor part occupies approximately the same range as and frequently crosses the tenor; it forms the third part, in addition to the discant or *cantus* or *superius* (the highest-sounding part) and tenor parts, of the typical three-part texture. The contratenor part is often more disjunct than the tenor and may give the impression of being supplementary to the structural pair formed by discant and tenor. With the emergence of four-part texture in the later 15th century, the functions of the contratenor were divided between two parts: the *contratenor altus* or simply *altus* (whence the term *alto), lying between the *superius* and the tenor, and the *contratenor bassus* or simply *bassus* (whence the term *bass), lying below the tenor.

Contra-violin. A large-sized violin introduced in 1917 by Henry Newbold to play the second-violin parts in chamber music.

Contraviolon [Ger.]. A large *violone; also called *grosse Bassgeige, Bassviolon,* [Fr.] *grande basse de violon,* and [It.] *violone grosso.* It was comparable in function, and sometimes identical in tuning, to the *double bass.

Contrebasse [Fr.]. *Double bass; *c. à pistons,* *tuba.

Contrebasson [Fr.]. Contrabassoon. See Bassoon.

Contredanse [Fr.; Ger. *Kontertanz, Contratanz;* It. *contraddanza;* Sp. *contradanza*]. A fast dance movement in duple meter (usually simple, but sometimes compound), constructed of a series of repeated eight-measure strains that maintain the simple motivic and textural qualities of dance music. English *country dances enjoyed a great vogue at the court of Louis XIV, where the name and style were Gallicized

before being disseminated across Europe. They spawned the quadrille and reached their height of bourgeois popularity in the late 18th century. Mozart wrote many for various ensembles, and Beethoven published a set of 12 in 1802 (WoO 14).

Converse, Frederick Shepherd (b. Newton, Mass., 5 Jan. 1871; d. Westwood, Mass., 8 June 1940). Composer. Studied with Paine at Harvard and with Rheinberger in Munich (1896–98). Taught at the New England Conservatory (1900–1902) and at Harvard (1903–7); later headed the theory department at New England and served as dean (1931–38). President of the Boston Opera Company (1908–14). Composed in a German Romantic style (*Flivver Ten Million,* 1926). Other works include operas, an oratorio, chamber music, piano music, songs.

Convertible counterpoint. See Invertible counterpoint.

Cook, Will Marion (b. Washington, D.C., 27 Jan. 1869; d. New York, 19 July 1944). Composer, conductor, and violinist. Studied violin at Oberlin and with Joachim in Germany. Devoted himself to musical comedy in New York; his *Clorindy, or the Origin of the Cakewalk* was the first Broadway musical composed and directed by blacks (1898). Composer-in-chief and conductor for the Williams/Walker productions (1900–1908) of black music theater. His "syncopated" symphony orchestra toured Europe and the U.S. (1918–21); his own music draws from black folklore and folk music, couched in a neo-Romantic style.

Cooke, Arnold (Atkinson) (b. Gomersal, Yorkshire, 4 Nov. 1906). Composer. Studied with Dent at Cambridge and with Hindemith at the Berlin Hochschule für Musik. Taught at the Royal Manchester College of Music, 1933–38 and at Trinity College of Music (London) in 1947. Works include the comic opera *The Invisible Duke* (1975–76); 6 symphonies (1946–84); concertos; piano music; songs and other vocal music.

Cool jazz. A subdued adaptation of *Bebop. Players suppressed highly emotional elements in favor of medium volume, gentle tone colors, legato phrasing, dense harmonies, moderate tempos, and middle registers of instruments. Emerging in the Miles Davis nonet's "Birth of the Cool" recordings of 1949–50 and also associated in New York with teacher-pianist Lennie Tristano, the label became synonymous with *West Coast jazz in the 1950s.

Cooper, Kenneth (b. New York, 31 May 1941). Harpsichordist. Studied with Sylvia Marlowe at Mannes College; coached by Fernando Valenti; studied musicology at Columbia Univ. (Ph.D., 1971). Taught at Barnard College, 1967–71; at Brooklyn

College, 1971–73; at Mannes College from 1975. Performed and recorded widely in ensembles and as a soloist.

Coperto [It., pl. *coperti*]. Covered; in music for kettledrum, muted by the placing of a cloth on the head.

Copla [Sp.]. (1) Any of several Spanish verse types, including as many as 12 lines with varying rhyme schemes, in use from the 14th century. (2) A four-line octosyllabic strophe rhymed abcb, as found in the *romance;* poetry of similar construction used in popular song. (3) A part of the *villancico.*

Copland, Aaron (b. Brooklyn, 14 Nov. 1900; d. Westchester, N.Y., 2 Dec. 1990). Composer, conductor, pianist, and writer on music. Following piano lessons as a child studied with Goldmark and with Boulanger at Fontainebleau. Returned to New York in 1924, lectured at the New School for Social Research (1927–37). Made several trips abroad and to Mexico; twice toured Latin America (1941, 1947); taught at Harvard during Piston's leaves (1935, 1944) and was Charles Eliot Norton lecturer (1951–52). Encouraged younger composers through his cosponsorship of the Copland–Sessions Concerts (New York, 1928–31) and his long association with the Berkshire Music Center (1940–65). In the mid-1920s cultivated an interest in jazz (Piano Concerto, 1926) which he abandoned in the early 1930s to explore a more austere style (*Short Symphony,* 1932–33; Piano Variations, 1930); a few works employ serial procedures (Piano Quartet, 1950; *Inscape,* 1967). After the mid-1930s frequently composed in a more accessible style, making use of New England hymnody, folk music (*El *Salón México*), and jazz; in the *Lincoln Portrait* (1942) borrowed tunes are blended in Ivesian fashion. Perhaps best known for his ballets, especially *Billy the Kid,* *Rodeo,* and *Appalachian Spring* (awarded a Pulitzer Prize). Wrote film scores during the 1940s. Copland was active as conductor, lecturer, and pianist on American and British television and on tour. Other works include operas (*The Second Hurricane,* 1936; *The *Tender Land*); film scores; orchestral works (*Fanfare for the Common Man,* brass and percussion, 1942; Symphony no. 3, 1944–46; Clarinet Concerto, 1947–48); chamber music; piano works; choral music and songs. Writings include *What To Listen for in Music* (1939, 2nd ed., 1957); *Copland on Music* (1960).

Coppélia. A ballet in three acts with music by Léo Delibes, choreography by Arthur Saint-Léon, and book by Saint-Léon and Charles Nuitter after a story by E. T. A. Hoffmann, first produced in Paris in 1870. Later versions have included choreography by Lev Ivanov, Enrico Cecchetti, and Nicholas Sergeyev.

Coprario [Coperario, Cooper, Cowper], **John** [Giovanni] (b. ca. 1575; d. London, ca. June 1626). Composer. Supported by various noble patrons; from 1622 or earlier closely associated with Charles, Prince of Wales, who in 1625 became King Charles I. Almost all of his works are secular. Instrumental works include over 100 fantasias and fantasia-suites for viol ensembles or violin (solo or duet), often with organ; and pieces for 1–3 lyra viols. Also wrote songs and 3-part *villanelle.*

Copula. [Lat., also *copulatio*] A grammatical term first used by 12th-century writers on music to describe the joining of two voices in a cadential accord. In the 13th century, Johannes de Garlandia used the word for a kind of polyphony between *organum and *discant, distinguished from the former by the modal [see Modes, rhythmic] organization of the second voice *(duplum).*

Coq d'or, Le [Fr.]. See *Golden Cockerel, The.*

Cor [Fr.]. *Horn; *c. anglais,* *English horn; *c. à pistons, c. d'harmonie,* valve horn; *c. de basset,* *basset horn; *c. de chasse,* hunting horn.

Coranto. See Courante.

Corbetta, Francesco [Corbette, Francisque] (b. Pavia, ca. 1615; d. Paris, 1681). Guitarist and composer. Active as a guitar teacher in Italy by 1639. A teacher and performer at the royal courts in Paris (where he taught Louis XIV) and, after the Restoration, in London. A great virtuoso, he wrote exclusively for 5-course guitar. Published 5 collections, 3 in Italian style (1639, 1643, 1648), 2 in French style (1671, 1674).

Corda [It.], **corde** [Fr.]. String; *snare; *corda vuota, corde à vide,* open string. See also *Una corda.*

Corder, Frederick (b. London, 26 Jan. 1852; d. there, 21 Aug. 1932). Composer and teacher. Studied at the Royal Academy of Music, 1873–75; with Hiller in Cologne, 1875–78; and in Milan, 1878–79; conductor at the Brighton Aquarium, 1880–82. With his wife translated all of Wagner's librettos (from *Lohengrin* onwards) into English. Composed in many genres, but more important historically as a teacher. Professor of composition at the Royal Academy from 1888; pupils include Bax, Bantock, and Holbrook.

Cordero, Roque (b. Panama, 16 Aug. 1917). Composer. Studied in Panama; in 1938 appointed conductor of the orchestra that later became the Symphony Orchestra of Panama. In 1943 traveled to the U.S and studied with Krenek in Minneapolis. Professor (1950–66) and director (1953–64) at Panama's National Institute of Music; from 1966 taught at Indiana Univ.; from 1972 at Illinois State Univ. Works include ballets; orchestral works (3 symphonies; *Cir-

cunvoluciones y móviles, 57 instruments, 1967); chamber music (*Variations and Theme for 5,* 1975); piano works.

Cordier, Baude (b. Rheims; fl. early 15th cent.). Composer. His identity is unclear. It has been hypothesized that he was the harpist and organist Baude Fresnel, who served at the court of Philip the Bold from 1384 and died in 1397 or 1398. One ballade, 9 rondeaux, and 1 Mass movement are extant; some employ complex notation and rhythms.

Corea, Chick [Armando Anthony, Jr.] (b. Chelsea, Mass., 12 June 1941). Jazz pianist, composer, and bandleader. Played Latin dance music (1962–63) and hard bop (1964–66) before joining Stan Getz's group (1967) and Miles Davis's jazz-rock band (1968–70). Led Circle with Dave Holland and Anthony Braxton (1970–71). In 1971 recorded 2 unaccompanied albums (both called *Piano Improvisations*), rejoined Getz, then formed Return to Forever; it was a delicate Latin jazz group (–1973), an intense jazz-rock group (1973–76, reunion tour in 1983), and finally a 13-piece ensemble incorporating brass and a string quartet (–1979). Played in duos with Burton and Hancock; led a quartet, the group Trio Music with Roy Haynes and Miroslav Vitous (intermittently from 1981), and the trio Elektric Band (from 1985).

Corelli, Arcangelo (b. Fusignano, 17 Feb. 1653; d. Rome, 8 Jan. 1713). Composer and violinist. In 1666 went to Bologna, where he studied with Giovanni Benvenuti and Leonardo Brugnoli; by 1675 was in Rome. Trips to Spain and France have been postulated but not documented. By 1675 he appears in Roman payment documents as a violinist; by 1679 had begun to lead Roman orchestras. From 1681 until his death was in Rome, making only a few trips. Active as a performer and leader of small and large instrumental ensembles in Roman homes and churches and at public celebrations; composed sinfonias and concertos for these occasions, often as introductions to large concerted works by others. In 1684 Corelli and Alessandro Scarlatti became members of the Congregazione dei Virtuosi di S. Cecilia; Corelli was head of the instrumental section in 1700. Retired from public view after 1708. Compared to other violinist-composers Corelli eschewed virtuosity. His collections maintain a traditional distinction between sacred and secular pieces, but dance movements may appear in church sonatas and fugal movements in chamber works. Published only five volumes during his lifetime. In the late 17th and 18th centuries his sonatas were widely performed and often reprinted; his works remained especially popular in England. For the op. 5 sonatas there are several extant sets of ornaments, some attributed to the composer himself (Walsh, 1710). Works (many probably composed well before publication): *Sonate a tre* op. 1 (Rome, 1681); *Sonate da camera a tre* op. 2 (Rome, 1685); *Sonate a tre* op. 3 (Rome, 1689); *Sonate a tre* op. 4 (Rome, 1694); *Sonate a violino e violone o cimbalo* op. 5 (Rome, 1700); Concerti grossi op. 6 (Amsterdam, 1714). Also a handful of other attributed works, some of them doubtful.

Corelli, Franco (Dario) (b. Ancona, 8 Apr. 1921). Dramatic tenor. Entered Pesaro Conservatory, 1947; operatic debut as Don José at Spoleto, 1952. La Scala debut with Callas, 1954. Debut at Covent Garden, 1957, as Cavaradossi; at the Met, 1962, as Manrico; at the Paris Opéra and Vienna Staatsoper, 1970.

Corigliano, John (Paul) (b. New York, 16 Feb. 1938). Composer. Studied with Luening at Columbia and with Giannini and Creston. Producer at CBS Television (1959–72), taught at the Manhattan School (from 1971) and at Lehman College at CUNY (from 1974). Composer in residence, Chicago Symphony (1987–90). Compositions are in a relatively conservative, largely tonal, and accessible style, only occasionally employing serial procedures and atonality. Works include a clarinet concerto (1977); the opera *The Ghosts of Versailles* (1991); Symphony no. 1 (1989); *Phantasmagoria,* cello and piano (1993); *The Cloisters,* mezzo-soprano and orchestra (1965).

Coriolan Overture. An orchestral work by Beethoven, op. 62 (1807), composed as an overture to a play by Heinrich Joseph von Collin on the same subject as Shakespeare's *Coriolanus.*

Cori spezzati [It., broken choirs]. See Polychoral.

Corista [It.]. (1) *Tuning fork. (2) *Concert pitch. (3) A singer in a chorus.

Cornago, Johannes (fl. ca. 1455–85). Composer. Active chiefly at the Aragonese court of the Kingdom of Naples but also in Spain in the chapel of Ferdinand V in 1475. Compositions include 4 sacred and 11 (or 12) secular works.

Cornamusa, cornemuse [It., Lat.]. (1) A wind instrument mentioned but not described in 16th-century sources. It was probably a capped *shawm, perhaps identical with the *dolzaina. (2) A *bagpipe of the Abruzzi mountains of Italy.

Cornelius, (Carl August) Peter (b. Mainz, 24 Dec. 1824; d. there, 26 Oct. 1874). Composer and writer. From 1844 to 1852 lived in Berlin, moving in literary circles; music lessons from Dehn (1844–46). In 1852 moved to Weimar and became Liszt's secretary and translator; wrote articles supportive of the New German School. Composed 5 Masses (1852–55), Lieder (1853–62), and the comic opera *Der Barbier von Baghdad* (1855–58); the difficulties accompanying its production under Liszt were factors in Liszt's leaving Weimar in 1861. Cornelius lived in Vienna as a private music teacher (1859–65), then in 1865 moved to Munich as part of the Wagnerian circle gathered by Ludwig II. From 1867 taught music theory and rhetoric at the new conservatory and was one of Wagner's closest associates.

Cornemuse [Fr.]. *Bagpipe.

Cornet [formerly also cornopean; Fr. *cornet à pistons;* Ger. *Kornett;* It. *cornetta;* Sp. *corneta, cornetín*]. A soprano brass instrument very similar to the modern trumpet but having a slightly more conical bore [see ill. under Brass instruments]. Its sound is somewhat more mellow than that of the trumpet (depending on the player). It is used in European and American military, community, and school bands. The cornet first appeared in France about 1828 when valves were applied to the *cornet simple* or *post horn. Its agility and flexibility were exploited in brilliant popular solos during the last half of the 19th century. In the 1920s, it was largely replaced by the trumpet in jazz and popular music. Its written range is from f♯ to c''' or higher, sounding a whole tone lower on the common B♭ instrument. The soprano E♭ cornet has been widely used as a solo instrument and in *brass bands.

Corneta [Sp.]. (1) *Cornet. (2) *Bugle. (3) *Cornett.

Cornett [Fr. *cornet à bouquin;* Ger. *Zink;* It. *cornetto;* Sp. *corneta*]. A wooden (or occasionally ivory) instrument of the brass family with a wide conical bore and side holes for a thumb and six fingers. It was used in church and chamber music, sometimes with very elaborate parts, from about 1550 to 1700. The English spelling of "cornet" was altered to "cornett" to avoid confusion with the modern *cornet. The most common type is the curved treble instrument, which is about 60 cm. (2 ft.) long with a range from a (which can be lipped down to g) to d'''. It is made of two hollowed-out wood halves glued together and covered with leather. See ill. under Brass instruments.

Cornetta [It.]. *Cornet.

Cornetto [It.]. *Cornett.

Cornett-ton [Ger.]. See Pitch (4).

Corno [It.]. (1) *Horn; *c. a macchina, a pistone, cromatico, ventile,* valve horn; *c. a mano,* natural horn; *c. da caccia,* hunting horn; *c. di bassetto,* *basset horn; *c. inglese,* *English horn; *c. storto,* *crumhorn. *Corno da tirarsi,* an instrument specified in some cantatas by Bach, perhaps a slide *trumpet. (2) [Sp.] Horn.

Cornu [Lat.]. (1) A horn of ancient Rome. It was curved in the shape of a G and held vertically with the tubing passing around the player's shoulder and the bell pointing forward. See ill. under Instrument. (2) *Horn.

Cornysh, William (d. 1523). Composer, actor, and writer. Active at the English court before late 1493. Master of the Children of the Chapel Royal from 1509 until his death. Acted in, devised, or wrote many plays and entertainments presented at court. Wrote numerous sacred works and many secular polyphonic pieces.

Coro [It., Sp.]. (1) Chorus. (2) *Course. See also *Cori spezzati.*

Corona [Lat., It.]. *Fermata.

Coronach, corranach [Gael.]. In Scotland from the 16th century through the early 19th, a funeral lament sung over the corpse principally by women and including praise for the deceased and highly emotional wailing. It is thought to have been the equivalent of the Irish *caoine.*

Coronation Anthems. (1) Four anthems for chorus and orchestra by Handel, composed for the coronation of George II in 1727: "Zadok the priest," "The King shall rejoice," "My heart is inditing," and "Let thy hand be strengthened." (2) An anthem for chorus and orchestra, "My heart is inditing," composed by Purcell for the coronation of James II in 1685.

Coronation Concerto. Mozart's Piano Concerto in D major K. 537 (1788), so called because he performed it (together with the Concerto in F major K. 459) at the coronation of the Emperor Leopold in Frankfurt in 1790.

Coronation Mass. Popular name for Mozart's Mass in C major K. 317 (1779), traditionally believed to have been composed for the annual crowning of the statue of the Virgin Mary at the shrine of Maria Plain near Salzburg, Austria.

Corps [Fr.]. (1) The resonating body of a stringed instrument. (2) *Corps de rechange,* a *tuning slide or *crook of a brass instrument.

Correa de Arauxo [Correa de Araujo], **Francisco** (b. ca. 1576; d. Segovia, ca. 31 Oct. 1654). Organist and composer. Organist at the Church of S. Salvador in Seville from 1599 until 1636, then at Jaén Cathedral until 1640, finally at Segovia Cathedral until his death. In 1626 published a collection of 62 *tientos* and 7 other pieces for organ.

Corrente [It.]. See Courante.

Corrette, Michel (b. Rouen, 1709; d. Paris, 22 Jan. 1795). Composer and author of method books.

Worked intermittently as an organist between 1737 and about 1780 and as a teacher. Traveled to England sometime before 1773. A large proportion of his numerous works are arrangements. The nearly 20 methods (some published in facs. in the 1970s) provide invaluable information on performance practice of the 18th century.

Corrido [Sp.]. A type of narrative ballad found in several countries of Latin America, derived from the Spanish *romance. It is especially important in Mexico, where it treats heroic figures and episodes of legend and history as well as contemporary events.

Corsi, Jacopo (b. Florence, 17 July 1561; d. there, 29 Dec. 1602). Patron and composer. Sponsored and participated in discussions and experiments that led to the beginnings of opera; the most prominent patron of music in Florence after the Medicis. With Peri composed the musical setting of *Dafne, and sponsored and played harpsichord in the first performance of Peri's *Euridice.*

Corteccia, (Pier) Francesco (b. Florence, 27 July 1502; d. there, 7 July 1571). Composer. A choirboy at S. Giovanni Battista in Florence in 1515; associated with this church until 1522, again from 1527 (as chaplain), from 1535 until 1539 (as organist), and from 1540 until his death (as *maestro di cappella*). Organist at the chapel of the Medici family for a year, beginning in 1531. From 1540 *maestro di cappella* at the court of the Duke of Florence and at Florence Cathedral. Secular works include over 100 madrigals and several *intermedi;* sacred works include 2 early Passions and 36 motets.

Cortège [Fr.]. A solemn procession; a composition appropriate to such a procession.

Cortés, Ramiro (Jr.) (b. Dallas, 25 Nov. 1938; d. Salt Lake City, 2 July 1984). Composer. Studied with Cowell (1952), at Yale with Donovan (1953–54), and at USC with Dahl and Stevens (1954–56); also with Petrassi in Rome (1956–58), and with Sessions (1958) and Giannini (1961–62). Taught at UCLA (from 1966), at USC (1967–72), and at the Univ. of Utah (from 1973). His early works were largely serial; later music became more flexibly chromatic. Compositions include operas (*The Eternal Return,* 1981); musicals; film and incidental music; orchestral works (*Movements in Variation,* 1972); choral and vocal works; chamber works.

Cortot, Alfred (Denis) (b. Nyon, Switzerland, 26 Sept. 1877; d. Lausanne, 15 June 1962). Pianist, conductor, and educator. Studied piano with Emil Descombes and Diémer at the Paris Conservatory; assistant at Bayreuth, 1898–1901. Formed various organizations to conduct Wagner's works. Formed trio with Casals and Thibaud, 1905. Taught piano at the Paris Conservatory, 1907–17. With Adolphe Mangeot founded École normale de musique, 1918; director, 1918–62. His work under the Nazi occupation during World War II was followed by a restricted role in French musical culture during the last 15 years of his life.

Coryell, Larry (b. Galveston, Tex., 2 Apr. 1943). Jazz guitarist and bandleader. Worked as an electric guitarist with Chico Hamilton (1966) and then played jazz-rock with the Free Spirits (1966), Gary Burton (1967–68), and his own groups (1969–75); his album *Spaces* (1970) included duets with John McLaughlin. Playing acoustic guitar, toured in a duo with Philip Catherine and a trio with McLaughlin and Paco De Lucia. Mainly played the electric instrument in the 1980s.

Così fan tutte, ossia La scuola degli amanti [It., All Women Act That Way, or The School of Lovers]. Comic opera in two acts by Mozart (libretto by Lorenzo da Ponte), produced in Vienna in 1790. Setting: Naples, 18th century.

Costa, Michael (Andrew Agnus) [Michele Andrea Agniello] (b. Naples, 4 Feb. 1808; d. Hove, England, 29 Apr. 1884). Conductor and composer. Studied at the Naples Conservatory under Furno, Tritto (his grandfather), Zingarelli, and Crescentini; had 4 operas performed in Naples, 1826–29; in 1829 settled in London. *Maestro al piano* at King's Theatre, 1830; music director there, 1832; conductor, 1833–46, apparently the first to unite that orchestra's direction under a single conductor using a baton; conductor of the Philharmonic Society, 1846–54; at Covent Garden, 1847–68; music director, Her Majesty's Theatre, 1871–81; also conducted choral societies and festivals. As a composer best known for his oratorios (*Eli,* 1855; *Naaman,* 1864). Knighted in 1869.

Costeley, Guillaume (b. Fontanges, Auvergne, 1530 or 1531; d. Evreux, 28 Jan. 1606). Composer. By 1560 appointed composer and organist to the court of Charles IX. Closely associated with Baïf and his Académie de poésie et de musique. Settled in Evreux in 1570; retained his position at court but seems to have stopped composing at this time. Retired from court between 1577 and 1588. Wrote over 100 chansons, 3 motets, and a very brief (perhaps only a fragment) organ fantasy. The chansons, of which he was a leading exponent, include 1 microtonal piece and a number of *airs.*

Costello, Elvis [McManus, Declan Patrick] (b. London, 25 Aug. 1954). Rock singer, songwriter, and guitarist. His first record (*My Aim Is True,* incl. "Alison," 1977) was produced by songwriter Nick Lowe, with whom he remained associated; since 1978 has released a large number of albums (*Impe-*

rial Bedroom, 1982; *King of America,* 1986; *All This Useless Beauty,* 1996) and toured extensively with his band, The Attractions. Though initially associated with the British New Wave, his music has assimilated many styles, including country, soul, and early rock-and-roll.

Cosyn, Benjamin (b. ca. 1570; d. London?, after 1652). Composer and organist. Worked as an organist from 1622 until 1643, first for two years at Dulwich College, then at Charterhouse. Wrote mostly highly ornamented and difficult keyboard music; was greatly influenced by John Bull.

Cotillon [Fr.], **cotillion.** (1) A social dance of the 18th and 19th centuries, related to the *contredanse and quadrille and often performed at the end of a ball. Music for such a dance might include the waltz, polka, mazurka, and galop. (2) A formal occasion for social dancing, especially for young people.

Cottage piano. A small upright piano, especially the design made by Robert Wornum in 1813.

Coulé [Fr.]. (1) Slurred; often used as a noun for a pair of notes connected by a slur. In 18th-century France, it seems sometimes to have meant a pair of notes played unequally (long-short or short-long) according to the convention of *notes inégales. (2) In the French Baroque, a descending *appoggiatura. (3) A single-note ornament filling in a descending third *(coulé de tierce),* slurred to the second note but often taking its value from the first. See Ornamentation.

Coulisse [Fr.]. (1) The slide of a trombone or slide trumpet. (2) The *tuning slide of a brass instrument.

Council of Trent. A council of the Roman Catholic Church that was convened by Pope Paul III to meet in the city of Trento (now northern Italy) and that met intermittently from 1545 through 1563. Its work embodied the spirit of the Counter-Reformation and, among many other topics, dealt with the reform of liturgical music. It prohibited the use of *tropes and all but a few *sequences and considered prohibiting the use of all polyphony in the liturgy. The story that Palestrina's *Marcellus Mass saved polyphony from this prohibition is without foundation. More closely associated with the Council was the music of Jacobus de Kerle (1531 or 1532–91), whose *Preces speciales* for four voices (Venice, 1562) were dedicated to the Council's members. A principal aim of the reforms and of the music composed with them in view was the intelligibility of the liturgical texts.

Counter. *Countertenor.

Counterexposition. In a *fugue, a second, complete exposition in the tonic and dominant.

Counterfugue. A *fugue in which the answer is an inversion of the subject, e.g., nos. 4, 5, and 6 of Bach's *The *Art of Fugue.* The technique dates from the 16th century and is sometimes described with the phrase *per arsin et thesin* [see Arsis and thesis (3)].

Countermelody. In a piece whose texture consists clearly of a melody with accompaniment, an accompanying part with distinct, though subordinate, melodic interest.

Counterpoint [Lat. *contrapunctus,* fr. *contra punctum,* against note; Fr. *contrepoint;* Ger. *Kontrapunkt;* It. *contrappunto;* Sp. *contrapunto*]. The combination of two or more melodic lines; the linear consideration of melodic lines sounding together; the technical principles governing such consideration.

The essence of contrapuntal perception is that, at one and the same time, horizontal motion of one part may be perceived and differentiated from the simultaneous horizontal motion of another. The very elementary fragment of music in Ex. 1 has a notationally horizontal component, the moving upper part (x), and a vertical component, the interval of a third (y), which changes to a fourth (z). The notation expresses the temporal dimension: the B comes after the A in time (a melodic succession), and the fourth comes after the third (an intervallic succession). The A can be perceived as moving to the B, and the F can be perceived as remaining stationary underneath the moving part. Alternatively, both of these parts can be perceived simultaneously; or the third can be perceived as changing to a fourth. In either case, the perception of the horizontal and vertical relationships simultaneously is the perception of counterpoint.

Although counterpoint is a property of *polyphony, its nature is indissolubly linked to the nature of melody. A melody must have coherence; its tones follow one another in a musically sensible way, and this is true for melodies combined contrapuntally no less than for those that are not. This is not to say that every melody used in counterpoint must be as distinctive as a theme or as memorable as a song, but it must be perceptible as a continuity, not just as a succession of isolated tones.

Counterpoint is a feature of all music in which combinations of two or more simultaneously sounding pitches are regularly employed. The term and its adjective form contrapuntal, however, are often used to distinguish from one another musical *textures in which each of the several lines sounding together retains its character as a line and textures in which one line predominates and the remainder are clearly subservient, retaining little or no distinct character as lines. In this sense, a fugue of Bach is contrapuntal whereas a nocturne of Chopin is not, even though careful analysis might reveal that the two are equally well worked out in linear terms. Similarly, counterpoint, with its emphasis on the linear or horizontal aspect of music, is sometimes contrasted with *harmony, which concerns primarily the vertical aspect of music embodied in the nature of the simultaneously sounding combinations of pitches employed. Counterpoint and harmony are, nevertheless, fundamentally inseparable.

Contrapuntal motion is regulated by direction, by rhythmic differentiation, and by separation. Direction [see also Motion] refers to the way in which the parts may move with respect to each other: by contrary motion, that is, in opposite directions, one part moving up while the other moves down; and by similar motion, the parts moving in the same direction. Parallel motion is similar motion in which the parts keep the same interval between them as they move. Oblique motion, one voice moving while the other remains fixed, is illustrated by Ex. 1; it is the basis for rhythmic differentiation between parts, for the ear tends to follow the moving part in preference to the slower one. Separation refers to the intervals formed between simultaneous tones in the different parts. These intervals may be consonant or dissonant [see Consonance and dissonance]. Dissonant intervals in tonal counterpoint are those that are treated as requiring resolution to consonant intervals; resolution is characteristically achieved by the stepwise motion of one of the tones in the dissonant interval.

The principles usually taught under the heading of counterpoint (also called the principles of voice-leading) describe the types of motion permitted in individual lines with respect to one another and the types of dissonance and resolution permitted between two or more lines. One of the most important principles governing motion is the prohibition against motion in parallel fifths and octaves [see Parallel fifths, octaves]. The principal types of dissonance (sometimes called *nonharmonic tones or embellishing tones) occurring in tonal counterpoint are as follows:

1. Passing tone [Ex. 2], which connects two consonant pitches by stepwise motion and normally occurs in a metrically weak position. When it occurs in a metrical position stronger than that of its resolution [see Accent], it is called an accented passing tone.

2. Neighboring tone or auxiliary tone, a tone a step above (upper neighbor; Ex. 3) or a step below (lower neighbor; Ex. 4) a consonant tone. Upper and lower neighbors are sometimes combined to form double neighbors [Exx. 5 and 6], to which the term cambiata [see 7 below] is also sometimes applied [see also échappée, 6 below]. Single neighboring tones may be either strong or weak metrically.

3. Suspension [Ex. 7], normally a dissonant tone occurring in a strong metrical position, having been sustained (or "suspended" or "prepared") from an initial attack as a consonance and converted to a dis-

sonance as a result of motion in another voice. It is most often resolved downward by step.

4. Appoggiatura [Ex. 8], a metrically strong dissonance, normally arrived at by leap and resolved by descending step. The term is also applied to accented dissonances similar to the suspension [Ex. 9], in which case it is said to be a prepared appoggiatura, and more loosely to any accented dissonance that is resolved by step in either direction.

5. Anticipation [Ex. 10], a metrically weak dissonant tone that is immediately reharmonized as a consonance.

6. Échappée or escape tone [Ex. 11], a metrically weak dissonance approached by step and left by leap in the opposite direction. Such formations can also be understood as incomplete neighboring tones.

7. Cambiata (or nota cambiata), properly a five-note figure [Ex. 12], the second note of which is dissonant and the third of which is consonant. The term is also applied, however, to a similar figure moving in an upward direction [Ex. 13] and to several related shorter figures [Exx. 14 and 15] as well as to the double neighboring tones described above [Exx. 5 and 6], to which the term changing notes is sometimes applied. All of these are common in music of the 15th and 16th centuries. The term cambiata has sometimes been further extended to include another figure [Ex. 16], the principal feature of which is

that the motion to the dissonance is in the same direction (unlike the motion of the *échappée*) as the motion between the initial and final consonances.

Although all of the above formations serve primarily to introduce dissonance into an otherwise consonant succession, some of them, particularly the first three, may on occasion be entirely consonant. See also Species counterpoint.

The term counterpoint did not come into use until the 14th century, but the principles that form the basis for counterpoint even into the period of tonality were formulated in 13th-century treatises on what was termed *discant. These principles include criteria for simultaneous, vertical combinations and for horizontal motion. The former consists in its essence of a list of intervals to be treated as consonant, the latter in a preference for contrary motion, especially when approaching a perfect consonance, and the banning of motion in parallel perfect intervals. Much of the history of counterpoint that follows, at least through the late 15th century, consists in redefinition, first in practice and then in theory, of the list of consonances, and the increasing strictness in practice of adherence to the prohibition against motion in parallel perfect intervals, which had been formulated by about 1300 [see Parallel fifths, octaves].

Countersubject. In a *fugue, a subordinate subject that accompanies statements of the principal subject.

Countertenor. (1) *Contratenor. (2) A male alto who sings *falsetto.

Country dance. Any of numerous English dances of folk origin (shared, however, by all classes of society) known since the 16th century and usually danced by a line of women and a line of men facing one another. The music for such dances included folk tunes and usually consisted of a series of eight-measure phrases. Such dances, including specific English examples, were taken up in France around 1700 as the *contredanse, which in turn spread through Europe.

Country and western music. A mass-disseminated product of the present century in America, derived from traditional oral music brought by nonliterate immigrants from the British Isles. Commercial recording companies began to tap rural Southern music in the early 1920s as part of a larger strategy to capitalize on the culture of various ethnic and minority groups. The musicians who gave the most important definition to the new genre were the Carter family and Jimmie Rodgers. The label hillbilly, a derogatory term for rural white Southerners, was now put on this music, taken from the name of a popular recording group from the vicinity of Galax, Virginia, the Hillbillies.

This music at first represented a cross section of the traditional repertory of the rural South. There were old narrative *ballads brought to America from Britain and newer American ballads of the same sort, usually accompanied by banjo, fiddle, guitar, or some combination of these instruments. Many other songs had passed into oral tradition from the composed, popular song literature of the 19th-century American parlor. There was also dance music: two-strain pieces played by one or more fiddles sometimes accompanied by banjo or guitar. The introduction of the guitar and other chord-playing instruments in the latter part of the 19th century, and the assimilation of pieces from the composed popular repertory at the same time, brought an increasing trend toward a tonal, triadic style.

By the middle of the 1930s, a mainstream style had crystallized, blending elements of traditional and more recent urban music. Roy Acuff was recognized as the first important practitioner of this consensus style, which has endured to the present day in the music of a small number of performers. Singing styles retain the nasal, "high-country" sound of older music; instrumentation consists of one or two fiddles, a banjo, guitars (including a Hawaiian or steel instrument capable of producing a characteristic sliding sound [see Steel guitar]), and usually a bass; texts are often concerned with such harsh realities as death, alcoholism, desertion, crime, and thwarted love; and both melody and accompaniment reflect a solid harmonic foundation.

Dissemination soon spread from the South, first to other areas with substantial populations descended from nonliterate British immigrants, and then to virtually all parts of the U.S. Regional dialects emerged, all eventually encompassed under the term country and western.

Coup d'archet [Fr.]. Bow stroke.

Coup de langue [Fr.]. In the playing of wind instruments, a movement of the tongue so as to articulate a sound.

Couperin, Armand-Louis (b. Paris, 25 Feb. 1727; d. there, 2 Feb. 1789). Organist, harpsichordist, and composer. Organist at St. Gervais, eventually additional posts at Notre Dame, the Sainte Chapelle, the French royal chapel, and at least three other churches. Regarded as an uncommonly fine organist; his improvisations were especially prized. His relatively few compositions include both secular and sacred pieces for keyboard alone or with other instruments; also works for chorus and chorus and orchestra.

Couperin, François ["le grand"] (b. Paris, 10 Nov. 1668; d. there, 11 Sept. 1733). Composer, organist, and harpsichordist. Came from a family of prominent musicians. Probably studied with his father and with the royal organist Jacques Thomelin. Possibly studied with Lalande, whose post at St. Gervais he assumed in 1685. In 1693 was named one of the four *organistes du roi* for the royal chapel; soon he was tutoring the royal family in harpsichord. Became chamber musician for the court, perhaps filling in for the ailing d'Alembert. During the next two decades established himself as one of the leading harpsichordists of his day; also composed church and chamber music during the king's final years. In 1717 was finally appointed to d'Alembert's post as *maître de clavecin du roi*. By that time there was a new king, however, and Couperin had begun to withdraw from court duties, continuing to edit his music for publication. Increasing ailments hindered his activities during the 1720s, and in 1730 he passed on his position as royal harpsichordist to his daughter.

Works: *Vocal music.* Some 40 sacred motets; secular vocal works, mostly *airs sérieux;* sacred cantatas (lost).

Instrumental music. Nouveaux concerts nos. 5–14, instruments not specified, in *Les goûts-réünis ou Nouveaux concerts* (1724); *Les nations: Sonades et suites de simphonies en trio* (Paris, 1926); *Pièces de violes avec la basse chifrée* (Paris, 1928).

Harpsichord works. Pièces de clavecin . . . premier livre (Paris, 1713); *L'art de toucher le clavecin* (Paris, 1716; rev. 2nd ed., 1717); *Second livre de pièces de clavecin* (Paris, 1716–17); *Troisième livre* (Paris, 1722); *Quatrième livre* (Paris, 1730).

Theoretical writings include *L'art de toucher le clavecin* (Paris, 1716; rev. 2nd ed., 1717) and *Regle pour l'accompagnement.*

Couperin, Louis (b. Chaumes, ca. 1626; d. Paris, 29 Aug. 1661). Composer, harpsichordist, and organist, uncle of François "le grand." Came to Paris by 1651 and spent the rest of his short life there, except for visits to Meudon in 1656 and Toulouse in 1659. In 1653 acquired the post of organist at St. Gervais in Paris; played treble viol and possibly organ in the French royal chapel. Some 200 instrumental works survive, including about 130 for harpsichord, about 75 for organ, and fewer than 10 for small ensembles.

Coupler. A mechanical device in organs and harpsichords for connecting one keyboard to another at unison pitch, and in electric-action organs, often at octave and suboctave pitches as well.

Couplet [Fr.]. (1) Two successive lines of poetry forming a pair, often within a larger form. (2) In French poetry, any of the strophes in a poem that includes a refrain [for the related Spanish *copla,* see *Villancico*]. (3) In the late 17th and 18th centuries (e.g., in the music of François Couperin), the sections between recurrences of the main theme of a **rondeau;* also the similar sections of a **rondo.* (4) In light opera of the 18th and 19th century and in derivative genres since, a humorous strophic song with refrain. (5) **Duplet.*

Courante [Fr.; It. *corrente;* Eng. corant, coranto]. A Baroque dance movement in triple meter. It originated in the 16th century and became a regular member of the solo **suite,* following the allemande, by ca. 1630. Two versions, ultimately considered French and Italian, coexisted; most composers used

1. Arcangelo Corelli, Corrente from Trio Sonata op. 2 no. 10 (1685).   2. Louis Couperin, Courante (ca. 1660).

courante and *corrente* interchangeably as titles, however. The Italian type uses fast triple meter (3/4 or 3/8), often with triadic or scalar figuration in even eighth or sixteenth notes [see Ex. 1]. It generally has homophonic texture, but imitative openings are not uncommon. The mature French courante was described by contemporary theorists as solemn and grave, having the same pulse as a *sarabande. It is usually notated in 3/2, with a strong proclivity toward *hemiola figures that combine 6/4 and 3/2 accent patterns as well as related syncopated figures [see Ex. 2]. Somewhat contrapuntal texture or *style brisé is the norm, and phrase structures are often ambiguous, as is the harmonic scheme. Both types are usually in binary form, although early examples may have three strains. Both begin with upbeats and end on the strong beat.

The dance was courtly and was known in the 16th century, becoming important in the 17th. In Italy, it was a cheerful courtship dance. French choreography survives only from the 18th century, so that the early relationship of the courante to the corrente is unknown. The courante was danced infrequently on the stage in France, but was one of the most important dances at court balls under Louis XIV, subsisting as late as 1725.

The courante/corrente was of central importance to solo and chamber suites. Music for both types is found in both France and Italy as early as the first third of the 17th century. From the middle of the 17th century to the end of the Baroque era, the Italians showed a distinct preference for the straightforward (and fast) corrente in the *sonata da camera, as well as in solo music. In France, the courante was first significant in lute music. By the middle of the century, the complex type in 3 (i.e., 3/2) was used almost exclusively and was relatively slow. There are more courantes than any other dance type in French harpsichord music of the 17th century

In the first half of the 18th century, the distinction between corrente and courante was sometimes explicit. Bach specified "corrente" in the harpsichord partitas nos. 1, 3, 5, and 6; nos. 2 and 4 have "courantes" in style and title. The dance form died out completely at the end of the Baroque period.

Course [Fr. *choeur, rang;* Ger. *Chor, Saitenchor;* It. *coro;* Sp. *orden*]. A set of one, two, or three strings tuned and played as one; the term is usually used in reference to 16th-, 17th-, and 18th-century plucked instruments such as the lute, theorbo, archlute, guitar, bandora, and cittern. Multiple strings in a course are tuned in unison or in octaves.

Courtaut, courtaud. A 17th-century double-reed woodwind instrument of cylindrical bore. It was constructed with two bore channels in a single block of wood and was usually played with a *wind cap.

Cover version. In popular music, a recording that remakes an earlier, sometimes very successful, recording.

Covered fifths, octaves. See Parallel fifths, octaves.

Cow horn [Ger. *Stierhorn*]. A lip-vibrated wind instrument made from the horn of a cow, often used by herdsmen. The parts specified by Wagner for such instruments in the *Ring* and in *Die Meistersinger* are usually played on specially made straight brass instruments with perfectly conical bore.

Coward, Noël (Pierce) (b. Teddington, Middlesex, 16 Dec. 1899; d. Blue Harbour, Jamaica, 26 Mar. 1973). Songwriter, playwright, and actor. His first play was produced in 1920. Self-taught in music, his light, sophisticated songs had to be dictated to an assistant who notated them. His best-known successes were the comedies *Private Lives* (1930) and *Blithe Spirit* (1942); also composed operettas, musicals, and ballets. Knighted in 1970.

Cowbell [Sp. *cencerro*]. A metal bell, usually with straight sides and a slightly expanding, nearly rectangular cross section. The type with clapper, associated with cattle, is sometimes specified in orchestral works. A type without clapper and played with a drumstick is widely used in Latin American popular music. See ill. under Percussion instruments.

Cowell, Henry (Dixon) (b. Menlo Park, Calif., 11 Mar. 1897; d. Shady Hill, N.Y., 10 Dec. 1965). Composer, pianist, and writer on music. A composer who never lost an early curiosity for new approaches and sounds; an advocate for new music who was an active lecturer, performer, and writer. Studied from 1914 with Samuel Seward and Charles Seeger; two quartets written during this period exploit his procedures for relating rhythm and pitch to the overtone series and employ a complex rhythmic language (*Romantic* and *Euphometric,* 1914–15). In 1916 studied at the Institute of Musical Art (Damrosch); in 1917 was an assistant at Berkeley. A concert of his music presented in New York (1919) launched an international career; made several European tours as composer-pianist (1923–33); in 1929 was the first American composer invited to the U.S.S.R. The piano works he presented in these concerts and lectures employed tone clusters ("The Tides of Manaunaun," 1917?) and new means of sound production on the piano ("Aeolian Harp," 1923; "Sinister Resonance," 1930; Piano Concerto, 1928). Continued experimenting in the 1930s, and pursued an interest in non-Western music by studying in Berlin with Hornbostel. Also wrote in a more conservative idiom; between 1935 and 1950 made extensive use of traditional and folk models and produced music that was more tonal and rhythmically regular. His studies of world music are reflected in several works of the 1950s and later (2 concertos for koto and orchestra, 1961–62 and 1965). Throughout his career advocated new American music: in 1927 founded the *New Musical Quarterly,* a journal that published works of American composers and some Europeans; co-founded the Pan-American Association of Composers. From 1941 to 1963 taught courses on non-Western music at the New School for Social Research; also taught at Peabody (1951–56) and Columbia (1949–65) and lectured in the U.S., Europe, and Asia. Cage and Harrison are among his pupils.

Cowen, Frederic Hymen [Hymen Frederick] (b. Kingston, Jamaica, 29 Jan. 1852; d. London, 6 Oct. 1935). Conductor and composer. Came to England in 1856; lessons with Goss and Benedict; studied in Leipzig (1860–66) and at the Stern Conservatory in Berlin (1867). Returned to London, established himself as a pianist and composer. Conductor of the Philharmonic Society, London (1888–92; 1900–07); of the Hallé Orchestra, Manchester (1896–99); of the Liverpool Philharmonic (1896–1913). Knighted in 1911. Works include 4 operas, 6 symphonies (no. 3, "Scandinavian," 1880); songs and cantatas.

Cox, Ida [née Prather] (b. Toccoa, Ga., 25 Feb. 1896; d. Knoxville, 10 Nov. 1967). Blues singer. Toured theater circuits (1910–44), starring in her own revues from 1929. From 1925 often worked with her second husband, the pianist Jesse Crump. Recordings include "Ida Cox's Lawdy Lawdy Blues" and "I've Got the Blues for Rampart Street" (1923); in 1939 sang in New York at Cafe Society and in the Spirituals to Swing Concert at Carnegie Hall.

Cps. Abbr. for cycles per second. See Hertz.

Crab motion. *Retrograde.

Cracovienne [Fr.]. *Krakowiak.

Craft, Robert (Lawson) (b. Kingston, N.Y., 20 Oct. 1923). Conductor and author. Studied composition and conducting at Juilliard; founded and led New York's Chamber Art Society (1947–50), and conducted the Los Angeles Monday Evening Concerts and Evening-on-the-Roof Series (1950–68). Led premieres of works by Stravinsky and Varèse; his recording of Webern's complete works (1957) was a milestone when released. His meeting with Stravinsky (1948) led to an extraordinarily intimate creative association; while living in the composer's home (1949–71) helped stimulate Stravinsky's production of specific works in a new manner. From 1959 Craft edited several volumes of "conversations" that portray Stravinsky in a flattering light.

Cramer, Johann [John] **Baptist** (b. Mannheim, 24 Feb. 1771; d. London, 16 Apr. 1858). Pianist and composer. Studied piano with Schroeter and Clementi (1783–84), and theory with Abel (from 1785). A frequent performer from 1783; beginning in 1788 embarked on a number of tours of France, Germany, the Netherlands, and Austria; recognized as a leading pianist, keyboard composer, and teacher. From 1805 involved in music publishing in a series of firms leading to J. B. Cramer. One of the first teachers at the Royal Academy of Music (1823). Mostly remembered for his didactic works, including *Studio per il piano forte,* 84 etudes in 2 vols. (London, 1804–10).

Crawford (Seeger), Ruth (Porter) (b. East Liverpool, Ohio, 3 July 1901; d. Chevy Chase, Md., 18 Nov. 1953). Composer, teacher, and folk music collector. Studied piano as a child; earned her B.Mus. (1923) and M.Mus. (1929) at the American Conservatory in Chicago. Early compositions were indebted to Scriabin and Debussy (Preludes for Piano, 1925–28); also explored polytonality and the use of tone clusters. After a summer at the MacDowell Colony (1929) studied composition with Charles Seeger, whom she married in 1931. Her String Quartet (1931) employed twelve-tone procedures. When the family moved to Washington, D.C., began to transcribe folk music at the Library of Congress; wrote very little after 1932. Other works include *Study in Mixed Accents* (piano, 1930); a violin sonata (1926); 2 sets of Preludes (1924–25, 1927–28).

Cray, Robert (b. Columbus, Ga., 1954). Blues guitarist and singer. Led a blues band in Tacoma, Wash., and Eugene and Portland, Oreg., then accompanied the blues guitarist Albert Collins (1976) and performed at the San Francisco Blues Festival (1977). From around 1980 Cray was the group's singer. One of the most popular blues musicians since B. B. King; recordings include *False Accusations* (1985) and *Strong Persuader* (including "Smoking Gun," 1986).

Creation, The [Ger. *Die Schöpfung*]. An oratorio by Haydn for soloists, chorus, and orchestra, Hob. XXI:2 (1796–98). It is a setting of a poem compiled by an unknown Mr. Lidley (Lindley?) from Milton's *Paradise Lost,* the whole project having been suggested to Haydn by the concert manager Johann Peter Salomon during the composer's second stay in London (1794–95). Upon Haydn's return to Vienna, the text was translated into German by Baron Gottfried van Swieten as *Die Schöpfung.* The work was first performed in Vienna in 1798 and in this translation.

Creation Mass. Popular name for Haydn's Mass in B♭ major Hob. XXII:13 (1801), so called because a theme from his oratorio The *Creation appears in the "Qui tollis."

Creatures of Prometheus. See *Geschöpfe des Prometheus.*

Crécelle [Fr.]. *Cog rattle.

Crecquillon [Créquillon], **Thomas** (b. between ca. 1480 and ca. 1500; d. Béthune? probably early 1557). Composer. Member of the chapel of Charles V in the 1540s; subsequently a canon in Namur, Termonde (1552–55), and Béthune (1555 until his death). Almost 200 chansons, including a handful of *chansons spirituelles,* survive, many also in arrangements for instruments. Sacred works consist of over 100 motets, 12 Masses, and 2 Lamentations cycles.

Credo [Lat., I believe; Eng. Creed]. The third item of the *Ordinary of the Roman Catholic *Mass, except on certain feasts when it is omitted. Its text is the Nicene Creed. In performance, the celebrant begins with the phrase "Credo in unum Deum," and the choir continues with the phrase "Patrem omnipotentem," with which most polyphonic settings therefore begin. For the complete text and translation, see Mass.

Crescendo, decrescendo [It., growing, decreasing; abbr. *cresc., decresc., decr.*]. As *performance marks, increasing and decreasing loudness, respectively; sometimes indicated with the signs ⎯⎯⎯ and ⎯⎯⎯. See also *Diminuendo.*

Crescendo pedal. In electric- or pneumatic-action organs, a device for bringing on each of the stops and couplers, from the softest to the loudest.

Crescent. *Turkish crescent.

Crespin, Régine (b. Marseilles, 23 Feb. 1927). Soprano. Studied at the Paris Conservatory; opera debut at Reims, 1949; sang Elsa *(Lohengrin)* at Mulhouse, 1950. Debut at Opéra-comique as Tosca (1951); at Paris Opéra as Elsa (1951). Sang Kundry at Bayreuth (1958); Met debut as the Marschallin (1962). From 1974 sang French operas exclusively.

Creston, Paul [Guttoveggio, Giuseppe] (b. New York, 10 Oct. 1906; d. San Diego, 24 Aug. 1985). Composer and keyboard player. Studied piano and organ; an autodidact in composition. Served as a church organist (1934–67), taught at Swarthmore (1956), the New York College of Music (1963–67), and then at Central Washington State College. His special interest in rhythm is attested by his compositions (also characterized by lush harmonic language and classical forms) and by his writings. Works include Symphony no. 6 (organ and orchestra, 1981); many concertos (for marimba, saxophone, piano, violin, accordion) and other works with soloists; a Piano Trio (1979), *Ceremonial* (percussion ensemble, 1972), and other chamber music; piano music; choral and solo vocal music.

Crist, Bainbridge (b. Lawrenceburg, Ind., 13 Feb. 1883; d. Barnstable, Mass., 7 Feb. 1969). Composer. Studied voice, theory, and orchestration in Berlin and London. Taught voice in Boston (1915–21), Washington (1922–23), and Florence (1927–38), then settled on Cape Cod. As a composer primarily known for his sensitive treatment of voice and text; his songs were performed and broadcast frequently in the 1940s and 1950s. Works for voice and orchestra include *Drolleries from an Oriental Doll's House,* 1920.

Cristofori, Bartolomeo (b. Padua, 4 May 1655; d. Florence, 27 Jan. 1731). Maker of keyboard instruments. From 1688 employed in Florence as a member of the court of Prince Ferdinand de' Medici, and later as custodian of musical instruments at the court. Constructed many different sorts of instruments but is remembered chiefly as the designer and maker of the first piano, developed in the course of work begun in about 1698. An article by Maffei published in 1711 describes and illustrates its action, which was quickly adopted and modified by a number of other instrument makers.

Criticism. The elucidation and interpretation, based on the experience of an informed listener, of a work or performance. Its fundamental aim is the illumination of the individual work or performance as heard rather than the discovery of structural or other features common to many works. In this respect it sometimes stands in contrast to *analysis, though the two are not rigidly separable, and criticism inevitably makes use of some of the methods most often associated with analysis. Criticism focuses its energies on the work or performance as perceived and thus is likely to give greater weight to temporal factors and to the detailed musical surface than does much analysis. It is concerned with the underlying structural features of works to the extent that they bear directly on the listener's response. It does not necessarily aim to judge value. Here a distinction must be made between writing about the works in a widely accepted canon and writing about (often termed reviewing) recent performances and works whose status with respect to the canon, perhaps because of their novelty, is itself the subject of discussion. In criticism of the former type, the critic's evaluative judgment is likely to be expressed principally in the mere choice of subject. Criticism of the second type, especially as written for the mass media, often aims explicitly to report the critic's judgment of quality for readers or listeners who may wish to use it as a guide. Distinguished practitioners of both types share the same qualities: thorough technical training in music, broad experience of repertories and performances, gifted use of language, respect for the art of music, and respect for their readers.

Croce, Giovanni (b. Chioggia, ca. 1557; d. Venice, 15 May 1609). Composer. Worked for most of his life at the Church of S. Maria Formosa. Assistant *maestro di cappella* at St. Mark's, Venice, from the early 1590s; became *maestro* there in 1603. Wrote both secular and sacred works in conservative styles. Many of the secular compositions were printed in translation in England and were highly influential there.

Croche [Fr.]. Eighth *note.

Croft [Crofts], **William** (b. Nether Ettington, Warwickshire, bapt. 30 Dec. 1678; d. Bath, 14 Aug. 1727). Composer. A chorister in the Chapel Royal and a student of John Blow; subsequently Gentleman (from 1700) and organist (from 1704) of the Chapel Royal. In 1708 succeeded Blow as composer and Master of the Children of the Chapel Royal and organist of Westminster Abbey. Wrote secular vocal and instrumental music but concentrated chiefly on sacred compositions after the first few years of the 18th century. Of these works, the anthems in particular show a grasp of late Baroque idiom that was new to England; an interest in an older polyphonic choral style is also evident.

Croiser les mains [Fr.]. An instruction to cross the hands in piano playing; also indicated with the forms *croisez, croisement.*

Croma [It.]. Eighth *note.

Cromatico [It.]. *Chromatic. For *madregali cromatici*, see *Note nere.*

Cromorne [Fr.]. *Crumhorn.

Crook. (1) [Fr. *corps de rechange;* Ger. *Aufsatzbogen, Stimmbogen;* It. *ritorto;* Sp. *tonillo, cuerpo de recambio*]. A curved segment of tubing that can be inserted into a brass instrument, especially a *natural horn or trumpet, in order to alter its fundamental pitch. See also Shank. (2) On the bassoon or English horn, the curved metal tube to which the reed is affixed.

Croon. To sing relatively softly and with inflections of pitch as in the style of such singers of sentimental popular songs as Rudy Vallee, Bing Crosby, Perry Como, and Frank Sinatra.

Crosby, Bing [Harry Lillis] (b. Tacoma, Wash., 2 May 1901; d. Madrid, 14 Oct. 1977). Popular music singer and actor. Between 1926 and 1930 performed jazz with the Paul Whiteman Orchestra as one of the Rhythm Boys. After 1930 began singing popular music; hosted radio shows and appeared in over 50 films between 1930 and 1966 (including the *Road* series films, 1940–62); made numerous successful recordings. His most famous recordings were associated with films, including Irving Berlin's "White Christmas" (in *Holiday Inn,* 1942) and "Swinging on a Star" (in *Going My Way,* 1944).

Cross fingering. (1) On an instrument with finger holes, a fingering requiring a closed hole or holes below an open one. The *Boehm system was in part developed in order to obviate the need for many of the fingerings of this type that would otherwise be necessary in order to produce chromatic pitches. See also Fork fingering. (2) The use of a "cross" key to produce the semitones outside the basic scale of a wind instrument. The first key to which the name applied, the short F key of the flute, lay across the body of the instrument. Later any key that produced a note one semitone higher than the natural fingering below it was so termed.

Cross flute. The transverse *flute as distinct from the *recorder.

Cross, Joan (b. London, 7 Sept. 1900; d. 12 Dec. 1993). Soprano. Studied with Peter Dawson at Trinity College, London. Solo debut as Cherubino at Old Vic Theatre (1924). Covent Garden debut as Mimi, 1931; returned 1934–35, 1947–54. First soprano (1931–46) and director (1931–46) of Sadler's Wells Opera. Sang Ellen Orford in *Peter Grimes* and developed a close artistic association with Britten, subsequently performing in other premieres of his operas. Co-founded the National School of Opera in 1948; retired from the stage in 1955.

Cross, Lowell (Merlin) (b. Kingsville, Tex., 24 June 1938). Composer. Studied at Texas Technological Univ. (1956–63) and established an electronic music studio there (1961); studied electronic music at the Univ. of Toronto (Schaeffer, Ciamaga). Directed the Mills College Tape Music Center (1968–69); from 1971 taught at the Univ. of Iowa, where he also directed the recording studios in the School of Music. Often collaborated with Tudor and others on works involving electronic musical and visual devices (*Reunion,* 1968, with Cage, Tudor, and others; *Video/Laser I–IV,* with Tudor and others).

Crosse, Gordon (b. Bury, Lancashire, 1 Dec. 1937). Composer. Studied with Wellesz and Rubbra at Oxford, and with Petrassi in Rome (1962). From 1966 professor at Birmingham Univ., from 1969 at the Univ. of Essex, and from 1973 at King's College, Cambridge. His early works follow serialism; more recent works show influence of contemporaries such as Davies. Compositions include operas (*Holly from the Bongs,* 1974); orchestral works (*Array,* trumpet and strings, 1986); anthems and hymns; chamber music (a piano trio, 1986).

Crossover. A recording that is intended to appeal to the audience for one style of popular music or jazz but that becomes popular with another audience as well; also an artist with an established reputation in one genre of popular music or jazz who makes recordings in another genre in an attempt to appeal to a new audience.

Cross-relation, false relation [Fr. *fausse relation;* Ger. *Querstand*]. The succession of a pitch in one voice by a chromatic alteration of that pitch (or its equivalent in another octave) in another voice. A simultaneous or vertical cross-relation is the simultaneous occurrence of two pitches related in this way. Such relations, especially between outer voices, are normally prohibited by the academic formulations of 18th- and 19th-century harmony and counterpoint on the grounds that such chromatic motion is most intelligible when it occurs within a single voice. Their appearance in music of this period, however, often mitigated by placement in inner voices or by accompanying passing tones, is not infrequent.

Cross-rhythm. A rhythm in which the regular pattern of accents of the prevailing meter is contradicted by a conflicting pattern and not merely by a momentary displacement that leaves the prevailing meter fundamentally unchallenged. See also Syncopation, Polyrhythm.

Crotal. (1) *Crotalum.* (2) *Pellet bell.

Crotales [Fr., also *cymbales antiques,* antique cymbals]. Small, rather thick cymbals of definite pitch ranging in size from about 5 to 12.5 cm. in diameter, now manufactured as a chromatic set mounted on a board. See ill. under Percussion instruments.

Crotalum [Lat., pl. *crotala;* Gr. *krotalon*]. *Clappers or *castanets of ancient Greece and Rome, made of wood, bone, bronze, etc. They were often used by dancers.

Crotch, William (b. Norwich, 5 July 1775; d. Taunton, 29 Dec. 1847). Composer. Exhibited by his mother as a child prodigy on tours of England and Scotland from age 3 to 9; played his own harpsichord concerto in London (1785); in 1786 published his first compositions and began composing an oratorio. In 1789 became organist at Christ Church and from about 1792 director of orchestral concerts of the Oxford Music Room. Professor of music at Oxford (from 1797); also named organist at St. John's College, University Church, and the Theatre. In 1804 gave first of several lecture courses at the Royal Institution in London; moved to London the following year, giving private lessons, playing organ, conducting, and lecturing. In 1811 completed his most important work, the oratorio *Palestine;* in 1822, named principal of the new Royal Academy of Music.

Crotchet. In British terminology, the quarter note [see Note, Notation].

Crouth, Crowd. See Crwth, *Rote.*

Crucible, The. Opera in four acts by Robert Ward (libretto by B. Stambler after Arthur Miller's play), produced in New York in 1961. Setting: Salem, Mass., 1692.

Crucifixus [Lat., crucified]. The portion of the Credo of the *Mass dealing with the crucifixion, often set as a separate movement in large-scale polyphonic settings of the Mass text.

Crüger, Johannes [Johann] (b. Gross-Breesen, near Guben, Lower Lusatia, 9 Apr. 1598; d. Berlin, 23 Feb. 1662). Composer and theorist. Studied music under Paul Homberger, then traveled widely, finally settling in Berlin. Kantor of the Nicolaikirche in Berlin from 1622 until his death. Wrote a few works for conventional choral forces, but is remembered chiefly for his work with Lutheran chorales, including the chorale book *Praxis pietatis melica* (1647, subsequently revised and reissued many times). His various theoretical works synthesized many of the new ideas of the time.

Cruit [Gael.]. A plucked stringed instrument of medieval Ireland. From the 12th to the 14th century, *cruit* denoted the *Irish harp, but the word may also have referred to plucked *lyres. See also *Rote, Tiómpán.*

Crumb, George (Henry) (b. Charleston, W.Va., 24 Oct. 1929). Composer. Studied at Mason College of Music and Fine Arts in Charleston, the Univ. of Illinois, and the Univ. of Michigan under Finney; worked with Blacher at the Berkshire Music Center (1955) and in Berlin (1956). Taught at the Univ. of Colorado (1964–69) and SUNY–Buffalo (1964–65) before moving to the Univ. of Pennsylvania. In 1968 received the Pulitzer Prize for *Echoes of Time and the River.* Crumb's music is particularly concerned with sonority and timbre; his scores often employ ingenious forms of notation, frequently including aleatoric sections. Early works reflect indebtedness to Bartók and Debussy; in *Variazioni* for orchestra (1959) he experimented with twelve-tone procedures. His mature style is evident in *Ancient Voices of Children* (mezzo-soprano, amplified piano, exotic instruments, 1970) and *Black Angels* (electric string quartet, 1970). Medieval cosmology and numerology play a part in many of Crumb's designs. Other works include *Makrokosmos II,* amplified piano, 1971; *Lux Aeterna,* 5 masked musicians, 1971; *Madrigals* (4 books), soprano and ensemble, 1964–69; *A Haunted Landscape,* orchestra, 1984; *Apparition,* soprano and piano, 1979.

Crumhorn [Fr. *cromorne, tournebout;* Ger. *Krummhorn;* It. *storto, piva torta;* Sp. *orlo*]. A *wind-cap, double-reed wind instrument of the 16th and 17th centuries. It has a narrow cylindrical bore and is shaped like the letter J. There are several sizes. The fingering of the instrument is similar to that of the *recorder, though the lack of direct control of the reed prevents *overblowing. The larger sizes were provided with keys, usually protected with perforated metal covers. Unfingered tuning holes are present in the curve of the tube. See ill. under Reed.

Cruz, Ivo (b. Corumbá, Brazil, 19 May 1901; d. Lisbon, 8 Sept. 1985). Composer and conductor. Studied music theory and piano in Lisbon and composition with Mors and Reuss in Munich (1925–30). Returned to Portugal and founded the Lisbon Philharmonic (1937); became director of the Lisbon Conservatory (1938). Compositions are strongly tonal and employ Portuguese folk tunes.

Crwth, crowd [Welsh, pronounced "crooth"]. A bowed *lyre of Wales, now obsolete. It was rectangular in shape, the lower portion being a flat sound box, the upper part consisting of two arms and a yoke to which the strings were held by pegs. A fingerboard with three or four strings above it passed from the center of the yoke to the sound box. Two additional strings were sometimes added to one side. The *crwth* was known in England, Ireland, and on the Continent, but it was above all the instrument of the Welsh *bards.

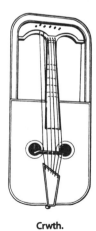

Crwth.

C.s. [It.]. Abbr. for *colla sinistra,* with the left hand.

Csárdás [Hung.]. A Hungarian dance first documented ca. 1835 and closely related to the fast *(friss)* part of the *verbunkos. It is typically in fast duple meter (though a slow, *lassu,* form was also developed) and was a fashionable ballroom dance

throughout the 19th century. Examples occur in the *Hungarian Rhapsodies* of Liszt.

Cuatro [Sp.]. A small, four-stringed guitar of Latin America, especially Venezuela. Many examples have strings in courses of two. The Puerto Rican *cuatro* adds a single fifth string pitched below the others.

Cue. (1) In an individual part, an extract from some other, prominent part, usually printed in smaller notes, serving to alert the performer to an approaching entrance, especially after a long rest. (2) A gesture given by a conductor to signal the entrance of a player or section; to give such a gesture.

Cueca [Sp.]. The national dance of Chile, also found in Bolivia and Argentina, descended from the *zamacueca (zambacueca)* of colonial Peru. In rural Chile, it is sung with guitar, harp, and, most commonly today, accordion; this accompaniment is frequently supplemented with drumming on a wooden box or the side of the guitar. It is typically in the major mode, in rapid tempo, and with compound duple accompaniments to melodies combining patterns in 6/8, 3/4, and 2/4.

Cuénod [Cuenod], **Hugues (Adhémar)** (b. Corseaux-sur-Vevey, Switzerland, 26 June 1902). Tenor. Studied at the Ribaupierre Institute in Lausanne, the Geneva Conservatory, and the Basel Conservatory, and with Singer-Burian in Vienna. Paris debut, 1928; performed in Coward's *Bitter Sweet* in London and the U.S. Back in Switzerland he concertized with Clara Haskil; taught at the Geneva Conservatory (1940–46). Created Sellem in *The Rake's Progress,* thereafter sang premieres in other Stravinsky works. From 1954 through the 1980s sang small roles at Glyndebourne.

Cui, César [Kyui, Tsezar Antonovich] (b. Vilnius, 18 Jan. 1835; d. Petrograd, 26 Mar. 1918). Composer and critic. Befriended all the members of the "Mighty Handful." Early works were influenced by Balakirev, who in 1857–58 supervised the orchestration of the overture to Cui's first opera, *A Prisoner in the Caucasus* (first performed 1883). Composed other operas but better known as a miniaturist: the bulk of his output consists of songs and short piano pieces. Also wrote a modest amount of orchestral music, chamber music, and choral music.

Cuivre [Fr.]. A player of a brass instrument; *les cuivres,* the brass instruments or section; *cuivré,* a harsh or brassy tone, especially on the horn.

Cumbia [Sp.]. An Afro-Hispanic dance-music genre of Panama and the Atlantic coastal region of Colombia, now widely disseminated. It is performed by small ensembles with, e.g., accordion, drums, and other percussion instruments. Distinctive traits include moderate to rapid duple meter, short, syncopated melodic phrases, and sharp off-beat accompanimental accents.

Cunning Little Vixen, The [Cz. *Příhody Lišky Bystroušky*]. Opera in three acts by Leoš Janáček (libretto by the composer after Rudolf Těsnohlídek), produced in Brno in 1924. Setting: a mythical woodland.

Cup. See Mouthpiece and ill. under Brass instruments.

Cupo [It.]. Gloomy, sombre.

Cursive and tonic. In *Gregorian and other Western liturgical chant, cadential melodic formulas that are, respectively, applied to a fixed number of the final syllables of the text without regard for accentuation or that are adjusted to the accentuation of the text by the addition or suppression of notes. The most prominent examples of the former are found in the tones for the great responsories; for the latter in the tones for the antiphonal psalmody of the Office [see Psalmody, Psalm tone].

Curtain tune. *Entr'acte.*

Curtal. An English double-reed wind instrument of conical bore, used in the 16th and 17th centuries, equivalent to the German *Dulzian* or *chorist Fagott*. It was constructed of a single piece of wood containing two parallel bores connected at the bottom and had a small integral or separate bell at the top. The curtal was made in two sizes, the single (tenor) and the double (bass). The bass instrument is the precursor of the modern *bassoon. See ill. under Reed.

Curtin, Phyllis (Smith) (b. Clarksburg, W.Va., 3 Dec. 1922). Soprano. Studied voice with Olga Avierino, Joseph Regneas, and Boris Goldovsky. Stage debut in Boston, 1946; performed with New York City Opera, 1953–64; with Vienna Staatsoper, 1959–63; the Met, 1961–74. Praised for her Salome. Taught voice at Yale School of Music, 1974–83. Appointed Dean, School of the Arts, Boston Univ., 1983.

Curzon, Clifford (Michael) (b. London, 18 May 1907; d. there, 1 Sept. 1982). Pianist. Studied with Charles Reddie and Katherine Goodson at the Royal Academy of Music; further studies with Matthay, Schnabel, Landowska, and Boulanger while teaching at the Royal Academy of Music, 1926–32. U.S. debut, 1939. Performed in a quartet with Szigeti, Primrose, and Fournier beginning in 1952. Renowned for his Mozart. Knighted in 1977.

Custer, Arthur (b. Manchester, Conn., 21 Apr. 1923). Composer. Studied at the Univ. of Conn., Univ. of Redlands with Pisk, Univ. of Iowa with Bezanson, and with Boulanger in Paris (1960–61). Assistant

dean of Fine Arts, Univ. of Rhode Island, 1962–65. Dean of Philadelphia Music Academy, 1965–67.

Custos [Lat.]. *Direct.

Cut time. The *meter indicated by the sign ₵, equivalent to 2/2.

Cuzzoni, Francesca (b. Parma, 2 Apr. 1696; d. Bologna, 1778). Soprano. One of the finest singers of her era and particularly successful for a time in London. Studied with Lanzi; sang in numerous Italian cities between 1716 and 1722. A highly successful lead singer in Handel's Royal Academy in London (1722–28); from 1726 involved in an intense rivalry with Bordoni. After 1728 Cuzzoni performed in Vienna and in Italy and for London's Opera of the Nobility (1734–36). Thereafter performed in other European cities, with progressively less success.

Cycle. (1) In *acoustics, one complete vibration of a vibrating system such as a string, the number of such vibrations per unit of time (usually described in cycles per second, or *Hertz) being the frequency of vibration and the principal determinant of pitch. (2) Any system of *tuning or *temperament in which the octave is divided into intervals of equal size. (3) See Song cycle. (4) The sequence or pattern of movements in a multimovement work such as a symphony or suite. (5) In discussions of polyphonic Masses of the 14th and 15th centuries, and to some extent of liturgical chant as well, settings of individual texts of the Mass (especially the Ordinary) that are intended to form a single work, whether or not unified musically. See also Cyclic form.

Cyclic form. Any musical form consisting of discrete movements in two or more of which the same or very similar thematic material is employed. The first large-scale works of this type were the cyclic Masses of the 15th century, in which a single *cantus firmus is employed in all movements or in which all movements begin in the same way ("motto beginning") [see Mass]. The 19th century saw a steady increase in their use, well-known early examples from this period including Schubert's *Wanderer-Fantasie and Berlioz's *Symphonie fantastique. Other composers to make considerable use of the technique, sometimes in association with the *transformation of themes, are Schumann, Liszt, and Franck.

Cylinder. See Valve.

Cymbalon [Hung.]. *Cimbalom.

Cymbals [Fr. *cymbales;* Ger. *Becken;* It. *piatti;* Sp. *platillos*]. Broad-rimmed circular plates of indefinite pitch, slightly convex so that only the edges touch when two are struck together. In the center of each is a small hump, or boss, pierced by a hole, through which a holding strap is attached. Modern orchestral cymbals, made of copper and tin alloy with a touch of silver, are heavier and flatter than their predecessors and come in a variety of sizes, typically between 44 and 55 cm. (17 and 22 in.) in diameter. Thickness and hence tone color vary as well. In orchestral music, they are most often held vertically and clashed together, the sound being damped if necessary against the chest. Cymbals can also be suspended and struck with some sort of beater or a pair of drum sticks; or one can be fastened to the top of a bass drum and hit with the other. For cymbals used in jazz and popular music, including hi-hat, ride, crash, and sizzle cymbals, see Drum set; for antique cymbals, see Crotales. See ill. under Percussion instruments.

Cymbals probably originated in Asia Minor as ritual instruments. They are mentioned frequently in the Bible and are widely disseminated. Cymbals came to Europe during the Middle Ages.

Cymbalum. (1) [Lat., pl. *cymbala*] In antiquity, *cymbala* were small cymbals. In the Middle Ages, they were a set of three to eight small, tuned bells, hung in a row and struck with a wooden rod or a small hammer. These were used in churches and monasteries to give intervals to singers and to accompany plainsong. (2) [Fr.] *Cimbalom.

Cymbasso [Ital.]. *Cimbasso.

Cythara [Lat.]. *Kithara.

Czardas [Hung.]. *Csárdás.

Czerny, Carl (b. Vienna, 20 Feb. 1791; d. there, 15 July 1857). Piano teacher and composer. An admirer of Beethoven, whom he met around 1800 and studied with; also studied the techniques of Hummel and Clementi. After 1806 gave most of his time to teaching; played in public infrequently, apparently mainly in chamber music, although in 1812 gave the poorly received Vienna premiere of Beethoven's Fifth Concerto. His writings and remarks on the performance of Beethoven's music are of considerable historical importance. His students included Kullak, Heller (briefly), and, most notably, Liszt (1821–23), although he disapproved of the theatricality of Liszt's virtuosity. Retired from teaching in 1836 but seems to have had occasional later students. His 800 compositions includes both ephemeral salon piano music and symphonies, piano concertos, Masses, and chamber music. Best remembered for his didactic works, including courses for almost every element of piano technique, collections of etudes for 2 or more hands, and treatises on composition.

Czimbalom [Hung.]. *Cimbalom.

D

D. (1) See Pitch names, Letter notation, Hexachord, Pitch. (2) In *harmonic analysis, *dominant. (3) In 16th-century sources, *discantus*. (4) Abbr. for Otto Erich Deutsch's (with Donald R. Wakeling) *Schubert: Thematic Catalogue of All His Works in Chronological Order.*

Da capo [It., abbr. *D.C.*]. From the beginning, and hence an indication that a piece is to be repeated from the beginning to the end, to a place marked *fine (da capo al fine),* or to a place marked with a specified sign (e.g., *da capo al segno,* or *al* 𝄋, or *al* 𝄌). On reaching the sign in the last case, the player is to skip ahead to the next occurrence of the same sign, often marking the beginning of a *coda. This may occur in conjunction with or as an alternative to the direction *da capo e poi la coda* (from the beginning, and then the coda). In the course of the repetition, other internal repetitions are normally omitted, as in the case of the minuet or scherzo with trio. This is sometimes made explicit with the direction *da capo senza repetizione.* The practice of omitting internal repetitions seems to have begun, however, only in the course of the 19th century. See also *Dal segno.*

Da capo aria. See Aria.

Dactyl, dactylic. See Prosody.

Daff, duff [Ar.]. A Middle Eastern *frame drum. It may be round, square, or octagonal and may have one head or two and sometimes jingles or snares. See ill. under Instrument.

Dafne. Opera in a prologue and six scenes by Jacopo Peri (libretto by Ottavio Rinuccini, after the classical story of Daphne and Apollo), first performed at the house of Jacopo Corsi, with whom Peri collaborated, in Florence at Carnival in 1598. This work, for which only some of the music survives, is the first opera. A revision of this libretto was set by Marco da Gagliano and produced in Mantua at Carnival in 1608. Giulio Caccini also claimed to have set this text. An adaptation by Martin Opitz of Rinuccini's libretto was set by Heinrich Schütz and performed in 1627. The music for this work, the first German opera, does not survive.

Dahl, Ingolf (b. Hamburg, 9 June 1912; d. Frutigen, Switzerland, 6 Aug. 1970). Composer, conductor, and pianist. Studied in Cologne and Zurich (1930–36); conducted and coached the Zurich Opera; moved to the U.S. in 1938 and composed, conducted, and remained active as a pianist; studied with Boulanger in 1944. Taught at USC (1945–70) and the Berkshire Music Center (1952–56); collaborated with Stravinsky, arranging some works for keyboard. With the Piano Quartet (1957) began to serialize material. Works include *Aria Sinfonica,* orchestra, 1965; Sinfonietta, wind ensemble, 1961; piano works; a few songs.

Dal segno [It., abbr. *D.S.*]. From the sign, and hence an indication that a piece is to be repeated beginning at the place marked with the sign 𝄋. See also *Da capo.*

Dal segno aria. See Aria.

Dalayrac [D'Alayrac], **Nicolas-Marie** (b. Muret, Haute-Garonne, 8 June 1753; d. Paris, 26 Nov. 1809). Composer. In 1781 composed the stage works *Le petit souper* and *Le chevalier à la mode.* His first successes were *Nina* (1786), and *Azémia* (1786), followed by more than 20 other stage works, mostly opéras comiques.

Dalcroze method. A system of musical education developed by Émile Jaques-Dalcroze (1865–1950), based on the idea of experiencing music and developing musical abilities through rhythmic movement.

Dalcroze, Émile Jaques. See Jaques-Dalcroze, Émile.

Dall'Abaco, Evaristo Felice (b. Verona, 12 July 1675; d. Munich, 12 July 1742). Composer. Perhaps studied cello and violin with Torelli. Went to Modena in 1696 and performed there alongside Vitali and others; by 1704 a cellist, later *Konzertmeister,* at the Bavarian court, which he accompanied to Brussels (1704), Mons (1706), Compiègne (1709), and back to Munich (1715). Works include chamber and church sonatas along with concertos; early indebtedness to Corelli later yields to *galant* and French-derived elements.

Dallapiccola, Luigi (b. Pisino d'Istria, 3 Feb. 1904; d. Florence, 19 Feb. 1975). Composer and pianist. Graduated from the Florence Conservatory; from 1926 active as a pianist, including a 40-year collaboration with violinist Sandro Materassi. Taught at the Florence Conservatory (1934–67) and toured

Europe, which allowed him to hear new music and to meet Berg, Webern, Milhaud, Poulenc, and others. The first Italian composer to adopt the twelve-tone method, first used strictly in *Liriche greche* (soprano, instrumental ensemble, 1942–45); in *Job* (1950) limited himself to a single series. Self-quotation, eye music, and word painting are frequent expressive devices (*Sicut umbra,* 1970). His international reputation developed after the war. Taught at the Berkshire Music Center (1951); lectured and performed widely in western Europe and the U.S. until 1972. Other works include 3 operas; a ballet; choral works (*Canti di prigionia,* 1938–41); orchestral works (*2 pezzi,* 1947); chamber music (*Ciaccona, intermezzo, e adagio,* cello, 1945); piano pieces; songs. Authored several monographs on music.

Dame blanche, La [Fr., The White Lady]. Opera in three acts by Adrien Boildieu (libretto by Eugène Scribe after Sir Walter Scott's novels *Guy Mannering* and *The Monastery*), produced at the *Opéra comique* in Paris in 1825. Setting: 17th-century Scotland.

Damnation de Faust, La [Fr., The Damnation of Faust]. "Dramatic legend" in four parts by Berlioz (libretto by the composer with Almire Gandonnière after Gérard de Nerval's translation of Goethe's *Faust*). Described by Berlioz as a "concert opera," it was given a concert performance in 1846 and staged in Monte Carlo in 1893.

Damoreau, Laure Cinti-. See Cinti-Damoreau, Laure.

Da Motta, José Vianna. See Vianna da Motta, José.

Damp. To cause the vibrations of a string or other vibrating system to stop.

Damper [Fr. *étouffoir;* Ger. *Dämpfer;* It. *sordina, smorzatore;* Sp. *apagador, sordina*]. In the action of a piano, a felt-covered device that prevents the string or strings associated with any one key from vibrating except when that key or the *damper pedal is depressed. In the harpsichord (which lacks a damper pedal), this function is served by a felt attached to each jack. See ills. under Harpsichord, Piano.

Damper pedal. On the piano, the rightmost pedal, which removes all of the *dampers from contact with the strings; also sustaining pedal, loud pedal.

Dämpfer [Ger.]. (1) *Damper. (2) *Mute.

Damrosch, Frank (Heino) (b. Breslau, 22 Jun. 1859; d. New York, 22 Oct. 1937). Emigrated to the U.S. in 1871. Studied conducting with his father, Leopold; led the Denver Choral Club, 1882–85, then became chorusmaster at the Metropolitan Opera. In 1905 founded and until 1926 served as dean of the Institute of Musical Art; from 1926 to 1933 dean of the newly merged Institute of Musical Art of the Juilliard Foundation (reorganized in 1945 as the Juilliard School).

Damrosch, Leopold (b. Posen, 22 Oct. 1832; d. New York, 15 Feb. 1885). Conductor. A professional violinist and part of Liszt's Weimar circle. Conducted in Breslau; from 1871 a prominent figure in New York music as choral and later orchestral conductor; 1884–85, director of the Metropolitan Opera, turning it to German opera and introducing Wagner's later works to the U.S.

Damrosch, Walter (Johannes) (b. Breslau, 30 Jan. 1862; d. New York, 22 Dec. 1950). Conductor and composer. Studied with his father Leopold and with Hans von Bülow before emigrating to the U.S. in 1871. Conductor of the Newark Harmonic Society from 1881; musical director with the Symphony Society of New York from 1885; conducted some German works at the Met. With the Damrosch Opera Company (1895–1900) brought first-rate productions of operas to many U.S. cities. With the Symphony Society from 1903. When his orchestra merged with the New York Philharmonic (1927), became musical counsel to NBC. Some of his operas were performed by his company and by the Met.

Dan, Ikuma (b. Tokyo, 7 Apr. 1924). Composer. Graduated from the Tokyo Music School in 1945; subsequently taught composition there (1947–50). His first symphony (1950) launched a successful career; in 1952 his first opera *Yūzuru* (The Twilight Heron) was received with acclaim in Japan and abroad. His music is diatonic, tending toward the lush and exotic. Works include 5 operas; vocal music; 5 symphonies; chamber works.

Dance band. A band that plays for social dancing; often synonymous with *big band.

Dancla, (Jean-Baptiste-) Charles (b. Bagnères de Bigorre, Hautes-Pyrénées, 19 Dec. 1817; d. Tunis, 9 or 10 Nov. 1907). Violinist, teacher, composer. Studied at the Paris Conservatory, 1828–40; played in Paris orchestras and as soloist and chamber musician; from 1855 taught violin at the Conservatory, professor 1860–92. Composed much instrumental music, including 14 string quartets.

Dandelot, Georges (Édouard) (b. Paris, 2 Dec. 1895; d. St.-Georges-de-Didonne, 17 Aug. 1975). Composer and pianist. His teachers included Diémer, d'Indy, Roussel, Widor, and Dukas; taught piano at the École normale de musique from 1919 and harmony at the Paris Conservatory from 1942. Composed operas (*Midas,* 1948) and ballets; a piano concerto (1934), a symphony (1941), an oratorio (*Pax,* 1937); chamber music; piano works.

Dandrieu, Jean-François (b. Paris ca. 1682; d. there, 17 Jan. 1738). Composer. Both he and his sister Jeanne Françoise were pupils of Moreau. Served as organist at St. Merry (from 1704) and at St. Barthélemy; in 1721 became one of the royal chapel organists. Highly regarded as a harpsichord composer, he issued several books of suites beginning about 1704; also produced trio sonatas, organ noëls, and airs.

D'Anglebert, Jean-Henri (b. Paris, 1635; d. there, 23 Apr. 1691). Composer. Served as organist to the Duke of Orléans and to the Jacobins in the rue St. Honoré; from 1662 until his death served as *ordinaire de la chambre du Roy pour le clavecin*. His collection *Pièces de clavecin* (Paris, 1689) established him as the major clavecinist before Couperin; the publication includes the most detailed table of ornaments from the period.

Daniel-Lesur [Lesur, Daniel Jean Yves] (b. Paris, 19 Nov. 1908). Composer, pianist, and organist. Studied with Tournemire and attended the Paris Conservatory (1919–29); assisted Tournemire as organist at Ste. Clotilde (1927–37), then organist of the Benedictine abbey in Paris (1937–44). Taught counterpoint at the Schola cantorum (from 1935) and served as director (1957–64). From 1939 associated with French Radio, where he created the series *Nouvelles musicales*. His compositions remained rather traditional and often had a modal flavor.

Dankworth, John [Johnny] **(Philip William)** (b. London, 20 Sept. 1927). English saxophonist, bandleader, composer, and arranger. Studied at the Royal Academy of Music (1944–46); led a bop group, The Johnny Dankworth Seven (1950–53), and a big band from 1953; also wrote film scores. From 1971 led a group to accompany his wife, Cleo Laine. From the early 1980s his regular ensemble was a quintet, though he led a big band occasionally.

Danse macabre [Fr.]. (1) The dance of death. (2) A symphonic poem by Saint-Saëns, op. 40 (1874), based on a poem of the same name (which he had earlier set as a song) by Henri Cazalis. Saint-Saëns's work depicts Death playing the violin and dancing in a graveyard at midnight. The music incorporates the *"Dies irae."

Dante Symphony [Ger. *Eine Symphonie zu Dantes Divina commedia*]. An orchestral work with choral ending by Liszt (1855–56), based on Dante's *Divina commedia*. It is in two movements, entitled "Inferno" and "Purgatorio," to which are added a choral Magnificat.

Danza tedesca [It.]. *Ländler,* *waltz.

Danzi, Franz (Ignaz) (b. Schwetzingen, 15 June 1763; d. Karlsruhe, 13 Apr. 1826). Composer. Studied in Mannheim with Vogler and played cello at the National Theater, where his first German opera was produced in 1780; in 1783 became cellist in the Munich orchestra. Toured widely with his wife, singer Margarethe Marchand. Deputy Kapellmeister in Munich (1798); Kapellmeister at Stuttgart (1807) and Karlsruhe (1812). The most widely performed of his many singspiels was *Die Mitternachtsstunde* (1788); other works include a large body of chamber music.

Daphnis et Chloé [Fr.]. Ballet by Ravel (book, after the classical story by Longus, and choreography by Michel Fokine; décor by Léon Bakst), produced by Diaghilev's Ballets russes in Paris in 1912. Ravel arranged two concert suites from the ballet in 1911 and 1913, the second of which, like the ballet, includes a wordless chorus.

Da Ponte, Lorenzo (b. Ceneda [Vittorio Veneto], 10 Mar. 1749; d. New York, 17 Aug. 1838). Poet and librettist. Born Emmanuele Conegliano; assumed the name of the Bishop of Ceneda, Lorenzo Da Ponte, in 1763 when his Jewish father converted to Christianity. Ordained a priest in 1770; in 1774 became professor of literature at Tiepolo but dismissed two years later; in 1779 banned from the Republic of Venice altogether for adultery. Settled in Gorizia and then in Vienna where Joseph II appointed him court poet for Vienna's Italian theater (1783–91). Authored a series of extraordinary libretti for Mozart (*Le *nozze di Figaro, *Don Giovanni, *Così fan tutte*), Salieri, Martín y Soler (*Una cosa rara,* 1786), and others. In 1793 served as librettist for the King's Theatre, London. Emigrated to New York in 1805 where he taught Italian language and literature at Columbia College, wrote his celebrated *Memorie* (New York, 1823–27), and strove to establish Italian opera in the city.

Daquin, Louis-Claude (b. Paris, 4 July 1694; d. there, 15 June 1772). Composer. Studied with Marchand (organ) and Bernier (composition); named organist at Petit St. Antoine (1706), at St. Paul (1727), and at the Cordeliers (1732). *Organiste du Roi* in 1739; served at Notre Dame beginning in 1755. Regarded as the best organist of his generation. Extant works are contained in the *Premier livre de pièces de clavecin* (1735) and the *Nouveau livre de noëls* (ca. 1740).

Darabukkah, darabuka, darbouka [Ar.]. A goblet-shaped drum of the Islamic world with a single head and made of clay, wood, or metal; see ill. under Instrument.

Dargomïzhsky, Alexander Sergeyevich (b. Troitskoye, Tula district, 14 Feb. 1813; d. St. Petersburg, 17 Jan. 1869). Composer. Met Glinka, who inspired him to compose his first opera, *Esmeralda* (1841). After travel to Brussels and Paris returned to Russia in 1845; made studies of Russian folk song and the intonation of Russian speech, the results of which are evident in the opera *Rusalka* (1855). His setting of Pushkin's *The Stone Guest* was completed by Cui and Rimsky-Korsakov (premiered 1872). Compositions include several orchestral works, numerous songs, and pieces for piano.

Darke, Harold (Edwin) (b. London, 29 Oct. 1888; d. Cambridge, 28 Nov. 1976). Organist and composer. Studied with Parratt (organ), Sharpe (piano), and Stanford (composition) at the Royal College of Music. Taught organ there (1919–69) and served as organist at St. Michael's, Cornhill, in London (1916–69). Founded the St. Michael's Singers (1919) and the City of London Choral Union (1924). Fellow of King's College, Cambridge (1945–49). Composed much church music; also orchestral music, chamber music, songs, and organ pieces.

Dart, (Robert) Thurston (b. Kingston, Surrey, 3 Sept. 1921; d. London, 6 Mar. 1971). Musicologist and harpsichordist. Studied music at the Royal College of Music (1938–39) and musicology with van den Borren in Brussels. Taught at Cambridge (from 1947) and at King's College, London (1964–71). Wrote an influential book on performance practice, *The Interpretation of Music* (London, 1954); published numerous articles and editions. In 1955 founded the Philomusica of London; with them and other artists and as a soloist recorded much music of the Baroque.

Daseian notation. A system of musical notation used in *Musica enchiriadis* (ca. 900) and related treatises that employs modified versions of the Greek aspirate sign to indicate pitches. The four signs designating the tetrachord of *finales* (the finals of plainchant), d e f g, are inverted, reversed, and otherwise modified to provide the signs for the remaining pitches in the system [see fig.].

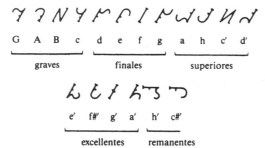

Dastgāh [Per., pattern or scheme]. The principal modal unit of Persian classical music, comprising a diatonic scale, a main cadential motif, a group of constituent melodies called *gusheh*, and ascribed musical character. There are seven main and five secondary *dastgah*s.

Dauer, dauernd [Ger.]. Duration, lasting.

Daughter of the Regiment. See *Fille du régiment, La*.

Dauprat, Louis-François (b. Paris, 24 May 1781; d. there, 16 or 17 July 1868). Horn player, teacher, composer. Studied the horn (1794–98), later theory and composition (1801–5, 1811–14) at the Paris Conservatory; played in military bands, then in theater orchestras (Grand Théâtre, Bordeaux, 1806–8; from 1808, Paris Opéra, in 1817–31 as first horn); 1828, founding member of the Conservatory orchestra; from 1802 to 1842 taught at the Conservatory. Composed concertos, chamber music, an important horn method, many exercises.

Dauvergne [D'Auvergne], **Antoine** (b. Moulins, 3 Oct. 1713; d. Lyons, 11 Feb. 1797). Composer and violinist. From 1739 was chamber musician for the royal court; from 1744 played in the orchestra of the Opéra. *Les amours de Tempé* (ballet, 1752) was the first in a series of successful stage works. Served as court composer (from 1755), *Maître du chambre du roi* (from ca. 1755), director of the Concert spirituel (from 1762) and the Opéra (from 1769), and finally musical *surintendant* of the court. Other theater works include *Les troqueurs* (1753); also composed motets and instrumental music.

David, Félicien (-César) (b. Cadenet, Vaucluse, 13 Apr. 1810; d. St.-Germain-en-Laye, 29 Aug. 1876). Composer. From spring 1830 studied a year at the Paris Conservatory (Benoist, Fétis, Reber). In 1832 joined the Saint-Simonian cult, withdrawing with the faithful to the cult's community at Ménilmontant outside Paris; with other "apostles" visited Istanbul, Smyrna, Jerusalem, and Egypt (1833–35). Published 22 *Mélodies orientales* for piano (1836); became an overnight celebrity with his ode-symphony *Le désert*, which he conducted in Paris (1844) to tremendous acclaim; subsequently toured France, northern Italy, central Europe, and Germany conducting it. *Lalla Roukh* (1862) was his only successful opera. In 1869 succeeded Berlioz at the Institute and as librarian of the Paris Conservatory. Other works include chamber music, vocal music, piano pieces.

David, Ferdinand (b. Hamburg, 19 Jan. 1810; d. Klosters, Switzerland, 18 July 1873). Violinist, composer, teacher. In 1823 studied in Kassel with Spohr (violin) and Hauptmann (theory); 1823–25, toured with his sister, a pianist; 1826–29, violinist, Königstadt Theater, Berlin; 1829–35; 1836–73, concertmaster, Gewandhaus Orchestra, Leipzig, and at the

Stadttheater; also director of Leipzig church music. From 1843 headed the violin department at the new Leipzig Conservatory (pupils include Joachim, Wilhelmj, Wasielewski). Advised Mendelssohn on his Violin Concerto and played its premiere (1845); published widely used *Violinschule* (1863) and etudes; edited much violin music. A prolific composer.

Dávid, Gyula (b. Budapest, 6 May 1913; d. there, 14 Mar. 1977). Composer. At the Budapest Academy of Music studied composition with Kodály (from 1938); conducted at the National Theater (1945–49). Professor of wind chamber music at the academy, 1950–60; professor of chamber music at the Budapest Conservatory from 1964 and at the teachers' training college of the academy from 1967. His music reflects the influence of folk song, and contains elements of pre-Baroque music and serial composition. Works include 4 symphonies (1947–70); *Four Madrigals* (1966); a piano trio (1972).

David, Johann Nepomuk (b. Eferding, Upper Austria, 30 Nov. 1895; d. Stuttgart, 22 Dec. 1977). Composer. Studied composition with Joseph Marx in Vienna (1920–23); for the next decade was organist and choirmaster in Wels. Teacher (from 1934) and director (from 1942) of the Leipzig Landeskonservatorium; director of the Salzburg Mozarteum (1945–48) and of the Stuttgart Hochschule für Musik (1948–63). Remained committed to conventional methods of compositions, but used more and more chromaticism, and even a twelve-tone series in compositions with a strong tonal center (Violin Concerto, 1957). Works include 8 symphonies (1936–65), an organ concerto (1965), and other orchestral music; organ music; choral music.

Davidovsky, Mario (b. Buenos Aires, 4 Mar. 1934). Composer and teacher. Studied in Buenos Aires and with Babbitt at the Columbia–Princeton Electronic Music Center (1960). After several visiting appointments taught primarily at City College of New York (1968–80), Columbia (1981–95, where he directed the Electronic Music Center), and Harvard (beginning 1995). Composer-in-residence at the Berkshire Music Festival, 1981. Best known for his combination of electronic and traditional instrumental sounds, especially in the series of pieces titled *Synchronism* (1963–74); *Synchronism* 6 (piano, tape) won the Pulitzer Prize in 1971. Works for conventional instruments have dominated his later output. Other compositions include 4 string quartets (1954–80); Divertimento for Cello and Orchestra (1984); *Shulamits' Dreams* (1993).

Davidsbündlertänze [Ger., Dances of the David-Leaguers]. A cycle of 18 *character pieces by Schumann, op. 6 (1837). Schumann frequently wrote of an imaginary League of David that was to oppose the Philistines of his day. In the first edition, each piece is signed E. or F. (or both) for Eusebius and Florestan, who represented, respectively, Schumann's pensive, introverted and impulsive, extroverted sides. Both characters, along with a "March of the David-Leaguers against the Philistines," also appear in his *Carnaval.*

Davies, Dennis Russell (b. Toledo, Ohio, 16 Apr. 1944). Conductor. Studied piano and conducting at Juilliard (1962–72) and taught there (1968–71); music director, Norwalk Symphony Orchestra (1968–72). With Berio founded the Juilliard Ensemble (later called the Ensemble). Conductor of the St. Paul Chamber Orchestra, 1972–80; music director of the American Composers Orchestra from 1977; music director of the Württemberg State Opera from 1980; *Generalmusikdirektor* of the city of Bonn, 1987–1995; music director, Brooklyn Academy of Music, and principal conductor, Brooklyn Philharmonic, from 1990.

Davies, Fanny (b. Guernsey, 27 June 1861; d. London, 1 Sept. 1934). Pianist. Studied at the Leipzig Conservatory (1882–83) and at the Frankfurt Conservatory (1883–85) with Clara Schumann. From 1885 prominent in England as soloist and chamber player; from 1887 played much on the Continent. A pioneer in the revival of English virginal music.

Davies, (Henry) Walford (b. Oswestry, Shropshire, 6 Sept. 1869; d. Wrington, Somerset, 11 Mar. 1941). Organist and composer. At St. George's Chapel, Windsor, studied organ with Parratt and was organist from 1885 to 1890. From 1890 studied at the Royal College of Music with Parry and Stanford. From 1891 organist at Christ Church, Hampstead; from 1898 at the Temple Church, London; returned to St. George's Chapel in 1927; taught at the Royal College (from 1895), and at the Univ. of Wales (1919–26). In 1934 was made Master of the King's Musick. Knighted in 1922.

Davies, Peter Maxwell (b. Manchester, 8 Sept. 1934). Composer. Studied at the Royal Manchester College of Music (from 1952), at Manchester Univ., and with Petrassi in Rome. From 1962 to 1964 was at Princeton. His interest in pre-Baroque music found expression in works such as the 2 orchestral fantasias (1962 and 1964) on an *In nomine* by John Taverner and in the opera *Taverner* (1970). In 1966 was composer-in-residence at the Univ. of Adelaide in Australia. Returned to England and collaborated with Birtwistle in forming the Pierrot Players, a chamber ensemble similar to that required to play *Pierrot lunaire.* Composed many of his subsequent works for this ensemble (reorganized in 1970 as the Fires of London), including *Miss Donnithorne's Maggot* (1974) and the well-known *Eight Songs for a Mad*

King (1969) as well as film scores. Knighted in 1987. Appointed Associate Conductor/Composer of the BBC Philharmonic in Manchester and of the Royal Philharmonic in 1992. Other works include a number of chamber operas; choral works; 5 symphonies (1976–94); 2 trumpet concertos (1988, 1990); *Strathclyde concerto no. 10* (orchestra, 1995); chamber works and pieces for solo instruments, some based on or evoking music of the Middle Ages and Renaissance.

Davis, Andrew (Frank) (b. Ashridge, Hertfordshire, 2 Feb. 1944). Conductor and organist. Studied organ with Hurford and Kee at the Royal Academy of Music and at Kings College, Cambridge, 1963–67; conducting with Franco Ferrara at the Accademia di S. Cecilia in Rome, 1968. Associate conductor of the BBC Scottish Orchestra, 1970–71; of the New Philharmonia, 1973–74. Musical director of the Toronto Symphony, 1975–88; chief conductor of the BBC Symphony from 1988; music director of the Glyndebourne Festival from 1989.

Davis, Anthony (b. Paterson, N.J., 20 Feb. 1951). Jazz and avant-garde pianist and composer. Studied music at Yale and played jazz with George Lewis (1973) and Leo Smith (1974–77). Joined Leroy Jenkins's trio (1977–79) and worked with James Newton (beginning 1978) in duos, trios, quartets, and Davis's octet Episteme, formed in 1981. *X*, an opera about Malcolm X, was given in Philadelphia (1985) and New York (1986). Other works include music to Kushner's *Angels in America: Millennium Approaches* (1993); *ESU Variations,* orchestra (1995).

Davis, Colin (Rex) (b. Weybridge, Surrey, 25 Sept. 1927). Conductor. Assistant conductor, BBC Scottish Orchestra, 1957–59. Principal conductor, Sadler's Wells, 1961–64; chief conductor, BBC Symphony, 1967–71. Appointed guest conductor of the London Symphony, the Boston Symphony, and the Amsterdam Concertgebouw Orchestra, 1971. Musical director, Covent Garden, 1971–86. Music director, Bavarian Radio Symphony from 1983. Appointed music director of the London Symphony, 1995. Acclaimed for his interpretations of Berlioz and Sibelius. Knighted in 1980.

Davis, Eddie "Lockjaw" (b. New York, 2 Mar. 1922; d. Culver City, Calif., 3 Nov. 1986). Jazz tenor saxophonist. After joining the big bands of Cootie Williams (1942–44), Lucky Millinder (1944), Andy Kirk (1945–46), and Louis Armstrong, was a principal soloist with Count Basie (1952–53, 1957); also led combos. Rejoined Basie's big band (1964–73), then worked again in combos, sharing leadership with Harry Edison in a quintet (1975–82).

Davis, Miles (Dewey, III) (b. Alton, Ill., 25 May 1926; d. Santa Monica, Calif., 28 Sept. 1991). Jazz trumpeter and bandleader. Played bop with Charlie Parker (1945–48) before leading his own bands. His nonet (1949–50) pioneered cool jazz. His hard bop quintet (1955–56) included John Coltrane, Red Garland, Paul Chambers, and Philly Joe Jones. Beginning 1958 his sextets included Coltrane, Adderley, Chambers, Jones or Jimmie Cobb, and Garland, Bill Evans, or Wynton Kelly. Recorded as a trumpeter and flugelhorn soloist with Gil Evans's orchestra. In 1963 formed a quintet with Hancock, Carter, Williams, and Coleman; later personnel included Corea, Jarrett, and Moreira. After a retirement forced by serious ailments (1975–80) returned to lead jazz-rock groups through the 1980s. His brooding tone, achieved with a stemless harmon mute (from 1954), and his use of the flugelhorn were widely imitated.

Davison, Wild Bill [William Edward] (b. Defiance, Ohio, 5 Jan. 1906; d. Santa Barbara, Calif., 14 Nov. 1989). Jazz cornetist. Worked in Chicago (1927–32) and Milwaukee. Led a group at Nick's in New York in 1941 and in Boston and St. Louis before returning to play and record with Eddie Condon regularly from 1945. After working on the West Coast in the early 1960s, played as a free-lance, frequently performing in Europe.

Davul [Turk.]. A cylindrical, double-headed bass drum of Turkey [see ill. under Instrument]. It is paired with the *zurna* for dance, processional, and wedding music.

Davy, John (b. Upton Hellions, Devonshire, 23 Dec. 1763; d. London, 22 Feb. 1824). Composer and violinist. By 1790 had moved to London, where he was violinist in various theaters. His opera *What a Blunder!* (1800) had some success at the Little Haymarket Theatre. Contributed music to at least 15 subsequent stage works and composed madrigals, sacred vocal works, and works for harp.

Dawson, William Levi (b. Anniston, Ala., 23 Sept. 1899; d. Tuskegee, Ala., 2 May 1990). Composer and conductor. Studied at Tuskegee Institute, the Horner Institute of Fine Arts in Kansas City, and the American Conservatory in Chicago. Played trombone in the Chicago Civic Orchestra and became director of music at Tuskegee; toured extensively in the U.S. and Europe with the college's choir before retiring in 1955. His style was neo-Romantic and made use of African American song idioms. Works include the *Negro Folk Symphony* (1934) and *Out in the Fields* (soprano and orchestra, 1928).

DB. Abbr. for *decibel.

D.C. Abbr. for *Da capo.

Deaconing. *Lining (out).

Dead interval. An interval formed between the last pitch of one phrase and the first pitch of the next and thus not strictly subject to the normal principles of melodic construction and voice leading.

Death and the Maiden. See *Tod und das Mädchen.*

Death and Transfiguration. See *Tod und Verklärung.*

Death in Venice. Opera in two acts by Britten (libretto by Myfanwy Piper after the story by Thomas Mann), produced at the Aldeburgh Festival in Suffolk in 1973. Setting: Munich, Venice, and the Lido, 1911.

Debole [It.]. Weak.

Debussy, (Achille-) Claude (b. St. Germain-en-Laye, 22 Aug. 1862; d. Paris, 25 Mar. 1918). Composer and writer. In 1872 was admitted to piano (Marmontel) and theory (Lavignac) classes at the Paris Conservatory. In 1880 joined Guiraud's composition class and four years later won the Prix de Rome. Visited Bayreuth in 1888 and 1889, and was fascinated by the Javanese gamelan at the Paris Exposition of 1889. The *Prelude to "The Afternoon of a Faun"* was performed in 1894, but it was the 1902 premiere of *Pelléas et Mélisande* that brought him significant recognition. By then had composed several songs, orchestral works including the *Fantaisie* (with piano, 1889–90), *Nocturnes,* piano works, and the string quartet (1893). Traveled frequently as conductor and performer of his own music in England, Russia, and throughout Europe; a music critic from 1901. Between 1902 and 1913 composed *La *Mer, *Images, *Jeux,* more songs, piano pieces, and chamber music. In 1909 appointed to the board of the Conservatory. His last trip to England was in 1914, after which he produced the *Études* for piano (1915) and three of six planned sonatas for chamber ensembles (cello and piano, 1915; flute, viola, and harp, 1915; violin and piano, 1916). Through his uses of archaic modes and whole-tone or pentatonic scales, as well as his subordination of chords to melody rather than to the demands of functional harmonic progressions, Debussy cultivated a style known as impressionism, although the composer himself objected to the term. His influence on 20th-century music is unmatched by any of his contemporaries. Writings are collected in *Debussy on Music,* trans. and ed. Richard Langham Smith (1977).

Other works include: *Orchestral music. Printemps* (lost; reorchestrated from a 1904 4-hand piano version); *Danse sacrée et danse profane* (harp and orchestra, 1904)

Works for voices and orchestra. La damoiselle élue (soprano, female chorus, and orchestra, 1887–88, reorchestrated in 1902).

Chamber music. Piano trio (ca. 1879); *Rapsodie* (alto saxophone and piano, 1901–8); *Première rapsodie* (clarinet and piano, 1909–10); *Syrinx* (flute, 1913, originally incidental music for *Psyché*);

Piano music. Rêverie (1890); *Suite bergamasque* (1890, rev. 1905); *Estampes* (including *Clair de lune); L'isle joyeuse* (1904); *Children's Corner* (including Golliwogg's Cake-Walk); *Préludes* (bk. 1, 1910; bk. 2, 1912–13).

Songs. Cinq poèmes de Baudelaire (1887–89); *Trois poèmes de Mallarmé* (1913).

Decani and cantoris [Lat.]. In English churches, the two halves of the choir, one seated on the dean's side of the altar (the right side when facing it), the other on the cantor's side (the left).

Decay. In *acoustics, the decline in intensity that results as the vibrations producing a sound are damped, whether artificially or by internal friction of the vibrating system.

Deceptive cadence. See Cadence.

Déchant [Fr.]. *Discant.

Decibel [abbr. dB]. A unit of measurement of the difference in intensity of two sounds (or the difference in power of two signals). The difference between the threshold of hearing and the threshold of pain is approximately 120 decibels. One decibel is approximately the minimum difference in intensity that the ear can detect.

Décidé [Fr.]. *Deciso.

Deciso, decisamente [It.]. Decisive, resolutely.

Declamation. That aspect of the musical setting of a text that corresponds to the purely sonorous quality of the text itself. Since about the 16th century, good declamation has usually been said to require that musical *accent and textual accent coincide, both at the level of individual words and syllables and at the level of phrases and sentences.

Decrescendo [It., abbr. *decr., decresc.*]. Becoming softer [see also *Diminuendo, Crescendo*].

Deering, Richard. See Dering, Richard.

DeFranco, Buddy [Boniface Ferdinand Leonardo] (b. Camden, N.J., 17 Feb. 1923). Jazz clarinetist. Played in the big bands of Gene Krupa (1941–42), Charlie Barnet (1943–44), and Tommy Dorsey (1944–48); joined Count Basie's octet (1950), led a bop quartet including Art Blakey and Kenny Drew (1952–53), toured Europe with Billie Holiday (1954). Led a bop quartet (1960–63) and directed the memorial Glenn Miller Orchestra (1966–74); in the 1980s led a quintet.

DeGaetani, Jan (b. Massillon, Ohio, 10 July 1933; d. Rochester, N.Y., 15 Sept. 1989). Mezzo-soprano. Studied voice at Juilliard; taught theory and solfège there and gave master classes at the Univ. of Wisconsin. Performed with the Waverly Consort, the Pro Musica Antiqua, and the Abbey Singers. Taught at SUNY–Purchase (1972–73) and Eastman (from 1973). Premiered Crumb's *Ancient Voices of Children* (1970) and became one of the most sought-after singers of 20th-century scores. A number of composers wrote works for her; she also recorded music of Stephen Foster and Hugo Wolf.

Degree. See Scale degrees.

Dehors, en [Fr.]. Prominent, standing out.

DeJohnette, Jack (b. Chicago, 9 Aug. 1942). Jazz drummer, pianist, and bandleader. Played drums in Charles Lloyd's quartet (1966–68), with Miles Davis's jazz-rock group (1969–71), later in a trio with Keith Jarrett and Gary Peacock (1983–), and with Ornette Coleman and Pat Metheny. Beginning in the 1970s regularly doubled as a drummer and pianist. Member of John Abercrombie's trio (1975–77); led the quartet Directions, and from 1979 Special Edition.

De Koven, (Henry Louis) Reginald (b. Middletown, Conn., 3 Apr. 1859; d. Chicago, 16 Jan. 1920). Composer, conductor, and critic. Studied in Stuttgart, Florence, Vienna, and Paris; graduated from Oxford. From 1882 critic for *Harper's Weekly* and New York and Chicago newspapers; founded the Washington Symphony (1902–4). Known for his operettas (*Robin Hood,* Chicago, 1890); also wrote 2 grand operas, ca. 400 songs.

Delage, Maurice (Charles) (b. Paris, 13 Nov. 1879; d. there, 19 Sept. 1961). Composer. Worked with Ravel and was a close friend of Stravinsky. Exoticism in his music arose from his travels to India (*Poèmes hindous,* soprano, nine instruments, 1913) and Japan (*7 haï-kaï,* voice and ensemble, 1929).

Delalande, Michel-Richard. See Lalande, Michel-Richard de.

Delannoy, Marcel (b. La Ferté-Alais, Seine-et-Oise, 9 July 1898; d. Nantes, 14 Sept. 1962). Composer. Sought instruction from Jean Gallon, Gédalge, and Roland-Manuel but was mainly self-taught. Works illustrate his interest in polytonality, instrumental color, and folklike melodies; the opera *Puck* (1945) employs varying vocal styles, ranging from speech to song.

De Lara [Cohen], **Isidore** (b. London, 9 Aug. 1858; d. Paris, 2 Sept. 1935). Composer. Studied at the Milan Conservatory and with Lalo; composed many operas (*Amy Robsart,* 1893; *Messaline,* 1899), the last in 1933; also a singer and conductor.

De Larrocha, Alicia. See Larrocha, Alicia de.

Delden, Lex van (b. Amsterdam, 10 Sept. 1919; d. there, 1 July 1988). Composer. After the war became a critic in Amsterdam. Works include the cantata *Rubayat,* oratorios, 8 symphonies (1952–64), choral works, chamber music, songs.

Delibes, (Clément-Philibert-) Léo (b. St. Germain du Val, Sarthe, 21 Feb. 1836; d. Paris, 16 Jan. 1891). Composer. Studied at the Paris Conservatory under Benoist (organ), Bazin (harmony), and Adam (composition). From 1853 accompanist at the Théâtre-lyrique; assistant chorusmaster at the Opéra (1865–72). In 1856 began producing light operas, but his most enduring works are the ballets *Coppélia (1870) and *Sylvia (1876), as well as the opéra comique *Lakmé (1883). Professor of composition at the Conservatory from 1881.

Delicato [It.]. Delicate.

Délié [Fr.]. (1) Detached, not *legato. (2) Free.

Delius, Frederick [Fritz] **(Theodor Albert)** (b. Bradford, Yorkshire, 29 Jan. 1862; d. Grez-sur-Loing, near Paris, 10 June 1934). Composer. In 1884 embarked for the U.S., where he had formal music instruction in Jacksonville. In 1885 became a music teacher in Danville, Virginia; the following year began studies with Jadassohn, Sitt, and Reinecke at the Leipzig Conservatory. In 1888 moved to Paris, where he remained for most of the rest of his life. Performances of his works took place chiefly in Germany until Beecham began to perform the opera *A Village Romeo and Juliet* (1900–01) and other works. Compositions include 6 operas or "lyric dramas"; incidental music (*Hassan,* 1920–23); vocal works (*Sea Drift,* baritone, chorus, orchestra, 1903–4; *Songs of Sunset,* 1906–7); orchestral music (*Florida,* suite, 1887–89; *Brigg Fair (An English Rhapsody),* 1907; *North Country Sketches,* 1913–15; Violin Concerto, 1916); chamber music; piano music; songs.

Della Casa, Lisa (b. Burgdorf, Switzerland, 2 Feb. 1919). Soprano. Debuted in Solothurn-Biel (1941); leading roles with the Zurich Stadttheater (1942–50) and Vienna Staatsoper (from 1947); a *Kammersängerin* from 1953. Performed at the Salzburg Festival, Munich, Bayreuth, Glyndebourne, and the Met. An outstanding interpreter of Strauss, was particularly noted for her Arabella.

Deller, Alfred (b. Margate, Kent, 31 May 1912; d. Bologna, 16 July 1979). Countertenor. More than anyone else he stimulated the revival of interest in the countertenor voice and its music. Soloist and choir director at St. Paul's Cathedral in London, 1947–61.

In 1948 formed the Deller Consort to perform music written before 1750, particularly by Englishmen. In 1960 created the part of Oberon in *A Midsummer Night's Dream.*

Dello Joio, Norman (b. New York, 24 Jan. 1913). Composer. Studied at City College (1932–34), Juilliard (Wagenaar, 1939–41), and at Tanglewood and Yale under Hindemith (1941). Taught at Sarah Lawrence (1945–50) and Mannes College (1956–72); dean of the School of Fine and Applied Arts at Boston Univ. (1972–78). Works reflect his interest in Italian opera, Roman Catholic religious music, and jazz; variation technique is prominent in several works (*Meditations on Ecclesiastes,* orchestra, 1955–56, awarded the Pulitzer Prize). Compositions include other orchestral works (*Variations, Chaconne, and Finale,* 1947; *Homage to Haydn,* 1969); operas (*The Triumph of St. Joan);* many choral works (*Nativity,* soloists, chorus, orchestra, 1987); chamber music; songs.

Del Monaco, Mario (b. Florence, 27 July 1915; d. Mestre, near Venice, 16 Oct. 1982). Tenor. In 1939 entered the conservatory at Pesaro and made his debut there as Turridu *(Cavalleria rusticana).* Professional debut at La Scala, 1941; Covent Garden debut, 1946; from 1950 one of the most popular artists at the Met. Admired for dramatic Verdi roles such as Radames, Alvaro, and Otello.

De los Angeles, Victoria [Gomez Cima, Victoria] (b. Barcelona, 1 Nov. 1923). Soprano. Studied voice and piano at the Barcelona Conservatory, 1940–42. Debut in Barcelona, 1944; subsequently performed in Paris, at Covent Garden, and at the Met (1951–61). Her wide repertory includes operas by Purcell, Vivaldi, Mozart, Wagner, Verdi, Massenet, Puccini, Mascagni, and Debussy, as well as Spanish and Catalonian music.

Del Tredici, David (Walter) (b. Cloverdale, Calif., 16 Mar. 1937). Composer. Studied with Sessions and Kim at Princeton. Taught at Harvard (1966–72), SUNY–Buffalo (1973), Boston Univ. (1973–84), and City College, CUNY (beginning 1984). Composer-in-residence with the New York Philharmonic (1988–90) before joining the faculty of Manhattan School (1991) and Juilliard (1993). In 1980 awarded the Pulitzer Prize for *In Memory of a Summer Day.* Works before 1968, primarily settings of texts by Joyce, employ serial techniques in the tradition of Webern. Beginning in 1968 produced a number of "Alice" works on texts of Lewis Carroll in a style reminiscent of Richard Strauss (*An Alice Symphony,* 1969; *Final Alice,* 1976; *Virtuoso Alice,* 1987, all for amplified soprano and orchestra, some with popular or folk instruments). Other works include *Tattoo* (orchestra, 1988); *Brass symphony,* brass quintet

(1992); instrumental chamber music; songs with piano or chamber ensemble.

De Luca, Giuseppe (b. Rome, 25 Dec. 1876; d. New York, 26 Aug. 1950). Baritone. Studied at the Accademia di S. Cecilia. Debut in Piacenza, 1897. Created Michonnet in Cilea's *Adriana Lecouvreur* (1902) and Sharpless in *Madama Butterfly* (1904). Also sang at the Teatro Colón in Buenos Aires (1906–10); at Covent Garden (1907–10); at the Vienna Hofoper (1909). Performed 52 different roles in 928 performances at the Met (1915–46).

De Lucia, Fernando (b. Naples, 11 Oct. 1860; d. there, 21 Feb. 1925). Tenor. Studied at the Conservatorio S. Pietro a Majella in Naples. Debut in Naples, 1885; sang in Bologna, Florence, Buenos Aires, and London. 1893 debut with the Met as Don José. In the 1890s turned to heavier verismo roles, including Turiddu in *Cavalleria rusticana* and Canio in *Pagliacci.* Regarded as the best tenor of the generation before Caruso.

Delvincourt, Claude (b. Paris, 12 Jan. 1888; d. Orbetello, Tuscany, 5 Apr. 1954). Composer. Studied with Widor at the Paris Conservatory; won the Prix de Rome in 1913. Directed the conservatory at Versailles from 1931, the Paris Conservatory from 1941 until his death. Composed in a style drawn from Debussy, Ravel, and earlier French traditions.

Démancher [Fr.]. In string playing, to shift the left hand from one position to another.

Demi- [fr. Lat.]. Half. For demisemiquaver, *demi-pause, demi-soupir,* see Note; *demi-ton,* semitone; *demi-voix,* **mezza voce.*

Demus, Jörg (Wolfgang) (b. St. Pölten, Austria, 2 Dec. 1928). Pianist. Studied at the Vienna Academy (1940–45), in Paris (1951–53), with Gieseking in Saarbrücken (1953), and briefly with Fischer, Kempff, and Benedetti-Michelangeli. Public debut, Vienna, 1943; subsequently performed in Europe and the U.S. First prize in the Busoni Competition, 1956. Also well known as an accompanist to Fischer-Dieskau and duo pianist with Badura-Skoda.

Demuth, Norman (b. South Croydon, London, 15 July 1898; d. Chichester, 21 Apr. 1968). Composer and music critic. Studied with Dunhill and Parratt at the Royal Academy of Music; from 1917 organist in several London churches. Taught composition at the Royal Academy from 1930; in 1936 founded the academy's New Music Society. Works include operas, 3 symphonies and 2 "symphonic studies," chamber music.

Dencke, Jeremiah (b. Langenbilau, Silesia, 2 Oct. 1725; d. Bethlehem, Pa., 28 May 1795). Composer. Organist at Gnadenfrei and, from 1748, at Herrnhut;

held other Moravian church posts at Gnadenberg and Zeist, Holland, before emigrating to America in 1761. Settled near Nazareth, Pa.; warden at Bethlehem, 1772–84, thereafter pastor at Bethlehem, Lititz, Nazareth, and once again at Bethlehem. Apparently the first to compose and perform concerted vocal music in America; wrote arias as well as anthems.

Denisov, Edison Vasilevich (b. Tomsk, Siberia, 6 Apr. 1929); d. Paris, 23 Nov. 1996). Composer and theorist. Studied piano in Tomsk; studied with Vissarion Shebalin at the Moscow Conservatory (1951–56); in 1959 completed graduate studies there under Shebalin and Nikolai Peiko. Joined the faculty of Moscow Conservatory in 1959. Used serial and other experimental techniques to develop a style noted for its transparency, motivic interplay, and restrained lyricism; in the 1980s his music exhibited a shift toward a neo-Romantic aesthetic. Works include operas (*The Four Girls,* 1986); a ballet; a symphony (1988); concertos, and other orchestral music; much chamber and vocal music; choral music (Requiem, 1980).

Denza, Luigi (b. Castellammare di Stabia, 24 Feb. 1846; d. London, 26 Jan. 1922). Composer. From 1862 studied at the Naples Conservatory. His opera *Wallenstein* (1876) was only moderately successful; best known for the song "Funiculì-funiculà," which Richard Strauss mistook for a folk song, introducing it into his *Aus Italien* (1886). From 1898 taught at the Royal Academy of Music.

De Peyer, Gervase (Alan) (b. London, 11 Apr. 1926). Clarinetist. Studied at the Royal College of Music and the Paris Conservatory. Principal clarinet of the London Symphony, 1955–71. Founding member of the Melos Ensemble. Director of the London Symphony Wind Ensemble; conductor of the Haydn Orchestra of London. Professor at the Royal Academy of Music from 1959.

Déploration [Fr.]. A poem, or the musical setting of such a poem, that is a *lament on someone's death.

De profundis [Lat.]. Psalm 129 (130). See Penitential Psalms.

Derb [Ger.]. Robust, rough.

De Reszke [Mieczislaw], **Édouard** (b. Warsaw, 22 Dec. 1853; d. Garnek, Poland, 25 May 1917). Bass. Studied in Warsaw, Italy, Paris; 1876, debut in Paris; 1879, at La Scala; 1880, Covent Garden; 1885, Paris Opéra; U.S. and Met debuts, 1891. Celebrated roles were Mephistopheles, Sachs, Hagen, Leporello.

De Reszke [Mieczislaw], **Jean** [Jan] (b. Warsaw, 14 Jan. 1850; d. Nice, 3 Apr. 1925). Tenor. Debuted as a tenor in Madrid, 1879. Quickly became the leading tenor of his time, performing at Drury Lane (1887),

Covent Garden (1888–1900), and the Met (1891–1901). Renowned in French roles (Faust, Roméo, Des Grieux, Raoul) and from around 1895 the heavier Wagner roles (Tristan, Siegfried).

Dering [Deering, Dearing], **Richard** (b. Kent, ca. 1580; d. London, buried 22 Mar. 1630). Composer. Graduated from Oxford in 1610; may have been in Italy by 1612; by 1617 was an organist in Brussels. In 1625 became organist to Queen Henrietta Maria, wife of Charles I, and served as a royal musician for the rest of his life. The majority of his works are Latin (Catholic) motets and Italian madrigals and canzonettas, which display a familiarity with contemporary Italian music. Also wrote some English music, including pieces for viol consort, 2 madrigals, and Anglican church music.

Dernesch, Helga (b. Vienna, 3 or 13 Feb. 1939). Soprano, mezzo-soprano. Studied at the conservatory in Vienna (1951–57) and joined the Bern Opera (1961). Sang Wagner with the Wiesbaden (1963–66) and Cologne Operas (1966–70), as well as at Bayreuth (from 1965). In 1969 von Karajan invited her to sing Brünnhilde and Isolde on stage and for his recordings, roles which eventually overtaxed her voice. Debuted as a mezzo in 1979; in addition to Wagnerian roles sang Herodias *(Salome)*.

De Rogatis, Pascual (b. Teora, Italy, 17 May 1880; d. Buenos Aires, 2 Apr. 1980). Composer. Studied at the Conservatory of Music in Buenos Aires. His opera *Huémac* (1916) was performed throughout Latin America and in Europe; other works include songs, piano pieces, and the tone poem *Atipac* (1928).

Des, deses [Ger.]. D-flat, D-double-flat. See Pitch names.

De Sabata, Victor (b. Trieste, 10 Apr. 1892; d. Santa Margherita Ligure, 11 Dec. 1967). Conductor and composer. A virtuoso pianist and violinist up to his last days, he concentrated on conducting and composition at the Milan Conservatory. Conductor at the Monte Carlo Opera (1918–29); U.S. debut in 1927. In 1929 began an affiliation with La Scala that lasted to the end of his career; also conducted in Florence (1933–42), Vienna (1936–37), and Bayreuth (1939). Retired unexpectedly in 1953. Artistic superintendent at La Scala, 1954–61. Works include operas (*Lisistrata,* 1920) and symphonic poems (*Juventus,* 1919; *Gethsemani,* 1925).

Descant [fr. Lat. *discantus*]. (1) *Discant. (2) A high-pitched (sometimes the highest) member of some families of instruments, e.g., the *recorder and *viol; the descant clef is the soprano *clef. (3) In hymn singing, a high ornamental part lying above the melody.

Descort [Prov.]. *Lai.

Deses [Ger.]. See *Des, deses.*

Des Marais, Paul (Emile) (b. Menominee, Mich., 23 June 1920). Composer. Studied at Harvard and in Paris with Boulanger (1949–51); taught at UCLA from 1960. Early compositions were neoclassical; later works have employed serial techniques but remained relatively diatonic. Compositions include the chamber opera *Epiphanies* (1964–68); the theater piece *Orpheus* (narrator and instruments, 1987); choral music; chamber music.

Desmond, Paul [Breitenfeld, Paul Emil] (b. San Francisco, 25 Nov. 1924; d. New York, 30 May 1977). Jazz alto saxophonist. Most of his career parallels that of Dave Brubeck, including rehearsal groups from 1946, the quartet of 1951–67, and subsequent reunions in duos and combos. Apart from Brubeck, as a leader Desmond recorded with Gerry Mulligan or Jim Hall, and he performed in New York with Hall (1974) and in Toronto (1974–75).

Désormière, Roger (b. Vichy, 13 Sept. 1898; d. Paris 25 Oct. 1963). Conductor. Studied with Koechlin at the Paris Conservatory. Conducted the Swedish Ballet in Paris, 1924–25; the Ballets russes, 1925–29; the Opéra-comique, 1936–44; the Grand Opéra, 1945; the BBC Symphony, 1946–47. An admirer of Satie in his youth, he remained attentive to new music.

Desprez, Josquin. See Josquin Desprez.

Dessau, Paul (b. Hamburg, 19 Dec. 1894; d. East Berlin, 27 June 1979). Composer. After the war was appointed music director and composer of the Hamburg Kammerspiele Theater. Coached and conducted at the Cologne and Mainz operas; in 1925 appointed principal conductor at the Berlin Städtische Oper. Studied twelve-tone music in Paris in the mid-1930s; in 1939 moved to the U.S., met and collaborated with Brecht (*Mutter Courage und ihre Kinder,* 1946). Lived in Hollywood and wrote film music; in 1948 returned with Brecht to East Berlin; directed music in a local upper school from 1960. In his prewar compositions interests in twelve-tone method and Jewish folk music are evident; later works are often filled with political commentary (*Einstein,* opera, 1971–73).

Dessus [Fr.]. *Treble, i.e., the normally highest part or member of a group of instruments. A still higher instrument is called a *pardessus,* e.g., the *pardessus de viole.*

Destinn, Emmy [Kittlová, Emilie Pavlína; Destinnová, Ema] (b. Prague, 26 Feb. 1878; d. České Budějovice [Budweis], 28 Jan. 1930). Soprano. Debut at the Dresden Hofoper, 1897; performed at the Berlin Hofoper (from 1898). Sang the first Bayreuth Senta in 1901. Covent Garden debut in 1904 (Donna Anna); U.S. debut 1908 at the Met (Aida). Sang every season at Covent Garden until 1914; at the Met until 1916, when her government interned her. Returned to the Met in 1919. Frequently cast opposite Caruso. Created many roles, including Minnie in *La fanciulla del West.*

Destouches, André Cardinal (bapt. Paris, 6 Apr. 1672; d. there, 7 Feb. 1749). Composer. Probably studied with Campra, for whose opera-ballet *L'Europe galante* (1697) he wrote airs. Became *sur-intendant de la musique de chambre* in 1718, *maître de la musique de chambre* in 1727; directorship of the Académie royale, 1728–30. Began a series of *concerts spirituels* for the queen at Versailles in 1725, presiding over them until 1745.

Destra [It.]. The right hand *(mano destra).*

Détaché [Fr.]. See Bowing (2).

Dett, R(obert) Nathaniel (b. Drummondsville, Ontario, 11 Oct. 1882; d. Battle Creek, Mich., 2 Oct. 1943). Composer, pianist, and conductor. Studied at Oberlin, Columbia (1915), with Boulanger in Paris (1929), at Harvard (1920), and at Eastman (M.Mus., 1932). Taught at various institutions, including Hampton Institute (1913–31). Noted for his piano suites and rags and was an important advocate for African American music, which he employed in most of his own compositions.

Deuterus [Gr.]. See Mode.

Deutlich [Ger.]. Clear, distinct.

Deutscher Tanz [Ger., German dance; pl. *Deutsche (Tänze)*]. In the late 18th and early 19th centuries, especially in South Germany and Austria, a dance for couples in a fast triple meter; not to be confused with the earlier *allemande, which was sometimes called a *Teutscher Tanz.* The term was eventually superseded by *waltz.

Deutsches Requiem, Ein [Ger., A German Requiem]. A work for soprano, baritone, chorus, and orchestra by Brahms, op. 45 (1857–68). Its seven movements are settings of texts freely adapted from the Bible.

Deutschland über alles [Ger.]. See *Einigkeit und Recht und Freiheit.*

Deux [Fr.]. Two; *à deux, a *due.

Deux journées, Les [Fr., The Two Days; also produced in English as The Water Carrier; Ger. *Der Wasserträger*]. Opera in three acts by Luigi Cherubini (libretto by Jean Nicolas Bouilly), produced in Paris in 1800. Setting: Paris and environs, 1617.

Development. (1) Structural alteration of musical material, as opposed to the exposition or statement of material. Development may affect any parameter of a theme; typical examples would include significant modification of pitch contour or rhythm, formal expansion or contraction, textural change, melodic fragmentation, and melodic or contrapuntal combination with other themes.

(2) The central section of a movement in sonata, sonata-rondo, or ritornello-sonata form [see Sonata form, Rondo, Concerto].

Devil and Daniel Webster, The. Opera in one act by Douglas Moore (libretto by the composer after Stephen Vincent Benét), produced in New York in 1939. Setting: New Hampshire in the 1840s.

Devil's Trill Sonata. A violin sonata in G minor by Tartini, probably composed no earlier than 1745 and first printed in 1798. It was said to have been inspired by a dream in which the devil appeared and, at the composer's request, played the violin. Among its many virtuosic effects, the work includes a long trill, for which it is named, in the last movement.

Devin du village, Le [Fr., The Village Soothsayer]. An *intermède* in one act by Jean-Jacques Rousseau (libretto by the composer), produced at Fontaine-bleau in 1752.

Devisenarie [Ger.]. See Motto.

Devoto [It.]. Devoutly.

De Waart, Edo (b. Amsterdam, 1 June 1941). Oboist and conductor. Studied at the Music Lyceum in Amsterdam; principal oboe with the Concertgebouw Orchestra beginning in 1963. Debut as conductor with Netherlands Radio Philharmonic, 1964; assistant conductor of the New York Philharmonic, 1965–66; founding conductor of the Netherlands Wind Ensemble, 1966–67; conductor (1966–73) and artistic director (1973–79) of the Rotterdam Philharmonic; principal guest conductor (1974–77) and music director (1977–85) of the San Francisco Symphony. Music director of the Minnesota Orchestra (1986–95); chief conductor and artistic director of the Sydney Symphony (from 1995).

Diabelli Variations [Ger. *33 Veränderungen über einen Walzer von Anton Diabelli,* 33 Variations on a Waltz by Anton Diabelli]. Beethoven's op. 120 (1819, 1822–23) for piano.

Diabelli, Anton (b. Mattsee, near Salzburg, 5 or 6 Sept. 1781; d. Vienna, 7 or 8 Apr. 1858). Publisher, composer. Had lessons with Michael Haydn at Salzburg cathedral; settled in Vienna as music teacher, composer, and music publisher's proof-reader. In 1818 was a founding partner in the publishing firm of Cappi & Diabelli, which became Diabelli & Cie. in 1824. The firm published great quantities of light music, the first published works of Schubert, and several works by Beethoven, including the Diabelli Variations.

Diabolus in musica [Lat., the devil in music]. In the late Middle Ages, the *tritone, the use of which was prohibited by various theorists. See *Mi-fa.*

Diaghilev, Sergei (Pavlovich) (b. Gruzino, Novgorod district, 31 Mar. 1872 [o.s. 19 Mar.]; d. Venice, 19 Aug. 1929). Impresario. Excelled at bringing leading innovators together into fruitful collaborations. The vehicle for his ambitions was the Ballets russes; he encouraged his choreographer, Fokine, and scenic designer, Bakst, to strike out on new paths with a bold and savage version of *Prince Igor.* For subsequent seasons commissioned new music (from Stravinsky, Debussy, Richard Strauss, Satie, Falla, Prokofiev, and Poulenc, among others) and scenic design (from Picasso, Matisse, Rouault, Chirico, and others). Above all stimulated and supported Fokine, Nijinsky, Massine, and Balanchine in their efforts to revolutionize ballet choreography.

Dialogues des Carmélites [Fr., Dialogues of the Carmelites]. Opera in three acts by Francis Poulenc (libretto by Ernest Lavery after the play by Georges Bernanos), produced in Milan in 1957. Setting: France, 1789.

Diamond, David (Leo) (b. Rochester, N.Y., 9 July 1915). Composer. Worked with Rogers at Eastman and with Paul Boepple and Sessions in New York (1934–36), then with Boulanger in France (1938). Taught in Rome (1951) and lived in Florence (1953–65); taught or lectured at various schools and festivals (Salzburg, Aspen, Harvard, SUNY–Buffalo, Manhattan School, Juilliard from 1973). A prolific composer in the classical tradition; his *Sinfonietta* (1935) and *Psalm* (orchestra, 1937) won prizes early in his career; other works include *Rounds,* string orchestra, 1944; 11 symphonies (1941–93); 10 string quartets (1940–68); piano works; choral music; songs.

Diapason [fr. Gr.]. (1) In Greek and medieval theory, the octave. (2) In English and American organs, the main open flue stop of the Great manual, at 8′ or 16′ pitch, depending on the size of the organ. (3) The range of a voice or instrument. (4) [Fr., It.; Sp. *diapasón*] Tuning fork. (5) [Fr.] *Diapason normal,* standard or concert *pitch.

Diapente [Gr.]. In ancient Greek and medieval theory, the interval of a fifth; *epidiapente,* the fifth above; *hypodiapente, subdiapente,* the fifth below.

Diaphonia [Gr.]. (1) In ancient Greek theory and in some medieval writings, dissonance, as opposed to *symphonia, consonance. (2) In theoretical works of the Middle Ages, two-part polyphony, for which *discant [Lat. discantus] became the preferred term in the 13th century.

Diastematic. Of or pertaining to notation that is precise with respect to pitch. See Neume.

Diatessaron [Gr.]. In ancient Greek and medieval theory, the interval of a fourth; epidiatessaron, the fourth above; hypodiatessaron, subdiatessaron, the fourth below.

Diatonic. (1) A *scale with seven different pitches (heptatonic) that are adjacent to one another on the *circle of fifths; thus, one in which each letter name represents only a single pitch and which is made up of whole tones and semitones arranged in the pattern embodied in the white keys of the piano *keyboard; hence, any major or pure minor scale and any church *mode, as distinct from the *chromatic scale, which employs only semitones. (2) Melody or harmony that employs primarily the pitches of a diatonic scale. (3) The genus of the music of ancient Greece [see also Chromatic, Enharmonic] that employs a *tetrachord constructed from a whole tone, a semitone, and a whole tone. See also Pandiatonicism.

Dibdin, Charles (b. Southampton, bapt. 15 Mar. 1745; d. London, 25 July 1814). Composer. singer, playwright, poet, and writer on the theater. In 1764 his operetta The Shepherd's Artifice was performed at Covent Garden. With librettist Isaac Bickerstaffe collaborated on successful operas. From 1768 engaged at Drury Lane; also composed for the Little Haymarket and Ranelagh theaters. Spent 1776 to 1778 in France. The first manager of the Royal Circus Theatre (1782–84); after 1785 devoted much time to memoirs and novels. Composed over 60 operas, pantomimes, and "dialogues"; also composed hundreds of songs, catches, and glees.

Dice music. See Aleatory music.

Dichterliebe [Ger., Poet's Love]. A *song cycle by Schumann, op. 48 (1840), consisting of settings of 16 poems by Heinrich Heine.

Dichtung [Ger.]. Poem; symphonische Dichtung, *symphonic poem.

Didjeridu. An Australian aboriginal trumpet made of wood or bamboo. The player maintains a low-pitched drone that is punctuated with bursts of higher partials. In addition, the player sings into the instrument while blowing, thus producing a great variety of pitches, timbres, and rhythms.

Dido and Aeneas. Opera in three acts by Purcell (libretto by Nahum Tate after Book 4 of Virgil's Aeneid), produced at Josias Priest's boarding school for young ladies in Chelsea, London, in 1689. Setting: Carthage, after the fall of Troy.

Diepenbrock, Alphons (Johannes Maria) (b. Amsterdam, 2 Sept. 1862; d. there, 5 Apr. 1921). Composer. From 1894 gave private lessons in Greek and Latin and devoted himself to music, including Renaissance music as well as works of Beethoven, Wagner, and Debussy. His large output, which consists almost exclusively of choral and solo vocal music (Fünf Gesänge nach Goethe, 1884; Te Deum, 1897) is characterized by Wagnerian harmony and Debussian modality.

Dieren, Bernard van (b. Rotterdam, 27 Dec. 1887; d. London, 24 Apr. 1936). Composer and writer on music. Studied composition in Germany; in 1909 resettled in the Netherlands, and from 1910 devoted himself chiefly to composition. His music, characterized by polyphonic complexity, include a comic opera; choral works (Balsazar, 1908); orchestral works (Anjou, 1935); chamber music; some 70 songs.

Dies irae [Lat., Day of wrath]. A rhymed *sequence, the text of which is attributed to Thomas of Celano (d. ca. 1250). One of four sequences retained by the *Council of Trent, it was officially made part of the *Requiem Mass in the 16th century. From the early 16th century, composers have often set it polyphonically. It has also been used in works such as Berlioz's *Symphonie fantastique, Liszt's Totentanz and *Dante Symphony, and Saint-Saëns's *Danse macabre.

Dièse [Fr.]. The sharp sign [see Accidental, Pitch names]. In the 17th century, the term was also used to indicate the major mode.

Diesis. (1) [It.] The sharp sign [see Accidental, Pitch names]. The term is used in this sense as early as the Renaissance. See also Dièse. (2) [Gr.] In Pythagorean writings, the minor semitone, i.e., the difference between a perfect fourth (4:3) and two whole tones (each 9:8). Thus $4:3 - (9:8)^2 = 256:243$, or 90.2 *cents. The diesis was later called limma.

Dietrich, Marlene [Maria Magdalene] (b. Weimar, 27 Dec. 1901; d. Paris, 6 May 1992). Popular singer and actress. Studied at the Berlin Hochschule für Musik and at the drama school of Max Reinhardt; achieved international fame with her performance of Friedrich Hollaender songs in the film Der Blaue Engel. Moved to the U.S., appeared in films and recorded a repertory of Tin Pan Alley, art, and folk songs.

Dieupart, Charles [François?] (b. ca. 1670; d. ca. 1740). Violinist, harpsichordist, and composer. Active in London from the early 1700s; worked with

Haym and Clayton on *Arsinoe* (1705), the first London venture in Italian-style opera, and also with Haym on Bonocini and Scarlatti operas and with Matteux on other stage works. Bach and Walter copied out some of his compositions.

Diferencia [Sp.]. In Spanish instrumental music of the 16th century, *variation. See also *Glosa,* Division.

Difference. **Differentia* [see Psalm tone].

Difference tone, differential tone. See Combination tone.

Differentia [Lat.]. Any of the various final cadences of the antiphonal *psalm tones.

Diluendo [It.]. Dying away.

Di Meola, Al (b. Jersey City, N.J., 22 July 1954). Jazz guitarist. Played jazz-rock with Barry Miles (1972–74), Chick Corea's Return to Forever (1974–76), and his own groups (beginning 1976). In the early 1980s formed a trio with John McLaughlin and Paco de Lucia, all playing acoustic guitar. His later groups combined acoustic and electric jazz fusion.

Dimeter. See Prosody.

Diminished interval. See Interval.

Diminished seventh chord. See Seventh chord.

Diminished triad. See Triad.

Diminuendo [It., abbr. *dim., dimin.*]. Becoming softer, *decrescendo* [see *Crescendo, decrescendo*].

Diminution. See Augmentation and diminution; Diminutions.

Diminutions. Also *divisions, *coloratura, passages. The division of the notes of a melody into shorter ones for the purpose of ornamentation, either written out or improvised. The terms diminutions and divisions are also sometimes used for fast-moving counterpoint to a slower *cantus firmus.* In the 17th century, the verb "break" meant to improvise diminutions. By extension, diminutions and divisions designate ornamental passages, especially at cadences, that do not strictly "divide" any existing rhythmic units.

The term diminution is used most characteristically for the arithmetical division of melody notes into steadily running passages and simple rhythmic figures.

Di molto [It.]. Very; e.g., *allegro di molto,* very fast.

D'India, Sigismondo. See India, Sigismondo d'.

D'Indy, Vincent. See Indy, Vincent d'.

Di nuovo [It.]. Again.

Direct [Lat. *custos;* Fr. *guidon;* Ger. *Kustos;* It. *guida;* Sp. *custos*]. A sign placed on the staff at the end of one line of music to indicate the first pitch of the next. Among its various forms, two of the most common are signs similar to a check mark and a mordent.

Direct fifths, octaves. See Parallel fifths, octaves.

Dirge [fr. Lat. *dirige,* the first word in an antiphon from the Office for the Dead]. A mournful song or hymn, usually slow and often with a repetitive quality, to accompany burial or memorial rites.

Dirigent, dirigieren [Ger.]. Conductor, to conduct.

Dis, disis [Ger.]. D-sharp, D-double-sharp; as late as the early 19th century, *Dis* may also mean E-flat. See Pitch names.

Discant [also descant, deschant; fr. Lat. *discantus,* singing apart]. Medieval polyphony, improvised or notated, in which all voices move at essentially the same speed. Discant may also refer to the added or newly composed voice of a polyphonic complex, to the highest part of such a complex, or to the highest register of certain instruments. See also *Clausula, Conductus, Organum, Notre Dame.*

Discant Mass. A *Mass or Mass section of the 14th or 15th century in which the *cantus firmus,* usually paraphrased, is presented in the uppermost voice or discant rather than in the tenor.

Disco. (1) [fr. Fr. *discothèque*] A nightclub at which there is dancing to recorded rather than live music. (2) A type of urban American dance music that achieved enormous popularity worldwide in the late 1970s. Disco is characterized less by its musical forms, which are extensions of basic pop formulas, than by its recording "mix," which emphasizes percussion, particularly the *hi-hat, and a thumping bass beating a straight 4/4 pattern in quarter notes.

Discography. (1) The description and cataloging of sound recordings in general. (2) A catalog of a specific category of sound recordings.

Discord. Dissonance. See Consonance and dissonance.

Disinvolto [It.]. Free, easy, jaunty.

Disis [Ger.]. See *Dis, disis.*

Disjunct. See Conjunct, disjunct.

Dissonance. See Consonance and dissonance.

Dissonant (Dissonance) Quartet. Popular name for Mozart's String Quartet in C major K. 465 (1785), so called because of the prominent dissonances in the slow introduction to the first movement.

Di Stefano, Giuseppe (b. Motta Santa Anastasia, near Catania, 24 July 1921). Tenor. Stage debut in Milan in 1946; sang with the Met (1948–68) but greatest successes occurred at La Scala beginning in 1951. From 1954 added heavier dramatic roles (Don José, Radames, Alvaro) to his repertory. Often cast with Callas in the 1950s; considered the outstanding Italian lyric tenor of the day.

Distler, Hugo (b. Nuremberg, 24 June 1908; d. Berlin, 1 Nov. 1942). Composer, organist, and choral conductor. Studied at the Leipzig Conservatory; organist at the Jacobikirche in Lübeck (1931–36); taught at the Württemberg Hochschule für Musik in Stuttgart (from 1937) and at the Staatliche Akademische Hochschule für Musik in Charlottenberg, Berlin (from 1940); director of the Berlin State and Cathedral Choir in 1942, the same year he took his own life. His harmonically bold compositional style draws especially on models from Bach and Schütz. Works include many organ pieces (including suites and trio sonatas), some orchestral and chamber music.

Dital harp. A harp with a lutelike soundbox and buttons for raising the pitch of individual strings by a semitone, invented by Edward Light in 1819. See also Harp lute.

Dithyramb [Gr. *dithyrambos*]. In ancient Greece, a song in honor of the god Dionysus.

Ditonus [Lat.]. In the Middle Ages, the interval of a major third, which consists of two whole tones.

Dittersdorf, Carl [Karl] **Ditters von** (b. Vienna, 2 Nov. 1739; d. Červená Lhotta, Bohemia, 24 Oct. 1799). Composer and violin virtuoso; born Carl Ditters. In 1750 was hired by Prince Joseph Friedrich von Sachsen-Hildburghausen for his court orchestra; there Dittersdorf studied with Francesco Trani (violin) and Bonno (composition). In 1761 became violinist for the imperial court theater; traveled to Bologna with Gluck in 1763. Served as *Kapellmeister* for the court of the Hungarian nobleman Adam Patachich (1764–69); in 1770 or 1771 appointed court composer to the Prince-Bishop of Breslau's court at Johannisberg (near Javorník, Czechoslovakia), and remained there 20 years. From the early 1780s began making frequent appearances in Vienna, where 6 of his 12 programmatic "Ovid" symphonies were performed as well as his oratorio *Hiob*. In 1786 his comic opera *Der Apotheker und der Doktor* became a huge success in Vienna, quickly traveling to nearly every major theater in Europe. Composed 8 more German comic operas during the next 5 years, 4 of which achieved international fame. From 1795 lived in southern Bohemia. Composed some 45 operas *(Il finto pazzo per amore; Die Liebe im Narrenhause)*, sacred vocal music, at least 120 symphonies, chamber music (including string quartets), and keyboard music.

Div. [It.]. Abbr. for **Divisi.*

Diva [It.]. See *Prima donna.*

Divertimento [It.]. In the second half of the 18th century, especially in Austria, any of a wide variety of secular instrumental works for chamber ensemble or soloist. In the period ca. 1750–80, the term was applied both to lighter entertainment music of an occasional nature [see Cassation, Notturno, Partita, Serenade] and to more serious genres such as the **string quartet and keyboard **sonata. For example, all of Haydn's string quartets through op. 20 (1772), and most of his keyboard sonatas through ca. 1770, were entitled divertimento by the composer. Hence, at least for the period ca. 1750–80 in Austria, the traditional association of the term divertimento with entertainment and especially occasional music, as well as with specific cycles such as the five-movement fast–minuet–slow–minuet–fast plan, cannot be justified. After ca. 1780, the term divertimento, when it appeared at all, generally designated works that were light or informal (e.g., Mozart's Divertimento/String Trio K. 563, in a six-movement cycle with two minuets). It is in the latter sense that 20th-century composers have utilized the term. See also *Divertissement.*

Divertissement [Fr.]. (1) A musical potpourri, frequently in the form of pieces extracted from an opera. (2) A group of musical pieces (dances, vocal solos, or ensembles) inserted within the acts or between the acts of an opera, play, or ballet. The genre originated in France at the end of the 17th century. (3) A French Baroque work on a mythological or allegorical subject, produced to enhance a celebration. (4) **Divertimento.*

Divided stop. In organs, the separation of a **stop into treble and bass halves in such a way that the two halves of the keyboard could use different registrations. See *Medio registro.*

Divine Liturgy. The Byzantine Mass. See also Byzantine chant.

Divine Office. See Office.

Divisi [It., abbr. *div.*]. Divided; hence, an indication in ensemble music that a group of players normally playing the same part (e.g., the first violins of an orchestra) are to be divided so as to play different parts, sometimes notated on the same staff. See also *Due, a.*

Division. In 17th- and 18th-century England, a type of **variation, often improvised, normally of a bass or *ground (whence "divisions on a ground"), performed by dividing the bass itself into running passages or other figuration in smaller note-values, by playing such figuration above the bass, or by a mixture of the two. See also Diminutions.

Division viol [It. *viola bastarda*]. An English bass *viol, smaller than the normal bass, but larger than the *lyra viol, used in playing *divisions.

Dixie. (1) Popular song by Daniel D. Emmett (1815–1904), written for Bryant's Minstrels traveling show and first published in 1860. (2) *Dixieland jazz.

Dixieland jazz. *New Orleans jazz and adaptations thereof; or that style only when played by white musicians. Included among the adaptations are *Chicago jazz of the 1920s, the small combo music of white New York contemporaries (Red Nichols, Miff Mole, the Dorsey brothers, et al.), and since the 1940s, a somewhat integrated international revival.

Dixon, (Charles) Dean (b. New York, 10 Jan. 1915; d. Zurich, 3 Nov. 1976). Conductor. Studied conducting with Albert Stoessel at Juilliard; founded the New York Chamber Orchestra (1938), the American Youth Orchestra (1944). The first African American to lead the New York Philharmonic (1941); subsequently conducted the Boston Symphony, the NBC Orchestra, the Philadelphia Orchestra, the Israel Philharmonic (1950–51), the Göteborg Symphony (1953–60). Principal conductor of the Hesse Radio Symphony at Frankfurt am Main (1961–70) and of the Sydney Symphony (1964–67).

Dlugoszewski, Lucia (b. Detroit, 16 June 1934). Composer. Studied piano (Sultan) and composition (Varèse) in New York. Beginning in 1951 composed for "timbre piano," using bows and plectra directly on the strings; invented some 100 percussion instruments prominent in works from the 1950s (*Eight Clear Places*, 1958–60). Compositions often employ a technique of "leaping" structures based on surprise and speed (*Strange Tenderness of Naked Leaping*, orchestra, 1977); other concepts include "elusivity" and "tilt" (*Wilderness Elegant Tilt*, concerto for 11 instruments and orchestra, 1981–84).

Do, doh. See Pitch names, Solmization, Tonic Sol-fa.

Dobro. A guitar with a large, circular, metal resonator under the bridge. It has been manufactured in the U.S. since the 1920s and is used in Hawaiian and in country and western music.

Dobrowen, Issay (Alexandrovich) [Barabeichik, Ishok Israelevich] (b. Nizhni-Novgorod, 27 Feb. 1891; d. Oslo, 9 Dec. 1953). Conductor. Studied piano with Igumnov at the Moscow Conservatory, with Godowsky in Vienna. Obtained a post at the Moscow Conservatory, 1917; conducting debut at the Bolshoi,

1919. Led the Vienna Volksoper, 1924–27; the Royal Opera at Sofia, 1927–28; the Oslo Philharmonic, 1927–31; associate conductor of the New York Philharmonic, 1932–33; conductor of the San Francisco Symphony, 1933–35, the Budapest Opera, 1936–39, the Palestine Symphony from 1937, the Göteborg Symphony, 1939–41, the Stockholm Opera, 1941–45. After World War II conducted opera at major houses throughout Europe, sometimes also acting as stage director.

Doctrine of affections. See Affections, doctrine of.

Doctrine of figures. See Figures, doctrine of.

Dodds, Baby [Warren] (b. New Orleans, 24 Dec. 1898; d. Chicago, 14 Feb. 1959). Jazz drummer; brother of Johnny Dodds. Played on Mississippi riverboats with Fate Marable (1918–21), then joined King Oliver in San Francisco (1922). In Chicago became a leading jazz drummer. Worked with Oliver (1922–23), Freddie Keppard (1924), and Johnny (1924, 1927–29, intermittently 1930–40) and also recorded with Louis Armstrong and Jelly Roll Morton. Active in the revival of New Orleans jazz in Chicago, New Orleans, and New York, worked with Jimmie Noone (1940–41), Bunk Johnson (1944–45), and Sidney Bechet.

Dodds, Johnny [John M.] (b. New Orleans, 12 Apr. 1892; d. Chicago, 8 Aug. 1940). Jazz clarinetist; brother of Baby Dodds. Played with Kid Ory in New Orleans (intermittently ca. 1912–17, 1919) and King Oliver in Chicago (1920–21, 1922–23) and California (1921–22). One of the finest blues soloists among clarinetists, led the band at Kelly's Stables in Chicago (1924–29) while also recording with Louis Armstrong, Jelly Roll Morton, ad hoc small groups, and as a leader.

Dodecaphonic. *Twelve-tone.

Dodge, Charles (Malcolm) (b. Ames, Iowa, 5 June 1942). Composer. Studied at the Univ. of Iowa, Columbia (with Chou and Luening), and Princeton (with Winham, 1969–70); has taught at Columbia (1970–77) and at Brooklyn College (from 1977), directing the Center for Computer Music. Wrote some works for traditional performers (*Distribution, Redistribution*, clarinet, violin, and piano, 1982), but his main interest has been in computer music (*The Voice of Binky*, 1989), some with live performers and often involving synthesized voices (*He Met Her in the Park*, 1983).

Dodgson, Stephen [Cuthbert Vivian] (b. London, 17 March 1924). Composer. Studied with R. O. Morris at the Royal College of Music, then taught there (1964–82). Wrote many works for solo guitar as well as 2 concertos for guitar and chamber orchestra (1959, 1972) and a quintet for guitar and strings. Other works include the opera *Margaret Catchpole* (1979); concertos for bassoon (1969), clarinet (1983), and trombone (1986); a Magnificat (1975); other vocal works; chamber music; 3 piano sonatas (1959, 1975, 1983).

Dohnányi, Christoph von (b. Berlin, 8 Sept. 1929). Conductor. Grandson of Ernst von Dohnányi, he studied at the Berlin Hochschule für Musik and in Munich. Chorusmaster, then conductor at the Frankfurt Opera, 1952–56. Conductor of the Lübeck Orchestra, 1957–63; of the Kassel Orchestra, 1963–64; of the West German Radio Orchestra at Cologne, 1964–68. Chief conductor of the Frankfurt Opera, 1968–77. Musical director of the Hamburg Opera, 1977–83; of the Cleveland Symphony from 1984.

Dohnányi, Ernő [Ernst von] (b. Pozsony [Bratislava], 27 July 1877; d. New York, 9 Feb. 1960). Composer, pianist, and conductor. Studied in Pozsony and at the Budapest Royal Academy (1894–97). Brahms recommended his Piano Quintet for performance in Vienna. Dohnányi studied piano briefly with Eugen d'Albert in Berlin, then concertized extensively in Europe and the U.S. Professor of piano at the Berlin Hochschule für Musik (1908–15); director of the Royal Academy in Budapest (1918–20) and conductor of the Budapest Philharmonic (from 1921); guest lecturer and conductor at American universities (1925–27); director of piano and composition at the Franz Liszt Royal Academy in Budapest. From 1949 taught at Florida State Univ. in Tallahassee. Dohnányi forged a Brahmsian style in his compositions; they include operas; 2 symphonies (1900–1901, 1943–44); 2 piano concertos (1897–98, 1946–47); *Variationen über ein Kinderlied* (piano and orchestra, 1914); 2 piano quintets (1895, 1914), 3 string quartets; piano works.

Doigté [Fr.]. *Fingering; *d. fourchu, *cross fingering.

Dolce [It.]. Sweet; usually also soft; *dolcemente,* sweetly, softly; *dolcissimo,* extremely sweet, soft.

Dolcian, dolcino. *Dulzian* [see Curtal], dulcian.

Dolente [It.]. Sad.

Doles, Johann Friedrich (b. Steinbach-Hallenberg, Thuringia, 23 Apr. 1715; d. Leipzig, 8 Feb. 1797). Composer. Enrolled at the Univ. of Leipzig in 1739 and directed the city's Grosses Konzert; studied with Bach. From 1744 Kantor in Freiberg; from 1755 Kantor of the Thomaskirche in Leipzig. Composed many sacred works, including some 175 cantatas, 35 motets, 8 Passions, 5 Masses, sacred lieder, more than 200 4-part chorales, and chorale preludes.

Dolmetsch, (Eugène) Arnold (b. Le Mans, 24 Feb. 1858; d. Haslemere, 28 Feb. 1940). Performer and historian of early music. Studied violin with Vieuxtemps in Brussels (1881–83) and with Henry Holmes at the Royal College of Music (1883–85). While teaching at Dulwich (1885–89) collected, repaired, and played old instruments. Founded the Dolmetsch Trio and devoted himself to performances on original instruments. Toured the U.S. in 1902; settled in Boston (1904–11), where he concertized and supervised the building of virginals and harpsichords at Chickering & Sons; similarly in Paris (1911–14) for Gaveau. Published *The Interpretation of the Music of the 17th and 18th Centuries* (1915; 2nd ed., 1946; R: 1969), a pioneering text. Moved to Haslemere in 1917. From 1928 the Dolmetsch Fund supported him and the spread of his teaching.

Doloroso [It.]. Painful, sorrowful.

Dolphy, Eric (Allan) (b. Los Angeles, 20 June 1928; d. Berlin, 29 June 1964). Jazz alto saxophonist, bass clarinetist, and flutist. Joined Chico Hamilton (1958–59) and Charles Mingus (1959–60), played on Ornette Coleman's album *Free Jazz* (1960), and with the trumpeter Booker Little led a quintet (1961). Played intermittently with Coltrane (1961–63), Mingus, and as a leader. Dolphy's music ranged from bop to free jazz; singlehandedly established the bass clarinet as a convincing vehicle for jazz improvisation.

Dolzaina [It.]. A wind instrument of the 16th and 17th centuries, perhaps a *shawm and possibly very similar to the earlier *douçaine.* See also *Dulzaina.*

Dömbra, domra [Russ.]. A *long-necked lute of Soviet Central Asia and an antecedent of the *balalaika. It has either two or three strings and may or may not have frets.

Domchor [Ger.]. The choir of a German cathedral *(Dom).*

Domestic Symphony. See *Symphonia domestica.*

Dominant. (1) The fifth *scale degree of the major or minor scale. The *triad and the *seventh chord built on this degree as root are the dominant triad and dominant seventh, respectively. As part of a *cadence, both of these chords are most often resolved to the tonic triad because of the presence in both of the leading tone and the supertonic. The relationship of dominant and tonic expressed in such a cadence, which is a function of both *counterpoint and *harmony, is the most powerful in *tonal music and is fundamental to the structure of tonal melodies and of both small- and large-scale forms [see Binary and ternary form, Sonata form]. When serving as the root of a chord, the fifth scale degree is identified in *harmonic analysis by the numeral V or the letter D (for dominant). Secondary dominants [see also Toniciza- tion] are the dominants of degrees other than the tonic and are designated as follows: V of II (or simply V/II; e.g., in the key of C, the fifth above D, namely A), V of III (V/III), etc. (2) For the dominant of the modes, see Mode, Psalm tone.

Dominant seventh chord. See Seventh chord, Dominant.

Domingo, Plácido (b. Madrid, 21 Jan. 1941). Tenor and conductor. Studied at the Mexico City Conserva- tory and with Carlo Morelli. Debuted as Alfredo with the Monterrey Opera in 1960; U.S. debut in 1960, singing with Joan Sutherland. Sang with the Hebrew Opera in Tel Aviv (1962–65); Met debut 1966. One of the two or three best lyric and bel canto tenors of his generation, has also sung dramatic roles such as Otello; conducted the New York City Opera and at the Met; appointed artistic director of the Washing- ton Opera in 1994. The 1994 telecast of the second "Three Tenors" concert (with Pavarotti and Carreras) was seen by over a billion people worldwide.

Dominica [Lat.]. Sunday. See also *Feria.*

Domino, Fats [Antoine] (b. New Orleans, 26 Feb. 1928). Rock-and-roll singer and pianist. Worked in the band of trumpeter Dave Bartholomew; between 1950 and 1960 released several singles that helped establish rock-and-roll with white audiences ("Ain't That a Shame," 1955; "Blueberry Hill," 1956). After a decline in popularity began to tour again in the late 1970s.

Domp(e). See Dump.

Don Carlos. Opera in five acts by Verdi (libretto in French by François Joseph Méry and Camille Du- Locle, based on Schiller's play), produced in Paris in 1867. A revised version in four acts and in Italian was produced in Milan in 1884. Setting: Spain, mid-16th century.

Don Giovanni [It., Don Juan]. Opera *(*dramma gio- coso)* in two acts by Mozart. The libretto, by Lorenzo da Ponte, has literary predecessors in Tirso de Molina's *El burlador de Sevilla,* Molière's *Le festin de pierre,* Goldoni's *Don Giovanni Tenorio ossia Il dissoluto,* and most directly Giovanni Bertati's li- bretto *Don Giovanni Tenorio, ossia Il convitato di pietra.* The opera was first produced in Prague in 1787 under the title *Il dissoluto punito, ossia Il Don Giovanni* (The Rake Punished, or Don Giovanni). Mozart made a few changes in the work for the first performance in Vienna in 1788. Setting: Seville, 17th century.

Don Juan. Symphonic poem by Richard Strauss, op. 20 (1888–89), based on a verse play of the same name by Nicolaus Lenau.

Don Pasquale. Opera in three acts by Donizetti (li- bretto by the composer and Giovanni Ruffini after Angelo Anelli's libretto *Ser Marc' Antonio*), pro- duced in Paris in 1843. Setting: Rome in the early 19th century.

Don Quixote. (1) "Fantastic Variations on a Theme of Knightly Character" for orchestra by Richard Strauss, op. 35 (1896–97), based on the novel by Cervantes. Don Quixote and Sancho Panza are often represented musically by prominent solo cello and viola parts, respectively. (2) Ballet by Léon Minkus (book and choreography by Marius Petipa), pro- duced in Moscow in 1869. A version with choreogra- phy revised by Alexander Gorsky was produced in Moscow in 1900. A revival of the latter, with some new music and dances, was produced in Moscow in 1940 and has remained in the repertory. (3) Opera [Fr. *Don Quichotte*] in five acts by Massenet (libretto by Henri Cain after Jacques Le Lorrain's play based on Cervantes's novel), produced in Monte Carlo in 1910. (4) Three songs [Fr. *Don Quichotte à Dul- cinée*] by Ravel on poems by Paul Morand composed in 1932–33 for baritone and chamber orchestra (also in a version with piano) intended for use in a film.

Don Rodrigo. Opera in three acts by Alberto Gina- stera (libretto by Alejandro Casona), produced in Buenos Aires in 1964. Setting: Spain in the 8th cen- tury.

Donato, Anthony (b. Prague, Nebr., 8 Mar. 1909). Composer and violinist. Attended Eastman (compo- sition with Rogers and Hanson; violin with Tinlot; conducting with Goossens); taught at Drake Univ., Iowa State Teachers College, the Univ. of Texas, and Northwestern (1947–76). Works include *Centennial Ode* (1967); an opera; orchestral works; chamber and piano music; choral music; songs.

Donatoni, Franco (b. Verona, 9 June 1927). Com- poser. Studied at the Milan (1946–47) and Bologna conservatories (1948–51); further composition study with Pizetti in Siena. In 1952 met Maderna, and the next year attended the Darmstadt lectures; taught at conservatories in Bologna, Turin, and Milan, as well as at the Univ. of Bologna (from 1971) and the Ac- cademia Chigiana summer courses in Venice. Early works are indebted to Bartók; serial works from the late 1950s were influenced by Webern, Boulez, and Stockhausen. Beginning 1961 employed aleatory procedures and constructed permutable forms (*Black and White,* 37 strings, 1964). In works of the late 1960s continued to search for new instrumental ef- fects and reintroduced traditional notation. Other works include *Ecco* (chamber orchestra, 1986); *Cloches III* (two pianos, two percussionists, 1991).

Donizetti, (Domenico) Gaetano (Maria) (b. Bergamo, 29 Nov. 1797; d. there, 8 Apr. 1848). Composer. Studied music at the school of J. S. Mayr (1806–14) and with Mattei at the Bologna Conservatory. Composed several operas before the opera seria *Zoraide di Granata* (1822) established his career. From 1822 worked much in Naples; *Anna Bolena* (Milan, 1830) moved him into the front rank of Italian composers and put him in demand everywhere; his next great success was *L'*elisir d'amore*. Made his first visit to Paris in 1835; in 1836–38 composed one opera a year for Venice. During this period produced only four new operas at the San Carlo in Naples, but these included three of his most important (*Maria Stuarda*, 1834; **Lucia di Lammermoor; Roberto Devereux*, 1837). Appointed counterpoint and composition professor (1834) and acting director (1837) at the Naples Conservatory. In Paris his *La *fille du régiment* was highly popular, as was *La favorite* (1840). The success of *Linda di Chamounix* (1842) in Vienna led to Donizetti's appointment as *maestro di cappella e di camera e compositore* at the imperial court. In 1843 produced his greatest comic opera, **Don Pasquale*. Besides the 60 operas performed in his lifetime, works include much sacred and instrumental music.

Donnermaschine [Ger.]. **Thunder machine.

Donostia, José Antonio de (b. San Sebastián, 10 Jan. 1886; d. Lecároz, Navarra, 30 Aug. 1956). Composer. Studied composition with Eugene Cools and Roussel in Paris and spent time in both Latin America and France. His compositions encompass sacred works, such as staged cantatas and a Requiem Mass (1945), as well as solo and chamber music; also made important contributions to Basque folk music.

Donovan, Richard Frank (b. New Haven, 29 Nov. 1891; d. Middletown, Conn., 22 Aug. 1970). Composer and organist. Studied at Yale, and at the Institute of Musical Art in New York, and with Widor in Paris. Taught at Smith College, in New York, and at Yale (1928–60); conducted the New Haven Symphony (1936–51) and was organist and choirmaster at Christ Church (1928–65). Composed works for orchestra (*Epos,* 1963); chamber and keyboard music; a Mass, Magnificat, and other choral works; songs (*Five Elizabethan Lyrics,* 1963).

Doppel [Ger.]. Double; *Doppel-Be,* double flat; *Doppelchörig,* for double chorus, with a course of two strings; *Doppelgriff,* double stop; *Doppelkreuz,* double sharp; *Doppelpedal,* double pedal, double action pedal (as in the harp); *Doppelpunkt,* double dot; *Doppelschlag,* turn; *Doppelstrich,* double bar; *Dop-*

pelzunge, double tonguing; with reference to instruments such as the horn, duplex.

Doppelt so schnell [Ger.]. Twice as fast.

Dopper, Cornelis (b. Stadskanaal, 7 Feb. 1870; d. Amsterdam, 18 Sept. 1939). Composer and conductor. From 1877 to 1890 studied at the Leipzig Conservatory with Karl Wendling (piano), Jadassohn (theory), and Reinecke (composition). Conducted the Netherlands Opera from 1896. Assistant conductor of the Concertgebouw Orchestra (1908–31). Compositions manifest a late-Romantic outlook, with special care for details of orchestration.

Doppio [It.]. Double; *d. bemolle,* double flat; *d. diesis,* double sharp; *d. movimento,* twice as fast; *d. pedale,* double pedal.

Dorati, Antal (b. Budapest, 9 Apr. 1906; d. Gerzensee, near Bern, 13 Nov. 1988). Conductor and composer. Studied with Léo Weiner, Bartók, and Kodály at the Franz Liszt Academy. Répétiteur and conductor at the Budapest Opera, 1924–28; assistant conductor at the Dresden Opera (1928–29); musical director and conductor at the Münster Opera (1930–32); conductor and music director of the Ballet russe de Monte Carlo (1933–41); music director, American Ballet Theater (1941–45); director of New Opera Company in New York (1941–42). Music director, Dallas Symphony (1945–49); conductor and then music director, Minneapolis Symphony (1949–60); chief conductor of the BBC Symphony (1962–66); principal conductor of the Stockholm Philharmonic (1966–70); musical director of the National Symphony (1970–77); senior conductor of the Royal Philharmonic, London (1975–78); music director of the Detroit Symphony (1977–81). Composed works in large forms; made more than 500 recordings.

Doret, Gustave (b. Aigle, Vaud, Switzerland, 20 Sept. 1866; d. Lausanne, 19 Apr. 1943). Composer and conductor. Studied with Joachim in Berlin (1885–87) and with Dubois and Massenet in Paris; began an active conducting career in Paris and in 1894 (when he also led the premiere of Debussy's *Faun*) was appointed director of the Opéra-comique; established the Théâtre du Jorat in Mezières (near Lausanne), for which he wrote many lighter stage works with René Morax. His light works were popular in France, Switzerland, and Belgium. Wrote mainly vocal music.

Dorian. See Mode. The Dorian sixth is the interval of a major sixth formed above the tonic in a minor key (e.g., D–B♮ in D minor), since in the conventional description of the church modes, the Dorian mode differs from the pure minor scale only in having a major sixth above the tonic.

Dorian Toccata and Fugue. Popular name for Bach's Toccata and Fugue in D minor for organ BWV 538 (composed during Bach's Weimar years, 1708–17), written without Bb in the key signature and thus having the appearance of a composition in the *Dorian mode. Bb is consistently specified as an accidental, however, in keeping with a common practice in the 17th and early 18th centuries.

Dorn, Heinrich (Ludwig Egmont) (b. Königsberg, 14 Nov. 1800 or 1804; d. Berlin, 10 Jan. 1892). Conductor, composer, and teacher. Studied in Berlin with Berger (piano), Zelter and Klein (composition). From 1828, theater conductor, Königsberg; 1829–32, music director and theater conductor, Leipzig, where Schumann and Clara Wieck studied with him; 1832, conductor, Hamburg; 1832–42, music director, St. Peter's cathedral, Riga, where he met Wagner and formed the basis for his later opposition to him and his music; 1843, music director and theater conductor, Cologne; 1844–47, directed Lower Rhine Music Festival; 1845, founded Rheinische Musikschule, which in 1850 became the Cologne Conservatory; 1849–69, conductor, Berlin Opera. Published a 7-volume collection of memoirs and opinions, *Aus meinem Leben* (1870–86).

Dorsey, Jimmy [James] (b. Shenandoah, Pa., 29 Feb. 1904; d. New York, 12 June 1957). Jazz and popular clarinetist, alto saxophonist, and bandleader. Brother of Tommy Dorsey. Played dixieland jazz with Red Nichols; formed the Dorsey Brothers Orchestra (1934), taking over sole leadership after a dispute with Tommy (1935–53); the band's greatest hit record was "Green Eyes" (1941). The Dorsey Brothers Orchestra re-formed in 1953, with Jimmy briefly assuming control of the big band after Tommy's death.

Dorsey, Thomas A(ndrew) [Georgia Tom; Barrelhouse Tommy] (b. Villa Rica, Ga. 1 July 1899; d. Chicago, 23 Jan. 1993). Blues and gospel pianist, singer, and songwriter. Accompanied Ma Rainey (1924–28), then made influential recordings with many blues players, especially guitarist Tampa Red (1928–32), under several names including The Hokum Boys. Contributed numerous blues songs to the standard repertory before turning exclusively to gospel music ca. 1932; composed many gospel songs.

Dorsey, Tommy [Thomas] (b. Shenandoah, Pa., 19 Nov. 1905; d. Greenwich, Conn., 26 Nov. 1956). Jazz and popular trombonist and bandleader; brother of Jimmy Dorsey. After an argument with Jimmy, left the Dorsey Brothers big band (1934–35) to form his own, which at times included Bunny Berigan, Buddy Rich, and Frank Sinatra. From 1953 again led a big band with Jimmy.

Dot [Fr. *point;* Ger. *Punkt;* It. *punto;* Sp. *puntillo*]. (1) In modern musical *notation, a sign placed after a note so as to increase its duration by one-half. For its antecedents, see Mensural notation, *Punctus.* See also Dotted notes. (2) A sign placed above or below a note to indicate *staccato. (3) In some keyboard music of the early 16th century, a sign placed above or below a note to indicate chromatic alteration. See also Tablature.

Dotted notes. Notes written with a dot of addition (other uses of the dot are discussed under Notation, Staccato, *Notes inégales,* Lombard rhythm). A dot written after a note increases its value by half. A second dot adds a quarter of the value and a third dot, an eighth [Ex. 1]. Double dotting is rare before the 19th century, but may be found as early as *Les pièces de Clavessin* (Paris, 1670) of Jacques Champion de Chambonnières [Ex. 2]. Triple dotting is very rare but occurs in the music of Robert Schumann. In mu-

Dotted notes.   2. Chambonnières, Courante, *Les pièces de clavessin,* bk. 1 (1670).   3. Bach, Toccata in G minor BWV 915.

sic before 1800, dots were often written as in Ex. 2, that is, they were positioned where a note of equivalent value would come in the measure, even if a bar line separated them from the parent note. Such dots are easy to mistake for staccato dots pertaining to another part.

Although early theory and instruction books almost invariably define dotted notes as above, dots were in practice very frequently used to prolong the value of a note as long as necessary to fill in the time preceding the complementary short note or group. If the short notes were played slowly or quickly, according to the discretion of the executant, then the dotted note was curtailed or lengthened to compensate.

From the 17th to the early 19th century, dotted figures were commonly used against triplets, as in Ex. 3a, instead of the notation in Ex. 3b. Ordinarily, the short note of the dotted figure should coincide with the last note of the triplet, as clearly it must in Ex. 3. But J. F. Agricola reported that Bach taught his pupils to distinguish between the dotted figure and the triplet rhythm, and Quantz agreed. Yet assimilation to triplets was recommended by C. P. E. Bach.

Double. (1) To perform or to specify the performance of the same note or notes by two parts, either at the same pitch level or in octaves. Two identical instruments may double one another, as well as two different instruments, an instrument and a voice, or even two lines of a keyboard composition. (2) To play two instruments in a single piece; to be capable of playing two different instruments; to sing two roles (or to sing one and understudy another) in an opera. (3) Instruments of low pitch, usually an octave below the normal pitch, e.g., *double bass, double bassoon; thus often a synonym for *contra. (4) Two instruments combined in one, e.g., *double clarinet, double *horn. A double *harpsichord has two manuals. For the double action harp, see Harp. (5) [Fr.] A variation, particularly in French harpsichord suites, usually characterized by consistent motion in note-values twice (or three times) as fast as the original movement.

Doublé [Fr.]. In 17th- and 18th-century French harpsichord music, *turn.

Double action. See Harp.

Double appoggiatura. Any of the three ways in which two *appoggiaturas can be used: (1) two appoggiaturas performed simultaneously, at the interval of a third or a sixth; (2) two conjunct appoggiaturas approaching the main note from the interval of a third above or below it [see Slide]; (3) two disjunct appoggiaturas, one being placed below the main note, the other above it [see *Anschlag*].

Double ballade. In 14th-century French poetry and music, a poem consisting of two *ballades or a musical work in which two *ballades* are set simultaneously.

Double bar. Two parallel lines drawn vertically through a staff or the staves of a score to indicate the end of a composition or a section of it.

Double bass [Fr. *contrebasse;* Ger. *Kontrabass;* It. *contrabbasso;* Sp. *contrabajo*]. The lowest-pitched member of the family of bowed stringed instruments and a hybrid of the *viol and *violin families; also bass viol, contrabass, string bass, bass. Its four strings are tuned $E_1 A_1 D G$, notated one octave higher. Some instruments have a fifth string tuned C_1 (in jazz and popular music more often c), and in orchestras, the E string of the four-stringed instrument is often fitted with an extension that, by means of levers along the fingerboard, permits playing down to C_1. The highest pitch in orchestral works is rarely above a (notated a'). Tuning is by means of a mechanism incorporating worm gears. The overall length of instruments in current use ranges from 180 to 200 cm. (71 to 79 in.), the length of the vibrating string being from 105 to 110 cm. (41 to 43 in.). The sloping shoulders and flat back of most instruments testify to ancestry in the viol family, as does the tuning in fourths rather than fifths [see ill. under Violin]. Two types of bow are used: the French type, held with the palm downward, and the German type, held with the palm upward as in viol playing [see Bow, Bowing].

Shape, size, number of strings, and tuning varied considerably into the 20th century. The instrument's earliest ancestors were 16th-century members of the viol family, whence the term double-bass viol. The Italian term *violone was and is applied to some of these ancestors. As late as the late 18th century, the most common instrument of this general type in use in Austria seems to have been one with five strings, tuned $F_1 A_1 D F\sharp A$, and frets, though writers of the period also mention four- and three-stringed instruments without frets. Three-stringed instruments, tuned $A_1 D G$, $G_1 D G$, or $G_1 D A$, were well known in the 18th century and common throughout Europe in the 19th, persisting into the 20th. The modern tuning of the four-stringed instrument originated in the late 17th century but became standard only in the 19th as the four-stringed instrument itself began its rise to prominence. The first consistent extensions of the range down to C_1 also took place in the 19th century.

Double-bass clarinet. Contrabass *clarinet.

Double C (D, etc.). See Pitch names.

Double cadence [Fr.]. See Turn.

Double chorus. Two choruses that perform in a single work, often in alternation. See Polychoral.

Double clarinet. A wind instrument consisting of two cane or wooden pipes, side by side, with a single reed at the top of each. In some, the finger holes of the two pipes are next to one another, each pair of holes being covered by one finger. Other examples have holes in one pipe only, the other pipe being a drone. In a few cases, the pipes are separate, each fingered with one hand.

Double concerto. A *concerto for two solo instruments and orchestra.

Double counterpoint. *Invertible counterpoint in two parts.

Double croche [Fr.]. Sixteenth *note.

Double cursus. In some types of medieval music, the repetition (to new words with the same poetic form) of a section that may itself consist of repeated elements, as in some examples of the *sequence (e.g., AABBCC AABBCC).

Double dot, double dotting. A second dot adds a quarter of the value of the plain written note to its dotted value; e.g., a double-dotted quarter note equals seven sixteenth notes. See Dotted notes.

Double flat. See Accidental.

Double fugue. (1) A *fugue in which two subjects are first given full and independent treatment, each in its own turn, and then treated in contrapuntal combination with one another. Fugues that treat three and four subjects in a similar way are termed triple and quadruple fugues, respectively. Examples of double fugues in the works of Bach include the fugue in G♯ minor in the second book of *The Well-Tempered Clavier* and the fugue from the Toccata and Fugue in F major for organ BWV 540. (2) A fugue in which the subject is accompanied consistently and from the outset by a countersubject, thus giving the impression of a fugue based on two subjects simultaneously.

Double horn. See Horn, Duplex instruments.

Double leading tone. In a *cadence (especially in music of the 14th and 15th centuries), two leading tones, one of which rises by half step to the primary cadential pitch, the other rising by half step to the fourth below or its equivalent in another octave.

Double motet. A *motet in which two different texts are set simultaneously in different voices.

Double pedal. On the organ, the playing of two pitches or parts simultaneously in the pedal.

Double reed. See Reed.

Double sharp. See Accidental.

Double stop. The execution of two (or more, in which case the terms triple or quadruple stop are sometimes employed) pitches simultaneously or in such a way as to create the effect of a simultaneity on a bowed, stringed instrument; also multiple stop. This is accomplished by means of stopping (i.e., fingering) strings with the left hand in such a way as to allow two or more pitches to sound simultaneously, even if the technique of *bowing [see also Bow], because of the curvature of the *bridge on such instruments, requires that they be bowed in succession.

Double-time. In jazz, a tempo twice as fast as the prevailing tempo, often introduced in the course of an improvised solo.

Double tonguing. See Tonguing.

Double trill. In keyboard music, two trills on two different pitches, often a third apart, performed simultaneously with the same hand.

Doubles cordes [Fr.]. *Double stop.

Doubling. See Double.

Douçaine [Fr.]. A wind instrument of the 14th and 15th centuries, perhaps a *shawm and possibly similar to the later *dolzaina.

Doucement [Fr.]. Gently, softly.

Douloureux [Fr.]. Painful, sorrowful.

Doux [Fr.]. Sweet, soft.

Dowland, John (b. London? 1563; d. there, buried 20 Feb. 1626). Composer and lutenist. In Paris from 1580 until about 1584; earned the B.Mus. from Oxford in 1588. After travels to Germany and Italy returned to England in late 1596 or early 1597; might have taken a court post in Kassel in 1598. Late that year became a court lutenist for Christian IV of Denmark, a post he retained until 1606, when an English nobleman gave him a position. In 1612 won a post at the English royal court. His compositions, widely known and popular both in England and on the Continent, include settings of Psalms or sacred songs and pieces for instrumental consort (*Lachrimae or Seven Teares,* London, 1604), as well as dances, arrangements, and compositions for solo lute. Most important are the secular lute songs or airs, the majority for 1 voice and lute or 4 voices.

Down in the Valley. Folk opera in one act by Kurt Weill (libretto by Arnold Sundgaard), produced in Bloomington, Indiana, in 1948. Setting: the U.S. in the 1940s.

Downbeat. (1) The first and thus metrically strongest beat of a measure [see Meter], usually signaled in *conducting with a downward motion. (2) The first beat of a piece and thus also the conductor's signal to begin a piece.

Down-bow. See Bowing (1).

Doxology. An expression of glory to God the Father and usually also to the Son and the Holy Ghost. The Greater Doxology is the *Gloria ("Gloria in excelsis Deo") of the Roman Catholic *Mass. The Lesser Doxology is the text "Gloria Patri et Filio et Spiritui Sancto; sicut erat in principio, et nunc, et semper, et in saecula saeculorum. Amen." (Glory be to the Father and to the Son and to the Holy Ghost; as it was in the beginning, is now, and ever shall be, world without end. Amen.) The Lesser Doxology is sung following the Psalms of the Office [see Psalmody], the verse of the introit, most canticles, and in a few other circumstances. In Protestant churches, the term may refer to the metrical text "Praise God from whom all blessings flow," often sung to the *Old Hundredth tune.

Draeseke, Felix (August Bernhard) (b. Coburg, 7 Oct. 1835; d. Dresden, 26 Feb. 1913). Composer. Studied at the Leipzig Conservatory and with Rietz; became a firm adherent of the New German School. Composed long symphonic poems and an opera. Moved to Lausanne in 1862 and to Dresden in 1876, teaching at the conservatory there (from 1884); from 1892 taught at the Univ. of Berlin. A prolific composer; works include the oratorio tetralogy *Christus* (1895–99); 5 symphonies and operas; chamber music; choral music.

Drag. A common stroke on the snare drum, the first two notes played with one hand, the concluding main note with the other: ♫♪

Draghi, Antonio (b. Rimini, ca. 1634; d. Vienna, 16 Jan. 1700). Composer and librettist. Perhaps served in the court orchestra at Mantua; possibly also studied at Venice, where he appeared as a bass singer in 1657. Served the Viennese court from 1658 to his death, first as a member of the dowager Empress Eleonora's Kapelle; took over as her Kapellmeister in 1669; director of dramatic music for the imperial court (from 1673) and imperial Kapellmeister (1682–1700). In addition to 124 stage works and 50 vocal chamber pieces, produced over a dozen oratorios, some 30 *sepolcri* and a variety of other sacred works, as well as many libretti.

Draghi, Giovanni Battista (b. Italy, ca. 1640; d. London, 1708). Keyboardist and composer. Brought to England in the 1660s by King Charles II; became organist at the queen's Catholic chapel (1673) and at the chapel of James II (1687). Composed songs for inclusion in plays and published collections along with suites and other keyboard music; provided the

setting for Dryden's *Ode for St. Cecilia's Day* in 1687.

Dragonetti, Domenico (Carlo Maria) (b. Venice, 7 Apr. 1763; d. London, 16 Apr. 1846). Double bassist and composer. Mostly self-taught, he became a phenomenal virtuoso. From 1794 a leading figure in London music as first double bassist in many orchestras. Composed concertos and much chamber music for bass, almost none of it published until recent times.

Drame lyrique [Fr.], **dramma lirico** [It.]. From the middle of the 19th century, the term *drame lyrique* has been used, with no great precision, to refer to French operas that cannot be comfortably accommodated by the designations *opéra comique* or *grand opéra*. Massenet called his opera *Werther* a *drame lyrique*, as did Debussy his *Pelléas et Mélisande*. *Dramma lirico* is used as a subtitle occasionally by Verdi (*Nabucco, I Lombardi, Ernani, Otello*, among others) and Puccini (*Manon Lescaut, Turandot*).

Dramma giocoso [It.]. A comic opera with some serious elements. The term was introduced in the middle of the 18th century by Carlo Goldoni to describe his librettos in which serious characters, from an aristocratic social class, interacted with comic servants and peasants. The most famous example of *dramma giocoso* is Mozart's *Don Giovanni*.

Dramma lirico [It.]. See *Drame lyrique*.

Dramma per musica [It.]. A designation that commonly follows the title in 17th- and 18th-century librettos, usually meaning that the text has been written expressly to be set to music.

Dramma sacro. [It.]. An *oratorio.

Drängend [Ger.]. Pressing on, quickening.

Drdla, František [Franz] Alois (b. Žďár nad Sázavou, Moravia, 28 Nov. 1869; d. Bad Gastein, Austria, 3 Sept. 1944). Composer and violinist. Studied at the Prague Conservatory (1880–82) with Foerster (composition) and Bennewitz (violin) and then at the Vienna Conservatory (1882–88) with Hellmesberger (violin) and Krenn and Bruckner (composition). Violinist in the Viennese Royal Opera (1890–93), concertmaster at the Theater an der Wien (1894–99). His lighter compositions achieved great popularity (Serenade no. 1 in A, 1901; *Souvenir in D*, 1904).

Dreher [Ger.]. A dance in 3/4 meter related to the *Ländler*.

Drehleier [Ger.]. *Hurdy-gurdy.

Drehorgel [Ger.]. *Barrel organ.

Dreigroschenoper, Die [Ger., The Threepenny Opera]. Opera in a prologue and eight scenes by Kurt

Weill (libretto by Bertolt Brecht after *The *Beggar's Opera*), produced in Berlin in 1928. An English adaptation by Marc Blitzstein was first produced in 1952.

Dreiklang [Ger.]. *Triad.

Dreitaktig [Ger.]. Three-beat.

Dresden, Sem (b. Amsterdam, 20 Apr. 1881; d. The Hague, 30 July 1957). Composer. Studied in Amsterdam and with Pfitzner in Berlin. From 1919 taught composition at the Amsterdam Conservatory, serving as director in 1924. Later directed the Royal Conservatory, The Hague (1937–41; 1945–49). After his retirement from teaching in 1949 was prolific, producing several of his best works, including the orchestral suite *Dansflitsen* (1951). His chiefly Romantic musical idiom is often infused with impressionistic sonorities. Other works include operas (*François Villon*, 1956–57); choral and vocal works; orchestral works (*Symphonietta*, clarinet, orchestra, 1938); chamber works; piano works.

Drigo, Riccardo (b. Padua, 30 June 1846; d. there, 1 Oct. 1930). Conductor and composer. Studied at the Venice Conservatory, 1860–64; from 1869 gradually became known as an opera conductor in northern Italy and on tour; 1878–79, conductor at the Teatro Manzoni, Milan; 1879–86, conductor at the Italian Opera, St. Petersburg; 1886–1919, at the Imperial Ballet, conducting the premieres of *Sleeping Beauty* and *Nutcracker;* composed additional and substitute music for ballets and several complete ones.

D'Rivera, Paquito (b. Havana, 4 June 1948). Jazz alto saxophonist. In 1967 helped form a jazz, pop, and salsa group called Orquesta cubana de música moderna. Several members remained together in the band Irakere (from ca. 1973), which began touring internationally. While in Spain, D'Rivera defected and moved to New York (1980); played with Gillespie and Tyner, then formed his own Afro-Cuban jazz combo.

Drone. (1) Any instrument that plays only a constant pitch or pitches. See *Tamburā.* (2) On a *bagpipe, those pipes that have no finger holes and thus sound a single pitch. They may be pitched above or below the *chanter, which plays the melody. (3) A long, sustained tone in a piece of music, often intended to imitate the sound of (1), usually pitched below the melody. See also *Bourdon,* Pedal point.

Drouet, Louis (-François-Philippe) (b. Amsterdam, 14 Apr. 1792; d. Bern, 30 Sept. 1873). Flutist. Child prodigy, invited to Paris by Napoleon and given a court appointment, making successful solo appearances. Toured widely in Europe, played in England and started flute manufacture; 1840–54, Kapellmeis-

ter at Coburg; 1854, visited U.S. Composer of 10 flute concertos and other flute music.

Druckman, Jacob (Raphael) (b. Philadelphia, 26 June 1928; d. New Haven, 24 May 1996). Composer. Studied with Copland at the Berkshire Music Center (1949) and with Wagenaar, Mennin, and Persichetti at Juilliard; attended the École normale in Paris (1954). Taught at Bard College (1961–67), Brooklyn College (1972–76), and Yale (from 1976), where he directed the electronic music studio. *Windows* (orchestra, 1972) won the Pulitzer Prize; composer-in-residence to the New York Philharmonic, 1982–87. Having explored serialism (String Quartet no. 2, 1966), in the mid-1960s began to combine recorded electronic music and live performers, often with elements of theater. Several works from the 1970s incorporate preexistent material; *Prism* (1980) quotes a different opera in each of its 3 movements. Other works include the opera *Medea* (1982); orchestral music (*Summer Lightning,* 1991; *Demos,* 1992); works for performers and tape (*Animus I–IV,* 1966–77); 3 string quartets (1948, 1966, 1981); *Counterpoise,* soprano, orchestra, 1994.

Drum [Fr. *tambour;* Ger. *Trommel;* It. *tamburo;* Sp. *tambor*]. Any of the instruments known as *membranophones, with skin (or plastic) stretched over a frame or vessel of, usually, wood or metal; a few instruments also termed drums are *idiophones (e.g., the *slit drum). While most drums are struck with the hand(s) or a beater, in some cultures they are also shaken (rattle drums), rubbed (*friction drums), or plucked (drums with a tensioned string attached [see String drum]). These instruments are found in a large variety of sizes and shapes ranging from bowls, cylinders, and barrels to cones, hourglasses, and simple frames. They have one or two heads that are either laced, nailed, or glued to the body, or in their modern form, held in place by a counterhoop and bolts. Drums are found throughout the world, from the most primitive African or South American tribal cultures to sophisticated cultures of China, India, and Muslim lands. In most musical cultures, drums are of indefinite pitch, though in Africa, the Near East, Southeast Asia, and elsewhere, the contrast of two or more higher and lower indefinite pitches on one, two, or more drums is a central feature of drumming. European *kettledrums, however, must be tuned to definite pitches, as must drums used in the art music of South Asia, such as the *tablā and *mṛdaṅgam.

Drums of indefinite pitch in Western art music [see ills. under Percussion instruments]. 1. Side drum, snare drum [Fr. *caisse claire, tambour militaire;* Ger. *kleine Trommel;* It. *tamburo militare;* Sp. *tambor, caja militar*]. A cylindrical shell made of wood or metal with two heads, the lower being furnished with snares—gut strings or wires running parallel to one another across the center of the head. When the upper or batter head is struck, the snares, if appropriately adjusted, vibrate against the lower or snare head. The instrument used in the modern orchestra and in the *drum set of jazz and popular music is about 35 cm. (14 in.) in diameter and about 13 cm. (5 in.) deep. It is mounted on a stand horizontally or at a slight angle. The instrument used in marching is about 30 cm. (12 in.) in diameter and about 38 cm. (15 in.) deep. It is suspended at an angle at the player's left side (whence the term side drum) from a strap worn over the right shoulder. The side drum is played with wooden sticks that taper to a slightly elongated knob at the tip. In jazz and popular music, the side drum may also be played with wire brushes. For characteristic strokes employed on the side drum, see Drag, Flam, Paradiddle, Roll, Ruff.

2. Tenor drum [Fr. *caisse roulante;* Ger. *Rührtrommel, Wirbeltrommel;* It. *cassa rullante;* Sp. *redoblante*]. A cylindrical drum, similar in diameter to the side drum, but rather deeper (25 to 30 cm. or more). Its construction is like that of the side drum except that it has no snares. It is played either with felt-headed or side-drum sticks and has always been primarily a military or marching instrument.

3. Bass drum [Fr. *grosse caisse;* Ger. *grosse Trommel;* It. *gran cassa;* Sp. *bombo*]. A large instrument, approximately 90 cm. (almost 36 in.) in diameter and 40 cm. (16 in.) deep, consisting of a cylindrical wooden shell with two heads tensioned as are those of the side drum. In the symphony orchestra, it is suspended from a swivel frame or placed on a stand and is hit with a large, felt-headed stick.

Drum-Roll Symphony. Popular name for Haydn's Symphony no. 103 in E♭ major Hob. I:103 (1795, the 11th of the *Salomon Symphonies), so called because of the timpani roll in the opening measure of the introduction to the first movement.

Drum set. A collection of percussion instruments played by a single player; characteristic of jazz, rock, and other forms of American popular music. It typically includes the following drums: a pedal-operated bass *drum, a snare drum, and two or more *tomtoms. The normal complement of cymbals includes a hi-hat: a pair of cymbals mounted horizontally on a stand and clashed together by a pedal mechanism. The drum set also usually includes one or more single cymbals, each mounted at an angle on a stand. These may include a ride cymbal, a crash cymbal, and a sizzle cymbal (a large cymbal with loose rivets inserted in a ring of holes near the edge). To all of these may be added *bongos, *timbales, *cowbells, *wood blocks, etc. The seated drummer plays with sticks, hard or soft mallets, and wire brushes. See ill. under Percussion instruments.

Drum Stroke Symphony. See *Surprise* Symphony.

D.S. Abbr. for *Dal segno.*

Dubensky, Arcady (b. Viatka, Russia, 15 Oct. 1890; d. Tenafly, N.J., 14 Oct. 1966). Composer and violinist. Trained at the Moscow Conservatory, played in the Imperial Opera Orchestra (1910–19); arrived in New York in 1921 and played in the New York Symphony (later Philharmonic, 1922–53). Compositions are in a diatonic style drawn from Russian Romanticism.

Dubois, (François-Clément-) Théodore (b. Rosnay, Marne, 24 Aug. 1837; d. Paris, 11 June 1924). Composer and teacher. Studied at the Paris Conservatory, winning the Prix de Rome in 1861. Organist at Ste.-Clotilde, choirmaster (1869–77) and organist (from 1877) at the Madeleine. Taught at the Conservatory from 1871. A prolific composer best known for his organ music (88 solo pieces; *Fantaisie triomphale,* organ and orchestra) and religious vocal music (including Masses and 71 motets).

Du Caurroy, (François-) Eustache (b. Gerberoy or Beauvais, bapt. 4 Feb. 1549; d. Paris, 7 Aug. 1609). Composer. From about 1570 associated with the French royal court, first as singer, then composer; later held ecclesiastical posts in provincial churches. Works include *Meslanges de musique* (Paris, 1610); a Requiem composed in 1606 was performed at the funeral in 1610 of Henry IV and at funerals of all French kings for some time thereafter.

Duct flute. A flute, also called a fipple flute or whistle flute, that is blown at one end through a mouthpiece that directs the air stream through a narrow passage across the sharp edge of a hole in the pipe. The upper end of the pipe is usually plugged by a block or fipple with only the duct left open. Examples are the *flageolet, *penny whistle, and *recorder.

Dudelsack [Ger.]. *Bagpipe.

Due [It.]. Two; *a due,* an indication in orchestral scores that a single part notated on a staff that normally carries parts for two different players (e.g., first and second flutes) is to be played by both players, or conversely, that two pitches or parts notated on a staff that normally carries only a single part (e.g., first violins) are to be played by different players or groups of players; also [Fr.] *à deux; a due corde,* on two strings [for the use of this phrase in piano music, see *Una corda*].

Duenna, The. (1) Comic opera in three acts by Thomas Linley, the son in collaboration with his father (libretto by Richard B. Sheridan), produced in London in 1775. (2) Opera [Russ. *Obrucheniye v monastïre,* Betrothal in a Monastery] in four acts by

Prokofiev (libretto by Prokofiev and Mira Mendelson after Sheridan), composed in 1940–41 and produced in Leningrad in 1946. Setting: Seville in the 18th century.

Duet [Fr. *duo;* Ger. *Duett, Duo;* It. *duetto;* Sp. *dúo, dueto*]. A composition for two performers, with or without accompaniment. The term is most frequently used in vocal music and for two performers on one piano [see Piano duet], while duets for two instruments are frequently called duos. See also *Bicinium.*

Dufay, Guillaume (b. ca. 1400; d. Cambrai, 27 Nov. 1474). Composer. Contemporaries regarded him as the greatest composer of their age. Most of his life was spent in association with Cambrai Cathedral, beginning as a choirboy from 1409. Apparently established connections with Italy and with the Malatesta family, and may have been in Constance, Rimini, and Laon, returning in 1426 or 1427 to Cambrai. Was in Rome with the papal chapel (1428–33), then at the court of Savoy (1433–35) before rejoining the papal chapel. From no later than 1439 until his death resided in Cambrai (but spent seven years in Savoy during the 1450s). From at least 1433 had some contact with the Este family in Ferrara. Busnois, Ockeghem, and Héniart composed lamentations on his death. His sacred music can be divided into works with a treble-dominated style (hymns, antiphons, many independent Mass movements, some motets), musically complex motets (often isorhythmic and/or polytextual), and Mass pairs, three-section sets of Mass movements, and Mass cycles (some loosely unified; later works are tenor Masses in four voices). The secular songs are nearly all in three parts, with French texts; the rondeau predominates. 9 Masses include *Missa *Ave regina caelorum, Caput Mass* (authenticity doubtful), *Missa L'*homme armé, Missa Se la face ay pale;* nearly 30 Mass movements or sets of movements; about 20 other Mass compositions; 15 antiphons; almost 30 hymns; over 30 motets (13 isorhythmic), including *Nuper rosarum flores;* almost 90 secular songs.

Duff [Ar.]. **Daff.*

Dugazon. See *Soubrette.*

Dukas, Paul (Abraham) (b. Paris, 1 Oct. 1865; d. there, 17 May 1935). Composer and critic. Studied at the Paris Conservatory from age 16; a member of Guiraud's composition class. Later taught orchestration (1910–13) and composition (from 1928) at the conservatory. By the 1890s had begun writing criticism for several publications; friendly with d'Indy and Debussy. Particularly admired for his skillful orchestration; some of his harmonic practices anticipated works of Debussy. Surviving compositions include an opera and a ballet; the Symphony in C

(1895–96); and his best-known work, *L'*Apprenti sorcier.*

Duke Bluebeard's Castle. See *Bluebeard's Castle.*

Duke, Vernon [Dukelsky, Vladimir Alexandrovich] (b. Parfianovka, near Pskov, Russia, 10 Oct. 1903; d. Santa Monica, Calif., 16 Jan. 1969). Composer and violinist. Studied at the Kiev Conservatory (1916–19); fled Russia for Constantinople (1920–21) and New York (1922); in Paris (1924–25) Diaghilev commissioned the ballet *Zephyr et Flore* for which the composer was praised as successor to Stravinsky. Went to London (ca. 1926–29) and composed stage music, then returned to New York. Best known for the stage music he wrote between 1932 and 1952 under the pseudonym Vernon Duke; as Dukelsky continued to write serious music and Russian poetry. Works include at least 12 musicals and revues (*Walk a Little Faster,* 1932, including "April in Paris"); 2 operas; chamber music; piano works (*Souvenir de Venise,* 1955); choral music and songs ("Autumn in New York," 1935).

Dulcimer. A *zither sounded by striking rather than plucking. Instruments of the dulcimer family usually have trapezoidal sound boxes and metal strings, in courses of two to four, divided into unequal lengths by high bridges. The strings run parallel to the long side, which is closest to the player, the instrument being placed horizontally. The strings are struck with light wooden hammers of various types. See ill. under Zither. In the U.S., the instrument is sometimes termed a hammered dulcimer to distinguish it from the *Appalachian dulcimer.

Dulcitone. A keyboard instrument similar to the *celesta, but which employs tuning forks rather than metal plates.

Dulzaina [Sp.]. A *shawm of Spain, made of wood or metal with seven finger holes. It is played in ensemble with a drum. See also *Chirimía, Dolzaina, Zūrnā.*

Dulzian [Ger.]. *Curtal.

Dumbarton Oaks. Popular name for a concerto for 15 instruments by Stravinsky, composed in 1937–38 in the style of a *concerto grosso. The name is that of the then residence of Mr. and Mrs. Robert Woods Bliss (who commissioned the work) in Washington, D.C.

Dumka [dim. of Ukrainian *duma,* pl. *dumky*]. Either of two types of folk music and poetry of Ukrainian origin taken up in Poland and Bohemia in the 19th century: a narrative type with features of the epic and the ballad, and a lament. Elements of the two were often combined. Examples include melismatic sections along with sudden alternation between slow-moving, melancholy sections and faster, livelier ones.

Dump, domp. A type of piece for lute or keyboard of which about 20 examples survive from the late 16th and early 17th centuries. Most are continuous variations on *ground basses that alternate tonic and dominant harmonies (e.g., for one measure each, TTDD or DTDT or TTDT) or on one of the familiar patterns such as the *romanesca.

Dunayevsky, Isaak Iosifovich (b. Lokhvitsa, province of Poltava, 30 Jan. 1900; d. Moscow, 25 July 1955). Composer. Studied at the Kharkov Music School (1910–15) and at the Kharkov Conservatory (1915–19). Music director of the Ermitazh and Korsh theaters in Moscow (1924–29); composer of the Moscow Theater of Satire (1926–29). From 1929 to 1941 music director of the Leningrad Music Hall, where he attempted an adaptation of jazz styles to Soviet popular music.

Duni, Egidio [Romualdo] (b. Matera, 9 Feb. 1709; d. Paris, 11 June 1775). Composer. His opera *Nerone* (Rome, 1735) eclipsed Pergolesi's *Olimpiade,* which it followed on the stage; other operas were presented at Rome, London, Milan, and Florence between 1736 and 1743; his last opera seria was *Olimpiade* (1755). *Maestro di cappella* at S. Nicola di Bari in Naples and at the court in Parma. The first to set Goldoni's *La buona figuola* (1757); moved to Paris and was important in the development of the opéra comique.

Dunstable [Dunstaple], **John** (b. ca. 1390; d. 24 Dec. 1453). Composer, mathematician, and astronomer. May have been in the service of the Duke of Bedford; nothing else is known of his career. His contemporaries and successors recognized him as the foremost English composer of the 15th century. The influence of his music and of the English style in general on the works of Dufay, Binchois, Ockeghem, and Busnois was noted in his own era. Works include three songs (only one definitely by him); twelve isorhythmic motets; almost 30 nonisorhythmic settings of liturgical texts outside the Ordinary; about 20 Mass cycles and Mass movements.

Duo. (1) *Duet. (2) An ensemble of two players. See also Duo sonata.

Duo sonata. In the Baroque period, a *sonata *a 2,* i.e., for one melody instrument and continuo.

Duole [Ger.], **duolet** [Fr.]. *Duplet.

Duparc [Fouques Duparc], **(Marie Eugène) Henri** (b. Paris, 21 Jan. 1848; d. Mont-de-Marsan, 12 Feb. 1933). Composer. Studied piano with Franck at the Jesuit College of Vaugirard in Paris; from 1869 made a series of trips to Germany to see productions of Wagner's operas; in 1878 founded the Concerts de musique moderne. An illness left him blind and paralyzed; composed little after 1885. Surviving works include 16 songs, many on texts by Gautier, Baudelaire, and other important French poets; other vocal music; instrumental music.

Dupla [Lat.]. (1) The ratio 2:1; hence, in early discussions of intervals, the octave; in the system of rhythmic *proportions, the diminution of durations by half. (2) Plural of *duplum.

Duple meter, time. See Meter.

Duplet [Fr. *duolet;* Ger. *Duole;* It. *duina;* Sp. *dosillo*]. A group of two notes of equal duration to be played in the time normally taken up by three notes of the same type, e.g., two eighth notes (marked with the figure 2) in the time of three eighth notes in 6/8, 9/8, or 12/8.

Duplex instrument. A brass instrument that combines two instruments in one, the player switching between the two by means of a valve. The two most common examples are the double-belled *euphonium and the double *horn.

Duplum [Lat., pl. *dupla*]. In music of the *Notre Dame repertory (except for the *motet, where it was termed the *motetus*), the part immediately above the tenor; *organum duplum,* *organum in two parts. See also *Triplum, Quadruplum.*

Duport, Jean-Louis (b. Paris, 4 Oct. 1749; d. Paris, 7 Sept. 1819). Cellist and composer. Studied with his older brother Jean-Pierre; debut at the Concert spirituel at age 19. Followed his brother to Potsdam, returning to France in 1806 to serve the exiled Charles IV of Spain (at Marseilles). Taught cello at the Paris Conservatory (1813–16); in 1813 published the most comprehensive cello method of the day.

Duport, Jean-Pierre (b. Paris, 27 Nov. 1741; d. Berlin, 31 Dec. 1818). Cellist and composer. Debuted at the Concert spirituel in 1761; from 1769 engaged at the court of the Prince of Conti. Toured throughout Europe; in 1773 invited to Berlin by Frederick the Great, where he served as chapel cellist and (from 1778) as chamber musician. Beethoven probably composed his first two cello sonatas with Duport in mind.

Dupré, Desmond (John) (b. London, 19 Dec. 1916; d. Tunbridge, 16 Aug. 1974). Lutenist and gambist. Studied with Ivor Jame and Herbert Howells at the Royal College of Music. Played cello, accompanied Alfred Deller on guitar; as a gambist concertized and recorded with Thurston Dart. During the 1950s and 1960s played with many prominent early music ensembles.

Du Pré, Jacqueline (b. Oxford, 26 Jan. 1945; d. London, 19 Oct. 1987). Cellist. Studied with Pleeth, Tortelier, Casals, and Rostropovich. Debut recital in 1961; U.S. debut in 1965. Married Daniel Barenboim in 1967. In 1972 her career was cut short by multiple sclerosis.

Dupré, Marcel (b. Rouen, 3 May 1886; d. Meudon, 30 May 1971). Organist and composer. At age 12 appointed organist at St. Vivien in Rouen and began study with Guilmant. At the Paris Conservatory studied piano (Diémer), organ (Guilmant and Vierne), and fugue (Widor). Assisted Widor at St. Sulpice from 1906, succeeding him in 1934. Toured England and the U.S.; world tour in 1939. A celebrated improviser; won the Prix de Rome in 1914. Among his compositions are 2 symphonies and a wealth of solo and ensemble music for organ.

Dur, moll [Ger., fr. Lat *durus,* hard, *mollis,* soft]. Major, minor. The terms originally denoted the two forms of the letter b in the *hexachord system of the Middle Ages and Renaissance: "hard" or "square" b for B-natural, and "soft" or "round" b for B-flat [see also Accidental].

Duramente [It.]. Harshly.

Durante, Francesco (b. Frattamaggiore, 31 Mar. 1684; d. Naples, 30 Sept. 1755). Composer. A violin pupil of Francone and possibly later of Pitoni and Pasquini. Studied (1702–5) and taught (1710–11) at S. Onofrio, Naples; *primo maestro* of the conservatory Poveri del Gesù Cristo, Naples, 1728–38, where Pergolesi studied with him. Took the same post at S. Maria di Loreto (1742–55); Anfossi and Traetta were among his pupils. Appointed *primo maestro* at S. Onofrio in 1744. His fame rests on his church music and his considerable reputation as a teacher.

Durastini, Margherita (fl. 1700–1734). Soprano. Appeared in Venice in 1700; served Prince Ruspoli in Rome from 1707, performing several of Handel's cantatas. Sang in Italy, Germany, and London (1720–21, 1722–24, 1733–34), and in premieres of operas by Caldara and Scarlatti; created roles in Handel's *Agrippa* (1709), *Radamisto* (1720), and *Giulio Cesare* (1724), among others.

Duration. The time that a sound or silence lasts. This can be measured in seconds or similar units, though for this purpose common musical notation employs *notes and rests of various shapes whose values are fixed with respect to one another. The absolute duration of individual notes and rests in the system is fixed either approximately, through the use of terms such as *allegro* (fast), or precisely, by the specification of the number of occurrences per minute of some particular value. See also Tempo, Performance marks, Metronome.

Durchbrochene Arbeit [Ger.]. A technique of composition, often encountered in works of the Classical period, in which melodic material is broken into fragments and distributed among two or more instruments or parts.

Durchdringend [Ger.]. Piercing, shrill.

Durchführung [Ger.]. (1) In a movement in *sonata form, the development. (2) In a *fugue, an exposition.

Durchkomponiert [Ger.]. *Through-composed.

Durey, Louis (Edmond) (b. Paris, 27 May 1888; d. St. Tropez, 3 July 1979). Composer. Studied at the Schola cantorum in Paris; a member of "Les six" from 1919 but dissociated himself from that group in 1921. The song cycle *L'offrande lyrique* (1914) is indebted to Schoenberg, but the music of Satie and Stravinsky became more influential. From the 1930s to the 1960s was the most important French communist musician; much of his music contains overt political content.

Durezza [It.]. (1) Harshness. (2) In 17th-century Italy, a dissonance, as in a *toccata di durezze e ligature.

Durón, Sebastián (bapt. Brihuega, 19 Apr. 1660; d. Cambó, 3 Aug. 1716). Composer. Organ pupil of de Sola, whom he served as assistant at Zaragoza in 1679; second organist at Seville Cathedral from 1680; organist at Burgo de Osma Cathedral from 1685, moving to Palencia Cathedral the following year. Appointed Capilla real organist at Madrid in 1691, becoming *maestro de capilla* and choir school rector in 1702. Exiled in 1706 as a result of the War of the Spanish Succession, he lived mainly in France for the rest of his life. His considerable output includes zarzuelas and operas, songs, sacred and secular *villancicos,* church music, and organ works.

Duruflé, Maurice (b. Louviers, 11 Jan. 1902; d. Paris, 16 June 1986). Organist and composer. Studied organ (Tournemire and Vierne) and composition (Dukas) at the Paris Conservatory. Appointed organist at the church of St-Étienne-du-Mont in Paris, 1930; assisted Dupré at the Paris Conservatory in 1942 and became professor of harmony there in 1943. In addition to organ works composed a large-scale Requiem and a Mass.

Dušek [Dussek], **František Xaver** (b. Chotěborky, Bohemia, baptized 8 Dec. 1731; d. Prague, 12 Feb. 1799). Composer and pianist. Studied music in Prague and with Wagenseil in Vienna. Settled in Prague around 1765, where for three decades was a popular keyboard player and an influential teacher. Mozart completed *Don Giovanni* at his Bertramka summer villa. Dušek was a leading composer of *galant* style instrumental music.

Dussek [Dusík], **Jan Ladislav** [Johann Ludwig] (b. Čáslav, Bohemia, 12 Feb. 1760; d. St.-Germain-en-Laye, 20 Mar. 1812). Composer and keyboard virtuoso. Studied in Prague (1776–78); during the 1780s performed as pianist in the Netherlands, St. Petersburg, and Germany. Moved to Paris in 1786; fled the Revolution and settled in London, gaining popularity as a piano virtuoso and performing frequently with Salomon and occasionally with Haydn. Fled to Hamburg in 1799 to escape debt; in 1804 entered the service of Prince Louis Ferdinand of Prussia. The prince's death in 1806 inspired Dussek's famous *Élégie harmonique*. In 1807 he returned to Paris and served as *maître du chapelle* for Prince Talleyrand. Recognized as a pioneer of the colorful, virtuosic sonorities of early 19th-century piano music. Works include over 40 piano sonatas; 18 piano concertos; nearly 90 accompanied keyboard sonatas; chamber music; vocal works.

Dutilleux, Henri (b. Angers, 22 Jan. 1916). Composer. Studied with Büsser at the Paris Conservatory (1933–38); won the Prix de Rome in 1938. Director of singing at the Paris Opéra (1942), subsequently served as director of music productions at French Radio (1945–63). Taught at the École normale (from 1961) and at the Conservatory (from 1970). His postwar style derives from the tradition of Ravel, Debussy, and Roussel. Works include *Timbres, espaces, mouvement,* orchestra, 1978; a violin concerto, 1982; *Ainsi la nuit,* string quartet, 1975–76; 4 sets of songs with orchestra or piano.

Dutoit, Charles (Edouard) (b. Lausanne, 7 Oct. 1936). Conductor. Studied at the Lausanne Conservatory and conducting with von Karajan in Lucerne (1955), with Samuel Baud-Bory at the Geneva Academy of Music, with Munch at the Berkshire Festival (1959). Assistant to von Karajan at the Vienna Opera, 1964; to Paul Kletzki with the Bern Symphony Orchestra, 1963–67. Music director, Zurich Radio Orchestra, 1964–66; Bern Symphony Orchestra, 1967–77; National Orchestra of Mexico, 1974–76; Göteborg Symphony Orchestra, 1975–78; Montreal Symphony Orchestra, from 1977; chief conductor of the Orchestre national de France beginning in 1990; principal conductor of the NHK Orchestra in Tokyo beginning in 1996.

Dux, comes [Lat.]. In compositions employing *imitation, such as the *canon and *fugue, the leading voice and the following or imitating voice, respectively.

Dvořák, Antonín (Leopold) (b. Nelahozeves, near Kralupy, 8 Sept. 1841; d. Prague, 1 May 1904). Composer. Studied at the Prague Organ School (1857–59) and supported himself as an orchestral violist. The third symphony was conducted by Smetana in 1874; the fourth (1874) and fifth symphonies (1875) quickly followed. In 1877 Brahms recommended Dvořák's music to his own publisher, Simrock, who in 1878–79 brought out several works, soon followed by the firms of Bote & Bock and Schlesinger. This led to performances; several works, especially the Slavonic Dances and Rhapsodies, began to be widely popular. In the 1880s English enthusiasm for his music was perhaps the most important factor in Dvořák's recognition; he made the first of nine visits in 1884 and began to conduct more widely, although not frequently; in 1891 began teaching at the Prague Conservatory (among his first pupils was his future son-in-law Josef Suk). Spent 1892 to 1895 in the U.S. as composition teacher and titular director of the National Conservatory of Music in New York; made a number of successful concert appearances. In 1893 composed his last symphony, "From the *New World," and summered in the Czech community of Spillville, Iowa, where he composed the "American" String Quartet. In 1895 resumed his post at the Prague Conservatory; the following year made his last visit to England for the premiere of his cello concerto. Completed his last chamber works at the end of 1895 and his last orchestral (and instrumental) works in 1896–97. The rest of his life was devoted to opera, including *Russalka* (1901) and *Armida* (1904). Other works include Stabat Mater (1877); many duets and songs; 9 symphonies (no. 7, 1884–85; no. 8, 1889); concertos for piano (1876) and violin (1879–80); Carnival Overture (1891); Slavonic Dances (1878, 1886–87); Symphonic Variations (1877); 2 serenades (strings, 1875; winds, cello, double bass, 1878); 14 string quartets; 3 string quintets; 4 piano trios (Dumky Trio, 1890–91); 2 piano quartets; 2 piano quintets.

Dyad. Two pitches, whether sounded simultaneously or successively. The term is used principally with reference to nontonal music.

Dykes, John Bacchus (b. Hull, 10 Mar. 1823; d. Ticehurst, Sussex, 22 Jan. 1876). Composer. A minor canon and precentor at Durham Cathedral (1849–62); composed many favorite Victorian hymn tunes (*Nicaea,* sung to "Holy, Holy, Holy"; *Saint Agnes,* "Come, Holy Spirit, heavenly dove"; *Horbury,* "Nearer my God to Thee"). From 1862 vicar of St. Oswald, Durham.

Dylan, Bob [Zimmerman, Robert] (b. Duluth, 24 May 1941). Folk and rock songwriter and singer. From 1961 performed folk songs, protest songs, and "talking blues" by Woody Guthrie and himself in New York; began recording in 1962. From 1965 played rock-oriented music, recording albums with electric instrumentation (*Blonde on Blonde,* 1966) and performing with members of the rock group The Band (*The Basement Tapes,* 1975); in the 1970s toured with folk singers Joan Baez and Jack Elliot in the Rolling Thunder Revue. Between 1979 and 1981 became a fundamentalist Christian and recorded religious songs; in 1983 worked with reggae musicians *(Infidels).* A central figure to both folk and rock music in the 1960s and early 1970s: his song "Blowin' in the Wind" (1963) became an anthem of the civil rights movement, while other pieces ("Mr. Tambourine Man," 1965; "All Along the Watchtower," 1968) were recorded by rock musicians.

Dynamic marks. Terms, abbreviations, and symbols used in musical notation to indicate degrees of loudness and transitions from one to another. See Performance marks.

Dynamics. (1) That aspect of music relating to degrees of loudness. (2) *Dynamic marks.

Dyson, George (b. Halifax, Yorkshire, 28 May 1883; d. Winchester, 28 Sept. 1964). Composer and writer on music. Studied at Oxford, at the Royal College of Music (1900–1904), and in Italy and Germany (1904–8). After 1908 held teaching posts at Osborne, Marlborough, and Rugby. Returning from war duty in 1921, he became director of music at Wellington College. Later taught at the Royal College, which he directed from 1938 to 1952; knighted in 1941. Works include choral music (the cantata *Nebuchadnezzar,* 1935); orchestral works (Concerto for Violin in E♭, 1942).

Dzerzhinsky, Ivan Ivanovich (b. Tambov, 9 Apr. 1909; d. Leningrad, 18 Jan. 1978). Composer. Studied piano with Yavorsky at the First Music Tekhnikum in Moscow (1925–29) and composition with Mikhail Gnesin at the Gnesin School (1929–30); also studied with Gavriil Popov and P. B. Ryazanov at the Leningrad Central Music Tekhnikum (1930–32) and with Asaf'yev at the Leningrad Conservatory (1932–34). Early works were influenced by Grieg, Rachmaninoff, and Ravel; by the early 1930s had come under the influence of Shostakovich, with whom he consulted while writing his opera *Tikhiy Don* (Quiet Flows the Don, 1936). Stalin recognized its worth as propaganda, and the opera was held up as a model of Soviet realism in music. Although written in an undistinguished musical style, it had 200 performances by May 1938. None of his later operas made their way into the Soviet repertory.

E

E. See Pitch names, Letter notation, Hexachord, Pitch.

Eames, Emma (Hayden) (b. Shanghai, 13 Aug. 1865; d. New York, 13 June 1952). Soprano. Studied in Boston and in Paris with Marchesi. Sang at Paris Opéra (1889–91), Covent Garden (1891–1901) and the Met (1891–1909). Roles include Marguérite, Micaëla, Desdemona, Aida, Tosca, and Mozart and light Wagner roles.

Ear training. Training intended to improve musical perception, including the ability to recognize by ear alone and reproduce in musical notation melodies, intervals, harmonies, rhythms, and meters and the ability to sing at sight. Practice in the former is often termed dictation; in the latter, sight-singing. See also Solfège, Sight-reading, Sight-singing.

Easdale, Brian (b. Manchester, 10 Aug. 1909; d. 30 Oct. 1995). Composer. Studied at the Royal College of Music. Composed operas; after 1936 composed chiefly incidental music and film scores (*The Red Shoes,* 1948). Works include orchestral music (*Dead March,* 1931); a piano concerto (1937); chamber music; songs.

East, Michael (b. ca. 1580; d. Lichfield, 1648). Composer. Provided a madrigal to *The Triumphs of Oriana* (1601); perhaps served the Hatton family; a clerk at Ely Cathedral, 1609–14. Master of the choristers at Lichfield by 1618. His 7 publications include madrigal books, consort songs, anthems, viol music.

Easton, Florence (b. Middlesborough-on-Tees, Yorkshire, 25 Oct. 1882; d. New York, 13 Aug. 1955). Soprano. Studied voice at the Royal Academy of Music and in Paris. Debut in 1903 at Newcastle-on-Tyne; U.S. debut in 1905 with the touring Savage English Grand Opera Company. Performed with the Berlin Royal Opera (1907–13), the Hamburg Opera (1913), the Chicago Opera Company (1915) and the Met (from 1917), where she created Lauretta in *Gianni Schicchi.* After appearances in England returned to the Met as Brünnhilde, 1936.

Eaton, John (Charles) (b. Bryn Mawr, Pa., 30 Mar. 1935). Composer and keyboard player. Studied at Princeton under Babbitt, Cone, and Sessions; early career as a jazz pianist. From 1971 taught at Indiana Univ., where he directed the Center for Electronic and Computer Music. Has performed on and composed especially for the Syn-ket, a synthesizer with pressure-sensitive key (*Concert Piece, for Syn-ket and Symphony Orchestra,* 1966); has also explored microtones (*Microtonal Fantasy,* 2 pianos tuned a quarter-tone apart, 1966). Other works include instrumental music and the opera *The Reverend Jim Jones* (1989).

Eberl, Anton (Franz Josef) (b. Vienna, 13 June 1765; d. there, 11 Mar. 1807). Composer and pianist. Possibly studied with Mozart; in 1784 gave his first public piano recitals in Vienna's Burgtheater. Wrote stage works and toured Germany and Russia as pianist and conductor (1795–1802). Compositions include the cantata *Bey Mozarts Grab* (1791); many keyboard pieces; instrumental music; chamber music; songs.

Eberlin, Johann Ernst (bapt. Jettingen, Bavaria, 27 Mar. 1702; d. Salzburg, 19 June 1762). Composer. Went to Salzburg in 1721, becoming fourth organist at the cathedral in 1724; subsequently court and cathedral organist (from 1729) and Kapellmeister (from 1749). Leopold Mozart, his former student, praised him in Marpurg's *Kritischer Beiträgen.* Music includes stage and dramatic works (many lost), church music, and keyboard pieces.

Eccard, Johannes (b. Mühlhausen, 1553; d. Berlin, 1611). Composer. Probably studied in Mühlhausen with Joachim a Burck, with whom he later published works jointly; sang in the chapel of the Weimar court from 1567 to 1571, then until late 1573 in the Bavarian Hofkapelle in Munich, where he was a pupil of Lassus. Served in the musical household of Jakob Fugger in Augsburg (1577 and 1578), became Vice-Kapellmeister (from 1579) then Kapellmeister (from 1586) of the Prussian Hofkapelle in Königsberg. From 1608 Kapellmeister to the Elector in Berlin. Composed simple 5-part chorale harmonizations as well as more elaborate chorale motets.

Eccles, John (b. probably London, ca. 1668; d. Hampton Wick, 12 Jan. 1735). Composer. Joined United Companies of Drury Lane as theater composer in 1693; when some actors formed a new troupe at Lincoln's Inn Fields in 1695 he became their music director. Produced many songs and masques along with incidental music; also served as musician-in-ordinary to the king and composed court odes. Took part in a composing contest on Congreve's *The Judgement of Paris* in 1701 and composed *Semele* (1707).

Échappée [Fr.]. See Counterpoint.

Échelette [Fr.]. Xylophone.

Échelle [Fr.]. Scale.

Échiquier [Fr.]. *Chekker.

Echo. (1) The acoustical phenomenon in which a sound is heard as having been repeated, usually from some distance, because of the reflection of the sound waves back toward the listener from some, often distant, surface. (2) A musical effect that imitates the acoustical phenomenon (1). Such effects have been created in numerous works since the 16th century. (3) An attachment to a brass instrument that permits the imitation of the acoustical phenomenon (1). On the *cornet it may take the form of a mechanically operated mute. (4) In organs, a division intended to imitate the acoustical phenomenon (1). Depending on the type of organ, it may be located within the main case or at some distance.

Echos [Gr.]. In Eastern chant, a system of melodic formulas that characterize the ecclesiastical *modes. Hence, the *oktoēchos* is the collection of eight modes that forms the compositional framework of Byzantine, Syrian, and Latin chant. Each mode comprises a restricted set of melody types peculiar to it, and these can be employed in many different combinations and variations. Byzantine theorists refer to the eight sets as Modes I–IV Authentic and I–IV Plagal, a terminology that is borrowed for early Western treatises.

The *oktoēchos* appears to have little in common, apart from nomenclature, with the ancient Greek tonal system. It does seem certain, however, that by the late 7th century, the eight-mode system had become established within the Greek liturgical world; its organization is perhaps attributable to St. John of Damascus (ca. 675–ca. 749). It is evident that the Byzantine *oktoēchos*, with its corresponding set of intonation formulas *(enēchēmata)*, reached the West shortly before the year 800.

Eckhardt-Gramatté, S(ophie)-C(armen) (b. Moscow, 6 Jan. 1899; d. Stuttgart, 2 Dec. 1974). Violinist, pianist, and composer. Studied at the Paris Conservatory; career as a virtuoso pianist and violinist began in 1911 in Berlin. From the 1930s devoted more time to composition, studying with Max Trapp in Berlin (1936–38); from 1957 lived in Canada. Confined to instrumental genres, her compositions from the 1920s and 1930s reflect her virtuosity as a performer; later she explored neoclassical and serial styles.

Éclatant [Fr.]. Brilliant, dazzling.

Eclogue. A poem in which shepherds converse. Such poems were written in classical antiquity by Theocritus and Virgil, and in the 16th century they were sometimes written as plays and staged. Thus, they form part of the pastoral tradition on which early opera drew.

École d'Arcueil, L'. A group of French musicians (Henri Sauguet, Roger Desormière, Maxime Jacob, Henri Cliquet-Pleyel) formed in 1923 around Erik Satie and taking their name from Arcueil, the working-class suburb of Paris that, after 1898, was Satie's home. See also *Les *six.

Écossaise [Fr., Scottish]. A type of *contredanse that was very popular in France in the late 18th century. It was related to the *country dance of the British Isles. The form cultivated elsewhere as well in the early 19th century, especially in Vienna, was in a lively 2/4.

Ecphonetic notation. Notation intended to guide the recitation or *cantillation of liturgical texts, especially those from the Bible; also lectionary notation. Such notation, of which there are various systems, occurs in Latin, Greek, Hebrew (in which the related system of *ta'amim* is still in use in Jewish music), Syriac, Armenian, and Coptic manuscripts, among others. Examples survive from as early as the 5th century and as late as the 15th. Some symbols represent accents or a rising and falling of the voice, and some may be chironomic [see Chironomy]. Their precise musical significance is in every case unknown. See also Byzantine chant, Neume.

Eddy, Nelson (b. Providence, R.I., 29 June 1901; d. Miami Beach, 6 Mar. 1967). Baritone. Professional debut with the Philadelphia Civic Opera (1924–30); sang in U.S. premieres of *Ariadne auf Naxos* (1928) and *Wozzeck* (1931). In 1933 appeared in the first of 18 operettas and musicals filmed by M.G.M. Achieved great popularity as partner to Jeanette MacDonald in 8 of these (*I Married an Angel*, 1942).

Edison, Harry "Sweets" (b. Columbus, Ohio, 10 Oct. 1915). Jazz trumpeter. Joined Count Basie's big band (1938–50), recording solos regularly. Toured with Jazz at the Philharmonic from 1950, joined Buddy Rich (1951–53) and Frank Sinatra (1952–78) intermittently, and played again with Basie (1966–81). Also led groups, including a quintet (1975–82).

Effinger, Cecil (b. Colorado Springs, 22 July 1914; d. Boulder, 22 Dec. 1990). Composer, oboist, inventor. Studied with Wagenaar (1938) and Boulanger (1939); taught music at Colorado College (1936–41, 1946–48), the American Univ. (Biarritz, 1945–46), and the Univ. of Colorado. In the 1930s played first oboe in the Colorado Springs Symphony and the Denver Symphony. Invented the Music Writer, a typewriterlike machine for producing musical notation. Compositions include a number of choral works (*2 Sonnets from the Portuguese,* 1985).

Egge, Klaus (b. Gransherad, 19 July 1906; d. Oslo, 7 Mar. 1979). Composer. Studied with Valen at the Oslo Conservatory and with Gmeindl in Berlin. Worked as a vocal coach in Oslo and as a journalist and editor; from 1946 to 1948 presided over the *Nordisk Komponistråd.* His music is characterized by harmony based on fourths and fifths, with shifting tonal centers, and melodies employing all 12 notes serially or nonserially. Works include 5 symphonies (no. 4, *Sinfonia seriale sopra B.A.C.H.—E.G.G.E.,* 1968); 3 piano concertos (1938–74); concertos for violin (1953) and cello (1966); choral works; chamber music.

Egk [Mayer], **Werner** (b. Auchsesheim, near Donauwörth, 17 May 1901; d. Inning, Bavaria, 10 July 1983). Composer and writer. Studied in Frankfurt and Munich with Orff; lived in Italy (1925–27), Berlin (1928), and Munich (1929–36). Guest conductor at the Berlin Staatsoper (1937–41) and director of the Berlin Hochschule für Musik (1950–53). In later years continued to write successfully for the stage. Works were influenced primarily by the French impressionist and Stravinsky; writings include two volumes of essays. Works include at least 7 operas (*Die Verlobung in San Domingo,* 1963); ballets; *Orchestersonate* 1 and 2 (1948, 1969), *Canzona* (cello and orchestra, 1982); choral and other vocal music.

Egmont. Incidental music by Beethoven, op. 84 (1809–10), composed for Goethe's play. The overture is frequently performed separately.

Eguale [It.]. See *Equale.*

Ehrling, Sixten (Evert) (b. Malmö, 3 Apr. 1918). Conductor and pianist. Studied conducting at the Stockholm Conservatory (1936–40) and with Böhm in Dresden (1941). Toured Europe as a concert pianist during the 1940s. Conductor (1944) and artistic director (1953–60) at the Royal Opera House in Stockholm. Led the Detroit (1963–73) and Göteborg Symphony (1973–75). Taught conducting at the Salzburg Mozarteum (1954) and at Juilliard (from 1973). Principal guest conductor of the Denver Symphony (1978–85); artistic adviser, San Antonio Symphony (1985–88).

Eighteen-Twelve Overture. A festival overture by Tchaikovsky, op. 49 (1880), for orchestra, carillon, and artillery, composed for the commemoration in 1882 of Napoleon's retreat from Moscow in 1812.

Eight-foot. See Foot.

Eilend, mit Eile, eilig [Ger.]. Hurrying.

Eimert, (Eugen Otto) Herbert (b. Bad Kreuznach, 8 Apr. 1897; d. Cologne, 15 Dec. 1972). Composer and critic. Studied musicology in Cologne; worked for German Radio there (1927–33; 1945–65) and founded an electronic music studio (1951); professor of electronic music at the Musikhochschule in Cologne (1965–71). Founded the periodical *Die Reihe* (1955). His essay *Atonale Musiklehre* (1924) contained the first systematic discussion of twelve-tone technique. Works include a ballet, orchestral, chamber, and choral pieces; electronic works.

Einem, Gottfried von (b. Bern, 24 Jan. 1918; d. Oberndürnbach, Austria, 12 July 1996). Composer. Educated in Austria and England; studied composition with Blacher in Berlin (1941–43). Musical adviser to the Dresden Opera; *Dantons Tod,* his first opera, was staged at the Salzburg Festival in 1947. Director of the Vienna Festival, 1960–64; from 1965 professor of composition at the Vienna Hochschule für Musik. His compositional style reflects expressionist, neoclassic, and jazz elements; Stravinsky, Egk, and Orff are other influences. Other works include the opera *Tulifant* (1990); Symphony no. 4 (1988); Trio for Strings (1985).

Einfach [Ger.]. Simple.

Eingang [Ger., entrance]. In a Classical concerto, a short cadenzalike passage for the soloist that precedes and leads into a solo section.

Einigkeit und Recht und Freiheit. The national anthem of the Federal Republic of Germany, sung to the "Emperor's Hymn" by Haydn [see *Emperor Quartet*]. The text is the third verse of a poem written in 1848 by August Heinrich Hoffmann von Fallersleben, the first line of which is "Deutschland, Deutschland über alles." The poem was adopted in 1922, but because the first line came to be associated with the Nazi party, the third verse was substituted for the first after World War II.

Einklang [Ger.]. *Unison.

Einleitung [Ger.]. Introduction.

Einsatz [Ger.]. (1) Entrance. (2) Attack.

Einstimmig [Ger.]. *Monophonic.

Eintritt [Ger.]. Entrance, as of a fugue subject or the soloist in a concerto.

Eis, eisis [Ger.]. E-sharp, E-double-sharp. See Pitch names.

Eisler, Hanns (Johannes) (b. Leipzig, 6 July 1898; d. Berlin, 6 Sept. 1962). Composer. Studied composition at the Vienna Conservatory under Weigl; Schoenberg and Webern taught him without fee (1919–23). *Palmström* (voice and ensemble, 1924) employs *Sprechstimme* and a twelve-tone series. Broke with Schoenberg in 1926, the year he joined the German Communist party. Subsequent works reflect his leftist political stance and his collaborations with Brecht and Ernst Busch. Lived in the U.S. (1938–48), teaching at the New School in New York and at USC, then taught at the Hochschule für Musik in East Berlin. His enormous output includes 38 stage works; 42 film scores; 15 orchestral works; 8 works for chorus and orchestra; some 80 works for voice and piano or other accompaniment ("Auferstanden aus Ruinen," the national anthem of the German Democratic Republic, 1949).

Eisteddfod [Welsh, session]. A gathering, originally of Welsh *bards, featuring competitions in music and poetry. Although the term was not established until the 18th century, such events are known to have taken place at least as early as the 12th century, and probably before. Through the 16th century, they were occasions for competition as well as for regulating the bards' complicated organization and procedures. A movement to revive the ancient traditions began in earnest in the 19th, leading to the establishment of a National Eisteddfod in 1880. These events now feature both solo and choral singing as well as *penillion, instrumental music, and dancing.

Eklund, Hans (b. Sandviken, 1 July 1927). Composer. Studied at the Stockholm Conservatory (1947–52) and with Lars-Erik Larssen and Ernst Pepping in Berlin. From 1964 taught at the Stockholm Conservatory. His music shows the influence of Hindemith and manifests an interest in Baroque and classical formal procedures. Compositions include 8 symphonies (1958–85); 6 sets of *Musica da camera* (1955–70); *Music for Orchestra* (1960); chamber music; piano music.

Ekphonetic. See Ecphonetic notation.

Élargissant [Fr.]. *Allargando.*

El-Dabh, Halim (Abdul Messieh) (b. Cairo, 4 Mar. 1921). Composer. Studied at Cairo Univ. (1941–44), with Copland and Fine at the Berkshire Music Center (1950), and at New England Conservatory and Brandeis. Has taught in Ethiopia (1962–64), at Howard Univ. (1966–69), and at Kent State, where he directed the Center for the Study of World Musics. Some of his compositions blend Egyptian and Western styles. Works include operas or opera-pageants, ballets, chamber and piano music, vocal and electronic music.

Eldridge, (David) Roy [Little Jazz] (b. Pittsburgh, 30 Jan. 1911; d. Valley Stream, N.Y., 26 Feb. 1989). Jazz trumpeter. A soloist in the big bands of Teddy Hill (1935), Fletcher Henderson (1935–36), Gene Krupa (1941–43), and Artie Shaw (1944–45). From 1935

led combos and big bands; from 1949 toured with Jazz at the Philharmonic and with Benny Goodman. Accompanied Ella Fitzgerald (1963–65), briefly joined Count Basie (1966), then resumed leading groups, playing at Jimmy Ryan's club in New York from 1970 through 1980; in the late 1970s played drums or piano.

Electric bass. A type of *electric guitar invented by Leo Fender to replace the *double bass. A standard electric bass has a solid body and four strings tuned like those of the double bass and thus an octave below the four lowest strings of the guitar (E A d g). Fretted and fretless models are both popular. It has been widely used in rock since the 1950s and is now used by some jazz players as well. See ill. under Guitar.

Electric guitar. A guitar or guitarlike instrument designed for electronic amplification. It is one component of a system that includes *pickups to translate string vibrations into electrical impulses, an amplifier to modify these impulses, and loudspeakers that turn the electrical impulses back into sound. Most electric guitars have six strings, a fretted neck, two or three pickups mounted under the strings, and knobs on the body for tone and volume control. Additional circuits and controls are often added to the system for special effects.

There are two types of electric guitar: electro-acoustic and solid-body. The electro-acoustic has a sound box like the conventional guitar, and the pickup is driven by both the strings and the sound box. A solid-body guitar has no sound box, only a usually guitar-shaped slab of wood or fiber glass. The pickup is driven by the vibration of the strings only. Because there is no sound box to disperse the vibrational energy of the strings, the solid-body guitar can sustain a tone much longer than other kinds of guitar. Because there is no feedback from the loudspeakers to the pickup (through a sound box), the solid-body guitar admits of much greater amplification than acoustic or electro-acoustic guitars. These two factors have contributed to the extraordinary success of the solid-body guitar in popular music. See ill. under Guitar.

Electric (electronic) piano. An electronic keyboard instrument designed to emulate to a greater or lesser extent the tone and playing characteristics of the piano. One type, developed in the 1920s, used piano strings and hammers plus *pickups activated by the motion of the strings. More successful designs generate the initial vibrations by other means, usually metal rods or reeds that are struck or plucked. In either case, the electrical impulses generated by the acoustical vibrations are modified by an amplifier and converted back into sound by loudspeakers. The term electronic (as distinct from electric) piano is sometimes reserved for an instrument in which the sounds are generated by wholly electronic means.

Electro-acoustic music. Music that is produced, changed, or reproduced by electronic means and that makes creative use of electronic equipment. Since 1948 several genres have emerged that are usually related to the artistic potential of specific electronic devices.

Musique concrète uses the phonograph and tape recorder to combine, modify, and store "natural sounds." *Electronic music* consists either wholly or partially of sounds produced by electronic oscillators and modifying devices such as synthesizers and then stored on magnetic tape. *Tape music* (U.S.A.) and *electrophonic music* (U.K.) combine *concrète* and electronic sounds on tape. *Computer music* is either composed or generated by a digital computer. *Live/electronic music* uses any of the equipment above for live performance. *Text-sound* compositions take spoken language as their literary and musical source. Such works can be created by tape techniques or computer synthesis of speech.

(1) *Musique concrète* [Fr., concrete music]. Music that stores, combines, and modifies natural sounds. This type is the historical source of electro-acoustic music and a continuing genre. The first examples were music for radio plays composed by Pierre Schaeffer at the studios of French radio in Paris in 1948. Composers of *musique concrète* were the first to develop techniques for manipulating sounds recorded on tape (cutting and splicing, loops, speed change, direction change, etc.). Schaeffer was joined by composers Pierre Henry, François Bayle, Bernard Parmegiani, Guy Reibel, and others who formed the *Groupe de recherches musicales*. Between 1948 and 1980, 935 works were composed in their studios, including pieces by Varèse, Messiaen, Berio, Stockhausen, Cage, and Boulez.

(2) *Electronic music.* Music that consists either wholly or partially of sounds produced by electronic oscillators and modifying devices such as synthesizers and then stored on magnetic tape. Composers Herbert Eimert, Karlheinz Stockhausen, György Ligeti, and Gottfried Michael Koenig, working at the West German Radio studio in Cologne, were attracted by the use of electronic sound as a means of extending the techniques of *serial music. There was also an early interest in realizing a complex music that exceeded the capacity of human performers. Tape techniques, similar to those of *musique concrète,* were used to create these compositions, which used oscillators instead of microphones for the original signal. In the U.S., John Cage, working with Louis and Bebe Baron, Earl Brown, and David Tudor, established the Project of Music for Magnetic Tape (1951). Although their work employed chance techniques in selecting sounds used, the equipment was the same as that used in the European works. Traditional instrumental sounds modified by tape techniques were used by Vladimir Ussachevsky and Otto Luening in 1952.

The late 1950s saw the creation of numerous special studios for the purpose of providing composers with the costly equipment required to produce electronic music. In Europe these studios were often affiliated with state radio stations. Most North American studios were established at universities in the early 1960s: Columbia-Princeton (New York), University of Illinois (Urbana), Mills College (Oakland, California), University of Michigan (Ann Arbor), and the University of Toronto. These studios usually contained several tape recorders, oscillator banks, microphones, mixing consoles, and modifying devices such as reverberation chambers, filters, and ring modulators.

The introduction of the *synthesizer brought about a fundamental change in the production of electronic music. Significantly greater control of existing sound-generating and modifying equipment was first achieved in the early 1950s by the RCA Synthesizer, used extensively by composer Milton Babbitt. In the mid-1960s, spurred by increased interest in electro-acoustic music and the availability of low-cost transistor technology, inventors Robert Moog and Donald Buchla manufactured the first voltage-controlled synthesizer. By interconnecting modules, voltages could be applied to amplifiers, oscillators, and filters, thereby creating continuously changing sound sequences without the need for tape splicing. These procedures uncovered a large new vocabulary of sounds that were the source for compositions by Morton Subotnik, Joel Chadabe, John Eaton, and others. Synthesizers have been used extensively for arrangements of Western art music (W. Carlos, Tomita), in rock (Pink Floyd), and for film and television scores. By the 1980s there were numerous commercial synthesizers, ranging from sophisticated studio models to pocket-sized devices used for entertainment.

(3) *Live/electronic music.* Music that uses any of the equipment described above for live performance. Because most electro-acoustic music existed on tape, a special genre was developed by composer-performers who sought "real time" performance of their music. Much early live/electronic music occurred in theatrical contexts. Gordon Mumma used special electronic circuits to produce music for the Merce Cunningham dance company; La Monte Young provided music for "happenings"; Salvatore Martirano, Alvin Lucier, Pauline Oliveros, and Robert Ashley created performance pieces, each with unique frames of reference. Several groups specializing in live/elec-

tronic performance were formed in the 1960s: The ONCE Group, The Sonic Arts Union, FLUXUS, and Musica elettronica viva. Works for traditional instruments and tape are often included in this category, for example, Milton Babbitt's *Vision and Prayer* (for soprano and tape, 1961), the several *Synchronisms* by Mario Davidovsky, and works by Jacob Druckman and Steve Reich. In the 1970s, Reich and Philip Glass created ensembles of electronic and amplified instruments to perform their music.

(4) *Text-sound.* Music in which spoken words, as opposed to sung words or wordless vocal sounds, are the primary musical material. Best known for work in this genre are the Swedish composers Lars-Gunnar Bodin, Bengt-Emil Johnson, and Sten Hanson. American composers Charles Amirkhanian and Charles Dodge have extended the genre.

(5) *Computer music.* Music that is either composed or generated by a digital computer. Computers have become the most important tool for composers of electro-acoustic music because they can be used for all the genres described above. The first use of computers was to compose or to assist composers in creating works for instruments or electro-acoustic performance. In his first experiments in 1956, Lejaren Hiller revealed the difficulty of programming algorithms that approach the complexity of compositional decisions made by human beings. He was followed by Herbert Brün, Gottfried Michael Koenig, and James Tenney.

The most significant use of computers has been to synthesize sound waves. Stored as numbers, the sound waves are converted into voltages that drive loudspeakers. Although computers can also be used to control analog synthesizers and other sound equipment such as mixers, direct digital synthesis has most interested composers because all sounds can be recorded, resynthesized, and modified in this way. Computer programs for sound synthesis were first written by Max Mathews at the Bell Telephone Laboratories and were developed further by Jean-Claude Risset, Barry Vercoe, Hubert Howe, and F. Richard Moore. These programs are run on large general-purpose computers. Composer John Chowning at Stanford University's Center for Computer Research in Music and Acoustics made important discoveries in the domain of timbre. Numerous research projects in sound synthesis have been carried out at the French Institut de recherche et de coordination acoustique/musique (IRCAM) directed by Pierre Boulez. The difficulty of translating musical ideas into computer programs and the length of time between specification and audition has limited the number of composers using these computer programs for composition.

In the 1970s, Jon Appleton and Sydney Alonso (Dartmouth College) and William Buxton (Toronto) created special-purpose computer systems designed to reduce the composer's input to musical specifications and to enable the composer to hear the sound output in "real time." This reduction was accomplished by presenting composers with a limited set of instructions that were sent to the computer by typing at a terminal, turning knobs or pushing buttons, or by playing on a keyboard. These developments led to the manufacture of commercial digital performance instruments such as the Synclavier and Fairlight machines and ultimately to devices varying widely in complexity and cost.

Electronic instrument. An instrument in which the tone is produced and/or modified by electronic means. There are two broad classes, in both of which sound is transmitted to the listener by means of loudspeakers.

(1) Instruments in which the sound is generated by mechanical systems, such as vibrating strings or reeds, and modified electronically. These include in the first instance conventional instruments, such as the guitar or saxophone, to which a *pickup or a microphone is attached for the sake of amplifying their sound and, in some cases, modifying their tone color.

(2) Instruments in which the sound is generated and produced entirely by electronic means. Many such instruments employ one or more oscillators to generate the signals from which a variety of pitches and tone colors is produced by means of frequency dividers, filters, *ring modulators, and the like. Some *electronic organs are purely electronic in this way. The most versatile of these instruments is the *synthesizer, of which various types are widely used. Some other instruments, however, make use of the techniques of generating sound with the aid of a computer [see Electro-acoustic music].

Among the first electronic instruments was the Telharmonium (ca. 1900). The first practical types began to appear in the 1920s. Historically important examples include the *Theremin, *Ondes Martenot, and *Trautonium.

Electronic music. See Electro-acoustic music.

Electronic organ. An *electronic instrument the first examples of which were designed to approximate the acoustic *organ in sustaining power, tone quality, and playing technique. Like the organ, such an instrument may have two manuals, a pedalboard, *stops or analogous devices for producing a variety of tone colors, and a swell pedal for controlling loudness. Various devices have been used to generate their sound. The first widely successful electronic organ was developed by Laurens Hammond by 1935. The widespread use of such instruments in popular music and in the home led to the development of specific playing styles and to the creation of instruments that do not claim to imitate the acoustic organ.

Electrophone. An *electronic instrument.

Electropneumatic action. In organs, a system introduced in the 1860s for connecting keys and stop controls to the wind-chest by means of pneumatic pouches and electric contacts.

Elegie für junge Liebende [Ger., Elegy for Young Lovers]. Opera in three acts by Hans Werner Henze (libretto by W. H. Auden and Chester Kallman), produced in Schwetzingen in 1961. Setting: the Austrian Alps in the early 20th century.

Elegy. (1) A sorrowful or melancholy poem, especially one of mourning for someone dead. (2) A musical work of similar character, whether a setting of such a poem or an instrumental work. Other terms for works of mourning include *lament, *planctus, *tombeau, *apothéose, and *dump.

Elektra. Opera in one act by Richard Strauss (libretto by Hugo von Hofmannsthal, after his own play, which is based on the drama by Sophocles), produced in Dresden in 1909. Setting: the royal palace of Mycenae, after the Trojan War.

Elevation [Lat. elevatio; It. elevazione]. In the Mass, the elevation of the elements of communion following their consecration, historically often accompanied by a motet or by organ music.

Eleventh. See Interval, Chord.

Elgar, Edward (William) (b. Broadheath, near Worcester, 2 June 1857; d. Worcester, 23 Feb. 1934). Composer. Worked as a violinist and band director. During the 1880s his compositions began to be performed in London; *Salut d'amour* became popular during the late 1880s. The success of the *Imperial March* (1897) led to other commissions, but it was the *Enigma Variations* that won him popularity in London, and the oratorio *The Dream of Gerontius* (1899–1900) that brought recognition from the rest of Europe. Other works of the period include the oratorio *The Apostles* and the first of the *Pomp and Circumstance* marches. He was knighted in 1904, and appointed professor of music at Birmingham Univ. (1905) and conductor of the London Symphony (1911–12). Composed little after his wife's death in 1920. Other works include incidental music (*Grania and Diarmid*, 1901; *The Starlight Express*, 1915; *Arthur*, 1923); music for chorus and orchestra (*The Light of Life (Lux Christi)*, 1896); orchestral music (*Cockaigne (In London Town)*, 1900–1901; *Introduction and Allegro*, 1904–5; 2 symphonies, 1907–8, 1903–11; *Elegy*, strings, 1909; concertos for violin (1909–10) and cello (1919); *Falstaff*, 1902–13); solo voice with orchestra (*Sea Pictures*, 1897–

99); chamber music (*Salut d'amour*, piano, 1888; violin sonata, 1918; String Quartet, 1918; Piano Quintet, 1918–19); some 40 songs for voice and piano.

Elijah [Ger. *Elias*]. Oratorio for soloists, chorus, and orchestra by Mendelssohn, op. 70 (completed in 1846, revised in 1847), to texts from the Old Testament. The English version was first performed at the Birmingham Festival in 1846, and the German version in Hamburg in 1847.

Elisir d'amore, L' [It., The Love Potion]. Opera in two acts by Donizetti (libretto by Felice Romani, after Eugène Scribe's libretto for Auber's *Le philtre*), produced in Milan in 1832. Setting: a small Italian village in the early 19th century.

Elkus, Albert (Israel) (b. Sacramento, 30 Apr. 1884; d. Oakland, 19 Feb. 1962). Composer and pianist. Studied at Berkeley and with Kaun in Berlin (1907–8) and Weil in San Francisco; subsequent studies in Paris, Berlin, and Vienna. Taught at the San Francisco Conservatory (1923–25, 1930–37; director, 1951–57), Mills College (1929–44), and at Berkeley (1931–59). Employed chromatic harmony and wrote in a style drawn from Brahms.

Ellington, Duke [Edward Kennedy] (b. Washington, D.C., 29 Apr. 1899; d. New York, 24 May 1974). Jazz bandleader, pianist, and composer. From 1923 led the Washingtonians, which became a 12-piece band at the Cotton Club (1927–31); in 1932 the group began a lifetime of touring. With few exceptions Ellington's compositions were tailored to the duration of a 78-rpm disc until the mid-1940s. He displayed an unrivaled gift for jazz orchestration, harmonization, and miniature form to compose a body of the finest big band recordings in jazz. From 1943 to 1948 gave concerts at Carnegie Hall and concentrated on suites, tone poems, ballets, and (from the mid-1960s) sacred music. Recordings include "Mood Indigo" (1930), "It Don't Mean a Thing" (1932), "Sophisticated Lady" (1933), "Take the 'A' Train" (1941), "Trumpets No End" (1946), and the albums *Ellington at Newport* (1956) and *The New Orleans Suite* (1970).

Elman, Mischa [Mikhail Saulovitch] (b. Talnoy, 20 Jan. 1891; d. New York, 5 Apr. 1967). Violinist. Studied in Odessa and with Leopold Auer in St. Petersburg (1901–4). Debut in 1899, toured Germany (1904) and England (1905); U.S. debut in 1908. With Heifetz and Zimbalist he brought to Auer's Russian school an unsurpassed prestige. Composed character pieces for violin.

Elmendorff, Karl [Carl] **Eduard Maria** (b. Düsseldorf, 25 Oct. 1891; d. Hofheim, 21 Oct. 1962). Conductor. Studied at the Cologne Conservatory; conducted in Düsseldorf (1916), Mainz, and Hagen. Conductor at the Berlin and Munich State Operas, 1925–32; at Bayreuth, 1927–42. General music director of the Hesse State Theater at Kassel-Wiesbaden, 1932. Musical director of the Mannheim National Theater, 1935; of the Dresden State Opera from 1942. Conducted in Kassel-Wiesbaden, 1948–56.

Eloy, Jean-Claude (b. Mont-St.-Aignan, near Rouen, 15 June 1938). Composer. Studied with Milhaud at the Paris Conservatory (1953–61), with Scherchen and Pousseur at Darmstadt, and with Boulez in Basel (1961–62). Taught for two years at Berkeley. His interest in Middle Eastern and Hindu musics began to be reflected in his own compositions (*Kamakala*, 3 choral and orchestral groups, 1971). At Stockhausen's invitation worked at the Cologne studio (1972), where he completed *Shanti* (6 voices, instruments, and electronics).

Elsner, Józef (Antoni Franciszek) [Joseph Anton Franciskus; Józef Ksawery; Joseph Xaver] (b. Gródkow, Silesia, 1 June 1769; d. Elsnerowo, near Warsaw, 18 Apr. 1854). Composer and teacher. Studied in Breslau (1781–88); theater conductor in L'vov (1792–99). In 1799 settled in Warsaw and became conductor at the Opera (1799–1824), where he had many works produced through 1821. Founded several schools, including the conservatory (1821–30) where Chopin, his most celebrated pupil, studied. Other works include much sacred music; oratorios, cantatas; 8 symphonies; 6 string quartets and other chamber pieces; piano pieces.

Elwell, Herbert (b. Minneapolis, 10 May 1898; d. Cleveland, 17 Apr. 1974). Composer and critic. Studied in New York with Bloch (1919–21) and in Paris with Boulanger (1921–24), after which he was at the American Academy in Rome (1924–27). Taught at the Cleveland Institute (1928–45); wrote program notes for the Cleveland Symphony (1930–36) and criticism for the *Cleveland Plain Dealer* (1932–65). Works include a ballet, *The Happy Hypocrite* (1925); orchestral pieces; chamber music; a few choral works; many songs.

Embellishment. See Ornamentation, Counterpoint.

Embouchure. (1) [Eng., Fr.; Ger. *Ansatz*] The placement of the lips, facial muscles, and jaw in the playing of wind instruments. (2) [Fr.] *Mouthpiece. (3) [Eng., Fr.] The mouth hole of a flute.

Emmanuel, (Marie François) Maurice (b. Bar-sur-Aube, 2 May 1862; d. Paris, 14 Dec. 1938). Composer and musicologist. In 1880 studied composition with Delibes at the Paris Conservatory. His *Overture pour un conte gai* (orchestra, 1890) made use of medieval modes and a free approach to rhythm, and

was criticized by Delibes. Taught art history at the Lycée Racine and Lycée Lamartine until 1904, when he was appointed *maître de chapelle* at Ste. Clotilde. From 1909 until 1936 taught at the Paris Conservatory, where his students included Casadesus and Messiaen. His 3 major stage works all reflect his knowledge of ancient Greek civilization.

Emmett, Dan(iel Decatur) (b. Mt. Vernon, Ohio, 29 Oct. 1815; d. there, 28 June 1904). Minstrel show musician and composer. From 1835 to 1842 was a blackface singer and banjoist in touring circuses. In 1843 was a member of one of the earliest minstrel companies, the Virginia Minstrels; they toured Great Britain, 1843–44. From 1844 to the 1870s worked as a minstrel performer. Published collections of minstrel songs (not all original) and many individual songs of his own, the best known being "Dixie," first performed in 1859.

Emperor Concerto. Popular name for Beethoven's Piano Concerto no. 5 in E♭ major op. 73 (1809). The name may have been added by pianist and publisher Johann Baptist Cramer (1771–1858).

Emperor Quartet [Ger. *Kaiserquartett*]. Popular name for Haydn's String Quartet in C major op. 76 no. 3, Hob. III:77 (1797). It is so named because the slow movement consists of variations on "Gott, erhalte [Franz] den Kaiser" (the so-called "Emperor's Hymn"), formerly the Austrian national anthem, which was composed by Haydn (originally as a solo song with keyboard, Hob. XXVIa:43) in 1796–97.

Empfindsam style [fr. Ger. *empfindsamer Stil*]. The north German "sensitive" or "sentimental" style of the mid-18th century. The noun form of *empfindsam* is *Empfindsamkeit,* sometimes translated as "sensibility" in its earlier meaning of emotional sensitiveness. The goal of *Empfindsamkeit* was the direct, natural, sensitive, and often subjective expression of emotion.

The *empfindsam* style may be considered a dialect of the international *galant* style, characterized by simple homophonic texture and periodic melody. Particular traits of the *empfindsam* style are the liberal use of appoggiatura or sigh figures, exploitation of dynamic nuance, and frequent melodic and harmonic chromaticism. C. P. E. Bach's lieder and his later keyboard pieces (especially the fantasies and sonatas) best represent its more intimate side [see also *Klavierlied*].

Empfindsamkeit [Ger.]. See *Empfindsam* style.

Empfindung, mit [Ger.]. With feeling.

Empressé [Fr.]. Eager, hastening.

Ému [Fr.]. Moved, with emotion.

En [Fr.]. For phrases beginning with this preposition, see the word following.

En Saga. See *Saga, En.*

Enchaînement [Fr.]. Voice leading.

Enchaînez [Fr.]. Continue without pause.

Enchiriadis, enchiridion [Lat., fr. Gr., handbook, manual]. Part of the titles of or references to several medieval treatises, particularly *Musica enchiriadis, Scolica enchiriadis.*

Encina [Enzina], **Juan del** [Fermoselle, Juan de] (b. Salamanca, 12 July 1468; d. León, late 1529 or early 1530). Writer and composer. Spent the first three decades of his life in or near Salamanca, as a singer in the cathedral choir from 1484, then from 1492 in the service of Fadrique, the second Duke of Alba. From 1498 until 1521 lived chiefly in Rome but retained connections with Spain. In 1519 the pope appointed him prior of León Cathedral, where he was resident from 1521 until his death. A central figure in the emergence of Spanish theater; his compositions (mostly *villancicos)* are all secular and polyphonic.

Enclume [Fr.]. *Anvil.

Encore [Fr., again]. When said by members of the audience (usually English-speaking), a request that the performer(s) repeat a composition or perform an additional one not on the program; also the work performed in response to such a request or to enthusiastic applause. On the Continent, the usual term is *bis* [Lat., twice].

End-blown flute. A *flute that is played by blowing directly across its open upper end. Examples are the *caval,* *nāy, quena,* and *shakuhachi.*

Endpin [Fr. *pique;* Ger. *Stachel;* It. *puntale;* Sp. *puntal].* An adjustable steel or wooden rod fastened in a wooden socket to the bottom block of the cello or double-bass. It is used to support the instrument's weight and control its height above the floor for the convenience and comfort of the player. While fixed supports were sometimes used in the 17th and 18th centuries, the adjustable endpin did not gain popularity until the last half of the 19th century.

Enescu, George [Enesco, Georges] (b. Liveni-Vîr-nav [now George Enescu], Romania, 19 Aug. 1881; d. Paris, 4 May 1955). Composer, conductor, and violinist. Studied with Hellmesberger, Robert Fuchs, and Sigismund Bachrich at the Gesellschaft der Musikfreunde in Vienna. Went to Paris in 1894, where he had lessons from Thomas, Dubois, Massenet, and Fauré. Became prominent as a conductor and violinist both in Paris and in his native country; established the Enescu Prize for composition in Bucharest (1912) and the George Enescu Symphony Orchestra

in Jassy (1917). Taught at the Accademia Chigiana in Siena and at the American Conservatory in Fontainebleau; from 1928 was an instructor of violin and composition at the École normale de musique. During the 1920s and 1930s toured the U.S. and Europe as violinist and conductor; in 1946 taught at the Mannes School of Music. Compositions include stage works (*Oedipe,* 1931); 5 symphonies (1906–41); 3 orchestral suites (1903, 1915, 1937–38); 2 Rumanian Rhapsodies (1901, 1902); *Vox maris* (soprano, tenor, voices, orchestra, 1955); 2 piano quintets and quartets; 2 string quartets and piano trios; 3 suites for piano.

Enfance du Christ, L' [Fr., The Childhood of Christ]. Oratorio for soloists, chorus, and orchestra by Berlioz, op. 25 (1850–54). Berlioz called the work a "trilogie sacrée" and, though the work is not an opera, included stage directions in the score to explain the events portrayed.

Enfant prodigue, L' [Fr., The Prodigal Son]. (1) "Lyric scene" by Debussy (libretto by Ernest Guinand) composed in 1884 (revised 1906–8) for the *Prix de Rome. It was produced as an opera in London in 1910. (2) Ballet by Prokofiev (choreography by George Balanchine), op. 46, produced in Paris in 1929. Most of the ballet music is contained in an orchestral suite arranged by Prokofiev in the same year.

Enfant et les sortilèges, L' [Fr., The Child and the Enchantments]. Opera *(fantaisie lyrique)* in two parts by Ravel (libretto by Colette), produced in Monte Carlo in 1925. Setting: a French country house.

Engel, (A.) Lehman (b. Jackson, Miss., 14 Sept. 1910; d. New York, 29 Aug. 1982). Composer and conductor. Studied at the Cincinnati College–Conservatory, with Goldmark at Juilliard and with Sessions. In the 1930s founded the Lehman Engel Singers and the Madrigal Singers; active as a composer from the 1920s through the 1950s; in later years turned away from atonality to compose in a diatonic idiom marked by sharp rhythms.

Engführung [Ger.]. *Stretto.

English discant. See Discant.

English flute. In late 18th-century England, the *recorder, as distinguished from the *transverse or *German flute.

English guitar. A type of *cittern popular in mid-18th-century Britain. It has six courses of metal strings (the top four double), tuned c e g c' e' g', and is plucked with the fingers.

English horn [Fr. *cor anglais;* Ger. *Englischhorn;* It. *corno inglese;* Sp. *corno inglés].* A double-reed woodwind instrument that is a lower-pitched member of the *oboe family. It is a *transposing instrument in F, a fifth below the oboe, with a sounding range of e to a'', a fifth lower than written. Late 18th-century instruments, which seem to be descended from the *oboe da caccia,* are curved and usually covered with leather. The modern instrument is straight, except for a curved *bocal. It has a hollow bulb-shaped bell, which is now known to have only a minimal effect on its tone. There are no satisfactory explanations for the origin of its name. See ill. under Reed.

English Suites. Six suites for harpsichord by Bach, BWV 806–11, usually considered to date from the Cöthen years (1717–23), but perhaps composed in Weimar ca. 1715. Each suite opens with an extended prelude. The title English Suites was not used by Bach himself, so far as is known, and its origins remain obscure.

English violet. A type of *viola d'amore described by Leopold Mozart (1756) as having 14 *sympathetic strings, but apparently unknown in England.

Enharmonic. (1) Of the three genera of tetrachords in the music of ancient Greece, all of which are bounded by a perfect fourth, the one in which the lower two intervals are quarter tones. (2) In modern theory, pitches that are one and the same even though named or "spelled" differently, e.g., G♯ and A♭ or E and F♭. Pitches related in this way are said to be the enharmonic equivalents of one another. In systems of tuning other than equal *temperament (in which all semitones are the same size), two pitches forming such a pair may not be absolutely the same. Singers and players of fretless stringed instruments may readily preserve such distinctions, and some believe that sharps should be consistently higher and flats consistently lower than their enharmonic equivalents. Much music since at least the 18th century, however, exploits enharmonic equivalence for purposes of *modulation and thus requires that enharmonic equivalents in fact be equivalent.

Enigma Variations. Popular name for *Variations on an Original Theme ("Enigma")* for orchestra by Elgar, op. 36 (1898–99). Each variation depicts a person identified by initials or a nickname.

Enigmatic scale. *Scala enigmatica.*

Enna, August (Emil) (b. Nakskov, Denmark, 13 May 1859; d. Copenhagen, 3 Aug. 1939). Composer. Played in orchestras in Finland; in 1884 returned to Denmark and composed his first opera, *Agleia.* The success of *Heksen* [The Witch] (1888–89) led to 14 more operas; also composed choral and orchestral works. His music shows the influence of Wagner, Richard Strauss, and Puccini.

Enríquez (Salazar), Manuel (b. Ocotlán, Jalisco, Mexico, 17 June 1926; d. Mexico City, 26 Apr. 1994). Composer. Concertmaster of the Guadalajara Symphony, 1949–55; studied with Galamian, Mennin, and Primrose at Juilliard (1955–57), and with Wolpe. Taught at the Music School of the National Univ. and at the National Conservatory in Mexico. His music contains serial as well as aleatory elements; compositions are predominantly instrumental, with works for both orchestra (*Encuentros,* 1971; *El y ellos,* violin and orchestra, 1972) and chamber ensembles (*Móvil II,* violin, tape, 1969).

Ensalada [Sp., salad]. A poem that mixes lines from other poems or in diverse meters, often in several languages and usually with humorous intent; also a musical setting of such a poem, particularly a composition that quotes other compositions or melodies and thus a type of *quodlibet.* The singing of such works was apparently common in 16th-century Spain.

Ensemble. (1) A group of performers who perform together, whether instrumentalists, singers, or some combination, e.g., a string ensemble, an early-music ensemble. (2) The degree to which a group of performers performs with appropriate balance and well-coordinated articulation; thus, a group may be said to perform with good or poor ensemble. (3) In opera, a set piece for more than two soloists, sometimes also including the chorus, as occurs frequently at the conclusion or finale of an act. (4) Of or pertaining to music intended for performance by more than one player; also music or a performance in which individual parts are performed by more than one performer, as distinct from solo or soloistic music or performance.

Entendre [Fr.]. To hear; *entendu,* heard.

Entfernt [Ger.]. Distant.

Entführung aus dem Serail, Die [Ger., The Abduction from the Seraglio]. *Singspiel in three acts by Mozart (libretto by Gottlob Stephanie, based on Christoph Friedrich Bretzner's libretto *Belmonte und Constanze*), produced in Vienna in 1782. Setting: Turkey in the 16th century.

Entr'acte [Fr.]. A piece, usually instrumental, performed between the acts of a play (e.g., Beethoven's compositions for Goethe's play *Egmont*) or an opera (Bizet's *entr'actes* in *Carmen*). The terms *entr'acte,* *intermède,* *intermezzo, and *incidental music are, for the most part, coextensive. In Purcell's works, the terms curtain tune and act tune are used.

Entrada [Sp.], **entrata** [It.]. See *Intrada.*

Entrée [Fr.]. (1) In 17th- and 18th-century France, a subdivision of a musico-dramatic work. In *ballet de *cour* an *entrée* is a self-contained group of dances, unified by subject, forming part of an act. The later *opéra-ballet* referred to entire acts as *entrées*. (2) The entrance on stage of a character or group of characters, or the music, often marchlike, accompanying such an entrance, or the first piece in a *divertissement*. (3) The first piece of an instrumental suite, having the function of a prelude or introduction. Such an *entrée* may have a marchlike character.

Entremés [Sp.]. A play, most often comic and sometimes with music, intended for performance between the acts of a larger work. The genre was cultivated by Cervantes and other 17th-century Spanish authors. See also Intermezzo.

Entremets [Fr.]. *Intermède.*

Entry. (1) The point in a composition at which a particular part begins or begins again after a rest; also the musical material with which the part begins at that point. (2) In a fugue, a statement of the subject.

Entschieden [Ger.]. Decided, resolute.

Entschlossen [Ger.]. Resolute, determined.

Envelope. In *acoustics, the characteristics (especially amplitude) of the attack, steady state, and decay of a sound.

Environment. See Mixed media.

Envoi, envoy [Fr.; Prov. *tornada;* It. *commiato*]. In some poetic forms of the Middle Ages such as the *chant royal* and the *ballade,* a concluding half-stanza that usually begins with some form of address such as "Prince," a reference to the prince presiding over a poetic competition.

Éoliphone [Fr.]. *Wind machine.

Epilogue. *Coda.

Épinette [Fr.]. Spinet, harpsichord.

Episema [Gr.]. A short horizontal stroke found in association with neumes in some 9th- and 10th-century manuscripts. Editions of *Gregorian chant prepared at Solesmes, which embody a particular theory of the rhythmic interpretation of chant, employ a "vertical episema" to mark the location of the *ictus. This is not found in medieval sources. See Neume.

Episode. A subsidiary passage occurring between passages of primary thematic importance; in a *fugue, a passage, often modulatory, occurring after the exposition of the subject or between subsequent principal statements of the subject [see also Codetta]; in a *rondo, a passage occurring between statements of the principal recurring theme.

Episodic form. *Rondo.

Epistle [Lat. *epistola*]. One of the New Testament Epistles, from which readings are taken for the *Mass of the Roman Catholic Church as well as for the analogous services of other Eastern and Western rites. In the Roman rite, these readings may be sung to a simple recitation formula or tone or they may be spoken.

Epistle sonata. An instrumental work intended for performance probably following the *Epistle of the *Mass. The term is especially applied to the 17 sonata-allegro movements by Mozart for various combinations of instruments and for organ.

Epithalamium [It. *epitalamio*]. A poem composed for a wedding, especially one to be sung on the wedding night.

Epstein, David M(ayer) (b. New York, 3 Oct. 1930). Composer, conductor, and theorist. Studied at Antioch, the New England Conservatory, Brandeis, and with Babbitt and Sessions at Princeton (Ph.D., 1968) and with Milhaud at Aspen (1955–56). Taught at Antioch (1957–62) and M.I.T. (from 1965); in 1984 became music director of the New Orchestra of Boston. His style, related to the serialism of Webern, is concise and complex; he is the author of several theoretical articles and of *Beyond Orpheus: Studies in Musical Structure* (1979). Works include orchestral music; *Ven-tures* (large wind ensemble, 1970); chamber and piano music; a song cycle (*The Seasons,* 1955); other choral and vocal works.

Epstein, Julius (b. Agram, Croatia, 7 Aug. 1832; d. Vienna, 1 Mar. 1926). Pianist and pedagogue. Studied in Agram and Vienna; professor of piano at the Vienna Conservatory (1867–1901), performed often with the Vienna Philharmonic. Edited Schubert's piano music, which he also performed frequently; his son Richard (1869–1919) taught piano at the Vienna Conservatory before becoming a well-known accompanist in London (1904–14) and New York (1914–19).

Equal voices. Voices of the same type when employed in a polyphonic work, e.g., all sopranos or all tenors; sometimes also merely all male or all female.

Equale [Lat., also *aequale;* It. *eguale*]. A piece for voices or instruments all of the same type, especially one for four trombones written for a funeral or other solemn occasion.

Equal temperament. See Temperament.

Erb, Donald (James) (b. Youngstown, Ohio, 17 Jan. 1927). Composer. Studied at Kent State Univ. then worked as a jazz trumpeter; worked briefly with Boulanger in Paris (1953), and with Marcel Dick at the Cleveland Institute and Bernard Heiden at Indiana Univ. (D.Mus., 1964). Taught at the Cleveland

Institute and Case Western Reserve (from 1965), Southern Methodist Univ. (1981–84), and Indiana Univ. (from 1984). His compositional style reflects jazz, neoclassical, and serial influences. Best known for his orchestral compositions and for concertos (piano, 1958; percussion, 1966; trombone, 1976; cello, 1976; keyboards, 1978; trumpet, 1980; clarinet, 1984; contrabassoon, 1984). Often combines electronically synthesized sound with traditional instruments (*The Devil's Quick Step,* winds, piano, percussion, strings, and tape, 1983). Other works include *Prismatic Variations* (1983); *Klangfarbenfunk I* (rock band, orchestra, tape, 1970); string quartet no. 2 (1990), Violin Sonata (1994), and other chamber music; choral works.

Erb, Karl (b. Ravensburg, 13 July 1877; d. there, 13 July 1958). Tenor. Debut with the Stuttgart Opera in 1907; sang with the Lübeck (1908–10), Stuttgart (1910–12), and Munich (1913–25) Opera houses. Roles included Parsifal, Pfitzner's Palestrina, which he created in 1917, and the Evangelist in Bach's Passions. Two accidents in the 1920s cut short his theatrical career, but he continued to sing recitals and perform as the Evangelist. The model for the tenor Erbe in Mann's *Doktor Faust.*

Ergriffen [Ger.]. Moved, stirred.

Erhaben, Erhabenheit [Ger.]. Lofty, noble, sublime; nobility, sublimity.

Erh-hu (erhu) [Chin.]. A Chinese *spike fiddle, about 75 cm. tall, with two silk strings and a small, hexagonal body covered with snakeskin. It has no fingerboard; the player stops the strings with finger pressure alone. The bow is threaded between the strings, but normally only one string at a time is played. See also *Ching-hu;* see ill. under Instrument.

Erhöhen, Erhöhungszeichen [Ger.]. To sharp, the sharp sign.

Erickson, Robert (b. Marquette, Mich., 7 Mar. 1917; d. Encinitas, Calif., 24 Apr. 1997). Composer. Studied with May Strong, La Violette, Krenek, and Sessions; taught at the College of St. Catherine in St. Paul (1953–54), Berkeley (1956–58), the San Francisco Conservatory (1957–66), and UC-San Diego; directed the Pacifica Foundation in Berkeley (1954–63). Early works were serial and contrapuntal; later works are more concerned with timbre and texture (*General Speech,* 1969). Other compositions include orchestral music (*Taffytime,* 1983; *Corona,* 1986); string quartets (*Corfu,* 1986), pieces for tube drums (the composer's invention), and other chamber music; piano works; choral and solo vocal music; electronic music, usually with live performers.

Erkel, Ferenc [Franz] (b. Gyula, Hungary, 7 Nov. 1810; d. Budapest, 15 June 1893). Composer and conductor. In 1835 appointed conductor at new Hungarian Theater, Buda; 1836–38, conductor, German Theater, Pest; then at new Hungarian National Theater, Pest. The capital's leading pianist until Liszt's appearances in 1839–40. Early compositions (*Duo brillant en forme de fantaisie sur des airs hongrois,* 1837) use Hungarian themes. Founded Hungarian opera with *Bátori Mária* (1840), followed by *Hunyadi László* (1844) and *Bánk Bán* (1861). In 1844 composed the Hungarian national anthem. Founded and conducted Philharmonic Concerts, and was first director of the Budapest Academy of Music (1875–87).

Erlanger, Camille (b. Paris, 25 May 1863; d. there, 24 Apr. 1919). Composer. Studied with Delibes at the Paris Conservatory (1881–89), winning the Prix de Rome. Her first great success came in 1900 with *Le juif polonais,* followed by *Aphrodite* (1906). Also composed a French Requiem; symphonic poems and other orchestral pieces; chamber and piano pieces.

Erlebach, Philipp Heinrich (baptized Esens, Ostfriesland, Lower Saxony, 25 July 1657; d. Rudolstadt 17 Apr. 1714). Composer. Served at the court of Count Albert Anthon von Schwartzburg-Rudolstadt, becoming Kapellmeister in 1681. J. C. Vogler was among his pupils. Extant works include dozens of cantatas along with 2 collections of arias and collections of overtures and sonatas.

Erlöschend [Ger.]. Dying out.

Ermattend [Ger.]. Tiring, weakening.

Ernani. Opera in four acts by Verdi (libretto by Francesco Maria Piave, after Victor Hugo's drama *Hernani*), produced in Venice in 1844. Setting: Spain and Aix-la-Chapelle, 1519.

Erniedrigen, Erniedrigungszeichen [Ger.]. To flat, the flat sign.

Ernst, ernsthaft [Ger.]. Earnest, serious.

Ernst, Heinrich Wilhelm (b. Brno, 6 May 1814; d. Nice, 8 Oct. 1865). Violinist and composer. Studied at the Vienna Conservatory; heard Paganini in 1828 and was inspired to become a great virtuoso, but was also a highly expressive and musicianly player. Paris debut in 1831; toured Europe continuously, visiting Russia in 1847; also composed.

Eroica. Beethoven's Symphony no. 3 in E♭ major op. 55 (1803). It was composed in homage to Napoleon, but when Napoleon took the title of emperor, Beethoven changed the work's title from *Sinfonia grande: Bonaparte* to *Sinfonia eroica composta per festeggiar il sovvenire d'un gran uomo* (Heroic symphony composed to celebrate the memory of a great man) and dedicated it to Prince Franz Joseph von Lobkowitz. The second movement is headed "Marcia funebre" (Funeral March). The last movement includes a series of variations based on a theme that Beethoven had used in three earlier compositions: *Contretanz* no. 7 in E♭ major WoO 14 (completed in 1802) [see *Contredanse*]; *Die *Geschöpfe des Prometheus;* *Eroica Variations.*

Eroica Variations. Variations and fugue in E♭ major op. 35 (1802), by Beethoven, so called because Beethoven later used the work's theme in the last movement of the *Eroica* Symphony. The variations are also called *Prometheus Variations,* after the ballet *Die *Geschöpfe des Prometheus,* in which the theme occurred for the first time.

Ersatz [Ger.]. Substitute; *Ersatzklausel,* substitute *clausula.

Ersterbend [Ger.]. Dying away.

Erwartung [Ger., Expectation]. Opera for soprano and orchestra in one act by Schoenberg (libretto by Marie Pappenheim), composed in 1909 and produced in Prague in 1924. Setting: a forest.

Erweitern [Ger.]. To extend, expand.

Erzähler [Ger.]. Narrator.

Es, eses [Ger.]. E-flat, E-double-flat. See Pitch names.

Escape note. *Échappée.* See Counterpoint.

Escapement. See Piano.

Eschaquier, eschiquier [Fr.]. *Chekker.

Escher, Rudolf (George) (b. Amsterdam, 8 Jan. 1912; d. De Koog, Texel, 17 Mar. 1980). Composer. Studied at the conservatory at Rotterdam and took composition lessons from Pijper (1934–37). Worked at electronic studios in Delft and Utrecht (1959–61) and taught at the Amsterdam Conservatory (1960–61) and Utrecht Univ. (1964–75). His music shows influences from Debussy and Ravel as well as Boulez. Works include 2 symphonies (1953–54, 1958–64); vocal music (*Univers de Rimbaud,* 1970); chamber music (string trio, 1959).

Esercizio [It.]. Exercise, etude.

Eses [Ger.]. E-double-flat. See Pitch names.

Eshpai, Andrei Iakovlevich (b. Kozmodemiansk, Mari A.S.S.R., U.S.S.R., 15 May 1925). Composer. Attended the Moscow Conservatory (1948–53) and pursued graduate studies there under Khachaturian. A prominent figure in Soviet musical life, his music incorporates the influences of Mari folklore and jazz into a highly melodic, accessible idiom.

Eslava (y Elizondo), (Miguel) Hilarión (b. Burlada, near Pamplona, 21 Oct. 1807; d. Madrid, 23 July 1878). Composer. Studied composition in Calahorra; choirmaster at Burgo de Osma (1828) and Seville Cathedral (1832). Appointed director of the Royal Chapel, Madrid (1844) and professor at Madrid Conservatory (1854). Best known for sacred music and his 10-volume anthology of Spanish sacred music, *Lira sacro-hispana* (1869).

Espinette [Fr.]. In the 16th century, harpsichord, *spinet.

Esplá (y Triay), Oscar (b. Alicante, 5 Aug. 1886; d. Madrid, 6 Jan. 1976). Composer. Studied in Munich and Meiningen with Reger (1912) and in Paris with Saint-Saëns (1913). Joined the faculty at the Madrid Conservatory in 1930, serving as director, 1936–39; in 1948 appointed music director of the Laboratoire musical scientifique, Brussels. Succeeded del Campo at the San Fernando Academy (1953) and Honegger at the Institut de France (1955); director of the Oscar Esplá Academy in Alicante in 1958. Musical influences include Debussy and Stravinsky; also integrated materials from the popular music of Spain's Mediterranean coast into some compositions.

Espressivo [It., abbr. *espr.*]. Expressive, with expression.

Espringale [OFr.]. A jumping dance, as distinct from the *carole,* a round dance.

Esser, (Karl?) Michael, Ritter von (b. Aachen, bapt. 3? Apr. 1737; d. ca. 1795). Violinist and composer. Solo violinist (from 1756) and director (from 1761) in the chapel orchestra at the Hessen-Kassel court. Embarked on a successful concert tour of Europe as soloist on violin and viola d'amore. Mozart praised his playing but criticized his overladen manner of ornamentation. Composed an opera and instrumental music.

Estampes [Fr., Prints]. A set of three piano pieces by Debussy, composed in 1903: "Pagodes" (Pagodas), "La soirée dans Grenade" (Evening in Granada), and "Jardins sous la pluie" (Gardens in the Rain).

Estampie [Fr.; Prov. *estampida;* It. *istanpita;* Lat. *stantipes*]. A textless musical composition of the 13th and 14th centuries; also a type of late medieval poem. The musical *estampie* may be one of the oldest surviving varieties of purely instrumental music composed in western Europe. Scholarly opinion is divided on whether the *estampie* is a dance (functional or stylized).

Musical compositions called *estampies* or *istanpite* in the original sources consist of from three to seven units *(puncta),* each repeated immediately, with first and second endings [Fr. *ouvert* and *clos;* It.

aperto and *chiuso;* Lat. *apertum* and *clausum*]. A single pair of endings (x,y) may serve for any number of units, as follows: AxAy, BxBy, CxCy, etc.

Estey organ. A suction-operated reed organ built in the second half of the 19th century by the firm of Jacob Estey in Brattleboro, Vermont.

Estinguendo [It.]. Dying away.

Estinto [It.]. Barely audible.

Estompé [Fr.]. Toned down.

Estribillo [Sp.]. *Refrain. See also *Villancico.*

Et in terra pax [Lat.]. See Gloria.

Éteindre [Fr., p.p. *éteint*]. To extinguish.

Ethnomusicology. A subdivision of musicology concerned primarily with the comparative study of musics of the world, music as an aspect of culture, and the music of oral tradition. According to other definitions that have been promulgated, ethnomusicology is the study of non-Western and folk music, or of the music of contemporary cultures, the anthropological study of music, or the study of a music by an outsider to its culture. Although there is disagreement on precise definition, it is clear that most ethnomusicologists do research in non-Western or folk music, take an interest in the role of music in culture, engage in field research, and use concepts developed by anthropology. As their subject is mainly music that lives primarily in oral tradition, they are for the most part limited to materials collected in recent or contemporary times, and as students of music outside their own culture, they are usually obliged to follow a comparative approach.

Ethos. In the music of ancient Greece, the ethical or moral character of music, or, by extension, simply its generalized emotion or mood, especially of the individual modes, each of which was regarded as embodying certain attributes (strength, manliness, passion, lasciviousness, etc.) and as capable of arousing those in the listener. Some writers of the Middle Ages and Renaissance connect the modes of their own day with such qualities, often employing (incorrectly) the Greek names for the modes (Dorian, Phrygian, etc.; see Mode).

Étouffé [Fr.]. Damped, muted; *étouffoir,* *damper.

Etude [Fr. *étude,* study; Ger. *Etüde, Studie;* It. *studio;* Sp. *estudio*]. A composition designed to improve the technique of an instrumental performer by isolating specific difficulties and concentrating his or her efforts on their mastery. A single etude usually focuses on one technical problem; etudes are usually published in groups more or less systematically covering a range of such problems in a range of keys. In present-day usage, the etude falls between the exercise, a short formula not worked out as a formal composition, and the concert etude, which can stand as a self-sufficient piece of music.

The concept of a series of etudes designed as a course of study combined with sufficient compositional interest and shaping to hold the student's attention is perhaps to be linked to needs arising from the explosion of bourgeois music-making in the late 18th and early 19th centuries. Beginning with Muzio Clementi, Johann Baptist Cramer, Carl Czerny, and others for the keyboard and Rodolphe Kreutzer, Pierre Rode, Charles-Auguste de Bériot, and others for the violin, the 19th century produced a large quantity of such courses. See also Capriccio.

Composers of the 19th century recognized wider musical possibilities in the etude, the development of which led to what is usually called the concert etude. The etudes of Chopin (op. 10, 1833; op. 25, 1837) are the earliest examples, followed by those of Scriabin (op. 8, 1894; op. 42, 1903; op. 65, 1912), Debussy (twelve in two books, 1915), and many others. In the Lisztian tradition (*Études d'exécution transcendante,* published 1852), the concert etude becomes as much, or perhaps more, a demonstration of triumphant virtuosity to the concert public as a means to its achievement.

Études d'exécution transcendante [Fr., Transcendental Etudes]. A set of 12 studies by Liszt. The first version was published in 1826 as op. 6 and included 11 pieces related to later versions. The second version was completed and published by 1839. The final version, the first to use the term *transcendante,* was published in 1852. Most of the pieces have descriptive or poetic titles ("Mazeppa," "Vision," "Harmonies du soir," etc.).

Études symphoniques [Fr., Symphonic Etudes]. A set of piano pieces by Schumann, op. 13 (1834–37 with the title *Etüden im Orchestercharakter für Pianoforte von Florestan und Eusebius;* revised in 1852 with the title *Études en formes de variations*), in the form of a theme (by Baron von Fricken, father of Ernestine, the young Schumann's sweetheart) with 12 variations and a finale. Five additional variations not included in either of the earlier versions were published posthumously in 1873.

Etwas [Ger.]. Somewhat.

Eugene Onegin [Russ. *Evgeny Onegin*]. Opera in three acts by Tchaikovsky (libretto by the composer and Konstantin Shilovsky, after Pushkin's poem), produced in Moscow in 1879. Setting: St. Petersburg, about 1820.

Eunuch flute [Fr. *flûte-eunuque*]. A type of *mirliton described and illustrated by Mersenne (1636).

Euouae. The vowels of the words "seculorum Amen," with which the Lesser *Doxology concludes; sometimes also spelled *evovae*. In books and manuscripts containing *Gregorian chant, these letters accompany the pitches of the final cadences or *differentiae* of certain melodic formulas [see Psalm tone]. When the letters and pitches are given together following a melody such as an antiphon, they serve to indicate which formula is to be used for the singing of verses in association with that melody.

Euphonium [Fr. *euphonium, basse à pistons;* Ger. *Euphonium, Baryton;* It. *eufonio;* Sp. *euphonium*]. A valved brass instrument in B♭, an octave lower than the *cornet or *trumpet. It has about 2.75 m. (9 ft.) of tube length, usually folded in tuba or upright form with the bell straight up or turned partly forward [see ill. under Brass instruments]. The euphonium has a large bore of bugle or flugelhorn proportions in contrast to the otherwise similar English baritone, which has more modest cornetlike dimensions. Both the euphonium and the baritone have been used extensively in military, community, and school bands since the middle of the 19th century. In bands of the late 19th century, the euphonium became a featured solo instrument with many fine band parts and virtuoso solos written for it.

Valved instruments at 9′ B♭ pitch first appeared in Germany in the 1830s. From almost the beginning there were at least two sizes. The wide-bore instrument was a euphonium in England, a *saxhorn basse* in France, a *Baryton* in Germany, and a *flicorno basso* in Italy. The smaller size was a baritone or Baryton in England, a *saxhorn baritone* in France, a *Baryton B* or *Barytonhorn* in Germany, and a *flicorno tenore* in Italy. In the U.S., several of these terms were used before the English practice of euphonium and baritone was accepted early in the 20th century. The instrument is also known in the U.S. as a tenor tuba.

The double-belled euphonium combines a euphonium or baritone and a valved trombone in the same instrument. Such duplex instruments in several sizes were first made in Europe in the mid-19th century and in the U.S. from the 1880s until well into the 20th century.

Eurhythmics. See Dalcroze method.

Euridice. (1) Opera in a prologue and six scenes by Jacopo Peri (libretto on the myth of Orpheus and Eurydice by Ottavio Rinuccini), produced in Florence in 1600. (2) Opera by Giulio Caccini (libretto by Rinuccini), published in 1600 and first produced in Florence in 1602.

Evangeliary [Lat. *evangeliarium*]. See Liturgical books.

Evangelist. In a *Passion, the narrator, whose text is taken from one of the Gospels.

Evangelisti, Franco (b. Rome, 21 Jan. 1926; d. there, 28 Jan. 1980). Composer. Studied music in Rome (D. Paris, 1948–53), Freiburg (Genzmer, 1953–56), and Darmstadt (Eimert, Stockhausen). In 1961 founded Nuova consonanza, an ensemble devoted to contemporary music and, from 1964, to group improvisation. Taught electronic music at the Accademia di S. Cecilia (1968–72), the Conservatorio dell'Aquila (1969–75), and the Conservatorio di S. Cecilia in Rome (1974–80). Composed little after 1962. Works include *Die Schachtel* (pantomime, 1962–63); 6 orchestral pieces (*Random or Not Random,* 1962); *Campi integrati* (1959, 1979), in which he applied aleatory procedures to electronic music.

Evangelium [Lat., Ger.]. Gospel.

Evans, Bill [William John] (b. Plainfield, N.J., 16 Aug. 1929; d. New York, 15 Sept. 1980). Jazz pianist. Began recording as a leader in 1956; came to prominence as a member of Miles Davis's sextet (1958–59) and composed "Blue in Green" for Davis's album *Kind of Blue* (1959). Also recorded in a duo with Jim Hall in 1959 and from that year made his principal contribution as a leader of trios. Founded in bop traditions, his original, influential piano playing involved a sensitive touch and an unusual approach to chordal substitution and voicing.

Evans, Geraint (Llewellyn) (b. Pontypridd, South Wales, 16 Feb. 1922; d. Aberystwyth, 19 Sept. 1992). Baritone. Studied voice at Cardiff, and in Hamburg, Geneva, and London. Covent Garden debut in 1948; sang Figaro there (1949) and with great success at La Scala (1960), the Vienna Staatsoper (1961), and the Salzburg Festival (1962). Met debut as Falstaff in 1964. Sang in a number of premieres, including *Billy Budd* and Vaughan Williams's *Pilgrim's Progress* (1951). Knighted in 1971; retired from opera in 1983.

Evans, Gil [Green, Ian Ernest Gilmore] (b. Toronto, 13 May 1912; d. Cuernavaca, Mexico, 20 Mar. 1988). Jazz arranger and bandleader. Arranged tunes as a member of Claude Thornhill's big band (1941–43, 1946–48); arranged "Boplicity" for Miles Davis's cool jazz nonet; later Davis recorded with Evans's orchestra. From the mid-1960s his orchestra turned toward rock music; from 1983 it held a residency in New York clubs.

Evensong. In medieval England, the canonical hour of Vespers. At the Reformation, the name was carried over into the Book of Common Prayer formally to designate what subsequently came to be called Evening Prayer.

Evirato [It.]. **Castrato.*

Evovae. See *Euouae.*

Ewing, Maria (Louise) (b. Detroit, 27 Mar. 1950). Mezzo-soprano. Studied at the Cleveland Institute and at Juilliard. Debut in 1973 at the Ravinia Festival; Met debut as Cherubino, 1976; at La Scala as Genevieve, 1976; at the Paris Opéra, 1981; at Covent Garden, 1988. Sang Poulenc's Blanche at the Met in 1981, and Monteverdi's Nero at the Glyndebourne Festival in 1984. Her 1985 Carmen at the Met was a great success.

Exaquier [Fr.]. *Chekker.

Exchange of voices. See Voice exchange.

Exequiae [Lat.], **Exequien** [Ger.]. Exequies, i.e., a funeral service.

Exposition. (1) In *sonata form, the first major section, incorporating at least one important modulation to the dominant or other secondary key and presenting the principal thematic material. (2) In a *fugue, the statement of the subject in imitation by the several voices; especially the first such statement, with which the fugue begins.

Expression marks. Symbols and words or phrases and their abbreviations employed along with musical notation to guide the performance of a work in matters other than pitches and rhythms. Such marks in general affect *dynamics, *tempo, and *articulation (including *bowing and *tonguing). The use of the term expression in this context is somewhat misleading, since whatever the nature of musical expression, it does not result exclusively or perhaps even principally from those aspects of music specified by "expression" marks. See Performance marks.

Expressionism. A movement in German visual art and literature of the early 20th century. The term is sometimes applied to Germanic music of the period, especially that of Schoenberg and his school. The expressionists believed that art should reflect the inner consciousness of its creator: rather than produce a physically accurate depiction of a scene, the painter or writer should "express" his personal feelings toward it. Thus, a major feature of the expressionist style is a restructuring of external reality through exaggeration and distortion. Schoenberg's abandonment of tonality and triadic harmony suggests interesting correspondences with these developments. His tonal works of the early 1900s reveal an analogous tendency to produce extreme expressive effects through distortion of traditional harmonic structures, emphasis upon nontriadic tones, and avoidance of unambiguous tonal regions. Soon thereafter Schoenberg composed the first atonal works, breaking completely with the conventions of triadic harmony and the major-minor tonal system.

Expressive organ [Fr. *orgue expressif*]. A pressure-operated *harmonium.

Extemporization. See Improvisation.

Extravaganza. A musical work characterized by extravagant fancy, often with satirical or parodistic intent. The term was often used in 19th-century Britain and the U.S. for a genre of popular musical stage work descended from the burlesque and itself one of the ancestors of the modern musical comedy.

Eybler, Joseph (Leopold) [von] (b. Schwechat, near Vienna, 8 Feb. 1765; d. Vienna, 24 July 1846). Composer. Studied with Albrechtsberger (1776–79); from 1782 a professional musician and composer in Vienna; assisted in rehearsals of *Così fan tutte*. He was given Mozart's Requiem to complete but felt unable to do so. Kapellmeister at the Carmelite Church from 1792; at the Schottenkloster from 1796; from 1801 music teacher to the imperial family. In 1824 succeeded Salieri as court Kapellmeister. Works include a famous Requiem (1803); 32 Masses and much other sacred music; orchestral, chamber, piano works.

Eye music [Ger. *Augenmusik*]. Music in which some purely graphic aspect of the notation conveys nonmusical meaning to the eye. Such techniques were used particularly in the 15th and 16th centuries, the most common being the use of blackened notes for texts expressing grief or lament. Black notes were sometimes also used for individual words such as night, dark, and the like, especially in *madrigals of the second half of the 16th century by composers such as Luca Marenzio. The term eye music is sometimes also applied to examples of *word painting such as the use of ascending or descending motion in conjunction with words such as up, down, heaven, and hell.

Eysler, Edmund (b. Vienna, 12 Mar. 1874; d. there, 4 Oct. 1949). Composer. Studied composition with Johann Nepomuk Fuchs, then taught piano and conducted theater orchestras. His operetta *Bruder Straubinger* (1903) was extremely successful; wrote more than 50 operettas, most before the First World War and performed in Vienna. Other works include a ballet, 2 operas, songs, dances, and piano works.

F

F. Abbr. (often in italics, *f*) for **forte*. See also Pitch names, Letter notation, Hexachord, Pitch, Clef, Sound hole.

Fa. See Pitch names, Solmization, Hexachord. *Fa fictum* is f″, i.e., the first pitch above the upper limit of the **gamut* of medieval and Renaissance theory; it is therefore part of **musica ficta*.

Fa fictum [Lat.]. See *Fa*.

Faburden. An English technique of polyphonic vocal improvisation, current from about 1430 until the Reformation in England and until the late 16th century in Scotland. Originally designating the lowest voice of such improvised polyphony, the term faburden was eventually applied to the technique itself and to the entire polyphonic complex [see also Burden (2)]. Singers would begin with a preexisting melody, usually a liturgical chant. This melody would be made the middle of three voices, and the others would be reckoned from it. One would consist of thirds and fifths below, another of parallel fourths above [see Sight]. Ends of phrases were slightly ornamented. The resulting sound, a series of sixth chords with an occasional octave harmonized by a fifth, is similar to that of Continental **fauxbourdon*, which, however, was principally a written technique.

Faccio, Franco [Francesco Antonio] (b. Verona, 8 Mar. 1840; d. Monza, 21 July 1891). Conductor. Studied at the Milan Conservatory, where he collaborated with Boito. Following the failure of his two operas, became a conductor at the Teatro Carcano (from 1868) and at La Scala (from 1869). Professor of composition, Milan Conservatory (1868–78).

Facile, facilmente [It.]. Simple, simply.

Fado, fadinho [Port.]. Since the 19th century, the most characteristic genre of urban popular song of Portugal, especially in Lisbon. It is sung in cafés and in the streets to the accompaniment of the guitar and related instruments.

Fag. [Ger., It.]. Abbr. for **Fagott, *fagotto*.

Fagott [Ger.]. **Bassoon*.

Fagottgeige [Ger.; It. *viola di fagotto*]. In the 17th and 18th centuries, a viola tuned like a cello and played on the arm. Its use of overspun strings produced a buzzing sound similar to that of the bassoon.

Fagotto [It.]. **Bassoon; fagottino, *tenoroon; fagottone,* contrabassoon.

Fairchild, Blair (b. Belmont, Mass., 23 June 1877; d. Paris, 23 Apr. 1933). Composer. Studied at Harvard under Paine and Spalding; lived in Turkey and Persia (1901–3), then Paris (from 1905). Orchestral works often reflect his interest in the Near East; also wrote chamber, piano, choral, and vocal music.

Fairlamb, James Remington (b. Philadelphia, 23 Jan. 1838; d. Ingleside, N.Y., 16 Apr. 1908). Composer. Studied at the Paris Conservatory and in Florence; organist and composer in Washington, Philadelphia, New Jersey; taught high school music in New York. Published sacred choral music and 2 chamber operas.

Fairy Queen, The. A **semi-opera* in a prologue and five acts by Purcell, the text of which is an anonymous adaptation of Shakespeare's *A Midsummer Night's Dream,* produced in London in 1692.

Fake-book. A collection of popular and jazz melodies with chord symbols (often rudimentary or simply incorrect) [see Fake-book notation] and sometimes words, used especially by musicians in restaurants, nightclubs, and the like as a basis from which to improvise or "fake" their own arrangements. Such books are most often reproduced in violation of copyright laws.

Fake-book notation. The symbols and abbreviations used to indicate the chords of jazz and popular music in **fake-books* and elsewhere. Their use is not entirely standardized and may be ambiguous in some cases. Nothing is implied about the inversion or spacing of a chord unless a bass note is specifically indicated (usually by a slash followed by its letter name). The root of a chord is specified by the appropriate letter of the alphabet. A major triad is indicated by a capital letter; a minor triad by a lowercase letter or by the addition of "min," "m," or "−"; an augmented triad by "aug" or "+"; a dominant seventh chord (i.e., a major triad with a minor seventh above the root) by a 7; a minor seventh chord (a minor triad with a minor seventh above the root) by "min 7" or "−7"; a major seventh chord (a major triad with a major seventh above the root) by "maj 7"; a diminished triad by "dim" or "°"; a diminished seventh chord by "dim 7" or "°7"; a half-diminished seventh chord (a diminished triad with a minor seventh above the root) by "ø7." A triad with a sixth added above the root is indicated by a 6, and ninth, eleventh, and thirteenth chords by the numerals 9, 11, and 13, respectively. In each of these cases, the top-most pitch may be specified as raised (by "♯" or "+") or lowered (by "♭" or "−") as compared with the major sixth, ninth, and thirteenth and the perfect eleventh that would ordinarily be formed above the root.

Fa-la, fa-la-la. Nonsense syllables that recur in some types of 16th-century song, especially the *balletto,* and thus pieces of this type, such as Thomas Morley's "Now is the month of Maying."

Falconieri, Andrea (b. Naples, 1585 or 1586; d. there, 19 or 29 July 1656). Composer and lutenist. At the court of Parma (1604–14), then elsewhere in Italy; travels in Spain and France (1621–28); from 1639 lutenist, from 1647 *maestro di cappella* at the royal chapel at Naples. Composed songs and instrumental music.

Fall, Leo(pold) (b. Olomouc, Moravia, 2 Feb. 1873; d. Vienna, 16 Sept. 1925). Composer and conductor. Studied at the Vienna Conservatory with Robert and Johann Nepomuk Fuchs; directed theater orchestras and wrote stage music in Berlin, Hamburg, and Cologne. In 1906 returned to Vienna, where his operettas had considerable success; also composed overtures, waltzes, and songs.

Falla (y Matheu), Manuel (María) de (los Dolores) (b. Cádiz, 23 Nov. 1876; d. Alta Gracia, Argentina, 14 Nov. 1946). Composer. Studied at the Madrid Conservatory, and pursued zarzuela composition. In Paris (1907–14) met Dukas, Ravel, Debussy, Stravinsky, and Albéniz. Published *Pièces espagnoles* for piano (1909), composed the opera *La *vida breve* (1913). In Madrid (1914–20) wrote some of his best-known works, including *El *amor brujo, *Noches en los jardines de España, El *sombrero de tres picos,* and *Fantasía bética* for piano (1919). Moved to Granada (1920); met and collaborated with Lorca (puppet theater piece *El retablo de maese Pedro,* 1923). Although evocative of the French milieu, his work is nonetheless viewed as the embodiment of Spanish nationalism.

Falsa [Sp., Port.]. Dissonance. For *tiento de falsas,* see *Tiento* and Toccata.

Falsa musica [Lat.]. See *Music ficta.*

False. False cadence, deceptive *cadence; false relation, *cross relation; false fifth (triad), diminished fifth (triad). See also Modulation.

Falsetto [It.; Fr. *fausset;* Ger. *Falsett, Fistelstimme;* Sp. *falsete*]. The male voice above its normal range, the latter usually called full or chest voice. It entails a special method of voice production that is frequently used by tenors to extend the upper limits of their range. Male *altos or countertenors use only this method of voice production. The falsetto voice has a distinctly lighter quality and is less powerful than the full voice. The practice of using male falsettists for the upper parts in vocal polyphony, especially the alto, is well documented, along with the term falsetto itself, from the 16th century. The use of falsetto voice is a prominent feature of some types of black American popular music, from which it and much else were taken up by rock musicians generally.

Falsobordone [It.; Sp. *fabordón*]. In its most characteristic form, a four-part, homophonic, vocal harmonization of a *psalm tone or similar liturgical chant, which may be placed in the tenor or in the uppermost part. It differs from *fauxbourdon, from which, because of the similarity of the names, it has sometimes been thought to derive, in that all four parts are written out and root-position triads predominate. It is often sung in alternation with chant [see *Alternatim*], principally for Psalm verses, the *Magnificat, and the *Lamentations. Most popular on the Continent around 1600, *falsobordone* has continued in use to the present day, and in England it has survived as *Anglican chant. The genre also gave rise to solo songs and purely instrumental pieces.

Falstaff. Opera in three acts by Verdi (libretto by Arrigo Boito based on Shakespeare's *The Merry Wives of Windsor* and *King Henry IV*), produced in Milan in 1893. Setting: Windsor, early 15th century.

Familiar style [It. *stile familiare*]. A style employing four-part vocal, syllabic, *homorhythmic texture such as characterizes simple hymn settings or *falsobordone.

Fanciulla del West, La [It., The Girl of the Golden West]. Opera in three acts by Puccini (libretto by Guelfo Civinini and Carlo Zangarini based on a play by David Belasco), produced in New York in 1910. Setting: a California mining camp during the gold rush of the late 1840s.

Fancy. The 16th- and 17th-century English manifestation of the *fantasia.

Fandango [Sp.]. A dance and dance-song of Spain in a moderately fast triple meter, appearing first in the early 18th century. Examples for keyboard by Soler and Domenico Scarlatti are characterized by regular alternation, in a minor key, of a measure of tonic and a measure of dominant harmony supporting a steadily unfolding upper part of improvisatory character. More recent examples in art music occur in Rimsky-Korsakov's *Capriccio espagnole* (1887), Granados's *Goyescas* (no. 3, 1912), and Falla's *Sombrero de tres picos* (1919). The folk dance of this name, which is widely disseminated and includes regional variants such as the *malagueña* (from Málaga) is danced by a couple with castanets and accompanied by guitars, and it includes sung couplets, similar to those of the *jota,* in alternation with instrumental interludes.

Fanfare. (1) Music played by trumpets or other brass instruments, sometimes accompanied by percussion, for ceremonial purposes, especially to call attention to the arrival of a dignitary or to the beginning of a public ceremony; also termed a flourish, as in the "Ruffles and Flourishes" played by military bands in the U.S. to announce the arrival of the President. The term is sometimes extended to include military and hunting signals of similar character.
    (2) [Fr.] A brass band.

Fantasia [It., fr. Gr. *phantasia,* product of the imagination; Eng. fantasia, fantasy, fancy; Fr. *fantaisie;* Ger. *Fantasie, Phantasie;* Sp. *fantasía*]. An ingenious and imaginative instrumental composition, often characterized by distortion, exaggeration, and elusiveness resulting from its departure from current stylistic and structural norms. Throughout its use, fantasia has often simply meant to improvise [Ger. *fantasieren,* It. *sonar di fantasia,* Sp. *tañer fantasía*]. By extension, it may be applied to a piece that attempts to give the impression of flowing spontaneously from a *player's* imagination and delight in dexterity. A fantasia may also be an esoteric work that evolves from a *composer's* technical manipulation and mental abstractions. The fantasia has often borrowed antithetical formal procedures and styles, and an inexact use of terminology sometimes compounds the problems in musical definition. In the 16th century, the terms fantasia and *ricercar* are often substituted for one another; since then, the fantasia has been equated with the *capriccio, automaton,* *voluntary,* *toccata,* *canzona,* *fuga,* *rhapsody,* and other genres.
    Fantasia has often been used for pieces that attempt to capture the character of improvisation as well as for didactic compositions by players wishing to illustrate their art. The Italian lutenist Francesco Canova da Milano (1497–1543) is the first master of the fantasia. His fantasias balance compositional methods drawn from vocal polyphony and the requirements of a purely instrumental idiom, employing the techniques of *cantus firmus,* parody, and *paraphrase.* Keyboard fantasias, especially those by organists, have always tended toward learnedness, though the element of improvisation is strong in some works of the English virginalists (who emphasize *divisions*) and Jan Pieterszoon Sweelinck (1562–1621). The Sweelinck tradition was cultivated in the Baroque by central Europeans such as Samuel Scheidt (1587–1654), Johann Jacob Froberger (1616–67), Johann Pachelbel (1653–1706), and Got-

tlieb Muffat (1690–1770). North German composers of the 18th century increased the sense of improvisational freedom. The contrasting moods, sudden deceptive cadences, instrumental recitative, and bold modulations of J. S. Bach's *Chromatic Fantasy and Fugue* BWV 903 illustrate the type. C. P. E. Bach and his father's other students extended it still further by abandoning the bar line and regular meter. Although the unmeasured fantasia did not survive the post-Bach generation, many features survive in Mozart's Fantasia in C minor K. 457 (1786, intended to preface the Sonata K. 475). But J. S. Bach's seven fantasias for organ and eight for harpsichord include both learned and improvisatory styles.
    The 19th and early 20th centuries were inundated with fantasias, capriccios, and rhapsodies that draw upon popular songs, pseudo–folk melodies, and patriotic airs to evoke exotic landscapes, or that quote themes from familiar operas. These range from modest salon pieces to virtuoso vehicles by and for showmen such as violinists Paganini, Bériot, Vieuxtemps, and Sarasate and pianists Thalberg, Gottschalk, Satter, and Tausig, as well as for ubiquitous cornet and piccolo band soloists. The genre also reflected important manifestations of musical Romanticism, as in works for piano by Chopin (Fantasie op. 49, 1841; Polonaise-Fantasie op. 61, 1845–46), for violin by Bruch (*Schottische Fantasie* op. 46, 1880), and for orchestra by Tchaikovsky (*Capriccio italien* op. 45, 1880), Rimsky-Korsakov (*Fantasia on Two Russian Themes* op. 33, 1886–87), and Richard Strauss (*Aus Italien* op. 16, 1886). Liszt was the consummate master of the potpourri, particularly in his operatic fantasias, capriccios, and *paraphrases de concert.*
    Other 19th-century works fuse the fantasia with the sonata. Such a *sonata quasi fantasia* deviates from the formal norms of the Classical sonata by joining movements together, rearranging their internal sequence, recalling previous ideas, or altering normal tonal and thematic relationships. Following Schubert's influential *Wandererfantasie* (D. 760, 1823), many fantasies favored thematic transformation over development. Sets of short ternary *Phantasiestücke* with widely varying moods and occasional programmatic titles such as "caprice," "night," and "soaring" represent another extreme in the Romantic fantasia. Examples include Chopin's *Fantaisie-Impromptu* op. 66 (1835); Schumann's *Phantasiestücke* op. 12 (1832–37); and Brahms's op. 116 for piano (1892). During the late 19th and early 20th centuries, there was a modest vogue for concerto fantasias that are closer in spirit and form to the symphonic fantasia than to the potpourri. Examples include works by Anton Rubinstein (op. 84, ca. 1886), Widor (op. 62, 1889), Debussy (1889–90), and Fauré (op. 111, 1919).

Fantasiestück [Ger.]. See Fantasia.

Fantastic Symphony. See *Symphonie fantastique.*

Fantasy. (1) *Fantasia, fancy. (2) The development section of a work in *sonata form.

Farandole [Fr.; Prov. *farandoulo*]. A dance of Provence performed by a chain of alternating men and women who follow the leader in a variety of winding patterns. The music is usually in moderate 6/8 and is played on the *pipe and tabor.

Farce [Fr., Eng., Ger.; It., Sp. *farsa*]. (1) A work of theater characterized by low comedy, often satirical, sometimes obscene, and frequently making use of sudden appearances and other visual humor; also humor of the type found in such works. The first works bearing the term occur in 15th-century France. (2) In 18th-century Italian opera, a comic scene interpolated into a serious work. The term was also used in the 18th century for comic operas performed, like *intermezzi, between the acts of an opera or as an afterpiece.

Farewell Symphony. Popular name for Haydn's Symphony no. 45 in F♯ minor Hob. I:45 (1772). The title stems from an episode recounted by Haydn and refers to the design of the closing section of the last movement, which permits players to leave one by one, concluding with only two violins. This jest was intended to dissuade Prince Esterházy, whom Haydn served as conductor and composer, from further prolonging his stay in the palace at Esterháza, allowing the members of the orchestra to return to their families in Eisenstadt instead.

Farina, Carlo (b. Mantua, ca. 1600; d. ca. 1640). Violinist and composer. *Konzertmeister* at the court of Dresden, 1626–29, alongside Schütz; in 1637 was in Danzig. His virtuosic music helped establish an idiomatic violin style.

Farinelli [Broschi, Carlo] (b. Andria, Apulia, 24 Jan. 1705; d. Bologna, 15 July 1782). Soprano castrato. Studied with Porpora; successful operatic performances in Naples and Rome (1722–24), then northern Italy, Vienna, and Munich (1724–32). In 1734 went to London, where his triumphs hastened Handel's withdrawal from operatic composition. Performed in Paris and London (1736–37); in Spain was a prized court performer and confidant to Philip V (until 1746) and Ferdinand VI (1746–59).

Farkas, Ferenc (b. Nagykanizsa, 15 Dec. 1905). Composer. From 1922 studied composition at the Budapest Academy, and with Respighi in Rome (1929–31). During the 1930s and 1940s composed scores for stage and films in Vienna, Budapest, and Copenhagen. Taught at the Higher Music School in Budapest (1935–41), at the Koloszvár Conservatory

(1941–46; director from 1943), and at the Budapest Academy (1949–75). Works include operas; orchestral works; vocal works; chamber music; songs; piano works.

Farmer, Art(hur Stewart) (b. Council Bluffs, Iowa, 21 Aug. 1928). Jazz flugelhorn player and trumpeter. Played trumpet in Hampton's big band (1952–53), then worked with Horace Silver, Gerry Mulligan, and George Russell. In 1959 founded the Jazztet, and began concentrating on flugelhorn. From 1962 led groups; toured with the Jazztet, re-formed in 1982.

Farmer, John (b. ca. 1570; fl. 1591–1601). Composer. From 1595 associated with Christ Church Cathedral, Dublin, but in 1599 was living in London. Best-known works are English madrigals, of which he wrote a complete volume (1599) and a single piece published in *The Triumphes of Oriana* (1601).

Farnaby, Giles (b. ca. 1563; d. London, buried 25 Nov. 1640). Composer. Received the B.Mus. from Oxford in 1592, then lived near Lincoln; around 1611 moved to London. Works include over 50 keyboard pieces (most in the *Fitzwilliam Virginal Book*), Psalms, and a book of canzonets.

Farrar, Geraldine (b. Melrose, Mass., 28 Feb. 1882; d. Ridgefield, Conn., 11 Mar. 1967). Soprano. 1901 debut at the Berlin Opera; Met debut as Gounod's Juliette (1906). Sang opposite Caruso at the Met premiere of *Madama Butterfly* (1907); from 1914 closely identified with the part of Carmen. Created Wolf-Ferrari's Susanna (1911) and Puccini's Suor Angelica (1918) for the Met; farewell performance in 1922.

Farrell, Eileen (b. Willimantic, Conn., 13 Feb. 1920). Soprano. Hosted her own show, *Eileen Farrell Presents,* 1941–46. Stage debut as Santuzza in Florida (1956); subsequently performed with the San Francisco Opera, the Chicago Lyric Opera, and at the Met (1960–66); many concert performances thereafter, often in Wagnerian roles. Taught at Indiana Univ. (1971–80) and the Univ. of Maine at Orono (1980–84).

Farrenc [née Dumont], **(Jeanne-) Louise** (b. Paris, 31 May 1804; d. there, 15 Sept. 1875). Composer, teacher. Studied with Reicha; settled in Paris in 1825 and published piano music in the salon genres and etudes; from the 1830s composed chamber and orchestral music. Professor of piano, Paris Conservatory (1842–73).

Farse [Lat. *farsa*]. A Latin or vernacular interpolation in a liturgical chant or text, especially in an epistle or other reading; a *trope.

Farwell, Arthur (b. St. Paul, Minn., 23 Apr. 1872; d. New York, 20 Jan. 1952). Composer, critic, and editor. Studied composition with Chadwick in Boston and with Humperdinck, Pfitzner, and Guilmant in Europe; returned to the U.S. in 1899 and taught at Cornell (1899–1901), Berkeley (1918–19), and Michigan State (1927–39), then returned to New York and taught privately. In 1901 founded the Wa-Wan Press, which published his own music and that of other American composers. Chief music critic of *Musical America* (1909–14). Remembered primarily as an Indianist; early works are Wagnerian in their harmonic language; later works are very chromatic.

Fasano, Renato (b. Naples, 21 Aug. 1902; d. Rome, 3 Aug. 1979). Conductor and composer. Studied piano and composition at the Naples Conservatory. Through the early 1940s best known as a composer. Director of the Cagliari Conservatory, 1931–39; of the St. Cecilia Academy in Rome, 1944–47, and its president, 1972–76; of the Rome Conservatory, 1960–72. In 1948 founded the Collegium musicum italicum; as I virtuosi di Roma (from 1952) they became widely known through recordings.

Fasch, Carl Friedrich Christian (b. Zerbst, 18 Nov. 1736; d. Berlin, 3 Aug. 1800). Composer. Studied with his father, Johann Friedrich. Second harpsichordist at the court of Frederick the Great in 1755, was promoted after C. P. E. Bach's departure for Hamburg (1767); directed the royal opera (1774–76). In later years devoted much time to choral music; founded the Berlin Singakademie (1789).

Fasch, Johann Friedrich (b. Buttstädt bei Weimar, 15 Apr. 1688; d. Zerbst, 5 Dec. 1758). Composer. Studied with Kuhnau in Leipzig, and with Graupner and Grünewald in Darmstadt. Worked in Bayreuth and Lukavec before accepting the post of Kapellmeister in Zerbst (1724), where he remained for the rest of his life. Fasch's modern reputation rests on his instrumental music, often considered an important link between Baroque and classical styles.

Fasola [contr. of fa-sol-la]. An early English system of *solmization, later called sol-fa or Lancashire sol-fa, in use from the end of the 16th century. Fasola, utilizing only the four syllables *fa-sol-la-mi,* is thus an abridged reconception of the hexachordal system *ut-re-mi-fa-sol-la* [see Hexachord]. See also Shape-note.

Fassbaender, Brigitte (b. Berlin, 3 July 1939). Mezzo-soprano. Studied voice at the Nuremberg Conservatory (1957–61). Debut in 1961 with the Bavarian State Opera; debuted at the San Francisco Opera, 1970 (Carmen); at Covent Garden, 1971 (Octavian); at the Paris Opéra, 1972 (Brangäne); at Salzburg, 1972 (Dorabella); at the Met, 1976 (Octavian). Praised for her Countess Geschwitz *(Lulu)* and for her solos in Bach Passions.

Fastoso [It.]. Pompous.

Fauré, Gabriel (Urbain) (b. Pamiers, 12 May 1845; d. Paris, 4 Nov. 1924). Composer. From 1854 to 1865 studied at the École Niedermeyer in Paris under Loret (organ), Wackerthaler (counterpoint, fugue), Dietsch (harmony), and Niedermeyer (singing, piano, plainsong); also studied piano with Saint-Saëns; composed his first works, including the choral *Cantique de Jean Racine.* Organist at St. Sauveur in Rennes (1866–70), returned to Paris as assistant organist at Notre Dame Clignancourt; subsequently assistant organist to Widor at St. Sulpice (from 1871) and choirmaster at the Madeleine (from 1877). Composed songs and, from about 1875, piano pieces and chamber music (2 violin sonatas; 2 piano quartets; 2 cello sonatas; the Second Piano Quintet; the Piano Trio); in 1887 began the Requiem, the most important of his sacred works; composed the song cycle *La bonne chanson* (1892–94). In 1896 appointed professor of composition at the Paris Conservatory (pupils included Ravel and Nadia Boulanger) and became organist at the Madeleine. From 1894 made several visits to England, leading to incidental music for Maeterlinck's *Pelléas et Mélisande* (1898). In 1901 became professor of composition at the École Niedermeyer; in 1905 appointed director of the Conservatory. Between 1907 and 1912 composed his only opera, *Pénélope* (1913). Other works: nearly 100 songs; piano pieces, including nocturnes, barcarolles, impromptus, valse-caprices; *Dolly Suite,* 4-hands; works for piano and orchestra (Ballade).

Faust. Opera in five acts by Gounod (libretto by Jules Barbier and Michel Carré, after Goethe's *Faust* part 1), produced in Paris in 1859. It was produced with recitatives instead of spoken dialogue in Strasbourg in 1860 and with the further addition of ballet at the Paris Opéra in 1869. Setting: Germany in the 16th century.

Faust-Symphonie, Eine [Ger., A Faust Symphony]. An orchestral work by Liszt (completed in 1857, though revised at various times thereafter) in three movements described by the composer as "character sketches" of Faust, Gretchen, and Mephistopheles, respectively. The last movement includes a setting for tenor, men's chorus, and orchestra of the final words of Goethe's drama.

Fauvel, Roman de. A long poem by Gervais du Bus that was completed in 1316 and is an allegorical satire of the church (the character Fauvel being a horse). One of the surviving copies, also probably not later than 1316, includes more than 100 musical additions.

Fauxbourdon [Fr.]. A 15th-century French technique of composition, employed in short pieces or sections within longer pieces. Two voices are notated, the upper a *cantus prius factus* (usually sacred) an octave higher than ordinary plainchant, the lower forming sixths and octaves below. The words *faux bourdon* or some variant thereof appear at the beginning of the piece or section, usually near the lower part. In the earliest and most widely accepted method of realization, a third voice paralleling the upper part at the fourth below is added in performance. Thus, three voices sound where parts for only two are written out, and the result is a series of first-inversion triads with an occasional octave with a fifth. There was also a method for producing four voices.

After the 15th century the term was increasingly confused with *falsobordone*. Although present knowledge of *fauxbourdon* necessarily rests in large part on written compositions, the technique was also used in extemporizing harmonizations of plainchant. In such improvisation, the preexisting melody is in the tenor, whereas in written *fauxbourdon* it is in the upper voice. The relationship of *fauxbourdon* to the English *faburden has been debated extensively.

Favola d'Orfeo, La [It., The Fable of Orpheus; also *L'Orfeo*]. Opera *(favola in musica)* in a prologue and five acts by Monteverdi (libretto by Alessandro Striggio on the myth of Orpheus and Eurydice), produced in Mantua in 1607. See also *Euridice.*

Fayrfax, Robert (b. Deeping Gate, Lincolnshire, 25 Apr. 1464; d. St. Albans?, Hertfordshire, 24 Oct. 1521). Composer. Gentleman of the Chapel Royal by 6 Dec. 1497, remaining in service to the English royal family until his death. Surviving works include Magnificats, motets, secular part songs, and a few instrumental compositions, but his Masses are most significant.

Feierlich [Ger.]. Solemn.

Felciano, Richard (James) (b. Santa Rosa, Calif., 7 Dec. 1930). Composer. Studied with Milhaud at Mills College and in Paris, at the Univ. of Iowa, and with Dallapiccola in Italy. Chaired the music department at Lone Mountain College (1959–67) and taught at Berkeley; composer-in-residence for the City of Boston (1971–73). Aleatoric, electronic, and dramatic elements are common in his music; he was among the first to use electronic music in a liturgical context (*Glossolalia,* baritone, organ, percussion, and tape, 1967). Works include a chamber opera and theater piece; orchestral pieces; *Salvador Allende* (string quartet, clarinet, percussion, 1983) and other chamber music; keyboard works.

Feldman, Morton (b. New York, 12 Jan. 1926; d. Buffalo, 3 Sept. 1987). Composer. Studied piano and took composition from Riegger and Wolpe; in 1950 met Cage and became associated with Tudor, Wolff,

and Brown in New York. Taught at SUNY–Buffalo from 1972. Feldman's music is characterized by soft dynamics and understated gestures (*In Search of an Orchestration,* 1967); he used aleatoric devices and graphic as well as conventional notation. Precise pitch is sometimes left to performer choice (*Projections,* 1950–51); after 1957 controlled pitch and direction of a line more precisely. Late in his career produced some very long pieces (the Second String Quartet, 1983, lasts for 6 hours). Other works include the monodrama *Neither,* soprano and orchestra, 1977; film scores; orchestral works (*Coptic Light,* 1986); chamber music (*For John Cage,* violin and piano, 1982); works for voice(s) and ensemble; a few songs.

Feldmusik [Ger.]. In the 17th and 18th centuries, music for winds to be played out-of-doors; also a band of musicians who perform out-of-doors.

Feldparthie [Ger.]. See Partita (3).

Feminine cadence. See Masculine, feminine cadence.

Fenby, Eric (William) (b. Scarborough, Yorkshire, 22 Apr. 1906; d. there, 18 Feb. 1997). Composer. Studied organ and served as amanuensis to Delius (1928–34). From 1948 to 1962 director of music at North Riding Training College; from 1964 professor of composition at the Royal Academy of Music. His overture *Rossini on Ilkley Moor* is his best-known piece.

Fennell, Frederick (b. Cleveland, 2 July 1914). Conductor. Studied at the Eastman School (1933–37, 1938–39) and at the Mozarteum (1938). Conducted the Eastman Symphonic Band, 1935–62. Music director of the Eastman Opera Theater, 1953–60. Founding conductor of the Eastman Chamber Orchestra and the Eastman Wind Ensemble, 1953–62. Associate conductor of the Minnesota Symphony, 1962–63. Conductor of the Univ. of Miami Symphony, 1965–80. Principal guest conductor at the Interlochen Arts Academy, 1980–83. Music director of the Tokyo Kosei Wind Ensemble from 1984.

Fennelly, Brian (b. Kingston, N.Y., 14 Aug. 1937). Composer and theorist. Studied at Yale (1963–68) with Mel Powell and at N.Y.U. Uses twelve-tone procedures as well as a freely atonal idiom (*Canzona and Dance,* clarinet, piano, violin, and cello, 1982–83), usually exhibiting instrumental virtuosity and rhythmic complexity. In later works particular pitch sequences are chosen from harmonic fields dependent on tone rows. Works include *Tropes and Echoes* (clarinet and orchestra, 1981), a brass quintet (1987), *Songs with Improvisations* (mezzo-soprano, clarinet, and piano, 1964).

Feo, Francesco (b. Naples, 1691; d. there, 28 Jan. 1761). Composer. Studied with Basso and Fago, perhaps also in Rome with Pitoni. *Maestro* of the Conservatorio di S. Onofrio, 1723–39, with Jommelli among his students; *maestro* of the Conservatorio dei Poveri di Gesù Cristo, 1739–43; *maestro di cappella* at the church of the Annunziata, 1726–45. Works include several operas; intermezzi; arias and duets; sacred music.

Ferguson, Howard (b. Belfast, 21 Oct. 1908). Composer. Studied at the Royal College of Music and piano with Harold Samuel. From 1948 to 1963 taught composition at the Royal College; after 1959 devoted himself to editing and writing about music. Compositions include *The Dream of the Rood* (tenor, chorus, orchestra, 1958–59); orchestral works; piano music; songs. Edited several music anthologies.

Ferguson, Maynard (b. Verdun, Canada, 4 May 1928). Jazz trumpeter and bandleader. Joined the big bands of Boyd Raeburn, Charlie Barnet, Jimmy Dorsey, and, in 1950–53, Stan Kenton; from 1956 led bands. His band turned toward rock and then disco; its biggest hit was "Gonna Fly Now" (1978), the theme song to the film *Rocky*. From the mid-1980s led a 10-piece band and then a combo.

Feria [Lat.]. (1) In classical antiquity, a festival day. (2) In the usage of the Roman and other Latin rites, any day of the week except Saturday and Sunday on which no feast falls [see Liturgy], Monday through Friday being numbered two through six, respectively.

Fermata [It., also *corona;* Fr. *point d'orgue;* Ger. *Fermate;* Sp. *fermata, calderón*]. The symbol ⌢, placed over a note or rest to indicate that it is to be prolonged beyond its normal duration (usually with a suspension of the regular metrical pulse) or placed over a bar or double-bar line to indicate the end of a phrase or section of a work; also called a pause or hold. In a *concerto, it marks the point at which the soloist is to play a *cadenza.

Fernández Caballero, Manuel (b. Murcia, 14 Mar. 1835; d. Madrid, 20 or 26 Feb. 1906). Composer. Studied at the Madrid Conservatory (under Albéniz, Eslava); from 1853 conducted theater orchestras, also beginning to compose zarzuelas and other theater music. From 1864 to 1870 conducted at a Cuban zarzuela theater; returned to Madrid and became a prolific zarzuela composer.

Ferne [Ger.]. Distance; *wie aus der Ferne,* as if from a distance.

Ferneyhough, Brian (b. Coventry, 16 Jan. 1943). Composer. Studied with Lennox Berkeley at the Royal Academy of Music, and with Ton de Leeuw in Amsterdam and Klaus Huber in Basel (1969–71).

Taught at the Hochschule in Freiburg, Germany (from 1971), at the Darmstadt summer courses (1976, 1978, 1980), and at UC/San Diego (from 1985). His music employs the total serialism and dense textures common to Boulez; more recent music shows the influence of Stockhausen and other Darmstadt figures. Works include 3 string quartets; *Mnemosyne* (bass flute, tape, 1986).

Ferrabosco, Alfonso (1) (b. Bologna, bapt. 18 Jan. 1543; d. there, 12 Aug. 1588). Composer. By 1562 was in England at the court of Queen Elizabeth I, where he served in the 1560s and 1570s, despite frequent visits to Rome, Paris, and Bologna; from no later than 1582 until his death was in Turin at the court of the Duke of Savoy. Extant works include nearly 80 sacred pieces, over 100 madrigals, and an important body of solo lute music.

Ferrabosco, Alfonso (2) (b. Greenwich?, before 1578; d. there, buried 11 Mar. 1628). Composer. Son of Alfonso Ferrabosco (1). From 1592 associated with the royal court as a musician and teacher. Between 1605 and 1622 several court masques by Ben Jonson with Ferrabosco's music were produced at Whitehall or Greenwich; other compositions include Latin motets, English anthems, songs and lute songs, music for viol consort, and nearly 70 technically demanding lessons for lyra viol.

Ferrabosco, Domenico Maria (b. Bologna, 14 Feb. 1513; d. there, Feb. 1574). Composer. Father of Alfonso Ferrabosco (1). Singer and later *maestro di cappella* at San Petronio; *magister puerorum* at the Cappella Giulia in Rome in 1546 and a singer in the papal chapel, 1551–55. His most important compositions are Italian madrigals, published between 1542 and 1600.

Ferrari, Luc (b. Paris, 5 Feb. 1929). Composer. Studied with Cortot, Honegger, and Messiaen (1951–54); taught in Cologne (1964–66) and Montreal (1966–67, 1969). Early works are atonal. In 1958 joined the Groupe de recherches musicales at French Radio; employed aleatory principles (*Spontanés,* 1962). Other works include orchestral music (*Symphonie inachevée,* 1963–66) and multimedia pieces (*Allo, ici la terre,* 1972).

Ferras, Christian (b. Le Touquet, 14 June 1933; d. Paris, 15 Sept. 1982). Violinist. Studied violin with Charles Bistesi at the Nice Conservatory (1941–44) and with René Benedetti at the Paris Conservatory (1944–46); also studied privately with Enescu. Recorded much of the standard concerto literature with von Karajan after 1964.

Ferretti, Giovanni (b. ca. 1540; d. after 1609). Composer. From 1575 until 1603, *maestro di cappella* at various Italian churches, beginning with Ancona Cathedral; resident in Rome by 1609. His most important works are *napolitane;* many were widely reprinted and exerted considerable influence. Also extant are a Mass and other sacred compositions.

Ferrier, Kathleen (b. Higher Walton, 22 Apr. 1912; d. London, 8 Oct. 1953). Contralto. She studied voice in London; created the title role in Britten's *The Rape of Lucretia.* Sang Gluck's Orpheus at Glyndebourne, 1946, and at Covent Garden, 1953. Britten wrote the alto part of his *Second Canticle* for her. Her career was cut short by cancer.

Fes, feses [Ger.]. F-flat, F-double-flat. See Pitch names.

Festa teatrale [It.]. A courtly musico-dramatic entertainment written and performed to commemorate a notable royal or dynastic event such as a birth, baptism, wedding, birthday, or nameday. The subject was usually mythological or allegorical. The genre was cultivated in the 17th and 18th centuries at the Hapsburg court in Vienna and at various Italian courts.

Festa, Costanzo (b. ca. 1490; d. Rome, 10 Apr. 1545). Composer. A few years at the French royal court may have preceded his entry into the papal choir in 1517, where he remained for the rest of his life. Composed various types of sacred music; his numerous madrigals are among the first of this genre and include the earliest pieces so titled.

Feste romane [It., Roman Festivals]. A symphonic poem by Respighi, composed in 1928, in four movements: "Circenses" (Circus Maximus Games), "Il giubileo" (The Jubilee), "L'ottobrata" (October Festival), "La Befana" (The Epiphany).

Festing, Michael Christian (d. London, 24 July 1772). Violinist and composer. Studied with Richard Jones and Geminiani; his own pupils included Arne. First played publicly in 1724; named Master of the King's Musick in 1735. Played in subscription concerts and garden performances; works include violin solos and concertos, cantatas, and songs.

Festoso [It.]. Festive.

Festspiel [Ger.]. Festival.

Feuer [Ger.]. Fire, passion; *mit feuer, feurig,* with fire, passionate.

Feuermann, Emanuel (b. Kolomea, Galicia [now Ukraine], 22 Nov. 1902; d. New York, 25 May 1942). Cellist. His family moved to Vienna in 1908; studied with Klengel in Leipzig, 1917–19; taught at the Gürzenich Conservatory in Cologne (from 1919) and at the Berlin Hochschule (from 1929). Returned to Vienna, then moved to the U.S. in 1938. Taught at Curtis, 1941–42. Formed famous trios with Goldberg

and Hindemith, with Schnabel and Huberman, and with Artur Rubinstein and Heifetz.

Févin, Antoine de (b. Arras?, ca. 1470; d. Blois, late 1511 or early 1512). Composer. Associated with the French royal court from no later than 1507; well regarded during his lifetime. Surviving works include Masses, motets and other sacred pieces, plus some French chansons.

Ff. Abbr. (often in italics, *ff*) for *fortissimo* [see *Forte*].

F-hole. See Sound hole.

Fiala, Joseph (b. Lochovice, Bohemia, 3 Feb. 1748?; d. Donaueschingen, 31 July 1816). Composer, oboist, gambist, and cellist. Studied oboe and cello in Prague and in Lochovice. Served at Prince Kraft Ernst's court at Oettingen-Wallerstein (1774–77) and at the Munich court of Maximilian Joseph (1777–78), where he encountered the Mozarts. Wolfgang apparently secured him positions in the Salzburg orchestra (1778) and with Prince Esterházy's regiment in Vienna (1785). Fiala later served at the St. Petersburg court (1786–90?); concertized in Berlin and Breslau for Friedrich Wilhelm II of Prussia; spent his last years at the Donaueschingen court.

Fiato [It.]. Breath; *stromenti da fiato* or *fiati,* wind instruments.

Fibich, Zdeněk [Zdenko] **(Antonín Václav)** (b. Všebořice, Bohemia, 21 Dec. 1850; d. Prague, 15 Oct. 1900). Composer. Attended schools in Vienna and Prague; studied in Leipzig (Moscheles, Richter, and Jadassohn, 1865–67), Paris (1868–69), and Mannheim (1869–70). In 1873 became a choral director in Vilnius, but returned to Prague the following year. Assistant conductor and chorusmaster, Provisional Theater (1875–78); choirmaster, Russian Orthodox Church (1878–81); dramaturg at the National Theater (1899–1900). Works include operas, melodramas, choral and instrumental music.

Ficher, Jacobo (b. Odessa, Russia, 15 Jan. 1896; d. Buenos Aires, 9 Sept. 1978). Composer and violinist. Studied at the Imperial Conservatory, St. Petersburg (1912–17); in 1919 became first violinist for the State Opera there. Emigrated to Argentina in 1923; taught at the Univ. of La Plata and at the Municipal and National Conservatories in Buenos Aires.

Ficta [Lat.]. See *Musica ficta*.

Fiddle. (1) Any bowed stringed instrument. (2) The *violin, especially in colloquial usage. (3) [Lat. *viella, viola;* Fr. *vielle;* Ger. *Fi(e)del;* Sp. *vihuela de arco*]. Any of a variety of medieval bowed stringed instruments, especially members of one of the two principal classes of such instruments (the other class being the medieval *viol). The term fiddle and its cognates are applied to a wide variety of instruments depicted in medieval art beginning in the 11th century, including instruments with bodies that may be elliptical or with slightly or deeply suppressed waists. The normal playing position was on the shoulder or arm, but instruments of this type are also shown being played upright in the lap, like the viol. See ill. under Violin.

Fi(e)del [Ger.]. *Fiddle.

Fidelio, oder Die eheliche Liebe [Ger., Fidelio, or Conjugal Love]. Opera in three acts by Beethoven, op. 72 (libretto by Josef Sonnleithner after Jean Nicolas Bouilly's *Léonore, ou L'amour conjugal*), first produced in Vienna in 1805 with *Leonore* Overture no. 2; revised in two acts (libretto recast by Stefan von Breuning) and produced in Vienna in 1806 with *Leonore* Overture no. 3; final version (libretto revised by Georg Friedrich Treitschke) produced in Vienna in 1814 with the *Fidelio* Overture. Setting: a state prison near Seville in the 18th century.

Fiedler, Arthur (b. Boston, 17 Dec. 1894; d. Brookline, Mass., 10 July 1979). Conductor. Studied violin at the Royal Academy in Berlin (1911–14); joined the Boston Symphony as a violinist (1915) and later violist. Founded Boston Sinfonietta (1924) and active as a choral conductor. Appointed music director of the Boston Pops in 1930, where his skillful amalgamation of light classics, American popular music, and commissioned works became the model for other musical organizations. Led annual concerts with the San Francisco Symphony, 1951–78.

Field holler. Solo singing by blacks in the fields of the southern U.S. Observers in the 19th century describe free rhythmic patterns and falsetto cries. It is often cited among the likely forerunners of country *blues.

Field, John (b. Dublin, 16 or 26 July 1782; d. Moscow, 23 Jan. 1837). Composer and pianist. Studied with Tommaso Giordani; moved to London in 1793 and apprenticed for 7 years to Clementi; from 1798 became prominent in London concert life. In 1802 Clementi took him to Paris, Vienna, and then to St. Petersburg, where their relations deteriorated. In Russia Field established a reputation as pianist and teacher, but composed sporadically. Returned to London in 1831, where he concertized, composed, and taught, then went back to Russia in 1835. Especially remembered for his elegant and expressive piano nocturnes.

Fier, Lubo (b. Prague, 20 Sept. 1935). Composer. Studied at the Prague Conservatory (1952–56) and Academy (1956–60). During the 1960s came to prominence in Prague; a traditional composing style gave way to more experimentalism during the late 1960s. In 1971 emigrated to the U.S. Works include operas (*Lancelot*, 1959–60); orchestral works (2 symphonies, 1956; 1958–60); chamber works; piano music (6 sonatas, 1955–78).

Fiero, fieramente [It.]. Proud, high-spirited, fierce.

Fife [Fr. *fifre;* Ger. *Querpfeife;* It. *piffero;* Sp. *pífano*]. A small *transverse flute of narrow cylindrical bore, sometimes associated with military music and played together with drums. Usually keyless with six finger holes, it exists in modern times with some improvements such as keys or holes to replace some of the fork fingerings. Fifes are usually made of wood, but other materials are known. See ill. under Flute.

Fifth. See Interval, Scale degrees, Circle of fifths, Parallel fifths.

Figlia del reggimento, La. See *Fille du régiment, La.*

Figural, figurate, figured [Lat. *figuratus;* Fr. *figuré;* Ger. *figuriert;* It. *figurato;* Sp. *figurado*]. (1) In the 15th and 16th centuries, mensural music *(musica figurata)* and thus polyphony as distinct from plainsong *(musica plana)*. (2) Florid counterpoint such as that codified in fifth-*species counterpoint; especially the florid polyphonic style of late-15th-century composers such as Ockeghem and Obrecht. (3) Music characterized by the use of *figuration. See also Figure, Figured bass, Figured chorale.

Figuration. Stereotyped *motives or patterns ("figures") that are ornamental in character, at least implying if not actually resulting from the embellishment of simpler, underlying melody or harmony, as in *variations. Figuration may include *diminutions and various types of *ornamentation as well as more mechanical passage work consisting of scales and arpeggios.

Figure. (1) A *motive or pattern that is ornamental in character. See Figuration. (2) A number placed below a bass part to indicate the accompanying harmony [see Thoroughbass].

Figured bass [Fr. *basse chiffrée;* Ger. *bezifferter Bass;* It. *basso figurato, cifrato;* Sp. *bajo cifrado*]. A bass part to which Arabic numbers ("figures") have been added to indicate the accompanying harmonies [see Thoroughbass]. The strict realization in four parts of figured basses is a regular feature of instruction in *harmony [see also Harmonic analysis].

Figured chorale. An *organ chorale in which a single motive or figure [see Figuration] is used continuously in the accompaniment to the chorale melody, which may itself remain largely unadorned. There are numerous examples in Bach's *Orgel-Büchlein, e.g., "Ich ruf' zu dir."

Figures, doctrine of [Ger. *Figurenlehre*]. Any of various attempts made in the 17th and 18th centuries to codify music according to classes of musical figures thought to be analogous to the figures of rhetoric.

Filar il suono [It.], **filer le son** [Fr.]. (1) In singing, to sustain a tone without interruption for breath and without a change in loudness; similarly in wind playing; in string playing, to sustain a tone without change of bow. (2) In the 18th century, *messa di voce.

Fill. In jazz, a brief, animated drum solo interpolated between phrases of melody and interrupting steady, accompanimental drum patterns.

Fille du régiment, La [Fr., The Daughter of the Regiment]. Opera in two acts by Donizetti (libretto by Jules Henri Vernoy de Saint-Georges and Jean François Alfred Bayard), produced in Paris in 1840; revised in Italian (libretto by C. Bassi) with recitatives by Donizetti instead of spoken dialogue and produced in Milan in 1840. Setting: the Swiss Tyrol about 1815.

Fils [Filtz, Filz], **(Johann) Anton** (b. Eichstätt, bapt. 22 Sept. 1733; d. Mannheim, buried 14 Mar. 1760). Composer and cellist. In 1754 became second cellist in the Mannheim orchestra; studied there with Johann Stamitz; died in Mannheim at age 26. Composed more than 40 symphonies; Masses; concertos; trio sonatas.

Fin [Fr., Sp.]. The end.

Fin' al segno [It.]. An instruction to play (usually to repeat) a piece "as far as the sign" (𝄋).

Final [Lat. *finalis*]. The pitch on which a melody in a given church *mode ends.

Finale [It.]. (1) The final movement of a *sonata or related form such as a symphony, concerto, or string quartet, usually in a fast tempo. (2) In opera, the concluding number of an act, especially an ensemble for the principal characters, perhaps with chorus, in which dramatic tension is created, elaborated, or resolved.

Finalmusik [Ger., final music]. In the Classical period, a type of piece belonging to the family also bearing names such as *cassation, *serenade, and *divertimento and performed at the end of a concert or, especially in the case of the works to which Leopold and W. A. Mozart referred with this term (e.g., K. 185 [167a], 251), at the end of the summer semester of the university in Salzburg.

Finck, Heinrich (b. Bamberg?, 1444 or 1445; d. Vienna, 9 June 1527). Composer. Lived chiefly in Poland, often serving in the royal court; after 1510 lived in Stuttgart, Salzburg, and Vienna. Most of his hymns and songs written after 1500 have survived intact, but many Masses and motets are missing parts.

Finck, Hermann (b. Pirna, 21 Mar. 1527; d. Wittenberg, 29 Dec. 1558). Theorist and composer. Great-nephew of Heinrich Finck; lived in Wittenberg from 1545; composed mostly motets. His major work is *Practica musica,* a treatise illustrated with nearly 100 compositions by some of the best composers of his time.

Fine [It.]. The end.

Fine, Irving (Gifford) (b. Boston, 3 Dec. 1914; d. there, 23 Aug. 1962). Composer and conductor. Studied with E. B. Hill and Piston at Harvard; with Boulanger in Cambridge, Mass., and in Paris; took conducting with Koussevitzky at the Berkshire Music Center. Taught at Harvard (1939–50) and Brandeis; wrote music criticism. Early works were in a neoclassical style derived from Stravinsky and Hindemith; with the String Quartet of 1952 began to employ the twelve-tone procedures that he regarded as secondary to matters of tonality, harmonic rhythm, and form. Compositions include 5 orchestral works (Symphony, 1962); chamber music; choral music; songs.

Fine, Vivian (b. Chicago, 28 Sept. 1913). Composer and pianist. Studied composition with Ruth Crawford (1925–28) and Adolf Weidig (1930–31); Cowell and Copland were important supporters of her work. Continued her studies at the Dalcroze School (1935–36) and with Sessions (composition, 1934–42), Szell (orchestration, 1942), and Whiteside (piano, 1937–45). Taught at NYU (1945–48), Juilliard (1948), SUNY–Potsdam (1951), the Connecticut College School of Dance (1963–64), and then at Bennington. Employed serial techniques to produce a dissonant counterpoint; after 1937 her style became more diatonic. Works include ballets, an opera (*The Women in the Garden,* 1978); orchestral and chamber works; choral works; piano music; songs.

Fingal's Cave. See *Hebriden, Die.*

Fingerboard. In stringed instruments, a strip of hardwood (often ebony) fixed to the neck, over which the strings are stretched and against which they are pressed (stopped) by the fingers to vary their pitch. The fingerboards of some early bowed instruments, such as members of the *viol family, and those of most Western plucked instruments, such as the guitar and lute, are fitted with *frets.

Fingering [Eng., for nonkeyboard instruments, also stopping; Fr. *doigté;* Ger. *Fingersatz, Applikatur;* It. *diteggiatura;* Sp. *digitación*]. (1) A system of symbols (usually Arabic numbers) for the fingers of the hand (or some subset of them) used to associate specific notes with specific fingers. In most 19th- and 20th-century editions of keyboard music, both thumbs are numbered *1*, both index fingers *2*, and so on. Most earlier alternatives denote the index fingers with *1*, the middle fingers with *2*, and so on. Much late 18th-, 19th-, and early 20th-century British keyboard music denotes the thumb with an *x*. In music for the violin and related instruments, the index finger is numbered *1*, the middle finger *2*, and so forth.

(2) Control of finger movement and position to achieve physiological efficiency, acoustical accuracy (or effect), and musical articulation. An aspect of instrumental technique, fingering is directly related to the manner in which vibration is initiated and the means by which its frequency is regulated. Some instruments (e.g., natural horns, slide trombones, pedal timpani) do not use finger articulations for these essential functions; plucked and keyboard instruments usually require them for both; bowed chordophones and most handheld aerophones use them to select pitch but not to initiate vibration.

Finke, Fidelio Friedrich (Fritz) (b. Josefstal, near Gablonz, Bohemia, 22 Oct. 1891; d. Dresden, 12 June 1968). Composer. Studied with Novák at the Prague Conservatory (1908–11); taught there (1915–26) and at the German Academy in Prague (1927–45); directed the Academy for Music and Theater in Dresden (1946–51); professor of composition at the Leipzig Musikhochschule (1951–59). Early works drew on Czech folk music and German Romanticism; later wrote expressionist and neoclassical works.

Finlandia. A symphonic poem by Sibelius, op. 26 (1899; revised 1900), from music for a pageant for press pension celebrations. Although it makes no use of folk music as such, it came to be regarded as the supreme musical embodiment of Finnish nationalism.

Finney, Ross Lee (b. Wells, Minn., 23 Dec. 1906; d. Carmel, Calif., 5 Feb. 1997). Composer. Studied composition with Donald Ferguson at the Univ. of Minnesota and at Carleton; studied with Boulanger (1927–28), Berg (1931–32), Sessions (1935), and Malipiero (1937). Taught at Smith (1929–48) and at the Univ. of Michigan (1949–73), where his students included Albright and Crumb. Won the Pulitzer Prize for his First String Quartet (1935). Works after 1950 combine serial and tonal approaches. Some earlier works exploit American themes, while orchestral compositions from the 1970s combine aleatoric procedures with quotes from folk songs (*Landscapes Remembered*, 1971).

Finnissy, Michael (b. London, 17 Mar. 1946). Composer. Studied with Bernard Stevens and Humphrey

Searle at the Royal College of Music, and with Roman Vlad in Rome. From 1968 taught at the London School of Contemporary Dance; his avant-garde music often employs aleatory and dense counterpoint. Works include stage music (*The Undivine Comedy*, 1988); vocal music; orchestral music (*Red Earth*, 1988); piano music.

Finzi, Gerald (b. London, 14 July 1901; d. Oxford, 27 Sept. 1956). Composer. Studied with Ernest Farrar (1915–16), Edward Bairstow (1917–22), and R. O. Morris (1925). In 1930 began teaching at the Royal Academy of Music; during the 1930s composed his first important works, including *Seven Part Songs* for chorus (1934–37). Moved to Aldbourne, Wiltshire, then to Ashmansworth. In 1939 formed the Newbury String Players, for which he composed a number of works. Compositions include concertos for cello (1951–55) and clarinet (1948–49); *Grand Fantasia* (orchestra, 1928); *Romance*, strings (1928); songs with orchestral or piano accompaniment; chamber music.

Fioritura [It., flowering]. Ornamental passages, improvised or written out. See Diminutions.

Fipple flute. *Duct flute.

Firebird, The. See *Oiseau de feu, L'*.

Fireworks Music. Handel's *Music for the Royal Fireworks*, an instrumental suite composed for performance at a fireworks display in London in 1749 celebrating the Peace of Aix-la-Chapelle.

Firkušný, Rudolf (b. Napajedla, 11 Feb. 1912; d. Straatsburg, N.Y., 19 July 1994). Pianist. Studied with Janáček from 1917, piano with Růzena Kurzová (1920–27), Vilém Kurz (1927–31), and Schnabel (1932, 1938); also took composition with Josef Suk (1929–30). Settled in the U.S. in 1938, concertized internationally after World War II; taught at Juilliard from 1965. Composed chamber music, song cycles, piano pieces.

Firsova, Elena Olegovna (b. Leningrad, 21 Mar. 1950). Composer. Studied at the Moscow Conservatory, 1970–75. Her works include symphonic scores; chamber concertos for flute (1978), cello (1982), piano (1985), horn (1987); 2 violin concertos (1976, 1983); chamber music. The poetry of Mandelstam has inspired many of her vocal scores.

First-movement form. *Sonata form. See also Sonata.

Fis, fisis [Ger.]. F-sharp, F-double-sharp. See Pitch names.

Fischer, Edwin (b. Basel, 6 Oct. 1886; d. Zurich, 24 Jan. 1960). Pianist and conductor. Studied piano with Hans Huber at the Basel Conservatory (1896–1904)

and with Martin Krause at the Stern Conservatory in Berlin (1904–5). Taught piano there (1905–14) and at the Berlin Hochschule (from 1931). Played new music but was most influential for his interpretations of Bach and Mozart; as a conductor explored neglected 18th-century pieces. Founded a famous trio with Kulenkampff (later Schneiderhan) and Mainardi.

Fischer, Johann Caspar Ferdinand (b. ca. 1665–70; d. Rastatt, 27 Mar. 1746). Composer. By 1695 was Hofkapellmeister to Margrave Ludwig Wilhelm of Baden, in residence at Schlackenwerth at this time. The court moved to Rastatt in 1716, Fischer presumably accompanying it; probably remained linked to the Baden court until his death. Led in establishing the French style of Lully in Germany; a cycle of preludes and fugues in various keys (*Ariadne,* 1702) prefigures J. S. Bach's work.

Fischer-Dieskau, Dietrich (b. Berlin, 28 May 1925). Baritone and conductor. Studied at the Berlin Musikhochschule, 1943; debut in 1947, active in opera from the late 1940s. Eventually recorded much of the lieder repertoire, including extensive collections of Schubert, Mendelssohn, Brahms, Schumann, and Wolf. Sang at Bayreuth (from 1954) and the Vienna State Opera (from 1957); 1965 debut at Covent Garden; soloist in the premiere of Britten's *War Requiem,* 1962. Conducting debut in 1973 with the English Chamber Orchestra. Retired from performing in 1993.

Fisk, Eliot (Hamilton) (b. Philadelphia, 10 Aug. 1954). Guitarist. Studied guitar with Oscar Ghiglia at Aspen, 1970–76; harpsichord with Ralph Kirkpatrick and Albert Fuller at Yale, 1972–77. Founded the guitar department at Yale in 1977, taught there until 1982; at Mannes College in New York, 1978–82; at the Cologne Hochschule für Musik from 1982.

Fitelberg, Jerzy (b. Warsaw, 20 May 1903; d. New York, 25 Apr. 1951). Composer. From 1922 to 1926 studied with Walther Gmeindl and Franz Schreker at the Musikhochschule in Berlin. After six years in Paris (1933–39) moved to New York and remained in the U.S. until his death. His music contains elements of the neoclassicism of the 1920s and 1930s and also of late Romantic expressiveness. Works include orchestral music (3 suites, 1925, 1928, 1930; cello concerto, 1931; clarinet concerto, 1948); chamber works; piano music.

Fitzgerald, Ella (b. Newport News, Va., 25 Apr. 1918; d. Beverly Hills, Calif., 15 June 1996). Jazz and popular singer. Sang with Chick Webb's big band (1935), giving it a hit song with "A-tisket, A-tasket" (1938). After Webb's death took over the band (1939–41). Worked through the 1980s as a so-

loist in varied settings, accompanied by her trio, the all-star cast of Jazz at the Philharmonic, big bands, and orchestras. Her work ranged from swing to bop scat singing to definitive versions of American popular songs.

Fitzwilliam Virginal Book. A manuscript copied by Francis Tregian between 1609 and 1619 containing nearly 300 works for *virginal dating from ca. 1562 to ca. 1612 and including dances, arrangements of songs and madrigals, preludes, and sets of variations by the principal English composers of keyboard works of the period, among them William Byrd, John Bull, and Giles Farnaby.

Five, The. A group of five Russian composers— César A. Cui (1835–1918), Alexander P. Borodin (1833–87), Mily A. Balakirev (1837–1910), Modest P. Mussorgsky (1839–81), and Nikolai A. Rimsky-Korsakov (1844–1908)—who joined together in St. Petersburg in about 1875 to create a Russian national music. A slightly larger group including these five were first referred to as The Mighty Handful (*moguchaya kuchka*) by the critic Vladimir Stasov in a newspaper article in 1867.

Five-three chord. A *triad in root position. See Inversion, Thoroughbass.

Fixed-do(h). See Movable do(h), Solmization.

Fl. Abbr. for flute.

Flagellant songs. See *Geisslerlieder.*

Flagello, Nicolas (b. New York, 15 Mar. 1928; d. New Rochelle, N.Y., 16 Mar. 1994). Composer, conductor, and pianist. Studied composition with Giannini at the Manhattan School, conducting with Mitropoulous and at the Accademia di S. Cecilia (Rome). Professional accompanist (1947–58); taught at the Manhattan School (1950–77); conducted and recorded operas. Works include 7 operas (1953–83) and vocal music; orchestral music; chamber music.

Flageolet. A *duct flute similar to the recorder. Two types are distinguished. The French flageolet, originating in the 16th century, has four front finger holes and two thumb holes [see ill. under Flute]. The English flageolet, originating in the early 19th century, has six (sometimes seven) front finger holes and one thumb hole.

Flageolet tones [Ger. *Flageolett-Töne*]. *Harmonics.

Flagg, Josiah (b. Woburn, Mass., 28 May 1737; d. Boston? 1795?). Psalmodist, bandmaster, and engraver. By the 1760s had settled in Boston; his two compilations of psalm tunes are among the most important tune-book publications before Billings. Organized a military band in 1769; later put on a concert of works by Handel and J. C. Bach.

Flagstad, Kirsten (Marie) (b. Hamar, Norway, 12 July 1895; d. Oslo, 7 Dec. 1962). Soprano. Studied voice in Oslo and Stockholm; debut at the Oslo opera in 1913. From 1919 to 1932 sang with the Mayol Theater and National Theater in Oslo and with the Storn Theater in Göteborg. Engaged at Bayreuth in 1933, returned in 1934 as Sieglinde *(Die Walküre)* and Gutrune *(Götterdämmerung)*. Met debut in 1935 as Sieglinde; based there, 1935–41, then in Norway (1941–45), the U.S. (1947–48), Covent Garden (1948–51). Director of the Oslo opera, 1958–60. One of the foremost Wagnerian soprano of her generation.

Flam. A common stroke on the snare drum played with the two hands in quick succession: ♪ ♪

Flamenco [Sp.]. A repertory of music and dance of Andalusia in southern Spain. Its origins remain much in dispute and have been variously attributed to Arabic-speaking peoples entering Spain from North Africa and to Gypsies arriving from the east or from the north (including the Low Countries, whence, according to some authorities, the name, which can mean Flemish), among others. On grounds of musical similarities, the strongest arguments point to Arabic and, to a lesser extent, Indian (by way of Gypsies) ties. Its association with Gypsies remains strong. The repertory incorporates characteristic styles of singing (including *cante hondo* or *jondo,* deep song, a term sometimes applied to the repertory as a whole), dancing (featuring erect posture, foot stamping, and finger snapping), and guitar playing (in which both strumming and passage work are prominent). Much of the music embodies the E or Phrygian mode, the descending phrase A, G, F, E being a characteristic concluding melodic gesture, but with significant microtonal inflections. Among the numerous individual musical types are the *seguidilla (siguiriya)* and *soleá.* The continuing evolution of the repertory has resulted in mixed genres and considerable interpenetration of flamenco traditions and other forms of folk and popular music.

Flanagan, Tommy (Lee) (b. Detroit, 16 Mar. 1930). Jazz pianist. Joined the tenor saxophonist Billy Mitchell's bop quintet and Kenny Burrell, with whom he moved to New York in 1956. Worked with Oscar Pettiford, J. J. Johnson (1956–58), Miles Davis (1956–57), and Coleman Hawkins (1960, 1962); recorded with Sonny Rollins and John Coltrane (1959). Accompanied Ella Fitzgerald (1956, 1963–65, 1968–78) and Tony Bennett (1966). From 1978 worked as a soloist, mainly leading trios.

Flanagan, William (Jr.) (b. Detroit, 14 Aug. 1923; d. New York, 31 Aug. or 1 Sept. 1969). Composer and critic. Worked with Bernard Rogers and Burrill Phillips at Eastman, with Barber, Honegger, and Copland at the Berkshire Music Center (1947–48), and with Diamond in New York; wrote music criticism. As a composer focused on small vocal forms, setting texts of Melville, Whitman, Stein, and others; also wrote operas and orchestral works.

Flat [Fr. *bémol;* Ger. *Be;* It. *bemolle;* Sp. *bemol*]. (1) The symbol ♭, which indicates the lowering of the pitch of a note by a semitone. See Accidental, Pitch names. (2) [adj.] Incorrectly sounded below the correct pitch.

Flatt, Lester (Raymond) (b. Overton County, Tenn., 28 June 1914; d. Nashville, 11 May 1979). Bluegrass singer and guitarist. In 1944 joined Bill Monroe's Bluegrass Boys, where he met banjo player Earl Scruggs. They left in 1948 to form the Foggy Mountain Boys; "The Ballad of Jed Clampett" (for the television series *The Beverly Hillbillies,* 1962) and Scruggs's "Foggy Mountain Breakdown" (1949) were very popular. After the group separated in 1969, Flatt led the Nashville Grass.

Flattement [Fr.]. (1) On Baroque woodwind instruments, a slow vibrato made by waving the finger over a hole that the written note requires to be open. (2) On Baroque stringed instruments, a two-finger vibrato above the pitch, the fingers being pressed together and rocked.

Flatterzunge [Ger.]. Flutter *tonguing.

Flautando, flautato [It., flutelike]. An instruction to bow a stringed instrument over the fingerboard. See Bowing (12).

Flautino [It.]. A small flute, either a small *recorder or *flageolet; not a *piccolo.

Flauto [It.]. (1) Flute; *f. a becco, diritto, dolce,* *recorder; *f. piccolo,* *piccolo; *f. traverso,* *transverse flute. (2) In the 18th century, *recorder.

Flautone [It.]. Alto *flute.

Flaviol [Cat.]. A *duct flute of Catalonia played in a *pipe and tabor combination, particularly in the *cobla* ensemble.

Flebile [It.]. Plaintive, mournful.

Flecha, Mateo (1) (b. Prades, near Tarragona, 1481; d. Poblet, Tarragona, 1553). Composer. Singer, then *maestro de capilla* at Lérida Cathedral until 1525; 1525–43, served in Spanish ducal courts; 1543–48, *maestro de capilla* at the court at Arévalo of the princesses of Spain. Wrote chiefly *ensaladas* (often macaronic).

Flecha, Mateo (2) (b. Prades, near Tarragona, ca. 1530; d. monastery of Portella, Lérida, 20 Feb. 1604). Composer. Nephew of Mateo Flecha (1). Chorister at Arévalo; from 1552 a Carmelite in Valencia; from 1564 a member of the imperial chapel in Vienna; from 1599 abbot of the (Benedictine) monastery of Portella in Spain. Works include a volume of Italian madrigals, 3 *ensaladas* published in 1581 along with those of his uncle, and several sacred pieces.

Fledermaus, Die [Ger., The Bat]. Operetta in three acts by Johann Strauss, Jr. (libretto by Carl Haffner and Richard Genée, after the French farce *Le reveillon* by Henri Meilhac and Ludovic Halévy, itself after a German comedy by Roderich Benedix), produced in Vienna in 1874. Setting: an Austrian city in the late 19th century.

Fleisher, Leon (b. San Francisco, 23 July 1928). Pianist and conductor. Studied with Schnabel, 1938–48; debut in 1942. In the 1960s carpal tunnel syndrome disabled his right hand; has since made several attempts at two-handed performance. Debut as conductor with the New York Chamber Orchestra, 1970. Associate conductor of the Baltimore Symphony, 1973–74; conductor, 1974–78; artistic director of the Tanglewood Music Center from 1985. Has taught at Peabody (from 1959), Curtis (from 1986), and Juilliard (from 1993).

Flemish school. See Renaissance.

Flesch, Carl (b. Wieselburg, Hungary, 9 Oct. 1873; d. Lucerne, 14 Nov. 1944). Violinist and pedagogue. Studied at the Vienna Conservatory (1886–90) and Paris Conservatory (1890–94). Taught violin at conservatories in Bucharest (1897–1902), Amsterdam (1903–8), Berlin (1908–23), Philadelphia (1924–34), Baden-Baden (1928–34). Taught in London (1934–43) and at the Lucerne Conservatory (1943–44). Played in a trio with Schnabel and Becker. His treatise on violin playing became a standard work.

Flex [Lat. *flexa*]. (1) See Psalm tone. (2) *Clivis* [see Neume].

Flexatone. A percussion instrument patented in the 1920s and consisting of a narrow sheet of flexible metal about 25 cm. long, on either side of which is mounted a wooden ball on a straight spring, all joined in a handle. When the instrument is shaken, the balls strike the metal sheet, producing a sound similar to that of the *musical saw.

Flicorno [It.]. See Flugelhorn, Euphonium.

Fliegende Holländer, Der [Ger., The Flying Dutchman]. Opera in three acts by Wagner (to his own libretto, after Heine's *Aus den Memoiren des Herren von Schnabelewopski*), first produced in Dresden in 1843 and revised in 1846, 1852, and 1860. Wagner originally intended to have the work presented in one continuous act, and present-day productions sometimes follow this practice. Setting: a Norwegian coastal village in the 18th century.

Fliessend, fliessender [Ger.]. Flowing, more flowing.

Florid. Ornamented, characterized by *figuration. In *species counterpoint, the fifth species is termed florid counterpoint.

Flos [Lat., pl. *flores*]. In the Middle Ages, ornament. See Ornamentation.

Flöte [Ger.]. Flute.

Flötenuhr [Ger., flute clock]. An *automatic instrument that combines a clockwork with a barrel organ to play music at fixed times of the hour.

Flothuis, Marius (b. Amsterdam, 30 Oct. 1914). Composer and musicologist. Studied in Amsterdam and Utrecht. From 1937 assistant manager of the Concertgebouw Orchestra; returned to the job after the war, subsequently became artistic director (1955–74) and professor of musicology at Utrecht. Compositions include orchestral and chamber works.

Flotow, Friedrich (Adolf Ferdinand) Freiherr von (b. Teutendorf, Mecklenburg-Schwerin, 27 Apr. 1812; d. Darmstadt, 24 Jan. 1883). Composer. Studied at the Paris Conservatory from 1828 (Pixis, piano; Reicha, composition); in the later 1830s lived mostly in Paris and composed operas. *Alessandro Stradella* (1844) was one of his two great successes, but limited mostly to German-speaking regions; the other, *Martha* (1847) was a worldwide success and is still occasionally performed. From 1853 to 1863 intendant, Schwerin court theater, for which he composed operas, ballets, and other theater music.

Flott [Ger.]. Lively, fast.

Flourish. (1) A *fanfare, especially for trumpets. (2) Any florid passage, especially one that calls attention to itself.

Floyd, Carlisle (b. Latta, S.C., 11 June 1926). Composer. Studied with Bacon at Converse College and Syracuse Univ.; taught piano at Florida State Univ. from 1947; from 1976 taught at the Univ. of Houston and directed the Houston Opera Studio. His opera *Susannah* (1953–54) won the New York Critics' Circle Award and later represented American opera at the Brussels World's Fair. By 1981 had written 7 other operas, most with American settings and in a conservative style.

Flue pipe. The main class of organ pipework, so called because the wind passes through a flue or opening between the languid and lower lip of the pipe. See diagram under Organ.

Flügel [Ger., wing]. The grand piano, so called because it is shaped like a wing; *Hammerflügel,* the piano as distinct from the *Kielflügel* or harpsichord.

Flugelhorn [also fluegelhorn; Ger. *Flügelhorn;* Fr. *bugle;* It. *flicorno;* Sp. *fiscorno*]. Originally, a half-round, 18th-century, German hunting horn of animal horn or bugle proportions; later, the large-bore German valved *bugle. The flugelhorn or valved bugle was the parent of whole families of similarly proportioned valve instruments that made up the brass bands of the mid-19th century. Soprano flugelhorns in Bb, whose range is the same as that of the cornet, are increasingly used in modern popular music and jazz. See ill. under Brass instruments.

Flüssig [Ger.]. Flowing.

Flüsternd [Ger.]. *Bisbigliando.

Flute [Fr. *flûte;* Ger. *Flöte;* It. *flauto;* Sp. *flauta*]. A woodwind instrument sounded without the aid of a reed. Instruments of this type may be classified in several ways, one of the most useful of which distinguishes instruments with whistle mouthpieces (*duct flutes) from those that use the mouth of the performer to direct air against the edge (embouchure-hole flutes) [see ill.]. *Penny whistles, *recorders, *czakans,* and *flageolets are examples of the former group; orchestral transverse flutes, *fifes, and *shakuhachis* are examples of the latter. Other classifications concern the ways in which flutes are held and blown and the geometry of the enclosed air column; e.g., *end-blown flute, *globular flute, *nose flute, *transverse flute.

The modern orchestral flute is a transverse flute with embouchure hole. It dates from ca. 1850 and was the work of Theobald Boehm (1794–1881). It is a cylindrical tube, usually of metal (silver, platinum, gold, or an alloy), with a number of side holes and a mechanism for the systematic covering of them. It is nontransposing and has a range of b or c' to c''''. There are several subsidiary sizes of the modern orchestral instrument. The *piccolo is a small instrument pitched an octave higher than the normal flute (sounding range d'' to d'''''', written an octave lower). The piccolo is sometimes pitched in keys other than C. The alto flute (formerly called bass) [Fr. *flûte alto;* Ger. *Altflöte;* It. *flautone;* Sp. *flauta baja*] is a larger transposing instrument in G, a fourth below the normal flute (sounding range g to d''', written a fourth higher). The true bass flute is in C (range c to

g''). More recently a contrabass instrument has been developed. This is not a true contrabass, however, but a large-bore bass flute with additional keys extending its range down to G. The *flûte d'amour* [Ger. *Liebesflöte*] of the late 18th and early 19th centuries was pitched in A, a third below the modern flute. See also Albisiphone, Giorgi flute.

Flutes are probably among the oldest and most widely disseminated instruments. Several sizes of transverse flute were produced during the Renaissance, but recorders retained the greater popularity until just after 1700. Beginning in the mid-17th century, woodwind instruments were all redesigned. The transverse flute acquired a key for D♯ (the only note not easily produced on the keyless Renaissance flute) and a reverse conical bore (smaller at the end away from the player). The recorder was given a more conical bore, and both instruments were typically decorated with ornate turnings. After midcentury, the recorder's use waned rapidly.

Additional keys were added to the transverse flute in the latter part of the 18th century. These were designed, not to increase the range, but to provide louder substitutes for some of the muffled *fork fingerings. The state of acceptance of these added keys was in such flux in the 1830s that a few players continued to play flutes with three or four keys, others played the then-standard eight-key instrument, and still others played instruments with a considerable number of doubled and alternate keys and/or foot sections that extended the range down to g.

Theobald Boehm redesigned the conical-bore flute and presented a new system featuring a separate tone hole for each note, thus avoiding the weaker (and, according to some writers, more expressive) forked notes [see Boehm system]. Boehm's instrument of 1832 became the basis from which many of the later innovations in the flute and other woodwind instruments derived. His development of the cylindrical-bore instrument in 1847 left the flute nearly in its present form.

Flûte [Fr.]. (1) *Flute; *f. à bec, douce,* *recorder; *f. allemande, traversière,* *transverse flute.

Flutter tonguing. See Tonguing.

Flying Dutchman, The. See *Fliegende Holländer, Der.*

Focoso [It.]. Fiery.

Foerster, Josef Bohuslav (b. Prague, 30 Dec. 1859; d. Nový Vestec, Bohemia, 29 May 1951). Composer and writer on music. Studied at the Prague Organ School; in 1882 became organist at St. Vojtěch, and in 1889 was made choirmaster at Panna Maria Sněžná. Moved to Hamburg in 1893, where he wrote music criticism and taught at the conservatory (from

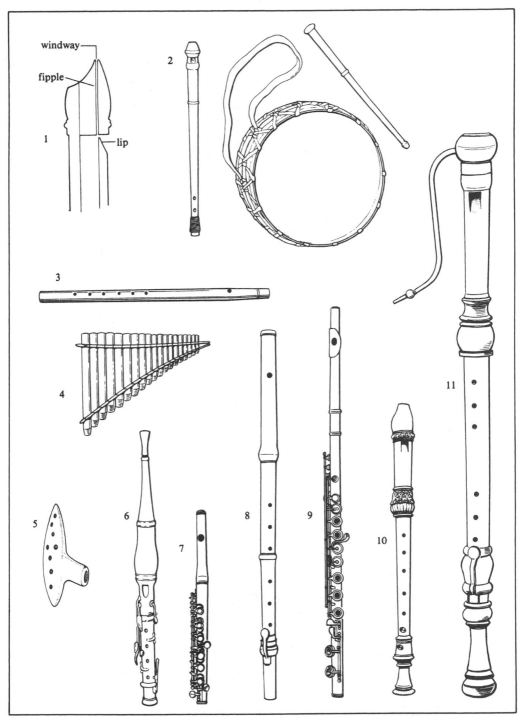

windway

fipple

lip

1

2

3

4

5

6

7

8

9

10

11

1. Cross section of fipple mouthpiece.   2. Pipe and tabor with drum stick.   3. Fife.   4. Panpipes.   5. Ocarina.
6. Flageolet (French).   7. Piccolo.   8. Baroque flute.   9. Flute (Boehm).   10. Alto recorder.   11. Bass recorder.

1901); in 1903 moved to Vienna and taught at the New Conservatory. Returned to Bohemia in 1918, taught at the Prague Conservatory and then at the Univ. of Prague (1920–36). Works include 6 operas, Masses and other large-scale choral works, 5 symphonies, chamber music, songs.

Folia [Port., It., insanity; Fr. *Folies d'Espagne*]. A dance and dance song first mentioned in Portuguese documents of the late 15th century and associated in Spain in the early 17th century with wild singing and dancing. From the last quarter of the 17th century, however, compositions on the *folia* have been art music based on a single isometric harmonic pattern, usually accompanied by the same discant tune [Ex.]. *Folia* variations were written by D'Anglebert, Marais, Corelli, Alessandro Scarlatti, J. S. Bach, C. P. E. Bach, Grétry, Cherubini, Liszt (*Rhapsodie espagnole,* 1867), and Rachmaninoff (*Variations on a Theme of Corelli* op. 42, 1931).

Folk music. Music in oral tradition, often in relatively simple style, primarily of rural provenance, normally performed by nonprofessionals, used and understood by broad segments of a population and especially by the lower socioeconomic classes, characteristic of a nation, society, or ethnic group, and claimed by one of these as its own. The concept of folk music is difficult to define precisely, and the lines between it and other types of music such as art, popular, religious, and tribal music are blurred. It is most useful in explicating the musical culture of Europe and the Americas before ca. 1920, but it is valid also in non-Western cultures such as those of East, South, and West Asia that have a sophisticated art music and make similar distinctions.

Folk rock. A combination of *folk music with the amplified instrumentation of *rock, usually including drums and electric stringed instruments.

Fonola. See Pianola.

Fontane di Roma [It., Fountains of Rome]. A symphonic poem by Respighi, composed in 1916. It is in four movements, each of which depicts a fountain in Rome: Valle Giulia at dawn, Triton in the morning, Trevi at midday, and Villa Medici at sunset.

Fontanelle [Fr.]. See Shawm.

Foot. (1) See Prosody. (2) In organ building, a measure of the pitch at which a pipe sounds. The termin-

ology derives from the fact that an open flue pipe sounding the pitch C (two octaves below middle C) measures about eight feet (2.44 m.) in length. This pipe is taken to represent all pipes or ranks of pipes, regardless of length (which will necessarily be different for every pitch), that sound the actual pitch represented by the individual keyboard key or keys to which they are connected. All such pipes are thus said to be at eight-foot (usually written 8-ft. or 8′) pitch. A pipe twice as long sounds an octave lower; one half as long sounds an octave higher, etc. [see Acoustics]. Hence, a pipe or rank that sounds an octave lower than the pitch represented by the key or keys that sound it is said to be at 16′ pitch; an octave higher, at 4′ pitch, etc., regardless of the particular pitch name in question. The system can be extended to include pipes or ranks that sound intervals other than one or more octaves from the standard 8′ pitch. These terms are also used to describe the relative pitch of the strings or choirs of strings of the *harpsichord; to classify other types of instruments; and to identify octaves within the total range of pitches (the 8′ octave proceeding upward from C, the 4′ from c, the 2′ from c′, etc.).

Foote, Arthur William (b. Salem, Mass., 5 Mar. 1853; d. Boston, 8 Apr. 1937). Composer, organist, pianist. Studied with Paine at Harvard, eventually receiving the first M.A. in music granted in the U.S. (1875); also studied organ with Benjamin Lang. Spent entire career in Boston as a teacher and performer: as organist and choirmaster at the Church of the Disciples (1876–77) and at the First Unitarian Church (1878–1910), and as instructor in piano at the New England Conservatory (1921–37). Compositions reflect his admiration for Brahms and Wagner.

Ford, Thomas (buried London, 17 Nov. 1648). Composer. Named one of the musicians to Prince Henry in 1611; later a lutenist and singer to Prince Charles. His *Musick of Sundrie Kindes* (London, 1607) contains many well-known ayres; other works include anthems, part songs, and viol fantasies.

Forefall. See Backfall, forefall.

Foreground. See Schenker analysis.

Fork fingering. On wind instruments with finger holes, a fingering in which the middle finger of either hand is lifted while the two fingers on either side cover their respective holes. See also Cross fingering.

Forlana, furlana [It.; Fr. *forlane*]. A lively dance from the northern Italian province of Friulia. Examples from the 16th century are in duple meter (2/4), in a style suggesting a folk dance. From the early part of the 17th century until well into the 18th, however, it flourished as an elegant French court dance, one with lascivious connotations. It was a gay dance, in a compound duple meter (6/8 or 6/4), with dotted rhythms. Forlanas have been composed from the 18th century to the present as abstract compositions, frequently as a part of a suite.

Form. The shape of a musical composition as defined by all of its pitches, rhythms, dynamics, and timbres. In this sense, there can be no distinction between musical form and specifically musical content, since to change even a single pitch or rhythm that might be regarded as part of the content of a composition necessarily also changes the shape of that composition, even if only in detail. The term form is also applied, however, to abstractions or generalizations that can be drawn from groups of compositions for purposes of comparing them with one another. A form in this sense is defined by a loose group of general features shared in varying degrees by a relatively large number of works, no two of which are in fact exactly the same. Only when form is used in this sense can a distinction be made between form and content. Any attempt to define forms of this kind too rigidly will be futile or will at the very least greatly diminish the usefulness of the definition by excluding too many specific compositions.

The years from about 1700 to about 1830 provide the bulk of the repertory on which classifications of form have been based, and many 20th-century discussions of form have their roots in writings of the late 18th and early 19th centuries.

On the largest scale, tonal works may be classified as either single or compound forms. Single (or simple) forms are tonally self-contained and formally complete, and they are not divisible into smaller, self-sufficient works. Compound (or composite) forms are those that include two or more single forms; compound forms thus include forms with more than one *movement, such as the *sonata, *symphony, *string quartet, and *suite. A compound form in which the same or similar music is used in two or more movements is said to be *cyclic. In principle, *opera, *cantata, and *oratorio are also compound forms, though the variety among such works and the considerable length of many examples make difficult the formulation of detailed definitions of them as forms.

With respect to tonality, a fundamental distinction is made between works in which a major section is incomplete tonally, ending in a key different from the one in which it begins and thus demanding continuation or resolution in a succeeding section, and works in which the principal components are self-contained tonally, beginning and ending in the same key. The former type is said to be open, the latter closed. Most binary forms are open in this sense; most ternary forms are closed [see Binary and ternary form, Sonata form, Aria]. Forms characterized by repetition or recurrence include *rondo, *variation (including

*chaconne and *passacaglia), and some types of *concerto movements.

Some types of works often described as forms are characterized more by procedures or techniques than by any well-defined pattern of larger elements. Such types include some cultivated long before the 18th century as well as some cultivated principally in the 18th and 19th centuries. Examples are *fugue, *ricercar, *canzona, *toccata, *fantasia, and the imitative *motet.

Vocal works from all periods may take the larger aspects of their form from their text. The principal types include the *formes fixes of early French secular music [see also Chanson], the *frottola and related forms, *bar form, the forms of *Gregorian chant, the *Mass, and *strophic songs and hymns.

The forms of tonal music inherited from the 18th century were considerably modified in the 19th, and with the abandonment of tonality by many composers early in the 20th century, the importance of these forms declined considerably. Composers of *twelve-tone and *serial music moved in the direction of forms that avoid repetition altogether and instead unfold continuously. Each new work thus defines its own form without reference to other works. This approach to form and musical time has important precedents in works by Debussy. Composers of *aleatory music, on the other hand, explored radical alternatives to the fixity of the individual *composition and thus to shared concepts of form. Works that can be realized in fundamentally different ways are sometimes termed mobile or open forms.

Formant. See Acoustics.

Formes fixes [Fr.]. A group of forms that dominated the secular poetry and music of France in the 14th and 15th centuries. The principal *formes fixes* are the *ballade,* the *rondeau,* and the *virelai.* A related form is the *bergerette,* popular especially in the latter half of the 15th century.

Forqueray, Antoine (b. Paris, 1672; d. Mantes, 28 June 1745). Viol player and composer. Louis XIV brought him into the court musical establishment and named him royal chamber musician in 1689. A favorite at court, where he was an associate of François Couperin and Robert de Visée, and a famed performer on the bass viol.

Forrester, Maureen (Katherine Stewart) (b. Montreal, 25 July 1930). Contralto. Debut with the Montreal Elgar Choir, 1951; operatic debut with the Operatic Guild of Montreal, 1953; Paris recital debut, 1955. Became widely known in 1957 after a performance of Mahler's Symphony no. 2 with Bruno Walter in New York followed by a well-received recital there. Sang Handel's Cornelia at the New York City Opera theater, 1966; San Francisco Opera debut in 1967, Met debut in 1974. Taught at the Philadelphia Academy of Music, 1966–71; at the Univ. of Toronto from 1971.

Fort. (1) [Fr.] **Forte,* strong. (2) [Ger.] Forth, onward; off, as with respect to an organ stop.

Forte [It., abbr. *f*]. Loud; *fortissimo* (abbr. *ff, fff*), very loud; *più forte* (sometimes abbr. *ff*), louder; *mezzoforte (mf),* moderately loud; *fortepiano (fp),* loud followed immediately by soft. See Performance marks.

Fortepiano [It.]. (1) See *Forte.* (2) Any of various early forms of the *piano.

Fortissimo [It., abbr. *ff*]. Very loud. See *Forte.*

Fortner, Wolfgang (b. Leipzig, 12 Oct. 1907; d. Heidelberg, 5 Sept. 1987). Composer. Attended the conservatory in Leipzig and studied musicology at the university. Taught composition and theory at the Heidelberg Institute of Church Music from 1931; at Darmstadt from 1946; at the Northwest German Music Academy in Detmold (1954–56), and at the conservatory in Freiburg (1957–72). In 1935 founded the Heidelberg Chamber Orchestra; directed the Musica Viva concerts from 1964 to 1978. During the 1930s and early 1940s wrote in a neoclassical style influenced by Hindemith and Stravinsky; from the mid-1940s began to compose according to twelvetone and, later, serial principles; *Immagini* (1967) and *Prismen* (1974) employ aleatoric methods.

Forty-eight, The. Popular name for Bach's **Well-Tempered Clavier.*

Forza [It.]. Strength, force.

Forza del destino, La [It., The Power of Fate]. Opera in four acts by Verdi (libretto by Francesco Maria Piave, after Ángel de Saavedra Duke of Riva's play *Don Álvaro, o La fuerza del sino* and Friedrich Schiller's *Wallensteins Lager*), produced in St. Petersburg in 1862; revised version (libretto revised by Antonio Ghislanzoni) produced in Milan in 1869. Setting: Spain and Italy about the middle of the 18th century.

Forzando, forzato [It., abbr. *fz*]. Forcing, forced, i.e., strongly accented.

Foss, Lukas (b. Berlin, 15 Aug. 1922). Composer, conductor, and pianist. Studied in Berlin and Paris until 1937; then attended Curtis, studying piano (Vengerova), composition (Scalero, Thompson), and conducting (Reiner); also studied with Koussevitzky at the Berkshire Music Center (1939–43) and with Hindemith at Yale (1939–40). Pianist for the Boston Symphony (1944–50); succeeded Schoenberg at UCLA, where in 1957 founded the Improvisation

Chamber Ensemble. Taught at SUNY–Buffalo (1963–70) and conducted the Buffalo Philharmonic; directed the Brooklyn Philharmonic (from 1971); conducted the Kol Israel Orchestra in Jerusalem (1972–76); music director of the Milwaukee Symphony (1981–86). Most of his earlier works are related to the neoclassicism of Hindemith and Stravinsky, often tinged with the Americanism of Copland. Later explored serialism in which composer and performers choose at will from material generated by the row (*Echoi,* 1961–63); minimalism (String Quartet no. 3, 1975); compositions based on recomposition of preexisting works (*Baroque Variations,* 1967). Some pieces involve competition between players or players and tapes. Other works include the opera *Griffelkin,* 1993; orchestral works (*Celebration,* 1990); chamber music; choral music; songs.

Foster, Frank (Benjamin, III) (b. Cincinnati, 23 Sept. 1928). Jazz tenor saxophonist, flutist, arranger, composer, and bandleader. Joined Count Basie's big band (1953–64); led a big band intermittently from 1964, joined Elvin Jones (late 1960s to mid-1970s), toured with the Thad Jones–Mel Lewis Orchestra (mid-1970s), and with Frank Wess led a hard bop quintet (1980s). In 1986 assumed the leadership of the memorial Count Basie orchestra.

Foster, Stephen Collins (b. Lawrenceville [now in Pittsburgh], 4 July 1826; d. New York, 13 Jan. 1864). Composer. Largely self-taught in music, he began to publish his first songs in 1844. Decided to become a full-time songwriter after the tremendous success of "Oh! Susanna" and "Uncle Ned" (both 1848). In 1850 arranged with E. P. Christy to introduce and have the rights to his minstrel show songs. Hits of this period include "Old Folks at Home" (1851), "Camptown Races" (1850), "My Old Kentucky Home" (1853). Most hits had appeared by 1855 (including "Hard Times Come Again No More"; thereafter only "Old Black Joe," 1860; "Beautiful Dreamer," 1864, his last song). By the end of the century had achieved legendary status as America's best-loved songwriter.

Fountains of Rome. See *Fontane di Roma.*

Four-foot. See Foot.

Four-line. See Pitch names.

Four Saints in Three Acts. Opera in a prelude and four acts by Virgil Thomson (libretto by Gertrude Stein), produced in Hartford, Connecticut, in 1934. The four saints of the title are Saint Theresa, Saint Settlement, Saint Ignatius Loyola, and Saint Chavez, though 30 or more saints appear in the course of the four (not three) acts. Although the historical subject matter is from 16th-century Spain, the libretto is not intended to reflect a coherent narrative.

Four Seasons, The [It. *Le quattro stagioni*]. The first four concertos of Vivaldi's *Il cimento dell'armonia e dell'inventione* op. 8 (published ca. 1725), a set of twelve concertos for solo violin, strings, and continuo. Each of the four is preceded by a sonnet describing a season, and some lines correspond to specific passages in the music.

Four-shape note. See Shape-note.

Fournier, Pierre (Léon Marie) (b. Paris, 24 June 1906; d. there, 8 Jan. 1986). Cellist. Studied at the Paris Conservatory. Debuted in Paris in 1928, then pursued an international career as soloist. Taught at the École normale de musique, 1937–39; at the Paris Conservatory, 1939–49. Concertized with Szigeti, Schnabel, and Primrose. Moved to Switzerland, 1973.

Fours, trade fours. In jazz, four-bar improvised solos by successive members of an ensemble, originally most often two in alternation. One or more choruses may be played in this way following the whole choruses by individual soloists and just before the return of the original tune.

Fourth. See Interval; Scale degrees; Consonance and dissonance; Tetrachord.

Fourth chord. A chord consisting entirely or principally of fourths (e.g., c–f–b♭), in contradistinction to the *chords built of thirds that characterize *tonal music. See also Quartal harmony.

Fox, Virgil (Keel) (b. Princeton, Ill., 3 May 1912; d. West Palm Beach, 25 Oct. 1980). Organist. Studied with Wilhelm Middelschulte in Chicago, 1928–29; with Louis Robert at the Peabody Conservatory, 1929–32; with Marcel Dupré in Paris, 1932–33. Professor of organ at Peabody Conservatory, 1938–42; organist at Riverside Church in New York, 1946–65. During the late 1960s toured with an electronic organ and a psychedelic light show.

Foxtrot. The enduring American social dance in 4/4. Introduced in 1913, it became a genre encompassing many patterns of steps. Dance-band musicians applied the name to thousands of popular tunes in 4/4 in moderate tempo with *two-beat or *walking bass-lines.

Fp [It.]. Abbr. for *fortepiano* [see *Forte*].

Frackenpohl, Arthur (Roland) (b. Irvington, N.J., 23 Apr. 1924). Composer. Studied with Bernard Rogers at Eastman and with Milhaud at the Berkshire Music Center (1948); with Boulanger (1950); and at McGill (1957). Taught at SUNY–Potsdam from 1949; composed in an eclectic style. Produced many works for high school band; a few works use graphic notation.

Frager, Malcolm (b. Clayton, Mo., 15 Jan. 1935; d. Lenox, Mass., 20 June 1991). Pianist. Studied with Carl Madlinger in St. Louis, 1942–49; with Carl Friedberg in New York, 1949–55. Soloist with the St. Louis Symphony, 1945. Studied at the American Conservatory in Fontainebleau, 1952. First tour of the U.S. and Europe, 1959. One of the earliest modern exponents of the fortepiano for performances of Haydn and Mozart.

Frame drum. A portable drum with one or sometimes two membranes stretched over a light, narrow, and usually circular frame. Some varieties have jingles attached to the frame, and some have a handle. They are most commonly held in one hand and struck with the other, but some varieties are beaten with a stick. See, e.g., *Daff*, Tambourine.

Frame harp. A *harp enclosed on all three sides. One side is a sound box, another a neck, the third a pillar. The strings are stretched between the neck and the sound box. The orchestral harp is of this type. See also Angle harp, Arched harp.

Française [Fr.]. In Germany, the English *country dance and its French derivative the *contredanse.

Françaix, Jean René (b. Le Mans, 23 May 1912; d. Paris, 25 Sept. 1997). Composer and pianist. Studied at the conservatories in Le Mans and Paris, and with Nadia Boulanger. His compositional style is influenced most by Ravel; as a pianist toured in Europe and the U.S. Works include 5 operas (*La princesse de Clèves*, 1965), 16 ballets, film scores, and incidental music; some 50 orchestral works (guitar concerto, 1983); choral music; chamber music (2 wind quintets, 1948, 1987); songs.

Francescatti, Zino [René] (b. Marseilles, 9 Aug. 1905; d. La Ciotat, France, 18 Sept. 1991). Violinist. Perfomed Beethoven's concerto at age 5. After further studies with Thibaud, made his Paris debut in 1925; toured England with Ravel, 1926. Began playing with Casadesus in 1942; their joint recordings include the complete Beethoven sonatas. The best-known French violinist of his generation.

Francesco Canova da Milano [Francesco da Milano] (b. Monza, 18 Aug. 1497; d. Milan, 15 Apr. 1543). Composer and lutenist. His contemporaries and successors ranked him among the finest of lutenists. Various popes and cardinals employed him in Rome (1516–39, with brief interruptions). Compositions include ricercars, fantasias, and intabulations of vocal pieces.

Franchetti, Alberto (b. Turin, 18 Sept. 1860; d. Viareggio, 4 Aug. 1942). Composer. Studied in Turin and Venice and in Germany with Draeseke and Rheinberger; directed the Florence Conservatory (1926–28). His operas *Asrael* (1888) and *Cristoforo Colombo* (1892) were successes, but afterwards his reputation declined. Also composed orchestral music; chamber music; songs.

Franchomme, Auguste (Joseph) (b. Lille, 10 Apr. 1808; d. Paris, 21 Jan. 1884). Cellist. Studied at the Paris Conservatory; prominent in Paris musical life as orchestral and chamber player and soloist; from 1846 professor at the Conservatory. Close friend of Chopin and dedicatee and first performer of his cello sonata.

Franck, César (-Auguste-Jean-Guillaume-Hubert) (b. Liège, 10 Dec. 1822; d. Paris, 8 Nov. 1890). Composer. Studied at the Liège Conservatory (1830–35); in Paris with Zimmermann (piano) and Reicha (composition), and later at the Paris Conservatory (1837–42). His 3 piano trios, op. 1 (1843) brought him favorable attention. Became a church organist (Notre Dame de Lorette; from 1853, St. Jean-St. François du Marais) and teacher. In 1858 appointed organist and precentor at the new Basilica of Ste. Clotilde; this post, which he held until his death, brought him considerable notice, especially for his improvisation. Composed some sacred works and organ pieces; in the later 1860s began to attract a circle of pupils and devotees. In 1872 appointed professor of organ at the Conservatory. Composed oratorios and operas, but best known for his orchestral works (Symphonic Variations, piano and orchestra, 1885; Symphony, 1886–88), chamber music (Piano Quintet, 1878–79; Violin Sonata, 1886; String Quartet, 1889), and solo keyboard works (*Prélude, choral et fugue,* 1884; *Trois piéces,* 1878; *Trois chorals,* 1890).

Franck, Melchior (b. Zittau, ca. 1579; d. Coburg, 1 June 1639). Composer. Possibly a student of Demantius and Gumpelzhaimer. Worked in Nuremberg, 1601–3; from 1603 until his death Kapellmeister in Coburg. Works include hundreds of German sacred works (many based on chorales), secular pieces, and instrumental dances.

Franco-Flemish school. See Renaissance.

Franco of Cologne (fl. 13th cent.). Theorist. Described as a papal chaplain and preceptor of the Knights Hospitallers of St. John of Jerusalem at Cologne; may have worked at the Univ. of Paris. Wrote *Ars cantus mensurabilis,* which proposed a notational system for rhythm that, in its essentials, remained in use for two centuries. His work is closely associated with the polyphonic music developed in Paris in the 13th century.

Franco, Hernando [Fernando] (b. Galizuela, near Alcántara in Extremadura, 1532; d. Mexico City, 28 Nov. 1585). Composer. A chorister at Segovia Cathedral from 1542 to 1549; probably went to the New World in 1554; *maestro de capilla* at Guatemala Cathedral by 1573; *maestro* at the cathedral at Mexico City from 1575. Compositions include 16 Magnificats, a Lamentations setting, and 20 motets.

Frank, Claude (b. Nuremberg, 24 Dec. 1925). Pianist. Studied in Paris with Louise Wacksmann-Field (from 1938), and in New York with Schnabel (1941–44, 1946–48, 1951). Taught at Bennington College (1948–55), Mannes (from 1963), Aspen (from 1970), and Yale (from 1972).

Franklin, Aretha (b. Memphis, Tenn., 25 Mar. 1942). Soul and gospel singer. From 1966 made recordings of rhythm-and-blues and popular songs, including "I Never Loved a Man (The Way I Love You)" (1967) and "Jump to It" (1982). Also recorded gospel music.

Franz [Knauth], **Robert** (b. Halle, 28 June 1815; d. there, 24 Oct. 1892). Composer. Studied in Halle and with Schneider in Dessau (1835–37). Church organist and choral conductor in Halle; in 1843 a set of 12 lieder was published on Schumann's recommendation. Became totally deaf by 1867, when he had to resign his various posts. Between 1843 and 1884 published the 279 songs on which his reputation rests; many are still part of the lieder repertory.

Frau ohne Schatten, Die [Ger., The Woman without a Shadow]. Opera in three acts by Richard Strauss (libretto by Hugo von Hofmannsthal after his story of the same title), produced in Vienna in 1919. Setting: the imaginary empire of the Southeastern Islands.

Frauenchor [Ger.]. Women's chorus.

Frauenliebe und Leben [Ger., Woman's Love and Life]. A cycle of eight songs for voice and piano by Schumann, op. 32 (1840), setting poems written by Adalbert von Chamisso and published with the same title.

Frauenlob [Heinrich von Meissen] (b. in or near Meissen?, between 1250 and 1260; d. Mainz, 29 Nov. 1318). Minnesinger. Many courts in northern and eastern Germany and a number of persons of high rank played a part in his life, though little biographical detail survives. Works include melodies in a traditional style and examples of the late courtly *Spruch.* An important predecessor to the Meistersingers.

Frederick II of Prussia [Frederick the Great] (b. Berlin, 24 Jan. 1712; d. Sanssouci, Potsdam, 17 Aug. 1786). Monarch, flutist, and composer. In 1740 ascended the throne, and soon after moved to found the Berlin opera; from 1742 until 1756 two major operas were produced each year, with Graun and Hasse the most prominent composers. Frederick hired C. P. E. Bach and Quantz; chamber concerts featured the music and performances of the king. Gradually the musical environment at court soured: Bach left in 1767, and the opera house was dark from 1756 until 1764. A skillful composer and flute player, Frederick also wrote several libretti.

Free jazz. Since the late 1950s, the esoteric jazz style. United mostly in their desire for freedom from the stylistic conventions of *bebop, players explored numerous alternatives: new types of collective improvisation, thematic variation, and motivic work, pantonality, drones, nontempered intonation, the melodic possibilities of the bass and of percussion instruments, open-ended forms, new timbres, extreme registers, abrupt rhythmic changes, unmetered pulses, and contrasting dynamics. The movement was heralded by pianist Cecil Taylor's recordings of 1956–58 and by saxophonist Ornette Coleman's controversial New York performances in 1959.

Freed, Isadore (b. Belorussia, 26 Mar. 1900; d. New York, 10 Nov. 1960). Composer. Studied with Bloch and Josef Hoffman, and in Europe with d'Indy and Vierne. Taught at Temple Univ. (1937–46) and at the Hartt School of Music (1947–60). Wrote *Harmonizing the Jewish Modes* (1958) and was known primarily for Jewish sacred music in a diatonic, neoclassical style.

Freeman, Bud [Lawrence] (b. Chicago, 13 Apr. 1906; d. there, 15 Mar. 1991). Jazz tenor saxophonist. His recordings of Chicago jazz with McKenzie and Condon's Chicagoans (1927) initiated an affiliation with Eddie Condon that extended into the 1960s. Joined Ben Pollack (1927–28), Red Nichols (1929), Tommy Dorsey (1936–38), and Benny Goodman (1938) before leading the Summa cum Laude Orchestra (1939–40). Over the next 50 years toured internationally as a soloist in small groups.

Freeman, Harry Lawrence (b. Cleveland, 9 Oct. 1869; d. New York, 21 Mar. 1954). Composer and conductor. Studied piano with Edwin Schonert and composition with Johann Beck; taught at Wilberforce Univ. (1902–4) and was active as a theater-orchestra conductor in Chicago and New York until 1910; then established the Freeman School of Music in New York. Conducted the Negro Choral Society and the Negro Grand Opera Company; his first opera (*The Martyr,* 1893) was performed in concert version in Carnegie Hall in 1947.

Freer, Eleanor Everest (b. Philadelphia, 14 May 1864; d. Chicago, 13 Dec. 1942). Composer. Studied voice and composition in Paris (1883–86); moved to Chicago in 1891 and studied with Bernard Ziehn

(1902–7). Works include 11 operas (most performed in Chicago); over 150 songs; piano pieces.

Frei [Ger.]. Free, freely.

Freischütz, Der [Ger., The Freeshooter]. Opera in three acts by Weber (libretto by Friedrich Kind after a folktale), produced in Berlin in 1821. Setting: Bohemia in the 17th century. In its use of folklike subject matter and melody (with spoken dialogue rather than recitative) and its treatment of the supernatural and nature, it is the paradigmatic German Romantic opera.

Freitas (Branco), Frederico (Guedes) de (b. Lisbon, 15 Nov. 1902; d. there, 12 Jan. 1980). Composer. Studied at the National Conservatory; conductor of the Portuguese Broadcasting Company's chamber orchestra and assistant director of its symphony; in 1940 created the Lisbon Choral Society, and from 1949 to 1953 led the Oporto Symphony. His music ranges from polytonal to nationalist and pictorial in character.

Freitas Branco, Luis de (b. Lisbon, 12 Oct. 1890; d. there, 27 Nov. 1955). Composer. Studied in Lisbon and with Humperdinck in Berlin and Grovlez in Paris; joined the National Conservatory faculty upon returning to Lisbon in 1916; played a major role in introducing then-current European musical styles into Portugal. Earlier music is impressionist in nature; works after the mid-1920s often contain neoclassical features.

French harp. *Mouth organ.

French horn. *Horn.

French overture. See Overture, Suite.

French sixth. See Sixth chord.

French Suites. Six *suites for harpsichord by Bach, BWV 812–17 (the first five of which were originally included in the *Clavierbüchlein* I, composed for Anna Magdalena Bach in the years 1722–25). The name French was not used by Bach himself, and its origins remain obscure, though it appears on some early copies. These works are not more French in character than other keyboard suites by Bach and his German predecessors.

French, Jacob (b. Stoughton, Mass., 15 July 1754; d. Simsbury, Conn., May 1817). Composer and singing master. In 1774 attended Billings's singing school in Stoughton; later served as singing master in Uxbridge, Mass., and in Providence, R.I. Best known for 3 published tunebooks which contain more than 100 of his own compositions as well as works by his contemporaries.

Freni, Mirella [Fregni] (b. Modena, 27 Feb. 1935). Soprano. Studied voice in Mantua; debut in 1955 in Modena as Micaëla. Sang at the Amsterdam Opera (1957), at Glyndebourne (1960) as Zerlina, at Covent Garden (1961) as Nannetta, at La Scala (1963) as Mimi. Met debut 1965; sang annually at Salzburg beginning 1968. Ill health interrupted her career in the 1970s; she returned as Liù *(Turandot)*.

Frequency. In *acoustics, the number of complete vibrations or cycles occurring per unit of time (usually per second; see Hertz) in a vibrating system such as a string or column of air. Frequency is the primary determinant of the listener's perception of *pitch.

Fresco, frescamente [It.]. Fresh, freshly.

Frescobaldi, Girolamo (b. Ferrara, mid-Sept. 1583; d. Rome, 1 Mar. 1643). Keyboardist and composer. Studied with Luzzaschi; appointed organist at the Accademia della Morte in 1597. Came under the patronage of Guido Bentivoglio, member of a powerful Ferrarese family. Went to Rome, was admitted to the Accademia di S. Cecilia in 1604 and became organist at S. Maria in Trastevere in 1607. Accompanied Guido to Flanders in 1607–8, summoned back to Rome and appointed organist of the Cappella Giulia, St. Peter's; also worked as a member of Enzo's household *musica*. By 1615 seems to have left the service of the Bentivoglio family for that of Cardinal Aldobrandini. During the next 13 years produced 2 books of toccatas, sets of ricercars, canzonas, and capriccios, and a collection of ensemble canzonas; his fame as a keyboardist continued to grow. Employed by the Medici in Florence, 1628–34. Returned again to Rome; resumed playing at St. Peter's and took a post with Cardinal Francesco Barberini, acquiring an international reputation. His compositions were central to keyboard study until well into the next century.

Fret [Fr. *touche, ton;* Ger. *Bund;* It. *tasto;* Sp. *traste*]. A strip of material placed across the fingerboard or neck of some bowed or plucked instruments, allowing the strings to be stopped at a predetermined pitch. Frets may be movable or fixed. Movable frets—of gut or cord—are tied around the neck (*sitār, viola da gamba,* lute, early guitar) and can be adjusted to vary the intervals of the pitches. Fixed frets—of metal, ivory, or wood—are inlaid into a groove in the fingerboard (banjo, cittern, modern guitar). The frets of Western instruments are usually placed a semitone apart. See Temperament.

Frettevole, frettoso, frettoloso [It.]. Hurried.

Fricassée [Fr.]. A type of *quodlibet* occurring among the chansons of the first half of the 16th century and in which quotations are mixed for humorous effect from sources that include polyphonic chansons, folk tunes, and street cries.

Fricker, Peter Racine (b. London, 5 Sept. 1920; d. Santa Barbara, Calif., 1 Feb. 1990). Composer. Studied at the Royal College of Music; met Tippett in 1939 at Morley College, later studying there with Mátyás Seiber (1946–48). In 1952 joined the Morley faculty; later taught at the Royal College (1955–64) and at UC/Santa Barbara (1964–84). His musical style, influenced by Bartók and Hindemith, occasionally employs twelve-note melodies and partial serialism. Compositions include stage works, film scores, radio operas, orchestral works (5 symphonies, 1948–76), choral music, songs, chamber works (4 string quartets, 1947–76), keyboard music.

Fricsay, Ferenc (b. Budapest, 9 Aug. 1914; d. Basel, 20 Feb. 1963). Conductor. Studied with Kodály and Bartók; conducted the symphony and opera in Szeged (1934–44); musical director of the National Philharmonic of Hungary. Conducted at Salzburg beginning in 1947; conductor at the Berlin State Opera, 1948–52; of the Berlin Radio Symphony, 1948–54; of the Houston Symphony, 1954–55. Music director of the Munich State Opera, 1955–59; of the West Berlin Opera, 1961–63.

Friction drum. A drum that is sounded by rubbing rather than striking. Most consist of a hollow body covered by a membrane through which passes a stick or string that the player pulls, turns, or rubs. See, e.g., *Zambomba.*

Friedheim, Arthur (b. St. Petersburg, 26 Oct. 1859; d. New York, 19 Oct. 1932). Pianist, conductor, and composer. Studied piano with Carl Siecke (1865–74) and Anton Rubinstein (1874–78). Student and companion of Liszt, 1880–86; respected thereafter as Liszt's most persuasive interpreter. Based in New York, 1891–97; in England, 1897–1908. Conducted in Munich, 1908–10. Toured North America and Europe, 1910–14; taught at the New York School of Music and Arts, 1917–32; at the Canadian Academy in Toronto, 1922–24.

Friml, (Charles) Rudolf (b. Prague, 7 Dec. 1879; d. Los Angeles, 12 Nov. 1972). Composer and pianist. Studied piano with Josef Jiránek and composition with Dvořák. Toured with violinist Jan Kubelík, emigrated to the U.S. (1906). Remained active as a pianist throughout his career; wrote serious and lighter music, the latter often under the pseudonym Roderick Freeman. His career as a composer of operettas was launched with *The Firefly* (1912); other successes were *High Jinks* (1913) and *The Three Musketeers* (1928). Also composed film scores and orchestral music.

Friss, friszka [Hung.]. See *Csárdás, Verbunkos.*

Frizzell, Lefty [William Orville] (b. Corsicana, Tex., 31 Mar. 1928; d. Nashville, 19 July 1975). Country singer and songwriter. Moved to Nashville, where he made recordings of original and borrowed material. His own "If You've Got the Money, Honey, I've Got the Time" (1950) was popular, as were his renditions of "Long Black Veil" (1959) and "Saginaw, Michigan" (1964).

Froberger, Johann Jacob (bapt. Stuttgart, 19 May 1616; d. Héricourt, near Belfort, France, 6 or 7 May 1667). Keyboardist and composer. Court organist at Vienna (from 1637); studied with Frescobaldi in Rome, 1637–41; returned to Vienna as organist, 1641–45. Perhaps visited Italy again in 1649; probably was in Brussels in 1650, in France in 1652, and also in England around this time. Reinstated as Viennese court organist in 1653 but dismissed in 1658; his final position was as tutor to Princess Sibylla of Württemberg-Montbéliard at Héricourt. Compositions, almost all for keyboard, reflect his mixed musical heritage: partitas, capriccios, ricercars, and toccatas are in a style close to Frescobaldi's, while his suites and programmatic works are based on the French usage.

Frog [Brit. nut; Fr. *hausse, talon;* Ger. *Frosch;* It. *tallone;* Sp. *talón*]. That portion of the *bow of a stringed instrument that is held in the player's hand and by means of which the tension of the hair is adjusted. See also Bowing.

Fröhlich [Ger.]. Joyous.

From My Life [Cz. *Z mého života*]. Smetana's first string quartet, in E minor (1876). Although both Smetana quartets are meant to be descriptive of his life (the second, composed in 1882–83, is also in E minor), Smetana himself seems to have applied the title only to the earlier quartet.

From the New World. See *New World* Symphony.

Front line. The wind instruments of a *New Orleans or *Dixieland jazz ensemble: clarinet (occasionally saxophone), trumpet (or cornet), and trombone.

Frosch [Ger.]. *Frog; *am Frosch,* an instruction to bow near the frog.

Frottola [It.]. A piece from a repertory of secular music written in northern Italy ca. 1480–1520. The word has popular, even rustic connotations, and poetic forms used for the written repertory of *frottole* were cultivated by improvisers at this time and probably a good deal earlier; but the *frottola* should not be thought of as popular or folklike music. Occasionally printers used *frottola* in a more specific sense as the equivalent of the verse form *barzelletta.*

The main body of *frottole* survives in manuscripts of northern Italian provenance and in the prints (1504–14) of Ottaviano Petrucci. Most of the music was the work of native Italians, centering in the Veneto, Ferrara, and especially Mantua, chief among whom were Bartolomeo Trombonino (ca. 1470–ca. 1535) and Marchetto Cara (ca. 1470–1525).

Poetic forms favored by the frottolists include the *barzelletta* (most popular of all); other multistanza forms used include the *oda and *capitolo.* The single-stanza *strambotto,* beloved of improvisers, was set often; but the *canzone stanza and the sonnet were rare until Petrucci's last books, either because they were too "literary" or because they had been the special province of improvisers. A few pieces, called *modo* or *aere,* provided models for singing any text in the form indicated.

In musical style, the *frottola* varies from near-homophony among the (usually four) voices to fairly elaborate melodic ornament (mainly in the top voice) and running figuration in the inner voices, serving as, or substituting for, polyphonic activity. Many *frottole* use rhythmic formulas suggestive of the dance-song; a favorite pattern (for eight-syllable trochaic verse) is shown in the accompanying example.

Frullato [It.]. Flutter *tonguing.

Fry, William Henry (b. Philadelphia, 10 or 19 Aug. 1813; d. Santa Cruz, Virgin Islands, 21 Dec. 1864). Composer. His *Leonora* is usually considered the first American grand opera to be staged (Philadelphia, 1845), followed by *Notre Dame de Paris* (1864). In 1846–52 was European correspondent for various American newspapers; from 1852, editorial writer and music critic, *New York Tribune.*

Frye, Walter (fl. ca. 1450–75). Composer. Probably never worked outside his native England. Extant compositions include three Mass cycles, a handful of motets and other short sacred compositions, and a few secular songs.

Fuchs, Joseph (Philip) (b. New York, 26 Apr. 1900; d. there, 14 Mar. 1997). Violinist. Brother of Lillian; studied violin with Franz Kneisel at the Institute of Musical Art, New York (diploma, 1918). Debut at Aeolian Hall in 1920; concertmaster of the Cleveland Orchestra, 1926–40, leader of the first Cleveland Quartet, 1930–34. Joined Juilliard faculty in 1946; toured widely.

Fuchs, Lillian (b. New York, 18 Nov. 1903; d. Englewood, N.J., 5 Oct. 1995). Violist. Sister of Joseph. At the Institute of Musical Art, studied violin with Louis Svečenski and Franz Kneisel and composition with Percy Goetschius. Founding violist with the Perolé Quartet, 1925–45. Taught at the Manhattan School from 1962, at Juilliard from 1971; composed numerous works for her instrument.

Fuchs, Robert (b. Frauenthal, Styria, 15 Feb. 1847; d. Vienna, 19 Feb. 1927). Composer and teacher. Studied at the Vienna Conservatory; 1875–1912, professor there, his pupils including Mahler, Wolf, Sibelius, and Zemlinsky. From 1875 conductor of the concerts of the Gesellschaft der Musikfreunde; 1894–1905, court organist. Compositions include operas, symphonies, chamber music, choral works, songs, keyboard works.

Fuenllana, Miguel de (b. Navalcarnero, near Madrid, early 16th cent.; d. after 1568). Vihuelist and composer. Employed in Spanish royal and noble courts, including those of Philip II and Elisabeth de Valois. His *Orphénica lyra* (Seville, 1554) presents intabulations for vihuela of works by other composers and nearly 70 original pieces.

Fuga [Lat., It., Sp.]. See Fugue.

Fugato [It.]. A fuguelike (and thus contrapuntal and imitative) passage occurring in a larger work or movement that is not itself a fugue, e.g., in the development section of a movement in sonata form; also a fuguelike piece that in one way or another does not incorporate the usual features of a *fugue.

Fughetta [It.]. A short fugue.

Fuging tune, fuge tune. A type of psalm or hymn tune cultivated in Great Britain and the U.S. from the 18th century on, involving contrapuntal writing and the overlapping of text in at least one phrase. It has always been most popular in rural areas.

The fuging tune, unrelated to the fugue, originated in England in the early 18th century, the first examples appearing in songbooks of itinerant singing masters; the genre reached its peak there around the middle of the century. It then declined in popularity in England, but was taken up enthusiastically in the U.S., receiving substantial attention from both composers and the general public. The peak of growth and popularity of the American fuging tune came in the 1790s.

American composers of early fuging tunes include William Billings (1746–1800), Supply Belcher (1752–1836), Lewis Edson (1748–1820), Daniel Read (1757–1836), Timothy Swan (1758–1842), and many others. The American fuging tune continued in vogue into the 20th century and has been kept alive in the southern and western *shape-note tradition long after its disappearance elsewhere.

Fugue [Fr. *fugue;* Ger. *Fuge;* Lat., It., Sp., *fuga*]. (1) The most fully developed procedure of imitative counterpoint, in which the theme is stated successively in all voices of the polyphonic texture, tonally established, continuously expanded, opposed, and reestablished; also a work employing this procedure. (2) In the Renaissance, *imitation. (3) In the Middle Ages, *canon.

Fugal texture requires a strict number of voices; two to six are practical, but the usual number is three or four. In a fugal *exposition, the *subject is presented alone in one voice (perhaps accompanied by a *basso continuo), then imitated or answered, usually in the dominant, by a second voice; this answer may be *tonal (modified) or *real (exact), depending on the characteristics of the subject and the composer's intentions with respect to modulation. Typically, the third voice enters with the subject in the tonic, the fourth in the dominant, and so on until all voices have entered. After stating the subject, each voice continues with a *countersubject or free counterpoint, usually moving to a *cadence. An exposition is normally followed by an *episode, the motivic material for which often derives from an aspect of the subject or countersubject. The episodic material is brought into an opposing or contrasting context, an effect often achieved by the use of harmonic sequences; once sufficient contrast has been established, the fugue subject reenters, as a single entry or as a reexposition, in the tonic or in a related key. The alternation of exposition and episode may occur only once or many times. The final section is usually a convincing exposition (complete or incomplete) in the tonic, often concluding with a *pedal point in the bass. See the accompanying example.

A fugue is fundamentally a monothematic work, although the subject itself may be varied by *augmentation, *diminution, *inversion, *retrograde, and other devices or opposed by various countersubjects. Bach's *Art of Fugue* is the comprehensive exemplar of these techniques. Some fugues present two or three subjects, in which case they are called *double or triple fugues. Here, each subject is normally set forth separately, but, later, the multiple subjects are usually combined, though there is considerable variety in these respects as well.

Fuga literally means flight, which suggests the fleeing and chasing characteristic of all fugues. In the Middle Ages, *fuga* was used synonymously with *chace* and *caccia* to denote canon. Early in the Renaissance, however, the principal meaning came to be *imitation. Although fugal expositions were common in both vocal and instrumental music of the Renaissance, it was particularly the instrumental forms—*ricercar, *canzona, and *fantasia—that proved important for subsequent development.

Early in the Baroque, the concept of predicating a whole fugue on a single subject superseded the polythematic conception of the Renaissance; and the idea of "working out" the thematic material was added. Fugues and fugal passages are to be found

Bach, Fugue in C minor (in three voices) from *The Well-Tempered Clavier*, bk. 1.

throughout the works of Bach and Handel, but Bach's *Well-Tempered Clavier* and *Art of Fugue* have come to be regarded as the supreme examples of fugal composition. By the end of the 18th century, however, fugue ceased to be a spontaneous, improvisatory procedure, as it had been from the late Renaissance to Bach, and became increasingly associated with academic study and with musical antiquarianism. But in works such as the finale of Mozart's *Jupiter* Symphony K. 551, the last movement of Beethoven's *Hammerklavier* Sonata op. 106, and Beethoven's quartets opp. 131 and 133, fugue in a sonata was elevated to a level of artistic accomplishment clearly comparable to that of the Baroque masters.

Fugue tune, fuguing tune. See Fuging tune, fuge tune.

Functional harmony. A theory of tonal harmony developed by Hugo Riemann according to which all harmonies can be analyzed as having one of three functions: tonic, dominant, and subdominant. The term functional harmony is sometimes loosely applied to tonal harmony in general as it is understood in prevailing methods of *harmonic analysis, which regard each of the seven diatonic scale degrees as having a separate function.

Fundamental, fundamental tone. In *acoustics, the lowest frequency or tone in a harmonic series and hence the first harmonic, i.e., the frequency of which all remaining frequencies in the series are integral multiples.

Fundamental bass [Fr. *basse fondamentale*]. In the theory of Jean-Philippe Rameau (*Traité de l'harmonie,* 1722), a bass line consisting of the roots of a succession of chords. Rameau's formulation of the principles of chord *inversion and of harmony as governed by a succession of roots underlies much of modern *harmonic analysis.

Fundamentum [Lat., foundation]. Any of a number of 15th- and 16th-century collections by German keyboard composers that contain works intended for use in the teaching of composition. The pieces consist of one or more florid contrapuntal parts over a *cantus firmus.* The most celebrated such collection is Conrad Paumann's *Fundamentum organisandi* (1452) for organ.

Funebre [It.]. Funereal, gloomy.

Funk(y). Earthy, sexual, danceable, *gospel-influenced. Equated with *soul jazz in 1954, it indicated a desire to unseat the prevailing intellectualized *West Coast style. The term is now applied to many recordings of black popular music, especially those with complex syncopations at the eighth-and sixteenth-note levels.

Fuoco, con [It.]. With fire.

Furiant [Cz.]. A Bohemian folk dance in a rapid tempo alternating 3/4 and 2/4 meters. Examples in art music are in 3/4 with strong accents forming pairs of beats resulting in occasional hemiola patterns.

Furioso [It.]. Furious.

Furlana [It.]. See *Forlana*.

Furtwängler, (Gustav Heinrich Ernst Martin) Wilhelm (b. Berlin, 25 Jan. 1886; d. Baden-Baden, 30 Nov. 1954). Conductor and composer. Studied theory and composition with Anton Beer-Walbrunn (1898), Josef Rheinberger (1900), and Max von Schillings (1902). Répétiteur (1908–9) and assistant conductor (1909–10) at the Munich Opera and at the Strasbourg Opera (1910–11). A revision of his *Te Deum* in 1910 established his reputation as a composer. Conductor of the Lübeck Philharmonic, 1911–15. Music director of the Mannheim Opera, 1915–20. Guest conductor of the Berlin Philharmonic, 1917. Succeeded Strauss in 1920 as conductor of symphony concerts at the Berlin State Opera; succeeded Nikisch in 1922 as conductor of the Leipzig Gewandhaus Orchestra and the Berlin Philharmonic. Stayed with Leipzig until 1928, with Berlin the rest of his life. Acclaimed U.S. debut with the New York Philharmonic in 1925, returned in 1926 and 1927. Conducted at Bayreuth, 1931–32. Director of the Berlin State Opera, 1933. Resigned all his posts in 1934; eventually returned to the Berlin Philharmonic and Opera; in 1944 fled with his family to Switzerland.

Fusion. A synthesis of *jazz and *rock. The style combines traditional jazz instruments and long, improvised melodies with electronic instruments, experimental tone colors, strong duple (not *swing) rock or Latin dance rhythms, and simple *ostinato harmonies. Fashionable since the late 1970s, the term applies to recordings made as early as 1968. See Jazz.

Fux, Johann Joseph (b. Hirtenfield, near St. Marein, Styria, 1660; d. Vienna, 16 Feb. 1741). Theorist and composer. Admitted to the Jesuit Univ. in Graz in 1680 and by 1683 was enrolled in a similar school at Ingolstadt, where he was also organist at St. Moritz in 1685–88. Organist at the Schottenkirche in Vienna (by 1696–1702), court composer (from 1698), Vice-Kapellmeister (from 1705) and then Kapellmeister (1712–15) at St. Stephen's. Appointed principal court Kapellmeister in 1715, he remained in this post the rest of his life. The main body of his work consists of church music but also includes some 20 operas and instrumental music. His *Gradus ad Parnassum* (1725), a tutor for species counterpoint, is the most influential book of its type, used by Mozart, Haydn, Beethoven, and Brahms among others.

Fz [It.]. Abbr. for *forzando, forzato.*

G

G. In French organ music, abbr. for **Grand orgue;* also G.O. See also Pitch names, Letter notation, Hexachord, Clef.

Gabriel, Peter (b. London, 13 May 1950). Rock songwriter, singer, keyboardist, and guitarist. Lead singer for the art rock band Genesis, 1969–75; popular recordings include "The Musical Box," 1971; *The Lamb Lies Down on Broadway,* 1974. Composed the score for Martin Scorcese's *Last Temptation of Christ.* Released solo albums *Security* (1982) and *So* (1986).

Gabrieli, Andrea [Andrea di Cannaregio] (b. Venice, ca. 1510; d. there, late 1586). Organist and composer. Uncle of Giovanni Gabrieli, who edited many of his works. Organist at St. Mark's from 1566 until his death. Among the first Venetian composers to depart from the Netherlandish style. Composed Masses, Psalms, motets (some polychoral), concerti; madrigals; other secular vocal works; canzonas, ricercars, *intonationi,* and toccatas, most for keyboard.

Gabrieli, Giovanni (b. Venice, ca. 1553–56; d. there, Aug. 1612). Composer. Nephew and pupil of Andrea Gabrieli. Court musician in Munich from 1575 or earlier until 1579; organist at St. Mark's, Venice, from 1584. Composed sacred vocal works, many of them polychoral and with specified instruments. Also composed keyboard works and instrumental ensemble pieces (canzonas, ricercars, sonatas). Schutz was among his pupils.

Gabrilowitsch, Ossip (Salomonovich) (b. St. Petersburg, 7 Feb. 1878; d. Detroit, 14 Sept. 1936). Conductor and pianist. At the St. Petersburg Conservatory studied piano with Tolstov and Rubinstein, composition with Lyadov and Glazunov; studied piano with Leschetizky in Vienna. Married the mezzo Clara Clemens, daughter of Mark Twain, in 1909; they gave frequent joint recitals. Conducted the Munich Konzertverein, 1910–14; the Detroit Symphony, 1918–36. Composed *Ouverture rhapsodie* for orchestra; piano pieces.

Gaburo, Kenneth (Louis) (b. Somerville, N.J., 5 July 1926; d. Iowa City, Iowa, 26 Jan. 1993). Composer. Studied with Bernard Rogers, with Petrassi, and at the Univ. of Illinois; taught there (1955–68) and at the Univ. of California at San Diego (1968–75). Founder/conductor of the New Music Choral Ensemble (1962–75). His style varies from tonal, to serial, to more experimental approaches incorporating theater and electronics. Based some works (*Lingua II: Maledetto,* 7 virtuoso speakers) on a "compositional linguistics" derived from his study of language. Works include an opera, mixed media (*Antiphony VI: Cogito,* 1972), theater pieces, and incidental music; orchestral, chamber, and piano music; electronic pieces; choral music and songs.

Gace Brulé (b. ca. 1160; d. after 1213). Trouvère. Active at several French noble courts, such as that of Marie de France, and may have participated in Crusades. His poems and melodies were often quoted in literary works, imitated by later trouvères and minnesingers, and used as the basis for Latin *contrafacta.*

Gade, Niels (Wilhelm) (b. Copenhagen, 22 Feb. 1817; d. there, 21 Dec. 1890). Composer. In 1844, became assistant conductor of the Leipzig Gewandhaus Orchestra and a teacher at the conservatory; succeeded Mendelssohn as conductor in 1847. Director of the Copenhagen Musical Society from 1849. Also active as an organist; from 1866, joint director with Paulli and Hartmann of the new Copenhagen Conservatory. Works include symphonies; incidental music and ballets (2 for Bournonville); concert overtures; chamber music (Octet for Strings op. 17, 1848); piano pieces; songs; choral cantatas (*Comala* op. 12, 1846).

Gaffurius [Gafurio, Gaforio, Gafori], **Franchinus** [Franchino] (b. Lodi, 14 Jan. 1451; d. Milan, 25 June 1522). Theorist and composer. *Maestro di cappella* in Milan from 1484. Composed Masses, motets, madrigals; wrote treatises on music, including *Theorica musicae,* 1492, and *Practica musicae,* 1496.

Gagaku [Jap., elegant music]. The traditional court music repertory of Japan codified in the Heian period (794–1185).

Gagliano, Marco da (b. Florence, 1 May 1582; d. there, 25 Feb. 1643). Composer. Student of Bati; his assistant at S. Lorenzo, Florence, from 1602; founded the Accademia degli Elevati, 1607. Composed for the Gonzagas of Mantua, 1607–8. *Maestro di cappella* at S. Lorenzo from 1608, and at the Medici court from 1609. Composed stage works (*Dafne,* 1608; libretto by Rinuccini); madrigals;

monodies; Masses, motets, responsories, and spiritual madrigals.

Gagliarda [It.; Fr. *gaillarde;* Sp. *gallarda;* Eng. *galliard*]. A gay, rollicking 16th-century court dance of Italian origin. The music is characterized by a predominantly compound duple (6/8) meter occasionally interspersed with hemiola (3/4) measures. The dance steps of the *gagliarda* are like those of the *saltarello;* both use variations of the same simple steps and the *cinque passi*. Either is frequently coupled to a *pavana* or a *pass'e mezo*. As a dance, the *gagliarda* survived well into the 17th century.

Gagnebin, Henri (b. Liège, 13 Mar. 1886; d. Geneva, 2 June 1977). Composer and organist. Studied with d'Indy in Paris. Directed the Geneva Conservatory (1925–28); founded and directed the Geneva International Competition for Musical Performance (1938–59). His music shows the influence of Franck, d'Indy, and Stravinsky. Works include orchestral and chamber music; piano and organ works; sacred choral music; songs.

Gai, gaiement [Fr., gay, lively]. *Allegro*.

Gaillarde [Fr.]. See *Gagliarda*.

Gaita [Sp., Port.; cf. Ar. *ghaytah*]. (1) A *bagpipe of Spain and Portugal. It is usually mouth-blown, with a double-reed *chanter, at least one bass *drone, and often a treble drone. It is still popular in northern Spain and Portugal, especially in Galicia. (2) *Shawm. (3) *Hornpipe (2). (4) In Colombia, a *duct flute.

Gál, Hans (b. Brunn, near Vienna, 5 Aug. 1890; d. Edinburgh, 4 Oct. 1987). Composer and musicologist. Studied with Mandyczewski in Vienna; taught there 1919–29; directed the Hochschule für Musik and the conservatory in Mainz (1929–33); conducted in Vienna until he was forced out by the Nazis. Taught at the Univ. of Edinburgh from 1945. His works, in tonal idioms similar to those of Brahms and Strauss, include 5 operas; orchestral music; chamber music; piano and organ music; oratorios and part songs for chorus. Published volumes on Brahms, Wagner, and Schubert as well as *The Golden Age of Vienna* (1948).

Galamian, Ivan (Alexander) (b. Tabriz, Persia, 5 Feb. 1903 [23 Jan. o.s.]; d. New York, 14 Apr. 1981). Violinist and teacher. Studied violin in Moscow and in Paris with Capet. Taught in Paris 1925–39; at the Curtis Institute, 1944–46; at the Juilliard School, 1946–81. Students included Pinchas Zukerman, Itzhak Perlman, Kyung-Wha Chung, Paul Zukovsky, Jaime Laredo. Published *Principles of Violin Playing and Teaching* (1962); *Contemporary Violin Technique* (1966).

Galán, Cristóbal (b. ca. 1630; d. Madrid, 24 Sept. 1684). Composer. Choirmaster at Segovia Cathedral (1664–67); later director of music at the Real Convento de Señoras Descalzas in Madrid; *maestro* of the royal chapel from 1680. Composed Masses, responses, a Passion, pieces with occasional texts, secular vocal works, and incidental music.

Galant style [fr. Fr. *style galant,* fr. *galer,* to amuse oneself, to enjoy; Ger. *galanter Stil*]. In 18th-century writings about music, the free or homophonic style as opposed to the strict, learned, or contrapuntal style. Traits include light texture, periodic phrasing with frequent cadences, liberally ornamented melody, simple harmony, and free treatment of dissonance. Historically, the *galant* is the principal style of the early *Classical period (as defined here). Some musicologists, however, have also applied the term *galant* style to French *rococo music of the early 18th century such as that of François Couperin.

Galanterie [Fr.]. A short, modish piece for harpsichord or other intimate medium, including chamber ensemble, especially in early 18th-century Germany. It implies French refinement and expressiveness.

Galilei, Vincenzo (b. S. Maria a Monte, near Florence, probably late 1520s; d. Florence, buried 2 July 1591). Theorist, lutenist, and composer. Father of the astronomer Galileo Galilei. Studied with Zarlino. His treatise *Fronimo* (Venice, 1568 and 1584) deals with lute intabulation; *Dialogo della musica antica et della moderna* (Florence, 1581) discusses the notion that monody might resemble ancient Greek music. Composed lute pieces, madrigals, and some monodies (now lost). Also wrote *Discorso intorno all'opere di Messer Gioseffo Zarlino* (Florence, 1589).

Galindo Dimas, Blas (b. San Gabriel, Jalisco, Mexico, 3 Feb. 1910; d. 19 Apr. 1993). Composer. Pupil of Chávez, Rolón, and Huízar in Mexico City, 1931–44. In 1934, formed the Grupo de los Cuatro with Ayala Pérez, Contreras, and Moncayo, aiming to develop a contemporary musical idiom using indigenous materials. Studied with Copland in 1941 and 1942. From 1947, directed the conservatory (until 1961) and the music department at the National Institute of Fine Arts. Music director of the Symphony of the Mexican Institute of Social Security, 1960–65. Works include orchestral music, concertos, ballets, chamber music, and vocal compositions.

Gallarda [Sp.]. See *Gagliarda*.

Galliard. See *Gagliarda*.

Galliard, John Ernest [Johann Ernst] (b. Celle, ca. 1685; d. London, 1749). Composer. Studied with Steffani; went to London in 1706. Translated Tosi's singing manual into English (1742). Works include operas, music for pantomimes, and sonatas and concertos for oboe and bassoon.

Gallican chant. The Latin chant of the churches in Gaul before the importation of *Gregorian chant under Pepin and Charlemagne. There were probably diverse local traditions rather than a single unified repertory. No notated manuscript survives.

Galli-Curci, Amelita (b. Milan, 18 Nov. 1882; d. La Jolla, Calif., 26 Nov. 1963). Soprano. Debut as Gilda *(Rigoletto)* at the Trani Municipal Theater, 1906. Sang with the Chicago Opera, 1916–18; with the Met, 1921–31. In 1936 she required an operation on her throat, which led to her retirement.

Gallus, Jacobus. See Handl, Jacob.

Galop [Fr.]. A fast dance in 2/4 that was extremely popular in the middle of the 19th century, when it was often used as the concluding number of a ball. It was sometimes made the finale of a *quadrille*. In the dance, embracing couples form a line and move rapidly with a galloping motion.

Galoubet [Fr.]. The pipe of the *pipe and tabor combination of southern France.

Galuppi, Baldassare (b. Burano, near Venice, 18 Oct. 1706; d. Venice, 3 Jan. 1785). Composer. Studied with Lotti. Collaborated on operas with Giovanni Battista Pescetti. Composed serious operas in London (1741–43); returned to Venice, composing opere buffe, mostly to librettos by Goldoni. *Vice-maestro* at St. Mark's from 1748; in 1762, he became *maestro*. At Catherine the Great's court in St. Petersburg 1765–68. Composed more than 100 stage works, as well as cantatas, oratorios, liturgical works, and keyboard sonatas.

Galway, James (b. Belfast, 8 Dec. 1939). Flutist. Studied with John Francis and Geoffrey Gilbert in London; with Jean Pierre Rampal in Paris. Principal flute in the Royal Philharmonic, 1966–69; in the Berlin Philharmonic, 1969–75. Taught at the Eastman School, 1975–76. Thereafter successful as a soloist in light classical and popular repertories.

Gamba [It.]. See Viol, Viola da gamba.

Gambang [Jav.]. A Javanese *xylophone with 16 to 21 wooden bars of varying length and thickness laid on a trapezoidal wooden frame and struck with two padded mallets. See ill. under Instrument.

Gambe [Ger.]. See Viol, Viola da gamba.

Gambenwerk [Ger.]. A *bowed keyboard instrument. See also *Geigenwerk,* Sostenente piano.

Game of Cards, The. See *Jeu de cartes.*

Gamelan [Indonesian, Malay, fr. Jav.]. Musical ensemble. In current international usage the term may refer to most Indonesian or Malay ensembles that have gongs, gong-chimes, metallophones, and drums. The usage closest to that found most often in Java encompasses ensembles that play Javanese music in the *slendro and *pelog tunings. These, however, include ensembles with few or no metallophones, gong-chimes, or gongs. See ill. under Instrument.

Gamma. The Greek letter Γ, the name of the lowest pitch (G) of the medieval *gamut [see also Hexachord]; by extension, the entire gamut, whence the Italian *gamma* and French *gamme* for scale.

Gamme [Fr.]. *Scale [see also *Gamma*].

Gamut. (1) A contraction of *gamma ut* [see Hexachord, Solmization]. (2) The entire range of diatonic pitches from G to e'' (with the addition of b♭ and b♭') forming the basis of discussions of pitch in the Middle Ages and Renaissance [see also Guidonian hand]. The pitches of the gamut constitute *musica recta,* the remainder *musica ficta.* (3) Range, compass.

Gandini, Gerardo (b. Buenos Aires, 16 Oct. 1932). Composer and pianist. Studied with Ginastera; founded the Grupo de experimentacion musical. He has held several teaching positions in Buenos Aires; instructor at the Juilliard School from 1970. Appeared widely as a pianist. Works include *Contrastes* (1968); *Fantasie-impromptu,* "an imaginary portrait of Chopin," piano and orchestra (1970); chamber music.

Ganz, Rudolph (b. Zurich, 24 Feb. 1877; d. Chicago, 2 Aug. 1972). Pianist, conductor, and composer. Studied piano with Busoni. Conductor of the St. Louis Symphony, 1921–27; of the New York Philharmonic's Young People's Concerts, 1938–49. At the Chicago College of Music from 1928; president, 1934–54. A champion of contemporary composers. Works include Piano Concerto op. 32 (1940) and the overture *Laughter—Yet Love* (1950).

Ganze Note, ganze Pause [Ger.]. Whole note, whole-note rest. See Note.

Ganzton [Ger.]. Whole tone; *Ganztonleiter,* whole-tone scale.

Gapped scale. A scale used in one piece, derived from some tone system, but omitting some of that system's tones.

Garant, (Albert Antonio) Serge (b. Quebec City, 22 Sept. 1929; d. Sherbrooke, Quebec, 1 Nov. 1986). Composer, conductor, pianist, and critic. Studied with Claude Champagne in Montreal; with Messiaen and Boulez in Paris. Many of his compositions employ serial techniques; other works allow controlled improvisation. Active as a performer and conductor of contemporary music in Montreal and in other Canadian cities. From 1969, taught composition at the Univ. of Montreal. Works include pieces for large ensembles or orchestra; chamber music; piano pieces; and vocal compositions.

Garbo, con; garbato [It.]. Graceful, elegant.

Garcia, Jerry [Jerome John] (b. San Francisco, 1 Aug. 1942; d. Forest Knolls, Calif., 9 Aug. 1995). Rock songwriter, singer, and guitarist. In the mid-1960s he formed The Grateful Dead, the leading band of the San Francisco psychedelic era. They produced studio albums (*American Beauty,* 1970) but were best known for live performances; their most famous songs ("Truckin'," 1970; "Sugaree," 1971) are by Garcia and lyricist Robert Hunter. They achieved new popularity in 1987 with the album *In the Dark.* Shortly after Garcia's death, the remaining members of The Grateful Dead dissolved the band.

Garcia, José Maurício Nunes. See Maurício, José.

García, Manuel (Patricio Rodríguez) (b. Madrid, 17 Mar. 1805; d. London, 1 July 1906). Singing teacher. Son of Manuel Garcia; made opera debut in 1825, but, lacking a good voice, left the stage in 1829. Pioneered the scientific study of the voice (invented laryngoscope, 1855); his *Traité complet de l'art du chant* (1840) was perhaps the most important singing treatise of the 19th century. Professor of singing, Paris Conservatory, 1847; Royal Academy of Music, London, 1848–95; pupils included Lind, Frezzolini, M. Marchesi.

García [del Popolo], **Manuel (Vicente Rodríguez)** (b. Seville, 21 or 22 Jan. 1775; d. Paris, 2 or 9 June 1832). Tenor. After success at the Théâtre-Italien, Paris, 1808, sang in leading Italian houses (1816, created Almaviva in Rossini's *Barbiere*); 1825–26, headed the first Italian opera company in the New World; after returning to Paris, gave up the stage for teaching. Father of Maria Malibran, Pauline Viardot, Manuel García. Composed operas and operettas.

García Morillo, Roberto (b. Buenos Aires, 22 Jan. 1911). Composer. Studied under Ugarte, André, and others at the National Conservatory, and later under Nat in Paris. Music critic for the Buenos Aires newspaper *La nación* from 1938; named to the faculty of both the municipal and national conservatories in 1942. Compositions include the pantomime drama *Usher* (1942), symphonies and other orchestral works, stage pieces, film music, cantatas, chamber music, and piano works.

Gardane [Gardano], **Antonio** (b. southern France, 1509; d. Venice, 28 Oct. 1569). Printer and composer.

Began printing music in Venice in 1538 using movable type and a single impression, as did Attaingnant. His publications include madrigals, Masses, and motets, by composers from Italy, the Netherlands, France, Spain, Germany, and the imperial court. Composed chansons, Masses, and motets.

Garden, Mary (b. Aberdeen, 20 Feb. 1874; d. there, 3 Jan. 1967). Soprano. Studied in Chicago with Mrs. Robinson Duff; in Paris with Jacques Bouhy, Mathilde Marchesi, Lucien Fugère, and Jules Chevalier. At the Opéra-comique 1900–1906, creating title roles in several French operas, most notably Debussy's *Pelléas et Mélisande.* Prima donna with the Chicago–Philadelphia Opera, 1910–31; director, 1921–22. Continued to perform until 1935. Her most important recordings were made with Debussy at the piano in 1903.

Gardiner, Henry Balfour (b. London, 7 Nov. 1877; d. Salisbury, 28 June 1950). Composer. Studied at the Charterhouse School, London; at the Musikhochschule in Frankfurt; and at New College, Oxford. His compositions manifest an interest in English folk tunes, which he spent time collecting, as well as in the music of Vaughan Williams. Among his works are pieces for orchestra (*Overture to a Comedy,* 1906?); choral works (*News from Whydah,* 1912; *April,* 1912–13); songs; chamber works; piano music.

Gardiner, John Eliot (b. Springhead, Dorset, 20 Apr. 1943). Conductor; great-nephew of composer Henry Balfour Gardiner. Studied conducting under George Hurst; in Paris with Nadia Boulanger; in London with Thurston Dart. Founder of the Monteverdi Choir (1964) and the English Baroque Soloists. Attracted widespread attention in 1967 with a performance of his own edition of Monteverdi's *Vespro della Beata Vergine* at Ely Cathedral; led his own editions of Rameau's operas in London, 1973–75. Music director of the Lyons Opéra, 1983–88; chief conductor of the North German Radio Symphony from 1991. Numerous recordings with historical instruments of instrumental and vocal works of the 17th, 18th, and early 19th centuries.

Gardner, John Linton (b. Manchester, 2 Mar. 1917). Composer. Studied at Oxford with Ernest Walker, Hugh Allen, and Thomas Armstrong. Assistant director at Covent Garden, 1946–52; thereafter taught at Morley College (director of its music program from 1965); and at the Royal Academy of Music from 1956. Composed operas (*The Moon and Sixpence,* 1954–57); and many choral works (*Cantata for Christmas,* 1966; *Cantata for Easter,* 1970); also chamber and instrumental works.

Gardner, Samuel (b. Elisavetgrad [now Kirovograd], 25 Aug. 1891; d. New York, 23 Jan. 1984). Violinist and composer. Studied violin with Loeffler and Winternitz in Boston; composition with Goetschius and violin with Kneisel in New York. Member of the Kneisel Quartet, 1914–15; of the Chicago Symphony, 1915–16. His String Quartet no. 1 won the Pulitzer Prize in 1918. Other compositions include the tone poem *Broadway* (1924), a violin concerto, chamber music, and *Country Moods* for string orchestra (1946). Taught at the Institute of Musical Art (which became the Juilliard School in 1926), 1924–41.

Garland, Red [William McKinley] (b. Dallas, 13 May 1923; d. there, 23 Apr. 1984). Jazz pianist. With Paul Chambers and Philly Joe Jones he formed the fiery rhythm section of Miles Davis's quintets and sextets (1955–58), while also recording his own albums *All Mornin' Long* and *Soul Junction* with Donald Byrd and John Coltrane (1957). Led hard bop trios and combos.

Garlandia, Johannes de. See Johannes de Garlandia.

Garner, Erroll (Louis) (b. Pittsburgh, 15 June 1921; d. Los Angeles, 2 Jan. 1977). Jazz pianist. Joined Slam Stewart's trio; recorded with Charlie Parker (1947), but mainly performed as a soloist. Characteristic of his style were unpredictable introductions to popular songs; tension between a steady chordal "four-beat" in his left hand and rhythmically freer melodies in his right. Recordings include "Fantasy on Frankie and Johnny" (1947) and his composition "Misty" (1954).

Garrido, Pablo (b. Valparaiso, Chile, 26 Mar. 1905; d. Santiago, 14 Sept. 1982). Composer. Did folkloric research throughout South America and in Spain, 1930–32; in Puerto Rico, 1949–51. His *Biografía de la cueca chilena* (1943) is the standard scholarly reference on that Chilean dance. His own music often draws on folk material; works include an opera, orchestral and chamber music, vocal pieces, and piano music.

Garrido Lecca, Celso (b. Piura, Peru, 9 Mar. 1926). Composer. Studied under Sas and Holzmann in Lima; attended the Univ. of Chile, Santiago; joined the faculty there in 1967. He integrated both international and indigenous elements into his music, the latter approach exemplified by his *Elegía a Machu Picchu* (1965) and the setting of the Quechua poem *Apu Inc Atahualpaman* (1971). Also composed chamber and piano music, as well as songs and some music with tape.

Gaspard de la nuit [Fr.]. Three piano pieces composed by Ravel in 1908 and inspired by poems of the same title by Aloysius Bertrand (subtitled *Histoires vermoulues et poudreuses du Moyen Age*), who described them as written by the devil, Gaspard. Ravel's pieces are titled "Ondine" (a water nymph), "Le gibet" (gallows), and "Scarbo" (a goblin appearing in a hallucination).

Gasparini, Francesco (b. Camaiore, near Lucca, 5 Mar. 1668; d. Rome, 22 Mar. 1727). Composer. Possibly a student of Legrenzi, Corelli, and Pasquini. Named *maestro di coro* at the Ospedale della pietà, Venice, in 1701; his important thoroughbass manual *L'armonico pratico al cimbalo* appeared there in 1709. Eventually became *maestro di cappella* at S. Lorenzo in Lucina, Rome. In addition to over 60 operas, he cultivated other secular and sacred vocal genres and was an influential teacher, with Marcello, Quantz, and Domenico Scarlatti among his pupils.

Gasparo da Salò [Bertolotti] (b. Salò, bapt. 20 May 1540; d. 14 Apr. 1609). Instrument maker. Among the finest makers of bowed stringed instruments, active in Brescia from 1562. His best work was in double basses and, particularly, tenor violas. These instruments remain in demand today, despite the considerable alterations many have undergone since their making.

Gassmann, Florian Leopold (b. Brüx, Bohemia, 3 May 1729; d. Vienna, 20 Jan. 1774). Composer. In 1763, succeeded Gluck as ballet composer to the Viennese imperial court. In 1770, during the meeting of Joseph II and Frederick II, Gassmann composed *La contessina;* appointed court Kapellmeister in 1772. Composed at least 22 operas; the oratorio *La Betulia liberata* (1772); sacred choral works; secular cantatas; symphonies; and chamber works.

Gastein or **Gmunden–Gastein Symphony.** A supposedly lost work by Schubert, D. 849 (1825–?), composed in Gastein, the Tyrolian region in which he vacationed in 1825. It is now thought that the symphony that Schubert worked on in Gastein is the Symphony in C major ("Great") D. 944, completed in 1828.

Gastoldi, Giovanni Giacomo (b. Caravaggio, 1550s?; d. 1622?). Composer. In the chapel of the Gonzaga family in Mantua, 1572–1608, eventually as *maestro di cappella;* then probably moved to Milan. Composed madrigals, sacred vocal music, and instrumental music; most prominent and influential are his 2 sets of *balletti.*

Gathering note. A note sounded by the organist to give the congregation the pitch for the singing of a hymn.

Gatti-Casazza, Giulio (b. Udine, Italy, 3 Feb. 1869; d. Ferrara, 2 Sept. 1940). Impresario. Took over the

Teatro comunale in Ferrara from his father in 1893; directed La Scala from 1898, with Toscanini on the podium. The two migrated to the Metropolitan Opera in New York in 1908, where Gatti-Casazza remained until 1935.

Gaultier, Denis (b. 1603; d. Paris, 1672). Lutenist and composer. Cousin of Ennemond Gaultier. Gained fame through salon playing. Three published collections of his music for the lute appeared later in his life: *La rhétorique des dieux* (1652), containing suites arranged into the 12 modes; *Pièces de luth sur trois différens modes nouveaux* (ca. 1670); and *Livre de tablature* (ca. 1672).

Gaultier, Ennemond (b. Villette, Dauphiné, 1575; d. Nèves, near Villette, 11 Dec. 1651). Lutenist and composer. Called "le vieux Gaultier" to distinguish him from his younger cousin Denis. Servant in French courts until 1631. Though his works (with those of his cousin) constitute a corpus of music influencing both other lutenists and later *clavecinistes,* they were not published during his lifetime; Denis brought out some of them in 1672.

Gauthier, (Ida Joséphine Phoebe) Eva (b. Ottawa, 20 Sept. 1885; d. New York, 26 Dec. 1958). Mezzosoprano. Studied voice with Auguste-Jean Dubulle in Paris, declamation with Sarah Bernhardt. Stage debut in Pavia in 1909 as Micaela *(Carmen).* Introduced new works by Ravel, Stravinsky, Bartók, Hindemith, Schoenberg, Satie, Honegger, and Poulenc. In 1923 she gave a recital of songs by Kern, Berlin, and Gershwin, accompanied by Gershwin.

Gautier de Coincy (b. Coincy-l'Abbaye, 1177 or 1178; d. Soissons, 25 Sept. 1236). Trouvère. Author of the long verse narrative *Miracles de Nostre-Dame,* which includes many songs with music, and of independent songs. Most of the music is drawn from earlier sources; his importance lies chiefly in his emphasis on sacred (especially Marian) texts, unusual in a trouvère of his time.

Gaveaux, Pierre (b. Béziers, 9 Oct. 1760; d. Charenton, near Paris, 5 Feb. 1825). Composer and singer. Sang at Montpellier, Bordeaux, and at the Théâtre de Monsieur in Paris (from 1789). Composed more than 30 operas (*Léonore, ou L'amour conjugal,* 1798; based on the same Bouilly libretto that Beethoven used for *Fidelio*). Also composed sacred vocal works, revolutionary songs, and instrumental music.

Gaviniès, Pierre (b. Bordeaux, 11 May 1728; d. Paris, 8 Sept. 1800). Violinist and composer. First performed at the Concert spirituel in 1741; became its director in 1773. In 1795 he was made professor of violin at the newly founded Paris Conservatory. Among his works is the opéra comique *Le prétendu*

(1760), orchestral and chamber works, and solo vocal music.

Gavotte [Fr., Eng., Ger.; It. *gavotta;* Sp. *gavota*]. A gracious Baroque dance movement in duple meter. Usually it has four-measure phrases that begin and end in the middle of the bar (that is, with a half-measure upbeat), and its meter is ¢ (or 2). It uses simple rhythmic motives, homophonic texture, and does not often have syncopations or other complications [Ex.]. It is generally moderate or sprightly in tempo, but slower than a *bourrée or *rigaudon. In the late 16th and early 17th centuries, the dance was a type of *branle. In the middle of the 17th century, a new dance with similar musical characteristics took the name and became popular at the court of Louis XIV. It quickly became an important form for independent music for instrumental ensembles and especially harpsichord and was frequently one of the movements following the sarabande in harpsichord *suites. As such it was mostly cast in *binary form. The gavotte is still known as a folk dance in Brittany.

Rameau, Gavotte from *Naïs* (1749).

Gay, John (bapt. Barnstaple, 16 Sept. 1685; d. London, 4 Dec. 1732). Poet and dramatist. Wrote the libretto to Handel's *Acis and Galatea* (1718), but is best known for the phenomenally successful *Beggar's Opera,* the first ballad opera. Wrote 2 other ballad operas, *Polly* (a sequel to the first, banned and not staged until 1779) and *Achilles* (1733).

Gaye [Gay], **Marvin** (b. Washington, D.C., 2 Apr. 1939; d. Los Angeles, 1 Apr. 1984). Soul singer and songwriter. From 1961 recorded for the Motown label, becoming popular with both black and white audiences for songs such as "How Sweet It Is To Be Loved by You" (1964), "I Heard It through the Grapevine" (1968), and "Sexual Healing" (1982).

Gaztambide (y Garbayo), Joaquín (Romualdo) (b. Tudela, Navarre, 7 Feb. 1822; d. Madrid, 18 Mar. 1870). Composer. Studied in Madrid; from 1848 prominent there as theater conductor; from 1862 directed orchestra concerts of the conservatory. Composed 44 zarzuelas, including *Catalina* (1854), *El* *valle de Andorra* (1852), *Los Magyares* (1857), and *El juramento* (1858).

Gazza ladra, La [It., The Thieving Magpie]. Opera ("melodramma") in two acts by Rossini (libretto by Giovanni Gherardini after the comedy *La pie voleuse* by d'Aubigny and Caignez), produced in Milan in 1817. Setting: a village near Paris.

Gazzaniga, Giuseppe (b. Verona, 5 Oct. 1743; d. Crema, 1 Feb. 1818). Composer. Studied with Porpora and Piccinni. *Maestro di cappella* at the cathedral at Crema from 1791. His *Don Giovanni Tenorio o sia Il convitato di pietra* (1787; text by Bertati) is generally recognized as a prototype for Da Ponte's and Mozart's *Don Giovanni*. Composed 47 known operas; liturgical and other sacred music.

Gazzelloni, Severino (b. Roccasecca Frosinone, 5 Jan. 1919; d. Cassino, 21 Nov. 1992). Flutist. Studied with Creati and Tassinari. Orchestral player in Belgrade and Rome; at the Darmstadt Festival from 1952. Known as an able exponent of the avant garde; over 150 works were written for him, by Messiaen, Boulez, Stockhausen, Berio, Nono, and others.

Gebrauchsmusik [Ger.]. Music for use, functional music. The term was coined in the 1920s for music that was intended to be immediately useful or accessible to a large public, e.g., music for films and the like, but especially music for performance by amateurs in the home, in schools, etc., as distinct from music for its own sake or as strictly a means to the composer's self-expression. It has most often been associated with some of the music of Paul Hindemith (who, however, later objected to the term, preferring *Sing- und Spielmusik,* music to sing and play) and Kurt Weill.

Gebrochen [Ger.]. Broken, *arpeggiated.

Gebunden [Ger.]. (1) *Legato. (2) With respect to the *clavichord, fretted.

Gédalge, André (b. Paris, 27 Dec. 1856; d. Chessy, 5 Feb. 1926). Composer. Studied with Guiraud in Paris. Taught counterpoint at the Conservatory; among his students were Ravel, Honegger, and Milhaud. Published didactic works, including *Traité de la fugue* (1901) and *L'enseignement de la musique par l'éducation de l'oreille* (1920). Composed dramatic works, symphonies, a piano concerto; chamber music; piano music and songs.

Gedämpft [Ger.]. Muted.

Gedda [Ustinoff], **Nicolai (Harry Gustaf)** (b. Stockholm, 11 July 1925). Tenor. Studied with C. M. Öhmann in Stockholm and Paola Novikova in New York. Debut at the Stockholm Royal Opera in 1952 as Chapelou (Adam's *Postillon*). Created Anatole in

Barber's *Vanessa* at the Metropolitan Opera. Best known for roles in French and Russian operas from Rameau's *Platée* to Shostakovich's *Lady Macbeth.*

Gedehnt [Ger.]. Prolonged; hence, slow.

Gefällig [Ger.]. Pleasing, pleasant.

Gefühlvoll [Ger.]. With feeling.

Gehalten [Ger.]. Sustained.

Gehaucht [Ger.]. Whispered.

Geheimnisvoll [Ger.]. Mysterious.

Gehend [Ger.]. *Andante.

Geige [Ger.]. Violin [see also Gigue (2)].

Geigenwerk [Ger.]. A *bowed keyboard instrument invented in 1575 by Hans Haiden of Nuremberg. Depressing a key caused a string to be pressed against one of several revolving, parchment-covered wheels that were activated by a treadle. See also Sostenente piano.

Geisslerlieder [Ger., flagellant songs]. Songs sung in the 13th and 14th centuries by flagellants. Penitential flagellation flourished in 13th-century Italy, from which a repertory of associated songs, *laude spirituali* [see *Lauda*], survives. The German repertory dates from the 14th century and has a relationship to broader repertories of folk song and to the later German *chorale.

Geistertrio [Ger., Ghost Trio]. Popular name for Beethoven's Piano Trio in D major op. 70 no. 1 (1808), so called with reference to passages in the second movement in which the pianist plays soft tremolo chords and "mysterious" chromatic scales.

Geistlich [Ger.]. Sacred; *geistliches Konzert,* sacred concerto, i.e., a sacred work for voices and instruments. The latter term is associated particularly with works by Schütz and other German composers of the 17th century. For *Geistliches Klavierlied,* see *Klavierlied.*

Gekkin [Jap.]. The Japanese "moon-shaped" lute, with flat, round body and short neck; similar to the Chinese *yüeh-ch'in. See ill. under Instrument.

Gekoppelt [Ger.]. Coupled.

Gelassen [Ger.]. Calm, tranquil.

Gelinek, Joseph (b. Sedlec, Bohemia, 3 Dec. 1758; d. Vienna, 13 Apr. 1825). Composer and pianist. Chaplain for Prince Nikolaus (II) Esterházy from ca. 1805. Composed chamber works, songs, and at least 120 sets of variations for piano. Published piano arrangements of works by Beethoven, Haydn, Mozart, and others.

Gemächlich [Ger.]. Comfortable, slow.

Gemässigt [Ger.]. Moderate.

Gemeindelied [Ger.]. Congregational hymn, *chorale.

Gemell. See Gymel.

Gemendo [It.]. Moaning, lamenting.

Gemessen [Ger.]. Measured.

Geminiani, Francesco (bapt. Lucca, 5 Dec. 1687; d. Dublin, 17 Sept. 1762). Violinist, composer, and theorist. Probably a pupil of Lonati, Alessandro Scarlatti, and Corelli. Active in England from 1714 and Ireland from 1733; Festing and Avison were among his pupils. Composed sonatas and concerti grossi. Writings include *A Treatise on the Art of Good Taste in Music* (1749), *The Art of Accompaniment* (ca. 1754), and *The Art of Playing on the Violin* (1754).

Gemischte Stimmen [Ger.]. Mixed voices.

Genau [Ger.]. Precise, strict.

Gender [Jav.]. A *metallophone of Java and Bali, with thin bronze bars 4 to 8 cm. wide suspended on cords in a wooden frame. Each bar has a tube resonator below it. The player strikes the keys with two disk-shaped mallets. See ill. under Instrument.

Gendhing. [Indonesian, fr. Jav.] (1) Any of the types of pieces that are played on large Javanese *gamelan. The term usually precedes the proper names of all *gamelan* pieces except those that have certain metric-melodic forms. This usage was derived in the first half of the 20th century from (2) below. (2) [Jav.] Any piece that is played on large Javanese *gamelan* but that does not use *kempul* (the highest-pitched hanging gongs).

Genera [Lat.]. Plural of *genus.

Generalbass [Ger.]. *Thoroughbass.

Generali, Pietro (b. Masserano, 23 Oct. 1773; d. Novara, 3 Nov. 1832). Composer. Began his career in Rome as a composer of sacred works; after 1800 composed mostly operas, including *Pamela nubile* (1804); *Le lagrime di una vedova* (1808); and *Adelina* (1810). Music director of the opera at Palermo ca. 1823–25; *maestro di cappella* at the Novara Cathedral from 1827.

Generalpause [Ger., abbr. G.P.]. General pause, a rest for the entire orchestra, especially one that occurs unexpectedly.

Género chico [Sp.]. See *Zarzuela*.

Genus [Lat., pl. *genera*]. In ancient Greek music, a tetrachordal tuning. The three categories of tuning were the *diatonic, *chromatic, and *enharmonic genera. Some composers and theorists of the Renaissance (e.g., Nicola Vicentino) attempted to revive the use of all three genera.

Genzmer, Harald (b. Blumenthal, near Bremen, 9 Feb. 1909). Composer. Pupil of Hindemith. Taught at the Musikhochschule in Freiburg (1946–57) and then in Munich. Has written several ballets; orchestral music; concertos for many instruments including trautonium; chamber music; keyboard works; and vocal music.

Gerhard, Roberto (b. Valls, Catalonia, 25 Sept. 1896; d. Cambridge, 5 Jan. 1970). Composer. Pupil of Pedrell and Schoenberg. Taught in Barcelona 1931–39; then emigrated to England. Made use of twelve-tone technique. Works include *Don Quixote* (ballet, 1940–41); *The Duenna* (opera, 1945–47); symphonies; concertos; film and incidental music; vocal works (*The Plague,* speaker, chorus, orchestra, 1963–64); Chamber music (*Libra,* 1968; *Leo,* 1969); pieces for tape (*Lament for the Death of a Bullfighter,* speaker, tape, 1959).

Gericke, Wilhelm (b. Schwanberg, near Graz, 18 Apr. 1845; d. Vienna, 27 Oct. 1925). Conductor. Opera conductor at Linz 1868–74; Vienna Opera, 1874–84. In the 1880s-90s, conducted concerts of the Gesellschaft der Musikfreunde, and the Boston Symphony. Composed chamber, choral, piano works; an operetta; songs.

Gerle, Hans (b. Nuremberg, ca. 1500; d. there, 1570). Compiler and arranger, especially of music for lute. His books contain intabulations, arrangements, and reprints of works by others; also music for bowed strings and essays on playing technique and on musical notation.

German dance. *Deutscher Tanz.

German flute. In the 18th century, the transverse flute, as distinct from the English flute or recorder.

German Requiem, A. See *Deutsches Requiem, Ein.*

German sixth. See Sixth chord.

German, Edward [Jones, German Edward] (b. Whitechurch, Shropshire, 17 Feb. 1862; d. London, 11 Nov. 1936). Composer. Pupil of Prout. Conductor at the Globe Theatre, 1888. Composed incidental music (*Richard III*); comic operas (*Merrie England,* 1902); songs (*Just So Stories,* 1903), 2 symphonies, 3 orchestral suites, and chamber and piano music.

Gero [Ghero], **Jhan** [Jan, Jehan] (fl. 1540–55). Composer. Active in Venice but probably of northern origin. Wrote or arranged many madrigals and chansons. Published books of *note nere* madrigals for 4 voices (1549) and 5-part motets (1555).

Gerschefski, Edwin (b. Meriden, Conn., 19 June 1909). Composer and pianist. Studied with Schnabel and Schillinger. Taught at Converse College from 1940 (dean of the music school, 1945–59); at the Univ. of Georgia (1960–80). Set "informal" texts such as news stories (*Border Raid* op. 57, 1966). Other works include a symphony, piano and violin concertos; chamber and piano music; film scores.

Gershwin, George (b. Brooklyn, 26 Sept. 1898; d. Hollywood, 11 July 1937). Composer, pianist, and conductor. Started as Tin Pan Alley pianist; later studied composition with Goldmark, Riegger, Cowell, and Schillinger. Composed musical comedies and popular songs, many with lyrics by his brother, Ira (*Funny Face,* 1927: "'S Wonderful"; *Girl Crazy,* 1930: "Embraceable You," "I Got Rhythm"). Inserted jazz and popular idioms into orchestral music (**Rhapsody in Blue; Concerto in F,* piano and orchestra, 1925; *An *American in Paris*) and opera (**Porgy and Bess*). Also composed film scores, including *Shall We Dance,* 1937 ("Let's Call the Whole Thing Off," "They Can't Take That Away from Me").

Gershwin, Ira [Gershvin, Israel] (b. New York, 6 Dec. 1896; d. Beverly Hills, Calif., 17 Aug. 1983). Lyricist. With his brother George Gershwin, wrote Broadway shows (*Of Thee I Sing,* 1931, won the Pulitzer Prize for drama), and songs for films. Later worked with other composers, including Weill, Kern, and Arlen.

Gervaise, Claude (fl. Paris, 1540–60). Composer, editor, and arranger. Worked for the printer Attaingnant. Composed dances for the *Danceries;* chansons.

Ges, geses [Ger.]. G-flat, G-double-flat. See Pitch names.

Gesamtkunstwerk [Ger., total artwork]. Richard Wagner's term for his mature operas, in which all the arts (including music, poetry, and visual spectacle) were to be perfectly fused [see Opera].

Gesang [Ger.]. Song; *gesangvoll,* songlike, cantabile.

Gesang der Jünglinge [Ger., Song of the Young Boys]. An electronic work by Karlheinz Stockhausen, composed in 1955–56, in which the voice of a boy speaking and singing the *Benedicite* is transformed and combined with purely electronic sounds. It is reproduced through five spatially separated groups of loudspeakers.

Geschöpfe des Prometheus, Die [Ger., The Creatures of Prometheus]. A ballet by Beethoven, op. 43 (choreography by Salvatore Viganò), produced in Vienna in 1801. The overture remains in the concert repertory. Beethoven used a theme from the finale in three other works [see *Eroica, Eroica Variations*].

Geschwind [Ger.]. Quick, fast.

Geses [Ger.]. See *Ges, geses.*

Gesteigert [Ger.]. Increased; hence, **crescendo* or **rinforzando.*

Gestopft [Ger.]. Stopped [see Stopped tones, Horn].

Gesualdo, Carlo, Prince of Venosa, Count of Conza (b. Naples?, ca. 1561; d. Gesualdo, Avellino, 8 Sept. 1613). Composer. Known mostly for polyphonic madrigals in a chromatic, often dissonant idiom, with great emphasis on text expression. Also composed sacred works.

Geteilt [Ger.]. **Divisi.*

Getragen [Ger.]. Sustained, slow, solemn.

Getz, Stan [Stanley] (b. Philadelphia, 2 Feb. 1927; d. Malibu, Calif., 6 June 1991). Jazz tenor saxophonist and bandleader. Played in big bands, including Woody Herman's, as one of the "Four Brothers" saxophone section (1947–48); thereafter led small groups. From ca. 1985 artist-in-residence at Stanford Univ. His most innovative albums were *Focus* (1961) and *Jazz Samba* (1962).

Gewandhaus [Ger.]. See Concert, Orchestra.

Gewandt [Ger.]. Agile.

Gewöhnlich [Ger.]. Usual; an instruction to the player to return to the usual way of playing after a previous instruction to play in a special way, e.g., after an instruction to bow over the fingerboard.

Gezupft [Ger.]. **Pizzicato.*

Ghedini, Giorgio Federico (b. Cuneo, 11 July 1892; d. Nervi, near Genoa, 25 Mar. 1965). Composer. Pupil of Bossi. Taught in Turin, Parma, and Milan (director of the conservatory, 1951–62). Arranged and edited works of Frescobaldi, Monteverdi, and others. Many of his own works adopt features of Baroque music (*Partita,* orchestra, 1926; *Concerto funebre per Duccio Galimberti,* 1948). Works such as *Architetture* (orchestra, 1940) show the influence of Stravinsky. Composed 6 operas, a ballet, film and incidental music; orchestral pieces; chamber and piano music; vocal works.

Ghent, Emmanuel (Robert) (b. Montreal, 15 May 1925). Composer and psychoanalyst. Pupil of Shapey. Taught and practiced psychoanalysis in New York. Works include *Hex* (trumpet, 11 instruments, and 4-track tape, 1966); works for dancers with computer-generated lighting, electronic and computer music, and live performers (*Phosphones,* 1971).

Gherardello da Firenze (b. ca. 1320–25; d. Florence, 1362 or 1363). Composer. Active in Florence; a member of the first generation of Florentine trecento composers. Works include monophonic *ballate,* a *caccia,* and 2-voiced madrigals and Mass movements.

Ghiglia, Oscar (Alberto) (b. Livorno, 13 Aug. 1938). Guitarist. Studied with Andrés Segovia; his assistant at the Accademia Chigiana in Siena and at the Univ. of California at Berkeley, 1964. Debut at the Spoleto Festival in 1961; in New York and London, 1966.

Ghironda [It.]. *Hurdy-gurdy.

Ghiselin [Verbonnet], **Johannes** (fl. early 16th cent.). Composer. Contemporary and associate of Josquin and Obrecht; active chiefly in Ferrara and at the French royal court. Works include 8 Masses (most based on secular chansons), motets, and chansons.

Ghislanzoni, Antonio (b. Lecco, 25 Nov. 1824; d. Caprino Bergamasco, 16 July 1893). Librettist. Published poetry, novels, and about 85 librettos (for Ponchielli, Catalani, Gomes, Petrella, among others); collaborated with Verdi on the revision of *La forza del destino* and on *Aida.*

Ghost trio. See *Geistertrio.*

Giacosa, Giuseppe (b. Colleretto Parella, near Turin, 21 Oct. 1847; d. there, 2 Sept. 1906). Librettist. Successful dramatist; collaborated with Luigi Illica on librettos for Puccini (*La bohème, Tosca, Madama Butterfly*).

Gianni Schicchi. See *Trittico.*

Giannini, Vittorio (b. Philadelphia, 19 Oct. 1903; d. New York, 28 Nov. 1966). Composer. Studied with R. Goldmark. Taught at Juilliard, the Manhattan School, the Curtis Institute (from 1956), and was appointed director of the North Carolina School of the Arts. Works include operas (*The Taming of the Shrew,* 1953); symphonies (*In Memoriam Theodore Roosevelt,* 1935), concertos, and other orchestral and band works; chamber music; piano works; sacred and secular vocal music.

Gibbons, Christopher (bapt. Westminster, London, 22 Aug. 1615; d. there, 20 Oct. 1676). Organist and composer. Son of Orlando Gibbons. Organist at Winchester Cathedral 1638–42; at the Chapel Royal and to King Charles II from 1660; later also at Westminster Abbey. Collaborated with Locke on the masque *Cupid and Death,* 1653. Compositions include sacred works, consort, and keyboard music. Blow was among his pupils.

Gibbons, Orlando (bapt. Oxford, 25 Dec. 1583; d. Canterbury, 5 June 1625). Composer and organist. Organist at the Chapel Royal from 1605; at Westminster Abbey from 1623. Became one of the king's private virginalists in 1619. Works include full and verse anthems; madrigals; fantasias and dances for consort or keyboard; consort songs.

Gibbs, Cecil Armstrong (b. Great Baddon, Essex, 10 Aug. 1889; d. Chelmsford, 12 May 1960). Composer. Pupil of Vaughan Williams and Adrian Boult at the Royal College of Music; instructor there after 1920. Works include *Dusk* (piano, 1946); stage works (*The Blue Peter,* 1923); orchestral works; cantatas; chamber music; some 200 choral works; 100 songs.

Gideon, Miriam (b. Greeley, Colo., 23 Oct. 1906; d. New York, 18 June 1996). Composer. Pupil of Saminsky and Sessions. Taught at Brooklyn College, the City College of New York, the Jewish Theological Seminary, and the Manhattan School (from 1967). Composed an opera; orchestral works; chamber and piano music; Jewish sacred music (Sabbath service, 1970); works for voices and orchestra; songs with piano or ensemble (*The Condemned Playground,* 1963; *Creature to Creature,* 1985).

Gielen, Michael (Andreas) (b. Dresden, 20 July 1927). Conductor and composer. Studied with J. Polnauer. Music director, Belgian National Orchestra, 1968–72; Frankfurt Opera, 1977–80; Cincinnati Symphony, 1980–86; and South-West Radio Symphony in Baden-Baden from 1986. Premiered works by Stockhausen, Ligeti, and others. Compositions include *Variations for 40 Instruments* (1959), orchestral, chamber and vocal music.

Gieseking, Walter (b. Lyons, of German parents, 5 Nov. 1895; d. London, 26 Oct. 1956). Pianist and composer. Studied piano with Karl Leimer, Hannover. First European tour, 1921; U.S. debut, 1926. His playing of Debussy won special admiration. Compositions include Concerto-Sonatina for cello and piano; a wind quintet; Serenade for string quartet.

Giga [It., Sp.]. *Gigue.

Gigault, Nicolas (b. Paris, ca. 1627; d. there, 20 Aug. 1707). Organist and composer. Held posts at several churches in Paris from 1646. Perhaps a teacher of Lully. Works include variations on French noëls, plainsong settings, *récits,* dialogues, preludes, and fugues.

Gigelira [It.]. *Xylophone.

Gigli, Beniamino (b. Recanati, 20 Mar. 1890; d. Rome, 30 Nov. 1957). Tenor. Studied with Agnese Bonucci, Antonio Cotogni and Enrico Rosati. Debut in Rovigo in 1914 as Enzo (*La gioconda);* in New York as Boito's Faust, 1920. Remained with the Met 13 seasons; then settled in Rome. Later favored recitals when on tour. Farewell U.S. tour in 1955. He appeared in 6 films, including *Mamma.*

Gigout, Eugène (b. Nancy, 23 Mar. 1844; d. Paris, 9 Dec. 1925). Organist and composer. Pupil of Saint-Saëns. Teacher at the École Niedermeyer (1863–85, 1900–1905). Organist at St. Augustin, 1863–1925; 1885, founded an organ school; from 1911, professor of organ, Paris Conservatory. Many organ compositions, especially the collections *Pièces brèves* (1889), *Album grégorien* (1895), *L'orgue d'église* (1904).

Gigue [Fr., fr. Eng. jig; Ger. *Gigue;* It. *giga;* Sp. *giga, jiga*]. (1) A fast Baroque dance movement in binary form, the last movement of the mature *suite. The details of rhythm and texture vary greatly, deriving from Italian and French models. The Italian *giga* features triadic, sequential running figures in even note-values in 12/8 at presto tempo. Its texture is mostly homophonic, and phrases are in four-measure units. French versions are less consistent, often having dotted rhythms in duple meter (usually compound, but also simple), syncopations, hemiolas, and cross rhythms. The most influential type opens each strain with imitation and has irregular phrase lengths. Many composers, especially in Germany, mixed elements of the two schools.

Bach, Gigue from French Suite no. 4.

The dance originated in Ireland and England [see Jig]. It was known in France by the 1650s and became an important part of the lute and harpsichord repertory. In the early 18th century in France, its tempo varied but was usually quick: faster than a *loure, slower than a *canarie. In Italy, it was much faster and was particularly common in violin music, often as the last movement of solo sonatas and trio sonatas. In Germany, most composers adopted French imitative texture, often making the thematic relationship between the strains closer by using an inversion of the opening motive as the subject of the second strain [see Ex.]. They often favored Italian flowing triplet motion.

(2) In the Middle Ages, a bowed stringed instrument: a fiddle or *rebec. The term is the root of the modern German word for violin, *Geige.*

Gilbert, Henry F(ranklin Belknap) (b. Somerville, Mass., 26 Sept. 1868; d. Cambridge, Mass., 19 May 1928). Composer. Pupil of MacDowell. Helped Farwell establish the Wa-Wan Press. Composed 2 operas; incidental and film music; orchestral works (*The Dance in Place Congo,* ca. 1908; rev. 1916; *Comedy Overture on Negro Themes,* ca. 1906; *The Intimate Story of Indian Tribal Life,* 1911); chamber and piano music; songs; folk song arrangements.

Gilbert, Kenneth (b. Montreal, 16 Dec. 1931). Harpsichordist, organist, and musicologist. Studied with Nadia Boulanger, Maurice Duruflé, and Gustav Leonhardt. Organist in Montreal, 1952–67, and an exponent of historical organ building; thereafter pursued a European-based concert career. From 1988, taught at the Salzburg Mozarteum and at the Paris Conservatory. Edited the complete keyboard works of François Couperin, Rameau, D'Anglebert, Dieupart, and Domenico Scarlatti.

Gilbert, William Schwenck (b. London, 18 Nov. 1836; d. Harrow Weald, Middlesex, 29 May 1911). Librettist. Collaborated with Sullivan from the 1870s; the success of their *H.M.S. Pinafore* (1878) led to more joint works (including *The Pirates of Penzance,* 1879; *The Mikado,* 1885; *The Gondoliers,* 1889). In 1890 this collaboration interrupted; resumed with less success 1893–96.

Gilboa, Jacob (b. Koice, 2 May 1920). Composer. Settled in Palestine 1938. Pupil of Tal, Ben-Haim and Stockhausen. From the 1960s, assimilated quarter tones, aleatory, and other new techniques into his "Mediterranean" style. Works include *The Twelve Jerusalem Glass Windows by Chagall,* soprano, voices, chamber ensemble, 1966; *Five Red Sea Impressions,* chamber ensemble, 1976; *Lament of Klonimos,* orchestra, 1974.

Gilchrist, William Wallace (b. Jersey City, 8 Jan. 1846; d. Easton, Pa., 20 Dec. 1916). Composer. Active as church musician, conductor, and singing teacher in Philadelphia; edited the official Presbyterian hymnal, 1895. Composed 2 symphonies, chamber music, piano pieces, songs; choral music, including *A Christmas Idyll* (1898), Psalm 46 (1882), *The Rose* (1887), *The Lamb of God,* oratorio (1909).

Gilels, Emil (Grigor'evich) (b. Odessa, 19 Oct. 1916; d. Moscow, 14 Oct. 1985). Pianist. Studied in Odessa and Moscow. Taught at the Moscow Conservatory from 1938. Best known for Mozart, Beethoven, Schubert, Schumann, and his Russian contemporaries.

Gilles, Jean (b. Tarascon, 8 Jan. 1668; d. Toulouse, 5 Feb. 1705). Composer. *Maître de musique* at cathedrals in Aix-en-Provence, Agde, and Toulouse (from 1697). His *Messe des morts* was widely performed, including at the funerals of Rameau and Louis XV. Other works include a Mass and motets.

Gillespie, Dizzy [John Birks] (b. Cheraw, S.C., 21 Oct. 1917; d. Englewood, N.J., 6 Jan. 1993). Jazz trumpeter, composer, and bandleader. Played in bands of Teddy Hill (1937), Cab Calloway (1939–41), and Billy Eckstine (1944–45). Led a combo with Oscar Pettiford (1943–44); his own bop big band; with Charlie Parker, a quintet that made the first mature bebop recordings (1945). His second big band (1946–50) established Afro-Cuban jazz. Later mainly led combos. Gillespie's playing was marked by unprecedented dexterity; also a hilarious scat singer. Among his recordings of his compositions are "Groovin' High" (1945), "A Night in Tunisia" (1946), "Manteca" (1947), and "Con Alma" (1957). Other recordings as a leader include "Salt Peanuts," "I Can't Get Started," "Hot House" (all 1945), "Oop-bop-sh'bam" (1946), and "Oop-pop-a-dah" (1947).

Gillis, Don (b. Cameron, Mo., 17 June 1912; d. Columbia, S.C., 10 Jan. 1978). Composer. Produced Toscanini's NBC radio broadcasts (1944–54). Administrative posts at Interlochen Music Camp (1958–61); Dallas Baptist College (1968–72); the Univ. of South Carolina (from 1973). His compositions draw on American sources such as jazz. Wrote operas and ballets; orchestral and band pieces (symphonies; *Tulsa, a Symphonic Portrait in Oil,* 1950); chamber music; vocal music.

Gilmore, Patrick S(arsfield) (b. Ballygar, Galway, 25 Dec. 1829; d. St. Louis, 24 Sept. 1892). Bandmaster. Settled in Boston 1849. Organized Massachusetts army bands in the Civil War; Peace Jubilee band concerts (Boston, 1869, 1872). From 1873 directed the New York 22nd Regiment Band. Composed songs and marches, including "When Johnny Comes Marching Home," published under a pseudonym.

Gilson, Paul (b. Brussels, 15 June 1865; d. there, 3 Apr. 1942). Composer. Studied at the Brussels Conservatory; taught there from 1899 and at Antwerp 1904–9. Composed operas (*Prinses Zonneschijn,* 1901); an oratorio (*Francesca da Rimini,* 1892); ballets; many pieces for orchestra (*La mer,* 1892) and band; cantatas; chamber and piano music. Also wrote *Le tutti orchestral,* 1913; *Traité d'harmonie,* 1919; artistic director of the Revue musicale belge.

Gimel. See Gymel.

Giménez (Jiménez) (y Bellido), Jerónimo (b. Seville, 10 Oct. 1854; d. Madrid, 19 Feb. 1923). Composer. Pupil of Savard, Alard, and Thomas at the Paris Conservatory. Director of the Teatro de la Zarzuela and the Madrid Concert Society. Composed zarzuelas, often drawing on Spanish folk material; titles include *De vuelta de vivero* (1895), *La tempranica* (1900), and *La boda de Luis Alonso* (1897).

Ginastera, Alberto (b. Buenos Aires, 11 Apr. 1916; d. Geneva, 25 June 1983). Composer. Pupil of Palma and Copland. Taught in Buenos Aires and La Plata; 1962–69 directed the Torcuato di Tella Institute. Used Argentine folk material in early works; later turned to "neo-expressionism." Compositions include ballets (*Panambí,* 1934–36); operas (*Don Rodrigo,* 1964); orchestral works (*Obertura para el "Fausto" criollo,* 1943; *Pampeana núm. 3,* 1954; concertos; *Iubilum,* 1980); chamber music; vocal music (3 *Cantatas dramáticas*); solo music for piano, organ, and guitar.

Gingold, Josef (b. Brest-Litovsk, 28 Oct. 1909; d. Bloomington, Ind., 11 Jan. 1995). Violinist and teacher. Pupil of Vladimir Graffman and Eugene Ysaÿe. New York debut 1926. Member of the NBC Symphony Orchestra, 1937–43. Concertmaster, Detroit Symphony, 1943–47; Cleveland Orchestra, 1947–60. Taught at Case Western Reserve Univ., 1950–60; at Indiana Univ. from 1960; at the Manhattan School of Music, 1980–81.

Gioconda, La [It., The Joyful Girl]. Opera in four acts by Amilcare Ponchielli (libretto by Arrigo Boito [pseud. Tobia Gorrio], after Victor Hugo's drama *Angelo, tyran de Padoue*), produced in Milan in 1876. Setting: Venice in the 17th century.

Giocoso [It.]. Jocose, humorous.

Gioioso [It.]. Joyous, merry.

Giordani, Tommaso (b. Naples, ca. 1730; d. Dublin, Feb. 1806). Composer. His family's traveling theater troupe performed his first opera, *La comediante fatta cantatrice,* at Covent Garden 1756. From 1769 he conducted at the King's Theatre, London; settled in Dublin around 1783. Among his theater works are *The Maid of the Mill* (1765), *L'eroe cinese* (1766); many songs for pasticcios. Also published instrumental music.

Giordano, Umberto (b. Foggia, 28 Aug. 1867; d. Milan, 12 Nov. 1948). Composer. Studied in Naples. Composed operas (*Mala vita,* 1892; *Fedora,* 1898; *Andrea Chénier; La cena delle beffe,* 1924); orchestral works; chamber and piano music; songs.

Giorgi flute. A vertically held version of the orchestral *flute, invented by Carlo Tomaso Giorgi and patented in 1896.

Giovannelli, Ruggiero (b. Velletri, near Rome, ca. 1560; d. Rome, 7 Jan. 1625). Composer. Active in

Rome from at least 1583; *maestro di cappella* of the Cappella Giulia at St. Peter's (1594–99, succeeding Palestrina) and singer at the Sistine Chapel (1599–1624); played a small role in the reform of the Gradual. Composed light madrigals, canzonettas, Masses, and numerous motets.

Giovanni da Cascia [Johannes de Florentia, Giovanni da Firenze] (fl. northern Italy, 1340–50). Composer. A colleague of Jacopo da Bologna and of Maestro Piero in Verona and Milan. Composed madrigals and cacce.

Giovanni da Firenze. See Giovanni da Cascia.

Gipps, Ruth (b. Bexhill-on-Sea, Sussex, 20 Feb. 1921). Composer, pianist, and conductor. Studied with Morris, Jacob, and Vaughan Williams at the Royal College of Music, where she was later professor. Choirmaster of the City of Birmingham Choir (1948–50); conducted the London Repertory Orchestra; founded the Chanticleer Orchestra 1961. Works include 5 symphonies; concertos; choral works (*The Cat,* 1947; *Goblin Market,* 1953; *Gloria in excelsis,* 1974); chamber music.

Giraffe piano. A grand *piano of the first half of the 19th century, the wing-shaped portion of which (and thus the plane of the strings) is set upright, perpendicular to the keyboard.

Giraut [Guiraut] **de Bornelh** [de Borneill] (b. Excideuil, near Périgeux, ca. 1140; d. ca. 1200). Troubadour. Traveled widely in southern France and northern Spain. Almost 80 poems, 4 with music (including "Reis glorios"), are ascribed to him.

Girl of the Golden West. See *Fanciulla del West, La.*

Gis [Ger.]. G-sharp. See Pitch names.

Giselle (ou Les Wilis). A ballet in two acts by Adolphe Adam (choreography by Jean Coralli and Jules Perrot, book by Vernoy de Saint-Georges, Théophile Gautier, and Jean Coralli, after a story by Heinrich Heine), first produced in Paris in 1841.

Gisis [Ger.]. G-double-sharp. See Pitch names.

Gitana, alla [It.]. See Gypsy music.

Gittern [also gyterne, gitt(e)ron; Fr. *guiterne;* Ger. *Quinterne;* It. *chitarra, ghiterra*]. (1) A small medieval plucked stringed instrument with a pear-shaped body, round back, and sickle-shaped pegbox. (2) Any of a variety of plucked stringed instruments of the Middle Ages and Renaissance thought to derive from the *guitarra latina* and *guitarra morisca* mentioned in Spanish literature beginning in the 14th century.

Giù [It.]. Down; *arcata in giù,* down-bow. See Bowing (1).

Giuffre, Jimmy [James Peter] (b. Dallas, 26 Apr. 1921). Jazz clarinetist, saxophonist, and composer. Played in the big bands of Boyd Raeburn, Jimmy Dorsey, Buddy Rich, and Woody Herman, for whom he wrote "Four Brothers" (1947). Played West Coast jazz with Howard Rumsey and Shorty Rogers. His trio of 1956–59 turned toward folk influences; that of ca. 1961–62 played free jazz. After exploring Eastern and African influences, he turned to bop in the 1980s. From 1978 taught at the New England Conservatory of Music.

Giuliani, Mauro (Giuseppe Sergio Pantaleo) (b. Bisceglie, near Bari, 27 July 1781; d. Naples, 8 May 1829). Guitarist and composer. Lived in Vienna 1806–19; in Rome until 1823 and thereafter in Naples, patronized by court and aristocracy. His guitar compositions include 3 concertos, chamber music, sonatas, etudes, variations, and dances.

Giulini, Carlo Maria (b. Barletta, Italy, 9 May 1914). Conductor. Studied with Bernardino Molinari. Conductor of the RAI Symphony in Milan, 1946–50. Assistant to De Sabata at La Scala, 1951–53; principal conductor, 1953–56. Conductor of the Vienna Philharmonic, 1973–76; of the Los Angeles Philharmonic, 1978–86.

Giulio Cesare in Egitto [It., Julius Caesar in Egypt]. Opera in three acts by Handel (libretto by Nicola Francesco Haym, after G. F. Bussani), produced in London in 1724. Setting: Egypt, 48 B.C.E.

Giustamente [It.]. *Giusto.

Giustiniana [It.]. A late 16th-century comic subgenre of the *villanella* in which three old men sing, with much written-in stammering, of love.

Giusto [It.]. Just, precise; *tempo giusto,* an appropriate tempo or the usual tempo for the type of work at hand, or a return to regular tempo after a passage in which tempo is flexible.

Glagolitic Mass [Cz. *Glagolská mše*]. A cantata composed in 1926 by Leoš Janáček for soprano, alto, tenor, and bass soloists, chorus, orchestra, and organ, with a text adapted by Miloš Weingart from Old Church Slavonic.

Glanville-Hicks, Peggy (b. Melbourne, 29 Dec. 1912; d. Sydney, 25 June 1990). Composer. Pupil of R. O. Morris, Vaughan Williams, N. Boulanger, and Wellesz. Lived in New York, 1942–59. Conducted musical research in the Aegean and in the Middle and Far East. Works include operas (*The Transposed Heads,* 1953); ballets; film scores; vocal works (*Thomsoniana,* 1949; *Letters from Morocco,* 1952); instrumental music (*Sinfonia da Pacifica,* 1953).

Glanz, glänzend [Ger.]. Brightness, brilliant.

Glarean, Heinrich [Glareanus, Heinricus; Loriti] (b. Mollis, canton of Glarus, June 1488; d. Freiburg, 28 Mar. 1563). Theorist and writer. Lived in Basel 1514–29; from 1529 taught at the university in Freiburg im Breisgau. His most influential treatise, the *Dodecachordon* (1547), advocates a system of 12 modes.

Glass (h)armonica. An instrument invented by Benjamin Franklin in 1761 and called "armonica." It consists of a row of glass bowls of graded sizes fixed concentrically on a horizontal spindle that is made to rotate by a treadle. Sound is produced by gently rubbing the fingers (slightly wetted or dipped in chalk) on the rims of the revolving glasses. Later models are fitted with a trough of water beneath the spindle to keep the glasses constantly wet, and some are fitted with a keyboard that rubs the glasses mechanically. It became very popular in connection with the Romantic movement of the late 18th and early 19th centuries. Mozart (Adagio in C major K. 356 [617a] and Adagio and Rondo in C minor with flute, oboe, viola, and cello K. 617), Beethoven, Hasse, Jommelli, and Padre Martini wrote for the glass harmonica. See also Musical glasses.

Glass harmonica.

Glass, Philip (b. Baltimore, 31 Jan. 1937). Composer. Pupil of Bergsma, Persichetti, Milhaud, and Boulanger. Exposure to Indian music caused him to adopt its rhythmic language and additive/repetitive construction; from 1965 composed in a minimalist idiom, favoring nonnarrative structures. Works include operas (*Einstein on the Beach,* 1975; *Akhnaten,* 1983; *The Fall of the House of Usher,* 1988) and other theatrical pieces; film and television scores; music for the Philip Glass Ensemble, using electronic and amplified instruments; symphonies; string quartets; chamber and piano music; works composed before 1965 have been withdrawn.

Glazunov, Alexander Konstantinovich (b. St. Petersburg, 10 Aug. 1865; d. Paris, 21 Mar. 1936). Composer. Pupil of Rimsky-Korsakov. A prominent member of the "Belyayev Circle." With Rimsky-Korsakov completed and revised Borodin's unfinished compositions. From 1899, professor at the St. Petersburg Conservatory (director 1905–30). Settled in Paris 1932. Composed ballets (*Raymonda,* 1896–97); 8 symphonies and other orchestral works (Violin Concerto, 1904); incidental music; choral music; 7 string quartets and other chamber music; piano pieces; songs.

Gleason, Frederick Grant (b. Middletown, Conn., 17 or 18 Dec. 1848; d. Chicago, 6 Dec. 1903). Composer. Studied with Dudley Buck. Organist in Connecticut; director of the Chicago Conservatory from 1900; music critic. Composed operas (*Otho Visconti,* 1876–77); cantatas; a piano concerto; symphonic poems (*Edris,* 1896); songs; keyboard works; sacred choral music.

Glee. An English composition for three or more voices, usually unaccompanied and male, popular in the 18th and early 19th centuries. The poem (and its music) may be either lighthearted or serious, since this usage of glee does not relate directly to the word's present meaning, but derives from their common Old-English source meaning entertainment, play, sport, and also musical entertainment, the playing of music, and music itself. Used in the sense of melody, it is found in *Beowulf.*

The glee was at its height in the second half of the 18th century, when it was a favorite for amateur music-making, and clubs devoted to singing glees and similar music and to encouraging their composition were formed in London (and elsewhere), including the Glee Club (1783–1857). The use of Glee Club as a name for American school choruses derives from their origin in such groups in the 19th century.

The 18th-century glee tended toward a vigorous style, rather simple in texture, less contrapuntal than most madrigals. In the 19th century, there was a tendency to even more homophonic texture and to sentimental melody, leading to the part song, which eventually replaced the glee. Samuel Webbe (1740–1816) is generally considered the leading glee composer.

Gleemen. See Minstrel.

Gleichmässig [Ger.]. Even, equal.

Gli scherzi [It.]. See *Scherzi, Gli.*

Glier, Ryngol'd Moritsevich [Glière, Reinhold] (b. Kiev, 11 Jan. 1875; d. Moscow, 23 June 1956). Composer. Studied with Taneyev, Arensky, Konyus, and Ippolitov-Ivanov at the Moscow Conservatory; professor there (1920–41). Compositions include operas (*Shakh-Senem,* 1923; *Gyul'sara,* 1936; *Leyli i Mej-*

nun, 1940), symphonies (Third Symphony, *Il'ya Muromets,* 1909–11), concertos (for harp, 1938), symphonic poems, overtures, ballets (*Krasniy tsvetok* [The Red Flower], 1949; *Medniy vsadnik* [The Bronze Horseman], 1948–49), chamber music, and songs.

Glinka, Mikhail Ivanovich (b. Novospasskoye, Smolensk district, 1 June 1804; d. Berlin, 15 Feb. 1857). Composer. Received an unsystematic musical education; 1824–28 held a bureaucratic post in St. Petersburg. Traveled widely in Europe. Named Kapellmeister of the imperial chapel following the 1836 premiere of his opera *Zhizn'za tsarya* (A *Life for the Tsar). Other works include the opera *Ruslan and Lyudmila* (1837–42); songs (*Adel'* [Adèle], *Zazdravniy kubok* [The Toasting Cup], both 1849; *Finskiy zaliv* [The Gulf of Finland], 1850); orchestral music (symphonies; 2 Spanish Overtures; *Kamarinskaya,* 1848).

Glissando [It., abbr. *gliss.;* fr. Fr. *glisser,* to slide]. A continuous or sliding movement from one pitch to another. On the piano, the nail of the thumb or of the third finger or the side of the index finger is drawn, usually rapidly, over the white keys or the black keys, thus producing a rapid scale. A similar effect is much used in harp playing. On stringed instruments such as the violin, on wind instruments (particularly, though not exclusively, the slide trombone), and on the pedal kettledrum, the sliding movement may produce a continuous variation in pitch rather than a rapid succession of discrete pitches. This is often indicated by a straight or wavy line drawn between the starting and ending pitches and is sometimes termed *portamento,* though glissando remains the prevalent term for this effect in musical scores.

Glissé [Fr.]. In *harp playing, *glissando.

Globokar, Vinko (b. Anderny, Meurthe-et-Moselle, 7 July 1934). Composer and virtuoso trombonist. Pupil of Leibowitz and Berio. Teacher at the Hochschule für Musik in Cologne from 1968. Compositions include vocal works (*Voie,* narrator, chorus, orchestra, 1965–66; *Accord,* soprano, chamber ensemble, 1966; *Traumdeutung,* 4 choruses, chamber ensemble, 1967); chamber works (*Discours I–IV,* various instrumental groupings, 1967–74; *Dos a dos,* 2 performers, 1988).

Globular flute. A *flute whose body is not a tube; also called a vessel flute. Globular flutes are particularly characteristic of Africa and pre-Columbian South America. A familiar example is the *ocarina.

Glocke [Ger.]. Bell (1).

Glockenspiel [Ger., also *Stahlspiel;* Eng., also bells, but see also Tubular bells; Fr. *carillon, jeu de tim-*

bres; It. *campanelli, carillon;* Sp. *carillón, campanólogo*]. (1) A percussion instrument of definite pitch consisting of metal bars of varying length arranged in two rows, somewhat in the fashion of a piano keyboard, on a frame, usually without resonators. It is mounted horizontally on a stand and played with two or more beaters with hard, small, round heads. Some instruments of this general type, which came into use in the mid-18th century, are played from a pianolike keyboard. Its range is notated from g to c'', and it sounds two octaves higher. A similar instrument used in military and marching bands has its bars arranged on a frame shaped like a Greek lyre and is thus often termed a bell lyra or bell lyre. See ill. under Percussion instruments. (2) [Ger.] *Carillon.

Gloria (in excelsis Deo) [Lat., Glory to God in the highest]. The second item of the *Ordinary of the Roman Catholic *Mass, except in Advent, Lent, and a few other occasions when it is omitted; also known as the Greater Doxology and the Angelic Hymn. In performance, the first phrase is intoned by the celebrant, and the choir continues with the phrase "Et in terra pax." Thus it is that most polyphonic settings begin with this phrase.

Gloria patri [Lat.]. See Doxology.

Glosa [Sp., ornamentation, gloss]. In 16th-century Spanish music, (1) ornamental figures and passages and (2) a musical gloss. *Glosa* and its adjectival form, *glosado,* may thus identify a composition, usually an *intabulation, that has been enlivened with nearly continuous, florid instrumental ornamentations or *divisions. Spanish and Portuguese collections of organ and *vihuela* music are full of such works, many important to the history of *variation. In Cabezón's works, *glosa* identifies short figural variations in *fabordón* style on psalm tones (cf. *intonatione*), in contrast to sets of variations called *diferencias.

Glover, Jane (Alison) (b. Helmsley, Yorkshire, 13 May 1949). Conductor and musicologist. Studied at St. Hugh's College, Oxford. Music director of the Glyndebourne Festival from 1981; of the London Choral Society from 1983; of the London Mozart Players from 1984.

Gluck, Alma [Reba Fiersohn] (b. Bucharest, 11 May 1884; d. New York, 27 Oct. 1938). Soprano. Studied voice with Arturo Buzzi-Peccia. Debut at the Met as Sophie *(Werther),* 1909. Later became a recording star; her nearly 120 recordings include "Carry Me Back to Old Virginny" and Rameau's "Rossignol amoureux" *(Hippolyte et Aricie).* Many of her records featured obbligato violin solos by her second husband, Efrem Zimbalist.

Gluck, Christoph Willibald (b. Erasbach, 2 July 1714; d. Vienna, 15 Nov. 1787). Composer. Pupil of Sammartini. Composed operas throughout Europe; by 1748 settled in Vienna. With librettist Raniero Calzabigi undertook to reform Italian opera: "to restrict music to its true office of serving poetry by means of expression." They collaborated on the ballet *Don Juan* (1761) and the operas **Orfeo ed Euridice* and **Alceste*. Gluck's other theater works include *La Semiramide riconosciuta* (1748); *Le cinesi* (1754); *L'innocenza giustificata* (1755); *La fausse esclave* (1758); *La rencontre imprévue* (1764); *Paride ed Elena* (1770); **Iphigénie en Aulide; Armide* (1777); **Iphigénie en Tauride; Echo et Narcisse* (1779). Also composed sacred vocal works, including *De profundis;* songs and odes; symphonies and trio sonatas.

Glückliche Hand, Die [Ger., The Fortunate Hand]. A "drama with music" by Schoenberg (to his own text) with one singing part, for baritone, two mimed parts, and chorus, composed in 1910–13 and produced in Vienna in 1924.

Gnattali, Radamés (b. Pôrto Alegre, Brazil, 27 Jan. 1906). Composer and conductor. Studied in Rio de Janeiro. Conductor of the Radio nacional orchestra. Works include *Rapsódia brazileira* (1931); 10 *Brasilianas* for piano solo or with orchestra (1944–62); the folk ballet *Negrinho do pastoreio* (1959); concertos for piano, guitar, and harmonica; chamber music; and songs.

Gnesin, Mikhail Fabianovich (b. Rostov-na-Donu, 2 Feb. 1883; d. Moscow, 5 May 1957). Composer. Pupil of Rimsky-Korsakov and Lyadov. An organizer of the Society of Jewish Folk Music in St. Petersburg; professor at Moscow and Leningrad Conservatories. Among his pupils were Khachaturian and Khrennikov. Compositions include works for the stage, orchestral music, chamber music, piano pieces, film scores, choral music, and songs.

Goat's trill [Fr. *chèvrotement;* Ger. *Bockstriller, Geisstriller;* It. *trillo caprino;* Sp. *trino de cabra*]. Usually, the rapid reiteration of a single pitch. For this ornament, see Tremolo. According to some 18th-century writers, a *Bockstriller* is a trill in which the two pitches are less than a semitone apart or are sung with unequal speed or loudness. Leopold Mozart terms a trill a *Geisstriller* if it is performed too fast and thus sounds like "bleating."

Gobbi, Tito (b. Bassano del Grappa, 24 Oct. 1913; d. Rome, 5 Mar. 1984). Baritone. Studied with Giulio Crimi. Debut in Rome, 1937, as Germont *(Traviata),* then joined the Rome Opera. Sang with the Chicago Lyric Opera, 1954–73; at the Met through 1976. Staged operas in Chicago, at Covent Garden and at the Met. Also appeared in 26 films.

God Save the Queen [King]. The British national anthem. Both words and music are anonymous and seem to have become popular in 1745. In the U.S., the melody is often sung to the words beginning "My country 'tis of thee."

Godard, Benjamin (Louis Paul) (b. Paris, 18 Aug. 1849; d. Cannes, 10 Jan. 1895). Composer. Studied with Reber. Composed salon and concert music, including descriptive symphonies; a dramatic symphony with voices, *Le Tasse,* 1878; 2 piano and 2 violin concertos; chamber music; piano pieces and songs. Also wrote operas (*Jocelyn,* 1888).

Godowsky, Leopold (b. Soshly, Russian Poland, 13 Feb. 1870; d. New York, 21 Nov. 1938). Pianist and composer. Pupil of Woldemar Bargiel and Saint-Saëns. Taught in the U.S., 1890–1900; in Vienna, 1909–14. Settled in the U.S., 1914. Composed mostly for piano, including *53 Studies on Chopin's Études* (1893–1914), *Triakontameron* (1920) [includes *Alt Wien*], *Phonoramas* (Java Suite, 1925).

Goeb, Roger (John) (b. Cherokee, Iowa, 9 Oct. 1914; d. Rockville Center, N.Y. , 3 Jan. 1997). Composer. Studied with Luening and Elwell. Taught at Bard College (1945–47). Works include at least 6 symphonies and other orchestral music (*Fantasia,* 1983); 4 woodwind quintets and other chamber music; a few vocal pieces.

Goehr, (Peter) Alexander (b. Berlin, 10 Aug. 1932). Composer. Son of Walter Goehr. Studied with Messiaen and Loriod. Has taught at New England Conservatory, Yale, Southampton Univ., Leeds Univ., and Cambridge (from 1976). Works include operas (*Arden Must Die,* 1966; *Arianna,* 1994–95); a triptych of music theater pieces; film music; orchestral works (symphonies; concertos; *Romanza,* 1968; *Metamorphosis/Dance,* 1973–74; *Colossos or Panic,* 1993); vocal works (*The Deluge,* 1957–58; *Eve Dreams in Paradise,* 1989); chamber music and piano pieces.

Goehr, Walter (b. Berlin, 28 May 1903; d. Sheffield, 4 Dec. 1960). Conductor and composer. Father of Alexander; studied with Schoenberg. Settled in England in 1933. Music director for the Columbia Recording Company; conducted the Morley College Concerts, 1943–60; the BBC Theatre Orchestra, 1945–48. Composed symphonic, chamber, and film music, including the score of the movie *Great Expectations.*

Goeyvaerts, Karel (August) (b. Antwerp, 8 June 1923; d. there, 3 Feb. 1993). Composer. Teachers included Messiaen, Milhaud, and Stockhausen. Worked in the West German Radio electronic studios. Taught at the Antwerp Conservatory, 1950–57. Composed electronic music (*Composition no. 5,* 1954), sometimes combined with instruments (*Pièce pour piano* with tape, 1964); orchestral pieces; works requiring improvisation (*Van uit de kern,* 2 players, 1969); pieces for mixed media; choral music; a ballet; works for chamber ensemble.

Goffriller, Matteo (b. Bressanone, ca. 1659; d. Venice, 23 Feb. 1742). String instrument maker. Arrived in Venice 1685; probably worked under Martin Kaiser and, by 1690, took over his business. Most renowned for his cellos, with Pablo Casals and Janos Starker two famous players of his instruments.

Gold, Arthur (b. Toronto, 6 Feb. 1917; d. New York, 3 Jan. 1990). Duo pianist. Studed with Rosina Lhévinne. Formed a duo with pianist Robert Fizdale, 1944–82. They expanded the 2-piano repertory by commissioning works from Milhaud, Poulenc, Rieti, Berio, and others.

Goldberg, Johann Gottlieb (bapt. Danzig, 14 Mar. 1727; buried Dresden, 15 Apr. 1756). Organist, harpsichordist, and composer. Student of J. S. and/or W. F. Bach and the central figure in Forkel's story concerning the *Goldberg Variations. Served Count Heinrich von Brühl from 1751. Composed cantatas, keyboard pieces, trio sonatas, *galant* works, and concertos.

Goldberg, Szymon (b. Włoclavek, 1909; d. northwestern Japan, 19 July 1993). Violinist and conductor. Studied violin with Carl Flesch in Berlin. Concertmaster of the Dresden Philharmonic, 1926–30; of the Berlin Philharmonic, 1930–34; played in a trio with Hindemith and Feuermann, and in duo with Lili Kraus. Conducted the Netherlands Chamber Orchestra from 1955 and the New Japan Philharmonic from 1990; taught at Yale, Juilliard, and Curtis; made many recordings.

Goldberg Variations. Popular name for Bach's *Aria mit* [30] *verschiedenen Veränderungen* (Aria with [30] Different Variations) BWV 988, named after Bach's pupil Johann Gottlieb Goldberg (1727–56). The work's plan is a series of threefold units, each consisting of two variations in free style (frequently highly virtuosic) followed by a canonic variation (nos. 3, 6, 9, etc.), the *canon occurring at successively larger intervals; the final variation is a *quodlibet.* The air is played at the beginning and end of the piece. Bach published the work as the fourth part of his *Clavier-Übung* (1741–42).

Golden Cockerel, The [Russ. *Zolotoy petushok;* Fr. *Le coq d'or*]. Opera in three acts by Rimsky-Korsakov (libretto by V. I. Bel'sky, after Pushkin), composed in 1906–7 and produced in Moscow in 1909. Michel Fokine created a version in French for Di-

aghilev's Ballets russes (libretto revised by Alexandre Benois) in which the characters were mimed by dancers and the singers were placed in boxes to the side. This version was produced in Paris in 1914. Setting: a mythical kingdom.

Golden Sequence. Popular name for the *sequence "Veni Sancte Spiritus."

Goldman, Edwin Franko (b. Louisville, Ky., 1 Jan. 1878; d. New York, 21 Feb. 1956). Bandmaster and composer. Studied with Dvořák. Played solo cornet for the Metropolitan Opera, 1899–1909. In 1911 he founded the New York Military Band (later the Goldman Band). Composed over 100 marches ("On the Mall," 1923) and other band works. Wrote technical methods and studies for the cornet and other winds, and for band.

Goldman, Richard Franko (b. New York, 7 Dec. 1910; d. Baltimore, 19 Jan. 1980). Composer, bandmaster, and writer on music. Son of Edwin Franko Goldman. Pupil of Nadia Boulanger. Assistant conductor to his father with the Goldman Band, succeeding him 1956–79. Taught at Juilliard and Princeton; director of the Peabody Conservatory from 1968. Works include *The Lee Rigg* (orchestra); chamber music; many pieces and arrangements for band (*A Sentimental Journey,* 1941).

Goldmark, Karl [Karoly] (b. Keszthely, Hungary, 18 May 1830; d. Vienna, 2 Jan. 1915). Composer. Played and taught violin in Vienna. Composed operas (*Die Königin von Saba,* 1875); orchestral works (*Sakuntala* Overture, 1865; the "Rustic Wedding" Symphony op. 26); chamber and choral works.

Goldmark, Rubin (b. New York, 15 Aug. 1872; d. there, 6 Mar. 1936). Composer and teacher. Studied with Robert Fuchs, Dvořák, and Joseffy. Directed the conservatory in Colorado Springs (1895–1901); taught at Juilliard from 1924. Copland and Gershwin were among his students. Works include a Piano Quintet (1909), *The Call of the Plains* (orchestra, 1925), other chamber and orchestral music, songs, and part songs.

Goldoni, Carlo (b. Venice, 25 Feb. 1707; d. Paris, 6 or 7 Feb. 1793). Librettist and playwright. Wrote for Venetian theaters, 1734–62; thereafter for the Comédie italienne in Paris. Created the *dramma giocoso;* contributed to the development of the ensemble finale as well. His libretti were set by Galuppi, Piccinni, and Haydn, among others.

Goldovsky, Boris (b. Moscow, 7 June 1908). Pianist, conductor, and opera producer. Studied with Kreutzer, Schnabel, and Dohnányi. Director of the Berkshire Music Center Opera Workshop; founding director of the New England Opera Company, 1946. Moderator for broadcasts of the Metropolitan Opera.

Goldschmidt, Otto (Moritz David) (b. Hamburg, 21 Aug. 1829; d. London, 24 Feb. 1907). Conductor. From 1848 based in London; husband (from 1852) of Jenny Lind, frequently accompanying her; founder and first conductor, London Bach Choir (1875–85); also composed, most notably the sacred pastoral *Ruth* (1867).

Goldsmith, Jerry [Jerrald] (b. Los Angeles, 10 Feb. 1929). Composer and conductor. Pupil of Rozsa. Wrote and conducted music for radio and television series, including *Gunsmoke, Perry Mason,* and *The Waltons;* film scores include *Lonely Are the Brave* (1961), *Planet of the Apes* (1967), *Chinatown* (1974), *Star Trek* (1979), *Poltergeist* (1982), and *Rambo* (1985).

Golestan, Stan (b. Vaslui, Moldavia, 7 June 1875; d. Paris, 21 Apr. 1956). Music critic and composer. Studied with Roussel, d'Indy, and Dukas. Music critic for *Le Figaro;* teacher at the École normale. His works incorporate Gypsy and other Romanian folk idioms; they include orchestral works (*Première rapsodie roumaine,* 1915); chamber music; songs; piano works (*Poèmes et paysages,* 1932).

Goliards. Wandering scholar-poets who flourished in England, France, and Germany in the 12th and 13th centuries. The terms goliardic verse and goliardic song have been applied to a large repertory of Latin secular song of the period (including the *Carmina burana*) that is frequently profane, satirical (often directed against the Church and the Pope), amorous (often obscene), and in praise of drink. Only a fraction of the repertory was written by the wandering goliards themselves, however.

Golschmann, Vladimir (b. Paris, 16 Dec. 1893; d. New York, 1 Mar. 1972). Conductor. Studied at the Schola cantorum, Paris. In 1919 established the Concerts Golschmann, which premiered music by "Les six," Ibert, Prokofiev, and Falla. Conductor of the Bilbao Symphony, 1923–28; of the Scottish Orchestra, 1928–30; of the St. Louis Symphony, 1931–58; of the Denver Symphony, 1964–70.

Golson, Benny (b. Philadelphia, 26 Jan. 1929). Jazz tenor saxophonist and composer. Joined Lionel Hampton (1953), Earl Bostic (1954–56), Dizzy Gillespie (1956–57), and Art Blakey's Jazz Messengers (1958–59). With Art Farmer led the Jazztet (1959–62; re-formed 1982). Composed "Stablemates," "I Remember Clifford," "Whisper Not," and "Blues March"; music for films and television.

Gomberg, Harold (b. Malden, Mass., 30 Nov. 1916; d. Capri, 7 Sept. 1985). Oboist. Brother of Ralph.

Pupil of Tabuteau. First chair in the National Symphony, the Toronto Symphony, the St. Louis Symphony (1939–43), and the New York Philharmonic (1943–77). Taught at Juilliard, 1948–77.

Gomberg, Ralph (b. Boston, 18 June 1921). Oboist. Brother of Harold. Pupil of Tabuteau. First chair in the Baltimore Symphony, 1945–49, and the Boston Symphony, 1949–85. Taught at the Peabody Conservatory, 1945–49; at Boston University, 1949–86.

Gombert, Nicolas (b. ca. 1495; d. ca. 1560). Composer. Served the imperial chapel of Charles V 1526–40. Works include 10 Masses, 8 Magnificats, motets, and chansons.

Gomes, (Antônio) Carlos (b. Campenas, Brazil, 11 July 1836; d. Belém, 16 Sept. 1896). Composer. Pupil of Lauro Rossi. Composed primarily operas (*Il Guarany,* 1870; *Lo schiavo,* 1889); also a large cantata (*Colombo,* 1892).

Gomez, Eddie [Edgar] (b. San Juan, Puerto Rico, 4 Nov. 1944). Jazz double bass player. Worked with Jim Hall, Marian McPartland, Paul Bley, and Gerry Mulligan in the mid-1960s. Joined Bill Evans's trio (1966–77). Later played with Jack DeJohnette, Hank Jones, JoAnne Brackeen, and Chick Corea. With Michael Brecker and others founded the fusion group Steps (later, Steps Ahead) in 1979–85.

Gomółka, Mikołaj [Nicolas] (b. Sandomierz?, ca. 1535; d. Jazłowiec, western Ukraine, in or after 1591). Composer. Chorister, then wind player, at the Polish royal court, 1545–63; subsequently a musician for various high-ranking persons in Poland; wrote *Melodie na Psalterz polski* (1580), a book of Psalm settings in Polish.

Gondola song [Ger. *Gondellied;* It. *gondeliera*]. See Barcarole.

Gong. A metal percussion instrument, usually circular, with its circumference turned over to form a lip. In some cases the lip is very deep, making the gong kettle-shaped. The center is often raised into a knob called a boss. A bossed gong has a definite pitch and may be tuned, while a flat gong, such as the *tam-tam,* is of indefinite pitch. Gongs are suspended, either horizontally or vertically, and struck with sticks or padded mallets. Tunable gongs may be assembled into sets, called gong chimes. The gong has found its greatest use and development in the Far East and Southeast Asia. In the Javanese *gamelan,* gong denotes the largest gong in the ensemble, the *gong ageng* [see ill. under Instrument].

Gonsalves, Paul [Mex] (b. Boston, 12 July 1920; d. London, 15 May 1974). Jazz tenor saxophonist. Played in the big bands of Count Basie, Dizzy Gillespie, and Duke Ellington (from 1950). Recordings include *Ellington at Newport,* 1956; Ellington's *Newport 1958;* and *Salt and Pepper* (with Sonny Stitt, 1963).

Goodall, Reginald (b. Lincoln, 13 July 1905; d. Canterbury, 5 May 1990). Conductor. At the Royal Academy of Music in London studied piano with Arthur Benjamin, violin with W. H. Reed. Assistant conductor under Furtwängler with the Berlin Philharmonic. At Covent Garden, 1936–39; 1946–71. Joined the Sadler's Wells Opera in 1944. Conducted and recorded Wagner to great acclaim. Knighted in 1985.

Goode, Richard (b. New York, 1 June 1943). Pianist. Studied with Claude Frank and Nadia Rosenberg at Mannes College, with Elvira Szigeti and Rudolf Serkin at the Curtis Institute. Participated in the Marlboro Festival, 1957–63; in the Spoleto Festival, 1964–66. Debut, New York, 1961. Numerous recordings, including the complete Beethoven sonatas.

Goodman, Benny [Benjamin David] (b. Chicago, 30 May 1909; d. New York, 13 June 1986). Jazz and classical clarinetist and jazz bandleader. Joined Ben Pollack (1925–29), Red Nichols (1929–31) and Joe Venuti and Eddie Lang (1931). Formed a big band, whose sensational reception in 1935 marks the beginning of the swing era. From 1935 he also led a racially integrated combo. Briefly led a band oriented toward bop (1947–49). An intense and imaginative improviser; also concentrated on intonation, technique, and a round timbre. Pursued a parallel career in classical music; commissioned and performed major works by Bartók, Hindemith, and Copland; recorded Mozart's Clarinet Concerto and other classical works. Jazz recordings include "Clarinetitis" (1928), "King Porter," "After You've Gone" (both 1935), "Lady Be Good," "Moonglow," "Stompin' at the Savoy" (all 1936), "Sing, Sing, Sing" (1937), "Don't Be That Way" (1938), "Benny Rides Again" (1940), and the album *Benny Goodman Today* (1970).

Goodrich, (John) Wallace (b. Newton, Mass., 27 May 1871; d. Boston, 6 June 1952). Organist, conductor, and educator. Studied with Rheinberger and Widor in Europe, and at the New England Conservatory, where he taught, 1897–1942 (director from 1931). Church organist in Boston, 1900–1909. Founding conductor of the Choral Art Society, 1901–7; conductor of the Boston Opera Company, 1909–12.

Goossens, (Aynsley) Eugene (b. London, 26 May 1893; d. Hillingdon, Middlesex, 13 June 1962). Conductor and composer. Studied at the Royal College with Stanford. Conductor of the Rochester Philharmonic, then of the Cincinnati Symphony (1931–46). Directed the New South Wales Conservatory (1947–

56) and conducted the Sydney Symphony. Works include operas (*Judith,* 1929; *Don Juan de Mañara,* 1937); incidental music; orchestral works; choral and other vocal works (*The Apocalypse,* oratorio, 1953); chamber works; piano music.

Gopak [Russ.], **hopak** [Ukr.]. A Belorussian and Ukrainian dance in rapid duple meter, of which there is an example in Mussorgsky's **Sorochintsy Fair.*

Gordon, Dexter (Keith) (b. Los Angeles, 27 Feb. 1923; d. Philadelphia, 25 Apr. 1990). Jazz tenor saxophonist. Played in the big bands of Lionel Hampton (1940–43), Louis Armstrong (1944), and Billy Eckstine (1944–46). Recorded with Dizzy Gillespie (1945). Led a group with Wardell Gray to 1952. Recordings include *Doin' Allright* (1961) and *Homecoming* (1976). Starred in the film *'Round Midnight* (1986).

Górecki, Henryk (Mikołaj) (b. Czernica, Poland, 6 Dec. 1933). Composer. Studied with B. Szabelski at Katowice and in Paris with Messiaen. Teacher at the Katowice Conservatory from 1968. His early, serial works show the influence of Webern; he later tended toward more flexible forms, with a tonal language akin to that of Messiaen. Works include 3 symphonies and other orchestral works (*Muzyka staropolska,* 1969); vocal music (3 *Monodrammas,* soprano, ensemble, 1963); chamber music (*Muzyczka I–IV,* 1967–70; string quartets).

Gorgia [It.]. Improvised *ornamentation, especially that associated with Italian vocal music of ca. 1600. A modern term for vocal ornamentation of this type, including rapid passage work, is *gorgheggio.*

Gospel. (1) [Lat. *evangelium*]. In all of the Christian liturgies, a reading or lesson from one of the four Gospels of the Bible. In the Roman Catholic *Mass, it may be chanted to a simple tone.

(2) Anglo-American Protestant evangelical hymns from the 1870s to the present; also gospel hymn, gospel song. In revival meetings, preacher Dwight Moody (1837–99) and singer Ira Sankey (1840–1908) popularized simple, strophic melodies set homophonically to strong tonal progressions in major keys. Texts are often in the first person and concern the Christian life and the anticipated joys of heaven. Among the best-known examples is George Bernard's "The Old Rugged Cross" (1913). More recent gospel music performed by white musicians draws heavily on contemporary styles of pop, country and western, or rock.

(3) Black American Protestant sacred singing and an associated 20th-century sacred genre; also gospel music, gospel song. In this style, vocalists radically embellish simple melodies in full and falsetto voice. Spontaneous or choreographed dancing, clapping,

and stomping may accompany the singing. Mingled functions, performing media, and repertories confuse stylistic distinctions within the genre "black gospel music." Musicians perform for religious stimulation and for commercial profit, in boisterous services and concerts or in silent recording studios.

Vocalists may be a preacher and congregation, soloists (Mahalia Jackson, Marion Williams), singer-guitarists (Blind Willie Johnson, Rev. Gary Davis, Rosetta Tharpe), quartets and quintets, or choirs. Accompanying instruments, if present, are piano, Hammond organ, or guitar, alone or with bass, drums, and tambourine. Performances may include open-ended ostinatos, in which a soloist's improvised comments alternate with a repeated phrase of text. After creating (through male quartets) the basis for *rhythm and blues and *soul, black gospel drew upon those secular genres for new material.

Goss, John (b. Fareham, England, 27 Dec. 1800; d. London, 10 May 1880). Composer. Studied with Attwood; church organist from 1813 at St. Paul's Cathedral; also a teacher (Sullivan, Cowen, Frederick Bridge). Noted for glees and church music. Knighted in 1872.

Gossec, François-Joseph (b. Vergnies, Belgium, 17 Jan. 1734; d. Passy, near Paris, 16 Feb. 1829). Composer. Studied in Antwerp. Settled in Paris, 1751. Founded the Concerts des amateurs, 1769; director of the Concert spirituel from 1773; *maître de musique* at the Opéra from 1775; after 1799, professor at the Conservatory. Composed operas (*Les pêcheurs,* 1766; *Sabinus,* 1733; *Rosine,* 1786); ballets (*Mirza,* 1779); many symphonies; *symphonies concertantes;* chamber works; Revolutionary songs; and sacred vocal music (*Messe des morts,* 1780).

Gothic music. See Middle Ages, music of the.

Gotovac, Jakov (b. Split, 11 Oct. 1895; d. Zagreb, 16 Oct. 1982). Composer. Studied in Zagreb and with Joseph Marx in Vienna. Music director of the Croatian National Opera from 1923. His music draws on Croatian folk melody. Composed operas (*Morana,* 1930; *Ero s onoga svijeta* [Ero from the World Beyond], 1935); orchestral music (*Pjesme i ples za Balkana,* 1939); vocal works (*Koleda,* 1925).

Götterdämmerung [Ger.]. See *Ring des Nibelungen.*

Gottschalk, Louis Moreau (b. New Orleans, 8 May 1829; d. Tijuca, Brazil, 18 Dec. 1869). Composer and pianist. Studied in Paris. Toured widely in Europe and the U.S., as well as Central and South America, where he organized "monster" concerts. Won popularity with piano compositions, especially *Bamboula, La savane, Le bananier,* and *The Last Hope* (1855).

Goudimel, Claude (b. Besançon, 1514–20; d. Lyons, 28–31 Aug. 1572). Composer. Associate of the Parisian publisher Nicolas du Chemin. Works include sacred Latin pieces, chansons, odes on texts by Horace, and especially Psalms in French.

Gould, Glenn (Herbert) (b. Toronto, 25 Sept. 1932; d. there, 4 Oct. 1982). Pianist. Studied in Toronto; debut as an organist there, 1945. In 1955, made his U.S. debut and an acclaimed recording of Bach's Goldberg Variations. Acquired a reputation for brilliant but idiosyncratic musicianship. In 1964 he retired from the concert stage.

Gould, Morton (b. New York, 10 Dec. 1913; d. Orlando, 21 Feb. 1996). Composer and conductor. Worked in radio as composer, arranger, and conductor from 1933. Early works tended to draw from vernacular styles, but in the 1950s Gould employed serial techniques. Composed ballets (*Interplay,* 1945, and *I'm Old Fashioned,* 1983, both choreographed by Jerome Robbins; *Fall River Legend,* Agnes De Mille); orchestral works (*Stephen Foster Gallery,* 1940; *Jekyll and Hyde Variations,* 1955; *Stringmusic,* Pulitzer Prize, 1994); musicals, film and television scores; pieces for symphonic band; chamber and piano music; and choral music.

Gounod, Charles (François) (b. Paris, 18 June 1818; d. St. Cloud, 18 Oct. 1893). Composer. Pupil of Reicha and Halévy. Conducted the male-voice chorus, the Orphéon de la ville de Paris, from 1852; the Royal Albert Hall Choral Society, 1871–72. Composed operas (*Le médecin malgré lui,* 1859; *Philémon et Baucis,* 1860; **Faust; Mireille,* 1864; *Roméo et Juliette,* 1867; *Polyeucte,* 1878); incidental music (*Le bourgeois gentilhomme,* 1857); much choral music (*Messe solennelle de Ste. Cécile,* 1855; the oratorios *Rédemption,* 1881, and *Mors et vita,* 1885); 12 Masses, Latin motets, and other sacred and secular choruses; also many solo songs; and 2 symphonies.

Goyescas [Sp.]. (1) Six piano pieces in two sets composed by Enrique Granados in 1911 and inspired by paintings by Francisco Goya (1746–1828). A seventh piece, "El pelele," is usually performed with the original six. (2) Opera in three scenes by Granados (libretto by Fernando Periquet y Zuaznabar), produced in New York in 1916. The opera makes use of the piano pieces of the same name.

G.P. (1) Abbr. for **Generalpause.* (2) In French organ music, abbr. for **Grand (orgue)* and **Positif,* indicating that the two divisions should be coupled.

Grace. In 16th- and 17th-century England, any musical ornament, whether written out in notes, indicated by sign, or improvised by the performer.

Grace note. A note printed in small type to indicate that its time value is not counted in the rhythm of the bar and must be subtracted from that of an adjacent note. Large groups of grace notes sometimes represent an exception to this rule in that together they fill up the time value of a single note that has been omitted from the score (as in works by Chopin and others), in which case the rhythm of the grace notes is flexible and not subject to a strict beat. Most grace notes are used to represent *graces or musical ornaments. See Ornamentation.

Gracieux [Fr.]. Graceful.

Gracile [It.]. Delicate.

Gradatamente [It.]. Gradually.

Gradevole [It.]. Pleasant, agreeable.

Gradito [It.]. Pleasing.

Gradual [Lat. *graduale*]. (1) In *Gregorian chant, the item of the *Proper of the *Mass that is sung following the reading of the Epistle. An example of responsorial *psalmody, it consists of a respond intoned by soloists and completed by the choir, a verse sung by the soloists, and a repetition by the choir of the last part of the respond. Its texts are most often drawn from the Psalms, and its melodies are highly *melismatic.
   (2) The *liturgical book containing the chants for the Mass.

Gradus ad Parnassum [Lat., Steps to Parnassus (a mountain sacred to Apollo and the Muses)]. (1) A treatise on counterpoint by Johann Joseph Fux (Vienna, 1725; 2nd ed., 1742). See also Species counterpoint. (2) A collection of piano etudes by Clementi, op. 44, in three volumes (1817, 1819, 1826).

Graener, Paul (b. Berlin, 11 Jan. 1872; d. Salzburg, 13 Nov. 1944). Composer and conductor. Taught at the New Conservatory in Vienna 1908; at the Leipzig Conservatory 1920–25; and at the Reichsmusikkammer 1935–41. Composed orchestral, chamber, and piano works, operas (*Friedemann Bach*, 1931), and songs.

Graffman, Gary (b. New York, 14 Oct. 1928). Pianist. Studied with Isabelle Vengerova, Horowitz, and Serkin. In the 1960s and 1970s performed chamber music with the Guarneri and Juilliard Quartets as well as Leonard Rose and Henryk Szeryng. After his right hand became disabled in 1979, he continued performing the solo and concerto literature for left hand. Taught at the Curtis Institute from 1980; artistic director from 1986.

Grail [archaic]. *Gradual.

Grainger, (George) Percy (Aldrige) (b. Melbourne, Australia, 8 July 1882; d. White Plains, N.Y., 20 Feb. 1961). Composer, pianist, folk song collector, and musical inventor. Studied with I. Knorr. Toured as a pianist from 1901; taught at the Chicago Musical College from 1918 and at New York Univ. 1932–33. Collected and arranged hundreds of folk songs. Invented electronic composition machines in order to produce "free music," characterized by small intervals, "gliding tones," and irregular rhythms. Composed piano pieces (*Molly on the Shore*, 1918; "Random Round," 1912–15); orchestral works (*The Warriors*, 1912–16); band pieces (*Colonial Song*, 1918); chamber music (*Free Music*, 1936, for a quartet of theremins); choral music (*Love Verses from "The Song of Solomon"*).

Gram, Hans (b. Copenhagen, 20 May 1754; d. Boston, 28 Apr. 1804). Composer, organist, and writer on music. Studied in Copenhagen. Settled in Boston 1785; organist at the Brattle Street Church. Composed and arranged sacred music and apparently co-edited the *Massachusetts Compiler*, a collection of psalm tunes containing a treatise on psalmody.

Gran cassa [It.]. Bass drum.

Gran tamburo [It.]. Bass drum.

Granados, Enrique (b. Lérida, Spain, 25 July 1867; d. at sea, English Channel, 24 Mar. 1916). Composer and pianist. Studied piano with Pujol and Bériot and composition with Pedrell. Performed widely as a pianist. Founded his Academia Granados in 1901; Pablo Casals, Ivan Manén, and Camille Saint-Saëns collaborated with him in recitals. Composed piano pieces (*Danzas españolas*, 1892–1900; *Goyescas*; *Escenas poéticas*, *Estudios expresivos*, *Valses poéticos*); zarzuelas (*Maria del Carmen*, 1898); operas (*Goyescas*, adapted from the piano piece, 1916); tone poems (*Divina commedia*, 1908; *Elisenda*, piano and orchestra, 1912); chamber music; songs (*Colleción de tonadillas escritas en estilo antiguo*).

Grand opera. In 19th-century France, a work suitable for performance at the Paris Opéra. This implied a serious work on a historical subject, in four or five acts, including chorus and ballet, with the text fully set musically (that is, without spoken dialogue). More loosely, any opera making lavish use of musical and theatrical resources. See Opera.

Grand orgue [Fr.]. The main division of a French organ.

Grand piano. A large, wing-shaped piano, in which the plane of the strings is horizontal.

Grandezza, con [It.]. With grandeur.

Grandi, Alessandro (b. ca. 1575–80; d. Bergamo, 1630). Composer. Possibly a student of G. Gabrieli. Active in Ferrara 1597–1617. Vice-*maestro* at St. Mark's, Venice, under Monteverdi from 1620. *Maestro* of S. Maria Maggiore in Bergamo from 1627. Composed motets, many with obbligato instrumental accompaniment; Masses and Psalms; secular cantatas, arias, and concertato madrigals.

Grandioso [It.]. Grandiose.

Grandjany, Marcel (George Lucien) (b. Paris, 3 Sept. 1891; d. New York, 24 Feb. 1975). Harpist. Studied with Henriette Renié. Organist at Sacré-Coeur, 1915–18. Taught harp at Fontainebleau, 1921–35; at Juilliard, 1938–75; also at the Montreal Conservatory and the Manhattan School of Music. Founded the American Harp Society in 1961. Composed songs and several dozen works for harp.

Graphic notation. In some works since the early 1950s, visual materials other than conventional musical notation (though sometimes combined with conventional notation) by means of which a composer instructs, guides, or merely hopes to inspire or motivate the activities of performers. The realization of works employing such notation typically allows a great deal of freedom to the performer [see Aleatory music; Notation].

Grappelli [Grappelly], **Stéphane** (b. Paris, 26 Jan. 1908; d. there, 1 Dec. 1997). Jazz violinist. With Django Reinhardt led the swing group the Quintette du Hot Club de France; recordings include "Dinah" and "Tiger Rag" (both 1934). Recorded the album *Violin Summit* with Svend Asmussen, Jean-Luc Ponty, and Stuff Smith (1966) and the *Stéphane Grappelli–Oscar Peterson Quartet* with Niels Henning Ørsted-Pederson and Kenny Clarke (1973). Also worked with Joe Venuti, Gary Burton, Earl Hines, and George Shearing.

Graun, Carl Heinrich (b. Wahrenbrück, 1703–4; d. Berlin, 8 Aug. 1759). Composer. Court musician in the Duchy of Braunschweig from 1725. From 1735 served as composer, performer, and instructor to Crown Prince Frederick of Prussia, who became king in 1740 and made Graun *Kapellmeister,* and organizer and principal composer at the new Berlin Opera. Produced many operas (*Montezuma,* libretto by Frederick, 1755); sacred and secular vocal music (the Passion oratorio *Der Tod Jesu,* 1755, libretto by Rammler; Te Deum, 1756); concertos, trio sonatas, and other chamber pieces. Pupils included Franz Benda, Nichelmann, and Kirnberger.

Graun, Johann Gottlieb (b. Wahrenbrück, ca. 1702–3; d. Berlin, 27 Oct. 1771). Violinist and composer. Student of Pisendel and Tartini; brother of Carl Heinrich Graun. Became *Konzertmeister* in Meres-

burg around 1726; joined the orchestra of Crown Prince Frederick of Prussia in 1732, moving with it to Berlin in 1740 when Frederick became king. Works include a great many sinfonias, overtures, concertos, and trio sonatas; sacred and secular concerted music. Wilhelm Friedemann Bach was among his pupils.

Graupner, (Johann) Christoph (b. Kirchberg, Saxony, 13 Jan. 1683; d. Darmstadt, 10 May 1760). Composer. Studied under Schelle and Kuhnau. In 1709 he became Vice-*Kapellmeister* at the court of Ernst Ludwig, Landgrave of Hessen-Darmstadt; *Kapellmeister* in 1712. He wrote many operas, 1,418 sacred cantatas, 24 secular cantatas, 113 symphonies, some 50 concertos, 80 suites, 36 chamber sonatas, and keyboard music.

Graupner, (Johann Christian) Gottlieb (b. Verden, Lower Saxony, 6 Oct. 1767; d. Boston, 16 Apr. 1836). Oboist, conductor, and composer. Played oboe in Haydn's orchestra in London 1791–92. Settled in Boston around 1797; cofounded a music publishing venture. Also a founder of the Boston Philharmonic Society (1810), and of the Handel and Haydn Society (1815). Published instructional books for the piano, clarinet, and flute.

Grave [It.]. (1) Grave, solemn. (2) Since the 17th century, slow, often equivalent to *adagio* [see Performance marks]. (3) With respect to pitch, low.

Gravicembalo [It.]. In 17th-century Italy, *harpsichord; perhaps a corruption of *clavicembalo.*

Grazioso [It.]. Graceful.

Great Fugue. See *Grosse Fuge.*

Great organ. The main division of an English or American organ. The corresponding French term is *Grand orgue,* the German *Hauptwerk.*

Grechaninov, Alexandr Tikhonovich (b. Moscow, 25 Oct. 1864; d. New York, 4 Jan. 1956). Composer. Studied at the Moscow Conservatory and with Rimsky-Korsakov. Taught at the Gnesin Institute and the Moscow Conservatory from 1906. Settled in Paris 1925; in New York 1940. Compositions include operas (*Dobrïnya Nikitich,* 1896–1901), orchestral music, incidental music, sacred choral music, songs, music for children, chamber music, and piano pieces.

Green, Ray (Burns) (b. Cavendish, Mo., 13 Sept. 1908). Composer and publisher. Studied with Bloch, Milhaud, and Monteux. Secretary of the American Music Center in New York (1948–61); in 1951 founded American Music Editions. Wrote for orchestra (*Sunday Sing Symphony,* 1939–40), chamber ensembles, chorus, voice, and piano; drew on shape-note hymnody and fuguing tunes (*Festival Fugues, An American Toccata,* 1934–35).

Greenberg, Noah (b. New York, 9 Apr. 1919; d. there, 9 Jan. 1966). Conductor and musicologist. With Bernard Krainis he founded and led the New York Pro Musica 1952–73. With the group he researched, performed, and recorded Renaissance and medieval music. His realizations of *The Play of Daniel* (1958) and *The Play of Herod* (1963) were particularly influential.

Greene, Maurice (b. London, 12 Aug. 1696; d. there, 1 Dec. 1755). Organist and composer. Sang under J. Clarke in the choir of St. Paul's; organist there from 1718; organist and composer of the Chapel Royal from 1727; Master of the King's Musick from 1735. Works include services, oratorios, and dozens of anthems, along with secular vocal music and keyboard works.

Greenfield, Elizabeth Taylor (b. Natchez, 1817? or 1819?; d. Philadelphia, 31 Mar. 1876). Singer. Born a slave; raised by a wealthy Quaker. Began concert career in 1851, causing a sensation because of her race and extraordinary vocal range; 1853–54, sang in England; later taught in Philadelphia.

Greghesca [It.]. A Venetian subgenre of the *villanella,* on texts written in a mixture of Venetian dialect and Greek.

Gregorian chant. The *plainsong or liturgical chant of the Roman Catholic Church. It is one of the five principal repertories of Latin liturgical chant of the Middle Ages, the others being *Old Roman, *Ambrosian, *Gallican, and *Mozarabic. As preserved in musical manuscripts beginning in the 10th century, it consists of unaccompanied melodies set to the Latin texts of the *liturgy (of which some understanding is essential to the understanding of the chant itself) including both the *Mass and the *Office. It is named for St. Gregory the Great, pope from 590 until 604, though his role in shaping the surviving repertory is a matter of conjecture and debate.

The Book of *Psalms is the principal source of texts for the Gregorian chant. Texts drawn from the Psalms and musical forms associated principally with the singing of the Psalms are termed psalmodic. Some texts are drawn from other parts of the Bible, however, particularly the lyrical passages that make up the *canticles, and a few are drawn from the lives of saints or other early Christian writings. Among the most important nonpsalmodic texts of the Mass are those of the Ordinary. All of these texts, both psalmodic and nonpsalmodic, are treated as prose. Poetic texts make up a much smaller part of the repertory. The most important to continue in use are the *hymns. In the Middle Ages and on through the 16th

century, however, *sequences with poetic texts were an important genre, and *rhymed Offices were composed in which forms such as antiphons and responsories that normally employ scriptural texts were set to poetic texts.

The forms and methods of performance of the chant repertory can be broadly divided into two groups: psalmodic (i.e., forms thought to derive from the various methods of singing the Psalms, even when employed with texts that are not taken from the Psalms) and nonpsalmodic. Three forms of psalmody are usually distinguished, though both medieval and modern practice often obscure the supposed differences among them [see Psalmody for a fuller discussion]: antiphonal psalmody, in which two halves of a choir or schola sing the verses of a Psalm or other text in alternation and in combination with a melody called an antiphon that serves as a refrain; responsorial psalmody, in which one or more soloists or cantors alternate with the schola in singing one or more verses and a refrain often called a respond; and direct psalmody, in which the cantor or cantors sing verses without alternation with the schola and without a refrain.

Nonpsalmodic forms include the strophic form of the hymn, in which a single melody is repeated for all strophes; the double-versicle form of the sequence, in which there is repetition within each couplet, though successive couplets are in general different; the repetitive forms of the *Kyrie and *Agnus Dei, which derive from the repetitive elements in their texts; and the essentially nonrepetitive forms of the *Sanctus and of the longer prose texts of the *Gloria and the *Credo. Thus, in the Mass, the chants of the Ordinary are all nonpsalmodic with respect to both text and form, whereas those of the Proper are (or were at one time) psalmodic in form if not always with respect to text. In modern practice, these nonpsalmodic forms too may employ alternation either between cantors and schola or between the two halves of the schola.

Three melodic styles are usually identified: syllabic, in which each syllable of text is borne by only a single note; neumatic (from *neume), in which single syllables are regularly borne by two to a dozen notes; and melismatic, in which single syllables may occasionally be borne by dozens of notes. In general, this range of styles from simple to complex is closely coordinated with the forms and methods of performance outlined above. The antiphonal psalmody of the Office is largely syllabic. The antiphonal psalmody of the Mass, except for the offertory, is neumatic. The responsorial psalmody of the Mass, the offertory, and the great responsories of the Office are most likely to be melismatic. Chants that are primarily choral, such as the Office antiphons and psalm tones, are the simplest and are often syllabic throughout. Chants that are intended for soloists, such as the great responsories of the Office and the gradual, alleluia, and tract of the Mass, are the most elaborate and may be highly melismatic. The sharing of melodic elements ranging from a very few notes to longer phrases or melismas is a prominent feature of most types of psalmodic chant [see Centonization].

Gregorian melodies are classified tonally according to a system of eight *modes adopted from Byzantine practice in the late 8th century and thus after the early core of the repertory was already formed, but before the earliest sources with musical notation. In the Middle Ages, melodies were listed by mode in *tonaries. Modern liturgical books also indicate the mode for each chant.

The rhythm of Gregorian chant is the subject of considerable controversy. In general, the notations [see Neume] of early sources do not indicate the duration of individual notes. In most modern interpretations, including that embodied in the official liturgical books prepared by the monks of Solesmes, the rhythm is regarded as essentially free and employing predominantly notes of equal length. Within this framework, however, many variations exist, often claiming to derive from one or another feature of the Latin texts such as their accentuation. Much less common are various mensuralist interpretations, in which notes of varied length are employed.

For much of the first 1,000 years of the Christian era, the specific character of liturgical chant in the West is a matter of speculation. It seems likely that Christian chant had its roots in the cantillation of Scripture in the Jewish synagogue. Whether specific musical forms and melodies can be traced to Jewish practice must be seriously questioned, however. Recent scholarship has also doubted that the origins for Christian chant lie in classical Greek musical culture. The formation of the Western rites and the musical forms peculiar to them probably began in the 4th century, by which time Latin had superseded Greek as the language of Christian worship in Rome. In this process, however, elements from Eastern Christendom, such as the churches of Antioch and Jerusalem, were probably incorporated. A document composed in France in the third quarter of the 8th century cites a series of popes, beginning with Damasus I (pope from 366 to 384) and including Gregory I (590–604), as having contributed to the formation of a repertory of chant for the liturgical year.

Roman practice began to spread north of the Alps by the 8th century, and during the reigns of Pepin the Short (752–68) and Charlemagne (768–814) its displacement of the native *Gallican rite was imposed. There is abundant testimony to this process of romanization in France and Germany from the 8th, 9th, and 10th centuries—the regions and the periods of the earliest musical documents and notational systems, from which the chant repertory surviving throughout Europe directly derives. The relationship of what is thus a Frankish redaction of the chant (evidently from oral transmission) to the actual practice of Rome at the time and in earlier centuries remains a matter of considerable debate, especially in view of manuscripts from the 11th through 13th centuries that show a somewhat different version of the repertory in use in Rome [see Old Roman chant].

Grétry, André-Ernest-Modeste (b. Liège, 8 Feb. 1741; d. Montmorency, Paris, 24 Sept. 1813). Composer. One of the founders of the opéra comique on the French stage. Titles include *Le huron* (Comédie italienne, 1768), *Zémire et Azor* (1771), *Colinette à la cour* (1783), *La caravane du Caire* (1783), *Richard Coeur-de-lion* (1784), and *Le casque et les colombes* (1801). His music shows concern for declamation and spare texture. Also published literary works.

Gr. Fl. [Ger.]. Abbr. for *Grosse Flöte*.

Grieg, Edvard (Hagerup) (b. Bergen, 15 June 1843; d. there, 4 Sept. 1907). Composer. Pupil of Moscheles, Hauptmann, E. F. E. Richter, and Reinecke. Settled in Christiana (now Oslo) 1866; 1867, helped found a Norwegian Academy of Music. Composed orchestral works (incidental music for Bjørnson's *Sigurd Jorsalfar,* 1872, and Ibsen's *Peer Gynt; Symphonic Dances,* 1896–97); chamber music (1 cello and 3 violin sonatas; String Quartet op. 27); piano pieces (sonatas; 10 collections of *Lyric Pieces,* 1867–1901; *Old Norwegian Romance with Variations,* 1891; *Slåtter,* arrangements of fiddle dances, 1903–5); songs (op. 26, to poems by Ibsen; op. 21 to Bjørnson lyrics); choral works (*Four Norwegian Psalms,* 1906).

Griffbrett [Ger.]. Fingerboard. See also *Am Griffbrett.*

Griffes, Charles T(omlinson) (b. Elmira, N.Y., 17 Sept. 1884; d. New York, 8 Apr. 1920). Composer and pianist. Pupil of Humperdinck. Director of music at the Hackley School (Tarrytown, N.Y.) from 1907. For a time influenced by Debussy and Ravel; later wrote in a more dissonant harmonic language. Works include 3 ballets; tone poems and arrangements of piano works for orchestra; chamber music; piano music (*The Pleasure Dome of Kubla Khan,* 1912; *Three Tone Pictures* op. 5, 1910–12; *Roman Sketches for Piano* op. 7, 1915–16); choral works; songs (*Five Poems of Ancient China and Japan,* 1917; *Three Poems of Fiona Macleod,* 1918).

Grigny, Nicolas de (bapt. Rheims, 8 Sept. 1672; d. there, 30 Nov. 1703). Organist and composer. Served at St. Denis, Paris, 1693–95; cathedral organist at Rheims thereafter. His *Premier livre d'orgue* (1699), copied out by J. S. Bach around 1710, contains music for liturgical use, marked by rich counterpoint, varied tone colors, and extensive pedal work.

Grillo, Frank Raul. See Machito.

Grisar, Albert (b. Antwerp, 26 Dec. 1808; d. Asnières, 15 June 1869). Composer. Pupil of Reicha and Mercadante. Composed many opéras comiques, including *L'eau merveilleuse*, 1839; *L'opéra à la cour*, 1840; *Gille ravisseur*, 1848; *Les porcherons*, 1850; *Bonsoir, Monsieur Pantalon*, 1851.

Grisi, Giulia (b. Milan, 22 May 1811; d. Berlin, 29 Nov. 1869). Soprano. Studied in Milan and Bologna; 1832, debut at Théâtre-Italien, Paris, becoming a principal factor in the Golden Age of Italian opera there in the 1830s and 1840s; also performed often in London 1834–61. In 1839 began long liaison and artistic partnership with the tenor Rubini.

Grocheo, Johannes de. See Johannes de Grocheo.

Grofé, Ferde [Ferdinand Rudolph von] (b. New York, 27 Mar. 1892; d. Santa Monica, Calif., 3 Apr. 1972). Composer, arranger, and pianist. 1917–33, associated with the Paul Whiteman band, for which he arranged Gershwin's *Rhapsody in Blue*. Taught at Juilliard 1939–42. Composed orchestral tone poems (*Grand Canyon Suite*, 1931); film scores (*Minstrel Man*, 1944); music for jazz and brass band; piano pieces; songs.

Grøndahl [née Backer], **Agathe (Ursula)** (b. Holmestrand, Norway, 1 Dec. 1847; d. Oslo, 4 June 1907). Composer and pianist. Pupil of von Bülow and Liszt; toured Scandinavia, Germany, and Britain as a pianist. Composed some 190 Norwegian art songs; piano pieces and etudes; Norwegian folk song arrangements for piano.

Groppo [It.]. See *Gruppetto.*

Gross [Ger. masc., sing.; other endings depending on case and gender]. (1) Great, large. (2) With respect to intervals such as the third or sixth, major; with respect to the fourth and fifth, perfect.

Grosse caisse [Fr.]. Bass drum.

Grosse Flöte [Ger.]. The ordinary flute, as distinct from the piccolo.

Grosse Fuge [Ger., Great Fugue]. Beethoven's fugue for string quartet op. 133 (1825–26), originally conceived as the last movement of his String Quartet op. 130. He composed a new finale to the quartet later in 1826 and published the *Grosse Fuge* as a separate composition in 1827.

Grosse Trommel [Ger.]. Bass drum.

Grosses Orchester [Ger.]. Full orchestra.

Ground, ground bass. A pattern of notes, most often a single melodic phrase set in the bass, that is repeated over and over again during the course of a vocal or instrumental composition. Although ground bass is usually used interchangeably with *basso ostinato* to describe this technique in the music of any period [see Ostinato], ground refers most particularly to English music of the late 16th and the 17th century, where it means either a repeating bass line or the entire composition in which that bass appears. The 17th century saw a lively tradition of improvisations, especially for viola da gamba, called *divisions on a ground.

Groven, Eivind (b. Lårdal, Telemark, 8 Oct. 1901; d. Oslo, 8 Feb. 1977). Composer and musicologist. Studied at Oslo Conservatory. His compositions incorporate Norwegian folk songs; also experimented with microtonal instruments. Works include 2 symphonies; symphonic poems; a piano concerto; choral works; songs; chamber music; works for Hardanger fiddles.

Groves, Charles (b. London, 10 Mar. 1915; d. there, 20 June 1992). Conductor. Studied at the Royal College of Music. Conducting posts with the BBC, Bournemouth Symphony, and Royal Philharmonic. Music director of the Welsh National Opera, 1961–63; of the Royal Liverpool Philharmonic, 1963–77; of the English National Opera, 1978–79.

Grovlez, Gabriel (Marie) (b. Lille, 4 Apr. 1879; d. Paris, 20 Oct. 1944). Composer, conductor, and pianist. Pupil of Gédalge and Fauré. Taught at the Schola cantorum 1899–1909; music director of the Paris Opéra from 1914; from 1939 professor at the Paris Conservatory. Wrote operas and ballets (*Le vrai arbre de Robinson,* New York, 1922); orchestral, chamber, and piano music; choral and solo vocal works.

Gr. Tr. [Ger.]. Abbr. for *Grosse trommel.*

Grua, Franz Paul [Paolo; Francesco da Paula] (b. Mannheim, 1 Feb. 1753; d. Munich, 5 July 1833). Composer and violinist. Pupil of Holzbauer, Padre Martini, and Traetta. From 1776 violinist at Mannheim; moved with the orchestra to Munich, where he became Kapellmeister in 1784. Composed an opera (*Telemaco,* Munich, 1780), Masses, sacred works.

Gruber, Franz Xaver (b. Unterweizburg, Austria, 25 Nov. 1787; d. Hallein, near Salzburg, 7 June 1863). Composer. While Kantor and organist at St. Nicholas's church, Oberndorf (1816–29), composed the Christmas hymn "Stille Nacht" (Silent Night). Also composed Latin church works.

Gruber, H(einz) K(arl) (b. Vienna, 3 Jan. 1943). Composer and double bass player. Pupil of Jelinek and von Einem. In 1967 he co-founded the MOBart & tonART ensemble. His works in the 1960s were serial and electronic, without entirely abandoning tonality. Compositions include stage works (*Die Vertreibung aus dem Paradies,* 1966; *Gomorra,* 1976; *Gloria: A Pigtale,* Munich, 1995); orchestral and ensemble pieces (*Revue,* 1968; concertos for violin, cello, and percussion); *Konjugationen,* tape, 1963.

Gruenberg, Louis (b. near Brest-Litovsk, 3 Aug. 1884; d. Beverly Hills, 10 June 1964). Composer and pianist. Raised in the U.S. Pupil of Busoni. Toured as a pianist in the U.S. and Europe; taught at the Vienna Conservatory. Drew on jazz and Negro spirituals. Compositions include dramatic works (*The Emperor Jones,* Metropolitan Opera, 1931); film scores (*All the King's Men,* 1949); an oratorio; 6 symphonies, symphonic poems, concertos for violin, cello, piano; the *Jazz-Suite,* orchestra, 1925; *Four Diversions,* string quartet; *The Daniel Jazz,* tenor, clarinet, trumpet, string quartet, 1924.

Grumiaux, Arthur (b. Villers-Perwin, Belgium, 21 Mar. 1921; d. Brussels, 16 Oct. 1986). Violinist. Pupil of Absil and Enescu. Toured Europe beginning 1945. Taught at the Brussels Conservatory from 1949. With Clara Haskil recorded the complete Beethoven violin sonatas. In 1967 he founded the Grumiaux Trio with Georges Janzer and Eve Czako.

Gruppen [Ger., Groups]. A work for three orchestras with three conductors composed by Stockhausen in 1955–57. Its use of spatial deployment of sound sources, a technique first explored in his electronic work *Gesang der Jünglinge,* was widely influential. See also Serial music.

Gruppetto, gruppo, groppo [It.]. In the 16th through 18th centuries, a variety of ornamental notegroups, often written out and often meant to be performed in time or at least not extremely quickly; most commonly, in the earlier part of this period, a trill ending in a *turn; sometimes a turn only. See Ornamentation.

Gsp. Abbr. for *glockenspiel.

Guadagni, Gaetano (b. Vicenza or Lodi, ca. 1725; d. Padua, Nov. 1792). Castrato. Sang in operas and theaters throughout Europe. Handel used him in *Messiah, Samson,* and *Theodora;* he created the title role in Gluck's *Orfeo* in 1762. Burney describes him as a "well-toned countertenor" and praises his acting.

Guajira [Sp.]. (1) A traditional song style of rural Cuba (which is generally referred to with the adjective *guajiro*), characterized by the prevalence of 3/4 and 6/8 meters, often in combination, and the singing

of *décima* texts. (2) A prominent Afro-Cuban urban popular genre, in duple meter and moderate tempo.

Guaracha [Sp.]. A Cuban song and dance-music genre, prominent in theatrical entertainments in the 19th century, and in the 20th century an important element in the repertories of urban popular dance ensembles.

Guárdame las vacas [Sp., watch over the cows for me]. The subject of several sets of 16th-century Spanish variations *(diferencias).* It is identical with the *romanesca.

Guarneri. Family of stringed instrument makers. The patriarch, Andrea (b. Cremona, ca. 1626; d. there, 7 Dec. 1698), was an apprentice of Nicola Amati. His violins are often marked by a lack of symmetry. Worked with two of his sons, Pietro Giovanni "de Mantova" (b. Cremona, 18 Feb. 1655; d. Mantua, 26 Mar. 1720) and Giuseppe Giovanni Battista (b. Cremona, 25 Nov. 1666; d. there, ca. 1739–40). Pietro apparently made few instruments; one was played by Szigeti. Giuseppe became one of the great builders, producing violins and cellos. After about 1715 his own sons Pietro "da Venezia" (b. Cremona, 14 Apr. 1695; d. there, 7 Apr. 1762) and Bartolomeo Giuseppe "del Gesù" (b. Cremona, 21 Aug. 1698; d. there, 17 Oct. 1744) were active in the shop. Pietro's production peaked in Venice in the 1740s. Giuseppe "del Gesù" ranks as one of the two greatest makers in history. His violins, legendary for their full tone, have been played by Paganini, Grumiaux, Heifetz, Stern, and Zukerman.

Guarnieri, (Mozart) Camargo (b. Tietê, São Paulo, 1 Feb. 1907; d. São Paulo, 13 Jan. 1993). Composer. Studied with Koechlin. Taught at the São Paulo Conservatory from 1927; conductor of the São Paulo Symphony. Brazilian nationalism is a common thread in his work. Compositions include *Pedro Malazarte* (comic opera, 1932); 3 symphonies; concertos for piano and violin; orchestral suites; *Homenajem a Villa-Lobos,* winds (1966), and other chamber music; piano music; songs.

Gubaidulina, Sofia Asgatovna (b. Chistopol, Tatar ASSR, 24 Oct. 1931). Composer. Pupil of Peiko and Shebalin. Rejected socialist realism, embracing the full panorama of contemporary musical discourse. Works include 2 symphonies; concertos; vocal-symphonic works (the cantata *Rubaiat,* 1969; *Hour of the Soul,* 1976; rev. 1988); 4 string quartets and other chamber music; music for percussion; vocal works; film music.

Gueden, Hilde (b. Vienna, 15 Sept. 1917; d. Klosterneuburg, 17 Sept. 1988). Soprano. Studied in Vienna. Debut in Zurich as Cherubino *(Nozze),* 1939. Sang with the operas of Munich, Rome, West Berlin,

Vienna (1947–73), and with the Metropolitan Opera (1951–60). Most often seen in German operas, especially those by Strauss.

Guédron, Pierre (b. province of Beauce, Normandy, ca. 1570; d. Paris?, 1619–20). Singer and composer. Musician at the French royal court from 1588; later composer and superintendant of the king's chamber music. Published many *airs de cour,* incl. "Est-ce que Mars," 1613.

Guerra Peixe, César (b. Retrópolis, Brazil, 18 Mar. 1914; d. Rio de Janeiro, 23 Nov. 1993). Composer. Studied in Rio de Janeiro with H. J. Koellreutter. Until 1950 wrote mainly twelve-tone chamber and piano works; thereafter turned toward a nationalist approach, composing many orchestral pieces as well.

Guerre des bouffons [Fr.], **guerra dei buffoni** [It.]. See *Bouffons, Querelle (guerre) des.*

Guerrero, Francisco (b. Seville, 4 Oct.? 1528; d. there, 8 Nov. 1599). Composer. Pupil of his brother Pedro Guerrero and of Morales. Musician at Seville Cathedral from 1542; *maestro de capilla* there from 1574. *Maestro* at Jaén Cathedral, 1546–49. Wrote 18 Masses, about 150 motets and other liturgical works, and secular songs, many published as sacred *contrafacta.*

Guézec, Jean-Pierre (b. Dijon, 29 Aug. 1934; d. Paris, 10 Mar. 1971). Composer. Studied with Milhaud and Messiaen at the Paris Conservatory, where he taught from 1969. Works include *Suite pour Mondrian* (orchestra, 1962); *Textures enchaînées* (winds, harp, and percussion, 1967); *Couleurs juxtaposées I & II* (various chamber groups with voice).

Guglielmi, Pietro (Alessandro) (b. Massa, 9 Dec. 1728; d. Rome, 19 Nov. 1804). Composer, principally of operas. Pupil of Durante. Lived in London, 1767–72. From 1793 *maestro di cappella* at St. Peter's, Rome, where he composed much sacred music. Stage works include *Il ratto della sposa* (1765); *La sposa fedele* (1767?); *La Quakera spirituosa* (1783?); *La bella pescatrice* (1789).

Guida [It.]. (1) *Direct. (2) The subject of a fugue. (3) An abbreviated orchestral score.

Guidon [Fr.]. *Direct.

Guidonian hand [Lat. *manus Guidonis (Guidonica), palma, manus*]. A diagram of the human hand with the notes and *solmization syllables of the *gamut [see also Hexachord] assigned to joints or fingertips, well known as a teaching aid by the beginning of the 12th century and continuing in widespread use into the 17th or 18th century. Although the hand is mentioned in none of the writings of Guido

d'Arezzo (d. after 1033), it is attributed to him by numerous contemporaneous and later writers.

Guillaume de Machaut. See Machaut, Guillaume de.

Guillaume li Vinier (b. Arras, ca. 1190; d. 1245). Trouvère. In addition to songs, wrote *jeux-partis* in conjunction with his brother Gille li Vinier, Adam de Givenci, and Andrieu Contredit. His works vary widely in genre, poetic form, and musical construction.

Guillaume Tell [Fr., William Tell]. Opera in four acts by Rossini (libretto by Victor Joseph Etienne de Jouy, Hippolyte Louis Florent Bis, and others, after Schiller's play), produced in Paris in 1829. Setting: Switzerland in the 14th century.

Guilmant, (Félix) Alexandre (b. Boulogne-sur-mer, 12 Mar. 1837; d. Meudon, 29 Mar. 1911). Organist and composer. From a family of organists and organ builders. Organist at several churches in Paris. Cofounder and teacher at the Schola cantorum; professor at the Paris Conservatory from 1896 (pupils included Nadia Boulanger, Jacob, Dupré). Composed and edited much organ music.

Guimbarde [Fr.]. *Jew's harp.

Guiraud, Ernest (b. New Orleans, 23 June 1837; d. Paris, 6 May 1892). Composer and teacher. Pupil of Marmontel and Halévy. From 1876 taught at the Paris Conservatory; pupils included Debussy, Dukas. Composed 6 opéras comiques; orchestral pieces, piano pieces, songs; recitatives for Bizet's *Carmen* (1875); orchestrated Offenbach's *Contes d'Hoffmann.*

Güiro [Sp.]. A *scraper of Latin America made from a hollow gourd in which notches are cut and across

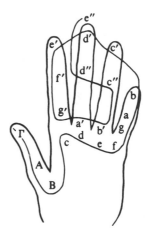

Guidonian hand.

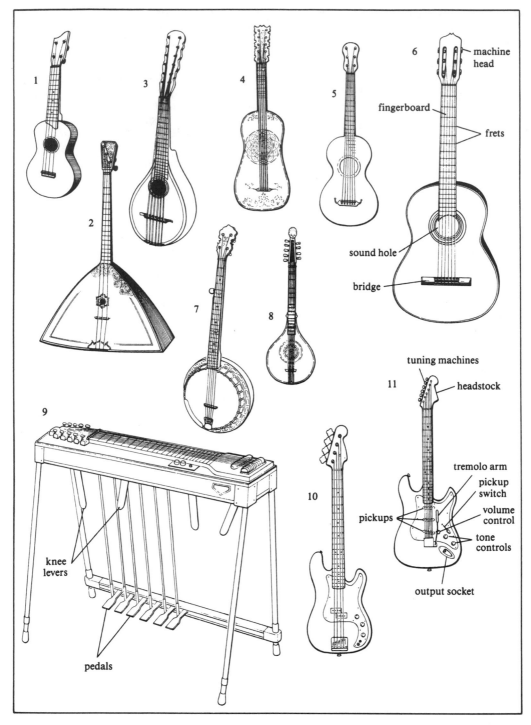

1. Ukulele.　2. Balalaika.　3. Bandurria.　4. 17th-century guitar.　5. Early 19th-century guitar.　6. Modern guitar (not to scale).　7. Banjo.　8. Cittern.　9. Pedal steel guitar.　10. Electric bass guitar.　11. Electric guitar.

which a stick is rubbed. See ill. under Percussion instruments.

Guitar [fr. Gr. *kithara;* Fr. *guitare;* Ger. *Gitarre;* It. *chitarra;* Sp. *guitarra;* Port. *violão*]. A plucked stringed instrument with a hollow resonating chamber, gently waisted sides, a flat or slightly curved back, and a fretted fingerboard. Guitars are widely used in folk and popular music, with a variety of modified shapes (e.g., f-shaped sound holes, solid bodies), stringings (differences including number, material, and tunings of strings), and performance techniques (e.g., the use of a plectrum) [see also Electric guitar, Guitar family, Steel guitar]. The modern or "classical" guitar has six strings tuned E A d g b e', geared tuning pegs, an open round sound hole, and normally 19 inlaid metal frets. The table or soundboard is almost always made of spruce or cedar, and the back and sides of a hardwood such as Brazilian rosewood. String length is typically 65 or 66 cm. Since ca. 1946, nylon strings have been employed (the lower three wrapped with fine wire); earlier, strings were made of gut and silk. Until the late 18th century, guitar music was notated in *tablature. Since then it has been written in the treble clef, one octave higher than sounded.

Precursors of the guitar are traceable to early Babylonian and Egyptian instruments, and words similar to guitar (*gitere,* *gittern, gittarra latina*) appear in medieval literature. The Renaissance four-course guitar appeared in the 15th century. Guitars of the 16th and 17th centuries were much smaller than their modern counterparts and featured an inlaid rose and four courses of strings. The earliest printed music appears in Alonso Mudarra's *Tres libros de música* (1546), a book devoted mainly to the six-course *vihuela.* The guitar was especially popular in 16th-century France.

The five-course guitar was widely played in the 17th century, particularly in Italy, where it was known as the *chitarra spagnola.* The most important composers for the five-course guitar were Francesco Corbetta (ca. 1615–81) and Robert de Visée (ca. 1660–ca. 1720), authors of numerous suites, and Gaspar Sanz, eight editions of whose *Instrucción* appeared between 1674 and 1697.

The six-string guitar probably originated in Italy before 1780 and spread throughout Europe by the early 1800s. The leading composer/performers were the Spaniard Dionysio Aguado (1784–1849), whose method-book (first published in 1825 in Madrid) helped to establish modern technique; Fernando Sor (1778–1839), another Spaniard who made his career in London and Paris; the Italian Mauro Giuliani (1781–1829), who established himself in Vienna; and Ferdinando Carulli (1770–1841), a prolific Ital-

ian who settled in Paris. Other significant 19th-century guitarists are Matteo Carcassi (1792–1853), Johann Kaspar Mertz (1806–56), Napoléon Coste (1806–83), and Francisco Tárrega (1852–1909). The Spanish luthier Antonio de Torres Jurado (1817–92) is credited with establishing the guitar's present dimensions after 1850.

Guitar family. A family of instruments that are variants of the guitar but adhere to its general shape [see Guitar; see also Electric guitar, Steel guitar]. The smaller four- and five-course guitars of the 16th through mid-18th centuries are considered the true ancestors of the modern instrument. Other early plucked stringed instruments are harder to classify, but several belong to the *cittern family [see Bandurria, Citole, Gittern, English guitar, Orpharion]. The 16th-century *vihuela is usually considered a member of the guitar family, as is the later Italian *chitarra battente.

The 19th-century *Terzgitarre* [It. *chitarrino*] is a small guitar tuned a minor third above the ordinary instrument. Many guitars with extra bass strings have been developed, and guitars with seven or eight strings were common in the later 19th century and into the 20th.

Numerous guitarlike instruments are used to play folk music in many parts of the world, particularly Latin America. These include the Andean *charango and the *cuatro of Venezuela. The *ukulele is a descendant of the Portuguese *machete* of the Azores.

Guitarrón [Sp.] (1) In Mexico, a very large guitar with four or five strings, used as the bass in a *mariachi ensemble. (2) In Chile, a guitar with 21 strings distributed into five courses and an additional four short strings passing over the body but not the fingerboard.

Gulda, Friedrich (b. Vienna, 16 May 1930). Pianist and composer. Pupil of Josef Marx. In the 1940s and 1950s toured Europe and the U.S. From 1956 he also played jazz piano, baritone saxophone, and flute. Founded the Eurojazz Orchestra in 1960; a school for improvisation at Ossiach in 1968. Compositions include *Galgenliedern,* baritone and 2 pianos (1954); *The Veiled Old Land,* jazz orchestra (1964); *Blues Fantasy,* piano (1971); *Concerto for Myself,* piano and orchestra (1986).

Guridi (Bidaloa), Jesús (b. Vitoria, Alava, 25 Sept. 1886; d. Madrid, 7 Apr. 1961). Composer and organist. Pupil of d'Indy and Jongen. Organist at churches in Bilbao; directed the Bilbao Choral Society, 1911–26. Taught at the Biscay Conservatory (1922) and the Madrid Conservatory (1944). Composed choral music, often based on Basque song; operas (*Mirentxu,*

1915; *Amaya,* 1920); zarzuelas (*El caserío,* 1926); orchestral works (*Una aventura de Don Quixote).*

Gurney, Ivor (Bertie) (b. Gloucester, 28 Aug. 1890; d. Dartford, near London, 26 Dec. 1937). Composer. Studied with Stanford and Vaughan Williams. Composed solo songs (*Five Elizabethan Songs,* 1913; *Ludlow and Teme,* 7 songs, 1919; *Six Songs,* 1918–25) and chamber music.

Gurrelieder [Ger., Songs of Gurre]. A cantata by Schoenberg on poems (originally in Danish) by Jens Peter Jacobsen, for five soloists, three male choruses, one mixed chorus, narrator, and large orchestra, begun in 1900–1901 and completed in 1911. Schoenberg began the setting of these texts as a song cycle for voice and piano.

Gusle [Serb.-Cro.; Bulg. *gusla*]. A bowed stringed instrument of Yugoslavia with a pear-shaped body, a single horsehair string, and no fingerboard. The player, a singer of epic poetry called a *guslar,* holds the instrument between the knees and holds a curved bow in the right hand.

Gusli [Russ.]. A *zither used by several nationalities of the former Soviet Union. Its 12 to 36 gut or metal strings are strung across a shallow, usually triangular box. See also Psaltery.

Gusto, con [It.]. With taste, style, relish.

Gutchë, Gene [Gutsche, Romeo Maximilian Eugene Ludwig] (b. Berlin, 3 July 1907). Composer. Studied with Busoni and Clapp; settled in the U.S. 1925. Composed in a neo-Romantic style, but explored polytonality, microtones, and serialism. Works include 6 symphonies, *Genghis Khan* (winds and double basses, 1964), *Akhenaten (Eidetic Images)* (1978), and other orchestral music; chamber music; choral works.

Guthrie, Woody [Woodrow Wilson] (b. Okemah, Okla., 14 July 1912; d. New York, 3 Oct. 1967). Folksinger and songwriter. Many of his over 1,000 folk songs concern his travels in the U.S. during the Great Depression. Recorded much of his repertory with Alan Lomax at the Library of Congress; performed with folksingers Pete Seeger, Leadbelly, and Cisco Houston. Songs include "This Land Is Your Land," "So Long, It's Been Good To Know Ya'," "Hard Travelin'," and "Union Maid." His son Arlo Guthrie (b. 1947) is a folk and rock musician.

Gutiérrez, Horacio (Tomás) (b. Havana, 28 Aug. 1948). Pianist. Moved to Los Angeles in 1962. Studied with Sergei Tarnovsky and Adele Marcus at Juilliard. Won the silver medal in the 1970 Tchaikovsky Competition in Moscow; the Avery Fisher Award in 1982.

Gutiérrez (y) Espinosa, Felipe (b. San Juan, Puerto Rico, 26 May 1825; d. there, 27 Nov. 1899). Composer. Largely self-taught; 1858–98, choirmaster of San Juan Cathedral; conducted at Teatro Tapia; ran a free music school. Composed several operas, of which only *Macías* survives; sacred music, an oratorio, 2 Passions.

Gymel, gimel, gemel [fr. Lat. *gemellus,* twin]. In English counterpoint of the 15th and 16th centuries, the temporary splitting of one voice part into two of equal range; also the name of each of these two parts. The historically inappropriate association of the term gymel with parallel motion in imperfect consonances is due largely to its use ca. 1470 by the Italian theorist Guillelmus Monachus.

Gymnopédies [Fr.]. Three piano pieces by Erik Satie composed in 1888. They take their name from a festival of ancient Sparta. Debussy orchestrated the first and third in 1896, Roland-Manuel the second.

Gypsy music. The itinerant people known as Gypsies are thought to have come from northern India and were known throughout Europe by the 15th century. They are widely distributed in the Near and Middle East and in America as well. Their music is correspondingly varied, and little is known of what may have constituted a purely Gypsy tradition. What is known as Gypsy music in various regions is most often music native to the region in question and that has been adapted and modified by Gypsy musicians. The *flamenco music of Spain is a prominent example. The music most widely thought of as Gypsy music, however, is the product of Hungarian Gypsies adapting a variety of local genres [see also *Csárdás, Verbunkos*]. By the late 18th century, the characteristic Hungarian Gypsy ensemble was already known, consisting of two violins, *cimbalom, and double bass. The scale c d e♭ f♯ g a♭ b c', found in much of the music played by Gypsy musicians in Hungary in the 19th century and since, is sometimes called the Gypsy scale.

Gyrowetz, Adalbert [Jírovec, Vojtěch Matyáš] (b. Česke Budějovice, 20 Feb. 1763; d. Vienna, 19 Mar. 1850). Composer. Traveled widely in Europe; 1804–31, imperial composer and Kapellmeister in Vienna. Works include stage music (*Robert,* 1815; *Il finto Stanislao,* 1818; *Hans Sachs im vorgerückten Alter,* 1834); symphonies and other orchestral works; chamber music; secular songs; 11 Masses and other sacred vocal works.

H

H. (1) Abbr. for horn. (2) [Ger.] B-natural. See Pitch names, Letter notation. (3) Abbr. for *Hauptstimme*.

Haas, Joseph (b. Maihingen, 19 Mar. 1879; d. Munich, 30 Mar. 1960). Composer. Pupil of Reger. Taught at the conservatory in Stuttgart from 1911; cofounded the Donaueschingen Festival in 1921; directed the Musikhochschule in Munich 1945–50. His compositions are in a late Romantic idiom; also make use of folk music. Works include 3 operas, 6 Masses, a Te Deum, and 6 folk oratorios; works for orchestra; chamber, piano, and organ music; choral music and songs.

Hába, Alois (b. Vizovice, Moravia, 21 June 1893; d. Prague, 18 Nov. 1973). Composer. Brother of Karel Hába. Pupil of V. Novák and Schreker. Taught at the National Conservatory in Prague 1924–51. Founded and led the Smetana Theater Opera 1945–49. Composed much tempered microtonal music, for which he designed and had built a piano and other instruments. His music also draws on folk music. Works include operas (*Matka* [The Mother] op. 35, 1927–29, 1/4 tone); orchestral works; concertos for violin and viola; 16 string quartets; 4 *Fantazies* and many sonatas and suites for conventional and microtonal instruments.

Habanera [Sp.]. A 19th-century Cuban song and dance form, its name derived from that of the country's capital city of Havana. It is in slow to moderate tempo and in duple meter, with a characteristic accompanimental figure:

$\frac{2}{4}$ 𝅘𝅥𝅭 𝅘𝅥𝅮 𝅘𝅥𝅮 𝅘𝅥𝅮

It was popular in Spain and Europe (where it was adapted by Bizet in *Carmen* in 1875) as well as elsewhere in Latin America.

Habeneck, François Antoine (b. Mézières, 22 Jan. 1781; d. Paris, 8 Feb. 1849). Conductor. Studied at the Paris Conservatory; taught there 1808–16 and 1825–48, and conducted the student orchestra 1806–15. Conductor of the Concert spirituel 1818–21; 1821–26, director and then chief conductor of the Opéra. Organized the Société des Concerts du Conservatoire 1828. Influential in the introduction of Beethoven's orchestral music into France; conducted premieres of Berlioz's *Symphonie fantastique* and Requiem.

Hackbrett [Ger.]. *Dulcimer.

Hackett, Bobby [Robert Leo] (b. Providence, 31 Jan. 1915; d. Chatham, Mass., 7 June 1976). Jazz cornetist. Performed with Benny Goodman (1938, 1962–63); recorded with Eddie Condon's groups 1938–62. Doubled on guitar with Glenn Miller's big band (1940–41), recording the cornet solo on "String of Pearls" (1941). Accompanied Louis Armstrong (1947) and Jackie Gleason (early 1950s). Recorded with Jack Teagarden; led an unusual octet (including alto horn, baritone saxophone, vibraphone, and tuba) 1956–58, and a quintet with Vic Dickenson 1968–70.

Haden, Charlie [Charles Edward] (b. Shenandoah, Iowa, 6 Aug. 1937). Jazz double bass player. As a member of Ornette Coleman's first quartet (1959–60) he defined the role of the free-jazz bassist. Worked with Archie Shepp (1966), Keith Jarrett (ca. 1967–76), and Coleman (from 1966). Led the Liberation Music Orchestra. With Don Cherry, Dewey Redman, and Ed Blackwell he formed Old and New Dreams, devoted to Coleman's music (from 1976).

Hadjidakis, Manos (b. Xanthi, Macedonia, 23 Oct. 1925; d. Athens, 15 June 1994). Composer. Founded the "ATI-Hadjidakis" composition contest (1962) and the Athens Experimental Orchestra (1964). Director general of the National State Opera from 1974 and of the Athens State Orchestra from 1976. His music incorporates elements as disparate as Greek folk music and Baroque styles. Works include ballets; the "folk opera" *Rinaldos kai Armída,* 1962; film and incidental music (his title song for the film *Never on Sunday* won an Oscar 1960); many song cycles; piano music.

Hadley, Henry (Kimball) (b. Somerville, Mass., 20 Dec. 1871; d. New York, 6 Sept. 1937). Composer and conductor. Studied with Chadwick and Thuille. Taught at St. Paul's School (Garden City, N.Y., 1895–1902); held conducting posts at the Mainz Stadttheater, the Seattle Symphony, the San Francisco Symphony (founder-conductor, 1911–15), the New York Philharmonic (1920–27), and the Manhattan Symphony. Founded the National Association of American Composers and Conductors (1933) and the Berkshire Music Festival (1934). His works, composed in a late Romantic style, include 14 operas and other dramatic works; symphonies and other orchestral works; chamber and piano music; oratorios, cantatas, anthems; over 200 songs.

Hadley, Patrick (Arthur Sheldon) (b. Cambridge, 5 Mar. 1899; d. King's Lynn, Norfolk, 17 Dec. 1973). Composer. Pupil of Vaughan Williams. Taught at the Royal College 1925–38 and at Cambridge from 1938. His music, essentially tonal and lyrical, shows influences from Delius and from folk music. Choral works include *The Trees So High* (1931) and *A Cantata for Lent* (1962); also composed vocal and orchestral works (*One Morning in Spring,* 1942).

Haefliger, Ernst (b. Davos, Switzerland, 6 July 1919). Tenor. Studied in Genf and Vienna. Debut in 1942 as a concert singer; first performed his acclaimed Evangelist in Bach's St. Matthew Passion, 1943. Engaged by the Zurich Stadttheater, 1943–52; by the Berlin Deutsche Oper, 1952–74. From 1971, professor at the Munich Musikhochschule.

Haffner Serenade. The Serenade in D major for orchestra by Mozart, K. 250 (1776), composed for a festive wedding in the family of Sigismund Haffner, burgomaster in Salzburg. The work consists of nine movements, including an opening march (K. 249) and several movements that feature a solo violin prominently.

Haffner Symphony. Mozart's Symphony no. 35 in D major K. 385 (1782), composed for the ennoblement of Sigismund Haffner in Salzburg. It was originally intended as a serenade with the March K. 408/2 (385a) and another minuet (now lost). The flute and clarinet parts were added later.

Hagegård, Håkan (b. Karlstad, Sweden, 25 Nov. 1945). Baritone. Studied with Tito Gobbi and Gerald Moore. Debut in 1968 as Papageno *(Zauberflöte)* at the Royal Opera, Stockholm; sang that role in Ingmar Bergman's film of the opera. Other roles include Rossini's Figaro, Wagner's Wolfram, Berg's Eisenstein, and Corigliano's Beaumarchais (*The Ghosts of Versailles*).

Hageman, Richard (b. Leeuwarden, Holland, 9 July 1882; d. Beverly Hills, 6 Mar. 1966). Composer, conductor, and pianist. Studied with Gevaert. Conducted at the Metropolitan Opera, 1908–22 and 1936; head of the opera department at the Curtis Institute in Philadelphia. Moved to Hollywood in 1938, where he provided music for films including *Stagecoach, Fort Apache, She Wore a Yellow Ribbon, The Howards of Virginia.* Also composed an opera (*Caponsacchi,* completed 1931), art songs, and popular songs.

Hagen, Francis Florentine (b. Salem, N.C., 30 Oct. 1815; d. Lititz, Pa., 7 July 1907). Composer. Ordained in 1844, he served Moravian churches in North Carolina and elsewhere. Composed 17 anthems, 6 choral pieces, a Christmas cantata, Overture in F for orchestra, songs, organ pieces and hymn arrangements, piano pieces; best known for the carol "Morning Star" (1836).

Hagen, Peter Albrecht von [van], **Sr.** (b. Netherlands, 1755; d. Boston, 20 Aug. 1803). Composer, violinist, and music publisher. Emigrated to the U.S. in 1774; by 1796, settled in Boston, where he composed and published some of his own songs. Organist at King's Chapel from 1798; conducted a theater orchestra. The attribution of works between him and his son of the same name (d. 1837) is virtually impossible to determine.

Hahn, Reynaldo (b. Caracas, 9 Aug. 1874; d. Paris, 28 Jan. 1947). Composer and conductor. Studied with Massenet. Conductor at the Paris Opéra from 1945. From 1934 wrote musical criticism for *Le Figaro.* Works include operas (*Le marchand de Venise,* Paris, 1935); operettas; musical comedies (*Mozart,* 1925); ballets; concertos and other orchestral music; string quartets and other chamber music; piano and organ works. The songs for which he is now best known set texts of Hugo, Verlaine, Daudet, Heine, and Lecomte de Lisle.

Haieff, Alexei (Vasilievich) (b. Blagoveshchensk, Siberia, 25 Aug. 1914; d. Rome 1 Mar. 1994). Composer. Studied with Jacobi, Goldmark, and Boulanger; 1960s, taught at SUNY–Buffalo, the Carnegie Institute of Technology, Brandeis, and at the Univ. of Utah. His music is often described as neoclassical; some jazz influence is also evident. Works include ballets; orchestral works (symphonies, concertos; *Caligula,* baritone, orchestra, 1971); chamber music (Serenade, oboe, clarinet, bassoon, piano, 1942; *Éloge,* 9 instruments, 1967); sonatas and other piano works; vocal music.

Hailstork, Adolphus Cunningham (b. Rochester, N.Y., 17 Apr. 1941). Composer. Studied with Nadia Boulanger, Nicholas Flagello, Vittorio Giannini, David Diamond, and H. Owen Reed. Has taught at Youngstown State Univ. in Ohio (1971–76) and Norfolk State Univ. in Virginia (from 1976). Composed works for orchestra (*Bellevue,* 1974; *Celebration,* 1975; *Epitaph: For a Man Who Dreamed,* 1979; Symphony no. 1, 1988); for band (Bagatelles for Brass, 1974; *American Landscape nos. 1–3*); choral works; chamber music; guitar pieces; sonatas and other piano pieces.

Haitink, Bernard (Johann Herman) (b. Amsterdam, 4 Mar. 1929). Conductor. Artistic director of the Concertgebouw Orchestra 1964–88; of the London Philharmonic, 1969–78. Music director at Glyndebourne, 1977–87; of the Royal Opera from 1987. His recorded legacy with the Concertgebouw Orchestra includes performances of Brahms, Bruckner, Mahler, and Strauss. In the theater he concentrated early on Mozart, but also gave much-admired performances of Stravinsky, Britten, Borodin, and Wagner.

Hakim, Talib Rasul [Chambers, Stephen Alexander] (b. Asheville, N.C., 8 Feb. 1940; d. New Haven, Conn., 31 Mar. 1988). Composer. Teachers included Robert Starer, William Sydeman, Hall Overton, Morton Feldman, Chou Wen-Chung, and Ornette Coleman. Taught at Pace College (1970–72), Nassau Community College (1972–88), and Morgan State Univ. (1978–79). Works include pieces for orchestra (*Shapes,* 1965; *Re/Currences,* 1975; *Concepts,* 1976; *Arkan-5,* with tape, 1980); piano and percussion music; concert works for jazz ensembles; vocal works; works for chamber ensembles.

Halbe Note, halbe Pause [Ger.]. Half note, halfnote rest. See Note.

Halévy, (Jacques François) Fromental (Elie) (b. Paris, 27 May 1799; d. Nice, 17 Mar. 1862). Composer. Pupil of Cherubini and Berton. Taught at the Paris Conservatory from 1816. From 1826, chief vocal coach at the Théâtre-Italien; at the Opéra 1829–40. Stage works include *Le dilettante d'Avignon* (1829) and *L'éclair* (1835), both at the Opéracomique; ballets; grand operas (*La juive,* 1835; *La reine de Chypre,* 1841; *Le juif errant,* 1852; *La magicienne,* 1858, all at the Opéra). Among his pupils were Bizet, Saint-Saëns, and Lecocq. From 1844 he published historical and critical essays on music.

Half cadence. A *cadence ending on the dominant.

Half close. Half *cadence.

Half-diminished seventh chord. See Seventh chord.

Half-fall. According to Thomas Mace (1676), an *appoggiatura that rises by a half step.

Half note. See Note.

Half shift. In violin playing, second *position.

Half step. *Semitone.

Half-stop. *Divided stop.

Half-tube. See Wind instruments.

Halffter (Jiménez), Cristóbal (b. Madrid, 24 Mar. 1930). Composer. Nephew of Ernesto and Rodolfo Halffter. Studied with del Campo and Tansman. Taught at the Madrid Conservatory 1960–67; conducted the Orquesta Manuel de Falla, 1955–63. His

works use a variety of contemporary techniques: twelve-tone, aleatory, exploration of new timbres, contrasting blocks of sonority, and electronic media; examples include *Variaciones sobre la resonancia de un grito* (instruments, tape, and live electronic transformation, 1977), the Violin Concerto (1980), and the *Sinfonía para tres grupos instrumentales* (1963). He has composed other orchestral works; sacred and secular choral music; pieces for chamber ensemble and solo instruments; and the opera *Don Quichotte* (1970).

Halffter (Escriche), Ernesto (b. Madrid, 16 Jan. 1905; d. there, 5 July 1989). Composer. Brother of Rodolfo Halffter; uncle of Cristóbal Halffter. Pupil of Falla and Ravel. Founded the Seville Conservatory in 1931; 1942–52 taught at the Instituto español in Lisbon. His compositions, which might be either adventurous in their modernism or evocative of the past, are usually tonal. Composed ballets, incidental and film music; orchestral works (*Amanecer en los jardines de España,* 1937; *Rapsodia portuguesa,* 1940, rev. 1951); sacred works (psalm settings; memorials for Pope John XXIII and Prince Pierre de Polignac; *Gozos de Nuestra Señora,* 1970); collections of songs; chamber music; and keyboard works.

Halffter (Escriche), Rodolfo (b. Madrid, 30 Oct. 1900; d. Mexico City, 14 Oct. 1987). Composer. Brother of Ernesto Halffter; uncle of Cristóbal Halffter. Settled in Mexico, 1939. Taught at the National Conservatory from 1940; director of the ballet group La paloma azul. His music is generally tonal in conception, though with some injections of parallel dissonance and polytonality; works include a lost opera, several ballets, and orchestral compositions; works for chorus, including the Easter piece *Pregón para una pascua pobre;* chamber music; works for both piano and guitar.

Hallé, Charles [Carl] (b. Hagen, Westphalia, 11 Apr. 1819; d. Manchester, 25 Oct. 1895). Pianist and conductor. Pupil of Rinck, Weber, and George Osborne. Performed and taught in Paris, championing Beethoven's piano sonatas. Settled in Manchester 1849, conducting the orchestra and organizing concerts. First principal of the Royal Manchester College of Music (1893). Active as pianist and conductor in the U.K. From 1888 toured with his second wife, the violinist Wilma Norman-Neruda (1839–1911).

Hallelujah [Heb., praise ye the Lord]. An expression of praise to God or of general rejoicing. For its occurrence in the Bible and its use in Gregorian chant, see Alleluia. In choral works of the 17th and 18th centuries, its occurrence in a text is often the occasion for an elaborate passage or movement for chorus, often employing imitation. Examples include the "Hallelujah Chorus" from Handel's *Messiah.*

Hallén, (Johannes) Andreas (b. Göteborg, 22 Dec. 1846; d. Stockholm, 11 Mar. 1925). Composer and conductor. Pupil of Reinecke, Rheinberger, and Rietz. Conductor of the Stockholm Philharmonic 1885–95; of the Royal Opera 1892–97; founder and conductor, Southern Swedish Philharmonic, Malmö 1902–7. Taught at the Stockholm Conservatory 1909–19. Works include 3 operas, incidental music, choral works, *Missa solemnis,* 3 symphonic poems, 2 rhapsodies, songs, chamber music.

Halling [Nor.]. A Norwegian folk dance in a moderately fast duple meter, usually danced by one dancer at a time and accompanied on the *Hardingfele.*

Hallström, Ivar (Christian) (b. Stockholm, 5 June 1826; d. there, 11 Apr. 1901). Composer and pianist. Court librarian for Oscar II from 1850; director of the Lindblad School of Music 1861–72. His music shows the influence of Gounod; it consists chiefly of stage works: operas (*The Enchanted Cat,* 1869; *The Bewitched One,* 1874); ballets; incidental music; also songs and folk song settings; piano works (*Variations on a Swedish Folksong "Sven i Rosengård"*).

Hambraeus, Bengt (b. Stockholm, 29 Jan. 1928). Composer, organist, and music scholar. On the staff of the Swedish Broadcasting Corporation from 1957. Taught at McGill Univ. in Montreal from 1972. A central figure in European electronic music. Works include operas; choral/instrumental works (*Symphonia sacra,* 1986; *Echoes of Loneliness,* 1988); orchestral works (*Rota,* 3 orchestras, tape, 1956–62; *Transfiguration,* 1963; *Rencontres,* 1971); solo vocal works; chamber music; works for organ and for piano; tape music (*Transit I,* 1963).

Hamerik [Hammerich], **Asger** (b. Fredericksberg, Denmark, 8 Apr. 1843; d. there, 13 July 1923). Composer. Brother of musicologist Angul Hammerich (1848–1931); father of Ebbe Hamerik. Studied with Gade, Hartmann, Bülow and Berlioz. Director and teacher at the Peabody Conservatory, Baltimore, 1871–98. Composed operas, 8 symphonies, 5 Nordic Suites, a Requiem, and many other choral works and cantatas.

Hamilton, Iain (Ellis) (b. Glasgow, 6 June 1922). Composer. Taught at Duke University. Used serial techniques. Composed works for the stage (*The Royal Hunt of the Sun,* 1967–69; *The Cataline Conspiracy,* 1972–73; *Tamburlaine,* 1979; *Anna Karenina,* 1981; *Raleigh's Dream,* 1984; *Lancelot,* 1985); sacred and secular vocal works (*The Bermudas,* baritone, chorus, orchestra, 1956; *Epitaph for This World and Time,* 1970, 3 choirs and organs; Te Deum, soprano, alto, tenor, bass, orchestra (1973–74); *The Morning Watch,* chorus, 10 winds, 1982; St. Mark's Passion, 4 soloists, chorus, orchestra, 1983; Re-

quiem, chorus; *Prometheus,* 4 soloists, chorus, orchestra); orchestral pieces (symphonies; Sinfonia, 2 orchestras, 1958; concertos for violin, for piano, and for jazz trumpet); string quartets, piano sonatas, and pieces for chamber ensembles.

Hammer(ed) dulcimer. In the U.S., the *dulcimer, as distinct from the *Appalachian dulcimer.

Hammerklavier [Ger.]. In the early 19th century, a name for the *piano. Beethoven subtitled his Piano Sonatas in A major op. 101 (1816) and B♭ major op. 106 (1817–18) "für das Hammerklavier"; the latter is popularly known as the *Hammerklavier* Sonata.

Hammerschmidt, Andreas (b. Brüx, 1611 or 1612; d. Zittau, 8 Nov. 1675). Composer. Organist at St. Petri, Freiberg (1635–39) and at St. Johannis, Zittau (1639 to his death). Composed German sacred concertos for a variety of vocal forces and continuo, sometimes with instruments; also dances, secular vocal pieces, and occasional music.

Hammerstein, Oscar (Greeley Clendenning), II (b. New York, 12 July 1895; d. Doylestown, Pa., 23 Aug. 1960). Lyricist and librettist. Produced musicals with composers Vincent Youmans, Rudolf Friml (*Rose-Marie,* 1924), Sigmund Romberg (*The Desert Song,* 1926), George Gershwin, and Jerome Kern (*Showboat,* 1927). In 1943 formed a partnership with composer Richard Rodgers, with whom he wrote *Oklahoma!,* 1943; *Carousel,* 1945; *South Pacific,* 1949; *The Sound of Music,* 1959. Wrote for television and film (*State Fair,* 1945), and adapted Bizet's *Carmen* for Broadway as *Carmen Jones* (1943).

Hammond organ. See Electronic organ.

Hampton, Lionel (b. Louisville, Ky., 20 Apr. 1909). Jazz vibraphonist, drummer, and bandleader. Began playing vibraphone during a recording session with Louis Armstrong (1930). Joined Benny Goodman's quartet (1936–40); their recordings include "Moonglow" (1936) and "The Blues in Your Flat" (1938). Led all-star swing groups for recordings, including "Hot Mallets" (1939). Formed a big band (1940) that helped establish the rhythm-and-blues style.

Hancock, Herbie [Herbert Jeffrey] (b. Chicago, 12 Apr. 1940). Jazz and popular keyboard player, composer, and bandleader. Has played with Miles Davis (1963–68), Freddie Hubbard, Ron Carter, Tony Williams, Wayne Shorter, Chick Corea, Wynton and Branford Marsalis, and Michael Brecker. Led a jazz sextet (1970–73) that explored African and Indian musics and electric instruments. Jazz compositions include "Watermelon Man" (1962); "Dolphin Dance" and "Maiden Voyage" (both 1965); the Oscar-winning score for the film *'Round Midnight* (1986), in which he acted and played. In pop music, has played in funk and disco styles; recordings include "Chameleon" on the album *Headhunters* (1973) and "Rockit" (1983).

Handel, George Frideric (b. Halle, 23 Feb. 1685; d. London, 14 Apr. 1759). Composer. Pupil of Zachow, friend of Telemann. Moved to Hamburg in 1703; played ripieno violin and later harpsichord in the opera orchestra. Befriended by Johann Mattheson. At Hamburg, composed the opera *Almira* (Hamburg, 1705), *Nero* (1705), *Florindo,* and *Daphne* (produced in 1708); also sonatas and vocal works, none of which survives.

Went to Italy 1706. Among his patrons there were the cardinals Colonna, Pamphili, and Ottoboni and the lay prince Francesco Ruspoli. Pamphili wrote the libretto for Handel's first oratorio, *Il trionfo del tempo e del disinganno* (probably May 1707). For Ruspoli's household (intermittently, 1707–9) produced weekly secular cantatas and the sacred drama *La Resurrezione* (1708). He also composed the three Psalms *Dixit Dominus, Laudate pueri,* and *Nisi Dominus* in mid-1707 at Rome.

Handel also served Prince Ferdinand in Florence annually during the autumn season. In 1707 the opera *Rodrigo* was given. His greatest Italian success came in Venice during Carnival 1709–10, with *Agrippina.* The score combines the reworked music of Mattheson, Keiser, and Handel himself with five new arias. Musical contacts in Italy included the Scarlattis, Corelli, Caldara, Pasquini, and perhaps Steffani in Rome, and Lotti and Gasparini as well as Vivaldi and Albinoni in Venice.

Kapellmeister at Hannover from 1710. He arrived in London late in 1710. He remained until at least June 1711, gaining success with the opera *Rinaldo* at the Queen's Theatre, Haymarket, also giving concerts at court and in the home of the coal trader Thomas Britten. In Hannover, wrote several vocal duets for Princess Caroline; in London 1712–16, produced theater works (*Il pastor fido,* 1712, revised with dances in 1734 as *Terpsichore; Teseo,* 1713; *Silla,* 1713; *Amadigi,* 1715) and occasional music (the Utrecht *Te Deum* and *Jubilate* as well as a Birthday Ode for Queen Anne, from whom he received a £200 pension; all 1713).

Upon Queen Anne's death in 1714, Handel's official employer, the Elector of Hannover, became George I of England. Handel accompanied the king to Hannover in 1716, visiting Halle and an old friend, Johann Christoph Schmidt, who became (as John C. Smith) the composer's secretary and copyist. In 1717 Handel composed his *Water Music* for a royal boat trip on the Thames. The same year he joined the service of the Duke of Chandos at Cannons, probably residing there until February 1719. His music from this period includes the 11 Chandos Anthems, a Te Deum, and *Acis and Galatea* and *Esther,* two masques.

In 1719 several nobles launched an operatic venture, the Royal Academy of Music, choosing Handel as musical director. *Radamisto* made the inaugural season a great success. Among the operas Handel contributed were *Floridante* (1721), *Ottone* (1723), *Flavio* (1724), *Giulio Cesare* (1724), *Tamerlano* (1724), *Rodelinda* (1725), *Scipione* (1726), *Alessandro* (1726), *Admeto* (1727), and *Siroe* (1728). His principal librettists were Rolli and Haym; Bononcini and Amadei each supplied one act for the composite *Muzio Scevola* (Apr. 1721). Handel published his *Suites de pièces pour le clavecin* in 1720; the anthems for the coronation of George II in 1727.

After the dissolution of the Royal Academy in 1728, Handel was hired to produce operas at the King's Theatre, with Heidegger as manager. New operas included *Lotario* (1729), *Partenope* (1730), *Poro* (1731), and *Ezio* (1732). Handel revived *Esther* in 1732 with new material in a quasi-concert setting, and *Acis and Galatea* under similar circumstances, foreshadowing his future triumphs with oratorio.

Handel's Italian operas of 1732–33 faltered in the face of competition from the short-lived English Opera at Lincoln's Inn Fields; he refused to attempt an English opera, but rather responded with *Orlando* (1733). His oratorio *Deborah* made an unsuccessful debut in 1733; in July, however, his oratorio *Athalia* received its premiere successfully. *Arianna in Creta* was his only new opera for the 1733–34 season, his last with Heidegger. Singers had defected to the Opera of the Nobility. Handel moved to Covent Garden and produced *Ariodante* and *Alcina,* the latter of which was one of his greatest public operatic triumphs. The setting of Dryden's *Alexander's Feast* (1736) was a success; *Atalanta* followed. Handel wrote three new operas and thoroughly revised his *Il trionfo* of 1707 for 1736–37, to no avail. He suffered a physical breakdown and temporary paralysis in April 1737, and in June both companies folded, deeply in debt.

In fall 1737 Heidegger hired him at the King's Theatre. *Farabundo* (1738) and *Serse* were far outdrawn by Lampe's Italian operatic parody *The Dragons of Wantley.* Handel began the oratorios *Saul* and *Israel in Egypt.* The op. 6 concertos date from 1739; they were played along with *L'Allegro, il Penseroso ed il Moderato* (libretto by Jennens, after Milton). Handel's last two operas, *Imeneo* and *Deidamia,* were prepared for the 1740–41 season; both failed, and oratorio revivals fared little better. For Dublin Handel composed *Messiah* on scriptural passages as arranged by Jennens, finishing the score in 24 days. The series began with *L'Allegro* on 23 Dec. 1742, to general acclaim; *Messiah* was first performed on 13 April. He returned to London in August, contracted for the Lenten concert series that he presented until his death. *Samson* was first performed 1743. He fell ill in April, but soon recovered, writing *Semele (1744), the *Dettingen Te Deum* and *Anthem* (1743), and *Joseph and His Brethren* (1744).

Handel planned a more ambitious King's Theatre season for 1745, with premieres of *Hercules* and *Belshazzar.* Low attendance forced him to shorten the schedule. The Second Jacobite Rebellion of 1745–46 called forth patriotic sentiment, and Handel responded with the *Occasional Oratorio* (1746), *Judas Maccabaeus* (1747), *Joshua* (1748), and *Alexander Balus* (1748), all with martial overtones. He produced *Susanna* and *Solomon* during the 1749 Lenten season, and in April of that year his *Music for the Royal Fireworks* in Vauxhall Gardens celebrated the Treaty of Aix-la-Chapelle. Handel's first association with the Foundling Hospital also dates from 1749; he later was named a governor, and from 1750 *Messiah* was given annually in the Hospital Chapel as a benefit.

Theodora was the only new offering for the 1750 Lenten concerts. He wrote no new oratorios for Lent 1751, presenting instead revivals and new organ concertos. In February 1751, while composing the chorus "How dark, O Lord, are thy decrees" from his last oratorio, *Jepthe,* he was struck with blindness in his left eye. He led *Jepthe*'s premiere in February 1752, but by January 1753 he was blind. Very few works date from after 1752; still, he played organ concertos until his final days.

Works: *Vocal Music.* 45 operas (some with new music for revivals), including pasticci with music by Handel (*Oreste,* 1734; *Alessandro Severo,* 1738); 9 adapted pasticci from Vinci, Hasse, and others; 31 oratorios and odes; sacred music, including several motets written for Italy, 11 *Chandos Anthems, 4 *Coronation Anthems, 5 *Te Deums, 2 Jubilates, and several other occasional pieces; over 100 cantatas composed in Italy, 1707–9; some 20 continuo duets and trios; English songs, many with new texts adapted to Handel's music (authentic songs include "Love's But the Frailty of the Mind," 1740, and "Stand Round My Brave Boys," 1745); French songs, including several from a "Cantate françoise" (1707); German songs, including 9 arias on Brockes texts (1724–27).

Instrumental Music. Orchestral concertos, including 6 Concerti grossi op. 3 (1734) and *12 Grand Concertos in 7 Parts* op. 6 (1740); organ, harp, and harpsichord concertos, including *6 Concertos* op. 4 (1738), *A Second Set of 6 Concertos* (keyboard only, 1740), *A Third Set of 6 Concertos* op. 7 (posthumous, 1761); *Concerti a due cori* (performed with 1748 oratorios); suites, including *Water Music* (1717, published later), *Music for the Royal *Fireworks*

(1749, originally for winds; strings added in published parts); several overtures; minuets, marches, and other movements (some dance-related) for orchestra and wind ensemble; chamber music, including 12 *Sonates* (ca. 1730; rev. ed. ca. 1732), *VI Sonates* op. 2 (ca. 1730; rev. ed. ca. 1732–33), and *7 Sonatas or Trios* op. 5 (1739) for 2 treble instruments and continuo, and several solo sonatas (original works and reworkings); and over 250 movements for keyboard solo, including some 25 suites along with sonatas ("lessons"), preludes, airs, allegros, chaconnes, sonatinas, and fugues.

Handel Variations. Twenty-five Variations and a Fugue on a Theme by G. F. Handel op. 24 composed by Brahms in 1861. The theme is the Air from Handel's Suite no. 1 in B♭ major for harpsichord, from the second set of suites, published in 1733. The fugue subject is freely derived from the initial notes of Handel's tune.

Handharmonika [Ger.]. *Accordion.

Handl, Jacob [Gallus, Jacobus] (b. probably at Ribniča, between 15 Apr. and 31 July 1550; d. Prague, 18 July 1591). Composer. Singer in the imperial chapel in Vienna from ca. 1574–75; ca. 1580–85, choirmaster to the Bishop of Olomouc; thereafter Kantor of St. Jan na Brzehu in Prague. Wrote Masses, motets, 3 Passions, and secular Latin songs.

Handorgel [Ger.]. *Accordion.

Handy, W(illiam) C(hristopher) (b. Florence, Ala., 16 Nov. 1873; d. New York, 28 Mar. 1958). Blues composer. Played cornet in and led ragtime and minstrel bands. Formed a music publishing company in Memphis with Harry Pace (1908–20), issuing his compositions "Mr. Crump" (1909; revised as "Memphis Blues," 1912), "St. Louis Blues" (1914), and "Beale Street Blues" (1916). Recorded with his blues- and jazz-oriented Memphis Orchestra in New York (1917–23); staged concerts of African American music, notably at Carnegie Hall (1928). Also wrote spirituals, popular songs, stage songs, and art songs.

Hänsel und Gretel. Opera in three acts by Engelbert Humperdinck (libretto by his sister, Adelheid Wette, after the fairy tale in the Grimm brothers' collection), produced in Weimar in 1893. Setting: a forest in Germany.

Hanson, Howard (Harold) (b. Wahoo, Nebr., 28 Oct. 1896; d. Rochester, N.Y., 26 Feb. 1981). Composer, conductor, and teacher. Pupil of Arne Oldberg and Respighi. Taught at the College of the Pacific in San José 1916–21; director of the Eastman School 1924–64. In Rochester founded the American Composers

Concerts and the Institute of American Music; often conducted his own and other American music in the U.S. and abroad. Composed in a neo-Romantic style; made use of northern folk styles, chorale melodies, and Gregorian chant. Composed 7 symphonies (No. 4, *The Requiem,* Pulitzer Prize, 1944; No. 5, *Sinfonia Sacra,* 1954; No. 7, *A Sea Symphony,* 1977); an opera (*Merry Mount,* 1934) and 2 ballets; tone poems, concertos and other orchestral works; works for band; chamber music; works for piano; choral works (*Song of Democracy,* Whitman, solo voices, chorus, and orchestra, op. 44, 1957); songs.

Happening. See Mixed media.

Harbison, John (b. Orange, N.J., 20 Dec. 1938). Composer and conductor. Pupil of Piston, Blacher, Sessions, and Kim. On the faculty at M.I.T. from 1969. His style has been influenced by his experience in jazz improvisation; early works employed twelve-tone procedures. Works include 2 operas (*A Winter's Tale,* 1974; *Full Moon in March,* 1977), ballets, and incidental music; 3 symphonies, concertos, and other orchestral works (*Four Hymns,* 1987; *The Most Often Used Chords,* 1993); *Deep Potomac Bells* (250 tubas, 1983); *Bermuda Triangle* (amplified cello, tenor saxophone, and electric organ; 1970), string quartets and other chamber and piano music; cantatas (*The Flower-Fed Buffaloes,* 1976; *The Flight into Egypt,* Pulitzer Prize, 1987) and other vocal music; *Three City Blocks* (band, 1991).

Hard bop. A mid-1950s resurgence of *bebop. Unlike other derivatives, it adopted unaltered the conventions of the parent style, except for intersections with *soul jazz. Its exponents included drummers Art Blakey and Max Roach, trumpeter Clifford Brown, and saxophonist Sonny Rollins.

Hardanger fiddle. *Hardingfele.*

Hardelot, Guy d' [Mrs. W. I. Rhodes, née Helen Guy] (b. Château Hardelot, near Boulogne, ca. 1858; d. London, 7 Jan. 1936). Composer. Published over 300 songs ("Sans toi," Victor Hugo; "Because"), some very popular in the 1890s and early 1900s and sung by Melba, Maurel, Calvé, and others. Later a singing teacher in London.

Hardi [Fr.]. Bold, rash.

Hardingfele [Nor.], **hardanger fiddle.** A folk fiddle of western Norway with four melody strings plus four or five metal *sympathetic strings running beneath the fingerboard.

Harfe [Ger.]. *Harp.

Harmon mute. Trade name for a type of *wa-wa mute. See also Mute.

Harmonic. See Acoustics, Harmonics.

Harmonic analysis. Analysis of harmonic functions and their relationship to the larger dimensions of a musical work. Analysis of Western tonal harmony, principally of the 18th and 19th centuries, includes elucidation of chord types and their functional basis (expressed by roman-numeral notation); evaluation of their relative harmonic strength and their patterns within the phrase; the relationship of these to the key and to changes of key; and ultimately the larger and smaller relationships of individual and assembled harmonies to the overall structure of the work [see Harmony].

The simplest chord is the triad, composed of three pitches: the root (also called the fundamental tone), a third (major or minor), and a fifth, as in Ex. 1, which illustrates a C major triad in its simplest form, without doubling voices. Any other arrangement of C's, E's, and G's would thus constitute some kind of C-major triad. A triad whose root is below the other pitches is said to be in root position. If some other pitch is in the bass, the chord is said to be inverted. See Triad, Inversion.

Example 2 shows triads formed on each scale degree in C major, including three major and three minor, which are made up only of consonant intervals and employ no tones from outside the C-major scale; the bracketed chord, formed on the seventh scale degree, is a diminished triad (so called because of the diminished fifth, a dissonant interval) and is the only other type of triad possible in the major mode. It is regarded by some theorists as having a weakened harmonic function and as being an incomplete dominant *seventh chord without the root. Each triad is identified by the roman numeral corresponding to the scale degree that is its root; the roman numeral is capitalized if the triad is major. (If a chord is more complex than a triad [see below] or if it is in some position other than root position, arabic numerals are added to the roman numerals in a variety of ways; for a description of this system of notation, see Thoroughbass.) Because of the variability of scale forms, the *minor mode demonstrates a more complicated set of triads, including augmented (+) and diminished (°) [Ex. 3].

Many different structural types are possible in the family of seventh chords, formed from triads surmounted by a seventh above the root [Ex. 4]. By far the most important of these is the dominant seventh chord (a). Other seventh chords include the major seventh (b), minor seventh (c), major-minor seventh (d), half-diminished seventh (e), and diminished seventh (f); all of these are distinguished from each other by their intervallic content. Next to the dominant seventh, the commonest seventh-chord structure is the diminished seventh; in its commonest usage it is variously described as based on the seventh scale degree or as a dominant ninth chord with the root omitted.

The harmonic weight of most of these seventh chords, as well as of the homologous ninth, eleventh, and thirteenth chords that can be constructed on paper, is attenuated by the nonharmonic values of the dissonant pitches; in most cases, in actual music, such structures arise only as momentary events in the ebb and flow of counterpoint. Late in the period of tonal harmony, however, these complex chords are used independently, for the sake of their particular sonic qualities, e.g., in the music of Debussy, Ravel, and others.

Altered chords are triads or seventh chords with one or more pitches that have been chromatically altered by application of accidental signs so as to include at least one tone not found in the major or minor scales of a particular key. They include the Neapolitan *sixth chord, shown in Ex. 5a, the various types of triads with raised or lowered fifth, particularly the dominant triad (b), the raised supertonic and submediant seventh chords (c), and the augmented sixth chords (d); in Ex. 5 these are shown with their normal resolutions. (Triads of secondary dominant function, discussed below, are considered not as chromatically altered chords, but rather as chords borrowed from other keys.) It is a general rule that resolutions of the altered pitches follow the direction of alteration: raised pitches resolve upward, and lowered pitches resolve downward.

In the key of C major, a D-major triad progressing to a G-major triad is usually considered to be not a major triad formed on the supertonic but rather the dominant of the dominant (i.e., the triad formed on the dominant or fifth degree of the scale in which G is tonic, described as V of V and often written V/V). Its tonal strength applies more immediately to G, in which key it is a primary triad, and accordingly with respect to C it is a secondary dominant. Since secondary dominants usually include at least one pitch from outside the scale (e.g., G♯ in V of VI in C major), these pitches are considered as borrowed from the scale of the secondary key and not as alterations of the primary scale. Secondary dominants (sometimes called applied dominants) create a tonal emphasis on the chords to which they apply; V of II, for example, is said to tonicize II (i.e., treat II as if it were tonic). *Tonicization is a temporary state, of short duration, as distinguished from *modulation, which persists long enough to create an actual sense of a new key.

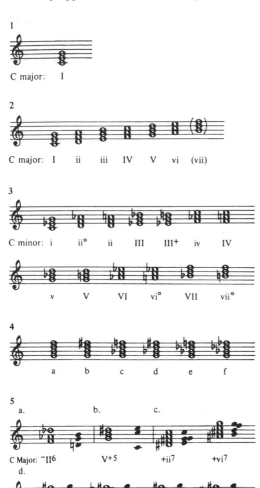

1

C major: I

2

C major: I   ii   iii   IV   V   vi   (vii)

3

C minor: i   ii°   ii   III   III⁺   iv   IV

v   V   VI   vi°   VII   vii°

4

a   b   c   d   e   f

5
a.   b.   c.

C Major: ⁻II⁶   V+5   +ii⁷   +vi⁷
d.

Italian   German   French

Harmonic inversion. See Inversion.

Harmonic minor (scale). See Scale.

Harmonic rhythm. The rhythm of the changes of harmony in time in a musical work.

Harmonic series. See Acoustics, Harmonics.

Harmonica. (1) *Mouth organ. (2) *Glass harmonica.

Harmonicon. (1) *Glass harmonica or *musical glasses in general.

Harmonics. (1) In acoustics, a series of frequencies, all of which are integral multiples of a single frequency termed the fundamental [see Acoustics]. The fundamental and its harmonics are numbered in order, the fundamental being the first harmonic and having the frequency 1f, the second harmonic having the frequency 2f, the third harmonic 3f, and so forth. Harmonics above the fundamental are sometimes termed overtones, the second harmonic being the first overtone, etc. The pitches represented by these frequencies, and thus the intervals formed among these pitches, are said to be acoustically pure. In some measure, they correspond to the pitches and intervals employed in much Western music. Most such music, however, requires the use of a tuning system in which relatively few intervals (always the octave and sometimes only the octave) are acoustically pure. Ex. 1 shows the pitches corresponding to the harmonic series for the fundamental C. The pitches shown in whole notes are in general judged to be sufficiently well in tune. Those in black notes are, by the standards of Western tonal music, quite out of tune, and thus their representation on the staff is only approximate. See also Interval, Temperament.

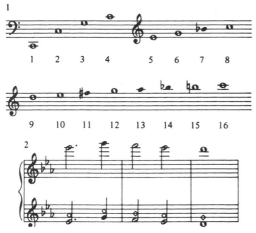

(2) [Fr. *flageolet, sons harmoniques;* Ger. *Flageolett-Töne;* It. *suoni flautati;* Sp. *sonidos del flautín*]. The general class of pitches that are produced by sounding the second or some higher harmonic of a vibrating system such as a string. In the playing of stringed instruments (including the harp and guitar), these are high tones of a flutelike timbre, sometimes called flageolet tones, produced by causing a string to vibrate in segments corresponding to a mode of vibration other than the fundamental and thus suppressing altogether the pitch that is produced when the string vibrates along its entire length [see Acoustics]. Harmonics are produced by touching the string lightly at a node for the desired mode of vibration at the same time that the string is bowed or plucked. Thus, if a string is bowed or plucked while being touched lightly at a point one-third of the distance from one end, it will produce the harmonic with a frequency three times that of the open string and with a pitch an octave and a fifth higher than that of the open string. This may be notated by placing a small circle above the desired pitch.

For instruments of the violin family, natural harmonics are those produced on open strings. Artificial

harmonics are those produced on stopped strings and are often notated by a normal note-shape, indicating the pitch for which the string is to be stopped, in combination with a lozenge placed a fourth above, indicating the point at which the string is to be touched lightly so as to produce the harmonic having a frequency four times that of the stopped string and having a pitch two octaves higher than that of the stopped pitch; in Ex. 2, the lower staff shows the notation and the upper staff the sounded pitch.

Harmonie [Fr., Ger.]. (1) Harmony. (2) Wind instruments or a band made up of wind instruments. In the late 18th and early 19th centuries, such bands of from two to a dozen instruments were often maintained by the aristocracy. (3) [Ger.] Also *Harmoniemusik.* In the late 18th century, a multimovement work for winds (after 1780 often two each of oboes, clarinets, horns, and bassoons) of a type related to the *divertimento and slightly earlier often termed *partita or *Parthie.*

Harmonie der Welt, Die [Ger., The Harmony of the World]. (1) Opera in five acts by Hindemith (to his own libretto), produced in Munich in 1957. Setting: central Europe between 1608 and 1630, the last years of Johannes Kepler's life. (2) A symphony in three movements composed by Hindemith in 1951 and derived from music that was intended ultimately for the opera of the same name.

Harmoniemesse [Ger., Wind-band Mass]. Popular name for Haydn's Mass in Bb major Hob. XXII:14 (1802) for soloists, chorus, and orchestra, so named because of its generous use of wind instruments.

Harmonika [Ger.]. (1) *Accordion. (2) *Mouth organ. (3) *Musical glasses.

Harmonious Blacksmith. Popular name attached in the 19th century to the air with five variations from Handel's Suite no. 5 in E major for harpsichord, from his first set of suites, published in 1720.

Harmonium. A keyboard instrument with free *reeds sounded by pedal-operated (later electric in some models) bellows; also called a reed organ, though unlike the *organ it has no pipes or resonators. In some instruments of this type (including the first instrument to bear the name harmonium as well as its predecessors the *orgue expressif* and the *physharmonica*) the bellows generate air pressure; in others (American organ, seraphine, melodeon, cottage organ) the bellows create suction. Stops above the keyboard activate different sets of reeds to provide various timbres. A special feature of many pressure-operated instruments is the "expression" stop, which bypasses the pressure-regulating mechanism and allows the player to control volume by means of foot pressure. The harmonium was developed in the first half of the 19th century. See also Regal.

Harmonium.

Harmony [fr. Gr., Lat. *harmonia;* Fr., Ger. *Harmonie;* It. *armonia;* Sp. *armonía*]. The relationship of tones considered as they sound simultaneously, and the way such relationships are organized in time; also any particular collection of pitches sounded simultaneously, termed a chord. See Harmonic analysis, Tonality, Counterpoint.

In principle, any chord may follow any other, constituting simply a harmonic succession. In practice, however, the vocabulary of tonal music is greatly limited in types of root motion, and these may be regarded variously as strong or weak harmonic progressions. The progression from V to I, dominant to tonic, especially in root position (with the root of each chord in the bass, i.e., as the lowest-sounding pitch), has evolved as not only the strongest progression but also by far the most common in tonal music [see also Cadence]. The subdominant in relation to the tonic, IV–I, is of comparable but lesser force.

Weak progressions are illustrated by triads whose roots are a third apart, such as I–iii or vi–I; such triads have two pitches in common and thus the progression between them involves a change in only one pitch. The weakness is relative, for in root position, the new root obtained by the downward bass motion of a third provides a useful contrast, with a change of harmonic color from major to minor or vice versa. On the other hand, if the bass remains stationary, the

progression may be so weak as to be perceived as the result of nonharmonic motion

Triads with roots a step apart have no common tones; the progression then involves a complete change of pitch collection. Such progressions are regarded as strong, but their usage evolved differently during the period of tonal harmony; IV–V and V–vi are commonly found, for example, while I–ii is found relatively seldom (though often in the 16th century), and ii–iii or IV–iii must be considered rare.

Harmony is vertical, as melody is horizontal; these popular conceptions arise in the Western notational system, which relates simultaneous events vertically on the staff and successive events along it. Counterpoint designates a generalized relationship of melodies together, or even of melody and harmonic bass.

Tastes in harmony have varied widely with time and place, though there have been numerous attempts to show that the particular harmonic style of Western music of the 18th and 19th centuries is ordained in nature [see Acoustics].

Harmony of the spheres. A Pythagorean belief that the distances between the earth and celestial bodies visible with the naked eye, as well as the speeds at which these bodies rotated around the earth, were related to one another according to the same numerical ratios that characterized the notes of the diatonic scale.

Harnoncourt, Nikolaus (b. Berlin, 6 Dec. 1929). Conductor and cellist. Played in the Vienna Symphony, 1952–69. In 1953, cofounded the Concentus musicus, dedicated to performances of Renaissance and Baroque music on original instruments; the ensemble recorded Bach's Brandenburg Concertos (1962), other works of Bach, Rameau, and masters of the Italian Baroque, and the extant Bach cantatas, the leadership alternating between Harnoncourt and Gustav Leonhardt. Began conducting and recording with the Amsterdam Concertgebouw Orchestra in 1981. Taught at the Mozarteum from 1972.

Harold en Italie [Fr., Harold in Italy]. A program symphony in four movements (after portions of Byron's *Childe Harold*) by Berlioz, op. 16 (1834), composed at Paganini's request for a work that would feature his newly acquired Stradivarius viola. Paganini never performed the work because the viola part was not sufficiently prominent.

Harp [Fr. *harpe;* Ger. *Harfe;* It., Sp. *arpa*]. A chordophone in which the plane of the strings is perpendicular to the soundboard. Triangular in shape, all harps have three basic structural elements, a resonator, a neck, and strings. Some have a forepillar or column. The resonator is topped with a soundboard and string holder. Strings are attached to the neck directly with special knots, or indirectly through tuning pegs (usually movable). Buzzing mechanisms, attached near either end of the string on the neck or the soundboard, and activated by the plucked string, were used on Renaissance European harps and are found today on most African harps. Harps have from one to 47 strings. Chromaticizing mechanisms range from manually operated hooks to complex pedal-activated systems. Strings are usually plucked, but may be strummed, struck by hand or with a plectrum, or slid upon. The resonator may also be used as a percussion instrument and struck by fingers, hand, or hooked rattles. The harp may be played with a single finger, with the thumb of one hand and the thumb and forefinger of the other, and with the thumb and first three fingers of both hands. The little fingers are usually not used.

The modern Western concert harp has 47 strings, 7 per octave, from C_1 to g''''. Each string (except C_1 and D_1) can be raised two semitones (double action) using a pedal-activated system. First patented by Sébastien Érard in 1810, the double action made the harp into an equal-tempered chromatic instrument. At the foot or base of the harp are seven pedals, each with three positions. These allow each diatonic pitch to be played flat, natural, or sharp. From left to right, D, C, and B pedals are on the left side, with E, F, G, and A on the right. When a pedal is depressed, all strings of the same note-name are changed in all octaves. With pedals in flat or uppermost position, each string is free to vibrate over its entire sounding length. When the pedals are depressed to the natural or middle position, forks in the upper of two rows rotate to tighten and shorten the strings, raising their pitch a semitone. When the pedals are depressed to the sharp or lowest position, the lower forks act in a similar way, raising the pitch of the strings a second semitone.

Basic harp notation is similar to keyboard notation. Strings are usually plucked at mid-length or near the soundboard, the latter producing a guitarlike timbre. A glissando (also termed *glissé* and *sdrucciolando*) is produced by strumming across the strings with the fleshy part of the fingers or thumb. Pedals can be set

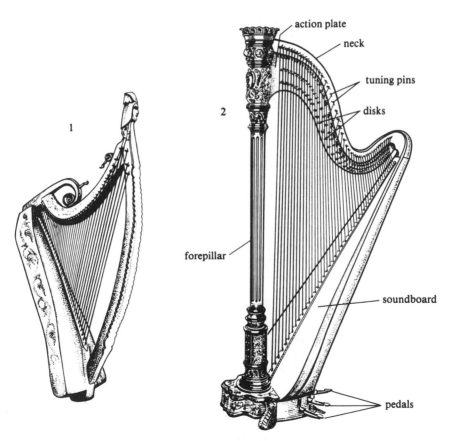

1. Irish harp.   2. Orchestral harp.

for a particular glissando scale or chord, eliminating all dissonances or extraneous tones with enharmonics. *Harmonics, often played by placing the heel of the hand lightly against the midpoint of the string while plucking above with the thumb, are a regular feature of harp technique.

The harp is an ancient and widely distributed instrument, and its usage ranges from religious ritual to pure entertainment and from solo to ensemble music to accompaniment played by singers of ballads and epic poetry.

The oldest extant harp, found at Ur in Sumer, dates from ca. 2600 B.C.E. See also Angle harp, Arched harp, Frame harp.

Harp lute. Any of a series of instruments invented and produced beginning in 1798 by Edward Light of London. They combine a triangular harp body with a guitar neck, the plane of the strings being parallel to the belly. Some later types incorporate "ditals," devices operated by the fingers for raising the pitch of the open strings.

Harp Quartet. Popular name for Beethoven's String Quartet in E♭ major op. 74 (1809), so called because of several pizzicato arpeggios in the first movement.

Harp stop. On the harpsichord, pads of buff leather or other absorbent material mounted on a sliding batten that can be brought into contact with one choir of strings, damping it slightly so as to produce a harp-like effect; also buff stop.

Harp way. One of several 17th-century tunings of the lyra *viol.

Harpsichord [Fr. *clavecin;* Ger. *Cembalo, Kielflügel, Clavicimbel;* It. *clavicembalo;* Sp. *clavicémbalo, clavecín*]. A stringed keyboard instrument in use from the 16th through 18th century and revived since the 1880s.

The harpsichord is similar in shape to the modern grand piano, the strings being roughly parallel to the long side of the case. Each string is plucked by a quill plectrum mounted in the pivoted tongue of a fork-shaped jack that stands at the rear end of the key lever. Depressing the key raises the jack until the horizontally projecting plectrum plucks the string, causing the tongue to rotate on its pivot. As the jack continues to fall, the plectrum is tilted upward and back until its point passes below the string. A spring (of boar bristle, brass wire, or plastic) mounted at the rear of the jack then returns the tongue to its original position, so that the jack is again ready to pluck. A cloth damper is inserted into a slot sawed in one tine of the forked jack, its bottom edge just above the level of the plectrum. When the key is at rest, the damper touches the string, but the slightest depression of the key raises the damper, leaving the string

free to vibrate. Thus a harpsichord string, like an organ pipe, can continue sounding only so long as the player holds a key down.

Each rank of jacks is carried in a pair of mortised battens mounted vertically over one another. The lower batten or guide is fixed, but the upper slide or register is movable, usually by means of stop levers located above the keyboard(s) or at the sides of the wrestplank. Some harpsichords, particularly Italian models, have so-called box slides, combining lower guide and slide in one assembly that moves integrally. In many Flemish harpsichords, registers extending through the cheekpiece can be moved in or out directly. Thus each rank of jacks can be moved slightly toward or away from its choir of strings, engaging or disengaging the plectra. In this way, stops or ranks of jacks can be silenced or added to the ensemble.

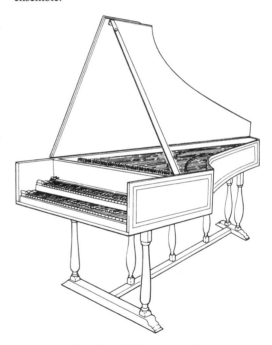

Harpsichord with two manuals.

The typical 18th-century harpsichord of northern Europe has three choirs of strings, two tuned to 8' pitch and one an octave higher at 4' pitch [see Foot]. (Very rarely in late German harpsichords, a fourth choir at 16' might be added.) Such a harpsichord ordinarily has three ranks of jacks, one for each choir. Frequently there are two keyboards, the upper sounding one 8' stop and the lower the other 8' stop and the 4' stop. The upper manual normally can be coupled to the lower, making all three stops available from the latter.

The more nasal sound of a string plucked near one

end is noticeable in the upper manual or front 8' stop of the typical harpsichord. It contrasts with the darker sound of the center-plucked lower manual or back 8'. Sometimes an alternative rank of jacks plucks the upper manual choir of 8' strings at its extreme end to produce an even more nasal timbre (lute stop). Buff leather pads mounted on a sliding batten can be used to damp one choir of 8' strings partially to give a harplike effect (buff stop).

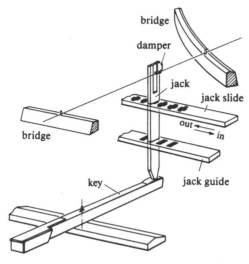

Harpsichord mechanism.

During the first years of the harpsichord's modern revival, there was a tendency to employ concepts of design and aesthetic more germane to the piano or organ than to the harpsichord itself. Thus many revival harpsichords did not resemble their antique prototypes in the most essential details. Some modernized instruments were of far heavier construction than the early ones, with longer treble strings and shorter bass strings, the latter often overspun like those of the piano. Plectra were of leather instead of the quill almost invariably used in earlier times. All these changes tended to produce a more sustained, but not necessarily stronger tone of less harmonic complexity than is typical of antique instruments.

The oldest surviving dated harpsichord is an Italian instrument dated 1515. In the 17th and 18th centuries, the harpsichord enjoyed a substantial solo literature and was the chief chord-playing instrument in the realization of the *thoroughbass. By the late 18th century the harpsichord had been superseded by the piano. See also Arpicordo, Chekker, Clavicytherium, Lute harpsichord, Pedal harpsichord, Spinet, and Virginal.

Harrell, Lynn (b. New York, 30 Jan. 1944). Cellist. Studied with Leonard Rose. Debut with the New York Philharmonic, 1960. Principal cellist with Cleveland Orchestra, 1965–71. Taught at Cincinnati College-Conservatory, 1971–76; at Juilliard from 1976; at the Univ. of Southern California from 1986. Appointed director of the Royal Academy of Music, 1993.

Harris, Barry (Doyle) (b. Detroit, 15 Dec. 1929). Jazz pianist. Played with Max Roach (1956) and Cannonball Adderley (1960). Settled in New York and later accompanied Coleman Hawkins (1965–69). Leading bop pianist and teacher. Albums with his own trio include *At the Jazz Workshop* (1960) and *Live in Tokyo* (1976).

Harris, Roy [LeRoy] **(Ellsworth)** (b. near Chandler, Okla., 12 Feb. 1898; d. Santa Monica, 1 Oct. 1979). Composer. Pupil of Farwell and Boulanger. Taught at Juilliard (summers, 1932–40), Westminster Choir School (1934–38), Cornell Univ., Colorado College (1943–48), the Pennsylvania College for Women (1952), UCLA (1961–73), and California State Univ. in Los Angeles (1973). His melodies are indebted to Anglo-American folk song, early hymnody, and monophonic chant; his own classification of chords based on overtones; asymmetrical rhythms. Works: 4 ballets, a film score, incidental music; symphonies (No. 4, *Folksong Symphony,* 1939), pieces with descriptive titles (*When Johnny Comes Marching Home,* 1934; *Epilogue to Profiles in Courage JFK,* 1964), and concertante works (mainly for piano or organ); pieces for band; chamber music, much of it for strings; some piano music (*American Ballads,* 1942–45); choral music; cantatas (*Abraham Lincoln Walks at Midnight,* 1953) and songs ("Fog," Sandburg, 1945).

Harrison, George (b. Wavertree, Liverpool, 25 Feb. 1943). Rock guitarist, sitarist, singer, and songwriter. Lead guitarist and backup vocalist for the Beatles 1962–70. Wrote songs including "Within You, Without You," on which he played sitar (*Sgt. Pepper's Lonely Hearts Club Band,* 1967). Solo albums include *All Things Must Pass* (1970) and *Cloud Nine* (1987).

Harrison, Lou (b. Portland, Oreg., 14 May 1917). Composer. Pupil of Cowell and Schoenberg. Has taught at Mills College (1936–39 and from 1980) and at San Jose State (from 1967). Composed much for dancers (Merce Cunningham and others). Whereas earlier works often employ a twelve-tone idiom or imitate Ives or Copland, his later compositional style reflects his interests in just intonation and Eastern culture. Works include several ballets, operas (*Rapunzel,* 1954; *Young Caesar,* puppets, 1971), incidental music and film scores; symphonies, a piano concerto, *A Parade* (1995) and other orchestral music, some requiring Eastern instruments (*Pacifika rondo,* chamber orchestra, 1963); many pieces for gamelan; instrumental music for ensembles or soloists, including much for percussion (*Summerfield Set*, piano, 1988); choral and solo vocal music (including *4 Strict Songs*, 8 baritones and orchestra, text in Esperanto, 1955).

Harsányi, Tibor (b. Magyarkanisza, 27 June 1898; d. Paris, 19 Sept. 1954). Composer and pianist. Pupil of Kodály. His compositional idiom derives from Hungarian folk music and from a lyrical Romanticism. Works include operas (*Les invités*, Paris, 1937; *Illusion*, radio, 1948); ballets; orchestral works (*Suite hongroise*, 1935; *Divertimento*, trumpet, strings, 1943); chamber works (*Nonette*, 1932); piano works (*Trois pièces de danse*, 1928).

Hart, Fritz (Bennicke) (b. Greenwich, 11 Feb. 1874; d. Honolulu, 9 July 1949). Conductor and composer. Director of the Melbourne Conservatory (1915–35) and artistic director of the Melbourne Symphony (from 1928). From 1936, conducted the orchestra in Honolulu and taught at the Univ. of Hawaii. Best known for vocal works, including over 500 songs and 22 operas.

Hart, Lorenz (Milton) (b. New York, 2 May 1895; d. there, 22 Nov. 1943). Lyricist and librettist. Collaborated with composer Richard Rodgers on Broadway musicals (including *A Connecticut Yankee*, 1927; *Babes in Arms*, 1937; *I Married an Angel*, 1942; *The Boys from Syracuse*, 1938; *Pal Joey*, 1940), as well as songs for films (beginning with *The Hot Heiress*, 1931).

Hartley, Walter S(inclair) (b. Washington, D.C., 21 Feb. 1927). Composer. Studied with Bernard Rogers and Howard Hanson; taught at the State Univ. College at Fredonia, N.Y. Works include Concerto for 23 winds (1957); concertos for soloists and orchestra; a series of sinfonias and other works for band; chamber music, especially for winds and brass.

Hartmann, Johan Peter Emilius (b. Copenhagen, 14 May 1805; d. there, 10 Mar. 1900). Composer. Son of a musician (and grandson of Johann Ernst Hartmann, 1726–93); 1828–70, a lawyer in government service; active throughout his life as composer, teacher, organist. In 1836, a founder of the Copenhagen Musical Society; 1867, a founder and co-director of Copenhagen Conservatory, teaching there until his death. Works: 3 operas (*Liden Kirsten*, 1846); ballets; incidental music; 2 symphonies; concert overtures; chamber music; many cantatas and choruses; church music; songs; much piano music.

Hartmann, Karl Amadeus (b. Munich, 2 Aug. 1905; d. there, 5 Dec. 1963). Composer. Pupil of Haas, Scherchen, and Webern. Compositional influences include works of Mahler and Bruckner, the Second Viennese School, Bartók, Stravinsky, and Blacher;

he revitalized the German symphonic tradition and composed works organized in large spans. Works include an opera (*Simplicius Simplicissimus*, 1934–35) and oratorios; symphonies, concertos (viola, piano, winds, and percussion, 1955) and other orchestral music; string quartets and other chamber music; piano music; *Ghetto* (alto, baritone, and small orchestra, 1960) and other vocal music.

Harty, (Herbert) Hamilton (b. Hillsborough, County Down, Ireland, 4 Dec. 1879; d. Brighton, 19 Feb. 1941). Composer, conductor, and pianist. Organist and violist in Ireland; noted accompanist in London after 1900; conductor of the Hallé Orchestra 1920–33. Works include *The Mystic Trumpeter* (baritone, chorus, orchestra, 1913); *Comedy Overture* (1906); *An Irish Symphony* (1924); *The Children of Lir* (symphonic poem, 1939); chamber music (Piano Quintet, 1904; *Irish Fantasy*, violin and piano, 1912); many songs (*Ode to a Nightingale*, Keats, 1907); arrangements of orchestral classics (e.g., Handel's *Royal Fireworks Music*).

Harvey, Jonathan (Dean) (b. Sutton Coldfield, Warwick, near Birmingham, 3 May 1939). Composer. Studied with Babbitt. Lecturer at Sussex University from 1977. Has composed large choral/instrumental works (*Cantata X: Spirit Music*, 1976; *Passion and Resurrection*, a "church opera," 1979; *Resurrection*, 2 choruses, organ, 1981); other vocal music (*Four Songs of Yeats*, 1965); orchestral works (a symphony, 1966; *Persephone's Dream*, 1972; *Inner Light*, 1976; *Madonna of Winter and Spring*, with synthesizers, 1986; *Timepieces*, 1987; *Lightness and Weight*, tuba and orchestra, 1987); works for tape (*Time-Points*, 1970; Toccata, organ and tape, 1980); 2 string quartets and other chamber music. He also authored a book on Stockhausen.

Harwood, Basil (b. Woodhouse, Gloucester, 11 Apr. 1859; d. London, 3 Apr. 1949). Composer and organist. Pupil of Reinecke and Jadassohn. Organist at Christ Church, Oxford (1892–1909); also conducted the orchestral society and Bach Choir. Composed chiefly sacred choral works (*Inclina domine*, 1898; *Ode on May Morning*, 1913; many other anthems) and organ music (2 sonatas; a concerto; *Dithyramb; Christmastide*).

Haskil, Clara (b. Bucharest, 7 Jan. 1895; d. Brussels, 7 Dec. 1960). Pianist. Pupil of Alfred Cortot; also an accomplished violinist. Performed in recitals with Ysaÿe and Casals. The onset of a muscular disorder thwarted her career until 1920, when a remission made possible piano recitals in Switzerland, Belgium, and the U.S. Recognized especially for performances of Mozart, Beethoven, and Schubert.

Hasse, Johann Adolf (bapt. Bergedorf, near Hamburg, 25 Mar. 1699; d. Venice, 16 Dec. 1783). Composer. Tenor with the Hamburg opera, 1718; then in Braunschweig-Wolfenbüttel. Settled in Naples 1722; studied with Porpora and Alessandro Scarlatti. *Maestro di cappella* at the electoral court in Dresden 1731–64 and at the Ospedale degli incurabili in Venice. Traveled widely in Europe to produce his operas. Worked closely with Metastasio from the 1740s. Works include about 80 operas, intermezzi, and other theater works, including *Artaserse* (Venice, 1730), *Alessandro nell'Indie* (also *Cleofide;* Dresden, 1731), *La clemenza di Tito* (2 versions: Pesaro, 1735; Naples, 1759), *Lucio Papirio* (Dresden, 1742), *Antigono* (Hubertusburg, 1743), *Semiramide* (Venice, 1744), *Il Rè pastore* (Hubertusburg, 1755), *Nitteti* (Venice, 1758), and *Ruggiero* (Milan, 1771); arias for revivals and pasticci; cantatas; church music, including Masses, motets, and antiphons.

Hassler, Hans Leo (b. Nuremberg, bapt. 26 Oct. 1564; d. Frankfurt am Main, 8 June 1612). Composer. Pupil of Andrea Gabrieli; 1586–ca. 1600, court organist in Augsburg; 1601–4, director of town music in Nuremberg; from 1608, organist and eventually Kapellmeister to the Saxon electoral chapel in Dresden. Composed sacred works (incl. Masses, motets, Psalms, and spiritual songs) for Catholic and later for Lutheran use. Secular compositions include Italian madrigals, German part songs, dance songs, and instrumental works for ensembles or for keyboard.

Hässler, Johann Wilhelm (b. Erfurt, 29 Mar. 1747; d. Moscow, 29 Mar. 1822). Pianist, organist, and composer. Pupil of his uncle Johann Christian Kittel. Concertized during the 1770s, 1780s and 1790s, making contacts with C. P. E. Bach and others. Settled in Moscow 1794. Published many keyboard works, including sonatas, fantasies, preludes, and the *Grand gigue* in D minor op. 31; also a Grand concert op. 50; a cantata; chamber works; and songs.

Hastig [Ger.]. Hurried.

Hastings, Thomas (b. Washington, Conn., 15 Oct. 1784; d. New York, 15 May 1872). Composer and educator. Settled in New York 1832; choirmaster, Bleecker Street Presbyterian Church. Published didactic works (*Dissertation on Musical Taste,* 1822), many collections of church music (*Musica sacra,* 1815); composed over 1,000 hymns, including "Rock of Ages."

Haubenstock-Ramati, Roman (b. Kraków, 27 Feb. 1919; d. Vienna, 3 Mar. 1994). Composer. Pupil of Artur Malawski and Józef Koffler. Music director at Kraków Radio, 1947–50. Taught at the Academy of Music in Tel Aviv and directed the State Music Library, 1950–56. Settled in Vienna 1957. Works such as his series of "Mobiles" (e.g. *Interpolation,* 1958) were influential experiments in aleatoric musical structure. Composed stage works (*Amerika,* 1962–64, after Kafka); vocal works (*Blessings,* soprano, chamber ensemble, 1951; rev. 1978; *Mobile for Shakespeare,* voice, 6 instruments, 1960); orchestral pieces (*Tableaux* I–III, 1967–71; *Symphonien,* 1977; *Sotto voce,* 1986; *Imaginaire,* 1989); other instrumental works (*Credentials,* 1960; 2 string quartets; pieces with tape).

Haubiel [Pratt], **Charles (Trowbridge)** (b. Delta, Ohio, 30 Jan. 1892; d. Los Angeles, 26 Aug. 1978). Composer and pianist. Pupil of Scalero and Josef and Rosina Lhévinne. Taught at the Institute of Musical Art (1920–30) and at New York Univ. (1923–47); founded the Composer's Press 1935. Works include 7 operas; incidental music; orchestral pieces (*Portraits,* 1935; *Pioneers,* a symphonic saga of Ohio, 1946; rev. 1956; *Metamorphoses,* variations on "Swanee River," 1926, piano or orchestra); 5 piano trios and other chamber music; piano music; choral works, 3 cantatas, song cycles, songs.

Hauer, Josef Matthias (b. Wiener Neustadt, 19 Mar. 1883; d. Vienna, 22 Sept. 1959). Composer. Formulated a "law of twelve notes" similar to Schoenberg's, but in terms of 44 unordered hexachords (which he called tropes) rather than ordered sets of 12 pitch classes. Composed an opera and a singspiel; 8 orchestral suites, violin and piano concertos, and other orchestral music; string quartets and other chamber music; choral and vocal music (*Wandlungen,* 6 solo voices, chorus, orchestra, 1927); many twelve-tone works without opus number (1939–59).

Haupt [Ger.]. Head, principal.

Hauptmann, Moritz (b. Dresden, 13 Oct. 1792; d. Leipzig, 3 Jan. 1868). Theorist, teacher. Pupil of Spohr. Violinist in the Kassel orchestra 1822–42; 1842–68, Kantor, Thomasschule, Leipzig; 1843–68, taught theory, Leipzig Conservatory. Cofounder (1850) and first president of the Bach Gesellschaft, also editing its first 3 volumes. Composed much sacred music, an opera, instrumental pieces, and songs; best known as a teacher and for his theoretical works, especially *Die Natur der Harmonik und Metrik* (1853).

Hauptsatz [Ger.]. The first theme or section in *sonata form. See also *Satz.*

Hauptstimme [Ger.]. (1) The principal or leading part, often the soprano. (2) In *twelve-tone and other nontonal works by Schoenberg, Berg, and others, a voice or part of particular importance, often indicated by brackets formed from the letter H.

Hausegger, Siegmund von (b. Graz, 16 Aug. 1872; d. Munich, 10 Oct. 1948). Conductor and composer. Conducting debut with the Graz Opera, 1895. Conducting posts in Munich, Frankfurt, Glasgow, Hamburg, and Berlin. As chief conductor of the Munich Philharmonic, 1920–38, he was one of the first to perform Bruckner's symphonies from the Haas editions.

Hausmusik [Ger.]. Music for informal performance by amateurs in the home. The term dates from the 17th century. In the 20th, it has been associated with *Gebrauchsmusik.*

Hausse [Fr.]. *Frog; *à la hausse,* an instruction to bow near the frog.

Haut, haute [Fr.]. (1) High, e.g., in pitch. (2) [It., Lat., Sp. *alta*]. In the late Middle Ages and Renaissance, instruments or music that was loud rather than soft *(bas, basse).* To the former group belonged the trumpet and especially the *shawm and the *sackbut, which often formed an ensemble [see *Alta* (2), *Basse danse*], and their music; to the latter belonged stringed instruments (both plucked and bowed), the *recorder, and the *crumhorn, and their music.

Hautbois, hautboy [Fr.]. *Oboe.

Haut-dessus [Fr.]. High treble or soprano, especially the higher of two treble parts, the lower being the *bas-dessus.*

Haute-contre [Fr., fr. Lat. *contratenor altus*]. In France in the late 18th and early 19th centuries, a male *alto or high tenor who sang in full voice rather than *falsetto, except perhaps in the highest register; also an alto part in an instrumental ensemble.

Hawaiian guitar. See Steel guitar.

Hawkins, Coleman (Randolph) [Bean; Hawk] (b. St. Joseph, Mo., 21 Nov. 1904; d. New York, 19 May 1969). Jazz tenor saxophonist. Became the first important jazz tenor saxophone soloist as a member of Fletcher Henderson's big band (1924–34); recorded in Europe with Benny Carter, Django Reinhardt, and others. Led a big band (1939–41), then small groups. From the mid-1940s he embraced bop; made powerful interpretations of blues in the 1950s. Recordings include "The Stampede" (1926), "Crazy Rhythm" (1937), "Body and Soul" (1939), and the album *Duke Ellington Meets Coleman Hawkins* (1962).

Hayasaka, Fumio (b. Sendai City, 19 Aug. 1914; d. Tokyo, 15 Oct. 1955). Composer. Cofounder of Shin Ongaku Renmei (New Music League). Composed nearly 100 scores for films, including for Kurosawa's *Rashōmon* (1951). Other works include a piano concerto (1946); orchestral pieces (*Kodai no bukyoku,* 1938; *Metamorphosis,* 1953; *Yūkara,* 1955); chamber music (including a string quartet, 1950).

Haydn, (Franz) Joseph (b. Rohrau, 31 Mar. 1732; d. Vienna, 31 May 1809). Composer. Boy chorister at St. Stephen's in Vienna from 1740. Haydn received instruction in voice, violin, and keyboard, but little general education except for a smattering of Latin. As Haydn's voice changed, his position as a chorister became increasingly untenable. In late 1749 he was dismissed peremptorily over a practical joke. He made ends meet by giving violin and keyboard lessons, working as a free-lance musician in churches, and performing in (and sometimes composing for) groups playing the open-air evening serenades so popular in Vienna. At the same time he began an intensive study of counterpoint (using the writings of Fux) and figured bass (using Mattheson).

Through Metastasio, he met Nicola Porpora. Haydn proposed to serve as Porpora's factotum in return for instruction; although this arrangement was undertaken for no more than three months, Haydn later credited Porpora with teaching him "the true fundamentals of composition." His first patron was Freiherr Karl Joseph von Fürnberg. In 1759 Count Karl von Morzin made the composer his music director. Haydn began the imposing series of symphonies and string quartets for which he is best known.

Count Morzin, early in 1761, decided to disband his costly orchestra. Apparent disaster turned into a stroke of luck when Prince Paul Anton Esterházy, himself a sometime composer and one of Europe's most lavish patrons of music, heard that Haydn was available and invited him to become the assistant music director. The prince died in 1762. Nikolaus, his brother and successor, possessed an appetite for music that was, if anything, even keener than his predecessor's. Daily music making often meant accompanying the prince in divertimentos for his favored instrument, the baryton, typically in concert with viola and cello (Haydn created a repertory of at least 126 such works in the years 1765–76); it sometimes meant playing solo keyboard works. Twice a week, orchestral "academies" were held.

In 1766 Prince Nikolaus moved his entourage into a palace, Esterháza. About the same time Haydn first encountered keyboard music by Carl Philipp Emanuel Bach. Haydn's remarkable musical development both before and after 1766 can be seen, above all, in the symphonies and keyboard sonatas. Beginning with his opus 9 string quartets of 1769, Haydn began writing some of his most challenging and original music for chamber groups as well. For Prince Nikolaus, more music lover than musician, Haydn's increasingly complex musical style seems to have brought challenges that were not always welcome. By the time of the move to Esterháza he had written for Prince Nikolaus five one-act operas and a two-act intermezzo. At Esterháza a 400-seat theater and a smaller marionette theater were built; Haydn wrote for both. During the same period he also composed a series of liturgical works for the prince's chapel.

By the early 1780s Haydn had become one of the best-known and most sought-after composers in Europe. For Lisbon he revised his oratorio; for Cadíz he wrote *Die sieben letzten Wörte unseres Erlösers am Kreuze;* for the King of Naples he penned several concertos; for Paris he revised *La vera costanza* (as *Laurette*) and composed six symphonies. During the 1780s Haydn composed operas, symphonies, and quartets that further expanded the horizons of those genres. When in Vienna he met and kept in touch with Mozart, whose music impressed him profoundly. In September 1790 Prince Nikolaus died. His son and successor, Anton, immediately disbanded the orchestra and opera at Esterháza.

The English entrepreneur Johann Peter Salomon convinced Haydn to visit London. He stopped in Bonn, where he was shown one of Beethoven's cantatas, and was sufficiently impressed to accept the young man as a student. In England Haydn wrote his last opera and his best-known symphonies, trios, and sonatas. All his London concerts were well received, but the public seems to have especially liked the symphony Hob. I:94 with its unexpected timpani outburst in the slow movement; the work was soon heard again at a benefit concert, christened "the Surprise" by the organizer of that occasion.

Haydn returned to Vienna in July 1792 only to set out for England again in January 1794. The second visit was, if possible, even more successful than the first, and King George III asked Haydn to move to London permanently. He returned to Austria in August 1795. A new Prince Nikolaus pressed Haydn back into limited service to provide an annual Mass for the Esterházy chapel. As it happened, Haydn's own thoughts had centered on choral music ever since he had attended the Handel commemoration at Westminster Abbey. In the last eight years of his creative life Haydn produced an unbroken series of masterpieces that constitute his most public and his most private utterances: on the one hand, two large-scale oratorios and six Masses in which Austrian choral tradition is fused with the classical symphony; on the other the quartets of opp. 76, 77, and 103.

Works: *Operas. Acide* (1762; rev. 1773), *La cantarina* (1766), *Lo speziale* (1768), *Le pescatrici* (1769), *L'infedeltà delusa* (1773), *L'incontro improvviso* (1775), *Il mondo della luna* (1777), *La vera costanza* (1779; rev. 1785), *La fedeltà premiata* (1780), *Orlando paladino* (1782), *Armida* (1783), *L'anima del filosofo* (1791).

Oratorios. Il ritorno di Tobia (1774–75; rev.

1784), *Die *Schöpfung* (1796–98), *Die *Jahreszeiten* (1799–1801).

Masses (15). Missa (*Nelsonmesse,* 1798).

Symphonies (107; Hob. I numbers in approximate order of composition, following Gerlach, 1969–70, and Larsen, 1988). 1761: 6 (Le *matin), 7 (Le midi); 1761–62: 3, 8 (Le soir); 1765: 31 (Hornsignal); 1768: 49 (La passione); 1770–71: 44 (*Trauersinfonie); 1772: 45 (*Farewell); 1775–76: 69 (Laudon); 1779: 63 (La Roxelane); 1782: 73 (La *chasse); 1785: 83 (La *poule), 85 (La *reine); 1786: 82 (L'*ours); 1789: 92 (*Oxford); (nos. 93–104, *London Symphonies) 1791: 94 (*Surprise), 96 (*Miracle); 1793–94: 100 (*Military), 101 (*Clock); 1795: 103 (*Drum-Roll), 104 (*London).

String quartets (in sets of 6, except as noted; publication date, then approximate composition date). Include: op. 20 (*Sun Quartets, 1774, 1772); op. 33 (*Russian Quartets, 1782, 1781); op. 50 (*Prussian Quartets, 1787, 1787); op. 51 (*Die 7 letzten Worte* [see Seven (Last) Words], 1787, 1787); op. 54, 1–3 (*Tost Quartets, 1789, 1788); op. 55, 1–3 (Tost Quartets, 1790, 1788); op. 64 (Tost Quartets, no. 5 *Lark, 1791, 1790); op. 71 (1795–96, 1793); op. 76 (Erdödy Quartets, no. 2 *Quintenquartett, no. 3 *Emperor, no. 4 Sunrise, 1799, 1797); op. 77; op. 103).

Keyboard trios (42) and sonatas (58).

Haydn, (Johann) Michael (b. Rohrau, Lower Austria, bapt. 14 Sept. 1737; d. Salzburg, 10 Aug. 1806). Composer. Brother of Franz Joseph. Chorister at St. Stephen's from about 1745; 1757, received a post at the court of the Bishop of Grosswardein (now northern Romania); 1763, *Konzertmeister* to Archbishop Schrattenbach in Salzburg. Mozart's successor as court and cathedral organist. From 1787, violin instructor for the court (succeeding Leopold Mozart). Composed more than 400 sacred works; stage works (*Die Wahrheit der Natur,* 1769; *Der englische Patriot,* ca. 1779; *Die Ährenleserin,* 1788; incidental music to Voltaire's *Zayre,* 1777); oratorios (*Oratorium de Passione Domini nostri Jesu Christi,* ca. 1775) and cantatas (*Ninfe in belli,* 1765; *Die Jubelfeyer,* 1787); some 40 symphonies; concertos; divertimentos and other ensemble works; chamber music (12 string quartets, string sonatas).

Haydn Quartets. Popular name for the six quartets by Mozart K. 387, 421, 428, 458, 464, and 465, composed in the years 1782–85 and dedicated to Haydn.

Haydn Variations. A set of eight variations and a finale by Brahms on a theme entitled "St. Anthony's Chorale," the second movement of a divertimento for winds Hob. II:46*, probably not by Haydn. Brahms's work was composed in 1873 and published in two versions: one for orchestra (op. 56a) and one for two pianos (op. 56b).

Haye, hay, hey, heye [Eng.; perhaps fr. Fr. *haie*]. A dance described in the 16th century as a type of *branle. It is a group dance using simple steps and one in which rows of dancers interweave in a serpentine fashion. In the 17th century, it was identified with the *canarie.

Haym, Nicola Francesco (b. Rome, 6 July 1678; d. London, 11 Aug. 1729). Cellist, librettist, and composer. Played under Corelli in Rome (1694–1700). Served the second Duke of Bedford in London, 1701–11, later the Duke of Chandos. An important figure in London's Italian opera. Wrote substitution arias for operas by Bononcini and Scarlatti, and various pasticcios, and adapted many libretti for Handel, including *Giulio Cesare* (1724). He also performed chamber music and was active as a teacher. His works include sacred and secular vocal music as well as sonatas.

Hayne van Ghizeghem (b. ca. 1445; d. between 1472 and 1497). Composer. Served Charles the Bold of Burgundy as a musician from boyhood until at least 1472; perhaps spent some years thereafter at the French royal court. Composed chansons ("Allez regrets," "De tous biens plaine").

Hays, Will(iam) S(hakespeare) (b. Louisville, Ky., 19 July 1837; d. there, 23 July 1907). Songwriter. Published more than 300 songs, including sentimental ballads ("Evangeline"), Irish songs ("Mollie Darling," "Nora O'Neal"), Civil War songs ("Drummer Boy of Shiloh"), pseudo-spirituals, and minstrel songs.

Hb. [Fr.]. Abbr. for *hautbois,* oboe.

Head arrangement. A collaborative, memorized composition for jazz ensemble. The early *big bands of Duke Ellington, Bennie Moten, and Count Basie performed such arrangements.

Head-motive. A motive occurring at the beginning of each of the movements of a work; also *motto. The term is especially applied to the *cyclic Masses of the 15th century and later.

Head voice. The higher register of the voice, as compared with chest voice. See Register, Voice.

Heavy Metal. A subgenre of *rock music characterized by sluggish rhythms and high amplification applied to *blues-derived musical forms. The style flourished in the late 1960s and 1970s in the U.S., England, and Europe, and was generally associated with drug-taking, working-class audiences. An early and important exponent was Jimi Hendrix. Heavy Metal enjoyed a renewed popularity in the 1980s.

Hebriden, Die, or **Fingals Höhle** [Ger., The Hebrides, or Fingal's Cave]. A concert overture by Mendelssohn, op. 26 (1830, revised in 1832). Originally called *Die einsame Insel* (The Lonely Island), it was inspired by a visit to the famous cave in Scotland during his first tour through the British Isles in 1829.

Heckelclarina [Ger. *Heckelklarina*]. A conical-bore, single-reed wind instrument devised in 1890 by the firm of Wilhelm Heckel of Biebrich to play the part of the shepherd's pipe in Wagner's *Tristan und Isolde* (1857–59). It is not certain if it was actually ever constructed.

Heckelphone [Ger. *Heckelphon*]. A wooden, conical-bore, double-reed woodwind instrument invented in 1904 by the firm of Wilhelm Heckel of Biebrich. It is similar to the bass (or barytone) oboe in range and construction, but it has a larger bore and produces a tone closer to that of the bassoon or saxophone than to the English-horn sound of the low oboes. The instrument has a bulb-shaped bell that is usually fitted with a floor support at the bottom, with the tone opening(s) moved to the side. The heckelphone was originally made in three sizes, but only the bass (pitched in C with range from A to g'') was much used. Works employing it include Richard Strauss's *Salome* (1905). See ill. under Reed.

Hefti, Neal (b. Hastings, Nebr., 29 Oct. 1922). Jazz, film, and television composer and arranger. Played trumpet with Woody Herman (1944–45), who recorded his "The Good Earth" and "Wild Root" (both 1945). From 1950, composed and arranged for Count Basie ("Li'l Darlin'" and "Whirlybird," 1957). Composed television and film soundtracks, including *Batman* (1965–68), *Lord Love a Duck* (1965), *Barefoot in the Park,* and *The Odd Couple* (both 1967).

Heftig [Ger.]. Violent, impetuous, passionate.

Hegar, Friedrich (b. Basel, 11 Oct. 1841; d. Zurich, 2 June 1927). Composer. Pupil of Hauptmann, Rietz, and David. Conductor of the Tonhalle Orchestra, Zurich, 1865–1906; of the mixed chorus, 1865–1901, and several other choruses; 1876–1914, director of the Music School (later Conservatory). His oratorio *Manasse* (1885; rev. 1888) was widely performed, but he is historically important for his male choruses, marking a stage in that genre's development.

Heiden, Bernhard (b. Frankfurt am Main, 24 Aug. 1910). Composer. Studied with Hindemith. Moved to the U.S. in 1935. Taught at Indiana Univ. to 1981. Composed an opera, music for dance and for Shakespearean plays, and a film score; 2 symphonies, concertos, and other orchestral works; much chamber music including string quartets, a woodwind quintet, sonatas for various instruments; choral and solo vocal music.

Heifetz, Jascha (b. Vilna, Lithuania, 2 Feb [20 Jan. Julian cal.] 1899; d. Los Angeles, 10 Dec. 1987). Violinist. Studied with Leopold Auer. Debut in Berlin, 1914. Emigrated to the U.S. in 1917. Cofounded the Hebrew Music Conservatory in Palestine, 1926. World tour, 1934. Played and recorded trios with Rubinstein and Piatigorsky. From 1959 taught at the Univ. of Southern California. Commissioned and played concertos by Walton, Korngold, Rozsa, and others. Published many transcriptions, including the *Hora staccato,* and popular songs, under the name Jim Hoyl.

Heinichen, Johann David (b. Krössuln, near Weissenfels, 17 Apr. 1683; d. Dresden, 16 July 1729). Theorist and composer. Student and assistant of Kuhnau. Opera director in Leipzig, 1709; journeyed to Italy in 1710, composing operas in Venice. Kapellmeister in Dresden from 1717. Composed a great variety of sacred and secular vocal music and instrumental works; best known for his treatise *Der Generalbass in der Composition* (1728, partially reworked from a publication of 1711), an account of continuo practice and of the technical and aesthetic aspects of composition.

Heinrich, Anthony Philip (b. Schönbüchel [now Krásný Búk], Bohemia, 11 Mar. 1781; d. New York, 3 May 1861). Composer. Emigrated to the U.S. by 1810; settled in Kentucky. In 1817 in Lexington, organized the first known U.S. performance of a Beethoven symphony. Lived in London, 1826–31; in New York, 1837–61. Composed songs and piano pieces published in his collections *The Dawning of Music in Kentucky* op. 1 (1820), *The Western Minstrel* op. 2 (1820), and *The Sylviad* op. 3 (1823–26); after 1831, produced large orchestral works, mostly on programmatic or descriptive American subjects.

Heiter [Ger.]. Serene, merry, cheerful.

Heldenleben, Ein [Ger., A Hero's Life]. An autobiographical symphonic poem by Richard Strauss, op. 40 (1897–98). It includes quotations of themes from other works by Strauss and depicts the composer's trials (e.g., hostile music critics) and triumphs.

Heldentenor [Ger., heroic tenor]. A tenor voice of considerable brilliance, power, and endurance, suitable for singing the roles of the heros in Wagner's operas, e.g., Tristan and Siegfried.

Helicon [Fr. *hélicon;* Ger. *Helikon;* It. *helicon, elicon;* Sp. *helicón*]. A circular brass instrument possibly first made in Russia about 1845. Ignaz Stowasser of Vienna made F, E♭, and BB♭ sizes in 1849. It was subsequently made in all sizes, sometimes with nonfunctional tubing, and was popular in European and American bands. Also called a cavalry horn, it rested

on the left shoulder and under the right arm and could be played comfortably with one hand. A later instrument embodying this idea was John Philip Sousa's *sousaphone.

Hellendaal, Pieter (b. Rotterdam, bapt. 1 Apr. 1721; d. Cambridge, 19 Apr. 1799). Composer, organist, and violinist. Pupil of Tartini. Settled in London, 1751. Organist at Pembroke Hall, Cambridge, from 1762; at Peterhouse Chapel from 1777. Works include violin sonatas; *Six Grand Concertos,* (1758); *Three Grand Lessons,* keyboard, violin, and continuo (ca. 1790); vocal works (including canons, catches, and glees).

Heller, Stephen [István] (b. Pest, 15 May 1813; d. Paris, 14 Jan. 1888). Composer. Lived in Augsburg, 1830–38; then moved to Paris. Friend of Berlioz. Composed almost exclusively for the piano, including 4 sonatas, many collections of character pieces and dances, variations, opera potpourris, etc.; best known for etudes, especially *L'art du phraser* op. 16 (1840?) and opp. 45, 46, 47 (1844?).

Hellermann, William (b. Milwaukee, 15 July 1939). Composer and guitarist. Pupil of Luening, Chou Wen-chung, Ussachevsky, and Wolpe. Taught at Columbia 1967–72. Has produced "Eyescores" (visually oriented works); performance art (*Squeak,* chair, 1977; *Progress in Music Demands Daily Drill,* tape and sculpture, 1982); pieces for orchestra, for variable ensembles (*Frozen Music Is Not Melted Architecture,* 1975), for guitar, piano, and voices; many works involve tape and mixed media.

Helm, Everett (Burton) (b. Minneapolis, 17 July 1913). Composer and writer on music. Taught in the U.S., 1940–50; then moved to Europe. Editor of *Musical America,* 1961–63. Authored several books, including German volumes on Liszt and Bartók, and, in English, *Composer, Performer, Public* (1970) and *Music and Tomorrow's Public* (1981). Compositions include operas (*Adam and Eve,* 1951; *The Siege of Tottenburg,* 1956); 2 piano concertos and other orchestral works; chamber music and songs.

Helps, Robert (Eugene) (b. Passaic, N.J., 23 Sept. 1928). Composer and pianist. Pupil of Sessions. Has taught at New England Conservatory, the Manhattan School, Princeton, and the Univ. of South Florida at Tampa (from 1980). Noted as an interpreter of contemporary piano music. His own works employ twelve-tone procedures; they include a symphony and other orchestral and chamber music; many piano works; and songs (*Gossamer Noons,* soprano and orchestra, 1977).

Hemidemisemiquaver. In British terminology, the sixty-fourth note. See Note.

Hemiola, hemiolia [Gr., Lat. *sesquialtera*]. The ratio 3:2. In terms of pitch, it is the ratio of the lengths of two strings that together sound a perfect fifth [see Interval]. In terms of rhythm, it refers to the use of three notes of equal value in the time normally occupied by two notes of equal value. In *mensural notation of the 14th century and later, it is often expressed with red notes if the prevailing notation is black, or black notes if the prevailing notation is white. The resulting rhythm can be expressed in modern terms as a substitution of 3/2 for 6/4 or as two measures of 3/4 in which quarter notes are tied across the bar, as shown in the example.

This rhythmic gesture is common in the music of 15th-century composers such as Dufay, is a characteristic feature of the French Baroque *courante and the Viennese *waltz, and occurs often in the music of Schumann and Brahms (e.g., the opening measures of the third symphonies of both composers).

Hemitonic [fr. Gr., Lat. *hemitonium*, semitone]. Characterized by or including semitones.

Henderson, Fletcher (Hamilton, Jr.) [Smack] (b. Cuthbert, Ga., 18 Dec. 1897; d. New York, 29 Dec. 1952). Jazz bandleader, arranger, and pianist. From 1924, led a group in New York which became the first important jazz big band; sidemen included Louis Armstrong, Coleman Hawkins, Benny Carter. Arranged for Benny Goodman ("King Porter Stomp," 1935) until 1941, then resumed bandleading (to 1950). Recordings include "Copenhagen," "Shanghai Shuffle" (both 1924), "Sugar Foot Stomp" (1925), "The Stampede" (1926), "King Porter's Stomp" [*sic*] (1933), "Wrappin' It Up" (1934).

Henderson, Joe [Joseph A.] (b. Lima, Ohio, 24 Apr. 1937). Jazz tenor saxophonist. Led a quintet with Kenny Dorham, 1962–64; member of Horace Silver's hard bop quintet, 1964–66; joined Herbie Hancock (1969–70), then led groups in San Francisco. Also worked with Freddie Hubbard in the 1980s. Led a quintet including Wynton Marsalis in *Lush Life,* a recording of works by Billy Strayhorn (1992).

Hendrix, Jimi [James Marshall] (b. Seattle, Wash., 27 Nov. 1942; d. London, 18 Sept. 1970). Guitarist and singer. Played for Little Richard and others; 1964, led Jimmy James and the Blue Flames; 1966, formed the Jimi Hendrix Experience in London. Pioneered the use of electronic sound modification through distortion devices and feedback; performances included guitar tricks, use of the guitar as a dramatic prop, and destruction of equipment. His most popular recordings were those of Bob Dylan's "All Along the Watchtower" (1968) and his own

"Purple Haze" (1967); appeared at the Monterey Pop Festival in 1967 and at Woodstock in 1969.

Henry, Pierre (b. Paris, 9 Dec. 1927). Composer. Pupil of Boulanger and Messiaen. At the electronic music studios of French Radio, led the Groupe de recherche de musique concrète (1950–58). Wrote the first electronic work for the stage (*Orphée,* Donaueschingen, 1953). Long collaboration with the choreographer Béjart (incl. *Nijinsky, clown de Dieu,* 1971). Other works include *Mise en musique du corticolart* (1971), *L'apocalypse de Jean* (1968), and *Pierre réfléchies* (1982).

Henschel, (Isidor) George [Georg] (b. Breslau, 18 Feb. 1850; d. Aviemore, Scotland, 10 Sept. 1934). Singer and conductor. Baritone soloist; debut in London, 1877. Conductor, Boston Symphony, 1881–84; married an American singer, Lillian Bailey (1860–1901), with whom he often appeared in joint recitals. Wrote *Personal Recollections of Johannes Brahms* (1907). Composed operas, sacred music, songs, instrumental pieces.

Hensel, Fanny (Cäcilie) Mendelssohn (Bartholdy) (b. Hamburg, 14 Nov. 1805; d. Berlin, 14 May 1847). Composer. Sister of Felix Mendelssohn. Pupil of Zelter; considered equal in musical talent to Felix, but her father (and later Felix) objected to a public career for her. Composed choral music, piano pieces, chamber music, songs.

Henselt, (Georg Martin) Adolf von (b. Schwabach, near Nuremberg, 9 May 1814; d. Bad Warmbrunn [now Cieplice], Silesia, 10 Oct. 1889). Composer and pianist. Studied with Hummel and Sechter. Toured Europe 1834–38; then settled in St. Petersburg, becoming a teacher and pianist to the empress. Works include a Piano Concerto op. 16; *12 études de concert* op. 2 (no. 6, "Si oiseau j'étais"), *12 études de salon* op. 5, and other piano pieces.

Henze, Hans Werner (b. Gütersloh, Westphalia, 1 July 1926). Composer and conductor. Pupil of Wolfgang Fortner and René Leibowitz. In 1953 he left Germany for Italy. Has made use of twelve-tone methods, blues and jazz progressions, taped sounds. Works include operas and music theater (*Boulevard Solitude,* 1952; *König Hirsch,* 1956, rev. 1962 as *Il re cervo; Der Prinz von Homburg,* 1960; *Elegie für junge Liebende,* 1961; *Der junge Lord,* 1965; *The Bassarids,* 1966; *We Come to the River,* 1976; *The English Cat,* 1983; *Das verratene Meer,* 1990); ballets (*Ondine,* 1957; *Orpheus,* 1978); film scores and incidental music; numerous orchestral pieces (including 8 symphonies; 2 violin concertos; *Sieben Liebeslieder,* cello and orchestra, 1985; *Allegro brillante,* 1989); 5 string quartets and other chamber music; a few works for piano or harpsichord; several works for chorus and instrumental ensemble or orchestra; solo vocal music (*Apollo et Hyazinthus,* alto, instruments, 1948; 5 Neapolitan songs, baritone and orchestra, 1956; *3 Auden Pieces,* voice and piano, 1983).

Heptachord. A collection of seven pitches, especially the diatonic *scale.

Herabstimmen [Ger.]. To tune down or lower the pitch, e.g., of a string.

Herabstrich [Ger.]. Down-bow. See Bowing (1).

Heraufstimmen [Ger.]. To tune upward or raise the pitch, e.g., of a string.

Heraufstrich [Ger.]. Up-bow. See Bowing (1).

Herbert, Victor (August) (b. Dublin, 1 Feb. 1859; d. New York, 26 May 1924). Composer, conductor, and cellist. Emigrated to the U.S., 1886. Conductor of the Pittsburgh Symphony, 1898–1904, after which he founded his own orchestra. Cofounder of the American Society of Composers, Authors, and Publishers (ASCAP). Works include 2 operas (*Natoma,* 1900; and *Madeleine,* 1914), over 40 operettas (*Babes in Toyland,* 1903; *Naughty Marietta,* 1910; *Sweethearts,* 1913); scenes for Ziegfeld's Follies; film scores (*The Fall of a Nation,* 1916; *Indian Summer,* 1919) and incidental music; 2 cello concertos, *Irish Rhapsody* (1892), *Columbus* (1903), and other orchestral music; *The Captive* (a symphonic poem for solo voices, chorus, and orchestra, 1891); chamber works; piano pieces; choral music; songs.

Herbig, Günther (b. Osti nad Labem, Czechoslovakia, 30 Nov. 1931). Conductor. Held several conducting posts, including at the East Berlin Symphony, 1966–72 (chief conductor, 1977–78). Music director of the Dresden Philharmonic beginning 1970; of the Detroit Symphony, 1984–90; of the Toronto Symphony from 1990.

Herbst, Johannes (b. Kempten, Swabia, 23 July 1735; d. Salem, N.C., 15 Jan. 1812). Composer. Fled to America, 1786; 1811, moved to Salem, N.C., as a bishop in the Moravian church. His personal library is an important early American music collection, containing nearly 1,000 songs and anthems; vocal/choral works by Haydn, Mozart, and others; and keyboard music. Among his own works are nearly 200 anthems and 150 solo songs.

Herman, Woody [Woodrow Charles] (b. Milwaukee, 16 May 1913; d. Los Angeles, 29 Oct. 1987). Jazz bandleader, clarinetist, alto saxophonist, and singer. From 1936, led big bands, beginning with a repertory of swing music and moving into newer styles. Among his sidemen were Stan Getz, Zoot Sims, Serge Chaloff (in the saxophone section of tenors and baritone, known as the "Four Brothers"). Recordings include "Woodchopper's Ball" (1939), "Caldonia" (1945), "Summer Sequence" (1946–47), "Four Brothers" (1947), "Early Autumn" (1948). Stravinsky composed the *Ebony Concerto* for Herman's First Herd (1945).

Hernando (y Palomar), Rafael (José María) (b. Madrid, 31 May 1822; d. there, 10 July 1888). Composer. Pupil of Carnicer, Albéniz, and Auber. Composed mainly zarzuelas (*Colegiales y soldados,* 1849; *El duende,* 1848); also sacred music. In 1852 became secretary, later professor, Madrid Conservatory.

Hero's Life, A. See *Heldenleben, Ein.*

Hérold, (Louis Joseph) Ferdinand (b. Paris, 28 Jan. 1791; d. there, 19 Jan. 1833). Composer. Son of a piano teacher and composer. Pupil of Méhul. Lived in Naples, 1813–15. Returned to Paris, becoming maestro al cembalo at the Théâtre-Italien; chief vocal coach at the Opéra from 1826. Composed operas, including *Marie* (1825), *Zampa* (1831), *Le pré aux clercs* (1832); also 2 symphonies, 4 piano concertos, 10 piano sonatas, much piano music, including many opera potpourris.

Herrmann, Bernard (b. New York, 29 June 1911; d. Los Angeles, 24 Dec. 1975). Composer and conductor. Pupil of Grainger, Philip James, Wagenaar, and Stoessel. Composed music for CBS radio programs including Welles's *The War of the Worlds,* 1938. His 61 film scores include *Citizen Kane* (1941); *Vertigo* (1958); *Psycho* (1960); *Fahrenheit 451* (1966); *All That Money Can Buy* (Oscar, 1941); *Anna and the King of Siam* (1946). Wrote the music for several television series (*The Alfred Hitchcock Hour, Twilight Zone*). Conducted the CBS Symphony (1940–45). Also composed ballets, 3 operas (*A Christmas Carol,* 1954); a musical; orchestral and chamber music; vocal works.

Herschel, William [Friedrich Wilhelm] (b. Hannover, 15 Nov. 1738; d. Slough, near Windsor, 25 Aug. 1822). Musician and astronomer. Settled in England, where he established a reputation as violinist and conductor; from 1766, organist at the Octagon Chapel, Bath. Discovered the planet Uranus in 1781. Among his works are 24 symphonies; concertos; trio sonatas; capriccios for solo violin; keyboard pieces.

Herstrich [Ger.]. Down-bow. See Bowing (1).

Hertz [abbr. Hz.]. In *acoustics, a measure of frequency equal to one cycle per second and named after the German physicist Heinrich R. Hertz (1857–94).

Hertz, Alfred (b. Frankfurt am Main, 15 July 1872; d. San Francisco, 17 April 1942). Conductor. Conducted opera in Germany, 1891–1902; 1902–15, at the New York Metropolitan Opera; there led the first American performances of *Parsifal* (without the approval of Bayreuth), *Salome, Rosenkavelier,* and the premiere of Humperdinck's *Königskinder.* Conductor, San Francisco Symphony, 1915–30; inaugurated Hollywood Bowl Concerts, 1922.

Hervé [Florimond Ronger] (b. Houdain, Pas de Calais, 30 June 1825; d. Paris, 3 Nov. 1892). Composer. Pupil of Auber. Worked as an organist and in the theater, often singing in his own musical comedies. From 1849, music director at the Odéon; ran his own theater, the Folies-concertantes (Folies-nouvelles), 1854–56. His operettas include *L'oeil crevé,* 1867; *Chilpéric,* 1868; *Mam'zelle Nitouche,* 1883. Worked in London, 1870–71 and 1886–92.

Hervorgehoben [Ger.]. Prominent, emphasized.

Hervortretend [Ger.]. Brought out, prominent.

Herz, Henri (b. Vienna, 6 Jan. 1803; d. Paris, 5 Jan. 1888). Pianist. Pupil of Reicha. Toured Europe from the 1830s, also North and South America (1845–51). Taught at the Paris Conservatory, 1842–74. Also a successful piano manufacturer; with brother Jacques Simon Herz (1794–1880) founded École spéciale de piano, Paris, which also housed a concert hall. Published over 200 works of piano salon music; also 8 concertos; a sonata; a piano trio; a collection of scales and exercises; piano method.

Herzlich [Ger.]. Heartfelt, affectionate.

Herzogenberg, (Leopold) Heinrich (Picot de Peccaduc), Freiherr von (b. Graz, 10 June 1843; d. Wiesbaden, 9 Oct. 1900). Composer. Conducted the Bach Society in Leipzig, 1875–85; from 1885, taught composition at the Berlin Hochschule für Musik. Composed much sacred music, oratorios, cantatas, part songs, solo songs, 3 symphonies, much chamber and piano music. Married Brahms's close friend Elisabeth von Stockhausen (1847–92).

Heseltine, Philip. See Warlock, Peter.

Heses [Ger.]. B-double-flat. See Pitch names.

Hesitation waltz. See Boston dip waltz, Boston waltz.

Hess, Myra (b. London, 25 Feb. 1890; d. there 25 Nov. 1965). Pianist. Studied with Tobias Matthay. Debut 1907 in London, playing Beethoven's Fourth Concerto. Later joined her cousin Irene Scharrer to concertize as a duo pianist. After World War II she excised many Baroque and contemporary pieces from her repertory, retaining Bach (often in her own transcriptions), Scarlatti, and the standard composers from Mozart to Brahms.

Heterophony. The simultaneous statement, especially in improvised performance, of two or more different versions of what is essentially the same melody (as distinct from *polyphony). It often takes the form of a melody combined with an ornamented version of itself, the former sung and the latter played on an instrument. The technique is widely found in musics outside the tradition of Western art music.

Heure espagnole, L' [Fr., The Spanish Hour]. Opera in one act by Ravel (libretto by Franc-Nohain [pseud. of Maurice Le Grand] after his own comedy), produced in Paris in 1911. Setting: Toledo, Spain, in the 18th century.

Hewitt, James (b. Dartmoor? 4 June 1770; d. Boston, 2 Aug. 1827). Composer, publisher, and conductor. Moved to New York, 1792. Organist at Trinity Church, Boston, 1811–16. As a publisher, issued some 650 compositions, including his own. Composed stage works (*The Tars from Tripoli,* 1806–7); ballets; orchestral overtures (*The Fourth of July,* 1801; *Yankee Doodle with Variations,* 1807–10; *Lafayette's Quick Step,* ca. 1824); sacred hymns and anthems; and many songs.

Hewitt, John Hill (b. New York, 12 July 1801; d. Baltimore, 7 Oct. 1890). Composer. Son of James Hewitt. Composed dance music, marches, the oratorio *Jepthah,* theater music, sentimental songs, Confederate songs. Also wrote plays, stories, and poetry.

Hexachord [fr. Gr., six string]. A collection of six pitches. Hexachords figure prominently in the history of *solmization and in twelve-tone theory. For their use in the latter, see Twelve-tone music.

Solmization by means of a system of hexachords, which prevailed in the 11th–16th centuries, was traditionally attributed to Guido of Arezzo, who in his *Epistola de ignoto cantu* (ca. 1028–29) refers to the pitches of the hexachord with the six vocables *ut, re, mi, fa, sol, la,* the initial syllables of the first six lines of the hymn "Ut queant laxis," which begin on the pitches c d e f g a, respectively. According to the "Guidonian" system, there were three main types of hexachord: those beginning on C's, F's, and G's. Each hexachord was built from the interval succession tone, tone, semitone, tone, tone, the six syllables being assigned to the six pitches in ascending order. The position of the semitone was critical, always occurring between the syllables *mi* and *fa.* Hexachords formed on C's (e.g., c d e f g a) were called natural hexachords *(hexachordum naturale);* those formed on G's (e.g., g a b♮ c' d' e') were called hard hexachords *(hexachordum durum),* since they contain B♮ (hard b or *b durum,* written with a square-shaped b, the origin of the modern natural sign [see Accidental]); those on F's (e.g., f g a b♭ c' d') soft hexachords *(hexachordum molle),* since they contain

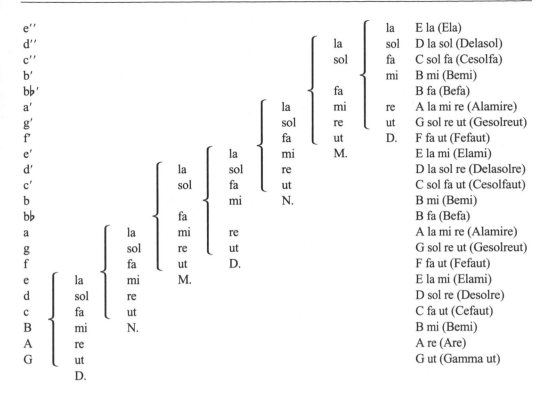

a B♭ (soft b or *b molle,* written with a rounded b, the origin of the flat sign). Using these three types of hexachord, theorists described the *gamut from G to e′′ as a complex of seven overlapping hexachords, as shown in the accompanying table (where D = *durum,* N = *naturale,* and M = *molle*). Pitches lying within the seven hexachords constituted *musica recta;* those lying outside were classed as *musica ficta.*

Each pitch of the gamut is identified by its pitch letter and the syllable or syllables corresponding to its position in one or more hexachords. Thus, middle C may be designated C *sol fa ut,* whereas C one octave below would be C *fa ut,* and C two octaves above that C *sol fa.* Where the same name occurs in two different octaves (e.g., G *sol re ut*), the two pitches are distinguished as high *(acutum)* or low *(grave).* In assigning single syllables to single pitches for purposes of singing, melodies that extend beyond the range of a single hexachord are accommodated by means of mutation, which allows free transfer from one hexachord to another by way of pitches common to both hexachords. Such pitches would have a solmization syllable in each hexachord. During the 15th century, increasing use of chromatic alteration prompted theorists to introduce hexachords starting on pitch classes other than C, F, and G. See Solmization, *Musica ficta.*

Heyden [Haiden], **Sebald** (b. Bruck, near Erlangen, 8 Dec. 1499; d. Nuremberg, 9 July 1561). Composer and theorist. From 1521 Kantor and school rector at the Spitalkirche in Nuremberg; from 1525 rector of the school of St. Sebald there. Published didactic treatises *Musicae stoicheiōsis* (1532) and *Musicae* (1537). Composed a Passion, Psalms, and other Protestant church music (including the chorale "O mensch, bewein dein Sünde gross").

Hichiriki [Jap.]. A small Japanese oboe with seven finger holes and two thumb holes, used in *gagaku* music. See ill. under Instrument.

Hidalgo, Juan (b. Madrid, 1612–16; d. there, 30 Mar. 1685). Composer. Entered the royal chapel around 1631. Composed the earliest extant Spanish opera, *Celos aun del aire matan* (Madrid, 1660) and other stage works with texts by Pedro Calderón de la Barca. Other works include 2 Masses, motets, and over 100 secular *villancicos* and *tonos humanos.*

Hidden fifths, octaves. See Parallel fifths, octaves.

Higgins, Billy (b. Los Angeles, 11 Oct. 1936). Jazz drummer. Member of Ornette Coleman's free jazz quartet, 1959–60. Toured with Thelonious Monk (1960) and Sonny Rollins (1962–63) and recorded extensively, most often with hard bop musicians. Worked with pianist Cedar Walton from 1966; occasionally rejoined Coleman. From 1981 a member of the Timeless All Stars sextet.

Highland bagpipe [Gael. *pìob mhór*]. The *bagpipe of the Scottish highlands. It is mouth blown, with a double-reed *chanter and three single-reed *drones.

Hi-hat. A pair of cymbals mounted horizontally on a stand and clashed by means of a pedal. It is a regular component of the *drum set used in jazz and popular music, having first appeared in 1927.

Hildegard of [von] **Bingen** (b. Bemersheim, near Alzey, Rheinhessen, 1098; d. Rupertsberg, near Bingen, 17 Sept. 1179). Abbess, mystic, writer, and composer. Founder of a monastery (Rupertsberg) near Bingen. Wrote a liturgical cycle of 77 lyric poems with monophonic music and *Ordo virtutum*, a morality play in verse with 82 melodies, in addition to non-musical writings.

Hill, Alfred (Francis) (b. Melbourne, 16 Nov. 1870; d. Sydney, 30 Oct. 1960). Composer. Studied at the Leipzig Conservatory. Active as a conductor in New Zealand and Australia. His over 500 works include 9 operas (*Tapu*, 1902, on Maori legend), 13 symphonies (no. 1, *Maori*, 1896–1900), 8 string quartets, choral music, *Hinemoa* (cantata, 1895), chamber music, and songs, including Maori settings. Taught at the Austral Orchestral College in Sydney.

Hill, Edward Burlingame (b. Cambridge, Mass., 9 Sept. 1872; d. Francestown, N.H., 9 July 1960). Composer. Studied with Paine, B. J. Lang, Arthur Whiting, Widor, and Chadwick. Taught at Harvard, 1908–40; his students included Bernstein, Thomson, Finney, and Carter. Composed 3 symphonies, a violin concerto, *Stevensonian Suites I and II* (1916–17, 1921–22), and other orchestral works; chamber and piano music (*Jazz Studies*, 1924 and 1935); a cantata (1907).

Hiller, Ferdinand (von) (b. Frankfurt am Main, 24 Oct. 1811; d. Cologne, 11 May 1885). Conductor, pianist, and composer. Pupil of Hummel; friend of Chopin and Berlioz. Lived in Paris (1828–36) and Italy (1836–42); conducted in Leipzig, Dresden, Düsseldorf. From 1850, music director of Cologne; director of the Cologne Conservatory. Wrote books representing a conservative, anti-Wagnerian position. Composed prolifically in most genres.

Hiller, Johann Adam (b. Wendisch-Ossig, near Görlitz, 25 Dec. 1728; d. Leipzig, 16 June 1804). Composer and writer on music. Pupil of Homilius. Hofmeister to Count Brühl in Dresden from 1754. Conducted Leipzig's principal orchestral society, the Grosses Konzert, 1763–71; edited the periodical *Wöchentliche Nachrichten*, 1766–70. With the poet

Christian Felix Weisse, established the first full-blown German singspiel; their collaboration produced *Die verwandelten Weiber oder Der Teufel ist los* (Leipzig, 1766), *Die Jagd* (1770), *Der Dorfbalbier* (1771), *Der Aerndtekranz* (1771), and others. Also composed sacred vocal works, secular cantatas, and song collections; authored a number of musical treatises.

Hiller, Lejaren A(rthur, Jr.) (b. New York, 23 Feb. 1924; d. Buffalo, 26 Jan. 1994). Composer. Pupil of Babbitt and Sessions. Taught chemistry at the Univ. of Illinois, 1952–58; in the music department there from 1958. From 1968, professor of composition at SUNY–Buffalo and co-director with Foss of the Center for Creative and Performing Arts. Wrote music in a variety of styles: twelve-tone and serial, microtonal, aleatory, electronic, and computer assisted. Composed stage works (*Blues Is the Antecedent of It*, an electronic theater fantasy, 1959; *John Italus*, opera, 1989); 2 symphonies and other orchestral works; 7 string quartets (*Illiac Suite*, composed on the computer with Leonard Isaacson, 1957) and other chamber music (*The Fox Trots Again*, 1985); works for piano; electronic music (*HPSCHD*, 1–7 harpsichords and 1–51 tapes, 1967–69, a collaboration with Cage); a few songs.

Hilton, John (1) (d. Cambridge, before 20 Mar. 1608). Composer. Musician at Lincoln Cathedral from at least 1584–94; then organist at Trinity College, Cambridge. Composed one known madrigal; most of the services and anthems attributed to "John Hilton" may be by either him or his son, John Hilton (2).

Hilton, John (2) (b. Cambridge? 1599; buried Westminster, 21 Mar. 1657). Composer. Organist at St. Margaret's, Westminster from 1628. Published songs and rounds (*Ayres or Fa-las for three voyces*, 1627; *Catch As Catch Can*, 1652). Other works, some of which may be confused with those of his father, include services, a Te Deum, anthems, and music for viols.

Himmel, Friedrich Heinrich (b. Treuenbrietzen, 20 Nov. 1765; d. Berlin, 8 June 1814). Composer. Pupil of Naumann. Appointed chamber composer in Berlin, 1792; Kapellmeister, 1795. Toured Russia, Scandinavia, Italy, and central Europe, where his operas were performed. Composed 8 known works for the stage (*Fanchon das Leyermädchen*, 1804; *Vasco da Gama*, 1801; *Frohsinn und Schwärmerey*, 1801; all Berlin); many oratorios and cantatas; nearly 200 songs; concertos and chamber works; clavier music.

Hindemith, Paul (b. Hanau, near Frankfurt am Main, 16 Nov. 1895; d. Frankfurt, 28 Dec. 1963).

Composer, theorist, violist, and conductor. Pupil of Arnold Mendelssohn and Bernard Sekles. Concertmaster of the Frankfurt Opera Orchestra, 1915–23; played in several chamber ensembles. Taught at the Berlin Hochschule für Musik 1927–35. Emigrated to Switzerland in 1938, and to New York in 1940. Taught composition, harmony, and theory at Yale 1940–53. In 1953 moved permanently to Switzerland.

His experience teaching amateurs contributed to his growing sense "of the danger of an esoteric isolationism in music" and his advocacy of music composed for a specific purpose, *Gebrauchsmusik; composed many works motivated by his desire to reduce the distance separating performing amateurs and professional musicians. Explored in turn Brahmsian late Romanticism, Impressionism, Expressionism, and "anti-Romanticism," before arriving at his mature, neoclassical language. The works from his middle period exploit a variety of neo-Baroque elements; in the last three decades of his life, Hindemith cultivated a more tonal idiom.

Works include 7 operas (*Cardillac, 1926; *Mathis der Maler, 1934–35; Die *Harmonie der Welt, 1956–57; The Long Christmas Dinner, 1960), ballets, film and radio scores, and other stage works; some 40 orchestral works, including concertos (for violin, viola, cello, viola d'amore, piano, organ, horn, clarinet), Concerto for Orchestra (1925), symphonies; chamber music for solo instruments, duets (including many sonatas with piano), 6 string quartets, a septet for winds (1948); *Ludus tonalis (1942), 3 sonatas (1936), and other piano music; 3 sonatas for organ (1938–40); Das Unaufhörliche (oratorio, 1931) and other accompanied choral music; Zwölfe Madrigale (à 5, 1958), Messe (1963), and other unaccompanied choral music; Das *Marienleben (1922–23) and other vocal music with ensemble or orchestra; songs with piano. Published books, including Unterweisung im Tonsatz, 3 vols. (1937; 1939; 1970), the first 2 vols. trans. as The Craft of Musical Composition (1941–45); Elementary Training for Musicians (1946); A Composer's World (1952).

Hines, Earl (Kenneth) [Fatha] (b. Duquesne, Pa., 28 Dec. 1903; d. Oakland, Calif., 22 Apr. 1983). Jazz pianist and bandleader. In Chicago worked with Louis Armstrong (1926–28; recording "Weather Bird") and Jimmie Noone (1927–28; "Apex Blues"). His "trumpet style" improvisations helped move jazz piano playing away from approaches based on ragtime. Formed a big band in 1928; in the early 1940s, when Billy Eckstine and Sarah Vaughan were his singers, the group turned toward bop, with Charlie Parker and Dizzy Gillespie among Hines's sidemen.

Joined Armstrong's All Stars (1948–51); led swing and Dixieland groups mainly in the San Francisco Bay area (to 1983); also performed alone, as on the album *Quintessential 1974.*

Hingeston [Hingston, Hinkson], **John** (b. early 17th cent.; buried London, 17 Dec. 1688). Composer. Musician to Cromwell, 1654–58; at court after the Restoration in 1660; later a member of the Chapel Royal. Blow was his pupil, Purcell his apprentice. His music, much of which is lost, includes works for viols, organ, and chorus.

Hinsterbend [Ger.]. Dying away.

Hinstrich [Ger.]. Up-bow. See Bowing (1).

Hinton, Milt(on John) [the Judge] (b. Vicksburg, Miss., 23 June 1910). Jazz double bass player. Worked with Zutty Singleton in Chicago, Cab Calloway (1936–51, recording "Ebony Silhouette," 1941), Count Basie, and Louis Armstrong. From 1951 recorded and performed prolifically as a freelance in New York. Also known for his photographs of jazz musicians.

His, hisis [Ger.]. B-sharp, B-double-sharp. See Pitch names.

Histoire du soldat, L' [Fr., The Soldier's Tale]. A play with music by Stravinsky (libretto by Charles-Ferdinand Ramuz), produced in Lausanne in 1918. The work combines a ballet d'action with a story told in dialogue by the characters and a narrator. The music consists of a number of distinct pieces, including "Marche," "Tango," "Valse," "Ragtime," "Petit Choral," and "Grand Choral," composed for an ensemble of clarinet, bassoon, cornet, trombone, violin, double bass, and percussion. Two suites of music from the work were arranged by the composer in 1919 and 1920, the first scored for piano, clarinet, and violin, the second for the original combination of instruments.

Historia [Lat.]. (1) A Biblical story or a musical setting of such a story. The Passion story was among the favored texts for musical works among German composers of the 16th–18th centuries [see also Passion music]. Works of this type, by Heinrich Schütz and others, are closely related to the *oratorio. (2) See Rhymed Office.

History of music. The history of Western art music has traditionally been divided into periods adapted from other branches of history. This is in part because the discipline of musicology was established somewhat after related humanistic disciplines and in part because many historians of the 19th and 20th centuries believed that the history of music must necessarily follow the outlines of cultural history generally, each period in history expressing itself equally in all political, social, and cultural spheres. The principal periods so identified are (with approximate and oft-debated dates) the *Middle Ages (500–1430), *Renaissance (1430–1600), *Baroque (1600–1750), *Classical (1750–1820), and *Romantic (1820–1910). (No comparable term has yet been widely adopted to describe the 20th century.) Each of these terms and associated dates has posed considerable problems in the attempt to relate their inherited meanings to specifically musical materials. The dates have usually had to be placed somewhat later than those employed in the fields from which the terms were borrowed. And subperiods, sometimes defined in more specifically musical terms, have been identified to cope with the more unwieldy expanses of time that include radically different kinds of music. The terms nevertheless remain in use at least as conveniences.

Hitch pin. On a stringed keyboard instrument, any of the pins to which the strings are affixed or around which they pass at the end opposite the tuning pins.

Hob. Abbr. for Anthony van Hoboken's thematic catalog of the works of Haydn: *Joseph Haydn: Thematisch-bibliographisches Werkverzeichnis.*

Hoboe [Ger., obs.] Oboe.

Höchst [Ger.]. In the highest degree.

Hocket [Lat. *hoquetatio, hoquetus, (h)ochetus;* Fr. *hocquet, hoquet;* It. *ochetti*]. In polyphony of the 13th and 14th centuries, a stylistic device or a self-contained composition characterized by the distribution of a melodic line between two voices in such a way that as one sounds the other is silent. As a device, it is first used in *conductus* and *motets* and later in Mass movements and certain of the vernacular forms, above all the *caccia* and the *chace.* As a genre, the hocket is intimately related to the discant *clausula.* Texture of this type is prominent in the musics of some non-Western cultures and is especially characteristic of some African musics.

Hoddinott, Alun (b. Bargoed, Wales, 11 Aug. 1929). Composer. Pupil of Arthur Benjamin. Taught at Welsh College of Music and Drama (from 1951) and at University College in Cardiff (1959–87). Often employs a highly chromatic, late Romantic tonal language, with large gestures and big climaxes. Among his works are 5 operas (*The Beach of Falesá,* Cardiff, 1974; *The Rajah's Diamond,* TV performance, 1979; *The Trumpet Major,* Manchester, 1981); choral works (*Sinfonia Fidei,* soprano, tenor, chorus, orchestra, 1977); orchestral works, including 7 symphonies, 4 sinfoniettas, many concertos, *Star Child* (1989), *Noctis Equi* (scena for cello and orchestra, 1989).

Hodges, Johnny [Hodge, Cornelius; Jeep; Rabbit] (b. Cambridge, Mass., 25 July 1907; d. New York, 11 May 1970). Jazz alto saxophonist. Joined Duke Ellington in 1928, remaining for most of his career; known for strong blues soloing and graceful use of slow glissandos in interpreting ballads (including "Warm Valley," recorded in 1940). Recorded under his own name from 1937 (including "Jeep's Blues," 1938, and "Passion Flower," 1941). Left Ellington, 1951–55, to lead a small group with Lawrence Brown and John Coltrane among his sidemen.

Hodkinson, Sydney (Phillip) (b. Winnipeg, 17 Jan. 1934). Composer, conductor, and clarinetist. Pupil of Rogers, Louis Mennini, Carter, Sessions, Babbitt, Bassett, Castiglioni, and Finney. Taught at the Univ. of Virginia (1958–63), Ohio Univ. (1963–66), the Univ. of Michigan (1968–73), and Eastman (from 1973). His compositional styles range from jazz-influenced to electronic. Works include orchestral compositions (*Frescoe,* Symphony no. 1, 1968; *The Edge of the Olde One,* electric English horn, strings, and percussion, 1976; Symphony no. 6, 1995); 4 operas (*The Wall,* 1980; *The Catsman,* 1985) and an oratorio; piano trios, brass and woodwind quintets, works for percussion ensemble, and other chamber music (string quartet no. 3, 1995); organ, vocal, and choral music.

Høffding, (Niels) Finn (b. Copenhagen, 10 Mar. 1899; d. 29 Mar. 1997). Composer. Pupil of Joseph Marx. Cofounded the Copenhagen School of Folk Music in 1931. Taught at the Copenhagen Conservatory from 1931; director from 1954. His later music tends toward dense, chromatic one-movement forms. Composed 2 operas; choral works (*Karlsvognen,* 1924; *Christofer Columbus,* 1937; *Kantate til Det kongelige danske Musikkonservatoriums årsfest,* 1948; *Giordano Bruno,* 1968); orchestral works (Symphony no. 1, Sinfonia impetuosa, 1923; no. 4, Sinfonia concertante, 1934; *Fantasia concertante,* 1965); chamber works (2 string quartets; a wind quintet). Also wrote pedagogical theory treatises.

Hoffman, Richard (b. Manchester, England, 24 May 1831; d. Mt. Kisco, N.Y., 17 Aug. 1909). Pianist and composer. Emigrated to New York 1847. Played in many New York Philharmonic concerts, 1847–92; toured with Jenny Lind, 1850–52; played with Gottschalk several times. Works include piano salon music (*La gazelle,* 1858?, especially popular), sacred anthems, songs.

Hoffmann, E(rnst) T(heodore) A(madeus) (b. Königsberg, 24 Jan. 1776; d. Berlin, 25 June 1822). Composer, author, conductor, and music critic. Pupil of Reichardt. Employed as attorney and later judge in Berlin. From 1808 conducted theater orchestras in Bamberg, Dresden, and Leipzig. Composed some 20 stage works (*Aurora,* 1811–12; *Undine,* 1816); sacred music; secular vocal works; orchestral works including a symphony; and chamber and piano music. Wrote essays on contemporary music. His literary works (including *Fantasiestücke in Callots Manier; Nachtstücke;* and *Die Serapions-Brüder*) have inspired many musical interpretations.

Hoffmeister, Franz Anton (b. Rothenburg am Neckar, 12 May 1754; d. Vienna, 9 Feb. 1812). Publisher and composer. In the 1780s began publishing music in Vienna; that firm published first editions of works by Haydn, Mozart, and Beethoven. In Leipzig with Ambrosius Kühnel, established the Bureau de musique, later to become C. F. Peters; they produced complete editions of Bach, Haydn, and Mozart. His own oeuvre includes 10 stage works; nearly 70 symphonies; 75 concertos; some 500 chamber works (57 string quartets).

Hofhaimer, Paul (b. Radstadt, 25 Jan. 1459; d. Salzburg, 1537). Composer and organist. Organist in Innsbruck (from 1478), to Maximilian I (1489–1519), and in Salzburg at the cathedral and to the archbishop. Extant works include chordal settings of classical odes; Tenorlieder; instrumental pieces, including 2 liturgical organ compositions.

Hofkapelle [Ger.]. See *Kapelle.*

Hofmann, Josef (Casimir) [Józef Kazimierz] (b. Podgorze, Poland, 20 Jan. 1876; d. Los Angeles, 16 Feb. 1957). Pianist and composer. Studied with Anton Rubinstein. First European tour 1883; New York debut 1887; first Russian tour 1896. Director of the Curtis Institute in Philadelphia, 1926–38. Many of his compositions, which include symphonic and concerted works, were published under the name Michel Dvorsky.

Hofmannsthal, Hugo von (b. Vienna, 1 Feb. 1874; d. there, 15 July 1929). Poet, dramatist, and librettist. Collaborated with Richard Strauss on **Elektra; Der *Rosenkavalier; *Ariadne auf Naxos; Die *Frau ohne Schatten; Die ägyptische Helena* (1924–27); **Arabella; Die Liebe der Danae* (completed by Gregor, 1938–40). Many aspects of the compositional process are preserved in their correspondence.

Hoftanz [Ger.]. A 16th-century German dance, a counterpart of the French **basse danse.* Like its Burgundian model, it was a slow, processional couple dance in a simple triple meter, and like its model it was frequently followed by a **Nachtanz.*

Hogwood, Christopher (Jarvis Haley) (b. Nottingham, 10 Sept. 1941). Conductor and harpsichordist. Pupil of Raymond Leppard, Thurston Dart, and Rafael Puyana. Harpsichordist in the Academy of St. Martins-in-the-Fields from 1966. With David Munrow founded the Early Music Consort of London in 1967. With Peter Woodland formed the Academy of Ancient Music in 1973; the recording of Mozart's symphonies established his reputation internationally. Artistic director of the Handel and Haydn Society of Boston from 1986; associated with the St. Paul Chamber Orchestra from 1988.

Hoiby, Lee (b. Madison, Wis., 17 Feb. 1926). Composer and pianist. Pupil of Menotti, Milhaud, and Petri. Works include operas (*The Scarf,* 1958; *Natalia Petrovna,* 1964, rev. as *A Month in the Country,* 1981; *Summer and Smoke,* 1972; *The Tempest,* 1986); ballets (*After Eden,* 1966); incidental music; an oratorio (*Galileo Galilei,* 1975); 2 piano concertos and other orchestral music; chamber music (Serenade, violin and piano, 1988); piano music; choral music (*Psalm 93,* 1985); songs.

Holborne, Antony [Anthony] (fl. from 1584?; d. between 29 Nov. and 1 Dec. 1602). Composer. Little about his life except his nationality (English) is known with any certainty. Of his roughly 150 compositions virtually all are for instruments alone, and the great majority are dances.

Holbrooke, Joseph [Josef Charles] (b. Croydon, 5 July 1878; d. London, 5 Aug. 1958). Composer. Pupil of Frederick Corder. Worked as a pianist and conductor. Composed operas, including the trilogy *The Cauldron of Annwyn,* based on a Welsh epic poem (1912–29), and *The Sailor's Arms;* choral works (*Homage to E. A. Poe,* Dramatic Choral Symphony, 1908); symphonic poems (*The Raven,* 1900); 8 symphonies; concertos; works for military brass band; chamber and piano music.

Hold. **Fermata.*

Holden, Oliver (b. Shirley, Mass., 18 Sept. 1765; d. Charlestown, Mass., 4 Sept. 1844). Composer and minister. Owned a music store in Charlestown from ca. 1790. Founded a church, taught in singing schools, compiled anthologies of anthems and hymns, and composed many of his own. Coauthored the *Massachusetts Compiler of Theoretical Principles* (1795).

Holiday, Billie [Fagan, Eleanora; Lady Day] (b. Baltimore, 7 Apr. 1915; d. New York, 17 July 1959). Jazz singer. Recorded with Teddy Wilson and under her own name 1935–42. Her free interpretation of melodies and blues-inflected delivery brought an emotional depth to popular songs in recordings such as "These Foolish Things" (1936), "He's Funny That Way" (1937), "Them There Eyes" (1939), "All of Me," and "God Bless the Child" (both 1941). Sang with Count Basie (1937–38) and Artie Shaw (1938); thereafter with small groups.

Holler. See Field holler.

Höller, York (b. Leverkusen, 11 Jan. 1944). Composer. Pupil of Eimert and Zimmermann. Member of the Cologne ensemble Gruppe 8. Succeeded Stockhausen as director of the WDR Electronic Studio in Cologne, 1990. Works include the opera *Der Meister und Margarita* (1989); *Aura* (1991–92) and other orchestral music (some with electronic sounds); *Décollage*, 2 speaking choruses, 3 amplified instruments, live feedback, and tape (1972); *Improvisation sur le nom de Pierre Boulez*, 17 instruments (1985), and other works for small ensemble; *Horizont*, tape (1971–72).

Holliger, Heinz (b. Langenthal, Switzerland, 21 May 1939). Oboist and composer. Pupil of Boulez. Professor of oboe at the Staatliche Musikhochschule in Freiburg from 1965. Works were written for him by Henze, Lutoslawski, Berio, Stockhausen, and others. Compositions include dramatic works (*Der magische Tänzer*, 1965; *Come and Go*, 1978, and *What Where*, 1989, both after Beckett; *NOT I*, 1980); orchestral works (*Tonscherben*, 1985; *Zwei Liszt-Transcriptionen*, 1986; *Gesänge der Frühe*, with choir and tape, 1987); compositions featuring oboe and harp; vocal works (*Variazioni su nulla*, 4 voices, 1988); chamber music (a string quartet, 1973; *Vier Stücke*, violin, piano, 1984); piano pieces; organ pieces.

Holloway, Robin (Greville) (b. Leamington Spa, 19 Oct. 1943). Composer. Choirboy at St. Paul's; pupil of Alexander Goehr. Taught at Cambridge from 1974. Works include the opera *Clarissa* (1976); *The Blackbird and the Snail* (melodrama, voice, piano, 1995); *Cantata on the Death of God*, 1973; *The Spacious Firmament* (chorus, orchestra, 1990); orchestral works (*Domination of Black*, 1974; *Second Idyll*, 1983; several concertos); chamber music (*Winter Music: Concertino no. 6*, mixed sextet, 1993); songs and song cycles.

Holly, Buddy [Holley, Charles Hardin] (b. Lubbock, Tex., 7 Sept. 1938; d. near Clear Lake, Iowa, 3 Feb. 1959). Rock-and-roll singer, songwriter, and guitarist. Began recording original country and rock-and-roll songs in 1956 with his band The Three Tunes (later renamed the Crickets). Popular recordings include "That'll Be the Day," "Oh, Boy," and "Peggy Sue" (all 1957); he has been credited with expanding the musical and emotional scope of rock-and-roll.

Holmboe, Vagn (b. Horsens, eastern Jutland, 20 Dec. 1909; d. 1 Sept. 1996). Composer. Pupil of Høffding and Toch. Studied Romanian folk music. Wrote music criticism for the Copenhagen *Politiken*. Taught at the Copenhagen Conservatory from 1950. His music shows influences from Nielsen, Hindemith, and Stravinsky. Works include theater music; choral works (*Requiem for Nietzsche*, 1963–64; *Liber canticorum*, 1951–67); symphonies (no. 8, *Sinfonia boreale*, 1951–52); concertos; ballets; other orchestral works (*Epitaph*, 1956); 14 string quartets; sonatas and other chamber works; piano works; organ music.

Holmès, Augusta (Mary Anne) (b. Paris, 16 Dec. 1847; d. there, 28 Jan. 1903). Composer. Pupil of Franck. Prominent figure in Paris salons. Composed 11 symphonic poems and dramatic symphonies (*Les Argonautes*, 1881); 4 operas (to her librettos, including *La montagne noire*, Opéra, 1895); over 100 songs, some very popular.

Holst, Gustav(us, Theodore von) (b. Cheltenham, 21 Sept. 1874; d. London, 25 May 1934). Composer. Pupil of Stanford; friend of Vaughan Williams. Taught at St. Paul's Girls School from 1905; at Morley College from 1907; at Reading College and the Royal College of Music, 1920–23. Works include operas (*The Perfect Fool*, 1923; *At the Boar's Head*, 1925; *The Wandering Scholar*, 1929–30); ballets and other stage works; choral/orchestral works (*Choral Hymns from the Rig Veda*, 1908–12; *The Hymn of Jesus*, 1917; *First Choral Symphony*, 1923–24); works for chorus alone (*Six Choral Folk Songs*, 1916; *The Evening Watch*, 1924); orchestral works (*The *Planets; Egdon Heath*, 1927; *Hammersmith*, 1930–31); 2 suites for military band (1909–11); chamber and piano music; many songs and smaller vocal works.

Holyoke, Samuel (Adams) (b. Boxford, Mass., 15 Oct. 1762; d. East Concord, N.H., 7 Feb. 1820). Composer and singing master. During the 1790s taught school at Groton, Mass., and organized singing-school concerts. Published numerous collections of his nearly 900 works, including *The Columbian Repository* (1803) and *The Christian Harmonist* (1804).

Holz [Ger.]. Wood; *Holzbläser*, woodwind player; *Holzblasinstrument*, woodwind instrument; *Holzblock, Holzblocktrommel*, wood block; *Holzharmonika, Holzstabspiel*, xylophone; *Holzschlegel*, wooden drumstick; *Holztrompete*, alphorn.

Holzbauer, Ignaz (Jakob) (b. Vienna, 17 Sept. 1711; d. Mannheim, 7 Apr. 1783). Composer. Engaged at the Viennese Imperial Theater around 1740. Kapellmeister in Stuttgart from 1751; in Mannheim 1753–78. Among his stage works are the German opera *Günther von Schwarzburg* (Mannheim, 1777), Italian operas, pantomimes, and ballets. Other works include sacred oratorios (*La Betulia liberata*, 1760); Masses and motets; some 70 symphonies; chamber

L'hom-me, l'hom-me, l'homme ar-   mé, l'homme ar- mé, L'homme ar-   mé doibt   on doub- ter, doibt on doub-

-ter.   On   a   fait par- tout cri-   er   Que chas- cun   se viegne ar-   mer D'un hau- bre- gon de   fer.____   *D.C. al*

L'homme armé. "The armed man, the armed man . . . One should fear the armed man. The warning has been shouted everywhere that everyone should be armed with a suit of mail."

and instrumental music (string quartets, notturni, sonate da camera, etc.).

Homer, Louise (Beatty) (b. Shadyside, Pa., 30 Apr. 1871; d. Winter Park, Fla., 6 May 1947). Contralto. Married to Sidney Homer. Debut in Vichy, 1898, as Léonor *(Favorite)*. Sang in New York, 1900–19 and 1927–29; Chicago, 1920–25; San Francisco, 1926. Commanded a broad repertoire of Italian, French, and Wagnerian roles.

Homer, Sidney (b. Boston, 9 Dec. 1864; d. Winter Park, Fla., 10 July 1953). Composer. Pupil of Chadwick and Rheinberger. Taught in Boston 1888–95; 1900, settled in New York with his wife, Louise Beatty. Wrote over 100 songs in a conservative diatonic style; also some chamber music.

Homilius, Gottfried August (b. Rosenthal, Saxony, 2 Feb. 1714; d. Dresden, 2 June 1785). Composer and organist. Pupil of Johann Schneider and J. S. Bach. Organist at the Frauenkirche in Dresden from 1742; from 1755, music director at the Kreuzkirche, the Sophienkirche, and the Frauenkirche. Composed Passions; more than 200 cantatas; some 60 motets; oratorios; 8 Magnificats; many organ works.

Homme armé, L' [Fr.]. A 15th-century melody [Ex.] that was widely used as a *cantus firmus* of polyphonic Masses from the second half of the 15th century through the first part of the 17th and of which there are also several polyphonic chanson settings.

Homophony. Music in which melodic interest is concentrated in one voice or part that is provided with a subordinate accompaniment, as distinct from *polyphony*, in which melodic interest is distributed among all parts of the musical texture. The term may refer to a variety of melody-plus-accompaniment textures as well as to texture, termed *homorhythmic*, in which all parts move with the same or similar rhythm.

Homorhythmic. Characterized by the same or very similar rhythm in all parts making up a musical texture, as in a simple hymn or chorale setting. Texture of this type is also described with the terms chordal

style, familiar style, note-against-note style, isometric, and homophonic [see Homophony].

Homs (Oller), Joaquín (b. Barcelona, 22 Aug. 1906). Composer. Pupil of Roberto Gerhard. Has employed serial techniques. His piano work *Présences* received a municipal award from Barcelona in 1967. Has composed in most standard genres except for stage music, with a focus on chamber ensemble and Catalan vocal compositions.

Honegger, Arthur (b. Le Havre, 10 Mar. 1892; d. Paris, 27 Nov. 1955). Composer. Pupil of Gédalge, Widor, d'Indy, and Capet. One of "Les six." Taught at the École normale in Paris. Among the influences obvious in Honegger's music are his Swiss Protestant heritage, Gregorian chant, impressionism, jazz, and the French and German symphonic and operatic traditions. Melodic and rhythmic relationships he considered of more importance than tonality in shaping his works. Composed operas *(Antigone, 1924–27)*, operettas, and other dramatic works *(Le *roi David; Jeanne d'Arc au bûcher,* Claudel, 1934–35, Basel, 1938); ballets; incidental music; film and radio scores; 5 symphonies, 3 *Mouvements symphoniques* (no. 1, *Pacific 231,* 1923; no. 2, *Rugby,* 1928), and other orchestral works; choral works; sonatas, string quartets, and other chamber music; keyboard works; several works for voice(s) and orchestra; some 50 songs.

Hook, James (b. Norwich, 3? June 1746; d. Boulogne, 1827). Organist and composer. Held several organ posts in London from 1763. Wrote more than 30 theater works *(The Double Disguise,* 1784); cantatas and odes; songs, catches, and canons; concertos and chamber works. Authored a treatise, *Guida di musica* (1785–94).

Hopak [Ukr.]. See *Gopak.*

Hopkins, (Charles) Jerome (b. Burlington, Vt., 4 Apr. 1836; d. Athenia [now Clinton], N.J., 4 Nov. 1898). Composer. From 1853, organist and choirmaster, New York. In 1861, founded Orpheon Free Schools to teach music to poor children. Composed operas *(Taffy and Old Munch,* children's opera, 1880); the oratorio *Samuel;* church music; the symphony *Life;* Serenade in E, orchestra; a piano concerto; chamber music; songs. Edited sacred anthologies.

Hopkinson, Francis (b. Philadelphia, 21 Sept. 1737; d. there, 9 May 1791). Musician, statesman, and inventor. Organist for Christ Church, Philadelphia, ca.1770. Signer of the Declaration of Independence. Compiled texts for a political oratorio, *America Independent, or The Temple of Minerva;* also books of psalm tunes. Among his own compositions are *Seven* [actually 8] *Songs for the Harpsichord or Forte Piano* (1788); his song "My Days Have Been So Wondrous Free," dated 1759, has been cited as the earliest surviving American secular composition.

Hoquet [Fr.], **hoquetus** [Lat.]. *Hocket.

Horenstein, Jascha (b. Kiev, 6 May 1898; d. London, 2 Apr. 1973). Conductor. Pupil of Max Brode and Schreker. Assistant to Furtwängler. Debut with the Vienna Symphony, 1924. Conducted in Berlin, 1924–28; music director of the Düsseldorf Opera, 1929–33. Emigrated to the U.S. 1940; later settled in Lausanne. Led the premiere of Berg's *Lyrische Suite,* 1929. Introduced *Wozzeck* and other modern operas in Düsseldorf, Paris, and the U.S. Championed symphonic scores of Bruckner, Mahler, Nielsen.

Horn [also French horn; Fr. *cor;* Ger. *Horn; Ventilhorn,* valve horn; *Waldhorn,* natural horn, hand horn; It. *corno;* Sp. *trompa*]. A circular brass instrument about 35 cm. (14 in.) in diameter with mouthpiece and valve levers at the top and a widely flared end or bell at the bottom. Three or four usually rotary valves, operated with the left hand, and associated extra tubing occupy the center area [see ill. under Brass instruments]. The instrument is usually made of brass and is sometimes nickel or silver plated. Horns made of German silver, copper, and—more rarely—silver also exist. The horn is a prominent solo instrument in European and American symphony orchestras, each of which has a horn section of four or more players. It is also used in bands and in chamber music ensembles such as woodwind and brass quintets.

The most common horn is a double instrument in F/B♭ incorporating a horn in F approximately 3.65 m. (12 ft.) in length with a horn in B♭ alto of about 2.75 m. (9 ft.). The longer or shorter instrument is selected by a left thumb valve. Three double valves for the left hand provide both horns with the usual additional lengths of tubing [see Valve]. Single horns in F are also encountered. Less often found are single instruments in B♭ alto, double horns in F/F alto or B♭/B♭ soprano, and triple horns in F/B♭/F alto.

The F/B♭ horn is the only survivor of a prestigious class of long brasses designed to play normally in the third octave or higher of the *harmonic series. Its tube lengths and fundamentals (lowest tones) are the same as those of the F tuba (F horn) and B♭ trombone (B♭ horn). Yet because of its smaller bore and much smaller mouthpiece it is played in the tenor and alto ranges.

Although small, the horn mouthpiece is long and cone-shaped. The main tube of the instrument is also conical for as much of its length as possible. The sound of the instrument is smooth, lyrical, and mellow in its most characteristic written range of f to f'' (sounding a fifth lower, B♭ to b♭'), more intense but gradually thinner on the increasingly difficult higher notes up to and above (written) c''', and more and more guttural on the extremely low notes down to c and below.

The horn is held with the right hand in the bell. Partially closing off the throat of the bell flattens the pitch; fully opening it raises the pitch, giving the player some control of pitches that may be out of tune. Closing the opening tightly with the hand produces a muted or stopped effect [Fr., *sons bouchés;* Ger., *gestopft;* It. *chiuso;* Sp. *tapada*], sometimes specified in musical notation with the sign + and requiring altered fingering. The effect may also be produced with a *mute, which, depending on its type, may or may not require altered fingering.

Instrument makers in Vienna began producing horns in F and *crooks for other keys in the first decade of the 18th century. In this period, Bohemian and Austrian horn players—especially in Vienna, Prague, and Dresden—established the range and technical capabilities of the horn to limits approaching what is known today. Hand stopping (partially or fully closing off the bell with the right hand) was developed as a technique for tuning and for providing notes not obtainable in the natural series. Invented later in the century were central crooks, attached by a slide, that allow a permanent mouth pipe and mouthpiece position more convenient for hand stopping. The use of this type of instrument, called the *Inventionshorn,* quickly spread throughout the Continent. The 19th century saw the invention of the *valve and its application to the horn. The increasing use of historical instruments in the performance of 18th-century music, however, has contributed to a revival of the natural horn, i.e., the horn without valves [see Performance practice].

Horn fifths. See Parallel Fifths.

Horn, Charles Edward (b. London, 21 June 1786; d. Boston, 21 Oct. 1849). Composer. Son and pupil of Karl Friedrich Horn (1762–1830); double bassist and cellist in London theater orchestras; singer in English opera. Composed English operas, musical comedies, and pasticcios (*The Devil's Bridge,* 1812); many popular songs and ballads ("Cherry Ripe"); the oratorio *The Remission of Sin* (New York, 1835). From

1827 lived mostly in the U.S.; conductor of the Handel and Haydn Society, Boston, 1847–49.

Horne, Lena (Calhoun) (b. Brooklyn, N.Y., 30 June 1917). Popular singer and actress. Sang and danced at the Cotton Club in Harlem; toured with Noble Sissle and Charlie Barnet. Appeared on Broadway (including *Blackbirds,* 1939; *Jamaica,* 1957) and in films (*Panama Hattie,* 1942; *Ziegfeld Follies,* 1946); recorded extensively ("Stormy Weather," 1943; the album *We'll Be Together Again,* 1993).

Horne, Marilyn (b. Bradford, Pa., 16 Jan. 1934). Mezzo-soprano. Studied with Lotte Lehmann. Stage debut in Los Angeles in Smetana's *Bartered Bride.* Dubbed Dorothy Dandridge's songs in the film *Carmen Jones,* 1954. Engaged by the Gelsenkirchen Stadttheater 1957–60. New York, 1962, sang Bellini's Agnes *(Beatrice di Tenda)* in the first of many performances with Joan Sutherland. Member of the Metropolitan Opera from 1970. Played an important role in the revival of Handelian opera seria and the works of Rossini.

Hornpipe. (1) A dance popular in England, Wales, and Scotland from the 16th to 19th centuries, related to the *jig and *country-dance families of dances. The country-dance type is found as a movement in harpsichord and orchestral music and is usually in animated 3/2 time (also 3/4, 2/4, and later 4/4). On the Continent hornpipes were sometimes called *angloises.* Most exploit Scotch-snap syncopations. As a solo dance, the hornpipe has often been associated with sailors. A type in duple meter is a prominent folk dance of Ireland.
(2) A reedpipe with a bell made of animal horn. Most are like *shawms, some are *double clarinets, and some are fitted with bags. Examples include the Scottish stock and horn and the Welsh *pibgorn.

Horowitz, Vladimir (b. Berdichev, 1 Oct. 1903; d. New York, 5 Nov. 1989). Pianist. Debut, Kiev, 1921. Concertized extensively in the U.S. and Europe 1928–36; 1939, moved to the U.S. and began touring once again until 1953. Returned to the concert stage in 1965 (Carnegie Hall); gave concerts in Russia in 1986. He was especially associated with the Third Piano Concerto of Rachmaninoff (a close friend), the concertos of Tchaikovsky, and works of Chopin, Schumann, and Liszt.

Horst, Louis (b. Kansas City, Mo., 12 Jan. 1884; d. New York, 23 Jan. 1964). Composer. Pupil of Riegger. Music director of the Denishawn Dance Company 1915–25; 1926–48, of Martha Graham's dance company, for which he provided numerous scores. Founded the *Dance Observer* 1934. Taught at Bennington (1934–45), Columbia University Teachers

College (1938–41), and the Juilliard School (1958–63). Authored 2 books on dance.

Horszowski, Mieczysław (b. Lemberg [now Lvov, Ukraine], 23 June 1892; d. Philadelphia, 22 May 1993). Pianist. Pupil of Leschetizky. Carnegie Hall debut, 1906. In 1957 gave a 12-concert cycle of Beethoven's complete solo piano works. Taught at the Curtis Institute from 1942. Continued to concertize and record until he was nearly 100; regularly took part in chamber music with Casals and others.

Hosanna [Lat., fr. Gr. and Heb., save, we beseech Thee]. An acclamation occurring in the phrase "Hosanna in excelsis" (Hosanna in the highest) in the Sanctus of the *Mass. In the Anglican Book of Common Prayer this is rendered "Glory be to Thee, O Lord, most High."

Hotteterre, Jacques(-Martin) ["Le Romain"] (b. Paris, 29 Sept. 1674; d. there, 16 July 1763). Woodwind player and maker, theorist, and composer. From a family of musicians and instrument makers. By 1708, bassoonist in the Grands Hautbois and "flute of the King's chamber." Writings include *Principes de la flûte traversière* (1707) and a method for the musette. Composed suites, duets, and sonatas for treble instruments and continuo.

Hours. See Office.

Hovhaness [Hovaness], **Alan** [Chakmakjian, Alan Hovhaness] (b. Somerville, Mass., 8 Mar. 1911). Composer. Pupil of Converse and Martinů. Organist at St. James Armenian Church, Boston, 1940–47; taught at Boston Conservatory 1948–51. Studied the musics of Armenia, India, Japan, and Korea, incorporating many elements into his own compositions; also used aleatory procedures. Works include operas (*The Frog Man,* 1987); incidental and dance music (*Ardent Song,* for Martha Graham, 1954); over 60 symphonies (no. 2, *The Mysterious Mountain,* 1955; no. 63, *Loon Lake,* 1988) and other orchestral works (*And God Created Great Whales,* with taped whale sounds, 1970; *3 Armenian Rhapsodies,* 1944); the oratorio *Revelations of St. Paul* (1981); chamber music (*Koke no niwa,* English horn, harp, and percussion, 1954); piano works; religious choral music; solo vocal music.

Howe, Mary (b. Richmond, Va., 4 Apr. 1882; d. Washington, D.C., 14 Sept. 1964). Composer and pianist. Pupil of Strube and Boulanger. Performed in piano duo with Ann Hull 1920–35. A founding member of the Association of American Women Composers (1926). Wrote 2 ballets, orchestral works (*Castellana,* 2 pianos and orchestra, 1930, based on Spanish folk songs); chamber music (*Three Pieces after Emily Dickinson,* string quartet, 1941); choral and vocal music.

Howells, Herbert (Norman) (b. Lydney, Gloucestershire, 17 Oct. 1892; d. Oxford, 24 Feb. 1983). Composer. Pupil of Stanford and Charles Wood. Taught at the Royal College from 1920; at St. Paul's Girls' School, Hammersmith, 1936–62; and at the Univ. of London, 1950–64. His lush, frankly Romantic style recalls the music of Elgar and Vaughan Williams. Composed sacred vocal music (including *Hymnus Paradisi*, 1938; *Stabat Mater*, 1963); many songs (*Peacock Pie*, 6 songs, 1919); 2 piano concertos and other orchestral works; band pieces; chamber and piano music; organ works.

Howlin' Wolf [Burnett, Chester Arthur] (b. West Point, Miss., 10 June 1910; d. Hines, Ill., 10 Jan. 1976). Blues singer, harmonica player, and guitarist. His aggressive, gravelly singing defined the rough side of Chicago blues and greatly influenced rock music through performances in Europe (1961–64) and recordings such as "Smoke Stack Lightning" (1956), "Sitting on Top of the World" (1957), "Back Door Man," "Spoonful" (both 1960), "The Red Rooster," and "I Ain't Superstitious" (both 1961).

Hr. Abbr. for horn.

Hrabovsky [Grabovsky], **Leonid Alexandrovich** (b. Kiev, 28 Jan. 1935). Composer. In the 1960s experimented with modern techniques and styles, becoming a pioneer of the Soviet avant garde. Works include symphonic scores (*Homeomorphia IV,* 1970); vocal-symphonic scores (*La Mer,* melodrama for narrator, chorus, and orchestra, 1970); works for chamber orchestra; vocal and choral music; much chamber music.

Hrisanidis [Hrisanide], **Alexandre** (b. Petrila, Romania, 15 June 1936). Composer and pianist. Pupil of Constantinescu, Vancea, and Boulanger; also studied at Darmstadt. From 1959 taught at the Bucharest Academy; from 1962 at the conservatory. Taught at the Univ. of Oregon 1972–74, then settled in the Netherlands. Among his works are cantatas; orchestral works (*Passacaglia,* 1959; *Vers antiqua,* 1960); chamber and piano works (sonatas; "Piano Pieces" nos. 1–13, 1955–64; *Volumes-Inventions,* cello, piano, 1963); works with tape.

Hubay [Huber], **Jenő** (b. Budapest, 15 Sept. 1858; d. there, 12 Mar. 1937). Violinist and composer. Pupil of Joachim and Vieuxtemps. Taught at the Brussels Conservatory (1882–86); then at the Budapest Conservatory (director from 1919); his violin pupils included Szigeti. His own works are in a strongly Romantic style; he composed 8 operas (*A falu rossza* [The Village Vagabond], Budapest, 1894; *Moharózsa* [The Moss Rose], Budapest, 1903; *Anna Karenina,* Budapest, 1915; *Az álarc* [The Mask], Budapest, 1931); 4 symphonies (no. 4, [Petőfi Symphony], so-

loists, chorus, orchestra, 1925); 4 violin concertos; solo violin pieces.

Hubbard, Freddie [Frederick Dewayne] (b. Indianapolis, 7 Apr. 1938). Jazz trumpeter, flugelhorn player, and bandleader. Joined Art Blakey's Jazz Messengers (1961–64); then led groups, initially playing hard bop and modal jazz, but turning to simpler danceable styles. Sidemen have included the pianist Kenny Barron and Joe Henderson. Has recorded with Herbie Hancock's quintet.

Huber, Hans (b. Eppenburg, Solothurn, Switzerland, 28 June 1852; d. Locarno, 25 Dec. 1921). Composer and pianist. Teacher and organist in Alsace, 1875–77; in 1877 he went to Basel; 1889–1902, directed the Choral Society there and taught at the music school (director from 1896). Works include operas, oratorios; 9 symphonies, 4 piano concertos; chamber music for strings, winds, and piano; choral works; and songs.

Huber, Klaus (b. Bern, 30 Nov. 1924). Composer. Pupil of Burkhard and Blacher. Taught at the Zurich Conservatory (1950s); at the Lucerne Conservatory (1960–63); then at the Music Academy in Basel, and in Freiburg. Employs serial procedures. Works include *Des Engels Anredung an die Seele* (tenor and ensemble, 1958); the opera *Jot, oder Wann kommt der Herr zurück* (1973); pieces for orchestra, some with tape; *Cantiones de circulo gyrante* (soloists, chorus, and 15 instruments, after Hildegard von Bingen and Heinrich Böll, 1985); *Von Zeit zu Zeit* (string quartet, 1985) and other chamber and keyboard music; choral and vocal music.

Hu-ch'in, huqin [Chin.]. (1) Any *spike fiddle. (2) The *ching-hu.

Hudson, George (d. London, before 1673). Violinist and composer. Court musician to Charles II from 1660. Composed music for The *Siege of Rhodes;* ayres; pieces for viols; other instrumental works.

Huguenots, Les [Fr., The Huguenots]. Opera in five acts by Giacomo Meyerbeer (libretto by Eugène Scribe, revised by Émile Deschamps and Meyerbeer), produced in Paris in 1836. Setting: Touraine and Paris in 1572.

Huízar (García de la Cadena), Candelario (b. Jérez, Zacatecas, Mexico, 2 Feb. 1883; d. Mexico City, 3 May 1970). Composer. Hornist in the Mexico Symphony, 1929–37. The *Imágenes* (orchestra, 1929) is indebted to Debussy; later works show a nationalist character, using indigenous melodies. Compositions include 4 symphonies, the symphonic poem *Pueblerinas,* a sonata for clarinet and bassoon (both 1931), a string quartet (1938), vocal music.

Hullah, John (Pyke) (b. Worcester, 27 June 1812; d. London, 21 Feb. 1884). Composer and educator. From 1837 a church organist (1858–84 at the Charterhouse); taught singing throughout Britain using a fixed-do system (from 1841 at Exeter Hall; 1849–60 at St. Martin's Hall; 1844–74 at King's College). Wrote textbooks and music history; edited musical anthologies; composed songs ("O That We Two Were Maying," "The Three Fishers") and English operas.

Hume, Tobias (b. ca. 1560s; d. London, 16 Apr. 1645). Viol player and composer. Served as a soldier. Published the collections *First Part of Ayres* (1605) and *Captaine Hume's Poeticall Musicke* (1607), containing dances, programmatic pieces, and accompanied songs, mainly for lyra viol.

Humfrey, Pelham (b. 1647; d. Windsor, 14 July 1674). Composer. Sang under Cooke in the Chapel Royal from 1660; later court lutenist and Gentleman of the Chapel Royal. Assistant for the Corporation of Music, 1670; a Warden, 1672. Master of the Children of the Chapel Royal from 1672; Purcell was among his pupils. Composed songs, court odes, masque music, and sacred works, including 17 verse anthems with instrumental ritornelli.

Hummel, hommel, humle [Swed.]. A fretted *zither of Sweden, Denmark, and the Low Countries. Today largely obsolete, it was similar in form and playing technique to the Norwegian *langleik.

Hummel, Johann Nepomuk (b. Pressburg [now Bratislava], 14 Nov. 1778; d. Weimar, 17 Oct. 1837). Composer and pianist. Pupil of Mozart, Albrechtsberger, Salieri, and Haydn. Concertmaster and later Kapellmeister to Prince Esterházy at Eisenstadt, 1804–11. Court Kapellmeister in Stuttgart, 1816–18; in Weimar from 1819. Toured Europe as a pianist, as a child and 1814–30. Composed sacred music (including 5 masses, a Te Deum, motets, mainly for Esterháza); operas; chamber music, including piano trios and the Septet in D minor op. 74 (ca. 1816); piano concertos; sonatas, salon music, and etudes for piano; dance music for orchestra; songs, choruses.

Humoreske [Ger.], **humoresque** [Fr.]. A title used by some composers of the 19th century for pieces of fanciful character. The term derives from humor in the sense of mood rather than wit. Works include Schumann's *Humoreske* in B♭ major for piano op. 20 (1838), which is in five sharply contrasting sections, and Dvořák's set of eight *Humoresques* for piano op. 101 (1894), of which the one in G♭ major is well known.

Humperdinck, Engelbert (b. Siegburg, 1 Sept. 1854; d. Neustrelitz, 27 Sept. 1921). Composer. Pupil of Hiller, Lachner, and Rheinberger. Assistant to

Wagner at Bayreuth. Taught at Barcelona Conservatory (1885–86) and Cologne Conservatory (1886–88); 1888–90, editor, Schott publishing house, Mainz; from 1891, taught at the Hoch Conservatory in Frankfurt; 1900–20, at the Berlin Hochschule für Musik. Composed operas (including *Hänsel und Gretel; Königskinder,* Metropolitan Opera, 1910); *Die Wallfahrt nach Kevelaar,* chorus and orchestra, 1878; incidental music for Max Reinhard's productions of Shakespeare and other dramas (Berlin, 1905–12); music for a pantomime, *The Miracle* (London, 1911); songs; 3 string quartets.

Hungarian Dances [Ger. *Ungarische Tänze*]. A collection of 21 dances for piano four-hands by Brahms, composed in 1852–69 and published in four volumes (two in 1869 and two in 1880). Brahms arranged nos. 1, 3, and 10 for orchestra in 1873 and nos. 1–10 for piano solo in 1872. Most are freely invented in imitation of the Hungarian *csárdás* and in the style of so-called *Gypsy music, rather than drawing on Hungarian folk music.

Hungarian Rhapsodies [Fr. *Rhapsodies hongroises*]. A group of 19 piano pieces by Liszt, composed in 1846–85 and published in 1851–86. They are based on an earlier set of 21 piano pieces (some of which were called Hungarian Rhapsodies) that draw on Hungarian Gypsy music and that were published by Liszt between 1840 and 1847. Many are freely invented or based on "Gypsy" melodies by various amateur composers and styled in imitation of the Hungarian *csárdás* or so-called *Gypsy music, rather than drawing on Hungarian folk music.

Hunnenschlacht, Die [Ger., The Battle (Slaughter) of the Huns]. A symphonic poem by Liszt completed in 1857 and inspired by a painting by Wilhelm von Kaulbach.

Hunt Quartet. Popular name for Mozart's String Quartet in B♭ major K. 458 (1784), no. 3 of the *Haydn Quartets; and for Haydn's String Quartet no. 1 in B♭ major Hob. III:1, composed by 1762. In both quartets, the name refers to the hunting-horn motif in the opening movement.

Hunt Symphony [Fr. *La chasse*]. Haydn's Symphony no. 73 in D major Hob. I:73 (completed by 1782). The title refers to the last movement, which was originally composed as an overture, depicting a hunting scene, to his opera *La fedeltà premiata* Hob. XXVIII:10 (1780).

Hünten, Franz (b. Coblenz, 26 Dec. 1793; d. there, 22 Feb. 1878). Composer. Pupil of Reicha and Cherubini; a fashionable teacher and salon composer in Paris, 1821–35 and 1839–48. Composed over 250 piano pieces, including variations, opera potpourris and fantasies, rondos, dances; a *Méthode de piano* op. 60 (1833); etudes; 4 piano trios.

Hunting horn. See Horn.

Hupfauf [Ger.]. See *Nachtanz.*

Hurdy-gurdy [Fr. *vielle à roue, chifonie;* Ger. *Drehleier, Leier, Radleier;* It. *ghironda;* Lat. *symphonia;* Sp. *zanfonía*]. A bowed stringed instrument, most often shaped like a viol, with a crank at the end opposite the pegbox. When the crank is turned, a rosined wooden wheel adjacent to the bridge and touching the strings rotates, causing the strings to sound. Two strings tuned in unison pass over the central bridge and through a long box under what would otherwise be the fingerboard. These strings are stopped by tangents that are connected to keys set into the side of the box. Two pairs of drone strings, tuned in some combination of fifths and octaves, pass over separate bridges, one on either side of the main bridge. The number of strings may vary.

The instrument was introduced into Latin Europe from the East and from Spain in the Middle Ages, when it was at first termed an *organistrum.* Its first depictions, in the 12th century, show a large instrument held and played by two players. The smaller size for a single player and the Latin name *symphonia* and its derivatives emerged in the 13th century. By the 17th century, it was regarded as an instrument of the lower classes, including beggars and itinerant musicians. In the 18th century, however, it was taken up along with the *musette by the French aristocracy. It continues in use as a folk instrument in France, Scandinavia, and Hungary. See ill. under Violin. The term is sometimes also applied to the *barrel organ and *barrel piano.

Hurford, Peter (John) (b. Minehead, Somerset, 22 Nov. 1930). Organist. Pupil of Harold Darke and André Marchal. Master of the Music at St. Albans Abbey 1958–78; founded the International Organ Festival there 1963. As a performer and recording artist he specialized in the music of Bach and 18th-century French music.

Hurt, Mississippi John (b. Teoc, Miss., 3 July 1893; d. Grenada, Miss., 2 or 3 Nov. 1966). Blues singer and guitarist. Recorded in Memphis and New York in 1928; for the Library of Congress in 1963, performing folk and country blues songs with nimble finger-picking guitar work in a style unchanged since the 1920s. Recordings include "Casey Jones," "Nobody's Dirty Business," and "Candy Man."

Hurtig [Ger.]. Quick, agile.

Husa, Karel (b. Prague, 7 Aug. 1921). Composer and conductor. Pupil of Rídký, Tálich, Honegger, Boulanger, and Cluytens. On the faculty at Cornell Univ.,

1954–92. Has employed twelve-tone and serial methods, quarter-tones, new string techniques, and aleatory procedures. Works include *Apotheosis of This Earth* (chorus and band/orchestra, 1970); *An American Te Deum* (baritone, band, and chorus, 1976); the ballet *The Trojan Women* (1980), 2 symphonies, concertos, and other works for orchestra (*Poem,* viola and orchestra, 1959; *Mosaïques,* 1961; *Serenade,* woodwind quintet and orchestra/piano, 1963; *Cayuga Lake [Memories],* 1992); music for wind ensemble (*Music for Prague,* 1968; *Al fresco,* 1975; *Five Poems,* 1994); chamber music (String Quartet no. 3, 1968, awarded the Pulitzer Prize; no. 4, 1989; *Landscapes,* brass quintet and piano, 1977; *Sonata a tre,* clarinet, violin, and piano, 1981); a few songs.

Huss, Henry Holden (b. Newark, N.J., 21 June 1862; d. New York, 17 Sept. 1953). Pianist and composer. Pupil of his father, George John Huss, and Rheinberger. Taught at Hunter College 1930–38. Composed a Rhapsody (op. 3, piano, orchestra, 1885); Piano Concerto (op. 10); the symphonic poem *Life's Conflicts* (1921); vocal music; chamber music.

Hüttenbrenner, Anselm (b. Graz, 13 Oct. 1794; d. Ober-Andritz, near Graz, 5 June 1868). Composer. Pupil of Salieri; friend of Schubert. Conductor at the Steiermärkischer Musikverein 1825–29 and 1831–39. Composed several operas performed in Graz; much church music; symphonies; chamber music; male part songs; songs; piano and organ pieces; 1854, wrote his somewhat unreliable recollections of Schubert.

Hydraulis [Gr.; Lat. *hydraulus*]. The organ of ancient Greece and Rome. Its invention is attributed to Ktesibios of Alexandria (ca. 300–250 B.C.E.). As described by ancient sources, it consisted of three components: a set of pipes, a keyboard mechanism, and a wind mechanism that used water to regulate air pressure.

Hymn [fr. Gr. *hymnos,* a song in praise of gods or heroes]. In Christian churches, a song in praise of God. St. Augustine (353–430) stipulates the essential presence of three elements—song, praise, and God—and thus distinguishes hymns from psalms or spiritual songs (mentioned in the Bible in Ephesians 5:19 and Colossians 3:16). The distinction is often blurred, however. The character and history of the hymn in the West are clearly distinguishable from those of the hymn of classical antiquity or of the closed *Byzantine repertory. From the beginning, the Western hymn has displayed, in varying measure, the influence of vulgar language, didactic (even evangelical) fervor, and congregational participation.

In its use of allegory and symbolism, the Jewish Psalter (first in Greek translation, then in Latin) was the model of the early Christian hymn in the West.

But by the fourth century, the hymn had defined itself by language (Latin), form (strophic verse), and manner of performance (some form of alternation) and had begun to relinquish the quantitative accent of classical Latin in favor of the rhythm and rhyme of typically medieval verse. The history of medieval hymnody begins with St. Ambrose (340–97), four of whose hymns ("Aeterne rerum conditor," "Deus creator omnium," "Iam surgit hora tertia," and "Veni redemptor gentium") were certified as genuine by St. Augustine. By the death of St. Gregory the Great (604), the form, language, and use of the medieval hymn were ordered. From the 14th through the 16th century there is a rich tradition of polyphonic settings of hymns in which successive verses alternate between polyphony and plainsong.

In the 16th century, the Lutheran German vernacular hymn *(Kirchenlied)* emerged as a congregational replacement for the corresponding sung Latin texts of Ordinary and Proper, then as general confessional and evangelical statement. The printed corpus of texts expanded slowly during Luther's lifetime from eight to over one hundred. Such texts, later known as *chorales, combine vernacular language, folk imagery, strophic form, and hortatory earnestness to make them prototypes of the modern congregational hymn.

Though Lutheran texts penetrated into the Anglo-American hymn repertory, particularly through 19th-century translation, the rhymed *Psalter translation of the Reformed church had far greater and more basic historical influence. The Elizabethan Injunctions of 1559 provided royal authority for the singing of hymns in the Anglican service; the 1562 Psalter of Thomas Sternhold (d. 1549) and John Hopkins (d. 1570)—the "Old Version"—contained, in addition to the rhymed Psalter translations, nine "original" hymns. In the 17th century the translation of George Wither (1623) and the *New Version* (1696) of Nahum Tate (1652–1715) and Nicholas Brady (1659–1726) virtually superseded Sternhold and Hopkins.

The Psalms of David Imitated in the Language of the New Testament (1719) by Isaac Watts aimed "rather to *imitate* than to translate, and thus to compose a *Psalm-book for Christians* after the manner of the Jewish Psalter." Most of his texts were formed in common, long, or short meter and thus lent themselves conveniently to the rhythmically equivalent melodies. The whole work of Watts marked the modernization of English hymnology. It was quickly followed by the texts of John Wesley (1703–91) and Charles Wesley (1707–88). These texts converged with others reflecting a heightened sense of liturgical order and blended with a corpus of new texts translated from Latin (e.g., those of John Mason Neale, 1818–66; John Keble, 1792–1866; and John Henry Cardinal Newman, 1801–90) producing *Hymns Ancient and Modern* in 1861.

Insofar as early North American denominational practices derived from European tradition, the histories of their hymnodies were also largely derivative. The first attempt to break away from this tradition was the *Bay Psalm Book (1640), which went through some 70 editions. In this period, lack of immediate contact with a performing tradition for congregational psalmody led to the widespread practice of *lining-out, and the skill of reading music consequently began to disappear.

This in turn led to the creation of the New England singing schools and led subsequently to the compositions of William Billings (1746–1800) [see Fuging tune] and later to the pedagogical work of Lowell Mason (1792–1872). Adaptation is visible in three areas: religious (the Great Awakening, its effect on the Separatist Baptists, their enthusiasm for experiential texts); notational (advent of the four- and seven-shape-notes as devices for teaching singing to the musically unlettered); and musical (the joining of secular folk song to religious text). There resulted white and black *spirituals, America's most distinctive contributions to hymnody, both bound to the 19th-century societies that nurtured them. White spirituals are found in *tune books (e.g., William Walker, *Southern Harmony,* 1835); black spirituals were collected in print after the Civil War. In style, the two are similar, reflecting personal religion, with shared textual sources, use of refrain, repetition, and chorus tag line; in tone, the black spirituals, viewed from the perspective of time, are generally far more eloquent.

The *gospel hymn associated with the urban evangelism of Dwight L. Moody (1837–99) and Ira Sankey (1840–1908), as in Percy P. Bliss and Sankey's *Gospel Hymns and Sacred Songs* (1875), flourished in the last quarter of the 19th century. Its textual and musical practices were not unlike those of the earlier spirituals, but resulted in styles distinctive to white and black congregations (e.g., Holiness and Pentecostal).

Hyper-, hypo- [Gr.]. Prefixes meaning literally over or above and under or below, respectively. In ancient Greek music, they were attached to the ethnic names of the *tonoi,* e.g., Hyperdorian, Hypodorian. The Hyperdorian *tonos* was a higher tuning of the Greater Perfect System than the Dorian *tonos;* the Hypodorian was a lower tuning than the Dorian. In the medieval modal system of paired modes (authentic and plagal), hypo- was attached to the low-lying plagal member of each pair [see Mode].

Hz. Abbr. for *Hertz.

I

Iamb, iambic. See Prosody; Modes, rhythmic.

Iberia. (1) A suite of 12 piano pieces by Albéniz, published in four sets of three in 1906–8. Their titles evoke Spanish places or scenes. Although Albéniz orchestrated two pieces himself, the five orchestrations by his friend Enrique Arbós are performed more often. (2) An orchestral work forming part of Debussy's *Images.*

Ibert, Jacques (François Antoine) (b. Paris, 15 Aug. 1890; d. there, 5 Feb. 1962). Composer. Pupil of Gédalge, Fauré, and Vidal. Director of the French Academy in Rome 1937–40, 1946–60; of the Paris Opéra and the Opéra-comique 1955–56. Related to "Les six" in style and temperament, but not officially associated with them. Works include 7 operas (*Angélique,* 1926; 2 collaborations with Honegger); 7 ballets (*Le chevalier errant,* after *Don Quixote,* 1935); incidental and film music, radio scores; 25 works for orchestra or large ensemble (*Escales,* 1922; *Bacchanale,* 1956; concertos); a string quartet, pieces for winds or strings; solo works for various instruments; piano music; choral works; songs.

Ichiyanagi, Toshi (b. Kobe, 4 Feb. 1933). Composer. Pupil of Ikenouchi; strongly influenced by Cage. In Japan founded the New Directions Group 1963, and the Orchestral Space Festival 1966. Works include *Appearance,* 3 instruments and 5 electronic devices (1967); *Extended Voices,* chorus (1967); *Music for Living Space,* chorus, computer (1969); *Theatre Music,* tape (1969); *Music for Living Process,* 2 dancers, chamber ensemble (1973); *Time Sequence,* piano (1976); a piano concerto (1988).

Ictus [Lat.]. (1) In prosody, and by analogy in music, a metrical *accent. (2) In the theory developed at Solesmes, the "rhythmic step" or "alighting point" that governs the rhythm of Gregorian chant.

Idée fixe [Fr., obsession]. Berlioz's term for the recurring musical idea linking the several movements of his *Symphonie fantastique* and associated in its program with the image of the beloved. See also Cyclic form.

Idiomatic. Of a musical work, exploiting the particular capabilities of the instrument or voice for which it is intended. These capabilities may include timbres, registers, and means of articulation as well as pitch combinations that are more readily produced on one instrument than another (e.g., a *glissando on the slide trombone as opposed to a valved brass instrument or an *Alberti bass on a keyboard instrument as opposed to a slide trombone).

Idiophone. Any musical instrument that produces sound by the vibration of its own primary material, i.e., without the vibrations of a string, membrane, or column of air.

Idomeneo, rè di Creta [It., Idomeneo, King of Crete]. Opera in three acts by Mozart (libretto by the Abbé Giovanni Battista Varesco, after a French libretto by Antoine Danchet), produced in Munich in 1781. Setting: Crete after the Trojan wars.

Idyll. (1) A short work in prose or verse depicting rustic life, sometimes synonymous with pastoral or *eclogue. (2) A musical work evoking the quality of pastoral or rural life.

Ikebe, Shin-Ichiro (b. Tokyo, 15 Sept. 1943). Composer. Pupil of Ikenouchi and Yashirō. Works include the opera *The Death Goddess* (1971); orchestral music (*Movements,* 1965; Piano Concerto; 3 symphonies; *Quadrants,* Japanese instruments, orchestra, 1974); chamber works: (*Raccontino,* violin, piano, 1967; *Energia,* 60 players, 1970); *Kusabi,* dancers, female chorus, and 11 players, 1972; *Oedipus' Pilgrimage,* joruri, male chorus, 10 players.

Ikenouchi, Tomojirō (b. Tokyo, 21 Oct. 1906). Composer. Pupil of Büsser. Taught at Nihon Univ. from 1936; at the National Univ. of Fine Arts from 1947; most Japanese composers of the postwar generation studied with him. His music reflects French influence; works include orchestral pieces (*Shiki* [The Four Seasons], 1938; *Symphony in Two Movements,* 1951); vocal music (*Yuya,* soprano, chamber orchestra, 1942); chamber works (3 string quartets; *Fantasy on a Japanese Folksong,* violin and piano, 1940; 3 "Sonatines").

Illica, Luigi (b. Castell'Arquato, near Piacenza, 9 May 1857; d. Colombarone, 16 Dec. 1919). Librettist, journalist, writer, and playwright. Wrote librettos for Catalani's *Wally* (1892), Giordano's *Andrea Chénier,* Mascagni's *Iris* (1898), among others; collaborated with Giocosa on Puccini's *Bohème, *Tosca,* and *Madama Butterfly.*

Im Takt [Ger.]. See *Takt*.

Images [Fr.]. (1) Six piano pieces by Debussy in two sets of three each: I (1905), "Reflets dans l'eau," "Hommage à Rameau," "Mouvement"; II (1907), "Cloches à travers les feuilles," "Et la lune descend sur le temple qui fut," "Poissons d'or." (2) *Images pour orchestre,* three symphonic poems by Debussy (1905–12): *Rondes de printemps, Ibéria, Gigues.* The second, *Ibéria,* consists of three movements: "Par les rues et par les chemins," "Les parfums de la nuit," and "Le matin d'un jour de fête."

Imbrie, Andrew (Welsh) (b. New York, 6 Apr. 1921). Composer and pianist. Pupil of Sessions. Teacher at Berkeley from 1949. Has made use of twelve-tone procedures. Works include 2 operas; 3 symphonies, concertos, and other orchestral music; chamber pieces (including string quartets; *Pilgrimage,* flute, clarinet, violin, cello, piano, and percussion, 1983); piano music; vocal works (including a Requiem, soprano, chorus, and orchestra, 1984).

Imbroglio [It.]. A scene, usually occurring in a comic opera, in which the illusion of confusion is created by means of polyphonic complexity and rhythmic, metric, and melodic diversity. Originating in 18th-century *opera buffa,* the imbroglio was brought to a high point of artfulness and intricacy in the end of the second act of Wagner's *Die Meistersinger.*

Imitation. The statement of a single motive or melody by two or more parts or voices in succession, each part continuing as the others enter in turn. If successive statements are at the same pitch level, the imitation is said to take place at the unison. Imitation often takes place at different pitch levels, however. Especially common is a regular alternation between statements at the original pitch level and statements at the interval of a fifth above or a fourth below. The distance in time between successive statements may vary, but it often remains constant within any one set of statements. Imitation is generally classified as belonging to one of three types—*canon, *fugue, and free imitation—depending upon the nature of the motive or melody and the preciseness of the restatements. Such techniques are found in all periods of Western art music from the 12th century to the present and in some non-Western musics as well.

In canon, each successive voice *(comes)* repeats the complete leading voice *(dux)* literally or in a given transformation (transposition, inversion, retrograde, augmentation, etc.) as prescribed by the "canon" or rule. In fugue, although the entire piece may be based on a single idea or subject (double fugues will have two, etc.), this idea may be developed, possibly reordering motives, and even integrated with new material (e.g., countersubjects, epi-

sodes). Furthermore, fugal imitations are often less strict than those in canon; characteristic intervals may be altered so long as the subject keeps its essential contour (e.g., *tonal versus real answers). The terms canonic imitation and fugato refer to sections of canon or fugue that appear within otherwise nonimitative pieces. Free imitation, however, is looser still, and in many cases the only material shared between voices is the opening motive. As in fugue, this motive may be modified in successive statements, so long as it remains recognizable. In all types of imitative counterpoint, the imitating voice may be accompanied by independent lines.

Although the term was probably not used until the 15th century, the various imitative techniques emerge as early as the 12th and 13th centuries. Some organa, *conductus,* and motets employ imitation (often in a form termed *voice exchange), and by the 14th century several canonic forms also appear: the *rota, the Italian *caccia, and the French *chace. During the 15th century, imitation became gradually more important (e.g., in both sacred and secular works by Dufay), but it was not until around 1500 that imitation became established as a paradigm of musical style in works by Josquin and his contemporaries. Composers of the middle and later 16th century, such as Gombert, Willaert, Clemens non Papa, and Palestrina, made still more extensive use of imitation, sometimes termed pervading imitation. Here, each line of text was set imitatively with a new melody, each such set of imitative entries termed a point of imitation, with successive points or sections overlapping one another. Pervading imitation was used in sacred genres (Masses, motets) and secular genres (madrigal, chanson) alike and also became the distinguishing feature of instrumental forms such as the *ricercar, *canzona, *fantasia, and *capriccio.

Imitation remained a basic technique of musical composition through the first half of the 18th century, not only in specifically imitative forms such as fugue and canon, but in a wide variety of vocal and instrumental music as well. The masters of the Classical style—Haydn, Mozart, and Beethoven—all make significant use of imitation also, though that style is usually thought to make distinctly less use of imitation and polyphony than do the styles of preceding centuries.

Imitative. Characterized by *imitation.

Immer [Ger.]. Always, continuously; e.g., *immer stärker,* continuously louder.

Imperfect. See Cadence, Interval, Mensural notation.

Imperfection. See Mensural notation.

Impetuoso [It.]. Impetuous.

Impressionism. A term principally applied to the style cultivated by Claude Debussy during the final decade of the 19th century and the first decade of the 20th. The term was originally introduced in the visual arts to characterize the work of a group of French painters of the late 19th century (e.g., Monet, whose painting *Impression: soleil levant* inspired critic Louis Leroy to coin the term in 1874) who exploited the suffusing effects of light, color, and atmospheric conditions to undermine sharply drawn contours. The subtle gradations produced by haze and smoke were especially favored, giving rise to softly focused, somewhat "blurred" images intended to convey the general "impression" of a scene rather than its precise visual equivalent.

Traditional descriptions of Debussy's style suggest a number of parallels with visual impressionism: finely graded instrumental colors; static, nonclimactic melodies, often circling around a single pitch; harmony conceived as a largely coloristic element; complex textures consisting of elaborate surface figurations, often suffusing whatever melodic material they contain; continuously evolving forms without sharp sectional divisions. First used as early as 1887, the term is not equally applicable to all of Debussy's works, and Debussy himself disapproved of the term in a letter to Jacques Durand in 1908.

Among Debussy's contemporaries, Ravel is often regarded as an impressionist; but despite corresponding emphasis on color and figuration, the more emphatic rhythm and phrase structure of much of Ravel's music sets it distinctly apart from that of Debussy.

Impromptu [Fr., unpremeditated]. In the 19th century and since, a composition, usually for piano, in an offhand or extemporized style or perhaps intended to suggest the result of sudden inspiration. The term was first used in 1822 by both Jan Václav Voříšek and Heinrich Marschner. The best-known examples are by Schubert (op. 90, D. 899, and op. 142, D. 935, for at least the first set of which the title was supplied not by Schubert but by his publisher), Chopin (opp. 29, 36, 51, 66), and Schumann (op. 5, actually a set of variations, and *Albumblätter* no. 9). Like other types of *character pieces, they are varied in form, though ternary form is common.

Improperia [Lat., reproaches]. In the Roman Catholic Rite, a series of chants sung at the Veneration of the Cross on Good Friday, expressing in alternation God's compassion for Israel and man's ingratitude as seen in the suffering of Christ.

Improvisation, extemporization. The creation of music in the course of performance. Even though it is tempting to distinguish simply between composed, or "precomposed," music (determined precisely in advance) and improvisation (created on the spot), the world of music actually comprises repertories and performances in which improvisation of quite different sorts is present in various degrees. Thus, music in oral tradition is normally composed by improvisation of a sort: the audible rendition of pieces (though usually without audience), whose components may then be altered and recombined and finally memorized. The performance of music in oral tradition, however, may or may not involve improvisation. In Western art music, which is heavily dependent on notation for transmission, improvisation includes phenomena such as the addition of extemporized ornaments as well as special improvised genres. Certain cultures with orally transmitted music such as those of South and West Asia also distinguish between improvised and memorized materials. Some improvisational systems are governed by theoretical rules strictly applied by performers. The degree to which a musician departs from a written or memorized work and the extent to which performances differ from each other may also be considered a function of improvisation. Thus, the presence or nature of improvisation is affected by, but does not depend upon, the concept of composition, the use of notation and oral tradition, and the nature of performance practice. But it seems most appropriate to reserve the term improvisation for cultures and repertories in which a distinction from nonimprovised or precomposed forms can be recognized.

In Western art music, improvisation has played its principal role in the supplementation and variation of written compositions. There was considerable emphasis on the art in the Baroque and Classical periods. Virtuosic genres such as the *toccata were sometimes improvised. Sweelinck, Frescobaldi, Buxtehude, Bach, and Handel were famed for their organ improvisations, and on the piano, Mozart and Beethoven. The practice of improvising Baroque forms such as fugues continued in the 19th century, constituting, well into the 20th, an academic requirement in certain European conservatories, and the performance of fugues based on themes given by the audience remained a special genre of modern organ virtuosos. But improvisation of works in contemporary styles continued in the 19th century; Mendelssohn, Liszt, Moscheles, Bruckner, Saint-Saëns, and Franck were famous for improvisations in the style of their own composed works.

An important improvisatory genre of the Classical and Romantic eras was the *cadenza of concertos, in which soloists combined thematic development and technical prowess.

Revival of improvisation came in the course of the 20th century as a result of several factors. Knowledge of non-Western music with its improvisatory systems stimulated composers, as did the development of jazz, a form principally improvised and in part indirectly derived from the improvised variation technique of West Africa. Complete domination by the musical score led, after 1950, to a reaction by composers such as Lukas Foss who required improvisation in sections of their works. In these, performers are typically directed to improvise for a specific amount of time on the basis of a stated group of tones. Composition with the use of aleatoric principles involves improvisation as well. The interest in authentic performance, especially of music from the 18th century and before, has also led to the development of improvisatory performance practice. In recent decades, improvisation has become an important factor in the music education of children. See also Aleatory music, Jazz, Performance practice.

The role of improvisation in non-Western musical cultures varies widely, the most developed improvisatory systems being those of India and the Middle East. Improvisation is not a major factor in Chinese and Japanese art music.

In Central Asia [Russ. *V sredney Azii*]. A "musical picture" for orchestra by Borodin (1880), evoking the journey of a caravan across the steppes.

In nomine [Lat.]. Any of over 150 English instrumental compositions of the 16th and 17th centuries, all using the *Sarum antiphon "Gloria tibi Trinitas" as a *cantus firmus.

Although a few examples are for lute and a few more for keyboard, most are for instrumental consort.

In the Steppes of Central Asia. See *In Central Asia.*

Incalzando [It.]. Pressing on, chasing.

Incatenatura [It.]. *Quodlibet.*

Incidental music. Music to be used in connection with a play. It may consist of instrumental music played before an act or between acts (*overture, *entr'acte, *interlude); it may be vocal or instrumental music accompanying the action of the play (songs and serenades, marches and dances, background music for monologues or dialogues, music for supernatural or transformation scenes); it may underscore the action or be a digression from the action.

Incoronazione di Poppea, L' [It., The Coronation of Poppea]. Opera in three acts by Monteverdi (libretto by G. F. Busenello, after Tacitus), produced in Venice in 1642. Setting: Rome during the reign of Nero, ca. 62 C.E.

Indeterminacy. See Aleatory music.

India, Sigismondo d' (b. Palermo, ca. 1582; d. Modena?, before 19 Apr. 1629). Composer. Director of chamber music at the ducal court of Savoy, 1611–

23; court musician in Modena from 1626. Composed a Mass, a sacred drama, and motets; many secular vocal compositions including polyphonic madrigals, villanellas, an opera, and many monodies.

Indian Queen, The. A *semi-opera in five acts by Purcell (play by John Dryden and Robert Howard, final masque by Daniel Purcell), produced in London in 1695. Setting: Peru and Mexico.

Indy, (Paul Marie Théodore) Vincent d' (b. Paris, 27 Mar. 1851; d. there, 2 Dec. 1931). Composer. Pupil of Franck. From 1872 worked as percussionist, church organist, piano accompanist, choral conductor. Taught at the Schola cantorum from 1897 (director from 1904; pupils included Roussel and Séverac); at the conservatory 1912–29. Appeared widely as a conductor in western Europe, Russia, and the U.S. Composed operas (*Fervaal,* 1887–95; *L'étranger,* Brussels, 1903; *La légende de Saint Christophe,* 1908–15); orchestral works (*Le chant de la cloche,* dramatic symphony with voices, after Schiller, 1884; *Symphonie sur un thème montagnard,* 1887; the *Istar* Variations, 1897; *Jour de l'été à la montagne,* 1906; Concerto for flute and cello, op. 89); 3 string quartets, String Sextet, 2 piano trios, Piano Quintet op. 81, Piano Quartet, violin and cello sonatas; choral music, songs; many piano pieces. Also an editor of early music and writer of criticism, essays, polemics.

Inégales [Fr.]. See *Notes inégales.*

Inflection, inflexion. (1) See Monotone, Psalm tone. (2) Deliberate deviation from the norm of a pitch. It is prominent in jazz [see Blue note] and popular music and is not unknown in Western art music.

Ingegneri, Marc'Antonio [Marco Antonio, Marc Antonio, Marcantonio] (b. Verona, ca. 1547; d. Cremona, 1 July 1592). Composer. Probably a student of Vincenzo Ruffo. Prefect of music (by 1578) and *maestro di cappella* (by 1579) at the Cremona cathedral. Composed Masses, motets, responsories, and numerous madrigals. Monteverdi was his pupil.

Inghelbrecht, Désiré Émile (b. Paris, 17 Sept. 1880; d. there, 14 Feb. 1965). Composer and conductor. Conducted at several theaters including the Ballets Suédois (1920–23) and the Paris Opéra (1945–50); 1934 founded the French National Radio Orchestra. Composed in the styles of Fauré and Debussy; some works employ folk songs. Wrote operas, operettas, and ballets; orchestral music (*Iberiana,* with solo violin, 1949); a Requiem; chamber music; piano pieces (*La Nursery,* 5 vols., 1905–11); choral music and songs.

Innig [Ger.]. Heartfelt, sincere, fervent.

Inno [It.]. Hymn.

Insieme [It.]. Together.

Instrument. (1) [Ger.] In Germany in the 17th and 18th centuries, a stringed keyboard instrument, especially the clavichord; in the early 19th century, the piano.

(2) Any means of producing sounds that are considered to be music by the persons producing them, except the human voice and body areas used for musical purposes. The scientific study of musical instruments is called organology.

The terms and classifications of instruments reflect the culture and needs of the classifier. They tend to fall into three general categories based on playing method, structure or material, and use or status. These can be either practical or theoretical.

Researchers' systems generally deal with (a) where and for what purpose an instrument is used, (b) how it is played, or (c) its physical features. The first category is favored by historians and anthropologists. Most organologists find physical features and performance practice more amenable to Western-style classifications. A system in wide use identifies four categories, shown below with their first layers of subclasses and a few examples.

1. Idiophone. Vibrations are produced, without stretching the basic material, by striking either one portion of the instrument against another (cymbals) or another object against the instrument (triangle), by scraping, by plucking *(sanza)*, by rubbing, or by bowing (nail violin or modern single cymbal).

2. Membranophone. Sound produced by vibrations of a stretched membrane that is struck or rubbed (drum). The mirliton (kazoo) is called a blown membranophone.

3. Chordophone. Sound produced by a vibrating (stretching) string activated by striking, plucking, or bowing (rubbing). Its four basic families are: (i) Lute. Strings are parallel to the soundboard and extend beyond it along a neck or fingerboard (guitar, violin, *sitār*). (ii) Zither. Strings are parallel to the soundboard and functionally its same length (piano, dulcimer, *koto*). (iii) Harp. Strings are at right angles to the soundboard. (iv) Lyre. Strings are parallel to the soundboard and are suspended beyond it on a crossbar of a yoke (Ethiopian *krar* and *beganna*).

4. Aerophone. Sound from a vibrating column of air. It may be activated from a blow hole (flute), a reed (single, double, or quadruple; clarinet, shawm, oboe), or buzzing lips (trumpet, horn).

Instrumentation. (1) *Orchestration. (2) The particular combination of instruments employed in any piece.

Intabulation [fr. It. *intabolatura, intavolatura;* Fr. *reducite en tablature;* Ger. *Intabulierung*]. An arrangement of a vocal or instrumental ensemble work

for keyboard or plucked string instrument, notated in *tablature. The earliest surviving notated keyboard music (ca. 1320) and that for lute, *vihuela,* guitar, etc. (ca. 1470–73), consists overwhelmingly of arrangements of vocal polyphony and (less frequently) ensemble dances and abstract pieces such as ricercars. Although the term intabulation is usually associated only with music before 1600, the procedure did continue into the Baroque.

Intavolatura [It.]. *Intabulation. On the title pages of keyboard music of the 16th and 17th centuries, the term often refers to the use of score format with two staves, as distinct from *tablatures of the usual sort.

Intensity. In *acoustics, the energy of a sound as measured in watts per square meter at some point. It is the principal property responsible for the sensation of loudness of a sound.

Interchange of voices. See Voice exchange.

Interference. In *acoustics, the result of the simultaneous presence in a medium of sound waves from two or more sources.

Interlude. Music played between sections of a composition or of a dramatic work [see also Act tune, *Entr'acte, Intermède, Intermedio, Intermezzo*]. In a dramatic work, it may be purely instrumental music or may include action or narration related to the principal work. In purely instrumental music, it may serve to connect larger movements or sections. In church music, the term is applied to music (often improvised) played between verses (sometimes between lines) of a hymn or Psalm.

Intermède [Fr.]. A work performed between the acts of a play or opera. Its beginnings in France in the 16th century are closely related to the Italian *intermedio*. The French *intermède,* however, like French opera, soon gave considerably greater play to ballet. In the 17th century, such works were often fully comparable to contemporaneous operas.

Intermedio [It.]. In the Renaissance, a work performed between the acts of a play. Such works were performed beginning in the late 15th century in Ferrara between the acts of plays by Terence and Plautus as well as by playwrights of the time and could consist of instrumental music alone or staged presentations of pastoral or mythological subjects with singers, dancers, and instrumentalists. The *moresca was an important ingredient of the early *intermedio*. For the related genre in France, see *Intermède;* for the related 18th-century phenomenon, see *Intermezzo*.

Intermezzo [It.]. (1) In the 18th century, a comic work performed between the acts of a serious opera. Its origins lie in the *intermedio* (to which the term is

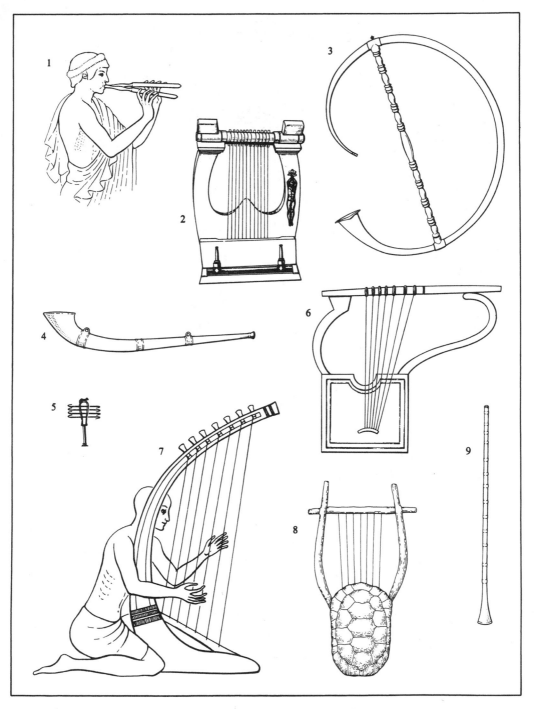

Ancient instruments: 1. Aulos (Greece).   2. Kithara (Greece).   3. Cornu (Rome).   4. Lituus (Rome).
5. Sistrum (Sumeria, Egypt, Rome).   6. Lyre (Egypt).   7. Bow harp (Egypt).   8. Lyra (Greece).   9. Tuba (Rome).

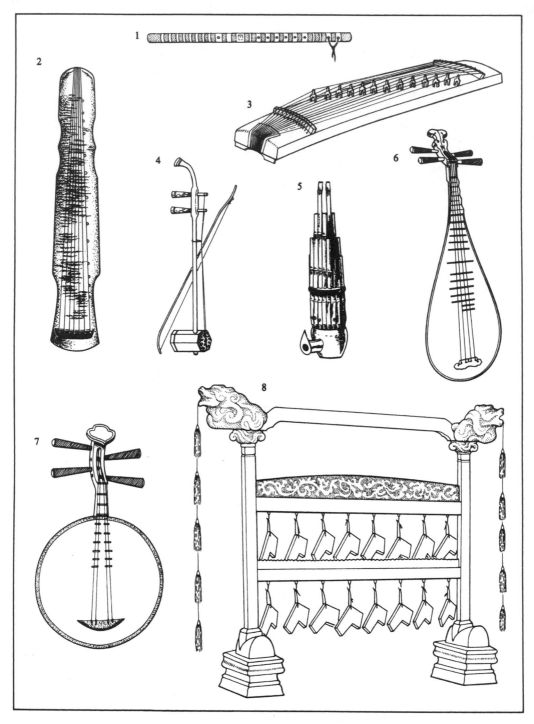

Chinese instruments: 1. Ti-tzu (not to scale). 2. Ch'in. 3. Cheng. 4. Erh-hu. 5. Sheng. 6. P'i-p'a. 7. Yüeh-ch'in.
8. Lithophone or ch'ing (not to scale).

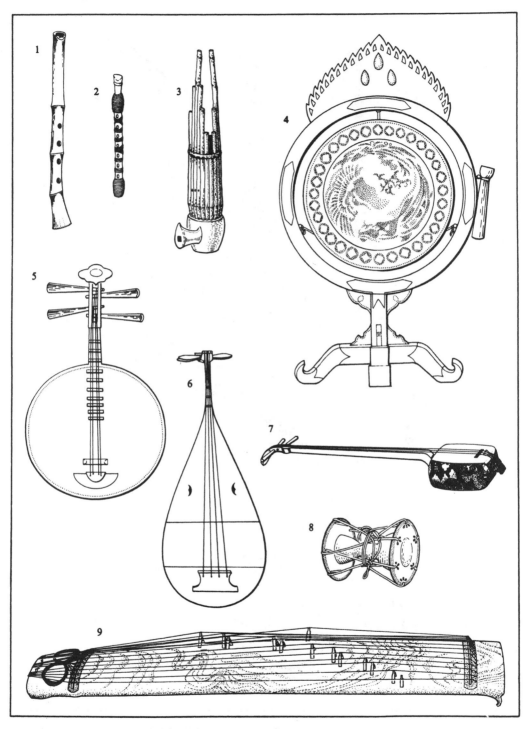

Japanese instruments: 1. Shakuhachi. 2. Hichiriki (shown twice its size in relation to others). 3. Sho.
4. Tsuridaiko. 5. Gekkin. 6. Biwa. 7. Shamisen. 8. Kotsuzumi. 9. Koto.

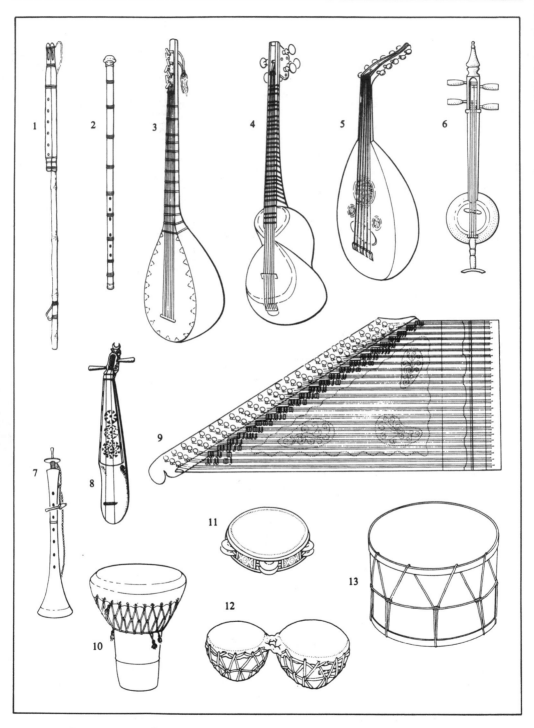

Instruments of the Near and Middle East: 1. Arghūl. 2. Nāy. 3. Saz. 4. Tār. 5. ʿŪd. 6. Kamānjah. 7. Zūrnā.
8. Rabāb. 9. Qānūn. 10. Darabukkah. 11. Daff. 12. Naqqārah. 13. Davul (shown half size in relation to others).

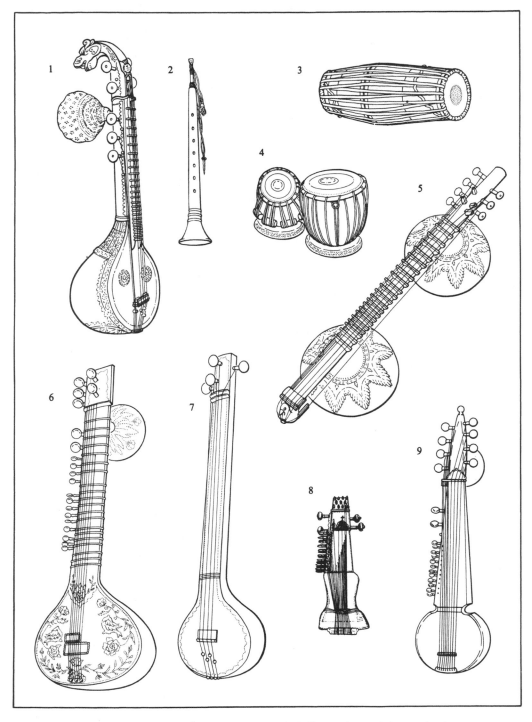

Instruments of South Asia: 1. Vīṇā.   2. Śahnāi (shown one and a half times size in relation to others).
3. Mṛdaṅgam   4. Tablā.   5. Bīn.   6. Sitār.   7. Tamburā.   8. Sāraṅgī.   9. Sarod.

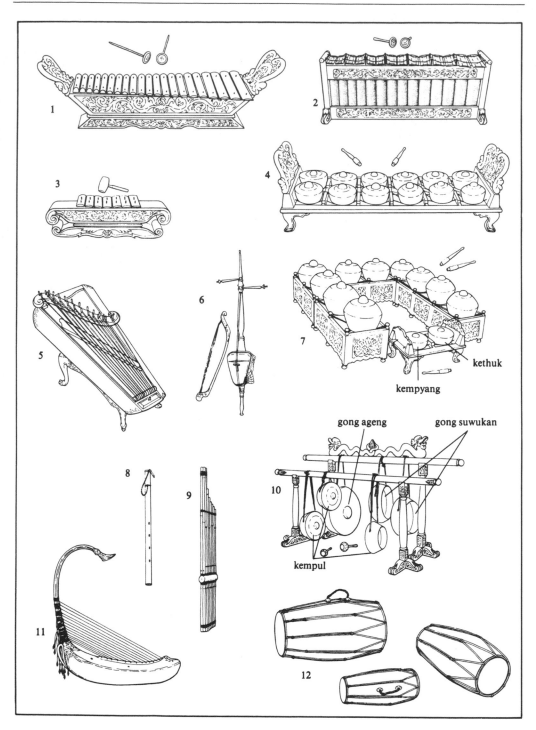

Instruments of Southeast Asia: 1. Gambang. 2. Gender. 3. Saron. 4. Bonang. 5. Clempung. 6. Rebab. 7. Kenong with kethuk and kempyang (shown half size in relation to others). 8. Suling (shown one and a half times size). 9. Khene. 10. Gong ageng, gong suwukan, and kempul (shown three-quarters size). 11. Saùnggauk. 12. Kendang.

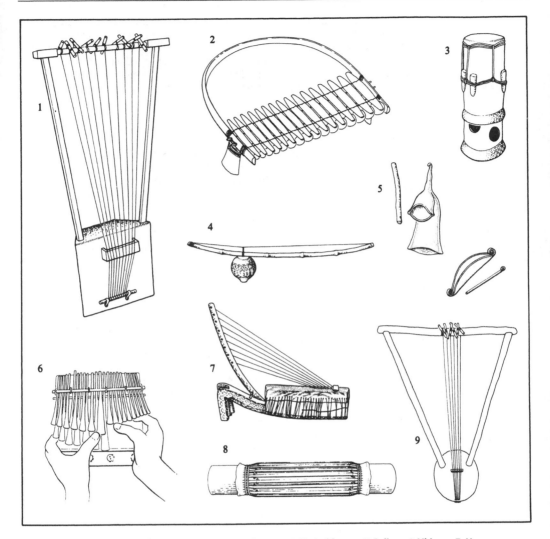

African instruments: 1. Bagana. 2. Xylophone. 3. Drum. 4. Musical bow. 5. Bells. 6. Mbira. 7. Harp. 8. Valiha. 9. Krar.

also sometimes applied) and in the comic scenes of 17th-century Italian opera.

(2) In the 19th and 20th centuries, a middle movement or section of a larger work, usually lighter in character than its surroundings; or an independent work of small scale, often a lyrical piece for piano of the general type termed *character pieces.

Interpretation. Those aspects of the performance of a work that result from the performer's particular realization of the composer's instructions as set down in musical notation. The boundary between notation and performance, however, is not as clear as it has sometimes seemed, for the notation of every period is in some degree incomplete and functions within a set of expectations or conventions that guides (or guided) its realization [see Performance practice]. Interpretation is often thought of as the individual performer's unique and personal contribution to the realization of a work. Used in this way, the term is likely to carry with it notions of expression.

Interval [Fr. *intervalle;* Ger. *Intervall;* It. *intervallo;* Sp. *intervalo*]. The relationship between two pitches [see Pitch (3)]. For purposes of Western tonal music, intervals are named according to (1) the number of diatonic scale degrees included, as represented in the letter names of the two pitches, and (2) the number of semitones (the smallest interval in the Western system) between the two pitches. The former is expressed as a number, determined by counting the letters of the alphabet beginning with that of the lower pitch and including that of the higher (remembering that only the first seven letters are used and then repeated). Thus, c–c is a prime or unison, c–d a second, c–e a third, c–f a fourth, c–g a fifth, c–a a sixth, c–b a seventh, c–c' an octave. Intervals larger than an octave can be named similarly (ninth, tenth, eleventh, etc.), though they are also known as compound intervals, since they can be thought of as consisting of an octave plus a smaller interval (e.g., a tenth is the same as an octave plus a third). For most purposes, compound intervals function as do their corresponding simple intervals (e.g., a tenth functions much as does a third, both being consonant [see Consonance and dissonance]). The number of semitones between the two pitches is indicated by a qualifying adjective (perfect, major, minor, diminished, or augmented), as illustrated in Table 1, where the number of semitones in each case is given in parentheses.

This table shows that the fourth, fifth, and octave above the tonic in a major scale (c–f, c–g, c–c', as illustrated here with the scale of C major) are called perfect. The remaining intervals above the tonic (c–d, c–e, c–a, c–b) are called major. A perfect interval if reduced by a semitone becomes diminished. A major interval if reduced by a semitone becomes minor, and a minor interval if reduced by a semitone becomes diminished. Both perfect and major intervals become augmented if increased by a semitone. Augmented and diminished intervals may become doubly augmented or doubly diminished by the addition or subtraction of yet another semitone, respectively. Interval types that contain the same number of semitones but have different names (e.g., the diminished third and the major second) are enharmonically equivalent [see Enharmonic] (though specific examples of each will be enharmonically equivalent only if the specific pitches in question are enharmonically equivalent).

Two intervals that form an octave when added together are the complements of one another, and the *inversion of an interval is its complement. Thus, the inversion of a major sixth (e.g., c–a) is a minor third

(a–c'), and these two intervals complement each other in that they form an octave when added together (c–a + a–c' = c–c'). This feature of inversion, like the function of compound intervals, derives from the phenomenon of octave equivalence, according to which pitches separated by one or more octaves are perceived as in some sense equivalent. Western pitch names reflect this perception in assigning the same letter name to all pitches separated by one or more octaves. All such pitches (e.g., all A's or all C's) are said to belong to the same pitch class (e.g., A or C). Thus, the octave enjoys a unique status among the intervals employed in Western music. Whether this derives from its acoustical properties [see Acoustics, Harmonics] is a matter of some debate.

Musical styles have up to now employed only a fraction of the intervals that the human ear can differentiate, and current nomenclature consequently allows a considerable latitude to the range of pitches subsumed by any particular term. Non-Western musical systems employ a wide variety of interval types, including intervals smaller than the smallest employed in Western tonal music. See also Microtone.

The interval between two pitches can be represented as the ratio of the two string lengths required to produce those two pitches. Thus, if a string is divided exactly in half, the shorter length will produce a pitch one octave higher than that of the undivided string, with the result that the octave may be represented by the ratio 2:1 [see Table 2]. The ratio of the sum of any two intervals is equal to the product of the ratios of those intervals. Thus, if a fifth (3:2) is added to a fourth (4:3), the result is an octave (3/2 × 4/3 = 2/1). Similarly, the ratio of the difference of any two intervals is equal to the quotient of the larger ratio divided by the smaller, which is the same thing as the product of the larger ratio and the reciprocal of the smaller. (String lengths given in Table 2 are in fact denominators in the ratio 200,000:length.)

The interval between two pitches can also be represented as the ratio of the two frequencies that produce the two pitches. Since the frequency of a vibrating string varies inversely with its length [see Acoustics], the inverse of the ratio of frequencies is

Table 1

	Diminished	Minor		Major	Augmented
Second	c#–db (0)	c–db (1)		c–d (2)	c–d# (3)
Third	c#–eb (2)	c–eb (3)		c–e (4)	c–e# (5)
Sixth	c#–ab (7)	c–ab (8)		c–a (9)	c–a# (10)
Seventh	c#–bb (9)	c–bb (10)		c–b (11)	c–b# (12)
			Perfect		
Fourth	c#–f (4)		c–f (5)		c–f# (6)
Fifth	c#–g (6)		c–g (7)		c–g# (8)
Octave	c#–c' (11)		c–c' (12)		c–c#9(13)

able 2

terval	Pitch	Pythagorean			Just intonation			Mean-tone			Equal temperament		
		Ratio	Log	Cents	Ratio	Log	Cents	String length	Log	Cents	String length	Log	Cents
rime or unison	C	1:1	.00000	0	1:1	.00000	0	200,000	.00000	0	200,000	.00000	0
Minor 2nd	D♭	256:243	.02263	90.2	16:15	.02803	111.7	—	—	—	188,775	.02509	100
ugm. prime	C♯	2187:2048	.02852	113.7	25:24	.01773	70.7	192,120	.01908	76.1	188,775	.02509	100
Major 2nd	D	9:8	.05115	203.9	9:8	.05115	203.9	178,885	.04806	193.2	178,180	.05017	200
Minor 3rd	E♭	32:27	.07379	294.1	6:5	.07918	315.6	167,188	.07783	310.3	168,179	.07526	300
Major 3rd	E	81:64	.10231	407.8	5:4	.09691	386.3	160,000	.09691	386.3	158,740	.10034	400
erfect 4th	F	4:3	.12494	498.0	4:3	.12494	498.0	149,533	.12629	503.4	149,831	.12543	500
ugm. 4th	F♯	729:512	.15346	611.7	45:32	.14806	590.2	143,108	.14537	579.5	141,421	.15051	600
erfect 5th	G	3:2	.17609	702.0	3:2	.17609	702.0	133,749	.17474	696.6	133,483	.17560	700
ugm. 5th	G♯	6561:4096	.20461	815.6	25:16	.19382	772.6	128,000	.19382	772.6	125,992	.20069	800
Minor 6th	A♭	128:81	.19873	792.2	8:5	.20412	813.6	—	—	—	125,992	.20069	800
Major 6th	A	27:16	.22724	905.9	5:3	.22185	884.4	119,626	.22320	889.7	118,921	.22577	900
Minor 7th	B♭	16:9	.24988	996.1	9:5	.25527	1017.6	111,801	.25258	1006.9	112,246	.25086	1000
Major 7th	B	243:128	.27840	1109.8	15:8	.27300	1088.3	107,002	.27165	1082.9	105,946	.27594	1100
Octave	C	2:1	.30103	1200.0	2:1	.30103	1200.0	100,000	.30103	1200.0	100,000	.30103	1200

the ratio of the two string lengths required to produce a given interval. Thus, given a pitch of some frequency, the pitch an octave above it will have a frequency equal to twice the frequency of the first pitch, i.e., in the ratio 2:1.

Intervals whose ratios are those occurring in the harmonic series [see Harmonics], that is, intervals produced by dividing the length of a string of constant tension and mass per unit of length successively by 2, 3, 4, 5, 6 and so forth, are said to be acoustically pure. Thus, the ratios 3/2, 4/3, 5/4, and 6/5 describe the acoustically pure perfect fifth, perfect fourth, major third, and minor third, respectively.

In the *Pythagorean scale, all intervals except the octave are multiples of the fifth (3:2). Let A♭–G♯ be a segment of the pitch continuum comprising twelve fifths. Then if C is arbitrarily assigned the ratio 1:1, the ratios of the remaining intervals can be calculated through multiplication or division of 1/1 by the requisite number of fifths. To bring the entire series into one octave, ratios to the right of the 1:1 octave must be divided by 2 the appropriate number of times; those to the left of this octave must be multiplied by 2 the appropriate number of times. In this way the standard ratios for the Pythagorean scale (as found in Table 2) are derived.

Intervals in *just intonation may be derived from the Pythagorean scale by keeping the latter's C (1/1, 2/1), F (4/3), G (3/2), and D (9/8); dividing C, G, and F by 16/15 to obtain B, F♯, and E; dividing C and F by 10/9 to obtain B♭ and E♭; multiplying G by 10/9 to obtain A; and, finally, multiplying C and G by 25/24 to obtain C♯ and G♯.

Intervals in *mean-tone temperament can be approximated by tempering each interval of the Pythagorean series by $37x/10,000$, where x equals the number of fifths needed to generate the Pythagorean ratio. Intervals to the left of 1:1 add this temperament; those to the right subtract it. For example, three fifths are needed to generate the Pythagorean E♭ (32/27), so mean-tone E♭ is approximately $32/27 + 3(37)/10000 = 32000/27000 + 11.1(27)/27000 \approx 32300/27000$ or $323/270$.

In equal *temperament, all semitones are of exactly the same size, and the sum of 12 semitones must be an octave with the ratio 2:1. Since the sum of two intervals is the product of their ratios, the ratio for the equally tempered semitone must be a number n that when raised to the 12th power equals 2. That is, given the starting point of 1:1 or simply 1, the semitone above will be $1 \times n$, the next semitone above will be $(1 \times n) \times n$ or n^2, and so forth. Since $n^{12} = 2$, $n = \sqrt[12]{2}$ or 1.05946. In terms of frequency, this means that given a pitch of a certain frequency, in equal temperament, the pitch a semitone above will have a frequency equal to the frequency of the first pitch multiplied by $\sqrt[12]{2}$.

For precise calculations of tempered intervals, musicians use a logarithmic scale in which the octave is given the value 1200 cents and in which each semitone in equal temperament is given the value 100 cents. Table 2 permits the comparison of intervals of various sizes in these terms.

Intonation. (1) The degree to which pitch is accurately produced in performance, especially among the players in an ensemble. (2) A system of tuning, such as *just intonation. (3) The first pitches of a *psalm tone or other form of plainchant.

Intonatione [It.]. A short liturgical piece for organ intended to establish the pitch and mode of a following vocal composition.

Intrada [Ger.; It. also *entrata;* Sp., Port. *entrada;* Fr. *entrée*]. A piece that accompanies the entrance of a character on the stage or of an important personage at an event; also music that introduces or marks the beginning of another work or of a dance [see also *Entrée*].

Introduction [Eng., Fr.; Ger. *Einleitung, Eingang;* It. *introduzione;* Sp. *introducción*]. A passage, usually in a slow tempo, at the beginning of a movement or work and preparatory to the main body of the form. Such passages vary widely in length and complexity. Movements in *sonata form, especially the first movements of symphonies, sonatas, and the like, often have slow introductions (e.g., Haydn, Symphony nos. 101 and 104; Beethoven, Symphony nos. 1 and 7).

Introit [Lat. *introitus*]. In *Gregorian chant, the first item of the *Proper of the *Mass, sung during the procession of the celebrant to the altar. It is an example of antiphonal *psalmody, in *neumatic style, consisting of an antiphon (A), a verse (V, abbr. "Ps." or the like for "Psalmus" in early manuscripts and in liturgical books), and the lesser *Doxology (D) as follows: A V D A. The verse and Doxology are sung to a *psalm tone.

Invention [Eng., Ger.; It. *invenzione;* Lat. *inventio*]. A discovery, an original product of the imagination. The term is associated with musical works beginning in the 16th century. It implies no particular musical characteristics for the works in question. Among German composers and theorists of the 17th and 18th centuries (who often prefer the Latin form), the term is closely tied to its use in rhetoric. Bach's use of the term is in this tradition. The works by Bach to which the term is generally applied are 15 in two-part counterpoint BWV 772–86 and 15 in three-part counterpoint BWV 787–801, all appearing in the *Clavier-Büchlein* for Wilhelm Friedemann Bach of 1723. No single form characterizes these works, nor do all employ imitation. They make significant use of *invertible counterpoint, and both sets are arranged in the following ascending key scheme (lowercase letters for minor keys): C, c, D, d, E♭, E, e, F, f, G, g, A, a, B♭, b.

Inventionshorn [Ger.]. See Horn.

Inversion. One interval is the inversion or complement of another if the sum of the two intervals forms

a third, fixed interval with respect to which the inversion takes place. Unless something to the contrary is specified, inversion is usually reckoned with respect to the octave. In this case, an interval is inverted by placing the lower pitch class above the upper one, that is, by raising the lower pitch class an octave. Thus, the inversion of the interval c–e is e–c'. Since the octave contains 12 semitones, the sum of two intervals related by inversion is 12 (in the preceding example, 4 + 8). With respect to the octave, therefore, the inversion of any interval of n semitones is the complement of n with respect to (with a modulus of) 12, or $12 - n$. In terms of the nomenclature of intervals employed in tonal music, the sum of the numbers associated with the two intervals will always be 9, perfect intervals yielding perfect intervals, major intervals yielding minor, and minor yielding major. Thus, the inversion of a perfect fifth is a perfect fourth; of a major third, a minor sixth; of a minor third, a major sixth; of a major second, a minor seventh; of a minor second, a major seventh.

If, as in some examples of *invertible counterpoint, the inversion takes place at an interval other than the octave, similar principles apply. Thus, in inversion at the twelfth, the lower pitch is raised a twelfth, e.g., c–g becomes g–g' or a fifth becomes an octave.

1. Triad in (a) root position, (b) first inversion, and (c) second inversion; seventh chord in (d) root position, (e) first inversion, (f) second inversion, and (g) third inversion.

Two chords are related by inversion if both contain the same pitch classes and have the same root, but have different pitch classes in the bass or lowest-sounding position. In the case of the *triad, a root-position chord has the root in the bass with the third and fifth above. If, however, the third is the lowest-sounding pitch, the chord is in first inversion, and if the fifth is the lowest, the chord is in second inversion. Thus, the root-position triad c–e–g becomes e–g–c' in first inversion and g–c'–e' in second inversion. For seventh chords, if the seventh is in the bass, the chord is in third inversion [see Ex. 1]. The nomenclature for chord inversions thus depends solely on the lowest-sounding pitch and is not affected by the particular disposition of the remaining pitches. Because the intervals formed above its lowest-sounding pitch are a sixth and a fourth, the second-inversion triad is termed a six-four chord; similarly, a first inversion triad is termed a six-three chord, or simply a six or sixth chord. See also Harmonic analysis, Thoroughbass.

The inversion of a melody is a melody whose contour is the mirror image of the original melody. Thus, where the original melody rises, the inversion falls and vice versa. The intervals between successive pitches may remain exact or, more often in tonal music, they may be the equivalents within the diatonic scale. Hence, c'–d'–e' may become c'–b–a (where the first descent is by a semitone rather than by a whole tone) instead of c'–b♭–a♭. In either case, the starting pitches need not be the same [see Ex. 2]. Melodic inversion has been common at least since the 15th century, particularly in imitative forms [see Canon, Fugue, Imitation]. Inversion may be indicated by phrases such as "per motu contrario" and "per arsin et thesin."

2. Bach, Fugue in G major from *The Well-Tempered Clavier*, bk. 1.

Inversion is one of the four basic operations used in *twelve-tone composition. Row inversion resembles melodic inversion. But since the crucial property of a row is the order in which pitch classes appear, the particular register in which any pitch class appears being independent of its position in the order, the relations of contour characteristic of melodic inversion need not be preserved between a row and its inversion. Thus, although a row can be inverted by preserving precisely the number of semitones between adjacent pitches while reversing their direction, a more general formulation of the process of inversion in twelve-tone music forms the inversion of a row by taking the complements mod 12 of the pitch numbers of that row. If the pitch classes from C up through B are numbered 0 through 11, respectively, the inversion of the row 0 1 2 3 4 5 6 7 8 9 10 11 (the trivial case of an ascending chromatic scale) can be found by subtracting each pitch number from 12, yielding 12 (= 0) 11 10 9 8 7 6 5 4 3 2 1 (a descending chromatic scale). Both forms may be transposed to begin on any of the 12 pitch classes by adding a constant (mod 12) to their pitch numbers. Thus, in the present example, the inversion transposed up a major third (4 semitones) would be 4 3 2 1 0 11 10 9 8 7 6 5.

Inverted canon. See Canon.

Inverted fugue. *Counterfugue.

Inverted mordent. See *Schneller.*

Invertible counterpoint. Counterpoint in which the lower voice or voices may also be placed above the higher (or the higher below the lower); thus, counterpoint in which the intervals or chords may be inverted [see Inversion] and remain correct as counterpoint. If for two voices, it is termed double counterpoint; if for three, triple; if for four, quadruple; etc. The inversion may take place at the octave or at some other interval; e.g., the inversion may be achieved by raising the lower voice or lowering the upper voice an octave, a tenth, a twelfth, etc.

Of primary concern in the composition of invertible counterpoint is that the inversion process not introduce parallel perfect intervals [see Parallel fifths] or dissonances that are incorrectly treated [see Counterpoint]. In the simplest case—double counterpoint at the octave—all consonances invert to consonances (thirds become sixths, sixths become thirds) except the perfect fifth, which becomes a perfect fourth; all dissonances invert to dissonances (seconds become sevenths, sevenths become seconds) except the perfect fourth, which becomes a perfect fifth; and all perfect intervals invert to perfect intervals. Thus, only the perfect fifth need be treated with special care, to avoid an incorrect dissonance. Inversion at some other interval is rather more complicated. In inversion at the twelfth, for example, sixths become sevenths, substituting dissonances for frequently used consonances. J. S. Bach's Two-part Invention no. 9, employs double counterpoint at the octave; Bach's Three-part Sinfonia no. 9, employs triple counterpoint at the octave. More complex examples occur in Bach's use of *canon, notably in the *Canonic Variations on Vom Himmel hoch* BWV 769 and in the **Art of Fugue,* and in the Confiteor of the *B-minor Mass.

Invitation to the Dance. See *Aufforderung zum Tanz.*

Invitatory [L. *invitatorium*]. Psalm 94 (95), "Venite, exsultemus Domino" (Oh come, let us sing unto the Lord, often referred to as "the *Venite*"), especially as sung with an antiphon at the opening of Matins in the *Office of the Roman Catholic Rite or in the Anglican rite as a component of Morning Prayer.

Ionian. See Mode.

Iphigénie en Aulide [Fr., Iphigenia in Aulis]. Opera in three acts by Gluck (libretto by F. L. G. le Bland du Roullet, after Racine's tragedy, based in turn on Euripides), produced in Paris in 1774.

Iphigénie en Tauride [Fr., Iphigenia in Tauris]. Opera in four acts by Gluck (libretto by N. F. Guillard and F. L. G. le Bland du Roullet, after Euripides) produced in Paris in 1779. Gluck revised the work for a German translation by J. B. von Alxinger that was produced in Vienna in 1781.

Ippolitov-Ivanov [Ivanov], **Mikhail Mikhaylovich** (b. Gatchina, 19 Nov. 1859; d. Moscow, 28 Jan. 1935). Composer and conductor. Taught at the Moscow Conservatory from 1893 (director, 1905–22). Students included Vasilenko and Glier. Conducted Bolshoi Theater from 1925. His music shows the influence of oriental folk song. Composed operas (*Ruf'* [Ruth], 1887; *Poslednyaya barrikada* [The Last Barricade], 1933); orchestral works (*Kavkazskiye eskizï* [Caucasian Sketches], 1894; Symphony in E minor op. 46, 1908; *Armyanskaya rapsodiya* [Armenian Rhapsody], 1895); choral works (*Gimn trudu* [Hymn to Labor], chorus, orchestra, brass band, op. 59, 1934); chamber music; songs.

Īqā' [Ar.]. The unit in the classical Arabic system of rhythmic modes.

Iradier [Yradier], **Sebastián** (b. Sauciego, Álava, Spain, 20 Jan. 1809; d. Vitoria, Spain, 6 Dec. 1865). Composer. Perhaps professor at the Madrid Conservatory; visited Cuba; 1850s, lived in Paris. Composed songs (including "La paloma," called a *canción americana,* "Ay Chiquita!" and "El arreglito," on which Bizet based Carmen's Habanera).

Ireland, John (Nicholson) (b. Bowdoin, Cheshire, 13 Aug. 1879; d. Rock Mill, Washington, Sussex, 12 June 1962). Composer and pianist. Pupil of Stanford. Organist and choirmaster at St. Luke's Church in Chelsea, 1904–26. Taught at the Royal College of Music from 1923; among his pupils were Moeran and Britten. Works include choral music (*These Things Shall Be,* 1936–37); services; part songs; song cycles; orchestral works (*The Forgotten Rite,* 1913; the Piano Concerto in E♭, 1930; *Legend,* piano and orchestra, 1933; *A London Overture,* 1936); chamber music (including string quartets, sonatas); organ music; piano works, including 40 "lyric pieces"; the score to the film *The Overlanders* (1947).

Irino, Yoshirō (b. Vladivostok, 13 Nov. 1921; d. Tokyo, 28 June 1980). Composer. Studied with Saburō Moroi. Taught at the Tōhō Gaknen School of Music (director from 1960) and at the Tokyo Music College (from 1973). Organized the Institute of Twentieth-Century Music 1957. Employed twelve-tone technique. Works include an opera (*Aya no Tsuzumi,* 1975), 3 dance dramas, and other dramatic works; choral pieces; orchestral/ensemble pieces (2 symphonies; *Sinfonietta,* 1953; *Wandlungen,* 2 shakuhachi and orchestra, 1973); chamber music (String Sextet, 1950; *Music for 2 Koto,* 1957; *Quintet,* clarinet, alto saxophone, trumpet, piano, and cello, 1958; *Duo concertante,* alto saxophone, koto, 1979).

Irish harp [Gael. *cláirseach*]. A *frame harp with a sound box carved from a single piece of wood, a pillar that curves outward, and 30 to 36 metal strings. An instrument of this type was played in 10th-century Ireland and remained popular until the late 18th century, especially as an accompaniment for songs. Although it became a national symbol, the playing tradition died out at the beginning of the 19th century. A modern version of the instrument employs gut or synthetic strings, each with a tuning hook for raising the pitch one semitone. See also Harp.

Isaac [Ysaac, Isaak], **Heinrich** [Henricus] [Arrigo il Tedesco] (b. Flanders, ca. 1450; d. Florence, 26 Mar. 1517). Composer. Court musician to the Medici in Florence from around 1485; to Maximilian I from 1497. Brought the Netherlandish style of music to German-speaking areas. Composed about 40 Mass Ordinaries; almost 100 cycles of the Proper of the Mass (published in the *Choralis constantinus); motets; French, Italian, and German secular songs.

Isamitt, Carlos (b. Rengo, Colchagua, Chile, 13 Mar. 1887; d. Santiago, 2 July 1974). Composer. Director of the Santiago School of Fine Arts, 1927–28; taught at the National Conservatory. Pursued ethnomusicological research among the Araucanian Indians; incorporated their music into his own work; also used twelve-tone techniques. Works include a ballet and other symphonic music, a violin concerto, chamber music, many piano pieces, and songs. Also a painter.

Ishii, Kan (b. Tokyo, 30 Mar. 1921). Composer. Pupil of Ikenouchi and Orff. Worked as pianist in his father's dance company. Professor at the Tōhō Gakuen School of Music from 1954; at the Aichi Prefectural Arts Univ. in Nagoya from 1966. His music shows the influence of Orff and Debussy. Has composed ballet scores (including *Kami to bayādere,* Tokyo, 1950; *Hakai* [Sin against Buddha], 1965); operas (*Kantomi,* 1981; *Aojishi* [The Blue Lion], operetta, 1989); orchestral works; film scores; choral/vocal music; instrumental music (piano and viola sonatas).

Ishii, Maki (b. Tokyo, 28 May 1936). Composer. Son of dancer Bac Ishii and brother of Kan Ishii. Pupil of Ikenouchi and Blacher. Has composed orchestral works (including *Kyō-ō,* piano, orchestra, tape, 1968; Violin Concerto, 1978; *Translucent Vision,* 1982; *Gioh,* 1984, and *Gedatsu,* 1985, Japanese flute, orchestra; *Intrada,* 1986); chamber music (*Nucleus,* biwa, harp, shakukachi, flute, 1973; *Anime amare,* harp, percussion, tape, 1974; *13 Drums,* solo percussion, 1986); tape works including the ballets *Samsara* (1968) and *Yukionna* (1971); many works for Japanese instruments alone.

Ísólfsson, Páll (b. Stokkseyri, Iceland, 12 Oct. 1893; d. Reykjavík, 23 Nov. 1974). Composer and organist.

Organ pupil of Karl Straube. From 1930, director of the Reykjavík College of Music and of the music department of Icelandic Radio; 1939–68, organist at Reykjavík Cathedral. His musical style is closely allied to that of the late Romantics. Works include the *Althing Festival Cantata* (1930); *Skálholtsljódh Cantata* (1956); *Lyric Suite,* orchestra; many organ works; songs, piano works.

Isometric. *Homorhythmic.

Isorhythm [fr. Ger. *Isorhythmie*]. The repetition of a rhythmic pattern throughout a voice part. The device is found in motets of the 14th and early 15th centuries and on occasion can be found in other genres as well. Most often the tenor of such a piece is isorhythmic, sometimes also the contratenor, and less frequently the upper voices.

An isorhythmic voice normally contains two patterns that are repeated, a rhythmic pattern or *talea* and a melodic pattern or *color.* The two patterns need not be of the same length, however, with the result that successive statements of the rhythmic pattern may occur with different pitches. The repetition of both rhythmic and melodic patterns has precedents in the tenors of 13th-century motets. Isorhythm based on the reiteration of a relatively long rhythmic pattern allowed the construction of compositions on a large scale. The earliest such works are early 14th-century motets in the *Roman de Fauvel.* Most of the motets by Guillaume de Machaut are isorhythmic.

Isouard, Nicolas [Nicolò] (b. Malta, 6 Dec. 1775; d. Paris, 23 Mar. 1818). Composer. Pupil of Nicola Sala. 1795–98, church organist in Malta; later settled in Paris. 1802, cofounded a publishing venture with Méhul, Cherubini, Boieldieu, and others. Composed some 40 opere serie, opere buffe, and opéras comiques (*La statue,* 1802; *Cendrillon,* 1810; *Le billet de loterie,* 1811; *Joconde,* 1814); sacred music; cantatas; solo vocal music, and vocal chamber music.

Israel in Egypt. An oratorio for soloists, chorus, and orchestra by Handel, first performed in London in 1739. The text is from the Bible and the Prayer Book Psalter.

Istampita, istanpitta [It.]. *Estampie.

Istar Variations. Seven symphonic variations by Vincent d'Indy, op. 42 (1896). Based on the sixth canto of the Assyrian epic poem of Izdubar, d'Indy's work depicts the voyage of self-discovery and gradual denudation of Istar, daughter of Sin. The most complex variation, presented first, is gradually stripped of its ornamentation to reveal the bare theme, presented last.

Istesso tempo, L' [It.]. The same tempo; hence, an indication that the tempo is to remain the same despite a change in meter and thus in the unit of metrical pulse. In a change from 4/4 to ¢, the half note of the latter will equal the quarter note of the former; in a change from 3/4 to 6/8, the dotted quarter note of the latter will equal the quarter note of the former.

Istomin, Eugene (George) (b. New York, 26 Nov. 1925). Pianist. Studied with Serkin and Horszowski. Debut with the Philadelphia Orchestra, 1943. Performed with the Adolf Busch Chamber Players; 1961, formed a trio with Isaac Stern and Leonard Rose.

Italian Concerto. A "Concerto in the Italian Manner" for solo harpsichord with two keyboards by Bach, BWV 971, published in 1735 as the second part of the *Clavier-Übung.* The work is so named because it is in the form and style of the Italian instrumental concerto of the early 18th century, the concerto's characteristic element of contrast being achieved through contrasting *registrations on the harpsichord's two keyboards.

Italian overture. See Overture.

Italian sixth. See Sixth chord.

Italian Symphony. Popular name for Mendelssohn's Symphony no. 4 in A major op. 90 (completed in 1833; many later revisions), begun during a trip to Italy in 1830–31 and containing allusions to Italian folk music, particularly in the last movement, entitled "Saltarello."

Italiana in Algeri, L' [It., The Italian Woman in Algiers]. Comic opera in two acts by Rossini (libretto by Angelo Anelli, previously set by Luigi Mosca), produced in Venice in 1813. Setting: Algiers in the 19th century.

Ite, missa est [Lat., Go, you are dismissed]. The concluding formula of the *Ordinary of the Roman Catholic *Mass, to which the response "Deo gratias" (Thanks be to God) is made. It is not normally a part of polyphonic settings of the Mass Ordinary except in the 14th century.

Iturbi, José (b. Valencia, Spain, 28 Nov. 1895; d. Hollywood, Calif., 28 June 1980). Pianist and conductor. Taught at the Geneva Conservatory 1919–23; toured Europe, South America, and the U.S. Conductor of the Rochester Philharmonic, 1936–44. He appeared in a number of films; his performances of Spanish music were especially noteworthy. Often appeared with his sister Amparo, also a pianist.

Iturriaga, Enrique (b. Lima, 3 Apr. 1918). Composer. Pupil of Honegger. Has taught at the Lima Conservatory (director, 1973) and at the Univ. of San Marcos. As a composer he has integrated European and indigenous elements. Works include *Preludio y* *danza* (1954), *Vivencias* (1965), and *Homenaje a Stravinsky* (1972), all for orchestra; vocal and chamber music.

Ives, Charles (Edward) (b. Danbury, Conn., 20 Oct. 1874; d. New York, 19 May 1954). Composer. Pupil of Parker and of his father, George E. Ives (1845–94), a conductor and music teacher. Held several church organ posts. Founded and ran an insurance company with Julian Myrick, 1906–30. In his music Ives explored atonality and serial procedures, polyrhythms, quarter-tones, use of space as an important compositional element, layered polyphony and multidimensionality. His music frequently quotes American tunes (hymns, marches, songs of Stephen Foster); his subject matter was often a nostalgic reflection on the New England of his boyhood. Works: 4 symphonies (the Third won the Pulitzer Prize in 1947), *The Unanswered Question* and *Central Park in the Dark* (1906), and many other works for orchestra and band; string quartets, violin sonatas, and other chamber music mainly for strings; organ and piano works (including the Second Piano Sonata "Concord, Mass., 1840–60," 1910–15, and 3 Quarter-Tone Pieces, 2 pianos, 1923–24); choral music and some 150 songs. Published *Essays before a Sonata and Other Writings.*

Ivey, Jean Eichelberger (b. Washington, D.C., 3 July 1923). Composer and pianist. Studied at the Peabody Conservatory, the Eastman School, and the Univ. of Toronto. Taught at Peabody and founded the electronic music studio there 1969. Has used serial procedures. Works include much vocal music, often setting her own texts (*Birthmark,* opera, after Hawthorne, 1980–82; *Hera Hung from the Sky,* mezzo-soprano, 7 woodwinds, 3 percussionists, piano, and tape, 1973); incidental and film music; orchestral works (*Forms in Motion,* 1972; a cello concerto, 1983–85); chamber music (*Ariel in Flight,* violin and tape, 1983); concert and teaching pieces for piano; electronic music.

J

Jácara [Sp.]. (1) A *romance* relating the adventures of a lowlife character, often sung, and in the 17th century forming the basis for entertainment between the acts of plays. Becoming more elaborate musically, these entertainments were antecedents of the *tonadilla.* (2) A dance in triple meter derived from the music for (1) and with rhythms similar to the sarabande, to which it was likened in the 17th century.

Jack. That part of the *harpsichord's action to which the plectrum is fixed and that moves past the string when the key is depressed.

Jackson, George K(nowil) (b. Oxford, bapt. 15 Apr. 1757; d. Boston, 18 Nov. 1822). Composer and organist. Educated in England. Emigrated to the U.S. around 1796; teacher and organist in New Brunswick, N.J., New York, and Hartford, Conn. Settled in Boston 1812. Published compilations of church music. Composed sacred vocal music; secular choral and solo vocal music; and keyboard works.

Jackson, Mahalia (b. New Orleans, 26 Oct. 1911; d. Chicago, 27 Jan. 1972). Gospel singer. Sang in Chicago churches; after 1932 toured with the Johnson Gospel Singers. Her repertory included "Precious Lord," "God's Gonna Separate the Wheat from the Tares" (recorded 1937), and "Move on Up a Little Higher" (1947). Hosted radio and television shows in the 1950s; appeared at the inauguration of John F. Kennedy and at the funeral of Martin Luther King, Jr.

Jackson, Michael (Joseph) (b. Gary, Ind., 29 Aug. 1958). Popular singer and songwriter. Began singing in a vocal group with his brothers, the Jackson Five; performed with them throughout the 1970s; began a concurrent solo career 1971. Released albums of his own songs, including *Off the Wall* (1979), *Thriller* (1982), and *Bad* (1987). Pioneered the use of music videos. Recent albums include: *Dangerous* (1991) and *HIStory: Past, Present and Future, Book I* (1995).

Jackson, Milt(on) [Bags] (b. Detroit, 1 Jan. 1923). Jazz vibraphonist. Joined Dizzy Gillespie's bop sextet (1945–46) and big band (1946–48); also worked with Howard McGhee, Thelonious Monk, Charlie Parker, and Woody Herman. Led the Modern Jazz Quartet (1952–74, 1981); from 1974 toured widely as a leader and a free-lance. Recorded his composi-

tion "Bags' Groove" with Miles Davis (1954) and an album with John Coltrane, *Bags and Trane* (1959).

Jacob, Gordon (Percival Septimus) (b. London, 5 July 1895; d. Saffron Walden, 8 June 1984). Composer. Pupil of Stanford and Howells. Taught at the Royal College 1924–54. Compositions include orchestral music (2 symphonies; *Variations on an Original Theme,* 1936; 3 suites); concertos for viola, piano, oboe, bassoon, horn, flute, trombone; Concerto for Band, 1970; songs; choral works; chamber music (String Quartet in C, 1928; Suite for Bassoon and String Quartet, 1969; Suite for Four Trombones, 1968; Sonata for Viola and Piano, 1978).

Jacobi, Frederick (b. San Francisco, 4 May 1891; d. New York, 24 Oct. 1952). Composer and conductor. Pupil of Goldmark, Bloch, and Juon. Assistant conductor of the Metropolitan Opera 1913–17; from 1924 taught at the Master School of United Arts; from 1936 at Juilliard. Included Pueblo Indian and Hebrew material in some compositions. Works include an opera; *Indian Dances* (1928), 2 symphonies, a violin concerto, and other orchestral music; string quartets, a woodwind quintet, other chamber music; works for piano and organ; a few songs.

Jacobs, Paul (b. New York, 22 June 1930; d. there, 25 Sept. 1983). Pianist and harpsichordist. Debut, New York, 1951; then worked in Europe for almost a decade; 1956, performed a complete cycle of Schoenberg's piano music in Paris. Taught at Mannes, the Manhattan School, the Berkshire Music Center, and Brooklyn College; pianist (from 1962) and harpsichordist (1974) with the New York Philharmonic. Best known for his performances and recordings of the 20th-century repertory.

Jacopo da Bologna [Jacobus de Bononia] (fl. northern Italy, 1340–60?). Composer. A member of the first generation of Italian trecento musicians; active at courts in Verona and Milan. His 34 surviving works include 2- and 3-voice madrigals, *cacce,* a *lauda-ballata,* and a motet.

Jacquet, (Jean Baptiste) Illinois (b. Broussard, near Lafayette, La., 31 Oct. 1922). Jazz tenor saxophonist and bandleader. With Lionel Hampton's big band (1941–42) recorded a widely imitated improvisation on "Flying Home" (1942). Joined Cab Calloway (1943–44) and Count Basie (1945–46), performed in the film *Jammin' the Blues* (1944), worked with Jazz at the Philharmonic, and led groups, including a big band from 1984.

Jacquet de La Guerre, Élisabeth-Claude (b. ca. 1666–67; d. Paris, 27 June 1729). Harpsichordist and composer. A child prodigy; encouraged by Louis XIV. In 1704–17, after the deaths of her husband and son, gave concerts at her home. Composed an opera, a ballet, cantatas, songs, a lost Te Deum, sonatas, and keyboard suites.

Jacquet [Jaquet, Jachet] **of Mantua** [Colebault, Jacques] (b. Vitré, 1483; d. Mantua, 2 Oct. 1559). Composer. *Maestro di cappella* in Mantua from 1534. The most significant of his works are his nearly 25 Masses, most parodies, and 5 books of motets, including a small number of secular pieces.

Jaffee, Stephen (Abram) (b. 30 Dec. 1954). Composer. Pupil of Crumb, Rochberg, and Wernick; has taught at Duke Univ. from 1981. Compositions include *Three Yiddish Songs,* soprano, chamber orchestra (1978); *Four Images,* orchestra (1982–83); Double Sonata, 2 pianos (1989) and other chamber music; *Pedal Point,* cycle of four songs (1994).

Jagdhorn [Ger.]. Hunting *horn.

Jagdmusik [Ger.]. Music for the hunt.

Jagger, Mick [Michael Philip] (b. Dartford, Kent, 26 July 1944). Rock singer and songwriter. In 1962, helped form the Rolling Stones; with Keith Richard authored their most successful songs, including "Satisfaction" (1965), "Jumpin' Jack Flash" (1969), and "Honky Tonk Woman" (1969). The band remained popular through the 1970s and continued to tour and record in the 1980s and 1990s. Jagger released the solo albums *She's the Boss,* 1985; *Primitive Cool,* 1987; *Wandering Spirit,* 1993.

Jahreszeiten, Die [Ger.]. See *Seasons, The.*

Jam. In jazz and rock, to improvise in an informal setting.

Jamal, Ahmad [Fritz Jones] (b. Pittsburgh, 2 July 1930). Jazz pianist. From 1951 he led groups, usually trios; recorded the album *Ahmad Jamal at the Pershing* (1958). Played in both fusion and bop styles. Miles Davis adopted several of his arrangements.

James, Harry (Hagg) (b. Albany, Ga., 15 Mar. 1916; d. Las Vegas, 5 July 1983). Jazz and popular trumpeter and bandleader. Joined Benny Goodman's big band 1937–38. His own big band played swing as well as novelty songs ("Flight of the Bumble Bee," 1940) and sentimental ballads, which he played with a sweet and wide vibrato ("You Made Me Love You," 1941). Acted and performed in films, including *The*

Benny Goodman Story (1955). From the 1960s led groups mainly in Las Vegas.

James, Philip (Frederick Wright) (b. Jersey City, 17 May 1890; d. Southampton, N.Y., 1 Nov. 1975). Composer, organist, and conductor. Pupil of Goldmark, Scalero, and Herbert. Taught at New York Univ. (1923–55) and at Columbia (1931–33). Founded the New Jersey Symphony (1922–29). His compositions in a late Romantic style include *Station WGZBX* (orchestra, 1931); 2 symphonies; band music; a string quartet and other chamber music; organ and piano works; several cantatas (*General William Booth Enters into Heaven,* 1932) and other vocal music.

Janáček, Leoš [Leo Eugen] (b. Hukvaldy, Moravia, 3 July 1854; d. Moravská Ostrava, 12 Aug. 1928). Composer. Son of a cantor and Kapellmeister. Studied in Brno, Prague, Leipzig, and Vienna. In 1881, helped found the Brno Organ School (later the Brno Conservatory). Taught at the Prague Conservatory from 1920. Collected folk songs in northern Moravia; published editions and collections of folk tunes, as well as writings on the subject, and incorporated Moravian folk music into his own compositions. Other influences on his musical style include those of Russians such as Mussorgsky and of French impressionists. Composed operas (including *Jenůfa; *Kát'a Kabanová; Příhody Lišky Bystroušky* [The *Cunning Little Vixen]; *Věc Makropulos* [The Makropulos Affair], 1923–25); ballets; sacred and secular choral music, including *Glagolská mše* [*Glagolitic Mass] (1926); orchestral works including *Taras Bulba* (1915–18) and *Sinfonietta* (1926); chamber, piano, and organ works; folk song settings.

Janequin [Jannequin], **Clément** (b. Châtellerault, ca. 1485; d. Paris, 1558). Composer. Held posts in various French cities, especially Angers during the 1530s. For a short time before his death in Paris, he was *chantre,* then *compositeur ordinaire du roi.* Best known for his chansons, including the descriptive pieces "Le chant des oiseaux"; "Les cris de Paris"; "La bataille de Marignan." Also composed French Psalms and *chansons spirituelles,* 2 Masses, motets.

Janigro, Antonio (b. Milan, 21 Jan. 1918; d. there, 1 May 1989). Cellist and conductor. Pupil of Casals. Debut 1933, followed by international concert tours. Taught at the Zagreb (1939–53) and Düsseldorf (from 1965) conservatories. Conducted orchestras in Zagreb, Milan, and the Saar. Formed the Solisti di Zagreb 1954.

Janis [Yanks, Yankelevitch], **Byron** (b. McKeesport, Pa., 24 Mar. 1928). Pianist. Pupil of the Lhévinnes and Horowitz; debuted in 1943 with the NBC Symphony in Rachmaninoff's 2nd Concerto. Toured the Soviet Union in 1960. His career suffered a number of setbacks owing to illness.

Janissary music. Music of the elite corps of soldiers known as Janissaries that formed the personal guard of Turkish sultans from the 14th century until 1826, or music of similar character performed on similar instruments; also termed Turkish music or *alla turca.* The typical Turkish ensemble included fifes, shawms, triangle, cymbals, kettledrums, *Turkish crescent, and bass drum and was widely imitated in Europe beginning in the early 18th century. Its influence on European military music lasted well into the 19th. Among works to draw on this idiom are Mozart's *Die *Entführung aus dem Serail* and Rondo *alla turca* from the Piano Sonata in A major K. 331.

Jaques-Dalcroze, Émile (b. Vienna, 6 July 1865; d. Geneva, 1 July 1950). Composer and pedagogue. Pupil of R. Fuchs, Bruckner, Delibes, and Fauré. From 1892 taught at the conservatory in Geneva. Developed "Eurythmics," a method of teaching music, especially rhythm, through coordinated body motions. Founded institutes to teach these techniques, first in Hellerau (near Dresden), 1910; later in Geneva. His compositions, which show strong influence from Swiss folk song, include operas; orchestral works; chamber music; many song collections. Published *La respiration et l'innervation musculaire* (1906), *Méthode Jaques-Dalcroze* (1906–17), and other writings on music and eurhythmics.

Jarnach, Philipp (b. Noisy, France, 26 July 1892; d. Bornsen, 17 Dec. 1982). Composer. Of Spanish and Flemish origin. Pupil of Lavignac. Close friend of Busoni. Taught at the conservatory in Zurich (1918–21), at the Hochschule für Musik in Cologne (1927–49) and at the Hochschule in Hamburg (1949–70; director to 1959). Weill was among his students. Composed in a neoclassical style. Works include orchestral pieces (*Musik mit Mozart,* 1935); chamber music; piano and organ works; choral music; songs.

Järnefelt, (Edvard) Armas (b. Viipuri [Vyborg, Finland], 14 Aug. 1869; d. Stockholm, 23 June 1958). Conductor and composer. Pupil of Busoni, Wegelius, and Massenet. Conductor of the Royal Opera in Stockholm 1907–32; 1932–36, of the Finnish National Opera; 1942–43, of the Helsinki Philharmonic. Composed choral/orchestral works (*Päivän poika* [Son of Day], 1939); orchestral music (*Berceuse,* 1904).

Jarre, Maurice (b. Lyons, 13 Sept. 1924). Composer. Pupil of Honegger. Percussionist under Boulez from 1946 at the Renaud–Barrault Theater Company, and at the Théâtre populaire. Composed many film scores (winning Oscars for *Lawrence of Arabia,* 1963, and

"Lara's Song" in *Doctor Zhivago,* 1965); theater and orchestral music. His concert works employ serial techniques.

Jarrett, Keith (b. Allentown, Pa., 8 May 1945). Jazz pianist and bandleader. Joined Art Blakey's Jazz Messengers (1965–66) and Miles Davis's jazz-rock group (1970–71). From 1966 led a trio (later a quartet) with Charlie Haden. From 1971 he began improvising unaccompanied. Led a European quartet 1974–79 and from 1983 a trio with Gary Peacock and Jack DeJohnette.

Järvi, Neeme (b. Tallinn, Estonia, 7 June 1937). Conductor. Studied at Leningrad Conservatory. Conductor of the Estonian Opera from 1963. Music director of the Scottish National Orchestra, 1984–88; of the Detroit Symphony from 1990. Made numerous recordings of unfamiliar repertory of the 19th and 20th centuries.

Jawbone [Sp. *quijada*]. A *rattle made from a horse's, mule's, or donkey's jawbone in which the teeth remain loosely attached. When one side of the open end is struck with the hand, it vibrates in the fashion of a tuning fork, causing the teeth to rattle. It was used in American minstrel shows and is still widely used in Latin American popular music.

Jazz. An eclectic, expanding collection of 20th-century styles, principally instrumental and of black American creation. *Swing and improvisation are essential to several styles. Jazz has always been linked to *blues through instrumental adaptations (derived equally from the black church) of improvisatory story telling, *call and response, and vocal inflections (*blue notes, cries, growls, hums, moans, shouts), as well as through performances with blues vocalists and variations on blues progressions. In its early years, jazz absorbed the instrumentation, multithematic structures, strong tonality, and rhythms of American marching band music and *ragtime, the harmonic colors of the piano music of such composers as Debussy and Ravel, the melodies and forms of American popular song, and the rhythms of Latin American dances [see also Afro-Cuban jazz]. Later it incorporated accompanimental figures and electronic innovations in *rock and *soul as well as non-Western musical procedures, especially with respect to African and Brazilian percussion.

As jazz emerged in the 1890s through the 1910s, the great majority of the most original players resided in New Orleans, whence the term *New Orleans jazz. A number of the features of this music were soon thereafter taken over into *Chicago jazz. A new style emerged in large ensembles in the 30s and 40s that became known as *swing. The early 40s began with reactions against the commercialization of jazz, which split into three styles: a resuscitated late New

Orleans jazz modified with swing rhythms, big-band swing, and *bebop. In the late 40s, *cool jazz emerged and in the 50s *West Coast jazz. At about this time attempts to bring jazz together with the tradition of concert music gave rise to *third-stream music. The late 50s saw the rise of *free jazz, the most radical alternative to bebop, which was neither a style nor free, but rather an amalgamation of individual efforts to replace stereotypes with new procedures. Later strains of jazz included the Brazilian-derived *bossa-nova and the amalgamation of jazz and *rock termed *fusion. All of the substyles enumerated here have in some degree continued to flourish simultaneously.

Jefferson, Blind Lemon (b. Couchman, Tex., July 1897; d. Chicago, Dec. 1929). Blues singer and guitarist. Began recording in Chicago in 1925, including gospel material (under the name Deacon L. J. Bates) and songs such as "Long Lonesome Blues" (1926), "Black Snake Moan," and "Match Box Blues" (1927).

Jehan des Murs [Johannes de Muris] (b. diocese of Lisieux, ca. 1300; d. ca. 1350). Astronomer and music theorist. Active in Paris and Normandy. Wrote treatises dealing with musical proportions, including *Notitia artis musicae* and *Musica speculativa secundum Boetium. Libellus cantus mensurabilis,* which is probably not by des Murs but merely conveys his late teachings, transmits an account of *ars nova* mensural notation. His work strongly influenced music theorists of the 14th and 15th centuries.

Jelinek [Elin], **Hanns** (b. Vienna, 5 Dec. 1901; d. there, 27 Jan. 1969). Composer. Pupil of Schoenberg. Worked under the pseudonym Elin as a bar pianist, bandleader, and film composer. From 1958 taught at the Vienna Musikhochschule. Composed jazz, popular, and electronic music, as well as an operetta; orchestral music; chamber and piano works (*Zwölftonwerk* op. 15, 1947–52 and *Zwölftonfibel* op. 21, 1953–54, designed to demonstrate twelve-tone methods); vocal music. Published *Anleitung zur Zwölftonkomposition.*

Jemnitz, Sándor [Alexander] (b. Budapest, 9 Aug. 1890; d. Balatonföldvár, 8 Aug. 1963). Composer, conductor, and critic. Pupil of Reger and Schoenberg. Taught at the Budapest Conservatory. Music critic for a number of newspapers in Germany and Hungary; published popular books on famous composers. Compositions include orchestral works; chamber music (trio, flute, violin, viola, 1923; 2 string trios); 5 sonatas and other keyboard works; songs and choral music.

Jena Symphony. A symphony in C major discovered in Jena, Germany, in 1909. Once thought to be an early work of Beethoven because his name appears on two of the parts found in Jena, it is now believed to be the work of Friedrich Witt (1770–1836) on the basis of two further copies with attributions.

Jenkins, John (b. Maidstone, 1592; d. Kimberley, Norfolk, 27 Oct. 1678). Composer. Served various wealthy families in England; theorbo player in the King's Musick from 1660. Famed as a lutenist and viol player, he was a major exponent of the English 17th-century viol fantasia; also wrote vocal music.

Jennings, Waylon (Arnold) (b. Littlefield, Tex., 15 June 1937). Country singer, guitarist, and songwriter. Played in Buddy Holly's Crickets 1958–59. Began recording with his band, the Waylors, 1965 (including "That's What You Get for Loving Me," 1966; "Good Ol' Boys," 1980). Incorporates elements of rock into his work. Has recorded with Willie Nelson and Jessi Colter (including *Wanted: The Outlaws,* 1976).

Jensen, Adolf (b. Königsberg, 12 Jan. 1837; d. Baden-Baden, 23 Jan. 1879). Composer. Pupil of Köhler; active as pianist, teacher, and theater conductor (in Brest-Litovsk, Copenhagen, Königsberg, Berlin). Works include an unperformed opera and choral works; best known for many piano pieces and songs.

Jenůfa [Cz. originally *Její pastorkyňa,* Her Foster Daughter]. Opera in three acts by Leoš Janáček (libretto by the composer, after Gabriela Preissová's play), produced in Brno in 1904. Setting: the Moravian mountains in the late 19th century.

Jephtha. (1) An oratorio by Handel (English text by Thomas Morell based on the Bible and George Buchanan's *Jepthes sive Votum*), produced in London in 1752. (2) [Lat. *Jephte*]. An oratorio by Carissimi (Latin text from the Bible), composed before 1650.

Jeritza [Jedlitzková, Jedlitzka], **Maria** [Mimi, Marie] (b. Brünn, Moravia [Brno, Czechoslovakia], 6 Oct. 1887; d. Orange, N.J., 10 July 1982). Soprano. Studied with Marcella Sembrich. Engaged by the Vienna Court Opera 1912–35. Created Strauss's Ariadne (Stuttgart, 1912) and Kaiserin (Vienna, 1919). After 1921, became the Met's leading soprano, introducing Jenůfa and Turandot to U.S. audiences.

Jessel, Léon (b. Stettin, 22 Jan. 1871; d. Berlin, 4 Jan. 1942). Composer. From 1894, theater conductor in several cities. Settled in Berlin, 1911; composed popular operettas, including *Schwarzwaldmädel* (1917). Best known for the piano piece *Parade der Zinnsoldaten* (Parade of the Tin Soldiers), 1905. The Nazis banned his works and later imprisoned him.

Jeté [Fr.]. See Bowing (5).

Jeu [Fr.]. An organ stop or stop knob; sometimes also a combination of stops.

Jeu de cartes [Fr., Card Game]. Ballet "in three deals" by Stravinsky (choreography by George Balanchine), composed in 1936 and produced in New York the following year. The dancers represent cards in a poker game.

Jeu de timbres [Fr.]. *Glockenspiel.

Jeune France, La [Fr.]. A group of French composers formed in 1936 by Olivier Messiaen (b. 1908), Yves Baudrier (b. 1906), André Jolivet (1905–74), and Daniel-Lesur (b. 1908). Their published manifesto proclaimed the wish to "propagate a living music, having the impetus of sincerity, generosity, and artistic conscientiousness" and to "return to the human" in the face of prevailing neoclassicism.

Jeu-parti [Fr.], **joc partit, partimen** [Prov.]. A poetic genre in dialogue form, practiced by the *troubadours and trouvères. Like the *tenso,* it consists of a debate on a question of love or some other subject.

Jeux [Fr., Games]. Ballet by Debussy (choreography by Vaslav Nijinsky, scenery and costumes by Léon Bakst), produced in Paris in 1913.

Jew's harp [also jew's trump, jaw's harp; Fr. *guimbarde;* Ger. *Maultrommel*]. A single tongue of wood or metal fastened at one end to the closed end of a U-shaped or keyhole-shaped frame. The narrow part of the frame is placed lengthwise between the player's lips and the free end of the tongue is then plucked. The player's mouth acts as a resonator; pitch is altered by changing the size of the oral cavity, thus reinforcing different partials. The name remains unexplained and seems to have no connection with the Jewish people. See ill. under Percussion instruments.

Jig. A vigorous dance popular in the British Isles from the 16th century onward. The word seems to come from the French *giguer* (to frolic, to leap); the term was repatriated as a musical form and developed specific musical characteristics on the Continent [see Gigue]. In England, it implied no particular rhythmic characteristics except in the hands of composers writing in imitation of Continental (usually Italian rather than French) style.

Jingling Johnny. *Turkish crescent.

Jirák, Karel Boleslav (b. Prague, 28 Jan. 1891; d. Chicago, 30 Jan. 1972). Composer and conductor. Pupil of V. Novák and J. B. Foerster. Conducted the Hamburg Opera 1915–18; professor at the Prague Conservatory 1920–30; music director of Czech Radio 1930–45. Taught at Roosevelt College, Chicago,

from 1947. His later music follows the Czech late Romantic style. Works include an opera, *Žena a bůh* [The Woman and the God] (1912–13); 6 symphonies and other orchestral works; choral works (Requiem, 1952); chamber works (7 string quartets); piano pieces.

Jitterbug. See Lindy.

Joachim, Joseph (b. Kittsee [now Köpcsény], near Poszony, 28 June 1831; d. Berlin, 15 Aug. 1907). Violinist. Pupil of Hellmesberger and David; associate of Mendelssohn, Schumann, and Brahms. Debut London, 1844. In 1850, concertmaster at Weimar under Liszt; 1852, violinist to the King of Hannover. Led a string quartet; directed the new Berlin Hochschule für Musik, 1868–1905; toured annually. Compositions include 3 concertos (Hungarian Concerto op. 11, 1857); 5 concert overtures; violin and viola pieces; cadenzas for concertos by Mozart, Beethoven, Brahms.

Jochum, Eugen (b. Babenhausen, 1 Nov. 1902; d. Munich, 26 Mar. 1987). Conductor. Pupil of Hausegger. Conducted the Hamburg Philharmonic 1934–49; held conducting posts with the Berlin Radio Orchestra, Berlin Civic Opera, and Hamburg Opera. Founding conductor of the Bavarian Radio Orchestra in Munich (1949–60); conductor of the Amsterdam Concertgebouw Orchestra (1961–64) and of the Bamberg Symphony (1969–71); laureate conductor of the London Symphony (1975–78). Best known as a champion of Bruckner's Masses and symphonies.

Joel, Billy [William Martin] (b. New York, 9 May 1949). Popular singer, songwriter, and pianist. From 1973, produced several albums of original songs, including "Piano Man" (1973), "Just the Way You Are" (1977), and "It's Still Rock and Roll to Me" (1980).

Johannes de Florentia. See Giovanni da Cascia.

Johannes de Garlandia [Johannes Gallicus] (fl. ca. 1240). Theorist. Wrote two influential treatises: *De plana musica* and *De mensurabili musica,* which treats the polyphony of the Notre Dame era, its rhythm, notation, consonances, and dissonances, and the 3 species discant, copula, and organum.

Johannes de Grocheo (fl. ca. 1300). Theorist. His *Ars musice* or *Theoria* describes musical practice in Paris around 1300, including secular monophony and the poetic and social functions of various sorts of music. Several types of *cantus* and cantilena are described; unfortunately, the descriptions are not always clear or congruent with extant compositions.

Johannes de Muris. See Jehan des Murs.

Johannesen, Grant (b. Salt Lake City, 30 July 1921). Pianist. Studied with Casadesus and Petri. Debut, New York, 1944. Toured Europe with the New York Philharmonic under Mitropoulos (1956–57); the U.S.S.R. with the Cleveland Orchestra under Szell (1968). Music director of the Cleveland Institute of Music from 1974; president, 1977–84. Often programmed French works, especially by Poulenc, Debussy, and Roussel.

John, Elton [Reginald Kenneth Dwight] (b. Pinner, Middlesex, 25 Mar. 1947). Rock singer, songwriter, and pianist. Studied music at the Royal Academy; 1970–76, collaborated with lyricist Bernie Taupin on songs including "Your Song" (1970), "Honky Cat" (1972), "Goodbye, Yellow Brick Road" (1973), and "Benny and the Jets" (1973). His "Little Jeannie" (1980) was very popular.

Johns, (Paul) (b. Kraków, ca. 1798; d. Paris, 10 Aug. 1860). Pianist and merchant. Settled in New Orleans by 1818; 1819, soloist in first known U.S. performance of a Beethoven piano concerto; ca. 1831–34, published *Album Louisiannais* (6 songs, 2 piano pieces); 1830–46, owned music shop; dedicatee of Chopin's Mazurkas op. 7.

Johnson, Bunk [Willie; William Geary] (b. New Orleans, 27 Dec. 1889; d. New Iberia, La., 7 July 1949). Jazz trumpeter and bandleader. Worked with the Eagle Band around 1910 and with other groups until 1934. From 1942 he became the central figure in the revival of New Orleans jazz, leading groups in New Orleans, New York, and elsewhere. Recordings include "Dusty Rag" (1942) and "Over in the Gloryland" (1945). His style was ragtime oriented.

Johnson, J. J. [James Louis] (b. Indianapolis, 22 Jan. 1924). Jazz trombonist. Joined the big bands of Benny Carter (1942–45) and Count Basie (1945–46). Moving to New York in 1946, he played trombone with a previously unimagined dexterity and began working with bop musicians; also with Illinois Jacquet (1947–49). Led a quintet with Kai Winding, as well as his own groups (1956–64); joined Miles Davis (1961–62). From 1956, wrote extended jazz compositions; later largely abandoned jazz performance to compose for films and television.

Johnson, James P(rice) (b. New Brunswick, N.J., 1 Feb. 1894; d. New York, 17 Nov. 1955). Pianist and composer. The foremost exponent of the stride piano style. Accompanied blues singers, including Bessie Smith. Wrote stage shows, including "Runnin' Wild" with Cecil Mack (their hit song "The Charleston" started that dance craze, 1923); *Keep Shufflin'* with Fats Waller (1928). Among his many songs was "If I Could Be With You One Hour Tonight" (1926); among piano compositions, "Carolina Shout" (1921). From 1927, composed orchestral works

drawing on jazz and classical sources (*Yamekraw,* piano and orchestra, 1927).

Johnson, Robert (b. ca. 1583; d. London, before 26 Nov. 1633). Lutenist and composer. Lutenist to King James I (from 1604) and Charles I. Composed songs for plays by Shakespeare and others, music for court masques, anthems, dances, and works for lute.

Johnson, Robert Sherlaw (b. Sunderland, Durham, 21 May 1932). Composer. Pupil of Boulanger and Messiaen. Taught at the Univ. of Leeds (from 1961), at the Univ. of York (1965–70), and at Oxford (from 1970). Has used serial techniques. Works include an opera; sacred choral/orchestral works; solo vocal (*Green Whispers of Gold,* soprano, piano, tape, 1971); 3 piano sonatas, 2 string quartets, and other chamber and piano music.

Johnston, Ben(jamin Burwell, Jr.) (b. Macon, Ga., 15 Mar. 1926). Composer and theorist. Pupil of Partch, Luening, Ussachevsky, and Cage. Taught at the Univ. of Illinois 1951–83. Has composed serial, electronic, aleatoric, and microtonal music, and worked with just intonation. Works include a rock chamber opera, theater pieces, ballets, film and incidental music; *Quintet for Groups* (orchestra, 1966); several string quartets, *12 Partials* (flute and retuned piano, 1981), Sonata for microtonal piano (1965), and other instrumental music; choral music and songs.

Jolas [Illouz], **Betsy** (b. Paris, 5 Aug. 1926). Composer and conductor. Studied with Milhaud and Messiaen. Has taught at the Paris Conservatory (from 1971), at Mills, the Berkshire Music Center, Yale, and the Univ. of Southern California. Her music is in a lyrical style, sometimes employing serial procedures. Compositions include operas (*Le cyclope,* after Euripides, 1986; *Schliemann,* 1988–89); works for orchestra; pieces for instrumental ensembles (*Points d'Aube,* viola, 13 winds, 1967; piano trio, 1989); choral and solo vocal music (*Quatuor II,* soprano and string trio, 1964).

Jolivet, André (b. Paris, 8 Aug. 1905; d. there, 20 Dec. 1974). Composer. Pupil of Le Flem and Varèse. With Baudrier, Daniel Lesur, and Messiaen, formed the group Jeune France, 1936. Director of music at the Comédie-Française, 1943–59; taught at the Paris Conservatory, 1966–70. Composed ballets and other dramatic works; several concertos, 3 symphonies, and other orchestral works; chamber music; *La vérité de Jeanne* (oratorio, 1956) and other choral works; solo works for various instruments (*Mana,* piano 1935); songs; didactic works; and incidental music.

Jolson, Al [Yoelson, Asa] (b. Srednike [now Seredzius], Lithuania, 26 May 1886; d. San Francisco, 23 Oct. 1950). Popular singer, actor. Raised in Washington, D.C. From 1911 sang in revues at the Shubert Brothers' Winter Garden Theatre. Appeared in the first successful sound film, *The Jazz Singer* (1927), performing songs from the Shubert revues including "My Mammy" and "Toot, Toot, Tootsie". Continued to appear in films and made many popular recordings ("Swanee," 1920; "Sonny Boy," 1928).

Jommelli, Niccolò [Nicolò] (b. Aversa, near Naples, 10 Sept. 1714; d. Naples, 25 Aug. 1774). Composer. Pupil of Feo, Fago, and probably Padre Martini. Director of the Ospedale degli incurabili in Venice, 1743–46; from 1749, *maestro coadiutore* of the papal chapel in Rome; 1754–68 court opera composer in Stuttgart; contributed operas for the court theater of José I of Portugal. Composed more than 60 opere serie; titles include *Ricimero rè dei Goti* (Rome, 1740); *Achille in Sciro* and *Didone abbandonata* (both Vienna, 1749); *Demofoonte* (Stuttgart, 1764); *Fetonte* (Ludwigsburg, 1768). Also composed comic operas (*L'errore amoroso,* Naples, 1737; *La critica,* Ludwigsburg, 1766); serenatas and pasticcios; oratorios, cantatas, and hundreds of other sacred works (including some 20 Masses); chamber works and concertos.

Jones, Hank [Henry] (b. Vicksburg, Miss., 31 July 1918). Jazz pianist. Worked with Hot Lips Page, Coleman Hawkins, and Billy Eckstine. Toured with Ella Fitzgerald and Jazz at the Philharmonic (1947–53); recorded with Charlie Parker ("Star Eyes," 1950). Joined Artie Shaw; worked with Benny Goodman before joining the staff of CBS (1959–ca. 1976). Conducted the show *Ain't Misbehavin';* led the Great Jazz Trio from 1976. Recordings include the album *Solo Piano* (ca. 1980).

Jones, Jo(nathan) (b. Chicago, 7 Oct. 1911; d. New York, 3 Sept. 1985). Jazz drummer. Joined Count Basie (1934–44, 1946–48; recordings include "One O'Clock Jump," 1937, and "Jumpin' at the Woodside," 1938). Toured with Jazz at the Philharmonic intermittently from 1947; joined Illinois Jacquet, Lester Young, and Teddy Wilson; led groups; had a featured role in the television show *The Sound of Jazz* (1957). On the album *The Drums* (1973) he demonstrates jazz drumming.

Jones, Philip (b. Bath, 12 Mar. 1928). Trumpeter. Served as first trumpet with most of the leading London orchestras, including the Royal Philharmonic (1956–60), the Philharmonia (1960–64), the London Philharmonic (1964–65), the New Philharmonia (1965–67), and the BBC Symphony (1968–71). In 1951, formed the Philip Jones Brass Ensemble, which performed and recorded widely. From 1983 taught at the Guildhall School of Music.

Jones, Philly Joe [Joseph Rudolph] (b. Philadelphia, 15 July 1923; d. there, 30 Aug. 1985). Jazz drummer. Joined Miles Davis's hard bop quintet and sextet (1955–58, 1962). Recorded as a free-lance, including John Coltrane's album *Blue Train* (1957). Led a group (1959–62); played and taught in Japan, the U.S., England, and France. Joined Bill Evans, 1967, 1976; led a jazz-rock group in Philadelphia from 1972; toured with Red Garland; formed Dameronia, a nonet devoted to Tadd Dameron's music (1981–85).

Jones, Quincy (Delight, Jr.) (b. Chicago, 14 Mar. 1933). Composer, arranger, conductor, producer, and bandleader. Played trumpet in Lionel Hampton's big band (1951–53); directed Dizzy Gillespie's big band on tours (1956); composed music for his own album *This Is How I Feel about Jazz* (1956); studied composition in Paris; directed his own all-star big band in the show *Free and Easy* in Europe (1959–60). Composed for films and television, including *The Pawnbroker* (1965), *In the Heat of the Night, In Cold Blood* (both 1967), *The Color Purple* (1985), and two Bill Cosby series. Produced and directed albums for Michael Jackson (*Thriller,* 1982) and Frank Sinatra (1984), as well as the song "We Are the World" (1986), which raised funds for Ethiopian famine relief.

Jones, Robert (fl. 1597–1615). Composer. Published 5 lute song collections, a book of madrigals (1607); wrote a madrigal for *The *Triumphes of Oriana* (1601). A leader of the Children of the Revells of the Queene 1610–15.

Jones [née Joyner], **(Matilda) Sissieretta** (b. Portsmouth, Va., 5 Jan. 1869; d. Providence, 24 June 1933). Soprano. Studied at New England Conservatory; 1888, began to tour widely with black concert companies (U.S., West Indies, Canada, Europe) or minstrel troupes. Sang at the White House 1892. Toured with her own vaudeville company, 1896–1915, Black Patti's Troubadours. Her repertory ranged from opera arias to popular songs.

Jones, Thad(deus Joseph) (b. Pontiac, Mich., 28 Mar. 1923; d. Copenhagen, 20 Aug. 1986). Jazz trumpeter, cornetist, flugelhorn player, composer, and bandleader; brother of Elvin and Hank Jones. Worked in Billy Mitchell's quintet in Detroit, accompanying leading bop musicians (1950–53). Worked with Charles Mingus; joined Count Basie's big band (1954–63). With Mel Lewis led a big band (1965–79); his compositions for it include *The Big Dipper* and *Central Park North* (1969). Led groups in Denmark from 1977; returned to the U.S. to direct the memorial Basie orchestra (1984–86).

Jongen, Joseph (Marie Alphonse Nicolas) (b. Liège, 14 Dec. 1873; d. Sart-lez-Spa, province of Liège, 12 July 1953). Composer. Brother of Léon Jongen. From 1902 taught at the Liège Conservatory; from 1920 at the Brussels Conservatory (director, 1925–39). During World War I led a piano quartet in England that performed some of his music. In Brussels conducted the Concerts spirituels. Wrote numerous pieces for orchestra (*Symphonie concertante*, 1926) and for chamber ensembles (string quartets; wind quintets; piano trios); the cantata *Comala* (1897) and other vocal works.

Jongen, Léon (Marie Victor Justin) (b. Liège, 2 Mar. 1884; d. Brussels, 18 Nov. 1969). Composer. Brother of Joseph Jongen. Organist at St. Jacques in Liège 1898–1904. Concertized as a pianist; conducted the Tonkin Opera in Hanoi (1927–29). Taught at the Brussels Conservatory, succeeding his brother as director, 1939–49. Works include 2 operas; 2 ballets; orchestral works (*Malaisie*, 1935; Violin Concerto, 1962); 4 works for chorus and orchestra; chamber music, songs, film music, and pieces for brass band.

Jongleur [Fr.]. See Minstrel.

Jonny spielt auf [Ger., Jonny Strikes up the Band]. Opera in two acts by Ernst Krenek (libretto by the composer), produced in Leipzig in 1927. Setting: the 1920s.

Joplin, Janis (Lyn) (b. Port Arthur, Tex., 19 Jan. 1943; d. Hollywood, 4 Oct. 1970). Blues and rock singer. In 1966, joined Big Brother and the Holding Company in San Francisco; later led the Kozmic Blues Band and the Full Tilt Boogie Band. A leading figure of the San Francisco psychedelic era; one of the first women to establish an independent image in rock music; famous for emotional, blues-oriented interpretations. Recordings include "Women Is Losers" (1968), "Me and Bobby McGee" (1971), and "Get It While You Can" (1971).

Joplin, Scott (b. near Marshall, Tex., or Shreveport, La., 24 Nov. 1868; d. New York, 1 Apr. 1917). Composer, pianist. Learned several instruments as a child; later had classical piano training from a local German immigrant. From his early teens he sang, played, and taught professionally; toured with vocal groups (Texas Medley Quartette, 1895) and as a bandleader playing cornet and piano. From 1896, studied at George R. Smith College for Negroes in Sedalia, Mo. and played at a prominent black dance hall, the Maple Leaf Club. With a local publisher, John Stark, issued his first original ragtime piece, the *Maple Leaf Rag*. Thereafter published some 40 piano rags, marches, and waltzes; also composed a ragtime ballet, *The Ragtime Dance*, 1899, and two ragtime

operas, *The Guest of Honor* (St. Louis, 1903; lost) and *Treemonisha* (1906–7). Settled in New York 1907.

Josquin Desprez [Juschino; Jodocus Pratensis; Joducus a Prato] (b. Picardy?, northern France, ca. 1440; d. Condé-sur-Escaut, Hainaut, 27 Aug. 1521). Composer. Singer at Milan Cathedral 1459–72; to Duke Galeazzo Maria Sforza 1474–76; thereafter served various patrons, possibly including King René of Anjou, Cardinal Ascanio Sforza, Louis XI and Louis XII. Singer at the papal chapel in Rome from 1486 to at least 1494. *Maestro di cappella* at the Ferrarese court 1503–4. Provost at Notre Dame in Condé after 1504. His music circulated widely throughout the 16th century, serving as models for parody composition and transcription. Of numerous compositions attributed to him, some 20 Masses are believed to be authentic, as well as 110 motets and some 75 secular works, primarily French chansons but with a handful of instrumental pieces and 3 compositions on Italian texts.

Josten, Werner (Erich) (b. Elberfeld, Wuppertal, Germany, 12 June 1885; d. New York, 6 Feb. 1963). Composer and conductor. Pupil of Jaques-Dalcroze. Taught at Smith College 1923–49. Composed in a neoclassic style, employing mild dissonance and some bitonality. Composed 3 ballets; orchestral works (*Jungle*, 1928; Symphony in F, 1936); chamber and piano music (a string quartet, piano trio, the *Canzona seria: A Hamlet Monologue*, flute, oboe, clarinet, bassoon, and piano, 1957); *Ode for St. Cecilia's Day* (1925) and other choral music; many songs.

Jota [Sp.]. A genre of song and dance especially characteristic of Aragón, in northern Spain, but widely disseminated through the Iberian peninsula. It is danced by one or more couples with castanets and is accompanied by guitars and *bandurrias. Some versions of the choreography require rather high leaps. As a quintessentially Spanish form of folk music, it has often been taken over into art music.

Jouer [Fr.]. To play.

Jouhikantele, jouhikannel, jouhikko [Finn.]. A bowed *lyre of Finland with from two to five horsehair strings, related to the *crwth*.

Jubilus [Lat.]. The melisma sung to the final syllable of the word *alleluia* in the *alleluia of Gregorian chant.

Judas Maccabaeus. Oratorio by Handel (libretto by Thomas Morell, based on 1 Maccabees of the Apocrypha and Josephus, Antiquities XII), produced in London in 1747.

Jug band. (1) A small folk ensemble of the U.S. that includes various homemade instruments (e.g., washtub, washboard, and jug), along with a few conventional pitched instruments, particularly guitar and harmonica. (2) An ensemble of a type formed among black musicians in the southern U.S. in the 1920s and 30s, including a jug (played by blowing across its opening) and associated with the blues and some currents of jazz.

Jukebox. An automatic phonograph containing a variety of recordings, principally of current popular music, and operated by inserting a coin and pressing a button to make a selection. Devices of this type date from the late 19th century and were widely disseminated through the middle of the 20th century in modest restaurants and bars.

Julius Caesar. See *Giulio Cesare.*

Juon [Yuon], **Paul** [Pavel Fedorovich] (b. Moscow, 6 Mar. 1872; d. Vevey, Switzerland, 21 Aug. 1940). Composer. Settled in Berlin, 1897; taught at the Hochschule 1906–34. His music combines elements of Russian folk song with the German tradition. Wrote 3 violin concertos, *Sinfonietta Capricciosa* (1940), *Psyche* (tenor, chorus, and orchestra, 1906), and other orchestral music; chamber music for winds, strings, and piano; piano works; choral music and songs. S. Wolpe and Jarnach were among his students.

Jupiter Symphony. Popular name for Mozart's Symphony in C major K. 551 (1788). Mozart's son attributed the name to Haydn's London impresario Johann Peter Salomon. The first edition to use it was Muzio Clementi's arrangement for piano published in London in 1823. The name is usually thought to refer to the majestic character of the opening of the first movement.

Jurinac, Sena [Srebrenka] (b. Travnik, Yugoslavia, 24 Oct. 1921). Soprano. Debut at the Zagreb Opera in 1942 as Mimì *(Bohème).* Joined the Vienna Staatsoper 1944; debut there as Cherubino *(Figaro),* 1945. At La Scala, the Teatro Colón in Buenos Aires, and the San Francisco Opera she achieved great success singing Mozart and Strauss heroines. Also distinguished for her Elisabeth *(Don Carlos)* and Butterfly.

Just intonation [Fr. *intonation juste;* Ger. *reine Stimmung;* It. *accordatura giusta;* Sp. *entonación justa*]. (1) The beatless tuning of an interval, one that brings it into agreement with some analogous interval in the *harmonic series. Such intervals are considered to be acoustically pure. They are expressed by ratios containing the smallest possible integers corresponding to the lowest analogous partials of the harmonic series. When an interval can be expressed by adjacent partials in the series it has the form $(x + 1){:}x$. See Interval.

(2) Any tuning that incorporates five or more acoustically pure types of interval within the octave; in the case of diatonic or chromatic scales, those based on acoustically pure major thirds and acoustically pure fifths. It is not possible to construct a diatonic scale in which both fifths and thirds are pure.

In the 18th century, just intonation was sometimes recommended for violin playing. There has been a modest resurgence of interest in the 20th century.

K

K., KV. Abbr. for *Köchel-Verzeichnis,* the thematic catalog of the works of Mozart first prepared by Ludwig von Köchel: *Chronologisch-thematisches Verzeichnis sämtlicher Tonwerke Wolfgang Amadé Mozarts* (Leipzig, 1862) and in various editions thereafter. Because Köchel numbers are intended to be chronological, advances in the study of the canon and chronology of Mozart's works have led to the reassignment of Köchel numbers for some works.

Kabalevsky, Dmitri Borisovich (b. St. Petersburg, 30 Dec. 1904; d. Moscow, 14 Feb. 1987). Composer, pianist, and writer on music. Pupil of Catoire and Myaskovsky. Taught at the Moscow Conservatory from 1932; editor of the journal *Sovremennaya muzïka* 1940–46. Member of the Communist party; wrote a number of large-scale patriotic works *(The Mighty Homeland,* cantata, 1941–42). Composed dramatic works (including *Colas Breugnon,* 1936–38, rev. 1953, 1969; *The Taras Family,* 1947, rev. 1950, 1967; *The Sisters,* 1967); orchestral music (symphonies; concertos for piano, violin, and cello; the *Comedians* suite, 1940); chamber music, including string quartets; sonatas, preludes and fugues, and other keyboard music; choral works; songs; film and incidental music.

Kabeláč, Miloslav (b. Prague, 1 Aug. 1908; d. there, 17 Sept. 1979). Composer. Pupil of Jirák. Music director of Czech Radio from 1932; at Prague Radio from 1945; taught at the Prague Conservatory 1958–62. Worked with early music, Chinese, Japanese, and Indian music, and electronic sounds. Works include 8 symphonies and other orchestral compositions; works for instrumental ensemble *(Osm invenci,* percussion, 1963); tape *(E fontibus bohemicis,* 1972); vocal works.

Kabuki [Jap.]. A major genre of Japanese music theater.

Kadenz [Ger.]. *Cadence, *cadenza.

Kadosa, Pál (b. Léva [now Levice, Czech Republic], 6 Sept. 1903; d. Budapest, 30 Mar. 1983). Composer and pianist. Pupil of Kodály. Taught piano at the Fodor Conservatory (1927–43) and the Budapest Academy (from 1945). Early compositions reflect the influence of Bartók and Stravinsky; later employed free twelve-tone elements. As a pianist, known for performances of Bartók. Composed 2

comic operas; 8 symphonies and other orchestral works; concertos for piano, violin, viola; cantatas *(Folksong Cantata,* 1939); songs; string quartets, other chamber music; various piano works.

Kaffeekantate [Ger.]. See *Coffee* Cantata.

Kagel, Mauricio (Raúl) (b. Buenos Aires, 24 Dec. 1931). Composer. Pupil of Paz. Worked at the Teatro Colón from 1949 (director, 1955). Settled in Cologne, 1957; there directed the Institute of New Music (from 1969) and taught at the Musikhochschule (from 1974). Lectured at the Darmstadt summer courses 1960–66. Has explored *musique concrète (Der Schall,* 1968), new vocal techniques *(Anagrama,* 1958), electronic composition *(Transición I–II,* 1958–60), and theatrical elements. Also wrote plays and films, including *Ludwig Van,* 1969, based on his musical work of the same name. Other works include the operas *Die Erschöpfung der Welt* (1980) and *Aus Deutschland* (1977–80); *Sankt-Bach-Passion* (1985); *Musik für Tasteninstrumente und Orchester* (1989).

Kahn, Robert (b. Mannheim, 21 July 1865; d. Biddenden, Kent, 29 May 1951). Composer. Pupil of Rheinberger. Coach at the opera and choral conductor, Leipzig, 1890–93; teacher, Berlin Hochschule, 1894–1930. Emigrated to England 1937. A respected conservative composer, especially of chamber music, choral music, songs, piano pieces. Brother of the American banker and patron of the arts Otto Kahn (1867–1934).

Kaiserquartett [Ger.]. See *Emperor* Quartet.

Kalafati, Vasily Pavovlich (b. Evpatoriya, Crimea, 10 Feb. 1869; d. Leningrad, 30 Jan. 1942). Composer. Pupil of Rimsky-Korsakov. Taught at the St. Petersburg Conservatory 1907–29; pupils included Stravinsky and Prokofiev. Composed the opera *Zygany* [The Gypsies] (1939–41), a symphony, an overture, 2 string quartets, piano pieces and choral works.

Kalevala. The Finnish national epic. Among the symphonic poems by Finnish composers based on portions of this epic, those by Sibelius include *Lemminkäinen Suite, *Pohjola's Daughter,* and *Tapiola.*

Kalimba. See *Mbira.*

Kalinnikov, Vasily Sergeyevich (b. Voina, Oryol district, 13 Jan. 1866; d. Yalta, 11 Jan. 1901). Composer. Best known for his Symphony no. 1 in G minor (1894–95); the work bears resemblances to Tchaikovsky and Borodin in its use of folklike melodies. Other works include the Symphony no. 2 in A (1895–97); *Tsar Boris* (incidental music, 1899); *The Cedar and the Palm* (orchestra, 1897–98); *Grustnaya pesenka* [Chanson Triste] (piano, 1892–93).

Kalish, Gilbert (b. Brooklyn, 2 July 1935). Pianist. Studied with Isabelle Vengerova. New York debut, 1962. Has promoted new works by American composers; also a noted interpreter of Haydn. Has appeared with the Juilliard String Quartet and mezzo Jan De Gaetani. Taught at Rutgers (1965–67), Swarthmore (1966–72), and SUNY–Stony Brook (from 1970).

Kalkbrenner, Friedrich Wilhelm (Michael) (b. near Kassel, between 2 and 8 Nov. 1785; d. Enghien-les-Bains, 10 June 1849). Pianist and composer. Son of the composer Christian Kalkbrenner (1755–1801); pupil of Albrechtsberger. Lived in London, 1814–24; toured as pianist, 1820s to 1830s; settled in Paris 1824. Part-owner of the Pleyel piano firm. Wrote sonatas; salon music; etudes; concertos; chamber music; a *Méthode* (1831); a *Traité* on piano improvisation (1849).

Kalliwoda, Johann Wenzel [Kaliwoda, Jan Křtitel Václav] (b. Prague, 21 Feb. 1801; d. Karlsruhe, 3 Dec. 1866). Composer. From 1821, toured as solo violinist. Kapellmeister to Prince von Fürstenberg, Donaueschingen 1822–48, 1857–66. Composed 2 operas, 7 symphonies, 18 overtures, chamber music, 10 Masses, piano pieces, songs.

Kallstenius, Edvin (b. Filipstad, Sweden, 29 Aug. 1881; d. Danderyd, 22 Nov. 1967). Composer. Studied at the Leipzig Conservatory; worked as music critic and music librarian in Sweden. Works include tone poems; 5 symphonies (*Sinfonia su temi 12-tonici*, 1960); Piano Concerto, 1922; choral music (*När vi dö* [When We Are Dying], requiem, 1919); chamber music (8 string quartets; clarinet quintet); solo vocal music.

Kálmán, Imre [Emmerich] (b. Siófok, Hungary, 24 Oct. 1882; d. Paris, 30 Oct. 1953). Composer. Studied at the Budapest Academy of Music. Lived in Vienna 1908–39; later in Paris and the U.S. Composed operettas, often on Hungarian subjects, including *The Gay Hussars* (Vienna, 1908); *Miss Springtime* (Budapest, 1915); *Riviera Girl* (Vienna, 1915).

Kalomiris, Manolis (b. Smyrna, Turkey, 14 Dec. 1883; d. Athens, 3 Apr. 1962). Composer. Studied in Athens, Constantinople, and Vienna. Taught at the Obolensky Lyceum in Russia (1906–10) and at the Athens Conservatory (1911–19). Founded and directed the Hellenic Conservatory (1919–26) and the National Conservatory (1926–48) in Athens; 1944–45, director of the National Opera. His compositions reflect his love of Greek folk song as well as his contact with German and Russian music. Composed operas (*O protomastoras* [The Master Builder], 1915, rev. 1929, 1940); vocal works; orchestral pieces; other instrumental works and concertos; many songs and arrangements of folk songs.

Kamieński, Mathias [Maciej] (b. Sopron? [Ödenburg], 13 Oct. 1734; d. Warsaw, 25 Jan. 1821). Composer. Composed operas including *Nędza uszczęśliwiona* [Poverty Made Happy] (1778), probably the first publicly performed Polish opera, and *Słowik czyli Kasia z Hanka na wydaniu* [The Nightingale, or Kasia and Hanka, Two Maidens] (1790), both Warsaw; a cantata; Masses; works for harpsichord.

Kaminski, Heinrich (b. Tiengen, near Waldshut, 4 July 1886; d. Ried, near Benediktbeuren, 21 June 1946). Composer. Pupil of Juon and Kaun. From 1914 lived and taught in Ried; Orff was among his students. Taught in Berlin 1930–33. Works include 2 operas, 5 orchestral pieces (*Orchesterkonzert mit Clavier*, 1936); 2 string quartets and other chamber music; piano and organ works; a Magnificat and other choral music; songs with organ or instrumental ensemble.

Kaminsky, Max (b. Brockton, Mass., 7 Sept. 1908; d. Castle Point, N.Y., 6 Sept. 1994). Jazz trumpeter. Worked in Eddie Condon's Chicago-style Dixieland groups, 1933–45; joined the big bands of Tommy Dorsey (1936, 1938) and Artie Shaw (1938, 1941–43); toured Europe with the Jack Teagarden and Earl Hines All Stars (1957); worked at Jimmy Ryan's club in New York (late 1960s–1983).

Kammer [Ger.]. Chamber; *Kammermusik*, chamber music; etc. For *Kammerton* see Pitch.

Kancheli, Giia [Giya] **(Alexandrovich)** (b. Tbilisi, 10 Aug. 1935). Composer. Studied at the Tbilisi Conservatory; taught there after 1972. From 1971, directed music at the Rustaveli Dramatic Theater. Works include musical theater; the opera *Music for the Living* (1984); 7 symphonies (1975, In Memoriam Michelangelo; 1977, In Memory of My Parents; 1986, Epilogue); *Bright Sorrow* (2 boy soloists, boys' choir, orchestra, 1985); *Mourned by the Wind* (solo viola, orchestra, 1987).

Kanon [Ger.]. *Canon.

Kantele [Finn.]. A Finnish *zither. The traditional instrument was a narrow trapezoid with 5 strings. The modern version has 12 to 46 metal strings tuned diatonically. It is mentioned in the *Kalevala* and is a national symbol.

Kantor [Ger.]. The chief musician of a German Protestant (Evangelical) church, whose duties comprised teaching school as well as selecting, composing, rehearsing, and performing music appropriate to liturgical celebrations and public municipal occasions. Bach was Kantor at the church of St. Thomas and its associated school in Leipzig from 1723 until his death. See also Cantor.

Kantorei [Ger.]. In German Protestant cities from the 16th through the 18th century, a voluntary group of townspeople who performed polyphonic music in church under the leadership of the *Kantor;* at Protestant courts in the 16th and 17th centuries, the professional singers and instrumentalists, usually known at Catholic courts as the *Kapelle.*

Kapelle [Ger.]. *Chapel; *Hofkapelle,* court chapel. In the 17th century, this came to mean the entire musical establishment of a court, both sacred and secular, including the opera. Ultimately, the term lost its sacred associations altogether and in the 19th century could refer to any orchestra or ensemble, including a military band *(Militärkapelle).* See also *Kapellmeister.*

Kapellmeister [Ger.]. The leader of a musical *chapel, which might provide both sacred and secular music. Bach held this title at the court at Cöthen from 1717 until 1723. In the 19th century, when the term *Kapelle* could refer to a wholly secular musical establishment, including an opera or any orchestra or ensemble, *Kapellmeister* came to mean simply conductor.

Kapr, Jan (b. Prague, 12 Mar. 1914; d. there, 29 Apr. 1988). Composer. Studied at the Prague Conservatory; music producer for Czech Radio 1939–46; taught at the Janáček Academy of Music 1961–70. Experimented with the folk song idiom; later works utilize serial procedures. Composed an opera; orchestral music (8 symphonies; *Marathon,* symphony scherzo, 1939; Piano concerto no. 1, 1938); string quartets and other chamber music; cantatas; film music.

Karajan, Herbert von (b. Salzburg, 5 Apr. 1908; d. Anif, Austria, 16 July 1989). Conductor. Pupil of Schalk. Debut 1928; conducting posts at Ulm 1929–34; at Aachen (where he was a member of the Nazi party); at the Berlin State Opera 1938–45. From 1947, recorded with the Vienna Philharmonic; appeared in London, at La Scala, and at Bayreuth (from 1951). U.S. debut 1955; that year succeeded Furtwängler as music director for life of the Berlin Philharmonic (resigned 1989). Led the Salzburg Festival

1956–60 and from 1964; the Vienna Opera 1957–64. Made over 800 recordings.

Karel, Rudolf (b. Plzeň, Czechoslovakia, 9 Nov. 1880; d. Terezín concentration camp, 6 Mar. 1945). Composer. Pupil of Dvořák. Taught at music schools in Russia and at the Prague Conservatory (1923–41). Later compositions use irregular rhythms and modal-based progressions. Works include operas (*Ilsa's Heart,* 1909); orchestral music (*Spring Symphony,* 1938); cantatas.

Karelia. An orchestral overture, op. 10, and a suite, op. 11, by Sibelius, both drawn from his incidental music to a historical pageant presented in 1893 by students at the university in Vyborg, Karelia (now Russia).

Karg-Elert [Karg], **Sigfrid** (b. Oberndorf-am-Neckar, 21 Nov. 1877; d. Leipzig, 9 Apr. 1933). Composer, theorist, and organist. Pupil of Reinecke. Taught at the Magdeburg and Leipzig (from 1919) conservatories. Composed some 250 organ works (*66 Chorale-Improvisationen,* 1908–10); pieces for harmonium; piano pieces and didactic works; orchestral and chamber pieces; choral and vocal music. Wrote volumes on the harmonium, the organ, and music theory.

Kasemets, Udo (b. Tallinn, Estonia, 16 Nov. 1919). Composer. Pupil of Scherchen and Krenek. Emigrated to Canada 1951; active as a teacher, music critic, concert organizer, and conductor. Early works are neoclassical (including orchestral, chamber, and vocal music); in the 1960s he adopted chance mixed-media procedures. Works include *Tt* (1968), *Colourwalk* (1971), *Music of the Eighth Moon of the Year of the Dragon* (recordings, tapes, mixers, reader, transparencies, 1976), *Vertical Music: In Remembrance of Morton Feldman* (any 7 instruments, 1987), *Portrait: Music of the 12 Moons of the I Ching* (various instruments, 1988).

Kastal'sky, Alexandr Dmitriyevich (b. Moscow, 28 Nov. 1856; d. there, 17 Dec. 1926). Composer and musicologist. Pupil of Tchaikovsky and Taneyev. From 1887 taught at the Moscow Synodal Academy and directed the Synodal Choir (1910–23); taught at the Moscow Conservatory from 1923. Composed mainly choral music; also a scholar of old Russian chant.

Kát'a Kabanová. Opera in three acts by Leoš Janáček (libretto by the composer, after A. N. Ostrovsky's tragedy *The Storm*), produced in Brno in 1921. Setting: Kalinov, a small town on the Volga, about 1860.

Katchen, Julius (b. Long Branch, N.J., 15 Aug. 1926; d. Paris, 29 Apr. 1969). Pianist. Appeared with the New York Philharmonic and the Philadelphia Orchestra at age 11. Formed a trio with Suk and Starker 1967. His repertory encompassed the classics, Slavic and contemporary music; particularly noted for his Brahms readings.

Katerina Izmaylova. See *Lady Macbeth of the Mtsensk District.*

Kauer, Ferdinand (b. Klein-Tajax, Znaim [now Znojmo], near Brno, bapt. 18 Jan. 1751; d. Vienna, 13 Apr. 1831). Composer. Settled in Vienna around 1777; church organist; violinist and later composer at the Leopoldstadt Theater; Kapellmeister at the Josefstadt Theater 1814–18. Composed some 200 stage works, including *Das Faustrecht in Thüringen* (1796), *Die Löwenritter* (1799), and *Das Donauweibchen* (1798). Also composed church music, symphonies, chamber and keyboard music.

Kaun, Hugo (b. Berlin, 21 Mar. 1863; d. there, 2 Apr. 1932). Composer and choral conductor. Studied in Berlin. Lived in Milwaukee 1886–1902. Taught at the Berlin Conservatory from 1922. Heavily influenced by Wagner. Composed operas; symphonies, piano concertos, and other orchestral music; string quartets and other chamber music; numerous choral pieces, songs, and piano works.

Kay, Hershy (b. Philadelphia, 17 Nov. 1919; d. Danbury, Conn., 2 Dec. 1981). Composer. Pupil of Randall Thompson. Orchestrated many Broadway musicals, including *On the Town* (1944), and other works by Bernstein. Composed many ballets, (*L'inconnue*, 1965, after Poulenc, and *Stars and Stripes*, 1958, after Sousa, for Balanchine; *The Clowns*, 1968, employing serial methods); film scores.

Kay, Ulysses (Simpson) (b. Tucson, 7 Jan. 1917; d. Englewood, N.J., 20 May 1995). Composer. Nephew of King Oliver; pupil of Hindemith. Taught at Lehman College, CUNY, 1968–88. His works are in a neoclassical idiom. Composed operas (*Frederick Douglass*, 1983), a ballet, film and television scores; *String Triptych* (1987) and other orchestral music; chamber music for strings, winds, and brass; works for voices and orchestra; piano (*2 Impromptus*, 1986) and organ music; choral music (*Festival Psalms*, baritone, mixed choir, piano, 1983); songs.

Kazoo. A voice-operated *mirliton of the U.S. and Europe. A membrane is attached over a hole in the side of a short wooden or metal tube and vibrates with a buzzing effect when the player sings or hums into the tube.

Keats, Donald (Howard) (b. New York, 27 May 1929). Composer. Pupil of Q. Porter, Hindemith, Luening, Cowell, and Jarnach. Has taught at Antioch College (1957–75) and the Univ. of Denver. Makes

occasional free use of serial procedures; lyricism is the dominant characteristic of his style. Works include 2 symphonies, a piano concerto, and other orchestral music; 2 string quartets, *Musica Instrumentalis I* (10 instruments, 1980); piano and choral music; *Tierras del alma* (song cycle for soprano, flute, guitar, 1979) and songs.

Keene, Christopher (b. Berkeley, Calif., 21 Dec. 1946; d. New York, 8 Oct. 1995). Conductor. General director of Menotti's Spoleto Festival from 1973; music director from 1976. Music director of the American Ballet Company, 1969–70; at ArtPark, 1975–89; of the Syracuse Symphony, 1976–87. Founding conductor of the Long Island Philharmonic, 1979–89. From 1989 director of the New York City Opera.

Keiser, Reinhard (b. Teuchern, 10 or 11 Jan. 1674; d. Hamburg, 12 Sept. 1739). Composer. Pupil of Schelle. Chamber composer at Braunschweig court, 1694. Moved to Hamburg, composing operas for the Oper am Gänsemarkt; its director, 1702–7. In 1728, succeeded Mattheson as *Canonicus minor* and cantor at the cathedral. Composed numerous operas (including *Der königliche Schäfer*, Braunschweig ca. 1693; *Der Karneval von Venedig*, Hamburg 1707). His 1712 setting of Brockes's Passion-oratorio text (later set by Handel) was central to the development of the genre.

Kelemen, Milko (b. Podravska Slatina, Croatia, 30 Mar. 1924). Composer. Pupil of Sulek, Messiaen, Aubin, and Fortner. Taught at the Zagreb Academy of Music, the Düsseldorf Conservatory (1970–72), and the Stuttgart Musikhochschule (from 1973). Has worked with folk materials and with serial and electronic sound techniques. Works include operas; ballets (*Apocalyptica*, 1983); orchestral music (*Phantasmes*, viola, orchestra, 1985; *Antiphonie*, organ, orchestra, 1985; *Drammatico*, cello, orchestra, 1984; *Archetypon*, 1986); chamber music (String Quartet no. 4, *Landschaftsbilder*, 1986); film scores.

Kéler, Béla [Keler, Adalbert Paul von] (b. Bártfa, Hungary [now Bardejov, Czech Republic], 13 Feb. 1820; d. Wiesbaden, 20 Nov. 1882). Violinist and composer. Theater violinist; dance orchestra conductor; Austrian military bandmaster; later conducted at Wiesbaden (1863–70) and Bad Spa (from 1870); also toured widely. Published very popular dances and marches; also 12 overtures (*Lustspiel-Ouverture* op. 73; *Ungarische Lustspiel-Ouverture* op. 108).

Kell, Reginald (Clifford) (b. York, 8 June 1906; d. Frankfort, Ky., 5 Aug. 1981). Clarinetist. First clarinet, London Philharmonic from 1932; London Symphony from 1937. Taught at the Royal Academy of Music from 1935. Emigrated to the U.S., 1948;

worked as a soloist and with ensembles such as the Fine Arts Quartet.

Kelley, Edgar Stillman [Stillman-Kelley, Edgar] (b. Sparta, Wis., 14 Apr. 1857; d. New York, 12 Nov. 1944). Organist, composer, and writer on music. Studied in Chicago and Stuttgart; studied Chinese music in San Francisco. Taught in Berlin (1902–10); and at the Cincinnati Conservatory (1911–34). Wrote stage music (*The Pilgrim's Progress*, 1917); *Aladdin: A Chinese Suite* (1887–93), Symphony no. 2, "New England" (1913), and other orchestral music; chamber and piano music; choral works ("O Captain! My Captain!," op. 19); songs (*A California Idyll*, soprano, orchestra, 1918).

Kelly, Michael (b. Dublin, 25 Dec. 1762; d. Margate [Kent], 9 Oct. 1826). Tenor, composer, and theater manager. Studied with Rauzzini and Arne and in Naples. From 1783 sang at the imperial theater, Vienna (created Don Basilio, *Figaro*); from 1787, at Drury Lane. Published *Reminiscences* (1826) on Viennese and London musical life. Composed stage works (*Blue Beard*, 1798).

Kelterborn, Rudolf (b. Basel, 3 Sept. 1931). Composer and conductor. Pupil of Blacher and Fortner. Taught at Darmstadt (1956–60), the Northwest German Music Academy, Detmold (1960–68), the Zurich Musikhochschule (1968–75), and the Karlsruhe Hochschule für Musik (from 1980). Has worked with serial and aleatory techniques. Works include 7 operas (*Ophelia*, 1984; *Julia*, 1991); a ballet; symphonies, *Kommunikationen* (6 groups of instruments, 1971–72), *Musica luminosa* (1985), and other orchestral music; large works for voices and orchestra; 4 string quartets and other chamber music; organ, piano, and harpsichord pieces; choral music and songs.

Kempe, Rudolf (b. Niederpoyritz, 14 June 1910; d. Zurich, 11 May 1976). Conductor. Oboist with the Leipzig Opera, 1929; debut as conductor there, 1935. Conducted opera at Chemnitz, 1943–48. Music director, Bavarian State Opera, 1952–54; Metropolitan Opera debut, 1954. Conductor of the Royal Philharmonic, 1961–75; of the Munich Philharmonic, 1967–76; of the BBC Symphony, 1975–76.

Kempff, Wilhelm (b. Jüterbog, 25 Nov. 1895; d. Positano, Italy, 23 May 1991). Pianist and composer. Pupil of R. Kahn. Director, Stuttgart Musikhochschule, 1924–29. Recorded all of Beethoven's concertos, piano sonatas, violin sonatas (with Schneiderhan and Menuhin), trios (with Szeryng and Fournier), and cello sonatas (with Fournier), as well as Schubert's piano sonatas. Composed operas, a ballet, concertos for piano and violin, symphonies, a tone poem, and chamber music.

Kennan, Kent (Wheeler) (b. Milwaukee, 18 Apr. 1913). Composer. Pupil of Hanson. Taught at Kent State Univ., Ohio State Univ., and the Univ. of Texas. Influences include Romanticism, impressionism, jazz, and neoclassicism similar to Hindemith's. Wrote books on orchestration and counterpoint; Works include orchestral pieces; chamber music (*Scherzo, Aria, and Fugato*, oboe, piano, 1948); piano music; *The Unknown Warrior Speaks* (male chorus, 1944).

Kenner und Liebhaber [Ger.; Fr. *connaisseur* and *amateur*]. In publications of the late 18th century (e.g., by C. P. E. Bach), a phrase often used to suggest that the music in question was suitable both for knowledgeable musicians and the growing number of amateur music-lovers.

Kent bugle, Kent horn. See Keyed bugle.

Kenton, Stan(ley Newcomb) (b. Wichita, Kans., 15 Dec. 1911; d. Los Angeles, 25 Aug. 1979). Jazz bandleader, pianist, and arranger. From 1941 led big bands, including the Progressive Jazz Orchestra (1949), Innovations in Modern Music (1950–51), and Los Angeles Neophonic (1965–66). Attempted to bring contemporary classical devices into jazz (arrangers included Pete Rugolo, Shorty Rogers, Bill Russo, Gerry Mulligan); from 1952 returned to swing and bop traditions; 1970s, used rock rhythms. From 1959 directed college workshops.

Kerle, Jacobus de (b. Ieper [Ypres], 1531 or 1532; d. Prague, 7 Jan. 1591). Composer and organist. Active in various Italian and German cities. Composed the *Preces speciales*, prayers sung at the Council of Trent; held a position at Augsburg Cathedral 1568–74. Surviving works include Masses, motets, and other liturgical genres.

Kerll [Kerl, Gherl], **Johann Kaspar** (b. Adorf, Saxony, 9 Apr. 1627; d. Munich, 13 Feb. 1693). Composer and organist. Pupil of Valentini, Carissimi and possibly Frescobaldi. Served Archduke Leopold Wilhelm in Brussels until 1656; Kapellmeister at Munich until 1673; organist at St. Stephen's, Vienna, 1674–77; imperial organist from 1677. Composed Masses and other sacred pieces, dramatic works, and keyboard and chamber music.

Kern, Jerome (David) (b. New York, 27 Jan. 1885; d. there, 11 Nov. 1945). Popular songwriter. Worked as a song plugger; wrote songs for revues. From 1911 wrote full-length musical shows, which fundamentally influenced the development of American musical theater. Collaborated with book writer Guy Bolton and lyricist P. G. Wodehouse (including *Very Good Eddie*, 1915; *Oh Boy!*, 1917) and with Oscar Hammerstein II (*Show Boat*, 1927, including "Ol' Man River," "Why Do I Love You?"). After 1935 wrote primarily for film ("The Way You Look To-night," in *Swing Time*, 1936; "The Last Time I Saw Paris," *Lady Be Good*, 1941).

Kerr, Harrison (b. Cleveland, 13 Oct. 1897; d. Norman, Okla., 15 Aug. 1978). Composer. Pupil of Boulanger. Taught at the Univ. of Oklahoma 1949–68. Compositions include an opera and a ballet; 3 symphonies, a concerto for violin, and other orchestral pieces; 2 string quartets and other chamber and piano music; choral music and songs.

Kertész, István (b. Budapest, 28 Aug. 1929; d. Kfar Saba, Israel, 16 Apr. 1973). Conductor. Conductor of the Györ Philharmonic, 1953–55; of the Budapest Opera, 1955–56. Music director at Augsburg, 1958–63, and at the Cologne Opera, 1964–73. Principal conductor of the London Symphony, 1965–68; of the Gürzenich Orchestra at Cologne, 1971–73.

Kessel, Barney (b. Muskogee, Okla., 17 Oct. 1923). Jazz guitarist. Performed in the film *Jammin' the Blues* (1944); joined Artie Shaw (1945); became a studio musician in Los Angeles. Recorded with Charlie Parker (1947); toured with Oscar Peterson (1952–53); recorded widely as a free-lance. Led groups, including Great Guitars with Charlie Byrd and Herb Ellis, from 1973.

Kesselpauke, Kesseltrommel [Ger.]. *Kettledrum.

Ketèlbey, Albert W(illiam) [Vodorinski, Anton] (b. Birmingham, 9 Aug. 1875; d. Cowes, Isle of Wight, 26 Nov. 1959). Composer and conductor. Music director of the Vaudeville Theatre from 1897. Published early songs and piano works under the name Anton Vodorinski. Composed a series of light narrative works for orchestra (beginning with *In a Monastery Garden*, 1915); songs; anthems; solo instrumental works; music to accompany silent films.

Kettledrum [also pl. timpani; Fr. *timbale;* Ger. *Pauke;* It. *timpano;* Sp. *timbal, atabal*]. The most important orchestral percussion instrument, and the only member of the drum family of Western art music capable of producing notes of definite pitch. It consists of a large hemispherical shell of metal or fiber glass across which is stretched a head, ordinarily of calfskin or plastic, mounted (lapped) on a hoop that is held in place by a metal ring (counterhoop) through which pass threaded screws or rods that allow the skin's tension to be varied. Kettledrums come in standard sizes, from 50 to 82 cm. (20 to 32 in.) in diameter, with a range from high bb to low D. Typical sets of four drums will include drums that are 58, 64, 71, and 76 cm. (23, 25, 28, and 30 in.) or now often 58, 66, 74, and 81 cm. (23, 26, 29, and 32 in.) in diameter, each with a range of approximately a perfect fifth, upward from d, Bb, F, and D or Eb, respectively. If only two drums are used, they are usually

the middle two. They are played with two wooden sticks with heads of felt or other material, varying in shape, size, weight, and texture. See ill. under Percussion instruments.

Key. (1) [Fr. *tonalité, ton;* Ger. *Tonart;* It. *tonalità, tono;* Sp. *tonalidad, tono*]. In tonal music [see Tonality], the pitch relationships that establish a single *pitch class as a tonal center or tonic (or key note), with respect to which the remaining pitches have subordinate functions. There are two types or modes of keys, *major and minor, and any of the twelve pitch classes can serve as a tonic. There are thus in principle 24 different keys. Because a pitch class may have more than one name, however (e.g., C♯ and D♭, which are said to be *enharmonic equivalents), the nomenclature of keys includes more than 24. The key of a composition or passage is described in terms of its tonic and its mode (e.g., C major, D minor), and a work or passage is said to be "in" a certain key.

The key of a work is defined in terms of the particular major or minor *scale from which its principal pitches are drawn. This is indicated in the first instance by a *key signature—an arrangement of sharps or flats (or the absence of both) at the beginning of each staff that specifies the principal pitches. (Other pitches may be used as well, producing *chromaticism.) The notion of scale embodies not only the selection of seven pitch classes from the available twelve, however, but also the organization of the seven in a hierarchy around the one that serves as tonic. When the pitches of a scale are arranged as a scale, the tonic is placed first. Furthermore, each key signature represents one major and one minor key that share the same basic pitch collection, but have different tonics. For example, the pitches of the white keys of the piano (represented by a key signature of no sharps and no flats) can be arranged in a scale with C first and thus as tonic (yielding C major) or with A first as tonic (yielding A minor). These two "modes" of presenting the same pitches differ in the arrangement of tones and semitones on either side of the tonic [for a discussion of these and other modes, see Mode]. Thus, in order to be in a given key, a composition must not only give prominence to the seven pitch classes of the appropriate scale, but it must also treat the tonic as the single pitch class of greatest stability and toward which all tonal movement ultimately tends. A piece in a given key will virtually always conclude with the tonic and will most often include a number of prominent *cadences on the tonic.

Although a tonal piece is usually described as being in a single key, it may incorporate passages in other keys before returning finally to the principal key. The process of moving from one key to another in the course of a piece is called *modulation [see

Key signatures.

also Key relationship]. Often, though not always, the key signature of a work is left unchanged throughout one or more modulations, the necessary changes of pitch being specified with *accidentals. Pieces consisting of more than one *movement may include one or more movements in a different key altogether [see, e.g., Sonata]. Such movements will have the appropriate key signature.

(2) [Fr. *touche;* Ger. *Taste;* It. *tasto;* Sp. *tecla*]. A lever by means of which the movement of a player's hand is transmitted to the action of an instrument, causing it to sound. A set of such levers arranged for ease of playing is a *keyboard, and instruments operated by such a device are keyboard instruments, e.g., the piano, organ, harpsichord, and clavichord.

(3) [Fr. *clef;* Ger. *Klappe;* It. *chiave;* Sp. *llave*]. On a woodwind instrument, a lever used to open or close a hole. The complete mechanism made up of such levers is the keywork.

Key relationship. The degree to which one *key is related to another is primarily a function of the number of pitches that the two hold in common. The most closely related keys are those adjacent to each other on the *circle of fifths. Their *key signatures differ by a single flat or sharp, and thus they share six of their seven pitches. Conversely, distant keys are those that are distant from each other on the circle of fifths and thus have relatively few pitches in common. Other important relationships are those between parallel keys, i.e., major and minor keys with the same tonic, and between relative keys, i.e., major and minor keys with the same key signature and thus the same basic pitch collection. The relative minor of any major key or scale, while sharing its key signature and pitches, takes as its tonic the sixth scale degree of that major key or scale; e.g., the relative minor of E♭ major is C minor. See also Modulation.

Key signature. In tonal music [see Tonality], an arrangement of sharps or flats (or the absence of both) at the beginning of each staff that defines the principal pitches employed in the composition in question. Each sharp or flat indicates, respectively, a raising or lowering by a semitone of all pitches (in whatever octave) with the letter name of the line or space on which it is placed. This may be countermanded in

individual cases by means of a natural sign or other *accidental.

Each key signature defines a diatonic *scale that can be employed in one of two modes, *major or minor, and thus with either of two tonics—one for a major *key and one for a minor key. Since there are twelve pitch classes altogether, there are in principle twelve different key signatures. Since, however, a pitch class can have more than one name (e.g., C♯ and D♭, which are *enharmonic equivalents), the number of key signatures available is greater than twelve. Fifteen are in common use. In the accompanying example, key signatures are presented in order from no sharps or flats through seven sharps and from one flat through seven flats. The whole note in each case indicates the tonic of the corresponding major key; the black note indicates the tonic of the corresponding minor key. Within each key signature, the sharps or flats are always arranged in the order and in the pattern on the staff presented here.

A comparison of this example with the *circle of fifths shows that the addition of sharps corresponds to movement through keys along the circle in a clockwise direction, whereas the addition of flats corresponds to movement through keys along the circle in a counterclockwise direction. The order in which sharps are added (F C G D A E B) can also be seen to be represented by adjacent pitch classes on the circle proceeding clockwise, as can the order in which flats are added (B E A D G C F), proceeding counterclockwise.

The consistent use of this system of key signatures associated with specific keys dates from the later 18th century, even though the tonal system had by then been well established for at least a century. Earlier in the 18th century, minor keys were often written with one less flat than is now usual. Less often, keys with sharp signatures were written with one less sharp.

Keyboard [Fr. *clavier;* Ger. *Klaviatur;* It. *tastiera;* Sp. *teclado*]. The whole set of levers in pianos, organs, harpsichords, clavichords, and similar instruments that actuate the tone-producing mechanism. Each octave consists of seven natural and five chromatic keys, arranged as in the accompanying figure. The intervals between the natural keys are whole tones except for the semitone steps E–F and B–C, where no chromatic key intervenes. The interval between any natural key and an adjacent chromatic key is a semitone [see Interval].

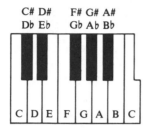

This arrangement of keys dates from the early 15th century and has survived various attempts at reform through adoption of a truly chromatic keyboard on which all scales beginning on either the lower or upper keys would have the same fingering. In Western tonal music, the primacy of the C-major scale, played entirely on the lower keys, must derive in some measure from the traditional keyboard design. The lower keys on the modern piano and organ are invariably made of ivory or white plastic, and the upper keys or sharps of ebony or black plastic. On many types of older keyboard instruments, however, the color scheme was the reverse, with dark-colored naturals and light-colored chromatic keys.

In the course of the late 17th century, the harpsichord compass first grew toward the bass, down to G_1 and F_1, and then inched its way from c''' to f'''. But only the largest clavichords could be extended down to the late 18th-century standard keyboard compass of five octaves (F_1 to f''). The early piano soon reached the full five-octave compass, expanding it to c'''' in the 1790s. By 1810 it was six octaves (F_1 to f'''' in Vienna, C_1 to c'''' in London), and shortly afterward six and one-half octaves (C_1 to f''''), the compass of Beethoven's last sonatas and Chopin's works. By mid-century, the seven-octave compass A_2 to a'''' had become common. The final three keys of today's standard A_2-to-c'''' 88-note piano keyboard were added after ca. 1870.

Experimental keyboards have been designed with six lower keys (C♯, D♯, F, G, A, and B) and six raised keys (C, D, E, F♯, G♯, and A♯) per octave to permit the use of identical fingerings in every tonality. Invented and then improved during the 19th century (most notably by Paul von Janko), they have never succeeded in displacing the standard type. Radiating keyboards in a fanlike shape (Clutsam, 1907, based on a Viennese design of 1824), intended to facilitate playing extreme bass and treble keys, have not gained favor either except on organ pedalboards of the modern type.

Keyboard instruments. Instruments sounded by means of a *keyboard, especially the *piano, *organ, *harpsichord, and *clavichord. The term is often used in the context of music composed before the late 18th century, some of which does not distinguish among the different types then in use.

Keyed bugle, Royal Kent bugle. A trumpet-shaped soprano brass instrument of large, conical bore with five to twelve woodwindlike side holes and keys. Joseph Haliday of Dublin patented the five-key prototype in 1810. By 1815, several inches in length and an additional open key near the bell had been added. The improved instrument was called the Royal Kent bugle in honor of the Duke of Kent, then commander-in-chief of British troops in Ireland. His six-key model in C (with a pigtail crook to B♭) was one of the first fully chromatic soprano brasses. By the 1820s, one more key to improve low E♭ brought the basic set of keys to seven—five for the right hand and two for the left.

Keyed trumpet. See Trumpet.

Keynote. *Tonic.

Khachaturian, Aram Il'yich (b. Tbilisi, 6 June 1903; d. Moscow, 1 May 1978). Composer. Pupil of Gnesin, Glier, and Myaskovsky. In 1948, along with Prokofiev and Shostakovich, came under attack by the Soviets for "following an antipopular, formalistic trend"; traveled to Armenia, where he wrote folk songs. From 1950 taught at the Gnesin School; later at the Moscow Conservatory. Works include ballets *(Gayane,* 1942; rev. 1957; *Spartacus,* 1954; rev. 1968); incidental music; orchestral works (3 symphonies; concertos and concert rhapsodies for piano, violin, and cello; *Song of Stalin,* chorus, orchestra, 1937); chamber and piano works (sonatas for unaccompanied cello, violin, and viola); film music.

Khan, Ali Akbar (b. Shibpur, Bengal, 14 Apr. 1922). Sarod player and composer. Studied with his father, Ustad Allauddin Khan; Ravi Shankar was a fellow pupil. Served the court of the Maharaja of Jodhpur. In 1955, made his U.S. debut and released the first Western recording of Indian art music. Established the Ali Akbar School of Music at Calcutta (1956) and a school at San Rafael, California. Has composed ragas, talas, and music for ballet, theater, and film.

Khovanshchina [Russ., The Khovansky Affair]. Opera in five acts by Mussorgsky (libretto by the composer), completed and orchestrated by Rimsky-Korsakov and produced in St. Petersburg in 1886. Setting: Moscow and environs, 1682–89.

Khrennikov, Tikhon Nikolaevich (b. Elets, Russia, 10 June 1913). Composer and pianist. Pupil of Shebalin. In 1948, joined Soviet condemnation of Shostakovich, Prokofiev, and other leading composers; leader of the Union of Composers for more than 40 years. Composed in a tuneful, highly accessible idiom. Works include operas and comic operas (*Into the Storm,* 1939; *Mother,* 1952–57; *Dorothea,* 1983; *The Golden Calf,* 1984; *The Naked King,* 1988); operettas; ballets; 3 symphonies; concertos, suites, and other orchestral music; choral music and songs; incidental and film music.

Kilar, Wojciech (b. Lwów, 17 July 1932). Composer. Pupil of Woytowicz and Boulanger. Best known in Poland for film scores; some compositions (e.g. *Diphthongos,* chorus, percussion, 2 pianos, strings, 1964) make use of unusual vocal techniques. Works include ballet; symphonies, 2 piano concertos, and other orchestral music; vocal works (*Angelus,* soprano, chorus, orchestra, 1984); instrumental pieces (*Orawa,* 15 string instruments, 1986).

Kilpinen, Yrjö (Henrik) (b. Helsinki, 4 Feb. 1892; d. there, 2 May 1959). Composer. Pupil of Hofmann, Heuberger, and Juon. Composed over 700 songs to German, Finnish, and Swedish words, characterized by simple melodies and ostinato accompaniments. Song cycles include *Reflexer* [Reflections] (1922); *Hochgebirgswinter* (1954).

Kim, Earl [Eul] (b. Dinuba, Calif., 6 Jan. 1920; d. Cambridge, Mass., 19 Nov. 1998). Composer. Pupil of Schoenberg, Bloch, and Sessions. Taught at Princeton (1952–67) and then at Harvard. Works include *Footfalls* (orchestra, 1983); a violin concerto; piano and chamber music; several large works for instruments, singers, actors, dancers, films, television, and lighting; *3 Poems in French* (soprano, string quartet, 1989) and other vocal music.

Kimball, Jacob (b. Topsfield, Mass., 15 Feb. 1761; d. there, 24 July 1826). Composer and tunebook editor. Taught at singing schools and compiled tunebooks containing many of his own compositions, including *The Village Harmony* (1798).

Kincaid, William (b. Minneapolis, 26 Apr. 1895; d. Philadelphia, 27 Mar. 1967). Flutist. Studied in New York. Played in the New York Symphony and Chamber Music Society. First chair in the Philadelphia Orchestra, 1921–60; taught at the Curtis Institute.

Kindermann, Johann Erasmus (b. Nuremberg, 29 Mar. 1618; d. there, 14 Apr. 1655). Composer. Pupil of Staden; church organist in Nuremberg from 1636. Composed organ works, cantatas, concertato pieces, arias, sonatas, and suites. Progressive traits include idiomatic instrumental writing, contrasting solo and choral movements, use of recitative.

Kinderszenen [Ger., Scenes from Childhood]. A collection of 13 short and simple pieces for piano by Schumann, op. 15 (1838), of which no. 7 is the familiar "Träumerei" (Dreams).

Kindertotenlieder [Ger., Songs on the Death of Children]. A cycle of five songs with orchestra or piano accompaniment by Mahler, composed in 1901–4. The poems, by Friedrich Rückert, are an elegy on the death of two of his children.

King David. See *Roi David, Le.*

King, B. B. [Riley B.] (b. Itta Bena, Miss., 16 Sept. 1925). Blues singer, guitarist, and bandleader. Moved to Memphis 1947; from 1953 led urban blues groups. Influenced rock guitarists (especially Eric Clapton). His full-bodied, tuneful singing and playing and command of blues effects are evident on his album *Live at the Cook County Jail* (1970).

King, E(lisha) J. (b. Wilkinson County, Ga., ca. 1821; d. near Talbotton, Ga., 31 Aug. 1844). Composer. Joint compiler (with B. F. White) of *The Sacred Harp* (1844), the most widely used collection of sacred songs in shape-note notation, of which he contributed the largest number

King, Karl L(awrence) (b. Paintersville, Ohio, 21 Feb. 1891; d. Fort Dodge, Iowa, 31 Mar. 1971). Bandmaster and composer of band music. Composed *Barnum & Bailey's Favorite* (1913), marches for universities, and many other band works. Led the Fort Dodge Military Band 1920–58. A founder and president of the American Bandmasters Association; inspired the musical *The Music Man.*

Kinnor [Heb.]. A *lyre of ancient Israel, similar to the Greek *kithara. The "harp" of King David was really a *kinnor.*

Kipnis, Igor (b. Berlin, 27 Sept. 1930). Harpsichordist. From 1959 toured internationally, playing fortepiano, clavichord, and harpsichord; taught at Fairfield Univ., Conn. (1971–77), and the Royal Northern College of Music, Manchester (from 1982); also active as an editor and writer on music.

Kirbye, George (d. Bury St. Edmunds, buried 6 Oct. 1634). Composer. Musician in various great houses. Composed madrigals (including a volume published 1597 and one piece in *The *Triumphes of Oriana*) and sacred vocal works, especially Psalm settings.

Kirche [Ger.]. Church; *Kirchengesang,* liturgical chant; *Kirchenjahr,* church or liturgical year; *Kirchenkantate,* church cantata; *Kirchenlied,* a *chorale or other church song in German rather than Latin; *Kirchenmusik,* church music; *Kirchenschluss,* plagal *cadence; *Kirchensonate,* *sonata da chiesa;* *Kirchenton,* church *mode.

Kirchgässner [Kirchgessner], **Marianne (Antonia)** (b. Bruchsal, 5 June 1769; d. Schaffhausen, 9 Dec. 1808). Glass harmonica player. Blind from age 4. From 1791, gave concert tours; Mozart composed for her the Quintet in C major K. 617 for glass harmonica, flute, oboe, viola, and cello.

Kirchner, Leon (b. Brooklyn, 24 Jan. 1919). Composer, pianist, and conductor. Pupil of Toch, Schoenberg, Bloch, and Sessions. Taught at Berkeley, Univ. of Southern California (1950–54), Mills College, and Harvard (from 1961). Active as a pianist and conductor of classical works and his own compositions. Influenced by the Second Viennese School. Works include an opera (*Lily,* 1973–76, after Saul Bellow); 2 piano concertos, *Music for Cello and Orchestra* (1992), and other orchestral music; String Quartet no. 3 (with tape, 1966, Pulitzer Prize) and other chamber and piano music; choral music; *The Twilight Stood* (song cycle, after Dickinson, 1983).

Kirkby, (Carolyn) Emma (b. Camberley, 26 Feb. 1949). Soprano. London debut, 1974. Toured the U.S., 1978. Specializes in Renaissance and Baroque music: solo songs (often accompanied on lute by Anthony Rooley), madrigals; operas, cantatas, and other concerted genres (with the Academy of Ancient Music and other groups).

Kirkpatrick, John (b. New York, 18 March 1905; d. Ithaca, N.Y., 8 Nov. 1991). Pianist and scholar. Studied at Princeton and with N. Boulanger. Premiered Ives's *Concord Sonata* 1939; later catalogued his manuscripts and edited his *Memos.* Taught at Mount Holyoke College (1943–46), and Cornell Univ. (1949–68). From 1968, curator of the Ives Collection at Yale Univ. Recordings include music of Ives and MacDowell.

Kirkpatrick, Ralph (Leonard) (b. Leominster, Mass., 10 June 1911; d. Guilford, Conn., 13 April 1984). Harpsichordist and scholar. Pupil of Landowska, Dolmetsch, and Tiessen. From 1940 taught at Yale Univ.; catalogued the works of Domenico Scarlatti. Promoted contemporary literature for harpsichord; introduced new works such as Carter's Double Concerto. Recorded the complete keyboard works of Bach.

Kirkpatrick, William J(ames) (b. Duncannon, Pa., 27 Feb. 1838; d. Germantown, Pa., 20 Sept. 1921). Hymn book compiler. From 1865, music director of Methodist churches. From 1880, published numerous gospel song collections, about 50 in collaboration with John R. Sweeney.

Kirnberger, Johann Philipp (bapt. Saalfeld, 24 Apr. 1721; d. Berlin, 26 or 27 July 1783). Theorist and composer. Pupil of J. S. Bach and champion of his teaching methods. Violinist at the royal chapel, Ber-

lin; from 1758 served Princess Anna Amalie. Theoretical writings include the 4-volume *Die Kunst des reinen Satzes in der Musik* (1771–79). Composed lieder, motets, cantatas, sonatas, and keyboard works.

Kit [Fr. *pochette;* Ger. *Tanzmeistergeige, Taschengeige;* It. *sordino*]. A small bowed stringed instrument without frets used primarily from the 16th to the 18th century by dance masters to accompany their students. The instrument's small size made it conveniently portable in a coat pocket; hence the names *pochette* and *Taschengeige.* Kits, with their origin in the medieval *rebec, appear in many varied shapes, usually with four strings tuned like the violin or in higher fifth relationships.

Kithara [Gr.; Lat. *cithara, cythara*]. A *lyre of ancient Greece and Rome, the most important stringed instrument of classical antiquity. It had a flat wooden sound box from which two arms rose. The arms, often hollow, were connected by a crosspiece to which were attached gut strings of equal length: 3 to 5 strings in early instruments, 11 or more by the 5th century B.C.E. The player held the instrument vertically, resting it against the left side of the body. The right hand plucked the strings from the front with a plectrum; the left hand remained behind the instrument, plucking or stopping the strings. The instrument is mentioned in the *Iliad* under the name phorminx. The classic seven-stringed kithara is depicted in Greek art from the 6th century B.C.E. It was exported to Rome, where it was popular both as an accompaniment to song and as a solo instrument. In the Middle Ages, the name *cithara* was applied to a variety of stringed instruments: lyre, harp, psaltery, and even the fiddle. See also Lyra.

Kitt, Eartha (b. North, S.C., 26 Jan. 1928). Popular singer, actress, dancer. From 1950 sang a multilingual repertoire in cabarets and nightclubs in Paris and New York. Appeared in films (*Time Runs,* 1950), musicals (*New Faces of 1952*), and on television, and made many recordings.

Kittel, Johann Christian (b. Erfurt, 18 Feb. 1732; d. there, 17 Apr. 1809). Organist and composer. Pupil of J. Adlung and J. S. Bach. Organist at Erfurt from 1756. Compiled a treatise on keyboard instruction (*Der angehende praktische Organist,* 1801–8) and chorale books. Composed chorale preludes and other keyboard works.

Kittl, Jan Bedřich [Johann Friedrich] (b. Orlík nad Vltavou, 8 May 1806; d. Lissa, Prussia [now Leszno, Poland], 20 July 1868). Composer. Pupil of Tomášek. Director, Prague Conservatory, 1843–65. Works include operas (*Bianca und Giuseppe,* Prague, 1848; libretto by Wagner); 4 symphonies (no. 2,

The Hunt, 1837), 3 concert overtures, choral and chamber music; songs; piano pieces.

Kiyōse, Yasuji (b. Yokkaichi, Ōita prefecture, Japan, 13 Jan. 1900; d. Tokyo, 14 Sept. 1981). Composer. Pupil of Yamada. Worked with Japanese folk material. Takemitsu was his pupil. Works include choral (*Itaziki-yama no yoru* [A Night at Mount Itaziki], 1957); chamber music (3 violin sonatas; Shakuhachi Trio, 1964); songs (*Mannyō kak-yoku-shū* [Songs from Mannyō], 1942); orchestral works.

Kjerulf, Halfdan (b. Christiania [now Oslo], 15 or 17 Sept. 1815; d. Grefsen, near Christiania, 11 Aug. 1868). Composer. Studied with Gade and at Leipzig. Worked with Norwegian folk song; composed many songs, male part songs, and piano pieces.

Kl. [Ger.]. Abbr. for *Klarinette,* clarinet. See also Kl. Fl., Kl. Tr.

Klagelied [Ger.]. Lament, elegy.

Klagend, kläglich [Ger.]. Plaintive.

Klagende Lied, Das [Ger., The Plaintive Song]. A cantata by Mahler (setting his own text) for soprano, alto, and tenor soloists, chorus, and orchestra, composed in 1880. Originally in three parts—*Waldmärchen* (Forest Tales), *Der Spielmann* (The Minstrel), and *Hochzeitsstück* (Wedding Piece)—it was revised in 1892–93 and 1898–99 omitting *Waldmärchen.*

Klami, Uuno (Kalervo) (b. Virolahti, Finland, 20 Sept. 1900; d. there, 29 May 1961). Composer. Pupil of Ravel. Utilized Finnish folk tunes in orchestral works such as the *Karelian Rhapsody, Fantaisie tschérémisse* (cello and orchestra, 1931), and *Kalevala Suite,* (1933; rev. 1943). Also composed symphonies, concertos, a ballet, vocal music.

Klang [Ger.]. Sound, sonority.

Klangfarbenmelodie [Ger., tone-color melody]. A succession of tone colors (even if with only a single pitch) treated as a structure analogous to a melody, which is a succession of pitches. The notion was proposed and the term coined by Arnold Schoenberg in his *Harmonielehre* of 1911. Anton Webern explored the concept extensively, e.g., in the first of his *Five Pieces for Orchestra* op. 10 (1913), and it has played an important role in the development of *serial music and in some *electro-acoustic music. The texture that results has sometimes been termed pointillism, by analogy with painting.

Klanglich [Ger.]. Sonorous.

Klappe [Ger.]. *Key (3); *Klappenhorn, -trompete,* keyed bugle, keyed trumpet.

Klar [Ger.]. Clear, distinct.

Klarinette [Ger.]. Clarinet.

Klavier [Ger.]. (1) Piano; *Klavierauszug,* piano reduction or arrangement, piano-vocal score; *Klavierkonzert,* piano concerto; *Klavierstück,* piano piece. (2) Keyboard, manual. (3) Keyboard instrument, especially though not necessarily stringed as distinct from the organ. Eighteenth-century titles such as *Clavier-Übung* and *Das *wohltemperirte Clavier* do not specify a particular keyboard instrument. (4) In the later 18th century (spelled *Clavier*), often though not always clavichord. See also Clavier.

Klavierlied [Ger.]. A song with keyboard accompaniment [see Lied, Berlin school]. The *Geistliches Klavierlied* was a nonliturgical lied on a sacred or devotional strophic text. *Geistliche Klavierlieder* were characteristic products of the north-German *Empfindsamkeit* [see *Empfindsam* style].

Klebe, Giselher (Wolfgang) (b. Mannheim, 28 June 1925). Composer. Pupil of Blacher. From 1957 taught at the Northwest German Music Academy, Detmold. Has worked with twelve-tone techniques. Works include 12 operas (*Die Räuber,* 1957; *Die Fastnachtsbeichte,* 1983) and other stage music; orchestral music (5 symphonies; *Herschläge: Furcht, Bitte, und Hoffnung,* rock group and orchestra, 1969); chamber and keyboard music; Masses and other choral works; vocal music.

Kleber, Leonhard (b. Göppingen, ca. 1495; d. Pforzheim, 4 Mar. 1556). Organist. Organist in Pforzheim from 1521. Compiled a large organ tablature consisting chiefly of arrangements of vocal works by Josquin, Isaac, Obrecht, and others.

Kleiber, Erich (b. Vienna, 5 Aug. 1890; d. Zurich, 27 Jan. 1956). Conductor and composer. Studied in Prague. Debut, 1911. General music director, Berlin Staatsoper, 1923–34 (produced Berg's *Wozzeck,* 1925); chief conductor, Deutsche Staatsoper, East Berlin, 1951–55; resigned both posts to protest government interference. Led the German Opera, Teatro Colón, Buenos Aires, 1937–49; the Havana Philharmonic, 1944–47. Composed orchestral works, chamber music, and songs.

Klein [Ger. masc. sing.; other endings depending on case and gender]. (1) Small. (2) With respect to intervals such as the third or sixth, minor.

Kleine Flöte [Ger.]. Piccolo.

Kleine Nachtmusik, Eine [Ger., A Little Night Music]. Mozart's title for his Notturno or Serenade in G major for string ensemble K. 525 (1787). It was originally in five movements, of which the second, a minuet, is now lost. Although it is often performed with orchestra, it was evidently intended for performance with one player on each part. See Divertimento, Notturno, Serenade.

Kleine Trommel [Ger.]. Side drum.

Kleinsinger, George (b. San Bernardino, Calif., 13 Feb. 1914; d. New York, 28 July 1982). Composer. Pupil of Bauer, Haubiel, James, Jacobi, and Wagenaar. Works include *I Hear America Singing* (Whitman, cantata, 1940); *Tubby the Tuba* (P. Tripp, narrator and orchestra, 1942) and other dramatic works; a symphony; concertos (for harmonica, 1947); chamber music.

Klemperer, Otto (b. Breslau, 14 May 1885; d. Zurich, 6 July 1973). Conductor and composer. Pupil of I. Knorr, Pfitzner, and Schoenberg. Associate of Mahler. Debut, Prague, 1907. Music director at Cologne, Wiesbaden, and the Kroll Opera, Berlin (1927–31); introduced Stravinsky's *Oedipus Rex,* Schoenberg's *Erwartung,* and other works. Conducted the Berlin Staatsoper, 1931–33. Emigrated to the U.S. 1933; led the Los Angeles Philharmonic until 1939. Musical director, Budapest Opera, 1947–50. From 1954 conducted and recorded with Legge's Philharmonia Orchestra.

Klenau, Paul (August) von (b. Copenhagen, 11 Feb. 1883; d. there, 31 Aug. 1946). Composer and conductor. Studied in Copenhagen and with Bruch, Thuille, and Schoenberg. Held posts at the Freiburg Opera and the Hofoper, Stuttgart. Conducted the Danish Philharmonic (1920–26) and the Vienna Konzerthausgesellschaft (1922–30). Works include operas (*Sulamith,* 1913; *Elisabeth von England,* 1939); ballets; orchestral and vocal music; piano pieces.

Klengel, August (Stephan) Alexander (b. Dresden, 29 Jan. or June 1783; d. there, 22 Nov. 1852). Composer. Studied and traveled with Clementi; settled in St. Petersburg, 1805–11; then toured Europe as a pianist. From 1817, organist at the Dresden court chapel. Composed much piano music, including salon music, 2 concertos, chamber pieces, and 48 canons and fugues (Leipzig, 1854).

Klengel, Julius (b. Leipzig, 24 or 29 Sept. 1859; d. there, 26 or 27 Oct. 1933). Cellist. Brother of conductor Paul Klengel (1854–1935); principal cellist, Leipzig Gewandhaus Orchestra, 1881–1924; toured Europe as soloist and with the Gewandhaus Quartet; 1881–1933, taught at the Leipzig Conservatory (pupils included Feuermann, Piatigorsky); also composed and edited, especially for cello.

Kl. Fl. [Ger.]. Abbr. for *kleine Flöte,* piccolo.

Klingen [Ger.]. To sound; *klingen lassen,* allow to sound, do not damp; *klingt wie notiert,* pitch sounds as notated.

Klose, Friedrich (b. Karlsruhe, 29 Nov. 1862; d. Ruvigliana, Lugano, 24 Dec. 1942). Composer. Pupil of V. Lachner and Bruckner. Taught in Switzerland (citizen, 1886); at the Munich Academy of Music, 1907–19. Composed a Mass in D minor (1889), symphonic poems, the opera *Ilsebill* (1903), an oratorio, chamber music, songs.

Klosé, Hyacinthe Eléonore (b. Corfu, 11 Oct. 1808; d. Paris, 29 Aug. 1880). Clarinetist. Military bandmaster; studied at the Paris Conservatory; taught there 1839–68; collaborated with the instrument maker L. A. Buffet on a Boehm-style key-ring clarinet (patented 1844); wrote a *Méthode complète* (1844), etudes, and exercises for clarinet, saxophone method and exercises.

Kl. Tr. [Ger.]. Abbr. for *kleine Trommel,* side drum.

Knab, Armin (b. Neuschleichach, Lower Franconia, 19 Feb. 1881; d. Bad Wörishafen, 23 June 1951). Composer and writer on music. Taught at the Berlin Academy of Music Education and Church Music, 1934–43. Composed an oratorio; music for theater and radio; orchestral works; chamber and piano music; cantatas and other vocal music; folk song arrangements. His writings, most concerned with the German youth movement, are collected in *Denken und Tun* (1959).

Knaben Wunderhorn, Des [Ger., The Youth's Magic Horn]. A group of German folk-song texts collected and published in three volumes (ca. 1805–8) by Ludwig Achim von Arnim and Clemens Brentano. Mahler composed settings of a number of these texts: nine songs with piano (1887–90), ten songs with piano or orchestra (1892–98), and two songs with piano or orchestra from the so-called "Seven Songs from the Last Years" (1899–1902). An additional three songs were set as parts of his symphonies: "Urlicht" (Primeval Light) in the Second or **Resurrection* Symphony (1888–94, rev. 1903), "Es sungen drei Engel" (Three Angels Were Singing) in the Third Symphony (1893–96, rev. 1906), and "Das himmlische Leben" (The Heavenly Life) in the Fourth Symphony (1892, 1899–1900, rev. 1901–10).

Knappertsbusch, Hans (b. Elberfeld, 12 Mar. 1888; d. Munich, 25 Oct. 1965). Conductor. Pupil of O. Lohse. Conductor at the Elberfeld Opera, at Leipzig, and at Dessau. Succeeded Walter as general music director at Munich (1922–36). Conducted the Philharmonic and the opera in Vienna (1937–45); at the Bayreuth Festivals from 1951. Championed Bruckner symphonies, but used Schalk's recompositions.

Knarre [Ger.]. **Rattle.

Kneisel, Franz (b. Bucharest, 26 Jan. 1865; d. New York, 26 Mar. 1926). Violinist. Pupil of Hellmesberger. Concertmaster, Boston Symphony, 1885–1903. In 1886, founded a quartet whose commitment to American composers contributed to the flowering of native chamber music in the U.S. From 1905 taught at the Institute of Musical Art, New York.

Kniegeige [Ger., obs.]. Viola da gamba.

Knight, Gladys (M.) (b. Atlanta, 28 May 1944). Soul singer. After singing gospel music with church choirs, formed the vocal group The Pips with family members (1952). Recordings include "Every Beat of My Heart," 1961; "I Heard It through the Grapevine," 1967; *Imagination,* 1973; *About Love,* 1980; *Life,* 1985).

Knipper, Lev Konstantinovich (b. Tbilisi, 3 Dec. 1898; d. Moscow, 30 July 1974). Composer. Pupil of Glier, Jarnach, and J. Weismann. Worked with folk materials. Composed operas (*Severniy veter* [The North Wind], 1929–30); ballets; 14 symphonies and other orchestral music; chamber and vocal music.

Knorr, Ernst-Lothar von (b. Eitorf, 2 Jan. 1896; d. Heidelberg, 30 Oct. 1973). Composer. Studied at Cologne. After World War I taught at Heidelberg and Mannheim; a founder of the Heidelberg Chamber Orchestra. Principal of music academies in Berlin, Frankfurt, Trossingen, Hannover, and Heidelberg. Works include a concerto for piano, chorus, and orchestra; string quartets and other chamber music; piano, organ, and harpsichord works; cantatas; choral music; songs.

Knorr, Iwan (Otto Armand) (b. Mewe, West Prussia, 3 Jan. 1853; d. Frankfurt am Main, 22 Jan. 1916). Composer and teacher. Studied at Leipzig. Taught in Kharkov 1874–83; from 1883, at the Hoch Conservatory, Frankfurt (director from 1908). Pupils include Pfitzner, Toch. Composed 3 operas; orchestral, chamber, choral, piano pieces; songs. Wrote books on Tchaikovsky, harmony, fugue.

Knorr, Julius (b. Leipzig, 22 Sept. 1807; d. there, 17 June 1861). Piano teacher. Friend of Schumann; an editor of the *Neue Zeitschrift für Musik* (1834); wrote collections of progressive exercises for piano and other didactic works.

Knussen, (Stuart) Oliver (b. Glasgow, 12 June 1952). Composer and conductor. Pupil of Gunther Schuller. From 1983 artistic director of the Aldeburgh Festival; from 1986 coordinator of contemporary music at Tanglewood. Early 1990s, composer-in-residence to the Chamber Music Society of Lincoln Center. Works include symphonies and other orchestral compositions; chamber works; Cantata, oboe, string trio (1977); with Maurice Sendak, 2 one-act operas, *Where the Wild Things Are* (1979–83) and *Higglety Pigglety Pop!* (1984–90).

Knyaz' Igor' [Russ.]. See *Prince Igor.*

Koch, (Sigurd Christian) Erland von (b. Stockholm, 26 Apr. 1910). Composer. Studied in Stockholm, Germany, and France. Taught at the Stockholm Musikhögskolan from 1953. Combines folk melodies with twelve-tone techniques. Works include operas; orchestral music (4 symphonies; *Impulsi-trilogen,* 1964–66; *Midvinterblot-Sommarsolstånd,* 1987); choral works; chamber music (6 string quartets); songs.

Koch, Heinrich Christoph (b. Rudolstadt, 10 Oct. 1749; d. there, 19 Mar. 1816). Theorist, composer, and violinist. Court musician at Rudolstadt from 1772. Influential writings include *Versuch einer Anleitung zur Composition* (1782–93), which deals with classical-period harmony, counterpoint, and forms, and *Musikalisches Lexikon* (1802), which defines terms such as *sonata, rondo,* etc., as they were viewed in the late 18th century.

Köchel-Verzeichnis [Ger.]. See K.

Koczwara, František (b. Prague? ca. 1750; d. London, 2 Sept. 1791). Composer. Active in London from about 1775; during the 1780s, in Ireland. Composed chiefly chamber music, including trio sonatas, string quartets, and solo keyboard music (including *The Battle of Prague,* 1788).

Kodály method. A system of music education for children developed by the Hungarian composer Zoltan Kodály (1882–1967). The method aims to achieve universal musical literacy by teaching children to sing from notes using a "movable do" *solfège system and a progressive repertory of songs and exercises based on Hungarian folk material.

Kodály, Zoltán (b. Kecskemét, Hungary, 16 Dec. 1882; d. Budapest, 6 Mar. 1967). Composer and ethnomusicologist. Pupil of Koessler. Associate of Bartók, with whom he compiled and edited *Magyar népdalok* (Hungarian Folk Songs), 1906. Taught at the Budapest Academy of Music from 1907; from 1930 lectured on folk music at the Univ. of Budapest. After 1946 toured internationally, conducting his own works. Composed stage works (*Háry János,* 1926; *Székely fonó* [The Transylvanian Spinning-Room], 1932); orchestral music (*Háry János,* suite, 1927; *Dances of Marosszék,* 1930; *Dances of Galánta,* 1933); sacred and secular choral works (*Psalmus hungaricus,* 1923); solo vocal music; chamber music; piano works; didactic pieces. Also a noted music educator.

Koechlin, Charles (Louis Eugène) (b. Paris, 27 Nov. 1867; d. Le Canadel, Var, 31 Dec. 1950). Composer and writer on music. Pupil of Massenet, Fauré, and Gédalge. In 1909, cofounded the Société musicale indépendante in opposition to d'Indy's conservative organizations. Among his students were Poulenc, Tailleferre, and Milhaud. Published books on theory, Fauré, Debussy, and orchestration. Composed ballets and other stage music; some 16 symphonic poems (the *Jungle Book Suite*, 1926–40, after Kipling) and other orchestral and band music; string quartets and other chamber music; many piano and organ works; film scores; choral music; songs; orchestrations.

Koellreutter, Hans Joachim (b. Freiburg im Breisgau, 2 Sept. 1915). Composer. Pupil of Hindemith. Taught at the Brazilian Conservatory, Rio de Janeiro (1937–52) and other music schools in Brazil. Lived briefly in New Delhi and Tokyo. Has used twelve-tone and aleatory techniques and indigenous instruments of Brazil, India, and Japan. Works include orchestral music (*Música*, 1947; *Mutações*, 1953; *Advaita*, sitar and orchestra, 1968); vocal and chamber music.

Koenig, Gottfried Michael (b. Magdeburg, 5 Oct. 1926). Composer. Studied in Detmold and Cologne. Worked at the Electronic Music Studio of the West German Radio, Cologne, 1954–64. Taught there at the Musikhochschule and the New Music courses, and at the Darmstadt summer courses. From 1964, director of the Instituut voor Sonologie, Utrecht Univ., where he has explored interactive computer music. Has written works for traditional instruments (*Orchesterstück 1–3*, 1960–63; *Beitrag*, orchestra, 1986) and tape music (*Funktion Grün*, 1967).

Kogan, Leonid (Borisovich) (b. Dnepropetrovsk, 14 Nov. 1924; d. Mytishcha, 17 Dec. 1982). Violinist. Studied with his father and at the Moscow Conservatory. Taught there from 1952. Formed a trio with Emil Gilels and Rostropovitch. U.S. debut, 1958.

Köhler, (Christian) Louis (Heinrich) (b. Brunswick, 5 Sept. 1820; d. Königsberg, 16 Feb. 1886). Teacher. Studied in Vienna. From 1845 lived in Königsberg, as conductor, piano teacher, and writer of didactic and critical works. Composed primarily piano pieces; widely used exercises and studies.

Kohn, Karl (George) (b. Vienna, 1 Aug. 1926). Composer, pianist, and conductor. Emigrated to the U.S., 1939. Pupil of Piston, Fine, and R. Thompson. Teacher at Pomona College and Claremont Graduate School from 1950. As a pianist, specialized in modern music. Some of his pieces borrow fragments from other works (*Introductions and Parodies*, clarinet, horn, bassoon, string quartet, piano, 1967). Works include *Concerto mutabile* (piano, orchestra, 1962); *Time Irretrievable* (orchestra, 1983); chamber music; keyboard works; vocal works (*Lions on a*

Banner, 7 Sufi texts for soprano, chorus, orchestra, 1988).

Kohoutek, Ctirad (b. Zábřeh, Czechoslovakia, 18 Mar. 1929). Composer. Pupil of Kvapil. Teacher at the Brno Academy of Music, the Janáček Academy (1965–80) and the Academy of Music Arts, Prague (from 1980). Artistic director, Czech Philharmonic, 1980–87. Has worked with folk song and twelve-tone techniques. Works include the opera *O Kohoutkovi a Slepičce* [About the Cock and the Hen] (1989); orchestral music (*Slavnosti světla* [Festivals of Light], 1974–75; *Pocta životu* [Homage to Life], 1989); chamber and keyboard music (*Panychida*, 2 violas, ensemble, tape, 1968); vocal works (*Od jara do zimy* [From Spring to Winter], children's chorus, 1962).

Kohs, Ellis (Bonoff) (b. Chicago, 12 May 1916). Composer. Pupil of Wagenaar and Piston. Taught at the Univ. of Southern California 1950–85. Wrote textbooks on theory and composition. Works include 2 symphonies and other orchestral works; an opera (*Amerika*, after Kafka, 1966–69); incidental music; 2 string quartets, a sonata for snare drum and piano (1966), and other chamber music; pieces for piano, organ, and harpsichord; *Psalm 23* (4 solo voices and chorus, 1957) and other choral music; songs with piano or orchestra.

Kol Nidre [Heb., All the vows]. (1) A prayer from the Jewish service on the eve of Yom Kippur (Day of Atonement). It was set, with some modifications, by Schoenberg for speaker, chorus, and orchestra in 1938. (2) *Kol Nidrei*. An adagio on Hebrew melodies for cello and orchestra by Max Bruch, op. 47 (1881).

Kolb, Barbara (b. Hartford, 10 Feb. 1939). Composer and clarinetist. Pupil of Foss and Schuller. Has taught at Brooklyn College (1973–75), Temple Univ. Has employed serial and chance procedures, quotation, and electronic sounds. Works include a film score (*Cantico*, 1982); a ballet *(New York Moonglow, 1995);* orchestral (*Yet That Things Go Round*, 1987; *All in Good Time*, 1993) and other instrumental works (*Millefoglie*, ensemble and computer-generated sound, 1984–85; *Extremes*, flute, cello, 1989); vocal music (*Chansons bas*, song cycle, Mallarmé, soprano, harp, and percussion, 1966).

Kolisch, Rudolf (b. Klamm, 20 July 1896; d. Watertown, Mass., 1 Aug. 1978). Violinist. Pupil of Otakar Ševčík and Schoenberg. 1922, founded a quartet to promote new music. Emigrated to the U.S., 1935; joined the Pro Arte Quartet, 1942. Taught at the Univ. of Wisconsin (1944–67), then at New England Conservatory, and at Darmstadt (summers). Unlike most violinists, held the instrument with his right hand and bowed with his left.

Kollmann, Augustus Frederic Christopher (b. Engelbostel, Hanover, 21 Mar. 1756; d. London, 19 Apr. 1829). Composer and theorist. Emigrated to England, 1782; organist at the Royal German Chapel in London. Composed a piano concerto, chamber and solo instrumental music, and songs. Published theoretical treatises, including *An Essay on Musical Harmony* (1796) and *An Essay on Practical Musical Composition* (1799). His harmonic theories expand on those of J. P. Kirnberger, using the music of J. S. Bach as a basis.

Kolęda, kolenda [Pol., pl. *kolędy*], **colindă** [Rom., pl. *colinde*]. A Christmas carol. With roots in pagan winter celebrations, songs of this type were known in Poland from the 12th century and survive in quantity with Polish texts from the 16th century, some in polyphonic settings and instrumental intabulations. The repertory expanded considerably in the 17th and 18th centuries.

Kondrashin, Kirill (Petrovich) (b. Moscow, 6 Mar. 1914; d. Amsterdam, 7 Mar. 1981). Conductor. Attended the Moscow Conservatory; taught there 1950–53, 1972–75. Conducted at theaters in Moscow and Leningrad, including the Bolshoi (1943–56). U.S. debut, 1958. Directed the Moscow Philharmonic 1960–75; the Concertgebouw Orchestra, Amsterdam, from 1979.

Konitz, Lee (b. Chicago, 13 Oct. 1927). Jazz alto saxophonist. A member of Miles Davis's nonet (1948–50) and Lennie Tristano's combo, which recorded "Subconscious-Lee" (1949). Lead alto saxophonist in Stan Kenton's big band (1952–53). Led a group with the tenor saxophonist Warne Marsh in Europe (1975–76) and a nonet (from 1975); played in duos, including one with Martial Solal (from 1974).

Kontakte [Ger., Contacts]. A four-track tape composition by Stockhausen composed in 1959–60 and used in the theater piece *Originale* in 1961. A second version of the work is for piano, percussion, and four-track tape.

Kontarsky, Alfons (b. Iserlohn, 9 Oct. 1932). Pianist. With his brother Aloys, won the 1955 Bavarian Radio Competition for piano duo; they subsequently went on a worldwide tour. Taught at the Darmstadt summer courses 1962–69; at Cologne from 1967. Introduced many contemporary works.

Kontarsky, Aloys (b. Iserlohn, 14 May 1931). Pianist. Studied at Cologne and Hamburg. Performed frequently with his brother Alfons; affiliated with the International Festival Series, Darmstadt, from 1960; appeared with cellist Siegfried Palm.

Kontertanz [Ger.]. *Contredanse*.

Kontra- [Ger.]. *Kontrabass*, double bass, or as a prefix in the names of instruments, contrabass or double-bass; *-fagott*, contrabassoon; *-faktur, contrafactum; -Oktave*, contra-octave; *-punkt*, counterpoint; *-subjekt*, countersubject.

Kontski [Kątski], **Antoine de** (b. Kraków, 27 Oct. 1817; d. Ivanichy, Novgorod district, 7 Dec. 1899). Pianist and composer. Pupil of Field. From childhood toured widely with his family; later on his own. Composed salon music (*Le réveil du lion, caprice héroique*, op. 115) as well as larger works. His brothers Charles (1815–67) and Apollinaire (1825–79) were violinists, Stanislas (b. 1820) a pianist.

Konzert [Ger.]. (1) Concert. (2) Concerto.

Konzertmeister [Ger.]. Concertmaster.

Konzertsinfonie [Ger.]. (1) Concert *symphony. (2) Ripieno concerto. See Concerto.

Konzertstück [Ger., concert piece]. See Concertino (2).

Koppel, Herman D(avid) (b. Copenhagen, 1 Oct. 1908; d. there, 14 July 1998). Composer and pianist. Concert debut, 1930. Taught at the Copenhagen Conservatory from 1949. Influences include Nielsen, Bartók, Stravinsky, and jazz. Composed *Tre-Davids-salmer* op. 48, chorus and orchestra; the opera *Macbeth* (1970); 7 symphonies; numerous concertos; chamber music; choral works; songs; film scores.

Korean temple block. See Temple block.

Korn, Peter Jona (b. Berlin, 30 Mar. 1922; d. Munich, 14 Jan. 1998). Composer, conductor, and writer on music. Pupil of Rubbra, Wolpe, Schoenberg, Toch, and Eisler. U.S. citizen, 1944. Founded and conducted the New Orchestra of Los Angeles (1948–56); director of the Strauss Conservatory, Munich, from 1967. Works include an opera (*Heidi*, 1963); symphonies, *Concerto classico* (harpsichord, orchestra, 1988), and other orchestral pieces; the cantata *Der Psalm von Mut* (1985); chamber music (mainly for brass and winds); piano and organ works; choral music and songs.

Kornauth, Egon (b. Olmütz, 14 May 1891; d. Vienna, 28 Oct. 1959). Composer and pianist. Led an orchestra in Sumatra, 1926–27. Taught at the Musikhochschule, Vienna, from 1940; at the Mozarteum, Salzburg, from 1945. Composed orchestral music; chamber music; piano pieces.

Kornett [Ger.]. Cornet.

Korngold, Erich Wolfgang (b. Brno, 29 May 1897; d. Hollywood, 29 Nov. 1957). Composer. Son of music critic Julius Korngold. In 1934, went to Hollywood, where he wrote 19 film scores (*Robin Hood* and *Anthony Adverse* won Oscars). Other works include 5 operas (*Die Tote Stadt,* 1920) and other dramatic works; concertos, a symphony, and other orchestral music; chamber and piano music; song cycles and songs.

Korte, Karl (Richard) (b. Ossining, N.Y., 25 Aug. 1928). Composer. Pupil of Copland, Mennin, Luening, Persichetti, and Petrassi. Has taught at SUNY– Binghamton (1964–70) and the Univ. of Texas at Austin (from 1971). Influenced by serialism, jazz, computer procedures, and neo-tonality. Works include an oratorio; symphonies and other orchestral and band music; *Matrix* (wind quintet, saxophone, percussion, piano, 1968) and other chamber music; *Hill Country Birds* (slides and tape, 1982); choral and vocal music.

Kósa, György (b. Budapest, 24 Apr. 1897; d. there, 16 Aug. 1984). Composer and pianist. Pupil of Bartók, Kodály, and Dohnányi. Taught at the Budapest music academy 1927–60. Influenced by Mahler; composed in an expressionist idiom. Works include operas; orchestral works (incl. 9 symphonies); chamber (incl. 8 string quartets); oratorios; cantatas; piano works; songs.

Köselitz, (Johann) Heinrich [pen name: Peter Gast] (b. Annaberg, Germany, 10 Jan. 1854; d. there, 15 Aug. 1918). Composer. Served as Nietzsche's secretary, literary executor, editor, and archivist. Composed 5 operas, instrumental works, and songs, attempting to embody Nietzschean, anti-Wagnerian principles.

Kostelanetz, André (b. St. Petersburg, 22 Dec. 1901; d. Port-au-Prince, 13 Jan. 1980). Conductor. Emigrated to the U.S., 1922. Hired by CBS Radio, 1930; his broadcasts mixed standard orchestral repertory with popular arrangements. Guest conducted many U.S. orchestras; commissioned works by Copland and others; initiated the New York Philharmonic's Promenade concerts. Made many popular recordings.

Kotík, Petr (b. Prague, 27 Jan. 1942). Composer and flutist. Pupil of Jelinek. At the Center for Creative and Performing Arts, SUNY–Buffalo, 1969–74; presented works of Marcel Duchamp and of Cage. American citizen, 1977. Has composed for live electronics, tape, and conventional instruments (*Solos and Incidental Harmonies,* flute, violin, 2 percussionists, 1983; rev. 1984); many settings of texts of Gertrude Stein (*There Is Singularly Nothing,* 21 instrumental and vocal solos that may be performed simultaneously, 1971–73).

Koto [Jap.]. A Japanese *zither. The term designates several historical zithers with 1 to 17 strings. The prevalent form today has a rectangular body about 80–90 cm. long and 24 cm. wide. Thirteen silk strings are stretched over movable bridges and tuned in a variety of pentatonic tunings. See ill. under Instrument.

Kotoński, Włodzimierz (b. Warsaw, 23 Aug. 1925). Composer. Studied at the Warsaw Conservatory and with Szeligowski. Worked at electronic studios in Cologne and Warsaw. From 1967 taught at the Warsaw Conservatory. Has worked with Polish folk music and serial techniques. Works include orchestral music (*Szkice baletowe* [Ballet Sketches], 1951; *Musique en relief,* 1959; *Terra incognita,* 1984); chamber music (*Birds,* clarinet, cello, piano, 1988); electronic music (*Etiuda na jedno uderzenie w talerz* [Study on a Cymbal Stroke], tape, 1959; *Textures,* computer, 1984); piano pieces.

Kotter, Hans [Johannes] (b. Strasbourg, ca. 1485; d. Bern, 1541). Organist and composer. Pupil of Hofhaimer. Church organist in Fribourg, Switzerland, 1514–30. His compositions and many arrangements by him of vocal pieces by Hofhaimer, Isaac, and others survive in 3 organ tablatures, which he helped to compile for Bonifacius Amerbach of Basel.

Kotzwara, Franz. See Kočžwara, František.

Koukouzeles, Johannes (b. Dyrrachium [Durrës], Albania, ca. 1280; d. Great Laura?, Mount Athos, 1360–75?). Composer. Educated at the imperial court in Constantinople; eventually settled at the monastery at Mount Athos. Composed one didactic piece and many liturgical chants, which are innovative in their presentation of texts and music.

Koussevitzky, Sergey (Alexandrovich) (b. Vyshni-Volochek, Russia, 26 July 1874; d. Boston, 4 June 1951). Conductor. Began a solo career as double bassist, 1896, composing some of his own music; conducting debut with the Berlin Philharmonic, 1908; conducted in Russia until 1920; then led the Concerts Koussevitzky in Paris. Conductor of the Boston Symphony 1924–49, for which he commissioned many new works. Throughout his career championed new music. Formed the Berkshire Music Center at Tanglewood, 1940, where Leonard Bernstein was among the first students.

Koutzen, Boris (b. Uman, near Kiev, 1 Apr. 1901; d. Mount Kisco, N.Y., 10 Dec. 1966). Composer and violinist. Studied in Moscow. Taught at the Philadelphia Conservatory (1925–62) and at Vassar College (1944–66). Composed 2 operas; *Valley Forge* (symphonic poem, 1931) and other orchestral works; 3 string quartets and other chamber music; piano and organ pieces; choral music and songs; arrangements, didactic works, and cadenzas.

Kozeluch [Koželuh], **Johann Antonin** [Jan Evangelista Antonín Tomáš] (b. Velvary [Welwarn, Bohemia], 14 Dec. 1738; d. Prague, 3 Feb. 1814). Composer. Pupil of Hasse, Gassmann, and Gluck. Kapellmeister, St. Vitus' Cathedral, Prague, from 1784. His cousin Leopold Kozeluch was among his pupils. Composed 2 operas (*Il Demofoonte,* 1771); oratorios, nearly 50 Masses, motets, other sacred works; symphonies and concertos. Known as a great contrapuntist.

Kozeluch [Koželuh], **Leopold** [Jan Antonín] (b. Velvary [Bohemia], 26 June 1747; d. Vienna, 7 May 1818). Composer, pianist, and music publisher. Pupil of his cousin Johann Antonin and of Dušek. Settled in Vienna, 1778; began publishing music, 1784. Succeeded Mozart as court composer, 1792. Composed more than 20 piano concertos, chamber music with piano, 50 piano sonatas, pioneering aspects of keyboard style and technique idiomatic to the fortepiano; also symphonies, operas, cantatas, oratorios, sacred works.

Kraft, Anton (b. Rokycany, Bohemia, 30 Dec. 1749; d. Vienna, 28 Aug. 1820). Cellist and composer. Cellist in court orchestras, including Prince Esterházy's chapel orchestra (1778–90). Haydn's D major Cello Concerto was composed for him. Composed cello concertos and chamber works with cello. His son Nikolaus (1778–1853) was also an important cellist in Vienna.

Kraft, Leo (Abraham) (b. Brooklyn, 24 July 1922). Composer. Pupil of R. Thompson and Boulanger. Taught at Queens College, 1947–89; at New York Univ. from 1989. Works include *Pacific Bridges* (clarinet, string orchestra, 1989), and other pieces for orchestra and band; string quartets, *Antiphonies* (piano 4-hands and tape, 1972), and other chamber and piano music; vocal music (*Spring in the Harbor,* soprano, flute, cello, and piano, 1970). Published theory and ear-training textbooks.

Kraft, William (b. Chicago, 6 Sept. 1923). Composer. Pupil of Luening, Ussachevsky, Beeson, Brant, and Cowell. Percussionist with the Los Angeles Philharmonic, 1955–81; composer-in-residence of that orchestra, 1981–85, and director of its new music group. Works include *Interplay* (1984) and other orchestral music; *Encounters II–X* and other chamber music; vocal works; pieces for percussion ensemble; *Kandinsky Variations* (1 or more instruments, slide, 1981); film scores.

Kräftig [Ger.]. Strong, energetic.

Krakowiak [Pol.; Fr. *cracovienne;* Ger. *krakauer Tanz*]. A Polish dance from the region of Kraków in rapid duple meter with syncopations. Pieces of this type survive in instrumental tablatures from the 16th century. The dance enjoyed considerable vogue in the 19th century, partly because of performances by the dancer Fanny Elssler, and was employed in art music by Chopin (*Krakowiak* in F op. 14, a rondo for piano and orchestra) and others.

Kramer, A(rthur) Walter (b. New York, 23 Sept. 1890; d. there, 8 Apr. 1969). Composer, critic, editor, and publisher. Editor-in-chief of *Musical America,* 1929–36; music supervisor for CBS Radio, 1927–28; managing director of Galaxy Music Corporation, 1936–56. Wrote orchestral and chamber works; piano and organ music; vocal music; and transcriptions.

Kramer, Jonathan D. (b. Hartford, 7 Dec. 1942). Composer and theorist. Pupil of Imbrie, Sessions, and Stockhausen. Has taught at Yale (1971–78), the Cincinnati College-Conservatory (1978–90), and Columbia (from 1988); composer-in-residence, Cincinnati Orchestra, from 1988. Has employed serial technique. Compositions include *About Face* (1989) and other orchestral music; instrumental and tape works; mixed-media and conceptual works (*Higher Education,* teacher with office, 1971; *En noir et blanc,* 2 actor-pianists, actor-dancer, 1988).

Kraus (Trujillo), Alfredo (b. Las Palmas, Canary Islands, 24 Sept. 1927). Tenor. Studied in Barcelona and Milan. Debut as the Duke of Mantua *(Rigoletto),* Cairo, 1956. Had special success in bel canto roles such as Donizetti's Edgardo *(Lucia)* and Gennaro *(Lucrezia),* Rossini's Count Almaviva *(Il barbiere).*

Kraus, Joseph Martin (b. Miltenberg am Main, 20 June 1756; d. Stockholm, 15 Dec. 1792). Composer. Court Kapellmeister to King Gustavus III of Sweden from 1787. Traveled widely in Europe. Composed operas (*Aeneas i Carthago,* Stockholm 1799); ballet and incidental music; cantatas (*Begravningskantata,* for Gustavus III, 1792); sacred choral works; symphonies; chamber works; piano music. Authored treatises on music.

Kraus, Lili (b. Budapest, 4 March 1905; d. Burnsville, N.C., 6 Nov. 1986). Pianist. Studied with Bartók, Kodály, Schnabel, and Steuermann. Taught at the Vienna Academy 1925–31. Touring in Java in 1942 she was interned by the Japanese army for three years. She focused particularly on Mozart, performing cycles of his complete concertos and sonatas in the 1960s.

Krauss, Clemens (Heinrich) (b. Vienna, 31 Mar. 1893; d. Mexico City, 16 May 1954). Conductor. Pupil of Heuberger. Conducted at the Vienna Opera (1922–24); at the Frankfurt Opera (1924–29); and at the Berlin Staatsoper (1934–36); music director of the Munich Opera (1937–40). Premiered *Arabella* (1933), *Capriccio* (for which he wrote a libretto after sketches by S. Zweig; 1942), and other works by Strauss.

Krebs, Johann Ludwig (bapt. Butterstedt, Weimar, 12 Oct. 1713; d. Altenburg, 1 Jan. 1780). Composer. Pupil of his father, Johann Tobias Krebs, and of J. S. Bach, whom he served also as a copyist. Church organist, 1737–56; then court organist at Altenburg-Gotha. Composed keyboard works, sinfonias, and church and chamber music.

Krebs, Karl August (b. Nuremberg, 16 Jan. 1804; d. Dresden, 16 May 1880). Conductor. Pupil of Seyfried. City Kapellmeister, Hamburg, 1827–50; 1850–72, succeeded Wagner as court Kapellmeister, Dresden; from 1872, music director of Dresden's Catholic church. Composed operas, church music, songs and part songs (his greatest successes), piano pieces.

Krebsgängig [Ger.]. Crabwise, retrograde.

Krebskanon [Ger.]. Crab or retrograde *canon.

Krein [Krayn, Kreyn], **Aleksandr Abramovich** (b. Nizhni-Novgorod, 20 Oct. 1883; d. Staraya Ruza, near Moscow, 21 Apr. 1951). Composer. Studied at the Moscow Conservatory; taught at the People's Conservatory of Moscow, 1912–17. Worked with Jewish and oriental folk songs (*Hebrew Sketches*, clarinet quintet, 1909–10); influenced by Scriabin and Debussy. Wrote music for many Jewish plays, the opera *Zagmuk* (1930), *Threnody in Memory of Lenin* (chorus, orchestra, 1925), orchestral and chamber music.

Krein [Krayn, Kreyn], **Grigory Abramovich** (b. Nizhni-Novgorod, 18 Mar. 1879; d. Komarovo, near Leningrad, 6 Jan. 1955). Composer. Brother of Aleksandr Krein. Pupil of Glier, Juon, and Reger. Influenced by Scriabin and the French impressionists. Works include a symphonic cycle on Lenin's life (1937), a symphony, a violin concerto, 2 piano sonatas, and a *Hebrew Rhapsody* (clarinet, orchestra, 1926).

Krein, Julian Grigor'yevich (b. Moscow, 5 Mar. 1913). Composer. Pupil of his father Grigory Krein and of Dukas. Taught at the Moscow Conservatory, 1934–37. Works include *Five Preludes*, orchestra (1927); a cello concerto, 1931; piano pieces; songs.

Kreisler, Fritz [Friedrich] (b. Vienna, 2 Feb. 1875; d. New York, 29 Jan. 1962). Violinist and composer. Studied at the Vienna and Paris Conservatories. Lived in the U.S. 1914–24 and from 1939. Composed violin pieces which he at first attributed to Vivaldi, Couperin, and other composers; also a string quartet; *Caprice viennois, Tambourin chinois, Liebesfreud, Schön Rosmarin*, and many other popular violin pieces; cadenzas for the Beethoven and Brahms concertos.

Kreisleriana [Ger.]. Schumann's cycle of eight pieces for piano op. 16 (1838). The title refers to Kapellmeister Johannes Kreisler, the protagonist of E. T. A. Hoffmann's autobiographical work of 1810.

Krejčí, Iša (František) (b. Prague, 10 July 1904; d. there, 6 Mar. 1968). Composer and conductor. Pupil of Jirák, Novák, and Talich. Music director of Radio Prague, 1934–45; artistic director of the Olomouc Opera, 1945–58, and of the Prague National Theater from 1957. Works include operas (*Antigona*, 1933–34; rev. 1963); orchestral music (4 symphonies); chamber music (*Kasace* [Cassation], flute, clarinet, bassoon, trumpet, 1925; 3 string quartets); songs; choral works.

Kremer, Gidon (b. Riga, 27 Feb. 1947). Violinist. Pupil of D. Oistrakh. In 1967, won bronze medal at the Queen Elisabeth of Belgium Competition, Brussels; first prize at the 1970 Tchaikovsky Competition.

Krenek [Křenek], **Ernst** (b. Vienna, 23 Aug. 1900; d. Palm Springs, Calif., 22 Dec. 1991). Composer and writer. Pupil of Schreker. Emigrated to the U.S., 1938; taught at Vassar (1939–42) and Hamline College, Minnesota (from 1942). After early radical and neo-Romantic (1926–31) periods, used serial, computer-generated, and chance procedures; influenced by Adorno. Works include 20 operas (*Jonny spielt auf; Karl V,* 1933; *Pallas Athene weint,* 1955; *Der goldene Bock,* 1963), ballets, and a film score; symphonies; concertos; other orchestral music (*Horizon Circled,* 1967); 8 string quartets, *Fibonacci Mobile* (string quartet and piano 4-hands, 1964), and other chamber music; music for organ, piano, and other solo instruments; choral works (*Opus sine nomine,* oratorio, 1990); solo vocal music; pieces for tape. Also wrote literary works including prose, poetry, musicological studies, and libretti.

Kreutzer, Conradin [Conrad] (b. Messkirch, Baden, 22 Nov. 1780; d. Riga, 14 Dec. 1849). Composer. Pupil of Albrechtsberger. Court Kapellmeister at Stuttgart, 1812–16; at Donaueschingen, 1818–22. Music director of the Vienna court opera 1822–40; of the Josefstadt Theater, 1833–35. Composed more than 30 operas (*Das Nachtlager in Granada*, Vienna 1834), incidental music to Raimund's play *Der Verschwender* (Vienna 1834), an oratorio, church music, chamber and piano pieces, male choruses and songs.

Kreutzer, Rodolphe (b. Versailles, 16 Nov. 1766; d. Geneva, 6 Jan. 1831). Violin virtuoso and composer. Pupil of A. Stamitz. Orchestra violinist from 1785. From 1815, *maître de la chapelle du roi;* chief conductor of the Opéra from 1817. Composed many successful stage works (*Jeanne d'Arc,* 1790; *Lodoïska,* 1791); 19 violin concertos; numerous *sym-*

phonies concertantes; 15 string quartets; string trios; duets; violin sonatas; and *42 études ou caprices* (1796). Dedicatee of Beethoven's op. 47 violin sonata (the Kreutzer).

Kreutzer Sonata. Popular name for Beethoven's Violin Sonata in A minor op. 47 (1802–3), dedicated to the French composer and violin virtuoso Rodolphe Kreutzer (1766–1831). It was originally composed for the English violinist George Bridgetower (1779?–1860), whom Beethoven accompanied at the first performance in 1803, but with whom he subsequently had a dispute, leading to the change in dedication.

Kreuz [Ger.]. Sharp.

Krieger, Adam (b. Driesen, 7 Jan. 1634; d. Dresden, 30 June 1666). Composer. Possibly a pupil of Scheidt. Chamber and court organist at Dresden from 1658. His lieder appear in the collections *Arien von einer, zwey, und drei Vocal-Stimmen* (1657) and *Neue Arien* (1667; assembled after his death); also composed cantatas and other sacred works.

Krieger, Armando (b. Buenos Aires, 7 May 1940). Composer and pianist. Pupil of Ginastera, Copland, Dallapiccola, Messiaen, and Malipiero. Conductor of the Teatro Colón, Buenos Aires. Works include a string symphony (1959); *Aleatoria I–II,* winds (1961); *Metamorphose d'aprés une lecture de Kafka,* piano and 15 instruments (1968); keyboard works; cantatas and solo vocal works.

Krieger, Edino (b. Brusque, Santa Catarina, Brazil, 17 Mar. 1928). Composer. Pupil of Koellreutter, Copland, Mennin, and L. Berkeley. Musical director of the National Symphony, Rio; active as a critic, teacher, and advocate for contemporary music. Has employed serial technique and some nationalist elements. Works include the oratorio *Rio de Janeiro* (1965), orchestral pieces, chamber and piano music, and songs.

Krieger, Johann (b. Nuremberg, 28 Dec. 1651; d. Zittau, 18 July 1735). Composer. Pupil of his brother Johann Philipp; succeeded him as organist at Bayreuth, 1672. Cantor at St. Johannis, Zittau from 1682. Published keyboard collections containing suites, fugues, and other types of pieces; also wrote sacred and secular vocal music.

Krieger, Johann Philipp (b. Nuremberg, 25 Feb. 1649; d. Weissenfels, 6 Feb. 1725). Composer. Pupil of Rosenmüller, Abbatini, and Pasquini. Organist at Bayreuth from 1670; chamber musician and organist at Halle from 1677 (Kapellmeister after the court moved to Weissenfels, 1680). Composed over 2,000 vocal works (especially cantatas), keyboard music, trio sonatas, and operas.

Krips, Josef (b. Vienna, 8 Apr. 1902; d. Geneva, 13 Oct. 1974). Conductor. Pupil of Weingartner. Music director of theaters at Aussig, Dortmund, and Karlsruhe before moving to the Vienna State Opera (1933–38 and after 1945). Principal conductor of the symphonies in London (from 1950), Buffalo (1954–63), San Francisco (1963–70), and Vienna.

Krommer, Franz (Vinzenz) [Kramář, František Vincenc] (b. Kamenice [Kamenitz], 27 Nov. 1759; d. Vienna, 8 Jan. 1831). Composer and violinist. Ballet master for the Hoftheater, Vienna, from 1810; imperial court composer and Kapellmeister from 1818. Composed symphonies, concertos, chamber music; Masses and other sacred works.

Krosnick, Joel (b. New Haven, Conn., 3 Apr. 1941). Cellist. Student of C. Adam. Held several teaching posts before joining the Juilliard Quartet and taking a faculty post at Juilliard (1974). Has also toured as soloist and with the New York Chamber Soloists.

Krumpholtz, Jean-Baptiste [Johann Baptist, Jan Křtitel] (b. Budenice, near Zlonice, 3 or 8 May 1742; d. Paris, 19 Feb. 1790). Harpist and composer. Served at Esterházy's court 1773–76; studied with Haydn. Worked with manufacturers toward improving the construction of the harp. His wife, Anne-Marie (1755–1824), was also a virtuoso harpist. Composed concertos and sonatas for harp and chamber music.

Krumpholtz, Wenzel [Václav] (b. Budenice?, ca. 1750; d. Vienna, 2 May 1817). Violinist. Brother of Jean-Baptiste Krumpholtz. Played in the Esterházy orchestra and from 1796 in the imperial opera orchestra. Close friend of Beethoven, who dedicated his *Gesang der Mönche* (WoO 104) to the violinist's memory.

Krupa, Gene (b. Chicago, 15 Jan. 1909; d. Yonkers, N.Y., 16 Oct. 1973). Jazz drummer and bandleader. Recorded with McKenzie and Condon's Chicagoans (1927) and Red Nichols (1929–31). Joined Benny Goodman, 1934; known for his unrelenting tom-tom drum rhythm on "Sing, Sing, Sing" (first recorded, 1937). Led big bands (1938–51), recording "Let Me Off Uptown" with Anita O'Day and Roy Eldridge (1941) and "Leave Us Leap" (1945). From 1951 toured with Jazz at the Philharmonic, led small groups, and taught.

Kubelík, Jan (b. Michle, Czechoslovakia, 5 July 1880; d. Prague, 5 Dec. 1940). Violinist and composer. Pupil of Ševčík. Debut, 1898. Toured widely; hailed as an equal of Paganini, but his playing declined in later years. Composed a symphony, 6 violin concertos, chamber music, cadenzas.

Kubelík, Rafael (Jeronym) (b. Býchory, Czechoslovakia, 29 June 1914; d. Lucerne, 11 Aug. 1996). Conductor and composer. Son of Jan Kubelík. Conducted the Prague Philharmonic (1936–38 and 1941–48); the Chicago Symphony (1950–53); the Covent Garden Opera (1955–58); the Bavarian Radio Symphony, Munich (1961–79); and the Metropolitan Opera (music director, 1973–74). Composed 5 operas (*Veronika,* 1947); 2 symphonies; *Orphikon* (orchestra, 1981); concertos for violin and cello; Requiems; 6 string quartets; music for piano and violin; songs.

Kubik, Gail (Thompson) (b. South Coffeyville, Okla., 5 Sept. 1914; d. Claremont, Calif., 20 July 1984). Composer. Pupil of B. Rogers, Sowerby, Piston, and Boulanger. Taught at Scripps College, 1970–80. Composed scores for radio, television, and film (*Gerald McBoing-Boing,* 1950); operas and other dramatic works; orchestral music (3 symphonies; *Symphony concertante,* piano, viola, trumpet, and orchestra, Pulitzer Prize, 1952); works for chorus and orchestra; chamber and piano music; choral pieces and songs.

Kuerti, Anton (Emil) (b. Vienna, 21 July 1938). Pianist and composer. Debut with the Boston Pops at age 9. Pupil of Serkin, A. Shepherd, and Cowell. Taught from 1965 at the Univ. of Toronto. Recorded an integral set of Beethoven sonatas. Has composed a symphony, string quartets and other chamber music, piano pieces.

Kuhlau, (Daniel) Friedrich (Rudolph) (b. Uelzen, near Hannover, 11 Sept. 1786; d. Copenhagen, 12 March 1832). Composer and pianist. Court *Kammermusiker* in Copenhagen from 1813; chorusmaster of the Royal Theater from 1816. Composed much piano music (sonatas and other solo pieces; works for piano 4-hands; a concerto); also operas (*Lulu,* 1824); chamber music (a string quartet; 3 piano quartets; works with flute).

Kuhnau [Kuhn], Johann (b. Geising, 6 Apr. 1660; d. Leipzig, 5 June 1722). Composer. Organist at the Thomaskirche, Leipzig, from 1684; Thomaskantor from 1701. Published keyboard collections of suites and sonatas, *Neue Clavier-Übung* (1689, 1692), *Frische Clavier-Früchte* (1696), and *Musicalischer Vorstellung einiger Biblischer Historien* (1700); also wrote cantatas, other church music, dramatic music, treatises, and literary works.

Kujawiak [Pol.]. A Polish dance from the region of Kujawy, in 3/4 and similar to the *mazurka, but slower. Examples in art music include Chopin's op. 6 no. 4, op. 30 no. 4, and op. 41 no. 1.

Kullak, Theodor (b. Krotoszyn, Poland, 12 Sept. 1818; d. Berlin, 1 Mar. 1882). Piano teacher. Pupil of Czerny, Sechter, and Nicolai. Court pianist in Berlin from 1846. In 1855, founded a conservatory. Composed a piano concerto, 2 sonatas, salon and character pieces; exercises (*Die Schule des Oktavenspiels* op. 48, 1848); edited much piano music. His son Franz (1844–1913) was also a noted teacher.

Kullman, Charles [Kullmann] (b. New Haven, Conn., 13 Jan. 1903; d. there, 8 Feb. 1983). Tenor. Debut, 1929, with the touring American Opera Company as Pinkerton (*Madama Butterfly).* At Salzburg from 1934, sang both Italian and German roles; sang at the Metropolitan 1935–60 (debut there as Gounod's Faust). Sang under Bruno Walter on the first recording of Mahler's *Das Lied von der Erde,* 1936.

Kummer, Friedrich August (b. Meiningen, 5 Aug. 1797; d. Dresden, 22 Aug. 1879). Cellist. From a family of wind musicians; from 1814, in the Dresden orchestra first as oboist, then as cellist; also a noted chamber player and a teacher at the conservatory. Composed much cello music and many studies, some still used.

Kunst der Fuge, Die [Ger.]. See *Art of Fugue, The.*

Kunstlied [Ger.]. Art song, as distinct from folk song *(Volkslied).*

Kunzel, Erich (b. New York, 21 March 1935). Conductor. Taught at Brown, 1958–65. Has conducted and recorded extensively with the Cincinnati Symphony and Pops Orchestras. Also conducted the Philharmonia Orchestra (1967–71) and the New Haven Symphony (1974–77). Active with the San Francisco Arts Commission Pops concerts beginning 1981.

Kupferman, Meyer (b. New York, 3 July 1926). Composer and clarinetist. Taught at Sarah Lawrence College from 1951. Works include 9 operas (*The Proscenium,* 1991), 9 ballets, 17 film scores, and other stage music; orchestral works (11 symphonies; concerto for cello, tape, and orchestra, 1974; *Savage Landscape,* 1989); over 170 chamber and instrumental pieces; choral and solo vocal music. *Cycle of Infinities* (begun 1961) includes more than 30 pieces for various ensembles based on a single twelve-tone set and incorporating jazz and chance elements.

Kuri-Aldana, Mario (b. Tampico, Mexico, 15 Aug. 1931). Composer. Pupil of R. Halffter, Ginastera, Malipiero, Messiaen, Dallapiccola, Copland, and Stockhausen. Directed several ensembles in Mexico; from 1972 taught at the Academy of Mexican Dance of the National Institute of Fine Arts. An active folklorist. Works include orchestral, choral, chamber, and solo vocal music in a variety of styles.

Kurka, Robert (Frank) (b. Cicero, Ill., 22 Dec. 1921; d. New York, 12 Dec. 1957). Composer. Pupil of

Luening and Milhaud. Taught at Queens College and Dartmouth. Composed the opera *The Good Soldier Schweik* (New York 1958), which is often compared to the operas of Weill; also symphonies, string quartets, violin sonatas, piano music, songs, and choral music.

Kurtág, György (b. Lugoj, Romania, 19 Feb. 1926). Composer. Pupil of Kadosa (piano), Veress, Farkas, Milhaud, and Messiaen. From 1967 taught at the Budapest Academy of Music. Has employed serial techniques. Works include String Quartet, op. 1 (1959); *Bornemisza Péter mondásai* [The Sayings of Péter Bornemisza] (concerto for soprano and piano, 1963–68); *Quasi una fantasia* (chamber orchestra, 1988); *Samuel Beckett: What is the Word . . .* (voices, ensemble, 1991).

Kurz [Ger.] Short; *Kurz-Oktave,* *short octave.

Kusser [Cousser], **Johann Sigismund** (bapt. Pressburg [now Bratislava], 13 Feb. 1660; d. Dublin, Nov. 1727). Composer. Pupil of Lully. Opera Kapellmeister at Brunswick from 1690; founded an opera company in 1696; Oberkapellmeister in Stuttgart, 1700–1704; held posts at Trinity College, Dublin, from 1711 and with the Crown in Ireland from 1716. Respected for his mastery of the French and Italian styles; surviving works include orchestral suites and arias from his operas *Erindo* and *Ariadne*.

Kuula, Toivo (Timoteus) (b. Vaasa, Finland, 7 July 1883; d. Viipuri, 18 May 1918). Composer and conductor. Pupil of Wegelius and Järnefelt. Conducted in Helsinki (1914–16) and Viipuri (1916–18). Employed Finnish folk tunes. Composed orchestral music (*Eteläpohjalainen sarja* [South Ostrobothnian Suite] no. 1, 1906–9; no. 2, 1912–14); choral-orchestral works; songs; instrumental works.

KV. See K.

Kvapil, Jaroslav (b. Fryták, Czechoslovakia, 21 April 1892; d. Brno, 18 Feb. 1959). Composer. Pupil of Janáček and Reger. Taught at the School of Organists and at the Janáček Academy of Music, Brno (1947–57); conductor and choirmaster of the Brno Beseda (1919–47). Works include an opera; orchestral music (4 symphonies; piano concerto); vocal music (*Lví srdce* [The Lionheart], oratorio, 1931); piano pieces; string quartets.

Kyrie eleison [Gr., Lord, have mercy]. In the Roman Catholic Rite, the first item of the *Ordinary of the *Mass. Its text consists of three petitions, "Kyrie eleison," "Christe eleison," and "Kyrie eleison" (Lord, have mercy; Christ, have mercy; Lord, have mercy), each stated three times. Its *Gregorian melodies often reflect this ninefold structure with forms such as AAA BBB CCC' or AAA BBB AAA', though other forms, some distinctly more complex, are also encountered.

Kyrieleis [Ger.]. See *Leise.*

L

L. Abbr. for left [Ger. *links*]; L.H., left hand [Ger. *linke Hand*].

La. See Pitch names, Solmization, Hexachord.

La Barbara, Joan (Linda) [née Lotz] (b. Philadelphia, 8 June 1947). Composer, vocal performer. Pupil of Helen Boatwright and of Curtin. Founding member of the New Wilderness Preservation Band; performed in ensembles of Glass and Reich in the 1970s. From 1981, teacher at the California Institute of the Arts. Has employed extended vocal techniques. Works include *Loose Tongues* (8 solo voices, tape, 1985); *The Solar Wind: I–III* (voices with various instruments and electronic sounds, 1983–84); *October Music: Star Showers and Extra Terrestrials* (amplified voice and tape, 1980).

L'abbé le fils [Joseph-Barnabé Saint-Sévin] (b. Agen, 11 June 1727; d. Paris, 25 July 1803). Composer. Pupil of Leclair. Violinist at the Paris Opéra, 1742–62; at the Concert spirituel; and at the Théâtre de la République et des arts during the Revolution. Works include several chamber music collections and a number of symphonies. His *Principes du violon* (1761) gives important information on the violin technique of the period.

Lablache, Luigi (b. Naples, 6 Dec. 1794; d. there, 23 Jan. 1858). Bass. Sang at La Scala, 1821–23, and San Carlo, 1823–30; 1830–56, a principal figure in the golden age of Italian opera at the Théâtre italien, Paris, and Covent Garden, London. Best known in comic roles, creating many, including Don Pasquale. Published a singing *Méthode* (1840).

La Borde [Laborde], Jean-Benjamin (-François) de (b. Paris, 5 Sept. 1734; executed there, 22 July 1794). Composer and writer. Pupil of Rameau and Dauvergne. Confidant and *premier valet de chambre* to Louis XV. Composed operas and chansons (some to his own texts); published the 4-volume *Essai sur la musique ancienne et moderne* (1780) and some trouvère songs. Often attacked Rousseau's views.

Labunski [Łabuński], Feliks Roderyk (b. Ksawerynów, Poland, 27 Dec. 1892; d. Cincinnati, 28 Apr. 1979). Composer. Pupil of Dukas and Boulanger. Emigrated to the U.S., 1936. Taught at the Cincinnati College of Music from 1945; active as a pianist and critic. Composed orchestral works; a ballet (*God's Man,* 1937); string quartets, a brass quartet, and other chamber, organ, and piano music; choral works and songs.

Labunski, Wiktor (b. St. Petersburg, 14 Apr. 1895; d. Kansas City, Mo., 26 Jan. 1974). Composer and pianist. Brother of Feliks Labunski. Taught at the Kraków Conservatory 1919–28. Carnegie Hall debut, 1928; taught at several U.S. colleges, including the Kansas City Conservatory (1937–71, director from 1941). Works include a symphony, pieces for piano and orchestra; piano music and songs.

Lacerda, Osvaldo (Costa de) (b. São Paulo, 23 Mar. 1927). Composer. Pupil of Guarnieri, Copland, and Giannini. Taught at the São Paulo Mozarteum Academy from 1966 and municipal music school from 1969. His music draws on Brazilian folk elements; works include the orchestral suite *Piratininga* (1962) and other symphonic music, chamber pieces, choral works, songs, and piano compositions.

Lachner, Franz Paul (b. Rain am Lech, Upper Bavaria, 2 Apr. 1803; d. Munich, 20 Jan. 1890). Conductor and composer. Pupil of Sechter and Stadler; associate of Schubert. From 1823, organist at the Lutheran church in Vienna. Chief conductor, Vienna Opera 1829–34; 1834–36, Kapellmeister, Mannheim; from 1836, conductor, Munich (*Generalmusikdirektor* from 1852). A prolific composer of operas, oratorios, 8 symphonies, 7 orchestral suites; chamber, piano, organ pieces; songs.

Lachner, Ignaz (b. Rain am Lech, Upper Bavaria, 11 Sept. 1807; d. Hannover, 24 Feb. 1895). Conductor and composer. Pupil of Molique and of his brother Franz, whom he succeeded at posts in Vienna and assisted at the Munich Opera (1842–53). From 1853, conductor, Hamburg Municipal Theater; from 1858, court Kapellmeister, Stockholm; 1861–75, chief conductor, Frankfurt. Composed opera, including *Alpenszenen;* church music; orchestral works; chamber and piano pieces; songs.

Lachner, Vinzenz (b. Rain am Lech, Upper Bavaria, 19 July 1811; d. Karlsruhe, 22 Jan. 1893). Conductor and composer. 1834, succeeded his brother Franz as conductor, Vienna Opera, and in 1836–73 as Kapellmeister at Mannheim; taught at the Karlsruhe conservatory from 1884; especially known for his male part songs.

Lacombe, Louis (Trouillon) (b. Bourges, 26 Nov. 1818; d. St-Vaast-la-Hougue, Manche, 30 Sept. 1884). Pianist and composer. Pupil of Czerny, Sechter, and Seyfried. Settled in Paris ca. 1840. Composed operas; dramatic symphonies with voices; sacred, orchestral, chamber works; many songs and piano pieces. Wrote criticism and essays.

Lacombe, Paul (b. Carcassonne, 11 July 1837; d. there, 5 June 1927). Composer. Associate of Bizet. Composed 3 symphonies, concert overtures; sacred and chamber music; many piano pieces and songs.

Lacrimoso, lagrimoso [It.]. Tearful, mournful.

Laderman, Ezra (b. Brooklyn, 29 June 1924). Composer. Pupil of Wolpe, Gideon, Luening, and Douglas Moore. Has taught at SUNY–Binghamton (1971–82); has worked at the National Endowment for the Arts; dean of the Yale School of Music from 1989. Has used twelve-tone and aleatory approaches. Has composed operas (*Marilyn*, 1993) and other dramatic music; 8 symphonies, several concertos, and other works for orchestra (*Citadels*, 1990); 8 string quartets and other chamber music; a few piano and organ works; *A Mass for Cain* (1983) and other choral and vocal works.

Ladmirault, Paul (Émile) (b. Nantes, 8 Dec. 1877; d. Kerbili en Kamoel, St. Nagoire, 30 Oct. 1944). Composer and critic. Pupil of Fauré and Gédalge. Professor and then director of the conservatory in Nantes. Works include ballets, opera, and incidental music; orchestral and band music; chamber and piano music; *Messe brève* (chorus and organ) and other sacred music; some 20 songs, including arrangements of Breton folk songs.

Lady Macbeth of the Mtsensk District [Russ., *Ledi Makbet Mtsenskovo uyezda*]. Opera in four acts by Shostakovich (libretto by the composer and A. Preys, after N. S. Leskov's story), produced in Leningrad in 1934 and in the same year in Moscow with the title *Katerina Izmaylova*. The work, and by implication all modern music, was officially condemned in *Pravda* in 1936. It was slightly revised beginning in 1956 with the title *Katerina Izmaylova* and produced in Moscow again in 1962.

LaFaro, Scott (b. Newark, N.J., 3 Apr. 1936; d. Geneva, N.Y., 6 July 1961). Jazz double bass player. Accompanied Chet Baker, Sonny Rollins, Barney Kessel, and Benny Goodman, but then redefined the role of the jazz bassist while working in Bill Evans's trio (1959–61), moving freely between timekeeping and contrapuntal dialogues with Evans. Also worked with Ornette Coleman and Stan Getz.

Lage [Ger.]. (1) In string playing, *position (erste,* first; *zweite,* second; etc.). (2) Of a chord, *spacing (enge,* close; *weite,* wide or open). (3) Of the voice or an instrument, *register (hohe,* high; *tiefe,* low).

La Guerre, Élisabeth-Claude Jacquet de. See Jacquet de La Guerre, Élisabeth-Claude.

La Guerre, Michel de (b. Paris, 1605–6; buried there, 13 Nov. 1679). Composer. Organist at the Sainte-Chapelle 1633–75; also referred to as *organiste du roi.* His "pastorale en musique" *Le triomphe de l'Amour sur des bergers et bergères* (1654) was likely the first attempt at French opera.

Lai, lay [Fr.]. A type of lyric poetry (the *lai lyrique,* as distinct from the *lai breton,* a narrative form), sometimes with music, cultivated chiefly in late medieval France, although perhaps originating elsewhere. Lyric *lais* are usually quite long; with only rare exceptions, the music of *lais* is monophonic. The German *Leich* is similar in history and formal traits.

In stanzaic *lais,* successive stanzas are in different forms and, consequently, are set to different music. Most *lais* of the 14th century fit into a standard pattern: usually 12 stanzas (double strophes, sometimes called double versicles), each having formally identical halves and in a pattern not used in the preceding stanza, with the first and last stanzas being related or identical in form and music. Throughout its history, the *lai* incorporated notably short lines. The *lai* probably originated around 1200 and was cultivated throughout the 13th century, first by the troubadours, then by the trouvères and their successors. The Provençal term is *descort,* though there has been some controversy about this term.

Laisse [Fr.]. See *Chanson de geste.*

Laisser [Fr.]. To allow; *laissez vibrer,* allow to sound, do not damp.

Lajtha, László (b. Budapest, 30 June 1892; d. there, 16 Feb. 1963). Composer. Taught at the National Conservatory in Budapest (1919–49), and from 1952 at the Budapest Academy. Directed the music department in the Hungarian Broadcasting Service from 1945. Worked with Hungarian folk materials. Works include ballets; film scores; 9 symphonies and other orchestral works; choral works; 10 string quartets and other chamber music; piano works; solo vocal works.

Lakmé. Opera in three acts by Léo Delibes (libretto in French by Edmond Gondinet and Philippe Gille), produced in Paris in 1883. Setting: India in the middle of the 19th century.

Lakner, Yehoshua (b. Bratislava, Czechoslovakia, 24 Apr. 1924). Composer. Pupil of Partos, Boskovich, Copland, Zimmermann, Koenig, Kagel, and Stockhausen. Taught at the Zurich conservatory from 1974. From 1965 he wrote a number of electronic music scores to accompany plays at the Theater an der Winkelwiese, in addition to film and television music.

Lalande, Michel-Richard de (b. Paris, 15 Dec. 1657; d. Versailles, 18 June 1726). Composer. Musician at the royal chapel from 1683; *surintendant de la musique de la chambre* from 1689 (*maître* from 1695). Composed over 70 *grands motets;* instrumental music (*Symphonies de noëls* and *Sinfonies pour les soupers du Roi);* ballets, airs, and sacred works.

Lalo, Édouard (Victoire Antoine) (b. Lille, 27 Jan. 1823; d. Paris, 22 Apr. 1892). Composer. Studied at Lille and Paris. A founding member (violinist) of the Armingaud Quartet (1856–67). Composed operas (*Le roi d'Ys,* 1875–81); ballets; orchestral works (*Symphonie espagnole,* 1874, and *Fantaisie norvégienne,* 1878, both violin and orchestra; Symphony in G minor, 1886; concertos for piano, violin, and cello); chamber and vocal music.

Lamb, Joseph F(rancis) (b. Montclair, N.J., 6 Dec. 1887; d. Brooklyn, 3 Sept. 1960). Ragtime composer. Along with Scott Joplin and James Scott, one of the greatest of ragtime composers; also wrote songs for Tin Pan Alley. Works include "Sensation" (1908), "American Beauty Rag" (1913), "The Ragtime Nightingale" (1915), and "Top Liner Rag" (1916).

Lambert, (Leonard) Constant (b. London, 23 Aug. 1905; d. there, 21 Aug. 1951). Composer, conductor, and writer on music. Pupil of Vaughan Williams and Morris. Conducted the Vic-Wells (later Sadler's Wells) Ballet, 1931–47. Composed ballets (*Romeo and Juliet,* for Diaghilev, 1926; *Pomona,* for the choreographer Nizhinska, 1927); orchestral works (*Elegiac Blues,* 1927); choral works (*The Rio Grande,* 1928); songs (8 poems of Li-Po, voice and instruments, 1926–29); incidental music; film scores; arrangements.

Lamellaphone. An instrument on which sound is produced by plucking one or more flexible tongues, usually of metal; also called a plucked *idiophone.* Examples are the *mbira* and the *music box.*

Lament. A poem or song of mourning; by extension, an instrumental piece of mournful character. Among Western countries, they have been especially important in the music of Ireland and Scotland, both as song and as music for the bagpipe [see also *Caoine, Coronach*].

Lamentabile, lamentoso [It.]. Sadly, plaintively.

Lamentations. Music for verses from the *Lamentations of Jeremiah* [Lat. *Threni, id est Lamentationes Ieremiae Prophetae*]. The Hebrew letter that precedes each verse in the Bible is retained in musical settings. In the Roman Catholic liturgy, nine groups

of these verses are sung, three each at Matins on Maundy Thursday, Good Friday, and Holy Saturday to the *tonus lamentationum,* whose use was prescribed by the Council of Trent (mid-16th cent.), or to a more elaborate Spanish tone. The development of polyphonic settings of the Lamentations began in the middle of the 15th century and ended at about the start of the 19th.

Lamento [It., lament]. A song of mourning or great sadness and an important element in Italian opera of the 17th century. The *lamento* rose to prominence along with *monody. Monteverdi's Lamento d'Arianna* of 1608 was the first celebrated example. The *lamento* was prominent in mid-17th-century Venetian operas and was often treated as variations on an *ostinato* bass of a descending tetrachord. Dido's lament from Purcell's *Dido and Aeneas* belongs to this tradition.

La Montaine, John (b. Chicago, 17 Mar. 1920). Composer. Pupil of Rogers, Hanson, Wagenaar, and Boulanger. Taught at Eastman, 1964–65. Influences on his work include serialism, medieval music, folk song, and jazz. Works include 5 operas; orchestral music (piano concerto, Pulitzer Prize, 1959); music for jazz band; chamber music; choral and vocal music.

Lamoureux, Charles (b. Bordeaux, 28 Sept. 1834; d. Paris, 21 Dec. 1899). Conductor. Studied at the Paris Conservatory. Underwrote and conducted the Société de l'harmonie sacrée (1873–74), which gave large sacred works; 1881–97, conducted his Concerts Lamoureux, which introduced Paris to much native and foreign instrumental music; conducted Paris premieres of *Lohengrin* (1887) and *Tristan* (1899).

Lampe, John Frederick (b. Saxony, ca. 1703; d. Edinburgh, 25 July 1751). Composer. Settled in London about 1725. Composed stage works (*The Dragon of Wantley,* 1737); other instrumental and vocal works. Associate of Wesley, many of whose hymns appear in a 1746 print set to Lampe's music. Wrote manuals on thoroughbass and harmony.

Lampugnani, Giovanni Battista (b. Milan, 1706; d. there, after late 1786). Composer. Worked mainly in Italy; 1743–44, at the King's Theatre, London. Played harpsichord at the opera in Milan from 1758. Composed stage works including *Alfonso* (London, 1744); arias and many sonatas and sinfonias.

Lancio, con [It.]. Bounding, springing.

Landi, Stefano (b. Rome, ca. 1586–87; d. there, 28 Oct. 1639). Composer. *Maestro di cappella* at S. Maria di Monte, Rome; associated with the Barberini family; sang in the papal choir from 1629. Composed

La morte d'Orfeo (opera, 1619); *Il Sant'Alessio* (sacred opera, 1632); books of arias; church music in both *stile antico* and *stile moderno,* madrigals, and dialogues.

Landini cadence, sixth. See Cadence.

Landini [Landino], **Francesco** [Francesco degli organi] (b. Fiesole? or Florence, ca. 1325; d. Florence, 2 Sept. 1397). Composer, organist, organ tuner and builder, poet. Blind from childhood. From 1365 *cappellanus* at the Church of SS. Annunziata, Florence. His over 150 compositions (mainly *ballate* and madrigals) constitute about a quarter of the extant music from the Italian trecento.

Ländler [Ger.]. A dance of Austria and southern Germany in a slow 3/4 time. It originated as a folk dance for couples and in the later 18th century became popular in the ballroom, enjoying a considerable vogue in the early 19th. It was eventually superseded by the *waltz. Mozart (K. 606), Beethoven (WoO 11), and Schubert (D. 378, 734, 790) composed sets of *Ländler,* and movements by Bruckner and Mahler draw on its style.

Landowska, Wanda [Alexandra] (b. Warsaw, 5 July 1879; d. Lakeville, Conn., 16 Aug. 1959). Harpsichordist and pianist. Studied in Warsaw, Berlin, and Paris. Taught at the Berlin Conservatory, 1913–19; at the École normale in Paris; at a school she founded with Alfred Cortot at Saint-Leu-la-Forêt (summers 1925–40); at the Curtis Institute, Philadelphia, 1925–28. Made the first recording of Bach's Goldberg Variations; commissioned and premiered Falla's Harpsichord Concerto and Poulenc's *Concert champêtre.*

Landowski, Marcel (b. Pont l'Abbé, Finistère, 18 Feb. 1915). Composer and writer on music. Pupil of Büsser. Directed music at the Comédie-Française, 1962–65; then at the Ministry of Cultural Affairs. Works include operas and ballets, film and incidental music; symphonies, symphonic poems, concertos; chamber and piano works; choral and solo vocal music. Writings include a book on Honegger.

Landré, Guillaume (Louis Frédéric) (b. The Hague, 24 Feb. 1905; d. Amsterdam, 6 Nov. 1968). Composer. Pupil of his father and of Pijper. Worked with serial techniques and jazz-influenced rhythms. Works include operas (*De snoek,* 1938); orchestral music (symphonies; concertos; *Permutazioni sinfoniche,* 1957); vocal works (*Piae memoriae pro patria mortuorum,* chorus, orchestra, 1942); 4 string quartets and other chamber music.

Lang, B(enjamin) J(ohnson) (b. Salem, Mass., 28 Dec. 1837; d. Boston, 3 or 4 Apr. 1909). From 1858 prominent in Boston musical life as pianist, organist (from 1862, Old South Church; from 1885, King's

Chapel), conductor, especially of choral societies (Apollo Club; Caecilia; Handel and Haydn Society), teacher, and composer. Conducted premiere of Tchaikovsky's First Piano Concerto.

Lang, Josephine (Caroline) (b. Munich, 14 Mar. 1815; d. Tübingen, 2 Dec. 1880). Composer. Daughter of Munich Kapellmeister Theobald Lang (1783–1834) and singer Regina Hitzelberger (1788–1827); pupil of Mendelssohn; sang in the court chapel. Settled in Tübingen on her marriage; resumed teaching and composing after her husband's death. Published 52 opuses of songs and piano pieces.

Lang, Margaret Ruthven (b. Boston, 27 Nov. 1867; d. there, 29 May 1972). Composer. Pupil of her father, B. J. Lang, Chadwick, and MacDowell. Best known for about 200 songs, some quite popular; also composed choral music, piano pieces, orchestral works. The first U.S. woman to have a work performed by a major orchestra (Dramatic Overture op. 12, Boston Symphony, 1893); stopped composing in about 1917.

Lange-Müller, Peter Erasmus (b. Frederiksborg, Denmark, 1 Dec. 1850; d. Copenhagen, 26 Feb. 1926). Composer. From 1879 to 1883, assistant conductor of a concert society that he had helped found, the only public post he ever held. Composed ca. 200 songs and part songs; also 4 operas and other stage music; 2 symphonies; 2 orchestral suites; a violin concerto; chamber music.

Langgaard, Rued [Rud] **(Immanuel)** (b. Copenhagen, 28 July 1893; d. Ribe, Denmark, 10 July 1952). Composer and organist. Debut as organist, 1905. After an experimental atonal phase (1916–24), composed in a Romantic style. Cathedral organist in Ribe from 1940. Works include the biblical opera *Antikrist* (1921–39), compositions for chorus and orchestra, 16 symphonies, 8 string quartets.

Langlais, Jean (b. La Fontenelle, 15 Feb. 1907; d. Paris, 8 May 1991). Composer and organist. Pupil of Dupré, Dukas, and Tournemire, whom he succeeded in 1945 as organist at Ste. Clotilde. Played and taught widely in Europe and the U.S. Composed ca. 100 organ works (including 3 concertos; *Prélude Gregorien,* 1979); pieces for orchestra; chamber works; vocal and choral pieces.

Langleik [Nor.]. A fretted *zither of Norway with a narrow trapezoidal body and four to eight metal strings.

Langsam [Ger.]. Slow; *langsamer,* slower; *sehr langsam,* very slow.

Langspil [Icel.]. A bowed *zither of Iceland; similar in form to the *langleik.*

Lanier, Nicholas (bapt. London, 10 Sept. 1588; buried there, 24 Feb. 1666). Composer. Joined the King's Musick as lutenist, 1616; collaborated with Jonson on masques; Master of the Musick of Prince Charles from 1618 (and of the king's music after Charles's accession in 1625). Active as an artist in Paris during the Commonwealth. Composed many songs; a few instrumental works also survive.

Lanner, Joseph (Franz Karl) (b. Vienna, 12 Apr. 1801; d. Oberdöbling, near Vienna, 14 Apr. 1843). Composer and dance orchestra conductor. Mostly self-taught in music; violinist-conductor of a popular dance orchestra; later divided into two orchestras, the other headed by Strauss, Sr. Published over 200 works, including many waltzes.

Lansky, Paul (b. New York, 18 June 1944). Composer. Pupil of Perle, Weisgall, Babbitt, Cone, and Kim. Taught at Princeton from 1969. Has worked with twelve-tone technique and computer-generated sounds. Works include a string quartet and other chamber music, *Modal Fantasy* (piano, 1970), *Six Fantasies on a Poem by Thomas Campion* (computer, 1978–79), and *As If* (string trio, computer, 1982).

Lantins, Arnold de (fl. ca. 1430). Composer. Probably from the region of Liège; 1431, sang with Dufay in the papal choir. Composed one cyclic Mass, other Mass movements, motets, ballades, and rondeaux.

Lantins, Hugo de (fl. 1420–30). Composer. Possibly related to Arnold de Lantins. Connected with Venice and the Malatesta family and with Dufay. Made extensive use of imitation. Composed Mass movements, motets, Italian secular songs, and French rondeaux.

Lanza, Alcides (b. Rosario, Argentina, 2 June 1929). Composer and pianist. Pupil of Ginastera, Copland, Messiaen, Malipiero, Maderna, and Ussachevsky. On the staff of the Teatro Colón, Buenos Aires, 1959–65; taught at the Electronic Music Center of Columbia and Princeton, 1965–71; at McGill Univ., Montreal, from 1971. Has made use of graphic notation and electronic sounds as well as traditional media.

Lap organ. A reed organ made in the U.S. in the second quarter of the 19th century in the form of a box held on the player's lap.

Lara, Agustín (b. Tlacotalpán, Mexico, 30 Oct. 1900; d. Mexico City, 6 Nov. 1970). Popular songwriter. His over 600 songs include "Mujer," "Maria Bonita," and "Rosa"; among his most popular were those on Spanish topics (including "Madrid," "Granada").

Largamente [It.]. Broadly.

Largando [It.]. *Allargando.*

Larghetto [It., dim. of *largo*]. Slightly less slow than *largo*. Heinrich Koch (1802) equated it with *andante*.

Largo [It., broad, large]. (1) Very slow; according to some 18th-century theorists, the slowest of the principal divisions of *tempo*, though then and later it was often placed between *adagio* and *andante*. (2) A movement whose tempo is *largo*. The piece popularly known as Handel's "Largo" and played in a variety of arrangements is the aria "Ombra mai fù" (Shade never was) from *Serse*, which, however, is actually marked *larghetto*.

Lark Quartet. Popular name for Haydn's String Quartet in D major Hob. III:63 (1790), so called because of the high passage played by the first violin at the opening of the first movement. Haydn arranged the fourth movement for *Flötenuhr* (Hob. XIX:30).

Larrocha (y de la Calle), Alicia de (b. Barcelona, 23 May 1923). Pianist. Studied in Barcelona; orchestral debut at age 12 with the Madrid Symphony. Toured internationally from 1947. Concertized with cellist Gaspar Cassadó from 1956; from 1959, director of the Marshall Academy, Barcelona. Esteemed interpreter of classical and Romantic works; made award-winning recordings of works by Granados and Albéniz.

Larsson, Lars-Erik (Vilner) (b. Äkarp, Skåne, Sweden, 15 May 1908; d. Hälsingborg, 27 Dec. 1986). Composer. Pupil of Berg. Composer and conductor for Swedish radio, 1937–53; taught at Stockholm Conservatory, 1947–59; music director at Uppsala Univ., 1961–66. Worked with neoclassicism, polytonality, and his own twelve-tone method.

La Rue, Pierre de (b. probably Tournai, c. 1460; d. Courtrai [Kortrijk], 20 Nov. 1518). Composer. Sang at Siena Cathedral, 1482–85; at the Burgundian *grande chappelle* in Brussels from 1492. Served Philip the Fair, his sister Margaret of Austria, and her son (later Emperor Charles V). In 1516, retired as abbot at Courtrai. Rich in canonic and imitative procedures, his works include 30 Masses and a Requiem, motets, and chansons. His name appeared variously translated as Petrus de Vico, Petrus Platensis, Peteren van Straeten; Pierchon, Pierrazon, etc.

Laserna, Blas de (b. Corella [Navarre], 4 Feb. 1751; d. Madrid, 8 Aug. 1816). Composer. From 1778, *compositor de compañía* for the two theaters in Madrid; from 1790, conductor, Teatro de la Cruz. Composed zarzuelas, some 700 tonadillas, in addition to *sainetes, melólogos,* and incidental music. Among his works are *El majo y la italiana fingida* (1778), *La gitana por amor* (1791), *Idomeneo* (1792).

Lassen, Eduard (b. Copenhagen, 13 Apr. 1830; d. Weimar, 15 Jan. 1904). Conductor. Studied at the Brussels Conservatory; 1858, succeeded Liszt as Kapellmeister at Weimar. Composed operas (*Landgraf Ludwigs Brautfahrt,* Weimar 1857); much incidental music, a ballet; orchestral works; songs.

Lassú [Hung.]. See *Verbunkos, Csárdás.*

Lassus, Orlande de [Orlando (di) Lasso, Orlandus Lassus, Roland Delattre] (b. Mons, Hainaut, 1532; d. Munich, 14 June 1594). Composer. Associate of the Gabrielis. By 1553, choirmaster at St. John Lateran, Rome. From 1556, at the court chapel of Duke Albrecht V of Bavaria, Munich (*maestro di cappella* from 1563). His output is characterized by a close connection between text and music. Composed approximately 530 motets (including religious, humorous, ceremonial, and didactic works, and settings of classical or humanistic texts, such as the *Prophetiae Sibyllarum*); almost 60 Masses (most parodies, modeled on his own sacred motets or other composers' secular works); other liturgical compositions including hymns, over 100 Magnificats, responsories for Holy Week, Passions. Compositions in the vernacular include about 175 Italian madrigals and villanellas, roughly 150 French chansons, and around 90 sacred and secular German lieder. Created hybrid forms (Latin chanson, double-choir drinking song, etc.).

Lateiner, Jacob (b. Havana, Cuba, 31 May 1928). Pianist. Pupil of Isabelle Vengerova and Schoenberg. Debut with the Philadelphia Orchestra in 1945. Commissioned and premiered Elliott Carter's Piano Concerto, 1967. His accounts of late Beethoven highly praised. From 1966 taught at Juilliard.

La Tombelle, (Antoine Louis Joseph Gueyrand) Fernand (Fouant) de (b. Paris, 3 Aug. 1854; d. Château de Fayrac, Dordogne, 13 Aug. 1928). Organist and composer. Pupil of Guilmant and Dubois; church organist in Paris; 1896–1904, taught at the Schola cantorum. Composed 2 operettas, orchestral works, songs, piano pieces; later primarily church music: Masses, oratorios, motets, organ pieces, settings of chant.

Laube Sonata [Ger.]. See *Moonlight* Sonata.

Lauda [It., pl. *laude;* or *laude,* pl. *laudi*]. A nonliturgical religious song, of greatest importance in the 13th and in the 15th–16th centuries, but in continuous use until the mid-19th century, with texts usually in Italian, less often in Latin; also *lauda spirituale.* In diction, subject matter, and musical setting, the *lauda* is familiar, not elite.

Laudon (Loudon) Symphony. Haydn's name for his Symphony no. 69 in C major Hob. I:69 (completed in 1779), composed in honor of the Austrian field marshal Baron von Laudon (1717–90).

Lauds [Lat. *laudes*]. The second of the services making up the *Office.

Launeddas. A triple clarinet of Sardinia consisting of three cane pipes. Two pipes, one held in each hand, have finger holes; the other is a bass drone.

Lauri-Volpi, Giacomo (b. Lanuvio, 11 Dec. 1892; d. Valencia, 17 Mar. 1979). Tenor. Studied in Rome. Debut, Viterbo, 1919. Sang at La Scala 1921–40; at the Metropolitan 1923–33. Roles included the Duke of Mantua *(Rigoletto),* Calaf *(Turandot),* and Rodolfo *(Luisa Miller).* Created Boito's *Nerone* (Rome, 1928).

Laut [Ger.]. (1) [adj.] Loud. (2) [n.] Sound.

Laute [Ger.]. Lute; *Lautenzug,* the buff or *harp stop of the harpsichord; for *Lautenclavicymbel,* see Lute harpsichord.

Lauto, laouto [Gr.]. A fretted *lute of Greece. Four pairs of gut strings are plucked with a quill or a plastic plectrum.

Lavallée, Calixa (b. Verchères, Quebec, 28 Dec. 1842; d. Boston, 21 Jan. 1891). Composer. Studied in Montreal and Paris; 1861–62, bandsman in a U.S. army regiment; settled in Boston, 1880. Composed *O Canada* (1880), now the national anthem; other works include a comic opera, *The Widow* (ca. 1881), a music comedy, the concert etude *Le papillon* op. 18.

Lavista, Mario (b. Mexico City, 3 Apr. 1943). Composer. Student of R. Halffter, Quintanar, Ligeti, Stockhausen, and Xenakis. His music combines traditional timbres and media with avant-garde elements; works include *5 Pieces,* string quartet (1969); *Cluster,* piano (1973); *Antifonia,* flute, 2 bassoons, and percussion (1974); and a piano trio (1976), as well as pieces employing radios, alarm clocks, prepared instruments, and electronic equipment.

Lavolta. See *Volta.*

Lavry, Marc (b. Riga, 22 Dec. 1903; d. Haifa, 24 Mar. 1967). Composer. Pupil of Glazunov. Emigrated to Palestine, 1935. Composed the symphonic poem *Emek* [The Valley] (1937); a number of works influenced by Jewish cantillation, such as *Shir ha'shirim* [The Song of Songs] (1940); the folk opera *Dan ha'shomer* [Dan the Guard] (1945); piano concertos; chamber music.

Law, Andrew (b. Milford, Conn., 21 Mar. 1749; d. Cheshire, Conn., 13 July 1821). Composer, singing master, minister, and tunebook compiler. Founded singing schools in Philadelphia, New York, Boston,

Charleston, and other cities. Around 1802–3 formulated a new form of staffless shape notation, which never became widely popular. Among compilations he published are *Select Harmony* (Cheshire, Conn., 1779); *The Art of Singing* (Cheshire, 1792–93).

Lawes, Henry (b. Dinton, 5 Jan. 1596; d. London, 21 Oct. 1662). Composer, brother of William Lawes. Gentleman of the Chapel Royal from 1626; member of the King's Musick from 1631; resumed these posts after the Restoration. Composed over 400 vocal works (collections include *Ayres and Dialogues*, 1653; *Choice Psaumes*, 1648); music for court entertainments (working with poets such as Milton); several anthems, and instrumental works.

Lawes, William (bapt. Salisbury, 1 May 1602; d. in battle, Chester, 24 Sept. 1645). Composer, brother of Henry Lawes. Pupil of Coprario; musician to Prince (later King) Charles. Composed vocal and instrumental music for many court masques and plays, much church music, chamber music, keyboard works, and suites for viol consorts.

Lay. *Lai.

Layer. In *Schenker analysis, any of the musical structures underlying a tonal work and understood as related to one another by certain techniques of elaboration.

Layolle, Francesco de (b. Florence, 4 Mar. 1492; d. Lyons, ca. 1540). Composer. Settled in Lyons, 1521; worked as music editor, particularly for the printer Moderne. Most of his sacred music is lost; his secular music includes many Italian madrigals and about a dozen French chansons.

Layton, Billy Jim (b. Corsicana, Tex., 14 Nov. 1924). Composer. Pupil of Q. Porter and Piston. Taught at Harvard 1957–66; thereafter at SUNY–Stony Brook. Opposed the constructivism of Boulez and aleatory procedures; influenced by jazz and popular idioms, as well as medieval music. Works include orchestral pieces; chamber music; a setting of Dylan Thomas poems for choir and brass.

Lazarof, Henri (b. Sofia, Bulgaria, 12 Apr. 1932). Composer. Studied in Jerusalem, with Petrassi in Rome, and at Brandeis. Taught at UCLA, 1962–87. Employs serial procedures. Works include a ballet (*Mirrors, mirrors . . .* , 1980); *Spectrum* (trumpet, orchestra, and tape, 1972–73), concertos, symphonies (no. 3, Choral, 1994), and other orchestral music; string quartets and other chamber music, some with tape; keyboard works; and *Canti* (chorus, 1971).

Lead sheet. In jazz and popular music, a shorthand score or part. It may provide melody, chord symbols [see Fake-book notation], accompanimental figures, or lyrics.

Leadback. *Retransition [see Sonata form].

Leadbelly. See Ledbetter, Huddie.

Leader. (1) Conductor. (2) [Brit.] Concertmaster.

Leading motive, motif. See *Leitmotif.*

Leading tone, note [Fr. *(note) sensible;* Ger. *Leitton;* It. *(nota) sensibile;* Sp. *(nota) sensible*]. The seventh degree of the major and harmonic or ascending melodic minor scales, which lies a semitone below the tonic and in tonal music often leads or resolves to the tonic [see Scale, Scale degrees]. Melodic motion from leading tone to tonic, especially when harmonized with the dominant and tonic harmonies (V–I), respectively, is one of the most characteristic gestures of tonal music [see Cadence]. In the major scale, the seventh degree lies naturally a semitone below the tonic. In the pure minor, it lies a whole tone below and is raised by means of an accidental in order to produce the leading-tone effect of the harmonic and melodic minor scales [see Major, minor]. In some of the *modes of early music, too, the seventh degree lies a whole tone below *(subtonium)* the final. Under certain circumstances, however, the seventh degree in such modes could be raised with an accidental to create a semitone below *(subsemitonium)* the final [see *Musica ficta*].

Leap. Melodic *motion from one pitch to another that is more than a whole tone away.

Lear, Evelyn (Shulman) (b. Brooklyn, 8 Jan. 1926). Soprano. Studied at Juilliard School and the Berlin Musikhochschule. Debut as the Composer *(Ariadne auf Naxos)*, Berlin 1957. Metropolitan Opera debut as Lavinia in Marvin Levy's *Mourning Becomes Electra*, 1967; sang there for 13 seasons, usually in works by Mozart, Strauss, and Berg.

Lebègue, Nicolas-Antoine (b. Laon, ca. 1630; d. Paris, 6 July 1702). Composer. Organist at St. Merry, Paris, from 1664; an *organiste du Roy* from 1678; Grigny was his pupil. Composed several types of sacred and secular organ works presenting a range of technical requirements.

Lebendig [Ger.]. Lively.

Lebhaft [Ger.]. Lively, *vivace.*

Lebrun, Ludwig August (b. Mannheim, bapt. 2 May 1752; d. Berlin, 16 Dec. 1790). Oboist and composer. Played in the Mannheim court orchestra from at least 1764. Toured extensively with his wife Franziska Lebrun. Extended the upper range of the oboe beyond the standard of the day. Composed incidental music; concertos and chamber works with oboe.

Lechner, Leonhard [Lechnerus, Leonardus Athesinus] (b. valley of Adige, Austrian Tirol, ca. 1553; d.

Stuttgart, 9 Sept. 1606). Composer. The foremost German writer of choral music in the late 16th century. Chorister in Munich under Lassus; court musician and eventually Kapellmeister in Stuttgart (from 1585). Composed sacred works (including Latin motets and liturgical pieces, a German motet-Passion); numerous vernacular songs and song-motets.

Leclair, Jean Marie [*l'aîné*] (b. Lyons, 10 May 1697; d. Paris, 22 Oct. 1764). Violinist and composer. Pupil of Somis. Debut at the Concert spirituel in 1728. *Ordinaire de la musique* to Louis XV, 1733–37; served Princess Anne of Orange, 1738–43. Composed many suites, sonatas, concertos, and an opera.

Leclair, Jean-Marie [*le cadet*] (b. Lyons, 23 Sept. 1703; d. there, 30 Nov. 1777). Violinist and composer. Brother of Jean-Marie *l'aîné*. From 1733, teacher at the Académie des Beaux-Arts, Lyons. Composed sonatas and several lost vocal and instrumental works.

Lecocq, (Alexandre) Charles (b. Paris, 3 June 1832; d. there, 24 Oct. 1918). Composer. Composed operettas and comic operas including *Fleur-de-thé* (Paris 1868), *Les cent vierges* and *La fille de Madame Angot* (both Brussels 1872), and *Giroflé-Girofla* (Paris 1874); also songs, salon music, and a few other works.

Lecuona, Ernesto (b. Guanabacoa, Cuba, 7 Aug. 1896; d. Sta. Cruz de Tenerife, 29 Nov. 1963). Composer. Pupil of Joaquín Nin. Toured South America and the U.S. with his dance band, Lecuona's Cuban Boys. His most famous melodies include "Malagueña," "Andalucía," "Siboney," and "Rosa la china."

Ledbetter, Huddie "Leadbelly" (b. Mooringsport, La., 21 Jan. 1885 [or 1888, 1889]; d. New York, 6 Dec. 1949). Folk and blues singer, guitarist, songwriter. Became a traveling musician in his teens, styling himself "King of the Twelve-String Guitar"; teamed briefly with Blind Lemon Jefferson. While in prison (1930–34), he was discovered by John Lomax, who recorded much of his repertoire for the Library of Congress. Thereafter settled in New York; toured and recorded extensively; songs include "Goodnight, Irene" and "Rock Island Line."

Ledger line. A short line parallel to and above or below the staff, representing a continuation of the staff and used to indicate pitches above or below the staff itself [see Notation].

Leduc, Alphonse (b. Nantes, 9 Mar. 1804; d. Paris, 17 June 1868). Music publisher and composer. Studied at the Paris Conservatory; 1841, founded a music publishing firm in Paris, which was carried on by his descendants. Composed salon music and didactic works for piano; songs; flute, guitar pieces.

Leduc, Simon [*l'aîné*] (b. Paris, 15 Jan. 1742; d. there, 20 Jan. 1777). Composer and violinist. Pupil of Gaviniès. From 1763 played at the Concert spirituel (co-director from 1773). Published symphonies, *symphonies concertantes,* concertos, and trio sonatas.

Lee, Dai-Keong (b. Honolulu, 2 Sept. 1915). Composer. Pupil of Sessions, Jacobi, Copland, and Luening. Some of his compositions use Polynesian elements. Has written stage works; film scores; orchestral music (*Polynesian Suite,* 1958); chamber and piano music, songs, and *Meleolili* (Joyful Songs based on Hawaiian chants; soloists, chorus, and orchestra, 1960).

Lee, Noël (b. Nanking, of American parents, 25 Dec. 1924). Composer and pianist. Pupil of Boulanger. Has recorded complete works of Debussy, Ravel, Stravinsky, and Copland. Compositions include a ballet, chamber music (*Convergences,* flute and harpsichord, 1972); piano music (including *3 Préludes néoclassiques,* 1951); *Devouring Time* (after Shakespeare, chorus and piano, 1957) and other vocal music.

Leere Saite [Ger.]. Open string.

Lees [Lysniansky], **Benjamin** (b. Harbin, Manchuria, 8 Jan. 1924). Composer. Pupil of Dahl and Antheil. Has taught at Peabody Conservatory, Queens College, the Manhattan School, and Juilliard (1976–77). His style involves expanded tonality and clear formal designs. Has written 3 operas and a ballet; 5 symphonies, concertos, *Echoes of Normandy* (tenor, tape, organ, orchestra, 1994), and other orchestral music; sonatas, *Fantasy Variations* (piano, 1984), and other instrumental music; choral music and songs.

Leeuw, Ton [Antonius Wilhelmus Adrianus] **de** (b. Rotterdam, 16 Nov. 1926). Composer. Pupil of Badings and Messiaen. Taught at the conservatories in Utrecht and Amsterdam and at Amsterdam Univ. (from 1963). Has worked with "static" music, serial methods, aleatoric and mathematical techniques, and Eastern music; experimented with spatial relations in his compositions. Has composed dramatic works (*Antigone,* opera, 1991); orchestral works (*Treurmuziek in memoriam Willem Pijper,* 1946; symphonies; *Spatial Music I,* 1966); instrumental music (string quartets; *Antiphony,* wind quintet, tape, 1960; *Spatial Music II,* percussion ensemble, 1967); songs; piano music.

LeFanu, Nicola (Frances) (b. Wickham Bishops, Essex, 28 Apr. 1947). Composer. Daughter of composer

Elizabeth Maconchy. Pupil of Petrassi and Davies. Taught at Morley College (1970–75) and at King's College, London, from 1977. Compositions include operas *(Blood Wedding,* 1992) and other theatrical works; orchestral works *(The Hidden Landscape,* 1973); chamber music; choral works; solo vocal music.

Lefébure-Wély, Louis James Alfred (b. Paris, 13 Nov. 1817; d. there, 31 Dec. 1869). Organist and composer. Organist at St. Roch, Paris, 1831–47; at the Madeleine, 1847–58; from 1863 at St. Sulpice. A celebrated improviser. Composed especially salon music for piano *(Les cloches du monastère* op. 54) and organ music, including the collections *L'organiste moderne* and *L'office catholique.*

Lefebvre, Charles Édouard (b. Paris, 19 June 1843; d. Aix-les-Bains, 8 Sept. 1917). Composer. From 1895, professor, Paris Conservatory. Composed much instrumental music (wind suites opp. 57, 122); operas *(Djelma,* 1894); cantatas; sacred music; choruses; songs.

Lefèvre, (Jean) Xavier (b. Lausanne, 6 Mar. 1763; d. Paris, 9 Nov. 1829). Clarinetist. Played in the Opéra orchestra; 1795–1825, taught at the Paris Conservatory, producing its official *Méthode de clarinette;* 1807–29, member of the imperial (later royal) chapel. Composed 7 concertos, chamber music with clarinet.

Le Flem, Paul (b. Lézardrieux, Côtes-du-Nord, 18 Mar. 1881; d. Trégastel, 31 July 1984). Composer and critic. Teacher at the Schola cantorum, 1923–39; conductor of the choir of St. Gervais; chorusmaster at the Opéra-comique; critic for *Comoedia,* 1921–37. Works include operas, the choral fable *Aucassin et Nicolette* (1908), radio and film scores; 3 symphonies and other orchestral and instrumental music; choral music; songs.

Legato [It., bound; Fr. *lié;* Ger. *gebunden;* Sp. *ligado*]. Played smoothly with no separation between successive notes; the opposite of *staccato. Although it is sometimes specified by means of a *slur, which on wind and bowed instruments calls for no articulation of successive notes (i.e., no tonguing or change of bow), the term itself does not necessarily imply the absence of articulation, but only a very smooth articulation. See Bowing, Performance practice.

Legende [Ger.], **légende** [Fr.]. Legend; in the 19th century, a title used for shorter instrumental works and for symphonic poems intended to depict specific legends.

Léger, légèrement [Fr.]. Light, lightly; in the 18th century, also fast.

Leger line. See Ledger line.

Legg(i)ero, leggermente [It.]. Light, nimble, quick; sometimes non-*legato.

Leggiadro, leggiadramente [It.]. Graceful, charming.

Legley, Vic(tor) (b. Hazebrouck, 18 June 1915). Composer. Pupil of Absil. Taught at the Brussels Conservatory from 1949; at the Chapelle musicale Reine Elisabeth from 1950. Works include an opera; 6 symphonies, concertos, and other orchestral music; 4 string quartets, *Middagmuziek* (winds, string quartet, and double bass, 1948), and other chamber music; piano music; a few songs and choral works.

Legno [It.]. Wood; *stromenti di legno* or *legni,* woodwinds; *col legno,* in string playing, to strike the strings with the bow stick rather than bow with the hair.

Legrand, Michel (b. Paris, 24 Feb. 1932). Popular composer and arranger. Worked with Maurice Chevalier, 1954–55. Several of his film scores earned Oscars (including *Les parapluies de Cherbourg,* 1965; *Summer of '42,* 1971); his songs "La valse des lilas" and "Comme elle est longue" were also popular.

Legrenzi, Giovanni (bapt. Clusone, 12 Aug. 1626; d. Venice, 27 May 1690). Composer. *Maestro di cappella* at the Accademia dello Spirito Santo, Ferrara, 1656–65. Settled in Venice about 1671; served at the Conservatorio dei mendicanti and the Oratorio S. Maria della Fava; maestro at St. Mark's from 1685. Composed operas, oratorios, church music, sonatas, and secular vocal works.

Lehár, Franz [Ferencz] **(Christian)** (b. Komáron, Hungary, 30 Apr. 1870; d. Bad Ischl, 24 Oct. 1948). Composer and conductor. Worked as military bandmaster and theater conductor. Founded the publishing house Glocken Verlag in 1935. Composed an opera, ca. 30 operettas *(Die lustige Witwe* [The Merry Widow], 1905; *Die Graf von Luxembourg,* Vienna, 1909; *Giuditta,* Vienna, 1934); 5 film scores; orchestral works; some 65 waltzes ("Gold und Silber" op. 79), marches, and dances; piano music; some 90 songs.

Lehmann, Hans Ulrich (b. Biel, canton of Bern, 4 May 1937). Composer and cellist. Pupil of Boulez and Stockhausen. Taught at the Basel Academy of Music (1964–72), at the Univ. of Zurich (from 1969), and at the Musikhochschule in Zurich (from 1972). Has employed serial procedures. Works include *Streuungen* (3 choruses and 2 orchestras, 1975–76); *Aphorismus* (chamber orchestra, 1985), and other orchestral music; *Stroiking* (percussion ensemble, 1982) and other instrumental music; vocal pieces.

Lehmann, Lilli (b. Würzburg, 24 Nov. 1848; d. Berlin, 16 May 1929). Soprano. Debut as Mozart's First Lady *(Magic Flute),* Prague, 1867. Sang at the Berlin Opera, 1870–86; at the Metropolitan until 1891, when she returned to Berlin. Known for Wagner and Mozart roles.

Lehmann, Lotte (b. Perleberg, 27 Feb. 1888; d. Santa Barbara, Calif., 26 Aug. 1976). Soprano. Sang German roles at the Hamburg Opera from 1910, at the Vienna Staatsoper from 1914. Created Strauss's Composer *(Ariadne,* 1916), Dyer's Wife *(Frau,* 1919), and Christine *(Intermezzo,* 1924). Emigrated to the U.S. 1933; sang with the Metropolitan, 1934–45. In later years she turned more to song.

Leibowitz, René (b. Warsaw, 17 Feb. 1913; d. Paris, 29 Aug. 1972). Musicologist, composer, and conductor. Pupil of Schoenberg, Webern, and Ravel. Founded the International Festival of Chamber Music, Paris. Published writings on the twelve-tone method; among his students were Boulez and Henze. Wrote 5 operas; a symphony, 3 piano concertos, and other works for orchestra; 4 string quartets and other chamber music; piano music; choral and solo vocal music.

Leich [Ger.]. See *Lai.*

Leicht [Ger.]. Light, nimble.

Leidenschaftlich [Ger.]. Passionately.

Leider, Frida (b. Berlin, 18 Apr. 1888; d. there, 4 June 1975). Soprano. Debut as Venus *(Tannhäuser),* Halle 1915. Sang at the Berlin Staatsoper (1923–40), Covent Garden (1924–38), Bayreuth (1928–38), Chicago, and the Metropolitan; roles included Wagner heroines, Leonore *(Fidelio),* and the Marschallin *(Rosenkavalier).* Taught at the Studio of the Berlin Staatsoper and the Musikhochschule, Berlin-Charlottenburg.

Leier [Ger.]. (1) Lyre. (2) Hurdy-gurdy; also *Drehleier, Radleier, Bettlerleier.* See also *Leierkasten.*

Leierkasten [Ger.]. *Barrel organ.

Leifs, Jón (b. Sólheimer Farm, Iceland, 1 May 1899; d. Reykjavík, 30 July 1968). Composer and conductor. Pupil of Scherchen, Lohse, and Graener. Conducted in Germany for several decades. Founded the Union of Icelandic Artists and the Icelandic Composers' Society; worked for Icelandic Radio (1934–37). Made use of Icelandic folk music. Works include orchestral music *(Baldur* op. 34; *Iceland Ouvertüre* op. 9, 1926); string quartets; sacred works; piano music.

Leigh, Walter (b. London, 22 June 1905; d. near Tobruk, Libya, 12 June 1942). Composer. Pupil of Hindemith. Musical director at the Festival Theater,

Cambridge, 1931–32. Best known for his stage music, including the 2 light operas *The Pride of the Regiment* (1932) and *The Jolly Roger* (1933).

Leighton, Kenneth (b. Wakefield, Yorkshire, 2 Oct. 1929; d. Edinburgh, 24 Aug. 1988). Composer. Pupil of Petrassi. Teacher at Edinburgh Univ. (from 1956) and Worcester College, Oxford (1968–70). Some works use serial techniques. Compositions include an opera; sacred and secular vocal works; orchestral works (symphonies; concertos); string quartets and other chamber music; piano pieces (sonatas; *Fantasia contrappuntistica,* 1956); organ music.

Leinsdorf [Landauer], **Erich** (b. Vienna, 4 Feb. 1912; d. Zurich, 11 Sept. 1993). Conductor. Studied in Vienna. Assistant to Bruno Walter and Toscanini at Salzburg; conducted at the Metropolitan Opera from 1937. Music director of the Cleveland Orchestra, 1943; of the Rochester Philharmonic, 1947–56; of the Boston Symphony, 1962–69. Director of the New York City Opera, 1956.

Leise [Ger.]. (1) Soft. (2) German sacred songs of the Middle Ages, so called because they included the phrase *Kyrie eleison,* which was contracted to *kirleis* or *leis.*

Leiter [Ger.]. (1) Scale *(Tonleiter).* (2) Leader, director; *Leitung,* direction.

Leitmotif, Leitmotiv [Ger., leading motive]. A musical fragment, related to some aspect of the drama, that recurs in the course of an opera. The term leitmotif is used most often in connection with Wagner's later works. Leitmotifs combine both dramatic and musical functions. They may simply emphasize aurally what is seen on stage, or suggest to the listener something unseen that is being thought by one of the characters—a recollection, intuition, or prediction. Beyond presenting an exegesis of the action, the leitmotifs are the material from which the musical substance is constructed, just as motifs would be for an instrumental composer. See also Transformation of themes.

Leitton [Ger.]. *Leading tone.

Le Jeune, Claude [Claudin] (b. Valenciennes, 1528–30; d. Paris, buried 26 Sept. 1600). Composer. From 1560 served French Huguenot nobles and at Huguenot courts. Belonged to Baïf's Académie de poésie et de musique from 1570. His works show a concern with text-music relationships, and Flemish as well as Parisian influences. Composed Psalm settings, *chansons mesurées,* Latin sacred music, sacred and secular chansons *non mesurées,* and Italian madrigals.

Lekeu, Guillaume (Jean Joseph Nicolas) (b. Heusy, near Verviers, Belgium, 20 Jan. 1870; d. Angers, 21 Jan. 1894). Composer. Pupil of Franck and d'Indy.

Works include Violin Sonata (1892, commissioned by Ysaÿe); *Fantaisie symphonique sur deux airs populaires angevins* (1892); vocal works.

Lemare, Edwin (Henry) (b. Ventnor, Isle of Wight, 9 Sept. 1865; d. Hollywood, 24 Sept. 1934). Organist and composer. Studied at the Royal Academy of Music; taught there from 1892. Held organ posts in England and the U.S. (San Francisco municipal organist, 1917); taught at Carnegie Institute, Pittsburgh, 1902–5. Composed some 200 works for organ, choir, or solo voice; numerous organ transcriptions.

Lemmens, Jacques Nicolas (b. Zoerle-Parwijs, near Antwerp, 3 Jan. 1823; d. Zemst, near Malines, 30 Jan. 1881). Organist and composer. Studied at the Brussels Conservatory; taught there, 1849–69. In 1879, established a school at Malines for church musicians. Wrote an *École d'orgue basée sur le plainchant romain* (1862); organ pieces, 2 symphonies, vocal works.

Lemminkäinen Suite [Finn. *Lemminkäis-sarja*]. Four symphonic poems by Sibelius, op. 22, on legends of the warrior Lemminkäinen from the *Kalevala.* Their titles are *Lemminkäinen and the Maidens of the Island* (1895; rev. 1897, 1939), *Lemminkäinen in Tuonela* (1895; rev. 1897, 1939), *The Swan of Tuonela* (1893; rev. 1897, 1900), and *Lemminkäinen's Return* (1895; rev. 1897, 1900).

Leningrad Symphony. Popular name for Shostakovich's Symphony no. 7 in C major op. 60, begun in Leningrad during the German siege in 1941 and completed in Kuibishev later in the year.

Lennon, John [Winston] (b. Liverpool, 9 Oct. 1940; murdered New York, 8 Dec. 1980). Rock singer, songwriter, pianist, and guitarist. Formed the Beatles with Paul McCartney (with whom he collaborated on most of their songs), George Harrison, and Ringo Starr. Albums include *Meet the Beatles* (1964); *Sgt. Pepper's Lonely Hearts Club Band* (1967); *Abbey Road* (1969). They experimented with non-Western musics, classical music, and advanced studio recording techniques; also made movies. After the group's dissolution in 1970 Lennon pursued a solo career, often collaborating with his wife, Yoko Ono.

Lenormand, René (b. Elbeuf, Normandy, 5 Aug. 1846; d. Paris, 3 Dec. 1932). Composer. Founded the Société "Du lied en tous pays." Composed dramatic works; *Le Lahn de Mabed* (violin and orchestra, on an Arabic theme) and other orchestral works; chamber and piano music; some 150 songs.

Lent, lentement [Fr.]. Slow [see Performance marks].

Lento, lentamente [It.]. Slow [see Performance marks]; *lentissimo,* extremely slow.

Lenya, Lotte [Blamauer, Karoline Wilhelmine] (b. Vienna, 18 Oct. 1898; d. New York, 27 Nov. 1981). Actress and singer. Became famous singing the music of her husband, Kurt Weill; created Jenny in the *Mahagonny Songspiel* (1927), Jenny in *Die Dreigroschenoper* (1928), and Anna in *Die Sieben Todsünden* (1933).

Leo, Leonardo [Lionardo] **(Ortensio Salvatore de)** (b. S. Vito degli Schiavi, 5 Aug. 1694; d. Naples, 31 Oct. 1744). Composer. Pupil of Fago. From 1713, an organist at the viceroyal chapel, Naples; served at the royal chapel from 1730 (*maestro di cappella,* 1744). Taught at the Conservatorio S. Onofrio and the Conservatorio dei Turchini, with Piccinni and Jommelli among his pupils. Wrote some 30 serious operas (several to Metastasian librettos), 20 comic operas, serenatas, and other shorter dramatic works; oratorios, church music, and instrumental compositions; several didactic manuals.

Leoncavallo, Ruggero (b. Naples, 23 Apr. 1857; d. Montecatini, 9 Aug. 1919). Composer. Student of Rossi. Toured the Near East; café pianist, songwriter, teacher, and accompanist in Paris, 1882–87. Composed operas, mostly to his own librettos (*I Medici,* 1893, the first in an unfinished trilogy; *I *pagliacci; La bohème,* Venice, 1897; *Zazà,* Milan, 1900; *Der Roland von Berlin,* Berlin, 1904); operettas and musical comedies; a Requiem; songs (*Mattinata,* 1904, for Caruso); occasional works; piano pieces.

Leonhardt, Gustav (Maria) (b. Graveland, Netherlands, 30 May 1928). Harpsichordist, organist, and conductor. Taught at the Vienna Academy of Music (1952–55) and at the Amsterdam Conservatory from 1954. Performed and recorded extensively on antique harpsichords; conducted Baroque choral and operatic music; founded the Leonhardt Consort, 1955. Edited keyboard music of Sweelinck.

Léonin [Leonius, Leo, Leoninus] (b. Paris, ca. 1135; d. there, in or shortly after 1201). Musician, canon, and poet. Wrote 2-voiced organum collected in the *Magnus liber organi.* See Notre Dame.

Leonore overtures. The overtures composed by Beethoven for his opera *Fidelio,* originally titled *Leonore,* prior to the composition of the work now known as the *Fidelio* Overture. *Leonore* no. 2 was composed for the first production of the opera in 1805. No. 3 is a revision of no. 2 for a revival of the opera in 1806. No. 1, op. 138 (1806–7), was for a proposed production of the opera in Prague that never materialized. The *Fidelio* overture was composed for the revival of the opera in 1814.

Leppard, Raymond (John) (b. London, 11 Aug. 1927). Conductor, harpsichordist, and editor. Taught at Trinity College, Cambridge (1957–67). Has appeared at Covent Garden, Glyndebourne, Sadler's Wells, the Metropolitan Opera. Conducted the English Chamber Orchestra, BBC Northern Symphony, and St. Louis Symphony; music director, Indianapolis Symphony, from 1987. Edited, revived, and recorded many 17th- and 18th-century Italian operas. Published a book on performance practice.

Lerdahl, Fred [Alfred] **(Whitford)** (b. Madison, Wis., 10 Mar. 1943). Composer and theorist. Pupil of Fortner. Taught at Berkeley, Harvard (1970–79), Columbia (1979–85), and the Univ. of Michigan (from 1985). Works include orchestral music (*Crosscurrents,* 1987); string quartets and other chamber music; *Eros* (Pound; mezzo-soprano, alto flute, viola, harp, piano, electric guitar, electric double bass, and percussion, 1975) and other vocal music. Published *A Generative Theory of Tonal Music* (1983) with linguist Ray Jackendoff.

Lerner, Alan Jay (b. New York, 31 Aug. 1918; d. there, 14 June 1986). Popular lyricist and librettist. From 1942 worked with composer Frederick Loewe, writing musicals (*Brigadoon,* 1947; *Paint Your Wagon,* 1951; *My Fair Lady,* 1956; *Camelot,* 1960) and films (*Gigi,* 1958). Also worked with Kurt Weill, Burton Lane, and Leonard Bernstein.

Le Roux, Maurice (b. Paris, 6 Feb. 1923). Composer and conductor. Pupil of Messiaen and Leibowitz. Conducted the Orchestre nationale of the French Radio, 1960–68. Most of his compositions are serial; they include the ballet *Le petit Prince* (1950); *Un koan* (orchestra, 1973); film scores for *The Red Balloon* and *A View from the Bridge.*

Leroux, Xavier (Henry Napoléon) (b. Velletri, Italy, 11 Oct. 1863; d. Paris, 2 Feb. 1919). Composer. From 1896, professor, Paris Conservatory. Composed operas (*Evangeline,* 1895; *Astarté,* Opéra, 1901; *La reine Fiammette,* Opéra-comique, 1903; *Le chemineau,* Opéra-comique, 1907); songs, piano pieces.

Le Roy, Adrian (b. Montreuil-sur-mer, ca. 1520; d. Paris, 1598). Music printer, composer, and writer. Artistic director of the firm Le Roy & Ballard, active 1551–98; printed most works of Lassus. Wrote chansons, accompanied songs, and pieces and pedagogical books for cittern, lute, and guitar.

Leschetizky, Theodor (b. Łańcut, near Lwów, 22 June 1830; d. Dresden, 14 Nov. 1915). Piano teacher. Pupil of Czerny and Sechter. Taught in Vienna and St. Petersburg (1852–78); toured as pianist and conductor. Pupils included Paderewski and Schnabel. Composed 2 operas, piano pieces.

Lessard, John (Ayres) (b. San Francisco, 3 July 1920). Composer, pianist, and conductor. Pupil of Boulanger, Dandelot, and Cortot. Taught at SUNY–Stony Brook, 1962–90. Works include orchestral music; *Drift, Follow, Persist* (horn, piano, percussion, 1988) and other chamber music; piano and harpsichord pieces; vocal music including *The Pond in a Bowl* (soprano, piano, marimba, vibraphone, 1984) and some 35 songs with piano.

Lesson. (1) [Lat. *lectio*]. In a liturgical service, a reading from Scripture or other source such as the church fathers. (2) In England from the late 16th century through much of the 18th, a piece for instrumental consort, for lute, or, especially, for keyboard. The term did not imply any particular style or form, and it rarely implied pedagogical aims.

Le Sueur [Lesueur], **Jean-François** (b. Drucat-Pleissiel, near Abbeville, 15 Feb. 1760; d. Paris, 6 Oct. 1837). Composer. *Maître de musique* at Dijon, Le Mans, and Tours. *Maître de chapelle* at Notre Dame, Paris, 1786; from 1804 at the Tuileries chapel. Inspector at the Conservatory from 1795; teacher there from 1818; taught Gounod and Berlioz. Composed stage works (*La caverne,* 1793; *Paul et Virginie,* 1794; *Ossian,* 1804); sacred music (Masses, motets, oratorios, cantatas); songs. Published theoretical writings.

Lesur, Daniel Jean Yves. See Daniel-Lesur.

Letelier (Llona), Alfonso (b. Santiago, Chile, 4 Oct. 1912). Composer. Student of Allende and del Campo. Cofounded the Escuela moderna de música, 1940. Taught at the National Conservatory from 1946; at the Univ. of Chile from 1953. Early compositions draw on indigenous Chilean music, impressionism, and modality; later works move toward serialism. Works include Masses; an opera/oratorio; film scores; orchestral works; choral music; chamber and piano works.

Letter notation. Musical notation that uses the letters of the alphabet to designate pitches. The *pitch names in current use constitute such a notation, especially if combined with a system (e.g., of superscripts and subscripts) to indicate the precise register of each of the pitch classes represented by the first seven letters of the alphabet and associated accidentals.

Leuto [It., obs.]. Lute.

Levalto. See *Volta.*

Levare, levate [It.]. Remove, referring to an organ stop or a mute; *si levano i sordini,* the mutes are removed.

Levatio [Lat.], **elevazione, levazione** [It.]. *Elevation.

Levi, Hermann (b. Giessen, Upper Hesse, 7 Nov. 1839; d. Munich, 13 May 1900). Conductor. Pupil of V. Lachner. Kapellmeister at Karlsruhe, 1864–72; at Munich, 1872–96. Championed the music of Brahms; later, despite being Jewish, became a leading figure at Bayreuth, conducting the premiere of *Parsifal.*

Levine, James [Lawrence] (b. Cincinnati, 23 June 1943). Conductor and pianist. Pupil of R. Lhévinne (piano) and J. Morel, A. Wallenstein, and Max Rudolf (conducting). Music director, Metropolitan Opera, from 1975; artistic director from 1986. Director, Ravinia Festival, 1973–93. First conducted at Bayreuth, 1982; active at the Salzburg Festival.

Levy, Alexandre (b. São Paulo, 10 Nov. 1864; d. there, 17 Jan. 1892). Composer. In 1891, with brother Luis (1861–1935), took over Casa Levy, a leading music store and center of musical life, founded by his father. Pioneer of Brazilian art music; made use of popular tunes. Works include *Suite brasileiro* for orchestra (1890); piano pieces, including *Tango brasileiro* (1890).

Levy, Marvin David (b. Passaic, N.J., 2 Aug. 1932). Composer. Studied with P. James and Luening. His style is atonal and characterized by rhythmic flexibility; many works are theatrical. Works include 4 operas (*Mourning Becomes Electra,* after O'Neill, Metropolitan Opera, 1967); *Arrows of Time* (1988) and other orchestral music; *Sacred Service* (1964) and other choral music; chamber music (*Chassidic Suite,* horn, piano, 1956); songs; incidental and film music.

Lewis, Anthony (Carey) (b. Bermuda, 2 Mar. 1915; d. Haslemere, 5 June 1983). Scholar, conductor, composer. Taught at the Univ. of Birmingham from 1947. Founder and general editor of Musica Britannica; edited works by Blow, Handel, and Purcell. Conducted the first commercial recordings of Monteverdi's *Vespers,* Purcell's *Fairy Queen,* and other Baroque vocal works. Compositions include concertos for trumpet (1947) and horn (1956). Knighted in 1972.

Lewis, Jerry Lee (b. Ferriday, La., 29 Sept. 1935). Rock-and-roll and country singer and pianist. His recordings played an important role in the rock-and-roll movement ("Whole Lotta Shakin' Goin' On," "Great Balls of Fire," both 1957), as did his performances, which featured his athletic piano style. Remained popular in the 1960s and 1970s, recording country music and country-rock ("Chantilly Lace," 1972).

Lewis, John (Aaron) (b. LaGrange, Ill., 3 May 1920). Jazz pianist and composer. Joined Dizzy Gillespie's bop big band (1946–48) and recorded with Charlie Parker (1948). Music director of the Modern Jazz Quartet (1952–74, from 1981), for which he composed *Three Windows* (1957), *The*

Comedy (ballet suite, 1962), and other works. Music director of the Monterey Jazz Festival (1958–82); a founder of Orchestra U.S.A. (1962–65) and the American Jazz Orchestra (from 1985).

Lewis, Meade (Anderson) "Lux" (b. Chicago, 4 Sept. 1905; d. Minneapolis, 7 June 1964). Boogie-woogie pianist. His "Honky Tonk Train Blues" (1927; rediscovered 1935) initiated a national craze for boogie-woogie. Formed a trio with Albert Ammons and Pete Johnson (1938–39); otherwise worked as a soloist.

Lewis, Mel [Sokoloff, Melvin] (b. Buffalo, 10 May 1929; d. New York, 3 Feb. 1990). Jazz drummer and bandleader. Played in big bands of Stan Kenton (1954–57), Gerry Mulligan (1960–63), Benny Goodman (1962), and others; studio musician in Los Angeles and New York. Cofounded the Thad Jones–Mel Lewis Orchestra (1965–79), which then continued under Lewis's leadership.

Lewis, Robert Hall (b. Portland, Oreg., 22 Apr. 1926). Composer, conductor, and trumpet player. Pupil of Rogers, Hanson, Boulanger, and Krenek. Taught at the Peabody Conservatory (from 1958) and at Johns Hopkins (1969–80). Early works are serial; from the 1970s explored spatial effects, electronic music, quotations, and aleatory techniques. Works include 4 symphonies and other orchestral music; the series *Combinazioni* for various ensembles, 4 string quartets, and other chamber music; *Serenades I* (piano, 1970); *Monophony X* (soprano, 1983) and other vocal music.

Ley, Salvador (b. Guatemala City, 2 Jan. 1907; d. there, 21 Mar. 1985). Composer. Studied in Berlin. Director of the National Conservatory in Guatemala 1934–37, 1944–53; then settled in the U.S. Concertized frequently; taught at the Westchester Conservatory, 1963–70. Works include orchestral pieces; piano and chamber music; many songs set to Spanish, German, and English poetry.

L.H. Abbr. for left hand [Ger. *linke Hand*].

Lhéritier, Jean [Johannes] (b. ca. 1480; d. after 1552). Composer. May have had contact with composers at the French royal court around 1501. Held posts in Ferrara (1506–8) and Rome (1521–22) and several benefices in the region of Avignon; perhaps lived in the region of Venice, 1550s. Composed nearly 50 motets, a Mass, Magnificats, a chanson.

Lhévinne, Josef (b. Orel, near Moscow, 13 Dec. 1874; d. New York, 2 Dec. 1944). Pianist. Pupil of Safonov; Rachmaninoff and Scriabin were fellow students. Debut, Moscow, 1889. Married pianist Rosina Bessie in 1898. Taught in Tiflis (1900–1902) and at the Moscow Conservatory (1902–6). Lived in Berlin, 1907–19. Taught at Juilliard from 1922.

Lhévinne, Rosina (Bessie) (b. Kiev, 29 March 1880; d. Glendale, Calif., 9 Nov. 1976). Pianist and educator. Studied with Safonov. Taught at Juilliard, 1924–76; Van Cliburn was among her pupils. After marrying Josef Lhévinne, subordinated her career to his; reappeared as a soloist in 1945.

L'homme armé [Fr.]. See *Homme armé, L'*.

Liadov, Anatol Konstantinovich. See Lyadov, Anatol Konstantinovich.

Libero, liberamente [It.]. Freely.

Liber usualis [Lat.]. See Liturgical books.

Libitum [Lat.]. See *Ad libitum*.

Libre, librement [Fr.]. Freely.

Libretto [It.]. The text of an opera or oratorio; originally, and more specifically, the small book containing the text, printed for sale to the audience. As a basic minimum, the libretto gives a list of the cast of characters and the words that are to be performed. In addition, it often gives stage directions and a description of scenes. The libretto may further give a summary of the plot or background information necessary for the comprehension of the plot (called an *argomento* in Italian libretti).

Licenza [It., licence]. (1) In the 17th and 18th centuries, a passage or *cadenza added to a composition by a performer. (2) In the 17th and 18th centuries, an epilogue to a stage work, honoring a dignitary on a festive occasion.

Liceo [It.]. School; *l. musicale,* music school, *conservatory.

Lié [Fr.]. (1) Legato. (2) Of the *clavichord, fretted.

Liebermann, Rolf (b. Zurich, 14 Sept. 1910; d. Paris, 2 Jan. 1999). Composer and administrator. Pupil and assistant of Scherchen; studied with Vogel. Worked in Swiss and German radio, 1945–59; general manager of the Staatsoper, Hamburg, 1959–73, 1985–87; of the Paris Opéra, 1973–80. Works include operas (*La forêt,* 1987); radio and incidental music; a concerto for jazz band and orchestra (1954); *Concert des échanges* (machines and performers, 1964); *Cosmopolitan Greetings* (music theater, 1988).

Lieberson, Goddard (b. Hanley, Staffordshire, 5 Apr. 1911; d. New York, 29 May 1977). Composer and recording executive. Pupil of Rogers. At Columbia Records, from 1939, was responsible for recording much American contemporary music. Composed a ballet and incidental music; a symphony; a string quartet and other chamber music; *Songs without Mendelssohn* and other piano music; and choral music.

Liebes- [Ger.]. As a prefix in the names of instruments, a translation of the Italian *d'amore; Liebesgeige,* *viola d'amore; Liebesoboe,* oboe d'amore [see Oboe]; *Liebesflöte, flûte d'amour* [see Flute].

Liebeslieder [Ger., Love Songs]. Two groups of 18 and 15 short songs, respectively, by Brahms, op. 52 (1868–69) and op. 65 (*Neue Liebeslieder,* 1874). Each is a waltz scored for vocal quartet and piano four-hands. Brahms arranged nine of the earlier set for voices and small orchestra in 1870 and later arranged all of them for piano four-hands alone, op. 52a (1874) and op. 65a (1877). The texts are taken from Georg Friedrich Daumer's *Polydora,* except for the last song in op. 65, the text of which is by Goethe.

Liebhaber [Ger.]. See *Kenner und Liebhaber.*

Lied [Ger., pl. *Lieder*]. A German poem, usually lyric and strophic; also a song having such a poem for its text; most commonly, a song for solo voice and piano accompaniment in German-speaking countries during the Classical and Romantic periods; more broadly, any song setting of a German poetic text for voice(s) alone or for voice(s) with instrument(s).

In German, *Lied* as a musical term means any song (e.g., folk, work, children's, political), whereas in English, lied commonly refers to the German "art song" *(Kunstlied)* of the 19th and late 18th centuries, a poem of literary pretension set to music by a composer. A *Kunstlied* is a consciously artistic creation, distinguished from the functional nature of other songs. The general term lied occurs throughout the recorded history of German music, from the earliest notated monophonic songs [see *Minnesinger, Meistersinger*], to the polyphonic songs of the 15th and 16th centuries by Isaac, Hofhaimer, and Senfl, and through the works of Franz Schubert (1797–1828), by whose songs the genre was established on a serious artistic level, and his successors in the later 19th century, including Brahms and Wolf.

Lied von der Erde, Das [Ger., The Song of the Earth]. A cycle of six songs by Mahler (who called it a symphony) for alto (or baritone), tenor, and orchestra, composed in 1908–9 and first performed in 1911, after Mahler's death. The texts are German translations by Hans Bethge of 8th- and 9th-century Chinese poems.

Lieder eines fahrenden Gesellen [Ger., Songs of a Wayfarer]. Four songs for low voice and orchestra or piano by Mahler (composed ca. 1883–85; revised ca. 1891–96; orchestrated in the early 1890s), setting his own poems. The second song was used as the basis of the first movement of his First Symphony, and the last song is quoted in the slow movement of this symphony.

Lieder ohne Worte [Ger., Songs without Words]. Forty-eight piano pieces in songlike texture and style by Mendelssohn, published in eight books of six each, opp. 19 (1830, originally published in London as *Melodies for the Pianoforte*), 30 (1835), 38 (1837), 53 (1841), 62 (1844), 67 (1845), 85 (1850), 102 (ca. 1846). A few isolated pieces not published during his lifetime were also titled *Lied ohne Worte*. The titles given to individual pieces in many editions are not Mendelssohn's except for *Venezianisches Gondellied* (Venetian Gondola-Song, nos. 6, 12, 29), *Duetto* (no. 18), and *Volkslied* (Folk Song, no. 23).

Liederbuch [Ger.]. Song book. Normally a reference to 15th-century manuscript collections of German monophonic and polyphonic songs [see Lied].

Liederkreis, Liederzyklus [Ger.]. *Song cycle.

Liederspiel [Ger.]. A 19th-century German dramatic entertainment in which songs, newly composed upon preexisting poems, are inserted in the drama. The originator and principal proponent of the genre was Johann Friedrich Reichardt (1752–1814). The *Liederspiel* was meant to appeal to a popular, bourgeois audience. By the third decade of the 19th century, the term *Liederspiel* was used more freely.

Liedertafel [Ger.]. Originally, a group of men gathered around a table [Ger. *Tafel*] for singing and refreshment; later an occasion for such singing and refreshment.

Liedform [Ger.]. *Song form.

Lieto, lietamente [It.]. Joyful, merry; *lieto fine*, happy ending, as of an opera.

Lieve, lievemente [It.]. Light, easy.

Life for the Tsar, A [Russ. *Zhizn' za tsarya*]. Opera in four acts and an epilogue by Mikhail Ivanovich Glinka (libretto by Georgy Rosen), produced in Moscow in 1836. It is the first historically important Russian opera. In the U.S.S.R., Glinka's original title, *Ivan Susanin*, is now often used. Setting: Russia and Poland in the winter of 1612.

Ligature. (1) Any of the notational symbols in use from the late 12th through the 16th centuries that combine two or more notes in a single symbol. They emerged as rectilinear forms (thus, sometimes called square notation) of the neumes with which liturgical chant was notated [for examples of these forms, see Neume]. Around 1200, they were taken up for the notation of the polyphony of the repertory of *Notre Dame, and they remained in use in *mensural notation through the 16th century.

(2) In modern notation, a *slur connecting two or more notes, indicating that all are to be sung to a single syllable.

(3) In instruments of the clarinet family, the adjustable metal band that attaches the reed to the mouthpiece.

Ligeti, György (Sándor) (b. Dicsöszentmárton, Transylvania, 28 May 1923). Composer. Pupil of Farkas, Kadosa, Veress, and Járdányi. Taught at the Budapest Academy, 1950–56; at the Darmstadt summer courses; at the Academy of Music in Stockholm; and at the Hamburg Musikhochschule from 1973. Has worked with electronics, microtones, and the concept of *Klangflächenkomposition* (composition with planes of sound); some vocal works use an invented language of phonetic sounds and inflections. Works include *Artikulation,* 4-track tape (1958); *Poème symphonique,* 100 metronomes (1962); orchestral works (*Apparitions,* 1958–59; *Atmosphères,* 1961; concertos for cello, piano, and violin; *Ramifications,* strings, 1968–69); vocal pieces (*Aventures* and *Nouvelles aventures,* 3 solo voices, 7 instruments, 1962–65; arr. stage, 1966; Requiem, 1963–65; *Le grand macabre,* music theater, Stockholm, 1978); String Quartet no. 2 (1968), *Loop* (solo viola, 1991), and other chamber music.

Limoges, school of. See St. Martial, repertory of.

Lind, Jenny [Johanna] **(Maria)** (b. Stockholm, 6 Oct. 1820; d. Wynds Point, Herefordshire, 2 Nov. 1887). Soprano. Studied with Garcia. Prima donna at Stockholm from 1838. Sang opera in Berlin, Vienna, and London through 1849; roles included Alice in *Robert le diable,* Norma, and Meyerbeer's *Ein Feldlager in Schlesien,* composed for her. American tour arranged by P. T. Barnum, 1850–51. Settled in England, singing concerts and oratorios; from 1883 taught at the Royal College of Music.

Lindy. A social dance of the U.S., originating in the late 1920s in New York City and at first associated with the Savoy Ballroom in Harlem. It was danced to music (later, principally *swing) in fast duple meter and was characterized especially by "breakaways," in which the partners in a couple separated and improvised steps individually. Known from the 1930s also as jitterbug, it was widely danced until well into the 1950s and the advent of rock and roll.

Linear analysis. See Schenker analysis.

Linguaphone. *Lamellaphone, plucked *idiophone.

Lining (out). In Protestant Psalm and hymn singing in England and America beginning in the 17th century, the practice of leading the congregation by having each line read or sung (sometimes both read and sung) first by the minister or some other person.

Linke Hand [Ger.]. Left hand.

Linley, Thomas, Sr. (b. Badminton, 17 Jan. 1733; d. London, 19 Nov. 1795). Composer and harpsichordist. Pupil of Chilcot. Director of the Drury Lane Theatre, London, from 1774. Composed and arranged operas, pastiches, pantomimes, and incidental music, including *The Royal Merchant* (opera, 1767); *The Gentle Shepherd* (pastoral, 1781).

Linley, Thomas, Jr. (b. Bath, 5 May 1756; d. Grimsthorpe, 5 Aug. 1778). Composer and violinist. Pupil of Boyce and Nardini. Traveled widely in Europe; settled in London, 1776. Composed theater and choral works, including an oratorio, *The Song of Moses,* and, with his father, Thomas Linley, Sr., the comic opera *The Duenna* (1775).

Linz Symphony. Popular name for Mozart's Symphony no. 36 in C major K. 425, composed in Linz, Austria, in 1783 and first performed there by the private orchestra of Count Johann Joseph Thun.

Lip. See Embouchure.

Lipatti, Dinu [Constantin] (b. Bucharest, 19 Mar. 1917; d. Geneva, 2 Dec. 1950). Pianist and composer. Studied piano with Cortot, conducting with Munch, and composition with Jora, Dukas, Boulanger, and Stravinsky. Concertized and recorded with his godfather, Georges Enescu in Romania, 1939–43; after World War II recorded for Walter Legge. Taught at the Geneva Conservatory from 1944. Works include *Concertino in the Classic Style* (1936), the Symphonie Concertante and 2-piano *Suite* (both 1938).

Lira, lirica, lyra [Gr.]. A bowed stringed instrument of Greece and the Balkans with three strings, a pear-shaped body, and a broad neck without fingerboard, the strings being stopped with the pressure of the fingers or fingernails alone. It is usually held vertically, resting on the player's knee.

Lira da braccio [It.]. A bowed stringed instrument of the late 15th and 16th centuries, shaped like a violin, with a flat, leaf-shaped pegdisk with front pegs, five strings over the fingerboard (tuned g g' d' a' e''), and two drone strings to the left (tuned d d'). It was held on the shoulder with the pegdisk down and was intended to play chords as well as melody. See ill. under Violin.

Lira da gamba [It.]. A bass *lira da braccio* developed in the 16th century, usually fretted, with 9–14 melody strings and 2 drones; also called a *lirone*. It was held between the legs.

Lira organizzata [It.]. See Hurdy-gurdy.

Lirone [It.]. *Lira da gamba.*

Liscio [It.]. Smooth, even.

Lissenko, Nikolai Vitalievich. See Lysenko, Nikolay Vitalyevich.

L'istesso tempo [It.]. See *Istesso tempo, L'.*

Liszt, Franz [Franciscus] (b. Raiding, Hungary [now Austria], 22 Oct. 1811; d. Bayreuth, 31 July 1886). Pianist and composer. Pupil of Czerny, Salieri, Reicha, and Paer. Associate of Chopin and (from 1841) Wagner, who dedicated *Parsifal* to him and married his daughter, Cosima. Became very popular as a virtuoso pianist, concertizing throughout Europe. Kapellmeister extraordinaire, Weimar, 1842–58. There became the center of the New German School, making Weimar a center for the performance of new music, including Berlioz and Wagner. Settled in Rome, 1861; 1865, took the four minor orders of the church. A founder and the first president of the National Academy of Music in Budapest (1875). Works include the one-act opera *Don Sanche* (Opéra, 1825); orchestral works (*Eine *Faust-Symphonie; *Dante Symphony;* symphonic poems including *Ce qu'on entend sur la montagne,* *Tasso, Les *Preludes,* *Mazeppa, Die *Hunnenschlacht, Von der Wiege bis zum Grabe,* 1881–82); works for piano and orchestra (*Malédiction,* 1833; two piano concertos; *Totentanz,* 1849); many piano pieces (*Album d'un voyageur,* 1835–38; *Études d'execution transcendante; Grand galop chromatique,* 1838; *Paganini Etudes;* *Hungarian Rhapsodies; Sonata in B Minor; two *Légendes,* 1863; *Années de pèlerinage;* arrangements of his own and others' orchestral music); sacred music, including the oratorios *Die Legende von der heiligen Elisabeth,* (Pest, 1865) and *Christus;* Masses and motets; organ pieces and sacred and secular choral music.

Litany [Lat. *litania*]. A prayer consisting of a series of invocations and petitions, each sung or recited by a deacon or other person and responded to by the congregation with a phrase such as *"Kyrie eleison" (Lord, have mercy) or "Ora pro nobis" (Pray for us); also a procession at which such a prayer is sung or recited. When sung, all invocations in the series employ the same syllabic melody.

Literes Carrión, Antonio (b. Artá, Majorca, 18 June 1673?; d. Madrid, 18 Jan. 1747). Composer. Court musician in Madrid from 1688. Composed dramatic works (*Accis y Galatea,* 1708); an oratorio based on St. Vicente's life (1720, lost); Masses and vespers music; sacred and secular cantatas.

Lithophone. A stone or set of stones that produces musical sounds on being struck. The stones are either laid on a frame or hung from cords. They are tuned by carving. See, e.g., *Ch'ing.*

Litolff, Henry Charles (b. London, 6 Feb. or 7 Aug. 1818; d. Bois-Colombes, near Paris, 5 or 6 Aug. 1891). Composer and pianist. Pupil of Moscheles. Appeared as pianist and conductor throughout Europe. From 1851, ran a music publishing firm in Brunswick; from 1855, court Kapellmeister, Saxe-Coburg-Gotha. Settled in Paris 1858. Composed operas, oratorios, orchestral and piano pieces; best known for his 5 piano concertos (Concertos Symphoniques).

Little Hours. See Office, Divine.

Little Richard [Penniman, Richard] (b. Macon, Ga., 25 Dec. 1935). Rock-and-roll singer, songwriter, and pianist. A central figure in the mid-1950s rock-and-roll movement; his recordings showcased a virtuosic vocal style ("Tutti Frutti," 1956; "Good Golly, Miss Molly," 1958). Also a Seventh-Day Adventist minister; recorded gospel and soul music.

Little Russian Symphony. See *Ukrainian* Symphony.

Little Walter [Jacobs, Marion Walter] (b. Marksville, La., 1 May 1930; d. Chicago, 15 Feb. 1968). Blues harmonica player. Joined Muddy Waters's band in Chicago, 1948–56; developed a rough amplified harmonica style. Recordings include "Long Distance Call" (1951) and "Juke" (1952).

Liturgical books. Books used for the performance of the liturgies or services of the Christian rites. The number and makeup of such books not only vary among rites, but within rites have changed considerably with time.

In the Roman Catholic rite, the liturgy antedating the Second Vatican Council (1962–65) was contained in seven fundamental books: the missal *(missale)*, containing all of the texts for the Mass, including those of the chants, but without music; the *gradual *(graduale)*, containing the chants for the Mass; the breviary *(breviarium)*, with the texts for the Office; the *antiphoner *(antiphonale, antiphonarium)*, with the chants for the Office (except for Matins, celebrated for the most part only in monastic communities); the martyrology *(martirologium)*, with the lives of the saints, read as part of the Office, presented in the order of the liturgical calendar; the pontifical *(pontificale)*, containing the ceremonies performed by a bishop, such as confirmation, ordination, and the consecration of a church; and the *rituale*, containing ceremonies performed by a priest in the administration of sacraments such as baptism, marriage, and extreme unction. Other modern books excerpted or derived from one or more of these include the *Kyriale*, with the chants of the Ordinary;

the *vesperale*, containing Vespers and sometimes Compline; and the *Liber usualis*, a modern creation combining elements of the missal, gradual, breviary, and antiphoner and thus providing both text and music for both Mass and Office (including Matins in a few cases) for the most important feasts (though with important omissions, such as the weekdays in Lent and the Ember Days). The *Liber responsorialis* includes chants, particularly responsories, for Matins and the *Processionale monasticum* chants for processions before Mass, both for use in monastic communities. In the Middle Ages, there were many more kinds of liturgical books, most arranged according to the liturgical calendar.

The Book of Common Prayer, first issued under Edward VI in 1549 (revised significantly in 1552 and 1662), is the basic Anglican liturgical text and contains the daily Offices of Morning and Evening Prayer, the order of Communion, other rites (Baptism, Matrimony, Burial), the Psalter, and the ordinal. *The Alternative Service Book 1980,* with a new liturgical psalter, sets forth services authorized for use in conjunction with the *Book of Common Prayer;* it is designed to supplement, not to supersede, the 1662 revision. The Protestant Episcopal Church in the U.S. issued its own *Book of Common Prayer* in 1789 (revised 1892, 1928, and 1979). Although the Anglican Church has never had an official hymnal, *Hymns: Ancient and Modern* (1861, rev. 1950), *The English Hymnal* (1906, rev. 1933), *Songs of Praise* (1925, rev. 1931), and *The Anglican Hymn Book* (1965) have been most widely used. *The Hymnal 1940* (rev. ed., 1976) has been authorized for use by the American Episcopal communions.

Liturgical drama. Medieval church drama created for or influenced by the liturgy. This vast repertory from the 10th to the 16th centuries is distinguished from spoken dramas such as the mystery plays, in which music was used only occasionally. Liturgical dramas were sung, mostly in Latin, and often borrowed texts, music, and forms of organization from the liturgy itself. The great majority of liturgical dramas were written for Easter or Christmas.

The first known Easter play or *Visitatio sepulchri*, from ca. 970, consists of the well-known "Quem quaeritis" dialogue between the women coming to the tomb of Jesus and the guarding angel.

Liturgy. The formally constituted services of the various rites of the Christian church; also the particular formal arrangement of any such service. In the West, the term is usually applied to all such services. In the Eastern Orthodox Church, the Divine Liturgy is specifically the analogue of the Mass of the Western rites. Some fundamental features are shared among the rites of both East and West, and some remained a part of the worship of non-Roman churches after the Reformation.

The principal services of the Roman Catholic Church are the *Mass or Holy Eucharist, at the heart of which is the reenactment of the Last Supper, and the Divine *Office, which consists of a series of services performed throughout the day. Although the general outline of these services, including the types of readings, prayers, and chants of which they consist, is largely constant, the specific content of services changes in the course of the liturgical year.

Two cycles of observances or feasts make up the calendar of the liturgical year. The first of these, called the Proper of the Time, the *Temporale,* or the feasts of the Lord, commemorates primarily events in the life of Christ and thus includes, for example, Christmas (the Nativity, 25 December) and Easter (the Resurrection, celebrated on the Sunday following the first full moon after the vernal equinox and thus between 22 March and 25 April). Feasts such as Easter that do not occur on the same date every year are said to be "movable" feasts. The second cycle of feasts, which overlaps the first, is the Proper of the Saints or the *Sanctorale.* These feasts occur on fixed dates and commemorate individual saints and, in some cases, particular events in their lives, e.g., the Nativity of John the Baptist (24 June) and the Assumption of the Blessed Virgin Mary (15 August).

In both Mass and Office, the texts of certain items of the liturgy remain the same for all feasts, though different melodies may be employed for those that are sung. These items make up the *Ordinary. Items that change from feast to feast make up the *Proper. Within the *Sanctorale,* however, some feasts, particularly those of lesser rank, have not been provided with their own complete Propers. For these saints, Propers are drawn from those that have been provided for certain classes of saints (martyrs, confessors, virgins, etc.). These Propers make up the Common of the Saints.

Liturgy of the Hours. See Office, Divine.

Lituus [Lat.]. (1) A trumpet of the ancient Etruscans and Romans, 75–160 cm. long, with its bell bent back in the shape of a J. See ill. under Instrument. (2) In the Renaissance, *cornett or *crumhorn. (3) In the 18th century, a brass instrument. The two *litui* requested by Bach in Cantata no. 118 may have been tenor trumpets.

Liuto [It.]. Lute.

Livret [Fr.]. Libretto.

Lloyd Webber, Andrew (b. London, 22 Mar. 1948). Composer. Studied at the Royal College of Music. Best known for musicals, including *Joseph and the Amazing Technicolor Dreamcoat* (lyrics by Tim Rice, 1967); *Jesus Christ Superstar* ("rock opera," Rice, 1970); *Evita* (Rice, 1976; stage version, 1978); *Cats* (T. S. Eliot, 1981); *Phantom of the Opera* (R. Stilgoe and C. Hart, 1986); *Sunset Boulevard* (1993). Other works include Requiem (1985); *Variations on a Theme of Paganini,* orchestra (1986).

Lobgesang [Ger.]. (1) Hymn of praise. (2) Mendelssohn's name for his symphony-cantata op. 2 (1840) in B♭ major, the last movement of which adds soloists, chorus, and organ to the orchestra in setting a Biblical text. Although there is no chronological justification, the work is also known as his Second Symphony.

Locatelli, Pietro Antonio (b. Bergamo, 3 Sept. 1695; d. Amsterdam, 30 Mar. 1764). Composer and violinist. Studied in Rome. *Virtuoso da camera* at Mantua from 1725; also performed in Venice, Berlin, and Kassel. Settled in Amsterdam 1729. Composed mainly sonatas and concertos; his caprices for solo violin in *L'arte del violino* (1733) at one time earned him the title "Paganini of the 18th century."

Locke, Matthew (b. Exeter, 1621–22; d. London, Aug. 1677). Composer. Traveled to the Netherlands in the 1640s. Associate of Playford, H. Lawes, Simpson, and Purcell. Composer to Charles II from 1661; organist to the queen from 1662. Composed dramatic music including *Cupid and Death* (with Christopher Gibbons, 1653); anthems, motets, and services; songs and dance music.

Lockwood, Normand (b. New York, 19 Mar. 1906). Composer. Pupil of Respighi and Boulanger. Taught at Oberlin (1932–43), Columbia and Union Theological Seminary (1945–53), the Univ. of Denver (1961–75), and elsewhere. Works include 5 operas; 2 symphonies, concertos for organ and brass, and other orchestral music; 7 string quartets and other instrumental music; many choral (*A Child's Christmas in Wales,* children's voices and piano, 1984) and solo vocal works.

Loco [It., place, abbr. *loc.*]. An instruction to return to the normal register or way of playing after an instruction to play, e.g., an octave higher or lower; also *al loco.*

Loeffler, Charles Martin (b. Mulhouse, Alsace, 30 Jan. 1861; d. Medfield, Mass., 19 May 1935). Composer. Pupil of Joachim, Massart, Guiraud, and H. Léonard. Emigrated to the U.S. 1881; 1882–1903, assistant concertmaster, Boston Symphony, also appearing as soloist. Works include a string quartet and other chamber music; orchestral music (*Nights in the Ukraine,* with solo violin, 1891; *La mort de Tintagiles,* 1897–1900, with 2 violas d'amore, later rev. for 1; *A Pagan Poem,* 1906); choral and solo vocal works.

Loeillet, Jean-Baptiste [John] (bapt. Ghent, 18 Nov. 1680; d. London, 19 July 1730). Composer. Brother of Jacques Loeillet (1685–1748). Moved to London around 1705; played oboe and flute in the Queen's Theatre orchestra; built a reputation as a harpsichord player and teacher. Composed suites of lessons for harpsichord and both trio and solo sonatas for flute, recorder, oboe, and violin.

Loesser, Frank (b. New York, 29 June 1910; d. there, 26 July 1969). Popular songwriter, lyricist, and librettist. From 1936 worked in Hollywood, writing lyrics for films with Hoagy Carmichael, Burton Lane, and Jimmy McHugh. After World War II, produced musicals on Broadway for which he wrote score, lyrics, and book, including *Where's Charley?* (1948), *Guys and Dolls* (1950), *Most Happy Fella* (1956), and *How To Succeed in Business without Really Trying* (1961), which won a Pulitzer Prize in drama.

Loewe, (Johann) Carl (Gottfried) (b. Löbejün, near Halle, 30 Nov. 1796; d. Kiel, 20 Apr. 1869). Composer. Pupil of Türk. From 1820, cantor and organist at St. Jacobus, Stettin; city music director from 1821. Toured widely as a singer (baritone). Composed 6 operas; ca. 16 oratorios; cantatas, part songs; chamber works; piano sonatas, piano tone poems; best known for ballads and other lieder, including *Erlkönig* (1818).

Loewe, Frederick (b. Berlin, 10 June 1901; d. Palm Springs, Calif., 14 Feb. 1988). Popular composer. Studied in Berlin; emigrated to the U.S. 1924. Composed at first in Viennese style. From 1947 wrote American musicals in collaboration with Alan Jay Lerner, including *Brigadoon* (1947, "Almost Like Being in Love"), *Paint Your Wagon* (1951, "They Call the Wind Maria"), *My Fair Lady* (1956, "Rain in Spain," "I Could Have Danced All Night," "On the Street Where You Live"), and *Camelot* (1960), and the film *Gigi* (1958).

Logothetis, Anestis (b. Pyrgos, Greece, 27 Oct. 1921). Composer. Pupil of Uhl. Before 1960 employed serial methods. Has composed musical plays and other stage music (*5 Porträte der Liebe*, ballet, 1960; *Das Urteil des Paris in Paris*, actor and piano, 1968, both in graphic notation); orchestral music; chamber works; piano pieces; some vocal music; tape pieces; many works for unspecified instrument(s) in graphic notation (*Reversible Bi-Junction*, 1965).

Logroscino, Nicola (bapt. Bitonto, 22 Oct. 1698; d. Palermo, after 1765). Composer. Studied in Naples; later taught at the Ospedale dei figliuoli dispersi, Palermo. An important figure in Neapolitan comic opera. Composed serious (*Il Quinto Fabio*, Rome,

1738) and comic operas (*Il governatore*, 1747); a small amount of church music.

Lohengrin. Opera in three acts by Wagner (to his own libretto, based on Wolfram von Eschenbach and medieval legends), produced in Weimar in 1850. Setting: Antwerp in the early 10th century.

Lolli, Antonio (b. Bergamo, ca. 1725; d. Palermo, 10 Aug. 1802). Violinist and composer. Solo violinist at the Württenburg court, Stuttgart, 1758–74. Concertized throughout Europe. Served Catherine the Great until 1783; may have served the King of Naples during the 1790s. Composed violin concertos and sonatas.

Lombard rhythm. Reversed dotting; a succession of dotted figures whose short notes come on the beat, especially characteristic of Italian music in the style of the 1740s. It also existed in Scottish music [see Strathspey] by this time, termed by John Burney the "Scots catch." It was a favorite rhythm in England in the second half of the 17th century.

Lombard style. A style mentioned with disfavor by certain 18th-century writers on music. It may include but is not limited to passages incorporating *Lombard rhythm.

London [Burnstein], **George** (b. Montreal, 30 May 1920; d. Armonk, N.Y., 24 Mar. 1985). Bass-baritone. Debut at the Hollywood Bowl as Dr. Grenvil *(La traviata)*, 1941. In 1947, formed the Bel Canto Trio with Mario Lanza and Frances Yeend. Roles included Amonastro *(Aida)*, Mozart's Figaro, Amfortas, and Boris Godunov. Sang at the Metropolitan Opera, 1951–66. Left the stage in 1967 when his vocal cords became partially paralyzed. Artistic director of the Kennedy Center in Washington, D.C., 1968–71; directed the Opera Society of Washington, D.C., 1975–80.

London Symphony. (1) Popular name for Haydn's Symphony no. 104 in D major Hob. I:104 (1795); also known as the *Salomon* Symphony [see Salomon Symphonies]. (2) Ralph Vaughan Williams's Symphony no. 2, composed in 1912–13 (rev. 1920, 1933). Although the work contains musical evocations of the Westminster chimes and other London sounds, it has no stated program.

Longa [Lat.], **long.** See Mensural notation.

Long-necked lute. Any of a family of plucked stringed instruments in which the length of the neck is substantially greater than the length of the body. A typical example has a very narrow neck, a wooden body shaped like a halved pear, and two to four strings or courses of strings. Fretted and unfretted models are both common. The pictorial record of long-necked lutes extends back to the 3rd millennium B.C.E. Today they are distributed most heavily in Eastern Europe and Asia. Examples include the *balalaika, *colascione, *dömbra, *saz, *shamisen, *sitār, *tanbur, and tār. See also Lute.

Longy, (Gustave-) Georges (-Leopold) (b. Abbeville, 28 Aug. 1868; d. Moreuil, France, 29 Mar. 1930). Oboist, conductor, and educator. Studied at the Paris Conservatory. First oboist of the Boston Symphony, 1898–1925. In Boston, founded the Longy Club to give concerts of chamber music in 1900, and the Longy School of Music (Cambridge) in 1911. Conducted the Boston Orchestral Club, the MacDowell Club, and the Cecilia Society chorus.

Lontano [It.]. Distant.

Loomis, Harvey Worthington (b. Brooklyn, 5 Feb. 1865; d. Boston, 25 Dec. 1930). Composer. Pupil of Dvořák. Worked with Native American melodies. Composed pantomimes (*Her Revenge*, libretto by E. S. Belknap); 4 comic operas; incidental music; a violin sonata; piano works (*Lyrics of the Red Man; Norland Epic);* and songs.

Lopatnikoff, Nicolai (Lvovich) (b. Reval, Estonia, 16 Mar. 1903; d. Pittsburgh, 7 Oct. 1976). Composer and pianist. Pupil of Toch. In 1939, moved to the U.S.; taught at Hartt College and Westchester Conservatory 1939–45; at the Carnegie Institute of Technology 1945–69. Works include an opera and a ballet; 4 symphonies, 2 piano concertos, and other orchestral music; chamber music; 2 pieces for mechanical piano.

Lopes-Graça, Fernando (b. Tomar, Portugal, 17 Dec. 1906). Composer, musicologist, and pianist. Studied in Lisbon and with Koechlin. Taught at the Academia de amadores de música, Lisbon 1941–54. Worked with folk materials. Compositions include stage works (*La fièvre du temps*, revue-ballet, 1938; *Dançares*, choreographic suite, 1984), orchestral music (2 piano concertos; *3 danças portuguesas*, 1941; *Sinfonia*, 1944; *Concerto da camera*, with cello obbligato, 1967; *Homenagem a Haydn*, 1980); string quartets and other chamber music; piano music (6 sonatas; 24 preludes); guitar music; vocal music, including settings of major Portuguese poets. Published numerous books on music.

López Capillas, Francisco (b. Andalusia?, ca. 1615; d. Mexico City, 18 Jan. or 7 Feb. 1673). Composer. Organist at Puebla (Mexico) Cathedral from 1641; organist and *maestro de capilla*, Mexico City Cathedral, from 1654. Works include Masses (several based on his own compositions as well as on those of composers such as Janequin and Palestrina), motets, Magnificats, and a St. Matthew Passion.

López Cobos, Jesús (b. Toro, 25 Feb. 1940). Conductor. Studied in Madrid and Vienna. Debut leading the Prague Symphony, 1969. Conducted opera at La Fenice, Venice; general music director of the Deutsche Oper in East Berlin, 1981–90. Director of the Spanish National Orchestra, 1984–89, of the Cincinnati Orchestra, 1986–90, of the Lausanne Chamber Orchestra from 1990.

Lord's Prayer. See *Pater noster.*

Lorenzani, Paolo (b. Rome, 1640; d. there, 28 Nov. 1713). Composer. *Maestro di cappella* at the Seminario romano from 1675. Lived in Paris 1678–94; thereafter maestro at the Cappella Giulia. Works include motets and Psalms; a Mass and Magnificat; the pastorale *Nicandro e Fileno* (1681); various airs and cantatas; and the opera *Orontée* (1688).

Lorenzo Fernândez, Oscar (b. Rio de Janeiro, 4 Nov. 1897; d. there, 27 Aug. 1948). Composer. Studied and later taught at the National Music Institute. Founded and directed the Brazilian Conservatory from 1936. Composed orchestral works (*Suite sinfônica sôbre 3 temas populares brasileiros*, 1925; the Amerindian tone poem *Imbapara*, 1928; 2 symphonies; violin and piano concertos; *Reisado do pastoreio*, 1930); the opera *Malazarte* (1931–33); chamber music, piano works, and songs.

Loriod, Yvonne (b. Houilles, Seine-et-Oise, 20 Jan. 1924). Pianist. Studied at the Paris Conservatory, where she taught from 1967. Married her composition professor, Olivier Messiaen; inspired and premiered many solo and concerted piano works by him. Also introduced works of Boulez, Barraqué, and Jolivet; gave first French performances of concertos by Bartók and Schoenberg.

Lortzing, (Gustav) Albert (b. Berlin, 23 Oct. 1801; d. there, 21 Jan. 1851). Composer. Conducted at theaters in Leipzig, Vienna, and Berlin. Composed comic operas including *Die beiden Schützen* (Leipzig, 1837), *Zar und Zimmermann* (Leipzig, 22 Dec. 1837), *Der Waffenschmied* (Vienna, 1846); the Romantic opera *Undine* (Magdeburg, 1845); *Rolands Knappen* ("magic opera," Leipzig, 1849). Also an oratorio, a few occasional pieces, many part songs for male or mixed voices.

Los Angeles, Victoria de. See De los Angeles, Victoria.

Lotti, Antonio (b. Venice?, ca. 1667; d. there, 5 Jan. 1740). Composer. Studied with Legrenzi. Sang at St. Mark's, from 1689; organist from 1692; *maestro di cappella* from 1736. Active at the Ospedale degli incurabili until 1726. Spent 1717–19 in Dresden. Composed sacred music; stage works (*Alessandro Severo*, 1716); many secular cantatas; sinfonias and solo sonatas. Galuppi and Marcello were among his pupils.

Loudness. The perceived characteristic of a sound that is a function of its intensity, i.e., of the physical energy that the sounding body transmits to the surrounding medium. The term volume is most often used synonymously. The human ear is not equally sensitive to changes in intensity throughout the range of audible frequencies, it being least sensitive at high and low extremes of frequency. This phenomenon is sometimes called the Fletcher-Munson effect, and some phonograph amplifiers are equipped with a "loudness" control (in addition to a "volume" control) that attempts to compensate for it by permitting some control of relative intensities of various ranges of frequencies independent of the intensity (or volume) with which the sound as a whole is reproduced.

Louise. Opera ("musical novel") in four acts by Gustave Charpentier (to his own libretto), produced in Paris in 1900. The work embodies a then novel naturalism. Setting: Paris, ca. 1900.

Lourd [Fr.]. Heavy.

Loure [Fr.]. (1) In the late Baroque period, a slow and majestic French *gigue, with heavy accents (François Couperin marked one *pesament*). It is usually in 6/4 meter, with upbeats, dotted figures, syncopations, and hemiolas, e.g.:

It may have contrapuntal texture and is found in orchestral and harpsichord *suites (Bach, Telemann). (2) In the 16th and 17th centuries, a type of bagpipe with no proven connection to the dance.

Louré [Fr.]. See Bowing (6).

Lourer [Fr.]. See *Notes inégales.*

Lourié, Arthur Vincent (b. St. Petersburg, 14 May 1892; d. Princeton, N.J., 12 Oct. 1966). Composer. Studied in St. Petersburg; appointed music commissar, 1918. In 1921, moved to Berlin; 1924, to Paris; 1941, settled in the U.S. In early works used serial techniques; later employed free atonality and sometimes quarter tones. Works include an opera (*Blackamoor of Peter the Great,* 1961) and an opera-ballet; 2 symphonies and other orchestral music; 3 string quartets and other chamber music; piano music; *Sonata liturgica* (alto voices and chamber orchestra) and vocal music.

Love for Three Oranges, The [Russ. *Lyubov k tryom apelsinam*]. Opera in a prologue and four acts by Prokofiev (libretto by the composer, after Carlo Gozzi's fable), produced in Chicago in French in 1921; produced in Leningrad in 1926. Setting: fairy tale. A suite, a march, and a scherzo from the opera were made into separate works by Prokofiev.

Low Mass. In the Roman Catholic Church, a simplified form of the *Mass, without singing, said by a single celebrant, sometimes in private.

Lowry, Robert (b. Philadelphia, 12 Mar. 1826; d. Plainfield, N.J., 25 Nov. 1899). Hymn writer and Baptist minister. Composed (usually both words and music) many hymns and gospel songs, including "Shall We Gather at the River?" (1865), "I Need Thee Every Hour" (1872, words by Annie S. Hawkes), "Low in the Grave He Lay" (1875); also compiled collections.

Lualdi, Adriano (b. Larino, Campobasso, 22 Mar. 1885; d. Milan, 8 Jan. 1971). Composer, conductor, and writer on music. Elected to Parliament, 1929. In the 1930s, led orchestras in South America, Germany, the U.S.S.R., and Italy. Directed the conservatories in Naples (1936–44) and Florence (1947–56). Composed *Euridikes Diatheke: Il Testamento di Euridice* (1963) and other operas and incidental music; works for chorus and orchestra; symphonic poems and other orchestral music; some instrumental chamber music; choral pieces and songs. His 17 books on music include *Viaggio musicale in Italia* (1927).

Lübeck, Vincent (b. Paddingbüttel, Land Wursten, Sept. 1654; d. Hamburg, 9 Feb. 1740). Organist and composer. Organist at SS. Cosmos and Damian, Stade, from 1675; at St. Nicolai, Hamburg, from 1702. Composed preludes and fugues for organ; chorale preludes; keyboard dances; sacred vocal works.

Lucia di Lammermoor. Opera in three acts by Donizetti (libretto by Salvatore Cammarano, after Sir Walter Scott's novel *The Bride of Lammermoor*), produced in Naples in 1835. Setting: Scotland at the end of the 17th century.

Lucier, Alvin (Augustus, Jr.) (b. Nashua, N.H., 14 May 1931). Composer. Pupil of Berger, Fine, Shapero, Copland, Foss, and Q. Porter. From 1963 taught at Brandeis; from 1969, at Wesleyan Univ. Music director of the Viola Farber Dance Company 1972–77. Works include dance scores; *Music for Solo Performer* (amplified brain waves and percussion, 1965); *Vespers* (performers and echo-location devices, 1967); *Music on a Long Thin Wire* (electronic monochord and audio oscillators, 1977); *Intervals* (voices and sound-sensitive lights, 1983); *Navigations* (string quartet, 1991); *Amplifier and Reflector I* (open umbrella, ticking clock, glass oven dish, 1991); a few orchestral pieces; incidental music, film and television scores.

Ludford, Nicholas (b. ca. 1485; d. Westminster?, in or after 1557). Composer. Worked at the Church of St. Stephens, Westminster, until 1547. Composed Masses, including 7 3-voiced *alternatim* Lady Masses; a Magnificat; motets.

Ludus tonalis [Lat., Play of Tonalities]. A work for piano composed by Hindemith in 1942, consisting of 12 fugues in different keys, linked by 11 modulating interludes, and preceded by a prelude in C that serves, in retrograde inversion, as a postlude. The fugues use many learned contrapuntal devices and are arranged according to Hindemith's principle of decreasing tonal relationship to the tonic of C: C, G, F, A, E, E♭, A♭, D, B♭, D♭, B♮, F♯.

Ludwig, Christa (b. Berlin, 16 Mar. 1928). Mezzo-soprano. Debut as Orlovsky *(Fledermaus),* Frankfurt, 1946. Joined the Vienna Staatsoper, 1955; sang at the Metropolitan Opera, Bayreuth, and Covent Garden. Roles included Mozart's Cherubino, Bizet's Carmen, Strauss's Marschallin, Beethoven's Leonore, Monteverdi's Octavia, Wagner's Kundry, Verdi's Lady Macbeth, and contemporary roles. Sought after as a singer of Mahler. Gave a series of farewell recitals in 1993–94.

Luening, Otto (Clarence) (b. Milwaukee, 15 June 1900; d. New York, 2 Sept. 1996). Composer, conductor, and flutist. Pupil of Jarnach and Busoni. Taught at Bennington College (1934–44); Barnard College (1944–64); Columbia (1944–70); and the Juilliard School (1971–73). Cofounded the American Music Center and the Columbia–Princeton Electronic Music Center. Early works were polytonal and atonal; 1928, formulated a theory of "acoustic harmony" concerned with the manipulation of overtones. Pioneered electronic music, collaborating with Ussachevsky on *Rhapsodic Variations* for orchestra and tape (1953–54) and on several other electronic pieces. Other works include *Evangeline* (after Longfellow, 1930–32; rev., 1947–48) and other stage works; *Symphonic Fantasia I–IX* (1924–88) and other orchestral music; string quartets, suites for solo flute, and much other chamber music; piano music; choral music and songs; and electronic music (*Fantasy in Space,* 1952). His students included Carlos, Chou Wen-chung, Davidovsky, and Wuorinen.

Luftpause [Ger.]. Breathing *pause.

Lugubre [Fr., It.]. Mournful.

Luigini, Alexandre (Clément Léon Joseph) (b. Lyons, 9 Mar. 1850; d. Paris, 29 July 1906). Composer. Studied at the Paris Conservatory. From 1877 conductor, Grand Théâtre, Lyons; teacher at the Lyons Conservatory. From 1897, conductor, Opéra-comique, Paris. Best known for ballets (*Ballet égyptien,* Lyons, 1875); also 3 comic operas; *Carnaval*

turc, symphonic poem, op. 51; instrumental pieces; songs.

Lullaby [Fr. *berceuse;* Ger. *Wiegenlied, Schlummerlied;* It. *ninna nanna;* Sp. *canción de cuna*]. A cradle song, usually with gentle and regular rhythm. A number of instrumental works of the 19th and early 20th centuries evoke such songs. See *Berceuse.*

Lully, Jean-Baptiste [Giovanni Battista Lulli] (b. Florence, bapt. 29 Nov. 1632; d. Paris, 22 Mar. 1687). Composer. Pupil of Gigault; associate of Michel Lambert. From 1652, active at the French court as a dancer and composer; from 1657 was responsible for most of the *ballets de cour;* directed the *Vingt-quatre violons du roi* and the 16-member "petits violons." Held the posts of *surintendant de musique et compositeur de la musique de chambre* (from 1661), *maître de la musique de la famille royale* (from 1662), and *secrétaire du Roi* (from 1681). Worked with Molière on machine plays and *comédies-ballets,* including *Le bourgeois gentilhomme* (1670). In 1672, Lully gained the sole privilege of presenting operas and formed the Académie royale de musique, which later took over the Palais Royal Theater. With the librettist Quinault and, initially, the machinist Vigarini, produced 13 *tragédies lyriques,* including *Cadmus et Hermione* (1673), *Alceste* (1674), *Thésée* (1675), *Atys* (1676), *Bellérophon* (1679), *Phaéton* (1683), *Amadis* (1684), *Roland* (1685), and *Armide* (1686); also some 30 ballets and *intermèdes,* including *Ballet des muses* (1666) and *Le triomphe de l'amour* (1681); incidental music; motets; instrumental marches and dances; and airs.

Lulu. Opera in three acts by Alban Berg (to his own libretto, after Frank Wedekind's plays *Erdgeist* and *Die Büchse der Pandora*). Setting: Germany, France, and England before World War I. At the time of Berg's death in 1935, acts 1 and 2 were entirely complete, and act 3 was complete in short score and partly orchestrated. The first production, in Zürich in 1937, included the first two acts plus two sections from act 3 (orchestrated by Berg for the *Symphonische Stücke aus der Oper "Lulu"*) that were used simply to accompany stage action. The composer's widow subsequently withheld act 3, and only after her death in 1976 did performance of the complete work become possible. The first complete production, based on Berg's materials for the entire work as realized by Friedrich Cerha, was given in Paris in 1979.

Lunetta, Stanley (b. Sacramento, 5 June 1937). Composer and percussionist. Pupil of Tudor, Cage, and Stockhausen. Many of his works incorporate slides, dance, theater, electronic devices, and sculpture (*The Unseen Force,* 1976); built several sound sculptures activated by changes in the environment. Compositions include *Many Things* (orchestra, 1966); *A Day in the Life of the Moosack Machines* (1972).

Lungo [It.]. Long; *lunga pausa,* prolonged pause or rest.

Lupi, Johannes [Leleu, Jehan] (b. ca. 1506; d. Cambrai, 20 Dec. 1539). Composer. Choirboy at Cambrai; from 1526 vicar, then master of the choirboys there. Composed Masses, motets, and chansons.

Lupo, Thomas (d. London, Jan. 1628). Composer. From an Italian family of musicians active at the English court from 1540. Thomas was at court from 1591; from 1621 "composer to the violins," later also "composer to the lutes and voices." Composed instrumental music, especially fantasias and dances; a few sacred and secular vocal pieces.

Lur [Dan.]. (1) A prehistoric bronze trumpet of Scandinavia, 1.5 to 2.5 m. long and shaped like a loose helix with a flat, ornamented disk for a bell. More than 40 specimens, dated between 1100 and 600 B.C.E., have been excavated, often in pairs, one a left spiral, the other a right spiral. There is no evidence concerning its use. See ill. under Brass instruments. (2) In Scandinavia and the Baltic region, a straight wooden trumpet up to 2 m. long and very similar to the *alphorn.

Lusingando [It.]. Flattering, coaxing.

Lustig [Ger.]. Merry, joyous.

Lustige Witwe, Die [Ger., The Merry Widow]. Operetta in three acts by Franz Lehár (libretto by Viktor Léon and Leo Stein, after Henri Meilhac's comedy *L'attaché d'ambassade*), produced in Vienna in 1905. Setting: Paris, early in the 20th century.

Lustigen Weiber von Windsor, Die [Ger., The Merry Wives of Windsor]. Opera in three acts by Otto Nicolai (libretto by S. H. Mosenthal, after Shakespeare's comedy), produced in Berlin in 1849. Setting: Windsor in the 15th century.

Lute [fr. Ar. *al 'ūd;* Fr. *luth;* Ger. *Laute;* It. *lauto, liuto, leuto;* Sp. *laúd*]. (1) A European plucked-string instrument with an oblong, rounded body, a flat soundboard featuring a rosette, and a short, fretted neck with nearly perpendicular pegbox [see ill.]. (2) In Sachs-Hornbostel terminology [see Instrument], a stringed instrument with a body and neck.

The lute's predecessors are the *pandoura* and *'ūd*. Moors and Saracens brought the 'ūd to Spain and Sicily, where it was later adopted by European musicians and taken north. During the Renaissance, the lute became the dominant musical instrument in Europe and England. It was gradually superseded in

popularity by the *theorbo, the violin, and the harpsichord in the 17th century, though it was cultivated in France until the early 18th century, in Italy until ca. 1750, and in Germany and Austria until the time of Mozart. Almost all its music after 1500 was written in *tablature.

The lute had four or five courses (each with one or two strings) in the 15th century; six became standard after 1500. The top string was usually single. The paired strings of the next two to four courses were tuned in unison, the lower ones in octaves, though national practice and string-making technology were responsible for much variation. Around 1580, more bass courses began to be added, and by 1640, 11 courses were the norm in France and Germany, 13 or 14 in Italy [see Archlute]. Thirteen courses became common in Germany by ca. 1720. In the Renaissance, the standard tuning was *vieil ton* (fourths between most courses but a third between the middle two), and the instrument was built in seven sizes, from the small octave lute (highest string or chanterelle at d'') to the contrabass lute (chanterelle at g). Italy retained the old tuning through the Baroque, but experiments during the early 17th century in France [see *Accords nouveaux*] led to the tuning C D E F G A d f a d' f', which prevailed in France and Germany through the 18th century.

Lute harpsichord [Fr. *clavecin-luth;* Ger. *Lautenclavicymbel, Lautenwerk, Lautenklavier*]. A harpsichord with gut strings (occasionally supplemented by a 4' choir of metal strings) intended to imitate the sound of the lute rather than the harp, as in the case of the *arpicordo. The lute harpsichord was primarily cultivated in Germany during the lifetime of J. S. Bach, whose estate included two of them. No historical example has survived.

Lute stop. On the harpsichord, a rank of jacks that plucks one choir of strings at the extreme end, thus producing a more nasal timbre.

Luth [Fr.]. Lute.

Lutherie [Fr.]. Lute making; by extension, the making and repair of any stringed instruments, especially those of the violin family.

Luthier [Fr.]. A lute maker; one who makes and repairs stringed instruments, especially those of the violin family.

Lutosławski, Witold (b. Warsaw, 25 Jan. 1913; d. Warsaw, 7 Feb. 1994). Composer. Studied at the Warsaw Conservatory. From the 1940s, composed for Polish Radio. Worked with twelve-tone and aleatory techniques and folk material. Orchestral works include 4 symphonies; Symphonic Variations (1938); *Mała suita* [Little Suite] (1951); Concerto for Orchestra (1954); *Funeral Music,* strings (1958); *Gry*

1. Chitarrone.   2. Mandolin.   3. Orpharion.   4. Descant lute.   5. Flat-back mandolin.   6. Bandora.
7. Baroque lute.   8. Colascione.

weneckie [Venetian Games], chamber orchestra (1961); *Preludes and Fugue,* strings (1972); concertos for piano and cello. Vocal works: *Tryptyk śląski* [Silesian Triptych], soprano, orchestra (1951); *20 Polish Christmas Carols,* voice, piano (1946); children's songs. Chamber music: *Preludia taneczne* [Dance Preludes], clarinet, piano (1954); String Quartet (1964); *Sacher Variation,* cello (1975). For piano: *Variations on a Theme of Paganini,* 2 pianos (1941); *Melodie ludowe* [Folk Melodies] (1945).

Luttuoso, luttuosamente [It.]. Mournful.

Lutyens, (Agnes) Elisabeth (b. London, 6 July 1906; d. there, 14 Apr. 1983). Composer. Studied in Paris and with Darke. Used serial techniques. Works include operas (*The Numbered,* 1965–67; *Time Off?—Not a Ghost of a Chance!* 1967–68; *Isis and Osiris,* 1969–70); music for voices and instruments ("O Saisons! O Châteaux!" 1946; *Quincunx,* 1959–60; *And Suddenly It's Evening,* 1966; *Essence of Our Happinesses,* 1968); orchestral music (Chamber Concerto no. 1 for nine instruments, 1939–40; *Music for Orchestra I-IV,* 1954–81); 13 string quartets and much other chamber music; piano pieces; organ pieces; guitar pieces; music for film and radio.

Luzzaschi, Luzzasco (b. Ferrara, 1545?; d. there, 10 Sept. 1607). Composer. Pupil of Rore. Served at the Este court, Ferrara, from 1561; organist at the Cathedral. Composed madrigals, some with keyboard accompaniment, written for virtuoso female singers at court; much keyboard music.

L'vov [Lvoff], **Aleksey Fyodorovich** (b. Reval [now Tallinn], Estonia, 5 June 1798; d. near Korno [now Kaunas], Lithuania, 28 Dec. 1870). Composer and violinist. Director of the imperial court chapel choir 1837–61. Composed *Bozhe, tsarya khrani* [God Save the Tsar] (1833), the Russian national anthem until 1917; also several operas; violin music; sacred music; secular songs.

Lyadov [Liadov], **Anatol** [Anatoly] **Konstantinovich** (b. St. Petersburg, 11 May 1855; d. Polïnovka, Novgorod district, 28 Aug. 1914). Composer. Pupil of his father and of Rimsky-Korsakov. From 1878 taught at the St. Petersburg Conservatory; among his students were Prokofiev, Asafiev, and Myaskovsky. Associated with the Moguchaya Kuchka ("The Five"). Composed orchestral music (*Baba-Yaga,* 1891?–1904; The *Enchanted Lake,* 1909; *Kikimora,* 1909); preludes, etudes, intermezzi, and miniatures for piano (*A Musical Snuffbox,* 1893); arrangements of Russian folk songs.

Lyapunov, Sergey (Mikhaylovich) (b. Yaroslavl, Russia, 30 Nov. 1859; d. Paris, 8 Nov. 1924). Pianist, composer, and conductor. Pupil of Tchaikovsky, Taneyev, and Balakirev. Taught at the St. Petersburg

Conservatory 1910–17; from 1923 ran a music school in Paris. Best known for piano compositions, including *12 études d'exécution transcendante* (1900–1905).

Lyatoshinsky, Boris (Nikolayevich) (b. Zhitomir, Ukraine, 3 Jan. 1895; d. Kiev, 15 April, 1968). Composer. Pupil of Glier. Taught at the Kiev Conservatory 1919–68; at the Moscow Conservatory 1935–38, 1941–44. Made use of Ukrainian folk melodies. Works include 2 operas, 5 symphonies, 4 string quartets, many folk song arrangements; orchestrations and editions of Glier's music.

Lybbert, Donald (b. Cresco, Iowa, 19 Feb. 1923; d. Norwalk, Conn., 26 July 1981). Composer. Pupil of Wagenaar, Carter, Luening, and Boulanger. Taught at Hunter College 1954–80. Works include 2 operas; *Zap* (chorus, 4 instrumental ensembles, and rock group, 1970); orchestral music; a concerto for piano and tape; *Lines for the Fallen* (soprano, 2 quarter tone–tuned pianos, ca. 1967).

Lydian. See Mode, Cadence.

Lynn [née Webb], **Loretta** (b. Butcher Hollow, Ky., 14 Apr. 1932). Country singer and songwriter. In 1948, moved to Washington State; from 1962, performed at the Grand Ole Opry, Nashville. Recordings include "Success" (1962), "Coal Miner's Daughter" (1970), "Somebody Somewhere" (1976), and several duets with Conway Twitty.

Lyon, James (b. Newark, N.J., 1 July 1735; d. Machias, Maine, 12 Oct. 1794). Composer and tune collector. Pastor of a church at Machias from 1774. Best known for his tunebook *Urania* (1761).

Lyra [Gr.; Lat. also *lira*]. (1) A *lyre of ancient Greece with a bowl-shaped, skin-covered resonator (originally a tortoise shell), curved arms, and 5 to 12 gut strings. Compared to the *kithara, another Greek lyre, the *lyra* was smaller and simpler and sounded at a lower pitch. It was considered an instrument of amateurs. See ill. under Instrument. (2) In the Middle Ages and Renaissance, any of several kinds of stringed instruments, including *fiddles and *hurdy-gurdies. (3) [Ger.] A portable *glockenspiel in the shape of a lyre. See also *Lira.*

Lyra piano. An upright piano of the early 19th century, with case shaped like a Greek lyre.

Lyra-way. The playing style and associated repertory of the lyra *viol.

Lyre [fr. Gr., Lat. *lyra*]. (1) A stringed instrument whose strings are parallel to the soundboard and attached to a crossbar between two arms extending beyond the soundboard [see Instrument]. (2) The Greek *lyra.* (3) A musical instrument or other device with curved arms similar to those of the Greek *lyra* or the Greek *kithara [see ill. under Instrument], including the clip attached to wind instruments for holding music.

Lyric. (1) Melodious. (2) For lyric soprano and lyric tenor, see Voice. (3) Lyrics [pl.]. The words of a popular song or number from a musical comedy.

Lyric Suite. (1) An orchestral work by Grieg arranged in 1904 from the first four of the six works in his *Lyric Pieces* [Ger. *Lyrische Stücke*], bk. 5, for piano op. 54. (2) A suite in six movements for string quartet by Alban Berg (1925–26), three movements of which were later arranged for string orchestra (1928). The pitch classes B, F, A, B♭ (German *pitch names H, F, A, B) play an important role and are derived from his own initials combined with those of Hanna Fuchs-Robettin.

Lysenko [Lissenko], **Nikolay (Vitalyevich)** (b. Grinki, near Kremenchug, Ukraine, 22 Mar. 1842; d. Kiev, 6 Nov. 1912). Composer, pianist, and folk song collector. Pupil of E. Richter, Reinecke, and Rimsky-Korsakov. In 1904, founded a Ukrainian School of Music in Kiev. Works include operas (*Taras Bulba,* 1880–90); orchestral works; choruses (*Vechny revolyutsioner* [The Eternal Revolutionary], 1905); chamber music; songs; piano pieces. Published some 600 folk songs and wrote treatises on Ukrainian folk music.

M

M. Abbr. for *manual, *manualiter, *main, *mano,* *metronome, *mezzo [see Dynamic marks].

Ma [It.]. But; *ma non troppo,* but not too much.

Ma, Yo-Yo (b. Paris, 7 Oct. 1955). Cellist. Pupil of his father and of Leonard Rose. Has appeared as soloist with major orchestras in the U.S. and Europe; recordings include the Beethoven cello sonatas with pianist Emanuel Ax, a frequent collaborator. Awarded the Avery Fisher Prize, 1978.

Maayani, Ami (b. Ramat-Gan, 13 Jan. 1936). Composer and conductor. Pupil of Ben-Haim and Ussachevsky. His music combines Near Eastern elements with European forms and French impressionist orchestration. Works include *Hebrew Requiem,* mezzo, chorus, orchestra, 1977; a concertino for harp and strings, 1980; Symphony no. 4, *Sinfonietta on Popular Hebraic Themes,* chamber orchestra, 1982; chamber music; songs; electronic music; music for harp.

Maazel, Lorin (Varencove) (b. Neuilly, 6 Mar. 1930). Conductor and violinist. Began to conduct complete programs at age 11. In 1960, became the first American to conduct at Bayreuth. Music director of the Berlin Deutsche Oper (1965–71) and Radio Symphony (1965–75); of the Cleveland Orchestra, 1972–82; of the Orchestre national de France, 1977–82; of the Pittsburgh Symphony, 1988–96. Artistic director and general manager, Vienna State Opera, 1982–84.

Macbeth. (1) Opera in four acts by Verdi (libretto by Francesco Maria Piave and Andrea Maffei, after Shakespeare's play), produced in Florence in 1847; revised version in French first produced in Paris in 1865. Setting: Scotland in the 11th century. (2) Opera in a prologue and three acts by Ernest Bloch (libretto by Edmond Fleg, after Shakespeare), produced in Paris in 1910.

McCabe, John (b. Huyton, 21 Apr. 1939). Composer. Pupil of Pitfield and Genzmer. Active in London as a recital pianist and as soloist in his own concertos. Principal of the London College of Music 1983–90. Has composed dramatic works (*The Lion, the Witch, and the Wardrobe,* children's opera, 1968; *The Teachings of Don Juan,* ballet, 1973); orchestral works (2 violin concertos; 3 symphonies; 3 piano concertos; *Notturni ed Alba,* soprano and orchestra, 1970; Concerto for Orchestra, 1984; *Fire at Durilgai,* 1989); choral and vocal works; chamber music (5 string quartets); music for piano and organ.

McCartney, (John) Paul (b. Liverpool, 18 June 1942). Rock singer, songwriter, bass guitarist, and keyboardist. One of the four Beatles; with John Lennon, a principal songwriter for them. When the group broke up he made recordings with his wife, Linda McCartney; 1971, they assembled the band Wings (albums include *Band on the Run,* 1974). From 1980 he worked as a solo artist; recorded a duet with Stevie Wonder, "Ebony and Ivory" (1982). In 1994 he reunited with the other surviving Beatles to record some new music based on tapes made by John Lennon. Founded a music school in Liverpool; composed an oratorio.

McCormack, John (b. Athlone, 14 June 1884; d. Dublin, 16 Sept. 1945). Tenor. Trained in Dublin and Milan. Covent Garden debut as Turiddù *(Cavalleria),* 1907. From 1910 sang Italian roles with the Boston, Philadelphia, and Chicago Operas, and at the Metropolitan; in 1918, turned to recitals and recordings, adding German lieder and popular songs to his repertory. Retired 1938.

McCracken, James (John Eugene) (b. Gary, Ind., 16 Dec. 1926; d. New York, 29 Apr. 1988). Tenor. Metropolitan Opera debut as Parpignol *(Bohème)* 1953. Otello was his most celebrated role. Remained with the Met until 1978; sang at most of the world's leading houses.

MacCunn, Hamish (James) (b. Greenoch, Scotland, 22 Mar. 1868; d. London, 2 Aug. 1916). Composer, conductor. Pupil of H. Parry and Stanford. Taught at the Royal Academy of Music 1888–94; later active as opera conductor. Composed works on Scottish subjects, especially the concert overture *Land of the Mountains and the Flood* (1887), 5 cantatas, and 2 Scottish operas (*Jeanie Deane,* after Scott, 1894); also other stage works and many songs.

McDonald, Harl (b. Boulder, Colo., 27 July 1899; d. Princeton, N.J., 30 Mar. 1955). Composer, pianist, and conductor. Taught at the Univ. of Pennsylvania 1926–46. His research in acoustics led to the book *New Methods of Measuring Sound,* with O. H. Schenck (1935). Compositions include many orchestral works (*My Country at War,* tone poem, 1945); some chamber music; much piano and choral music.

MacDonald, Jeannette (b. Philadelphia, 18 June 1903; d. Houston, 14 Jan. 1965). Soprano and film actress. Studied with Lotte Lehmann. Appeared on Broadway in the 1920s; in films, including 8 popular musicals with Nelson Eddy (*Naughty Marietta,* 1935; *Rose Marie,* 1936; *Sweethearts,* 1939). U.S. opera debut as Gounod's Juliette (Chicago Civic Opera, 1944).

MacDowell, Edward (Alexander) (b. New York, 18 Dec. 1860; d. there, 23 Jan. 1908). Composer. Studied with Marmontel and Raff. Taught at Columbia Univ. 1896–1904. Composed orchestral works (2 piano concertos; symphonic poems; *Indian Suite,* 1895); numerous piano pieces (2 *Modern Suites; Hexentanz,* 1883; 4 sonatas; *Woodland Sketches,* 1896; *Sea Pieces,* 1898); songs, part songs. After MacDowell's death, his wife made their farm in New Hampshire an artists' colony.

McDowell, John Herbert (b. Washington, D.C., 21 Dec. 1926; d. Scarsdale, 3 Sept. 1985). Composer and choreographer. Pupil of Luening and Beeson. Active as teacher; music director of Paul Taylor's and other dance companies. Composed numerous dance scores; theatrical works (*Tumescent lingam,* oboe, chorus, tape, 101 performers, dog, infant, visual effects, 1971); orchestral and chamber music; a few vocal works.

Mace, Thomas (b. Cambridge?, 1612 or 1613; d. there?, ca. 1706). Writer, singer, and lutenist. Joined the choir of Trinity College, Cambridge, 1635. His *Musick's Monument* (1676) defends English music against the French style and contains valuable information about performance practice. Composed a verse anthem and works for viol.

Macero, Teo [Allitio Joseph] (b. Glens Falls, N.Y., 30 Oct. 1925). Composer, conductor, and saxophonist. Pupil of Brant. Producer for Columbia Records 1957–75; then founded his own recording company (Teo Productions). Has composed many works for jazz ensembles (*A Jazz Presence,* with narrator, 1980); operas and over 80 dance scores (*Jamboree,* Joffrey Ballet, 1984); orchestral music; many television scores.

McEwen, John (Blackwood) (b. Hawick, 13 Apr. 1868; d. London, 14 June 1948). Composer. Pupil of Prout, Corder, and Matthay. Teacher at the Athenaeum School of Music, Glasgow; at the Royal Academy of Music from 1898. Works include *Three Border Ballades* (including *Grey Galloway,* orchestra, 1905–8); a symphony; 17 string quartets; 7 violin sonatas; piano pieces; songs.

Macfarren, George Alexander (b. London, 2 Mar. 1813; d. there, 31 Oct. 1887). Composer and teacher. Pupil of Potter at the Royal Academy; taught there 1837–47 and from 1851; at Cambridge from 1875. Composed English operas (*King Charles II,* 1849; *Robin Hood,* 1860); oratorios (*St. John the Baptist,* Bristol, 1873); cantatas (*May Day,* 1857); 9 symphonies and other orchestral works; much chamber music; Anglican church music; many songs and part songs.

McFerrin, Bobby (b. New York, 11 March 1950). Jazz and popular singer. Trained as a pianist. Usually sings unaccompanied, creating complex polyphonic textures; juxtaposes rock, jazz, and other styles. Recordings include the hit song "Don't Worry, Be Happy" (1988); has also recorded with Yo-Yo Ma. Appointed Creative Chair of the Saint Paul Chamber Orchestra, 1994.

McFerrin, Robert (b. Marianna, Ariz., 19 Mar. 1921). Baritone. Joined the New England Opera Company 1950. In 1953, became the first male black singer to join the Met; roles included Amonasro, Rigoletto, and Valentin. Sang the role of Porgy on the *Porgy and Bess* film soundtrack (1959); toured widely as a recitalist.

McGlaughlin, William (b. Philadelphia, 3 Oct. 1943). Conductor, composer, radio host. Studied trombone at Temple Univ. and conducting with William R. Smith and Max Rudolph. Trombonist with Philadelphia Orchestra (1967–68), Pittsburgh Symphony (1969–75), St. Paul Chamber Orchestra (1975–82). Held conducting posts with St. Paul Chamber Orchestra (1975–82); music director of symphony orchestras in Eugene, Ore. (1981–85), Tucson, Ariz. (1982–87), Kansas City, Mo. (1986–98). Host of radio programs *Saint Paul Sunday* from 1980; *Sprint Symphony Hour* from 1988; *Music from Marlboro* 1990–91. Compositions for orchestra include *Crooked Timber,* 1997; *Bela's Bounce,* 1998.

Machaut [Machault], **Guillaume de** (b. ca. 1300; d. Rheims?, 13 Apr. 1377). Composer and poet. In both arts the foremost figure of 14th-century France. Ca. 1323–40, traveled widely in Europe as secretary to the King of Bohemia. Settled in Rheims about 1340; patrons included Charles of Normandy and Jean, Duc de Berry. Composed *lais,* ballades, rondeaux, virelays, motets, 1 Mass, and 1 hocket. Wrote several narrative and numerous lyric poems, as well as the texts to his musical works, some of which are included as interludes in his long poems.

Machete [Port.]. See *Cavaquinho.*

Machine head. A mechanical device, typically employing worm gears, for controlling the tension of the strings on a stringed instrument, especially the guitar and double bass. Such devices have been in use since the 18th century.

Machito [Grillo, Frank Raul] (b. Tampa, Fla., 16 Feb. 1912; d. London, 15 Apr. 1984). Jazz and salsa bandleader, singer, and maraca player. Raised in Cuba; returned to the U.S. 1937. In 1940, formed his Afro-Cubans, a big band that soon moved toward jazz under the musical direction of the trumpeter Mario Bauza. Recordings included "Cubop City" (1949), "Okiedoke" (with Charlie Parker as soloist, 1949), and the album *Kenya* (1957).

Machover, Tod (b. New York, 24 Nov. 1953). Composer, conductor, and cellist. Pupil of Dallapiccola, Sessions, and Carter. Composer-in-residence and then director of musical research at IRCAM in Paris (1978–84); teacher at M.I.T. from 1985. Works include the opera *Valis* (1987); *Desires* (orchestra, 1983–84); *Soft Morning, City!* (after Joyce, soprano, double bass, computer-generated tape, 1980); *Song of Penance* (computer-enhanced viola, chamber ensemble, 1992).

McKenna, Dave [David J.] (b. Woonsocket, R.I., 30 May 1930). Jazz pianist. Worked with big bands of Charlie Ventura and Woody Herman, and with smaller ensembles of Gene Krupa, Stan Getz, Bobby Hackett, and others. From the late 1960s, lived on Cape Cod working as soloist; from the late 1970s, associated with the Concord label, playing and recording with other Concord artists.

Mackenzie, Alexander (Campbell) (b. Edinburgh, 22 Aug. 1847; d. London, 28 Apr. 1935). Composer, conductor, and educator. Studied at the Royal Academy of Music; principal there from 1888; active as conductor in London. Works include *The Bride* (cantata, 1881); *Colomba* (opera, London, 1883); *The Rose of Sharon* (oratorio, 1884); *Pibroch Suite* (violin and orchestra, 1889).

Mackerras, (Alan) Charles (MacLaurin) (b. Schenectady, N.Y., 17 Nov. 1925). Conductor and oboist. Studied in Australia and with Talich. During the 1950s, studied and revived authentic performance practice of 18th-century vocal music. Recordings include Handel's *Messiah* (1967); works by Janáček. Musical director, English National Opera, 1970–77; Welsh National Opera, 1987–92. Principal conductor, Sydney Symphony, 1980–85.

Mackey, Steven (b. Frankfurt, 1956). Composer. Has taught at the Univ. of California at Davis, Northeastern Univ., and Princeton Univ. Works include a string quartet (1983); *Banana/Dump Truck* (cello, orchestra, 1995) and other orchestral works; *Deal* (electric guitar, drum set, chamber ensemble, 1995).

McKinley, Carl (b. Yarmouth, Maine, 9 Oct. 1895; d. Boston, 24 July 1966). Composer and organist. Pupil of Goldmark, Hill, and Boulanger. Taught at the New England Conservatory. Works include *The Blue Flower* (symphonic poem, 1921); *The Man of Galilea* (oratorio, 1916); a string quartet (1941) and other chamber music; piano and organ music; songs.

McKinley, William Thomas (b. New Kensington, Pa., 9 Dec. 1938). Composer and jazz pianist. Pupil of Schuller, Powell, Wyner, and Moss. Has taught at the Univ. of Chicago and at New England Conservatory. Early works were influenced by expressionism; many later compositions borrow from jazz. Works include *Deliverance Amen* (oratorio, 1982–83), symphonies and concertos (clarinet, 1977); *Scarlet* (jazz band, 1983); string quartets and other chamber music; piano and choral music; songs.

McKuen, Rod (Marvin) (b. Oakland, 29 Apr. 1933). Composer, poet, and singer. Settled in New York 1959. Has composed more than 1,000 songs; film scores (*A Boy Named Charlie Brown*, 1970); ballets and a musical; 4 symphonies; concertos for harpsichords, guitar, piano, and cello; *I Hear America Singing* (soprano, narrator, and orchestra, 1973); piano and chamber music.

McLaughlin, John [Mahavishnu] (b. Yorkshire, England, 4 Jan. 1942). Guitarist and bandleader. Recorded with Miles Davis's jazz-rock groups. In 1970, formed the Mahavishnu Orchestra. Played acoustic guitar in Shakti, exploring a fusion of jazz and Indian improvisatory methods (1973–77), and in guitar duos and trios. In 1975, settled in France; acted and played in the film *Round Midnight* (1986).

McLean, Jackie [John Lenwood, Jr.; Abdul Kareem, Omar Ahmed] (b. New York, 17 May 1932). Jazz alto saxophonist. Worked with Sonny Rollins, Miles Davis, Charles Mingus, and Art Blakey. Acted and performed in the play *The Connection* in New York, London, and Paris (1959–61, 1963). Recorded the hard bop album *Bluesnik* (1961); mid-1960s, turned toward free jazz. From 1968, taught at the Hartt School of Music.

MacMillan, Ernest (Alexander Campbell) (b. Mimico, Ont., 18 Aug. 1893; d. Toronto, 6 May 1973). Conductor, composer, and organist. Studied in Toronto. Interned near Berlin during World War I. Organist at Timothy Eaton Memorial Church (Toronto) 1919–25; 1926–42, principal of the Toronto Conservatory; 1927–52, dean of the Faculty of Music of the university. Conducted the Toronto Symphony, 1931–56. Works include a ballad opera (1933); several pieces for orchestra; chamber and piano music; a Te Deum (1936); original songs and arrangements of folk songs.

Macon, Uncle Dave [David Harrison] (b. Smart Station, Tenn., 7 Oct. 1870; d. Murfreesboro, Tenn., 22 Mar. 1952). Country singer and banjo player. Played professionally from 1918; appeared on the W.S.M. Barn Dance (later the Grand Ole Opry) from 1925. Helped to introduce minstrel, vaudeville, and Tin Pan Alley material to the growing country movement. Recordings include "Keep My Skillet Good and Greasy" (1924) and "Wreck of the Tennessee Gravy Train" (1930).

Maconchy, Elizabeth (b. Broxbourne, Hertfordshire, 19 March 1907; d. Norwich, 11 Nov. 1994). Composer. Studied with C. Wood, Vaughan Williams, and Jirák. Works include 7 operas; 3 ballets; orchestral works, including concertos and concertante pieces; choral works, songs, and song cycles, some with orchestra; 14 string quartets and other chamber music; solo pieces for piano and other instruments. She is the mother of composer Nicola LeFanu.

Maconie, Robin (John) (b. Auckland, 22 Oct. 1942). Composer and writer. Pupil of Messiaen, Zimmermann, Eimert, and Stockhausen. Moved to England, 1969. Compositions include *Māui* (television ballet for speaker, mime, 6 male dancers, and orchestra, 1967–72); *Canzona* (chamber orchestra, 1962); String Quartet (1970); *A:B:A* (harp, 1964); *Basia Memoranda* (song cycle, 1962); *Ex evangelio Sancti Marci* (chorus, 1964); film scores; electronic incidental music for the NZBC.

McPartland, Jimmy [James Dougald] (b. Chicago, 15 Mar. 1907; d. Port Washington, N.Y., 13 Mar. 1991). Jazz cornetist. Replaced Bix Beiderbecke in the Wolverines (1924–25). While working with Ben Pollack, recorded with McKenzie and Condon's Chicagoans, including "Sugar" and "China Boy" (1927). Thereafter worked as a free-lance and a leader in New York and Chicago, playing Dixieland and traditional jazz. Married Marian Turner in 1945; though later divorced, they worked together occasionally.

McPartland [née Turner], **Marian (Margaret)** [Page, Marian] (b. Windsor, England, 20 Mar. 1920). Pianist. Came to the U.S. in 1946 after marrying Jimmy McPartland. Led trios, notable for an engagement at the Hickory House in New York (1952–60). From about 1978, hosted the nationally syndicated radio show *Piano Jazz*.

McPhee, Colin (Carhart) (b. Montreal, 15 Mar. 1900; d. Los Angeles, 7 Jan. 1964). Composer and writer on music. Studied piano with Friedheim; composition with Le Flem and Varèse. From 1934 to 1939, lived in Southeast Asia, studying the music of Java and Bali; published several books on this music, which also influenced his own compositions. Taught at UCLA 1958–64. Works include *Tabu-tabuhan* (2 pianos and orchestra, 1936) and 3 symphonies; *Balinese Ceremonial Music* (2 pianos, 1940); *From the Revelation of St. John the Divine* (male voices, 3 trumpets, 2 pianos, timpani, 1935).

McRae, Carmen (b. New York, 8 Apr. 1922; d. Beverly Hills, Calif., 10 Nov. 1994). Jazz singer. Sang with Benny Carter and Mercer Ellington (1946–47); played piano and sang in New York clubs. After recording as a leader in 1954, she mainly sang, accompanied by a bop-oriented trio. Her voice had a smoky timbre, and biting articulation gave her work an intense rhythmic quality.

Madama Butterfly. Opera in three acts (originally in two acts) by Puccini (libretto by Giuseppe Giacosa and Luigi Illica, based on David Belasco's dramatization of a story by John L. Long). It was first produced in Milan in 1904; the fourth and definitive version was produced in Paris in 1906. Setting: Japan, near Nagasaki, about 1900.

Maderna, Bruno (b. Venice, 21 Apr. 1920; d. Darmstadt, 13 Nov. 1973). Composer and conductor. Pupil of Malipiero and Scherchen. Taught at the conservatories in Venice (1948–52), Milan, and Rotterdam; at the Darmstadt summer courses from 1954; at the Mozarteum in Salzburg 1960–70. With Berio, founded the Electronic Music Studio at Milan Radio, 1955; from 1971 conducted the Milan Radio Orchestra. His early works are neoclassic, but he soon turned to twelve-tone and serial procedures and to electronic music. His *Musica su due dimensioni* (1951, rev. 1957 and 1963; flute and tape) was one of the earliest works to combine live and taped sound. Works include *Hyperion* (Venice, 1964), *Don Perlimplin* (radio opera, 1962), and other dramatic music; *Quadrivium* (4 percussionists and 4 orchestral groups, 1969), 3 oboe concertos, and other orchestral music; chamber music; vocal music; film scores; many transcriptions of Italian Baroque and other early music; arrangements of light music, jazz, and songs of Kurt Weill.

Madetoja, Leevi (Antti) (b. Oulu, 17 Feb. 1887; d. Helsinki, 6 Oct. 1947). Composer. Pupil of Sibelius, d'Indy, and Fuchs. Conducted the Helsinki Philharmonic Society (1912–14) and the orchestra of Viipuri (1914–16). Taught at the Helsinki music institute (later academy), 1916–39. Made extensive use of Finnish folk tunes. Works include 2 operas (*Pohjalaisia* [The Ostrobothnians], 1923); a ballet; *Tanssinäky* [Dance Vision] (orchestra, 1910); 3 symphonies; piano and chamber music; many choral pieces and songs; cantatas; violin music; incidental and film music.

Madonna [Ciccone, Madonna Louise] (b. Bay City, Mich., 16 Aug. 1958). Popular singer and songwriter. Worked briefly in dance (with Alvin Ailey); since 1983 has recorded original and co-written popular songs. Albums include *Like a Virgin* (1984, including "Material Girl"), *Like a Prayer* (1989), and *Bedtime Stories* (1994). Has made extensive use of music videos; has also acted in films.

Madrigal [It.]. (1) A poetic and musical form cultivated in 14th-century Italy. The poems, at first nearly always pastoral in theme but later more varied, usually consist of two or three stanzas of three lines followed by a ritornello of two lines (though the ritornello is sometimes lacking). Typical rhyme schemes are aba bcb dd, abb cdd ee, etc. Seven- and eleven-syllable lines are both used, but the latter predominate.

Musical settings of madrigals for two or (rarely) three voices survive in manuscripts of north Italian and Florentine provenance dating from ca. 1340 to ca. 1440; the sources are on the whole somewhat late in relation to the composition of the music. Composers include the north Italians Giovanni da Cascia and Jacopo da Bologna as well as a group of Florentines of whom the most famous was Francesco Landini (d. 1397). The upper lines of the madrigal show a good deal of melodic fioritura. The supporting tenors, though texted, are less elaborate. After ca. 1370, the madrigal lost popularity to the *ballata*, and few madrigals of this type were written after 1400.

(2) A poetic genre popular with 16th-century musicians, distantly if at all related to the 14th-century type. In the writings of 16th-century literary theorists, the madrigal was defined as a one-stanza poem of free rhyme scheme, using a free alternation of seven- and eleven-syllable lines. As such it is similar to a single stanza of a *canzone*. Petrarchan language is used a great deal, especially in the first half of the 16th century.

(3) A vocal setting, polyphonic and unaccompanied for most of its history, of any of various kinds of verse from ca. 1520 to the middle of the 17th century. The madrigal in its beginning stages was chiefly the work of Florentine composers (Bernardo Pisano, Philippe Verdelot, Jacques Arcadelt) and of men with strong Florentine connections (Costanzo Festa).This music, normally written for four fully texted voices, is closer to the French *chanson* of the early 16th century than to most examples of the *frottola*. The poetry is set line by line in a basically chordal style animated with points of imitation and without rhetorical extremes. But beginning about 1540, in the hands of Adrian Willaert, Cipriano de Rore, and their Venetian circle, the madrigal became denser in texture, declamatory in a more individual and less stereotyped manner, and in every way more serious. Petrarch's sonnets are favorite texts here; five-voice writing is the norm.

By 1550, the madrigal had become in part a vehicle for experiment; thus the chromaticism espoused by the theorist Nicola Vicentino and practiced to some degree by a number of composers, including Rore and the young Lassus, can be seen as an integral part of the history of the genre. A new generation of madrigalists, among them Palestrina, Lassus, Philippe de Monte, and Vincenzo Ruffo, came to prominence in the middle 1550s, and a talented group of composers including Giaches de Wert, Alessandro Striggio, Stefano Rossetto, and Andrea Gabrieli rose to prominence early in the 1560s.

About 1580, the center of activity changed from Venice to Rome, Mantua, and Ferrara (Wert and Luzzasco Luzzaschi). The greatest madrigal composer of the period, the Roman Luca Marenzio (d. 1599), whose work may be regarded as the classic manifestation of the later madrigal, never abandoned contrapuntal texture and made use of coloristic harmony and contrapuntal dissonance. In the 1580s and 90s, the epic and pastoral poetry of Tasso and especially the pastoral verse of Guarini was in vogue; some of the most impressive madrigals of the period set texts from Guarini's *Pastor fido*. The experimentalists of the 1590s, chief among them Pomponio Nenna, Carlo Gesualdo, Alfonso Fontanelli, and Luzzaschi, favored short, expressionistic texts that gave them occasion for extremes of melodic and tonal language—what was soon to be called the *seconda prattica* [see *Prima prattica, seconda prattica*]. But madrigals in a more conservative vein continued to be written throughout the 1580s and 90s, some of the music being of great distinction, such as the later work of Monte and Lassus.

About 1600, madrigals with continuo parts began to appear. Solo and few-voice pieces with continuo formed one new genre [see Monody]; concerted madrigals for a variety of vocal and instrumental forces formed another. Giulio Caccini, Sigismondo d'India, and Marco da Gagliano are among the notable figures in this new field. The unaccompanied madrigal continued to be written in the first half of the 17th century, but its vogue had passed and late examples lack conviction and energy.

Monteverdi published his first book of madrigals, for five voices, in 1587; his eight books, the last issued in 1638, are a microcosm of everything important in the final stages of the history of the genre, including the continuo (appearing for the first time in the fifth book of 1605) and concerted madrigal.

Outside Italy, the madrigal flourished in German-speaking lands, and the Netherlands was an important center of madrigal publication as well as composition. In England in the last years of Elizabeth's reign, an intense cultivation of the genre—chiefly imitative of Marenzio's earlier style and of the *canzonetta*—took place, led by Thomas Morley and carried to its highest point at the turn of the century by Thomas Weelkes and John Wilbye.

Related lighter forms are the *villanella and the *canzonetta.

Madrigal comedy. A modern term for a group of secular Italian vocal pieces in descriptive or naturalistic style, unified by some kind of plot. Descriptive madrigal cycles may be seen as early as the 1560s, but the greatest vogue for these pieces came in the last decade of the 16th century and the first few years of the 17th. Orazio Vecchi's *L'Amfiparnaso* (1597) is the most famous example.

Madrigale spirituale [It.]. A setting of a vernacular, nonliturgical religious text for general devotional use in Counter-Reformation Italy.

Madrigalism. A musical effect intended to illustrate, usually in a rather literal way, some aspect of the text in a vocal composition, as in many *madrigals of the later 16th century. See also Word painting.

Maegaard, Jan (Carl Christian) (b. Copenhagen, 14 Apr. 1926). Composer and musicologist. Studied at UCLA and at the Univ. of Copenhagen, where he taught from 1971. Early compositions are in a diatonic style; subsequent works have employed twelve-tone techniques (Serenade "O alter Duft aus Märchenzeit," piano trio, 1960), and total serialism (*Due tempi,* orchestra, 1961), sometimes with aleatoric elements (Chamber Concerto no. 2, 1961); has also experimented with nine-tone scales (*Triptykon,* violin, string orchestra, 1984). Has authored numerous studies of Schoenberg.

Maelzel, Johann[es] Nepomuk (b. Regensburg, 15 Aug. 1772; d. in the harbor of La Guiara, Venezuela, 21 July 1838). Inventor. Settled in Vienna, 1792; from 1808, was a court "mechanician" there. In 1816, began manufacturing the metronome in Paris. Also invented the Panharmonicon [See Automatic instruments].

Maestoso [It.]. Majestic.

Maestro [It.]. Master; a form of address used especially for conductors, but often for composers, soloists, or teachers of performance; for *m. de capilla, m. di cappella,* see Chapel master.

Magadis. A stringed instrument of ancient Greece, probably a triangular harp.

Magelone Romances. See Romanzen aus L. Tieck's Magelone.

Maggiore [It.]. Major mode.

Magic Flute, The. See *Zauberflöte, Die.*

Magnard, (Lucien Denis Gabriel) Albéric (b. Paris, 9 June 1865; d. Oise, 3 Sept. 1914). Composer. Pupil of d'Indy. Composed operas (*Bérénice,* Opéra-comique, 1911); symphonies and other orchestral music, chamber works, songs. Wrote his own librettos and used leitmotivs in the manner of Wagner.

Magnificat [Lat.]. The *canticle of the Virgin, Luke 1:46–55, the Latin text of which begins "Magnificat anima mea Dominum" (My soul doth magnify the Lord). The Magnificat is used in both Roman Catholic and Anglican services, at Vespers and Evening Prayer, respectively. Like the Psalms, its verses are sung in Roman Catholic services to one of a set of *psalm tones chosen according to the mode of its accompanying antiphon.

The 15th and 16th centuries saw the composition of numerous polyphonic settings of the Magnificat, often but not always incorporating the recitation formulas. Most were vocal, but some were instrumental. Notable examples were contributed by Dufay, Victoria, Lassus, and Palestrina. Such settings were often composed with *alternatim performance in mind; that is, polyphony was supplied for only every other verse (usually even-, sometimes odd-numbered), plainchant to be used for the rest.

In the Baroque and Classical periods, polyphonic settings of the Magnificat came to be divided into self-contained sections not necessarily congruent with verses. Usually, polyphony was supplied for the entire text. There are examples by Monteverdi, Schütz, Vivaldi, Bach (BWV 243 in D), and Mozart (last movements of the Vespers K. 321 and K. 339).

Magnus liber organi. A large book of *organum attributed by the 13th-century theorist Anonymous IV to Master Leonin, who was active in Paris in the late 12th century. Surviving manuscripts preserve a collection consisting of 13 organa based on responsorial chants from the Office and 33 Mass compositions. With the exception of two pieces, all of these are appropriate to the liturgies of *Notre Dame in Paris. While many of the compositions show signs of revision or modernization through the introduction of modally ordered passages in *discant, thought to be the work of Master Perotin at the beginning of the 13th century, the majority of the music is *organum purum, the style in which Leonin was said to have excelled.

Magrepha [Heb.]. An organ of the ancient Hebrews containing perhaps 100 pipes and used in the first centuries C.E. as a signaling instrument.

Mahler, Gustav (b. Kalischt [Kaliště], Bohemia, 7 July 1860; d. Vienna, 18 May 1911). Composer and conductor. Studied in Vienna with J. Epstein and

R. Fuchs; possibly attended some of Bruckner's lectures. Held conducting posts at the Prague Opera (1885–56); the Budapest Opera (1888–1891); Hamburg (1891–97); the Vienna Opera (1897–1907); the Vienna Philharmonic (1898–1901); the Metropolitan Opera (from 1908); the New York Philharmonic (1909–10). Works: *Das klagende Lied* (cantata, 1880); works for voice and orchestra (**Lieder eines fahrenden Gesellen; Des *Knaben Wunderhorn* songs, including "Revelge," 1899; five *Rückert Lieder,* 1901; **Kindertotenlieder; Das *Lied von der Erde);* 9 symphonies (including no. 1, *Titan, and no. 2, the *Resurrection Symphony) and an unfinished tenth; songs with piano.

Maid as Mistress, The. See *Serva padrona, La.*

Maillart, Aimé [Louis] (b. Montpellier, 24 Mar. 1817; d. Moulins-sur-Allier, 26 May 1871). Composer. Studied at the Paris Conservatory. Composed 6 comic operas (*Les dragons de Villars,* Paris, 1856); cantatas.

Main [Fr.]. Hand; *m. droite (gauche),* right (left) hand; *à deux (quatre) mains,* for two (four) hands; *m. dans le pavillon,* hand in the bell (of a brass instrument).

Mainardi, Enrico (b. Milan, 19 May 1897; d. Munich, 10 Apr. 1976). Cellist. Studied in Milan and Berlin. Formed duos with Dohnányi and E. Fischer, and a trio with Fischer and Kulenkampff (later Schneiderhan). Taught at the Accademia di S. Cecilia, Rome (from 1930), and in Berlin, Lucerne, and Salzburg; 1933, recorded *Don Quixote* with Strauss. Compositions include 4 cello concertos.

Mainstream jazz. In the 1980s, *bebop, *swing, and related jazz styles.

Maître de chapelle [Fr.]. *Chapel master [see also *Maîtrise*].

Maîtrise [Fr.]. A choir school attached to a church, under the direction of the chapel master; also a church choir.

Majeur [Fr.]. Major.

Majo, Gian Francesco (de) (b. Naples, 24 Mar. 1732; d. there, 17 Nov. 1770). Composer. Pupil of his father, Giuseppe de Majo (1697–1771) and of Feo and Martini. Harpsichordist and organist at the royal chapel, Naples. Composed about 20 serious operas (*Cajo Fabricio,* Naples, 1760; *Alcide negli orti Esperidi,* Vienna, 1764; *Ifigenia in Tauride,* Mannheim, 1764; *Didone abbandonata,* Venice, 1769); also oratorios, cantatas, Masses, and other sacred works.

Major [Fr. *majeur;* Ger. *Dur;* It. *maggiore;* Sp. *mayor*]. See Interval, Scale, Chord, Triad, Mode, Key, Tonality.

Major [Mayer], (Jakab) Gyula [Julius] (b. Kassa, Hungary [now Košice, Slovakia], 13 Dec. 1858; d. Budapest, 30 Jan. 1925). Composer and pianist. Pupil of Volkmann, Erkel, and Liszt. In 1889, co-founded the Hungarian Music School. Made use of folk material. Works include operas (*Mila,* 1913); 6 symphonies and other orchestral works; chamber music, piano sonatas (2 Hungarian sonatas, 1896); songs.

Maksymiuk, Jerzy (b. Grodno, Poland, 9 April 1936). Conductor, composer, and pianist. Pupil of Perkowski. Founder and music director, Polish Chamber Orchestra, from 1972; conductor, BBC Scottish Symphony, 1983–93. Debut at the English National Opera (*Don Giovanni),* 1991. Compositions include ballets, orchestral music, and choral works.

Malagueña [Sp.]. A variety of the **fandango* associated with the region of Málaga in southern Spain, but also known in the New World. As a type of *flamenco music, it is in free rhythm with texts composed of five-line octosyllabic strophes.

Malawski, Artur (b. Przemyśl, Poland, 4 July 1904; d. Kraków, 26 Dec. 1957). Composer, violinist, and conductor. Pupil of Sikorski. Taught in Kraków, and in Katowice; students included Penderecki and Schäffer. Works include 2 symphonies; *Etiudy symfoniczne* (piano, orchestra, 1947); string quartets; the ballet-pantomine *Wierchy* [The Peaks] (1942; rev. 1950–52) and other vocal works.

Malengreau [de Maleingreau], **Paul (Eugène)** (b. Trélon, Nord, France, 23 Nov. 1887; d. Brussels, 9 Jan. 1959). Composer and organist. Studied at the Brussels Conservatory; taught there from 1913. Works include an oratorio; *Symphonie de la Passion;* chamber and piano music; organ symphonies, preludes, and other organ music; Masses, motets, and songs.

Maler, Wilhelm (b. Heidelberg, 21 June 1902; d. Hamburg, 29 Apr. 1976). Composer. Pupil of Haas and Jarnach. Taught at the Cologne Musikhochschule and at the Univ. of Bonn (1931–44); directed music schools in Detmold and Hamburg (1959–71). Influenced by Hindemith's contrapuntal style, and by folk song and impressionism; works include concertos, piano and chamber music, choral works. Wrote a harmony textbook.

Malfitano, Catherine (b. New York, 18 Apr. 1948). Soprano. Debut, Central City Opera, 1972. Sang with the New York City Opera, 1973–79. Metropolitan Opera debut, 1979; Vienna Staatsoper debut, 1982; filmed *Tosca* with Domingo, 1992.

Malibran [née García], **María (Felicia)** (b. Paris, 24 Mar. 1808; d. Manchester, 23 Sept. 1836). Singer. Pupil of her father, Manuel García, and of Hérold; sister of Manuel García II and Pauline Viardot. Debut, London, 1825; then went to New York with her father's company. From 1828, sang in Europe. Had a son, Charles Wilfride Bériot, by the violinist Bériot. Her voice was said to have been naturally a contralto, extended into the soprano register. Composed some songs.

Malinconico [It.]. Melancholy.

Malipiero, Gian Francesco (b. Venice, 18 Mar. 1882; d. Treviso, 1 Aug. 1973). Composer and musicologist. Studied in Vienna and with Bossi. Teacher at the Liceo musicale, Venice, 1932–40; director, 1939–52. Departed from the conventions of 19th-century Italian music, often borrowing from procedures of the 17th and 18th centuries. Works include *Tre commedie goldoniane* (1920–22), *L'Orfeide,* (trilogy, including *Sette canzoni,* 1918–19), *Venere prigioniera* (1955), and over 30 other dramatic works; 11 symphonies, 8 *Dialoghi* for solo instruments and orchestra, and other orchestral music; oratorios and cantatas; 8 string quartets and other chamber music; works for 1 or 2 pianos; choral music and songs. Edited the complete works of Monteverdi; writings include studies of Stravinsky (1945) and Vivaldi (1958).

Mambo [Sp.]. An Afro-Cuban dance-music genre, developed by the early 1940s and quickly popularized internationally. It is performed by an ensemble with voices, trumpets, and extensive rhythm section or by larger, jazz-influenced dance bands in moderate to rapid tempo.

Mamelles de Tirésias, Les [Fr., The Breasts of Tiresias]. Comic opera in two acts and a prologue by Poulenc (libretto by Guillaume Apollinaire), produced in Paris in 1947.

Ma mère l'oye [Fr., Mother Goose (Suite)]. A suite by Ravel depicting characters in fairy tales by Charles Perrault (1628–1703) and others. Originally written for piano four-hands (1908–10), it was later orchestrated by Ravel and produced with additional movements and interludes as a children's ballet in 1912.

Man. Abbr. for *manual.

Mana Zucca [Zuckermann, Augusta; Zuckerman, Gussie] (b. New York, 25 Dec. 1885; d. Miami, 8 Mar. 1981). Composer and pianist. Played her piano concerto with the Los Angeles Symphony in 1919. Works include 2 operas, a violin concerto, chamber and choral music, and some 172 songs.

Mancando [It.]. Fading, dying away.

Manche [Fr.]. The neck of a stringed instrument.

Manchicourt, Pierre de (b. Béthune, ca. 1510; d. Madrid, 5 Oct. 1564). Composer. Held posts at the cathedrals of Tours, Tournai, and Arras. From 1559, led Philip II's Flemish chapel in Madrid; perhaps also his Spanish chapel. Composed about 20 Masses; over 60 motets; 9 Psalms; a Magnificat; and over 50 chansons.

Mancinelli, Luigi (b. Orvieto, 6 Feb. 1848; d. Rome, 2 Feb. 1921). Conductor and composer. Director, Bologna Conservatory (1881–86). Conducted at the Madrid Opera (1887–93), Covent Garden (1888–1905), Metropolitan Opera (1893–1903), S. Carlos, Lisbon (1901–20), Teatro Colón, Buenos Aires (from 1908). Composed operas, incidental and film music, orchestral pieces, sacred works, songs.

Mancini, Francesco (b. Naples, 16 Jan. 1672; d. there, 22 Sept. 1737). Composer. Succeeded A. Scarlatti as director of the royal chapel, Naples, 1725. Directed the Conservatory of S. Maria di Loreto, 1720–35. Works include over 20 operas; also cantatas, oratorios, and liturgical works.

Mancini, Henry (b. Cleveland, 16 Apr. 1924; d. Los Angeles, 14 June 1994). Popular composer, pianist, and arranger. Staff composer at Universal Studios 1952–58. His film and television scores won several Oscars and Grammys; they include *Breakfast at Tiffany's* ("Moon River"), *Peter Gunn* (1958), *The Pink Panther* (1964), and *Victor/Victoria* (1982).

Mandelbaum, (Mayer) Joel (b. New York, 12 Oct. 1932). Composer. Pupil of Blacher, Dallapiccola, Fine, Piston, and Shapero. Teacher at Queens College, CUNY, from 1961. Has explored microtonal tunings. Works include 3 operas; orchestral music; *Xenophony no. 2* (violin, cello, double bass, woodwind quintet, and organ, 1979) and other chamber music; keyboard music; choral and vocal works (*Light and Shade,* soprano, oboe, and piano, 1983).

Mandolin [Fr. *mandoline;* Ger. *Mandoline;* It. *mandolino;* Sp. *mandolina*]. A small pear-shaped instrument with a round back and short neck developed from the *mandora. The earliest had four to six courses of gut strings and were often finger plucked. After 1730, a version with four double courses intended for plectrum playing only was adapted for metal strings by means of metal frets, a deeply vaulted back, a downward bend in the top below the bridge, and fastenings for strings at the end of the body. The tuning g d' a' e'' for four double courses of wire strings is used today. One of the most characteristic playing styles on the mandolin produces sustained tones by means of a tremolo with the plectrum.

Although mandolins, like lutes, usually had round

backs built up of many ribs, some with flat backs were used in France and Portugal in the 1800s. Late in the 19th century, the American Orville Gibson invented a family of mandolins with carved tops and flat backs that were based on the principles of the Cremonese violins. In the U.S., flat-backed instruments were popular in mandolin bands around the turn of the 20th century and (including electric versions, some with a cut-out in the body similar to that of the electric guitar) are widely used in country and western music, both as solo instruments and in ensembles.

Other members of the mandolin family are the mandola, either an alto, tuned c g d' a', or a tenor, tuned G d a e'; the mandocello, a bass, tuned an octave below the alto, C G d a; the mandolone, a special 18th- and 19th-century bass, tuned F G a d g b e' a'; the mandobass, a modern contrabass, tuned C₁ G₁ D A. See ills. under Lute.

Mandora, mandore, mandola [Fr. *mandore;* Ger. *Mandoër, Mandürichen, Mandorlauten;* It. *mandola;* Sp. *vandola*]. (1) A lutelike instrument developed from the medieval *gittern. Mandoras are gut-strung and played with a plectrum. The name was adopted in the mid-16th century with a new tuning and playing method. Early mandoras were carved from solid wood and have three or four courses. By the 17th century, built-up mandoras were also made and the number of courses increased to four or five, later up to eight. A very large mandora was sometimes called a colachon.

(2) An 18th-century Austrian and German eight-course hybrid combining a lute body and pegbox with a guitar neck.

Maneria [Lat.]. In the church *modes of the Middle Ages, the pair of authentic and plagal modes associated with any of the four regular finals (D, E, F, G), but without regard for the distinction between authentic and plagal.

Manfred. (1) An overture and incidental music by Schumann, op. 115 (1848–49), to Byron's poetic drama of the same name. (2) A symphony in B minor by Tchaikovsky, op. 58 (1885), after Byron's work.

Manfredina. *Monferrina.

Manfredini, Vincenzo (b. Pistoia, 22 Oct. 1737; d. St. Petersburg, 16 Aug. 1799). Composer. Pupil of his father, Francesco Manfredini (1684–1762), and of G. Perti. Ca. 1758–69, *maestro di cappella,* St. Petersburg; director of the opera company there from 1762. Best known for his *Regole armoniche* (1775), which contains instructions for singing and keyboard accompaniment. Composed operas (*Semiramide,* 1760); ballets, cantatas, sacred music, chamber and keyboard works.

Mangione, Chuck [Charles Frank] (b. Rochester, N.Y., 29 Nov. 1940). Jazz flugelhorn player and bandleader. Studied at the Eastman School while leading a hard bop group. Joined Woody Herman, Maynard Ferguson, and Art Blakey (1965–67). Switched from trumpet to flugelhorn after forming his own quartet in 1968. Recordings include "Land of Make Believe" (1972) and the title track of the album *Feels So Good* (1977). Headed the jazz program at Eastman, 1968–72.

Manica [It.]. In string playing, shift; *mezza manica,* half shift [see Position].

Manico [It.]. The *neck of a stringed instrument.

Manicorde [Fr.], **manicordio** [Sp.], **manicordo** [It.]. Clavichord.

Manieren [Ger.]. In the 18th century, ornaments or *graces [see Ornamentation; see also Mannheim school].

Mann, Herbie (b. New York, 16 Apr. 1930). Jazz flutist. 1959, founded the Afro-Jazz Sextet and incorporated elements of African, Latin, and Middle Eastern styles; pioneered bossa nova in the U.S. During 1970s and 1980s, his group Family of Mann fused jazz with rock, funk, disco, and reggae. Appeared widely as soloist with pop orchestras.

Mann, Robert (Nathaniel) (b. Portland, Ore., 19 July 1920). Violinist and composer. Studied at Juilliard; joined the faculty there, 1946. Founding member (first violin), Juilliard Quartet, 1948; also founded the Mann Duo with his violinist son Nicholas, 1980. Has appeared as violin soloist and conductor and composed orchestral and chamber works.

Manne, Shelly [Sheldon] (b. New York, 11 June 1920; d. Los Angeles, 26 Sept. 1984). Jazz drummer and bandleader. Worked in big bands, including Stan Kenton's; recorded with Coleman Hawkins; toured with Jazz at the Philharmonic. In Los Angeles, formed the Poll-Winners with Barney Kessel and Ray Brown (1957–60); with André Previn recorded the album *My Fair Lady* (1956). Ran a nightclub, Shelly's Manne Hole (1960–74); formed the L.A. Four with Brown (1974–77).

Männerchor [Ger.]. Men's chorus.

Männergesangverein [Ger.]. Male choral society.

Mannerism. An aesthetic principle, recently associated with music from the mid-16th to the early 17th century, according to which individuation of local musical events may seem to take precedence over the exposition of clear and coherent musical structures. Mannerism is thus viewed as a countertendency to classicism. The Italian *madrigal is the genre most closely associated with the notion. The modern concept of mannerism emerged in German art criticism of the early 20th century. Its utility as a music-historical concept remains controversial.

The designation of the late 14th-century secular repertory at Avignon as manneristic has lost favor to the term *ars subtilior.

Mannheim school. A group of composers and performers active at the court of Mannheim in southwestern Germany during the 18th century. The importance of Mannheim as a musical and cultural center began in 1720 and lasted until 1778, when the Mannheim court moved to Munich. Its principal fame was achieved during the reign of Elector Carl Theodor (ruled in Mannheim 1742–78), who assembled some of the finest performers and composers in Europe. Of particular renown was the Mannheim orchestra, widely regarded as the finest in Europe.

Although some writers in the early 20th century thought the Mannheim school to be the creators of the Classical symphonic style, recent attention has centered on the debt of the Mannheim symphony to Italy, in particular to the opera overtures of composers such as Niccolò Jommelli and Baldassare Galuppi. For example, the extended crescendo passage or *Walze,* once considered to have been a Mannheim invention, unquestionably originated in Italian opera. The same may be said for the "Mannheim sigh" or melodic appoggiatura, the "Mannheim rocket" (an arpeggio theme rising through several octaves), and numerous other melodic figures once associated with Mannheim. The role of Mannheim may best be described as the adaptation and extension of the dramatic Italian overture style to the concert symphony. Other important contributions include the earliest consistent use of four movements in the symphony (in the works of Johann Stamitz after ca. 1745) and the idiomatic, frequently virtuosic treatment of the orchestra.

The modern concept of a compositional school is clearly inappropriate for the first generation of Mannheim symphonists, including Stamitz, Franz Xaver Richter, and Ignaz Holzbauer; their backgrounds and musical styles are too divergent. By contrast, the music of such second-generation Mannheimers as Anton Fils, Christian Cannabich (Stamitz's successor as concertmaster), and Carl Joseph Toeschi, all of whom were students of Stamitz, shows a rather stereotyped approach that conforms to the conventional notion of a "school" of composition.

Manns, August (Friedrich) (b. Stolzenberg, near Stettin, 12 Mar. 1825; d. Norwood, London, 1 Mar. 1907). Conductor. Conducted military bands in Königsberg and Cologne. Emigrated to London in 1854. From 1855, chief conductor, Crystal Palace, instituting the Saturday Concerts (1855–1901), designed to bring concert music to the masses.

Mano [It.]. Hand; *m. destra (sinistra),* right (left) hand.

Manon. Opera in five acts by Massenet (libretto in French by Henri Meilhac and Philippe Gille, after the novel by the Abbé Antoine François Prévost), produced in Paris in 1884. Setting: Amiens, Paris, and Le Havre about 1721.

Manon Lescaut. Opera in four acts by Puccini, produced in Turin in 1893. The libretto, which appeared without attribution, had been worked on by Ruggiero Leoncavallo, Mario Praga, Domenico Oliva, Giacomo Giacosa, and Luigi Illica as well as Giulio Ricordi and Puccini himself and was based on the Abbé Prévost's novel. Setting: France and Louisiana in the early 18th century.

Mansurian, Tigran (b. Beirut, 27 Jan. 1939). Composer. Moved to Armenia, 1947. Taught at Yerevan Conservatory from 1967. Early works used Armenian folk materials; later works were influenced by Webern and Boulez. Compositions include symphonic music (*Night Music,* 1980); concertos; chamber music (*Tovem,* chamber ensemble, 1979); vocal works.

Manual. A keyboard (other than the pedalboard) of an organ or harpsichord.

Manualiter [Lat.]. To be played on the organ keyboards (manuals) only, without use of the pedal keyboard.

Manzoni Requiem. The name sometimes given to Verdi's *Messa da Requiem,* which was composed and first performed in 1874 on the first anniversary of the death of the Italian novelist and poet Alessandro Manzoni.

Maqām [Ar., place, pl. *maqāmāt;* Turk. *makam*]. The main modal unit of Arabic music; hence, also Middle Eastern modal practice in general. A *maqām* consists of a diatonic scale (sometimes with 3/4 and 5/4 tones), the lower tetrachord being the most characteristic. Although typical tone sequences, motifs, and cadences as well as nonmusical characterizations are part of the concept, 20th-century practice stresses the scalar aspects.

Maraca. A Latin American rattle consisting of a round or oval-shaped vessel filled with seeds or similar material and held by a handle. An essential element of Latin American popular music, they are almost always played in pairs, one in each hand. See ill. under Percussion instruments.

Marais, Marin (b. Paris, 31 May 1656; d. there, 15 Aug. 1728). Composer and bass viol player. Pupil of

Lully. Court musician in Paris, 1676–1725. Composed 5 collections of music for 1–3 bass viols with figured bass, which include dance movements, fantaisies, rondeaux, tombeaux, and "pièces de caractère"; also trios for flutes or violins and figured bass and 4 operas.

Marazzoli, Marco (b. Parma, between 1602 and 1608; d. Rome, 26 Jan. 1662). Composer. Tenor in the papal chapel from 1637. Collaborated with Mazzocchi on one of the first comic operas, *Chi soffre speri* (1639); other operas include *Il capriccio* (1643); *La vita humana* (1656); *Dal male il bene* (with Abbatini, Rome, 1653); nearly 400 cantatas and oratorios.

Marcabru (b. Gascony, 1100–1110?; fl. 1128–50). Troubadour. His lyric poems (in Provençal) indicate that he served Guillaume X of Aquitaine and Alfonso VII of Castile until 1144. Of his 43 known chansons, 4 survive with melodies.

Marcato [It.]. Marked, stressed, emphasized, often with respect to a melody that is to be made prominent.

Marcello, Alessandro (b. Venice, 1684; d. there, 1750). Composer. Older brother of Benedetto Marcello. Published under the pseudonym Eterio Stinfalico. Best known for the Oboe Concerto in D minor (formerly attributed to his brother) that was transcribed for keyboard by J. S. Bach.

Marcello, Benedetto (b. Venice, 24 July or 1 Aug. 1686; d. Brescia, 24 or 25 July 1739). Composer. Brother of Alessandro Marcello. Pupil of his father and of Gasparini and Lotti. Held a number of political posts. Composed vocal music, including settings of Giustiniani's Italian paraphrases of the first 50 Psalms (1724–26); over 400 secular cantatas. Writings include *Il teatro alla moda* (ca. 1720), a satire on operatic manners.

Marcellus Mass [Lat. *Missa Papae Marcelli*]. A Mass in six voices by Palestrina composed about 1562–63 and published in his Second Book of Masses in 1567, where it was dedicated to Pope Marcellus II (d. 1555). Because of the clarity with which the text is treated, it was once thought to have been responsible for deterring the *Council of Trent from banishing polyphony from the liturgy.

March [Fr. *marche;* Ger. *Marsch;* It. *marcia;* Sp. *marcha*]. Music designed to keep the marching of troops or processions of nonmilitary groups uniform, usually through emphatic strong beats embodied in simple, repetitive rhythmic patterns. Military marches are categorized by the tempo of the drum beat, corresponding to military function, in ascending order of pace: the slow or parade march [Ger.

Parademarsch; Fr. *pas ordinaire*]; the quick march [Ger. *Geschwindmarsch;* Fr. *pas redoublé;* Sp. *paso doble*]; and the double-quick or attack march [Ger. *Sturmmarsch;* Fr. *pas de charge*]. The normal tempo for a military march in the U.S. is 120 beats per minute; school bands performing at football games are likely to march at a very much faster tempo.

By the early 16th century, the marching of European armies was ordered through standard drum patterns. The more musically developed march began to grow with the beginning of the modern military band around the mid-17th century. The expansion of the band and the improvement of many of its instruments in the 19th century ushered in a golden age of the military march that lasted into the early 20th century, the period of John Philip Sousa (1854–1932), the most notable among a considerable number of march composers popular in that period.

There has been at times a close connection between the march and popular dance music; the march was used for the two-step in the 1890s and was important as a source of *ragtime. The form that the march took in the 19th century was similar to that of contemporary dance music: a series of eight- or, more often, sixteen-measure strains, the principal strain or strains repeated later in the piece, with an introduction and one or more intermediate trios, often in the subdominant.

Marchal, André (Louis) (b. Paris, 6 Feb. 1894; d. St. Jean-de-Luz, 27 Aug. 1980). Organist. Blind from birth. Pupil of Gigout. Organist at St. Germain des Prés 1915–45; at St. Eustache 1945–63. Acclaimed for his improvisations; a significant force in the return to performance of Baroque music on Baroque-style instruments.

Marchand, Louis (b. Lyons, 2 Feb. 1669; d. Paris, 17 Feb. 1732). Organist and composer. Held several organ posts in Paris; *organiste du roi* from 1708. Composed mainly keyboard pieces; also an opera and other vocal works.

Marche [Fr.]. March; *m. harmonique (d'harmonie)*, sequence (1).

Marchesi, Blanche (b. Paris, 4 Apr. 1863; d. London, 15 Dec. 1940). Soprano, daughter of Salvatore and Mathilde Marchesi. Studied with her mother. London debut, 1896; operatic debut as Brünnhilde *(Die Walküre),* Prague, 1900. Performed a number of Wagnerian roles at Covent Garden; was a highly regarded teacher in London.

Marchesi (de Castrone) [née Graumann], **Mathilde** (b. Frankfurt am Main, 24 Mar. 1821; d. London, 17 Nov. 1913). Singing teacher. Studied with Nicolai and García. Concert debut as a mezzo-soprano, 1844. Taught at the conservatories of Vienna (1854–61;

1868–78) and Cologne (1865–68). In 1852, married Salvatore de Castrone Marchesi. Her students (mostly female) include Calvé, Eames, Garden, Melba, Sanderson.

Marchesi de Castrone, Salvatore (b. Palermo, 15 Jan. 1822; d. Paris, 20 Feb. 1908). Baritone and singing teacher. Studied with Lamperti and García. From a noble Sicilian family; had to leave Italy for taking part in the 1848 Revolution. Opera debut, New York (as Carlo in *Ernani*); had a career primarily in concerts, sometimes with his wife, Mathilde. From 1854 they were active as teachers in Vienna, Cologne, and Paris. He published singing exercises, songs.

Marchetti, Filippo (b. Bolognola, Macerata, 26 Feb. 1831; d. Rome, 18 Jan. 1902). Composer. Studied at Naples. Settled in Rome as a singing teacher and song composer; 1862, moved to Milan. Composed operas, including *Romeo e Giulietta* (Trieste, 1865), and *Ruy Blas* (La Scala, 1869). President of the Accademia di S. Cecilia, Rome, 1881–86; director of its conservatory 1886–1901.

Marchetto da Padova [Marchettus de Padua] (b. Padua, 1274?; fl. 1305–26). Theorist. *Maestro di canto*, Cathedral of Padua, 1305–7. His treatise *Lucidarium* covers traditional music theory and plainchant, and sets forth a division of the whole tone into five parts. The *Pomerium* deals with mensural music, emphasizing notation in the Italian manner.

Marcia [It.]. March; *m. funebre*, funeral march; *alla m.*, in the manner of a march.

Marco, Tomás (b. Madrid, 12 Sept. 1942). Composer. Studied in Madrid and with Stockhausen, Boulez, Ligeti, Kagel, Maderna, and Koenig. Worked for Spanish Radio from 1966. Works include *Piraña* (piano, 1965); *Jabberwocky* (actress, 4 percussionists, 6 radios, piano, tenor saxophone, and slides, 1967); *Vitral* (organ and strings, 1969); *Escorial* (orchestra, 1973); *Espacio sagrado* (piano, 2 choruses, orchestra, 1982); Symphony no. 3 (1986).

Marenzio, Luca (b. Coccaglio, near Brescia, 1553 or 1554; d. Rome, 22 Aug. 1599). Composer. One of the so-called virtuoso madrigalists of the late Renaissance in Italy. Served the Grand Duke Ferdinando de' Medici in Florence (1588–89); also various cardinals in Rome. Composed nearly 25 books of madrigals and related pieces; music for 2 *intermedi;* about 75 motets, many polychoral; perhaps a few Masses.

Mariachi. A traditional ensemble of western Mexico, and especially the state of Jalisco, now found throughout the country. Today, the typical *mariachi* ensemble consists of one or more trumpets and vio-

lins, five-string *vihuela*, guitar(s), and *guitarrón* (six-string bass guitar).

Marienleben, Das [Ger., The Life of Mary]. A song cycle for soprano and piano by Hindemith on 15 texts by Rilke, composed in 1922–23 and revised in 1936–48.

Marimba. (1) A *xylophone with resonators under each bar. Originally an African instrument, it spread to Latin America and remains popular in Mexico and Central America, especially in Guatemala, where it is considered the national instrument.

In Latin America, marimbas are typically mounted on stands. The resonators may be tubular or made from gourds or other material, sometimes with *mirliton devices. Marimba orchestras are popular in Mexico and Guatemala.

Marimbas have been manufactured in the U.S. since the early 20th century for use in popular and concert music, including the symphony orchestra. A typical orchestral instrument covers three to four chromatic octaves ascending from the C below middle C, the bars being arranged on the pattern of piano keys. See ill. under Percussion instruments.

(2) *Mbira.

Marimbaphone. A variety of *marimba with metal bars.

Marine shell trumpet. A trumpet made from a mollusk shell, most often a conch. The player blows through a hole pierced at or near the small end of the spiral. Today they are most common in Oceania.

Marine trumpet. *Tromba marina.

Marini, Biagio (b. Brescia, ca. 1587; d. Venice, 20 Mar. 1665). Composer and violinist. Played violin at St. Mark's, Venice, under Monteverdi, 1615–18. Kapellmeister at the Wittelsbach court at Neuburg, 1623–49; at S. Maria della Scala, Milan, 1649. Composed principally instrumental music, including some of the earliest Italian solo violin sonatas (*Affetti musicali*, 1617; *Sonate, symphonie*, 1629).

Mario, Giovanni Matteo, Cavaliere de Candia (b. Cagliari, Italy, 17 Oct. 1810; d. Rome, 11 Dec. 1883). Tenor. Studied in Paris; debut at the Opéra, 1838. From 1839 he had a romantic and artistic liaison with Giulia Grisi. They appeared at the Théâtre-Italien, Paris; Her Majesty's, London (from 1847 Covent Garden); also in St. Petersburg, Madrid, and on a U.S. tour (1854–55; he returned in 1872–73 with Patti). He created Ernesto in *Don Pasquale* (1843).

Marizápalos [Sp.]. A 17th-century Spanish dance in 3/4 time. Examples survive for guitar and for keyboard.

Markevitch, Igor (b. Kiev, 27 July 1912; d. Antibes, 7 Mar. 1983). Composer and conductor. Pupil of Cortot, Boulanger, and Scherchen. Taught in Salzburg (1948–56), Mexico, and at the Moscow Conservatory; conducted the Concerts Lamoureux, Paris, 1957–61. Diaghilev commissioned his piano concerto (1929) and the ballet *Rébus* (1930). Other works include an oratorio (*Le paradis perdu,* 1936); orchestral music; chamber and piano works; songs.

Markiert [Ger.]. *Marcato.

Markig [Ger.]. Vigorous.

Marley, Bob [Robert Nesta] (b. Rhoden Hall, St. Ann, Jamaica, 6 Feb. 1945; d. Miami, 11 May 1981). Reggae singer, songwriter, and guitarist. In 1961 formed the Rudeboys with Peter Tosh; they later became the Wailers. Albums include *Rastaman Vibrations* (1976), *Burnin'* (1973), and *Babylon by Bus* (1978). His son David "Ziggy" Marley later formed the reggae group The Melody Makers.

Marliani, Marco Aurelio, Count (b. Milan, Aug. 1805; d. Bologna, 8 May 1849). Composer. Studied in Siena. About 1830, fled to Paris for political reasons; taught singing there (pupils included Grisi). Encouraged by Rossini, produced the opera *Il bravo* (1834); best known for one-act *La xacarilla* (Opéra, 1839). Also composed songs, piano pieces.

Marmontel, Antoine François (b. Clermont-Ferrand, 18 July 1816; d. Paris, 16 or 17 Jan. 1898). Teacher. Pupil of Zimmermann; succeeded him at the Paris Conservatory (1848–87). Published piano pieces, etudes, exercises; writings include a *Histoire du piano* (Paris, 1885) and many biographical and critical essays.

Marpurg, Friedrich Wilhelm (b. Seehof, Brandenburg, 21 Nov. 1718; d. Berlin, 22 May 1795). Theorist and writer on music. Edited several periodicals about music (from 1749); authored important early assessments of the music of J. S. Bach; propagated the theories of Rameau in Germany. His most important treatise is the *Abhandlung von der Fuge nach den Grundsätzen der besten deutschen und ausländischen Meister* (1753–54), the best treatment of fugal practices of its day; also wrote on thoroughbass and other aspects of composition.

Marqué [Fr.]. *Marcato.

Marqués y García, Pedro Miguel (b. Palma de Mallorca, 20 May 1843; d. there 25 Feb. 1918). Composer. Pupil of Berlioz and Monasterio. Orchestra violinist in Madrid. Composed symphonies and other orchestral works; many zarzuelas, especially *El anillo de hierro* (1878), *El monaguillo* (1891).

Marriage of Figaro, The. See *Nozze di Figaro, Le.*

Marriner, Neville (b. Lincoln, England, 15 Apr. 1924). Conductor and violinist. Studied with A. Sammons and in Paris. Taught at the Royal College of Music, 1949–59; played in orchestras and chamber ensembles in London. Formed the Academy of St. Martin-in-the-Fields as a string orchestra, 1959; the Los Angeles Chamber Orchestra, 1969–77. Music director, Minnesota Orchestra, 1979–86; Stuttgart Radio Orchestra, 1983–89.

Marsalis, Branford (b. Breaux Bridge, La., 1960). Jazz tenor and soprano saxophonist. Worked with his brother, Wynton Marsalis, Art Blakey, Clark Terry, Herbie Hancock, and Miles Davis. Appeared in videos with the rock guitarist Sting; had his own video hit with a bop rendition of "Royal Garden Blues" (1987). Led the band on NBC's "Tonight Show."

Marsalis, Wynton (b. New Orleans, 18 Oct. 1961). Jazz and classical trumpeter, jazz bandleader. Brother of Branford Marsalis. Studied at Juilliard. Worked with Art Blakey and Herbie Hancock; led groups from 1981. In 1984, became the first musician to win Grammy awards in jazz and classical music, for the albums *Think of One* (1982) and *Haydn, Hummel, Leopold Mozart* (1983). Has composed works for big band (*Blood on the Fields,* 1994; Pulitzer Prize, 1997). Led the Lincoln Center Jazz Orchestra.

Marsch [Ger.]. March.

Marschner, Heinrich August (b. Zittau, 16 Aug. 1795; d. Hannover, 14 Dec. 1861). Composer. Pupil of Tomasek and Schicht. Weber's assistant at the Dresden court, 1823–26; music director at the Leipzig theater from 1827; at the Hannover court theater from 1831. Hannover court Kapellmeister, 1852–59. Composed operas, including *Der Vampyr* (Leipzig, 1828), *Der Templer und die Jüdin* (Leipzig, 1829), and *Hans Heiling* (Berlin, 1833); other stage works; many songs and piano pieces; sacred and secular choral works; chamber and orchestral music.

Marseillaise, La. The French national anthem, with words (beginning "Allons enfants de la patrie," Come, children of France) and music composed by Claude-Joseph Rouget de Lisle in 1792. It was adopted in 1795.

Marteau sans maître, Le [Fr., The Hammer without a Master]. A composition in nine movements by Boulez for alto, alto flute, viola, guitar, xylorimba, vibraphone, and percussion, composed in 1952–54 (rev. 1957) on a cycle of poems of the same name by René Char.

Martelé [Fr.]. See Bowing (3).

Martellato [It.]. (1) See Bowing (3). (2) In piano playing, a "hammered" touch.

Martellement [Fr., a hammering]. In the 17th century, a *mordent. In the 18th century, a mordent or a *Schneller;* occasionally a *trill.

Martenot, Maurice (Louis Eugène) (b. Paris, 14 Oct. 1898; d. there, 10 Oct. 1980). Musician and inventor. Studied at the Paris Conservatory. Taught at the École normale de musique, Paris; directed the École d'art Martenot, Neuilly. In 1928, demonstrated his electronic instrument, the ondes martenot.

Martha. Opera in four acts by Friedrich von Flotow (libretto in German by Wilhelm Friedrich [pseud. for Friedrich W. Riese], after a French ballet scenario by Vernoy de Saint-Georges), produced in Vienna in 1847. Setting: England in the early 18th century.

Martín y Soler, (Anastasio Martín Ignacio) Vicente (Tadeo Francisco Pellegrin) [lo Spagnuolo] (b. Valencia, 2 May 1754; d. St. Petersburg, 10 Feb. 1806). Composer. Pupil of Padre Martini. Court composer to the Infante (later Charles IV of Spain), Joseph II in Vienna, and Catherine the Great in St. Petersburg (from 1788). Composed operas, including *Ifigenia in Aulide* (Naples, 1779), *Il burbero di buon cuore* (1786), *Una cosa rara* (1786); ballets; other vocal and instrumental works.

Martín, Edgardo (b. Cienfuegos, Cuba, 6 Oct. 1915). Composer. Student of Ardévol; taught at the Univ. of Havana, 1945–68. An important cultural figure in the early days of the Castro regime. Works include *Soneras* and *Cuadros de Ismaelillo* for orchestra; chamber music; and vocal works, often political in nature.

Martin, Frank (b. Geneva, 15 Sept. 1890; d. Naarden, Netherlands, 21 Nov. 1974). Composer. Studied with Jaques-Dalcroze. Taught at the Dalcroze Institute, 1928–38; at the Cologne Musikhochschule, 1950–57; Stockhausen was among his pupils. Active as pianist and harpsichordist. Worked with folk materials and twelve-tone method but never abandoned extended tonality. Works include operas, ballets, and incidental music; oratorios (*Le vin herbé,* 1938–41); *Petite symphonie concertante* (1945), concertos, and other orchestral music; a string quartet and other chamber music; piano works; cantatas and other choral music; solo vocal music.

Martinelli, Giovanni (b. Montagnana, 22 Oct. 1885; d. New York, 2 Feb. 1969). Tenor. Studied in Milan; debut there, 1908. Puccini cast him as Dick Johnson in the European premiere of *La fanciulla del West* (Rome, 1911). Sang at the Metropolitan, 1913–46 (debut as Rodolfo, *Bohème),* often as partner to Rosa Ponselle. Roles included Ernani, Tristan, Radames, Canio, Eléazar *(La juive),* and Otello.

Martinet, Jean-Louis (b. Ste. Bazeille, Lot-et-Garonne, 8 Nov. 1912). Composer and conductor. Pupil of Leibowitz, Desormière, and Messiaen. Taught at the Montreal conservatory from 1971. Works include *Le triomphe de la mort* (symphonie dramatique, 1973) and other orchestral pieces; chamber and piano works; choral and solo vocal music.

Martinez, Marianne [Anna Katharina] **von** (b. Vienna, 4 May 1744; d. there, 13 Dec. 1812). Singer and composer. Pupil of Porpora, Haydn, and G. Bonno; encouraged by Metastasio. Performed in the courts of Vienna. Composed oratorios (*Isacco,* Vienna, 1782); cantatas (*La tempestà,* 1778); sacred works; a symphony; concertos; sonatas.

Martínez, Odaline de la (b. Matanzas, Cuba, 31 Oct. 1949). Composer and conductor. Studied with P. Patterson and R. Smith Brindle. Founding conductor, London Contemporary Chamber Orchestra, 1982. Influenced by Crumb, electronic music, minimalism, and Latin American music; works include *Sister Aimee* (opera, 1978–83); *Phasing* (chamber orchestra, 1975); *2 American Madrigals,* (chorus, 1979); a string quartet (1985); *Cantos de amor* (soprano, piano, string trio, 1985).

Martini, Giovanni Battista ["Padre Martini"] (b. Bologna, 24 Apr. 1706; d. there, 3 Aug. 1784). Writer on music, pedagogue, and composer. Pupil of Perti. From 1725, *maestro di cappella,* Church of S. Francesco, Bologna. Ordained, 1729. Among his pupils were J. C. Bach, Gluck, and Mozart. Authored treatises, including *Esemplare o sia saggio fondamentale pratico di contrappunto sopra il canto fermo* (1774–75). Composed oratorios; nearly 40 Masses; some 1,000 canons; sinfonias; concertos; sonatas; liturgical organ works.

Martini, Johannes [Zohane; Giovanni] (b. Brabant, ca. 1440; d. Ferrara, late 1497 or early 1498). Composer. Of Flemish origin but active in Italy; from 1473, a member of the ducal chapel in Ferrara. Works include 10 Masses; almost 70 Psalms; hymns, Magnificats, and motets; over 30 secular pieces, most settings of French texts.

Martino, Donald (James) (b. Plainfield, N.J., 16 May 1931). Composer. Pupil of Bacon, Sessions, Babbitt, and Dallapiccola. Has taught at Princeton, Yale, the New England Conservatory, and Harvard (from 1983). Has made use of serial procedures. Works include *The White Island* (after Robert Herrick, chorus and instrumental ensemble, 1987); works for solo instruments and orchestra; vocal works; chamber and piano music (*Notturno,* Pulitzer

Prize, 1974; string quartets); film scores, popular songs, and jazz arrangements.

Martinon, Jean (b. Lyons, 10 Jan. 1910; d. Paris, 1 Mar. 1976). Composer and conductor. Pupil of Roussel, Münch, and Desormière. Conducted the Concerts Lamoureux in Paris, 1951–57; the Chicago Symphony, 1963–69. Compositions include *Stalag IX* (*Musique d'exil* for jazz orchestra, 1941) and *Chants des captifs* (soprano, tenor, speaker, chorus, and orchestra, 1945), both composed in a Nazi labor camp; an opera and a ballet; 4 symphonies and other orchestral music; 2 string quartets and other instrumental music; piano pieces; songs.

Martinů, Bohuslav (Jan) (b. Polička, east Bohemia, 8 Dec. 1890; d. Liestal, Switzerland, 28 Aug. 1959). Composer. Pupil of Suk and Roussel. Taught at Princeton (1948–51), the Curtis Institute, and the American Academy in Rome. Worked with Czech folk materials, jazz and ragtime idioms, and Baroque formal principles. Works include operas (*Tři přání* [The Three Wishes], 1929; *Juliette,* Prague, 1938; *The Greek Passion,* Zurich, 1961); ballets (*Špaliček,* Prague, 1933); choral and solo vocal music; orchestral works (*Half-time,* 1924; *Memorial to Lidice,* 1943; 6 symphonies; works for solo instruments with orchestra); 7 string quartets and other chamber music; keyboard works.

Martirano, Salvatore (b. Yonkers, N.Y., 12 Jan. 1927; d. Urbana, Ill., 17 Nov. 1995). Composer. Pupil of Elwell, Rogers, and Dallapiccola. Taught at the Univ. of Illinois from 1963. Has employed the twelve-tone method and popular elements. Developed the Sal-Mar Construction, an instrument that permits simultaneous creation and performance of improvisatory compositions. Works include chamber and orchestral music; a Mass; theater pieces, including *L's G. A.* (1967–68); *Dance/ Players I and II* (video pieces, 1986); *3 not 2* (variable forms piece, 1987); *Phleu* (amplified flute, synthetic orchestra, 1988).

Marttinen, Tauno (b. Helsinki, 27 Sept. 1912). Composer. Pupil of Palmgren and Vogel. Conducted the city orchestra of Hameenlinna, 1949–59; directed the Music School, 1950–75. Early works were nationalistic; he later adopted twelve-tone techniques. Composed principally operas (*Poltettu oranssi* [Burnt Orange], 1968; *Häät* [The Wedding], 1986) and ballets; also 7 symphonies, concertos, chamber music, choral works, film music, and songs for solo voice and orchestra.

Martucci, Giuseppe (b. Capua, 6 Jan. 1856; d. Naples, 1 June 1909). Composer. Studied in Naples. Toured widely as concert pianist until 1880. Teacher,

Naples Conservatory (1880–86; director, 1902–9); 1886–1902, director, Bologna Conservatory. Conducted the Italian premiere of *Tristan,* Bologna, 1888. Composed salon piano pieces; 2 piano concertos; 2 symphonies; chamber music; songs; an oratorio.

Marx, Joseph (b. Graz, 11 May 1882; d. there, 3 Sept. 1964). Composer and critic. From 1914, taught at the Music Academy in Vienna; director from 1922. Published textbooks on harmony and counterpoint as well as 2 volumes of essays. Works include *Idylle* (1926) and other orchestral music; string quartets; numerous songs; *Verklärtes Jahr* (song cycle for mezzo-soprano or baritone and orchestra, 1935–36).

Mascagni, Pietro (b. Livorno, 7 Dec. 1863; d. Rome, 2 Aug. 1945). Composer. Pupil of Ponchielli. Directed the Pesaro Conservatory 1895–1903. Replaced Toscanini as director of La Scala, 1929. Composed operas, including *Cavalleria rusticana, L'amico Fritz* (Rome, 1891, with Calvé), *Iris* (Rome, 1898), *Isabeau* (Buenos Aires, 1911); also *Rapsodia satanica* (symphonic poem for the film *Alfa,* 1915), sacred and secular choral works, songs.

Mascherata [It.]. A masked Carnival performance in Renaissance Italy. Pieces for such occasions, like *villanelle* in style but for four or more voices, were also called *mascherate.*

Mascheroni, Edoardo (b. Milan, 4 Sept. 1852; d. Ghirla, 4 Mar. 1941). Conductor. Studied in Milan. Conductor at La Scala 1891–97 (including the premiere of *Falstaff,* 1893); also conducted in Spain and South America, retiring in 1925.

Masculine, feminine cadence. A cadence is termed masculine if its final pitch or chord occurs on a metrically strong beat [see Meter], feminine if on a metrically weak beat. Feminine cadences occur in both instrumental and vocal music, in the latter often when the final word to be set is accented on the penultimate syllable.

Masked Ball, A. See *Ballo in maschera, Un.*

Mason, Daniel Gregory (b. Brookline, Mass., 20 Nov. 1873; d. Greenwich, Conn., 4 Dec. 1953). Composer. Grandson of Lowell Mason; his father, Henry, co-founded the piano firm of Mason & Hamlin. Pupil of Chadwick and d'Indy. Taught at Columbia, 1905–42. Works include *Chanticleer* (overture, 1926), 3 symphonies, and other orchestral music; *String Quartet on Negro Themes* (1918–19) and other chamber music; piano and organ music; choral music and many songs. Published several books on music appreciation.

Mason. Lowell (b. Medford, Mass., 8 Jan. 1792; d. Orange, N.J., 11 Aug. 1872). Educator and composer. Pupil of O. Shaw. Choirmaster and organist in Boston, 1827–51; director, Handel and Haydn Society, 1827–32. In 1833, founded the Boston Academy of Music. Through his work, Boston public schools accepted music into the curriculum. Settled in New York 1853. Composed many hymns, including "Olivet" ("My faith looks up to thee") and "Bethany" ("Nearer, my God, to thee"). Published collections of hymns, glees, children's songs, and musical exercises.

Masque, mask. A form of entertainment, involving costumes, scenery, dances, music, and poetry, that flourished in England in Tudor and Stuart times. The subject matter was usually mythological, allegorical, or heroic. Models for the masque may be found in similar productions in Italy and France, such as the *ballet de cour.* The English court masque reached a literary and visual high point between 1601 and 1631 when Ben Jonson and Inigo Jones collaborated to produce more than 30 masques. Composers who contributed music to these masques included Alfonso Ferrabosco, John Coprario, Thomas Campion, Nicholas Lanier, and William Lawes. After the Commonwealth masquelike entertainments were performed in the theater, generally at the ends of acts of plays or *semi-operas. The greatest examples of such works may be found in Purcell's *Dioclesian, King Arthur,* and *The Fairy Queen.*

Mass [Fr. *messe;* Ger. *Messe;* It., Lat. *missa;* Sp. *misa*]. The most important service of the Roman rite, deriving from a ritual commemoration of the Last Supper. The term is taken from the words of dismissal of the congregation at the end of the ceremony ("Ite missa est"); an earlier name was *eucharistia.* By the 7th century, the Mass had developed an elaborate liturgy of chants, prayers, and readings placed before and after the central canon [see Canon (3)], and a distinction was made between those parts of the liturgy whose texts (and music) were appropriate only to a particular feast (the Proper) and those whose texts (and music) could be used on any day (the Ordinary) [see also Liturgy, Gregorian chant, *Missa*]. The division of the Mass into musical and nonmusical sections and Proper and Ordinary is shown in the accompanying table.

The liturgy of the Mass contains 11 musical items: 5 Proper and 6 Ordinary (the latter including the dismissal, Ite missa est). Proper chants are the oldest in the written tradition (beginning around the 9th century); they are divided among chants employing antiphonal *psalmody (*introit, *offertory, *communion), responsorial psalmody (*gradual, *alleluia), and direct psalmody (the *tract, which occasionally replaces the alleluia). The texts and chants of

	Sung		Spoken or recited	
Proper	Ordinary		Proper	Ordinary
1. Introit				
	2. Kyrie			
	3. Gloria			
			4. Collect	
			5. Epistle	
6. Gradual				
7. Alleluia or Tract				
			8. Gospel	
	9. Credo			
10. Offertory				
				11. Offertory Prayers
			12. Secret	
			13. Preface	
	14. Sanctus			
				15. Canon
				16. Pater noster
	17. Agnus Dei			
18. Communion				
				19. Postcommunion
	20. Ite missa est or Benedicamus Domino			

the Ordinary entered the liturgy at various times, the *Credo not becoming part of the Roman Mass until 1014.

The first five items of the musical Ordinary (i.e., not including the Ite missa est) have so often been set by composers of the polyphonic period that they are sometimes thought of as a unit. Liturgically, however, they are not, as the parts of the Ordinary (with the exception of the *Kyrie and *Gloria) are separated by other chants, readings, and prayers; chant composers made no attempt to make musical links among them in the many melodies created for each text. The chants of the Ordinary and certain chants of the Proper (particularly the introit and alleluia) were also troped [see Trope], and the application of texts to the extended melismas following the alleluia verse gave rise to a new member of the Mass liturgy known as the *sequence. In the 13th century, the Ordinary chants (with the exception of the Credo) were gathered together into plainsong Mass cycles, and they are presented in this way in modern *liturgical books; in modern publications, the cycles are identified by number (Mass IX, etc.), or by title (*Missa de Beata Virgine, Missa de Angelis,* etc.).

The responsorial items of the Proper and the sequence were the first Mass chants to inspire polyphonic elaboration, no doubt because they stressed soloistic singing. In the 11th and 12th centuries, the solo sections of the responsorial chants of the Mass and *Office were used by the composers of the *Notre Dame School as the basis of a complex polyphony known as *organum; the *Magnus liber organi, ascribed to Leonin, sets the graduals and alleluias of the *Temporale in two-part polyphony. Perotin, a younger colleague, is credited with composing three- and four-part organa. Eventually, though, the *clausula and its descendant the *motet became the focus of composition, and by the 13th century, interest in organum (hence, in the Mass) had declined.

The revival of Mass composition in the 14th century concerned the Ordinary rather than the Proper. Manuscripts connected with the papal court at Avignon (1305–78) contain many polyphonic elaborations of the first five elements of the Ordinary (the Ite is rarely set) arranged as groups of Kyries, Glorias, Credos, etc. These were composed in a number of styles. The first presentations of the parts of the Ordinary as a polyphonic cycle (perhaps emulating plainsong cycles) also appear in the 14th century. Machaut's Messe de Notre Dame, a setting of all six elements of the Ordinary, including the Ite, is often regarded as the first polyphonic cycle by a known composer, though it may not have been composed as a cycle.

Settings of individual Ordinary texts (with the exception of the Ite, which was by then ignored entirely) abound in the early 15th century, e.g., in the Old Hall Manuscript. In these and in other works, *paraphrase technique with Ordinary chants in the uppermost voice is quite common, though the chant could also be treated more strictly or could appear in the tenor. The continued concern with the Ordinary also fostered a desire to unite the elements by musical means; Masses so unified are called cyclic Masses. The simplest method of unification consisted of beginning each part of the Ordinary with the same music [see Motto]. More far-reaching was the attempt to unite the five-part Ordinary by basing each polyphonic setting on the same borrowed melody or *cantus firmus (hence the term cantus firmus Mass). The first cyclic Masses were composed by English composers.

The first great Continental exponent of the cyclic Mass was Dufay. He expanded the number of voices from three to four, adding a bass below the tenor. In the works of later composers the cyclic Mass became an important genre and many cyclic Masses were based on the tenors of French chansons (though Gregorian chants were by no means abandoned). Josquin wrote at least 20 cyclic Masses, forming a compendium of all techniques known in his time and introducing several new ones. In the Missa Pange lingua, a paraphrased cantus firmus moves from voice to voice within an imitative texture—a method of Mass construction that proved extremely attractive to 16th-

century composers. Equally novel and influential, the Missa Mater patris is based on a three-part motet and consistently quotes more than one voice of its model.

After 1500, the increase in the composition of motets in an imitative-homophonic style had a pronounced effect upon the Mass and gave rise to a new type of cyclic Mass, the *parody Mass. Parody Masses were first produced by Josquin's younger French contemporaries, and the type became very popular in the 16th century. But at the same time, interest in Mass composition itself seems to have declined. The cyclic Mass returned to prominence in the works of Palestrina, who composed 104 Masses, drawing principally on Gregorian chants and motets for his models. In this he differed from his great contemporary Lassus, who generally preferred chansons or madrigals. By far the most popular technique for Palestrina, as for his contemporaries, was parody. Palestrina's *Marcellus Mass, which is not clearly based on a model, renders the words of the Gloria and Credo particularly intelligible and is a notable example of classical Roman polyphony of the late 16th century embodying the ideals of the *Council of Trent.

The items of the Proper and plainsong Mass cycles (often in *alternatim style) were also set polyphonically during the 15th and 16th centuries. Heinrich Isaac produced many plainsong alternatim Mass cycles, settings of individual Ordinary texts, and a three-volume set of Proper cycles, the *Choralis constantinus.

Although the Latin liturgy was acceptable to Luther and his followers, there were many attempts to create a liturgy in German, leading eventually to Luther's Deutsche Messe und Ordnung des Gottesdienstes of 1526. The German liturgy stressed the *chorale over other elements; indeed, it soon became possible to substitute a chorale for any section of the Mass liturgy. The great emphasis placed on the chorale in Protestant countries tended to discourage composition of the Latin Mass. In England, after the break with Rome and the establishment of a liturgy in English, the elements of the Mass became part of the Communion Service, and the Latin Mass as such ceased to exist. The only important cyclic Masses composed by an Englishman in the late 16th century were those by Byrd, a Catholic, who did not intend them for the Anglican Church.

In the early 17th century, Masses were among those works assigned to the *prima prattica, partly because the Mass text (i.e., the Ordinary) was considered to be impersonal and not apt for expressing the affections. This essentially conservative manner of composition, also called stile antico, remained the most acceptable for Masses in the 17th century, particularly in Rome, though composers there worked for greater brilliance within the style by composing for many choruses (as in the Masses of Orazio Benevoli and others) [see also Palestrina style, Roman school]. Eventually, however, the new style, or *stile moderno*, was adopted for Mass settings.

In the 18th century, particularly in Italy, many Masses were written in a mixture of old and new styles, employing soloists and orchestra along with the chorus and borrowing techniques from instrumental music and opera. But the basic identification of the Mass with the *stile antico* was never lost; it can be seen in the settings of Antonio Caldara and some of those by Johann Joseph Fux. The greatest Mass embodying the early 18th century's mixed style is Bach's *B-minor Mass, with its *stile antico* choruses, fugues, arias, and duets. In the later 18th century, what might be called a symphonic Mass tradition developed, especially in Austria. Masses were usually written for orchestra, chorus, and four soloists, and new musical forms were introduced, as in the Masses of Haydn, Mozart, and Beethoven.

Early 19th-century composers continued writing symphonic Masses. But the most striking Masses of the 19th century were settings of the *Requiem, including those by Berlioz, Verdi, and Fauré. The perceived theatricality of Masses and other church music spurred a reaction in the later 19th century, evidenced in the Cecilian movement and in the pronouncements of church officials. These currents of thought are reflected in a number of Masses composed by Liszt and in the E-minor Mass of Bruckner, works attempting to recapture the feeling of Renaissance polyphony in a 19th-century musical context.

Although the Mass continued to decline in importance as a major musical genre, several composers of the 20th century completed important settings, e.g., Stravinsky's Mass (1944–48), the *Missa brevis* of Kodály (1947), and Hindemith's Mass (1963). Leonard Bernstein's *Mass* (1970–71) is not a Mass in any strict sense, but uses the Mass liturgy as the framework for a theater piece. The effect of the Second Vatican Council's introduction of vernacular and congregational singing into the Mass has yet to be measured.

Massart, (Joseph) Lambert (b. Liège, 19 July 1811; d. Paris, 13 Feb. 1892). Violinist. Pupil of Kreutzer, Zimmermann, and Fétis. Performed mainly in chamber music; occasionally appeared with Liszt. Taught at the Paris Conservatory, 1843–90 (pupils included Wieniawski, Sarasate, Kreisler). His wife, Louise Aglaé Masson, was a pianist and teacher at the Conservatory.

Massé, Victor [Félix Marie] (b. Lorient, 7 Mar. 1822; d. Paris, 5 July 1884). Composer. Studied at the Paris Conservatory, where he taught, 1866–76. Chorusmaster at the Opéra from 1860. Works include songs; opéras comiques, especially *Galathée* (1852) and *Les noces de Jeannette* (1853); *Paul et Virginie* (opera, 1876).

Masselos, William (b. Niagara Falls, N.Y., 11 Aug. 1920; d. New York, 23 Oct. 1992). Pianist. Studied at Juilliard and the Curtis Institute. Recital debut, New York, 1939. A champion of contemporary music; premiered Ives's *First Piano Sonata* (1948) and Copland's *Piano Fantasy* (1957). Taught at the Catholic Univ. of America (1965–71), at Georgia State Univ. (1972–75), at Juilliard from 1976.

Massenet, Jules (Émile Frédéric) (b. Montaud, near St. Étienne, 12 May 1842; d. Paris, 13 Aug. 1912). Composer. Pupil of Reber and A. Thomas. Taught at the Paris Conservatory, 1878–96. Composed operas (*Le roi de Lahore*, 1877; *Manon; Esclarmonde*, Opéra-comique, 1889; *Werther; Thaïs*, Opéra, 1894; *La navarraise*, Covent Garden, 1894); oratorios (*Marie Magdeleine*, 1873). Other works include much incidental music; orchestral pieces, especially 7 suites, Piano Concerto (1902); piano pieces; some 250 songs.

Mässig [Ger.]. Moderate, moderately.

Mastersingers. See Meistersinger.

Mastersingers of Nuremberg, The. See *Meistersinger von Nürnberg, Die*.

Masur, Kurt (b. Brieg, Silesia, 18 July 1927). Conductor. Studied in Breslau and Leipzig. Musical director, Komische Oper, Berlin, 1960–64; chief conductor, Dresden Philharmonic, 1955–58, 1967–72; conductor, Leipzig Gewandhaus Orchestra, 1970–98; music director, New York Philharmonic, from 1991.

Mata, Eduardo (b. Mexico City, 5 Sept. 1942; d. near Cuernavaca, 4 Jan. 1995). Composer and conductor. Pupil of R. Halffter, Chávez, Orbón, Schuller, and Leinsdorf. Conducted the orchestras of Guadalajara, the Univ. of Mexico, and Phoenix. Music director, Dallas Symphony, 1977–94. Compositions include 3 symphonies; chamber music, including several *Improvisaciones* and sonatas for various instruments; *Aires sobre un tema del siglo XVI* (mezzo-soprano and chamber ensemble); and the ballet *Los huesos secos* (tape).

Matasin, matassin [Fr.; It. *mattaccino;* Sp. *matachín*]. A dance known in Europe from the 16th through the 18th century and thereafter in Mexico and the southwestern U.S. It has most often been a dance in which combat is enacted, sometimes by buffoons or grotesque characters, sometimes with intricate swordplay.

Materna (-Friedrich), Amalie (b. St. Georgen, Styria, 10 July 1844; d. Vienna, 18 Jan. 1918). Soprano. Sang at the Vienna Opera 1869–94. Brünnhilde in the first complete *Ring* (Bayreuth, 1876); created Kundry in *Parsifal* (Bayreuth, 1882).

Mather, Bruce (b. Toronto, 9 May 1939). Composer and pianist. Pupil of Weinzweig, Morawetz, G. Ridout, Messiaen, and Milhaud. Taught at McGill from 1966. Has worked with microtones; recorded some of Wyschnegradsky's music for pianos tuned in quarter and sixth tones. Works include orchestral music (*Scherzo,* 1987); chamber music; Sonata for 2 pianos (1970) and other keyboard works; choral and vocal music (a series of madrigals for voices with instruments); film scores.

Mathews, Max V(ernon) (b. Columbus, Nebr., 13 Nov. 1926). Computer scientist and composer. Working with Boulez and other composers, developed languages for computer sound synthesis and some "intelligent instruments" (the Sequential Drum, electronic violins). Wrote several works for computer and a book on computer music.

Mathias, William (James) (b. Whitland, Dyfed, Wales, 1 Nov. 1934; d. Menai Bridge, Gwynedd, 29 July 1992). Composer. Pupil of I. Parrott and L. Berkeley. Taught at Univ. College of Wales, Bangor (1959–68, 1970–88), and the Univ. of Edinburgh. Works include an opera; concertos, symphonies, and other orchestral music; *Three Medieval Lyrics* (1966) and many other choral works; *Let the People Praise Thee O God* for the marriage of the Prince and Princess of Wales (1981); 3 string quartets and other chamber music; incidental, film, and television music.

Mathis der Maler [Ger., Mathis the Painter]. Opera in seven scenes by Hindemith (to his own libretto, after Matthias Grünewald's life), completed in 1934 and produced in Zürich in 1938. A three-movement symphony of the same name was drawn from the opera. Setting: Mainz, Germany, ca. 1525.

Matin, Le [Fr., The Morning]. Haydn's Symphony no. 6 in D major Hob. I:6. Like the Symphony no. 7 in C major Hob. I:7, *Le midi* (Noontime), and no. 8 in G major, *Le soir* (The Evening), it was composed about 1761. Haydn himself gave *Le midi* its name; the other titles are also probably authentic.

Matins [fr. Lat. *matutinus,* early morning]. A service forming part of the Divine *Office.

Matraca [Sp.]. A rattle, often a *cog rattle, of Spain, Portugal, and Latin America.

Matrimonio segreto, Il [It., The Secret Marriage]. Opera in two acts by Domenico Cimarosa (libretto by Giovanni Bertati, after the play *The Clandestine Marriage* by G. Colman and David Garrick), pro-

duced in Vienna in 1792. Setting: Italy in the 18th century.

Matsudaira, Yoritsune (b. Tokyo, 5 May 1907). Composer. Pupil of Tcherepnin. Has worked with twelve-tone technique, total serialism, gagaku, and improvisation. Works include *Theme and Variations* (piano, orchestra, 1951); *Music for 17 Performers: Tōei [Projection] Henkei [Metamorphosis]* (flute, oboe, clarinet, harp, piano, vibraphone, xylophone, 10 percussionists, 1967); *Rhapsody on a Gagaku Theme,* 1983; *Kashin* (female voices, orchestra, 1969).

Matsushita, Shin-ichi (b. Osaka, 1 Oct. 1922). Composer. Studied at Kyushu Univ. and in Germany and Sweden. Taught at the Univ. of Osaka City and at Nara Women's Univ. Has worked with electronic music. Works include *Correlazioni per 3 Gruppi* (chamber ensemble, piano, percussion, 1958); *Musique pour soprano et ensemble de chambre* (soprano solo or ondes martenot, piano, percussion, string quartet, 1962–63); keyboard pieces (*Konzentration for Organ,* 1973).

Mattei, Stanislao (b. Bologna, 10 Feb. 1750; d. there, 12 May 1825). Composer and theorist. Pupil of Padre Martini; succeeded him as *maestro di cappella,* Church of S. Francesco, 1784; *maestro di cappella,* S. Petronio, from 1789. In 1804, helped found the Liceo filarmonico; pupils included Rossini and Donizetti. Composed sacred works, symphonies, and chamber works; authored a book on figured bass.

Matteis, Nicola (b. Naples; d. London?, ca. 1707). Composer. Arrived in England after 1670. Works include 4 books of *Ayrs* (dance suites) for violin (1685); the prefaces to them contain information about performance practice. His son, Nicola (b. 1670s?; d. 1749?), gave Burney violin and French lessons.

Matteo da Perugia [Matheus de Perusio] (d. in or before Jan. 1418). Composer. Singer at Milan Cathedral, 1402–7 and 1414–16; at the papal court at Bologna, 1409–14. Composed Mass movements and motets, French songs, Italian *ballate.*

Matthay, Tobias (Augustus) (b. London, 19 Feb. 1858; d. High Marley, near Haslemere, 15 Dec. 1945). Pianist, composer, and teacher. Pupil of S. Bennett, Macfarren, and Sullivan. Taught at the Royal Academy of Music, 1876–1925. In 1900, founded a piano school in London; published didactic books, including *The Act of Touch in All Its Diversity* (1903). Composed much piano music.

Mattheson, Johann (b. Hamburg, 28 Sept. 1681; d. there, 17 Apr. 1764). Composer, theorist, and lexicographer. Pupil of J. N. Hanff. Associate of Handel.

Singer (from 1696), conductor, and composer at the Hamburg opera. Music director, Hamburg Cathedral, 1715–28. From 1719, Kapellmeister to the Duke of Holstein. Composed much sacred music and opera. Writings include *Der vollkommene Capellmeister* (1739); *Grundlage einer Ehren-Pforte* (1740), a biographical lexicon of 149 musicians; the first German music periodical, *Critica musica* (1722–25); *Grosse General-Bass-Schule* (1731).

Matton, Roger (b. Granby, Quebec, 18 May 1929). Composer and ethnomusicologist. Pupil of Champagne, Boulanger, and Messiaen. Teacher and folklore archivist at Laval Univ. 1956–76. Transcribed volumes of Acadian folk songs. Works include *Mouvement symphonique* (1962) and other orchestral music; chamber and keyboard works; choral music.

Maturana, Eduardo (b. Valparaiso, Chile, 14 Apr. 1920). Composer. Pupil of Allende. His music uses serial, aleatory, and electronic techniques. Works include the opera *Regreso a la muerte* (1963); *Responso para el Ché Guevara* (tape and orchestra, 1968) and other symphonic pieces; chamber and piano pieces; vocal music.

Mauceri, John (b. New York, 12 Sept. 1945). Conductor. Taught at Yale from 1968. Consultant for music theater, Kennedy Center, from 1981. Music director of the Washington Opera, 1980–82; of the American Symphony, 1984–87; of the Scottish Opera from 1987; of the Hollywood Bowl from 1990.

Maurel, Victor (b. Marseilles, 17 June 1848; d. New York, 22 Oct. 1923). Tenor. Opera debut, Marseilles, 1867. Sang at the Paris Opéra, 1868, 1879–94; in Italian houses from 1869; at Covent Garden (1873–79, 1891–95, 1904). Directed the Théâtre-Italien in Paris, 1883–85. Created Iago (La Scala, 1887), Falstaff (La Scala, 1893), and Tonio in *I pagliacci* (1892).

Maurício (Nunes Garcia), José (b. Rio de Janeiro, 20 Sept. 1767; d. there, 18 Apr. 1830). Composer. Ordained, 1792. *Mestre de capela* at the cathedral in Rio de Janeiro from 1798; at the royal chapel of Dom João VI from 1808. Composed Masses, Requiems, hymns, motets, antiphons; a *drama heróico* (*Ulissea*, 1809); orchestral works.

Má Vlast [Cz., My Fatherland]. A cycle of six symphonic poems composed by Smetana, ca. 1872–79, on subjects from his native Czechoslovakia: (1) *Vyšehrad* (a legendary castle; also, the old citadel of Prague); (2) *Vltava* (the River Moldau); (3) *Šárka* (an Amazon maiden in Czech legend); (4) *Z českých luhů a hájů* (from Bohemian fields and forests); (5) *Tábor* (an ancient city); (6) *Blaník* (a mountain near Prague where, according to legend, heroes slumber awaiting the moment when their country needs their help).

Mavra. Opera in one act by Stravinsky (libretto by Boris Kochno, after Pushkin's "The Little House at Kolomna"), produced in Paris in 1922. Setting: A Russian village long ago.

Maw, (John) Nicholas (b. Grantham, 5 Nov. 1935). Composer. Pupil of Berkeley and Boulanger. Resident composer, Trinity College, Cambridge, 1966–70. Has worked with serialism. Has composed 2 operas; orchestral works (*Odyssey*, 1974–79; *Shahnama*, 1992); vocal works (*Scenes and Arias*, 3 women's voices and orchestra, 1962); chamber music (3 string quartets; *Life Studies*, 15 solo strings, 1973).

Maxima [Lat.]. See Mensural notation.

Maxixe [Port.]. An urban dance-music genre of Brazil, originating as an adaptation of the European polka and popular in the late 19th and early 20th centuries. It is in rapid, syncopated, duple meter and is an important antecedent of the urban *samba.

Maxwell Davies, Peter. See Davies, Peter Maxwell.

Mayone [Maione], **Ascanio** (b. Naples, ca. 1565; d. there, 9 Mar. 1627). Composer. *Maestro di cappella*, Church of the Annunziata, Naples, 1595–1621. Organist at the Spanish viceregal chapel from 1602. Composed innovative works for keyboard; a few vocal pieces.

Mayr, Richard (b. Henndorf, Austria, 18 Nov. 1877; d. Vienna, 1 Dec. 1935). Bass. Sang at the Vienna Court Opera from 1902; at the New York Metropolitan Opera, 1927–30; at Covent Garden, 1924–31. Roles include Pogner *(Meistersinger)*, Baron Ochs *(Rosenkavalier)*; sang in the premieres of Mahler's Symphony no. 8 and Strauss's *Die Frau ohne Schatten* (1919).

Mayr [Mayer], **(Johannes) Simon** (b. Mendorf, Bavaria, 14 June 1763; d. Bergamo, 2 Dec. 1845). Composer. Pupil of Bertoni. From 1802, *maestro di cappella*, Bergamo Cathedral. Composed many operas (*Saffo*, 1794; *La Lodoiska*, Venice, 1796; *Ginevra di Scozia*, Trieste, 1801; *Medea in Corinto*, Naples, 1813; *La rosa bianca e la rosa rossa*, Genoa, 1813); oratorios; cantatas; Masses, Requiems, vespers, other sacred works; some instrumental works.

Mayuzumi, Toshirō (b. Yokohama, 20 Feb. 1929; d. Kawasaki, 10 April 1997). Composer. Pupil of Ikenouchi, Ifukube, and Aubin. Has worked with electronic music, jazz, Middle Eastern music, aleatoric devices, serialism, and traditional Japanese music. Works include an opera (*Kinkakuji* [The Golden Pavilion], 1976); musicals; symphonic works (*Ne-*

han Kōkyōkyoku [Nirvana Symphony], 1958; *Perpetuum mobile,* 1989); *Shūsaku I* (Study I, electronic, 1955); *Piece for Prepared Piano and String Quartet* (1957); *Shōwa Tenpuōraku* (gagaku ensemble, 1970); music for theater and films (*Tokyo Olympic,* 1964).

Mazas, Jacques Féréol (b. Lavaur?, 23 Sept. 1782; d. Bordeaux, 25 or 26 Aug. 1849). Violinist. Studied at the Paris Conservatory. Toured widely as a soloist; 1831, first violin, orchestra of the Théâtre du Palais Royal, Paris. Taught at Orléans and (1837–41) Cambrai. Published much-used violin methods and etudes.

Mazeppa. (1) A *symphonic poem by Liszt, composed in 1851 and revised in 1854 (orchestrated with Joachim Raff), based on a poem by Victor Hugo describing the insurrection (1708) and death of the Ukrainian Cossack hetman Mazeppa. (2) An etude for piano by Liszt from the *Études d'exécution transcendante* and of which the symphonic poem (1) is an expansion.

Mazurka [Pol.]. A Polish folk dance, in triple time, from the province of Mazovia near Warsaw. Mazurkas in art music, such as those of Chopin, exhibit strong differences in tempo and expressive character. This variability may reflect the subsuming under that name of several different folk dances of Mazovia: the mazurka proper (*mazur* or *mazurek* in Polish), fiery and warlike in character; the *obertas* or *oberek,* livelier in tempo and gayer in expression; and the *kujawiak,* originally from the neighboring province of Kujawy, partly slower in tempo and more sentimental and melancholy. These dances are linked by common rhythmic traits, such as strong accents unsystematically placed on the second or third beat and the tendency to end on the dominant pitch on an unaccented third beat. The 1830s and 1840s were the period of its greatest vogue as a drawing-room dance in Western Europe and thence in the New World.

Mazzinghi, Joseph (b. London, 25 Dec. 1765; d. Downside, Bath, 15 Jan. 1844). Composer and pianist. Pupil of J. C. Bach, Sacchini, and Anfossi. From 1786, director, King's Theatre; tutor to the Princess of Wales. Among his stage works are *Ramah Droog* (1798) and *Paul and Virginia* (1800) both in collaboration with William Reeve; also composed more than 20 ballets; some 75 clavier sonatas; overtures and chamber works.

Mazzocchi, Domenico (b. Veja, near Città Castellana, bapt. 8 Nov. 1592; d. Rome, 21 Jan. 1665). Composer. Ordained, 1619. Patrons included Cardinal Ippolito Aldobrandini, Pope Urban VIII, and Innocent X. Composed sacred and secular vocal music, including *Madrigali* (Rome, 1638) and the opera *La catena d'Adone* (Rome, 1626).

Mazzocchi, Virgilio (b. Città Castellana, bapt. 22 July 1597; d. there, 3 Oct. 1646). Composer. Pupil of his brother Domenico. *Maestro di cappella* at the Chiesa del Gesù, at St. John Lateran, and at the Cappella Giulia, St. Peter's (1629–46). Composed sacred and secular vocal music, including motets, madrigals, and oratorios; collaborated with Marazzoli on the comic opera *Chi soffre speri* (1639).

Mbira. An African instrument made of 5 to 30 or more thin metal or cane tongues attached to a board or a box resonator. The tongues, which are held in one or two rows by two bars, with one end left free to vibrate, are plucked with the thumbs and or forefingers. The soft sound is sometimes roughened by wrapping the tongues with wire or adding a mirliton device, or the sound may be amplified with a gourd. The instrument is widely distributed in sub-Saharan Africa and has been exported to Latin America. Other names for it are *kalimba, marimba, marimbula, sansa, sanza,* and thumb piano. See also Lamellaphone; see ill. under Instrument.

Meane, mene, mean. In English music of the 14th to 17th centuries, a middle part, usually the middle of three in a polyphonic piece; also, one of the *sights.

Mean-tone temperament. A scale in which justly tuned (i.e., acoustically pure) major thirds (ratio 5:4) above and below the tonic are made up of equal-sized whole tones whose value is thus the geometric mean of 5:4, whence the name.

Mean-tone temperament was widely used on keyboard instruments between ca. 1500 and ca. 1830. It replaced earlier *Pythagorean and *just tunings while preserving some features of both. Many artists now prefer mean-tone temperament to equal temperament when performing 15th-, 16th-, and 17th-century repertories. See also Interval, Temperament.

Measure [Fr. *mesure;* Ger. *Takt;* It. *misura;* Sp. *compás*]. A unit of musical time consisting of a fixed number of note-values of a given type, as determined by the prevailing *meter, and delimited in musical notation by two *bar lines; also (especially in British usage) bar. The absolute duration of a measure is a function of tempo, i.e., the rate at which any note-value is performed. Informally, a measure may be said to consist of a given number of *beats, with a given note-value receiving one beat. At very rapid tempos, however, the beating of time may occur at the rate even of one beat per measure, though the meter might be, e.g., 3/4. Thus, the number of beats or pulses perceived as occurring within a measure may also vary with tempo, though the number and type of note-values making up the measure remain fixed. For the arrangement of strong and weak beats or pulses within a measure, see Accent (1), Meter.

Mechanical instruments. *Automatic instruments.

Medesimo [It.]. Same; e.g., *m. tempo.*

Medial cadence. See Cadence.

Mediant. See Scale degrees; Psalm tone.

Mediation [Lat. *mediatio*]. See Psalm tone.

Medieval music. See Middle Ages, music of the.

Medio registro [Sp.]. A *divided stop. The practice of dividing organ stops into treble and bass halves between c′ and c♯′ became the norm in Castile from the second half of the 16th century.

Medium, The. Opera in two acts by Gian Carlo Menotti (to his own libretto), produced in New York at Columbia University in 1946. Setting: outside a large city in the present.

Medley. A succession of well-known melodies loosely connected to one another; sometimes synonymous with *potpourri.

Medtner, Nicolai. See Metner, Nikolay.

Meeresstille und glückliche Fahrt [Ger., Calm Sea and Prosperous Voyage]. (1) A cantata for chorus and orchestra by Beethoven, op. 112 (1814–15), setting two contrasting poems by Goethe. (2) An overture by Mendelssohn, op. 27 (1828), evoking the calm and storm of the same two poems by Goethe.

Méfano, Paul (b. Basra, Iraq, 6 Mar. 1937). Composer. Pupil of Dandelot, Messiaen, Milhaud, Boulez, Stockhausen, and Pousseur. Works include *À B. Maderna* (12 strings and tape, 1970); *Fragment* (chamber orchestra, 1975); *Micromégas* (solo voices, speakers, chorus, brass, and tape, 1979); and *Traits suspendus* (bass flute, 1980).

Mehr [Ger.]. More, several; *mehrchörig,* polychoral; *mehrsätzig,* in several movements; *mehrstimmig,* polyphonic; *Mehrstimmigkeit,* polyphony.

Mehta, Zubin (b. Bombay, 29 Apr. 1936). Conductor. Son of the violinist and conductor Mehli Mehta. Pupil of H. Swarowsky. Music director of the Montreal Symphony, 1960–67; of the Los Angeles Philharmonic, 1962–78; of the Hollywood Bowl Summer Festival, 1970–78; of the New York Philharmonic, 1978–91; of the Israel Philharmonic from 1981. Metropolitan Opera debut, 1965 *(Aïda);* Covent Garden, 1977 *(Otello).*

Méhul, Étienne-Nicolas (b. Givet, 22 June 1763; d. Paris, 18 Oct. 1817). Composer. Pupil of Jean-Frédéric Edelmann. Taught at the Institut national de musique from 1793; inspector at the new Paris Con-

servatory from 1795. Composed operas (*Euphrosine,* 1790; *Ariodant,* 1799; *Hélena,* 1803; *Joseph,* 1807); republican songs and hymns; many choral works (*Chant national du 14 juillet 1800,* soloists, triple chorus, and triple instrumental ensemble, 1800); "Napoleonic" cantatas; symphonies; chamber and keyboard music.

Mei, Girolamo (b. Florence, 27 May 1519; d. Rome, July 1594). Writer. Studied ancient Greek music, producing treatises and letters on the early development of monody and opera. His *De modis musicis antiquorum libri IV* (1567–73) discusses the Greek *tonoi* and the uses of music in Greek society and Greek drama. Among his other writings is *Discorso sopra la musica antica e moderna* (1602).

Meistersinger. A burgher belonging to one of the guilds of the 14th to 16th centuries formed to perpetuate or emulate the received or presumed artistic traditions of the *Minnesinger. Beginning in western Germany, these guilds spread eastward in the 15th century, reaching their zenith ca. 1500–1550, above all in Nuremberg, home of Hans Sachs (1494–1576), the best-known Meistersinger both in his day and since.

The Meistersinger conceived of melodies as necessary and specific complements to particular patterns of verse. Both melodies and poetic strophes are typically in *bar form, together constituting a model, or *Ton,* for the production of other songs. Meistersinger guilds included several classes of members. A member began as an apprentice *(Schüler),* next became a journeyman (*Geselle* or *Schulfreund*), and (it was hoped) ended as a master *(Meister).* By 1600, the canon had expanded to about 600 *Töne.* Every *Meistergesang* was governed by 24 rules, as set down in the *Tabulatur.* Meistersinger guilds held monthly concerts in town halls and churches and held major singing competitions, or *Singschulen,* during the feasts of Easter, Whitsuntide, and Christmas. By the middle of the 18th century, the guilds had virtually ceased to exist.

Meistersinger von Nürnberg, Die [Ger., The Mastersingers of Nuremberg]. Opera in three acts by Wagner (to his own libretto, drawn from several historical and literary sources), produced in Munich in 1868. Setting: Nuremberg in the 16th century. See also Meistersinger.

Melba, Nellie [Mitchell, Helen Porter] (b. Richmond, near Melbourne, 19 May 1861; d. Sydney, 23 Feb. 1931). Soprano. Pupil of Marchesi. Opera debut as Gilda, Brussels, 1887. From 1902, sang principally at Covent Garden and in New York; toured Australia with her own company, 1902 and 1911; from 1915 taught at the Melbourne Conservatory.

Her repertory included *Lucia, Traviata, Rigoletto, Faust, Hamlet, Bohème,* and lighter Wagner roles.

Melchior, Lauritz [Hommel, Lebrecht] (b. Copenhagen, 20 Mar. 1890; d. Santa Monica, 18 Mar. 1973). Tenor. Pupil of A. Bahr-Mildenburg. Opera debut as a baritone, Copenhagen, 1913; second debut (as a tenor) in *Tannhäuser,* 1918. Sang at Bayreuth, Covent Garden (1926–39), and the Metropolitan (1926–50); the outstanding Wagnerian tenor of his day. During 1940s and 1950s, appeared in films and operetta.

Melisma [Gr., melody]. A group of more than a few notes sung to a single syllable, especially in liturgical chant.

Melismatic. Characterized by the presence of *melismas; one of the three principal categories of style in *Gregorian chant.

Melkus, Eduard (b. Baden, near Vienna, 1 Sept. 1928). Violinist. Teacher at the Vienna Hochschule für Musik from 1958; 1965, founded the Vienna Capella Academica, an ensemble whose goal was to perform on 18th-century instruments. Has recorded 18th-century sonatas and some dance music.

Mellers, Wilfrid (Howard) (b. Leamington, 26 Apr. 1914). Composer and writer. Pupil of Wellesz and Rubbra. Has taught at Cambridge (1945–48), Birmingham Univ. (1948–59), the Univ. of Pittsburgh (1960–63), and the Univ. of York (from 1964). Has made use of popular elements and avant-garde techniques. Works include dramatic works; many choral and solo vocal works (Missa Brevis, 1962; *Cloud Canticle,* 1969); orchestral (*The Spring of the Year,* 1985) and chamber works (*The Key and the Kingdom,* dancing soprano, improvising flutes, harp or piano, 1974). Books include *Music in a New Found Land* (1964), *Caliban Reborn* (1967), and *The Masks of Orpheus* (1987).

Mellophone. See Alto horn.

Melodeon. A small, suction-operated reed organ of the first half of the 19th century [see Harmonium].

Mélodie [Fr.]. (1) Melody. (2) A solo song with accompaniment, usually the French art song of the 19th and 20th centuries, and thus the French counterpart of the German *lied. Forerunners include 17th-century *airs, early 18th-century solo *cantatas, and late 18th-century *romances. The last were simple, tuneful, strophic settings of poems, with square musical phrasing, corresponding to the regular line lengths of the verse, and subordinate keyboard accompaniment. The early 19th-century composers began to pull away from this model on their own artistic initiative and in response to the new French Romantic poetry and to Schubert's lieder, many of which appeared in French editions under the title *Mélodies.* General tendencies of French song through the 1800s are increasingly careful setting of the subtle rhythms and accents of the French language, growing harmonic freedom (e.g., chromaticism, idiosyncratic chord progressions), prominent, mellifluous keyboard accompanimental styles, and a certain elegance and reserve.

Gounod wrote approximately 200 songs and, in Ravel's opinion, established the character of the French *mélodie.* A new chapter in the history of the *mélodie* opens with the songs of Henri Duparc (1848–1933), who set poems by Baudelaire, Gautier, and Leconte de Lisle in a dissonant and unconventional harmonic style. The great master of French song was Fauré, who composed approximately 100 songs including many settings of Paul Verlaine. Debussy was the great innovator of French song, especially in settings of Verlaine and of Pierre Louÿs's prose lyrics.

The 20th-century composers known as *Les *six* contributed to the repertory of French song with their settings of poets like Guillaume Apollinaire, Stéphane Mallarmé, Jean Cocteau, Gérard de Nerval, and Paul Eluard. Their style, best represented by the prolific Poulenc, is an anti-Romantic, neoclassical one, in which humor, sarcasm, and impudence combine with serious lyricism and detachment.

Melodrama. A musico-dramatic technique in which spoken text alternates with instrumental music or, more rarely, is recited against a continuing musical background. There are examples of entire works using this technique (sometimes called monodrama if there is only one character or duodrama if there are two characters), but some of the best-known examples of melodrama appear as parts of a larger work such as an opera.

The first significant example of a work constructed entirely as a melodrama is *Pygmalion* (1770), with text by Jean-Jacques Rousseau and music by Rousseau and Horace Coignet. Rousseau called the work a *scène lyrique,* not a melodrama. The melodramas composed by Georg Benda were frequently performed and much admired in the late 18th century. Perhaps the most famous examples of melodrama are found in Beethoven's *Fidelio* (act 2, scene 1) and Weber's *Der Freischütz* (act 2, scene 2).

Melodramma [It.]. A text to be set as an opera, or the resulting opera; not the same as *melodrama. The term was used in the 17th century; in the 19th century, it was employed in connection with a variety of works, including *Rigoletto* and *Un ballo in maschera,* evidently without implying anything very specific apart from the combination of music and drama.

Melody [fr. Lat. *melodia*, fr. Gr. *melōidia*, fr. *melos*]. In the most general sense, a coherent succession of pitches. Here pitch means a stretch of sound whose frequency is clear and stable enough to be heard as not noise; succession means that several pitches occur; and coherent means that the succession of pitches is accepted as belonging together. The whole of music is often informally divided into three domains: melody, *harmony, and *rhythm. Melody is opposed to harmony in referring to successive rather than simultaneous sounds; it is opposed to rhythm in referring to pitch rather than duration or stress.

In a narrower sense, melody denotes a specific musical entity, and its meaning touches upon those of figure, motive, subject, theme, and, above all, tune; melody is in fact nearly synonymous with tune, though the latter perhaps implies more finitude and closure. Theme or subject denotes a fixed melodic entity that is used as the basis for a larger musical item. The terms motive and figure suggest melodic fragments: a motive is a configuration that forms part of a subject, theme, or melody but that is clearly recognizable in its own right if it recurs in another context; a figure is a protean configuration used for spinning out a melody begun more memorably.

All musical cultures have melody and melodies, and within bounds of larger stylistic consistencies, a culture's melodies resemble and differ from one another in ways easily perceivable, if not always so easily describable; yet the consideration of melodies in relatable groups is the quickest path to grasping their individual modes of coherence. A group of melodies that resemble one another in consistent ways is sometimes called a melody type. In some musics, melody types are named and are describable entities manipulated by musicians; the Indian *rāga* is the outstanding modern instance. The tune types of Anglo-American folk song, on the other hand, are not reified in this way in musical practice, though singers as well as scholars are perfectly conscious of the resemblances they embody.

It is obviously impossible to separate rhythm completely from melody, since every pitch must have a duration, and duration is part of rhythm. Furthermore, a motive, and therefore a theme or melody depending on it, is as likely to be recognizable from its attack pattern—its rhythm—as it is from its pitch contour. Similarly, in Western tonal music, melody is fundamentally inseparable from harmony, since melodies in this system clearly imply simultaneous combinations of sounds such as major and minor triads.

Melody chorale. An *organ chorale in which the chorale melody is clearly present in the uppermost part.

Melody type. The shared features or underlying pattern of a group of melodies regarded as resembling one another in consistent ways. The concept has been employed principally with respect to repertories transmitted anonymously and often orally and to musics in which the essential creative act lies with the performer rather than with a composer whose activity precedes performance. It may thus embrace, for example, the *tune families of Anglo-American folk song, the melodic families into which some scholars have classified genres of Gregorian chant such as *antiphons and *graduals, the *rāgas of Indian music, and the *maqāms of Turkish and Arabic music.

Melograph. A mechanical device for ethnomusicological *transcription usually producing a kind of graph.

Mélophon [Fr.]. A *reed organ in the shape of a large guitar or hurdy-gurdy, invented in France ca. 1837.

Melopiano. A mechanism, invented in 1873, for converting a piano into a sustaining instrument. The device, which could be installed in a conventional piano, contained metal springs that caused small hammers to bounce repeatedly against the strings, producing a tremolo effect.

Melopoeia [fr. Gr., Lat.]. The art or invention of melody.

Membranophone. An instrument in which sound is produced by the vibration of a membrane, traditionally a stretched animal skin, though now often a synthetic material. Most are *drums, but *mirliton instruments are also included in this category. The membrane may be made to vibrate by striking, rubbing (*friction drum), or, in a mirliton, by the action of sound waves. See also Instrument.

Memphis Slim [Chatman, Peter] (b. Memphis, 3 Sept. 1915; d. Paris, 24 Feb. 1988). Blues pianist, singer, songwriter. In Chicago (1937–61), worked with Big Bill Broonzy and others; as bandleader and soloist, often teamed with Willie Dixon. Appeared at Carnegie Hall and the Newport Festival, 1959. Settled in Paris 1961. Composed and recorded prolifically.

Mendelssohn, Fanny. See Hensel, Fanny (Cäcilie) Mendelssohn (Bartholdy).

Mendelssohn (Bartholdy), (Jakob Ludwig) Felix (b. Hamburg, 3 Feb. 1809; d. Leipzig, 4 Nov. 1847). Composer. Grandson of the noted thinker Moses Mendelssohn. In 1816 his father had his children converted to Christianity. Pupil of Zelter, who declared Mendelssohn at 15 a fully formed musician (early works include short comic operas, 13 string symphonies, concertos, chamber music, piano pieces, and songs). Revived interest in the music of J. S. Bach, and historically oriented concerts in general, by conducting the St. Matthew Passion with the Berlin Singakademie (1829); also revived several Handel oratorios. Music director of Düsseldorf, 1833–35; of the Leipzig Gewandhaus Orchestra, 1835–47. Royal Kapellmeister and later *General-musikdirektor*, Berlin, 1840–44. Established the Leipzig Conservatory, 1843. Married Cécile Jeanrenaud, 1837, and had three children. Works: operas (*Die Hochzeit des Camacho*, Berlin, 1827); oratorios (**St. Paul; *Elijah*); symphonies (**Lobgesang*, the **Scotch*, the **Italian*, the **Reformation*); overtures (**Midsummer Night's Dream; *Meeresstille und glückliche Fahrt; Die *Hebriden; Ruy Blas*, 1839); incidental music for plays (including Sophocles' *Antigone*, 1841; *A *Midsummer Night's Dream*); Violin Concerto, 1844; 2 piano concertos, 1831 and 1837; chamber pieces (including Octet in Eb, 1825; 2 piano trios; 6 string quartets; sonatas for violin, viola, clarinet, and cello; piano quartets; string quintets); organ and piano pieces (sonatas; *Rondo capriccioso; *Lieder ohne Worte;* preludes and fugues); cantatas; church music; part songs; solo songs.

Mene. See Meane.

Ménestrel [Fr.]. **Minstrel; ménestraudie,* the art of the minstrel, including music; *ménestrandise,* a guild of minstrels or their collective activity.

Mengelberg, (Josef) Willem (b. Utrecht, 28 Mar. 1871; d. Chur, Switzerland, 21 Mar. 1951). Conductor. Pupil of Jensen and Wüllner. Conductor, Amsterdam Concertgebouw, from 1895. Led annual Palm Sunday performances (from 1899); appeared regularly in Frankfurt, London, and New York. Noted for his performances of Mahler and Strauss. Barred from professional activities in Holland after 1945; retired to Switzerland.

Mennin [Mennini], **Peter** (b. Erie, Pa., 17 May 1923; d. New York, 17 June 1983). Composer and educator. Pupil of N. Lockwood, Rogers, and Hanson. Teacher at Juilliard, 1947–58 (president from 1962); director of the Peabody Conservatory, 1958–62. Works include 9 symphonies, concertos for cello, piano, and flute, *Concertato "Moby Dick"* (1952), and other orchestral music; *Canzona* (band, 1951); string quartets and other chamber music; piano pieces; choral works (*Cantate de virtute: Pied Piper of Hamelin*, 1969; *Reflections of Emily* 1978); solo vocal music (*Voices*, 1975).

Mennini, Louis (Alfred) (b. Erie, Pa., 18 Nov. 1920). Composer. Brother of Peter Mennin. Pupil of Rogers and Hanson. Teacher at Eastman, 1949–65; dean of

the School of Music at the North Carolina School of the Arts, 1965–71; chair of the music department, Mercyhurst College, until 1983; founder and head, Virginia School of the Arts, 1983–88. Has composed 2 operas and a ballet; 2 symphonies and other works for orchestra; chamber and piano music; and a *Proper of the Mass* (chorus, 1953).

Meno [It.]. Less; *meno mosso,* slower.

Menotti, Gian Carlo (b. Cadegliano, Varese, 7 July 1911). Composer and librettist. Pupil of Scalero; close friend of Samuel Barber, for whom he wrote librettos. Taught at Curtis, 1948–55; active as a stage director for his own and others' operas. Founder and artistic director of the Spoleto Festival of Two Worlds, 1958–93. From 1993, director of the Rome opera. Has composed many operas *(Amelia al ballo,* 1933; *The Old Maid and the Thief,* 1939; *The *Medium; The *Telephone; The *Consul,* Pulitzer Prize, 1950; **Amahl and the Night Visitors; The Saint of Bleecker Street,* Pulitzer Prize, 1955; *Le dernier sauvage,* 1963; *Help, Help, the Globolinks!,* 1971; *The Most Important Man,* 1971; *Tamu-Tamu,* 1973; *Goya,* 1987; *The Singing Child,* 1993); ballets (*Sebastian,* 1944); cantatas (*The Wedding,* 1988); a symphony and several concertos; chamber and piano music; *Gloria* (1995) and other choral and vocal music.

Mensur [Ger.]. Meter, mensuration.

Mensural (mensurable) music [Lat. *musica (cantus) mensurabilis*]. In the Middle Ages, music in which durations are fixed, as distinct from plainsong *(cantus planus);* thus, music written in **mensural notation.*

Mensural notation. A system of notating duration whose principles began to be established around 1260 and that, with various modifications, remained in use until about 1600. Franco of Cologne [see Theory] is usually credited with the first systematic exposition (ca. 1250) of the fundamental principles, and notation of this period embodying these principles is thus termed Franconian. Franco's system made use of three main note-values: long, breve, and semibreve. The long was normally equivalent to three breves and the breve equivalent to three semibreves. A duplex long, equivalent to two longs, was also available. In the first half of the 14th century, Philippe de Vitry and Jehan des Murs increased the number of note-values, extended Franco's principles to govern the relationship among these values, and placed the duple division of note-values on an equal footing with triple division. It is this fuller system that is described in what follows.

Four principal note-values and associated rests are employed: long, breve, semibreve, and minim. When

	Notes	Rests
Duplex long		
Long		or
Breve		
Semibreve		
Minim		
Semiminim		
Fusa		

written as single notes, these have the solid black shapes illustrated in the Ex. (a few longer and shorter note-values are also given). As in the Franconian system, longs, breves, and semibreves can be combined to form ligatures, but this does not affect their relationship to one another as note-values. The relationship between any two adjacent note-values in the system can be either triple (as with Franco) or duple. The relationship between long and breve is termed *modus* (mood) and is said to be major if there are three breves to the long and minor if there are two; the relationship between breve and semibreve is termed *tempus* (time) and may be perfect (triple) or imperfect (duple); and that between semibreve and minim is termed *prolatio* (prolation) and may be major (triple) or minor (duple). The particular combination of these relationships governing a composition is termed its mensuration and is roughly analogous to the concept of meter in current musical *notation. In mensural notation, however, the organization of the metrical pulse into recurring patterns of various kinds is not indicated by *bar lines [see also *Tactus*]. The four possible combinations of *tempus* and *prolatio* were termed by Philippe de Vitry the four prolations *(quatre prolacions)* and can be indicated by four signs formed as follows: a complete circle indicates perfect *tempus;* an incomplete circle (C) indicates imperfect *tempus;* a dot in the center of the circle indicates major *prolatio;* and absence of a dot indicates minor *prolatio;* see the accompanying table. These signs, of which the modern use of **C** for 4/4 is a survival, were not much used in sources of the 14th century, with the result that the mensuration of a piece must usually be determined from context.

If the relationship between two adjacent levels of note-values is triple, the particular duration of each note is determined according to the principles applied by Franco to the relationships of long to breve and breve to semibreve. The following summary is in terms of longs and breves but applies equally to other levels of the system. A long followed by a single breve is made imperfect (or imperfected) and has the value of two breves (thus creating the succession 2 + 1). If a long is followed by two breves that are in turn followed by a long, the first long remains perfect, the first breve retains its normal value (and is termed a *brevis recta*), and the second breve is altered (termed a *brevis altera*) to have the value of two normal breves (thus creating the succession 3 + 1 + 2). A long followed by three breves remains perfect, and all three breves have the normal value (thus, 3 + 1 + 1 + 1). If a long is followed by four or more breves, the first breve imperfects the long, and the remaining breves are divided into groups of three equal breves. If a single breve remains, it may imperfect a following long; if two breves remain, the second of the two is altered. A note preceding another note of the same type is always perfect. These rules governing imperfection and alteration clearly derive from a wish to notate the patterns of the rhythmic modes [see Modes, rhythmic].

A note can imperfect a following note as well as a preceding one, though not both. A note can also in effect imperfect a note that forms part of a higher value. For example, a long worth three breves, each worth three minims, may be "imperfected" by a minim, thus reducing its value to eight minims; the minim has in effect imperfected one of the three breves of which the long consists. Rests can cause imperfection and alteration, but their own values are fixed and not subject to imperfection and alteration. Notes written in red are imperfect. This is termed coloration and most often serves to introduce three notes of equal value into the time normally occupied by two notes of the same type; e.g., in imperfect *tempus* with major *prolatio,* three red semibreves occupy the same time as two black ones, an effect identical to the shift in 6/8 from two dotted quarters to three undotted quarters, termed *hemiola.

A dot may be placed between adjacent notes in order to prevent imperfection or alteration according to the usual rules. If the relationship between two note-values is duple, as in current notation, imperfection and alteration do not take place. The dot, however, may be used to cause a preceding note to be perfect, i.e., worth three of the next smaller value. Although its function, as most often in triple relationships, is to cause a note to be perfect, it was and is sometimes termed a dot of addition *(punctus additionis),* since it may be thought of as adding to a note a duration equal to half of its own value. By whatever

Tempus	Prolatio	Sign	Value	Examples
Imperfect	Imperfect	C	◧ = ♦ ♦ ♦ = ↓ ↓	C ◧ ♦ ↓ ↓ = 2/4 ♩ | ♩ ♫
Perfect	Imperfect	O	◧ = ♦ ♦ ♦ ♦ = ↓ ↓	O ◧ ♦ ↓ ↓ ♦ = 3/4 ♩. | ♩ ♫♩
Imperfect	Perfect	C·	◧ = ♦ ♦ ♦ = ↓ ↓ ↓	C· ◧ ♦ ↓ ↓ ↓ = 6/8 ♩. | ♩. ♫♫
Perfect	Perfect	O·	◧ = ♦ ♦ ♦ ♦ = ↓ ↓ ↓	O· ◧ ♦ ↓ ↓ ↓ ♦ = 9/8 ♩.♩. | ♩. ♫♫♩.

Mensural notation.

name, this is precisely the way in which the dot has continued to function.

In the course of the 15th century, hollow (or void) black notes were substituted for solid black notes as the norm, the earlier function of red notes being assumed by solid black notes. Except for the use of elaborate *proportions by some composers around 1500, mensural notation thereafter became steadily simpler, the need for the principles of imperfection and alteration being obviated in various ways.

Mensuration. See Mensural notation.

Mente, alla [It.]. Improvised.

Menuet [Fr.], **Menuett** [Ger.]. *Minuet.

Menuhin, Yehudi (b. New York, 22 Apr. 1916; d. Berlin, 12 Mar. 1999). Violinist. Pupil of L. Persinger and G. Enescu. In 1927, performed the Beethoven concerto in New York under Fritz Busch. Organized the Gstaad Festival in Switzerland (1956) and, after settling in London, the Bath Festival (1959). Conducted and toured with his own chamber orchestra; devoted much time to musical education. Often gave recitals with his sister, Hephzibah (1920–81), a pianist.

Mer, La [Fr., The Sea]. An orchestral work by Debussy consisting of three "symphonic sketches," composed in 1903–5: De l'aube à midi sur la mer (From Dawn to Noon on the Sea); Jeux de vagues (Play of the Waves); and Dialogue du vent et de la mer (Dialogue of the Wind and the Sea).

Merbecke [Marbeck], **John** (b. Windsor, ca. 1510 or earlier; d. ca. 1585). Composer and writer. Organist at St. George's Chapel, Windsor, from at least 1531. Authored many theological writings. Composed settings (often based on plainchant melodies) for The Booke of Common Praier Noted (1550), used in the newly mandatory English-language church services; also 1 Mass, 2 Latin motets, and 1 English anthem.

Mercadante, (Giuseppe) Saverio (Raffaele) (b. Altamura, near Bari, bapt. 17 Sept. 1795; d. Naples, 17 Dec. 1870). Composer. Pupil of Tritto and Zingarelli. Music director at Novara Cathedral 1832–40; from 1840, director of the Naples Conservatory. Composed operas (Elisa e Claudio, Milan, 1821; I giuramenti, La Scala, 1837; La vestale, Naples, 1840; Orazi e Curiazi, Naples, 1846); ballets; sacred works; cantatas; orchestral pieces (Il lamento del bardo, dictated after he became blind in 1862); chamber music; songs.

Mercer, Johnny [John Herndon] (b. Savannah, Ga., 18 Nov. 1909; d. Los Angeles, 25 June 1976). Popular lyricist, songwriter, and singer. Wrote musicals (including Li'l Abner, music by G. de Paul, 1956) and for many films. Collaborated with Jerome Kern, Hoagy Carmichael ("Skylark," 1942), Henry Warren, and Henry Mancini ("Blue Moon," 1961; "Moon River," 1961). Composed both music and words for songs, including "I'm an Old Cowhand" (1936) and "Dream" (1945). In 1942, cofounded Capitol Records.

Mercure, Pierre (b. Montreal, 21 Feb. 1927; d. Avallon, France, 29 Jan. 1966). Composer, bassoonist, and administrator. Pupil of Champagne, Milhaud, Boulanger, Dallapiccola, and P. Schaeffer. Bassoonist, Montreal Symphony, 1947–52. Composer and television producer (1952–66) for CBC. Works include Psaume pour abri (narrator, 2 choruses, brass quintet, string quartet, harpsichord, piano, harp, percussion, and tape, 1962); Lignes et points (orchestra, 1963; uses graphic notation); H₂O for Severino (4–10 flutes or clarinets, 1965); ballets (Incandescence, tape, 1961) and film scores.

Merengue [Sp.]. A folk and popular dance-music genre of the Dominican Republic. In rapid 2/4 meter, it typically alternates sections of stanza and refrain, with responsorial singing of short phrases common in both sections. Voices, accordion, guayo (metal scraper), and *tambora* (double-headed drum played with both bare hand and stick) form a characteristic ensemble. The accompanimental pattern, played by *tambora*, is also characteristic:

The *merengue* is also popular elsewhere in Latin America and is especially well established in Venezuela. The *méringue* of Haiti is a closely related but distinct dance-music tradition.

Merikanto, Aarre (b. Helsinki, June 29, 1893; d. there, 29 Sept. 1958). Composer. Son of the composer Oskar Merikanto (1868–1924). Studied with Reger and in Moscow. From 1936 taught at the Sibelius Academy, Helsinki. Works include an opera, *Juha* (1920–22); orchestral works (3 symphonies, piano and violin concertos); pieces for voice and orchestra (*Genesis,* soprano, chorus, orchestra, 1956); 2 string quartets and other chamber music.

Merkel, Gustav Adolf (b. Oberoderwitz, near Zittau, 12 Nov. 1827; d. Dresden, 30 Oct. 1885). Organist and composer. Pupil of Wieck, Schumann, and Reissiger. Church organist from 1858; director, Dreyssig Singakademie, 1867–73. Composed sonatas, chorale preludes, fantasies, and trios for organ; also didactic works and etudes.

Merrill, Robert (b. Brooklyn, 4 June 1917). Baritone. Sang at the Metropolitan, 1945–75 (debut as Germont in *La traviata*). Appeared frequently in recital and with major orchestras in the U.S.; recordings include *Traviata* and *Un ballo in maschera* under Toscanini.

Merriman, Nan [Katherine-Ann] (b. Pittsburgh, 28 Apr. 1920). Mezzo-soprano. Sang background music for Hollywood films; opera debut, Cincinnati, 1942. Worked with Toscanini; appeared at Glyndebourne, Edinburgh, and Aix-en-Provence. Roles included Dorabella, Meg *(Falstaff)*, Maddalena *(Rigoletto)*, Emilia *(Otello)*, and Baba the Turk *(The Rake's Progress)*.

Merry Widow, The. See *Lustige Witwe, Die.*

Merry Wives of Windsor, The. See *Lustigen Weiber von Windsor, Die.*

Mersenne, Marin (b. La Soultière, Maine, 8 Sept. 1588; d. Paris, 1 Sept. 1648). Music theorist and philosopher. Studied in Paris. Joined the Order of Minims, 1611; taught philosophy and theology at the monastery near Nevers (1615–18). His writings treat music as a scientific discipline; experimented with the physical properties of sound. His chief work: *Harmonie universelle* (Paris, 1636–37).

Merseybeat. A style of popular music that originated ca. 1959 in Liverpool, England. It combined elements of folk music and American rock-and-roll. Its most notable exponents were the Beatles.

Merula, Tarquinio (b. Cremona, 1594 or 1595; d. there, 10 Dec. 1665). Composer and organist. Church organist at Lodi and to the King of Poland (from at least 1624). *Maestro di cappella,* Laudi della Madonna, Cremona (1627–31, 1633–35, 1646–65); held positions in Bergamo during intervening years. Works include opera (*La finta savia,* in collaboration with five others, Venice, 1643); solo motets with string accompaniment; sacred concertos; secular monodies and accompanied madrigals.

Merulo [Merlotti], **Claudio** (b. Corregio, 8 Apr. 1533; d. Parma, 5 May 1604). Composer, organist, and music publisher. Organist at St. Mark's, Venice (1557–84) and in Parma (from 1586). Edited and published collections of his own works and of works by other Italian composers. Composed works for organ (especially toccatas, ricercars, organ Masses, and organ canzonas); sacred and secular vocal works (Masses, motets, and madrigals); *intermedi* for 2 dramas. Didactic treatises by his students transmit his contributions to organ technique.

Mescolanza [It.]. *Medley.

Mesotonic. *Mean-tone temperament.

Messa di voce [It.]. In singing, a gradual *crescendo* and *decrescendo* on a sustained note. It was first discussed by Giulio Caccini (*Le nuove musiche,* 1601–2). It later became one of the primary exercises of *bel canto* and is still often used in teaching. Many 18th-century arias begin with a long *messa di voce,* as did the Classical vocal cadenza.

Messager, André (Charles Prosper) (b. Montluçon, France, 30 Dec. 1853; d. Paris, 24 Feb. 1929). Composer and conductor. Pupil of Fauré and Saint-Saëns. Music director at the Opéra-comique (1898–1903, 1919–20), where he conducted the premiere of *Pelléas et Mélisande* (1902); director and conductor, Covent Garden (1901–17); co-director and conductor, Paris Opéra (1907–14); also a noted symphonic conductor. Composed ballets (*Les deux pigeons,* 1886); *opéras comiques* (*La basoche,* 1890; *Les p'tites Michu,* 1897; *Véronique,* 1898; *Béatrice,* 1914); operettas and musical comedies, including *Monsieur Beaucaire* in English (1919).

Messe [Fr., Ger.]. Mass; *Messe des morts* [Fr.], *Requiem Mass.

Messiaen, Olivier (Eugène Prosper Charles) (b. Avignon, 10 Dec. 1908; d. Paris, 27 Apr. 1992). Composer and organist. Pupil of Dupré and Dukas.

From 1931, organist, l'Église de la Sainte Trinité, Paris. Taught at the École normale de musique and at the Schola cantorum (1930s); at the Conservatory from 1942. In 1936, founded La jeune France with Jolivet, Daniel-Lesur, and Yves Baudrier. His students included Boulez, Barraqué, Stockhausen, and Goehr. Has worked with Greek meters, medieval rhythmic procedures, Hindu rhythms, bird songs, and other materials; his *Modes de valeurs et d'intensités* (piano, 1949) pioneered the serial treatment of pitch, duration, mode of attack, and intensity. Works: an opera, *Saint François d'Assise: Scènes franciscaines* (Paris, 1983); orchestral music (*Turangalîla-symphonie,* with piano, ondes martenot, 1946–48; *Chronochromie,* 1959–60; *Des canyons aux étoiles,* 1971–74); choral works (*Cinq rechants,* 1948; *Transfiguration de notre Seigneur Jésus-Christ,* 1965–69); chamber music (*Quatuor pour la fin du temps,* clarinet, violin, cello, and piano, 1940–41); piano works (*Vingt regards sur l'enfant Jésus,* 1944; *Catalogue d'oiseaux,* 1956–58); organ music (*La nativité du Seigneur: Neuf méditations,* 1935; *Livre d'orgue,* 1951); vocal works (*Poémes pour Mi,* text by Messiaen, 1936; *Harawi,* song cycle, 1945). Writings include *Technique de mon langage musical* (1944).

Messiah. An oratorio in three parts for soloists, chorus, and orchestra by Handel (text compiled by Charles Jennens from various passages in the Bible), first performed in Dublin in 1742. Portions of the work were later revised; the entire oratorio was first published in 1767, after Handel's death.

Mester, Jorge (b. Mexico City, 10 Apr. 1935). Conductor. Studied with Morel, Bernstein, and A. Wolff. Debut, Mexico City, 1955. Music director of the Louisville Orchestra (1967–79), Aspen Music Festival (from 1970), Casals Festival in Puerto Rico (from 1980), and the Pasadena Symphony (from 1984). With the Louisville Orchestra, conducted nearly 200 first performances and was the first to record many 20th-century works. Taught at Juilliard, 1957–67 and from 1980.

Mesto [It.]. Sad, mournful.

Mestres-Quadreny, Josep María (b. Manresa, Barcelona, 4 Mar. 1929). Composer. Cofounded the Conjunt català de música contemporània. Has worked with serialism, aleatory elements, multimedia, electronics, and computer composition. Has composed theater pieces, including *Concert per a representar* (6 singers, flute, clarinet, trumpet, trombone, percussion, bass, and tape, 1964) and *Suite bufa* (dancer, mezzo-soprano, piano, and electronic sound, 1966); ballets; *Ibemia* (chamber orchestra, 1969); *Double Concerto* (ondes martenot, percus-sion, and orchestra); chamber music, with and without electronics; sonatas for piano and organ.

Mesure [Fr.]. Meter; measure; *à la m., en m.,* in time or *a tempo.*

Mesuré [Fr.]. Measured.

Metallophone. A *percussion instrument consisting of a row of tuned metal bars, struck in most cases with a mallet. Examples include the *celesta, *gender, *glockenspiel, *saron, *tubular bells, *vibraharp. See also Idiophone.

Metamorphosis. See Transformation of themes.

Metastasio, Pietro [Trapassi, Antonio Domenico Bonaventura] (b. Rome, 3 Jan. 1698; d. Vienna, 12 Apr. 1782). Librettist. From 1724 wrote operatic librettos for Naples, Rome, and Venice. In 1729, succeeded Apostolo Zeno as Austrian court poet. Wrote librettos for 27 3-act heroic operas, including *Didone abbandonata* (1724); *Semiramide* (1729); *Alessandro nell'Indie* (1729; rev. 1753–54); *La clemenza di Tito* (1734); *Il re pastore* (1751). There are over 800 settings of his librettos, by composers including Handel, Gluck, Mozart, Hasse, and Porpora, making him the principal exponent of opera seria.

Meter [Fr. *mesure;* Ger. *Takt, Taktart;* It. *tempo, misura;* Sp. *tiempo, compás*]. The pattern in which a steady succession of rhythmic pulses is organized; also termed time. Most works of Western tonal music are characterized by the regular recurrence of such patterns. One complete pattern or its equivalent in length is termed a measure or bar and in musical notation is enclosed between two *bar lines. The meter of a work or of a passage within a work is indicated by a fraction or by the sign ₵ or ₵. The denominator of the fraction indicates the basic note-value of the pattern, and the numerator indicates the number of such note-values making up the pattern. Thus, a measure of the meter 3/4 consists of three quarter notes or their equivalent. The sign ₵ is the equivalent of 4/4; ₵ is the equivalent of 2/2. Informally, the numerator is sometimes taken as specifying the number of beats per measure, and the denominator as specifying the note-value to receive one beat. The perception of the beat or pulse, however, depends to some extent on tempo. Thus, 3/4 in a very fast tempo may be heard (or conducted) as having only one beat per measure, and 6/8 will be heard as having two beats per measure as often as six.

Meters in Western music are of two principal kinds: duple or triple, depending on whether the basic unit of pulse recurs in groups of two or three. The recurrence of groups of four pulses, as in 4/4, may be termed quadruple meter but is also a special case of duple meter. A meter in which this basic pulse is subdivided into groups of three, however, is said to be a compound meter. Thus, 6/8 is a compound duple meter because it consists of two groups of three eighth notes (three groups of two eighth notes would be written as 3/4 and would be a simple triple meter); 9/8 is a compound triple meter because it consists of three groups of three eighth notes. Before the 20th century, meters other than these are relatively rare, though there are some well-known exceptions such as the second movement of Tchaikovsky's Symphony no. 6, which is in 5/4 or quintuple meter. Composers of the 20th century have employed a variety of other meters as well, sometimes in rapid succession and sometimes simultaneously in different parts. And some music of the 20th century avoids regular meters and even regular pulse altogether.

The perception of meter is a function of the organization of pitch as well as duration. It consists in recognizing every nth pulse or beat as the first in a new recurrence of the metrical pattern. This first beat is thus said to be the strong beat (or downbeat) of the measure. Other beats are described as weak in varying degrees. Thus, in 4/4, the first beat is the strong beat, the third beat is the next strongest, and beats two and four are weak beats. To the extent that the strong beat is thought of as bearing an accent, it is a metrical accent and not one to be necessarily reinforced by increased loudness or sharper attack [see Accent (1)].

The concern for meter in Western music becomes explicit in the 13th century. The present basic scheme of meters, note-values, and their relationships to one another derives from 14th-century practice. See also Mensural notation, Notation, Note, Prosody, Rhythm.

Metheny, Pat [Patrick Bruce] (b. Lee's Summit, Mo., 12 Aug. 1954). Jazz guitarist, composer, and bandleader. Joined Gary Burton's group, 1974–77. From 1977, formed his own groups; his style combined elements of jazz, rock, country, and Latin music. Formed a trio with Charlie Haden and Billy Higgins (from 1983); recorded the free jazz album *Song X* with Ornette Coleman, 1985. Composed the soundtrack for the film *The Falcon and the Snowman* (1985; "This Is Not America").

Metner [Medtner], **Nikolay Karlovich** (b. Moscow, 5 Jan. 1880; d. London, 13 Nov. 1951). Composer and pianist. Pupil of Safonov, Arensky, and Taneyev. Taught at the Moscow Conservatory, 1909–10, 1914–21; then emigrated, settling first near Paris and then in London (1935). Composed chiefly for the piano; also about 100 songs and a few chamber works.

Metrical psalms. See Psalter.

Metronome. A device used to indicate the tempo of a composition by sounding regular beats at adjustable speed. It was invented ca. 1812 by Dietrich Nikolaus Winkler (ca. 1780–1826) of Amsterdam but takes its name from Johann Nepomuk Maelzel (1772–1838), who copied the device, adding a scale of tempo divisions, and patented it as a "metronome." The instrument is still sometimes called a Maelzel Metronome. The case of the Maelzel Metronome, still usually pyramid shaped, contains a mechanism based on the principle of the double pendulum, i.e., an oscillating rod with a weight at each end, the upper weight being movable along a scale. Clockwork maintains the motion of the rod and provides the ticking. By adjusting the movable weight away from or toward the axis, the pendulum's swinging, and the ticking, can be made slower or faster, respectively. Some modern electric metronomes do not rely on a pendulum, frequently supplementing or replacing the ticking with a blinking light. An indication in a musical score that some note-value is to be performed at M.M. = 80, for example, means that the pendulum oscillates from one side to the other (and ticks) 80 times per minute and that the note-value specified with the indication should be performed at the rate of 80 per minute.

Mettere [It.], **mettre** [Fr., imperative *mettez*]. To put on, e.g., a mute or an organ stop.

Meulemans, Arthur (b. Aarschot, 19 May 1884; d. Brussels, 29 June 1966). Conductor and composer. Directed the organ and song school at Harselt, 1916–30; 1930–42, conductor and director for Belgian Radio. Works include 3 operas; *Peter Breugel Suite* (orchestra, 1952) and several concertos; chamber and piano music; *Sanguis Christi* (solo voices, chorus, and orchestra, 1938); other choral music and songs; a *Serenata* for carillon (1950).

Meyerbeer, Giacomo [Jakob Liebmann] (b. Vogelsdorf, near Berlin, 5 Sept. 1791; d. Paris, 2 May 1864). Composer. Pupil of Zelter and Abbé Vogler. Successful as a virtuoso pianist and improviser; 1816, went to Italy to learn the Italian art of vocal writing. *Generalmusikdirektor* in Berlin from 1842. Composed operas, including *Il crociato in Egitto* (Venice, 1824); **Robert le diable; Les *huguenots; Le *prophète; Ein Feldlager in Schlesien* (1844), reworked as *Vielka* (Vienna, 1847); *L'étoile du nord* (Opéra-comique, 1854); *Le pardon de Ploërmel* (Opéra-comique, 1859); *L'*africaine*. Also wrote songs, sacred works, instrumental pieces.

Meyerowitz, Jan [Hans-Hermann] (b. Breslau, 23 Apr. 1913; d. France, 15 Dec. 1998). Composer, pianist, and conductor. Pupil of Respighi, Casella, and Molinari. Emigrated to the U.S., 1946. Has taught at the Berkshire Music Center, Brooklyn College (1954–61), and City College in New York (1962–80). Works include 8 operas (*The Barrier,* Langston Hughes, 1950); orchestral and band music; chamber and piano music; *Missa Rachel plorans* (1962), Hebrew Service Music (1962), and other choral music; songs.

Mezzo, mezza [It.]. Half, medium, middle; *mezzo forte* (abbr. *mf*), moderately loud, less loud than *forte; mezzo piano* (abbr. *mp*), moderately soft, louder than *piano* [see Performance marks]; *mezza voce,* with half voice, restrained (not the same as **messa di voce*); for mezzo-soprano, see Voice.

M.d. Abbr. for *main droite* [Fr.] or *mano destra* [It.], right hand.

Mf [It.]. Abbr. for **mezzo forte.*

M.g. [Fr.]. Abbr. for *main gauche,* left hand.

Mi. See Pitch names, Solmization, Hexachord, *Mi-fa.*

Mi contra fa [Lat.]. See *Mi-fa.*

Miaskovsky, Nicolai. See Myaskovsky, Nikolay.

Michael, David Moritz (b. Künhausen, near Erfurt, 21 Oct. 1751; d. Neuwied, near Koblenz, 26 Feb. 1827). Composer, violinist, and wind player. Taught and conducted in the Moravian communities in Nazareth and Bethlehem, Pa., 1795–1815. Composed *Parthien* for winds, two "water-music" suites, anthems, and other choral works.

Michelangeli, Arturo Benedetti (b. Brescia, 5 Jan. 1920; d. Lugano, Switzerland, 12 June 1995). Pianist. Studied in Milan; from 1939 taught at the Martini Conservatory, Bologna. London debut, 1946; toured widely thereafter. Founded the International Pianists' Academy in Brescia, 1964; from 1973 taught at the Villa Schifanoia near Florence.

Microtone. An interval smaller than a semitone. Microtones have served both melodic and intonational functions in Western music since antiquity and are fundamental to some non-Western music cultures, notably those of India and the Middle East. In the enharmonic tetrachord of ancient Greek music theory, an interval of a major third is combined with a pair of microtonal intervals that subdivide the tetrachord's remaining semitone. Since the Greek enharmonic scale is a series of such tetrachords, both conjunct and disjunct, its intervallic structure is only periodically microtonal, unlike modern microtonal scales. By the 2nd century, however, the microtonal genera were no longer used by musicians.

The only certain context for the medieval discussion of microtones is the incommensurability of intervals in rational proportions, and it is within this context that interest in microtones chiefly lay between Hellenistic times and the late 19th century. For example, Christiaan Huygens divided the octave into 31 equal tones in the late 17th century in order to permit transposition of diatonic scales in just intonation. The Renaissance, however, saw attempts by some theorists (principally Nicola Vicentino, *L'antica musica ridotta alla moderna prattica,* 1555) and composers (e.g., Guillaume Costeley and Anthoine de Bertrand) to reestablish the enharmonic genus of ancient music.

The modern resurgence of interest in microtonal scales coincided with the search for expanded tonal resources in much 19th-century music. Jacques Fromental Halévy was the first modern composer to subdivide the semitone, in his cantata *Prométhée enchaîné* (1847). In 1892, G. A. Behrens-Senegalden published an account of his patented quarter-tone piano; in 1907, Ferruccio Busoni proposed a sixth-tone scale that was realized in a two-manual harmonium built for him ca. 1911. Alois Hába composed his first quarter-tone piece, a Suite for String Orchestra, in 1917. In 1920, the Russian émigré composer Ivan Vishnegradsky began but was unable to complete a quarter-tone piano in France. Hába, who knew Vishnegradsky's instrument, had greater success building three types of quarter-tone piano in the years 1924–31. Hába became Europe's most effective advocate for the enrichment of the conventional twelve-tone scale by quarter, third, sixth, and finer divisions of the whole tone.

The Mexican composer Julián Carrillo began exploring microtonal intervals on the violin as early as 1895. By 1917, American composers as diverse as Hanson and Ives were experimenting with music for two pianos tuned a quarter tone apart. From 1924 on, Carrillo devoted himself almost exclusively to composing microtonal pieces for new or adapted instruments, and in 1930 he formed an ensemble, the Orquesta Sonido trece, to play them. Carrillo's designs for microtonal pianos, patented in 1940 and built in Germany during the 1950s, are the most successful thus far.

All of these composers adhered to the equal division of the octave. In the 1920s, the American composer Harry Partch followed a similar microtonal path. After 1929, however, he pursued an independent course that combined a concern for acoustic purity (manifested in a 43-tone just division of the octave) with a synthesis of ritual elements borrowed from several ancient and folk traditions. John Eaton has been a leading exponent of microtones and has employed them in several operas. Composers of **electro-acoustic music, because of the inherent flexibility and precision of some of the relevant equipment, have made the greatest use of microtones, though not necessarily as the result of a primary wish to employ such intervals for their own sake.

Middle Ages, music of the. Music of the period from about 500 until about 1430. Like most ideas traditionally employed in the periodization of the history of music, the idea of the Middle Ages was borrowed from other branches of historical study. Hence, both of the traditional boundaries cited above are problematical and subject to disagreement. The earlier boundary must remain necessarily vague, since musical *notation begins to be used in Western Europe only in the 9th century and is not transcribable until the 11th. The later boundary and the concept Middle Ages itself are most often defined with reference to the period following, namely the *Renaissance. Thus, general descriptions of the period often stress explicitly or implicitly the absence of features of later music, such as a particular kind of relationship between words and music and a more familiar type of concern on the part of composers for the harmonic as well as the contrapuntal organization of works. Nevertheless, the term Middle Ages continues in widespread use, at least as a convenience.

The term Gothic has sometimes been used to describe the period from ca. 1150 to ca. 1430, also by analogy with other branches of history, particularly of art and architecture. It has gained relatively little currency, however. Terms that have gained more acceptance for the designation of subperiods, largely because they are defined more specifically with respect to music, include *Ars antiqua, *Ars nova, and *Ars subtilior. For individual repertories and genres from the Middle Ages, see St. Martial, Notre Dame, Santiago de Compostela, Troubadour, Trouvère, Minnesinger, Meistersinger, Plainsong, Mass, Motet, Liturgical drama, Lauda, Cantiga, Chanson.

Middle C. The C that is closest to the center of the piano keyboard, notated on the first ledger line below the treble staff and the first above the bass staff. See Pitch names, Notation, Clef.

Middleground. See Schenker analysis.

Midi, Le [Fr.]. See Matin, Le.

Midsummer Night's Dream, A. (1) [Ger. Ein Sommernachtstraum] Incidental music by Mendelssohn, op. 61 (completed in 1842), to Shakespeare's play. The overture, op. 21, was composed in 1826. (2) Opera in three acts by Britten (libretto by the composer and Peter Pears, after Shakespeare's play), produced in Aldeburgh, England, in 1960. Setting: a wood near Athens and Theseus' palace in Athens in legendary times.

Mi-fa. In the theory of *hexachords used in the Middle Ages and Renaissance, a combination of *solmization syllables designating any of several dissonant intervals against which singers and composers were warned by theorists. Because each of the syllables could designate several pitches, the combination mi-fa could represent *tritones (called the diabolus in musica and to which the warning to avoid mi contra fa was particularly directed), minor seconds (as well as their inversions and compounds [see Interval]), and *cross relations.

Mignon. Opera in three acts by Ambroise Thomas (libretto in French by Michel Carré and Jules Barbier, after Goethe's Wilhelm Meisters Lehrjahre), produced in Paris in 1866. Setting: Germany and Italy in the late 18th century.

Mignone, Francisco (Paulo) (b. São Paulo, 3 Sept. 1897; d. Rio de Janeiro, 18 Feb. 1986). Composer. Studied in São Paulo and Milan. Taught at the São Paulo Conservatory, 1928–33; at the National School of Music, Rio de Janeiro, 1933–67. Toured Europe and the U.S. as a conductor. Worked with Brazilian musical materials. Works include operas (O contratador de diamantes, Rio, 1924; L'innocente, Rio, 1928); ballets (Maracatu de chico rei, 1933; Leilão, 1941); orchestral music (4 Fantasias brasileiras with piano, 1929–36; Festa das Igrejas, 1942; Sinfonia transamazônica, 1972); concertos; chamber music; choral music; piano pieces; songs.

Migot, Georges (b. Paris, 27 Feb. 1891; d. Levallois, near Paris, 5 Jan. 1976). Composer, painter, poet, and writer on music. Pupil of Guilmant, Gigout, Widor, and d'Indy. Curator of the Museum of Instruments at the Paris Conservatory, 1949–61. Worked with Asian music and French medieval polyphony. Works include Mystère orphique (polyphonie choréographique, 1948) and other stage works; 6 oratorios; 13 symphonies and other orchestral music; Le livre des danceries (flute, violin, and piano, 1929), 3 string quartets, and other chamber music; piano and organ music; De Christo (1971–72) and other choral music; songs.

Mihalovich, Ödön Péter József de (b. Feričance, Slovenia, 13 Sept. 1842; d. Budapest, 22 Apr. 1929). Composer and educator. Pupil of Mosonyi, Hauptmann, and Cornelius. Succeeded Liszt as head of the Budapest Academy of Music, 1887. Compositions include opera (Hagbart und Signe, Dresden, 1882; Toldi szerelme [Toldi's Love], Budapest, 1893), 4 symphonies, choral works, chamber music.

Mihalovici, Marcel (b. Bucharest, 22 Oct. 1898; d. Paris, 12 Aug. 1985). Composer. Studied in Bucharest and with d'Indy. Composed ballets (Une vie de Polichinelle, 1922) and operas (Les Jumeaux, based on Rostand, 1962); orchestral music (Caprice romanien, 1936; Overture tragique, 1957); chamber (sonatas and sonatinas; 3 string quartets) and piano music (*Cantus firmus,* 2 pianos, 1970; *Passacaille,* 1975).

Mihály, András (b. Budapest, 7 Nov. 1917; d. 19 Sept. 1993). Composer. Pupil of Weiner and Kadosa. After the war he was solo cellist at the State Opera; from 1950 taught at the Budapest Academy; 1978–87, directed the Hungarian State Opera. Works include the opera *Együtt és egyedül* [Together and Alone] (1964–65); 3 symphonies; concertos; *Monodia* (1970); *3 Movements* (ensemble, 1969); 2 string quartets; vocal music.

Mikrokosmos [Ger., Little World]. A collection of 153 piano pieces (plus supplementary exercises) in six volumes by Bartók, composed in 1926 and 1932–39 and arranged in order from very elementary works to very difficult ones.

Milán, Luis [Luys] **de** (b. ca. 1500; d. after 1561). Composer and writer. His books include *Libro de música de vihuela de mano intitulado El maestro* (1536), containing verbal instruction as well as original music (fantasias, *tientos,* and pavans for vihuela along with accompanied songs, *villancicos, romances, sonetos,* in various languages); also *El cortesano,* 1561, about courtly life at Valencia.

Milanese chant. *Ambrosian chant.

Milano, Francesco Canova da. See Francesco Canova da Milano.

Milanov [née Kunc; Ilić], **Zinka** (b. Zagreb, 17 May 1906; d. New York, 30 May 1989). Soprano. Studied with Milka Ternina. Debut, Ljubljana, 1927. Sang with the Zagreb Opera, 1928–35; with the Metropolitan Opera, 1937–66. Soloist in the Verdi Requiem under Toscanini, Salzburg, 1937. Best known for Verdi roles. Taught at Curtis from 1977.

Mildenburg, Anna. See Bahr-Mildenburg, Anna.

Milford, Robin (Humphrey) (b. Oxford, 22 Jan. 1903; d. Lyme Regis, Dorset, 29 Dec. 1959). Composer. Pupil of Holst, Vaughan Williams, and R. O. Morris. Composed choral, chamber, and vocal music (*A Book of Songs,* 1926); oratorio (*A Prophet in the Land,* 1931); orchestral works; opera (*The Scarlet Letter,* 1958–59).

Milhaud, Darius (b. Aix-en-Provence, 4 Sept. 1892; d. Geneva, 22 June 1974). Composer, conductor, and pianist. Pupil of Leroux, Dukas, Gédalge, Widor, and d'Indy. By 1920 was known as one of "Les six." Emigrated to the U.S., 1940; taught at Mills College and the Paris Conservatory (1947–71); 1949 helped to found the Aspen Music Festival. Oliveros, Reich, and Subotnik were among his students. Worked with popular and folk music of Provence, jazz, and polytonality. Composed prolifically, including 15 operas

(*Christophe Colomb; Bolivar,* 1943; *David,* 1952); 17 ballets (*Le boeuf sur le toit,* 1919; *La création du monde,* 1923); incidental music (*Les choëphores,* 1915); film (Renoir's *Madame Bovary,* 1933) and radio scores, and other dramatic works; 12 symphonies, concertos, and other orchestral music (*Cinq études,* with piano, 1920; *Saudades do Brasil,* 1921; *Music for San Francisco,* 1971); a few pieces for brass band; 18 string quartets and other chamber and solo instrumental music (*Trois rag caprices,* piano, 1922); choral music (*Service sacré,* 1947); many cantatas (*Adieu* op. 410, Rimbaud; voice, flute, viola, and harp, 1964); song cycles and songs for solo voice and ensemble or piano (*Poèmes juifs,* 1916); scores for children and amateurs (*Un petit peu de musique,* 1932); *Essai poétique* (tape, 1954).

Military Polonaise. Popular name for Chopin's Polonaise in A major for piano op. 40 no. 1 (1838, published in 1840).

Military Symphony. Popular name for Haydn's Symphony no. 100 in G major Hob. I:100 (1793–94; no. 8 of the *Salomon Symphonies). The second movement, marked *allegretto,* employs triangle, cymbals, and bass drum in imitation of Turkish military music [see Janissary music] and also includes a trumpet fanfare. This movement was originally the second movement of a concerto in G major for two *lire organizzate* [see Hurdy-gurdy] and orchestra Hob. VIIh:3*. After the symphony's success, Haydn made another setting of this movement for military band.

Miller, (Alton) Glenn (b. Clarinda, Iowa, 1 Mar. 1904; d. between London and Paris, 15? Dec. 1944). Jazz and popular bandleader, arranger, and trombonist. Joined Ben Pollack (1926–28). Helped Ray Noble organize a big band (1935–36) before forming his own (1937, 1938). Appeared in films and recorded "Moonlight Serenade," "In the Mood" (both 1939), "Tuxedo Junction," "Pennsylvania 6-5000" (both 1940), "Chattanooga Choo Choo," and "A String of Pearls" (both 1941). Enlisted in the Army Air Force; led a big band in the U.S. and England. Disappeared during a flight to Paris.

Millöcker, Karl (b. Vienna, 29 Apr. 1842; d. Baden, near Vienna, 31 Dec. 1899). Composer. Flutist in theater orchestras in Vienna; theater conductor in Graz, Budapest, and (1869–83) at Theater an der Wien. Composed operettas, including *Das verwunschene Schloss* (1878), *Gräfin Dubarry* (1879), *Der Bettelstudent* (1883), *Gasparone* (1884), and *Der arme Jonathan* (1890).

Milner, Anthony (Francis Dominic) (b. Bristol, 13 May 1925). Composer. Pupil of R. O. Morris and Seiber. Has taught at Morley College from 1947; at

London Univ. from 1954; at the Royal College of Music from 1962; at Goldsmith's College from 1971. Worked with Tippett in the performance of early choral music. Has composed much sacred choral music (*Cantata for Christmas 'Emanuel,'* 1974–75); solo songs (*Our Lady's Hours,* soprano, piano, 1957); Variations for Orchestra (1958); 3 symphonies; a concerto for string orchestra (1982).

Milnes, Sherrill (Eustace) (b. Hinsdale, Ill., 10 Jan. 1935). Baritone. Joined Goldovsky's New England Opera Company in 1960. New York City Opera debut as Valentin (*Faust*), 1964; Metropolitan Opera debut, 1965. Sang Verdi roles as well as Scarpia, Escamillo, and Don Giovanni; recorded widely.

Milonga [Sp.]. A traditional song genre of Argentina. In duple meter, but often with guitar accompaniment in 6/8, it is characteristically sung with wry and playful texts in *romance* or *décima* form; the alternation of passages between two singers in a kind of vocal combat (*payada*) is also a common trait. It became popular in Buenos Aires in the late 19th century and is generally regarded as a principal source of the Argentine **tango*.

Milstein, Nathan (Mironovich) (b. Odessa, 31 Dec. 1904; d. London, 21 Dec. 1992). Violinist. Studied with Auer. Debut, Odessa, 1920. Often appeared in recitals with Horowitz; both left the Soviet Union, 1925; at times performed as a trio with Piatigorsky. Milstein settled in the U.S., 1929. Successful as soloist and recording artist.

Milton, John (b. Stanton St. John, near Oxford, ca. 1563; d. London, buried 15 Mar. 1647). Composer. Father of the poet. Chorister at Christ Church, Oxford, from 1572. Moved to London, 1585; joined the Scriveners' Company. Composed madrigals, one printed in *The *Triumphes of Oriana,* anthems, Psalm settings, a motet, a 6-part *In nomine.*

Mimaroğlu, Ilhan (Kemaleddin) (b. Istanbul, 11 Mar. 1926). Composer. Settled in New York 1959. Studied with Ussachevsky, Beeson, Chou, Lang, Wolpe, and Varèse. From 1963 associated with the Columbia–Princeton Electronic Music Center. Taught at Columbia Teachers College, 1970–71. Has composed works for orchestra; chamber music (*Parodie sérieuse,* string quartet, 1947); a sonata (1964) and *Valses ignobles et sentencieuses* (1984) for piano; *2 x e.e.* (vocal quartet, 1963); electronic works (*Wings of the Delirious Demon,* 1969; *Immolation Scene,* with voice, 1983).

Mimodrame [Fr.]. Pantomime.

Minaccioso, minacciosamente [It.]. Threatening.

Mineur [Fr.]. Minor.

Mingus, Charles (Jr.) (b. Nogales, Ariz., 22 Apr. 1922; d. Cuernavaca, Mexico, 5 Jan. 1979). Jazz double bass player, composer, and bandleader. Joined the big bands of Louis Armstrong (ca. 1943) and Lionel Hampton, Red Norvo's trio, and Bud Powell's trio (1953). Formed Debut Records, 1952–57. In 1955, founded his Jazz Workshop. Its bop-inspired repertory included pieces by Mingus drawing upon New Orleans jazz, blues, and African American gospel music; arrangements of music associated with Duke Ellington; and jazz-rock (1970s). Compositions include "E's flat, Ah's flat too," "My Jelly Roll Soul," "Wednesday Night Prayer Meeting," "Fables of Faubus," "Goodbye Pork Pie Hat" (all recorded 1959), "The Black Saint and the Sinner Lady" (1963), and "Praying with Eric" (1964). In performance Mingus could maintain a bass line while adding inner harmonies and improvised countermelodies.

Minim. In British usage, the half note [see Note; but see also Mensural notation].

Minkus, Léon [Alois; Aloysius Ludwig] (b. Vienna, 23 Mar. 1826; d. there 7 Dec. 1917). Composer. From 1855, violinist, Bolshoi Theater, Moscow; from 1866, teacher, Moscow Conservatory; from 1870, ballet composer, imperial theaters, St. Petersburg, associating with Petipa and others. Composed ballets, including *Paquita* (1846, with Deldevez); *La source* (1866, with Delibes); *Don Quixote* (1869); *La bayadère* (1877).

Minnesinger [Ger., fr. *Minne,* love]. Any of the contributors to the corpus of Middle High German lyric verse on the topic of love, known as *Minnesang,* as well as to the related corpus of political and didactic verse, all dating from ca. 1150 to ca. 1325.

The Minnesinger probably originated in the Rhineland, but many of the most famous came from Bavaria and Austria. Almost all the first generation were nobles of high degree. By the late 12th century, some important Minnesinger were *ministeriales,* members of the lesser nobility, including Reinmar (ca. 1160–ca. 1210), Walther von der Vogelweide (ca. 1170–ca. 1230), and Neidhardt von Reuental (ca. 1180–ca. 1250). The *ministerialis* class (e.g., Tannhäuser, ca. 1230–ca. 1280) and the emerging burgher class (e.g., Konrad von Würzburg, ca. 1225–1287) dominated 13th-century *Minnesang,* as knightly *Minnesang* declined. Like Heinrich von Meissen (called *Frauenlob,* ca. 1260–1318), influential Minnesinger from the later 13th and the early 14th century were often burghers. Oswald von Wolkenstein (1377–1445) is sometimes considered the last of the Minnesinger.

Minnesang (love song) treats various topics of courtly love and was composed to be sung. The *Minnelied* is a man's love song; the *Frauenlied* a woman's. Both derive from the Provençal *canzo [see also Troubadour]. In the 12th-century Wechsel (exchange), a man and woman speak of their common situation in alternating stanzas. In the 13th-century Tagelied (dawn song), derived from the Provençal *alba, lovers part at daybreak. All such poetry is typically written in one or more stanzas of equal length and in *bar form. The Leich is a song in unequal stanzas influenced by the Provençal *lai and descort and by the Latin *sequence. The Spruch (or Sangspruch) is formally closer to the Minnesang but retains its own identity. Both the Leich and the Spruch are devoted primarily to political or to religious and secular didactic themes.

Minor. See Interval, Scale, Chord, Triad, Mode, Key, Tonality.

Minore [It.]. Minor; the term is sometimes used to label a section of a work, e.g., a variation, that is in minor mode.

Minstrel [Fr. ménétrier, ménestrel; Ger. Spielmann; It. menestrello; Sp. ministril; Lat. ministerialis, an officer of the court]. (1) In English-speaking lands since ca. 1570, a wandering singer of ballads; formerly, one skilled in the performance of music as opposed to its theoretical aspect. In medieval Europe, the term is interchangeable with ioculator [Lat., joker; ME. jogelour; Fr. jogleor, jongleur; It. gioccolatore; Sp. joglar]. Before ca. 1300, a minstrel might also be any sort of professional entertainer. Minstrels occupied several social stations. In the lowest was the mendicant on the fringe of society, unprotected by feudal or civic law. The moral norms and (frequently pagan) practices of his milieu were regularly condemned by the Church and by educated people. To counter such views, minstrels in the larger cities formed guilds.

Among the positions open to minstrels in the new bourgeois society of the late Middle Ages was that of town musician or *wait. Beginning with Florence (1291) and Lucca (1308) and spreading rapidly after 1400, many European cities guaranteed a minimum income to one or more minstrels to play for civic and religious functions. In feudal society, the minstrel attached to a noble household occupied a correspondingly elevated social station.

At the 13th-century English royal court, and in noble households, servant-minstrels were usually jestours, singers of gestes who accompanied themselves on the harp. Nonetheless, most minstrels are documented only as instrumentalists. In 14th- and 15th-century France and Burgundy, minstrels were especially those who performed on *haut (loud) instruments.

(2) In the U.S. since 1843, a member of a troupe of entertainers who, in his most characteristic role, amuses by portraying members of the underclasses, especially blacks, as stereotypes with fictional or comically exaggerated racial features. In February 1843, four "Ethiopian Delineators"—Billy Whitlock, Frank Pelham, Dan Emmett, and Frank Brouwer—left the circuses and appeared together in New York City as The Virginia Minstrels. They were a sudden sensation. Minstrel shows of the 1840s were conceived as musical revues spiced with a generous dose of comedy. This proportion of music to comedy was reversed during the 1850s, but the minstrel show remained the 19th century's premiere platform for American populist song. By the mid-1890s they were no longer the dominant form of American theatrical entertainment. Early in the 20th century, they were largely absorbed into vaudeville, the Broadway revue, and burlesque. In these new venues, men like Al Jolson continued for several decades to perform occasionally in blackface. The minstrel show itself became classicized and identified with its mid-19th-century origins.

Mintz, Shlomo (b. Moscow, 30 Oct. 1957). Violinist. Studied in Israel and at Juilliard. New York debut, 1973; settled in the U.S. Music adviser to the Israel Chamber Orchestra from 1989. Recordings include concertos of Mendelssohn, Bruch, and Prokofiev, and the Bach sonatas and partitas.

Minuet [Fr. menuet; Ger. Menuett; It. minuetto; Sp. minué, minuete]. An elegant dance movement in triple meter (usually 3/4) of enormous popularity ca. 1650–1800. It is usually in binary form, with very regular phrases constructed of four-measure units, beginning without upbeat and cadencing on the strong beat. The small, quick dance steps have a hemiola relationship to the meter; therefore, accented second beats and hemiola melodic figures are common in minuets. Such pieces were slower when danced, especially in France, and moderately quick as independent instrumental music, above all in Italy where they were often in 3/8 or 6/8.

The minuet is first known in the middle of the 17th century in France, where it was associated with the town of Poitou. It became a rage at the court of Louis XIV, himself an avid minuet dancer. It changed little in character when taken over into harpsichord and orchestral suites, although English composers were sometimes influenced by the quicker Italian version of the dance. From ca. 1700, pairs of minuets were commonly played *alternativement (ABA). The second one was often labeled trio and was written in a contrasting key and texture.

The minuet with trio was the only Baroque dance form that did not become obsolete as the Classical style emerged in the second third of the 18th century. The minuet often served as the closing movement of an opera overture and thus was one of the original elements of the symphony and related genres. The *binary (usually rounded binary) minuet with trio ultimately became the standard third movement of the Classical symphony (*Mannheim school, Mozart, Haydn). Haydn especially exploited the form, using canons, retrograde designs, unusual key relationships, or quicker tempos. This loosening of the minuet's definition led to the abandonment of the name in favor of *scherzo, most prominently by Beethoven.

Minute Waltz. Popular name for Chopin's Waltz in Db major op. 64 no. 1 (1846–47), so called because it lasts approximately one minute when played at an excessively fast tempo (dotted half note = 140).

Miracle play. See Liturgical drama.

Miraculous Mandarin, The [Hung. *A csodálatos mandarin*]. A pantomime in one act by Bartók (scenario by Menyhért Lengyel), composed in 1918–19, orchestrated and revised thereafter, and first produced in Cologne in 1926. Bartók arranged an orchestral suite from the work in 1919 and 1927.

Mirliton. A vibrating membrane that modifies a sound produced in some other way, adding a nasal or buzzing quality. It may be set in motion by the human voice (as in a *kazoo), or by the sound waves of an instrument to which it is attached (e.g., the *marimba, *mbira, and *ti-tzu).

Miroirs [Fr., Mirrors]. Five piano pieces by Ravel, composed in 1905: *Noctuelles* (Moths); *Oiseaux tristes* (Mournful Birds); *Une barque sur l'océan* (A Boat on the Ocean; orchestrated in 1906, rev. 1926); *Alborada del gracioso* (The Fool's Dawn Song; orchestrated in 1918); and *La vallée des cloches* (The Valley of the Bells).

Mirror composition. A composition that can be performed in *inversion with respect to the intervals of each part as well as the relationship of all of the parts to one another (thus, as if it were being performed from a mirror held below the notation) or one that can be performed in *retrograde (i.e., backward, as if from a mirror held at the end of the notation).

Mischakoff [Fischberg], **Mischa** (b. Proskurov, Ukraine, 16 Apr. 1896; d. Petoskey, Mich., 1 Feb. 1981). Violinist. Studied with Auer. Debut, Berlin, 1912. Concertmaster with the New York Symphony (1924–27), Philadelphia Orchestra (1927–30), Chicago Symphony (1930–37), NBC Symphony (1937–52), Detroit Symphony (1952–68). Taught at Juilliard, 1941–52; at Wayne State Univ., Detroit, from 1952; led the Mischakoff String Quartet.

Mise [Fr.]. Placing, setting; *m. en musique,* setting to music; *m. en scène,* staging.

Miserere [Lat.]. Psalm 50 [51], "Miserere mei, Deus, secundum magnam misericordiam tuam" (Have mercy upon me, O God, according to thy loving kindness). One of the *Penitential psalms, it is assigned in the Roman rite to Lauds of Maundy Thursday, Good Friday, Holy Saturday, and the Office of the Dead.

Misón [Missón], **Luis** (bapt. Mataró, Barcelona, 26 Aug. 1727; d. Madrid, 13 Feb. 1766). Composer. Musician the royal chapel, Madrid, from 1748; also at the Teatro del Buen Retiro. Composed more than 80 *tonadillas;* the intermezzo *La festa chinese* (1761); 12 sonatas for flute, viola, and bass.

Missa [Lat.]. *Mass. Missa solemnis* (solemn or High Mass) is the full form of the Mass with all musical items sung; Beethoven's *Missa solemnis* op. 123 (1818–23), however, like most polyphonic Masses, consists of settings of only the five main parts of the Mass Ordinary, in this case for soloists, chorus, and orchestra. *Missa brevis* (short Mass) in the 16th century refers to a relatively brief setting of all five main parts of the Ordinary; in the 17th century and after, it could also refer to a setting of the Kyrie and Gloria only. *Missa lecta* (read or Low Mass) is the Mass with all texts, including those of musical items, read. *Missa cantata* is sung Mass. *Missa pro defunctis* is Mass for the Dead or *Requiem Mass. For *Missa Papae Marcelli,* see Marcellus Mass. For *Missa L'homme armé,* see *Homme armé, L'*.

Missal [Lat. *missale*]. See Liturgical books.

Mistic(h)anza [It.]. *Quodlibet.

Misura [It.]. Meter, measure, beat; *alla m.,* in strict meter; *senza m.,* freely, without strict meter.

Mit [Ger.]. With. For phrases beginning with this word, see the second word of the phrase.

Mitchell, Red [Keith Moore] (b. New York, 20 Sept. 1927; d. Salem, Ore., 8 Nov. 1992). Jazz double bass player. From 1949 to 1954, played with Charlie Ventura, Woody Herman, Red Norvo, and Gerry Mulligan. During 1950s and 1960s, worked in Los Angeles as bandleader, collaborator, and studio bassist for MGM. In 1968, settled in Stockholm. Pioneered expanded double bass techniques and tuning in fifths (C₁ G₁ D A).

Mitropoulos, Dimitri (b. Athens, 1 Mar. 1896; d. Milan, 2 Nov. 1960). Conductor, composer, and pianist. Pupil of Gilson and Busoni. Conducted the Athens Symphony and Monte Carlo Opera; taught at the Athens Conservatory from 1930. Music director, Minneapolis Symphony, 1937–49; conducted the New York Philharmonic and Metropolitan Opera (1954–60; led the premiere of Barber's *Vanessa*).

Noted for interpreting scores of the late 19th and early 20th centuries, especially a recording of *Wozzeck.* Compositions include *Soeur Béatrice* (opera, 1919); orchestral works; chamber and solo piano music.

Mitte [Ger.]. Middle, e.g., of a drum head *(Fell).*

Mixed media. The merging of elements from different arts into a single, composite expression, usually as in recent works in which live sound (including music) and movement (including dance and dramatic action), film, tape, and setting are combined, often incorporating indeterminate elements [see Aleatory music] and audience participation; also multimedia.

Mixed voices. A combination of men's and women's voices, as distinct from *equal voices.

Mixolydian. See Mode.

Mixture. An organ stop with two or more pipes for each note, always sounding pitches at the octave and twelfth.

Miyagi [Wakabe; Suga], **Michio** [Nakasuga Kengyō] (b. Kobe, 7 Apr. 1894; d. Kariya, 25 June 1956). Composer and performer of the zoku-sō (13-string koto). Blind by the age of 7. Taught in Korea from 1907; at the Tokyo Music School from 1930; at the National Univ. of Fine Arts and Music from 1950. His music integrates European forms and genres with Japanese musical traditions. Has constructed Japanese instruments, including 17-string and 80-string variants of the koto. Works include choral music; solo vocal and chamber music (*Yamato no haru* [Spring in Yamato], voice, koto, ensemble, 1940).

Miyoshi, Akira (b. Tokyo, 10 Jan. 1933). Composer. Studied with Ikenouchi and in Paris. Taught at the Toho Gakuen School of Music, Tokyo, from 1965. Works include dramatic works (*Ondine,* 1959); symphonies, concertos, and other orchestral music; chamber music (sonata for flute, cello, piano, 1955; *IV,* string quartet, 4 Japanese instruments, 1972); *Transit,* electronic and concrete sounds, percussion, keyboard instruments, 1969; vocal music (*Torse II,* chorus, piano, tape, 1961; *Duel,* soprano, orchestra, 1964).

Mizmār [Ar.]. Any reedpipe, especially the *zūrnā and similar instruments.

Mizuno, Sūhkō (b. Tokushima, 24 Feb. 1934). Composer. Studied with Shibata. Taught at Chiba Univ., 1968–71; at the National Univ. for Fine Arts and Music from 1971. Has worked with sound clusters, aleatoric devices, graphic notation, jazz, and improvisation. Works include *Remote Control* (tape, 1962); *Dies Irae* (chorus, electronics, 1972); *Jazz Orchestra '73* (1973); *Tenshukaku Monogatari* (opera, 1977).

Młynarski, Emil (b. Kibarty, near Suwałki, 18 July 1870; d. Warsaw, 5 Apr. 1935). Composer. Studied violin with Auer, piano with Rubinstein, and composition with Lyadov. From 1898, active as conductor in Warsaw; 1904–7, director, Warsaw Conservatory; conducted the Scottish Symphony, 1910–16, and at the Bolshoi Theater through 1917. Taught at the Curtis Institute 1929–31. Used some folk elements. Composed dramatic music (*Noc letnia* [Summer Night], opera, 1914); orchestral music (a symphony; 2 violin concertos); chamber music.

M.M. Abbr. for Maelzel *Metronome.

Mobile form. See Aleatory music.

Modal. Characterized by the use of a *mode or modes, especially the church modes of the Middle Ages and Renaissance [see also Modality], or by the use of the rhythmic modes [see Modes, rhythmic].

Modal jazz. See Jazz.

Modal notation. Notation, especially that in the sources for the repertory of *Notre Dame, designed to represent the rhythms of the rhythmic modes [see Modes, rhythmic; Notation].

Modal rhythm. The rhythm of the rhythmic modes [see Modes, rhythmic].

Modality. A musical system based on the use of a *mode or modes, as distinct especially from *tonality; also that quality of a work that is attributable to its use of a specific mode. For the use of the modes in monophonic and polyphonic music of the late Middle Ages and Renaissance, see Mode. The term modality is often applied to the presence within predominantly tonal works of features describable in terms of the modes or to music that is diatonic to a significant degree but not clearly an example of tonality. In such cases the use of the term does not necessarily imply a direct connection with the historical modes, only that any music employing diatonic scales and/or harmonies based on them can be described with the terminology of the modes. Folk music is sometimes described in these terms and in consequence so is art music based on folk music of this type. Features that may suggest the term include, for example, a whole tone below the tonic in a scale that is otherwise major (as in the Mixolydian mode); a major sixth above the tonic in a scale that is otherwise minor (Dorian); an augmented fourth above the tonic in a scale that is otherwise major (Lydian); a semitone above the tonic in a scale that is otherwise minor (Phrygian).

Mode [Lat. *modus*]. (1) In *mensural notation, the relationship between the long and the breve. (2) Any of the rhythmic patterns making up the set of rhythmic modes [see Modes, rhythmic] employed in certain repertories of medieval music. (3) In the writings of some early medieval theorists, interval. (4) In *acoustics, any of the ways in which vibrating systems such as strings and columns of air can be made to vibrate, e.g., in the case of a string, vibration in segments of one-half, one-third, one-fourth, etc., of its total length.

(5) Any of a series of loosely related concepts employed in the study and classification of both scales and melodies. The term is often restricted to scale types defined as collections of pitches arranged from lowest to highest, each including one pitch that is regarded as central. At another extreme, some concepts of mode emphasize melody types; any given mode is defined principally by characteristic melodic elements. Other concepts of mode range between these extremes. No single concept usefully embraces all that has been meant by the term throughout the history of Western music as well as all that is meant by the terms associated with non-Western music that have at one time or another been translated as mode.

The essentials of the system of modes, termed the church modes, used in the classification of Gregorian chant were formulated by ca. 1000. Eight modes are defined, each according to final (i.e., the pitch on which melodies in that mode end), the intervallic relationship of other pitches to the final (i.e., the scale type), and ambitus (i.e., the range of pitches available from the scale type). From this period onward, the final is regarded as the most important criterion of mode, though the gamut of diatonic pitches (which, however, could include b♭) is a prior assumption, and thus the intervallic relationship of other pitches to the final is in large measure inseparable from the definition of the final itself.

There are four finals—d, e, f, and g—and for each final there is a high ambitus, termed authentic, and a low one, termed plagal, thus yielding the total of eight modes. Definitions of ambitus vary somewhat. In the authentic modes, the ambitus stretches from the pitch below the final to the octave above the final; in the plagal modes, the ambitus stretches from the fifth below the final to the sixth above the final. Some accounts, however, define each ambitus as an octave, either above the final or from the fourth below to the fifth above, and regard pitches above or below as additional. The pitch below the octave is sometimes termed the *subtonium* or, in the case of an authentic mode, the *subfinalis*. Actual melodies present a more varied picture, however.

In the 11th century, theorists began to regard the tenors of *psalm tones as essential characteristics of the modes themselves (and thus sometimes termed dominants of the modes) rather than merely as features of particular types of melodies. The location of these tenors is sometimes described as follows. In

authentic modes the tenor lies a fifth above the final and in plagal modes a third above, except that the pitch b is replaced by c′ (in the authentic mode with final on e and the plagal with final on g), and in the plagal mode with final on e, g is replaced by a. Early practice as regards the tenors was a good deal more varied, however, and thus their identity was clearly not essential to the earliest conceptions of the modes.

Some early sources number the four finals in ascending order with terms derived from the Greek ordinal numbers: *protus, deuterus, tritus,* and *tetrardus,* distinguishing authentic and plagal forms for each. They employ the term *tonus.* In the 9th century, Hucbald proposed the numbering 1 through 8 that remains in use, and, like some other theorists, he used the terms *modus* and *tropus* along with *tonus.* The 9th-century treatise *Alia musica* brought together the eight Latin church modes with Boethius's account of octave species and applied the Hellenistic names that have also remained in use in some contexts (though the terms were not used in the way they had been used in Greek theory). These three forms of nomenclature and the characteristics of the modes described above are summarized in the accompanying table.

Important features of early descriptions of the modes are the characteristic melodies or phrases associated with each mode. These include melodic formulas (derived from Byzantine chant) termed *noeane and the like and model antiphons not taken from liturgical books but with texts from the Bible that incorporate the numbering of the modes. Early writers often assign a melody to a specific mode on the grounds of its similarity to other melodies in that mode. Thus, the early history of the church modes reveals a reliance on concepts of melodic type as well as on the concepts of scale type and final that ultimately became dominant.

Beginning in the late 15th century, theorists described polyphony in modal terms as well. Some regard the tenor as the crucial voice for determining the mode of a polyphonic work as a whole and in this way maintain the distinction between authentic and plagal modes. It is in this context that the traditional system of eight modes is expanded to twelve, first by Heinrich Glarean (*Dodecachordon,* 1547). He adds authentic and plagal modes with finals on a (numbered 9 and 10 and termed Aeolian and Hypoaeolian, respectively) and c′ (numbered 11 and 12 and termed Ionian and Hypoionian, respectively). All modal theorists devoted attention to the set of cadential pitches appropriate to each mode. More difficult to establish is concern by composers for the supposed ethical or affective qualities of the modes. The attribution of such qualities to the modes has its origins in classical antiquity and persists through the Middle Ages. Writers of the Renaissance, under the influence of antiquity, take up the matter with renewed vigor. Throughout the Middle Ages and the Renaissance, however, there is steady (though not complete) disagreement on what these qualities are for individual modes.

By the early 18th century, theorists regard the twelve pitches within each octave as each capable of supporting two scale types distinguished by major and minor thirds. The result is the system of 24 major and minor keys. By the early 19th century, major and minor are seen as the only two survivals of the twelve modes of earlier practice. Although it persists, such a view is at odds with the complex history of the modes, especially in the 17th century. See also Tonality, Modality.

The concepts that have been associated with the term mode in the study of music outside the tradition of Western art music (principally that of the Middle Ages and Renaissance) vary considerably in the relative strength of three elements: scale or pitch collection, usually with some internal hierarchy; melody type; and emotive or other "nonmusical" characteristics. With respect to some repertories, especially of *folk music, these concepts do not form an explicit part of musical practice, but are tools for study and classification by scholars. In some non-Western art musics, on the other hand, such concepts may explicitly underlie a largely improvisatory practice. The latter include the *maqām and *dastgāh of musics of the Near and Middle East and the *rāga of South Asia. In *jazz, the term mode has been applied to scales other than the major or minor scale that may serve as the basis for sometimes extended improvisation over a single harmony, as in some music by Miles Davis.

	Mode		Final	Ambitus	Tenor
1.	Protus authentic	Dorian	d	d–d′	a
2.	Protus plagal	Hypodorian	d	A–a	f
3.	Deuterus authentic	Phrygian	e	e–e′	c′
4.	Deuterus plagal	Hypophrygian	e	B–b	a
5.	Tritus authentic	Lydian	f	f–f′	c′
6.	Tritus plagal	Hypolydian	f	c–c′	a
7.	Tetrardus authentic	Mixolydian	g	g–g′	d′
8.	Tetrardus plagal	Hypomixolydian	g	d–d′	c′
9.		Aeolian	a	a–a′	e′
10.		Hypoaeolian	a	e–e′	c′
11.		Ionian	c	c–c′	g
12.		Hypoionian	c	g–g	e′

Moderato [It.]. Moderate with respect to tempo; allegro m., not as fast as allegro; andante m., not as slow as andante.

Moderator. A pedal or knee lever found on pianos beginning in the late 18th century that causes a strip of cloth to be inserted between the hammers and the strings, thus softening the tone color.

Modéré [It.]. Moderate with respect to tempo. Rousseau (1768), however, equates it with *adagio.

Modern jazz. In the 1950s, *bebop and its derivatives, including *cool jazz. With the advent of *free jazz in the late 1950s, these styles ceased to be regarded as modern, and the term lost currency.

Moderne, Jacques (b. Pinguente, ca. 1495–1500; d. Lyons, 1562 or later). Printer. Settled in Lyons by 1523. Published principally newly composed music, much of it by French or Franco-Flemish composers. Publications include the Motteti del fiori (4 vols.); Le parangon des chansons (11 or more vols.); other books of motets, chansons, Masses, noëls, and instrumental music.

Modes, rhythmic. Patterns of temporal order abstracted by 13th-century theorists from *Notre Dame polyphony; above all, the *discant *clausula. There are six modes, each with its own characteristic foot or combination of long (L) and short (B) notes [see Ex.]. The value of the normal breve or short note (brevis recta) is one temporal unit (tempus), and that of the normal long (longa recta) is two. The modes that make use of these values only (the first, second, and sixth) are known as modi recti; in them each foot contains a total of three tempora. The basic values may be altered to accommodate patterns of greater length—the so-called modi ultra mensuram—to the ternary rhythm of the shorter ones. Thus, in the third, fourth, and fifth modes the longs have three tempora, while in the third and fourth the first breve has one and the second two. Each pattern could be repeated a number of times to produce a phrase or ordo (pl. ordines).

Modal rhythm governed not only the clausula but also the *conductus and, in its early stages, the *motet. Scholars have differed on the degree to which the rhythmic modes are applicable to the conductus, however, and to repertories such as those of the trouvères, troubadours, Minnesinger, Meistersinger, cantigas, and laude. The latter half of the 13th century saw the gradual dissolution of the modes as the breve was broken down, in the triplum of the motet, into ever smaller values—at times up to seven semibreves. If the tenor and the duplum still appeared on the page as modal, the ear did not perceive them as such, so extended had both the longs and the breves become.

1. L B
2. B L
3. L B B
4. B B L
5. L L
6. B B B

The six rhythmic modes.

Since the late 13th century, Greek names have sometimes been used to identify the rhythmic modes, as follows: (1) trochaic; (2) iambic; (3) dactylic; (4) anapestic; (5) spondaic; (6) tribrachic.

Mödl, Martha (b. Nuremberg, 22 Mar. 1912). Soprano and mezzo-soprano. Studied in Nuremberg and Milan. Sang mezzo roles at the Düsseldorf Opera, 1945–49; there grew into a dramatic soprano. Joined the Hamburg Opera, 1949; sang often at Bayreuth from 1951. Roles include Isolde, Brünnhilde, Carmen, Strauss's Clytemnestra. Created characters in Fortner's *Elisabeth Tudor* (1972) and Cerha's *Baal* (1981).

Modo [It.]. Mode; manner.

Modulation. In tonal music, the process of changing from one *key to another, or the result of such change [see Tonality, Key relationship; for the term as used in electronics, see Modulator]. Modulation may take the form of a simple modulation to a closely related key and back again (for example, from C major to G major and back to C) in a short piece, or it may occur as part of a whole series of complex modulations involving many keys in larger works. The capacity for modulation, even more than the establishment of key, is the most distinctive and powerful property of the tonal system in Western music, especially since the community of twelve major and twelve minor keys was made intonationally practical by equal *temperament.

Modulation characteristically is accomplished by means of a pivot chord, having a particular harmonic function in the initial key but a different function in the second. The harmony following the pivot chord is then a distinct harmony of the new key. The process is shown schematically in the accompanying example; in actual music, modulation requires some musical time, at least a phrase, to be carried out. A strong authentic cadence in the new key then helps to con-

firm the modulation, so that the ear's perception of the old key yields to that of the new. A modulation of no longer than a phrase, allowing for one strong cadence, followed then by a reversion to the old key, still fresh in mind, is called an intermediate modulation (or sometimes false modulation). This state must be distinguished from *tonicization, which is of shorter duration, occurs anywhere within the phrase, and generally affects only primary triads [see Harmonic analysis]. Gray areas between these three defined states abound, so a distinction between them may be difficult or arbitrary.

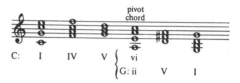

C: I   IV   V { vi
       G: ii   V   I

The most common modulations are between closely related keys: tonic and dominant, tonic and subdominant, tonic and relative minor or major. The modulation to the key of the dominant (in major mode), or to that of the relative major (in minor mode), is at the heart of the sonata principle, being the most basic tonal aspect of the sonata exposition [see Sonata form]. Nevertheless, modulations between any and all keys are possible, and modulations between distantly related keys, involving complex pivot-chord relationships, can be found everywhere throughout the period in which tonality was the norm for Western art music.

A succession of transient modulations (sometimes called passing modulations), traversing several keys before reaching a well-established one, is called a modulation chain. The individual keys are established only briefly, sometimes by as few as two chords, before moving on to the next. Modulation chains [see also Sequence (1)] are commonly found in the keyboard fantasies of the late Baroque and in the development sections of the Classical sonata form. In the 19th century, continuous chromatic modulation over a very long musical time, with an apparent main key occurring but seldom, is a distinguishing characteristic of several composers, especially Wagner in his mature operas, and Liszt, Franck, and Bruckner in their orchestral works. The later intensification of this practice, in the late works of Mahler and the early works of Schoenberg, was one of the factors that led to the breakdown of functional tonality altogether [see Atonality].

Modulator. (1) An electronic device for varying some characteristic (e.g., frequency, amplitude) of a carrier wave for the purpose of transmitting a signal; the process is termed modulation and is the basis for radio and television transmission, whence the terms amplitude modulation (AM) and frequency modulation (FM). See also Ring modulator. (2) See Tonic Sol-fa.

Modus [Lat.]. (1) *Mode. (2) Any of the rhythmic *modes. (3) In *mensural notation, the relationship between the *longa* and the *brevis* (also termed *modus longarum, modus minor*); *modus maximarum* or *modus major* denotes the relationship of the *maxima* to the *longa*. English theorists such as Thomas Morley (1597) sometimes translate these terms as lesser and greater mood, respectively.

Moeran, E(rnest) J(ohn) (b. Heston, Middlesex, 31 Dec. 1894; d. near Kenmare, Ireland, 1 Dec. 1950). Composer. Studied with Ireland. Collected folk songs in Norfolk. Composed a symphony, a violin concerto, and other orchestral works (*Whythorne's Shadow*, 1931; *Rhapsody*, with piano, 1943); chamber music (*Bank Holiday, Summer Valley*, piano, 1923; sonatas; a string quartet).

Moeschinger, Albert (b. Basel, 10 Jan. 1897; d. Thun, 25 Sept. 1985). Composer. Taught at the Bern Conservatory, 1937–43. Worked with twelve-tone technique from the mid-1950s. Works include a ballet and a radio opera; 5 symphonies, 5 piano concertos, and other orchestral works; string quartets, wind trios, and other chamber music; piano and organ works; sacred and secular vocal music.

Moevs, Robert (Walter) (b. La Crosse, Wis., 2 Dec. 1920). Composer and pianist. Pupil of Boulanger and Piston. Teacher at Harvard (1955–63) and Rutgers (from 1964); composer-in-residence at the American Academy in Rome, 1960–61. Works include the ballet *Endymion* (1948); *Symphonic Piece* no. 5 (1984); *Dark Litany* (wind ensemble, 1987); *Paths and Ways* (dancer and saxophone, 1970); string quartets; piano and organ music; sacred choral works; songs.

Moffo, Anna (b. Wayne, Pa., 27 June 1932). Soprano. Debut at the Spoleto Festival as Norina *(Don Pasquale)*, 1955. Sang Verdi roles at La Scala, the Salzburg Festival, and Covent Garden; at the Metropolitan, Violetta *(Traviata)*, Pamina *(Zauberflöte)*, Verdi's Luisa Miller, Gounod's Juliette, Debussy's Mélisande, and other French and Italian roles.

Möglich [Ger.]. Possible; *wie m.*, as possible (e.g., as fast, as loud).

Mohaupt, Richard (b. Breslau, 14 Sept. 1904; d. Reichenau, Austria, 3 July 1957). Composer. Toured as a pianist and conductor in eastern Europe and Asia; lived in New York, 1939–55. Composed much light and film music; 4 operas (*Double Trouble*, 1954); ballets; orchestral music (*Stadtpfeifermusik*, 1939; rev. for winds, 1953); chamber and piano music; vocal and choral music with orchestra; songs and children's songs.

Moins [Fr.]. Less.

Moiseiwitsch [Moyseivich], **Benno** (b. Odessa, 22 Feb. 1890; d. London, 9 Apr. 1963). Pianist. Studied with Leschetizky. Debut, Reading, England, 1908. Toured widely from 1919. Acclaimed for his performances of Rachmaninoff.

Moldau, The. See *Má Vlast.*

Mole, Miff [Irving Milford] (b. Roosevelt, N.Y., 11 Mar. 1898; d. New York, 29 Apr. 1961). Jazz trombonist and bandleader. During the 1920s, pioneered a new soloistic role for the trombone in jazz. Associated with Bix Beiderbecke, Red Nichols, and the Memphis Five; with NBC studios and Paul Whiteman (1930s); and with Benny Goodman (1943). Thereafter led combos, often with cornetist Mugsy Spanier.

Molique, (Wilhelm) Bernhard (b. Nuremberg, 7 Oct. 1802; d. Cannstadt, near Stuttgart, 10 May 1869). Violinist and composer. Concertmaster of the Munich orchestra; of the Stuttgart court orchestra, 1826–49. Toured Germany as soloist from 1822. Settled in London 1849; taught at the Royal Academy of Music from 1861. Composed 6 violin concertos; a cello concerto; an oratorio, *Abraham* (1860); chamber music.

Moll [Ger.]. Minor.

Moller, John Christopher [Möller, Johann Christoph] (b. Germany, 1755; d. New York, 21 Sept. 1803). Composer, organist, and concert organizer. During 1790s, church organist in Philadelphia; 1793, established a music press with Henri Capron. From 1796, managed the New York City Concerts. Composed chamber music, a sinfonia; a cantata; piano works.

Molnár, Antal (b. Budapest, 7 Jan. 1890; d. there, 7 Dec. 1983). Composer. Studied in Budapest. From 1910, played viola with chamber groups. Taught at the Budapest Academy of Music 1919–59. Published writings on Bartók and Kodály, and about the aesthetics and teaching of music. Composed chamber and keyboard works, songs, and folk song arrangements.

Molto [It.]. Very.

Moment form. See *Momente.*

Momente [Ger., Moments]. A work by Stockhausen for soprano, 4 choral groups, and 13 instrumentalists, composed in 1962–64. It is based on the combination of what he termed moments: brief units of musical time defined by a particular process. In a work in what is termed moment form, such moments may be combined in a variety of ways, perhaps at the discretion of the performers.

Moments musicaux [Fr., Musical Moments]. The title given by the publisher in 1828 to Schubert's six piano pieces D. 780 (op. 94; 1823–28). The original title page uses the spelling *Momens musicals.*

Mompou, Federico (b. Barcelona, 16 Apr. 1893; d. there, 30 June 1987). Composer. Studied with I. Philipp. Lived in Paris, 1911–14 and 1921–41. Made use of popular themes. Composed many piano pieces (*Scènes d'enfants,* 1915–19; *Cants magics,* 1917–19; *Cançons i dansas* I–XII, 1921–62; *Preludes* I–X, 1927–51; *Variaciones sobre un tema de Chopin,* 1938–57; *Música callada,* 1959–67); choral works; songs; *Suite compostelana* (guitar, 1963); *Perlimplinada* (ballet, 1956).

Monacordio [Sp.]. Clavichord.

Monasterio, Jesús (b. Potes, near Santander, Spain, 21 Mar. 1836; d. Casar del Periedo, 28 Sept. 1903). Violinist. Studied with Bériot. In 1854, honorary violinist, Spanish Royal Chapel. From 1857, taught at the Madrid Conservatory (director, 1894–97). Founder, Quartet Society; conductor, Sociedad de conciertos, 1869–76; published violin pieces *(Adiós a la Alhambra)* and etudes.

Moncayo García, José Pablo (b. Guadalajara, 29 June 1912; d. Mexico City, 16 June 1958). Composer. Pupil of Huízar and Chávez; formed the "Group of Four" with Galindo, Ayala, and Contreras. Led the National Symphony, 1949–52. Works include *La mulata de Córdoba* (opera, 1948); *Huapango* (orchestra, 1941); *Homenaje a Cervantes* (2 oboes and strings, 1947); choral works; piano compositions.

Mondonville, Jean-Joseph Cassanéa de (b. Narbonne, bapt. 25 Dec. 1711; d. Belleville, 8 Oct. 1772). Violinist and composer. Performed at the Concert spirituel from 1734; intendant of the royal chapel from 1744. Composed operas (*Titon et l'Aurore,* Paris, 1753) and *grands motets; Pièces de clavecin en sonates* (1734); *Pièces de clavecin avec voix ou violon* (1748); *Les sons harmoniques* (1738, including a manual on playing violin harmonics).

Mondscheinsonate [Ger.]. See *Moonlight* Sonata.

Monferrina. A country dance in 6/8 from the Piedmont of northern Italy, popular in England around 1800; also manfredina, monfreda, monfrina.

Moniuszko, Stanislaw (b. Ubiel, near Minsk, 5 May 1819; d. Warsaw, 4 June 1872). Composer. Studied in Warsaw and Berlin. Organist at St. John's, Vilnius, 1840–58. Conductor at the Grand Theater, Warsaw,

from 1859; taught at the conservatory from 1864. Composed operas (*Halka,* 1848, called the first Polish opera); operettas; sacred music; cantatas; some 360 Polish songs, published in his *Home Song Book.*

Monk, Meredith (Jane) (b. Lima, Peru, 20 Nov. 1942). Composer and singer. In 1968, founded the Meredith Monk Vocal Ensemble. Employs extended vocal techniques; elements of minimalism and popular music. Active as filmmaker, choreographer, and director of her theater pieces. Works include *Juice* (theater cantata, 85 solo voices, 85 jew's harps, and 2 violins, 1969); *Book of Days* (film score, 10 voices, cello, shawm, synthesizer, hammered dulcimer, bagpipe, hurdy-gurdy, 1988); *Atlas* (opera, 1991).

Monk [Mönch] **of Salzburg** (fl. late 14th cent.). Poet and composer. Author of both words and music for almost 50 sacred, monophonic songs and over 55 secular songs (a few polyphonic; the earliest such pieces from Germany to survive). His patron was the Archbishop of Salzburg, Pilgrim II.

Monk, Thelonious (Sphere) [Thelious Junior] (b. Rocky Mount, N.C., 10 Oct. 1917; d. Weehawken, N.J., 17 Feb. 1982). Jazz pianist, composer, and bandleader. In 1940s, worked with Coleman Hawkins and Dizzy Gillespie. Led quartets including tenor saxophonists John Coltrane (1957), Johnny Griffin (1958), and Charlie Rouse (1959–70). In 1971–72, toured with the Giants of Jazz, including Gillespie and Art Blakey. Characteristic of his piano playing were unpredictable rhythmic placement, sparse but colorful voicings of chords, and motivic development. Recordings of his compositions include "Well You Needn't," "'Round about Midnight" (both 1947), "Misterioso" (1948), "Brilliant Corners" (1956), and "Straight, No Chaser" (1966–67).

Monn [Mann], **Matthias Georg** [Georg Matthias] (b. Vienna, 9 Apr. 1717; d. there, 3 Oct. 1750). Composer and organist. From 1738, at the Karlskirche, Vienna. Albrechtsberger was among his pupils. Composed symphonies (including one cited as the first known 4-movement symphony with a third-movement minuet), concertos, chamber works (including 6 string quartets), keyboard music, and vocal works. Wrote a treatise on thoroughbass.

Monochord [Gr. *kanōn*]. A *zither with a single string stretched over a rectangular sound box. Calibrations are marked on the sound box to indicate divisions of the string according to mathematical ratios corresponding to various intervals [see Interval]. Usually a movable bridge is provided. The player holds the string firmly against the bridge with one hand and plucks the string with the other. In this way, precisely tuned pitches can be obtained one at a time. The monochord was the principal instrument of ancient Greek music theorists, who used it to investigate the precise relationships among intervals. Its invention was attributed to Pythagoras. In the Middle Ages, it was used for theoretical demonstrations, for the training of singers, and for tuning instruments.

Monocordo [It.]. In string playing, a direction to play a work or passage on a single string.

Monodrama. See Melodrama.

Monody. (1) Music consisting of a single melodic line [see Monophony]. (2) Any of various types of Italian solo song with instrumental accompaniment that flourished during the first half of the 17th century. Although the years around 1600 (which witnessed the performance of the first operas and the publication of Giulio Caccini's important collection of lyric monodies, *Le nuove musiche,* 1602) have usually been considered the starting point of monody, a thriving tradition of accompanied solo song may be traced in Italy at least back to the 15th century.

Two more or less distinct sorts of monody may be discerned: lyric and dramatic. Collections of lyric monodies proliferated after Caccini's path-breaking publication. While Caccini and other composers often referred to their monodies simply as *musiche* (musical works) on their title pages, the contents of the collections usually fall into two distinct genres: the madrigal *(madrigale)* and the air *(aria)*. Madrigals for solo voice and continuo are typically either through-composed settings of freely structured poetry or settings of such poetry with a final section repeated, and they borrow many devices of text expression—unprepared or extreme dissonance, chromaticism, sequential repetition of important phrases, etc.—from their polyphonic precursors. Airs, meanwhile, set strophic poetry, or poetry in fixed forms such as the sonnet. They may consist of repeating musical units adaptable to any example of a particular poetic form; these derive from 16th-century formulas for poetic recitation. More often they employ *strophic variation, in which the strophes of poetry are set to altered versions of the same music, frequently employing the same bass. Perhaps most often they display strict strophic form.

Dramatic monody—the *stile rappresentativo* or *recitative—is the fundamental musical novelty of the earliest opera. It attempts to imitate speech, and to this end, its rhythmic pace is freely declamatory, following closely the accentual patterns of the text. Its melodies are less tuneful than those of the monodic madrigal, often declaiming several words on a single pitch. It generally avoids the virtuosic embellishments of lyric monody.

Monophony, monophonic. Music consisting of a single line or melody without an accompaniment that is regarded as part of the work itself, as distinct from

*polyphony and homophony. For repertories of Western monophonic music see Plainsong, Trouvère, Troubadour, Minnesinger, Meistersinger, *Cantiga, Lauda*. Most folk song is also monophonic in principle, though it may often be sung with improvised accompaniment.

Monothematic, polythematic. A composition based on one or on several themes, respectively. Most *fugues are monothematic, being based on a single subject. Earlier imitative forms such as the *ricercar, *canzona, and *fantasia may be either monothematic or polythematic, however. Examples of *sonata form are often polythematic, having different themes associated with each of the principal tonal areas of the exposition. Some composers, however (e.g., Haydn), have composed monothematic sonata forms.

Monotone. A single tone on which a liturgical text, most often a prayer or passage of Scripture, is recited. An inflected monotone is a formula for recitation in which a single tone predominates but in which divisions in the text may be marked by brief deviations from the principal tone. See Tone, Psalm tone.

Monroe, Bill [William] **(Smith)** (b. near Rosine, Ky., 13 Sept. 1911; d. Springfield, Tenn., 9 Sept. 1996). Country singer, songwriter, and mandolin player. In 1938, formed the Blue Grass Boys; joined the Grand Ole Opry 1939. With guitarist Lester Flatt and banjo player Earl Scruggs (from 1945), this group established the classic bluegrass sound, featuring Monroe's high harmony singing and a string texture of mandolin, guitar, banjo, and fiddle. Monroe's compositions include "Mule Skinner Blues" (1940), "Blue Moon of Kentucky" (1947), and "Cheyenne" (1955).

Monsigny, Pierre Alexandre (b. Fauquembergues, 17 Oct. 1729; d. Paris, 14 Jan. 1817). Composer. Moved to Paris, 1749. *Maître d'hôtel* for the Duke of Orleans, 1768–84; succeeded Piccinni as Inspector of Musical Education, 1800. Composed operas, many with the librettist Sedaine, including *Le roy et le fermier* (1762); *Rose et Colas* (1764); *Aline, reine de Golconde* (1766); *Le déserteur* (1769); *Félix ou L'enfant trouvé* (1777).

Monte, Philippe de [Filippo di, Philippus de] (b. Mechlin, 1521; d. Prague, 4 July 1603). Composer. Lived mainly in Naples and Rome, 1542–68. Kapellmeister to the Habsburg court, Vienna and Prague, from 1568. Secular works include chansons (most with texts by Ronsard) and over 1,100 madrigals. Also composed spiritual madrigals; some 40 Masses (parodies of motets, madrigals, and chansons); motets.

Montéclair, Michel Pignolet [Pinolet] **de** (b. Andelot, bapt. 4 Dec. 1667; d. Aummont, 22 Sept. 1737).

Composer and theorist. Pupil of Moreau. Settled in Paris, 1687. Played *basse de violon* in the Opéra orchestra around 1699. Composed stage works (*Les festes de l'été*, 1716; *Jephté*, 1732); cantatas; some instrumental music. Published the first French violin method (1711–12) and several practical theory books.

Montemezzi, Italo (b. Vigasio, near Verona, 31 May 1875; d. there, 15 May 1952). Composer. Studied in Milan. Lived in California, 1939–49. Composed operas (*Giovanni Gallurese*, Turin, 1905; *L'amore dei tre re*, Milan, 1913; *La nave*, Milan, 1918); a few orchestral, chamber, and choral pieces (*Italia mia, nulla fermerà il tuo canto*, symphonic poem, 1944).

Monter [Fr.]. To raise, e.g., the pitch of an instrument.

Monteux, Pierre (b. Paris, 4 Apr. 1875; d. Hancock, Maine, 1 July 1964). Conductor. Studied at the Paris Conservatory. Founding conductor of the Concerts Berlioz (1910). With the Ballets russes (1911–14 and 1917), led premieres of Ravel's *Daphnis et Chloé*, Debussy's *Jeux*, Stravinsky's *Petrushka, Rite of Spring*, and *Rossignol*. Conducted the Metropolitan Opera (1917–19, 1954–58), the Boston Symphony (1919–24, 1949–62), the Amsterdam Concertgebouw Orchestra (1924–34). Founding conductor of the Orchestre symphonique de Paris (1929–38). Organized and led the NBC Symphony Orchestra (1937). Music director, San Francisco Symphony, 1935–52; chief conductor, London Symphony, 1961–64.

Monteverdi [Monteverde], **Claudio (Giovanni** [Zuan] **Antonio)** (bapt. Cremona, 15 May 1567; d. Venice, 29 Nov. 1643). Composer. Pupil of Marc'Antonio Ingegneri. By 1592–1612, served Duke Vincenzo I of Mantua. *maestro di cappella* of St. Mark's, 1613. Took holy orders, 1632. In 1600 G. M. Artusi attacked the contrapuntal licences taken by some of Monteverdi's madrigals; see *prima prattica, seconda prattica; stile concitato*. Monteverdi was perhaps the first composer to envision opera as a drama in music. Composed operas (*La *favola d'Orfeo; L'Arianna*, Mantua, 1608, most music lost; *Il *ritorno d'Ulisse in patria; L'*incoronazione di Poppea;* ballets (*Il ballo delle ingrate*, Mantua, 1608; *Tirsi e Clori*, Mantua, 1616); spiritual madrigals, Masses, and other sacred vocal works; secular vocal works, including 9 books of madrigals (the fifth, 1605, was the first to include basso continuo; the eighth contains *Combattimento di Tancredi e Clorinda*). His best-known madrigals include "A quest'olmo, a quest'ombre" (1619); "Con che soavità" (1619); "Cruda Amarilli" (1605); "Non si levav'ancor" (1590); "O come sei gentile, caro augellino" (1619); "Tempro la cetra" (1619); "Zefiro torna" (1632).

Montezuma. Opera in three acts by Sessions (libretto by G. A. Borgese), produced in Berlin in 1964. Setting: Mexico, 1519–20.

Montgomery, Wes [John Leslie] (b. Indianapolis, 6 March 1923; d. there, 15 June 1968). Jazz guitarist. Worked with Lionel Hampton (1948–50), his brothers (1955–62), John Coltrane (1961–62), and Wynton Kelly (1959–60, 1963–64), made a series of jazz albums; from 1964 concentrated on pop-oriented albums with orchestral accompaniment.

Montirandé [Fr.]. A 16th- and 17th-century variety of the *branle*, in 4/4 meter and with dotted rhythms.

Montoya, Carlos (b. Madrid, 13 Dec. 1903; d. Wainscott, N.Y., 3 Mar. 1993). Guitarist, principally in the flamenco style. Toured with the dancer La Argentina (Antonia Merce) and later as soloist. Improvised a number of works, including *Suite flamenca* (guitar and orchestra, 1966); made recordings.

Montsalvatge, Xavier (b. Gerona, 11 Mar. 1912). Composer. Studied with Millet, Morera, Costa, and Pahissa. Music critic and teacher in Barcelona (at the conservatory from 1970). Employed West Indian and Catalan folk materials. Composed operas (*El gato con botas*, 1948); ballets for the Goubé–Alexander ballet company (*La muerte enamorada*, 1943; *Manfred*, 1945; *La Venus de Elna*, 1946); orchestral works (*Poema concertante*, with violin, 1951; *Desintegración morfológica de la Chacona de Bach*, 1962; rev. 1972; *Bric-à-brac*, 1993); vocal works (*5 Canciones negras*, 1945; *Canciones para niños*, 1953; *Sinfonía de réquiem*, soprano, orchestra, 1985); chamber works (*Cuarteto indiano*, string quartet, 1952).

Mood. *Modus* (3) [see also Mensural notation].

Moog, Robert A(rthur) (b. Flushing, N.Y., 23 May 1934). Engineer and inventor. In 1954, founded the R. A. Moog Co. (later Moog Music, Inc.; it became a subsidiary of Norlin Industries in 1973) to manufacture theremins. From 1965 the company focused on producing synthesizers. Has worked with composers Wendy (formerly Walter) Carlos, Ussachevsky, Cage, and others. Worked with Kurzweil Music Systems of Boston 1984–89.

Moon guitar (lute). See *Yüeh-ch'in*.

Moonlight Sonata. Popular name for Beethoven's Piano Sonata no. 14 in C♯ minor op. 27 no. 2 (1801), marked *Sonata quasi una fantasia*. The name probably derives from a review written by Heinrich Rellstab (1799–1860) in which the first movement was likened to "a boat visiting, by moonlight, the primitive landscapes of Vierwaldstättersee [Lake Lucerne] in Switzerland." The work has also been called the *Laube-Sonate* [Ger., Bower Sonata].

Moór, Emanuel (b. Kecskemét, 19 Feb. 1863; d. Mont Pélerin, Switzerland, 20 Oct. 1931). Composer and pianist. Studied in Prague, Budapest, and Vienna. Toured Europe and the U.S. as pianist, conductor, and accompanist. Invented the Emanuel Moór Pianoforte, a double-keyboard piano. Works include 5 operas, 8 symphonies, violin concertos and sonatas, string quartets, and many songs.

Moore, Dorothy Rudd (b. New Castle, Del., 4 June 1940). Composer, poet, and singer. Studied with Boulanger and Chou Wen-chung. Has taught at the Harlem School of the Arts, New York Univ., and Bronx Community College, CUNY. Works include an opera (*Frederick Douglass,* 1979–85); a symphony; *Ih Celebration* (baritone, chorus, and piano, 1977); chamber music; piano works; and many songs and song cycles.

Moore, Douglas S(tuart) (b. Cutchogue, N.Y., 10 Aug. 1893; d. Greenport, N.Y., 25 July 1969). Composer. Studied at Yale and with Boulanger, d'Indy, Tournemire, and Bloch. Taught at Columbia, 1926–62. Employed elements of American folk and popular music. Works include 12 operas (*The *Devil and Daniel Webster; Giants in the Earth,* Pulitzer Prize 1951; *The *Ballad of Baby Doe*); a ballet; incidental and film music; *The Pageant of P. T. Barnum* (1924), Symphony no. 2 (1945), and other orchestral music; chamber music; organ (*4 Museum Pieces,* 1922) and piano works; choral music; songs.

Moore, Gerald (b. Watford, 30 July 1899; d. Buckinghamshire, 13 Mar. 1987). Pianist. Served as accompanist to numerous singers, including Fischer-Dieskau and Schwarzkopf, especially in the lieder of Schubert and Wolf. Published a number of musical studies (*The Schubert Song Cycles,* 1975).

Moore, Grace (b. Nough, Tenn., 5 Dec. 1901; d. Copenhagen, 26 Jan. 1947). Soprano and actress. Performed on Broadway; then studied in Paris. Joined the New York Metropolitan Opera, 1928 (debut as Mimi, *Bohéme*). Appeared in eight films, including *One Night of Love* (1934) and *I'll Take Romance* (1937).

Moore, Mary (Louise) Carr (b. Memphis, 6 Aug. 1873; d. Inglewood, Calif., 9 Jan. 1957). Composer and singer. Studied in San Francisco. Taught in Los Angeles at the Olga Steeb Piano School (1926–43) and Chapman College (1928–47). Works include 10 operas (*Narcissa, or the Cost of Empire,* 1910–11); a piano concerto and other orchestral pieces; string quartets, piano trios, and other chamber pieces; many

piano works; choral pieces; a song cycle (*Beyond These Hills,* 4 solo voices and piano, 1923–24) and about 250 songs.

Moore, Thomas (b. Dublin, 28 May 1779; d. Sloperton Cottage, near Devizes, 25 Feb. 1852). Poet. Studied at Trinity College, Dublin; from 1799, sang in London salons. Published songs (*Irish Melodies,* 1808–34), glees, and poetry, set by many composers, including Berlioz and Schumann; his oriental poem *Lalla Rookh* (1817) was used by several composers. Also wrote opera librettos.

Moorman, (Madeline) Charlotte (b. Little Rock, Ark., 18 Nov. 1933; d. New York, 8 Nov. 1991). Cellist and video and performance artist. Studied with Leonard Rose. Founded the Annual New York Avant Garde Festival, 1963; worked closely with performance artist Nam June Paik.

Morales, Cristóbal de (b. Seville, ca. 1500; d. Málaga?, between 4 Sept. and 7 Oct. 1553). Composer. Studied in Seville. *Maestro de capilla* at Avila from 1526; at Plasencia, 1528–30. Sang in the papal choir in Rome 1535–45. *Maestro de capilla* in Toledo (1545–47), Marchena (1548–51), and Málaga (from 1551). Composed Masses; Magnificats and Lamentations; many motets; a few secular vocal works.

Morales, Melesio (b. Mexico City, 4 Dec. 1838; d. there, 12 May 1908). Composer. Studied in Mexico City. In Europe, 1865–68. Organized and headed a composition department at the Mexico City Conservatory. Works include Italian operas (*Romeo e Giulietta,* 1863; *Ildegonda,* 1865); orchestral pieces.

Moran, Robert (Leonard) (b. Denver, 8 Jan. 1937). Pianist and composer. Pupil of Apostel, Berio, Milhaud, and Haubenstock-Ramati. From 1959 to 1972, often directed the New Music Ensemble at San Francisco State Univ. His works are often aleatory and improvisatory. They include stage and mixed-media works (*Erlösung dem Erlöser,* tape loops and performers, 1982; *The Juniper Tree,* children's opera with Glass 1985; *From the Towers of the Moon,* opera, 1992); works for one or more orchestras; "city pieces" (*Hallelujah,* 20 bands, 40 choruses, organ, carillon, 1971, for Bethlehem, Pa.); and *L'Après-midi du Dracula* (any instruments, 1966).

Moravec, Ivan (b. Prague, 9 Nov. 1930). Pianist. Studied in Prague. U.S. debut with the Cleveland Orchestra under George Szell (1964). Teacher at the Prague Academy of the Arts from 1967. His repertory ranges from Mozart to Debussy.

Morawetz, Oskar (b. Světlá nad Sázavou, Czechoslovakia, 17 Jan. 1917). Composer. Studied in Prague and Toronto. Works include orchestral music (symphonies; concertos; *Carnival Overture,* 1946; *Memorial to Martin Luther King,* with cello, 1968; *From the Diary of Anne Frank,* with soprano, 1970; *The Railway Station,* 1980); *Sinfonietta for Winds* (1965); 5 string quartets, *3 Improvisations* (brass quintet, 1977), and other chamber music; piano music (*Sonata Tragica; 10 Preludes,* 1966); choral music and many songs.

Morceau [Fr.]. Piece, composition.

Mordent [also beat; Ger. *Mordant;* Fr. *martellement, pincement, battement, pincé, agrément;* It. *mordente, tremolo;* Sp. *quiebro*]. An ornament, especially a single or multiple alternation of the principal note with its lower auxiliary [Ex.]. The mordent is one of the oldest ornaments for which a description, a sign, and a term exist. The form of the ornament as defined here seems to have crystallized first in England and France in the 17th century. English writers give a "shaked beat" (a "prepared" and continuous mordent, i.e., one beginning on the auxiliary); and a short, prepared mordent is also known in France in the 17th century. Later examples generally begin on the main note and are identified with the terms *pincement, pincé,* and beat. Except in connection with the **port de voix,* the mordent was used much more in instrumental music, especially keyboard music, than in singing. During most of the 18th century, the short and the long mordent were recognized in England, France, and Germany; in Germany, the long "prepared" mordent was called *battement.* Normally, all these ornaments took their value from the note they embellished. They went out of fashion with the rise of the Classical style.

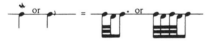

Moreau, Jean-Baptiste (b. Angers, 1656; d. Paris, 24 Aug. 1733). Composer. *Maître de musique* at the cathedrals of Langres and Dijon; *musicien ordinaire* at the royal school of St. Cyr, Paris, 1686–94. Composed recitatives and choruses for Racine's *Esther* (1689) and *Athalie* (1691); settings of Racine's *Cantiques spirituels* (1695) and Laînez's *Zaïre* (lost); sacred works.

Morel Campos, Juan (b. Ponce, Puerto Rico, 16 May 1857; d. there, 12 May 1896). Composer. Pupil of M. G. Tavárez. Church organist; director of military and dance bands; conductor of a zarzuela company. Composed 3 zarzuelas; sacred and orchestral music; nearly 300 *danzas,* mostly for piano.

Morel, (Joseph Raoul) François (d'Assise) (b. Montreal, 14 Mar. 1926). Composer. Studied with Champagne and Varèse. Composed incidental music

for the CBC, 1956–70. Directed the Académie de musique de Québec, 1972–78; then taught at the universities of Montreal and Laval. Has employed serial techniques. Works include orchestral music (*L'étoile noire,* 1962; *Jeux,* 1976); *Prisme anamorphoses* (winds, harp, celesta, piano, and percussion, 1967) and other chamber music; solo works for piano, guitar, flute, and organ; a few songs.

Morel, Jean (b. Abbeville, France, 10 Jan. 1903; d. New York, 14 Apr. 1975). Teacher and conductor. Studied with I. Philipp, M. Emmanuel, and G. Pierné. Taught at the American Conservatory in Fontainebleau (1921–36), Brooklyn College (1940–43), and at Juilliard (1949–71), where his students included James Levine and Leonard Slatkin. Appeared (from 1956) with the Metropolitan Opera.

Morendo [It.]. Dying, fading away.

Moreno Torroba, Federico (b. Madrid, 3 Mar. 1891; d. there, 12 Sept. 1982). Composer. Pupil of del Campo. Composed zarzuelas *(Luisa Fernanda,* 1932; *Maravilla,* 1941; *Orgullo de Jalisco,* 1947; and *Maria Manuela,* 1953); music for guitar; orchestral music (*Cuadros castellanos,* ca. 1920); operas (*La virgen del Mayo,* 1925; *María la tempranica,* 1930; *El poeta,* 1980).

Moresca, morisca [It.]. (1) A dance of Renaissance Europe, performed by dancers with blackened faces and with bells attached to their legs, sometimes depicting combat between Moors and Christians. The fool or buffoon was also frequently represented in such dances. (2) A subgenre of the **villanella* caricaturing Africans or Moors.

Morgan, Justin (b. West Springfield, Mass., 28 Feb. 1747; d. Randolph, Vt., 22 Mar. 1798). Composer. Settled in Vermont, 1788; traveled as a singing master. His works appeared in *Federal Harmony* (1790); he is known especially for the fuguing tune "Montgomery."

Morlacchi, Francesco (Giuseppe Baldassare) (b. Perugia, 14 June 1784; d. Innsbruck, 28 Oct. 1841). Composer. Pupil of Zingarelli and Mattei. Assistant director, Italian Opera, Dresden, 1810; Kapellmeister from 1811. Remembered for his rivalry with Weber. Composed operas, oratorios, and much sacred music.

Morley, Thomas (b. Norwich, 1557 or 1558; d. London, Oct. 1602). Composer, theorist, and editor. Pupil of Byrd. Organist at St. Paul's by 1591; Gentleman of the Chapel Royal, 1592. From 1598 he possessed a monopoly over printing music; publications include anthologies of popular light Italian pieces, collections of original lute songs and consort music, and *The *Triumphes of Oriana,* as well as his treatise *A Plaine and Easie Introduction to Practicall Musicke*

(1597). Composed English madrigals, canzonets, and songs; a few keyboard works; Latin motets; English sacred music (services, anthems, Psalms); various instrumental pieces.

Mormorando [It.]. Murmuring, whispering.

Moroi, Makoto (b. Tokyo, 17 Dec. 1930). Composer. Pupil of his father, Saburō Moroi, and of Ikenouchi. From 1968, taught at the Osaka Univ. of Art and Science. His music uses electronics, serialism, and traditional Japanese elements. Has composed dramatic works (*Gyosha Paeton* [Phaeton the Charioteer], solo voices, chorus, orchestra, tape, 1965); orchestral music (piano concertos; Symphony, 1968; *3 Movements,* shakuhachi, strings, percussion, 1970); chamber and solo music for both Japanese and Western instruments.

Moroi, Saburō (b. Tokyo, 7 Aug. 1903; d. there, 24 Mar. 1977). Composer. Studied with Trapp and Schmidt in Berlin. Directed the Senzoku Gakuen Academy of Music in Tokyo from 1967. Composed 5 symphonies, concertos for piano and violin, and other orchestral music; chamber music; songs and choral works (*Taiyō no otozure* [A Visit of the Sun], fantasy oratorio, 1968).

Moross, Jerome (b. Brooklyn, 1 Aug. 1913; d. Miami, 25 July 1983). Composer. Studied at Juilliard and New York Univ. From 1940, worked in Hollywood as an orchestrator. From 1948 composed film scores (*The Big Country,* 1958) and music for television. Employed American popular and folk elements. Other works include 3 operas (*Sorry, Wrong Number!,* 1977); 3 ballets (*Frankie and Johnny,* 1937–38; *The Last Judgement,* 1953), and 4 ballet-operas; a symphony and other orchestral pieces; chamber music.

Morris dance. A type of English folk dance danced by six men, in two groups of three, with bells attached to their legs and each holding a white handkerchief or a stick. At times the tradition has also included dancing with blackened faces. There are numerous morris dances, and the term is sometimes extended to include the sword dance as well. Its historical relationship to the **moresca* and the origins of its name (often said to derive from the representation of Moors) are matters of some dispute.

Morris, Harold (b. San Antonio, 17 Mar. 1890; d. New York, 6 May 1964). Composer and pianist. Studied with Scalero. Taught at Juilliard (1922–39) and Columbia Univ. Teachers College (1935–46). Worked with southern folk music and African-American rhythms. Works include 3 symphonies; *Piano Concerto on 2 Negro Themes* (1927); *Passacaglia, Adagio, and Finale* (orchestra, 1955); 2 string quartets; piano trios and quintets; piano music.

Morris, Joan (Clair) (b. Portland, Ore., 10 Feb. 1943). Mezzo-soprano. Studied at Gonzaga Univ. A celebrated interpreter of American popular song and art song; often performed and recorded with her husband, William Bolcom. From 1981, a faculty member of the Univ. of Michigan.

Morris, R(eginald) O(wen) (b. York, 3 Mar. 1886; d. London, 14 Dec. 1948). Composer and writer. Pupil of C. Wood. Taught at the Royal College of Music; at the Curtis Institute, 1926–28. Published textbooks in harmony and counterpoint. Compositions include orchestral works and concertos, solo songs, folk song settings, and choral works.

Morris, Robert (Daniel) (b. Cheltenham, England, 19 Oct. 1943). Composer and theorist. Has taught at Yale, the Univ. of Pittsburgh, and the Eastman School (from 1980). Has worked with twelve-tone methods, medieval isorhythmic procedures, the songs of Stephen Foster, and Korean court music. Works include *Hagoromo* (voices, ensemble, 1977); orchestral works; chamber works (*Arci,* string quartet, 1988); piano music; electronic music; choral pieces and songs; incidental music.

Mortari, Virgilio (b. Passirana di Lainate, Milan, 6 Dec. 1902; d. Rome, 5 Sept. 1993). Composer and pianist. Pupil of Bossi and Pizzetti. Taught at the conservatories of Venice (1933–40) and Rome (1940–73). Works include operas and ballets; orchestral music (*Prospettive,* 1986; and many concertos); a piano trio (1924); choral and solo vocal music; editions of early Italian operas and other vocal music.

Mortelmans, Lodowijk (b. Antwerp, 5 Feb. 1868; d. there, 24 June 1952). Composer and conductor. Studied and taught (from 1902) at the Conservatory of Music in Antwerp (director, 1924–33). Works include an opera (*De kinderen der zee,* Antwerp, 1915); symphonic poems and other orchestral music; chamber and piano music; settings of Flemish poetry by Gezelle; choral pieces; arrangements of Flemish folk songs.

Mortensen, Finn (Einar) (b. Oslo, 6 Jan. 1922; d. there, 21 May 1983). Composer. Pupil of Egge and Bentzon. Taught at the Oslo Conservatory, 1970–73; and then at the Oslo Musikkhøgskolen. Worked with twelve-tone and aleatoric devices. Works include much chamber music (String Trio, 1950; *Constellations* op. 34, accordion, guitar, percussion, 1971); orchestral pieces; vocal and piano music (several sonatas; Nocturne op. 22, 1968).

Morton, Jelly Roll [Lemott [La Menthe, La Mothe], Ferdinand Joseph] (b. New Orleans, 20 Oct. 1890; d. Los Angeles, 10 July 1941). Jazz composer, bandleader, and pianist. Made his first recordings in 1923, including his "King Porter–A Stomp" and

"New Orleans Joys" [New Orleans Blues], in a rag-time-based style infused with jazz improvisation and swing. With his Red Hot Peppers, recorded "Black Bottom Stomp," "The Chant," "Dead Man Blues," "Grandpa's Spells" (all 1926), and "The Pearls" (1927). In 1938, made a collection of recordings for the Library of Congress.

Morton, Robert (b. ca. 1430; d. 1475 or later). Composer. Of English origin; served in the Burgundian court chapel, 1457–75. Of his works, only a few secular rondeaux survive, including "Le souvenir" and "N'aray je jamais."

Moscheles, Ignaz (b. Prague, 23 May 1794; d. Leipzig, 10 Mar. 1870). Teacher, pianist, composer. Pupil of Albrechtsberger and Salieri; associate of Beethoven and Mendelssohn. Toured as a piano virtuoso from 1816; also a renowned improviser. Settled in London, 1825, teaching at the Royal Academy of Music and conducting the Philharmonic Society. Soloist in Mendelssohn's first Gewandhaus concert, 1835; from 1846, taught at the Leipzig conservatory. Published much piano and salon music; sonatas; etudes; works for piano and orchestra, including 8 concertos; a symphony; concert overture; chamber music with piano; songs.

Moses und Aron [Ger.]. Opera in three acts, of which only the first two were completed (1930–32), by Schoenberg (to his own libretto), performed in concert in Hamburg in 1954 and staged in Zürich in 1957. Setting: Egypt and Mt. Sinai in Biblical times.

Mosolov, Alexandr Vasil'yevich (b. Kiev, 29 July/11 Aug. 1900; d. Moscow, 12 July 1973). Composer and pianist. Pupil of Glier, Myaskovsky, and Prokofiev. Collected folk music in northern Russia and other parts of the Soviet Union. Works include operas (*Geroy* [The Hero], 1927); oratorios *(Narodnaya oratoriya* [People's Oratorio], 1970); 6 symphonies, 2 piano concertos, and other orchestral works; string quartets; 5 piano sonatas; choruses; songs.

Mosonyi, Mihály [Brand, Michael] (b. Boldogasszonyfalva, Hungary [now Frauenkirchen, Austria], 4 Sept. 1815; d. Pest, 31 Oct. 1870). Composer. Associate of Liszt. From 1842, taught and played the contrabass in Pest; focused on developing a native style for Hungarian music. Composed 3 operas, 2 symphonies, a piano concerto, 7 string quartets, 5 Masses and other sacred works, cantatas, choral works, piano pieces, and songs.

Moss, Lawrence K(enneth) (b. Los Angeles, 18 Nov. 1927). Composer. Pupil of Dahl and Kirchner. Taught at Mills College (1956–59), Yale (1960–68), and the Univ. of Maryland (from 1969). Works include multi-media pieces (*Blackbird,* clarinet, mime/

dancer, tape, 1987); opera (*The Queen and the Rebels,* 1989); a symphony for brass quintet and chamber orchestra (1977); *Portals* (tenor, ensemble, 1983); *Violaria, una dramma per musica* (viola, tape, 1988).

Mosso [It.]. Moved, agitated.

Moszkowski, Moritz (b. Breslau, 23 Aug. 1854; d. Paris, 4 Mar. 1925). Composer and pianist. Studied in Dresden and at Kullak's school, Berlin, where he later taught. Retired to Paris, 1897. Works include piano music (*Spanische Tänze; Album espagnol; Gondoliera*); violin pieces; an opera; Piano Concerto (1898).

Moten, Bennie [Benjamin] (b. Kansas City, Mo., 13 Nov. 1894; d. there, 2 Apr. 1935). Jazz bandleader and pianist. By 1918 he was leading a trio, which expanded into a big band, eventually including Count Basie, Hot Lips Page, Jimmy Rushing, Walter Page, and Ben Webster. In 1932, the group made recordings in the Kansas City jazz style, including "Toby" and "Moten Swing." After Moten's death, his band formed the nucleus of Count Basie's orchestra.

Motet. A major musical genre from the 13th through the 18th century, of minor importance thereafter. Because no single definition can encompass the characteristics of the motet during the entire course of its development, it is helpful to distinguish three major phases. In the first (ca. 1200–1450), the term motet denoted a particular structure: a tenor derived from chant that serves as the foundation for newly composed upper voices; the resulting composition is heterogeneous both in the musical style of the individual voices and in their texts. In the second phase (ca. 1450–1600), motet denoted a genre: a polyphonic setting of a sacred Latin text. In the third phase (after 1600), the term, while retaining its basic meaning as a type of sacred music, became associated with a particular style *(stilus motecticus):* the serious, imitative style of church polyphony derived from Palestrina.

In the 13th century, the term motet had two meanings: first, a brief composition for two or three voices, in which the tenor, drawn from chant, serves as the foundation for one or more upper voices with French or Latin texts; and second, one of the texted upper voices (*motetus,* from the Fr. *mot,* word, and thus, a voice or part to which words have been put) of such a composition. If there is a third voice, it is termed the *triplum.* The principal features of the early compositions of this type are a sharp differentiation in style between the tenor, which consists of a short, repeated rhythmic pattern, and the rhythmically active upper voices and, in works for three voices, the frequent setting of independent texts (sometimes in different languages) in the two upper parts. The earliest motets were *clausulae, drawn from the repertory of *Notre Dame, with text added to the upper voice or voices.

The motet was at the center of the fundamental changes occurring in rhythmic notation during the second half of the 13th century (in the work of theorist Franco of Cologne and in compositions attributed to Petrus de Cruce) and the beginning of the 14th century (in both the theory and compositions of Philippe de Vitry). A technique known today as *isorhythm became the the the most prominent organizing principle for the motet. Despite these innovations, the motet lost its place of predominance in the 14th century as composers cultivated instead a new genre of secular music, though Guillaume de Machaut composed important examples. By the end of the century, the motet typically had a Latin rather than a French text, employed isorhythm, and consisted of four rather than three voices.

During the first half of the 15th century, the interest in rhythmic organization continued, extending at times to all of the voices (panisorhythm, e.g., in Dunstable) and often involving proportional relationships among the sections (e.g., in Dufay). At the same time, composers were finding different ways of setting short sacred texts in Latin intended for devotional or liturgical use. Some of these settings, now called cantilena-motets or song-motets, employed a style similar to that found in contemporaneous secular music: a two-voice framework between the uppermost voice and the tenor to which a third voice was added; others employed a simple homophony perhaps related to contemporaneous practices of improvisation.

The period from ca. 1450 to 1600 witnessed a remarkable flowering of the motet. The motet occupied a central position in the work of all the leading composers of the period: Josquin, Willaert, Lassus, Palestrina, and Byrd. In this phase of its development, the motet was generally understood to be a polyphonic setting of a sacred Latin text; the titles of many of the collections of motets published in the 16th century explain *motectus (mottetto,* etc.) as the common translation of *cantio sacra* (sacred song). Purely by convention, scholars today exclude from consideration as motets all settings of sacred texts in the vernacular (e.g., anthems, spiritual madrigals) as well as certain categories of liturgical music (e.g., hymns, canticles, lamentations).

In addition to the traditional texts from the liturgy, composers chose passages taken directly from the Bible (including entire Psalms). Fewer texts, but still a significant number, come either from classical or humanist Latin poetry; many of the newly composed texts honor a particular person or event. In this period, motets served a paraliturgical function as an ornament to the liturgy, not an essential part of it. The motet was also part of the musical entertainments at the princely establishments.

Many motets employ the same techniques as settings of the Mass: canon, ostinato, *cantus firmus,* paraphrase. The technique most characteristic of the motet and indeed of the musical language of this period was imitation, though the use of imitation in relation to homophonic texture was an important feature of text setting. This coincided with the establishment of the four-voice ensemble, in which all of the voices participate equally in presenting motivic material, allowing the composer freedom to fit the music to the individual phrase.

After 1600, the term motet became both more specific and more general in its meaning. In the more specific sense, the word came to be associated with a particular style. "Motet-style" (*stilus moteticus* or *ecclesiasticus*) meant imitative polyphony in the manner of Palestrina, a serious, solemn style considered appropriate for church use [see Palestrina style]. In its general sense, the term motet meant simply a sacred vocal composition intended for liturgical or devotional use; the term no longer had specific connotations concerning language, style, or the nature of the performing forces. In addition to motet, composers also employed a variety of other terms, such as *concerto ecclesiastico* or *symphonia sacra.* The subsequent development of the motet throughout Europe reflects the divisions between Catholics and Protestants and differences among national styles. At the most basic level, the differences in practice are evident in language: Latin continued to be employed by Catholics, while Protestants used the vernacular.

In Italy composers applied the techniques of the *seconda prattica.* Lodovico Viadana's motets, for one, two, three, or four voices with organ accompaniment, employ basso continuo. Giovanni Gabrieli's monumental motets designed for Venetian ceremony exploited the principle of contrast in several ways, including harmonic structure and performing forces. Between these two extremes lies a whole range of compositions for many different performance ensembles by composers such as Alessandro Grandi, Giacomo Carissimi, Maurizio Cazzati, Alessandro Scarlatti, and Vivaldi.

Many elements of the Italian development are also evident elsewhere, perhaps most conspicuously in the work of Schütz, who composed polychoral motets in the Venetian manner as well as sacred vocal concertos employing both large and small performing forces. The six motets of Bach (four for double chorus, one for five voices, one for four voices and continuo) represent the peak of the German development. In France, the *grand motet,* cultivated by composers such as Henry Du Mont, Lully, Marc-Antoine

Charpentier, Michel-Richard de Lalande, André Campra, François Couperin, and Rameau, was designed primarily for use at the royal court; it had a large-scale episodic structure (many elements of which were drawn from contemporary opera) and employed a large ensemble (soloists, choir, orchestra). In England, the development of sacred music—despite the many points of contact with Continental practices—is traditionally considered under the separate category of *anthem.

After 1750, major composers no longer derived their income from churches or courts, and the composition of church music thus became incidental to their main output. Furthermore, the vogue for the "antique," exemplified by the Cecilian movement, as well as the restrictions imposed by the Catholic Church (e.g., the *Motu proprio* of Pope Pius X, 1903) dictated an artificial style removed from current practice. Motets continued to be written by major composers (including Mozart, Schubert, Brahms, Berlioz, Franck, Liszt, Bruckner, and Verdi), but the absence of unifying elements makes it difficult to characterize the motet after 1750.

Motet-chanson. A polyphonic work of the Renaissance that combines a Latin sacred text in one voice, usually the tenor or bass, often in relatively longer note-values, with a secular text in the vernacular in another voice or voices.

Motetus [Lat., fr. Fr. *mot*, word]. (1) *Motet. (2) In the 13th century, the second voice of a *clausula*, to which words have been set [see Motet]; the first (texted) voice above the tenor in a motet.

Mother Goose Suite. See *Ma mère l'oye*.

Motion. Movement from one pitch to another within a single part or simultaneously in two parts. Within a single part, motion is said to be conjunct or by step if it is by an interval not larger than a second; disjunct or by leap if by an interval larger than a second. Motion in two parts simultaneously is parallel if the interval between the two parts remains constant, at least within the general type, e.g., third, sixth, etc. [see also Parallel (consecutive) fifths, octaves]; contrary if one part moves up while the other moves down; similar if both move in the same direction but by different intervals. Motion is oblique if one part remains stationary while the other moves.

Motive, motif. A short rhythmic and or melodic idea that is sufficiently well defined to retain its identity when elaborated or transformed and combined with other material and that thus lends itself to serving as the basic element from which a complex texture or even a whole composition is created. The term is used rather flexibly but is usually taken to refer to something less than a *phrase. A motive may consist of as few as two pitches, or it may be long enough to be seen to consist of smaller elements, themselves termed motives or perhaps cells. The potential for generating more extended material is most often regarded as essential. Passages that modulate are often constructed from a motive, perhaps repeated in a sequence [see Sequence (1)]. Music characterized by the pervasive use of a motive is said to be highly or very motivic, and some works of Beethoven, e.g., the Fifth Symphony, are regarded as paradigms of the technique. Development sections of movements in *sonata form are especially likely to be built from motives introduced earlier in the work. See also Leitmotif.

Moto [It.]. Movement, motion; often, as in *andante con m.,* to indicate more movement, i.e., a slightly faster tempo, than ordinarily called for by the term being modified.

Moto perpetuo [It.]. See *Perpetuum mobile.*

Motown [fr. Motortown, i.e., Detroit, Michigan]. A fusion of black *gospel, pop, and *rhythm and blues that began to flourish commercially in the U.S. in the early 1960s. Producer Berry Gordy, Jr., and numerous staff songwriters forged the style, and Gordy's Detroit-based record labels Motown, Tamla, and Gordy and Soul provided the outlet for the numerous black recording artists employed, including Smokey Robinson and the Miracles, Diana Ross and the Supremes, Marvin Gaye, Stevie Wonder, and the Temptations.

Motte, Diether de la (b. Bonn, 30 Mar. 1928). Composer. Studied with Leibowitz, Krenek, Fortner, and Messiaen. From 1950, taught in Düsseldorf; from 1962, at the Musikhochschule in Hamburg. Has worked with gamelan, Gregorian chant, and gesture or "visible music"; works include opera; 2 concertos for orchestra; *Klänge fur zwei Orchester* (1981); chamber, vocal, choral, and tape pieces.

Mottl, Felix (Josef) (b. Unter-St. Veit, near Vienna, 24 Aug. 1856; d. Munich, 2 July 1911). Conductor. Pupil of Bruckner; associate of Wagner and Liszt. In 1876, helped prepare first Bayreuth Festival; conducted there often from 1886. Directed the Karlsruhe Opera and Philharmonic from 1881 (*Generalmusikdirektor,* 1893); the Munich Opera and conservatory from 1903; the Vienna Philharmonic, 1904–7. Works include the opera *Agnes Bernauer* (Weimar, 1880).

Motto. (1) In Masses of the 15th and 16th centuries, a musical idea that recurs at the beginning of each major section; also head-motive. (2) In *arias of the 17th and 18th centuries, the opening gesture of the melody when sung at the outset and followed immediately by an instrumental ritornello, which is then followed by the principal entrance of the voice. Such an aria is termed a motto aria [Ger. *Devisenarie*].

Motu proprio [Lat., by one's own initiative]. Two such statements on the music of the church were issued by Pius X in 1903 and 1904. Among various prohibitions and recommendations, it specified Palestrina's music as the appropriate model for polyphony, disapproved the use of music of a theatrical character, ordered the restoration of *Gregorian chant under the leadership of the monks of Solesmes, restricted the role of the organ, and largely suppressed other forms of instrumental music.

Motus [Lat.]. *Motion; a *canon *per motu contrario* is one by inversion.

Mount of Olives, The. See *Christus am Ölberge*.

Mouret, Jean-Joseph (b. Avignon, 11 Apr. 1682; d. Charenton, 20 Dec. 1738). Composer. *Surintendant de la musique* at the court of Sceaux from 1708 or 1709. Directed the orchestra of the Paris Opéra (1714–18), the New Italian Theater (1717–37) and the Concert spirituel (1728–34). Stage works include *Le mariage de Ragonde* (Sceaux, 1714); *Les fêtes ou Le triomphe de Thalie* (Opéra, 1714); also composed motets, airs, and instrumental music.

Mouth organ [Fr. *harmonica à bouche;* Ger. *Mundharmonika;* It. *armonica a bocca;* Sp. *armónica*]. A wind instrument consisting of several free *reeds that may be sounded individually or in combination by means of blowing and or sucking. Instruments of this type consisting of vertical pipes, each containing a reed, have been known in the Far East since at least 1000 B.C.E. Modern examples there include the Chinese *sheng* and the Japanese *sho*. The Western instrument often called a harmonica (sometimes also mouth harp) was invented in the 19th century. In the most common models, each opening along the edge of the instrument contains two brass reeds pitched a *diatonic scale-degree apart, one activated by blowing, one by sucking. Openings can be blown or sucked singly or in combination, producing the diatonic scale as well as some intervals and chords derived from it. There are also chromatic instruments.

Mouthpiece [Fr. *embouchure* (of brasses), *bec* (of single reeds); Ger. *Mundstück* (of brasses), *Schnabel* (of single reeds); It. *bocchino;* Sp. *boquilla*]. That part of a wind instrument that forms the juncture of the instrument with the player's mouth. Brass instrument mouthpieces are made of brass and are roughly bell-shaped. See ill. under Brass instruments. Clarinet and saxophone mouthpieces are made of wood, metal, rubber, plastic, or glass and are shaped like a narrow hollow cone sliced off at an angle near the small end to leave a flat surface or table for the reed. See ill. under Reed.

Mouton, Jean [Jehan] (b. Holluigue [now Haut-Wignes], near Samer, ca. 1459; d. St. Quentin, 30 Oct. 1522). Composer. A singer in Nesle from 1477, *maître de chapelle* there from 1483; subsequently active in Amiens (from 1500), then in Grenoble (from 1501). From 1502 associated with the French royal court. Works include chansons, Masses, Magnificats, and over 100 motets, many of them occasional works.

Mouvement [Fr.]. (1) Movement. (2) Tempo. (3) Motion.

Movable do(h). A system of *solmization in which the syllable *do* represents the first scale-degree of the major scale regardless of its transposition and is thus "movable" to any pitch.

Movement [Fr. *mouvement;* Ger. *Satz;* It. *movimento, tempo;* Sp. *movimiento, tiempo*]. Any self-contained and thus at least potentially independent section of a larger work such as a sonata, symphony, concerto, string quartet, suite, cantata, oratorio, or even Mass. In performance, successive movements are usually separated by a brief pause (during which the audience customarily does not applaud). Composers occasionally specify, however, that a movement is to succeed another without pause [see *Attacca*], as in the fourth movement of Beethoven's Fifth Symphony.

Movimento [It.]. (1) Movement. (2) Tempo; *doppio m.,* twice as fast. (3) Motion.

Moyzes, Alexander (b. Kláštor pod Znievom, Slovakia, 4 Sept. 1906; d. Bratislava, 20 Nov. 1984). Composer. Son of composer Mikuláš Moyzes. Studied with Ostrčil, Karel, and Novák. Taught at the Bratislava Academy of Music and Drama, then at the College of Musical Arts in Bratislava (director, 1965–71). Worked for Bratislava Radio 1937–48. His music synthesized nationalistic Slovak elements with international avant-garde techniques. Composed much orchestral and vocal music; chamber works; music for film and radio.

Mozarabic chant. The liturgical chant of the Christian church of Spain until its suppression in favor of the Roman rite in 1085. The term Mozarabic refers to Christians living and practicing their own religion under Muslim political rule. It is not, therefore, entirely appropriate, since the rite existed well before the Muslim invasion of the Iberian peninsula in 711. It has many features in common with Gregorian chant and related repertories.

Mozart, (Johann Georg) Leopold (b. Augsburg, 14 Nov. 1719; d. Salzburg, 28 May 1787). Composer, violinist, and writer on music. Father and teacher of W. A. Mozart. Violinist to the Salzburg court chapel from 1743; Vice-Kapellmeister by 1763. Took Wolfgang and his sister, Nannerl, on extensive concert tours of Europe. Wrote a large number of sacred works; many symphonies; serenades and divertimentos; concertos; chamber and keyboard music; a violin method, *Versuch einer gründlichen Violinschule* (1756).

Mozart, (Johann Chrysostom) Wolfgang Amadeus (b. Salzburg, 27 Jan. 1756; d. Vienna, 5 Dec. 1791). Composer. Pupil of his father, Leopold Mozart. Wolfgang demonstrated his musical ability at the age of 4; his earliest known compositions are from 1761, the date of his first public performance. From 1762 Leopold took his children on the first of a succession of concert tours of the musical centers of Europe, during which he became acquainted with J. C. Bach, Haydn, G. B. Sammartini, and others.

In 1769 Niccolò Piccinni arranged for the composition and performance of Mozart's opera *Mitridate, ré di Ponto* (Milan, 1770). The next five years included trips to Italy, Vienna, and Munich, and performances of the operas *Lucio Silla* and *La finta giardiniera*. Leopold's hopes of a position for his son at the imperial court were not fulfilled, and Mozart returned to Salzburg; the years 1775–77 saw the composition of the violin concertos.

In September 1777 Mozart toured with his mother, Anna Maria, to Mannheim, where he met the Weber family, and to Paris. His mother died in July 1779. Mozart returned to Salzburg, where he had been appointed court organist, and composed his most ambitious serious opera, *Idomeneo,* on commission from the Elector of Bavaria (first performance Munich, 1781). In 1781 Mozart was called to Vienna for coronation ceremonies for the new emperor, Joseph II. In May 1781 he petitioned for release from service to the archbishop and became a free composer and piano teacher in the imperial capital.

The Weber family, who had relocated to Vienna, took him in as a boarder; he married Constanze Weber in August 1782. An imperial commission resulted in the Singspiel *Die Entführung aus dem Serail* (1782). During the early 1780s Mozart joined a Masonic lodge. He continued to compose piano concertos for himself and his pupils. In 1785 he began work on *Le nozze de Figaro* with the librettist Lorenzo da Ponte; its first performance, in May 1786, was a success.

Leopold died in May 1787. At the time Mozart was composing *Don Giovanni* (first performance Prague, October 1787). He accepted a position as *Kammermusikus* at the court in Vienna. In 1789 King Friedrich Wilhelm II, a cellist, commissioned a set of string quartets (the Prussian quartets). *Così fan tutte* had its first performance in 1790.

Despite illness, Mozart was productive during his last year; *La clemenza di Tito* and *Die Zauberflöte* both had their premieres in September 1791. In November he struggled to complete the Requiem, commissioned by Count Walsegg-Stuppach. Mozart died before finishing the work, but reportedly left instructions with Franz Süssmayr for its completion.

Works: [Initial "K" nos. are from Köchel, 6th ed.; those in parentheses are from the original edition of 1862.] Major stage works (dates are of first performance): *Bastien und Bastienne; Mitridate, rè di Ponto* (opera seria, Milan, 1770); *Lucio Silla* (opera seria, Milan, 1772); *La finta giardiniera* (opera buffa, Munich, 1775); *Il rè pastore (dramma per musica,* Salzburg, 1775); *Idomeneo; Die *Entführung aus dem Serail; Der Schauspieldirektor* (singspiel, Schönbrunn, 1786); *Le *nozze di Figaro; *Don Giovanni; *Così fan tutte; Die *Zauberflöte; La *clemenza di Tito.* Numerous scenes and concert arias for voice and orchestra; songs and vocal canons. Oratorios. Sacred music: Masses, including the *Coronation; Requiem in D minor, K. 626 (1791; completed by Joseph Eybler and F. X. Süssmayr); litanies, vespers, and other sacred works; *Ave verum corpus* in D, K. 618 (1791); church sonatas (2 violins, bass, organ). 41 symphonies: *Paris, *Haffner, *Linz, *Prague; no. 40 in G minor, K. 550 (1788); *Jupiter. Concertos: 27 for piano and orchestra, incl. no. 10 in E♭ (2 pianos), K. 316a (365) (1779); 5 for violin and orchestra; *Sinfonia concertante* in E♭, violin, viola, orchestra, K. 364 (1779); 4 concertos for horn, orchestra; concertos for clarinet, bassoon, and flute. Cassations, divertimentos, and serenades, incl. *Ein *musikalischer Spass; Eine *kleine Nachtmusik;* serenades for wind ensemble; marches, minuets, *Ländler,* and contredanses, for various instrumental ensembles. Chamber music: string quintets; quintets for clarinet and strings, for piano and winds; quartets for piano and strings, for oboe and strings; string quartets, including the *Haydn quartets, K. 458 in B♭ (Hunt, 1784), K. 465 in C (Dissonant, 1785); K. 590 in F (the Prussian quartets, 1789–90); piano trios; more than 30 sonatas for clavier and violin; sonatas and variations for clavier solo (most for fortepiano).

Mp [It.]. Abbr. for *mezzo piano.*

Mravinsky, Evgeny (Alexandrovich) (b. St. Petersburg, 4 June 1903; d. Leningrad, 19 Jan. 1988). Conductor. Studied at the Leningrad Conservatory. Conducted the Leningrad Academic Opera and Ballet Theater, 1932–38; the Leningrad Philharmonic from 1938. Best known for his interpretations of Soviet composers; premiered a number of symphonies by Shostakovich.

Mṛdaṅgam. A double-headed, barrel-shaped, wooden drum of South India, held horizontally on the player's lap. The right head is damped permanently with a mixture of iron filings, lampblack, and wax to produce a fixed, high pitch. The left head is damped before and during play by a paste of flour and water, producing low and indefinite pitches that vary with the pressure of the heel of the left hand as the fingers strike the head. See ill. under Instrument.

M.s. [It.]. Abbr. for *mano sinistra,* left hand.

Muck, Carl [Karl] (b. Darmstadt, 22 Oct. 1859; d. Stuttgart, 3 Mar. 1940). Conductor. Kapellmeister of the Deutsches Landestheater, Prague, from 1886; of the Berlin Opera from 1892 (general music director there, 1908). Director of the Boston Symphony, 1906–8, 1912–18; conducted the Hamburg Philharmonic, 1922–33. Best known for performances of Wagner; led *Parsifal* at Bayreuth, 1901–30.

Mudanza [Sp.]. See *Villancico.*

Mudarra, Alonso (b. ca. 1508; d. Seville, 1 Apr. 1580). Composer. From 1546 active at the cathedral in Seville. His *Tres libros de música en cifras para vihuela* (1546) contains compositions for vihuela, guitar, harp, organ, or voice and vihuela, including fantasias, *tientos,* dances, variation sets, intabulations of Mass sections and motets, and accompanied songs with Spanish, Galician, Italian, and classical Latin texts.

Muddy Waters [Morganfield, McKinley] (b. Rolling Fork, Miss., 4 Apr. 1915; d. Downers Grove, Ill., 30 Apr. 1983). Blues singer, guitarist, and bandleader. Recorded for the Library of Congress, 1941–42. In Chicago, his band, including Little Walter from 1948, made recordings such as "I'm Your Hoochie Coochie Man" (1954) and "Got My Mojo Working" (1956). Played with Chris Barber in England, 1958; toured widely from the mid-1960s. Influenced the development of rock.

Mueller, Johann Christoph (b. Württemberg, 1777; d. Bridgewater, Pa., 1845). Pianist, violinist, and flutist. Cofounder and music director of religious colonies in Pennsylvania and Indiana. Compiled and printed hymns, waltzes, overtures, and other music by European and American composers. Formed an orchestra in Economy, Pa.

Muffat, Georg (b. Mégève, Savoy, bapt. 1 June 1653; d. Passau, 23 Feb. 1704). Composer. Pupil of Lully and Pasquini. Served Archbishop Max Gandolf, Salzburg. From 1690, Kapellmeister to Johann Philipp von Lamberg, Bishop of Passau. Composed concerti grossi, orchestral suites, sonatas, organ works, and operas.

Muffat, Gottlieb [Theophil] (b. Passau, bapt. 25 Apr. 1690; d. Vienna, 9 Dec. 1770). Composer and organist. Georg Muffat's son; studied with Fux. Court organist in Vienna from 1717. His students included the

future empress Maria Theresia. Composed mainly keyboard music (toccatas, *ciaccona,* fugues). His *Componimenti musicali per il cembalo* (ca. 1739) includes an explanatory table of ornamentation symbols.

Mugnone, Leopoldo (b. Naples, 29 Sept. 1858; d. there, 22 Dec. 1941). Conductor and composer. Studied at the Naples Conservatory. As conductor of the Teatro Costanzi in Rome, led the premieres of Mascagni's *Cavalleria rusticana* (1890) and Puccini's *Tosca* (1900). Also appeared in Paris, at Covent Garden, and at La Scala. In addition to Italian stage works, conducted French operas and *Götterdämmerung.*

Mühlfeld, Richard (Bernhard Herrmann) (b. Salzungen, 28 Feb. 1856; d. Meiningen, 1 June 1907). Clarinetist. From 1873, violinist and then clarinetist, Saxe-Meiningen court orchestra; from 1890, music director of the court theater; 1884–96, first clarinetist, Bayreuth Festival. Inspired and premiered Brahms's Trio op. 114 and Quintet op. 115 (1891), and the 2 sonatas op. 120 (1894).

Muldowney, Dominic (b. Southampton, 19 July 1952). Composer. Studied with Birtwistle, Rands, and Blake. From 1976, resident composer at the National Theatre, London. Has used twelve-tone techniques, jazz, and popular elements. Works include music for a BBC production of Brecht's play *Baal;* 3 song cycles using Brecht's texts; a piano trio (1980); piano and saxophone concertos; a sinfonietta (1986); *A First Show* (percussion, tape, 1979); film music.

Mulè, Giuseppe (b. Termini Imerese, near Palermo, 28 June 1885; d. Rome, 10 Sept. 1951). Cellist, conductor, and composer. Directed the conservatory in Palermo, 1922–24; the Conservatory of Saint Cecilia in Rome, 1925–43. Leader in the Sindacato dei musicisti, 1929–33. Worked with Sicilian folk materials. Works include operas (*La baronessa di Carini,* Palermo, 1912); *Tema con variazioni* (cello and orchestra, 1940); a string quartet and other chamber music for violin and cello; songs; incidental and film music.

Müller, Georg Gottfried [George Godfrey] (b. Gross Hennersdorf, 22 May 1762; d. Lititz, Pa., 19 Mar. 1821). Composer, violinist, and minister. After 1784, Moravian minister in Lititz and in Beersheba, Ohio. Eight of his anthems survive.

Müller, Wenzel (b. Trynau [Trnava], Moravia, 26 Sept. 1767; d. Baden, near Vienna, 3 Aug. 1835). Composer. Pupil of Dittersdorf. Theater violinist in Brno from 1782. Kapellmeister at the Leopoldstadt-Theater, Vienna, from 1786; at the German Theater in Prague, 1807–13. Composed singspiels and other theater works, including *Das Sonnenfest der Brami-*

nen (1790); *Das Neusonntagskind* (1793); and *Die Teufelsmühle am Wienerberg* (1799).

Mulligan, Gerry [Gerald Joseph; Jeru] (b. New York, 6 Apr. 1927; d. Darien, Conn., 20 Jan. 1996). Jazz baritone saxophonist, arranger, and bandleader. Helped found Miles Davis's cool jazz nonet (1948–50), for which he composed "Jeru" and arranged "Godchild" (both recorded 1949). In 1952, formed a "pianoless" quartet with Chet Baker; recordings include "Bernie's Tune" and "Line for Lyons" (both 1952). Led diverse groups (including the thirteen-piece Concert Jazz Band, 1960–64), working with Bob Brookmeyer, Zoot Sims, and others. Joined Dave Brubeck, 1968–72.

Multimedia. See Mixed media.

Multimetric. Characterized by frequent changes of meter, as in much music of the 20th century. See also Polymeter.

Multiphonics. Two or more pitches sounded simultaneously on a single wind instrument.

Multiple stop. In the playing of bowed stringed instruments, the stopping of two or more strings simultaneously [see Double stop].

Mumma, Gordon (b. Framingham, Mass., 30 Mar. 1935). Composer and performer of electronic music. Worked with the Merce Cunningham Dance Company, 1966–74. For certain compositions (*Hornpipe*, 1967; *Beam*, 1969), constructed special electronic equipment to modify and produce sounds in reaction to the performers' instrumental sounds or movements ("cybersonic music"). Has collaborated with Tudor, Cage, and Oliveros. Other works include *Some Voltage Drop*, variable-duration theater piece, 1974; pieces for tape (*Pontpoint*, 1980); *Schoolwork* (crosscut saw, psaltery, piano, melodica, 1970); *Mesa* (bandoneon and electronics, 1965); *Aleutian Displacement* (chamber orchestra, 1987); *Ménage à deux* (violin, piano, vibraphone, marimba, 1989).

Munch [Münch], Charles (b. Strasbourg, 26 Sept. 1891; d. Richmond, Va., 6 Nov. 1968). Conductor and violinist. Studied with Carl Flesch and Lucien Capet. Taught at Strasbourg and Leipzig. Concertmaster of the Strasbourg orchestra; of the Gewandhaus under Furtwängler (1926–33). From 1938, conductor, Société des Concerts du Conservatoire de Paris; 1949–62, succeeded Koussevitzky as principal conductor, Boston Symphony. In 1967, helped found the Orchestre de Paris.

Münchinger, Karl (b. Stuttgart, 29 May 1915; d. there, 13 Mar. 1990). Conductor. Studied with Clemens Krauss. In 1945, founded the Stuttgart Chamber Orchestra to perform Baroque music, especially that of Bach, on modern instruments, later adding works by Mozart, Dvořák, Hindemith, and others to its repertory. In 1966, founded the Stuttgart Classical Philharmonia.

Mundharmonika [Ger.]. *Mouth organ.

Mundstück [Ger.]. *Mouthpiece.

Mundy [Munday], John (b. ca. 1555; d. Windsor, 29 June 1630). Composer. Son of William Mundy. Studied at Oxford. Organist at St. George's Chapel, Windsor. Works include *Songs and Psalms* (1594), English anthems, Latin motets, keyboard pieces, and instrumental works (including 5 In Nomines).

Mundy [Munday], William (b. ca. 1529; d. London?, 1591?). Composer. Father of John Mundy. Held positions in a number of churches; Gentleman of the Chapel Royal, 1564. Composed services, English anthems, 2 Mass settings, much other Latin sacred music, and 1 In Nomine.

Munrow, David (John) (b. Birmingham, 12 Aug. 1942; d. Chesham Bois, Buckinghamshire, 15 May 1976). Performer on early winds. Taught in South America, at Leicester Univ., and at the Royal Academy of Music, London. In 1967, formed the Early Music Consort of London to perform medieval and Renaissance music.

Munter [Ger.]. Lively, merry.

Muradeli, Vano Il'ich (b. Gori, Georgia, 6 Apr. 1908; d. Tomsk, 14 Aug. 1970). Composer. Studied at the Tbilisi Conservatory and with Myaskovsky. His 1947 opera *Velikaya druzhba* [The Great Friendship] led to official sanctions against composers such as Myaskovsky, Prokofiev, and Shostakovich. Best known for choral music and nationalist songs ("Bukhenval'dskiy nabat" [The Buchenwald Alarm]); other works include 2 symphonies; *Put' pobedï* [The Way of Victory] (symphonic poem, chorus, orchestra, 1950); cantatas *(S nami Lenin* [Lenin Is with Us], 1960); and more than 200 songs.

Muris, Johannes de. See Jehan des Murs.

Murky [Ger. also *Murki*]. In keyboard music of the 18th century, a piece employing a left-hand or bass part consisting of broken octaves played on a relatively slowly changing succession of pitches, sometimes notated as a *Brillenbass;* also a bass part of this type, termed a murky bass.

Murrill, Herbert (Henry John) (b. London, 11 May 1909; d. there, 25 July 1952). Composer. Studied with Bush and at Oxford. From 1936 worked with the BBC (head of the music division, 1950). Taught at the Royal College of Music, 1933–52. Works include *Man in Lage* (jazz opera, London, 1930); orchestral music (including 2 cello concertos), solo piano works, and solo songs.

Muselar [Du.]. A type of *virginal.

Musette [Fr.]. (1) A small French *bagpipe, very popular in aristocratic circles in the 17th and 18th centuries. In its most developed form, it consisted of a bellows-inflated windbag, two double-reed *chanters with keys for semitones, and a set of four to six double-reed *drones cylindrically arranged. (2) A pseudopastoral dance piece of the 18th century, usually characterized by a drone in the bass imitating the instrument of the same name.

Musgrave, Thea (b. Barnton, Midlothian, Scotland, 27 May 1928). Composer and conductor. Studied at the Univ. of Edinburgh and with Gál, Boulanger, and Copland. Taught at London Univ. in Teddington, 1958–65; at the Univ. of California, Santa Barbara, 1970–78; at Queens College, CUNY, from 1987. Has composed operas (*The Decision,* 1964–65; *The Voice of Ariadne,* 1972–73; *Mary, Queen of Scots,* 1975–77; *Harriet, the Woman Called Moses,* 1982–84; *Simón Bolívar,* 1993); ballets; orchestral music (Concerto for Orchestra, 1967; solo concertos; *Night Music,* 1969; *Rainbow,* 1990); vocal music (*Sir Patrick Spens,* tenor, guitar, 1961); instrumental music (piano sonatas; String Quartet, 1958; pieces with tape).

Music box. See Automatic instruments.

Music drama. See Opera.

Music theater. In 20th-century music, the combination of elements from music and drama in new forms distinct from traditional opera. Although some action is usually specified, music theater is normally nonrealistic and often nonrepresentational. An early example is Schoenberg's *Pierrot lunaire* (1912). Stravinsky, however, was the most active of the early 20th-century composers in developing alternative musico-theatrical approaches, beginning with *Renard* (1916) and later with *Histoire du soldat* (1918).

Music theater flourished especially in the latter half of the 20th century, during which time a number of composers came to view much of their work, including purely instrumental music, in essentially dramatic terms. Singers or instrumentalists may be required to wear masks (e.g., George Crumb's *Vox balaenae,* 1971) or full costume (Peter Maxwell Davies's *Eight Songs for a Mad King,* 1969), or the musical performance itself may be treated as a "staged" dramatic event (Luciano Berio's *Recital I,* 1972, and numerous works by John Cage and Mauricio Kagel). See also Mixed media.

Music therapy. The clinical use of music in the treatment especially, though not exclusively, of mental illness or disability. Although healing powers of music are attested from ancient times and in numerous cultures, the scientific understanding of such powers remains limited. The nature of musical perception itself remains imperfectly understood. Nevertheless, music has been found useful in working with patients with a variety of disorders, including autism, cerebral palsy, brain damage, and mental retardation.

Music video. A film or video tape made to be shown to the accompaniment of a recording of a rock or pop song; also rock video. It may present a live or staged performance, a direct interpretation of the song's words, or a much more loosely related series of images. Music videos were developed in the mid-1970s by recording companies as an aid to marketing popular music.

Musica [Lat., Gr.]. Music. Four important classifications of music are transmitted by ancient and medieval texts. (1) Theoretical and practical. This distinction is encountered in late antiquity, and it was widely employed by writers beginning in the 13th century. (2) *Musica mundana, musica humana, musica instrumentalis* (the harmony of the universe, the harmony of the body and of the soul, and music produced by instruments, including the voice). For music history, the direct source of this classification is Boethius (ca. 480–ca. 524). (3) Harmonics, rhythmics, metrics. This classification appears clearly for the first time in the writings of Aristides Quintilianus, and Isidore of Seville (ca. 559–636) passes it on to later ages. Aurelian makes this a subclassification of *musica humana.* (4) Natural and artificial. This dichotomy is made by Aristotle and transmitted to medieval writers, some of whom use it to distinguish between vocal and instrumental music.

Musica ficta [Lat., feigned music]. In music theory before the end of the 16th century, notes outside of the *gamut or *Guidonian hand. Notes in the gamut or hand constitute *musica recta* or *musica vera* (right or true music). The term *musica falsa* (false music) is an earlier equivalent.

The term *musica ficta* is now often used loosely to describe intended accidentals left unwritten in the original manuscripts or prints of music from before about 1600 but added in performance or editing. In modern editions, added accidentals are often placed above the staff. Sometimes they are placed on the staff but are printed in a different typeface from that of accidentals found in the sources.

Although the theoretical definition of *musica ficta* remained constant in the years before 1600, the degree to which unwritten accidentals were admitted into practice and sanctioned by theorists changed greatly over time. No single formula for applying accidentals to all types of music has been found, nor is one likely to be.

Certain guidelines for adding accidentals are commonly used. Employing terms used by theorists as early as the 13th century, these are often summed up under the two headings *causa necessitatis* (by reason of necessity) and *causa pulchritudinis* (by reason of beauty). Under the former heading are guidelines resulting in perfect intervals, under the latter those pertaining to imperfect intervals. Some bear principally on melody, others on harmony.

Most modern writers and editors would agree on the following procedures : (a) Sharp lower neighboring tones or other melodic leading tones. (b) Avoid the melodic tritone between F and B when the melodic line turns down from B. (c) Flat upper returning notes (specifically single notes above *la*) when not doing so would cause a tritone to be outlined melodically; by the 16th century, this principle had been formulated in the Latin rhyme "una nota super *la*, semper est canendum *fa*" (a note above *la* is always to be sung *fa*). (d) Avoid *mi* against *fa* in fourths, fifths, and octaves; that is, make those intervals perfect (some writers exclude fourths). (e) Avoid cross-relations. (f) Approach a perfect consonance from the nearest imperfect consonance; specifically, when the upper voice ascends by step, make a sixth before an octave or a third before a fifth major, and when the upper voice descends by step, make a third before a unison or fifth minor. (g) When a piece ends on a complete minor triad, raise the third of that triad to make it major. See also Conflicting signatures, Hexachord, Solmization.

Musica reservata [Lat., also *m. riservata*]. A term occurring (sometimes in vernacular cognates) in about 15 treatises or documents from 1552 until 1625, but for which scholars have been unable to agree on a single and precise meaning. It has variously been thought to refer to the whole range of techniques applicable to text expression, to the sociological phenomenon of music for a limited and privately informed audience, and to cultural currents sometimes described with the term *mannerism.

Musical (comedy). A popular form of musical theater of the 20th century, developed chiefly in the U.S. and England. In structure and general style, it is similar to European *operetta, with spoken dialogue developing dramatic situations appropriate for song, ensemble numbers, and dance. The harmonic and melodic vocabulary is similar to that of the *Tin Pan Alley period of songwriting in America and Britain, and in fact, many of these composers were writers of musical comedy.

The first indigenous American musical theater took the form of the *minstrel show and *vaudeville, similar to products of the 19th-century music hall in consisting of a string of musical and comedy acts without dramatic unity. Extended stage pieces unified by common characters and a semblance of a plot appeared only in the 1880s. The "musical plays"

of George M. Cohan (1878–1942), including *Little Johnny Jones* (1904) and *Forty-five Minutes from Broadway* (1906), were an important step toward indigenous musical theater, with their American subject matter, aggressive patriotism, and memorable songs in the style of popular American song of the day.

The first decades of the 20th century were still dominated by variety shows, vaudeville, and *revues, as opposed to book musicals. Irving Berlin (b. 1888) was typical of the young songwriters who created songs and skits drawing on the rhythms of *ragtime and other syncopated dances and depicting uniquely American characters. Jerome Kern (1885–1945) worked in both London and New York, writing first single songs for interpolation into stage works, then a complete show (*The Red Petticoat*, 1912), and eventually a successful and influential series of musical comedies.

American musical comedy took its definitive form in the 1920s with a series of shows built on fast-paced librettos, into which songs and other musical numbers were smoothly integrated, contributing to plot and character development. Settings were usually contemporary and urban, and musical style was squarely in the stream of popular songwriting of the day. Typical shows were *La La Lucille* (George Gershwin, 1919), *Lady, Be Good* (Gershwin, 1924), *No, No, Nanette* (Vincent Youmans, 1925), and *The Girl Friend* (Richard Rodgers, 1926). Later in the decade, musical comedy became a less parochial product, with characters and plots drawn from American life outside of New York and with music sometimes reflecting nonurban styles. Jerome Kern's *Show Boat* (1927) became the first hugely successful "populist" show; the following two decades brought the American musical stage to its peak, with such shows as *Strike Up the Band* (George Gershwin, 1930), *Oklahoma!* (Richard Rodgers, 1943), *Carousel* (Rodgers, 1945), and *Annie Get Your Gun* (Berlin, 1946).

When rock-and-roll altered the course of American popular music in the 1950s, musical comedy at first clung to its own musical style and stage conventions, with *My Fair Lady* (Frederick Loewe, 1956), *The Sound of Music* (Richard Rodgers, 1959), and *Funny Girl* (Jule Styne, 1964). Some attempts were made to integrate the music and culture of the rock age with the traditions of musical comedy (Galt MacDermot's *Hair* of 1967 and Andrew Lloyd Webber's *Jesus Christ Superstar* of 1971). But even though many musicals thereafter dealt with contemporary characters and problems (Stephen Sondheim's *Company* of 1970 and director Michael Bennett's *A Chorus Line* of 1975 are prime examples), the form has remained essentially oriented toward a prerock musical vocabulary strongly influenced by

European styles. The single most prominent composer of musicals of the late 20th century is Andrew Lloyd Webber (*Evita*, 1978; *Cats*, 1981; *Phantom of the Opera*, 1986; *Sunset Boulevard*, 1993).

Musical bow. An instrument consisting of a string held taut by a flexible, curved stick. The player plucks or strikes the string to make it vibrate. A resonator is often added to amplify the sound, the simplest resonator being the player's mouth held to one end of the bow. Gourds, coconut shells, and tin cans are also used as resonators. The musical bow is distributed worldwide except Australia. See ill. under Instrument.

Musical clock. See Automatic instruments.

Musical glasses. Drinking glasses tuned by being filled with varying amounts of water and played either by striking with small sticks or rubbing the rims with wetted fingers. See Glass harmonica.

Musical Joke, A. See *Musikalischer Spass, Ein.*

Musical Offering. See *Musikalisches Opfer.*

Musical saw [Fr. *lame musicale;* Ger. *singende Säge*]. A handsaw that is bowed on the smooth edge with a violin or cello bow or struck on the flat side with a soft mallet. The player places one end of the saw between the legs and holds the other with the left hand. Bending the saw raises its pitch, which can be varied continuously.

Musicology [Fr. *musicologie;* Ger. *Musikwissenschaft, Musikforschung;* It. *musicologia;* Sp. *musicología*]. The scholarly study of music, wherever it is found historically or geographically. The methods of musicology are any that prove fruitful with respect to the particular subject of study. Because musicology has become steadily more diverse in both subject and method, certain traditional boundaries among its subdisciplines have been blurred. Nevertheless, in practical terms, several disciplines are usually distinguished.

(1) *Ethnomusicology. In the broadest terms, ethnomusicology is concerned with music in its human context. In this respect, the discipline is as broad as musicology itself, and it has been argued that all musicology aims ultimately to be ethnomusicology. In practice, however, ethnomusicology is usually thought of as the study of any music, especially in its cultural context, outside the tradition of Western art music.

(2) Musicology, historical musicology. The great majority of scholars who describe themselves as musicologists (as distinct from ethnomusicologists) are students of Western art music. Most would also describe themselves as historians, and most specialize in the music of one or a few historical periods. The

subjects of study and the methods brought to bear on these subjects are increasingly diverse, however.

(3) *Theory. Two general approaches to the study of music theory may be distinguished: the study of the history of theory, and the study and development of theories of existing repertories. (Allied with composition is the development of speculative theory that explores the bases for future works.) Both approaches are essential to the work of the musicologist even simply as historian, and many musicologists resist regarding the theory of music as the subject of a separate discipline.

(4) Other subjects of study. A number of diverse subjects, including theory, have sometimes been grouped under the heading of systematic musicology, a term that has not retained the currency of the parallel historical musicology. These subjects have included acoustics, aesthetics, psychology and physiology of music, sociology of music, and education or pedagogy. Other subjects that cut across traditional historical and geographical boundaries include iconography and organology, or the study and classification of musical *instruments.

Musikalischer Spass, Ein [Ger., A Musical Joke]. A divertimento by Mozart, K. 522 (1787), for strings and two horns, that caricatures the work of undistinguished composers and performers by the deliberate use of incorrect dissonances, parallel fifths, etc.

Musikalisches Opfer [Ger., Musical Offering]. A work by Bach, BWV 1079 (composed and published in 1747), dedicated to Frederick the Great of Prussia. It consists of 13 compositions—a three-voice ricercar, a six-voice ricercar, ten canons, and a trio sonata—all based on a theme invented by Frederick and on which Bach had improvised during a visit to Potsdam in 1747. The dedication copy bears the inscription "Regis Iussu Cantio Et Reliqua Canonica Arte Resoluta" (Upon the King's Demand, the Theme and Additions Resolved in Canonic Style), which forms the acrostic RICERCAR. Extended controversies have arisen as to the proper order of the pieces and the intended medium of performance.

Musique concrète [Fr.]. See Electro-acoustic music.

Musique mesurée [Fr.]. Music composed in France in the late 16th century in which long and short syllables of text were set by note-values in the ratio 2:1, respectively, without regard for any regular musical meter. Music of this type was at first composed to set poetry, termed *vers mesurés,* written by Jean Antoine de Baïf and his followers in the Académie de poésie et musique (founded in 1570) with the aim of adapting to French the quantitative principles of Latin and Greek poetry (whence the terms *vers mesurés à l'antique* and *musique mesurée à l'antique*). The principal composers concerned were Guillaume Costeley (ca. 1530–1606), Nicolas de la Grotte (1530–ca. 1600), Claude Le Jeune (ca. 1530–1600), Eustache Du Carroy .(1549–1609), and Jacques Mauduit (1557–1627). The style of this music was taken up by composers of the *air de cour for conventional rhymed poetry and persisted into the 17th century.

Mussorgsky [Moussorgsky, Musorgsky], **Modest Petrovich** (b. Karevo, Pskov district, 21 Mar. 1839; d. St. Petersburg, 28 Mar. 1881). Composer. Pupil of Balakirev. Held various bureaucratic posts. One of the "Moguchaya Kuchka" [Mighty Handful] of Balakirev, Borodin, Cui, Mussorgsky, and Rimsky-Korsakov. Works: operas (*Boris Godunov; *Khovanshchina; Sorochinskaya yarmarka [*Sorochintsky Fair] (1874–80, completed by Lyadov and others); orchestral works (*Night on Bald Mountain); choral music; songs ("Seminarist" [The Seminarist] 1866; "Evreyskaya pesnya" [Hebrew Song] 1867; the cycles Detskaya [The Nursery] and Pesni i plyaski smerti [Songs and Dances of Death]); piano pieces (Intermezzo in modo classico, 1860–61; *Pictures at an Exhibition).

Mustel organ. A *harmonium with an expression stop, invented by Victor Mustel in Paris in 1843.

Muta, mutano [It., imperative and 3rd person plural]. Change, e.g., of instrument and or tuning. Thus, in a timpani part, "muta in G/d" means that the tuning of the timpani should be changed to G and d. In a flute part, "muta in flauto piccolo" means that the player should change to the piccolo.

Mutation. In *solmization, the change from one hexachord to another.

Mutation stop. An organ stop sounding the fifth or its octaves (5 1/3′, 2 2/3′, 1 1/3′, etc.) or the third or its octaves (1 3/5′, etc.) above normal pitch. Thus, a mutation stop 2 2/3′ will sound g′ if the c key is depressed.

Mutazione [It.]. See Ballata.

Mute [Fr. sourdine; Ger. Dämpfer; It. sordino; Sp. sordina]. A device for reducing the volume and or altering the tone color of an instrument. On the violin and related instruments it produces a veiled, soft tone; on brass instruments a nasal, penetrating tone. In instruments of the violin family, the mute is a comb-shaped clamp that is fastened to the top of the bridge. It damps the vibration of the bridge and thus hinders transmission of vibrational energy from the strings to the sound box. In brass instruments, the mute is a hollow, conical stopper of metal, cardboard, or similar material that fits into the bell. [For the use of the hand to produce stopped tones in the French horn, see Horn.] Such a mute reduces the amount of

vibrating air that leaves the bell and at the same time eliminates lower partials and reinforces higher partials. Various types are used for brass instruments, especially in jazz and popular music, including straight, cup, and *wa-wa (or Harmon) mutes [see ill. under Brass instruments]. Jazz trombonists often use a rubber plunger or similar mute that is held in the left hand and moved in front of and away from the bell while playing.

On the piano, a muted effect is produced by the *una corda pedal. A related purpose was served by the *moderator on some early pianos. Some confusion has resulted from the fact that the German and Italian words for mute can also mean *damper. Thus, Beethoven's instruction senza sordini in the first movement of the Moonlight Sonata means that the passage should be played without dampers, i.e., with the damper pedal depressed. The result on the modern piano is inappropriately different from that on the pianos of Beethoven's day.

Muti, Riccardo (b. Naples, 28 July 1941). Conductor. Studied at the Naples and Milan Conservatories. Music director of the Maggio musicale, Florence, 1969–82; principal conductor, Florence Teatro comunale, from 1970. American debut, 1972. Music director of the Philadelphia Orchestra, 1980–92, succeeding Ormandy; of the New Philharmonia (later the Philharmonia), London, 1978–82; at La Scala from 1986.

Mutter, Anne-Sophie (b. Rheinfelden, 29 June 1963). Violinist. In 1977, Karajan invited her to perform and record with the Berlin Philharmonic. Engagements with orchestras under Dohnányi, Sawallisch, and Mehta followed. Taught at the Royal Academy of Music (1986). Formed a trio with Bruno Giuranna (viola) and Rostropovich.

Muzak. A trade name for music intended solely for use as background in work or public places. Several companies provide music of this type as a commercial service, and it is made available through both radio and closed-circuit broadcast.

Muzio, Claudia [Claudina] (b. Pavia, 7 Feb. 1889; d. Rome, 24 May 1936). Soprano. Studied in Turin and Milan. Debut, 1910. Roles include Puccini's Manon, Violetta (Traviata), Desdemona (Othello), and Fiora (L'amore dei tre ré). Appeared at La Scala from 1913. Sang at the Met, 1916–22, 1934 (created Puccini's Giorgietta there, 1918); with the Chicago Lyric Opera, 1922–32.

M.v. [It.]. Abbr. for mezza voce [see Mezzo, mezza].

My Country (Fatherland). See Má Vlast.

Myaskovsky, Nikolay Yakovlevich (b. Novogeorgiyevsk, 20 Apr. 1881; d. Moscow, 8 Aug. 1950). Composer. Studied with Glier, Lyadov, and Rimsky-

Korsakov. From 1921 taught at the Moscow Conservatory; among his pupils were Kabalevsky, Khachaturian, and Shebalin. Although he won the title of People's Artist (1946), he was accused of "formalism" during the cultural purge of 1948. Works include 27 symphonies; symphonic poems; concertos; *Kirov s nami* [Kirov Is with Us] (cantata, 1942); 13 string quartets; 2 cello sonatas; 9 piano sonatas; other piano pieces; songs.

Mysliveček, Josef (b. Horní-Šárka, near Prague, 9 March 1737; d. Rome, 4 Feb. 1781). Composer. Studied in Prague and with Pescetti. Composed operas (*Il Bellerofonte*, Naples, 1766; *Montezuma,* Florence, 1771; and *Ezio,* Naples, 1775); oratorios (*Abramo ed Isacco,* 1777); cantatas; symphonies, concertos, and chamber works; keyboard sonatas.

Mystery play. See Liturgical drama.

Mystic chord. A chord used by Scriabin consisting of various types of fourths: c–f♯–b♭–e′–a′–d″. It occurs prominently in his tone poem *Prométhée* op. 60 (1908–10) and his Seventh Piano Sonata op. 64 (1911). Other similar chords are used in his works as well.

N

Nabokov, Nicolas [Nikolay] (b. Lyubcha, near Minsk, 17 Apr. 1903; d. New York, 6 Apr. 1978). Composer and writer. Studied in St. Petersburg and with Juon and Busoni. In 1933, emigrated to the U.S. where he taught at several institutions including the Peabody Conservatory. Cultural adviser to the American ambassador in Berlin 1944–47; 1960–63, to the mayor of West Berlin. Works include 2 operas (*The Holy Devil*, Louisville, 1958) and 5 ballets; orchestral pieces; a string quartet and other chamber and piano works; 3 marches for band; oratorios and cantatas (*Symboli chrestiani*, performed 1956); and songs.

Nabucodonosor [It., Nebuchadnezzar; usually referred to as *Nabucco*]. Opera in four parts by Verdi (libretto by Temistocle Solera, after a French play of the same name by Auguste Anicet-Bourgeois and Francis Cornue), produced in Milan in 1842. Setting: Jerusalem and Babylon in the 6th century B.C.E.

Nacchera, naccherone [It.]. (1) *Naqqārah.* (2) [pl. *nacchere*] *Castanets.

Nachdrücklich [Ger.]. Energetic, emphatic.

Nachlassend [Ger.]. Slackening, slowing.

Nachschlag [Ger., after-beat]. (1) In modern German terminology, the suffix of a *trill. (2) The class of ornaments that follow and take their value from the notes they are understood to embellish. The principal ornaments of this class are the *accent* [Ex. 1;

1

Tris-   tes ap- prêts

2   3

Types of *Nachschlag.* **1.** Accent, from Rameau, *Hyppolyte et Aricie* (1733). **2.** Springer. **3.** Cadent.

see *Accent* (3)], *springer [Ex. 2], and perhaps the 17th-century English cadent [Ex. 3].

Nachspiel [Ger.]. Postlude.

Nachtanz [Ger.]. *After-dance; in German instrumental collections of the 16th and 17th centuries, the second of a pair of dances meant to be played and danced in succession. The *Nachtanz* was in a fast tempo that contrasted with the slow movement of its predecessor, and it used the melodic/harmonic material of the first dance, recomposed into a form of triple meter (3/4 or 6/8). The dance appears under a variety of titles and spellings: *Hopp tancz, Hopper dancz, Hopeldantz, Hupfauf, Hupf auff, Proportz, Proportio,* and *Sprung(k).*

Nachtmusik [Ger.]. *Serenade.

Nachtstück [Ger.]. *Nocturne.

Nāgasvaram [Tamil]. A large *shawm of South India, about 75 cm. long with seven finger holes and a metal bell.

Nagauta [Jap., long song]. A major lyrical genre connected with the *kabuki* theater, also performed in concert.

Nagelgeige [Ger.]. *Nail violin.

Nail violin, nail fiddle, nail harmonica [Ger. *Nagelgeige, Nagelharmonica*]. An instrument of the late 18th and early 19th century consisting of a flat, semicircular sound box with nails or U-shaped iron pins of varying lengths driven in around the circumference. It was held in the left hand, and the nails were set into vibration with a violin bow. A concert model with sympathetic strings was introduced in the late 18th century as the *violino-harmonico.*

Naker. A kettledrum. See *Naqqārah.*

Nancarrow, Conlon (b. Texarkana, Ark., 27 Oct. 1912; d. Mexico City, 10 Aug. 1997). Composer. Pupil of Slonimsky, Piston, and Sessions. Moved to Mexico City, 1940. After the late 1940s composed only for one or more player pianos, creating an effect of virtuosity beyond the capability of a human performer. Works include Studies for player piano(s) (No. 27 Canon–5%/6%/8%/11%; No. 30 for Prepared Player Piano), chamber music (String Quartet no. 3, 1987), piano music (*Prelude and Blues for Acoustic Piano,* 1984).

Nänie [Ger., elegy]. A composition for chorus and orchestra by Brahms, op. 82 (1880–81), setting a poem by Friedrich von Schiller.

Nanino, Giovanni Maria (b. Tivoli, 1543 or 1544; d. Rome, 11 Mar. 1607). Composer. Pupil of Palestrina; succeeded him, ca. 1567, as *maestro di cappella* at S. Maria Maggiore, Rome; *maestro* at S. Luigi dei Francesi in Rome from 1575. Joined the papal choir, 1577; from 1591, with his brother, Giovanni Bernardino, taught the choirboys of S. Luigi. Works include madrigals, canzonettas, and many sacred works, especially motets.

Napolitana [It.]. See *Villanella.*

Nápravník, Eduard (Francevič) (b. Býšt, near Hradec Králové, 24 Aug. 1839; d. Petrograd, 23 Nov. 1916). Conductor and composer. Studied with Kittl. Settled in St. Petersburg, 1861; from 1869, directed the imperial theaters. Conducted the premiere of *Boris Godunov* (1874). Works include 5 Russian operas (*Dubrovsky,* 1895), 4 symphonies, chamber music, vocal pieces.

Naqqārah [Ar.; Eng. naker; Fr. *nacaire;* It. *nacchera, naccherone;* Sp. *nácara*]. A *kettledrum of the Middle East made of metal, clay, or wood and almost always played in pairs tuned to different pitches. Such drums are played with padded sticks, sometimes while riding a horse or camel. The instrument was brought to Europe by the 13th century. The word *naqqārah* and its cognates denote various sizes of kettledrums from England to Ethiopia *(nagarit)* to India *(nāgarā).* See ill. under Instrument.

Nardini, Pietro (b. Livorno, 12 Apr. 1722; d. Florence, 7 May 1793). Violinist and composer. Studied with Tartini. Solo violinist and leader of the court orchestra in Stuttgart, 1762–65. From 1770, music director of the court orchestra in Florence. Noted for cantabile playing and purity of sound. Works include violin concertos, sonatas, and chamber works.

Nares, James (b. Stanwell, Middlesex, bapt. 19 Apr. 1715; d. London, 10 Feb. 1783). Composer and organist. Pupil of Pepusch. From 1735, organist at York Minster; from 1756, of the Chapel Royal; Master of the Children there from 1757. Composed a dramatic ode (*The Royal Pastoral*); much sacred music, including services and anthems; catches, canons, glees; also published instructional works.

Narváez, Luys [Luis] **de** (b. Granada; fl. 1530–50). Composer. Musician at the Spanish royal court. Published *Los seys libros del delphin* (1538), containing fantasias, *diferencias, villancicos, romances,* and

intabulations of vocal works by Josquin and others for vihuela.

Nationalism. The use in art music of materials that are identifiably national or regional in character. These may include actual folk music, melodies or rhythms that merely recall folk music, and nonmusical programmatic elements drawn from national folklore, myth, or literature. This concept of musical nationalism has most often been employed to describe music of the later 19th and early 20th centuries by composers from what were regarded as peripheral countries. It rests in the main on a view that the music of German-speaking countries, and to a lesser extent Italy and France, constitutes the central tradition of Western art music. Nevertheless, much German music, especially of the Romantic period, could be understood as nationalistic in precisely this way.

Natural. (1) A note that is not affected by either a sharp or a flat, e.g., D-natural as distinct from D-sharp or D-flat. (2) The accidental sign ♮, used to cancel a previous sharp or flat or to warn against the possible use of either [see Accidental].

Natural horn, trumpet. Brass instruments that lack *valves or keys and thus produce only the tones available in the *harmonic series. Such instruments may employ additional lengths of tubing (termed crooks) that can be substituted for one another so as to alter the fundamental and with it the pitches of the harmonic series produced. See also Brass instruments.

Natural tones. The pitches of the *harmonic series; especially those produced on a *wind instrument without the aid of *valves or keys.

Naturhorn, Naturtrompete [Ger.]. *Natural horn, natural trumpet.

Naumann, Johann Gottlieb (b. Blasewitz, near Dresden, 17 Apr. 1741; d. Dresden, 23 Oct. 1801). Composer. Studied in Dresden and with Tartini, Hasse, and Padre Martini. Court composer at Dresden, 1764; by 1766, Kapellmeister. From 1767 composed operas in Stockholm for Gustav III; *Oberkapellmeister,* Dresden, from 1786. Composed nearly 30 operas (*Cora och Alonzo,* 1782; *Gustav Wasa,* 1786; *Medea in Colchide,* 1788; *Orpheus og Eurydike,* Copenhagen, 1786); oratorios, sacred cantatas, Masses, lieder, symphonies, chamber works, and 12 sonatas for glass harmonica.

Navarro, Juan (b. Seville or Marchena, ca. 1530; d. Palencia, 25 Sept. 1580). Composer. *Maestro de capilla* at Avila (from 1563), Salamanca (from 1566), and Palencia (from 1578). At Salamanca collaborated with Salinas. Works include much sacred music

(*Psalmi, hymni ac Magnificat totius anni,* 1590); a few secular songs.

Nāy [Per., Ar.], **ney** [Turk.]. An *end-blown flute of the Middle East. Most are 60 to 70 cm. long, made from cane, and have six finger holes and a thumb hole. It is much used in Persian, Arabic, and Turkish art music, in folk music, and in the religious music of the Sufi orders. See ill. under Instrument.

Naylor, Edward (Woodall) (b. Scarborough, 9 Feb. 1867; d. Cambridge, 7 May 1934). Composer. Studied composition with his father, John Naylor, and at the Royal College of Music and at Emmanuel College, Cambridge, where he played organ and lectured from 1908. Works include much sacred choral music, frequently for male chorus, as well as some chamber music.

Nazareth (Nazaré), **Ernesto (Julio de)** (b. Rio de Janeiro, 20 Mar. 1863; d. there, 4 Feb. 1934). Composer and pianist. Worked for the publisher Carlos Gomez from 1921; played alongside Villa-Lobos at the Odeon cinema, 1920–24. Composed 200-odd tangos, waltzes, polkas, and other dance compositions for piano.

Neapolitan school. A group of 18th-century composers, known chiefly for their operas, who studied in Naples or were active there for some significant portion of their careers. Nicola Porpora (1686–1768), Leonardo Vinci (ca. 1690–1730), Francesco Feo (1691–1761), Leonardo Leo (1694–1744), Nicola Logroscino (1698–1765), Giovanni Battista Pergolesi (1710–36), Gaetano Latilla (1711–91), Domingo Terradellas (1713–51), Tommaso Traetta (1727–79), Pietro Guglielmi (1728–1804), Niccolò Piccinni (1728–1800), Antonio Sacchini (1730–86), Giacomo Tritto (1733–1824), Giovanni Paisiello (1740–1816), and Domenico Cimarosa (1749–1801) all studied at one or another of the several musical conservatories in Naples. Feo, Leo, Tritto, and Francesco Provenzale (1627–1704, sometimes called the founder of the Neapolitan school) taught in these conservatories. Alessandro Scarlatti (1660–1725) and Niccolò Jommelli (1714–74) are included in the Neapolitan school although they, as well as many of the composers mentioned above, were also active in a number of other cities.

Neapolitan sixth. See Sixth chord.

Nebenstimme [Ger.]. Subsidiary voice or part, sometimes indicated in works by Schoenberg and others with brackets formed from the letter N [see also *Hauptstimme*].

Nebra (Blasco), José (Melchor de) (b. Calatayud, bapt. 6 Jan. 1702; d. Madrid, 11 July 1768). Composer. Organist of the Descalzas Reales convent and the royal chapel in Madrid from 1724; head of the royal choir school from 1751. Composed nearly 60 stage works; sacred music (Salve Reginas, Masses, orchestral Lamentations, a Requiem for Queen Maria Bárbara).

Neck. (1) [Fr. *manche;* Ger. *Hals;* It. *manico;* Sp. *cuello, mango, mástil*] The portion of a stringed instrument that projects from the body, over which the strings pass (usually over a *fingerboard), and by which the instrument is held. (2) The curved, uppermost side of the harp, along which the strings are attached to their tuning pins. (3) The curved, uppermost section of the alto and larger saxophones, to which the mouthpiece is attached.

Neefe, Christian Gottlob (b. Chemnitz, 5 Feb. 1748; d. Dessau, 26 Jan. 1798). Composer. Studied with J. A. Hiller. Court organist in Bonn from 1782; Beethoven's instructor in clavier and composition. From 1796, directed the theater in Dessau. Composed singspiels, including *Die Apotheke* (Berlin, 1771); *Amors Guckkasten* (Leipzig, 1772); *Adelheit von Veltheim* (Frankfurt, 1780); and 10 songs in Hiller's *Der Dorfbarbier* (Leipzig, 1771).

Nehmen [Ger., third person sing. *nimmt*]. To take up, as in an instruction for the flutist to take up or prepare to play the piccolo.

Neidhart [Neidhardt] **von Reuental** [Reuenthal] (b. ca. 1180; d. after 1237). Minnesinger. Served a Duke of Bavaria and later a Bishop of Salzburg; participated in a Crusade; from 1232 lived in Austria. Of his poems 68 survive, 17 with music; his work was widely imitated.

Neighboring tone, neighbor note. See Counterpoint.

Neikrug, Marc (Edward) (b. New York, 24 Sept. 1946). Composer and pianist. Studied with G. Klebe and at SUNY–Stony Brook. Has composed dramatic works (*Through Roses,* 1979–80; *Los Alamos,* 1988); concertos for piano, violin, flute; 2 string quartets; *Sonata concertante* (1994), and numerous instrumental works. Has performed with Pinchas Zukerman.

Nelhýbel, Václav (b. Polanka nad Odrou, Czechoslovakia, 24 Sept. 1919; d. Scranton, 22 Mar. 1996). Composer and conductor. Studied in Prague and at Fribourg Univ., where he later taught. Conducted the Czech Philharmonic (1945–46) and for Radio Free Europe (1950–57). In 1957, emigrated to the U.S. Works include 3 operas; 3 ballets; orchestral and band works; 2 string quartets and other chamber music; piano and organ music; *Let There Be Music* (baritone, chorus, orchestra, 1982); *Dies ultima* (3 solo voices, chorus, jazz band, orchestra, 1967); anthems for choir; songs.

Nelson Mass, Lord Nelson Mass. Popular name for the Mass in D minor by Haydn Hob. XXII:11 (1798). Particularly striking is the use of three trumpets in the Benedictus, sometimes said to have been inspired by news of Lord Nelson's victory in the Battle of the Nile. It is also called the *Imperial* or the *Coronation* Mass.

Nelson, Ron(ald Jack) (b. Joliet, Ill., 14 Dec. 1929). Composer. Studied at Eastman and in Paris. Taught at Brown Univ. from 1956. Has worked with aleatoric procedures. Works include 2 operas; *Savannah River Holiday* (orchestra, 1953; arr. band, 1973); *5 Pieces after Paintings by Andrew Wyeth* (1 voice, rock and jazz ensembles, 1976); *Te Deum Laudamus* (chorus, wind ensemble, 1985); songs; film scores.

Nelson, Willie (Hugh) (b. Abbot, Tex., 30 Apr. 1933). Country singer, songwriter, and guitarist. From 1960 wrote songs in Nashville. With Waylon Jennings developed the "Redneck Rock" style; recordings include "Blue Eyes Cryin' in the Rain" (on the album *Redheaded Stranger,* 1975). He and his songs were featured in films, including "Mamas, Don't Let Your Babies Grow Up To Be Cowboys" (in *Electric Horseman,* 1979), and "On the Road Again" (in *Honeysuckle Rose,* 1980).

Nelsova [Katznelson], **Zara** (b. Winnipeg, 23 Dec. 1918). Cellist. Studied in London and with Casals. London debut, 1932; formed the Canadian Trio with her sisters (a violinist and a pianist). American citizen, 1955. Often performed with her pianist husband, Grant Johannesen.

Nenna, Pomponio (b. Bari, near Naples, ca. 1550–55; d. Rome?, by late Oct. 1613). Composer. Served Gesualdo in Naples 1594–99; by 1608 he was in Rome. Composed 9 books of madrigals, responsories, a Psalm, villanellas, ricercares.

Neoclassical. A stylistic classification most commonly applied to the works of Stravinsky from *Pulcinella* (1920) to *The Rake's Progress* (1951). Its chief aesthetic characteristics are objectivity and expressive restraint, its principal technical ones, motivic clarity, textural transparency, formal balance, and reliance upon stylistic models. In Stravinsky's music, these models may be specific compositions (e.g., *Pulcinella* and *Le baiser de la fée,* based, respectively, upon actual compositions of the 18th and 19th centuries) or, more commonly, general stylistic traits (e.g., the Piano Concerto and Symphony in C, which contain explicit stylistic references to the Ba-

roque concerto and the Classical symphony, respectively).

As a more general stylistic attribution, neoclassical is also applied to other music of the period between the wars, especially music that—like Stravinsky's—preserves a degree of tonal centricity, as well as characteristics of clarity and expressive detachment. In this broadest sense, it pertains to much music of this period, not only in France (where Stravinsky lived from 1920 until 1939 and had an especially strong influence), but in other countries as well—e.g., Germany (Hindemith), Italy (Casella), Russia (Prokofiev), Spain (Falla), and the U.S. (Copland). Moreover, if a still broader stylistic characterization is accepted, the term even applies to the Schoenberg school, whose postwar *twelve-tone music reflects a more rational and systematic compositional approach and a closer affinity to traditional musical forms than did its prewar *expressionistic music.

Neo-Gallican chant. Chant composed for any of the reformed liturgies of the Catholic Church in France from the mid-17th century through much of the 19th. See also *Plain-chant musical.*

Nepomuceno, Alberto (b. Fortaleza, Brazil, 6 July 1864; d. Rio de Janeiro, 16 Oct. 1920). Composer. Studied with his father and in Europe. Taught at the National Institute in Brazil from 1895 (director, 1902, 1906–16); conducted the Sociedade de concertos populares from 1896. Worked with Brazilian folk materials. Works include operas (*Abul,* 1899–1905); *Série brasileira* (1892) and other orchestral works; chamber music, sacred choral works, songs.

Neri [Negri], **Massimiliano** (b. Brescia?, 1615?; d. Bonn, 1666). Composer and organist. Organist of St. Mark's, Venice, 1644–64; at SS. Giovanni e Paolo, 1644–46, 1657–64. Kapellmeister to the Elector of Cologne from 1664. Composed sonatas for various instruments; canzonas; motets.

Netherlands schools. See Renaissance, music of the.

Neubauer [Neubaur], **Franz Christoph** (b. Melník, 21 Mar. 1750; d. Bückeburg, 11 Oct. 1795). Composer and violinist. Studied in Prague. Kapellmeister for the Prince of Weilburg from 1790; 1795, succeeded J. C. F. Bach as Kapellmeister in Bückeburg. Composed an opera, sacred works, symphonies, string quartets and other chamber music, songs.

Neuhaus, Max (b. Beaumont, Tex., 9 Aug. 1939). Composer and percussionist. Studied with Krupa; played under Boulez and Stockhausen. In 1968, began to compose electronic music. His works are sound installations (for example in New York, Toronto, Kassel, Chicago, and Pistoia); swimming pool pieces (*Underwater Musics,* 1975–78); participatory radio pieces that combine material called in by listeners.

Neukomm, Sigismund Ritter von (b. Salzburg, 10 July 1778; d. Paris, 3 Apr. 1858). Composer and pianist. Pupil of Michael Haydn. Taught in Vienna; Mozart was among his students. Kapellmeister at the German Theater, St. Petersburg, 1804–9. Moved to Paris 1809. Introduced music of Haydn and Mozart to South America (1816–21). Compositions include Quintet for clarinet and string quartet; organ voluntaries; 10 operas; incidental music; 48 Masses; 8 oratorios; motets; piano pieces; some 200 songs.

Neuma [Lat., also *pneuma, neupma*]. (1) *Neume. (2) Any melisma in liturgical chant, but especially those of the *alleluia [see also *Jubilus*], those added to great responsories, and the untexted melodies of *sequences. (3) Any of the melismas attached to the Western adaptations of the Byzantine modal intonation formulas in order to form the melodies *(*noeane)* used in *tonaries and related treatises of the 9th through the 12th century to characterize the *modes.

Neumann, Václav (b. Prague, 29 Oct. 1920; d. Vienna, 2 Sept. 1995). Conductor. Studied at the Prague Conservatory. Played in the Smetana Quartet; appeared with the Berlin Komische Oper, 1956–64. Gewandhaus-Kapellmeister, Leipzig, 1964–68; chief conductor, Czech Philharmonic, 1968–89; music director, Stuttgart Staatsoper, 1970–73. Metropolitan Opera debut, 1985 (*Jenůfa*).

Neumatic [fr. *neume]. Characterized by the presence of groups of five or six notes sung to single syllables; one of the three principal categories of style in *Gregorian chant.

Neume [Lat. *neuma,* fr. Gr.]. Any of the signs employed in the notation of plainsong beginning in about the 9th century. The accompanying table gives the names and shows the forms of the principal neumes as they are found in modern liturgical books and in several of the major regional notations of the Middle Ages, together with an approximate equivalent for each (at least in terms of pitch contour) in modern notation. The extent to which neumes represent duration or rhythm has been the subject of considerable controversy [see Gregorian chant].

Until the 11th century, individual neumes of two or more notes indicated only the general pitch contour of the notes contained, and the relationship of the pitch of one neume to that of the next was most often not implied in their placement on the page. Such neumes are variously described as nondiastematic, staffless, oratorical, and *in campo aperto* (in an open field). The 11th century saw the development of diastematic neumes, the first examples of which are Aquitanian. These specify pitch precisely by their careful arrangement above and below an imaginary line. The earliest type of actual line to be used is termed a dry-point line because it was scratched into the parchment of manuscripts without the use of ink. The use of one or more lines drawn with ink and clefs led in time to the standard practice of using four-line staves with C or F clefs. The square shapes on which those of modern liturgical books are modeled emerged in the 12th century.

	a	b	c	d	e
Punctum					
Virga					
Podatus or Pes					
Clivis or Flexa					
Scandicus					
Climacus					
Torculus					
Porrectus					
Scandicus flexus					
Porrectus flexus					
Torculus resupinus					
Pes subpunctis					

Neumes. a. Modern liturgical books. b. Pitch contour. c. St. Gall (10th century). d. Aquitanian (11th century). e. Gothic or *Hufnagel* (15th century).

Neusidler [Newsidler], **Hans** (b. Pressburg, ca. 1508–9; d. Nuremberg, 2 Feb. 1563). Composer and lutenist. Wrote 8 lute books (1536–49) containing arrangements of German, French, and Italian sacred and secular vocal works; German and Italian dances;

and some original preludes; also a didactic introduction on lute playing and many fingering indications.

Nevin, Arthur (Finlay) (b. Edgeworth, Pa., 27 Apr. 1871; d. Sewickley, Pa., 10 July 1943). Composer, educator, and conductor. Brother of Ethelbert Nevin. Pupil of Klindworth and Humperdinck. Studied Blackfoot Indian folklore in Montana. Taught at the Univ. of Kansas, Lawrence, from 1915. Directed orchestras in Memphis, Tenn., 1920–22. Works include operas, piano pieces, chamber pieces, 2 cantatas, 2 orchestral suites.

Nevin, Ethelbert (Woodbridge) (b. Edgeworth, Pa., 25 Nov. 1862; d. New Haven, 17 Feb. 1901). Composer. Brother of Arthur Nevin. Pupil of B. J. Lang and Klindworth. During 1890s taught, studied, and composed in Boston and Europe. Composed mainly short pieces, including the songs "The Rosary" and "Mighty Lak' a Rose."

New German School [Ger. *Neudeutsche Schule*]. A group of musicians initially gathered around Liszt during his Weimar years (1849–61) and including Hans von Bülow, Peter Cornelius, Joachim Raff, and Carl Taussig. They championed the program music of Berlioz and the music dramas of Wagner.

New Orleans jazz. The first jazz style. The most characteristic features of New Orleans jazz are ensemble passages with dense textures resulting from overlapping rhythms and dissonant clashes among one or two cornets (or trumpets), trombone, clarinet, and perhaps saxophone. See also Chicago jazz, Dixieland, Jazz.

New wave. A general designation for the *rock music played by numerous English and American bands after the late 1970s. The term is applied to a variety of styles whose direct antecedent was *punk rock but whose forms and rhythms derive directly from the *rock-and-roll of the 1950s and 60s. Notable exponents include Elvis Costello, Graham Parker, Dave Edmunds, Patti Smith, the Talking Heads, and Brian Eno.

New World Symphony [Cz. *Z Nového světa*, From the New World]. Dvořák's Ninth Symphony (formerly no. 5) in E minor op. 95 (1893). It was composed during Dvořák's residence in the U.S. and employs some melodies modeled on traditional Afro-American melodies but does not actually quote any.

Newman, Alfred (b. New Haven, 17 Mar. 1900; d. Los Angeles, 17 Feb. 1970). Composer and conductor. Pupil of Goldmark and Schoenberg. Conducted on Broadway from 1920. From 1930, music director for United Artists in Hollywood; 1940–60, head of the music division of 20th Century Fox. Worked on more than 230 films (*Street Scene*, 1931; *The Robe*,

1953; *Airport*, 1969); received 9 Academy Awards. Established the Romantic symphonic style in Hollywood and developed a system for synchronizing music and film.

Newman, Anthony (b. Los Angeles, 12 May 1941). Harpsichordist, organist, conductor, and composer. Studied with Boulanger, Berio, and Kirchner. Has taught at Juilliard (1968–73), SUNY–Purchase (1968–75), and Indiana Univ. (1978–81). Performs mainly Baroque repertory, in particular works of J. S. Bach. Has composed works for organ, piano, orchestra, and various instrumental ensembles.

Nibelungenring [Ger.]. See *Ring des Nibelungen, Der.*

Nichelmann, Christoph (b. Treuenbrietzen, 13 Aug. 1717; d. Berlin, 1761 or 1762). Composer. Studied under J. S. Bach, W. F. Bach, Telemann, Mattheson, Quantz, and Graun. Court harpsichordist in Berlin (along with C. P. E. Bach), 1745–56. Best known for his keyboard works, especially sonatas and concertos.

Nichols, Red [Ernest Loring] (b. Ogden, Utah, 8 May 1905; d. Las Vegas, 28 June 1965). Jazz cornetist and bandleader. Made a series of influential Dixieland recordings with his Five Pennies (including *That's No Bargain*, 1926; *Imagination, Feelin' No Pain*, both 1927; and *Shim-me-sha-wabble*, 1928). Worked with Miff Mole, Jimmy Dorsey, and others. Led mainly small groups, except for a swing big band (mid-1930s).

Nicodé, Jean Louis (b. Jercik, near Poznań, 12 Aug. 1853; d. Langebrück, near Dresden, 5 Oct. 1919). Composer, pianist, and conductor. Studied with Kullak. Taught at the Dresden Conservatory, 1878–85. Compositions include the symphonic odes *Das Meer* (1880) and *Gloria!* (1905); the symphonic poem *Maria Stuart* (1880); other orchestral and vocal works; chamber and piano music.

Nicolai, Otto (Ehrenfried) (b. Königsberg [Kaliningrad], 9 June 1810; d. Berlin, 11 May 1849). Composer, conductor. Pupil of Zelter and B. Klein. Organist at the Prussian embassy chapel, Rome, 1833–36. Conducted the Vienna Court Opera, 1837–38 and from 1841; 1842, began concerts that eventually became the Philharmonic. Kapellmeister, Berlin Opera and at the cathedral, 1848. Wrote operas (*Enrico II*, Trieste, 1839; *Il templario*, Turin, 1840; *Die *lustigen Weiber von Windsor*); part songs, songs, piano pieces; essays and music criticism.

Niedermeyer, (Abraham) Louis (b. Nyon, 27 Apr. 1802; d. Paris, 14 Mar. 1861). Composer. Pupil of Moscheles, Foerster, and Zingarelli. Settled in Paris, 1823. Reopened the church music school of Choron, renaming it École Niedermeyer; Saint-Saëns was on the faculty, Fauré was one of its first students. Works include 4 operas; much sacred music; piano and organ works.

Nielsen, Carl (August) (b. Nörre-Lyndelse, near Odense, 9 June 1865; d. Copenhagen, 3 Oct. 1931). Composer. Studied with Gade. First worked as a violinist with the Royal Chapel Orchestra. Conductor at the Royal Theater 1908–14; 1916–19, taught at the Copenhagen Conservatory; 1915–27, head of the Music Society in Copenhagen. From 1914, compiled Danish songs. Works include 2 operas (*Saul og David* [Saul and David], 1898–1901; *Maskarade*, 1904–6) and music for plays; 6 symphonies (no. 2, The 4 Temperaments, 1901–2) and other orchestral works (Violin Concerto, 1911; Flute Concerto, 1926); vocal works (cantatas; pieces for chorus and orchestra; a cappella works; solo songs, often in a simple folklike setting; hymn tunes); chamber works (4 string quartets; Wind Quintet, 1922; pieces for solo instruments); piano and organ works.

Nielsen, Riccardo (b. Bologna, 3 Mar. 1908; d. Ferrara, 30 Jan. 1982). Composer. Studied in Bologna; 1946–50, superintendent of the Teatro Communale there; from 1952, director of the conservatory in Ferrara. Works include the expressionist monodrama *L'incubo* (1948); *La via di Colombo* (radio opera, 1953); 2 symphonies and other orchestral, chamber, and piano music; *Requiem nella miniera* (1958) and other vocal music.

Nigg, Serge (b. Paris, 6 June 1924). Composer. Pupil of Messiaen and Leibowitz. Works include radio operas; ballets (*L'étrange aventure de Gulliver à Lilliput*, 1958); *Le Chant du dépossédé* (1944) and other oratorios and cantatas; *Jérôme Bosch-Symphonie* (1960), *Millions d'oiseaux-d'or* (1980–81), and other orchestral music; piano music; songs.

Night on Bald Mountain [Russ. *Ivanova noch' na Lisoy Jore*, St. John's Night on the Bare Mountain]. A symphonic poem by Mussorgsky, inspired by the witches' Sabbath in Nikolai Gogol's story "St. John's Eve." Composed in 1867, it was revised and eventually incorporated into his unfinished opera *Sorochintsy Fair*. It is now usually performed in an orchestral adaptation by Rimsky-Korsakov of Mussorgsky's original music.

Nightingale, The [Russ. *Solovey;* Fr. *Le rossignol*]. Opera ("musical fairy tale") in three acts by Stravinsky (libretto by the composer and Stepan Mitusov, after Hans Christian Andersen), produced in Paris (in French) in 1914. Setting: China. Stravinsky adapted it for the ballet *Le chant du rossignol* (The Song of the Nightingale; choreography by Leonide Massine,

scenery and costumes by Henri Matisse), produced in Paris in 1920.

Nights in the Gardens of Spain. See *Noches en los jardines de España.*

Nikisch, Arthur (b. Lébényi Szent Miklós, 12 Oct. 1855; d. Leipzig, 23 Jan. 1922). Conductor. Studied with Dessoff and Hellmesberger; played violin under Wagner at Bayreuth (1872). Conducted the Boston Symphony Orchestra (1889–93), Budapest Opera (1893–95), Leipzig Gewandhaus, and Berlin Philharmonic. Director, Leipzig Conservatory (1902–7), Stadttheater (1905–6).

Nilsson [Svennsson], **(Märta) Birgit** (b. Västra Karups, Sweden, 17 May 1918). Soprano. Debut, Stockholm Royal Opera, as Agathe *(Der Freischütz),* 1946. Sang often at Bayreuth, 1959–70, as Elsa, Isolde, Sieglinde, and Brünnhilde. Metropolitan Opera debut, 1959. Other roles included Elisabeth *(Tannhäuser),* Beethoven's Leonore, Electra *(Idomeneo),* Turandot, Strauss's Elektra and Salome.

Nilsson, Bo (b. Skellefteaa, Sweden, 1 May 1937). Composer. Has worked with serialism, electronic music, and jazz. Works include *Séance* (orchestra, tape, 1963); *Nazm* (voices, jazz group, orchestra, 1973); *Reaktionen,* 1–4 percussionists, 1960); *Wendepunkt* (brass, live electronics, 1981); *Szenes I–IV: IV,* saxophone, orchestra, chorus, 1974–75); music for film and television.

Nimmt [Ger.]. See *Nehmen.*

Nin (y Castellanos), Joaquín (b. Havana, 29 Sept. 1879; d. there, 24 Oct. 1949). Composer and pianist. Studied in Spain and at the Schola cantorum, where he taught, 1905–8. Composed works for piano, violin and piano, and voice. Edited and performed Spanish Baroque music.

Nin-Culmell, Joaquín (María) (b. Berlin, 5 Sept. 1908). Composer and pianist. Son of Joaquín Nin. Pupil of Dukas, de Falla, Cortot, and R. Viñes. Taught at Williams College, 1940–50; at Univ. of California, Berkeley, until 1974. Works include *La Celestina* (opera, 1965–80); ballets; *Diferencias* (orchestra, 1962); *The Ragpicker's Song* (men's chorus, piano, 1988); chamber, piano, and guitar music (*Doce danzas cubanas,* piano, 1984); 2 Masses, Spanish songs, and other vocal music.

Ninth. See Interval, Chord.

Nivers, Guillaume Gabriel [Guilaume] (b. Paris?, ca. 1632; d. there, 30 Nov. 1714). Composer and organist. Organist of St. Sulpice from the early 1650s; of the royal chapel from 1678. Master of music to the queen from 1681; music director of the convent school Maison Royale de St. Louis from

1686. Published 3 *Livres d'orgue* (1665, 1667, 1675), containing versets that combine sacred and secular styles.

No drama. See *Noh.*

Noble, (Thomas) Tertius (b. Bath, 5 May 1867; d. Rockport, Mass., 4 May 1953). Composer. Pupil of Parratt, Bridge, and Stanford. Church organist in Cambridge and Colchester; cofounder and conductor, York Symphony Orchestra, 1898–1912; then organist at St. Thomas's Episcopal Church, New York, where he helped establish a choir school. Composed music for the Anglican service and some orchestral and chamber music.

Nobre, Marlos (b. Recife, 18 Feb. 1939). Composer. Pupil of Koellreutter, Guarnieri, Ginastera, Asuar, and Ussachevsky. Music director of the National Symphony of Brazil, 1971–76. Works include orchestral pieces (*Concerto breve,* with piano, 1969; *Mosaico,* 1970; Guitar concerto, 1980); vocal works (*Ukrinmakrinkrin,* soprano, ensemble, 1964); instrumental pieces (Piano Trio, 1960; *Variações ritmicas,* piano, percussion, 1972; *Sonata on a Theme of Bartók,* piano, 1980).

Noces, Les [Fr., The Wedding; originally Russ. *Svadebka*]. Four choreographic scenes by Stravinsky (choreography by Bronislava Nijinska; text by Stravinsky, after traditional Russian poems), produced in Paris in 1923. Two early orchestrations of the work were abandoned by Stravinsky; the published version is scored for chorus, soloists, 4 pianos, and 17 percussion instruments (including 4 timpani).

Noches en los jardines de España [Sp., Nights in the Gardens of Spain]. Three symphonic impressions for piano and orchestra by Falla, composed in 1911–15: (1) *En el Generalife* (In the Generalife); (2) *Danza lejana* (Distant Dance); (3) *En los jardines de la Sierra de Córdoba* (In the Gardens of the Sierra de Córdoba).

Nocturn. A component of the Office of Matins [see Office, Divine].

Nocturne [Fr., of the night; Ger. *Nachtstück;* It. *notturno*]. The title for certain instrumental works of the 19th and 20th centuries, typically for solo piano; such works do not in general derive from the 18th-century genre of ensemble music termed the *notturno.* The title was first used in 1812 by John Field, whose 18 Nocturnes employed the texture commonly associated with the repertory: a lyrical melody accompanied by broken chords pedaled to collect the harmonies. Chopin's 21 Nocturnes are the best-known examples. Many other pieces whose titles connect them with evocations of night lie outside this

tradition of piano writing, e.g., Debussy's *Nocturnes* for orchestra.

Nocturnes. Three symphonic poems by Debussy, composed in 1897–99: *Nuages* (Clouds); *Fêtes* (Festivals); *Sirènes* (Sirens), with women's voices. Debussy's use of the term nocturnes is borrowed from paintings by Whistler.

Noeane, noeagis. Combinations of syllables and the melodies set to them found in *tonaries and related treatises of the 9th through the 12th centuries where they serve to characterize each of the eight *modes. Both syllables and melodies are derived from the eight modal intonation formulas or *enechemata* [see *Echos*] of *Byzantine chant.

Noël [Fr., fr. Lat. *natalis,* of birth]. (1) A semireligious Christmas song or *carol of French origin, its text strophic, written in the vernacular, and popular in character. From the 16th century onward, most *noëls* were associated with the Nativity, although their antecedents and relatives include songs used in pre-Christian celebrations and pieces connected with other Christian feasts.

(2) From the latter half of the 17th century, an instrumental piece in the spirit of a vocal *noël,* commonly designed to be played during the Christmas service. Most such *noëls* are for keyboard instruments, particularly the organ; a few are for instrumental ensembles. Many consist chiefly of variations on currently popular *noël* melodies.

Noh [Jap., ability]. A Japanese music and dance theater based on philosophical concepts drawn from Zen Buddhism and founded by Zeami Motokiyo (1363–1443). A *noh* play is performed by *shite* (principal actor), *waki* (supporting actor), several minor actors (*tsure* and *wakizure*), a chorus of about eight who sit on stage left, and an accompanying instrumental ensemble *(hayashi).* The *hayashi,* whose members sit on the stage, play various instruments: a *nōkan* (transverse bamboo flute with seven holes), a *kotsuzumi* (shoulder-held hourglass drum), an *ōtsuzumi* (side-held hourglass drum), and a *taiko* (shallow barrel drum played with two sticks). *Noh* plays are divided into five basic categories according to their plots and characters: god plays, warrior plays, woman plays, madwoman plays, and plays on miscellaneous subjects.

Noire [Fr.]. Quarter *note.

Nola, Giovanni [Giovan] **Domenico del Giovane da** (b. Nola, ca. 1510; d. Naples, May 1592). Composer. *Maestro di cappella* at SS. Annunziata, Naples, from 1563. Composed motets; light vocal works *(villanesche, mascheratas, napolitane);* and many madrigals, some with texts by Petrarch.

None. See Office, Divine.

Nonet [Fr. *nonette;* Ger. *Nonett;* It. *nonetto;* Sp. *noneto*]. (1) A composition for nine solo performers. (2) An ensemble of nine solo performers.

Nonharmonic tones. In *harmonic analysis, dissonant tones understood as embellishing otherwise consonant harmonies; also embellishing tones. Such tones can almost always be explained in terms of the dissonance treatment embodied in the principles of counterpoint [for examples of specific types, see Counterpoint] and are components of some of the most conventional harmonies of Western tonal music, e.g., the seventh in dominant seventh chords.

Nonnengeige [Ger., nun's fiddle]. *Tromba marina.

Nono, Luigi (b. Venice, 29 Jan. 1924; d. there, 8 May 1990). Composer. Studied with Malipiero, Maderna, and Scherchen. In 1955, married Schoenberg's daughter, Nuria. Lectured at Darmstadt, 1957–60. Employed serial techniques, concrete sounds, nontraditional vocal techniques, and political texts. Works include 3 operas (*Intolleranza*, 1960; *Prometeo: Tragedia dell'ascolto*, Venice, 1984); a ballet and incidental music; orchestral music; chamber music (*Incontri*, 24 instruments, 1955); choral music (*Il canto sospeso*, 1955–56; *Caminantes . . . Ayacucho*, with electronics, 1986–87); works for solo voice; electronic music (*La fabbrica illuminata*, 1964; *Contrappunto dialettico alla mente*, 1967–68).

Nordheim, Arne (b. Larvik, 20 June 1931). Composer. Pupil of Holmboe. Worked as a music critic until 1968; later as a performer of electronic music. Works include *Respons I* (2 percussion groups and tape, 1966–67); *Solitaire* (tape, 1968, based on texts by Baudelaire); *Warszawa* (4-track tape, 1967–68); *Sturm* (ballet, 1979); *Aurora* (4 soloists, chorus, 2 percussionists, tape, 1984); *Creo* (orchestra, 1989).

Nordoff, Paul (b. Philadelphia, 4 June 1909; d. Herdecke, Germany, 18 Jan. 1977). Composer and music therapist. Pupil of Goldmark. Taught at Philadelphia Conservatory, 1938–48; Michigan State College, 1945–49; Bard College, 1948–59. Composed 6 operas and ballets as well as orchestral (*Winter Symphony*, 1954), chamber, and vocal music (several song cycles); music for performance by handicapped children. Wrote several books with Clive Robbins on music therapy.

Nordraak [Nordraach], **Rikard** (b. Christiania [now Oslo], 12 June 1842; d. Berlin, 20 Mar. 1866). Composer. Studied with Kullak and Kiel, and in Copenhagen and Christiania. Associate of Grieg. Wrote the Norwegian national anthem (1863–64).

Nørgård, Per (b. Gentofte, near Copenhagen, 13 July 1932). Composer. Pupil of Holmboe, Høffding, and Boulanger. Has taught at the Copenhagen Conservatory, 1960–65; at the Århus Conservatory. Has worked with serialism, coloristic pointillism, quarter tones, metric modulation, and graphic notation. Works include the series *Fragmenter* (1960–61; I-IV, for piano; V, for piano and violin; VI, for orchestra); ballets (*Den unge mand skal giftes* [The Young Man Is To Marry] after Ionesco, 1964); 4 operas; 3 oratorios; orchestral music (4 symphonies; *Voyage into the Golden Screen*, 1968); string quartets and other chamber music; vocal works (*Entwicklung*, alto, chamber ensemble, 1986).

Norma. Opera in two acts by Bellini (libretto by Felice Romani, after Alexandre Soumet's play *Norma*), produced in Milan in 1831. Setting: Gaul during the Roman occupation, ca. 50 B.C.E.

Norman, Jessye (b. Augusta, Ga., 15 Sept. 1945). Soprano. Studied at the Univ. of Michigan and the Peabody Conservatory. Debut at the Berlin Deutsche Oper as Elisabeth *(Tannhäuser)*, 1969. Recital debuts in London and New York, 1973; Metropolitan Opera debut, 1983. Recordings include lieder of Schubert and Mahler.

Norrington, Roger (Arthur Carver) (b. Oxford, 16 Mar. 1934). Conductor. Pupil of Boult. Performed as a tenor. Has conducted the Heinrich Schütz Choir and Chorale; Kent Opera, 1969–84; Bournemouth Sinfonietta, 1985–89. In 1984, formed the Early Opera Project with his wife, choreographer Kay Lawrence. With the London Baroque and the London Classical Players, has conducted period instrument performances; recordings include the complete Beethoven Symphonies and the Berlioz *Symphonie fantastique.*

North, Alex (b. Chester, Pa., 4 Dec. 1910; d. 8 Sept. 1991). Composer and conductor. Studied at Curtis, Juilliard, and the Moscow Conservatory. Taught at Bennington and elsewhere in the U.S. Works include *Revue* (clarinet and orchestra, 1946; performed by Benny Goodman); incidental music for Arthur Miller's *Death of a Salesman* (1949); numerous film scores (*A Streetcar Named Desire*, 1951; *Prizzi's Honor,* 1985; *Good Morning, Vietnam!,* 1988); music for television; ballets, children's works with narrator; cantatas and songs.

Northcott, Bayan (Peter) (b. Harrow-on-the-Hill, 24 Apr. 1940). Music critic and composer. Studied at Oxford and the Univ. of Southampton. Music critic for the *Sunday Telegraph* (1976–86); then for the *Independent.* Works include Fantasia for Guitar (1982–83), *Hymn to Cybele* (1983), a sextet (1985).

Norvo, Red [Norville, Kenneth] (b. Beardstown, Ill., 31 Mar. 1908). Jazz xylophonist, vibraphonist, and bandleader. Worked with Paul Whiteman (early

1930s); in swing groups with Mildred Bailey (his wife, 1933–45). Played vibraphone in Benny Goodman's sextet, 1944. Brought together swing and bop musicians in recordings with Charlie Parker, Dizzy Gillespie, and Teddy Wilson (1945). During 1950s led trios (the first with Tal Farlow and Charles Mingus); then mainly worked in California and Nevada; in 1980s, toured Europe regularly.

Nose flute. A flute blown through the nose instead of the mouth. The player blows with one nostril only, plugging the other with a finger or some material.

Noskowski, Sigismund (Zygmunt von) (b. Warsaw, 2 May 1846; d. there, 23 July 1909). Composer. Studied in Warsaw and with Kiel. Created a music notation for the blind. In Warsaw, directed the Music Society, 1881–92; taught at the Conservatory from 1888; conducted the Opera and Philharmonic Society. Collected 2 editions of folk melodies. Works include 3 operas, 3 symphonies, symphonic poems, and vocal works.

Nota cambiata [It.]. See Counterpoint.

Notation. Any means of writing down music. The system of musical notation now most widely in use for Western music specifies in varying degrees all four of the components of any musical sound: pitch (or lack of it), duration (and thus rhythm as well as some aspects of *articulation), timbre, and loudness (including changes in loudness over time and some aspects of articulation). The system is principally concerned with pitch and duration, which are represented along a kind of graph. Pitch is notated on the vertical axis, corresponding to its intuitive perception as high or low, and duration along the horizontal axis from left to right. Degrees of pitch are marked on the vertical axis by means of five horizontally parallel lines termed a *staff (pl. staves). Two or more parallel staves increase the range of pitches specifiable (or separate different strands of the composition, termed voices, perhaps played or sung by different performers; see Score). On each staff, a *clef fixes the location of one particular pitch and thus, by extension, determines that of each line or space. *Ledger lines locate pitches lying above or below any staff. The lines and spaces of the staff, in combination with any clef, indicate only the *diatonic scale that underlies Western tonal music. The structure and importance of this scale are reflected in the design of the piano *keyboard, where the scale is embodied in the white keys, and in the nomenclature for pitch, which assigns the first seven letters of the alphabet to the repeating pattern of the white keys alone. Pitches corresponding to the black keys must be indicated with reference to one or another white key by means of an *accidental or a *key signature. Thus, the lines or spaces alone can specify only pitches with the

names A through G; e.g., a pitch such as B-flat must be indicated on the staff with the aid of a flat sign ($\flat$).

When any given pitch is to be notated, the rounded head of a symbol termed a *note is placed on the appropriate line or space, preceded by an accidental if necessary. The duration of the pitch is determined by the particular shape and coloring of the note. Silence is specified by means of a rest [see Note]. There are seven basic values of notes and rests, each twice as long as the next smaller value. Other durations are created in a variety of ways. A dot following a note or rest increases its value by one-half. Two or more different values may be joined together by means of curved lines termed ties in order to form a single duration. Notes may be grouped together to form subdivisions other than duple subdivisions of some larger value, e.g., groups of three equal notes are termed triplets and are indicated by placing the number 3 above or below the group. For ease of reading, groups of notes of the same value that ordinarily employ one or more flags may be written with a corresponding number of beams (relatively thick, solid lines) connecting their stems. Partly for ease of reading, but principally because Western tonal music employs both pitch and duration in such a way as to produce recurring patterns of *meter, vertical lines, termed *bar lines, running through the staff or staves mark off a fixed number of some note-value or the equivalent duration. The total duration between adjacent bar lines is termed a *measure or bar.

This system fixes durations only with respect to one another. The absolute duration of any note or rest is a matter of *tempo, i.e., the rate per unit of time at which some particular value (and thus each of the remaining values) is to be performed. This rate is often indicated rather informally by words in Italian or other languages, e.g., *allegro, langsam,* slow. It may, however, be made precise by a *metronome marking, e.g., quarter note = 120 per minute. Tempo, however, may be varied [see Rubato] even over short spans, and tradition and taste will often dictate greater or lesser departures from the precise durations reflected in the available notes and rests. In these respects, duration in Western art music is considerably more susceptible of nuance in performance than pitch, with the result that the notation of duration is, with respect to actual performance, rather crude. The principal respect in which pitch in performance is likely to deviate from its notation is in *ornamentation, generally the addition of notes to those specified as notes. Although there are many supplementary symbols for specifying ornaments rather unambiguously, the practice of unnotated ornamentation has been widespread in some periods. Musical notation, therefore, is like any other sort of text in requiring realization by a reader who brings to bear on it an accumulation of habits and experience.

In music, this accumulation is termed *performance practice.

The specification of timbre is largely a matter of specifying the intended instruments or voices. Some instruments, however, have traditionally been capable of a variety of timbres, and 20th-century composers have demanded greatly expanded timbral variety on instruments in general. The organ and harpsichord achieve considerable variety by means of *registration. Bowed stringed instruments have traditionally employed techniques of *bowing for this purpose, as well as *mutes. Brass instruments regularly make use of mutes, and the French horn in addition employs *stopped tones.

Loudness is least precisely specified, being left in the main, like tempo, to a relatively small number of words and abbreviations. Those employed for loudness, together with some related symbols, are termed *dynamic marks. These and other *performance marks, along with the principal elements of the notation of pitch and duration, are illustrated in the accompanying table.

The notation of classical Greece was a *letter notation, and notations of this type were again used, principally for theoretical and pedagogical purposes, in the Middle Ages. They are related to systems of *solmization and pitch names [see also Gamut, Guidonian hand, Hexachord]. The earliest surviving notation to employ a staff for fixing pitch occurs in the treatise *Musica enchiriadis* of ca. 900. The history of current musical notation, however, begins in the 11th century with the development of a diastematic notation (i.e., notation that is precise with respect to pitch) that represents pitch on a vertical axis by means of the precise spacing of notational symbols. This development and the related pitch nomenclature are often associated with Guido d'Arezzo. Since about the 9th century, various types of *neume had been employed in the notation of liturgical chant. In general, neumatic notations indicated the approximate contour of a melody and thus served as an aid to the memory. Aquitanian neumes of the 11th century, however, arranged dots carefully around a real or imagined horizontal line. In time more lines were added, and the staff with four lines and a clef became common. By about 1200, square-shaped neumes similar to those still employed in some liturgical books became standard [see ill. under Neume].

Neumatic notations seem not to have indicated durations precisely, though this has been a subject of controversy [see also Gregorian chant]. By the 13th century, however, square neumes began to be used for polyphony and for secular melodies [see especially Troubadour, Trouvère]. In sacred polyphony, especially that of *Notre Dame, certain of the neumes, termed *ligatures, were employed to indicate durations based on the rhythmic modes [see

Modes, rhythmic]. This is the first Western notation to indicate durations with any precision. Only in the later 13th century, however, did a set of notes with precisely assigned values emerge. This marks the beginning of *mensural (i.e., measurable) notation, a development most often associated with the theorist Franco of Cologne.

Franco's notation relied on a triple subdivision of note-values. Early in the 14th century, Philippe de Vitry extended the system to include more note-values and both duple and triple subdivisions [see also *Ars nova*]. This formed the basis of the mensural notation in use through the 16th century and of the system of note-values still in use. By the early 17th century, most of the remaining features of mensural notation that distinguish it from the notation now in use had largely disappeared. The 15th and 16th centuries also saw the rise of *tablatures, notations designed for certain instruments. Some 20th-century music has required the creation of numerous new notational symbols, as yet standardized to only a limited degree. The notation of some electronic music has necessarily gone further afield (though it does not usually serve as the basis for performance, as conventional notation does). *Graphic notations may make little or no use of conventional symbols.

Western art music has relied on notation much more than any other music. Cultures that distinguish between art music and popular music and those that have a body of music theory are most likely to have notation, if only for theoretical or didactic purposes, as in Arabic-speaking cultures. Perhaps the earliest to survive is from Mesopotamia. The musical cultures of China, Japan, Korea, and India have all made extensive use of notation, often based on solmization syllables of a kind, sometimes with supplementary signs for duration and performance technique, and with instrumental tablatures playing a prominent role.

Note. A symbol used in musical notation to represent the duration of a sound and, when placed upon a staff, to indicate its pitch; more generally (especially in British usage), the pitch itself. Types of notes are classed and named according to the relationship of their durations to one another and are sometimes termed note-values. The symbol for indicating silence of a certain duration is termed a rest. The accompanying table gives the notes and rests in current use from largest to smallest, together with their names. Each note or rest is twice as long as the next smaller one. The European names for these notes are as follows. Whole: Brit. semibreve, Fr. *ronde,* Ger. *Ganze (Note),* It. *semibreve,* Sp. *redonda.* Half: Brit. minim, Fr. *blanche,* Ger. *Halbe (Note),* It. *bianca,* Sp. *blanca.* Quarter: Brit. crotchet, Fr. *noire* (quarter rest, *soupir*), Ger. *Viertel,* It. *nera,* Sp. *negra.*

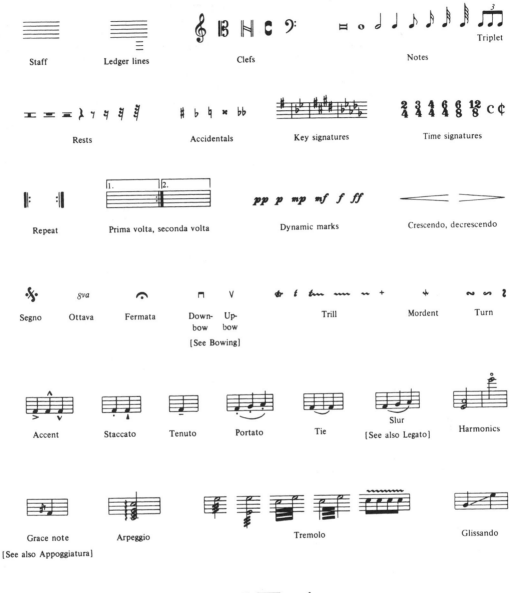

Commonly used notational symbols [see separate entry for each].

Eighth: Brit. quaver, Fr. *croche,* Ger. *Achtel,* It. *croma,* Sp. *corchea.* Sixteenth: Brit. semiquaver, Fr. *double-croche,* Ger. *Sechzehntel,* It. *semicroma,* Sp. *semicorchea.* Thirty-second: Brit. demisemiquaver, Fr. *triple-croche,* Ger. *Zweiunddreissigstel,* It. *bis-croma,* Sp. *fusa.* Sixty-fourth: Brit. hemidemisemiquaver, Fr. *quadruple-croche,* Ger. *Vierundsechzigstel,* It. *semi-biscroma,* Sp. *semifusa.*

	Note name	Note	Rest
1.	Whole	o	—
2.	Half	♩	—
3.	Quarter	♩	♩
4.	Eighth	♪	♪
5.	Sixteenth	♬	♬
6.	Thirty-second	♬	♬
7.	Sixty-fourth	♬	♬

For ways in which the durations and shapes of notes are sometimes modified and for the history of the notational and metrical systems to which they belong, see Notation, Mensural notation.

Note-against-note style. See Homophony.

Note nere [It., black notes]. A notational development seen in madrigals of the 1530s and 1540s. Under the mensuration sign C (instead of the normal ₵) the tactus is here on the semibreve rather than the breve; there are many semiminims and *fusae,* giving the page a "blackened" appearance. The notation was also called *cromatico* (colored).

Note sensible [Fr.]. *Leading tone.

Noter. See Appalachian dulcimer.

Notes inégales [Fr., unequal notes]. A performing convention that renders divisions of the beat in alternating long and short values, even if written in equal values, to add grace or liveliness to the music. It is documented in over 85 French treatises from 1550 to ca. 1810, the great majority and the most detailed dating 1690–1780. In 18th-century France, the verbs *pointer, piquer, lourer, passer,* and *inégaliser* could all mean "to make unequal," but all except the last had other meanings as well, and their application to inequality was a matter of disagreement. The de-

gree of inequality (the ratio of lengths of the notes of each pair) varied, according to expression and tempo, from sharply dotted to barely perceptible. Occasionally specified, this was usually left to the performer, for whom it was one of the chief problems in taste and expression. French inequality was normally long-short, but the short-long variety also existed [see Lombard rhythm]. Theorists do not discuss whether inequality was to be maintained throughout a piece, but the evidence is that here, too, there was much disagreement and individuality in playing styles. Although there was little disagreement between 1690 and 1780 that inequality was the norm in French music for eligible notes and equality the exception, its character was governed by the style and expressive message of the music and the taste of the moment. The rule with the most theoretical support stated that inequality applied only to predominantly conjunct passages and not to predominantly disjunct ones. See also Dotted notes.

Notker (Balbulus) (b. near St. Gall, ca. 840; d. St. Gall, 6 Apr. 912). Author. Wrote *sequence texts, preserved in the *Liber hymnorum* of 884, constructed with great attention to classical literary values; also histories of Charlemagne and of St. Gall, a *Martyrologium,* and a few other poems.

Notre Dame, repertory of. A body of music dedicated above all to the polyphonic categories of *organum, *clausulae, *conductus,* and *motet but including as well a small number of monophonic *conductus* and *rondeaux* [see also *Magnus liber organi*], written between ca. 1150 and ca. 1240. The chant-based organa, of which there are 110 for two voices *(dupla),* 28 for three *(tripla),* and 2 for four *(quadrupla),* are, with few exceptions, appropriate to liturgies of the 12th and 13th centuries at the Cathedral of Notre Dame in Paris.

Notturno [It.]. (1) *Nocturne. (2) An instrumental (occasionally vocal) work intended for performance at night. In the 18th century, most instrumental notturnos were evidently meant to be performed by soloists rather than orchestrally, including Mozart's K. 286/269a (for four sextets, each consisting of two horns and strings) and his *Eine kleine Nachtmusik* (*Nachtmusik* being the German equivalent of *notturno*). Notturnos range in length from two to six or more movements, one or more of which is usually a minuet. See also Serenade.

Nourri, bien [Fr., well nourished]. With a rich, full sound.

Nourrit, Adolphe (b. Montpellier, 3 Mar. 1802; d. Naples, 8 Mar. 1839). Tenor. Studied with Manuel García. Opéra debut in Gluck's *Iphigénie en Tauride,* 1821; 1826–36, succeeded his father as leading tenor there. Taught at Paris Conservatory from 1827. In 1836, went to Italy. Sang premieres of many works including *Guillaume Tell* (1829), *Robert le Diable* (1831), *Les Huguenots* (1836), *Norma* (1839).

Nováes [Pinto], Guiomar (b. São João da Boa Vista, Brazil, 28 Feb. 1895; d. São Paulo, 7 Mar. 1979). Pianist. Studied in São Paulo and with I. Philipp. Recital debuts in Paris (1911), London (1912), and New York (1915). Particularly celebrated for her performances of Schumann and Chopin.

Novák, Vítězslav [Viktor], (Augustín Rudolf) (b. Kamenice nad Lipou, Czechoslovakia, 5 Dec. 1870; d. Skuteč, 18 July 1949). Composer. Studied with Dvořák. Works include operas; ballet pantomimes; orchestral music (*Jihočeská svita* [South Bohemian Suite], 1936–37; *Svatováclavský triptych* [St. Wenceslas Triptych], 1941); choral works (*Bouře* [The Storm], cantata, 1910; *Podzimní symfonie* [Autumn Symphony], 1931–34); chamber (3 string quartets) and piano music (*Sonata eroica*, 1900; *Pan,* tone poem, 1910); songs and folk song arrangements (*Songs on Moravian Folk Texts,* 1897–98).

Novelette [Fr.; Ger. *Novellette*]. A title first used by Schumann for his *Novelletten* op. 21 for piano (1838), eight short pieces without further title that he thought of as constituting a story representing Clara Wieck, his future wife. The title implies no particular form, and works bearing it belong in general to the tradition of the *character piece.

Novello, Vincent (b. London, 6 Sept. 1781; d. Nice, 9 Aug. 1861). Organist, conductor, composer, and publisher. Pupil of Webbe. Organist at Portuguese embassy, 1797–1822. Founded Novello and Company, 1811. Published *The Fitzwilliam Music* (1825); 5 volumes of Purcell's music (1829). His son (Joseph) Alfred Novello (1810–96) took over the firm 1847.

Nowak, Lionel (b. Cleveland, 25 Sept. 1911). Pianist and composer. Pupil of Elwell, Sessions, and Q. Porter. Has taught at Converse College, Syracuse Univ., and Bennington College (from 1948). Music director for the Doris Humphrey–Charles Weidman Modern Dance Company 1938–42. Active as a music educator. Has used serial techniques. Works include orchestral music (*Concert Piece,* timpani, strings, 1961); chamber and piano music (Suite, flute, harpsichord, 1989); and songs.

Nozze di Figaro, Le [It., The Marriage of Figaro]. Comic opera in four acts by Mozart (libretto by Lorenzo da Ponte, after Beaumarchais's play *La folle journée, ou Le mariage de Figaro*), produced in Vienna in 1786. Setting: a castle near Seville in the 18th century.

Number opera. Opera that makes a pronounced distinction between self-contained pieces—arias, ensembles, or choruses—and recitative or spoken dialogue. These numbers may on occasion be excerpted and published or performed as separate units.

Nunc dimittis [Lat.]. The *canticle of Simeon (Luke 2:29–32, beginning "Lord, now lettest thou thy servant depart in peace"). In the Roman rite, it is sung at Compline; in the Anglican rite, at Evensong.

Nuove musiche, Le [It., The New Musical Works]. (1) A collection of works by Giulio Caccini, published in 1601 (1602 new style), containing strophic songs, madrigals, and dramatic scenes in the then new style of *monody. (2) Music of the period around 1600 employing the new monodic style and including the first operas, cantatas, and oratorios.

Nut. (1) A slightly raised ridge fastened to the upper end of the neck of a stringed instrument, serving to raise the strings over the fingerboard. (2) In British usage, the *frog of a bow.

Nutcracker, The [Russ. *Shchelkunchik;* Fr. *Casse-noisette*]. A ballet by Tchaikovsky (based on a Christmas story by E. T. A. Hoffmann, choreography by Marius Petipa), op. 71, completed in 1892 and produced that year in St. Petersburg. The orchestral suite op. 71a drawn from the ballet was also first performed in 1892.

Nyckelharpa [Swed.; Ger. *Schlüsselfiedel*]. A keyed *fiddle of Sweden. Shaped like a large viola with a broad neck, it has 2 gut melody strings, 1 or 2 bass strings, and 6 to 13 metal sympathetic strings. Protruding from one side of the neck are 9 to 24 wooden keys. When depressed, the keys raise brass tangents to stop the melody strings.

Nystroem, Gösta (b. Silvberg, Dalarna, 13 Oct. 1890; d. Särö, 9 Aug. 1966). Composer, painter, and music critic. Studied with Hallén in Stockholm, in Copenhagen, and with d'Indy in Paris. Composed an opera and a ballet; 2 suites; incidental music; symphonies and concertos; chamber music and many solo songs.

O

Oakeley, Herbert (Stanley) (b. Ealing, London, 22 July 1830; d. Eastbourne, 26 Oct. 1903). Composer. Studied at Oxford, in Leipzig with Moscheles, in Dresden, and in Bonn. Taught at Edinburgh Univ., 1865–91. Works include *Suite in the Olden Style* op. 27 (1893); songs, hymns, piano pieces.

Obbligato [It., obligatory]. An accompanying part that is nevertheless of considerable importance and thus not to be omitted; the opposite of *ad libitum. In the Baroque era, the term often referred to keyboard parts that were written out in full rather than realized from a *thoroughbass part. Since that time it has often referred to prominent but largely ornamental accompanying parts such as countermelodies [see also Accompaniment].

Oberek [Pol.]. A round dance for couples, in quick triple meter, and related to the *mazurka; originally *obertas*.

Oberlin, Russell (Keys) (b. Akron, Ohio, 11 Oct. 1928). Countertenor. Studied at Juilliard. Founding member of the New York Pro Musica with Noah Greenberg (1952). Has appeared with numerous opera companies, orchestras, and ensembles, and in recitals. Has taught at Hunter College from 1971.

Obertas [Pol.]. *Oberek.

Obligat [Ger.]. *Obbligato.

Oblique motion. See Motion.

Oboe [Fr. *hautbois;* Ger. *Oboe;* It., Sp. *oboe*]. A conical-bore, double-reed woodwind instrument. The modern oboe family includes the oboe itself (in C, range bb to a′′′), the *oboe d'amore* [It.; Fr. *hautbois d'amour;* Ger. *Liebesoboe*] (in A, range ab to e′′′), the *English horn [Fr. *cor anglais;* Ger. *Englischhorn;* It. *corno inglese;* Sp. *corno inglés*] (in F, range e to a′′), and the baritone (or bass) oboe [Fr. *hautbois baryton, basse de hautbois*] (in C, range B to e′′). The bell of the oboe proper is flared. Other members of the family have hollow, bulb-shaped bells [Ger. *Liebesfuss*]. All oboes are now usually constructed of grenadilla (African blackwood). See ill. under Reed.

The oboe is descended from the Renaissance *shawm. It seems to have made the transition to its modern form at the hands of 17th-century Dutch makers, though it is often said to have been devel-

oped in France, along with all the other Baroque woodwinds. However the instrument developed, it was rapidly introduced into the French court just after the middle of the 17th century. The instrument had keys for C and Eb and an additional Eb key that allowed it to be played with either hand uppermost. The bell retained the unfingered tuning holes of the shawm. These were reduced from several to two, however.

Early in the 19th century, the oboe acquired cross keys for G# and sometimes F, as well as a *speaker key. Additional keys for low C, B, Bb, and a cross key for the upper C were added, and some players used a few more. By 1825, the 13-key instrument of the celebrated oboist Josef Sellner (1787–1843) was enjoying success. With little change, this is the Viennese oboe of today.

The history of the oboe diverges at this point into the Viennese and French types. The French oboe had become somewhat narrower in bore, and key placement had begun to diverge slightly. New styles of construction (such as ring-keys and axles) were incorporated, and the fingering system was modified. Such changes eventually obliterated most traces of the connection between the French and Viennese types. At first these changes were merely improvements of a mechanical nature. But by 1880, successive adoption of the Bb and C mechanisms of Apollon Barret (1804–79) and of the Triébert family's *Système A6* completely transformed the oboe. This system, somewhat revised, is in use today throughout most of the world, excepting only Vienna. It is usually known as the conservatory system, but sometimes is called the Gillet system, after Georges Gillet (1854–1934), who first introduced *Système-A6* oboes at the Paris Conservatory. Although many of Theobald Boehm's improvements to the flute influenced the development of the Triéberts' oboe designs, Boehm's ideas did not become a part of the established French oboe.

Obouhov, Nicolas [Obukhov, Nikolay] (b. Kursk, Russia, 22 Apr. 1892; d. Paris, 13 June 1954). Composer. Studied with Tcherepnin and Ravel. Developed and composed for the electric "croix sonore" (similar to the ondes martenot). Worked with twelve-tone methods and his own notation system. Composed the stage work *Le livre de vie* for solo voices, piano 4-hands, and orchestra.

Obra [Sp.]. Work.

Obrecht [Hobrecht], **Jacob** (b. Bergen op Zoom? or Sicily?, 22 Nov. 1450 or 1451; d. Ferrara, 1505). Composer. a priest by 1480. Held posts at churches in Utrecht (1476–78; in Bergen op Zoom (1479–84 and 1496–97); in Cambrai (1484–85); in Bruges (1486–91 and 1499–1500); in Antwerp at Notre Dame (1494–95 and 1498). Travelled to Ferrara, 1487–88 and 1504–5. Composed 29 known Masses, all based on preexisting material (Gregorian chant, popular tunes, or other composers' motets or chansons); motets (many with cantus firmi); secular vocal and instrumental works.

Ocarina. A *globular flute invented in the 19th century by Giuseppe Donati; also called a sweet potato or sweet-potato whistle. Made of porcelain, clay, or plastic, and in various sizes, it has a *duct-type mouthpiece, eight finger holes, and two thumb holes. See ill. under Flute.

Ochetus [Lat.]. *Hocket.

Ockeghem, Johannes [Jean] (b. ca. 1410–20; d. Tours, 6 Feb. 1497). Composer. Singer (bass) at Notre Dame in Antwerp, 1443–44; 1446–48, a member of the chapel of Charles I, Duke of Bourbon. Served Charles VII of France from around 1450; Louis XI, 1461–83; Charles VIII, 1483–97. Canon at Notre Dame, Paris, 1463–70. Busnois was likely a student. Visited Spain in 1470, Flanders in 1484. Composed 14 Mass cycles (*Missa prolationum; Au travail suis* and others based on chansons; a *L'homme armé* Mass; the *Missa mi-mi;* and a polyphonic Requiem); motets; chansons.

Octave. (1) An *interval bounded by two pitches with the same pitch names and the higher of whose frequencies is twice the lower. See also Pitch names. (2) In liturgical contexts, the eighth day or the entire week following a feast.

Octave equivalence. The feature of musical perception according to which all pitches separated by one or more perfect octaves (i.e., all pitches whose frequencies are related by powers of 2) are regarded as belonging to the same class [see Pitch class] or as being in some sense equivalent. This is reflected in the system of Western *pitch names, in which the seven letters employed are repeated for each octave.

Octave species. The particular arrangement of tones and semitones occurring in any given octave of the *diatonic scale. This arrangement is different for the octaves bounded by each of the seven diatonic scale degrees. For example, starting on C and proceeding upward along the white keys of the piano, tones (t) and semitones (s) occur in the order t t s t t t s, whereas proceeding upward from D they occur in the

order t s t t t s t. This is an important element in the Western concepts of *mode and *tonality. It also played an important role in the theory of ancient Greek music.

Octet [Fr. *octette, octour;* Ger. *Oktett;* It. *otteto;* Sp. *octeto*]. (1) A chamber composition for eight solo performers. (2) An ensemble of eight solo performers.

Octobasse [Fr.]. A large double bass, about 4 m. high, first made by Jean-Baptiste Vuillaume in Paris in 1849. Its three strings, tuned $C_1 G_1 C$, are stopped by levers.

Octoechos [Gr.]. See *Ēchos.*

Oda [It.]. A verse form used by composers of the *frottola. It consists of four-line stanzas rhyming aaab, bccc, etc., or abbc cdde, etc. The first three lines of each stanza are of seven syllables; the last varies from four to eleven.

O'Day, Anita [Colton, Anita Belle] (b. Kansas City, Mo., 18 Oct. 1919). Jazz singer. Sang with the big bands of Gene Krupa (1941–43, 1945–46) and Stan Kenton (1944–45), then worked as a soloist. Drug addiction interrupted her career; she revived it at the Newport Jazz Festival, 1958. Toured Japan periodically from 1964; 1972, formed her own record company; gave a concert at Carnegie Hall, 1985.

Ode [Gr. *ōdē*, fr. *aeidein*, to sing; Lat. *oda*]. (1) In current usage, a lyric poem of considerable length and complexity, often written for a ceremonial occasion. Poems of this type reflect the tradition of the Greek odes of Pindar (522–442 B.C.E.), which were intended to be performed with song and dance in the theater and on public occasions and whose form is a complex and variable arrangement of irregular lines. The Latin odes of Horace (65–68 B.C.E.), on the other hand, consist of regular stanzas in a few meters and are contemplative rather than ceremonial or public. Horace's odes were set polyphonically by several composers of the Renaissance.

The Pindaric ode was cultivated in England in the 17th century by Ben Jonson, and this period marks the beginning of the ode in England as a work for an occasion in the life of the monarch or for St. Cecilia's Day, set to music in the fashion of a cantata. Among composers who set such poems were Matthew Locke, Henry Cooke, Pelham Humfrey, John Blow, Purcell, and Handel (settings by Handel including Dryden's "Ode for St. Cecilia's Day").

In north Germany in the mid-18th century, numerous odes were set to music by composers of the first Berlin lieder school and others. Goethe and Schiller wrote odes, and Schiller's "Ode to Joy" was set by Beethoven in the finale to the Ninth or *Choral Symphony.

(2) In Byzantine chant, one of the nine sections of the *kanōn.*

Ode to Napoleon Buonaparte. A composition by Schoenberg, op. 41 (1942), based on Byron's poem on the downfall of dictators, scored for string quartet (later string orchestra), piano, and reciting voice.

Odhecaton. Abbreviated title of the anthology of polyphony published in 1501 by the printer Ottaviano Petrucci as *Harmonice musices odhecaton A* (100 Songs of Harmonic Music, vol. A; collections titled *Canti B* and *Canti C* followed). It is the first publication of polyphonic music printed with movable type and contains 96 (not 100) pieces, mostly French chansons published without texts, by composers such as Agricola, Busnois, Compère, Hayne van Ghizeghem, Isaac, and Josquin.

Odington, Walter [Walter Evesham] (fl. 1298–1316). Theorist. Wrote treatises on astronomy, arithmetic, geometry, and alchemy, as well as music. His *Summa de speculatione musice* contains discussion of the mathematical bases of music, sections on chant, including a tonary, and on discant, especially modal rhythm and the genres of polyphonic music.

Odo of Arezzo (fl. Arezzo, late 10th cent.). Theorist. Wrote a tonary and prefatory treatise, which influenced 11th-century Italian theory and practice. Parts of it were incorporated into the anonymous *Dialogus* on music. Guido of Arezzo based his theories in part on Odo's ideas.

Odo of Cluny (b. the Maine, 878/79; d. Tours, 18 Nov. 942). Abbot of Cluny from 927. Wrote 3 hymns and a dozen antiphons, as well as sermons and biblical commentaries. Has often been confused with Odo of Arezzo. Neither the *Dialogus* on music nor any tonary is his work.

Oedipus Rex [Lat., Oedipus the King]. An opera-oratorio in two acts by Stravinsky (libretto by Jean Cocteau, translated into Latin by J. Daniélou, after Sophocles' tragedy), performed as an oratorio in Paris in 1927 and staged in Vienna in 1928. Setting: ancient Thebes.

Oeuvre [Fr.]. Work, *opus.

Offenbach, Jacques (b. Cologne, 20 June 1819; d. Paris, 5 Oct. 1880). Composer. Pupil of Halévy. Lived in Paris from 1833; worked as a cellist. Conductor at the Théâtre-Français from 1850; 1855, opened his own theater, the Bouffes Parisiens. Managed the Théâtre de la Gaîté, 1873–75. Produced his works in England, Vienna, and Germany; conducted concerts in the U.S., 1876. Composed operettas, including *Orphée aux enfers, La belle Hélène* (1864), *La vie parisienne* (1866), *La *Périchole;* the opera *Les *contes d'Hoffmann.*

Offertory [Lat. *offertorium*]. In *Gregorian chant, the item of the *Proper of the *Mass sung during the presentation of the offering (originally the bread and wine to become the elements of communion). Even though its opening section is consistently identified as an *antiphon, the earliest sources present both antiphons and verses in an extremely ornate or *melismatic style unlike that of other antiphonal pieces. The verses were gradually discarded beginning in the 12th century and were formally removed in the 16th century by the *Council of Trent, except in the *Requiem Mass.

Office, Divine [Lat. *officium*]. The daily series of services of the Western Christian rites, as distinct from the *Mass. In the Roman Catholic Church, until the reforms following the Second Vatican Council of 1962–65, eight services made up this series for each day. The precise arrangement of the services within this series and of the series throughout the liturgical year followed one plan (the Roman cursus) in churches and another (the monastic cursus) in monastic communities. The single most influential document in the establishment of the round of eight services, especially in their observance in monastic communities, was the Rule of St. Benedict, written in about 535. It incorporates an outline according to which the entire Psalter is recited every week. The eight services or "hours" are as follows:

(1) Matins [Lat. *ad matutinum,* early in the morning], also called the *Night Office* and originally called *Vigils,* a long service held principally in monastic communities at about 3 A.M., though sometimes as early as midnight. (2) Lauds [Lat. *laudes,* praises], held at daybreak. (3) Prime [Lat. *ad primam,* at the first hour of the day, according to the division of the daylight hours into twelve], at 6 A.M., (4) Terce [Lat. *ad tertiam*], at 9 A.M., (5) Sext [Lat. *ad sextam*], at noon, and (6) None [Lat. *ad nonam*], at 3 P.M., all of which together make up the Little Hours. (7) Vespers [Lat. *ad vesperas,* in the evening], held at twilight. (8) Compline [Lat. *ad completorium,* from *completus,* completed], held before retiring, which in modern practice includes one of the four Marian antiphons, *"Alma Redemptoris Mater," *"Ave Regina caelorum," *"Regina caeli laetare," and *"Salve Regina," chosen according to the season of the year.

The Second Vatican Council called for a thorough reform of the Office, and this was promulgated in 1972 as the Liturgy of the Hours *(Liturgia horarum).* In the Anglican rite, the corresponding services are Morning Prayer (also called Matins and derived from the Matins of the Middle Ages) and Evening Prayer (also called Evensong and derived from Vespers and Compline of the Middle Ages).

Ogdon, John (Andrew Howard) (b. Mansfield Woodhouse, 27 Jan. 1937; d. London, 1 Aug. 1989).

Pianist and composer. Studied piano with Petri; composition with Hall, Pitfield, and G. Lloyd. London debut, 1958. Formed a piano duo with Brenda Lucas, whom he married, 1960. Compositions include piano concertos. Taught at Indiana Univ., 1976–80.

Ohana, Maurice (b. Casablanca, 12 June 1914; d. Paris, 13 Nov. 1992). Composer and pianist. Studied with Daniel-Lesur, Casella, Schaeffer, and Dutilleux. Taught at the École normale. Works include opera (*Célestine,* 1988); radio and film scores; an oratorio (*Llanto per Ignacio Sanchez Mejias,* Lorca, 1950); instrumental music (*Signes,* flute, piano, zither in one-third tones, percussion, 1965; string quartets; concertos); piano music; and vocal music (*Cantigas,* 1953–54; *Lux Noctis–Die Solis,* 4 choral groups, 2 organs, 1981–88).

Ohlssohn, Garrick (Olof) (b. Bronxville, N.Y., 3 Apr. 1948). Pianist. Pupil of R. Lhévinne. Has made frequent tours of Poland, and has appeared with major orchestras in Europe, the U.S., Japan, and New Zealand. Recordings include music of Brahms, Liszt, Chopin, and Scriabin.

Ohne [Ger.]. Without.

Oiseau de feu, L' [Fr., The Firebird]. A ballet by Stravinsky (choreography by Michel Fokine, scenery and costumes by Alexander Golovine and Léon Bakst), produced at the Ballets russes in Paris in 1910. Three versions of a suite taken from the ballet music were made by the composer in 1911, 1919, and 1945, the last two for smaller orchestra.

Oistrakh, David (Fyodorovich) (b. Odessa, 30 Sept. 1908; d. Amsterdam, 24 Oct. 1974). Violinist. Studied at the Odessa Conservatory; debut, Leningrad, 1928. Played at the front during the war, then gave concerto programs, 1946–47. London and Paris debuts, 1953; New York, 1955. Dedicatee and first performer of both Shostakovich violin concertos (1955 and 1967). Taught at the Moscow Conservatory from 1934.

Oketus [Lat.]. *Hocket.

Oktave [Ger.]. Octave; *Oktavflöte,* piccolo; *Oktavfagott,* contrabassoon.

Oktoēchos [Gr.]. See *Ēchos.*

Old Hundred(th). A hymn tune used in Bèze's *Genevan Psalter* (1551) for the 134th Psalm, in Knox's *Anglo-Genevan Psalter* (1556) for the 3rd Psalm, and in Sternhold and Hopkins's *Psalter* (1562) for the 100th Psalm (hence its name). It is often used to sing the Doxology.

Old Roman chant. A repertory of liturgical chant preserved in five Roman manuscripts (three graduals and two antiphoners) dating from the 11th through the 13th century. Nonmusical manuscripts attest to the presence of this tradition in Rome from the 8th century. The liturgy is for the most part that of the *Gregorian chant, and the melodies are in many respects similar as well, though there are significant variants even among the Old Roman manuscripts themselves. There has been considerable debate concerning the origins of both traditions and their relationship to each other.

Oldberg, Arne (b. Youngstown, Ohio, 12 July 1874; d. Evanston, Ill., 17 Feb. 1962). Composer. Pupil of Leschetizky and Rheinberger. Taught at Northwestern Univ., 1899–1941. Works include 5 symphonies and several concertos (2 for piano); *S. Francis of Assisi* (baritone and orchestra, 1954); chamber and piano music.

Oliphant [fr. OFr. *cor d'olifant*]. A trumpet made from an elephant's tusk, usually elaborately carved, and regarded in the Middle Ages as a symbol of authority.

Oliveira, Jocy de (b. Curitiba-Parana, Brazil, 11 Apr. 1936). Composer. Studied in São Paulo and with Marguerite Long. Appeared as a piano soloist with major orchestras in Europe and the U.S. Compositions include *Probabilistic Theater I, II,* and *III* (musicians, actors, dancers, television, traffic conductor); *Polinteracões I, II, III;* sambas; also a fantasy novel and a play.

Oliver, Henry Kemble (b. Beverly, Mass., 24 Nov. 1800; d. Salem, 12 Aug. 1885). Organist and composer. Organist at several churches in Boston and Salem. Studied at Dartmouth and Harvard. Wrote many hymns and other church music.

Oliver, King [Joe] (b. in or near New Orleans, 11 May 1885; d. Savannah, Ga., 8 or 10 Apr. 1938). Jazz cornetist and bandleader. Played in New Orleans and (from 1918) Chicago, where he formed King Oliver's Creole Jazz Band, with Louis Armstrong among his sidemen. Recordings include *Chimes Blues, Snake Rag, Dipper Mouth Blues,* and *Riverside Blues* (all 1923). Led the 10-piece Dixie Syncopators, 1925–27.

Oliver, Stephen (b. Liverpool, 10 Mar. 1950; d. London, 29 Apr. 1992). Composer. Studied with Kenneth Leighton and Robert Sherlaw Johnson. Taught at the Huddersfield School of Music. Composed stage works (*The Duchess of Malfi,* 1971; *Tom Jones,* 1974–75; *Euridice,* 1981; *Waiting,* 1985); cantatas and other vocal works; a symphony and other orchestral works; a string quartet and other chamber music.

Oliver, Sy [Melvin James] (b. Battle Creek, Mich., 17 Dec. 1910; d. New York, 27 May 1988). Jazz arranger and trumpeter. With Jimmie Lunceford

(1933–39), recorded his composition "For Dancers Only" (1937) and his arrangements of others' compositions. Arranged for Benny Goodman, 1934–39; joined Tommy Dorsey. Served as a music director for several recording companies. During 1970s and 1980s, played trumpet again, leading a nonet.

Olivero, Magda [Maria Maddalena] (b. Saluzzo, near Turin, 25 Mar. 1913 or 1914). Soprano. Pupil of Ghedini. Debut, Turin, 1933; then sang in Parma, Rome, Naples, Florence, and Venice. Had great success as Cilea's Adriana. London debut, 1952; Metropolitan debut, 1975.

Oliveros, Pauline (b. Houston, 30 May 1932). Composer and performer. Pupil of Robert Erickson. Cofounded the San Francisco Tape Music Center, 1961; its director at Mills College, 1966–67. Taught at the Univ. of California at San Diego 1967–81. Works include theater and ceremonial pieces (*Bonn Feier,* actors, dancers, performers, 1977); film scores; music for acoustic instruments (*Variations for Sextet,* flute, clarinet, horn, trumpet, cello, and piano, 1961) and voices (*Sound Patterns,* chorus, 1962); mixed media and electronic works (*The Wheel of Times,* string quartet, electronics, 1982).

Ondeggiando [It.]. See Bowing (14), Tremolo.

Ondes Martenot. An *electronic instrument introduced by Maurice Martenot in 1928. It generates a single tone whose pitch can be controlled either by a keyboard or by a sliding metallic ribbon that makes the pitch continuously variable. Additional circuits are provided to control volume, timbre, and *envelope. Honegger, Varèse, Milhaud, Messiaen, and Boulez have composed works for it. See also Electroacoustic music.

Ondulé [Fr.]. See Bowing (14), Tremolo.

O'Neill, Norman (Houstoun) (b. London, 14 Mar. 1875; d. there, 3 Mar. 1934). Composer and performer. Pupil of Somervell and Knorr. Music director, Haymarket Theatre, from 1908; St. James' Theatre, 1919–20. From 1924 taught at the Royal Academy of Music. Composed incidental music, including *The Pretenders* (Ibsen; 1913); *Henry V* (Shakespeare; 1933); descriptive orchestral pieces; vocal and chamber works.

One-line. The octave proceeding upward from middle C (c'), or any pitch in that octave [see Pitch names].

One-step. A fast social dance of the decade 1910–20; also a piece for such a dance. It was danced to ragtime and popular songs in 2/4 at about 132 quarter notes per minute.

Ongarese, all' [It.]. In the Hungarian *Gypsy style.

Onion flute. *Mirliton.

Onslow, (André) Georges (Louis) (b. Clermont-Ferrand, 27 July 1784; d. there, 3 Oct. 1853). Composer. Studied with Dussek, Cramer, and Reicha. Composed comic operas (*Le Colporteur,* Paris, 1827); 34 string quintets; 35 string quartets; music for piano 4-hands; chamber music with piano; orchestral works.

Op. Abbr. for *opus.

Open fifth, open triad. A perfect fifth or a triad without the third, e.g., c–g–c'.

Open forms. See Aleatory music.

Open harmony. See Spacing.

Open note. (1) On wind instruments, a note played without depressing any key or valve or covering any finger hole. (2) On stringed instruments, a note played on an *open string.

Open position. See Spacing.

Open string. On stringed instruments, a string that is not stopped. Its use may be indicated by a zero where a fingering number might otherwise occur.

Opera. A drama that is primarily sung, accompanied by instruments, and presented theatrically. That opera is primarily sung distinguishes it from dramatic pieces in which music is incidental or clearly subsidiary to the drama. That it is presented theatrically distinguishes it from *oratorio, which has similar musical components.

Opera has had a history of almost 400 years; in that time, it has exhibited many different forms and styles. Thus, overtures, choruses, ballets, and ensembles are present in operas of certain times and places, but they do not define the genre. Likewise, an opera may be accompanied by an orchestra or by a small group of instruments; it may be sung throughout or it may be interspersed with spoken dialogue. The text of an opera, called a *libretto, may be newly created or may be based on one or more purely literary antecedents; the author of a libretto may be primarily a poet, a dramatist, or simply an adapter.

Operatic history, in the sense of a continuous, unbroken tradition of works related to one another, begins in Italy at the end of the 16th century. The theoretical preparations for the new art form were made in the three decades before 1600 by a group of poets, musicians, and classical scholars active in Florence, some of them at first under the sponsorship of Count Bardi in a group later called the *Camerata. The immediate results were three operas: *Dafne and two settings of *Euridice. The librettos for these works were written by Ottavio Rinuccini. *Dafne,* composed by Jacopo Peri in collaboration with Jacopo Corsi, was first performed in Florence in 1598. Peri's *Euridice,* with some additions by Giulio Caccini, was performed and published in Florence in 1600. Caccini's full setting of the text was first published in 1600 but was not performed until 1602.

The subjects of these operas derive from Greek myth, and the Florentines were much concerned with the manner in which ancient Greek drama was performed. But the language and the dramatic presentation of Rinuccini's librettos are largely indebted to contemporary pastoral poetic dramas and to the **intermedio.* The music itself consisted of songs, madrigal-like choruses, dances, instrumental pieces, and most important, a new manner of reciting in music: a type of **monody termed the **stile rappresentativo* or **recitative.* The vocal music was written in an abbreviated fashion in which only the outer voices—the melody and the bass line—were written down, while the harmonies supported by the bass line were improvised [see Thoroughbass].

Celebrations at the court of Mantua in 1607 and 1608 brought forth three new operas: *La *favola d'Orfeo* (1607, libretto by Alessandro Striggio) and *Arianna* (1608, libretto by Rinuccini), both by Monteverdi, and *Dafne* (1608, libretto by Rinuccini, an adaptation of the libretto set by Peri in 1598), by Marco da Gagliano. In *Orfeo,* Monteverdi realized more fully than before the expressive and musical power of the *stile rappresentativo. Orfeo* is also more elaborately scored than its operatic predecessors and shows a much greater richness in the variety and complexity of its musical forms, including instrumental **toccatas* and **ritornellos,* strophic and ternary **arias,* and madrigal-like choruses.

Rome became an operatic center in the second quarter of the 17th century. Indeed, in 1600, several months before the production of Peri's *Euridice,* Emilio de' Cavalieri produced a dramatic work making use of the new style, **Rappresentatione di Anima, et di Corpo,* sometimes referred to as the first oratorio because of its allegorical characters, didactic intent, and place of presentation—the oratory of St. Philip Neri. A theater capable of holding 3,000 spectators opened in 1632 with *Il Sant'Alessio,* music by Stefano Landi. Giulio Rospigliosi, who was later to reign as Pope Clement IX, wrote the libretto for *Il Sant'Alessio* and for several other operas (*Chi soffre speri,* 1639; *Dal male il bene,* 1653). Recitative, the great discovery of the Florentines and the expressive heart of the earlier operas, became less important in Roman operas; arias, choruses, and instrumental preludes received a more expansive musical treatment. To the pastoral and mythological subjects preferred in Florence and Mantua were added stories from saints' lives, chivalric epics, fantasy, and comic subjects. An interest in spectacular scenic effects, which was a part of opera from its earliest days, was taken to even more lavish heights in Rome.

It was in Venice that the first commercial, public opera house was opened in 1637. Several changes accompanied the transformation of a courtly entertainment to a business venture. Spectacular stage effects—flying machines, ships crossing the stage, scenic transformations—were still important but were not always as lavish as in courtly entertainments. Librettos were often constructed to make use of stock scenic devices, and comic scenes were regularly incorporated. Choruses were de-emphasized, and recitative tended to be more formulaic. Arias, on the other hand, of which there might be 30 or more in an opera after mid-century, began to undergo a fuller musical development, tending toward standardized forms such as ABB and, by the final decades of the century, the da capo **aria,* which would remain dominant through much of the 18th century. The leading composers of public opera in Venice initially were Monteverdi, his student Pier Francesco Cavalli, and a younger contemporary, Pietro Antonio Cesti. Prominent through the 1680s was Giovanni Legrenzi.

The sources of French opera can be found in several indigenous French dramatic genres—tragedy, ballet, and **pastorale*—reshaped under the impact of Italian opera. The librettos of French opera were taken seriously as literature and judged by standards similar to those of spoken tragedy. **Ballet de cour,* a courtly entertainment involving dance, song, prose recitation, and costume, had enjoyed not only the support but the active participation of French royalty and nobility. Ballet was an important part of serious French opera from its beginnings through the 19th century. Also important were works in the pastoral tradition. The librettist Pierre Perrin received the permission of Louis XIV to form an Academy of Opera. Italian opera was most enthusiastically supported and encouraged in Paris by Cardinal Mazarin, Richelieu's successor. Between 1645 and 1662, the year of Mazarin's death, Italian operas by Cavalli, Luigi Rossi, Francesco Sacrati, and Carlo Caproli were performed at court.

The most significant figures for the creation and standardization of French opera (called *tragédie en musique* or *tragédie lyrique*) were the composer Jean-Baptiste Lully and the librettist Phillipe Quinault. Lully produced 15 operas between 1672 and 1686, all but three in collaboration with Quinault. These operas are typically in five acts (a form taken over from the theater) with subjects based on classical or chivalric stories. They begin with an **overture in two or more parts, the first stately with dotted rhythms, the second lively and imitative. There follows a prologue in which mythical or allegorical characters, who normally make no further appearance in the opera, make flattering references or allusions to the king, his court, and his policies. French recitative and airs did not contrast strongly with one another. Instead, choruses, ballets, and instrumental pieces, often grouped in *divertissements,* were the pieces in which purely musical expansion was likely to take place.

Lully's operas remained in the repertory of the Académie de musique and continued to be performed well into the 18th century. His principal successors were André Campra, Marc-Antoine Charpentier, and André Destouches. Their works show a lessening of the importance of a central dramatic idea, manifested in an increased use of more or less irrelevant dances and *divertissements.* Still more loosely organized is the *opéra-ballet,* in which each act contains a separate set of characters. Italian influence on French opera after Lully is seen in the appearance of vocally ornate da capo arias called *ariettes.* The culminating master of *tragédie-lyrique* and *opéra-ballet* was Rameau.

Many 17th-century English musicians and writers were aware of operatic developments in Italy and France. In 1617, Ben Jonson's *Lovers Made Men* "was sung after the Italian manner, *stylo recitativo,* by Master Nicholas Lanier," but its music is not extant. In *The Siege of Rhodes* (1654) all of the dialogue was set as recitative; the music, by Henry Lawes, Matthew Locke, and others, is also lost. John Blow's *Venus and Adonis* (ca. 1684) is often cited as a significant influence on Purcell's *Dido and Aeneas* (1689, libretto by Nahum Tate), arguably the greatest English opera until the 20th century. These works remained more or less isolated experiments. In general, English audiences preferred either operas that were entirely foreign, that is, set to non-English texts by non-English composers, or dramatic works in which the music was clearly subsidiary or at most separate but equal. Purcell's *Dioclesian* (1690), *King Arthur* (1691), and *The Fairy Queen* (1692), sometimes called *semi-operas,* show a close relation to the *masque in that the music is used more for decorative than for dramatic purposes.

Rinuccini's *Dafne,* translated into German by Martin Opitz and set to music by Heinrich Schütz, was performed in Torgau in 1627. This, so far as is known, was the first German opera, though its music is lost. After the middle of the 17th century, Italian opera was performed at court in Dresden, Munich, Hanover, and Dusseldorf, as well as in Innsbruck and Vienna. Hamburg, a commercial port-city, attempted commercial opera starting in 1678. Performances were most often in German, but performances of

Italian, French, and polyglot opera (part German, part Italian) were also given. Handel was briefly associated with opera in Hamburg, but the towering figure of Hamburg opera was Reinhard Keiser, who combined the roles of director and manager of the theater with that of its chief composer, writing well over 100 operas in 40 years (1694–1734). His works show a blending of Italian, French, and German stylistic features, French influence emerging most clearly in the overtures and dances.

Toward the end of the 17th century a group of Roman aristocrats and writers, calling themselves the Arcadian Academy, sought to ennoble and purify the exuberantly popular art form opera had become. For ideals they turned to the theories of Aristotle; for models they turned to the French classical theater of Corneille and Racine. The most important authors of the newly reformed libretto, the librettos of *opera seria,* were Apostolo Zeno and his successor as Caesarean poet for the Hapsburg court, Pietro Metastasio. A Metastasian libretto is typically in three acts with each act divided into numerous (from 10 to 20) scenes, a scene being defined by the entrance or exit of a character. There are usually six characters. The subject matter may be drawn from classical history or from legend. Comic elements are purged from the libretto as being inappropriate to the generally noble tone. The happy resolution of the drama, the *lieto fine,* reaffirmed for the audiences the value of moral and virtuous behavior. Each of Metastasio's librettos was set dozens of times.

Opera seria is dominated by the da capo aria. The importance of the aria is a reflection of the significance of the virtuoso singer, particularly the *castrato.* The heroic roles of *opera seria* were written for soprano or alto *castrati,* or for women playing male roles. Ensembles are rare, and the brief homophonic chorus with which an opera may close is often musically negligible. Except for the overture, the instrumental role is largely accompanimental. Most of the text of the libretto is set as simple, continuo-accompanied recitative *(recitativo semplice).* Recitative accompanied by strings or other instrumental groupings *(recitativo stromentato, accompagnato,* or *obbligato)* is reserved for the most dramatic moments and the most important characters in the opera. Although *opera seria* used Italian texts, the musical style was international. Only France maintained its own national style of opera.

The composers of 18th-century Italian opera were strikingly prolific. Alessandro Scarlatti, who made important contributions to the development and expansion of the aria, composed approximately 115 operas between about 1680 and 1720, of which some 50 are extant. Among the most important composers in the generation following Scarlatti are Leonardo

Vinci (40 operas), Leonardo Leo (ca. 60 operas), Francesco Feo (14 operas), Nicola Porpora (44 operas), and Antonio Vivaldi (ca. 46 operas, 21 extant). For many of Italy's most prominent opera composers of the 18th century, Naples was an important center of activity [see Neapolitan school]. Handel, a German composer writing Italian operas for an English audience in London, exemplifies the international aspects of *opera seria*. That he was active away from the mainstream did not prevent him from producing some of the finest examples of the genre (e.g., *Giulio Cesare in Egitto, 1724).

The middle of the 18th century saw a trend toward greater musical expansion with the appearance of longer, more richly accompanied arias. Johann Adolf Hasse, active at the court at Dresden and one of Metastasio's preferred composers, was widely admired. At the same time, serious opera underwent certain changes that tended to increase its dramatic component. The major composers in this operatic reform, Niccolò Jommelli, Tommaso Traetta, and Gluck, brought about a certain rapprochement of Viennese, French, and Italian operatic traditions. This led to a reduction in importance of the aria as a static, purely lyrical entity and an increase in importance of accompanied recitative, of choruses, and of instrumental writing—both in the accompaniments of arias and in separate instrumental pieces; there was also greater flexibility in the formal construction of arias. Gluck's prominence as a reformer is due in part to his operas *Orfeo ed Euridice* (Vienna, 1762) and *Alceste* (Vienna, 1767) and in part to his statements on reform, most notably his preface to *Alceste*.

The 18th century also saw the vigorous development of comic opera. Comic scenes—e.g., scenes with comic servants—were found in operas before the middle of the 17th century and were also a feature of entertainment provided between the acts of operas. By the end of the 17th century, such scenes had begun to decline in number and were often placed at the ends of acts. The reforms of this period leading to *opera seria* removed the comic scenes altogether, confining them to independent works termed *intermezzi that were played between the acts of serious operas. It is from these intermezzi that Italian comic opera or *opera buffa* arose as a wholly independent genre. Unlike serious opera, comic opera made considerable use of duets, trios, quartets, and larger ensembles, particularly as *finales of acts.

Several national varieties of comic opera arose. Italian *opera buffa,* French *opéra comique,* English *ballad opera, and German *Singspiel have in common that they were in the language of the audience and were popular, commercial works. *Opéra comique,* Singspiel, and ballad opera are alike in their alternation of musical numbers with spoken dia-logue; *opera buffa* continued to set dialogue as recitative. Comic opera also tended to use contemporary, plebeian characters. An exception to this is Singspiel, which showed a preference for exotic, oriental, or fantastic settings.

Mozart's operatic production includes three genres—*opera seria, opera buffa,* and Singspiel. *Idomeneo* (1781) and La *clemenza di Tito* (1791) are both examples of *opera seria,* composed for courtly occasions. *La clemenza di Tito* is a setting of a much-adapted Metastasian libretto. Mozart's three mature *opere buffe, Le *nozze di Figaro* (1786), *Don Giovanni* (1787, a work with more serious overtones), and *Così fan tutte* (1790), are notable for the subtlety and penetration of characterization, the integration of vocal and instrumental factors, and the adaptation of classical symphonic style in their ensemble finales. Mozart's final opera, *Die *Zauberflöte,* is a Singspiel that fuses the most diverse musical and dramatic features.

French opera at the end of the 18th and beginning of the 19th century responded to the cataclysmic social and political changes taking place in that country. The Opéra (Académie royale de musique, descended from Perrin's academy), previously supported by royal and aristocratic patronage, was largely neglected, while *opéra comique* increased in importance. At the same time *opéra comique* changed significantly in character; lightheartedness and naïve charm were replaced by moral earnestness and explorations of the darker sides of human personality. *Rescue opera came into vogue at this time. Characteristic examples are Jean-François Le Sueur's *La caverne* (1793; heroine rescued from bandits in a cave) and Cherubini's *Les *deux journées* (1800; hero saved from unjust arrest). During Napoleon's reign, the Opéra resumed an important role, producing heroic and grandiose works such as Gaspare Spontini's *La vestale* (1807) and *Fernand Cortez* (1809). At this time Paris could boast three major active opera houses, one producing grand opera (the Opéra), one *opéra comique* (the Opéra-comique), and one Italian opera (the Théâtre italien).

Grand opera, as it developed in the second and third quarters of the 19th century, produced significant works in its own right and influenced the course of Italian and German opera as well. Initiated by Rossini's *Le siège de Corinthe* (1826) and *Guillaume Tell* (1829) and Daniel-François-Esprit Auber's *La muette de Portici* (1828), grand opera reached its apex in the collaborations of Meyerbeer and the librettist Eugène Scribe—*Robert le diable* (1831), Les *Huguenots* (1836), Le *prophète* (1849), and L'*africaine* (1865). These works derive their energy from large-scale conflicts—not just of individuals but of whole national or religious groups—that are frozen at climactic moments into striking, massed tableaux in which all possible aural and visual forces—soloists, chorus, orchestra, ballet, costumes, scenery—contribute to achieve a maximum effect.

Somewhere between the Opéra and Opéra-comique, and a rival to both, was the Théâtre lyrique, which, in the 21 or so years between its founding and its failure in 1870, produced such works as Gounod's *Faust (1859) and *Roméo et Juliette (1867), Bizet's Les *pêcheurs de perles (1863) and La jolie fille de Perth (1867), and a portion of Berlioz's Les *troyens (1863). The term lyric opera, though frequently used, does not indicate a distinct genre, though the works given at the Théâtre lyrique (despite the example of Les troyens) were generally smaller in scale and more intimate in style than grand opera.

The dominating figure in Italian opera at the beginning of the 19th century was Rossini. His best-known works are the comic opera Il *barbiere di Siviglia (Rome, 1816) and the grand opera Guillaume Tell (Paris, 1829). Although he retired from operatic production early (in 1829, at the age of 36), he remained the model for a succeeding generation of composers. The most important composers of Italian opera of the 1830s were Bellini (La *sonnambula, 1830; *Norma, 1831) and Donizetti (L'*elisir d'amore, 1832; *Lucia di Lammermoor, 1836).

In the works of Rossini, Donizetti, and Bellini, several significant trends emerge. One is the development of a new set of character stereotypes based on vocal types. The heroic voice became the tenor (rather than the alto or soprano as it had been in 18th-century opera seria); the baritone became the rival in love, the villain, or sometimes a father or older adviser. Another trend is the increasing somberness of plots. Tragic endings replaced happy ones in serious operas; comic operas represented the smaller share of Rossini's output and were composed less and less frequently after the first third of the century. Furthermore, the aria, with introductory scena, became longer, incorporating more and more action; a leading character was likely to have no more than one aria in an act.

After 1840, Italian opera was dominated by the work of Verdi. From the start of his career, Verdi's operas were associated in the public's mind with hopes for the unification and independence of Italy—an association that Verdi fostered with stirring settings of librettos dealing with the struggle against personal or national oppression. Vital to this new conception was the emergence of the Verdian baritone, a voice type often set against the hero (tenor) or heroine (soprano). *Rigoletto (1851), Il *trovatore (1853), and La *traviata (1853) mark Verdi's full maturity and assured his lasting international reputation. Later works such as *Don Carlos (1867) and

*Aida (1871) show the important influence of grand opera. The last operas, *Otello (1887) and *Falstaff (1893), often singled out for their musico-dramatic continuity, have a chromatically expanded harmonic palette and a new subtlety of scoring, but nevertheless remain essentially true to the Italian tradition.

Among the composers of operas on German texts at the beginning of the 19th century were Beethoven, Spohr, E. T. A. Hoffmann, Weber, and Heinrich August Marschner. On the whole, they preferred a form that alternated spoken dialogue with set numbers, that is, *Singspiel. The librettos of the operas of this period show Romantic features such as an interest in folk elements, an emphasis on nature as it impinges on man or anthropomorphically reflects his state of mind, and the intrusion of the supernatural upon the everyday world. Examples are Hoffman's Undine (1816), Spohr's Faust (1816), Weber's Der *Freischütz (1821), and Marschner's Der Vampyr (1828).

Although Wagner, especially in his early years, was very much an eclectic, borrowing ideas, themes, and visual impressions wherever he found them, his operas nevertheless represent a new era. One category of changes worked in the direction of avoiding small musical units; ends of phrases were obscured by eschewing conventional cadences, and arias and ensembles were merged into the flow of action or replaced by expressive arioso. With Der *fliegende Holländer (1843) and Das Rheingold (1869), Wagner experimented with merging the acts into one continuous unit, the opera; with Der *Ring des Nibelungen (first performed complete in 1876), he suggested that even the single opera was too small a unit, the complete work being no less than a cycle of four operas. As a means of organizing his new structures, Wagner developed the very flexible use of the *Leitmotif.

Wagner's mature works may be divided into Romantic operas—Der fliegende Holländer, *Tannhäuser (1845, revised 1861 and 1865), *Lohengrin (1850)—and music dramas—Das Rheingold, Die Walküre, Siegfried, Götterdämmerung [see Ring des Nibelungen, Der], *Tristan und Isolde (1865), Die *Meistersinger (1868), and *Parsifal (1882). In these works, Wagner recognized that the apposite subject matter for his operas was legend and myth, subjects that simultaneously emphasized the national (German and Nordic) in their settings and the universal in their issues.

One result of 19th-century *nationalism was the appearance of operas using a broader range of languages and musical idioms, particularly in eastern Europe. A significant 19th-century school of opera developed in Czechoslovakia with the works of Smetana (The *Bartered Bride, 1866; Dalibor, 1868) and Dvořák (Rusalka, 1901). Even more important was the development of opera in Russia. The first of the Russian operatic composers to achieve resounding fame in Russia (and international recognition as well) was Mikhail Glinka. He composed only two operas, A *Life for the Tsar (1836) and *Ruslan and Lyudmila (1842), but with these two he explored patriotic subjects drawn from earlier Russian history and Russian myth, and legend or fairy tale, particularly as told by the great poet Pushkin. A concern for apt Russian declamation was the overriding musical concern of Glinka's younger contemporary Alexander Dargomïzhsky.

In the second half of the 19th century, Russian opera followed two courses. The self-proclaimed nationalistic manner was pursued by Borodin, Mussorgsky, and Rimsky-Korsakov. Of this group, only Rimsky-Korsakov was a professional musician, and it was he who completed, revised, and reorchestrated the works of the other two. He composed more than a dozen operas, of which The *Golden Cockerel (1909) is perhaps the best known. The Russian opera that has achieved the most enduring international fame is Mussorgsky's *Boris Godunov (1874). The operas of Tchaikovsky were not so overtly nationalistic, although some, such as *Eugene Onegin (1879) and The *Queen of Spades (1890), made use of texts by Pushkin.

Opera in the century since the death of Wagner has exhibited abundant diversity in terms of subject matter, musical styles, philosophical viewpoints, and social aims. The first operatic masterpiece of the 20th century was Debussy's *Pelléas et Mélisande (1902), a setting of Maurice Maeterlinck's symbolist play. In Germany, as elsewhere in Europe, Wagner's operas had profound influence but few true successors. Richard Strauss was greeted as Wagner's heir apparent after *Salome (1905) and *Elektra (1909), but his later works—Der *Rosenkavalier (1911), *Ariadne auf Naxos (1916), Die *Frau ohne Schatten (1919), *Arabella (1933)—did not pursue the same paths of intense chromaticism and emotionalism. The operas composed in Italy at the turn of the century maintained clear links with the Romantic tradition. The *verismo movement helped launch the careers of Mascagni (*Cavalleria rusticana, 1890) and Leoncavallo (*Pagliacci, 1892) and also had an effect on some of Puccini's operas such as *Tosca (1900) and Il tabarro (1918) [see Trittico]. Many of Puccini's works—e.g., La *bohème (1896) and *Madama Butterfly (1904)—have enjoyed enduring success.

Composers from Czechoslovakia, Hungary, and Russia produced works that have joined the international repertory. Among these works are Janáček's *Kát'a Kabanová (1921), The *Cunning Little Vixen (1924), and The Makropoulos Case (1926); Prokofiev's The *Love for Three Oranges (1921) and War and Peace (1945–55); Shostakovich's The Nose (1930) and *Lady Macbeth of the Mtsensk District

(1934, revised 1963); Bartók's *Bluebeard's Castle (1918); and Kodály's Háry János (1926). England experienced a significant operatic renaissance through the works of Britten—*Peter Grimes (1945), *Billy Budd (1951), The *Turn of the Screw (1954), A *Midsummer Night's Dream (1960), and *Death in Venice (1973)—and Tippett—The Midsummer Marriage (1952), The Knot Garden (1969), and The Ice Break (1976).

Jazz was reflected in some operas composed after World War I, notably Krenek's *Jonny spielt auf (1927) and Weill's Die *Dreigroschenoper (1928) and Aufstieg und Fall der Stadt Mahagonny (1930), the latter two works written in collaboration with Bertolt Brecht and reflecting his ideas of Epic Theater. Two American operas that make use of jazz are Scott Joplin's Treemonisha (1911–15) and Gershwin's *Porgy and Bess (1935). Operas in which the organizing powers of tonality are either severely challenged or else replaced by the twelve-tone system are Berg's *Wozzeck (1925) and *Lulu (1937) and Schoenberg's *Moses und Aron (first staged performance in 1957). Serial writing is also important in Dallapiccola's Volo di notte (1940), Il prigioniero (1950), and Ulisse (1968), and in Sessions's *Montezuma (1964). More widely performed, however, have been some operas that follow more traditional lines, including works of Menotti (The *Medium, 1945; The *Consul, 1949; *Amahl and the Night Visitors, 1951) and others. The most frequently performed neoclassical opera is Stravinsky's The *Rake's Progress (1951). Among more recent innovative works are two operas by minimalist composer Philip Glass, Einstein on the Beach (1975) and Satyagraha (1980).

Opéra-ballet [Fr.]. A musico-dramatic form that flourished in France starting in the late 17th century. The principal composers were Campra, Mouret, and Montéclair. The genre makes use of musical types found in ballet (instrumental pieces, dances) and in opera (recitatives, arias, choruses), but the dramatic premise linking the musical numbers is likely to be tenuous.

Opéra bouffe [Fr.]. A type of French comic opera. The term was used by Offenbach starting in 1858 with *Orphée aux enfers. See Operetta.

Opera buffa [It.]. Comic opera. See Opera.

Opéra comique [Fr.]. (1) An opera on a French text with musical numbers separated by spoken dialogue. In the 18th century, the treatment of the subject matter of an opéra comique was likely to be lighthearted or sentimental. In the 19th century, opéra comique plots incorporated serious or tragic events. In such works, e.g., Bizet's *Carmen, the adjective comique is divorced from the notion of the comic or humorous and refers only to the presence of spoken dialogue.

(2) Opéra-comique. The company established by the French government in Paris in 1801 for the purpose of producing *opéra comique*. It was formed from two earlier companies, one with an intermittent history dating to 1715, at times known by this name.

Opera semiseria [It.]. An operatic genre, arising in the second half of the 18th century, in which both comic and serious elements are present. An *opera semiseria* is likely to have ornate arias, such as would not be out of place in *opera seria*, as well as ensemble finales more characteristic of *opera buffa*.

Opera seria [It.]. A form of opera prevalent through the 18th century. Set to Italian librettos, notably those of Apostolo Zeno and Pietro Metastasio, operas of this type were composed by Italians, Austrians, and Germans and were performed in all the major countries of Europe with the exception of France. The characters of *opera seria* are usually drawn from ancient history. An *opera seria* is generally in three acts. Its basic musical components are simple recitative and da capo exit arias—perhaps 25 in the course of an opera. The term was also used early in the 19th century for some works by composers such as Rossini, Bellini, and Donizetti. See Opera.

Operetta. In the 17th and 18th centuries, an operatic work of small scale and pretensions, one that could equally well be classified as *intermezzo, opera buffa* [see Opera], *opéra comique,* or *Singspiel*. Starting in the middle of the 19th century, operetta developed as a distinct genre, first in France and then in the Austro-Hungarian empire, Germany, England, and the U.S. Operetta is an essentially popular form of entertainment made up of spoken dialogue, song, and dance, whose tone may range from sentimental comedy, through satire and parody, to outright farce.

The originator of the modern operetta is Jacques Offenbach. He composed over 90 works in one, two, three, or four acts; some of these, starting with *Orphée aux enfers* (1858), are designated as *opéras bouffes* and have a pronounced satirical strain. The success of Offenbach's operettas in Vienna provided the impetus for the composition of similar works first by Franz von Suppé and later by Johann Strauss the younger. Strauss composed about 16 operettas, mostly in three acts, the most successful of which is *Die *Fledermaus* (1873). After Strauss, the Viennese tradition was continued in Franz Lehár's *Die *lustige Witwe* (1905). A characteristically English form of operetta was developed by Gilbert and Sullivan. Sullivan's musical style, occasionally parodistic but more often simply eclectic, complemented Gilbert's witty social satire.

The operettas performed in the U.S. in the 19th century were mainly importations from Europe or imitations of such works. Victor Herbert, Rudolf Friml, and Sigmund Romberg, all European born and trained, perpetuated the genre in the first two decades of the 20th century. By the 1920s and 1930s, the terms musical comedy, musical drama, or simply musical came to be preferred to operetta, although it is debatable whether the new terms indicate new genres. See also Musical comedy.

Ophicleide [Fr. *ophicléide;* Ger. *Ophikleide;* It. *oficleide;* Sp. *figle*]. An alto or bass brass instrument, tall and narrow in shape, with nine to twelve woodwindlike side holes and keys. Ophicleides were invented in Paris about 1817 by Jean-Hilaire Asté, known as Halary. They were intended to be the lower members of a brass-instrument family based on the *keyed bugle. In addition to keyed bugles in E♭ and B♭, which Halary called *clavitubes,* this family included *quinticlaves* (alto ophicleides) in six-foot F and E♭ and ophicleides in eight-foot C and B♭. The bass ophicleide was by far the most successful and found use in symphony and opera orchestras as well as in military bands of the 1830s and 1840s and even later. Its parts are now played on the tuba. See ill. under Brass instruments.

Oppens, Ursula (b. New York, 2 Feb. 1944). Pianist. Studied at Juilliard. Active as a soloist and recitalist. A founding member of Speculum musicae. Has performed with the Chamber Music Society of Lincoln Center and the Center for Creative and Performing Arts. Carter, Wuorinen, and others have composed works for her.

Opus [Lat., pl. *opera;* Fr. *oeuvre;* Ger. *Opus;* It. *opera,* pl. *opere;* Sp. *opus*]. Work; often abbreviated op. (pl. opp.). The term is most often used with a number to designate a work in its chronological relationship to a composer's other works. These numbers are often unreliable guides to chronology, however. Some genres, notably vocal works and operas, were often not assigned such numbers. In the cases of Haydn and Mozart, they are so unreliable that they are rarely used, the numbering of scholarly thematic catalogs being used instead [see K., Hob.]. In the 17th and 18th centuries, an opus often included at first 12 and later 6 separate works, each identified by number, e.g., op. 20 no. 3

Oratio [Lat.]. Prayer, *collect.

Oratorio. An extended musical drama with a text based on religious subject matter. The oratorio originated in the 17th century. Throughout most of its history it was intended for performance without scenery, costume, or action. As a result, most oratorios place special emphasis on narration, on contemplation, and, particularly in the 18th, 19th, and 20th centuries, on extensive use of a chorus.

Oratorio originally meant prayer hall, a building normally located adjacent to a church and carefully designed as a setting for community experiences that are distinct from the regular liturgy. Such buildings were brought into existence under the auspices of the Congregation of the Oratory, a religious reform movement in the Catholic Church that had been founded by Saint Philip Neri (1515–95). In these buildings the oratorio as a musical genre was born.

Emilio de' Cavalieri's *Rappresentatione di Anima, et di Corpo* (Rome, 1600) was a bold attempt to create a religious opera. But because it ill suited the needs and expectations of the oratorio community, it did not lead to further works of its kind. More indicative of the music that was current in the Roman oratorio in the first decades of the 17th century is Giovanni Francesco Anerio's *Teatro armonico spirituale di madrigali* for five to eight voices (Rome, 1619). All of the texts in this collection are based on biblical passages or the lives of the saints, and many of the texts employ dialogue. Because the oratorio reflected the Counter-Reformation zeal to attract the broad populace to the Church, most oratorios were written in the Italian language (the *oratorio volgare*). But Latin is the language set by the greatest composer of oratorios of the mid-17th century, Giacomo Carissimi. Most of his 13 surviving works involve a narrator *(historicus)* and a story drawn from the Old Testament. The chorus plays an important role in most of Carissimi's oratorios, which is contrary to the norm in Italian oratorios of the 17th century.

In the latter half of the 17th century, oratorios of strongly Roman character were produced in other Italian cities (Venice, Bologna, Modena, Florence, Naples), and trends toward secularization became evident. Oratorios were now regularly performed in locations other than the traditional oratorio buildings, including public theaters. They acquired a length similar to operas, and the stories often involved the lives of the saints and sometimes had a distinctly erotic quality. Female singers were regularly employed, and a strong emphasis was placed on arias, especially the da capo aria. There was little use of a chorus, and the function of the narrator was assumed by the recitatives of the various characters in the story. Principal Italian composers of oratorios in the late 17th century and the first half of the 18th include Bernardo Pasquini, Alessandro Melani, Alessandro Stradella, Alessandro Scarlatti, and Vivaldi. Most of the well-known opera composers of the period also composed oratorios [see, e.g., Neapolitan school], and the two genres remained closely linked. The oratorio was distinguished from opera principally by its subject matter, its division into two parts rather than three acts, and the absence of staged action (though there were occasional exceptions).

In Vienna, under the patronage of Leopold I (1658–1705), the genre thrived. In addition to oratorios based on Italian models, there existed in Vienna the *sepolcro*, a shorter work, also with an Italian text, sometimes captioned "rappresentazione sacra." These did involve scenery, costume, and action, and they depicted events surrounding the death of Christ. In Vienna, oratorio texts were written by such significant opera librettists as Apostolo Zeno and Pietro Metastasio, whose works were set in Italy and elsewhere as well. The leading oratorio composers in Vienna in the late 17th and early 18th centuries were Antonio Draghi, Johann Joseph Fux, and Antonio Caldara. Cultivation of the Italian oratorio persisted in Vienna into the second half of the century, producing works by Salieri among others. But Italian oratorio also spread wherever Italian opera took root, especially in Roman Catholic centers, e.g., Dresden, where Johann Adolf Hasse set librettos by Metastasio for both operas and oratorios.

In Protestant Germany, the idea of a sacred musical drama was rooted in the Lutheran *historia*, a story of Christ (often associated with Christmas, with Christ's Passion, or with Easter) taken from the Bible, set to music, and performed in the church. The musical format was austere, involving an alternation of unaccompanied liturgical reciting tones sung by soloists with unaccompanied choral polyphony. The greatest master of this repertory was Schütz. During the 17th century, dramatic music composed for performance in the Lutheran Church increasingly came under the influence of the Italian oratorio, especially with the introduction of basso continuo [see Thoroughbass] and the interpolation of non-Biblical texts. The resulting genre has been called the oratorio passion. The genre culminated in the great examples by Bach, especially his *St. John Passion (first version, 1724) and *St. Matthew Passion (first version, 1727 or 1729). In such works there is a free alternation of dramatic material that employs text drawn verbatim from Scripture with contemplative material that employs newly created poetry. Soloists and chorus are involved in both of these functions.

In England during the 17th century, there were sporadic attempts at the production of sacred dialogues, but with no significant later continuity. The flourishing of oratorio in that country in the period 1732–52 was almost exclusively based on the work of Handel. The Handelian oratorio flourished largely as a result of the vacuum created by the London audience's disaffection with Italian opera. An English nationalistic spirit is particularly evident in such works as *Israel in Egypt* (1738), *Judas Macabbeus*

(1746), *Joshua* (1747), and *Solomon* (1748). Although Handel's **Messiah* (first version, 1741) is obviously the best-known oratorio ever composed, Handel remarked that his own favorite work in this genre was *Theodora* (1749).

Many German oratorios of the second half of the 18th century show close parallels with the Italian oratorios of the period. The German oratorio of the Classical period culminates in Haydn's *The *Creation* (1798) and *The *Seasons* (1801).

In the 19th century, the oratorio was influenced by the massive choral ensembles of the contemporaneous grand opera. Oratorios in this era provided an increasingly secular society with a quasi-religious experience, usually outside the setting of the church. National trends are again apparent. In 19th-century France, Roman Catholic mysticism was reflected in such oratorios as Berlioz's *L'*enfance du Christ* (1850–54) and Franck's *Redemption* (1871–74). Romantic interest in the legendary, the supernatural, and the apocalyptic was reflected in such 19th-century German oratorios as Carl Loewe's *Die Zerstörung Jerusalems* (1829) and Liszt's *Die Legende von der heiligen Elisabeth* (1857–62). Other German oratorios still drew on Biblical stories, as in Schubert's *Lazarus* (1820) and Mendelssohn's *Paulus* (1834–36) and **Elijah* (1844–46).

The cultivation of the oratorio in the 19th and 20th centuries has been most consistent in England, largely because of the national interest in choral festivals. In this setting, not only have works of Continental composers been performed over the generations, but numerous new works have been commissioned.

Although it has occasionally produced works that draw on the basic idea of the oratorio (e.g., Honegger's *Le *roi David,* 1923, and Stravinsky's **Oedipus Rex,* 1927), the 20th century in general lacks the institutions and the strong traditions that would stimulate the regular production of large choral works based on religious texts, with or without a plot. The historical function of the oratorio as a vehicle for propaganda—originally religious, then nationalistic—made it an apt genre for cultivation in socialist countries.

Orbison, Roy (Kelton) (b. Vernon, Tex., 23 Apr. 1936; d. Hendersonville, Tenn., 6 Dec. 1988). Rock-and-roll singer, songwriter, and guitarist. Joined Sun Records in Memphis, 1956; released singles in Nashville, including "Only the Lonely" (1960) and "Oh, Pretty Woman" (1964). Albums include *The Traveling Wilburys* (1988), a collaboration with Bob Dylan and George Harrison, and *Mystery Girl,* 1989.

Orbón (de Soto), Julián (b. Avilés, Spain, 7 Aug. 1925; d. Miami Beach, 20 May 1991). Composer. Studied with Ardévol and Copland. Directed his father's Orbón Conservatory in Havana, 1946–60; taught at the National Conservatory in Mexico City, 1960–63. Settled in New York, 1964; taught at Columbia Univ. Used some folk elements. Composed music for orchestra, chamber ensemble, chorus, and solo piano and guitar.

Orchestra [fr. Gr. *orchēstra,* dancing area; Fr. *orchestre;* Ger. *Orchester;* It. *orchestra;* Sp. *orquesta*]. A performing body of diverse instruments. The term orchestra may be applied to any such group, such as the *gagaku* orchestra of Japan or the *gamelan* orchestras of Indonesia and Bali. In the context of Western art music, it refers to the symphony orchestra, an ensemble consisting of multiple strings plus an assortment of woodwinds, brass, and percussion instruments. Major orchestras usually include three of each woodwind instrument (with possible use of piccolo, English horn, bass clarinet, saxophone, and contrabassoon), four horns (sometimes five with the first horn doubled), three trumpets, three trombones, tuba, two harps, a keyboard player (for piano, celesta, or possibly organ), timpani, three percussion players, and strings. The number of strings in contemporary orchestras varies considerably, but the best include at least twelve first violins, twelve second violins, ten violas, ten cellos, and eight double basses. Most orchestras, however, will reduce somewhat the size of the string sections in performances of 18th-century music.

The first established ensembles in this tradition were the court orchestras of 17th-century England and France [see *Vingt-quatre violons du roi*], though these at first contained only strings (but without double basses, which were not fully accepted into the orchestra until the advent of the 18th century). These prototypical string orchestras generally contained a core membership of 10 to 25 players that could be augmented when occasions demanded. By 1700, woodwinds were also to be found in certain court orchestras, and by the end of the Baroque era (ca. 1750), composers had come to specify in some detail the composition of the orchestras for which they wrote. The core of such an ensemble consisted of strings (usually in four parts, with each part modestly doubled) and two oboes, with the addition of a continuo part realized by varied combinations of harpsichord (organ for church performances), harp, lute, violoncello solo, or bassoon [see Thoroughbass]. Other instruments (flutes, horns, trumpets, timpani) were often added, and occasionally the oboes were omitted.

In the 18th century, the members of the viol family gave way to stringed instruments more closely approximating those in use today, the recorder was replaced by the transverse flute, and the *oboe da caccia* was replaced by the English horn. Trumpets and horns, previously limited in theory to the harmonics of the key in which they were pitched, soon acquired crooks—varied lengths of tubing that could be inserted quickly into the instruments, thereby altering their key and thus their concomitant pitch capacities. Clarinets were accepted as full-fledged members of the woodwind section by 1800. Shortly before, the bassoon had divorced itself from the continuo and joined the woodwinds as an equal partner.

In the late 18th century a pair of horns was added to the Baroque core group of two oboes, strings, and continuo, and it was for this combination that Haydn composed a number of his early and middle-period symphonies. He often made use of flutes, either singly or in pairs, as well as two trumpets and a pair of timpani (one rarely occurring without the other). Following Mozart's lead, he also came to employ clarinets in certain of his late symphonies. The symphony orchestra had also dispensed with the continuo by the first decade of the 19th century, although the tradition of a harpsichord accompaniment for recitative continued in *opera buffa* into the early 1800s. The scoring of Haydn's *London* Symphony no. 104 (1795) well represents the composition of a full high-Classical orchestra: two flutes, two oboes, two clarinets, two bassoons, two horns, two trumpets, a pair of timpani, and strings. Though the number of string players per part varied with the nature of the ensemble, it was not unreasonable to expect at least three players per part. The cello section, however, seems to have been surprisingly small at that time.

It was Beethoven who secured a place for trombones in the early 19th-century orchestra, as he did for the piccolo as well. And it was largely through the works of Beethoven and Weber that the standard number of horn parts was increased from two to four. With few exceptions, most early 19th-century orchestras were not appreciably larger than those of the previous century. Although the primary duties of such orchestras were operatic performances, they were hired for symphonic programs as well. But by mid-century, a number of municipal concert orchestras had been established. Notable among them were the orchestras of the Gewandhaus of Leipzig (founded 1781), the Paris Conservatoire (1800), the Philharmonic Society of London (1813), and the Philharmonic Society of New York (1842).

In the first decades of the 1800s the introduction of the ophicleide (later replaced by the bass tuba) assured the presence of a bass brass instrument in the orchestra. While the core group of two flutes, two oboes, two clarinets, two bassoons (sometimes four in France), four horns, two trumpets, three trombones, tuba or ophicleide, three or four timpani, and strings (the last increasing in number throughout the century) remained sufficient for more conservative composers such as Mendelssohn, Schumann, and

Brahms, other more radical figures demanded larger forces. Following in Berlioz's footsteps, Wagner substantially enlarged the orchestral apparatus he required. Large forces are also necessary for the late symphonies of Bruckner, Mahler, and Scriabin as well as for late 19th- and early 20th-century symphonic poems, operas, ballets, and choral works by Richard Strauss, Schoenberg, Stravinsky, and others. Although the size of the typical symphony orchestra was reduced somewhat in the period following World War I, composers of the second half of the 20th century sometimes called for substantially larger percussion sections.

Orchestration. The art of employing instruments in various combinations, most notably the orchestra; sometimes also termed scoring. Orchestration includes the concept of instrumentation—the study of the properties and capabilities of individual instruments.

The assignment of specific instruments to specific parts was rare before 1600, an early example being Monteverdi's suggestion of certain instrumental combinations for his opera *Orfeo* (1607). By 1750, a fully orchestrated Baroque concert work might include parts for one or more flutes, oboes (or other members of the oboe family), bassoons, horns, trumpets, timpani, and continuo, plus a body of three- or four-part strings with several players per part. Baroque orchestration frequently featured both contrasts between given orchestral choirs (such as winds versus strings) and simple homophonic doublings (winds plus strings). Equally common was a polyphonic approach that achieved homogeneity through the counterpoint of individual, balanced lines. Though doubling sometimes occurred between strings and winds in this context, independent lines requiring equal levels of dexterity were often given to them as well as to trumpets and horns.

Since most of the music of the early Classical period was based on a simpler melody-and-accompaniment texture, the first violins became the focus of the orchestrator's attention, with lower strings often assigned a rhythmically simple background. Winds—mostly pairs of oboes and horns—were employed to sustain the harmony, resulting in parts substantially less complex and demanding than those common in the late Baroque. Mozart allotted the woodwinds a much enlarged melodic function, however, as did Haydn in his later works. In addition to pioneering the symphonic use of the clarinet, which he had come to appreciate at *Mannheim, Mozart was vital in returning to the woodwinds a role more in balance with that of the strings while also providing them parts requiring greater agility than in the early Classical period. Beethoven continued this trend toward soloistic writing, increasing the importance not only of woodwinds (including piccolo), but of brass as well.

In Berlioz, the Romantic era produced perhaps the most important figure in the history of symphonic orchestration. Unlike his predecessors, for whom orchestration was sometimes in effect applied after the fact to completed music, or was largely a matter of convention, Berlioz considered orchestration an integral part of the original compositional process, thus elevating it to the status of other musical elements. To Berlioz and his aesthetic successors, the orchestration of a musical idea was inseparable from the idea itself. He undertook substantial timbral experimentation, pioneering the symphonic use of string techniques such as *col legno* and *sul ponticello* [see Bowing], string and harp *harmonics, muted and *stopped horn tones, flute glissandos, chordal writing for multiple timpani, and the use of percussion instruments in a role other than the provision of "Turkish" color typical in earlier scores. In addition, Berlioz secured places for the harp, English horn, E♭ clarinet, cornet, and valved trumpet in the symphony orchestra.

The invention of valved horns and trumpets in the first decades of the 19th century was of major importance to composers. These instruments' new-found abilities to play complete chromatic scales throughout their ranges with comparative ease closely followed improvements in the construction of woodwinds. It was Wagner who contributed the most to orchestration and to the brass section's role within the orchestra. Though some of Wagner's orchestration favored a homogeneous approach involving substantial doubling between orchestral choirs, lengthy solos for various wind instruments, often without string accompaniment, signaled a new importance for those instruments. Horns, trumpets, and trombones, both soloistically and sectionally, became central to the orchestral concept, as did the bass trumpet, contrabass trombone, bass tuba, and the special Wagner tubas invented for the four operas of *Der Ring des Nibelungen*.

Although Wagner's orchestration had a great influence on Mahler, Richard Strauss, Schoenberg, and Berg, other traditions evolved as well. The first, typified by Schubert, Mendelssohn, and Brahms, maintained the fundamental aesthetic of Beethoven: an often heterogeneous blend of orchestral choirs with strings dominant, followed in importance by woodwinds, brass, and percussion. The second, typified by Bruckner and imitated to some extent by Franck and Saint-Saëns (all of whom were organists), favored full orchestral choirs either juxtaposed or contrasted in a fashion reminiscent of the movement to or from various organ manuals. The third, a direct outgrowth of Berlioz's timbral experiments, featured a virtuosic and color-oriented style that encompassed every-

thing from piquantly scored chamber combinations to brilliant tuttis replete with much exotic percussion. This approach reached its zenith during the Romantic era in the middle-period works of Rimsky-Korsakov (e.g., *Capriccio espagnol*) and the later works of Bizet (particularly *Carmen, 1873–74*).

Debussy's highly subtle orchestration elevates woodwinds, more often scored soloistically than sectionally, to the level of dominance. Imitated by Scriabin (in his later works) and to some extent by Ravel, Debussy preferred the brass section muted and provided equally understated parts for percussion. Most noticeable of all is the greatly reduced role of strings. Such orchestration entrusts them with a largely accompanimental role, making much use of tremolo, coloristic performing techniques such as *sul ponticello* and *sul tasto* [see Bowing], and (again following Berlioz's lead) substantial division of individual sections into two or more parts.

The 20th century brought such a plethora of orchestrational approaches that no one or two can be said to dominate, although a general increase of percussion scoring and an interest in new percussion instruments are clearly observable. Perhaps most novel was the technique of Webern and many composers of the American and European *serial school who sought to fragment lines through a constantly shifting array of colors in which each instrument or instrumental section plays only a small number of articulations at a given time, sometimes termed pointillism by analogy with the technique of some painters [see also *Klangfarbenmelodie*]. Some later 20th-century composers called for increasing numbers and types of percussion instruments and for unconventional performances techniques on traditional instruments [see, e.g., Multiphonics].

Orchestrion. An *automatic instrument that imitates the sound of an entire orchestra, employing organ pipes and other devices controlled by a barrel-and-pin, perforated-paper, or similar mechanism.

Ordinario [It., abbr. *ord.*]. Ordinary, normal; an instruction to return to the ordinary way of playing after a passage in which some special technique has been specified, e.g., bowing *col legno*.

Ordinary. Those items of the *Mass and Office of the Roman rite whose texts remain the same throughout the liturgical year; as distinct from items making up the *Proper, whose texts vary with the occasion. In musical contexts, the term most often refers to the *Kyrie, *Gloria, *Credo, *Sanctus, and *Agnus Dei of the Mass.

Ordonez, Carlo d' (b. Vienna, 19 Apr. 1734; d. there, 6 Sept. 1786). Composer and violinist. Held a bureaucratic position in Vienna; by the 1770s was known there as a violinist. Composed stage works

(*Diesmal hat der Mann den Willen,* 1778); more than 70 symphonies (*Sinfonie périodique,* 1764; *Sinfonia solenne);* some 35 string quartets and many other chamber works; concertos; a cantata.

Ordre [Fr.]. (1) A series of harpsichord or instrumental ensemble pieces in the same key. François Couperin coined the term in his four harpsichord books (1715, 1717, 1722, 1730) and in *Les nations* (1726). It is not certain whether he conceived these groups of 4 to 24 pieces as performance units [see Suite]. A few French followers used the term in place of suite, and some modern editors have supplied it in the works of other composers. (2) *Course.

Orfeo. See *Favola d'Orfeo, La* (Monteverdi); *Orfeo ed Euridice* (Gluck); *Orphée aux enfers* (Offenbach).

Orfeo ed Euridice [It., Orpheus and Eurydice]. Opera ("azione teatrale") in three acts by Gluck (libretto by Raniero de Calzabigi), produced in Vienna in 1762. It was revised, with added music and the part of Orpheus, originally a contralto, rewritten for tenor, for a French production (text by Pierre Louis Moline) given in Paris in 1774. Setting: legendary Thrace and Hades.

Orff, Carl (b. Munich, 10 July 1895; d. there, 29 Mar. 1982). Composer and music educator. Pupil of Kaminski. From 1915 to 1919, held posts as Kapellmeister in Munich, Mannheim, and Darmstadt. With Dorothee Günther, founded and taught at the Güntherschule for gymnastics, music, and dance, 1924–43; designed a variety of simple percussion instruments for use with children. Conductor of the Munich Bach Society, 1930–33. Taught at the Staatliche Hochschule für Musik, 1950–60. Works include *De temporum fine comoedia* (Salzburg, 1973; rev. 1980) and many other dramatic works; *Carmina burana, Dithyrambi für gemischten Chor und Orchester* (1981), and other choral works; *Entrata* (orchestra in 5 groups, after Byrd's *The Bells*); arrangements of Monteverdi's "Lamento d'Arianna," *Orfeo,* and *Ballo delle ingrate.* Published *Schulwerk* collections of student improvisations (1930, 1954).

Orff-Schulwerk. A system of music education developed by the German composer Carl Orff (1895–1982). It is intended for groups of children singing and playing together, and it emphasizes the development of creativity and the ability to improvise. Orff designed a special set of instruments—mainly *xylophones, *metallophones, and other percussion instruments—for which he composed five volumes of "Music for Children" embodying his ideas.

Orgad, Ben-Zion (b. Gelsenkirchen, 21 Aug. 1926). Composer. Pupil of Ben-Haim, Copland, Fine, and Shapero. Employed by the Ministry of Education and Culture, Jerusalem. Often utilizes Jewish religious texts and vocal traditions. Has composed orchestral music (*Melodic Dialogues on Three Scrolls,* violin, oboe, percussion, string quartet, string orchestra, 1969); chamber music (*Min He'afar* [Out of the Desert], voice, flute, bassoon, viola, cello, 1956; *She'arim,* brass orchestra, 1986); choral music (*Sh'ar Larashut,* 1988).

Organ [Fr. *orgue;* Ger., Du. *Orgel;* It. *organo;* Sp. *órgano*]. A wind instrument consisting of from one to many sets of pipes controlled by one or more keyboards. The simplest organ has a single keyboard, one pipe for each key, and a wind-chest fed by a bellows. All but the smallest *portative organs have several stops or sets of pipes for each keyboard. Stop actions, moved by knobs, enable the player to combine the sounds of more than one set of pipes as appropriate for the music being played. The English term stop [Fr. *jeu;* Ger. *Register*], although it is of uncertain origin, suggests a means for stopping air from reaching pipes. Disposition refers to the manner in which stops are disposed over several keyboard divisions and pedal, each with its own wind-chest and keyboard. The essential components of the traditional organ are its pipework (properly scaled and voiced), wind supply and wind-chests, key and stop actions, and case.

Organ pipes fall into two general classes, depending on how their sound is generated. Flue pipes sound on the same principle as a penny whistle or recorder. Wind, admitted through the toe hole in the foot of the pipe, passes through the flue (an opening between the languid and lower lip), striking the upper lip and setting in vibration a column of air in the body of the pipe [see Fig. 1]. A pipe that is stopped (closed at the top) sounds an octave lower than an open pipe of the same length, because of the doubling back of the standing wave. Flue pipes make up the majority of organ stops and produce different timbres, depending on their voicing and scaling.

Reed pipes sound on the same principle as a clarinet and supply voices of great variety and often brilliance. Their sound is generated by a thin metal tongue, acting as a reed, which vibrates against the open side of a metal or wood shallot (much like a clarinet mouthpiece) when air is forced into the wind-tight housing (boot) surrounding the reed assembly. Resonators may be cylindrical, flared, open, or partially covered and are often of exotic configuration, all of these variations affecting tone quality.

Pitch for an organ stop is indicated by the length (in feet) of the longest pipe. In a unison open flue stop, this pipe, at C, is eight feet long. Since pipe lengths halve at each octave, a 4' (pronounced "four-foot") stop sounds an octave above the 8', a 2' stop two octaves above, and a 16' stop an octave below.

Flue Pipes   Reed Pipe

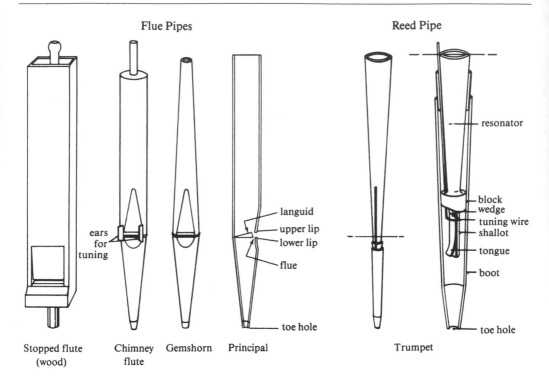

ears
for
tuning

languid
upper lip
lower lip
flue

toe hole

resonator

block
wedge
tuning wire
shallot

tongue

boot

toe hole

Stopped flute   Chimney   Gemshorn   Principal   Trumpet
(wood)   flute

Fig. 1. Organ pipes.

The same system applies to stops sounding intervals other than octaves: 5 1/3' produces the fifth, 2 2/3' the twelfth, 1 3/5' the seventeenth, and so on. These off-unison pitches enrich the harmonic series and are often referred to as mutations. For stopped pipes, the sounding pitch for C is used, although the actual length of the C pipe at 8' C is only 4'. For reed pipes, pitch is determined by the length of the reed, and sounding pitch at C is always used, although some reed resonators may be half-length or even less.

Scaling refers to the diameters of pipes in relation to their length, and this determines their basic tone family. For flue pipes, relatively narrow scaling produces a bright quality known as Principal tone, the distinctive sound of the organ. Wider scaling produces a less complicated harmonic series known as Flute tone; stopping a pipe further reduces harmonic development and produces the most characteristic Flute registers. Extremely narrow scaling of open pipes gives a variant of Principal tone known as String tone. There is considerable variety within the Principal and Flute families.

Voicing is the regulation of each pipe's tone quality, loudness, and promptness of speech. It is begun at the workbench and completed (finishing) where the organ is to be heard, to ensure proper balance among all the stops. For flue pipes, critical voicing factors include the sizes of the toe hole and flue opening, the

position of upper and lower lips, the precise contour and position of the languid, and the distance (cut-up) between upper and lower lips. For reed pipes, the thickness and degree of curvature of the reed tongue are the voicer's most important concerns.

The tuning of open flue pipes is accomplished by slightly increasing or decreasing the resonating length of the pipe, by adjusting a tuning slide or a slot in the back of the pipe, or by using a metal cone to increase or decrease the opening at the top. Stopped flue pipes are tuned by moving their stoppers or caps, reed pipes by moving a spring wire that bears against the reed tongue or by adjusting a slot near the top of the resonator.

The traditional wind supply consists of a pair or more of wedge-shaped bellows, raised by hand and collapsed in sequence by their weighted tops, the wind reaching the wind-chest through rectangular wooden ducts. By the late 18th century, single or multifold reservoirs were interposed, located as close as possible to the wind-chests. Other changes made by 19th-century builders included the development of tiered reservoirs capable of supplying different pressure for different stops (especially reed registers) or for treble and bass of the same stop. Because of the freer quality of the earlier system, many builders have returned to it, filling the bellows either by hand or with an electric blower, but omitting spring-loaded stabilizers, which are detrimental to voicing in the traditional styles.

Wind-chests of various types were designed during the organ's long history, but by the mid-17th century, the slider chest emerged as the norm. This consists of a rectangular wooden box filled with wind, with the pipes located on its top in rows roughly parallel to the keyboards. A thin wooden strip or slider runs from left to right underneath the pipes of each row or stop. The slider has one hole for each pipe and can be positioned so that the slider holes either are or are not in line with the pipe holes above them. All the pipes for each note stand over a single wind channel or groove (perpendicular to the keyboard), to which air is admitted by a pallet valve connected to the key. By moving the sliders, the player determines which pipes receive wind from their wind channel and thus whether one or more stops will be heard.

All organs have two distinct actions, one connecting the keys to valves under the pipes, and another to control the stops. Traditional key action employs a direct mechanical connection (by means of a thin wooden tracker, hence tracker action) between each key and the corresponding pallet valve in the wind-chest [see Fig. 2]. The stop action consists of strong wooden connections from the sliders to knobs located near the player, who may place each slider in the on or off position by moving the knob. When the key is depressed, the valve opens, admitting wind to the wind channel for that note and to the pipes with which slider holes are aligned, i.e., to pipes belonging to the stops that have been drawn. Because all the pipes for any note receive their wind from the same note channel, an important blending of combined sounds is achieved.

Various modifications of the traditional actions were tried during the 19th century involving pneumatic means for operating key valves and sliders, most notably the pneumatic lever (Barker machine) used by Cavaillé-Coll and others. The introduction of electricity led to replacement of the traditional actions by either direct electromagnetic valves or a combination of magnets and pneumatic motors. This allowed keyboards to be separated from wind-chests, since no mechanical linkage was required but only an electric cable. For most American builders, the pitman electropneumatic wind-chest became the standard, along with adjustable combination actions controlled by thumb pistons underneath the keyboards. These systems accounted for practically all the organs built in the U.S. from the early 20th century through the 1960s. Since that time there has been a considerable revival of the tracker action.

The late 20th century has also seen a revival of the traditional organ case, which involves placing the pipes for each division in a separate, shallow, wooden enclosure, open at the front, with keyboards located in the center of the main case. Traditional practice places the pipes for the main Principal stop for each division in the facade of its case, suggesting the size and resources of the organ and filtering out the less desirable high-frequency content of organ pipe sound.

Swell boxes, which consist of enclosures with louvered shutters at the front, are usually installed in the main case. Opening and closing the shutters controls the loudness and harmonic development of the pipes contained within the enclosure. Swell divisions became important in 18th-century English organs and from the 19th century in France, although they were not a part of classical designs in France or northern Europe.

Stop names ideally are based on the sound, shape, pitch, or location of the pipes. Some nomenclature describes only the general tone family (Principal 8', Flute 4'), while some suggests the instrument being imitated (Trumpet, *Cromorne*). Other names arise from the appearance of the pipe: *Gedeckt* [Ger., covered]; *Spitzflöte* [fr. Ger. *spitz,* tapering]; Chimney flute (with its cap pierced by a chimneylike cylinder). Still others imply, by custom, both tone family and pitch: Quint, for Principal 2 2/3'; *Nazard,* for Flute 2 2/3'. *Prestant* [fr. Lat. *praestare,* to stand before] is used in northern Europe to mean the main Principal stop, which is displayed in the facade, while *Montre* [Fr., to show] has the same meaning in France. For some reed voices, names are associated with full- or half-length pipes: *Posaune* or *Bazuin,* full-length; *Fagott,* half-length.

Mixtures are Principal-scaled stops, having two or more pipes per note, sounding octaves and fifths. Their function is to complete the full flue chorus of the organ [Fr. *Plein jeu*] by reinforcing the harmonic series of 16', 8', and 4' flue registers. A mixture's name traditionally indicates its pitch, which is given for the longest pipe at C. Mixtures for a 16' *Grand orgue* in the classical French tradition are called *Fourniture* (2') and *Cymbale* (1'), with the number of ranks (pipes per note) varying with the size of the organ and the acoustics of the building. In northern Europe, the terms are *Mixtur* and *Scharff* [Ger.], and *Mixtuur* and *Scherp* [Du.]; comparable Spanish terms are *Lleno* and *Címbala.*

Registration is the selection and combination of stops by the player, according to the style of the music and the design of the organ. The first and oldest principle of all registration practice in any style is the use of the complete flue chorus [Fr. *Plein jeu*], consisting of Principals at 16', 8', 4', 2 2/3', and 2' pitches, plus mixtures. In northern European style, the reeds may be added, but couplers are not used, nor are pitches doubled, while in the classical French practice, keyboards are coupled, thereby doubling pitches. Reeds are reserved for the *Grand jeu,* which

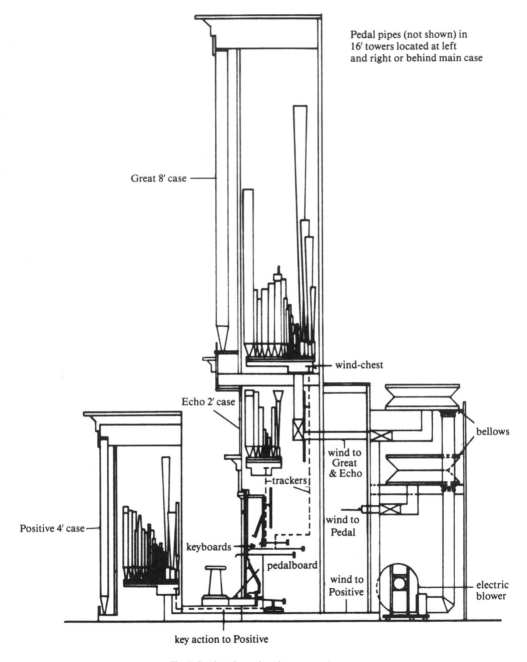

Great 8' case

Pedal pipes (not shown) in
16' towers located at left
and right or behind main case

wind-chest

Echo 2' case

bellows

wind to
Great
& Echo

trackers

Positive 4' case

wind to
Pedal

keyboards

pedalboard

wind to
Positive

electric
blower

key action to Positive

Fig. 2. Section through a three-manual organ.

also includes the *tierces* and flue stops at all pitches, but without the mixtures. It is essential for the player to be aware of such fundamental distinctions in different styles. Registration instructions are often minimal, although French composers usually give clear directions, often including indications in the title of a piece.

Although the concept of an instrument with several fixed-pitch pipes blown by a single player (such as the *panpipes, or oriental *sheng*) goes back to primitive times, the history of the organ actually begins in the Graeco-Roman period, probably in the 3rd century B.C.E. An early instrument said by Hero (*Pneumatika,* ca. 120 B.C.E.) to have been invented by Ktesibios of Alexandria was the first to possess the basic components of the modern organ—a mechanism to supply air under pressure, a wind-chest to store and distribute it, keys and valves to admit wind to the pipes, and one or more graded sets of fixed-pitch pipes.

In the primitive organ, wind pressure was regulated by water (hence the name *hydraulis) and admitted to the pipes by spring-loaded slides pulled by the player. It was a melodic instrument, secular in usage, sometimes employed for signaling purposes, and frequently used outdoors. Its use spread to Byzantium and Arabian lands; it acquired ceremonial functions and was often a prized possession of rulers and organizations.

In the 6th or 7th century, organs began to be made in which wind was supplied by a bellows similar to a smith's bellows. Organs are recorded in western European churches as early as the 8th century, but their usage is open to speculation. By the 10th century, however, definite records appear of the introduction of organs and bells into ritual use, at least on feast days and other special occasions, by the Benedictines. By the end of this century, writers describe large and loud organs in churches of France, England, Spain, Germany, and the Low Countries. By the early 11th century, learned treatises were being written on their construction and the scaling of their pipes by the Benedictine monk Theophilus and many others. In the 12th century, there are indications of a definite liturgical function for the organ, which by this time was technically capable of being played in at least two parts.

The proliferation of organs was rapid between the 12th and 15th centuries, and their use spread to south central Europe and the Slavic countries. Technical progress was steady during this period, and by the end of the 15th century the organ could be said to possess most of the technical and tonal attributes of its modern successors. Large church organs had become immense mixtures *(Blockwerk)* of several ranks of open flue pipes at unison and quint pitches. Parallel to the development of these large stationary church organs was that of the small portable or semi-portable instruments known as *portatives, *positives, or *organetti.

The most important developments of the 15th and 16th centuries were the division of the tonal resources of the organ into separate stops of varying pitches and colors and the multiplication of sections (divisions) controlled by separate keyboards, particularly in northern Europe. By the 17th century, organs already possessed virtually all of the varieties of tone and of flue and reed pipe construction found in modern organs. After the early 16th century, the Reformation and Counter-Reformation, along with the more rigid national boundaries engendered by the political climate, tended to polarize the liturgical use of the organ along regional lines. This, in turn, had a marked effect on both the tonal and physical development of the instrument in various geographic regions in the 17th and 18th centuries, often regarded as the golden age of the organ. Regional variation continued to be important into the 20th century, though builders in all countries in the later 20th century returned increasingly to 17th- and 18th-century principles. See also Electronic organ.

Organ chorale [Ger. *Orgelchoral*]. A polyphonic prolongation, elaboration, or working out of a Protestant *chorale tune on the organ, for use as a prelude to a congregational chorale, in *alternatim style, as an interlude between verses, as an independent piece elsewhere in the service, or as a concert piece. Typically, the chorale tune is presented complete in one voice, and/or its motives form the basis of a polyphonic texture. Bach's more than 140 organ chorales represent exemplary achievements in the form.

Organ chorales are generally classified according to whether the chorale tune is presented in strict form (i.e., in its entirety, even if ornamented) or free form. Strict forms include the chorale motet, chorale variations, and chorale prelude; free forms include the chorale fantasia and chorale fugue. Both long and short forms of these types are possible.

In the *chorale motet, each line of the chorale serves as the subject of a point of imitation; the overall form is a series of such points analogous to the Renaissance motet (e.g., BWV 686). In a set of *chorale variations, the chorale melody is elaborated several times in contrasting styles (BWV 768, 769). The chorale prelude, intended to serve as the prelude for the singing of a chorale, includes the following types: (1) melody chorale, a short form in which the chorale tune appears as a continuous melody in the soprano accompanied by contrapuntal parts (BWV 644 and many other pieces in the *Orgel-Büchlein); (2) ornamental chorale, in which the chorale is presented with elaborate ornamentation (BWV 622 and 641, short; 659, long); (3) *cantus firmus* chorale, a long form in which the chorale tune is presented in long notes (often in the pedal) and its successive phrases are separated by interludes (BWV 661); and (4) chorale canon, in which the chorale tune appears in canon supported by accompanying voices (BWV 608 and 634, short; 678 and 682, long). In the chorale fantasia, free treatment of the chorale tune prevails (BWV 615, short; 718, long). Two types of chorale fugue are possible, the short fughettas on the first phrase of the chorale (BWV 677, 679, 681) and the larger free fugues (BWV 680, 733). The accompanying voices in all these forms except the fugue most frequently serve only as modest support for the chorale tune. In the larger examples by Bach, however, the accompaniment is often cast in a clear, self-sufficient structure—invention, fugue, motet, canon, fantasia, duet, aria, trio sonata—to which the chorale tune is added.

Organ hymn. A set of organ pieces intended to be substituted for the odd-numbered verses of a Latin hymn [see *Alternatim*].

Organ Mass. A set of organ pieces intended to be substituted for portions of plainchant in a *Mass. Organists improvised *versets to alternate [see *Alternatim*] with phrases of sung plainchant in both the Proper and the Ordinary, but usually only Ordinary sections were written down (because they were not limited to a particular liturgical occasion). The possible uses of the organ at Mass were standardized by 1600.

From ca. 1400 to 1650, organ versets were based closely on the chants they replaced. The *cantus firmus* might be presented unadorned as part of the polyphonic texture, or it might be embellished considerably and used thematically. Composers in the 17th century made little more than slight references to a *cantus firmus,* being careful only to end on the appropriate harmony to give the pitch for the next phrase to be sung. In the 18th century, a type of Christmas organ Mass became popular in which each verset is based on a familiar *noël.* Composers also returned then to writing simple versets based on chants, a style that continued in the 19th century in unpretentious collections of service music. The Church tolerated this decimation of the liturgical texts until 1903, when *alternatim* organ music was discouraged. Some writers call the third part of Bach's *Clavier-Übung* an organ Mass, but it has neither the form nor the liturgical function outlined here. In 20th-century music, the term is sometimes used for liturgical organ music (Messiaen), but the choice of movements has not been standardized, and *alternatim* performance is not usually assumed.

Organ point. *Pedal point [cf. Fermata].

Organetto [It.]. (1) A *portative organ, small enough to be carried by a shoulder strap, with a range of less than three octaves, and usually only one set of pipes; small enough also to be pumped by the player's left hand while played with the right. (2) *Barrel organ.

Organillo [Sp.]. *Barrel organ, *barrel piano.

Organista. (1) [Lat., It., Sp.] Organist. (2) [Lat.] In the late 13th-century treatise of Anonymous IV, composer of *organum. The composer Leonin is there described as the "optimus organista" (the greatest composer of organum).

Organistrum [Lat.]. *Hurdy-gurdy.

Organology. The study of musical instruments. See Instrument.

Organum [Lat.]. Medieval polyphony most often based on a *cantus firmus. Initially improvised, with the added voice (or voices) duplicating the preexistent melody at a given consonant interval, the organum was eventually to be characterized by a sharp distinction, both melodic and temporal, between the original voice and the newly composed material.

The Latin word *organum,* from the Greek *organon,* meaning tool or instrument, was used from the patristic age forward to refer to any musical instrument and, more particularly, to the organ. How it came to be associated with polyphony is not entirely clear. The early history of organum is known from theoretical treatises written before the crystallization of a viable system of notation. The oldest of these are the *Musica enchiriadis* and the closely related *Scolica enchiriadis,* both from the 9th century. The anonymous authors describe three kinds of organum or what they prefer to call diaphony, that is, music composed of distinct but harmonious lines. The first of these is organum at the octave. The second has the added or "organum-making voice" *(vox organalis)* moving parallel with the chant *(vox principalis)* at the fifth below. This simple, two-voiced complex can be expanded to three or four voices by doubling one or both of the lines at the octave. The third kind of organum is described as being at the fourth. The difference between this and the first two types arises from the need to avoid the *tritones that almost inevitably occur in the course of an uninterrupted succession of parallel fourths. Mention of parallel organum in theoretical treatises from as late as the 13th and 14th centuries makes it clear that the early practice was by no means abandoned when composers began to cultivate polyphony of greater complexity and sophistication.

The oldest of the practical sources of organum is the Cambridge version of the Winchester Troper, a manuscript from the middle of the 11th century that contains the organal or newly composed voices for nearly 160 liturgical melodies. While the organal voice sometimes moves at the fourth below the chant, crossing of the voices is not uncommon. Pitch repetition may occur in the newly composed voice, resulting in a drone effect. Late 11th- and early 12th-century additions to three Chartres manuscripts include polyphony that has much in common with that of Winchester. Motion is sometimes contrary, sometimes parallel, and there is some crossing of voices; but the drone created by oblique movement does not occur. Perfect consonances, including the octave, appear consistently at phrase beginnings and endings, but elsewhere thirds and seconds are prominent, and there are even occasional sixths.

cap-   ti-   vi-   ta-

All. ℣ Ascendens Christus

Organum.

A group of four Aquitanian manuscripts ranging in date from the end of the 11th century to just past the beginning of the 13th contain nearly 100 pieces for two voices, only about half of which are based on *cantus firmi*. A sizable number of the newly composed *versus* are in note-against-note counterpoint, but the preference is now for the melismatic type, with several notes in the added voice for each note of the *cantus firmus*. The use of the term organum to describe this particular kind of polyphony is an anticipation of 13th-century theoretical practice. The same two types of polyphony appear in that part of the late 12th-century Codex Calixtinus devoted to the Offices for St. James [see Santiago de Compostela, repertory of].

The *Notre Dame repertory of organa is dominated by compositions for two voices (110) but includes as well a goodly number (28) for three, and a pair for four. Like those from Chartres, they are based on responsorial chants, of which only the soloistic portions are set polyphonically. The choral portions, though omitted from the manuscripts in the interest of saving time and parchment, were sung monophonically. The earliest layer of the repertory for two voices, attributable in part, perhaps, to Master Leonin, shows a marked preference for the florid or *organum purum* style, which is interrupted from time to time by short *discant sections or *clausulae [Ex.]. What distinguished the latter from the surrounding material is not only the faster movement of the *cantus firmus* or *tenor, but the precise rhythmic measurement of the voices. Successive layers of organum composition show an ever-increasing preoccupation with the discant *clausula* and with its measurement according to one or more of the rhythmic *modes.

The three- and four-voiced organa (*tripla* and *quadrupla,* respectively), cultivated in all probability from the last decade of the 12th century, were almost of necessity precisely measured even in the sustained-tenor passages. Both of the *quadrupla* and several of the *tripla* are attributed by the English Anonymous IV (ca. 1272) to Master Perotin.

It is not known how far into the 13th century organum composition continued. By 1230 or at the very latest 1240, however, it had been superseded by the *motet.

Orgel [Ger., Du.]. *Organ.

Orgel-Büchlein [Ger., Little Organ-Book]. An unfinished collection by Bach containing 46 *organ chorales on 45 chorale tunes. Numerous pages of the original manuscript are empty except for the title of a chorale tune, indicating that Bach intended to include a total of 164 pieces. All of the compositions are short settings, mostly of the melody-chorale type. The collection, BWV 599–644, was, with few exceptions, probably made toward the end of Bach's stay in Weimar (1708–17).

Orgue [Fr.]. *Organ.

Orgue de Barbarie [Fr.]. *Barrel organ; the term derives from a corruption of the name of an 18th-century instrument maker from Modena, Giovanni Barberi.

Orgue expressif [Fr.]. *Harmonium.

Ó Riada, Seán [Reidy, John] (b. Cork, 1 Aug. 1931; d. London, 3 Oct. 1971). Composer. Studied at the University College, Cork; taught there, 1963–71. Music director, Abbey Theatre, Dublin, 1955–62. Performed Irish folk music, but based his own compositions in serialism. Works include 2 ballets; orchestral music (*Nomos* no. 4, with piano, 1957–58); choral music (*Nomos* no. 2, Sophocles, baritone, chorus, orchestra, 1963); chamber and keyboard works; songs.

Ormandy, Eugene [Blau, Jenö] (b. Budapest, 18 Nov. 1899; d. Philadelphia, 12 Mar. 1985). Conductor. Studied and taught at the Budapest Royal Academy. In 1921, moved to New York. Conducted the Capitol Theater Orchestra; the Minneapolis Symphony, 1931–36; the Philadelphia Orchestra, 1936–80 (with Stokowski, 1936–38). Conducted premieres of Rachmaninoff's *Symphonic Dances*, Bartók's Piano Concerto no. 3.

Ornamentation. In the Western tradition of art music, the modification of music, usually but not always through the addition of notes, to make it more beautiful or effective, or to demonstrate the abilities of the interpreter. Often, substantial liberty for the performer is implied, though this liberty operates within certain conventions for each period. Although the concept may seem to imply the existence of unadorned compositions representing the pure intentions of their composers, ornamentation, particularly in the 17th and 18th centuries, is often an indispensable feature of a musical work, even when its details are not fully specified by the composer. The resources of this type of ornamentation may be classified as follows:
   I. Graces: (1) additional notes in stereotyped figures; (2) alterations or shifts of the written note-values; (3) dynamic, color, and pitch ornaments.
   II. Diminutions, paraphrase, variation.
   III. The elaboration of pauses, cadenzas.
In this dictionary, separate articles are devoted to the principal kinds of ornament as follows: I, 1: *Acciaccatura, Anschlag,* Appoggiatura, *Coulé,* Grace note, Mordent, *Nachschlag, Port de voix,* Relish, *Ribattuta (di gola), Schneller,* Slide, *Tirade,* Trill, Turn. I, 2: Arpeggio, Rubato, Suspension. I, 3: *Balancement, Bebung, Messa di voce, Portamento,* Vibrato. II: Diminutions. III: Cadenza. In addition, articles will be found on the following terms, which apply to more than one kind of ornament: *Accent, Aspiration, Battement, Chûte, Gruppetto, Martellement, Plainte,*

Redoble. For the early Baroque *trillo* (an accelerating repetition of a note, usually the penultimate one in a cadence) see Tremolo, Trill.
   What is and what is not ornamental in a piece of music depends very much upon the style and period or upon the point of view of the observer. In the 17th century, for example, the string vibrato, the shortening of a note, and a *crescendo* and *decrescendo* on a single note were all considered to be ornaments; today they are considered aspects of playing technique, articulation, or expression.
   Some notations of the Middle Ages (including some for liturgical chant) call for special techniques of performance that could be classed with ornamentation. By the 16th century, the subject is widely discussed. Treatises of this period are unanimous in asserting that there was no difference between the practices of singers and instrumentalists; the same vocabulary of embellishment served both. This vocabulary can be divided roughly into two categories: the graces, more or less stereotyped ornaments applied to single notes, and *diminutions, or passaggi,* which embellished intervals and melodies. Either type could be written out or improvised; the use of signs to indicate ornaments not written out in notes was limited to a few repertories and was generally vague and rudimentary by comparison with the elaborate codes of the 18th century. The graces of the 16th century fell mainly into the classes of mordents, trills, and *gruppetti.* This unity of ornamental practice was broken in the 17th century with the increasing differentiation of instrumental styles and changing fashions in vocal music.
   The first repertory to make lavish use of ornament signs was that of the English virginalists, beginning in the mid-16th century and extending to the mid-17th. Two signs were employed, a double and a single diagonal stroke through the stem of the note to be ornamented (above or occasionally through the note if there was no stem). The meanings of these signs have never been adequately explained, and the inconsistency with which they occur in different sources of the same music suggests that they had no universally recognized meaning.
   The use of ornament signs continued in 17th-century lute music, though it is clear from written descriptions of lute ornamentation that the variety and frequency of ornaments played was very much greater than the signs written in the tablatures would indicate. An important factor in the restraint with which ornament signs were used up to the mid-17th century was the lack of appropriate printer's characters (Mersenne) and the complexity of typesetting they entailed. When engraving became more common, ornament signs proliferated, and scores, particularly of French viol and keyboard music (Marais, D'Anglebert, François Couperin), grew so charged

that reading them with attention to every sign is laborious in the extreme.

An elaborate code and a terminology for vocal ornaments were developed in connection with Italian monody of the early Baroque period and elaborated by both Italians and Germans during the 17th century. What is known about French vocal ornamentation in the 17th century applies mainly to the *air de cour*. Although the diminution of successive strophes played the largest role, certain codified ornaments such as the trill and *port de voix* were essential to the style. But throughout this period, neither the signs nor the terminology of ornaments remained the same from teacher to teacher or medium to medium.

The first large table of ornament-symbols was included in Christopher Simpson's *The Division-Violist* (1659), where it was credited to Charles Coleman. French composers for the solo viol from Du Buisson (1666) to Antoine Forqueray (1747) also had a code of signs and terms, which maintained a certain consistency over the years, though it was considerably less elaborate than Simpson's. One of the most elaborate and influential ornament tables was included by D'Anglebert in his harpsichord pieces of 1689. Bach copied this table, and it served as the basis for the ornamental practice of many French harpsichord composers, including Rameau. The ornaments of 18th-century French instrumental music, termed *agréments,* represent the most elaborate practice of its kind in Western art music.

One of the most detailed and certainly the best-known discussion of ornaments occupies most of the

↗ ↘	Appoggiaturas from below and above; slides.
↗	In English virginal music, uncertain and probably variable; late 17th-century English, a dotted slide (rare).
↗	*Aspiration;* curtailment of note-value.
↯ ↯	Separation beginning with bottom or top note, respectively. On thirds, it may include intermediate note (*coulé de tierce*).
↯ ↯	Rising or falling arpeggio.
♪	In England, late 17th and early 18th century, a trill.
♪	In English and Dutch music of late 16th and early 17th century, meaning uncertain but probably different kinds of trills.
∧ ∨	Various meanings; the second often a *port-de-voix* in 17th-century French vocal music.
+ ×	Most common sign for trill of any type in French vocal and instrumental (not keyboard) music in 17th and 18th century. Occasionally a mordent. English 17th century, a slide.
⸙	In French Baroque keyboard music, appoggiatura.
⸙⁾	In French Baroque keyboard music, a mordent.
(⸙⁾)	Appoggiatura from below and mordent (prepared mordent).
(⸙	Upward slide with lower note held (D'Anglebert).
⸙⁾	Downward slide, upper note held.

 Upward/downward figured arpeggio (single intermediate note added in one of the intervals).

 Upward or downward appoggiatura (Bach).

 Turns.

 Trills. Length sometimes shows how long trill is to be continued. Short sign also *Schneller.* In England around 1700, mordent or prepared mordent.

 Vibrato, possibly with pulsations corresponding to note-values. Also a long trill.

Compound trills with appoggiatura and initial or final turns.

✣ ✤ ✢ Mordent.

⌣ Slide. Also custos.

 Arpeggio. Upward and downward arpeggios.

ᴧ *Suspension* (delayed attack, François Couperin).

 Trills.

Examples of ornamentation.

second chapter of C. P. E. Bach's *Versuch* (1753). Although the number of signs and basic types was fewer than ten, these were elaborated into an infinity of variants and subtypes through the lavish use of small notes and the explanation of examples. The 1750s also saw other major treatises as well, and these established a tradition aspects of which extended well into the 19th century. Even Chopin continued to insist upon trills beginning with the auxiliary and appoggiaturas on the beat. Modern doctrine concerning music of the 18th and 19th centuries is based on the mid-18th-century code as modified by Hummel (1828), Spohr (1832), and others. Principal among the modifications are the preference for trills beginning on the main note and the shift of most other ornaments ahead of the beat so as to leave the written note in its notated position. The entire subject is surrounded by considerable scholarly controversy, however.

One 18th-century ornament, the long appoggiatura, so exploited in the *empfindsamer Stil* of C. P. E. Bach and other German composers of his time, was assimilated into the harmonic language of the 19th century, becoming a salient characteristic of the music of Wagner, Brahms, and especially Mahler. Also, Italian opera continued to be modified and added to by singers, especially at cadences and fermatas. Although musicians are often taught in school today that the score is sacrosanct and may be neither added to nor subtracted from, a rich and living practice of unwritten ornamentation can be observed in popular music. This practice has yet to be studied in any systematic way.

Ornstein, Leo (b. Kremenchug, Ukraine, 2 Dec. 1892). Composer and pianist. Studied in New York. Debut, 1911. From 1920 taught at the Philadelphia Music Academy; then founded the Ornstein School of Music. Works include a Piano Concerto (1923); string quartets and other chamber music; many piano pieces (*Suicide in an Airplane*, ca. 1913; *2 Legends*, 1982); and songs.

Orpharion. A wire-strung plucked instrument with a festooned outline like a *bandora, but smaller, tuned like the *lute (G c f a d' g'), and possibly derived from the *cittern. See ill. under Lute.

Orphée aux enfers [Fr., Orpheus in the Underworld]. Operetta in two acts by Offenbach (libretto by Hector Crémieux and Ludovic Halévy), produced in Paris in 1858. A revision in four acts was produced in Paris in 1874. Setting: Greek legend.

Orphéon [Fr.]. A male choral society; the first to bear this name was established in Paris about 1830. Such societies multiplied rapidly, principally among the working classes, and by 1900 there were more than 2,000.

Orpheoreon. *Orpharion.

Orpheus in the Underworld. See *Orphée aux enfers*.

Orr, Robin [Robert] **(Kemsley)** (b. Brechin, Scotland, 2 June 1909). Composer. Studied in London and with Casella and Boulanger. Organist at St. John's College, Cambridge, 1938–50; taught at Cambridge, 1965–76. Chairman of the Scottish Opera, 1962–76; director of the Welsh National Opera, 1977–83. Works include operas (*On the Razzle*, 1988); symphonies and other orchestral music; chamber music; music for the Anglican service.

Orrego-Salas, Juan (b. Santiago, 18 Jan. 1919). Composer. Pupil of Allende, Santa Cruz, Thompson, and Copland. Taught at the Univ. of Chile from 1947; at Indiana Univ., 1961–87. Editor, *Revista musical chilena*, 1949–61. Has drawn on traditional Iberian and Latin American music. Works include operas (*El retablo del rey Pobre*, 1950–52; *Windows*, 1990); oratorio; ballets, film scores, and incidental music; orchestral works, including 4 symphonies; chamber music; *Canciones Castellanos* (soprano, chamber orchestra, 1948), cantatas, songs, and choral pieces; piano and guitar pieces.

Ortiz, Diego (b. Toledo, ca. 1510; d. Naples?, after 1570). Composer. *Maestro de capilla* of the Spanish viceregal chapel in Naples from 1558. Composed sacred music (Psalms, hymns, motets, etc., in *Musices liber primus*, 1565); *Trattado de glosas* (1553), containing secular music and an ornamentation manual for bowed stringed instruments.

Ory, Kid [Edward] (b. La Place, La., 25 Dec. 1886; d. Honolulu, 23 Jan. 1973). Jazz trombonist and bandleader. Led bands in New Orleans (1912–19) and California (1919–25). In Chicago (1925–30), worked with King Oliver, Louis Armstrong (recording Ory's *Muskrat Ramble*, 1926), and Jelly Roll Morton. After 1942, active in the traditional jazz revival.

Osanna. See *Hosanna*.

Osborne, Nigel (b. Manchester, 23 June 1948). Composer. Pupil of Leighton, Wellesz, and Rudziński. Has worked with serialism, electronics, and microtones. Works include chamber music (*Kerenza at the Zawn*, oboe, tape, 1978; Chamber Concerto, flute, 1980); operas (*Terrible Mouth*, 1992); orchestral music (Cello Concerto, 1977; *Stone Garden*, 1988); and vocal music (*The Sickle*, soprano, orchestra, 1975; *Pornography*, mezzo-soprano, ensemble, 1985).

Osiander, Lucas [Lukas] (b. Nuremberg, 15 or 16 Dec. 1534; d. Stuttgart, 17 Sept. 1604). Theologian and composer. A Protestant cleric in Stuttgart and elsewhere. Published *Fünffzig geistliche Lieder und Psalmen* (1586), the first book of German chorales in cantional style.

Ossia [It.]. Or; used to indicate an alternative (often easier) version of a passage.

Osten, Eva von der (b. Heligoland, 19 Aug. 1881; d. Dresden, 5 May 1936). Soprano. Studied in Dresden; sang at the Dresden Hofoper, 1902–27; thereafter an assistant producer at the Dresden Staatsoper. Sang at Covent Garden, 1913–14; toured the U.S. with the German Opera Company, 1922–24. Created Oktavian in *Der Rosenkavalier,* 1911.

Osterc, Slavko (b. Veržej, Slovenia, 17 June 1895; d. Ljubljana, 23 May 1941). Composer. Pupil of Novák, Jivák, and Hába. Taught at the conservatory and the academy in Ljubljana. Made use of twelve-tone and quarter-tone techniques. Works include 6 operas (*Krst pri Savici* [Baptism at the Savica], 1921; *Salome,* 1919–30); ballets (*Maska rdeče smrti,* 1930); works for orchestra (Symphony, 1922; *Mati,* symphonic poem, 1940); vocal, chamber, and piano music.

Ostinato [It., obstinate]. A short musical pattern that is repeated persistently throughout a performance or composition or a section of one. Repetition of this type is found in the music of cultures throughout the world and is especially characteristic of the music of Africa, whence its presence in much folk and popular music elsewhere (e.g., *rock) and in some 20th-century Western art music.

Although any musical element may figure as an ostinato, the most memorable patterns in Western art music, where the device is found as early as the Middle Ages, result when it is a melody, a chord progression, a rhythm, or some combination of these. Melodic-harmonic ostinatos were most prevalent in the Baroque period, while melodic-rhythmic ostinatos appear most often in the 20th century.

A repeating melodic phrase set in the bass is called a basso ostinato, or *ground bass, and is usually from one to eight measures in length, as in Bach's Passacaglia in C minor for organ BWV 582. Although a close relationship often exists between a melodic ostinato and the harmonies associated with it, as in the Bach example, harmonies are by no means fixed in a piece with basso ostinato. Harmonic ostinatos, on the other hand, have no fixed repeating melody, but do permit occasional new chords. Melodic and harmonic variations may give rise to a set of continuous variations that develops irresistible momentum when the upper parts are varied with each repetition of the ostinato unit, as in Pachelbel's Canon in D major [see also Variation, Ground, Chaconne, Passacaglia].

Ostrčil, Otakar (b. Smichov, near Prague, 25 Feb. 1879; d. Prague, 20 Aug. 1935). Composer and performer. Pupil of Fibich. Conducted Prague's Orchestral Association, 1908–22; at the National Theater and the Prague Vinohrady Theater; the Prague Opera, 1920–35. Taught at the Prague Conservatory, 1925–29. Influenced by expressionism and folk music. Works include 5 operas (*Honzovo království* [Honza's Kingdom], Brno, 1934); orchestral music (*Symfonietta,* 1921); vocal music, including 2 melodramas, 2 ballads, and a cantata.

Oswald von Wolkenstein (b. Schöneck in Pustertal, the Tirol, ca. 1377; d. Merano, 2 Aug. 1445). Poet and composer. Travelled widely in Europe and the Near East; served King (later Emperor) Sigismund. Wrote poems with monophonic melodies and others with polyphonic settings, some of them *contrafacta.* Created close text-music relationships.

Otello. Opera in four acts by Verdi (libretto by Arrigo Boito, after Shakespeare's *Othello*), produced in Milan in 1887. Setting: Cyprus in the late 15th century.

Ôter, ôtez [Fr.]. To remove, e.g., a stop or a mute.

Othmayr, Caspar (b. Amberg, 12 Mar. 1515; d. Nuremberg, 4 Feb. 1553). Composer. Studied at Heidelberg. Associated with the monastery in Heilsbronn. From 1547, canon, and later provost, at the monastery of St. Gumbertus, Ansbach. Composed almost exclusively vocal works, in most sacred and secular genres of his time except the Mass.

Ottava [It.]. The interval of an octave; abbr. *8va.* *All'ottava, ottava alta, ottava sopra,* or *8va* written above a passage indicates that it should be played an octave higher than written; *ottava bassa, ottava sotto,* or *8va* written below a passage indicates that it should be played an octave lower than written; *coll'ottava* indicates doubling at the octave, either above or below. In arias of the 18th century, *all'ottava* may indicate that the vocal line is to be accompanied only in unison or octaves, without other harmony.

Ottava rima [It.]. See *Strambotto.*

Ottavino [It.]. *Piccolo.

Ottoni, stromenti d'ottoni [It.]. Brass instruments.

Ours, L' [Fr., The Bear]. Popular name for Haydn's Symphony no. 82 in C major Hob. I:82 (1786), the first of the *Paris Symphonies, so called because of the series of "growling" pedal points at the opening of the last movement.

Ouseley, Frederick Arthur Gore (b. London, 12 Aug. 1825; d. Hereford, 6 Apr. 1889). Organist, pianist, and composer. Studied at Oxford; taught there,

1855–89, establishing standards for degrees in music. Ordained as priest, 1849. Founded St. Michael's College, Tenbury. Works include services; cantatas; oratorios; anthems; 1 opera; songs; chamber music; organ preludes and fugues; piano songs without words. Published theoretical treatises.

Ouvert, clos [Fr., open, closed; Lat. *apertum, clausum;* It. *aperto, chiuso*]. In secular music of the Middle Ages, especially the *formes fixes,* the first and second endings, respectively, of a section to be repeated; hence, the equivalent of the modern *prima* and *seconda volta.*

Ouverture [Fr.]. Overture.

Overblowing. The process by which a wind instrument is made to sound a harmonic higher than the fundamental (first harmonic) [see Acoustics] and thus the process by which the second and higher registers are produced. For some instruments, such as the flute or brass instruments, a change in *embouchure and/or wind pressure produces the change in mode of vibration from the first to the higher harmonics. In other instruments the transition is aided by a *speaker key.

Overdotting. See Dotted notes.

Overstrung. An arrangement of the strings of a piano such that those of the bass pass diagonally over those of the middle register.

Overton, Hall (b. Bangor, Mich., 23 Feb. 1920; d. New York, 24 Nov. 1972). Composer and jazz performer and arranger. Pupil of Persichetti, Riegger, and Milhaud. After 1945, played in prominent jazz groups and arranged for Thelonious Monk. Taught at Juilliard (1960–71), the New School (1962–66), and Yale (1970–71). Works include the opera *Huckleberry Finn* (1971) and other stage music; 2 symphonies and other orchestral music; chamber music; piano pieces; songs.

Overtones, overtone series. See Harmonics, Acoustics.

Overture [fr. Fr. *ouverture*]. (1) A composition for orchestra intended as an introduction to an opera or other dramatic or vocal work. During the 17th and much of the 18th century, the most common designations for overtures were *sinfonia* and (less often) *introduzione.* During the same period, overtures to operas and other large dramatic works often served as preludes to acts other than merely the first.

The earliest operas often had no overtures. Later 17th-century overtures, generally called *sinfonie* in the sources, ranged from brief chordal introductions to multisectional *sonata- and *canzona-like pieces. By 1700 the three-movement overture had become the norm for Italian opera. This type is now sometimes termed an Italian overture.

In France, overtures were of a specific sort consisting of two parts: first a stately slow section in duple meter with pervasive dotted rhythms, then a faster fugal section, usually in triple or compound meter. A return near the end of the second section to the style and often the material of the opening is common, especially in later examples. Double-dotting [see Dotted notes] is expected in the opening section; this section ends on (or in) the dominant or relative major, and both sections are repeated in toto. Hence, the form represents a type of binary or rounded binary form with contrasting parts [see Binary and ternary form].

Overtures of the type just described, known as French overtures *(ouvertures à la française),* appeared for the first time in Lully's ballet *Alcidiane* (1658). Their basis was the processional entrée of the early *ballet de cour,* which by about 1640 often bore the title *ouverture.* The French overture remained the standard type in France during the reign of Louis XIV and was quickly adopted by composers in Germany, England, and elsewhere. In Germany, a French overture often stood at the head of an ensemble or keyboard *suite. Such a suite was usually called an *Ouverture* or *Ouvertüre,* as are Bach's four "suites" for orchestra, which are actually called *ouvertures* in the sources.

The Italian overture of the early Classical period was generally in three movements. First movements from early in the period often disclose a tri-ritornello structure in which the first section moves to the dominant, the second moves to the submediant or other related key, and the third remains throughout in the tonic. During the 1730s, however, a variant of this scheme began to appear in certain Neapolitan overtures in which the middle section was either omitted entirely or reduced to a short retransition: the result resembles an unrepeated sonata-form exposition followed directly by the recapitulation. The similarity to sonata form without development becomes even closer with the introduction of thematic differentiation (including use of a contrasting secondary theme) beginning in approximately the mid-1730s; this and other stylistic elements of the Italian overture were influential during the early Classical period [see Symphony].

The movement structure just outlined remained the norm until fairly late in the 18th century. It also formed the basis for the most characteristic type of the so-called da capo or reprise overture, in which the usual dancelike finale is replaced by a restatement of all or part of the opening allegro. The da capo overture, found in Italy as early as the 1730s, represents a halfway stage in the shift from three- to one-movement overtures. True one-movement overtures appear sporadically throughout the first half of the 18th century. Gluck began to utilize the one-movement type in the 1750s, and by approximately the 1770s it had supplanted the three-movement type as the norm. A related trend was the more intimate connection of the overture with the work it introduced, either by incorporation within the overture of musical material from the opera or by anticipation in it of the action or mood of the first scene. In other respects, late Classical overtures tend to resemble the first movements of contemporaneous symphonies, employing sonata forms (without repeats) and often slow introductions.

These trends culminated in the overture of the Romantic period, as in Weber's overture to *Der Freischütz* (1821), which presents the most important thematic material of the opera. An extension of this principle may be seen in the "potpourri" or "medley" overture of comic opera, operetta, and musical comedy from Auber to the present day. An alternative type to the independent overture was the *prelude or introduction in free form, found in Italian opera from Bellini and Donizetti onward and in Wagner beginning with the *Ring*. With numerous exceptions, this type became standard after ca. 1850.

(2) A composition of the 19th and 20th centuries similar to a dramatic overture but intended for independent concert performance. A preliminary stage in the development of the concert overture is represented by the overture to a spoken drama and the overture written for a specific occasion. The most characteristic concert overtures, however, are works with generalized programs inspired by literature, history, nature, and the like.

Oxford Symphony. Popular name for Haydn's Symphony no. 92 in G major Hob. I:92 (1789). It was performed at Oxford in 1791 when the university awarded Haydn the honorary degree of Doctor of Music.

Oxyrhynchos Hymns. The earliest surviving Christian hymns with music, preserved on fragments of papyrus from the third century found at Oxyrhynchos in Egypt.

Ozawa, Seiji (b. Fenytien [now Shenyang, Liaoning, China], 1 Sept. 1935). Conductor. Studied in Tokyo, at the Berkshire Music Center, and with Karajan. Conducted in Japan; assistant conductor of the New York Philharmonic under Bernstein, 1961–65. Music director of the Ravinia Festival, 1964–68; of the Toronto Symphony, 1965–69; of the San Francisco Symphony, 1970–76; of the Boston Symphony from 1973. Appointed artistic director of the Berkshire (later Tanglewood) Music Festival, 1970; music director from 1973. Has conducted opera companies at Salzburg, Covent Garden, La Scala, Vienna, and the Paris Opéra.

P

P. Abbr. for *piano [see also Performance marks]; in organ and piano music, pedal.

Pablo, Luis de (b. Bilbao, 28 Jan. 1930). Composer. Studied in Madrid and at Darmstadt; had contact with Boulez and Messiaen. Has taught at the Madrid Conservatory. At first influenced by Falla, Stravinsky, and Bartók; after 1953 embraced serialism and experimental timbres. Works include operas (*El viajero indiscreto,* 1990); music theater works; choral music; orchestral music (*Tombeau,* 1963; *Iniciativas,* 1966; *Senderos del aire,* 1988); chamber music (*Ejercicio,* string quartet, 1965; *Modulos III,* 17 instruments, 1967); piano and vocal music (*Malinche,* soprano, piano, 1985–86); electronic works.

Pacato [It.]. Calm.

Paccagnini, Angelo (b. Castano Primo, Milan, 17 Oct. 1930). Composer and writer. Studied with Berio at the electronic music studio in Milan and at the Milan Conservatory; taught there, 1969–80; directed the conservatories in Mantua (1980–83) and Verona. Employed serial procedures. Works include operas; *Il Dio di oro* (soloists, chorus, and orchestra, 1964); music for orchestra (*Flou VII,* flute, harpsichord, and strings, 1981), chamber ensemble, chorus and solo voice, tape.

Pachelbel, Johann (b. Nuremberg, bapt. 1 Sept. 1653; d. there, buried 9 Mar. 1706). Composer and organist. Held organ posts at St. Stephen's Cathedral, Vienna (1673–77); Eisenach; the Protestant Predigerkirche, Erfurt (1678–90); Stuttgart; Gotha; and St. Sebald, Nuremberg (1695–1706). Pupils included Johann Christoph Bach, who later taught Johann Sebastian. Composed works for organ (*Acht Choräle zum Praeambulieren,* 1693; *Hexachordum Apollinis,* 1699), harpsichord, and chamber ensembles (*Canon and Gigue* in D, 3 violins and basso continuo); sacred concertos, motets, and other vocal works.

Pacini, Giovanni (b. Catania, Sicily, 17 Feb. 1796; d. Pescia, 6 Dec. 1867). Composer. Studied in Bologna and Venice. Music director at the San Carlo, Naples, from 1825. Established a music school in Viareggio; from 1837, ducal music director in Lucca, moving his school there. Composed numerous operas (*Saffo,* San Carlo, 1840); much sacred music, oratorios,

secular cantatas; *Sinfonia Dante* (piano and orchestra, 1863); chamber music; songs.

Pacius, Fredrik [Friedrich] (b. Hamburg, 19 Mar. 1809; d. Helsinki, 8 Jan. 1891). Composer. Studied with Spohr and Hauptmann. Violinist in the Stockholm court orchestra, 1828–34. Teacher at Univ. of Helsinki from 1835. Composed the first Finnish opera, *Kung Karls jakt* (1852) and the Finnish national anthem, *Vårt land* (1843; translated into Finnish 1848); also a violin concerto, songs, orchestral pieces, cantatas.

Paderewski, Ignacy Jan (b. Kuryłówka, Poland, 18 Nov. 1860; d. New York, 29 June 1941). Pianist, composer, premier. Studied at the Warsaw Conservatory, in Berlin, and with Leschetizky in Vienna. Debut, Vienna, 1888; from 1891 frequently toured the U.S. In 1919 became premier and foreign minister of the new Polish state, which he represented at the Versailles Peace Conference; from 1940, president of the parliament of Polish government in exile. Composed piano pieces (Minuet op. 14, no. 1; Sonata, ca. 1903); a piano concerto; *Fantaisie polonaise* for piano and orchestra; a symphony; *Manru* (opera, Dresden, 1901).

Padiglione [It.]. The bell of a wind instrument; *p. in alto,* with the bell raised.

Padilla, Juan Gutiérrez de (b. Málaga, ca. 1590; d. Puebla, Mexico, before 22 Apr. 1664). Composer. *Maestro de capilla* at Cádiz Cathedral, 1616–ca. 1620; singer at Puebla Cathedral from 1622 and *maestro* from 1629. Works include 2 parody Masses on his own motets, *Ave Regina* and *Joseph fili David;* *chanzonetas* and *villancicos.*

Padovana, padoana [It., from Padua; Fr. *padouenne*]. (1) In the first half of the 16th century, a generic term for the dances of the *pavana-**pass'e mezo* species. (2) Toward the middle and in the second half of the 16th century, usually a quick dance in a quadruple compound meter (12/8) resembling a **piva.*

Paean. An exuberant song, as of praise or thanksgiving; originally, one addressed to Apollo.

Paer, Ferdinando (b. Parma, 1 June 1771; d. Paris, 3 May 1839). Composer. Studied in Parma. From 1797, director of the Kärntnertortheater, Vienna;

1804–6, court Kapellmeister, Dresden. *Maître de chapelle* to Napoleon from 1807; director of the Théâtre-Italien, 1812–27, and of the chapel of Louis Philippe from 1832. Composed operas, including *Camilla* (Vienna, 1799); *Griselda* (Padua, 1798); *Achille* (Vienna, 1801); *Le maître de chapelle* (Paris, 1821); also cantatas, oratorios, symphonies, concertos, and chamber music.

Paganini Etudes. (1) Six concert etudes (*Études d'exécution transcendante d'après Paganini*) for piano by Liszt, composed in 1838 and based on Paganini's *Capricci* for solo violin op. 1 (except no. 3, "La campanella," which is after Paganini's "Rondo à la clochette," the last movement of his Concerto in B minor for violin and orchestra op. 7). (2) Two sets of six etudes for piano by Schumann, op. 3 (1832) and op. 10 (1833), on themes from Paganini's *Capricci*.

Paganini, Niccolò (b. Genoa, 27 Oct. 1782; d. Nice, 27 May 1840). Violinist, composer. Pupil of Paer. Soloist and teacher at the court of Napoleon's sister in Lucca, 1805–9. Toured Italy as a soloist 1810–28. First appearance in Vienna, 1828; thereafter toured Europe, becoming extremely popular for a time for his viruosity and showmanship. In 1834, settled in Parma; spent his last years mainly in Nice. Composed many solo violin works, including the 24 capricci op. 1; concertos and other pieces for violin and orchestra; chamber works; pieces for guitar; vocal works.

Paganini Variations. Two sets of variations for piano by Brahms, op. 35 (1862–63), on a theme from Paganini's *Capricci* for solo violin op. 1, the same theme employed by Liszt in no. 6 of his *Paganini Etudes.

Pagliacci [It., The Clowns]. Opera in a prologue and two acts by Leoncavallo (to his own libretto), produced in Milan in 1892. Setting: a village in Calabria on the Feast of the Assumption in the late 1860s.

Pahissa, Jaime (b. Barcelona, 7 Oct. 1880; d. Buenos Aires, 27 Oct. 1969). Composer. Pupil of Morera. Taught at the Municipal Music School, Barcelona. Emigrated to Argentina, 1937. Works include about a dozen operas (*La presó de Lleida,* 1906); overtures, tone poems, and other orchestral music, often based on Catalan folk material; incidental music; chamber works; piano pieces; and songs. Published a biography of Manuel de Falla (1947).

Paik, Nam June (b. Seoul, 20 July 1932). Composer. Studied at the Univs. of Tokyo, Munich, and Cologne, with Fortner at Freiburg, and at Darmstadt. Has taught at SUNY–Stony Brook (1968) and at the California Institute of the Arts, Los Angeles, from 1970. Works include *Hommage à John Cage* (2 pianos, which are destroyed during the performance, 3

tape recorders, projections, live actions with eggs, toy cars, etc.; Düsseldorf, 1959); *TV Bra for Living Sculpture* (1969), in which the images on miniature television sets (placed over Charlotte Moorman's breasts) vary with the notes she produces on the cello.

Paine, John Knowles (b. Portland, Maine, 9 Jan. 1839, d. Cambridge, Mass., 25 Apr. 1906). Composer, teacher, and organist. Studied at the Berlin Hochschule für Musik. Harvard University organist, 1862–82. From 1862, first instructor in the newly established Harvard music department. Works include a Mass; the oratorio *St. Peter;* 2 symphonies; *As You Like It* (concert overture, 1876); *The Tempest* (symphonic poem, 1876?); incidental music to *Oedipus Rex* (1880–81); *Azara* (grand opera, 1886–1900); 2 piano trios, and a violin sonata.

Paisiello, Giovanni (b. Roccaforzata, near Taranto, 9 May 1740; d. Naples, 5 June 1816). Composer. Studied in Taranto and Naples. *Maestro di cappella* to Catherine II of Russia, 1776–84. In Naples, served as court composer and music director to Ferdinand IV, 1784–99 and from 1815, as well as to the intervening republican governments. Director of Napoleon's chapel music, Paris, 1802–4; of the state college of music, Naples, 1807–13. Composed over 80 operas, including *Il *barbiere di Siviglia, Il re Teodoro in Venezia* (Vienna, 1784), *Antigono* (Naples, 1785), *Nina* (Caserta, 1789), and *Proserpine* (Paris, 1803); also oratorios, cantatas, Masses and other liturgical pieces, occasional works, concertos, string quartets, and violin sonatas.

Paladilhe, Émile (b. near Montpellier, 3 June 1844; d. Paris, 8 Jan. 1926). Composer. Pupil of Halévy and Marmontel. Composed operas (*Patrie,* 1886); the cantata *Le Czar Ivan IV* (1860); a Stabat Mater (1905); *Messe solenelle de la Pentecôte* (1889); *Messe de St. François d'Assise* (1905); songs; piano and organ works; a symphony.

Palau (Boix), Manuel (b. Alfara de Patriarca, Spain, 4 Jan. 1893; d. Valencia, 18 Feb. 1967). Composer. Studied with Koechlin and Ravel. Taught at the Valencia Conservatory from 1932 (director from 1952); also active as a conductor and musicologist. Influences include impressionism, folk music, and atonality. Composed orchestral works (*Homenaje a Debussy,* 1929; 3 symphonies; concertos for piano and guitar); chamber works; local-color piano pieces; and songs.

Palester, Roman (b. Śniatyń, 28 Dec. 1907; d. Paris, 25 Aug. 1989). Composer. Pupil of Sikorski. Taught at the Warsaw Conservatory, 1945–48; then settled in Paris. Worked with Polish folk materials and serial techniques. Works include 1 opera and 2 ballets; orchestral music (concertos, symphonies, and one-movement works); chamber music; choral and solo vocal music (*Kołacze* [Country Cakes], 1942; *Sonette an Orpheus,* 1951); theater and radio music.

Palestrina. Opera ("musical legend") in three acts by Hans Pfitzner (to his own libretto), produced in Munich in 1917. Setting: Rome and meetings of the *Council of Trent.

Palestrina, Giovanni Pierluigi da (b. probably Palestrina, near Rome, between 3 Feb. 1525 and 2 Feb. 1526; d. Rome, 2 Feb. 1594). Composer. Choirboy at S. Maria Maggiore; 1544–50, organist at S. Agapito Cathedral in Palestrina. *Maestro di cappella* at the Capella Giulia in Rome, 1551–55 and from 1571; at St. John Lateran, 1555–60. Briefly joined the papal choir, 1555. Served at S. Maria Maggiore 1560–66. From 1567 to 1571, was employed by Cardinal Ippolito II d'Este and taught at the Seminario romano. Associated with Guglielmo Gonzaga, Duke of Mantua. Composed 104 Masses, including many parody Masses; at least 250 motets; offertories, hymns, Magnificats, Lamentations, and Litanies; secular and spiritual madrigals. For centuries after his death theorists set him up as a model; one legend credits the *Missa Papae Marcelli* [see Marcellus Mass] with saving church polyphony during the Counter-Reformation.

Palestrina style. The style of unaccompanied, largely diatonic, polyphonic vocal music embodied in the works of Giovanni Pierluigi da Palestrina (1525 or 1526–1594). Palestrina's music has often been regarded as the model of classical Renaissance polyphony, especially in its controlled treatment of dissonance. See also Roman school.

Pallavicino, Benedetto (b. Cremona, 1551; d. Mantua, 26 Nov. 1601). Composer. Active by 1584 at the Gonzaga court in Mantua, as *maestro di cappella* from 1596. Composed Masses, motets, Psalms, and numerous madrigals.

Pallavicino [Pallavicini], **Carlo** (b. Salò, Lake Garda; d. Dresden, 29 Jan. 1688). Composer. *Organista ai concerti* at S. Antonio, Padua, 1665–66; *maestro dei concerti* there, 1673. Vice-Kapellmeister at the Dresden court under Schütz from 1667; Kapellmeister, 1672 and from 1685. *Maestro di coro* of the Ospedale degli incurabili, Venice 1674–85. Composed many operas, including *Vespasiano* (Venice, 1678).

Palm, Siegfried (b. Wuppertal, 25 April 1927). Cellist. Pupil of Mainardi. Played with orchestras in Lübeck, Hamburg, and Cologne. From 1962, taught at the Cologne Hochschule (director from 1972). Administrator of the Deutsche Oper, Berlin, 1976–81.

Known as a soloist and chamber player in performances of avant-garde music.

Palma, Athos (b. Buenos Aires, 7 June 1891; d. Miramar, 10 Jan. 1951). Composer. Studied at the National Conservatory; later professor there. Lived in Europe, 1904–14. Official with both the Teatro Colón and the National Council of Education. Works include operas (*Los hijos del sol,* 1928; based on Inca myth); tone poems; a string quartet; sonatas; and songs. Published 2 music textbooks.

Palmer, Robert (Moffat) (b. Syracuse, N.Y., 2 June 1915). Composer. Pupil of Rogers, Copland, Harris, and Q. Porter. Taught at the Univ. of Kansas (1940–43) and at Cornell (1943–80). Works include 2 symphonies, *Centennial Overture* (1965), and a concerto (2 pianos, 2 percussionists, strings, and brass, 1984); sonatas and other chamber music (String Quartet no. 2, 1942; Piano Quintet, 1950); piano music (*Toccata ostinato,* 1945, inspired by boogie-woogie); *Nabuchodonosor* (tenor, bass, male choir, woodwinds, percussion, and 2 pianos, 1964) and other vocal music.

Palmgren, Selim (b. Björneborg [now Pori], 16 Feb. 1878; d. Helsinki, 13 Dec. 1951). Composer and pianist. Pupil of Wegelius and Busoni. Appointed to faculty of Eastman, 1923; taught at the Sibelius Academy, Helsinki, 1936–51. Works include 1 opera, 5 piano concertos, a violin concerto, and other one-movement works; some 260 pieces for piano (*Fantasy* op. 6; *24 Etudes* op. 77; around 200 songs.

Palmieri, Eddie [Eduardo] (b. New York City, 1936?). Salsa bandleader and pianist. From 1961 to 1968, led the salsa band La Perfecta. During 1970s, experimented with rhythm-and-blues and jazz idioms. Recordings include "Muñeca" (1965), *Justicia* (1969), and *Sun of Latin Music* (1974).

Pandereta, pandero [Sp.]. Tambourine.

Pandiatonicism. The predominance in some 20th-century music of the pitches of the diatonic scale (often forming dissonances), as distinct from the chromaticism of late 19th-century music and of 20th-century *atonal and *twelve-tone music.

Pandora. See Bandora.

Pandoura [Gr.], **pandura** [Lat.]. The long-necked *lute of ancient Greece and Rome.

Pange lingua [Lat.]. (1) The Passiontide hymn "Pange lingua gloriosi proelium certaminis" (Sing, my tongue, the glorious battle) by Venantius Fortunatus (d. ca. 600). (2) The hymn for Corpus Christi "Pange lingua gloriosi corporis mysterium" (Sing, my tongue, the mystery of the glorious body) by Thomas Aquinas (d. 1274).

Panharmonicon. See Automatic instruments.

Paniagua y Vasques, Cenobio (b. Tlalpujahua, 30 Oct. 1821; d. Córdoba, Veracruz, 2 Nov. 1882). Composer. Violinist in cathedral orchestras of Morelia and Mexico City. Composed the first Mexican opera, *Catalina de Guisa* (Mexico City, 1859); one other opera, *Pietro d'Abano* (1863); about 70 Masses and other sacred music.

Panpipes. A wind instrument consisting of a number of small pipes held vertically and blown across the top. Each pipe sounds a single pitch; the longer a pipe, the lower its pitch. The tubes may be arranged in a bundle or in a row. If in a row, they are often arranged from longest at one end to shortest at the other. They are an ancient instrument and are found nearly worldwide, especially in the Andean highlands, East Africa, Oceania (except Australia), and Romania. See ill. under Flute.

Pantaleon, pantalon. (1) A large *dulcimer with up to 275 strings covering five or more octaves, invented ca. 1690 by Pantaleon Hebenstreit. It enjoyed a vogue in the first half of the 18th century, but passed out of use in the 1770s. (2) In the late 18th century, a square piano, especially one with a down-striking action. (3) On a clavichord, a stop that divides the strings from the damping felt, thus permitting them to vibrate sympathetically as well as after a key has been released.

Pantonal, pantonality. The free use of all twelve pitch classes, as distinct from their restricted use according to the principles of *tonality; hence, synonymous with atonal, *atonality.

Panufnik, Andrzej (b. Warsaw, 24 Sept. 1914; d. Twickenham, 27 Oct. 1991). Composer. Pupil of his mother, Sikorski, and Weingartner. Conducted the Kraków Philharmonic and the Warsaw Philharmonic. In 1954, settled in England. Worked with serial techniques, quarter tones, and graphic notation. Composed 1 ballet; orchestral music (*Tragic Overture*, 1942; *Sinfonia rustica*, 1948, rev. 1955; Symphony no. 10, 1988; concertos); choral music (*5 Polish Peasant Songs*, 1940; *Universal Prayer*, soloists, chorus, 3 harps, organ, 1968–69); chamber works (String Quartet no. 3, Wycinanki, 1990); piano music (*12 Miniature Studies*, 1947).

Paolo da Firenze [Paolo Tenorista, Paulus de Florentia] (d. Arezzo, Sept. 1419). Composer and theorist. Composed madrigals, *ballate*, and 2 sacred compositions. His surviving works reveal an awareness of both Italian and French styles; many are stylistically similar to the works of Landini.

Papaioannou, Yannis Andreou (b. Cavala, 6 Jan. 1911; d. Athens, 11 May 1989). Composer. Studied at the Hellenic Conservatory, where he taught from 1953, and with Honegger. Worked with folk materials, serialism, sound clusters, and quarter tones. Composed orchestral music (symphonies, concertos, descriptive works); chamber music; choral- orchestral works; pieces for chamber ensemble and solo voice (*To kardhiochtypi* [The Heartbeat], 1959).

Papillons [Fr., Butterflies]. Schumann's set of 12 short piano pieces op. 2 (1829–31). It was inspired by a masked ball in a work of Jean-Paul Richter.

Papineau-Couture, Jean (b. Montreal, 12 Nov. 1916). Composer. Pupil of Q. Porter and Boulanger. Taught at the provincial conservatory in Montreal (1946–63) and at the Univ. of Montreal (from 1951; dean, 1968–73). Founding member and later president of the Canadian Music Center. Early works were tonal and neoclassical; later he explored atonality. Composed music for pantomimes and puppet shows; orchestral works (a symphony; concertos; *Clair-obscur*, 1986); chamber music (*Le débat du coeur et du corps du Villon*, speaker, cello, and percussion, 1977; Suite for solo violin, 1956); piano and harpsichord pieces; choral music and songs.

Paradiddle. A characteristic series of strokes played on the snare drum with hands alternating as follows: L R L L R L R R or R L R R L R L L.

Paradies [Paradisi], **(Pietro) Domenico** (b. Naples, 1707; d. Venice, 25 Aug. 1791). Composer. Reportedly studied with Porpora. Taught voice, keyboard, and harmony in London from 1746. Composed 12 harpsichord sonatas (1754), concertos, and other keyboard works; operas (*Fetonte*, London, 1747); songs for pasticcios.

Paradis [Paradies], **Maria Theresia von** (b. Vienna, 15 May 1759; d. Vienna, 1 Feb. 1824). Composer, pianist, and singer. Blinded as a child. Pupil of L. Kozeluch, Salieri, and Abbé Vogler. Received a pension from the imperial court; toured widely (Concert spirituel, 1784). Founded a school of music in Vienna. Composed German operas; cantatas; songs; piano music. Mozart probably composed his K. 456 piano concerto for her.

Parallel chords. A succession of chords all having the same interval structure and number of parts, the parts thus moving parallel to one another. Because classical *tonal theory prohibits motion in *parallel fifths and octaves, it allows only first-inversion triads [see also Sixth chord, Sixth-chord style] and diminished seventh chords in parallel motion. Composers of tonal music have sometimes employed otherwise prohibited parallels to evoke a rustic or primitive quality or in conjunction with folk or folklike melodies. In the 20th ceentury, the technique is often associated with the music of Debussy (e.g., *Danse sacrée*

[Ex. 1]) and with *impressionism generally. It is also encountered in some works of Bartók and of early and middle-period Stravinsky (e.g., *Petrushka* [Ex. 2]). Jazz and rock music have also used parallel chords [Ex. 3], often as a result of repeated reliance on characteristic keyboard or fingerboard idioms.

Parallel (consecutive) fifths, octaves. The simultaneous statement of the same melodic interval in two otherwise independent parts of a polyphonic complex at the distance of a perfect fifth [Ex. 1] or octave [Ex. 2] or equivalent compound interval. *Motion of this type is prohibited in classical tonal harmony and *counterpoint. A related phenomenon is variously termed hidden, direct, or covered fifths or octaves. Here a fifth or octave is approached in similar motion in two parts. These are in general avoided when both parts move by leap, especially when the two parts are the outermost voices. A familiar type of direct fifth is sometimes termed horn fifths [Ex. 3] because it occurs frequently in parts composed for natural horns.

Some early forms of *organum make extensive use of parallel fifths and octaves. The prohibition against their use first occurs around 1300.

Parallel key. See Key relationship.

Parallel motion. See Motion.

Paraphrase. (1) A metrical rendition in the vernacular of Scripture or the Psalms, set to music. (2) In music of the 14th–16th centuries, a melody borrowed from another source (usually chant) and then ornamented or elaborated. The technique was used in polyphonic settings of the Ordinary of the Mass and also in settings of hymns, sequences, and antiphons. Paraphrased chants sometimes serve as the *cantus firmi* of early *cyclic Masses. In the 16th century, a highly paraphrased *cantus firmus* might migrate from voice to voice within an imitative structure. (3) In the 19th century, a solo work of great virtuosity in which popular melodies, usually from operas, were elaborated (as in Liszt's *Rigoletto: Paraphrase de concert,* 1860); such pieces could also be called Fantasia or Reminiscences and were distinguished from works attempting to be faithful transcriptions.

Paray, Paul (M. A. Charles) (b. Le Tréport, 24 May 1886; d. Monte Carlo, 10 Oct. 1979). Conductor and composer. Studied at the Paris Conservatory. Conducted the Concerts Lamoureux (1923–28), the Monte Carlo Orchestra (1928–33), the Concerts Colonne (1933–40, 1944–52), and the Detroit Symphony (1952–63). Works include *Mass of Joan of Arc* (1931); 2 symphonies; the ballet *Artemis troublée* (1922); chamber and piano works.

Pardessus de viole [Fr.]. A descant *viol of the 17th and 18th centuries [see also *Dessus*], with five strings tuned g c' e' a' d''.

Paris Symphonies. Haydn's Symphonies nos. 82–87 Hob. I:82–87 (1785–86), composed for the *Concert de la Loge olympique* in Paris. Three of them have popular names: L'*ours (no. 82), La *poule (no. 83), and La *reine (no. 85).

Paris Symphony. Popular name for Mozart's Symphony in D major K. 297 (1778), composed during a stay in Paris and performed there at the *Concert spirituel.*

Parish Alvars, Elias [Parish, Eli] (b. Teignmouth, 28 Feb. 1808; d. Vienna, 25 Jan. 1849). Harpist and composer. Pupil of Bochsa and Labarre. Associate of Mendelssohn. Toured the Far East, 1838–42; chamber musician to the emperor in Vienna, 1847. Composed 2 concertos and other pieces for solo harp; a symphony; 2 piano concertos; an opera.

Parisot, Aldo (Simoes) (b. Natal, Brazil, 30 Sept. 1920). Cellist. Studied in Rio and at Yale. Has taught at Yale (from 1958), at Mannes College, at the New England Conservatory, at Banff, and at the Manhattan and Juilliard schools.

Parkening, Christopher (William) (b. Los Angeles, 14 Dec. 1947). Guitarist. Pupil of Segovia, Castelnuovo-Tedesco, and Pepe and Celedonio Romero. Debut, 1963. Has taught at the Univ. of Southern California. Has toured and recorded extensively and published guitar transcriptions.

Parker, Charlie [Charles, Jr.; Bird; Yardbird] (b. Kansas City, Kans., 29 Aug. 1920; d. New York, 12 March 1955). Jazz alto saxophonist and bandleader. Played in jam sessions in New York from which the bop style emerged. Worked with Dizzy Gillespie, 1945–46; recordings include *Groovin' High, Salt Peanuts* (both 1945). From 1947 led small groups; among his sidemen were Miles Davis, Kenny Dorham, and Max Roach. Composed original melodies based on borrowed chord progressions (*Now's the Time, Ornithology, Scrapple from the Apple);* improvised solos of extreme rhythmic and harmonic complexity, sometimes inserting quotations from completely unrelated genres. Often drew on blues-based Kansas City jazz. Recordings include *Yardbird Suite, A Night in Tunisia* (both 1946), *Klactoveedsedstene* (1947), *Au Privave* (1951).

Parker, Horatio (William) (b. Auburndale, Mass., 15 Sept. 1863; d. Cedarhurst, N.Y., 18 Dec. 1919). Composer, teacher. Pupil of Chadwick and Rheinberger. Organist and choirmaster, Trinity Church, Boston, 1893–1902. Teacher, Yale School of Music, from 1894; dean from 1904. Founded and conducted the New Haven Symphony, 1895–1918. Organist and choirmaster, St. Nicholas's, New York, 1902–10. Composed operas (*Mona,* Metropolitan Opera, 1912; *Fairyland,* Los Angeles, 1915); oratorios (*Hora novissima,* New York, 1893), cantatas (*A Wanderer's Psalm,* Hereford, 1900); and other choral works; a few orchestral and chamber works (Organ Concerto, 1902); much organ music, songs, hymns. Charles Ives was his pupil.

Parlando [It., speaking]. Speechlike; also *parlante.* The term is used principally with respect to singing, but sometimes also with respect to instrumental music.

Parlante [It.]. (1) *Parlando.* (2) In 19th century Italian opera, music in which continuity is maintained by the orchestra, sometimes employing a recurrent motive, while the voice proceeds in a less melodic and more speechlike fashion.

Parlato [It.]. (1) *Parlando.* (2) Spoken rather than sung, e.g., the dialogue of certain types of comic opera.

Parody. (1) A work that, with humorous or satirical aims, makes distorted or exaggerated use of the features of some other work or type of work. The history of opera includes numerous examples, beginning with comic interludes in otherwise serious operas of the 17th century and including contemporaneous parodies of the operas of Lully, comic operas intended for performance between acts of serious operas of the early 18th century, some features of *ballad opera, Wagner's portrayal of Beckmesser in *Die *Meistersinger,* and many passages in the works of Gilbert and Sullivan.

(2) A work in which a new text has been substituted for the original, often without humorous intent. A work of this type from the Middle Ages or Renaissance is usually termed a *contrafactum.

(3) A composition that seriously reworks the musical material of another composition. Compositions of this type were common in the 16th and early 17th centuries, the principal genre being the *parody Mass.

Parody Mass [Lat. *missa parodia*]. A cyclic Mass based on a polyphonic model, making use of the model's motivic construction and quoting more than one of its voices. The first parody Masses were produced by the younger French contemporaries of Josquin Desprez, whose own *Missa Mater patris* is sometimes regarded as a parody Mass.

Parratt, Walter (b. Huddersfield, 10 Feb. 1841; d. Windsor, 27 Mar. 1924). Organist. Studied at Oxford. Organist at Magdalen College, Oxford (1872); at St. George's Chapel, Windsor (1882). Taught at the Royal College of Music from 1883. Master of the Queen's Musick, 1893. Chair of Music at Oxford, 1908–18; dean of music at London Univ., 1916.

Parris, Robert (b. Philadelphia, 21 May 1924). Composer. Pupil of Mennin, Bergsma, Copland, Ibert, and Honegger. Taught at George Washington University from 1963. Music critic for Washington, D.C., newspapers, 1958–78. Has employed serial procedures. Works include concertos (*The Phoenix,* timpani, 1969) and other orchestral music; chamber works (*The Book of Imaginary Beings II,* 1983; 3 duets for electric guitar and amplified harpsichord, 1984); choral music; songs.

Parry, (Charles) Hubert (Hastings) (b. Bournemouth, 27 Feb. 1848; d. Rustington, near Littlehampton, 7 Oct. 1918). Composer, teacher. Pupil of Bennett, Macfarren, Pierson, and Dannreuther. From 1883, taught at the Royal College of Music (director from 1894); professor at Oxford, 1900–1908. Composed oratorios (*Job,* Gloucester, 1892), cantatas (*Blest Pair of Sirens,* 1887) and other choral works; orchestral works (4 symphonies; Symphonic Variations, 1897); incidental music; an opera; songs; chamber and keyboard music. Published several books on music, including *The Art of Music* (1893).

Pars [Lat., pl. *partes*]. A self-contained section of a work, especially of a Renaissance motet.

Parsifal. Opera ("stage-dedication festival play" [Ger. *Bühnenweihfestspiel*]) in three acts by Wagner (to his own text, after Wolfram von Eschenbach), produced in Bayreuth in 1882 at the dedication of the festival theater. Setting: Monsalvat, Spain, in the Middle Ages.

Part. (1) [Fr. *voix;* Ger. *Stimme;* It. *voce;* Sp. *voz*] In a polyphonic work for voices or instrument(s), any of the individual lines or melodies making up the texture; sometimes also *voice or voice part, though not usually with respect to works for instrumental ensemble. In keyboard music, some genres, such as the *fugue, adhere to a fixed number of parts for any work, while others may employ textures in which a fixed number of parts is not readily distinguishable. (2) The music for any single voice or instrument in an ensemble. (3) A section of a larger work or form [see, e.g., Binary and ternary form].

Pärt, Arvo (b. Paide, 11 Sept. 1935). Composer. Studied at Tallinn Conservatory. Worked at Estonian Radio 1958–67. In 1982, moved to West Berlin. Has worked with serial techniques and aleatoric devices; quoted from specific works or musical styles of the past. Works include orchestral pieces (3 symphonies; *Perpetuum mobile,* 1963; *Silovans Song,* 1991); choral music (*Laul armastatule* [Song for the Beloved], cantata, 1973; *Johannespassion,* 1981; *Te Deum,* 1985; *Litany,* 1994); chamber works (*Kriips ja punkt* [Dash and Dot], 1967).

Partbook. A separately bound manuscript or printed book containing the music for only a single voice or instrument in an ensemble. The term is applied chiefly to what was one of the principal formats for the dissemination of ensemble music of the 16th and early 17th centuries [see also Choirbook, Score].

Part song. (1) An unaccompanied secular choral work of relatively modest length. The repertory of such works grew strikingly in the 19th century with the spread of amateur choral societies and has continued to grow in the 20th. (2) Any unaccompanied secular vocal work, including genres from the Middle Ages and Renaissance such as the chanson and madrigal.

Part writing. *Voice leading.

Partch, Harry (b. Oakland, Calif., 24 June 1901; d. San Diego, 3 Sept. 1974). Composer, instrument maker, and performer. Developed a tuning system based on a scale with 43 pitches to the octave and invented instruments adapted to it. Drew on a variety of folk materials. Works include *17 Lyrics by Li Po* (voice and adapted viola, 1930–33); dance scores

(*The Bewitched,* 1955); music for films; *Delusion of a Fury* (large ensemble, including actors and dancers, 1955–56). Published his theories of tuning in *Genesis of a Music* (1949).

Parte [It.]. (1) *Part; *colla parte,* an indication that the accompaniment should follow the free rhythmic interpretation of the principal melodic part or that one player is to double the part of another. (2) In the 17th century, a variation [see Partita].

Parthia, Parthie, Partia [Ger.]. *Partita.

Partial. In acoustics, *harmonic.

Partial signature. *Conflicting signature.

Particella [It.; Ger. *Particell*]. A detailed sketch or draft of a composition written on relatively few staves.

Partie. (1) [Fr.] *Part. (2) [Fr., Ger.] See Partita.

Partimento [It., division]. In the 18th and early 19th centuries, a thoroughbass part with occasional melodic suggestions on the basis of which a complete composition rather than simply an accompaniment was to be improvised.

Partita [fr. It. *parte,* part], **Parthia** [Ger.; also *Parthie, Partie, Partia*]. (1) In the late 16th and the 17th century, a variation, usually one on a traditional melody such as the *romanesca or *passamezzo. This meaning was continued in the chorale partitas of Georg Böhm and Bach.

(2) In the late Baroque period, a *suite.

(3) In the early Classical period, a type of multi-movement instrumental work consisting of either a mixture of dance and abstract (nondance) movements or of a succession of only abstract movements. In Austria during this period, partita was the most common designation for all multimovement chamber works until the 1750s, when it was replaced as the title of choice by *divertimento. After about 1760, the term generally designated a work for winds, often entitled *Feldparthie* (partita for outdoor performance). After about 1780, works of this latter type were more often termed *Harmonie.*

Partition [Fr.], **Partitur** [Ger.], **Partitura** [It., Sp.]. *Score.

Parton, Dolly (b. Locust Ridge, Tenn., 19 Jan. 1946). Country singer and songwriter. Recordings of her own songs include "Coat of Many Colors" (1971) and "9 to 5" (1980). From 1977, has achieved success with popular audiences; has acted in a number of films.

Partos, Oedoen [Ödön] (b. Budapest, 1 Oct. 1907; d. Tel Aviv, 6 July 1977). Composer, conductor, violinist. Pupil of Kodály. Conducted the Budapest

Konzertorchester, 1926–27 and from 1937. Lived in Germany, 1927–33. Director, Tel Aviv Academy of Music, from 1951. Worked with Jewish folk music and with serialism. Composed orchestral music (*Yizkor* [In Memoriam], strings, 1947; *Tehilim* [Psalms], 1960; concertos); chamber works (*Arpiliyot* [Nebulae], 1966); vocal music.

Pas [Fr.]. A dance step; *pas de deux,* a dance for two dancers; for *pas de Brabant,* see *Saltarello.*

Pasacalle [Sp.]. (1) Literally, music for walking in the streets. See Passacaglia. (2) In Andean South America, any of various kinds of dance music.

Pasatieri, Thomas (b. New York, 20 Oct. 1945). Composer. Pupil of Giannini, Persichetti, and Milhaud. Has composed mainly vocal music in the tradition of Puccini and Menotti. Works include operas (*Calvary,* 1971; *The Trial of Mary Lincoln,* 1972; *The Seagull,* 1974; *Maria Elena,* 1983); over 400 songs (*3 Poems of James Agee,* 1974); cantatas; a Mass; *Invocations* (orchestra, 1968); piano music.

Pasdeloup, Jules Étienne (b. Paris, 15 Sept. 1819; d. Fontainebleau, 13 Aug. 1887). Conductor. Studied and later taught at the Paris Conservatory. Organized concerts of the Société des jeunes élèves du Conservatoire, 1853, and Concerts populaires de musique classique, 1861. Co-directed Paris Orphéon; founded Paris Oratorio Society, 1868.

Pashchenko, Andrey Filippovich (b. Rostov-on-Don, 3 Aug. 1885; d. Moscow, 16 Nov. 1972). Composer. Pupil of Vītols. Co-founded the Society for the Promotion of Contemporary Russian Music, 1923. His works, often on Soviet topics, include 17 operas (*The Eagle Revolt,* 1925); choral music; symphonies and other orchestral works; string quartets; romances; incidental and film music.

Pasillo [Sp.]. A dance originally derived from the European waltz, cultivated in the ballrooms and salons of 19th-century Colombia and Ecuador and practiced since in these countries and elsewhere in Latin America as an urban social dance.

Paso doble [Sp., double step]. One of the most characteristic national social dances of Spain, in moderately fast duple meter with a somewhat marchlike character.

Paspy. *Passepied.*

Pasquini, Bernardo (b. Massa da Valdinievole [now Massa e Cozzili], Lucca, 7 Dec. 1637; d. Rome, 21 Nov. 1710). Composer and keyboard player. Pupil of Cesti; associate of Corelli and A. Scarlatti. Organist at several churches in Rome (S. Maria Maggiore, ca. 1663); harpsichordist to Prince Giambattista Borghese. His pupils included Gasparini, Georg Muffat,

and possibly D. Scarlatti. Composed keyboard works (suites, variations, sonatas, toccatas); oratorios, operas, and cantatas.

Pass, Joe [Passalaqua, Joseph Anthony Jacobi] (b. New Brunswick, N.J., 13 Jan. 1929; d. Los Angeles, 24 May 1994). Jazz guitarist. Toured with Oscar Peterson, as accompanist to Ella Fitzgerald and Sarah Vaughan, and as a soloist. Played occasionally in Count Basie's small groups.

Passacaglia. A continuous variation form, principally of the Baroque, whose basso ostinato formulas originally derived from *ritornellos to early 17th-century songs. These passacaglias or ritornellos were played on the guitar between stanzas or at the ends of songs, where they were repeated many times, probably with improvised variations; the practice began in Spain [Sp. *pasacalle*] and quickly moved to Italy and France. The passacaglia then developed in a way quite similar to the *chaconne. Its four-bar *ostinato became the basis for long sets of continuous variations as well as vocal pieces (e.g., by Frescobaldi). Early differences between chaconne and passacaglia were the particular chord progressions: the passacaglia tended to be in minor, with a I–IV–V or I–IV–V–I pattern. The bass lines themselves might change in successive phrases, or extra harmonies might be inserted, but these variants fell within a limited set of formulas. One of these formulas is the descending tetrachord used in so many operatic laments but appearing as well in pieces titled passacaglia. Bach's Passacaglia in C minor for organ BWV 582, employing an eight-bar ostinato, is perhaps the best-known 18th-century passacaglia and was used as a model by many later composers.

Passage. (1) Any section of a work, of indefinite length and not necessarily self-contained. (2) A succession of scales, arpeggios, or similar figures, often of considerable technical difficulty and intended to display virtuosity, but without particular musical substance; also passage work.

Passaggio [It.]. (1) Transition, modulation. (2) *Passage work. (3) An ornamental melodic passage, written or improvised; also the introductory flourishes on manual or pedals in German Baroque toccatas. See Diminutions.

Passamezzo [Eng., also passing measures, passymeasures], **Pass'e mezo** [It., also *pass'e mezzo, passo e mezo, passomezo*]. An Italian dance of the 16th and early 17th centuries similar to a *pavana;* indeed, the musical style of the common *pavana* cannot be distinguished from that of a *pass'e mezo.* In all probability, the *pass'e mezo* was a type of *pavana.* Like the *pavana,* it was usually coupled to a *saltarello,* a *gagliarda,* or a *padovana.* Dances coupled together were composed on the same melodic and/or harmonic patterns. A large proportion of the *pass'e mezi,* a few *pavane,* and at least one-fifth of all 16th-century dances (including *saltarelli, gagliarde, padovane,* etc.) are composed on two harmonic patterns known as the *pass'e mezo antico* [Ex. 1] and the *pass'e mezo moderno* (*commune, novo*) [Ex. 2]. No particular discant was associated with the two patterns.

or

Passamezzo.

Passecaille [Fr.]. *Passacaglia.

Passepied [Fr.]. A lively, simple Baroque dance in triple meter (often 3/8). It has an upbeat, regular two- or four-measure phrases, and homophonic texture. The dance steps encourage the exploitation of a hemiola figure, e.g., a 3/4 measure formed from two measures in the midst of 3/8 motion. It was popular in French stage and harpsichord music of the late 17th and early 18th centuries.

Passer [Fr., pass]. In timpani parts, to retune from one specified pitch to another.

Passing chord. A chord occurring within the prolongation of some harmony and introduced over a passing tone [see Counterpoint] in the bass; also any chord whose function is clearly subordinate to those preceding and following and one or more of whose elements is introduced as a passing tone.

Passing tone. See Counterpoint.

Passion music. A musical setting of Jesus' sufferings and death as related by one of the four Evangelists. In the Roman Catholic liturgy the *Passio Domini nostri Jesu Christi* is enacted or performed on Palm Sunday (Matthew 26:36–75; 27:1–60), Tuesday (Mark 14:32–72; 15:1–46), Wednesday (Luke 22:39–71; 23:1–53), and Good Friday (John 18:1–40; 19:1–42) of Holy Week. The parts of Christ, the narrating

Evangelist, and direct speakers other than Christ (Pilate, Judas, etc.) are taken, respectively, by the celebrant, the deacon, and the subdeacon; the part of the crowd (*turba*) is usually taken by the congregation. Since the Second Vatican Council, chanting of the Latin Passion has been replaced in virtually all North American Catholic dioceses by reading of the vernacular Passion.

Plainsong Passions, like other Scriptural readings, are chanted on specific reciting tones, or *tubae.* Between ca. 1450 and ca. 1550, the monophonic Passion tone was either augmented or replaced by polyphony. The manner in which a polyphonic Passion sets its text is closely coordinated with the nature of the text employed.

Responsorial Passions are so named because they preserve both the traditional Passion narratives (according to the Vulgate or Luther's German) and the tripartite division of their recitation. At first, polyphony was restricted to the speeches of the crowds. A more developed approach is found in late 15th-century English Passions, in which the *turba* speeches are set for six to eight voices or in which all direct speeches are set with four-voice polyphony. This anticipates a north Italian repertory that begins with two four-voice Passions (St. Matthew and St. John) written before 1541 by Gasparo Alberti. These works set all direct speech, including Christ's, in polyphonic textures. This north Italian Passion was soon introduced into German-speaking lands, where the new Lutheran chorale style was integrated with the motet style prevalent in the responsorial Passion. Johann Walter had set Luther's translation of the Vulgate narratives (St. Matthew and St. John) before ca. 1530, however, and in so doing adapted the Latin Passion tones to the requirements of German.

Dramatic Passions are 17th-century settings that follow the text of Luther's Bible, but may be compilations of several Evangelists. The vocal writing is unaccompanied but borrows elements of operatic recitative and aria. These contrast with more conservative melodic elements related to both plainsong and the chorale. The result is a new and vivid kind of unaccompanied Passion that is quite independent of the older Passion tones. The three Passions of Schütz (St. Luke, St. John, and St. Matthew; 1665–66) are the outstanding specimens of this genre.

Motet or through-composed Passions conflate the four Gospel narratives into a single condensed text that is then treated like any other motet text. Works of this type were composed throughout the 16th century.

Oratorio Passions interpolate non-Biblical texts and set the Evangelist's narrative in *recitative style with continuo accompaniment [see also Oratorio]. When an instrumental ensemble is specified, it is used for interpolated sinfonias, arias, and choruses, written in imitation of the latest Italian operatic styles. Another important feature after 1650 is the inclusion of chorale tunes. The apex of the oratorio Passion is reached in the settings of *St. John (BWV 245) and *St. Matthew (BWV 244) by Bach.

Passion oratorios set poetic paraphrases of the Biblical accounts that were written under the influence of the early 18th-century Pietist movement. Keiser was the first (1712) of many (including Handel, Telemann, and Mattheson) to set Barthold Heinrich Brockes's *Der für die Sünde der Welt gemarterte und sterbende Heiland Jesus*. The most popular Passion oratorio of the later 18th and the 19th century was *Der Tod Jesu* (1755) by Carl Heinrich Graun. Despite its title, this account completely omits the trial and death of Jesus.

Composers of Passions in the 20th century, including Distler, Pepping, Pinkham, and Penderecki, have drawn on various of the historical types.

Passy-measures. *Passamezzo.

Pasta [née Negri], **Giuditta (Maria Costanza)** (b. Saronno, near Milan, 28 Oct. 1797; d. Blevio, Como, 1 Apr. 1865). Soprano. Studied at the Milan Conservatory. Debut, Brescia, 1815. Sang first performances of *La sonnambula* (Amina, 1831), *Norma* (1831), and *Anna Bolena* (1830).

Pasticcio [It., hodgepodge], **pastiche** [Fr.]. (1) Any work assembled from bits of other works and, at least by implication, therefore lacking artistic coherence. (2) A composite vocal work, usually an opera, containing music by several different composers or music originally intended for several different works. Most often in the 18th century, a *pasticcio* was a product of accretion, with several composers and poets making their contributions over an extended period of time. The term is also used to describe works written by several composers at the same time, such as *Muzio Scevola* (act 1 by Mattei, act 2 by Bononcini, act 3 by Handel) and to works that borrow parts of previously existing works.

Pastoral Symphony. Beethoven's Symphony no. 6 in F major op. 68 (1808), published in 1809 with the title *Sinfonie pastorale*. Beethoven's inscriptions for the five movements are (in translation): (1) Awakening of Cheerful Feelings on Arrival in the Country; (2) Scene by the Brook; (3) Merrymaking of the Country Folk; (4) Storm; (5) Song of the Shepherds, Joy and Gratitude after the Storm. His comment on a violin part used at the first performance in 1808 reads, "Mehr Ausdruck der Empfindung als Malerei" (more expression of feeling than painting).

Pastorale [Fr., It., pastoral]. A work of literature or music that represents or evokes life in the countryside, especially that of shepherds. Pastoral poetry provided the texts for numerous madrigals of the late 16th century, and the tradition of staged pastoral plays was central to the development of *opera in both Italy and France. Pastoral themes also provided the subjects for numerous cantatas of the 17th and 18th centuries. In instrumental works of the period, pastoral life was evoked by such features as drone basses [see also *Musette*], dotted rhythms in moderate or slow 6/8 or 12/8 as in the *siciliana, and the use of double-reed instruments and flutes. Some of these features are still present in the final movement of Beethoven's *Pastoral* Symphony. Perhaps because of the tradition of Italian shepherds [see *Piffero*] playing bagpipes and shawms in the cities at Christmas, such music was often associated with the pastoral element in the Christmas story and thus with Christmas itself. Works in this tradition include Corelli's *Christmas Concerto, the *Pifa* of Handel's *Messiah,* and the opening sinfonia of Bach's *Christmas Oratorio.*

Pastorella [It.]. In the 17th and 18th centuries, a vocal and or instrumental work for Christmas drawing on pastoral elements of the Christmas story and often employing the associated musical conventions [see *Pastorale*].

Pastourelle [Fr.], **pastorela** [Prov.]. A strophic genre of the troubadours and the trouvères, whose subject is an amorous debate between a shepherdess [Prov. *pastora*] and a knight who wishes to seduce her.

Pater noster [Lat., Our Father]. The Lord's Prayer. In the Roman Catholic Church it has formed part of the Mass and of the hours of Lauds and Vespers. The text was set polyphonically in the Renaissance by Josquin, Willaert, Palestrina, and others, sometimes with the use of an associated liturgical melody.

Patetico [It.]. Pathetic, with great emotion.

Pathet [Jav., fr. constraint, limit]. A system of categories for tonal use in *slendro and *pelog *gendhing and pathetan for central Javanese *gamelan; often rendered *mode.

Pathétique [Fr., pathetic]. (1) Beethoven's Piano Sonata no. 8 in C minor op. 13 (completed ca. 1797–98). The first edition (1799) bears the title *Grande sonate pathétique*, which is possibly Beethoven's title or one sanctioned by him. (2) Tchaikovsky's Symphony no. 6 in B minor op. 74 (1893), titled *Symphonie pathétique* at his brother Modest's suggestion.

Pathetisch [Ger.]. Pathetic, with great emotion.

Patter song. A song whose text, usually humorous, is sung very rapidly. Numerous examples occur in the works of Gilbert and Sullivan.

Patterson, Paul (b. Chesterfield, 15 June 1947). Composer. Studied at the Royal Academy of Music, where he later taught, and with Bennett. Has worked with serial technique and electronic sound sources. Works include orchestral music (*Sinfonia,* 1983; concertos); choral music (*Mass of the Sea,* 1986; *Te Deum,* 1988); chamber music (*At the Still Point of the Turning World,* 1980; string quartet, 1986).

Patti, Adelina [Adela] **(Juana Maria)** (b. Madrid, 19 Feb. 1843; d. Craig-y-Nos, near Brecon, Wales, 27 Sept. 1919). Soprano. From a family of singers; moved to New York as a child. Debut, New York, 1859. Sang at Covent Garden 1861–85. Toured widely in Europe and the U.S. Roles included Lucia, Aida, Amina (*La sonnambula).* Farewell concert, Albert Hall, 1906.

Pauke [Ger.]. Kettledrum.

Paul, Les [Polfus, Lester] (b. Waukesha, Wis., 9 June 1915). Popular guitarist, inventor. Played on country, jazz, and popular recordings, sometimes with his wife, Mary Ford ("How High the Moon," 1951). Invented the solid-body electric guitar and several forms of electric guitar pickup; pioneered multitrack recording and overdubbing.

Paulus, Stephen (Harrison) (b. Summit, N.J., 24 Aug. 1949). Composer. Pupil of Argento. Works include operas (*The Postman Always Rings Twice,* St. Louis, 1982; *The Woman at Otowi Crossing,* 1995); orchestral pieces; chamber music (*American Vignettes,* cello, piano, 1988); choral music (*Voices,* 1980; *Whitman's Dream,* 1995); songs and song cycles (*Letters from Colette,* 1986).

Pauman, Conrad [Konrad] (b. Nuremberg, ca. 1410; d. Munich, 24 Jan. 1473). Organist, lutenist, and composer. Blind from birth. By 1446, organist at St. Sebald, Nuremberg; from 1447 town organist. From 1450, served Dukes of Bavaria in Munich. Traveled widely in Europe. Works include 1 Tenorlied and 4 didactic *fundamenta* for organ. Credited with inventing German lute tablature.

Paumgartner, Bernhard (b. Vienna, 14 Nov. 1887; d. Salzburg, 27 July 1971). Composer, conductor, and musicologist. Studied with Adler. During World War I, collected soldiers' songs. Director, Salzburg Mozarteum, 1917–38; 1945–59; president, Salzburg Festival, 1960–71. Wrote several biographies and other books on music; edited works of Haydn, Mozart, and Corelli. Composed operas, ballets, incidental music, orchestral music, and songs.

Paur, Emil (b. Czernowitz, Bukovina, 29 Aug. 1855; d. Mistek, Moravia, 7 June 1932). Violinist, conductor. Pupil of Hellmesberger. Conductor of the Leipzig Stadttheater, 1891; Boston Symphony, from 1893; New York Philharmonic Society, 1898–1902; Pittsburgh Symphony, 1904–10. Director of the National Conservatory, New York, 1898–1902.

Pauroso [It.]. Timid, fearful.

Pausa [It., Sp.]. Rest.

Pause. (1) *Fermata. (2) A breathing pause [Ger. *Atempause, Luftpause*], often indicated by an apostrophe above the staff; it is a slight break in the musical line to allow the singer or player to draw breath or merely to mark the end of a phrase. (3) [Fr., Ger.] Rest. See also *Generalpause.*

Pavan. *Pavana.*

Pavana [It., Sp.; Fr. *pavane, pavenne;* Eng. *pavan, paven, pavin*]. A 16th-century court dance of Italian provenance. The word is derived from Pava, a dialect form of Padua; music and literature as well as dances from Pava or in the Paduan style were described as *alla pavana.* The dance became popular early in the century and quickly spread throughout Europe. It attained its highest point of artistic perfection under the aegis of the English virginalists, including William Byrd, John Bull, Orlando Gibbons, Thomas Tomkins, Thomas Morley, Giles Farnaby, Peter Philips, and John Dowland. Under the title *paduana,* it flourished briefly in the early 17th century in Germany, where it was used as the introductory movement of the German suite. More recent examples, actually re-creations of the earlier idealized dance form, have been written by Saint-Saëns, Ravel ("Pavane pour une infante défunte"), and Vaughan Williams.

The *pavana* is a slow, processional type of dance, for the most part employing a continuous repetition of basic step patterns. Usually, the *pavana* is followed by one of the faster dances, the *saltarello,* the *gagliarda,* the *padovana,* or the *piva.* Most dances in the genre are in a simple quadruple meter (4/2 or 4/4). Musically they resemble the *pass'e mezo* [see Passamezzo].

Pavaniglia [It.]. An instrumental dance and dance song of uncertain origin, most popular in Italy from the late 16th to the mid-17th century. Non-Italian sources refer to it as the "Spanish pavana," perhaps because it is one of the variant harmonic-melodic patterns that led to the *folia.*

Pavarotti, Luciano (b. Modena, 12 Oct. 1935). Tenor. Debut, Reggio Emilia, 1961. First sang at La Scala, 1965; Metropolitan Opera debut, 1968. Has made numerous recordings of operas (mainly Italian), as well as of light repertory, and has appeared often on television, sometimes as one of the "Three Tenors" (with Carreras and Domingo).

Pavillon [Fr.]. (1) The bell of a wind instrument; *p. en l'air,* an instruction to play with the bell raised. (2) *Pavillon chinois,* *Turkish crescent.

Payne, Anthony (b. London, 2 Aug. 1936). Composer. Music critic for the *Daily Telegraph.* Works include *Concerto for Orchestra* (1974); chamber music (*Echoes of Courtly Love,* brass quintet, 1987; *Sea Change,* flute, clarinet, harp, string quartet, 1988); cantatas and other choral music (*Hoquetus David,* 1987).

Paz, Juan Carlos (b. Buenos Aires, 5 Aug. 1901; d. there, 25 Aug. 1972). Composer. Pupil of d'Indy. Worked with twelve-tone technique. Composed orchestral works (suite for Ibsen's *Juliano Emperador,* 1931; *Passacaglia,* 1936; rev. 1953; *Música para piano y orquesta,* 1964); chamber music (2 concertos for winds and piano; string quartets; *Continuidad 1953,* percussion); piano works (3 sonatas; *Tres movimientos de jazz,* 1932; *Diez piezas sobre una serie dodecafónica,* 1936); the song "Abel" (1929; his only vocal composition). Published several books on 20th-century music.

Peacock, Gary (b. Burley, Idaho, 12 May 1935). Jazz double bass player. Joined Bill Evans, 1962–63. In Albert Ayler's group, carried free jazz bass playing to the extreme, abandoning timekeeping in favor of improvised melody. Toured Japan with Paul Bley, 1976; 1977, began recording as a leader. In 1983, formed a trio with Keith Jarrett and Jack DeJohnette.

Peal. See Change ringing.

Pears, Peter (Neville Luard) (b. Farnham, 22 June 1910; d. Aldeburgh, 3 Apr. 1986). Tenor. Attended the Royal College of Music. Beginning in 1937, often appeared in recital with Britten, who wrote principal tenor roles in many operas for him. Operatic debut, London, 1942; 1943, joined Sadler's Wells opera troupe, where he premiered *Peter Grimes,* 1945. Cofounded the Aldeburgh Festival, 1948. Also a renowned interpreter of lieder and of the part of the Evangelist in Bach's Passions.

Peasant Cantata. See *Bauernkantate.*

Pêcheurs de perles, Les [Fr., The Pearl Fishers]. Opera in three acts by Bizet (libretto by Michel Carré and Eugène Cormon) produced in Paris in 1863. Setting: legendary Ceylon.

Ped. Abbr. for *pedal.

Pedal. (1) On the piano, any of several levers operated by the foot, especially the one that removes all of the dampers from contact with the strings [see Piano]; hence, as a verb, to use the damper pedal [for associated symbols, see Notation]. (2) In organs, the pedal keyboard; also the entire Pedal Division, consisting of wind-chests and pipes [see also Pedalboard]. (3) *Pedal point. (4) *Pedal tone. See also Harp, Harpsichord, Kettledrum, Pedal harpsichord, Pedal piano.

Pedalboard. The pedal keyboard of the organ, with a modern range of C–f' or g'.

Pedalcembalo [Ger.]. *Pedal harpsichord.

Pedal clarinet. Contrabass *clarinet.

Pedal drum. Pedal *kettledrum.

Pedalflügel [Ger.]. *Pedal piano.

Pedal glissando. On the *kettledrum, a glissando produced by striking the drum and operating the pedal to vary its pitch.

Pedal harp. Double-action *harp.

Pedal harpsichord [Ger. *Pedalcembalo*]. A *harpsichord equipped with a pedalboard like that of an organ. A number of Italian 16th- and 17th-century harpsichords, even spinets, exist that can be seen formerly to have had pedalboards attached by cords to the corresponding manual keys, the lowest 8 to 15 notes from the low C (*short octave). Separate instruments to be placed under the harpsichord on the floor are known to have existed in 17th- and 18th-century France and Germany.

Pédalier [Fr.]. Pedal keyboard.

Pedaliter [Lat.]. To be played on the pedalboard of an organ.

Pedalklavier [Ger.]. *Pedal piano.

Pedalpauke [Ger.]. Pedal *kettledrum.

Pedal piano [Fr. *piano à pédalier;* Ger. *Pedalflügel, Pedalklavier;* It. *pianoforte con pedaliera;* Sp. *piano con pedalero*]. A piano equipped with a pedalboard similar to that of an organ. In some 18th-century instruments, a single set of strings was used for both pedalboard and manual keyboard. The norm in the 19th century was for a wholly independent instrument to be placed on the floor under a grand piano. Schumann (opp. 56, 58), Alkan (opp. 66, 69), and Gounod composed pieces for such instruments.

Pedal point [Fr. *pédale;* Ger. *Orgelpunkt;* It. *pedale;* Sp. *bajo de órgano, nota pedal*]. A sustained tone in the lowest register, occurring under changing harmonies in the upper parts; also pedal, organ point. In tonal music, pedal points may occur on any scale degree (and are often identified by the name of the scale degree), but the most common are those on the dominant, preparing a climactic return to the tonic, and on the tonic, as the final, summarizing statement of the tonic at the conclusion of a work.

Pedal steel guitar. An electric *zither, much used in *country and western music. Six or more strings are set over an unfretted fingerboard in a rectangular frame mounted on a stand. String tunings can be quickly changed by means of pedals and knee levers. The seated player uses a metal bar to stop the strings, sliding it along to produce a characteristic *portamento. See ill. under Guitar.

Pedal tone. On a brass instrument, the fundamental tone of a harmonic series, of which there will in principle be one for each slide position or combination of valves [see Acoustics]. On some instruments such as the trumpet, however, pedal tones are not easily produced because of the shape and size of the mouthpiece, which is intended to facilitate playing the higher harmonics.

Pedreira, José Enrique (b. San Juan, 2 Feb. 1904; d. there, 25 Dec. 1959). Composer. Studied in San Juan and New York. Taught in San Juan; accompanied visiting artists in recital. Composed piano works (2 sonatas, waltzes, *Capricho ibérico,* many *danzas*); the ballet *Jardin de piedra;* a piano concerto; chamber music and songs.

Pedrell, Felipe (b. Tortosa, Spain, 19 Feb. 1841; d. Barcelona, 19 Aug. 1922). Scholar, composer. Choirboy at the cathedral; moved to Barcelona, 1873. Studied in Rome, 1876–77. Taught at the Madrid Conservatory, 1895–1903. Worked at bringing to light Spain's musical past and encouraging contemporary composition of a recognizable Spanish character. Compositions include the operatic trilogy *Los Pirineos* (1890–91). Published scholarly editions, biography, a collection of Spanish folk songs, essays on contemporary and folk music.

Peer Gynt Suite. Either of two orchestral suites by Grieg, op. 46 (1888) and op. 55 (1891–92), arranged from his incidental music op. 23 (1874–76; rev. 1885) to Ibsen's play *Peer Gynt.*

Peerce, Jan [Perelmuth, Jacob Pincus] (b. New York, 3 June 1904; d. there, 15 Dec. 1984). Tenor. Sang on Radio City Music Hall broadcasts. Debut, 1938, in Beethoven's Ninth Symphony with Toscanini. Joined the Metropolitan Opera, 1941–68; sang with many other U.S. and European companies, including the Bolshoi Opera, Moscow. Played Tevye in *Fiddler on the Roof* on Broadway, 1971.

Peeters, Flor (b. Tielen, near Antwerp, 4 July 1903; d. Antwerp, 4 July 1986). Composer and organist. Pupil of Dupré and Tournemire. Organist at the Mechelen Cathedral from 1925. Taught at the Lemmens Institute and the conservatories of Ghent, Tilburg, and Antwerp (director, 1952–68). Published didactic organ works, including *Ars organi* (1952–54) and an accompaniment method for Gregorian chant

(1943). Influenced by early Flemish polyphony and Flemish folk song. Composed numerous organ works (*Hymn Preludes for the Liturgical Year,* 24 vols., 1959–64; pieces with orchestra); piano and chamber music; sacred choral works.

Pegbox [Fr. *chevillier;* Ger. *Wirbelkasten;* It. *cassetta dei bischeri, cavigliera;* Sp. *clavijero*]. In stringed instruments, a continuation of the neck, into which are inserted the tuning pegs that control the tension of the strings; especially the type found in the violin and related instruments in which the pegs are inserted from the side. When the pegs are inserted from above or below (i.e., perpendicular to the plane of the strings), as on the *ukulele and some *banjos, the terms pegdisc and pegboard are sometimes used. See also Machine head.

Pegdisc. See Pegbox.

Peiko, Nikolay Ivanovich (b. Moscow, 12 Mar. 1916). Composer. Pupil of Myaskovsky. Taught at the Moscow Conservatory, 1942–59; from 1954 at the Gnesin Institute. Assistant to Shostakovich, 1944. Works include operas, ballets, 8 symphonies, other orchestral works, chamber music, vocal works, incidental music, and film and radio scores.

Peine entendu, à [Fr.]. Barely audible.

Peixinho, Jorge (Manuel Rosado Marques) (b. Montijo, Portugal, 20 Jan. 1940). Composer and pianist. Pupil of Boulez, Stockhausen, Koenig, and Nono. Taught at the Oporto Conservatory, Brazil, and at the New University of Lisbon. Works include *Recitativo II* (music theater, 1966–70); *Kinetofonias* (25 strings, 3 tape recorders, 1965–69); *Sucessões simétricas II* (orchestra, 1971); many vocal, chamber, and piano pieces.

Peking Opera. A type of Chinese musical theater combining speech, stylized gestures, and acrobatics, which has dominated the national stage since the 19th century. The genre uses a repertory of about 30 preexistent tune types. Each of the individual tune types is named and may be easily recognized. By setting the same tune to different texts, new arias are produced. The orchestra, which sits on stage left, is divided into two ensembles. The melodic ensemble, consisting of an *erh-hu (erhu) and a *ching-hu (two-stringed spike fiddles of different sizes), a *yüeh-ch'in (yueqin, a moon-shaped, four-stringed plucked lute), and a san-hsien (sanxian, a three-stringed plucked lute), accompanies the singing in heterophony. The percussion ensemble, consisting of a pan-ku (bangu, a one-headed drum resting on a wooden tripod, played with two sticks), a pan (ban, wooden clappers), a t'ang-ku (tanggu, a large barrel-drum played with two sticks), and large and small gongs and cymbals, plays conventional rhythmic patterns of varying length and complexity to indicate dramatic situations and changes of mood as well as to provide rhythmic drive for the action. In addition, a *sona* (oboe) is used for special sound effects or in military scenes.

Pelham, Peter, III (b. London, 9 Dec. 1721; d. Richmond, Va., 28 Apr. 1805). Organist and composer. His family settled in Boston, 1726. Studied with the son of Johann Pachelbel. Taught in Charleston, S.C., 1740–42. Organist at Trinity Church, Boston, from 1743; at Bruton Church, Williamsburg, after 1755. Appeared as soloist and theater accompanist.

Pelissier, Victor (b. ?Paris, ca. 1750; d. prob. New Jersey, ca. 1820). Composer and horn player. Joined the Old American Company, New York, 1793, as horn player, composer, and arranger. Composed songs and piano pieces (*Pelissier's Columbian Melodies,* 12 vols., 1811–12); operas (*Edwin and Angelina,* New York, 1796); pantomimes; melodramas (*Ariadne,* New York, 1797 [lost]); instrumental pieces.

Pelléas et Mélisande [Fr., Pelléas and Mélisande]. (1) Opera in five acts by Debussy (to his abridgment of the play by Maurice Maeterlinck), begun in 1893 and produced in Paris in 1902. Setting: the fictional kingdom of Allemonde in legendary times. (2) A symphonic poem by Schoenberg, op. 5 (1902–3), based on Maeterlinck's play. (3) A suite of incidental music to Maeterlinck's play by Fauré, op. 80 (1898).

Pellet bell. A small, rounded, metal vessel with slits or other openings and containing a loose pebble or bit of metal that rattles when the bell is shaken; also called a crotal. *Sleigh bells are of this type. See also Idiophone.

Pelletier, (Louis) Wilfrid (b. Montreal, 20 June 1896; d. New York, 9 Apr. 1982). Conductor and pianist. Pianist and later conductor (1929–50) at the Metropolitan Opera. Cofounded the Montreal Symphony, 1934; the Quebec Conservatoire, 1942.

Pelog [Indonesian, fr. Jav.]. One of the two major tunings (the other being *slendro*) that serve as background tunings for the interpretation of melodies performed by *gamelan* instrumentalists and singers in central and east Java.

Peñalosa, Francisco de (b. Talavera de la Reina, ca. 1470; d. Seville, 1 Apr. 1528). Composer. Singer in the chapel of Ferdinand V from 1498. Canon at the Cathedral of Seville from 1505. *Maestro de capilla* to Prince Ferdinand in Burgos, 1511–16; member of the papal chapel, 1517–21. Composed Masses, Magnificats, motets, hymns, and a few secular vocal works.

Penderecki, Krzysztof (b. Dębica, 23 Nov. 1933). Composer. Pupil of Malawski and Wiechowicz. Taught at the Kraków Conservatory. Has worked with serialism, electronic sound production, and graphic notation. Works include the operas *Diably z Loudun* [The Devils of Loudun] (1969); *Paradise Lost* (1978); *Die schwarze Maske* (1984–86); *Ubu Rex* (1990–91); choral music (*St. Luke Passion,* 1963–65; *Utrenia* [The Laying in the Tomb], 1971–72; *Veni creator; Song of Cherubim,* 1987); orchestral works (*Anaklasis,* 1960; *Threnody for the Victims of Hiroshima,* strings, 1960; 4 symphonies; cello concerto; *Sinfonietta,* 1991); chamber works (*Die unterbrochene Gedanke,* string quartet, 1988); works for electronic tape.

Penillion [Welsh]. An improvised Welsh song sung to the accompaniment of the harp and forming part of the tradition of the *bards.

Penitential psalms. Psalms 6, 31 [32], 37 [38], 50 [51], 101 [102], 129 [130], and 142 [143] [for the numbering of the Psalms, see Psalter].

Pennario, Leonard (b. Buffalo, 9 July 1924). Pianist. Studied with Vengerova and at the Univ. of Southern California. Recorded chamber music with Piatigorsky and Heifetz; toured and recorded as recitalist and orchestral soloist, playing a wide repertory. Rozsa wrote a concerto for him.

Penniman, Richard. See Little Richard.

Penny whistle. A small, metal *duct flute with six finger holes; also called a tin whistle.

Pentachord. A collection of five pitches; the arrangement of intervals that defines the structure of a collection of five pitches. *Octave species are often defined as consisting of one pentachord plus one *tetrachord.

Pentatonic. A scale consisting of five pitches or pitch classes; music based on such a scale. Scales of this type, of which there are many, are widely distributed geographically and historically. Western writers have sometimes given prominence to two types that can be (but, in other cultures, have not necessarily been) derived from the Western diatonic scale: (1) a scale of the form C D E G A or some reordering (or mode, depending on which pitch is taken as central) of this relationship (embodied, e.g., in the black keys of the piano), which, because it lacks semitones, is sometimes termed anhemitonic and which, because it seems to omit members of the seven-tone (heptatonic) diatonic scale, is sometimes inappropriately termed a gapped scale; (2) scales that do include semitones in the forms C E F G B or C E F A B. Pentatonic scales, especially of this first type, have sometimes been used in 19th- and 20th-century Western art music.

Pentland, Barbara (b. Winnipeg, 2 Jan. 1912). Composer and pianist. Pupil of Jacobi, Wagenaar, and Copland. Taught at the Toronto Conservatory from 1943; at the Univ. of British Columbia, 1949–63. Has worked with serialism, aleatoric procedures, and microtones. Works include a chamber opera and a ballet, incidental music, radio and film scores; orchestral music (*Symphony for Ten Parts*, 1957); string quartets; *Tides* (violin, marimba, and harp, 1984); piano music; choral pieces; *Disasters of the Sun* (mezzo-soprano, 9 instruments, and tape, 1976); songs.

Pépin, (Jean-Josephat) Clermont (b. St. Georges-de-Beauce, Quebec, 15 May 1926). Composer and pianist. Pupil of Champagne, Scalero, Jolivet, Honegger, and Messiaen. Taught at the Quebec Conservatory, Montreal, 1955–64 (director, 1967–72). Has employed serial techniques. Works include ballets and incidental music; *Guernica* (symphonic poem, 1952), symphonies (no. 3, *Quasars*, 1967); string quartets; piano music; vocal music (*Trois Incantations*, 1987).

Pepper, Art [Arthur Edward, Jr.] (b. Gardena, Calif., 1 Sept. 1925; d. Panorama, Calif., 1 June 1982). Jazz alto saxophonist. Joined the big bands of Benny Carter (1943) and Stan Kenton (1943, 1946–51). Recorded with Miles Davis's hard bop rhythm section, 1957. A leading soloist in the West Coast jazz style; from 1977, incorporated elements of free jazz.

Pepping, Ernst (b. Duisburg, 12 Sept. 1901; d. Berlin, 1 Feb. 1981). Composer. Studied at the Berlin Hochschule for Music; taught there, 1953–68. Composed much music for the German Protestant church (*Spandauer Chorbuch*, 1934–41; rev., 1962; *Grosses Orgelbuch*, 1939); organ music (preludes, fugues, concertos, partitas); sacred and secular choral music (Te Deum, 1956); 3 symphonies; chamber and piano music; songs. Published 2 books on music.

Pepusch, Johann Christoph [John Christopher] (b. Berlin, 1667; d. London, 20 July 1752). Composer. Served the Prussian court from 1681; settled in London by 1704. Musician at Drury Lane; organist and composer to the Duke of Chandos. In 1710, co-founded the Academy of Ancient Music. Arranged music for the *Beggar's Opera*. Composed stage works (*Venus and Adonis*, 1715); church music; cantatas (*Alexis*, 1710); instrumental works. Published a *Treatise on Harmony* (1730).

Perahia, Murray (b. New York, 19 Apr. 1947). Pianist and conductor. Debut, 1972, with the New York Philharmonic. Artistic director at the Aldeburgh Festival from 1982. Best known for his renditions of Mozart piano concertos, many of which he conducts from the keyboard.

Percussion instruments [Fr. *instruments à percussion* (of the orchestra, *batterie*); Ger. *Schlaginstrument, Schlagzeug;* It. *percussione;* Sp. *percusión, batería*]. Musical instruments that produce sound by being struck or, less often, scraped, shaken, or plucked. In more formal classifications of musical *instruments, they are usually divided between *membranophones and *idiophones, with both categories including instruments of definite as well as indefinite pitch. Percussion instruments, including those illustrated here, are described in this dictionary in separate entries; see especially Drum.

Perdendosi [It.]. Dying away.

Pérez, David [Davide] (b. Naples, 1711; d. Lisbon, 30 Oct. 1778). Composer. From 1738, served the Royal Chapel at Naples; *maestro di cappella,* 1741. From 1752, served King José I in Lisbon. Composed operas for Naples, Rome, Vienna, and Lisbon (*Demofoonte,* 1752; *Solimano,* 1757; *Creusa in Delfo,* 1774); also sacred and secular vocal works (cantatas; 8 Masses; and an oratorio).

Perfect. See Cadence, Interval, Mensural notation, Absolute pitch.

Performance marks. Words, abbreviations, and symbols employed along with the notation of pitch and duration to indicate aspects of performance. These may be tempo indications, dynamic marks, technical instructions, marks for *phrasing and articulation, and designations for the character of the piece or section.

Tempo marks indicate the speed, and frequently the character, of the music [see also Tempo]. The most commonly used terms are Italian: *grave* (very slow, serious), *largo* (broad), *lento* (slow), *adagio* (slow; literally, at ease), *andante* (literally, walking), *moderato* (moderate), *allegretto, allegro* (fast; literally, cheerful), *vivace* (lively), *presto* (very fast), *prestissimo* (as fast as possible). Gradual and relative changes of tempo are indicated by *ritardando,* abbreviated *rit.* (slowing), *accelerando* (quickening), and *più mosso* (faster). Prior to the 17th century, tempo designations are rare. In music of the 14th through 16th centuries, tempo is indicated principally by the mensuration signs and *proportions of *mensural notation in conjunction with the concept of *tactus or fixed pulse [see Tempo]. In the early 17th century, *tardo* (slow), *presto* (fast), *lento, adagio,* and *allegro* appeared with increasing regularity in Italian and other music. Although Italian markings have predominated, non-Italian composers have always to some degree retained their vernaculars for musical terminology. During the late 17th and early 18th cen-

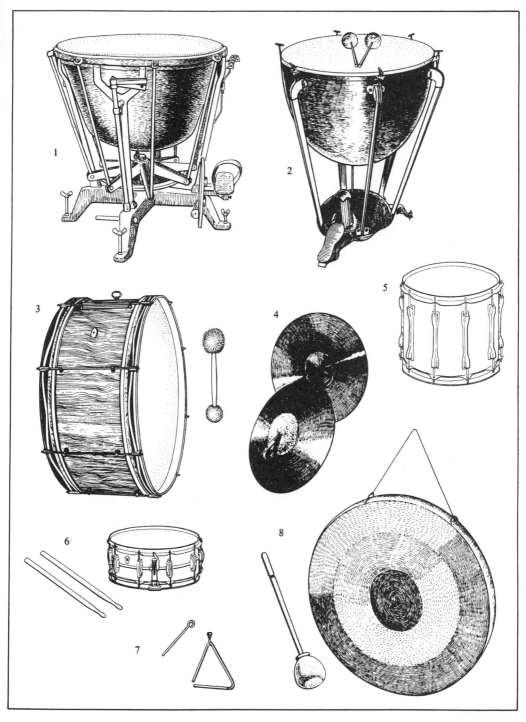

Percussion instruments: 1. Kettledrum: Ringer type. 2. Kettledrum: Professional model. 3. Bass drum. 4. Cymbals. 5. Tenor drum. 6. Side (snare) drum. 7. Triangle. 8. Tam-tam.

Percussion instruments: 1. Glockenspiel.   2. Xylophone.   3. Marimba.   4. Crotales.   5. Celesta.   6. Tubular bells.

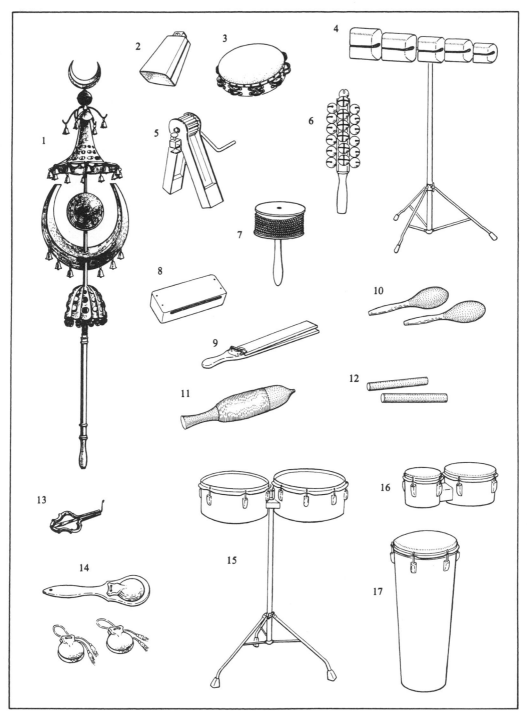

Percussion instruments (not all drawn to same scale): 1. Turkish crescent. 2. Cowbell. 3. Tambourine.
4. Temple blocks. 5. Ratchet. 6. Sleigh bells. 7. Cabaça. 8. Wood block. 9. Slapstick. 10. Maracas. 11. Güiro.
12. Claves. 13. Jew's harp. 14. Castanets. 15. Timbales. 16. Bongos. 17. Conga.

Drum set.

turies, the French developed a system of terms as comprehensive as the Italian. During the 19th century, German terms were codified into an elaborate system as well.

Dynamic marks indicate degrees of loudness and are also customarily written in Italian, usually abbreviated: *pianissimo, pp* (very soft); *piano, p* (soft); *mezzo piano, mp* (moderately soft); *mezzo forte, mf* (moderately loud); *forte, f* (loud; literally, strong); *fortissimo, ff* (very loud). Continuous change from one degree of loudness to another may be specified by the terms *crescendo* (getting louder) and *diminuendo* or *decrescendo* (getting softer) or by the symbols ⟨ and ⟩, respectively. Dynamic changes were almost certainly a part of performance earlier, but, like tempos, only came to be notated with any regularity in the 17th century. Until the late 18th century, however, such notations were far from extensive.

Further performance marks include verbal technical instructions, e.g., *con sordino* (play with mute), *tutti* (the whole ensemble plays), *arco* (play with the bow); symbols denoting *phrasing and articulation like slurs, dots, lines, accent symbols, wedges, terms like *sforzato, sf,* and strokes over notes—symbols that, like tempo designations, generally have rather different interpretations for different periods and styles; *fingerings for stringed and keyboard instruments, *tonguings for wind instruments, *bowings for stringed instruments, and pedalings for piano, all affecting articulation and phrasing; directions concerning the general character of a piece or section, e.g. *dolce* (sweet), *cantabile* (singing), *con spirito* (spirited), *sostenuto* (sustained), *marcato* (marked, emphasized). For the symbols employed, see Notation; for many of the terms mentioned here, see separate entries. See also Performance practice.

Performance practice [Ger., *Aufführungspraxis*]. The conventions and knowledge that enable a performer to create a performance. In the context of notated music, performance practice is usually thought to encompass everything about performance that is not unambiguously specified in notation. This, however, implies a distinction that is not readily made between what is notated and what is not notated. All notation requires an informed reader for its realization, and thus all notation is fundamentally incomplete. In this respect, performance practice is equally important in written and oral musical traditions. The status of the concept *composition in Western art music has sometimes obscured this similarity among diverse musical cultures and thus among the methods of study appropriate to them. The aspects of performance specified in Western *notation have, in general, steadily increased since the beginnings of this system in the Middle Ages. Historically, the study of performance practice has concentrated on periods and repertories in which the gap between what was notated and what was thought necessary for a performance (especially a historically authentic performance) was greatest. The recent history of this study has seen the extent and importance of this gap recognized in repertories ever closer to the present. Important topics in the study of performance practice for most periods through the 19th century have been *ornamentation and/or *improvisation, the changing character of musical instruments [see, e.g., Piano, Violin, Bow], tuning and temperament, the size and composition of ensembles [see, e.g., Orchestra, Chorus, Chapel (2)], *tempo, *articulation, *dynamics and other performance marks, and the nature of voice production and *singing styles.

Pergolesi, Giovanni Battista (b. Iesi, Marche, 4 Jan. 1710; d. Puzzuoli, near Naples, 16 Mar. 1736). Composer. Pupil of Vinci and Durante. *Maestro di cappella* to Prince Ferdinando Colonna Stigliano, 1732; to the Duke of Maddaloni from 1734. Composed dramatic works (*Lo frate 'nnamorato*, 1732; *Il prigionier superbo*, 1733, including *La *serva padrona; Adriano in Siria*, 1734; *Il Flaminio*, 1735); sacred dramas and oratorios; sacred vocal works (Masses; Psalms; Salve Regina and Stabat Mater, both 1736); chamber cantatas and other vocal works; a few instrumental pieces.

Peri, Jacopo ["Zazzerino"] (b. Rome, 20 Aug. 1561; d. Florence, 12 Aug. 1633). Composer and singer. Pupil of Malvezzi. Organist and singer in Florence from 1579. Probably participated in discussions of the "Camerata" during the 1580s. Composed dramatic works, often collaborating with other composers (*Dafne; *Euridice; La Flora*, 1628, with Marco Gagliano; *intermedi* and ballets); oratorios; songs (*Le varie musiche*, 1609); ricercars.

Périchole, La. Comic opera in two acts by Offenbach (French libretto by Henri Meilhac and Ludovic Halévy, after a play by Mérimée), produced in Paris in 1868, and in a three-act revision, in 1874. Setting: Peru.

Period. (1) A complete musical utterance, defined in tonal music by arrival at a cadence on some harmony that does not immediately require further resolution. In this sense, which is necessarily somewhat flexible, the musical term corresponds to the sentence (or period) in language. In the music of the late 18th and early 19th centuries especially, a period usually consists of two *phrases (an *antecedent and a consequent), each of which may be made up of still shorter subphrases. Periods may be joined to form larger periods.

(2) A musical element that is in some way repeated..

Perkins, Carl (b. Lake City, Tenn., 9 Apr. 1932; d. Jackson, Tenn., 19 Jan. 1998). Rock-and-roll and country singer, songwriter, and guitarist. His "Blue Suede Shoes" (1956) joined the recordings of Elvis Presley and Jerry Lee Lewis in establishing rock-and-roll. Toured with Johnny Cash, 1965–76.

Perkins, John Macivor (b. St. Louis, Mo., 2 Aug. 1935). Composer. Pupil of Boulanger, Rubbra, and Gerhard. Taught at the Univ. of Chicago (1962–65), Harvard (1965–70), and Washington Univ. (St. Louis, from 1970). Has used serial procedures. Works include a chamber opera; *Music for Orchestra* (1964); *Music for 13 Players* (mezzo-soprano and chamber ensemble, 1964–66); and *Caprice* (piano, 1963).

Perkinson, Coleridge-Taylor (b. New York, 14 June 1932). Composer and conductor. Pupil of Giannini, Mills, and Kim. Cofounder and conductor of the Symphony of the New World, 1965–75. Works include ballets (*To Bird with Love,* for Alvin Ailey, 1984); incidental music, film, and television scores; *Lamentations: A Black Folk Song Suite* (cello, 1973); *The Legacy* (narrator, solo voice, chorus, orchestra, 1982).

Perkowski, Piotr (b. Oweczacze, 17 Mar. 1901; d. Otwock, near Warsaw, 12 Aug. 1990). Composer. Pupil of Szymanowski and Roussel. Head of the Toruń Conservatory, 1936–39; 1945–49, of the Polish Composers' Union. Taught at the Warsaw and Wrocław Conservatories. Used elements of Polish folk music. Composed orchestral music, several ballets, choral and chamber music, and many songs.

Perle, George (b. Bayonne, N.J., 6 May 1915). Composer and theorist. Pupil of LaViolette and Krenek. Has taught at the Univ. of Louisville, the Univ. of California at Davis, and Queens College

(1961–84). Works include orchestral music (*Three Movements for Orchestra*, 1960; Cello Concerto, 1966; *Sinfonietta II*, 1990; 2 piano concertos); chamber music (Wind Quintet no. 4, Pulitzer Prize, 1986; Sonata a cinque, 1987; 8 string quartets); piano music (*6 New Etudes*, 1984; *Sonatina*, 1986); vocal music. Wrote books on his theory of twelve-tone composition and on the music of Schoenberg, Berg, and Webern.

Perlemuter, Vlado (b. Kaunas, Lithuania, 26 May 1904). Pianist. Pupil of Moszkowski and Cortot; had contact with Ravel, recording all of his piano music. Taught at the Paris Conservatoire from 1950; also known as an interpreter of Chopin.

Perlman, Itzhak (b. Tel Aviv, 31 Aug. 1945). Violinist. Stricken by polio at age 4. Appeared on the *Ed Sullivan Show*, 1958; settled in New York. Studied with Galamian and Dorothy DeLay. Debut, 1963. Has toured widely as orchestral soloist and in recital; appeared on television with Stern, Zukerman, and others. Has also performed jazz and ragtime. Teaches at Brooklyn College and at the City Univ. of New York.

Permutation fugue. A type of fugue or fugal passage, often found in the choral works of Bach, in which every voice enters with the same succession of a number of musical ideas equal to the number of voices, the second idea in each voice serving to accompany the first in the succeeding voice, etc.

Perosi, Lorenzo (b. Tortono, 21 Dec. 1872; d. Rome, 12 Oct. 1956). Composer and church musician. Studied in Rome, Milan, and Regensburg. From 1894, choirmaster of San Marco (Venice); 1898–1915 and from 1923, music director of the Sistine Chapel. Composed over 20 oratorios; Masses and many other sacred pieces; orchestral works; 18 string quartets and other chamber music; and organ music.

Pérotin [Perotinus Magnus] (fl. Paris, ca. 1200). Composer. Known through references by the theorists Anonymous IV and Johannes de Garlandia. He is said to have revised Léonin's *Magnus liber organi*, writing new clausulas. Also wrote 3- and 4-voiced organum (*Viderunt omnes; Sederunt principes; Alleluia, Posui adiutorium)* and conductus.

Perpetuum mobile [Lat., perpetual motion; It. *moto perpetuo*]. A composition in which rhythmic motion, often in a single note-value at rapid tempo, is continuous from beginning to end. Among composers who have used the term as a title for such a piece are Paganini (op. 11), Weber (Piano Sonata op. 24, last movement), Mendelssohn (op. 119), and Johann Strauss, Jr. (op. 257). The technique is also encountered in some Chopin etudes.

Perrin, Pierre (b. Lyons, ca. 1620; d. Paris, buried 26 Apr. 1675). Poet and librettist. In 1669, received a privilege to establish academies for the development of a French national opera. With Cambert, wrote *Pomone* (1671) for the inaugural production. Surrendered his privilege to Lully, 1672.

Perry, Julia (Amanda) (b. Lexington, Ky., 25 Mar. 1924; d. Akron, Ohio, 24 Apr. 1979). Composer. Pupil of Boulanger and Dallapiccola. Taught at Florida A.&M. (Tallahassee) and at Atlanta Univ. Employed black folk idioms in some works. Composed 3 operas and an opera-ballet; 12 symphonies, 2 piano concertos, and other orchestral works; pieces for voices and orchestra; chamber music; songs and arrangements of spirituals.

Perséphone. A *melodrama in three scenes for speaker, tenor, choruses, and orchestra by Stravinsky, after a poem by André Gide, first performed in Paris in 1934 and revised in 1949.

Persichetti, Vincent (b. Philadelphia, 6 June 1915; d. there, 15 Aug. 1987). Composer. Pupil of R. Harris and Nordoff. Taught at the Coombs Conservatory, Philadelphia, and at Juilliard School (from 1947). Works include a one-act opera; 9 symphonies, concertos, and other orchestral music; band pieces; Serenades and Parables for various solo instruments and ensembles; sonatas and other works for piano and for harpsichord; organ works; sacred and secular choral music (*Hymns and Responses for the Church Year*, 1955; a Mass; cantatas; *The Creation*, oratorio, 1969); songs; many pieces for amateurs. Published the book *Twentieth-Century Harmony*.

Perti, Giacomo Antonio (b. Bologna, 6 June 1661; d. there, 10 Apr. 1756). Composer. *Maestro di cappella* at the Cathedral of S. Pietro, Bologna, 1690–96; at S. Petronio, 1696–1756; at S. Domenico, 1704–55; at S. Maria, Galliera, 1706–50. His pupils included Torelli and G. B. Martini. Composed much sacred vocal music, often with strings; operas and oratorios.

Pertile, Aureliano (b. Montagnana, 9 Nov. 1885; d. Milan, 11 Jan. 1952). Tenor. Debut, Vicenza, 1911. Toured South America, 1918. Sang at the Metropolitan Opera (1921–22), La Scala (1922–37), and Covent Garden (1927–31). Taught in Rome from 1940; in Milan from 1946. Roles include those of Verdi (Otello and Radames) and Wagner (Lohengrin).

Pesante [It.]. Weighty, with emphasis.

Pescetti, Giovanni Battista (b. Venice, ca. 1704; d. there, 20 Mar. 1766). Composer and keyboardist. Pupil of Lotti. Directed the Opera of the Nobility, London, from 1736. By 1747, returned to Venice; second organist at St. Mark's from 1762. Works include *Siroe re di Persia* (with Galuppi, Venice, 1731); *Demetrio* (Florence, 1732); *Il Farnaspe* (Siena, 1750); *Artaserse* (Milan, 1751).

Peter and the Wolf [Russ. *Petya i volk*]. A work for small orchestra and narrator by Prokofiev, op. 67 (1936), in which each of the characters of the children's story being narrated is associated with a specific instrument and tune.

Peter Grimes. Opera in a prologue and three acts by Britten (libretto by Montagu Slater, after George Crabbe's poem "The Borough"), produced in London in 1945. Setting: the Borough, a fishing village on the east coast of England, about 1830.

Peter, Johann Friedrich [John Frederik] (b. Heerendijk, Holland, 19 May 1746; d. Bethlehem, Pa., 13 July 1813). Composer. From 1770, active in Moravian communities in America (1780–90, musical director of the congregation, Salem, N.C.). Works include concerted anthems; solo songs; and 6 quintets (1789), the oldest surviving chamber music composed in America.

Peters, Carl Friedrich (b. Leipzig, 30 March 1779; d. Sonnenstein, Bavaria, 20 Nov. 1827). Music publisher. In 1814, bought Kühnel's and Hoffmeister's Bureau de Musique, calling it Bureau de Musique C. F. Peters. In 1828, Carl Gotthelf Siegmund Böhme took over the firm and brought out works by J. S. Bach. From 1855 to 1860, the firm was run by the Leipzig town council and then by Julius Friedländer and Max Abraham, who became sole owner in 1880 and built a worldwide reputation for C. F. Peters by publishing first editions of important works, launching Edition Peters (1867), opening the Musikbibliothek Peters to the public (1894), and publishing the *Jahrbuch der Musikbibliothek Peters* from 1895.

Peters, Roberta (b. New York, 4 May 1930). Soprano. Sang at the Metropolitan Opera, 1951–85 (debut as Zerlina). Has appeared in concert and musical theater, on radio and television (as both singer and actress), and at other opera houses, including Covent Garden and the Vienna Staatsoper. Sang Violetta at the Bolshoi Opera, 1972.

Peterson, Oscar (Emmanuel) (b. Montreal, 15 Aug. 1925). Jazz pianist. Performed with Jazz at the Philharmonic from 1949. Formed a trio, 1951; among his sidemen have been Ray Brown, Barney Kessel, and Joe Pass. In 1974–75, recorded a series of duos with trumpeters, including Dizzy Gillespie and Roy Eldridge. Performed as an unaccompanied soloist from the 1970s.

Peterson-Berger, (Olaf) Wilhelm (b. Ullånger, Ångermanland, 27 Feb. 1867; d. Östersund, 3 Dec. 1942). Composer. Studied at the Stockholm Conservatory and in Dresden. Music critic for *Dagens nyheter*, Stockholm, 1896–1930; worked with the Stockholm Opera, 1908–10. Used Swedish folk materials. Composed music dramas (*Arnljot*, 1907–9); orchestral music (Symphony no. 3, "Lapland," 1913–15); choral pieces (*Sveagaldrar*, cantata, 1897); music for men's quartets; many songs (*Jämtlandsminnen* [Jämtland Memories], 1893); and piano music (*Färdminnen* [Travel Memories], 1908). Translated the writings of Wagner and Nietzsche.

Petrassi, Goffredo (b. Zagarola, near Palestrina, Italy, 16 July 1904). Composer and conductor. Attended the Conservatory of S. Cecilia; taught there from 1934. Has employed serial devices. Works include 2 operas (*Morte dell'aria*, 1948), ballets, and incidental music; 8 concertos, *Partita* (1933), and other orchestral music; choral works (*Salmo IX*, 1934; *Noche oscura*, 1951); chamber music (*Sonata da camera*, harpsichord and 10 instruments, 1948; *Sestina d'autunno* "Veni, creator Igor," 1982); a few piano pieces; solo vocal music; film scores.

Petrella, Errico (b. Palermo, 10 Dec. 1813; d. Genoa, 7 Apr. 1877). Composer. Studied with Costa, Zingarelli, and Bellini. Musical director at the Teatro Nuovo, Naples, from 1851. Composed operas, including *Elena di Tolosa* (1852), *Marco Visconti* (1854); *Jone* (1858); *I promessi sposi* (1869).

Petri, Egon (b. Hannover, 23 March 1881; d. Berkeley, Calif., 27 May 1962). Pianist. Pupil and protégé of Busoni. Taught at Royal Manchester College (1905–11) and the Berlin Hochschule (1921–26); toured Europe. Moved to the U.S., 1939; taught at Cornell (1944–46), Mills College (1947–57), and the San Francisco Conservatory (from 1957).

Petridis, Petros (John) (b. Nigde, Turkey, 23 July 1892; d. Athens, 17 Aug. 1977). Composer. Studied in Constantinople and in Paris with Wolff and Roussel. Taught at King's College, 1918–19. Music critic for Greek and British periodicals. Incorporated elements of Greek folk songs and Byzantine music. Works include concertos; symphonies (no. 1, "Greek," 1928–29; no. 4, "Doric," 1941–43); the opera *Zefyra* (1923–25; rev. 1958–64); the oratorio *Hayos Pavlos* (1950).

Petrov, Andrei Pavlovich (b. Leningrad, 2 Sept. 1930). Composer. Studied at the Leningrad Conservatory; taught there, 1961–63. Has composed popular songs and film scores; his concert music often draws on jazz and popular styles. Works include ballets (*The Creation of the World*, 1971); operas (*Peter the First*, 1975; *Mayakovsky Begins*, 1985); symphonic works (*The Master and Margarita*, 1985); chamber music.

Petrov, Osip (Afanas'yevich) (b. Elizavetgrad [now Kirovograd], 15 Nov. 1806 or 1807; d. St. Petersburg, 12 Mar. 1878). Bass-baritone. Pupil of Cavos. Debut, St. Petersburg, 1830. Roles written for him include Glinka's *A Life for the Tsar* (1836) and *Ruslan* (1842); Varlaam in Mussorgsky's *Boris Godunov* (1874); the Mayor in Tchaikovsky's *Vakula the Smith* (1876).

Petrovics, Emil (b. Nagybecskerek [now Zrenjanin], 9 Feb. 1930). Composer. Pupil of Sugár, Viski, and Farkas. Taught at the Academy of Dramatic Arts, Budapest, from 1964; directed the Hungarian State Opera, 1986–90. Has employed serial techniques and folk materials. Works include operas (*C'est la guerre*, 1960–61; *Crime and Punishment*, 1969); choral pieces; songs and folk song arrangements; chamber music (*Passacaglia in Blues*, bassoon, piano, 1964; *Nocturne*, cimbalom, 1972; *Rhapsody no. 2*, viola, 1983).

Petrucci, Ottaviano (dei) (b. Fossombrone, 18 June 1466; d. Venice, 7 May 1539). Printer. Developed the first method of printing polyphonic music from movable type. Printed music in Venice, 1501–9; in Fossombrone, 1511–36. Publications include collections of chansons (beginning with *Harmonice musices odhecaton A*, 1501), frottolas, Masses, and motets, and books in lute tablature; volumes of the works of single composers (e.g., Josquin, Obrecht, Isaac) as well as anthologies.

Petrus de Cruce [Pierre de la Croix] (fl. ca. 1290). Theorist and composer. Composed motets employing a mensural notation slightly different from that of Franco of Cologne, allowing the breve to be subdivided into as many as seven equal semibreves. Also authored a treatise, *Tractatus de tonis*, on the modes.

Petrushka. Ballet by Stravinsky (choreography by Michel Fokine), produced in Paris in 1911 by Diaghilev's Ballets russes. It was revised in 1946.

Pettersson, (Gustaf) Allan (b. Västra Ryd, Uppsala län, 19 Sept. 1911; d. Stockholm, 20 June 1980). Composer and violist. Pupil of Blomdahl, Honegger, and Leibowitz. Works include 15 symphonies (no. 12, *De döda på torget* [The Dead in the Square], 1974); concertos; *Vox humana* (soloists, chorus, string orchestra, 1973–74); *24 Barfotasånger* [24 Barefoot Songs] (1943–45); chamber music.

Pettiford, Oscar (b. Okmulgee, Okla., 30 Sept. 1922; d. Copenhagen, 8 Sept. 1960). Jazz double bass player and bandleader. In 1943, worked with Charlie Barnet, Roy Eldridge, Coleman Hawkins, and Thelonious Monk. Co-led a group with Dizzy Gillespie (1943–44). Joined the big bands of Duke Ellington (1945–48) and Woody Herman (1949), where he began using amplified cello as a solo instrument. Mid-

1950s, led bop combos and recorded with a large ensemble.

Petzoldt, Johann Christoph. See Pezel, Johann Christoph.

Peu [Fr.]. Little; *un peu*, a little; *peu à peu*, little by little.

Peuerl [Peyerl, Bäuerl], **Paul** (b. Stuttgart?, bapt. 13 June 1570; d. after 1625). Composer and organ builder. Held organ posts in Upper and Lower Austria; built or renovated organs in those and other churches. Composed the first German variation suites (*Newe Padouan, Intrada, Däntz und Galliarda*, 1611).

Pevernage, Andreas [Andries, André] (b. Harelbeke, near Courtrai, 1543; d. Antwerp, 30 July 1591). Composer. Choirmaster at St. Salvator, Bruges, 1563; at Notre Dame, Courtrai, 1563–78 and 1584; from 1585 at Notre Dame, Antwerp. Works include Masses, motets, elegies, and chansons.

Pezel [Petzel, Petzoldt, Pecelius, Bezel(d), Bezelius], **Johann Christoph** (b. Glatz, Silesia, 5 Dec. 1639; d. Bautzen, 13 Oct. 1694). Composer. Musician in the Leipzig town band from 1664. Composed music for brass ensembles (*Hora decima musicorum*, 1670; *Fünff-stimmigte blasende Music*, 1685); sacred works.

Pezzo [It.]. Piece, composition.

Pf. (1) Abbr. for pianoforte, i.e., the piano. (2) Abbr. for the dynamics *piano* followed immediately by *forte*.

Pfeife [Ger.]. Fife, pipe, organ pipe.

Pfitzner, Hans (Erich) (b. Moscow, 5 May 1869; d. Salzburg, 22 May 1949). Composer, conductor, and writer. Pupil of I. Knorr. Taught at the Stern Conservatory, Berlin; directed the conservatory and conducted both orchestra and opera in Strasbourg, 1908–17. Taught at the Prussian Academy of Arts from 1920; at the Academy of Music in Munich, 1920s to early 1930s. Works include 5 operas (**Palestrina*); incidental music; 3 symphonies, concertos, and other orchestral music; 3 string quartets, a piano trio and quintet, other chamber and piano music; *Von deutscher Seele* (cantata, 1915–16) and other vocal music and songs. Published writings on musical composition and aesthetics; remained opposed to atonality.

Phalèse, Pierre (b. Louvain, ca. 1510; d. there?, 1573–76). Music publisher. From 1551, produced high-quality prints of music from movable type. His output includes Masses, motets, and chansons (by Clemens non Papa, Lassus, Rore, and others), and pieces in French lute tablature. In 1570, formed a partnership with Jean Bellère, a printer in Antwerp.

Phantasie [Ger.]. *Fantasia. Related terms or titles include *Phantasiestücke* (Fantasy Pieces; Schumann, opp. 12, 111) and *Phantasiebilder* (Fantasy Pictures; Schumann, *Faschingsschwank aus Wien* op. 26); *phantasieren*, to improvise.

Phantasy. The title of one-movement works composed for the Cobbet competitions, established in England in 1905.

Phasing. A technique developed by Steve Reich in which two subgroups of an ensemble begin by playing the same rhythmic pattern, but with one gradually accelerating until, after a period of being "out of phase," the two are again playing the pattern simultaneously or "in phase." His works incorporating the technique include *Piano Phase* (1967), *Four Organs* (1970), and *Drumming* (1971).

Philharmonic [fr. *phil-*, loving, plus *harmonic*, related to music]. A name taken by various kinds of musical organizations, especially *orchestras.

Philidor [Filidor], **François-André Danican** (b. Dreux, 7 Sept. 1726; d. London, 31 Aug. 1795). Composer and champion chess player. From a family of musicians; his half-brother, Anne (1681–28), founded the Concert spirituel. Pupil of Campra. Moved to Paris, 1740. Lived in London, 1745–54 and from 1771. Composed opéras comiques (*Le Sorcier*, 1764; *Tom Jones*, 1765); serious operas (*Ernelinde*, 1767; *Persée*, 1780); sacred and secular choral works (*Carmen saeculare*, 1779).

Philipp, Isidor (b. Budapest, 2 Sept. 1863; d. Paris, 20 Feb. 1958). Pianist. Student of Heller and Saint-Saëns; Taught at the Paris Conservatoire, 1893–1934; in New York and Montreal, 1941–55. Played chamber as well as solo music; published many 2-piano arrangements.

Philippot, Michel Paul (b. Verzy, 2 Feb. 1925; d. 1996). Composer. Pupil of Dandelot and Leibowitz. From 1949, associated with ORTF in Paris. From 1970, taught at the Paris Conservatory; later at the Univ. of São Bernardo do Campo, Brazil. Has employed serial procedures. Works include *Commentariolus Copernicae* (9 instruments, 1973); piano quintet (1986); Concerto for viola and violin (1987); electronic music.

Philips, Peter (b. London?, 1560–61; d. Brussels, 1628). Composer. Organist at the English College in Rome from 1582. Served Lord Thomas Paget, who settled in Brussels, 1585–89. Organist to Archduke Albert, Brussels, from 1597. Composed keyboard works (many included in the Fitzwilliam Virginal

Book); Italian madrigals; numerous motets; some instrumental ensemble music; other sacred pieces.

Phillips, Burrill (b. Omaha, 9 Nov. 1907; d. Berkeley, 22 June 1988). Composer and pianist. Pupil of Hanson and Rogers. Taught at Eastman, 1933–49; at the Univ. of Illinois, 1949–64. Used serial procedures. Works inlcude an opera (*The Unforgiven*, 1981), ballets and incidental music; orchestral, chamber, organ, and piano music; and vocal music (*The Return of Odysseus*, baritone, narrator, chorus, orchestra, 1956).

Phillips, Harvey (Gene) (b. Aurora, Mo., 2 Dec. 1929). Tuba player. Played in the Ringling Brothers band. Studied at Juilliard and the Manhattan School. Taught at the Univ. of Hartford, Mannes College, and Indiana Univ. (1971–94). Performed in many ensembles and in solo recital; has founded innovative programs for tuba players.

Phoebus and Pan. See *Streit zwischen Phöbus und Pan.*

Phonola. See Pianola.

Phorminx [Gr.]. A stringed instrument of ancient Greece, probably a *kithara.

Phrase. By analogy with language, a unit of musical syntax, usually forming part of a larger, more complete unit sometimes termed a *period. A phrase is the product, in varying degrees, of melody, harmony, and rhythm and concludes with a moment of relative tonal and/or rhythmic stability such as is produced by a *cadence. Phrases may also be defined by the repetition of a rhythmic pattern or melodic contour. In tonal music generally, phrases are often composed of multiples of two measures, and in the late 18th and early 19th centuries, the four-measure phrase became especially common. When a phrase is constructed so as to require response or resolution by a following phrase, the two are said to be *antecedent and consequent phrases, respectively. Often pairs of phrases are joined at more than one level to produce a hierarchy: e.g., four pairs of two-measure phrases may form two pairs of four-measure phrases, which in turn form a pair of eight-measure phrases. In such a context, the boundary between what constitutes a phrase as distinct from a larger period is necessarily informal. Elements shorter than the shortest phrase are termed *motives. The analysis of phrase structure in this way has often been a tool of style analysis. See also Phrasing.

Phrasing. The realization, in performance, of the *phrase structure of a work; the phrase structure itself. The realization of phrase structure is largely a function of the performer's *articulation. Apart from rests, musical notation employs a variety of symbols as guides to phrasing, principally an arc above the staff, similar to a *slur and termed a phrase mark, an apostrophe or comma placed above the staff to indicate a breathing *pause, and two short parallel lines inclined slightly to the right and crossing the top line of the staff to indicate a caesura or brief interruption of the musical line. In music for the piano, the use of the damper pedal is crucial to phrasing, and the notation of its use is thus sometimes a guide to phrasing as well. See also Notation, Performance practice.

Phrygian. See Mode, Cadence.

Physharmonica. An antecedent of the *harmonium.

Piacere, a [It.]. At the pleasure of the performer, especially as regards tempo and the use of *rubato.

Piacevole [It.]. Pleasing, agreeable.

Piaf [Gassion], **Edith (Giovanna)** (b. Paris, 19 Dec. 1915; d. there, 11 Oct. 1963). Popular singer and songwriter. From 1930, performed in nightclubs in Paris. After World War II, became known internationally through films and recordings, including those of her own songs ("La vie en rose," 1950).

Piangendo [It.]. Crying, plaintive.

Pianino [It.]. A small, upright piano.

Pianissimo [It., abbr. *pp*]. Very soft [see Performance marks].

Piano. (1) [It., abbr. *p*] Soft [see Performance marks]. (2) [Fr., It., Sp.; Eng., also pianoforte; Ger., also *Klavier;* fr. It. *fortepiano* or *pianoforte,* loudsoft, soft-loud]. A large stringed keyboard instrument. Its *keyboard is a set of keys or levers that operate a system of hammers. When the keys are pressed or driven down at their outer ends by the player's fingers, their inner ends cause the hammers to strike tuned, vibratable strings. In the wing-shaped grand piano [Fr. *piano à queue;* Ger. *Flügel;* It. *pianoforte a coda;* Sp. *piano de cola;* see Fig. 1], the strings, the soundboard over which they are

stretched, the iron frame to which these are fastened, and the mechanism of keys and hammers (collectively called the action) occupy a horizontal space whose enclosing case usually rests on three legs. The greatest width, at the keyboard end, is about 1.4 m. (4 ft. 8 in.). The total length ranges from 1.6 m. (5 ft. 3 in.) for a "baby" grand to 3 m. (9 ft. 10 in.) for a concert grand. The musical range or compass is 7 1/3 octaves, from A_2 to c'''''. Smaller pianos are made with soundboard and strings cased vertically and combined with a special action that places the keyboard along one side. These instruments range in size from spinets, as low as 1 m. (39 in.) and with compass reduced to under six octaves, through slightly larger console versions with nearly full compass, to studio and larger heavy uprights 1.5 m. (5 ft.) or more high. The large uprights were by far the commonest pianos in the first third of the 20th century.

Fig. 1. Grand piano.

The piano's sound originates in taut wire strings bearing on a large thin soundboard by way of one or

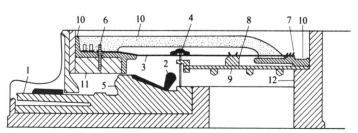

Fig. 2. Cross section of typical modern grand piano. Early instruments are similar but lack the iron frame. Moving parts are shown in outline; shaded areas are fixed members; solid black is cloth, felt, or leather. (Action details are shown in Figs. 3 and 5.) Key (1) propels hammer (2) to string (3) and lifts damper (4) via action mechanism (5). Vibrations of string, stretched from tuning pin (6) to hitch pin (7), pass via bridge (8) into soundboard (9). Iron frame (10) carries tension of strings, positioning pin block (11), and rim of wooden frame and case (12).

more elevated wooden ribs or bridges [see Fig. 2]. Its two distinctive features are its tone and the great effect of the "loud" or damper pedal. The strings are struck near their ends with soft, blunt hammers. This is structurally convenient as well as acoustically efficient in producing a rich, complex sound without high, metallic overtones. The energy in a vibrating string is made audible by the soundboard, but a portion is lost by passing from the string to the bridge and back into unplayed strings kept mute by their dampers. These leave their strings only when the corresponding keys are depressed or when the damper pedal is used to disengage all dampers at once. This frees all the strings to prolong, assist, and enrich the sound of the played notes.

The piano is the heir of the harpsichord and clavichord. It differs from these in its ability to produce widely varying degrees of loudness thanks to the use of hammers that strike the strings and immediately fall away from them. Bartolomeo Cristofori (1655–1730) of Florence first perfected a true piano with controllable hammers, termed a *gravicembalo col piano e forte* (harpsichord with soft and loud). The making of such instruments was soon taken up in Germany by Gottfried Silbermann (1683–1753).

The rudimentary piano had at least (a) hammers hinged to be tossed or snapped only through the first part of their strokes by key levers with motion suitably limited, and (b) dampers as in the harpsichord. Between 1760 and 1775, limited but musically usable instruments made commercial debuts, among them the little rectangular pianos of Johann Zumpe (fl. 1735–83) in England; these were not much more than clavichords with minuscule hammers and dampers. In these and other primitive pianos, fast playing is erratic or impossible, because the hammers rebound after the keys are released. If a hammer is still bobbling from the previous stroke, its motion can unpredictably aid or oppose both the loudness and the timing of the repeated note. If played too forcefully, the hammers can even bounce high enough to strike the strings a second time on one stroke of a key.

In the Cristofori and similar Silbermann pianos this problem is solved. The hammer is freed before it strikes the string, recoiling to a rest position even when the key is held. By the time the key is released and ready to play again, the hammer is motionless and is unable to affect the repetition in any way. The length of the fall assures that there will be no restriking bounces. A workable, simplified version of this action was patented in England in 1777, and in short order the great harpsichord firm of Shudi and Broadwood launched their excellent and successful grand pianos.

In due course the problem of repetition was solved by instrument makers on the Continent as well. The effect is called escapement action and assures that the hammer is motionless or nearly so when the key is ready to repeat. This action is lighter and repeats faster than the English one, and it quickly gained supremacy in Austria and Germany. The invention is attributed to Johann Andreas Stein (1728–92) of Augsburg, and by 1780 there were many Austrian and German makers offering good grand pianos with this so-called Viennese action [see Fig. 3].

Whether from London or Vienna, the pianos of 1780 are more similar to the harpsichord than they are to the modern piano or even to the pianos of Schubert and Schumann. Their compass, like that of the harpsichord, is five octaves (F_1 to f'''), and they are capable of only slightly more sound than the harpsichord. But their sounds are expressively controllable by touch and have an instrumental color that was truly new when they appeared. The hammers of the earliest Viennese pianos weigh about half a gram and travel at 12 to 16 times the velocity of the player's fingers. Many of these instruments quite naturally took their shape and general design from the harpsichord. Such an instrument is now usually termed a fortepiano and is often encountered in per-

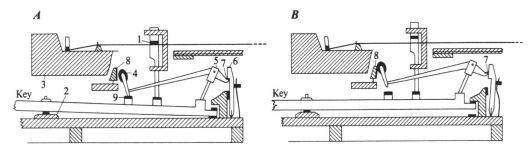

Fig. 3. Viennese action. A: (1) damper; (2) balance rail; (3) pin block. Key raises hammer (4) via pivot in fork or *Kapsel* (5). Beak (7) slips free of overhang on hopper (6) just before hammer strikes string. B: Head of hammer falls, stopping on back check (8), having shifted left while pivoting about balance point at (2). On release, beak reengages hopper (6); hammer head is freed and falls to rest (9).

formances of the works of Haydn, Mozart, Beethoven, and their contemporaries [see Fig. 4].

Fig. 4. Fortepiano, an early form of the piano.

The limit on the amount of sound a hammer can generate in a string is reached when the amplitude of the traveling wave of energy it produces is great enough to overcome the bearing force holding the string in contact with the bridge, through which the energy must pass to the soundboard. To absorb more energy from the hammers, strings should therefore be more like gongs or bells, i.e., stiffer. Since pulling them tighter and making them longer to maintain the pitches would result in an oversized, overstressed instrument, the preference is for shorter, thicker strings that are stiffer, have more bearing force on the bridge, and can be struck harder with heavier, slower-moving hammers for more sound. In pianos of the second generation, the hammer weights are roughly double, the key leverage ratios half, and the strings one and a half times thicker. Somewhat more sound is available, and it is more easily controlled.

In the Viennese action, heavier hammers are more subject to the rebounding problem, making their re-engagement with the escapement uncertain. The solution is the back check, which the English makers inherited from Cristofori and used in grand pianos from the beginning. The earliest, very delicate Viennese actions manage without it, but it is universal in the second generation, which indeed it defines. The back check is shaped to engage the falling hammer at a very flat angle and, owing to friction, stops it dead upon collision. The hammer is freed for another stroke when the key release disengages it by changing the relative positions.

Pianos grew rapidly, first in compass, then in power and action weight. As a result, soon after 1810 a significant sacrifice was made in the fast actions that skilled players specially cherished in the early instruments. This was because the stiffer strings cannot give the heavier hammer (which has farther to fall) much help on the rebound. The problem was mitigated by thick, resilient hammer coverings (many layers of leather, and eventually felt), which improve the bounce at the expense—because of the larger radii and softer surfaces—of some brilliance in the tone. What was needed to serve the ever more florid virtuosos and preserve the tonal ideal was a faster and more powerful action. This was furnished by Sébastien Érard (1752–1831), whose invention, an elaboration on the original English grand action, was patented in 1821. It permits a note to be repeated at once from any point of partial release. Érard's action spread slowly, as the original English and Viennese actions held their own through most of the 19th century. Since then, its descendants have been the undisputed world standard [see Fig. 5].

Pianos acquired musical accessories very early, at first operated by hand or knee levers, later by pedals. The first was the device for raising and disengaging the dampers. This was soon followed by the moderator, which interposes tongues of soft cloth between hammers and strings, yielding a soft, sweet, dark tone contrasting with the basic brilliant tone. Shortly before 1800 in England, and soon after on the Continent, grand pianos included a pedal for shifting the action sideways so that hammers can strike only one (hence, *una corda*) or two of the two or three strings for each note. The soft and loud pedals survive today, but the moderator is gone, since modern, thickly felted hammers produce *only* a dark round tone when played *pianissimo*. In the Empire period (1804–14), other exotic stops had brief vogues. There were effects simulating distant harps, bassoons, bells, and even drums. The third or center pedal in modern pianos, called the *sostenuto* pedal, keeps undamped only the notes being held at the moment it is pressed. It is a relatively recent and mainly American accessory.

The piano continued to grow along the same lines until by 1860 it reached approximately its modern form and compass of seven octaves. The single most important addition in this period was the one-piece, cast-iron frame, first patented by Alpheus Babcock of Boston in 1825 and improved by Jonas Chickering (1840 and 1843) and Steinway and Sons (1859). The iron frame eliminates the structural need for a closed bottom, thus releasing more of the available sound. Because it takes all the tension of the strings, the iron frame has in principle no bad effect on soundboard design. This led makers to use still thicker strings to obtain more sound; hammer design had to follow.

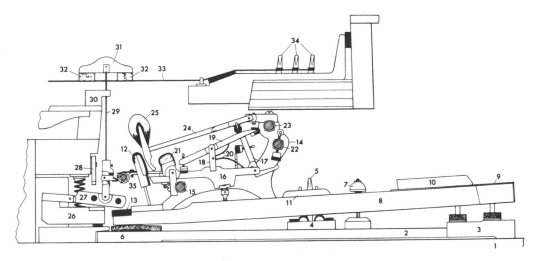

Fig 5. Cross section of modern grand piano action: 1. Keybed. 2. Keyframe. 3. Front rail. 4. Balance rail. 5. Balance rail stud. 6. Back rail. 7. Key stop rail. 8. White key. 9. Key covering. 10. Black key. 11. Key button. 12. Back check. 13. Underlever key cushion. 14. Action hanger. 15. Support rail. 16. Support. 17. Fly. 18. Support top flange. 19. Balancer. 20. Repetition spring. 21. Hammer rest. 22. Regulating rail. 23. Hammer rail. 24. Hammer shank. 25. Hammer. 26. Underlever frame. 27. Underlever. 28. Damper stop rail. 29. Damper wire. 30. Damper guide rail. 31. Damper head. 32. Damper felts. 33. String. 34. Tuning pin. 35. Sostenuto rod. (Courtesy of Steinway & Sons)

All this contributed to more evolution of the tonal ideal—away from the quickly decaying, brilliant transparency of the early instruments toward the robust, long-sustaining, fundamental-rich sound of today's piano.

During their first century, pianos were made in a great variety of sizes and shapes, of which the commonest was the so-called square piano with horizontal strings. American makers concentrated on this design, which, while retaining the action of the English square, grew large and powerful; after 1860 it was eclipsed by the fine grands of Chickering, Steinway, and their followers. Important European pianos were always of grand shape. In fact, all musically first-rate pianos are of horizontal grand shape and are at least 160 cm. (5 ft. 3 in.) long.

Piano accordion. An *accordion with pianolike keyboard as distinct from the *concertina and similar instruments with buttons only.

Piano arrangement. An arrangement for piano of a work intended for another medium.

Piano concerto. A *concerto for piano and orchestra.

Piano duet. A composition for two pianists, playing either one instrument or two. Music to be played on a single instrument is usually described as being for piano four hands.

Pianoforte. (1) Piano. (2) As a dynamic mark, *piano* followed immediately by *forte* (abbr. *pf*).

Pianola. (1) The trade name for a *player piano [see also Automatic instruments] manufactured by the Aeolian Piano Company. (2) Any player piano, including such instruments as the Duo-Art, Fonola, Phonola, and Welte-Mignon.

Piano-organ [Fr. *piano organisé, piano-orgue;* Ger. *Orgelklavier*]. An instrument popular in the late 18th century combining a piano, controlled from one manual, with an organ, controlled from another.

Piano quartet. Most often, a *quartet consisting of piano and strings; a work for such a quartet; rarely, a quartet of four pianos.

Piano reduction. An arrangement for piano of a work for orchestra or other ensemble.

Piano score. A score of a work for orchestra or other ensemble arranged on two staves in the fashion of piano music, sometimes with indications of the instruments intended for salient parts.

Piano trio. A *trio consisting of piano, violin, and cello; a work for such a trio.

Piano-vocal score. A score of an opera, oratorio, or other work for voices and orchestra in which the vocal parts are given in full while the orchestral music is reduced or arranged for piano.

Piatigorsky, Gregor (b. Ekaterinoslav, Ukraine, 17 Apr. 1903; d. Los Angeles, 6 Aug. 1976). Cellist. Joined the Imperial Opera orchestra and the Lenin Quartet, 1919. First cellist, Berlin Philharmonic, from 1924. Began a solo career, 1928. Taught at the Curtis Institute, 1942–44; at the Univ. of Southern California from 1962. Formed trios with Schnabel and Flesch in Berlin, Heifetz and Rubinstein in the U.S.; premiered concertos of Hindemith, Walton, and others.

Piatti [It.]. *Cymbals.

Piatti, Alfredo (Carlo) (b. Bergamo, 8 Jan. 1822; d. Crocetto di Mozzo, 18 July 1901). Cellist and composer. Pupil of Molique. Debut, Milan, 1837. After 1846, lived in London; joined Italian Opera and taught at the Royal Academy of Music. Wrote many pieces for cello, including 12 caprices (1875) and 2 concertos.

Piave, Francesco Mario (b. Murano, 18 May 1810; d. Milan, 5 Mar. 1876). Poet and librettist. Wrote libretti for works by Mercadante, Pacini, Ponchielli, and 10 of Verdi's operas, including *Ernani, *Macbeth, *Rigoletto, La *traviata, *Simon Boccanegra, La *forza del destino.

Pibgorn, pibcorn. A *hornpipe of Wales consisting of a single-reed *chanter with a bell and a mouthpiece of cow's horn. It was used from the Middle Ages into the 18th century.

Pibroch [Gael. *pìobaireachd,* piping]. A type of solo Scottish bagpipe music, also termed *ceòl mor* (great music), consisting of highly figured variations on a theme called an *urlar.* A form of solmization used for didactic purposes with this repertory is termed *canntaireachd.*

Picardy third [Fr. *tierce de Picardie*]. The raised or major third of the tonic triad as the final chord in a work otherwise in the minor mode. Its use begins by about 1500 and is very nearly universal in late Renaissance and Baroque music.

Picchettato [It.]. In string playing, *spiccato* [see Bowing (4)].

Piccinni [Piccini], **(Vito) Niccolò** [Nicola] **(Marcello Antonio Giacomo)** (b. Bari, 16 Jan. 1728; d. Passy, near Paris, 7 May 1800). Composer. Pupil of Leo and Durante. Composed operas for Naples, Rome, and other Italian cities, 1758–73. Second *maestro di cappella* at the Naples cathedral; from 1771, second organist at the royal chapel. Settled in Paris, 1776. Held up as representative of Italian opera, in opposition to Gluck's French style. Returned to Naples, 1791–98. Dramatic works include *La Cecchina, ossia La buona figliuola* (Rome, 1760); *Iphigénie en Tauride* (1781); *Didon* (1783); *Atys* (1780); *Pénélope* (1785).

Piccolo [It., small]. (1) [Fr. *petite flûte, flûte piccolo;* Ger. *Pikkoloflöte, kleine Flöte, Pickelflöte, Ok-*

tavflöte; It. *ottavino, flauto piccolo;* Sp. *flautín*] A small *flute pitched an octave higher than the ordinary flute. Its normal range is from d'' to d''''', written one octave lower. It normally lacks a foot joint and may be made of wood or metal. It is sometimes pitched in keys other than C, for bands often in D♭. See ill. under Flute. (2) The smallest or highest-pitched member of a family of instruments, e.g., *violino piccolo,* piccolo *clarinet, piccolo *cornet, piccolo *trumpet.

Pick. (1) *Plectrum. (2) To pluck a stringed instrument, especially a guitar or banjo, rather than strum it; thus, to play melodies as well as chords. The use of one or more plectra is often implied.

Pickelflöte [Ger.]. Piccolo (1).

Picker, Tobias (b. New York, 18 July 1954). Composer and pianist. Pupil of Wuorinen and Carter. Works include a violin concerto, 2 piano concertos, a symphony; *Encantados* (narrator and orchestra, 1983); chamber music (*New Memories,* string quartet, 1987), piano, and vocal music; and piano pieces for students.

Pickett, Wilson (b. Prattville, Ala., 18 Mar. 1941). Soul singer and songwriter. Joined the Falcons in 1959. His solo recordings, which are seminal to the history of soul music, include "It's Too Late" (1963), "Land of 1,000 Dances" (1966), and "Don't Knock My Love, Pt. 1" (1971).

Pickup. (1) One or more notes preceding the first metrically strong beat (usually the first beat of the first complete measure) of a phrase or section of a composition; anacrusis, upbeat. (2) A device, usually consisting of one or more electromagnetic coils, for converting the movement of a vibrating string (or other object) into electrical impulses. On the *electric guitar and similar instruments, one or more pickups are located on the face of the instrument, directly beneath the strings.

Pictures at an Exhibition [Russ. *Kartinki s vïstavki*]. A suite of descriptive pieces for piano by Mussorgsky, composed in 1874. Each piece is inspired by one of the paintings by the Russian artist Victor A. Hartmann (1834–73) shown at a memorial exhibition in 1874. The work is often performed in an orchestral arrangement by Ravel (1922).

Piece [Fr. *pièce, morceau;* Ger. *Stück;* It. *pezzo;* Sp. *pieza*]. A composition, especially but not necessarily an instrumental one. The term, as used informally, implies nothing about length or character. As a title or part of a title, however, it is likely to imply a relatively short composition. In French keyboard music of the 17th and 18th centuries, it frequently occurs in the phrase *pièces de claveçin.* The German term is often part of compounds [see *Stück*].

Piedi [It.]. See *Ballata.*

Pieno [It.]. Full; *organo pieno,* full organ; *voce piena,* full voice.

Pierce, Webb (b. near West Monroe, La., 8 Aug. 1926; d. Nashville, Tenn., 24 Feb. 1991). Country singer, songwriter, guitarist, and publisher. Joined the Louisiana Hayride, 1950; the Grand Ole Opry, 1952. Recordings include "Wondering" (1952); "More and More" (1954); a duet album with Willie Nelson (1982). Introduced the pedal steel guitar to country music.

Pierné, (Henri-Constant-) Gabriel (b. Metz, 16 Aug. 1863; d. Ploujean Finestère, 17 July 1937). Composer and conductor. Pupil of Franck and Massenet. Organist, Ste. Clothilde, 1890–98; conductor, Concerts Colonne, 1903–34. Composed dramatic works (*Fragonard,* Paris, 1934); ballets, pantomimes, and incidental music; oratorios; cantatas (*Edith,* 1882); orchestral music (*Fantaisie basque,* with solo harp, 1927); chamber and piano music; choral pieces and songs.

Pierrot lunaire [Fr., Moonstruck Pierre]. A work consisting of 21 short pieces by Schoenberg, op. 21 (1912), for a narrator employing *Sprechstimme and five instrumentalists (three of whom double: flute/piccolo, clarinet/bass clarinet, violin/viola, cello, piano), on poems by Albert Giraud in a German translation by Otto Erich Hartleben.

Pierson [Pearson], **Henry Hugo** [Hugh] (b. Oxford, 12 Apr. 1815; d. Leipzig, 28 Jan. 1873). Composer. Pupil of Attwood, Rinck, Reissiger, and Tomašek. Professor at Edinburgh Univ., 1844. Published under the pen name Edgar Mansfeldt. Works include 99 songs; incidental music to Goethe's *Faust,* pt. 2 (1854); operas (*Leila,* 1848); oratorios (*Jerusalem,* 1852); overtures; choral works.

Pifa [fr. It. *piffero or *piva*]. The instrumental *pastorale in Handel's *Messiah.*

Piffero, piffaro [It.]. Shawm; hence, *pifferari* for south Italian shepherds who travel to Rome during Advent to play shawms and bagpipes in the streets in imitation of the shepherds of the Christmas story. See *Pastorale.*

Pijper, Willem (b. Zeist, 8 Sept. 1894; d. Leidschendam, 18 Mar. 1947). Composer. Pupil of Wagenaar. Wrote music criticism in Utrecht and taught at the Amsterdam Conservatory, 1918–30. From 1930, head of the Rotterdam Conservatory. Explored multiple tonal centers; developed a "germ cell" approach to composition, by which a motive is unfolded over

the course of a composition. Works include symphonies; chamber and piano music (Septet, 1920; Piano Sonata, 1930); vocal works (*Romances sans paroles,* 1916; *Heer Halewijn,* chorus, 1929); operas (*Halewijn,* 1933).

Pikkoloflöte [Ger.]. *Piccolo flute.

Pilkington, Francis (b. ca. 1570; d. Chester, 1638). Composer. Held various posts at Chester Cathedral from 1602; active in the choir. Published 2 books of madrigals (1613–14, 1624) and a volume of lute songs (1605).

Pimsleur, Solomon (b. Paris, 19 Sept. 1900; d. New York, 22 Apr. 1962). Composer and pianist. Studied with Daniel Gregory Mason, with Goldmark, and in Salzburg. Operated an artists' agency and production company with his sister, Susan Pimsleur Puma. Wrote over 120 instrumental and vocal works (*Heart Rending Sonata for String Sextet* op. 77).

Pin block. In the *piano and related instruments, the piece of wood into which the tuning pins are inserted.

Pincé [Fr., plucked]. (1) *Pizzicato. (2) In the later 17th and 18th centuries, *mordent.

Pini di Roma [It., Pines of Rome]. A symphonic poem by Respighi composed in 1924, depicting four forested landscapes near Rome: the Villa Borghese, a catacomb, the Janiculum (a hill named after the god Janus), and the Appian Way.

Pini-Corsi, Antonio (b. Zara, Dalmatia, 19 June 1858; d. Milan, 22 Apr. 1918). Baritone. Debut, Cremona, 1878. Created the role of Ford in *Falstaff* (1906); Happy in Puccini's *La fanciulla del West* (1910). Sang at the Metropolitan Opera, 1909–14. Specialized in comic roles of Rossini and Donizetti.

Pinilla, Enrique (b. Lima, 3 Aug. 1927). Composer. Pupil of Sas, Koechlin, Honegger, del Campo, and Ussachevsky. Taught at the National Conservatory, Lima, from 1961; later at the Univ. of Lima. Has worked with folk idioms, atonality, serialism, and electronic music. Works include *Festejo* (1965); *Evoluciones* (1967); chamber works; music for theater, film, and television; piano and vocal pieces.

Pinkham, Daniel (Rogers, Jr.) (b. Lynn, Mass., 5 June 1923). Composer, organist, and harpsichordist. Pupil of Piston, Copland, Honegger, Barber, and Boulanger. Studied organ with Biggs and harpsichord with Landowska. Taught at Simmons College, Boston Univ., Harvard, and (from 1959) the New England Conservatory. Director of music at King's Chapel (Boston) from 1958. Has worked with serial procedures and with electronic music. Works include stage works; 3 symphonies and other orchestral pieces; film scores; chamber and keyboard music

(*Toccatas for the Vault of Heavens,* organ and tape, 1972; Sonata da chiesa, viola and organ, 1988); many choral pieces; and solo vocal music (*Three Latin Motets,* 1998).

Pinnock, Trevor (b. Canterbury, 16 Dec. 1946). Harpsichordist and conductor. Studied at the Royal College of Music. Founded the period instrument ensemble The English Concert, 1972. Has recorded Rameau's complete keyboard music, Bach's Goldberg Variations, and orchestral music of J. S. Bach, Handel, Vivaldi, and C. P. E. Bach.

Pinto, George Frederick (b. Lambeth, England, 25 Sept. 1785; d. Chelsea, 23 Mar. 1806). Composer and violinist. Pupil of Salomon. Concertized widely in London, 1798–1803; performed with Field, 1800. Also an accomplished pianist. Compositions include 2 Grand Sonatas for piano (1803).

Pinza, Ezio (Fortunato) (b. Rome, 18 May 1892; d. Stamford, Conn., 9 May 1957). Bass. Studied in Ravenna and Bologna. Debut, 1914. Sang at the Metropolitan Opera, 1926–48, as well as in Rome, London, and Vienna. Roles included Don Giovanni and Boris Godunov; appeared on Broadway in *South Pacific* and in films.

Pìobaireachd [Gael.]. *Pibroch.

P'i-p'a (pipa) [Chin.]. A pear-shaped, fretted, short-necked *lute of China. Its four silk (more recently nylon) strings are usually tuned A d e a. The traditional model has 16 frets extending well up onto the body of the instrument; on more recent models there may be as many as 24. It is held upright, with its lower end resting on the player's lap. The strings are plucked with the fingernails of the right hand. See ill. under Instrument.

Pipe. Any wind instrument in the form of a tube. See also Aerophone, Bagpipe, Organ, Pipe and tabor, Reed, Woodwinds.

Pipe and tabor. A *duct flute with three finger holes and a small snare drum, both played by a single player who holds the pipe in the left hand and beats the tabor with a stick held in the right. The tradition of *galoubet* and *tambourin* survives in southern France and that of *flaviol* and *tamboril* (Catalan), *txistu* and *tamboril* (Basque), and *pito* and *tambor* (Castilian) in Spain. See ill. under Flute.

Pique Dame [Fr.]. See *Queen of Spades, The.*

Pirouette [Fr., Sp. *tudel*]. A wooden disc or cylinder that holds and partly covers the reed of the shawm and similar double-reed instruments.

Pisador, Diego (b. Salamanca, ca. 1509; d. after 1557). Vihuelist and composer. Took minor orders in 1526. Published a book in vihuela tablature (1552),

which includes some original fantasias together with intabulations of Masses by Josquin, motets, Spanish and Italian songs, and madrigals.

Pisano [Pagoli], **Bernardo** (b. Florence, 12 Oct. 1490; d. Rome, 23 Jan. 1548). Composer. *Maestro di cappella* at the Cathedral of Florence; from 1514, singer in the papal chapel. Works include responsories, canzonettas, *ballate,* and some of the earliest true 16th-century madrigals.

Pisendel, Johann Georg (b. Cadolzburg, 26 Dec. 1687; d. Dresden, 25 Nov. 1755). Violinist and composer. Pupil of Torelli, Heinichen, and Vivaldi. Director of the Collegium musicum and opera orchestra, Leipzig, 1710. Court violinist, Dresden, from 1712; *Konzertmeister* from 1728. Works include 7 violin concertos and a solo violin sonata. Vivaldi, Albinoni, and Telemann dedicated violin works to him.

Pisk, Paul Amadeus (b. Vienna, 16 May 1893; d. Hollywood, 12 Jan. 1990). Composer, musicologist. Studied with Schreker and Schoenberg. Taught at the Volkhochschule, 1922–34; in the U.S. at the Univ. of the Redlands (1937–51), the Univ. of Texas (Austin), and Washington Univ. (1963–72). Composed ballets, orchestral (*3 Ceremonial Rites,* 1958) and chamber music; choral music and over 150 songs.

Piston. (1) *Valve. (2) On the organ, a button that controls preset stops.

Piston, Walter (Hamor, Jr.) (b. Rockland, Maine, 20 Jan. 1894; d. Belmont, Mass., 12 Nov. 1976). Composer and teacher. Pupil of Boulanger and Dukas. Taught at Harvard, 1926–60. His pupils included Bernstein and Carter. Wrote textbooks on harmony, counterpoint, and orchestration. Composed orchestral works, including 8 symphonies (no. 3, 1947, and no. 7, 1960, won Pulitzer prizes), concertos, suites, fantasies, Variations (with solo cello, 1966), and *Three New England Sketches,* 1959); the ballet *The Incredible Flutist* (1938); a few band pieces; chamber and piano works (5 string quartets; Divertimento, 9 instruments, 1946; *Partita,* violin, viola, and organ, 1944; *Improvisation,* piano, 1945); 2 vocal works.

Pitch [Fr. *hauteur;* Ger. *Tonhöhe;* It. *intonazione;* Sp. *entonación*]. (1) The perceived quality of a sound that is chiefly a function of its fundamental frequency—the number of oscillations per second (called *Hertz, abbr. Hz) of the sounding object or of the particles of air excited by it [see Acoustics]. In general, pitch is regarded as becoming higher with increasing frequency and lower with decreasing frequency. Pitches may be quantitatively expressed either directly by the value of their frequencies, or indirectly by the ratios their frequencies make with some reference frequency. Unimpaired ears detect frequencies from 16 Hz to ca. 20,000 Hz (as high as

25,000 Hz for young people; as low as 10,000 Hz for those over 40). Musically useful frequencies extend from ca. 20 Hz to ca. 5,000 Hz.

(2) [Fr. *ton;* Ger. *Ton;* It., Sp. *tono*]. Any point on the continuum of musical pitch. This continuum is analogous to the domain of musically useful frequencies, and each point on it corresponds to some definite frequency within that domain. For the nomenclature employed with the pitches used in Western music, see Pitch names.

(3) The position of a point or, in early writings, of a set of points (e.g., a particular range of the scale or staff) on the musical pitch continuum. This position is described as being higher when the corresponding frequency is greater and as being lower when the frequency is smaller.

(4) [Fr. *diapason;* Ger. *Kammerton, Stimmung;* It. *diapason;* Sp. *diapasón*]. The standardized association of some particular frequency and some pitch name (e.g., c' = 256 Hz). Letter names refer essentially to elements of ordered interval collections (called tunings, scales, etc.) and by extension to the relationships that inhere in such collections. In the 20th century, the standard a' = 440 Hz has been widely used, especially since its endorsement by the British Standards Institution Conference in May 1938 and by the International Organization for Standardization in 1955.

In most times and places, the identification of letter names with specific frequencies has varied. In the 16th–18th centuries, some writers asserted that it does not matter which particular pitch is called (say) a' so long as players can tune together to it. In practice, by the early 17th century, organs (outside of France, at least) tended to be tuned a tone or more higher than either singers or gut strings could tolerate. At the same time, makers of various instruments favored particular—and differing—pitch compasses. It consequently became common during the 17th and 18th centuries to speak of several pitch standards and to identify their interrelations. The terminology was not systematic, and its scope varied in different regions.

The oldest and stablest term is choir pitch [Fr. *ton de choeur, ton de chapelle;* Ger. *Chorton;* It. *tuono chorista*]. This was often contrasted with a chamber pitch [Fr. *ton de chambre;* Ger. *Kammerton*] lying a whole tone lower. Several north German authors described a second chamber pitch a semitone lower still. During Bach's tenure at Leipzig, singers, woodwinds, and strings tuned to *Kammerton;* the organ and trumpets were pitched in *Chorton* a whole tone

Mean pitch of	Frequency of a'	Sample pitches, 1495–1812
	506	Halberstadt organ, 1495
	489	Hamburg organ, 1688
15 German organs, 1495–1716	487	
14 Silbermann organs, 1717–50	484	
8 Austrian organs, ca. 1550–1700	466	
48 Venetian *cornetto*s, 16th–17th c.	466	
33 German *Zinck*s, 16th–17th c.	465	
	464	Störmthal organ, 1723
25 *cornetto*s of unknown provenance, 16th–17th c.	461	
	455	Hamburg organ, 1749
	454	Amati violins, high resonance, ca. 1650
	454	London tuning fork, ca. 1720
7 English organs, 1665–1708	450	
32 Italian (non-Venetian) *cornetto*s, 16th–17th c.	448	
	440	Paris Conservatoire fork, 1812
	435	Hamburg choir tuning fork, 1761
5 French *cornets,* 16th–17th c.	431	
	427	Sauveur's standard, 1713
	426	Praetorius's *Cammerton,* 1619
	≈ 425	Padua pitch pipe, 1780
	424	Amati violins, low resonance, ca. 1650
	423	"Handel's" tuning fork, 1751
13 English and American organs, 1740–1843	421	
	415	Dresden choir tuning fork, ca. 1754–1824
6 German organs, 1693–1762	412	
92 French oboes, ca. 1670–1750	411	
	408	Hamburg organ, 1762
	405	Deslandes-Sauveur organ, 1704
13 French organs, 1601–1789	399	
	394	De Caus's standard, 1612

above. Other terms denoted standard pitch for high winds (*Cornett-Ton, Zinck-Thon, Feldton,* etc.) and for opera (*Opernton*). The accompanying table gives the mean pitches of 13 collections of instruments, whose original pitches can be reliably ascertained. They should be compared with the particular historical pitches also included in the table.

No concerted effort was made to promulgate a single pitch standard until 1834, when the German scientific society accepted Scheibler's recommendation of a' = 440 Hz. This had little effect on 19th-century concert halls and opera houses, which used progressively higher pitch standards, until in 1885 an international conference (not including the United Kingdom or United States) at Vienna urged the adoption of the French *Diapason normal,* a' = 435 Hz, as recommended in 1859 by a French governmental commission as the pitch least taxing to singers. The Viennese conference's a' = 435 remained the most widely used pitch standard until its replacement by a' = 440 in the 20th century. Performers on 18th-century instruments are likely to adopt the lower pitch of that period, however.

Pitch aggregate. In discussions of 20th-century music, a collection of pitches, whether or not sounded simultaneously.

Pitch class. A pitch without reference to the octave or register in which it occurs; hence, e.g., the class of all C's as distinct from the pitch c'. Western tonal music uses twelve pitch classes, each of which is represented in each octave of the entire range of pitches. The term is used particularly (though not exclusively) with respect to *twelve-tone and *serial music. See also Octave equivalence.

Pitch names. The accompanying table gives the systems for naming pitch classes in English, French, German, Italian, and Spanish. Exceptions to the model for the addition of suffixes in German include *B* for B-flat (B-natural being represented by *H*), *Es* for E-flat, and *As* for A-flat.

English	C	D	E		F	G	A	B
German	C	D	E		F	G	A	H
French	ut	ré	mi		fa	sol	la	si
Italian	do	re	mi		fa	sol	la	si
Spanish	do	re	mi		fa	sol	la	si

English	C-sharp	C-flat
German	Cis	Ces
French	ut dièse	ut bémol
Italian	do diesis	do bemolle
Spanish	do sostenido	do bemol

English	C-double-sharp	C-double-flat
German	Cisis	Ceses
French	ut double-dièse	ut double-bémol
Italian	do doppio diesis	do doppio bemolle
Spanish	do doble sostenido	do doble bemol

Several competing schemes for the designation of specific octaves are in use. The one employed in this dictionary and widely used elsewhere is the first of the three illustrated here, in which middle C (the C occurring roughly in the middle of the piano keyboard) is designated c'. In all three, the form of the name changes with each C, proceeding upward. Thus, the B above middle C in the first scheme is b', and the B below middle C is b. For terminology derived from organ building, see Foot (2).

1. C_1	C	c	c'	c''	c'''	c''''
2. CCC	CC	C	c	c'	c''	c'''
3. C_2	C_1	C	c	c^1	c^2	c^3

Pitch pipe [Fr. *choriste, flûte d'accord, diapason à bouche;* Ger. *Stimmpfeife;* It. *corista, diapason a fiato;* Sp. *diapasón de boca*]. A small wind instrument used to give an initial pitch to singers or to tune instruments. Pitch pipes from the 18th century were *duct flutes with calibrated movable plungers. Since the 19th century, they have usually been free reeds arranged in a row or a disc.

Pitfield, Thomas B(aron) (b. Bolton, 5 April 1903). Composer and visual artist. Studied at the Royal Manchester College of Music; taught there, 1947–73. Works include orchestral pieces; *Adam and the Creatures: Morality with Music* (speaker, chorus, organ, percussion, 1965); songs, chamber works, and folk-song arrangements.

Pito [Sp.]. (1) Whistle. (2) A *duct flute of the *pipe and tabor of central Spain.

Più [It.]. More; *più allegro,* faster; *più tosto,* more quickly.

Piuttosto [It.]. Rather; *piuttosto allegro,* rather fast.

Piva [It.]. (1) *Bagpipe. (2) The fastest measure (*misura*) or step unit of the *basse dance (*bassadanza*). It consists of a series of rapid steps (*passetti presti*) embellished by leaps and turns. (3) One of the fastest dances of the early 16th century. Some early examples appear as the third dance of a suite that includes a *pavana, a *saltarello, and a *piva*. All are in a compound quadruple (12/8) meter.

Pivot chord. See Modulation.

Pixis, Johann Peter (b. Mannheim, 10 Feb. 1788; d. Baden-Baden, 22 Dec. 1874). Pianist and composer. Pupil of Albrechtsberger. Settled in Munich, 1809; in Paris, 1823; in Baden-Baden, 1840. Composed mainly piano works, including a concerto, sonata, and many smaller pieces. With Chopin, Liszt, Czerny, Thalberg, and Herz, he contributed to a set of variations on a theme from *I puritani*.

Pizzetti, Ildebrando (b. Parma, 20 Sept. 1880; d. Rome, 13 Feb. 1968). Composer, conductor, and writer on music. Studied at the Parma Conservatory and taught there, 1907. Taught at the Florence Conservatory from 1908 (director, 1917–24). From 1924, directed the Milan conservatory; 1936–58, taught at the Academy of S. Cecilia in Rome. Signed a manifesto with Respighi and others recommending a return to tradition in music. Works include many operas (*Fedra,* 1909–12; *Debora e Jaele,* 1915–21; *Assassinio nella cattedrale,* 1957; *Ifigenia,* 1950); incidental music (*La sacra rappresentazione di Abram e d'Isaac,* 1915–17); choral works (*Messa di Requiem,* 1922); film scores; concertos, a symphony, and a few other orchestral pieces; some chamber and piano music; songs.

Pizzicato [It., abbr. *pizz.*]. In the playing of bowed stringed instruments, an indication that notes are to be plucked rather than bowed. Typically the player uses the right forefinger for pizzicato while continuing to hold the bow. If the passage of pizzicato notes is long enough and an immediate return to bowing (usually indicated by the word *arco*) is not required, the bow may be laid aside. Sometimes all four strings are strummed, and in such a case the thumb may be used.

Placido [It.]. Placid, tranquil.

Plagal cadence. See Cadence.

Plagal mode. See Mode.

Plagius [Lat.]. Plagal [see Mode]; *primus plagius,* the first plagal mode, i.e., mode 2.

Plainchant. *Plainsong.

Plain-chant musical [Fr.]. A repertory of liturgical chant composed and performed in France from the 17th through the 19th century. It aimed to correct what were regarded as the deficiencies of the received Gregorian repertory by eliminating melismas, introducing fixed rhythmic values and otherwise revising melodies in such a way as to reflect current norms of Latin declamation, and introducing accidentals, including the sharp. The repertory, which varied from place to place, was accompanied by the organ or the serpent and served as the basis for organ *versets.

Plainsong [fr. Lat. *cantus planus*]. Monophonic Christian liturgical chant in free rhythm, as distinct from measured music [Lat. *musica mensurabilis*]; also plainchant. The principal repertories of Western plainsong are the *Ambrosian, *Gallican, *Gregorian (to which the term is most often applied), *Old Roman, and *Mozarabic. The principal Eastern repertories are the Armenian, *Byzantine, and *Syrian.

Plainsong Mass. (1) The *Mass in *Gregorian chant. (2) A polyphonic *Mass in which the music for each liturgical item is based on the corresponding liturgical chant.

Plainsong notation. The notation employed for liturgical chant, especially the square-shaped forms that became prominent in the 12th century and were sometimes employed for secular repertories as well. See Neume.

Plainte [Fr.]. (1) *Lament. (2) In Baroque music, a rare term for any of several ornaments: *accent or *aspiration; in viol playing, a one-finger vibrato; vocal pulsations; downward *glissando.

Plaisanterie [Fr.]. In the first half of the 18th century, a cheerful and unpretentious movement in a harpsichord suite. The term was also used to refer to *galanteries in general.

Plançon, Pol (Henri) (b. Fumay, Ardennes, 12 June 1851; d. Paris, 11 Aug. 1914). Bass. Studied with Sbriglia. Debut, 1877, Lyons. His best-known role was Mephistopheles in Gounod's *Faust.* Sang regularly at Covent Garden, 1891–1904. Sang at the Metropolitan Opera, 1893–1908.

Planctus [Lat.]. *Lament.

Planets, The. A suite for orchestra by Holst, op. 32 (1914–16), describing in successive movements the astrological nature of seven planets: Mars, Venus, Mercury, Jupiter, Saturn, Uranus, and Neptune (with women's chorus).

Planquette, (Jean) Robert (b. Paris, 31 July 1848; d. there, 28 Jan. 1903). Composer. Studied at the Paris Conservatory. Composed 20 operettas, including *Les cloches de Corneville* (1877), *Rip van Winkle* (1882), and *Mam'zelle Quat'sous* (1897).

Plaqué [Fr.]. An instruction to play the notes of a chord simultaneously rather than as an *arpeggio.

Platti, Giovanni Benedetto (b. Padua, 9 July 1697; d. Würzburg, 11 Jan. 1763). Composer. From 1722 to 1761, served at the court of the Würzburg bishops as teacher, composer, tenor, and virtuoso instrumentalist. Composed 57 sonatas for various instruments; concertos; vocal works.

Player piano. An *automatic instrument consisting of a piano and a mechanical device that plays it. In some early examples, from the late 19th century, a separate device with fingerlike levers was placed in front of a piano. More characteristic of the player piano's period of greatest popularity in the 1920s were self-contained models. In either case, a perforated roll of paper passes over a bar with holes corresponding to each of the keys of the piano. When a perforation coincides with a hole, the suction created by a pedal mechanism draws air through the hole, activating the pneumatically powered action that causes the instrument to sound. Among the most widely known trade names was *Pianola, and this was often used as a generic term.

Playford, John (b. Norwich, 1623; d. London, Nov. 1686). Music publisher and bookseller. In 1647, opened a shop in the porch of the Temple Church, where he was clerk from 1653. From 1651 to 1684, dominated the music publishing trade, producing lesson books, song and instrumental collections, and hymns. Publications include *The English Dancing Master* (1651); *Catch that Catch Can* (1652); *A Breefe Introduction to the Skill of Musick* (1654).

Plectrum [Fr. *plectre, médiator;* Ger. *Plektrum, Spielblatt, Kiel* (quill); It. *plettro;* Sp. *plectro*]. A piece of some material such as horn, tortoise shell, plastic, quill, or ivory used to pluck a stringed instrument. The *mandolin, *ʻūd, *biwa, *zither, and often the *guitar are played with a plectrum. In guitar and *banjo playing, the term pick is more common, and in some styles, picks may be worn on more than one finger.

Plein-jeu [Fr.]. In the classic French organ, the full sound of the *Grand orgue and Positif [see Positive].

Plenary Mass. A setting of the *Mass that includes both Ordinary and Proper.

Pleyel, Ignace Joseph [Ignaz Josef] (b. Ruppersthal, Austria, 18 June 1757; d. Paris, 14 Nov. 1831). Composer, music publisher, and piano maker. Pupil of Haydn and possibly Vanhal. Kapellmeister to Count Ladislaus Erdödy from around 1776; of Strasbourg Cathedral from 1789. Conducted the Professional Concerts in London 1791–92. From 1795, ran a music shop and a publishing house, the Maison Pleyel, in Paris. Issued Haydn's complete string quartets, 1801, and the first miniature scores, 1802. Founded a piano firm, 1807. Composed about 45 symphonies; concertos and *symphonies concertantes;* 70 string quartets; numerous quintets, trios, and duos; the opera *Ifigenia in Aulide* (Naples, 1785).

Plica [Lat., fold]. A notational symbol derived from the liquescent *neume and employed in both texted and nontexted music until the early 14th century. It represents two pitches, the second of which is usually a step above or below the first. A plica could also be joined to a *ligature by the addition of an upward or downward stroke to the final note of the ligature, representing a single note a step above or below. It is the convention of modern editions of early music to reproduce this second note in a smaller size or with a slash through the stem. There is some doubt whether it implies a special or ornamental vocal technique.

Plötzlich [Ger.]. Suddenly.

Plus [Fr.]. More.

Pneuma [Gr., Lat.]. *Neuma.

Poche, pochette [Fr.]. *Kit.

Poco [It.]. Little in amount; *un poco,* a little; *poco a poco,* little by little; *fra poco,* shortly; *pochettino, pochetto,* very little; *pochissimo,* extremely little.

Podatus [Lat.]. See Neume.

Poetic meter. See Prosody.

Poglietti, Alessandro [Boglietti, Alexander de] (b. Tuscany?, 1st half of the 17th century; d. Vienna, July 1683). Composer and teacher. Settled in Vienna, 1661, as Kapellmeister in a Jesuit church; then court organist to Leopold I. Composed sacred vocal music and keyboard works, including 12 ricercars; experimented with imitation of natural sounds such as birdcalls. Authored a treatise on keyboard playing and composition.

Pohjola's Daughter [Finn. *Pohjolan Tytär*]. A symphonic fantasia by Sibelius, op. 49 (1906), based on an episode from the *Kalevala.

Poi [It.]. Then, afterward; *poi la coda,* then (play) the coda, e.g., after the final repetition of the scherzo in a scherzo with trio.

Point. (1) The tip of the violin or similar bow, at the end opposite the one at which it is held. (2) Point of *imitation. In a work making consistent use of imitation, a passage made up of statements of a single subject by each voice in succession. Many polyphonic works of the Renaissance consist of a series of such passages, each on a new subject and often overlapping, a new point of imitation beginning as the last voices to enter in the preceding point conclude. (3) [Lat. *punctus*] The point or dot of perfection [see Mensural notation].

Point d'orgue [Fr.]. (1) *Fermata. (2) *Cadenza, often signaled in notation by a fermata. (3) In the 17th century, rarely, *pedal point (for which the standard term since the 19th century has been *pédale*).

Pointer [Fr.]. To dot [see *Notes inégales*].

Pointillism. By analogy with the technique of this name employed by painters such as Georges Seurat (1859–91), a musical texture in which pitches are presented in varying timbres and largely in linear isolation from one another rather than in successions to be perceived as melodies. See *Klangfarbenmelodie.*

Pokorny [Pokorn, Pockorný], **Franz** [František] **Xaver (Thomas)** (b. Mies, Bohemia, 20 Dec. 1729;

d. Regensburg, 2 July 1794). Composer. Pupil of Riepel, Stamitz, Richter, and Holzbauer. In 1766, joined the Kapelle of the court of Thurn and Taxis, Regensburg. Composed many symphonies, about 50 harpsichord concertos, and some chamber music.

Polacca [It.]. *Polonaise; *alla polacca,* in the Polish style.

Poldini, Ede (Eduard) (b. Budapest, 13 June 1869; d. Corseaux, Vaud, 28 June 1957). Composer. Studied in Budapest and Vienna. In 1908, settled in Bergeroc, Vevey. Used some folk elements. Composed many stage works (*Vagabund und Prinzessin,* 1903; *Hochzeit im Fasching,* 1924; *Himfy,* 1938; all Budapest); piano works, choral music, and songs.

Poldowski [Irene Regine Wieniawska; Lady Dean Paul] (b. Brussels, 18 Mar. 1879; d. London, 28 Jan. 1932). Composer. Daughter of Henryk Wieniawski; pupil of Gevaert, d'Indy, and Gedalge. Wrote principally songs in the tradition of Fauré (she set 21 texts for Verlaine) and chamber works. Works include *Dimanche d'avril* (published 1911), *Colombine* and *Mandoline* (both published 1913).

Polka. A Bohemian dance originating ca. 1830 and becoming extremely popular throughout Europe and in America in the course of the 19th century. It is in a moderately fast 2/4, often incorporating the rhythm shown in the example.

Pollarolo, Carlo Francesco (b. ca. 1653; d. Venice, 7 Feb. 1723). Composer. Held various posts in Brescia from 1676. Second organist at St. Mark's, Venice, 1690; vice-*maestro di cappella* from 1692. Musical director of the Ospedale degli incurabili. Composed about 85 operas and 13 oratorios.

Pollini, Maurizio (b. Milan, 5 Jan. 1942). Pianist. Attended the Milan Conservatory. Has performed and recorded solo piano music and works with orchestra. His repertory extends from Bach to 20th-century compositions.

Polo [Sp.]. (1) A song and dance of southern Spain originating in the 18th century and popular into the 19th. (2) A type of *flamenco music belonging to the genre of *cante hondo* and related to the *soleá.*

Polonaise [Fr.]. (1) A festive, processional, couple dance of Polish origin in a moderate tempo. The polonaise, not so named until the 17th century, stems from Polish folk dances accompanied by singing, such as the *chodzony,* the *wolny,* and the *wielki.* Most of the extant music for these dances is in triple meter,

lacks upbeats, and has internal short repeated sections.

(2) An instrumental piece, originating in accompaniment to the courtly dance and largely developed outside of Poland. Pieces called Polish dances (*polnischer Tanz, chorea polonica, polacca*) are found in sources of the late 16th century. But these lack the features that characterize the later polonaise, which emerged in the 17th century. In the 18th century, the stylized instrumental polonaise acquired the characteristics thereafter considered typical: moderate tempo, triple meter, lack of upbeats, and repetition of rhythmic figures. Certain initial and final rhythmic patterns are less consistently present. A common initial rhythm, often accompanimental rather than melodic, is shown in Ex. 1. Endings of polonaises are usually feminine, the accents occurring after the downbeat. Characteristic final rhythms are shown in Ex. 2.

The first polonaises showing all these features (except the initial rhythm) include those of Bach (French Suite no. 6, Orchestral Suite no. 2). The genre was particularly admired and cultivated in the 18th century by Germanic composers, including Telemann, Wilhelm Friedemann Bach, Johann Philipp Kirnberger, Johann Schobert, and Mozart. After 1800, the instrumental polonaise began to be cultivated by Polish composers, and the popularity of polonaises by some of these men contributed greatly to the spread of the genre throughout Europe, in the guise of salon pieces in particular. The greatest and most prominent composer of polonaises was Chopin, whose works for piano made the dance a symbol of Poland. Notable examples include those in A major op. 40 no. 1 (the so-called *Military* Polonaise, 1838) and Ab major op. 53 (1842). Other composers of polonaises include Beethoven, Schubert, Schumann, Weber, Liszt, Mussorgsky, and Tchaikovsky.

Polovtsian Dances. A choral and orchestral interlude in the second act of Borodin's opera *Prince Igor.* The Polovtsy are nomadic invaders of Russia who, in the opera, capture the Russian warrior Prince Igor Svyatoslavich (1151–1202).

Polska. Any of several dances, at first in triple meter, but subsequently also in duple meter, thought to derive from early Polish dances [see Polonaise] and popular elsewhere in Europe, especially in Scandinavia, from the 16th century. The Swedish dance of this name is similar in character to the *mazurka.

Polychoral. Composed with parts for two or more choirs, most often separately positioned; sometimes also termed antiphonal. In principle, though not always in practice, music of this type exploits an element of contrast or tension between the choirs rather than mere alternation or duplication. It is particularly associated with the *Venetian school of the later 16th century, where the terms *coro battente* and *coro spezzato* (broken choir, pl. *cori spezzati*) were used. The architecture of the Basilica of St. Mark particularly facilitated its performance. Venetian composers with whom the technique is closely associated were Adrian Willaert and especially Andrea and Giovanni Gabrieli. The technique was by no means limited to Venice, however. Works that deploy choral and/or instrumental forces spatially have been composed regularly since and include Bach's *St. Matthew Passion* and Berlioz's *Requiem*. A resurgence of such techniques in the 20th century can be credited in large part to Henry Brant and Karlheinz Stockhausen.

Polychord. In music of the 20th century, a chord made up of two or more simpler, usually familiar types of chord such as a triad, e.g., the so-called *Petrushka* chord, which consists of a C-major triad and an F♯-major triad.

Polymeter. The simultaneous use of two or more meters. The term is sometimes applied, however, to the successive use of different meters in one or more parts.

Polyphony [Fr. *polyphonie;* Ger. *Mehrstimmigkeit;* It. *polifonia;* Sp. *polifonía*]. Music that simultaneously combines several lines, as distinct from *monophony, which consists of a single melody; more narrowly, music combining several lines, each of which retains its identity as a line to some degree, as distinct from *homophony, in which melodic interest is concentrated in one line. In the broader sense, polyphony characterizes most of Western art music and much of Western popular music; in the narrower sense, it characterizes the music of certain periods (especially the *Middle Ages [see Discant, Organum] and *Renaissance), genres (e.g., *canon and *fugue), and techniques (e.g., *imitation). In this narrower sense, the terms polyphony and polyphonic can be synonymous with counterpoint and contrapuntal. The latter pair of terms is perhaps more often applied to tonal music and the former to music from before about 1600, but this chronological distinction is informal, when it exists at all. More often, the term counterpoint is reserved for any codified form of polyphony in the narrow sense, e.g., 16th-century or modal counterpoint, Baroque counterpoint, etc.

Polyrhythm. The simultaneous use of two or more rhythms that are not readily perceived as deriving from one another or as simple manifestations of the same meter; sometimes also *cross-rhythm. Familiar examples in tonal music are the simultaneous use of triple and duple subdivisions of the beat, and the simultaneous use of 3/4 and 6/8 or similarly related pairs of meters (whether or not explicitly indicated), termed *hemiola. Western art music of the 20th century offers numerous examples, often notated explicitly with conflicting meters. Such techniques are especially prominent in some music of Elliot Carter. Traditional African music abounds in polyrhythm, and it is evident in African-derived musics of the New World.

Polytextuality. The simultaneous use of two texts in a vocal work. It is a prominent feature of the *motet in the 13th and 14th centuries, and it occurs occasionally in genres of secular music of the 14th and 15th centuries as well [see Double *ballade*].

Polythematic. See Monothematic, polythematic.

Polytonality. See Bitonality, polytonality.

Pommer, Pomhart [Ger.]. See *Bombard*.

Pomp and Circumstance. Five concert marches for orchestra by Elgar, op. 39 (nos. 1–4 composed in 1901–7, no. 5 completed by 1930). The title is taken from a phrase in Shakespeare's *Othello,* act 3, sc. 3: "Pride, pomp, and circumstance of glorious war!"

Pomposo [It.]. Pompous.

Ponce, Manuel (María) (b. Fresnillo, Zacatecas, 8 Dec. 1882; d. Mexico City, 24 Apr. 1948). Composer. Pupil of Bossi and Dukas. Taught at the Mexico City Conservatory from 1909; conducted the National Symphony, 1917–19. Lived in France, 1925–33. Works include orchestral music (*Balada mexicana,* with solo piano, 1914; *Ferial,* 1940; a guitar concerto); guitar music; piano pieces; numerous songs ("Estrellita," 1914) and folk song arrangements; an opera; vocal-orchestral pieces; chamber music.

Ponchielli, Amilcare (b. Paderno Fasolaro [now Paderno Ponchielli], near Cremona, 31 Aug. 1834; d. Milan, 16 Jan. 1886). Composer. Studied at the Milan Conservatory. Church organist, theater and band conductor in Cremona and Piacenza. From 1880, teacher at the Milan Conservatory (pupils included Puccini, Mascagni); from 1881, also music director, S. Maria Maggiore, Bergamo. Composed operas (*I promessi sposi,* Milan, 1872; *La *gioconda*); ballets; much sacred music; occasional cantatas; band pieces; songs.

Poniridis, Giorgios [Poniridy, Georges] (b. Constantinople, 8 Oct. 1892; d. Athens, 29 Mar. 1982). Composer. Pupil of Ysaÿe, Gilson, d'Indy, and Roussel. From 1954, head of the Music Division of the Greek Ministry of Education in Athens. Employed traditional Greek and Byzantine music and serial techniques. Works include symphonies, *Triptyque symphonique* (Athens, 1937), and many arrangements of Greek folk songs.

Pons, Lily (Alice Joséphine) (b. Draguigon, near Cannes, 12 Apr. 1898; d. Dallas, 13 Feb. 1976). Soprano. Studied at the Paris Conservatory. Debut, 1927. Sang at the Metropolitan Opera, 1931–61 (debut as Lucia). Renowned for her coloratura singing; made many recordings and appeared in films.

Ponselle, Rosa (b. Meriden, Conn., 22 Jan. 1897; d. Baltimore, 25 May 1981). Soprano. Began as vaudeville singer. Sang at the Metropolitan Opera, 1918–37 (debut opposite Caruso). From 1950, directed the Baltimore Civic Opera Company; also performed in recital and on radio. Sherrill Milnes and William Warfield were among her students.

Ponticello [It.]. The *bridge of a stringed instrument [for *sul ponticello,* see Bowing (11)].

Ponty, Jean-Luc (b. Avranches, France, 29 Sept. 1942). Jazz violinist and bandleader. Until 1964, pursued a career in classical music; then devoted himself to jazz. Recorded the swing album *Violin Summit,* with Stephane Grappelli and others, 1966; an album of Frank Zappa's jazz-rock music, 1969. Led a free-jazz group, ca. 1970–72; later a jazz-rock group. Also plays electric violin and synthesizer.

Poot, Marcel (b. Vilvoorde, near Brussels, 7 May 1901; d. Brussels, 12 Jan. 1988). Composer. Pupil of Gilson, with whom he cofounded *La Revue musicale belge,* and Dukas. Taught at the Brussels Conservatory from 1938 (director, 1949–66). Works include operas; ballets (*Paris in verlegenheid,* 1925); oratorios; orchestral works (*Charlot,* 1926; 5 symphonies; *Jazz Music,* 1933; *Vrolijke ouverture,* 1935); chamber music; many pieces for duos and solo piano; music for silent films.

Popov, Gavriil Nikolayevich (b. Novocherkassk, 12 Sept. 1904; d. Repino, 17 Feb. 1972). Composer and pianist. Studied at the Leningrad Conservatory. Composed works for the stage, 7 symphonies, choral works, chamber music, songs, and film scores.

Popp, Lucia (b. Uhorská Vez, Czechoslovakia, 12 Nov. 1939; d. Munich, 16 Nov. 1993). Soprano. After an early film career, studied at the Bratislava Academy. Debut there as the Queen of the Night, 1963. Covent Garden debut, 1966; Metropolitan Opera debut, 1967; sang throughout Europe.

Popper, David (b. Prague, 9 Dec. 1843; d. Baden, Vienna, 7 Aug. 1913). Cellist and composer. Studied at the Prague Conservatory. First tour, 1863; later appeared with Bülow. Member of Hellmesberger Quartet. First cellist, Vienna Court Orchestra, 1868–73. Taught at the Budapest Conservatory, 1896–1913. Wrote character pieces for cello and piano; a string quartet; 4 cello concertos; Requiem (3 cellos and orchestra, 1891); other orchestral and chamber works.

Porgy and Bess. Opera in three acts by George Gershwin (libretto by DuBose Heyward with lyrics by Ira Gershwin, after the play *Porgy* by DuBose and Dorothy Heyward), produced in New York in 1935. Setting: Charleston, South Carolina, in the 1920s.

Porpora, Nicola (Antonio) (b. Naples, 17 Aug. 1686; d. there, 3 Mar. 1768). Composer and singing teacher. Studied in Naples. *Maestro di cappella* to the Prince of Hessen-Darmstadt, 1711–25. Composer to the Opera of the Nobility, London (in competition with Handel), 1733–36. Kapellmeister, Dresden, 1748–51. Moved to Vienna, ca. 1752; Haydn was his pupil, valet, and keyboard accompanist. Taught at various institutions in Naples and Venice; pupils included Farinelli and Caffarelli. Composed over 40 operas (*Didone abbandonata,* Reggio, 1725; *Arianna in Nasso,* London, 1733); many solo cantatas and oratorios; Masses and a few instrumental works.

Port de voix [Fr.]. A compound vocal ornament beginning below the principal note (most often, a step lower) and "carrying the voice" up to a resolution that is itself ornamented, the whole being sung to the syllable of the principal note; also an *appoggiatura. It seems to have been developed in the mid-17th century by singer-composers of the *air de cour,* in which it was one of the principal embellishments and whence it spread rapidly to other repertories, both instrumental and vocal. It could be introduced whenever a shorter note was followed by a longer, higher one on a strong part of the measure, except following a cadential trill. To execute the *port de voix* on a given note, the singer divided the preceding note in half and began the ornament on the second half, pronouncing the syllable belonging to the principal note. Players of melody instruments seem to have imitated the singers' *ports de voix,* interpreting them according to the nature of their instruments.

Porta, Costanzo (b. Cremona, 1528–29; d. Padua, 19 May 1601). Composer. A member of the Franciscan Minorites. Pupil of Willaert. *Maestro di cappella* of Osima Cathedral from 1552; held similar positions at Padua (1565–67 and from 1589), Ravenna (1567–74 and 1580–89), and Loreto (1574–80). Composed sacred and secular vocal polyphony.

Portamento [It.]. A continuous movement from one pitch to another through all of the intervening pitches, without, however, sounding these discretely. It is principally an effect in singing and string playing, though for the latter and for other instruments capable of such an effect, the term glissando is often used [for distinctions between the two terms, see Glissando]. In vocal music, the portamento may be indicated by connecting with a slur two pitches that are sung to different syllables. If two pitches are sung to the same syllable, with the slur simply indicating this fact, a portamento is indicated by the term itself.

Portative organ. An organ small enough to be carried or placed on a table, usually with only one set of pipes. See also Organetto, Positive organ.

Portato [It.]. See Bowing (6).

Porter, Cole (Albert) (b. Peru, Ind., 9 June 1891; d. Santa Monica, Calif., 15 Oct. 1964). Popular songwriter and lyricist. Studied at Yale, Harvard, and in Paris. Composed musicals (*Anything Goes,* 1934, including "You're the Top"; *Kiss Me, Kate,* 1948, including "Wunderbar"; *Can-Can,* 1953, including "I Love Paris"); music for films (*Rosalie,* 1937); numerous songs ("Night and Day," 1932; "In the Still of the Night," 1937; "Begin the Beguine," 1935).

Porter, (William) Quincy (b. New Haven, 7 Feb. 1897; d. Bethany, Conn., 12 Nov. 1966). Composer. Pupil of Parker, D. S. Smith, Capet, d'Indy, and Bloch. Taught at the Cleveland Institute of Music, 1923–28 and 1931–32; at Vassar College from 1932. From 1938, dean of New England Conservatory; taught at Yale, 1946–65. Works include incidental music to Shakespeare and other plays; orchestral works (2 symphonies; *Concerto concertante,* 2 pianos and orchestra, Pulitzer Prize, 1954; *New England Episodes,* 1958); chamber and piano music (9 string quartets; sonatas; Piano Quintet, 1927; Quintet, harpsichord, strings, 1961; Oboe Quintet, 1966); many songs.

Porter, Walter (b. ca. 1587 or ca. 1595; d. London, buried 30 Nov. 1659). Composer. Perhaps studied with Monteverdi. Gentleman of the Chapel Royal from 1617. Sang and played theorbo in masques. Master of the choristers of Westminster Abbey from 1639. Composed madrigals and motets.

Portugal [Portogallo], **Marcos Antônio (da Fonseca)** (b. Lisbon, 24 Mar. 1762; d. Rio de Janeiro, 7 Feb. 1830). Composer. Pupil of Carvalho. From 1800, *mestre de capela* of the royal chapel and director of the S. Carlos Opera, Lisbon; 1811, rejoined the Portuguese court, which had fled to Rio de Janeiro. Composed 21 Portuguese comic operas (*A castanheira,* 1787); Italian operas, both seria and buffa (*Le confusioni,* Florence, 1793; *Demofoonte,* Milan, 1794; *Fernando nel Messico,* Venice, 1798); sacred music.

Portuguese hymn. See *Adeste fideles.*

Pos. Abbr. for **Posaune, positif,* *position.

Posaune [Ger.]. Trombone.

Position. (1) In harmony, the proximity in register of the several parts to one another, e.g., close position, open position [see Spacing]. (2) In string playing, the location of the hand on the fingerboard. In first or natural position on the violin, the first or index finger stops the pitch a whole tone above the open string, the fourth or little finger reaching a perfect fifth above the open string. Successively higher positions are numbered in order as the first finger is used to stop successively higher pitches of the diatonic scale. A movement from one position to another is termed a shift. Because of their larger size, the cello and double bass employ somewhat different systems. See also Fingering. (3) On the *trombone, any of the seven locations at which the slide is normally held. In first position, the slide is fully retracted, providing the shortest possible length of tubing and the fundamental tone by which the instrument is named (typically B♭). Successive positions lower the fundamental by a semitone.

Positive organ [Fr. *positif (à dos); Ger. Positiv, Rückpositiv;* It., Sp. *positivo*]. (1) The secondary division of an organ, with its pipes located behind the player, the key and stop actions running under the floor; also called Chair, because it is located behind the organist's chair or bench. (2) A small, one-manual organ, usually without independent Pedal stops, rarely with a pedalboard.

Post horn [Fr. *cornet de poste;* Ger. *Posthorn;* It. *cornetta da postiglione;* Sp. *corneta de postillón*]. A small horn sometimes straight or curved but usually coiled in a circle only a few inches across with mouthpiece and bell ends protruding at approximately a right angle to each other. From the beginning of postal service in the 16th century, small horns were used to signal the approach of the mail wagon.

Postlude. A work forming the conclusion of a larger work or one performed at the end of a ceremony; especially a piece played (sometimes improvised) on the organ at the conclusion of a church service.

Poston, Elizabeth (b. near Walkern, Hertfordshire, 24 Oct. 1905; d. Highfield, Hertfordshire, 18 Mar. 1987). Composer. Studied at the Royal Academy of Music. During 1930s, traveled often, collecting folk songs. Worked for the BBC 1939–45. Composed film music (*Howards End,* 1970) and choral and chamber music; edited collections of folk songs and carols.

Potpourri [Fr., "rotten pot," a stew of various meats and vegetables]. A composition based on selections from other works; sometimes also a *medley. The term was used early in the 18th century for miscellaneous collections of songs and by the end of the century for medleys of opera melodies.

Potter, (Philip) Cipriani (Hambly) [Hambley] (b. London, 3 Oct. 1792; d. there, 26 Sept. 1871). Composer and pianist. Pupil of Attwood, Callcott, Crotch, and Foerster; advised by Beethoven. Taught at the Royal Academy of Music from 1822. Introduced Beethoven's Piano Concertos nos. 1, 3, and 4 to England. Composed 9 symphonies; overtures; at least 3 piano concertos; many piano pieces; chamber works.

Poule, La [Fr., The Hen]. Popular name for Haydn's Symphony no. 83 in G minor Hob. I:83 (1785; no. 2 of the *Paris Symphonies), so called because the repeated woodwind figures accompanying the second theme of the first movement suggest the cackling of a hen.

Poulenc, Francis (Jean Marcel) (b. Paris, 7 Jan. 1899; d. there, 30 Jan. 1963). Composer. Studied piano with Viñes; composition with Koechlin. One of "Les six." From around 1936, worked with singer Pierre Bernac, whom he accompanied, often in premieres of his own songs. Works include the operas *Les *mamelles de Tirésias*, *Dialogues des carmélites, La voix humaine* (after Cocteau, 1958); ballets (*Les biches*, 1923, for the Ballets Russes); incidental music to works by Cocteau, Shakespeare, Anouilh, Molière, and others; orchestral works (*Concert champêtre*, harpsichord, orchestra, 1927–28; Concerto in D minor, 2 pianos, orchestra, 1932); sacred and secular choral works (Mass in G major, 1937; Gloria, 1959); numerous songs for voice and piano (*Tel jour, telle nuit*, song cycle, Eluard, 1936–37); chamber music (Sextet for piano and winds, 1932–39); piano pieces (*15 Improvisations*, 1932–59).

Poussé [Fr.]. Up-bow [see Bowing (1)].

Pousseur, Henri (Léon Marie Thérèse) (b. Malmédy, Belgium, 23 June 1929). Composer. Pupil of Souris; associate of Boulez, Stockhausen, Berio, and Maderna. Has taught at Darmstadt, Cologne, and Liège Conservatory (from 1970; director, 1975). Has employed serial and aleatory techniques. Works include electronic music (*Scambi*, 1957; *Electre*, ballet, 1960); orchestral music (*Couleurs croisées*, 1967); chamber works (*Symphonies à 15 soloistes*, 1954–55; *Quintette à la mémoire d'Anton Webern*, 1955); works for organ, piano, and other solo instruments;

dramatic works (*Votre Faust*, 1960–67); vocal music (*Traverser la forêt*, cantata, 1987).

Powell, Bud [Earl] (b. New York, 27 Sept. 1924; d. there, 1 Aug. 1966). Jazz pianist. Joined Cootie Williams's big band, 1942–44; worked in bop groups in New York, 1940s–1950s. Lived in Paris, 1959–64; played in a trio with Kenny Clarke. Recordings include *Bud's Bubble*, 1947; *Dance of the Infidels*, with Sonny Rollins, 1949; *Hallucinations*, 1950. Powell's playing defined the bop piano style.

Powell, John (b. Richmond, Va., 6 Sept. 1882; d. there, 15 Aug. 1963). Pianist and composer. Pupil of Leschetizky. Toured Europe as a pianist before World War I; in the U.S. after 1912. Collected and made use of songs from the rural South. Works include orchestral music (*Rapsodie nègre*, with piano, 1918; "Virginia" Symphony, 1951); vocal music (*The Babe of Bethlehem*, chorus, 1934; *5 Virginia Folk Songs*, baritone, piano, 1938); chamber and piano music.

Powell, Mel (b. New York, 12 Feb. 1923; d. Valencia, Calif., 24 Apr. 1998). Composer. Played as a jazz pianist with Benny Goodman and Glenn Miller. Pupil of Hindemith. Taught at Yale, 1957–69. From 1969, dean of the School of Music, California Institute of the Arts. Made use of twelve-tone and improvisational techniques. Works include *Immobiles I–IV*, tape and/or orchestra, 1967; *Settings*, jazz band, 1982; *Duplicates*, 2 pianos and orchestra, Pulitzer Prize, 1990); vocal music (*Haiku Settings*, 1961); chamber and piano works (*Filigree Setting*, string quartet, 1959); electronic music (*Inscape*, ballet, 1976).

Power, Leonel [Lionel, Lyonel, Leonelle] (d. Canterbury, 5 June 1445). Composer. Served Thomas, Duke of Clarence. From 1423, at Christ Church, Canterbury, directing the Lady Chapel choir, 1439–45. Composed Mass cycles, Mass movements, and settings of Marian texts. One of the first to write paired Mass movements and Mass cycles unified throughout by musical means. Authored a treatise on discant.

Pownall, Mary Ann (b. London, Feb. 1751; d. Charleston, S.C., 11 Aug. 1796). Singer and composer. Known first as Mrs. James Wrightson. Sang at Vauxhall, 1776–88. Moved to the U.S. 1792; sang in Boston, New York, Philadelphia, and Charleston. Among the first women to have her songs published in the U.S.

Pozo, Chano [Pozo y Gonzales, Luciano] (b. Havana, 7 Jan. 1915; murdered New York, 2 Dec. 1948). Cuban jazz conga player and singer. As a member of Dizzy Gillespie's big band (1947–48), brought authentic Afro-Cuban rhythms into jazz. Recordings include *Cubana Be/Cubana Bop* and *Manteca* with Gillespie (1947) and *Jahbero* with Tadd Dameron (1948).

Pp. Abbr. for *pianissimo,* very soft [see *Piano*]. Sometimes three or more *p*s are used to specify even softer playing.

Prado, Pérez (b. Mantanzas, Cuba, 1922; d. Mexico City, 15 Sept. 1989). Popular pianist and bandleader. From 1951, popularized the Latin mambo sound in the U.S. with a series of recordings, including "Anna" (1953), "Cherry Pink and Apple Blossom White" (1955), and "Patricia" (1958).

Praeambulum [Lat.]. *Prelude.

Praefatio [Lat.]. *Preface.

Praeludium [Lat.]. *Prelude.

Praetorius [Schulz, Schulze], **Hieronymus** (b. Hamburg, 10 Aug. 1560; d. there, 27 Jan. 1629). Composer and organist. Son of Jacob Praetorius (1); father of Jacob Praetorius (2). Organist at Hamburg from 1582. Wrote Masses, Magnificats (most for organ), and motets. Compiled books of church music.

Praetorius [Schulze], **Jacob** [Jacobus] (1) (b. Magdeburg, ca. 1530; d. Hamburg, 1586). Organist and editor. Father of Hieronymus Praetorius. By 1550, associated with St. Jacobi, Hamburg. Compiled books of monophonic and polyphonic sacred music.

Praetorius [Schulz], **Jacob** [Jacobus] (2) (b. Hamburg, 8 Feb. 1586; d. there, 21 or 22 Oct. 1651). Organist and composer. Son of Hieronymus Praetorius. Pupil of Sweelinck. Organist at St. Petri, Hamburg, from 1603. Composed sacred and secular vocal pieces; organ works.

Praetorius [Schultheiss], **Michael** (b. Creuzburg an der Werra, near Eisenach, 15 Feb. 1571; d. Wolfenbüttel, 15 Feb. 1621). Composer and theorist. Served dukes of Brunswick-Wolfenbüttel as organist (from 1595) and Kapellmeister (from 1604). Also worked in Dresden and Magdeburg. Composed over 1,000 sacred vocal works, most based on Protestant hymns or Lutheran liturgical texts, some with continuo; many were published with instructions for their use in church services. Also wrote chorale settings for organ and instrumental dances. His treatise on music theory and practice, *Syntagma musicum* (1614–20), includes a supplement which describes and pictures the instruments in use at that time.

Prague Symphony. Popular name for Mozart's Symphony no. 38 in D major K. 504, composed in Vienna in 1786 and first performed in Prague in 1787. Its three movements do not include a minuet.

Pralltriller [Ger.]. See *Schneller.*

Pran Nath (b. Lahore, India [now Pakistan], 3 Nov. 1918; d. Berkeley, 13 June 1996). Classical Indian vocalist and composer. The leading modern exponent of the Kirana style of north Indian singing. Performed on All India Radio from 1937; from 1960, taught at Delhi Univ. In 1971, established the Kirana Center for Indian Classical Music, New York. Taught at the Univ. of California, San Diego, and Mills College; disciples included Terry Riley and LaMonte Young. Produced innovations in instrumental design, notably for the classical tambūrā (drone lute).

Pratella, Francesco Balilla (b. Lugo di Romagna, 1 Feb. 1880; d. Ravenna, 17 May 1955). Composer. Pupil of Mascagni. Directed the Licei musicali of Lugo di Romagna (1910–29) and Ravenna (1927–45). Made use of Italian folk music; for a time advocated futurism. Composed 7 operas (*La Sina 'd Vargöun,* 1906–8; *L'aviatore Dro,* 1911–14); operettas; incidental and film music; orchestral music (*Romagna,* 1903–4); chamber music; many songs (*I canti del cammino,* 1958).

Pratt, Silas Gamaliel (b. Addison, Vt., 4 Aug. 1846; d. Pittsburgh, 30 Oct. 1916). Composer. Pupil of Dorn and Liszt. From 1895, principal, West End Music School, New York. In 1906, founded Pratt Institute of Music and Art, Pittsburgh. Composed dramatic works (*Zenobia,* 1883; *The Triumph of Columbus,* 1892); symphonies; symphonic poems; *Centennial Ode* (1876); many songs, choruses, and piano pieces; a cantata.

Préambule [Fr.], **preambulum** [Lat.]. *Prelude.

Precentor. In an Anglican cathedral, the cleric who directs the singing; in some Protestant churches, the person who leads the congregational singing by *lining out.

Preces [Lat., prayers]. In the Roman rite, prayers consisting of a series of supplications in alternating *versicles and responses. In form and origin they are closely related to the *litany.

Precipitato [It.]. Rushed.

Preface [Lat. *praefatio*]. The introduction, together with the immediately following Sanctus, to the Canon [see Canon (3)] of the *Mass.

Preghiera [It.]. In opera, especially of 19th-century Italy, an aria or chorus in which the character or characters plead for divine assistance.

Prelude [fr. Lat. *praeludere,* to play beforehand; Fr. *prélude;* Ger. *Präludium, Preambel, Vorspiel;* It., Sp. *preludio;* also Lat. *preambulum*].

(1) A composition establishing the pitch or key of a following piece. In France and northern Europe, prelude has been a preferred title for pieces that have

been equated with, and are virtually identical in style and function to, the *tiento, *toccata, *ricercar, *fantasia, arpeggiata, tastata, entrada, etc. All feature an idiomatic virtuosity, rhythmic freedom, and loose thematic construction, reflecting frequent contemporaneous observations that they were usually improvised, particularly when serving a preludial function [Fr. préluder, Ger. preludieren, It. sonar di fantasia, etc., to play impromptu]. The improvisatory element is particularly evident in the unmeasured preludes (préludes non mesurés) of 17th-century French lutenists and clavecinistes. More fully written-out preludes (e.g., those in Bach's Das Orgel-Büchlein; see Chorale prelude, Organ chorale) may serve the dual purposes of instructing the novice in the art of a famed composer-improviser and providing music for the composer's own performance. Most are thematically unrelated to the piece or pieces they preface. Accordingly, collections of preludial pieces will often provide a selection with one in each of the 8 (or 12) modes, or 24 major and minor tonalities. This practical consideration has produced a long tradition of cycles of preludial pieces in all current keys. The crowning work is Bach's Das wohltemperirte Clavier (The *Well-Tempered Clavier), with its 48 preludes and fugues in all major and minor tonalities.

(2) A short work for piano. Since Chopin's op. 28, prelude has connoted for many composers a tightly constructed, unattached, evocative miniature for piano that grows (as do many of the preludes of Bach and Chopin) from small, pervasive melodic or rhythmic fragments. Some of these essay programmatic moods, as in the two books of preludes by Debussy (1910, 1913, each piece being followed by a descriptive phrase).

(3) An introductory orchestral piece that elides with the opening scene of a drama, such as an opera. Pieces termed *overture most often come to a rousing close before the curtain rises and are often unrelated thematically to the work following. A prelude is integrated into the whole and draws upon thematic ideas and motives from the opera to evoke an essence of the drama's mood and conflicts.

Prelude to "The Afternoon of a Faun" [Fr. Prélude à "L'après-midi d'un faune"]. A symphonic work by Debussy inspired by Stéphane Mallarmé's poem L'après-midi d'un faune, completed and performed in 1894. In 1912, it was choreographed and danced by Vaslav Nijinsky for Sergei Diaghilev's Ballets russes in Paris.

Préludes, Les [Fr.]. A symphonic poem by Liszt, composed in 1848 (revised in 1852–54). It was orchestrated by Joachim Raff and originally served as an introduction to Liszt's unpublished choral work Les quatre élémens (The Four Elements). When Liszt decided to use the introduction as a separate work, he attached Alphonse de Lamartine's poem Les préludes as a "programme."

Prendere [It.], **prendre** [Fr.]. Take up, prepare to play; e.g., prendere il flauto, take up the flute (after a passage for piccolo).

Preparation. The introduction of some pitch as a consonance immediately preceding its statement as a dissonance, especially as part of a suspension [see Counterpoint].

Prepare [Fr. préparer; Ger. vorbereiten; It. preparare; Sp. preparar]. In harp playing, to set the pedals in the appropriate positions for a passage to follow, e.g., prepare F-sharp minor; in organ playing, to ready a combination of stops.

Prepared piano. A piano whose sound has been altered by inserting material such as bolts, rubber, cloth, and paper between the strings, thus altering pitch, loudness, and especially timbre. The preparation is usually carried out according to the instructions of a composer, who for each composition specifies the materials and their exact placement in relation to individual strings. The prepared piano was introduced by John Cage, who has composed numerous works for it, including Bacchanale (1938), A Book of Music (for two pianos, 1944), and Sonatas and Interludes (1946–48).

Près [Fr.]. Near; près de la touche, an instruction in string playing to bow near or over the fingerboard; près de la table, an instruction in harp playing to pluck the strings at a point near the soundboard.

Presa [It.]. In a *canon, the sign, often shaped somewhat like an S, that indicates the point reached by one voice when the succeeding voice begins.

Presley, Elvis (Aaron) [Aron] (b. East Tupelo, Miss., 8 Jan. 1935; d. Memphis, Tenn., 16 Aug. 1977). Rock-and-roll singer and guitarist, actor. Initially popular with country audiences (recordings include "Mystery Train," 1955); then made many successful rock-and-roll recordings ("Love Me Tender," 1956; "Jailhouse Rock," 1957). During 1960s, became famous for lyrical songs such as "Are You Lonesome Tonight" (1960); later returned to rock-and-roll. Appeared in numerous musical films. The first prominent white artist to incorporate black idioms into his style; also the first to associate rock-and-roll with rebellious feelings among American youth, through aggressive and sexually suggestive stage behavior.

Pressante [It.], **en pressant** [Fr.]. Hurrying.

Pressler, Menahem (b. Magdeburg, 16 Dec. 1923). Pianist. Emigrated to Palestine as a child. Toured and recorded with the Beaux Arts Trio, which he cofounded, 1955, and as a soloist. Taught at Indiana Univ. from 1955.

Presto [It.]. Very fast, i.e., faster than *allegro; prestissimo,* as fast as possible. Before the late 18th century, however, *presto* could be the equivalent of *allegro* or could indicate simply the normal, moderately fast tempo [see Tempo, Performance marks].

Preston, Simon (b. Bournemouth, 4 Aug. 1938). Organist. Studied at Cambridge. Organist and conductor of the Bach Choir at Oxford Univ., 1970–81. Organist and chorusmaster at Westminster Abbey from 1981.

Previn, André (b. Berlin, 6 Apr. 1929). Conductor, pianist, and composer. Pupil of Castelnuovo-Tedesco and Monteux. Worked at MGM Studios as composer, arranger, and conductor, winning several Academy Awards. Conductor of the London Symphony (1969–79), Pittsburgh Symphony (1976–84), Royal Philharmonic (from 1985), and Los Angeles Philharmonic (1985–89). Has recorded 20th-century solo piano music and jazz. Works include film scores, concertos, chamber music, Broadway musicals, and songs.

Prévost, André (b. Hawkesbury, Ontario, 30 July 1934). Composer. Pupil of Pépin, Messiaen, Philippot, Copland, Kodály, Schuller, and Carter. Taught at Montreal Univ. Works include orchestral pieces (*Fantasmes,* 1963; *Pyknon,* with solo violin, 1966); choral works (*Terre des hommes,* cantata, 1967); chamber music.

Prey, Hermann (b. Berlin, 11 July 1929; d. Munich, 22 July 1998). Baritone. Studied at the Berlin Hochschule. Recital debut, 1951; operatic debut, 1952. Joined the Hamburg Opera, 1953; appeared at major houses in Europe and the U.S. A much-admired interpreter of lieder; made many recordings.

Price [née Smith], **Florence Bea(trice)** (b. Little Rock, Ark., 9 Apr. 1888; d. Chicago, 3 June 1953). Composer. Pupil of Chadwick, Converse, and Sowerby. Head of the music department at Clark Univ., Atlanta, from 1910. In 1927, moved to Chicago. The first black woman to attain recognition as a symphonic composer; her Symphony no. 1 (1931–32) was performed by the Chicago Symphony. Other works include "Songs to the Dark Virgin" (1941); these draw on traditional black melodies and rhythms.

Price, (Mary Violet) Leontyne (b. Laurel, Miss., 10 Feb. 1927). Soprano. Studied at Juilliard. From 1952 to 1954, sang Bess in a new production of *Porgy and Bess.* Sang often at the Metropolitan Opera, 1961–85. Roles included Aida and Tosca; created Cleopatra

in Barber's *Antony and Cleopatra,* 1966. Performed widely in recital and with orchestras.

Prick song. In England from the late 15th through the early 17th centuries, music notated in mensural notation and thus polyphony as distinct from plainsong.

Prima donna [It.]. The singer of the principal female role in opera, or the leading female singer in an opera company. The corresponding male designation, less frequently used, is *primo uomo.* It connotes a performer of overbearing temperament and arrogance.

Prima prattica, seconda prattica [It., first practice, second practice]. In the early 17th century, the musical practice of 16th-century polyphony as codified by Zarlino, and the new styles of *monody and dissonance treatment, respectively. The guiding principle of the *seconda prattica* was that the words should govern the music, thus justifying previously unacceptable dissonance treatment and the like.

Prima vista [It.]. At first sight, i.e., *sight-reading.

Prima volta, seconda volta [It., first time, second time]. The first and second endings of a passage that is repeated. These are usually numbered 1 and 2, respectively, and marked off by horizontal brackets above the staff [see Notation]. In music of the Middle Ages, the terms *ouvert and *clos* were sometimes used.

Primary triads (chords). The tonic, subdominant, and dominant triads in any key; in the view of Schenker theory, the tonic and dominant triads only.

Prime. (1) The *interval of a unison. (2) The third hour of the *Office. (3) In *twelve-tone music, the original form of a row.

Primo, secondo [It., first, second]. In a duet (e.g., for piano four-hands), the two parts, the *primo* usually being the leading part; in an orchestra, the two parts into which a section has been divided (e.g., first and second violins); *primo tempo,* the tempo with which a work began; *primo uomo,* the leading male singer in an opera.

Primrose, William (b. Glasgow, 23 Aug. 1903; d. Provo, Utah, 1 May 1982). Violist. Pupil of Ysaÿe. Played in the London String Quartet, NBC Symphony, and Festival Piano Quartet. Founded the Primrose Quartet, 1939. Taught at several U.S. institutions, including Indiana Univ. (1965–72). Participated in the Heifetz–Piatigorsky Concerts, early 1960s. Bartók, Britten, and Milhaud wrote concertos for him.

Prince [Nelson, Prince Rogers] (b. Minneapolis, 7 June 1958). Soul and rock singer, instrumentalist, songwriter, and producer. Albums include *1999*

(1982, including "Little Red Corvette"), *Purple Rain* (1984, including "When Doves Cry"; also a film), and *Batman* (film soundtrack, 1989). In 1994, changed his name to a graphic symbol.

Prince Igor [Russ. *Knyaz' Igor'*]. Opera in a prologue and four acts by Borodin (libretto by the composer on a scenario by Vladimir Stasov, after the Russian chronicle *The Story of Igor's Army*), composed in 1869–70 and 1874–87. It was completed by Rimsky-Korsakov and Glazunov and first produced in St. Petersburg in 1890. Setting: semilegendary Russia in the 12th century. See also *Polovtsian Dances.*

Principal. (1) The characteristic tone of the organ, produced by open *flue pipes of medium scale. (2) In an orchestra or large wind ensemble, the leader of any section (e.g., trumpets, violas, but not the first violins, whose leader is called the *concertmaster); also called the first chair.

Principale [Ger., also *Prinzipal(e)*]. The principal or lower register of the natural trumpet, as distinct from the *clarino.

Pritchard, John (Michael) (b. London, 5 Feb. 1921; d. Daly City, Calif., 5 Dec. 1989). Conductor. Worked at the Glyndebourne Opera from 1947; musical director, 1969–77. Led the Royal Liverpool Philharmonic, 1957–63; the London Philharmonic, 1962–66; the BBC symphony from 1982. Appeared at the Cologne, Belgian National, and San Francisco Operas.

Prix de Rome. A prize awarded on the basis of a competition held by the Académie des Beaux-Arts in Paris from 1803 until 1968. The competition entailed the composition of a cantata on a prescribed libretto, and the first prize or Grand Prix de Rome was a four-year stay at the Villa Medici in Rome. There is also a Belgian Prix de Rome, and the American Academy in Rome awards fellowships to composers as well.

Processional. A work performed during a procession at the beginning of some ceremony.

Prodaná Nevěsta [Cz.]. See *Bartered Bride, The.*

Prodigal Son, The. See *Enfant prodigue, L'.*

Program music [fr. Fr. *musique à programme;* Ger. *Programmusik*]. Music that attempts to express or depict one or more nonmusical ideas, images, or events. The composer usually indicates the "program" (the subject or subjects being evoked) by a suggestive title or preface, which may be quite vague or may be specific and detailed. A seemingly simple title—e.g., *Romeo and Juliet* (Tchaikovsky)—may suggest a rather precise sequence of characters and events. Other titles do little more than label a piece's mood, style, or dance characteristics or suggest an image that is not essential to an understanding of the music's spirit. Many pieces not supplied with programs by their composers were given inauthentic but enduring nicknames (e.g., Beethoven's *Moonlight Sonata* op. 27 no. 2).

The predominant genres of Romantic program music were the *program symphony and the *symphonic poem, followed by *concert overtures, *character pieces for piano or small ensemble, and, later, even an occasional string quartet such as Smetana's *From My Life* (1876). The symphony orchestra was a particularly fertile medium for program music, and Liszt and Richard Strauss were among its leading exponents. Examples can be found throughout the history of music and for all media, however.

Program symphony. An orchestral work in the form of a *symphony and bearing a descriptive title or program, like that of a *symphonic poem; also called descriptive or poematic symphony. A few 18th-century symphonies were programmatic, in large or small degree, but the Sixth Symphony of Beethoven (*Pastoral, 1808) became the principal model. Later examples include works by Berlioz (*Symphonie fantastique, 1830), Liszt (*Faust-Symphonie, 1857; *Dante, 1855–56), and Richard Strauss (*Ein Heldenleben, 1897–98).

Progression. A succession of two or more chords; also chord progression, harmonic progression; in jazz and popular music also termed changes.

Progressive jazz. A jazz style heralded by Stan Kenton's "Progressive Jazz Orchestra" of 1947–48. Its complex, often loud, brassy, densely voiced *bigband arrangements were usually intended for concert performance.

Prokofiev, Sergei Sergeievich (b. Sontsovka, near Ekaterinoslav, Ukraine, 27 [not 23] April 1891; d. Moscow, 5 March 1953). Composer and pianist. Studied with Glier and at the St. Petersburg Conservatory with Liadov, Rimsky-Korsakov, and N. Tcherepnin. In 1917, left Russia to tour Japan and America. Lived in Paris 1922–36; gave frequent European concert tours. In 1936, settled in Moscow, where his Western tendencies aroused political suspicion. During Stalin's "Zhdanov purge" (1948), he was severely criticized and many of his works were banned. Works: operas (incl. *The Gambler,* 1917; *Love for Three Oranges; The Fiery Angel,* 1919–23, rev. 1926–27; *The *Duenna* [Betrothal in a Monastery] 1941; *War and Peace,* 1941–43, rev. 1946–52; the socialist-realistic *Semyon Kotko,* 1939, and *Story of a Real Man,* 1947–48); ballets (incl. *Chout* [The Tale of the Buffoon], 1915, rev. 1920; *Le pas d'acier,* 1926, for Diaghilev, choreography by Massine;

*L'*Enfant prodigue; *Romeo and Juliet,* 1934; *Cinderella; Tale of the Stone Flower,* 1948–50); orchestral works (incl. *Scythian Suite,* 1915; 7 symphonies, incl. the *Classical; 6 piano concertos; concertos for violin and for cello; suites; overtures; children's pieces, incl. *Peter and the Wolf);* film scores (incl. *Lieutenant Kijé,* 1933; *Alexander Nevsky; Ivan the Terrible,* 1942–48, with Eisenstein); 10 sonatas and other piano pieces; choral pieces with and without orchestra, some Soviet-inspired; songs with piano (incl. *The Ugly Duckling,* 1914; many settings of poems of Balmont).

Prolation [Lat. *prolatio*]. See Mensural notation.

Prologue. The preface or introduction to a dramatic work, often serving to give the audience either background or a frame of reference.

Prolongation. See Schenker analysis.

Prolongement [Fr.]. The sostenuto pedal of the piano.

Prometheus. (1) See *Geschöpfe des Prometheus.* (2) A symphonic poem by Scriabin, *Prométhée, le poème du feu* (Prometheus: The Poem of Fire) op. 60 (1908–10), for large orchestra, piano, organ, choruses, and *color organ. The music is based on the so-called *mystic (Promethean) chord.

Pronto, prontamente [It.]. Quick(ly).

Prooemium [Lat.]. *Prelude.

Proper. Those items of the Mass and Office of the Roman rite whose texts and melodies vary with the occasion, as distinct from those whose texts remain the same throughout the liturgical year and thus make up the *Ordinary.

Prophète, Le [Fr., The Prophet]. Opera in five acts by Meyerbeer (libretto by Eugène Scribe), produced in Paris in 1849. Setting: the Anabaptist uprising in 16th-century Münster.

Proportion [Lat. *proportio*]. In *mensural notation, a ratio expressing the relationship between the note-values following the ratio and those preceding it or between the note-values of a work or passage and an assumed normal relationship of note-values to metrical pulse or *tactus. When the proportion is written as a fraction, the numerator (the first term when written as a ratio) expresses the number of notes of a certain value that are to occupy the same time as was previously occupied by the number of notes of the same value expressed in the denominator. In the accompanying example, four semibreves following the proportion are to take the time occupied by three semibreves preceding it. A proportion thus specifies diminution or augmentation. Among the most common proportions are 2:1 (or simply 2, also expressed

by a line, usually vertical, through the mensuration sign C or O, thus ¢ or Ø, or by turning the mensuration sign C backward, thus Ɔ; termed *proportio dupla* or simply *dupla* or *diminutio*), 3:1 (or simply 3; *proportio tripla* or *tripla*), and 3:2 (*sesquialtera,* which is equivalent to the use of coloration [see Mensural notation]).

Proportions first occur in the 14th century and increase in variety and complexity through the 15th century, reaching a peak around 1500 in works by composers such as Johannes Ockeghem and Heinrich Isaac.

Proportz, proportio [Ger.]. See *Nachtanz.*

Proposta [It.]. The subject of a fugue, as distinct from the answer or *riposta.*

Prosa [Lat.], **prose** [Fr.]. A term used in many medieval sources, especially those of French or English origin, for the text added to the extended melisma, or *sequentia,* that followed the verse of the Alleluia in the Mass [see Sequence]. Although the resulting combined form of words and music is usually referred to today as a sequence by writers in English, the word *prose* is still frequently found in French literature on the subject.

Prosody. Originally versification alone, but currently extended to refer to all features of a language involving stress, pitch, and length of syllables. Variations in prosodic features occur in the sound-structure (phonology) of every known language. In any given language, variation in one or more aspects of prosody may, although phonetically present, be nonsignificant in determining structural contrasts, whereas in another language the same variation may have structural (phonemic) significance.

For example, stress (also termed *accent) is the amount of force involved in expelling air from the lungs in speaking, and it may vary from quite weak to quite strong. In Hungarian, this phonetic contrast is present in extreme form, but since stress falls automatically on the first syllable of each word, it is not phonemically significant. In French, there is very little phonetic contrast in stress between syllables, but since the last syllable of each breath-group automatically has slightly stronger stress than those preceding, stress is likewise not phonemic. In languages in which stress is structurally significant (e.g., the Germanic languages and the Romance languages except for French), levels of significant stress may vary from four (as in English) to three (Italian) or two (Spanish). Languages having phonemically significant stress are often termed accentual. Similar distinctions exist among languages with respect to the pitch and duration of syllables or groups of syllables.

Versification in each language is a function of the phonological prosodic resources available to its speakers. Poetry over much of its history has depended upon the recurrence of certain prosodic features in a predetermined and hence predictable pattern or meter, e.g., a specific alternation of long and short syllables, or the presence of a certain number of stresses or syllables, in each verse. (In normal conversational prose, on the other hand, the speaker is not bound in advance to any specific prosodic pattern.) In longer verses of any type, there is normally a break in the prosodic structure, corresponding to a break in the sense, termed caesura, in the middle of the line.

Classical Latin and Greek verse prosody was quantitative, i.e., dependent on the relation of long (−) and short (⌣) syllables in each line of a poem. A unit of two or three syllables was a foot. A verse consisted of anywhere from two to six feet (dimeter, trimeter, tetrameter, pentameter, hexameter). The main types of foot were the iamb (⌣ −), the trochee (− ⌣), the anapaest (⌣ ⌣ −), the dactyl (− ⌣ ⌣), the spondee (− −), and the tribrach (⌣ ⌣ ⌣). Verse types were named according to the type of foot and the number of feet in each line. The most common classical verse types were iambic pentameter and dactylic hexameter. In classical Greek and Latin, word stress was not correlated with the type of syllable contained in a foot. Skillful poets used this absence of correlation to create a tension between word stress and the structure of the metrical feet in the middle of each line, resolving the tension by bringing the two into harmony again at the end.

In the Germanic languages, stress is the major factor in versification, involving a sequence of stressed syllables in regular rhythm (in accordance with the stress-timed nature of the language), with unstressed syllables (usually one or two at a time) falling in between. Common to all Germanic languages is a four-stressed line, with a caesura after the second stress. In contrast, versification in the Romance languages is primarily syllable-timed, i.e., based on the number of syllables (often miscalled feet, in imitation of classical terminology) in each line. Verses are found with any number of syllables from two (exceptionally) to twelve. In modern French, which has no phonemic stress, the favorite longer verse is the twelve-syllable or Alexandrine, with the possibility of a caesura after the fourth, sixth, or eighth syllable and of subdivisions within a six-syllable sequence, thus forming a very flexible type of line.

Musical sounds are, of course, also describable in terms of stress, pitch, and duration, and in setting poetic texts in their own languages, composers since at least the 16th century have naturally tended to follow their native prosodic patterns. A composer can often depart from the minor details of prosody (e.g., stress or pitch contours) with resultant beneficial tension between habitual speech patterns and a special emphasis attained by their violation, but the basic prosodic patterns of the language are generally followed. That is, the stress, pitch, and duration of the musical setting of a syllable should not in general contradict the stress, pitch, and duration of the syllable as it would be spoken or recited by a native speaker of the language in question. The same is true of performance: a singer or chorus should not introduce into a rendition features that are not characteristic of the language being sung (e.g., heavy stress on the first beat of each measure in a French art song). In some music of the late 20th century, however, texts may be treated as raw sonorous material and used in ways that have little to do with the text as normally spoken.

A special problem is posed by settings of languages no longer spoken and for which no native-speaker models are available, such as Latin, Old French, and Old Provençal. Composers have tended to treat Latin texts in accordance with the prosodic patterns of their own native language: for instance, French composers have usually paid little or no attention to Latin word stress in settings of liturgical texts; in contrast, greater care has been shown by native speakers of languages in which word stress is significant.

Prosula [Lat.]. The medieval term for the texts added to the internal melismas of certain liturgical chants of the Mass and less frequently of the Office. The creative process involved—that is, the addition of words to a preexistent melody—is related to that of the *sequence or *prosa, the word itself being a diminutive form of *prosa,* The titles of certain Kyrie prosulae are still used in modern chant books to identify the Kyries to which they were originally attached.

Prout, Ebenezer (b. Oundle, 1 Mar. 1835; d. Hackney, 5 Dec. 1909). Scholar, editor, critic. Taught at the National Training School for Music, 1876–82; the Royal Academy of Music, 1879–1909; and Trinity College, Dublin, from 1894. Edited Handel's *Samson* (1880) and *Messiah* (1902). Composed cantatas, an organ concerto, symphonies, church music. Wrote treatises on instrumentation, harmony, counterpoint, and musical form.

Provenzale, Francesco (b. Naples, ca. 1626; d. there, 6 Sept. 1704). Composer. From 1663, chief maestro at the Conservatorio S. Maria di Loreto, Naples; at S. Maria della Pietà dei Turchini, 1675–1701. *Maestro di cappella* of the city of Naples from 1665; at S. Gennaro, 1686–99. *Maestro di cappella di camera* at the viceregal court from 1688. One of the founders of the Neapolitan opera school. Composed operas, including *Il schiavo di sua moglie* (Naples, 1671) and *La Stellidaura vendicata* (Naples, 1674); sacred works.

Prussian Quartets. (1) A set of three string quartets by Mozart, K. 575 in D major, K. 589 in B♭ major, and K. 590 in F major, composed in 1789–90, possibly at the suggestion of Friedrich Wilhelm II of Prussia, who in 1789 had invited Mozart to Berlin. The monarch played the cello, and the cello parts are unusually elaborate. (2) Haydn's six string quartets op. 50, Hob. III:44–49 (1787). The title page of the Artaria first edition of 1787 bears a dedication to Friedrich Wilhelm II.

Pryor, Arthur (Willard) (b. St. Joseph, Mo., 22 Sept 1870; d. West Long Branch, N.J., 18 June 1942). Trombonist and bandleader. Joined Sousa's band, 1892; assistant conductor until 1903. Then formed his own band, touring and making hundreds of recordings. His many compositions include marches and rags (often trombone showpieces), songs, and piano music.

Ps. (1) Abbr. for *Psalm. (2) [Ger.] Abbr. for *Posaune* (trombone).

Psalm [Gr. *psalmos;* Lat. *psalmus;* Fr. *psaume;* Ger. *Psalm;* It., Sp. *salmo*]. A sacred poem or song; specifically, one of the 150 such poems making up the Book of Psalms of the Bible, also termed the *Psalter. For the methods of Psalm singing employed in the Gregorian and other repertories of plainsong, see Psalmody, Latin.

Psalm tone. A melodic formula to which the verses of the Psalms and certain other texts are sung [see Psalmody, Latin]. The use of such tones in the Western Christian rites is linked to Byzantine practice [see Byzantine chant] as is the system of eight *modes with which the Gregorian tones described here are inextricably linked.

The following items of the Gregorian liturgy employ psalm tones for their verses, each item having its own set of eight tones, one for each mode: the Psalms, canticles, and great responsories of the Office, and the introit of the Mass. The Invitatory at Matins also employs psalm tones for its verses, though modes 1 and 8 are not represented, and the number of tones for other modes varies. The communion of the Mass, as long as it retained verses, shared the tones of the introit. Within the appropriate set, the psalm tone is chosen according to the mode of the accompanying antiphon (for the Psalms, canticles, and Invitatory), responsory, or introit.

The underlying scheme for the tones, which may be seen to underlie other types of chants as well, is generally bipartite. In the first half, an intonation formula (*initium* or *inchoatio*) leads to a reciting tone (tenor or *tuba*), and this is followed by a cadence (mediant or *mediatio*). If the first half of the verse is sufficiently long, the tenor is inflected (flex or *flexa*) before proceeding to the mediant. The second half may begin with another intonation, returns to a reciting tone, and ends with a final cadence (termination or *terminatio*). In the tones for the Office Psalms, the final cadences are varied so as to smooth the transition to the beginning of the antiphon. These variations are termed differences (*differentiae,* each identified in modern books by the letter of the pitch on which it ends and, if more than one ends on any single pitch, a number as well). In modern books, antiphons for the Office are usually preceded by the number of their mode and this designation for the difference and followed by the musical notation for

Psalm 111, Tone 7.c.

the difference placed over the final syllables of the lesser *Doxology (E u o u a e, from *seculorum Amen*), with which the singing of a Psalm concludes. Because in the simpler tones much of the text is sung to the reciting tone, psalm tones are often said to be inflected monotones or recitatives. The pitch of the reciting tone is sometimes said to be a fundamental feature of the mode in question. These pitches have nevertheless varied somewhat with time and liturgical type. The separate sets of tones modify the general scheme in other ways as well. The accompanying example adapts two verses of Psalm 111 to tone 7 (i.e., the tone used with antiphons in mode 7) for the Office Psalms.

The *tonus peregrinus* (wandering or foreign tone) lies outside the system of eight tones but is found in the earliest sources (though the name is slightly later) and is similar to the other tones in design except for its use of different pitches for the reciting tones of the two halves. It is used principally for the singing of Psalm 113 (114–15), *In exitu Israel.*

Psalmodikon. A bowed *zither of Scandinavia with one to four melody strings over a fret board and several drone strings. It was used in the 19th century to accompany choral singing in the absence of an organ or piano, but passed out of use with the advent of the harmonium. See also *Langleik.*

Psalmody, British and North American. In the English-speaking Protestant and Reformed churches of the 17th, 18th, and 19th centuries, the singing of Psalms according to published metrical *psalters; by extension, the performance of any concerted sacred vocal music either for worship or for recreation. In the Anglican- and Calvinist-rooted denominations, psalmody provided an approximate equivalent to the slightly older use of *chorales in the German Lutheran Church. It gradually gave way after about 1790 to the increased use of hymns and choral singing in the Anglican cathedral style (anthems, responses, etc.), features that persist today in these churches. A few metrical Psalms still survive as hymns, e.g., "Old Hundredth" ("All people that on earth do dwell").

Psalmody, Latin. The singing of the Psalms in the Western Christian rites; also the several musical forms associated principally, though not exclusively, with the singing of Psalms. The psalmodic forms have often been thought to derive from the earliest practices of Psalm singing in Biblical times. The form of individual Psalm verses, which consist of two parallel elements, and the form of some whole Psalms, such as Psalm 135 (136), in which all verses conclude with the same words, suggest possible models for the surviving forms of psalmody. Attempts to find their specific origins in Jewish practice, however, have been seriously questioned. Formally constituted psalmody as a part of the Christian liturgy perhaps dates from as late as the 4th century, and regular psalmody in the synagogue is perhaps later still. All of the Western Christian chant repertories share these forms. The following descriptions refer principally to the Gregorian chant [see also Ambrosian chant, Gallican chant, Mozarabic chant; for Eastern practice see Byzantine chant]. Three forms of psalmody are usually distinguished, though both medieval and modern practice often obscure the supposed differences among them.

In antiphonal psalmody, the verses of a Psalm are sung alternately by the two halves of a choir or schola seated facing one another in front of and on opposite sides of the altar. The singing of the Psalm itself, to a relatively simple melodic formula called a *psalm tone that is adapted and repeated for each verse, is preceded and followed by the singing of a separate melody with a brief text usually drawn from the Psalm and called an *antiphon. The principal examples of antiphonal psalmody in the Office are the Psalms, canticles, and the *Invitatory. Of these, only the Invitatory preserves a scheme in which the antiphon is sung following verses other than the last. In modern practice for the Psalms and canticles, the antiphon is sung only at beginning and end, the lesser Doxology being divided and treated as two verses sung to the same psalm tone as the verses themselves. The antiphon is begun by a soloist and continued by the choir. The first half of each verse is also often sung by the soloist and the second half by the choir. Thus, alternation between soloist and choir is substituted for the original practice of alternation between the two halves of the choir. In the Mass, the *introit is the clearest example of this type of psalmody. The *offertory and the *communion of the Mass are also usually regarded as antiphonal chants, though the style of surviving offertories and their verses is quite different from that of other antiphonal pieces, and both offertory and communion were ultimately stripped of all verses, as early as the 12th century in some sources. According to this classification, all of the antiphonal chants of the Mass are associated with actions: the entrance at the beginning of the Mass, the offering, and the communion.

In responsorial psalmody, one or more soloists or cantors sing one or more verses, and a choir sings a refrain or respond at the beginning and end and perhaps following each of the verses. Although the earliest forms of responsorial psalmody may have incorporated whole Psalms, surviving examples include only one or a very few verses. It is unlikely that the surviving examples (even the few with more than one verse) are the remnants of pieces that at one time included many more verses or whole Psalms. The principal examples of responsorial psalmody in the Office are the great *responsories, the verses of which are sung to relatively elaborate psalm tones, and the brief responsories. The responsorial chants of the Mass are the *gradual and the *alleluia. In both Mass and Office, responsorial chants are associated with readings.

In direct psalmody, a Psalm is sung without alternation among singers and without the refrainlike additions found in antiphonal and responsorial psalmody. In the Mass this is usually said to be represented by the elaborate melodies of the *tract. In modern practice, successive verses of the tract are usually sung in alternation either between the soloists and the choir or between the two halves of the choir rather than by soloists alone.

Psalmus [Lat.]. *Psalm.

Psalter. The collected Book of Psalms of the Old Testament, as an independent entity or as a section of a liturgical book (with or without separate pagination). The authorship of David (King of Israel ca. 1012–ca. 972 B.C.E.) is no longer assumed.

The numeration of the Psalter in the Latin (Vulgate) and the King James Version (1611, which corresponds to the Hebrew and Lutheran numeration), is as follows:

Latin (Vulgate)	King James Version
1–8	1–8
9	9, 10
10–112	11–113
113	114, 115
114, 115	116
116–145	117–146
146, 147	147
148–150	148–150

Thus, of a total of 150 Psalms, only the first eight and the last three have the same number in both numerations. In all versions, the ordering of the Psalms is identical: five books, each of the first four concluding with a brief doxology, and the final Psalm 150 constituting the doxology to the entire Psalter. In the numeration of the King James Version, the doxologies conclude Psalms 41, 72, 89, and 106. The Latin numbering is employed in this dictionary, followed by the King James numbering in parentheses if it is different.

The entire Psalter is incorporated into the Roman Breviary and the Book of Common Prayer. The rubrics of the former direct its recitation once a week (a practice embodied in the Rule of St. Benedict, ca. 535), and those of the latter once a month. For the methods of Psalm singing employed in Gregor-

ian chant and related repertories, see Psalmody, Latin.

The Psalter has always been privileged in liturgy and worship, but during the Reformation of the 16th century, it acquired special and renewed importance, particularly in the liturgies of the Reformed (Calvinist) and related churches. Calvin held that only singing of unaccompanied Psalm texts in the vernacular (thus being immediately intelligible) was proper to his Reformed liturgy. The 1562 editions of the so-called Geneva (Huguenot) Psalter (*Les Psaumes mis en rime francois . . .*), comprising 152 texts set to 125 different melodies, were the first containing rhymed paraphrases in French of the complete Psalter (plus the Decalogue and Canticle of Simeon).

The Genevan experiment, in which a series of smaller collections culminated in the complete 1562 Psalter, became the prototype for a plethora of similar complete rhymed paraphrases, termed metrical Psalters, in other languages—notably, in English, the so-called 1562 Old Version of Thomas Sternhold (d. 1549), John Hopkins (d. 1570), and others; the 1612 Psalter of Henry Ainsworth (1571–1622?) brought to North America by the Pilgrims in 1620; and the New England Version or so-called *Bay Psalm Book of 1640, the first indigenous Psalter to be published in the colonies. The first Dutch metrical Psalter, the *Souterliedekens, was published in Antwerp in 1540 by Symon Cock and employed Dutch and French folk songs.

Through rhymed translations into German by the Lutheran Ambrosius Lobwasser (1515–85), which were designed to fit Genevan tunes, the Genevan melodies also penetrated deeply into German-speaking lands, both Reformed and Lutheran (provoking, in turn, the opposing Lutheran translation of Cornelius Becker in 1602, later set by Schütz). They were published in Dutch translation by Petrus Dathenus in 1566. There are over 2,000 polyphonic settings of the Genevan Psalms from the 16th century. These are in a variety of styles, from simple homophony to elaborate motets, many making use of the Genevan melodies. Such settings were not intended for use in church. Harmonized Psalters in England included Thomas East's *The Whole Booke of Psalmes* of 1592, with settings of the whole of Sternhold and Hopkins, and Thomas Ravenscroft's *The Whole Booke of Psalmes* of 1621, which introduced a great many new tunes.

The history of the rhymed English Psalter leads away from literal toward more poetic translations, marked by the "New Version" (1696) of Nahum Tate (1652–1715) and Nicholas Brady (1659–1706), and beyond that to the paraphrases, literary and evangelical distortions, and expansions of the 1719 collection of Isaac Watts (1674–1748), *The Psalms of*

David Imitated in the Language of the New Testament.
The unrhymed translation of the Psalter by Miles Coverdale (1488–1568), taken from the Great Bible of 1539, was incorporated into the Book of Common Prayer in 1549 and persists beneath all subsequent Anglican and American revisions to 1979.

Psalterium [Lat.; Gr. *psaltērion*]. In ancient Greece, any stringed instrument, but especially the harp; in the Middle Ages, any of a variety of stringed instruments, including the *harp, *crwth, and *psaltery; in the Renaissance, almost always the *psaltery.

Psaltery [Lat. *psalterium;* Fr. *psaltérion;* Gr. *Psalterium;* It., Sp. *salterio*]. A plucked *zither of medieval Europe with a flat, wooden sound box and a variable number of strings. Medieval illustrators and commentators identified the Biblical *psalterium* with frame harps and triangular zithers. Sometime in the 11th or 12th century, the Arabic *qānūn* reached Europe (whence the Latin term *canon*), and thereafter the vernacular term psaltery referred primarily to this instrument and its variants. They were made in several shapes: trapezoidal like the *qānūn*, square, triangular, and "pig's snout" (a trapezoid with inward-curving sides). The psaltery seems to have been extremely widespread from the 12th through the 15th century, but its popularity declined thereafter. See ill. under Zither.

Ptaszyńska, Marta (b. Warsaw, 29 July 1943). Composer and percussionist. Studied in Warsaw, in Paris with Boulanger, and at the Cleveland Institute of Music. Has taught at Bennington College, the Univ. of California, Berkeley, and Indiana Univ. Works include a television opera; an oratorio; *Helio, centricum, musicum,* a multimedia spectacle (1973); *Marimba Concerto* (1985); *Holocaust Memorial Cantata* (1992).

Puccini, Giacomo (Antonio Domenico Michele Secondo Maria) (b. Lucca, 22 Dec. 1858; d. Brussels, 29 Nov. 1924). Composer. Worked as organist in churches in and around Lucca. Studied at the Instituto musicale Pacini in Lucca, and at the Milan Conservatory with Bazzini and Ponchielli. Composed 12 operas, including *Le villi* (1883); *Manon Lescaut; La *bohème; *Tosca; *Madama Butterfly; La *fanciulla del West; La rondine* (1917); *Il *trittico; *Turandot;* sacred vocal music, songs, several orchestral works, music for string quartet, a violin sonata, and several keyboard works.

Puente, Tito [Ernest Anthony] (b. New York, 20 Apr. 1923). Jazz and salsa percussionist, vibraphonist, and bandleader. Studied at Juilliard. Formed his own band, The Piccadilly Boys, 1947; worked with small jazz groups. With Pérez Prado and Tito Rodríguez, helped popularize the mambo with recordings such as *Dance Mania* (1958). Continued to record Latin and jazz; won several Grammys.

Pugnani, (Giulio) Gaetano (Gerolamo) (b. Turin, 27 Nov. 1731; d. there, 15 July 1798). Violinist and composer. Pupil of G. B. Somis and Ciampi. Conductor at the King's Theatre, London, 1767–69. From 1770, first violinist of the King's Music, Turin; later also had conducting duties there. Pupils included Viotti. May have consulted with Tourte on the development of his bow. Composed works for violin solo, operas, chamber music, trio sonatas, and 7 symphonies.

Pugno, (Stéphane) Raoul (b. Montrouge, near Paris, 23 June 1852; d. Moscow, 3 Jan. 1914). Pianist and composer. Pupil of Niedermeyer and Thomas. Musical director, Paris Opéra, from 1871; choirmaster, St. Eugène Church, 1878–92. Taught at the Paris Conservatory, 1892–1901. Toured as a pianist; gave recitals with Ysaÿe from 1896. Composed comic operas and other dramatic works, an oratorio, piano pieces, songs.

Pui [OFr.]. See *Puy.*

Pujol (Vilarrubí), Emilio (b. Granadella, 7 Apr. 1886; d. Barcelona, 16 Nov. 1980). Guitarist, vihuelist, and musicologist. Pupil of Tárrega. Combined performance with historical research into guitar and vihuela. Taught at the Lisbon Academy (1946–69) and in Siena and Paris. Also wrote and arranged music for guitar.

Pujol, Juan (Pablo) (b. Barcelona, ca. 1573; d. there, May 1626). Composer. *Maestro de canto,* Tarragona Cathedral, from 1593; organist, Nuestra Señora del Pilar, Saragossa, from 1596. From 1612, choirmaster, Barcelona Cathedral. Composed Masses, motets, and other sacred and secular vocal works.

Pulcinella. A ballet with song by Stravinsky for soloists and chamber orchestra, commissioned by Sergei Diaghilev (choreography by Leonide Massine, decor and costumes by Pablo Picasso) and produced in Paris, 1920. The music makes free use of numerous passages from works by Pergolesi and works formerly attributed to him.

Punctum [Lat.]. See Neume, Punctus.

Punctus [Lat.]. (1) The dot employed in *mensural notation. (2) [pl. *puncta*] A section of an *estampie.*

Punk rock. A subgenre of *rock music that evolved as a form of social protest among English and working-class youths in the mid-1970s. Punk groups rejected rock's emphasis on technique and professionalism and relied instead upon sheer volume and rhythmic energy applied to rhythms and forms derived from *rock-and-roll of the early 1960s. Their dress and behavior were often intended to shock. The Sex Pistols, an English quartet, are credited with initiating the genre; by the time of their breakup in 1977, punk had already fallen prey to the same commercial aesthetic it was meant to criticize [see New wave].

Punta [It.]. Point; *p. d'arco,* the point or tip of the violin or similar bow.

Punteado [Sp.]. The style of guitar playing in which individual strings are plucked, as distinct from that in which all are strummed [see also *Rasgado, rasgueado*].

Punto, Giovanni [Stich, Johann Wenzel (Jan Václav)] (b. Zehušice, near Čáslav, 28 Sept. 1746; d. Prague, 16 Feb. 1803). Horn player, violinist, and composer. Served various nobles in Mainz, Paris, and elsewhere. Traveled widely in Europe. Violinist-conductor, Théâtre des variétés amusantes, Paris, 1789–99. Composed concertos and chamber music, most of it for horn. Beethoven composed the Horn Sonata op. 17 for him.

Purcell, Daniel (b. London, ca. 1660; d. 12 Dec. 1717). Composer. Brother of Henry Purcell. Organist of Magdalen College, Oxford, 1688–95; of St. Andrew's, Holborn, London, from 1713. Composed music for the final masque of his brother's *The Indian Queen;* also songs and incidental music for many plays; anthems, cantatas, odes, and sonatas.

Purcell, Henry (b. London, ca. 1659; d. Westminster, London, 21 Nov. 1695). Composer. Boy chorister in the Chapel Royal; presumably studied with Cooke, Humfrey, and Blow. At age 8, contributed a three-part song to Playford's *Catch That Catch Can.* Composer-in-ordinary for the violins from 1677. Organist of Westminster Abbey from 1679; at the Chapel Royal from 1682. From 1683, organ maker and keeper of the king's instruments. Composed operas and semi-operas (incl. *Dido and Aeneas; Dioclesian,* 1690; *King Arthur,* Dryden, 1691; *The *Fairy Queen,* after Shakespeare's *A Midsummer Night's Dream,* 1692; *The *Indian Queen,* Dryden, final masque by D. Purcell, 1695; *The Tempest,* after Shakespeare, ca. 1695); incidental music and songs for over 40 plays; other secular music, including solo songs, songs for 2 or more voices and continuo, over 50 catches; anthems, services, and other sacred works; court odes and welcome songs for solo voices, chorus, and orchestra; instrumental music, including fantasias, overtures, pavans, airs, hornpipes, works for harpsichord and organ, as well as

chamber music for viol consort or two violins and continuo. Wrote a treatise on descant.

Purfling [Fr. *filet;* Ger. *Einlage;* It. *filetto;* Sp. *filete*]. The inlaid borders of the belly and back of the violin and some related instruments.

Puritani di Scozia, I [It., The Puritans of Scotland]. Opera in three acts by Bellini (libretto by Carlo Pepoli after the play *Têtes rondes et cavaliers* by François Ancelot and Xavier Boniface Saintine, in turn loosely related to Sir Walter Scott's *Old Mortality*), produced in Paris in 1835. Since the story has nothing to do with Scotland, the title is sometimes given simply as *I Puritani.* Setting: near Plymouth, England, early in the 1650s.

Puy, pui [OFr.]. A French literary or musical society of the period from the 12th century through the early 17th. Such societies, which existed in a number of French cities and in London, were presided over by an elected *prince du puy* (sometimes addressed as such in poems; see *Envoi*) and held regular competitions at which the winning poet was crowned.

Puyana, Rafael (b. Bogotá, 14 Oct. 1931). Harpsichordist. Pupil of Landowska. New York debut, 1957; toured Europe and the Americas and released recordings. Settled in Paris; built a collection of period keyboard instruments.

Pylkkänen, Tauno (Kullervo) (b. Helsinki, 22 Mar. 1918; d. there, 13 Mar. 1980). Composer. Pupil of Madetoja, Palmgren, and Ranta. Worked for the Finnish Broadcasting Company until 1961; as music critic for the daily *Uusi Suomi,* 1941–69. During 1960s, artistic director, Finnish National Opera. From 1967 taught at the Helsinki Academy of Music. Works include operas (*Varjo* [The Shadow], 1952; *Tuntematon stilas* [The Unknown Soldier], 1967); song cycles; choral, orchestral, and chamber works.

Pyramid piano. An upright grand piano in the shape of a truncated pyramid. Such pianos, which at first had curved sides, were made beginning in the first half of the 18th century and were popular until about 1825.

Pythagorean hammers. Elements of a myth, first appearing in the 2nd century, that ascribes to Pythagoras the discovery of the numerical characterization of basic musical intervals. He was said to have discovered that four blacksmith's hammers, weighing 12, 9, 8, and 6 pounds, produced musical intervals when struck in pairs: octave (12:6), fifth (12:8 and 9:6), fourth (12:9 and 8:6), and whole tone (9:8). Although these numbers correctly represent the ratios of frequencies of the intervals, the myth is unsound acoustically.

Pythagorean scale. A diatonic scale characterized by pure fifths (3:2), pure fourths (4:3), and whole tones defined as the difference between a fifth and a fourth (3:2 − 4:3 = 9:8). The earliest complete presentation occurs in Plato's *Timaeus*. There, each fourth is subdivided into two whole tones and a remainder, called *diesis* (difference) and later, *limma* (remnant). Thus, 4:3 − (9:8)^2 = 256:243. Thus, the diatonic scale from c to c′ would consist of five whole tones, each with the ratio 9:8, and two semitones (e–f and b–c′), each with the ratio 256:243. The same scale can be derived by assuming a series of perfect fifths, beginning with F. If this series, F c g d′ a′ e″ b″, is collapsed into a single octave, the Pythagorean scale is produced.

Q

Qānūn [Ar.; fr. Gr. *kanōn;* Turk. *kanun*]. A plucked *zither of the Middle East. Its 50 to 100 strings of metal, gut, or nylon are strung in courses of three over a shallow trapezoidal or half-trapezoidal box. The player holds it horizontally in the lap and plucks or strums the strings with plectra on the fingers of both hands. It is distributed from India to the Maghrib and is particularly favored in the art music of Turkey and the Arab countries. See ill. under Instrument; see also Psaltery.

Quadrat [Ger.]. The natural sign (♮).

Quadrivium [Lat.]. In the Middle Ages, the subjects making up the mathematical or upper group of the seven liberal arts: arithmetic, music, geometry, and astronomy. The rhetorical or lower group, known collectively as the *trivium,* were grammar, logic, and rhetoric.

Quadruple counterpoint. See Invertible counterpoint.

Quadruple-croche [Fr.]. Sixty-fourth *note.

Quadruple fugue. See Double fugue.

Quadruple meter, time. *Meter consisting of recurring groups of four pulses.

Quadruplet. A group of four notes of equal value occurring in the time normally occupied by three notes of the same value and identified by the figure 4.

Quadruplum [Lat.]. In music of the *Notre Dame repertory, the fourth or uppermost part of an *organum in four parts; *organum quadruplum,* an organum in four parts.

Quantz, Johann Joachim (b. Oberscheden, Hannover, 30 Jan. 1697; d. Potsdam, 12 July 1773). Flutist, composer, and flute maker. Pupil of J. D. Zelenka and Gasparini. Member of the Dresden town band; of the Polish chapel orchestra of Augustus II from 1718; of the Dresden court Kapelle from 1727. Flute instructor to Prince Frederick from 1728; court composer and chamber musician in Berlin after Frederick became king. His treatise, *Versuch einer Anweisung die Flöte traversiere zu spielen* (1752), discusses nearly all aspects of performance practice. Composed over 200 flute sonatas and 300 flute concertos; trio sonatas; some vocal music.

Quarrel of the Buffoons. See *Bouffons, Querelle des.*

Quartal harmony. Harmony based on combinations of the interval of a fourth, as distinct from tertian harmony (e.g., Western tonal harmony), which is based on combinations of the third.

Quarte [Ger.]. The interval of a fourth. As a prefix (*Quart-*) to the name of an instrument, it indicates that the instrument is pitched a fourth above or below the standard instrument.

Quarter note. See Note.

Quarter tone. An interval equal to half of a semitone [see Microtone].

Quartet [Fr. *quatuor;* Ger. *Quartett;* It. *quartetto;* Sp. *cuarteto*]. (1) A composition for four solo performers, with or without accompaniment. (2) An ensemble of four solo performers.

Four parts replaced three as the normal texture of vocal composition in the 15th century, with soprano, alto, tenor, and bass established as the standard distribution in the 16th century. Considerable Renaissance secular vocal and instrumental music is in four parts, usually performed by soloists.

Four-part texture is again prominent in Classical chamber music, especially in the *string quartet. Quartets combining strings and winds were also fairly common, but all-wind quartets less so than quintets. After ca. 1750, the quartet for keyboard and strings also began to be cultivated, first for harpsichord, two violins, and cello (Haydn, 11 extant quartets), then for the standard later ensembles of piano, violin, viola, and cello (Mozart, K. 478, 493). Later examples are relatively few but include notable works by Schumann, Brahms, and Fauré.

Use of the quartet as an operatic ensemble with orchestral accompaniment began in the early 18th century. The unaccompanied vocal quartet (male, female, or mixed) was very popular, especially as social music, in the 19th century, and remained so in popular music, especially black, in the 20th century [see also Barbershop singing].

Quartfagott [Ger.]. A *bassoon pitched a fourth below the normal bassoon; sometimes, however, a bassoon pitched a fourth above the normal bassoon.

Quartflöte [Ger.]. In the 17th and 18th centuries, a recorder with the lowest pitch c'', a fourth above the normal alto on g'.

Quartgeige [Ger.]. *Violino piccolo.

Quartole [Ger.], **quartolet** [Fr.]. *Quadruplet.

Quartposaune [Ger.]. In the 17th and 18th centuries, a bass trombone in F, a fourth below the normal tenor trombone.

Quasi [It.]. Almost, as if.

Quattro [It.]. Four; *quattro mani*, four hands; *quattro voci*, four voices.

Quatuor [Fr.]. *Quartet.

Quaver. In British terminology, the eighth *note.

Queen, The. See *Reine, La*.

Queen of Spades, The [Russ. *Pikovaya dama;* Fr. *Pique dame*]. Opera in three acts by Tchaikovsky (libretto by Modest Tchaikovsky and the composer, after Pushkin), produced in St. Petersburg in 1890. Setting: St. Petersburg at the end of the 18th century.

Queler, Eve (b. New York, 1 Jan. 1936). Conductor. Pupil of Susskind and Slatkin. Worked with the New York City Opera and the Metropolitan; 1968, formed the Opera Orchestra of New York, which she directed in a number of rarely performed operas. The first woman to conduct the symphony orchestras of Philadelphia, Cleveland, and Montreal.

Querelle des bouffons [Fr.]. See *Bouffons, Querelle des*.

Querflöte [Ger.]. Transverse flute.

Querpfeife [Ger.]. Fife.

Queue [Fr.]. Tail or stem, e.g., of a note; *piano à queue*, grand piano.

Quickstep. (1) Since the 18th century, a fast military march. (2) A fast version of the *foxtrot, introduced in London in 1923.

Quijada [Sp.]. *Jawbone.

Quilt canzona. A *canzona made up of short sections in contrasting styles.

Quilter, Roger (b. Brighton, 1 Nov. 1877; d. London, 21 Sept. 1953). Composer. Pupil of I. Knorr. Composed numerous songs (incl. *Three Shakespeare Songs*, 1905; *Three Songs of William Blake*, 1917), many of which were performed by popular singers; orchestral music (*A Children's Overture*, 1919); an opera; chamber music.

Quinault, Philippe (b. Paris, bapt. 5 June 1635; d. there, 26 Nov. 1688). Dramatist, librettist, and poet.

From 1671 collaborated with Lully on works including *Cadmus et Hermione* (1673); *Alceste* (1674); *Thésée* (1675); *Atys* (1676); *Isis* (1677); *Le triomphe de l'amour* (1681); *Persée* (1682); *Amadis* (1684); *Roland* (1685); *Armide* (1686).

Quinet, Marcel (b. Binche, 6 July 1915; d. Woluwé-St. Lambert, Brussels, 16 Dec. 1986). Composer. Pupil of Jongen and Absil. Taught at the Brussels Conservatory, 1943–79; at the Chapelle musicale Reine Elisabeth from 1956. Works include *Les deux bavards* (chamber opera, 1966); *La nef des fous* (ballet, 1969); *La vague et le sillon* (cantata, 1945); 3 piano concertos, a symphony, and other orchestral works; chamber music.

Quint. (1) [Fr. *quinte*] An organ stop of Principal scale sounding the interval of the fifth or its octaves. (2) [Ger.] A prefix in the names of some instruments, indicating that they sound a fifth above or below the standard instrument. See also *Quinte, Quintsaite*.

Quinta, quinta vox [Lat.]. In Renaissance polyphony, a fifth voice or part in addition to the normal complement of *superius, altus, tenor,* and *bassus*.

Quintanar, Héctor (b. Mexico City, 15 Apr. 1936). Composer. Studied with Galindo, R. Halffter, Jiménez Mabarak, and in New York and Paris. Joined and then directed (1965–72) the Composition Workshop of Carlos Chávez; established the Mexico City Conservatory electronic music facility, 1970. Works include symphonies and other orchestral music; *Aclamaciones* (orchestra, chorus, and tape, 1967); chamber music; *Sideral I,* tape (1968); *Símbolas,* 8 instruments, tape, slides, and lights; and *Diágolos,* piano and tape.

Quinte [Fr., Ger.]. (1) The interval of a fifth. (2) *Quint. (3) [Fr.] *Quinte (de violon),* viola.

Quintenquartett [Ger., Fifths Quartet]. Popular name for Haydn's String Quartet in D minor op. 76 no. 2, Hob. III:76 (1797), so called because of the descending fifths in the first theme of the opening movement.

Quintet [Fr. *quintette,* formerly *quintuor;* Ger. *Quintett;* It. *quintetto;* Sp. *quinteto*]. (1) A composition for five solo performers, with or without accompaniment. (2) An ensemble of five solo performers.

Five-part writing was highly favored in the 16th century and appears in much vocal and instrumental music of the period. In the 17th century, it continued to be common in music for orchestra and certain types of solo ensemble (e.g., the viol consort), but otherwise it was not much used again until the Classical period. The string quintet is less common than the string quartet, but there are notable examples by Mozart, Beethoven, Dvořák, Bruckner, and Brahms.

These employ the usual ensemble of string quartet with extra viola. An extra cello appears in most of the quintets of Boccherini, as well as in Schubert's great String Quintet in C major D. 956.

Quintets for string quartet and a woodwind instrument were popular in the Classical period. Brahms's Clarinet Quintet is the best-known later example. The usual wind quintet includes flute, oboe, clarinet, bassoon, and horn. Brass quintets (usually two trumpets, horn, trombone, and tuba) have become popular in North America in recent decades. The piano quintet (usually for piano and string quartet) seems to have arisen out of the many Classical concertos whose accompaniments could be played by a string quartet. Some piano quintets of this period do achieve a genuine chamber-music texture. Romantic composers (Schumann, Brahms, Dvořák, Franck, Fauré) produced several important examples. Mozart's Quintet in E♭ major K. 452 for piano and winds was the model for Beethoven's op. 16 but had few later followers.

Quintfagott [Ger.]. In the 17th century, a bassoon pitched a fifth below the ordinary bassoon; in the 18th and 19th centuries, also a bassoon pitched a fifth above the normal instrument.

Quintole [Ger.], **quintolet** [Fr.]. *Quintuplet.

Quinton [Fr.]. (1) In the 17th century, the *pardessus de viole*. (2) In the late 18th century, a hybrid of the viol and violin with a body similar, except for its sloping shoulders, to that of the violin and with its neck fretted like that of the viol. Its five strings were tuned g d' a' d'' g''.

Quintsaite [Ger.]. (1) The highest string of the lute, even if the instrument is of six courses. (2) The E-string of the violin.

Quintuor [Fr.]. *Quintet.

Quintuple meter. *Meter consisting of recurring groups of five pulses. In Western art music, it has been relatively rare, though by no means unknown, until the 20th century. Often the five pulses are in

effect subdivided into two plus three, as in the third movement of Tchaikovsky's Symphony no. 6, or three plus two.

Quintuplet. A group of five notes of equal value to be played in the time normally occupied by four notes of the same value and indicated by the figure 5.

Quintus [Lat.]. *Quinta pars, quinta vox.*

Qui tollis [Lat.]. A section of the *Agnus Dei of the Mass.

Quodlibet [Lat., what you please]. A composition in which well-known melodies or texts are presented simultaneously or successively, the result being humorous or displaying technical virtuosity. Examples date from the late Middle Ages to the present.

Quodlibets can be categorized as catalog, successive, or simultaneous. The texts of catalog quodlibets are lists or series of items classifiable under a single heading (e.g., noses, proverbs about drinking, or chanson refrains); their music is most often newly composed. The principal voice of a successive quodlibet is a string of textual and musical quotations. The other voices form a homophonic accompaniment and may be textless or may carry the same text as the principal voice. The type was popular as entertainment music throughout the 16th, 17th, and 18th centuries, as was its descendant, the *potpourri, in 19th-century Vienna. In a simultaneous quodlibet, two or more voices make use of preexisting musical material (and perhaps its text) at the same time, each consisting of either a patchwork of quotes or a single preexisting melody. A famous simultaneous quodlibet is the last variation of Bach's *Goldberg Variations, in which two German songs are set against each other as well as against the theme's harmonic framework.

Terms designating compositions similar to the quodlibet (but commonly not exact equivalents) include *farrago* [Lat.], *fricassée* [Fr.], *ensalada* [Sp.], and *messanza, misticanza, centone,* and *incatenatura* [It.].

R

R. Abbr. for *ripieno, *récit, *responsory (℞/), *ritardando.

Raaff, Anton (b. Gelsdorf, near Bonn, bapt. 6 May 1714; d. Munich, 28 May 1797). Tenor. Studied in Munich and Bologna. Sang in Vienna, Italy, Lisbon, Madrid, and Naples (1759–70). In 1770, joined Elector Carl Theodor's court in Mannheim. Mozart wrote the role of Idomeneo and the aria "Se al labbro mio" (K. 295) for him.

Rääts, Jaan (b. Tartu, Estonia, 15 Oct. 1932). Composer. Studied with Eller at the Tallinn Conservatory; taught there, 1968–70 and from 1978. Worked at Estonian Radio; 1966–74, musical director of Estonian Television. Works include 8 symphonies; concertos for piano, violin, 2 pianos; chamber music; sonatas and other piano pieces.

Rabāb [Ar.; related spellings in other languages]. Any of several distinct bowed, stringed instruments of the Islamic world, most of them held upright and bowed. It is described in Arabic theory of the 10th century, and one member of the group plays a leading role in the Javanese gamelan. See ills. under Instrument.

Rabaud, Henri (Benjamin) (b. Paris, 10 Nov. 1873; d. there, 11 Sept. 1949). Composer and conductor. Pupil of Gédalge and Massenet. Conductor of the Paris Opéra and the Opéra-comique from 1908; director, 1914–18. Director of the Paris Conservatory, 1922–41. Composed operas (Mârouf, savetier du Caire, 1914); film scores; 2 symphonies and other orchestral music; choral works (Job, oratorio, 1900); chamber music; piano pieces; songs.

Rabbia, con [It.]. With rage, fury.

Rabel [Sp.]. (1) *Rebec. (2) A fiddle of Spain and Latin America with one to four strings.

Rachmaninoff, Sergei (Vassilievich) (b. Semyonovo, 1 Apr. 1873; d. Beverly Hills, 28 Mar. 1943). Composer, pianist, and conductor. Studied at the St. Petersburg Conservatory and at the Moscow Conservatory with Ziloti, Taneyev, and Arensky. Concertized widely as a pianist and conductor. Conductor at the Bolshoi Opera, 1904–6; first American tour, 1909. Settled in the U.S., 1918. Recorded with the Victor Talking Machine Company. Composed operas (Aleko, 1892; The Miserly Knight, 1903–5;

Francesca da Rimini, 1900–5); orchestral works (3 symphonies; 4 piano concertos, incl. no. 2 in C minor, 1900–1; The Isle of the Dead, 1909; Rhapsody on a Theme of Paganini, with solo piano, 1934; Symphonic Dances, 1940); solo piano music (Prelude in C♯ minor, 1892; Études-tableaux, 1916–17; choral works (The Bells, cantata, 1913; All-Night Vigil, 1915); chamber music; songs on texts of Pushkin and other Russian Romantics.

Racket [Fr. cervelas, cervelat; Ger. Rankett, Rackett]. A small, cylindrical, double-reed woodwind instrument of the 16th and 17th centuries. The bore of the instrument is constructed of a number of parallel channels connected within a cylinder of solid ivory or wood to effect a long bore [see ill. under Reed]. In the 18th century, the racket was redesigned and renamed the racket bassoon [Fr. cervelat à musique, basson à serpentine; Ger. Rackettenfagott, Stockfagott, Wurstfagott (Eng. sausage bassoon)].

Raddolcendo [It.]. Becoming softer, sweeter.

Raddoppiare [It.]. To *double, often at the octave.

Radical bass. *Fundamental bass.

Radleier [Ger.]. *Hurdy-gurdy.

Raff, (Joseph) Joachim (b. Lachen, near Zurich, 27 May 1822; d. Frankfurt am Main, 24 or 25 June 1882). Composer. Associate of Liszt, whose works he may have helped to orchestrate. From 1877, director and teacher, Frankfurt Conservatory (pupils included MacDowell). Works include an oratorio, sacred music, male part songs, solo songs; 11 symphonies, concertos, and other orchestral pieces; much chamber music, many piano pieces.

Raffrenando [It.]. Slowing down.

Rāg(a) (-am) [Hin., Skt., Tel.]. *Mode in Indian music. In addition to scale, the concept may include notions of pitch ranking, characteristic ascent and descent patterns, motives, use of ornaments, performance time, and emotional character.

Ragtime. A composed instrumental genre, primarily for piano and principally created by black Americans, that combines syncopated melodies with the forms of the march; the syncopated style of this genre. Classic rags of Scott Joplin (1868–1917), James Scott (1886–1938), and Joseph Lamb (1887–

1960) present three or four distinct 16-bar themes (strains) in duple meter. Tempos are most often moderate, suitable for dances such as the *cakewalk, *two-step, *one-step (in a fast tempo), or *polka.

Raimondi, Pietro (b. Rome, 20 Dec. 1786; d. there, 30 Oct. 1853). Composer. Pupil of Tritto. Director of the royal theaters of Naples from 1824. Taught at the Naples Conservatory, 1824–32; Palermo Conservatory, 1832–52. *Maestro di cappella* at St. Peter's, Rome, from 1852. Composed fugues for up to 64 voices; 3 oratorios which may be performed simultaneously; 62 operas, sacred music, ballets.

Raindrop Prelude. Popular name for Chopin's Prelude in D♭ major op. 28 no. 15 (the 24 preludes of op. 28 dating from 1836–39), so called because the continuously repeated A♭ (G♯ in the middle section) suggests the sound of raindrops.

Rainey, Ma [Gertrude Pridgett] (b. Columbus, Ga., 26 Apr. 1886; d. Rome, Ga., 22 Dec. 1939). Blues singer. From 1904, toured the South and Midwest, singing in circuses and minstrel and vaudeville shows. The first great blues singer. Recordings include "Bo-weavil Blues," "Barrelhouse Blues," and "Moonshine Blues" (all 1923). Later recorded with Louis Armstrong, Fletcher Henderson, and Coleman Hawkins.

Rainier, Priaulx (b. Howick, Natal, 3 Feb. 1903; d. Besse-en-Chandesse, Auvergne, 10 Oct. 1986). Composer. Studied with McEwen at the Royal Academy of Music, where she taught 1943–61, and with Boulanger in Paris. Made use of Zulu music. Her works include orchestral music (Concertante for Two Winds and Orchestra, 1977–80), vocal music (Requiem, 1955–56), and chamber music (Grand Duo for Cello and Piano, 1980–82).

Raisa, Rosa [Burschstein, Raisa; Rose] (b. Białystok, Poland, 23 May 1893; d. Los Angeles, 28 Sept. 1963). Soprano. Studied in Naples; concert debut, Rome, 1912. Sang in Chicago in 1913 (Aida) and 1916–36. In 1937, opened a singing school there with her husband, baritone Giacomo Rimini. Created Puccini's Turandot at La Scala.

Raison, André (b. before 1650; d. Paris, 1719). Composer. Organist of the royal abbey of Ste. Geneviève, Paris, from about 1666, and at Jacobins de St. Jacques. Published 2 volumes of organ music, containing 5 Masses. Clérambault was his pupil.

Rake's Progress, The. Opera in three acts by Stravinsky (libretto by W. H. Auden and Chester Kallman, inspired by William Hogarth's series of prints of the same name), produced in Venice in 1951. Setting: England in the 18th century.

Rákóczi March. A Hungarian national air set down ca. 1810 by János Bihari in homage to Prince Ferenc Rákóczi II (1676–1735), leader of the Hungarian revolt against Austria. The melody was used by Berlioz in *La *damnation de Faust* and by Liszt in the *Hungarian Rhapsody* no. 15.

Raksin, David (b. Philadelphia, 4 Aug. 1912). Composer. Pupil of I. Freed and Schoenberg. Taught at the Univ. of Southern California from 1956 and at UCLA. Wrote mainly film scores, including the theme song "Laura" and *Modern Times* (Charlie Chaplin, 1935). Other works include symphonic suites; incidental music; a band instrumentation of Stravinsky's *Circus Polka* for Balanchine's production with the Barnum and Bailey Circus; *Oedipus memneitai* (1986).

Ralentir [Fr.]. To slow down.

Rallentando [It., abbr. *rall.*]. Slowing down.

Rameau, Jean-Philippe (b. Dijon, bapt. 25 Sept. 1683; d. Paris, 12 Sept. 1764). Composer and theorist. Held organ posts in Clermont, 1702–5 and 1715–22; Paris, 1706–9 and from 1732; Dijon, 1709; Lyons, 1713–15. Settled in Paris, 1722. Dramatic works (various genres, including the *tragédie lyrique,* the *opéra-ballet,* and *comédie-ballet)* include *Hippolyte et Aricie* (1733); *Les Indes galantes* (1735); *Castor et Pollux* (1737); *Les fêtes d'Hébé* (1739); *La princesse de Navarre* (Voltaire, 1745); *Platée* (1745); *Zaïs* (1748); *Pigmalion* (1748); *Naïs* (1749). Also composed secular cantatas (*Les amants trahis,* by 1721; *Le berger fidèle,* by 1728); sacred vocal music; several collections of solo harpsichord music; other instrumental works. Published important theoretical works, including *Traité de l'harmonie* (1722).

Ramey, Samuel (Edward) (b. Colby, Kans., 28 Mar. 1942). Bass-baritone. Studied in New York. New York City Opera debut, 1973; Metropolitan debut, 1984. Roles include Don Giovanni, Leporello, Figaro, Mephistopheles (Gounod's *Faust*), and Philip II (Verdi's *Don Carlos*); a leading figure in the revival of Handel and Rossini operas.

Rampal, Jean-Pierre (Louis) (b. Marseilles, 7 Jan. 1922). Flutist. Studied at the conservatories of Marseilles and Paris, where he taught from 1968. Joined the Paris Opéra orchestra, 1956–62. From 1947 toured as a soloist and made many recordings. Founded the Quintette à vent française (1945) and the Ensemble baroque de Paris (1953). Poulenc and others have written works for him.

Ran, Shulamit (b. Tel Aviv, 21 Oct. 1949). Composer and pianist. Pupil of Boskovich, Ben-Haim, Dello Joio, Reisenberg, and Shapey. In 1967, performed her own Capriccio for piano and orchestra (1963) with Bernstein and the New York Philharmonic. Works include Symphony no. 1 (1990; Pulitzer Prize) and other orchestral works; a concerto and other pieces for piano and orchestra; chamber and piano music (*Invocation*, horn, chimes, timpani, 1995).

Randall, James K(irtland) (b. Cleveland, 16 June 1929). Composer. Pupil of Elwell, Sessions, and Babbitt. Has taught at Princeton (from 1958) and the U.S. Naval School of Music. Has made use of computer-synthesized sounds. Works include *Slow Movement*, piano (1959); *Improvisation on a Poem by e. e. cummings*, voice, chamber ensemble (1960); *Lyric Variations*, violin, computer (1967); music for the film *Eakins* (1972).

Randegger, Alberto (b. Trieste, 13 Apr. 1832; d. London, 18 Dec. 1911). Composer and conductor. Pupil of L. Ricci. Directed theaters in Brescia and Venice, 1852–54. Moved to London, 1854. Taught at the Royal Academy of Music and Royal College of Music; directed at Covent Garden and Drury Lane (1887–98). Promoted Wagner's early works. Composed operas (*The Rival Beauties*, 1864) and other vocal works. Wrote a textbook on singing.

Rands, Bernard (b. Sheffield, 2 Mar. 1934). Composer. Pupil of Vlad, Dallapiccola, Boulez, Maderna, and Berio. Has taught at the Univ. of California, San Diego (from 1975), the California Institute of the Arts, Boston Univ., Juilliard, and Harvard. Works include orchestral music (*Wildtrack 1*, 1969; *Mésalliance*, with solo piano, 1972; *Ology*, jazz ensemble, 1973; Symphony, 1994); 2 string quartets and other chamber music; music for voice (*Serena*, voice, mime, tape, 1972; *Canti del sole*, tenor, orchestra, 1982; Pulitzer Prize, 1984).

Range. The span of pitches between highest and lowest of an instrument, voice, or part; also compass. See also Tessitura.

Rangström, (Anders Johan) Ture (b. Stockholm, 30 Nov. 1884; d. there, 11 May 1947). Composer. Pupil of Pfitzner. Worked as a music critic for several papers; taught singing. Conducted the Göteborg Symphony, 1923–25. Works include around 250 songs; dramatic music; 4 symphonies and other orchestral works; chamber and choral works.

Rank. A row of pipes, one for each note of the organ keyboard, making up a stop. Mixture stops have two or more pipes for each note.

Rankett [Ger.]. *Racket.

Rankl, Karl (b. Gaaden, near Vienna, 1 Oct. 1898; d. Salzburg, 6 Sept. 1968). Conductor and composer. Pupil of Schoenberg and Webern. Conducted at the Kroll Opera, Berlin, and the German Theater, Prague. Music director, Covent Garden, 1946–51; conductor, Scottish Orchestra, 1951–56. Composed the opera *Deirdre of the Sorrows* and 8 symphonies.

Ranta, Sulho (b. Peräseinäjoki, 15 Aug. 1901; d. Helsinki, 5 May 1960). Composer. Studied with Melartin and in Vienna and Paris. Taught at the Sibelius Academy, 1934–56. Edited biographical dictionaries of Finnish musicians. Works include orchestral music (Symphony No. 4, *Oratorio volgare*, 1951), concertos, songs, and chamber works (*Suite symphonique*, flute, clarinet, horn, string quartet, piano, 1926–28).

Ranz des vaches [Fr.; Ger. *Kuhreigen*, *Kuhreihen*]. A type of Swiss melody, sometimes sung, but most characteristically played on the *alphorn by herdsmen to call their cows; also *Lobetanz*, after the opening words of some examples "Lobet, o lobet" (fr. *loba*, cow).

Rape of Lucretia, The. Opera in two acts by Britten (libretto by Ronald Duncan after André Obey's play *Le viol de Lucrèce*, in turn after Shakespeare and Livy), produced in Glyndebourne in 1946. Setting: in or near Rome, ca. 510 B.C.E.

Raphael, Günter (Albert Rudolf) (b. Berlin, 30 Apr. 1903; d. Herford, Germany, 19 Oct. 1960). Composer. Pupil of R. Kahn. Taught in Leipzig until 1934; later at the Duisburg Conservatory, the Mainz Conservatory, and the Cologne Hochschule für Musik (from 1957). Used twelve-tone technique. Composed many orchestral works (5 symphonies; 2 violin concertos); vocal pieces (*Geistliche Chormusik*, 12 motets, 1938); 4 string quartets and other chamber music; piano and organ music.

Rappresentatione di Anima, et di Corpo [It., Representation of the Soul and the Body]. A work for the stage by Emilio de' Cavalieri (text in part from a dialogue by Agostino Manni), first performed in Rome in 1600 and published there in the same year (the first publication to include a *basso continuo*). Because of its religious themes, it is sometimes regarded as the first *oratorio. It was, however, staged with scenery, costumes, and dancing, the music consisting of recitatives, strophic airs, madrigals, and short homophonic choruses intended for dancing.

Rappresentativo [It.]. See *Stile rappresentativo.*

Rappresentazione sacra, sacra rappresentazione [It.]. In the 16th century, a religious play with music and thus an antecedent of *oratorio, especially of Cavalieri's *Rappresentatione di Anima, et di Corpo.*

Rapsodie espagnole [Fr., Spanish Rhapsody]. A suite for orchestra by Ravel, composed in 1907–8 and evoking Spanish themes. Its four movements are titled "Prélude à la nuit," "Malagueña," "Habanera," and "Feria." The "Habanera" was originally part of Ravel's *Sites auriculaires* (1895–97) for two pianos.

Rasch [Ger.]. Quick, lively.

Rascher, Sigurd (Manfred) (b. Elberfeld [now Wuppertal], Germany, 15 May 1907). Saxophonist. Studied in Stuttgart. Taught in Copenhagen and Sweden, 1930s. American debut, 1939; performed as soloist with many orchestras in the U.S. and Europe. Founded the Rascher Saxophone Quartet, 1969. Ibert, Hindemith, and Glazunov wrote works for him.

Rasgado, rasgueado [Sp.]. A style of guitar playing in which the strings are strummed, as distinct from *punteado*, in which individual strings are plucked.

Rasi, Francesco (b. Arezzo, 14 May 1574; d. Mantua, by 9 Dec. 1621). Composer and tenor. During 1590s, served Grand Duke Ferdinando I of Tuscany, Gesualdo, and the Duke of Mantua. Sang in the first performance of Peri's *Euridice* and almost certainly created the title role in Monteverdi's *Orfeo* (1607). Composed sacred and secular monodies; an opera.

Rasumovsky Quartets. Beethoven's three string quartets op. 59 (1805–6), dedicated to the Russian Count Andreas Rasumovsky; also termed the Russian Quartets. In nos. 1 (fourth movement) and 2 (third movement), Beethoven used Russian folk songs (labeled in each case "Thème russe") taken from a collection first published by Johann Gottfried Pratsch (Ivan Prach) in 1790.

Ratchet. *Cog rattle.

Rathaus, Karol (b. Tarnopol, 16 Sept. 1895; d. New York, 21 Nov. 1954). Composer. Pupil of Schreker. Settled in the U.S., 1938; from 1940 taught at Queens College. Works include *Fremde Erde* (opera, 1930); ballets (*Der letzte Pierrot*, 1927; *Le lion amoureux*, 1937); 3 symphonies, a piano concerto, and other orchestral works; vocal music (*3 Calderon Songs*, 1931; *XXIII Psalm*, 1945); chamber and piano works (5 string quartets; sonatas; *Trio Serenade*, piano trio, 1953); film music (*The Brothers Karamazov*, 1931).

Ratsche [Ger.]. *Cog rattle.

Rattenando, rattenuto [It.]. Holding back.

Rattle. An instrument that is shaken to produce sound. One familiar type consists of a vessel filled with seeds, pebbles, or pellets and often provided with a handle. In rattles of the stick and frame type, rattling or jingling objects are fastened or strung together, attached to a rigid object, and shaken against one another.

Rattle, Simon (Denis) (b. Liverpool, 19 Jan. 1955). Conductor. Studied at the Royal Academy of Music. Held conducting posts in Bournemouth, Liverpool, and with the BBC Scottish Symphony. From 1979 to 1998, principal conductor of the City of Birmingham Symphony; from 1981, principal guest conductor of the Los Angeles Philharmonic. C.B.E., 1987; knighthood, 1994.

Rauscher [Ger.]. *Batterie* (4).

Rauschpfeife [Ger.]. A 16th-century German *shawm made in various sizes, with and without a *wind cap.

Rautavaara, Einojuhani (b. Helsinki, 9 Oct. 1938). Composer. Pupil of Merikanto, Copland, Persichetti, and W. Vogel. From 1966, taught at the Sibelius Academy. Has worked with serialism. Works include operas (*Kaivos* [The Mine], 1963; *Thomas*, 1982–85; *Vincent*, 1987–88); a ballet; orchestral pieces (*A Requiem in Our Time*, 1953); chamber works; and choral music (*The Water Circle*, 1972).

Rauzzini, Venanzio (b. Camerino, near Rome, bapt. 19 Dec. 1746; d. Bath, 8 Apr. 1810). Male soprano, composer, and harpsichordist. Served the electoral court, Munich, 1766–72. In Italy sang Mozart's *Lucio Silla* (1772); inspired the motet *Exsultate, jubilate* (K. 165/158a). Sang at the King's Theatre, London, 1774–77. Composed chamber music, arias for pasticcios, and operas. Pupils included Nancy Storace and Michael Kelly.

Ravel, (Joseph) Maurice (b. Ciboure, Basses Pyrénées, 7 March 1875; d. Paris, 28 Dec. 1937). Composer. Studied at the Paris Conservatory with Fauré and Gédalge. Left the Conservatory in 1905 amid controversy over his failure to win the Prix de Rome. During 1920s, toured Europe and America. Made use of exotic scales and modes; often imitated historical or national styles. Among his few pupils were Vaughan Williams and Roland-Manuel. Works: operas (*L'*heure espagnole; *L'*enfant et les sortilèges); ballets (*Daphnis et Chloé; *Boléro*, 1928; *Ma mère l'oye; *Valses nobles et sentimentales; La *valse); orchestral works (incl. *Rapsodie espagnole; Une barque sur l'océan*, 1906, rev. 1926; *Pavane pour une infante défunte*, 1910; *Alborada del gracioso*, 1918; *Le tombeau de Couperin*, 1919; Piano Concerto for the left hand, 1929–30; Piano Concerto in G, 1929–31; an orchestral version of Mussorgsky's *Pictures at an Exhibition)*; works for voice and orchestra (incl. cantatas; *Schéhérazade; Don Quichotte à Dulcinée*, 1932–33; *Ronsard à son âme*, 1935); for voice and ensemble (incl. *Trois poèmes de Stéphane Mallarmé*, 1913); numerous works for voice with piano (incl. the cycle *Histoires naturelles*, 1906); chamber music (incl. 2 violin sonatas; String Quartet, 1902–3; *Introduction et allegro*, harp, flute, clarinet, string quartet, 1905; Piano Trio, 1914; *Le tombeau de Claude Debussy*, violin, cello, 1920; Sonata, violin, cello, 1920–22; *Berceuse sur le nom de Gabriel Fauré*, violin, piano, 1922; *Tzigane*, violin, piano, 1924); piano pieces (incl. *Jeux d'eau*, 1901; **Gaspard de la nuit; Menuet sur le nom d'Haydn*, 1909; **Ma mère l'oye*, 4 hands, 1908–10; *Valses nobles et sentimentales*, 1911).

Ravenscroft, John (d. not later than 1708). Composer. English, but resided in Italy; probably studied with Corelli. May have served Prince Ferdinando of Tuscany. Composed trio sonatas; sonatas for 2 violins.

Ravenscroft, Thomas (b. ca. 1582?; d. ca. 1635). Composer and editor. Chorister at Chichester Cathedral and at St. Paul's. Music master at Christ's Hospital, 1618–22. Edited *Pammelia* (1609), the earliest English printed collection of rounds and catches. Published the treatise *A Briefe Discourse* (1614) and *The Whole Booke of Psalmes* (1621), an important psalter of the period; both include some of his own works.

Ravvivando [It.]. Quickening.

Rawsthorne, Alan (b. Haslington, Lancaster, 2 May 1905; d. Cambridge, 24 July 1971). Composer. Studied at the Royal Manchester College of Music with Merrick and in Berlin with Petri. From 1932 taught at the Dartington Hall School. Employed serialistic devices. Compositions inlcude 1 ballet; orchestral music (3 symphonies; 2 piano concertos; 2 violin concertos); vocal works (*A Canticle of Man; Four Romantic Pieces*, 1953; *Practical Cats*, 1954; *Carmen vitale*, 1963); and chamber works (string quartets; Oboe Quartet, 1970).

Raxach, Enrique (b. Barcelona, 15 Jan. 1932). Composer. Pupil of Boulez, Messiaen, Maderna, and Stockhausen. Settled in the Netherlands, 1962. Works include orchestral pieces *(Metamorphose I, II, and III*, 1956, 1958, 1959; *Equinoxial*, 1967–68; *Erdenlicht*, 1975; *Calles y sueños—in Memoriam Federico García Lorca*, 1986); vocal music (*Sine nomine*, 1973; *Soirée musicale*, 1978); chamber works.

Razor Quartet. Popular name for Haydn's String Quartet in F minor op. 55 no. 2, Hob. III:61 (1788), so called because the English publisher John Bland claimed that Haydn jokingly gave him the autograph manuscript in exchange for an English razor. The work was not published by Bland, however.

Re. See Pitch names, Solmization, Hexachord.

Read, Daniel (b. Attleboro, Mass., 16 Nov. 1757; d. New Haven, Conn., 4 Dec. 1836). Composer. May have studied with Law and Billings. Settled in New Haven, 1782. Composed numerous hymn tunes, some of which became fixtures in the American psalmody repertory. Published *The American Singing Book* (1785), a collection of his own works; *The Columbian Harmonist* (1793–95); an instructional work on psalmody; and the first American music periodical.

Read, Gardner (b. Evanston, Ill., 2 Jan. 1913). Composer. Pupil of Hanson, Rogers, Pizzetti, and Copland. Has taught at the Cleveland Institute of Music and Boston Univ. (1948–78). Works include an opera, *Villon* (1965–67); orchestral music (4 symphonies; concertos; *Sketches of the City*, 1933; *Pennsylvania*, 1946–47; *Sonoric Fantasia no. 3*, winds, percussion, 1971); choral music (*Jesous Ahatonhia*, 1950; *The Prophet*, 1960); many songs; chamber music; piano and organ music. Has published books on orchestration and notation.

Reading Rota. **"Sumer is icumen in."*

Real. See Tonal and real.

Rebab [Jav.]. See *Rabāb*.

Rebec [Fr. *rebec, rebecq, rebecquet;* Ger. *Rubebe, Rebec;* It. *rebeca, ribeca;* Sp. *rabel*]. A bowed instrument derived from the ancient Arab **rabāb* and documented in Europe by the 13th century. Used during the Middle Ages and the Renaissance, in the 16th century it inspired the development of the dance master's fiddle or **kit*. The rebec generally bears an arched back with a pear-shaped body, a short, narrow neck, and an open pegbox. The three gut strings, tuned in fifths, pass over a flat bridge and are often played in pairs with the middle string acting as a drone. A typical tuning would be g d' a'. Iconographic sources show the rebec played either vertically on the lap or on the shoulder, with an outcurved bow held in the overhand position. See ill. under Violin.

Reber, (Napoléon-) Henri (b. Mulhouse, 21 Oct. 1807; d. Paris, 24 Nov. 1880). Composer. Studied with Reicha and Le Sueur at the Paris Conservatory; taught there from 1851. Works include operas (*Le père Gaillard*, 1852); the ballet *Le diable amoureux* (1840); a cantata; vocalises; 4 symphonies; string quartets and other chamber music; character pieces and dances for piano. Wrote *Traité d'harmonie* (1862).

Rebikov, Vladimir Ivanovich (b. Kresnoyarsk, Siberia, 31 May 1866; d. Yalta, 4 Aug. 1920). Composer. Studied at Moscow Conservatory with Klenovsky and in Berlin. Used whole-tone techniques. Works include musico-psychological dramas (*Alfa i omega*, 1911); operas (*V grosu*, 1894; *Snow-White*, 1909; *Narcissus*, 1913); *Mélomimiques* for voice and piano; many short piano pieces; some liturgical music; orchestral works.

Recapitulation. See Sonata form.

Recercada [Sp.], **recercar** [It.]. See Ricercar.

Récit [Fr.]. In French music of the 17th and 18th centuries, a passage or a complete composition (e.g., an aria) for solo voice or, in the later part of this period and beyond, for a solo instrument; not the same as *recitative, though a *récit* may be in recitative style.

Recital. A concert given by a small number of performers, most often a soloist, perhaps with an accompanist. The term was first used in this way in an advertisement for a performance on the piano by Liszt in London in 1840.

Recitative [Fr. *récitative;* Ger. *Rezitativ;* It., Sp. *recitativo*]. A style of text setting that imitates and emphasizes the natural inflections, rhythms, and syntax of speech. Such a setting avoids extremes of pitch and intensity and repetition of words, allowing the music to be primarily a vehicle for the words. The term recitative is used most often in connection with dramatic music—opera, oratorio, and cantata—but this type of text setting is far more widespread historically and geographically than are these genres. Recitative became a particular concern of composers from the beginning of the 17th century onward [see also Monody, Baroque]. Peri, Caccini, Cavalieri, Gagliano, and Monteverdi all proclaimed a new style of declamation, valued for its expressivity, that is variously referred to as *stile rappresentativo* and *stile recitativo.*

By the end of the 17th century in Italy, a simpler and more perfunctory style of setting text evolved, *recitativo semplice.* The sparse texture and slow harmonic rhythm of the accompaniment, played by continuo instruments only, allowed for the clear and rapid presentation of a large amount of text. The dramatic function was expository or narrative, advancing the action. The term *recitativo secco,* now used interchangeably with *recitativo semplice,* came into use in the 19th century, after that style of recitative was no longer being composed.

Recitativo semplice is accompanied by continuo instruments. Orchestrally accompanied recitative is called *recitativo accompagnato* or *recitativo stromentato.* When the accompanying instruments not only provide harmonic support but also present prominent motivic or melodic material, the term *recitativo obbligato* may be used. Fully accompanied recitative was reserved, in 18th-century opera, for the most important characters at climactic moments in the drama.

An urge for greater continuity of music and action—a desire to lessen the musical disparity between recitative and aria—was one of the principal concerns of Gluck in his reform operas. By the third decade of the 19th century, recitative accompanied by continuo alone had largely disappeared except in Italian comic opera. A motivically constructed orchestral part could provide the musical continuity of a whole scene, while the voice parts were declamatory and of lesser musical interest, a method termed *parlante.* The works of Wagner achieve the goal of blending recitative and aria into an endless melody supported by a motivically rich orchestral part. A 20th-century addition to techniques of recitative is the practice of *Sprechstimme* or *Sprechgesang.*

Reciting tone, note. See Psalm tone.

Recorder [Fr. *flûte à bec, f. douce;* Ger. *Blockflöte, Schnabelflöte;* It. *flauto diritto, f. dolce;* Sp. *flauta de pico*]. A *duct flute—end-blown with a fipple mouthpiece—used from the Middle Ages through the Baroque era. In England, this instrument was called a recorder in the Renaissance and a flute in the Baroque era. On the Continent, it was known throughout both periods as the *Blockflöte, flûte,* or *flauto.* The *transverse or cross flute was specifically identified as such (with terms such as German flute, *flauto traverso*) to distinguish it from the recorder or English flute. The English name perhaps derives from the Italian *ricordo* (a keepsake). See ill. under Flute.

The modern recorder family is regarded as including only instruments in C, no matter what the individual ranges or basic scales of its members. It includes the sopranino (lowest pitch f''), the soprano (in Britain, descant, c''), the alto (in Britain, treble, f'), the tenor (c'), the bass (f), the great bass (c), and the contrabass (F). All normally have a range of two octaves and a whole step. Music for the two highest members of this family is often notated an octave lower than it sounds. Because of their length, the two lowest instruments are provided with a curved mouth pipe similar to that of the bassoon. Basses, and sometimes the tenor, are also provided with a single key for the lowest pitch. The single lowest hole may also be replaced, especially on modern instruments, by two small holes placed beside one another to facilitate the playing of the lowest semitone.

Reco-reco, reso-reso [Port.]. A *scraper of Brazil made of notched bamboo and scraped with a stick. See also *Güiro.*

Recoupe [Fr.]. The first *after-dance of the *basse dance commune* in Pierre Attaingnant's collections.

Recte et retro [Lat.]. Forward and in *retrograde.

Recueilli [Fr.]. Contemplative.

Reda, Siegfried (b. Bochum, 27 July 1916; d. Mülheim, 13 Dec. 1968). Composer. Pupil of Pepping and Distler. Teacher and director, Institute for Evangelical Church Music, Essen Folkwangschule, from 1946. From 1953, director of church music, Mülheim. Composed 3 concertos and much other organ music; many choral works (*Chormusik für das Jahr Kirche*, 1947–58; *Requiem*, 1963).

Redding, Otis (b. Dawson, Ga., 9 Sept. 1941; d. near Madison, Wis., 19 Dec. 1967). Soul singer and songwriter. Helped establish a "Memphis" soul sound. Songs include "These Arms of Mine" (1963), "I've Been Loving You Too Long" (1965), and "(Sittin' on) The Dock of the Bay" (1967). His songs were recorded by rock groups including the Rolling Stones.

Redford, John (b. ca. 1485; d. London, late 1547). Composer and organist. Master of the choristers and probably organist at St. Paul's Cathedral. Composed organ settings of plainsong melodies, to be used in church services in alternation with sung chants; a few vocal works.

Redoble [Sp.]. In Spanish keyboard music of the Renaissance, a trill-like ornament of several repercussions that may be begun or ended with turns or other figures. Its use was not very different from that of *quiebro* [see also Ornamentation].

Redoute [Fr.]. See **Ridotto.*

Redowa [fr. Cz. *rejdovák*]. A social dance that became popular in Paris and elsewhere ca. 1840. Its Czech antecedents were the *rejdovák*, in 3/4 and similar to the *mazurka, and its following *rejdovačka*, in 2/4.

Reduction [Fr. *réduction*]. An arrangement, especially for piano (piano reduction, *réduction pour le piano*), of a work originally for orchestra or other ensemble.

Reed [Fr. *anche;* Ger. *Rohrblatt;* It. *ancia;* Sp. *lengüeta, caña*]. A thin, elastic strip, fixed at one end and free at the other, set into vibration by moving air. Reeds are the sound generators in *woodwind instruments (except flutes) and many other *aerophones [see ill.]. Woodwinds generally use reeds made from cane, particularly from the *arundo donax* grown in southern France. Plastic reeds have recently found limited acceptance, however. Organs and accordions have steel or brass reeds.

Cane reeds are constructed as either double reeds or single reeds. A double reed, used in the oboe, the bassoon, and *shawms, consists of two pieces of cane carved and bound into a hollow, round shape at one end and flattened out and shaved thin at the other.

The single reed of the clarinet or saxophone is a flat strip of cane shaved at one end and fastened at the other to a mouthpiece.

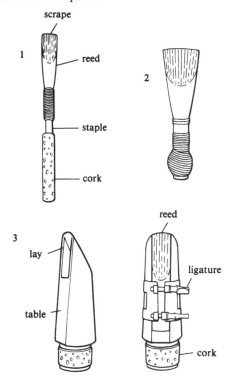

1. Oboe reed.   2. Bassoon reed.   3. Clarinet reed.

In woodwinds, a reed and a pipe constitute a coupled system with a soft reed. The vibrating reed sets the air column in motion, but, because the reed is capable of vibrating over a wide range of frequencies, the length of the pipe determines the frequency of the system. Metal reeds, on the other hand, are hard: they vibrate at one pitch only. Thus metal-reed instruments characteristically have many reeds and, except in the organ, no pipes (e.g., the *mouth organ and *harmonium). Metal reeds, except in the organ, are usually free reeds: they do not strike the frame that holds them and do not interrupt the flow of air. Cane reeds usually act as beating reeds: they beat against the frame that holds them (or, in the case of double reeds, the two halves beat against one another), periodically cutting off the air stream and producing a sharper sound, rich in upper partials. The reeds of organ pipes behave in this way as well, though they are made of metal.

Woodwind instruments such as the oboe, bassoon, clarinet, and saxophone are played by setting the lips directly onto the reed, thus damping it slightly and enabling fine tuning. In many reedpipes, however,

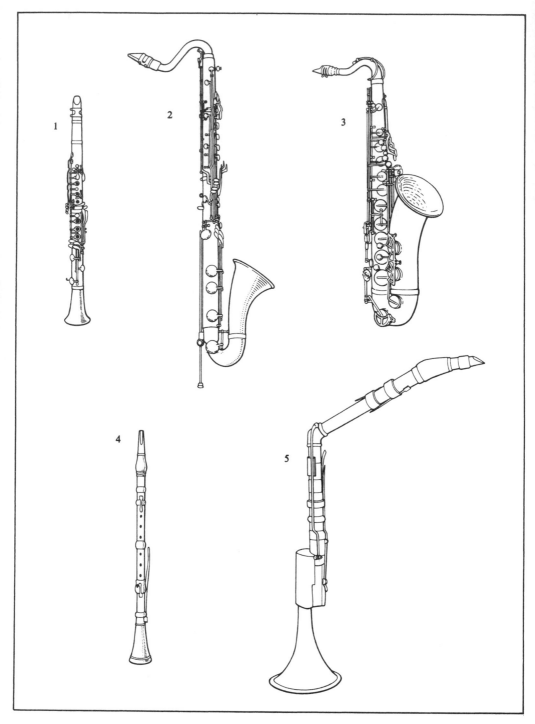

Reed instruments: 1. B♭ clarinet. 2. Bass clarinet. 3. Tenor saxophone. 4. Late 18th-century clarinet. 5. Basset horn.

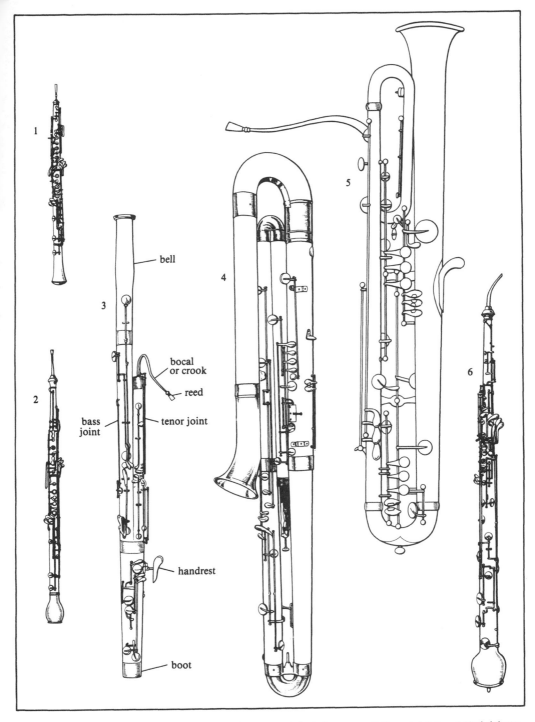

Reed instruments: 1. Oboe. 2. English horn. 3. Bassoon. 4. Contrabassoon. 5. Sarrusophone. 6. Heckelphone.

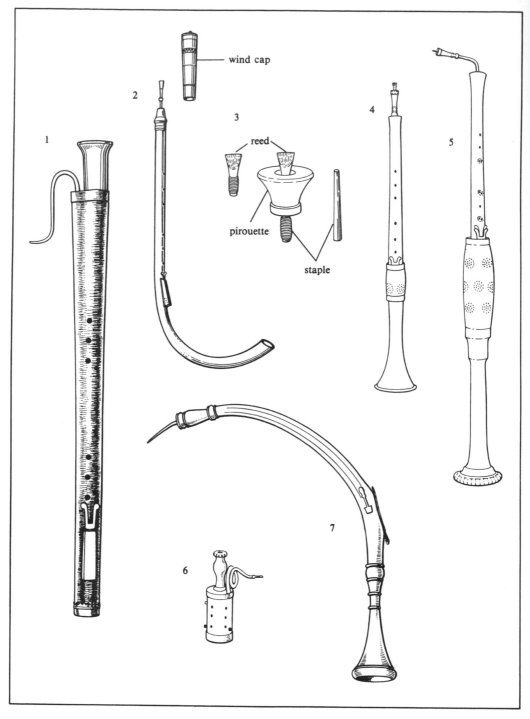

Reed instruments: 1. Curtal. 2. Crumhorn (with wind cap removed). 3. Shawm reed and pirouette (not to scale).
4. Alto shawm. 5. Tenor shawm. 6. Racket. 7. Oboe da caccia.

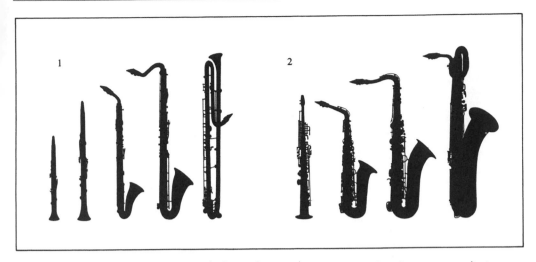

Reed instruments: 1. Clarinets: E♭ soprano, B♭, E♭ alto, B♭ bass, BB♭ contrabass. 2. Saxophones: soprano, alto, tenor, baritone.

the reed is removed from the player's control and enclosed in a *wind cap, producing a harsher, "reedier" sound.

Reed cap. *Wind cap.

Reed, H(erbert) Owen (b. Odessa, Mo., 17 June 1910). Composer. Pupil of Hanson, Rogers, Harris, Copland, and Bernstein. Taught at Michigan State Univ., 1939–76. Explored the folk music of Mexico, the Caribbean, and Scandinavia. Compositions include dramatic works (*The Masque of the Red Death,* ballet-pantomime, 1936; *Peter Homan's Dream,* opera, 1955); a symphony and other orchestral and band works. Has published textbooks on music.

Reed organ. An *organ in which all notes sound by means of blown reeds rather than flue pipes. See also Harmonium, Regal.

Reel. A dance for couples, usually four to eight, documented in Scotland as early as the 16th century and disseminated in Scandinavia, Ireland, and the U.S., where the Virginia reel is familiar in square dancing. Its music is in a moderately fast duple meter.

Refice, Licinio (b. Patrica, near Rome, 12 Feb. 1885; d. Rio de Janeiro, 11 Sept. 1954). Composer and conductor. Studied in Rome. Taught at the Scuola pontificia di musica sacra, 1910–50. *Maestro di cappella* at S. Maria Maggiore, 1911–47. Works include religious operas (*Cecilia,* 1922–23); oratorios, cantatas, over 40 Masses, hymns, motets, and Psalms; some secular songs and instrumental pieces.

Reformation Symphony. Mendelssohn's Symphony no. 5 in D minor op. 107 (1829–30), com-

posed for a proposed celebration in 1830 of the 300th anniversary of the adoption of the Augsburg Confession as the articles of faith of the Lutheran Church; not performed until 1832, however. The work makes recurring use of the Dresden Amen (composed in the late 18th century by J. G. Naumann), and the last movement is based on Luther's chorale "Ein' feste Burg."

Refrain [Fr. *refrain;* Ger. *Kehrreim;* It. *ritornello, ripresa;* Sp. *estribillo*]. Text or music that is repeated at regular intervals in the course of a larger form; also burden. In music with text, the refrain (both text and music) typically recurs following each of a series of strophes of identical structure also sung to recurring music. The alternation between strophes and refrain is sometimes associated with an alternation between soloist(s) and chorus.

Regal(s). A small portable reed organ used in the 16th and 17th centuries. A small regal that could be folded like a book for storage was called a bible regal.

Reger, (Johann Baptist Joseph) Max(imilian) (b. Brand, Bavaria, 19 Mar. 1873; d. Leipzig, 11 May 1916). Composer. Pupil of Riemann. Taught at the Munich conservatory (1905–6) and Leipzig Univ. (from 1907). From 1911 conducted the Meiningen court orchestra. Settled in Jena, 1915. Toured as a pianist and organist. Composed orchestral works (incl. *Symphonischer Prolog zu einer Tragödie,* 1908; Sinfonietta, 1904–5; Serenade, 1905–6; Violin Concerto, 1907–8; Piano Concerto, 1910; Variations and Fugue on a Theme of Mozart, 1914); sacred choral works; string quartets, sonatas, piano quartets, and other chamber music; lieder; piano pieces (incl.

dances, character pieces, Variations and Fugue on a Theme of J. S. Bach, 1904); sonatas, chorale preludes, and other organ works.

Reggae. Any of several styles of urban Jamaican popular music. Reggae appeared in the mid-1960s, and its musical style is a synthesis of American *rhythm and blues, traditional African and Jamaican folk musics, and *ska. Its texture is characterized by a constant emphasis on offbeat rhythmic patterns and chanted vocals; the lyrics predominantly reflect aspects of the religious movement known as Rastafarianism and the social unrest of Jamaica's lower classes.

Regina caeli laetare [Lat., Rejoice, Queen of Heaven]. One of the four *antiphons for the Blessed Virgin Mary, sung in modern practice at Compline from Easter Sunday through Friday after Pentecost. In the Renaissance, it was often set polyphonically and was the basis of many polyphonic *Masses.

Regisseur [Fr.]. The stage manager of a theatrical production.

Register. (1) A specific segment of the total range of pitches available to a voice, instrument, or composition. It may often be described loosely simply as high, low, etc. For the nomenclature of registers of the voice, see Voice. (2) In *serial music, the specific location of a pitch, as opposed simply to its designation as a member of a *pitch class. (3) Organ *stop.

Registration. In organ and harpsichord playing, the selection and combination of *stops (registers) employed in the performance of a work.

Regnart, Jacob [Jacques] (b. Douai, ca. 1540; d. Prague, 16 Oct. 1599). Composer. From 1557 served the Habsburgs in Prague and Vienna. Vice-Kapellmeister in Prague from at least 1579 to 1582 and from 1596; in Innsbruck, 1582–84. Kapellmeister in Innsbruck, 1585–96. Composed Masses, motets, and much other sacred music; secular songs, many in Italian styles but with German texts.

Regola dell'ottava [It.]. *Rule of the octave.

Rehfuss, Heinz (Julius) (b. Frankfurt am Main, 25 May 1917; d. Rochester, N.Y., 27 June 1988). Bassbaritone. Debut, 1938. Appeared at the Zurich Opera, 1940–52, and a number of European houses. Roles included Don Giovanni and Boris Godunov. Taught at the Montreal Conservatory, Eastman, and SUNY–Buffalo.

Reich, Steve [Stephen] **(Michael)** (b. New York, 3 Oct. 1936). Composer. Pupil of Overton, Bergsma, Persichetti, Milhaud, and Berio. Has studied African drumming in Ghana, Hebrew cantillation in Jerusa-

lem, and gamelan. Taught at the New School for Social Research, 1969–71. A proponent of musical minimalism. Has worked with electronic music, using tape loops that move in and out of phase with one another; also simulating this effect with live performers. Works include *Violin Phase,* violin, tape (1967); *Pulse Music,* phase-shifting pulse gate (1969); *Four Organs,* 4 electric organs, maracas (1970); *Impact,* dance music (1985); *The Four Sections,* orchestra (1987); *The Cave,* music theater, with Beryl Korot, (1990–93); *Proverb,* 3 sopranos, 2 tenors, 2 vibraphones, 4 synthesizers (1995); film scores.

Reicha [Rejcha], **Antoine(-Joseph)** [Antonín, Anton] (b. Prague, 26 Feb. 1770; d. Paris, 28 May 1836). Composer and theorist. Played alongside Beethoven in the Hofkapelle, Bonn. Taught in Hamburg, 1795–99. Associate of Beethoven and Haydn and pupil of Albrechtsberger and Salieri, Vienna, 1801–8. Taught at the Paris Conservatoire from 1818; at the Académie from 1835. Berlioz, Liszt, and Franck were among his pupils. Published treatises, including the *Traité de haute composition musicale* (1824–26). Composed operas, sacred and secular vocal works, symphonies, overtures, concertos, and many chamber works for winds and strings.

Reichardt, Johann Friedrich (b. Königsberg, 25 Nov. 1752; d. Giebichenstein, near Halle, 27 June 1814). Composer and writer. Studied at Königsberg Univ. and with Kirnberger and Homilius. Kapellmeister, Royal Berlin Opera, 1775–94. In 1783, founded the Berlin Concert spirituel. Served Jérôme Buonaparte in Kassel, 1807–8. Composed some 1,500 songs; singspiels, including *Claudine von Villa Bella* (with Goethe, 1789) and *Die Geisterinsel* (after Shakespeare's *The Tempest,* Berlin, 1798); orchestral, chamber, and keyboard works. Published numerous books on music.

Reichardt, Louise (b. Berlin, 11 Apr. 1779; d. Hamburg, 17 Nov. 1826). Composer. Daughter of Johann Friedrich Reichardt. Settled in Hamburg by 1813; directed a women's chorus. Translated texts and prepared choruses for performances of Handel oratorios. Composed sacred and secular vocal works.

Reimann, Aribert (b. Berlin, 4 March 1936). Composer and pianist. Pupil of Blacher and Pepping. Has accompanied singers, including Fischer-Dieskau. Taught at the Hamburg Hochschule für Musik, 1974–83; then at the Berlin Hochschule für Künste. Worked with serialism until 1967. Works include 6 operas (*Ein Traumspiel,* 1964; *Lear,* 1976–78; *Das Schloss,* 1992); 2 ballets; orchestral music; vocal music (*Requiem,* 1980–82; *Denn Bleiben ist nirgends, Sprechstimme,* 1986); chamber music.

Rein [Ger.]. (1) With respect to the tuning of intervals, acoustically pure; *reine Stimmung,* *just intonation. (2) With respect to types of intervals, perfect.

Reinagle, Alexander (b. Portsmouth, bapt. 23 Apr. 1756; d. Baltimore, 21 Sept. 1809). Composer. Pupil of R. Taylor. Settled in the U.S., 1786. Active as a conductor, teacher, and partner in a theater company in New York, Philadelphia, and Baltimore. Composed much dramatic music (almost all lost); 4 piano sonatas (the earliest piano pieces written in the U.S.); choral pieces and songs; orchestral music.

Reincken [Reinken, Reinike], **Johann Adam** [Jan Adams] (b. Wildeshausen, near Bremen, 27 Apr. 1623; d. Hamburg, 24 Nov. 1722). Composer and organist. Pupil and assistant of H. Scheidemann, and his successor (1663) as organist at St. Catherine's, Hamburg. Compositions include organ music and a set of suites for strings, *Hortus musicus* (1687), from which J. S. Bach made keyboard arrangements (BWV 954, 965, 966).

Reine, La [Fr., The Queen]. Popular name for Haydn's Symphony no. 85 in Bb major Hob. I:85 (1785?; no. 4 of the *Paris Symphonies), so called because Queen Marie Antoinette was said to have been particularly fond of it. The title first appears in the Imbault edition of 1788.

Reinecke, Carl (Heinrich Carsten) (b. Altona, 23 June 1824; d. Leipzig, 10 Mar. 1910). Teacher, pianist, composer. Associate of Mendelssohn, the Schumanns, and Liszt. Taught at the Cologne Conservatory, 1851–54. Conductor in Barmen, 1854–59; of the Leipzig Gewandhaus Orchestra, 1860–95. Taught at the Leipzig conservatory, 1860–1902; Grieg was among his pupils. Composed operas; cantatas; 3 symphonies; concertos; chamber music; songs; many piano pieces; a piano method and studies; music for children. Wrote several books on music.

Reiner, Fritz (b. Budapest, 19 Dec. 1888; d. New York, 15 Nov. 1963). Conductor. Pupil of Bartók. Conducted the People's Opera, Budapest, and the Dresden Hofoper (1914–22). Music director, Cincinnati Symphony, 1922–31. Taught at the Curtis Institute, 1931–41; pupils included Bernstein and Foss. Conducted opera in Philadelphia, San Francisco, and at the Metropolitan Opera (1948–53). Music director, Pittsburgh Symphony, 1938–48; Chicago Symphony, 1953–62.

Reinhardt, Django [Jean Baptiste] (b. Liberchies, near Luttre, Belgium, 23 Jan. 1910; d. Fontainebleau, 16 May 1953). Jazz guitarist. Formed the Quintette du Hot Club de France with Stephane Grappelli (later replaced by a clarinetist); recordings include "Lady

Be Good" (1934), "Djangology" (1935), and "Limehouse Blues" (1936). Worked with Duke Ellington, Coleman Hawkins, and other American jazz musicians. Made use of Gypsy guitar traditions.

Reinken, Johann Adam. See Reincken, Johann Adam.

Reissiger, Karl Gottlieb (b. Belzig, 31 Jan. 1798; d. Dresden, 7 Nov. 1859). Composer and conductor. Studied in Leipzig and with Salieri and Winter. *Hofkapellmeister,* Dresden, from 1828; directed first performance of *Rienzi.* Composed over 60 songs; 9 operas (*Die Felsenmühle,* 1831); an oratorio; Masses and other sacred works; chamber and piano music.

Reizenstein, Franz (Theodor) (b. Nuremberg, 7 June 1911; d. London, 15 Oct. 1968). Composer and pianist. Pupil of Hindemith, Lambert, Vaughan Williams, and Solomon. Taught at the Royal Academy of Music, 1958–68; the Royal Manchester College of Music, 1962–68. Works include *Voices of Night,* chorus (1951); 2 radio operas (*Anna Kraus,* 1952); an oratorio; concertos and other orchestral music; much chamber and piano music.

Rejdovák [Cz.]. See *Redowa.*

Related key, relative key. See Key relationship.

Relative pitch. The ability to identify specific intervals or to notate music by ear alone, without the ability to identify individual pitches independent of context (termed *absolute pitch).

Release. In jazz and popular music, *bridge.

Relish. An ornament used in performing early English music for lute, viol, and keyboard. The term *single relish* was used for any ornament formed by the alternation of two adjacent notes. The double relish consists essentially of a trill upon each of two successive notes.

Remettre, remettez [Fr.]. In French organ music, an instruction to take off a stop.

Renaissance, music of the. Music of the period from about 1430 until about 1600. Like others of the principal concepts employed in the periodization of the *history of Western art music, the concept Renaissance [Fr., rebirth] was borrowed from other branches of the study of history. The attempt to incorporate this view into the history of music met with several difficulties from the outset, however.

On purely musical grounds, the boundary of about 1430, represented by the music of Dufay, Binchois, and Dunstable, is undeniably important, largely because of an increasing reliance in this music on imperfect consonances and a more narrowly restricted use of dissonance [see Counterpoint]. But many of the genres in which they worked and the formal techniques that they employed (e.g., secular works in the *formes fixes* and sacred works based on a *cantus firmus*) belong to unbroken traditions stretching from the 14th century to the very end of the 15th century. And the late 15th century saw changes in musical style and structure (e.g., the adoption of four-voice texture as a norm, the increased use of *imitation, and abandonment of the *formes fixes*) that made themselves felt through the end of the 16th century.

The 15th century saw the emergence of a musical language that ultimately spread throughout all of Western Europe. This language and its dissemination was due in large measure to the work and travels of musicians from the Low Countries, including what is now part of northern France. These musicians, whose culture was principally French, were especially prominent in Italy in the 15th century. They have sometimes been described as constituting one or more schools spanning the 15th and 16th centuries. Raphael Georg Kiesewetter, in 1826, defined three "Netherlands schools," the first headed by Guillaume Dufay (ca. 1400–74), the second by Johannes Ockeghem (ca. 1410–97) and Jacob Obrecht (ca. 1450–1505), and the third by Josquin Desprez (ca. 1440–1521). In part because the term Netherlands is misleading with respect to the geographic and cultural origins of these composers, some more recent writers have preferred to term the first of these *Burgundian and the second and third variously as Flemish and Franco-Flemish, respectively, or simply (combining the second and third) Flemish, Netherlandish, or Franco-Netherlandish. Each such label, however, entails its own compromises.

For the principal genres of the period, see Mass, Motet, Chanson, Madrigal, *Frottola, Lauda, Villancico,* Canzona, Ricercar, Intabulation; see also Mode, Theory, Council of Trent, Roman school, Venetian school, Mannerism.

Renard [Fr., The Fox; Russ. *Bayka*]. Burlesque in one act for dancers, singers, and small orchestra by Stravinsky (libretto by Stravinsky, after Russian folktales; original choreography by Bronislava Nijinska; later versions by Serge Lifar and George Balanchine), produced by Diaghilev's Ballets russes in Paris in 1922.

Renforcer [Fr.]. To reinforce, make louder.

Repeat [Fr. *reprise;* Ger. *Wiederholung;* It. *replica;* Sp. *repetición*]. To play a passage again; repeat sign, either of the symbols (||: and :||) used to mark the beginning and end, respectively, of a passage that is to be repeated. In the absence of a sign like the first, the repetition is from the beginning of the work or

movement. Unless otherwise indicated, these symbols call for a single repetition. If the first and second statements of the passage have different endings, these are identified by number and termed *prima volta* and *seconda volta,* or first and second endings, respectively [see ill. under Notation].

Répétiteur [Fr.]. Coach; one who rehearses singers or soloists apart from general rehearsals.

Repetition. (1) The restatement of a musical idea or section of a work. The perception of repetition is one of the principal elements in the perception of musical *form. (2) The characteristics of the action of a piano that permit the rapid repetition of notes [see Piano].

Répétition [Fr.]. Rehearsal; *répétition générale,* dress rehearsal.

Repiano [fr. *ripieno*]. In some bands, a cornet or clarinet player other than the principal player [see Brass band].

Replica [It.]. *Repeat; *senza r.,* without repeat, as when a minuet or similar piece is played *da capo.

Répons [Fr.]. *Responsory.

Reports. In the 17th century, imitation; also contrapuntal texture generally.

Reprise [Fr.; also Eng., Ger.]. *Repeat, repetition. The term may refer to either literal or varied repetitions; in 17th- and 18th-century French keyboard music, the second section of a *binary form, the refrain of a *rondeau,* or a short phrase repeated at the end of a movement; in some accounts of *sonata form, the recapitulation; in musicals or operettas, an abbreviated repetition of a prominent number, usually after some intervening dialogue.

Reproaches. *Improperia.

Requiem [Lat.]. The Mass for the Dead (*Missa pro defunctis*), called Requiem after the first word of its introit ("Requiem aeternam dona eis Domine," Grant to them eternal rest, O Lord). The term has also been used in the 20th century in works not strictly liturgical but written in honor of the dead, as in Britten's *War Requiem* (1962) and Stravinsky's *Requiem Canticles* (1965–66). German Requiems, such as the *Musikalische Exequien* (1636) of Schütz or Brahms's *Ein Deutsches Requiem* op. 45 (1868), employ German texts drawn from the Bible or from chorales.

The Latin Requiem Mass, though part of the liturgy from the earliest times, was not actually standardized until after the Council of Trent (1545–63) in the Missal of Pius V (1570), which prescribed the following *Proper and *Ordinary items: introit ("Requiem aeternam"), Kyrie, gradual ("Requiem aeternam"), tract ("Absolve Domine"), sequence ("Dies irae"), offertory ("Domine Jesu Christe"), Sanctus and Benedictus, Agnus (with "Dona eis requiem" and "Dona eis requiem sempiternam" in place of "Miserere nobis" and "Dona nobis pacem"), and communion ("Lux aeterna"). The absolution (the responsory "Libera me Domine"), set by a few composers of Requiems, belongs not to the Mass itself but to the burial service. Polyphonic settings of the Requiem Mass begin in the 15th century. The polyphonic Requiem always includes some of the Proper (particularly, the introit) but does not always set all of the Ordinary.

After the Requiem Mass was liturgically fixed, the number of settings increased dramatically. During the 17th century, they were often written in *stile antico*—as were Masses generally—but new styles were eventually incorporated. Many important Requiems were composed in the 18th and 19th centuries (by Mozart, Berlioz, and Verdi, to name but a few); in these works, the formerly neglected "Dies irae" became the central musical event. Just as dramatic is Verdi's *Manzoni Requiem* (1874), with its offstage trumpets at the "Tuba mirum" and agitated soprano recitative in the "Libera me." Other 19th-century composers were more restrained, particularly Liszt, whose *Requiem* (1867–68) is written in *a cappella* style, and Fauré, who even chose not to set the "Dies irae" (1887). The Requiem by Maurice Duruflé (1947) is perhaps the best known example from the 20th century..

Rescue opera. A category of opéra-comique in which the hero or heroine, threatened by a natural catastrophe (e.g., avalanche or volcano), a villainous outlaw, or an unjust ruler, is rescued at the last moment by a person showing great personal courage and heroism. The genre was popular in France in the decade between the fall of the monarchy and the rise of Napoleon. Afterward it was taken up in Italy and Germany. The best-known example of a rescue opera is Beethoven's *Fidelio.*

Reservata [Lat.]. See *Musica reservata.*

Resnik, Regina (b. New York, 30 Aug. 1922). Soprano, mezzo-soprano. Joined the Metropolitan Opera, 1944. Roles included Leonora *(Il trovatore),* Donna Anna, Donna Elvira, Leonora *(Fidelio),* Alice *(Falstaff),* and Sieglinde. From 1955, took on mezzo-soprano roles, including Princess Eboli *(Don Carlos)* and Mistress Quickly *(Falstaff).* Has performed at Bayreuth, Covent Garden, Salzburg, and Vienna.

Resolution. A progression from a dissonant tone or harmony to one that is consonant; the consonant tone or harmony itself. In classical tonal counterpoint,

every dissonant tone must be resolved, normally by stepwise motion [see Counterpoint].

Resonator. A device that amplifies or reinforces a musical sound by vibrating at the same frequency. A resonator may be a column of air such as that contained in an organ pipe, or it may be an elastic surface such as the piano soundboard. Often it is both, for example, the sound box of a guitar. A resonator like the *marimba tube is specific—i.e., its natural frequency matches exactly the frequency of the driving sound. Other resonators (e.g., the sound box of the violin) are general—they vibrate in response to many different pitches.

Reso-reso [Port.]. *Reco-reco.*

Respighi, Ottorino (b. Bologna, 9 July 1879; d. Rome, 18 Apr. 1936). Composer. Pupil of Martucci and Rimsky-Korsakov. From 1913 taught at the Conservatorio di S. Cecilia (director, 1924–26). Toured as a pianist and conductor. Composed operas *(La bella dormente nel bosco,* 1916–21; *Maria Egiziaca,* 1929–32; *La fiamma,* 1930–33; *Lucrezia,* completed by Elsa Respighi, 1936); orchestral works *(*Fontane di Roma; *Pini di Roma; Impressioni brasiliane,* 1928; *Feste romane,* 1928); works for voice and ensemble *(Aretusa,* 1910; *Lauda per la Natività del Signore,* 1928–30); for voice and piano: *(Nebbie, Nevicata, Stornellatrice, 5 canti all'antica,* 1906); string quartets and other chamber music; organ and piano music.

Respond. *Responsory; also the refrain of a responsory as distinct from its verse.

Response. A short text (often preceded by the abbreviation ℞), spoken or sung by congregation or choir, in reply to a versicle (another short text spoken or sung by the officiant, identified by the abbreviation ℣), occurring as a single pair (℣ Benedicamus domino, ℞ Deo gratias) or in more elaborate sets (℣ Lord have mercy upon us, ℞ Lord have mercy upon us, ℣ Christ have mercy upon us, ℞ Christ have mercy upon us, etc.). The most elaborate form of versicle and response is the *litany.

Responsorial singing. Singing, especially in liturgical chant, in which a soloist or group of soloists alternates with a choir [see Psalmody]; in nonliturgical contexts, synonymous with *call and response.

Responsory. A type of liturgical chant common to the *Gregorian and other Western chant repertories and an example of responsorial *psalmody. As a general category within the repertory of Gregorian chant, it may be said to include the great and short responsories described here as well as the *gradual.

The great responsories or *responsoria prolixa* are a

prominent feature of Matins in the Office, where they are associated with lessons or readings from Scripture. They are also sung at Vespers on solemn feasts and in processions. In general, each consists of two parts: a respond (R, with R' representing its last part, called the *repetendum*) intoned by the soloists and continued by the choir, and a verse (V) sung by the soloists. To this the first half of the lesser *Doxology (D) may be added, as follows: R V R' D R'. The responds are moderately elaborate melodies with occasional long *melismas. The verses and the lesser Doxology are most often sung to one or another of a set of eight *psalm tones, according to the mode of the respond.

The short responsories or *responsoria brevia* are sung following the short readings or chapters of the lesser hours and Compline in the secular Office and at Lauds and Vespers as well in the monastic Office. Both verse and respond sometimes have the character of a psalm tone, though there is no fixed set of eight such tones.

Rest. A span of time in which there is silence; a notational symbol specifying a silence of some duration. For examples and nomenclature, see Note.

Restringendo [It.]. Becoming faster.

Resultant tone. See Combination tone.

Resurrection Symphony. Popular name for Mahler's Symphony no. 2 in C minor, composed in 1888–94 (rev. 1903). The fourth movement is a setting for alto and orchestra of "Urlicht" (Primeval Light, a song from Des *Knaben Wunderhorn*); the fifth and last movement is a setting of Friedrich Gottlieb Klopstock's poem "Auferstehung" (Resurrection) for soprano, chorus, and orchestra.

Retard. To slow down; a slowing down; *ritardando.*

Retardation [obs.]. Suspension [see Counterpoint].

Retenu [Fr.]. Held back.

Rethberg, Elisabeth [Sattler, Lisbeth] (b. Schwarzenberg, Germany, 22 Sept. 1894; d. Yorktown Heights, N.Y., 6 June 1976). Soprano. Studied in Dresden. Sang with the Dresden Opera, 1915–22; with the Metropolitan Opera, 1922–42. Appeared at Covent Garden, Salzburg, and Italian houses. Roles include the Mozart and Verdi heroines, and Wagner's Elsa, Eva, Sieglinde, and Elisabeth.

Retransition. A passage that leads to a restatement of some element of a musical form; specifically, in *sonata form, a passage that concludes the development and prepares the return to the tonic and the original thematic material in the recapitulation.

Retrograde [Lat. *cancrizans,* crab motion, *recte et retro;* Ger. *Krebsgang;* It. *al rovescio*]. Backward,

i.e., beginning with the last note and ending with the first.

Retrograde inversion. The *inversion of a series of notes presented from last to first.

Reubke, (Friedrich) Julius (b. Hausneindorf, near Quedlinburg, 23 Mar. 1834; d. Pillnitz, near Dresden, 3 June 1858). Composer, pianist, and organist. Pupil of Kullak, A. B. Marx, and Liszt. Works include sonatas and other solo compositions for piano and organ.

Reusner [Reussner], **Esaias** (b. Löwenberg, Silesia [now Lwówek Śląski, Poland], 29 Apr. 1636; d. Cölln, Berlin, 1 May 1679). Composer and lutenist. Served the Duke of Silesia, 1654–72, and the Elector of Brandenburg in Berlin, 1674–79. Published 2 collections of lute suites in the French style.

Reutter, (Johann Adam Joseph Karl) Georg (von) (b. Vienna, bapt. 6 Apr. 1708; d. there, 11 Mar. 1772). Composer. Pupil of Caldara. Court composer in Vienna from 1731; second court Kapellmeister from 1747; Kapellmeister from 1769. Succeeded his father as Kapellmeister at St. Stephen's Cathedral, 1738; engaged Haydn as a boy chorister there. Composed numerous operas and sacred works.

Reutter, Hermann (b. Stuttgart, 17 June 1900; d. there, 1 Jan. 1985). Composer. Studied at the Munich Academy of Music. Accompanied singers, including Onegin, Schwarzkopf, and Fischer-Dieskau. Taught at the Stuttgart Musik Hochschule, 1932–36; directed the Hoch Conservatory, Berlin, 1936–45. Teacher at the Staatliche Hochschule für Musik, Stuttgart, from 1952; director from 1956. Works include numerous songs; operas (*Saul,* 1928; rev. 1947; *Hamlet,* 1980); orchestral works; ballets, choral music, chamber and piano music.

Revolutionary Etude. Popular name for Chopin's Etude in C minor op. 10 no. 12 for piano (1831?), so called because Chopin supposedly composed it on hearing that Warsaw had been captured by the Russians, crushing the Polish Revolution of 1830–31. There is no evidence for the anecdote, and the etude may in fact have been composed in the previous year.

Revue. Beginning in the 19th century, a theatrical production featuring a series of songs, dances, and other entertainments, often humorous and usually without any unifying dramatic element.

Revueltas, Silvestre (b. Santiago Papasquiaro, Durango, 31 Dec. 1899; d. Mexico City, 5 Oct. 1940). Composer and violinist. Studied at Mexico City and with Borowski in the U.S. Concertized in Mexico, often with Chávez at the piano. Assistant conductor of the Mexico Symphony 1929–35. Worked with folk materials. Composed symphonic poems (*Sensemayá*, 1937–38) and other orchestral works; ballets (*El renacuajo paseador,* 1933); film scores; vocal/orchestral works; chamber music; songs.

Reyer [Rey], **(Louis-Etienne-) Ernest** (b. Marseilles, 1 Dec. 1823; d. Le Lavandon, Var, 15 Jan. 1909). Composer. Lived in Algiers, 1839–48; then moved to Paris. Works include 5 operas; *Messe pour l'arrivée du Duc d'Aumale à Alger* (1847); cantatas and other vocal pieces, and piano works. Published music criticism, travel journals, essays.

Reynolds, Roger (Lee) (b. Detroit, 13 July 1934). Composer. Pupil of Finney and Gerhard. Fellow of the Institute of Current World Affairs in Japan 1966–69. From 1969 taught at the Univ. of California, San Diego. Has worked with electronic and computer-generated sounds, serial techniques, graphic notation, and musical quotation. Works include, for the stage, *The Emperor of Ice Cream* (1962), *I/O: A Ritual for 23 Performers* (1970); for orchestra, *Graffiti* (1964); *Between,* with electronics (1968); *Transfigured Wind II,* flute, orchestra, computer (1984); *Whispers Out of Time* (1988; 1989 Pulitzer Prize); much chamber and vocal music.

Rezniček, E(mil) N(ikolaus) von (b. Vienna, 4 May 1860; d. Berlin, 2 Aug. 1945). Composer and conductor. Pupil of Reinecke. Court conductor at Mannheim, 1896–99. Settled in Berlin in 1902; conducted the Comic Opera, 1909–11. Taught at the Berlin Conservatory from 1906; at Hochschule für Musik, 1920–26. Director of Warsaw Opera and Philharmonic Orchestra, 1907–9. Compositions include 4 symphonies; operas *(Donna Diana,* 1894); an operetta; organ works; piano pieces; songs.

Rf., Rfz. Abbr. for *rinforzando.*

R.H. In keyboard music, abbr. for right hand.

Rhapsodie (Fragment aus Goethe's Harzreise im Winter) [Ger.]. Brahms's op. 53 (1869) for alto, men's chorus, and orchestra, setting a fragment of Goethe's *Harzreise im Winter* (Winter Journey through the Hartz Mountains); also known as the *Alto Rhapsody.*

Rhapsodies hongroises [Fr.]. See *Hungarian Rhapsodies.*

Rhapsody. (1) [fr. Gr. *rhapsōidos,* a singer or reciter of epic poetry] A section of an epic poem that is separately recited. (2) In the 19th and 20th centuries, a title chiefly for instrumental pieces. Borrowed from 18th-century literature, it implied no particular form, content, or compositional method. The piano was the principal medium for the repertory until the last quarter of the 19th century. See also Character (characteristic) piece.

Rhapsody in Blue. Rhapsody for piano and dance band by Gershwin, composed in 1924. Both the original version and the later version for piano and symphony orchestra were orchestrated by Ferde Grofé.

Rheinberger, Joseph (Gabriel) (b. Vaduz, Liechtenstein, 17 Mar. 1839; d. Munich, 25 Nov. 1901). Teacher, composer, organist. Studied in Munich with F. Lachner and at the conservatory, where he taught from 1859. Pupils included Humperdinck and Furtwängler. Court Kapellmeister from 1877. Composed 20 sonatas, 2 concertos, and other organ music; Masses and other sacred and secular choral works; operas; symphonies and other orchestral pieces; chamber works; piano pieces; songs.

Rheingold, Das [Ger.]. See *Ring des Nibelungen, Der.*

Rhenish Symphony. Popular name for Schumann's Symphony no. 3 in E♭ major op. 97 (1850, and thus the fourth in order of composition), composed after his arrival in Düsseldorf and in some measure inspired by the region along the Rhine. The fourth movement, originally inscribed "In the Style of an Accompaniment to a Solemn Ceremony," evokes a service for the elevation of a cardinal attended by Schumann in the cathedral in Cologne.

Rhumba. See *Rumba.*

Rhymed Office. A set of the services making up the *Office for some feast, most often that of a local saint, in which the antiphons and responsories have rhymed, metrical texts; also termed *historia.* The melodies for such Offices frequently follow one another in the order of the eight modes.

Rhythm [fr. Gr. *rhythmos;* Lat. *rhythmus;* Ger. *Rhythmus;* Fr. *rhythme;* Sp., It. *ritmo*]. That aspect of music concerned with the organization of time. As such it is a function primarily of the *duration of the sounds and silences of which music consists, though emphases created by means of *loudness as well as *harmony and melodic *motion also affect rhythm. Most Western music organizes time by means of regularly recurring pulses or beats that are in turn arranged in regularly recurring groups consisting of multiples of two or three pulses. The number of pulses per group and the internal organization of individual groups determine the *meter of a composition. The rate at which pulses or groups of pulses proceed is the *tempo. Although metrical regularity is a fundamental feature of much Western music, certain kinds of departures from regularity do occur frequently, e.g., *syncopation, *hemiola, and a wide variety of rhythmic patterns that may serve to contradict momentarily some metrical scheme. Such departures, however, derive their meaning from the prevailing regularity within which they occur. Similarly, the rhythm of much Western music is dependent upon a largely regular or steady tempo, but momentary departures from the prevailing tempo, whether specified by the composer or introduced by the performer in appropriate ways, are also an essential feature of much Western music.

Rhythmic organization of the type described began to be an important part of Western music at least as early as the 13th century, when musical *notation first included the means to notate rhythm unambiguously. Repertories from earlier periods, e.g., *Gregorian and other types of liturgical chant, may have been characterized by substantially greater rhythmic freedom, principally the lack of regular metrical structure. This absence of regular meter is also a feature of much music of the 20th century and of the music of various non-Western musical cultures. The term "free rhythm" is sometimes used in these contexts, though such music often relies on some fundamental unit of duration employed to mark off a regular pulse.

Although all music consisting of sounds and silences ordered in time is by definition rhythmic, the term *rhythmic* usually implies the use of particularly striking rhythmic patterns. See also Accent; Modes, rhythmic; Isorhythm; Polyrhythm; Rubato.

Rhythm and blues [also rhythm 'n' blues, R 'n' B]. Black American popular music from the late 1940s through the early 1960s. It was predominantly a vocal genre, often used for dancing, that featured lead singers (e.g., Clyde McPhatter, Sam Cooke) who worked independently or as members of a (usually male) vocal quartet or quintet (e.g., the Ravens, the Orioles, the Drifters, the Coasters). Other group members harmonized using nonsense syllables ("ooo," "doo-wop") and catchy phrases ("shake, rattle, and roll"). A bass voice sometimes provided an independent lower line. Lyrics, increasingly oriented toward teenagers through the 1950s, concerned love life. Singers were often accompanied by piano, electric guitar, bass, and drums, with a prominent, honking tenor saxophone. Harmonic and metric structures were clearly derived from 32-bar popular song forms and 12-bar *blues.

"Rhythm and blues" was as much an economic, sociological, and chronological designation as a musical one, however. *Billboard* magazine's R 'n' B Top 40 listed records by black artists that were hits in black communities from 1949 through 1964. Hence, urban bluesmen (Joe Turner, B. B. King) became R 'n' B artists by virtue of increased sales. Conversely, some R 'n' B hit singles with a female lead singer (Dinah Washington, Ruth Brown), a backup group, or a prominent tenor saxophone were otherwise identical to urban blues.

In the mid-1950s, one branch of R 'n' B became *rock-and-roll, as white musicians took up black creations and as black innovators (Chuck Berry, Fats Domino, Little Richard) reached white audiences. In the late 1950s, another branch merged with pop music, as producers introduced plush arrangements with strings. In the early 1960s, a third branch became *soul music, as impassioned, screaming singing (Ray Charles, James Brown) gained widespread popularity.

Rhythm section. The chord-playing, bass, and percussion instruments in a jazz group; the players of those instruments. A standard rhythm section comprises keyboard and or guitar, double bass (played pizzicato) or electric bass, and drums.

Rhythmic modes. See Modes, rhythmic.

Ribattuta [It.]. In Italian and German music of the 17th and 18th centuries, a trill in dotted rhythm (long-short) beginning on the main note. It usually accelerates to end either on a *tremolo* (in early Italian vocal music, *ribattuta di gola*) or in an ordinary trill.

Ricci, Federico (b. Naples, 22 Oct. 1809; d. Conegliano, near Treviso, 10 Dec. 1877). Composer. Pupil of his brother Luigi, Zingarelli, Raimondi, and Bellini. *Maître de chapelle,* Imperial Theaters, St. Petersburg, 1853–69. Composed operas, incl. *Crispino e la comare* (with his brother, 1850); *Corrado d'Altamura* (1841); *Une folie à Rome* (opéra bouffe, 1869); 2 Masses, 3 cantatas, smaller sacred pieces, songs.

Ricci, Luigi (b. Naples, 8 June or 8 July 1805; d. Prague, 31 Dec. 1859). Composer. Brother of Federico Ricci, with whom he collaborated on 4 operas. Pupil of Zingarelli and Generali. *Maestro di cappella* at Trieste and conductor of the Teatro grande from 1836. Directed the premiere of Verdi's *Il corsaro;* directed seasons in Odessa and Copenhagen. Composed 30 operas, incl. *Chiara di Rosembergh* (1831); more than 20 Masses, other sacred music, songs.

Ricci, Ruggiero [Roger; Rich, Woodrow Wilson] (b. San Bruno, Calif., 24 July 1918). Violinist. Pupil of Persinger and Kulenkampff. Carnegie Hall debut, 1929. Has toured Europe and the Soviet Union; world tour, 1957. Premiered Paganini's rediscovered Fourth Concerto, and concertos of Ginastera and von Einem. Taught at Indiana Univ. and Juilliard.

Rice, Thomas Dartmouth ("Daddy") (b. New York, 20 May 1808; d. there, 19 Sept. 1860). Minstrel performer. His "Jim Crow" act (Louisville, ca. 1828) created the genre of "Ethiopian opera," featuring blackface performers and songs, and included the first American song to become an international hit.

Other hit shows included *Otello* (1845), a parody on Shakespeare.

Ricercar, ricercare [fr. It. *ricercare,* to seek; also It. *ricercata;* Fr. *recherché;* Ger. *Ricercar;* Sp. *recercario, recercada*]. An instrumental composition of the 16th and 17th centuries, of which two varieties existed concurrently: a rhapsodic type in homophonic texture and a polyphonic type that exploits learned contrapuntal artifices and is a precursor of the *fugue. In the 16th century, both types frequently appear in German, English, Spanish, and French sources titled, respectively, *prelude, *fancy, *tiento, and *fantasia. They have sometimes served as *etudes or studies. The ricercar often had a preludial function, "seeking out" the key or mode of a following song, *intabulation, dance, motet, psalm, or portion of the Mass. Frescobaldi specified toccatas before the Mass and ricercars (some preceded by a toccata) before the Eucharist. Although ricercars do not always stand directly before the piece they are intended to introduce, they are often arranged and identified by mode or key, simplifying selection of one to match the following piece. Ricercars may follow an intabulation of vocal music or other work. In many such cases the term seems to refer to "searching out" (using *paraphrase and *parody procedures) permutations and combinations of thematic materials drawn from the model. In the 17th century, ricercars could appear in sets with a preceding *toccata and following *canzona, or with just a toccata, anticipating the later prelude and fugue.

The earliest ricercars of the homophonic rhapsodic type appear in lute manuscripts of the late 15th century and Petrucci prints from the beginning of the 16th. These were followed by organ works of Marco Antonio Cavazzoni (Venice, 1523) and of Claudio Maria Veggio (ca. 1510–after 1544). These thin-textured pieces lack formal organization and thematic unity and freely mingle chords with running passagework as in an improvisation. They are usually attached to a following intabulation or dance. Some are clearly intended as codas. Others, such as those by Joan Ambrosio Dalza (fl. 1508), are preceded by a *tastar de corde*.

After mid-century, the terms *tasteggiata, tastata,* and *toccata* ousted *ricercar* as a designation for preludial improvisationlike pieces. The term appears very frequently through the 18th century, however, being equated with testing the tuning of an instrument, cadential flourishes and difficult passages, or toccatalike compositions.

Instruction manuals such as those of Sylvestro di Ganassi dal Fontego (Venice, 1535), Diego Ortiz (Rome, 1553), and Giovanni Bassano (Venice, 1585) use *recercata* to identify either ornate pieces, for a single-line instrument, that explore a technical device such as trill-like figures, running sequences, or double stops, or pieces that illustrate procedures for embellishing a line in a vocal ensemble work or for improvising over a *cantus firmus* or bass pattern [see *Glosa*].

The polyphonic ricercar is sometimes (perhaps incorrectly) described as an instrumental counterpart to the motet. Many Renaissance instrumental genres were influenced by parallel vocal ones, but they were generally separate in development. Early works by lutenists Marco Dall'Aquila (Milan, 1536) and Francesco Canova da Milano (1536ff.) and by organists Giacomo Fogliano (composed ca. 1530) and Girolamo Cavazzoni (Venice, 1543) and ensemble ricercars by Adrian Willaert and his circle printed in *Musica nova* (Venice, 1540) and by the publisher Antonio Gardane (Venice, 1551ff.) are all remarkable for their reconciliation of compositional procedures of the Josquin generation with the needs of idiomatic instrumental styles. Compared with the motet, thematic materials are generally more animated rhythmically and more angular melodically, the individual lines more sweeping. Even the earliest ricercars tend to divide into sections developing short points of imitation in a considerable number of entries, separated by episodes of running passagework and harmonic sequences that anticipate the fugue.

Mid-century lute ricercars approach the part-writing complexities of the ensemble and keyboard ones, especially those by Bálint Bakfark (Lyons, 1553) and Melchior Neusidler (Venice, 1566; Strasbourg, 1574) and the 24 in all modes by Vincenzo Galilei (Rome, 1563). The ensemble ricercars of Giuliano Tiburtino (Venice, 1549) and Annibale Padovano (Venice, 1556) and those of Jacques Buus (Venice, 1547, 1549) for organ and for ensemble sometimes derive subsequent subjects from the opening one, heralding the monothematic ricercar. The ricercars of Andrea Gabrieli (ca. 1560–70; publ. Venice, 1589, 1595, 1596, 1605) are generally built from a few subjects; five of them are monothematic and treat the subject in augmentation, in contrary motion, and with regular countersubjects. These devices—as well as syncopation, diminution, and subjects that are chromatic, move only by leap, or are founded in solmization syllables—permeate the ricercars of Frescobaldi (Rome, 1615; Venice, 1635), turning the genre into a font of learned counterpoint, which it was to remain.

By 1632, ensemble ricercars disappeared, and by mid-century keyboard ones had taken on increasing severity and archaic connotations, the term being reserved for fugal compositions in long notes and *alla breve* meter—"in stile antico e grave," as Fabrizio Fontana (Rome, 1677) called his. Such works were composed by, among others, Johann Jacob Froberger (1616–67), whose ricercars are all monothematic. Bach's *Musical Offering* (1747) contains two ricercars that are thought to serve as preludes to the first and second parts. The connotation of a learned fugal piece continued into the 19th century. Twentieth-century neoclassicism produced ricercars that evoke a similar meaning.

Rich, Buddy [Bernard] (b. New York, 30 June 1917; d. Los Angeles, 2 Apr. 1987). Jazz drummer and bandleader. Played intermittently with the big bands of Harry James (1938–66), Artie Shaw (1939), and Tommy Dorsey (1939–55). Toured with Jazz at the Philharmonic from 1947; recorded with Charlie Parker, 1949–50. Led a big band from 1966; then small groups.

Richafort, Jean (b. probably in Hainaut, ca. 1480; d. Bruges?, ca. 1548). Composer. *Maître de chapelle* at St. Rombaud of Mechelin, 1507–9; then associated with the French royal chapel. *Maître de chapelle* at St. Gilles, Bruges, 1542–47. Works include Masses (parodies); Magnificats; motets; chansons; 2 secular Latin motets.

Richard [Richards], **Keith** (b. Dartford, Kent, 18 Dec. 1943). Rock guitarist and songwriter. With Mick Jagger formed The Rolling Stones, 1962; served as lead guitarist, coauthor of many songs, and architect of their distinctive hard rock sound. Released a solo album, *Talk Is Cheap* (1988).

Richter, Ernest Friedrich (Eduard) (b. Gross-Schönau, Lausitz, 24 Oct. 1808; d. Leipzig, 9 Apr. 1879). Composer and theorist. Studied at the Univ. of Leipzig; taught at the Leipzig Conservatory from 1843. Organist at several churches; Kantor of Thomasschule from 1868. Composed a cantata, chamber music, keyboard pieces, sacred music, songs. Published textbooks on counterpoint and *Lehrbuch der Harmonie* (1853).

Richter, Franz Xaver (b. Holleschau?, 1 Dec. 1709; d. Strasbourg, 12 Sept. 1789). Composer and singer. From 1740, Vice-Kapellmeister to the Prince-Abbot in Kempten, Allgäu. By 1747, court musician in Mannheim; chamber composer from around 1768. Kapellmeister at Strasbourg Cathedral from 1769. Gave concert tours in France, the Netherlands, and England. Composed many symphonies, string quartets, and sacred music (including 39 Masses). Wrote a composition treatise. Pupils included J. M. Kraus and C. Stamitz.

Richter, Hans (b. Raab, 4 Apr. 1843; d. Bayreuth, 5 Dec. 1916). Conductor. Studied at Vienna Conservatory. Associate of Wagner. Worked under Bülow as conductor of Munich Opera. Conductor at Pest (1871–75), of Birmingham Festival (1885–1909), Hallé Orchestra (1897–1911), London Symphony Orchestra (1904–11). Led first performances of the complete *Ring* cycle at Bayreuth (1876) and of

Bruckner's symphonies 1, 3, 4, 8. Played trumpet for premiere of *Siegfried Idyll* (1876).

Richter, Karl (b. Plauen, 15 Oct. 1926; d. Munich, 15 Feb. 1981). Organist, harpsichordist, and conductor. Pupil of K. Straube. Choirmaster of the Christuskirche, Leipzig, from 1946; organist of the Thomaskirche from 1947. Taught at the Hochschule für Musik, Munich, from 1951. Recorded and toured extensively with the Munich Bach Choir and Orchestra, which he founded, 1953.

Richter, Sviatoslav (Teofilovich) (b. Zhitomir, Ukraine, 20 Mar. 1915; d. Moscow, 1 Aug. 1997). Pianist. Studied at the Moscow Conservatory. Performed widely in Eastern and Western Europe, China, and the U.S. Made chamber recordings with Oistrakh and Rostropovich; also noted as a vocal accompanist.

Ricochet [Fr.]. See Bowing (5).

Řídký, Jaroslav (b. Liberec, 25 Aug. 1897; d. Poděbrady, 14 Aug. 1956). Composer. Pupil of Jirák, Foerster, and Křička. Played harp with the Czech Philharmonic, 1924–38; 1925–30 conducted the Czech Philharmonic choir. Taught at the Prague Conservatory, 1928–49; at the Prague Academy of Music from 1948. Used Czech folk materials. Works include 7 symphonies, concertos, 2 cantatas, and chamber works.

Ridotto [It.]. (1) Reduced, arranged, e.g., for piano, from a work for ensemble. (2) [Fr. *redoute*] An 18th-century entertainment consisting of music and dancing.

Ridout, Alan (John) (b. West Wickham, Kent, 9 Dec. 1934; d. Caen, France, 19 Mar. 1996). Composer. Pupil of Jacob, Howells, Fricker, Tippett, and Badings. Taught at the Royal College of Music from 1960; at Cambridge Univ., 1963–75. Worked with serialism, modality, and microtonality. Works include operas (*The White Doe*, church opera, 1987); 6 symphonies; concertos; much vocal music, often for Canterbury Cathedral (6 cantatas; Christmas Oratorio); organ works.

Ridout, Godfrey (b. Toronto, 6 May 1918; d. there, 24 Nov. 1984). Composer. Studied and later taught at the Toronto Conservatory and the Univ. of Toronto. Works include *Exile*, melodrama (1984); *La Prima Ballerina*, ballet (1966); orchestral works *(Fall Fair,* 1961; Concerto grosso, 1974); vocal-orchestral works (*Esther*, 1952; *Cantiones mysticae: Nos. 1–3*, 1953–72; *In Memoriam Anne Frank*, 1965); band music, chamber and vocal music. Reconstructed the earliest known North American comic opera, *Colas et Colinette*, composed by Joseph Quesnal, 1788.

Riduzione [It.]. *Reduction.

Riegger, Wallingford (Constantin) (b. Albany, Ga., 29 Apr. 1885; d. New York, 2 Apr. 1961). Composer. Pupil of R. Haussmann and Bruch. Conducted in Berlin and Würzburg, 1910–17. Taught at Drake Univ. in Iowa from 1917. Composed dance scores for Martha Graham, Doris Humphrey, and others (*New Dance*, 1940); orchestral works (4 symphonies; *Dichotomy*, 1931–32; *Canon and Fugue*, 1942; *Quintuple Jazz*, 1959); chamber and piano music (Piano Trio, 1920; *Study in Sonority*, 10 violins, 1926–27; string quartets; Nonet, brass, 1951); vocal music (*Eternity*, 1942; *In Certainty of Song*, 1950).

Rienzi [Ger. *Cola Rienzi, der letzte der Tribunen*, Cola Rienzi, the Last of the Tribunes.]. Opera in five acts by Wagner (to his own libretto, based on a drama by Mary Russell Mitford and a novel by Edward Bulwer-Lytton), produced in Dresden in 1842. Setting: Rome, about 1350.

Ries, Ferdinand (b. Bonn, bapt. 28 Nov. 1784; d. Frankfurt am Main, 13 Jan. 1838). Pianist and composer. Pupil of his father, Franz (Anton) Ries, B. H. Romberg, Beethoven, and Albrechtsberger. Toured widely in Europe. From 1813 to 1824, lived in London, appearing in the Philharmonic Concerts. Composed many works for piano, chamber music, symphonies, concertos, and several operas. With F. G. Wegeler wrote a biography of Beethoven.

Ries, Franz (Anton) (b. Bonn, 10 Nov. 1755; d. Godesberg, 1 Nov. 1846). Violinist. Pupil of J. P. Salomon. Performed in Vienna, 1779. Served Elector Maximilian in Bonn, 1779–94. Beethoven was his pupil. His eldest son was Ferdinand Ries.

Rieti, Vittorio (b. Alexandria, Egypt, 28 Jan. 1898; d. New York, 19 Feb. 1994). Composer. Studied in Milan and with Casella and Respighi in Rome. Taught at the Peabody Conservatory (1948–49), the Chicago Musical College (1950–53), Queens College (1955–60), and the New York College of Music (1960–64). Composed ballet music for Diaghilev (incl. *Barabau*, 1925) and Balanchine (incl. *Night Shadow*, 1941); operas; incidental music; symphonies, concertos, and other orchestral music; chamber works; piano music (*Second Avenue Waltzes*, 2 pianos, 1942); choral music; songs.

Rietz, (August Wilhelm) Julius (b. Berlin, 28 Dec. 1812; d. Dresden, 12 Sept. 1877). Cellist, composer, and conductor. Pupil of F. Schmidt and B. H. Romberg. Mendelssohn's assistant at Düsseldorf, 1834; became city's music director. Conductor of Leipzig Opera and Singakademie from 1847. Edited the B minor Mass and St. Matthew Passion for the Bach Gesellschaft. City music director of Dresden, 1860. Composed theater music, symphonies, a cello concerto, lieder.

Riff. In jazz, a brief, relaxed, tuneful phrase repeated over changing harmonies. It may serve as accompaniment or as melody.

Rigaudon, rigodon [Fr.; Eng. rigadoon]. A cheerful Baroque dance movement in duple meter. It typically has a quarter-note upbeat, four-measure phrases in ₵ (or 2), and binary form. Often phrases begin with half-note motion, increasing to no more than eighths. Like a *bourrée (from which it is sometimes indistinguishable), it is moderately quick, faster than a gavotte.

Righini, Vincenzo (b. Bologna, 22 Jan. 1756; d. there, 19 Aug. 1812). Composer. Studied in Bologna. Joined an opera troupe in Prague as a tenor, 1776. From 1780, singing master to the Princess of Württemberg and director of the Italian Opera, Vienna. Court Kapellmeister in Mainz from 1787; in Berlin from 1793 (also director of the Italian Opera there); of the court theater, Berlin, from 1811. Works include operas, sacred works, songs, and instrumental music.

Rigoletto. Opera in three acts by Verdi (libretto by Francesco Maria Piave, after Victor Hugo's drama *Le roi s'amuse*), produced in Venice in 1851. Setting: Mantua and environs in the 16th century.

Rigoroso [It.]. Rigorous, in strict time.

Rihm, Wolfgang (Michael) (b. Karlsruhe, 13 March 1952). Composer. Pupil of Searle, Stockhausen, and K. Huber. Taught at the Karlsruhe Hochschule, 1973–78. Works include 6 operas (*Jakob Lenz*, 1978; *Die Eroberung von Mexico*, 1987–89); orchestral music (3 symphonies; *Abgesangsszene nos. 1–5*, 1979–80; *Doppelgesang nos. 1–2*, 1980–83; *Tugurie I–VII*, 1981–82; *Gesungene Zeit*, violin, orchestra, 1991–92); music for voices and orchestra (*Hölderlin-Fragmente*, 1977; *Dies*, 1984); 8 string quartets and other chamber music (*Fremde Szene I–III*, piano trio, 1982–83; *Gejagte Form*, 11 instruments, 1989); songs; piano and organ music.

Riisager, Knudåge (b. Port Kunda, Estonia, 6 Mar. 1897; d. Copenhagen, 26 Dec. 1974). Composer. Studied in Copenhagen and in Paris with Roussel and LeFlem. Head of the Copenhagen Conservatory, 1956–67. Works include 1 opera (*Susanna*, Copenhagen, 1950), ballets (*Fruen fra havet*, New York, 1960; *Galla-variationer*, Copenhagen, 1967); orchestral music (5 symphonies; concertos); 6 string quartets and other chamber music; and music for film.

Rilasciando [It.]. Slowing down.

Riley, Terry (Mitchell) (b. Colfax, Calif., 24 June 1935). Composer and performer. Pupil of Erickson, Shifrin, and Pran Nath. Taught at Mills College,

1971–80. Has made use of "minimalist" techniques and Indian music. Works include *Mescalin Mix,* tape (1962–63); *Keyboard Studies* (1963); *In C,* any melodic instruments (1964); *Cadenza on the Night Plain,* string quartet (1984); improvisational works for various instruments and electronics (*Dorian Reeds,* 1964; *Do You Know How It Sounds?,* 1983); works with synthesizer, many with Indian instruments (*Song of the Emerald Runner,* 1983).

Rim. The hoop affixing the head of a drum to the shell. Percussion parts may direct that the drum be struck at or on the rim. A rim shot is a loud stroke produced by striking the rim and the head simultaneously.

Rimsky-Korsakov, Nikolay Andreyevich (b. Tikhvin, Novgorod govt., 18 Mar. 1844; d. Lyubensk, St. Petersburg govt., 21 June 1908). Composer. Pupil of Balakirev and one of "The Five." Served in the Russian navy, as Inspector of Naval Bands from 1873. From 1871 taught at the St. Petersburg Conservatory; dismissed in 1905 for his involvement in the political unrest that culminated in "Bloody Sunday." From 1883, assistant musical director of the imperial chapel. Composed many operas (incl. *The Maid of Pskov,* 1868–72; *Snegurochka* [Snow Maiden], 1881; *Mlada,* 1889–90; *Christmas Eve,* 1894–95; *Sadko,* 1894–96; *Barber of Baghdad,* 1895; *Mozart and Salieri,* 1897; *The Tsar's Bride,* 1898; *The Tale of Tsar Saltan,* 1899–1900; *Kaschchey the Immortal,* 1901–2; *Kitezh,* 1903–5; *The *Golden Cockerel); orchestral works (4 symphonies, incl. no. 2, *Antar,* 1868; *Capriccio espagnol; *Sheherazade; the overture *Russian Easter Festival,* 1888); choral works; songs; chamber music. Published a book on orchestration. Completed and orchestrated Mussorgsky's *Boris Godunov and *Khovanshchina and Borodin's *Prince Igor. Among his students were Lyadov, Glazunov, Myaskovsky, Stravinsky, Prokofiev, and Respighi.

Rinaldo di [da] **Capua** (b. Capua or Naples, ca. 1705; d. Rome?, ca. 1780). Composer. Active chiefly in Rome. Composed operas, including *La commedia in commedia* (1738), *Vologeso re de' Parti* (1739), and *La libertà nociva* (1740), all for Rome; some opera serie for Lisbon (1740–42); *La zingara* (Paris, 1753), which became involved in the *querelle des bouffons.*

Rinck, Johann Christian Heinrich (b. Elgersburg, Thuringia, 18 Feb. 1770; d. Darmstadt, 7 Aug. 1846). Organist and composer. Pupil of J. C. Kittel. Organist at Giessen from 1790. From 1805, teacher at the music school in Darmstadt, and organist and *Kammermusiker* to the Grand Duke. Gave concert tours. Composed organ works and sacred music.

Rinforzando [It., abbr. *r., rf., rfz., rinf.*]. Becoming stronger, i.e., louder, usually over a shorter span of time than is called for by *crescendo;* also (sometimes *sforzato*) a sudden accent on a single note, similar to *sforzando.*

Ring des Nibelungen, Der [Ger., The Ring of the Nibelung]. A cycle of four operas by Wagner (to his own "poems," after Scandinavian, Icelandic, and Germanic sagas, including the *Nibelungenlied*), intended for performance on a preliminary evening and the following three days, respectively: (1) *Das Rheingold* (The Rhine Gold) in four scenes (composed in 1853–54), which serves as the prelude (*Vorspiel;* also termed the *Vorabend,* preparatory evening) to the entire cycle. (2) *Die Walküre* (The Valkyrie) in three acts (1854–56). (3) *Siegfried* in three acts (1856–71). (4) *Götterdämmerung* (The Twilight of the Gods) in a prologue and three acts (1869–74). The entire cycle was first performed in Bayreuth in 1876. The first poem to be completed, in 1848, was titled *Siegfrieds Tod* (Siegfried's Death). This was followed by *Der junge Siegfried* (The Young Siegfried), *Die Walküre,* and *Das Rheingold,* in that order. *Siegfrieds Tod* and *Der junge Siegfried* were then revised as *Götterdämmerung* and *Siegfried,* respectively, the entire poem in its present order being completed in 1852. Sketches of the music for *Siegfrieds Tod* were undertaken in 1850.

Ring modulator. An electronic device named for the characteristic arrangement in its circuitry of four diodes in a ring. It accepts two signals as input and produces as output frequencies that are the sum and difference of the two input frequencies [see also Electro-acoustic music, Electronic instrument].

Rinuccini, Ottavio (b. Florence, 20 Jan. 1562; d. there, 28 Mar. 1621). Librettist and poet. Associated with some members and goals of the Camerata. Works include *Dafne* (set by Peri and Corsi, 1598); *Euridice* (Peri, 1600; with a preface commenting on their collaboration). Monteverdi set his *Arianna* and *Ballo delle ingrate* (both 1608) as well as some madrigals.

Ripa (da Mantova), Alberto da [Rippe, Albert de] (b. Mantua, ca. 1500; d. Paris, 1551). Lutenist and composer. Served Cardinal Ercole Gonzaga of Mantua before 1529, then entered the French court of François I. Works include fantasias, dances, and intabulated chansons and motets.

Ripetizione [It.]. Repetition; rehearsal.

Ripieno [It.]. (1) Played with doubled parts; *tutti. (2) In a Baroque concerto grosso, the larger ensemble, as distinct from the soloists [see Concerto; see also Repiano].

Riposato [It.]. With repose.

Riprendere [It.]. To resume (the original tempo).

Ripresa [It.]. (1) Repeat, repetition. (2) Refrain [see *Ballata, Barzeletta*]. (3) In some 16th- and 17th-century dances and songs, a short instrumental passage occurring in conjunction with the repetitions of the principal sections; also termed ritornello.

Riquier (de Narbona), Guiraut (b. Narbonne, ca. 1230; d. Rodez, 1292). Troubadour poet, composer, singer. Served Alfonso X of Castile, 1269–79, then Henry II, Count of Rodez. The last of the true Provençal langue d'oc troubadours. Of his 89 extant poems, 48 survive with melodies.

Riservata [It.]. See *Musica reservata.*

Risoluto [It.] Resolute, energetic.

Risset, Jean-Claude (b. Le Puy, 13 March 1938). Composer. Pupil of Jolivet. Moved to New York, 1964. Associate of Varèse and Mathews. Taught at the Centre universitaire de Marseille-Luminy; directed the Institut de recherche et de coordination acoustique/musique in Paris. Works include orchestral and chamber music; *Sketches: Duet for One Pianist* (1989); pieces for tape, with and without instruments (*Little Boy*, incidental music, 1968; *Mutations I–II*, 1969, 1973).

Ritardando [It., abbr. *rit., ritard.*]. Slowing down gradually; also indicated by *rallentando* [see also *Ritenuto*].

Rite of Spring, The. See *Sacre du printemps, Le.*

Ritenuto [It.]. Held back, slowed down; usually a more sudden reduction in tempo than called for by *ritardando* and *rallentando.*

Ritmico [It.]. Rhythmic.

Ritmo [It.]. Rhythm; for *ritmo di tre (quattro) battute*, see *Battuta.*

Ritornello [It., little return]. (1) In the 14th-century *madrigal and *caccia, the final couplet of the 8- or 11-line poem. The ritornello is set to different music and is often in a meter different from that of the preceding strophes of three lines. Despite the name ritornello, this final couplet is not a refrain, because it is stated only once. (2) In the 17th century, an instrumental section of an opera, cantata, strophic aria, or other vocal work. Ritornellos may be either recurrent, functioning as refrains, or nonrecurrent; in the latter case, the term probably refers to the "return" of the instrumental ensemble, not the thematic material. (3) In the late 17th and 18th centuries, the recurring tutti section of a concerto movement or a da capo aria [see Concerto; Aria]. See also *Ritournelle.*

Ritornello form. The characteristic form of the first and often the last movement of a late-Baroque or Classical concerto, based on an alternation of tutti (ritornello) and solo sections [see Concerto]. Ritornello form also occurs in concerto-based movements such as the choruses of many Bach cantatas, in which the choir functions as the "soloist," as well as in movements of works without tutti/solo contrast (e.g., sonatas and ripieno concertos of the late Baroque) in which the principal formal event is the recurrence of the main theme in various keys.

Ritorno d'Ulisse in patria, Il [It., The Return of Ulysses to His Country]. Opera in a prologue and five acts by Monteverdi (libretto by Giacomo Badoaro, after Homer's *Odyssey*), produced in Venice in 1640.

Ritournelle [Fr.]. (1) *Ritornello. (2) In French stage music from the late 17th to the early 19th century, an instrumental prelude to an air or vocal ensemble, or a similar passage that serves as an interlude or conclusion [see also Ritornello].

Ritter, Alexander [Sachsa] (b. Narva, Estonia, 27 June 1833; d. Munich, 12 Apr. 1896). Composer and violinist. Pupil of Ferdinand David and E. F. Richter. Second *Konzertmeister* of Weimar Orchestra; conductor of Stettin Opera, 1856–58. Violinist in Meiningen under Bülow, 1882–86. Wrote 2 operas, tone poems, string quartet, piano pieces, songs.

Ritter, Hermann (b. Wismar, Mecklenberg, 16 Sept. 1849; d. Würzburg, 22 Jan. 1926). Violist and instrument maker. Studied in Berlin and Heidelberg. Taught in Würzburg from 1879. Formed the Ritter Quartet, 1905. Created a large viola, the "viola alta," which was played at Bayreuth; arranged much music for the instrument and published a history of it.

Riverso [It.]. Reversed; either *inversion or *retrograde.

Rivier, Jean (b. Villemomble, Seine, 21 July 1896; d. La Penne sur Huveaune, 6 Nov. 1987). Composer. Studied at the Paris Conservatory; taught there, 1947–66. Works include concertos (piano, 1940; for Brass, Timpani, and Strings, 1963), 7 symphonies, and other orchestra pieces; an opera, *Vénitienne* (Paris, 1937); 2 string quartets and other chamber music; choral music; piano music; songs; scores for radio.

Rivolto [It.]. *Inversion.

Roach, Max [Maxwell] (b. Elizabeth City, N.C., 10 Jan. 1924). Jazz drummer and bandleader. Joined the bop combos of Dizzy Gillespie (1944) and Charlie Parker (intermittently from 1945); Miles Davis's cool jazz nonet (1948–50). With Clifford Brown, founded a hard bop quintet, 1954. From the late

1950s became active in artistic contributions to the civil rights movement. Also composed for musicals, films, television, and symphony orchestra. During 1970s-80s, led the group M'Boom Re: Percussion; taught at the Univ. of Massachusetts.

Robert le diable [Fr., Robert the Devil]. Opera in five acts by Meyerbeer (libretto by Eugène Scribe), produced in Paris in 1831. Setting: Palermo in the 13th century.

Robeson, Paul (b. Princeton, N.J., 9 Apr. 1898; d. Philadelphia, 23 Jan. 1976). Bass-baritone and actor. First concert, 1925. Appeared in London as Othello (1930); films include *The Emperor Jones* (1933) and *Show Boat* (1936). His American career ended in the 1940s with his espousal of communism, but he continued to perform elsewhere.

Robinson, Anastasia (b. Italy, ca. 1692; d. Southampton, Apr. 1755). Soprano, contralto. Studied with Croft. Around 1718 her voice dropped from soprano to contralto. Performed in many Handel operas, including *Amadigi* (creating the part of Oriana, 1715) and *Giulio Cesare* (1724); Handel composed the soprano part in *Ode for Queen Anne's Birthday* for her.

Robinson, Smokey [William] (b. Detroit, Mich., 19 Feb. 1940). Soul singer, songwriter, and record producer. His vocal group The Miracles became Motown Records' first success, with songs written and produced by Robinson and Berry Gordy, Jr. ("Shop Around," 1960). Produced groups such as The Temptations. From 1972, made many solo recordings.

Rochberg, George (b. Paterson, N.J., 5 July 1918). Composer. Pupil of Szell, L. Mannes, Scalero, and Menotti. Taught at Curtis, 1948–54; at the Univ. of Pennsylvania, 1960–83. Music editor, Presser Company, 1951–60. Has used serial techniques and musical quotation. Works include *The Confidence Man,* opera (1982); orchestral music (5 symphonies, incl. no. 1, 2nd movement: *Night Music,* 1948; 3rd movement: *Capriccio,* 1949; *Time-Span I-II,* 1960, 1962); chamber works (7 string quartets; *Contra mortem et tempus,* 1965; *Muse of Fire,* flute, guitar, 1991); keyboard music and vocal pieces.

Rock. A genre of mass-disseminated music emerging in the 1960s, related to but distinct from *rock-and-roll.

The musical and expressive features of rock were forged in California, by the Byrds and a number of bands in the San Francisco area (the Charlatans, the Great Society, Quicksilver Messenger Service, Big Brother and the Holding Company). The Jefferson Airplane, featuring singer Grace Slick, was most influential in popularizing this style elsewhere, with live performances across the country and a recording contract with a major company in 1966–67.

Rock is electrical, in its use of amplification, distortion, and eventual production of sound. The electric guitar is the most important melodic instrument and is played with a sustained and florid style made possible by electronic technology. The lyrics are usually intensely personal or political and are often obscure in poetical style. Formally, rock was the first popular genre to develop extended and often complex structures, made possible by its origins in live performance and its later dissemination on long-playing records. Socially, rock was aligned from the beginning with a mostly white and young constituency claiming to be at odds with traditional American attitudes toward drug use, sex, and the work ethic.

The Beatles heard this music while touring the U.S. in 1966 and immediately incorporated some of its elements into their *Revolver* (1966) and *Sgt. Pepper's Lonely Hearts Club Band* (1967). It quickly became an Anglo-American music, with equally important performers on both sides of the Atlantic, including the Rolling Stones, Eric Clapton, and the Who in Britain and the Doors, Jimi Hendrix, the Grateful Dead, and Janis Joplin in the U.S. Unlike rock-and-roll, it had little appeal for black and rural white audiences in America. In a global reflection of its strong ties to white middle-class youth, rock spread to the Continent and throughout the English-speaking world but had little impact on the Third World.

Some aspects of the style and substance of rock spread to other genres of music, resulting in musical dialects labeled jazz rock, art rock, *folk rock, country rock, and *heavy metal. By 1970, the term rock had become virtually synonymous with popular music. It was used by audiences and critics to encompass not only the music described above but also various types of Afro-American music (*Motown, for instance), the music of the singer-songwriters so popular at the beginning of the decade (Carole King, James Taylor, Cat Stevens, Elton John), and even music firmly rooted in older Tin Pan Alley styles (Barry Manilow, Billy Joel).

Gradually, however, the term came to be understood again as appropriate for a single dialect of the pluralistic media-disseminated popular music of the 1970s and 80s, characterized by a basic instrumentation of electric guitars, bass, keyboard, and drums (increasingly augmented or replaced by synthesized sounds); a fast, driving rhythm punctuated by prominent and often dominant drums and bass; and provocative dress and behavior by performers and audience, dramatizing rock's continuing alliance with attitudes at variance with those of mainstream Anglo-American culture. The Rolling Stones, Jefferson

Starship, the Who, Steve Miller, and other bands formed in the 1960s continued to be at the center of this music, joined by younger performers favoring a generally similar musical and expressive style: Bruce Springsteen, Kiss, the Eagles, Bob Seger, Rod Stewart, ZZ Top, and many others with equally individual styles derived from mainstream rock.

The later 1970s brought new dialects of rock, chiefly *punk and *new wave, referring back to the early days of the genre, simpler and more direct in style and less reliant on complex electronic technology and sophisticated mixing than had become the norm, yet equally associated with white, urban, disaffected youth.

Rockabilly. A form of American popular music that combined the plucked-string sounds of *country and western music with the song-forms and lyrics of *rock-and-roll. The genre flourished from about 1954 to 1960 in the southern U.S. and for somewhat longer in England. Its essential representatives include Gene Vincent, Carl Perkins, Johnny Cash, and the young Elvis Presley.

Rock-and-roll. A type of American popular music of the 1950s, based chiefly on elements of vernacular Afro-American music and enjoying a brief but spectacular worldwide dissemination. Rock-and-roll became the dominant popular style in 1955 with "Rock Around the Clock" by Bill Haley and his Comets. Pieces in a similar style, performed by both white performers (Elvis Presley, Jerry Lee Lewis, the Everly Brothers) and black (Chuck Berry, Little Richard, Fats Domino), were the most successful items of American popular music for several years.

Rock-and-roll is essentially a form of rhythmicized *blues. Most pieces were cast in some variation of the 12-bar blues form. Instrumentation was dominated by amplified and electric guitars, saxophones, and a prominent rhythm section of drums, piano, and bass giving powerful emphasis to the first beat of each 4/4 bar (hence the name "Big Beat" given to it in Europe). The tempo was fast and driving; the texts were mostly concerned with sex, openly or by innuendo; the dynamic level was uniformly high; and vocal styles were rough and raucous, with the text often delivered in a semishouted fashion.

Prototypes existed for at least a decade before 1955. Black popular music, labeled *rhythm and blues, offered pieces with all the elements of rock-and-roll, lacking only the label. Some white country and western singers also performed and recorded rhythmic blues during this time.

The term was soon adopted as an umbrella for popular music of the late 1950s, embracing not only pieces of the sort defined above but also others in quite different styles. Rock-and-roll was revitalized briefly in the early 1960s with the popularity of the twist, a dance based on rhythmicized blues, and with the emergence of new performers basing their styles on basic rock-and-roll, most notably the Beach Boys in the U.S. and various British groups—the Beatles, the Rolling Stones, the Who. But Anglo-American popular music soon began moving in somewhat different directions, and a related but different style, *rock, captured the energy and interest of most performers and audiences.

Rocket. See Mannheim school.

Rocking melodeon. *Lap organ.

Rococo [fr. Fr. *rocaille,* rockwork, possibly combined with *coquille,* shellwork]. In the visual arts, a style originating in France in the last decade of the 17th century and extending to approximately the 1760s. It is characterized by ornamental delicacy, graceful elegance, and (often) sophisticated wit; it shows a general lightening in color and tone and a reduction in scale by comparison with the more serious, monumental Baroque. Recent scholars, however, have stressed the formal kinship of the Baroque and rococo styles, a kinship especially obvious in south German and Austrian architecture and in large-scale allegorical and religious painting such as that of Tiepolo.

In the study of music, the term rococo has been used in various ways, not always judiciously. Its most appropriate application is to French music of the same period as the rococo in the visual arts, particularly small-scale lute and harpsichord works (e.g., descriptive pieces of François Couperin), works for chamber ensemble (especially with flute), and *opéra-ballets,* as well as to comparable music by French-influenced composers such as Telemann. Such works provide direct equivalents for rococo art, not only in style—including retention of Baroque traits such as motivic play and relatively linear bass lines—but also in content (often amorous or witty) and patronage (aristocratic and upper-class).

Periodic attempts by musicologists to extend the term rococo to all European music of the time and, in particular, to the subperiod designated in this dictionary as early *Classical have met with a number of difficulties.

Rode, (Jacques) Pierre (Joseph) (b. Bordeaux, 16 Feb. 1774; d. Château de Bourbon, near Damazon, 25 Nov. 1830). Violinist and composer. Pupil of Viotti. Taught at the Paris Conservatory from 1795. Solo violinist at the Opéra from 1799; to Napoleon, 1800; to the tsar in St. Petersburg, 1804–8. Gave the premiere of Beethoven's Violin Sonata op. 96 in Vienna, 1812. Works include 13 violin concertos, 12 string quartets, duos for 2 violins, caprices, and *airs variés.*

Rodeo. A ballet in two scenes by Copland (book and choreography by Agnes de Mille) produced in New York in 1942. Copland excerpted and arranged four dance episodes from the work for orchestra.

Rodgers, Jimmie [James Charles] (b. Meridian, Miss., 8 Sept. 1897; d. New York, 26 May 1933). Country singer, songwriter, and guitarist. Often referred to as the "Father of Country Music." Wrote many songs with his sister-in-law Elsie McWilliams. Particularly popular were his "blue yodels" ("T for Texas," 1928), and the songs "Waiting for a Train" (1929) and "Roll Along, Kentucky Moon" (1932).

Rodgers, Richard (Charles) (b. Hammels Station, N.Y., 28 June 1902; d. New York City, 30 Dec. 1979). Popular songwriter. Studied at Columbia and the Institute of Musical Art. Collaborated with lyricist Lorenz Hart on musicals including *Babes in Arms* (1937, including "The Lady Is a Tramp"), and *Pal Joey* (1940, "Bewitched"). From 1943, worked with Oscar Hammerstein II; their collaborations included *Oklahoma!* (1943, "Oh, What a Beautiful Mornin'"), *Carousel* (1945), *South Pacific* (1949, "Some Enchanted Evening"), *The King and I* (1951) and *Sound of Music* (1959, "My Favorite Things"). Also wrote songs for film, symphonic music, and the score for the documentary *Victory at Sea* (1952).

Rodrigo, Joaquín (b. Sagunto, Spain, 22 Nov. 1901; d. Madrid, 6 July 1999). Composer. Blind from childhood. Studied in Valencia and with Dukas. Associate of Falla. Taught at the Madrid Conservatory from 1947. Works include pieces for guitar and orchestra (*Concierto de Aranjuez,* 1940; *Fantasia para un gentilhombre,* 1954; *Concierto Andaluz,* 4 soloists, 1967; *Concierto madrigal,* 2 soloists, 1968; *Concierto para una fiesta,* 1982); concertos for piano, for violin, for cello, for harp, and other orchestral music; a ballet, a zarzuela, and an opera; vocal works; chamber and piano music.

Rodrigues Coelho, Manuel (b. Elvas, ca. 1555; d. probably Lisbon, ca. 1635). Organist, composer. Studied at Elvas Cathedral. Organist at Badajoz, 1573–77, at Elvas until 1602, and at the Lisbon court until 1633. Published a volume of keyboard music (Lisbon, 1620), containing *tientos* and versets. Influenced by both Cabézon and the English-Dutch virginalists.

Rodríguez (Amador), Augusto (Alejandro) (b. San Juan, Puerto Rico, 9 Feb. 1904). Chorusmaster, conductor, and composer. Pupil of E. B. Hill and Piston. Established the Puerto Rico Philharmonic, 1932. Taught at the Univ. of Puerto Rico from 1934, organizing and touring with its chorus. Composed over 100 choral and some orchestral works.

Rodriguez, Robert Xavier (b. San Antonio, Tex., 28 June 1946). Composer. Pupil of H. Johnson, Kennan, Stevens, Dahl, Boulanger, Maderna, Carter, and Druckman. Has taught at the Univ. of Texas, Dallas, from 1975. Works include operas (*Le diable amoureux,* 1978; *Suor Isabella,* 1982; *Tango,* 1985); *Estampie,* ballet (1980); orchestral pieces (Concerto III, piano, orchestra, 1974; *Oktoechoes,* 1983; *Trunks,* with narrator, 1983; *A Colorful Symphony,* with narrator, optional visual effects, 1988); chamber and vocal music.

Rodríguez de Hita, Antonio (b. ca. 1724; d. 21 Feb. 1787). Composer and theorist. *Maestro de capilla* at Palencia Cathedral (ca. 1740–57) and at the Madrid Convento real de la Encarnación. Composed zarzuelas (some in collaboration with the dramatist Ramón de la Cruz); liturgical Latin works, *villancicos,* and part songs. His *Diapasón instructivo* (1757) attacks the musical conservatism still prevalent in Spain.

Rodzinski, Artur (b. Spalato, 1 Jan. 1892; d. Boston, 27 Nov. 1958). Conductor. Pupil of J. Marx, Schreker, Schalk, and Sauer. Assistant conductor, Philadelphia Orchestra, under Stokowski (1926). Taught at the Curtis Institute. Conductor, Los Angeles Philharmonic, from 1929; Cleveland Orchestra, 1933–43; New York Philharmonic, 1943–47; Chicago Symphony, 1947–48. Thereafter conducted in concert and opera in Europe.

Roger-Ducasse, Jean (Jules Aimable) (b. Bordeaux, 18 Apr. 1873; d. Taillan-Médoc, Gironde, 19 July 1954). Composer. Pupil of Fauré, Gédalge, and de Bériot. Taught at the Paris Conservatory, 1929–40. Works include *Cantegril,* opera (Paris, 1931); *Orphée,* monodrama (1914); *Au jardin de Marguerite,* soloists, chorus, orchestra (1901–5); *Suite française,* orchestra (1907); chamber and keyboard music.

Rogers, Benjamin (b. Windsor, bapt. 2 June 1614; d. Oxford, June 1698). Organist and composer. Chorister and later lay clerk at St. George's Chapel, Windsor. Organist of Christ Church Cathedral, Dublin, 1638–41; of Eton College, 1660–64; of Magdalen College, Oxford, 1664–86 (also *informator choristarum).* Composed anthems and some instrumental works.

Rogers, Bernard (b. New York, 4 Feb. 1893; d. Rochester, N.Y., 24 May 1968). Composer. Pupil of Farwell, Bloch, Bridge, and Boulanger. Taught at Eastman, 1929–67. Among his students were Mennin, Argento, Diamond, and Ussachevsky. Works include 5 operas (*The Marriage of Ande,* 1931; *The Warrior,* 1944); choral-orchestral works *(The Passion,* 1942; *A Letter from Pete,* 1947); 5 symphonies and other orchestral works (*To the Fallen,* 1918); 2

string quartets and other chamber music; and songs. Published *The Art of Orchestration*, 1951.

Rogers, Shorty [Rajonsky, Milton M.] (b. Great Barrington, Mass., 14 Apr. 1924; d. Van Nuys, Calif., 7 Nov. 1994). Jazz composer, arranger, trumpeter, flügelhorn player, and bandleader. Joined Woody Herman, 1945–49; wrote for Stan Kenton, 1950–51; then became active in West Coast jazz. Composed and arranged music for films and television.

Rogowski, Ludomir Michel (b. Lublin, 3 Oct. 1881; d. Dubrovnik, 14 Mar. 1954). Composer. Pupil of Noskowski, Młynarski, Nikisch, and Riemann. Founder-conductor of the Vilnius Symphony, 1910. Toured western Europe as a conductor. Settled in Dubrovnik, 1926. Used unusual scales (Persian, "Slavonic," whole-tone) and folk materials. Works include operas and ballets; 7 symphonies; vocal music (*Fantasmagorie*, voice, orchestra, 1920; cantatas); and chamber music.

Rohrblatt [Ger.]. *Reed; *Rohrblattinstrumente*, reed instruments.

Röhrenglocken [Ger.]. *Tubular bells.

Roi David, Le [Fr., King David]. Opera ("Dramatic Psalm") in two parts by Honegger (libretto by René Morax), produced in Mézières, Switzerland, in 1921. It was revised and performed as an oratorio in New York in 1925. Setting: the lifetime of the Biblical King David.

Roland-Manuel [Lévy, Roland Alexis Manuel] (b. Paris, 22 Mar. 1891; d. there, 2 Nov. 1966). Composer. Pupil of Roussel and Ravel. Taught at the Paris Conservatory from 1947. Works include 5 operas (*Isabelle et Pantalon*, 1920), ballets (*L'écran des jeunes filles*, 1928), orchestral music, choral and chamber music, and songs. Writings include *Plaisir de la musique*, based on his radio show (1947–55), and 3 books on Ravel.

Roldán, Amadeo (b. Paris, 12 July 1900; d. Havana, 2 Mar. 1939). Composer. Studied at the Madrid Conservatory, and with del Campo and Sanjuan. Concertmaster, assistant conductor, and (from 1932) music director of the Havana Philharmonic. Founded the Havana String Quartet, 1927; the Escuela nacional de música, 1931. From 1935 taught at the Havana Conservatory (director, 1936–38). Used Afro-Cuban musical elements. Works include ballets (*La Rebambaramba*, 1928); orchestral music (*Tres toques*, 1931); chamber music (*Rítmicas V–VI*, percussion ensemble, 1930); vocal works (*Motivos de son*, 1934); and piano music.

Roll. On a drum, a rapid and continuous succession of indistinguishable strokes produced by the alternation of two sticks, on the side drum usually L L R R,

etc. It may be notated with the diagonal strokes of a *tremolo* or with the abbreviation *tr* (for trill).

Rolle [Ger.]. A *turn beginning on the main note, also called a *Walze* or *geschnellter Doppelschlag*.

Rollins, Sonny [Theodore Walter; Newk] (b. New York, 7 Sept. 1930). Jazz tenor saxophonist and bandleader. From 1949 to 1954, recorded with Charlie Parker, Thelonious Monk, the Modern Jazz Quartet, and Miles Davis (including his own bop themes "Doxy" and "Oleo"). Joined the Clifford Brown–Max Roach Quintet (1955–57); subsequently led groups. His strengths were as a bop soloist and in a fusion of bop with calypso music. Mid-1960s, turned toward free jazz and unaccompanied performance. From 1972 often worked with rhythm sections oriented toward African American dance music.

Rollschweller [Ger.]. On an organ, a roller pedal for obtaining a *crescendo*. See Crescendo pedal.

Rolltrommel [Ger.]. Tenor *drum.

Rolón, José (b. Jalisco, 22 June 1883; d. Mexico City, 3 Feb. 1945). Composer. Studied in Paris with Moszkowski, Gédalge, Boulanger, and Dukas. Founded and directed a music school in Mexico, 1907–27. Taught at the Mexican National Conservatory, 1930–38. Used Mexican folk idioms. Works include *El festín de los enanos*, ballet (1925); *Cuauhtémoc*, orchestra (1929); a piano concerto; chamber music and songs.

Roman, Johan Helmich (b. Stockholm, 26 Oct. 1694; d. Haraldsmåla, near Kalmar, 20 Nov. 1758). Composer. Served the royal chapel, 1711–15 and 1721–45 (chief master from 1727). Probably studied with Pepusch in England. Traveled widely in Europe. Works include sacred and secular vocal music; the orchestral suite *Drottningholmsmusiquen* (1744); chamber music.

Roman Carnival, The. See *Carnaval romain, Le*.

Roman chant. See Gregorian chant, Old Roman chant.

Romance. (1) [Sp.] *Ballad. The most characteristic type is in stanzas of four eight-syllable lines, with assonance in the even-numbered lines. Examples from the later 16th century and since sometimes include a refrain. *Romances* have been transmitted in large numbers both orally and in writing from the Middle Ages to the present. The repertory includes anonymous popular poetry, poems on epic and historical subjects (sometimes thought to be the earliest types), and learned poetry by known poets. They were sung from the earliest times, though relatively few melodies survive in early sources. The 17th century saw a flowering of polyphonic secular and sacred *romances,* similar in character to the polyphonic *villancico* of the period.

(2) [Fr.] Beginning in the 18th century, a lyrical, strophic poem on an amorous or epic subject; also a musical setting of such a poem. The character of the genre changed considerably in the early 19th century, and it ultimately merged with the *mélodie,* though the term continued in use. See also *Romanza, Romanze.*

Roman de Fauvel [Fr.]. See *Fauvel, Roman de.*

Romanesca. A harmonic bass, widely used for the composition of *arie per cantar* and dance variations from the middle of the 16th through the 17th centuries [see Ex.]. Because in *arie per cantar* singers improvised discant tunes to the bass pattern, many different discant melodies are found in extant versions of the *romanesca.* The earliest extant appearances of the title *Romanesca* with the bass pattern are in Alonso Mudarra's *Tres libros de música* (1546, "Romanesca, o Guárdame las vacas") and in Pierre Phalèse's *Carminum pro testudine liber III* (1546). In the 17th century, keyboard variations were written by Giovanni Maria Trabaci, Ascanio Mayone, and Frescobaldi; strophic bass arias [see Aria] by Caccini, Monteverdi, Stefano Landi, and Kaspar Kittel; and violin variations by Biagio Marini and Salomone Rossi. The pattern was also used for countless compositions for the guitar.

Romani, Felice (b. Genoa, 31 Jan. 1788; d. Mareglia, 28 Jan. 1865). Librettist. Studied at the Univ. of Pisa. Wrote libretti for nearly 100 operas, among them operas by Rossini (including *Il turco in Italia,* 1814), Donizetti (including *Anna Bolena,* 1830; *L'*elisir d'amore*), Bellini (including *La *sonnambula; *Norma*), Verdi (*Un giorno di regno,* 1840), Meyerbeer (including *Margherita d'Anjou,* 1820), Mayr, Mercadante, and Pacini.

Roman school. Composers of sacred polyphonic music active in Rome in the late 16th and early 17th centuries; principal among them is Giovanni Pierluigi da Palestrina (1525 or 1526–94), whence the term *Palestrina style to describe their music. Their unaccompanied or *a cappella* vocal music, with its controlled treatment of dissonance, is often regarded as representing a fundamental and conservative contrast with the instrumentally accompanied *polychoral works of the so-called *Venetian school of the period. Neither style, however, was limited to the city for which it is named. Composers sometimes identified as members of a Roman school include

Giovanni Maria Nanino (1543 or 1544–1607), Francesco Soriano (1548 or 1549–1621), Ruggiero Giovanelli (ca. 1560–1625), Felice Anerio (ca. 1560–1614), Gregorio Allegri (1582–1652), and Virgilio Mazzocchi (1597–1646).

Romantic. A period in European music history usually considered to have lasted from the early 19th century until the modernist innovations of the early 20th and sometimes subdivided, with an early phase before about 1850 and a late one from about 1890. Terms such as pre-Romantic and neo-Romantic have been used for historical prefigurations and survivals of Romantic traits.

German Romanticism arose in the late 18th century in opposition to the declining *Classical tradition. Romanticism encouraged the breaking down of traditions of subject matter, artistic conventions, limits set to genres, canons of taste and beauty—all fundamental to Classical aesthetics. Romantic form often embodied the Romantic emphasis on the indefinable and the infinite, weakening Aristotelian concepts of beginning, middle, and end. Works were often intentionally given the character of a fragment or an improvisation. Music reached new extremes of lengthiness and brevity (the latter often found in the newly prominent genres of short piano piece and art song). The exploration of distant harmonic and tonal relations (previously used with great caution) and new kinds of texture and instrumental sonority contributed to the creation of new Romantic effects. Performers were no longer encouraged to add creatively to a composition through ornamentation; rather they became conveyors of the composer's "intentions."

Romantic music became tied even more closely than before to literature and other extramusical elements through the belief that it could express their indefinable essence. This belief led to such typically Romantic musical genres as the *symphonic poem of Liszt and the *program symphony of Berlioz as well as to aspects of Wagner's music dramas and the subtle relations between poem and music in many *lieder.

Early Romantic writers, such as E. T. A. Hoffmann, found Romantic traits in the works of 18th-century composers such as Haydn and Mozart. Beethoven's music was even more fertile ground. In the later 19th century, however, a school of Romantic composers directly and consciously influenced by Romantic thought and literature was usually said to begin with Weber (1786–1826), regarded as the founder of German Romantic opera, followed by Schubert (1797–1828), Berlioz (1803–69), Mendelssohn (1809–47), Chopin (1810–49), Schumann (1810–56), and Liszt (1811–86), although whether these men were all true Romantics was debated.

Beethoven, nevertheless, continued to be regarded as a seminal influence by figures as diverse as Berlioz and Wagner (1813–83).

As with other such terms, the use of Romanticism as a general period designation in music remains problematic.

Romantic Symphony. (1) Bruckner's Symphony no. 4 in E♭ major, the original version of which was composed in 1874 and the revised version in 1878–80. (2) Howard Hanson's Symphony no. 2, completed in 1930.

Romanza [It.]. *Ballad. The term was used by Rossini, Donizetti, and Verdi, though not always consistently, for a somewhat more intimate and less elaborate piece than an aria [see also *Romance, Romanze*].

Romanze [Ger.]. (1) *Ballad. The term was often used interchangeably with *Ballade*. Examples from the 18th century were similar in character to the French *romance*. The *Romanze* was often folklike and was frequently found in *Singspiel (e.g., Mozart's *Die Entführung aus dem Serail*) and opera (e.g., Weber's *Der Freischütz*). (2) In the 18th and 19th centuries, an instrumental work of lyrical character in a slow tempo, often in ABA, rondo, or variation form and sometimes part of a symphony or other multimovement work. In the 19th century, the term was often taken as a title for *character pieces in a variety of forms.

Romanzen aus L. Tieck's Magelone [Ger.]. A cycle of 15 songs for voice and piano by Brahms, op. 33 (1861–ca. 1868), setting poems from Ludwig Tieck's *Liebesgeschichte der schönen Magelone und des Grafen Peter von Provence* (The Love Affair of the Beautiful Magelone and Count Peter of Provence).

Romberg, Andreas Jakob (b. Vechta, near Münster, 27 Apr. 1767; d. Gotha, 10 Nov. 1821). Violinist and composer. With his cousin, the cellist Bernhard Heinrich Romberg (1767–1841), gave several concert tours. Both joined the court orchestra in Bonn (1790) and an opera orchestra in Hamburg (1793); in Vienna, 1796, they met Haydn and played with Beethoven. Andreas later became *Hofkapellmeister* in Gotha; composed operas, choral music (*Das Lied von der Glocke*, Schiller), symphonies, concertos, string quartets, and other chamber music.

Romberg, Sigmund (b. Nagy Kaniga, Hungary, 29 July 1887; d. New York, 9 Nov. 1951). Composer, conductor. Moved to New York, 1909. From 1913, composed musical reviews for the Shubert brothers. During 1940s, toured with his own orchestra. Composed Viennese-style operettas, including *Blossom Time* (1921, using melodies of Schubert) and *The Student Prince* (1924); musicals; Hollywood film scores; popular songs, including "Deep in My Heart" and "Lover, Come Back to Me."

Romeo and Juliet. Works inspired by or based on Shakespeare's play include (1) A dramatic symphony for soloists, chorus, and orchestra by Berlioz, op. 17 (1839). (2) An opera in five acts by Gounod (1867). (3) A fantasy overture by Tchaikovsky (1869; rev. 1870, 1880). (4) A ballet by Prokofiev, op. 64 (1935–36).

Romero, Mateo [Rosmarin, Mathieu; "El Maestro Capitán"] (b. Liège, 1575 or 1576; d. Madrid, 10 May 1647). Composer. Royal choirboy in Madrid, 1586–93; then joined the Flemish chapel, becoming *maestro de capilla,* 1598–1634. Chaplain to Philip III, 1605; to John IV of Portugal from 1644. Composed sacred and secular vocal music.

Ronde [Fr.]. (1) Whole *note. (2) Round dance.

Rondeau [Fr., pl. *rondeaux*]. (1) One of the three *formes fixes, prominent in the poetry and music of France in the 14th and 15th centuries. It had become distinct from the others (*ballade and *virelai) by the early 13th century. In its most common form in the late 13th and 14th centuries, the *rondeau* has eight lines in the pattern ABaAabAB (capital letters indicating a refrain). Music is provided for A and B and is repeated according to this pattern. In the 14th and, especially, later centuries, A or B might have two or three poetic lines, the latter never having more than the former.

The earliest surviving *rondeaux* in French are monophonic insertions in the *Roman de la rose ou de Guillaume de Dole* by Jean Renart (early 13th century). Adam de la Halle (1245/50–85/88 or after 1306) wrote the first polyphonic settings of *rondeaux,* in a note-against-note style in three voices. Guillaume de Machaut (ca. 1300–77) composed 22 polyphonic settings, with one texted part and, most often, two untexted parts. In the 15th century, the *rondeau* (its text now at times having 21 lines) was by far the most popular of lyric forms, numerous examples being composed by Dufay, Binchois, and many others.

(2) In the Baroque era, a simple refrain form, usually employed in dance movements. The term is sometimes used alone as a title but does not have implications of tempo, meter, or texture. The first strain closes in the tonic (rather than the dominant or the relative minor) and serves as a refrain or *grand couplet* to be repeated following the succeeding strains or *couplets* [see Rondo]. When a dance usually in binary form was so treated, it was said to be *en rondeau.*

Rondellus [Lat.]. (1) In Continental medieval treatises, the Latin equivalent of *rondeau*. (2) In 13th-century England, a technique of composition for three voices based on *voice exchange; a piece exhibiting this technique. The lowest voice (the tenor or *pes*) of an English *rondellus* may be an independent part made up of a repeated phrase, or it may participate equally with the upper voices in voice exchange. The parts begin together. Excluding any independent part, the voices of a *rondellus* all have the same melodic material (in phrases that remain intact throughout) but present it in different orders.

Rondo [It.]. (1) A multisectional form, movement, or composition based on the principle of multiple recurrence of a theme or section in the tonic key.

In a standard rondo, the principal theme or section (usually symbolized A), known also as the refrain or rondo, alternates with subsidiary sections called couplets or episodes (symbolized B, C, etc.); it then returns at or near the end to complete the movement. All statements of the refrain are normally in the tonic key, whereas the couplets or episodes favor contrasting tonalities. Thus, rondo form differs fundamentally from *ritornello form, in which the refrain recurs in various keys. The refrain itself is frequently in binary or rounded binary form and may be shortened or otherwise varied in appearances after the first; the systematic application of variation may produce a hybrid form known as a variation rondo [see Variation]. Transitions and (especially) retransitions between sections are common, as are codas in all but the earliest examples.

Typical rondo designs include the two-couplet ABACA (common throughout the history of the rondo and its predecessor, the French Baroque *rondeau*), the multicouplet or serial ABACADA type (also characteristic of the *rondeau* as well as of early Classical rondos), the symmetrical or arched ABACABA scheme, and truncated forms such as ABACBA (a favorite of Mozart). Some writers also consider ABA (ternary) forms to be rondos (the "first rondo form" of 19th-century theory; see also Binary and ternary form).

The greatest importance of the rondo lies in its use as one movement of a larger work, in which function it provided the principal alternative to sonata and related forms. After ca. 1770, the rondo became the standard finale of the concerto and *symphonie concertante*, and it occurs in the same capacity in many sonatas, chamber works, and symphonies.

As the name indicates, sonata-rondo is a mixed form incorporating the sonata and rondo principles in varying degrees. Typical sonata-rondos follow an ABACAB′A plan in which the first A and B are treated as the primary and secondary themes of an exposition (i.e., B is generally in the dominant or relative major), the C section becomes a development, and the second A and B (AB′) are treated as a recapitulation (i.e., both A and B are in the tonic [see Sonata form]). Nevertheless, sonata-rondos cover a broad range of structural types.

Sonata-rondos appeared as early as 1768 in London and subsequently became a favorite type for Viennese Classical finales. They continued to appear throughout the 19th century in instrumental finales by conservative Romantic composers (e.g., the finales of Brahms's Second and Third Symphonies).

(2) A two-section aria of the latter half of the 18th century, the first section slow, the second fast; both sections are usually repeated. In this meaning, the term is often spelled *rondò*.

Ronger, Florimond. See Hervé.

Röntgen, Julius (b. Leipzig, 9 May 1855; d. Bilthoven, near Utrecht, 13 Sept. 1932). Composer, conductor, and pianist. Pupil of Hauptmann, E. F. Richter, and Reinecke. Taught in Amsterdam, 1877–1925. Cofounder, Amsterdam Conservatory, 1884; director, 1914–24. Conductor, Amsterdam Toonkunstkoor, 1886–98. Accompanied Messchaert and Casals. Formed piano trio with his sons Julius (1881–1951) and Engelbert (1886–1958). Composed symphonies, concertos, piano trios, piano quintets, sonatas.

Root. In tonal harmony, the fundamental or generating pitch of a triad or *chord. If the pitches of a chord are arranged as a series of superimposed thirds, the lowest pitch is the root. A chord sounded with the root as the lowest pitch (even if the remaining pitches are not sounded as superimposed thirds) is said to be in root position. Otherwise, the chord is in *inversion. In *harmonic analysis, the root of a chord is represented by a roman numeral that designates it as a particular *scale degree in the prevailing key.

Root, George Frederick (b. Sheffield, Mass., 30 Aug. 1820; d. Bailey Island, Maine, 6 Aug. 1895). Composer. Studied in Boston and Paris. Assistant at Lowell Mason's public school music classes. Taught at Union Theological Seminary. Joined his brother's music publishing firm. Composed several cantatas. Published songs under the pseudonym G. Friedrich Wurzel.

Rootham, Cyril Bradley (b. Bristol, 5 Oct. 1875; d. Cambridge, 18 Mar. 1938). Composer and organist. Pupil of Stanford and Parratt. From 1902, organist at St. John's College, Cambridge. Compositions include 1 opera (*The Two Sisters*, 1920); symphonies; choral-orchestral works (*Ode on the Morning of Christ's Nativity*, 1928); vocal music.

Ropartz, Joseph Guy (Marie) [Guy-Ropartz, Joseph] (b. Guingamp, Brittany, 15 June 1864; d.

Lanloup, Brittany, 22 Nov. 1955). Composer and conductor. Pupil of Dubois, Massenet, and Franck. Directed the Nancy Conservatory (1894–1919) and the Strasbourg Municipal Orchestra (1919–29). Composed an opera, *Le pays* (1910); ballets and incidental scores; symphonies; symphonic poems *(La cloche des morts,* 1887, *La chasse du Prince Arthur,* 1912); chamber and piano music; organ pieces; songs.

Rore, Cypriano de (b. Machelen, Flanders, Mechelen, or Ronse, 1515 or 1516; d. Parma, Sept. 1565). Composer. Lived in Brescia, 1541–45. *Maestro di cappella* to Ercole II of Ferrara from at least 1546–59. Served Margaret of Parma at Brussels, 1560, and her husband, Ottavio Farnese, at Parma, 1561–63. In 1563–4, succeeded Willaert at St. Mark's in Venice. Monteverdi named Rore as the founder of the *seconda prattica* (see *prima prattica, seconda prattica).* Works include 5 Masses; a St. John Passion; motets; 4 books of 5-voice madrigals (the last shared with several composers) and 2 books for 4 voices (the second shared with Palestrina).

Rorem, Ned (b. Richmond, Ind., 23 Oct. 1923). Composer, pianist, and author. Pupil of Sowerby, Virgil Thomson, and Copland. Lived in Morocco (1949–51), then in Paris. Taught at the Univ. of Buffalo (1959–60), Univ. of Utah (1966–67), and Curtis Institute (1980–86). Works include song cycles with piano or small ensemble *(Poems of Love and the Rain,* 1965; *Last Poems of Wallace Stevens,* 1974; *Women's Voices,* 1979; *The Nantucket Songs,* 1981; *Songs of Sadness,* 1994); vocal works with orchestra *(Sun,* 1969; *Swords and Plowshares,* 1990; *More Than a Day,* 1995); over 80 individual songs; choral works; 11 operas; orchestral works, including symphonies, concertos, and tone poems *(Air Music,* 1975, Pulitzer Prize); string quartets and other chamber works; piano, harpsichord, and organ pieces. Published several diaries and other books.

Rosa [Rose], **Carl (August Nikolaus)** (b. Hamburg, 22 Mar. 1842; d. Paris, 30 Apr. 1889). Violinist and conductor. Studied in Leipzig and Paris. *Konzertmeister* in Hamburg, 1863–65. Toured widely as a violinist. With his wife, soprano Euphrosyne Parepa, formed a touring opera company. In 1875, opened a company in London that performed operas in English.

Rosalia [It., fr. the song "Rosalia mia cara"; Ger. *Schusterfleck*]. A pejorative term for a sequence [see Sequence (1)] that embodies exact transposition up a step.

Rosamunde. Incidental music by Schubert, D. 797 (1823), for the play *Rosamunde, Fürstin von Zypern* (Rosamunde, Princess of Cyprus) by Helmina von Chézy, produced in Vienna in 1823. Schubert composed no overture specifically for this work, using at various times instead the overtures to *Die Zauberharfe* (now called the *Rosamunde* overture) and *Alfonso und Estrella.*

Rosbaud, Hans (b. Graz, 22 July 1895; d. Lugano, 29 Dec. 1962). Conductor. Pupil of Sekles. From 1921, directed the Städtische Musikschule, Mainz. Musical director, Frankfurt Radio, 1928–37. *Generalmusikdirektor* at Münster, 1937–41; at Strasbourg, 1941–44; of the Munich Philharmonic, 1945–48. Principal conductor, Southwest German Radio Orchestra and Zurich Tonhalle Orchestra. Conducted premieres of works by Schoenberg (including *Moses und Aron)* and Bartók.

Rose. In lutes and related instruments and in harpsichords, a round *sound hole in which a decorative, openwork carving has been inserted.

Rosé, Arnold (Josef) (b. Iaşi, Romania, 24 Oct. 1863; d. London, 25 Aug. 1946). Violinist. Studied at the Vienna Conservatory. Debut, Leipzig, 1879. Leader of the Vienna Court Opera (later Staatsoper) orchestra and Vienna Philharmonic, 1881–1938; often led the orchestra at Bayreuth. In 1882, founded the Rosé Quartet, which premiered works by Brahms, Pfitzner, Reger, and Schoenberg. Taught at the Vienna Academy of Music, 1893–1924. Moved to England, 1938.

Rose, Leonard (Joseph) (b. Washington, 27 July 1918; d. White Plains, N.Y., 16 Nov. 1984). Cellist. Studied at the Curtis Institute. Principal cellist, Cleveland Orchestra, 1939–43; played with the New York Philharmonic, 1943–51; then toured as a soloist and formed a trio with Stern and Istomin. Taught at the Cleveland Institute, Juilliard, Oberlin, and Curtis; among his pupils were Lynn Harrell and Yo-Yo Ma.

Roseingrave, Thomas (b. Winchester, 1688; d. Dunleary, 23 June 1766). Organist and composer. Traveled to Italy, ca. 1709–15; met D. Scarlatti. Organist of St. George's, Hanover Square, from 1725. Composed an opera, keyboard works, cantatas, and anthems. Published an edition of Scarlatti's 42 sonatas, 1739.

Rosen, Charles (Welles) (b. New York, 5 May 1927). Pianist and writer on music. Studied at Juilliard and Princeton, and with Moriz Rosenthal and Weigl. Debut as a pianist, New York, 1951. His performance and recorded repertory ranges from Bach to Elliott Carter and Boulez. From 1971, taught at SUNY–Stony Brook; later at the Univ. of Chicago. Writings include *The Classical Style* (1971) and *The Romantic Generation* (1995).

Rosenberg, Hilding (Constantin) (b. Bosjökloster, Ringsjön Skåne, 21 June 1892; d. Stockholm, 19 May 1985). Composer. Pupil of Stenhammar. Conductor of the Royal Opera, Stockholm, from 1934. Made use of Scandinavian folk music and of serialism. Composed operas (*Joseph and His Brothers,* opera-oratorio, 1946–48); choral-orchestral dramatic works (a Christmas oratorio, 1936); ballets; song cycles and other vocal music; orchestral music (8 symphonies, including no. 4, The Revelation of St. John, 1940) and concertos; much chamber music; film music; incidental music for some 40 plays.

Rosenboom, David (b. Fairfield, Iowa, 9 Sept. 1947). Composer; designer and maker of electronic instruments. Studied at the Univ. of Illinois with Binkerd, Martirano, and Hiller. Director of electronic media research at York Univ., Toronto, 1970–77; teacher at Mills College from 1979. Has studied the relationship between aesthetics and information processing in the brain and developed a programming language for computer music systems.

Rosenkavalier, Der [Ger., The Knight of the Rose]. Opera ("comedy for music") in three acts by Richard Strauss (libretto by Hugo von Hofmannsthal), produced in Dresden in 1911. Setting: Vienna, about 1745.

Rosenmüller, Johann [Rosenmiller, Giovanni] (b. Oelsnitz, near Zwickau, ca. 1619; d. Wolfenbüttel, buried 12 Sept. 1684). Composer. Studied at Leipzig. Teacher, Thomasschule, from 1642; organist, Nikolaikirche, 1651–55. From 1658, trombonist, St. Mark's, Venice; 1678–82, composer, Ospedale della Pietà. Court Kapellmeister, Wolfenbüttel, from 1682. Works include instrumental dance suites; *Sonate da camera* (1667); sacred concertos and other vocal music.

Rosenthal, Manuel [Emmanuel] (b. Paris, 18 June 1904). Conductor and composer. Studied at the Paris Conservatory and with Ravel. Has conducted the French Radio Orchestra (1934–47), the Seattle Symphony Orchestra (1949–51), the Liège Symphony Orchestra (1964–67), and at the Metropolitan Opera. Teacher at the Paris Conservatory from 1962. Compositions include several stage works, many orchestral pieces, chamber pieces, choral works, and songs.

Rosenthal, Moriz (b. Lemberg, 17 Dec. 1862; d. New York, 3 Sept. 1946). Pianist. Pupil of Joseffy and Liszt. Recital debut, Vienna, 1876. Toured the U.S., 1888–89, some of the time with Kreisler. Cowrote a piano method, *Schule des höheren Klavierspiels* (1892). Taught at the Curtis Institute, 1928–29.

Rosetti [Rösler, Rosety, Rossetti, Rössler], **(Francesco) Antonio** [Franz Anton, František Antonín] (b. Leitmeritz [now Litoměřice], ca. 1750; d. Lud-wigslust, 10 June 1792). Composer and double bass player. Has been confused with F. A. Rössler, a cobbler, and with 5 other musicians named Antonio Rosetti. Served the Prince of Oettingen-Wallerstein as bassist (from 1773), deputy Kapellmeister (1780), and Kapellmeister (1785). Kapellmeister to the Duke of Mecklenburg-Schwerin from 1789. Composed much orchestral and chamber music.

Rosin, resin. A hard, brittle substance derived from oil of turpentine. Rubbed on the hair of the bow of a stringed instrument, it leaves a white, powdery deposit that helps to create the friction required to set the strings in motion when the bow is drawn across them.

Roslavets, Nikolay Andreyevich (b. Dushatino, Chernigov region, Ukraine, 5 Jan. 1881; d. Moscow, 23 Aug. 1944). Composer. Studied with Vasilenko at the Moscow Conservatory. By 1915, developed a twelve-tone system independently of Schoenberg. Worked as an editor at the Moscow State Music Publishing House. His views on new music led to conflicts with the Association of Proletarian Musicians. Works include orchestral music, string quartets and other chamber music, piano pieces, choral music, and songs.

Rospigliosi, Giulio, Pope Clement IX (b. Pistoia, 28 Jan. 1600; d. Rome, 9 Dec. 1669). Librettist. Served the Barberini family in Rome. Became a cardinal, 1657; elected to the papacy, 1667. Wrote librettos for sacred operas, creating that genre (incl. *Il Sant'Alessio,* 1632; *La comica del cielo,* 1668), and for some of the earliest comic operas (incl. *Chi soffre speri,* 1639; *Dal male il bene,* 1653).

Ross, Diana (b. Detroit, Mich., 26 Mar. 1944). Soul and popular singer. From 1961 to 1969, recorded as a member of The Supremes (with Florence Ballard and Mary Wilson), including "Baby Love" (1964) and "Reflections" (1968). Solo recordings include "Ain't No Mountain High Enough" (1970), "Upside Down" (1980), and "Endless Love" (with Lionel Ritchie, 1981).

Rosseter, Philip (b. 1567 or 1568; d. London, 5 May 1623). Composer and theater manager. Associate of Campion, some of whose songs he published in *Book of Ayres* (1601). From 1603, lutenist at the court of James I; published arrangements for broken consort of his own and others' compositions. Managed the Children of the Queen's Revels, 1610–17.

Rossi, Lauro (b. Macerata, 19 Feb. 1812; d. Cremona, 5 May 1885). Composer and conductor. Pupil of Zingarelli. Moved to Mexico in 1835 to compose for and conduct an Italian opera troupe. In 1837, established a new troupe, with which he toured. Director of the Milan Conservatory, 1850–70; of the

Naples Conservatory, 1870–78. Composed 29 operas; cantatas, 1 Mass, an oratorio, fugues.

Rossi, Luigi (b. Torremaggiore, ca. 1597; d. Rome, 20 Feb. 1653). Composer. Studied with Giovanni de Macque in Naples. Served the Borghese in Rome, ca. 1621–41; Cardinal Antonio Barberini from 1641. Organist of S. Luigi dei Francesi from 1633. Composed operas, including *Il palazzo incantato* (Rome, 1642) and *Orfeo* (Paris, 1647); some 300 cantatas.

Rossi, Michelangelo [Michel Angelo del Violino] (b. Genoa, 1601 or 1602; d. Rome, buried 7 July 1656). Composer, violinist, and organist. Pupil of Frescobaldi. Served Cardinal Maurizio of Savoy in Rome from around 1624. Associate of d'India. Known as a virtuoso violinist. Composed operas (*Erminia sul Giordano,* 1633; *Andromeda,* 1638); toccatas and other keyboard music.

Rossi, Salamone [Salomone, Salamon de', Shlomo] (b. Mantua?, 19 Aug.? 1570; d. there?, ca. 1630). Composer. Associated with the Gonzaga court. Composed madrigals, including the first published continuo madrigals (1602); instrumental works, including the earliest published trio sonatas (1607); polyphonic settings of Psalms, hymns, and synagogue songs (*The Songs of Solomon,* 1623).

Rossignol, Le [Fr.]. See *Nightingale, The.*

Rossini, Gioachino (Antonio) (b. Pesaro, 29 Feb. 1792; d. Passy, near Paris, 13 Nov. 1868). Composer. Moved to Bologna, 1802 or 1803; worked there and in Ravenna as a singer in churches and in minor opera roles and as keyboardist. Studied at the Bologna conservatory, teachers including Padre Mattei. Beginning in 1810, composed operas for Venice, Rome, and Milan. Music director and composer at the San Carlo and Fondo theaters, Naples, 1815–23. In 1822–23, engaged at the King's Theatre, London; 1824–26, codirector with Paer of the Théâtre-Italien, Paris; from 1826, First Composer to the King and Inspector General of Singing in France. Consultant and acting director to the Bologna Conservatory 1839–42. Moved to Florence, 1848; to Paris, 1855. Composed operas, including *Il cambiale di matrimonio* (Venice, 1810); *L'inganno felice* (Naples, 1812); *La pietra del paragone* (La Scala, 1812); *L'*italiana in Algeri; Tancredi* (Venice, 1813); *Sigismondo* (La Fenice, 1814); *Il turco in Italia* (La Scala, 1814); *Elisabetta, regina d'Inghilterra* (Naples, 1815); *Otello* (1816); *La *gazza ladra; La donna del lago* (Naples, 1819); *Maometto II* (1820; rev. as *Le siège de Corinthe,* 1826); *Mosè in Egitto* (1818; rev. as *Moïse et Pharaon,* 1827). *Il *barbiere di Siviglia; La *cenerentola; *Semiramide; Il viaggio a Reims* (Paris, 1825); *Le comte Ory* (Paris 1828); *Guillaume Tell.* Other works include cantatas; orchestral

and chamber music; *Stabat Mater* (1832–41); *Péchés de vieillesse,* a large collection of songs and piano pieces (1857–68); *Petite Messe solennelle* (1863).

Rössler, Anton. See Rosetti, Antonio.

Rostropovich, Mstislav (Leopoldovich) (b. Baku, Azerbaidjan, 27 Mar. 1927). Cellist, conductor. Studied with Shostakovich and Shebalin at the Moscow Conservatory; taught there from 1956. Toured extensively from the 1950s. Conducting debut, Bolshoi Theater, 1968 *(Eugene Onegin).* From 1977 to 1996, music director of the National Symphony (Washington, D.C.). As a pianist, accompanied his wife, soprano Galina Vishnevskaya. Shostakovich, Britten, Prokofiev, and others wrote cello works for him.

Rota [Lat.]. A *round. The term is found only in the manuscript copy of *"Sumer is icumen in." See also Rote.

Rota [Rinaldi], **Nino** (b. Milan, 3 Dec. 1911; d. Rome, 10 Apr. 1979). Composer. Pupil of Pizetti, Casella, Scalero, and Reiner. Taught at the Liceo musicale di Bari from 1939 (director, 1950–77). Works include some 80 film scores for Zefirelli (*Romeo and Juliet,* 1968), Coppola (*The Godfather,* 1972), Fellini (incl. *La dolce vita,* 1960), and others; 11 operas (*Il cappello di paglia di Firenze,* 1946); 4 ballets; incidental music; 3 symphonies; concertos; Masses, oratorios, and cantatas; chamber and piano music; and songs.

Rote. In the Middle Ages, any of several stringed instruments, including plucked and bowed *lyres and the *psaltery. The word *rote* and a whole family of cognates occur from the 8th through the 16th century in literary texts: *cruit* and *crot* in Gaelic, *crwth* in Welsh, crowd and rote in English, *chrotta, rota,* and *rotta* in Latin, *Rotte* in German, *rote* and *rota* in French. In most of these texts, it is clear that the word refers to a stringed instrument, but it is seldom clear just which instrument is meant.

Rotta. (1) [Lat.] A medieval stringed instrument [see Rote]. (2) [It.] In 14th-century Italian dances, an *after-dance, a metrical variant of the main dance. (3) In the 16th century, a rare term used to designate dances.

Roulade [Fr.]. An ornamental passage of melody, especially a vocal melisma in music of the 18th century. See Diminutions.

Round. A perpetual canon at the unison [see Canon]. One singer or group begins an appropriately composed melody (e.g., "Three blind mice") and, on reaching a certain point, is joined by a second group that begins the melody. When the second reaches the same point, a third begins, and so on until all voices or parts have entered, which will have occurred before the first singer or group reaches the end and is itself ready to begin the melody again. On reaching the end, each part may return to the beginning immediately, and the piece may continue indefinitely or until one part has made an agreed-upon number of repetitions. See also Catch.

Round O. An anglicization of *rondeau (2), found mostly in harpsichord and chamber ensemble music around 1700.

Rounded. A composition consisting of two sections, the second ending with a return to the material of the first, as in rounded binary form [see Binary and ternary form]; also a composition in which the two principal sections conclude with the same material, as in many French *ballades, the latter termed rounded chansons [see also Rundkanzone].

Roundelay [fr. Fr. rondelet]. In the 14th century, *rondeau.

Rouse, Christopher (Chapman) (b. Baltimore, 15 Feb. 1949). Composer. Pupil of Crumb, Husa, and Palmer. Taught at the Univ. of Michigan, 1978–81; then at the Eastman School. Works include orchestral music (incl. 2 symphonies; The Infernal Machine, 1981; Phaeton Overture, 1986; trombone concerto, 1991, awarded the 1993 Pulitzer Prize); The Surma Ritornelli (11 players, 1983); Morpheus (cello, 1975); Bonham (percussion, 1988); Karolju (chorus, orchestra, 1990).

Roussakis, Nicolas (b. Athens, 10 June 1934; d. New York, 23 Oct. 1994). Composer and clarinetist. Pupil of Luening, Beeson, Ussachevsky, Cowell, Jarnach, Stockhausen, Boulez, Ligeti, and Berio. Taught at Columbia, 1968–77; at Rutgers from 1977. Worked with serial procedures, Greek folk music, and chance. Works include orchestral pieces (Fire and Earth and Water and Air, 1980–83; Hymn to Apollo, 1989); chamber music (Ephemeris, string quartet, 1977–79); vocal works (God Abandons Antony, cantata, 1987).

Rousseau, Jean-Jacques (b. Geneva, 28 June 1712; d. Ermenonville, 2 July 1778). Philosopher, author, and composer. Largely self-taught in music. Visited Venice, 1743. Composed dramatic works, including Le devin du village (Fontainebleau, 1752) and Pygmalion (Lyons, 1770). Participated in the querelle des bouffons as a partisan of Italian opera buffa. Writings on music include Dissertation sur la musique moderne (1743); Lettre sur la musique française (1753); articles for the Encyclopédie, later incorporated into his Dictionnaire de musique (1768).

Roussel, Albert (Charles Paul Marie) (b. Tourcoing, 5 Apr. 1869; d. Royan, 23 Aug. 1937). Composer.

After serving in the navy, studied with Gigout and d'Indy at the Schola cantorum. Taught there, 1902–14; Satie was among his pupils. Works include Padmâvatî (an opera-ballet based on a Hindu legend and using Hindu scales; Paris, 1923); ballets (Le festin de l'araignée, 1913; Bacchus et Ariane, 1930); incidental music; orchestral music, including Pour une fête de printemps (1920), 4 symphonies, and concertos for piano and cello; choral music (Evocations, 1910–11; Psalm 80, 1931); chamber music (Divertissement, wind quintet and piano, 1906); music for solo piano, harp, and guitar; and songs.

Rovescio [It.]. Either *retrograde (i.e., from the end to the beginning, as in the minuet of Haydn's Piano Sonata in A major Hob. XVI:26) or *inversion (as in the trio to the minuet of Mozart's Serenade in C minor K. 388 [384a]).

Row. An ordered set of the twelve pitch classes, as employed in the composition of *twelve-tone music.

Roxelane, La [Fr.]. Haydn's Symphony no. 63 in C major Hob. I:63 (completed by 1781). Haydn so named the work because the second movement is a set of variations on the French tune of that name.

Rózsa, Miklós (b. Budapest, 18 Apr. 1907; d. Los Angeles, 27 July 1995). Composer. Studied at the Leipzig Conservatory. Moved to Paris by 1931; to London, 1935; to the U.S., 1940. Wrote numerous film scores in London and at MGM in Hollywood (1948–62). Taught at the Univ. of Southern California, 1945–65. Drew on Hungarian folk song style. Concert works include concertos; Nottorno ungherse, orchestra (1964); 2 string quartets; Bagatellen, piano (1932); To Everything There Is a Season, 8 voices, organ (1945).

Rubato [It. tempo rubato, stolen time]. In performance, the practice of altering the relationship among written note-values and making the established pulse flexible by accelerating and slowing down the tempo; such flexibility has long been an expressive device.

Two varieties of rubato are usually discussed. In the first, the underlying pulse remains constant while the rhythmic values are minutely inflected. This was extensively done as an expressive nuance in the 18th century, especially in the solo part or melody of slow movements (the instrumental adagio and vocal cantabile) while the accompaniment held the beat steady.

The second type is the more common, present-day understanding of rubato. Changes in tempo and rhythmic figuration (*accelerando and *ritardando) are made in all parts at the same time without any compensation; the original tempo is simply resumed at the performer's discretion. Even though this expressive rhythmic freedom is frequently associated with the playing styles of 19th-century virtuosos such as Liszt, it is discussed by 17th- and 18th-century writers.

Rubbra, (Charles) Edmund (b. Northampton, 23 May 1901; d. Gerrard's Cross, 13 Feb. 1986). Composer. Pupil of Cyril Scott, Ireland, Goossens, Holst, and R. O. Morris. Taught at Oxford, 1947–68; at the Guildhall School of Music from 1961. Works include 11 symphonies (no. 9, Sinfonia sacra, 1971–72) and other orchestral music; choral works (*Songs of the Soul*, 1953); 4 string quartets and other chamber music; and vocal works.

Rubeba [Lat.], **Rubebe** [Ger.]. See Rebec.

Rubini, Giovanni Battista (b. Romano, near Bergamo, 7 Apr. 1794; d. there, 3 Mar. 1854). Tenor. Debut, Pavia, 1814. Sang many Rossini roles in Naples and Paris. Created leading roles in *Anna Bolena* (1830), *La sonnambula* (1831), and *I puritani* (1835), among others. Performed often in Paris and London, 1831–43; toured with Liszt, 1843. Published *12 Lezioni di canto moderno per soprano o tenore*.

Rubinstein [Rubinshteyn], **Anton (Grigor'yevich)** (b. Vikhvatinets, Podolia, 28 Nov. 1829; d. Peterhof, near St. Petersburg, 20 Nov. 1894). Pianist and composer. Brother of Nikolay Rubinstein. Studied with S. Dehn in Berlin. Moved to Vienna, 1846; settled in St. Petersburg, 1848. Founder, St. Petersburg Conservatory, 1862; its director, 1862–67 and 1887–91. Gave frequent concert tours in Europe; conducted the Philharmonic Concerts in Vienna, 1871–72; toured America as a soloist and with Wieniawski, 1872–73. Compositions include 6 symphonies; 5 piano concertos; Russian operas; chamber, piano, and vocal works.

Rubinstein, Artur [Arthur] (b. Łódź, 28 Jan. 1887; d. Geneva, 20 Dec. 1982). Pianist. Pupil of Joachim and Paderewski. Debut, Berlin, 1900. New York debut, 1906. During World War I, lived mainly in London, accompanying Ysaÿe. In 1932, withdrew from concert life to work on his technique and repertory. Toured America, 1937. Chamber music partners included Heifetz, Piatigorsky, Szeryng, and the Guarneri Quartet. Retired from the stage, 1976.

Rubinstein [Rubinshteyn], **Nikolay (Grigor'yevich)** (b. Moscow, 14 June 1835; d. Paris, 23 Mar. 1881). Pianist, composer, and conductor. Brother of Anton Rubinstein. Pupil of Kullak and Dehn. Founded the Moscow Conservatory, 1866, and was director to 1881. A strong proponent of music of the new nationalist Russian school during the 1860s and 1870s.

Rückpositiv [Ger.]. The *Positive division of an organ, whose pipes and wind-chest are in a wooden case located behind the player.

Rudel, Julius (b. Vienna, 6 Mar. 1921). Conductor. Studied at the Vienna Academy of Music and at the Mannes College of Music. Conducting debut, New York City Opera, 1944; the company's director, 1957–79. Music director of the Kennedy Center, 1971–75; of the Buffalo Philharmonic, 1979–85.

Rudhyar, Dane [Chennevière, Daniel] (b. Paris, 23 Mar. 1895; d. Palo Alto, 13 Sept. 1985). Composer and writer. Studied at the Sorbonne and at the Paris Conservatory. Moved to the U.S., 1916. Influenced by Asian music. Composed orchestral music including *Cosmic Cycle* (1977) and *Encounter* (with solo piano, 1977); string quartets (*Crisis and Overcoming*, 1979); piano music (*Transmutation*, 1976); and a few songs. Writings on music include *Culture, Crisis, and Creativity*, 1977; *The Magic of Tone and the Art of Music*, 1982; *The Rhythm of Wholeness*, 1983.

Rudolf, Max (b. Frankfurt am Main, 15 June 1902; d. Philadelphia, 28 Feb. 1995). Conductor. Studied in Frankfurt. Conducting debut, Freiburg, 1923; held posts there and in Darmstadt and Prague. Moved to the U.S., 1940. Conducted the Metropolitan Opera, 1945–58; the Cincinnati Symphony, 1958–70. Taught at the Cleveland Institute (1970–73) and the Curtis Institute. Wrote *The Grammar of Conducting* (1950).

Rue, Pierre de la. See La Rue, Pierre de.

Ruff. A common stroke on the snare drum, executed by the two hands in rapid alternation: ♫♪

Ruffo, Titta [Titta, Ruffo Cafiero] (b. Pisa, 9 June 1877; d. Florence, 6 July 1953). Baritone. Debut, Rome, 1898. Appeared in Rio de Janeiro, Vienna, Paris, London, and the principal Italian theaters. Sang often with the Chicago–Philadelphia Grand Opera Company, 1912–26; with the Metropolitan Opera, 1922–29. Appeared in several early sound films and at the opening of Radio City Music Hall in 1932.

Ruffo, Vincenzo (b. Verona, ca. 1508; d. Sacile, near Pordenone, 9 Feb. 1587). Composer. Court musician in Milan 1542–46. From 1554 to 1563, *maestro di cappella* at Verona Cathedral, where he had received his training; 1563–72, maestro at Milan Cathedral; thereafter held posts at Pistoia, Verona, and Sacile. Works include Masses and other sacred music, 9 books of madrigals, and a book of instrumental *capricci*.

Ruggiero [It.]. A harmonic bass of Italian provenance, popular from the mid-16th through the 17th century [see Ex.]. The word *Fedele* is sometimes substituted for *Ruggiero* and the piece labeled *Aria sopra Fedele*. Many different discant melodies are found associated with this bass, and numerous settings of the *ruggiero* have survived. An early example is the final *recercada* for viola da gamba and harpsichord in Diego Ortiz's *Tratado de glosas* of 1553. Others include keyboard variations by Giovanni de Macque, Giovanni Maria Trabaci, Ascanio Mayone, Ercole Pasquini, and Frescobaldi. Lute settings are found in tablatures by Vincenzo Galilei and in English collections from ca. 1600.

Ruggles, Carl [Charles] **(Sprague)** (b. East Marion, Mass., 11 Mar. 1876; d. Bennington, Vt., 24 Oct. 1971). Composer and painter. Pupil of John Knowles Paine. Taught and founded an orchestra in Winona, Minnesota, 1907–17; then moved to New York. Taught at the Univ. of Miami, 1938–43. Made some use of twelve-tone technique. Works include *Toys,* voice, piano (1919); *Vox clamans in deserto,* soprano, small orchestra (1923); *Portals,* strings, (1925); *Sun Treader,* orchestra (1932); *Evocations,* piano (1935–43); *Exaltation* (voices, organ, 1958).

Ruhig [Ger.]. Calm, peaceful.

Rührtrommel [Ger.]. Tenor *drum.

Ruinen von Athen, Die [Ger., The Ruins of Athens]. Incidental music by Beethoven, op. 113 (1811), for a play by August von Kotzebue, produced in Budapest in 1812. It contains an overture, choruses, an aria, and a Turkish March (this last adapted from Beethoven's variations for piano op. 76, composed in 1809).

Rule of the octave [It. *regola dell'ottava*]. In 18th-century *thoroughbass practice, a scheme for harmonizing a bass line consisting of a scale that ascends and descends through an octave. Various such schemes were discussed by the theorists of the period.

Rumba [Sp.]. An Afro-Cuban recreational event, dance, and accompanying music. The *rumba,* of which there are several named subtypes (e.g., *guaguancó, yambú, columbia*), is secular but contains elements from African-derived sacred traditions. It is performed by a vocal soloist and chorus with an accompaniment of percussion instruments. Adopted and transformed by Cuban urban popular ensembles, the *rumba* became known internationally in the 1930s. Although the term has been loosely applied, the popular *rumba* is most typically dance music in rapid duple meter, with the energetic character, emphasis on call-and-response patterns, and intricate percussion playing.

Rundkanzone [Ger., rounded chanson]. A *bar form in which the *Abgesang* concludes with most or all of the material of the *Stollen*. The whole piece is in the form AABA.

Ruslan and Lyudmila [Russ. *Russlan i Lyudmila*]. Opera in five acts by Glinka (libretto by Valeryan Fedorovich Shirkov and others, after Pushkin's poem), produced in St. Petersburg in 1842. Setting: Russia in legendary times.

Russell, Pee Wee [Charles Ellsworth] (b. St. Louis, 27 March 1906; d. Alexandria, Va., 15 Feb. 1969). Jazz clarinetist. In 1920s, played with Jack Teagarden, Bix Beiderbecke, and Red Nichols. Played intermittently with Eddie Condon, 1937–67. Joined Bobby Hackett, Bud Freeman, and other Dixieland and traditional musicians. From 1962, also explored newer styles; 1963, performed with Thelonious Monk.

Russian and Slavonic chant. The medieval, sacred plainsong of Russia and of the South Slavic lands. Both were entirely indebted to Byzantine forms that were brought over by Greek missionaries in the 9th century.

The monumental work of Saints Cyril and Methodios, who translated the Greek service books into Slavonic, also involved the transmission of *Byzantine chant, its notation, and its *oktoēch* [see *Ēchos*] organization. The earliest Russian musical manuscripts date from the late 11th century. In common with other chant dialects, Russian and Slavonic chant is entirely vocal, monodic, and unaccompanied.

By the late 15th century, there emerged a new school of notation different in character from the Byzantine tradition. Neumatic nomenclature was arranged in alphabetic lists called *azbuki,* among which appear the terms *krjuk* (hook) and *znamya* (sign). Eventually the new chant received the name *Znamenny raspev* (chanting by signs), and it followed an independent development in Russia.

The year 1219 marks the independence granted to the Serbian Church under its first archbishop, St. Sava, by the Patriarch of Nicaea. Although there is a lack of musical documents from the earliest period, evidence from written sources suggests an active use of sung Offices in the new Serbian Church. The bulk of surviving documents of or connected with Serbian chant comes from the 15th to the 18th centuries.

Russian bassoon. A tall narrow variety of the *serpent with two parallel tubes in sections joined at the bottom in a wooden, bassoonlike butt joint. A mouthpiece and gracefully curved or looped mouth pipe or *bocal of brass leads into the top of the narrow tube. The upper part of the larger tube ends in either a wooden or metal bell or a fanciful dragonhead. Several varieties were made by at least 1788. They were more convenient to hold than the serpent, but they shared the serpent's playing technique and compass.

Russian Quartets. See *Rasumovsky* Quartets; *Scherzi, Gli.*

Russolo, Luigi (b. Portogruaro, 30 Apr. 1885; d. Cerro di Laveno, Varese, 4 Feb. 1947). Composer, inventor, painter. Associated with the Italian futurist movement first as a painter and then as signer of the manifesto *L'arte dei rumori* (1913). Invented numerous machines (intonarumori, scoppiatori, ronzatore, rumorarmonio) for futurist music. Lived in Paris 1927–32. His music for machines was a precursor of *musique concrète.*

Rust, Friedrich Wilhelm (b. Wörlitz, near Dessau, 6 July 1739; d. Dessau, 28 Feb. 1796). Composer, violinist, and pianist. Pupil of W. F. Bach, F. Benda, and C. P. E. Bach. Served Prince Leopold II of Anhalt-Dessau. In Dessau, promoted public concerts and founded a theater for opera and spoken drama (1774); became court music director (1775). Works include chamber music and keyboard pieces.

Rute [Ger.]. A birch brush used in playing drums of various kinds. Introduced to Europe in the 18th century along with *Janissary music, it has been largely replaced in the 20th century by the wire *brush.

Rutini, Giovanni Marco [Giovanni Maria, Giovanni Placido] (b. Florence, 25 Apr. 1723; d. there, 22 Dec. 1797). Composer. Studied in Naples. Went to Prague (1748 and 1753), under the protection of the Electress of Saxony. Traveled widely in Europe. Settled in Florence, 1761. *Maestro di cappella* to the Duke of Modena from 1769. Works include at least 14 operas, harpsichord music, and several oratorios.

Ruyneman, Daniel (b. Amsterdam, 8 Aug. 1886; d. there, 25 July 1963). Composer. Studied at the Amsterdam Conservatory. A leader in the Dutch avant-garde. Worked with neoclassicism and serialism, and explored vocal and timbral capabilities. Works include operas, orchestra music, chamber music (*Réflections I-IV,* various instruments, 1958–61); choral and solo vocal music.

Rysanek, Leonie (b. Vienna, 14 Nov. 1926; d. there, 7 Mar. 1998). Soprano. Studied at the Vienna Conservatory with A. Jerger. Debut, Innsbruck, 1949. Sang at Saarbrücken and Munich. Covent Garden debut, 1953; her Metropolitan Opera debut, 1959. Known especially for her roles in the operas of Verdi, Wagner, and Strauss.

Rzewski, Frederic (Anthony) (b. Westfield, Mass. 13 Apr. 1938). Composer and pianist. Pupil of Thompson, Piston, Sessions, Babbitt, Dallapiccola, and Carter. Active in Europe, 1960s, as a pianist in performances and recordings of contemporary music. Taught at Cologne (1963, 1964, 1970). Lived in New York, 1971–76. Teacher at the Royal Conservatory of Belgium from 1977. Has made use of folk and popular music and improvisation. Works include *Chains* (3 short television operas; premiered 1987); works for orchestra and jazz band; *Work Songs* (1967–69); *Moutons de Panurge* (any ensemble, 1969); several mixed-media works and tape works (1960s).

S

S. (1) In current musical notation, abbr. for *segno, *sinistra, *soprano, *subito. (2) In liturgical books, abbr. for *schola. (3) In music of the 16th century, abbr. for *superius. (4) In the analysis of *functional harmony, abbr. for subdominant. (5) Abbr. for Wolfgang Schmieder's catalog of the works of Bach. See BWV.

Sacabuche [Sp.]. Sackbut [see Trombone].

Saccadé [Fr.]. Jerked, abrupt, especially with respect to a bow stroke.

Sacchini, Antonio (Maria Gasparo Gioacchino) (b. Florence, 14 June 1730; d. Paris, 6 Oct. 1786). Composer. Pupil of Durante. Taught at the Naples Conservatory S. Maria di Loreto, 1756–62. Lived in Rome, 1765–68. From 1768, directed the Conservatorio dell'Ospedaletto, Venice. Moved to London, 1772; to Paris, 1781. Composed operas, including *Olimpiade* (Padua, 1763); *Il Cid* and *Tamerlano* (both London, 1773); *Chimène* (Paris, 1783); *Oedipe à Colone* (1785); *Arvire et Evelina* (completed by Rey; Paris, 1788); also oratorios, sacred vocal pieces, and some chamber music.

Sacher, Paul (b. Basel, 28 Apr. 1906). Conductor. Pupil of Weingartner and Nef. Formed the Basel Chamber Orchestra, 1926. Founded the Schola cantorum basiliensis, 1933; it later became part of the Musikakademie, which he directed until 1969. Commissioned works including Bartók's *Music for Strings, Percussion, Celesta* and Stravinsky's Concerto in D. Established the Sacher Foundation, acquiring musical source material (Stravinsky's *Nachlass;* Webern estate).

Sachs, Hans (b. Nuremberg, 5 Nov. 1494; d. there 19 Jan. 1576). Meistersinger and poet. Traveled throughout Germany, 1511–16. After 1520, became a leader in the Nuremberg Meistersingers' guild, making it a model for others in Germany. Devised 13 *Töne* (see *Meistersinger), among them the *Silberweise* (1513). Wrote 4,300 Meisterlieder as well as didactic poems and plays.

Sackbut. The early *trombone.

Sackgeige [Ger.]. *Kit.

Sackpfeife [Ger.]. *Bagpipe.

Sacre du printemps, Le [Fr., The Rite of Spring; Russ. *Vesna svyashchennaya,* Sacred Spring]. Ballet ("Scenes of Pagan Russia") by Stravinsky (choreography by Vaslav Nijinsky, book and décor by Nicholas Roerich), produced in Paris in 1913 by Sergei Diaghilev's Ballets russes. It is in two parts, titled *L'adoration de la terre* (The Adoration of the Earth) and *Le sacrifice* (The Sacrifice), each divided into several scenes.

Sadai, Yizhak (b. Sofia, 13 May 1935). Composer. Emigrated to Israel, 1949. Studied with Boskovich and Haubenstock-Ramati; taught at the music academies in Tel Aviv and in Jerusalem. Has worked with serialism, elements of Middle Eastern music, and electronic media. Works include *Hazvi Israel,* cantata (1960); *Canti fermi,* orchestra, synthesizer (1986); *Reprises,* nonet (1986); *Impressions d'un chorale,* piano (1960).

Saeta [Sp., arrow]. In Andalusia, Spain, a song sung to a passing religious statue or float (usually the Virgin Mary or Jesus) during the processions of Holy Week.

Saeverud, Harald (Sigurd Johan) (b. Bergen, 17 Apr. 1897; d. 27 Mar. 1992). Composer. Studied at the Berlin Musikhochschule. From 1953 was supported by a Norwegian State Salary of Art. Made some use of Norwegian folk music. Works include 9 symphonies; concertos for piano and for cello; descriptive pieces and incidental music (*Peer Gynt,* 1947); chamber and piano music.

Safonov, Vasili (b. near Itsyursk, Terek, Caucasus, 6 Feb. 1852; d. Kislovodsk, Caucasus, 27 Feb. 1918). Pianist and conductor. Pupil of Leschetizky. Taught at the conservatories of St. Petersburg (1880–85) and Moscow (director, 1889–1905). Principal conductor, Russian Musical Society (Moscow), 1889–1905, 1909–11; New York Philharmonic Society, 1906–9. Wrote a book on piano technique.

Saga, En [Finn., A Saga]. A symphonic poem by Sibelius, op. 9 (1892; revised in 1902). Despite its title, the work has no known program.

Sainete [Sp.; Fr. *saynète*]. A type of Spanish comedy originating in the late 18th century, portraying scenes from everyday life and sometimes set to music or including a few musical numbers. The term was borrowed for a similar genre in France. See also *Tonadilla, Zarzuela.*

St. Anne's Fugue. Popular name for Bach's organ fugue in E♭ BWV 552 from the *Clavier-Übung* III (published in 1739), so called because its theme is similar to the beginning of the English hymn tune "St. Anne" (sung to the text "O God, our help in ages past").

Saint-Georges [Saint-George], **Joseph Boulogne, Chevalier de** (b. near Basse Terre, Guadeloupe, ca. 1739; d. Paris, 9 or 10 June 1799). Composer and violinist. From 1773, led the Paris Concert des Amateurs. In 1781, founded the Concert de la Loge Olympique, for which Haydn's Paris symphonies were commissioned. Moved to Lille, 1791, as a captain of the National Guard. Returned to Paris about 1797; directed the Cercle de l'harmonie. Composed operas, symphonies, *symphonies concertantes,* violin concertos, and string quartets.

St. John Passion [Lat. *Passio secundum Joannem*]. Bach's setting BWV 245 of the Passion story according to St. John (with free poetic texts by Barthold Heinrich Brockes and others for arias and large choruses) for soloists, chorus, and orchestra, first performed in Leipzig in 1724 and revised at various times thereafter. See also Passion music.

Saint-Marcoux, Micheline Coulombe (b. Notre Dame-de-la-Doré, Quebec, 9 Aug. 1938; d. Montreal, 2 Feb. 1985). Composer. Pupil of Champagne, Tremblay, Pépin, Aubin, and Schaeffer. Taught at the Conservatoire in Montreal. Used some aleatoric techniques. Works include orchestral pieces (*Modulaire,* 1967; *Hétéromorphie,* 1970); electronic works (*Arksalalartôq,* tape, 1971).

St. Martial, repertory of. A body of music of the 9th through 12th centuries transmitted in manuscripts that by historical accident all came to be held in the library of the monastery of St. Martial of Limoges (southwest France). Of these manuscripts, only a few (none containing polyphony) originated there. The repertory might more accurately be called Aquitanian.

The monophony of St. Martial is notable for its *tropes and *sequences. The well-known repertory of polyphony associated with St. Martial dates from the 11th and 12th centuries and includes both *discant (note-against-note or neume-against-neume) and *organum (with long tenor notes set against a florid upper part). A prominent form in St. Martial manuscripts, cultivated as both monophony and polyphony, is the *versus.

St. Matthew Passion [Lat. *Passio secundum Matthaeum*]. Bach's setting BWV 244 of the Passion story according to St. Matthew (with free poetic texts

by Picander [pseudonym of Christian Friedrich Henrici] for arias and large choruses) for soloists, two choruses, and orchestra, first performed in Leipzig in 1727 and revised for a performance in 1736. See also Passion music.

St. Paul (Paulus). An oratorio for soloists, chorus, and orchestra by Mendelssohn, op. 36, completed in 1836 and first performed in Düsseldorf in that year. The text is from the Bible's Acts of the Apostles.

Saint-Saëns, (Charles) Camille (b. Paris, 9 Oct. 1835; d. Algiers, 16 Dec. 1921). Composer. Pupil of Halévy. Associate of Pauline Viardot, Rossini, and Liszt. Debut as pianist at Salle Pleyel, 1846. From 1853, held church organ posts, most notably at the Madeleine, 1857–76; well known as an improviser. In 1871, cofounded the Société nationale de musique, designed to foster new French music; later lost control of it to D'Indy and the Franckists. After 1888 traveled frequently, including visits to the U.S. in 1906 and 1915. Works: Operas (incl. *Samson et Dalila; Henry VIII,* 1883; *Ascanio,* 1890; *Phryné,* 1893); incidental music; a ballet; many sacred works (incl. a Mass; motets; *Le déluge,* oratorio, 1875); symphonies (incl. no. 3, "Organ," 1886); 4 symphonic poems (incl. *Danse macabre); 5 piano concertos; 3 violin concertos; 2 cello concertos; *Le *carnaval des animaux;* chamber works (incl. 2 string quartets; 2 piano trios; a piano quartet; 2 violin sonatas; 2 cello sonatas; sonatas for oboe, clarinet, and bassoon); piano works (Variations on a Theme of Beethoven for two pianos, 1874); a film score. Published writings on astronomy, classical antiquity, and the natural sciences, a volume of poems, musical essays, a book of philosophical musings (1894; enlarged, 1922, as *Divagations sérieuses*), and memoirs. Edited works of Rameau, Gluck, and others.

Saite [Ger.]. String; *Saitenchor, *course of strings; *Saiteninstrument,* stringed instrument; *leere Saite,* open string.

Salieri, Antonio (b. Legnago, 18 Aug. 1750; d. Vienna, 7 May 1825). Composer. Pupil of Pescetti and Gassmann; received advice from Gluck. In 1774, succeeded Gassmann as court composer and conductor of the Italian opera in Vienna; 1788, became court Kapellmeister. Among his pupils were Beethoven, Schubert, Czerny, Hummel, Liszt, and Moscheles. Composed over 40 operas, incl. *Armida* (Vienna, 1771) and *Tarare* (Paris, 1787; revised for Vienna as *Axur, Re d'Ormus);* oratorios, Masses, and other sacred vocal music; vocal and instrumental chamber music; several concertos. There is no foundation for the rumor that Salieri poisoned Mozart.

Sallinen, Aulis (b. Salmi, 9 Apr. 1935). Composer. Pupil of Merikanto and Kokkonen. Head manager of the Finnish Radio Symphony 1960–70; 1963–76, teacher at Sibelius Academy. Appointed arts professor by the Finnish state, 1976–81. Used serial techniques and Finnish folk materials. Works include operas (*The Red Line*, 1977–78; *The King Goes Forth to France*, 1987; *Kullervo*, 1988); ballets (*Midsommernatten*, 1984; *Himlens hemlighet* [Secret of Heavens], 1986); orchestral works (6 symphonies; concertos; *Kaksi myytillistä kuvaa* [Two Mystical Scenes], 1956); vocal works; 5 string quartets and other chamber music.

Salmanov, Vadim (Nikolayevich) (b. St. Petersburg, 4 Nov. 1912; d. Leningrad, 27 Feb. 1978). Composer. Pupil of Gnesin. Taught at the Gnesin Institute and from 1946 at the Leningrad Conservatory. From 1968, secretary of the RSFSR (Russian State) Composers' Union. Works include folkloristic symphonic poems, songs, and choral pieces (*Lebyodushka* [The Hen Swan], 1970); 3 symphonies; 6 string quartets.

Salmo [It., Sp.]. *Psalm.

Salmond, Felix (b. London, 19 Nov. 1888; d. New York, 19 Feb. 1952). Cellist. Attended the Royal College of Music. Debut, 1909. Introduced several of Elgar's works, including the Cello Concerto (1919). Taught at Juilliard from 1924 and at the Curtis Institute, 1925–42. Leonard Rose was among his students.

Salò, Gasparo da. See Gasparo da Salò.

Salome. Opera in one act by Richard Strauss (libretto translated into German by Hedwig Lachmann from Oscar Wilde's play of the same name), produced in Dresden in 1905. Setting: the terrace of Herod's palace in Galilee, about 30 C.E.

Salomon, Johann Peter (b. Bonn, bapt. 20 Feb. 1749; d. London, 28 Nov. 1815). Violinist, impresario, conductor, and composer. Court musician at Bonn from 1758. Ca. 1764–80, served Prince Heinrich of Prussia at Rheinsberg; then settled in London. From 1783, promoted concerts; secured Haydn's visits to London (1791–92 and 1794–95), for which the "London" symphonies were written. A founder and member of the Philharmonic Society. Works include operas, other vocal music, violin concertos, and chamber music.

Salomon Symphonies. Haydn's Symphonies nos. 93–104 Hob. I:93–104 (1791–95), named for the impresario Johann Peter Salomon, who brought Haydn to London in 1791–92 and 1794–95. Only the first nine symphonies (93–101) were actually composed for Salomon's concerts; the last three (102–4) received their first performances in 1795 at a new series, the Opera Concerts. The twelve are also termed the *London* Symphonies, though the name *London*

Symphony specifically applies to no. 104 (sometimes also called the *Salomon* Symphony). Others are the *Surprise (no. 94), *Military (no. 100), *Clock (no. 101), and *Drum-Roll (no. 103).

Salón México, El. A descriptive piece for orchestra by Copland composed in 1933–36 and named for a dance hall in Mexico City that he had visited in 1932. In evoking this atmosphere, he made use of folk songs gathered in collections by Francis Toor and Rubén M. Campos (especially "El mosco," no. 84 in Campos's collection).

Salsa [Sp., sauce, connoting spiciness or soul]. A collective label for contemporary Latin American dance music, based principally on the styles and forms of Afro-Cuban urban popular tradition. The designation first began to be employed consistently in the late 1960s in Puerto Rico and among Latin musicians in New York and other cities in the U.S.

Saltarello [It.]. A gay, sprightly dance of Italian provenance.
(1) 14th century. The music of four *saltarelli* without choreographies is preserved. In varying meters (3/8, 3/4, 6/8, 4/4), all are monophonic pieces cast in the four-repeated-phrase form of the *estampie.
(2) 15th century [Fr. *pas de Brabant;* Sp. *altadanza*]. One of the faster measures (*misura*) or step units of the *basse danse (bassadanza).
(3) 16th century [Fr. *sauterelle, tordion, *tourdion;* Ger. *Hopp tancz, Hupfauf, Proportz, *Nachtanz, Sprung*]. In the 16th century, the music of the *saltarello* was indistinguishable from that of the *gagliarda. The difference is in the style of the dancing, the *gagliarda* being simply a more vigorous version of the *saltarello.* A *saltarello* or a *gagliarda* is usually coupled to either a *pavana* or a *pass'e mezo,* and the coupled dances are composed on the same musical material (harmonic patterns, melodies, etc.).
The *saltarello* continued in vogue until late in the 19th century. Indeed, its steps are still used in folk dances. By the 17th century, however, any function it had as an elegant court dance waned. As a folk dance, its movements were executed more rapidly and with greater violence.

Saltato, saltando [It.]. *Sautillé* [see Bowing (4)].

Salve Regina [Lat., Hail, Queen]. One of the four *antiphons for the Blessed Virgin Mary, sung in modern practice at Compline from the Feast of the Trinity through Saturday before the first Sunday in Advent. It was formerly attributed to Hermannus Contractus (d. 1054).

Salzedo [Salzédo], **Carlos (León)** (b. Arcachon, France, 6 Apr. 1885; d. Waterville, Maine, 17 Aug. 1961). Composer and harpist. Studied at the Bordeaux and Paris Conservatories. Harpist at Monte Carlo (1905–9) and the Metropolitan Opera (1909–13). Formed the Trio de Lutèce (harp, flute, piano); the Salzedo Harp Ensemble, 1917. Taught at Juilliard and the Curtis Institute. Works include the tone poem *The Enchanted Isle* (1919), harp concertos, and many harp solos. With Varèse, formed the International Composers' Guild, 1921.

Salzman, Eric (b. New York, 8 Sept. 1933). Composer and writer on music. Pupil of Beeson, Luening, Ussachevsky, Babbitt, Sessions, Petrassi, Scherchen, Stockhausen, and Nono. Music critic for the *New York Times* (1958–62) and the *New York Herald Tribune* (1963–66). Has taught at Queens College, Brooklyn College, and New York Univ. (from 1982). Works include music theater pieces; *Civilization and Its Discontents,* 1980; *Toward a New American Opera* (mixed media, 1985); *Larynx Music* (soprano, guitar, tape, 1966–67).

Samazeuilh, Gustave (b. Bordeaux, 2 June 1877; d. Paris, 4 Aug. 1967). Composer and writer on music. Pupil of Chausson, d'Indy, Bordes, and Dukas. Translated texts in works by Strauss, Schumann, Schubert, and Liszt; published music criticism and books on Dukas and Chausson. Works include orchestral music (*Le cercle des heures,* with women's voices, 1933); chamber and piano music; and songs.

Samba [Port.]. An Afro-Brazilian dance and dance-music form. Varieties of *samba* include the rural *sambas de roda,* round dances formerly widespread and still important in northeastern Brazil; the *sambas de morro* of the hillside slums (*favelas*) of Rio de Janeiro, prominent in the city's annual Carnival celebrations; and the internationally known urban popular *samba,* established in Rio by the 1920s. Characteristics shared among *samba* types include duple meter, verses for solo singer alternating with choral refrain, syncopated and often disjunct melodic lines, and accompaniments that combine layers of patterns over marchlike bass figures.

Saminsky, Lazare (b. Vale-Hotzulovo, Ukraine, 8 Nov. 1882; d. Port Chester, N.Y., 30 June 1959). Composer, conductor, and writer on music. Pupil of Liadov and Rimsky-Korsakov. Settled in the U.S., 1920; music director of Temple Emanuel, New York, 1924–56. Composed operas and opera-ballets; 5 symphonies; Hebrew service music; choral works (*By the Rivers of Babylon,* 1926); chamber and piano music. Collected traditional chants of the Transcaucasian Jews and wrote a book on Jewish music.

Sammartini [St. Martini, San Martini, San Martino, Martini, Martino], **Giovanni Battista** (b. 1700 or 1701; d. Milan, 15 Jan. 1775). Composer. *Maestro di cappella* at numerous churches in Milan, including

the Jesuit Church of S. Fedele and the ducal chapel. From 1730, taught at the Collegio de' Nobili; pupils included Gluck. His 68 symphonies placed him at the forefront of the first symphonic school in Europe. Also composed 3 operas, sacred and secular vocal music, concertos, and sonatas, string quartets, and other chamber and solo works.

Sammartini [S. Martini, St. Martini, San Martini, San Martino, Martini, Martino], **Giuseppe** [Gioseffo] **(Francesco Gaspare Melchiorre Baldassare)** (b. Milan, 6 Jan. 1695; d. London, ? between 17 and 23 Nov. 1750). Composer and oboist. Brother of Giovanni Battista Sammartini. Settled in London, ca. 1728; played in opera orchestras of Bononcini and Handel; known as a virtuoso. From 1736, served the Prince of Wales. Composed concerti grossi, solo concertos, overtures, sonatas.

Samson et Dalila [Fr., Samson and Delilah]. Opera in three acts by Saint-Saëns (libretto by Ferdinand Lemaire, after the Biblical story), first produced in Weimar in 1877 in German. Setting: Gaza, Palestine, ca. 1150 B.C.E.

Sanctorale [Lat.]. In the liturgical year, the feasts of the saints [see Liturgy].

Sanctus [Lat., holy]. The fourth item of the *Ordinary of the Roman *Mass, beginning with the threefold acclamation "Sanctus, sanctus, sanctus" and sung by the choir following the *Preface. The first part of its text is from Isaiah 6:3, and it is one of the oldest parts of the Mass. Up to the word "Benedictus," the text is retained in English in the Anglican service of Holy Communion.

Sanderling, Kurt (b. Arys, 9 Sept. 1912). Conductor. Active at the Berlin City Opera, 1931–36. Led the Moscow Radio Symphony, 1935–41; the Leningrad Philharmonic, 1941–60; the (East) Berlin Symphony, 1960–77; the Dresden Kapelle, 1964–67.

Sanders, Pharoah [Farrell] (b. Little Rock, Ark., 13 Oct. 1940). Jazz tenor saxophonist and bandleader. Joined John Coltrane, 1965–67. In his own groups from 1969, contrasted free-jazz improvisatory techniques with tuneful melodies and serene ostinatos. After briefly turning toward disco (1977–78), led stylistically wide-ranging jazz groups.

Sanders, Samuel (b. New York, 27 June 1937; d. there, 9 July 1999). Pianist. Studied at Hunter College and at Juilliard. Teacher there from 1963; also at the Peabody Conservatory. Accompanied Perlman, Rostropovich, Sills, Norman, and many others; also a chamber music performer. Founded the Cape and Islands Chamber Music Festival (1980) and the Musica Camerit of New York Hebrew Arts School (1983).

Sanderson, Sibyl (b. Sacramento, Calif., 7 Dec. 1865; d. Paris, 15 May 1903). Soprano. Pupil of Massenet, Sbriglia, and Mathilde Marchesi. Debuted under the name Ada Palmer at The Hague, 1888. Metropolitan Opera debut, 1895. Known for her large vocal range (g to g′′′). Works written for her include Massenet's *Esclarmonde* (1889), *Thaïs* (1894), and Saint-Saëns's *Phryné* (1893).

Sándor, György (b. Budapest, 21 Sept. 1912). Pianist. Pupil of Bartók and Kódaly. Debut, Budapest, 1930. Moved to the U.S., 1939. Taught at the Univ. of Michigan and at Juilliard. Has toured Europe, the U.S., Asia, and Australia. Best known for his interpretations of Bartók and Prokofiev; premiered Bartók's Third Concerto, 1946.

Sanft [Ger.] Soft.

Sanjuán, Pedro (b. San Sebastián, 15 Nov. 1886; d. Washington, D.C., 18 Oct. 1976). Composer. Pupil of Turina. Went to Havana, where he established the Havana Philharmonic. Returned to Spain, 1932–36; taught at Converse College (Spartanburg, S.C.) from 1942. Works include the orchestral *Rondo fantástico* (1926), *Castilla* (1947), *Macumba* (1951), and Symphonic Suite (1965); vocal and piano music. Roldán was among his pupils.

Sankey, Ira David (b. Edinburgh, Pa., 28 Aug. 1840; d. Brooklyn, N.Y., 13 Aug. 1908). Singer and composer. Instrumental in the popularization of gospel music. In 1870, formed a 30-year partnership with Dwight L. Moody. Composed about 1,200 songs and collected many more gospel hymns. President of the publishing firm Biglow and Main 1895–1908.

Santa Cruz, Domingo (b. La Cruz, Valparaiso, Chile, 5 July 1899; d. Santiago, 6 Jan. 1987). Composer. Pupil of Soro and del Campo. Founded numerous arts organizations in Chile. Taught at the National Conservatory, 1928–53 (dean, 1932–51 and 1962–68). Works include *Cantata de los rios de Chile* (1941); *Oratio Ieremiae prophetae* (1970); 4 symphonies; orchestral music, including *Variaciones* (1943, with piano solo); 3 string quartets and other chamber music; piano music, including *Viñetas* (1925–27); and songs, including *Canciones del Mar* (1952).

Santiago de Compostela, repertory of. A repertory of 20 polyphonic pieces and various monophonic pieces contained in the so-called *Codex Calixtinus* in Santiago de Compostela, Spain. The nonmusical parts of the manuscript are largely associated with pilgrimage to the shrine of St. James in Santiago and include a letter falsely attributed to Pope Calixtus II (1119–24). The manuscript and its music originated in central France, however, reaching Santiago by 1173.

Santoro, Claudio (b. Manáos, Brazil, 23 Nov. 1919; d. Brasilia, 27 Mar. 1989). Composer. Pupil of Koellreutter and Boulanger. Helped found the Brazilian Symphony. Taught at Santos Conservatory, 1953–56; at the Univ. of Brasilia from 1962; in Heidelberg, 1970–78. Worked with dodecaphony, Brazilian national elements, serialism, aleatory, and graphic notation. Works include 8 symphonies; several ballets; concertos; chamber music, including 7 string quartets; pieces for ensemble and tape; vocal works, including *Cantata elegíaca* (1970) and *Cantate* (1987); and piano music.

Santur [Per., Turk.]. A *dulcimer of the Middle East with a shallow, trapezoidal sound box, 12 to 18 courses of metal strings, and two rows of movable bridges. The player strikes the strings on either side of the bridges with light wooden hammers.

Sanz, Gaspar (b. Calanda, Aragon, mid-17th century; d. early 18th cent.). Composer and guitarist. Studied at the Univ. of Salamanca and in Italy. Published *Instrucción de música sobre la guitarra española* (1674), a treatise for a 5-course guitar tuned a/a–d′/d′–g/g–b/b–e′. Included are an introductory tutor, an essay on figured bass accompaniment, and 90 pieces of varying difficulty, mostly based on dance forms.

Sanza, sansa. See *Mbira.*

Sapp, Allen Dwight (b. Philadelphia, 10 Dec. 1922). Composer. Pupil of Piston, Thompson, Copland, and Boulanger. Has taught at Harvard, 1950–58; Wellesley College, 1958–61; SUNY–Buffalo, 1961–75; Florida State Univ., 1976–78; and the Cincinnati College-Conservatory (dean, 1978–80). Works include *Imaginary Creations* (harpsichord, orchestra, 1980); 4 string quartets; 7 piano sonatas; 5 toccatas (harpsichord, 1981); choral and solo vocal music.

Sarabande [Fr.; also Ger.; It. *sarabanda;* Sp. *zarabanda*]. A Baroque dance movement in triple meter. In France and Germany, it was usually slow and majestic, characterized by an accented dotted note on the second beat, beginning without upbeat, and cadencing on the third beat. It was normally in binary form, with fairly regular four- or eight-bar phrases and simple melodies that invited profuse ornamentation, sometimes written out or following as a *double.* It became a regular member of the solo and chamber *suite, following the courante.

The *zarabanda* is first known as a fast and wildly erotic dance in Mexico and Spain in the 16th century, accompanied by castanets and guitar. It was banned in Spain in 1583, but it nevertheless survived both there and in Italy as a fast dance until the end of the Baroque era. The earliest extant examples are in Italian guitar sources from the early 17th century. The sarabande was conceived primarily as a harmonic scheme until the middle of the century, when metric features (e.g., straightforward triple meter, not necessarily including an accented second beat) became the distinguishing characteristics. In solo and chamber sonatas of the mature Baroque, tempo markings are often given, usually *allegro* or *presto,* but sometimes *largo* or *adagio.* It was in France that the sarabande was transformed into an essentially slow dance.

German composers generally followed French rather than Italian models, adopting their slow tempo and accented second beat in music for harpsichord, lute, and chamber ensembles. Here the sarabande was almost always part of the core of a dance suite (allemande, courante, sarabande, gigue).

Sāraṅgī [Hind.]. A bowed stringed instrument of northern India and Pakistan. Three gut strings pass down a broad, unfretted neck and over a waisted, skin-covered belly. Ten to forty metal *sympathetic strings run beneath the melodic strings. It is held upright and the strings are stopped with the fingernails of the left hand. It is a favorite instrument for accompanying the voice. See ill. under Instrument.

Sarasate (y Navascuéz), Pablo (Martín Melitón) de (b. Pamplona, 10 Mar. 1844; d. Biarritz, 20 Sept. 1908). Violinist. Studied at the Paris Conservatory with Alard and Reber. Saint-Saëns, Bruch, and others composed works for him; historically a new type of player, with dazzling technique and singing tone; also a devoted chamber player. Published many concert show pieces for violin, including arrangements of Spanish airs, *Zigeunerweisen* (1878), and *Carmen Fantasy* (?1883).

Sardana [Sp.]. The national dance of Catalonia, in rapid 6/8 meter and danced in a circle to music performed by a *cobla.*

Sargent, (Harold) Malcolm (Watts) (b. Ashford, Kent, 29 Apr. 1895; d. London, 3 Oct. 1967). Conductor. Studied at Durham Univ. Taught at the Royal College from 1923. Held conducting posts with the Hallé Orchestra, Manchester (1939–42), the Liverpool Philharmonic (1942–48), and the BBC Symphony (1950–57); conducted the Promenade concerts in London from 1947. Appeared often with the London Symphony. Introduced works of Martinù, Walton (*Belshazzar's Feast,* 1932), Vaughan Williams (Ninth Symphony, 1958), and Bloch.

Sarod [Hind.]. A plucked, stringed instrument of northern India. Four or five melody strings plus three to five drone strings and 11 to 16 *sympathetic strings, all of metal, pass down a broad, unfretted, metal-covered neck and over a bowl-shaped, skin-covered sound box. A round, metal-covered resonator is attached to the underside of the pegbox.

Plucked with a plectrum, it is most often a solo instrument, accompanied by *tablā and *tamburā. See ill. under Instrument.

Saron [Jav.]. An Indonesian *metallophone. Thick bronze or iron bars are set on top of a wooden frame and struck with wooden mallets. Most contain six or seven bars and encompass one octave. They are important in many *gamelan* ensembles. See ill. under Instrument.

Sarrusophone [Eng., Fr.; Ger. *Sarrusophon;* It. *sarrusofono;* Sp. *sarrusofón*]. A family of brass, conical-bore, double-reed woodwind instruments invented by the French bandmaster W. Sarrus and constructed for him by P. L. Gautrot, Sr., of Paris. The sarrusophone was patented by Gautrot in 1856. The instruments exist in eight sizes, ranging from sopranino to subcontrabass. The smaller instruments resemble the straight soprano *saxophone, while the lower members of the family are constructed with vertical loops and an upward-facing bell. See ill. under Reed.

Sarti [Sardi], **Giuseppe** (b. Faenza, bapt. 1 Dec. 1729; d. Berlin, 28 July 1802). Composer. Pupil of Vallotti and Padre Martini. Court Kapellmeister, Copenhagen, 1755–65 and 1770–75. *Maestro di coro,* Pietà Conservatory, Venice, 1766–67. *Maestro di cappella,* Milan Cathedral, 1779–84. Court musician in St. Petersburg from 1784. Composed over 70 dramatic works (incl. *Le gelosie villane,* La Scala, 1776; *The Early Reign of Oleg,* St. Petersburg, 1790); sacred vocal works, symphonies, and sonatas. Cherubini was among his pupils.

Sarum Use. The modification of the Roman Catholic rite developed and used at the Cathedral of Salisbury between the 13th and the 16th century, adopted throughout much of the British Isles and influential elsewhere. The Sarum Use had substantial effects on the makeup of the Anglican Book of Common Prayer. In 1559, it was officially abolished in England.

Sassofono [It.]. Saxophone.

Satie, Erik [Eric] **(Alfred Leslie)** (b. Honfleur, 17 May 1866; d. Paris, 1 July 1925). Composer, pianist, and writer. Studied at the Paris Conservatory and the Schola cantorum. Worked as a café pianist; became the official composer for the Rosicrucian society; then withdrew to form his own religion. Associated at various times with Ravel, Debussy, Cocteau, "Les six," and l'École d'Arcueil. Works: 4 ballets (*Parade,* with Cocteau, Picasso, and Massine, 1917; *Mercure,* 1924; *Relâche,* 1924) and other stage music; *Socrate* (*drame symphonique,* Plato; voice(s) and piano/ orchestra, 1918); many piano pieces (*3 Sarabandes,* 1887; *3 *Gymnopédies; Sonatine bureaucratique,*

1917); instrumental music (*3 morceaux en forme de poire,* piano 4-hands, 1890–1903; *Musique d'ameublement,* with Milhaud; piano, 3 clarinets, trombone, 1920); songs.

Sattel [Ger.]. *Nut (1).

Satz [Ger.]. (1) Movement, e.g., of a sonata. (2) *Phrase, *period. (3) Theme; *Hauptsatz* and *Seitensatz* or *Nebensatz,* the first and second themes, respectively, in *sonata form. (4) The structure, fundamental style, or texture of a work; e.g., *strenger (freier) Satz,* strict (free) style.

Sauer, Emil von (b. Hamburg, 8 Oct. 1862; d. Vienna, 27 Apr. 1942). Pianist. Pupil of N. Rubinstein and Liszt. Toured the U.S., 1898–99 and 1908. Taught at the Meisterschule für Klavierspiel in Vienna, 1901–7 and 1915–36. Composed 2 piano concertos, 2 piano sonatas, etudes; edited the piano works of Brahms and several pedagogical works.

Sauget [Poupard], **Henri (-Pierre)** (b. Bordeaux, 18 May 1901; d. Paris, 22 June 1989). Composer and organist. Pupil of Canteloube and Koechlin. A member of the École d'Arcueil. Composed more than 25 ballets (*La chatte,* 1927; *Les forains,* 1945); operas (*La chartreuse de Parme,* 1927–36); film, radio, and television scores; 4 symphonies and other orchestral music; chamber music, including 3 string quartets; solo works for piano, organ, accordion, harpsichord, and guitar; choral music and many song cycles.

Saul. An oratorio for soloists, chorus, and orchestra by Handel, first performed in London in 1739. The text, compiled by Charles Jennens, is from the Bible (I Samuel 17–II Samuel 1) and Abraham Cowley's *Davideis.*

Sausage bassoon. See Racket (bassoon).

Sauterelle [Fr.]. *Saltarello.

Sautillé [Fr.]. See Bowing (4).

Saw, musical. See Musical saw.

Sawallisch, Wolfgang (b. Munich, 26 Aug. 1923). Conductor and pianist. Attended the Munich Academy. Led the Vienna Symphony (1960–70), the Hamburg Philharmonic (1961–73), and the Suisse Romande Orchestra (1972–80). Music director of the Bavarian State Opera, Munich, 1971–92; of the Philadelphia Orchestra, 1993–94. Appeared as a pianist in chamber music and lieder recitals.

Sax, Adolphe [Antoine Joseph] (b. Dinant, Belgium, 6 Nov. 1814; d. Paris, 4 Feb. 1894). Instrument maker. Studied at the Brussels Conservatory. To 1842, worked in the shop of his father, the instrument maker Charles Joseph Sax (1791–1865); 1842, set up shop in Paris, supported by Berlioz and others. De-

veloped and patented families of new instruments: the saxhorns (1845), saxotrombas (1845), and saxophones (1846). Persuaded the French government to reorganize its military bands, incorporating his new instruments. Taught at the Paris Conservatory, 1857–71; published a *Méthode complète pour saxhorn et saxotromba.*

Sax tuba. A valved brass instrument in circular form. Adolphe Sax made 15 of them in various sizes for Halévy's opera *Le juif errant* in 1852.

Saxhorn. A valved brass instrument, usually in upright tuba form, made in uniformly proportioned sizes from sopranino to contrabass. Saxhorns were an early attempt to create a uniform and complete family of brass instruments, an attempt made possible by the invention of the *valve. They were first produced about 1845 by (Antoine-Joseph) Adolphe Sax (1814–94) in Paris and were widely used by military and community bands in France, Belgium, England, and the U.S. during the last half of the 19th century. Some sizes of present-day band instruments—notably *alto horns, *euphoniums, and baritones—are direct descendants of the corresponding saxhorns.

Saxophone [Eng., Fr.; Ger. *Saxophon;* It. *sassofono;* Sp. *saxofón*]. A family of metal, conical-bore, single-reed woodwind instruments invented by Adolphe Sax (1814–94) of Brussels in 1841 and patented by him in 1846 after he settled in Paris. From the beginning, the instruments have been made in two shapes. Smaller saxophones are made in straight form, while larger ones have the bell bent up and toward the front and the neck bent back toward the player. Because Sax intended the instruments for both orchestral and band use, the family actually comprises two parallel groups. The orchestral group has seven sizes, pitched alternately in C and F. The band (or military) group also has seven sizes, pitched alternately in B♭ and E♭. In 1904, the firm of C. G. Conn in Elkhart, Indiana, added a subcontrabass. From the orchestral group only the C tenor (called the melody saxophone) is in use today.

All saxophones are notated in the treble clef and have a written range of b♭ to f‴, though some instruments may have additional keys for extending the range downward to written a or below, and skilled players may extend the range upward considerably. Saxophones used today include the sopranino in E♭ (sounding a minor third higher than written), soprano in B♭ (a major second lower), alto in E♭ (a major sixth lower), tenor in B♭ (or, less often, C, sounding a major ninth or an octave lower than written), baritone in E♭ (an octave and a major sixth lower), bass in B♭ (two octaves and a major second lower), contrabass in E♭ (two octaves and a major sixth lower), and subcontrabass in B♭ (three octaves and a major second lower). The principal instruments of the family are the alto in E♭, the tenor in B♭, and the baritone in E♭ [see ill. under Reed]. The saxophone has a fingering system similar to that of the Boehm flute in the right hand [see Boehm system]; the left hand retains some characteristics of the earlier *simple system.

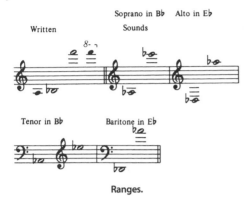

Ranges.

The instrument has been used extensively in jazz and popular music and in military bands and other large wind ensembles. It has been used to some extent in orchestral and chamber music as well.

Saxotromba. A valved brass instrument in upright tuba form for mounted military use. Saxotrombas, which were patented in 1845 by Adolphe Sax, have narrower bore proportions than the instruments of his *saxhorn family. They were not successful.

Saygun, Ahmet Adnan (b. Izmir, 7 Sept. 1907; d. Istanbul, 6 Jan. 1991). Composer and ethnomusicologist. Studied in Italy and with Le Flem and d'Indy. Taught at the conservatory in Ankara from 1946. Works include the opera *Köroğlu* (1973); the *ballet-féerie Gilgames;* 4 symphonies; concertos; chamber music; oratorios, cantatas, and songs. Published writings on Turkish folk music.

Saynète [Fr.]. See *Sainete.*

Saz [Turk.]. A *long-necked lute of Turkey with three courses of metal strings (tuned E D A or G D A, the middle string thus sounding lowest), a fretted neck, and a bulging, pear-shaped body. Of the instruments of varying size that make up the family of this name, the most common is the *bağlama.* The performer uses a flexible plectrum to play a melody on the highest string, adding accompaniment on the others. The *saz* is considered the Turkish national instrument and is used to accompany many kinds of songs and dances. See ill. under Instrument.

Scacchi, Marco (b. Gallese, near Viterbo, ca. 1600; d. there, between 1681 and 1687). Composer and theo-

rist. Pupil of G. F. Anerio. Royal musician in Warsaw, 1626–49. Composed Masses in the *stile antico,* operas, sacred concertos, and madrigals with continuo. Writings include *Breve discorso sopra la musica moderna* (1649), a defense of modern music. Classified music into 3 types: church, chamber, and theatrical.

Scala [It.]. *Scale.

Scala enigmatica [It.]. The scale c d♭ e f♯ g♯ a♯ b c', employed by Verdi in his *Ave Maria* ("Scala enigmatica armonizzata a quattro voci miste") for mixed chorus (original version, 1889; revised version, 1898).

Scale. (1) [Fr. *gamme, échelle;* Ger. *Tonleiter, Skala;* It. *scala, gamma;* Sp. *escala, gama*]. A collection of pitches arranged in order from lowest to highest or from highest to lowest. The pitches of any music in which pitch is definable can be reduced to a scale. The concept and its pedagogical use have been especially prominent in the history of Western art music. The importance of the concept in non-Western systems varies considerably and is often associated with concepts of melody construction and internal pitch relationships that go well beyond any simple ordering of pitches from lowest to highest [see also Mode, Melody type]. Even in Western tonal music, however, scales are only a reflection of compositional practice that includes notions of appropriate melodic progression and the functions of individual pitches in relation to one another. With respect to nontonal Western music, a scale is likely to be simply an arbitrary representation of pitch content that contributes little to an understanding of a given work.

The total pitch world of Western tonal music [see Tonality] is defined by the chromatic scale—a scale in which each pitch is separated from its neighbors by a semitone, the smallest *interval in use in the system. This scale thus includes twelve different pitch classes or pitch names, and by convention, as with other scales, the starting pitch name is repeated at the top of the scale [see the accompanying table]. A scale of this structure may be formed beginning on any of the twelve possible pitch classes and may be repeated through any number of octaves. It is embodied in all of the white and black keys of the piano keyboard taken together.

Central to the structure of Western tonal music is the *diatonic scale—a scale that includes two semitones (s) and five whole tones (t) arranged in the pattern embodied in the white keys of the piano: taking C as the starting point, t t s t t t s. In principle, any of the seven pitches of such a scale can be taken as the starting point, thus rearranging the order in which the tones and semitones occur, though not the underlying pattern from which the order derives.

There are thus seven different versions of the diatonic scale, termed octave species, since, by convention in Western tonal music, every scale is understood as being bounded by an octave. In historical practice, however, only some of these octave species have been important. By the end of the Renaissance, six (all but the one produced by starting upward from B) were recognized in both theory and practice, forming a central part of the system of modes. For a discussion of this system, see Mode.

Chromatic	c	c♯	d	d♯	e	f	f♯	g	g♯	a	a♯	b	c′
Major	c		d		e	f		g		a		b	c′
Minor, natural	c		d	e♭		f		g	a♭		b♭		c′
Minor, melodic													
ascending	c		d	e♭		f		g		a		b	c′
descending	c		d	e♭		f		g	a♭		b♭		c′
Minor, harmonic	c		d	e♭		f		g	a♭			b	c′
Whole tone	c		d		e		f♯		g♯		a♯		c′
Gypsy	c		d	e♭			f♯	g	a♭			b	c′
Pentatonic	c		d			f		g		a			c′
Octatonic	c	c♯		d♯	e		f♯	g		a	a♯		c′
Blues	c		d	e♭	e	f	g♭	g		a	b♭	b	c′

In tonal music, from the late 17th century on, only two octave species or modes are at work: major and minor. The major mode or major scale takes the pattern produced by starting upward through the diatonic scale from C. The natural or pure minor mode or scale takes the pattern starting upward from A: t s t t s t t. The distinction among starting points and the resulting orders of tones and semitones reflect a feature of compositional practice, namely, that pitches are treated in a hierarchical relationship and that each pitch in a tonal composition has a particular function with respect to the others. Each step or degree of a particular scale is thus numbered and named [see Scale degrees]. The starting pitch is of the greatest importance in the hierarchy, and since major and minor scales can be formed on any of the twelve available pitch classes, any given example is named for its starting pitch or tonic, e.g., C major, G minor, etc. A composition based primarily on a given scale is said to be in the *key of that scale, e.g., C major, G minor, etc. An important property of these scales is that the twelve different starting points or tonics produce twelve different scales, no two of which contain precisely the same pitch classes and each of which is uniquely and precisely related to all of the others. For the nature of this relationship, see Key relationship, Circle of fifths.

Compositions in the minor mode often approach the tonic from below by semitone, thus raising the seventh scale degree of the natural minor scale by a semitone to produce what is termed the harmonic minor scale [see table, where all scales are illustrated starting on c]. This produces an interval of three

semitones between the sixth and seventh scale degrees—an interval called an augmented second that is regarded as melodically awkward. Hence, in approaching the tonic from below, compositions in the minor mode often raise both the sixth and seventh scale degrees by a semitone. This results in what is termed the melodic minor scale, which, however, when descending from the tonic is identical with the natural minor scale. Here again, scales are simply abstractions from musical practice rather than musical objects with prior or independent standing.

Some kinds of Western music can be understood to employ scales that are largely modifications of major or minor scales (or perhaps one of the other octave species or modes), the music in question being essentially tonal, e.g., *Gypsy music, the *blues, and most 19th- and 20th-century examples of *modality. Among the most familiar nontonal scales is the whole-tone scale, which includes no semitones. This scale includes only six pitch classes, and there are only two different pitch collections reducible to a scale of this structure. *Pentatonic scales, found in both Western and non-Western music, include five pitches in differing patterns of intervals. The octatonic scale includes eight pitches per octave arranged in a pattern of alternating whole tones and semitones. There are only three different pitch collections reducible to a scale of this structure. This scale figures prominently in music by Stravinsky and others.

(2) For the scale of organ pipes, see Scaling.

Scale degrees. The numbered positions of individual pitches within a major or minor *scale. Because in Western *tonality each pitch of a scale functions in a particular way with respect to the others, scale degrees are both numbered (traditionally with roman numerals) and named, as follows: I tonic, II supertonic, III mediant, IV subdominant, V *dominant, VI submediant, VII *leading tone or *subtonic. The numbering and nomenclature are extensively used in *harmonic analysis.

Scalero, (Bartolomeo Melchiorre) Rosario (b. Moncalieri, near Turin, 24 Dec. 1870; d. Settimo Vittone, Ivrea, 25 Dec. 1954). Composer. Studied in Turin, London, and Vienna. Taught at the Academy of S. Cecilia in Rome from 1908; at the David Mannes School, 1919–28; and at the Curtis Institute, 1924–33, 1935–46. Among his students were Barber, Foss, Menotti, and Rota. Works include orchestral music; chamber and piano music; songs; and transcriptions of earlier music.

Scaling [Fr. *diapason;* Ger. *Mensur;* It. *misura;* Sp. *mensura*]. (1) The diameter of organ pipes in relation to their length. Scales for organ pipes are determined with regard for the size of the instrument and the acoustics of the space in which it is to be heard. Wide scaling of *flue pipes produces varieties of flute tone (characterized by few audible harmonics), and narrow scaling produces Principal tone. Extremely narrow scaling produces a variant known as string tone. (2) [Fr. *taille, mesure*] The length of the strings of a stringed keyboard instrument in relation to their pitch. Since, in addition to length, mass and tension are variables in the determination of the pitch of a string [see Acoustics], the length of lower-sounding strings on such instruments is usually made somewhat shorter than it would have to be if length were the only variable.

Scarlatti, (Pietro) Alessandro (Gaspare) (b. Palermo, 2 May 1660; d. Naples, 22 Oct. 1725). Composer. Went to Rome 1672. May have studied with Carissimi. *Maestro di cappella* to Queen Christina of Sweden, from at least 1680 to 1684; to the Viceroy of Naples, 1684–1702, 1708–18, and 1722–25. Assistant music director at S. Maria Maggiore, Rome, from 1703; *maestro* there, 1706–8. Works: about 115 operas (including *La Statira*, 1690; *Il Pirro e Demetrio*, 1694; *La caduta de' Decemviri*, 1697; *Il Tigrane*, 1715; *Il trionfo dell'onore*, 1718; *Telemaco*, 1718; *Marco Attilio Regolo*, 1719; *La Griselda*, 1721; and many now lost); over 600 cantatas; serenatas; oratorios; numerous Masses, motets, and other sacred and liturgical works (St. John Passion, ca. 1680); madrigals; orchestral works (incl. 12 Sinfonie de concerto grosso, 1715–?); chamber sonatas; keyboard pieces (incl. toccatas; variations on "La follia," 1715).

Scarlatti, (Giuseppe) Domenico (b. Naples, 26 Oct. 1685; d. Madrid, 23 July 1757). Composer. From 1701 to 1704, *organista e compositore di musica* of the Naples royal chapel, where his father, Alessandro Scarlatti, was maestro. *Maestro di cappella* to the Queen of Poland, 1709–13; of the Cappella Giulia, St. Peter's, 1714–19; at the court in Lisbon, from 1723. There taught the Infanta Maria Barbara; remained in her service in Madrid after she married the Spanish Crown Prince. In a legendary contest in virtuosity, Scarlatti is said to have bested Handel on the harpsichord, while the latter prevailed on the organ. Works: 555 single-movement keyboard "sonatas" (characterized by binary form, eccentric gestures, irregular phrases, extensive use of the acciaccatura, unusual modulations, and virtuoso technique); operas, oratorios, and serenatas (mostly lost); cantatas; Masses, motets, and other sacred vocal works; 17 sinfonias.

Scat singing. A *jazz solo of vocal nonsense syllables. First recorded by Louis Armstrong on "Heebie Jeebies" (1926), scat came to be represented after 1944 by virtuosic interpretations (by, e.g., Ella Fitzgerald, Eddie Jefferson, and Jon Hendricks) of rapid *bebop instrumental improvisation.

Scena [It.]. (1) Stage, or the scene represented on the stage. (2) A subdivision of an act of an opera. (3) In formulations such as *scena ed aria* or *scena e duetto*, which appear frequently in the scores of 19th-century operas, the recitative portion of the number. A setting of a portion of a libretto for concert performance by a solo singer plus orchestra, e.g., Beethoven's "Ah! perfido" or Mozart's "Misera, dove son," may also be called *scena ed aria*.

Schaeffer, Pierre (b. Nancy, 14 Aug. 1910; d. 19 Aug. 1995). Composer, theorist, and writer. Worked in radio. Taught at the Paris Conservatory from 1968. Credited with originating *musique concrète* (see Electro-acoustic music) in 1948. Compositions (all for tape alone) include *Étude violette* (1948); *Orphée 53* (opera; collaboration with Pierre Henry, 1953); String Quartet (1968); ballets, film scores, incidental music. Published writings on *musique concrète*, as well as novels and essays.

Schafer, R(aymond) Murray (b. Sarnia, Ont., 18 July 1933). Composer and writer on music. Studied at the Toronto Conservatory. Taught at Simon Fraser Univ., 1965–75. Works include dramatic works (*Loving*, 1965; *The Princess of the Stars*, ritual drama, performers and canoeists, 1981; *Patria V: The Crown of Ariadne*, 1992); orchestral music (*Son of Heldenleben*, 1968); string quartets and other chamber music; choral music (*Apocalypsis*, 12 choirs, brass, percussion, homemade instruments, tape, 1977); pieces for students and amateurs.

Schäffer, Bogusław (b. Lwów, 6 June 1929). Composer and theorist. Pupil of Malawski and Nono. Teacher at Kraków Conservatory from 1963; at the Salzburg Mozarteum from 1986. Worked at Polish Radio, 1965–68. Has used Polish folk idioms, serial techniques, microtones, graphic notation, and indeterminacy. Works include stage and action music (*TIS MW2*, 1963); orchestral music (*Scultura*, 1960; Sinfonia, 1993; concertos); Stabat Mater (1983); ensemble and piano music (*6 Models for Piano*, 1954–93; *Gasab*, Gasab-violin, piano, 1983); electronic and tape music (Open Music nos. 2–4, piano, tape, 1983; *Acontecimiento*, 3 pianos, computer, 1988). Books include *Nowa muzyka* (1958; enlarged, 1969).

Schalkhaft [Ger.]. Roguish.

Schall [Ger.]. Sound.

Schallbecher [Ger.]. *Bell (2).

Schallbecken [Ger.]. Cymbals.

Schalloch [Ger.]. *Sound hole.

Schallstück [Ger.]. *Bell (2).

Schalltrichter [Ger.]. *Bell (2); *S. auf*, an instruction to brass players to play with the bell raised.

Schalmei [Ger.]. *Shawm.

Scharwenka, (Ludwig) Philipp (b. Samter, 16 Feb. 1847; d. Bad Nauheim, 16 July 1917). Composer. Studied at the Kullak Academy of Music, Berlin; taught there from 1868. With his brother Xaver founded the Scharwenka Conservatory. Composed symphonic poems; overtures; string quartets, sonatas, and other chamber music; choruses and songs.

Scharwenka, (Franz) Xaver (b. Samter, 6 Jan. 1850; d. Berlin, 8 Dec. 1924). Pianist and composer. Pupil of Kullak. Debuted at the Singakademie, 1869. Toured Europe, the U.S., and Canada. Opened the Scharwenka Conservatory in Berlin, 1881, and a branch in New York, 1891. Works include 1 opera; a symphony; 4 piano concertos; a piano quintet and other chamber pieces; sonatas and shorter piano works. Published a piano method (1907).

Schat, Peter (b. Utrecht, 5 June 1935). Composer. Pupil of van Baaren, Seiber, and Boulez. Has made use of serialism, elements of chance, and electronic media. Works include operas (*Labyrinth*, 1966; *Symposium*, 1994); a ballet; instrumental music (*Inscripties*, piano, 1959; *Entelechie I & II*, 1961; *Clockwise and Anticlockwise*, 1967; Symphony no. 1, 1978); *To You*, 9 electric guitars, 4 electric pianos, 2 electric organs, 6 electric humming tops (1972).

Schauspieldirektor, Der [Ger., The Impresario]. *Singspiel in one act by Mozart (libretto by Gottlieb Stephanie), performed at the Orangery of the Schönbrunn Palace in Vienna in 1786. Setting: Salzburg, 1786. The music consists only of an overture, two arias for sopranos, a terzett, and a finale.

Scheherazade. See *Sheherazade.*

Scheibe, Johann Adolph (b. Leipzig, 3 May 1708; d. Copenhagen, 22 Apr. 1776). Composer and theorist. Self-taught in music. Moved to Hamburg, 1736; worked as a music critic. Kapellmeister to the Margrave of Brandenburg-Culmbach from 1739; to the Danish court, 1740–47 and after 1766. Composed cantatas, sonatas, Masses, and many other instrumental and vocal works; 150 flute concertos and numerous church pieces listed in his autobiography have been lost. Published progressive writings on music theory.

Scheidemann, Heinrich (b. Wöhrden, Holstein, ca. 1595; d. Hamburg, early 1663). Composer. Pupil of Sweelinck. Associate of Praetorius. From 1629, organist at the Catharinenkirche, Hamburg; from 1633 also clerk there. Composed many organ works; extended Sweelinck's keyboard style and helped develop the monodic organ chorale and the virtuosic chorale fantasia.

Scheidt, Samuel (b. Halle, bapt. 3 Nov. 1587; d. there, 24 Mar. 1654). Composer. Pupil of Sweelinck, Praetorius, and Schütz. From 1609, court organist to the Margrave of Brandenburg in Halle; also court Kapellmeister from 1619 or 1620. *Director musices* of the city of Halle, 1628–30. Composed numerous sacred vocal works, including sacred concertos (*Liebliche Krafft-Blümlein*, 1635), motets and madrigals; keyboard music (*Tabulatura nova*, 3 vols., 1624, containing various sacred and secular pieces; *Görlitzer Tabulatur-Buch*, 1650, containing organ chorales); instrumental music (*Ludi musici*, 4 vols., 1621–27; sinfonias).

Schein, Johann Hermann (b. Grünhain, near Annaberg [now Annaberg-Bucholz], 20 Jan. 1586; d. Leipzig, 19 Nov. 1630). Composer. Boy chorister in Dresden from 1593. Studied at the Univ. of Leipzig. Kapellmeister at Weimar, 1615. From 1616, *Thomaskantor* at Leipzig; teacher at the Thomasschule. Associate of Scheidt and Schütz. Composed sacred vocal works (*Opella nova*, 1618, 1626; *Fontana d'Israel*, 1623; *Cantional*, 1627, 1645); Italian-style secular vocal music in German; occasional music; instrumental music (*Banchetto musicale*, 1617).

Scheitholt, Scheitholz [Ger.]. A rectangular *zither, now obsolete, similar in playing technique to the Norwegian *langleik*, Swedish *hummel*, and *Appalachian dulcimer.

Schelle [Ger., pl. *Schellen*]. *Pellet bell, *sleigh bells.

Schellenbaum [Ger.]. *Turkish crescent.

Schell(en)trommel [Ger.]. *Tambourine.

Schelomo [Heb., Solomon]. A rhapsody for cello and orchestra by Ernest Bloch composed in 1915–16, inspired by the Book of Ecclesiastes, which is attributed to Solomon.

Schenk, Johann Baptist (b. Wiener Neustadt, 30 Nov. 1753; d. Vienna, 29 Dec. 1836). Composer. Pupil of Wagenseil. Mid-1790s, Kapellmeister to Prince Auersperg. Composed singspiels (*Der Dorfbarbier*, 1796), symphonies, vocal and choral works, and chamber music. In 1793 Beethoven took lessons in counterpoint and composition from him.

Schenker analysis. A method of analysis for tonal music, developed over some 30 years by the Austrian theorist Heinrich Schenker (1868–1935); sometimes also called linear analysis or layer analysis. Applied to a given work, Schenker's analytical technique aims to discover and reveal tonal relationships by their intrinsic linear connections in a hierarchy of structural levels (*Schichten*) or layers. The most immediate level of a composition, called the foreground (*Vordergrund*), includes all of the composition's most prominent note-to-note motions (Schenker sometimes employed the term to refer to the work itself). The second general level of a work is the middleground (*Mittelgrund,* of which there may be several specific levels), in which the linear relationships between the pitches of structurally important harmonies within and between phrases become apparent and in which structurally important melodic elements may be retained from the foreground. The third general level of a work is the background (*Hintergrund*), in which only the most fundamental harmonies of the piece are shown in their linear relationship; at this stage even an entire modulation lasting for several phrases may be symbolized by a single triad. Ultimately even the background is considered an elaboration of the tonal projection through time of a tonic triad, which is arpeggiated in the bass by a leap from tonic to dominant and back (*Bassbrechung*) so as to support in the upper part a linear, stepwise motion from the third, fifth, or eighth degree of the scale down through the intermediate degrees to the first degree or tonic. This fundamental structure is called the *Ursatz* by Schenker (who sometimes, however, equated this with the background); the upper part, the *Urlinie* (fundamental line).

Schenker, Heinrich (b. Wisniowczyki, Galicia, 19 June, 1868; d. Vienna, 13 Jan. 1935). Theorist. Pupil of Bruckner. Worked in Vienna as a private teacher, editor, critic, chamber music performer, and accompanist. His students included W. Furtwängler and F. Salzer. Schenker's principal theoretical work was the multivolume *Neue musikalische Theorien und Phantasien,* including (1) *Harmonielehre* (Stuttgart, 1906), (2/1) *Kontrapunkt* (1910), (2/2) *Kontrapunkt* (1922), and (3) *Der freie Satz* (1935). Other writings include *Der Tonwille,* 10 issues (1921–24); *Das Meisterwerk in der Musik,* 3 vols. (1925–30). Edited works of J. S. Bach, Handel, C. P. E. Bach, and Beethoven's piano sonatas. See Schenker analysis.

Schenker's theories show that in a well-composed tonal work, overall structural-harmonic design can be analyzed contrapuntally at various levels of complexity *(Schichten)*. The simplest, most fundamental level *(Ursatz)* consists of a melodic stepwise descent to the tonic note *(Urlinie)* supported by a bass I–V–I arpeggiation *(Bassbrechung)*. Other harmonic and melodic features of the work are hierarchically subordinate elaborations or "diminutions" that arise from a "composing-out" *(Auskomponierung)* of the *Ursatz*. Schenker devised an elaborate musicographical system to represent these concepts visually.

Traditional principles of form and vertical harmony play a lesser role in Schenker's analysis. He applied his theories mainly to music of the period from Bach to Brahms (ca. 1700–1900); later adherents have extended its application.

Scherchen, Hermann (b. Berlin, 21 June 1891; d. Florence, 12 June 1966). Conductor. Schoenberg's assistant for the premiere of *Pierrot lunaire* (1912). Held conducting posts in Riga, Leipzig, Frankfurt, and Königsberg; conducted the Zürich Radio Orchestra (from 1933) and Beromünster Radio Orchestra (1944–50). Founded the journals *Melos* and *Musica viva,* as well as the Scherchen Quartet, the Ars Viva Orchestra, and the Gravesano electro-acoustic research studio (1954). Authored 3 books on conducting. Known for interpretations of Schoenberg, Berg, Webern, Dallapiccola, Hindemith, Prokofiev, and Stravinsky.

Scherzando [It.], **Scherzhaft** [Ger.]. Playful.

Scherzi, Gli [It.]. Popular name for Haydn's six String Quartets op. 33, Hob. III:37–42 (1781), so called because the minuets are headed "Scherzo." The quartets are also known as the *Russian* Quartets because later editions bear a dedication to the Grand Duke Pavel Petrovich, who visited Haydn while in Vienna in 1781; and as the *Maiden* Quartets [Ger. *Jungfern Quartette*] because the title page of the Hummel edition of 1782 shows a female figure.

Scherzo [It., joke]. (1) In the Baroque period, a vocal or instrumental work of lighter character. Most uses of the term before about 1650 refer to vocal pieces of the *balletto type, while after 1650, the term usually signifies an instrumental work.

(2) In the 18th century, one movement of a suite or other multimovement work, quick in tempo and light in style. Scherzos of this sort are most often in 2/4 time.

(3) From the late 18th century to the present, a standard movement-type introduced as a replacement for the minuet in multimovement cycles. Scherzos are normally in rapid 3/4 time; they range in character from the light and playful to the sinister and macabre. Most scherzos are in rounded *binary form. As in the minuet, there is usually a contrasting trio, after which the scherzo is restated.

Haydn employed the term scherzo for the dance movements of his String Quartets op. 33 of 1781; these movements do not, however, differ greatly from the usual minuet and trio. Beethoven began to write true scherzos early in his career (see the Wind Octet of 1792–93, published posthumously as op. 103, and the Piano Trios op. 1 of 1794–95). His introduction of the scherzo within the symphony was especially influential; scherzos are found in every Beethoven symphony but the First and Eighth, though in the former case the movement is a scherzo in all but name. The scherzo was a standard component of the Romantic and post-Romantic symphony and related genres.

Schibler, Armin (b. Kreuzlingen, Lake Constance, 20 Nov. 1920; d. Zurich, 7 Sept. 1986). Composer and writer on music. Studied with Rubbra, Tippett, Fortner, Leibowitz, Krenek, and Adorno. Taught in Zurich from 1944. Wrote books on Mahler and on contemporary music. Worked with twelve-tone procedures, jazz, and popular music. Works include the 1986 opera trilogy *Amadeus und der graue Bote, Königinnen von Frankreich, Schlafwagen Pegasus;* music theater pieces and ballets; choral works; 3 symphonies; chamber and piano music; songs; film scores, and educational music.

Schickele, Peter (b. Ames, Iowa, 17 July 1935). Composer and writer. Pupil of Harris, Persichetti, and Milhaud. Taught at Juilliard, 1961–65. He is the creator of P. D. Q. Bach and a satirical oeuvre that includes *Iphigenia in Brooklyn,* cantata (1965), and the operas *The Abduction of Figaro* (1984), *Oedipus Tex* (1988), and *Prelude to Einstein on the Fritz* (1989). Under his own name Schickele has also composed orchestral and chamber works, film music, and popular songs.

Schicksalslied [Ger., Song of Destiny]. A setting for chorus and orchestra by Brahms, op. 54 (1868–71), of a poem from Johann Hölderlin's *Hyperion.*

Schidlowsky, León (b. Santiago, 21 July 1931). Composer. Studied with Allende and in Europe. Has taught at the Hebrew Institute, Santiago (1955–61), the Univ. of Chile and the National Conservatory (1962–68), and the Rubin Academy in Israel (from 1970). Has worked with serialism, graphic notation, and aleatory techniques. His works, many of which commemorate the Holocaust, include *Die Menschen,* opera (1970); choral-orchestral works (*La noche de cristal,* 1961); chamber music; orchestral works (*Kaddish,* 1967; *Laudatio,* 1988); vocal works (*Invocación,* 1964; *Chanson,* 1988); and tape compositions.

Schietto, schiettamente [It.]. Open(ly), sincere(ly).

Schiff, Andras (b. Budapest, 21 Dec. 1953). Pianist. Attended the Liszt Academy; won the 1974 Tchaikovsky Competition. Has pursued a career as recitalist and soloist, performing a repertory ranging from Bach to 19th-century composers.

Schifrin, Lalo [Boris] (b. Buenos Aires, 21 June 1932). Composer and jazz pianist. Pupil of Messiaen. Joined Dizzy Gillespie's quintet in New York, 1960–62. Music director, Paris Philharmonic, from 1988. Has composed for television (the series *Mission Impossible,* 1966–73) and films (*Cool Hand Luke,*

1967; *Dirty Harry,* 1971). Other works include *Songs of the Aztecs,* soloist, orchestra (1988).

Schikaneder, Emanuel (Johann Joseph [Baptist]) (b. Straubing, 1 Sept. 1751; d. Vienna, 21 Sept. 1812). Writer and composer. Studied in Regensburg; worked as an actor. Directed theaters in Vienna from 1783. In 1801, opened the new Theater an der Wien; 1806–9, directed the Brno Theater. Commissioned settings of his texts by Mozart (*Die Zauberflöte,* with Schikaneder as Papageno) and others. Wrote many librettos and plays and composed several theater scores.

Schildt, Melchior (b. Hannover, 1592–93; d. there, 18 May 1667). Composer. Pupil of Sweelinck. Organist at the Hauptkirche, Wolfenbüttel, 1623–26; to King Christian IV in Copenhagen, 1626–29; at the Marktkirche, Hannover, from 1629. Composed chorale-based organ works and other keyboard music, and the chorale concerto *Ach mein herzliebes Jesulein.* A founder of the so-called north German organ school.

Schillinger, Joseph (Moiseyevich) (b. Kharkov, Russia, 31 Aug. 1895; d. New York, 23 Mar. 1943). Composer and theorist. Studied in St. Petersburg. Taught and conducted in the U.S.S.R. until 1928; then taught at the New School for Social Research, New York Univ., and Columbia Univ. Teachers College. Among his pupils were Tommy Dorsey, George Gershwin, and Glenn Miller. Works include *Oktyabr* (1927) and *The People and the Prophet* (ballet, 1931). Published writings on his mathematically based theories of harmony and rhythm.

Schillinger system. A theory that proposes a mathematical basis for music (and other arts), introduced by Joseph Schillinger (1895–1943) and published posthumously in 1946 as *The Schillinger System of Musical Composition.* His methods were most influential in the 1930s and 40s, especially in popular music, where his ideas on orchestration and thematic and rhythmic variation were widely used. Schillinger's pupils included Benny Goodman, George Gershwin, and Glenn Miller.

Schillings, Max von (b. Düren, 19 Apr. 1868; d. Berlin, 24 July 1933). Composer and conductor. Studied in Bonn and Munich. Associate of R. Strauss. From 1892, assistant stage conductor at Bayreuth. Teacher at the Univ. of Munich 1903–8; then took a post at the Stuttgart Royal Opera; general music director there, 1911–18. Intendant at the Berlin Opera 1918–25. Works include 6 operas (*Mona Lisa,* 1915); Violin Concerto (1910); Piano Quintet (1917); choral music and songs.

Schindler, Anton Felix (b. Meedl, Moravia, 13 June 1795; d. Bockenheim, near Frankfurt, 16 Jan. 1864).

Violinist, conductor, writer on music. Beethoven's secretary from 1820. Conducted at theaters in Vienna; under Beethoven's supervision, conducted all 9 symphonies, 1823–24. Choirmaster at Münster Cathedral, 1831–35; at Aachen, 1835–40. Published a biography of Beethoven (1840; trans. D. MacArdle as *Beethoven As I Knew Him,* 1966).

Schindler, Kurt (b. Berlin, 17 Feb. 1882; d. New York, 16 Nov. 1935). Composer, conductor, and editor. Studied in Berlin and Munich. Assistant at the Metropolitan Opera from 1905. Founder-conductor of the MacDowell Chorus (later Schola Cantorum of New York), 1909–26. Worked for G. Schirmer from 1907; 1912–25, music director, Temple Emanuel. Taught at Bennington College from 1933. Collected and edited folk songs from Spain, Russia, and Louisiana. Works include *The Mummers' Revel* (1934) and songs.

Schipa, Tito (b. Lecce, Italy, 2 Jan. 1888; d. New York, 16 Dec. 1965). Tenor. Studied in Milan; debut, 1910. Appeared at La Scala, 1915; created Ruggiero in Puccini's *La rondine,* 1917. Sang at Chicago (1919–32), San Francisco (1925–40), the Metropolitan Opera (1932–35, 1941), and throughout Italy.

Schippers, Thomas (b. Kalamazoo, Mich., 9 Mar. 1930; d. New York, 16 Dec. 1977). Conductor. Studied at the Curtis Institute. Associate of Menotti. Led premieres of *Amahl and the Night Visitors* (1951) and of works by Barber and Falla. Metropolitan Opera and La Scala debuts, 1955; Bayreuth debut, 1963. Directed the Spoleto Festival, 1958–75. From 1970 led the Cincinnati Symphony; taught at the Cincinnati Conservatory from 1972.

Schlag [Ger.]. (1) Beat, blow; *Schlaginstrumente, Schlagzeug,* percussion instruments. (2) A popular song hit.

Schlägel [Ger.]. See *Schlegel.*

Schlegel [Ger.]. Drumstick.

Schleifer [Ger.]. *Slide (3).

Schleppen [Ger.]. To drag; *nicht schleppen(d),* do not drag.

Schlick, Arnolt (b. Heidelberg?, ca. 1460; d. there?, after 1521). Organist and composer. Blind from youth. Organist to the Count Palatine in Heidelberg. Played for the 1486 coronation of Maximilian I, the 1495 Diet of Worms, and possibly the 1520 coronation of Charles V. Wrote a treatise on organ building (1511) and organ tabulature (1512). Other works include *Ascendo ad patrem meum,* antiphon.

Schlummerlied [Ger.]. Lullaby.

Schluss [Ger.]. Conclusion, *cadence; *Schlusssatz,* concluding movement.

Schlüssel [Ger.]. *Clef.

Schmachtend [Ger.]. Languishing, pining.

Schmeichelnd [Ger.]. Flattering, coaxing.

Schmelzer [Schmeltzer, Schmelzer von Ehrenruef], **Johann Heinrich** (b. Scheibbs, Lower Austria, ca. 1620–23; d. Prague, between 29 Feb. and 20 Mar. 1680). Composer. Court musician in Vienna from 1635. Vice-Kapellmeister there from 1671; Kapellmeister from 1679. Influential in the development of the suite and the sonata (*Sonatae unarum fidium,* violin, continuo, 1664). Other works include ballets; vocal works.

Schmerzlich [Ger.]. Sad, painful.

Schmetternd [Ger.]. Blaring, brassy, especially in horn playing.

Schmidt, Franz (b. Pressburg, 22 Dec. 1874; d. Perchtoldsdorf, near Vienna, 11 Feb. 1939). Composer, conductor, pianist, and cellist. Pupil of Leschetizky. Cellist in the Vienna Court Opera orchestra, 1896–1911; teacher at the Gesellschaft der Musikfreunde, 1901–8. From 1914, teacher at the Vienna Staatsakademie; its director, 1925–27. Directed the Musikhochschule, 1927–31. Works include 2 operas and an oratorio; 4 symphonies; Piano Concerto (left-hand, 1934); chamber, piano, and organ music.

Schmidt-Isserstedt, Hans (b. Berlin, 5 May 1900; d. Holm-Hostein, near Hamburg, 28 May 1973). Conductor. Studied in Berlin. Led the Hamburg Opera, 1935–42; the Berlin State Opera, 1943–45; the Hamburg Radio Symphony, 1945–71; and the Stockholm Philharmonic, 1955–64. An advocate of 20th-century music and also a Mozart specialist.

Schmitt, Florent (b. Blamont, Meurthe-et-Moselle, 28 Sept. 1870; d. Neuilly-sur-Seine, Paris, 17 Aug. 1958). Composer. Pupil of Dubois, Gédalge, Massenet, and Fauré. Directed the Lyons Conservatory, 1922–24. Works: 3 ballets (*La tragédie de Salomé,* incl. "La danse de l'effroi," 1907; rev. as symphonic poem, 1910); incidental music; film scores; symphonies and other orchestral music; chamber music including *Sonate libre en deux parties enchaînées* (violin, piano, 1918–19); piano and organ music; choral music (*Psalm 47,* 1904) and songs.

Schnabel [Ger., beak]. The mouthpiece of the recorder or clarinet.

Schnabel, Artur (b. Lipnik, Austria, 17 Apr. 1882; d. Axenstein, Switzerland, 15 Aug. 1951). Pianist. Pupil of Leschetizky; debut, 1890. Toured Europe as soloist and chamber musician; U.S. debut, 1921. Presented the entire piano sonata cycles of Beethoven (1927) and Schubert (1928); 1931–35, recorded the first complete Beethoven sonatas. Taught at the Univ. of Michigan, 1940–45. Edited Beethoven's sonatas and Diabelli Variations; also composed.

Schnabelflöte [Ger.]. *Recorder.

Schnarre [Ger.]. *Rattle.

Schnarrsaite [Ger.]. Snare.

Schnebel, Dieter (b. Lahr, Baden, 14 Mar. 1930). Composer, writer on music, and theologian. Studied in Tübingen and Freiburg. Has worked as a curate and vicar, taught religious studies, and published writings on contemporary music. Has worked with serialism, unconventional vocal sounds, electronics, and audience participation. Works include *für stimmen für;* the series *visible music* (II: *nostalgie.* solo for conductor, 1962); *mo-no, musik zum lesen* (1968–69); *Missa: Dahlemer Messe* (4 soli, 2 choruses, orchestra, organ, 1984–87); *Zeichen-Sprache* (music theater, 1989); *Chili "Music and Pictures on Kleist"* (3 narrators, 4 singers, instruments, 1989–91); educational pieces.

Schneider, (Abraham) Alexander (b. Vilnius, 21 Oct. 1908; d. New York, 2 Feb. 1993). Violinist. Studied in Frankfurt; worked as a violinist there and at Saarbrücken and Hamburg. Joined the Budapest Quartet, 1932–44 and 1955–67. Settled in the U.S., 1938, playing chamber music, organizing concert series, and conducting. Taught at the Univ. of Washington and Royal Conservatory in Toronto.

Schneider, (Johann Christian) Friedrich (b. Alt-Waltersdorf, near Zittau, 3 Jan. 1786; d. Dessau, 23 Nov. 1853). Composer and conductor. Studied with his father, Johann Gottlob (1753–1840), and at the Univ. of Leipzig. Organist at St. Thomas's Church, Leipzig, from 1812; later Hofkapellmeister at Dessau. May have premiered Beethoven's Piano Concerto no. 5 (Leipzig, 1811). Composed operas, Masses, oratorios, cantatas, symphonies, piano concertos, sonatas, songs, piano works.

Schnell [Ger.]. Fast.

Schneller [Ger.]. An 18th-century ornament involving alternation of the written note with the note immediately above it, to be performed as a short, rapid trill beginning on the beat; sometimes also termed an inverted mordent. The *Schneller* was not one of the French *agréments,* having been introduced after 1750 by C. P. E. Bach, who always indicated it by two small grace notes [Ex. 1]. Later composers often designated the *Schneller* with a short wavy line [Ex. 2], which originally indicated a somewhat different ornament called a *Pralltriller.* This is a rapid trill of four notes, beginning with the upper auxiliary, as was

customary with trills in that period. This trill was used only on the lower note of a descending second and tied to the preceding note, sometimes giving the erroneous impression that the *Pralltriller* begins with the main note. The *Schneller,* on the other hand, can occur only on a detached note, that is, the upper note of a descending second, so that the position of the sign [Ex. 2] usually indicates whether a *Schneller* [Ex. 3] or a *Pralltriller* [Ex. 4] is meant.

After 1800, the *Pralltriller* dropped out of use; hence, the sign [Ex. 2] always indicates the *Schneller.* Simultaneously, however, the name *Schneller* dropped out of use and the ornament illustrated in Ex. 3 became known as a *Pralltriller,* the current German term for the *Schneller.* The former restriction regarding its position on the first note of a descending second has, of course, been long abandoned, and the *Schneller* is frequently found in connection with skips. About 1830, the *Schneller* began to be performed before the main note, and today this is generally considered the proper manner of execution.

Schnittke [Shnitke], **Alfred (Garrievich)** (b. Engels, near Saratov, Russia, 24 Nov. 1934; d. Hamburg, 3 Aug. 1998). Composer and theorist. Studied at the Moscow Conservatory; taught there, 1962–72. In 1960s, was among the first Soviets to experiment with serial and other formerly forbidden techniques; later developed "polystylistics," a synthesis of historical styles. Taught at Hamburg Conservatory from 1989. Works include ballets *(Peer Gynt,* 1986); *Yellow Sound,* after Kandinsky (1973–74); operas *(Life with an Idiot,* 1992; *Gesualdo,* 1993–94; *Historia von D. Johann Fausten,* 1995); symphonies, concertos, and other orchestral music; works for soloists and chorus; string quartets, sonatas, and other chamber and piano music; much film music.

Schnorr von Carolsfeld, Ludwig (b. Munich, 2 July 1836; d. Dresden, 21 July 1865). Tenor. Studied at Leipzig. Debut, Karlsruhe, 1855. Leading tenor at Dresden from 1860. Known especially for his performances of Tannhäuser and Lohengrin; also sang lieder and oratorios. With his wife, Malvina Garrigues, sang the premiere of *Tristan und Isolde* (1865).

Schobert, Johann [Jean] (b. Silesia?, ca. 1735; d. Paris, 28 Aug. 1767). Composer. Settled in in Paris by 1760 or 1761. During the 1760s, had a significant influence on the young Mozart, who imitated his sonatas and drew on material from them in his earliest piano concerto. Works include keyboard sonatas, some with accompanying violins and horns; keyboard concertos; a comic opera.

Schoeck, Othmar (b. Brunnen, 1 Sept. 1886; d. Zurich, 8 Mar. 1957). Composer, conductor, and pianist. Studied at the Zurich Conservatory and in Leipzig with Reger. Conducted various choruses in Zurich, 1909–17; led the orchestra at St. Gall until 1944. Composed nearly 400 songs, including the cycles *Das Wandsbecker Liederbuch* (1936) and *Das holde Bescheiden* (ca. 1950). Other works include 5 operas (*Penthesilea*, 1924–25); a few orchestral works; string quartets and other chamber and piano music; choral works.

Schoenberg, Arnold (b. Vienna, 2 Sept. 1874; d. Los Angeles, 13 July 1951). Composer and theorist. Pupil of Zemlinsky. Associate of R. Strauss, Mahler, and Kandinsky (after a 1910 exhibition of Schoenberg's paintings). In 1902, taught at the Stern Conservatory, Berlin; 1903, returned to Vienna, where his pupils included Berg, Webern, and Wellesz. In 1910, taught at the Vienna Academy; then once again at the Stern Conservatory. With his students founded the Society for Private Musical Performances (1919–21). Taught at the Prussian Academy of Arts, Berlin, succeeding Busoni, 1925–33. In 1933, settled in the U.S. Taught at the Univ. of Southern California, at UCLA until 1944 (Kim and Cage were among his students), then briefly at the Univ. of Chicago. Early in his career Schoenberg composed within the German Romantic tradition influenced by both Brahms and Wagner, but by 1907 was ready to abandon tonality. He developed the twelve-tone method and first employed it between 1920 and 1923. Works: stage works (*Erwartung; Die *glückliche Hand; Von heute auf morgen*, 1928–29; *Moses und Aron*); orchestral music including *Pelleas und Melisande*, Chamber Symphony nos. 1 and 2 (1906–16), *Five Orchestral Pieces* (1909), Variations (1926–28); concertos; chamber music including *Verklärte Nacht*, 4 string quartets (1905–36), Serenade (8 instruments, 1920–23), Phantasy (violin and piano, 1949); piano and organ music; *Gurrelieder, *Kol Nidre, A Survivor from Warsaw* (narrator, male voices, orchestra, 1947), and other choral music; *Pierrot lunaire; Das Buch der hängenden Garten* (1909), *Ode to Napoleon Bonaparte*, and other songs with piano or instruments; canons and arrangements. Writings include *Style and Idea* (London, 1950); *Harmonielehre* (Vienna, 1911); *Structural Functions of Harmony* (completed 1948; New York, 1954).

Schola (cantorum) [Lat., school of singers]. (1) The body of singers of the papal court in Rome, founded perhaps as early as the papacy of St. Gregory (590–604). It was dissolved in the late 14th century and its functions taken over by the papal chapel. (2) A choir that performs Gregorian chant. (3) An institution founded in Paris in 1894 by Vincent d'Indy, Alexandre Guilmant, and Charles Bordes, at first dedicated to instruction in church music, especially Gregorian chant, but subsequently concerned with early music generally and with thorough training in counterpoint.

Schöne Müllerin, Die [Ger., The Fair Maid of the Mill]. A cycle of 20 songs by Schubert, op. 25, D. 795 (1823), setting poems by Wilhelm Müller.

Schöpfung, Die [Ger.]. See *Creation, The.*

Schöpfungsmesse [Ger.]. See *Creation* Mass.

Schorr, Friedrich (b. Nagyvárad, Hungary, 2 Sept. 1888; d. Farmington, Conn., 14 Aug. 1953). Baritone. Studied in Brno. Sang at Graz (1912–16), Prague (1916–18), Cologne (1918–23), the Berlin State Opera (1923–31), Bayreuth (1925–31), Covent Garden (1925–33), and the Metropolitan (1924–43). Taught at the Univ. of Hartford. Roles included Wagner's Wotan, Hans Sachs, and the Dutchman, Beethoven's Pizarro, and Strauss's Orestes.

Schottisch [Ger.]. A round dance of the 19th century in the nature of a slow polka and not the same as the *écossaise*. In England it was termed the German polka.

Schreker, Franz (b. Monaco, 23 Mar. 1878; d. Berlin, 21 Mar. 1934). Composer and conductor. Studied at the Vienna Conservatory. From 1912 to 1920, teacher at the Music Academy and founder-conductor of the Philharmonic Choir, which premiered Schoenberg's *Gurrelieder*. Head of the Berlin Hochschule für Musik 1920–32; then taught briefly at the Prussian Academy of Arts. Worked with bitonality and polytonality. Works include 9 operas (*Der ferne Klang*, 1901–12; *Der Schatzgräber*, 1920) and other stage music; orchestral music; choral music; a few chamber and piano works; and songs.

Schrittmässig [Ger.]. Measured; *andante.*

Schröder-Devrient, Wilhelmine (b. Hamburg, 6 Dec. 1804; d. Coburg, 26 Jan. 1860). Soprano. Debut, Vienna, 1821. Appeared at Dresden (1823–47), Paris (1830–32), London (1832, 1833, 1837). Created 3 Wagner roles: Adriano (*Rienzi*, 1842), Senta (*Der fliegende Holländer*, 1843), and Venus (*Tannhäuser*, 1845). Schumann dedicated "Ich grolle nicht" (1840) to her. Roles included Donna Anna, Norma, Romeo, and Rossini's Desdemona.

Schröter, Corona Elisabeth Wilhelmine (b. Gruben, 14 Jan. 1751; d. Ilmenau, 23 Aug. 1802). Singer and composer. Pupil of J. A. Hiller; appeared in his Grand Concerts in Leipzig from 1765. Served at the court of Duchess Anna Amalia in Weimar, 1776–88; there created leading roles in Goethe's early dramas. Composed lieder, including the first setting of Goethe's "Der Erlkönig" (1786).

Schubart, Christian Friedrich Daniel (b. Obersontheim, Swabia, 24 Mar. 1739; d. Stuttgart, 10 Oct. 1791). Composer. Organist and court musician in Ludwigsburg, 1769–73. His political writings, published in his periodical, *Deutsche Chronik,* led to imprisonment, 1777–87. From 1787, was court and theater poet in Stuttgart. Wrote many lieder, most to his own texts. Schubert set his poems "Die Forelle" and "An mein Klavier."

Schubert, Franz (b. Dresden, 22 July 1808; d. there, 12 Apr. 1878). Violinist and composer. Pupil of C. P. Lafont. Friend of Chopin. Joined the Royal Orchestra at Dresden, 1823; leader from 1861. Compositions include works for violin and piano.

Schubert, Franz Peter (b. Vienna, 31 Jan. 1797; d. there 19 Nov. 1828). Composer. Received early instruction from his father, Franz Theodor Florian, and his brother Ignaz. Sang in the imperial chapel choir and studied at the Stadtkonvikt school from 1808, playing in the orchestra and becoming a pupil of Salieri. Taught elementary pupils at his father's school, 1814–16. Music teacher to the Esterházy family in the summers of 1818 and 1824. Moved to Wieden, 1825. Presented a concert of his works in Vienna in March 1828; continued to compose until shortly before his death, apparently from syphilis.

Stage works include *Die Zwillingsbrüder* (*Singspiel,* Vienna, 1820); the operas *Alfonso und Estrella* (1822; Weimar, 1854) and *Fierabras* (after Calderón, 1823; Karlsruhe, 1897); the melodrama *Die Zauberharfe* (Vienna, 1820); incidental music to *Rosamunde.* Symphonic music includes 10 symphonies (no. 8, the *"Unfinished";* no. 9, the "Great," in C major, 1828); 7 overtures. Choral works include 6 Latin Masses, a German Mass, and other sacred and secular works. Chamber music includes 15 string quartets (*Der *Tod und das Mädchen);* string trio in B♭ major, 1817; the *"Trout" Quintet; octet in F major for winds and strings, D. 803, 1824; piano trios in B♭ major, D. 898, and E♭ major, D. 929, both 1827; quintet in C major for 2 violins, viola, 2 cellos, 1828; works for violin and piano, including 3 sonatinas (1816), sonata in A major (1817), *Rondo brillant* in B minor (1826), *Phantasie* in C major (1827); sonata in A minor for arpeggione and piano, 1824. Piano

works include 22 sonatas; **Wanderer-fantasie;* minuets, waltzes, **Ländler,* *Écossaises,* *Moments musicaux,* *Impromptus,* and other short pieces; sonatas in B♭ major (1818) and C major ("Grand Duo," 1824), marches, and other pieces for piano four-hands. Vocal music includes *Der Hirt auf dem Felsen* (voice, piano, clarinet or cello, 1828); over 600 songs, including the cycles *Die *schöne Müllerin, Die *Winterreise,* and *Schwanengesang,* and the individual songs "Erlkönig" (1814), "Gretchen am Spinnrade" (1814), "Der Wanderer" (1816), "Die Forelle" (1817), "Der Tod und das Mädchen" (1817).

Schübler Chorales. Popular name for a collection of six chorale preludes for organ by Bach, BWV 645–50, published ca. 1748–49 by Johann Georg Schübler. Five of the chorale preludes are arrangements of arias from Bach's cantatas.

Schuller, Gunther (b. New York, 22 Nov. 1925). Composer, conductor, author, educator. Studied at Manhattan School of Music. Played horn in the Cincinnati Orchestra, 1943; in the Metropolitan Opera Orchestra, 1945–59; also in jazz ensembles and on recordings with Miles Davis, John Lewis, and others. From 1963 taught at the Berkshire Music Center; its director, 1974–84. Taught at Yale, 1964–67. President of the New England Conservatory, 1967–77. Has worked with twelve-tone techniques and elements of jazz; coined the term "Third Stream" to refer to such efforts at combining jazz and "classical" music. Works include the opera *The *Visitation* (Hamburg, 1966); orchestral music (*Seven Studies on Themes of Paul Klee,* 1957; *Spectra,* 1958; Concertino for Jazz Quartet and Orchestra, 1959; *Variants for Jazz Quartet and Orchestra,* 1960; *American Triptych,* 1965; *Museum Piece,* 1970, with Renaissance instruments; *Deai [Encounters],* 3 orchestras and 8 voices, 1978; *Of Reminiscences and Reflections,* Pulitzer Prize, 1994); chamber works (*Twelve by Eleven,* 1955, for the Modern Jazz Quartet; *Music for Brass Quintet,* 1961); band pieces (*Eine kleine Posaunenmusik,* with trombone, 1980; *In Praise of Winds—Symphony,* 1981). Has published books on jazz and on horn technique.

Schulz [Schultz], Johann Abraham Peter (b. Lüneburg, 31 Mar. 1747; d. Schwedt an der Oder, 10 June 1800). Composer. Pupil of Kirnberger. Musical director to the Berlin French theater from 1776. Hofkapellmeister in Copenhagen, 1787–95. Composed lieder (incl. the collections *Gesänge am Clavier,* 1779; *Lieder im Volkston,* 1782); stage works (*Clarissa,* Berlin, 1775); oratorios; cantatas; instrumental pieces. Writings include music articles for J. G. Sulzer's *Allgemeine Theorie der schönen Künste* and (with Kirnberger) *Die wahren Grundsätze zum Gebrauche der Harmonie* (1773).

Schuman, William (Howard) (b. New York, 4 Aug. 1910; d. New York, 16 Feb. 1992). Composer, educator, administrator. Pupil of Haubiel and R. Harris. Taught at Sarah Lawrence College, 1935–45. From 1945 to 1962, president of the Juilliard School, where he created a dance division and established the Juilliard String Quartet. President of Lincoln Center 1962–68, bringing the Juilliard School, the New York City Ballet, and the New York City Opera there. Works include the operas *The Mighty Casey* (Hartford, Conn., 1953) and *A Question of Taste* (1981); ballets, including *Night Journey* (1947) and *Judith* (1949), both for Martha Graham; 10 symphonies (no. 9, *Le Fosse Ardeatine,* 1968) and other orchestral works (*New England Triptych,* 1956; *In Praise of Shahn,* 1969); string quartets and other chamber music; choral music, including *A Free Song,* cantata on texts by Whitman (1942; Pulitzer Prize, 1943), *Carols of Death* (1958), *The Young Dead Soldiers* (1975), and *On Freedom's Ground* (1985).

Schumann [née Wieck], **Clara (Josephine)** (b. Leipzig, 13 Sept. 1819; d. Frankfurt am Main, 20 May 1896). Pianist, composer. Beginning in 1830, toured widely in Europe as a concert pianist. Continued to perform after she married Robert Schumann in 1840, becoming a major factor in his growing reputation as a composer. Taught at the Hoch Conservatory, Frankfurt, 1878–92. Maintained a close friendship with Brahms. Composed piano pieces, songs, a Concerto, and Piano Trio (1846).

Schumann, Elisabeth (b. Meeresburg, 13 June 1888; d. New York, 23 Apr. 1952). Soprano. Studied in Dresden, Berlin, and Hamburg. Debut, Hamburg, 1909. Sang there until 1919; at the Vienna Opera, 1919–37. Appeared at the Metropolitan Opera (1914–15), Salzburg (1922–35), and Covent Garden (1924–31); toured the U.S. with R. Strauss, 1921. Moved to the U.S., 1938.

Schumann, Robert Alexander (b. Zwickau, 8 June 1810; d. Endenich, near Bonn, 29 July 1856). Composer. Pupil of Friedrich Wieck (whose daughter, Clara, he married in 1840) and Dorn. Associate of Heine, Chopin, Moscheles, and Mendelssohn; close associate of Brahms. An injury to his right hand ended his career as a pianist in 1832. In 1834, launched the journal, *Neue Zeitschrift für Musik;* its editor until 1844. Appointed professor at the new Leipzig Conservatory in 1843; soon thereafter moved his family to Dresden, where he conducted a choral society. After 1850, town music director in Düsseldorf. In 1854 was placed in a sanatorium for the rest of his life.

Works include *Genoveva* (opera, 1847–49); incidental music to Byron's *Manfred;* 4 symphonies (no. 1, *Spring;* no. 3, *Rhenish*); overtures; works

for piano and orchestra, including concerto in A minor (1841–45), *Konzertstück* (1849), Introduction and Allegro (1853); cello concerto in A minor (1850); *Fantasia* for violin and orchestra (1853) and violin concerto in D minor (1853); choral works; chamber music, including 3 string quartets, 3 piano trios, *Fantasiestücke* for piano trio, a piano quartet and a piano quintet, 3 violin sonatas. Piano works include 3 sonatas; *Abegg Variations;* *Papillons;* *Davidsbündlertänze;* *Carnaval;* *Fantasiestücke* (1837, 1851); *Études symphoniques;* *Kinderszenen;* *Kreisleriana;* *Humoreske;* *Novelletten* (1838); *Faschingsschwank aus Wien: Fantasiebilder* (1839); *Album für die Jugend* (1848); pieces for piano four-hands. Numerous songs, including the cycles *Frauenliebe und Leben* and *Dichterliebe.*

Schusterfleck [Ger., cobbler's patch]. *Rosalia.*

Schütteln [Ger.]. To shake.

Schütz, Heinrich [Henrich] [Sagittarius, Henricus] (b. Köstritz [now Bad Köstritz], near Gera, bapt. 9 Oct. 1585; d. Dresden, 6 Nov. 1672). Composer. Choirboy at the court of Landgrave Moritz of Hessen-Kassel from 1599; second organist there, 1613. Pupil of G. Gabrieli. From 1614 served the Elector Johann Georg I of Saxony at Dresden; named Kapellmeister, 1619. Served intermittently until 1656. Visited Italy in 1628, studying with Monteverdi. Kapellmeister to King Christian IV of Denmark, 1633–35 and 1642–44; 1639–41, to Georg of Calenberg in Hildesheim. 1644–45, active at the Wolfenbüttel court. Pupils included C. Bernhard, J. Theile, and M. Weckmann. Composed the first German opera, now lost. Other works include *Psalmen Davids* (1619); *Symphoniae sacrae* (3 parts, published 1629, 1647, 1650); sacred works in Latin and German; *Musikalische Exequien* (1636); Easter and *Christmas oratorios; Passions according to Matthew, Luke, and John (1666); Die Sieben Wörte Christi am Kreuz;* Italian madrigals.

Schwach [Ger.]. Weak, soft; *schwächer,* weaker, softer.

Schwanda the Bagpiper. See *Švanda Dudák.*

Schwanengesang [Ger., Swan Song]. A collection (not properly a cycle) of Schubert's last songs, D. 957 (1828), setting seven poems by Ludwig Rellstab, six by Heinrich Heine, and one by Johann Gabriel Seidl, published in Vienna by Tobias Haslinger, who chose the title.

Schwantner, Joseph (b. Chicago, 22 Mar. 1943). Composer. Pupil of A. Donato and A. Stout. Teacher at Eastman from 1970. Has used twelve-tone techniques. Works include *Through Interior Worlds* (ballet, 1992); orchestral music (*Aftertones of Infinity,*

1978, Pulitzer Prize, 1979; *Freelight,* 1989; *A Play of Shadows,* with solo flute, 1990; *Evening Land Symphony,* with soprano, 1995); *And the Mountains Rising Nowhere* (band, 1977); chamber works (*In Aeternum,* 1973); songs, many with instrumental accompaniment, including *Wild Angels of the Open Hills* (1974) and *Sparrows* (1979).

Schwärmer [Ger.]. *Bombo (3) [see also Tremolo].

Schwarz, Gerard (b. Weehawken, N.J., 19 Aug. 1947). Trumpeter and conductor. Studied at Juilliard. Played with the American Brass Quintet, 1965–73; with the New York Philharmonic, 1973–77. Director of the Los Angeles Chamber Orchestra, 1978–86; of the Mostly Mozart Festival from 1984; of the Seattle Symphony from 1985. Has commissioned many trumpet works, and has recorded widely.

Schwarzkopf, Elisabeth (b. Jarotschin, Poland, 9 Dec. 1915). Soprano. Studied in Berlin, training initially as an alto. Debut, Berlin, 1938. Sang with the Vienna Staatsoper, 1942 and 1946; at Covent Garden, 1947–53; with the San Francisco Opera, 1955–64. Appeared at Salzburg (1947–64) and La Scala (1948–63). Created Anne Trulove in Stravinsky's *The Rake's Progress* (1951). Roles included the Marschallin *(Rosenkavalier).*

Schweigen [Ger.]. To be silent.

Schweitzer, Anton (b. Coburg, bapt. 6 June 1735; d. Gotha, 23 Nov. 1787). Composer. Studied in Bayreuth and Italy. From 1769, Kapellmeister to the Seyler theater company, settling in Weimar, 1771. Directed the ducal chapel in Gotha from 1778. Composed dramatic works, including the first German melodrama, *Pygmalion* (text by Rousseau, 1772; now lost); *Die Dorfgala* (singspiel, 1772); *Alkeste* (opera, 1773); ballets.

Schweller, Schwellkasten [Ger.]. The organ *swell box.

Schwellwerk [Ger.]. The *swell division of an organ.

Schwer [Ger.]. Heavy, ponderous; difficult; grave.

Schwindend [Ger.]. Dying away, becoming softer.

Schwungvoll [Ger.]. Spirited, energetic.

Sciolto [It.]. Free, unconstrained.

Scordatura [It., from *scordare,* to mistune]. Unconventional tuning of stringed instruments, particularly lutes and violins, used to facilitate or make available otherwise difficult or impossible pitch combinations, alter the characteristic timbre of the instrument to increase brilliance, reinforce certain sonorities or tonalities by making them available on open strings, imitate other instruments, etc. Scordatura appeared early in the 16th century and became common in the 17th, but much less so after about 1750.

Violin scordatura occurs often in 17th-century violin music. The German violin repertory of the 17th century, particularly the works of Heinrich Ignaz Franz von Biber, contains its most thorough exploration. Scordatura is far less prevalent in 18th-century German music; two famous examples are Bach's Fifth Suite for unaccompanied cello in C minor BWV 1011, in which the highest string is lowered from a to g, and Mozart's *Sinfonia concertante* K. 364 (320d), in which all the strings of the solo viola are tuned a semitone sharp. It is more common in 18th-century French and Italian music. Examples from the 19th and 20th centuries include works by Paganini, Schumann, and Bartók.

Score. (1) [Fr. *partition;* Ger. *Partitur;* It., Sp. *partitura*]. The notation of a work, especially one for ensemble, presented in such a way that simultaneous moments in all voices or parts are aligned vertically. In a full score, each voice or part is notated on its own staff (though two parts for instruments of the same kind, e.g., two flutes or two oboes, may be placed on a single staff). In a short or condensed score, related parts (e.g., woodwinds, brass) may be combined on a single staff. A piano-vocal score (usually of an opera, oratorio, or similar work) presents vocal parts on individual staves, with orchestral parts reduced to two staves and arranged so as to be performable on the piano. A single set of all of the necessary staves running across a page is termed a system and is linked at the left and right margins by a continuous bar line. Otherwise, bar lines, while drawn through each individual staff, may run between the staves only of related instruments. There may be several systems on a page if space permits; for ease of reading, they may be separated at the left margin by a pair of bold diagonal strokes.

Although practice has varied somewhat even since the mid-19th century, the normal arrangement of parts from top to bottom in an orchestral full score places choirs of related instruments together and, within these groups, arranges individual instruments from highest down to lowest in register.

Notation in score format was employed in the sources for the polyphonic repertories of *Notre Dame and *St. Martial, especially for the *conductus. By the middle of the 13th century and the rise to prominence of the *motet, however, it was abandoned for vocal music except in England, where it survived into the 15th century. *Choirbook format in the case of larger manuscripts, remained common for polyphonic music through the 16th century. *Partbooks were the other principal format for ensemble music of the 16th century. Score format was employed for keyboard music as early as the 14th century and was widespread in printed sources for keyboard music of the early 16th century [see also *Intavolatura*, Tablature]. In the later 16th and the 17th century, the term *partitura* could refer to keyboard scores in which each part of a polyphonic complex was notated on a separate staff. Manuscript scores of vocal music do not reappear until the second half of the 16th century, but steadily increase in number in this period. The first independent publications of vocal music in score date from 1577 and include madrigals by Cipriano de Rore. By the 17th century, score format was the norm for both vocal and instrumental music.

(2) [v.] To create a score, often from a more abbreviated form of notation; to orchestrate [see Orchestration]; to arrange [see Arrangement].

(3) A work such as would normally be notated in score.

Scoring. *Orchestration; the combination of instruments employed in a work or the character of their use.

Scorrendo, scorrevole [It.]. Flowing.

Scotch snap. *Lombard rhythm.

Scotch (Scottish) Symphony. Popular name for Mendelssohn's Symphony no. 3 in A minor op. 56 (begun in 1830, completed in 1841–42), inspired by a visit to Scotland in 1829.

Scott, Cyril (Meir) (b. Oxton, Cheshire, 27 Sept. 1879; d. Eastbourne, 31 Dec. 1970). Composer. Pupil of Humperdinck and Knorr. Settled in Liverpool, 1898. Works include numerous descriptive piano works and songs; 3 operas (*Maureen O'Mara*, 1946); the oratorio *Hymn of Unity* (1947); 3 symphonies, concertos, and other orchestral music; chamber music (4 string quartets); 3 piano sonatas. Published poetry, plays, and writings on Eastern Indian philosophy and occultism.

Scott, James (Sylvester) (b. Neosho, Mo., 12 Feb. 1885; d. Kansas City, Kans., 30 Aug. 1938). Ragtime composer and pianist. Worked in a local music store, which published his first rags, "A Summer Breeze" and "The Fascinator," 1903. Other compositions include "Frog Legs Rag" (1906) and "Grace and Beauty" (1909). Moved to Kansas City, Kans., 1920.

Scotto, Renata (b. Savona, 24 Feb. 1934). Soprano. Studied in Milan; debut there, 1953. Understudied Callas during a La Scala tour in 1959. Debuts at Chicago, 1960; Covent Garden, 1962. Sang with the Metropolitan Opera, 1965–87. Made many recordings, chiefly of Italian opera.

Scraper. An instrument made by cutting notches in a stick, bone, gourd, piece of bamboo, etc., and scraping with a stick or metal rod. See also Cog rattle, *Güiro, Reco-reco.*

Scriabin, Alexander Nikolaevich (b. Moscow, 6 Jan. 1872; d. there, 27 Apr. 1915). Composer. Pupil of Taneyev, Arensky, and Safonov; associate of Belyayev. Toured widely as a concert pianist; known as a performer of his own music and that of Chopin. Taught at the Moscow Conservatory, 1898–1903. Lived in Switzerland and Brussels, 1904–9. Made use of the *mystic chord. Composed numerous piano works, including preludes, etudes, mazurkas, waltzes, impromptus, nocturnes, fantasies; 10 sonatas; *Poème satanique* (1903); *Vers la flame* (1914). Also composed orchestral works (symphonies, incl. no. 3, *Le divin poème*, 1902–4; *Le poème de l'extase*, 1905–8; *Prometheus*); a few vocal and chamber pieces.

Scribe, (Augustin) Eugène (b. Paris, 24 Dec. 1791; d. there, 20 Feb. 1861). Librettist. Works include libretti for operas by Auber (38 works), Bellini (incl. *La sonnambula*, 1831), Boildieu (*La dame blanche*, 1825), Cherubini, Donizetti (5, incl. *L'elisir d'amore*, 1832), Gounod, Halévy (6, incl. *La Juive*, 1835), Meyerbeer (5, incl. *Les Hugenots*, 1836; *L'Africaine*, 1865), Offenbach, Rossini (*Le Comte Ory*, 1828), Suppé, and Verdi (*Les vêpres siciliennes*, 1855).

Scroll. The coiled ornamental carving above the pegbox of the violin and related instruments.

Scruggs, Earl (Eugene) (b. Flint Hill, N.C., 6 Jan. 1924). Bluegrass and country banjo player, songwriter, and singer. Joined Bill Monroe's Bluegrass Boys, 1945. In 1948, formed the Foggy Mountain Boys with guitarist Lester Flatt; recordings include "Foggy Mountain Breakdown" (1949) and "The Ballad of Jed Clampett" (1962). After 1969 performed country and rock with his sons. Credited with introducing the banjo technique characteristic of bluegrass music.

Scucito [It.]. Detached, *non legato.*

Sculthorpe, Peter (Joshua) (b. Launceston, Tasmania, 29 Apr. 1929). Composer. Pupil of Wellesz and Rubbra. Teacher at the Univ. of Sydney from 1963. Has worked with elements of Australian aboriginal culture and the music of eastern Asia. Works include *Rites of Passage*, opera (1972–74); radio scores; orchestral music (*Sun Music I-IV*, 1965–67; *Child of Australia*, with soprano, narrator, chorus, 1988); and chamber music (string quartets; *Irkanda I-III*, 1955–61; *Nourlangie*, guitar, percussion, strings, 1989; *Sun Song*, percussion, 1989).

Sdrucciolando [It.]. In harp playing, *glissando.

Sea Symphony, A. Vaughan Williams's Symphony no. 1, composed in 1903–9 (final revisions, 1923), for soloists, chorus, and orchestra, based on texts from Walt Whitman's *Leaves of Grass*.

Searle, Humphrey (b. Oxford, 26 Aug. 1915; d. London, May 12, 1982). Composer. Pupil of Jacob, Ireland, R. O. Morris, and Webern. Producer at the BBC from 1938. Teacher at the Royal College of Music from 1965. Made use of serial techniques. Works include 3 operas (*Hamlet*, 1965–68); 5 symphonies, concertos, and other orchestral music; chamber music; and vocal music (*The Shadow of Cain*, speakers, male chorus, orchestra, 1951; *Ophelia*, voice, piano, 1969; *Dr. Faustus,* soloists, chorus, orchestra, 1977).

Seasons, The. An oratorio for soloists, chorus, and orchestra by Haydn, Hob. XXI:3 (1799–1801), with a German libretto (*Die Jahreszeiten*) by Gottfried van Swieten, based on an English poem by James Thomson translated by Barthold Heinrich Brockes. Its four parts portray spring, summer, fall, and winter. See also *Four Seasons, The.*

Sec [Fr.]. Dry, staccato.

Secco recitative. See Recitative.

Sechszehntel, Sechszehntelnote, Sechszehntel-pause [Ger.]. See Note.

Sechter, Simon (b. Friedberg, Bohemia, 11 Oct. 1788; d. Vienna, 10 Sept. 1867). Teacher, theorist. Pupil of Kozeluch. Worked as a music teacher in Vienna from 1804. Court organist there from 1825. Professor, Vienna Conservatory, 1851–67 (succeeded by his pupil Bruckner). Writings include 3 volumes of *Die Grundsätze der musikalischen Komposition* (1853–54). His many compositions include operas, oratorios, Masses and other sacred works, chamber music, piano and organ works.

Second. See Interval, Scale degrees.

Seconda prattica [It.]. See *Prima prattica, seconda prattica.*

Seconda volta [It.]. See *Prima volta, seconda volta.*

Secondary dominant. See Dominant, Tonicization.

Secunda, Sholom (b. Alexandria, Russia, 4 Sept. (n.s.) 1894; d. New York, 13 June 1974). Composer. Moved to the U.S. in 1907; studied at Columbia Univ. and the Institute of Musical Art. Music critic for the Yiddish-language daily *Vorwärts.* Composed Yiddish-language operettas (*I Would If I Could,* 1933, incl. "Bei mir bist du schoen"); oratorios (*Yizkor, In Memory of the Six Million,* 1967); orchestral and chamber works; and much Jewish liturgical music.

Seefried, Irmgard (b. Köngetried, 9 Oct. 1919; d. Vienna, 24 Nov. 1988). Soprano. Debut, Aachen,

1940. Joined the Vienna Opera, 1943. Sang at the Metropolitan Opera (1953–54), La Scala (from 1949), and Covent Garden (from 1948). Roles ranged from Mozart to Berg. Also gave frequent recitals.

Seeger, Ruth Crawford. See Crawford, Ruth.

Seelenamt [Ger.]. *Requiem Mass.

Seelenvoll [Ger.]. Soulful.

Segni, Julio [Julio da Modena, Biondin] (b. Modena, 1498; d. Rome, 23 July 1561). Organist and composer. Pupil of G. Fogliano. Organist at St. Mark's, Venice, 1530–33. Thereafter served the Cardinal of Santa Fiore in Rome. Composed ricercars for lute and for keyboard.

Segno [It.]. A sign (𝄋) used to mark the beginning or end of a repeated section of a work. If the former, the end of the section bears the instruction *dal segno* (from the sign, often abbreviated *D.S.*); if the latter, the beginning of the section bears the instruction *al segno* (to the sign), *sin' al segno* (until the sign), or *fin' al segno* (end at the sign). See also *Da capo.*

Segovia, Andrés (b. Linares, 21 Feb. 1893; d. Madrid, 2 June 1987). Guitarist. Mainly self-taught. Debut, Granada, 1909. From the mid-1920s, toured throughout Europe; U.S. debut, 1928. Taught at Santiago de Compostela, Siena, Berkeley, and Los Angeles, with John Williams, Christopher Parkening, and Oscar Ghiglia among his pupils. Commissioned works by Falla, Roussel, Villa-Lobos, and others, and arranged much music for guitar. Recorded extensively.

Segue [It., follows]. (1) An indication that the next section of a work is to follow immediately without interruption, e.g., *segue l'aria, segue la coda.* (2) An instruction to continue a manner of execution that is at first written out in full, but thereafter abbreviated, e.g., a pattern of broken chords [for abbreviations of this type, see Notation].

Seguidilla [Sp.]. (1) A Spanish verse form consisting of one or more strophes of four or seven lines each, as follows: 7.5.7.5 or 7.5.7.5.5.7.5, with assonance within the pair(s) of five-syllable lines. Originally a form of popular poetry, it was taken up increasingly by poets in the later 16th century. Musical settings occur from around 1600 through the *zarzuelas of the 19th and 20th centuries. (2) [pl. *seguidillas*] A couple dance, widely distributed in Spain, done to the singing of a text of the type described under (1), accompanied by guitar, and in a moderately fast triple meter. (3) [*siguiriya, seguidilla gitana*] One of the principal types of *flamenco music, also termed *playera*, with a text (perhaps derived from (1) above) often of four lines, 7.5.11.5, with assonance between lines 2 and 4. The guitar accompaniment freely alternates measures of 6/8 and 3/4 under the flexible rhythm of the vocal part.

Sehnsucht [Ger.]. Longing; *Sehnsuchtvoll,* filled with longing.

Sehr [Ger.]. Very.

Seiber, Mátyás (György) (b. Budapest, 4 May 1905; d. Kruger National Park, South Africa, 24 Sept. 1960). Composer. Pupil of Kodály. Taught at the Hoch Conservatory, Frankfurt, 1928–33. Settled in England, 1935. Made use of jazz and folk elements. Composed operas, radio and film scores, and other dramatic music; orchestral works (*Fantasia Concertante,* violin, strings, 1943–44); vocal music (*Ulysses,* cantata, 1946–47; *Three Fragments,* speaker, chorus, ensemble, 1957); chamber music (3 string quartets).

Seidl, Anton (b. Pest, 7 May 1850; d. New York, 28 Mar. 1898). Conductor. Studied at the Leipzig Conservatory. Associate of Wagner. Conducted the Metropolitan Opera from 1885; the New York Philharmonic from 1891. Conducted the premiere of Dvorák's New World Symphony (1893); American premieres of *Die Meistersinger* (1886), *Tristan und Isolde* (1886), and *Siegfried* (1887).

Seises [Sp.]. From the 16th through the 19th century in the cathedrals of Seville and a few other cities of Spain and the New World, a group of six (*seis*) choirboys who sang polyphony and who, in Seville, danced in elaborate costumes, sometimes to specially composed music, on the feasts of Corpus Christi and the Immaculate Conception.

Seixas, (José António) Carlos de (b. Coimbra, 11 June 1704; d. Lisbon, 25 Aug. 1742). Composer. Organist at Coimbra Cathedral, 1718–20; at the royal chapel in Lisbon from 1720. Associate of D. Scarlatti. Composed numerous keyboard sonatas, employing a variety of styles and experimenting with motivic development; also choral works.

Selby, William (b. England, ca. 1738; d. Boston, 12 Dec. 1798). Composer and organist. Held organ posts in England before emigrating to America in 1771. Organist at King's Chapel, Boston, and Trinity Church in Newport, R.I. Compositions include sacred and secular choral works, keyboard pieces.

Selle, Thomas (b. Zörbig, near Bitterfeld, 23 Mar. 1599; d. Hamburg, 2 July 1663). Composer. Studied in Leipzig, perhaps with Calvisius. Kantor at the Johanneum in Hamburg (from 1641); civic director of church music in Hamburg. Wrote vocal music exclusively, including a Johannespassion (1641), sacred concertos, some secular pieces.

Semele. A dramatic oratorio by Handel (libretto based on a play by William Congreve), first performed in London in 1744. Setting: classical mythology.

Semi- [Lat.]. Half; for *semibiscroma, semibreve (semibrevis), semicroma, semifusa, semiminima, semiquaver,* see Note, Mensural notation; *semidiapente,* diminished fifth; *semiditonus,* minor third.

Semi-opera. In England in the late 17th century and the first years of the 18th, a dramatic work in which the principal characters employed only speech but in which there were elaborate musical scenes for lesser characters. The first such work was Thomas Betterton's version of Shakespeare's *The Tempest,* produced in 1674 with music by Pelham Humfrey, Matthew Locke, and others. The best-known examples are Purcell's *Dioclesian* (1690), *King Arthur* (1691), *The *Fairy Queen* (1692), and *The *Indian Queen* (1695).

Semiramide. Opera in two acts by Rossini (libretto by Gaetano Rossi, based on Voltaire's tragedy), produced in Venice in 1823. Setting: ancient Babylon.

Semitone. The smallest interval in use in the Western musical tradition. There are twelve such intervals to the octave, i.e., between two pitches with the same pitch name. The semitone is represented on the piano keyboard by the distance between any two immediately adjacent keys, whether white or black. See Interval.

Semplice [It.]. Simple, without ornament. For *recitativo semplice,* see Recitative.

Sempre [It.]. Always, continuously.

Senaillé [Senallié, Senaillié, Senallier, Senaillier], **Jean Baptiste** (b. Paris, 23 Nov. 1687; d. there, 15 Oct. 1730). Composer. Joined the Vingt-quatre Violons du Roi, 1713. Soloist at the Concert spirituel 1728–30. Composed 50 sonatas for violin and continuo (1710–27), combining Italian and French instrumental styles.

Sender, Ramon (b. Madrid, 29 Oct. 1934). Composer. Pupil of Carter and R. Erickson. With Subotnick, founded the San Francisco and Mills (College) Tape Music Centers. Works include *Thrones,* tape, colored lights (1963); *Desert Ambulance,* amplified accordion, tape (1964); chants for paraprofessional performers (after 1966); the choral work *I Have a Dream* (1984).

Senesino [Bernardi, Francesco] (b. Siena, ca. 1680; d. there?, by 27 Jan. 1759). Alto castrato. From 1707 to 1716, sang in Venice, Bologna, Genoa, and Naples, in operas by A. Scarlatti and others. Sang at Dresden, 1717–20; with the Royal Academy in London, 1720–28; with the second academy, 1730–33. Joined the rival Opera of the Nobility, 1733–36. Sang in Florence, 1737–39. Handel wrote 17 operatic roles for him.

Senfl [Sennfl, Sennfli], **Ludwig** (b. Basel?, ca. 1486; d. Munich, between 2 Dec. 1542 and 10 Aug. 1543). Composer. Court musician to Maximilian I from 1496. Isaac's amanuensis from at least 1507, succeeding him as *maestro di cappella,* 1517–19. *Maestro* to the Duke of Bavaria from 1523. Published the first German anthology of motets (1520); collaborated on other collections with Hofhaimer and Isaac. Works include 300 motets (2 commissioned by Martin Luther), 6 or 7 Masses, 8 Magnificats, 40 Latin classical odes, and nearly 300 lieder.

Sennet [perhaps fr. It. *sonata;* also senet, sennate, signate, synnet, cynet]. In the stage directions of Elizabethan plays, music played by trumpets or cornetts to signal the entrance or exit of a group of actors. See also Tuck, tucket.

Sensible [Fr.]. Leading tone.

Sentito [It.]. Felt, expressive.

Senza [It.]. Without; *s. tempo, s. misura,* without strict measure; for *s. sordini,* see Mute.

Septet [Fr. *septour;* Ger. *Septett;* It. *septetto;* Sp. *septeto*]. (1) A chamber composition for seven solo performers. (2) An ensemble of seven solo performers. Most compositions of this type employ mixed winds and strings, as does Beethoven's Septet op. 20; some include a piano.

Septuor [Fr.]. *Septet.

Septuplet. A group of seven notes of equal value to be played in the time normally occupied by four or six notes of the same value.

Sepulchrum play. A *liturgical drama set at the holy sepulchre.

Sequence. (1) The repetition of a phrase of melody (melodic sequence) and or a harmonic progression (harmonic sequence) at different pitch levels, the succession of pitch levels rising or falling by the same or similar intervals. In a melodic sequence (as distinct from *imitation), the repetition occurs within a single voice. A melody may be transposed exactly, retaining its precise interval content and thus probably effecting a change of key, or the sequence may

proceed diatonically, the melody retaining only its general contour and remaining in the same key. Many sequences mix the two procedures, and sequences are often employed to bring about modulations. In the case of a melodic sequence, the harmony may or may not remain the same in relationship to the melody. Sequences occur frequently in the music of Baroque composers such as Handel [see Ex.] and in the development sections of works in sonata form and similar modulatory passages of the Classical period. The sequential treatment of *leitmotifs is a prominent feature of the musico-dramatic technique of Wagner. See also *Rosalia.*

(2) [Lat. *sequentia*] In medieval music, one of the most important types of addition to the official liturgical chant of the Latin church [see also Trope]. It was usually sung in the Mass after the alleluia, to which it might be related melodically. The form was basically literary in origin. At first it consisted of a text added to the extended version of the *jubilus,* or alleluia melisma, which, in the Middle Ages, was sung after the alleluia verse. In medieval sources, the melodic expansion of the *jubilus* was often called a *sequentia.* The term *prosa* was applied to the added words, with reference to the prose style of the text, and the total production thus became *sequentia cum prosa,* i.e., melody with text. In modern times, however, both the terms sequence and prose have been applied somewhat misleadingly to the form as a whole, with sequence now being favored by most writers in English.

The sequence first appears in the course of the 9th century at approximately the same time as the trope. The sequence as a form, although its importance declined appreciably after the 13th century, survived until the 16th century and the Council of Trent, and a handful of sequences remain in the official liturgy of the Roman Catholic Church today. These include "Victimae paschali" (traditionally attributed to Wipo of Burgundy, d. 1050), which is still sung in the Mass for Easter Day, and the late medieval *"Veni sancte spiritus," *"Stabat mater dolorosa," and *"Dies irae."

Throughout the various stages of its history, the sequence had certain formal characteristics that were more or less constant, especially (1) the structural principle of paired repetition, according to which each unit of melody, whether single phrase or whole hymnlike stanza, was repeated with new text before the introduction of the next melodic unit; and (2) the

[ex-] al-   - ted

Sequence.

largely syllabic setting of the text. With the 12th century, the sequence reaches its final form, exemplified above all in the works of the Parisian monk Adam of St. Victor (d. 1192?). These late sequences, now completely disassociated from any specific alleluias, are quite hymnlike, with the paired versicles of the earlier form replaced by regular paired strophes of rhythmic and rhymed verse.

Serafin, Tullio (b. Rottanova di Cavarzere, near Venice, 1 Sept. 1878; d. Rome, 2 Feb. 1968). Conductor. Studied at the Milan Conservatory. Debut, Ferrara, 1900. Principal conductor at La Scala from 1909. Held posts at the Metropolitan Opera (1924–34); the Teatro reale, Rome (1934–43); the Chicago Opera (1956–58); and the Teatro dell'Opera, Rome (from 1962). Aided the careers of many singers, including Ponselle, Callas, and Sutherland.

Serebrier, José (b. Montevideo, 3 Dec. 1938). Composer, conductor. Pupil of Copland, Monteux, and Dorati. Associate conductor, American Symphony Orchestra, 1962–67; conductor, Cleveland Philharmonic, 1968–71. Founder (1984) and first artistic director, International Festival of the Americas. Works include Partita, orchestra (1963); Saxophone Quartet (1969); *Colores mágicos,* harp, chamber orchestra, and lights (1971); Symphony for percussion (1972).

Serenade. A vocal or instrumental work intended for performance in the evening and usually addressed to a lover, friend, or person of rank. In its most traditional form, an admirer sings beneath a lady's window, though part songs are also common.

The most important type of serenade during the 18th century was that for instruments. Such works were often commissioned for a specific occasion. Mozart's six Salzburg serenades are festive, large-scale pieces for orchestra, while his three Viennese serenades are for six to thirteen winds. Serenades for a small chamber ensemble were also common, however, especially in Vienna; scoring of this type is still found in Beethoven's Serenades op. 8 (for string trio) and op. 25 (for flute, violin, and viola).

The overall form of the 18th-century serenade is usually based on the standard three-movement (fast–slow–fast) succession of Classical instrumental music, to which are added marches (often as a processional or recessional), minuets (usually two or three), and often movements featuring one or more soloists. It should be noted that the terms *notturno and *cassation were used interchangeably with serenade by many composers of the 18th century. The serenade continued to be cultivated during the 19th century, examples including two by Brahms and the Dvořák and Tchaikovsky serenades for strings.

Serenata [It.]. (1) *Serenade. (2) In the Baroque period, a cantata composed to celebrate a special occasion such as the name-day of a prince or the arrival of an important visitor. Serenatas were often performed in the evening and outdoors, hence the name. They were usually longer and more elaborate than solo cantatas, with several characters, a plot of pastoral, mythological, or allegorical content, and impressive costumes and scenery but no stage action. Important composers of serenatas include Alessandro Stradella and Alessandro Scarlatti in Italy and Johann Joseph Fux and Antonio Caldara in Vienna.

Serial music. Music constructed according to permutations of a group of elements placed in a certain order or series. These elements may include pitches, durations, or virtually any other musical values. Strictly speaking, serial music encompasses *twelve-tone music as well as music employing other types of pitch series, i.e., those containing fewer than twelve pitches. Normally, however, the term is reserved for music that extends classical Schoenbergian twelve-tone pitch techniques and, especially, applies serial control to other musical elements, such as duration. Such music, mainly developed after World War II, is often distinguished from twelve-tone serialism as "integral" or "total" serialism.

The leading figures in the early development of integral serialism were Stockhausen and Boulez in Europe and Babbitt in the U.S. The earliest composition to control both pitch and nonpitch components through serial means was Babbitt's *Three Compositions for Piano,* written in 1947. In this and others of Babbitt's works of this period, the rhythmic and pitch series are essentially independent structures. Subsequently, however, Babbitt developed a "time-point" rhythmic system enabling him to translate pitch relationships into durational ones.

Series. See Twelve-tone music, Serial music.

Serioso [It., serious]. Beethoven's String Quartet in F minor op. 95 (1810), described by Beethoven on the title page of the autograph manuscript as a "Quartett[o] serioso."

Serkin, Peter (b. New York, 24 July 1947). Pianist. At 14 played a Mozart 2-piano concerto with his father, Rudolf Serkin, at Cleveland. Has recorded sonatas and the Diabelli Variations of Beethoven, Mozart piano concertos, Schubert works, and 20th-century music. Teacher at Juilliard and Mannes College.

Serkin, Rudolf (b. Eger, Bohemia, 28 March 1903; d. Guilford, Vt., 8 May 1991). Pianist. Pupil of Schoenberg. Appeared with the Vienna Symphony, 1915; with the New York Philharmonic under Toscanini, 1936. Played sonata recitals for many years with the violinist Adolf Busch. Taught at the Curtis Institute from 1938 (its director, 1968–75). In 1950, established the Marlboro Festival.

Serly, Tibor (b. Losonc, Hungary, 25 Nov. 1901; d. London, 8 Oct. 1978). Violist, composer, conductor. Studied in New York and in Budapest with Hubay and Kodály. Played viola in several U.S. orchestras. Made use of Hungarian folk song. Close associate of Bartók; completed his Third Piano Concerto and Viola Concerto. Works include orchestral music (Viola Concerto, 1929; *Six Dance Designs,* 1933; *Lament,* 1955–58); Piano Sonata (1947); chamber and vocal music.

Sermisy, Claudin [Claude] **de** (b. ca. 1490; d. Paris, 13 Oct. 1562). Composer. Held various musical and clerical posts at the Saint-Chapelle, in the private chapel of Louis XII, in Rouen, in Cambron, and at Ste. Catherine, Troyes. Composed chansons, mostly in 4 voices, with homophonic, folklike settings; sacred music including parody Masses and a St. Matthew Passion.

Serocki, Kazimierz (b. Toruń, 3 Mar. 1922; d. Warsaw, 9 Jan. 1981). Composer. Pupil of Sikorski, Boulanger, and Levy. Late 1940s, toured Europe as a concert pianist. Made use of twelve-tone techniques, graphic notation, and theatrical effects. Works include orchestral (*Segmenti,* 1961; *Freski symfoniczne,* 1964; *Pianophonie,* with piano, electronics, 1976–78), vocal (*Nioke,* speakers, chorus, orchestra, 1966), chamber, and piano music (*Suita preludiów,* 1952).

Serov, Alexander (Nikolaievich) (b. St. Petersburg, 23 Jan. 1820; d. there, 1 Feb. 1871). Composer and critic. Largely self-taught in music. Held government posts until 1851; then began writing music criticism. An advocate for Wagner's music and ideas in Russia. Awarded a pension by the czar, 1865. Made use of Russian folk idioms. Composed operas (incl. *Judith,* St. Petersburg, 1863; *Rogneda,* 1865; *Vrazhya sila* [Malevolent Power], completed by his widow and Soloviev).

Serpent [Fr. *serpent;* Ger. *Serpent, Schlangenrohr, Schlangenbass;* It. *serpentone;* Sp. *serpentón*]. A wide-bore, lip-vibrated wind instrument made in an undulating serpentine shape of wood covered with leather; a relative of the *cornett. It has six finger holes, a short brass mouth pipe, and an ivory or wood mouthpiece. It is usually about 2.45 m. (8 ft.) long, pitched in C or D, and plays from a note or two below this fundamental upward about three octaves. The serpent first appeared in France in the late 16th century. It was used in orchestras and bands through the first half of the 19th century. See ill. under Brass instruments.

Serrano (Simeón), José (b. Sueca, Valencia, 14 Oct. 1873; d. Madrid, 8 Mar. 1941). Composer. Pupil of Bretón and Chapí. Composed about 100 zarzuelas, including *El motete* (1900), *Moros y cristianos* (1905), *Alma de Dios* (1907), *El carro del sol* (1911, in collaboration with Vives), *Los de Aragón* (1927), and *La dolorosa* (1930); also an opera, a Mass and other sacred music, songs, and keyboard pieces.

Serrant [Fr.]. Becoming faster.

Serse [It., Xerxes]. Opera in three acts by Handel (libretto adapted from one by Niccolò Minato for Cavalli in 1654 and revised for Bononcini in 1694), produced in London in 1738. Setting: Persia in the 5th century B.C.E.

Serva padrona, La [It., The Maid as Mistress]. Comic opera in two acts by Pergolesi (libretto by Gennaro Antonio Federico), composed as an *intermezzo* to be played between the three acts of his serious opera *Il prigioner superbo* (The Haughty Prisoner), produced in Naples in 1733. Setting: 18th-century Naples.

Service. In religious use, worship, especially public worship according to form and order; also a musical setting of those portions of public worship that are sung; more particularly, in the Anglican Church, settings of certain texts used for Morning and Evening Prayer and Holy Communion.

The musical service of the Anglican Church (as applied to music, the term service is not current until the 17th century) generally implies settings of three groups of texts taken from three principal services of the Anglican liturgy as found in the Book of Common Prayer (from 1552): Morning Prayer, Holy Communion, and Evening Prayer. The long list of polyphonic settings of some or all of them commences with John Day's publication *Certaine notes set forth in foure and three parts to be song at the morning Communion and evening praier* (1560, reprinted 1565), in which musical settings by Thomas Caustun (d. 1569) are identified. The next and far more important printed collection is that of John Barnard in 1641: *The First Book of Selected Church Musick, consisting of services and anthems, such as are now used in the cathedrall, and collegiat churches of this Kingdome,* which preserves all or parts of 15 services by 11 deceased composers, including three by William Byrd and two each by Orlando Gibbons and Thomas Morley.

The three services by Byrd, along with a fourth (the Great Service), all employing organ, may be taken as typical. Two of them, the so-called Short Service and the Great Service, set the same seven texts (Venite, Te Deum, Benedictus, Kyrie, Creed, Magnificat, Nunc dimittis), the difference between them thus lying in the degree of elaborateness of treatment of the texts. Byrd's so-called Second Service (called in *The First Book of Selected Church Music* "service with verses to the organ") is the earliest surviving example of the use of solo voices and instrumental accompaniment in an Anglican liturgical context and is thus the prototype of the "verse" style that spread through later services and anthems. In a given service, all the text settings tended to use a single tonal center, often designated as a key or mode (e.g., Service in B♭, Dorian Service).

Despite liturgical constraints, the musical possibilities inherent in the various combinations of choir, organ, and solo voices (the number of written parts often masking the performing forces required) have led to a long series of liturgical settings, among them those of John Blow, Pelham Humphrey, Henry Purcell, Maurice Green, Samuel S. Wesley, John Stainer, Ralph Vaughan Williams, Herbert Howells, Michael Tippett, and Benjamin Britten.

Sesqui- [Lat.]. A prefix denoting a fraction whose numerator is larger by one than its denominator, e.g., *sesquialtera* (3/2, in some contexts equivalent to *hemiola), *sesquitertia* (4/3), *sesquiquarta* (5/4), *sesquioctava* (9/8). The terms were used especially by writers of the Middle Ages and Renaissance in discussions of *proportions and *intervals.

Sessions, Roger (Huntington) (b. Brooklyn, 28 Dec. 1896; d. Princeton, N.J., 16 Mar. 1985). Composer. Pupil of H. Parker and Bloch. Taught at Smith College, 1917–21; then at the Cleveland Institute of Music. Lived in Europe, 1926–33. Coproduced the Copland-Sessions Concerts of Contemporary Music. Taught at Princeton Univ., 1935–44 and 1953–65; at the Univ. of California at Berkeley, 1944–52 and 1966–67; at Harvard, 1968–69; at Juilliard until 1983. Worked with twelve-tone techniques. Works include operas (*Montezuma; The *Trial of Lucullus*); orchestral works (9 symphonies; concertos; incidental music for *The Black Maskers,* 1923; arranged as a suite 1928; Concerto for Orchestra, 1981); vocal works (*Idyll of Theocritus,* soprano, orchestra, 1954; *When Lilacs Last in the Dooryard Bloom'd,* cantata, 1970); string quartets and other chamber music; piano pieces (sonatas; *Pages from a Diary,* 1939; rev. 1940). Writings include *The Musical Experience of Composer, Performer, Listener* (1950); *Harmonic Practice* (1951); *Questions about Music* (1970).

Sestetto [It.]. *Sextet.

Set. In the context of *twelve-tone music, *row.

Seter, Mordecai (b. Novorossiysk, 26 Feb. 1916; d. Tel Aviv, 8 Aug. 1994). Composer. Pupil of Dandelot, Levy, Dukas, Boulanger, and Stravinsky. Made use of Jewish liturgical music, Palestinian folk music,

and serialism. Composed ballets, including 3 for Martha Graham; orchestral music; sacred and secular vocal works; string quartets and other chamber music.

Set-piece. (1) In Anglo-American sacred music of the 18th and 19th centuries, a through-composed setting of a metrical text. (2) In a musico-dramatic work, a composition such as an aria that is musically self-contained; also termed a number.

Seul [Fr.]. Solo.

Seven (Last) Words, The. The seven last words (actually phrases) of Christ, compiled from the four Gospels, which have been used as a text for *Passion music, e.g., by Schütz (*Die sieben Wörte* SWV 478, composed ca. 1645), Haydn, and Gounod (*Les sept paroles de N. S. Jésus-Christ sur la croix,* 1858). Haydn's composition, commissioned by the Bishop of Cádiz, was originally a series of seven instrumental "sonatas," one to be played after the recitation of each of the seven "words," plus a musical depiction of an earthquake. As such, its title was *Musica instrumentale sopra le sette ultime parole del nostro redentore in croce o sieno sette sonate con un introduzione ed al fine un teremoto* (Instrumental Music on the Seven Last Words of Our Savior on the Cross, or Seven Sonatas with an Introduction and at the End an Earthquake). It appeared in four versions: (1) for orchestra, Hob. XX/1 A (1785); (2) for string quartet, Hob. XX/1 B (also Hob. III:50–56; 1787); (3) for harpsichord or piano, Hob. XX/1 C (1787; a version not actually by Haydn but approved by him); and (4) an oratorio version for soloists, chorus, and orchestra, Hob. XX/2 (appearing by 1796), choral parts having first been added by Joseph Friebert to his own text, which was later revised by Haydn and Baron Gottfried van Swieten.

Seventh. See Interval, Scale degrees.

Seventh chord. A chord formed by the addition of pitches a third, a fifth, and a seventh above the lowest pitch or root. Such a chord can be formed on any of the seven *scale degrees of the major or minor scale, the intervals above the root varying by type (i.e., major, minor, etc.) accordingly. For the various types of seventh chords that can result, see Harmonic analysis; for inversions of seventh chords, see Inversion; for the types and nomenclature of seventh chords used in jazz and popular music, see Fakebook notation. Since the seventh is dissonant with the root (forming a seventh or, in inversion, a second), all seventh chords are dissonant. In tonal harmony and counterpoint, therefore, the seventh chord requires resolution through the resolution of the dissonant pitch, usually downward by step, as in Ex. 1. This dissonant pitch is most often introduced as a passing tone [Ex. 2], neighboring tone [Ex. 3], or suspension [Ex. 4], according to the principles of voice leading or counterpoint. It is from these principles that the seventh chord derives its force [see Counterpoint].

When formed on the fifth scale degree or dominant, the chord is termed a dominant seventh. Because of the presence in this chord of both the fourth and the seventh scale degrees, any given dominant seventh chord can exist in only one key. It therefore strongly implies a single tonic and is often resolved by the tonic triad. The progression from dominant seventh to tonic is termed a dominant-seventh *cadence and is one of the most familiar and powerful progressions in tonal music.

A diminished seventh chord consists of a diminished triad with a diminished seventh added above the root. It is thus made up of only minor thirds placed above one another. In tonal music, it occurs most often formed on the seventh scale degree. In the minor mode, this occurs when the seventh scale degree is raised; in the major mode, the sixth scale degree must be lowered. The diminished seventh chord is sometimes interpreted to be a dominant ninth chord with the root omitted. Because diminished seventh chords can be resolved in a variety of directions, they are especially useful as pivot chords in *modulations. A diminished triad with a minor seventh added above the root is termed a half-diminished seventh.

Séverac, (Marie-Joseph-Alexandre) Déodat de (b. St. Félix de Caraman en Laurangais, 20 July 1872; d. Céret, 24 Mar. 1921). Composer. Pupil of d'Indy, Magnard, and Albéniz, whose piano piece *Navarra* he completed in 1909. Used folk music from southwestern France. Works include the operas *Héliogabale* (Béziers, 1910) and *Le coeur du moulin* (Paris, 1909); incidental music; piano music (*Le chant de la terre,* 1901; *En Languedoc,* 1903–4; *Baigneuses au soleil,* 1908); orchestral, choral, and chamber works.

Sevillanas [Sp.]. A slightly faster variant from Andalusia of the *seguidillas* [see *Seguidilla* (2)]; also a type of *flamenco* music derived from this variant.

Sextet [Fr. *sextette, sextuor;* Ger. *Sextett;* It. *sestetto;* Sp. *sexteto*]. (1) A composition for six solo performers, with or without accompaniment. (2) An ensemble of six solo performers. Compositions of this type for winds or mixed winds and strings occur primarily among Classical divertimentos. The string sextet (usually paired violins, violas, and cellos) was used by Brahms, Dvořák, Schoenberg, and others. There are sextets with piano by Mendelssohn, Poulenc, and Copland. The sextet as an operatic ensemble is first found in 18th-century *opera buffa,* but later also in serious opera.

Sextolet, sextuplet [Fr. *sextolet;* Ger. *Sextole;* It. *sestina;* Sp. *seisillo*]. A group of six notes of equal value to be played in the time normally occupied by four notes of the same value and identified by the figure 6. The effect may be the same as two triplets of appropriate value or as three groups of two notes each. Beams may be drawn so as to distinguish between these effects.

Sextuor [Fr.]. *Sextet.

Seyfried, Ignaz (Xaver) von (b. Vienna, 15 Aug. 1776; d. there, 27 Aug. 1841). Composer. Pupil of Mozart, Kozeluch, Albrechtsberger, and Winter. Conducted in Schikaneder's theater, 1797–1801; at the Theater an der Wien, 1801–27. Composed stage works (*Der Wundermann am Rheinfall,* 1799); instrumental works; and church music. A friend of Beethoven, he conducted the premiere of *Fidelio.* Published theoretical works of other writers and his own articles on music.

Sf. Abbr. for *sforzando, sforzato.

Sfogato [It.]. With respect to expression, vented, unburdened, unrestrained.

Sforzando, sforzato [It., abbr. *sf., sfz.*]. Forcing, forced; accented (usually a single pitch or chord) at least with respect to the prevailing dynamic, but often simply loud.

Sfp. [It.]. Abbr. for *sforzando* followed immediately by *piano,* i.e., a sudden (often loud) accent followed immediately by a soft continuation.

Sfz. Abbr. for *Sforzando, sforzato.

Shake. Formerly, *trill. A shaked beat is a repeated lower *appoggiatura; a shaked cadent is a repeated *Nachschlag.

Shakuhachi [Jap.]. An *end-blown bamboo flute of Japan with four finger holes and one thumb hole. A notch is cut in the lip to facilitate sound production. Originally an instrument of Buddhist monks, it is now also played in ensembles with the *shamisen and the *koto. See ill. under Instrument.

Shamisen [Jap.]. A *long-necked lute of Japan. Three strings of silk or nylon pass down an unfretted neck and over a small, square sound box covered front and back with cat or dog skin. The strings are plucked with a large, triangular plectrum. See ill. under Instrument.

Shank. A relatively short, straight piece of tubing that can be inserted in a brass instrument to receive the mouthpiece and alter the instrument's fundamental pitch. See also Crook.

Shankar, Ravi (b. Varanasi, Uttar Pradesh, India, 7 Apr. 1920). Sitar player and composer. Studied with Ustad Allauddin Khan. Led the instrumental ensemble of All-India Radio, 1949–56. Toured internationally from 1956. Has worked with Yehudi Menuhin and George Harrison. Founded a music school in Bombay in 1962. Compositions include ballet and film music, 2 sitar concertos, and many ragas.

Shanty, chanty, chantey [perhaps fr. Fr. *chanter*, to sing]. A work song sung by sailors, especially one that rhythmically coordinates strenuous effort.

Shape-note. A type of notation employed in tune books and hymnals in the U.S. (especially in the South and Midwest) from the 19th century until the present in which the shape of the note head indicates the solmization syllable corresponding to the note in question; also termed buckwheat-note or character notation. The first such system, introduced in 1801 in *The Easy Instructor* of William Little and William Smith, was based on *fasola solmization and assigned a different shape to each of the four syllables employed (hence, four-shape notation): *fa, sol, la,* and *mi* [Ex. 1]. By the mid-19th century, the use of seven shapes (of which there were at first several competing systems) corresponding to seven syllables began to supersede the four-shape system [Ex. 2]. Rhythmic values were indicated with stems and flags in the conventional way.

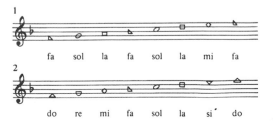

Shapero, Harold (Samuel) (b. Lynn, Mass., 29 April 1920). Composer, pianist. Pupil of Slonimsky, Krenek, and Piston. Worked as an arranger for Benny Goodman. Teacher at Brandeis Univ. from 1952. Has worked with twelve-tone techniques, electronic instruments, and jazz-derived idioms. Works include orchestral music (Symphony for Classical Orchestra, 1947; Credo for Orchestra, 1955; Partita in C, with solo piano, 1960); *On Green Mountain,* jazz ensemble (1957); String Quartet (1941) and other chamber music; sonatas and other piano pieces, some with synthesizer; vocal works.

Shapey, Ralph (b. Philadelphia, 12 Mar. 1921). Composer and conductor. Pupil of Wolpe. Taught at the Univ. of Chicago, 1964–91. In 1969 withdrew all of his compositions and did not release any new works until 1976. Awarded a MacArthur fellowship, 1982. Has composed orchestral works (*Ontogeny,* 1958; Double Concerto, violin, cello, 1983; *Concerto fantastique,* 1991); *Praise,* oratorio (1971); 8 string quartets; piano and organ pieces; vocal works (*The Covenant,* soprano, tape, chamber ensemble, 1977; *Song of Songs I-III,* soprano, bass, tape, chamber ensemble, 1979–80).

Shaporin, Yuri (Alexandrovich) (b. Glukhov, Ukraine, 8 Nov. 1887; d. Moscow, 9 Dec. 1966). Composer. Studied at the St. Petersburg Conservatory with Steinberg and Tcherepnin. Cofounder (1919) and later music director of the Grand Drama Theater. From 1939 taught at the Moscow Conservatory; pupils included Shchedrin, Volkonsky, and Khachaturian. Composed the opera *The Decembrists* (1920–53); oratorios, cantatas, and songs; orchestral works; piano pieces; film scores.

Sharp [Fr. *dièse;* Ger. *Kreuz;* It. *diesis;* Sp. *sostenido*]. (1) The sign ♯, which indicates the raising of the pitch of a note by a semitone. See Accidental, Pitch names. (2) [adj.] Incorrectly tuned above the correct pitch.

Shaw, Robert (b. Red Bluff, Calif., 30 Apr. 1916; d. New Haven, 25 Jan. 1999). Conductor. Pupil of Monteux and Rodzinski. Orchestral debut, Naumburg, 1946. Formed the Robert Shaw Chorale, 1948. Held posts with the San Diego Symphony (1953–58), the Cleveland Orchestra (as Szell's associate, 1956–67), and the Atlanta Symphony (1967–88). His ideas on choral development have been widely adopted.

Shawm [fr. Lat. *calamus,* reed; Fr. *chalemie;* Ger. *Schalmei;* It. *cennamella;* Sp. *chirimía*]. A conical-bore, double-reed woodwind instrument used in Europe from the 13th through the 17th century with many close relatives still in use elsewhere [see *Hichiriki, Nāgasvaram, Zūrnā*]. It survives as a folk instrument in some parts of Europe as well [see *Chirimía, Ciaramella, Dulzaina*]. See ill. under Reed. The older European instrument exists in at least seven sizes, as described by Michael Praetorius (1619). A disk called a pirouette is usually provided below the reed to support the player's lips. Shawms were used in early European music with other "loud" instruments [see *Haut*], often in outdoor settings.

Shchedrin, Rodion Konstantinovich (b. Moscow, 16 Dec. 1932). Composer and pianist. Pupil of Shaporin. Taught at the Moscow Conservatory, 1965–69; from 1973, head of the Union of Composers of the Russian Federation. Made use of folk tunes. Works include operas (*Not Love Alone,* 1961; rev. 1971; *Dead Souls,* 1976); ballets (incl. *The Little Humpbacked Horse,* 1955; *Anna Karenina,* 1971; *The Lady with a Dog,* 1985); 2 symphonies and other works for orchestra; 3 piano concertos; vocal-symphonic music; chamber works (*Geometry of Sound,* 18 soloists, 1987); music for piano; incidental and film music.

Shcherbachov, Vladimir Vladimirovich (b. Warsaw, 25 Jan. 1889; d. Leningrad, 5 Mar. 1952). Composer. Pupil of Lyadov and Steinberg. Worked as a pianist for Diaghilev's ballet company. Taught at Leningrad Conservatory, 1923–31 and 1944–48. Works include 5 symphonies (no. 4, History of the Izhorsky Factory, 1932–34; no. 5, "Russian," 1942–48); symphonic poems; film scores; the opera *Anna Kolosova* (1939); smaller theater pieces; songs; and piano works.

Shearing, George (Albert) (b. London, 13 Aug. 1919). Jazz pianist and bandleader. Emigrated to the U.S., 1947. Led quintets, 1949–67; among his sidemen were Cal Tjader and Joe Pass. Recordings include "Sorry, Wrong Rhumba" (1949) and his composition "Lullaby of Birdland" (1952). From the 1980s, accompanied Mel Torme.

Shebalin, Vissarion Yakovlevich (b. Omsk, 11 June 1902; d. Moscow, 28 May 1963). Composer. Pupil of Myaskovsky. Taught at the Moscow Conservatory from 1928; its director, 1942–48. Students included Khrennikov. Works include 2 operas (*The Taming of the Shrew,* 1946–56); ballets; scores for theater, film, and radio; 5 symphonies, concertos, and other orchestral works; choral works, songs, folk song arrangements; 9 string quartets and other chamber and piano works; guitar pieces.

Sheherazade. (1) A symphonic suite by Rimsky-Korsakov, op. 35 (1888), based on tales from the *Thousand and One Nights* and named for the woman who tells the stories. In 1910, it was presented in Paris as a ballet by the Ballets russes (choreography by Michel Fokine). (2) [Fr. *Shéhérazade*] A cycle

of three songs for voice and piano or orchestra by Ravel, composed in 1903, on poems by Tristan Klingsor inspired by the *Thousand and One Nights*.

Sheng [Chin.]. A Chinese *mouth organ consisting of a bowl-shaped wind-chest around the perimeter of which 12 to 19 bamboo pipes are inserted vertically. Each sounding pipe has a brass reed at its lower end and a hole that must be covered to produce a sound. The player holds the *sheng* cupped in both hands and inhales and exhales through a mouthpiece, covering several holes at a time to produce chords. See ill. under Instrument; see also *Sho.*

Shepherd, Arthur (b. Paris, Idaho, 19 Feb. 1880; d. Cleveland, 12 Jan. 1958). Composer, conductor, teacher. Pupil of Chadwick. Moved to Salt Lake City in 1897. Teacher at the New England Conservatory from 1909; at Case Western Reserve Univ., 1927–50. Assistant conductor, Cleveland Orchestra, 1920–26. Works include *Five Songs on Poems of James Russell Lowell* (1909); piano sonatas; string quartets; *Overture to a Drama* (1919); *Triptych* (soprano, string quartet, 1925).

Sheppard [Shepherd], **John** (b. ca. 1515; d. London?, 1559 or 1560). Composer. *Informator choristarum* at Magdalen College, Oxford, 1543–48; Gentleman of the Chapel Royal from at least 1552. Took part in the coronation of Elizabeth I, 1559. Works include both Latin service music (5 Masses, 2 Magnificats, motets, Psalms, hymns, and responsories) and post-Reformation English music (3 services, canticles, anthems, Psalm tunes).

Sheriff, Noam (b. Tel Aviv, 7 Jan. 1935). Composer. Pupil of Ben Haim and Blacher. Has worked with elements of traditional Jewish liturgical music and electronic media. Works include the ballet *Cain* (tape, 1969–70); orchestral music (*Fest-prelude,* 1957; *Song of Degrees,* 1960; *Ashrei [Psalms],* 1961; *La Follia,* 1984); String Quartet (1973); *A Little "Ligur"* (violin, cello, 1984); *Mechaye Hametin* (male voices, orchestra, 1987).

Shield, William (b. County Durham, 5 Mar. 1748; d. London, 25 Jan. 1829). Violinist and composer. Pupil of Avison. Joined the King's Theatre orchestra, London, about 1773. Composer to Covent Garden, 1778–91 and 1792–97; Master of the King's Music from 1817. Composed about 40 operas (*The Flitch of Bacon,* 1778); pantomimes, songs, and some instrumental works. Published treatises on harmony and thoroughbass.

Shifrin, Seymour (b. Brooklyn, 28 Feb. 1926; d. Boston, 26 Sept. 1979). Composer. Pupil of Schuman and Luening. Taught at the Univ. of California, Berkeley, 1952–66; at Brandeis Univ. from 1966. Composed orchestral works (*3 Pieces,* 1958); choral-orchestral works (*Cantata to Sophoclean Choruses,* 1957–58); string quartets and other chamber music; vocal works (*Satires of Circumstance,* mezzosoprano, ensemble, 1964); piano pieces (*Trauermusik,* 1956).

Shift. In the playing of stringed instruments, the movement from one *position to another.

Shimmy. A dance popular in the U.S. in the 1910s and 1920s whose characteristic motion is the rapid movement of the two shoulders in opposite directions, forward and backward. It was danced to music in a relatively fast tempo.

Shinohara, Makoto (b. Osaka, 10 Dec. 1931). Composer. Pupil of Ikenouchi, Messiaen, Zimmerman, and Stockhausen. Has worked in the Utrecht Univ. and Columbia–Princeton electronic music studios. Associated with Tokyo Radio. Works include *Alternance* (percussion ensemble, 1962); *Vision* (tape, 1965); *Kyūdō* (shakuhachi, harp, 1973); *Tabiyuki* (chamber ensemble, 1984); *Evolution* (cello, 1986).

Shnitke, Alfred. See Schnittke, Alfred.

Sho [Jap.]. A Japanese *mouth organ, very similar to the Chinese *sheng. It is used in *gagaku music. See ill. under Instrument.

Shofar [Heb.]. A ram's-horn trumpet of ancient Israel and modern Jewish worship. It produces primarily two pitches, corresponding to the second and third harmonics and thus a fifth apart, though other pitches may be produced by lipping. Today it is sounded on Rosh Hashanah (New Year) and Yom Kippur (Day of Atonement).

Short octave. In keyboard instruments, the omission of one or more pitches from the lowest octave, the keys corresponding to the omitted pitches causing other, usually lower pitches to sound instead. The practice began with the earliest keyboards and lasted well into the 18th century in Europe and even later in Mexico and Spanish America. It was justified by the lack of need for certain low pitches (especially accidentals); in organs, there was a substantial saving when large bass pipes could be omitted. The resulting reassignment of lower pitches to higher keys also made larger intervals reachable under the player's hand.

Short score. A *score in which parts are consolidated on relatively few staves. See also Particella.

Shorter, Wayne (b. Newark, N.J., 25 Aug. 1933). Jazz tenor and soprano saxophonist, composer, and bandleader. Studied at New York Univ. Joined Art Blakey (1959–64) and Miles Davis (1964–70). With Joe Zawinul led the jazz-rock group Weather Report (1970–85); toured with Herbie Hancock (1976–77).

Performed in the film *Round Midnight* (1986); co-led a band with Carlos Santana (1988). Compositions include "E.S.P." (1965), "Nefertiti" (1967), and "Sanctuary" (1969).

Shostakovich, Dmitri Dmitrievich (b. St. Petersburg, 25 Sept. 1906; d. Moscow, 9 Aug. 1975). Composer. Studied at the Petrograd Conservatory under Steinberg. Active as a pianist, winning honorable mention in the First International Chopin Competition in Warsaw in 1927. Taught at the Leningrad Conservatory, 1937–41, and at the Moscow Conservatory, 1943–48; returned to both in the 1960s. Awarded the Stalin Prize, 1941; the Order of Lenin, 1946. A decree of 1948 censured Shostakovich, Prokofiev, and other prominent Soviet composers for "formalistic perversions and anti-democratic tendencies." From 1957 he was secretary of the U.S.S.R. Composers' Union, and from 1962 a member of the Supreme Soviet. Traveled widely within and outside the U.S.S.R., including four trips to Britain and three to the U.S.

Works include operas (*The Nose,* 1930; *Lady Macbeth of Mtsensk*); ballets (*The Golden Age,* 1920); incidental music to plays; 15 symphonies (no. 7, *"Leningrad,"* 1941; no. 10, 1953; no. 13, "Babi Yar," with chorus and texts by Yevtushenko, 1962); other orchestral works; 2 concertos each for piano, violin, and cello; choral works; chamber music, including 15 string quartets, 2 piano trios, a piano quintet, and sonatas for violin, viola, and cello; piano pieces (sonatas, 1926 and 1942; 24 preludes and fugues, 1951); numerous songs and song cycles on texts by English, Jewish, and Russian poets; music for films; reorchestrations of Mussorgsky's *Boris Godunov* and *Khovanshchina.*

Shostakovich, Maxim (b. Leningrad, 10 May 1938). Conductor and pianist. Son of Dmitri Shostakovich. Studied at the Leningrad and Moscow Conservatories. Assistant conductor from 1966 of the U.S.S.R. State Symphony, with which he toured the U.S. in 1969; director of the U.S.S.R. State Radio Orchestra from 1971. Defected in 1981. Held posts with the Hong Kong Philharmonic (1983–85), Hartford Symphony (1985–86), and New Orleans Symphony (1986–91).

Shout. (1) Ring shout. (2) In jazz, a vigorous tune played by a *stride pianist (e.g., James P. Johnson's "Carolina Shout"); the performer of such a piece may be termed a shout pianist. (3) In blues, jazz, and rhythm and blues, a shout singer (e.g., Jimmy Rushing) is one who shouts more than sings the lyrics.

Si. See Pitch names, Solmization.

Sibelius, Jean [Johan] (**Julius Christian**) (b. Hämeenlinna, 8 Dec. 1865; d. Järvenpää, 20 Sept.

1957). Composer. Pupil of Wegelius, Busoni, Goldmark, and Fuchs. Employed some elements of Finnish folk song. Works: Stage works, including the opera *The Maid in the Tower;* incidental music (*Peléas et Mélisande,* 1905; *The Tempest,* 1925); *Scaramouche,* music for a pantomime (1913). Orchestral music, including *Karelia; *Lemminkäinen Suite; *Finlandia; En *Saga; 7 symphonies (an 8th was apparently destroyed); Violin Concerto (1903; rev. 1905); *The Bard* (1913; rev. 1914); Humoresques nos. 1–6, violin and orchestra (1917); *Pohjola's Daughter; *Tapiola. Choral works, including *Kullervo* (1892); *Sandels* (1898; rev. 1915); *The Liberated Queen,* cantata (1906); *Väinö's Song* (1926). Songs, including *Seven Songs of Runeberg* (1891–92); "Jubal" (1907–8); "Svarta rosor" [Black Roses] (1899); "Var det en dröm?" [Was It a Dream?] (1898–1902); "På verandan vid havet" [On a Balcony by the Sea] (1902–4). String quartets and other chamber music; piano works, mainly for amateurs.

Siciliana, siciliano [It., Eng., Ger.; Fr. *sicilienne;* Sp. *siciliana*]. (1) A late Baroque instrumental movement or an aria that evokes a gentle pastoral mood [see also *Pastorale*], usually through slow 6/8 or 12/8 time and simple phrases with repeated dotted figures (♩. ♪♩), often beginning with an upbeat. It frequently appears as a slow movement in sonatas and dance suites (Bach, Telemann) and was considered to be a sort of slow *gigue, though little is known of it as an actual dance. Arias with the same characteristics, as well as the use of the Neapolitan sixth chord at cadences, are very common (Alessandro Scarlatti, Handel), but they are rarely labeled *siciliano* by the composers.

(2) In the early 17th century, a musical setting of the Sicilian version of a *strambotto.

Sicilianos, Yorgo (b. Athens, 29 Aug. 1922). Composer. Pupil of Varvoglis, Pizzetti, Milhaud, Aubin, Messiaen, Piston, Blacher, and Persichetti. Head of the music division of the Greek National Broadcasting Institution (1960–61, 1979). Made use of native folk elements and of serialism. Works include ballets, orchestral music (*The Revelation of the Fifth Seal,* 1952; Concerto for Orchestra, 1954), choral music (*Epitaphion: In Memoriam Nikos Marangopoulos,* 1971), and chamber music.

Side drum. Snare *drum.

Sideman. Any member of a jazz or popular-music ensemble other than the leader.

Siefert [Syfert, Sivert, Sibert], **Paul** (b. Danzig, 28 June 1586; d. there, 6 May 1666). Composer. Pupil of Sweelinck. Organist of the principal church in Königsberg, 1611–16; at the Warsaw court; at the Marienkirche in Danzig from 1623. Involved in a feud with Marco Scacchi. Works include *Psalmen Davids* (1640; containing Psalm settings and vocal concertos).

Siege of Rhodes, The. The first English opera, with a libretto in five entries by William Davenant and music (now lost) by Henry Lawes, Henry Cooke, Matthew Locke, George Hudson, and Charles Coleman; produced in London in 1656.

Siegfried. See *Ring des Nibelungen, Der.*

Siegfried Idyll. A composition for small orchestra by Wagner, composed in 1870 and first performed on his wife Cosima's birthday at their home Tribschen (hence, also the *Tribschen Idyll*), near Lucerne. It is named for their son Siegfried, then a year old, and includes themes from the opera *Siegfried* as well as the lullaby "Schlaf, Kindlein, schlaf" (Sleep, baby, sleep).

Siegmeister, Elie (b. New York, 15 Jan. 1909; d. Manhasset, N.Y., 10 Mar. 1991). Composer. Pupil of Bingham, Riegger, and Boulanger. Collected, performed, and arranged American folk songs, integrating some into his own works. Composed operas, including *The Lady of the Lake* (New York, 1985); symphonies and other orchestral works (*Western Suite,* 1945; *Figures in the Wind,* 1990); choral music (*Abraham Lincoln Walks at Midnight,* 1937; *I Have a Dream,* cantata, 1967); songs ("The Strange Funeral in Braddock," 1933; *Four Langston Hughes Songs,* 1990); string quartets and other chamber and piano music.

Siepi, Cesare (b. Milan, 10 Feb. 1923). Bass. Debut at Schio, 1941. Sang at La Scala (1946–50, 1955–58) and at the Metropolitan Opera (1950–74); appeared also at Salzburg, San Francisco, and Covent Garden. Roles included Don Giovanni and Figaro. Recorded the Mozart operas and Verdi's Requiem (with Toscanini, 1951).

Sight, sighting. In English discant treatises of the 15th century, a system of improvising counterpoint while visualizing it on the same staff as a given liturgical melody sung by the tenor. Each improvised part or sight (or "degree of discant") is allowed to sound consonances within a certain range reckoned from the tenor, the parts from highest to lowest being quadreble, treble, mene (meane), countertenor (moving both above and below the tenor), and counter (countir, lying always below the tenor). *Faburden is a special application of sights.

Sight-reading, sight-singing [Fr. *lecture à vue;* Ger. *Blattspiel;* It. *suonare a prima vista;* Sp. *lectura a primera vista*]. The performing of a piece of music on seeing it for the first time. The ability to sing at sight requires the ability to imagine the sound of pitches or intervals without the aid of an instrument, and training in this skill forms an important part of instruction in basic musicianship or *ear training. *Solfège and other systems of *solmization are among the principal means for carrying out this training. Performing at sight on an instrument requires the ability to grasp the meaning of musical notation quickly and call upon the relevant technical skills for execution; this should be accompanied by the skills of the ear as well. The ability to perform efficiently at sight and the ability to give finished performances of distinction do not necessarily go together, and both should be among the goals of musical instruction.

Signature. See Key signature, Time signature, Conflicting signatures.

Silence [Fr.]. Rest.

Sillet [Fr.]. *Nut.

Sills, Beverly [Silverman, Belle] (b. Brooklyn, 25 May 1929). Soprano. Operatic debut, Philadelphia, 1946. Joined the New York City Opera, 1955; its director, 1979–89. Appeared at Vienna, La Scala, and Covent Garden; Metropolitan Opera debut, 1975. Roles included Donizetti heroines and Mozart's Constanze and Queen of the Night; created the title role in Menotti's *La loca* (San Diego, 1979). Recorded widely and appeared often on television.

Silver, Horace (Ward Martin Tavares) (b. Norwalk, Conn., 2 Sept. 1928). Jazz pianist, composer, and bandleader. Joined Stan Getz (1950–51) and Art Blakey, with whom he led the hard bop group the Jazz Messengers (1953–55). From 1956 led his own groups. Recordings of his compositions include "Opus de Funk" (1953), "The Preacher" (1955), "Señor Blues" (1956), and the title track of the album *Song for My Father* (1964).

Silvestrov, Valentin Vasilevich (b. Kiev, 30 Sept. 1937). Composer. Pupil of Lyatoshinsky. Taught at various music schools in Kiev, 1963–70. Has worked with serial, aleatoric, and other techniques. Works include 5 symphonies; works for solo instrument and orchestra; choral works; vocal works (*Quiet Songs*, 1974–75); chamber music (*Drama*, piano trio, 1970–71; String Quartet, 1974); piano works; film scores.

Simandl, Franz (b. Blatna, 1 Aug. 1840; d. Vienna, 13 Dec. 1912). Double bass player and composer. From 1869, played in the Vienna Court Opera orchestra and the Vienna Philharmonic, and taught at the Vienna Conservatory. Wrote a double bass method; various pieces for double bass. The German-style bow for the double bass, held with the palm upward, is named for him.

Similar motion. See Motion.

Simile, simili [It.]. An instruction to continue in the same manner of execution as has just been indicated explicitly.

Simon Boccanegra. Opera in a prologue and three acts by Verdi (libretto by Francesco Maria Piave and Giuseppe Montanelli, based on a play by Antonio García Gutiérrez), produced in Venice in 1857; revised version (libretto revised by Arrigo Boito) produced in Milan in 1881. Setting: Genoa and environs in the mid-14th century.

Simon, Paul (b. Newark, N.J., 13 Oct. 1941). Folk and rock songwriter, singer, and guitarist. Recorded many of his songs with vocalist Art Garfunkel, including "Sounds of Silence" (1965), "Mrs. Robinson" (1968), and "Bridge over Troubled Water" (1970). Solo recordings include the album *Graceland* (1986), recorded with South African musicians. Made soundtracks for *The Graduate* (with Garfunkel, 1968) and *One Trick Pony,* in which he starred (1980).

Simple system. Any of the most common types of woodwind fingering used prior to the innovations of Theobald Boehm (1794–1881); also called old system. The term is applied most often to the flute, but is applicable to other woodwinds as well. The simple system can be distinguished by the large number of *cross fingerings and *fork fingerings and by the production of a major scale when the six principal finger holes are opened sequentially.

Simpson [Sympson], **Christopher** (b. Westonby?, near Egton, Yorkshire, ca. 1605; d. Holborne?, London, between 5 May and 29 July 1669). Composer, theorist, and viola da gamba player. employed by Sir Robert Bolles. Published a viol method, *The Division-Violist* (1659), and the *Compendium of Practical Musick* (1667). Composed airs and other works for viol, with and without other instruments.

Sims, Ezra (b. Birmingham, Ala., 16 Jan. 1928). Composer. Pupil of Q. Porter, Kirchner, and Milhaud. Has worked with twelve-tone techniques and with microtones. Works include *Chamber Cantata on Chinese Poems* (1954); *Elegie nach Rilke* (soprano, instruments, 1976); *Grave Dance* (piano, 1958); string quartets; the string trio *This Way to the Egress—or—Manners Makyth Man* (1984); electronic tape pieces, many for dance performances (*Two Toby Minutes, I-III,* 1971).

Sims, Zoot [John Haley] (b. Inglewood, Calif., 29 Oct. 1925; d. New York, 23 Mar. 1985). Jazz tenor saxophonist. Joined the big bands of Benny Goodman (intermittently, 1940s–70s) and Woody Herman (1947–49, forming a part of the first "Four Brothers" saxophone section). Worked with Stan Kenton (1953) and Gerry Mulligan (1954–56; 1960); co-led a quintet with Al Cohn (1957–early 1980s). Also led groups, toured with Jazz at the Philharmonic, and recorded with Count Basie (1975).

Simultaneity. Any two or more pitches sounded simultaneously.

Sin' al fine (segno) [It.]. Until the end (or the *segno*); usually in conjunction with the instruction to repeat *da capo* or *dal segno*.

Sinatra, Frank [Francis Albert] (b. Hoboken, N.J., 12 Dec. 1915; d. Los Angeles, 14 May 1998). Popular singer, actor. Joined the Harry James Band, 1939. Hired by Tommy Dorsey, 1940 (recordings include "I'll Never Smile Again," 1940). During 1950s, became the most popular male vocalist in the U.S.; solo recordings include "Young at Heart," 1954; "Strangers in the Night," 1966; the signature "My Way," 1969. Acted in numerous films, including *From Here to Eternity* (1953), for which he won an Oscar.

Sinding, Christian (August) (b. Kongsberg, Norway, 11 Jan. 1856; d. Oslo, 3 Dec. 1941). Composer. Studied in Leipzig, Munich, Berlin, Dresden. From 1880, was subsidized by the Norwegian government. Lived much in Germany. Composed many songs and piano pieces (*Rustles of Spring,* no. 3 of *6 Pieces,* 1896); also a German opera, 4 symphonies, concertos, chamber music (Piano Quintet, 1889), sonatas and other violin works, cantatas, part songs.

Sinfonia [It., pl. *sinfonie*]. (1) Symphony. (2) In the Baroque period, an alternate designation for *sonata* or *canzona*, especially a trio or other ensemble sonata [see also *Sonata da chiesa*]. This meaning reflects the derivation of sinfonia from the Greek word for "sounding together" [see Symphony] and probably explains Bach's use of the term for his three-part inventions. Sinfonias for keyboard or instrumental ensemble also served during this period as preludes to Mass and motet sections and to sets of dances. (3) In operas and other extended vocal works of the 17th and 18th centuries, an instrumental piece serving as a prelude or *overture*, interlude, or postlude.

Sinfonia concertante [It.]. See *Symphonie concertante.*

Sinfonie pastorale [Fr.]. See *Pastoral* Symphony.

Sinfonietta [It.]. An orchestral work similar to a symphony but on a smaller scale; sometimes also a small orchestra.

Sinfonische Dichtung [Ger.]. *Symphonic poem.

Singend [Ger.]. In a singing style.

Singhiozzando [It.]. Sobbing.

Singing style. In ethnomusicology, those aspects of singing not normally indicated in Western notation, including timbre, tessitura, nasality, and tension.

Singspiel [Ger.]. A musico-dramatic work with a German text, especially a work written in the 18th or early 19th century in which spoken dialogue alternates with songs and sometimes with ensembles, choruses, or more extended musical pieces. The setting of such works is frequently rural, sometimes fantastic or exotic; the characters are often artisans or from the lower middle class and exhibit simpler or humbler virtues than characters from serious opera. There were two principal schools of Singspiel composition in the 18th century, the Viennese and the north German. The Leopoldstadt Theater in Vienna was the home of German plays interspersed with music from early in the 18th century. In 1778, Joseph II sought to encourage the growth of native German-language operas by the foundation of a national theater. The experiment lasted only a decade, but among its most successful products was Mozart's *Die *Entführung aus dem Serail* (1782, text by Stephanie). Other significant composers of Viennese Singspiel were Ignaz Umlauf, Karl Ditters von Dittersdorf, Wenzel Müller, Johann Schenck, and Joseph Weigl. Mozart's *Die *Zauberflöte* (1791, text by Schikaneder) represents a culmination of the genre.

North German Singspiel may be said to have begun in 1752 with the performance in Leipzig of a German adaptation of Charles Coffey's *ballad opera *The Devil to Pay* (*Der Teufel ist los,* text by Christian Friedrich Weisse, music by Johann C. Standfuss). For much of its history, north German Singspiel was susceptible to influences from English and French comic opera. The most notable composer of north German Singspiel was Johann Adam Hiller, who composed about 14 Singspiele between 1766 and 1779, most to librettos adapted by Weisse and almost all produced in Leipzig. Georg Benda was also a significant contributor to the genre.

Sinigaglia, Leone (b. Turin, 14 Aug. 1868; d. there, 16 May 1944). Composer. Studied with Giovanni Bolzoni, Mandyczewski, and Dvořák. Collected and arranged 6 volumes of *Vecchie canzoni popolari del Piemonte* (1914–27). A Jew, he died after being arrested by the Fascist police in 1944. Works include Violin Concerto (1900); *Rapsodia piemontese* (violin and orchestra, 1904); *Le baruffe chiozzotte* (overture, 1908); chamber works.

Sinistra [It.]. Left (hand).

Sinopoli, Giuseppe (b. Venice, 2 Nov. 1946). Composer and conductor. Studied composition with Stockhausen, Maderna, and Donatoni and conducting with Swarowsky; formed the Bruno Maderna Ensemble in 1975. Operatic conducting debut in 1978 in Venice, later appearing at Covent Garden, Hamburg, Bayreuth, and the Metropolitan Opera. Held conducting posts with the Philharmonia Orchestra (1983–95), St. Cecilia Orchestra, Rome (1983–87), and Dresden Staatskapelle (1991–92). Works include the opera *Lou Salome* (1981); *Opus Daleth* and *Opus Ghimel,* orchestra (1971); a piano concerto (1974); chamber and choral works; and electronic music.

Sistre [Fr.]. *Cittern.

Sistrum [Lat.]. A *rattle of ancient Sumeria, Egypt, and Rome. Heavy wires are set loosely into a U-shaped frame with a handle, and jingles are sometimes threaded onto the wires. It was sacred to the goddess Isis and traveled from Egypt to Rome with her cult. It is still used in the Coptic church. See ill. under Instrument.

Sitār [Hind.]. A *long-necked lute of northern India. It has a wide fingerboard with movable frets, a pear-shaped gourd body, and a gourd resonator at the top of the neck. There are 7 principal strings—4 melody strings and 3 drones—all made of metal, plus 12 to 20 *sympathetic strings. The player plucks the strings with a wire plectrum. The *sitār* is a solo instrument, usually accompanied by the **tablā* and the **tamburā.* See ill. under Instrument.

Sitole. *Citole.

Six, Les [Fr., The Six]. A name given by Henri Collet in 1920 to a group of six French composers—Louis Durey, Arthur Honegger, Darius Milhaud, Germaine Tailleferre, Georges Auric, and Francis Poulenc—who shared the aesthetic ideals of Erik Satie and for whom Jean Cocteau subsequently became an advocate.

Six-four chord. A *triad in second *inversion (i.e., with the fifth as the lowest-sounding pitch, e.g., g–c'–e'), so called because the third of the triad then forms a sixth with the lowest-sounding pitch while the root forms a fourth; it is notated in *thoroughbass notation and in *harmonic analysis with the figures $^6_4$. Because the interval of a fourth sounds above the lowest pitch, such a chord is normally treated in tonal music as a dissonance and must be resolved. It is often introduced as a suspension [see Counterpoint]. An especially familiar cadence resolves the tonic six-four chord to the dominant, which in turn moves to the tonic in root position (I^6_4–V–I). The *cadenza in concertos is often an elaboration of the progression from tonic six-four to dominant.

Sixteen-foot. See Foot.

Sixth. See Interval; Scale degrees; Consonance and dissonance; Added sixth.

Sixth chord. A *triad in first *inversion (i.e., with the third as the lowest-sounding pitch, e.g., e–g–c'), so called because the root then forms a sixth with the lowest-sounding pitch while the fifth of the triad forms a third; hence, also termed a six-three chord. It is notated in *thoroughbass notation and in *harmonic analysis with the figures $^6_3$. Because the sixth chord is wholly consonant when formed from a major or minor triad, it is freely used in tonal music [see Sixth-chord style].

Five chromatically altered sixth chords are also often found in tonal music. These are shown with their most common resolutions in Exx. 1–5. The names given are widely used, but have no historical or geographic significance. The first is the first inversion of a triad formed on the lowered second scale degree in either major or minor and most often resolves to the dominant; the root position of this triad is sometimes employed as well. The remaining four are termed augmented sixth chords because they are characterized by the interval of an augmented sixth above the lowest-sounding pitch. This interval is typically formed between the lowered sixth scale degree and the raised fourth scale degree, resolving in each case to an octave on the fifth scale degree or dominant. In consequence, these chords most often function as dominants to the dominant. Because of their interval content and the corresponding figures, these four chords are sometimes termed, respectively, augmented sixth, augmented six-five-three, augmented six-four-three, and doubly augmented fourth. See also Added sixth.

Sixth-chord style. A manner of composition characterized by the use of successions of *sixth chords, i.e., first-inversion triads. Passages made up of sixth chords have occurred occasionally in tonal music since the 18th century. The persistent use of sixth chords (though they are not described as such in contemporaneous theory) is more striking, however, in some music of the Middle Ages and Renaissance. In the 15th century, *fauxbourdon and *faburden rely almost exclusively on such harmonies, and the music of composers such as Dunstable, Dufay, and Binchois gives them a prominent place. Like the significant use of imperfect consonances generally, sixth chords first appear in quantity in English music of the late 13th century and after.

Sizzle cymbal. See Drum set.

Ska. A popular urban dance music that flourished in Jamaica between 1960 and 1965. The form originated from the imitation by black Jamaican musicians of the *rhythm and blues styles (notably that of Fats Domino) broadcast from New Orleans in the 1950s. A slower version of ska known as rock steady became popular ca. 1965; it was this latter style that developed into the internationally popular *reggae.

Skalkottas [Scalcotas], **Nikolaos** [Nikos, Nicos] (b. Halkis, Evia, 8 Mar. 1904; d. Athens, 19 Sept. 1949). Composer. Studied violin in Athens and Berlin, and composition with Schoenberg and Weill. Orchestral violinist in Athens from 1933. Most of his music was written during the last decade of his life; includes neoclassical, atonal, and serial styles, the latter being more fully worked out in late works such as the Fourth String Quartet (1940) and the Third Piano Concerto (1938–39). Works include Concertino op. 20, 2 pianos, orchestra (1935); Violin Concerto op. 22 (1937–38); I Epistrophi tou Odysseus [The Return of Ulysses], overture (1942–43); 4 string quartets; 4 piano suites.

Skiffle. A folklike English popular music of the 1950s in which guitars, bass, and drums were used to accompany simple songs. Skiffle groups provided training grounds for many future rock stars.

Skilton, Charles Sanford (b. Northampton, Mass., 16 Aug. 1868; d. Lawrence, Kans., 12 Mar. 1941). Composer. Studied at Yale and with Dudley Buck and Bargiel. Taught at Salem Academy, N.C. (1893–96), Trenton State Normal School, N.J. (1897–1903), Univ. of Kansas (from 1903). In 1915 came to know Native American music and musicians through association with the Haskell Institute, a national school for American Indians in Lawrence, Kans. His best-known works are adaptations and orchestrations of Native American songs and dances: Kalopin (opera, 1927); The Sun Bride (opera, 1930); Suite Primeval (orchestra, 1920); 3 Indian Sketches (piano, 1919); Shawnee Indian Hunting Dance (piano, 1929).

Skip. *Leap.

Skolie [Ger., fr. Gr. skolion]. A drinking song.

Skrowaczewski, Stanislaw (b. Lwów, 3 Oct. 1923). Conductor and composer. Studied piano; after injury to his hands during a bombing raid, turned to conducting. Led the Wrocław Philharmonic in 1946 and 1947; studied in Paris with Boulanger and Kletski; held posts with the orchestras of Katowice (1949–54), Kraków (1954–56), and Warsaw (1956–59). U.S. debut, 1958; 1960–79, music director of the Minneapolis Symphony; 1984–91 conducted the Hallé Orchestra, Manchester. Introduced many important Polish works to U.S. audiences, including Szymanowski's Second Symphony, Lutosławski's Funeral Music, and Penderecki's St. Luke Passion. His own works include 4 symphonies; concertos; film music; chamber and piano music; and songs.

Skryabin, Alexander. See Scriabin, Alexander.

Slancio [It.]. Dash, impulse, impetus.

Slapstick. Two narrow, flat pieces of wood about 30 cm. long, hinged so that they can be slapped together, producing a sound like the cracking of a whip; also termed a whip. See ill. under Percussion instruments.

Slargando [It.]. Broadening, slowing down.

Slatkin, Felix (b. St. Louis, 22 Dec. 1915; d. Los Angeles, 8 Feb. 1963). Conductor and violinist. Joined St. Louis Symphony in 1931; moved west in 1937, becoming concertmaster of the 20th-Century Fox studio orchestra. From 1947 to 1961 he led the Hollywood String Quartet, in which his wife, Eleanor Aller, was cellist, and worked as a free-lance studio musician.

Slatkin, Leonard (b. Los Angeles, 1 Sept. 1944). Conductor. Son of Felix Slatkin. Studied at Indiana Univ., Los Angeles City College, and Juilliard School. Assistant conductor (1968–71), associate (1971–74), and music director (1979–96) of the St. Louis Symphony. Also associated with the Minneapolis Orchestra and Oakland Symphony. Music director of the Great Woods Performing Arts Center (summer home of the Pittsburgh Symphony) from 1990 and of the Blossom Music Center (summer home of the Cleveland Orchestra) from 1991. In 1996 succeeded Rostropovich as music director of the National Symphony Orchestra. An advocate of American composers, his own works include Dialogue for 2 cellos and orchestra, The Raven for narrator and orchestra, and 4 string quartets.

Sleeping Beauty, The [Russ. Spyashchaya krasavitsa]. A ballet by Tchaikovsky, op. 66 (1888–89; choreography by Marius Petipa), produced in St. Petersburg in 1890.

Sleigh bells. In musical performance, small *pellet bells mounted in rows on a piece of wood with a protruding handle. See ill. under Percussion instruments.

Slendro [Indonesian, fr. Jav.]. One of the two major tunings (the other being *pelog) that serve as background systems for the interpretation of melodies performed by *gamelan instrumentalists and singers in central and east Java.

Slentando [It.]. Becoming slower.

Slezak, Leo (b. Schönberg, Moravia, 18 Aug. 1873; d. Egern am Tegernsee, Bavaria, 1 June 1946). Tenor. Debut at Brno in 1896 as Lohengrin; sang in Berlin (1898–99), Breslau (1900–1), Vienna (until the mid-1920s); guest appearances at Metropolitan Opera (1909–13). Specialist in German heldentenor roles. Retired from the stage in 1933 and became a film comedian; wrote several volumes of memoirs.

Slide. (1) On the *trombone and slide *trumpet, a U-shaped segment of cylindrical tubing fitted over two straight segments of tubing in such a way as to be able to slide easily in and out, thus changing the instrument's effective total length, and with it, its fundamental pitch. On brass instruments generally, a tuning slide is a much shorter device of similar design intended for minor adjustments of the instrument's pitch. Instruments with *valves may permit in this way the adjustment of the instrument as a whole as well as of each of the segments of tubing controlled by a valve.

(2) In the playing of bowed stringed instruments, movement from one pitch to another by sliding the finger that has stopped the first pitch toward the second pitch, which is then stopped by an adjacent finger at the rhythmically appropriate moment, an effect sometimes also termed a *portamento; also, any movement from one pitch to another or through a series of discrete pitches by sliding the finger (or fingers, in the case of double stops) from one to the next. The technique was developed early in the 19th century.

(3) [Ger. *Schleifer*] An ornament consisting most commonly of two notes ascending stepwise to the principal note and slurred to it. It is very often written out in full notes, but can also be indicated by small notes, a sign, or not at all.

Slide guitar. *Bottleneck.

Slit drum. A length of wood or bamboo hollowed out through a slit on one side and beaten with a stick.

Slonimsky, Nicolas (b. St. Petersburg, Russia, 27 Apr. 1894; d. Los Angeles, 25 Dec. 1995). Conductor and writer on music. Studied piano and composition at the Petersburg Conservatory. Accompanist for Koussevitzky in Paris. In 1923 moved to the U.S. to teach at Eastman School of Music. Conducted the Harvard Univ. Orchestra (1927–30) and the Boston Chamber Orchestra (1927–34), among others. Edited 4 editions of Thompson's *International Cyclopedia of Music and Musicians* (1946–58); editor-in-chief of *Baker's Biographical Dictionary of Musicians* for its 5th–8th editions (1958–92). Also author of *Music since 1900* (1st ed., 1937); *Thesaurus of Scales and Melodic Patterns* (1947), *Lexicon of Musical Invective* (New York, 1952; rev. 1965), and an autobiography, *Perfect Pitch* (1988).

Slonimsky, Sergei Mikhailovich (b. Leningrad, 12 Aug. 1932). Composer. Studied piano and composition at the Leningrad Conservatory; taught composition there from 1959. His music reflects his interest in Russian folklore. In the late 1960s and early 1970s experimented with serial, aleatoric, and other advanced techniques, subsequently returning to more traditional styles. Works include operas (*Virineia,* 1967 [rev. 1976]; *Master and Margarita,* 1973; *Mary Stuart,* 1980); ballet (*Icarus,* 1971); 9 symphonies; other symphonic music; a violin concerto (1983); cantatas; chamber music; choral works; vocal music.

Slur. A curved line placed above two or more notes of different pitch to indicate that they are to be performed *legato. In the case of bowed instruments, this generally means in a single bow; in the case of wind instruments, without *tonguing or taking breath [see also Articulation]. In vocal music, notes sung to a single syllable or in a single breath may be notated in this way. See also Bowing; Tie. Slurs may also be used to indicate phrasing on a larger scale, as distinct from detailed articulation of notes within a *phrase.

Sly Vixen, The. See *Cunning Little Vixen, The.*

Smalley, Roger (b. Swinton, Manchester, 26 July 1943). Composer. Studied at the Royal College of Music with Fricker and White. In the early 1960s studied with Goehr, performing the music of Boulez, Maxwell Davies, Schoenberg, and Stockhausen. In 1970 cofounded the new-music group Intermodulation. In 1976 joined the research faculty at the Univ. of Western Australia. Compositions incorporate improvisation, electronic media, and quotation, as well as popular musical style and minimalistic devices. Works include *Missa brevis* (16 solo voices, 1966–67); *Missa parodia I* and *II* (1967); *Zeitebenen* (ensemble, tape, 1973); Symphony in One Movement (1981); *The Narrow Road to the Deep North* ("journey" for baritone, 6 players, 1983); *Wind Chimes for Tape* (tape, 1987).

Smareglia, Antonio (b. Pola, Istria, 5 May 1854; d. Grado, Istria, 15 Apr. 1929). Composer. Studied at Milan Conservatory with Faccio. After becoming blind, appointed honorary artistic director of the Tartini Conservatory in Trieste in 1921. Composed 9 operas; orchestral works; piano music; vocal pieces.

Smart, George (Thomas) (b. London, 10 May 1776; d. there, 23 Feb. 1867). Organist, composer, and conductor. One of the founders of the Philharmonic Society of London, 1813 (conductor, 1813–44); introduced many works of Beethoven and Schumann. Named organist at Chapel Royal, 1822. Introduced Mendelssohn's oratorio *St. Paul* and Beethoven's Ninth Symphony to England, 1826. Knew Beethoven; Weber died in his house. Edited Gibbons's madrigals (1841) and other works. His compositions are primarily small sacred pieces. His brother was the violinist Henry Smart (1778–1823).

Smetana, Bedřich (b. Litomyšl, Bohemia, 2 Mar. 1824; d. Prague, 12 May 1884). Composer. Studied with Jozef Proksch. Dedicated his op. 1, piano pieces, to Lizst. In 1856 went to Göteberg, Sweden; composed tone poems following Lizst, Wagner, and Berlioz. Returned permanently to Prague, 1861; reopened his music school, 1863; published music criticism from 1864. In 1866 premiered his second opera, *The Bartered Bride,* which eventually overshadowed his other works. Appointed conductor at the Provisional Theater, 1866; began to be accused of musical radicalism. Became completely deaf in 1874 and resigned from conducting, but continued to compose. Suffering from the advanced stages of syphilis, taken to the Prague insane asylum three weeks before his death.

Works: operas include *Braniboři v Čechách* (The Brandenburgers in Bohemia, 1863), *Prodana nevěsta* (The *Bartered Bride, 1866), *Dalibor* (1868), *Dvě vdovy* (The Two Widows, 1874), *Hubička* (The Kiss, 1875–76), *Libuše* (1881), *Čertove stěna* (The Devil's Wall, 1879–82); orchestral works include Triumphal Symphony (1853–54), *Má vlast* (My Fatherland, 1874–75, 1878–79), *Prague Carnival* (1883); chamber music includes Piano Trio in G minor (1855), String Quartet in E minor (*From My Life, 1876), Second String Quartet (1882–83).

Sminuendo [It.]. *Diminuendo.*

Smit, Leo (b. Philadelphia, 12 Jan. 1921). Pianist and composer. Studied piano with Isabella Vengerova and José Iturbi and composition with Nicholas Nabokov. Accompanist at Balanchine's American Ballet (1936–37); taught at SUNY–Buffalo 1962–84. Works include *Virginia Sampler* (ballet, 1947); *American Graffiti* (voice, clarinet, cello, piano, percussion, 1959); Concerto for Orchestra and Piano (1968); operas *The Alchemy of Love* (1969) and *Magic Water* (1978); sonata for piano 4-hands (1987).

Smith, Bessie (b. Chattanooga, Tenn., 15 Apr. 1894; d. Clarksdale, Miss., 26 Sept. 1937). Blues singer. From 1912 toured in minstrel and vaudeville shows. Recorded widely, including "Down-Hearted Blues" (1923), "St. Louis Blues" (1925, with Louis Armstrong), "Back Water Blues" (1927, with James P. Johnson), "Empty Bed Blues" (1928, with trombonist Charlie Green), and "Gimme a Pigfoot" (1933, with Jack Teagarden, Benny Goodman, and Chu Berry). Starred in the pioneering African American film *St. Louis Blues* (1929).

Smith, Hale (b. Cleveland, 29 June 1925). Composer. Attended the Cleveland Institute of Music; worked in New York as a music editor for various publishers and as an arranger for jazz musicians such as Chico Hamilton, Abbey Lincoln, and Eric Dolphy. Taught at the Univ. of Connecticut, 1970–84. Works include *In Memoriam Beryl Rubinstein,* chorus and chamber orchestra (1953); *Contours,* orchestra (1961); jazz cantata *Comes Tomorrow* (1972; rev. 1976); *Rituals and Incantations,* orchestra (1974).

Smith, John Christopher [Schmidt, Johann Christoph] (b. Ansbach, 1712; d. Bath, 3 Oct. 1795). Composer and organist. Son of Johann Christoph Schmidt, who served as Handel's treasurer and principal copyist; both father and son used the name John Christopher Smith. The younger Smith moved to London in 1720 and produced English-language operas (*Ulysses* 1733), 2 Shakespearean operas (1755 and 1756). In 1754 became organist at the Foundling Hospital, where he directed performances of *Messiah* (1759–68). Also composed oratorio *Paradise Lost* (1757–58).

Smith, Julia (Frances) (b. Denton, Tex., 25 Jan. 1911; d. New York, 27 Apr. 1989). Pianist and composer. Studied at North Texas State Univ., Juilliard, and New York Univ. Wrote works based on American folk materials (*American Dance Suite,* orchestra, 1936, rev. 1963; *Folkways Symphony,* 1948; *Cynthia Parker,* opera, 1939) and more abstract compositions (*Characteristic Suite,* piano, 1949; String Quartet, 1964). Involved in efforts to gain recognition and performances for women composers. Author of *Aaron Copland: His Work and Contribution to American Music* (New York, 1955) and editor of *Directory of American Women Composers* (1970).

Smith, Leland (Clayton) (b. Oakland, 6 Aug. 1925). Composer and teacher. Studied with Milhaud, Sessions, and Messiaen. Taught at Univ. of Chicago and Stanford Univ. As director of the computer music center at Stanford beginning in the late 1960s, developed computer software for composing and printing music; author of numerous articles on computer music. Compositions include 6 Bagatelles for piano

(1965) and *Machines of Loving Grace*, narrator, bassoon and tape (1970).

Smith, Russell (b. Tuscaloosa, Ala., 23 Apr. 1927). Composer. Studied with Luening and worked with Copland at Tanglewood and with Varèse. Composer-in-residence with the Cleveland Orchestra (1966–67) and the New Orleans Philharmonic (1969–71). In 1975 moved to Germany. Works include comic opera *The Unicorn in the Garden*, based on the story by Thurber (1957); *Tetrameron*, orchestra (1957); Percussion Concerto (1979), Piano Sonata (1981), Symphony (1982).

Smith, William (Overton) (Bill) (b. Sacramento, 22 Sept. 1926; d. Havertown, Pa., 24 Mar. 1993). Composer and clarinetist. A jazz clarinetist since his teens, studied at Juilliard and with Milhaud and Sessions. Performed with the Dave Brubeck Octet. Taught at the Univ. of Southern California (1958–60) and Univ. of Washington (beginning 1966). Works include Concertino (trumpet and jazz ensemble, 1948); *Elegy for Eric* (1964); *Quiet Please* (jazz orchestra, 1982); Concerto for Jazz Soloist and Orchestra (clarinet and orchestra, 1962); *Theona* (jazz ensemble and orchestra, 1975); *Musings* (3 clarinets and 3 dancers); numerous works for unaccompanied clarinet.

Smith, Willie "the Lion" [William Henry Joseph Bonaparte Bertholoff] (b. Goshen, N.Y., 24 Nov. 1897; d. New York, 18 Apr. 1973). Jazz pianist and composer. Spent most of his career as a solo pianist in New York; also recorded with Mamie Smith (1920) and Sidney Bechet (1941); toured Europe and performed at many jazz festivals. Compositions include "Echoes of Spring," "Fading Star," and "Rippling Waters."

Smith Brindle, Reginald (b. Bamber Bridge, 5 Jan. 1917). Composer. Studied with Pizzetti and Dallapiccola. In 1967 joined the faculty at University College in Bangor; 1970, professor at the Univ. of Surrey. Later compositions used electronic media and percussion instruments. Author of *Contemporary Percussion* (1970); *The New Music: The Avant-Garde since 1945* (1975, 1987); *Musical Composition* (1986); *Serial Composition* (1966). Works include *Antigone* (chamber opera, 1969); orchestral music; chamber and vocal works; works for solo guitar and guitar ensemble.

Smorzando [It.]. Dying away.

Smyth, Ethel (Mary) (b. Marlebone, 22 Apr. 1858; d. Woking, 9 May 1944). Composer. Studied at Leipzig Conservatory with Reinecke and Jadassohn, later with Heinrich von Herzogenberg; met Grieg, Joachim, Clara Schumann, and Brahms. Returned to England in 1888; in 1890 premiered Serenade for Orchestra and the overture *Antony and Cleopatra;* 1893 performance of Mass in D at the Albert Hall brought acclaim. Operas include *Fantasio* (Weimar, 1898) and *Der Wald* (Berlin, 1902), both to her own German librettos; *The Wreckers,* originally written to a French libretto as *Les naufrageurs* and premiered in Leipzig in 1906 as *Strandrecht.* Other works include *March of the Women* (1911), the battle song of the Women's Social and Political Union; theater works.

Snare [Fr. *timbre;* Ger. *Schnarrsaite, Trommelsaite;* It. *corda, bordoniera;* Sp. *bordón*]. Heavy strings or wires, now often overspun with metal, stretched across the center of one head of the snare or side *drum (and sometimes of larger drums) so as to vibrate against it when the other head is struck.

Snare drum. See Drum.

Snello [It.]. Nimble, graceful.

Soave [It.]. Sweet, gentle.

Sobolewski, (Johann Friedrich) Eduard [Edward] (b. Königsberg, 1 Oct. 1804; d. St. Louis, Mo., 17 May 1872). Violinist, composer, and conductor. Studied with Zelter and Weber. Director of music at the Königsberg Theater, 1830; founded and conducted Philharmonische Gesellschaft, 1838. Critic for *Ostpreussische Zeitung* and *Neue Zeitschrift für Musikwissenschaft.* Music director of theater in Bremen from 1854. In 1859, settled in Milwaukee; there staged his first opera, *Mohega,* based on a tale of the American Indians (1859). Founder and conductor of Milwaukee Philharmonic Society Orchestra. Conductor of Philharmonic Society, St. Louis, 1860–66. Compositions are primarily for solo voice or chorus.

Söderström, Elisabeth (b. Stockholm, 7 May 1927). Soprano. Debut Stockholm, 1947. Joined Royal Opera in 1949; sang also at Salzburg (from 1955), Glyndebourne (from 1957), and the Metropolitan Opera (1959–63 and 1983–87). Sang in the premiere of Ligeti's *Le grand macabre* (Stockholm, 1978); other roles range from Nero in *L'incoronazione di Poppea* to the Marschallin in *Der Rosenkavalier* and Marie in *Wozzeck.* In 1990 became artistic director of the Drottningholm Court Theater.

Sofort [Ger.]. Immediately, *attacca.

Soft pedal. See *Una corda,* Piano.

Soggetto [It.]. Subject, theme. In the 16th century, the term referred to the entirety of a melody forming the basis of a canon. By the 18th century, it referred to a fugue subject of the type found in the early *ricercar, consisting of relatively few notes of relatively long duration.

Soggetto cavato (dalle parole) [It., subject carved from the words]. A musical subject or *cantus firmus* derived from a text by employing *solmization syllables whose vowels correspond to the vowels in the text.

Soir, Le [Fr.]. See *Matin, Le.*

Sol. See Pitch names, Solmization, Hexachord.

Solage (fl. 1370–90). Composer. Wrote 10 chansons (7 ballades, 2 virelays, 1 rondeau) preserved in the Chantilly manuscript, Musée Condé 564. Was perhaps active in the court of Jean, Duke of Berry. His 3-voice writing exhibits rhythmic and harmonic complexities of the *ars subtilior.*

Solares, Enrique (b. Guatemala City, 11 July 1910). Composer and pianist. Studied piano in his home city as well as in San Francisco; composition in Prague (with Krioka), Rome (with Casella), and Brussels (with Joseph Jongen and Raymond Moulart). Taught piano in Guatemala from 1943 before becoming a diplomat, serving in Rome, Brussels, Madrid, and Paris. Much of his music uses Baroque and classical formal procedures; later pieces venture into serial composition. Works include orchestral works; chamber music; ricercares (including 1 on B-A-C-H), toccatas, preludes, and other piano works; and songs.

Soldier's Tale, The. See *Histoire du soldat, L'.*

Soleá [Sp., pl. *soleares*]. One of the principal general categories of *flamenco music, incorporating many subtypes. The most prominent types of text or *copla* are the *grande* (great), consisting of four octosyllabic lines, with lines 2 and 4 rhyming, and the *corta* (short), consisting of three octosyllabic lines, with lines 1 and 3 rhyming. The guitar accompaniment employs a variety of patterns in 6/8 and 3/4.

Solenne [It.]. Solemn.

Solennel [Fr.]. Solemn.

Soler (Ramos), Antonio (Francisco Javier José) (bapt. Olot Gerona, 3 Dec. 1729; d. El Escorial, 20 Dec. 1783). Composer. Became *maestro di capilla* at Lérida around 1750, and at El Escorial in 1757. Took holy orders in 1752. Studied in Madrid with Domenico Scarlatti between 1752 and 1757. Remembered mainly for his keyboard works, which include 120 sonatas; 6 double organ concertos; 6 quintets for organ, 2 violins, viola, and cello; and liturgical organ works. Other compositions include 9 Masses, 5 Requiems, 136 *villancicos,* numerous sacred vocal works. Author of a theoretical treatise, *Llave de la modulación (1762).*

Sol-fa. See Tonic Sol-fa.

Solfège [Fr.], **solfeggio** [It.]. (1) In the 17th century and subsequently, a textless vocal exercise (first Italian, later also French).

(2) Particularly from the late 18th century to the present, the singing of scales, intervals, and melodic exercises to *solmization syllables. The term has also been used to encompass all aspects of the teaching of basic musical skills; in France particularly, extensive courses of solfège (in this sense) were developed. Currently, the (revised Guidonian) syllables *do, re, mi, fa, sol, la, si* (*ti*) are applied to notes in two different ways, called fixed *do* and movable *do.* In fixed *do,* the syllables are equivalent in meaning to letter names: *do* = C, *re* = D, *mi* = E, and so forth; they are assigned without regard to accidentals. In movable *do,* the syllables indicate the scale degrees of a major scale (e.g., in D major, *do* = D, *re* = E, *mi* = F♯, and so forth). Chromatic notes are assigned syllables in various ways. German *Tonwort* systems combine characteristics of both types of solmization: fixed correspondence between letter names and syllables, but variation of syllables according to chromatic alteration.

Solfegietto [It. also *solfeggieto*]. A short piece similar in character to an etude or study.

Sollberger, Harvey (b. Cedar Rapids, Iowa, 11 May 1938). Flutist, composer, conductor. Studied flute in New York with Samuel Baron and Betty Mather, composition at Columbia Univ. with Jack Beeson and Otto Luening. In 1962, with Charles Wuorinen, founded the Group for Contemporary Music. Taught at Columbia (1965–83) and at the Manhattan School of Music (1972–83); at Indiana Univ. from 1983. Pioneer in the development of "extended" techniques for the flute, featured in his compositions: *Divertimento* (flute, cello, piano, 1970), *Angel and Stone* (flute, piano, 1981), *Riding the Wind I–IV* (1973–74) for flute and various instruments. Other works include *Persian Golf* (string orchestra, 1987); *Quodlibetudes* (flute, 1988).

Solmization. The designation of pitches by means of conventional syllables rather than letter names. Many of the principal musical cultures of the world have systems of solmization, which may be employed in oral transmission or in the teaching or reading of music. The syllables most commonly used in Western cultures today are *do* (*doh*), *re, mi, fa, sol, la,* and *si* (or *ti*). These are derived from the Guidonian system.

The system that has survived into modern Western use, first recorded in the early 11th century, is traditionally associated with Guido of Arezzo. Guidonian solmization is based on a set of interlocking *hexachords. The system is based on the text and tune of the hymn *Ut queant laxis,* in which each of the first six lines begins one step higher than the previous line; the six initial tones of these lines constitute a hexachord. The syllables sung to the notes of the hexachord in the hymn tune, and associated with them in Guidonian solmization, are *ut, re, mi, fa, sol,* and *la.* Between *mi* and *fa* is a semitone; a whole tone separates other adjacent syllables. Solmization was conceived as a method for *sight-reading. To solmize a melody, one gives a syllable to each written note and sings the pitch associated with that syllable.

In the Guidonian system, regular hexachords begin on C, F, and G, within the range G to g'; the notes of these hexachords constitute the gamut, which reaches from G to e''. Early in the 15th century, hexachords beginning on every note, altered or unaltered, were described by theorists. When a melody to be solmized moves beyond the limits of a single hexachord (regular or *ficta*), the device of mutation is used to change from one hexachord to another.

Most theorists of the 16th century advanced no substantial changes in Guidonian solmization but simply tried to make it easier to use. Around the year 1600 the syllable *si* was added to the original six, so that the series could encompass an octave. Otto Gibelius both adopted Guido's syllables for the diatonic notes and, following Italian writers of the 16th century, used *do* in place of *ut.* Since then, many methods of using Guidonian solmization and of expanding it to include extra syllables, particularly for chromatically altered notes, have been advanced [see Solfège (2)]. None has become universal. In the 18th century, a simplified method called *fasola was widely used in the U.S. Recently, several systems, including *Tonic Sol-fa (especially in England) and Zoltán Kodály's method (developed in Hungary, now used elsewhere as well), have achieved considerable currency.

Solo [It., alone]. (1) A work for a single instrument without accompaniment or one in which a single instrument is prominently featured throughout, even if with accompaniment. (2) In a work for ensemble, a passage to be played by a single player instead of an entire section or one in which a single player has an especially prominent part. (3) In a concerto, a passage featuring the soloist, as distinct from a *tutti, in which the orchestra predominates.

Solti, Georg (b. Budapest, 21 Oct. 1912; d. Antibes, 5 Sept. 1997). Conductor. Attended the Liszt Academy, Budapest, a pupil of Bartók and Dohnányi in piano and Kodály in composition. Coach and accompanist for the Budapest State Opera, then Toscanini's assistant at the 1936 and 1937 Salzburg festivals; conducting debut in Budapest, 1938. In Switzerland when World War II broke out; in 1944 conducted Swiss Radio Orchestra. Appointed music director at the Bavarian State Opera, after the war, moving to

Frankfurt as music director in 1952. Music director, Covent Garden, 1961–71. Took British citizenship, and was knighted in 1972. Music director, Chicago Symphony, 1969–91; held similar posts with L'Orchestre de Paris (1972–75) and the London Philharmonic (1979–83); in 1992 became artistic director of the Salzburg Music Festival. Recorded extensively, including the first complete *Ring* cycle.

Sombrero de tres picos, El [Sp., The Three-Cornered Hat]. A ballet by Manuel de Falla (choreography by Leonide Massine; décor by Pablo Picasso; based on a novel by Pedro Antonio de Alarcón), produced in London in 1919. It is an expanded version of Falla's unpublished "farsa mímica" *El corregidor y la molinera* (The Magistrate and the Miller's Daughter), composed in 1916–17.

Somers, Harry (Stewart) (b. Toronto, 11 Sept. 1925). Composer. Studied piano with Reginald Godden and Weldon Kilburn, composition with John Weinzweig in Toronto. In 1940s gave piano recitals; after 1948 devoted himself to composition. Earlier works include *North Country* (string orchestra, 1948), Symphony no. 1 (1951), *Five Songs for Dark Voice* (alto and chamber orchestra, 1956). Later works employed serial techniques and electronic music: *The Fisherman and His Soul* (ballet, 1956), *12 x 12: Fugues for Piano* (1951); *Louis Riel* (opera, 1967). Other works include *Voiceplay* (solo singer-actor, 1971); *Kyrie* (soloists, choir, chamber ensemble, 1972) *Mario and the Magician* (opera, 1992).

Somervell, Arthur (b. Windermere, 5 June 1863; d. London, 2 May 1937). Composer. Studied with Stanford and Parry. Lecturer at the Royal College of Music from 1894; inspector of music for the Board of Education 1901–28. Music predominantly vocal, including the song cycles *Maud* (1898), *The Shropshire Lad* (1904), and *A Broken Arc* (1923); vocal works (Passion of Christ, 1913) and orchestral music (*Symphonic Variations 'Normandy,'* 1912).

Somis, Giovanni Battista (b. Turin, 25 Dec. 1686; d. there, 14 Aug. 1763). Composer and violinist. Violinist in the Turin ducal orchestra by 1699. Studied with Corelli and may have received instruction from Vivaldi. Solo violinist and leader of the Turin chapel from 1707; appeared in Paris in 1733. Violin pupils included Leclair, Guillemain, Guignon, and Pugnani. Reputed to have composed over 150 concertos and 75 violin sonatas; most of his music has not survived.

Son. (1) [Fr.] Sound; *s. bouché, étouffé,* in horn playing, *stopped tone; *s. ouvert,* an open or natural tone on a wind instrument; *s. harmonique,* harmonic. (2) [Sp.] In Cuba, a rural song and dance-music style combining Hispanic and African-derived elements. In moderate to rapid tempo, syncopated, and in duple meter, *sones* are varied in structure; a typical form alternates two sections, one with verses sung to a short repeated phrase, the other with a repeated *call-and-response refrain. In the early 20th century, the *son* became an important urban popular form, performed by ensembles that gradually modified its traditional instrumentation and musical style. (3) [Sp.] Any of a number of types of pieces of traditional dance music in several regions of Mexico.

Sonata [It.]. A work for one or more solo instruments, usually in several movements, and prevalent from the 17th century on. This definition must be refined for each historical period and must allow for exceptions, since the term sonata has at times been used for instrumental works that include a part for voice or, in the 17th and 18th centuries, for works that could also be performed by orchestra [see Trio sonata]. The term has a long history before 1600, but has always denoted instrumental music. See also Sonata form.

In the Baroque period, the term sonata was applied in Italy not only to dance collections but also to a new type of instrumental work in an abstract style. Sonatas in an abstract style were composed for a variety of instruments, both keyboard and ensemble, and in a variety of settings, from unaccompanied solo to polychoral works for as many as 22 parts grouped in five instrumental choirs. Giovanni Gabrieli's two sonatas in his *Sacrae symphoniae* (Venice, 1597) are the earliest examples in this abstract style.

Most common were ensemble sonatas for one to four melody instruments and basso continuo. Their appearance heralds the rise to prominence of the violin family, and they were the main vehicle for the development of a style appropriate to these instruments. The names applied to these works are misleading as to the number of performers involved. A solo sonata, for example, requires three: the solo instrument, usually a violin; a chord-producing instrument, usually either organ or harpsichord, to realize the harmonies of the continuo [see Thoroughbass]; and a bass instrument, usually stringed, to reinforce the bass line. The most common scoring, however, was to be that of the trio sonata.

Through the 1650s, it is often difficult to distinguish between the canzona and the sonata stylistically. Both have a number of sections contrasting in tempo, meter, and character, though the sonata tends to be more virtuosic and exploits such special effects for the violin as *double stops and *scordatura. Prominent composers include Carlo Farina (ca. 1600–ca. 1640), Biagio Marini (ca. 1587–1663), Johann Heinrich Schmelzer (ca. 1620–80), and Heinrich Biber (1644–1704).

The first half of the 17th century saw the gradual fusion of the canzona and sonata and the emergence of a concern with the uses of the sonata. Both trends crystallized in the 1650s in the sonatas of Giovanni Legrenzi (1626–90) and others, which are of two types, *sonata da chiesa* and *sonata da camera, differentiated in both style and function. The former, suitable for use in the church, employs an abstract style; the latter, intended for use in the chamber, is most often a collection of dances. By the 1650s, the number of contrasting sections in the two precursors of the *sonata da chiesa* had decreased, and those that remained took on the character of independent movements, normally three to five. Further standardization in format for both types is evident in the works of Corelli at the end of the 17th century.

In the 18th century, such non-Italian composers as Telemann, Bach, Handel, and Jean-Marie Leclair *l'aîné* were to write numerous sonatas that employed the format prevalent in Corelli's *sonate da chiesa*. These include solo sonatas and trio sonatas and often specify wind instruments such as recorder, flute, or oboe instead of the violin. Italian composers during these same years often favored either fewer or more movements. Francesco Veracini (1690–1768) wrote sonatas having from five to eight movements, whereas both Giuseppe Tartini (1692–1770) and Pietro Locatelli (1695–1764) preferred the three-movement format that was to become the norm in the Classical period.

The rise to prominence of solo sonatas for stringed keyboard instruments in the 1740s is one sign of the beginnings of Classical style, especially in the works of such eminent composers as Domenico Scarlatti and Carl Philipp Emanuel Bach. The former probably composed primarily for the harpsichord, the preferred instrument through the 1760s. The latter early in his career favored the clavichord; in the 1760s, Emanuel Bach turned to the more powerful fortepiano.

Scarlatti's sonatas are one-movement *binary forms. Emanuel Bach, on the other hand, composed sonatas in a three-movement format, fast–slow–fast, that was to become standard for the Classical sonata, regardless of instrumentation, though other plans are found as well. Solo sonatas of this type were extremely popular with the three late Classical Viennese composers: Haydn, Mozart, and Beethoven.

More popular initially than the solo keyboard sonata, and first appearing at about the same time, was the *accompanied keyboard sonata, which was of two types: the first included the violin, the second both violin and cello. In both types, the stringed instruments either reinforce the melody (or melody and bass) of the keyboard part or supply sustained notes against it.

The formal conventions employed for individual movements of the Classical sonata, regardless of instrumentation, were shared with other contemporary kinds of chamber music and with the symphony. Most evolved in some fashion from the *binary form associated with the dance. Most often, the first movements of such works are in *sonata form. The slow middle movements, normally in a different key, often also employ sonata form, occasionally with a short retransition replacing the development. Other conventions used for this movement include the simple binary form (common in Haydn), a ternary design (favored by Mozart and Beethoven), the variation set, and—rarely—the *rondo. If a fourth movement is present (and it was seldom included before Beethoven), it most often relates to the dance and is normally placed between the slow movement and the finale. In early Classical sonatas it is commonly a *minuet and trio; in Beethoven's works it is usually a *scherzo. For final movements, the two most common conventions are the dance (again a minuet and trio) and the rondo. The former was more popular with early Classical composers, the latter with the three Viennese masters, who often furnished their rondos with a development, creating what is commonly called a sonata-rondo [see Rondo]. Other possibilities for the final movement include sonata form and the variation.

During Beethoven's last years, such early Romantic composers as Schubert, Weber, and Mendelssohn wrote numerous sonatas, mainly for piano solo or for piano and violin. Though infused with a new spirit, these works still employ Classical conventions for the number of movements and their formal schemes. Following Beethoven's death in 1827, however, there was a marked decline in interest in the genre, even by such major composers as Schumann, Chopin, Liszt, and Brahms.

Yet the fact that Schumann, Chopin, Liszt, and Brahms all chose, early in their careers, to compose examples of the sonata testifies to the continuing high regard for the genre.

Interest in the sonata continued in the 20th century in a limited fashion, though the genre was often transformed in both style and general form. Between 1920 and 1940, many composers wrote sonatas that have been somewhat misleadingly labeled *neoclassical, since they reintroduce not only Baroque formal conventions but often rhythms and counterpoint of that period as well. After 1940, composers increasingly turned to other names for chamber works that earlier might have been called sonatas.

Sonata da camera [It., chamber sonata or court sonata]. A work for instrumental ensemble, prevalent from the 1650s through the 1740s. Written for one or more melody instruments, normally of the violin family, and basso continuo [see Thoroughbass], it was associated with the dance throughout the 17th century. The earliest examples, by Giovanni Legrenzi (op. 4, 1656), consist of a single binary form. Later examples by Giovanni Maria Bononcini (op. 2, 1667) consist solely of dances [see also Suite]. The format associated later with Corelli included an introductory free movement followed by two to four dances. After Corelli the genre was less favored, though new examples were being published at least through 1744 by Francesco Veracini.

Sonata da chiesa [It., church sonata]. A work for instrumental ensemble, prevalent from the 1650s through the 1770s. It has one to seven or more sections or movements, contrasting in meter, tempo, and texture, and is written for one or more melody instruments, normally of the violin family, and basso continuo [see Thoroughbass]. Though called simply sonata in most 17th-century publications, suggesting use outside the church as well, it is identifiable by a serious style, manifest in much fugal writing, by the relative scarcity of the dance movements characteristic of the *sonata da camera, and by the common specification of organ as the continuo instrument. With Corelli the form of the church sonata became standardized. Most have four movements: slow–fast–slow–fast. Composers employing this format in the 18th century—still under the name sonata—include Vivaldi, Handel, Bach, Telemann, and Jean-Marie Leclair l'aîné. The church sonata, in part or as a whole, was used in Italy, and doubtless elsewhere, in the Mass of the Roman rite as a substitute for the gradual and communion, and at Vespers for Psalm *antiphons.

Sonata form. The most characteristic form for an individual movement (as distinct from a complete, multimovement work) in instrumental music from the Classical period to the 20th century. Sonata form occurs not merely (or even most typically) in sonatas, but also in a wide variety of other orchestral and chamber genres—symphonies, overtures, string quartets, and so forth. Because this form is common in slow movements and finales as well as opening fast movements, the more general term sonata form is preferable to such designations as sonata-allegro form and first-movement form.

The basis for sonata form is the open modulatory plan of *binary form, in which an initial modulation from the tonic to a new key (normally the dominant in a movement in major) is answered by a complementary modulation from the new key back to the tonic. This scheme results in two large divisions or parts.

The first part, which modulates to the new key, is known traditionally as the exposition. It is repeated in most Classical and many Romantic examples. The second part, which leads eventually back to the tonic, was also generally repeated until the late 18th century, when composers began to omit this repetition,

(Intro.)	Part 1 Exposition			Part 2 Development		Recapitulation		(Coda)
⫼	⫴: Pr.　Tr.　｜Sec.　Cl.　:⫸(:)	(Pr.)		Retr.	｜Pr.　Tr.　｜Sec.　Cl.　(:⫸)	⫼
(I)	I ⟶ N ⟶┤	N or other ⌇⌇⟶ (V)	I ⟶ (IV) ┤

Sonata form.

especially in large-scale works. The second part is usually more extended than the first; it consists of two large sections, each of which may rival the exposition in size and importance: the development and the recapitulation. The development section ordinarily modulates still farther afield and provides varied and often dramatic treatment of material already heard in the exposition. This combination of tonal instability and intensive thematic development can create a high degree of tension at the midpoint of the movement. The recapitulation, the second section of part 2, is based thematically upon the exposition but now ends as well as begins in the tonic. (In minor-key movements, however, a shift to the tonic major may occur at any point in the recapitulation.) Once again tonality and thematic process coordinate, for the re-entry of the tonic coincides with the return to original material in its approximately original form and order. Moreover, the material formerly heard in the new key now recurs in the tonic, providing a long-range resolution of the tonal tension created by the modulation in the exposition.

Expositions vary widely in structure, revealing a highly flexible interaction of tonality, thematic material, and large-scale rhythmic motion. In one typical pattern, the tonic is established by means of a harmonically clear-cut primary theme or themes. After this section comes a more vigorous or brilliant transition that accomplishes the modulation to the new key. At this point, in order to confirm or stabilize the new key, the composer may introduce one or more contrasting secondary themes, often *piano*. The exposition then closes with cadential material, which may range from conventional chordal passages to full-fledged themes.

Construction of the development section follows no stereotyped plan. Most early development sections, and many later ones, begin with a restatement of the primary theme in the new key—an obvious vestige of their binary origin. Others introduce new or related material at this point, frequently transitional in character. Conventional descriptions of development sections emphasize the intensive, concentrated character of their thematic treatment. A majority of the development sections in mature Haydn, late Mozart, Beethoven, and Brahms do indeed fit this description, applying such techniques as melodic variation, fragmentation, expansion or compression, contrapuntal combination, textural and contextual change, reharmonization, and reorches-

tration to one or many themes of the exposition [see Development]. Others, however, from all chronological periods, merely restate material from the exposition with little change other than the key, or are basically episodic in nature. Yet even these sections often represent the dramatic culmination or high point of the movement, if only because of their more extensive modulatory excursions. A majority of development sections conclude with a passage known as a retransition, which sets the stage for the simultaneous return of the tonic key and original thematic material at the beginning of the recapitulation, usually by suspensefully stressing the dominant.

Recapitulations run the gamut from nearly exact restatement of the material of the exposition, the only alteration being transposition to the tonic of the new-key material, to thoroughgoing recomposition involving extensive compression or expansion.

In addition to the three obligatory sections, exposition, development, and recapitulation, a movement in sonata form may begin with an introduction and end with a coda, the latter generally returning once again to the primary theme and emphasizing the subdominant at some point. An entire movement in full sonata form might therefore proceed as in the accompanying figure (N = new key, arrows = modulations; Pr. = primary material, Tr. = transitional material, Sec. = secondary material, Cl. = closing material; Retr. = retransition).

Sonata-rondo. See Rondo.

Sonatina [It., dim. of sonata]. A work with the formal characteristics of a *sonata (usually of the type cultivated in the Classical period), but on a smaller scale and often less technically demanding for the performer.

Sondheim, Stephen (Joshua) (b. New York City, 22 Mar. 1930). Popular composer and lyricist. Studied at Williams College and with Milton Babbitt; wrote songs and lyrics under the direction of Oscar Hammerstein II. Rose to prominence with lyrics for Leonard Bernstein's *West Side Story* (1957) and Jule Styne's *Gypsy* (1959); first score was *A Funny Thing Happened on the Way to the Forum* (1962). In the 1970s collaborated with director Hal Prince on Broadway musicals *Company* (1970), *A Little Night Music* (1972), *Pacific Overtures* (1976), *Sweeney Todd* (1979). *Sunday in the Park with George* (1984, with James Lapine) won a Pulitzer Prize; other works include *Into the Woods* (1987), *Assassins* (1990), and *Passion* (1994, with James Lapine).

Song. A form of musical expression in which the human voice has the principal role and is the carrier of a text; as a generic term, any music that is sung; more specifically, a short, simple vocal composition consisting of melody and verse text. In this latter, narrower sense, song would exclude, for example, the ornate Baroque solo *cantata or the extended opera *aria. (In German, the generic and specific meanings are distinguished as, respectively, *Gesang* and *Lied*.) This article is limited primarily to Western secular art song.

Song verse most commonly is strophic poetry with short, regular line lengths, simple rhyme schemes, and often some kind of refrain. Subjects of song verse vary greatly, with love probably the most common. Judged as poetry, song verse may be inferior or of the highest literary achievement.

A song is most commonly for a solo voice, and its music may be considered to be primarily its melody or tune, whether accompanied or unaccompanied. In some periods, *polyphonic song, with no single voice predominating, is prevalent. A musical setting may be composed to an existing text, a text may be written to fit a melody, or the two may be created together. The authors of the text and music may be the same or different persons.

The music of a song may be related to its text in terms of form (or structure), sound, and meaning. Gross form is a matter of how the overall structure of the poem is manifested in the music: e.g., whether a setting of a strophic poem is musically *strophic (or modified strophic) or *through-composed. Particular form concerns the relation between the line structure of the text and the phrase structure of the music. Form and sound overlap, since sound elements such as meter and rhyme in poetry and rhythm and *cadences in music articulate structure. On a level of finer detail, the sound qualities of the text may be related to musical elements in a variety of ways. Song may also reflect, enhance, or construe the meaning of the text through mode, tempo, dynamics, word-painting, sets of conventionalized or personal musical symbols, and musical analogs to emotional effects. Changes in texture or in the pace of declamation may correspond to structural, phonetic, or semantic features of the text.

Almost no songs from ancient Greece and Rome have survived with their melodies intact or transcribable, but surviving epic and lyric poetry abundantly attests to the prominence of song in classical cultures. The largest body of medieval song is Christian liturgical *plainsong, within which the Latin *hymns are closest to the narrow definition of song. The secular monophonic song of the early Middle Ages may

have constituted just as vast a repertory. The little that survives includes *Goliard songs from the 12th century, the most famous of which are the *Carmina burana*. At the same time, the paraliturgical *conductus* existed also as a secular strophic Latin song.

The high Middle Ages developed a significant repertory of vernacular song: the epic *chansons de geste,* *troubadour and *trouvère songs in France, the Minnesang (and later Meistergesang) in German-speaking areas [see Minnesinger, Meistersinger], *laude and *cantigas in Italy and Spain, respectively, *minstrel songs (and later *carols) in England.

In the 14th century, France and Italy saw a great burgeoning of secular polyphonic song. In the French *ars nova,* the huge variety of trouvère genres was largely narrowed to the *formes fixes:* *rondeau, *virelai,* and *ballade (as in the works of Guillaume de Machaut). Three-part texture was most common, one part sung and two probably instrumental. In trecento Italy, the *madrigal and *ballata* predominated (composed by, e.g., Jacopo da Bologna and Francesco Landini); two sung parts, often joined by an instrumental one, were the norm. Elaborate *canonic songs were also composed (the *chace in France, the *caccia in Italy), and some genres remained partly or wholly monophonic (e.g., the *lai). English song tradition remained relatively separate from that of the Continent, and the sources transmit a smaller repertory, including the first *round (*"Sumer is icumen in") and the *carol, which was often purely secular and was not originally associated only with Christmas.

In the 15th century, the standard number of parts in polyphonic song gradually increased from three to four, *imitation among the parts began to be common, and the *formes fixes gave way to freer verse (though vestiges remained, as in the *bergerette,* a one-strophe virelai). The Franco-Flemish or Burgundian *chanson flourished in the mid-15th century (by, e.g., Binchois, Dufay).

In the early 16th century, pervasive imitation became the norm, as did the texting and singing of all parts (e.g., in the works of Josquin Desprez). The Parisian chanson (Claudin de Sermisy, Clément Janequin) and Italian *frottola (Marchetto Cara, Bartolomeo Trombonico) and *madrigal (Jacques Arcadelt, Philippe Verdelot, Cipriano de Rore) were the most common genres. A growing body of German-texted polyphonic songs, especially the *Tenorlied (Heinrich Isaac, Ludwig Senfl), set a preexisting monophonic popular or folk song in the tenor part, surrounded by other composed parts.

Later, the texture of polyphonic songs (e.g., by Adrian Willaert) was enriched to five and sometimes six voices. The Italian madrigal of the late 16th and early 17th centuries (Luca Marenzio, Claudio Monteverdi, Carlo Gesualdo) was the leading song genre of its time. English composers (Thomas Weelkes, John Wilbye, Thomas Morley) subsequently produced English madrigals that, though modeled on the Italian, maintained a distinct identity.

In the early 17th century, there was a widespread revival of interest in setting texts for solo voice, often in a speechlike manner over a simple, chordal accompaniment [see Monody, Thoroughbass], as cultivated in the new *opera (Jacopo Peri, Giulio Caccini), but also in the solo madrigal (Caccini, Sigismondo d'India). In Elizabethan England, lute songs or *ayres flourished, written by madrigal composers such as Morley and lutenists such as John Dowland. In France, analogous songs were *airs de cour and *vaudevilles.

Purcell integrated Italian and English vocal styles in a significant body of solo songs in the late 17th century. In a lighter vein, Purcell and his contemporaries produced humorous and bawdy *part songs called *catches and *glees.

During the 17th century, the solo songs or *arias in opera, largely following Italian models, became more complex in range and rhythm, more gymnastic vocally, and increasingly oriented toward projection of the emotion or *affect of the text as much as toward clear and straightforward setting of the words. This trend reached its height in arias of Alessandro Scarlatti (opera), Handel (opera and oratorio), and Bach (cantata) in the 18th century.

In the 18th century, a variety of musical and social factors helped produce the modern keyboard-accompanied solo song. At approximately the same time, the collection and printing of folk songs provided a body of accessible song as well as a style to be assimilated into the artistic tradition. Folk melodies were given keyboard accompaniments by Beethoven and Haydn, among others, and left their mark on original compositions.

In the late 18th and early 19th centuries, national traditions were important in the development of solo song. Foremost was the German, giving rise to the *lied, of which the chief exponents were Schubert and Schumann (followed later by Brahms, Wolf, Mahler, and Richard Strauss). The French art song, the *mélodie, shares some features of the lied, but embodies the unmistakably French style of its composers (e.g., Berlioz, Fauré, Henri Duparc).

In quantity, popular song completely overshadowed art song in the 20th century (e.g., folk, jazz, show tunes, rock-and-roll). The art song, nevertheless, continued strong in the music of such composers as Debussy, Ravel, Poulenc, and Messiaen in France; Vaughan Williams, Britten, and Tippett in England; Schoenberg, Berg, Webern, and Hindemith in Germany and Austria; and Ives, Copland, Barber, and Rorem in the U.S.

Song cycle [Ger. *Liederkreis, Liederzyklus*]. A group of songs, usually for solo voice and piano, constituting a literary and musical unit. The song cycle is associated primarily with the 19th-century German *lied.

The poems of a song cycle are usually by a single poet and often exist as a poetic cycle, taken over in whole or in part by the composer. The poems may be related in general theme and sometimes suggest a narrative outline. Many of the most familiar song cycles are examples: Beethoven's *An die ferne Geliebte* (Alois Jeitteles), Schubert's *Die schöne Müllerin* and *Winterreise* (Wilhelm Müller), Schumann's *Frauenliebe und Leben* (Adalbert von Chamisso). In other cases, the song texts are the composer's selection and arrangement of poems by a single poet, from a single source, or, less commonly, from different poets.

The songs in a cycle are sometimes drawn together by musical means. Beethoven's use of connective piano interludes between the songs of *An die ferne Geliebte* is unique, but his reprise of music from the beginning of the cycle at the end had imitators (e.g., Schumann in *Frauenliebe und Leben*), as did his writing the songs in closely related keys and ending the cycle in the key in which it had begun. Songs may also be related by common musical motives. However, Schubert's cycles, for example, manifest none of these traits.

Song form [Ger. *Liedform*]. Ternary form, ABA [see Binary and ternary form].

Song of Destiny. See *Schicksalslied*.

Song of the Earth, The. See *Lied von der Erde, Das*.

Songs of a Wayfarer. See *Lieder eines fahrenden Gesellen*.

Songs without Words. See *Lieder ohne Worte*.

Sonnambula, La [It., The Sleepwalker]. Opera in two acts by Bellini (libretto by Felice Romani, based on Eugène Scribe's scenario for a ballet), produced in Milan in 1831. Setting: a Swiss village early in the 19th century.

Sonnerie [Fr.]. A signal sounded by trumpets or bells.

Sonore [Fr.], **sonoro, sonoramente** [It.]. Sonorous(ly).

Sonority. (1) In discussions of 20th-century music, a sound defined by some combination of timbres or registers, especially one that plays a significant role in a work. (2) The tonal quality produced by a performer on an instrument. (3) Simultaneity.

Sopra [It.]. Above; *come sopra,* as above; *M. s.* (or *M. d.*) *sopra,* left (or right) hand above the other in piano playing.

Sopranino [It., dim. of and thus higher in pitch than soprano]. In the modern *recorder family, the highest pitched instrument; in the *clarinet family, an instrument pitched between the highest-pitched member, in A♭, and the clarinet in C.

Soprano. (1) The highest-pitched general type of human voice, normally possessed only by women and boys [for subtypes and ranges, see Voice; see also *Castrato,* Falsetto]. (2) In music for the conventional combination of four vocal parts, the highest part. (3) In some families of wind instruments, notably the *saxophone and *recorder, the highest-pitched conventional member [but see also Sopranino].

Soprano clef. See Clef.

Sor [Sors], **(Joseph) Fernando (Macari)** (bapt. Barcelona, 14 Feb. 1778; d. Paris, 10 July 1839). Composer and guitarist. Works for the guitar include many solo pieces (sonatas, divertimentos, variations, waltzes, fantasias, studies) and many *seguidillas* and boleros for voices with guitar or piano accompaniment. Also wrote an opera, ballets, and other vocal and instrumental works. Published a guitar method in 1830.

Sorabji, Kaikhosru Shapurji [Leon Dudley] (b. Chingford, 14 Aug. 1892; d. Dorchester, England, 15 Oct. 1988). Composer and performer. Mostly self-taught. Toured as a pianist and worked as a music critic. In 1940 issued a ban on the performance or publication of his music. During the 1960s recorded some of his own performances of his works and by the mid-1970s allowed performances by the pianists Michael Habermann and Yonty Solomon. Most of his music still remains in manuscript form. He composed works for piano and orchestra and for piano solo (100 *Transcendental Studies,* 1940–44), as well as songs.

Sorcerer's Apprentice, The. See *Apprenti sorcier, L'.*

Sordino [It.]. (1) *Mute. (2) *Damper. (3) *Kit. (3) *Clavichord.

Sorge, Georg Andreas (b. Mellenbach, Schwarzburg, Thuringia, 21 Mar. 1703; d. Lobenstein, Thuringia, 4 Apr. 1778). Composer and theorist. Court and civic organist and teacher at Lobenstein from 1722. Theoretical writings include the *Vorgemach der musicalischen Composition* (1745–47) and the *Anleitung zur Fantasie* (1767), a guide to keyboard improvisation. Keyboard music includes sonatas, preludes, toccatas, and fugues.

Soriano [Suriano, Suriani, Surianus], **Francesco** (b. Soriano, nr. Viterbo, Italy, 1548 or 1549; d. Rome, 1621). Composer. Teachers included Annibale Zoilo, Bartolomeo Roy, G. B. Montanari, and Palestrina. In 1580 became *maestro di cappella* of S. Luigi dei Francesi, Rome; director of music at the Gonzaga court in Mantua (1581–86). Returned to Rome, serving as *maestro di cappella* at S. Maria Maggiore (1587–99 and 1601–3), St. John Lateran (1599–1601), and the Cappella Giulia, St. Peter's (1603–20). In 1611 appointed with Felice Anerio to complete the revision of chant books begun in 1577 by Palestrina and Zoilo; the *Editio medicaea* was completed the following year (published 1614). Considered one of Palestrina's most distinguished successors; secular music includes several books of madrigals.

Soro, Enrique (b. Concepción, Chile, 15 July 1884; d. Santiago, 2 Dec. 1954). Composer. Studied in Milan; toured Italy and France. Returned to Chile in 1905, joining the piano and composition faculty at the National Conservatory in 1906; later assistant director (1907–19) and director (1919–28). Also toured throughout the Americas. *Sinfonia romántica* (1920) was the first full-scale symphonic work composed in Chile; other works include orchestral suites; *Impresiones líricas* and a Gran concerto, piano and orchestra (1919); chamber music; much piano music, including 3 sonatas; and songs.

Sorochintsy Fair [Russ. *Sorochinskaya Yarmarka*]. Unfinished comic opera by Mussorgsky (libretto by the composer, after Gogol), composed in 1874–80 and edited and completed by various composers after Mussorgsky's death. One version was produced in Moscow and St. Petersburg in 1913. A version by Nicolas Tcherepnin was produced in Monte Carlo in 1923. Setting: Ukraine in the mid-19th century.

Sospirando [It.]. Sighing.

Sostenente (sostinente, sustaining) piano. Any keyboard-operated stringed instrument that, unlike a piano or harpsichord, can sustain a pitch indefinitely. Many such instruments, all more or less ephemeral, have been invented, following three basic designs. In the *anémocorde,* the strings are set into vibration by currents of air. In the *melopiano,* they are struck repeatedly by spring-operated hammers. The most successful approach to the problem is found in the family of *bowed keyboard instruments. In many of these, the strings are "bowed" by revolving cylinders, a design similar to that of the *hurdy-gurdy.

Sostenido [Sp.]. (1) The sharp sign [see Accidental, Pitch names]. (2) Sustained.

Sostenuto, sostenendo [It., abbr. *sost.*]. Sustained, sustaining in duration; sometimes with the implication of a slowing in tempo.

Sostenuto pedal. On a modern piano with three pedals, the center pedal, which causes to remain undamped only those strings whose keys are depressed at the moment that the pedal itself is depressed.

Sotto [It.]. Under, below; *sotto voce,* in an undertone, subdued; *M. s.* (or *M. d.) sotto,* with left (or right) hand below the other in keyboard playing.

Soubrette. In opera, particularly comic opera of the 18th century, a clever female servant or lady's maid, often given to flirtation or intrigue.

Soul. A type of black American popular music that emerged in the mid-1960s. Featured vocalists (e.g., Ray Charles, James Brown, Aretha Franklin, Stevie Wonder, Otis Redding, Wilson Pickett, Gladys Knight, Sam and Dave, the O'Jays) or saxophonists who function by analogy as vocalists (Junior Walker, King Curtis, Grover Washington, Jr.) bring to this secular singing the impassioned improvisatory vocal devices of black *gospel music (sudden shouts, falsetto cries, moans, etc.) and a collection of church-derived, idiomatic formulas ("feel all right," "have mercy baby"). Songs are built on brief tonal progressions corresponding to alternating verses and refrains, on open-ended, hypnotic, interlocking one- or two-chord ostinatos, or, less often, on traditional 32-bar popular song forms and 12-bar blues.

Soundboard [Fr. *table d'harmonie;* Ger. *Resonanzboden;* It. *piano armonico, tavola armonica;* Sp. *caja armónica*]. On the *piano and related stringed instruments, a thin sheet of wood over which the strings pass and that is largely responsible for transmitting the vibrations of the strings to the surrounding air. On the *harp, the strings are attached to the soundboard and are stretched in a plane perpendicular to it. The analogous part of the *violin and related instruments is termed the belly or table.

Sound box. In stringed instruments, the hollow body, which is responsible for enhancing and transmitting the vibrations of the strings to the surrounding air.

Sound hole [Fr. *ouïe;* Ger. *Schalloch;* It. *occhio;* Sp. *abertura acústica*]. In stringed instruments, an opening or openings, both ornamental and functional, cut into the table to amplify sound and help focus musical quality. Instruments of the violin family traditionally have two sound holes, in the shape of an *f* and thus known as F holes, one on either side of the bridge. Viols similarly have such holes, usually in the shape of a *c* or an elaborate *f.* The guitar, lute, and other plucked instruments usually have one or more round sound holes beneath the strings between the fixed bridge and fingerboard. In early plucked strings, these sound holes are often carved with elaborate geometric patterns or are inlaid with decorative parchment to form rose holes.

Sound post [Fr. *âme;* Ger. *Stimmstock;* It. *anima;* Sp. *alma*]. In the *violin and other bowed strings, a slender movable dowel placed inside the instrument body behind the treble bridge foot connecting the table with the back. It functions to support string and bridge pressure on the table while transmitting and balancing string vibrations between the table and back. The sound post is fitted just snugly enough to be held in place without string tension, and its location and adjustment play an important role in sound production.

Soupir [Fr.]. A quarter rest [see Note].

Soupirant [Fr.]. Sighing.

Sourd [Fr.]. Muffled, muted.

Sourdine [Fr.]. *Mute.

Souris, André (b. Marchienne-au-Pont, Belgium, 10 July 1899; d. Paris, 12 Feb. 1970). Composer, conductor, teacher, musicologist. Studied composition with Paul Gilson and conducting with Hermann Scherchen. Around 1923 became involved with the group of surrealist writers and artists led by Paul Nougé in Brussels; works of this period include *Musique* (1925), a collage for orchestra, and *Les dessous des cartes* (1926). From the late 1920s through the 1930s many of his works had political themes (*Hommage à Babeuf,* woodwinds, 1934; *Hourra l'Oural,* incidental music to a play by Aragon, 1934). He also wrote scores for many movies. Taught at Charleroi Conservatory (1925–37) and Brussels Conservatory (1948–64). Conducted the orchestra of Radio Belgium 1937–46. Pursued musicological research into the lute repertory of the Renaissance, editing several collections.

Sousa, John Philip (b. Washington, D.C., 6 Nov. 1854; d. Reading, Pa., 6 Mar. 1932). Composer, conductor. His father played in the Marine Band. Studied the violin and other instruments; apprentice member of the Marine Band 1867–74, also studying theory and composition. Played in or conducted theater orchestras, 1874–76; in 1876 played under Offenbach in the American Centenary celebration. Remained in Philadelphia, 1876–80, playing in theater orchestras, also composing and teaching; 1879–80, conducted operetta companies, also composing his first operettas. Conductor of the Marine Band, 1880–92; the sobriquet "The March King" dates from this period, during which he composed some of the best known of his 136 marches *(Semper Fidelis, The Washington*

Post). Formed Sousa's Band in 1892, which toured the U.S. and Canada yearly; also toured Europe and made many recordings. Works include operettas, especially *El capitan* (1896); many songs in various genres; band fantasias and suites; dance music; many band arrangements.

Sousaphone. A circular tuba in BB♭ or E♭ with a large bell pointing forward above the player's head and coils of tubing balanced on the left shoulder and against the right hip for ease of carrying while marching. John Philip Sousa (1854–1932) suggested its design to J. W. Pepper of Philadelphia. Either Pepper or one of his suppliers made the first model in 1892. The bell, which originally pointed straight up, was turned forward by the C. G. Conn Company of Elkhart, Indiana, in 1908. See ill. under Brass instruments.

Souster, Tim(othy Andrew James) (b. Bletchley, Buckinghamshire, 29 Jan. 1943; d. 12 Mar. 1994). Composer. Studied at Oxford with Rose, Lumsden, Wellesz, and Bennett. Worked with representatives of the avant-garde while associated with the BBC (1965–67) and with Stockhausen. Helped found the electronic new-music groups Intermodulation (1969) and OdB (1976). His music employs avant-garde techniques such as electronics, serialism, and aleatory processes. Works include *Tsuwanonodomo,* soprano, 3 choirs, 3 orchestras, piano, prepared piano, harp (1968); *Pelvic Loops,* tape (1969); *Surfit,* tape, electric organs, percussion, electronics (1976); concerto for trumpet, live electronics, orchestra (1988).

Soutenu [Fr.]. Sustained.

Souterliedekens [Du., little Psalter-songs]. The first Dutch metrical *Psalter, published in Antwerp in 1540 by Symon Cock. Preexisting melodies were employed (and printed), including chiefly Dutch folk songs, but also some French and German folk songs.

Souzay [Tisserand], **Gérard (Marcel)** (b. Angers, 8 Dec. 1920). Baritone. Pupil of Bernac, Croiza, Marcoux, and Lotte Lehmann; attended the Paris Conservatory, making his recital debut in 1945. Sang in the 1956 Venice premiere of Stravinsky's *Canticum sacrum.* Operatic debut as Monteverdi's *Orfeo* in 1960; in 1965 sang Count Almaviva in *Nozze di Figaro* at the Metropolitan Opera. Artist-in-residence at the Univ. of California, Davis (1984); taught at Indiana University and at the Univ. of Texas, Austin (from 1986).

Sowerby, Leo (b. Grand Rapids, 1 May 1895; d. Port Clinton, Ohio, 7 July 1968). Composer and organist. Studied piano with Calvin Lampert and Percy Grainger, theory with Arthur Olaf Andersen. Early compositions premiered by the Chicago Symphony. Spent 1921–24 at the American Academy in Rome. Several compositions from the 1920s have a jazz flavor, such as *Syncopata* (1924) and *Monotony* (1925), both written for Paul Whiteman and his orchestra. From 1927 until 1962 organist and choirmaster at St. James Episcopal Cathedral in Chicago; taught at the American Conservatory in Chicago, 1932–62. Dean at the National Cathedral (Washington, D.C.) and founding director of the College of Church Musicians (1962–68). Works commissioned by the Chicago Symphony, Indianapolis Symphony, and the National Cathedral. Many of his works are for organ. *The Canticle of the Sun* (1944) won a Pulitzer Prize.

Sp. [Ger.]. Abbr. for *Spitze.

Spacing. The registral placement of the elements of a chord. In traditional four-part harmony, assuming all three elements of a triad to be present, a chord is said to be in close position if the three uppermost parts lie as close to one another as possible; otherwise it is in open position.

Spagna [It.]. The most famous of the 15th-century Italian *bassedanze* [see *Basse danse*] tenors. In the 16th century and early 17th, it was widely used as a *cantus firmus* for instrumental music and even for a few vocal compositions.

Spalding, Albert (b. Chicago, 15 Aug. 1888; d. New York, 26 May 1953). Violinist. Studied at the Bologna Conservatory; toured France, London, and Vienna. U.S. debut at Carnegie Hall (1908). During World War II directed Radio Rome. One of the first Americans to build an international reputation; his playing was praised by Saint-Saëns, Ysaÿe, and Joachim. Composed 2 concertos and much other music for the violin; works for orchestra, string quartet, piano, and voice; author of a 1943 autobiography and a 1953 novel about the composer Tartini.

Spanisches Liederbuch [Ger., Spanish Song Book]. A collection of 44 songs by Hugo Wolf, composed in 1889–90 to German translations (by Emanuel Geibel and Paul Heyse) of 16th- and 17th-century Spanish poetry. Wolf later arranged five of the songs for voice and orchestra.

Spanish Rhapsody. See *Rapsodie espagnole.*

Spanish Song Book. See *Spanisches Liederbuch.*

Spasshaft [Ger.]. Jocose.

Speaker key. On a woodwind instrument, a key that facilitates *overblowing. The hole for a speaker key is usually small and so placed that when uncovered it prevents the formation of one or more of the lower harmonics. Most modern woodwind instruments use some form of the key.

Speaks, Oley (b. Canal Winchester, Ohio, 28 June 1874; d. New York, 27 Aug. 1948). Composer and singer. Studied voice with Emma Thursby and composition with Will C. MacFarlane and Max Spicker. Wrote well over 100 songs, including "On the Road to Mandalay" (1907), "Morning" (1910), "Sylvia" (1914), and "The Lord Is My Light" (1914).

Species counterpoint. A method of instruction in 16th-century counterpoint, based on a categorization of contrapuntal relationships into five species, first promulgated by Johann Joseph Fux in his *Gradus ad Parnassum* of 1725. Haydn, Mozart, Beethoven, and several 19th-century composers studied from Fux's *Gradus* or taught from it; the method has been reinvigorated in the 20th century, with some modifications adapting it to the major and minor scale systems [see also Counterpoint].

Fux's method of instruction is based on exercises consisting of a given *cantus firmus,* represented in whole notes, for which a counterpoint is to be constructed. This begins with a single melody above or below the cantus firmus; at a later stage, exercises in three or more parts are introduced.

In the first species, also called note-against-note [Lat. *punctus contra punctum*], one note of the counterpoint is matched to one of the *cantus firmus.* This is the most restrictive species. All intervals must be consonant; parallel motion of perfect intervals is forbidden, nor may any perfect interval be approached by similar (direct) motion; disjunct motion (i.e., by skip) is used sparingly; certain formulas are required at the end of the phrase. In the second species, two notes are matched to one of the *cantus firmus.* All the first-species rules apply to the first note of each pair; the second note may be a passing tone, the only dissonance allowed in this species. The third species, or four against one, introduces further flexibilities, including the cambiata, the dissonant neighbor note, and the double neighbor note (changing tone, disallowed by Fux but allowed by others; see Counterpoint). The fourth species consists of two notes against one, like the second species, but the second note of each pair is tied to the first of the next, thus introducing the possibility of suspensions. The fifth species, called florid, allows the most melodic freedom and includes all the conditions of the first four species, but only with their appropriate note-values.

Speech song. *Sprechstimme.*

Sperdendosi [It.]. Fading away.

Speyer [Speier]**, Wilhelm** (b. Offenbach, 21 June 1790; d. there, 5 Apr. 1878). Violinist and composer. Studied violin in Paris with Baillot. In 1818 took over his father's banking business in Frankfurt, where he became friendly with Liszt, Mendelssohn, Spohr, Weber, Hauptmann, Meyerbeer, Pixis, and Mayr. Wrote for *Allgemeine musikalische Zeitung.* Many of

his compositions are for violin; other works include chamber music, choral pieces, and songs.

Spezzato [It.]. Divided, broken; for *coro spezzato,* see Polychoral; *registro spezzato,* *divided stop.

Spianato [It.]. Smooth, even.

Spiccato [It.]. See Bowing (4).

Spiegando [It.]. Spreading out, becoming louder.

Spiegel, Laurie (b. Chicago, 20 Sept. 1945). Composer. Studied at Juilliard and with Jacob Druckman at Brooklyn College. Early compositions for guitar, her own instrument; from 1970 increasingly involved with electronic and computer music and with videotape. Works include *The Expanding Universe* (1975), *Voices Within* (1979), *A Living Painting* (videotape, 1979), *Passage* (electronics, 1987), *3 Movements for Harpsichord* (1990).

Spiegelman, Joel (Warren) (b. Buffalo, 23 Jan. 1933). Composer, pianist, harpsichordist. Studied with Arthur Berger, Harold Shapero, and Irving Fine, and at the Paris Conservatory with Nadia Boulanger (1956–60). Taught at Brandeis 1961–66. In 1965 visited the Soviet Union; returning to the U.S., played concerts of 18th-century Russian harpsichord music and avant-garde Russian piano music. Taught at Sarah Lawrence College beginning in 1966. Also involved in electronic composition, using both tapes and synthesizers. Works include *Sacred Service* (cantor, choir reader, and tape, 1970), *Astral Dimensions* (violin, viola, cello, piano, percussion, 1973), *A Cry, a Song, and a Dance* (string orchestra, 1978), *Cicada Images: Moltings* (soprano, flute, piano, pipa, erhu, percussion, 1983).

Spieldose [Ger.]. Music box.

Spieloper [Ger.]. In the 19th century, a comic opera with spoken dialogue.

Spies, Claudio (b. Santiago, Chile, 26 Mar. 1925). Composer, theorist. Moved to the U.S. in 1942 and studied at the New England Conservatory and at Harvard with Walter Piston and Irving Fine. Taught at Swarthmore College (1958–70) and Princeton Univ. (beginning 1970). From the 1960s on his compositions were based on serial procedures: *Impromptu,* piano (1963), *Anima, vagula, blandula,* vocal quartet (1964), and *Five Sonnet Settings,* vocal quartet and piano (1977).

Spike fiddle. A bowed stringed instrument with a neck that pierces the body and emerges from the lower end. Spike fiddles commonly have two or three strings, no frets, and are held vertically. They are distributed through North Africa, the Middle East, Central Asia, and East and Southeast Asia. Examples include the *ching-hu and *rabāb.

Spinacino, Francesco (b. Fossombrone, Italy, fl. 1507). Lutenist and composer. Renowned in his day as a virtuoso of the lute; his only surviving publications are the *Intabulatura de lauto libro primo* and *libro secondo* (both Venice, 1507; facs., Geneva, 1978), the first printed lute music.

Spinet [Fr. *épinette;* Ger. *Spinett, Querflügel;* It. *spinetta, cembalo traverso;* Sp. *espineta*]. (1) A small *harpsichord, almost always with a single keyboard and set of jacks, strung diagonally from left to right with the bass strings at the rear. The jacks are arranged in pairs in the register, back to back, with plectra pointing in opposite directions. As in a harpsichord, one bridge rests on the wrest plank, the other on the soundboard, rather than having both on the latter, as in a *virginal. The design imposes an irregular trapezoidal shape on the instrument, as seen in early 17th-century spinets. This was later modified to the wing shapes, similar but distinct, seen in English, German, and French spinets built in the second half of the 18th century. (2) A small upright piano.

Spinto, lirico spinto [It.]. A lyric soprano or tenor voice, but one capable of being "pushed," i.e., of some dramatic power.

Spirito, spiritoso [It.]. Spirit, spirited, usually in association with a fast tempo; in the 18th century, however, the terms were sometimes closer in meaning to spiritual and called for a relatively slow tempo.

Spiritual. A religious folk song of the U.S. Related types were cultivated by both whites and blacks throughout the 19th century and into the 20th, and scholars have differed on the relationship between the two repertories. Among whites, the term referred especially to songs used in revival meetings as early as the late 18th century, as distinct from *metrical psalms and traditional hymns. These white spirituals were gathered in *shape-note publications. The term now most often refers to the religious songs of blacks beginning in the 19th century, a repertory genuinely Afro-American in character and largely transmitted orally. Such songs, hundreds of which were collected in the later 19th century, often have words of a melancholy character with regularly recurring refrain lines. Their original contexts included work as well as religious meetings, and contemporaneous accounts describe singing in unison, sometimes with heterophonic or polyphonic and rhythmic accompaniment, in *call-and-response patterns. Their introduction to large, white audiences in the U.S. and Europe by the Fisk [University] Jubilee Singers beginning in 1871 led to the production of numerous choral arrangements in the 20th century that are widely sung by whites and blacks alike.

Spitze [Ger., point]. (1) In violin playing, the tip of the bow. (2) In organ playing, the toe of the foot.

Spohr, Louis [Ludwig] (b. Brunswick, 5 Apr. 1784; d. Kassel, 22 Oct. 1859). Composer, violinist. Pupil of Franz Eck. Appointed concertmaster in Gotha, 1805–12. In 1806 married a harpist, Dorette Scheidler (1787–1834); wrote two concertos and six sonatas for violin and harp for their joint concerts. Conducted festivals at Frankenhausen (1810–11) and Erfurt (1811–12). Engaged in 1813–15 as conductor at the Theater an der Wien (with Dorette as harpist); composed some notable chamber works— including Nonet op. 31 and Octet op. 32—and his first important opera, *Faust* (1813). In 1816 at La Scala premiered his eighth and perhaps best-known concerto, op. 47. Music director of the Frankfurt theater (1817–19), producing there his *Faust* and *Zemire und Azor* (1819). In 1822 appointed Kapellmeister at Kassel (from 1847 *Generalmusikdirektor*). Produced further operas: *Jessonda* (1823), his most popular; *Der Berggeist* (1825); *Pietro von Abano* (1827); *Der Alchymist* (1830). Retired in 1857. Spohr was popular in Britain, especially for his oratorios (*Die letzten Dinge,* 1826; *Des Heilands Letzte Stunde,* 1835; *Der Fall Babylons,* 1840). Published an important violin method (1832).

Spontini, Gaspare (Luigi Pacifico) (b. Maiolati, near Iesi, Italy, 14 Nov. 1774; d. there, 24 Jan. 1851). Composer. Produced at least ten operas in Italy before emigrating to Paris in 1802; presented opéras comiques there. Empress Josephine helped get his serious opera *La vestale* (libretto by Jouy) accepted and staged at the Paris Opéra in 1807; it became the most successful French opera of its time and made Spontini famous. Appointed music director of the Théâtre-Italien, 1810–12. Director of the king's private music (1814) and the Théâtre-Italien (1814). A new version of *Fernand Cortez* (1817) won popularity nearly equal to that of *La vestale.* From 1820 to 1841 *Generalmusikdirektor,* Berlin. Career ended with a conviction for lèse-majesté for statements he had made in the press. Pardoned by the new king, left Berlin in 1842, retiring to Paris and then to his birthplace.

Sprechstimme, Sprechgesang [Ger., speaking voice, speech-song]. A use of the voice midway between speech and song. In general, it calls for only the approximate reproduction of pitches and in any case avoids the sustaining of any pitch. It is often notated with x's as note heads, their placement on a staff indicating at least a pitch contour, and stems and flags being used in the conventional way to indicate rhythm. Schoenberg made the greatest use of it.

Sprezzatura [It.]. The lack of regular rhythm in the performance of *monody around 1600.

Spring Sonata. Popular name for Beethoven's Sonata for Violin and Piano in F major op. 24 (1800–1801).

Spring Symphony. Schumann's Symphony no. 1 in B♭ major op. 38 (1841).

Springbogen [Ger.]. See Bowing (4).

Springer. An unaccented *échappé* or auxiliary note coming at the very end of the note-value on which it is placed; hence, the same as the French **accent* [see also *Nachschlag* (2)].

Square dance. A folk dance of the U.S. danced by groups of four couples forming a square; also, an occasion on which such dances are danced. The dance itself was derived from the French *quadrille* in the 19th century. It employs music in moderately fast duple meter performed by a fiddle and or various other instruments while the steps are called out to the dancers by a caller.

Square piano. A **piano* whose case is a horizontal rectangle. Pianos of this type were common from the late 18th through the 19th century and varied in size from quite small instruments similar to clavichords to quite large and elaborately decorated instruments of the 19th century.

St. Abbr. for (and alphabetized as) Saint.

Stabat Mater dolorosa [Lat. The pained Mother stood]. A sequence often attributed to the Franciscan Jacopone da Todi (d. 1306) and adopted in the Roman Catholic rite in 1727.

Stabile, Mariano (b. Palermo, 12 May 1888; d. Milan, 11 Jan. 1968). Baritone. Pupil of Cotogni at Rome; debut at Palermo in 1909; appeared in Italy, Spain, and Latin America before Toscanini cast him as Falstaff for the 1921 reopening of La Scala, a role he sang more than 1,000 times to 1961. Performed at Chicago (1924–29), Covent Garden (1926–31), Salzburg (1931–39), Glyndebourne (1936–39), and at La Scala until 1955.

Stabreim [Ger.]. **Alliteration.

Stabspiel [Ger.]. **Xylophone.

Staccato [It., abbr. *stacc.*]. Detached. Notes to be played in this fashion, marked by a dot (now most common), a solid black wedge, or a vertical stroke above or below, are decisively shortened in duration and thus clearly separated from the note following. A light accent is also implied. The term is thus the opposite of **legato*. For various related techniques of execution on the violin, see Bowing. *Staccatissimo* indicates an extreme form of such shortening.

Stade, Frederica Von. See Von Stade, Frederica.

Staden, Johann (b. Nuremberg, bapt. 2 July 1581; d. there, buried 15 Nov. 1634). Composer. By 1604 appointed court organist at Bayreuth. Published *Neue teutsche Lieder* and *Neue teutsche geistliche Gesäng* in Kulmbach in 1609. In 1611 became organist at the Spitalkirche and at St. Lorenz in Nuremberg; from 1618 organist at St. Sebald. Teacher of his son, Sigmund Theophil. Founder of the so-called Nuremberg school of the 17th century. His *Harmoniae sacrae* (1616) is notable for including some of the earliest sacred concertos in Germany.

Staden, Sigmund Theophil [Gottlieb] (b. Kulmbach, bapt. 6 Nov. 1607; d. Nuremberg, buried 30 July 1655). Composer. Studied with his father, Johann Staden, and with Jakob Paumann in Augsburg. In 1623 became a city instrumentalist in Nuremberg; in 1634 appointed organist of St. Lorenz. Published 2 books of vocal music, comprising 47 works, and a number of strophic songs. His singspiel *Seelewig* (1644; ed. 1881) is the earliest extant example of the genre.

Stadler, Anton (Paul) (b. Bruck an der Leitha, 28 June 1753; d. Vienna, 15 June 1812). Clarinetist and basset horn player; it was for his "basset clarinet," a clarinet with a downward extension, that Mozart's Quintet K. 581 and Concerto K. 622 were written. Stadler and his brother Johann, also a clarinetist, became the court orchestra's first regular clarinetists in 1787.

Stadler, Maximilian [Johann Karl Dominik] (b. Melk, 4 Aug. 1748; d. Vienna, 8 Nov. 1833). Composer, keyboard player, and music historian. In 1772 ordained as a Benedictine priest. Wrote mainly vocal music, much of it sacred (oratorio *Die Befreyung von Jerusalem,* ca. 1813); also chamber music and keyboard pieces. Author of a history of music in Austria, *Materialen zur Geschichte der Musik unter den österreichischen Regenten.* A friend of Mozart's, with Georg Nissen he catalogued Mozart's manuscripts.

Stadtpfeifer [Ger.]. Town piper, **wait; a musician, usually one of a group, employed by a municipality to perform music on public occasions of various kinds. Such musicians, especially wind players, were used in Germany from the 14th century.

Staff, stave [Fr. *portée;* Ger. *Liniensystem, System;* It. *sistema, rigo;* Sp. *pentagrama, pauta*]. A group of equidistant horizontal lines, now always five, on which notes are placed in such a way as to indicate pitch. Successive lines and spaces from lowest to highest represent rising steps of the diatonic **scale (embodied in the white keys of the piano) and bear the corresponding letter names, the first seven letters of the alphabet. Notes are sharped or flatted (to produce the pitches of the black keys of the piano) by means of *accidentals. The assignment of specific lines and spaces to specific letter names is made by means of a *clef placed at the beginning of each staff. Pitches lying above and below the lines of the staff proper are notated with the aid of *leger lines. Two or more staves connected by a brace are termed a system. Piano music is notated on two staves connected by a brace, the upper with a treble clef, the lower with a bass clef; this arrangement is sometimes termed the great or grand staff. See also Notation; Score.

Stage band. *Big band.

Stahlspiel [Ger.]. *Glockenspiel.

Stainer, John (b. London, 6 June 1840; d. Verona, 31 Mar. 1901). Musicologist and composer. Appointed organist at Christ Church, Oxford, 1859; founded Oxford Philharmonic Society, 1866. Organist at St. Paul's, 1872; organist and principal at National Training School for Music, 1881. Professor of music at Oxford from 1889. Compositions include oratorios, services, songs, anthems. Edited sacred music and wrote *A Theory of Harmony* (1871) and *Music in Relation to the Intellect and Emotions* (1892).

Stamitz, Anton (Thadäus Johann Nepomuk) (b. Německý Brod, 27 Nov. 1750; d. Paris or Versailles, between 1796 and 1809). Composer, violinist, and violist. Son of Johann Stamitz and brother of Carl. Played with the Mannheim orchestra from 1764, at the Concert spirituel in 1772, in the Royal Chapel Orchestra in Versailles, 1782–89. Among his compositions are 12 symphonies, 2 *symphonies concertantes,* 5 keyboard and over 20 violin concertos, over 50 string quartets, and numerous other chamber works.

Stamitz, Carl (Philipp) (bapt. Mannheim, 8 May 1745; d. Jena, 9 Nov. 1801). Composer, violinist. Son of Johann Stamitz and brother of Anton. Joined the Mannheim orchestra in 1762, performed with Anton at the Concert spirituel in 1772. Wrote more than 50 symphonies; at least 38 *symphonies concertantes;* and more than 60 concertos for violin, viola, viola d'amore, cello, clarinet, flute, and other instruments, as well as chamber music.

Stamitz, Johann (Wenzel Anton) (bapt. Německý Brod, 19 June 1717; d. Mannheim, buried 30 Mar. 1757). Composer and violinist. Educated in Jihlava and Prague; arrived in Mannheim probably by 1741. Became *Konzertmeister* in 1745 or 1746 and director of instrumental music in 1750. In Paris 1754–55, appeared at the Concert spirituel. One of the foremost early classical symphonists, his contributions include regular use of the 4-movement cycle and a transfer of features of Italian opera-overture style. Among his pupils were his sons Carl and Anton,

Christian Cannabich, Ignaz Fränzl, and Wilhelm Cramer. Best known for his symphonies, of which nearly 60 are extant, and his 10 orchestral trios; also wrote many solo concertos (for violin, flute, oboe, clarinet, and keyboard), a Mass, liturgical vocal music, and chamber works.

Stampita [It.]. See *Estampie.*

Standard. A popular song that has retained its popularity over a period of years; especially one that has been taken over into the jazz repertory.

Ständchen [Ger.]. *Serenade.

Stanford, Charles Villiers (b. Dublin, 30 Sept. 1852; d. London, 29 Mar. 1924). Composer, teacher. Studied at Cambridge (organist of Trinity College, 1873–82) and in Leipzig and Berlin. In 1883 became first professor of composition and orchestra conducting at the new Royal College of Music; 1885–1902, conductor, London Bach Choir; 1887–1924, professor, Cambridge Univ.; 1901–10, conductor, Leeds Festival. Students included Vaughan Williams, Holst, Bridge, Bliss, Benjamin. A highly prolific composer, his music grew increasingly old-fashioned after the turn of the century. Works include operas (*The Veiled Prophet of Khorossan,* 1877; *Shamus O'Brien,* 1896); 6 Irish Rhapsodies for orchestra; the Irish Symphony (3rd of 6) op. 28 (1887); also 3 piano concertos, 2 violin concertos, clarinet concerto; piano and organ pieces; chamber music; Anglican church music; many part songs and solo songs. Author of the textbook *Musical Composition* (London, 1911; 6th ed., 1950).

Stanley, John (b. London, 17 Jan. 1712; d. there, 19 May 1786). Composer and organist. An early accident left him blind; he became organist at the Church of All Hallows, Bread Street, London, before he was 12 and followed William Boyce as Master of the King's Band of Musicians in 1779. Composed opera (*Teraminta*) and oratorios patterned on those of Handel; also cantatas, court odes, sacred vocal music, concertos, organ voluntaries, and songs.

Stantipes [Lat.]. See *Estampie.*

Starer, Robert (b. Vienna, 8 Jan. 1924). Composer. Studied in Vienna; fled to Palestine and studied at the Jerusalem Conservatory with Joseph Tal, Odeon Partos, and Solomon Rosowsky. Moved to the U.S. in 1947; studied at Juilliard with Frederick Jacobi. Introduced as a composer by New York performances of his First Piano Concerto (1947), *Prelude and Dance,* orchestra (1949), and *Kohelet (Ecclesiastes),* soloists, chorus, orchestra (1952). Taught at Juilliard 1949–74; at Brooklyn College (CUNY) beginning 1963. Composed in a variety of genres, including symphonies, concertos, ballets, chamber music, band music, songs, and several operas. Works include Trio for clarinet, cello, and piano (1964); *Mutabili Variants for Orchestra* (1965); *Pantagleize* (opera, 1967; Brooklyn, 1974); *The Last Lover* (opera, New York, 1985); *Samson Agonistes* (ballet, 1961), *Holy Jungle* (ballet, 1974); 3 symphonies; 3 piano concertos; Violin Concerto (1980); Cello Concerto (1988); *Symphonic Prelude,* orchestra (1984); 2 piano sonatas.

Stark [Ger.]. Strong, loud; *stärker werdend,* becoming louder.

Starker, Janos (b. Budapest, 5 July 1924). Cellist. Studied at the Liszt Academy under Cziffer; played in the Budapest Philharmonic in 1945 and 1946, then left Hungary for the U.S. Principal cellist of the Dallas Symphony (1948–49), the Metropolitan Opera orchestra (1949–53), and the Chicago Symphony (1953–58). Joined the faculty of Indiana Univ. in 1958. Member of the Roth Quartet (1950–53) and the Suk, Starker, and Katchen Trio (1967–69). Published editions of the Bach cello suites and Beethoven cello sonatas and *An Organized Method of String Playing* (New York and Hamburg, 1985).

Starokadomsky, Mikhail Leonidovich (b. Brest-Litovsk, 13 June 1901; d. Moscow, 24 April 1954). Composer. Studied composition with Miaskovsky and organ with Aleksandr Goedicke at the Moscow Conservatory; remained there as professor of orchestration. Works include the opera *Sot* (1933), several operettas, orchestral works, incidental and film music, choral works, chamber music, and songs, especially children's songs.

Starr, Ringo [Starkey, Richard] (b. Liverpool, England, 7 July 1940). Rock drummer, singer, and songwriter. In 1962 he replaced Pete Best as the Beatles' drummer; songwriting contributions included "Octopus's Garden" (1969). Released first solo album in 1970 *(Sentimental Journey);* the later *Ringo* (1973) featured performances by all of the former Beatles as well as songs co-written with George Harrison. Appeared in films and on television. In 1994 reunited with the other surviving Beatles to record new music based on tapes made by John Lennon before he was murdered.

Star-Spangled Banner, The. The national anthem of the United States of America, officially adopted in 1931. The words were written by Francis Scott Key (1779–1843) in September 1814 as he watched the British bombardment of Fort McHenry, near Baltimore. The melody, for which Key intended his words, is by the English composer John Stafford Smith (1750–1836) and was sung in Anacreontic Societies in England and America to the words "To Anacreon in Heaven."

Starzer, Josef (b. 1726 or 1727; d. Vienna, 22 Apr. 1787). Composer. Violinist in the orchestra of the Viennese Burgtheater. An established composer of ballets, he became concertmaster and court composer in St. Petersburg, ca. 1759. Returned to Vienna ca. 1768. Helped found the Viennese Tonkünstler Sozietät in 1771, which performed much of his music. Works include more than 30 ballets (*Roger et Bradamate,* 1771; *Gli Orazi e gli Curiazi,* 1774); a singspiel, *Die drei Pächter;* an oratorio; symphonies, concertos, and chamber music.

Steber, Eleanor (b. Wheeling, W. Va., 17 July 1916; d. Langhorne, Pa., 3 Oct. 1990). Soprano. Studied at New England Conservatory and in New York; debut at Boston, 1936. Appeared at the Metropolitan Opera 1940–66, specializing in Mozart roles but also singing Verdi, Wagner, Strauss, and Berg; created the lead role in Barber's *Vanessa* (1958). Taught at the Cleveland Institute, 1963–72; from 1971 to her retirement at Juilliard and New England Conservatory. In 1963 was the first American to appear at Bayreuth after the war.

Steel drum. A percussion instrument made from an oil drum. The drum is cut to a relatively shallow depth, and the end is made concave, subdivided by grooves, and hammered into shape so as to create up to 30 segments, each of which produces a tuned pitch when struck with a rubber-headed stick. Steel drums are made in a variety of sizes and played in ensembles called steel bands. The instrument was developed in Trinidad in the 1940s and has since spread through the Caribbean and to other areas where there are West Indian populations.

Steel guitar. A guitar with metal strings that is held horizontally with the belly up and played by sliding a metal bar along the strings with the left hand, plucking with the right, rather than by pressing the strings against the frets; also called a Hawaiian guitar. It is now typically an electric instrument lacking a sound box, rectangular rather than guitar-shaped, and mounted on a stand. See also Pedal steel guitar.

Steffani [Staffani, Steffano, Stefani, Stephani], **Agostino** (b. Castelfranco, near Venice, 25 July 1654; d. Frankfurt am Main, 12 Feb. 1728). Composer. He probably attended a municipal school in Padua, and may have learned to sing at an early age. Studied organ in Munich with J. K. Kerll, and composition in Rome with Ercole Bernabei, *maestro di cappella* at St. Peter's. Became court organist in Munich, 1674; 1681, director of chamber music; 1688, Kapellmeister to Duke Ernst August of Hannover. Among his compositions, most of which are vocal, his operas and chamber duets were most influential.

Steg [Ger.]. The *bridge of a stringed instrument; *am Steg*, an instruction to bow at the bridge.

Steibelt, Daniel (b. Berlin, 22 Oct. 1765; d. St. Petersburg, 20 Sept. 1823). Composer and pianist. Studied piano and theory with Kirnberger; 1790–96, lived in Paris. He spent the next years in London; 1808, settled in St. Petersburg; 1810, became *maître de chapelle* to Czar Alexander I. Works include operas, ballets, piano concertos, a harp concerto, string quartets, keyboard music, songs.

Steiger, Rand (b. New York, 18 June 1957). Composer and conductor. Studied composition and percussion at the Manhattan School of Music and California Institute of the Arts. Taught at Cal Arts (1982–87) and Univ. of California at San Diego (from 1987); first Composer-Fellow of the Los Angeles Philharmonic (1987–88). Conducted new music ensembles including SONOR (UCSD), the Los Angeles Philharmonic's New Music Group, and the California E.A.R. Unit (Cal Arts). Works include numerous pieces for experimental chamber and orchestral groups, often employing electronic or computerized elements.

Steigern [Ger.]. To intensify, increase; *Steigerung, crescendo.*

Steinberg, Maximilian (Osseievich) (b. Vilna, 4 July 1883; d. Leningrad, 6 Dec. 1946). Composer. Teachers at St. Petersburg Conservatory included Rimsky-Korsakov, Lyadov, and Glazunov. In 1908 married Rimsky-Korsakov's daughter and began teaching at the conservatory. Edited a number of his father-in-law's compositions for posthumous publication and completed Rimsky's *Principles of Orchestration* (St. Petersburg, 1913). Compositions include ballet music; orchestral music (Symphony no. 4, "Turksib," 1933; *In Armenia,* symphonic picture, 1940); choral music; chamber music; songs.

Steinberg, William [Hans Wilhelm] (b. Cologne, 1 Aug. 1899; d. New York, 16 May 1978). Conductor. Klemperer's assistant at the Cologne Opera from 1920; principal conductor by 1924. Worked at the German Opera, Prague (1925–29), and the Frankfurt Opera (1929–33); dismissed by the Nazis, led a Jewish orchestra until 1936, when he emigrated to Palestine. In 1938 became Toscanini's assistant with the NBC Symphony; directed the Buffalo Symphony (1945–52) and the Pittsburgh Symphony (1952–76), appearing also with the London Philharmonic (1958–60), the New York Philharmonic (1966–68), and the Boston Symphony (1969–72).

Steiner, Max (Maximilian Raoul Walter) (b. Vienna, 10 May 1888; d. Beverly Hills, 28 Dec. 1971). Composer and conductor. Moved to New York in 1916 and worked in musical theater; 1929, moved to Hollywood, where he wrote for the movies well into the 1960s. Among his most famous scores are *Symphony of Six Million* (1932), *King Kong* (1933), *Gone with the Wind* (1939), *Casablanca* (1943), *Mildred Pierce* (1945), *The Big Sleep* (1946), and *A Summer Place* (1959).

Stem. The vertical line attached to a note head [see Note].

Stendendo [It.]. Stretching out, slowing.

Stenhammar, (Karl) Wilhelm (Eugen) (b. Stockholm, 7 Feb. 1871; d. there, 20 Nov. 1927). Composer. Studied piano with Andersson and theory with Dente, Sjögren, and Hallén. Held conducting posts with the Stockholm Philharmonic Society, the Royal Opera, the New Philharmonic Society, and the Göteborgs Orkesterförening; beginning in 1902 also toured as a concert pianist. His own music was influenced by Wagner and Liszt as well as by Scandinavian folk and art music traditions. Works include opera and stage music; orchestral music (2 piano concertos, 2 symphonies), choral works (*Ett Folk,* cantata, 1904–5), and many songs.

Stentando, stentato [It.]. Labored, halting.

Step. (1) A *scale degree. (2) The interval between one scale degree and the next, whether a semitone or a whole tone [see also Motion].

Stepwise. *Motion from one scale degree to an adjacent one.

Sterbend [Ger.]. Dying away.

Stern, Isaac (b. Kremnets, Ukraine, 21 July 1920). Violinist. Brought to the U.S. as an infant; studied at the San Franciso conservatory and with Persinger and Blinder. After the war made his European debut, 1948; played at the Casals Festival 1950–52 and toured the U.S.S.R. in 1956. Formed an acclaimed trio with Istomin and Rose in 1961; toured and recorded very extensively both as chamber musician and soloist. Encouraged various U.S.–Israeli student exchanges, and conceived the idea of the Jerusalem Music Center (opened 1975); in the U.S. was involved with saving Carnegie Hall and establishing the National Endowment for the Arts.

Stern, Julius (b. Breslau, 8 Aug. 1820; d. Berlin, 27 Feb. 1883). Violinist, composer, and conductor. Studied in Berlin, Dresden, and Paris. Founded the Sternscher Gesangverein in Berlin, 1847. With Kullak and Marx he founded a conservatory in Berlin (now called the Stern Conservatory) in 1847. Conducted the Berlin Sinfonie-Kapelle (1869–71). Wrote primarily songs and choruses.

Steso [It.]. Stretched, slow.

Stesso [It.]. Same [see *Istesso tempo*].

Steuermann, Edward (b. Sambor, near L'vov, 18 June 1892; d. New York, 11 Nov. 1964). Pianist and composer. Studied piano with Vilem Kurz in L'vov and with Busoni in Berlin, composition with Schoenberg. Became an important member of Schoenberg's circle, playing piano at the premieres of many works, including Schoenberg's *Pierrot lunaire* in 1912, Berg's Piano Sonata in 1911, and several pieces by Webern. During the 1920s and 1930s toured widely in Europe; 1936, emigrated to the U.S. Taught piano at Juilliard (1952–64) and at the Darmstadt summer courses (1954, 1957, 1958, 1960). Most of his own compositions are atonal and/or serial. Works include *Variations* (orchestra, 1958), Suite for Chamber Orchestra (1964), string quartets, solo piano works.

Stevens, Halsey (b. Scott, N.Y., 3 Dec. 1908; d. Long Beach, Calif., 20 Jan. 1989). Composer and musicologist. Studied piano and composition at Syracuse Univ.; also studied with Ernest Bloch. Taught at Dakota Wesleyan (1937–41), Bradley Univ. (1941–43), Univ. of Redlands (1946), and Univ. of Southern California, where he stayed for the remainder of his career. His First Symphony (1945) was premiered by the San Francisco Symphony in 1948. Author of *The Life and Music of Béla Bartók* (New York, 1953; rev. 1963). Works that show Bartók's influence include *12 Slovakian Folk Songs* (1962) and *Eight Yugoslavian Folk Songs* (1966); other works include sonatas for horn (1953), trumpet (1956), and cello (1958); *Sinfonia breve* (1957), *The Ballad of William Sycamore,* chorus and orchestra (1955), *Symphonic Dances* (1958); concertos for cello, clarinet, viola; *Dittico* (alto sax and piano, 1972).

Stevens [Steenberg], **Risë** (b. New York, 11 June 1913). Mezzo-soprano. Studied with Anna Schoen-René at Juilliard, making her debut in 1931; appeared at Prague in 1936. Performed with the Metropolitan Opera 1938–61; sang also at Chicago, San Francisco, Paris, London, and Milan. In the film *Going My Way* performed "Habanera" from *Carmen*. Co-director of the Metropolitan Opera's National Company 1965–67; 1975–78 president of Mannes College.

Stewart, Slam [Leroy Elliott] (b. Englewood, N.J., 21 Sept. 1914; d. Binghamton, N.Y., 10 Dec. 1987). Jazz double bass player. Formed Slim and Slam with singer and multi-instrumentalist Slim Gaillard (b. 1916), recording "The Flat Foot Floogie" in 1938. Accompanied Fats Waller in the film *Stormy Weather* (1943), played with Art Tatum (intermittently 1943 to early 1950s), Red Norvo (1944–45), Roy Eldridge (1953), and Benny Goodman (1945, 1973–75); also led groups from 1944, with Erroll Garner and Billy

Taylor among his sidemen. From 1971 taught at SUNY–Binghamton. Noted for solos in which he bowed a melody while humming it an octave higher; recorded examples include a duo with Don Byas, "I Got Rhythm" (1945).

Stich, Johann. See Punto, Giovanni.

Stich-Randall, Teresa (b. West Hartford, Conn., 24 Dec. 1927). Soprano. Attended the Hartford Conservatory and Columbia, appearing in the premieres of Thomson's *The Mother of Us All* (1947) and Luening's *Evangeline* (1948); sang with Toscanini and the NBC Symphony in 1949 and 1950, and in Florence, Vienna, and Salzburg in 1952. First appeared at Chicago in 1955, and at the Metropolitan Opera in 1961; also sang in recital and concerts, focusing on the Baroque and classical repertory.

Stick zither. A *zither whose strings are stretched along a solid stick as distinct from a resonating body. A resonator of some type is often attached.

Stierhorn [Ger.]. *Cow horn.

Stil [Ger.], **stile** [It.]. *Style.

Stile antico [It.]. See Palestrina style.

Stile concertante [It.]. See *Concertant, concertante;* Concerto.

Stile concertato [It.]. See *Concertato.*

Stile concitato [It.]. See *Concitato.*

Stile familiare [It.]. *Familiar style.

Stile rappresentativo [It.]. The dramatic or theatrical style of *recitative used in the earliest operas and semidramatic works of the first decades of the 17th century. It is characterized by freedom of rhythm and irregularity of phrasing; the vocal line readily forms dissonances with an accompaniment improvised by one or several chordal instruments reading from a figured bass.

Still, William Grant (b. Woodville, Miss., 11 May 1895; d. Los Angeles, 3 Dec. 1978). Composer. Studied music at Oberlin College and composition with George W. Chadwick and Edgard Varèse. Worked in New York as a conductor and arranger. His early compositions were in a modernist idiom; in the mid-1920s he began to search for a self-consciously African American style of composition. *Levee Land* (soprano and chamber ensemble, 1925) incorporated jazz elements; *From the Black Belt* (orchestra, 1926) was based on African American folk material, *Sahdji* (choral ballet, 1930) on an African subject. The success of *Afro-American Symphony* (1930) established Still as a significant American composer and an important voice in African American culture. Additional works of the 1930s and 1940s in this direction include *Kaintuck'* (piano and orchestra, 1935), *Lenox Avenue* (ballet, 1937), *Symphony in G minor (Song of a New Race)* (1937), and 2 operas, *Troubled Island* (1938) and *A Bayou Legend* (1940). Other works were less specifically African American in character. Still lived in Los Angeles after 1934. Notable works from his later years include *Songs of Separation* (voice and piano, 1949), *Ennanga* (harp and orchestra, 1956), *The Peaceful Land* (orchestra, 1960), *Highway 1, USA* (1-act opera, 1962).

Stimmbogen [Ger.]. *Crook; tuning *slide.

Stimme [Ger.]. (1) Voice. (2) *Part. (3) Organ *stop.

Stimmen [Ger.]. (1) Plural of *Stimme.* (2) To tune.

Stimmgabel [Ger.]. Tuning fork.

Stimmstock [Ger.]. (1) *Sound post. (2) *Pin block.

Stimmung [Ger.]. (1) Mood; *Stimmungsbild* (mood picture), a piece intended to express some particular mood. (2) Tuning, intonation; *reine Stimmung,* *just intonation.

Stimmzug [Ger.]. (1) Tuning slide. (2) The slide of the trombone.

Stinguendo [It.]. Fading away.

Stiracchiando, stiracchiato, stirando, stirato [It.]. Stretching out, slowing down.

Stitt, Sonny [Edward] (b. Boston, 2 Feb. 1924; d. Washington, D.C., 22 July 1982). Jazz alto and tenor saxophonist and bandleader. Played the alto instrument in Billy Eckstine's bop big band (1945) and Dizzy Gillespie's sextet and big band (1945–46); co-led groups with Gene Ammons (1950–52, 1960–62). Apart from periods with Gillespie (late 1950s) and Miles Davis (1960) and a tour with the Giants of Jazz (including Gillespie, Thelonious Monk, and Art Blakey, 1971–72), led bop groups; among his scores of albums is *Stitt Plays Bird* (1963).

Stock, Frederick [Friedrich August] (b. Jülich, Germany, 11 Nov. 1872; d. Chicago, 20 Oct. 1942). Conductor. Studied violin and composition at the Cologne Conservatory; joined the Theodore Thomas Orchestra (later the Chicago Symphony) in 1895; became assistant conductor in 1899, and conductor from 1903 until his death. Programmed new works by Debussy, Mahler, Ravel, Schoenberg, and Hindemith; Prokofiev premiered his Third Piano Concerto with him in 1921. The Chicago Symphony under Stock issued some of the earliest commercial orchestral recordings. His compositions include 2 symphonies and a violin concerto.

Stock and horn. See Hornpipe (2).

Stockfagott [Ger.]. See Racket.

Stockhausen, Julius (Christian) (b. Paris, 22 July 1826; d. Frankfurt am Main, 22 Sept. 1906). Baritone and conductor. Son of harpist Franz (Anton Adam) Stockhausen (1789–1868) and soprano Margarethe Stockhausen (1803–77). First concert success in performance of *Elijah* in Basel (1848); gave public premiere of *Die schöne Müllerin* (Vienna, 1856). At the Opéra-comique, Paris, 1856–59. Director of Hamburg Philharmonic Concerts and Choir, 1863–67. Taught at Hoch Conservatory, Frankfurt, 1878–80, 1883–84. Sang in the premiere of Brahms's German Requiem (1884); *Magelone Lieder* was written for him.

Stockhausen, Karlheinz (b. Mödrath, Germany, 22 Aug. 1928). Composer. Orphaned during World War II; at the Hochschule für Musik in Cologne studied piano with Hans Otto Schmidt-Neuhaus, harmony with Hermann Schroeder, and composition with Frank Martin. In 1952 went to Paris to study with Messiaen, composing works that extended ultraserial procedures; worked in the electronic studios of the French radio (ORTF). In 1953 returned to Cologne to work in the electronic music studio at North German Radio. *Gesang der Jünglinge* (1956), released as a record in 1958, became one of the first widely popular pieces of electronic music. A leading figure in the European avant-garde by 1957; visited the U.S. in 1958 and in 1962. Works from the late 1950s and the mid-60s explore spatial arrangements, serial operations, chance procedures, mixing human players and electronics in live performance. From the late 1960s tended toward increasing grandeur of scale and ideological ambition: the score of *Aus den Sieben Tagen* (1968) consists of nothing but verbal instructions, for example, "Play the rhythm of the universe." From 1978 on worked on the *Licht* series, a succession of large-scale stage works that combine elements of opera, dance, and ritual.

Works include *Kreuzspiel* (oboe, bass clarinet, piano, and percussion, 1951); *Gruppen (3 orchestras, 1955–57); *Carré* (1959–60); *Momente* (soprano, 4 choirs, chamber ensemble, 1964); *Mikrophonie I* (1964); *X i für Flöte* (1987); *Drachenkampf und Argument* (trumpet, trombone, synthesizer, tenor, bass, 2 dancers, percussion, 1987); *Eva's Erstgeburt* (1988); Helicopter Quartet (string quartet, 4 helicopters, 1995).

Stoessel, Albert (Frederic) (b. St. Louis, 11 Oct. 1894; d. New York, 12 May 1943). Violinist, conductor, and composer. Studied at the Hochschule für Musik in Berlin. Succeeded Walter Damrosch as conductor of the Oratorio Society of New York in 1921. Head of the music department at New York Univ. 1923–30; director of opera and orchestra departments at Juilliard Graduate School, 1927–43. Works include *Garrick,* opera (New York, 1937);

Cyrano de Bergerac, orchestra (1922); Concerto grosso, piano and string orchestra (1935).

Stokowski, Leopold (Anthony) (b. London, 18 April 1882; d. Nether Wallop, Hampshire, 13 Sept. 1977). Conductor. Studied at Royal College of Music and Oxford (B.Mus., 1903). Organist at St. James, Piccadilly, 1902–5; in 1905 moved to New York. Engaged in 1909 by the Cincinnati Symphony; 1912–38 director of the Philadelphia Orchestra, turning the orchestra into a world leader. Frequently programmed new music; recorded prolifically and became a popular public figure. Involved with the Disney movie *Fantasia* (1940), All-American Youth Orchestra (1940–41), NBC Symphony (1941–44) and New York City Symphony Orchestra (1944–45), and Hollywood Bowl Concerts (1945–46). Principal conductor of the Houston Symphony 1955–60. Organized and conducted the American Symphony Orchestra 1962–72; continued to conduct until 1975 and to record until 1977. Wrote *Music for All of Us* (New York, 1943).

Stollen [Ger.]. See Bar form.

Stoltzer, Thomas (b. Schweidnitz, Silesia, ca. 1475; d. near Znaim, Moravia, early 1526). Composer. From 1522 *magister cappellae* to the Hungarian royal court at Ofen under Ludwig II; drowned in the Taja River. His music circulated widely throughout Germany through the 1570s; his 150 extant works include 4 Masses, 5 Magnificats, 18 Psalm motets, many shorter motets and hymns, lieder, 8 fantasias.

Stoltzman, Richard (b. Omaha, 12 July 1942). Clarinetist. Studied with his father and at Ohio State Univ. and Yale. Was associated with the Marlboro Festival; cofounded the chamber ensemble Tashi with Peter Serkin. Taught at California Institute of the Arts (1970–75), then pursued an international concert career, maintaining a wide repertory of classical music and jazz including many transcriptions and commissions.

Stolz, Robert (Elisabeth) (b. Graz, Austria, 25 Aug. 1880; d. Berlin, 27 June 1975). Composer and conductor. Studied at the Vienna Conservatory and with Humperdinck in Berlin. Conducted at Theater an der Wien in Vienna (1905–12). In 1924 went to Berlin, where he composed for film musicals (*Zwei Herzen im Dreivierteltakt,* 1930). Fled Berlin in 1936; settled in the U.S. (1940–46), where he wrote for Hollywood films. Returned to Austria in 1946, continued to compose operettas and to conduct. His many operettas include *Studentenulke* (Marburg, 1899), *Der Tanz ins Gluck* (1921).

Stomp. A term common in jazz titles of the 1920s and 30s, as in "Jelly Roll" Morton's "King Porter Stomp." Such pieces are often characterized by ener-getic, sharply defined rhythms, especially in a climactic concluding section.

Stop. (1) In *organs, a row of pipes, one for each key, that can be made to sound when the stop knob is drawn by the player. Each keyboard and pedal division of the organ has its own wind-chest, on which one or more such rows of pipes are placed. Mixture stops have two or more pipes for each key, sounding octaves and fifths. (2) In *harpsichords, a set of jacks that can be brought into play or retired by the player in order to sound one or another choir of strings. The choirs of strings may be at different pitch (usually 8′ and 4′), and the timbre produced by each stop varies according to the point along the length of the strings at which they are plucked by the jacks. A buff stop, however, is simply a set of buff leather pads or a similar device that partially damps one choir of strings while it is being played.

Stopped pipe. (1) A pipe that is closed at one end. Such a pipe (including those on organs; see below) sounds a pitch an octave lower than an open pipe of the same length. See Acoustics, Wind instruments. (2) In organs, a *flue pipe whose top is closed by a metal cap or wooden stopper.

Stopped tones. Tones produced on the French horn by closing the opening in the bell with the hand or with a mute [see Horn]. In addition to producing a change in tone color, the technique may produce a change in pitch, requiring altered fingerings.

Stopping. (1) On a stringed instrument, altering the vibrating length of a string by pressing it against the fingerboard. See also Double stop. (2) On the French *horn, the production of *stopped tones.

Stop-time. In tap dancing, jazz, and blues, accompaniment consisting of a regular pattern of attacks (e.g., on the first beat of each measure) separated by silences.

Storace, Nancy [Ann Selina; Anna] (b. London, 27 Oct. 1765; d. there, 24 Aug. 1817). Soprano. Sister of composer Stephen Storace. Studied with Sacchini and Rauzzini in London. Sang in Florence, Milan, Parma, Vienna (1783–87); returned to London in 1787. Mozart wrote the role of Susanna in *Le nozze di Figaro* for her.

Storace, Stephen (John Seymour) (b. London, 4 Apr. 1762; d. there, 19 Mar. 1796). Composer. Son of Stephen Storace (b. Torre Annunziata, ca. 1725; d. ca. 1781), a double bass player. Studied with his father and at the Conservatorio S. Onofrio in Naples. Joined his sister Nancy in Vienna, where 2 comic operas were produced: *Gli sposi malcontenti* (1785) and *Gli equivoci* (1786); became friendly with Mozart. In 1787 returned to London and continued to write operas, including *The Haunted Tower* (1789). Works include other operas and adaptations of operas by other composers; vocal works (*Lamentation of Marie Antoinette on the Morning of Her Execution*, voice, strings, and bassoon); a ballet; chamber works.

Storm and stress. **Sturm und Drang.*

Storto [It., crooked]. **Crumhorn.

Stout, Alan (b. Baltimore, 26 Nov. 1932). Composer. Studied at Johns Hopkins Univ. and the Peabody Conservatory. Pupil of Henry Cowell, Wallingford Riegger, Vagn Holmboe, and John Verrall. During the 1950s worked intermittently as a music librarian. In 1963 moved to Chicago to teach at Northwestern Univ. Works include 3 symphonies; 10 string quartets (1953–62); Clarinet Quintet (1958); Cello Sonata (1966); *Nocturnes* (narrator, contralto, and chamber ensemble, 1970); *Suite* (saxophone and organ, 1973); Passion (1975); *Nimbus* (string orchestra, 1978); Brass Quintet (1984); songs.

Stradella, Alessandro (b. Nepi, ca. 1639; d. Genoa, 25 Feb. 1682). Composer. Was in Rome by 1667; wrote stage works, oratorios, prologues and intermezzos to operas, and motets on commission. In 1669 left Rome after an embezzlement scandal. *Il Biante*, an *azione drammatica*, performed in honor of Pope Clement X about 1670–72. In 1677 went to Venice to teach Alvise Contarini's mistress; absconded with her to Turin; was pursued and escaped to Genoa, narrowly avoiding death at the hands of Contarini's assassins. Following an intrigue with a married woman in the Lomelli family of Genoa, was murdered by a hired assassin. Vocal works include 7 operas, prologues, intermezzos, a Mass, motets, cantatas, arias, and canzonettas; 27 instrumental works, mostly *sonate da chiesa*. The Sonata di viole is the earliest known concerto grosso.

Stradivari, Antonio (b. Cremona?, 1644; d. there?, 18 Dec. 1737). Instrument maker. Pupil of Nicolo Amati in Cremona by 1666. Two of his six children, Francesco (b. 1 Feb. 1671; d. 11 May 1743) and Omobono (b. 14 Nov. 1679; d. 8 June 1742), became coworkers. Before 1680, in addition to violins Stradivari probably produced harps, lutes, mandolins, guitars, and a tromba marina. In 1680 began to distance himself from Amati's style and increased his output of violins and cellos. Fame spread beyond Cremona following Amati's death in 1684. After 1690 further refined his style and devised the "Long Strad" design; generally considered to have produced his greatest instruments in the period from about 1700 to 1720. Began making smaller cellos in response to the emergence of the virtuoso cellist, which have served

as models for makers since the early 19th century. Continued to make violins until his death.

Straff [Ger.]. Tense, rigid, strict.

Strambotto [It.]. A verse form popular among Italian improvisers in the 15th century and taken over into the repertory of the **frottola*. It consists of a single stanza of eight hendecasyllabic lines, normally rhyming abababcc (*strambotto toscano*), less often abababab. Musical settings of the *strambotto* often have only two phrases, each to be repeated four times in alternation; a separate phrase for the final couplet may be included.

Strang, Gerald (b. Claresholm, Alberta, 13 Feb. 1908; d. Loma Linda, Calif., 2 Oct. 1983). Composer, acoustician. Studied at Stanford Univ. and Univ. of California, Berkeley. In 1935 became acquainted with Schoenberg, serving him as teaching assistant at UCLA (1936–38) and as editor and factotum (1938–50). Works from the 1940s and 1950s, heavily influenced by Schoenberg and twelve-tone techniques, still contain many references to tonal harmonies (Symphony no. 1, 1954; Concerto grosso, orchestra, 1950). During 1950s and 1960s worked as an acoustical consultant on the design of auditoriums, studios, and other music facilities. In 1963 stopped composing for traditional instruments and turned to electronic and computer music exclusively. Taught at UCLA 1969–74.

Stransky, Josef (b. Humpolec, Bohemia, 9 Sept. 1872; d. New York, 6 Mar. 1936). Conductor. Conducted the Hamburg Opera (from 1903) and the Blüthner Orchestra, Berlin (from 1910). Succeeded Mahler at the New York Philharmonic, 1911–23; conducted the New York State Symphony until 1924, when he left music for a career as an art merchant.

Strascicando, strascinando [It.]. Dragging.

Stratas, Teresa [Strataki, Anastasia] (b. Toronto, 26 May 1938). Soprano. Studied at the Royal Conservatory, Toronto. Debut, 1958; performed frequently at the Metropolitan Opera from 1959; sang in the posthumous premiere of Falla's *Atlántida* at La Scala in 1962 and appeared with major orchestras and at festivals. Took title role in the 1979 premiere of the 3-act version of *Lulu;* played Violetta in Franco Zeffirelli's film of *La traviata;* in 1991 created the role of Marie Antoinette in Corigliano's *The Ghosts of Versailles.*

Strathspey. A type of Scottish **reel, slower in tempo, in duple meter, and characterized by dotted rhythms, including the inverted dotting termed the Scotch snap [see Lombard rhythm].

Straus, Oscar (b. Vienna, 6 Mar. 1870; d. Bad Ischl, Austria, 11 Jan. 1954). Composer. Studied with Hermann Grädener in Vienna and Max Bruch in Berlin.

From 1893 to 1899 conducted theater orchestras in various Austrian and German cities; in 1900 became pianist and resident composer at the Überbrettl, the famous Berlin cabaret. Returning to Vienna, composed a string of operettas, of which *Ein Walzertraum* (1907), *Der tapfere Soldat* (1908), *Der letzte Walzer* (1920), and *Drei Walzer* (1935) were particularly successful. Fled Vienna in 1939 for France, then New York and Hollywood; returned to Austria in 1948.

Strauss, Eduard (b. Vienna, 15 Mar. 1835; d. there, 28 Dec. 1916). Composer and conductor. Youngest son of Johann Strauss, Sr. Studied theory with Gottfried Preyer and Simon Sechter, violin with Amar, harp with Parish-Alvars and Zamara. Replaced brother Johann Jr. as conductor on a tour of Russia in 1865. Co-conducted the Strauss Orchestra with brother Josef until 1870. Director of Court Balls 1872–78. Composed over 300 waltzes and polkas.

Strauss, Johann (Baptist), Sr. (b. Vienna, 14 Mar. 1804; d. there, 25 Sept. 1849). Composer, dance orchestra director. Largely self-taught as a musician; in 1824 became violinist-director of a dance orchestra. By 1826 began to compose waltzes and galops, publishing them from 1827; from 1832 music director of a local regiment, for which he composed marches. From 1833 to 1838, toured with his orchestra: Budapest (1833), Austria-Germany (1834–35), Germany, Holland, Belgium (1836), Paris (1837–38), Great Britain (1838). In the 1840s his compositions expanded to include polkas and quadrilles, brought back from Paris and made popular in Vienna. In 1846 given the newly created title Director of Music for Court Balls. Compositions run to 250 opus numbers, mostly waltzes; his most famous work is the *Radetzky-Marsch,* still played at every Vienna Philharmonic New Year's Concert.

Strauss, Johann (Baptist), Jr. (b. Vienna, 25 Oct. 1825; d. there, 3 June 1899). Composer, dance orchestra director. Son of Johann Strauss, Sr. In 1844, organized his own dance orchestra; its popularity rivaled that of his father's orchestra, which was combined with his after the elder man's death. From 1853 directed the music of court balls; given his father's title of Director of Music for Court Balls in 1863. From 1846, toured with his orchestra throughout Europe; in 1853 joined as co-director by his brother Josef and in 1862 by their youngest brother, Eduard.

By 1860 he had published over 200 waltzes, polkas, quadrilles, marches. The 1860s began the period of his great symphonic waltzes. Resigned his court post in 1871 to capitalize on his international celebrity by guest-conducting his music throughout Europe. After 1870, composed relatively few instrumental dances, though some of his best-known

waltzes (*Wiener-Blut* op. 354, 1873; *Frühlingsstimmen* op. 410, 1883; *Kaiser-Waltz* op. 437, 1889). Devoted himself mainly to operetta from 1871 through 1887; his most enduring are *Die Fledermaus* (1874) and *Der Zigeunerbaron* (1884).

Strauss, Johann (Maria Eduard) (b. Vienna, 16 Feb. 1866; d. Berlin, 9 Jan. 1939). Composer and conductor. His father was Eduard Strauss. Served as Director of Court Balls, 1901–5, then moved to Berlin. Compositions include the operetta *Katze und Maus* (1898); the "polka schnell" *Schlau-Schlau* op. 6; other dance pieces.

Strauss, Josef [Joseph] (b. Vienna, 22 Aug. 1827; d. there, 21 July 1870). Composer and conductor. Son of Johann Strauss, Sr. Studied with Franz Dolleschal and Franz Amon. Co-conductor of the Strauss Orchestra; collaborated with his brother Johann Jr. on a few works. Composed over 200 waltzes and polkas, 8 marches, 11 quadrilles.

Strauss, Richard (Georg) (b. Munich, 11 June 1864; d. Garmisch-Partenkirchen, Bavaria, 8 Sept. 1949). Composer. Son of Franz Joseph Strauss, a horn player and composer. In 1877 joined his father's orchestra as a violinist; met Hans von Bülow in Berlin, 1883. In 1885 succeeded von Bülow as conductor at Meiningen and became third conductor at the Munich Court Opera; left Meiningen for Munich in 1886. Répétiteur at Bayreuth, 1889; after the premiere of *Don Juan* hailed as the greatest German composer since Wagner. In 1896 became chief conductor of the Munich Opera; 1897, conducted his own works in Holland, Spain, France, and England; 1898, became chief conductor of the Royal Court Opera in Berlin. Increasingly turned his attention to writing operas; *Salome* caused an uproar; *Der Rosenkavalier* was his greatest public success. Worked with librettists Hugo von Hofmannsthal, Stefan Zweig, Josef Gregor, Clemens Kraus; wrote his own libretto to *Intermezzo.*

Appointed by Goebbels as president of the National Socialist state music bureau, the Reichsmusikkammer; ordered to resign for insisting that Zweig (a Jew) be given credit on posters and programs for *Die schweigsame Frau.* In 1941 moved to Vienna; in 1945 went to Switzerland to avoid a denazification tribunal; returned to Garmisch in May 1949, his name having been cleared. Last work was four songs with orchestra (1948), published posthumously as *Vier letzte Lieder.*

Works: *Aus Italien,* symphonic fantasy (1886); incidental music to *Le bourgeois gentilhomme* (1912); tone poems *Macbeth* (1886–88), **Don Juan, *Tod und Verklärung, *Till Eulenspiegels lustige Streiche, *Also sprach Zarathustra, *Don Quixote, Ein *Heldenleben, Eine *Alpensinfonie;* operas *Feuersnot*

(1900–1901), *Salome, *Elektra, Der *Rosenkavalier, *Ariadne auf Naxos, Die *Frau ohne Schatten, *Intermezzo, Die ägyptische Helena (1923–27), *Arabella, Die schweigsame Frau (1933–34), Friedenstag (1935–36), Daphne (1936–37), Die Liebe der Danae (1938–40), *Capriccio, Metamorphosen (1945).

Stravinsky, Feodor (b. Voviÿ Dvor, Minsk, 20 June 1843; d. St. Petersburg, 4 Dec. 1902). Bass. Studied at St. Petersburg Conservatory. Engaged at Kiev until 1876. Had a repertory of over 60 roles; created roles in Tchaikovsky's *Mazeppa* and Rimsky's *Sadko.*

Stravinsky, Igor Fyodorovich (b. Oranienbaum, near St. Petersburg, 17 June 1882; d. New York, 6 Apr. 1971). Composer. Third of four sons of Feodor Stravinsky. Studied privately with Rimsky-Korsakov from 1902. Received acclaim for *Zhar'-ptitsa,* or *L'oiseau de feu* (The Firebird), commissioned by Sergei Diaghilev for the 1910 Paris season of the Ballets russes. Settled in Switzerland and continued to compose ballets; the first performance of *Le sacre du printemps* (The Rite of Spring), in Paris on 29 May 1913, incited a colorful riot. After the Bolshevik coup, eschewed Russian nationalism and composed works for smaller forces, including *L'histoire du soldat* (The Soldier's Tale, 1918). Moved to France after the war.

Neoclassical style began evolving in the early 1920s; also began appearing as conductor and pianist. *Apollon musagète,* or *Apollo* (1927–28) was the first of many collaborations with choreographer George Balanchine. In 1934 took French citizenship. American tours in 1935–36 brought new commissions; 1939, delivered the Charles Eliot Norton lectures at Harvard and filed for U.S. citizenship (granted in 1945); settled in Hollywood. Symphony in Three Movements, the ballet *Orphée,* and the Mass for choir and winds crown his neoclassical symphonic, balletic, and liturgical oeuvres, respectively.

A comic opera in English, *The Rake's Progress,* with a libretto by W. H. Auden and Chester Kallman, won wide acclaim and rejuvenated his standing in Europe. After 1948 Robert Craft became his amanuensis and close associate. Began to study serialism in 1951; compositions after *The Rake* show a growing concern with serial techniques. Also wrote a number of choral-orchestral sacred works. From 1951 conducted internationally and recorded frequently, increasingly with Craft's aid; in 1957 Craft collaborated in a series of interview-memoirs. Made only visit to the U.S.S.R. since 1914 on the occasion of his 80th birthday in 1962 at the invitation of the Composers' Union.

Works include ballets: *Zhar'-ptitsa,* or *L'*oiseau de feu* [The Firebird] (1909–10); *Vesna sviashchen-naia,* or *Le *sacre du printemps* [The Rite of Spring] (1911–13); *Svadebka,* or *Les *noces* [The Wedding], *Pulcinella* (1919–20), *Apollon musagète,* or *Apollo* (1927–28), *Le baiser de la fée,* or *The Fairy's Kiss* (1928), *Jeu de cartes* [The Card Party] (1935–36), *Orphée,* or *Orpheus* (1947), *Agon* (1953–57); operas: The *Nightingale,* The *Rake's Progress* (1948–51); other works: *L'*histoire du soldat* [The Soldier's Tale] (1918); *Ragtime* (1918); Symphonies of Wind Instruments (1920); wind Octet (1922–23); Concerto for piano and winds (1923–24); *Capriccio,* piano and orchestra (1928–29); Concerto for two pianos (1935); Violin Concerto in D (1931); opera-oratorio *Oedipus Rex* (1926–27); *Symphony of Psalms* (1930); *Perséphone* (1934); Concerto in E♭ ("*Dumbarton Oaks," 1937–38); Symphony in C (1938–40); Symphony in Three Movements (1942–45); Mass (1944–47); Cantata (1952); *3 Songs from William Shakespeare* (1953); *Canticum sacrum* (1955); *Movements,* piano and orchestra (1958–59); *A Sermon, a Narrative, and a Prayer* (1960–61); *The Flood* (1961–62), for CBS Television; *Anthem, "The Dove Descending"* (1962, text by T. S. Eliot); orchestral *Variations (Aldous Huxley in memoriam)* (1963–64); *Elegy for J.F.K.* (1964, text by Auden); *Introitus (T. S. Eliot in memoriam)* (1965); *Requiem Canticles* (1966).

Writings: *Chroniques de ma vie* (Paris, 1935–36; 2nd ed., 1962); trans. as *An Autobiography* (1936). *Poétique musicale* (Cambridge, Mass., 1942); trans. as *Poetics of Music* (1947).

Strayhorn, Billy [William; Swee' Pea] (b. Dayton, Ohio, 29 Nov. 1915; d. New York, 31 May 1967). Jazz composer, arranger, and pianist. From 1939 until his death wrote for Duke Ellington's orchestra and collaborated in recording sessions led by Ellington's sidemen, often playing piano. Composed the orchestra's theme "Take the 'A' Train" (first recorded 1941), "Lush Life," "Passion Flower," "Chelsea Bridge," and others.

Straziante [It.]. Agonizing, heart-rending.

Street organ. See Barrel organ, Barrel piano.

Streich [Ger.]. Bow; *Streichinstrumente,* bowed stringed instruments; *Streichorchester,* string orchestra; *Streichquartett,* string quartet; *Streichklavier,* *bowed keyboard instrument.

Streit zwischen Phöbus und Pan, Der [Ger., The Contest between Phoebus and Pan]. A secular cantata ("dramma per musica") by Bach, BWV 201 (1729?). The text by Picander is based on Ovid's account of the musical contest between Phoebus Apollo and Pan. The character Midas may satirize one of Bach's critics, Johann Scheibe (1708–76).

Streng [Ger.]. Strict.

Strepitoso [It.]. Noisy, boisterous.

Strepponi, Giuseppina [Clelia Maria Josepha] (b. Lodi, 8 Sept. 1815; d. Sant'Agata, near Busseto, 14 Nov. 1897). Soprano. Studied piano and singing at Milan Conservatory; La Scala debut, 1839. Donizetti wrote *Adelia* (1841) for her. Created the role of Abigaille in *Nabucco* in 1842. Retired in February 1846; married Verdi in 1859.

Stretta [It.]. *Stretto* (2).

Stretto [It., narrow, close]. (1) In a *fugue, the imitative treatment of the subject at a shorter interval of time than is employed in the initial exposition. (2) In nonimitative works, a climactic, concluding section in a faster tempo; often *stretta*. Examples occur in the finales of Italian opera.

Strich [Ger.]. Bow stroke. See also Bowing.

Strict composition. Composition in a predetermined, usually historical, form. For strict counterpoint, see Species counterpoint.

Stride. An accompanimental technique perfected by Harlem jazz pianists of the 1920s, including James P. Johnson, Fats Waller, and Willie "the Lion" Smith. Modifying the two-beat ("oom-pah") style of *ragtime, the left hand flows between bass note and chord in *swing rhythms, often sounding a tenth with the bass note on strong beats.

Striggio [Strigi, Strigia], **Alessandro** (1) (b. Mantua, ca. 1540; d. there, 29 Feb. 1592). Composer and instrumentalist, father of Alessandro Striggio (2). By the 1560s principal composer at the court of Cosimo I de' Medici. Wrote music for the anthology *Trionfo di musica di diversi*. In 1584 employed at the Gonzaga court. Admired as a performer (probably of the *lirone*, a bass *lira da braccio*); his music for *intermedi* typically contains a mixture of homophony and counterpoint.

Striggio, Alessandro [Alessandrino] (2) (b. Mantua, 1573?; d. Venice, 15? June 1630). Librettist and viol player, son of Alessandro Striggio (1). In 1589 played at the wedding of Grand Duke Ferdinand I in Florence; in 1596–97 published the last 3 books of his father's madrigals. Wrote the libretto of Monteverdi's *Orfeo* (Mantua, 1607).

String band. See Bluegrass music.

String bass. *Double bass.

String drum. A *friction drum in which a string that passes through a membrane is rubbed to produce sound.

String quartet. A composition for an ensemble consisting of four solo stringed instruments, normally two violins, viola, and cello; the ensemble itself [see also Quartet]. Since the second half of the 18th century, the string quartet has been the most widely cultivated and influential chamber-music genre.

The string quartet was a creation of the Classical era. Early in that period the textural ideal of four relatively independent solo performers began to supplant the polarized continuo texture of the Baroque trio sonata and related genres. Four-part writing for string orchestra had long been utilized in such Baroque genres as the overture, concerto grosso, and ripieno concerto [*concerto a 4;* see Concerto] and in a more modern idiom in the early Classical symphony *a 4*. The same four-part texture, but now for solo strings with continuo, may be found in the late Baroque period in occasional solo passages within ripieno concertos and in the four-part concertino sections of concerti grossi by Geminiani, Locatelli, Giuseppe Sammartini, and others.

The most important precursors of the string quartet were, however, Austro-Bohemian—namely the various informal chamber genres of the early Classical period such as the string *trio and quintet and the sextet for string quartet and two horns. Austrian chamber music of this type was not only soloistic, but it seems generally to have been performed without a keyboard continuo, the latter circumstance owing in part to the custom of playing these works outdoors [see Serenade].

It is within this context that Joseph Haydn created his first string quartets. Haydn's early quartets are in five movements with a minuet and trio in both second and fourth place. Haydn's next sets, opp. 9, 17, and 20 (ca. 1769–72), brought a change to four longer movements with the minuet in second place. This is also the form of four of the six quartets of op. 33 (1781) and three from Mozart's principal set, the quartets dedicated to Haydn (1782–85). Thereafter the standard symphonic cycle, with the minuet in third place, became the norm.

Beethoven's early quartets op. 18 (1798–1800) inevitably show the strong influence of Haydn. The five middle quartets (the *Razumovsky* Quartets op. 59, the *Harp* op. 74, and the *Serioso* op. 95, 1805–10) echo the extraordinary increase in dramatic intensity and time span heralded by Beethoven's *Eroica* Symphony (1803). At the same time, the expanded pitch range and technical difficulty of these works reflect the fact that they were written for performance by a professional quartet. Beethoven's late quartets (opp. 127, 130–32, and 135, 1823–26) employ large-scale forms, which range from the four movements (with scherzo) of opp. 127 and 135 to the seven connected movements of op. 131 and embody an enormous range of contrasts.

The Romantic period brought a gradual decline in interest in the string quartet. The more radical Romantic composers such as Berlioz, Liszt, and Wagner turned almost entirely from chamber music. There are notable examples, however, by Schubert, Mendelssohn, and Schumann.

The string quartet experienced a minor renascence in the latter part of the 19th century in the works of Dvořák, Brahms, and Smetana. In France, César Franck's single quartet spurred the composition of similar works by his student Vincent d'Indy and others. Before Franck the only significant 19th-century composer of string quartets in France was Luigi Cherubini. In Russia, the first noteworthy quartets were by Anton Rubinstein, followed somewhat later by Tchaikovsky and Alexander Borodin.

The rather modest repertory of string quartets from the 20th century begins with the Debussy and Ravel quartets. Shortly thereafter, Vienna saw the production of Schoenberg's first two quartets and one by Berg. These were followed much later by Schoenberg's last two quartets (1927–36) and Webern's op. 28 (1936–38), all three dodecaphonic. By contrast, a neoclassical approach characterizes many of Darius Milhaud's 18 string quartets, as it does the very different quartets of Ernst Toch and Paul Hindemith.

Among the most important quartets of the century are Bartók's set of six (1908–39). Somewhat similar in style, but programmatic in content, are Leoš Janáček's two quartets (1923–28). In Russia, the leading composers of string quartets in the 20th century were Nikolay Myaskovsky, Prokofiev, and Shostakovich (15 quartets), in Poland Karol Szymanowski and later Krzysztof Penderecki.

Of numerous British string quartets, those of Michael Tippett, Alan Rawsthorne, and Benjamin Britten are worthy of mention. American composition in this genre may be said to begin with Charles Ives's two quartets. More recent quartets include those by Walter Piston, Roger Sessions, Samuel Barber, Elliott Carter, Milton Babbitt, and George Rochberg.

String quintet. See Quintet.

String trio. See Trio.

Stringed instrument. An instrument in which one or more strings constitute the principal vibrating system; also chordophone. The string or strings may be set in motion by bowing, plucking, or striking. For the various types, see Instrument. The term is often used informally to refer to instruments of the violin family.

Stringendo [It.]. Pressing, becoming faster.

Strings. The stringed instruments (string section) of an orchestra.

Strisciando [It.]. *Glissando.

Stromentato [It.]. Accompanied by instruments. In *recitativo stromentato,* the standard continuo instruments are reinforced by others, usually strings. See Recitative.

Stromento [It.]. See *Strumento.*

Strong beat. See Meter.

Strong, George Templeton (b. New York, 26 May 1856; d. Geneva, 27 June 1948). Composer. Studied at Leipzig with Jadassohn (counterpoint), Hofmann (orchestration), and Grempert (horn). Moved to Frankfurt in 1881, then to Weimar, where he knew Liszt, Szigeti, and Raff; symphonic poem *Undine* op. 14 (1882–83) dedicated to Liszt. In Wiesbaden in 1886 became friends with MacDowell. Taught at New England Conservatory, 1891–92, then returned to Europe. Compositions include 7 symphonic poems; other orchestral works; choral works; chamber works; piano pieces; songs.

Strophic. (1) With respect to a poem, made up of units (strophes), all with the same number of lines, rhyme scheme, and meter. (2) With respect to a musical setting of a strophic text, characterized by the repetition of the same music for all strophes, as distinct from *through-composed.

Strophic variations. (1) In 17th-century vocal music, an aria or song whose bass line remains the same (or very nearly the same) for every stanza of text, while different melodies are set to it at each repetition; also called strophic bass. (2) In instrumental music of the 17th, 18th, and 19th centuries, a sectional theme-and-variations form in which the variations retain the structure of the theme; the melodies of the variations may or may not resemble or ornament that of the theme, though the harmonic structure, at least at cadences, is quite similar.

Strozzi, Barbara (b. Venice, 6 Aug. 1619; d. there?, 1664 or later). Composer and singer. Adopted daughter of and pupil of Cavalli. Commissioned the first 2 sets of Nicolò Fontei's *Bizzarrie poetiche* (1635, 1636); principal singer at the Accademia degli Unisoni. Works include *Il primo libro de madrigali* (1644), other madrigals and ariettas.

Strozzi, Piero (b. Florence, ca. 1550; d. there, after 1 Sept. 1609). Composer. Related to the poet and librettist Giulio Strozzi (1583–1652). Member of Count Giovanni de' Bardi's Camerata and Jacopo Corsi's circle; wrote music for the celebration of Francesco I de' Medici's marriage (1579), and Caccini's *Il rapimento di Cefalo* (1600). Only 3 of his compositions survive.

Strube, Gustav (b. Ballenstedt, Germany, 3 Mar. 1867; d. Baltimore, 2 Feb. 1953). Violinist, composer, conductor, teacher. Studied violin, piano, and composition at the Leipzig Conservatory. Invited by Nikisch to join the Boston Symphony, played there 1890–1913; from 1898 to 1912 conducted the Boston Pops, for which he composed many waltzes, marches, and lighter works. Taught music theory at the Peabody Conservatory of Music in Baltimore 1913–46; conducted the Baltimore Symphony 1916–30. Works include symphonies and other orchestral works; 2 concertos for violin (1924, 1930); sonatas for violin (1923), viola (1924), and cello (1925); string quartets.

Strumento [It., sometimes also *instrumento, stromento*]. A musical instrument; *s. d'arco,* bowed instrument; *s. a corde,* stringed instrument; *s. a fiato,* wind instrument; *s. di legno,* woodwind instrument; *s. d'ottone,* brass instrument; *s. a percussione,* percussion instrument; *s. da tasto,* keyboard instrument.

The *strumento d'acciaio* (steel instrument) specified in Mozart's *The Magic Flute* has been variously thought to be the *glockenspiel or a keyboard instrument like the *celesta.

Strungk [Strunck], **Nicolaus Adam** (b. Brunswick, bapt. 15 Nov. 1640; d. Dresden, 23 Sept. 1700). Composer, violinist, and organist. Violinist at the Wolfenbüttel court chapel in 1660. Served Emperor Leopold I in Vienna and Elector Johann Friedrich at Hannover. Director of music at Hamburg 1678–82; there his operas *Esther* and *Semiramis* (1681) were heard. Founded an opera company in Leipzig (1693). Composed operas, vocal works, instrumental compositions.

Stück [Ger.]. Piece, composition.

Stucky, Steven (b. Hutchinson, Kans., 7 Nov. 1949). Composer. Studied at Baylor Univ. with Richard Willis, at Cornell Univ. with Robert Palmer and Karel Husa. Taught at Lawrence Univ. in Wisconsin (1978–80), then at Cornell (beginning 1980). Composer in residence and new-music adviser with the Los Angeles Philharmonic (1988–91). Works include *Kennigar* (Symphony no. 4) (1978); Double Concerto (violin, oboe, chamber orchestra, 1985; rev. 1989); *Dreamwaltzes* (1986); *Son et lumière* (1988); *Angelus* (orchestra, 1990); woodwind quintet (1990); *Fanfares and Arias* (1995). Author of *Lutosławski and His Music* (New York, 1981).

Study. *Etude.

Sturgeon, N(icholas?) (d. between 31 May and 8 June 1454). Composer. In 1399 elected a scholar of Winchester College; canon at St. Paul's from 1432 (precentor from 1442). Sturgeon's 7 surviving compositions, including the motet "Salve mater Domini," are known only from the Old Hall Manuscript.

Sturm und Drang [Ger., storm and stress]. A movement in German literature of the second half of the 18th century that had as its goal the powerful, shocking, even violent expression of emotion. The most appropriate parallels between music and the literary *Sturm und Drang,* which might be bounded by publications appearing in 1773 and 1781, can be drawn with German opera and other stage music of the 1770s, notably the melodrama. Certain earlier works such as Gluck's ballets and operas of the 1760s, with their scenes of terror, have also been cited as examples of the *Sturm und Drang.* Yet such works antedate the *Sturm und Drang* proper. The same may be said for a series of minor-key instrumental pieces of the period ca. 1765–75, including symphonies, overtures, string quartets, and sonatas by Haydn, Mozart, Johann Vanhal, Carl Ditters von Dittersdorf, Johann Christian Bach, and others, which are commonly designated as *Sturm und Drang* compositions.

Stürmend, stürmisch [Ger.]. Stormy, impetuous.

Stürze [Ger.]. The bell of a wind instrument; *S. hoch,* an instruction to play with the bell raised.

Style [Fr. *style;* Ger. *Stil;* It. *stile;* Sp. *estilo*]. The choices that a work or performance makes from among the possibilities available. Style thus comprehends all aspects of a work or performance. As often used with respect to music, the concept style is borrowed from a rhetorical tradition (reaching back at least to Aristotle) that distinguishes style from content—the manner in which something is said as distinct from what is being said. Such a distinction is difficult to sustain even with respect to language. Its application to music is still more problematic, because music is essentially nonrepresentational. The pitches and durations that define the style of a composition also constitute its content. In this sense, music has only style.

The concept style is employed principally for the sake of comparing works or performances with one another and identifying the significant characteristics that distinguish one or more works or performances from others. Style may thus refer to features that characterize the works or performances of a period, region, genre, or individual composer or performer. An individual work may also be described as having a style that distinguishes it from other works by the same composer. In all of these cases, the attempt to define a style requires consideration of all aspects of the music being studied. Thus, the analysis of style makes use of all of the techniques of *analysis (including, e.g., the analysis of form) and *criticism. It is more likely, however, to concentrate on the establishment of normative categories against which to test the individual work than it is to concentrate on the uniqueness of the individual work.

Style brisé [Fr., broken style]. A texture in which melodic lines are subservient to the broken chords and composite rhythms they create. Voices merge and change roles frequently, and even melody notes are delayed to create continuous rhythmic presentation of the harmony. The term *style brisé* is most often used to describe an essential feature of 17th-century French lute music (whence the term *style luthé*) that was imitated by French harpsichordists (Chambonnières, d'Anglebert), as well as by Germans in harpsichord suites (Froberger, Bach). The term itself is modern.

Style galant [Fr.]. See *Galant* style.

Style luthé [Fr.]. *Style brisé.

Styne, Jule [Stein, Julius] (b. London, 31 Dec. 1905; d. New York, 20 Sept. 1994). Composer. During the 1920s, played in dance bands and wrote songs. In 1937 moved to Hollywood; with lyricist Sammy Cahn wrote songs such as "I've Heard That Song Before," "I'll Walk Alone," and "Time After Time," many performed by Frank Sinatra. Broadway shows include *High Button Shoes* (1947), *Gentlemen Prefer Blondes* (1949); with the lyricists Betty Comden and Adolph Green, *Two on the Aisle* (1951), *Bells Are Ringing* (1956), *Gypsy* (1959), *Do Re Mi* (1960), and *Funny Girl* (1964).

Subdominant. The fourth *scale degree of a major or minor scale, so called because it lies the same distance below the tonic as the *dominant lies above the tonic, namely a perfect fifth. In *harmonic analysis it is identified by the roman numeral IV or by the letter S [see also Functional harmony].

Subito [It.]. Suddenly, quickly.

Subject. A melody or melodic fragment on which a composition or a major portion of one is based. The term is now used principally with respect to the *fugue and other imitative forms such as the *ricercar and with respect to *sonata form (where it may be synonymous with theme).

Submediant. The sixth *scale degree.

Subotnick, Morton (b. Los Angeles, 14 Apr. 1933). Composer. Studied composition with Leon Kirchner and Darius Milhaud. Taught at Mills College (1959–66); founded and co-directed the San Francisco Tape Music Center (1961–65). Composed pieces in which traditional instruments were combined with electronic tape. In 1967 moved to New York and taught at New York Univ. Produced a series of all-electronic pieces expressly for recordings, using a Buchla syn-

thesizer: *Silver Apples of the Moon* (1967), *The Wild Bull* (1967), *Sidewinder* (1970), *Four Butterflies* (1971). In 1969 returned to California to teach at the California Institute of the Arts. His music moved back toward live performance (*Before the Butterfly,* orchestra and electronics, 1975), some computer-directed (*Parallel Lines,* orchestra, electronics, 1978; *Ascent into Air,* instrumental ensemble, electronics, 1981). Other works include *The Double Life of Amphibians* (theater piece, 1984); *In Two Worlds* (concerto, sax, electronic wind controller, orchestra, 1987–88); *Jacob's Room* (opera, 1993).

Subsemitonium modi [Lat.]. The pitch lying a semitone below the final of a *mode.

Substitution chord. A chord that can be substituted for another while retaining its harmonic function [see Functional harmony]. Jazz makes use of a variety of such chords (often chromatically altered), especially in the performance of popular songs or "standards" that are taken into the jazz repertory from outside. For example, the dominant or dominant seventh chord is often replaced in some styles of jazz by a seventh or ninth chord on the lowered supertonic.

Subtonic. The *scale degree immediately below the tonic, especially when it lies a whole tone below the tonic; otherwise the term *leading tone is preferred.

Subtonium modi [Lat.]. Originally, the pitch lying immediately below the lowest pitch of the normal ambitus of a *mode; in the case of the authentic modes, this is the pitch below the final. In the 16th century, the term was applied to the pitch below the final in both authentic and plagal modes when this occurred naturally at the interval of a whole tone, thus, in all modes except those with finals on C and F. See also *Subsemitonium modi.

Succentor. In some Anglican cathedrals, the deputy of the *precentor.

Suchoň, Eugen (b. Pezinok, Slovakia, 25 Sept. 1908; d. Bratislava, 5 Aug. 1993). Composer. Studied with Kafenda and Novák; taught at Bratislava Academy, Bratislava School for Education, and Bratislava Univ. (1959–74), and served composers' organizations in Czechoslovakia. His compositions drew on Slovakian folk themes and modalities; during the late 1950s he experimented with serialism. Works include stage music (*Krútňava* [The Whirlpool], 1949), orchestral music (*Symfonická fantázia na BACH,* organ, strings, percussion, 1971), and vocal works.

Suite [Fr., succession, following]. A series of disparate instrumental movements with some element of unity, most often to be performed as a single work.

The number of movements in a suite may be just large enough to constitute a series (three) or may be so great as to suggest that the work was intended to be treated as an anthology from which to make selections (e.g., 24 pieces in François Couperin's second *ordre*). Individual movements are almost always short and contrasting. A suite's unity may result from nothing more than a common key or from its origins in a larger work, such as an opera or ballet, from which it is excerpted; unity may occasionally involve thematic connections and some sense of overall form. In some suites, the relationship among movements is defined by an extramusical program. The Baroque solo suite came close to having a specific pattern of dance movements at its core (*allemande-*courante-*sarabande-*gigue), but even then looseness of definition and variability of design were implicit in the term.

The origins of the suite are found in dance music pairing two contrasting dances. By the 16th century, pairs of this type were commonplace, usually consisting of a slower gliding dance in duple meter followed by a faster leaping dance in triple meter (e.g., *Tanz* and *Nachtanz,* *pavan* and *galliard*; see also After-dance). Groups of three dances appeared during the 16th century as well, such as Joan Ambrosio Dalza's lute arrangements, in which he calls attention to the *pavana–saltarello–piva* groupings. In such groups, the dances are often thematically related, placing them as much in the history of variations as in that of the suite.

In the last quarter of the 16th century and the beginning of the 17th, dances for instrumental ensemble and for lute were published with varying contents, generally grouped by key, sometimes without overt thematic connections. The first composer to adopt a consistent pattern and thus demonstrate a concept of the suite as a coherent musical whole was Paul Peuerl (1611), using the order *paduana–intrada–Dantz–galiarda.*

Bach wrote nearly 40 suites (some called *partitas) for solo instruments (harpsichord, lute, violin, cello, and flute), a little over half of which have the following pattern: prelude–allemande–courante–sarabande–optional–gigue (henceforth P–A–C–S–O–G). This has given rise to the notion that the Baroque suite was by definition the sequence A–C–S–G, which might be prefaced by a nondance movement and which could allow optional dances to intervene before the gigue. Although the core of A–C–S–G did evolve to be the most frequent pattern in solo suites, the suite was less an architecturally conceived whole than a series of separate units.

The solo suite is principally a harpsichord genre. German harpsichordists in the second third of the 17th century imitated several aspects of French lute style, including A–C–S sequences. Johann Jakob Froberger created a norm (ca. 1650) of A–G–C–S, but virtually all succeeding composers in Germanic areas placed the gigue at the end. The large body of German harpsichord suites includes music by Johann Erasmus Kindermann, Dietrich Buxtehude, and Georg Böhm. The last composer in this tradition was Bach, whose works include partitas as well as "French" and "English" suites (the nicknames are not from Bach and carry no stylistic implications).

In French harpsichord music, the suite was more an ordering of pieces for publication or performance than a compositional form. Preexisting movements were compiled by composers or performers to create groupings in a single key. Often suites were put together from the music of more than one composer. In Italy, pieces were usually grouped together by type, not as multimovement forms. Harpsichord dances were occasionally placed in suitelike sequences, though the patterns were more closely related to the *sonata da camera.*

In the second half of the 17th century, the popularity of French ballet and especially of the music of Lully surged. With this came the practice of excerpting dances and airs from stage works, presenting the aggregate as an independent work for orchestra. By the 1680s, such extract-suites inspired composers to write original suites in a similar style. Bach wrote four masterly examples (BWV 1066–69), but the most famous are Handel's *Water Music* (ca. 1717) and *Music for the Royal Fireworks* (1749). Most orchestral suites begin with a French overture, and thus *ouverture* may stand as the title of a complete suite (Bach). Dances follow in no particular order, but in the same key (except for pairs of dances to be played alternatively, in which the second might be in a closely related key). The choice of dances emphasizes those popular in stage works and in the ballroom (e.g., minuet, bourrée, gavotte, passepied) and does not usually include the older forms of allemande and courante. Pieces with descriptive titles are also common.

As dances gave way to sonata designs in the middle of the 18th century, the dance suite all but disappeared for a time. Genres such as the *divertimento had the same looseness of definition as the Baroque suite without the strong attachment to dance forms [see also Partita]. The dance suite then assumed a retrospective gesture for composers, even as early as Mozart (K. 399/385i). Neoclassicists of the 19th and 20th centuries (Saint-Saëns, Hindemith) created a large corpus of such suites, and others contributed to a major revival of the orchestral suite (Debussy, Sibelius). Sometimes the title suite is used for collections of movements that could be considered multimovement tone poems (Massenet, Holst), often with a nationalistic flavor.

Beginning in the middle of the 19th century, the

extract-suite regained nearly the popularity it had enjoyed in the 17th century. Composers sometimes merely assemble coherent excerpts from larger works such as ballets, or may weave them together into a continuous whole, making key and orchestration changes as necessary. Famous examples include the *Nutcracker Suite* by Tchaikovsky and the *Firebird Suite* of Stravinsky.

Suite bergamasque [Fr.]. A suite for piano by Debussy in four movements: Prélude, Menuet, Clair de lune, and Passepied, composed in 1890 (revised in 1905). Its title is probably derived from a phrase in Paul Verlaine's poem "Clair de lune": "masques et bergamasques."

Suivez [Fr., imp., follow]. (1) *Attacca. (2) An instruction for the accompaniment to follow the lead of the soloist.

Suk, Josef (1) (b. Křečovice, 4 Jan. 1874; d. Benešov, near Prague, 29 May 1935). Composer. Studied violin and theory at the Prague Conservatory and worked with Wihan and Dvořák. With Wihan, played in the Bohemian String Quartet. In 1898 married Dvořák's daughter Otilie; Dvořák died in 1904 and Otilie in 1905. Joined the faculty at the Prague Conservatory in 1922; served as its head, 1924–26 and 1933–35. Compositions highly influenced by Dvořák, utilizing traditional forms and genres. His musical language became increasingly self-referential and complex and moved close to atonality. Works include *Serenade* (strings, 1892); *Pohádka* [Fairytale] (suite from "Radúz a Mahulena," 1899–1900); *Asrael* (symphony, 1905–6); *Zrání* [The Ripening] (symphonic poem, 1912–17); *Epilog* (symphonic piece, soprano, baritone, bass, 2 choirs, orchestra, 1920–29); *Sousedská* (chamber ensemble, 1935).

Suk, Josef (2) (b. Prague, 8 Aug. 1929). Violinist. Grandson of the composer Josef Suk (1). Pupil of Jaroslav Kocian; studied at the Prague Conservatory and Academy and led the Prague National Theater orchestra (1953–55). Member of the Prague Quartet 1951–52; founded the Suk Trio 1952. Toured with the Czech Philharmonic beginning in 1959. Performed chamber music with Starker and Katchen (1967–69); recorded extensively.

Sul, sulla [It.]. At, on, on the; *sul G*, an instruction in music for stringed instruments to play on the G string (or, similarly, another string identified by letter or by roman numeral); *sul ponticello*, to bow at the bridge; *sul tasto, sulla tastiera*, to bow over the fingerboard [see Bowing].

Sullivan, Arthur (Seymour) (b. London, 13 May 1842; d. there, 22 Nov. 1900). Composer. Son of Thomas Sullivan (1805–66), a London theater clari-

netist. Studied at the Royal Academy of Music and the Leipzig Conservatory. In April 1862 his music to *The Tempest* made him one of the rising stars of English music; his Irish Symphony and Cello Concerto were premiered in 1866, the same year as his first venture into operetta, *Cox and Box*. After 1867 composed very little instrumental music; from the mid-1860s through the 1870s produced most of his solo songs ("The Lost Chord," 1877), part songs and hymns ("Onward Christian Soldiers," 1872).

First collaboration with W. S. Gilbert was the comic opera *Thispis* (1871); *Trial by Jury* (1875) was their first success, leading Richard D'Oyly Carte in 1876 to form a company to produce further collaborations, including *H.M.S. Pinafore* (1878). Gilbert, Sullivan, and Carte traveled to the U.S. in November 1879, where they staged *The Pirates of Penzance* in New York (31 December 1879). *Patience* (1881) inaugurated the new Savoy Theatre in London, which Carte had built for them, followed by *Iolanthe* (1882), *Princess Ida* (1883), *The Mikado* (1885), *Ruddigore* (1887), and *The Gondoliers* (1889). Sullivan conducted the triennial Leeds Festival 1880–98. In 1890 the collaboration came to rupture when Gilbert went to court against Carte. After the failure of Sullivan's grand opera *Ivanhoe* (1891) to establish itself, he returned to musical comedy, including an anticlimactic reconciliation with Gilbert (*Utopia Unlimited*, 1893; *The Grand Duke*, 1896).

Sulzer, Salomon (b. Hohenems, 30 Mar. 1804; d. Vienna, 17 Jan. 1890). Cantor and composer. *Obercantor* in Vienna, 1826–81. His voice was admired by Schumann, Liszt, and Meyerbeer. Music for solo cantor and men's chorus published as *Schir Zion* in 2 volumes (1838–40; 1855–66). His son Julius Salomon Sulzer (1834–91) was a violinist and director of the Hofburgtheater in Vienna (1875–91).

Sumer is icumen in. A mid-13th-century infinite *canon or round at the unison for four voices over a texted two-voice *pes* involving *voice exchange; also known as the Summer Canon and the Reading Rota (from Reading, England, the probable place of composition).

Summation(al) tone. See Combination tone.

Sun Quartets [Ger. *Sonnenquartette*]. Popular name for Haydn's six string quartets op. 20, Hob. III:31–36 (1772). The Hummel edition of 1779 had an engraving of the rising sun as part of its frontispiece.

Sun Ra [Blount, Herman ("Sonny"); Le Sony'r Ra] (b. Birmingham, Ala., May 1914; d. there, 30 May 1993). Jazz bandleader, composer, and keyboard player. In Chicago in 1953 founded a band later known as Myth-Science (or Solar) Arkestra. Moved to New York 1960. The Arkestra, based in Philadelphia beginning in the 1970s, toured the U.S. and Europe. Albums include *Angels and Demons at Play* (1955–57), *The Magic City,* and *The Heliocentric Worlds of Sun Ra* (1965). The film *Sun Ra: A Joyful Noise* (1980) presented his "Egyptian-galactic" costumed performances and free-jazz improvising.

Suor Angelica [It.]. See *Trittico.*

Superdominant. The *scale degree above the dominant, normally termed the submediant.

Superius [Lat.]. In polyphonic vocal music of the 16th century, the highest part.

Supertonic. The second *scale degree.

Suppé [Suppè], **Franz (von)** [Francesco Ezechiele Ermenegildo Cavaliere Suppé Demelli] (b. Spalato, Dalmatia, 18 Apr. 1819; d. Vienna, 21 May 1895). Composer. Studied in Vienna with Seyfried and Sechter. In 1840 became third Kapellmeister at the Theater in der Josefstadt, for which from 1841 to 1845 he wrote over 20 theatrical scores, including *Marie, die Tochter des Regiments* and *Ein Morgen, ein Mittag und ein Abend in Wien* (both 1844), and music for *A Midsummer Night's Dream.* Between 1845 and 1862 he was Kapellmeister at the Theater an der Wien. *Das Pensionat* (1860) was the first successful Viennese operetta. Suppé moved to the Kaitheater (1862), then to the Carltheater (1865). His most successful scores were *Gervinus* (1849), *Flotte Bursche* (1863), *Fatinitza* (1876), and *Boccaccio* (1879). After his retirement from the Carltheater in 1882 he continued to compose. Aside from over 200 stage works, his compositions include sacred and secular vocal music, symphonies, overtures (*Poet and Peasant, Light Cavalry,* and *Morning, Noon, and Night in Vienna*), songs, dances, and string quartets.

Supplying. See Verset.

Sur [Fr.]. On, over; *sur le chevalet,* an instruction in music for stringed instruments to bow at the bridge; *sur la touche,* to bow over the fingerboard [see Bowing].

Suriano, Francesco. See Soriano, Francesco.

Surinach, Carlos (b. Barcelona, 4 Mar. 1915; d. New Haven, 12 Nov. 1997). Composer and conductor. Studied piano and music theory in Barcelona with José Caminals and composition with Enrique Morera; also at the Robert Schumann Conservatory in Düsseldorf and the Academy of Fine Arts in Berlin with Max Trapp. Returned to Barcelona in 1942; 1947–50 lived in Paris; 1950 moved to the U.S. For Martha Graham he wrote *Embattled Garden* (1958), *Acrobats of God* (1960), and *The Owl and the Pussycat* (1978). He also wrote for the José Limón Company, the Joffrey Ballet, the Paul Taylor Dance Com-

pany, and others. Works that reflect his Spanish heritage include Symphony no. 2 (1949), *Feria mágica* (orchestra, 1956), Concertino for Piano and Strings (1957), *Symphonic Variations* (1963), *Melorhythmic Dances* (orchestra, 1966).

Surprise Symphony. Popular name for Haydn's Symphony no. 94 in G major Hob. I:94 (1791, no. 2 of the *Salomon Symphonies), so called because of a loud chord in the middle of the quiet first theme of the second movement. Haydn later incorporated this celebrated second movement into his oratorio *The *Seasons,* in the aria "Schon eilet."

Susannah. Opera in two acts by Carlisle Floyd (to his own libretto), produced in Tallahassee, Florida, in 1955. Setting: the mountains of Tennessee.

Suspension. (1) See Counterpoint. (2) An ornament described in the 18th century by François Couperin and others as the delaying of a note by a short rest of flexible duration.

Suspirum [Lat.]. A rest equal in value to a *minima* [see Mensural notation].

Susskind, (Jan) Walter (b. Prague, 1 May 1913; d. Berkeley, Calif., 25 Mar. 1980). Conductor. Szell's assistant at the German Opera, Prague, 1934–38; member of the Czech Trio in London (1938–41) and director of the Carl Rosa Opera (1943–45). Led the Scottish Orchestra (1946–52); the Victoria Symphony, Melbourne (to 1955); the Toronto Symphony (1956–65); the Aspen Festival (1962–68); the St. Louis Symphony (1968–75); and the Cincinnati Symphony (from 1978).

Süssmayr, Franz Xaver (b. Schwanenstadt, Upper Austria, 1766; d. Vienna, 17 Sept. 1803). Composer. Pupil of Mozart; after Mozart's death Constanze engaged him to complete the unfinished Requiem K. 626. Continued his studies with Salieri; Kapellmeister of the German opera at the National Theater in Vienna from 1794 until his death. Works include over 20 operas; the singspiel *Der Spiegel von Arkadien* (1794); ballets; sacred and secular vocal pieces; 2 symphonies, 1 piano concerto, 2 clarinet concertos, and other orchestral pieces; and chamber music.

Sussurando [It.]. Whispering.

Sustaining pedal. The *sostenuto pedal of the piano; sometimes also the *damper pedal.

Sutherland, Joan (b. Sydney, 7 Nov. 1926). Soprano. Studied in her home city and at the Royal College of Music, London, with Clive Carey. Appeared at Covent Garden in *Die Zauberflöte* in 1952, sang there opposite Callas in *Norma* in 1953; also appeared in several new productions of Handel operas. Gained fame for her portrayal of Lucia at Covent Garden in 1959; in 1961 began a lasting association with the Metropolitan Opera. Toured Australia with her Sutherland–Williamson Opera Company, 1965. Her husband since 1954, Richard Bonynge, often conducted the orchestra for her performances and extensive recordings. Retired 1991.

Sutherland, Margaret (Ada) (b. Adelaide, 20 Nov. 1897; d. Melbourne, 12 Aug. 1984). Composer. Studied at the Melbourne Univ. Conservatorium, in London with Bax, and in Vienna; returned to Melbourne 1925. She continued to work as a pianist, teacher, and composer. Music influenced by Bax, Bartók, and Hindemith. Works include stage music (*The Young Kabbarli,* opera, 1965), orchestral music (*Haunted Hills,* 1950; Concerto grosso, 1955), vocal music (*Six Australian Songs,* voice, piano, 1967), and chamber music.

Suzuki method. A system of musical instruction for children developed by Shinichi Suzuki (1898–1998). The child begins at an early age (preferably 3–4 years) with lessons on an instrument, usually the violin, learning a fixed repertory of pieces (most, except the most elementary ones, by composers of the 18th and 19th centuries), arranged in order of increasing difficulty. Instruction is by ear and by rote, often aided by listening to recordings of the assigned pieces; emphasis is on correct technique and musicality from the beginning; practice entails substantial repetition and active participation of a parent until the student is quite advanced; note reading is not introduced until the child has acquired a basic technique. The method is also used to teach piano, cello, and flute.

Suzuki, Shinichi (b. Nagoya, 18 Oct. 1898; d. Matsumoto, 26 Jan. 1998). Violinist and teacher. Son of Masakichi Suzuki (1859–1944), instrument builder and founder of the Suzuki Seizō Co. Studied violin in Japan and in Berlin; in 1930 founded the Suzuki Quartet with three brothers and became head of the Teikoku Music School; later formed the Tokyo String Orchestra. Beginning in 1933 developed a teaching method based on creating a proper learning environment and using a process of repetition. Founded institutes and traveled widely, including to the U.S., to promulgate his technique.

Švanda Dudák [Cz., Schwanda the Bagpiper]. Opera in two acts by Jaromír Weinberger (libretto by Miloš Kareš and Max Brod, after the tale by Tyl), produced in Prague in 1927. Setting: fairy tale.

Svelto [It.]. Quick, nimble.

Svendsen, Johan (Severin) (b. Christiania [now Oslo], 30 Sept. 1840; d. Copenhagen, 14 June 1911). Violinist, composer, and conductor. Studied at the Leipzig Conservatory with Hauptmann, Ferdinand David, E. F. Richter, and Reinecke. Traveled to Paris, London, and Weimar, where he met Liszt. From 1872 to 1877 conducted and taught in Norway; joint conductor with Grieg of the Music Society concert and from 1883 court conductor at Copenhagen. Compositions include 2 symphonies; violin concerto and cello concertos; other orchestral and chamber works; piano works; songs.

Svetlanov, Evgeny (b. Moscow, 6 Sept. 1928). Conductor, composer, and pianist. Attended the Gnessin Institute and the Moscow Conservatory; from 1953 led concerts of the Moscow Radio Symphony; joined the Bolshoi Theater in 1955 (principal conductor 1962–64); named conductor of the U.S.S.R. State Orchestra, 1965. Works include a symphony (1956), a piano concerto (1951), the *Fantasia siberiana* for orchestra (1953), and film and piano music.

Sviridov, Georgy Vasilevich (b. Fatezh, near Kursk, 16 Dec. 1915; d. Moscow, 5 Jan. 1998). Composer. Studied at the Leningrad Conservatory with Shostakovich; concertized as a pianist. Best known as a composer of choral and vocal music, both of patriotic and of folk content. Works include the *Pathetic Oratorio* on texts of Mayakovsky for soloists, mixed chorus, and orchestra (1959), *Kursk Songs,* cantata, mixed chorus and orchestra (1964), and other vocal-symphonic music; choral music; many songs and song cycles; chamber music; works for piano; incidental and film music.

Sw. Abbr. for the *Swell division of an organ.

Swados, Elizabeth (b. Buffalo, 5 Feb. 1951). Composer. Studied at Bennington College; worked with La Mama Experimental Theater in New York and the International Theater Group. Musicals include *Runaways* (1978); *Doonesbury* (1983) and *Rap Master Ronnie* (1984), with the cartoonist Garry Trudeau. Other works include vocal and choral works and scores for theater, dance, and films. Author of *Listening Out Loud: Becoming a Composer* (New York, 1988).

Swallow, Steve [Stephen W.] (b. New York, 4 Oct. 1940). Jazz bass player and composer. Joined pianist Paul Bley in 1959, and with him Jimmy Giuffre (1961–63); recorded George Russell's album *Ezzthetics* (1961). Played with the Art Farmer–Jim Hall quartet (1963–64), Stan Getz (1965–67), Gary Burton (electric bass, 1967–70, from 1973), and Carla Bley (from late 1970s). Compositions include "Hotel Hello" (recorded 1974) and "Home" (recorded 1980).

Swan Lake [Russ. *Lebedinoye ozero*]. A ballet in four acts by Tchaikovsky, op. 20 (1875–76), produced in Moscow in 1877 with choreography by

Wenzel Reisinger. The choreography by Marius Petipa (acts 1 and 3) and Lev Ivanov (acts 2 and 4) that has remained in the repertory was for a new production in St. Petersburg in 1895.

Swan Song. See *Schwanengesang.*

Swan of Tuonela. See *Lemminkäinen Suite.*

Swanson, Howard (b. Atlanta, 18 Aug. 1907; d. New York, 12 Nov. 1978). Composer. Attended the Cleveland Institute of Music; studied with Nadia Boulanger. In 1941 moved to New York and became known for songs on poems by Langston Hughes—"The Negro Speaks of Rivers" (1942), "Joy" (1946), and "Montage" (1947). *Short Symphony* (1948) introduced by the New York Philharmonic. Lived in Europe 1952–66, then returned to New York. Later works include *Fantasy Piece,* soprano saxophone and string orchestra (1969); *Trio,* flute, oboe, piano (1975).

Swarowsky, Hans (b. Budapest, 16 Sept. 1899; d. Salzburg, 10 Sept. 1975). Conductor. Studied with Schoenberg, Webern, Weingartner, and Strauss. In the 1930s conducted opera at Stuttgart, Hamburg, Berlin, and Zurich. Managed the Salzburg Festival, 1940–44; from 1946 taught at the Vienna Academy of Music (Abbado and Mehta among his pupils) and conducted the Vienna Symphony (1946–48) and Graz opera (1947–50). From 1957 conducted at the Vienna Staatsoper and directed the Scottish National Orchestra.

Sweelinck [Swelinck, Zwelinck, Sweeling, Sweelingh, Sweling, Swelingh], **Jan Pieterszoon** (b. Deventer, May? 1562; d. Amsterdam, 16 Oct. 1621). Composer. By 1580 (possibly 1577), organist at the Oude Kerk; became known for his improvisations. An influential teacher, his pupils included Andreas Düben, Peter Hasse, Samuel and Gottfried Scheidt, Paul Siefert, Ulrich Cernitz, Jacob Praetorius, and Heinrich Scheidemann. Sweelinck's 254 vocal works, which were all printed, include 33 chansons, 19 madrigals, 39 motets (*Cantiones sacrae,* 1619), 153 Psalm settings; 70 keyboard works including fantasias *(Fantasia chromatica),* toccatas, and variations.

Sweet potato. *Ocarina.

Swell. In organs, a keyboard division whose pipes are placed within a large wooden box with Venetian louvres that enable variations in loudness as controlled by the Swell pedal.

Swift, Kay (b. New York, 19 Apr. 1897; d. Southington, Conn., 28 Jan. 1993). Pianist and composer. Studied at the Institute of Musical Art in New York and at the New England Conservatory with Charles

Loeffler and Percy Goetschius. Worked as a rehearsal pianist for Broadway shows; with her husband, James Warburg, as lyricist wrote "Can't We Be Friends?" (1929), "Can This Be Love?" (1930), and "Up among the Chimney Pots" (1930). Continued composing songs, musicals, ballets, film scores, and piano music well into the 1970s.

Swift, Richard (b. Middlepoint, Ohio, 24 Sept. 1927). Composer. Studied at the Univ. of Chicago with Leland Smith and Grosvenor Cooper. In 1956 joined the faculty at the Univ. of California, Davis. Works include concertos for chamber orchestra; 5 string quartets; *Domains I* (baritone, chamber ensemble, 1963); *Specimen Days* (soprano and orchestra, 1977); *A Stitch in Time* (guitar, 1989).

Swing. (1) The popular, dance-oriented, *big band jazz style that first flourished in the 1930s [see also Jazz]. Featured are combinations such as five saxophones, four trumpets, and four trombones, and often a vocalist, with a rhythm section of piano, guitar, bass, and drums. Based on popular songs (especially 32-bar AABA forms) and 12-bar *blues, the repertory ranges from complex, entirely written arrangements to impromptu *head arrangements in which simple *riffs provide thematic material and accompaniment to improvisations.

(2) An intangible rhythmic momentum in jazz. Swing defies analysis, but it is meaningful as a general stylistic concept in, e.g., swing [see (1) above] and *bebop, where "swinging" triplet subdivisions of quarter notes (or of eighths at slow tempos, halves at fast tempos) contrast with duple subdivisions of pulses in, e.g., *ragtime, Latin-American dances, rock, and soul.

Sydeman, William (Jay) (b. New York, 8 May 1928). Composer. Studied at Mannes with Felix Salzer and Roy Travis, at Hartt with Roger Sessions and Arnold Franchetti. Taught composition at Mannes 1959–70. In 1970 began a period of travel and philosophical study. Works include 3 *Studies for Orchestra* (1959, 1963, 1965); 3 Concerti da camera, violin and chamber ensemble (1959, 1960, 1965); *In memoriam—John F. Kennedy,* narrator and orchestra (1966); *18 Duos,* 2 violins (1976); *Songs of Milarepa,* violin, narrator, dancer (1980); *Calendar of the Soul,* chorus (1982).

Syllabic. Characterized by the singing of only one note for each syllable.

Sylphide, La [Fr., The Sylph]. A ballet in two acts by Jean Schneitzhoeffer (choreography by Filippo Taglioni), first produced in Paris in 1832. A Danish production of 1836 employed music by Herman

Løvenskjold and choreography by Auguste Bournonville.

Sylphides, Les [Fr., The Sylphs]. A ballet in one act with choreography by Michel Fokine, employing music by Chopin (orchestrated by Glazunov), first produced in Paris in 1909.

Sylvia, ou La nymphe de Diane. A ballet in three acts by Delibes (choreography by Louis Mérante), first produced in Paris in 1876.

Sympathetic string. A string that is not normally played upon directly but that is set in motion by the acoustical phenomenon of resonance [see Acoustics]. Such a string thus vibrates "in sympathy" with the strings played upon directly, contributing to the tone color of the instrument. Instruments incorporating sympathetic strings include the *viola d'amore, *baryton, and *sitar. Some pianos include such strings, termed *aliquot strings.

Symphonia [Gr.]. (1) In Greek theory, the unison. (2) In late Greek and medieval theory, consonance, as distinct from *diaphonia,* dissonance. (3) In the Middle Ages, any of several instruments, including the drum, *hurdy-gurdy or *chifonie,* and *bagpipe. (4) From the 17th century, *sinfonia.

Symphonia domestica. A "domestic symphony" for orchestra by Richard Strauss, op. 53 (1902–3), depicting a typical day spent at home by the composer, his wife, and young son.

Symphonic band, concert band. An ensemble of as many as 50 or more woodwind, brass, and percussion instruments, sometimes with the addition of a double bass. These terms, together with wind ensemble, all of which are roughly synonymous, are employed in schools and universities in the U.S. to distinguish ensembles devoted to performing in concert from those that march or otherwise perform at athletic events and the like. The full instrumentation of such an ensemble may now include the following parts: piccolo; flutes 1, 2, and 3; oboe 1 and 2; English horn; E♭ clarinet; B♭ clarinets 1, 2, and 3; E♭ alto clarinet; B♭ bass clarinets 1 and 2 (or contrabass clarinet); bassoons 1 and 2 (contrabassoon); alto, tenor, and baritone saxophones; cornets solo, 1, 2, and 3; trumpets 1, 2, and 3; French horns 1, 2, 3, and 4; euphoniums or baritone horns 1 and 2; trombones 1, 2, and 3 (bass trombone); tuba; 4–6 percussion; double bass. Historically, however, the repertory has not been standardized, nor is this instrumentation fully represented in every band. The flute, clarinet, and brass sections are likely to have several players for each part in most school and university bands; in some cases, the clarinet section is by far the largest, in part as a result of a tradition of transcriptions of orchestral

music in which the clarinets serve the function of the violins of the orchestra.

The repertories of these ensembles are widely varied, including marches, popular music of various kinds, transcriptions of orchestral works, and newly composed works intended specifically for this medium. Newly composed works are themselves varied, many drawing on the idioms of popular music and jazz (especially for school consumption), but with a significant number by composers of concert music generally. Among the first classics of the repertory are Gustav Holst's Suite no. 1 in E♭ (1909) and Suite no. 2 in F (1911) and Ralph Vaughan Williams's *English Folk Song Suite* (1923) and *Toccata marziale* (1924). Composers who have contributed to the repertory since include Paul Hindemith, Sergei Prokofiev, Ernst Krenek, Arnold Schoenberg, Darius Milhaud, Igor Stravinsky, Samuel Barber, Morton Gould, William Schuman, Vincent Persichetti, and Karel Husa.

Symphonic etudes. See *Études symphoniques.*

Symphonic poem [Fr. *poème symphonique;* Ger. *symphonische Dichtung*]. An orchestral piece whose music is accompanied by a program, i.e., a text, generally poetic or narrative in nature, which is meant to be read by the audience before listening to the work. As is true for other types of *program music, the program may be rather brief and vague (and may even consist merely of a suggestive title), or it may be long and detailed. Similarly, the music may be related to the program only very generally or in a myriad of specific ways. Usually the term is reserved for a composition in one movement, as opposed to the multimovement *program symphony; though many symphonic poems do contain several contrasting sections, these sections tend to flow into one another (through transitional passages) and are usually unified by tonal or motivic interrelationships. The term tone poem was preferred by Richard Strauss, and it has sometimes been used to refer to all works in the genre. The symphonic poem, by its very freedom of form, has also lent itself to hybridization with other genres, e.g., the solo concerto (Strauss, *Don Quixote,* 1896–97; Bloch, *Schelomo,* 1915–16), cantata (Franck, *Psyché,* 1887–88), or art song (Barber, *Knoxville: Summer of 1915,* 1947).

The term symphonic poem was coined by Liszt for a performance of his *Tasso* in 1854, and he subsequently applied it to all of his other works in the genre, including earlier ones, originally described as overtures. Many composers after Liszt eagerly seized upon this new, archetypally Romantic genre. Like him, they tended to avoid highly detailed musical depictions, but their programs were sometimes quite lengthy, especially if the work dealt with events or characters unlikely to be familiar to an audience (e.g., the six symphonic poems of Smetana, *Má Vlast, 1872–79). The symphonic poems of Dvořák, Franck, Saint-Saëns, Tchaikovsky, Balakirev, Mussorgsky, Rimsky-Korsakov, Borodin, and Scriabin contain some of these composers' finest music. Wagner's *Siegfried Idyll (1870) is also closely related to the Lisztian symphonic poem.

With Richard Strauss, the genre reached its culmination, in such works (termed tone poems) as *Till Eulenspiegels lustige Streiche (1894–95) and *Also sprach Zarathustra (1895–96). Contemporary with Strauss, many other composers—Debussy, Ravel, Loeffler, Sibelius, Elgar, Delius, Rachmaninoff, Ives, and others—composed important one-movement orchestral works that may be regarded as symphonic poems.

Around 1920, the anti-Romantic prejudices of the modernist movement led many composers away from the symphonic poem. It nevertheless flourished for a time in the hands of more traditional composers, such as Honegger, Milhaud, Villa-Lobos, Gershwin, and Copland. In the late 20th century, composers of varied stylistic persuasions—Jacob Druckman, Hans Werner Henze, David Del Tredici—composed works that are effectively symphonic poems, though not always so named.

Symphonic variations. See *Variations symphoniques.*

Symphonie concertante [Fr.; It. *sinfonia concertante*]. In the 18th and early 19th centuries, a type of concerto for two or more solo instruments (normally strings or winds) and orchestra. Though called *symphonies,* these works belong, with few exceptions, to the history of the concerto. They are in two or three movements, the first in Classical ritornello or ritornello-sonata form [see Concerto], the last typically in rondo form. The style tends generally toward the light and popular rather than the heroic or grand.

The earliest *symphonies concertantes* date from the late 1760s. From 1770 through the first decades of the 19th century the *symphonie concertante* experienced an exceptional vogue, centered primarily on Paris. The masterwork of the genre, however, is Mozart's *Sinfonia concertante* for violin and viola K. 364 (320d), written in Salzburg in 1779. In the 19th century the term *symphonie concertante* fell into disuse.

Symphonie fantastique [Fr., Fantastic Symphony]. A symphony by Berlioz, op. 14 (1830; revised 1831–45), an important example of *program music. The work (subtitled *Épisode de la vie d'un artiste*) consists of five movements—"Rêveries-Passions"; "Un bal" (A Ball); "Scène aux champs" (Scene in the Country); "Marche au supplice" (March to the Gallows); "Songe d'une nuit du sabbat" (Dream of a Witches' Sabbath)—which are united by a recurring theme, called an *idée fixe.* The final movement includes the *"Dies irae" from the Requiem Mass.

Symphonie pathétique [Fr.]. See *Pathétique* (2).

Symphony [fr. Gr. *symphōnia,* Lat. *symphonia,* sounding together, concord]. A work for orchestra in multiple movements (or occasionally one movement with multiple sections). Though symphonies are normally abstract or absolute in content, many from the 19th and 20th centuries, and some from the 18th, have more or less explicit programs [see Program music, Program symphony]. Likewise, although most symphonies are for orchestra alone, many later examples include parts for voice, chorus, or solo instrument.

Numerous earlier genres contributed to the formation of the concert symphony. The most important precursor seems to have been the late Baroque ripieno concerto (*concerto ripieno, concerto a 4* or *a 5; see Concerto). These works, though called concertos, did not generally contain solo parts and were scored for the same ensemble as early symphonies—string orchestra plus continuo. In addition, beginning with Giuseppe Torelli's *Concerti musicali* op. 6 (1698), ripieno concertos frequently utilized the standard formal cycle of the early symphony, three movements in a fast–slow–fast pattern, the last a binary dance or dance-related movement.

The three-movement Italian opera *sinfonia or *overture, established by Alessandro Scarlatti as early as the 1680s, furnished another important avenue for development. In addition to being one source for the name symphony, these pieces were frequently detached from their operas for independent performance.

The earliest symphonist of importance was the Milanese composer Giovanni Battista Sammartini (1700/1701–75). His works continue the tradition of the ripieno concerto in their scoring (string orchestra) and use of a three-movement cycle, but depart from it both in their increasingly Classical style and their adoption of a rounded binary or early sonata form for most of their fast movements. At about the same time, Italian opera composers, particularly such Neapolitans as Leonardo Vinci, Giovanni Battista Pergolesi, Leonardo Leo, and Niccolò Jommelli and the Venetian Baldassare Galuppi, were developing a fundamentally new style for their overtures that by the 1740s manifested the following Classical characteristics: use of a larger, more powerful orchestra (strings, pairs of oboes or flutes and horns, often trumpets and timpani); homophonic texture with blocklike rather than linear treatment of the winds; slow harmonic rhythm and extensive use of pedal point; reliance upon dynamic effects, especially the *crescendo* passage; and use of thematic contrast in first-movement expositions [see Sonata form].

Perhaps the most striking example of the assimilation of these traits occurred at the German court of Mannheim [see Mannheim school]. The Mannheim symphonists generally extended and enhanced each of the elements they borrowed from the overture. Orchestration, for instance, is much more varied and challenging to the performer in a Mannheim symphony than in an Italian overture. Clarinets appear beginning in the 1750s, and exposed passages for winds are frequent.

Mannheim also deserves credit for expansion of the symphonic cycle from three movements to four by insertion of a minuet and trio before the finale. Four-movement symphonies appeared from approximately the mid-1740s on in the works of Johann Stamitz (1717–57), concertmaster at the court and the most important Mannheim symphonist. However, later Mannheim composers returned eventually to the three-movement type, for example Stamitz's successor Christian Cannabich (1731–98).

The earliest Viennese symphonists such as Matthias Georg Monn (1717–50) and Georg Christoph Wagenseil (1715–77) were on the whole more conservative. The symphonies of the next generation, including Leopold Hofmann (1738–93), Carl Ditters von Dittersdorf (1739–99), and Johann Vanhal (1739–1813), are usually in four movements, some with slow introductions to the first movement, and rondo finales occur beginning in the 1760s. Similar traits are found in the symphonies of such later Viennese contemporaries of Mozart as Franz Anton Hoffmeister (1754–1812) and Paul Wranitzky (1756–1808).

The symphonies of Haydn range from the modest works of the late 1750s to the 12 great *"London" symphonies of 1791–95. The remarkable diversity of his symphonies encompasses form at every level, choice and use of instruments, texture (often contrapuntal), rhythm and phrase structure, and theme (often folklike). Most of Mozart's early symphonies show an Italianate orientation in their smooth and uncomplicated flow, clear thematic contrasts, choice of formal types, and use of three movements. The small number of symphonies from Mozart's Viennese period, especially the *Prague* of 1786 (K. 504) and the great trilogy of 1788 (K. 543, K. 550 in G minor, and K. 551, the *Jupiter*), are remarkable for their synthesis of strict and free counterpoint within the symphonic idiom as well as for their adoption of the intensive developmental techniques of Haydn.

The nine symphonies of Beethoven represent a culmination of the Classical symphony.

The principal German Romanticists, including Schubert, Mendelssohn, and Schumann, were for the most part conservative in their approach to the symphony. Brahms's four symphonies consciously return to the symphonic technique of Beethoven.

The generally conservative trend within the symphony was carried on by composers in other countries such as Russia, where works include the symphonies of Tchaikovsky (6 symphonies, 1866–93). Though Tchaikovsky occasionally quoted Russian folk material in his symphonies, his style is for the most part cosmopolitan or personal rather than specifically national. The growth of *nationalism in 19th-century orchestral music took place primarily in genres other than the symphony, notably the *symphonic poem. Among nationalist composers of symphonies, the most important were the Russian Alexander Borodin (2 symphonies, 1867–76) and the Czech Antonín Dvořák (9 symphonies, 1865–93).

In opposition to the conservative continuum, Romantic composers such as Berlioz, Liszt, and Wagner advocated the creation of new forms and a more radical union of music and poetic content. Although this approach led some composers away from the symphony (notably Wagner), others could not resist the challenge it presented. Berlioz's three most important symphonies are all programmatic in one sense or another. The most obvious successors to the symphonies of Berlioz were Liszt's *Faust* and *Dante* symphonies (1854–57, the former with tenor soloist and male chorus in the finale), though in both, the "program" consists primarily of the movement titles. In turn, Liszt's technique of thematic *transformation affected numerous symphonies within the French orbit, notably Vincent d'Indy's *Symphony on a French Mountain Air* (1886, with piano) and César Franck's Symphony in D minor (1889).

Anton Bruckner's nine numbered symphonies (1865–96; no. 9 incomplete, plus the early "no. 0") are a highly individual blend of Wagnerian proportions and dynamic range and eschew both explicit programs and the use of voices. The symphonies of Gustav Mahler are very different, though they doubtless owe something of the vastness of their conception to Bruckner. Of Mahler's nine symphonies (ca. 1884–1909; no. 10 incomplete), four utilize voices, ranging from the single soloist of the finale of the Fourth to the huge ensemble of the Eighth (*Symphony of a Thousand*).

Though Jean Sibelius (7 symphonies, 1899–1924) and Carl Nielsen (6 symphonies, 1894–1925) are often classified as Post-Romanticists, the later works of Sibelius in particular show a more compact and objective approach than do such symphonies as Mahler's, Rachmaninoff's (3, 1895–1936), and Elgar's (2, 1910–12)—not to mention Richard Strauss's *Symphonia domestica* (1902–3) and *Alpensinfonie* (1911–15).

World War I marked the beginning of an overt reaction to both the form and content of the Romantic symphony. A *neoclassical view of the symphony may be seen in Prokofiev's parody of Mozart and Haydn in the Symphony no. 1 (*Classical*, 1916–17) and in symphonies by two members of *Les *Six*, Darius Milhaud (6 chamber symphonies of 1917–23) and Arthur Honegger (Symphony no. 1, 1930; 4 later symphonies, 1941–51). Stravinsky's symphonies fall in varying degrees within the neoclassical orbit, at least if one disregards his early Symphony in Eb (1905–7) and understands neoclassical to include neo-Baroque: the *Symphonies of Wind Instruments* (1920), the choral *Symphony of Psalms* (1930), and the Symphony in C (1939–40) and Symphony in Three Movements (1945). The same may be said for the symphonies of Hindemith, though the tonal system differs and the forms are generally more traditional. The Viennese serialists showed little interest in the symphony.

The Russian proclivity for the symphony, evident already in the 19th century, continued in the 20th in works by Scriabin (3 symphonies, 1900–1904), Nikolay Myaskovsky (27 symphonies, 1908–50, many on political themes), Prokofiev (7 symphonies, 1916–52), and Shostakovich (15 symphonies, 1924–71). The symphony in both Britain and the U.S. shows a history of early domination by the German academic-Romantic tradition followed by assertion of a more national approach. In Britain the former trend is exemplified by the symphonies of Charles Villiers Stanford (7, 1875–1911), the latter by the symphonies of Ralph Vaughan Williams (9, 1903–57). Other symphonists of the Vaughan Williams generation are Arnold Bax (7 symphonies, 1922–39) and Havergal Brian (32 symphonies, ca. 1907–68), while later composers include William Walton, Benjamin Britten, Michael Tippett, Peter Maxwell Davies, and Oliver Knussen.

The late 19th-century German Romantic school is represented in the U.S. by John Knowles Paine (2 symphonies, 1875–80) and George Chadwick (3 symphonies, 1882–94). Against this background the symphonies of Charles Ives (4, 1895–1916, plus a fifth, the *Universe Symphony*, left incomplete) seem startling, especially the Fourth, with its synthesis of transcendental program, collage technique, and an incongruously wide range of styles. The establishment of a distinctively American school of symphonists had to await a second generation: Aaron Copland (3 symphonies, 1925–46, plus *A Dance Symphony*, 1930), Roy Harris (11 completed symphonies with orchestra, 1933–75), and Walter Piston (8 symphonies, 1937–65). To this generation of symphonists may be added Howard Hanson (7 symphonies, 1922–77); Roger Sessions (8 symphonies, 1927–68); Wallingford Riegger (4 symphonies, 1935–57); and Henry Cowell (20 symphonies of 1938–65, plus one student work). More recent American composers

notable for their symphonies include Samuel Barber (2 symphonies, 1935–44), William Schuman (10 symphonies, 1935–76), Alan Hovhaness (46 symphonies, 1937–82), Paul Creston (5 symphonies, 1940–55), David Diamond (8 symphonies, 1940–60), Peter Mennin (8 symphonies, 1941–73), Vincent Persichetti (8 symphonies, 1942–70), Elliott Carter (2 symphonies, 1942–77), and George Rochberg (5 symphonies, 1949–85). Many contemporary composers, however, prefer to give descriptive or evocative titles to works that might earlier have been called symphonies.

Symphony of Psalms. A work for chorus and orchestra (without violins or violas) by Stravinsky, composed in 1930 (rev. 1948). Its three movements are based on Latin Psalms.

Symphony of a Thousand. Popular name for Mahler's Symphony no. 8 in Eb major, composed in 1906. The impresario Emil Guttmann, who organized the Munich premiere of the work, so named it in a publicity slogan because of the extremely large orchestral and choral forces required. The first part is a setting of the hymn "Veni, creator spiritus"; the second part a setting of the closing scene of Goethe's *Faust*.

Syncopation. A momentary contradiction of the prevailing *meter or pulse. This may take the form of a temporary transformation of the fundamental character of the meter, e.g., from duple to triple or from 3/4 to 3/2 [see Hemiola], or it may be simply the contradiction of the regular succession of strong and weak beats within a measure or a group of measures whose metrical context nevertheless remains clearly defined by some part of the musical texture that does not itself participate in the syncopation. The former type may have the effect of "shifting the bar line," e.g., of causing one of the weak beats to function as a strong beat. It is frequently encountered in the music of Beethoven, among many others. The latter type may entail attacks between beats rather than on them and is particularly common in ragtime, blues, and some styles of jazz. Elaborate examples are found in French secular music of the late 14th century [see *Ars subtilior*]. The accompanying example includes some common types of syncopation. Syncopation may be created by the types of note-values themselves or by accentuation, articulation, melodic contour, or harmonic change in the context of an otherwise unsyncopated succession of note-values.

Synthesizer. An instrument that produces sounds, modifies them, and in some circumstances orders them in time by purely electronic means. In principle, such an instrument can create, or synthesize, any sound whose characteristics can be precisely specified in acoustical terms. That is, it generates electronically and permits independent control of the frequency, waveform, intensity, and envelope that together make up a musical sound [see Acoustics]. It consists of a collection of modular components that can be connected in a great variety of ways, the electronic output of one component serving as the input of the next, until the signal reaches a loudspeaker and is turned into sound.

Machines for synthesizing sounds electronically were introduced as early as 1929. The first synthesizer of consequence was the RCA Music Synthesizer developed early in the 1950s and installed at the Columbia–Princeton Electronic Music Center in New York. But not until the introduction of the principle of voltage control by Robert Moog around 1964 did synthesizers become commercially viable. At first they were used primarily in the studio in conjunction with tape recorders to create recorded electronic compositions. Transistors soon made it possible to build small, flexible, and relatively inexpensive synthesizers suitable for live performance. Computer technology has led to automated control of many synthesizer functions and to direct digital synthesis of sound. See Electro-acoustic music.

Syrinx [Gr.]. The *panpipes of ancient Greece and Rome.

System. Two or more staves connected by means of braces or bar lines for the purpose of allowing notation of music not readily accommodated on a single staff [see also Score].

Szabó, Ferenc (b. Budapest, 27 Dec. 1902; d. there, 4 Nov. 1969). Composer. Studied with Kodály, Siklós, and Weiner. Joined the Communist party in 1927; moved to the U.S.S.R. in 1932 and was involved with the Union of Soviet Composers. Returned to Hungary and in 1945 joined the faculty at the Budapest Academy (head, 1958–67). Works include stage music; orchestral music (*Lyric Suite,* 1936; *Ludas Matyi,* 1950; vocal music (*Föltámadott a tenger* [In Fury Rose the Ocean], oratorio, 1955); chamber works.

Szalonek, Witold (b. Katowice, 2 Mar. 1927). Composer. Studied in Katowice and with Boulanger in Paris. Joined the faculty at the State College in Katowice (head 1972). In 1974 moved to West Berlin and taught at the Hochschule für Musik. His music uses various European avant-garde techniques; works include orchestral (*Mutazioni,* chamber orchestra, 1966), vocal (*Ziemio miła* [O Pleasant

Earth], cantata, voice, orchestra, 1969), and chamber music (*Inside? Outside?,* bass clarinet, string quartet, 1988).

Szamotuł [Szamotulczyk, Szamotulski], **Wacław z** (b. Szamotuły, near Poznań, ca. 1524; d. Pińczów?, near Kielce, 1560?). Composer and poet. Studied at the Collegium Lubranscianum at Poznań and at the Univ. of Kraków; in 1547 appointed composer at the court of King Sigismund II August. Involved in the Polish Protestant movement; active at the Calvinist court of the Lithuanian Duke Mikołaj Radziwiłł. Works (much now lost) include principally sacred polyphony with Latin and Polish texts.

Székely, Endre (b. Budapest, 6 Apr. 1912; d. there, 14 Apr. 1989). Composer. Studied at the Budapest Academy of Music with Sikorski. Joined the Communist party, which was illegal at that time; wrote and conducted workers' music and, after the war, was associated with the Hungarian Musicians' Union. Edited the Hungarian periodicals *Éneklő nép* and *Éneklő munkás.* After 1960 served on the faculty of the Budapest Training College for Teachers. Wrote stage, orchestral, and chamber music.

Szelényi, István (b. Zólyom, 8 Aug. 1904; d. Budapest, 31 Jan. 1972). Composer. Studied composition with Kodály and piano with Laub and Székely at the Budapest Academy of Music; by 1945 joined the faculty at the Budapest conservatory. From 1956 to 1976 taught theory at the Budapest Academy. Early works were controversial in their incorporation of avant-garde techniques; later works moved closer to traditional Hungarian symphonic style. Works include pantomimes, orchestral music (*Egy gyár szimfóniája* [Symphony of a Factory], 1946; *Hommage à Bartók,* 1947), vocal music, chamber and piano works.

Szeligowski, Tadeusz (b. Lwów, 13 Sept. 1896; d. Poznań, 10 Jan. 1963). Composer. Studied in Lwów and Kraków, and in Paris with Boulanger. Returned to Poland; after the war, worked with the Polish Composers' Union. Works include stage music (operas, ballets), orchestral music (*Suita lubelske,* small orchestra, 1945), vocal music (*Karta serc* [The Charter of the Hearts], cantata, soprano, choir, orchestra, 1952), chamber music.

Szell, George (b. Budapest, 7 June 1897; d. Cleveland, 29 July 1970). Conductor. Studied piano with Richard Robert (debut with the Vienna Symphony, 1908) and with Reger and Prohaska. Assistant to Strauss at the Berlin State Opera from 1915; later worked at Strasbourg (1917–18), Prague (1919–21), Darmstadt (1921–22), and Düsseldorf (1922–24), returning to Berlin to lead the State Opera and Radio Orchestra (1924–30). Directed the German Opera,

Prague, 1930–36. Settled in the U.S.; conducted radio concerts of the NBC Symphony (1941), the Metropolitan Opera (1942–46), and the Cleveland Orchestra (music director from 1946 to his death), molding the ensemble into one of the world's finest.

Szervánsky, Endre (b. Kistétény, 27 Dec. 1911; d. Budapest, 25 June 1977). Composer. Studied clarinet and composition at the Budapest Academy of Music. Worked for Hungarian Radio as an orchestrator; from 1942 to 1948 taught at the National Conservatory; thereafter on the composition faculty of the Budapest Academy. Compositions influenced by the music of Kodály and Bartók; by the late 1950s engaged serial techniques. Works include the Clarinet Serenade (1950), Flute Concerto (1952–53), Concerto for Orchestra (1954), *Six Orchestral Pieces* (1959), Requiem (1963), and Clarinet Concerto (1965).

Szeryng, Henryk (b. Zelazowa Wola, near Warsaw, 22 Sept. 1918; d. Kassel, Germany, 3 Mar. 1988). Violinist and diplomat. Studied with Flesch in Berlin; in 1933 he made debuts in Warsaw, Bucharest, Vienna, and Paris. Studied composition with Boulanger in Paris. During World War II played over 300 concerts for Allied troops; helped 4,000 Polish refugees resettle in Mexico. Took Mexican citizenship in 1946 and taught at Mexico City Univ. 1948–56. From 1954 resumed extensive concertizing and recording, winning renown as an interpreter of Bach and Mozart. Adviser to UNESCO from 1970.

Szigeti, Joseph (b. Budapest, 5 Sept. 1892; d. Lucerne, 19 Feb. 1973). Violinist. Studied at the Budapest Academy (debut at age 11); lived in London 1906–13; toured Europe in 1913 and 1914. Taught at Geneva until 1924; moved to Paris, 1925; with the onset of war left for the U.S., settling in California; in 1960 went back to Switzerland. Composers such as Bartók, Busoni, Prokofiev, and Bloch wrote works for him; he recorded extensively.

Szokolay, Sándor (b. Kúnágota, 30 Mar. 1931). Composer. Studied with Szabó and Farkas at the Bu-dapest Academy of Music. Worked for Hungarian Radio 1957–61; in 1966 became professor at the Budapest Academy. His operas and oratorios saw great success; works of the late 1960s incorporated serial techniques. Works include *Istár pokoljárása* [Isthar's Descent into Hell], oratorio (1960); *Vérnász* [Blood Wedding], opera (1962–64); *Hamlet,* opera (1965–68); *Az áldozat* [The Sacrifice], oratorio-ballet (1970–71); *Ecce homo,* Passion opera (1987).

Szymanowska [née **Wołowska**], **Maria Agata** (b. Warsaw, 14 Dec. 1789; d. St. Petersburg, 24 July 1831). Pianist and composer. Studied with Antonio Lisowski and Tomasz Gremm; debut in Warsaw, 1810. Concertized 1815–28; first pianist to the Russian court, 1822. Cherubini dedicated his Fantasia in C major to her. Compositions include a fanfare; waltzes, piano 3-hands; *Sérénade,* cello and piano (1820); mazurkas, exercises, nocturnes, and other solo piano music; songs.

Szymanowski, Karol (Maciej) (b. Tymoszówska, Ukraine, 6 Oct. 1882; d. Lausanne, 29 Mar. 1937). Composer. Studied in Warsaw with Zawirski and Noskowski. In 1905 helped found the Young Polish Composers' Publishing Company in Berlin. Traveled widely before the war. In 1917 his family's home was destroyed; settled temporarily in Elisavetgrad and began work on his opera *Król Roger* [King Roger] (first perf. 1926). By 1920 returned to Warsaw; became an ardent proponent of nationalism in the tradition of Chopin. In 1927 appointed director, Warsaw Conservatory of Music; in 1930 head, Warsaw Academy of Music (resigned 1932); died of tuberculosis, 1937.

Early piano works were in the tradition of German Romantic composers such as Chopin and Schumann; orchestral works reflected Wagner's influence. Later Szymanowski considered it crucial for new music to move from a Romantic idiom to a modern one. Compositions include dramatic works (*Harnasie,* pantomime-ballet, 1923–31); orchestral works (Symphony no. 4 [Symphony Concertante], piano, orchestra, 1932); chamber and vocal works.

T. Abbr. for *tenor, *tonic, *trill, toe (in pedal parts for organ), *tutti.

Ta'amim [Heb.]. See Ecphonetic notation.

Tabarro, II [It.]. See *Trittico.*

Tabatière de musique [Fr.]. Music box.

Ṭabl [Ar.]. (1) Drum. (2) A cylindrical drum with two heads, widely distributed in various sizes in the Islamic world. (3) In the Maghrib, a kettledrum, usually played in pairs [pl. *aṭbāl,* whence Sp. *atabal].

Tablā [Hind., fr. Ar.]. A pair of drums of North India. The conical right-hand drum (*tablā* or *dāhinā*) is made of wood and is tuned to a definite pitch. The kettle-shaped left-hand drum *(bāyā)* is made of metal or clay and is tuned to a lower but indefinite pitch. See ill. under Instrument.

Tablature [fr. Lat. *tabula,* table, score; Fr. *tablature;* Ger. *Tabulatur;* It. *intavolatura;* Sp. *tablatura, cifra*]. Musical notation using letters, numerals, or diagrams to specify pitch in terms of the playing technique of a given instrument (e.g., which strings to stop at which frets, which keys to depress, which finger holes to cover) rather than abstractly, as in conventional Western staff notation. Systems of tablature are as old as notated music itself and are widely distributed. They include the principal notations of East Asia and are familiar to a large audience in the form of the guitar and ukulele chord symbols published with Western popular music since the 1920s.

From the late 15th century through the 18th, music for lute was notated in several systems of tablature that were also applied to other plucked and bowed stringed instruments such as the *vihuela,* guitar, orpharion, theorbo, cittern, bandora, mandora, viola da gamba, lyra viol, baryton, and violin. All systems entail some method of specifying the string on which a pitch is to be played and the fret (if any) at which that string is to be stopped, assuming some particular tuning of the instrument. Tunings for individual instruments varied considerably.

Italian, French, and Neapolitan (or "Spanish") lute tablatures employ six horizontal lines (sometimes five in French tablature) to represent the courses of the instrument arranged from the highest-pitched down to the lowest, except in Italian tablature, where the order is reversed, the bottom line denoting the highest-pitched string. Ciphers (letters in French and numerals in the other tablatures) indicate open and stopped courses that are plucked individually: *0* (sometimes *1* in Neapolitan) or *a* = open course, *1* or *b* = first fret, *2* or *c* = second fret, *3* or *d* = third fret, etc. [see Ex. 1 and Ex. 2, the opening of a ricercar for lute by Francesco Canova da Milano that was printed during the 16th century in four types of lute tablature]. Since frets were placed chromatically (though some cittern tablatures have frets placed diatonically), the ciphers represent notes a semitone, tone, minor third, major third, etc., above an open course. Notes or note stems above the lines show durations separating successive attacks, sometimes recurring only when the note-value changes. The tablature thus gives only the beginning of each pitch, not how long it is to be sustained. Hence, the performer or transcriber must assign note-values to individual pitches. This may entail reconstructing a polyphonic texture consisting of several individual lines. Dots under some individual ciphers tell the player to pluck the string upward with the index finger.

1. Note-values.

During the 16th century, Italian tablature was also used in Spain, southern France, and Bavaria; Neapolitan in southern Italy; and French in England and the Low Countries. After ca. 1600, French tablature gained international ascendancy except in Italy and Spain.

German lute tablature was devised for the five-course lute of the 15th century and notates the open strings with numbers, 1–5 starting with the lowest, and the frets with letters in like succession. Hundreds of 17th- and 18th-century guitar books assign letters and other symbols to represent specific *rasgado

2. Four types of lute tablature with transcription.

chords, strummed upward or downward as indicated in a variety of ways. In Spanish, such a notation is termed an *alfabeto*. Some tablatures combine *alfabeto* with French or Italian lute tablature.

From the 14th through the 18th century, much keyboard music was notated in systems employing numerals, letters of the alphabet, and combinations of letters and the staff. In letter tablature, keys of the organ or harpsichord are designated by the conventional a to g with some modifications. In other systems, the keys are numbered. In tablatures using numbers and letters, rhythmic values are indicated with diamond-shaped notes, or more frequently with the flagged note stems used in lute tablature.

Two systems of German keyboard tablature are generally recognized. One, called Old German, was in use in many parts of Europe from the 14th century until replaced in the late 16th century by the New

German system, which remained common, particularly in northern lands, until well into the 18th century. Old German tablature notates the upper part(s) on a staff and the lower with letters. New German tablature uses only letters.

Spanish keyboard tablatures are of three types. In two, numerals are placed on two to six horizontal lines, each of which represents one part in the polyphonic complex. The third type distributes the numerals above and below a line that divides notes for the right hand from those for the left. Italian, French, and English keyboard tablatures are not true tablatures, since they employ notation either on two staves with from five to eight lines each or on a single staff with as many as 13 lines. A preferable modern term for these is keyboard score, though this may be confused with keyboard *partitura,* a format in which each part is given a separate staff.

Table. (1) The belly or upper plate of the sound box of stringed instruments such as the violin and guitar. (2) [Fr.] The *soundboard of the harp [see also *Près*].

Tabor, taborel, tabour, tabourin, tabret [Eng., Fr.]. A small, shallow drum of Europe, often with a snare. See Pipe and tabor, Tambourin, Tambourine.

Tabulatur [Ger.]. *Tablature.

Tace [It.], **tacet** [Lat.]. Be (is) silent. The terms are used in parts and scores for ensemble music to indicate extended passages or movements in which a part remains silent.

Tactus [Lat.]. In the 15th and 16th centuries, beat. This was marked by a falling and rising motion of the hand, and in the 16th century, one *tactus* was equal to the value of a normal semibreve (or the corresponding value in cases of augmentation and diminution; see Mensural notation, Proportion).

Tafelmusik [Ger., table music; Fr. *musique de table*]. Music to be performed at a banquet or at dinner.

Tagelied [Ger.]. A song of the *Minnesinger related to the *alba*.

Taille [Fr.]. From the 16th century through the 18th, tenor, with respect to both voices and families of instruments (e.g., *taille des hautbois, taille de violon,* etc.).

Tailleferre, Germaine (b. Parc-Saint-Maur, France, 19 Apr. 1892; d. Paris, 7 Nov. 1983). Composer. Studied at the Paris Conservatory; with her classmates Milhaud, Honegger, and Auric, became a member of "Les *six." Remained active as a composer, performer, and public figure through the 1970s. Works include operas (*Il était un petite navire,* 1951), ballet and theater music, orchestral works, a piano concerto and solo piano works, songs and other vocal works, chamber music, and music for film, radio, and television.

Tailpiece [Fr. *cordier;* Ger. *Saitenhalter;* It. *cordiera;* Sp. *cordal*]. On the *violin and related instruments, a piece of wood (often ebony) to which the strings are attached below the bridge.

Tāl(a)(am) [Hin., Skt., Tel.]. In Indian music, meter, an abstract pattern of beats serving as a time frame for musical composition and improvisation.

Takahashi, Yuji (b. Tokyo, 21 Sept. 1938). Composer. Studied at the Toho School, at Tanglewood, and with Xenakis. Compositions influenced by Xenakis and stochastic techniques. Also toured as a virtuosic pianist of new music. Works include *Kaga-i* (piano, chamber orchestra, 1971), *Three Poems of Mao Tse-Tung* (piano, 1979), *Ye-guen,* (18-track tape, laser beams, 1970).

Takemitsu, Tōru (b. Tokyo, 8 Oct. 1930; d. there, 20 Feb. 1996). Composer. Largely self-taught, experimented with Euro-American avant-garde trends including serialism, aleatory, extended instrumental techniques, mixed-media performances, graphic notation, and electronic and tape music. In the early 1960s began to work with Cage; also incorporated traditional Japanese instruments into his compositions. Works include *November Steps* (biwa, shakuhachi, orchestra, 1967, commissioned by the New York Philharmonic), *From Me Flows What You Call Time* (percussion quintet, orchestra, 1990), *Fantasma/Cantos* (clarinet, orchestra, 1991), concertos, works for small and large ensembles; also happenings, film music, television scores.

Takt [Ger.]. (1) Beat; *Taktmesser,* metronome. (2) Measure; *Taktstrich,* bar line. (3) Meter (also *Taktart*); *im Takt, taktmässig,* in strict meter or tempo; *Taktvorzeichnung, Taktzeichen,* time signature.

Tal [Gruenthal], **Josef** [Joseph] (b. Pinne, near Poznań, 18 Sept. 1910). Composer. Studied with Tiessen and Trapp in Berlin; emigrated to Palestine, 1934. After 1950 taught at Hebrew Univ.; founded Center for Electronic Music, 1961. Compositions draw on avant-garde trends such as serialism and electronic media and Jewish tradition. Works include operas (*Massada 967,* 1972), orchestral music, vocal music, chamber music, music for tape (*Min hameitzar* [From the Depths], ballet, tape, 1971), dramatic scene (*Die Hand,* soprano, cello, 1987).

Talea [Lat.]. See Isorhythm.

Tales of Hoffmann, The. See *Contes d'Hoffmann, Les.*

Talharpa [Swed.]. A bowed *lyre of Sweden with three or four gut or metal (formerly horsehair) strings, related to the *crwth.

Tallis [Tallys, Talles], **Thomas** (b. ca. 1505; d. Greenwich, 23 Nov. 1585). Composer. Organist at Canterbury Cathedral (1541–42). By 1543 Gentleman of the Chapel Royal (organist and composer for the royal chapels); served during the reigns of Henry VIII, Edward VI, Mary I, and Elizabeth I. In 1575 Queen Elizabeth granted Tallis and Byrd one of the first letters patent to print and publish music. Works include antiphons, more than 20 English anthems (Tallis was one of the first to set texts of the new Anglican liturgy), more than 50 motets. The 40-voice motet *Spem in alium* was perhaps written for the 40th birthday celebration for Elizabeth in 1573. Other works include consort and keyboard music.

Tallone [It.]. *Frog.

Talma, Louise (Juliette) (b. Arcachon, 31 Oct. 1906; d. near Saratoga Springs, N.Y., 13 Aug. 1996). Composer. Studied at the Institute of Musical Art in New York and with Nadia Boulanger. Teacher at Hunter College in New York from 1928. Compositions from 1950s on used serial techniques. *The Alcestiad* (1962), opera with libretto by Thornton Wilder, was a critical success. Other works include *The Tolling Bell* (baritone, orchestra, 1969); *Summer Sounds* (clarinet, string quartet, 1973); *Diadem* (tenor and chamber orchestra, 1979).

Talon [Fr.]. *Frog.

Talvela, Martti (Olavi) (b. Hiitola, Finland, 4 Feb. 1935; d. Juva, Finland, 22 July 1989). Bass. Made his debut at the Stockholm Royal Opera House, 1961; performed at Bayreuth, the Deutsche Oper in Berlin, the Metropolitan, and at Covent Garden . Best known for his Wagnerian bass roles and for his Boris.

Tambor [Sp.]. Drum.

Tambour [Fr.]. Drum, drummer; *t. de Basque,* *tambourine; *t. militaire,* snare drum.

Tambourin [Fr.]. (1) A long, two-headed drum of Provence (sometimes called a *tambourin provençal*) played with the *galoubet as a *pipe and tabor. (2) *Tambourine. (3) An 18th-century French dance found in the theatrical works of Rameau and others, perhaps based on a Provençal folk dance, and often employing a texture imitating the *galoubet* and *tambourin* [see (1) above].

Tambourine [Fr. *tambour de basque;* Ger. *Schellentrommel, Tamburin;* It. *tamburello, tamburino;* Sp. *pandereta*]. A shallow, single-headed frame drum with a wooden frame in which metal disks or jingles are set; also sometimes timbrel. It is most often held in one hand and struck with the other; sometimes the head is rubbed along the perimeter with the thumb, producing a continuous sound from both head and jingles. See also *Tambourin;* see ill. under Percussion instruments.

Tamburā, tānpura [Hin.]. A *long-necked lute of India used exclusively as a drone. It has a hollow neck, a pear-shaped body, and four metal strings. See also *Tanbur;* see ill. under Instrument.

Tamburello [It.]. *Tambourine.

Tamburin [Ger.]. *Tambourine.

Tamburino [It.]. Tenor *drum; *tambourine.

Tamburo [It.]. Drum; *t. grande, grosso,* bass drum; *t. rullante,* tenor drum; *t. militare,* snare drum.

Tampon. A drumstick with a soft head on each end, used with the bass drum and permitting the execution of a roll by means of rapid, rotary oscillations of the hand.

Tam-tam. A percussion instrument of indefinite pitch consisting of a broad circular disk of metal, slightly convex, with the rim turned down, giving the appearance of a shallow plate with low vertical sides. It is hung vertically and struck in the center with a soft-headed beater. See also Gong; see ill. under Percussion instruments.

Tanbur [Turk.; Per. *ṭanbūr;* also *danbura, tambur, tambura, tamburica, ṭunbūr*]. A *long-necked lute distributed from the Balkans through the Middle East to Central Asia. A typical member of this family has a small pear-shaped body, a long fretted neck, and two or three metal strings.

Taneyev, Sergei (Ivanovich) (b. Vladimir district, 25 Nov. 1856; d. Dyudkovo, 19 June 1915). Composer, pianist, educator. Studied with Tchaikovsky and Nikolai Rubinstein. A lifelong friend of Tchaikovsky's, he premiered all of the latter's works for piano and orchestra. Teacher at the Moscow Conservatory 1878–1906; director 1885–89; students included Scriabin, Rachmaninoff, Lyapunov, and Glier. Compositions include opera, *Oresteya* [The Oresteia] (1887–94); symphonies; choral music; chamber music; songs; keyboard music. Published *Podvizhnoy kontrapunkt strogovo pis'ma* [Invertible Counterpoint in the Strict Style] (1909); trans. Eng. (1962).

Tangent. In a *clavichord, the metal blade attached to each key that both strikes the string and determines its vibrating length when the key is depressed.

Tango [Sp.]. An Argentine genre of urban song and dance that has remained popular throughout the 20th century. It is generally regarded as originating in the poor neighborhoods of Buenos Aires in the late 19th century, with important antecedents in the traditional Argentine *milonga* and in Cuban dances such as the *habanera, then in vogue. The dance, for couples in tight embrace, is characterized by almost violent movement. The often lengthy texts of the sung *tango* are emotional, sentimental, and sometimes intensely negative in tone, and the music of the *tango,* frequently in minor mode, is one of abrupt rhythmic and dynamic contrasts. In a typical *tango* accompaniment, a prevailing pattern in which all beats are sharply accented will be occasionally interrupted by sudden pauses and by emphatically syncopated passages [see Ex.]. Traditional performance media include solo voice with guitar accompaniment; trios with violin, flute, and guitar or *bandoneon (accordion); and ensembles of various sizes with *bandoneones,* strings, and piano.

Tannhäuser und der Sängerkrieg auf Wartburg [Ger., Tannhäuser and the Song Contest at the Wartburg]. Opera in three acts by Wagner (to his own libretto, based on a conflation of several medieval legends). First produced in Dresden in 1845, it was revised for a production in Paris in 1861. Setting: Venusberg and the Wartburg (near Eisenach) in the early 13th century.

Tannhäuser, Der (b. ca. 1205; d. ca. 1270). Minnesinger poet-composer. Of noble birth, probably Bavarian; "Der Tannhäuser" perhaps an assumed name. His extant works, 6 *Leiche* and 10 lieder (melodies lost), attest to a life of travel and adventure. From the 1400s he became identified with the legendary knight Tannhäuser.

Tansman, Alexandre (b. Łódź, 12 June 1897; d. Paris, 15 Nov. 1986). Composer. Studied in Warsaw; in 1919 settled in Paris; lived in the U.S. 1941–46. Works include operas; symphonies; concertos; string quartets; piano sonatas; film scores.

Tans'ur [Tansur, le Tansur, Tanzer], **William** (b. Dunchurch, Warwickshire, 1700; d. St. Neots, Huntshire, 7 Oct. 1783). Composer and psalmodist. *The Royal Melody Compleat* (1754–55) became *The American Harmony* (Newburyport, 1771). Besides 100 Psalm and hymn tunes, Tans'ur's output includes anthems and other sacred works.

Tanto [It.]. So much; *non tanto,* not so (too) much, e.g., *allegro non tanto.*

Tanz [Ger.]. Dance.

Tape music. See Electro-acoustic music.

Tapiola. A symphonic poem by Sibelius, op. 112 (1926), named for Tapio, the forest god of Finnish legend [see *Kalevala*].

Taqsīm [Ar., division; Turk. *taksim*]. A major improvised instrumental form in Arabic and Turkish music, usually nonmetric, one to ten minutes in length and often used to open a performance.

Tarantella [It.]. A folk dance of southern Italy that takes its name from the town of Taranto (not, as is often said, from the tarantula or from a dance to cure its bite). It is in a rapid, accelerating 6/8 with shifts between major and minor. The tarantella was taken up by various composers of the 19th century (Chopin, Liszt, Heller, Weber), often as a piece with continuous eighth notes (or eighth-note triplets in simple meters) and of some technical difficulty.

Tarchi, Angelo [Angiolo] (b. Naples, ca. 1760; d. Paris, 19 Aug. 1814). Composer. Wrote approximately 50 Italian operas and several opéras comiques. He apparently partially rewrote the third and fourth acts of Mozart's *Le nozze di Figaro* for a Milan performance in 1787.

Tardo, tardamente [It.]. Slow, slowly; *tardando,* slowing.

Tárogató [Hung.]. (1) A Hungarian woodwind instrument similar to the soprano saxophone, with a single reed and a conical bore, but made of wood. (2) A double-reed instrument, similar to the *zūrnā,* in use in Hungary from the 13th century through the 18th. The modern *tárogató* was inspired by this instrument.

Tarp, Svend Erik (b. Thisted, 6 Aug. 1908). Composer. Studied in Denmark, Germany, Holland, and Austria; taught at the Copenhagen Conservatory, the Statens Larerhøjskole, and the Univ. of Copenhagen. Compositions include stage works, vocal music, orchestral music, and some 40 film scores.

Tarr, Edward H(ankins) (b. Norwich, Conn., 15 June 1936). Trumpeter and musicologist. Pupil of Voisin and Herseth. In 1967 founded the Edward Tarr Brass Ensemble to perform Renaissance and Baroque music on period instruments. Taught at the Schola cantorum basiliensis (from 1972) and the Basel Musikakademie (from 1974). Edited trumpet music, including the complete trumpet works of Torelli; wrote *Die Trompete* (Basel, 1977).

Tárrega (y Eixea), Francisco (b. Villarreal, Castellón, 21 Nov. 1852; d. Barcelona, 15 Dec. 1909). Guitarist and composer. Laid the foundations of the dominant modern technique for the classical guitar. Composed works for guitar; transcribed music of Gottschalk, Mendelssohn, Chopin, Beethoven, Albéniz, and Granados.

Tartini, Giuseppe (b. Pirano, Istria, 8 Apr. 1692; d. Padua, 26 Feb. 1770). Composer, violinist, and theorist. Studied law in Padua and music in exile in Assisi. "Primo violino e capo di concerto" at St. Antonio in Padua 1721–1765. Taught violin until at least 1767; pupils included J. G. Graun, Nardini, J. G. Naumann, Paganelli, and Pagin. Materials from his treatise on violin playing, *Traité des agréments,* used by Leopold Mozart in his *Violinschule* (1756). Published his acoustical findings in the *Trattato di musica* (Padua, 1754; trans. Eng., 1985). Compositions include about 125 violin concertos; concertos for other instruments; numerous trio sonatas; and about 175 violin sonatas, including the "Trillo del Diavolo" [Devil's Trill].

Tartini's tone. See Combination tone.

Taschengeige [Ger.]. *Kit.

Tasnif [Per.]. The most important genre of composed, metric vocal music in 20th-century Iran, with lyrical, satirical, and sometimes political texts. In popular music, the term refers to songs in general.

Tasso. A symphonic poem by Liszt, after a poem by Byron, first performed in 1849 (orchestrated by August Conradi) as an overture to Goethe's drama *Torquato Tasso*. It was revised in 1850–51 (reorchestrated by Joachim Raff) and 1854.

Taste [Ger.]. A key of a keyboard; *Tasteninstrument,* keyboard instrument; *Tastenmusik,* keyboard music; *Obertaste,* upper or accidental key; *Untertaste,* lower or natural key.

Tastiera [It.]. (1) Keyboard; *t. per luce,* *color organ. (2) Fingerboard; *sulla t.,* an instruction to bow over the fingerboard [see Bowing (12)].

Tasto [It.]. (1) A key of a keyboard; *t. solo,* in *thoroughbass parts, an instruction to play the bass note only, without chords. (2) Fingerboard; *sul t.,* an instruction to bow over the fingerboard [see Bowing (12)].

Tattoo. A call sounded on bugles, drums, or fifes to summon soldiers to their quarters at night.

Tatum, Art (Arthur, Jr.) (b. Toledo, Ohio, 13 Oct. 1909; d. Los Angeles, 5 Nov. 1956). Jazz pianist. Despite near-blindness and limited formal training developed a technical command of the instrument. Preferred to work unaccompanied, but in the 1950s made albums with Benny Carter, Lionel Hampton, and Ben Webster.

Taubert, (Carl Gottfried) Wilhelm (b. Berlin, 23 Mar. 1811; d. there, 7 Jan. 1891). Pianist, composer, and conductor. Music director, Berlin Royal Opera, 1845–48; court conductor at Berlin, 1845–69; taught at Royal Academy of the Arts from 1865. Composed 6 operas, 4 symphonies, overtures, concertos, chamber works, piano pieces, and over 300 songs (incl. *Kinderlieder*).

Tauriello, Antonio (b. Buenos Aires, 20 Mar. 1931). Composer. Studied piano with Spivak and Gieseking and composition with Ginastera. Assistant director of the Chicago Lyric Opera; led performances for the New York City Opera, the Washington Opera Society, and the American Opera Center. Works include orchestral pieces; opera (*Escorial,* 1966); concertos; chamber works (*Impromptus,* 1980).

Tausig, Carl [Karol] (b. Warsaw, 4 Nov. 1841; d. Leipzig, 17 July 1871). Pianist and composer. Pupil of Liszt; taught piano in Berlin. Compositions include piano exercises *(Tägliche Studien)* and transcriptions.

Tavárez, Manuel Gregorio (b. San Juan, 28 Nov. 1843; d. Ponce, 1 July 1883). Composer. Studied in San Juan and with D'Albert in Paris. Published 2 collections of Puerto Rican music, *Album filharmónico* (1863) and *El delirio puertorriqueño* (1867–69); wrote primarily short character and salon pieces, including waltzes and marches.

Tavener, John (Kenneth) (b. London, 28 Jan. 1944). Composer. Studied with Berkeley and Lumsdaire. His biblical cantata *The Whale* (1965–66) was recorded in 1970 by Apple Records. Early music influenced by Stravinsky; later works combined his interest in religious subjects and symbolism. *The Protecting Veil* (solo cello, strings, 1989), a paean to the Virgin Mary, vaulted the composer to wide prominence. Works include *Cain and Abel* (cantata, 1965); *In memoriam Igor Stravinsky* (1971); *Thérèse* (opera, 1973–76); *Funeral Ikos* (chorus, 1981); *Towards the Son: Ritual Procession* (orchestra, 1983); *Ikon of Light* (double choir, string trio, 1984); *Akathist of Thanksgiving: Glory Be to God for Everything* (soli, chorus, orchestra, 1988); *St. Mary of Egypt* (opera, 1991).

Taverner, John (b. near Boston, Lincolnshire, ca. 1490; d. there, 18 Oct. 1545). Composer. First instructor of choristers at Cardinal Wolsey's new Cardinal College (later Christ Church), Oxford; by 1537 had apparently retired from music. Taverner's works represent the culmination of English late medieval polyphony before the Reformation. They include 8 Masses, 9 Mass segments, Magnificats, a Te Deum, motets, and songs. The highly melismatic *In nomine* segment of the Mass *Gloria tibi Trinitas* spawned the English *In nomine* consort genre.

Tavola [It.]. The table or belly of a stringed instrument; *t. armonica,* soundboard; *presso la t., sulla t.,* an instruction in harp music to pluck near the soundboard.

Taylor, Billy [William] (b. Greenville, N.C., 24 July 1921). Jazz pianist, broadcaster, educator, and author. Studied music at Virginia State College and the Univ. of Massachusetts. Worked in New York with Ben Webster and Stuff Smith, and in 1951 was the house pianist at Birdland. Directed the National Public Radio show *Jazz Alive* (ca. 1977–80) and contributed to CBS Television's *Sunday Morning.* Artistic adviser to the John F. Kennedy Center for the Performing Arts in Washington, D.C., 1994. Wrote *Jazz Piano: History and Development* (Dubuque, Iowa, 1982).

Taylor, Cecil (Percival) (b. New York, 15 Mar. 1933). Jazz pianist, composer, and bandleader. Played at the Five Spot club in New York (1956) and the Newport Jazz Festival (1957), and with Jimmy Lyons, Sunny Murray, and Albert Ayler. From the mid-1970s he toured as a soloist and leader, especially in Europe.

Albums include *Unit Structures* (1966), *Silent Tongues* (1974), and *Three Phasis* (1978).

Taylor, (Joseph) Deems (b. New York, 22 Dec. 1885; d. there, 3 July 1966). Composer and critic. Mostly self-taught as a musician. Radio commentator for the Metropolitan Opera and New York Philharmonic (1931–43); president of ASCAP (1942–48). Compositions include *Through the Looking Glass* (chamber orchestra, 1919; full orchestra, 1922) and the operas *The King's Henchman* (1927) and *Peter Ibbetson* (1931).

Taylor, Raynor (b. London, ca. 1747; d. Philadelphia, 17 Aug. 1825). Composer and organist. Named music director and composer at Sadler's Wells Theatre in 1765. Emigrated to the U.S. in 1792; appointed organist at St. Peter's Church in Philadelphia in 1793. Helped found the Musical Fund Society there in 1820. Compositions include an opera, *The Ethiop* (1814), vocal works (*Monody of the Death of Washington*, 1799), incidental music, songs, anthems, glees, and keyboard pieces.

Tchaikovsky, Piotr Ilyich (b. Votkinsk, Viatka Province, Western Central Urals, 7 May 1840; d. St. Petersburg, 6 Nov. 1893). Composer. Trained at an elite school and entered the civil service; began study with Anton Rubinstein at the St. Petersburg Conservatory in 1862, and resigned his post in 1863 to become a full-time music student. Taught harmony at Moscow Conservatory beginning 1866; served as music critic for a Moscow paper 1872–76. Beginning in 1876 was supported by commissions and then an annuity from Nadezhda von Meck, with whom he had a close epistolary relationship although they never met. Following an ill-advised marriage in 1877, attempted suicide by wading into the Moscow River. After resigning from his conservatory post in 1878 spent much time away from Moscow or abroad, notably in Paris and Florence. Toured as a conductor domestically and abroad from 1887. Mme. von Meck ended their relationship in 1890. Contracted cholera and died in 1893.

Compositions include operas (*Oprichnik*, 1870–72; *Evgeniy Onegin* [*Eugene Onegin], 1877–78; *Orleanskaya deva* [The Maid of Orleans], 1878–79; *Mazepa*, 1881–83; *Pikovaya dama* [The *Queen of Spades], 1890); 6 symphonies; concertos for piano and violin; ballets (*Lebedinoe ozero* [*Swan Lake], 1876; *Spiashchaya krasavitsa* [The *Sleeping Beauty], 1888–89; *Shchelkunchik* [The *Nutcracker], 1891–92); other orchestral works (*Romeo and Juliet*, 1869; *Serenade for Strings*, 1880; *1812 Overture*, 1880; *Manfred*, 1882); chamber music (*Souvenir de Florence*, string sextet, 1890); songs; and liturgical choral music.

Translated Schumann's *Musikalische Haus- und Lebensregeln* and J. C. Lobe's *Katechismus der Musik* and wrote 2 pedagogical volumes on harmony.

Tcherepnin, Alexander (b. St. Petersburg, 20 Jan. 1899; d. Paris, 29 Sept. 1977). Composer and pianist. Studied in Petersburg and Paris; debuted as a pianist in London in 1922. From 1926 through 1933 toured as a pianist in Europe, the U.S., and the Middle East. Taught at the Shanghai Conservatory 1934–37. Settled in Paris 1937; moved to the U.S. to teach at De Paul Univ. in Chicago (1949–64). Compositions include operas (*The Farmer and the Fairy*, 1952; *The Lost Flute*, 1954); 4 symphonies, piano concertos, a Harmonica Concerto (1953), and works for solo piano.

Tcherepnin, Ivan (b. Issy-les-Moulineaux, nr. Paris, 5 Feb. 1943; d. Boston, 11 Apr. 1998). Composer. Studied with his father, Alexander Tcherepnin, and with Stockhausen and Pousseur. Taught at the San Francisco Conservatory of Music, 1969–72, and at Harvard from 1972. Most of his works involve electronic instruments, electronic processing, or both (*Watergate Suite*, electronic tape, 1973; *Santur Opera*, santur and synthesizer, 1977; *New Rhythmantics IV*, string quartet, trumpet, electronics, 1987; *Concerto for 2 Continents*, synthesizer, wind orchestra, 1989).

Tcherepnin, Nicholas (b. St. Petersburg, 14 May 1873; d. Issy-les-Moulineaux, nr. Paris, 26 June 1945). Composer and conductor. Studied with Rimsky-Korsakov; taught at the Petersburg Conservatory 1905–17. Toured Europe with Diaghilev and the Ballets russes; ballets include *Pavillon d'Armide* (1907) and *Narcisse et Echo*. Director of the National Conservatory at Tiflis (1918–21), then the Russian Conservatory in Paris (1925–29, 1938–45). Works include operas *Swat* (1930) and *Vanka* (1935), songs, and much Russian Orthodox liturgical music.

Tcherepnin, Serge (b. Paris, 2 Feb. 1941). Composer. Studied with his father, Alexander Tcherepnin, and with Stockhausen, Eimert, and Nono. Taught electronic music at New York Univ. (1968–70) and California Institute of the Arts (1970–75). Designed the "Serge," a modular synthesizer. Most of his compositions involve electronics.

Teagarden, Jack [Weldon Leo] (b. Vernon, Tex., 29 Aug. 1905; d. New Orleans, 15 Jan. 1964). Jazz trombonist, singer, and bandleader. Played with Ben Pollack and Paul Whiteman and recorded with Eddie Condon, Louis Armstrong, Benny Goodman, Red Nichols, and Bud Freeman. Led a swing big band (1938–46); joined Armstrong's All Stars (1947–51), including the recording *St. James Infirmary*, 1947). Co-led a band with Earl Hines (1957); recorded the album *Coast Concert* with Bobby Hackett (1955).

Teagarden's siblings were also jazz musicians: pianist Norma (b. 1915), trumpeter Charlie (1913–84), and drummer Cub (1915–69).

Tebaldi, Renata (b. Pesaro, 1 Feb. 1922). Soprano. Studied with Carmen Melis in Parma and made her debut in 1944. Appeared as Desdemona in Covent Garden (1950) and Metropolitan Opera (1955) debuts. Considered one of the leading sopranos of her generation, she performed under Toscanini at La Scala from its reopening in 1946, for 17 seasons at the Metropolitan (roles included Tosca, Mimì, Gioconda, Manon Lescaut, Violetta), and at most of the leading houses before her retirement in 1976.

Tecla [Sp.]. Key, keyboard, keyboard instrument.

Tedesca [It.]. (1) In the 17th century, *allemande. (2) Around 1800, *Deutscher Tanz. (3) In the German style (alla tedesca).

Te Deum [Lat.]. A song of praise to God ("Te Deum laudamus," We praise thee, O God) sung in the Roman rite at the end of Matins on Sundays and feast days, in the Middle Ages following the last responsory, in modern practice replacing it. As a "Hymn of Thanksgiving" (as it is termed in modern liturgical books), it has also long been sung at both religious and secular ceremonies such as coronations and celebrations of victory in battle. In the Anglican rite, it is a canticle at Morning Prayer. Although attributed in the Middle Ages to St. Ambrose (whence sometimes termed Ambrosian Hymn), its authorship remains in doubt. There are polyphonic settings from the late Middle Ages and Renaissance, and the 17th century saw the beginning of a tradition of elaborate choral and orchestral settings. Luther's German translation, "Herr Gott dich loben wir," led to settings by Michael Praetorius and organ works by Scheidt, Buxtehude, and Bach (BWV 725). English settings include those by Purcell, Handel (for the Peace of Utrecht, 1713; for the victory at Dettingen, 1743), Sullivan, Parry, Stanford, and Walton (for the coronation of Elizabeth II in 1953).

Teitelbaum, Richard (Lowe) (b. New York, 19 May 1939). Composer. Studied at Yale Univ. and with Luigi Nono and Goffredo Petrassi. Founded Musica elettronica viva in Rome. Further studies at Wesleyan Univ. from 1970 and in Japan 1976–77. After 1980 worked mainly with computers and synthesizers. Works include In Tune (amplified brain waves, heartbeats, breathing, and synthesizer, 1967); Threshold Music (instruments and environmental sounds, 1974); Blends (shakuhachi and synthesizers, 1977); Reverse Polish Notation (keyboards and computers, 1983).

Te Kanawa, Kiri (b. Gisborne, Auckland, 6 Mar. 1944). Soprano. Studied in New Zealand and with Vera Rozsa in London. Joined Royal Opera Company and made her Covent Garden debut in 1970; Metropolitan Opera debut in 1974. Roles included the Countess in The Marriage of Figaro, Donna Elvira, Fiordiligi, Desdemona, and Mimì. Has toured widely and made many recordings. In 1982 made a Dame Commander of the British Empire.

Telemann, Georg Philipp (b. Magdeburg, 14 Mar. 1681; d. Hamburg, 25 June 1767). Composer. In 1701 appointed music director of the Leipzig Opera; in 1704 organist at the Neue Kirche; in 1705 Kapellmeister to the court of Count Erdmann II of Promnitz at Sorau. In 1708 or 1709 moved to Eisenach, where he probably met J. S. Bach; he was godfather to C. P. E. Bach in 1714. In 1712 appointed city director of music at Frankfurt am Main and Kapellmeister at the Barfüsserkirche; 1717 Kapellmeister at Gotha; 1721 Kantor of the Johanneum in Hamburg and music director of the city's five main churches; 1722–38 music director of the Hamburg Opera. Published many of his own works, including sacred cantatas and the three-part Musique de table. Turned in his later years to the oratorio.

Works: Sacred vocal music includes about 50 Passions (mostly lost); oratorios; Masses; about 1,400 cantatas; motets; Psalms; occasional music. Secular vocal works include operas; intermezzos; about 50 cantatas; serenades; occasional music; about 100 songs. Instrumental compositions include over 100 French overtures; 47 solo concertos (21 for violin); 40 concertos for 2 or more instruments; 8 concerti grossi; over 200 solo and trio sonatas; quartets and quintets; keyboard works; lute music.

Telephone, The. Comic opera in one act by Gian Carlo Menotti (to his own libretto), written to precede performances of The *Medium and produced in New York in 1947. Setting: a city apartment in the present.

Tellefsen, Thomas (Dyke Acland) (b. Trondheim, Norway, 26 Nov. 1823; d. Paris, 6 Oct. 1874). Pianist and composer. Pupil of Kalkbrenner and Chopin; became top interpreter of Chopin's music. Compositions include 2 piano concertos, 2 violin sonatas, mazurkas, Norwegian dances, and other works.

Telyn [Welsh]. A gut-strung *frame harp of Wales. Known as early as the 11th century, it was displaced in the 18th century by the triple harp. See also Harp.

Tema [It.]. Theme, subject.

Temperament [Fr. tempérament; Ger. Temperatur; It. temperamento, sistema participato; Sp. temperamento]. (1) The slight modification of an acoustically pure or just interval [see Just intonation, Interval]. (2) Any scale or system of tuning employing intervals that have been so modified. Tempered intervals sometimes deviate from just intervals by more than 3 percent. For more than two millennia, most theorists have taken the desirability of acoustical purity to be self-evident. Temperaments have thus been practical compromises made necessary by the fact that the desire for acoustical purity and for musical transposition or modulation are not compatible in any closed system, be it a tuning theory or an instrument that lacks a convenient means of varying intervallic size with changing melodic or harmonic contexts.

The chromatic scale can be expressed as a linear series of 12 fifths bounded by the pitch class A♭ and its enharmonic equivalent, G♯: A♭–E♭–B♭–F–C–G–D–A–E–B–F♯–C♯–G♯. If these fifths are kept acoustically pure (as happens in the Pythagorean tuning), then enharmonic pitch classes such as A♭ and G♯ will differ by an amount known as the Pythagorean or ditonic comma, equivalent to 23.5 *cents. The remedy for this is temperament, which dilutes the acoustic discrepancy by distributing it among several intervals. The distribution may be in 12 or fewer parts and may be equal or unequal.

In the 20th century, a temperament with 12-part equal distribution has predominated. In this, each of the Pythagorean scale's fifths (3:2, worth 702 cents) is diminished by about 2 cents so as to eliminate over the sum of 12 fifths the accumulation of the nearly 24 cents of the Pythagorean comma. If the 12 pitch classes are arranged in a chromatic scale within a single octave, the result is a succession of 12 semitones of equal size. Since the frequency of the higher of two pitches an octave apart must be two times the frequency of the lower pitch, the frequency of the higher of two pitches separated by such a semitone must be $\sqrt[12]{2}$ or about 1.05946 times the frequency of the lower one.

The first evidences of temperament come from northern Italy. In 1496, Franchinus Gaffurius testified that organists were subjecting fifths to a small diminution known as *participata*. Pietro Aaron used this same term in 1523 in describing *mean-tone temperament. The earliest source for a temperament that attempts to distribute the comma equally is Giovanni Lanfranco's *Scintille di musica* (Brescia, 1533). Equal temperament did not become the norm for another 300 years.

The tuning and construction of fretted instruments gave a strong practical impetus to the creation of equal temperament. Because the frets of such instruments intersect all strings and must produce, for example, an A at the seventh fret of a string tuned to D that is in tune with the A produced at the second fret of a string tuned to g′ (and, of course, many other such combinations), the frets must be positioned so as to produce semitones as nearly equal as possible, and the open strings must be tuned to reflect the size of the semitones.

Another class of temperaments begins with just intonation instead of the Pythagorean scale and equally distributes the syntonic comma. Indeed, the most widely used of all keyboard temperaments before the 19th century narrows each of the scale's 12 fifths by 1/4 of a syntonic comma [see Mean-tone temperament]. Francisco Salinas described (1577) an influential temperament that narrows each fifth by 1/3 of a syntonic comma.

The relative circumscription of modulation schemes before ca. 1765 allowed for the use of various unequal or irregular temperaments. Little-used keys can be tempered more. This works best if they lie a semitone or tritone away from the key of the tuning. Historically, the most important unequal distributions are those that eliminate the *wolf fifth. A number of these "circulating" temperaments were propagated during the 17th and 18th centuries, and it is to them rather than to equal temperament that the term well-tempered (as in Bach's *Das Wohltemperirte Clavier*) rightly refers. The most famous of these was given by Andreas Werckmeister in his *Musikalische Temperatur* (Frankfurt and Leipzig, 1691). In this, the Pythagorean comma is distributed equally to fifths on C, G, D, and B. See also Tuning.

Temperatur [Ger.]. *Temperament; *gleichschwebende, ungleichschwebende T.*, equal, unequal temperament.

Tempest, The. Popular name for Beethoven's Piano Sonata in D minor op. 31 no. 2 (1802). When Anton Schindler asked Beethoven to explain the "meaning" of this sonata and the sonata op. 57 (*Appassionata*), Beethoven cryptically suggested that Schindler read Shakespeare's *Tempest*. The title has been associated only with the earlier sonata, however.

Tempestoso [It.]. Tempestuous, stormy.

Temple block. A percussion instrument carved from hardwood into a round or oval shape and made hollow, with a slit spanning most of the lower half; also called a Chinese or Korean temple block (and sometimes confused with the rectangular *Chinese block). It is usually played in a set of five of differing pitches (approximating a pentatonic scale) with soft-headed mallets or drum sticks. See ill. under Percussion instruments.

Templeton, Alec (b. Cardiff, Wales, 4 July 1909; d. Greenwich, Conn., 28 Mar. 1963). Pianist and composer. Blind from birth. Studied at the Royal Academy of Music and the Royal College of Music; musical programs for the BBC 1921–35. Settled in the U.S. in 1935 and performed widely with orchestras and on the radio. Most famous works include humorous musical sketches and parodies ("Mozart Matriculates," "Debussy in Dubuque," "Bach Goes to

Town"); also wrote serious works (*Gothic Concerto,* 1954).

Tempo [It., time]. (1) The speed at which music is performed, i.e., the rate per unit of time of metrical pulses in performance; *a tempo,* an instruction to return to the original tempo after a temporary departure specified by **ritardando* or a similar term. Speeds of performance may range from quite slow to quite fast and, in Western art music beginning in the 17th century, are usually indicated on a score in words, or sometimes *metronome markings. Most pieces have a range of acceptable tempos, and even seemingly absolute metronome markings are seldom unchangeable. While performance speeds are often a matter of taste, tempos should be selected with a view to the date and style of the music.

Until the introduction of words or phrases to specify tempo in the 17th century, tempo was expressed in notation by the combination of mensuration or meter [see Mensural notation], the prevailing note-values in a given work, and the concept of **tempus* or **tactus*—a pulse of fixed rate assigned to some particular note-value. Although writers as late as the 18th century continued to discuss tempo in these terms, the system was not wholly unambiguous even in the 16th, especially as regards the fixity of the *tactus.* Every period has had its conventions of tempo expressed in combinations of meter and note-value.

By the 18th century, Italian terms for tempo were widespread, and theorists such as Quantz (1752) attempted to relate them to conventions based on meter and note-value. There was general agreement about the relative position of some basic tempos, e.g., from slowest to fastest, *adagio, andante, allegretto, allegro,* and *presto.* But disagreements about the precise meanings of these terms and, especially, those for intervening tempos were widespread. Conventions with respect to their use have changed steadily since. For a survey of the terms used to designate tempo, see Performance marks; see also Rubato.

(2) [It.] *Movement.

Tempo giusto [It.]. See *Giusto.*

Tempo marks. See Performance marks.

Tempo ordinario [It.]. (1) Common time, 4/4. (2) A tempo neither particularly fast nor slow.

Tempo primo [It.]. An instruction to return to the original tempo after some temporary departure.

Tempo rubato [It.]. See *Rubato.*

Temporale [Lat.]. In the liturgical year, the feasts of the Time, i.e., principally those commemorating (or organized around the commemoration of) events in the life of Jesus [see Liturgy].

Temps [Fr.]. Beat.

Tempus [Lat.]. In *mensural notation, the relationship (whether duple or triple) between the *brevis* and the *semibrevis.*

Ten. [It.]. Abbr. for **tenuto.*

Tender Land, The. Opera in two acts by Copland (libretto by Horace Everett), produced in New York in 1954 (revised in three acts in 1955; orchestral suite arranged in 1956). Setting: a Midwestern farm in the early 1930s.

Tendre, tendrement [Fr.]. Tender(ly).

Tenebrae [Lat., darkness]. In the Roman rite, the service made up of Matins and Lauds on Thursday, Friday, and Saturday of Holy Week, so called because a candle is extinguished after each Psalm, the final portion being conducted "in tenebris" (in darkness). The *Lamentations and **Miserere* form prominent parts of the service.

Teneramente [It.]. Tenderly.

Tenney, James (b. Silver City, N.M., 10 Aug. 1934). Composer, pianist. Studied at Juilliard, Bennington College with Carl Ruggles, and Univ. of Illinois. Worked on electronic and computer music at Bell Labs in New Jersey, at Yale Univ., and at the Polytechnic Institute of New York; played with the ensembles of Steve Reich and Philip Glass (1967–70). Taught at California Institute of the Arts 1970–75; at York Univ. in Ontario from 1977. Author of *A History of Consonance and Dissonance* (New York, 1988).

Tennstedt, Klaus (b. Merseburg, 6 June 1926; d. Kiel, 12 Jan. 1998). Conductor. Studied piano and violin at the Leipzig Conservatory; held conducting posts at the Halle Municipal Theater, Dresden opera, and Schwerin orchestra. In 1971, left for Sweden; conducted in Göteborg and Stockholm.. Chief guest conductor of the Minnesota Orchestra 1979–83; chief conductor of the Norddeutscher Rundfunk Symphony in Hamburg 1979–81; principal guest conductor of the London Philharmonic 1980–83, and principal conductor 1983–87. Retired 1994.

Tenor [fr. Lat. *tenere,* to hold]. (1) In medieval polyphony up to the 15th century, the part that "holds" or is based on a preexistent melody or **cantus firmus,* most often a liturgical chant [see Organum, Clausula, Motet]. This was in general the lowest sounding part. (2) In three-voice secular polyphony of the 14th and 15th centuries, the lowest part structurally (though often crossed by the *contratenor), forming at times a structural pair with the uppermost part. (3) In vocal textures for four parts, the part immediately above the lowest part or bass. This usage was established in the late 15th century, at which time the tenor still sometimes retained the function of presenting the *cantus firmus* in long note-values. By the 16th century, however, it was most often not distinguished from the other voices in the character of its music. Since the 18th century, it has formed part of the most characteristic texture for polyphonic vocal music, namely (from highest to lowest) soprano, alto, tenor, and bass. (4) The highest naturally occurring voice type in adult males. See Voice. (5) In some families of instruments, by analogy with the voice, one of the lower members (e.g., in the *trombone, the one immediately above the bass; in the *saxophone, the one immediately above the baritone). (6) In a *psalm tone, the reciting note. See also Clef.

Tenor cor [Fr. *cor alto*]. A brass instrument with piston valves operated by the right hand, round in shape like the French horn, and pitched in F an octave above the French horn. It was introduced by the firm of Besson in Paris ca. 1860.

Tenor drum. See Drum.

Tenorgeige [Ger.]. *Tenor violin.

Tenor horn. See Alto horn.

Tenorlied [Ger.]. A German polyphonic song of the 16th century in which a preexistent song is placed in the tenor [see Lied].

Tenor Mass. A polyphonic *Mass of the Renaissance based on a *cantus firmus* placed in the tenor.

Tenoroon. A 19th-century tenor member of the *bassoon family. It is a transposing instrument, sounding a fourth or a fifth higher than the normal bassoon.

Tenth. See Interval.

Tento [Port.]. *Tiento.

Tenuto [It., abbr. *ten.*]. Held, sustained. In the 18th century, notes so marked were to be held to their full value rather than detached somewhat, as was the norm. In music of the 19th century and since, the term may call for a delay of the beat following. It may be indicated by a short horizontal stroke over or under the note.

Ternary form. See Binary and ternary form.

Terradellas, Domingo Miguel Bernabe [Terradeglias, Domenico] (b. Barcelona, bapt. 13 Feb. 1713; d. Rome, 20 May 1751). Composer. Studied in Barcelona and Naples. Held posts in Padua and London. Compositions include operas (*Merope,* 1743; *Sesostri re d'Egitto,* 1751), oratorios, and other sacred vocal works.

Terry, Clark [Mumbles] (b. St. Louis, 14 Dec. 1920). Jazz trumpeter, flügelhorn player, and bandleader. Joined Charlie Barnet (1947), Count Basie (1948–

51), Duke Ellington (1951–59), and Quincy Jones (1959–60). Worked in New York studios, notably for NBC's *Tonight Show,* and led bands. Nickname derives from his mumbling version of blues scat singing. Headed Thelonious Monk Institute of Jazz at Duke Univ. from 1990.

Terry, Sonny [Terrell, Sanders] (b. Greensboro, Ga., 24 Oct. 1911; d. Mineola, N.Y., 11 Mar. 1986). Blues singer and harmonica player. Blinded at age 16. Teamed with Blind Boy Fuller, 1934–39; appeared at Carnegie Hall in 1939. In 1939 created a long-lived blues act with Brownie McGhee that was acclaimed into the 1980s.

Tertian harmony. Harmony based on combinations of the interval of a third, such as characterizes Western tonal harmony.

Tertis, Lionel (b. West Hartlepool, 29 Dec. 1876; d. London, 22 Feb. 1975). Violist. Studied violin at the Hochschule für Musik in Leipzig and the Royal Academy of Music in London; switched to viola and toured Europe and the U.S. as a soloist. Author of *My Viola and I: A Complete Autobiography* (1974); helped design a large viola.

Terz [Ger.]. (1) The interval of a third. (2) *Terzflöte, Terzfagott,* a flute and a bassoon, respectively, pitched a minor third above the standard instrument.

Terzett [Ger.], **terzetto** [It.]. A vocal work for three voices with or without accompaniment (a work for three instruments being a *trio).

Terzina [It.]. Triplet.

Terzo suono [It.]. See Combination tone.

Tessarini, Carlo (b. Rimini, ca. 1690; d. Amsterdam?, after 15 Dec. 1766). Composer. Violinist at St. Mark's in Venice; held posts at the Venetian conservatory SS. Giovanni e Paolo and Urbino Cathedral. Performed in Rome and the Netherlands. Compositions are almost all for strings; published a violin treatise, *Grammatica di musica* (1741).

Tessitura [It.]. The particular range of a part (especially a vocal part) that is most consistently exploited, as opposed to the total range or compass of such a part. Thus, a soprano part may have a high or a low tessitura.

Testo [It.]. In an *oratorio, *Passion, or similar work, the narrator, whose part is often set in recitative.

Testudo [Lat., tortoise]. (1) In ancient Rome, the Greek *lyra. (2) In the Middle Ages and Renaissance, the *lute. See also *Chelys.

Tetrachord. Four pitches. In ancient Greek music, the tetrachord spanned the interval of a perfect fourth and was the smallest system commonly used. Larger systems were constructed by combining tetrachords, culminating in the Greater Perfect System. See also Genus, Diatonic, Chromatic, Enharmonic.

Octave species are often defined as consisting of one pentachord (five pitches) plus one conjunct tetrachord, e.g., c–g and g–c', or, in the case of a plagal *mode, A–d and d–a. Both monophonic and polyphonic music of the Middle Ages and Renaissance has sometimes been analyzed in these terms. Similarly, the major scale is sometimes described as consisting of two disjunct tetrachords separated by a whole tone, e.g., c–f and g–c'.

Tetrazzini, Luisa [Luigia] (b. Florence, 29 June 1871; d. Milan, 28 Apr. 1940). Soprano. Studied in Florence with Ceccherini; toured in South America, eastern Europe, and Mexico. Her Covent Garden debut as Violetta in 1907 caused a sensation. Performed at Covent Garden until 1912; with the Metropolitan Opera (1911–12) and the Chicago Grand Opera (1911–13). Taught in Milan and performed concert tours in later years; published *My Life of Song* (1921) and *How To Sing* (1923).

Texture. The general pattern of sound created by the elements of a work or passage. For example, the texture of a work that is perceived as consisting of the combination of several melodic lines is said to be contrapuntal or polyphonic [see Counterpoint, Polyphony]. A work consisting primarily of a succession of chords sounded as such is said to have a chordal or homophonic texture [see Homophony]. Between these two extremes, there are numerous gradations for which there is no very precise terminology. A familiar texture in much non-Western music is *heterophony. Other aspects of texture include *spacing, *tone color [see also Orchestration], loudness, and *rhythm. The terms used with respect to these aspects of texture are most often rather imprecise adjectives such as sparse, thin, dense, and thick.

Although the control of texture and the creation of textural contrast within works has been a significant part of compositional technique in Western art music since the Middle Ages, a concern with texture comparable to that with other, more traditional concerns such as melody and harmony came to the fore only in the 20th century.

Teyte [Tate], **Maggie** (b. Wolverhampton, 17 Apr. 1888; d. London, 26 May 1976). Soprano. Studied in England, and in Paris with Jean de Reszke. In 1908 appeared at Monte Carlo and at the Opéra-comique in Paris. Debussy chose her for the role of Mélisande and accompanied her in recitals. Sang with the Chicago Grand Opera (1911–14), the Boston Opera (1914–17), the British National Opera (1922–23), and the New York City Opera (1948); also performed in operettas and musical comedies and gave recitals

of French songs. In 1958 named Dame of the British Empire.

Thalberg, Sigismond (Fortuné François) (b. Pâquis, near Geneva, 8 Jan. 1812; d. Posillipo, Naples, 27 Apr. 1871). Pianist, composer. Studied in Vienna; engaged Liszt in a celebrated pianistic duel in Paris in 1835. Toured Russia, Spain, Brazil, the U.S.; after 1858 lived in semiretirement. Devised new ways of writing for the piano, including a technique of figuration calculated to sound as if 3 hands must be playing.

Theater music. See Incidental music, Music theater.

Thebom, Blanche (b. Monessen, Pa., 19 Sept. 1918). Mezzo-soprano. Studied in New York with Margarete Matzenauer and Edyth Walker. Metropolitan Opera debut in 1944; remained with the company until 1967, performing mainly Wagnerian roles. Also performed at Glyndebourne and Covent Garden. Retired 1970.

Theile, Johann (b. Naumburg, 29 July 1646; d. there, buried 24 June 1724). Composer. Pupil of Schütz sometime between 1666 and 1672. Kapellmeister at Gottorf and Wolfenbüttel; employed by Duke Christian I at Merseburg. Known as "the father of contrapuntists" by his contemporaries, Theile wrote operas (lost), Passions, Masses, motets, and secular vocal and instrumental works.

Thematic transformation. See Transformation of themes.

Theme [Fr. *thème;* Ger. *Thema;* It., Sp. *tema*]. A musical idea, usually a melody, that forms the basis or starting point for a composition or a major section of one. Although the terms theme and *subject are sometimes used interchangeably, as in the context of *sonata form, theme often (though only since the 19th century) implies something slightly longer and more self-contained than subject. In the context of theme and *variations, it usually refers to an entirely self-contained melody or short piece. See also Transformation of themes.

Themenaufstellung [Ger.]. *Exposition.

Theodorakis, Mikis (Michael George) (b. Khios, 29 July 1925). Composer. Student at the Athens and Paris conservatories. Early compositions based in traditional Greek folk music. In the 1960s belonged to the Communist party and served as a member of the Greek parliament; his music was banned and he was arrested after the coup of 1967; eventually was freed and moved to Paris. Works include dramatic music (*Epiphania Averoff,* oratorio, 1968; *Dionysos,* religious drama, voice, choir, chamber ensemble, 1984; *Zorbas,* opera-ballet, 1988), orchestral music

(*Oedipus Tyrannus*, 1946; 7 symphonies), and film music (*Zorba the Greek; Z*).

Theorbo [Fr. *théorbe;* Ger. *Theorbe;* It., Sp. *tiorba*]. A large six-course bass lute to which have been added seven or usually eight diatonically tuned contrabass courses held in a second pegbox glued to an extension of the first. Developed late in 16th-century Italy to provide accompaniment for a new style of singing, *musica recitativa,* the theorbo was quickly adopted throughout Europe as an important *thoroughbass instrument. See also *Chitarrone.*

Theory. The abstract principles embodied in music and the sounds of which it consists. With respect to Western music, theory has traditionally encompassed the properties of single sounds—*pitch, *duration, *timbre—and those of collections of sounds: *acoustics, *tuning and *temperaments, *intervals, *consonance and dissonance, *scales, *modes, *melody, *harmony, *counterpoint, *rhythm, *meter, *form, and *analysis. Today the term also refers specifically to the teaching of the fundamentals or rudiments of music—e.g., elementary harmony and counterpoint, general musicianship, *ear training, *solfège. Non-Western musical cultures with rich traditions of explicit formulation and study of music theory include those of East Asia and South Asia.

Therapy. See Music therapy.

Theremin. An *electronic instrument invented in the 1920s by Leon Theremin. It generates a single tone whose pitch and loudness are controlled by the proximity of the player's hands to a straight antenna and a loop, respectively, that protrude from it.

Thérémin, Léon (b. St. Petersburg, 15 Aug. 1896; d. Moscow, 3 Nov. 1993). Inventor. Studied physics at Petrograd Univ., and in 1919 became director of the Laboratory of Electrical Oscillators there. Invented an electronic instrument (the aetherophone or theremin) that changed pitch and volume based on the proximity of the player's hands to an antenna and a loop on the device. Traveled to the U.S. in 1927 and gave a number of concert demonstrations; in 1938 returned to Russia.

Theresienmesse [Ger., Theresa's Mass]. Popular name for Haydn's Mass in B♭ major Hob. XXII:12 (1799), often supposed (without conclusive evidence) to have been written for Empress Maria Theresa.

Thesis. See Arsis and thesis.

Thibaud, Jacques (b. Bordeaux, 27 Sept. 1880; d. Mont Cemet, 1 Sept. 1953). Violinist. Studied at the Paris Conservatory with Martin Marsick. Solo debut was in 1898; toured widely in Europe and the U.S.; collaborated with Casals and Cortot.

Thibaut IV (b. Troyes, 30 May 1201; d. Pamplona, 7 July 1253). Trouvère. Count of Champagne and Brie; became King of Navarre in 1234. In 1239 visited Jerusalem while heading a Crusade. Nearly 50 compositions have been identified, including *chansons courtoises, chansons de croisade, jeux-partis, débats,* and religious works.

Thielemans, Toots [Jean Baptiste] (b. Brussels, 29 Apr. 1922). Jazz harmonica player, guitarist, and whistler. Toured Europe with Benny Goodman (1950); emigrated to the U.S. and joined George Shearing (1953–59); recorded *Man Bites Harmonica* (1957) and "Bluesette," playing guitar and whistling (1961). Often recorded with Quincy Jones, including the soundtrack to *Midnight Cowboy* (1969).

Third. See Interval; Scale degree; Consonance and dissonance; Tertian harmony; Picardy third; Just intonation.

Third-stream. Music that combines elements of jazz and of 20th-century art music. In the late 1950s, Gunther Schuller, who coined the term, and John Lewis led an effort to compose complex forms without destroying the vitality of jazz improvisation.

Thirteenth. See Interval, Chord.

Thirty-two foot. See Foot.

Thomas, (Charles Louis) Ambroise (b. Metz, 5 Aug. 1811; d. Paris, 12 Feb. 1886). Composer. Student at the Paris Conservatory; produced a number of works at the Opéra and Opéra-comique before the great success of *Le caïd* (1849), which remained in the theater's repertory until 1866 and along with *Le songe d'une nuit d'été* (1850) made him one of the principal figures in French light opera. Professor of composition at the Conservatory after 1852; appointed director in 1871. His greatest success was *Mignon* (1866), which remained widely popular well into the twentieth century, followed by the grand opera *Hamlet* (1868).

Thomas, Arthur Goring (b. Ratton Park, Sussex, 20 Nov. 1850; d. London, 20 Mar. 1892). Composer. Educated for the civil service; studied music in Paris with Sullivan and Prout, and in Berlin with Bruch. Died insane in an asylum. Operas include *Esmeralda* (1883), based on Hugo's *Notre-Dame de Paris,* though with a happy ending; *Nadeshda* (1885); *The Golden Web* (1893), completed by Waddington. Other works include choral pieces; works for violin, piano, cello; songs, romances, and lyrics.

Thomas, John Charles (b. Meyersdale, Va., Sept. 1891; d. Apple Valley, Calif., 13 Dec. 1960). Baritone. Studied with Adelin Fermin; debut 1924 in Washington, D.C., as Amonasro in *Aida.* Sang with the Théatre de la Monnaie in Brussels (1925–28),

San Francisco Opera, Chicago Opera, Metropolitan Opera 1934–43. Toured the U.S.; sang on the Bell Telephone radio program.

Thomas, Kurt (Georg Hugo) (b. Tonning, Germany, 25 May 1904; d. Bad Oeynhausen, 31 Mar. 1973). Choral conductor and composer. Student of Karl Straube at the Leipzig Conservatory; appointed to the faculty, 1925. The a cappella performance style of his chamber choir was widely influential. Professor at the Hochschule für Musik in Berlin from 1934; founded and directed the Musisches Gymnasium in Frankfurt (1939–45). After the war Kantor at the Frankfurt cathedral; director of the Thomasschule in Leipzig 1955–61; 1961, returned to Frankfurt. Author of the standard text *The Choral Conductor* (Leipzig, 1935; rev. 1948; trans. Eng. 1971). Compositions include a cappella choral works (Mass in A, 1925; St. Mark Passion, 1926), works for chorus and orchestra, instrumental works.

Thomas, Michael Tilson [Tomashevsky] (b. Los Angeles, 21 Dec. 1944). Conductor. Attended the Univ. of Southern California; studied composition with Ingolf Dahl, harpsichord with Alice Ehlers, piano with John Crown. In 1967, assisted Boulez at the Ojai Festival. Named assistant conductor of Boston Symphony, 1969; associate conductor, 1970; principal guest conductor, 1972–74. Music director of the Buffalo Philharmonic (1971–79), principal guest conductor of the Los Angeles Philharmonic (1981–85), conductor of the London Symphony (1988–95), and music director of the San Francisco Symphony (from 1995).

Thomas, Theodore (Christian Friedrich) (b. Esens, East Friesland, 11 Oct. 1835; d. Chicago, 4 Jan. 1905). Conductor. Played violin in the New York Philharmonic Orchestra from 1854; elected conductor, 1877–91. Founded a chamber series (1854–71), which premiered Brahms's Piano Trio in B minor op. 8. Formed his own orchestra, 1862; made a major tour, 1869. First conductor of the Chicago Symphony Orchestra, 1891–1905. Popularized German music and the music of many American composers. Author of *A Musical Autobiography* (Chicago, 1904; R: 1964).

Thompson, Randall (b. New York, 21 Apr. 1899; d. Boston, 9 July 1984). Composer and educator. Studied at Harvard with Archibald Davison and with Ernst Bloch in New York. In Rome 1922–25; returned to the U.S. in 1925, where his Second Symphony (1931) was a critical success. Taught and conducted choruses at Wellesley College (1927–29, 1936–37); Univ. of California, Berkeley (1937–39); Curtis Institute (1939–41); Univ. of Virginia (1941–46); Princeton Univ. (1946–48); Harvard Univ. (from 1948). *Americana,* chorus and piano (or orchestra) (1932), *The Peaceable Kingdom,* chorus a cappella (1936), *Alleluia,* chorus a cappella (1940), and *The Testament of Freedom,* male chorus and piano (or orchestra) (1943), became mainstays of American choral repertory; other works include *The Passion According to St. Luke,* oratorio (1965); *A Concord Cantata,* voices and orchestra (1975); orchestral and chamber works.

Thomson, Virgil (b. Kansas City, Mo., 25 Nov. 1896; d. New York, 30 Sept. 1989). Composer and critic. Studied at Harvard Univ. with Edward Burlingame Hill and Archibald Davison; in New York with Chalmes Clifton and Rosario Scalero; with Nadia Boulanger in Paris, where he became acquainted with Satie, Cocteau, and "Les six." Lived in Paris 1925–40, composing and writing music criticism; collaborated with the poet Gertrude Stein on an opera, *Four Saints in Three Acts* (1928), whose performance in the U.S. in 1934 by an all-black cast secured Thomson's American reputation. Also wrote instrumental music, and began a series of "portraits"—instrumental depictions of his friends and acquaintances.

Wrote music for two government-sponsored documentary films, *The Plow That Broke the Plains* (1936) and *The River* (1937), whose scores make use of American hymns, ballads, and popular songs, as does *Filling Station,* ballet (1937). Returned to the U.S.; influential music critic at the *New York Herald Tribune* 1940–54. Works from this period include *The Mayor La Guardia Waltzes* (orchestra, 1942), film scores (*Louisiana Story,* 1948; Pulitzer Prize, 1949), and a second opera, *The Mother of Us All* (1946), based on the life of Susan B. Anthony, with text by Gertrude Stein.

After resigning from the *Herald Tribune,* toured Europe and South America as a conductor and lecturer; visited universities on one-year appointments; continued to compose larger works (*Lord Byron,* opera, 1968), and added to his by now vast collection of portraits.

Writings include *The State of Music* (New York, 1939); *The Art of Judging Music* (New York, 1948); *Virgil Thomson* (autobiography, New York, 1966); *American Music since 1910* (New York, 1971); *A Virgil Thomson Reader* (New York, 1981); *Music with Words: A Composer's View* (New Haven, 1989).

Thorne, Francis (b. Bay Shore, N.Y., 23 June 1922). Composer and administrator. Studied music at Yale; worked as a banker in New York until 1955. Worked as a jazz pianist in New York; 1958, moved to Florence and studied composition with David Diamond. Returned to the U.S. in 1964; used family money to set up the Thorne Music Fund (1964–74) to commission new works and offered fellowships to composers. President of the American Composers' Orchestra (beginning 1976) and executive director of the American Composers' Alliance (beginning 1975). Works include *Elegy for Orchestra* (1963); 5 symphonies; *Liebesrock* (3 electric guitars and orchestra, 1969); *Fanfare, Fugue, and Funk* (3 trumpets and orchestra, 1972); *Mario and the Magician* (opera, 1994); string quartets and other chamber works.

Thornhill, Claude (b. Terre Haute, Ind., 10 Aug. 1909; d. Caldwell, N.J., 1 July 1965). Jazz bandleader and pianist. Attended the Cincinnati Conservatory and the Curtis Institute; worked as arranger and led recording and touring bands (1937–38). His big band (1940–42, 1946–48) was noted for using orchestral winds. Composed "Snowfall," the band's theme (recorded 1941); Gil Evans and Gerry Mulligan arranged for the group. Continued leading bands into the early 1960s.

Thoroughbass, figured bass [Fr. *basse continue, chiffrée, figurée;* Ger. *Generalbass, bezifferter Bass;* It. *basso continuo;* Sp. *bajo cifrado*]. An independent bass line continuing throughout a piece (whence the Italian *continuo*), on the basis of which harmonies are extemporized on keyboard or other chord-playing instruments. Individual chords may be specified by figures written above, below, or beside the bass notes (whence, figured bass and related terms). The thoroughbass method was essential to ensemble music in Europe from about 1600 to about 1750, the period sometimes being called the thoroughbass period [see also Baroque]. The technique reflects a conception of music as embodying a polarity between a foundation, consisting of a bass line with its implied harmonies, and one or more supported melodic parts above. The creation of a complete texture from a figured-bass part is termed its realization. The realization of figured basses in four parts (sometimes at sight at the keyboard) is still often part of instruction in harmony.

In historical practice, the conventions governing the use of figures and the completeness of figures in specifying the intended harmonies has varied considerably. Generally, arabic numbers are used to specify intervals formed above the bass note, much as they are used with roman numerals in *harmonic analysis. Unless modified, the figures specify the intervals occurring naturally above the bass note in the prevailing key signature. If chromatic alteration is required, an accidental is placed immediately before the figure. The sharp may also be indicated by a small stroke drawn through some part of the figure. The pitches specified can be played in any register and doubled at will, though in general the principles of correct voice leading should be observed. Hence, figures for intervals larger than a ninth are not normally used. If no figure is given, the chord is assumed to be in root position. If only an accidental is given, it is assumed

to modify the pitch a third above the bass and thus the third in a triad in *root position. The figure 0 indicates that only the bass note is to be played (termed *tasto solo*).

Example 1 shows the root position and first and second *inversions of a triad with the appropriate figures. The figures in brackets are most often omitted by way of abbreviation. Example 2 illustrates the figures for a seventh chord and its inversions in similar fashion. (In harmonic analysis, in the absence of a notated bass part, these harmonies would be notated with the same arabic numbers placed following a roman numeral designating the *scale degree of the root. In Ex. 1, in C major, this would be I; in Ex. 2, also in C major, V.) Figures may also be used to specify details of voice leading, including dissonances. For example, suspensions or appoggiaturas [see Counterpoint] in which a fourth above the bass resolves to a third are often indicated by the horizontal placement of the figures 4 and 3 connected by a dash; similar successions may be notated in similar fashion [Ex. 3]. A horizontal line following a figure and over changing bass notes indicates that the pitch or pitches originally specified are to be sustained. Diagonal slashes with changing bass notes indicate that the last figure given is to be applied to each succeeding bass note.

The realization of a thoroughbass part in performance normally requires at least two instruments: a harpsichord, organ, or other chord-playing instrument to realize the harmonies, and a melody instrument such as the cello or viola da gamba to play the bass line itself. Although the bass line is not to be modified, the player realizing the harmonies has considerable freedom and is not bound by the rhythm of the bass line or the simplest form of the harmonies specified. Within the bounds of historically informed taste, a realization may entail elaborate improvisation that interacts prominently with the written-out melody parts.

Three-Cornered Hat, The. See *Sombrero de tres picos, El.*

Three-line. The octave proceeding upward from c′′′, or any pitch in that octave [see Pitch names].

Three-part form. Ternary form, sometimes also termed song form [see Binary and ternary form].

Threepenny Opera, The. See *Dreigroschenoper, Die;* Ballad opera.

Threni [Lat.]. *Lamentations.

Threnody [Gr. *thrēnos;* Lat. pl. *threni*]. *Lament.

Through-composed [Ger. *Durchkomponiert*]. Without internal repetitions, especially with respect to the setting of a *strophic or other text that might imply the repetition of music for different words; thus, e.g., a song in which new music is composed for each stanza of text.

Thuille, Ludwig (Wilhelm Andreas Maria) (b. Bozen, the Tirol, 30 Nov. 1861; d. Munich, 5 Feb. 1907). Composer. Studied at Innsbruck, and with Rheinberger in Munich; taught at Königliche Musikschule from 1883. Friend of Richard Strauss and Alexander Ritter. Wrote *Harmonielehre* with Rudolf Louis (1907). Compositions include 3 operas, Symphony in F major (1886), Wind Sextet in B♭ op. 6 (1886–88), Piano Quintet in E♭ op. 20 (1897–1901), other chamber pieces, choral pieces, songs.

Thunder machine. A drum containing hard balls that strike the heads when it is rotated, thus producing a sound reminiscent of thunder. A sound like that of thunder is also sometimes produced by a long metallic sheet (termed a thunder sheet) that is shaken.

Thunder stick. *Bull-roarer.

Thus Spake Zarathustra. See *Also sprach Zarathustra.*

Tibbett [Tibbet], **Lawrence** (b. Bakersfield, Calif., 16 Nov. 1896; d. New York, 15 July 1960). Baritone. Studied with Basil Ruysdael and Frank La Forge; Metropolitan Opera debut in 1923, achieved great success there in 1925 singing Ford in *Falstaff.* Remained at the Metropolitan until 1950; premiered roles in Taylor's *The King's Henchman,* Hanson's *Merry Mount,* and J. L. Seymour's *In the Pasha's Garden;* sang in the first Metropolitan performances of *Simon Boccanegra* (title role), *Peter Grimes,* and *Khovanshchina.* Made several films.

Tibia [Lat.]. A reedpipe of ancient Rome, identical to the Greek *aulos.

Tie, bind. A curved line connecting two successive notes of the same pitch, indicating that the second note is not to be attacked, but that its duration is to be added to that of the first. It is identical in appearance to a *slur.

Tiento [Sp., fr. *tentar,* to feel, try out; Port. *tento*]. A Spanish or Portuguese composition for harp, *vihuela,* or keyboard from the 16th through the early 18th century. In style and function, the *tiento* has at times resembled pieces called *ricercar, *fantasia, *toc-cata, or *prelude, and varies from short flourishes of chords mixed with running scales to long and complex contrapuntal works. These appear first in collections of *vihuela* music, where they are sometimes preludes to longer pairs of fantasias and *intabulations. A high point in the early *tiento* is reached with Antonio de Cabezón's works, some of which use themes from sacred and secular part-music and liturgical chant and display sectional structure, thematic transformation, and polarities of restrained counterpoint and florid coloratura. The *tientos* of slightly later composers use features common to the Italian toccata and fantasia, such as elaborate figuration, sudden changes of mood, episodic sections, and punctuating passages in brilliant improvisatory style. Some *tientos* are monothematic in the manner of the ricercar or are styled after the canzona. The *tientos* of Juan Bautista José Cabanilles (1644–1712) are the final flowering of the genre and are large works of great stylistic diversity, some with programmatic content.

Tierce [Gr.]. The interval of a third. For *tierce picarde (de Picardie),* see Picardy third; for *tierce coulé,* see Coulé.

Till Eulenspiegels lustige Streiche [Ger., Till Eulenspiegel's Merry Pranks]. A symphonic tone poem by Richard Strauss, op. 28 (1894–95), in the words of the title, "based on the old rogue's tale [the 16th-century folktale of Till Eulenspiegel], set for large orchestra, in rondo form."

Timbal [Sp.]. *Kettledrum, timpani. See also *Timbales.*

Timbale [Fr.]. *Kettledrum, timpani.

Timbales [Sp., pl.]. (1) *Kettledrums. (2) A pair of single-headed, shallow cylindrical drums of Cuban origin that are tuned to different pitches, clamped side by side to a waist-high stand, and played with two sticks. One or two *cowbells are often attached to the same stand. *Timbales* are an essential element in Latin American urban popular music and have found some use in concert music as well. See ill. under Percussion instruments.

Timballo [It.]. *Kettledrum, timpani.

Timbre [Fr.]. (1) *Tone color. (2) A melody, especially an anonymous or popular one, that is used for different texts. The term, which came into use in the late 18th century, has been employed in connection with the *sequences of Adam of St. Victor and some other liturgical chant, the *noël of the 16th century and after, *vaudeville, and *opéra comique.

Timbrel. (1) *Tambourine. (2) A *frame drum. (3) The English translation of the Biblical Hebrew *toph.*

Time. See Meter, *Tempus,* Tempo, Duration.

Time signature. The sign placed at the beginning of a composition to indicate its meter. This **most often** takes the form of a fraction, but a few other **signs with** origins in the system of *mensural notation and **pro**portions are also employed [see Meter].

Timpan. (1) In the Middle Ages, *kettledrum. (2) *Tiómpán.*

Timpani [Eng. sing. and pl.; It., sing. *timpano*]. *Kettledrum; *t. coperti, t. sordi,* muted or muffled kettledrums.

Tinctoris, Johannes (b. Braine l'Alleud, near Nivelles, ca. 1435; d. ca. 1511). Composer and theorist. Served under Dufay at Cambrai as a *petit vicaire* in 1460; joined the court of Ferdinand I of Naples around 1472 as instructor of the king's daughter Beatrice, for whom he probably oversaw the compilation of the Mellon Chansonnier. Among his compositions are 5 Masses (including one based on *L'homme armé*) and several motets and chansons. Best known for his theoretical writings, including a dictionary of musical terms (*Terminorum musicae diffinitorium,* Treviso, 1495); treatises on mensural notation (*Proportionale musices,* ca. 1473–74), the modes (*Liber de natura et proprietate tonorum,* 1476), and counterpoint (*Liber de arte contrapuncti,* 1477); and descriptions of practical music making.

Tin Pan Alley. The popular music business in the U.S. from the late 19th century through the 1950s; its geographical center, beginning in the 1920s, around West 28th Street in New York City; also the style of U.S. popular song of the period. Often sentimental in character, such songs were at first usually in verse-and-chorus form. By the 1920s, the verse was often less prominent and the chorus in 32-bar AABA form [see Ballad (3)].

Tin whistle. *Penny whistle.

Tinel, Edgar (Pierre Joseph) (b. Sinaai, East Flanders, 27 Mar. 1854; d. Brussels, 28 Oct. 1912). Pianist and composer. Studied at Brussels Conservatory with Brassin and Gevaert. Director of Institute for Church Music at Malines, 1881; inspector of music education, 1889; professor of counterpoint and fugue at Brussels Conservatory from 1896. Wrote much sacred music including *Missa in honorem BMV de Lourdes* op. 41 (1905), cantatas, keyboard and orchestral works, Psalms, songs.

Tintinnabulum [Lat.]. A small *bell; in the Middle Ages, often synonymous with *cymbalum.*

Tiomkin, Dmitri (b. Poltava, 10 May 1894; d. London, 11 Nov. 1979). Composer. At the St. Petersburg Conservatory studied piano with Felix Blumenthal,

composition with Alexander Glazunov; in Berlin with Ferruccio Busoni and Egon Petri. Toured the U.S. as a pianist in 1925 and 1928; in 1929 went to Hollywood, where he composed scores for movie musicals and background music for films, including *Lost Horizon* (1937), *It's a Wonderful Life* (1947), *High Noon* (1952), *The Alamo* (1960). In 1968 moved to London.

Tiómpán, timpán [Gael.]. A stringed instrument of medieval Ireland, most likely a *lyre like the Welsh *crwth.*

Tiorba [It.]. *Theorbo.

Tiple [Sp.]. (1) Treble, soprano. (2) A small guitar of Spain and Latin America with varying stringings and tunings. A typical Colombian *tiple* has four courses (three of which are triple) tuned like the highest four strings of the guitar. (3) A treble *shawm of the Catalan *cobla* ensemble. See also *Chirimía.*

Tippett, Michael (Kemp) (b. London, 2 Jan. 1905; d. there, 8 Jan. 1998). Composer. At the Royal College of Music studied composition with Wood, Kitson, and R. O. Morris; conducting with Sargent and Boult. Head of the music department at Morley College 1940–51; then became a broadcaster with the BBC, and continued to work as a conductor and to compose.

Early works evinced interest in classical, symmetrical forms; later work explored modal harmonies and irregular rhythms and incorporated elements such as African American spirituals and English folk song: the oratorio *A Child of Our Time* (1939–41) uses spirituals, and the opera *The Midsummer Marriage* (1946–52) incorporates dance as an integral part of the drama. Other late works experimented with avant-garde terchniques and forms.

Works include operas (*The Midsummer Marriage,* 1946–52; *The Knot Garden,* 1966–69; *New Year,* 1985–88); vocal music (*The Vision of St. Augustine,* baritone, chorus, orchestra, 1963–65; *The Mask of Time,* chorus, orchestra, 1981–84); orchestral music (4 symphonies; *Festal Brass with Blues,* brass band, 1984; *Byzantium,* soloist, orchestra, 1991); chamber music.

Tirade [Fr.], **tirata** [It.]. A Baroque ornament consisting of a scale passage of more than three notes serving as a transition between two principal melody notes. It could be either written out or indicated by a sign, but it was often improvised to fill in large intervals

Tirando [It.]. Dragging.

Tirare [It., to draw]. (1) Down-bow. See Bowing (1). (2) To draw an organ stop; *tiratutti,* a *coupler.

Tirasse [Fr.]. In organs, a *coupler for connecting a keyboard to the pedalboard.

Tirer, tirez, tiré [Fr., to draw, draw, drawn]. (1) Down-bow. See Bowing (1). (2) To draw an organ stop.

Tishchenko, Boris Ivanovich (b. Leningrad, 23 Mar. 1939). Composer. At the Leningrad Conservatory studied with Salmanov, Voloshinov, and Evlakhov; graduate studies with Shostakovich. Beginning 1965, taught at the Leningrad Conservatory. Works include ballets (*Yaroslavna,* 1974); 6 symphonies (*The Siege Chronicle,* 1984); concertos; vocal-symphonic works; 5 string quartets and other chamber music, including *Concerto allamarcia,* 16 performers (1989); piano music; songs and choral works; film and incidental music.

Titan. Mahler's Symphony no. 1 in D major (1885–88, rev. 1893–96), originally termed a symphonic poem and including five movements with programmatic titles, which, like *Titan* itself, are after a novel by Jean Paul Richter. The Andante "Blumine" was subsequently removed, as were the titles of the other movements.

Titelouze, Jehan (b. St. Omer, ca. 1562–63; d. Rouen, 24 Oct. 1633). Composer. Became organist at St. Jean in 1585; organist of the cathedral from 1588; 1610, canon at the cathedral. Involved in the installation and renovation of important organs, 1588–1623. Besides organ works, wrote several sacred vocal compositions (lost).

Titov, Alexey [Alexei] **Nikolayevich** (b. St. Petersburg, 23 July 1769; d. there, 20 Nov. 1827). Composer and violinist. Major general in the cavalry before he retired. Wrote primarily stage music, including operas, ballets, and incidental music. Operas produced in St. Petersburg include *Andromeda and Perseus* (1802); *Yam, or The Post Station* (1805); *The Winter Party, or The Sequel to Yam* (1808); *The Cossack Woman* (1810); *Maslenitsa* (1813).

Titov, Nicolai Alexeyevich (b. St. Petersburg, 10 May 1800; d. there, 22 Dec. 1875). Composer. Son of violinist and composer Alexei Titov (1769–1827). Had no formal training in music; held a military position, 1817–67. Began composing in 1819; later advised by Glinka and Dargomyzhsky. Nicknamed "the father of Russian song." Wrote some 60 songs; also marches and piano music. His uncle Sergei Titov (1770–1825) composed works for the stage; cousin Nicolai Sergeyevich Titov (1798–1843) also composed songs, some of which have been attributed to him.

Ti-tzu (dizi) [Chin.]. A transverse bamboo flute of China with six finger holes. Near the mouth hole is another hole that is covered with a skin or paper *mirliton, giving a penetrating, reedy sound.

Toccata [fr. It. *toccare,* to touch; to hit or tap, e.g., a drum or bell; Ger. *Tokkata*]. (1) A virtuoso composition for keyboard or plucked string instrument featuring sections of brilliant passage work, with or without imitative or fugal interludes. The principal elements of toccata style are quasi-improvisatory disjunct harmonies, sweeping scales, broken-chord figuration, and roulades that often range over the entire instrument. In some periods, this style is also found in pieces called *prelude, *tiento, *ricercar, and *fantasia.

Toccatas first appeared in a 1536 Milanese anthology as codas to sets of lute dances. These short pieces by Francesco Canova da Milano and Pietro Paolo Borrono are virtually indistinguishable from earlier homophonic preludial ricercars and *tastar de corde* and from *tientos* by Alonso Mudarra. Only toward the century's end did Venetian organists firmly establish the toccata and its style, which spread quickly throughout Europe, becoming one of the most influential keyboard genres. In works by Giovanni Gabrieli (Venice, 1597, 1615) and especially Claudio Merulo (Rome, 1594–1604), sustained pedal tones and chords animated by passage work alternate with brief protofugal episodes, resulting in a homophonic/polyphonic duality that characterizes the toccata throughout most of its history.

The toccatas of Giovanni Maria Trabaci (Naples, 1603) and other Neapolitans link the Renaissance toccata, with its evenly flowing figuration, and the more articulated sectional toccata of the early Baroque. The genre's first high point was reached with Frescobaldi. His longer toccatas frequently juxtapose many segments that contrast greatly in figuration, meter, tempo, and texture, yet balance fugal elements with dramatic harmonic clashes and agitated virtuosity. Frescobaldi's disciples Froberger, Michelangelo Rossi, and Johann Kaspar Kerll often emphasize the fugal sections by unifying them with thematic transformation and other contrapuntal devices drawn from the variation ricercar and canzona, a procedure favored by north German organists through the time of Bach.

In Protestant north Germany, the toccatas of composers such as Matthias Weckmann, Dietrich Buxtehude, Johann Adam Reincken, Georg Böhm, and Bach often attain great heights of virtuosity, and many include several lively and thematically related fugues and contrasting recitativelike adagios, framed and interspersed with brilliant passage work. Others approach the sonata by having distinct movements, as do Bach's for harpsichord (BWV 912–16) and his organ toccata in C major (BWV 564, sometimes incorrectly called Toccata, Adagio, and Fugue). Terminology being inexact, numerous preludes (or fanta-sias) and fugues are cast in the usual toccata structure of toccata–fugue–toccata, e.g., Franz Tunder and early Bach (BWV 550–51, 561).

After 1750, the term toccata fell into disuse. The continuous drive of the late Italian harpsichord toc-cata was transferred to virtuoso etudes, some sub-titled toccata. The Bach revival in the 19th century inspired multimovement toccatas modeled on the C-major toccata. There are examples of such pieces in the 20th century as well, along with single-move-ment toccatas by Debussy, Prokofiev (op. 11, 1912), Ravel, Krenek, Holst, Poulenc, and Petrassi (1933), among others.

(2) A processional fanfare for trumpets and tim-pani for the entrances and departures at coronations, royal weddings, state banquets, and the like. From as early as 1393 through the late 18th century, literary sources refer to the *toccata de trompettes, tocade de guerra,* etc. Seldom notated, most were improvised by members of courtly trumpeters' guilds, who closely guarded their art. The term probably refers to the striking of the drums [see Tuck, Toccato].

(3) In *clarino trumpet playing, the fifth partial of the harmonic series.

Toccatina [It.]. A short toccata, often introducing further movements.

Toccato [It., struck, hit]. In 17th- through 19th-cen-tury music for trumpets, the tenor (usually fourth) trumpet part, which may be doubled or replaced with timpani in the performance of processional fanfares and other pieces; also *touquet.* See Toccata (2).

Toch, Ernst (b. Vienna, 7 Dec. 1887; d. Los Angeles, 1 Oct. 1964). Composer. At the Frankfurt Conserva-tory studied piano with Willy Rehberg and composi-tion with Ivan Knorr. In 1913 appointed professor of composition at the Musikhochschule in Mannheim; with String Quartet no. 9 (1919) adopted a dissonant, modernist idiom. In 1929 moved to Berlin and was forced to emigrate in 1933. In 1934 arrived in New York to teach at the New School for Social Research; 1936, moved to Los Angeles, where he wrote scores for movies and composed chamber music. Taught at UCLA 1940–48. Works include 7 symphonies (Symphony no. 3 [1955] won the 1956 Pulitzer Prize); sinfoniettas and other orchestral works (*Big Ben,* 1934; *Hyperion,* 1947); *Valse* (speaking chorus and percussion, 1961); string quartets.

Tod und das Mädchen, Der [Ger., Death and the Maiden]. Popular name for Schubert's String Quartet in D minor D. 810 (1824), the second movement of which consists of variations on his song of the same name, D. 531 (1817).

Tod und Verklärung [Ger., Death and Transfigura-tion]. A symphonic poem in four sections by Richard Strauss, op. 24 (1888–89). The work depicts a dying artist, his visions, his painful death, and the transfigu-ration of his soul. The poem by Alexander Ritter printed at the head of the score was written after the work was completed.

Toda, Kunio (b. Tokyo, 11 Aug. 1915). Composer. Career diplomat. Studied composition with Saburō Moroi; was influential in introducing serialism to Japan. Taught music at the Tōhō Gakuen College, the Gakuen School of Music (1964–76), and Senzoku Gakuen College (1977–88). Works include operas, ballets, orchestral works (*Song of the River,* mezzo-soprano, baritone, orchestra, 1989), piano works.

Toeschi, Carl Joseph (bapt. Ludwigsburg, 11 Nov. 1731; d. Munich, 12 Apr. 1788). Composer and vio-linist. Son of Alessandro Toeschi, composer and vio-linist in the Mannheim orchestra. Studied with Jo-hann Stamitz and Anton Fils; joined the Mannheim orchestra, 1752 (*Konzertmeister,* 1759); moved to Munich, 1778. A representative of the second gen-eration of the "Mannheim school," wrote more than 60 symphonies, many ballets, about 20 flute concer-tos, over 30 flute quartets, and other chamber works.

Tomášek, Václav Jan Křtitel (b. Skuteč, 17 Apr. 1774; d. Prague, 3 Apr. 1850). Composer. In part self-taught. In 1790 moved to Prague and taught mu-sic; in 1824 started his own music school (J. H. Voříšek and E. Hanslick were among his pupils). Met Haydn and Beethoven in Vienna; also knew Hum-mel, Dussek, and Clementi. Compositions include 2 operas, several *scenas,* Masses and other sacred works, symphonies, orchestral pieces, chamber works, songs, and much solo keyboard music.

Tomasi, Henri (b. Marseilles, 17 Aug. 1901; d. Paris, 13 Jan. 1971). Composer and conductor. Studied at the Marseilles and Paris conservatories. His music characterized by non-European subjects, rhythmic intensity, colorful orchestration, and sympathy with colonial and third world peoples. Music director at a radio station in French Indochina 1930–35; after World War II established as a conductor and opera composer (*Atlantide,* 1954; *Miguel de Mañara,* 1956). Also wrote concertos for trumpet, trombone, guitar; *Symphonie du Tiers-Monde* (1967), *Chant pour Vietnam* (symphonic poem, 1968).

Tomasini, Alois Luigi (b. Pesaro, 22 June 1741; d. Eisenstadt, 25 Apr. 1808). Composer and violinist. Became friend and possible pupil of Haydn while in Prince Paul Anton Esterházy's orchestra (1756–90); in 1802 named director of chamber music to the Esterházy family. Haydn dedicated violin concertos to him. Works include a few symphonies and violin concertos, string quartets, 24 baryton trios (for Prince Anton, a baryton player), *duos concertants* for violin, violin sonatas.

Tombeau [Fr., tombstone]. See Lament.

Tomkins, Thomas (b. St. Davids, Pembrokeshire, 1572; d. Martin Hussingtree, Worcester, buried 9 June 1656). Composer. *Instructor choristarum* at Worcester Cathedral, 1596; may have studied with Byrd. By 1620 Gentleman in Ordinary of the Chapel Royal choir; 1621, organist there; probably senior organist with the death of Orlando Gibbons in 1628. Active at Worcester Cathedral until 1646. Wrote 5 services; over 100 anthems (95 are in *Musica Deo sacra et ecclesiae anglicanae*, London, 1668); madrigals (including *When David Heard*); about 70 instrumental works.

Tommasini, Vincenzo (b. Rome, 17 Sept. 1878; d. there, 23 Dec. 1950). Composer. Studied violin, piano, and composition at the Liceo di S. Cecilia in Rome and at the Hochschule für Musik in Berlin with Max Bruch. Early works show Debussy's influence; during the 1930s was influenced by the neoclassical movement. Best remembered for *The Good-Humored Ladies* (1916), a ballet suite arranged from the harpsichord music of Domenico Scarlatti.

Tom-tom. (1) A cylindrical drum without snares, usually double headed, used in *drum sets, often in more than one size. Typical examples are 20 to 50 cm. high, 15 to 25 cm. in diameter, and are played with sticks, mallets, and brushes. (2) In colloquial usage, any African or American Indian drum, or the steady beating of such a drum.

Ton [Fr.]. (1) Pitch, tone. (2) Mode, key. (3) Whole tone. (4) Crook of a horn (*ton du cor, ton de rechange*). (5) Pitch pipe.
[Ger.]. (6) Pitch, tone. (7) See Meistersinger.

Tonabstand [Ger.]. Interval.

Tonada [Sp.], **toada** [Port.]. Melody, tune. The term is widely applied in Spanish-speaking Latin America and in Brazil to a variety of lyrical song types.

Tonadilla escénica [Sp.]. A short, one-act popular or comic Spanish opera, usually performed between the acts of a larger work. The word *tonadilla* is the diminutive form of *tonada* (from *tono*), meaning song. The *tonada* became important in the latter half of the 17th century as a long, strophic set piece that generally dominated an entire scene within a musical court play.
   In the 18th century, the *tonadilla* began as a self-contained solo song (literally, "little song") appended as the epilogue to a minor theatrical piece such as a *sainete*. When more than one character was intro-

duced into the *tonadilla,* an independent short theatrical form, the so-called *tonadilla escénica,* was born. Antonio Guerrero (ca. 1700–1776) and Luis Misón (d. 1766) were the first composers to cultivate the new genre enthusiastically around 1750. It reached its apogee in the compositions of Pablo Esteve y Grimau (ca. 1730–94) and Blas de Laserna (ca. 1751–1816). Its immense popularity lasted through the first decade of the 19th century.

Tonal. Exhibiting the principles of tonic-dominant or triadic *tonality, as distinct from *modality and other systems of organizing pitch. See also Atonality.

Tonal and real. Two types of answer that may be employed in a *fugue or related imitative work. An answer is termed tonal if it modifies the intervallic content of the subject in certain ways while preserving its essential contours. The most characteristic modification is the answering of a leap of a perfect fifth from tonic to dominant in the subject by a leap of a perfect fourth from dominant to tonic in the answer, as in the accompanying example from Bach's *The *Art of Fugue.* An answer is termed real if the subject is simply transposed to another scale degree, usually the dominant, thus preserving its intervallic content precisely.

Tonality. In Western music, the organized relationships of tones with reference to a definite center, the tonic, and generally to a community of *pitch classes, called a *scale, of which the tonic is the principal tone; sometimes also synonymous with *key. The system of tonality (sometimes termed the tonal system) in use in Western music since about the end of the 17th century embraces twelve major and twelve minor keys, the scales that these keys define, and the subsystem of triads and harmonic functions delimited in turn by those scales [see Harmonic analysis], together with the possibility of interchange of keys (*modulation). A piece embodying this system is said to be tonal. A particular tonality or key is defined and reinforced by the presence of a tonal center, embodied harmonically in the tonic triad; by harmonic progressions pointing to the tonic, especially by strong *cadences; by *pedal points and *ostinato basses; and by essential diatonicism as opposed to chromaticism.

Tonart [Ger.]. *Key (1).

Tonary [Lat. *tonarium, tonarius, tonale*]. A medieval *liturgical book (often incorporated into other books such as the antiphoner or gradual or into theoretical treatises) in which chants of the *Gregorian repertory are classified and listed by *mode.

Tondichtung [Ger.]. Tone poem [see Symphonic poem, Program music].

Tone [Fr. *ton;* Ger. *Ton;* It., Sp. *tono*]. (1) A sound of definite pitch; a pitch. (2) The interval of a whole tone. (3) The character of the sound achieved in performance on an instrument. (4) [Lat. *tonus*] A *psalm tone or other formula for the chanting of a liturgical text.

Tone cluster. A highly dissonant, closely spaced collection of pitches sounded simultaneously, at the piano usually by striking a large number of keys with the hand or arm. The term was coined by Henry Cowell, who made considerable use of tone clusters in his own music from at least 1912.

Tone color [Fr. *timbre,* also Eng.; Ger. *Klangfarbe;* It. *timbro, colore;* Sp. *timbre, color*]. The character of a sound, as distinct from its pitch; hence, the quality of sound that distinguishes one instrument from another. It is largely, though not exclusively, a function of the relative strengths of the harmonics (and sometimes nonharmonic frequencies) present in the sound. See Acoustics.

Tone poem [Ger. *Tondichtung*]. *Symphonic poem.

Tone row. See Twelve-tone music.

Tonfarbe [Ger.]. *Tone color.

Tongeschlecht [Ger.]. Mode, type, as between major and minor.

Tonguing. The use of the tongue for articulation in the playing of wind instruments. The tongue releases the wind stream for an initial attack and interrupts it for successive notes that are separately articulated. Single tonguing, the simplest type, consists in using the tongue as if to pronounce the letter *t* one or more times. On brass instruments and the flute, rapid notes in duple divisions may be played with double tonguing (*t–k, t–k* . . .). Similarly, rapid notes in triple divisions may be played with triple tonguing (*t–t–k, t–t–k* . . . or *t–k–t, t–k–t* . . .). In flutter tonguing [Ger. *Flatterzunge;* It. *frullato*], the tongue is fluttered or trilled against the roof of the mouth, just behind the front teeth.

Tonhöhe [Ger.]. *Pitch (1).

Tonic. See Scale, Scale degrees, Tonality.

Tonic accent. An accent produced by a rise in pitch. See also Accent.

Tonic Sol-fa. A type of musical notation and its associated method of sight-singing, developed in England in the 19th century. Similar systems have been adopted in many countries (e.g., *Tonika-Do* in Germany and the *Kodály method in Hungary and elsewhere).

The system was developed by the Rev. John Curwen (1816–80), beginning in 1841, with the aim of teaching beginners to sing accurately. Adopting many aspects of the method advocated and used by Sarah Glover of Norwich, Curwen employed the *solmization syllables *doh, ray, me, fah, soh, lah,* and *te* for the ascending pitches of the major scale. *Doh* is movable to any pitch, depending on the key of the piece in question [see also Solfège]. For purposes of notation, each syllable is represented by its initial consonant, and the precise pitch is specified in the form "Key C" or "Doh is C." In a minor scale, the tonic is represented by *lah.* If a modulation occurs within a piece, the location of *doh* is shifted. Octaves above and below the central octave are represented, respectively, by superscript and subscript vertical strokes following the consonants; sharped notes add the vowel *e* (pronounced *ee*) to the initial consonant; and flatted notes add the vowel *a* (pronounced *aw*). For drill with students, the teacher may point to a chart, termed a Modulator, that arranges the notation for the scale pattern vertically.

Tonicization [Ger. *Tonikalisierung*]. The momentary treatment of a pitch other than the tonic as if it were the tonic, most often by the introduction of its own leading tone or fourth scale degree or both. The resulting harmony is most likely to be the dominant of the tonicized pitch and is in such a case often termed a secondary or applied *dominant. The triad formed on the leading tone of the tonicized pitch may also function in this way. Tonicization, which may be prolonged beyond a single chord or two, is nevertheless a local phenomenon, as distinct from *modulation, which implies an actual change in tonic. The boundary between the two, however, is not always easily fixed in practice.

Tonika [Ger.]. Tonic; for *Tonika-Do,* see Tonic Sol-fa.

Tonkunst [Ger.]. Music; *Tonkünstler,* composer.

Tonleiter [Ger.]. Scale.

Tono [It., Sp.]. (1) Tone, pitch. (2) Key. (3) Mode. (4) Whole tone. (5) [Sp.] Tune, melody (especially in the period around 1600).

Tonsatz, Tonstück [Ger.]. Composition, piece.

Tonschrift [Ger.]. Notation.

Tonus [Lat., fr. Gr. *tonos*]. (1) Whole tone. (2) Any of the formulas to which liturgical texts are chanted, especially the *psalm tones (including the *tonus peregrinus*) [see also Psalmody]. (3) *Mode. (4) Tone, pitch.

Tordion [Fr.]. See *Tourdion*.

Torelli, Giuseppe (b. Verona, 22 Apr. 1658; d. Bologna, 8 Feb. 1709). Composer and violinist. May have studied with Giuliano Massaroti in Verona. Became a violinist in the Accademia filarmonica in Bologna, 1684; probably in 1692 elevated to the rank of *compositore*. Studied composition with G. A. Perti and played viola at S. Petronio 1686–96; appointed *maestro di concerto* to the Margrave of Brandenburg at Ansbach, 1698; returned to S. Petronio, 1701 until his death. Compositions primarily chamber and orchestral works, the majority for strings. Publications include trio sonatas; sinfonias *(Sinfonie à tre e Concerti à quattro* op. 5, 1692, containing 6 ripieno concertos, the earliest published examples of the genre); concertos and concerti grossi (*Concerti musicali* op. 6, 1698, containing the first 2 published examples of the solo violin concerto); also wrote a large number of unpublished instrumental works.

Tormé [Torme], **Mel** [Melvin Howard] (b. Chicago, Ill., 13 Sept. 1925; d. Los Angeles, 5 June 1999). Popular singer and songwriter. Performed with Chico Marx's band and led the vocal group the Mel-Tones; became successful after World War II singing both jazz and popular songs. Recordings include "Careless Hands" (1949) and "Bewitched" (1950). Also worked as an arranger; composed many songs, including "The Christmas Song (Chestnuts Roasting on an Open Fire)" (1940).

Tornada [Prov.]. See *Envoi*.

Torroba, Federico Moreno. See Moreno Torroba, Federico.

Tortelier, Paul (b. Paris, 21 Mar. 1914; d. Villarceaux, France, 18 Dec. 1990). Cellist and composer. Studied with Gérard Hekking at the Paris Conservatory. Played with the Orchestra of Monte Carlo (1935–37), Boston Symphony (1937–39), and Paris Conservatory Orchestra (1946–47). Embarked on a solo career (American debut at Carnegie Hall, 1955); 1957, appointed professor at the Paris Conservatory. Compositions include several cello concertos and a sonata. Author of *How I Play, How I Teach* (London, 1975).

Tosar, Héctor (b. Montevideo, 18 July 1923). Composer. Studied in the U.S. with Copland and Honegger, and at the Paris Conservatory with Rivier and Milhaud. Taught at the Montevideo and Puerto Rico conservatories. Works include 3 symphonies; *Concertino* (1941) and *Sinfonia concertante* (1957), piano and orchestra; *Aves errantes,* baritone and 11 instruments (1964); *Recitativo y variaciones* (1967) and *A 13* (1970), orchestra; vocal and choral works; chamber music; piano pieces; and songs.

Tosca. Opera in three acts by Puccini (libretto by Giuseppe Giacosa and Luigi Illica, based on Victorien Sardou's drama of the same name), produced in Rome in 1900. Setting: Rome in June of 1800.

Toscanini, Arturo (b. Parma, 25 March 1867; d. New York, 16 Jan. 1957). Conductor. At the Parma Conservatory studied cello, piano, and composition; engaged as a professional cellist. Spent the early years of his conducting career at Italian theaters; music director at the Turin Teatro regio 1895–98. Conducted the premieres of *Pagliacci* in Milan (1892) and *La bohème* in Turin (1896). Artistic director at La Scala in Milan, 1898–1903, 1906–8, 1920–29; returned in 1946 to conduct the first concert at the restored theater. Artistic director of the Metropolitan Opera 1908–15; gave world premiere of *La fanciulla del West* and American premieres of *Boris Godunov* and *Armide;* resigned in 1915. The first non-German to conduct at Bayreuth (1930–31); subsequently refused to conduct there in reaction to Hitler's condemnation of Jewish artists. In 1928 became conductor of an orchestra that combined forces from the New York Symphony and the New York Philharmonic; European tour, 1930; resigned in 1936. From 1937 to 1954 directed the NBC orchestra, a group formed especially for him and with which he made most of his recordings. Considered one of the greatest conductors of modern times, particularly in works of Wagner, Verdi, and Beethoven. Retired in 1954.

Tosi, Pier Francesco (b. Cesena, 13 Aug. 1654; d. Faenza, on or after 16 July 1732). Theorist, composer, castrato singer. From 1693 sang and taught singing in London; 1705–11 composer at the Viennese court; later in Dresden, Bologna, and London. His treatise on singing, *Opinioni de' cantori antichi e moderni* (1723), contains valuable information on late 17th- and early 18th-century performance practice.

Tost Quartets. Popular name for the 12 string quartets by Haydn dedicated to the Viennese merchant and violinist Johann Tost: op. 54, Hob. III:57–59 (completed in 1788); op. 55, Hob. III:60–62 (completed in 1788); and op. 64, Hob. III:63–68 (1790).

Tosti, (Franceso) Paolo (b. Ortano sul Mare, 9 Apr. 1846; d. Rome, 2 Dec. 1916). Composer and singing teacher. Studied violin with Pinto and composition with Conti and Mercadante in Naples. Singing teacher to Princess Margherita of Savoy; settled in London in 1880, appointed singing teacher to the royal family. Composed many Italian, French, and English songs.

Tosto [It.]. Quickly, at once; *più tosto, *piuttosto*, rather, somewhat.

Totenmesse [Ger.]. *Requiem Mass.

Touch. In piano playing, the way in which the keys are depressed so as to produce the desired qualities of sound; also the particular characteristics of any keyboard action according to which greater or lesser force is required in order to depress the keys.

Touche [Fr.]. (1) A key of a keyboard. (2) Fingerboard; *sur la touche,* an instruction to bow over the fingerboard. (3) In the 16th century, fret. (4) Toccata (2).

Touquet [Fr.]. See *Toccato.*

Tourdion, tordion [Fr.]. A 16th-century dance most commonly found as an *after-dance to the *basse danse commune.* Some writers in the 16th century describe it as a kind of *gaillarde* (*gagliarda*), but lighter, faster, and without its vigorous movements.

Tourel [Davidovich], **Jennie** (b. Vitebsk, Belorussia, 22 June ?1900; d. New York, 23 Nov. 1973). Mezzosoprano. Probably fled Russia at the time of the Revolution; settled in Paris and studied with Anna El Tour. Debut in Paris at the Opéra russe, 1931; Metropolitan Opera debut, 1937. Sang Baba the Turk in the premiere of *The Rake's Progress,* 1951; premiered several songs of Hindemith and Poulenc.

Tournemire, Charles (b. Bordeaux, 22 Jan. 1870; d. Arcachon, 3 Nov. 1939). Organist and composer. Studied with César Franck and Charles-Marie Widor at the Paris Conservatory. Organist at Ste. Clothilde in Paris from 1898 to the end of his life. Taught at the Conservatory from 1919. Best known for his organ works, inluding *Triple Choral* (1910), *7 Poèmes-Chorales* (1935), *Suite évocatrice* (1938), and the massive *L'orgue mystique* (1927–32); *5 Improvisations for Organ* (1958) were transcribed by his student Maurice Duruflé from a recorded performance.

Tourte bow. A *bow of the type developed and made beginning in the 1780s by François Tourte (1747–1835).

Tourte, François (b. Paris, 1747; d. there, 26 Apr. 1835). Bow maker. Member of a family of bow makers; François, the most famous, is generally regarded as the "creator" of the design of the modern bow. His bow design (which bow makers have copied for about 200 years) reached its standard probably around 1785; it combined and developed features of earlier bows, including a concave bowstick and a higher, larger head. Credited with a method for obtaining the curvature of the stick by heating and bending it and with the invention of the ferrule, a piece at the end of the frog that spreads the hair and increases the amount of playing surface. The first to use pernambuco wood consistently; standardized the length of the bow; derived a mathematical formula for optimum weight distribution and balance.

Tovey, Donald (Francis) (b. Eton, 17 July 1875; d. Edinburgh, 10 July 1940). Music scholar, composer, and pianist. Studied with Sophie Weisse (piano), Walter Parratt (counterpoint), and James Higgs (composition). In 1894 began a long association with Joachim, often appearing as pianist with the latter's quartet; performed his own works in London, Vienna, and Berlin. In 1914 named Reid professor of music at Edinburgh Univ., and in 1917 founded the Reid Orchestra; program notes for these concerts were later incorporated into *Essays in Musical Analysis.* Continued to concertize and compose (*The Bride of Dionysus,* opera, 1929; cello concerto written for Casals, 1935) but best known for his analytical writings, which remain influential to this day. Writings (all published in London) include *A Companion to the Art of Fugue* (1931), *Essays in Musical Analysis* (1935–39; R: 1981), *Essays in Musical Analysis: Chamber Music* (1944; R: 1972), *Beethoven* (1944), *Essays and Lectures on Music* (1949).

Tower, Joan (b. New Rochelle, N.Y., 6 Sept. 1938). Composer, pianist. Studied at Bennington College and at Columbia Univ. with Otto Luening and Chou Wen-chung. While in school organized the Da Capo Chamber Players, a contemporary music ensemble; most of her early compositions were written for this group. *Amazon II* (1979), her first orchestral work, was a revision of an earlier piece for chamber ensemble (*Amazon I,* 1977). Works include *Sequoia* (orchestra, 1981); *Noon Dance* (chamber ensemble, 1982); *Silver Ladders* (orchestra, 1986); *Fanfare for the Uncommon Woman no. 4* (orchestra, 1990); concerto for orchestra (1991); piano, clarinet, flute, and violin concertos; chamber music.

Toy(e). A light piece for lute or virginals from the end of the 16th century or the first half of the 17th.

Toy Symphony. A composition often attributed to Haydn (Hob. II:47*) and scored for violins, violas, horns (in some versions), and continuo, and for such instruments as toy drum, rattle, wind machine, whistle, cuckoo, quail (in some versions a screech owl), toy trumpet, and *cimbelstern* (an organ stop with a continuous tinkling sound). The piece, completed by 1786, is now variously attributed to Leopold Mozart (whose attributed version contains additional movements), Michael Haydn, and P. Edmund Angerer.

Tpt. Abbr. for trumpet.

Tr. Abbr. for trill, treble, transpose.

Trabaci, Giovanni Maria (b. Monte Pelusio [now Irsina], ca. 1575; d. Naples, 31 Dec. 1647). Composer. Tenor at the Church of the Annunziata, Naples, 1594; 1601, organist at the Spanish viceregal chapel in Naples; 1614, *maestro di cappella* there. Compositions include over 200 sacred and secular vocal works and 165 works for keyboard.

Tracker action. The traditional key action of the organ, in which the key is directly connected by a thin wooden strip, called a tracker, to the valve beneath the pipe. See Organ.

Tract [Lat. *tractus*]. In *Gregorian chant, an item of the *Proper of the *Mass that is sung before the Gospel, in the place of the *alleluia, on certain days during the season from Septuagesima Sunday through Lent to Holy Saturday, on certain of the Ember Days, and in the *Requiem Mass. Its texts consist of from two to ten or more verses, usually from the Psalms. Since it is sung without any refrain or response, it is an example of direct *psalmody.

Traetta [Trajetta], **Tommaso (Michele Francesco Saverio)** (b. Bitonto, near Bari, 30 Mar. 1727; d. Venice, 6 Apr. 1779). Composer. Studied in Naples with Porpora and Durante. First opera, *Il Farnace,* performed in Naples in 1751. In 1758 became *maestro di cappella* to the court of Parma; 1760–63 wrote operas for Turin, Vienna, and Mannheim; had great success with *Ifigenia in Tauride* (1763). In 1765 became director of the Conservatorio dell'Ospedaletto at Venice; 1768, employed as singing instructor and opera director by Catherine II of Russia in St. Petersburg, where his greatest opera, *Antigone,* was performed in 1772. Settled permanently in Venice by 1777. In addition to over 40 operas, wrote a number of other sacred and secular vocal works.

Tragédie lyrique [Fr.]. French serious opera of the 17th and 18th centuries; synonymous with *tragédie en musique.* It normally contains a prologue plus five acts and draws its subject from Greek mythology or chivalric romance.

Tragic Overture. See *Tragische Ouvertüre.*

Tragic Symphony. Schubert's title for his Symphony no. 4 in C minor D. 417 (completed in 1816); also the popular name for Mahler's Symphony no. 6

in A minor (1903–4, rev. 1906 and after) and Bruckner's Symphony no. 5 in B♭ major (1875–76).

Tragische Ouvertüre [Ger., Tragic Overture]. An orchestral composition by Brahms, op. 81 (1880, rev. 1881). It may have arisen from a request for incidental music to a new production of Goethe's *Faust* at the Vienna Burgtheater, a production that failed to materialize.

Traîner [Fr.]. To drag; *sans traîner,* without dragging.

Trampler, Walter (b. Munich, 25 Aug. 1915; d. Port Joli, Nova Scotia, 27 Sept. 1997). Violist. Studied with his father and at the State Academy of Music in Munich. Debut in Munich as a violinist in Beethoven's Concerto, 1933; played viola in the orchestra of Radio Deutschlandsender (1935–38) before immigrating to the U.S. Joined the orchestra of the City Center in New York (1946–48); played in the New Music Quartet (1947–55); appeared with the Juilliard, Guarneri, Budapest, and Emerson Quartets and the Beaux Arts Trio. In 1969 joined the Chamber Music Society of Lincoln Center. Premiered many works, made solo and chamber recordings, and held appointments at Juillard, Yale, and Boston Univ.

Tranquillo [It.]. Tranquil, calm.

Transcendental Etudes. See *Études d'exécution transcendante.*

Transcription. (1) The adaptation of a composition for a medium other than its original one, e.g., of vocal music for instruments or of a piano work for orchestra; also the resulting work [see also Arrangement, Intabulation]. (2) The translation of music from one notational system into another, especially from earlier systems into the system in current use. (3) The reduction of music from live or recorded sound to written notation.

Transfigured Night. See *Verklärte Nacht.*

Transformation of themes. The alteration of themes for the sake of changing their character while

Transformation of themes. Berlioz, *Symphonie fantastique.*

retaining their essential identity. It differs from *development in that the resulting theme is likely to be treated with as much independence as the original. The term normally excludes such abstract devices as *augmentation and diminution. Although the technique is found early in the history of the *suite of dance movements, the term is most often applied to music of the 19th century. The first characteristic use of the technique occurs in Berlioz's treatment of the *idée fixe* in his *Symphonie fantastique* [see Ex.]. Liszt used it extensively in his symphonic poems. Wagner's use of the *Leitmotif* is at the least very closely related.

Transition. *Bridge (2).

Transposing instruments. Instruments whose notated pitch is different from their sounded pitch. Except for those whose notated and sounded pitches differ by one or more octaves (usually for the sake of avoiding the use of multiple ledger lines), most such instruments are identified by the letter name of the pitch class of their fundamental, e.g., trumpet in B♭. The letter name identifies the pitch class that is sounded when a notated C is played. Thus, when the alto saxophone in E♭ plays a notated C, an E♭ a sixth below sounds. A few nontransposing instruments are also identified in this way, however: e.g., the tenor trombone in B♭ and the tuba in BB♭, which sound as notated. The direction of transposition may be up or down and may exceed an octave. For precise intervals of transposition, see the entries on individual instruments.

Transposition. The rewriting or performance of music at a pitch other than the original one. This entails raising or lowering each pitch of the original music by precisely the same interval. In tonal music, it results in changing the key of the original. Works are often transposed to accommodate the ranges of singers. The player of an instrument at one pitch will be required to transpose in order to perform a part written at another pitch; e.g., the player of a trumpet in B♭ will be required to transpose in order to perform from a part for trumpet in C or D, in the first case by raising every pitch a whole tone, in the second by raising every pitch a major third. See also Transposing instruments.

Transverse flute. A *flute in which the air stream is directed across the axis of its length rather than along it; thus, e.g., the modern flute as distinct from the *recorder.

Trapp, Max (b. Berlin, 1 Nov. 1887; d. there, 29 May 1971). Composer. At the Hochschule für Musik in Berlin studied piano with Ernst von Dohnányi, composition with Paul Juon. Taught at the Berlin Hochschule (1920–34), the Dortmund Conservatory

(1924–30), the Prussian Academy (1934–45), and the Berlin Conservatory (1950–53). Musical style emulated the late Romantic manner of Richard Strauss. Works include *Der letzte König von Orplid* (incidental music, 1922); 7 symphonies; 3 concertos for orchestra; concertos for violin, piano, and cello; many songs and piano pieces.

Traps. *Drum set; also the nondrum items used in such a set by theater drummers.

Traquenard [Fr., ambling gait]. A *gavottelike dance movement in some late 17th-century German orchestral suites (Georg Muffat, J. C. F. Fischer).

Trascinare, trascinando [It.]. To drag, dragging; *senza trascinare*, without dragging.

Traste [Sp.]. Fret.

Trattenuto [It.]. Held back, *ritardando*.

Tratto [It.]. Drawn out.

Traubel, Helen (Francesca) (b. St. Louis, Mo., 20 June 1899; d. Santa Monica, 28 July 1972). Soprano. Studied with Vetta Karst; operatic debut at the Metropolitan Opera, 1937, as Mary in Walter Damrosch's *The Man without a Country*. Concentrated on Wagnerian roles; during the 1940s regarded as the leading Wagnerian soprano at the Metropolitan; left in 1953 after disagreements with the management over her nightclub appearances.

Trauermarsch [Ger.]. Funeral march.

Trauermusik [Ger.]. Funeral music.

Trauernd [Ger.]. Mourning, lamenting.

Trauer-Ode [Ger., Funeral Ode]. A secular cantata by Bach, BWV 198 (1727), composed on the death of the Electress Christiane of Saxony. The text, beginning "Lass, Fürstin, lass noch einen Strahl," is an ode by Johann Christoph Gottsched.

Trauer-Symphonie [Ger., Mourning Symphony]. Popular name for Haydn's Symphony no. 44 in E minor Hob. I:44 (completed by 1772), apparently so called because the third movement (Adagio) was performed at a memorial concert in Berlin in September 1809.

Träumerisch [Ger.]. Dreamy.

Traurig [Ger.]. Sad, mournful.

Trautonium. An *electronic instrument exhibited in 1930 by Friedrich Trautwein. It produced, by entirely electronic means, only one pitch at a time, though its timbre could be varied widely. The performer controlled pitch by varying the point at which a wire was pressed against a metal bar. It was popular in the

1930s, and Richard Strauss, Hindemith, and Paul Dessau composed works for it.

Traverso [It.], **traversière** [Fr.], **Traversflöte** [Ger.]. *Transverse flute.

Traviata, La [It., The Strayed One]. Opera in three acts by Verdi (libretto by Francesco Maria Piave, after the play *La dame aux camélias* by Alexandre Dumas), first produced in Venice in 1853. Setting: Paris and environs, about 1700 (now more often set about 1850).

Travis, Roy (Elihu) (b. New York, 24 June 1922). Composer. Studied at Columbia and Juilliard, and in Paris with Darius Milhaud. Taught at Columbia (1952–53) and Mannes College of Music (1952–57). In 1957 joined the faculty at UCLA; at the Institute of Ethnomusicology there became acquainted with African music. Works include *African Sonata* (piano, 1968), *The Passion of Oedipus* (opera, Los Angeles, 1968), *The Black Bacchants* (opera, 1982), *Switched-on Ashanti* (flute and tape, 1973).

Tre [It.]. Three; *a tre voci*, for three voices; for *tre corde*, see *Una corda*.

Treble [fr. Lat. *triplum*]. The highest part; the highest range of voices; the highest-pitched members of some families of instruments, e.g., treble *viol or *recorder (in this case not the single highest). With respect to voices, the term is now generic for high voices, having been displaced as the specific term by soprano. See also Clef, Descant, Sight, Voice.

Trecento [It.]. The 14th century [see *Ars nova*].

Treibend [Ger.]. Driving, hurrying.

Tremblay, Gilles (b. Arvida, Quebec, 6 Sept. 1932). Composer and pianist. Studied at the Montreal Conservatory with Germaine Malépart (piano) and Claude Champagne (composition) and at the Paris Conservatory with Messiaen and Yvonne Loriod. Also studied ondes martenot and worked at the RTF. First major work, *Cantique de durées* (1960), reflects influence of Messiaen. Taught at the Montreal Conservatory from 1962. During the 1960s explored rhythmic textures and instrumental sonorities in chamber works, including the *Champs* series and *Kékoba* (voices, percussion, ondes martenot, 1965; rev. 1967); during the 1970s composed large pieces for orchestra, including *Jeu de solstices* (1974) and *Vers le soleil* (1978). Other works include *Un 9*, mime, 2 percussion instruments, 2 trumpets (1987); *Cèdres en voiles*, cello (1989).

Tremblement [Fr.]. In the 17th and 18th centuries, the *trill, the most important French ornament of the period.

Tremolando [It.]. With *tremolo.

Tremolo [It.]. Usually, the quick and continuous reiteration of a single pitch. On stringed instruments, it is produced by a rapid up-and-down movement of the bow, indicated as in Ex. 1. This effect is called for in violin music of the early 17th century, and is a feature of Monteverdi's *stile *concitato*. It has remained in continuous use. Eighteenth-century names for the string tremolo are [It.] *bombo* and [Ger.] *Schwärmer.* The term tremolo also refers, however, to a succession of repeated notes slightly articulated without a change in direction of the bow, as in Ex. 2, this being termed a slurred tremolo and sometimes indicated by a wavy line, and to a rapid alternation between two pitches of a chord, as in Ex. 3, this being termed a fingered tremolo because it is produced by rapid movement of a finger on the fingerboard rather than by rapid movement of the bow.

In violin music of the 18th century, a tremolo known as the undulating tremolo [It. *ondeggiando;* Fr. *ondulé*] occurs frequently. It is produced by an undulating motion of the bow arm, resulting in alternate bowing on two strings (or more when the technique is applied to the playing of arpeggios). This bowing can be used to produce either a reiteration of a single pitch alternately on a stopped string and an open string (in which case it is called *bariolage,* Ex. 4) or an alternation between two (or more) pitches. It is indicated by a wavy line, as in Ex. 5. The addition of a slur indicates that several notes are to be taken in a single bow stroke, i.e., without a change in the direction of the bow. The term tremolo was also used in the 18th century for *vibrato produced by the left hand, and this too could be indicated by a wavy line. Finally, the term could also mean *trill.

The tremolo of strings is sometimes imitated on the piano by the rapid alternation of a pitch and its octave, or of the several pitches of a chord. In organ music, the term tremolo is applied to the effect produced by the *tremulant stop. This effect, however, more nearly approximates the string player's *vibrato. In singing, the term now usually refers to excessive vibrato that leads to deviations in pitch. The rapid repetition of a single pitch, however, termed a *trillo,* is an effect widely used in the 17th century and was usually written out in small note-values. During this period, *tremolo* referred to various kinds of *trill or *mordent. In the 18th century, the rapid repetition of a single pitch in vocal music fell into disuse and began to be known by such pejorative terms as [Fr.] *chevrotement* and [Ger.] *Bockstriller* (goat's trill). See also Ornamentation, Bowing.

Tremulant. A mechanical device applied to the wind supply of organs to cause regular fluctuations of pressure to the wind-chests, thus producing a *vibrato.

Trenchmore. An English country dance of the 16th and 17th centuries in fast triple meter with dotted rhythms.

Trent Codices. Six manuscript volumes (Codice 87–92) of 15th-century polyphonic music in the National Museum in the Castello del Buonconsiglio at Trent, Italy. A seventh volume (Codice 93) is almost identical to the fourth. The six volumes contain 1,585 compositions from the first 74 years of the 15th century by English, Flemish, French, German, and Italian composers.

Trent, Council of. See Council of Trent.

Trepak [Russ.]. A Cossack dance in fast duple meter. An example occurs in Tchaikovsky's *Nutcracker.*

Tres [Sp.]. A small guitar of Latin America with three courses, which are sometimes double or triple.

Triad [Fr. *triade, accord parfait;* Ger. *Dreiklang;* It. *triade, accordo perfetto;* Sp. *triada, acorde perfecto*]. A chord consisting of three pitches, the adjacent pitches being separated by a third, and thus the whole capable of notation on three adjacent lines or three adjacent spaces of the staff; also termed the common chord. There are four types [Ex.]: (1) the major triad, in which the interval between the lower two pitches is a major third and that between the upper two a minor third, the interval between the lowest and highest pitches thus being a perfect fifth; (2) the minor triad, in which the lower interval is a minor third and the upper a major third, the outer interval being a perfect fifth; (3) the diminished triad, in which both internal intervals are minor thirds and the outer interval is a diminished fifth; and (4) the augmented triad, in which both internal intervals are major thirds and the outer interval is an augmented fifth. The major and minor triads include only consonant intervals and are thus consonant chords. The diminished and augmented triads both include a dissonant interval and are thus dissonant chords [see Consonance and dissonance]. For the various positions in which triads can be stated, see Inversion; see also Harmony, Harmonic analysis.

Triads can be formed on any *scale degree of the major or minor scale (i.e., with any degree as the lowest pitch), those on degrees I, IV, and V being termed the primary triads. Together these three include all of the pitches of the scale in question. In a major scale, the triad on the tonic is major; in a minor scale it is minor. The concepts triad and triad inversion have been central to discussions of tonality since the 18th century, the first explicit theoretical accounts of them dating from around 1600. The major and minor triads themselves occur regularly in English music beginning in the 13th century. They are prominent in Continental music from the 15th century on.

Trial of Lucullus, The. Opera in one act by Sessions (libretto by Bertolt Brecht), produced in Berkeley, California, in 1947.

Triangle [Fr. *triangle;* Ger. *Triangel;* It. *triangolo;* Sp. *triángulo*]. A percussion instrument made from a steel rod bent into the shape of a triangle but with the ends of the rod not joined at the corner. It is struck with a metal beater, producing a sound of high but indefinite pitch. Known in Europe since the Middle Ages (then usually with rings on the lowest side), it became especially prominent in the 18th century under the influence of *Janissary music. See ill. under Percussion instruments.

Tribrach, tribrachic. See Prosody.

Trichord. A collection of three pitches, especially any one of the four making up a *twelve-tone row.

Tricinium [Lat.]. A three-voice vocal or instrumental composition of the 16th and 17th centuries, especially one related in some measure to the didactic repertory of the *bicinium.

Trill [also shake; Fr. *tremblement, cadence;* Ger. *Triller;* It. *trillo, tremolo, groppo;* Sp. *trino, quiebro reyterado, redoble*]. An ornament consisting of the more or less rapid alternation of a note with the one next above it in the prevailing key or harmony. In current musical notation, it is often indicated by the abbreviation *tr,* but the signs used have varied in the course of its history, as have such conventions of its execution as whether it begins on the main note or the ornamenting note, whether it is preceded by an auxiliary ornamenting note, and whether any preceding note is to be played on the beat or before it.

Trill-like ornaments for both voice and organ were described by Jerome of Moravia toward the end of the 13th century, those for voice perhaps being more like a violent vibrato and those for organ requiring that the main note be held while the upper one was reiterated [see Ornamentation, Mordent]. Ornament signs in 14th- and 15th-century keyboard tablatures may have indicated trills as well as mordents. Written models for trills and trill-like ornaments appeared in treatises beginning with Ganassi (1535). These were generally known by some variant of the name *tremolo* or, when followed by a suffix (turn), *groppo; tremolo* was also applied to mordents and *groppo* to ornamental passages containing trill elements, but winding around two or more notes [Exx. 1–3]. *Trillo* was used by Caccini (in *Le nuove musiche*, Florence, 1601/2) and others for the rapid or accelerating reiteration of a single pitch, but the meanings of *trillo* and *tremolo* were sometimes reversed, and there was no consistency in the use of any of these terms. The Spanish *quiebro* and *redoble* were roughly analogous in range of meaning to the Italian (and later, German) *tremolo* and *groppo*, respectively. *Groppi* were often written out by 16th- and 17th-century composers, but performers were expected to supply others, especially at cadences. Simpler trills were ordinarily left to the performer.

1. Giovanni Luca Conforti, *Breve et facile maniera* (1593?).
2, 3. Girolamo Diruta, *Il transilvano* (1593).

Signs for the trill were rare until the mid-17th century. Not until the second half of the 17th century are trills indicated by signs whose meaning is spelled out in tables, prefaces, or treatises, and this growing precision of usage narrowed options and engendered the elaborate codes of the 18th century. Much was still left to the performer, however. In the Baroque period, except for certain short trills (accent trills, like the *Schneller* and *martellement*, and trills resolving appoggiaturas, the *Pralltriller*, etc.), which never exceeded two or three repercussions, the longer the trill the better, whatever the symbol.

The speed of a trill is important to its effect and was often mentioned. The *groppi* in 16th-century music were apparently very fast. In the Baroque period, keyboard trills were normally rapid and even, though some writers allowed a slight broadening in slow, expressive pieces. Vocal trills evidently varied considerably. A few writers seem to imply an uneven execution, with the main notes receiving more emphasis than the auxiliaries. Unevenness was an essential characteristic of the *ribattuta* [see Ex. 4]. Accelerating trills other than the *ribattuta* were common in

the Baroque period, but may have become unfashionable later. Instruction books for melody instruments generally fall between voice and keyboard. Leopold Mozart's violin treatise (1756) divided trills into slow, medium, fast, and accelerating, and warned against too much speed. Trills in 19th- and 20th-century music are usually fast.

4. Mattheson, *Der vollkommene Capellmeister* (1739).

The issue that has most engaged modern scholarship is whether the starting note should be the main note or the auxiliary. In the 16th century, *tremoli* (which included trills and mordents) began on the main note, while cadential *groppi* (trills on the leading note with suffixes and sometimes additional figures) generally began on the auxiliary, sometimes after dwelling on the main note [Ex. 1]. Usage in the 17th century appears to have varied greatly according to time, place, and medium, and sources are inadequate to establish common practices within this diversity. It appears that a preference for upper-note starts developed in French and English instrumental music during the second half of the century, and that by 1700 it had spread to Germany and perhaps to Italy.

The upper-note, on-beat start was clearly normal for trills from the late 17th to the early 19th century, in all countries and all media [Ex. 5]. Within this common practice, however, there was the greatest possible diversity of subspecies, conflicting terminology, and contradictory descriptions. Certainly, many trills were begun on the main note. Most fell into one of two types: trills following a written note a step above a trilled one, which was felt to do duty as the initial upper auxiliary (but even here, many writers preferred a repetition of the auxiliary, where time allowed, or a delay of the main note to give the effect of a tie to a downbeat auxiliary) [Ex. 6], and short, main-note trills that served as accents (*martellement*, *Schneller*).

5. Bach, *Clavier-Büchlein vor Wilhelm Friedemann Bach* (begun 1720).   6. Rameau, "De la méchanique des doigts," in *Pièces de clavecin* (1724).

The terms preparation, *Vorbereitung*, and *appuy*, all of which refer to the initial auxiliary of a trill, were used with the greatest inconsistency to mean either the simple presence of this first note or its prolongation, which might vary from a slight dwelling to half the value of the written note to nearly all its value. In the absence of a clear description or table, there is no way to be sure which was meant. The same is true of a small note indicating the auxiliary; this may or may not mean a prolongation. Thus, a trill *sans appuy* (without preparation) or without the auxiliary shown by a small note does not necessarily start on the main note.

The upper-note start was gradually abandoned during the first half of the 19th century, though Chopin preferred it, and it evidently persisted in Italian opera. Hummel and Czerny may have established the norm of the main-note start, which still persists and is applied by many pianists and orchestral players to 18th-century repertory. When the upper auxiliary is written as a small note, it is now normally played before the beat so that the trill may begin with the main note.

It is often more difficult to decide how to end a trill than how to begin it. One may stop, usually with a slight acceleration or "snap" (C. P. E. Bach) on the main note, early if the trill is short, or just for an instant at the end if it is long (François Couperin's *point d'arrêt*). One may stop, then very lightly anticipate the following note (Bacilly's *liaison*). One may trill smoothly into the following note (unavoidable if the trilled note is very short). Finally, one may add a "suffix" (*Nachschlag*), a dip to the lower auxiliary before the final main note [Exx. 1 and 7]. (The resemblance to an appended mordent or turn is reflected in two of the signs for a trill with suffix; Ex 8.) Normally one trills smoothly into the suffix, which connects without a break to the following note, but occasionally the suffix is separated from the trill by a pause or rest. The suffix is also used to end a trill that is not immediately followed by another note, e.g., a trilled fermata. Suffixes are indicated by signs or (more commonly) written out. They may also be added by the performer when not indicated.

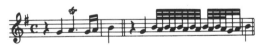

7. Johann Gottfried Walther, "Praecepta der musicalischen Composition" (1708).

8.

Triller [Ger.]. *Trill; *Trillerkette*, chain or series of trills.

Trillo [It.]. In 17th-century Italy, a vocal *tremolo (rapid repetition of the same pitch); later, a *trill [see also Ornamentation].

Trimble, Lester (b. Bangor, Wis., 29 Aug. 1920; d. New York, 21 Dec. 1986). Composer. Studied with Nikolai Lopatnikoff at Carnegie Institute of Technology and in Paris with Honegger, Milhaud, and Boulanger. Music critic at the *New York Herald Tribune* 1952 to the early 1960s. From 1963 to 1968 taught composition at the Univ. of Maryland, from 1971 at Juilliard. From 1970 to 1976 composed a series of "Panels" for various ensembles, consisting of independently composed modules, assembled by the performers. Other works include string quartets, symphonies, violin concerto.

Trinklied [Ger.]. Drinking song.

Trio [It.]. (1) In dance movements from the 17th century onward, a contrasting second or middle section appearing between the principal dance and its repetition (e.g., minuet–trio–minuet da capo). Trios are also found in *scherzos and *marches. The term derives from the 17th-century practice of scoring the second of two alternating dances for three instruments, frequently two oboes and bassoon. See also *Alternativo*.

(2) In the Baroque period, a strict contrapuntal composition in three parts without continuo.

(3) From the Classical period to the present, a composition for three solo instruments.

(4) During the same period, an ensemble of three solo instruments. The most important types of trio are the piano trio, for piano, violin, and cello, and the string trio, for violin, viola, and cello or two violins and cello. The piano trio derives from the *accompanied sonata for keyboard and violin [see also Sonata], the cello being added initially as simplified doubling for the bass line of the keyboard part. In the earliest examples, the violin is also subsidiary. In Haydn's many piano trios, the violin achieves considerable independence; the cello, however, continues its doubling function for the most part. Mozart's six late piano trios give the cello somewhat greater freedom, and in Beethoven's opp. 70 and 97 (the *Archduke Trio*) and Schubert's opp. 99–100, both string instruments attain true obbligato status.

The piano trio remained popular throughout the 19th century, with notable contributions by Mendelssohn (2), Franck (4), Schumann (3), Brahms (3), Smetana (1), and Dvořák (3). Examples from the 20th century include single works by Roussel, Ives, Ravel, and Fauré.

The string trio is a descendant of the *trio sonata of the Baroque; indeed, for many early Classical "trios," a keyboard continuo was doubtless intended. However, Haydn's many early string trios—some evidently dating from before 1760—are probably analogous to his early string quartets in dispensing with continuo [see String quartet]. A special mid-18th-century type of trio was the so-called orchestral trio for two violins and bass, which could be performed either with doubled parts or with a single player on each part. The small repertory of later Viennese string trios, nearly all for violin, viola, and cello, includes Mozart's K. 563, Beethoven's four trios opp. 3 and 9, and two trios by Schubert (one incomplete). The later 19th century generally neglected the string trio, but the 20th century has produced works by Hindemith, Webern, Roussel, Schoenberg, and Milhaud.

(5) A composition for three solo voices with or without accompaniment (more properly termed a *terzett; see also *Tricinium*).

(6) An ensemble of three solo voices.

Trio sonata. The commonest type of Baroque instrumental chamber music. Written in three parts—two upper lines, normally in the same register, and basso continuo [see Thoroughbass]—it often includes a *concertante* bass as well. It requires four performers: two melody instruments for the top lines, normally violins; a melody bass instrument (bass viol, violone, cello) that either reinforces the bass line of the continuo part or, as a *concertante* part, participates in imitations with the upper parts; and a chord-playing instrument such as organ, harpsichord, or theorbo to realize the harmonies of the continuo. Until the 1660s, occasional options in instruments were offered, such as *cornetto* for the violin, and trombone or bassoon for the stringed bass instrument. In the 18th century, flutes were often alternatives to the violin.

The origins of the genre lie in the adaptation to instruments of the three-part scoring common in Italian vocal music at the end of the 16th century. The earliest published trio sonatas are by Salomone Rossi (titled sinfonia, 1607) and Giovanni Paolo Cima (1610). At mid-century, two different types appeared: the *sonata da camera* and the *sonata da chiesa*. Corelli composed examples of both (first published between 1681 and 1694). From the 1750s, the term was often equated with *trio, *partita, *divertimento, and, as it had been since the 17th century, *sinfonia. During the 1760s, the continuo was increasingly abandoned, and by 1775 the trio sonata had largely disappeared.

The term has also been applied to Bach's organ sonatas for two manuals and pedal BWV 525–30 and to sonatas for violin and harpsichord by Bach and Jean-Joseph Cassanéa de Mondonville (1711–72) in which the keyboard supplies two obligatory parts—the second upper part and the bass.

Triole [Ger.], **triolet** [Fr.]. Triplet.

Trionfo di Dori, Il [It.]. See *Triumphes of Oriana, The.*

Tripla [Lat.]. (1) Plural of *triplum. (2) With respect to *proportions, triple. (3) *Proportz* [see *Nachtanz*].

Triple concerto. A concerto for three solo instruments and orchestra, e.g., Beethoven's op. 56 for violin, cello, and piano with orchestra.

Triple counterpoint. See Invertible counterpoint.

Triple-croche [Fr.]. Thirty-second *note.

Triple fugue. See Double fugue.

Triple meter, time. See Meter.

Triple tonguing. See Tonguing.

Triplet [Fr. *triolet;* Ger. *Triole;* It. *terzina;* Sp. *tresillo*]. Three notes of equal value to be played in the time normally occupied by two notes of the same value, indicated by the figure 3, often with a slur, above or below the group. See also Dotted notes.

Triplum [Lat., pl. *tripla*]. In music from the *Notre Dame repertory until the 15th century, the third part above the tenor; *organum triplum,* *organum in three parts.

Tristan chord. The first chord sounded in Wagner's *Tristan und Isolde* and prominent elsewhere in the work: f–b–d♯′–g♯′. Although it can be described as a half-diminished *seventh chord, its function in the terms of *harmonic analysis has been a matter of dispute.

Tristan und Isolde. Opera ("music drama") in three acts by Wagner (to his own "poem," based on Gottfried von Strassburg), composed between 1856 and 1859 and produced in Munich in 1865. Setting: aboard a ship, Cornwall, and Brittany, in legendary times.

Tristan Schalmei [Ger.]. A shawm pitched in F built by the firm of Wilhelm Heckel to play the part of the shepherd's pipe at the opening of act 3 of Wagner's *Tristan und Isolde.* See also Heckelclarina.

Tristano, Lennie [Leonard Joseph] (b. Chicago, 19 March 1919; d. New York, 18 Nov. 1978). Jazz pianist, teacher, and bandleader. Blind from childhood. Studied at the American Conservatory, Chicago; worked as a teacher. In New York led a sextet which included his pupils Lee Konitz, tenor saxophonist Warne Marsh, and guitarist Billy Bauer (1948–49). Recorded "Subconscious-Lee" and "Crosscurrent" (both 1949), establishing a manner of playing cool jazz identified with him. Reunited with Konitz and Marsh intermittently, 1958–66.

Tritone [Lat. *tritonus*]. An interval consisting of three whole tones; hence, the augmented fourth (e.g., f–b) or, because in equal temperament the inversion of this interval yields an interval of the same size, the diminished fifth (e.g., b–f′). It has been regarded as a dissonance since the Middle Ages, when it was nicknamed the *diabolus in musica* (the devil in music) and was the object of prohibitions by theorists [see also *Mi-fa*, *Musica ficta*, Hexachord]. Its role as a dissonance in tonal music has been principally as part of the dominant *seventh chord, in which it represents the fourth and seventh scale degrees.

Tritonius, Petrus [Treybenreif, Peter] (b. Bozen [Bolzano], ca. 1465; d. Hall [Solbad Hall]?, probably 1525). Composer. Studied at Vienna Univ. and Ingolstadt Univ. Under the humanist Conradus Celtis composed widely admired 4-voiced settings of Horatian odes; taught at Vienna Univ. under Celtis until the latter's death in 1508. Returned to the Tirol, where he taught at Bozen, Schwaz, and Hall. His bilingual Latin-German *Hymnarius* (Schwaz, 1524) is the first-known printed Catholic hymnbook.

Trittico, Il [It., The Triptych]. A cycle of three independent one-act operas by Puccini, first produced in New York in 1918. (1) *Il tabarro* (The Cloak), libretto by Giuseppe Adami, after Didier Gold's play *La Houppelande*. Setting: a barge on the Seine, early in the 20th century. (2) *Suor Angelica* (Sister Angelica), libretto by Giovacchino Forzano. Setting: a convent in Italy at the end of the 17th century. (3) *Gianni Schicchi*, libretto by Giovacchino Forzano, developed from a few lines in Dante's *Inferno*, canto 30. Setting: a bedroom in a house in Florence in 1299.

Tritto [Tritta], **Giacomo (Domenico Mario Antonio Pasquale Giuseppe)** (b. Altamura, 2 Apr. 1733; d. Naples, 16 or 17 Sept. 1824). Composer. Studied at the Pietà dei Turchini conservatory; later taught there (pupils included Bellini, Conti, Mercadante, Spontini, and Meyerbeer). Wrote upwards of 50 operas, sacred works, cantatas, other small pieces.

Triumphes of Oriana, The. A collection of 25 English madrigals in five and six voices by Morley, Weelkes, and 21 others, in praise of Elizabeth I and published by Thomas Morley in 1601. Each piece concludes with the line "Long live fair Oriana."

Trojans, The. See *Troyens, Les*.

Tromba [It.]. Trumpet; *t. a macchina (ventile)*, valved trumpet; *t. bassa*, bass trumpet; *t. da tirarsi, t. spezzata*, slide trumpet.

Tromba marina [It., marine trumpet or trumpet marine; Fr. *trompette marine;* Ger. *Nonnengeige, Trumscheit*]. A one-stringed, bowed instrument, common in Europe from the 15th through the 18th century. In its most developed form it was about two meters long with a narrow, slightly tapered sound box; the bridge had one leg shorter than the other so that it vibrated against the instrument's belly. The origin of its name is not known. See ill. under Violin.

Tromboncino, Bartolomeo (b. Verona, ca. 1470; d. Venice?, 1535 or later). Composer. Played trombone at the Gonzaga court in Mantua; served the Florentine Medici court, 1489–94, then returned to Mantua. Killed his wife for adultery in 1499, and fled Mantua permanently in 1501. In February 1502 he was engaged in Ferrara by Lucrezia Borgia; remained in her service until at least 1508. From at least 1521 lived in Venice. A great early frottolist; some 176 frottole are attributed to him, nearly all in print by 1520. Also composed sacred works.

Trombone [Fr., It.; Ger. *Posaune;* Sp. *trombón*]. A long, narrow brass instrument with tube ends folded to overlap in the center. One resulting U-shaped section is a cylindrical telescoping slide that begins with a mouthpiece. The other section is more conical and ends with an expanded opening or bell. About one-third of the tube length is conical, the rest cylindrical. Trombones are used in European and American symphony orchestras and bands as well as in many types of jazz and popular music. They are most often made of brass (sometimes plated with nickel or silver), but have also been made of German silver and, more rarely, of copper. Special chromium alloys are now used in the slide to lessen friction. See ill. under Brass instruments.

The most common trombone is a tenor instrument in B♭ (fundamental note B♭$_1$) folded to about 1.2 m. in length with approximately 2.75 m. (9 ft.) of tubing. The slide when extended provides enough additional length to lower the pitch of the instrument by up to six half-steps. The seven harmonic series of pitches [see Harmonics (1)] made possible by these seven positions (including the first or fully retracted position) together provide every chromatic note from low E to b♭' and, depending on the player's ability, above as high as f''. Other sizes of trombone, although not often used today, include the soprano or treble in B♭, alto in F or E♭, bass in G$_1$, bass in F$_1$ or E♭$_1$ (*Quart-* or *Quintposaune*), and contrabass in B♭$_2$. Bass trombones are now made with the same tube length as the tenor but with a larger bore and one or two valves, which add enough tubing to lower the pitch a fourth to a sixth. Since the invention of the valve, trombones having valves and no slide have also been made.

Music for tenor or bass trombone is written at concert pitch in the bass clef, switching freely to the tenor clef (c' fourth line) for higher passages. Alto trombone parts are most often written in the alto clef (c' center line).

The earliest evidence suggests that trombones first appeared in southern France or northern Italy sometime in the 15th century. Their ancestry, though vague, probably lies with the longer medieval trumpet, the *buisine* or *tromba*. A larger *tromba* in Italian was a *trombone*, while *buisine* gradually through varied spellings probably became *Posaune* in German. Spanish (*sacabuche*) and French (*saqueboute*) origins are suggested for the English term sackbut, thought to mean literally draw pipe, draw out, or push-pull. By the 16th century, the trombone was well established in England and on the Continent, and Nuremberg, Germany, had become a center of trombone making.

During the 16th and 17th centuries, trombones were regular members of town and court bands. With cornetts they were the principal instruments used to support singing in many churches and were most effectively used in works of Giovanni Gabrieli and Schütz. The earlier part of the 18th century saw a general decline in the use of the instrument. But this trend was reversed later in the century when military bands found the trombone useful and when its ecclesiastical and supernatural associations drew it into the opera orchestras of Gluck and Mozart.

By the 1830s, valve instruments flourished in most military bands. The valve trombone without slide was made as early as the late 1820s, and F valve attachments for the tenor slide instrument were invented by 1839. Slide trombones in alto, tenor, and bass sizes were regular members of the symphony orchestra by the mid-1800s, though even then the alto part was sometimes played on a tenor. The use of a larger-bore B♭ trombone with valve attachment to F or E♭ bass instead of the regular bass trombone began in Germany in the early 20th century. This, together with the neglect of the alto, led to the present practice of using two B♭ tenor instruments and a B♭/F or E♭ bass trombone for the usual three orchestral parts. The second and sometimes even the first player may also have a valve attachment to F because of its technical advantage as an alternate to the lower slide positions. The soprano trombone was revived briefly in the early 20th century for dance-band and novelty use, but was not very successful.

Trommel [Ger.]. *Drum; *Trommelschlegel,* drumstick.

Trompete [Ger.], **trompette** [Fr.]. Trumpet; *trompette à coulisse,* slide trumpet.

Trompetengeige [Ger.]. *Tromba marina.*

Tronca [It.]. Cut off, accented.

Trop [Fr.]. Too much.

Trope [Lat. *tropus*]. In the Middle Ages, a type of addition to an official liturgical chant of the Latin church, consisting of newly composed words or music or both and occurring most characteristically in connection with certain chants of the Mass. The term *tropus* was applied in the Middle Ages only to certain specific categories of additions, principally the type described under (3) below. Modern writers, however, have tended to use the word in a broader, generic

sense for all paraliturgical chants, assigning only the *sequence a separate category.

Three basic kinds of addition are found in the medieval sources:

(1) Addition of melody alone. Wordless melismas were on occasion added to the ends of phrases of various Mass chants, such as the introit or Gloria. This practice, however, seems not to have been widespread, except in the case of the very long melisma that was added to the repetition of the alleluia after its verse [see Sequence].

(2) Addition of words to a preexistent melody. Texts could be added to the melismas of the official chant itself, as was the case, for example, with the *prosulae added to the melismatic sections of graduals, alleluia verses, offertory verses, and so forth. Texts could also be added to melodies that were themselves additions. The most familiar example of textual addition of this latter type occurs in connection with the sequence. Whether or not the so-called Kyrie trope should be included in this general category is still the subject of scholarly debate.

(3) Addition of both words and music. This category contains by far the largest number of tropes. The earliest practice seems to have been the addition of a newly composed introduction to a chant of the Mass, most characteristically the introit. A familiar example of this type of introductory trope is the Easter introit trope "Quem queritis in sepulchro" in its simplest, predramatic form [see also Liturgical drama]. The apparent popularity of these introductory tropes led to an extension of the practice, with line-by-line introductions or interpolations before each of the phrases of a given chant. Tropes of this type occur above all in connection with the antiphonal or action chants of the Proper of the Mass—that is, introit, offertory, and communion—and with the nonmelismatic Ordinary chants—especially the Gloria, Sanctus, and Agnus Dei. The trope texts served the purpose of amplifying and interpreting the received texts of the liturgy and making the ancient words relevant to the needs and understanding of the contemporary listeners—that is, the monastic communities that gave rise to this practice. The added texts could be in prose or in poetry. They could quote Scripture or imitate the meters of classical Latin poetry, especially the dactylic hexameter. Much less frequently, they were written in rhymed or rhythmic Latin verse, but this type of poetry was much more characteristic of the sequence.

Appearing as early as the 9th century, the trope flourished primarily from the 10th through the 12th century. After the 12th century, troping seems to have fallen into disuse, and only the sequence and certain categories of tropes to the Ordinary of the Mass continued to develop beyond that date. By the time of the *Council of Trent in the 16th century, very little of this type of interpolation remained to be purged from the liturgy.

Troppo [It.]. Too much; *(ma) non troppo,* (but) not too much.

Tropus [Lat.]. (1) *Mode, octave species. (2) *Trope.

Troubadour. Any of the composer-poets of southern France who flourished in the 12th and 13th centuries. The troubadours established the first tradition of lyric poetry in a European vernacular tongue. Their works were composed in Old Occitan (i.e., *langue d'oc,* or Old Provençal), a language distinct from that of their northern counterparts, the *trouvères. Various etymologies for their Old Occitan name, *trobador,* have been proposed.

The subject matter of this poetry is closely associated with the doctrine of *fin' amor* [Prov., refined love]—popularly known since the 19th century as courtly love—in which the lover's emotions are progressively ennobled through his subjection to the lady. Arabic-Spanish models and medieval Latin material (both sacred and secular) have been cited along with indigenous factors as possible sources of "the courtly experience."

Noblemen, commoners, and bourgeois all figure in the ranks of the troubadours. Troubadours whose music has been preserved in part include Jaufre Rudel (fl. 1125–48), Marcabru (fl. 1130–49), Bernart de Ventadorn (fl. 1147–70), Giraut de Bornelh (fl. 1162–99), Raimbaut de Vaqeiras (fl. 1180–1205), and Guiraut Riquier (fl. 1254–92). The troubadours were primarily composers who in most cases also performed their works. Early in the extant tradition, however, *jongleurs* [Fr., minstrels; Prov. *joglars*] appear to constitute an inferior class of performers who occasionally composed as well.

The *canzo is the best known of the troubadour poetic forms, but their poetry covers a broad range of genres, including the dawn-song (*alba), poems of political or social satire (*sirventes*), funereal laments (*planh*), dialogue forms (*tenso, partimen*), and poems recounting the fictive encounter of knight and shepherdess (*pastorela). The melodies of several Old Occitan *lais and of various devotional compositions also survive. Although the precise delineation of the melodic corpus is still open to discussion, roughly 10 percent of the 2,500 surviving poems exist with melodies. The tunes are short monophonic compositions, which, with the exception of the *lais,* are repeated for each strophe of the poem.

Trough zither. A *zither in which a single string is laced a variable number of times across the opening of a wooden trough or bowl and plucked. It is found in Central and East Africa.

Trout Quintet. Popular name for Schubert's Quintet in A major op. 114, D. 667 (1819), for violin, viola, cello, double bass, and piano, in five movements, the fourth being a set of variations on his song "The Trout" [Ger. "Die Forelle"] D. 550a–e (several versions, ca. 1817–21).

Trouvère. Any of the poet-musicians of northern France who, in the latter part of the 12th century and in the 13th, following the model of the Old Provençal *troubadours, created a substantial repertory of largely strophic, monophonic songs in the Old French language. The troubadour forms and style spread to the northern regions at least in part as a result of the travels of the troubadours themselves and of their *jongleurs* [Prov. *joglars;* see Minstrel]. Also important were such powerful and influential patrons as Eleanor of Aquitaine, who brought her love of courtly entertainment to the north, where an analogous social context and the presence of indigenous artistic talent fostered the development of the Old French lyric repertory.

The earliest trouvères—such as Blondel de Nesle (fl. 1180–1200) and the Chastelain de Couci (ca. 1165–1203)—worked in an aristocratic environment, as did their southern counterparts. The opening phase of the trouvères' art flourished above all at the court of Champagne with such composers as Conon de Béthune (ca. 1160–1219 or 1220) and Gace Brulé (ca. 1160–after 1213), and reached its high point in the first half of the 13th century with the works of Thibaut de Navarre (d. 1253). In the course of the 13th century, however, the center of gravity of trouvère music shifted gradually away from the court toward the city and to bourgeois patronage. Guilds of trouvères were established in various northern towns—particularly in Arras—and assemblies known as *puys were held in which the middle-class trouvères could compete. In this final phase of trouvère music, the composer Adam de la Halle (d. 1285–88?) is noted not only for his monophonic compositions but also for his contributions to the history of polyphony and of the theater.

Over two-thirds of the more than 2,000 trouvère poems have been preserved with their tunes. The themes and genres of trouvère poetry are to a large extent those of the troubadours. As in the Old Provençal repertory, the chanson [Prov. *canzo] holds a central place. Other forms inherited from the troubadours, including the *jeu-parti, *pastourelle, and *aube* [Prov. *alba], are also found in the north.

Trovatore, Il [It., The Troubadour]. Opera in four parts by Verdi (libretto by Salvatore Cammarano completed by Leone Emanuele Bardare, based on a play by Antonio García Gutiérrez), produced in Rome in 1853. Setting: Spain, 1409.

Troyanos, Tatiana (b. New York, 12 Sept. 1938; d. there, 21 Aug. 1993). Mezzo-soprano. Studied at Juilliard School and with Hans Heinz. Debut, 1963, with the New York City Opera as Hippolyta in Britten's *A Midsummer Night's Dream*. Created the role of Jeanne in Penderecki's *The Devils of Loudun* (Hamburg, 1969); also appeared at Covent Garden, the Paris Opéra, Salzburg, and the Edinburgh, Munich, and Aix-en-Provence festivals. Sang the title role in Handel's *Ariodante* at the opening of the Kennedy Center in Washington, D.C., 1971; Metropolitan Opera debut as Octavian, 1976. Other roles include the Composer from *Ariadne auf Naxos,* Poppaea, Jocasta, and Carmen.

Troyens, Les [Fr., The Trojans]. Opera in five acts by Berlioz (libretto by Berlioz, after Virgil's *Aeneid* and a passage in Shakespeare's *The Merchant of Venice,* act 5), composed in 1856–58, revised and enlarged in 1859–60, and divided into two parts in 1863: *La prise de Troie* and *Les troyens à Carthage.* Part 2 was produced in Paris in 1863; the first complete production took place in Karlsruhe, Germany (in German), in 1890. Setting: Troy and Carthage.

Trumpet [Fr. *trompette;* Ger. *Trompete;* It. *tromba;* Sp. *trompeta*]. A soprano brass instrument commonly about 1.4 m. (4 1/2 ft.) in tube length folded twice to a narrow rectangular shape about 35 cm. (14 in.) long. A mouth pipe with mouthpiece protrudes from one end of the rectangle, and an expanded opening or bell extends from the other. The center of the rectangle is occupied by three valves and associated extra tubing. The bore of the trumpet is mostly cylindrical, though like the *cornet it expands just before the bell. Most trumpets are now made of brass, either lacquered or plated with silver, nickel, or more rarely gold. Other materials occasionally used besides brass include German silver, copper, silver, and very rarely gold. See ill. under Brass instruments.

Trumpets are commonly available in several sizes named according to the pitch class of their fundamental. Instruments in B♭, C, D, E♭, F, and piccolo B♭ or A have actual fundamentals B♭, c, d, e♭, f, and b♭ or a. The B♭ instrument is used mostly in school bands and popular music. The C trumpet is the favorite among professional orchestra players. The higher trumpets are becoming more common and find use in certain segments of the repertory written for instruments in those keys or demanding an extremely high register. For the latter use, piccolo trumpets are made in a variety of shapes, some (occasionally called Bach trumpets) straight except for the valves and their associated tubing, and some with four rather than three valves. American trumpets are now almost invariably equipped with Périnet piston valves for the right hand, though orchestra players sometimes use instruments with rotary valves. Better-quality instruments also have levers or rings for adjusting the length of the first and third valve tubes [see also Valve].

Most trumpet parts since about 1900 are written either for B♭ trumpet, sounding one tone lower, or for C trumpet at concert pitch. Orchestral parts from earlier periods were written for trumpets that could be put in the appropriate key for the composition to be played by means of crooks (small loops of extra tubing). These parts were commonly in B♭, C, D, E♭, and F, sounding from a tone lower to a fourth higher than written. Some late 19th-century parts were written for trumpets with an extra valve or slide to put them in A, sounding a minor third lower. Orchestra players today usually play all of these parts on B♭ or C instruments, making the necessary transposition as they play.

The trumpet has a very long history, having been used in ancient Egypt, the Near East, and Greece. During much of that time, however, it was a signaling device sounding only one or two tones. It was not until the 14th and 15th centuries that the more musical possibilities of the long trumpet began to be recognized and used, and the instrument acquired its characteristic folded form. The instruments of this period were natural trumpets, on which only the tones of the *harmonic series were available. Evidence exists that toward the end of this period, however, some instruments may have been fitted with a single slide at the mouth pipe, theoretically providing a chromatic scale, except for one pitch, from the fourth harmonic upward. Such an instrument was called a *tromba da tirarsi.*

The 16th century saw increasing use of the trumpet in a variety of more musical situations in addition to court ceremony and military communication. Craftsmen in Nuremberg, Germany, began to excel in trumpet making during this period and supplied instruments to most of Europe. During the 17th and 18th centuries, the natural trumpet reached its peak of development and was used with brilliant effect by Bach, Handel, and many other composers. The instruments were from about 1.8 to 2.5 m. (6 to 8 ft.) in total length, folded to traditional form, and pitched usually in D and C for court use and in E♭ and F for the military. Players specialized in different registers, allowing the *clarino* or high-range players to concentrate on the top dozen or so tones where melodic playing is possible. This type of playing reached its zenith in the mid-1700s and gradually declined toward the end of the century. The lower range was called the *principale.*

The orchestral trumpet of the late 18th and the early 19th century was in F, with crooks for lower keys down to C or B♭ to match the key of the composition played. Its sound was not as loud as the modern trumpet's, and it balanced well with other instruments in smaller ensembles. Hand stopping, used on horns since about 1750, was tried on specially constructed trumpets [Ger. *Inventionstrompete*] beginning in the 1770s. The keyed trumpet was tried with limited success by several makers and players in the last 30 years of the century. Four or five keys like those on clarinets of the time provided pitches missing in the natural harmonic series. Concertos by Haydn and Hummel exploited the capabilities of these instruments. The slide trumpet, never completely forgotten since the 16th century, was revived again in England about 1800. The improved slide mechanism was fairly successful in that country throughout the 19th century, and such instruments continued to be made into the 20th century in the U.S. as well.

The most important mechanical improvement, however, was the invention of the *valve for brass instruments about 1814. Valves were very quickly applied to the trumpet. By the mid-19th century, the orchestral trumpet in F had two or three valves instead of the crooks used earlier in the century. Late in the 19th century, as larger orchestras played for larger audiences, the long F trumpet was finally given up in favor of shorter valved trumpets in Bb and C. After the mid-1920s, the trumpet also replaced the cornet in dance bands.

Trumpet marine. *Tromba marina.*

Trumpet Voluntary. A work often played in an arrangement for trumpet, organ, and drums and misattributed to Purcell. The original is by Jeremiah Clarke (ca. 1674–1707) and survives in a version for harpsichord titled *The Prince of Denmark's March* as well as in a suite for winds. See also Voluntary.

Trumscheit [Ger.]. *Tromba marina.*

Trythall, Richard Aaker (b. Knoxville, Tenn., 25 July 1939). Composer and pianist. Brother of the composer Gilbert Trythall (b. 1930). Studied with David Van Vactor at Univ. of Tennessee, with Roger Sessions and Earl Kim at Princeton, and with Boris Blacher at the Hochschule für Musik in Berlin. Moved to Rome, 1964; served as music liaison at the American Academy in Rome from 1974. As a pianist performed his own works and those of other contemporary composers in Italy and in the U.S. Works include *Coincidences* (piano, 1969); *Omaggio a Jerry Lee Lewis* (tape, 1975); *Variations on a Theme by Haydn* (woodwind quintet and tape, 1976).

T.s. Abbr. for *tasto solo.*

Tuba. (1) [Lat.] A *trumpet of ancient Rome. A straight tube of bronze or iron, 1.25–1.6 m. long, with a slightly flaring bell, it was first and foremost a military instrument, sounding the attack and retreat in battle. In civilian life it was heard in funeral processions, at games and gladiatorial contests, and in religious rituals, particularly sacrifices.

(2) [Lat.] The reciting tone of a *psalm tone.

(3) [Eng., Fr., Ger., It., Sp.] The largest and lowest of the brass instruments, with a widely expanding tube as long as 5.5 m. (18 ft.). Tubas are usually wrapped in a rectangular shape about 45 cm. wide by 75 cm. tall. The narrow end with *mouthpiece points back from high on one side of the rectangular body, while the expanded end or bell rises above the body of the instrument either straight up or, less often, turned forward. Three or four *valves for the right hand are provided. The instrument is commonly used in European and American symphony orchestras as well as in school, community, and military bands. Tubas are usually made of brass or, less often, of German silver. Brass is usually lacquered but is sometimes plated with silver or nickel. In marching bands, circular tubas called *sousaphones are also common. See ill. under Brass instruments.

Tubas are now made mostly in four sizes, BBb (pronounced "double B-flat"), CC, Eb, and F (*fundamental tones Bb_2, C_1, Eb_1, and F_1). The first two sizes are the most common, with Eb a distant third, and F a rather remote last. There are also smaller tubas at baritone or *euphonium pitch. They are commonly used in brass bands as well as in some French orchestras and usually have additional valves for lower notes. A few larger tubas have been made a fifth or even an octave below the BBb instrument (11 m. in tube length, fundamental tone Bb_3).

Tubas are nontransposing bass-clef instruments except in brass bands where occasionally parts are written in treble clef, the Bb instrument sounding two octaves and a tone lower, the Eb sounding one octave and a major sixth lower. The most characteristic and dependable range of the BBb and CC tubas is from E_1 or $F\#_1$ to bb or c'. Lower pitches produced by additional valves or as pedal tones are slow to respond, but useful at least down to C_1. Upper pitches are increasingly difficult, but useful to f' or g'. The smaller tubas in Eb and F have correspondingly higher ranges, but can often play just as low as the larger ones if provided with additional valves.

Tubas belong to the bugle or cornet families [see Brass instruments], instruments having widely expanding bores and round mellow tone qualities. The earliest examples were bass tubas and *bombardons* in F and Eb designed and made in Berlin by Wilhelm Wieprecht (1802–72) and Johann Gottfried Moritz (1777–1840, founder of the firm later operated and known by the name of his son C[arl] W[ilhelm] Moritz, 1811–55); the first was patented in 1835. These instruments were the logical result of attempts to complete a choir of valved brasses for use in military bands. Predecessors of the tuba include a number of bass instruments using side holes to alter their sounding length. The earliest of these is the *serpent, dating from the late 16th century. Late in the 18th century and on into the 19th, a number of improved serpents were built, including the *bass horn, several so-called *Russian bassoons, the keyed serpent, and the *ophicleide.

Tubaphone. An instrument similar to the *glockenspiel, but with a softer sound, being made with metal tubes rather than solid bars.

Tubb, Ernest (Dale) (b. near Crisp, Tex., 9 Feb. 1914; d. Nashville, Tenn., 6 Sept. 1984). Country singer, songwriter, and guitarist. First recording success was "Walking the Floor over You" (1941); 1943, joined the Grand Ole Opry; further recordings included "Try Me One More Time" (1943) and "Thanks a Lot" (1963). Recorded duets with Loretta Lynn; from 1947 hosted the radio show "Midnight Jamboree," which introduced many rock-and-roll artists.

Tube zither. A wooden or bamboo tube with one or more strings running its length above its surface. It is widely distributed in Africa and Asia.

Tubular bells [Fr. *cloches tubulaires;* Ger. *Röhrenglocken, Glocken;* It. *campane tubolari;* Sp. *campanólogo*]. A set of metal tubes of varying length, hung vertically in a frame in an arrangement similar to that of the piano keyboard, and struck at the top with one or two rawhide mallets; also called chimes. They are tuned chromatically, usually from c' to f'', notated at pitch. Tubular bells were introduced in the 1880s and have become a standard part of the orchestral percussion section. See ill. under Percussion instruments.

Tuck, tucket [possibly fr. Ar. *tuqā,* alarm, or It., Sp., Fr., and Eng. *tocco, toc-toc, toque, tick-tack,* imitation of the sounds of bells or percussion instruments when hit]. A flourish on trumpets and kettledrums, often used as a fanfare or military signal from the 14th through the 18th century [see also *Tusch,* Toccata (2)]. The earliest usage of the term refers only to drums, though it is later encountered frequently as a stage direction upon the entrance of a noble (compare *sennet, used when a group of ordinary people enters or exits). In 17th-century military music, a *tucquet* is a march for trumpets, fifes, and drums.

Tucker, Richard [Ticker, Reuben] (b. Brooklyn, 28 Aug. 1913; d. Kalamazoo, 8 Jan. 1975). Tenor. Studied with Paul Althouse. Debut, 1943, with the Salmaggi Company in New York as Alfredo in *La traviata.* Associated with the Metropolitan Opera from 1945 on; specialized in the Italian repertory and performed as many as 30 roles. Also performed in Verona, Milan, Florence, London, Vienna, Buenos Aires and in concert with major orchestras.

Tuckwell, Barry (Emmanuel) (b. Melbourne, 5 Mar 1931). Horn player. Studied with Alan Mann at the Sydney Convervatorium. Went to England in 1950; met Dennis Brain and joined the Hallé Orchestra in Manchester (1951–53), Scottish National Orchestra (1953–54), Bournemouth Symphony (principal, 1954–55) and London Symphony (principal, 1955–68). Embarked on a solo career, becoming a leading player; composers who wrote works for him include Musgrave, Hoddinott, Richard Rodney Bennett, and Don Banks. Conductor of the Tasmanian Symphony (1980–83); music director of the Maryland Symphony (from 1982).

Tudor, David (b. Philadelphia, 20 Jan. 1926; d. Tomkins Cove, N.Y., 13 Aug. 1996). Pianist and composer. Studied piano with Josef Martin and Irma Wolpe, composition with Stefan Wolpe. Organist until 1948; in the early 1950s began performing piano works by John Cage and other avant-garde composers, notably Pierre Boulez's Second Piano Sonata in 1950 and the premieres of Cage's *Music of Changes* (1951) and *4'33''* in 1952. From 1953 associated with the Merce Cunningham Dance Company; performances on tour with Cage in Europe in 1954 inspired Silvano Bussotti's *Five Pieces for David Tudor* (1959) and Karlheinz Stockhausen's *Klavierstück VI* (1955). During the 1960s turned toward live performance of electronic music, such as Cage's *Cartridge Music* (1960); also participated in collaborative compositions (*Reunion,* 1968, with Cage, Lowell Cross, David Behrman, Gordon Mumma, and Marcel Duchamp). Many compositions involve multiple media: *Bandoneon!* (1966); *Video/Laser I–II* (1969), with Lowell Cross and Carson Jeffries; *Rainforest I,* live electronics (1968); *Toneburst,* live electronics (1974).

Tudway, Thomas (b. ca. 1650; d. Cambridge, 23 Nov. 1726). Composer. Chorister at the Chapel Royal, 1668; organist of King's College, Cambridge (1670–80 master of choristers); university organist and organist of Pembroke College. Between 1714 and 1720 assembled a 6-volume anthology of cathedral music. Compositions consist mainly of verse anthems.

Tuna [Sp.]. In Spain and several countries of Latin America, a student ensemble of singers and instrumentalists dedicated to the performance of folk and popular song, typically in serenades.

Ṭunbūr [Ar.]. A fretted, long-necked lute with a variable number of strings. Two types are described in the 10th century. Instruments still in use that derive from these include perhaps the *buzuq* and the larger *ṭunbūr al turkī* (Turkish), with four strings or double courses. See also *Tanbur; Bouzouki, Saz.*

Tunder, Franz (b. Bannesdorf, near Burg, Fehmarn, 1614; d. Lübeck, 5 Nov. 1667). Composer. Court organist at Gottorf in 1632; may have studied organ with Johann Heckelauer. Organist at the Marienkirche, Lübeck, from 1641 until his death; son-in-law Buxtehude succeeded him. His chorale cantatas mark the beginning of the Lutheran church cantata's evolution, and his organ preludes influenced those of Buxtehude. Surviving compositions include 17 vocal works (motets, solo and chorale cantatas, sacred arias), 14 organ pieces, sinfonia for strings.

Tune. (1) *Melody. (2) To adjust the pitch of an instrument.

Tune book. An 18th- or 19th-century collection of psalm tunes, printed in America (the British colonies, later the U.S.), oblong in shape, having a didactic preface, and designed for use in singing schools. Tune books originated in New England as a part of the clerical attempt to counter the shrinking repertory of psalm tunes in use. Until about 1770, their musical content was mostly British, though in a few it was entirely American; later it was commonly mixed.

Consistent with their original purpose, many use a simplified musical notation. One of the most influential early tune books, *An Introduction to the Art of Singing Psalm-Tunes* (Boston, 1721) by John Tufts (1689–1750), uses four letters corresponding to the solmization syllables *fa, sol, la,* and *mi* placed on a staff with either of two clefs and with dots to indicate duration. Eventually conventional note heads differently shaped for each syllable replaced the letters. The first book using the resulting four-shape *shapenote notation was *The Easy Instructor* (Philadelphia, 1801), compiled by William Little and William Smith. Subsequent collections offered borrowed and original tunes, harmonized in three and four parts; the tunes might be spiritual folk songs (folk hymns), fuging tunes, or psalm tunes.

The advocacy by some northern composers of seven-syllable solmization encouraged the development in the mid-19th century of seven-shape notations, which gradually supplanted four-shape notation in most areas. The first appeared in Jesse B. Aikin's *Christian Minstrel* of 1846, in which the four established shapes were retained and three new ones added. This system eventually prevailed over the several others introduced during the next 20 years. With the change in notation came an increase in European music in tune books.

In the Northeast, shape-note notation was never used extensively, but many tune books in standard notation were published. The most important early tune books from that area include William Billings's *New-England Psalm-singer* (1770, entirely original), Andrew Law's *Select Harmony* (1779, eclectic mix of British and American tunes), and Simeon Jocelyn

and Amos Doolittle's *Chorister's Companion* (1782, eclectic). Later tune books, especially those published after 1810 by reformers including Lowell Mason, tended to emphasize European music, even to the exclusion of American tunes. Beginning with the *Stoughton Collection* (1829), however, some American tunes were reprinted in new tune books using standard notation. Others were preserved in shapenote repertories.

Tuning [Fr. *accord;* Ger. *Stimmung;* It. *accordatura;* Sp. *afinación*]. (1) The act of adjusting the fundamental sounding frequency or frequencies of an instrument, usually in order to bring it or them into agreement with some predetermined pitch. When two pitches are slightly out of tune, the ear experiences fluctuations in intensity, or *beats. Tuners listen closely to the beats between upper partials, especially those in the range of 100–1600 Hz. Guitarists and some other string players frequently tune by harmonics and thus avoid fundamentals altogether.

(2) Any ordered interval collection all of whose members can be expressed precisely by rational numbers [see Pythagorean scale, Just intonation]. Interval collections not displaying this property are *temperaments.

Tuning fork [Fr. *diapason;* Ger. *Stimmgabel;* It. *corista;* Sp. *diapasón*]. A two-pronged metal fork that sounds a given pitch when struck. Such forks are used to provide reliable pitches (especially $a' = 440$ *Hz. [see Pitch, Acoustics]) for tuning instruments and for acoustical experiments.

Tuning pin. On the *piano and related instruments, including the harp, a short piece of metal of round cross section at one end, which is fitted into a hole in the pin block, and square or rectangular in cross section at the other, so as to fit into a wrench or "hammer" by means of which it is turned; also termed a wrest pin. Each of the instrument's strings is wrapped around such a pin at one end, and its pitch is adjusted by turning the pin so as to increase or decrease its tension.

Tuning slide. (1) On a brass instrument, a length of tubing, usually U-shaped, that can be made to slide in such a way as to alter the instrument's effective length, thus making it possible to adjust its pitch slightly. (2) An adjustable metal collar fitted to the top of an organ *flue pipe, by means of which the pipe is tuned.

Tuono [It.]. *Tono.

Turandot. Opera in three acts by Puccini, left unfinished at his death and completed by Franco Alfano (libretto by Giuseppe Adami and Renato Simoni, based on Carlo Gozzi's play of the same name), produced in Milan in 1926. Setting: Peking in legendary times.

Turba [Lat., crowd]. In *Passion music, the words spoken by crowds, often set in the works of Bach and others as short, imitative choral movements in a fast tempo; also, such a movement.

Turca, alla [It.]. In the Turkish style, i.e., in the style of *Janissary music.

Turchi, Guido (b. Rome, 10 Nov. 1916). Composer, critic, and administrator. Studied piano at the Rome Conservatory and the Accademia di S. Cecilia with Ildebrando Pizzetti. Works from the 1940s and early 1950s reflect the influences of Pizzetti, Bartók, and Hindemith. Taught at the Rome Conservatory (from 1941); director, Parma Conservatory (1967–69) and Florence Conservatory (1970–72); artistic director of the Accademia filarmonica of Rome (1963–66), Teatro comunale of Bologna (1968–70), Accademia musicale chigiana (from 1978), and Teatro angelicum in Milan (from 1988). Wrote music criticism for the *Corriere della sera*. Works include *Il buon soldato Svejk* (opera, Milan, 1962); *Rapsodia* (orchestra, 1969).

Tureck, Rosalyn (b. Chicago, 14 Dec. 1914). Pianist and scholar. Studied in Chicago with Jan Chiapusso and with Olga Samaroff at Juilliard. Toured extensively from 1937. Best known for recitals and recordings of Bach, on harpsichord, clavichord, and Moog synthesizer as well as piano. Founded the International Bach Institute (1966) and Tureck Bach Institute (1981); published the 3-volume anthology *An Introduction to the Performance of Bach* (London, 1960). Taught at the Univ. of Maryland, Mannes, Juilliard, and the Univ. of California, San Diego.

Turetzky, Bertram (Jay) (b. Norwich, Conn., 14 Feb. 1933). Double bass player and composer. Studied with Joseph Iadone and Josef Marx at the Hartt School and with Curt Sachs at New York Univ. Since 1964 has given recitals and recorded music for solo double bass, including works written for him by Erb, Perle, Martino, Barney Childs, and Ben Johnston. Compositions include *Reflections on Ives and Whittier,* double bass, tape, 1978–81; *In memoriam Charles Mingus,* 2 singers, 3 jazz groups, double bass choir, tape, film, 1979. Author of *The Contemporary Contrabass* (Berkeley, 1974; R: 1989).

Turina, Joaquín (b. Seville, 9 Dec. 1882; d. Madrid, 14 Jan. 1949). Composer. Studied piano at the Madrid conservatory and in Paris with Moszkowsky; composition with D'Indy at the Schola cantorum. With Falla and Albéniz, resolved to write music in a national vein. Returned to Madrid, 1914; conductor for the Ballets russes and choirmaster at the Teatro real. Joined the faculty at the Madrid Conservatory,

1930; named head of the Ministry of Education's general music commission, 1941. Works include *La procesión del Rocio* (symphonic poem, 1913), *Sinfoniá sevillana* (1920), *Jardin de oriento* (opera, 1923); chamber works, piano music, songs. Author of *Enciclopedia musical abreviada* (1917; with a prologue by Falla) and *Tratado de composición* (1947).

Türk, Daniel Gottlieb (b. Claussnitz, near Chemnitz, 10 Aug. 1750; d. Halle, 26 Aug. 1813). Theorist and composer. Studied with G. A. Homilius in Dresden and J. A. Hiller in Leipzig. Kantor at the Halle Ulrichskirche, 1774; 1779, music director at Halle Univ.; 1787, music director and organist at the Liebfrauenkirche in Halle. Wrote important treatises and theoretical works; composed an opera (now lost), cantatas, about 48 keyboard sonatas, other keyboard pieces, lieder.

Turkish crescent [also Jingling Johnny, Chinese pavilion or hat; Fr. *pavillon (chapeau) chinois;* Ger. *Schellenbaum;* It. *mezzaluna, cappello cinese;* Sp. *chinesco, sombrero chino*]. A long stick hung with bells and jingles suspended from symbolic shapes, especially crescents and conical hats. It is sounded by shaking. Originally part of the Turkish *Janissary band, it was adopted by European military bands in the 18th century. See ill. under Percussion instruments.

Turmmusik, Turmsonate [Ger., tower music (sonata)]. In Germany in the 16th through the 18th century, music for brasses, often in four or five parts, played from a tower by town musicians (*Stadtpfeifer*).

Turn [Fr. *double cadence, doublé, tour de gosier;* Ger. *Doppelschlag;* It. *groppo, circolo mezzo, gruppetto;* Sp. *grupeto*]. An ornament that "turns around" the main note. It consists most often of a stepwise descent of three notes beginning with the upper auxiliary, followed by a return to the principal note [Ex. 1]. But there are also "rising turns" and turns that begin with the main note and descend to the third below [Exx. 3a and 2]. The principal note may be prefixed as part of the ornament, and the return may be included as well [Ex. 3b]. If the turn connects a note to one a third higher, the passing note can be added to the ornament. A turn may be added to the beginning, middle, or end of a *trill, producing various compound ornaments.

Turns may come at the beginnning, middle, or end of a note, or they may occupy its whole value; in some cases they may also anticipate the note they are meant to embellish. Turns seem to have been generally performed in notes of equal value, but C. P. E. Bach (1753) recommended playing the first two notes of a turn beginning on the upper auxiliary faster than the third in slow tempos [Ex. 4].

Turns.   2. Chambonnières, *Les pièces de clavessin* (1670). 3. Wagner, *Götterdämmerung*.   4. C. P. E. Bach, *Versuch* (1753).   5. Loulié, *Eléments ou principes de musique* (1696).

Various kinds of turns are found written out in 16th-century *diminutions, most often in association with trills. They can be found also among the "figures" in 17th-century German treatises. The first appearance of the turn in a table of signs and terms seems to be in Chambonnières's *Pièces de clavessin* (1670), where it is indicated by the reverse curve that has remained the normal sign ever since [Ex. 2]. The melodic figure itself differs from the norm, however, as shown in the example; the same melodic figure is given by Saint-Lambert (1702) for cases in which the turn is followed by a trill on the same note, while the usual melodic figure is used in other circumstances. The sign for a turn is often placed between the note it embellishes and the following note, showing that the turn is to be delayed until the principal note has sounded for a while; this execution may be desirable even when the sign is over the note [Ex. 5]. In the 18th and increasingly in the 19th century, turns are indicated by small notes or notes of full value. Wagner, who employed this melodic figure often, used the sign in *Rienzi,* but used small or large notes in the late operas.

Turn of the Screw, The. Opera in two acts and a prologue by Britten (libretto by Myfanwy Piper, adapted from the story by Henry James), produced in Venice in 1954. Setting: Bly, an English country house, in the mid-19th century.

Turnaround, turnback. In jazz, a passage occurring at the end of one section of a form leading harmonically or melodically to the next, especially to the repetition of the section or of the entire form, e.g., the repetition of the A section in AABA song forms or the repetition of the 12-bar *blues pattern (in which bar 12 may turn to the dominant).

Turner, Tina [Bollock, Annie Mae] (b. Brownsville, Tenn., 26 Nov. 1939). Popular and rock singer. Began singing with Ike Turner in 1956; married to him 1958–76. Recordings include "River Deep, Mountain High" (1966), "Proud Mary" (1971), and Tina's "Nutbush City Limits" (1973). Also recorded solo albums (*Private Dancer,* 1984) and appeared in films.

Turrentine, Stanley (William) (b. Pittsburgh, 5 Apr. 1934). Jazz tenor saxophonist and bandleader. Toured with Ray Charles in Lowell Fulson's rhythm-and-blues group; joined his brother, the trumpeter Tommy Turrentine (b. 1928), in groups led by Earl Bostic (1953–54) and Max Roach (1959–60). In the 1960s made albums of his own, including *A Chip off the Old Block* with the organist Shirley Scott (1963); also played on recordings by Scott and Jimmy Smith. Reached wider audiences from 1970, when he recorded "Sugar."

Tusch [Ger., fanfare; fr. Fr. *touche,* stroke]. In the 18th century, a noisy, improvised flourish of arpeggios, runs, and high, sustained notes, performed on trumpets and kettledrums, usually over a single harmony.

Tutte le corde [It.]. See *Una corda.*

Tutti [It., all]. In a *concerto, the ensemble as distinct from the soloist(s); a passage for the ensemble.

Twelfth. See Interval.

Twelve-tone music. Music based on a serial ordering of all twelve chromatic pitches. The series of twelve pitches (also known as the row), whose form is uniquely determined for each composition, serves as the referential basis for all pitch events in that composition (in distinction to the seven-note diatonic basis used in tonal music). The term is most commonly applied to music by Arnold Schoenberg and his followers, though Josef Matthias Hauer actually developed a somewhat different type of twelve-tone composition shortly before Schoenberg.

Schoenberg experimented with twelve-tone structures; and in a number of movements from the Five Piano Pieces op. 23, the Serenade op. 24, and the

Schoenberg, Piano Suite op. 25.

Piano Suite op. 25, all published in 1923–24 but individually dating back as far as 1920, he gradually developed a systematic approach to twelve-tone composition. Each of these three works contains portions that are twelve-tone, and op. 25 is composed exclusively in the new system.

In Schoenberg's twelve-tone music, the twelve pitches of the chromatic scale are ordered into a row, or series, that provides the basic pitch structure for a given composition and is thus an essential element in the work's fundamental conception. Any order may be chosen, with different orderings normally used for different pieces. The entire pitch structure of the composition is then derived from the row, including its melodic, contrapuntal, and harmonic features. The row thus represents an abstract structure that is fleshed out in the actual music: it supplies the sequences of pitch classes, for example, but not their registers or durations; nor does it determine (though it may influence) the formal or textural aspects of the music.

In addition to the principal or prime form of the row (designated P), new forms may be derived through three basic operations: the row can be reversed (the retrograde, designated R), inverted (the inversion, I), and both reversed and inverted (the ret-

rograde-inversion, RI). Moreover, each of these four basic versions may be transposed to begin on a different pitch. In analysis, transpositions are designated by an arabic numeral following the row designation, indicating the number of half-steps upward from the prime form in the transposition: thus, P-0 indicates the untransposed principal form, and P-6 indicates the principal form transposed up six half-steps, or a tritone (though some analysts now prefer to number pitch classes from C upward starting with 0 and identify transpositions by the number of the pitch class on which they begin). The four basic forms, multiplied by the twelve possible transpositions of each, produce a total of 48 possible versions in all. Rarely, however, are all forms used in a single work; more commonly, a small collection is chosen for particular compositional reasons. The example gives the four basic forms of the row used in Schoenberg's Piano Suite op. 25 and presents the opening measures of the Trio of the fifth movement.

Schoenberg also developed a technique, known as combinatoriality, for controlling the relationship between two different forms of a row used simultaneously. A row is combinatorial if half of one of its forms (i.e., one of this form's two hexachords) can be combined with half of one of its other forms without producing any pitch duplications between the two halves. Thus, the two hexachords, one from each row form, combine to create a new twelve-tone aggregate (as, of course, do the remaining two hexachords from the same two row forms). Not all twelve-tone rows are combinatorial (except for the limited case that the first half of every row can be combined with the first half of its own retrograde to produce a twelve-tone aggregate). Many rows do have this property, however, and Schoenberg came to favor them almost exclusively, since they enabled him to combine rows without pitch duplication.

The twelve-tone system lends itself to markedly different compositional realizations, even within Schoenberg's own output. His pupils Berg and Webern, both of whom adopted the twelve-tone technique, brought radically different conceptions of the method.

Among the many composers of the generation following Schoenberg and his school who eventually adopted the twelve-tone system (and adapted it for their own personal use) were Krenek, Dallapiccola, and Sessions. After World War II, twelve-tone music continued to flourish both independently and as a component of integral *serial music. It has played a significant role in the music of such important postwar figures as Babbitt, Boulez, and Nono; and even Stravinsky adopted the system in his final years. Babbitt has also been a leading theorist of twelve-tone music.

Twilight of the Gods, The. See *Ring des Nibelungen, Der.*

Twitty, Conway [Jenkins, Harold Lloyd] (b. Friars Point, Miss., 1 Sept. 1933; d. Springfield, Mo., 5 June 1993). Country and rock-and-roll singer and songwriter. Played country music, then rock-and-roll after World War II ("It's Only Make Believe," 1958). Returned to country in the late 1960s; recorded solo ("You've Never Been This Far Before," 1973; "Happy Birthday, Darlin'," 1979) and with Loretta Lynn ("Mississippi Woman, Louisiana Man," 1973).

Two-beat. In jazz, emphasis on beats 1 and 3 (as when the bass plays only on these beats) in 4/4; music characterized by such rhythm.

Two-foot. See Foot.

Two-line. The octave proceeding upward from c'', or any pitch in that octave [see Pitch names].

Two-part form. See Binary and ternary form.

Two-step. The most popular pattern in social dancing ca. 1893–1913. Initially in 6/8 and associated with John Philip Sousa's march of 1889 "The Washington Post" (the title of which became a name for the dance in Europe), the simple steps came to be danced to music in duple meters at ca. 60 bars per minute. See also One-step.

Tye, Christopher (b. ca. 1505; d. 1572?). Composer. Studied at Cambridge; associated with King's College. Lifelong friendship with Dr. Richard Cox led to associations with Oxford Univ., the Chapel Royal, and Ely Cathedral. Latin church music includes motets, Magnificats, and 3 Masses (one on "Western Wind"); English church music includes anthems and service music. Also composed over 20 *In nomines* and other consort music.

Tympani. Timpani [see Kettledrum].

Tympanon [Gr.], **tympanum** [Lat.]. (1) A *frame drum of ancient Greece and Rome, usually round with two heads. (2) In the Middle Ages, any of several instruments including the *dulcimer, the *psaltery, and the Irish *tiómpán*. (3) [Fr. *tympanon*] *Dulcimer.

Tyner, (Alfred) McCoy [Saud, Sulaimon] (b. Philadelphia, 11 Dec. 1938). Jazz pianist and bandleader. Played in Art Farmer and Benny Golson's Jazztet (1959–60) and John Coltrane's quartet (1960–65). Albums with Coltrane include *Selflessness* (1963, 1965) and *A Love Supreme* (1964). From 1965 led his own groups, recording albums such as *Sahara* (1972) and *Supertrios* (1977) and touring into the 1990s. Member of the Milestone Jazzstars, a quartet including Sonny Rollins and Ron Carter (1978).

Tyrolienne [Fr.]. A Tyrolean folk song and dance similar to the *Ländler* and sung with a *yodel. Tyrolean folk music became popular in the U.S. and Europe in the 19th century and was often evoked in piano pieces and ballets (e.g., in Rossini's *Guillaume Tell,* act 3) titled *tyrolienne.*

Tzigane [Fr.]. *Gypsy.

U

Über [Ger.]. Over, above; *überblasen,* to overblow; *Übergang, Überleitung,* transition, bridge passage; *übergreifen,* to cross the hands in piano playing; *übermässig,* augmented (interval); *übersetzen,* to pass one finger over another; *übertragen,* to transcribe; *Übertragung,* transcription.

Übung [Ger.]. *Etude.

U.c. Abbr. for *una corda.*

Uccellini, Marco (b. ca. 1603; d. Forlimpopoli, near Forli, 10 Sept. 1680). Composer. Studied in Assisi; settled in Modena before 1639. Head of instrumental music at the Este court, 1641; 1647–65 *maestro di cappella* at the cathedral; *maestro di cappella* at the Farnese court in Parma until his death. Extant compositions, all instrumental, include 7 printed collections: Opp. 2–5 contain virtuosic sonatas for 1–4 violins; later collections consist of dances and sinfonias.

'Ūd [Ar., also *oud*]. A Middle Eastern, short-necked, fretless *lute with a pegbox set back at an angle, a bulging, pear-shaped body, and strings in double courses. The most common model has five double courses of gut or nylon strings tuned g a d' g' c''. A sixth course is sometimes added and tuned to f''. The 'ūd has a shorter neck than the European lute, is played with a plectrum rather than with the fingers, and is played in monophonic rather than polyphonic style. Known to the Arabs since the 7th century, it spread from Muslim Spain through Europe, where it became the lute. See ill. under Instrument.

Ugarte, Floro M(anuel) (b. Buenos Aires, 15 Sept. 1884; d. there, 11 June 1975). Composer. Studied in Argentina and at the Paris Conservatory with Fourdrain; 1913, returned to Buenos Aires. Taught at the National Conservatory; directed the Teatro Colón and the Buenos Aires Municipal Conservatory. Works include the opera *Saika* (1918); the ballet *El junco* (1944); orchestra pieces (*De mi tierra,* 1923, 1934; *La Rébelión del agua,* based on his own poetry, 1931); a symphony (1946); chamber music; piano works; and songs.

Uguale [It.]. Equal, uniform.

Uhl, Alfred (b. Vienna, 5 June 1909; d. there, 8 June 1992). Composer. Studied with Franz Schmidt at the Hochschule für Musik in Vienna. Traveled abroad and composed music for films; returned to Austria in 1938; taught at the Hochschule from 1945 on. Works include Violin Concerto (1963); *Der mysteriöse Herr X* (opera, Vienna, 1966); *Sinfonietta* (orchestra, 1977); *Konzertante Musik für Violine und Orchester* (1986); chamber works.

Uilleann pipe. *Union pipe.

Ukrainian Symphony. Popular name for Tchaikovsky's Symphony no. 2 in C minor op. 17 (1872, rev. 1879–80), so called because it incorporates Ukrainian folk songs; also termed *Little Russian* (Little Russia being another name for the Ukraine).

Ukulele, ukelele. A small *guitar of Hawaii with four gut or nylon strings tuned g' c' e' a' (or some transposition thereof). A larger, baritone model is tuned like the highest four strings of the guitar, d g b e'. The ukulele was developed in the late 19th century from the *cavaquinho* brought to Hawaii by Portuguese sailors, and it became very popular in the U.S. during and after World War I and again in the 1940s and 50s. See ill. under Guitar.

Umfang [Ger.]. Compass, range.

Um Kalthoum [Kalthum, Ibrahim Um] (b. Tamayet el Zahayra, Sinbellawein, Egypt, 1898; d. Cairo, 3 Feb. 1975). Singer. From 1922 worked in Cairo, where she assembled a group of instrumentalists; from 1936 appeared in many musical films; a major figure in Middle Eastern music in the 1950s and 1960s. Sang a wide repertory of traditional and newly composed music.

Umkehrung [Ger.]. Inversion.

Umlauf, Ignaz (b. Vienna, 1746; d. Meidling, 8 June 1796). Composer and violinist. By 1775 principal violist in the German Theater Orchestra. Known mainly as a composer of singspiels; in 1778 wrote the first work for Joseph II's German National Singspiel in Vienna, *Bergknappen.* Other singspiels (all for Vienna) include *Die Insul der Liebe* (ca. 1772), *Die Apotheke* (1778), *Das Irrlicht* (1782), *Der Ring der Liebe* (1786).

Umstimmen [Ger.]. To retune to another pitch.

Un ballo in maschera [It.]. See *Ballo in maschera, Un.*

Un peu [Fr.], **un poco** [It.]. See *Peu, Poco.*

Una corda [It., one string, abbr. *u.c.*]. In piano playing, an instruction to depress the leftmost or soft pedal [Ger. *Verschiebung*], which, on a grand piano, reduces loudness by shifting the keyboard and action in such a way that the hammers strike only one string (usually two on modern instruments) for each pitch instead of the usual two or three provided for all but the extreme bass. The instruction may be canceled with the phrases *tre corde* (three strings) and *tutte le corde* (all strings, abbr. *t.c.*).

Unbetont [Ger.]. Unaccented.

Unequal voices. Mixed voices, i.e., men's and women's.

Unfinished Symphony. Popular name for Schubert's Symphony no. 8 in B minor D. 759 (1822), so called because only the first two movements are complete. Schubert sketched a considerable part of the third movement, a Scherzo. In 1823, he sent the two completed movements to his friend Josef Hüttenbrenner as a gift to Josef's brother Anselm. The work was first performed in 1865 and published in 1867. Why Schubert failed to complete the work remains a matter of controversy.

Ungaresca [It.]. In lute and keyboard music of the 16th century, a dance tune of Hungarian origin, usually consisting of repeated phrases over a drone.

Ungarische Tänze [Ger.]. See Hungarian Dances.

Ungebunden [Ger.]. Free, unrestrained.

Ungeduldig [Ger.]. Impatient.

Ungerader Takt [Ger.]. Triple *meter.

Ungestüm [Ger.]. Turbulent, violent.

Ungezwungen [Ger.]. Free, unbridled.

Unheimlich [Ger.]. Sinister, uneasy.

Union (uilleann) pipe. A bellows-blown bagpipe of Ireland, developed in the 18th century and still popular. It includes three kinds of pipes: a double-reed, keyed *chanter, tuned chromatically with a range of two octaves, three single-reed *drones, and three or four regulators, which produce chords when opened by means of keys. See ill. under Bagpipe.

Unis [Fr.]. In orchestral music, together (after a passage in which a section has been divided).

Unison [It. *unisono*]. (1) [Ger. *Prim*]. The *interval formed by two statements of the same pitch and hence consisting of zero semitones; also termed prime. (2) Simultaneous performance at the same pitch, or sometimes at one or more octaves. This may be specified by the phrase *all'unisono*. An *all'unisono* aria is one in which the accompaniment consists exclusively of instruments playing in unison.

Unisono, all' [It.]. See Unison.

Uniti [It.]. United, together.

Unmerklich [Ger.]. Imperceptible.

Unruhig [Ger.]. Restless.

Unter [Ger.]. Under, below; *Unterdominante,* subdominant; *Unterklavier,* lower manual; *Untermediante,* submediant; *untersetzen,* to pass the thumb under in piano playing; *Unterstimme,* lower or lowest voice; *Untertaste,* white key; *Unterwerk,* *choir organ.

Upbeat [Fr. *anacrouse;* Ger. *Auftakt;* It. *anacrusi;* Sp. *anacrusa*]. One or several notes that occur before the first bar line and thus before the first metrically accented beat (downbeat) of a work or phrase; anacrusis, pickup.

Up-bow. See Bowing (1).

Uribe Holguín, Guillermo (b. Bogotá, 17 Mar. 1880; d. there, 26 June 1971). Composer. Studied in Bogotá at the National Academy and with Narciso Garay, in Paris at the Schola cantorum under D'Indy and alongside Satie and Turina. Returned to Colombia; director of the National Conservatory, 1910–35 and 1942–47. The leading Colombian composer of his time, his works include 11 symphonies; symphonic poems; violin and viola concertos; orchestral dances and other nationalist tableaux; 10 string quartets; 7 violin sonatas; the opera *Furatena* op. 76; church music, including a Requiem; hundreds of piano pieces; songs.

Urio, Francesco Antonio (b. Milan, 1631? or 1632; d. there, 1719 or later). Composer. *Maestro di cappella* at Spoleto Cathedral (1679), Urbino (1681–83), Assisi, and Genoa; also at the Basilica de' Santi Dodici Apostoli, Rome (1690); I Frari, Venice (1697); and S. Francesco, Milan (1715–19). Two collections of his compositions were published; among his other surviving works are an oratorio and a Te Deum, Urio's most famous composition. Handel may have seen the latter work in Florence and borrowed from it in his *Dettingen Te Deum, Saul, Israel in Egypt,* and *L'allegro ed il penseroso.*

Urlar [Gael.]. See *Pibroch.*

Urlinie, Ursatz [Ger.]. See Schenker analysis.

Urrutia Blondel, Jorge (b. La Serena, Chile, 17 Sept. 1905; d. Santiago, 5 July 1981). Composer. Studied in Santiago with Allende and Santa Cruz, in Paris with Boulanger, Koechlin, and Dukas, and in Berlin with Hindemith and Meresmann. Returned to Chile, became professor at the National Conservatory; also served as a dean at the Univ. of Chile. Contributed many articles to the *Revista musical chilena* and collaborated on a history of music in Chile. Works include the ballet *La guitarra del diablo* (1942); *Música para un cuento de antaño,* orchestra (1948); a piano concerto (1950); chamber music; choral music; songs.

Urtext [Ger.]. A text in its presumed original state, without subsequent alterations or additions by an editor; an edition purporting to present a work in such a state.

Usandizaga, José María (b. San Sebastián, 31 Mar. 1887; d. there, 5 Oct. 1915). Composer. Studied at the Schola cantorum, Paris, with D'Indy, Grovlez, Trícon, and Séré. Returned to Spain, 1906; produced music in many genres, generally with a strong Basque nationalist profile. Greatest successes were operas *Mendi mendigan* (1910), *Las golondrinas* (1914), and *La llama* (1915, completed by his brother Ramón). Other works include orchestra and band music; chamber music; sacred and secular vocal pieces.

Uspensky, Viktor Alexandrovich (b. Kaluga, 31 Aug. 1879; d. Tashkent, 9 Oct. 1949). Composer and ethnomusicologist. Studied with Lyadov at the St. Petersburg Conservatory. In 1918 cofounded the Tashkent Conservatory and taught there; also taught at the Uzbek Music Technical School. Conducted and published ethnomusical research in Turkmenistan and Uzbekistan. Compositions include *Farkhad i Shirin,* a music drama of 1936 revised as an opera in 1940, considered the first national Uzbek dramatic work with actual folk tunes.

Usper [Sponga, Spongia, Sponza], **Francesco** (b. Parenzo, Istria, before 1570; d. Venice, early 1641). Composer. Studied in Venice with Andrea Gabrieli. From 1596 until his death served the confraternity of S. Giovanni Evangelista; by 1614 organist at the Church of S. Salvatore. Collaborated with Giovanni Battista Grillo and Monteverdi on a Requiem Mass (lost) for the Medici Grand Duke Cosimo II, 1621. Vocal compositions include motets, Psalms, and madrigals; instrumental music includes some of the earliest Venetian ensemble canzonas as well as sinfonias, and capriccios.

Ussachevsky, Vladimir (b. Hailar, Manchuria, 3 Nov. 1911; d. New York, 2 Jan. 1990). Composer. Family moved to the U.S. from China in 1930. Studied at Pomona College and the Eastman School of Music with Bernard Rogers and Howard Hanson. Lecturer at Columbia Univ. after the war. In 1951, with Otto Luening, began to explore compositional possibilities of tape-recording and altering sounds of traditional instruments; the October 1952 performance of *Sonic Contours* at the Museum of Modern Art in New York was the first public performance of electronic music in the U.S. Further compositions combined electronic music on tape with live performance, and environmental sounds and vocal sounds with electronic sounds. In 1959 with Luening, Milton Babbitt, and Roger Sessions founded the Columbia–Princeton Electronic Music Center in New York. Worked with computers during the late 1960s and 1970s; also composed for traditional instruments played in traditional ways. Retired from Columbia, 1980; continued to teach at the Univ. of Utah. Works include *Transposition, Reverberation, Composition* (tape, 1951); *Rhapsodic Variations,* with Luening (orchestra and tape, 1954); *A Piece for Tape Recorder* (environmental and electronic sounds, 1955); *Creation Prologue* (4 choruses and tape, 1961); *Of Wood and Brass* (tape, 1965); *Computer Piece no. 1* (1968); *Missa brevis* (soprano, chorus, brass, 1972).

Ustvolskaia, Galina Ivanovna (b. Petrograd, 17 July 1919). Composer. Studied with Shostakovich at the Leningrad Conservatory. Taught at the Conservatory preparatory school; students included Boris Tishchenko. Indifferent to contemporary trends, embraced an uncompromising style of obsessive rhythms and expressive contrapuntal dissonance. Works include 5 symphonies; a piano concerto (1946); works for instrumental ensembles (Composition no. 1, *Dona nobis pacem,* piccolo, tuba, and piano, 1970–71; Composition no. 2, *Dies irae,* 8 double basses, percussion, and piano, 1972–73; Composition no. 3, *Benedictus qui venit,* 4 flutes, 4 bassoons, and piano, 1974–75); 6 piano sonatas.

Ut. See Hexachord, Pitch names, Solmization.

Ut supra [Lat.]. As above, as before.

Uttini, Francesco Antonio Baldassare (b. Bologna, 1723; d. Stockholm, 25 Oct. 1795). Composer. Studied with Padre Martini; member of the Accademia dei filarmonici in Bologna, 1743. Conductor for an Italian traveling opera company, for which he wrote his operas *L'olimpiade* and *Zenobia;* made Master of the King's Music in Stockholm, 1767. *Thetis och Pelée* (1773) was the first large-scale opera set in Swedish. *Aline* (1776) was also set in Swedish; wrote other operas with French and Italian texts. Other compositions include cantatas, oratorios, symphonies, harpsichord sonatas, arias, trio sonatas.

V

V. Abbr. for *versicle (℣), verso, *vide,* violin (also V°, VV), *voce (pl. voci), *vox.

Va. Abbr. for viola.

Vaccai, Nicola (b. Tolentino, 15 Mar. 1790; d. Pesaro, 5 Aug. 1848). Composer. Studied at Accademia di S. Cecilia in Rome and with Paisiello in Naples. Composed first opera for the Teatro nuovo, Naples; taught singing in Trieste (1821); moved to Parma in 1823. Taught in Paris in 1830, then in England to 1833. Returned to Italy; taught at Milan Conservatory from 1838. Wrote *Metodo pratico di canto italiano per camera* (1832), still in use. Composed 17 operas (*Giuletta e Romeo,* 1825), 5 cantatas, ballets, 1 Mass, other Mass movements, sacred music, arias, songs.

Vaet, Jacobus (b. Courtrai or Harelbeke, ca. 1529; d. Vienna, Jan. 8, 1567). Composer. Chorister at Notre Dame in Courtrai from 1543, singer in the imperial chapel of Charles V from 1550; from at least 1554 Kapellmeister to Archduke Maximilian of Austria (later Emperor Maximilian II). Works include 9 or 10 Masses; 2 volumes of motets (*Modulationes,* Venice, 1562), and several independent motets; sacred and secular vocal music.

Vaghezza, con [It.]. With longing, with charm.

Vainberg [Weinberg], **Moisei** [Mieczyslaw] **Samuilovich** (b. Warsaw, 8 Dec. 1919; d. Moscow, 26 Feb. 1996). Composer. Studied piano with Turczyn'ski at the Warsaw Conservatory, composition with V. Zolotarev at the Minsk Conservatory. Lived in Tashkent, 1941–43; in Moscow from 1943. Works include 7 operas (including *Madonna and the Soldier,* 1970; *The Idiot,* 1986); ballets and operettas; 19 symphonies, instrumental concertos, and other symphonic music; chamber music; piano music; vocal music; incidental and film music.

Valderrábano, Enríquez de (b. Peñaranda de Duero, ca. 1500; d. after 1557). Vihuelist and composer. Served Francisco de Zúñiga, fourth Count of Miranda. Published a 7-volume tabulature for vihuela, *Silva de Sirenas* (1547), containing transcriptions of sacred and secular works of Josquin, Morales, Gombert, Willaert, and others; fantasias, *sonetos,* and pavans.

Valen, (Olav) Fartein (b. Stavanger, Norway, 25 Aug. 1887; d. Haugesund, 14 Dec. 1952). Composer. Studied with Catharinus Elling in Oslo and with Max Bruch and Karl Leopold Wolf at the Hochschule in Berlin. Returned to Norway, 1916; moved to Oslo, 1924; to Valevåg, 1938. By the 1930s arrived at a novel individual style, atonal but rigorously contrapuntal. Works include 5 symphonies; *Ave Maria,* soprano and orchestra (1921); *Nenia* (1932) and *Le cimetière marin* (1934), both for orchestra; Violin Concerto (1940); string quartets; songs.

Valkyrie, The. See *Ring des Nibelungen, Der.*

Vallee [Vallée], **Rudy** [Hubert Prior] (b. Island Pond, Vt., 28 July 1901; d. Hollywood Hills, Calif., 3 July 1986). Popular bandleader, singer, saxophonist, publisher. Attended Univ. of Maine and Yale; many of his later recordings were of college songs. From 1928 led his own band, The Connecticut Yankees; appeared in films; from the 1930s ran Vallee Publications and later Ruval Music. Recordings include "Stein Song" (1930), "Brother, Can You Spare a Dime" (1932), and "As Time Goes By" (1943).

Valls, Francisco (b. Barcelona, 1665; d. there, 2 Feb. 1747). Composer. *Maestro de capilla* at Mataró parish church before 1688; held posts at Gerona Cathedral (1688) and S. María del Mar, Barcelona (1696). In 1696 became assistant to the *maestro de capilla* at Barcelona Cathedral; maestro, 1709; retired, 1740. Compositions include 12 Masses, 22 responsaries, 16 Magnificats, 12 Psalms, 2 Miserere, about 35 motets, and about 120 *villancicos.*

Valse [Fr.], **vals** [Sp.]. Waltz; *valse à deux temps* [Fr.], a form of waltz popular in the 19th century in which two steps (the first occupying two beats) are taken per measure. Its tempo is faster than the usual waltz.

Valse, La. "Poème choréographique" (dance poem) for orchestra by Ravel, composed in 1919–20 (arranged for two pianos in 1921) and evoking the Viennese waltz. It has been choreographed by Bronislava Nijinska, Michel Fokine, Harald Lander, Frederick Ashton, and George Balanchine.

Valse triste [Fr., Sad Waltz]. A waltz for orchestra by Sibelius, originally composed in 1903 as part of his incidental music op. 44 to the play *Kuolema* and revised in 1904.

Valses nobles et sentimentales [Fr., Noble and Sentimental Waltzes]. A set of waltzes for piano by Ravel, composed in 1911 and later orchestrated by the composer to serve as music for his ballet *Adélaïde, ou Le langage des fleurs* (Adelaide, or The Language of Flowers), produced in Paris in 1912. The title of the waltzes alludes to Schubert's *Valses nobles* op. 77, D. 969 (composed by 1826), and *Valses sentimentales* op. 50, D. 779 (ca. 1823), both for piano.

Valve [Fr. *piston, cylindre;* Ger. *Ventil;* It. *pistone, cilindro;* Sp. *pistón*]. A mechanical device used on brass instruments to change rapidly their sounding length. The two most common types are the piston valve, used on most American trumpets, and the rotary valve, more often seen on horns. In the modern piston valve, a piston moves up and down within a cylindrical casing. In a modern rotary valve, a rotor rotates on its own axis within a cylindrical casing. In both cases, when the valve is at rest or in "open" position, where it is held by a spring mechanism, the air column passes through one passage; but when the finger button or key controlling the valve is pressed, holes or depressions in the piston or rotor are aligned so as to bring another longer or sometimes shorter passage into play. A basic set of three valves is arranged so that the first adds enough tubing to lower the pitch of the instrument two semitones, the second a single semitone, and the third three semitones. Combinations of these can be used to lower the pitch an additional three semitones. Without some means of changing its length, a brass instrument can sound only a series of pitches corresponding approximately to the *harmonic series. The three-valve system provides every chromatic pitch from the second harmonic upward.

Because the amount of additional tubing needed to vary the pitch of an instrument by a semitone varies over the range of the instrument as the effective length of the instrument varies, the fixed lengths of tubing associated with each valve will not produce pitches that are equally well in tune over the instrument's entire range. Thus, most instruments provide for some method of varying the length of the tubing associated with one or more of the valves. Trumpets often have levers or rings that enable the player to lengthen the third and sometimes also the first valve slides. On lower-pitched instruments, a fourth valve is often provided.

Valves for brass instruments were first conceived in 1814–15 by Heinrich Stölzel of Breslau and Friedrich Blühmel of Silesia. A conical rotary valve, square piston valves, and tubular piston valves were tried. In 1818, Stölzel bought Blühmel's rights and patented his tubular piston valve, which then was widely produced throughout the 19th century. The modern rotary valve was a result of work by Blühmel in 1828. The Berlin valve.*(Berliner-Pumpe)* was developed in 1833 by Wilhelm Wieprecht of Berlin with ideas from an improved Stölzel design and from Blühmel's conical rotary valve. The Berlin valve was a short, fat piston valve copied by Adolphe Sax [see Saxhorn] and many other 19th-century makers. The modern piston valve was invented by Etienne François Périnet of Paris in 1839.

Valve instruments. Brass instruments provided with *valves, as distinct from natural instruments [see Natural horn, trumpet], instruments fitted with slides, such as the slide trombone and slide trumpet, and instruments with keys for covering side holes.

Valverde, Joaquín (b. Badajoz, 27 Feb. 1846; d. Madrid, 17 Mar. 1910). Composer. Studied flute and composition at Madrid Conservatory. Conducted in various Madrid theaters (1871–91). His most successful work was the operetta *La gran via* (1886; performed in England as *Castles in Spain*). Wrote *La flauta: Su historia, su estudio* (Madrid, 1886); composed some 30 zarzuelas, instrumental works, songs. His son Quinito [Joaquín] Valverde Sanjuán (1875–1918) was also a composer.

Vamp. A simple introductory or accompanimental phrase or chord progression that can be repeated indefinitely until a soloist enters; hence, the expression "vamp till ready."

Van Beinum, Eduard (b. Arnheim, 3 Sept. 1900; d. Amsterdam, 13 Apr. 1959). Conductor. Studied viola, piano, and composition. In 1927, named conductor of the Haarlem orchestra; 1931, second conductor of the Concertgebouw Orchestra; conductor, 1945. Guest conductor with the London Symphony, the Leningrad Philharmonic, and the Philadelphia Orchestra. In 1956 appointed musical director of the Los Angeles Philharmonic in addition to his post with the Concertgebouw; returned to Amsterdam, 1959.

Van Hagen. See Hagen, Peter Albrecht von.

Vanhal [Wanhal], **Johann Baptist** [Jan Křtitel Vaňhal; Jan Ignatius] (b. Nové Nechanice, Bohemia, 12 May 1739; d. Vienna, 20 Aug. 1813). Composer. Studied in Vienna with Dittersdorf; 1769–71 traveled in Italy. Pupils included Pleyel. Works include over 70 authentic symphonies; concertos, orchestral pieces, string and keyboard chamber music, keyboard sonatas, programmatic works, variations, divertimentos, fantasias; songs.

Van Heusen, Jimmy [James; Babcock, Edward Chester] (b. Syracuse, 26 Jan. 1913; d. Rancho Mirage, Calif., 6 Feb. 1990). Popular pianist and songwriter, publisher. Pianist and song plugger in New

York; wrote for Cotton Club revues; composed musicals and songs for films, primarily with lyricists Johnny Burke ("Swingin' on a Star," *Going My Way*, 1944) and Sammy Cahn ("High Hopes," *A Hole in the Head*, 1959); won several Oscars.

Van Vactor, David (b. Plymouth, Ind., 8 May 1906; d. Los Angeles, 24 Mar. 1994). Composer, conductor, flutist. Studied flute and composition at Northwestern Univ. and in Europe. Joined the Chicago Symphony as a flutist, 1931; 1943, flutist and assistant conductor with the Kansas City Philharmonic; 1947, conductor of the Knoxville Symphony Orchestra. Taught at the Univ. of Tennessee 1947–76. Compositions include 5 symphonies; Concerto, 3 flutes, harp, and orchestra (1935); *Economy Band* no. *1* (1966) and no. *2* (1969), brass and percussion.

Van Vleck, Jacob (b. New York, 1751; d. Bethlehem, Pa., 3 July 1831). Composer. A Moravian clergyman; director of several girls' schools; succeeded Johannes Herbst as bishop of Salem in 1812. Works include Moravian hymns and liturgies.

Vanessa. Opera in four acts by Samuel Barber (libretto by Gian Carlo Menotti), produced in New York in 1958. Setting: Vanessa's castle, in a northern country about 1905.

Varèse, Edgard (Victor Achille Charles) (b. Paris, 22 Dec. 1883; d. New York, 6 Nov. 1965). Composer. Admitted to the Schola cantorum with the assistance of his cousin, the pianist Alfred Cortot; studied there with Albert Roussel, Vincent d'Indy, and Charles Bordes, and at the Conservatory with Charles-Marie Widor. Departed in 1907 for Berlin; became friend of Ferruccio Busoni, Richard Strauss, and Hugo von Hofmannsthal. *Bourgogne* provoked a scandal at its 1910 performance. Returned to Paris, 1914; 1915 departed for the U.S.; became an American citizen, 1926. Conducted modern music in New York and Cincinnati, 1918–19; 1921, with Carlos Salzedo, founded the International Composers' Guild.

The premiere of *Hyperprism* (1923), which provoked a vigorous reaction from the audience and the press, added to Varèse's notoriety. Returned to Paris, 1928–33. Composed *Ionisation*, in which 41 percussion instruments (including 2 anvils, bongos, sleigh bells, lions' roar, and 2 sirens) are used to develop timbres, textures, and masses of sound. Became increasingly interested in the possibilities for electronic generation of sounds and worked with the inventor Léon Thérémin; returned to the U.S., 1933, but composed little until the advent of the tape recorder in the 1950s. *Déserts*, with taped passages created by the methods of *musique concrète*, was acknowledged as a masterpiece of electronic music.

Works include *Bourgogne*, symphonic rhapsody (1907); *Amériques*, orchestra with 20 percussion instruments and siren (1921); *Hyperprism*, winds and percussion (1923); *Arcana*, large orchestra (1927); *Ionisation*, percussion ensemble (1931); *Ecuatorial*, bass voice, brass, percussion, 2 theremins (1934; rev. 1961); *Densité 21.5*, solo flute (1936); *Dance for Burgess* (chamber orchestra, 1949); *Déserts*, winds, percussion, 2-channel tape (1954); *La procession de Vergès* (tape, 1955); *Le poème électronique*, 3-track tape (1958); *Nocturnal*, soprano, bass chorus, chamber orchestra (unfinished; completed by his student Chou Wen-chung).

Variation. A technique of modifying a given musical idea, usually after its first appearance; a form based on a series of such modifications. Variation is one of the most basic and essential of musical techniques and is widely distributed, playing an important role in, for example, the musics of South Asia, Southeast Asia, and Africa. In the context of Western art music, the term commonly means elaboration of melody or accompaniment; other kinds of modifications, such as *development or *transformation, are often considered to be outside the scope of variation. Variation form, in its simplest sense the "theme and variations," embodies a principle of strophic repetition: a theme with a particular structure is followed by a series of discrete pieces with the same or very similar structure. In each variation, some elements of the theme remain constant while others change.

Variation forms are not necessarily always sectional and strophic. If the theme is a short *ostinato or *ground bass, its repetitions will generate a continuously unfolding piece over which figuration and textures change with each statement of the theme; this is known as continuous variation. If variations recur after intervening material, the form will not be strophic because recurrence rather than repetition becomes the structural principle. The resulting hybrid variation forms include rondo-variations and alternating variations, in which the theme and its variations alternate with rondo couplets or with another theme and its own variations, respectively. There is an essential stylistic opposition between stricter variation sets, in which variations are relatively faithful to the structure and some elements of the theme, and freer variations, which may diverge considerably from the theme.

The material to be varied may be a bass line, chord progression, melody, or thematic complex that includes these and other elements. In the continuous variation types, the theme is a melodic pattern set in the bass (that is, a ground bass or ostinato) and is rarely more than eight bars long. The harmonies suggested by or accompanying the theme may stand in for it if the ostinato disappears but are not considered part of the theme except in certain dance types. Continuity is assured by the brevity of the theme and its typical conclusion on the dominant rather than on the tonic; a strong cadence is delayed until the end of the piece. In sectional variations, at least until the later 19th century, the theme is most often a two-reprise structure, about 16 to 32 bars in length, with a relatively clear phrase structure, a simple or affecting melody, and a cadence in the tonic at the close. But within this sectional structure, the actual theme may in essence be the bass line or chord progression, as in Bach's Goldberg Variations. In such pieces, the melody of the theme is the feature least likely to be retained or embellished in the variations that follow.

As a complex of elements, the theme presents the primary constructive features—bass, chords, phrase structure, melody—and their attendant characterizing elements—rhythm, meter, tempo, mode, texture, instrumentation, and dynamics. In individual variations, one or more of the constructive elements are usually retained, together with one or more of the characterizing elements. In strophic variations on a single theme, however, every characterizing element of the theme is subject to variation.

Because every variation retains elements of the theme while artfully altering or replacing others, the degree of relationship may be expressed in what is constant, modified, or new. Most important in these respects are the constructive elements (bass, harmony, structure, melody); because they offer the clearest lines of resemblance, most composers of variations retain at least one. But even "retention" allows considerable freedom. The following list of variation types is based primarily on the constant constructive elements within each set, because these chart the history of the form and point up the most consistent distinctions. Only type 1 is normally continuous; only type 6 regularly dispenses with the theme's structure.

1. Basso ostinato or ground bass variation. The theme, a short bass line, repeats essentially unchanged in each variation, resulting in a continuous variation form (e.g., Bach, Passacaglia in C minor for organ).

2. Constant-melody variation. The theme's melody remains the same and, although usually retained in the highest voice, may move from voice to voice and be reharmonized as well (e.g., Haydn, String Quartet in C major op. 76 no. 3, second movt.).

3. Constant-harmony variation. The harmonic structure is fixed, although changes in mode and some substitutions in chords are possible (e.g., Bach, Goldberg Variations). A subcategory is the constant-bass variation, in which the bass line of the theme remains the same (e.g., Haydn, String Quartet in B♭ major Hob. III:12, "op. 2 no. 6," first movt.).

4. Melodic-outline variation. The theme's melody is recognizable despite figuration, simplification, or rhythmic recasting. In a figured melodic-outline vari-

ation, the principal melodic notes of the theme appear within a highly elaborated melodic line. Simplified or rhythmically changed melodic-outline variation is usually unfigured, with a melodic outline similar to that of the theme. In the late 18th century, melodic-outline variation is often found in conjunction with retention of the theme's harmony (e.g., Mozart, variations on "Ah! vous dirai-je, Maman" K. 300e [265]).

5. Formal-outline variation. Aspects of the theme's form and phrase structure remain constant in this predominantly 19th-century type of variation. Nonetheless, phrase lengths may expand or contract within the general outline. Harmonies usually refer to the theme at the beginning and end of a variation (e.g., Beethoven, Diabelli Variations op. 120; Brahms, Handel Variations op. 24).

6. Fantasy variation. In this product of the 19th century, the variations only allude to the constructive elements, especially the structure and melody; the format may be sectional or "developmental." Sometimes the relationship is purely incidental, whereas at other times constructive elements of the theme come to the fore. Examples include most late 19th-century variations except those of Brahms, but sometimes this type is difficult to distinguish from formal-outline variation (e.g., Strauss, *Don Quixote;* Elgar, *Enigma* Variations).

7. Serial variation. Modifications of a serial theme (a twelve-tone row or some slightly longer or shorter configuration) in which figuration and accompaniment are derived from the row. The structure of the theme usually remains the same. Serial variation thus differs from serial pieces in which variation technique means manipulation of the row, not the theme (e.g., Schoenberg, Serenade op. 24, third movt.; Webern, Symphony op. 21, second movt.).

The history of the variation proper begins in Italy and Spain in the early 16th century and develops from the practice of repeating several times a strain of dance music, retaining the bass and varying or changing the upper line(s), as in the *passamezzo and *romanesca [see also *Diferencia*].

Later in the 16th century, English keyboard composers brought these techniques to a high point (see the many examples in the *Fitzwilliam Virginal Book, e.g., Byrd's "Jhon come kisse me now").

Sweelinck and his pupils wrote many sets of song variations, using either constant-melody or melodic-outline techniques. Sweelinck also wrote variations on sacred themes, usually chorales, the melodies of which are accorded constant-melody treatment in a contrapuntal setting. Song variations and chorale variations continued through Pachelbel and Buxtehude, Muffat and Biber. The dance-bass variation developed into *ostinato types on the one hand and sectional constant-bass types on the other. In Italy, dance basses and songs predominate as sources of variations, and both Italian and French composers began to write varied versions of suite movements (*doubles*), a purely ornamental melodic-outline type.

J. S. Bach's variations sum up the possibilities of the late Baroque in the constant-harmony type (Goldberg Variations), melodic-outline type (*Aria variata alla maniera italiana*), ornamental and figurative melodic-outline (B minor Partita for solo violin), ostinato variations (Passacaglia in C minor for organ, Chaconne in D minor for solo violin), and chorale variations ("Vom Himmel hoch"). Handel was known more for his figurative melodic-outline style than Bach (e.g., the "Harmonious Blacksmith" variations in the Harpsichord Suite in E major).

Haydn's variations span the range of possibilities of the Classical variation. At first writing only constant-bass and constant-harmony sets, he gradually added greater numbers of melodic-outline variations until this type began to predominate around 1770 (e.g., Symphony no. 47, second movt.). Mozart's variations reflect his virtuoso career in 14 independent sets mostly on popular themes (as opposed to Haydn's four or five on original themes), with their melodic-outline figurations and cadenzas. His variation movements equal the seriousness and complexity of Haydn's, with greater contrast and diversity of techniques afforded by the larger number of variations within a movement (e.g., finale of the C minor Piano Concerto K. 491).

Beethoven's variations occupy a central role in his oeuvre and in the history of the form as well. His early piano variations reflect his career as a virtuoso, whereas his later variation movements continue in Haydn's path. Notable in his strophic sets after the 1790s is the return of the constant-harmony variation (*Eroica* Variations for piano op. 35) and a marked increase in the number of characterizing elements that are altered in individual variations. His Diabelli Variations op. 120 are usually considered the successor to the Goldberg Variations as the summit of the variation form to that time. In this formal-outline set, Beethoven freely changed harmony, structure, and character.

Schubert's variations reflect his preoccupation with beautiful melody, especially in the prominent place accorded constant-melody technique in conjunction with melodic-outline technique (*Trout* Piano Quintet D. 667). Schubert contributed the first example of fantasy variation in the slow movement of the *Wanderer* Fantasy D. 760, with its melody richly arrayed in different keys and figurations without a strict structural frame. Other 19th-century composers tried their hand at variations, notably Mendelssohn (*Variations sérieuses*) and Schumann, but the true inheritor of Beethoven's variation mantle is Brahms. He identified the bass as the essence of the theme and

used the bass to control the structure and character of individual variations and the entire set. He interpreted the concept of the bass rather broadly, however; and together with variations clearly inspired by earlier models (String Sextet op. 18; Handel Variations op. 24; Haydn Variations op. 56), he also made use of more formal-outline and even fantasylike constructions (Schumann Variations op. 9; String Quintet op. 111).

The trend toward greater freedom in the later 19th-century variation meant fewer constant elements. Fantasy variations came to the fore in such works as Elgar's *Enigma* Variations and Franck's Symphonic Variations. This freedom extended toward variation movements as well, such as the alternating variations in Mahler's Fourth Symphony. Long continuous programmatic pieces, such as Strauss's *Don Quixote* (subtitled "Fantastic Variations"), stretch the limits of the form.

A stricter approach to thematic elements, especially structure and melody, reemerged in the 20th century, together with a striking resurgence of interest in the *passacaglia. Notable composers of variations in this period include Schoenberg, Webern, Stravinsky, and Carter.

Variations on a Theme by Diabelli (Handel, etc.). See Diabelli Variations, Handel Variations, etc.

Variations symphoniques [Fr., Symphonic Variations]. A work for piano and orchestra by Franck, composed in 1885.

Varnay, Astrid (Ibolyka Maria) (b. Stockholm, 25 Apr. 1918). Soprano. Studied with her mother, Maria Yavor, Paul Althouse, and the conductor Hermann Weigert, whom she later married. Metropolitan Opera debut as Sieglinde, 1941; remained at the Met until 1956, singing Wagnerian soprano roles as well as Venus, Kundry, Elektra, Salome, and Amelia *(Boccanegra)*. Also appeared at Bayreuth (1951–67) and most of the leading houses; returned to the Met in 1974 in mezzo roles, including Strauss's Herodias and Clytemnestra, and Begbick *(Mahagonny)*.

Varsovienne [Fr.]. A dance popular in Paris in the period 1850–70, named for the city of Warsaw and similar to a slow mazurka, with an accented note on the first beat of the second and fourth measures.

Vasilenko, Sergei (Nikiforovich) (b. Moscow, 30 Mar. 1872; d. there, 11 Mar. 1956). Composer. Studied with Taneyev, Ippolitov-Ivanov, and Safonov at the Moscow Conservatory; joined the faculty, 1906 (chair of composition department 1907–41, 1943–56); students included Khachaturian, Polovinkin, and Titov. Compositions drew from Russian and Asian folk melodies as well as French impressionism. In

1938 collaborated with Ashrafi on the first Uzbek opera, *Buran* [The Snowstorm].

Vasquez [Vázquez], **Juan** (b. Badajoz, Spain, ca. 1510; d. Seville? ca. 1560). Composer. Singer at Badajoz and Palencia cathedrals; *maestro de capilla* at Bajadoz (1545–50). In 1551 entered the service of the Sevillian nobleman Don Antonio de Zúñiga. Best known as a composer of *villancicos;* publications include *Villancicos i canciones,* 3–5 voices (1551); *Recopilacion de sonetos y villancicos,* 4–5 voices (1556); a volume of sacred music, *Agenda defunctorum* (1556).

Vater unser [Ger., Our Father]. The German version of the Lord's Prayer, sung to a 16th-century *chorale melody (perhaps by Luther) and made the basis of numerous vocal and instrumental works (e.g., *organ chorales and variations by Bach and others).

Vaudeville [Fr.]. In the 16th century, a lyrical or amatory strophic poem sung to a simple melody, often with chordal accompaniment. In this period, the form *voix de ville* was preferred. Some melodies also served as dance tunes, and some were employed in polyphonic chansons, in either the tenor or the uppermost voice. In a publication of 1571, Adrien Le Roy equates the *vaudeville* with the *air de cour.* In the 17th century, *vaudeville* increasingly referred to light or satirical texts sung most often to preexistent melodies [see *Timbre* (2)]. In the first half of the 18th century, such songs were the principal type of music in the genre of comedy (*comédie en vaudevilles*) that led to both *ballad opera and *opéra comique.* By the 19th century, the term referred to light comedies interspersed with music; in the later 19th century and well into the 20th, throughout Europe and America it came to designate variety shows or revues featuring singers of popular song, dancers, comedians, and acrobats.

Vaughan, Sarah (Lois) (b. Newark, N.J., 27 Mar. 1924; d. Hidden Hills, 3 Apr. 1990). Jazz singer. Won amateur night at Harlem's Apollo Theater in 1942 and soon joined Earl Hines's big band as pianist and vocalist. In 1944–45 sang with Billy Eckstine's band, working with Dizzy Gillespie and Charlie Parker. From 1946 performed with jazz and pop-orchestral groups, toured worldwide, and recorded extensively. Appeared at the 1974 Monterey Jazz Festival; continued to perform through the 1980s with leading jazzmen and major symphony orchestras.

Vaughan Williams, Ralph (b. Down Ampney, Gloucestershire, 12 Oct. 1872; d. London, 26 Aug. 1958). Composer. Studied at the Royal College of Music and Trinity College, Cambridge, with Parry, Wood, and Stanford; also with Bruch in Berlin and Ravel in Paris. Worked as a church organist, music editor, and researcher and arranger of folk songs; in 1905 became conductor of the newly established Leith Hill Musical Festival (to 1953). Joined the faculty of the Royal College of Music, 1919; worked with the Bach Choir 1920–28; taught with the English Folk Dance and Song Society. Frequently served as conductor for his own music; in the late 1930s began to compose music for film. His compositions utilized styles and techniques from contemporary Continental European music but deployed them in the context of a language born directly from his own English cultural experience; he avoided Schoenbergian serialism and its consequents. His later symphonies explored the use of percussion and nonstandard instrumentation.

Works include: Operas: *Riders to the Sea* (1925–32); *The Pilgrim's Progress* (1949; rev. 1951–52). 9 symphonies: A *Sea Symphony, no. 1, soprano, baritone, chorus, orchestra (1903–9; rev. 1923); A London Symphony, no. 2 (1912–13; rev. 1920, 1933); Pastoral Symphony, no. 3 (1921); *Sinfonia antarctica,* no. 7 (1949–52). Orchestral works: *Fantasia on a Theme by Thomas Tallis,* 2 string orchestras (1910; rev. 1919); Piano Concerto (1926–31); *Fantasia on "Greensleeves,"* flute, harp, strings (1934); *Five Variants of "Dives and Lazarus,"* string, harp (1939); Bass Tuba Concerto (1954). Choral works: *Six Choral Songs To Be Sung in the Time of War,* chorus, orchestra (1940); *The First Nowell,* Nativity play, soloists, chorus, small orchestra (1958, completed by Douglas). Also songs, chamber music, and music for film (*49th Parallel,* 1940–41; *The Vision of William Blake,* 1957), theater, and radio.

Vc., Vcl. Abbr. for violoncello.

Vecchi, Orazio [Horatio] **(Tiberio)** (b. Modena, bapt. 6 Dec. 1550; d. there, 19 Feb. 1605). Composer. *Maestro di cappella* at cathedrals of Salò (from 1581), Modena (from 1584), Reggio Emilia Cathedral (1586). Canon and then archdeacon, Correggio Cathedral, 1586–93; returned to Modena, where he composed *L'Amfiparnaso* (1594), a madrigal comedy with a pastoral setting, his best-known work. In 1598 became maestro of the Este court. Sacred music includes motets, hymns, Lamentations, Magnificats, and Masses; secular works include canzonette, madrigals, and the large-scale works *Selva di varia ricreatione* (1590), *Il convito musicale* (1597), and *Le veglie di Siena* (1604).

Vega, Aurelio de la (b. Havana, 28 Nov. 1925). Composer. Pupil of Frederick Kramer in Havana and Ernst Toch in Los Angeles, where he was a cultural attaché. Returned to Cuba and studied with Harold Gramatges; director of the music school at the Univ. of Oriente (1953–59). Compositions of this period were modernist, moving eventually toward serial techniques. After the Cuban revolution in 1959 moved to California; taught and directed the electronic music studio at San Fernando Valley State College from 1959. Later compositions incorporated electronics and aleatoric procedures. Works include *Elegy,* string orchestra (1954); String Quartet "In memoriam Alban Berg" (1957); *Para-Tangents,* trumpet, tape (1973); *Infinite Square* (1974); *Inflorescencia,* soprano, bass clarinet, tape (1978); *Odissea,* orchestra (1988); *Metamorphoses,* wind ensemble (1989).

Vejvanovský, Pavel Josef [Weiwanowski, Wegwanowskij, Paul Josep] (b. Hukvaldy or Hlučín, ca. 1633? or ca. 1639; d. Kroměříž, buried 24 Sept. 1693). Composer. Appointed principal trumpeter and Kapellmeister to Prince-Bishop Karl Liechtenstein-Kastelkorn at Kroměříž in 1664; director of the choir at St. Mořice. Compositions are influenced by Moravian folk music and make extensive use of trumpets and trombones; works include Masses, offertories, motets, vespers, litanies, and many instrumental pieces.

Velato [It.]. Veiled.

Veloce, velocemente [It.]. Fast.

Venegas de Henestrosa, Luis (b. ca. 1510; d. ca. 1557 or later). Composer. Served the Cardinal of Toledo, Juan Tavera (1534 or 1535–45). His *Libro de cifra nueva* (1557), which used a new type of tablature notation later employed by Antonio de Cabezón and Francisco Correa de Arauxo, includes works by Palero, Soto, and Venegas himself, as well as transcriptions of sacred and secular music.

Venetian school. A group of northern and Italian composers active in Venice in the late 16th and early 17th centuries, many associated with the Basilica of St. Mark. The first of the group was Adrian Willaert (ca. 1490–1562), who became chapel master at St. Mark's in 1527. Others include Cipriano de Rore (1515 or 1516–65), Andrea Gabrieli (ca. 1510–86), Baldassare Donato (ca. 1525–1603), Gioseffo Guami (ca. 1540–1611), Giovanni Gabrieli (ca. 1555–1612), Giovanni Croce (ca. 1557–1609), the organ composers Jacques Buus (ca. 1500–1565), Annibale Padovano (1527–75), and Claudio Merulo (1533–1604), and the theorists Nicola Vicentino (1511–ca. 1576) and Gioseffo Zarlino (1517–90). Their music has often been contrasted with that of a so-called *Roman school of the period in its use of instruments (especially by Giovanni Gabrieli; see Canzona) and *polychoral style and was influential in the work of German composers such as Jacob Handl (1550–91), Hieronymus Praetorius (1560–1629), Hans Leo Hassler (1562–1612), Michael

Praetorius (ca. 1571–1621), and Heinrich Schütz (1585–1672).

Vengerova, Isabelle [Isabella Afanasyevna] (b. Minsk, 1 Mar. 1877; d. New York, 7 Feb. 1956). Pianist. Studied in Vienna with Joseph Dachs and in St. Petersburg with Anna Essipoff. Taught at the St. Petersburg Conservatory (1906–20); moved to the U.S. in 1923. One of the founders of the Curtis Institute; taught at Mannes College. Students include Samuel Barber, Lukas Foss, Gilbert Kalish, and Leonard Bernstein.

Veni Sancte Spiritus [Lat., Come, Holy Spirit]. The *sequence for Pentecost; also called the Golden Sequence.

Venite exsultemus [Lat.]. The *Invitatory.

Vent` [Fr.]. Wind; *instruments à vent,* wind instruments.

Ventil [Ger.], **ventile** [It.]. *Valve; *Ventilhorn* [Ger.], valve horn.

Venuti, Joe [Giuseppe] (b. Lecco, Italy, 16 Sept. 1903; d. Seattle, 14 Aug. 1978). Jazz violinist. Worked with Eddie Lang, together joining Adrian Rollini (1927) and Paul Whiteman (1929–30). Recordings include "Stringing the Blues" (1926) and "Raggin' the Scale" (1933). Led a big band 1935–43, then worked mainly on the West Coast and in Nevada. After 1968 returned to prominence, touring Europe and recording with Zoot Sims (*Joe and Zoot,* 1974), Marian McPartland, Earl Hines, Dave McKenna, and others.

Veracini, Francesco Maria (b. Florence, 1 Feb. 1690; d. there, 31 Oct. 1768). Composer. Studied with his uncle Antonio Veracini, and with Giovanni Maria Casini, Francesco Feroci, and G. A. Bernabei. In 1711 and 1712 played violin in Venice; oratorio *Il trionfo della innocenza patrocinata da S. Niccolò* performed in Florence, 1712. After time in London, Düsseldorf, and Venice, employed at the Dresden court in 1717; in Florence 1723–33; returned to London in 1733, where Opera of the Nobility presented his first 3 operas. In 1744 published the *Sonate accademiche* op. 2. Returned to Florence in the 1750s; *maestro di cappella* at S. Pancrazio from 1755. Compositions include 4 operas, 8 oratorios (lost), sacred music, cantatas, songs, sonatas, and concertos.

Veränderungen [Ger.]. Variations.

Verbunkos [Hung., fr. Ger. *Werbung,* recruiting]. A Hungarian dance originating in the second half of the 18th century and used in the recruitment of soldiers until the advent of conscription in 1849; the dance and its associated music have nevertheless survived, principally in the closely related *csárdás.* Music was provided by Gypsy bands, who added their characteristic performing style to a repertory of folk tunes. The result was a central part of what is usually termed *Gypsy music. The *verbunkos* itself typically includes an alternation between a slow introductory section (*lassú*) and a section in a fast tempo (*friss*). Composers of art music drawing on this tradition include Liszt (**Hungarian Rhapsodies*), Brahms, Bartók, and Kodály.

Verdelot, Philippe (b. Verdelot, Les Loges, Seine-et-Marne, between 1470 and 1480; d. before 1552). Composer. In Florence by 1522; *maestro di cappella* at the Baptisterium S. Giovanni (1523–25) and at the Cathedral (1523–27). Between December 1523 and January 1524 performed for Clement VII in Rome; nothing is known of his subsequent fate. Sacred music includes 2 Masses and nearly 60 motets; other works include chansons and madrigals.

Verdi, Giuseppe (Fortunino Francesco) (b. Le Roncole, near Parma, 9 or 10 Oct. 1813; d. Milan, 27 Jan. 1901). Composer. Denied admission to the Milan Conservatory; studied privately with Vincenzo Lavigna, underwritten by Antonio Barezzi, whose daughter he married in 1836 (she died in 1839). In 1838 moved to Milan; *Oberto* produced at La Scala in 1839. *Nabucco,* commissioned by La Scala, was a great success and made Verdi a major figure. Began to compose operas prolifically, traveling to supervise their productions around Europe. *Ernani* was the most widely popular of his early operas; after *Giovanna d'Arco* refused to work with La Scala. In 1847 conducted the premiere of *I masnadieri* with Jenny Lind as prima donna to great success.

In Paris renewed his acquaintance with the former prima donna Giuseppina Strepponi, who became his companion and eventually his wife. Composed *Jérusalem* (a French version of *I Lombardi*) and *Les vêpres siciliennes* for the Paris Opéra. Composed the patriotic opera *La battaglia di Legnano,* inspired by the 1848 Italian uprising against the Austrians. Returned to Italy with Strepponi in 1849, settling first in Busseto and then withdrawing to Sant'Agata; operatic output began to decrease. *Luisa Miller* and *Rigoletto* were successes; the Venice premiere of *La traviata* was a fiasco because of an inadequate cast. In Paris 1853–55 and 1856-57, where *Les vêpres siciliennes* had its premiere. Returned to Italy, where *Un ballo in maschera* had its premiere after conflicts with the censor led to a change of the opera's setting from Sweden to Boston. Thereafter worked only intermittently. Married Strepponi in 1859.

In 1861 *La forza del destino* commissioned by St. Petersburg, and premiered there in 1862. *Don Carlos* commissioned by the Paris Opéra and premiered there in 1867. The revised *Forza del Destino* brought Verdi back to La Scala in 1869. In 1870 accepted an invitation to compose an opera for Cairo to celebrate the opening of the Suez Canal; *Aida* had its premiere there in 1871 and went on to great success. The Requiem, conceived as a tribute to Manzoni and first performed in Milan on 22 May 1874, the first anniversary of the writer's death, was acclaimed in Paris, London, and Vienna. Giulio Ricordi suggested collaboration with the librettist Boito, leading to a creative relationship that produced *Otello* and *Falstaff,* both triumphs. Afterward Verdi felt unequal to another opera; his final compositions were the *Four Sacred Pieces.*

Operas include *Oberto, Conte di San Bonifacio* (1839); **Nabucco* (1841); *I Lombardi alla prima crociata* (1843); **Ernani* (1844); *I due Foscari* (1844); *Giovanna d'Arco* (1845); *Attila* (1846); **Macbeth* (1847); *I masnadieri* (1847); *Jérusalem* (1847); *La battaglia di Legnano* (1849); *Luisa Miller* (1849); *Stiffelio* (1850); **Rigoletto* (1851); *Il *trovatore* (1853); *La *traviata* (1853); *Les vêpres siciliennes* (1854–55); **Simon Boccanegra* (1857); *Un *ballo in maschera* (1859); *La *forza del destino* (1861); **Don Carlos* (1866); **Aida* (1871); **Otello* (1886); **Falstaff* (1892). Choral works include Requiem (1874); *Four Sacred Pieces* (1898).

Verdoppeln [Ger.]. To *double.

Veress, Sándor (b. Kolozsvár [now Cluj], Romania, 1 Feb. 1907; d. Bern, Switzerland, 4 Mar. 1992). Composer. Studied at the Budapest Academy of Music with Bartók and Kodály. Collected, transcribed, and analyzed Hungarian folk music; began to attract attention as a composer during the 1930s. Taught at the State Academy of Music, Budapest, 1943–48; Bern Conservatory, 1950–68; Bern Univ. from 1968. During the 1950s music became increasingly influenced by serialism. Works include *Divertimento* (chamber orchestra, 1935); *Térszili Katica* (ballet, 1942); *Hommage à Paul Klee* (2 pianos, strings, 1952); *Passacaglia concertante* (oboe, strings, 1961); *Musica concertante* (strings, 1966); *Deux essais* (orchestra, 1986); *Stories and Fairy Tales* (2 percussion, 1987); *Concerto Tilinko* (flute, orchestra, 1988–89).

Verhallend [Ger.]. Fading away.

Verismo [It.]. A style of operatic composition, prevalent in Italy in the 1890s, with repercussions extending to other European countries and later decades. *Verismo* in Italy began as a literary movement, exemplified by the novels and plays of Giovanni Verga, showing analogies with the naturalism of Zola and de Maupassant. The landmark veristic opera, Mascagni's **Cavalleria rusticana* (1890), is based on a story by Verga. The veristic operas that followed, such as Leoncavallo's **Pagliacci* (1892), Giordano's *Mala vita* (1892), and Puccini's *Il tabarro* (1918) [see *Trittico*], have certain traits in common. The settings are contemporary; the characters are often rural and generally impoverished; the passions run high and lead to violence. There is a tendency in these works to wed the sordid with the sensational.

Verismo is also used, more loosely, to describe any of the operas by Mascagni, Leoncavallo, Puccini, Giordano, and Cilea, who were also collectively referred to as the young school (*nuove giovane*). A number of these works are alien to ideals of realism or naturalism, however.

Verkaufte Braut, Die [Ger.]. See *Bartered Bride, The*.

Verklärte Nacht [Ger., Transfigured Night]. A work in one movement for two violins, two violas, and two cellos by Schoenberg, op. 4 (1899), inspired by a poem of Richard Dehmel. It was later arranged for string orchestra (1917, rev. 1943), and it has served as the basis for many ballets, including *Pillar of Fire* (1942, choreography by Antony Tudor).

Verlöschend [Ger.]. Dying away.

Vermindert [Ger.]. Diminished.

Verrall, John (Weedon) (b. Britt, Iowa, 17 June 1908). Composer. Studied at Univ. of Minnesota with Donald Ferguson, the Royal College of Music in London, and the Liszt Conservatory in Budapest with Kodaly. Taught at Hamline Univ. in St. Paul 1934–42, at Univ. of Washington in Seattle 1948–73. Many compositions of the period 1948–54 are based on a 9-note scale of his own devising; later switched to modal harmonies. Works include Symphony no. 1 (1939); String Quartet no. 4 (1949); *The Wedding Knell,* opera (1952); Nonet (1970); Flute Sonata (1972). Author of *Fugue and Invention in Theory and Practice* (1966) and *Basic Theory of Scales, Modes, and Intervals* (1969).

Verrett [Carter], **Shirley** (b. New Orleans, 31 May 1931). Mezzo-soprano, later soprano. Studied in Los Angeles with Anna Fitziu and Hall Johnson, and with Marion Székely-Fresski at Juilliard. New York City Opera debut as Irina (Weill's *Lost in the Stars*), 1958. Received critical acclaim for her Carmen in Spoleto (1962); repeated the role at the Bolshoi (1963), the City Opera (1964), La Scala (1966), the Metropolitan Opera (debut, 1968), and Covent Garden (1973). Beginning in the late 1970s sang soprano roles, including Tosca and Norma; also sang Didon *(Troyens),* Gluck's Orpheus, Amneris, Lady Macbeth, and Selika *(L'africaine).*

Vers mesuré [Fr.]. See *Musique mesurée.*

Verschiebung [Ger.]. See *Una corda.*

Verschwindend [Ger.]. Disappearing, fading away.

Verse. (1) Poetry; a line of poetry. (2) A group of lines making up a unit of a poem, usually one of several based on the same meter and rhyme scheme; strophe, stanza. Several such units may be separated by a recurring *refrain. (3) In one of the most typical forms of American popular song of the mid-20th century, words and music preceding the chorus or refrain, which constitutes the body of the song itself. The form and nomenclature derive from verse-and-refrain form [see (2)], but in practice there may be only one set of words for the verse, and it is often not performed at all [see Ballad (3)]. (4) The small units into which chapters and books of the Bible (including the Psalms) are divided, often identified in liturgical books with the symbol ℣. For the singing of Psalm verses and related texts, see Psalmody, Latin; Psalm tone. (5) *Versicle.

Verset [Fr.; Ger. *Versett, Versetl;* It. *verso, versetto;* Sp. *versillo*]. A brief organ piece intended to replace a verse of plainchant in the liturgy. Organists customarily played in place of the odd-numbered verses of a liturgical item, the even-numbered verses being sung by the choir. Such pieces were improvised in virtually all Roman Catholic countries from ca. 1400 to 1903 [see Organ Mass]. Composers wrote out versets for liturgical items that were most frequently used, such as the Mass Ordinary, Magnificat, Te Deum, and certain Latin hymns. The practice of substituting organ music for plainsong is sometimes termed supplying.

Versetto [It.]. *Verset.

Versetzung [Ger.]. Transposition; *Versetzungszeichen,* accidental.

Versicle [abbr. ℣.]. (1) In the Western Christian rites, a phrase or sentence, often from Scripture, said or sung by the officiant and to which the choir or congregation answers with a phrase called a response (abbr. ℟.). (2) In the *sequence, either of the two parallel lines that make up a couplet or "double versicle."

Verstärken [Ger.]. To reinforce, amplify.

Verstovsky, Alexei Nikolayevich (b. Seliverstovo, Tambov, 1 Mar. 1799; d. Moscow, 17 Nov. 1862). Composer. Studied piano with Steibelt and Field, violin with Franz Böhm and Maurer. Named inspector of theaters in Moscow, 1825; director of Moscow theaters, 1842–60. Composed 6 operas, music for more than 30 vaudevilles, incidental music; cantatas; hymns, choruses, songs.

Versus [Lat.]. (1) Verse, as of a Psalm or some forms of liturgical chant [see Psalmody, Psalm tone]. (2) A line of poetry. (3) Rhymed, rhythmic, strophic Latin poetry set to music (both monophonic and polyphonic) beginning in the late 10th century and especially prominent in the repertory of *St. Martial.

Verzierung [Ger.]. Ornament, *ornamentation.

Vespers [fr. Lat. *vesper,* evening]. A service forming part of the Divine *Office.

Vessel flute. *Globular flute.

Via [It.]. Away; *via sordini,* remove mutes.

Viadana [Grossi da Viadana], **Ludovico** (b. Viadana, near Parma, ca. 1560; d. Gualtieri, near Parma, 2 May 1627). Composer. *Maestro di cappella,* Mantua Cathedral (1594–ca. 1597); convent of S. Luca, Cremona (1602); Concordia, near Venice (1608–9); and Fano Cathedral (1610–12). His *Cento concerti ecclesiastici* op. 12 (1602) is one of the earliest publications of sacred music with basso continuo. Works include Masses, motets, Psalms, Magnificats, Lamentations, canzonettas, pieces for 2 instrumental choirs.

Vianna da Motta [Viana da Mota], **José** (b. S. Tomá, 22 Apr. 1868; d. Lisbon, 31 May 1948). Pianist and composer. Studied in Berlin with Xaver Scharwenka (piano) and Philipp Scharwenka (composition), in Weimar with Liszt, and in Frankfurt with Hans von Bülow. Appeared in Europe and South America as a concert artist; director of the Lisbon Conservatory 1919–38. Published compositions include a symphony, a string quartet, piano pieces, and songs.

Viardot, (Michelle Ferdinande) Pauline (b. Paris, 18 July 1821; d. there, 18 May 1910). Mezzo-soprano. Daughter of Manuel García, sister of Maria Malibran and Manuel García. Studied piano with Meysenberg and Liszt, composition with Reicha. Concert debut 1837 in Brussels; stage debut 1839 in London, later Paris, as Desdemona (Rossini's *Otello*). Married Louis Viardot, manager of the Théâtre-Italien in Paris, 1840. Sang Fidès in the first performance of Meyerbeer's *Le prophète* (1849); premiered Brahms's *Alto Rhapsody* op. 53 (1869). Taught at the Paris Conservatory 1871–75. Compositions include operettas; vocal transcriptions of Chopin mazurkas.

Vibraharp, vibraphone. A percussion instrument of definite pitch consisting of graduated metal bars arranged horizontally in a fashion similar to that of the piano keyboard. Beneath each bar is a vertical resonating tube, in the upper part of which is a flat disk. The disks for each of the two rows of resonators (one for diatonic pitches, the other for chromatic) are connected by a rod that can be rotated by a motor, causing the disks to open and close the resonators, thus producing a *vibrato. The instrument may be played either with the motor on or off and is struck with

beaters of various hardnesses. It is also fitted with dampers controlled by a pedal. Its normal compass is f–f′′′.

Vibrare [It.]. To vibrate; *lasciar vibrare,* allow to vibrate, do not damp.

Vibrato [It., from Lat. *vibrare,* to shake]. A slight fluctuation of pitch used by performers to enrich or intensify the sound. In modern string playing, vibrato is produced by rocking the left hand as a note is played; in modern wind playing, it is effected by regulating the air flow into the instrument or by varying the tension of the lips or the pressure of the mouth on the reed or mouthpiece. Since the early years of the 20th century, vibrato, particularly on bowed stringed instruments, has become essentially an organic feature of tone production, a means of adding continuous intensity to the sound; vibrato has become a standard feature of the unchanging legato sound most often taught at present.

Until the 20th century, vibrato, or *tremolo, as it was generally termed, was produced in a number of ways and was considered to be an ornament, an expressive device that, like many others available to the performer, was used sparingly. Mace (1676), using the term sting, described lute vibrato. Vibrato on the viola da gamba is discussed by authors like Ganassi (1543), who found it appropriate for "sad and aggrieved" music, Simpson (1659), Marais (1686), and Jean Rousseau (1687). These writers distinguish between two-finger vibrato—a kind of microtonal trill—and the more familiar one-finger variety. Two-finger vibrato is variously termed close shake, *tremblement sans appuyer, battement,* and *flattement.* One-finger vibrato, termed *langeur* and *plainte,* is recommended for notes played with the fourth finger, when two-finger vibrato was impossible. Quantz (1752) mentions vibrato, calling it *Bebung, only to say that it is appropriate when swelling and diminishing a long-note *messa di voce.*

Eighteenth-century violin treatises by Tartini (MS; ca. 1752; pub. 1771) and Leopold Mozart (1756), who repeats much of Tartini's material, recommend specific and limited use of violin vibrato. Only Geminiani, who calls vibrato close shake, wrote that "it should be made use of as often as possible." But Leopold Mozart speaks disapprovingly of players who "tremble upon every note as though they had palsy," and subsequent editions of Geminiani's treatise delete the advice to use it as often as possible. Spohr (1832) and other 19th-century violinists continue to recommend limited, deliberate use of vibrato. In general, vibrato is said to be useful on long notes and to highlight expressive moments.

Vocal vibrato is more difficult to define. What is often termed vibrato and widely cultivated is at least as much a fluctuation in intensity as in pitch; some authorities maintain that it is entirely a fluctuation in intensity. An excessive fluctuation in pitch (sometimes termed in this context tremolo) is agreed by all to be undesirable. In general, vocal vibrato is the norm in Western art music today, its momentary restraint or absence serving an expressive purpose. Singers attempting to recreate the performing styles of some early music may employ vibrato sparingly or not at all, however. For vocal ornaments consisting of the rapid repetition of a pitch, see Tremolo; see also Voice, Performance practice.

Vibrer [Fr.]. To vibrate; *laissez vibrer,* allow to vibrate, do not damp.

Vicentino, Nicola (b. Vicenza, 1511; d. Milan, ca. 1576). Composer and theorist. Studied with Willaert; served Cardinal Ippolito II d'Este in Ferrara. First book of 5-voice madrigals appeared in Venice in 1546; followed the cardinal to Rome. In 1551 engaged in a famous debate with the Portuguese musician Vicente Lusitano concerning the ancient Greek genera (diatonic, chromatic, and enharmonic); published the treatise *L'antica musica ridotta alla moderna prattica* (Rome, 1555). By 1561 had constructed an arcicembalo and an arciorgano, keyboard instruments capable of playing chromatic and enharmonic genera. Around 1563 became *maestro di cappella* at Vicenza Cathedral.

Vickers, Jon(athan Stewart) (b. Prince Albert, Saskatchewan, 29 Oct. 1926). Tenor. Studied at the Royal Conservatory of Music in Toronto with George Lambert. Appeared at the 1956 Stratford Festival; in 1957 joined the Covent Garden Opera (debut as King Gustavus [Riccardo] in *Un ballo in maschera*). Other Covent Garden roles included Metropolitan Opera debut, 1960 (as Canio in *Pagliacci*). Performed with many of the world's major opera houses; important roles include Aeneas, Don Carlos, Don José, Radamès, Siegmund, Parsifal, and Peter Grimes.

Victimae paschali laudes [Lat., Praises to the Paschal victim]. The *sequence for Easter.

Victoria, Tomás Luis de (b. Ávila, 1548; d. Madrid, 20 Aug. 1611). Composer and organist. Entered the Jesuit Collegium germanicum, Rome, 1565; may have studied with Palestrina. Taught at the Collegium from 1571; *maestro di cappella* there 1573 to 1576 or 1577. Chaplaincy at S. Girolamo della Carità 1578–85. In 1587 appointed by King Philip II of Spain as chaplain to the Dowager Empress María in Madrid; maestro of the Monasterio de las Descalzas de S. Clara convent choir and then organist until his death. The greatest Spanish composer of the Renaissance, Victoria succeeded in publishing nearly his entire oeuvre during his lifetime. Works include motets,

Masses *(Missa Papae Marcelli),* Magnificats, Psalms, an *Officium defunctorum* (1605, composed on the death of Empress María), hymns, Marian antiphons, music for Holy Week.

Vida breve, La [Sp., The Brief Life]. Opera in two acts by Falla (libretto by Carlos Fernández Shaw), produced (in French) in Nice in 1913. Setting: the Gypsy quarter of Granada.

Vide. (1) [Fr.] Empty; *corde à vide,* open string. (2) [Lat.] See. The instruction to proceed directly from one point in a score to some other may be indicated by placing the syllable *Vi-* at the first and *-de* at the second.

Vieil ton [Fr., old tuning]. The Renaissance tuning in fourths for lute, *vihuela,* viola da gamba, and related instruments. The G tuning (G c f a d′ g′) is most frequently encountered in the sources, though the tuning on A was favored by some German lutenists. Renaissance lute tunings are "nominal," however, since the actual pitch would be determined by the instrument's size. The *vieil ton* was gradually displaced after 1600 by the many *accords nouveaux.

Vielle [Fr.]. Any of a variety of bowed stringed instruments of the Middle Ages, including both the medieval *viol and *fiddle; *v. à roue,* *hurdy-gurdy.

Viennese classical school. The principal composers of the *Classical period, Haydn, Mozart, and Beethoven, the major part of whose activity was in Vienna. The term is sometimes broadened to include their contemporaries and immediate predecessors.

Viennese school, second. Arnold Schoenberg (1874–1951) and his two pupils Anton Webern (1883–1945) and Alban Berg (1885–1935), the first major exponents of *twelve-tone music.

Vierhändig [Ger.]. For four hands, i.e., for two players at a single piano.

Vierne, Louis (b. Poitiers, 8 Oct. 1870; d. Paris, 2 June 1937). Organist and composer. Blinded at the age of 6; studied organ at the Paris Conservatory with César Franck, Charles Marie Widor, and Félix Guilmant. Organist at Notre Dame Cathedral from 1900 until his death. Performed recitals and toured Europe and the U.S. in the 1920s and 1930s. Compositions include 6 organ symphonies, a violin sonata, a quintet for piano and strings, works for organ.

Viertel [Ger.]. Quarter; *Viertelnote,* quarter *note; *Viertelton,* quarter tone.

Vieru, Anatol (b. Iaşi, 8 June 1926; d. Bucharest, 8 Oct. 1998). Composer. Studied at the Bucharest Conservatory with Constantinescu, Rogalski, Klepper, and Silvestri; at the Moscow Conservatory with Khachaturian and Rogal-Levitsky. Conductor at the

Bucharest National Theater 1947–50; taught at the Bucharest Conservatory and briefly in the U.S. at Sarah Lawrence College and the Composers' Forum at Juilliard. In 1982 and 1983 taught at the Rubin Academy for Music and Dance in Jerusalem. His compositions combine advanced modern techniques with characteristics of Romanian folk music. Works include opera (*Iona*, 1976; *Praznicul Calicilor,* 1980); orchestral works (Symphony no. 5, chorus and orchestra, 1984–85; *Clepsidra I,* 1968); vocal music (*Quatre angles pour regarder Florence,* voice, keyboard, percussion, 1973); chamber music (*Tara de piatra* [Land of Stones], tape, 1972; String Quartet no. 6, 1986).

Vieuxtemps, Henri (b. Verviers, 17 Feb. 1820; d. Mustapha, Algeria, 6 June 1881). Violinist and composer. Studied in Paris and Vienna, where his performance of Beethoven's Violin Concerto op. 61 in 1834 revived interest in the work. In 1835 studied composition with Reicha in Paris; toured Russia in 1838, the U.S. in 1844. Court violinist and professor of violin in St. Petersburg, 1846–52; professor of violin at Brussels Conservatory, 1871–73. Brother of the pianist (Jean-Joseph-) Lucien Vieuxtemps (1828–1901) and the cellist Jules Joseph Ernest Vieuxtemps (1832–96). Compositions include 7 violin concertos (no. 4, op. 31 [ca. 1850] still frequently performed); 2 cello concertos, a violin sonata, 3 piano quartets; 6 *Études de concert* op. 16, violin solo (ca. 1845); many pieces for violin and piano.

Vif [Fr.]. Lively, fast.

Vigil [Lat. *vigilia,* wakefulness, watchfulness]. A liturgical service held in anticipation of a given feast, especially on the night preceding.

Vihuela [Sp.]. A waisted, stringed instrument of medieval and Renaissance Spain. Three varieties are most often encountered: *vihuela de arco,* a bowed *vihuela; vihuela de peñola,* played with a quill; *vihuela de mano,* plucked with the fingers. By the 16th century, the unqualified term meant the *vihuela de mano.*

The *vihuela (de mano),* often seen in Renaissance sources, is a large instrument, quite like a modern guitar in size and appearance. It has a flat top and back, rather shallow sides, a narrow neck (with ten gut frets) and peghead, an elaborate rosette, and sometimes decoration. The peghead is bent slightly back with pegs inserted from the rear. Only one example from the period is known to survive, and it is thought to be abnormally large.

Six unison courses of double gut strings are typical, though printed music for five- and seven-course instruments is preserved. The *vihuela's* tuning uses intervals identical to the lute's: fourth, fourth, major

third, fourth, fourth. The *vihuela* repertory includes accompaniment to songs of the **romance* and **villancico* types, solo pieces (**fantasias, *diferencias,* and **tientos*), and **intabulations of vocal works and a few dances. It is printed in a variety of **tablature forms. Composers include Luis de Milán, Luys de Narváez, Miguel de Fuenllana, and Alonso Mudarra. By the beginning of the 17th century, the *vihuela* had been largely replaced by the four-course guitar.

Villa-Lobos, Heitor (b. Rio de Janeiro, 5 Mar. 1887; d. there, 17 Nov. 1959). Composer. Studied cello, guitar, and clarinet; as a youth played in *chôro* ensembles and the Recreio Theatre opera orchestra. Traveled throughout Brazil, collecting and studying folk music, before settling in Rio in 1912. A concert of his works in 1915 provoked critical debate. Met Milhaud in 1917; Artur Rubinstein became an advocate of his work. Based in Paris, 1923–30, where his circle included Prokofiev, d'Indy, Roger-Ducasse, Schmitt, and Varèse, and where concerts established his international reputation. Returned to Brazil in 1930 and became an important official in public education; produced folk song arrangements to be used in schools and a solfège method and founded a Ministry of Education conservatory (1942) and the Brazilian Academy of Music (1945). Toured widely in Europe and the Americas as a conductor of his own works, making U.S. appearances in Boston, New York, Chicago, Philadelphia, and Los Angeles. Continued to travel, conduct, record, and compose until his final days.

Works include: operas *Izhat* (1914, rev. 1932), *Magdalena* (1948), and *Yerma* (1955); ballets *Dança da terra* (1939), *Rudá* (1951), *Genesis* (1954), and *Emperor Jones* (1955); 12 symphonies, 2 sinfoniettas, and symphonic poems, including *Amazonas* (1917) and *Madona* (1945); 9 *Bachianas brasileiras* for various forces (1932–44); 14 *Chôros;* concertos for cello, piano, guitar, and harp; fantasias for various instruments with orchestra, 1 for at least 32 cellos (1958); 17 string quartets, other chamber works; 4 violin sonatas, 2 cello sonatas; choral music, including the *Canto orfeónico* (1940, 1950) and much sacred music; works for guitar; piano music, including *Danças características africanas* (1915), *Cielo brasileiro* (4 pieces, 1936), *Hommage à Chopin* (1949); and many songs.

Villancico [Sp.]. In the 15th and 16th centuries, a form of Spanish poetry consisting of a refrain (*estribillo*) that alternates with one or more strophes (*coplas* or *pies*), each of which is made up of a *mudanza* (change, i.e., of rhyme) and a *vuelta* (return, i.e., to the rhyme of the refrain). The number of lines and the rhyme scheme of these components are variable; the most common line length is of eight syllables. The accompanying diagram gives two common schemes. In the first, the rhyme scheme of the *vuelta* agrees with that of the refrain. In the second, a rhyme from the *mudanza* is carried over into the *vuelta,* with the result that the return to the music of the refrain begins before the return to its rhymes. In some examples, the *vuelta* repeats literally the last line or two of the refrain, thus contracting the two. The form is employed, though not so termed, in the 13th century *cantigas;* and it is closely related to the 12th-century Hispano-Arabic *zajal,* the French *virelai,* and the Italian *ballata* (the terminology for which is similar to that for the *villancico*). The repertory includes courtly, popular, and sacred elements and many poems in the feminine voice.

	Estribillo (refrain)	Copla (strophe)	
		Mudanza	Vuelta
Music	A	BB	A
Text	ABB	cdcd	abb
	ABB	cdcd	dBB

The first large collections are *cancioneros* from around 1500. These contain polyphonic settings in three and four voices by Juan del Encina (1468–1529 or 1530; the principal exponent of the genre in this period), Francisco Millán, Francisco de Peñalosa, Francisco de la Torre, Juan de Anchieta, and others. Some works employ polyphonic textures reminiscent of the 15th-century French chanson (sometimes with text supplied in only the uppermost of three voices), whereas others are largely homophonic (sometimes with text in all voices). Composers cultivating the genre later in the 16th century include Juan Vázquez and Francisco Guerrero. In this period, the number of voices is often reduced (sometimes to one) for the *mudanza,* and there is a growing repertory of sacred works, including *contrafacta.* Composers for the *vihuela* contributed settings.

The vast repertory of *villancicos* from the 17th century remains largely unpublished and unexplored. It includes secular works that continue the traditions of the 16th century, but by mid-century some *villancicos* had instrumental accompaniment. At the same time, the addition of refrains (*estribillos*) to the form of the *romance* leads to a merging of the musical forms of the *villancico* and *romance.* Such works may also be termed *tonada* or *tono humano.* This period also saw the rapid expansion of a repertory of increasingly elaborate sacred works. Such works were composed by chapel masters all over Spain for the principal religious feasts, especially Christmas. In the first half of the 18th century, the *villancico*

increasingly took on the character of the Italian cantata in its use of arias, recitatives, and instrumental movements. In 1765, the performance in church of works of this type with vernacular texts was suppressed.

The *villancico* followed a similar course in Latin America in the 17th and 18th centuries. Juan Gutiérrez de Padilla (ca. 1590–1664) composed cycles of *villancicos* for the Cathedral of Puebla, Mexico. The foremost poet of the repertory was Mexico's Sor Juana Inés de la Cruz (1651–95).

The term is now sometimes simply synonymous with Christmas carol.

Villanella [It., a country girl]. A form of vocal music popular in Italy from ca. 1530 to the end of the 16th century. The earliest examples, called *canzone villanesche alla napolitana,* are stanzas similar in poetic form and content to a chain of *strambotti* but have a refrain placed between adjacent couplets (abR abR abR ccR). The material is often but not invariably rustic; parodies of high-flown poetic language are common, and many proverbial expressions are used. The music, for three voices in homophonic style and with the chief tune in the top voice, is simple and rhythmically lively, with dancelike syncopations and well-marked cadences. The celebrated parallel fifths in the texture may be a deliberate rusticity and may also imitate the effect of a strumming instrument. Neapolitan composers such as Giovanni Domenico da Nola (1541 and after) and Giovan Tomaso di Maio (1546) wrote quantities of these pieces, the popularity of which soon spread throughout Italy.

The *villanella* was taken up by Adrian Willaert (1544) and other Venetian composers; they paraphrased the originals, adding a fourth voice, moving the tune to the tenor, and smoothing out the counterpoint. In the 1550s, the term *villanella* began to replace the older *villanesca.* Subgenres such as the *moresca* (Moorish song), *mascherata,* and *todesca* (German soldier's song) in the music of Lassus and others are *villanelle* in form and style. The three-voice, simple-textured *villanella* continued to flourish in the later 16th century, with Venetian subgenres such as the *giustiniana* and *greghesca* adding to its variety of subject matter. Three-voice *villanelle* of a more polished nature were also being written. Some multivoice *villanelle* are really identical to the *canzonetta.*

Villanesca [It., countrified, fr. *canzone villanesca alla napolitana*]. The term used for the early repertory of the *villanella.*

Villano [Sp., peasant; It. *vallan di Spagna*]. A sung dance of Spain, also popular in Italy in the 16th and

17th centuries. Music based on the harmonic progression I–IV–I–V–I was provided in numerous Spanish and Italian guitar tablatures.

Villotta [It.]. A type of vocal music popular in Venice and Padua during the early 16th century. The poems, of one or more stanzas varying in length and form, are of a rustic, unsentimental character and often include portions of popular song texts. The music of the *villotta* is for four voices, often with a popular tune in the tenor. The texture is basically chordal, although there are points of imitation.

Vīṇā. A South Indian *long-necked lute. Four playing strings and three drone strings are stretched over a broad neck that extends from its pear-shaped body. The neck has 24 frets, and a gourd resonator and backward-curving pegbox are attached to its upper end. The body and pegbox make it a long-necked lute in contrast to the North Indian *bīn, which is a stick zither. See ill. under Instrument.

Vincent, John (b. Birmingham, 17 May 1902; d. Santa Monica, 21 Jan. 1977). Composer and teacher. Studied with Frederick Converse and George Chadwick at New England Conservatory, also with Walter Piston and Nadia Boulanger. Taught at Western Kentucky Teachers College (1937–46) and UCLA (1946–69). Compositions employ "paratonality," the use of diatonic elements within an atonal context. Works include Symphony in D (1954; rev. 1956); *Symphonic Poem after Descartes* (1959); *Nude Descending a Staircase* (string orchestra, 1966); *Mary at Calvary* (chorus and organ, 1972); 2 string quartets.

Vinci, Leonardo (b. Strongoli, Calabria, ca. 1690 or ca. 1696; d. Naples, 27 or 28 May 1730). Composer. Studied with Gaetano Greco at the Conservatorio dei Poveri di Gesù Cristo; in 1719 *maestro di cappella* to the Prince of Sansevero; from 1725 *pro-vicemaestro* of the royal chapel. Wrote operas and directed their premieres throughout Italy. In 1728 became *maestro di cappella* at the Conservatorio dei Poveri (pupils included Pergolesi). Works include some 40 operas, commedie composed 1719–24 and opere serie composed 1722–30; also cantatas, sonatas, a serenata, and an oratorio.

Viñes, Ricardo (b. Lérida, 5 Feb. 1875; d. Barcelona, 29 Apr. 1943). Pianist. Studied with Juan Pujol in Barcelona and with Bériot, Godard, and Lavignac in Paris. Settled in Paris and toured extensively; friends included Debussy, Ravel, Albéniz, and Séverac. Best known for playing contemporary French and Spanish music. Poulenc was among his pupils.

Vingt-quatre violons du roi. A string ensemble of 24 players in five parts (6, 4, 4, 4, 6) at the French court under Louis XIII, Louis XIV, and Louis XV (1626–1761); this ensemble was famous throughout Europe under the directorship of Lully. It was also termed *La grande bande.*

Viol [fr. It. *viola da gamba;* Fr. *viole;* Ger. *Gambe;* Sp. *viola de gamba*]. Any of a family of fretted, bowed stringed instruments in use from the 16th through much of the 18th century; also viola da gamba, gamba. The Italian term *viola da gamba* (leg viol) distinguishes the instruments of this family, which are played upright, resting on or between the legs, from instruments termed *viola da braccio,* which are played on the arm. In addition to its seven gut frets, the usual distinguishing features of the viol are sloping shoulders, a flat back with a section that slopes toward the neck, deep ribs, *sound holes in the shape of a *c* rather than an *f,* six strings tuned in fourths except for a major third between the two middle strings, and relatively wide and flat bridge and fingerboard [see ill.]. The shape of the viol varied considerably, however. Like other instruments of its period, including the violin, its strings are lighter and under less tension than those of the modern violin family. The bow is held with the palm upward, and its stick curves slightly away from the hair [see also Bow, Bowing].

Terminology and tunings were often inconsistent for the viol, especially in the 16th century. In the 17th and 18th centuries, however, there were in general three standard sizes: the treble [Fr. *dessus de viole*], tuned d g c′ e′ a′ d′′ and supported on the knees; the tenor [Fr. *taille de viole*], tuned G c f a d′ g′ and held between the legs; and the bass [Fr. *basse de viole*], tuned D G c e a d′ and also held between the legs. A *chest of viols ordinarily included two of each type. The terms viola da gamba and gamba now usually refer to the bass. Other sizes and types included a smaller, higher-pitched instrument, often with five strings tuned g c′ e′ a′ d′′, termed a descant or *pardessus de viole;* bass viols with a seventh string tuned A_1; the double-bass viol [Fr. *contre-basse de viole;* It. *violone*], tuned an octave below the bass; the division viol [It. *viola bastarda*], a bass viol slightly smaller than the normal consort viol and used for playing *divisions; and the lyra viol, a still smaller bass viol with a somewhat flatter bridge, played in a variety of tunings, and for which a considerable literature in a polyphonic style was composed in 17th-century England. More distant relatives include the *viola d'amore and the *baryton. The viol is a contemporary and not an ancestor of the violin. See also Double bass.

The end of the 16th century saw the viol lose ground to the violin, especially in Italy. But the viol was well established in England by this time and

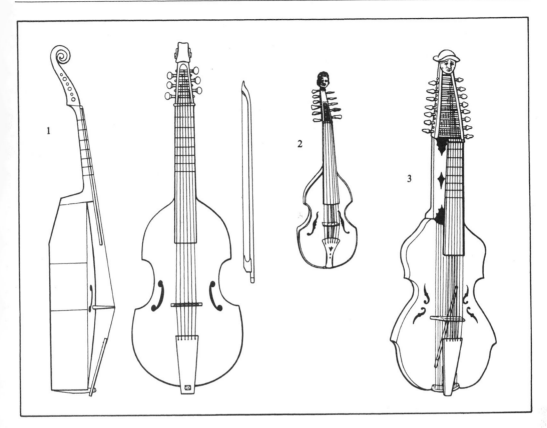

1. Viola da gamba (bass viol).   2. Viola d'amore.   3. Baryton.

gave rise to a large and varied repertory there [see Consort, Division, Fantasia, In nomine]. In the late 17th century and most of the 18th, French performers and composers of viol music were the most celebrated in Europe. These included Marin Marais (1656–1728), Antoine Forqueray (1671 or 1672–1745), Louis de Caix d'Hervelois (d. ca. 1760), and Jean-Baptiste Forqueray (1699–1782). Perhaps the last great performer and composer of viol music, however, was the German Carl Friedrich Abel (1723–87), active from 1758 in London (where he produced concerts jointly with J. C. Bach). By the mid-18th century, the bass viol gave way to the cello in ensembles, and it soon ceased to be cultivated widely as a solo instrument.

Viola. (1) [It., Sp.; Fr. *alto;* Ger. *Viola, Viole, Bratsche*]. The second highest member of the violin family. Its four strings are tuned c g d' a', a fifth below those of the violin, and its music is normally notated in the alto clef. The viola varies in size, with a body length of from 38 to 44 cm. (15 to 17 1/4 in.). It is thus larger than the violin (which has a normal body length of 35.5 cm.), but not as much larger as would be necessary if the violin's ratio of size to pitch were to be maintained. This facilitates its being played on the shoulder but results in tonal characteristics different from the violin's, notably a less rich and powerful sound in the extreme low register. The viola is otherwise similar in construction to the violin. For the early history of the viola and relatively recent designs of larger size, see Violin.

Although it has played an important role in orchestral and chamber music since the 18th century, its solo repertory remains limited. Orchestral works with solo viola include Mozart's *Sinfonia concertante* K. 364 (320d), Berlioz's **Harold en Italie,* and Richard Strauss's **Don Quixote* and concertos by Walton, Bartók (posthumous), Hindemith (himself a violist), and Piston.

(2) [It.] In the 16th and 17th centuries, any bowed stringed instrument. If played on the arm, such an instrument was a **viola da braccio* (whence the German *Bratsche*); if played on or between the legs, it was a **viola da gamba.*

Viola alta [It.; Ger. *Altgeige*]. A large viola (body length about 48 cm. with the exact proportions of the violin) built by Karl Adam Hörlein according to the specifications of the violist Hermann Ritter and exhibited in 1876.

Viola bastarda [It.]. *Division viol.

Viola d'amore [It.; Fr. *viole d'amour;* Ger. *Liebesgeige*]. A bowed stringed instrument prominent in the late 17th and 18th centuries, approximately the size of the viola and played on the shoulder, but with the body of a viol and most often provided with *sympathetic strings. The pegbox terminates in the figure of a head, the fingerboard is fretless, and the sound holes are in the shape of flaming swords [see ill. under Viol]. Typical 18th-century examples have seven gut playing strings and seven metal sympathetic strings that pass through the bridge and under the fingerboard to the pegbox. Early in the century, tunings varied considerably. By the end of the century, a widely used tuning was A d a d' f♯' a' d'', the sympathetic strings being tuned in unison or at the octave with the playing strings.

Viola da braccio [It. *braccio,* arm]. In the 16th and 17th centuries, a bowed stringed instrument played on the arm, as distinct from one played on or between the legs (*viola da gamba); thus, any of several instruments of the violin family, as distinct from viols. See also Viola.

Viola da gamba [It. *gamba,* leg]. In the 16th and 17th centuries, a bowed stringed instrument played on or between the legs, as distinct from one played on the arm (*viola da braccio); thus, any of the members of the *viol family.

Viole [Fr.]. *Viol; *viole d'amour,* *viola d'amore.

Violet [dim. of viol]. In the 16th century, the violin. See also English violet.

Viole-ténor [Fr.]. A large viola, held like a cello, constructed by R. Parramon of Barcelona in 1930; also termed *alto moderne.*

Violetta [It.]. Any of a variety of bowed stringed instruments. At the time of the emergence of the violin, Lanfranco in 1533 uses the term *violetta* to describe what is probably an early form of the violin, i.e., a three-string instrument without frets. In the 17th and 18th centuries, *violetta* refers to the viola, particularly in Germany; *violetta marina* to the viola d'amore.

Violin [Fr. *violin;* Ger. *violine, Geige;* It. *violino;* Sp. *violín*]. A bowed stringed instrument consisting of a hollow resonating wooden body with an attached neck and pegbox. Its four strings are tuned in fifths, g d' a' e''. The body is distinguished by rounded shoulders where it joins the neck and by indented center bouts, which allow free bow clearance when playing

on the outer strings. An extended, fretless fingerboard over the neck is used to stop the strings with fingers of the left hand. A *bow, with its ribbon of rosined horsehair, sets the strings in motion, and this string vibration is transmitted through the bridge to the table (top, belly) and resonating body, thereby creating the instrument's characteristic sound [see Fig. 1].

The table and back are carved and shaped to form archings and then hollowed inside to maximize vibrations, while retaining sufficient strength to sustain string tension. The edges extend slightly beyond the ribs to allow a delicate rounding of the form and to accentuate the shape of the body. *Sound holes, called F holes, are cut in the spruce top both for beauty and for sound production. The body is ornamented with an inlay of *purfling to emphasize the outline of the table and back and to aid in preventing cracks on the edges from continuing into the body of the instrument. Purfling also affects sound by increasing edge flexibility.

The spruce *bass-bar is fitted longitudinally beneath the left or g-string side beneath the bridge foot and glued in place under mild tension. It influences sound while strengthening the table against string pressure exerted by the bridge. The *sound post, also of spruce, is fitted between the table and back, near the right or treble bridge foot, and is held in place by string pressure. The sound post is readily movable, and its adjustment has a significant influence on musical quality and bow response, transmitting vibration of the strings to the maple back.

The *bridge is fitted to the arching of the table between the inner notches of the F holes and is held in place by string tension. From the button (endpin), which is set into the bottom block for strength, a tailgut of gut or nylon passes over a protective saddle and is secured to the tailpiece. The strings, fastened to the tailpiece, pass over the bridge, above the fingerboard, along fixed notches in the top-nut, and onto the four tuning pegs. Modern strings are usually of lamb gut wound with silver wire on the g and aluminum wire on the d' and a', and plain steel of considerable tension for brilliance of sound on the e''. Pegs, button, and tailpiece are usually of ebony, rosewood, or boxwood. The fingerboard, top-nut, and saddle are of ebony.

Varnish preserves the wood and protects it from wear and dirt while providing a flexible penetrating "blanket" that has a profound influence on sound. Excessively hard and brittle varnishes tend to emphasize brightness of tone, whereas overly soft varnish inadequately resists wear and abrasion. During the 17th century in northern Italy, especially in Cremona, varnish was developed with a nearly perfect combination of flexibility, texture, and lustrous depth of color. The basic formula was common knowledge in

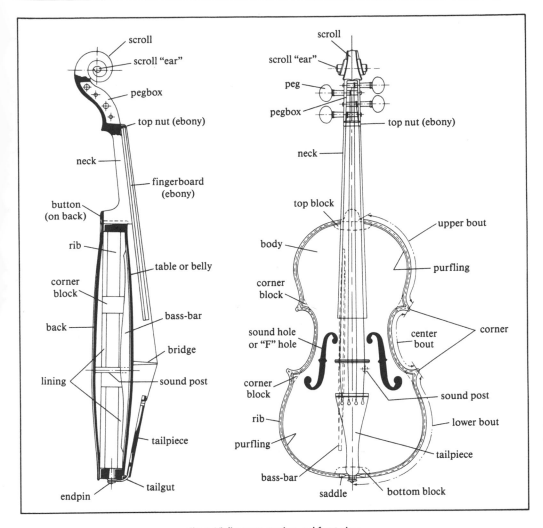

Fig. 1. Violin: cross section and front view.

the 17th and early 18th centuries, but by 1750 it was lost. Research and experimentation by makers and scientists since then have failed to rediscover the process and ingredients for making the classical varnish and to explain the exact means by which it influences sound.

The violin's antecedents include the medieval *fiddle, *rebec, and *lira da braccio. By at least 1520, the violin with only three strings was in existence. By 1550, the fourth string, the top e″, had been added. Between 1520 and 1550, the viola and cello also emerged, completing the family of bowed stringed instruments still in use.

The violin probably emerged in Cremona and Brescia. Andrea Amati (before 1511–before 1580), who founded violin making in Cremona and established its preeminence there, developed the basic propor-

tions of the violin, viola, and cello. His sons Antonio (ca. 1540–?) and Girolamo (Hieronymous) (1561–1630) continued his work, refining the style of the body outline, F holes, purfling, and scroll. In 1562, Gasparo da Salò (1540–1609) moved from Salò to Brescia, where there already existed a tradition of lute, viol, and keyboard instrument making. Here Gasparo produced many fine tenor violas, violins, and double basses.

Before 1600, instruments with body lengths both larger and smaller than the eventual standard of 14 inches (35.5 cm) were being produced. Bridge placement and vibrating string length also varied as makers sought to improve the quality of sound produced by strings of plain gut. Although twisted plain gut worked reasonably well for the top two strings, e″ and a′, it was much too slack for the lower d′ and g

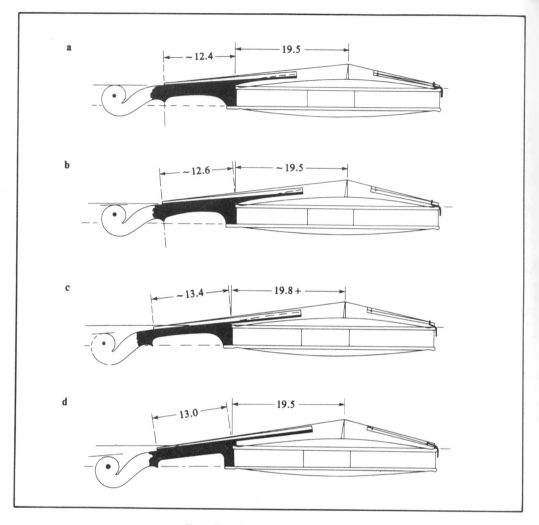

Fig. 2. Changing geometry of the violin.

strings. Roped strings from multiple strands of twisted gut, called Catlines, were more successful than plain gut, but spoke slowly under the bow and lacked focus and concentration of sound. The violin neck was short and simply extended in a straight projection from the upper edge of the table. The fingerboard was also short and wedge-shaped to allow string elevation for a low bridge that exerted only gentle downward string pressure onto the table of the instrument [see Fig. 2a]. Bass-bars were frequently small and short, and the sound post is believed to have been quite thin, probably less than 5 mm. in diameter. Plain gut strings did not make heavier structuring necessary, and instruments tended to be warm and resonant in musical quality, though somewhat lacking in power and projection.

The early cello was unusually large, with a body length that exceeded 31 inches (79 cm.) and was required to concentrate sound volume on the highly flexible C and G strings of roped Catline gut. With an overly long vibrating string length, fingering was difficult and a very heavy bow was required to achieve articulation. The viola also emerged as a large instrument, the tenor. With a body length of more than 18 inches (46 cm.), the tenor viola had a short neck, a feature allowing the instrument to be held on the shoulder with the left arm almost completely extended. The instrument was tuned c g d' a', an octave above the cello.

Violin proportion became largely standardized as we know it today in the 17th century, with a body length of roughly 14 inches (35.5 cm.). The viola and

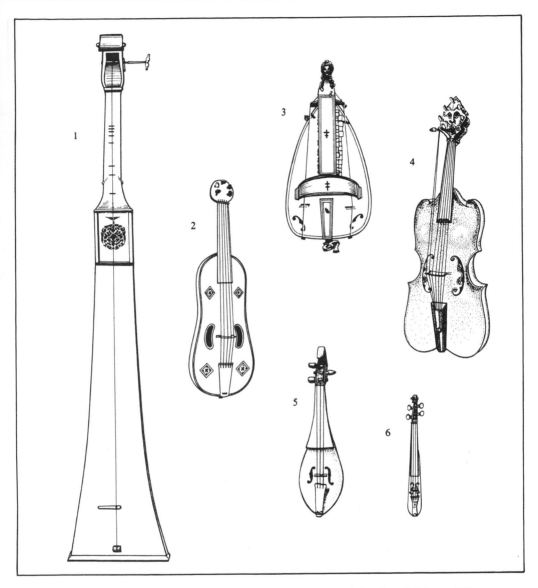

1. Tromba marina.   2. Medieval fiddle.   3. Hurdy-gurdy.   4. Lira da braccio.   5. Rebec.   6. Kit.

cello were, however, still in development. It was probably the brothers Amati who reduced the size of the tenor viola to the contralto, still with tenor tuning (c g d' a') but with a body length under 17 inches. Such an instrument from their hand emerged as early as 1616 and had a body 16 1/4 inches long. The small cello, destined to become a guide for the great Venetian makers in the late 17th and 18th centuries, was possibly created in the first quarter of the 17th century by Giovanni Paolo Maggini (ca. 1580–ca. 1632) in Brescia. The short body length (less than 30

inches) of the small cello was compensated with a broadening of the outline and higher ribs to retain interior volume.

After Girolamo Amati's death in 1630, his son Nicolo (1596–1684) became the most prominent maker in Italy. His influence as a teacher created a new generation of gifted makers, including Andrea Guarneri, Francesco Rugeri, and Antonio Stradivari. Jacob Stainer may also have received his training in part from Nicolo Amati.

New richness of sound resulted in part from highly

1. Violoncello.   2. Violin.   3. Viola.   4. Double bass (reduced in size).

built archings of the table and back. Instruments of great reputation with such archings were made by Jacob Stainer (ca. 1617–83), of Absam in the Austrian Tyrol. His instruments of German model rivaled and in many ways surpassed the instruments of the brothers Amati in Cremona. Until the 19th century, Stainer violins were considered among the very best and were widely imitated throughout Europe.

It was Antonio Stradivari (1644–1737), however, who refined and finalized the form, symmetry, and beauty of the violin. He is universally recognized as the greatest violin maker in history. After 1690, he departed from the popular Amati models, creating the "long-pattern" (14 5/16 inches) violin. In the same decade, string technology leapt forward as plain gut and Catline strings were covered with metal wire. Covered strings created quicker response and concentration of sound with increased mass and tension, allowing the lower register to become greatly focused with shorter vibrating length. With covered strings, the cello and tenor could be reduced in size

without sacrifice of musical quality. The tenor violin disappeared in favor of the smaller contralto viola; large cellos were also replaced with instruments of less than 30-inch body length.

Aware of the implications of concentrating sound with the new covered strings at higher tension, Stradivari abandoned the "long-pattern" after 1700, creating a new model of exactly 14 inches (35.5 cm.), with strong, flatter archings. He also applied these proportions to a smaller cello of 29 7/8 inches. Both models in this new form have remained the standard of excellence to the present. What has become known as Stradivari's golden period extended from 1700 until after 1724.

By 1675, makers were experimenting with instrument tension, finding that setting the neck back at an angle from the body and correspondingly increasing the bridge height were helpful in concentrating the sound of plain gut strings [Fig. 2b]. The neck also became longer to increase overall vibrating string length. The advent of covered. strings by 1700 spurred further experimentation with neck angles and length of vibrating string. In Prague and Mittenwald, in the course of work on models influenced by Stainer, the neck length increased slowly to 12.8 cm., and the neck tilt continued to increase. The new string tensions created the need for longer and higher bass-bars and thicker sound posts. Makers experimented widely with bass-bar location and grain direction, seeking to amplify violin sound.

Paris in the 18th century exerted a strong influence on the development of violin sound. Claude Pierray, Jacques Boquay, and Jean Baptiste Salomon continued experiments with violin tension and neck placement and with others evolved a French neck that was by 1740 even longer (13.4 cm.) than the established standard today [Fig. 2c], with an extended string length and thin body graduations producing unusual clarity, response, and brilliance.

Despite change and innovation, the violins of Nicolo Amati and Jacob Stainer remained the most sought-after instruments until the end of the 18th century. Although golden-period Stradivari were acclaimed for their perfection of form, the increased projection of flatter archings on these and the violins of Giuseppe Guarneri ("del Gesù," 1698–1744) was not truly appreciated until the 19th century, when bigger sound and projection were required for larger concert halls and the new, demanding concerto literature.

The 19th century firmly established the basic violin in use today. The modern *bow had been invented by François Tourte (1747–1835) with a weight, length, and balance capable of achieving increased power on the higher tensions of the violin. Instruments from the 17th and 18th centuries were already being "modernized" with respect to neck and bassbar by the great maker and connoisseur J. B. Vuillaume (1798–1875). Stradivari's reputation gained momentum through the musicianship of Viotti, and the playing of Paganini brought acclaim to the work of Guarneri.

The combined thickness of neck and fingerboard, difficult for the player to negotiate in the 17th century because it increased toward the body, had become virtually uniform on the modern instrument, and this, together with Spohr's invention of the chin rest around 1820, made holding the instrument and shifting positions with the left hand easier and cleared the way for modern playing technique. In the 20th century, the plain gut d' and a' have been wound with aluminum, and the e'' has been fabricated of steel wire to provide clarity, power, and projection. The geometry of the neck [Fig. 2d] in relation to the height of the bridge has remained largely unchanged in this century. Although instruments by Stainer are no longer widely popular, their delicacy of sound is being sought after again by specialists in the recreation of Baroque music, who use original instrumentation and Baroque performance practice.

Violino piccolo [It.; Ger. *Quartgeige, Terzgeige*]. A small violin with a body length of roughly 33 cm. (13 in.), similar to a 3/4-size child's instrument. It is known to have been used in the 16th and 17th centuries and was tuned a third or fourth higher than the normal violin.

Violon [Fr.]. Violin.

Violoncello, cello [It., diminutive of *violone;* Ger.; Fr. *violoncelle;* Sp. *violoncelo, violonchelo*]. The bass instrument of the violin family. Its four strings are tuned C G d a, an octave below those of the viola. The cello has a body length of 74–76 cm. (29–30 in.) and an overall length of ca. 120 cm. (47 in.). It is played between the legs, its weight being supported on the floor by the *endpin, and it is bowed with the palm downward. Except for its deeper ribs, it is similar in proportions and construction to the violin [see ill. under Violin].

The cello emerged in the early 16th century along with the violin and viola and was first distinguished as the bass member of this family by terms such as *basso di viola da braccio, Bass-Klein-Geig,* and *basse de violon.* The terms *violoncino* and *violoncello* date from the mid-17th century. In the 18th century in Austria and southern Germany, it was often termed *Bassetl* or *Bassett.* The modern tuning is described by 16th-century writers, as is a tuning a whole step lower that survived into the 18th century in England and France. Throughout the 17th century and into the early 18th, the cello sometimes had five strings tuned F₁ C G d a [see also *Violoncello piccolo;* for the early history of the cello, see Violin]. In the late 18th and the 19th century, it underwent modifications similar to those of the violin to produce a larger, more powerful tone. The last step in the development of the modern instrument was the widespread adoption of the adjustable endpin in the second half of the 19th century.

Violoncello piccolo [It.]. A small cello, perhaps with four strings tuned like the ordinary cello or perhaps with five strings tuned C G d a e'. Bach calls for a *violoncello piccolo* in several works, and his Sixth Suite for unaccompanied cello was written for an instrument with five strings, but it is not known if these are the same instrument. J. C. Hoffmann of Leipzig built a five-stringed instrument 76 cm. long for Bach in 1732.

Violoncino [It.]. In the 17th century, violoncello.

Violone [It.]. Now usually the double-bass *viol and thus the immediate ancestor of the *double bass. The term has designated a variety of instruments, however. In the 16th century, it referred to any viol as distinct from a violin. From about 1600 onward, it was applied to bass or contrabass viols. In Italian publications of the first half of the 18th century, it sometimes designated the violoncello. By the mid-18th century, it was falling out of use and referred increasingly to the double bass.

Viotti, Giovanni Battista (b. Fontanetto da Po, 12 May 1755; d. London, 3 Mar. 1824). Violinist and composer. Studied with Pugnani and toured with him in 1780. Played at the Concert spirituel in Paris, 1782; employed by Marie Antoinette, 1784; 1788, opened Théatre de Monsieur (later Théatre Feydeau). Left for London in 1792; appeared at Salomon's Hanover Square Concert, 1793; appointed musical director of the Opera Concerts, 1795, and the King's Theatre, 1797. Director of the Paris Opéra 1819–21; returned to England in 1823. Most influential works are 29 violin concertos; other works include 2 *symphonies concertantes;* string quartets, trios, and duos; 15 violin sonatas; 13 arias. Wrote *Méthode théorique et pratique de violon* (ca. 1835).

Virdung, Sebastian (b. Amberg, 19 or 20 Jan. ca. 1465). Theorist and composer. Studied in Heidelberg with Johannes von Soest; Kapellmeister at the Palatine court chapel there. Singer at the Württemberg court chapel in Stuttgart (1506–7); succentor at Konstanz Cathedral (1507–8). His treatise *Musica getutscht* (1511) is the oldest printed manual on musical instruments.

Virelai [Fr.]. One of the three *formes fixes,* prominent in the poetry and music of France in the 14th and 15th centuries. Except in popular or colloquial terminology, it was called *chanson balladée* before the latter half of the 15th century. In outline, the poetic structure of a virelai stanza is AbbaA (capital letters indicating the refrain) and the musical structure XYYXX. Each letter stands for several lines; the exact number is quite variable. The section b (Y) often has different endings on its two occurrences (*ouvert* and *clos*). Ordinarily there are three stanzas. The form of the Italian *ballata* is similar, as are the forms of the Galician-Portuguese *cantiga* and the Spanish *villancico,* all of which are in turn similar to the Hispano-Arabic *Zajal.*

The first polyphonic song in the form of a *virelai* was composed in the late 13th century by Adam de la Halle. The poetico-musical form as it came to be practiced in the 14th century becomes distinct in some monophonic works of Jehannot de l'Escurel (d. 1304). Guillaume de Machaut (ca. 1300–1377) wrote numerous *virelais.* In the 15th century, the *virelai* was rare, even as poetry without music. The late 15th-century *bergerette,* however, has the form of a *virelai* with only one stanza.

Virga [Lat.]. See Neume.

Virginal [Fr. *virginale, épinette;* Ger. *Virginal, Instrument;* It. *virginale, spinetta, spinettina;* Sp. *virginal*]. A small *harpsichord, almost always with one set of strings and jacks and a single keyboard. The strings run at right angles to the keys rather than obliquely as in the *spinet. In 17th-century England, virginal or pair of virginals referred to any quilled keyboard instrument. The origin of the term virginal is not known.

Virginal.

Unlike the spinet, the virginal has its long bass strings at the front, so that instruments could be built in various shapes, rectangular and polygonal, with inset or projecting keyboards. Typically the jacks are arranged in pairs in the register, back to back, plucking in opposite directions, and run in a line from the left front to the right rear of the virginal. Thus, the key levers in the bass are much shorter than in the treble, giving the instrument a characteristic but uneven touch. The earliest references to the virginal in the 15th and 16th centuries are to rectangular instruments. To judge from 16th- and 17th-century works of graphic art, virginals seem to have been far more numerous than harpsichords during this period.

By the 1560s, the thick-cased rectangular virginal was displacing the earlier thin-cased type. Three models of Flemish virginal were made: with their keyboards to the left (confusingly termed *spinett*), in the center (by 1600, only in octave virginals at 4′ pitch [see Foot]), and to the right (*muselar*), respectively. *Muselar*s, whose strings are plucked near the center, have a fairly uniformly flutelike sound from bass to treble, whereas *spinetten,* like harpsichords, change gradually from flutelike at the top to reedy at the bottom of the compass. English virginals all have the keyboard at the left, vaulted lids, and a shorter scale than Flemish models. Except in Italy, the virginal seems by the close of the 17th century to have been replaced by the spinet of wing shape. The compass of virginals paralleled that of contemporary harpsichords and spinets of the 16th and 17th centuries.

Virginalist. Any of the English composers of music for *virginal and related keyboard instruments of the late 16th and early 17th centuries, including William Byrd (1543–1623), Thomas Morley (1557 or 1558–1602), Peter Philips (1560 or 1561–1628), Giles Farnaby (ca. 1563–1640), John Bull (ca. 1562–1628), Thomas Weelkes (1576–1623), Thomas Tomkins (1572–1656), and Orlando Gibbons (1583–1625). Their repertory includes dances, *variations, *preludes, *fantasias, arrangements of songs and madrigals, and liturgical pieces.

Virtuoso [It.]. A performer of great technical ability. The term is now most often associated with the tradition of celebrated soloists that began in the 19th century with performers such as Paganini and Liszt and is applied to conductors and singers as well as to instrumentalists.

Visée, Robert de (b. ca. 1650; d. ca. 1725). Guitarist, theorbo and viol player, singer, and composer. May have studied with Corbetta; about 1680 became a chamber musician to Louis XIV, and in 1719 became guitar teacher to the king. Published 2 books of guitar music, *Livre di guittarre dédié au roy* (1682) and *Livre de pièces pour la guittarre* (1686); also wrote works for Baroque lute and theorbo.

Vishnegradsky, Ivan. See Wyschnegradsky, Ivan.

Vishnevskaya, Galina (Pavlovna) (b. Leningrad, 25 Oct. 1926). Soprano. Studied in Leningrad with Vera Garina; made her debut in operetta, 1944. Joined the Bolshoi Theater in Moscow, 1952. Non-Russian roles include Aida, Violetta, Tosca, Cio-cio-san, Leonore *(Fidelio),* and Cherubino. Metropolitan Opera debut (Aida), 1961; Covent Garden, 1962; La Scala (Liù), 1964. Toured Europe, the U.S., Australia, and New Zealand. In 1955 married the cellist Mstislav Rostropovich, with whom she performed (he on piano); left the Soviet Union in 1974 and settled in the U.S. Directed Rimsky-Korsakov's *The Tsar's Bride* in Washington, D.C., 1987.

Visitation, The. Opera in three acts by Gunther Schuller (libretto by the composer, after Franz Kafka), produced in Hamburg in 1966. Setting: the American South in the 20th century.

Vista [It.]. Sight; *a prima vista,* at sight, *sight-reading.

Vitali, Filippo (b. Florence, ca. 1590; d. there?, after 1 Apr. 1653). Composer. Until at least 1631 probably in Florence. His *Aretusa* (1620) was the first opera performed in Rome. Priest in the services of Cardinal Francesco Barberini and Cardinal Antonio Barberini (1637–42) in Rome, singer in the papal choir (1633), and *maestro di cappella* at S. Lorenzo, Florence (1642) and at S. Maria Maggiore, Bergamo (1648–49). Wrote both sacred and secular vocal music.

Vitali, Giovanni Battista (b. Bologna, 18 Feb. 1632; d. there, 12 Oct. 1692). Composer. Pupil of Cazzati, *maestro di cappella* of S. Petronio, Bologna. Joined the Accademia filarmonica, 1666. *Maestro di cappella* of S. Rosario, Bologna (1673); from 1674 served Duke Francesco II at the Este court in Modena (*maestro di cappella* 1684–86). Member of the Accademia dei Dissonati in Modena. Published 12 collections of instrumental music important in the history of the Baroque sonata, including *Artificii musicali* (1689); also wrote sacred and secular cantatas, oratorios, Psalms, and hymns.

Vitali, Tomaso Antonio (b. Bologna, 7 Mar. 1663; d. Modena, 9 May 1745). Composer and violinist. Went with his father, Giovanni Battista Vitali, to Modena in 1674. Studied composition with Pacchioni; employed at the Este court orchestra 1675–1742. Pupils include Dall'Abaco and Senaillé. Works are all instrumental; solo and trio sonatas reveal the influences of his father and Corelli.

Vite, vitement [Fr.]. Fast; in the 18th century, the fastest of the principal divisions of *tempo.

Vitry, Philippe de [Vitriaco, Vittriaco] (b. Paris, 31 Oct. 1291; d. there, 9 June 1361). Theorist and composer. Attended the Sorbonne in Paris; held clerical posts in Cambrai, Clermont, St. Quentin, and Soissons; Archbishop of Brie. In service to Duke Jean of Normandy from 1346, remaining in his service when the duke became king in 1350; appointed Bishop of Meaux by Pope Clement VI in 1351. A number of early motets appear in the *Roman de Fauvel,* but his fame rests primarily on the treatise *Ars nova* (ca. 1322–23), which established a new theory of mensural notation.

Vivace [It.]. Lively, brisk. In isolation, the term may indicate a *tempo equivalent to *allegro* or faster. It has also been used to modify various terms (e.g., *allegro vivace*), usually, but not always, implying a faster tempo than the term modified. The intensifiers *vivacissimo* and *vivacissimamente* are also used.

Vivaldi, Antonio (Lucio) (b. Venice, 4 Mar. 1678; d. Vienna, 28 July 1741). Composer. Taught violin by his father, Giovanni Battista; ordained as a priest in 1703. *Maestro di violino* at the Pio Ospedale della Pietà orphanage in Venice, 1703–9; publication of *L'estro armonico* op. 3 (1711) earned Vivaldi fame across Europe (Bach transcribed five of the concertos for keyboard). Returned to the Pietà in 1711 (1716, appointed *maestro de'concerti*); composed oratorios, concertos, and operas. From 1718 to 1720 *maestro di cappella da camera* to Prince Philipp of Hessen-Darmstadt in Mantua; spent three Carnival seasons in Rome (1723–25); returned to S. Angelo, Venice, as composer and impresario (1726–28). Traveled from 1729 to 1733; continued to publish instrumental concertos. After 1735 confined his operatic activities to Verona, Ancona, Reggio, and Ferrara; *maestro di cappella* at the Pietà 1735–38. Died in Vienna in 1741. Most influential as a composer of instrumental music, particularly concertos (including *Le quattro stagioni* [The *Four Seasons], op. 8).

Works: *Secular vocal.* Over 40 operas (21 extant, including *Orlando furioso,* 1727; *La fida ninfa,* 1732); serenatas *(Mio cor povero cor); about 40 cantatas (mostly for solo voice). *Sacred vocal.* Masses and Mass movements; oratorios *(Juditha triumphans,* 1716); Psalms *(Nisi Dominus); motets (Invicti bellate); Magnificat; Stabat mater. Instrumental.* Over 500 concertos, including over 20 "chamber concertos"; about 60 ripieno concertos and sinfonias; about 80 concertos for 2 or more solo instruments; over 230 solo violin concertos; over 110 solo concertos for other instruments; 26 trio sonatas; about 60 solo sonatas for violin, cello, and wind instruments.

Vivanco, Sebastián de (b. Ávila, ca. 1551; d. Salamanca, 26 Oct. 1622). Composer. *Maestro de capilla* at Lérida, Segovia, Ávila, and Salamanca cathedrals; 1603 appointed professor of music at Salamanca Univ. One of the leading composers of his day; his sacred music includes the *Liber magnificarum* (1607), 10 Masses (1608), and 36 motets (1610).

Vivement [Fr.]. Lively.

Vives, Amadeo (b. Collbató, near Barcelona, 18 Nov. 1871; d. Madrid, 1 Dec. 1932). Composer. Studied with Ribera and Pedrell in Barcelona. With Luis Millet formed the chorus Orteó Català; moved to Madrid and composed operas and zarzuelas admired by connoisseurs and the public alike, among them *Doña Francisquita* (1923). Author of the play *Jo no sabía que el món era eixi,* staged in 1920. Other compositions include piano pieces and songs.

Vivo, vivamente [It.]. Lively, brisk.

Vl. Abbr. for violin.

Vla. Abbr. for viola.

Vlad, Roman (b. Cernauti, Romania, 29 Dec. 1919). Composer and critic. Studied at the Cernauti Conservatory and with Alfredo Casella at Santa Cecilia in Rome. Became an Italian citizen in 1951. Early compositions drew on Romanian heritage; by the 1950s embraced serialism. Composed scores for films and

wrote extensively about 20th-century music. Works include *Sinfonietta,* (orchestra, 1941); *Storia di una mamma* (opera, Venice, 1951); *Variazioni concertanti su una serie di 12 note dal Don Giovanni di Mozart* (piano and orchestra, 1955); *Il dottore di vetro* (radio opera, 1960); *Cadenze michelangiolesche* (tenor and orchestra, 1967); *Il sogno* ("azione musicale," Bergamo, 1973); *Musica per archi* no. 2 (1988). Writings include *Luigi Dallapiccola* (1957), *Storia della dodecafonia* (1958).

Vladigerov, Pantcho (b. Zurich, 13 Mar. 1899; d. Sofia, 8 Sept. 1978). Composer. Studied at the Sofia Music School and in Berlin with Juon, Gernsheim, and Schumann. Conductor and composer at the Deutsches Theater, 1921–32; returned to Sofia and taught at the Academy of Music until 1972. Compositions infuse Romanian folk elements into late Romantic language of western Europe. Works include *Tsar Kaloyan* (opera, 1936); 2 symphonies; 2 violin concertos; suites and tone poems (*Essenna elegiya* [Autumn Elegy], 1922; *Deveti septemvri* [September 9], heroic overture, 1949); chamber and vocal pieces.

Vlc. Abbr. for violoncello.

Vlijmen, Jan van (b. Rotterdam, 11 Oct. 1935). Composer. Studied with van Baaren at the Utrecht Conservatory. Head of the Amersfoort Music School 1961–65; taught at the Utrecht Conservatory 1965–67; then deputy director at the Conservatory of The Hague (director from 1971). General manager of the Netherlands Opera 1985–88. Compositions explore serialism and incorporate improvisation. Works include *Serie* (woodwinds, trumpet, piano, 1960); *Reconstructie* (opera, collaboration, 1966); *Omaggio a Gesualdo* (violin, 6 instrument groups, 1971); *Axel* (opera, collaboration, 1975–77); *Un malheureux vêtu de noir* (opera, 1990).

Vocalise [Fr.]. A composition for voice without text. Numerous such pieces, often with piano accompaniment, were published beginning in the 19th century as exercises in vocal technique or in *solfège. The term has sometimes also been used to refer to any melismatic passage in a vocal work with text.

Vocalization, to vocalize. To sing without text, often for didactic purposes or to warm up before performance, thus often arpeggios or other exercises.

Voce [It., pl. *voci*]. Voice, part; *voce di petto,* chest voice; *voce di testa,* head voice; *a due (tre,* etc.) *voci,* for two (three, etc.) voices; *voci pari* or *eguali, *equal voices. See also *Colla, Mezzo, Sotto.

Voces [Lat.]. Plural of *vox.

Vogel, Wladimir (b. Moscow, 29 Feb. 1896; d. Zurich, 19 June 1984). Composer. Studied in Berlin with Heinz Tiessen and Ferruccio Busoni. Frequently works combined spoken and sung delivery of text; also experimented with serialism. Fled Berlin in 1933 and settled in Switzerland. Works include *Drei Sprechlieder* (bass and piano, 1922); *Wagadu's Untergang durch die Eitelkeit* (soloists, chorus, speaking chorus, 5 saxophones, 1930); *Epitaffio per Alban Berg* (piano, 1936); *Arpiade* (soprano, speaking chorus, chamber ensemble, 1954).

Vogelweide, Walther von der. See Walther von der Vogelweide.

Vogl, Heinrich (b. Au, near Munich, 15 Jan. 1845; d. Munich, 21 Apr. 1900). Tenor and composer. Studied with Lachner in Munich. Debut in Munich (1865) as Max in *Der Freischütz;* created Loge in *Das Rheingold* (1869) and Siegmund in *Die Walküre* (1870). Sang at Bayreuth, 1876–77. London debut, 1882; New York Metropolitan Opera debut, 1890. Wrote the opera *Der Fremdling* (1889) and sang in the premiere. Known for his great vocal stamina. Married to soprano Therese Thoma (1845–1921).

Vogl, Johann Michael (b. Ennsdorf, near Steyr, Austria, 10 Aug. 1768; d. Vienna, 19 Nov. 1840). Baritone. Studied at Kremsmünster; classmate of Süssmayr. Member of Vienna Court Opera, 1795–1822. Sang in premiere of revised version of *Fidelio* (1814). Close friend of Schubert; first to sing the cycle *Winterreise* (1827). Also composed Masses and songs.

Vogler, Georg Joseph [Abbé Vogler] (b. Pleichach, near Würzburg, 15 June 1749; d. Darmstadt, 6 May 1814). Composer and theorist. Studied in Italy with Padre Martini among others. In 1775 named Vice-Kapellmeister at the Mannheim court and founded the Mannheimer Tonschule. Appointed Kapellmeister in Munich, 1784; in 1786 to King Gustavus III of Sweden; in 1807 *Hofkapellmeister* to the Grand Duke of Hessen-Darmstadt. Traveled widely as teacher, performer, and organ reformer; students included Carl Maria von Weber, Giacomo Meyerbeer, Peter Winter, and Joseph Kraus. Wrote theoretical and pedagogical treatises, including *Tonwissenschaft und Tonsetzkunst* (1776) and *Betrachtungen der Mannheimer Tonschule*. Constructed a portable organ, the "orchestrion," and published *Système de simplification pour les orgues* (1798). Compositions include operas, ballets, other incidental stage music, sacred vocal pieces, secular cantatas, 33 symphonies, piano concertos, chamber music.

Voice. (1) The human mechanism for producing sound from the mouth. Every musical culture has its own distinct *singing style, with characteristic ranges and timbres. Thus, even the most basic terms and categories for describing vocal sound in one cul-

ture may not be relevant to others. What follows concerns the voice as employed in Western art music.

Since the 19th century, voices have usually been classified in six basic types, three male and three female, according to their range, roughly as shown in the accompanying example. Most voices, especially untrained ones, fall into the intermediate ranges, baritone and mezzo soprano, the extremes being more rare. The limits of range vary among individuals, although trained singers often much exceed those given in the example. Voices of similar range may be unlike in tessitura—that part of the range that is most comfortable for the singer and sounds best. The voice categories also differ in timbre, with the result that singers of different categories can be distinguished even on the same pitch. In practice, however, singers of one type often have an admixture of the timbre of another, such as a tenor with some baritonal quality.

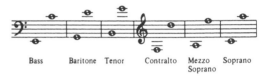

Bass   Baritone Tenor   Contralto Mezzo   Soprano
                                         Soprano

Ranges.

Kinds of voices and ranges now unusual have been cultivated at other times, for example, Russian basses of very low range; the male alto, countertenor, or falsettist [see Falsetto], who, after long employment in European music, went out of favor in the 19th century, regaining some of it in the 20th; or the *castrato*, a dominant figure in Italian singing from the 16th to the early 19th century.

In singing, register refers to series of pitches that are of like tonal character because of a consistent vocal production. The question of registers has been subject to profound disputes, and the terminology to considerable confusion. Sometimes two, sometimes three principal registers are recognized in the classically trained voice. Often, but not invariably, these are called chest, head, and falsetto in men, and chest, middle, and head in women. The terms chest and head reflect the tonal quality of those registers and, sometimes, sensations felt in singing them. But it is now generally held that registral differences do not depend on the resonating cavities, but result from different functions within the laryngeal mechanism itself. For this reason some now prefer the terms heavy and light register to chest and head, though the latter remain in common use.

Difference of registral emphasis is one of the principal factors distinguishing types of singers. The coloratura soprano is characterized by very light registration, high tessitura, and agility. Most young tenors and sopranos use a predominantly light registration; this makes them, in standard terminology, lyric voices. Some remain in this category, but others adopt heavier registration and more powerful sound with age and experience. A *lirico spinto* is a voice of basically lyric quality that can "push" (the meaning of *spinto*) the voice more powerfully in climaxes; a tenor of this sort is called a *tenore di forza*. The dramatic soprano sings more powerfully and with heavier registration more of the time and throughout her range. *Tenore robusto* is the tenor equivalent, *Heldentenor* that for Wagnerian singing. Basses and contraltos sing mainly in chest voice, the bass using falsetto only for comic effect. The *basso profondo* [Fr. *basse profonde*] emphasizes a rich, low tessitura, the *basso cantante* [Fr. *basse chantante*] a higher one, of lighter register and more flexibility.

(2) In American usage, the study of singing (e.g., "voice teacher").

(3) A single melodic line or part in polyphonic music, as in a four-voice fugue. Used in this way, voice implies no specific manner of performance, vocal or instrumental, solo or doubled. Part and voice part are also used in this sense. *Voice leading is derived from this usage.

Voice exchange [Ger. *Stimmtausch*]. The exchange between two voices (sometimes also among three voices) of phrases that are sounded simultaneously; thus, the first voice takes the phrase just sung by the second, while the second takes the phrase just sung by the first; also termed part exchange.

Voice leading. The conduct of the several voices or parts in a polyphonic or contrapuntal texture [see Counterpoint].

Voice part. See Voice (3).

Voicing. (1) The adjustment of the general tonal quality of a stringed keyboard instrument or of individual pitches to produce consistency throughout. On the piano, this entails principally the use of needle-like tools to prick the felt of the hammers and reduce their hardness. On the harpsichord, it entails modifying the shape and flexibility of the plectra. (2) The adjustment of organ pipes for proper speech, loudness, and tone quality.

Voilé [Fr.]. Veiled, subdued.

Voisin, Roger (b. Angers, 26 June 1918). Trumpeter. Immigrated to the U.S., 1927, settling in Boston. Instructed by his father, Georges Mager, and Marcel La Fosse. Member of the Boston Symphony 1935–73 (first trumpet 1949–67). Taught at Boston Univ., New England Conservatory, and the Berkshire Music Center.

Voix [Fr.]. Voice.

Voix de ville [Fr.]. See *Vaudeville*.

Vokal [Ger.]. (1) Vowel. (2) Vocal; *vokalisieren,* to vocalize; *Vokalise,* *vocalization, *vocalise.

Volante [It.]. Flying, rushing. See also Bowing (7).

Volkmann, (Friedrich) Robert (b. Lommatzsch, near Dresden, 6 Apr. 1815; d. Budapest, 29 Oct. 1883). Composer. Studied with his father, music director in Lommatzsch, and with Friebel and Anacker in Leipzig, where he met Schumann and Mendelssohn. Taught in Prague (1839–41), Pest (1841–54), and Vienna (1854–58); named professor of harmony and counterpoint at the Budapest Academy of Music in 1875. Compositions include an overture and interludes to *Richard III;* 2 Masses; 2 symphonies; a cello concerto; chamber music; piano solos and duets; songs.

Volkonsky, Andrey Mikhaylovich (b. Geneva, 14 Feb. 1933). Composer, conductor, and harpsichordist. Studied piano with Auber at the Geneva Conservatory, with Boulanger and Lipatti in Paris; moved to the U.S.S.R. in 1947 and studied at the Moscow Conservatory with Shaporin. Expelled from the school in 1954 after a performance of his Concerto for Orchestra; later expelled from the Composers' Union after the performance of his serial work *Musica stricta* (piano, 1956). Turned to pointillistic works (*Serenade for an Insect,* chamber orchestra, 1958), and experiments with aleatoric writing (*Games for Three,* flute, violin, harpsichord, 1962). Emigrated to Switzerland in 1973.

Volkslied [Ger.]. Folk song.

Volkstümliches Lied [Ger.]. The folklike lied cultivated by composers such as Schulz, Reichardt, and Zelter beginning in the later 18th century. Such songs were often marked *im Volkston.*

Volonté, à [Fr.]. *Ad libitum.*

Volta [It.]. (1) [Fr., Ger. *Volte*] A dance from Provence popular in much of Europe around 1600, similar to the *gagliarda*. Examples are notated in compound duple meter. It was danced in an embrace and included a step in which the man helped the woman to execute a high jump. Shakespeare and others used the terms lavolta or levalto. (2) A component of the *ballata*. (3) Time, occasion [see *Prima volta, seconda volta; Ouvert, clos*].

Volteggiando [It.]. Crossing the hands in keyboard playing.

Volti [It.]. Turn (the page); *volti subito* (abbr. *v.s.*), turn quickly.

Volume. *Loudness [see also Acoustics].

Voluntary. An English organ piece performed or improvised before, during (in earlier practice), or after an Anglican church service. The musical term is derived from one of the word's general definitions: "growing wild or naturally; of spontaneous growth." It was applied in this sense to musical improvisations. The term came to be most firmly attached to the organ music, whether improvised or not, played before (sometimes called In-Voluntary) and after (Out-Voluntary) the Anglican service.

The earliest known organ composition designated as a voluntary, by Richard Alwood in the Mulliner Book (ca. 1560), is in an imitative, ricercarlike style. Fugal writing remained the most common texture in the organ voluntary, often prefaced by a preludelike movement or section, but the voluntary is not limited to any style or form, being ultimately defined by its function more than by its materials. Voluntaries of the period of Byrd and Tomkins are often similar to pieces called fantasia, verse, or the like by the same or other early 17th-century composers. Later examples can resemble the suite, concerto, or sonata, or consist of arrangements or variations of hymn tunes. Exploitation of organ stops led to standard types such as the diapason voluntary and the cornet or trumpet voluntary [see also *Trumpet Voluntary*]. The voluntary had its last great flowering in the 18th and early 19th centuries.

Von Stade, Frederica (b. Somerville, N.J., 1 June 1945). Mezzo-soprano. Studied with Sebastian Engleberg at the Mannes School in New York. Metropolitan Opera debut, 1970; major roles there include Siebel in Gounod's *Faust*, Cherubino, Lola in *Cavalleria rusticana*, Zerlina, and Suzuki in *Madama Butterfly;* particularly known for Cherubino and Octavian, from *Der Rosenkavalier.* Has performed widely in Europe and the U.S., often in recital and concert, and made many recordings.

Von Tilzer, Harry [Gumm, Harold] (b. Detroit, 8 July 1872; d. New York, 10 Jan. 1946). Popular songwriter, publisher. Began as a vaudeville performer in Detroit and New York; founding publishing firm, 1902. Important to the early Tin Pan Alley music industry; aided Gershwin and Irving Berlin and helped form ASCAP in 1914. Songs include "My Old New Hampshire Home" (1898), "A Bird in a Gilded Cage" (1900), and "Wait 'Til the Sun Shines, Nellie" (1905).

Voormolen, Alexander Nicolas (b. Rotterdam, 3 Mar. 1895; d. there, 12 Nov. 1980). Composer. Studied at the Utrecht School of Music with Wagenaar and Petri, and in Paris with Ravel and Roussel. Returned to The Hague and worked as a music critic, music librarian, and composer. Compositions show French influence and occasionally incorporate elements of Dutch folk music. Works include music for orchestra (2 *Baron Hop Suites*, 1923, 1931; *Kleine*

Haagse Suite, chamber orchestra, 1939; Chaconne and Fugue, 1958) and chamber ensembles (*Tableaux des Bays-Pas,* 1921, 1926); vocal music (*Obsession,* voice, piano, 1952; *Aux baigneurs,* chorus, 1967).

Vorbereiten [Ger.]. *Prepare.

Voříšek, Jan Václav [Worzischek, Johann Hugo] (b. Vamberk, northeast Bohemia, 11 May 1791; d. Vienna, 19 Nov. 1825). Composer. Studied with Tomášek in Prague and with Hummel in Vienna, where he became acquainted with Beethoven and Spohr. In 1818 appointed conductor at the Gesellschaft der Musikfreunde; 1822, assistant court organist (later principal). Works include 1 symphony; 4 orchestral pieces that feature piano; piano rhapsodies, impromptus, and other solo pieces; secular and sacred vocal pieces.

Vorschlag [Ger.]. *Appoggiatura; *grace note.

Vorspiel [Ger.]. (1) Prelude, overture. (2) Audition, performance; *vorspielen,* to perform before an audience.

Vortrag [Ger.]. Interpretation, performance; *mit freiem Vortrag,* in a free style; *Vortragszeichen, Vortragsbezeichnung,* *performance mark.

Vorwärts [Ger.]. Forward, continue; *vorwärtsdrängend,* *accelerando.

Vorzeichen [Ger.]. (1) Accidental. (2) [also *Vorzeichnung*] Key signature (*Tonartvorzeichen*), time signature (*Taktvorzeichen*).

Votive antiphon. Any of the four *antiphons for the Blessed Virgin Mary sung at Compline or a polyphonic setting of one of these [see also Votive Mass].

Votive Mass [Lat. *missa votiva*]. A Mass for some special circumstance (e.g., in time of war, the consecration of a bishop, a wedding) or devotion (e.g., to the Blessed Virgin Mary, the Trinity, certain saints).

Vox [Lat., pl. *voces*]. (1) Pitch, note, solmization syllable. (2) In polyphonic music, voice part. (3) Voice, either the human voice or the "voice" of an instrument.

V.s. Abbr. for *Volti subito.

Vuillaume, Jean-Baptiste (b. Mirecourt, 7 Oct. 1798; d. Paris, 19 Mar. 1875). Violin maker. From a family of violin makers; worked for François Chanot in Paris and established his own business there in 1828. A pioneer of imitation, his best violins were modeled on old Italian instruments. Bought the collection of the dealer Luigi Tarisio in 1855 and made copies of the instruments of Amati, Maggini, and Stradivari.

Vulpius [Fuchs], **Melchior** (b. Wasungen, near Meiningen, ca. 1570; d. Weimar, buried 7 Aug. 1615). Composer. In 1592 became Kantor at Schleusingen; from 1596 Kantor and teacher at the Weimar Lateinschule. Output includes nearly 200 motets and some 400 hymns, all written for the Lutheran service.

Vuoto [It.]. Empty, void; *corda vuota,* open string.

VV. Abbr. for violins, voices.

Vycpálek, Ladislav (b. Prague, 23 Feb. 1882; d. there, 9 Jan. 1969). Composer. Studied with Novák; their friendship ruptured in 1917 because of Vycpálek's criticism of his teacher's work. Established Prague Univ. music department in 1922 (head through 1942). Around 1950 the performance of his music underwent a decline when it was criticized by the political establishment. Works—mostly choral music, frequently inspired by or using folk music—include *Kantáta o posledních věcech člověka* [Cantata of the Last Great Things of Man] (soprano, baritone, chorus, orchestra, 1920–22); *České requiem "Smrt a spasení"* [Czech Requiem "Death and Redemption"] (soprano, alto, baritone, chorus, orchestra, 1940); *Září* [September] (solo voices, chorus, 1951; rev. 1953).

Vyshnegradsky, Ivan. See Wyschnegradsky, Ivan.

W

Waart, Edo de. See De Waart, Edo.

Wachsend [Ger.]. Growing, increasing.

Wacław z Szamotuł. See Szamotuł, Wacław z.

Waelrant [Waelrand], **Hubert** [Huberto] [Waelrandus, Hubertus] (b. between 20 Nov. 1516 and 19 Nov. 1517; d. Antwerp, 19 Nov. 1595). Composer, music editor, and singer. Soloist at Antwerp Cathedral (1544–45) and teacher at a music school operated by Gregorius de Coninck (1553–56). From 1554 served as music editor for the printer Jean de Laet, producing 16 volumes of mostly sacred music, including one devoted to his own motets (1556?). Surviving compositions also include a volume of 5-part madrigals and chansons (1558).

Wagenaar, Bernard (b. Arnhem, Netherlands, 18 July 1894; d. York Harbor, Maine, 19 May 1971). Composer. Studied violin and piano at the Utrecht Conservatory, then taught and conducted in the Netherlands. In 1920 came to the U.S.; played violin in the New York Philharmonic 1921–23; 1925–27, taught composition at the Institute of Musical Arts in New York and at its successor institution, the Juilliard School of Music, to 1968. Works include 4 symphonies; Triple concerto (flute, cello, harp, and orchestra, 1935); Divertimento no. 2 (orchestra, 1953); violin and piano sonatas; 3 string quartets; *Four Vignettes* (harp, 1965).

Wagenaar, Johan (b. Utrecht, 1 Nov. 1862; d. The Hague, 17 June 1941). Composer. Studied in Utrecht with Hol and in Berlin with Herzogenberg. Head, Utrecht Music School, 1887–1904; 1887–1919, organist at the Utrecht Cathedral; 1919–37, director of the Conservatory of The Hague. Compositions are in a late Romantic Germanic idiom. Works include 2 operas (*De Doge van Venetie,* 1901; *De Cid,* 1915), orchestral music (*Cyrano de Bergerac,* overture, 1905; *Elverhoi,* symphonic poem, 1939), vocal and organ music.

Wagenseil, Georg Christoph (b. Vienna, 29 Jan. 1715; d. there, 1 Mar. 1777). Composer. Pupil of J. J. Fux and Matteo Palotta. Court composer from 1739; in 1749 also appointed *Hofklaviermeister* to the imperial archduchesses. Mozart and Haydn were both familiar with his music; F. X. Dušek, Leopold Hoffmann, and J. A. Štěpán were among his pupils. Compositions include operas, 3 oratorios, Masses, cantatas, other sacred vocal music, symphonies, harpsichord concertos, other solo concertos, chamber music, solo keyboard pieces. Wrote *Rudimenta panduristae oder Geig-Fundamenta* (1751).

Wagner, (Wilhelm) Richard (b. Leipzig, 22 May 1813; d. Venice, 13 Feb. 1883). Composer and author. Studied piano with Humann in Dresden, at that time residence of Weber, Spohr, and Marschner; composition with Christian Gottlieb Müller and Christian Theodor Weinlig in Leipzig. Early works include an overture whose 1832 performance marked Wagner's debut as a conductor and a symphony whose performances in Leipzig and Prague brought favorable notice as far away as London. Began composing operas; became involved with the Young Germans and published "Die Deutsche Oper" (1834). Appointed music director of a theatrical company in Magdeburg; made his debut as an opera conductor and began an association with the singer Wilhelmine Schröder-Devrient that would include premieres of three subsequent operas.

In 1836 became conductor at a theater in Königsberg and married the actress Christine Wilhelmine "Minna" Planer; 1837–39, appointed music director at the theater in Riga, where he began work on *Rienzi.* After a disappointing stay in Paris (1839–42) returned to Dresden for successful premiere of *Rienzi;* appointed co–music director at the Dresden court. *The Flying Dutchman* premiered in Dresden in 1843, *Tannhäuser* in 1845. Reading of Wolfram von Eschenbach's *Parzifal* inspired *Parsifal* and *Lohengrin;* the latter, premiered under Liszt at Weimar in 1850, became by the end of the century Wagner's most-performed opera. After the uprising of 1849, fled to Zurich; published *Die Kunst und die Revolution* (Art and Revolution), *Die Kunst der Zukunft* (The Artwork of the Future), and *Oper und Drama.* Began work on *Der Ring des Nibelungen;* by 1851 arrived at the overall conception of the tetralogy. Between 1856 and 1859 composed *Tristan und Isolde,* which became his most influential and most analyzed work.

In 1857 returned briefly to Paris, where a performance of *Tannhäuser* was a fiasco; then relocated to Karlsruhe and turned to work on *Die Meistersinger.* In 1864 Ludwig II, King of Bavaria, became his patron; Cosima von Bülow, daughter of Liszt and wife of the Munich music director Hans von Bülow, became his companion. Premiere of *Tristan,* 1865; moved to Tribschen, on Lake Lucerne, 1867; Munich premiere of *Meistersinger,* 1868, a complete success that led to the king's commanding a production of the *Ring*'s first two parts (1869, 1870). In 1866 Minna died in Dresden; in 1870 married Cosima and wrote the *Siegfried Idyll* for her.

In 1871 began planning the "consecrated" festival theater in Bayreuth for the performance of his operas; moved there, 1872; theater opened in 1876 with a production of the *Ring.* Premiere of *Parsifal* there in 1882 received with reverence. Died in Venice in 1883.

Operas include *Die Feen* (1834); *Das Liebesverbot* (1836); **Rienzi, der Letzte der Tribunen* (1840); *Der *fliegende Holländer* (The Flying Dutchman, 1841); **Tannhäuser und der Sängerkrieg auf Wartburg* (Tannhauser and the Contest of Singers on the Wartburg, 1845); **Tristan und Isolde* (1859); **Lohengrin* (1848); *Die *Meistersinger von Nürnberg* (1867); *Der *Ring des Nibelungen,* comprising *Das Rheingold* (1854), *Die Walküre* (1856), *Siegfried* (1871), and *Götterdämmerung* (1874); **Parsifal* (1882). Other works include *Faust* overture (1840, rev. 1855); *Fünf Gedichte* (*Wesendonck Lieder,* 1857); **Siegfried Idyll* (1870).

Wagner tuba. A type of tuba developed for use in Wagner's *Der *Ring des Nibelungen;* also tuben. It uses a French horn mouthpiece and was intended to be played by horn players. The tubing, which has a wide conical bore, is coiled in an upright ellipse. Four rotary valves are arranged at the center in such a way as to be operated with the left hand. A tenor size is pitched in B♭ (sounds E♭ to f'') and a bass size is pitched in F (sounds B♭₁ to a').

Wagner-Régeny, Rudolf (b. Szász-Régen, Romania, 28 Aug. 1903; d. East Berlin, 18 Sept. 1969). Composer. Studied in Leipzig and in Berlin at the Hochschule für Musik. In 1935 achieved sudden success with the opera *Der Günstling; Die Bürger von Calais* (1939) was criticized and *Johanna Balk* (1941) was banned. After World War II turned to twelve-tone methods and Boris Blacher's system of "variable meters." Works include *2 Klavierstücke* (1950); *5 französische Klavierstücke* (1951); *Divertimento* (winds and percussion, 1954); *Das Bergwerk zu Falun* (opera, Salzburg, 1961).

Wait. (1) Beginning in the 13th century, a town or castle watchman, who signaled with a horn. By the late 13th century, those in noble households were sometimes *minstrels and played the shawm, whence the beginning of the association of this instrument with the term wait or wayte. (2) In the 15th

through the 18th century, a town musician, analogous to the German **Stadtpfeifer.*

Walcha, Helmut (b. Leipzig, 27 Oct. 1907; d. Frankfurt, 11 Aug. 1991). Organist. Studied with Ramin at the Leipzig Conservatory; although blind, recorded all the organ music of Bach, composed many chorale preludes, and edited works of Bach and Handel. Taught at the Frankfurt Music Institute from 1929; organist at Three Kings Church from 1981.

Waldhorn [Ger.]. *Horn, especially the natural horn, but also the modern French horn with valves.

Waldstein Sonata. Popular name for Beethoven's Piano Sonata in C major op. 53 (1803–4), dedicated to his patron Count Ferdinand von Waldstein.

Waldteufel [Lévy], **(Charles) Emile** (b. Strasbourg, 9 Dec. 1837; d. Paris, 12 Feb. 1915). Pianist, composer, and conductor. His father, Louis (1801–84), and brother Léon (1832–84) were both violinists and composers. Studied at the Paris Conservatory; in 1865 named court pianist. Appeared at Covent Garden, 1885 and in Berlin as a conductor, 1889. Majority of his compositions were waltzes; his first, *Joies et peines,* was a big success (1859); *Les patineurs* (The Skater's Waltz) remains his most famous.

Walker, George (Theophilus) (b. Washington, D.C., 27 June 1922). Pianist and composer. Studied at Oberlin College, the Curtis Institute, the American School in Fontainebleau, and the Eastman School; teachers included Clifford Curzon, Rudolf Serkin, and Robert Casadesus for piano, Normand Lockwood, Rosario Scalero, and Nadia Boulanger for composition. Piano debut, New York, 1945. Lived in Paris during the late 1950s; returned to the U.S. and taught at Smith College (1961–68) and Rutgers Univ. (from 1969). Works integrate serial techniques, jazz rhythms, and folk-derived melodies. Compositions include *Address for Orchestra* (1959); Cello Sonata (1957); *Perimeters* (clarinet and piano, 1966); *Variations* (orchestra, 1971); Piano Concerto (1975); Piano Sonata no. 3 (1975); *In Praise of Folly* (orchestra, 1980); Cello Concerto (1982); *Lilacs* (cantata, 1996; Pulitzer Prize).

Walker, T-Bone [Aaron Thibeaux] (b. Linden, Tex., 28 May 1910; d. Los Angeles, 17 Mar. 1975). Blues singer and guitarist. Accompanied Ida Cox and recorded "Wichita Falls Blues" (1929); after moving to California took up electric guitar around 1935; toured with Les Hite's big band as a singer. Thereafter led bands, visiting Europe regularly from 1962 to 1971. Recordings include an influential guitar solo on the rhythm-and-blues song "Call It Stormy Monday" (1947).

Walking bass. A type of bass line in which rhythmic motion is predominantly in one note-value, often quarters or eighths when the pulse is equal to the quarter note. Stepwise melodic motion is characteristic and pitch repetition is generally avoided. The term is applied to Baroque music as well as to jazz in which the bass sounds a pitch on each beat in 4/4 (as distinct from *two-beat), often with a sustained or legato sound.

Walküre, Die [Ger.]. See *Ring des Nibelungen, Der.*

Wallace, (William) Vincent (b. Waterford, 11 Mar. 1812; d. Château de Haget, Vieuzos, Hautes-Pyrénées, 12 Oct. 1865). Composer and performer. Violin debut, Dublin, 1834; 1835, emigrated to Tasmania; opened an academy of music in Sydney. Later traveled to South America and the U.S.; in 1845 in London produced his first of 6 completed operas, *Maritana,* which was received with considerable success as was his third opera, *Lurline.* Also composed songs, duets, and piano solos.

Wallace, William (b. Greenock, 3 July 1860; d. Malmesbury, 16 Dec. 1940). Composer. Served in the Royal Army Medical Corps before enrolling at the Royal Academy of Music; published monographs on musicality and was active in the establishment of the legal rights of composers in England. Works include symphonic poems (*Passing of Beatrice,* 1892; *To the New Century,* 1901), the symphony *The Creation* (1899), and an orchestral suite based on *Pelléas et Mélisande* (1900).

Wallenstein, Alfred (b. Chicago, 7 Oct. 1898; d. New York, 8 Feb. 1983). Conductor and cellist. Studied with Julius Klengel. Principal cellist with the Chicago Symphony (1922–29) and the New York Philharmonic (1929–36) under Toscanini, who encouraged him to conduct; in 1933 founded the Wallenstein Sinfonietta. First American music director of the Los Angeles Philharmonic (1943–56); taught at Juilliard from 1968.

Waller, Fats [Thomas Wright] (b. New York, 21 May 1904; d. Kansas City, Mo., 15 Dec. 1943). Jazz and popular pianist, organist, singer, bandleader, and composer. Studied piano with James P. Johnson; by 1923 was a soloist (recording discs and piano rolls, broadcasting), blues accompanist, jazz composer, songwriter ("Squeeze Me"). Recorded with Fletcher Henderson's big band and others; composed for and performed in the musical revues *Keep Shufflin'* (1928), *Load of Coal* (1929; including "Honeysuckle Rose"), and *Hot Chocolates* (1929; including "Ain't Misbehavin'," "Black and Blue"). From 1929 recorded solo versions of his stride piano compositions (including "Handful of Keys," 1929) and popular songs; from 1934 broadcast, toured, and recorded

with a swing combo, Fats Waller and His Rhythm. Hit recordings included "I'm Gonna Sit Right Down and Write Myself a Letter" (1935) and "Your Feet's Too Big" (1939). Appeared in films, including *Stormy Weather* (1943).

Walmisley, Thomas Attwood (b. London, 21 Jan. 1814; d. Hastings, 17 Jan. 1856). Organist and composer. Son of Thomas Forbes Walmisley, editor of *Cathedral Music: A Collection of Services and Anthems* (1875). Organist at Croydon Church and at Trinity and St. John's Colleges (Cambridge); named professor of music at Cambridge Univ., 1836. Composed 2 symphonies, 4 overtures, an organ concerto, 3 string quartets; anthems, services, odes, part songs, and solo songs.

Walter, Bruno [Schlesinger, Bruno Walter] (b. Berlin, 15 Sept. 1876; d. Beverly Hills, 17 Feb. 1962). Conductor. First conducting appointment with the Cologne Opera, 1893; Mahler's assistant at the Hamburg Opera, 1894, and at the Vienna Opera from 1901. Music director of the Munich Opera (1913–22), Covent Garden (1924–31), Charlottenburg Opera, Leipzig Gewandhaus, and Vienna Staatsoper; appeared widely in Europe and in the U.S. as guest conductor. Settled in the U.S. in 1939; conducted the Metropolitan Opera, the Los Angeles Philharmonic, the NBC Symphony, the New York Philharmonic, and the Philadelphia Orchestra. Known for interpretations of Mozart, Mahler, and Bruckner; conducted the premieres of Mahler's "Das Lied von der Erde" and Ninth Symphony. Compositions include orchestral and choral works, chamber music, and songs. Author of a biography of Mahler (1936) and *Theme and Variations: An Autobiography* (New York, 1947; rev. 1960).

Walter [Walther], **Johann** (b. Kahla, Thuringia, 1496; d. Torgau, 25 Mar. 1570). Composer and poet. In 1524 published the first Protestant collection of choral music, the *Geystliches gesangk Buchleyn;* the following year summoned by Luther to Wittenberg to assist in the composition of the German Mass. Cantor of the Municipal Latin School in Torgau and director of the Stadtkantorei, 1526–48; Kapellmeister of the court chapel in Dresden, 1548–54.

Walther, Johann Gottfried (b. Erfurt, 18 Sept. 1684; d. Weimar, 23 Mar. 1748). Composer and theorist. Studied organ with Johann Bernhard Bach and Johann Andreas Kretschmar, and composition with Buttstett and Wilhelm Hieronymus. Appointed organist at the Thomaskirche, Erfurt, 1702; from 1707 organist at the Church of St. Peter and St. Paul, Weimar, where he taught music to Duke Wilhelm Ernst and Prince Johann Ernst and befriended J. S. Bach. Joined the duke's court orchestra as *Hof-musicus,* 1721. Wrote sacred vocal works and numerous organ pieces, consisting mostly of chorale preludes; writings include the *Musicalisches Lexicon oder Musicalische Bibliothec* (1732), the first dictionary of musicians and musical terms.

Walther von der Vogelweide (b. ca. 1170; d. Würzburg?, ca. 1230). Minnesinger. Considered the greatest lyric poet of medieval Germany; active at the Vienna court at the time of the Babenbergs Leopold V and his son Friedrich (1190–98). After Friedrich's death wandered through Europe and appeared at the courts of, among others, Philip of Swabia, Wolfger von Ellenbrechtskirchen, Margrave Dietrich von Meissen, Duke Bernhard von Kärten, and the Count of Katzenellenbogen; beginning around 1214 was associated with Friedrich of Sicily (later Emperor Friedrich II). Although many poetic works survive, only a single complete melody, the *Palästinalied*, is extant.

Walton, William (Turner) (b. Oldham, 29 Mar. 1902; d. Ischia, Italy, 8 Mar. 1983). Composer. Studied at Oxford; lived with Osbert and Sacheverell Sitwell until the early 1930s; settled on Ischia in the late 1940s. Music performed frequently; composed for films (*Major Barbara*, 1941; *Next of Kin*, 1941; *Went the Day Well?*, 1942) and worked with Laurence Olivier (*Henry V*, 1943–44; *Hamlet*, 1947; *Richard III*, 1955). Toured as composer and conductor in the U.S., Australia, New Zealand, England, and the U.S.S.R. Early works bore the imprint of Schoenberg and postwar French composers and also experimented with jazz and popular dances; later moved toward a more introspective style. Works include operas *Troilus and Cressida* (1950–54), *The Bear* (1965–67); ballets *The Wise Virgins* (1940) and *The Quest* (1943); orchestral music (Symphony no. 1, 1932–35; Violin Concerto, 1938–39; *The Wise Virgins*, suite, 1940; Symphony no. 2, 1959–60; *Variations on a Theme by Hindemith*, 1962–63; *Improvisations on an Impromptu of Benjamin Britten*, 1969; *Passacaglia*, cello, orchestra, 1982); choral music (*Belshazzar's Feast*, baritone, chorus, orchestra, 1930–31; *Set Me As a Seal upon Thine Heart*, unaccompanied chorus, 1938; *Missa brevis*, chorus, organ or orchestra, 1966); vocal and chamber music.

Waltz [Ger. *Walzer,* fr. *walzen,* to turn about; Fr. *valse;* It. *valzer;* Sp. *vals*]. A couple dance in triple time, popular in various versions since the late 18th century. The waltz is the most long-lived and continuously favored among modern ballroom dances. It grew out of southern German and Austrian country dances known generally as **Deutscher* or German Dances (and having no connection with the *allemande of the Baroque suite). The **Ländler* and waltz were originally closely related, but the *Ländler* retained a slower tempo and more rustic character,

whereas the waltz in the late 18th century took on a faster tempo and greater refinement, keeping the turning movements that had given it its name. By the 1780s, the waltz had achieved considerable popularity across Europe, and this increased in the early years of the next century, though it was still considered daring and, by some, morally objectionable because of the close embrace in which the couple danced.

The popularity of the waltz across Europe was given a new impetus in the middle decades of the 19th century by the vogue of the Viennese waltz. This vogue was stimulated by waltz-composing Viennese dance-orchestra leaders, beginning with Joseph Lanner (1801–43) and climaxing with the Strauss family.

Walze [Ger.]. (1) The *crescendo pedal of an electric-action organ. (2) In the 18th century, a stereotyped accompaniment figure such as the *Alberti bass. (3) A roll for a player piano.

Wanderer-fantasie [Ger., Wanderer Fantasy]. Popular name for Schubert's Fantasy in C major op. 15, D. 760 (1822), for piano, actually a sonata in four movements played without pauses, so called because the second movement is a set of variations on a theme from his song "Der Wanderer" D. 489a–c (1816). Portions of this theme are also used in the other three movements.

Wanhal, Johann Baptist. See Vanhal, Johann Baptist.

War of the Buffoons. See **Bouffons, Querelle des.*

War Requiem. Britten's setting of the Requiem Mass with interpolated poems by Wilfred Owen, for soprano, tenor, baritone, boys' choir, chorus, organ, orchestra, and chamber orchestra, completed in 1961 and first performed in Coventry Cathedral in 1962.

Ward, John (b. Canterbury, bapt. 8 Sept. 1571; d. before 31 Aug. 1638). Composer. Served as household musician to the family of Sir Henry Fanshawe in London, composing both sacred and secular music for their use. Works include a volume of madrigals dedicated to his patron (1613), 22 verse anthems, and music for viol consort.

Ward, Robert (Eugene) (b. Cleveland, 13 Sept. 1917). Composer. Studied at Eastman with Bernard Rogers, Howard Hanson, and Edward Royce and at Juilliard with Frederick Jacobi and Bernard Wagenaar. Taught at Juilliard, 1946–56; 1956–67, vice president and managing editor of Galaxy Music in New York; 1967–72, chancellor, North Carolina School of the Arts; 1979–87, taught at Duke Univ. Achieved wide recognition with his opera *The Crucible* (1961; Pulitzer Prize, 1962). Other works include *Jubilation: An Overture* (1946); *Sacred Songs for*

Pantheists (soprano and orchestra, 1951); *He Who Gets Slapped* (opera, 1956); Piano Concerto (1968); *Canticles of America* (Symphony no. 5; soprano, baritone, chorus, orchestra, 1976); *Claudia Legare* (opera, 1977); *Sonic Structures* (orchestra, 1980); *Minutes till Midnight* (opera, 1982).

Ward-Steinem, David (b. Alexandria, La., 6 Nov. 1936). Composer. Studied at Florida State Univ. and the Univ. of Illinois, and in Paris with Nadia Boulanger. In 1961 joined the faculty at San Diego State College. Music of the 1960s emphasizes instrumental colors; beginning in the 1970s, most works involve electronics. Compositions include *Prelude and Toccata for Orchestra* (1962), *Song of Moses* (oratorio, 1964), *Antares* (orchestra and electronics, 1971), Sonata for Fortified Piano (1972), *Tamar* (mixed media opera, 1977), *Children's Corner Revisited* (voice, piano, 1985); *What's Left* (piano, left-hand, 1987); *Gemini* (2 guitars, 1988); *Cinnabar Concerto* (viola, chamber orchestra, 1993).

Warfield, William (Caesar) (b. Helena, Ark., 22 Jan. 1920). Baritone. Studied at the Eastman School. Recital debut, 1950 at Town Hall in New York. Toured internationally as a soloist; appeared in musicals in the U.S. and Europe, including the role of Porgy in Gershwin's *Porgy and Bess* and Joe in Jerome Kern's *Showboat*. From 1952 to 1972 married to the soprano Leontyne Price. Joined faculty at the Univ. of Illinois, 1974; 1984, named president of the National Association of Negro Musicians.

Warlock, Peter [Heseltine, Philip (Arnold)] (b. London, 30 Oct. 1894; d. there, 17 Dec. 1930). Composer. Met Delius in 1910; decided to pursue composition. Worked as a music critic and arranger under his original name, but published musical compositions under the name Peter Warlock. Works are primarily vocal. Songs for voice and piano include *Lillygay: The Distracted Maid, Johnny Wil the Tye, The Shoemaker, Burd Ellen and Young Tamlane, Rantum Tantum* (1922); *The Lover's Maze* (1927); and *The Frostbound Wood* (1929); choral works include *Bethlehem Down* (1927). Also wrote chamber music.

Wärme, mit [Ger.]. With warmth, passionately.

Warren, Harry [Guaragna, Salvatore] (b. Brooklyn, 24 Dec. 1893; d. Los Angeles, 22 Sept. 1981). Popular songwriter. Published first song in 1922; wrote revues with Billy Rose (*Sweet and Low*, 1930); from 1930 composed principally for films. Among his songs are "Absence Makes the Heart Grow Fonder" (1929), "Jeepers Creepers" (1938), "Chattanooga Choo-Choo" (1941), and "On the Atchison, Topeka and the Santa Fe" (1946).

Warwick(e), (Marie) Dionne (b. East Orange, N.J., 12 Dec. 1941). Popular singer. From 1960 worked with composer Burt Bacharach and lyricist Hal David; popularized their songs including "Anyone Who Had a Heart" (1963) and "Do You Know the Way to San Jose" (1968). In the 1970s worked with various artists; in 1985 was successful with "That's What Friends Are For" by Bacharach and Carole Bayer Sager.

Washboard. A *scraper consisting of the domestic laundry implement (a piece of corrugated metal set in a wooden frame) scraped with a metal rod or with thimbles worn on the fingers. It has been used as a rhythm instrument to accompany blues singing and in *jug, *string, and jazz bands.

Washington, Dinah [Jones, Ruth] (b. Tuscaloosa, Ala., 29 Aug. 1924; d. Detroit, 14 Dec. 1963). Popular singer. Sang gospel and blues in Chicago; in 1943 joined Lionel Hampton's band. From 1946 worked as a solo artist; recordings include "Teach Me Tonight" (1954) and "What a Difference a Day Makes" (1959).

Washtub bass. A folk string bass of the U.S. made from a metal washtub. A single string is affixed at one end to the center of the tub (which is turned upside down) and at the other end to a stick approximately four feet long. Bracing the free end of the stick against the rim of the tub, the player pulls on the stick in such a way as to vary the tension of the string and thus the pitch produced when the string is plucked.

Water Music. Popular name for three orchestral suites by Handel in F, D, and G major, the original order of movements of which is, however, uncertain. Some or all movements were presumably performed during a royal procession on the River Thames on 17 July 1717.

Water organ. *Hydraulis.

Waters [née Howard], **Ethel** (b. Chester, Pa., 31 Oct. 1896; d. Chatsworth, Calif., 1 Sept. 1977). Popular singer, actress. Began recording in 1921; "Am I Blue" (1929) and her signature "Stormy Weather" (1933) were very popular. Appeared in Cotton Club revues, musicals (*As Thousands Cheer*, 1933), and drama (*Member of the Wedding*, 1950); in the 1960s performed with evangelist Billy Graham.

Waters, Muddy. See Muddy Waters.

Watts, André (b. Nuremberg, 20 June 1946). Pianist. Studied in Philadelphia with Genia Robiner; appeared at early ages with the Philadelphia Orchestra and the New York Philharmonic under Bernstein. World tour, 1967, sponsored by the U.S. State Department. Toured and recorded extensively; in 1976 played the first live network television broadcast of a solo recital.

Wa-wa [also wah-wah, wow-wow]. An undulating musical sound obtained by mechanical or electronic means. Jazz and dance-band trumpeters and trombonists produce the effect with a Harmon or wa-wa *mute by covering and uncovering the bell-like opening in the end of the mute with the fingers of the left hand. A related effect is produced by covering and uncovering the bell of the instrument itself with a plunger (sometimes the domestic plumbing implement). On electric pianos and guitars, the effect is produced electronically and activated by a pedal.

Waxman [Wachsmann], **Franz** (b. Königshütte, Silesia, 24 Dec. 1906; d. Los Angeles, 24 Feb. 1967). Composer and conductor. Studied at the Dresden Music Academy and the Berlin Conservatory; worked in the German film industry as orchestrator (*The Blue Angel*, 1930), and composer (*Liliom*, 1933). Moved to the U.S. in 1934 and worked in Hollywood for over 30 years; among his best-known scores are *Rebecca* (1940), *Suspicion* (1941), *Sunset Boulevard* (1950), *The Spirit of St. Louis* (1957). Also composed works for the concert stage and conducted frequently in the U.S. and Europe.

Wayte. See Wait.

Webbe, Samuel (1) (b. ?London, 1740; d. there, 15 May 1816). Composer. Regarded by some as the leading composer of glees; first collection of vocal music came out in 1761. Associated with the Glee Club (secretary from 1794). In addition to many collections of glees, catches, canons, etc., wrote keyboard sonatas, Latin and English sacred vocal music, and organ pieces.

Webbe, Samuel (2) (b. London, ca. 1770; d. there, 25 Nov. 1843). Composer. Son of Samuel Webbe (1). From ca. 1798 to 1817 organist of the Unitarian chapel in Liverpool; from 1817 at the Spanish embassy chapel in London. Works include a musical comedy, *The Speechless Wife* (London, 1794), Masses, motets, many glees and catches, and instrumental music.

Weber, Ben (William Jennings Bryan) (b. St. Louis, Mo., 23 July 1916; d. New York, 9 May 1979). Composer. Briefly studied voice and piano at De Paul Univ.; mostly self-taught as a composer. In 1945 moved to New York; worked as a music copyist and composed works that combine the serial and the traditional. From 1965 taught composition at New York Univ. Works include *Two Pieces for String Orchestra* (1952); *Prelude and Passacaglia* (orchestra, 1954); *Rhapsodie concertante* (viola and orchestra, 1957); Piano Concerto (1961); *The Ways* (song cycle for soprano, tenor, and piano, 1964); *The Enchanted*

Midnight (orchestra, 1967); *Concert Poem* (violin and orchestra, 1970); *Sinfonia Clarion* (chamber orchestra, 1973); *Capriccio* (cello and piano, 1977); string quartets.

Weber, Carl Maria (Friedrich Ernst) von (b. Eutin, Germany, ?18 Nov. 1786; d. London, 5 June 1826). Composer. Son of Franz Anton von Weber (?1734–1812), manager of a touring theatrical company; cousin of Constanze (Weber) Mozart. Took lessons from Michael Haydn in Salzburg; studied in Munich with J. E. Wallishauser (known as Valesi) and J. N. Kalcher, and in Vienna with Abbé Vogler. Music director at the Breslau theater 1804–6; in 1806 at the court of the Duke of Württemberg-Öls at Karlsruhe; 1807, became secretary to Duke Ludwig, younger brother of the King of Württemberg, at Stuttgart. In 1809 a financial imbroglio led to expulsion from the kingdom. Resumed studies with Vogler in Darmstadt; with Meyerbeer formed the Harmonische Verein; 1811 conducted the successful premiere of his singspiel *Abu Hassan* in Munich and met the clarinetist Heinrich Bärmann, for whom he composed his two clarinet concertos, the Clarinet Concertino, and other works. Toured with Bärmann; premiered *Silvana* in Berlin, 1812; music director of the Prague Opera, 1813–16. In 1816 appointed music director of the new German Opera in Dresden (later Royal Kapellmeister). Collaborated with Friedrich Kind on *Der Freischütz*, whose Berlin premiere (1821) made Weber an international celebrity. Composed *Euryanthe* on commission from the Vienna Opera; *Oberon* for London; died there after conducting the first 12 performances.

Operas include *Das Waldmädchen* (1800), *Peter Schmoll und seine Nachbarn* (1803), *Silvana* (1808–10), *Abu Hassan* (singspiel, 1811), *Fidelio* (1814), *Der *Freischütz* (1817–21), *Euryanthe* (1823), *Oberon* (1826). Other works include *Der erste Ton* (cantata, 1809), Piano Quartet (1809), 2 clarinet concertos, Clarinet Quintet (1815), Grand Duo Concertant (1816), *Konzertstück* (piano and orchestra, 1821).

Webern, Anton (Friedrich Wilhelm von) (b. Vienna, 3 Dec. 1883; d. Mittersill, Austria, 15 Sept. 1945). Studied musicology at Univ. of Vienna with Guido Adler, harmony with Hermann Graedener, and counterpoint with Karl Navrátil. In 1904 met Arnold Schoenberg; became his loyal disciple, with Alban Berg, Egon Wellesz, Heinrich Jalowetz, and a few others. Conducted light opera and operetta in Danzig (1910–11), Stettin (1912–13), and elsewhere; produced first works under Schoenberg's influence, a group of songs written in 1908 and 1909 on texts by Stefan George. Tendency toward brevity and concision became pronounced during 1910–14; most works between 1914 and 1926 were songs, many settings of devotional verses. Worked with So-ciety for Private Musical Performances, founded by Schoenberg and devoted to the performance of new music (1918–22); conducted choruses. Adopted Schoenberg's twelve-tone method in the early 1920s. Toured Germany and England as a composer and conductor, 1929. Turned to instrumental composi-tions and larger forms; works employed an exceed-ingly high degree of serial organization. In 1938 per-formance and publication of his works banned by the Nazis, although he continued to compose; in 1945, fled to the American zone of Austria; as an innocent bystander, shot and killed by an American soldier.

Works include *Passacaglia* op. 1 (orchestra, 1908), *Entflieht auf leichten Kähnen* op. 2 (chorus a capella, 1908), *Six Pieces for Orchestra* op. 6 (1909; rev. 1928), *Six Bagatelles* op. 9 (string quartet, 1913), *Five Pieces for Orchestra* op. 10 (1913), *Three Little Pieces* op. 12 (cello and piano, 1914), *Five Sacred Songs* op. 15 (1917–22), String Trio op. 20 (1927), Symphony op. 21 (1928), *Das Augenlicht* op. 26 (chorus and orchestra, 1935), *J. S. Bach: Fuga (Ricercata) a 6 voci* (arrangement from the *Musical Offering*, orchestra, 1935), *Variations* op. 30 (orches-tra, 1940).

Webster, Ben (Benjamin Francis) (b. Kansas City, Mo., 27 March 1909; d. Amsterdam, 20 Sept. 1973). Jazz tenor saxophonist. Played in big bands of Ben-nie Moten (1931–33), Andy Kirk (1933), Fletcher Henderson (1934, 1937), and Duke Ellington (1940–43); thereafter mainly led small groups. Rejoined Ellington (1948–49) and toured with Jazz at the Phil-harmonic (1950s); based in Europe from 1964. Re-corded with Art Tatum (1956), Coleman Hawkins (1957), Oscar Peterson (1959), Harry Edison (1962), and Don Byas (1968).

Wechsel [Ger.]. Change; *wechseln*, in harp playing, to change the key of the instrument by adjusting the pedals (e.g., *wechseln in D-dur*, change to D major).

Weckmann, Matthias (b. Niederdoria, near Mühl-hausen, 1619 or earlier; d. Hamburg, 24 Feb. 1674). Composer. Pupil of Schütz and Praetorius. Became organist at the electoral chapel, Dresden, 1637; 1642, followed Schütz to Nykøbing, Denmark; organist at the chapel there until 1647. Returned to Dresden; organist at the Jacobikirche, Hamburg, from 1655. Extant works include cantatas, choral works, can-zonas, sonatas, and keyboard music.

Wedge fugue. Popular name for Bach's organ fugue in E minor BWV 548 (composed between 1727 and 1731), so called because the subject consists of in-creasingly wider intervals around a central axis.

Weelkes, Thomas (b. Elsted?, Sussex, ca. 1575; d. London, 30 Nov. 1623). Organist and composer. In 1598 appointed organist of Winchester College; 1601 or 1602, joined the choir of Chichester Cathedral as organist and *informator choristarum;* dismissed, 1617. Published 4 volumes of madrigals (1597, 1598, 1600, 1608); also composed other secular vo-cal music, anthems, services, and a few instrumental pieces.

Weerbeke [Werbeke, Werbeck], **Gaspar van** (b. Oudenaarde, ca. 1445; d. after 1517). Composer. Ac-tive at the Sforza court in Milan by 1471; served as *vice-abbate* to the *cantori de camera* (the other half of the choir, the *cantori de cappella,* included Josquin, Compère, and Johannes Martini). Served in the papal choir in Rome, 1481–89 and 1500–9; also at the court of Duke Ludovico Sforza, "il Moro," in Milan and the court choir of Philip the Fair; in 1517 canonicus of the Church of S. Maria ad Gradus in Mainz. Composed Masses and motets.

Wegelius, Martin (b. Helsinki, 10 Nov. 1846; d. there, 22 Mar. 1906). Composer. Studied in Helsinki, Vienna, and Leipzig. Conductor at the Finnish Op-era, 1878–79; first director of the Helsinki Music College, 1882 (students included Sibelius and Palmgren). Compositions include an overture, canta-tas, piano music, and songs. Author of texts on music theory, history, and composition.

Wehmütig [Ger.]. Sad, melancholy.

Weich [Ger.]. Soft, delicate.

Weigl, Joseph (b. Eisenstadt, 28 Mar. 1766; d. Vi-enna, 3 Feb. 1846). Composer. Son of Joseph Franz Weigl, a cellist in Prince Esterházy's orchestra. Stud-ied in Vienna with Albrechtsberger and Salieri; dep-uty Kapellmeister to Salieri at the court theater by 1790; named court Vice-Kapellmeister, 1827. Wrote over 30 operas, including *La Principessa d'Amalfi* (1794) and *L'amor marinaro* (1797); 18 ballets; 2 oratorios, 11 Masses, over 20 cantatas; orchestral music, chamber music, lieder.

Weigl, Karl (b. Vienna, 6 Feb. 1881; d. New York, 11 Aug. 1949). Composer. Studied with Alexander von Zemlinsky and with Guido Adler at the Univ. of Vi-enna. Opera coach under Mahler (1904–6); taught at the New Vienna Conservatory (1918–28) and the Univ. of Vienna (1930–38); emigrated to the U.S. and taught at Hartt School of Music (1941–42) and Philadelphia Academy of Music (1948–49). Works include 6 symphonies; 2 piano concertos (one for left-hand alone, 1925); 8 string quartets; 2 violin so-natas; viola sonata.

Weihe des Hauses, Die [Ger., The Consecration of the House]. An overture by Beethoven, op. 124 (1822), composed for the opening of the Josephstadt Theater in Vienna.

Weihnachts Oratorium [Ger.]. See *Christmas Oratorio.*

Weill, Kurt (Julian) (b. Dessau, 2 Mar. 1900; d. New York, 3 April 1950). Composer. Studied briefly at the Berlin Hochschule für Musik; 1919, conductor at the municipal theater in the Westphalian town of Lüdenscheid. In 1920 accepted into Ferruccio Busoni's master class in composition at the State Academy of the Arts in Berlin and became Busoni's favorite pupil; compositions earned him a contract with Universal Publishers. First success with premiere in Dresden in 1926 of *Der Protagonist,* a one-act opera written with the playwright Georg Kaiser; much greater sensation was *Die Dreigroschenoper,* opened in 1928 in Berlin, written with the communist poet and playwright Bertold Brecht. Collaborated with Brecht on further works, including the opera *Aufstieg und Fall der Stadt Mahagonny;* broke with him, 1931. After the February 1933 opening of *Silbersee* was disrupted in Magdeburg by storm troopers, fled to Paris; wrote *Die sieben Todsünden,* his last work in collaboration with Brecht.

Arrived in New York, 1935; worked with Franz Werfel and Max Reinhardt on *The Eternal Road,* a theatrical pageant of Jewish history; began composing Broadway musicals, including *Knickerbocker Holiday* with Maxwell Anderson (yielded the hit "September Song"); *Lady in the Dark* with Moss Hart and Ira Gershwin; and others.

Works include *Die Zaubernacht* (ballet-pantomime, 1922); Concerto for Violin and Wind Orchestra (1924); *Der Protagonist* (one-act opera, 1925); *Royal Palace* (opera, 1926); *Mahagonny-Songspiel* (1927); *Die *Dreigroschenoper* [Threepenny Opera] (1928); *Kleine Dreigroschenmusik* (wind orchestra, 1928); *Das Berliner Requiem* (1928); *Der Lindberghflug* (1929); *Happy End* (opera, 1929); *Aufstieg und Fall der Stadt Mahagonny* (opera, 1929); *Die Burgschaft* (1931); *Der Silbersee: Ein Wintermärchen* (1932); *Die sieben Todsünden* (ballet with songs, 1933); Broadway musicals *Johnny Johnson* (1936), *Knickerbocker Holiday* (1938), *Lady in the Dark* (1941), *One Touch of Venus* (1943); *Street Scene* (1947), *Love Life* (1948), *Lost in the Stars* (1949).

Weinberger, Jaromír (b. Prague, 8 Jan. 1896; d. St. Petersburg, Fla., 8 Aug. 1967). Composer. Studied at the Prague Conservatory and with Max Reger in Leipzig. Early works based on Czech folk tunes harmonized in the tradition of Smetana, including *Schwanda, The Bagpiper* (opera, 1927), *Six Bohemian Songs and Dances* (1930), *Die geliebte Stimme* (opera, 1931). Emigrated to the U.S. in 1939; turned to American sources in works such as *Prelude and Fugue on "Dixie"* (1939) and *The Legend of Sleepy Hollow* (orchestra, 1940); later works, such as *Prel-*

udes réligieuses et profanes (orchestra, 1953), aimed at a more international style.

Weiner, Lazar (b. Cherkassy, near Kiev, 17 Oct. 1897; d. New York, 10 Jan. 1982). Composer. Studied piano at the Kiev Conservatory; 1917, emigrated to New York; studied with Frederick Jacobi and Joseph Schillinger and was drawn into the Yiddish cultural revival movement. Directed Workman's Circle Chorus (1930–65); music director of Central Synagogue in New York (1930–75); lectured widely on Jewish music. Wrote several piano pieces, an opera (*The Golem,* 1956), instrumental works; the bulk of his compositions are songs and choral music in Yiddish and liturgical music in Hebrew.

Weiner, Léo (b. Budapest, 16 Apr. 1885; d. there, 13 Sept. 1960). Composer. Studied at the Budapest School of Musical Art with Koessler; 1908, joined the faculty. Compositions are in a late Romantic style, with some use of native folk music. Works include dramatic music (*Csongor és Tünde,* ballet, 1930), orchestral music (*Preludio, notturno e scherzo diabolico,* 1950), and chamber pieces (*Magyar népi muzsika* [Hungarian Folk Music], piano, 1953).

Weingartner, (Paul) Felix, Edler von Münzberg (b. Zara, Dalmatia, 2 June 1863; d. Winterthur, 7 May 1942). Conductor, composer, author. Studied with W. A. Rémy in Graz, and with Reinecke, Jadassohn, and Paul at the Leipzig Conservatory; met Liszt, who recommended production of his first opera, *Sakuntala* (1884). Conducted at the Königsberg Opera and in Danzig, Hamburg, and Mannheim; in 1891 named conductor at the Berlin Opera; director of the Kaim concerts in Munich (1898–1903). Succeeded Mahler at the Vienna Court Opera (1908–11); remained with the Vienna Philharmonic until 1927. Director, Vienna Volksoper (1919–24); director, Basel Conservatory (1927–33). Appeared in England and the U.S. with the Royal Philharmonic, the London Symphony, the New York Philharmonic, and the Boston Opera. Composed several operas (*Genesius,* 1892); wrote on musical subjects.

Weinzweig, John (Jacob) (b. Toronto, 11 Mar. 1913). Composer. Studied at the Univ. of Toronto with Healey Willan and Sir Ernest MacMillan and at Eastman with Bernard Rogers. Became acquainted with twelve-tone theory and practice and composed serial works for concert and for radio and film; taught at the Toronto Conservatory of Music (1939–43, 1945–60) and at the Univ. of Toronto (1951–78); founded the Canadian League of Composers in 1951 (president 1951–57, 1959–63). Works include *Suite for Piano* (1939); orchestral suites *Our Canada* (1943), *Red Ear of Corn* (1949); *Divertimento no. 1* (flute and string orchestra, 1946); Cello Sonata ("Israel," 1949); Violin Concerto (1954); *Divertimento no. 3* (bassoon and strings, 1960); Piano Concerto (1966); Concerto for Harp and Chamber Orchestra (1967); *Dummiyah/Silence* (orchestra, 1969); *Riffs* (flute, 1974).

Weir, Judith (b. Cambridge, 11 May 1954). Composer. Played oboe and studied composition with Tavener at North London Collegiate. Worked on computer music under Vercoe at the Massachusetts Institute of Technology; 1975, attended Tanglewood and met Gunther Schuller, a key influence; 1976, worked with Holloway and was commissioned by Peter Maxwell Davies for his group The Fires of London. Composer-in-residence for the Southern Arts Association; 1979–82, Cramb Fellow in composition at Glasgow Univ. Works include *Out of the Air* (flute, oboe, clarinet, bassoon, horn, 1975); *Wunderhorn* (orchestra, 1978); cello sonata (1980); *Thread!* (speaker, flute/alto flute/piccolo, clarinet/bass clarinet, string quartet, piano, percussion, 1981); *A Night at the Chinese Opera* (opera, 1987); *Narcissus* (flute, digital delay, 1988); *Heaven Ablaze in His Breast* (opera, 1989); *The Vanishing Bridegroom* (1990); *Music, Untangled* (orchestral overture, 1991); *Blond Eckbert* (opera, 1994).

Weisgall, Hugo (David) (b. Ivančice, Czechoslovakia, 13 Oct. 1912; d. Baltimore, 13 Mar. 1997). Composer. Studied at Johns Hopkins Univ., Peabody Conservatory, and Curtis Institute of Music with Rosario Scalero and Fritz Reiner; also with Roger Sessions. During World War II served as military attaché in London, then as cultural attaché in Prague, continuing to compose. Returned to the U.S., 1948; taught at the Jewish Theological Seminary in New York beginning 1952, at Juilliard 1957–68, and at Queens College 1961–83. Works include ballets *Quest* (1938), *Outpost* (1947); one-act operas *The Tenor* (1950), *The Stronger* (1952); operas *Six Characters in Search of an Author* (1956), *Purgatory* (1958), *The Gardens of Adonis* (1959), *Athaliah* (1963), *Nine Rivers from Jordan* (1968), *Jennie, or The Hundred Nights* (1976), *Will You Marry Me* (1989); *Fancies and Inventions* (baritone and chamber ensemble, 1970); *Translations* (mezzo-soprano and piano, 1972); *Lyrical Interval* (voice and piano, 1985); *Esther* (1993).

Weiss, Adolph (b. Baltimore, 12 Sept. 1891; d. Van Nuys, Calif., 21 Feb. 1971). Composer and bassoonist. Played with the New York Symphony and the Chicago Symphony; in 1925 went to Berlin to study with Arnold Schoenberg at the Akademie der Künste. Adopted Schoenberg's twelve-tone methods. Returned to the U.S.; continued to work as a bassoonist in Hollywood studios and in the Los Angeles Philharmonic. Works include 2 string quartets (1925,

1926); Chamber Symphony (1927); *American Life, orchestra* (1928); *The Libation Bearers* (1930), a "choreographic cantata"; *Theme and Variations,* orchestra (1933).

Weiss, Silvius Leopold (b. Breslau, 12 Oct. 1686; d. Dresden, 16 Oct. 1750). Composer and lutenist. By 1706 employed in Breslau by Count Carl Philipp of the Palatinate; in Rome with the Polish Prince Alexander Sobiesky, 1708–14, where he probably worked with the Scarlattis; in 1715 at the courts of Hessen-Kassel and Düsseldorf; from 1717 at Dresden. Wrote more music for the lute—almost 600 pieces—than any other composer in the history of the instrument.

Weissenberg, Alexis (Sigismund) (b. Sofia, Bulgaria, 26 July 1929). Pianist. Studied with Pancho Vladigerov in Bulgaria; fled from Nazi occupation to Palestine; after the war moved to New York; attended Juilliard and studied with Schnabel, Samaroff, and Landowska. In 1947 won the Leventritt International Competition; resumed career in 1966 after a lengthy absence from the stage. Recorded the Beethoven concertos with Karajan and toured widely with Maazel and the New Philharmonic.

Weldon, John (b. Chichester, 19 Jan. 1676; d. London, 7 May 1736). Composer. Studied with John Walter and Purcell. Organist at New College, Oxford (1694–1702), St. Bride's (from 1702), the Chapel Royal (1708), and St. Martin-in-the-Fields (1714). Became Gentleman Extraordinary of the Chapel Royal, 1701; second composer to the Chapel Royal, 1715. Compositions include stage works (*The Judgement of Paris,* 1701; *The Tempest,* ca. 1712), anthems, services, odes, songs, and instrumental works.

Welk, Lawrence (b. Strasburg, N.D., 11 Mar. 1903; d. Santa Monica, Calif., 17 May 1992). Popular bandleader and accordionist. Formed his first groups in the 1920s; from 1951 appeared on television. Termed his characteristic sound "Champagne Music"; repertory featured light classical arrangements and dance music. Published music in California and made several successful recordings ("Calcutta," 1960).

Wellesz, Egon (Joseph) (b. Vienna, 21 Oct. 1885; d. Oxford, 9 Nov. 1974). Composer and musicologist. Studied musicology at the Univ. of Vienna with Guido Adler and composition with Arnold Schoenberg. Close associate of Schoenberg and Anton Webern. Published studies of 17th-century opera and ballet, Middle Eastern and Byzantine music; scholarly activity influenced compositions. In 1929 became professor of music history at the Univ. of Vienna; 1938, fled to England; taught music history at Oxford 1943–72.

Works include *Die Prinzessin Girnara* (opera,

1921), *Alkestis* (opera, 1924), *Achilles auf Skyros* (ballet, 1926), *Der Opferung des Gefangenen* (opera, Cologne, 1926); *Die Bakchantinnen* (opera, Vienna, 1931); *Incognita* (English-language opera, 1951); 9 symphonies (1945–71); 4 Masses; 10 string quartets (1912–68); other chamber works; songs. Writings include *Arnold Schönberg* (1921); *Byzantinische Kirchenmusik* (1927); *A History of Byzantine Music and Hymnography* (1949; rev. 1963).

Wellingtons Sieg [Ger., Wellington's Victory]. A "battle symphony" [see *Battaglia*] by Beethoven (full title, *Wellingtons Sieg, oder Die Schlacht bei Vittoria*), op. 91 (1813), written in celebration of Wellington's victory over Napoleon. It depicts battle scenes and quotes English and French fanfares, "Rule Britannia," "Marlborough s'en va-t-en guerre," and "God Save the King." The second part was originally composed for Maelzel's panharmonicon [see Automatic instruments], but the entire work was later orchestrated by Beethoven for strings, "opposing" wind bands, and miscellaneous artillery.

Wells, Junior [Blackmore, Amos, Jr.; Wells, Amos, Jr.] (b. West Memphis, Ark., 9 Dec. 1934; d. Chicago, 15 Jan. 1998). Blues harmonica player and singer. Moved to Chicago, 1946; formed a band with David and Louis Myers and Fred Below, Jr., called, variously, the Little Boys, Three Deuces, and Four Aces. In 1952 replaced Little Walter in Muddy Waters's group; recordings include "Eagle Rock" (1953) and "So All Alone" (1954). In the late 1960s began performing and recording with Buddy Guy.

Wells, Kitty [Muriel Ellen Deason] (b. Nashville, 30 Aug. 1919). Country singer and songwriter. In 1937 began to tour with her husband, Johnny Wright, and his Tennessee Mountain Boys; appeared on radio shows including the *Louisiana Hayride* (1947–52) and the Grand Ole Opry (from 1952). Recordings include "It Wasn't God Who Made Honky-Tonk Angels" (1952), "I Can't Stop Loving You" (1958), and "Heartbreak U.S.A." (1965). The first female country singer to achieve success as a soloist.

Well-Tempered Clavier, The [Ger., Das wohltemperirte Clavier]. Bach's collection of 48 preludes and fugues, grouped in two parts, BWV 846–69 and 870–93 (assembled in 1722 and 1738–42), each of which contains 24 paired preludes and fugues, one prelude and fugue for each major and minor key beginning with C major and ascending chromatically. The pieces making up the collections date from various periods in Bach's life and employ a variety of styles. The title refers to the use of a *temperament in which all keys are satisfactorily in tune, but not necessarily an absolutely equal temperament. These collections are the first to exploit such a possibility fully.

Welsh harp. See *Telyn.*

Wenig [Ger.]. Little, slightly; *ein wenig*, a little; *weniger,* less.

Werner, Gregor Joseph (b. Ybbs an der Donau, 28 Jan. 1693; d. Eisenstadt, Burgenland, 3 Mar. 1766). Composer. Organist at Melk Abbey, 1715 to 1716 or 1721; 1728 became Kapellmeister at the Esterházy court at Eisenstadt. After Haydn became Vice-Kapellmeister there in 1761, as *Oberhofkapellmeister* remained in control of sacred music. Resentment of the younger composer is evident in a petition to Prince Nikolaus von Esterházy in 1765 that blames Haydn for the decline of the Esterházy musical establishment. Compositions include Masses, oratorios, smaller sacred vocal works, symphonies, and trio sonatas.

Wernick, Richard (b. Boston, Mass., 16 Jan. 1934). Composer. Studied at Brandeis Univ. with Irving Fine, Arthur Berger, and Harold Shapero and at Mills College with Leon Kirchner. Composer and conductor, Winnipeg Ballet, 1956–58; 1958–64 in New York, composing music for documentary films and television and also for the public schools. Taught at Univ. of Chicago (1965–68) and Univ. of Pennsylvania (from 1968). Best-known works are settings of political and/or religious texts, often based on music of the past. Compositions include *Haiku of Bashō* (soprano, chamber ensemble, and tape, 1968); *A Prayer for Jerusalem* (mezzo-soprano and percussion, 1971); *Kaddish-Requiem, a Secular Service for the Victims of Indo-China* (mezzo-soprano, chamber ensemble, and tape, 1971); *Visions of Terror and Wonder* (mezzo-soprano and orchestra; Pulitzer Prize, 1977); *Introits and Canons,* chamber orchestra (1977); *A Poison Tree* (soprano and chamber ensemble, 1980); Piano Sonata (1982); Symphony no. 1 (1987); String Quartet no. 3 (1988); Concerto for Piano and Orchestra (1989); Symphony no. 2 (1995); *. . . And a Time for Peace* (mezzo-soprano, orchestra, 1995).

Wert [Vuert, Werth], **Giaches** [Jaches] **de** (b. Weert?, near Antwerp, 1535; d. Mantua, 6 May 1596). Composer. By 1558 employed by Count Alfonso Gonzaga at Novellara; 1565, appointed *maestro di cappella* at the ducal chapel of S. Barbara in Mantua; also had contact with the Este court at Ferrara. Succeeded by Gastoldi in 1592. Madrigals praised by, among others, Palestrina, Artusi, and Berard; Monteverdi cited him, along with Rore, Marenzio, Ingegneri, and Luzzaschi, as a composer of the *seconda prattica.*

Werther. Opera in four acts by Massenet (libretto in French by Édouard Blau, Paul Milliet, and Georges Hartmann, after Goethe's novel), first produced in

German in Vienna in 1892 and in French in Paris in 1893. Setting: Wetzlar, Germany, in 1772.

Wesley, Charles (b. Bristol, 11 Dec. 1757; d. London, 23 May 1834). Composer, organist. Brother of Samuel Wesley. Studied organ with Joseph Kelway and eventually had a position at St. Marylebone; studied composition with William Boyce. Published compositions include 6 concertos for organ or harpsichord, 6 string quartets, other keyboard music, hymns, anthems, and songs.

Wesley, Samuel (b. Bristol, 24 Feb. 1766; d. London, 11 Oct. 1837). Composer, organist. Younger brother of Charles Wesley. Regarded as one of the leading organists of his day, but held few permanent appointments and was often close to poverty. Greatly admired Bach's music and figured prominently in the England Bach revival. Wrote Latin sacred vocal music, hymns, anthems, secular vocal pieces, some orchestral and chamber works, and many organ and other keyboard works.

Wesley, Samuel Sebastian (b. London, 14 Aug. 1810; d. Gloucester, 19 Apr. 1876). Composer, organist. Son of Samuel Wesley. Pupil of his father; 1826–32, organist and conductor in London; served as cathedral organist at Hereford, Exeter, Winchester, and Gloucester. Highly regarded for playing and improvising; from 1850, professor at the Royal Academy. Produced few written organ compositions; best known for Anglican church music (Service in E, 1841–44), ca. 38 anthems, and hymns.

West Coast jazz. Small-combo *cool jazz in California in the 1950s. Although performances increasingly emphasized complex arrangements in this restrained style derived from *bebop, the most innovative sounds came in clear, contrapuntal improvisations by the pianoless Gerry Mulligan–Chet Baker Quartet and in the Dave Brubeck Quartet's experiments in meters other than 4/4.

Westergaard, Peter (Talbot) (b. Champaign, Ill., 28 May 1931). Composer and theorist. Studied at Harvard with Walter Piston, at Princeton with Roger Sessions, and in Freiburg with Wolfgang Fortner. Taught at Columbia Univ. (1958–66), Amherst College (1967–68), Princeton Univ. (beginning 1968). Compositions are in a serial idiom; as a theorist concerned with both tonal and atonal music. Works include *The Plot against the Giant (Cantata I),* female chorus, clarinet, cello, harp (1956); *Mr. and Mrs. Discobolos,* chamber opera (1966); *The Tempest* (opera, 1970–90); *Ode* (soprano, 5 instruments, 1989).

Whip. *Slapstick.

Whistle. A small, end-blown pipe, usually a *duct flute, made of wood, cane, metal, or plastic. Whistles may produce only a single pitch or they may produce several with the aid of finger holes or a plunger that varies the effective length of the pipe. The pipe may be open or stopped. See also Penny whistle.

Whistle flute. *Duct flute.

White, Clarence Cameron (b. Clarksville, Tenn., 10 Aug. 1880; d. New York, 30 June 1960). Violinist and composer. Attended Howard Univ. and Oberlin Conservatory and studied with Samuel Coleridge-Taylor in London and with Raoul Laparra in Paris. Toured widely in the U.S.; taught at several black schools and conservatories, including the Washington Conservatory of Music (1903–7), West Virginia State College (1924–30), and Hampton Institute (1932–35). Most compositions based on black folk music. Works include virtuoso violin pieces *Bandanna Sketches* (1918), *From the Cotton Fields* (1920); *A Night in Sans Souci* (ballet, 1929); *Ouanga* (opera, 1932); orchestral pieces *Kutamba Rhapsody* (1942), *Elegy* (1954); arrangements of spirituals.

White [Whyte], **Robert** (b. ca. 1538; d. London, Nov. 1574). Composer. Cantor at Trinity College, Cambridge; 1562, appointed master of the choristers at Ely Cathedral, a position previously held by his father-in-law, Christopher Tye. By 1567 master of the choristers at Chester Cathedral; held a similar post at Westminster Abbey. One of the first English composers to write fantasias; his hymns served as models for two of Byrd's settings of *Christe qui lux es.*

Whiteman, Paul (b. Denver, 28 March 1890; d. Doylestown, Pa., 29 Dec. 1967). Popular bandleader. In 1919 formed a dance orchestra; hit recordings included "Whispering" (1920) and "Three O'Clock in the Morning" (1922). When instrumentation grew to include a big band, orchestral winds, and strings, promoted his music as "symphonic jazz"; soloists included Bix Beiderbecke, Joe Venuti, and Jack Teagarden. Commissioned and first performed Gershwin's *Rhapsody in Blue* (1924); also commissioned Grofé's *Metropolis* (ca. 1928) and Stravinsky's *Scherzo à la russe* (1942).

Whithorne [Whittern], **Emerson** (b. Cleveland, 6 Sept. 1884; d. Lyme, Conn., 25 Mar. 1958). Composer. Studied in Europe with Theodor Leschetizky and Artur Schnabel. From 1907 to 1915 lived in London; wrote music criticism and composed exoticist works. After return to the U.S. in 1915, compositions drew on American sources such as Negro spirituals and Western lore. Works include *The Rain* (orchestra, 1912); *Greek Impressions* (string quartet, 1914); *New York Days and Nights* (piano, 1922; orchestrated 1923); *Saturday's Child* (mezzo-soprano, tenor, and chamber orchestra, 1926); *El Camino Real* (piano,

1937); *Sierra Morena* (orchestra, 1938); 2 symphonies (1929, 1935); violin concerto (1931).

Whiting, Arthur Battelle (b. Cambridge, 20 June 1861; d. Beverly, Mass., 20 July 1936). Pianist and composer. Studied at New England Conservatory with William Hall Sherwood and George Chadwick and at the Munich Conservatory with Joseph Rheinberger. Returned to Boston, 1885; moved to New York, 1895. Active as a concert pianist and also performed on harpsichord. Most compositions in the style of German Romanticism. Works include *Concert Overture* (1886); Piano Concerto (1888); *Fantasia* (piano and orchestra, 1897); *The Rubaiyát of Omar Kayyám* (baritone and piano, 1901).

Whiting, George E(lbridge) (b. Holliston, Mass., 14 Sept. 1842; d. Cambridge, 14 Oct. 1923). Organist and composer. Studied in New York with George W. Morgan, then in Liverpool. Organist in Hartford, Albany, and Boston; in 1874 went to Berlin to study with Haupt and Radecke. Organist at the Immaculate Conception Church in Boston, 1876–1910; head of the organ department at New England Conservatory until 1898. Published several collections of organ music.

Whitney, Robert (Sutton) (b. Newcastle upon Tyne, 9 July 1904; d. Louisville, Ky., 22 Nov. 1986). Conductor and composer. Studied at the American Conservatory of Music in Chicago and with Eric DeLamarter. During the 1920s played piano in Chicago nightclubs and on the radio; conducting debut with the Chicago Civic Orchestra, 1932. In 1937 engaged as conductor of the Louisville Orchestra; from 1948, the orchestra commissioned a new work for every program, and from 1953 through the 1980s produced over 200 "First Edition" recordings. Served as dean of the Univ. of Louisville Music School from 1956 to 1972; retired from the orchestra in 1967. Compositions include Concerto grosso (orchestra, 1934), Symphony in E minor (1936), Concertino (orchestra, 1960).

Whittern, Emerson. See Whithorne, Emerson.

Whizzer. *Bull-roarer.

Whole note. See Note.

Whole tone. An *interval consisting of two semitones (e.g., C–D or E–F♯).

Whole-tone scale. A *scale consisting only of whole tones. Such a scale includes six pitches in each octave, and only two different examples can be constructed from the twelve pitch classes of Western music: C D E F♯ G♯ A♯ and C♯ D♯ F G A B (or their enharmonic equivalents).

Whythorne, Thomas (b. Ilminster, England, 1528; d. London 31? July 1596). Lutenist and composer. Matriculated at Magdalen College, Oxford; served John Heywood and the Duchess of Northumberland. Traveled on the Continent 1553–55; inspired by the popularity of madrigal books in Italy, composed *Songes for Three, Fower and Five Voyces* (1571), the first work of its kind published in England. The 1955 rediscovery of Whythorne's autobiography (ca. 1576) has revealed much about musical and social practice of the time.

Widor, Charles Marie (Jean Albert) (b. Lyons, 21 Feb. 1844; d. Paris, 12 Mar. 1937). Organist, composer, teacher. Studied at the Brussels Conservatory with Fétis and Lemmens. From 1860 organist at St. François, Lyons; 1870–1934, at St. Sulpice, Paris. Organ professor, Paris Conservatory, 1890–96, succeeding Franck; from 1896, composition professor; pupils included Tournemire, Vierne, Schweitzer, Dupré, Honegger, Milhaud. A noted improviser and prolific composer; best known for organ music, especially the 10 organ symphonies, nos. 1–4 published as op. 13 (1876), nos. 5–8 as op. 42 (1880?), *Symphonie gothique* op. 70 (1895), *Symphonie romain* op. 73 (1900). Other works include 3 operas (*Les pêcheurs de Saint Jean,* 1905), a ballet and incidental music, 3 numbered symphonies and other orchestral works, much chamber music, piano pieces, sacred works, songs. Writings include *Technique de l'orchestre moderne* (1904).

Wie [Ger.]. As, as if, like [see *Ferne*].

Wieck, Clara. See Schumann, Clara.

Wieniawski, Henryk [Henri] (b. Lublin, Poland, 10 July 1835; d. Moscow, 31 Mar. 1880). Violinist, composer. Brother of Józef Wieniawski. Studied at the Paris Conservatory with Massart. In 1848 gave concerts in Paris, St. Petersburg, Moscow, and Warsaw. Began to publish virtuoso violin pieces from ca. 1850; from 1851 was a touring virtuoso. In St. Petersburg 1860–72, serving as solo violinist to the tsar (1859), concertmaster of St. Petersburg orchestra, and leader of Russian Musical Society quartet. In 1872–74 toured North America (with Rubinstein the first year); then toured Europe and taught at the Brussels Conservatory (1875–77). Considered one of the great violinists of his time. Compositions for violin still played include the 2 polonaises opp. 4 and 21; *Souvenir de Moscou* op. 6; the second concerto (1862); *L'école moderne,* 10 etudes-caprices op. 10, and *Etudes-Caprices* op. 18.

Wieniawski, Józef [Joseph] (b. Lublin, 23 May 1837; d. Brussels, 11 Nov. 1912). Pianist and composer. Brother of Henryk Wieniawski. Studied with Zimmermann and Marmontel at the Paris Conservatory and with Lizst in Weimar and Adolf Bernhard Max in Berlin. Concertized with his brother in Russia, 1851–53; named to the piano faculty at Moscow Conservatory when it was founded in 1866; 1878, became professor of piano at Brussels Conservatory. Compositions include the Symphony in D op. 49, Piano Concerto in G minor op. 20, Violin Sonata op. 24, Cello Sonata op. 26, String Quartet op. 23, Piano Trio op. 40, and many short piano pieces.

Wigglesworth, Frank (b. Boston, 3 Mar. 1918; d. New York, 19 Mar. 1996). Composer. Studied in New York with Otto Luening and Henry Cowell and with Edgard Varèse. Beginning 1954 taught at the New School for Social Research, New York. Compositions draw from diverse sources, including American hymnody and French Ars nova. Works include 3 symphonies; *Telesis* (orchestra, 1951); *Ballet for Esther Brooks* (1961); Concertino (viola and orchestra, 1965); *The Willowdale Handcar* (opera, 1969); 2 Short Masses (1961, 1970); *Duets* (mezzo-soprano and clarinet, 1978); *Music for Strings* (1981); *The Police Log of the Chronicle* (opera, 1984).

Wilbye, John (b. Diss, Norfolk, bapt. 7 Mar. 1574; d. Colchester, between Sept. and Nov. 1638). Composer. By 1598, the year of his first volume of madrigals, in the employ of Sir Thomas Kytson at Hengrave Hall, outside Bury St. Edmunds; remained at Hengrave for nearly three decades; only other collection of madrigals appeared in 1609. After the death of Lady Kytson in 1628 moved to Colchester to serve her daughter, Lady Rivers. One of the finest and most expressive of the English madrigalists.

Wild, Earl (b. Pittsburgh, 26 Nov. 1915). Pianist and composer. Studied at Carnegie Technical College and with Selmar Jansen, Egon Petri, and Paul Doguereau. Pianist with the NBC Symphony; in 1942 invited by Toscanini to appear as soloist. Premiered Marvin David Levy's First Piano Concerto and Paul Creston's Piano Concerto op. 43. Taught at Juilliard (from 1977), the Manhattan School (1981–83), and Ohio State Univ. (from 1987); in 1978 became artistic director of the Wolf Trap Chamber Group. Best known for performances of the Romantic repertory and music of Gershwin; compositions include orchestral music, an oratorio, and many piano transcriptions.

Wilder, Alec [Alexander] **(Lafayette Chew)** (b. Rochester, 16 Feb. 1907; d. Gainesville, Fla., 24 Dec. 1980). Composer. Studied briefly at the Eastman School but was largely self-taught. During the 1930s and 1940s did arrangements for several bands; songs recorded by Tommy Dorsey, Mildred Bailey, the Mills Brothers, Frank Sinatra ("Where Is the One?" 1948), and others. Experimented with blending popular and classical music in a series of *Octets* for winds, harpsichord, and rhythm section (1939); by the 1950s turned primarily to concert music, writing 12 wind quintets, 8 brass quintets, and sonatas for a great variety of wind instruments. Continued to write songs and works for the stage: *Kittiwake Island* (1955) and *The Truth about Windmills* (opera, 1975).

Willaert, Adrian (b. Bruges or Roulaers, ca. 1490; d. Venice, 17 Dec. 1562). Composer. Pupil of Jean Mouton; served at the court of Louis XII and Francis I; from 1515 in the retinue of Cardinal Ippolito I d'Este; in the employ of Duke Alfonso 1520–27. In 1527 appointed *maestro di cappella* at St. Mark's in Venice, which under him became one of the most prestigious chapels in Europe. Pupils included Rore, Vicentino, Parabosco, Andrea Gabrieli, Porta, Buus, Barré, and Zarlino. Compositions show an interest in theoretical questions. Works include Masses, motets, hymns, Psalms, madrigals, *villanesche,* chansons, and a lute intabulation of Verdelot's madrigals. Best-known publication is *Musica nova* (1559), dedicated to Alfonso II d'Este.

Willan, (James) Healey (b. London, 12 Oct. 1880; d. Toronto, 16 Feb. 1968). Composer and organist. Studied organ with William Stevenson Hoyte, piano with Evlyn Howard-Jones. Beginning in 1898, held series of posts as organist and choirmaster; from 1913, taught at the Toronto Conservatory of Music and was organist at St. Paul's Anglican Church in Toronto; 1921, moved to St. Mary Magdalene. Taught at Univ. of Toronto 1937–50. Works for organ include *Epilogue* (1908), *Prelude and Fugue in C minor* (1908), *Introduction, Passacaglia and Fugue in E♭ minor* (1916), *Six Chorale Preludes, Set I* (1950) and *Set II* (1953), *Passacaglia and Fugue no. 2* (1959). Other works include *Healey Willan Song Album* (no. 1, 1925; no. 2, 1926); ballad operas (*L'ordre de Bon Temps,* 1928); 2 symphonies (1936, 1941) and a piano concerto (1944; rev. 1949); *Deirdre of the Sorrows* (opera, 1944); *Coronation Suite* (chorus and orchestra, 1953); much liturgical music; incidental music for plays; works for radio.

Willcocks, David (Valentine) (b. Newquay, 30 Dec. 1919). Composer and organist. Studied at the Royal College of Music and King's College, Cambridge. Organist at Salisbury Cathedral 1947–50; 1950–57, at Worcester Cathedral; also conducted choral works. In 1957 returned to King's College Chapel in Cambridge as organist and choirmaster; 1960, appointed conductor of the London-based Bach Choir; 1974, director of the Royal College of Music

William Tell. See *Guillaume Tell.*

Williams, Alberto (b. Buenos Aires, 23 Nov. 1862; d. there, 17 June 1952). Composer. Attended the Colegio S. Martin and the Provincial Music School; studied at the Paris Conservatory under Franck and Bériot. Returned to Argentina, 1889; 1893, founded a conservatory (later named for him) in Buenos Aires, directing it until 1941. Musical language merged European models with Argentine nationalism. Compositions include 9 symphonies, 3 Argentine Suites (1923), *Aires de la Pampa* (1944), and other orchestral music; 3 violin sonatas and other chamber works; much piano music; choral pieces and songs.

Williams, Cootie [Charles Melvin] (b. Mobile, 24 July 1908; d. Long Island, 15 Sept. 1985). Jazz trumpeter and bandleader. Joined Duke Ellington (1929–40), playing the growling, plunger-muted style developed by Bubber Miley. Recorded Ellington's "Concerto for Cootie," 1940. Joined Benny Goodman's big band and small groups (1940–41); formed a big band (1941–48) which at times included Charlie Parker, Bud Powell, and Thelonious Monk, whose "Round Midnight" he recorded (1944). Rejoined Goodman (1962) before returning to Ellington's orchestra (1962–1970s).

Williams, Hank [Hiram] (b. near Georgiana, Ala., 17 Sept. 1923; d. Oak Hill, W.Va., 1 Jan. 1953). Country singer, songwriter, and guitarist. Performed in honky-tonks and on radio in Alabama; from 1946 worked with songwriter and producer Fred Rose. Recordings with his band The Drifting Cowboys include "Hey, Good Lookin'" (1951) and "Your Cheatin' Heart" (1953); appeared on the *Louisiana Hayride* (from 1947) and the Grand Ole Opry (from 1949). His music was seminal to the development of country music in the 1950s and 1960s.

Williams, Joe [Goreed, Joseph] (b. Cordele, Ga., 12 Dec. 1918; d. Las Vegas, 29 Mar. 1999). Jazz and blues singer. In Chicago sang with bands led by Jimmie Noone (1937), Coleman Hawkins (1941), and Lionel Hampton (1943); toured to New York with Andy Kirk (1946). Joined Count Basie's big band (1954–61), recording "Everyday I Have the Blues" on the album *Count Basie Swings & Joe Williams Sings* (1955); joined Harry Edison's quintet (1961–62); worked as a soloist and performed with Basie intermittently into the 1980s. Appeared regularly as an actor on the *Bill Cosby Show* on television.

Williams, John (Christopher) (b. Melbourne, Australia, 24 Apr. 1941). Guitarist. Studied with Segovia in Siena and at the Royal College of Music in London; debut at Wigmore Hall in London, 1958. Toured the U.S., the U.S.S.R., Japan, South America, and Europe. Repertoire includes non-Western, jazz, and folk musics, and works by composers such as Takemitsu, André Previn, Leo Brouwer, and Stephen Dodgson written for him.

Williams, John (Towner) (b. New York, 8 Feb. 1932). Pianist, composer, and conductor. Studied in Los Angeles with Bobby van Eps and at Juilliard with Rosina Lhévinne; also played in clubs and recording studios in New York and Los Angeles. Took composition lessons with Arthur Olaf Andersen and Mario Castelnuovo-Tedesco. During the 1960s composed music for television *(Gilligan's Island)* and for films *(Valley of the Dolls,* 1967) and concert music *(Essay,* string orchestra, 1966; *Sinfonietta,* winds, 1968). Achieved great success with film scores for *Jaws* (1975), *Close Encounters of the Third Kind* (1977), George Lucas's *Star Wars* trilogy (1977, 1980, 1983), and *Schindler's List* (1993); received numerous Academy Awards. Conducted the Boston Pops, 1980–95; recent works include a cello concerto (1995) written for Yo-Yo Ma.

Williams, Mary Lou [née Scruggs, Mary Elfrieda] (b. Atlanta, 8 May 1910; d. Durham, 28 May 1981). Jazz pianist, arranger, and composer. Joined Andy Kirk's big band (1929–42); recordings of her compositions include "Walkin' and Swingin'" (1936) and "Mary's Idea" (1938). Also wrote arrangements for Benny Goodman, Earl Hines, Tommy Dorsey, and Duke Ellington ("Trumpets No End," 1946). Wrote the "Zodiac Suite" (1945) and began playing with bop musicians; worked in Europe 1952–54; retired until 1957. Later concentrated on writing sacred works while maintaining a career as a soloist.

Williamson, Malcolm (Benjamin Graham Christopher) (b. Sydney, 21 Nov. 1931). Composer. Studied composition with Goossens and piano with Sverjensky at the Sydney Conservatory and composition with Lutyens and Stein in London. Influenced by the organ works of Messiaen; worked as a church organist, 1955–60. Composer-in-residence at Westminster Choir College in 1970; 1977, became president of the Royal Philharmonic Orchestra. Instrumental works through the 1960s and 1970s utilized techniques from serialism and modalism, in standard genres; by the mid-1960s began to explore dramatic music. Works include operas *(Our Man in Havana,* 1963; *The Violins of Saint-Jacques,* 1966; *The Growing Castle,* chamber opera, 1968; *The Red Sea,* 1972); orchestral music (Symphony no. 1, *Elevamini,* 1957; 3 piano concertos; Violin Concerto, 1965; *The Icy Mirror,* 1972, libretto by Ursula Vaughan Williams, also known as Symphony no. 3; Symphony no. 5, *Aquero,* 1980; Symphony no. 7, 1984; *Three Poems of Borges,* 1985); choral works *(A Young Girl,* chorus, 1964; *In Place of Belief,* chorus, piano 4-hands, 1970; *The Musicians of Bremen,* cantata, 1972; *Mass of Christ the King,* chorus, orchestra, 1977); chamber works, songs, and pieces for organ (Symphony, 1960; *Vision of Christ-Phoenix,*

1961; *Elegy—J.F.K.*, 1964; *Peace Pieces*, 1971; *The Lion of Suffolk*, 1977).

Wills, Bob [James Robert] (b. near Kosse, Tex., 6 Mar. 1905; d. Ft. Worth, 13 May 1975). Country singer, songwriter, fiddler, and bandleader. In 1931 helped form the Light Crust Doughboys and in 1934 founded the Texas Playboys, both important to the early history of western swing. Popular recordings include "Steel Guitar Rag" (1936) and his own "San Antonio Rose" (1938); repertory included popular and jazz tunes as well as country.

Willson, (Robert Reiniger) Meredith (b. Mason City, Iowa, 18 May 1902; d. Santa Monica, 15 June 1984). Flutist, composer, conductor. Studied flute with Georges Barrère and composition with Henry Hadley at the Institute of Musical Art in New York. Played in John Philip Sousa's band (1921–23) and in the New York Philharmonic under Toscanini (1924–29). In 1929 went to Seattle, where he conducted the Seattle Symphony and did radio work; 1932, became musical director of NBC's Western Division. Remained with NBC until 1956, conducting and performing on radio and later television; wrote songs, including "You and I" (1941) and "May the Good Lord Bless and Keep You" (1950). Also composed some concert music, including 2 symphonies, and some film scores (*The Great Dictator*, 1940). From 1952 to 1957 worked on the book and score to a musical based on his Iowa boyhood; *The Music Man* opened on Broadway in 1957 and logged over 1,300 performances. Subsequent musicals include *The Unsinkable Molly Brown* (1960); *Here's Love* (1963).

Wilson, John (b. Faversham, Kent, 5 Apr. 1595; d. Westminster, London, 22 Feb. 1674). Composer, lutenist, and singer. Active in London at court and in the theaters from 1614, became a city wait in 1622, and entered the King's Musick among the lutes and voices in 1635. Professor of music at Oxford Univ. 1656–61; became a Gentleman of the Chapel Royal, 1662. Most notable works are songs, many written for plays.

Wilson, Olly (Woodrow) (b. St. Louis, Mo., 7 Sept. 1937). Composer. Studied at Washington Univ. in St. Louis, the Univ. of Illinois, and the Univ. of Iowa; taught at Florida A & M (1960–65), Oberlin (1965–70), and the Univ. of California at Berkeley (beginning 1970). Music combines avant-garde procedures with rhythms and sonorities drawn from black traditional and popular music and the music of Africa. Works include *Piece for Four* (flute, trumpet, piano, bass, 1966); *Black Martyrs* (chorus and electronic tape, 1972); *Akwan* (piano and orchestra, 1974); *Sometimes* (tenor and tape, 1976); *Sinfonia* (orchestra, 1984); *Expansions II* (orchestra, 1987).

Wilson, Teddy [Theodore Shaw] (b. Austin, 24 Nov. 1912; d. New Britain, Conn., 31 July 1986). Jazz pianist and bandleader. Founding member of Benny Goodman's racially integrated small groups (1936–39); their recordings include "Body and Soul" (1935). His widely imitated swing style served as a bridge to the bop piano style. From 1935 to 1939 directed recording sessions featuring Billie Holiday; led a swing big band (1939–40) and sextet (1940–44); rejoined Goodman (1944–45). Played in small groups (including the album *Pres and Teddy* with Lester Young, 1956) and unaccompanied (including the album *Striding after Fats*, 1974); toured as a soloist and in reunions with Goodman (1950s–80s).

Wind band. See Band.

Wind-band Mass. See *Harmoniemesse*.

Wind cap [Ger. *Windkapsel*]. A wooden cover enclosing and concealing the double reed of certain woodwind instruments of the 14th through the 17th century. A blowing hole was provided at the top or rear edge of the cap. The lack of direct lip contact with the reed prevented such instruments from being *overblown, and thus limited their range to pitches of the first *harmonic. The principal example of such instruments is the *crumhorn. See ill. under Reed.

Wind ensemble. See Symphonic band.

Wind instruments. A class of instruments having an enclosed mass of air, especially those sounded by means of the breath. The technical term for such instruments is *aerophone, which, however, properly refers to all instruments in which air or wind is the primary agent of sound production, whether or not the vibrations produced are those of an enclosed column of air and whether or not the player's breath is the wind supply. As the term wind instruments is often used, this group usually excludes keyboard instruments such as the *organ, *accordion, and related instruments but occasionally includes a few instruments in which a bellows has replaced the lungs (Irish *union pipes, *musette).

Wind instruments are generally divided into two classes, called *woodwinds and *brass winds. The terms woodwind and brass originated at a time when *flutes, *oboes, *clarinets, and *bassoons were all commonly made of wood, and when *trumpets, *horns, *trombones, *ophicleides, and *tubas were made of brass. The names of both classes persist, though in current practice several instruments of the woodwind class are usually made of metal (flute, *saxophone), and some revived early instruments related to the present-day brass group are usually made of wood (*cornett, *serpent).

With respect to sounding method, the brass winds

are a homogeneous group. All are sounded by the vibration of the player's lips, which are supported by a cup- or funnel-shaped *mouthpiece. Woodwind instruments are homogeneous in terms of pitch-changing apparatus. All have side holes that can be covered or left open so as to vary the sounding length of the tube. But they are diverse in sounding method and are thus often classed according to the method by which the air column is set into motion, whether by single reed, double reed, or no reed. These classes can be further divided [see Reed, Flute, Woodwinds].

Wind machine [Fr. *Éoliphone;* Ger. *Windmaschine*]. A device for imitating the sound of wind, usually a horizontally mounted large wooden cylinder with spaced slats that rub against canvas or other material when it is rotated.

Winter [von Winter], **Peter** (bapt. Mannheim, 28 Aug. 1754; d. Munich, 17 Oct. 1825). Composer. Played violin in Karl Theodor's orchestra; named director when the court moved to Munich in 1778; became Vice-Kapellmeister in 1787, court Kapellmeister in 1798. *Das unterbrochene Opferfest* (1796) and subsequent operas achieved wide recognition. Wrote operas for Munich, Vienna, Naples, Venice, Milan, Paris, and London; other compositions include ballets, Masses, cantatas, symphonies, various solo concertos, and chamber music.

Winterreise, Die [Ger., Winter Journey]. A cycle of 24 songs by Schubert, D. 911 (1827), in two parts, setting poems by Wilhelm Müller.

Wirbel [Ger.]. A tuning peg of a stringed instrument; *Wirbelkasten,* *pegbox. (2) A drum roll; *Wirbeltrommel,* tenor *drum.

Wirén, Dag (Ivar) (b. Striberg, Närke, 15 Oct. 1905; d. Danderyd, 19 Apr. 1986). Composer. Studied with Ellberg at the Stockholm Conservatory and with Sabaneyev in Paris. Returning to Sweden, worked for the Swedish Composers' Association, the Swedish Composers' International Music Agency, and as a music critic for *Svenska Morgonbladet.* Works include dramatic music (*Oscarbalen* [The Oscar Ball], ballet, 1949; *Hamlet,* incidental music, 1960), orchestral music (Serenade for Strings, 1937; 5 symphonies, 1932–64; concertos); and chamber music.

Wise, Michael (b. Salisbury?, ca. 1647; d. there, 24 Aug. 1687). Composer. In 1668 appointed organist and instructor of the choristers at Salisbury Cathedral; became a Gentleman at the Chapel Royal (1676) and almoner and master of the choristers at St. Paul's Cathedral (1687). Compositions include 4 services, 30 anthems *(The Ways of Sion Do Mourn),* and a few songs and catches.

Witt, Friedrich (b. Niederstetten, Württemberg, 8 Nov. 1770; d. Würzburg, 3 Jan. 1836). Composer and cellist. Played in the Prince of Oettingen-Wallerstein's orchestra from ca. 1789; became Kapellmeister for the Prince Bishop of Würzburg in 1802 and held a similar position at the Würzburg theater from 1814. Composed symphonies, concertos, oratorios, Masses, cantatas, chamber music; remembered today for his Jena Symphony, which was misattributed to Beethoven.

Wizlâv [Wizlaw] **III von Rügen** (b. 1265–68; d. Barth, near Stralsund, Germany, 8 Nov. 1325). Minnesinger, Prince of Pomerania and Rügen (from 1302), brother of Queen Eufemia of Norway. A well-known patron of literature; Frauenlob and other poets visited his court. Fourteen *Minnelieder* and 13 *Sprüche* survive; 17 have melodies.

Wohltemperirte Clavier, Das [Ger.]. See *Well-Tempered Clavier, The.*

Wolf. (1) On any bowed stringed instrument, a pitch whose quality or loudness differs in an undesirable way from others. (2) A perfect fifth that is noticeably out of tune with respect to others in a given *tuning system or *temperament, especially the fifth that results from a succession of 11 acoustically pure fifths; also the Pythagorean *comma.

Wolf, Hugo (Filipp Jakob) (b. Windischgratz, Styria, 13 Mar. 1860; d. Vienna, 22 Feb. 1903). Composer. Studied at the Vienna Conservatory with Fuchs, Schenner, and Krenn. Became a fervent Wagnerian; left the school and tried to make a living in Vienna as a private teacher. In 1884–87 music critic for the *Wiener Salonblatt;* attracted attention for attacks on Brahms. During 1888–89 produced more than half his songs, including the *Mörike Lieder,* most of the *Eichendorff Lieder,* the *Goethe Lieder,* and 26 songs of the *Spanish Songbook;* began to receive public recognition. Composed the *Italian Songbook* in 1890–91 and 1896. During 1895 wrote opera *Der Corregidor;* premiered successfully in Mannheim (1896) but did not establish itself. In September 1897 had a complete mental collapse, and was confined in an asylum; discharged in January 1898, but in October had a relapse and never again emerged.

Other works include *Penthesilea,* symphonic poem (1883–85); Italian Serenade, string quartet (1887; arranged for string orchestra, 1892); choral works, especially *6 Geistliche Lieder* (Eichendorff, 1881); *Der Feuerreiter* (arranged from a solo song), incidental music, especially for Ibsen's *Das Fest auf Solhaug* (1890–91).

Wolff, Christian (b. Nice, 8 Mar. 1934). Composer. Studied classics and comparative literature at Harvard Univ.; studied piano but had no other formal musical training. Began to compose as a teenager; associated with a group of avant-garde composers in New York that included John Cage, David Tudor, Morton Feldman, and Earle Brown. Taught classics at Harvard (1962–70); classics and music at Dartmouth College (from 1970). Earliest published compositions used a severely restricted number of pitches, and included long periods of silence; beginning with *Duo for Pianists 1* in 1957, introduced elements of choice and chance; from the mid-1960s much music explicitly related to left-wing political themes. Works include *Duo for Pianists 2* (1958); *Burdocks* (multiple ensembles, 1971); *Changing the System* (chamber ensemble, 1972); *I Like To Think of Harriet Tubman* (female voice and 3 instruments, 1984).

Wolf-Ferrari, Ermanno (b. Venice, 12 Jan. 1876; d. there, 21 Jan. 1948). Composer. Studied painting, then music at the Akademie der Tonkunst in Munich with Joseph Rheinberger and Ludwig Abel. Lived alternately in Munich and Venice except during World War I, spent in Switzerland; returned to Munich, 1922. Early works in German Romantic tradition; later turned to a neoclassical style. Best known for the 1-act opera *Il segreto di Susanna* (1909); other operas include *Cenerentola* (1900), *Le donne curiose* (1903), *I quattro rusteghi* (1906), *Sly* (1927), *Il Campiello* (1936). Other works include *La vita nuova* (cantata, 1901), *Idillio-concertino* (oboe and chamber orchestra, 1933), *Suite veneziano* (chamber orchestra, 1936), Violin Concerto (1946), String Quintet (1942), and *duo,* viola d'amore and viola da gamba (1946).

Wölfl [Woelfl, Wölffl], **Joseph** (b. Salzburg, 24 Dec. 1773; d. London, 21 May 1812). Composer and pianist. Studied in Salzburg with Leopold Mozart and Michael Haydn; met Mozart in Vienna in 1790; settled there permanently in 1795. Thought by some to be a rival to Beethoven. Arrived in Paris, 1801; moved to London, 1805. Wrote 7 operas, 2 ballets, 7 piano concertos, 2 symphonies, chamber music, 30 solo piano sonatas, other keyboard music, some vocal music.

Wolkenstein, Oswald von. See Oswald von Wolkenstein.

Wolle, John Frederick (b. Bethlehem, Pa., 4 Apr. 1863; d. there, 12 Jan. 1933). Conductor and organist. Grandson of Peter Wolle. Studied with Rheinberger in Munich. Organist at Central Moravian Church in Bethlehem, 1885–1904; with Bethlehem Choral Union (conductor 1885–92) gave first complete performance of the St. John Passion (1888) and St. Matthew Passion (1892). Organized Bethlehem Bach Choir; founding member of American Guild of Organists; director of music at the Univ. of California, 1905–11.

Wolle, Peter (b. New Herrnhut, St. Thomas, West Indies, 5 Jan. 1792; d. Bethlehem, Pa., 14 Nov. 1871). Composer. Grandfather of John Frederick Wolle. Moved to Pennsylvania, 1800; Moravian minister at Nazareth (bishop, 1845). May have studied with David Moritz Michael (1751–1827) and Johannes Herbst (1735–1812), two important composers in the Moravian congregation. Composed anthems and hymns, including "Sing Hallelujah, Christ Doth Live"; edited the *Moravian Tune Book* (1836).

Wolpe, Stefan (b. Berlin, 25 Aug. 1902; d. New York, 4 Apr. 1972). Composer and teacher. Studied briefly at the Berlin Hochschule für Musik with Paul Juon; came into contact with Ferruccio Busoni, Hermann Scherchen, the Novembergruppe, and the Bauhaus movement. Member of the Communist party of Germany, 1925–33; in 1933 fled to Vienna and studied with Anton Webern; then to Palestine and taught at the Jerusalem Conservatory, 1934–38. In 1938 emigrated to the U.S. and settled in New York. Works of the late 1930s and early 1940s show the influence of Middle Eastern music; after study of Schoenberg, arrived at style based on manipulation of motivic cells. Taught in New York, Philadelphia, and at Black Mountain College in North Carolina; students included Ralph Shapey, Morton Feldman, and David Tudor. Works include *The Man from Midian* (ballet, 1942); *Yigdal* (cantata, 1945); *Battle Piece* (piano, 1947); Violin Sonata (1949); *Enactments* (3 pianos, 1953); Symphony (1956); *Form for Piano* (1959); *Trio in 2 Parts* (flute, cello, and piano, 1964); *Chamber Piece* no. *1* (14 instruments, 1964); *Chamber Piece* no. *2* (13 instruments, 1967).

Wonder, Stevie [Judkins, Steveland; Morris, Steveland; Hardaway, Steveland] (b. Saginaw, Mich., 13 May 1950). Soul and popular singer, songwriter, and keyboardist. Blind from birth. Made successful recordings with Motown Records as a teenager; from 1971 produced albums of his own songs (*Talking Book,* including "You Are the Sunshine of My Life," 1972; *Songs in the Key of Life,* 1976; *In Square Circle,* 1985). One of the first to use electronic synthesizers in popular music.

WoO. In the thematic catalog of Beethoven's works compiled by Georg Kinsky and Hans Halm, abbr. for *Werk ohne Opuszahl* (work without opus number).

Wood block. *Chinese block.

Wood, Charles (b. Armagh, 15 June 1866; d. Cambridge, 12 July 1926). Composer. Studied with T. O. Marks at Armagh Cathedral and at the Royal College of Music with Stanford and Bridge. Taught harmony at the Royal College of Music from 1888; professor of conducting at Cambridge Univ. Music Society, 1888–94; lecturer in harmony and counterpoint at Cambridge, 1897–1924; professor of music from 1924. Compositions include 3 operas (*The Pickwick Papers,* 1922), incidental music, 3 string quartets, anthems, part songs, and solo songs. Also known as the composer of the chimes for the clock at Gonville and Caius Colleges, Cambridge.

Wood, Henry J(oseph) (b. London, 3 Mar. 1869; d. Hitchin, Hertfordshire, 19 Aug. 1944). Conductor. Studied with Prout, Steggall, Macfarren, and García at the Royal Academy of Music. Conducted in theaters; in 1895 initiated the Queen's Hall Promenade Concerts (the "Proms") and continued to direct them until 1940. Founded the Nottingham Orchestra in 1899; conducted at various music festivals. Made arrangements under the pseudonym Paul Klenovsky, including Chopin's *Marche Funèbre* and "Purcell's" [actually Clarke's] *Trumpet Voluntary;* in 1923 appointed professor at the Royal Academy of Music. Published books about singing and conducting.

Woodbury, Isaac Baker (b. Beverly, Mass., 23 Oct. 1819; d. Columbia, S.C., 26 Oct. 1858). Composer, editor, and writer on music. Studied in Boston with Lowell Mason and in Paris and London. Taught privately and held positions as organist, choral conductor, and trainer of music teachers in Boston. Corresponding editor of *World of Music* (1846–48), *American Monthly Musical Review* (1850–53), and other journals. In 1849 settled in New York; with his cousin Benjamin Baker founded the National Musical Convention school. Compositions include 3 oratorios, 4 secular cantatas, choruses, glees, piano works, numerous pedagogical works.

Woodwinds. Wind instruments that have an enclosed, vibrating air column set into motion by a *reed or by blowing across or through an aperture [see Flute]; as distinct from *brass instruments, in which the air column is set into motion by the vibration of the player's lips. Keyboard instruments sounded by the same means as woodwinds (e.g., the *organ) are excluded. Despite the name woodwind, this group of instruments is no longer composed only of wooden-bodied instruments. See Wind instruments.

Worcester, repertory of. A repertory of over 100 polyphonic works (mostly in three parts) preserved on leaves and fragments thought to have originated and most still preserved at Worcester, England (whence the term Worcester fragments), and dating from the 13th and early 14th centuries. They include examples of *rondellus, *conductus, *motets, and settings of various types of liturgical items; many

employ *voice exchange and make extensive use of imperfect consonances, complete triads, and first-inversion triads or six-three chords.

Word painting. The musical illustration of the meaning of words in vocal music, especially the literal meaning of individual words or phrases. It is a prominent feature of some music of the late Renaissance (especially some *madrigals, whence the synonym madrigalism) and of the Baroque, but examples occur throughout the history of music. The devices used rely principally on the relationship between qualities of the thing illustrated and certain characteristics of music. In the simplest cases, natural sounds, such as those of birds, thunder, sighing, and sobbing, are imitated. Otherwise, music that is high, low, ascending, descending, loud, soft, fast, or slow may be associated, respectively, with these same concepts in the abstract or with concepts or things that share these qualities. Thus, for example, the word heaven may be associated with music that is high or ascending in pitch.

Wordsworth, William (Brocklesby) (b. London, 17 Dec. 1908; d. Kingussie, Scotland, 10 Mar. 1988). Composer. Studied with Oldroyd and at Edinburgh Univ. with Tovey. Active in establishment of the Scottish Composers' Guild (1966). Musical language generally conservative. Works include 8 symphonies, 3 concertos (piano, violin, cello), chamber music (6 string quartets, 1941–64).

Work song. A song synchronizing the rhythm of group tasks. Such songs are distributed throughout the world and include many types (e.g., the sea *shanty). West African work songs contributed, under slavery, to the emergence of blues and jazz.

Work, Henry Clay (b. Middletown, Conn., 1 Oct. 1832; d. Hartford, 8 June 1884). Composer. Worked as a printer in Hartford and Chicago (from 1855) and for the periodical *Song Messenger of the Northwest.* Composed over 75 songs, including "Marching through Georgia" (1865) and "Grandfather's Clock" (1876).

Work, John Wesley (II) (b. Nashville, 6 Aug. 1872; d. there, 7 Sept. 1925). Singer, conductor, musicologist. Attended Fisk Univ. and Harvard Univ. From 1898 to 1923 taught history and Latin at Fisk, conducted the school choir, and toured with the Fisk Jubilee Quartet. Active as a collector of black folk songs, particularly spirituals; published several collections of arrangements and the scholarly treatise *Folk Song of the American Negro* (1915).

Work, John Wesley, III (b. Tullahoma, Tenn., 15 June 1901; d. Nashville, 17 May 1967). Composer, conductor. Son of John Wesley Work II. Attended Fisk Univ., the Juilliard School (then called the Institute of

Musical Art), Columbia Univ. Teachers College, and Yale Univ. Beginning in 1927 taught at Fisk; conducted and sang with university ensembles, lectured on music, and collected, arranged, and wrote about black folk song. Compositions deeply influenced by black folk and traditional music. Works include *Yenvalou* (orchestra, 1946); *The Singers* (cantata, 1941); *Appalachia* (piano, 1954); *From the Deep South* (organ, 1936).

Wormser, André (Alphonse-Toussaint) (b. Paris, 1 Nov. 1851; d. there, 4 Nov. 1926). Composer. Studied with Bazin and Marmontel at the Paris Conservatory. Most successful work was the pantomime *L'enfant prodigue* (1890); other compositions include operas, the ballet *L'étoile, Suite tsigane, Diane et Endymion*, choruses, and songs.

Wozzeck. Opera in three acts by Berg (libretto in German by Berg, adapted from Georg Büchner's play of the same name), produced in Berlin in 1925. Setting: Germany in the early 19th century.

Wranitzky [Vranický, Wraniczky, Wranizky], **Anton** (b. Nová Říše, Moravia, 13 June 1761; d. Vienna, 6 Aug. 1820). Composer, violinist. Studied with brother Paul Wranitzky, and in Vienna with Mozart, Haydn, and Albrechtsberger. Kapellmeister for the Prince J. F. Maximilian Lobkowitz (1797), orchestral director for the Viennese court theater (1807), orchestral director at the Theater an der Wien (1814). Wrote 15 symphonies, 15 violin concertos, other solo concertos, overtures, serenades, notturnos, a great deal of chamber music, vocal music.

Wranitzky [Vranický, Wraniczky, Wranizky], **Paul** [Pavel] (b. Nová Říše, Moravia, 30 Dec. 1756; d. Vienna, 26 Sept. 1808). Composer. Brother of Anton Wranitzky. Studied in Vienna with Joseph Kraus and Haydn. Became a violinist in Prince Esterházy's orchestra at Eisenstadt around 1780; head orchestral director of the Viennese court theaters about 1790; secretary of the Viennese Tonkünstler Sozietät. Well known as a conductor; directed the first performance of Beethoven's First Symphony. Singspiel *Oberon, König der Elfen* (1789) enjoyed great success. Compositions include about 9 other operas, ballets, 51 symphonies, several solo concertos, many string quartets, quintets, and trios.

Wrest pin. *Tuning pin.

Wrest plank. *Pin block.

W.T.C. Abbr. for *Well-Tempered Clavier, The*.

Wuchtig [Ger.]. Weighty, vigorous.

Wüllner, Franz (b. Münster, 28 Jan. 1832; d. Braunfels, 7 Sept. 1902). Composer and conductor. Father of the singer Ludwig Wüllner (1858–1938). Studied

at Brussels, Bremen, Cologne, Leipzig, and Munich; teachers included Joachim, Brahms, and Jahn. Named professor of piano at the Munich Conservatory, 1856; court conductor in 1864; music director at Aix-la-Chapelle from 1858. In 1871 succeeded Bülow as director of the Munich Opera. Director of the Dresden Conservatory from 1877 and the Cologne Conservatory from 1884. Conducted the premieres of *Das Rheingold* (1869), *Die Walküre* (1870), *Till Eulenspiegel* (1895), and *Don Quixote* (1898).

Wunderlich, Fritz (b. Kusel, Rheinland-Pfalz, 26 Sept. 1930; d. Heidelberg, 17 Sept. 1966). Tenor. Studied at the Freiburg Hochschule für Musik; debut as Tamino (*Die Zauberflöte*) with the Stuttgart Opera, 1955. Remembered for his Mozart roles; also premiered the role of Tiresias in Orff's *Oedipus der Tyrann* (1959) and Christoph in Egk's *Die Verlobung in San Domingo*. Engaged by the opera companies in Frankfurt (1958–60) and Munich (1960–66).

Wuorinen, Charles (b. New York, 9 June 1938). Composer. Studied with Vladimir Ussachevsky and Jack Beeson. Joined Columbia faculty, 1964. By early 1960s his music was receiving considerable attention from the press. With Harvey Sollberger founded in 1962 the Group for Contemporary Music. Early music nondiatonic, sometimes atonal, sometimes serial; beginning about 1961 became more rigorously serial; by 1966 worked out a "time-point system," also applied to electronic composition; during the 1970s modified serial technique and used preexisting musical materials. Left Columbia in 1971; taught at the Manhattan School of Music (1972–79); 1984 moved to Rutgers.

Works include *Orchestral and Electronic Exchanges* (orchestra and tape, 1965); *Duo* (violin and piano, 1966); *Time's Encomium* (synthesizer, 1969; Pulitzer Prize, 1970); *Grand Bamboula* (string orchestra, 1971); Violin Concerto no. 2 (amplified violin and orchestra, 1972); *A Reliquary for Igor Stravinsky* (orchestra, 1975); *The W. of Babylon* ("baroque burlesque," New York, 1975); *Percussion Duo* (mallet instruments and piano, 1979); *Spinoff* (violin, bass, conga drums, 1984); *Miami Bamboula* (orchestra, 1988); *Machault non chou* (1989); string quartets.

Würdig [Ger.]. Dignified, stately.

Wurstfagott [Ger.]. Sausage bassoon [see Racket].

Wütend [Ger.]. Raging, furious.

Wyner, Yehudi (b. Calgary, 1 June 1929). Pianist and composer. Son of composer Lazar Weiner. Studied at Juilliard, at Yale with Richard Donovan and Paul Hindemith, and with Walter Piston at Harvard. During the 1950s active as a pianist, composer, and conductor in New York. Taught at Yale (1963–73), the Berkshire (Mass.) Music Center (1975–78), and SUNY–Purchase (from 1978; dean of music, 1978–82). Most instrumental music for piano and/or chamber ensemble; wrote for his wife, soprano Susan Davenny Wyner (b. 1943); also composed Jewish liturgical music. Works include Piano Sonata (1954), *Concert Duo* (violin and piano, 1957), *Three Short Fantasies* (piano, 1963), *Intermedio* (soprano and string orchestra, 1974), *Fragments from Antiquity* (soprano and orchestra, 1981), *On This Most Voluptuous Night* (soprano and chamber ensemble, 1982), String Quartet (1984–85), *Composition* (viola, piano, 1986), *Sweet Consort* (flute, piano, 1988).

Wynette, Tammy [Pugh, Virginia Wynette] (b. Itawamba County, near Tupelo, Miss., 5 May 1942; d. Nashville, 6 Apr. 1998). Country singer and songwriter. From 1966 made numerous successful recordings with producer Billy Sherrill (including "D-I-V-O-R-C-E" and "Stand by Your Man," both 1968). From 1969 sang duets with husband, George Jones ("Take Me," 1971); remained among the most popular female country performers throughout the 1970s and 1980s.

Wyschnegradsky [Vishnegradsky], **Ivan Alexandrovich** (b. St. Petersburg, 16 May 1893; d. Paris, 29 Sept. 1979). Composer. Studied composition with Nicolas Sokoloff. Early work influenced by Scriabin; went on to explore microtonal intervals. Settled in Paris in the early 1920s; pursued interest in quarter tone music; in the mid-30s devised system of tuning several pianos at microtonal intervals from one another. Works include string quartets (1924, 1932), *Ainsi parlait Zarathoustra* (orchestra, 1930), Preludes (2 pianos, 1934), *Acte choréographique* (baritone, chorus, and 4 pianos, 1940). Writings include *Manuel d'harmonie à quarts de ton* (Paris, 1932).

X

Xenakis, Iannis (b. Braila, Romania, 29 May 1922). Composer, architect. Trained in Greece as an engineer; blinded in one eye during World War II. Denounced as a communist, fled to Paris in 1947; worked for the architect Le Corbusier until 1959 and studied music with Honegger, Milhaud, and Messiaen. Compositions focus on realizing mathematical structures or processes as musical sound; in *Pithoprakta* (orchestra, 1956) the individual instruments of the orchestra are conceived as molecules obeying the Maxwell–Boltzmann law of molecular velocities in a gas. Established as a major figure in the European avant-garde with the premieres of *Pithoprakta* and *Achorripsis* (chamber ensemble, 1957). After 1959 supported by commissions, grants, and teaching activities; 1950s–1970s experimented with *musique concrète* (*Diamorphoses,* 1958), electronic music (*Analogique B,* 1959), elements of performer choice (*Duel,* 2 orchestras, 1959; *Stratégie,* 2 orchestras, 1962), and space and light (*Le diatope,* incandescent light, laser light, tape, 1978); also began to use computers in composition (*ST/4,* string quartet, 1962; *ST/48,* orchestra, 1962; *Mycenes Alpha,* 1978). Works include: *Oresteia* (incidental music, chorus and orchestra, 1966); *Nomos gamma* (orchestra, 1968); *Nuits* (vocal ensemble, 1968); *Anaktoria* (chamber ensemble, 1969); *Noomena* (orchestra, 1975); *Cendrées* (chorus and orchestra, 1974); *Khoaï* (amplified piano, 1976); *Jonchaies* (orchestra, 1977); *Ais* (baritone, percussion, orchestra, 1980); *Nekuia* (choir, orchestra, 1981); *Chants des soleils* (mixed choir, children's choir, brass, percussion, 1983); *Tetras* (string quartet, 1983); *Keqrops* (piano, 92-piece orchestra, 1986); *Horos* (89-piece orchestra, 1986); *Akea* (string quartet, piano, 1987); *Jalons* (orchestra, 1988). Writings include *Musiques formelles* (1963); trans. as *Formalized Music* (1971), *Musique architecture* (1971; rev. 1976).

Xerxes. See *Serse.*

Xylophone [fr. Gr. *xylon,* wood; Fr. *xylophone,* also obs. *claquebois;* Ger. *Xylophon;* It. *xilofono;* Sp. *xilófono*]. A percussion instrument of definite pitch consisting of suspended wooden bars struck with a beater. The modern orchestral instrument has bars made of hardwood or a synthetic material suspended horizontally on a frame and arranged in the fashion of a keyboard. Beneath each bar is a vertical tubular resonator whose length corresponds to the pitch of the bar. The instrument is mounted on a stand and struck with two (or more) beaters of various hardnesses. The back of each bar is longitudinally concave, a feature that contributes to definition of pitch. The pitch of a bar is determined by both its length and thickness; a decrease in length raises pitch, a decrease in thickness lowers it. The range of the modern instrument varies, the largest being four octaves upward from c′ to c′′′′′, another standard size being from f′ or g′ to c′′′′′. It is normally notated on a single treble staff an octave below sounding pitch. See ill. under Percussion instruments.

Y

Yamada, Kōsaku [Kôsçak] (b. Tokyo, 9 June 1886; d. there, 29 Dec. 1965). Composer. Studied vocal music, cello, and theory at the Tokyo School of Music, composition at the Hochschule für Musik in Berlin with Bruch and Karl Wolf. Returned to Japan, 1913; established and conducted the Tokyo Philharmonic (predecessor to the later orchestra). Beginning in 1917 toured the U.S. as a conductor. Established the Japanese Association for Music Drama in 1920; 1922 with the poet Kitahara founded the journal *Shi to ongaku* [Verse and Music]. Music influenced by Wagner and Strauss; moved toward a more Japanese aesthetic in the settings and subjects of vocal works. Compositions include operas (*Ochitaru tennyo* [The Depraved Heavenly Maiden], 1912; *Kurofune* [The Black Ships], 1939); orchestral music (*Yajin sōzō* [The Creation of the Rustics], dance poem, 1916; *Meiji shōka* [Ode to the Meiji], 1921; *Shukuten jokyoku* [Festival Overture], chorus, orchestra, 1940); choral music (*Tsuki no tabi* [A Journey of the Moon], voices, violin, 1914); chamber music, many songs, and film scores.

Yancey, Jimmy [James Edwards] (b. Chicago, 20 Feb. 1898; d. there, 17 Sept. 1951). Boogie-woogie pianist. Toured the U.S. and Europe as a vaudeville singer and dancer; settled in Chicago, 1915. Mainly worked as a baseball groundskeeper; taught Albert Ammons and Meade "Lux" Lewis and was invited to record after they had initiated the craze for boogie-woogie in the late 1930s. Recordings include "Yancey Stomp," "State Street Special" (both 1939), and "Yancey's Bugle Call" (1940). Performed with his wife, the singer Mama Yancey, at Carnegie Hall in 1948.

Yankee Doodle. A tune of unknown origin first published, with this title but without words, in James Aird's *A Selection of Scotch, English, Irish, and Foreign Airs* (Glasgow, ca. 1778). It has been associated with various words and was sung during the Revolutionary period by both British and American troops. In the U.S., it has come to represent the American revolutionaries.

Yannay, Yehuda (b. Timişoara, 26 May 1937). Composer. Immigrated to Israel, 1951; studied with Boscovich at the Rubin Academy in Tel Aviv and in the U.S. with Berger, Shapero, and Schuller. Joined the faculty at the Univ. of Wisconsin and created the new-music performance group Music from Almost Yesterday Ensemble. Compositions, many associated with this ensemble, are avant-garde in form, style, and message. Works include *Incantations* (voices, keyboard, piano interior, 1964), *Per se* (chamber concerto, 1968), *Houdini's 9th* (double bass, escape artist, and 2 hospital orderlies, 1969); *A Noiseless Patient Spider* (women's chorus, 1975), *Celan Ensembles* (tenor, ensemble, 1986); *Jidyll* (film score, 1988).

Yardumian, Richard (b. Philadelphia, Pa., 5 April 1917; d. Bryn Athyn, Pa., 15 Aug. 1985). Composer. Mostly self-taught, with some formal training in composition and piano. In 1945 *Desolate City* premiered by Eugene Ormandy and the Philadelphia Orchestra; designated "composer laureate" of the orchestra (1949–64). Compositions colored by his Armenian heritage and his Swedenborgian religious beliefs. During the 1940s worked out his own harmonic system; from the 1950s on also influenced by medieval and Renaissance modality. Works include *Armenian Suite* (orchestra, 1937); 2 symphonies; Violin Concerto (1949; rev. 1960); *The Story of Abraham* (oratorio, 1972); *Mass "Come Creator Spirit"* (1966); *Cantus animae et cordis* (string quartet, 1955).

Yodel [Ger. *Jodel*]. A style of folk singing, to a succession of vowels, characterized by rapid shifts between full voice and *falsetto combined with rapid alternation between two pitches or the arpeggiation of several.

Yon, Pietro Alessandro (b. Settimo Vittone, near Turin, 8 Aug. 1886; d. Huntington, N.Y., 22 Nov. 1943). Organist and composer. Studied in Milan with Fumagalli and at the Accademia di S. Cecilia in Rome with Remigio Renzi and Sgambati. Assistant organist at St. Peter's in Rome; in 1907 became organist and choir director of St. Francis Xavier Church in New York (1907–19, 1921–26); later served as organist at St. Patrick's Cathedral (1927–43). Became a U.S. citizen, 1921. *Gesù Bambino* (1917) his most popular work; also wrote an oratorio, *The Triumph of St. Patrick* (1934), and over 20 Masses.

Yonge [Young, Younge], **Nicholas** (b. Lewes?; d. London, buried 23 Oct. 1619). Singer and music editor. Sang in the choir at St. Paul's Cathedral (1594–1618); edited 2 anthologies of Italian madrigals published with English texts, both entitled *Musica transalpina* (1588, 1597). The earlier collection, which contains nearly 60 works by 18 composers, was one of the most influential volumes of Italian madrigals to appear in England at the time.

Youmans, Vincent (Millie) (b. New York, 27 Sept. 1898; d. Denver, 5 Apr. 1946). Popular songwriter. Between 1921 and 1927 wrote 4 successful musicals (*Two Little Girls in Blue*, 1921; *The Wildflower*, 1923; *No, No, Nanette*, 1925; *Hit the Deck*, 1927); a large number of songs from these and later productions became standards ("Tea for Two," 1925; "Through the Years," 1932).

Young, La Monte (Thornton) (b. Bern, Idaho, 14 Oct. 1935). Composer and performer. Played jazz clarinet and saxophone; studied at UCLA with Stevenson, and at the Univ. of California, Berkeley, with Shifrin and Imbrie; also worked with Leonard Stein and with Maxfield at the New School for Social Research. Studied Indian classical folk music with Pran Nath. Edited *An Anthology* (1963; R: 1970), a major stimulant to the Fluxus movement. Early compositions influenced by interest in organum and in the drones of non-Western music and are seen as forerunners of minimalism; during the early 1960s experimented with works that consisted solely of verbal instructions (*Composition 1960*). Studied intonation and founded the Theatre of Eternal Music, for which he began to compose *The Tortoise, His Dreams and Journeys*, a multisectional work in which performers improvise in just intonation over electronic and acoustic drones; just intonation also used in *The Well-Tuned Piano* (begun in 1964). Has frequently collaborated with his wife, the artist and illustrator Marian Zazeela. Compositions include action and text works (*arabic numeral (any integer) to H.F.*, piano or gong, 1960); electronic and mixed media (*The Big Dream*, 1984); works for conventional instruments (*For Brass*, 2 horns, 2 trumpets, 2 trombones, 2 tubas, 1957; Trio for Strings, 1958; *For Guitar*, 1958; *Orchestral Dreams*, orchestra, 1985).

Young, Lester (Willis) [Pres; Prez] (b. Woodville, Miss., 27 Aug. 1909; d. New York, 15 Mar. 1959). Jazz tenor saxophonist. Played with Walter Page (1930), Bennie Moten (1933), an early Count Basie group (1934), and Fletcher Henderson's big band (1934). Joined Basie (1936–40), recording solos with small groups and with the big band. Recorded many accompaniments to Billie Holiday's singing (1937–41); led groups and recorded with Nat "King" Cole. Rejoined Basie (1943–44). From 1946 toured with Jazz at the Philharmonic and led groups. Recordings include "These Foolish Things" (1945) and

the album *Pres and Teddy* with Teddy Wilson (1956); influenced the playing of Stan Getz, Zoot Sims, Al Cohn, Brew Moore, and others.

Young, Victor (b. Chicago, 8 Aug. 1900; d. Palm Springs, 10 Nov. 1956). Popular songwriter, conductor, and violinist. From 1922 led popular and movie orchestras; began composing in the late 1920s and moved to Hollywood in 1935. Works include songs for revues ("A Hundred Years from Today," 1933), musicals, and films ("My Foolish Heart," 1949), many film scores (*Gulliver's Travels*, 1939; *For Whom the Bell Tolls*, 1943; *Shane*, 1953), and instrumental compositions (mainly excerpted from film scores).

Young [Jough], **William** (d. Innsbruck, 23 Apr. 1662). Composer and viol player. An Englishman, one of the chief transmitters of the English style of viol playing to Continental courts. By 1652 employed by Archduke Ferdinand Karl of Innsbruck; accompanied him to Italy in 1652 and 1654. By 1655 his reputation had spread across Europe. His compositions, many of which are for lyra-viol, include sonatas, fantasies, and dances.

Youth's Magic Horn, The. See *Knaben Wunderhorn, Des.*

Yradier, Sebastián de. See Iradier, Sebastián de.

Ysaÿe, Eugène(-Auguste) (b. Liège, 16 July 1858; d. Brussels, 12 May 1931). Violinist, conductor, and composer. Studied at the Liège Conservatory with Heynberg and Rodolphe Massart; later with Wieniawski at the Brussels Conservatory and with Vieuxtemps in Paris. In 1879 became leader of the Bilse orchestra in Berlin; toured Scandinavia and Russia with Anton Rubinstein. In Paris 1883–86; met Franck, Saint-Saëns, Debussy, d'Indy, and Fauré. From 1886 to 1898 taught at the Brussels Conservatory and initiated the Concerts Ysaÿe, devoted to contemporary Belgian and French music. Made many tours of England and the U.S. as soloist and conductor; conductor of the Cincinnati Symphony 1918–22. Also composed a number of works in post-Romantic style, including 8 violin concertos.

Ysaÿe, Théophile (b. Verviers, 22 Mar. 1865; d. Nice, 24 Mar. 1918). Pianist, composer, and conductor. Brother of Eugène Ysaÿe. Studied at the Liège Conservatory, with Kullak at the Neue Akademie der Tonkunst in Berlin, and with Franck in Paris; frequently accompanied his brother. Professor of piano at the Geneva Academy of Music, 1889–1900. After returning to Belgium served as rehearsal conductor for the Concerts Ysaÿe. Compositions include a piano concerto (1909); Symphony no. 1 in F major op. 14 (1908); Requiem Mass (ca. 1906); Piano

Quintet op. 20 (1913); Variations op. 10, 2 pianos (ca. 1910).

Yüeh-ch'in (yueqin) [Chin.]. A short-necked lute of China; also called a moon guitar. Its round sound box is flat in back and front, and it has four strings tuned in pairs a perfect fifth apart and stretched over ten frets that are distributed along the neck and well onto the body. See ill. under Instrument.

Yun, Isang (b. Tongyong, 17 Sept. 1917; d. Berlin, 3 Nov. 1995). Composer. Studied in Korea and Japan, with Revel at the Paris Conservatory, and with Blacher, Rufer, and Schwarz-Schilling at the Berlin Hochschule für Musik. Settled in Berlin; in 1967 abducted and imprisoned in Seoul on political charges. After protests from the government of West Germany and from prominent composers, granted amnesty and returned to Berlin in 1970. Taught at the Hannover Hochschule für Musik (1970–71) and the Berlin Hochschule (from 1970). From the 1960s works began to combine Korean musical idioms with Western instruments.

Works: opera (*Der Traum des Liu-Tung*, 1965; *Die Witwe des Schmetterlings*, 1968; *Geisterliebe*, 1970; *Sim Tjong*, 1972); orchestral (5 symphonies; *Dialogue between Butterfly and Atom Bomb*, violin, orchestra, 1983); chamber (*Loyang*, flute, oboe, clarinet, bassoon, harp, 2 percussion, violin, cello, 1962; *Images*, flute, oboe, violin, cello, 1968; *Mugung Dong*, chamber ensemble, 1987; *Kammersinfonie I*, 2 oboes, 2 horns, strings, 1988); instrumental (*Garak*, flute, piano, 1963; *Tuyaux sonores*, organ, 1967; *Duo*, viola, piano, 1976; *In Balance*, harp, 1987); vocal works (*Teile Dich, Nacht*, soprano, orchestra, 1980).

Z

Zabaleta, Nicanor (b. San Sebastián, 7 Jan. 1907; d. Puerto Rico, 31 Mar. 1993). Harpist. Studied in Madrid and in Paris with Marcel Tournier; toured the U.S., Europe, and South America. Brought solo harp playing before a wide audience through resurrection of previously forgotten works and performance of new works. Halffter, Krenek, and Tailleferre wrote solo works for him; Ginastera, Milhaud, Piston, Virgil Thomson, Villa-Lobos, and Josef Tal wrote concertos for his use. Also made a number of recordings.

Zacher, Gerd (b. Meppen, Germany, 6 July 1929). Organist and composer. Studied at the Northwest German Academy of Music in Detmold, with Theodor Kaufmann in Hamburg, and with Messiaen at the Darmstadt summer courses. Organist at the German church in Santiago, Chile (1954–57), and at the Lutherkirche in Hamburg (1957–70). In 1970 appointed professor at the Folkwangschule in Essen. Became known as an advocate and interpreter of avant-garde music on the organ, introducing works by György Ligeti, Mauricio Kagel, John Cage, Silvio Bussotti, and others; his own compositions make use of many new organ techniques and sonorities.

Zachow [Zachau], **Friedrich Wilhelm** (b. Leipzig, bap. 14 Nov. 1663; d. Halle, 7 Aug. 1712). Composer. Probably studied with Johann Hildebrand in Eilenburg. From 1684 until his death organist at the Marienkirche in Halle; among his pupils were Handel and Johann Gotthilf Krieger. About 30 sacred cantatas as well as numerous chorale preludes and fugues for organ survive.

Zador, Eugene [Zádor, Jenő] (b. Bátaszék, Hungary, 5 Nov. 1894; d. Hollywood, 4 Apr. 1977). Composer. He learned piano and began composing as a child. Studied at the Vienna Conservatory with Richard Heuberger, with Max Reger in Leipzig, and at the Univ. of Münster. Taught at the New Vienna Conservatory 1922–28; emigrated to the U.S. in 1938. Worked as an orchestrator in New York, then in Hollywood, where he orchestrated over 100 movies. Remained active as a composer of orchestral music and opera. Works include *The Inspector General* (opera, 1928); *Hungarian Caprice* (orchestra, 1935); *Christopher Columbus* (New York, 1939); *The Magic Chair* (1955); *Festival Overture* (1964); Cimbalom Concerto (1969); Accordion Concerto (1971).

Zählzeit [Ger.]. Beat.

Zambra [Sp.]. A lively party with *flamenco* music and dancing.

Zambomba [Sp.]. A *friction drum of Spain and Latin America, now often made from a tin can rather than the traditional earthenware and particularly associated with the Christmas season.

Zampogna, cornamusa [It.]. A *bagpipe of southern Italy and Sicily. It has two separate *chanters, one fingered with each hand. It is played by shepherds and itinerant musicians, particularly during the Christmas season and usually in ensemble with the *piffero.

Zampoña [Sp.]. A *bagpipe of Spain, particularly the Balearic Islands.

Zandonai, Riccardo (b. Sacco di Rovereto, in the Trentino, 30 May 1883; d. Pesaro, 5 June 1944). Composer and conductor. Studied with Pietro Mascagni at the Liceo musicale in Pesaro; early operas *Il grillo del focolare* (1908), *Conchita* (1911), and *Francesca da Rimini* (1914) established him as Puccini's heir apparent. Later operas did not become popular outside of Italy. Active as a conductor; also composed orchestral music, including *Tra gli alberghi delle Dolomiti* (1922) and *Rapsodia trentina* (1936).

Zapateado [Sp. fr. *zapato,* shoe]. Any of various, sometimes quite intricate, patterns of stamping of the feet that characterize certain dances of Spain and Latin America.

Zappa, Frank [Francis Vincent] (b. Baltimore, 21 Dec. 1940; d. Los Angeles, 4 Dec. 1993). Rock songwriter and guitarist, composer. In 1964 joined the band which became known as the Mothers of Invention; released albums with them from 1966 to the mid-1970s, and under his own name from 1969. Among his better-known recordings are the albums *Freak Out* (1966), *We're Only in It for the Money* (1967, a parody of the Beatles' *Sgt. Pepper's Lonely Hearts Club Band*), and *Joe's Garage*, and the singles "Don't Eat the Yellow Snow" (1973) and "Valley Girl" (1982). Around 1980 became increasingly involved in avant-garde composition and performance; conducted concerts of Varèse's music and had his works recorded by the Ensemble intercontemporain

(*The Perfect Stranger,* 1984). Wrote works for orchestra, orchestra and chorus, synclavier, and various chamber ensembles.

Zarabanda [Sp.]. *Sarabande.

Zarlino, Gioseffo [Gioseffe] (b. Chioggia, 31? Jan. 1517; d. Venice, 4 Feb. 1590). Music theorist and composer. Pupil of Francesco Maria Delfico; singer (1536) and organist (1539–40) at Chioggia Cathedral, then *capellano* and *mansionario* of the Scuola di S. Francesco in Chioggia. Continued his musical training with Willaert in Venice (1541); in 1565 succeeded Rore as *maestro di cappella* at San Marco. Also served as chaplain of S. Severo from 1565; students included Artusi, Vincenzo Galilei, and Claudio Merulo. Author of *Le istitutioni harmoniche,* a seminal work in the history of music theory, and *Dimostrationi harmoniche.* Attacked by Galilei in his *Dialogo* (1581); responded with *Sopplimenti musicali.* Also composed motets and madrigals. Writings: *Le istitutioni harmoniche* (1558–59); *Dimostrationi harmoniche* (1571); *Sopplimenti musicali* (1588).

Zart [Ger.]. Delicate, soft.

Zarzuela [Sp. from *zarza,* bramble bush]. A Spanish theatrical genre characterized by a mixture of singing and spoken dialogue. Throughout its history, the *zarzuela* has included elements from the Spanish popular tradition. The term *zarzuela* originated in the 17th century with the musical court plays intended for performance at the royal hunting lodge or Palace of the Zarzuela outside of Madrid. Both the two-act pastoral *zarzuelas* and the three-act mythological spectacle plays by Pedro Calderón de la Barca (1600–1681) and contemporary dramatists were hybrids, consisting of a mixture of sung and spoken dialogue and incorporating elements from the native tradition and forms from opera. Although the earliest works called *zarzuelas* date from 1657, recitative was introduced for the speech of the gods as early as 1652 in Calderón's *La fiera, el rayo, y la piedra.*

The classical theatrical genre and the musical style developed by Juan Hidalgo (1614–85) remained essentially stable to the last decade of the 17th century, when the *zarzuela* adapted to a change in literary fashion and a new interest in contemporary foreign musical styles. These were reflected in *zarzuelas* by Sebastián Durón (1660–1716) and Antonio Literes (1673–1747). *Zarzuelas* by Durón and especially Literes include longer and more elaborate set pieces, a clearer distinction between recitative and air, and some da capo arias. From ca. 1710 to 1750, the *zarzuela* increasingly approximated the musical styles and conventions of contemporary *opera seria,* which quickly replaced *zarzuela* as the favorite court entertainment.

Around 1760, Spanish composers gained public support by self-consciously cultivating a popular native style and returning to Spanish theatrical conventions. In this nationalistic movement, the importance of the dramatist Ramón de la Cruz (1731–94) and the influence from the smaller comic forms (the *sainete* and the *tonadilla*) cannot be overestimated. The first important work of this type (*zarzuela burlesca*) performed in Madrid was *El tío y la tía* (1767) by the composer Antonio Rosales (ca. 1740–1801) to a one-act *sainete*-like text by Ramón de la Cruz. This was followed in 1769 by the production of a two-act work with music by Antonio Rodríguez de Hita (ca. 1724–87) on a text by Ramón de la Cruz, *Las labradoras de Murcia.* The latter work can be defined as the first extant *zarzuela de costumbres,* because the plot is not only injected with popular humor but devoted to local customs.

The first 19th-century *zarzuela* production in Madrid took place in 1839 with the one-act *El novio y el concierto* (termed *zarzuela-comedia*) by the Italian Basilio Basili (1803–95) and the poet Manuel Bretón de los Herreros (1796–1873), a declared enemy of Italian opera. By the middle of the century, the resurgence of *zarzuela* was fired by a nucleus of young Spanish composers, the "grupo de los cinco" (group of five), who, in essence, founded the modern *zarzuela* genre: Francisco Asenjo Barbieri (1823–94), Rafael Hernando (1822–88), Joaquín Gaztambide (1822–70), Cristóbal Oudrid y Segura (1825–77), and José Inzenga (1828–91).

Barbieri was behind the founding of Madrid's Teatro de la Zarzuela in 1856, and his efforts in support of the genre were crucial to the future of Spanish musical theater. The 19th-century *zarzuela* was inextricably linked to Madrid, which provided its typical subjects and characters and whose working middle class was its principal audience.

The *zarzuela* was an ephemeral entertainment, and the continual demand for new works made the one-act *zarzuelas* referred to as *género chico* (small genre) more practical. Federico Chueca (1846–1908) was a leading exponent of this genre, and his *La Gran Vía* (1886) is still one of the most frequently performed works of the period. Several works by Ruperto Chapí (1851–1909), including *La tempestad* (1882) and *La revoltosa* (1897), have remained favorites in the standard repertory as well. The high point of the *género chico,* however, was reached by Tomás Bretón (1850–1923) with *La verbena de la paloma* (1894), which has enjoyed unflagging popularity.

In the opening decades of the 20th century, the *zarzuela* continued as popular theater and attracted many talented composers, most notably Amadeo Vives (1871–1932), whose reputation was established with *Bohemios* (1904) and whose *Doña Francisquita* (1923) is the archetype of the sentimental *zarzuela.* Among the most respected and revered works of the entire genre is Federico Moreno Torroba's (1891–1982) *Luisa Fernanda* (1932). Although performances of established works continue to appeal to a wide audience in Spain (and to have some appeal in the Western Hemisphere), the production of new works has virtually ceased.

Zauberflöte, Die [Ger., The Magic Flute]. Opera (*Singspiel) in two acts by Mozart (libretto by Emanuel Schikaneder, after various sources, including Liebeskind's fairy tale "Lulu, oder Die Zauberflöte," published by Wieland in 1786–89), produced in Vienna in 1791. Setting: ancient Egypt.

Zawinul, Joe [Josef Erich] (b. Vienna, 7 July 1932). Jazz keyboard player, composer, and bandleader. Immigrated to the U.S.; played with Maynard Ferguson (1959) and then joined Dinah Washington (1959–61). Played electric piano in Cannonball Adderley's group (1961–70), for which he composed the title track of the album *Mercy, Mercy, Mercy* (1966). In 1969–70 recorded with Miles Davis and composed the title track of Davis's album *In a Silent Way* (1969). Co-led with Wayne Shorter the jazz-rock group Weather Report (1970–85), for which he composed the hit tune "Birdland" (on the album *Heavy Weather,* 1976). Renaming the group Weather Update, Zawinul continued as sole leader; by 1989 was leading a new jazz-rock quartet.

Zeitlin, Zvi (b. Dubrovna, 21 Feb. 1923). Violinist. Studied at the Hebrew Univ. in Jerusalem and then at the Juilliard School. Professional debut with the Palestine Orchestra, 1940. Toured widely; known for his support of contemporary music. Joined faculty of the Eastman School in 1967. Also active in research; discovered 6 concertos by Pietro Nardini.

Zeitmass [Ger.]. (1) Tempo; *im ersten Z., *tempo primo; im früheren Z., a *tempo; im freien Z.,* in free tempo. (2) *Zeitmasse* [pl.], Stockhausen's work no. 5 for flute, oboe, English horn, clarinet, and bassoon, which simultaneously combines independent tempos.

Zeitmesser [Ger.]. Metronome.

Zelenka, Jan Dismas [Johann Dismas, Jan Lukáš] (b. Lounovice, Bohemia, 16 Oct. 1679; d. Dresden, 22 Dec. 1745). Composer. Served Count Hartig in Prague (1709–10); from 1710 played double bass in the royal orchestra at Dresden. Studied with J. J. Fux in Vienna and A. Lotti in Venice; returned to Dresden in 1719; in 1735 became *Kirchen-compositeur.* Compositions include Masses, oratorios, cantatas, motets, other sacred vocal works, 6 trio sonatas, various orchestral works.

Zelter, Carl Friedrich (b. Berlin, 11 Dec. 1758; d. there, 15 May 1832). Composer. In 1779, violinist in the Doebblin Theater orchestra; studied composition with Carl Fasch and joined his Singakademie in 1791. Director of the group, 1800; started a companion orchestral ensemble, the Ripienschule, 1808. In 1809 joined the faculty of the Royal Academy of the Arts in Berlin and started the Liedertafel, a men's singing society; in 1822 established the Royal Institute for Church Music. Goethe admired Zelter's settings of his poems; the two became friends and correspondents. Composed primarily vocal works; remembered for his lieder (around 200). Also composed cantatas, other sacred and secular choral works, a viola concerto, keyboard music. Author of pedagogical works on singing and composition.

Zemlinsky, Alexander (von) (b. Vienna, 14 Oct. 1871; d. Larchmont, N.Y., 15 Mar. 1942). Composer and conductor. Studied at the Vienna Conservatory and enjoyed early success with chamber music. Acquainted with Brahms, Mahler (who introduced his opera *Es war einmal* at the Hofoper in 1900), and Schoenberg. Conductor at the Carltheater (1899–1903), the Volksoper (1904–7, 1909–11), and the Hofoper (1907–8). With Schoenberg founded the Vereinigung Schaffender Tonkünstler to promote new music. In 1911 moved to Prague as principal conductor of the Deutsches Landestheater, but remained close to Schoenberg and to Viennese contemporary music circles. Stylistic evolution paralleled that of Schoenberg but he declined to follow Schoenberg into atonality. Moved in 1927 to Berlin; conducted at the Kroll Opera (1927–30) and taught at the Musikhochschule (1927–33). Returned to Vienna in 1933; fled to the U.S. in 1938. Works include *Sarema* (opera, 1897); *Eine florentinische Tragödie* (opera, 1917); *Der Zwerg* (opera, 1922); 2 symphonies; *Sinfonietta* (orchestra, 1934); string quartet no. 4 (1936); "Maeterlinck Songs" (mezzo-soprano or baritone and piano, 1913; also orchestrated); *Symphonische Gesänge* (voice and orchestra, 1929).

Zender, Hans (b. Wiesbaden, 22 Nov. 1936). Conductor and composer. Studied at the Frankfurt Musikhochschule and the Freiburg Musikhochschule with Wolfgang Fortner. Held conducting posts in Freiburg (1959–63), at the theaters in Bonn (1964–68) and Kiel (1969–71), and with the Radio Orchestra of the Saar (1971–77); music director at the Hamburg Opera (1977–88). Compositions include *Schachspiel* (2 orchestras, 1970); *Zeitströme* (orchestra, 1974); *Hölderlin lesen* (string quartet, ad lib Sprechstimme, 1979); *Die Wüste hat zwölf Dinge* (mezzo-soprano and orchestra, 1986); *Five Haiku* (flute and strings, 1982); *Happy Band* (trumpet, 1989).

Zeno, Apostolo (b. Venice, 11 Dec. 1668; d. there, 11 Nov. 1750). Librettist. Founder of the Accademia degli Animosi (1691) and the *Giornale dei letterati d'Italia* (1710). First success as a librettist in 1700 with *Lucio Vero,* set by C. F. Pollarolo and performed in Venice; later collaborated with Pietro Pariati. From 1718 until 1729 "poeta e istorico di S. M. Cesarea" in Vienna, succeeded by Metastasio. Wrote about 70 librettos.

Zeuner, Charles (Heinrich Christoph) (b. Eisleben, 20 Sept. 1795; d. Philadelphia, 7 Nov. 1857). Pianist, organist, and composer. Studied with Hummel at Weimar. Emigrated during the late 1820s or in 1830 to Boston. Organist for the Handel and Haydn Society, 1830; president, 1838–39. Moved to Philadelphia, 1839, and was organist at several churches. Composed oratorios, Masses, cantatas, organ works (including many fugues), band marches, choral works, songs.

Zhizn' za tsarya [Russ.]. See *Life for the Tsar, A.*

Ziani, Marc'Antonio (b. Venice, ca. 1653; d. Vienna, 22 Jan. 1715). Composer. Probably taught by his uncle Pietro Andrea Ziani. In 1686 appointed *maestro di cappella* at S. Barbara, Mantua; while there taught Caldara. Became successful as an opera composer in the 1690s in Vienna, Bologna, and Venice. In 1700 appointed *vice-Hofkapellmeister* to Emperor Leopold I in Vienna; 1712, *Hofkapellmeister.* Works include about 45 operas, 16 oratorios, over 20 Masses, 3 Requiem Masses, more than 100 other sacred vocal works, secular cantatas, and arias.

Ziani, Pietro Andrea (b. Venice, probably before 21 Dec. 1616; d. Naples, 12 Feb. 1684). Composer. Uncle of Marc'Antonio Ziani. Organist at S. Salvatore, Venice; *maestro di cappella* at S. Maria Maggiore, Bergamo (1657–59). In 1662 appointed *vice-Kapellmeister* to the Dowager Empress Eleonora in Vienna; 1669, succeeded Cavalli as first organist of St. Mark's, Venice. Taught at the Conservatorio S. Onofrio, Naples; appointed *maestro di cappella* at court, 1680. Wrote about 30 operas, oratorios, other sacred vocal works, madrigals, canzonettas, cantatas, and sonatas.

Ziehharmonika [Ger.]. Accordion.

Zieleński [Zelenscius], **Mikołaj** (fl. 1611). Composer. Organist and director of music to Wojciech Baranowski, Archbishop of Gneizno and primate of Poland from 1608. His two publications, the *Offertoria* and the *Communiones* (both 1611), contain polychoral sacred music as well as the earliest examples of Polish monody, concertato, and music specifically written for instruments.

Ziemlich [Ger.]. Rather.

Zigeunerbaron, Die [Ger., The Gypsy Baron]. Operetta in three acts by Johann Strauss, Jr. (libretto by Ignaz Schnitzer, after a story by Mor Jókai), produced in Vienna in 1885. Setting: the Austro-Hungarian Empire in mid-18th century.

Zigeunermusik [Ger.]. *Gypsy music.

Zilcher, Hermann (b. Frankfurt, 18 Aug. 1881; d. Würzburg, 1 Jan. 1948). Pianist, composer, and teacher. Studied at the Hoch Conservatory in Frankfurt with James Kwast and Iwan Knorr. Toured as a pianist; taught at the Akademie der Tonkunst in Munich 1908–20; 1920–44 director of the Würzburg Conservatory. Works include *Fitzebutze* (opera, 1903); *Doktor Eisenbart* (opera, 1922); 4 symphonies; 2 piano concertos; concertos for 1 and 2 violins; chamber works and many songs.

Zillig, Winfried (Petrus Ignatius) (b. Würzburg, 1 Apr. 1905; d. Hamburg, 17 Dec. 1963). Composer and conductor. Studied at the Würzburg Conservatory with Hans Zilcher and with Arnold Schoenberg; adopted twelve-tone techniques. Kleiber's assistant at the Berlin Staatsoper (1927–28); conductor at Düsseldorf, Essen, and Poznań. Remained committed to Schoenberg and to twelve-tone music during the Nazi period; important in the revival of modern music in Germany after the war. After World War II conducted in Germany and on German radio. Works include *Rosse* (opera, 1933); *Das Opfer* (opera, 1937); *Das Verlobnis* (opera, 1963); Concerto for Orchestra (1930); Violin Concerto (1955); many songs. Author of *Variationen über neue Musik* (1959).

Zimbalist, Efrem (Alexandrovich) (b. Rostov-na-Donu, Russia, 21 Apr. 1889; d. Reno, 22 Feb. 1985). Violinist and composer. Studied violin with his father and with Leopold Auer at the St. Petersburg Conservatory. Performed in Europe; settled in the U.S. after debut with the Boston Symphony, 1911. Taught at the Curtis Institute (director, 1941–68). Compositions include the opera *Landara* (1956); concertos for piano, cello, and violin; orchestral and chamber works; solo violin music.

Zimbalon. *Cimbalom.

Zimmermann, Bernd Alois (b. Bliesheim, Germany, 20 Mar. 1918; d. Königsdorf, 10 Aug. 1970). Studied at the Cologne Hochschule für Musik with Heinrich Lemacher and Philipp Jarnach. Works of the late 1940s and early 1950s influenced by the expressionism of Berg, Schoenberg, and Stravinsky, as well as non-Western music and American jazz. Work with Wolfgang Fortner and René Leibowitz at the Darmstadt summer courses (1948–50) plus intense study of the works of Anton Webern led by the mid-50s toward serialism. Taught at the Univ. of Cologne (1950–52), and the Cologne Musikhochschule from 1957; active at West German Radio in Cologne. Achieved international stature with 1965 premiere in Cologne of opera *Die Soldaten,* which combines many musical styles in a texture he called "pluralistic" and linked with a philosophical notion of time. *Requiem für einen jungen Dichter* (speakers, singers, jazz ensemble, orchestra, and electronic sounds, 1969) is an aural collage of European history from 1920 to 1969. Other works include *Dialoge* (2 pianos and orchestra, 1960; rev. for 2 pianos solo, 1965); Cello Concerto (1966); *Musique pour les soupers du roi Ubu* (ballet, 1966); *Tratto* (tape, 1966); *Stille und Umkehr* (orchestra, 1970); *Ich wandte mich und sah an alles Unrecht . . .* (speakers, baritone, orchestra, 1970).

Zimmermann, Udo (b. Dresden, 6 Oct. 1943). Composer. Studied at the Dresden Hochschule für Musik with Johannes Paul Thilman and at the Akademie der Künste in Berlin with Günther Kochan. Returned to Dresden in 1970; associated with the Dresden Opera and the Studio for New Music (from 1974). Appointed professor of composition at the Dresden Hochschule, 1987; 1986, director, Dresden Zentrum für Zeitgenössische Musik and artistic adviser to the opera workshop of the Bonn Opera; 1990, intendant for the Leipzig Opera. Many works are serial; some employ aleatory elements. Compositions include *Die weisse Rose* (dramatic cantata, 1967); *Die zweite Entscheidung* (opera, 1970); *Mutazione* (orchestra, 1973); *Der Schuhu und die fliegende Prinzessin* (opera, 1976); Concerto (percussion and orchestra, 1980); *Mein Gott, wer trommelt denn da?* (orchestra, 1985); *Canticum Marianum* (12 cellos, 1985); *Die Sündflut* (1988); Horn Concerto (1987); *Gantebein Gesänge* (baritone, orchestra, 1988); *Nouveau divertissement* (viola concerto, 1988).

Zingarelli, Niccolò Antonio (b. Naples, 4 Apr. 1752; d. Torre del Greco, near Naples, 5 May 1837). Composer. Studied at the Conservatorio Santa Maria di Loreto with Fenaroli, Sacchini, Anfossi, and Speranza. Named *maestro di cappella* of the Milan Cathedral in 1793, at Loreto in 1794, at St. Peter's in Rome in 1804; 1813, took charge of the conservatory S. Pietro a Majella in Naples; 1816, musical director at the Naples Cathedral. Teacher of Mercadente and Bellini. Wrote at least 41 operas and a large amount of church music, including oratorios (*La passione di Gesù Cristo,* 1787), Masses, about 55 Magnificats, 23 Te Deums, Psalms; secular vocal music; over 50 symphonies; sonatas, string quartets, pastorales for keyboard, duets.

Zingarese, alla [It.]. In the *Gypsy style.

Zink [Ger.]. *Cornett.

Zinman, David (Joel) (b. New York, 9 July 1936). Conductor. Studied at Oberlin Conservatory and the Univ. of Minnesota and with Pierre Monteux. Music director of the Netherlands Chamber Orchestra (1964–77), Rochester Philharmonic (1974–85), Rotterdam Philharmonic (1979–82); principal guest conductor and then director (from 1985) of the Baltimore Symphony.

Zipoli, Domenico (b. Prato, 16 or 17 Oct. 1688; d. Santa Catalina, near Córdoba, Argentina, 2 Jan. 1726). Composer. Studied with Giovanni Maria Casini in Florence, Alessandro Scarlatti in Naples, Lavinio Felice Vannucci in Bologna, and Bernardo Pasquini in Rome. In 1715 appointed organist at the Jesuit church in Rome. Published keyboard collection *Sonate d'intavolatura* (1716); settled in Córdoba in 1717. Works include oratorios, Masses, and cantatas.

Zither. (1) Any of a class of stringed instruments in which the string or strings run the length of the body [see ill.]. The body is usually the principal *resonator, and the strings are stretched above it over bridges. Zithers may be plucked, struck, bowed, or set into vibration by the wind (as in *aeolian harps). They are widely distributed, especially in Europe, Asia, and Africa, and take a great variety of forms, ranging from the simple *trough zither to the refined *koto to the technically intricate *piano. Zithers may be divided into broad classes on the basis of shape, construction, and playing technique: *trough zither, *stick zither, *tube zither, long zither, and board or box zither (the latter incorporating a *sound box).

(2) A box zither native to Austria and southern Germany. It has four or five metal melody strings passing over a chromatically fretted fingerboard that runs along the straight side closest to the player. Parallel to these are 30 to 40 gut or nylon accompaniment strings stretched over a flat sound box with sound hole and an outward curve opposite the player. The player stops the melody strings with the left hand and plucks them with a plectrum worn on the right thumb. The remaining fingers of the right hand add accompaniment on the open strings. This type of zither was developed in the 19th century and has been used as both a solo and an ensemble instrument.

Zitternd [Ger.]. *Tremolando.

Znamenny chant. A type of Russian chant originating in the 15th century and characterized by the nondiastematic *krjuki* or hook notation that superseded the Byzantine neumes. See also Russian and Slavonic chant.

Zögern [Ger.]. To hesitate, to retard.

Zoilo, Annibale (b. Rome, ca. 1537; d. Loreto, 1592). Composer and singer. Choirmaster of S. Luigi

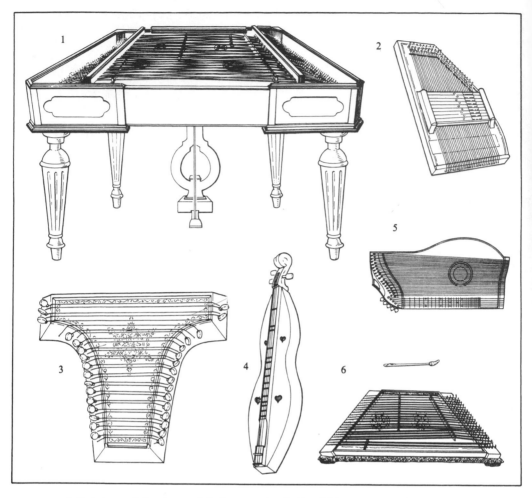

1. Cimbalom.   2. Autoharp.   3. Psaltery.   4. Appalachian dulcimer.   5. Zither.   6. Dulcimer.

dei Francesi (1561–66) and St. John Lateran (1567–70); employed by Cardinal Guglielmo Sirleto and joined the choir of the Sistine Chapel (1570–77). Appointed choirmaster of Todi Cathedral, 1581; from 1584 at Santa Casa, Loreto. Works are similar in style to those of Palestrina.

Zöllner, Heinrich (b. Leipzig, 4 July 1854; d. Freiburg, 8 May 1941). Composer and conductor. Son of composer Carl Friedrich Zöllner (1800–1860). Studied at Leipzig Conservatory; lived in the U.S., 1890–98. Music director, Leipzig University, 1898; professor of composition, Leipzig Conservatory, from 1902. Conductor at Flemish Opera in Antwerp, 1907–14; taught at Freiburg, 1914. Served as editor of *Leipzig Tageblatt,* 1903–6. Cantata *Die neue Welt* won a prize at the Cleveland Sängerfest in 1892. Other works include 5 symphonies, overtures, 5 string quartets, solo piano works, piano 4-hand pieces, music for men's chorus, songs.

Zoppa, alla [It., lame, limping]. A typical rhythm of the 18th-century **galant* style consisting of a syncopated quarter note between two eighths in 2/4 time, usually preceded by an anacrusis.

Zu [Ger.]. To, too, toward, for; *zu 2, a *due.*

Zug [Ger.]. (1) Slide; *Zugposaune,* slide trombone; *Zugtrompete,* slide trumpet. (2) Organ stop.

Zukerman, Pinchas (b. Tel Aviv, 16 July 1948). Violinist, violist, and conductor. Studied at the Tel Aviv Academy of Music with Ilona Feher, and at the Juilliard School. Won the Leventritt Competition, 1967; New York debut at Lincoln Center, 1969; appeared as soloist with American and European orchestras. Conducting debut with the Philharmonia Orchestra,

London, 1974; conductor of the St. Paul Chamber Orchestra, 1980–86. Many of his collaborations with orchestras feature him as both soloist and conductor.

Zukofsky, Paul (b. Brooklyn, 22 Oct. 1943). Violinist. Studied with Ivan Galamian at the Juilliard School; Carnegie Hall debut, 1956. Known for his activity in contemporary music; has premiered works by Babbitt, Sessions, Carter, Crumb, and others. Many recordings include an anthology of American violin music written between 1940 and 1970. Taught at the New England Conservatory and SUNY–Stony Brook and elsewhere. Conductor of the Contemporary Chamber Ensemble at Juilliard from 1984; director of the Arnold Schoenberg Institute from 1992.

Zumsteeg, Johann Rudolf (b. Sachsenflur [Odenwald], 10 Jan. 1760; d. Stuttgart, 27 Jan. 1802). Composer. He studied at the Karlsschule in Stuttgart and with Agostino Poli, the court Kapellmeister. In 1781 became a member of the court orchestra as a cellist; 1785, music teacher at the Karlsschule; 1791, music director at the court theater; 1793, court *Konzertmeister*. Remembered chiefly for about 300 songs, said to have had an influence on Schubert; published 7 volumes of *Kleine Balladen und Lieder* (1800–5). Other compositions include 10 cello concertos (1777–92); operas; cantatas; orchestral works; chamber pieces.

Zūrnā [Ar., also *ghaytah, mizmār, zamr;* Turk. *zurna;* Per. *surnāy*]. A *shawm of the Middle East and regions influenced by Islam. A typical example is a wooden tube 30 to 35 cm. in length with a conical bore, a flared bell, and seven finger holes plus a thumb hole. It has a small reed, often with a metal lip-disk below it. The whole reed is usually taken into the mouth and circular breathing is used so as to produce a continuous sound. See ill. under Instrument.

Zurückhalten [Ger.]. To hold back, *rallentando.*

Zusammen [Ger.]. Together, as after a passage in which a section of the orchestra has been divided.

Zusammenschlag [Ger.]. *Acciaccatura.

Zwilich, Ellen Taaffe (b. Miami, 30 Apr. 1939). Composer. Studied violin with Richard Burgin in Tallahassee and Ivan Galamian in New York, composition at Juilliard with Elliott Carter and Roger Sessions. By the mid-70s her works—tonal, lyrical, and formally clear—were getting performances and winning prizes; in 1983 Symphony no. 1, a Romantic work in the vein of Mahler and Shostakovich, was awarded the Pulitzer Prize. Joined the Juilliard faculty in 1993; 1995, became the first composer appointed to Carnegie Hall's Composer's Chair. Works include *Symposium for Orchestra* (1973); Sonata in Three Movements (violin, 1973), written for her husband, the violinist Joseph Zwilich; Chamber Symphony (1979); *Passages* (soprano and chamber ensemble, 1981); String Trio (1982); Double Quartet (2 string quartets, 1984); Symphony no. 2 (1985); trombone concerto (1988); *Symbolon* (orchestra, 1989); flute concerto (1990); clarinet quintet (1990); Double Concerto (1992); Symphony no. 3 (1993); Concerto for Horn and String Orchestra (1993); *A Simple Magnificat* (chorus, organ, 1994); *American Concerto* (trumpet, orchestra, 1994); Triple Concerto (1996).

Zydeco [fr. Fr. *les haricots,* French beans]. A type of music originating among blacks in Cajun Louisiana and combining elements of French Cajun traditions with blues, rhythm and blues, rock-and-roll, Caribbean music, and country and western music. The closely related music as performed by white musicians is usually termed Cajun. Traditional instruments are the accordion and washboard, to which have been added electric guitar, bass, and drums. Its first exponent to achieve widespread recognition was Clifton Chenier (b. 1925).

Zyklus [Ger.]. Cycle.